Jürgen Nöhring
Wörterbuch Medizin
Deutsch-Englisch

Dr. med. Jürgen Nöhring

Dictionary of Medicine

German-
English

containing approximately 75 000 terms

1987
Verlag Harri Deutsch · Thun · Frankfurt/M.

Dr. med. Jürgen Nöhring

Wörterbuch Medizin

Deutsch-
Englisch

Mit etwa 75 000 Wortstellen

1987
Verlag Harri Deutsch · Thun · Frankfurt/M.

Fachgutachter: MR Prof. Dr. med. habil. *L. Pickenhain*

Eingetragene (registrierte) Warenzeichen sowie Gebrauchsmuster und Patente sind in diesem Wörterbuch nicht ausdrücklich gekennzeichnet. Daraus kann nicht geschlossen werden, daß die betreffenden Bezeichnungen frei sind oder frei verwendet werden können.

CIP-Kurztitelaufnahme der Deutschen Bibliothek:

Nöhring, Jürgen:
Wörterbuch Medizin : dt.-engl. ; mit etwa 75 000
Wortstellen / Jürgen Nöhring. — Thun ; Franfurt/M.:
Deutsch, 1987.
  Parallelsacht.: Dictionary of medicine
  ISBN 3-87144-957-1
NE: HST

ISBN 3 87144 957 1

Lizenzausgabe für den Verlag Harri Deutsch, Thun
© VEB Verlag Technik, Berlin, 1987
Printed in the German Democratic Republic
Satz: Lichtsatz Druckerei Neues Deutschland Berlin
Offsetdruck und buchbinderische Verarbeitung:
Druckerei „Thomas Müntzer", Bad Langensalza

VORWORT

Das nunmehr vorliegende deutsch-englische WÖRTERBUCH „Medizin" ergänzt das im gleichen Verlag herausgegebene englisch-deutsche Wörterbuch zu einem Gesamtwerk.
Bei der Auswahl des medizinischen Wortbestandes wurden sowohl die deutschen Fachbegriffe als auch die lateinischen Termini berücksichtigt. Die Terminologie des englisch-deutschen Bands wurde nach fachlichen und lexikografischen Gesichtspunkten bearbeitet, anhand moderner deutscher Fachliteratur nochmals überprüft, und es wurden einige Ergänzungen vorgenommen. Die IUPAC-Schreibung für chemische Benennungen wurde in Form von Verweisen eingefügt; die IPUAC-Nomenklatur für chemische Verbindungen, die besonders die Art und die Form von Stellungsangaben betrifft, ist noch nicht durchgängig aufgenommen worden. Ein Anhang mit Hinweisen und Literaturangaben zur Anwendung der IUPAC-Nomenklatur bietet dem Nutzer weitere Informationsmöglichkeiten. Anregungen und Hinweise, die uns zum englisch-deutschen Band zugingen, sind teilweise mit berücksichtigt worden.
Das zweisprachige Wörterbuch „Medizin" wendet sich sowohl an wissenschaftlich und klinisch tätige Ärzte als auch an Studenten der Medizin in den vorklinischen und klinischen Semestern, an das mittlere medizinische Personal sowie an Sprachmittler und all jene, welche in ihrer täglichen Praxis mit der Übersetzung deutschsprachiger medizinischer Begriffe in die englische Sprache konfrontiert werden. Dabei berücksichtigt dieses Wörterbuch sowohl die Belange des deutschsprachigen als auch die des der deutschen Sprache unkundigen Nutzers.
Besonderer Dank gilt an dieser Stelle den Mitarbeitern des Wörterbuchlektorats des Verlags für ihre unermüdlichen kritischen Hinweise und Anregungen zur Manuskriptgestaltung.
Infolge des hohen Spezialisierungsgrads wird auch dieses Wörterbuch nicht frei von Unzulänglichkeiten sein. Autor und Verlag sind deshalb für sachdienliche kritische Hinweise zur weiteren Verbesserung dieses Fachwörterbuchs dankbar. Wir bitten, diese an den Verlag Harri Deutsch, Gräfstr. 47, D-6000 Frankfurt (Main) 90, zu richten.

Jürgen Nöhring

BENUTZUNGSHINWEISE

1. Beispiele für die alphabetische Ordnung

Kanüle*
● eine ~ einführen
~/weitlumige
Kehlkopf
Kehlkopfkrampf
Kehlkopf- und Rachenentzündung
Kiefer
Kieferanomalie
Klappe
Klappengeräusch
Klappenplastik
Kneippkur
Knochenmark
Knorpelhaft
Kolon*
~/irritables
Kolon-Duodenum-Fistel
Krabbe-Syndrom I*
~ II
krank*
● sich ~ fühlen
● unheilbar ~ sein
kränkeln
Krankheit*
~/akute
~/Basedowsche
~/chronische
~/Letterer-Siwesche
Krankheitsbild

O.
O-Agglutination
Oat-cell-Karzinom
O_2-Aufsättigung des Bluts
o.B.
Obduktion
obduzieren
O-Bein
Oberarm
Oculus*
~ caesius
~ purulentus
Ödem*
~/alimentäres
~ der Gliedmaßenenden
~/pulmonales
ödematös
Oedema*
~ neonatorum
Okular
Okularnystagmus
Ollier-Syndrom
Ovar
Ovarialruptur
Oxydation
β-Oxydation
oxydieren*
~/zu Nitrat
Ozaena

*Ein hier mit * gekennzeichnetes Stichwort ist ein sog. Nestwort. Alle mit diesem Nestwort vorhandenen Wortverbindungen sind alphabetisch geordnet im Anschluß an das Nestwort aufgeführt, wobei dieses mit Tilde wiedergegeben wird.*

2. Bedeutung der Zeichen

/		Gelenkfortsatz/oberer = oberer Gelenkfortsatz
( )		asthmaartige (asthmatoide) Atmung = asthmaartige Atmung *oder* asthmatoide Atmung
		Refsum's disease (syndrome) = Refsum's disease *or* Refsum's syndrome
[ ]		Blinden[punkt]schrift = Blindenpunktschrift *oder* Blindenschrift
		mastoid [air] cell = mastoid air cell *or* mastoid cell
( )		Diese Klammern enthalten Erklärungen.
		These brackets contain explanations.
f	Femininum/feminine noun	s. siehe/see
m	Maskulinum/masculine noun	s. a. siehe auch/see also
n	Neutrum/neuter noun	z. B. zum Beispiel/for example
pl	Plural/plural	

A

AAK s. Antigen-Antikörper-Komplex
AAR s. Antigen-Antikörper-Reaktion
Aaron-Zeichen n Aaron's sign *(Appendizitiszeichen)*
Aasernährung f necrophagia *(von Mikroorganismen)*
abakteriell abacterial, without bacteria
abapikal abapical, away from the apex, opposite the apex
Abarognosis f abarognosis, baragnosis
Abart f variation, variety
abartig abnormal, anomalous; deviated
~/psychisch psychopathic
Abartiger m/psychisch psychopath
Abartigkeit f/geschlechtliche sexual deviation (abnormality)
~/psychische psychopathy
abartikulär abarticular, remote from the joint; not connected with the joint
Abasia f trepidans trembling abasia
Abasie f abasia
Abbau m decomposition, catabolism; dissimilation
abbauen to catabolize; to dissimilate
Abbauprodukt n catabolite, catabolic (decomposition) product
Abbaustoffwechsel m catabolism, catabiosis; dis[as]similation, devolution ● **dem ~ unterliegen** to catabolize; to dissimilate
abbildbar sein/röntgenologisch to cast an X-ray shadow
abbildend/gleichartig (gleichgroß) isoiconic
~/nicht punktförmig astigmatic *(z. B. Linse)*
~/punktförmig anastigmatic *(z. B. Linse)*
Abbildung f/nicht punktförmige astigmatism *(durch Hornhautverkrümmung)*
~/punktförmige anastigmatism
Abbildungsfehler m s. Aberration
abbinden to ligate, to tie off (up) *(z. B. Blutgefäß)*; to apply a tourniquet to *(z. B. Extremität)*
Abbinden n ligation, ligature *(z. B. von Blutgefäßen)*
Abbindungsfaden m ligature
abblättern to exfoliate, to scale [off], to desquamate *(z. B. Haut)*
abblätternd exfoliative, scaling, desquamative
Abblätterung f exfoliation, scaling, desquamation
Abbruchblutung f withdrawal bleeding
abdecken[/steril] to drape, to cover with sterile sheets
Abdecktest m cover test *(Schielddiagnostik)*
Abdecktuch n[/steriles] drape, sterile sheet (towel)
Abderhalden-Fanconi-Syndrom n s. 1. Abderhalden-Kaufmann-Lignac-Syndrom; 2. Debré-de Toni-Fanconi-Syndrom
Abderhalden-Kaufmann-Lignac-Syndrom n Abderhalden-Kaufmann-Lignac syndrome, cystinosis, cystine storage disease

Abdominoperinealresektion

Abdomen n abdomen, belly, venter *(Zusammensetzungen s. unter Bauch)*
Abdomenröntgenaufnahme f abdominal roentgenogram (X-ray photograph), X-rays of the abdomen
Abdomenübersichtsaufnahme f plain abdominal roentgenogram, plain X-rays of the abdomen, scout film of the abdomen
abdominal abdominal
Abdominal... s. a. Bauch...
Abdominalarterie f abdominal artery
Abdominalatmung f abdominal breathing (respiration)
Abdominalbegleitverletzung f concomitant abdominal injury
Abdominalchirurgie f abdominal surgery
Abdominalechotomographie f abdominal echotomography
Abdominalfistel f abdominal fistula
Abdominalganglion n abdominal ganglion
Abdominalgia f abdominalgia, abdominal pain
Abdominalgravidität f abdominal pregnancy (gestation, gravidity)
Abdominalhernie f abdominal (ventral) hernia
Abdominalhöhle f abdominal cavity
Abdominalhysterotomie f abdominal hysterotomy, abdominohysterotomy, abdominouterotomy
Abdominalinzision f abdominal incision (section)
Abdominalisation f abdominalization *(Spaltung des Zwerchfells zur Herzentlastung)*
Abdominalkolik f abdominal colic
Abdominalkompression f abdominal compression
Abdominalkrampf m abdominal cramping
Abdominallinie f abdominal line
Abdominalnephrektomie f abdominal nephrectomy
Abdominalorgan n abdominal viscus
Abdominalpalpation f abdominal touch
Abdominalparazentese f abdominal paracentesis (puncture), abdominocentesis, coelioparacentesis
Abdominalptose f abdominal ptosis, visceroptosis
Abdominalpuls m abdominal pulse
Abdominalreflex m abdominal reflex
Abdominalretraktor m abdominal retractor
Abdominalsauger m abdominal suction tube
Abdominalschere f abdominal scissors
Abdominalsyndrom n abdominal syndrome
Abdominaltumor m abdominal tumour
Abdominalzyste f abdominal cyst
abdomino-anterior abdominoanterior *(z. B. Geburtslage)*
Abdominohysterektomie f abdominal hysterectomy, abdomino-hysterectomy
abdomino-lumbal lumbo-abdominal
abdomino-pelvin abdominopelvic
abdomino-perineal abdominoperineal
Abdominoperinealresektion f abdominoperineal resection *(Rektum)*

abdomino-posterior

abdomino-posterior abdominoposterior *(z. B. Geburtslage)*
Abdominoskopie *f* abdominoscopy
Abdruck *m* [dental] impression *(Stomatologie)*
Abdruckmaterial *n* disclosing material
Abduktion *f* abduction
Abduktionslähmung *f* abduction paralysis
Abduktionsmuskel *m* abductor [muscle]
Abduktionsmuskellähmung *f* abductor paralysis
Abduktionsschiene *f*/**Magnusonsche** Magnuson splint *(bei Oberarmbrüchen zur Ruhigstellung)*
Abduktor *m* abductor [muscle]
Abduktoreninsuffizienz *f* abductor insufficiency
Abduktorenparalyse *f* abductor paralysis
Abduzens *m* abducens, abducent nerve
Abduzenskern *m* abducent nucleus
Abduzenslähmung *f* abducent nerve paralysis
abduzieren to abduct
abduzierend abducent
Abendtemperatur *f* evening temperature
abenterisch abenteric, outside the intestine
Abercrombie-Syndrom *n* Abercrombie's syndrome (degeneration) *(bei Amyloidose)*
Aberratio *f* **temporis** heterochronia *(Gewebsentstehung zu ungewöhnlicher Zeit)*
Aberration *f* aberration *(Ophthalmologie)*
~/chromatische chromatic aberration
~/longitudinale longitudinal aberration
~/sphärische spherical aberration
~/visuelle visual aberration
Aberrationswinkel *m* aberration angle, angle of aberration
aberrierend aberrant
A-Beta-Globulinämie *f* abetaglobulinaemia
A-Beta-Lipoproteinämie *f* abetalipoproteinaemia, Bassen-Kornzweig syndrome
Abfallen *n* drop *(z. B. der Temperatur)*
abfallend/im Fieber allmählich lytic
Abflachung *f* applanation *(der Hornhaut)*
abfließen to drain
~ lassen to drain
Abfluß *m* runoff *(bei Gefäßplastik)*
Abflußrohr *n* drain, drainage tube
abfühlen to palpate, to touch
Abfühlen *n* palpation, dipping, touch
abfühlend palpatory
abführen to purge away (off), to act as an aperient; to purge, to cause purgation (catharsis), to evacuate (cleanse, loosen) the bowels
Abführen *n* purgation, catharsis
abführend 1. purgative, laxative, evacuant, cathartic, aperient, aperitive; 2. *s.* **herausführend**
Abführmittel *n* purgative, laxative [agent], evacuant [agent], cathartic [agent], aperient [agent], aperitive
~/salinisches saline [agent], saline purgative (cathartic)
Abführmittelmißbrauch *m* purgative abuse
Abgang *m* 1. discharge; passage *(von Steinen, Stuhl)*; 2. decease, passing [away] *(durch Tod)*; 3. flux *(von Patienten)*
abgebaut werden to be catabolized; to be dissimilated

abgeflacht oblate *(an den Polen)*
abgehen 1. to discharge, to pass *(z. B. Stuhlwürmer)*; 2. to break loose, to come off *(z. B. Thrombus)*; 3. to branch off *(z. B. Gefäße)*
~ lassen/Flatus (Winde) to pass flatus
abgekapselt encapsul[at]ed
abgemagert emaciated
abgeplattet flattened; oblate *(an den Polen)*
abgerissen incoherent *(Sprache)*
abgeschilfert scaly, exfoliated, branny, pityroid
abgeschwächt weak[ened] *(z. B. Viren)*; diminished *(z. B. Atmung)*; mitigated *(z. B. Schmerz)*
Abgespanntheit *f* languor, lassitude; fatigue; exhaustion; ponopathy
abgestiegen/nicht undescended *(z. B. Hoden)*
abgestorben dead; necrotic *(z. B. Gewebe)*; numb *(z. B. Körperglied)*; devitalized *(z. B. Nerven)*
abgezehrt cachectic, emaciated, haggard
abgrenzen to demarcate, to [de]limit, to mark off
Abgrenzungsperkussion *f* definitive percussion *(von Organen)*
Abguß *m* 1. cast, mould *(z. B. aus Gips)*; die *(Stomatologie)*; 2. cast *(z. B. in den Harnkanälchen)* ● **einen ~ machen** to make a cast
abhängig dependent; addicted ● **~ sein** to be addicted (habituated) *(z. B. von Drogen)*
~ von Luftsauerstoff aerobic
~ von Sauerstoff/absolut obligately aerobic
abhärten to inure to, to harden [against], to toughen [against]
~ abheben/die Haut to elevate the skin
abheilen to heal [up]; to close *(z. B. Wunde)*
~/narbig to scar over
abhorchend auscultatory
abhören to auscult[ate] *(z. B. Herztöne)*
Abhustemittel *n* expectorant [agent]
abhusten to expectorate *(Sputum)*
abhustend expectorant
Abiosis *f*, **Abiotrophie** *f* abiosis, abiotrophy, abiotrophic disease *(1. embryonale Defekte; 2. normale Bildungen mit reduzierter Lebensenergie)*
abiotrophisch abiotic, abiotrophic
abkapseln/sich to become encapsulated
Abkapselung *f* encapsulation
Abklatschgeschwür *n* contact ulcer
Abklatschkrebs *m* contact cancer
Abklatschmetastase *f* contact (drop) metastasis
Abklatschung *f* tapotement *(Massage)*
abklemmen to clamp [off]
Abklemmung *f* **von Blutgefäßen** forcipressure
abklingen to disappear *(z. B. Symptom)*; to ease off *(z. B. Schmerzen)*; to decrease, to go down, to defervesce, to die away *(z. B. Fieber)*; to defloresce *(z. B. Exanthem)*; to wear off *(z. B. Wirkung einer Droge)*
Abklingen *n* subsidence; disappearance *(z. B. von Symptomen)*; defervescence, remission *(z. B. von Fieber)*; decrease *(z. B. einer An-*

8

schwellung); deflorescence *(z. B. von Hautausschlag)*
abklingend subsiding; remittent
Abklingquote *f* subsidence rate
abklopfen/die Körperoberfläche to percuss
Abklopfen *n* **der Körperoberfläche** *s.* Perkussion
Abknickung *f* flexion
Abkömmling *m* offspring
abkratzen to scrape (scratch) off
Abkratzung *f* scraping, raclage, raclement
Abkühlung *f* cooling, chilling; refrigeration *(unter den Gefrierpunkt)*
abladieren to ablate, to remove by cutting *(s. a. amputieren)*
abladierend ablative
ablagern/Melanin to melanize *(in Geweben oder Organen)*
~/Mineralien to mineralize
Ablagerung *f* 1. deposition; sedimentation, hypostasis *(Vorgang)*; 2. deposit; sediment, hypostasis *(Substanz)*
Ablaktation *f* ablactation
Ablaktationsdyspepsie *f* ablactation dyspepsia
ablassen to let (blow) off *(Gase)*; to drain off, to run off *(Flüssigkeiten)*; to tap *(Flüssigkeiten durch Punktion einer Körperhöhle)*; to vent *(z. B. Ärger)*
Ablatio *f* **chorioideae** choroid detachment, detachment of the choroid
~ corporis vitrei detachment of the vitreous body
~ mammae mammary (breast) amputation, mammectomy
~ retinae retinal detachment (non-attachment), detachment (separation) of the retina
Ablation *f* ablation, amputation, sublation *(Zusammensetzungen s. unter Amputation)*
ablativ ablative
ableitbar drainable
ableiten 1. to drain [off], to run off *(z. B. Flüssigkeiten)*; 2. to derive, to lead *(EKG)*
ableitend draining *(z. B. Flüssigkeiten)*; efferent *(z. B. ein Lymphgefäß)*; excretory *(z. B. ein Drüsengang)*; deferent *(z. B. ein Samenkanälchen)*; secretory *(z. B. ein Kapillargefäß)*; revulsive, revulsant *(z. B. Blut)*
Ableitung *f* 1. leading off, diversion, drainage; revulsion *(z. B. von Blut)*; 2. derivation, lead *(EKG)*
~/Goldbergersche Goldberger (augmented unipolar) limb lead
~/intrakardiale intracardial electrode lead
~/präkordiale precordial lead (electrocardiogram)
Ableitungsbronchus *m* drainage bronchus
Ableitungselektrode *f* lead *(EKG)*
Ableitungspunkt *m* lead position *(EKG)*
Ableitungsrohr *n* drain, [drainage] tube
ablenkbar divertable, defractable, distractable
Ablenkung *f* deviation; deflection *(z. B. von Strahlen)*; distraction *(Zerstreuung)*
~/seitliche laterodeviation

Ablenkungswinkel *m* deviation angle, angle of deviation
Ablepharie *f* ablepharia
ablepharös ablepharous
Ablepsie *f* ablepsia
ablösen to detach, to remove; to ablate, to amputate; to strip; to scale off *(z. B. Schorf)*
~/die Haut to elevate the skin
~/sich to break loose, to come off *(z. B. Thrombus)*; to peel off *(z. B. Haut)*
ablösend ablative
Ablösung *f* detachment, removal; ablation, sublation, amputation; diastasis *(z. B. von Knochen)*
abmagern to grow lean, to fall off, to lose weight, to grow thin, to emaciate; to atrophy
abmagernd emaciating; atrophic
Abmagerung *f* falling off, emaciation; atrophy
~ bis auf die Knochen skeletization
Abmagerungsdiät *f*, **Abmagerungskost** *f* reducing (obesity, low-caloric) diet
Abmagerungskur *f* reducing cure, course of slimming
Abnabelung *f* omphalotomy, exumbilication, cutting of the umbilical cord
Abnabelungsmesser *n* omphalotome
abnehmend decrescent
Abneigung *f* **gegen Haare** trichophobia
~ gegen Neues (Veränderungen) neophobia, misoneism, horror of novelty (change)
abnerval abnerval
abnorm abnormal, anomalous
~/geistig-seelisch psychopathic
Abnormität *f* abnorm[al]ity, anomaly; deformity *(z. B. Extremität)*; monstrosity
~/geschlechtliche sexual perversion, sexual deviation (abnormality)
Abnutzung *f* attrition *(z. B. eines Gelenks)*; detrition *(z. B. der Zähne)*
Abnutzungspigment *n* wear-and-tear pigment
Abnutzungsprozeß *m* wearing process *(z. B. am Knorpel)*
AB0-Blutgruppensystem *n*, **AB0-System** *n* AB0 [blood group] system, blood group AB0 system
aboral aboral, caudal
Abort *m* 1. abortion, miscarriage, foetus loss *(s. a. unter Abortus und Fehlgeburt)*; 2. abortion, abort[us], aborted foetus ● **einen ~ bewirkend** abortient, abortifacient ● **einen ~ haben** to abort, to miscarry
~/afebriler afebrile abortion
~/eingeleiteter induced abortion
~/infektiöser contagious (infectious) abortion
~/künstlicher artificial abortion, foetus wastage
~/natürlicher natural abortion
~/therapeutischer therapeutic abortion
~/unvermeidlicher inevitable abortion
abortauslösend producing abortion, ecbolic
Abortbazillus *m* abortus bacillus
abortbewirkend abortient, abortifacient
abortieren to abort, to miscarry
Abortin *n* abortin
Abortinhautreaktion *f s.* Abortinreaktion

Abortin-Intrakutan-Test

Abortin-Intrakutan-Test *m* abortin test
Abortinprobe *f* abortin test
Abortinreaktion *f* abortin reaction
abortiv abortive
Abortivmitose *f* abortive mitosis
Abortivum *n* abortifacient [agent], ecbolic [agent]
Abortlöffel *m* ovum scoop
Abortus *m s.* Abort
~ **completus** complete abortion
~ **habitualis** habitual abortion
~ **imminens** imminent (threatened, impending) abortion
~ **incipiens** incipient (beginning) abortion
~ **incompletus** incomplete abortion
AB0-Unverträglichkeit *f* [blood group] AB0 incompatibility
abpuffern to buffer
abpunktieren to tap, to puncture
Abpunktion *f* tapping, puncture
Abrachie *f* abrachia, armlessness
Abrachius *m* abrachius, armless individual
Abrasio *f* 1. abrasion, curettage, curettement *(mittels Instruments);* 2. abrasion, excoriation *(durch Reibung);* 3. *s.* ~ dentis
~ **dentis** [dental] abrasion, wearing away (down) of the teeth, odontotripsis
Abräumzelle *f* scavenger cell
Abreagieren *n,* **Abreaktion** *f* abreaction *(Enthemmung eines Affekts)*
abreiben 1. to rub off, to rub down, to chafe; to rub in[to], to embrocate; 2. to rub, to scour, to chafe
Abreibung *f* 1. rub[bing]-down, towelling; rubbing in, embrocation *(Hauteinreibung);* 2. attrition, rubbing (chafing) of the skin *(Abnutzung)*
Abrikosow-Tumor *m* Abrikosoff's tumour, granular-cell myoblastoma (schwannoma) *(granuläres Neurom)*
Abriß *m* avulsion, evulsion, divulsion, disinsertion *(einer Sehne);* disinsertion, retinodialysis *(der Netzhaut)*
Abrißfissur *f* avulsion fissure *(z. B. der Schienbeinrauhigkeit)*
Abrißfraktur *f* avulsion fracture
Abruptio *f* **placentae** premature detachment of the placenta
absaugen to aspirate, to draw by suction, to suck[le]; to pump
~/**die Trachea** to suck out the trachea
Absauggerät *n* suction apparatus (machine)
Absaugkatheter *m* suction catheter
Absaugschlauch *m* suction tube
Absaugung *f* 1. suction, sucking, aspiration; 2. *s.* Absauggerät
~/**tracheobronchiale** tracheobronchial suction (aspiration)
Absaugungsdekompression *f* suction decompression *(z. B. des Darms)*
Absaugvorrichtung *f* secretion suction unit
abschaben to scrape [off], to abrade *(Haut);* to exfoliate
Abschabung *f* abrasion; exfoliation
abscheiden to separate, te segregate; to precipitate, to deposit *(z. B. festen Bodensatz);* to secrete *(z. B. Körpersäfte);* to excrete *(z. B. Stuhlgang)*
Abscheidung *f* 1. separation, segregation; precipitation, deposition, secretion; excretion; 2. precipitate, deposit; secretion; excretion
Abscheidungsthrombus *m* stratified (mixed, fibrolaminar) thrombus
Abscherfraktur *f* shearing fracture
Abscheu *m(f)* abhorrence; aversion
abschilfern to desquamate, to exfoliate, to scale [off]
abschilfernd desquamative, exfoliative
Abschilferung *f* desquamation, exfoliation, scaling
abschleifen to dermabrade *(z. B. die Haut);* to grind down *(z. B. Zähne)*
abschließen to occlude, to close, to shut *(z. B. eine Öffnung);* to obstruct *(z. B. ein Hohlorgan);* to stop up *(z. B. eine Zahnöffnung);* to close in *(z. B. Zahnflächen);* to bring into occlusion *(z. B. das Gebiß)*
~/**sich** to seclude; to keep aloof, to retire
Abschlußcholangiographie *f* completion cholangiography
abschnallen/eine Prothese to doff a prosthesis
abschneiden *s.* amputieren
Abschnitt *m* 1. segment[um]; 2. phase, stadium
~/**gekrümmter** flexion
abschnüren to ligate *(z. B. Gefäße);* to tie up *(z. B. Extremität);* to strangulate *(z. B. Eingeweidebruch)*
Abschnürung *f* 1. ligation; strangulation; 2. ligation, ligature
Abschnürungslähmung *f* tourniquet paralysis
abschreckend repellent, repellant
Abschreckmittel *n* repellent [agent] *(z. B. gegen Insekten)*
abschuppen to desquamate, to scale [off]
abschuppend desquamative
Abschuppung *f* desquamation
~/**kleieförmige** defurfuration *(bei Masern)*
abschürfen to excoriate, to scrape, to abrade
~/**sich die Haut** to chafe (graze) the skin
Abschürfung *f* excoriation, abrasion, attrition; erosion
abschwächen to weaken, to diminish *(Wirkungen);* to alleviate, to mitigate, to deaden, to moderate *(z. B. Schmerzen);* to attenuate *(z. B. die Virulenz pathogener Keime)*
~/**sich** to decline *(z. B. Körperkräfte)*
Abschwächung *f* weakening; mitigation; attenuation; declining
abschwellen to shrink, to decongest; to detumesce
Abschwellung *f* detumescence, subsidence of swelling *(z. B. der Schwellkörper)*
Absence *f s.* Absentia
Absentia *f* absence
~ **epileptica** absence attack (seizure)

absetzen 1. to sediment, to deposit *(z. B. Substanzen)*; 2. *s.* amputieren
~/Kot (Stuhlgang) to defaecate, to egest, to pass stool
Absetzen *n* sedimentation, deposition
Absetzgeschwindigkeit *f* sedimentation rate
Absetzung *f s.* Amputation
Absiedlung *f s.* Metastase
Absinthvergiftung *f* absinthism
Absolutakkommodation *f* absolute accommodation
absondern to secrete *(z. B. Körpersäfte)*; to exude *(z. B. Flüssigkeit)*; to excrete *(z. B. Stuhlgang)*
~/einen Kranken to isolate
~/Milch to lactate
~/Schweiß to perspire
~/Speichel to salivate
~/Transsudat to transudate
absondernd secretory; excretory; apocrine *(Drüsen)*
~ ins Körperinnere incretory
Absonderung *f* 1. secretion *(Vorgang)*; 2. isolation, sequestration *(von Infektionskranken)*; 3. secretion; excrement, excretion
~ phosphoreszierenden Schweißes phosphor[h]idrosis
~ von Drüsenprodukten excretion
~ von dunkelgefärbtem Schweiß melanephidrosis
~ von Schweiß/gestörte par[h]idrosis, parahidrosis
Absorbat *n* absorbate, absorbed substance
Absorbens *n*, **Absorbentium** *n* absorbent [agent], absorbing substance
absorbierbar absorbable
~/nicht non-absorbable
Absorbierbarkeit *f* absorbability
absorbieren to absorb
absorbierend absorbent, absorbefacient, absorbing
Absorption *f* absorption
~/mangelhafte malabsorption *(aus dem Magen-Darm-Kanal)*
Absorptionsatelektase *f* absorption atelectasis
Absorptionslinse *f* absorption lens
Absorptionsmittel *n s.* Absorbens
Absorptionsoberfläche *f* absorptive surface
Absorptionsspektrum *n* absorption spectrum *(Radiologie)*
abspalten/Amidogruppen to deamidate, to deamidize
~/Aminogruppen to deaminate
~/Kohlendioxid to decarboxylate
~/Methylgruppen to demethylate
~/Wasser to dehydrate
~/Wasserstoff to dehydrogenate, to dehydrogenize
abspreizen to abduct
Abspreizung *f* abduction
Absprengung *f* divulsion
Absprengungsfraktur *f* chip fracture

abstammen to descend, to be descended from
~/aus dem Ektoderm to be ectodermal in origin
abstammend descendent
~/vom Gewebe histogenous
~/von drei Keimblättern tridermic
~/von pluripotentem Gewebe teratogenous
~/von totem Gewebe necrogenic, necrogenous
abstehen to stick out *(Ohren)*
absteigend descending, descendent
absterben 1. to die off; to mortify; to necrotize, to necrose *(z. B. Organe)*; 2. to get numb *(z. B. Körperglied)*
Absterben *n* mortification; necrosis *(z. B. von Organen)*; necrobiosis *(von einzelnen Zellen in einem Gewebeverband)*
absterbend/langsam necrobiotic
Abstieg *m* descent, descensus *(eines Organs)*
Abstilldyspepsie *f* ablactation dyspepsia
abstillen to wean *(Säugling)*
Abstillen *n* weaning, ablactation, delactation
Abstinenz *f* abstinence
Abstinenzdelir[ium] *n* abstinence delirium
Abstinenzerscheinung *f* abstinence phenomenon (symptom)
Abstinenzsyndrom *n* abstinence syndrome
abstoßen to reject *(z. B. körperfremdes Gewebe)*
~/Nekrosen to slough, to cast off necrotic tissue
Abstoßung *f* extrusion, expulsion, repulsion; rejection *(z. B. von Transplantat)*; sequestration *(z. B. des Fetus)*
~ eines demarkierten Organteils sequestration
Abstoßungsreaktion *f* rejection
Abstrich *m* smear *(z. B. aus der Scheide)*; swab *(z. B. der Tonsillen)* ● **einen ~ machen** to take a smear; to take a swab
Abstrichöse *f* platinum loop
Abstrichröhrchen *n* culture (specimen) tube
Abstrichzytologie *f* brush cytology *(zur Zellluntersuchung)*
abstumpfen to stupefy *(z. B. Empfindungen)*
Abstumpfung *f* stupefaction, obtusion
abszedierend abscess-forming
Abszedierung *f* abscess formation, suppuration
Abszeß *m* abscess[us], apostasis, apostema *(s. a. unter Eiteransammlung)*
~ der Bartholinischen Drüsen Bartholinian abscess
~/embolischer embolic abscess
~/epiduraler epidural abscess
~/extraduraler extradural abscess
~/hämorrhagischer haemorrhagic abscess
~/hypostatischer hypostatic abscess
~ im Ligamentum latum uteri broad ligament abscess
~/intrasellärer intrasellar abscess
~/käsiger caseous abscess
~/kleiner microabscess, small abscess
~/lymphatischer lymphatic abscess
~/parametrischer parametric abscess
~/pelviner pelvic abscess
~/perianaler perianal abscess
~/periapikaler periapical abscess

Abszeß

~/**perityphlitischer** perityphlitic abscess, periappendicular (appendix) abscess
~/**pyämischer** pyaemic abscess
~/**retromammärer** retromammary abscess
~/**retrotonsillärer** retrotonsillar abscess
~/**retrovesikaler** retrovesical abscess
~/**subgalealer** subgaleal abscess
Abszeßbildung f abscess formation
Abszeßhöhle f abscess cavity
Abszeßlanzette f abscess lancet
Abszeßmembran f abscess membrane
Abszeßmesser n abscess knife
abtasten 1. to palpate, to touch (mit der Hand); 2. to scan (mit einem Elektronenstrahl)
Abtasten n 1. palpation, dipping, touch (mit der Hand); 2. scanning (mit einem Elektronenstrahl)
abtastend 1. palpatory; 2. scanning
Abteilung f ward (Krankenhaus)
abtragen to amputate, to ablate, te resect, to cut off (away) (z. B. Gliedmaßen); to remove
abtragend amputating, ablative, resecting, cutting off
Abtragung f amputation, ablation, resection, cutting off (von Gliedmaßen) (s. a. unter Amputation)
~ **mit der elektrischen Schlinge** electrodesiccation
~ **nekrotischen Gewebes** escharotomy
abtreiben 1. to expel, to purge off (Würmer); 2. to abort
abtrennen to detach; to ablade; to resect; to separate; to sequester
Abtrennung f sublation; detachment; ablation; resection; abscission; separation; sequestration
Abtropfmetastase f drop metastasis
Abulie f aboulia, aboulomania, abul[e]ia
Abusus m abuse, misuse; wrong use
Abwärtsnystagmus m down-beat nystagmus
Abwärtsschielen n hypotropia
~/**latentes** cataphoria
abwärtsschielend/latent cataphoric
Abwaschzange f dressing (washing) forceps (z. B. vor Operationen)
Abwehr f **gegen Infektionen/natürliche** phylaxis
~/**zelluläre** cellular defence
abwehren/eine Infektion to repel an infection
Abwehrmittel n repellent [agent] (z. B. gegen Insekten)
Abwehrspannung f rebound tenderness
~/**lokale** local tenderness (Bauchdecken)
Abwehrstoff m 1. antitoxin; repellent; 2. antibody, immune body (des Körpers)
abweichend aberrant; heterologous
~/**vom Mittelpunkt** eccentric
~/**von der Regel** abnormal, anomalous
Abweichung f 1. deviation; 2. aberration (Ophthalmologie); 3. atypia (z. B. von Zellen)
~ **nach hinten** retrodeviation
~ **vom Normalen** anomaly
Abweisung f repulsion; refusal

abwendend prophylactic; preven[ta]tive
Abwesenheit f/**geistige** absence
abzapfen to drain (z. B. Eiter); to draw (Blut)
abzehrend consumptive, wasting, tabescent
Abzehrung f 1. consumption, wasting, emaciation, tabefaction, tabes[cence] (Vorgang); 2. cachexia, marasmus (Zustand)
Abziehen n abduction
Abzieher[muskel] m abductor [muscle]
Abzugskanal m emissary
Acanthocephaliasis f acanthocephaliasis (Darminfektion)
Acanthosis f **juvenilis** juvenile acanthosis
Acardi[ac]us m acardiac[us], acardius
Acarus m **scabiei (siro)** Acarus scabiei
Accouchement n accouchement, parturition
ACD-Stabilisatorlösung f ACD solution, anticoagulant acid citrate dextrose solution (zur Blutkonservierung)
Acephalus m **athorus** acephalus athorus, pseudohemiacardius
Acervulus m **[cerebri]** acervulus, brain sand
Acetabulum n s. Azetabulum
Aceton... s. Azeton...
Acetyl... s. Azetyl...
Achalasie f achalasia
Acheilie f ach[e]ilia, absence of the lips
Acheilus m ach[e]ilus
Acheirie f ach[e]iria
Acheirus m ach[e]irus
Achilie f ach[e]ilia
Achillessehne f Achilles (calcaneal) tendon, tendon Achilles
Achillessehnendurchtrennung f[/**operative**] achillotenotomy
Achillessehneninzision f achillotomy
Achillessehnennaht f achillorrhaphy
Achillessehnenreflex m Achilles tendon reflex, Achilles (ankle) jerk, ankle reflex
Achillessehnenriß m achillorrhexis
Achillessehnenschleimbeutel m Achilles bursa
Achillessehnenschmerz m achillodynia
Achillessehnenverletzung f Achilles tendon lesion
Achillessehnenzeichen n Achilles tendon sign
Achillobursitis f achillobursitis, superficial calcaneal bursitis
Achillodynie f achillodynia
Achillorrhaphie f achillorrhaphy
Achillorrhexis f achillorrhexis
Achillotenotomie f achillotenotomy
Achillotomie f achillotomy
Achlorhydria f **gastrica** gastric achlorhydria
Achlorhydrie f achlorhydria; anacidity
achlorhydrisch achlorhydric
Achloroblepsie f, **Achloropsie** f achloro[ble]psia
Achluophobie f achluophobia, nyctophobia (krankhafte Angst vor Dunkelheit)
Acholie f acholia
acholisch acholic
Acholurie f acholuria
acholurisch acholuric

Achondroplasie f achondroplasia, achondroplasty, chondrodystrophy
achondroplastisch achondroplastic
Achorese f achoresis
Achor-Smith-Syndrom n Achor-Smith syndrome, nutritional deficiency with hypokalaemia
Achreozythämie f achreocythaemia, achroiocythaemia, hypochromic anaemia
Achroazytose f achroacytosis
achrom achromic, achromous
Achromasie f 1. achromasia, achromia, achromatosis, achromoderm[i]a *(Haut)*; 2. achromasia, achromia, achromatosis *(Histologie)*
Achromat m achromate
Achromatin n achromatin, linin *(nicht färbbarer Teil des Zellkerngerüsts)*
achromatisch 1. achromatic, rod-monochromatic *(Ophthalmologie)*; 2. colourless, uncoloured, achromatic; non-pigmented
Achromatismus m 1. achromatism *(Ophthalmologie)*; 2. colourlessness, achromatism
Achromatolyse f achromatolysis *(Herauslösen des Achromatins aus der Zelle)*
achromatophil achromatophil
Achromatophiler m achromatophil *(z. B. Mikroorganismus)*
Achromatophilie f achromatophilia
Achromatopsie f achromatopsia, acritochromacy, total colour blindness
Achromatosis f achromatosis *(z. B. bei Albinismus)*
Achromatozyt m achroma[to]cyte
Achromaturie f achromaturia
Achromazyt m achroma[to]cyte
Achromie f achrom[as]ia, achromatosis
Achromoderma n achromoderma
Achromodermie f achromoderma
Achromotrichie f achromotrichia, trichopoliosis, canities, greyness (whiteness) of the hair
Achse f axis, centre line *(s. a. unter Axis)* ● in Richtung der ~ axial ● sich in einer ~ bewegend uniaxial *(Gelenk)*
~/elektrische electrical (QRS) axis *(Herz)*
~/optische optic axis *(gedachte Linie zwischen Horn- und Netzhautmittelpunkt des Auges)*
~/pelvine pelvic axis, axis of the pelvis
Achsel f s. Achselhöhle
Achselabszeß m axillary abscess
Achselarterie f axillary artery
Achselausräumung f axillary nodal removal (Lymphknoten)
Achselbereich m axillary region
Achselfalte f axillary fold (plica)
~/hintere posterior axillary fold (plica)
~/vordere anterior axillary fold (plica)
Achselhaare npl hirci, axillary hair
Achselhöhle f axilla, armpit, axillary fossa, ala
Achselhyperhidrose f axillary hyperhidrosis
Achsellinie f axillary line
Achsellymphknoten m axillary lymph (lymphatic) node, axillary glands
Achsellymphknotenbeteiligung f axillary nodal involvement
Achsellymphknotenentfernung f axillary nodal removal
Achsellymphknotenmetastase f axillary lymph node metastasis
Achselnerv m axillary (circumflex) nerve
Achselschweißbildung f/**vermehrte** axillary hyperhidrosis
Achselvene f axillary vein
Achselvenenstau m/**akuter** Paget-Schroetter's syndrome, effort thrombosis
Achselvenenthrombose f axillary vein thrombosis
Achselvenenverschluß m/**thrombotischer** s. Achselvenenstau/akuter
Achsenabweichung f axis deviation
Achsendrehung f torsion
Achsenfaden m 1. axial fibre *(im Spermium)*; 2. s. Achsenzylinder
achsengerecht 1. axial; 2. synclitic *(Geburtsvorgang)*
~/nicht asynclitic *(Geburtsvorgang)*
Achsenhyperopie f axial hyperopia
Achsenstab m notochord *(Embryologie)*
Achsenstrom m axial stream (current) *(der Blutkörperchen)*
Achsentomogramm n axial tomogram (tomography scan)
Achsenzugzange f axis-traction forceps
Achsenzylinder m axis cylinder [process], axial (nerve) fibre, [neur]axon, neurite
Achsenzylinderentzündung f neuraxitis
Achsenzylinderfortsatz m s. Achsenzylinder
Achsenzylinder[neuro]plasma n axoplasm
Achsenzylinderschwellung f axonal swelling
Achter[touren]verband m figure-of-eight bandage *(Wundverband)*
Achylie f achylia, achylosis
achylisch achylic
achym achymous
Achymie f achymia
Acne f acne *(Hauterkrankung mit Knötchen- und Pustelbildung)*
~ agminata acne agminata, acnitis *(Form der Hauttuberkulose)*
~ disseminata disseminated acne
~ erythematosa s. ~ rosacea
~ hypertrophica hypertrophic acne
~ indurata scleracne
~ pustulosa pustulous acne
~ rosacea rosacea, facial teleangiectasis; brandy face (nose), rosy drop
~ seborrhoeica seborrhoeic acne
~ simplex common acne
~ teleangiectodes [kaposi] disseminated follicular lupus
~ varioliformis varioliform (lupoid) acne
~ vulgaris common acne
Acrodermatitis f **chronica suppurativa, ~ continua** Hallopeau's disease (acrodermatitis), continuous (chronic suppurative) acrodermatitis, pustular psoriasis

ACTH

ACTH s. Adrenokortikotropin
Actinobacillus m **mallei** glanders bacillus
Actinomyces m **israelii** Actinomyces israeli *(Erreger der Strahlenpilzkrankheit)*
ad lib. (libitum) ad lib. (libitum), at pleasure, the amount desired, to any extent
Adair-Dighton-Syndrom n **[der blauen Skleren]** Adair-Dighton syndrome, osteogenesis imperfecta with deafness
Adaktylie f adactyly
Adaktylus m adactyl[us]
Adamantin n adamantine, [dental] enamel
Adamantinokarzinom n adamantinocarcinoma
Adamantinoma n adamantinoma, adamanto[blasto]ma, enameloblastoma
Adamantoblast m adamantoblast, ameloblast, enameloblast, ganoblast
Adamantoblastenfortsatz m ameloblastic (Tomes's) process
Adamantoblastoma n s. Adamantinoma
Adamkiewicz-Probe f Adamkiewicz reaction *(Proteinnachweis)*
Adamsapfel m Adam's apple, laryngeal prominence (protuberance), thyroid eminence
Adamsit n adamsite *(nasen- und rachenreizender Kampfstoff)*
Adams-Stokes-Anfall m Stokes-Adams attack
Adams-Stokes-Syndrom n Stokes-Adams disease (syndrome), Adams-Stokes disease
Adaptation f adaptation
Adaptationsbreite f amplitude of adaptation
Adaptationsbrille f adaptation goggles
Adaptationshypertrophie f adaptive hypertrophy
Adaptationskrankheit f adaptation disease
Adaptationskurve f adaptation curve *(Dunkelanpassung des Auges)*
Adaptationsnaht f coapting suture; coaptation suturing
Adaptationsstörung f dysadaptation *(z. B. der Netzhaut)*
Adaptationssyndrom n/**allgemeines (Selyesches)** Selye's (general) adaptation syndrome
Adaptationsverhalten n adaptive behaviour
Adaptationszeit f adaptation time
adaptieren 1. to adapt; 2. to coapt *(z. B. Knochenbrüche)*
Adaptometer n adaptometer
Adaptometrie f adaptometry *(Bestimmung der Dunkelanpassungsfähigkeit des Auges)*
adde add, adde *(Rezeptur)*
Addis-Harnsediment n s. Addis-Sediment
Addisonismus m addisonism
Addison-Krise f Addisonian (adrenal) crisis, acute adrenal insufficiency
Addison-Syndrom n Addison's disease (syndrome), chronic adrenal insufficiency, adrenal cortical insufficiency
Addis-Sediment n Addis count *(Untersuchung des Harnsediments)*
Adduktion f adduction
Adduktionsmuskel m s. Adduktor

Adduktor m adductor [muscle]
Adduktorenkanal m adductor canal [of Hunter], subsartorial (Hunter's) canal
Adduktorenkanalöffnung f/**untere** adductor hiatus
Adduktorenmuskulatur f adductor musculature
Adduktorenparalyse f adductor paralysis
Adduktorenreflex m adductor reflex
Adduktorenschlitz m adductor hiatus
Adduktorensyndrom n adductor syndrome
Adduktorentuberkulum n adductor tubercle
adduzieren to adduct
adelomorph adelomorphic, adelomorphous *(z. B. Drüsenzellen des Magens)*
Adenalgie f adenalgia, adenodynia
Adenasthenie f adenasthenia, hypoadenia, deficient glandular activity
adendritisch adendritic
Adenektomie f 1. adenectomy, adenotomy; 2. adenoidectomy
Adenektopie f adenectopia, displacement (malposition) of a gland
Adenie f adenia
Adenin n adenine, 6-aminopurine
Adenindesoxyribonukleosid n deoxyadenosine
Adeninnukleotid n adenine nucleotide
Adenitis f adenitis, glandular inflammation, inflammation of a gland
~ **phlegmonosa** phlegmonous adenitis; adenophlegmon
Adenoakanthom n adenoacanthoma, adenocancroid, adenoid squamous cell carcinoma
Adenoameloblastom n adenoameloblastoma
Adenoangiosarkom n adenoangiosarcoma
Adenoblepharitis f adenoblepharitis
Adenochondrom n adenochondroma *(Geschwulst aus Drüsen- und Knorpelgewebe)*
Adenochondrosarkom n adenochondrosarcoma *(Geschwulst aus Drüsen-, Knorpel- und Muskelgewebe)*
Adenocystoma n **lymphomatosum** Warthin's tumour
Adenodynie f adenodynia, adenalgia
Adenofibrom n adenofibroma, fibroadenoma
Adenofibrose f adenofibrosis *(1. Fibrose einer Drüse; 2. fibrozystische Brustkrankheit)*
adenogen adenogenic, adenogenous
Adenogenese f adenogenesis, gland development
Adenohypophyse f adenohypophysis, antehypophysis
adenohypophyseal adenohypophyseal, adenohypophysial
adenoid adenoid, adenose
Adenoide npl adenoids *(lymphatisches Gewebe im Nasenrachen)*
Adenoidenentfernung f[/**operative**] adenoidectomy, adenotomy
Adenoidgesicht n adenoid facies
Adenoiditis f adenoiditis, inflammation of the adenoids
Adenoidmesser n adenoid curette

Adenokankroid n s. Adenoakanthom
adenokarzinoid adenocarcinoid
Adenokarzinom n adenocarcinoma, glandular carcinoma
adenokarzinomartig, adenokarzinomatös adenocarcinomatous
Adenokystom n adenocystoma, cystadenoma
Adenoleiomyofibrom n adenoleiomyofibroma
Adenoleiomyom n s. Adenomyom
Adenolipom n adenolipoma
Adenolymphom n adenolymphoma
Adenolymphozele f adenolymphocele
Adenom n adenoma (s. a. unter Adenoma)
~/**basophiles** basophilic adenoma, basophilic tumour of the pituitary
~/**bösartiges** malignant adenoma
~/**chromophobes** chromophobe adenoma [of the anterior lobe], chromophobe tumour
~ **der Brunnerschen Drüsen** Brunner's gland adenoma
~ **der Meibomschen Drüse** Meibomian adenoma
~/**eosinophiles** eosinophilic adenoma
~/**schleimiges** myx[o]adenoma
Adenoma n adenoma (s. a. unter Adenom)
~ **macrofolliculare** macrofollicular adenoma
~ **malignum** malignant adenoma
~ **mammae** mastadenoma
~ **microfolliculare** microfollicular adenoma
~ **sebaceum** Pringle's adenoma sebaceum, sebaceous naevus
~ **sudoriparum** sudoriparous (sweat gland) adenoma
adenomähnlich adenomatoid, adenomatous
Adenomalazie f adenomalacia, softening of a gland
Adenomanhäufung f s. Adenomatose
adenomartig adenomatous, adenomatoid
Adenomatoidtumor m adenomatoid tumour
adenomatös s. adenomartig
Adenomatose f adenomatosis
~/**endokrine** endocrine adenomatosis
Adenomektomie f adenomectomy
Adenomyohyperplasie f adenomyohyperplasia
Adenomyom n adeno[leio]myoma (Geschwulst aus Muskulatur und Epithel des weiblichen Genitals)
Adenomyomatose f adenomyomatosis (Ausbreitung eines Adenomyoms auf Nachbargewebe)
Adenomyometritis f adenomyometritis
Adenomyosalpingitis f adenomyosalpingitis, endosalpingiosis, isthmic nodular salpingitis, adenomyosis of the Fallopian tube
Adenomyosarkom n adenomyosarcoma (bösartiger embryonaler Tumor)
Adenomyosis f adenomyosis (Geschwulst aus Endometrium und Muskulatur des weiblichen Genitals)
Adenomyositis f adenomyositis (entzündliche Gebärmuttervergrößerung)
Adenomyxochondrosarkom n adenomyxochondrosarcoma
Adenomyxom n adenomyxoma

Adenomyxosarkom n adenomyxosarcoma
adenoneural adenoneural
Adenopathie f adenopathy, glandular disease
~/**inguinale** inguinal adenopathy
Adenopharyngitis f adenopharyngitis, pharyngotonsillitis
Adenophlegmone f adenophlegmon, phlegmonous adenitis
Adenophthalmie f adenophthalmia
Adenosalpingitis f adenosalpingitis
Adenosarkom n adenosarcoma, glandular sarcoma
Adenosarkorhabdomyom n adenosarcorhabdomyoma
Adenose f adenosis
Adenosin n adenosine, adenine riboside
Adenosindiphosphatase f adenosine diphosphatase (Enzym)
Adenosindiphosphorsäure f adenosine diphosphate, ADP, adenosinediphosphoric acid
Adenosinmonophosphat n s. Adenosinmonophosphorsäure
~/**zyklisches** cyclic adenosine monophosphate, cAMP
Adenosinmonophosphatase f adenosine monophosphatase, AMPase
Adenosinmonophosphorsäure f adenosine monophosphate, AMP, adenosine monophosphoric acid, adenylic acid, AA
Adenosin-5'-monophosphorsäure f adenosine 5'-monophosphate, AMP, adenosine 5'-phosphoric acid, adenylic acid
Adenosin-3-phosphatase f adenosine-3-phosphatase (Enzym)
Adenosintriphosphat n s. Adenosintriphosphosäure
Adenosintriphosphatase f adenosine triphosphatase, ATPase, adenylpyrophosphatase (Enzym)
Adenosintriphosphorsäure f adenosine triphosphate, ATP, adenosinetriphosphoric acid, adenyl pyrophosphoric acid
Adenosis f adenosis
Adenosklerose f adenosclerosis, hardening of a gland
Adenotom n adenotome
Adenotomie f adenotomy
adenotonsillär adenotonsillar
Adenotonsillektomie f adenotonsillectomy
Adenovirus n adenovirus, APC virus
Adenoviruspharyngitis f adenoviral pharyngitis
Adenozele f adenocele (zystischer Drüsentumor)
Adenozellulitis f adenocellulitis
adenozystisch adenocystic
Adenozystosarkom n adenocystosarcoma
Adenylpyrophosphorsäure f s. Adenosintriphosphorsäure
Adenylzyklase f adenyl cyclase (Enzym)
Adephagie f adephagia, boulimia
Adeps m(f) adeps
~ **lanae** wool fat (Dermatologie)

Ader

Ader f 1. [blood] vessel; 2. vein *(Zusammensetzungen s. unter Vena)*; 3. artery *(Zusammensetzungen s. unter Arteria)* ● **zur ~ lassen** to bleed, to venesect
Äderchen n small blood vessel; veinlet, veinule
Aderfigur f/**Purkinjesche** Purkinje image
Adergeflecht n 1. plexus; 2. choroid plexus [of the brain]
~ **der dritten Hirnkammer** choroid plexus of the third ventricle
~ **der seitlichen Hirnkammer** choroid plexus of the lateral ventricle
~ **der vierten Hirnkammer** choroid plexus of the fourth ventricle
Adergeflechtarterie f anterior choroid artery
adergeflechtartig plexiform
Adergeflechtentfernung f[/**operative**] choroid plexectomy
Adergeflechtpapillom n choroid papilloma
Aderhaut f choroid, chorioid[ea], choroid coat (membrane) ● **über der ~** suprachoroid[al] ● **unter der ~** subchoroid[al]
Aderhaut... *s. a.* Chorioidea...
Aderhautablösung f choroid detachment, detachment of the choroid
Aderhautanschwellung f choroid oedema
Aderhautatrophie f choroid atrophy, choroideremia
Aderhautblutung f choroid haemorrhage
Aderhautdegeneration f choroid degeneration
Aderhautdurchblutung f choroid blood flow
Aderhauteinblutung f choroid haemorrhage
Aderhautentzündung f choroiditis *(Zusammensetzungen s. unter Chorioiditis)*
Aderhautgefäß n choroid blood vessel
Aderhautgefäßanordnung f choroid vasculature
Aderhautgefäßtumor m choroid angioma
Aderhautgefäßversorgung f choroid vascularization
Aderhautgranulom n choroid granuloma
Aderhautinfarkt m choroid infarction
Aderhautkapillare f choroid capillary
Aderhautkapillarschicht f choroid capillary layer
Aderhautkolobom n choroid coloboma
Aderhautkonus m choroid crescent
Aderhautkrebs m choroid cancer
Aderhautnekrose f choroid necrosis
Aderhautneurilemmom n choroid neurilemmoma
Aderhautschwellung f choroid oedema
Aderhautschwund m choroideremia
Aderhautsklerose f choroid sclerosis
Aderhautspalte f coloboma, choroid fissure
Aderhauttumor m choroid tumour (angioma)
Aderhaut- und Irisentzündung f choroidoiritis
Aderhaut- und Netzhautentzündung f choroidoretinitis, retinochoroiditis
Aderhaut- und Ziliarfortsatzentzündung f choroidocyclitis
Aderhautzerreißung f choroid rupture
Aderlaß m bleeding, blood-letting, venesection, phlebotomy ● **einen ~ durchführen** to bleed, to venesect

~/**unblutiger** bloodless phlebotomy, phlebostasis
Adermin n adermin[e], pyridoxine, vitamin B_6
Adermogenese f adermogenesis
Adernegel m schistosome
Adernegelbefall m/**Ägyptischer** Egyptian splenomegaly *(durch Schistosoma mansoni) (s. a. unter Schistosomiasis)*
Adernegellarve f cercarian
Aderpresse f tourniquet
aderreich venose
ADH s. 1. Alkoholdehydrogenase; 2. Hormon/antidiuretisches
Adhaesio f **interthalamica** intermediate massa, interthalamic (soft, middle) commissure
adhärent adherent
Adhäsion f adhesion ● **Adhäsionen durchtrennen** to cut (sever) adhesions ● **Adhäsionen lösen** to loosen adhesions, to detach (free) adhesions
Adhäsionsileus m adhesion ileus
Adhäsionsphänomen n adhesion phenomenon
Adhäsiotomie f adhesiotomy *(Lösung oder Durchtrennung von Verwachsungen)*
Adhäsivprozeß m adhesive process *(z. B. in der Mittelohrschleimhaut)*
ADH-Test m, **ADH-Verfahren** n alcohol dehydrogenase test *(enzymatische Blutalkoholbestimmung)*
adiabetisch adiabetic
Adiadochokinese f adiadochokinesis *(Unfähigkeit zu schnellen entgegengesetzten Bewegungen)*
Adiaphorese f adiaphoresis
adiaphoretisch adiaphoretic, reducing (checking, preventing) perspiration
Adiastole f adiastole
adiatherm adiathermic, impervious to radiant heat
adiathetisch adiathetic
Adie-Syndrom n Adie's syndrome, Adie's [tonic] pupil, pseudo Argyll-Robertson pupil
Adipektomie f adipectomy
Adipocire f adipocere, lipocere
Adipokinese f adipokinesis
adipokinetisch adipokinetic
Adipom n adipoma, lipoma, pimeloma, steatoma
Adiponecrosis f **subcutanea neonatorum** subcutaneous necrosis of the newborn, subcutaneous fat necrosis
Adiponekrose f adiponecrosis
adipös adipose, obese, fat[ty], liparous
Adiposis f **hepatica** fatty degeneration of the liver
~ **orchalis** s. Adipositas hypogenitalis
~ **tuberosa simplex** Anders' disease
Adipositas f 1. adiposity, obesity, adiposis, fatness; corpulence; 2. adiposis, fatty infiltration *(z. B. der Leber)*
~ **corneae** corneal adiposis
~ **dolorosa** Dercum's disease, adiposis (neurolipomatosis) dolorosa
~ **hypogenitalis** adiposogenital dystrophy (syn-

drome), Froehlich's syndrome, Babinski-Froehlich disease
~/**hypothalamische** hypothalamic obesity
Adipositis f adipositis, panniculitis
Adiposurie f adiposuria, lipuria, pimeluria
Adipozele f adipocele, lipocele
adipozellulär adipocellular
Adipozyt m adipocyte, lipocyte, adipose (fat) cell (im Fettbindegewebe)
Adipozytendifferenzierung f adipocyte differentiation
Adipsie f adipsia, aposia
Aditus m aditus, entrance, inlet, opening, passage for entrance, iter
~ **ad antrum [mastoideum]** entrance to the mastoid antrum
~ **glottidis inferior** inferior entrance to the glottis
~ **glottidis superior** superior entrance to the glottis
~ **laryngis** laryngeal inlet, inlet of the larynx, entrance to the larynx
~ **orbitae** orbital opening
Adiuretin n vasopressin, antidiuretic hormone
Adjuvans n adjuvant, adjunct (Pharmazie)
Adjuvans-Arthritis f adjuvant arthritis
Adlernase f aquiline nose
Adnexe mpl 1. adnexa, annexa, appendages; 2. [uterine] adnexa, uterine appendages
Adnexeanheftung f adnexopexy
Adnexeentfernung f[/operative] adnexectomy
Adnexeentzündung f adnexitis
Adnexefixierung f adnexopexy
Adnexektomie f adnexectomy .
Adnexitis f adnexitis, inflammation of the adnexa uteri
Adnexopathie f adnexopathy, adnexal disease
Adnexopexie f adnexopexy
Adoleszentenalbuminurie f adolescent albuminuria
Adoleszentendepression f adolescent depression
Adoleszentenkrise f adolescent crisis
Adoleszentenkyphose f adolescent kyphosis
Adoleszentenskoliose f adolescent scoliosis
Adoleszentenstruma f adolescent goitre
Adoleszenz f adolescence, youth [period] (zwischen Pubertät und Reife)
Adontie f adontia, toothlessness
adoptieren to adopt, to affiliate
Adoption f adoption, affiliation
adoral adoral, near the mouth; toward the mouth
adorbital adorbital, near the orbit; toward the orbit
ADP s. Adenosindiphosphorsäure
adrenal adrenal, suprarenal
Adrenaldrüse f adrenal [gland]
Adrenalektomie f adrenalectomy, epinephrectomy, suprarenalectomy
adrenalektomieren to adrenalectomize
Adrenalin n adrenalin[e], suprarenin, epinephrine; sympathetic hormone
Adrenalinämie f adrenalinaemia, epinephrinaemia

Adrenalinausscheidung f im Urin adrenalinuria
adrenalinbedingt adrenergic
Adrenalinbildung f adrenalinogenesis
adrenalineffektauslösend adrenergic
adrenalineffekthemmend adrenolytic
Adrenalinmangel m s. Adrenalinspiegelverminderung
Adrenalinspiegelerhöhung f [im Blut] hyperadrenal[in]aemia, suprarenalaemia
Adrenalinspiegelverminderung f [im Blut] hypoadrenal[in]aemia
Adrenalintest m adrenaline test
Adrenalismus m adrenalism, suprarenalism
Adrenalitis f adren[al]itis, epinephritis, inflammation of the adrenal glands
Adrenalopathie f adren[al]opathy
adrenalotrop adrenalotropic
Adrenalsystem n adrenal (chromaffin) system
Adrenarche f adrenarche
adrenerg[isch] adrenergic, adrenomimetic
Adrenochrom n adrenochrome (Oxydationsprodukt des Adrenalins)
adrenogen adrenogenous
adrenogenital adrenogenital
Adrenogramm n adrenogram
Adrenographie f adrenography
adrenokortikal adrenocortical, adrenal cortical, adrenocorticoid
Adrenokortikoid n adrenocorticoid
adrenokortikolytisch adrenocorticolytic
adrenokortikomimetisch adrenocorticomimetic
adrenokortikotrop adrenocorticotrop[h]ic, adrenotrop[h]ic
Adrenokortikotropin n adrenocorticotrop[h]in, adrenotrop[h]in, adrenocorticotrophic hormone, ACTH, corticotrop[h]in
Adrenolytikum n adrenolytic agent (blocker, blocking agent)
adrenolytisch adrenolytic
adrenomedullär adrenomedullary
adrenomimetisch adrenomimetic, adrenergic, sympathomimetic
Adrenopause f adrenopause
adrenopriv adrenoprival
Adrenosteron n adrenosterone (androgenes Hormon)
adrenosympathisch adrenosympathetic
adrenotrop s. adrenokortikotrop
Adrenotrophin n s. Adrenokortikotropin
Adson-Syndrom n Naffziger's (scalenus anterior) syndrome
Adsorbat n adsorbate, adsorbed substance
Adsorbens n, **Adsorbentium** n adsorbent [agent], adsorbing substance
adsorbierbar adsorbable
~/**nicht** non-adsorbable
Adsorbierbarkeit f adsorbability
adsorbieren to adsorb
adsorbierend adsorbent, adsorptive, adsorbing
Adsorption f adsorption
~/**immunologische** immunoadsorption

Adsorption

~ **von Viren** attachment
Adsorptionschromatographie f adsorption chromatography
adsorptionsfähig adsorbable
Adsorptionsfähigkeit f adsorptive power (capacity)
Adsorptionsmittel n s. Adsorbens
adsorptiv adsorptive
adsternal adsternal, near the sternum; toward the sternum
Adstringens n, **Adstringentium** n remedium astringent [agent]
Adstringenz f astringency, astringent power
adstringieren to astringe
adstringierend astringent
Adtorsion f adtorsion *(Schielstellung beider Augen in Richtung Nase)*
Adultizid n adulticide
Adultparasitismus m adult parasitism
Adventitia f [tunica] adventitia
~ **degeneration** adventitial degeneration
Adventitiaentzündung f adventitial inflammation, exarteritis
Adventitiahülle f adventitial coat
adventitial adventitial
Adventitialzelle f adventitial cell
Adventitiascheide f adventitial sheath *(z. B. einer Arterie)*
adventitiell adventitial
Adversivanfall m adversive seizure *(bei Epilepsie)*
Adversivfeld n adversive field
Adynamie f adynamia, lack of vital strength; loss of muscular power; asthenia; debility; weakness
adynamisch adynamic
AE, A. E. s. Antitoxin-Einheit
Aëdes f **aegypti** Aëdes [aegypti] *(Gelbfieberüberträger)*
Aëdesmücke f yellow-fever mosquito
Aequator m **bulbi** [oculi] aequator of the eye [ball]
~ **lentis** aequator of the lens
Aerämie f aeraemia *(z. B. bei Taucherkrankheit)*
Aerasthenie f aerasthenia *(Nervenschwäche bei Piloten)*
Aeroatelektase f aeroatelectasis *(bei reiner Sauerstoffatmung in großen Höhen)*
aerob aerobic, aerobiotic, aerophil[e]
~/**obligat** obligately aerobic
Aerobier m aerobe
Aerobierkultur f aerobe culture
Aerobilie f aerobilia, aerocholia
Aerobiologie f aerobiology
Aerobiont m aerobe
Aerobiose f aerobiosis
aerobiotisch aerobiotic
Aerocholie f aerocholia, aerobilia
Aerodontalgie f aerodontalgia
Aeroembolie f aeroembolism *(durch Druckabfall oder -erhöhung)*
Aeroemphysem n aeroemphysema *(bei Fliegern)*
Aerogastrie f aerogastria

aerogen 1. aerogenic, aerogenous, gas-producing, forming gas; 2. air-borne *(z. B. Krankheitserreger)*
Aerogramm n aerogram
Aerographie f aerography
aerographisch aerographic
Aerohydrotherapie f aerohydrotherapy
Aeroionotherapie f aeroionotherapy
Aerokolie f aerocoly, colon meteorism
Aerokolpos m aerocolpos
Aeromedizin f aeromedicine, aviation (air) medicine
Aeroneurosis f aeroneurosis, air pilot's disease
Aeropathie f aeropathy *(Krankheitszustand infolge Luftdruckänderung)*
Aerophagie f aerophagy, air swallowing
aerophil aerophil[e], aerophilic, aerophilous
Aerophobie f aerophobia *(krankhafte Angst vor Luft)*
Aeroplethysmograph m aeroplethysmograph
Aerosialophagie f aerosialophagy
Aerosinusitis f aerosinusitis, barosinusitis
Aerosolapplikation f aerosol administration
Aerosolgerät n atomizer, hydroconion
Aerosolspray m(n) aerosol spray
Aerosoltherapie f aerosol therapy
Aerotaxis f aerotaxis *(Induktion von Bakterienbewegungen durch Luft)*
Aerotherapie f aerotherapy, aerotherapeutics
Aerothermotherapie f aerothermotherapy, treatment with heated air
Aerotitis f aerotitis, barotitis
~ **media** aerotitis (barotitis) media, otic barotrauma
Aerotonometer n aerotonometer
Aerotonometrie f aerotonometry *(Bestimmung der Blutgaspartialdrucke)*
aerotrop aerotropic
Aerotropismus m aerotropism *(Anziehung von aeroben Bakterien durch Luft)*
aerotympanal aerotympanal
Aerourethroskop n aerourethroscope
Aerourethroskopie f aerourethroscopy
Aerozele f aerocele
Aerozystoskop n aerocystoscope
Aerozystoskopie f aerocystoscopy *(zur Aufdehnung)*
Aether m **pro narcosi** anaesthetic ether
afebril afebrile, feverless, without fever
afetal afoetal, without a foetus
Affekt m affect[ion], emotion, passion ● **im** ~ under the urge of passion, in the heat of passion
Affektabbau m, **Affektabstumpfung** f blunted affect
Affektamenorrhoe f emotional amenorrhoea
Affektausbruch m affective crisis (explosion)
affektbedingt affective; catathymic
affektbetont affective, emotional
Affektdepression f affective (reactive) depression
Affektentzugssyndrom n anaclytic depression
Affektepilepsie f affective (reactive) epilepsy

affektgebunden emotional, affective, reactive
affektgemindert hypoaffective
affektgeneigt hyperthymic
affektgesteigert hyperaffective
Affekthandlung f affective (emotional) act
~/isolierte monomania, monopsychosis
Affektinkontinenz f affective (emotional) incontinence
Affektion f 1. s. Affekt; 2. affection; lesion (krankhafter Zustand)
~ der Hautlymphgefäße lymphodermia
affektiv affective
Affektivität f 1. affectivity, emotionality; 2. affectivity, susceptibility to emotional stimuli
Affektkrampf m affective (emotional) spasm
Affektlabilität f affective instability
Affektlosigkeit f apathy
Affektminderung f hypoaffectivity
Affektneigung f/**gesteigerte** hyperthymia
Affektpsychose f affective (emotional) insanity, affective[-reaction] psychosis, reactive psychosis
Affektreaktion f affective reaction
Affektreflex m affective reflex
Affektschizophrenie f affective (reactive) schizophrenia
Affektschock m s. Affektstupor
Affektstau m affective (emotional) block
Affektsteigerung f hyperaffectivity
Affektstörung f affective disorder, emotional disturbance
Affektstupor m affective (emotional) stupor
Affektsyndrom n affective syndrome
Affektverödung f blunted affect
Affektzustand m affective condition
Affenfurche f simian crease, four-finger line
Affenhand f ape (monkey, simian) hand (bei Medianusnervenlähmung)
Affenkopf m cebocephalus
affenköpfig cebocephalic, cebocephalous
Affenköpfigkeit f cebocephalia
Affenpocken pl monkey (simian) pox
Affenspalte f simian cleft (Störung der Hirnentwicklung)
afferent afferent
Afferentopathie f afferent loop syndrome
Afferenz f/**sensorische** sensory afference
Afferenzsynthese f afference synthesis
Affinität f affinity, avidity (z. B. in Antigen-Antikörper-Bindungen)
Affinitätschromatographie f affinity chromatography
affizieren to affect, to infect
affiziert affected (infected) with
Afflux m afflux[ion] (Zufluß)
Afibrinogenämie f afibrinogenaemia, factor I deficiency [syndrome]
Aflatoxikose f aflatoxicosis
Aflatoxin n aflatoxin (Mykotoxin von Aspergillus flavus)
After m anus, anal orifice (s. a. unter Anus) ● **durch den ~** per anum, by the anus

~/faltenloser infundibuliform anus
~/fehlender proctatresia
~/künstlicher artificial (praeternatural) anus, enteroproctia
After... s. a. Anal... und Anus...
Afterbucht f proctodaeum, anal pit
After-Damm-Plastik f proctoperineoplasty
Afterdehner m procteurynter, anal dilator
Afterdivertikel n anal diverticulum
Afterentzündung f proctitis, anusitis
Aftererweiterung f proctectasia, anal ectasia
Afterfurche f glutaeal furrow, anal cleft
Afterheber m levator ani [muscle]
Afterjucken n, **Afterjuckreiz** m anal pruritus
Afterkrampf m proctospasm, anal spasm
afterlos aproctous
Aftermuskel m anal sphincter, sphincter ani [muscle]
Afterplastik f anoplasty
Afterreflex m anal reflex
Afterschleimhaut f anal mucosa (skin)
Afterschleimhautfalte f[/quere] anal valve
Afterschließmuskel m anal sphincter, sphincter ani [muscle] ● **über dem ~** supralevator
~/äußerer external anal sphincter [muscle], sphincter ani externus [muscle]
~/innerer internal anal sphincter [muscle], sphincter ani internus [muscle]
Afterschließmuskelfunktion f anal sphincteric function
Afterschließmuskelspiegel m anal sphincteroscope
Afterschließmuskelspiegelung f anal sphincteroscopy
Afterschmerz m proctalgia, proctodynia, sphincteralgia
~/plötzlicher proctagra
Afterschrunde f anal fissure, fissure of the anus
Afterspiegel m anoscope, anuscope
Afterspiegelung f anoscopy
After- und Dammnaht f proctoperineorrhaphy
After- und Dammrekonstruktion f proctoperineoplasty
After- und Rektumrekonstruktion f proctoplasty
Afterverengung f anal stenosis
Afterverschluß m/**angeborener** s. Analatresie
Aftervorfall m anal prolapse
Agalaktie f agalactia, agalaxy, agalaxia, non-secretion of milk
agalaktisch agalactous
A-Galle f A bile (Galle aus dem Gallengang)
Agalorrhoe f agalorrhoea, cessation of the milk flow
Agamet m agamete
agamisch agamous, agamic, asexual, sexless
Agammaglobulinämie f agammaglobulinaemia
~/alymphozytäre (lymphopenische) [autosomal recessive] alymphocytic agammaglobulinaemia, Swiss type agammaglobulinaemia, alymphocytosis
agammaglobulinämisch agammaglobulinaemic
Agamogonie f agamo[cyto]gony, agamogenesis, asexual reproduction

Agamospermie

Agamospermie f agamospermia
aganglionär aganglionic
Aganglionose f aganglionosis
~/kongenitale congenital aganglionosis, Hirschsprung's disease
Agar[-Agar] m (n) agar[-agar] (Bakteriennährboden)
Agardilutionsmethode f agar dilution method
Agargeldiffusionstest m agar gel diffusion test
Agargelelektrophorese f agar gel electrophoresis
Agarplatte f agar plate
Agarsäule f agar column
Agastrie f agastria
agastrisch agastric, without alimentary canal
Agenesie f agenesis, agenesia, failure of development
agenetisch agenetic
Ageniozephalie f ageniocephalia (milde Form der Otozephalie)
Ageniozephalus m ageniocephalus (Mißgeburt)
Agenitalismus m agenitalism (mit Sexualhormonausfällen)
Agenosomie f agenosomia (Fehlentwicklung der Genitalien)
Ageusie f ageusia, taste blindness, loss (impairment) of the sense of taste
~/zentrale central ageusia
Agglomerat n agglomerate
Agglomeration f agglomeration, conglomeration
agglomerieren to agglomerate, to cluster
Agglugen n s. Agglutinogen
Agglutinat n agglutinate
Agglutination f agglutination; clumping ● ~ bewirkend haemagglutinative
Agglutinationsbeobachtungsgerät n agglutinoscope
agglutinationsfreundlich agglutinophilic
agglutinationshemmend anti-agglutinating, anti-agglutinant
Agglutinationshemmungsreaktion f agglutination inhibiting reaction
Agglutinationsphänomen n agglutination phenomenon
Agglutinationsreaktion f agglutination reaction
Agglutinationstest m agglutination test
agglutinierbar agglutinable
~/nicht inagglutinable
Agglutinierbarkeit f agglutinability
agglutinieren to agglutinate, to fuse, to cohere, to adhere; to aggregate, to form clumps
~/Erythrozyten to agglutinate erythrocytes
agglutinierend agglutinative, agglutinating, agglutinant; haemagglutinative
~/leicht (sofort) agglutinophilic
Agglutinin n agglutinin (Blutantikörper)
agglutininbildend agglutinogenic
agglutininfrei agglutinin-free
agglutinogen agglutinogenic
Agglutinogen n agglutinogen (Blutantigen zur spezifischen Antikörperbildung)
Agglutinogramm n agglutinogram

Agglutinoid n agglutinoid (inkompletter Antikörper)
agglutinophil agglutinophilic
agglutinophor agglutinophoric
Agglutinoskop n agglutinoscope
Aggravation f aggravation, exacerbation, augmentation (z. B. von Symptomen)
Aggravationstest m aggravation test
aggravieren to aggravate
Aggregat n aggregate
~/heterologes heterologous aggregate
~/heterotypisches heterotypic aggregate
~/homologes homologous aggregate
~/homotypisches homotypic aggregate
Aggregation f aggregation
Aggregationshemmer m aggregation inhibitor
Aggressin n aggressin
Aggressinbildner m, **Aggressinogen** n aggressinogen
Aggression f aggression
Aggressionsdelikt n aggressive delict (crime)
Aggressionshandlung f aggressive act
Aggressionstrieb m aggressive instinct
aggressiv aggressive
Aggressivität f aggressivity, aggressiveness (z. B. eines Parasiten)
Agitatio[n] f agitation
agitieren to agitate
agitiert agitated, excited
Agitographie f agitography (schnelles und fehlerhaftes Schreiben)
Agitolalie f, **Agitophasie** f agitolalia, agitophasia (schnelles und fehlerhaftes Sprechen)
aglandulär aglandular, eglandular
aglomerulär aglomerular, without glomeruli (Niere)
Aglossie f aglossia, absence of the tongue
Aglossus m aglossus (Mißgeburt)
Aglukon n aglycon[e]
Aglukosurie f aglycosuria, absence of sugar in the urine
aglukosurisch aglycosuric, without urinary sugar; free from glycosuria
Aglutition f aglutition, inability to swallow; difficulty in swallowing
Aglykämie f aglycaemia
aglykämisch aglycaemic
Aglykon n aglycon[e]
agnath agnathous
Agnathie f agnathia, absence of the yaws
Agnathozephalie f agnathocephalia (Form der Otozephalie)
Agnathozephalus m agnathocephalus (Mißgeburt)
Agnathus m agnathus
Agnosie f agnosia
~/akustische acoustic agnosia, mind deafness
~/optische visual agnosia, mind (psychic) blindness, psychanopsia
~/physiognomische prosopagnosia
~/räumliche [visual-]spatial agnosia
~/taktile tactile agnosia, astereocognosy, astereognosis, stereoagnosis; stereoanaesthesia

agnostisch agnostic
Agomphiasis f agomphiasis, agomphosis *(1. Zahnlockerung; 2. Fehlen von Zähnen)*
Agon n agon, prosthetic group *(nichteiweißartiger Proteidbestandteil)*
agonadal agonadal
Agonadismus m agonadism, gonadal aplasia
agonal agonal
Agonie f agony, death struggle
Agonist m agonist, agonistic muscle
Agoraphobie f agoraphobia *(krankhafte Angst vor offenen Plätzen)*
Agrammaphasie f s. Agrammatismus
Agrammatismus m agrammaphasia, agrammatism *(ungrammatische Ausdrucksweise)*
~/partieller dysgrammatism
agranulär agranular
agranuloplastisch agranuloplastic
Agranulozyt m agranulocyte, non-granular leucocyte
agranulozytär agranulocytic
Agranulozytenangina f agranulocytic angina
Agranulozytose f agranulo[cyto]sis, agranulocythaemia, malignant (pernicious) leucopenia *(z. B. durch Medikamentenwirkung)*
Agraphie f agraphia, logagraphia, inability to write
~/absolute absolute agraphia
~/akustische acoustic agraphia
~/amnestische amnemonic agraphia
~/ataktische atactic (absolute) agraphia
~/motorische motor agraphia
~/musikalische musical agraphia
~/optische optical agraphia
~/sensorische sensory agraphia
~/verbale verbal agraphia
~/zerebrale cerebral (mental) agraphia
agraphisch agraphic
Agromanie f agromania
Agrypnie f agrypnia, ahypnosis, ahypnia, insomnia, sleeplessness, [abnormal] wakefulness
AGS s. Syndrom/adrenogenitales
Agyrie f agyria, absence of cerebral convulsions
Ahämopexinämie f ahaemopexinaemia
Ahaptoglobulinämie f ahaptoglobulinaemia
AHG s. Globulin/antihämophiles
Ahlfeld-Wiederbelebung f Ahlfeld's resuscitation *(des Neugeborenen)*
Ahnenmerkmal n/wiederauftretendes atavism
Ahornrindenkrankheit f maple bark [stripper's] disease, Towey disease
Ahornsirupkrankheit f maple syrup [urine] disease, branched-chain ketoaciduria (oxoacid aciduria), intermittent branched-chain ketonuria
Ährenverband m spica [bandage]
AIDS AIDS *(Kurzwort für: a*cquired *i*mmuno-*d*eficiency *s*yndrome*)*
Ainhum n ainhum *(Tropenkrankheit mit spontaner Abschnürung von Zehen und Fingern)*
Air-Block-Methode f air block technique *(bei Krampfaderverödung)*

Ajmalin n ajmaline *(Alkaloid)*
Akalkulie f acalculia *(bei aphasischem Symptomenkomplex)*
Akalzinose f acalcinosis
Akanthästhesie f acanthaesthesia
Akanthoameloblastom n acanthoameloblastoma
Akanthocheilonema-perstans-Befall m acanthocheilonemiasis, dipetalonemiasis
Akanthokeratodermie f acanthokeratodermia
Akanthokeratom n s. Keratoakanthom
Akantholyse f acantholysis
akantholytisch acantholytic
Akanthom n acanthoma
Akanthopelvis n acanthopelvis, spinous pelvis
Akanthorrhexis f acanthorrhexis
Akanthose f acanthosis
~/juvenile juvenile acanthosis
akanthotisch acanthotic
Akanthozyt m acanth[r]ocyte
Akanthozytose f acanth[r]ocytosis
Akapnie f acapnia, absence of carbon dioxide [in the blood]
akapsulär acapsular
akardial acardiac
Akardie f acardia, absence of the heart
Akardier m acardiac[us], acardius
Akardiohämie f acardiohaemia, lack of blood in the heart
Akardiotrophie f acardiotrophia, atrophy of the heart
Akari[di]asis f, **Akarinose** f acariasis, acari[n]osis
akarizid acaricide, acarotoxic, miticidal
Akarizid n acaricide [agent], miticide
Akarodermatitis f acarodermatitis
Akarophobie f acarophobia *(krankhafte Angst vor Milbenbefall)*
akarotoxisch acarotoxic, poisonous to acarids
akaryot acaryote
Akatalasämie f acatalasaemia, catalase deficiency in the blood
Akatalasie f acatalasia
Akatalepsie f acatalepsia *(1. Unfähigkeit, etwas zu verstehen; 2. Ungewißheit einer Diagnose)*
akataleptisch acataleptic
Akatamathesie f acatamathesia, inability to understand conversation
Akataphasie f acataphasia, inability to construct sentences
Akathexie f acathexia, inability to retain bodily secretions
Akathisie f acathisia, inability to sit down
akaudal acaudal, acaudate
Akeratose f akeratosis, absence of horny tissue *(z. B. der Nägel)*
AKG s. Apexkardiogramm
Akinese f akinesia, immobility
~/zerebrale cerebral akinesia
akinetisch akinesic, akinetic
Akinospermie f akinospermia
Akklimatisation f acclimatization

akklimatisieren

akklimatisieren to acclimatize
~/sich to become acclimatized
Akkommodation f accommodation, adaptation (adjustment) of an organ
Akkommodationsamplitude f accommodation amplitude, amplitude (range) of accommodation
Akkommodationsastigmatismus m accommodative astigmatism
Akkommodationsbereich m, **Akkommodationsbreite** f s. Akkommodationsamplitude
Akkommodationsermüdung f accommodative fatigue
Akkommodationsfähigkeit f accommodative capacity
Akkommodationshemmung f accommodation impairment
Akkommodationskonvergenz f accommodation convergence
Akkommodationskrampf m accommodative spasm, spasm of accommodation
Akkommodationslähmung f accommodative paralysis, paralysis of accommodation
Akkommodationsmangel m accomodative failure
Akkommodationsmechanismus m accommodation mechanism
Akkommodationsmuskel m accommodation muscle
Akkommodationsphosphen n accommodation phosphene
Akkommodationsprüfung f accommodation test
Akkommodationsquotient m accommodation quotient
Akkommodationsreflex m accommodation (near) reflex
Akkommodationsschielen n accommodative squint (strabismus)
Akkommodationsschwäche f accommodative asthenopia (insufficiency), ill-sustained accommodation, dysadaptation, hypocyclosis
Akkommodationsstörung f accommodation disturbance (difficulty)
Akkommodationsüberschuß m accommodative excess
akkommodativ accommodative
akkommodieren to accommodate
Akkommodometer n accommodometer
Akkretion f accretion, accumulation of foreign matter
Akkretionslinie f accretion (incremental) line
Aklasie f aclasia
aklastisch aclastic, not refracting
Akme f acme, crisis, critical stage (z. B. in einem Krankheitsverlauf)
Akne f acne (Hauterkrankung mit Knötchen- und Pustelbildung) (Zusammensetzungen s. unter Acne)
akneartig acne[i]form
akneauslösend acnegenic
Aknebakterium n acne bacillus
Aknekeloid n folliculitis sclerotisans nuchae

Aknelanzette f acne lancet
Aknemie f acnemia (1. Atrophie der Waden; 2. angeborenes Fehlen der Beine)
Aknitis f acnitis (Form der Hauttuberkulose)
Akoasma n acoasm[a], acousma, auditory hallucination
Akonin n aconine (Alkaloid)
Akonitase f aconitase (Enzym)
Akonitin n aconitine (Alkaloid)
Akonitinvergiftung f aconitism, aconitine poisoning, aconite intoxication
Akonitsäure f aconitic acid
Akorie f 1. acoria, akoria, polyphagia; 2. acorea, absence of the pupil
Akormus m acormus (Mißgeburt)
akral acral, pertaining to the extremities
akranial acranial
Akranie f acrania, absence of the cranium
Akranius m acranius (Mißgeburt)
Akrasie f acrasia, lack of self-control, intemperance
Akratie f acratia, impotence, loss of power
Akremoniose f acremoniosis (Pilzinfektion durch Acremonium potroni)
Akren fpl acra
Akrenschwellung f acrooedema
Akrenvergrößerung f acromegaly
Akrenverkleinerung f acromicria
Akridin n acridine
Akridinfarbstoff m acridine dye
Akriflavin n acriflavine (Antiseptikum)
Akriflavinhydrochlorid n acriflavine hydrochloride, acid acriflavine
Akroagnosis f acroagnosis
Akroanästhesie f acroanaesthesia
Akroarthritis f acroarthritis, arthritis of the extremities
Akroasphyxie f acroasphyxia (Blauverfärbung der Gliedmaßen infolge Gefäßspasmus)
Akroästhesie f acroaesthesia, pain in the hands or feet
Akroataxie f acroataxia, muscle incoordination of the fingers and toes
Akroblast m acroblast (Rest des Golgi-Apparates)
Akrobrachyzephalie f acrobrachycephalia (Mißbildung des Kopfes)
Akrochordon n acrochordon (Hautpolyp an Augenlidern)
Akrodermatitis f acrodermatitis (entzündliche Hauterkrankung der Extremitäten)
~ chronica atrophicans [Herxheimer] atrophic chronic acrodermatitis, Pick-Herxheimer disease, diffuse idiopathic atrophoderma (atrophy of the skin)
~/persistierende persistent (recalcitrant pustular) acrodermatitis
Akrodermatose f acrodermatosis
Akrodolichomelie f acrodolichomelia
Akrodynie f[/infantile] acrodynia, pink (Feer's, Swift's) disease, Feer's syndrome, dermatopolyneuritis

Akrodysplasie f acrodysplasia
Akrodystonie f acrodystonia
Akroerythrose f acroerythrosis
Akrogerie f acrogeria *(Kleinheit der Hände und Füße bei vorzeitiger Vergreisung der Haut)*
Akrognosis f acrognosis
Akrohyperhidrose f acrohyperhidrosis, excessive sweating of the hands or feet
Akrohypothermie f acrohypothermy, coldness of the extremities
Akrokeratose f acrokeratosis
Akrokinese f acrokinesia, acrokinesis, excessive motion of the limbs
Akrokontraktur f acrocontracture
Akromanie f acromania *(unheilbare Geisteskrankheit)*
Akromastitis f acromastitis, inflammation of the nipple
akromegal acromegalic
Akromegalie f acromegaly, Marie's disease (syndrome)
akromegaloid acromegaloid
Akromelalgie f s. Erythromelalgie
akromial acromial
Akromialreflex m acromial reflex
Akromikrie f acromicria
akromiohumeral acromiohumeral
akromioklavikulär acromioclavicular
Akromioklavikularband n/**unteres** inferior acromioclavicular ligament
Akromioklavikulargelenk n acromioclavicular joint
akromiokorakoid[al] acromiocoracoid, coracoacromial
Akromion n acromion [process] ● **über dem** ~ supra-acromial ● **unter dem** ~ subacromial
Akromionektomie f acromionectomy
akromioskapular acromioscapular
akromiothorakal acromiothoracic, thoracoacromial
Akromykose f acromycosis
Akromyotonie f acromyotonia
Akroneuropathie f acroneuropathy
Akroneurose f acroneurosis
~/**trophische** acrotrophoneurosis
Akroödem n acrooedema
Akroosteolyse f acroosteolysis *(atrophische Defekte der Endphalangen)*
Akropachie f acropachy, hypertrophic pulmonary osteoarthropathy
Akropachyderma n, **Akropachydermie** f acropachyderma, Brugsch's syndrome
Akroparalyse f acroparalysis, paralysis of the hands or feet
Akroparästhesie f acroparaesthesia
Akropathie f acropathy
Akropathologie f acropathology *(Lehre von den Extremitätenerkrankungen)*
Akrophobie f acrophobia, batophobia *(krankhafte Angst vor Höhen)*
Akropigmentation f acropigmentation
Akroposthitis f acroposthitis, inflammation of the prepuce

Akroskleroderma n acroscleroderma
Akrosklerose f acrosclerosis
Akrosom n acrosome, idiosome *(Spermienteil)*
akrosomal acrosomal
Akrosomensystem n acrosomal system *(des Spermiums)*
Akrosomenvesikel f acrosomal vesicle
Akrostealgie f acrostealgia
akrot acrotic
Akrotie f, **Akrotismus** m acrotism, imperceptibility of the pulse
Akrotrophoneurose f acrotrophoneurosis
akrozentrisch acrocentric
akrozephal acrocephalic, acrocephalous
Akrozephalie f acrocephalia, oxycephalia; steeple-head, tower-head
Akrozephalopagus m acrocephalopagus
Akrozephalosyndaktylie f acrocephalosyndactylism, Apert's syndrome *(Mißbildung von Kopf und Extremitäten)*
Akrozyanose f acrocyanosis, Crocq disease
akrozyanotisch acrocyanotic
Akrylatklebstoff m, **Akrylkleber** m acrylate adhesive *(Wundklebstoff)*
Aktin n actin *(Muskelprotein)*
aktiniform actiniform
Aktinismus m actinism
Aktinodermatitis f actinodermatitis, actinic dermatitis
Aktinodermatose f actinodermatosis
aktinogen actinogenic
Aktinograph m actinograph *(Gerät zur Strahlenaufzeichnung)*
Aktinometer n actinometer *(Gerät zur Strahlenmessung)*
Aktinometrie f actinometry
aktinometrisch actinometric
Aktinomykom n actinomycoma
Aktinomykose f actinomycosis, lumpy yaw *(durch Actinomyces israelii)*
~/**gastrointestinale** gastro-intestinal actinomycosis
~/**kavernöse** cavernous (cavitary) actinomycosis
~/**pulmonale** pulmonary actinomycosis
~/**renale** renal actinomycosis
aktinomykotisch actinomycotic
Aktinomyzesknoten m s. Aktinomykom
Aktinomyzet m actinomycete, ray fungus
aktinomyzetisch actinomycetic, actinomycetous, actinomycelial
Aktinomyzetom n actinomycetoma
Aktinomyzin n actinomycin *(Zytostatikum)*
Aktinoneuritis f actinoneuritis
Aktinophytose f actinophytosis
aktinotherapeutisch actinotherapeutic
Aktinotherapie f actinotherapy, actinotherapeutics *(z. B. mittels UV- oder Röntgenstrahlung)*
Aktionspotential n action (spike) potential
Aktionsstrom m action current
Aktionsstromaufzeichnung f electrography
Aktionsstromkurve f electrogram
Aktionszeit f action time

Aktivator

Aktivator *m* activator
~/inaktiver proactivator
Aktivatorvorstufe *f* proactivator
aktivieren to activate, to render active
aktivierend/die Milchdrüsen lactogenic
Aktivierungsanalyse *f* activation analysis *(Radiologie)*
Aktivierungsfaktor *m* activation factor *(Blutgerinnung)*
Aktivierungsmittel *n* activator
Aktivität *f*/**antibakterielle** antibacterial activity
~/geistige mental activity, cerebration
~/gesteigerte hyperactivity; hyperpraxia, restlessness of movement
~/hämolytische haemolytic activity
~/katalytische catalytic activity
~/optische optical activity, rotary polarization *(von Substanzen)*
~/psychische mental activity
~/verminderte hypoactivity, deficient activity; hypopraxia
Aktivitätsanreicherung *f* activity enrichment *(Radiologie)*
Aktivitätshypertrophie *f* work hypertrophy; adaptive hypertrophy
Aktivitätssteigerung *f*/**hypomane** hyperthymia
Aktivitätsverminderung *f* activity decrease
Aktivkohle *f* activated (active) charcoal
Aktivkohle-Hämoperfusion *f* charcoal haemoperfusion
Aktomyosin *n* actomyosin *(Eiweißkomplex des Muskels)*
Akuästhesie *f* ac[o]uaesthesia
Akumeter *n* ac[o]umeter
akumetrisch ac[o]umetric
Akuphonie *f* acouophonia, auscultatory percussion
Akupressur *f* acupressure *(Kompression eines Blutgefäßes mit Nadeln)*
Akupunktur *f* acupuncture
Akusektor *m* acusector
Akusmatagnosis *f* acousmatagnosis
akustikofazial acousticofacial *(zum VII. und VIII. Hirnnerven gehörend)*
akustikomotorisch acousticomotoric
akustikopalpebral acousticopalpebral
Akustikophobie *f* acousticophobia *(krankhafte Angst vor Tönen)*
Akustikus *m* acusticus, auditory (acoustic) nerve, eighth [cranial] nerve
Akustikusgeschwulst *f* acoustic nerve tumour
Akustikusneurinom *n* acoustic nerve neurinoma (neurilemmoma, neuroma)
Akustikustaubheit *f* auditory (acoustic nerve) deafness, eighth-nerve deafness
akut acute
~/ganz hyperacute, superacute
~/nicht ganz subacute
Akutdialyse-Abteilung *f*, **Akutdialyse-Einheit** *f* renal failure unit
Akute-Phase-Protein *n* acute phase protein
Akzeleration *f* acceleration
Akzelerator *m* accelerator
Akzeleratorglobulin *n* accelerator globulin, Ac globulin, AcG, accelerin, cothromboplastin
Akzeleratorglobulinmangel *m* accelerator globulin deficiency
akzelerieren to accelerate
Akzelerin *n s.* Akzeleratorglobulin
akzessorisch accessory, supernumerary
Akzessorius *m* [spinal] accessory nerve
Akzessoriusnervenverletzung *f* [spinal] accessory nerve injury
akzident[i]ell accidental
Ala *f* ala, wing
~ auris auricle, pinna [of the ear]
~ cristae galli alar process
~ major ossis sphenoidalis greater sphenoidal wing
~ minor ossis sphenoidalis smaller sphenoidal wing
~ nasi wing (ala) of the nose
~ ossis ilii (ilium) ala of the ilium
~ ossis sacri ala of the sacrum
~ parva ossis sphenoidalis lesser sphenoidal wing
~ vomeris wing (ala) of the vomer
Alaktie *f* agalactia, agalaxia, agalaxy, non-secretion of milk
Alaktoflavinose *f* ariboflavinosis
Alalie *f* alalia *(Artikulationsstörung)*
~/mentale mental (relative) alalia
Alanin *n* alanine, α-aminopropionic acid
Alaninaminotransferase *f* alanine aminotransferase (transaminase), ALAT, glutamic-pyruvic transaminase, GPT, glutamic-alanine transaminase *(Enzym)*
Alarmreaktion *f* alarm reaction *(erstes Stadium des Adaptationssyndroms)*
Alastrim *n* alastrim, minor variola, paravariola, pseudovariola, pseudosmallpox, milk (white) pox, glasspox, amaas
Alastrimvirus *n* alastrim virus
ALAT *s.* Alaninaminotransferase
Alaunhämatoxilin *n* alum haematoxilin
Albarren-Drüse *f* Albarran's (subcervical) gland
Albarran-Krankheit *f* Albarran's disease
Albarran-Test *m* Albarran's (polyuria) test
Albee-Knochensäge *f* Albee's saw
Albee-Repositionstisch *m* Albee's fracture table
Albert-Krankheit *f* 1. Albert's disease, painful heel; 2. achillodynia
Albinismus *m* albinism, leucopathy *(mit Astigmatismus, Nystagmus und Photophobie)*
Albino *m* albino *(Individuum ohne Pigmentbildung)*
albinotisch albinotic
Albinurie *f* 1. albinuria, albiduria, passage of colourless urine; 2. *s.* Chylurie
Albright-Syndrom *n* Albright's disease, Albright-McCune-Sternberg syndrome *(polyostotische Form der fibrösen Dysplasie)*
Albuginea *f* albuginea *(derbfibröse weißliche Bindegewebshaut um ein Organ)*

Albugineadurchtrennung f [/operative] albugineotomy
Albugineotomie f albugineotomy
Albuginitis f albuginitis, inflammation of the albuginea
albuginös albugineous
Albugo m albugo, leucoma of the cornea
Albumin n albumin *(Sammelbezeichnung für eine Gruppe einfacher Eiweiße)*
~/mit Jod 131 markiertes iodine-131-tagged albumin
Albuminämie f albuminaemia
albuminartig album[in]oid, albuminous
Albuminat n albuminate
Albuminauflösung f albuminolysis
Albuminausscheidung f albuminorrhoea
~ im Urin s. Albuminurie
Albuminbestimmung f albuminometry
albuminbildend albuminogenous, albuminiparous
albuminenthaltend albuminous
Albuminfraktion f albumin fraction
Albumin-Globulin-Quotient m albumin-globulin ratio
albuminhaltig albuminiferous
Albuminimeter n albuminometer
Albuminimetrie f albuminometry
Albuminmangel m [im Blut] analbuminaemia, hypoalbuminaemia, hypoalbuminosis
albuminogen albuminogenous
albuminoid album[in]oid, albuminous
Albuminoid n albuminoid, scleroprotein
Albuminolyse f albuminolysis
Albuminolysin n albuminolysin
Albuminorrhoe f albuminorrhoea
albuminös albuminous
albumino-zytologisch albuminocytologic
albuminproduzierend albuminiparous, albuminogenous
albuminuretisch albuminuretic
Albuminuria f s. Albuminurie
~ acetonica anoxaemic albuminuria
Albuminurie f albuminuria, albiduria ● **~ bewirkend** albuminuretic
~/alimentäre alimentary albuminuria
~/falsche false (adventitious) albuminuria
~/hypostatische hypostatic albuminuria
~/nächtliche nocturnal albuminuria, noctalbuminuria, nyctalbuminuria
~/orthostatische ortho[sta]tic albuminuria
~/paroxysmale paroxysmal (cyclic) albuminuria
~/physiologische physiological albuminuria
~/renopalpatorische palpatory albuminuria
albuminurisch albuminuric
Albumose f albumose *(Eiweißabbauprodukt bei der Proteolyse)*
Albumosurie f albumosuria *(Ausscheidung von Bence-Jones-Protein im Urin)*
Alcock-Kanal m Alcock's (pudendal) canal
Alcohol m s. Alkohol
Aldehyddehydrogenase f aldehyde dehydrogenase

Aldehydmutase f aldehyde mutase *(Enzym)*
Aldehydoxydase f aldehyde (xanthine) oxidase
Alder-Granulationsanomalie f, **Alder-Keilly-Anomalie** f Alder's anomaly (phenomenon)
Aldohexose f aldohexose
Aldolase f aldolase, zymohexase *(Enzym)*
Aldosteron n aldosterone *(Nebennierenrindenhormon)*
Aldosteronausschüttung f aldosterone excretion (secretion)
Aldosteronismus m aldosteronism
~/primärer primary [hyper]aldosteronism, Conn's syndrome
Aldosteronmangel m hypoaldosteronism
Aldosteronspiegelerhöhung f im Blut [hyper]aldosteronism
Aldosteron[spiegel]verminderung f im Blut hypoaldosteronism
Aldrich-Syndrom n Aldrich syndrome
Aleppobeule f Aleppo boil (button) *(Hautleishmaniase)*
Aleukämie f aleukaemia
aleukämisch aleukaemic
Aleukie f aleukia, aleukaemic myelosis (lymphadenosis)
~/hämorrhagische malignant thrombocytopenia
Alexander-Adams-Operation f Alexander's operation, shortening of the round ligaments *(des Uterus)*
Alexie f alexia, word blindness
~/kortikale cortical alexia
~/motorische motor alexia
~/musikalische musical alexia
~/sensorische optical (sensory, visual) alexia
Alexin n alexin
Algenpilzinfektion f phycomycosis
Algesie f 1. algesia, algaesthesia, pain sensibility; 2. algesia, hyperaesthesia
Algesimeter n algesimeter
Algesimetrie f algesimetry
Algizid n algicide
algogen 1. algogenic, pain producing; 2. algogenic, cold (chill) producing
Algolagnie f/**aktive** active algolagnia, sadism
~/passive passive algolagnia, masochism
Algolagnist m algolagnist
Algometer n algometer
Algometrie f algometry
Algophilie f algophilia *(krankhafte Schmerzfreude)*
Algophobie f algophobia *(krankhafte Angst vor Schmerzen)*
Algor m algor, coldness; chill; rigor
Algospasmus m algospasm, painful cramp (spasm)
algospastisch algospastic
Alice-im-Wunderland-Syndrom n Alice in Wonderland syndrome
Alienation f 1. alienation, mental derangement; insanity; 2. self-alienation
aliform aliform, wing-shaped
alimentär alimentary, nutritional *(Stoffwechsel und Ernährung betreffend)*

Alimentation

Alimentation *f* alimentation, feeding, nourishment, nourishing with food
Alimentotherapie *f* alimentotherapy, alimentary therapy
Aliquorrhoe *f* aliquorrhoea
Alizarin *n* alizarin *(Farbstoff)*
Alkalämie *f s.* Alkalose
Alkalialbuminat *n* alkali albuminate
Alkaliausscheidung *f* im Urin alkalinuria
Alkalibehandlung *f* alkalitherapy, alkalotherapy *(bei peptischen Geschwüren)*
alkali[gehalts]bestimmend alkalimetric
Alkaligehaltsmeßgerät *n* alkalimeter
Alkalimangel *m* alkali deficiency, hypoalkalinity
Alkalimeter *n* alkalimeter
Alkalimetrie *f* alkalimetry
alkalimetrisch alkalimetric
Alkalinurie *f* alkalinuria
Alkalireserve *f* alkali reserve *(Puffersystem des Blutes)*
Alkaliresistenz *f* alkali resistance
alkalisch/schwach alkalescent, slightly (faintly) alkaline
~/stark superalkaline, strongly alkaline
alkalisieren to alkal[in]ize, to render alkaline
alkalisierend alkalescent, alkalizing
Alkalisierung *f* alkal[in]ization
Alkalität *f* alkalinity, basicity
Alkaliüberschuß *m* base excess; excess alkalinity
Alkaloid *n* alkaloid *(stickstoffhaltiges pflanzliches Gift)*
alkaloidisch alkaloidal
Alkalose *f* alkalosis, alkalaemia
~/dekompensierte uncompensated alkalosis
~/hypochlorämische hypochloraemic alkalosis
~/metabolische metabolic alkalosis
~/respiratorische respiratory alkalosis
alkalotisch alkalotic
Alkapton *n* alcapton, alkapton, homogentisic acid
Alkaptonausscheidung *f* im Urin alcaptonuria
Alkohol *m* alcohol
~/absoluter absolute (dehydrated) alcohol
~/denaturierter denatured alcohol
~/reiner *s.* **~/absoluter**
~/vergällter denatured alcohol
Alkoholabhängigkeit *f* alcoholism
Alkoholabreibung *f* alcohol rub
Alkoholämie *f* alcoholaemia
Alkoholase *f* alcohol dehydrogenase, alcoholase *(Enzym)*
Alkoholataxie *f* alcoholic ataxia
Alkoholausscheidung *f* im Urin alcoholuria
Alkoholbestimmung *f* alcoholometry
Alkoholdehydrogenase *f* alcohol dehydrogenase, alcoholase *(Enzym)*
Alkoholdelir[ium] *n* alcohol delirium, delirium tremens
Alkoholdemenz *f* alcoholic dementia (insanity)
Alkoholembryopathie *f* alcoholic embryopathy
Alkoholentzugserscheinung *f* alcohol withdrawal symptom

26

Alkoholepilepsie *f* alcoholic epilepsy
alkoholfrei non-alcoholic
Alkoholgastritis *f* alcoholic gastritis
Alkoholgehalt *m* alcohol content, alcoholic strength
Alkoholgehaltbestimmung *f* alcoholometry
alkoholgetränkt soaked in alcohol
Alkoholhalluzinose *f* alcoholic hallucinosis
alkoholhaltig alcoholic, containing alcohol
Alkoholhepatitis *f* alcoholic hepatitis
Alkoholiker *m* alcoholic, potator, alcohol addict, drunkard; dipsomaniac
alkoholisch alcoholic
alkoholisieren to alcoholize
Alkoholismus *m* alcoholism
Alkoholkoma *n* alcoholic coma
Alkoholleberzirrhose *f* alcoholic (portal) cirrhosis; hobnail (gin-drinker's) liver
alkohollöslich alcohol-soluble
Alkoholmesser *m* alcoholometer
Alkoholmißbrauch *m* alcohol abuse, abuse in alcohol
Alkoholmyokardiopathie *f* alcoholic myocardiopathy
Alkoholneuritis *f* alcoholic neuritis
Alkoholometer *n* alcoholometer
Alkoholometrie *f* alcoholometry
Alkoholophilie *f* alcoholophilia
Alkoholparalyse *f* alcoholic paralysis
Alkoholparanoia *f* alcoholic paranoia
Alkoholparaplegie *f* alcoholic paraplegia
Alkoholpolyneuropathie *f* alcohol polyneuropathy
Alkoholpsychose *f* alcoholic psychosis
Alkoholschmerz *m* alcoholic pain
Alkoholsyndrom *n***/embryofetales** *s.* **Alkoholembryopathie**
Alkoholtupfer *m* alcohol sponge (swab)
Alkoholumschlag *m* alcohol compress (pack, bandage, dressing)
Alkoholunverträglichkeit *f* alcoholic intolerance
Alkoholvergiftung *f* alcoholic intoxication, alcohol poisoning, alcoholism
Alkoholzirrhose *f s.* **Alkoholleberzirrhose**
Allantiasis *f s.* **Botulismus**
Allantochorion *n* allantochorion
allantoenterisch allantoenteric
Allantogenese *f* allantogenesis
allantoid allantoid
Allantoin *n* allantoin *(Purinstoffwechselprodukt)*
Allantois *f* allantois *(Embryologie)*
allantoisartig allantoid
Allantoisbildung *f* allantogenesis
Allantoisblase *f* allantoic vesicle (sac)
Allantoisdivertikel *n* allantoic diverticulum
Allantoisfehlbildung *f* allantoic dysgenesis
Allantoisflüssigkeit *f* allantoic fluid
Allantoisgang *m* allantoic (allantoenteric) duct
Allantoiskreislauf *m* allantoic circulation
Allantoisparasit *m* allantoic parasite
Allantoissack *m* allantoic sac (vesicle)
Allantoisvene *f* allantoic vein

Allantoiszyste f allantoic cyst
allel allelic, allelomorphic
Allel n allel[e], allelomorph
allelomorph allelomorphic
Allelomorphie f allelomorphism
Allelotaxie f allelotaxis, allelotaxy *(Organentwicklung aus verschiedenen Embryonalanlagen)*
Allen-Trakt m Allen's tract, tractus solitarius
allergen allergenic
~/**nicht** anallergenic
Allergen n allergen
Allergendesensibilisierungstherapie f allergendesensitizing treatment
Allergenextrakt m allergen extract
Allergenhauttest m allergen skin test
Allergen[iz]ität f allergenicity
Allergenstandardisierung f allergen standardization
Allergie f allergy, hypersensitivity, hypersensitiveness *(Krankheitszustand nach Antigen-Antikörper-Reaktion)*
~/**angeborene** hereditary (spontaneous) allergy
~/**bakterielle** bacterial allergy
~/**latente** latent allergy
~/**provozierte** induced allergy
~/**sofortige** immediate allergy
~/**verzögerte** delayed allergy
~/**zellübertragene** cell-mediated allergy
allergieauslösend allergenic
~/**nicht** anallergenic
Allergiebereitschaft f allergic diathesis
Allergiebestimmung f allergometry
Allergiedermatitis f allergic dermatitis (dermatosis)
Allergiediathese f allergic diathesis
Allergieekzem n allergic (atopic) eczema
Allergiegleichgewicht n allergic balance
Allergiekatarakt f allergic (atopic) cataract
Allergiekonjunktivitis f allergic conjunctivitis
Allergiekontaktdermatitis f allergic contact dermatitis
Allergiereaktion f allergic reaction
Allergiespezialist m allergist
Allergiesteigerung f allergic increase
Allergietestung f allergometry
Allergieübertragung f/**passive** passive transfer of hypersensitivity, Prausnitz-Küstner reaction
Allergieumkehr f allergic transformation
Allergieveranlagung f allergic constitution
Allergiezustand m allergic state
Allergiker m allergic person
allergisch allergic, hypersensitive; anaphylactic; hyperergic ● ~ **sein gegenüber** to be hypersensitive to
allergisieren to allergize, to sensitize
allergisierend allergenic
Allergisierung f allergization, sensitization
Allergogastroenteropathie f allergic gastroenteropathy
Allergologe m allergist
allergologisch allergological

Allergose f allergosis, allergic disease; allergic state
Allescheriasis f allescheriasis *(durch Allescheria boydii)*
allesfressend omnivorous *(z. B. Bakterien)*
Alles-oder-Nichts-Gesetz n all-or-non law *(Physiologie)*
Allgemeinanästhesie f general anaesthesia
Allgemeinanästhetikum n general anaesthetic
Allgemeinarteriosklerose f generalized arteriosclerosis
Allgemeinausbreitung f generalization *(z. B. einer Infektion)*
Allgemeinbefinden n general [state of] health, general condition
Allgemeinbehandlung f general treatment
Allgemeinchirurg m general surgeon
Allgemeinchirurgie f general surgery
allgemeinchirurgisch general surgical
Allgemeindisposition f general disposition
Allgemeinempfinden n general sensation
Allgemeinerkrankung f generalized disease, systemic illness
Allgemeinhypothermie f general hypothermia
Allgemeininfektion f generalized (systemic) infection
Allgemeinkrankenhaus n general hospital
Allgemeinlähmung f general paresis, polyparesis
Allgemeinmedizin f general practice; family medicine
Allgemeinmediziner m general practitioner; family physician
allgemeinmedizinisch general medical
Allgemeinnarkose f general anaesthesia
Allgemeinpraktiker m s. Allgemeinmediziner
Allgemeinpraxis f general practice
Allgemeinreaktion f general reaction
Allgemeinsklerose f general sclerosis
Allgemeinsymptom n general symptom
Allgemeinuntersuchung f general examination
Allgemeinvergiftung f general poisoning (intoxication)
Allgemeinzustand m general condition (state of health)
Allheilmittel n panpharmacon, cure-all, heal-all, panacea
Allingham-Operation f Allingham's operation *(inguinale Kolostomie über dem Leistenband)*
Allis-Klemme f Allis forceps
Alliteration f alliteration *(Sprachstörung)*
Alloalbuminämie f allo-albuminaemia
Alloantigen n allo-antigen *(durch Allele gesteuerte Antigenstrukturen)*
Alloantikörper m allo-antibody *(wirkt gegen Alloantigene)*
Alloarthroplastik f allo-arthroplasty *(künstlicher Gelenkersatz)*
Allobiose f allobiosis *(Verhaltensänderungen von Organismen bei Umweltveränderungen)*
Allocheirie f alloch[e]iria *(fehlerhafte Lokalisation eines Tastreizes oder Stiches in die kontralaterale Hand)*

Allochezie

Allochezie f allochezia, allochetia *(1. Stuhlentleerung an anomaler Stelle; 2. Entleerung von Blut bzw. Urin mit dem Stuhl)*
Alloerotismus m alloeroti[ci]sm
allogen allogen[e]ic
Allogenese f allogenesis
Allograft n allograft, homograft, allogeneic graft (homograft)
Alloiogenesis f alloiogenesis *(Form des Generationswechsels)*
Allokortex m allocortex, heterogenetic (heterotypical) cortex *(Großhirnrindenabschnitt)*
Allopathie f allopathy *(unwissenschaftliche Therapieform; Gegenteil: Homöopathie)*
Allophanamid n allophanamide, carbamyl urea, biuret *(Harnstoffderivat)*
Alloplasma n alloplasm
Alloplastik f alloplasty *(Einheilung körperfremden leblosen Materials bei plastischer Operation)*
alloplastisch alloplastic
Allorhythmie f allorhythmia *(Herzrhythmusstörung)*
Allosom n allosome, sex (heterotypical) chromosome, heterochromosome
allotherm allothermic, poikilothermic
Allotopie f dystopia, dystopy
Allotransplantat n allotransplant
Allotransplantation f allotransplantation
Allotriogeusie f allotriogeusia, perverted sense of taste
Allotriophagie f allotriophagy, eating of injurious substances
Allotyp m allotype
Allotypie f allotypia *(Genetik)*
Alloxandiabetes m alloxan diabetes
Alloxurie f alloxuria *(Vorhandensein von Purin im Urin)*
alloxurisch alloxuric
Allschichtennaht f all-coats stitch *(chirurgische Nahtform)*
Allschichten[naht]verschluß m all-layers closure *(chirurgische Wundverschlußtechnik)*
Allylmorphin n allylnormorphine, nalorphine *(Morphinantagonist)*
Almeida-Krankheit f [Lutz-Splendore-de] Almeida disease, South American blastomycosis
Alopecia f alopecia, baldness
~ **adnata** congenital alopecia (baldness)
~ **areata** alopecia areata, pelada, pelade
~ **atrophicans** alopecia atrophicans, pseudopelade
~ **capitis totalis** complete baldness
~ **celsi** s. ~ areata
~ **cicatrisata** cicatricial alopecia, pseudopelade
~ **circumscripta** circumscript alopecia
~ **congenitalis** congenital alopecia
~ **diffusa (disseminata)** disseminated alopecia
~ **genitalis** genital alopecia
~ **hereditaria** hereditary alopecia
~ **prematura (presenilis)** premature (presenile) alopecia
~ **seborrhoeica** seborrhoeic alopecia
~ **senilis** senile alopecia
~ **symptomatica** symptomatic alopecia
~ **syphilitica** syphilitic (luetic) alopecia
Alopezie f alopecia, baldness *(s. a. unter Alopecia)*
~ **der Lider** palpebral alopecia
Alpdrücken n nightmare, incubus, night terrors; passive oneirodynia
Alpers-Syndrom n Alpers' disease, progressive cerebral poliodystrophy
Alpha-1-Antitrypsin n alpha-1-antitrypsin *(Glykoprotein)*
Alpha-Chymotrypsin n alpha-chymotrypsin *(Enzym)*
Alpha-1-Chymotrypsin n alpha-1-chymotrypsin (Proteinaseinhibitor)
Alpha-Fetoprotein alpha foetoprotein
Alpha-Globulin n alpha globulin
Alpha-Granula npl alpha granules *(1. im Hypophysenvorderlappen; 2. in der Bauchspeicheldrüse)*
Alpha-Hämolyse f alpha haemolysis
Alpha-Hämolysin n alpha haemolysin
Alpha-Index m alpha index
Alpha-Keratin n alpha keratin
Alpha-Lysin n alpha lysin
Alpha-Methyldopa n alpha methyldopa *(Antihypertensivum)*
alpha-mimetisch alpha-mimetic
Alpha-Motoneuron n alpha motor neuron
Alpha-Rezeptor m alpha[-adrenergic] receptor
Alpha-Rezeptorenblocker m alpha-adrenergic blocker, alpha-adrenergic [receptor] blocking agent
Alpha-Rhythmus m alpha rhythm (wave) *(EEG)*
Alpha-Spastizität f alpha spasticity
Alphastrahlen mpl alpha rays
Alpha-Streptokokkus m alpha streptococcus
Alpha-Tokopherol n alpha tocopherol
Alphavirus n alpha virus
Alphawelle f alpha wave *(EEG)*
Alpha-Zelle f alpha cell *(1. im Hypophysenvorderlappen; 2. in der Bauchspeicheldrüse)*
Alphodermie f alphodermia, alphosis
Alport-Syndrom n Alport's syndrome, hereditary nephritis
Alptraum m s. Alpdrücken
alt senile; aged ● ~ **werden** to grow old, to age
Alter n/**gebärfähiges** childbearing period, reproductive age
~/**geistiges** mental age
~/**kritisches** 1. critical stage (age) *(von Jugendlichen)*; 2. s. Klimakterium
altern to age, to grow old
Altern n ag[e]ing, growing old, senescence
~/**pathologisches** pathological aging
~/**physiologisches** physiological aging
~/**vorzeitiges** senilism, presenility, premature old age
alternd ag[e]ing, senescent
Altersabnutzung f senile attrition

Altersamyloidose f senile amyloidosis
Altersangiom n senile angioma, papillary varix
Altersappendizitis f senile appendicitis
Altersarteriosklerose f senile arteriosclerosis
Altersarthrose f senile arthrosis
Altersatrophie f senile atrophy
Altersbeschwerden pl geriatric complaints
Altersbrand m senile (Pott's) gangrene
Alterschirurgie f geriatric surgery
Altersdegeneration f senile degeneration
Altersdemenz f senile dementia, presbyophrenia
Altersdepression f involutional (senile) depression
Altersdiabetes m maturity-onset diabetes, adult-onset diabetes
Altersdiabetiker m maturity-onset diabetic
Altersektropion n senile ectropion
Altersemphysem n senile (aging-lung) emphysema
Altersentropion n senile entropion
Alterserscheinung f symptom (sign) of old age
Altersforschung f gerontology, [scientific] study of aging
Altersfürsorge f old-age assistance
Altersgebrechlichkeit f senility
Altershaut f presbyderma
Altersheilkunde f geriatrics, geriatric medicine, presby[ti]atrics
Altersherz n presbycardia; senile heart disease
Altersinvolution f senile involution
Altersjucken n senile pruritus
Alterskeratose f senile keratosis
Altersmarasmus m senile marasmus, geromarasmus
Altersmelancholie f involution melancholia, involutional depression
Altersmiose f senile miosis
Altersosteoporose f senile osteoporosis
Alterspemphigus m senile pemphigus
Alterspigment n aging pigment
Alterspsychiatrie f gerontopsychiatry
Alterspsychose f senile psychosis (insanity), geriopsychosis
Alterspurpura f senile purpura
Altersring m senile arch (der Augenhornhaut)
Altersrückbildung f senile involution
Altersschlaflosigkeit f senile agrypnia
altersschwach senile, decrepit, infirm
Altersschwäche f decrepitude, old-age infirmity; senility, senile decay (debility, marasmus)
Altersschwachsinn m presbyophrenia, senile dementia
altersschwachsinnig presbyophrenic, senile
Altersschwerhörigkeit f presbyac[o]usia, presbycusis
alterssichtig presbyopic, presbytic
Alterssichtiger m presbyope
Alterssichtigkeit f presbyopia, presbytism, senopia, old sightedness
~/gesteigerte hyperpresbyopia
Altersstar m senile cataract, phacoscleroma
Alterstrübungsring m senile arch

Alterstuberkulose f senile tuberculosis
Alterswarze f senile wart
Altersweitsichtigkeit f s. Alterssichtigkeit
Alterszahnheilkunde f gerodontia
Alterszittern n senile tremor
Alterungsarthritis f senescent arthritis, degenerative joint disease
Alterungspsychose f degenerative (senescent) psychosis
Althausen-Test m Althausen test
Altinsulin n regular (amorphous) insulin
Altruismus m altruism
Alttuberkulin n old (original) tuberculin
Aluminiumstaublunge[nerkrankung] f aluminium (bauxite fume) pneumoconiosis
Aluminose f aluminosis
Alveobasilarlinie f alveobasilar line
alveolar, alveolär alveolar
Alveolar... s. a. Alveolen...
Alveolarabszeß m alveolar (dentoalveolar) abscess, dental abscess
Alveolarbogen m alveoiar arch
~/oberer dental arch of the upper teeth
~/unterer dental arch of the lower teeth
Alveolardruck m alveolar pressure
Alveolardrüse f saccular gland
Alveolardysplasie f/kongenitale congenital alveolar dysplasia
~/zystische cystic alveolar dysplasia
Alveolarektasie f alveolar ectasia
Alveolareminenz f alveolar eminence
Alveolarepithel n alveolar (respiratory) epithelium
Alveolarepithelschicht f alveolar epithelial layer
Alveolarfortsatz m alveolar (dental) process
Alveolarfortsatzresektion f alveolectomy (am Ober- oder Unterkiefer)
Alveolargas n alveolar air
Alveolarhöhle f alveolar cavity
Alveolarindex m alveolar index
Alveolarkamm m alveolar crest (ridge)
Alveolarkanal m alveolar (dental) canal
~/unterer inferior alveolar canal
Alveolarknochen m alveolar bone
Alveolarkrebs m alveolar cancer (carcinoma)
Alveolarlinie f alveolar line
Alveolarluft f alveolar air
Alveolarmakrophage m alveolar macrophage
Alveolarmukosa f alveolar mucosa
Alveolarperiost n alveolar periosteum (Knochenhaut der Zahnfächer)
Alveolarphagozyt m alveolar phagocyte
Alveolarplastik f alveoloplasty
Alveolarplateau n alveolar plateau
Alveolarpore f alveolar pore
Alveolarproteinose f alveolar proteinosis
Alveolarpunkt m alveolar point
Alveolarrand m alveolar margin
Alveolarraum m alveolar space
Alveolarsack m alveolar (air) sac
Alveolarsarkom n alveolar sarcoma
Alveolartasche f periodontal pocket

Alveolartumor

Alveolartumor *m* alveolar tumour
Alveolarventilation *f* alveolar ventilation
Alveolarvolumen *n* alveolar volume
Alveolarwand *f* alveolar wall
Alveolarwandzelle *f* alveolar lining cell
Alveolarwinkel *m* alveolar angle
Alveolarzange *f* alveolar forceps
Alveolarzellkarzinom *n* alveolar [cell] carcinoma
Alveole *f* 1. pulmonary (lung) alveolus, air sac; 2. alveolus, tooth socket; 3. alveolus, acinus *(Drüsen)*
Alveolektomie *f* alveolectomy *(am Ober- oder Unterkiefer)*
Alveolen... *s. a.* Alveolar...
Alveolenbelüftung *f* alveolar ventilation
Alveolenbeteiligung *f* alveolar involvement *(Pneumonie)*
Alveolendarstellung *f*[/radiologische] alveolography
Alveolenentzündung *f s.* Alveolitis
Alveolengang *m* alveolar duct
Alveolengeschwulst *f* alveolar tumour
Alveolitis *f* alveolitis, dry socket *(des Kiefers)*
~/**allergische** allergic alveolitis *(der Lunge)*
Alveoloklasie *f* alveoloclasia *(führt zur Zahnlockerung)*
Alveolotomie *f* alveolotomy
Alveolus *m* [dentalis] alveolus, tooth socket
Alvinolith *m* alvinolith, enterolith; intestinal calculus
Alvus *m* alvus, abdomen
Alymphie *f* alymphia, absence (deficiency) of lymph
Alymphoplasie *f* alymphoplasia, thymic aplasia
Alymphozytose *f* alymphocytosis
Alzheimer-Zelle *f* Alzheimer cell *(bei hepatolentikulärer Degeneration)*
Alzianblau-Färbung *f* Alcian blue stain
amakrin amacrine, amacrinal
Amalgamfüllung *f* amalgam filling *(eines Zahns)*
Amalgamträger *m* amalgam carrier
Amastie *f* amastia, amazia, [congenital] absence of the mammae
Amaurose *f* amaurosis, blindness
~/**transitorische** transitional amaurosis (blindness), blackout [of vision]
Amaurosis *f* centralis central amaurosis
Amaurot[ik]er *m* amaurotic
amaurotisch amaurotic
Amaxophobie *f* amaxophobia *(krankhafte Angst vor Wagenfahrten)*
Amazie *f s.* Amastie
ambidexter ambidextrous
Ambidexter *m* ambidexter
Ambidexteritie *f* ambidexterity
ambilateral ambilateral
Ambitendenz *f* ambitendency *(Neurose mit Entschlußlosigkeit infolge Antriebsstörung)*
ambivalent ambivalent
Ambivalenz *f* ambivalence *(Nebeneinanderbestehen von entgegengesetzten Gefühlen)*
Ambiversion *f* ambiversion *(Gleichgewicht zwischen Introversion und Extroversion)*
Amblyakusie *f* amblyacousia
Amblychromasie *f* amblychromasia
amblychromatisch amblychromatic
amblyop amblyopic
Amblyopia *f* **ex anopsia** amblyopia of disuse
Amblyopie *f* amblyopia, dimness of vision
~/**myope anisometrope** myopic anisometropic amblyopia
Amblyoskop *n* amblyoscope *(Apparat zur Schielbehandlung)*
ambomalleal ambomalleal
Amboß *m* incus, anvil *(Gehörknöchelchen)*
Amboßentfernung *f*[/**operative**] incudectomy
Amboß-Hammer-Gelenk *n* ambomalleal articulation (joint)
Amboßschenkel *m*/**kurzer** short crus of the incus
~/**langer** long crus of the incus
Amboß-Steigbügel-Gelenk *n* incudostapedial articulation (joint)
Ambozeptor *m* amboceptor, interbody *(Immunkörper)*
Ambozeptoreinheit *f* amboceptor unit
ambulant ambulant, ambulatory
Ambulanz *f* ambulance, outpatient's department
AMCA *s.* Aminokapronsäure
amegakaryozytär amegakaryocytic
Ameiose *f* ameiosis *(Ausbleiben der Kernreduktionsteilung)*
Ameisenlaufen *n* formication
amelanotisch amelanotic
Amelie *f* amelia, [congenital] absence of the extremities
Ameloblast *m* ameloblast, adamantoblast, enameloblast, ganoblast
Ameloblastenfibrom *n* ameloblastic fibroma
Ameloblastenfortsatz *m* ameloblastic process
Ameloblastenodontom *n* ameloblastic odontoma
ameloblastisch ameloblastic
Ameloblastom *n* ameloblastoma, adamantinoma, enameloblastoma
Ameloblastosarkom *n* ameloblastosarcoma *(bösartiger Tumor)*
Amelogenese *f* amelogenesis, formation of enamel
Amelus *m* amelus *(Mißgeburt ohne Extremitäten)*
Amenorrhoe *f* amenorrhoea, amenia
~/**erworbene** *s.* ~/**sekundäre**
~/**pathologische** pathologic amenorrhoea
~/**primäre** primary amenorrhoea
~/**sekundäre** secondary amenorrhoea
amenorrhoisch amenorrhoeal
Amentia *f* amentia, idiocy *(Zusammensetzungen s. unter* Idiotie)
Ametastasis *f* ametastasis
Ametrie *f* ametria, [congenital] absence of the uterus
Ametrohämie *f* ametrohaemia, deficiency (lack) of uterine blood supply

ametrop ametropic
Ametroper m ametrope
Ametropie f ametropia, refractive error, error of refraction
Amid n amide
Amidase f amidase *(Enzym)*
Amidopyrin n amidopyrine *(Antipyretikum, Analgetikum, Antiphlogistikum)*
amikrobiell amicrobic
amikroskopisch amicroscopic
Amimie f amimia *(Verlust des Mienenspiels);* mask[-like] face, masked facies
Amin n amine
Aminausscheidung f im Urin amin[os]uria
Aminazidurie f s. Aminoazidurie
Aminoalkohol m amino alcohol
Aminoazidurie f aminoaciduria, acidaminuria
~/gesteigerte hyperaminoaciduria, hyperacidaminuria
~/renale renal (transport) aminoaciduria
p-Aminobenzolsulfonamid n aminobenzenesulphonamide, sulphanilamide *(bakteriostatische Substanz)*
2-(p-Aminobenzolsulfonamido)-pyridin n sulphapyridine, sulphadiazine
p-Aminobenzolsulfonsäure f sulphanilic acid
p-Aminobenzolsulfonylguanidin n sulphaguanidine
α-Aminobenzylpenizillin n α-aminobenzyl penicillin, ampicillin *(Antibiotikum)*
α-Aminobernsteinsäure f α-aminosuccinic acid, aspartic (asparaginic) acid
α-Aminobernsteinsäuremonoamid n α-aminosuccinamic acid, asparagine
Aminoessigsäure f aminoacetic acid
Aminoglukose f aminoglucose, glucosamine, glycosamine
α-Aminoglutarsäure f α-aminoglutaric acid, glutam[in]ic acid
α-Amino-σ-guanidyl-n-valeriansäure f α-amino-σ-guanidovaleric acid, arginine
α-Amino-β-hydroxybuttersäure f α-amino-β-hydroxybutric acid, threonine
α-Amino-β-hydroxypropionsäure f α-amino-β-hydroxypropionic acid, serine
α-Amino-β-imidazolylpropionsäure f α-amino-β-imidazolylpropionic acid, histidine
α-Aminoisokapronsäure f α-aminoisocaproic acid, leucine
α-Aminoisovaleriansäure f α-aminoisovaleric acid, 2-amino-3-methylbutanoic acid, valine
Aminokapronsäure f aminocaproic acid *(blutungshemmende Substanz)*
ε-Aminokapronsäure f epsilon-aminocaproic acid
α-Amino-δ-Karbamidovaleriansäure f α-amino-δ-ureido-valeric acid, citrulline
Aminolipid n aminolipid
α-Amino-β-merkaptopropionsäure f α-amino-β-mercaptopropionic acid, cysteine
Aminomethanamidin n aminomethanamidine, iminourea, guanidine, carbamidine

8-(4'-Amino-1'-methylbutylamino)-6-methoxychinolin n 8-(4-amino-1-methylamino)-6-methoxy-quinoline, primaquine *(Antimalariamittel)*
α-Amino-γ-methyl-thiobuttersäure f α-amino-γ-methylthiobutyric acid, methionine *(essentielle Aminosäure)*
Aminooxydase f amine oxidase *(Enzym)*
Aminopeptidase f aminopeptidase *(Enzym)*
Aminophenazon n amidopyrine *(Antipyretikum, Analgetikum, Antiphlogistikum)*
α-Amino-β-phenylpropionsäure f α-amino-β-phenylpropionic acid, phenylalanine
Aminophyllin n aminophylline, theophylline ethylene-diamine
Aminopolypeptidase f aminopolypeptidase *(Enzym)*
α-Aminopropionsäure f α-aminopropionic acid, alanine
6-Aminopurin n 6-aminopurine, adenine
Aminosalizylsäure f aminosalicylic acid
Aminosäure f amino acid
Aminosäureausscheidung f im Urin s. Aminoazidurie
Aminosäurebelastungstest m amino-acid tolerance test
Aminosäuredehydratase f amino-acid dehydratase *(Enzym)*
Aminosäuredekarboxylase f amino-acid decarboxylase *(Enzym)*
Aminosäurediabetes m [Debré-de Toni-]Fanconi syndrome, de Toni-Fanconi[-Debré] syndrome, amino diabetes, renal amino-acid diabetes
Aminosäuregemisch n amino-acid mixture
Aminosäuregleichgewicht n amino-acid balance
Aminosäureinkorporation f amino-acid incorporation
Aminosäurekarboxylase f amino-acid carboxylase *(Enzym)*
Aminosäurelösung f amino-acid solution
Aminosäuremalabsorption f amino-acid malabsorption
Aminosäureoxydase f amino-acid oxidase *(Enzym)*
Aminosäurepool m amino-acid pool
Aminosäureresorption f amino-acid resorption
Aminosäuresequenz f amino-acid sequence
Aminosäurespiegel m im Blut amino-acid blood level
~ im Urin amino-acid urine level
Aminosäurespiegelerhöhung f im Blut hyperaminoacidaemia, hyperacidaminaemia
Aminosäurespiegelverminderung f im Blut hypoaminoacidaemia
Aminosäuretoleranztest m amino-acid tolerance test
Aminosäuretransport m amino-acid transport
Aminosäureverwertungsstörung f amino acidopathy
α-Amino-γ-thiobuttersäure f α-amino-γ-mercaptobutyric acid, homocysteine

α-Amino-β-thiopropionsäure

α-Amino-β-thiopropionsäure f 2-amino-3-mercaptopropanoic acid, cysteine
Aminotoluol n aminotoluene, toluidine
Aminotransferase f aminotransferase *(Enzym)*
Aminozucker m amino sugar
Amitose f amitosis
amitotisch amitotic
Amme f [wet-]nurse, nutrix
Ammoniak n ammonia
ammoniakalisch ammoniacal
Ammoniakausscheidung f im Urin ammoniuria
Ammoniakbildung f[/bakterielle] ammonification
Ammoniakfermentation f ammoniacal fermentation
ammoniakhaltig ammoniacal
Ammoniakspiegel m ammonia level
Ammoniakspiegelerhöhung f im Blut hyperammoniaemia
Ammoniämie f ammoniaemia
Ammoniumbromid n ammonium bromide *(Beruhigungsmittel)*
Ammoniumchlorid n ammonium chloride
Ammoniumkarbonat n ammonium carbonate
Ammoniumtoleranztest m ammonium tolerance test
Ammoniumverbindung f/quaternäre quaternary ammonium compound *(Desinfektionsmittel)*
Ammonshorn n Ammon's horn, hippocampus
Ammonshornsklerose f Ammon's horn sclerosis, sclerosis of the hippocampus
Ammonurie f ammoniuria
Amnesie f amnesia
~/**anterograde** anterograde amnesia
~/**auditorische** auditory amnesia, word deafness
~/**kortikale** cortical amnesia
~/**olfaktorische** olfactory amnesia
~/**organische** organic amnesia
~/**posthypnotische** posthypnotic amnesia
~/**psychogene** psychogenous amnesia
~/**retrograde** retrograde amnesia
~/**taktile** tactile amnesia, astereognosis
~/**verbale** verbal amnesia
~/**visuelle** visual amnesia, word blindness
amnestisch amnestic, amnesic
amniochorial amniochorial
amnioembryonal amnioembryonic
Amniofetographie f s. Amniographie
Amniogenese f amniogenesis
Amniographie f amniography *(Röntgendarstellung des Feten in der Gebärmutter)*
Amnion n amnion, amnios
Amnionadhäsion f amniotic adhesion
Amnionbänder npl amniotic bands
Amnionbildung f amniogenesis
Amnionentzündung f amnionitis
Amnionepithel n amniotic epithelium
Amnionflüssigkeit f amniotic fluid (liquor), waters
Amnionhöhle f amniotic cavity, bag of waters
Amnioninzision f amniotomy
Amnionitis f amnionitis, amniotitis, inflammation of the amnion
Amnionpunktion f amniocentesis, amniotic puncture
Amnionruptur f amniorrhexis, amniotic sac rupture
Amnionsack m amniotic sac
amnionspiegelnd amnioscopic
Amnionspiegelung f amnioscopy
Amnionzelle f amniotic cell
Amnionzellkultur f amniotic cell culture
Amnionzyste f amniotic cyst
Amniorrhexis f amniorrhexis, amniotic sac rupture
Amniorrhoe f amniorrhoea, [premature] discharge of amniotic fluid
Amnioskopie f amnioscopy
amnioskopisch amnioscopic
amniotisch amniotic, amnionic
Amniotom n amniotome
Amniozentese f amniocentesis, amniotic puncture
Amöbe f amoeba
Amöbenabszeß m [end]amoebic abscess, tropical abscess
~ **der Leber** amoebic liver abscess
amöbenartig amoeboid
Amöbenausscheidung f im Urin amoeburia
Amöbenbefall m der Leber hepatic amoebiasis
Amöbenchemotherapie f antiamoebic chemotherapy
Amöbendysenterie f s. Amöbiasis
Amöbenenzephalitis f amoebic encephalitis
Amöbengangrän f amoebic gangrene
Amöbengift n amoebicide, antiamoebic [agent]
Amöbengranulom n amoebic granuloma, amoeboma
Amöbenhepatitis f amoebic hepatitis
Amöbenkeratitis f amoebic keratitis
Amöbenkolitis f amoebic colitis
Amöbenleberabszeß m amoebic liver abscess
Amöbenmeningoenzephalitis f amoebic meningoencephalitis
Amöbenmittel n antiamoebic [agent], amoebicide
Amöbenpneumonie f amoebic pneumonia
Amöbenruhr f s. Amöbiasis
amöbentötend antiamoebic
Amöbentrophozoit m amoebic trophozoite *(vegetatives Amöbenstadium)*
Amöbenzelle f amoebocyte
Amöbenzyste f amoebic cyst
Amöbiasis f [intestinal] amoebiasis, amoebic (tropical) dysentery, loeschiasis *(durch Entamoeba histolytica)*
amöbisch amoebic
amöbizid antiamoebic
amöboid amoeboid
Amöbom n amoeboma, amoebic granuloma
Amok m amok, amuck *(Zustand einer Besessenheit)* ● ~ **laufen** to run amok
Amoklaufen n amok, amuck
amorph amorphic, amorphous
Amorphie f amorphism, amorphia

Amorphinismus m amorphinism *(bei Süchtigen)*
Amorphismus m amorphism, amorphia
Amorphus m amorphus, amorphous foetus, anideus
Amotio f **chorioideae** choroid detachment, detachment of the choroid
~ **corporis vitrei** detachment of the vitreous body
~ **retinae** retinal detachment, detachment of the retina
AMP/zyklisches s. Adenosinmonophosphat/zyklisches
AMPase f s. Adenosinmonophosphatase
Amphiarthrose f amphiarthrosis, mixed joint
amphiarthrotisch amphiarthrotic
Amphiaster m amphiaster *(Mitosefigur)*
amphiblastisch amphiblastic
amphibol amphibolic *(z. B. Typhusfieber)*
Amphigastrula f amphigastrula *(Eiteilungsstadium)*
amphigenetisch amphigenetic
Amphigonie f amphigony
Amphikaryon m amphikaryon
Amphikranie f amphicrania
Amphimixis f amphimixis *(Erbanlagenvereinigung bei der Befruchtung)*
Amphimorula f amphimorula *(Ungleichheit der beiden Morulahälften)*
amphitrich amphitrichous
Amphizyt m amphicyte
Amphodiplopie f ampho[tero]diplopia
amphophil amphophil[ic]
amphorisch amphoric
Amphoterodiplopie f ampho[tero]diplopia
Ampizillin n ampicillin, α-aminobenzyl penicillin *(Antibiotikum)*
Ampulla f ampulla *(blasenförmige Erweiterung von Hohlorganen)*
~ **canaliculi lacrimalis** ampulla of the lacrimal canaliculus (duct)
~ **ductus deferentis** ampulla of the ductus deferens, Henle's ampulla, seminal capsule
~ **hepatopancreatica** s. ~ Vateri
~ **membranacea** membranous ampulla
~ **membranacea anterior** anterior membranous ampulla
~ **membranacea lateralis** lateral membranous ampulla
~ **membranacea posterior** posterior membranous ampulla
~ **ossea** osseous ampulla *(der knöchernen Bogengänge)*
~ **recti** rectal ampulla
~ **tubae uterinae** ampulla of the uterine tube, pavilion of the oviduct
~ **Vateri** Vater's ampulla, hepatopancreatic ampulla
Ampulle f 1. ampoule, ampul[e], vial, phial *(Glasgefäß)*; 2. s. Ampulla
ampullenförmig ampullate
Amputatio f **femoris supracondylica osteoplastica** s. Amputation/Grittische
~ **pedis osteoplastica** Pirogoff's amputation

Amputation f amputation, ablation, abscission
● **bei der** ~ in amputation
~/**blutsparende** bloodless (dry) amputation
~/**Callandersche** Callander's amputation
~/**Chopartsche** Chopart's amputation *(Vorfußamputation)*
~/**Grittische** Gritti-Stokes amputation, supracondylar amputation
~ **im Lisfrancschen Gelenk** Lisfranc's amputation
~ **in Blutleere** bloodless (dry) amputation
~/**Lisfrancsche** Lisfranc's amputation
~/**partielle** partial amputation
~/**pathologische** pathologic amputation
~/**supravaginale** supravaginal amputation *(der Gebärmutter)*
~/**Symesche** Syme's amputation
Amputationslappen m amputation flap
Amputationsmesser n amputation (amputating) knife
~/**Listonsches** Liston's knife
Amputationsneurom n amputation neuroma, pseudoneuroma
Amputationsrate f amputation rate
Amputationsretraktor m amputation retractor
Amputationssäge f amputation saw
Amputationsstumpf m amputation stump
~/**Chopartscher** Chopart's [amputation] stump
Amputationsstumpfneurom n amputation (stump) neuroma
Amputationsstumpfschmerz m stump neuralgia, amputation stump pain
amputieren to amputate, to ablate, to dismember
~/**im Gelenk** to disarticulate
amputierend ablative
Amputierter m amputee
Amusie f amusia, note blindness
~/**motorische** motor amusia, tonaphasia
~/**sensorische** sensory amusia, tone deafness
Amydriasis f amydriasis
Amyelenzephalus m amyelencephalus
Amyelie f amyelia, [congenital] absence of the spinal cord
amyelin amyelinic, unmyelinated, non-medullated
amyelisch amyelic, amyelous
amyeloisch 1. amyelonic, without bone marrow; 2. amyelonic, without a spinal cord
Amyelus m amyelus
Amygdalektomie f amygdaloidectomy
Amygdalin n amygdalin *(Glykosid)*
Amygdalitis f amygdalitis, inflammation of a tonsil
Amygdalolith m amygdalolith, tonsillar calculus
Amygdalotomie f amygdalotomy
Amylase f [pancreatic] amylase, amylolytic enzyme
α-Amylase f α-amylase
β-Amylase f β-amylase
Amylasebestimmung f amylase estimation
Amylaseerhöhung f **im Blut** hyperamylasaemia
Amylase[spiegel]senkung f **im Blut** hypoamylasaemia

Amylodextrin 34

Amylodextrin *n* amylodextrin
Amylodyspepsie *f* amylodyspepsia, inability to digest starch
amyloid amyloid
Amyloid *n* amyloid *(im Gewebe abgelagerte glasige Eiweißsubstanz)*
~**/atypisches** atypical amyloid, paramyeloid
Amyloidablagerung *f* 1. amyloid deposition; 2. *s.* Amyloidose
~ **in der Niere** amyloid nephrosis
Amyloidangiopathie *f* amyloid angiopathy
Amyloiddegeneration *f* amyloid (bacony, lardaceous) degeneration, glassy swelling
Amyloideinlagerung *f* amyloid deposition
Amyloidentartung *f s.* Amyloidose
Amyloidkörper *m* amyloid body
Amyloidlarynx *m* amyloid larynx
Amyloidleber *f* amyloid (albuminoid) liver, lardaceous (waxy) liver
Amyloidmilz *f* amyloid spleen, lardaceous (waxy, sago) spleen
Amyloidnephropathie *f* amyloid nephropathy
Amyloidnephrose *f* amyloid nephrosis
Amyloidneuropathie *f* amyloid neuropathy
Amyloidniere *f* amyloid (lardaceous, waxy) kidney
Amyloidose *f* amyloidosis, amyloid disease
~**/atypische** atypical amyloidosis
~**/perikollagene** pericollagenous amyloidosis
~**/periretikuläre** perireticular amyloidosis
~**/primäre** primary amyloidosis
~**/sekundäre** secondary amyloidosis
Amyloidschrumpfniere *f s.* Amyloidniere
Amyloidspeicherkrankheit *f* amyloid thesaurismosis
Amyloidstein *m* amyloid body
Amyloidtumor *m* amyloid tumour
Amyloidzylinder *m* waxy cast *(im Urin)*
amylolytisch amylolytic
Amylopektin *n* amylopectin
Amylopektinose *f* amylopectinosis, Andersen's disease, brancher deficiency glycogenosis [type IV of Cori]
Amylophosphorylase *f* amylophosphorylase *(Enzym)*
Amylose *f* amylose
Amylum *n* amylum, starch
Amylurie *f* amyluria, presence of starch in the urine
Amyoästhesie *f* amyoaesthesia, amyoaesthesis, lack of the muscle sense
Amyoplasie *f* amyoplasia, lack of muscle formation
amyoplastisch amyoplastic
amyostatisch amyostatic
Amyosthenie *f* amyosthenia, myasthenia
Amyotaxie *f* amyotaxia
Amyotonia *f* **congenita** congenital atonic pseudoparalysis
Amyotonie *f* amyotonia, lack of muscular tone; floppiness
amyotroph amyotrophic

Amyotrophie *f* amyotrophia, muscular atrophy, myatrophy *(Zusammensetzungen s. unter Muskelatrophie)*
amyotrophisch amyotrophic
Amyxie *f* amyxia, absence (deficiency) of mucous secretion
Amyxorrhoe *f* amyxorrhoea
ana [partes] ana [partes aequales], $\overline{aa}$, $\overline{AA}$, the same quantity of each
anabiotisch anabiotic
anabol[isch] anabolic
Anabolismus *m* anabolism, synthetic (constructive) metabolism
Anadenie *f* 1. anadenia, absence of glands; 2. anadenia, deficiency of glandular activity
Anadidymus *m* anadidymus *(Mißgeburt)*
Anadipsie *f* anadipsia, polydipsia, excessive thirst
Anaemia *f* **perniciosa [Biermer]** *s.* Anämie/perniziöse
~ **pseudoleucaemica infantum** *s.* Anämie/Jaksch-Hayemsche
anaerob an[a]erobic, anaerobiotic
~**/obligat** obligately anaerobic
Anaerobier *m* anaerobe
Anaerobierantitoxin *n* anaerobic antitoxin
Anaerobierinfektion *f* anaerobic infection
Anaerobiont *m* anaerobe
Anaerobiose *f* anaerobiosis
anaerobiotisch anaerobiotic
anaerogen anaerogenic
Anaesthesia *f s.* Anästhesie
~ **olfactoria** *s.* Anosmie
Anaklisis *f* anaclisis
Anakroasie *f* anacroasia, auditory aphasia
Anakrotie *f*, **Anakrotismus** *m* anacrotism *(Auftreten von Wellen im aufsteigenden Teil der Pulskurve)*
Anakusie *f*, **Anakusis** *f* anacousia, anacousis, complete deafness
anal anal
Anal... *s. a.* After... *und* Anus...
Analatresie *f* anal atresia, proctatresia, aproctia; imperforate anus
Analbuminämie *f* analbuminaemia
Analbuminurie-Syndrom *n* analbuminuria syndrome
Analchirurgie *f* anal surgery
Analdivertikel *n* anal diverticulum
Analdreieck *n* anal (rectal) triangle
Analdrüse *f* anal gland
Analektopie *f* anal ectopy
Analekzem *n* anal eczema
Analeptikum *n* analeptic [agent]
analeptisch analeptic
Analerotik *f*, **Analerotismus** *m* anal erotism
Analfissur *f* anal fissure, fissure of the anus
Analfistel *f* anal fistula
Analgeschwür *n* anal ulcer
Analgeschwürstrias *f* anal ulcer triad
Analgesie *f* analgesia, alganaesthesia
~ **der unteren Körperhälfte** para-analgesia

analgesieren to analgize
Analgesiestadium n analgesic state
Analgetikum n analgesic, antalgic [agent]
analgetisch analgetic, analgesic, an[t]algic
Analgie f analgia, analgesia, alganaesthesia
Analhaut f anal skin
Analhöcker m anal tubercle (hillock)
Analinkontinenz f anal incontinence
Analkanal m anal canal, anal part of the rectum
Analkarzinom n anal carcinoma, anus cancer
Analkrypte f anal crypt (sinus)
anallergen anallergenic
anallergisch anallergic
Analmanometrie f anal manometry
Analmembran f anal membrane (plate)
Analmukosa f anal mucosa (skin)
Analöffnung f anal orifice (apertura, opening)
~/definitive definitive (secondary) anal opening
~/fehlende imperforate anus
~/sekundäre s. ~/definitive
Analpapille f anal papilla, papilla of Morgagni
Analphalipoproteinämie f/**familiäre** familial analphalipoproteinaemia
Analplastik f anoplasty
Analplatte f anal plate (membrane)
Analpolyp m anal polyp
Analpruritus m anal pruritus
Analrand m anal rim; anocutaneous line
Analreflex m anal reflex
Analrhagade f anal rhagade
Analring m anal ring
Analsinus m anal sinus (crypt)
Analsperrer m procteurynter, anal dilator
Analsphinkter m anal sphincter
Analsphinkterdehnung f anal sphincteric dilatation
Analsphinkterfunktion f anal sphincteric function
Analsphinkterspasmus m anal sphincteric spasm
Analspiegel m anoscope, anuscope
Analspiegelung f anoscopy
Analstenose f anal stenosis
Analstriktur f anal constriction, proctencl[e]isis
Analtuberkel m anal tubercle (hillock)
Analvenenthrombose f anal venous thrombosis
Analvorfall m anal prolapse
Analyse f analysis, assay
~/chromatographische chromatographic analysis
analysieren to analyze, to assay
Anämie f anaemia, haemophthisis, oligocythaemia, exsanguinity
~/achlorhydrische achlorhydric anaemia
~/achrestische achrestic anaemia
~/achylische achylic anaemia
~/Addisonsche s. ~/**perniziöse**
~/akute hämolytische acute haemolytic anaemia
~/anoxische anoxaemia, oxygen want
~/aplastische aplastic (atrophic) anaemia, panmyelopathia
~/aregeneratorische aregeneratory (primary refractory) anaemia

~/asiderotische s. ~/**sideroprive**
~/chronische hypochrome chronic hypochromic anaemia
~/Cooleysche Cooley's anaemia (disease), Mediterranean anaemia, erythroblastic (target cell) anaemia, thalassaemia major
~/drepanozytäre s. Sichelzellenanämie
~/essentielle hypochrome essential hypochromic anaemia
~/Fabersche Faber's anaemia (Eisenmangelanämie bei Achlorhydrie)
~/familiäre hämolytische s. ~/**konstitutionelle hämolytische**
~/Fanconische Fanconi's anaemia (disease)
~/hämolytische haemolytic anaemia
~/hämorrhagische haemorrhagic anaemia
~/hyperchrome hyperchromic anaemia, hyperchromaemia (Blutfärbeindex über 1)
~/hypochrome hypochromic anaemia, hypochromaemia, achreocythaemia, achroiocythaemia (Blutfärbeindex unter 1)
~/hypochrome mikrozytäre hypochromic microcytic anaemia
~/Jaksch-Hayemsche infantile pseudoleukaemia (pseudoleukaemic anaemia), von Jaksch's anaemia
~/konstitutionelle hämolytische constitutional haemolytic anaemia, chronic acholuric jaundice, chronic familial icterus (jaundice), congenital haemolytic anaemia
~/kryptogene cryptogenic anaemia
~/makrozytäre macrocytic anaemia
~/megalozytäre megalocytic anaemia
~/metastatische metastatic anaemia (infolge Knochenmarkzerstörung durch Tochtergeschwülste)
~/mikrozytäre microcytic anaemia
~/myelopathische myelopathic (myelophthisic) anaemia
~/normochrome normochromic anaemia
~/normozytäre normochrome normocytic normochromic anaemia
~/normozytische normocytic anaemia
~/osteosklerotische osteosclerotic anaemia
~/ovalozytäre ovalocytic anaemia
~/perniziöse pernicious (Addison's) anaemia, Biermer's disease (anaemia)
~/physiologische physiological anaemia
~/pleochrome pleochromic anaemia
~/posthämorrhagische posthaemorrhagic anaemia
~/primäre primary anaemia
~/refraktäre refractory anaemia
~/sekundäre secondary anaemia
~/siderochrestische siderochrestic anaemia
~/sideroprive asiderotic (nutritional hypochromic, iron-deficiency) anaemia
~/splenogene splenogenic anaemia
~/toxische toxic anaemia
~/von Jaksch-Hayemsche s. ~/**Jaksch-Hayemsche**
Anämieblässe f anaemic pallor

Anämiefaktor

Anämiefaktor m extrinsic factor
Anämiesymptom n anaemic symptom
anämisch anaemic, oligocythaemic, bloodless, exsanguine, exsanguinate
Anamnese f anamnesis, case (medical) history, history of the patient
~/**epidemiologische** epidemiologic history
Anamneseerhebung f exploration
anamnestisch anamnestic
Anandrie f anandria, lack of virility; impotence
anangioplastisch anangioplastic
Anankasmus m anankastia, anankasm
Anankast[iker] m anankastic (compulsive) personality
anankastisch anankastic
Anaphase f anaphase *(Kernteilungsphase)*
Anaphie f anaphia *(1. Fehlen des Berührungssinns; 2. abnorme Berührungsempfindlichkeit)*
Anaphorese f anaphoresis *(Elektrophorese)*
anaphoretisch anaphoretic
Anaphorie f anaphoria, hyperphoria
Anaphrodisiakum n anaphrodisiac
Anaphrodisie f anaphrodisia, sexual anaesthesia
Anaphylaktin n anaphylactin *(Anaphylaxieantikörper)*
anaphylaktisch anaphylactic; hypersensitive
anaphylaktogen anaphylactogenic
Anaphylaktogen n anaphylactogen *(Anaphylaxieantigen)*
Anaphylaktogenese f anaphylactogenesis
anaphylaktoid anaphylactoid
Anaphylatoxin n anaphylatoxin, serotoxin
Anaphylaxie f anaphylaxis, immediate hypersensitivity [reaction]; immediate allergy, hypersensivity, hypersensitiveness
~/**aktive** active anaphylaxis
~/**invers-passive kutane** reversed passive cutaneous anaphylaxis
~/**lokale** local anaphylaxis
~/**passive** passive anaphylaxis
Anaphylaxieantikörper m anaphylactic antibody
anaphylaxieauslösend anaphylactogenic
Anaphylaxieauslösung f anaphylactogenesis
Anaphylaxiegift n anaphylatoxin, serotoxin
Anaphylaxiereaktion f anaphylactic reaction
Anaphylaxieschock m anaphylactic shock
Anaplasie f anaplasia *(Zellumbildung in weniger differenzierte Zellen)*
Anaplastik f anaplasty, [ana]plastic surgery
anaplastisch anaplastic
Anarithmie f anarithmia, inability to count
~ **literalis** stuttering, stammering
Anarthrie f anarthria, inability to articulate
Anasarka f anasarca
anasarkös anasarcous
Anastase f anastasis, recovery, convalescence
anastatisch anastatic
Anästhekinesie f anaesthekinesia
Anästhesie f anaesthesia, narcosis *(s. a. unter Narkose)*
~ **der unteren Körperhälfte** para-anaesthesia
~/**intraneurale** intraneural anaesthesia

36

~/**iontophoretische** iontophoretic anaesthesia
~/**lokale** local anaesthesia
~/**paravertebrale** paravertebral anaesthesia (block)
~/**partielle** partial anaesthesia
~/**taktile** tactile anaesthesia
~/**traumatische** traumatic anaesthesia
Anästhesieabteilung f anaesthetic department
Anästhesieäther m anaesthetic ether
Anästhesiebügel m anaesthetic frame
Anästhesieeinleitung f induction of anaesthesia
Anästhesiegas n anaesthetic gas
Anästhesieindex m anaesthetic index
Anästhesiemeter n anaesthetometer, anaesthesimeter
Anästhesieparalyse f anaesthesia paralysis
anästhesieren to anaesthetize, to render anaesthetic; to induce anaesthesia
anästhesierend anaesthetic
Anästhesierisiko n anaesthetic risk
Anästhesierung f anaesthetization
Anästhesiespritze f anaesthetic syringe
Anästhesietubus m anaesthetic airway
Anästhesieverfahren n anaesthetic technique
Anästhesiologe m s. Anästhesist
Anästhesiologie f anaesthesiology
Anästhesist m anaesthesist, anaesthesiologist
Anästhetikum n anaesthetic
anästhetisch 1. anaesthetic, causing anaesthesia; 2. anaesthetic, insensible to pain (touch)
Anästhetometer n anaesthetometer, anaesthesimeter
Anastigmat m anastigmat, anastigmatic lens
anastigmatisch anastigmatic
Anastigmatismus m anastigmatism
Anastomose f anastomosis ● **durch die** ~ transanastomotic
~/**anisoperistaltische** anisoperistaltic anastomosis
~/**aortokoronare** aortocoronary anastomosis
~/**aortopulmonale** aort[ic]opulmonary artery anastomosis; Pott's operation, Pott's and Smith procedure *(Verbindung zwischen großer Körperschlagader und Lungenschlagader bei Fallotscher Tetralogie)*
~/**arteriovenöse** arteriovenous anastomosis
~/**biliodigestive** biliodigestive anastomosis
~/**Blalock-Taussigsche** Blalock-Taussig anastomosis
~/**einschichtige** single-layer anastomosis
~/**enterokolische** enterocolic anastomosis, enterocolostomy
~/**isoperistaltische** isoperistaltic anastomosis
~/**kolorektale** colorectal anastomosis
~/**laterolaterale** side-to-side anastomosis
~/**lateroterminale** side-to-end anastomosis
~/**portokavale** portocaval anastomosis (shunt)
~/**portorenale** portorenal anastomosis (shunt)
~/**portosystemische** portosystemic anastomosis (shunt)
~/**rektokolische** colorectal anastomosis
~/**terminolaterale** end-to-side anastomosis

~/terminoterminale end-to-end anastomosis
Anastomosenaneurysma n anastomotic aneurysm
Anastomosenbogen m anastomotic arch
Anastomosengeschwür n anastomotic ulcer
Anastomoseninsuffizienz f anastomotic leak
Anastomosenklemme f anastomosis clamp (forceps)
Anastomosenödem n anastomotic oedema
Anastomosenstenose f anastomotic stenosis
Anastomosenulkus n anastomotic ulcer
anastomosieren to anastomose, to inosculate (z. B. Blutgefäße, Nerven)
Anastomosierung f anastomosis, inosculation (z. B. von Blutgefäßen)
Anastomosierungsoperation f anastomotic operation
Anastomosis f s. Anastomose
Anastomositis f anastomositis, anastomotic inflammation
anastomotisch anastomotic
Anatom m anatomist
Anatomie f 1. anatomy, anat. (Wissenschaft); 2. anatomy department (Institut); 3. s. Anatomiesaal
~/allgemeine general anatomy
~/beschreibende descriptive anatomy
~ des Mannes andranatomy, anatomy of the male
~ des Nervensystems neuroanatomy
~/makroskopische macroscopic (gross) anatomy, macroanatomy
~/mikroskopische microscopic (minute) anatomy, microanatomy
~/pathologische pathologic (morbid) anatomy, patho-anatomy
~/physiognomonische physiognomonic anatomy
~/physiologische physiologic anatomy
~/systematische systematic anatomy
~/topographische topographic anatomy
~/vergleichende comparative anatomy
Anatomiesaal m anatomic theatre, dissecting room
anatomisch anatomic[al]
Anatoxin n anatoxin (entgiftetes Toxin)
anatrikrot anatricrotic (Pulswelle)
Anatrikrotismus m anatricrotism
Anatropie f anatropia (Aufwärtsdrehung der Augen in Ruhe)
anätzen to cauterize
anazid anacid
Anazidität f anacidity
~ des Magens achlorhydria
Anazoturie f anazoturia
Anbaulinie f accretion line (Stomatologie)
anbohren/den Schädel to trepanize, to trephine
Anchipodie f anchipody (Mißbildung)
Ancylostoma n duodenale Ancylostoma duodenale, Old World hookworm (Erreger der Ankylostomiasis)
ändernd/die Ernährung[sweise] metatrophic
~/die Reizschwelle des Herzens bathmotropic

andersartig 1. heterogenetic, different [from]; 2. s. abartig
Andersen-Krankheit f 1. s. Amylopektinose; 2. Andersen's disease (syndrome), cystic fibrosis of the pancreas
Andrang m afflux, congestion (z. B. von Blut); accumulation (z. B. von Zellen)
Andr[ei]oblastom n andrei[oblast]oma, androblastoma (Ovarialtumor)
Androgalaktosämie f androgalactosaemia
Androgamon n androgamone (Keimzellenwirkstoff)
androgen androgenic
Androgen n androgen, androgenic agent (männliches Geschlechtshormon)
Androgenese f androgenesis, male parthogenesis (Entwicklung ohne mütterlichen Kernanteil)
Androgenizität f androgenicity
Androgenmangel m hypoandrogenism
Androgenresistenz f androgen resistance
Androgenstoffwechsel m androgen metabolism
Androgensynthese f androgen synthesis
Androgenüberschuß m hyperandrogenism
Androgenwirksamkeit f androgenicity
androgyn androgynous, androgynic
Androgynie f androgyny, androgyneity, androgynism, male pseudohermaphroditism
androgynoid androgynoid
android android[al]
Andrologie f andrology, andriatrics
andrologisch andrologic[al]
Andromanie f andromania, nymphomania, metromania
andromorph andromorphous
androphil androphilic, androphilous (z. B. Stechmücken)
Androphobie f androphobia (krankhafte Angst vor Menschen)
Androphonomanie f androphonomania, homicidal insanity
Androstendiol n androstenediol (männliches Keimdrüsenhormon)
Androstendion n androstenedione (männliches Keimdrüsenhormon)
Androsteron n androsterone (männliches Keimdrüsenhormon)
Androtrichie f androtrichia (männlicher Behaarungstyp bei Frauen)
androtrop androtropic
aneinanderlegen to appose, to adapt (z. B. Knochenbruchstücke)
aneinanderliegend adjacent (z. B. Organe); apposed (z. B. Knochenbruchstücke)
anelektrotonisch anelectrotonic
Anelektrotonus m anelectrotonus
Anemophobie f anemophobia (krankhafte Angst vor Wind)
anenzephal anencephalic, anencephalous
Anenzephalie f anencephalia
Anenzephalus m anencephalus, toad head (Mißgeburt)
Aneosinophilie f aneosinophilia (Fehlen der eosinophilen Leukozyten)

Anephrie

Anephrie f anephria
Anergasie f anergasia
Anergie f anergy, hyposensi[ti]vity, hyposensitiveness
anergisch anergic, hyposensitive ● ~ **machen** to hyposensitize
anerkannt/als Arzneimittel officinal
Anerythroplasie f anerythroplasia, inadequate formation of erythrocytes
Anerythropoese f anerythropoiesis, defective formation of erythrocytes
Anerythropsie f anerythro[ble]psia, red blindness, protanopia
Anerythrozyt m anerythrocyte
Anetodermia f [maculosa] anetoderma, dermatitis atrophicans maculosa
aneuploid aneuploid *(Chromosomensatz)*
Aneuploidie f aneuploidy
Aneurie f aneuria, lack of nervous energy
Aneurin n s. Thiamin
Aneurinase f s. Thiaminase
Aneurysma n aneurysm, aneurism
~/**angeborenes** congenital (developmental) aneurysm
~/**arteriovenöses** arteriovenous aneurysm (fistula), phlebarteriodialysis
~/**bakterielles** bacterial aneurysm
~ **der absteigenden Körperschlagader** descending thoracic aortic aneurysm
~ **der Aorta** aortic aneurysm
~ **der Bauchaorta** abdominal aortic aneurysm
~ **des Gehirns** cerebral aneurysm
~ **des Herzens** cardiac aneurysm; cardiocele
~ **dissecans der Aorta** dissecting aortic aneurysm, double-barrelled aorta
~/**dissezierendes** dissecting (intramural) aneurysm
~/**echtes** true (circumscribed) aneurysm
~/**embolisches** embolic aneurysm
~/**endogenes** endogenous aneurysm
~/**falsches** false (spurious, consecutive) aneurysm, pseudoaneurysm
~/**hirsekorngroßes** miliary aneurysm
~/**intrakranielles** intracranial aneurysm
~/**intramurales** intramural aneurysm
~/**murales** mural aneurysm
~/**mykotisches** mycotic aneurysm
~/**partielles** partial aneurysm
~/**primäres** primary aneurysm
~/**rankenförmiges (razemöses)** racemose (cirsoid) aneurysm
~/**sackförmiges** saccular (sacculated) aneurysm, ampullary (saclike) aneurysm
~/**serpentinöses** serpentine aneurysm
~/**spindelförmiges** fusiform (spindle-shaped) aneurysm
~/**spontanes** spontaneous aneurysm
~/**syphilitisches** syphilitic (luetic) aneurysm
~/**traumatisches** traumatic (exogenous) aneurysm
~/**valvuläres** valvular aneurysm
~/**venöses** venous aneurysm
~/**ventrikuläres** ventricular aneurysm
~/**zylindrisches** cylindroid (tubular) aneurysm
Aneurysmaentfernung f[/operative] s. Aneurysmektomie
Aneurysmaeröffnung f[/operative] s. Aneurysmotomie
Aneurysmaerweiterung f aneurysmal dilatation
Aneurysmagröße f size of aneurysm
Aneurysmanadel f aneurysm needle
Aneurysmanaht f aneurysmorrhaphy
Aneurysmaplastik f aneurysmoplasty
Aneurysmaresektion f s. Aneurysmektomie
Aneurysmaröntgen[kontrast]bild n aneurysmogram
Aneurysmasack m aneurysmal sac
Aneurysmaschatten m shadow of aneurysm *(Radiologie)*
Aneurysmaschwirren n aneurysmal thrill
Aneurysmasymptomatik f aneurysmal symptoms
aneurysmatisch aneurysmatic, aneurysmal
Aneurysmawand f wall of the aneurysm
Aneurysmektomie f aneurysmectomy, aneurysmal resection
Aneurysmorrhaphie f aneurysmorrhaphy
Aneurysmotomie f aneurysmotomy, incision of the aneurysm
Anfall m attack, fit, seizure *(z. B. bei Krampfleiden)*; paroxysm *(z. B. bei Atemnot)*; crisis, relapse *(z. B. bei Fieberrückfall)*; stroke, insult *(z. B. bei Hirnschlag) (s. a. unter* Insult*)*; spasm, cramp *(z. B. bei Muskelkrampf)* ● **zwischen zwei Anfällen** interparoxysmal
~/**abortiver epileptischer** petit mal
~/**epileptischer** epileptic seizure (fit)
~/**großer epileptischer** grand mal
~/**hysterischer** hysterical attack (psychosis, neurosis), hysterics
~/**kleiner motorischer** minor motor seizure
~/**plötzlicher** ictus, seizure *(z. B. Gehirnschlag)*
~/**psychomotorischer** psychomotor attack
~/**psychosensorischer** psychosensory attack
~/**tonischer epileptischer** tonic epileptic seizure
~ **vom Jacksontyp/epileptischer** Jacksonian seizure (convulsion), Jacksonian epileptic fit
anfallartig paroxysmal
anfällig susceptible, disposed, cranky, sickly *(z. B. für Krankheiten);* labile *(psychisch)* ● ~ **sein** to be susceptible ● **nicht ~ sein** to be resistant
~/**für Koliken** colicky, colic
Anfälligkeit f susceptibility, disposition *(z. B. für Krankheiten)*; lability *(psychisch)*
Anfallsauslösung f s. Anfallsprovokation
Anfallsbereitschaft f predisposition [to an attack]
Anfallshäufigkeit f frequency of attacks
Anfallskoupierung f interruption of an attack
Anfallsleiden n convulsive disorder (disease)
Anfallsprovokation f provocation of an attack
Anfallsrhythmus m rhythm of attack
Anfallsunterbrechung f interruption of an attack

Anfangsdosis *f* initial dose
Anfangsstadium *n* initial stage
Anfangssymptom *n* initial symptom
anfärben to dye; to stain *(histologische Präparate)*
anfertigen/nach Rezept to dispense
anfeuchten to moisten, to humidify, to wet
anfrischen to freshen, to clean, to refresh, to revivify *(Wunde)*
~/die Hautränder to debride (trim) the skin edges
angeboren 1. congenital, inborn, intrinsic, indigenous, innate, genetous; hereditary, inherent, protal *(Vererbung)* 2. connatal *(bei Geburt)*; 3. instinctive, instinctual *(Instinkt)*; 4. native, indigenous
angegriffen shaken, poor, in a bad condition *(Gesundheit)*; involved, affected *(Organ)*
angelegt/embryonal preformed
Angelhakenharnleiter *m* fishhook ureter
Angelhakenmagen *m* J (fishhook) stomach
Angelhakenschnitt *m* J (fishhook) incision
Angepaßtsein *n*/**soziales** social adjustment (adaptation)
angereichert enriched
angeschoppt turgid, congested; hyperaemic
angeschwollen swollen, turgid, tumefacient, tumid
angesteckt sein to be infected
~ werden [mit] to become infected [with]
angewachsen attached, adherent *(z. B. Bauchfell)*
angezeigt sein to be indicated
~ sein/nicht to be contraindicated
angezogen werden/vom Gebiet der Verletzung to be attracted to areas of injury *(z. B. Leukozyten)*
Angialgie *f* angialgia, angiodynia
Angiasthenie *f* angiasthenia, vascular instability
Angiektasie *f* angiectasia
angiektatisch angiectatic
Angiektid *n* angiectid
Angiektomie *f* 1. angiectomy, arteriectomy; 2. angiectomy, venectomy
angiektopisch angiectopic
Angiektopie *f* angiectopia, displacement (abnormal position) of a blood vessel
angiektopisch angiectopic
Angiitis *f* angi[i]tis, vasculitis, inflammation of a vessel
Angina *f* 1. angina, tonsillitis, tonsillar inflammation; 2. sore throat, pharyngitis; 3. s. ~ pectoris
~ abdominalis abdominal (intestinal) angina
~/agranulozytäre agranulocytic angina
~/akute acute angina
~ cruris intermittent claudication
~/eitrige suppurative angina
~/follikuläre follicular tonsillitis
~/gangränöse gangrenous tonsillitis
~/lakunäre lacunar tonsillitis
~ Ludovici Ludwig's angina *(Zellgewebsentzündung des Mundbodens und der oberen Halsgegend)*

Angiogramm

~/mykotische mycotic tonsillitis
~/oberflächliche superficial tonsillitis
~/parenchymatöse parenchymatous tonsillitis
~ pectoris angina [pectoris], anginal syndrome, cardiac angina (neuralgia), stenocardia, sternalgia, breast pang
~ pectoris/instabile unstable angina pectoris, preinfarction angina
~ pectoris vasomotorica vasomotor angina, false (spurious, mock) angina, pseudo-angina
~/phlegmonöse phlegmonous angina
~ Plaut-Vincenti Plaut's angina, Vincent's angina (infection), trench throat, ulceromembranous stomatitis
~/pseudomembranöse pseudomembranous angina
~ ulceromembranacea s. ~ Plaut-Vincenti
anginaartig anginoid
Angina-pectoris-Daueranfall *m* anginose state
Angina-pectoris-Syndrom *n* anginal syndrome, Heberden's disease
Anginaschmerz *m* anginal pain
Anginasyndrom *n* anginal syndrome
anginiform anginiform, anginoid
anginoid anginoid, resembling angina
Anginophobie *f* anginophobia *(krankhafte Angst vor Angina pectoris)*
anginös anginose, anginous
Angioblast *m* angioblast
angioblastisch angioblastic
Angioblastom *n* angioblastoma
angioblastomatös angioblastomatous
Angiocheiloskop *n* angiocheiloscope *(Instrument zur Beobachtung der Lippenblutgefäße)*
Angiochondrom *n* angiochondroma
Angiodensitometrie *f* angiodensitometry
Angiodermatitis *f* angiodermatitis
Angiodiathermie *f* angiodiathermy
Angiodynie *f* angiodynia, angialgia
Angiodysplasie *f* angiodysplasia
~/intestinale intestinal angiodysplasia
Angiodystrophie *f* angiodystrophy
Angioektasie *f* angioectasia
Angioelephantiasis *f* angioelephantiasis *(Ansammlung von Gefäßgeschwülsten im Unterhautgewebe)*
Angioendotheliom *n* angioendothelioma *(Blutgefäßgeschwulst)*
Angiofibroblastom *n* angiofibroblastoma *(Gefäßgeschwulst mit Fasergewebsanteil)*
Angiofibrom *n* angiofibroma
~/juveniles juvenile angiofibroma
Angiofibromatose *f* angiofibromatosis
Angiofibrose *f* angiofibrosis
angiogen angiogenic
Angiogenese *f* angiogenesis, development of blood vessels
Angiogliom *n* angioglioma
Angiogliomatose *f* angiogliomatosis *(multiple Angiombildung)*
Angiogramm *n* angiogram
~/zerebrales cerebral angiogram

Angiographie

Angiographie f angiography
~/**intrakranielle** intracranial angiography
~/**renale** renal angiography
~/**selektive** selective angiography
~/**semiselektive** semiselective angiography
~/**spinale** spinal angiography
~/**superselektive** superselective angiography
~/**zerebrale** cerebral angiography
Angiographiekatheter m angiography catheter
angiographisch angiographic
Angiohämophilie f angiohaemophilia, vascular haemophilia
Angiohelminthen fpl angiohelminthes
Angiohypertonie f angiohypertonia
Angiohypotonie f angiohypotonia
angioid angioid
Angioidstreifen mpl angioid streaks *(des Augenhintergrunds)*
Angiokardiogramm n angiocardiogram
Angiokardiographie f angiocardiography, cardioangiography
~ **in einer Ebene** single-plane angiocardiography
~/**venöse** venous angiocardiography
angiokardiographisch angiocardiographic
Angiokardiopathie f angiocardiopathy
Angiokavernom n angiocavernoma
angiokavernös angiocavernous
Angiokeratom n angiokeratoma; angiokeratosis
Angiokeratoma n **corporis diffusum [universale]** Fabry's disease, Andersen-Fabry disease, diffuse angiokeratosis
Angiokinematographie f angiocinematography
Angiokymographie f angiokymography
Angiolipom n angiolipoma
Angiolith m angiolith
angiolithisch angiolithic
Angiologe m angiologist
Angiologie f angiology *(Lehre von den Gefäßen und Gefäßkrankheiten)*
angiologisch angiologic[al]
Angiolupoid n angiolupoid *(Teleangiektasien der Gesichtshaut)*
Angiolymphangiom n angiolymphangioma
Angiolyse f angiolysis
Angiom n 1. angioma, haemangioma; 2. angioma, lymphangioma *(s. a. unter Angioma)*
~/**gestieltes** pedunculated angioma
~/**kapillares** capillary angioma, strawberry haemangioma (mark)
~/**kavernöses** cavernous angioma, angiocavernoma
~/**lymphatisches** lymphangioma, angiolymphoma *(gutartige Lymphgefäßgeschwulst)*
Angioma n s. Angiom
~ **myoneuroarteriale** glomus tumour, glomangioma, angiomyoneuroma, angioneuromyoma
~ **retinae** angioma of the retina
~ **serpiginosum** serpiginous angioma
Angiomalazie f angiomalacia, softening of the blood vessels
angiomartig, angiomatoid angiomatoid
angiomatös angiomatous, resembling an angioma

Angiomatose f angiomatosis
~/**enzephalo-trigeminale** encephalotrigeminal (encephalofacial) angiomatosis, Sturge-Weber syndrome, naevoid amentia
~/**hereditäre hämorrhagische** hereditary haemorrhagic angioma (telangiectasia), haemorrhagic familial angiomatosis, Osler-Weber-Rendu disease
~/**meningokutane** meningocutaneous angiomatosis
Angiomatosis f **retinae** s. Krankheit/Lindausche
Angiombildung f/**multiple** s. Angiomatose
Angiomegalie f angiomegaly, enlargement of the blood vessels
Angiometer n angiometer *(Instrument zur Messung des Gefäßlumens)*
Angiomyolipom n angiomyolipoma *(Blutgefäßgeschwulst mit Muskel- und Fettgewebeanteil)*
Angiomyom n angiomyoma
Angiomyoneurom n angiomyoneuroma, glomus tumour, glomangioma, angioneuromyoma
Angiomyopathie f angiomyopathy
Angiomyosarkom n angiomyosarcoma *(Mischgeschwulst)*
Angiomyositis f angiomyositis
Angionekrose f angionecrosis
Angioneoplasma n angioneoplasm
Angioneuralgie f angioneuralgia
Angioneurektomie f angioneurectomy
Angioneurom n angioneuroma *(Mischgeschwulst)*
Angioneuromyom n s. Angiomyoneurom
Angioneuropathie f, **Angioneurose** f angioneurosis, vasoneurosis, vasomotor neurosis, angiospastic syndrome
angioneurotisch angioneurotic
Angioneurotomie f angioneurotomy
Angioödem n angioneurotic oedema
Angioparalyse f angioparalysis
angioparalytisch angioparalytic
Angioparese f angioparesis
angioparetisch angioparetic
Angiopathie f angiopathy
~/**diabetische** diabetic angiopathy
angiopathisch angiopathic
Angiopathologie f angiopathology
Angiophakomatose f angiophacomatosis
Angioplastik f angioplasty
angioplastisch angioplastic
Angiopneumogramm n angiopneumogram
Angiopneumographie f angiopneumography
angiopneumographisch angiopneumographic
Angiopoese f angiopoiesis, formation of blood vessels
angiopoetisch angiopoietic
Angioretikulom n angioreticuloma *(Hirngeschwulst)*
Angioretinogramm n angioretinogram
Angioretinographie f angioretinography
angioretinographisch angioretinographic
Angiorezeptor m angioreceptor
Angioröntgenologe m angiographer

Anilinkrebs

Angiorrhaphie f angiorrhaphy
Angiorrhexis f angiorrhexis, vascular rupture
Angiosarkom n angiosarcoma, vascular sarcoma
Angiose f angiosis
Angiosklerose f angiosclerosis
angiosklerotisch angiosclerotic
Angioskop n angioscope
Angioskopie f angioscopy
Angioskotom n angioscotoma *(Sehstörung durch Blutgefäßschatten)*
Angioskotometer n angioscotometer
Angioskotometrie f angioscotometry
Angiospasmus m angiospasm
angiospastisch angiospastic
Angiostenose f angiostenosis
angiostenotisch angiostenotic
Angiostratigraphie f s. Angiotomographie
Angiostrongyliasis f angiostrongyliasis *(eosinophile Meningitis durch Angiostrongylus cantonensis)*
Angiotelektasie f angiotelectasia
angiotelektatisch angiotelectatic
Angiotensin n angiotensin, angiotonin, hypertensin *(blutdruckerhöhende Substanz)*
Angiotensinase f angiotensinase *(Enzym)*
Angiotensinogen n angiotensinogen, hypertensinogen, renin substrate
Angiotomie f angiotomy
Angiotomogramm n angiotomogram
Angiotomographie f angiotomography
~/simultane simultaneous angiotomography
angiotomographisch angiotomographic
Angiotonin n s. Angiotensin
angiotonisch angiotonic
angiotroph angiotrophic
Angiovideodensitometrie f angiovideodensitometry *(zur Bestimmung der Herzfunktion)*
angleichen to assimilate *(z. B. Nährstoffe) (s. a. anpassen)*
Angophrasie f angophrasia *(Auftreten unartikulierter Laute beim Sprechen)*
angrenzend limitrophe
Angst f anxiety, dread, fear; fright; horror; terror; pavor; dysphoria *(s. a. unter Pavor)*
~/krankhafte phobia, morbid fear
Angstanfall m anxiety attack
Angstdepression f anxiety depression
Angsthierarchie f anxiety hierarchy
Angsthysterie f anxiety hysteria
Angstkomplex m anxiety complex
angstlösend anxiolytic
Angstneurose f anxiety (fright, phobic) neurosis
Angstreaktion f anxiety reaction
Angstschweiß m cold sweat
Angstsyndrom n anxiety syndrome
Angsttraum m anxiety dream; nightmare
Angstzustand m anxiety state
Anguilluliasis f strongyloidiasis, strongylosis, anguilluliasis, anguillulosis, intestinal capillariasis
angulär angular
Angularissyndrom n Gerstmann's syndrome
Angulus m angle

~ acromialis acromial angle
~ arcuum costarum s. ~ infrasternalis
~ costae angle of the rib
~ infectiosus perleche
~ inferior scapulae inferior angle of the scapula
~ infrasternalis infrasternal (costal, epigastric) angle
~ iridocornealis iridocorneal (iris, iridian) angle
~ lateralis scapulae lateral angle of the scapula
~ mandibulae mandibular angle, angle of the mandible (jaw)
~ mastoideus ossis temporalis mastoid angle of the temporal bone
~ medialis scapulae medial angle of the scapula
~ oculi lateralis lateral (temporal) angle of the eye
~ oculi medialis (nasalis) medial (nasal) angle of the eye
~ oculi temporalis s. ~ oculi lateralis
~ oris angle of the mouth (lips), labial angle
~ pontocerebellaris pontocerebellar angle
~ pubis angle of the pubes
~ scapulae angle of the scapula
~ sterni angle of the sternum, angle of Louis (Ludwig)
~ subpubicus subpubic angle
~ superior scapulae superior angle of the scapula
~ venosus venous angle
anhaftend adherent
anhaltend persistent, prolonged *(z. B. Medikamentenwirkung)*
~/das ganze Leben lifelong
anhämolytisch anhaemolytic
Anhämopoese f anhaemopoiesis, anhaemato[poie]sis
anhämopoetisch anhaemopoietic
Anhang m appendix, appendage
~/schnabelförmiger rostrum
Anhangsgebilde npl [menschlicher Organe] s. Adnexe 1.
anhäufen to agglomerate; to accumulate
anheben to disimpact *(Knochenimpression)*
anheften to attach, to affix *(z. B. chirurgisch)*
Anheftung f anchorage, pexis *(z. B. eines Organs)*; attachment *(z. B. der Netzhaut)*
anhepatisch anhepatic
anhepatogen anhepatogenic
Anhidrose f anhidrosis, absence of sweat secretion
~/tropische tropical (heat) anhidrosis
anhidrotisch anhidrotic
Anhydrämie f anhydraemia
anhydrämisch anhydraemic
Anhydrase f anhydrase *(Enzym)*
Anideus m anideus, amorphus, amorphous foetus
anikterisch anicteric, non-icteric, non-jaundiced
Anilinismus m anilinism, anilism, aniline poisoning
Anilinkrebs m aniline carcinoma, dye-worker's cancer *(der Harnblase)*

Anilinvergiftung

Anilinvergiftung f s. Anilinismus
animal[isch] animal
Animal-Protein-Faktor m s. Vitamin B_{12}
Anionenaustauscher m anion exchanger
Anionenaustausch[er]harz n anion-exchange resin
Aniridie f aniridia, absence of the iris
Aniseikometer n aniseikometer, eikonometer (Ophthalmologie)
Aniseikonie f aniseikonia (Größenabbildungsfehler des Auges)
aniseikonisch aniseikonic
anisochrom[atisch] anisochromic
Anisochromie f anisochrom[as]ia (z. B. der roten Blutkörperchen)
anisodaktyl anisodactylous
anisodont anisodont
Anisodontie f anisodontia
anisogam anisogamous
Anisogamet m anisogamete
Anisogamie f anisogamy
anisognath anisognathous (Gebiß)
Anisokaryose f anisokaryosis (unterschiedliche Zellkerngröße bei gleichartigen Zellen)
Anisokorie f anisocoria (unterschiedliche Pupillengröße)
anisolezithal anisolecithal
Anisomakrozytose f anisomacrocytosis
anisometrop anisometropic
Anisometroper m anisometrope
Anisometropie f anisometropia, anisopia (Refraktionsfehler des Auges)
Anisomikrozytose f anisomicrocytosis
anisomorph anisomorphic, anisomorphous
Anisonukleose f anisonucleosis (unterschiedliche Zellkerngröße)
Anisophorie f anisophoria (Horizontalabweichung der Sehachsen)
Anisopoikilozytose f anisopoikilocytosis
Anisosphygmie f anisosphygmia (Pulsunterschied an symmetrischen Arterien)
anisosthen[isch] anisosthenic, not of equal power (Muskeln)
Anisothrombozytose f anisothrombocytosis
Anisotonie f anisotonia, unequal osmotic pressure
anisotonisch anisotonic
anisotrop anisotropic, anisotropous (Muskelfasern)
Anisotropie f anisotropy
Anisozytose f anisocytosis (Vorhandensein von roten Blutkörperchen ungleicher Größe)
Anisurie f anisuria (Wechsel von Polyurie und Oligurie)
Anitschkow-Zelle f Anitschkow cell (myocyte)
ankleben to adhere
anklebend adherent
anknacken to fracture partially (z. B. Knochen)
Ankopplung f/elektromechanische electromechanical coupling (Physiologie)
ankündigend premonitory
Ankyloblepharon n ankyloblepharon (Verwachsung der Augenlidränder)
~ **filiforme adnatum** filiform adnatum ankyloblepharon
~/**laterales partielles** lateral partial ankyloblepharon
~/**mediales partielles** medial partial ankyloblepharon
Ankylocheilie f ankylocheilia, synch[e]ilia
Ankylodaktylie f ankylodactyly (1. Verwachsung der Finger; 2. Verwachsung der Zehen)
Ankyloglossie f ankyloglossia; ankyloglosson (Verwachsung der Zunge mit dem Mundboden)
Ankyloglossum-superius-Syndrom n ankyloglossum superius syndrome
Ankylokolpos n ankylokolpos, atresia of the vagina
Ankylophobie f ankylophobia (krankhafte Angst vor Gelenkversteifung)
Ankylose f ankylosis, stiffness of a joint, acampsia
~/**angeborene** congenital ankylosis
~/**echte** true ankylosis
~/**extrakapsuläre** extracapsular ankylosis
~/**falsche** false ankylosis, pseudoankylosis
~/**fibröse** fibrous ankylosis
~/**intrakapsuläre** intracapsular ankylosis
~/**knöcherne** bony (osseous) ankylosis
~/**künstliche** s. Arthrodese
~/**ligamentäre** ligamentous ankylosis
~/**partielle** partial ankylosis
ankylosebewirkend ankylopoietic
ankylosieren to ankylose (operativ oder auf natürlichem Wege)
ankylosierend ankylosing, ankylopoietic
Ankylosierung f/operative s. Arthrodese
Ankylostoma n Ankylostoma, hookworm
Ankylostomainfestation f s. Ankylostomiasis
Ankylostomenei n hookworm egg
Ankylostomiasis f ancylostomiasis, ankylostomiasis, brickmaker's anaemia, Egyptian chlorosis, miner's anaemia (sickness), tunnel anaemia, Saint Gotthard's disease
Ankylotie f ankylotia (Verwachsung beider Ohrmuscheln)
ankylotisch ankylotic
Ankylotom n ankylotome (krummes chirurgisches Messer)
Ankylotomie f ankylotomy (operative Beseitigung einer Ankyloglossie)
Anlage f 1. anlage, primordium (Embryologie); 2. [pre]disposition, inclination, constitution, tendency; aptitude, talent (Genetik)
anlagebedingt constitutional
Anlagebild n genotype
Anlagen fpl/**vererbte** heritage, heredity
anlagern to adsorb; to accumulate
~/**sich** to juxtapose (z. B. Organe)
anlagernd adsorbent
Anlagerung f adsorption; accumulation
Anlagerungs[knochen]span m onlay graft, bone onlay
Anlaß m cause, motive, occasion
Anlasser m **für Zahnbohrer** floor control for the dental engine

anlegen/die Ekg-Elektroden to attach the ECG leads
~/ein Tracheostoma to perform a tracheostomy
~/eine Bandage to apply a bandage, to bandage, to bind
~/eine Schiene to splint
~/einen Gips[verband] to put into plaster
~/einen Heftpflasterverband to strap [up]
~/einen Verband to dress [up], to bandage
annähen to sew, to suture, to attach
Annähen n suturing, pexis (z. B. von Organen bei Lageänderung)
Annahme f take, acceptance (von Transplantaten)
annehmen to adopt, to take, to accept (z. B. Transplantate)
annehmend/nicht Farbe achromatophil
Annexe mpl s. Adnexe
Annexitis f adnexitis, annexitis
Anochromasie f anochromasia (Hämoglobinanhäufung am Erythrozytenrand)
Anodenöffnungsklonus m anodal opening clonus
Anodenöffnungstetanus m anodal opening tetanus
Anodenöffnungszuckung f anodal opening contraction
Anodenschließungstetanus m anodal closure tetanus
Anodenschließungszuckung f anodal closure contraction
Anodontie f anodontia, anodontism, absence of teeth
Anodynie f anodynia, absence of pain
anogenital anogenital
Anoia f anoia, idiocy
anokokzygeal anococcygeal
anokutan anocutaneous
Anokutanlinie f anocutaneous line
anomal anomalous, abnormal, irregular
Anomalie f anomaly, abnormality, abnormalism
~/anorektale anorectal anomaly
~/Ebsteinsche Ebstein's anomaly (disease, syndrome), Ebstein's malformation [of the tricuspid valve]
Anomalität f s. Anomalie
Anomaloskop n anomaloscope (Farbsinnuntersuchungsgerät) ,
Anomie f anomia, nominal aphasia (Verlust der Namensfindung)
Anonychie f anonychia, absence of the nails
Anonyma f s. Arteria brachiocephalica
anopelvisch anopelvic
anoperineal anoperineal
Anopheles[mücke] f anopheles, anopheline [mosquito]
anophelestötend anophelicide
Anophelesvernichtungsmittel n anophelicide [agent]
Anophelesvertreibungsmittel n anophelifuge [agent]
anophthalm anophthalmic

Anophthalmie f anophthalmia, absence of the eyes
anophthalmisch anophthalmic
Anopie f 1. anop[s]ia, blindness; 2. anop[s]ia, anoopsia, upward strabismus
~/zentrale central blindness
Anoplastik f anoplasty
Anopsie f s. Anopie
Anorch[id]ie f, **Anorchismus** m anorchia, anorchi[di]sm, absence of testes
Anorchus m anorchus
anorektal anorectal
Anorektalabszeß m anorectal abscess
Anorektalanomalie f anorectal anomaly
Anorektalchirurgie f anorectal surgery
Anorektalerkrankung f anorectal disease
Anorektalfistel f anorectal fistula
Anorektalinkontinenz f anorectal incontinence
Anorektallinie f anorectal line
Anorektalplastik f anorectoplasty
Anorektalsyndrom n anorectal syndrome
Anorektikum n anorexiant [agent], anorectic [agent]
Anorektum n anorectum
Anorexie f anorexia, absence of appetite
~/falsche pseudoanorexia
Anorgasmie f anorgasm[ia], failure to experience orgasm
anormal s. anomal
Anormalität f s. Anomalie
Anorthographie f anorthography
Anorthopie f 1. anorthopia (Störung des symmetrischen Sehens); 2. s. Strabismus
Anoskop n anoscope, anuscope
Anoskopie f anoscopy
Anosmie f anosmia, olfactory anaesthesia, absence of the sense of smell
~/afferente afferent anosmia
~/obstruktive obstructive anosmia
~/organische organic anosmia
~/periphere peripheral anosmia
~/respiratorische respiratory anosmia
~/zentrale central anosmia
Anosognosie f anosognosia, nosoagnosia (subjektives Nichterkennen von krankhaften Veränderungen)
anospinal anospinal
Anosteoplasie f anosteoplasia, cleidocranial dysostosis (dysplasia)
Anostose f anostosis (fehlerhafte Knochenentwicklung)
Anotie f anotia (Fehlen der Ohrmuschel)
Anovarie f, **Anovarismus** m anovarism (Fehlen der Eierstöcke)
anovesikal anovesical
Anovulation f anovulation (Fehlen des Eisprungs)
anovulatorisch anovular, anovulatory
Anoxämie f anoxaemia, oxygen want
anoxämisch anoxaemic
Anoxie f anoxia
~ des Gehirns cerebral anoxia
~ des Neugeborenen anoxia of the newborn

anoxisch

anoxisch anoxic, anoxaemic
anpassen to adapt, to adjust, to accommodate; to acclimatize, to acclimate *(z. B. an Klima)*; to coapt *(z. B.Knochenbrüche)*
~/sich to adapt, to adjust, to accommodate; to acclimatize, to acclimate
Anpassen n coaptation *(z. B. von Knochenbrüchen)*; fitting *(z. B. eines Verbandes)*
anpassend[/sich] adaptable, adjustable, accommodative
Anpassung f adaptation, adjustment, accommodation *(z. B. des Auges)*
~/berufliche professional adaptation
~/klimatische acclima[tiza]tion
~/mangelnde maladjustment, maladaptation *(z. B. an die Umwelt)*
~/soziale social adaptation
anpassungsfähig adaptable
~/beschränkt monotropic
~/stark polytropic
Anpassungshypertrophie f adaptive hypertrophy
Anpassungsreaktion f adjustment reaction (response)
Anpassungsstörung f pathergasia, adaptation disturbance
Anpassungssyndrom n adaptation syndrome
~/kardiopulmonales cardiopulmonary adaptation syndrome
Anpassungstest m adaptation test
Anpassungsverhalten n adaptive behaviour
Anpassungsvermögen n adaptability
Anpassungszeit f adaptation time; presphygmic interval *(des Herzens)*
anregen to excite, to stimulate, to activate, to animate; to promote *(z. B. den Kreislauf)*; to bring about *(z. B. die Harnausscheidung)*; to induce *(z. B. den Schlaf)*; to dope *(mit Dopingmittel)*; to innervate *(durch Nervenreize)*
anregend exciting, stimulating, stimulative, stimulant; analeptic; tonic
~/den Speichelfluß ptyalogogue
~/die Körperwärmebildung thermoexcitory
~/die Milchbildung galactogenous
~/die Milchdrüsen lactogenic
~/die Pepsinsekretion pepsigogue
~/die Retikulozytenbildung reticulocytogenic
Anregung f excitation, excitement, stimulation; innervation *(durch Nervenreize)*
Anregungsbad n stimulating bath
Anregungsmittel n stimulant [agent], analeptic [agent]; dope
anreichen/die Instrumente to pass the instruments
anreichern/mit Sauerstoff to oxygenate; to arterialize *(venöses Blut)*
~/mit Vitaminen to vitaminize
Anreicherung f enrichment; concentration
~ mit Sauerstoff oxygenation; arterialization
anreizend stimulant
anrühren to mix *(z. B. Gips)*
Anrührplatte f mixing slab *(zahnmedizinische Behandlung)*

ANS s. Atemnotsyndrom
Ansa f ansa, loop
~ cervicalis cervical ansa
~ lenticularis (lentiformis) lenticular loop
~ nephroni Henle's loop, loop of Henle *(Teil des Hauptstücks der Nierenkanälchen)*
~ peduncularis peduncular ansa, ansa of Reil
~ subclavia ansa of Vieussens
~ vitellina vitelline ansa
Ansatz m insertion, attachment *(Anatomie)*
Ansatzpunkt m insertion, point of attachment *(z. B. eines Muskels am Knochen)*
Ansatzsehne f tendon of insertion *(eines Muskels)*
ansäuern to acidify, to acidulate
Ansäuern n acidification, acidulation
ansaugen to suck, to aspirate
Ansaugung f suction, aspiration
Anschauungsbilder npl/**eidetische** eidetic (primary memory) images
Anschlagsperre f im Gelenk arthroereisis, arthrorisis
anschnallen/eine Prothese to don a prosthesis
Anschnallgurt m strap *(am Operationstisch)*
Anschoppung f congestion, engorgement, stasis
~/rote [red] engorgement of the lung *(bei Lungenentzündung)*
~/venöse venosity, venous stasis
Anschoppungsherzversagen n congestive cardiac (heart) failure
anschwellen to swell [up], to tumefy; to enlarge *(Drüsen)*
anschwellend swelling, [in]tumescent, tumefacient, turgescent
Anschwellung f swelling, enlargement, [in]tumescence, intumescentia, tumefaction, turgescence
~ der kleinen Schamlippen nymphoncus
anschwemmen to store, to deposit *(z. B. im Knochenmark)*
ansetzen 1. to insert, to attach *(z. B. Muskel)*; 2. to incubate *(z. B. Bakterienkulturen)*; 3. to put on weight *(zunehmen)*; 4. to apply *(z. B. Blutegel)*
ansiform ansiform, loop-shaped, ansate
anspannen to contract, to tense, to strain *(Muskel)*; to exert *(z. B. Kräfte, Verstand)*
Anspannung f 1. tension, stretch[ing] *(Muskelkontraktion)*; 2. exertion, strain[ing], effort
ansprechbar sein to be responsive *(Patient)*
~ sein/nicht to be resistant *(z. B. auf eine Therapie)*
ansprechen to react, ro respond, to be responsive
~/auf Antibiotika to respond to antibiotics *(Krankheitserreger)*
~/auf die Behandlung to respond to treatment *(therapy)*
~/auf Penizillin to be responsive (susceptible) to penicillin
~/nicht to be ineffective *(z. B. Medikament)*
Anstalt f home, hospital, clinic; sanatorium

Anstaltsbehandlung f institutional (hospital) treatment
Anstaltsinsasse m inpatient
anstechen to puncture, to lance
Ansteckbarkeit f infectivity, infectiosity; infectiousness; contagiousness *(z. B. einer Krankheit)*
anstecken to infect, to contaminate
~/neu to reinfect
~/sich to infect, to catch [infection], to become (get) infected, to be catching
ansteckend infectious, infective, contagious, morbiphor, pestilential; virulent; zymotic
Ansteckung f infection, contamination *(z. B. mit Bakterien)*; infestation *(z. B. mit Parasiten)*
~/bakterielle bacterial contamination
ansteckungsfähig infectable, infectious, contagious; virulent
Ansteckungsfähigkeit f infectiosity, infectivity, contagiousness *(z. B. einer Krankheit)*; infectiosity, virulence *(z. B. eines Krankheitserregers)*
ansteckungsfrei free from infection
Ansteckungsgefahr f danger of infection
Ansteckungsherd m focus [of infection]
Ansteckungskrankheit f infectious disease, contagious (communicable) disease
Ansteckungsstoff m contagion
ansteigen to rise, to increase, to go up *(z. B. Fieber, Blutdruck)*
Anstieg m rise, increase
Anstrengung f effort, exertion, strain[ing]
Anstrengungsasthma n exercise induced asthma
antagonisieren to antagonize, to counteract, to act in opposition; to neutralize
Antagonismus m antagonism, antagonistic action, counteraction, opposition
Antagonist m 1. antagonist, antagonistic muscle; 2. antagonist, antagonistic tooth; 3. antagonist, competitor, opponent *(Pharmakologie)*
Antagonistendurchtrennung f/**operative** equilibrating operation
antagonistisch antagonistic, opposing
Antalgikum n antalgic [agent], analgesic, analgetic
Antaphrodisiakum n antaphrodisiac
Antarthritikum n antarthritic [agent]
antazid antacid, antiacid
Antazidabehandlung f antacid therapy *(bei peptischen Geschwüren)*
Antazidum n antacid [agent]
ante cibum ante cibum, a. c., before meals
~ mortem antemortem, ante mortem, premortal, before death
~ partum s. antepartal
antebrachial antebrachial
Antebrachium n s. Unterarm
antefebril antefebrile
Antefixationsgeburt f antefixation delivery
Antefixationsoperation f **der Gebärmutter nach Baldy-Webster** Baldy-Webster operation

anteflektieren to anteflect
Anteflexio f **uteri** anteflexion of the uterus
Anteflexion f anteflexion
antekolisch antecolic
antekubital antecubital
Antekurvation f, **Antekurvatur** f antecurvature
antemenstruell premenstrual
Antemenstrum n antemenstrum
Antemetikum n antemetic [agent]
antenatal antenatal, prenatal
antepartal antepartal, ante partum, antepartum, before delivery (birth), prepartal
Antepartumblutung f antepartum haemorrhage
Anteposition f anteposition, forward displacement *(z. B. des Uterus)*
anterior anterior, anticus, a.
anteroparietal anteroparietal
anteroposterior anteroposterior
anterosuperior anterosuperior
anterotransversal anterotransverse
Antesystole f antesystole
antethorakal antethoracic
Antetorsion f antetorsion
Anteversion f anteversion
antevertieren to antevert *(z. B. Gebärmutter)*
Anthelix f anthelix *(Ohrmuschelwindung)*
Anthelminthikum n anthelmintic [agent], helminthagogue
anthelminthisch anthelmint[h]ic
Anthracosis f **pulmonum** s. Anthrakose
Anthrakofibrose f anthracofibrosis
Anthrakose f anthracosis, black phthisis, miner's lung
Anthrakosilikose f anthracosilicosis, miner's asthma (phthisis), coal miner's disease *(Kombination von Anthrakose und Silikose)*
anthrakotisch anthracotic
Anthrax m anthrax, malignant (contagious) anthrax, splenic fever, tanner's (woolsorter's, ragsorter's) disease, malignant pustule, milzbrand, charbon
~/intestinaler intestinal anthrax
~/pulmonaler pulmonary anthrax
~/symptomatischer symptomatic anthrax
~/zerebraler cerebral anthrax
Anthrax... s. Milzbrand...
anthrazid anthracidal
Anthropodesoxycholsäure f chenode[s]oxycholic acid *(Gallensäure)*
Anthropogenese f anthropogenesis, anthropogeny *(Phylogenese und Ontogenese)*
anthropogenetisch anthropogen[et]ic
Anthropoid m anthropoid [ape]
Anthropologie f anthropology, science of man
anthropologisch anthropologic[al]
Anthropometer n anthropometer
Anthropometrie f anthropometry *(Bestimmung der menschlichen Körpermaße)*
anthropometrisch anthropometric
Anthroponose f anthroponosis
Anthropophagie f anthropophagy, cannibalism *(sexuelle Abnormität)*

anthropophil

anthropophil anthropophilic, androphilous *(z. B. Insekten)*
anthropophob anthropophobic
Anthropophobie *f* anthro[po]phobia *(Abneigung gegen Menschen)*
Anthroposomatologie *f* anthroposomatology *(Lehre vom menschlichen Körper)*
Anthroposoziogenese *f* anthroposociogenesis
Anthropozoonose *f* anthropozoonosis, zooanthroponosis
Anti-A *n* anti-blood group A antibody *(Blutserologie)*
Antiabstoßungsbehandlung *f* antirejection therapy *(bei Transplantation)*
antiadrenerg[isch] antiadrenergic, sympathicolytic
Antiagglutinin *n* antiagglutinin
Antiaggressin *n* antiaggressin *(Antikörper)*
Antiallergikum *n* antiallergic [agent]
Antiallertikum *n s.* Antihistaminikum
Antiamöbi[ati]kum *n* antiamoebic [agent], amoebicide
antiamöbisch antiamoebic
Antiamylase *f* antiamylase
Antianämie-Faktor *m* antianaemia factor (principle)
Antianämikum *n* antianaemic [agent]
antianämisch antianaemic
Antianaphylaktikum *n* antianaphylactic [agent]
Antianaphylaxie *f* antianaphylaxis *(Unempfindlichkeit gegenüber Antigenen)*
Antiandrogen *n* antiandrogen
Antiantikörper *m* antiantibody
Antiarrhythmikum *n* antiarrhythmic [agent]
antiarrhythmisch antiarrhythmic
Antiarthritikum *n* antiarthritic [agent]
antiarthritisch ant[i]arthritic
Antiasthmatikum *n* antiasthmatic [agent]
antiasthmatisch ant[i]asthmatic
Antiatelektasefaktor *m* surface-active agent, surfactant
antiazid ant[i]acid
Antiazidum *n* antacid [agent]
Anti-B *n* anti-blood group B antibody *(Blutserologie)*
Antibabypille *f* anti-baby pill
Antibasalmembran-Glomerulonephritis *f* antibasement-membrane glomerulonephritis
Antiberiberivitamin *n* antiberiberi vitamin, vitamin B₁
Antibiogramm *n* antibiotic (antibacterial) spectrum
Antibiose *f* antibiosis *(Hemmwirkung eines Mikroorganismus auf einen anderen)*
Antibiotikaära *f* antibiotic era
Antibiotikabehandlung *f* antibiotic therapy
~/hochdosierte high-dose antibiotic treatment
Antibiotika-Dilutions-Test *m* antibiotic dilution test
Antibiotikapräparat *n* antibiotic preparation
Antibiotikaprophylaxe *f* antibiotic prophylaxis
antibiotikaresistent resistant to antibiotics

Antibiotikaresistenz *f* antibiotic resistance
Antibiotikasalbe *f* antibiotic ointment
Antibiotikaschutz *m* antibiotic cover
Antibiotikaspray *m(n)* antibiotic spray
Antibiotikastrategie *f* antibiotic strategy
Antibiotikatestung *f* antibiotic testing
Antibiotikaunempfindlichkeit *f* antibiotic resistance
Antibiotikaverordnung *f* antibiotic prescribing
Antibiotikaverschreibung *f* antibiotic prescribing
Antibiotikawirkung *f* antibiotic action
Antibiotikum *n* antibiotic [agent], antibiotic preparation
~ der Wahl antibiotic of choice
antibiotisch antibiotic
Antibotulismusserum *n* antibotulinus serum, botulism (botulinus) antitoxin
Anticandidaserum-Präzipitin *n* anticandida serum precipitin
Anticholeraserum *n* anticholera serum
Anticholinergikum *n* anticholinergic [agent]
anticholinergisch anticholinergic, parasympathicolytic
Anticholinesterase *f* anticholinesterase *(Enzym)*
Antidekubitusbett *n* hydrostatic bed
antidepressiv antidepressive, antidepressant
Antidepressivum *n* antidepressant [agent]
Antidermatitisvitamin *n* antidermatitis vitamin, vitamin B₆
Antidiabetikum *n* antidiabetic [agent]
antidiabetisch antidiabetic
Antidiarrhoikum *n* antidiarrhoeal [agent], costive [agent]
antidiarrhöisch antidiarrhoeal
Antidiphtherieserum *n* antidiphther[it]ic serum
Antidiurese *f* antidiuresis
Antidiuretikum *n* antidiuretic [agent]
antidiuretisch antidiuretic
Antidot *n* antidote
Anti-D-Prophylaxe *f* anti-D prophylaxis
Anti-D-Serum *n* anti-D serum
antiekzematisch antieczematic
Antiemetikum *n* antiemetic [agent]
antiemetisch antiemetic
antientzündlich anti-inflammatory
Antienzym *n* antienzyme
antiepidemisch antiepidemic
Antiepileptikum *n* antiepileptic [agent], anticonvulsant [agent]
antiepileptisch antiepileptic
Antierysipeloidserum *n* antierysipeloid serum
antierythrozytär antierythrocytic
antifebril *s.* antipyretisch
Antifebrilium *n s.* Antipyretikum
Antiferment *n* antiferment *(gärungshemmendes Mittel)*
antifermentativ antifermentative, antizymotic
antifibrillatorisch antifibrillatory
Antifibrinolysin *n* antifibrinolysin
Antifibrinolytikum *n* antifibrinolytic [agent]
antifibrinolytisch antifibrinolytic
Antifilarienmittel *n* antifilarial [agent]

antifungiell antifungal, antifungoid, suppressing (destroying) fungi
antigen antigenic
Antigen n antigen, immunogen
~/**artfremdes** xenoantigen
~/**fetopankreatisches** foetopancreatic antigen
~/**heterogenetisches** heterogenetic antigen
~/**inkomplettes** incomplete antigen, hapten
~/**karzinoembryonales** carcinoembryonic antigen
~/**onkofetales** oncofoetal antigen
~/**ubiquitäres** ubiquitous antigen
Antigenämie f antigenaemia *(Vorhandensein von Antigen im Blut)*
Antigen-antibody-crossed-Elektrophorese f antigen-antibody-crossed electrophoresis
Antigen-Antikörper-Komplex m antigen-antibody complex
Antigen-Antikörper-Nephritis f antigen-antibody nephritis
Antigen-Antikörper-Reaktion f antigen-antibody reaction
Antigenbehandlung f antigenotherapy
Antigendeterminante f antigenic determinant
Antigendrift f antigenic drift
Antigeneiweiß n antigenic protein
Antigenformel f antigenic formula
Antigenhierarchie f antigenic hierarchy
Antigenität f antigenicity
Antigenlokalisation f antigenic localization
Antigenmodulation f antigenic modulation
Antigennachweistest m antigen provocation test
Antigenshift f antigenic shift
Antigenstärke f antigenic strength
Antigenstruktur f antigenic structure
antigentolerant anergic
Antigentoleranz f anergy
Antigenwirkung f antigenicity
antiglaukomatös antiglaucomatous
Antiglaukombehandlung f antiglaucomatous therapy
Antiglobulin n antiglobulin
Antiglobulinkonsumptionstest m antiglobulin consumption test
Antiglobulinserum n antiglobulin (Coombs) serum
Antiglobulintest m antiglobulin test, [Race-] Coombs test, antihuman globulin (serum) test, direct Coombs (developing) test
~/**indirekter** indirect Coombs test
Anti-Glomerulum-Basalmembran-Antikörper m antiglomerular basement membrane antibody *(Niere)*
Antigonorrhoikum n antigonorrhoeic [agent]
Anti-Graue-Haare-Faktor m anti-grey-hair factor *(Vitamin-B-Komplex)*
Antihämagglutinin n antihaemagglutinin
Antihämolysin n antihaemolysin
antihämolytisch antihaemolytic
Antihämophilieglobulin n antihaemophilic globulin (factor), AHF
Antihämophiliepräparat n antihaemophilia preparation

Antihämorrhagikum n antihaemorrhagic [agent], haemostatic [agent]
antihämorrhagisch ant[i]haemorrhagic, haemostatic, haemostyptic
Antihämorrhoidenmittel n antihaemorrhoidal [agent]
Antiheparinfaktor m antiheparin factor
Antihidrotikum n antihidrotic [agent]
Antihistaminikum n antihistaminic [agent], antihistamine [drug]
antihistaminisch antihistaminic
Antihistaminliberation f antihistamin liberation
Antihormon n antihormone
Antihumanglobulin n antihuman globulin
Antihumanglobulinkonsumptionstest m antihuman globulin consumption test
Antihuman-IgA-Antiserum n antihuman IgA antiserum
Antihumanimmunglobulin n antihuman immunglobulin
Antihyaluronidase f antihyaluronidase
antihypertensiv antihypertensive
Antihypertensivum n, **Antihypertonikum** n antihypertensive [agent], hypotensor
Antihypnotikum n antihypnotic [agent]
Antihypotensivum n, **Antihypotonikum** n antihypotensive [agent], hypertensor
Antiimmunoglobulin n anti-immunoglobulin
antiinfektiös anti-infective, anti-infectious
antiinflammatorisch anti-inflammatory
antikachektisch anticachectic
antikariös anticariogenic, anticarious
antiketogen antiketogen[et]ic
Antiketogenese f antiketogenesis
Antikoagulans n anticoagulant
Antikoagulantienbehandlung f anticoagulant therapy (treatment)
Antikoagulantienüberwachung f anticoagulant [therapy] control
Antikoagulation f anticoagulation
Antikoagulationsmittel n anticoagulant
antikoagulierend anticoagulant, anticoagulative
Antikodon m anticodon *(in Transfer-RNS)*
Antikollagenase f anticollagenase
Antikomplement n anticomplement
Antikomplementaktivität f anticomplementary activity
antikomplementär anticomplementary
Antikomplementtitration f anticomplementary titration
antikonvulsiv anticonvulsive, anticonvulsant
Antikonvulsivatherapie f anticonvulsant therapy (treatment)
Antikonvulsivum n anticonvulsant [agent], anticonvulsive
Antikonzeption f contraception
antikonzeptionell anticonceptive, contraceptive
Antikonzeptionsmittel n s. Antikonzeptivum
antikonzeptiv anticonceptive, contraceptive
Antikonzeptivum n contraceptive [agent]
Antikörper m antibody, immune body
~/**agglutinierender** agglutinating antibody

Antikörper 48

~/anaphylaktischer anaphylactic antibody
~/antierythrozytärer antierythrocytic antibody
~/antimikrosomaler antimicrosomal antibody
~/artfremder xenoantibody, xenogenic antibody
~/bivalenter s. ~/kompletter
~/blockierender s. ~/inkompletter
~/fluoreszierender fluorescent antibody
~ gegen Bruzellen antibrucella antibody
~ gegen eigenes Gewebe autoantibody
~/inkompletter incomplete (blocking) antibody
~/kompletter complete (bivalent) antibody
~/natürlicher natural antibody
~/neutralisierender neutralizing antibody
~/präzipitierender precipitable antibody
~/sessiler sessile antibody
~/zellständiger cell-bound antibody
~/zytophiler cytophilic antibody
Antikörperbildung f antibody formation (production)
Antikörpergehalt m antibody titer
Antikörperinzidenz f antibody incidence
Antikörpermangelsyndrom n antibody-deficiency syndrome
Antikörperprävalenz f antibody prevalence
Antikörperproduktion f antibody formation (production)
Antikörperreaktion f antibody response
Antikörpertiter m antibody titer
Antikörpertitration f antibody titration
Antikörperübertragung f immunotransfusion
Antikrampfbehandlung f anticonvulsant therapy
Antikrampfmittel n anticonvulsant [agent]
Antikrotalusserum n anticrotalus serum
Antilepraserum n antileprous serum
Antilepravakzine f antileprosy vaccine
Antileprotikum n antileprotic [agent]
Antileukämikum n antileukaemic [agent] (Zytostatikum)
antileukämisch antileukaemic
Antileukozytenserum n antileucocytic serum
antilipotrop antilipotropic
Antilymphoblastenglobulin n antilymphoblast globulin
Antilymphozytenglobulin n antilymphocytic globulin
Antilymphozytenserum n antilymphocytic serum
antilymphozytisch antilymphocytic, antilymphocyte
Antilyse f antilysis
Antilysin n antilysin
Antimakrophagenglobulin n antimacrophage globulin
Antimakrophagenserum n antimacrophage serum
Antimalariamittel n antimalarial [agent]
Antimelanomantikörper m antimelanoma antibody
Antimeningokokkenserum n antimeningococcic (meningitis) serum
antimesenteriell, antimesenterisch antimesenteric
Antimetabolit m antimetabolite

Antimetabolitentherapie f antimetabolite therapy
Antimetropie f antimetropia (entgegengesetzte Refraktion beider Augen)
Antimilzbrandserum n anti-anthrax serum
Antimineralokortikoid n antimineralocorticoid
Antimitotikum n antimitotic [agent]
Antimonvergiftung f antimony poisoning, stibialism
Antimutagen n antimutagen
Antimykotikum n antimycotic [agent], antifungal [agent], fungicide [agent]
antimykotisch antimycotic, antifungal, fungicidal
Antinarkotikum n antinarcotic [agent]
antineoplastisch antineoplastic
Antineuralgikum n antineuralgic [agent]
antineuralgisch antineuralgic
Antineuritikum n antineuritic [agent]
antineurotisch antineurotic
Antiopsonin n antiopsonin
antiparalytisch antiparalytic
Antiparasitenmittel n antiparasitic [agent]
antiparasitisch antiparasitic
Antiparkinsonikum n antiparkinson[ian] agent
Antipathie f antipathy, aversion
Antipediculosum n lousicide
Antipellagravitamin n pellagra preventive factor, PP factor
Antiperistaltik f antiperistalsis, anastalsis
antiperistaltisch antiperistaltic, anastaltic
Antiperniziosa-Faktor m antipernicious-anaemia [liver] factor, erythrocyte-maturing factor, vitamin B_{12}
Antipertussisserum n antipertussis serum
Antiphagenserum n antiphage serum
antiphagozytär antiphagocytic
Antiphlogistikum n antiphlogistic [agent]
antiphlogistisch antiphlogistic
Antiplasmin n antiplasmin
antiplasmodisch antiplasmodial, malariacidal
Antiplättchenfaktor m antiplatelet factor
Antipräzipitin n antiprecipitin
Antiprothrombin n antiprothrombin
Antiprothrombinantikörper m antiprothrombin antibody
Antiprotozoikum n antiprotozoal [agent]
antipruriginös antipruriginous
Antipruritikum n antipruritic [agent]
antipruritisch antipruritic
Antipsoria[ti]kum n antipsor[iat]ic [agent]
Antipyrese f antipyresis
Antipyretikum n antipyretic [agent], febrifuge [agent]
antipyretisch antipyretic, febrifugal, febrifuge, antifebrile, antithermic, reducing fever
Antipyrinum n antipyrine (Fiebermittel)
Antirabiesgammaglobulin n antirabies gammaglobulin
Antirabiesvakzination f antirabies vaccination
Antirabiesvakzine f antirabies vaccine
Antirabikum n antirabic [agent]
Antirachitikum n antirachitic [agent]

antirachitisch antirachitic, rickets-preventing
Antirefluxoperation *f*, **Antirefluxplastik** *f* antireflux operation
Antirefluxverfahren *n* antireflux procedure
Antirejektionstherapie *f* antirejection therapy
Anti-Rh-Agglutinin *n* anti-Rh agglutinin, anti-rhesus agglutinin
Antirheumatikum *n* antirheumatic [agent]
antirheumatisch antirheumatic
Anti-Rh-Serum *n* anti-Rh serum, anti-rhesus serum
Antiriboflavin *n* antiriboflavin
Anti-ribonukleoprotein-Antikörper *m* antiribonucleoprotein antibody
Antischafzellen-Hämolysin *n* anti-sheep-cell haemolysin
Antischarlachserum *n* antiscarlatinal serum
Antischistosomenmittel *n* antischistosomal [agent]
Antischwerkraftreflex *m* antigravity reflex
antiseborrhoisch antiseborrhoeic
Antisepsis *f*, **Antiseptik** *f* antisepsis, degermation
Antiseptikum *n* antiseptic [agent], germicide [agent]
antiseptisch antiseptic, germicidal
Antiserum *n* antiserum
Antiserumtherapie *f* antiserum therapy (treatment)
Antiskabikum *n*, **Antiskabiosum** *n* antiscabetic [agent], scabicide [agent]
antiskorbutisch antiscorbutic
Antiskorbutmittel *n* antiscorbutic [agent]
Antisomatogen *n* antigen
Antispastikum *n* antispasmodic [agent]
antispastisch antispastic, antispasmodic
Antispirochätenmittel *n* antispirochaetic [agent], spirochaeticide [agent]
Antistaphylo[hämo]lysin *n* antistaphylo[haemo]lysin
Antisterilitätsvitamin *n* antisterility vitamin, vitamin E
Antistreptodornase *f* antistreptodornase
Antistreptohämolysin *n* antistrepto[haemo]lysin
Antistreptokinase *f* antistreptokinase
Antistreptolysin *n* antistrepto[haemo]lysin
Antistreptolysintiter *m* antistrepto[haemo]lysin titre
Antisyphilitikum *n* antisyphilitic [agent], antiluetic [agent]
antisyphilitisch antisyphilitic, antiluetic
Anti-T-Antikörper *m* anti-T antibody
Antitetanikum *n* antitetanic [agent]
antitetanisch antitetanic
Antitetanus-Gammaglobulin *n*/**humanes** human antitetanus gamma globulin
Antitetanusglobulin *n* antitetanus globulin
Antitetanusserum *n s.* Tetanusserum
Antitetanusspritze *f* antitetanus injection
Antithenar *n* antithenar, hypothenar [eminence]
Antithrombin *n* antithrombin
Antithrombinmangel *m* antithrombin deficiency

Antithromboplastin *n* antithromboplastin
Antithrombotikum *n* antithrombotic [agent]
antithrombotisch antithrombotic
Antithrombozytenserum *n* antiplatelet serum
Antithymozytenglobulin *n* antithymocyte globulin
Antithymozytenserum *n* antithymocyte serum
Antithymusserum *n* antithymus serum
Antitoxin *n* antitoxin, toxinicide, toxolysin, immunotoxin, counterpoison
antitoxinbildend antitoxigenic
Antitoxin-Einheit *f* antitoxic unit
Antitoxinexanthem *n* antitoxin rash
Antitoxinserum *n* antitoxin serum
Antitoxintherapie *f* antitoxin therapy (treatment), toxitherapy
antitoxisch antitoxic
Antitragus *m* antitragus
Anti-Trendelenburg-Lage *f* anti-Trendelenburg position *(Operationslagerung)*
antitrichomonal antitrichomonal, trichomonacidal
antitrypanosomal antitrypanosomal, trypanocidal
Antitrypsin *n* antitrypsin, antitryptase
Antitrypsinmangel *m* antitrypsin deficiency
Antitrypsintest *m* antitrypsin test
antitryptisch antitryptic
Antituberkulin *n* antituberculin
antituberkulös antituberculous
Antituberkulotikum *n* tuberculostatic [agent]
Anti-Tubulus-Basalmembran-Antikörper *m* antitubular basement membrane antibody
Antitumorogramm *n* oncobiogram
antitussiv antitussive
Antitussivum *n* antitussive [agent]
Antityphusmittel *n* antityphoid [agent]
Antityphusserum *n* antityphoid serum
Antivenin *n* antivenin, antivenene
antiviral antiviral
Antivirus *n* antivirus
Antivitamin *n* antivitamin
antixerophthalmisch antixerophthalmic
Antizestodikum *n* anticestode [agent]
Antizipation *f* anticipation
Antizytolysin *n* anticytolysin
Anti-Zytomegalovirus-Antikörper *m* anticytomegalovirus antibody
Anton-[Babinski-]Syndrom *n* Anton's syndrome, hemiasomatognosis
Antrektomie *f* antrectomy, antrum resection
antriebslos athymic
antriebssteigernd thymoleptic
Antritis *f* antritis, maxillary sinusitis
Antrodynie *f* antrodynia
Antroskop *n* antroscope
Antroskopie *f* antroscopy *(Spiegelung des Sinus maxillaris)*
Antrostomie *f* antrostomy
Antrotomie *f* antrotomy; antrectomy
antrotympanal antrotympanic
Antrotympanitis *f* antrotympanitis

Antrozele

Antrozele f antrocele *(Flüssigkeitsansammlung in der Kieferhöhle)*
Antrum n antrum, sinus; cavity
~ **cardiacum** cardiac antrum
~ **Highmori** s. ~ maxillare
~ **mastoideum** mastoid (tympanic) antrum, antrum of the ear, Valsalva's antrum
~ **maxillare** maxillary sinus, antrum of Highmore
~ **pyloricum** pyloric (gastric) antrum, pylorus vestibule, pyloric gland area
~ **tubae uterinae** antrum of the uterine tube
Antrumaufmeißelung f antrotomy
Antrumdrainage f antrostomy
Antrumentzündung f antritis
Antrumfistelung f anstrostomy
Antrumgastritis f antrum gastritis
Antrumperforation f antrum perforation
Antrumresektion f antrum resection, antrectomy
Antrumschmerz m antrodynia
Antrum- und Paukenhöhlenentzündung f antrotympanitis
anular anular, ring-shaped
Anuloplastik f annuloplasty
Anulorrhaphie f annulorrhaphy
Anulotomie f annulotomy
Anulozyt m pessary cell (form) *(Erythrozyt in Pessarform)*
Anulozytose f annulocytosis
Anulus m ring, a[n]nulus
~ **conjunctivae** conjunctival ring
~ **femoralis** femoral (crural) ring
~ **fibrocartilagineus** fibrocartilaginous ring
~ **fibrosus** fibrous ring
~ **fibrosus cordis** fibrous ring of the heart valve
~ **fibrosus disci intervertebralis** fibrous ring of the intervertebral disk
~ **inguinalis** inguinal ring
~ **inguinalis profundus** internal inguinal (abdominal) ring, deep (abdominal) inguinal ring
~ **inguinalis superficialis** superficial (subcutaneous) inguinal ring, external inguinal (abdominal) ring
~ **iridis major** greater ring of the iris, ciliary zone
~ **iridis minor** lesser ring of the iris, pupillary zone
~ **migrans** annulus migrans, erythema chronicum migrans
~ **tendineus communis** ligament of Zinn
~ **tympanicus** tympanic ring
~ **umbilicalis** umbilical ring
~ **urethralis** urethral ring
Anurie f anuria, anuresis
~/**physiologische** physiological anuria
~/**postrenale** postrenal anuria
~/**prärenale** prerenal anuria
~/**reflektorische** reflex anuria
~/**renale** renal anuria
anurisch anur[et]ic
Anus m anus, anal orifice *(s. a. unter* After*)*
~ **imperforatus** imperforate anus
~ **praeter/einläufiger** single-barrelled colostomy
~ **praeternaturalis** preternatural (artificial) anus, enteroproctia

Anus... s. a. After... *und* Anal...
Anuschirurgie f anal surgery
Anusdilatation f proctectasia, anal ectasia
Anusdivertikel n anal diverticulum
Anusfistel f anal fistula
Anusheber m levator ani [muscle]
Anusitis f anusitis
Anuskrebs m anus cancer, anal carcinoma
Anus-praeter-Beutel m colostomy bag
Anus-praeter-Pflege f colostomy care
Anusprolaps m anal prolapse
Anus-Rektum-Plastik f proctoplasty
Anusulkus n anal ulcer
anwachsen to adhere, to grow to[gether], to grow on *(z. B. Transplantat)*
Anwachsen n 1. adhesion; 2. increase
anwendbar applicable *(z. B. Medikament)*; practicable *(z. B. Therapie)*; adaptable *(z. B. Zahnfüllung)*
anwendend/Arzneimittel medicamentous
Anwendung f s. Applikation
Anwendungsweise f mode of application, method of administration *(z. B. von Medikamenten)*
Anxiolytikum n anxiolytic [agent]
Anzapfsyndrom n steal syndrome
Anzeichen n symptom, sign
Anzeige f indication *(z. B. für Heilverfahren)*
anzeigen/eine Infektion to indicate an infection
anzeigend indicative, indicatory, prodromal, prodromic, symptomatic, semeiotic
Anzeigepflicht f notification *(z. B. einer Infektionskrankheit)*
anzeigepflichtig notifiable
anziehen 1. to adduct *(z. B. Muskeln)*; 2. to absorb, to draw [in] *(z. B. Flüssigkeiten)*
anziehend adducent *(Muskeln)*
~/**Feuchtigkeit** hygroscopic
~/**Tumorzellen** oncotropic
Anziehmuskel m adductor [muscle]
Anziehung f 1. adduction *(z. B. Muskelbewegung)*; 2. absorption *(z. B. von Flüssigkeiten)*
AO s. Arbeitsgemeinschaft für Osteosynthesefragen
AO-Besteck n, **AO-Instrumentarium** n AO instruments
AO-Osteosynthese f AO osteosynthesis
Aorta f aorta ● **durch die** ~ transaortic ● **neben der** ~ para-aortic ● **oberhalb der** ~ supra-aortic ● **unter der** ~ subaortic
~/**abdominale** abdominal aorta
~/**absteigende** descending aorta
~/**aufsteigende** ascending aorta
~/**kinking** kinking of aorta
~/**reitende** [over]riding of the aorta, biventricular origin of aorta
~/**thorakale** thoracic (dorsal) aorta
Aorta... s. a. Aorten...
Aorta-descendens-Aneurysma n descending thoracic aortic aneurysm
Aortaexklusionsklemme f aorta-exclusion clamp
Aortageräusch n aortic murmur

Aorta-Herzkranzgefäß-Anastomose f aortocoronary bypass surgery
aortal aortic, aortal
Aortalgie f aortalgia
Aortamedianekrose f medial necrosis of the aorta
Aortanervengeflecht n aortic plexus
Aortaröntgen[kontrast]bild n aortogram
Aorta-Speiseröhren-Fistel f aorto-oesophageal fistula
Aortektomie f aortectomy
Aorten... s. a. Aorta...
Aortenabklemmung f aortic [cross-]clamping, cross-clamping of the aorta
Aortenabknickung f kinking of aorta
Aortenaneurysma n aortic aneurysm
~/dissezierendes dissecting [aortic] aneurysm
Aortenaneurysmaklemme f aortic aneurysm clamp
Aortenatresie f aortic atresia; interrupted aorta
Aortenbifurkation f aortic bifurcation, bifurcation of the aorta
Aortenbifurkationsbereich m aortic bifurcation area
Aortenbifurkationsprothese f aortic bifurcation graft
Aortenbifurkationssyndrom n aortic bifurcation syndrome, Leriche syndrome
Aortenbogen m aortic arch, arch of the aorta
Aortenbogenaneurysma n aortic arch aneurysm
Aortenbogenanomalie f aortic arch anomaly
Aortenbogensyndrom n aortic arch syndrome (arteritis, occlusive disease), young female syndrome, Takayasu's arteritis (syndrome), pulseless disease
Aortenbulbus m aortic bulb, bulb of the heart
Aortenchirurgie f aortic surgery
Aortendiastole f aortic diastole
Aortendreieck n aortic triangle
Aortendruck m/**mittlerer systolischer** aortic mean systolic pressure
Aortendruckkurve f aortic pressure curve
Aortenektasie f aortectasia
Aortenembolie f aorta embolism
Aortenenge f isthmus of aorta
Aortenentfernung f[/**operative**] aortectomy
Aortenentzündung f aortitis, inflammation of the aorta
Aorteneröffnung f[/**operative**] aortotomy, cutting of the aorta
Aortenersatz m aortic replacement
Aortenerweiterung f aortectasia, dilatation of the aorta
Aortenfenster n aortic window
Aortenfreigabe f aorta declamping (nach Abklemmung)
Aortengabelung f s. Aortenbifurkation
Aortenherz n sabot (wooden-shoe) heart
Aortenhiatus m aortic hiatus
Aortenhypoplasie f aortic hypoplasia
Aorteninsuffizienz f aortic insufficiency (incompetence), aorta valve regurgitation

Aortenintimaentzündung f endaortitis
Aorteninzisur f aortic incisure
Aortenisthmus m aortic isthmus
Aortenisthmusstenose f aortic coarctation, coarctation of the aorta
Aortenisthmusstenosenresektion f resection of coarctation
Aortenklappe f aortic valve • **unter der** ~ subaortic
~/künstliche aortic valve prosthesis
~ vom Kugel-Käfig-Typ aortic ball valve prosthesis
Aortenklappenatresie f aortic atresia
Aortenklappenauskultationspunkt m Erb's point
Aortenklappenbypass m aortic valve bypass
Aortenklappenersatz m aortic valve replacement
Aortenklappenfehler m aortic valve disease
Aortenklappengeräusch n aortic [valve] murmur
Aortenklappenhomotransplantat n aortic valve homograft
Aortenklappeninsuffizienz f aortic valvular insufficiency (incompetence), aortic (aorta valve) regurgitation, incompetence of the aortic valve, Corrigan's disease
Aortenklappenprothese f aortic valve prosthesis
Aortenklappensegel n aortic valve cusp (leaflet)
Aortenklappensklerose f/**aufsteigende** Mönckeberg's sclerosis
Aortenklappenstenose f s. Aortenstenose
Aortenklappentransplantat n aortic valve graft
Aortenklemme f aortic clamp
Aortenknopf m aortic knob
Aortenkompression f aortic compression
Aortenkompressorium n aortic compressor
Aortenkonfiguration f aortic configuration
Aortenläsion f aortic lesion
Aortenmessung f aortometry
Aortenmitteldruck m mean aortic pressure
Aortennaht f aortorrhaphy
Aortenöffnung f aortic orifice
Aortenplastik f aortoplasty
Aortenplexus m aortic plexus
Aortenprothese f aorta prosthesis (graft)
Aortenrekonstruktion f aorta reconstruction
Aortenruptur f aortic rupture, rupture of the aorta
Aortenschmerz m aortalgia
Aortenschwirren n aortic thrill
Aortensegel n aortic valve cusp (leaflet)
Aortenseptum n aortic septum
Aortensinus m aortic sinus, sinus (aorta) of Valsalva
Aortensinusaneurysma n aortic sinus aneurysm
Aortensklerose f aortic sclerosis
Aortenstamm m aortic trunk
Aortenstenose f 1. aortic [valvular] stenosis, aorta valve stenosis; 2. aortarctia, aortostenosis
~/subvalvuläre subvalvular aortic stenosis, subaortic stenosis
~/supravalvuläre supravalvular aortic stenosis
~/valvuläre valvular aortic stenosis

Aortenstriktur

Aortenstriktur f aortic stricture (constriction)
Aortenteilentfernung f [/operative] partial aortectomy
Aortentransplantat n aorta graft
Aortentransposition f aortic transposition, transposition of the aorta
Aortentrauma n aortic trauma
Aortenursprung m aortic origin
Aortenvereng[er]ung f aortarctia, aortostenosis
Aortenverletzung f aortic lesion
Aortenverschluß m/**abdominaler** abdominal aortic occlusion, Leriche syndrome
Aortenwiederherstellung f [/operative] aortoplasty
Aortenwurzel f aortic root, root of the aorta
Aortenwurzelaneurysma n aortic root aneurysm
aortikopulmonal aorticopulmonary, aorticopulmonic
aortikorenal aorticorenal
Aortitis f aortitis, inflammation of the aorta
Aortoarteriographie f aortoarteriography
Aortogramm n aortogram
Aortographie f aortography
~/**retrograde** retrograde aortography
~/**thorakale** thoracic aortography
~/**transseptale** transseptal aortography
aortographisch aortographic
Aortointestinalfistel f aortointestinal fistula
aortokoronar aortocoronary, aortic-coronary
Aortoösophagealfistel f aorto-oesophageal fistula
Aortopathie f aortopathy
aortopulmonal aorticopulmonary, aorticopulmonic
Aortorrhaphie f aortorrhaphy
Aortotomie f aortotomy, cutting of the aorta
apallisch apallic
aparalytisch aparalytic
Aparathyreose f aparathyr[e]osis, aparathyroidism, absence of the parathyroid glands
Apathie f apathy, listlessness; indifference
apathisch apath[et]ic, listless; indifferent
apathogen apathogenic, non-pathogenic
Apathogenität f apathogenicity
APC-Virus n s. Adenovirus
Apektomie f s. Apikotomie
aperiosteal aperiosteal
Aperistaltik f aperistalsis
Apertognathie f apertognathy, anterior open bite
Apert-Syndrom n Apert's syndrome, acrocephalosyndactylia
Apertura f **externa aquaeductus vestibuli** external aperture of the aqueduct of the vestibule
~ **lateralis ventriculi quarti** lateral aperture of the fourth ventricle, foramen of Luschka *(Verbindungsloch zwischen 4. Hirnkammer und dem Subarachnoidalraum)*
~ **mediana ventriculi quarti** median aperture of the fourth ventricle, foramen of Magendie *(unpaare Verbindungsöffnung des vierten Ventrikels)*
~ **pelvis inferior** lower aperture of the pelvic canal, lower opening of the true pelvis, pelvic outlet, outlet of the pelvis
~ **pelvis superior** upper aperture of the pelvic canal, upper opening of the true pelvis, pelvic inlet, inlet of the pelvis
~ **thoracis inferior** inferior aperture of the thoracic cavity
~ **thoracis superior** superior aperture of the thoracic cavity
Apex m apex
~ **auriculae [Darwini]** Darwin's (ear) tubercle
~ **capitis fibulae** apex of the head of the fibula
~ **cartilaginis arytenoideae** upper extremity of the arytenoid cartilage
~ **cordis** cardiac apex, apex of the heart
~ **linguae** tip of the tongue
~ **nasi** tip of the nose
~ **ossis sacri** caudal end of the sacrum
~ **partis petrosae** petrous apex
~ **pulmonis** apex of the lung
Apexgeräusch n apex murmur
Apexkardiogramm n apex cardiogram
Apexpneumonie f apex pneumonia
Apexschwirren n thrill at apex *(am Herzen)*
Apfelsäure f malic acid
Apfelsäuredehydr[ogen]ase f malic acid dehydrogenase, malate dehydrogenase *(Enzym)*
Apfelschalensyndrom n apple-peel syndrome *(z. B. bei Dünndarmatresie)*
Apfelsinenileus m orange ileus
Apfelsinenschalenphänomen n orange-skin phenomenon, orange-peel appearance *(bei Brustkrebs)*
Apgar-Schema n Apgar rating (score) *(zur Beurteilung eines Neugeborenen)*
Aphagie f aphagia, inability to swallow
aphak aphakial, aphakic
Aphakie f aphakia, absence of the lens
~/**angeborene** congenital aphakia
~/**erworbene** secondary aphakia
Aphakieglaukom n aphakic glaucoma
aphakisch aphakial, aphakic
Aphalangie f aphalangia *(z. B. bei Lepra)*
Aphasie f aphasia *(zentrale Sprachstörung)*
~/**akustische** acoustic (auditory) aphasia
~/**amnestische** amnes[t]ic aphasia, autonomasia, inability to remember words
~/**assoziative** associative aphasia
~/**ataktische** ataxic aphasia
~/**Brocasche** Broca's aphasia
~/**frontokortikale** frontocortical aphasia
~/**frontolentikuläre** frontolenticular aphasia
~/**funktionelle** functional aphasia
~/**globale** global aphasia
~/**graphomotorische** graphomotor aphasia
~/**ideokinetische motorische** ideokinetic motor aphasia
~/**kombinierte** combined aphasia
~/**komplette** complete aphasia
~/**kortikale** cortical aphasia
~/**lentikuläre** lenticular aphasia
~/**motorische** motor (oral expressive) aphasia, aphemia, word dumbness

~/musikalische amusia, musical aphasia
~/nominale nominal aphasia
~/optische s. ~/visuelle
~/parietookzipitale parieto-occipital aphasia
~/psychosensorische psychosensory aphasia
~/semantische semantic aphasia
~/sensorische sensory (receptive) aphasia, impressive aphasia, word deafness
~/subkortikale subcortical aphasia
~/syntaktische syntactic[al] aphasia, acataphasia *(Unfähigkeit zur Satzkonstruktion)*
~/taktile tactile aphasia
~/temporoparietale temporoparietal aphasia
~/verbale verbal aphasia
~/visuelle visual (optic) aphasia
~/zentrale central aphasia
Aphasiologie *f* aphasiology *(Lehre von der Aphasie)*
aphasisch aphasic, aphemic
Aphemie *f s.* Aphasie/motorische
aphon aphonic, aphonous
Aphonie *f* aphonia, loss of voice
~/paralytische paralytic aphonia
aphonisch aphonic, aphonous
Aphrasie *f* aphrasia
Aphrodisiakum *n* aphrodisiac [agent]
Aphrodisie *f* 1. aphrodisia, sexual excitation (excitement); 2. aphrodisia, sexual union (congress)
Aphtha *f epizootica* aphthous fever, [hand-]foot-and-mouth disease
Aphthe *f* aphtha *(in der Mundschleimhaut)*
Aphthen *fpl*/**Bednarsche** Bednar's aphthae
~/kachektische cachectic aphthae
~/tropische tropical aphthae (sprue)
aphthenartig aphthous
Aphthenseuche *f s.* Aphtha epizootica
aphthoid aphthoid
Aphthongie *f* aphthongia *(Sprachstörung infolge Zungenkrampfes)*
aphthös aphthous
Aphthosis *f* aphthosis *(Geschwürbildungen an den Genitalien)*
apikal apical
Apikalabszeß *m* apical abscess *(Stomatologie)*
apikokaudal apicocaudal
Apikolyse *f* apicolysis *(Lösung der Lungenspitzen aus der Pleurakuppel)*
Apikostomie *f* apicostomy
Apikotomie *f* apicotomy, apicectomy, apiceotomy
Apiophobie *f* apiophobia *(krankhafte Angst vor Bienen)*
Apiotherapie *f* apiotherapy, treatment with bee venom
Apizitis *f* apicitis, inflammation of an apex
Aplanatio *f corneae* flattening of the cornea
Aplasie *f* aplasia
aplastisch aplastic
aplazental aplacental
Apleurie *f* apleuria, ecostatism, absence of the ribs

APN-Beatmung *f* alternating positive-negative pressure breathing
Apneumatose *f* apneumatosis *(nach Geburt)*
Apneusis *f* apneusis
Apnoe *f* apnoea, respiratory arrest (standstill), cessation of breathing
~/weiße pale asphyxia
apnöisch apnoeic
apodal apodal, ap[od]ous
Apodemialgie *f* apodemialgia
Apodie *f* apodia, absence of feet
Apoenzym *n* apoenzyme, bearer protein *(Enzymanteil)*
Apoerythrein *n* apoerythrein
Apoferritin *n* apoferritin *(eisenspeicherndes Protein)*
Apokamnose *f* apocamnosis *(z. B. bei Myasthenia gravis)*
Apokarteresis *f* apocarteresis, suicide by self-starvation
apokrin apocrine
Apolipoprotein *n* apolipoprotein
Apomorphin *n* apomorphine *(Morphinabkömmling)*
Aponeurektomie *f* aponeurectomy
Aponeurorrhaphie *f* aponeurorrhaphy
Aponeurose *f s.* Aponeurosis
Aponeurosenentzündung *f* aponeurositis
Aponeurosenexstirpation *f* aponeurectomy
Aponeuroseninzision *f s.* Aponeurotomie
Aponeurosennaht *f* aponeurorrhaphy, suturing of an aponeurosis
Aponeurosis *f* aponeurosis ● **unter der ~** subaponeurotic
~ *epicranialis* epicranial (galeal) aponeurosis, aponeurosis of the occipitofrontalis muscle
~ *linguae* lingual aponeurosis (fascia)
~ *musculi bicipitis [brachii]* bicipital aponeurosis
~ *nuchae* nuchal aponeurosis
~ *palmaris* palmar aponeurosis, deep palmar fascia
~ *plantaris* plantar aponeurosis (fascia)
Aponeurositis *f* aponeurositis, inflammation of an aponeurosis
aponeurotisch aponeurotic
Aponeurotomie *f* aponeurotomy, incision of an aponeurosis
Apophyse *f s.* Apophysis
Apophysenentzündung *f* apophysitis
Apophysenfuge *f* apophyseal plate
Apophysenlösung *f*, **Apophyseolyse** *f* apophyseal fracture
Apophysis *f* apophysis
~ *cerebri* cerebral apophysis, pineal body
~ *mamillaris* mamillary apophysis
Apophysitis *f* apophysitis, inflammation of an apophysis
~ *calcanei* calcaneal apophysitis
apoplektiform apoplectiform
apoplektisch apoplectic
Apoplex *m s.* Apoplexie 1.
apoplexartig apoplectiform, apoplectoid

Apoplexia

Apoplexia f cerebri s. Apoplexie 2.
~ **retinae** retinal apoplexy
Apoplexie f 1. apoplexy *(allgemein)*; 2. [cerebral] apoplexy, [apoplectic] stroke, cerebrovascular accident, cerebral [vascular] accident, cerebral infarct[ion]
~/**falsche** pseudoapoplexy
~/**hämorrhagische** sanguineous apoplexy
~/**leichte** parapoplexy
~/**uteroplazentare** uteroplacental (uterine) apoplexy
apoplexieartig apoplectoid, apoplectiform
Aposie f aposia, adipsia
Apostasis f, **Apostema** n abscess[us], apostasis, apostem[a]
Aposthie f aposthia, absence of the prepuce
Apotheke f dispensary, chemist's shop, pharmacy
Apothekenschrank m medicine cabinet
Apotheker m dispensing chemist, pharmaceutist, pharmacist
Apothekergewicht n apothecaries' weight
Apparat m 1. apparatus, system *(Anatomie)* (s. a. unter Apparatus); 2. apparatus, appliance, device *(Gerät)*
~/**juxtaglomerulärer** juxtaglomerular apparatus
~ **zur künstlichen Beatmung** pulmotor, lungmotor
Apparatus m **digestorius** digestive system
~ **lacrimalis** lacrimal apparatus
~ **respiratorius** respiratory system
~ **urogenitalis** urogenital system (tract)
Appendalgie f appendalgia
Appendektomie f append[ic]ectomy
~ **durch McBurneyschen Schnitt** McBurney's operation
Appendektomieklemme f appendectomy clamp
Appendicitis f s. Appendizitis
Appendicopathia f **oxyurica** oxyuric appendicopathy
~ **verminosa** verminous (helminthic) appendicopathy
Appendiklausis f appendiclausis, obstruction (obliteration) of the vermiform appendix
Appendikoenterostomie f appendicoenterostomy
Appendikographie f appendicography *(Röntgendarstellung des Wurmfortsatzes)*
Appendikolith m appendicolith
Appendikopathie f appendicopathy
Appendikostomie f appendicostomy
Appendix f 1. appendix, appendage; 2. s. ~ vermiformis
~ **epididymidis** epididymal appendage
~ **epiploica** epiploic appendage
~ **testis** appendix of the testicle, hydatid of Morgagni, [stalked] hydatid
~ **vermiformis** appendix, vermiform appendix (process), caecal appendage, epityphlon
Appendix... s. a. Wurmfortsatz...
Appendixkalkulus m appendicolith
Appendixkolik f appendicular colic

Appendixobstruktion f s. Appendiklausis
Appendixschutzklemme f appendix protection forceps
Appendizismus m appendicism, pseudoappendicitis
Appendizitis f appendicitis, epityphlitis, perityphlitis
~/**akute** acute appendicitis
~/**chronische** chronic appendicitis
~/**eitrige** suppurative (purulent) appendicitis
~/**foudroyante** foudroyant appendicitis
~/**gangränöse** gangrenous appendicitis, gangrene of the appendix
~/**intrauterine** intrauterine appendicitis
~/**katarrhalische** catarrhal appendicitis
~/**maskierte** masked appendicitis
~/**obliterierende** obliterative (protective) appendicitis
~/**perforierende** perforating (perforative) appendicitis
~/**phlegmonöse** phlegmonous appendicitis
~/**retrozökale** retrocaecal (lumbar) appendicitis
~/**scheinbare** pseudoappendicitis
~/**subakute** subacute appendicitis
~/**traumatische** traumatic appendicitis
Appersonifikation f appersonification *(unbewußte Identifikation mit anderen Personen)*
Apperzeption f apperception, mental perception
Appetit m appetite
appetitanregend appetizing, aperitive, orexigenic, stimulating the appetite
Appetitanreger m appetizer
appetitlos anore[c]tic, anorectous, inappetent
Appetitlosigkeit f anorexia, inappetence, want of appetite
Appetitsstörung f dysorexia
appetitsteigernd s. appetitanregend
appetitszügelnd anorexiant, anorexigenic, antiobesic
Appetitszügler m anorexiant [agent], anorectic [agent], antiobesic [agent]
appetitverringernd s. appetitszügelnd
Applanatio f applanation *(z. B. der Hornhaut)*
Applanationsdruck m applanation pressure
Applanationsspannung f applanation tension
Applanationstonometer n applanation tonometer, applanometer
Applanationstonometrie f applanation tonometry
Applanometer n s. Applanationstonometer
Applikation f application, administration; medication
~/**bukkale** buccal application
~/**intraarterielle** intraarterial application
~/**intraartikuläre** intraarticular application
~/**intrakutane** intracutaneous application
~/**intramuskuläre** intramuscular application
~/**intravenöse** intravenous application
~/**orale** oral medication
~/**parenterale** parenteral application
~/**rektale** rectal application
~/**sublinguale** sublingual application

Applikationsintervall n application interval
Applikator m applicator, medicator
applizieren to apply, to administer
~/durch intramuskuläre Injektion to give by intramuscular injection
~/eine Injektion to give an injection
~/Kurare to curarize (zur Muskelerschlaffung)
~/oral to give by mouth, to administer orally
Approbation f license to practice, [medical] registration
approbiert licensed, registered, certificated
Approximalfläche f approximal surface (Stomatologie)
Approximalkaries f approximal caries
Apragmatismus m apragmatism
Apraxie f apraxia
~/ideokinetische ideokinetic apraxia
~/ideomotorische ideomotor apraxia
~/innervatorische innervation apraxia
~/kinetische kinetic apraxia
~/konstruktive constructive apraxia
~/kortikale cortical apraxia
~/motorische motor apraxia
~/okulomotorische oculomotor apraxia
~/sensorische sensory apraxia
~/verbale verbal apraxia
aproktisch aproctous
Aprosexie f aprosexia
Aprosopie f aprosopia
Aprosopus m aprosopus
Apselaphesie f apselaphesia, loss of the tactile sense
Aptyalismus m aptyalism, aptyalia, asialia
APUD = aminoacid precursor uptake decarboxylation
APUD-Zellsystem n APUD cell system
Apus m apus
Apyrexie f apyrexia
apyrogen apyrogen[et]ic
Aqua f **ad injectionem** [sterile] water for injection
~ destillata distilled water
Aquädukt m s. Aquaeductus
Aquäduktdrainage f aqueduct drainage
Aquäduktstenose f aqueductal stenosis, atresia of iter
Aquädukt-Syndrom n Sylvian aqueduct syndrome
Aquaeductus m aqueduct
~ cerebri cerebral (Sylvian) aqueduct, aqueduct of Sylvius (the midbrain)
~ cochleae cochlear aqueduct, aqueduct of the cochlea
~ Falloppii Fallopian aqueduct (canal)
~ mesencephali (Sylvii) s. **~ cerebri**
~ vestibuli vestibular aqueduct, aqueduct of Cotunnius (the vestibule)
Aquaphobie f aquaphobia, hydrophobia (krankhafte Angst vor Wasser)
Äquationsteilung f equational division, homeotypic mitosis

Äquatorialplatte f, **Äquatorialscheibe** f [a]equatorial plate (disk), nuclear plate (Chromosomenanordnung bei der Zellkernteilung)
Äquatorialteilung f equatorial cleavage (Zellteilung)
Äquivalent n**/epileptisches** epileptic (convulsive) equivalent, psychomotor epilepsy
~/kalorisches caloric equivalent
~/klinisches clinical equivalent
~/pharmazeutisches pharmaceutical equivalent
~/psychisches psychomotor equivalent
~/therapeutisches therapeutic equivalent
~/toxisches toxic equivalent
Äquivalentdosis f equivalent dose
Äquivalent-Einzeldosis f equivalent single dose
Äquivalenttemperatur f equivalent temperature
Arabinose f arabinose (Pentose)
Arachidonsäure f arachidonic acid (essentielle Fettsäure)
Arachnidismus m arachn[o]idism, spider venom poisoning
Arachnitis f s. Arachnoiditis
Arachnodaktylie f arachnodactyly; spider fingers
Arachnoentomologie f arachnoentomology (Bereich der Parasitologie)
Arachnogastrie f arachnogastria (bei Bauchwassersucht)
arachnoidal arachnoidal, arachnoid[ean]
Arachnoidalzotten fpl arachnoid granulations
Arachnoidalzyste f arachnoidal cyst
Arachnoidea f arachnoid [membrane], arachnoidea ● **unter der ~** subarachnoid
~ encephali arachnoid [mater] of the brain
~ spinalis arachnoid [mater] of the spinal cord, spinal arachnoid
Arachnoideaentzündung f s. Arachnoiditis
Arachnoideamesser n arachnoid knife
Arachnoiditis f arachn[oid]itis, inflammation of the piarachnoid
~ chronica adhaesiva basilar (chronic adhesive) arachnoiditis
~/optico-chiasmatica opticochiasmatic (optic-chiasmatic) arachnoiditis
Arachnopathia f **cerebellaris** cerebellar arachnopathy
~ cerebralis cerebral arachnopathy
~ optico-chiasmatica opticochiasmatic arachnopathy
~ pontocerebellaris pontocerebellar arachnopathy
~ spinalis spinal arachnopathy
Arachnophobie f arachnephobia (krankhafte Angst vor Spinnen)
Aräometer n areometer, densimeter
Araphie f araphia, dysraphism
Arbeitsbefreiungsschein m certificate of disablement
Arbeitsdermatologie f industrial dermatology
Arbeitsdermatose f industrial dermatosis
Arbeitsfähigkeit f fitness for work; working capacity

Arbeitsgemeinschaft ...

Arbeitsgemeinschaft *f* **für Osteosynthesefragen** Association for the study of internal fixation
Arbeitshygiene *f* industrial hygiene
Arbeitshyperämie *f* active hyperaemia
Arbeitshyperglykämie *f* active hyperglycaemia
Arbeitshyperthermie *f* active hyperthermy
Arbeitshypertrophie *f* compensatory (work) hypertrophy
Arbeitshypoglykämie *f* active hypoglycaemia
Arbeitsleistungsmessung *f* ergometry *(z. B. der Muskeln)*
Arbeitsmedizin *f* industrial (occupational) medicine
Arbeitsmediziner *m* occupational physician
Arbeitsneurose *f* occupational neurosis
Arbeitsphysiologie *f* physiology of effort
Arbeitsplatz *m***/geschützter** sheltered workshop
Arbeitsplatzkonzentration *f***/maximale** industrial threshold limit value *(von Schadstoffen)*
Arbeitspsychologie *f* industrial psychology
Arbeitsschutz *m* industrial safety
Arbeitstherapie *f* work (occupational) therapy, ergotherapy
arbeitsunfähig unfit for work, incapable of working; permanently disabled; invalid
Arbeitsunfähigkeit *f* disablement, inability to work, incapacity [of working]; invalidism *(ständig)*
Arbeitsunfähigkeitsbescheinigung *f s.* Arbeitsbefreiungsschein
Arbeitsunfall *m* industrial accident, occupational injury
Arborisation *f* arborization *(baumartige Anordnung)*
Arborisationsblock *m* arborization block *(EKG)*
Arbovirus *n* arbovirus, arthropod-borne virus, encephalovirus
Arbovirusenzephalitis *f* arbovirus encephalitis
Archenteron *n* archenteron, archigaster, progaster, primary (primitive) gut
Archenzephalon *n* archencephalon *(Embryologie)*
Archoplasma *n* archoplasm
Arcus *m* arch, arcus
~ **alveolaris** alveolar arch
~ **anterior atlantis** anterior arch of the atlas
~ **aortae** aortic arch, arch of the aorta
~ **corneae** corneal arcus
~ **costae (costarum)** costal arch, arch of the rib
~ **dentalis inferior** inferior dental arch, dental arch of the lower teeth
~ **dentalis superior** superior dental arch, dental arch of the upper teeth
~ **juvenilis** anterior embryotoxon
~ **lipoides cornealis** lipoid arch [of the cornea]
~ **palatini** palatal arch
~ **palatoglossus** palatoglossal (glossopalatine) arch, anterior pillar of the fauces
~ **palatopharyngeus** palatopharyngeal (pharyngopalatine) arch, posterior pillar of the fauces
~ **palmaris** palmar (volar) arch
~ **palmaris profundus** deep palmar (volar) arch
~ **palmaris superficialis** superficial palmar (volar) arch
~ **palpebralis inferior** inferior palpebral (tarsal) arch, arterial arcade of the lower eyelid
~ **palpebralis superior** superior palpebral (tarsal) arch, arterial arcade of the upper eyelid
~ **pedis longitudinalis** longitudinal arch [of the foot]
~ **pedis transversalis** metatarsal arch
~ **plantaris** plantar [arterial] arch
~ **posterior atlantis** posterior arch of the atlas
~ **pubicus** pubic arch
~ **senilis [lentis]** senile arch
~ **superciliaris** superciliary arch (ridge), supraorbital arch (ridge)
~ **tarseus inferior** *s.* ~ palpebralis inferior
~ **tarseus superior** *s.* ~ palpebralis superior
~ **tendineus fasciae pelvis** tendinous arch [of the pelvic fascia] *(Verstärkungszug der Beckenfaszie)*
~ **tendineus musculi levatoris ani** arcuate line
~ **venosus juguli** jugular [venous] arch
~ **vertebrae** vertebral arch
~ **zygomaticus** zygomatic arch, inferior temporal arcade
Area *f* 1. area, field; region *(Anatomie)*; 2. area *(Hirnrinde)*
~ **acustica** acoustic area
~ **cribrosa** cribriform area
~ **germinativa** germinal area (spot), embryonic disk (shield)
~ **olfactoria** olfactory area
~ **parolfactoria** parolfactory area
~ **striata** striate area (cortex)
~ **subcallosa** parolfactory area
~ **vestibularis** vestibular area, acoustic eminence (tubercle)
~ **vestibularis inferior** inferior vestibular area
~ **vestibularis superior** superior vestibular area
Areal *n s.* Area
Areflexie *f* areflexia
aregeneratorisch aregeneratory, aregenerative
Arenovirusgruppe *f* arenovirus group
Areola *f* areola
~ **mammae** mammary areola
areolär areolar
Areolitis *f* areolitis, inflammation of the mammary areola
argentaffin argentaffine
Argentaffinität *f* argentaffinity
argentophil argentophil[e], argentophilic
Arginase *f* arginase
Arginin *n* arginine
Argininglutamat *n* arginine glutamate *(gegen Ammoniakvergiftung)*
Argininosukzinaturie *f* argininosuccinic aciduria
Argininprovokationstest *m* arginine provocation test
Argonlaser-Photokoagulation *f* argon laser photocoagulation *(z. B. in Ophthalmologie)*
Argyll-Robertson-Phänomen *n* Argyll Robertson phenomenon (sign, pupil)

Argyrie f, **Argyrismus** m s. Argyrose
argyrophil argyrophil[e], argyrophilic
Argyrophilie f argyrophilia
Argyrose f argyrosis, argyria, argyrism
Argyrosiderose f argyrosiderosis
Arhinie f s. Arrhinie
Ariboflavinose f ariboflavinosis
Arithmomanie f arithmomania
Arizona-Bakterien npl, **Arizona-Gruppe** f Arizona bacteria
Arm m arm, brachium, upper extremity, pectoral (thoracic) limb
Armabweichungstest m arm deviation test
Armamputation f arm amputation, brachiotomy
Armani-Ebstein-Nephropathie f Armani-Ebstein nephropathy *(bei Diabetes mellitus)*
Armani-Ebstein-Zelle f Armani-Ebstein cell *(bei Diabetes mellitus)*
Armarterie f/**tiefe** deep brachial artery, profunda brachii artery
Armaturenbrettverletzung f dashboard injury
Armbad n arm bath
Armbeuge f bend of the elbow (arm)
Armbeuger m brachialis [muscle]
Armentwicklung f liberation of the arms *(bei der Geburt)*
Armgelenk n brachial joint
Armhöcker m deltoid tuberosity
Armhypertrophie f arm hypertrophy
Armhypotrophie f arm hypotrophy
Armkopfarterie f innominate artery
Armkopfvene f innominate vein
Armlagerung f positioning of the arm
Armlähmung f brachial paralysis (palsy)
Armlappen m/**gekreuzter** cross-arm flap *(bei Transplantation)*
Armlosigkeit f abrachia
Armlösung f liberation (freeing) of the arms *(bei der Geburt)*
Arm-Lunge-Zeit f arm-to-lung time [test]
Armlymphödem n arm lymphoedema
Armmanschette f armlet
Armmuskel m brachial muscle
~/**dreiköpfiger** triceps brachii muscle
~/**zweiköpfiger** biceps brachii [muscle]
Armmuskulatur f muscles of the arm
Armnebenarterie f/**untere ellenseitige** inferior ulnar collateral artery
Armnerv m brachial nerve
Arm-Ohr-Kreislauf-Zeit f arm-to-ear circulation time [test]
Armorthese f artificial arm
Armplexus m brachial plexus
Armplexusblockade f brachial plexus block
Armplexuskompressionssyndrom n brachial plexus compression syndrome
Armplexuslähmung f brachial plexus palsy (paralysis)
~ **bei der Geburt** brachial birth palsy
~/**obere** upper brachial plexus paralysis, upper arm [type of] paralysis, upper radicular syndrome, Erb's (Erb-Duchenne's) paralysis, Duchenne-Erb palsy (syndrome)
~/**untere** lower brachial plexus paralysis, lower arm [type of] paralysis, lower radicular syndrome, Déjerine-Klumpke's paralysis (syndrome), Klumpke's palsy
Armplexusneuralgie f brachial plexus neuralgia
Armplexustumor m brachial plexus tumour
Armplexusverletzung f brachial plexus injury (trauma)
Armprothese f artificial arm
Armschiene f arm splint
Armschlinge f [arm] sling, mitella; collar-and-cuff sling
Armschmerz m brachialgia *(neuritischen oder vasomotorischen Ursprungs)*
Armstrecker m triceps brachii muscle
Armstütze f arm rest (support)
Armtonusreaktion f arm deviation test
Armtragetuch n mitella, [arm] sling
Arm- und Kopfvene f/**linke** left brachiocephalic vein
~/**rechte** right brachiocephalic vein
Armvergrößerung f/**abnorme** macrobrachia
Armverkleinerung f/**abnorme** microbrachia
Armvorfall m arm presentation *(bei der Geburt)*
Arm-Zunge-Zeit f arm-tongue time [test]
Arnold-Chiari-Syndrom n Arnold-Chiari malformation (syndrome) *(Hemmungsmißbildung des Kleinhirns)*
Arnold-Realy-Syndrom n Arnold-Realy syndrome, extraglandular hyperaldosteronism
Arrector m arrector, erector [muscle]
Arrest-Reaktion f arrest reaction *(plötzliches Erstarren des Organismus)*
Arrest-Verhalten n arrest behaviour *(Abbruch von Umweltbeziehungen)*
Arrhenoblastom n arrheno[blasto]ma *(Ovarialtumor)*
Arrhenotokie f arrhenotoky *(Bildung ausschließlich männlicher Nachkommen)*
Arrhinenzephalie f arrhinencephalia
Arrhinie f ar[r]hinia, absence of the nose
arrhinisch ar[r]hinic
Arrhythmie f a[r]rhythmia
~/**absolute** absolute (continuous) arrhythmia
~ **des Herzens** heart (cardiac) arrhythmia
~ **des Pulsschlags** irregularity of the pulse
~/**respiratorische** respiratory arrhythmia
~/**ventrikuläre** ventricular arrhythmia
Arrhythmieanalysator m arrhythmia analyzer
Arrhythmiecomputer m arrhythmia computer
arrhythmieerzeugend arrhythmogenic
arrhythmisch arrhythmic[al]
arrhythmogen arrhythmogenic
Arrosionsaneurysma n arrosion aneurysm
Arrosionsblutung f arrosion haemorrhage (bleeding)
Arsenamblyopie f arsenic amblyopia
Arsenbehandlung f arsenotherapy
Arsendermatitis f arsenical dermatitis
Arsenenzephalopathie f arsenical encephalopathy
Arsengegenmittel n arsenic antidote

arsenhaltig

arsenhaltig arseniferous, arsenical
Arsenhyperkeratose f arsenical [hyper]keratosis
Arsenik n arsenic *(Kapillargift)*
Arsenikkrebs m arsenical carcinoma
arsenisch arsenic
Arsenkeratose f arsenical [hyper]keratosis
Arsenkrebs m arsenical carcinoma
Arsenlähmung f arsenical paralysis
Arsennachweis m/**Bettendorffscher** Bettendorff's test
Arsenpolyneuritis f arsenical polyneuritis
Arsenpolyneuropathie f arsenical polyneuropathy
Arsenpräparat n arsenical preparation
Arsentremor m arsenical tremor
Arsentrioxid n arsenic trioxide, arsenous oxide, arsenic *(Kapillargift)*
Arsenvergiftung f arsenical poisoning
Arsenwasserstoffvergiftung f arsine poisoning
Arsonvalisation f [d']arsonvalization *(Behandlung mit Hochfrequenzströmen)*
Art f[/**biologische**] species
~/männliche masculinity
~/weibische feminism
Artantigen n specific antigen
Artefakt n artefac[t], artifact
artefiziell artificial *(z. B. Organe)*
arteigen specific; characteristic *(z. B. Symptom)*
Arterenol n arterenol *(Sympathikuswirkstoff)*
Arteria f artery, arteria, a.
~ **abdominalis** abdominal artery
~ **acetabuli** acetabular artery
~ **alveolaris inferior** inferior alveolar artery
~ **alveolaris superior anterior** superior anterior alveolar artery
~ **alveolaris superior posterior** superior posterior alveolar artery
~ **angularis** angular artery *(Endast der Gesichtsschlagader)*
~ **anonyma** s. ~ brachiocephalica
~ **appendicis vermiformis** appendicular artery
~ **appendicularis** appendicular artery
~ **arcuata** arcuate artery
~ **arcuata pedis** arcuate artery of the foot
~ **auditiva interna** internal auditory artery
~ **auricularis anterior** anterior auricular artery
~ **auricularis posterior** posterior auricular artery
~ **auricularis profunda** deep auricular artery
~ **axillaris** axillary artery
~ **basilaris** basilar artery
~ **brachialis** brachial artery
~ **brachialis superficialis** superficial brachial artery
~ **brachiocephalica** brachiocephalic (innominate) artery, anonyma
~ **bronchialis** bronchial artery
~ **bronchialis inferior** inferior bronchial artery
~ **bronchialis superior** superior bronchial artery
~ **buccalis** buccal artery
~ **bulbi penis** artery of the bulb of the penis
~ **bulbi vestibuli vaginae** artery of the bulb of the vestibule of the vagina

58

~ **caecalis anterior** anterior caecal artery
~ **caecalis posterior** posterior caecal artery
~ **canalis pterygoidei** artery of the pterygoid canal
~ **carotis** carotid [artery], carotis, cervical artery
~ **carotis communis** common carotid artery
~ **carotis communis dextra** right common carotid artery, R.C.C.
~ **carotis communis sinistra** left common carotid artery, L.C.C.
~ **carotis externa** external carotid artery
~ **carotis interna** internal carotid artery
~ **centralis retinae** central artery of the retina, Zinn's central artery
~ **cerebelli inferior anterior** anterior inferior cerebellar artery
~ **cerebelli inferior posterior** posterior inferior cerebellar artery
~ **cerebelli superior** superior cerebellar artery
~ **cerebri** cerebral artery
~ **cerebri anterior** anterior cerebral artery
~ **cerebri media** middle cerebral artery
~ **cerebri posterior** posterior cerebral artery
~ **cervicalis** cervical artery
~ **cervicalis ascendens** ascending cervical artery
~ **cervicalis profunda** deep cervical artery
~ **cervicalis superficialis** superficial cervical artery
~ **chorioidea [anterior]** anterior choroid artery
~ **ciliaris anterior** anterior ciliary artery
~ **ciliaris posterior breve** short posterior ciliary artery
~ **ciliaris posterior longa** long posterior ciliary artery
~ **circumflexa femoris lateralis** lateral femoral circumflex artery
~ **circumflexa femoris medialis** medial femoral circumflex artery
~ **circumflexa humeri anterior** anterior humeral circumflex artery
~ **circumflexa humeri posterior** posterior humeral circumflex artery
~ **circumflexa ilium profunda** deep iliac circumflex artery
~ **circumflexa ilium superficialis** superficial iliac circumflex artery
~ **circumflexa scapulae** circumflex scapular artery
~ **clitoridis** clitoridal artery
~ **colica** colic artery
~ **colica dextra** right colic artery
~ **colica media** middle colic artery
~ **colica sinistra** left colic artery
~ **collateralis media** medial collateral artery
~ **collateralis radialis** radial collateral artery
~ **collateralis ulnaris inferior** inferior ulnar collateral artery
~ **collateralis ulnaris superior** superior ulnar collateral artery
~ **comitans nervi ischiadici** accompanying sciatic nerve artery
~ **communicans** communicating artery

- ~ **communicans anterior [cerebri]** anterior communicating artery of the cerebrum
- ~ **communicans posterior [cerebri]** posterior communicating artery of the cerebrum
- ~ **conjunctivalis anterior** anterior conjunctival artery
- ~ **conjunctivalis posterior** posterior conjunctival artery
- ~ **coronaria** coronary artery
- ~ **coronaria circumflexa sinistra** left circumflex coronary artery
- ~ **coronaria [cordis] dextra** right coronary artery
- ~ **coronaria [cordis] sinistra** left coronary artery
- ~ **corticalis radiata renis** interlobular artery of the kidney
- ~ **cremasterica** s. ~ spermatica externa
- ~ **cystica** cystic artery
- ~ **digitalis dorsalis manus** dorsal digital artery of the hand
- ~ **digitalis dorsalis pedis** dorsal digital artery of the foot
- ~ **digitalis palmaris communis** common palmar digital artery
- ~ **digitalis palmaris propria** proper palmar digital artery
- ~ **digitalis plantaris communis** common plantar digital artery
- ~ **digitalis plantaris propria** proper plantar digitalis artery
- ~ **digitalis volaris communis** common volar digital artery
- ~ **digitalis volaris propria** proper volar digital artery
- ~ **dorsalis clitoridis** dorsal artery of the clitoris
- ~ **dorsalis nasi** dorsal nasal artery
- ~ **dorsalis pedis** dorsalis pedis [artery], dorsal pedal artery
- ~ **dorsalis penis** dorsal artery of the penis
- ~ **ductus deferentialis (deferentis)** deferential artery
- ~ **epigastrica inferior** inferior epigastric artery
- ~ **epigastrica superficialis** superficial epigastric artery
- ~ **epigastrica superior** superior epigastric artery
- ~ **episcleralis** episcleral artery
- ~ **ethmoidalis** ethmoid artery
- ~ **ethmoidalis anterior** anterior ethmoid artery
- ~ **ethmoidalis posterior** posterior ethmoid artery
- ~ **facialis** facial (external maxillary) artery
- ~ **femoralis** femoral artery
- ~ **fibularis** fibular artery
- ~ **frontalis** frontal artery
- ~ **gastrica brevis** short gastric artery
- ~ **gastrica dexta** right gastric (stomach coronary) artery
- ~ **gastrica sinistra** left gastric (stomach coronary) artery
- ~ **gastroduodenalis** gastroduodenal artery
- ~ **gastroepiploica dextra** right gastroepiploic artery
- ~ **gastroepiploica sinistra** left gastroepiploic artery
- ~ **genus descendens** descending genicular artery
- ~ **genus inferior lateralis** lateral inferior genicular artery
- ~ **genus inferior medialis** medial inferior genicular artery
- ~ **genus media** middle genicular artery
- ~ **genus superior lateralis** lateral superior genicular artery
- ~ **genus superior medialis** medial superior genicular artery
- ~ **glutaea inferior** inferior gluteal artery
- ~ **glutaea superior** superior gluteal artery
- ~ **haemorrhoidalis** ... s. ~ rectalis ...
- ~ **helicina penis** coiled artery of the penis
- ~ **hepatica** hepatic artery
- ~ **hepatica accessoria** accessory hepatic artery
- ~ **hepatica communis** common hepatic artery
- ~ **hepatica propria** proper hepatic artery
- ~ **hyaloidea** hyaloid artery
- ~ **hypogastrica** s. ~ iliaca interna
- ~ **ileocolica** ileocolic artery
- ~ **iliaca communis** common iliac artery
- ~ **iliaca externa** external iliac artery
- ~ **iliaca interna** hypogastric (internal iliac) artery
- ~ **iliolumbalis** iliolumbar artery
- ~ **infraorbitalis** infraorbital artery
- ~ **intercostalis** intercostal artery
- ~ **intercostalis posterior** posterior intercostal artery
- ~ **interlobaris renis** interlobar artery of the kidney
- ~ **interlobularis** interlobular artery
- ~ **interlobularis hepatis** interlobular artery of the liver
- ~ **interlobularis renis** interlobular artery of the kidney
- ~ **interossea anterior** anterior interosseous artery
- ~ **interossea communis** common interosseous artery
- ~ **interossea posterior** posterior interosseous artery
- ~ **interossea recurrens** recurrent interosseous artery
- ~ **interossea recurrens dorsalis** dorsal interosseous recurrent artery
- ~ **intestinalis** intestinal artery
- ~ **iridis** long posterior ciliary artery
- ~ **labialis anterior** anterior labial artery
- ~ **labialis inferior** inferior labial artery
- ~ **labialis posterior** posterior labial artery
- ~ **labialis superior** superior labial artery
- ~ **lacrimalis** lacrimal artery
- ~ **laryngea inferior** inferior laryngeal artery
- ~ **laryngea superior** superior laryngeal artery
- ~ **lienalis** splenic artery
- ~ **ligamenti teretis uteri** artery of the round ligament of the uterus
- ~ **lingualis** lingual artery
- ~ **lumbalis** lumbar artery
- ~ **lumbalis ima** lowest (fifth) lumbar artery
- ~ **malleolaris anterior lateralis** anterior lateral malleolar artery

Arteria

- ~ malleolaris anterior medialis anterior medial malleolar artery
- ~ malleolaris posterior lateralis posterior lateral malleolar artery
- ~ malleolaris posterior medialis posterior medial malleolar artery
- ~ mammaria interna internal thoracic artery
- ~ masseterica masseteric artery
- ~ maxillaris [internal] maxillary artery, Vidian artery
- ~ maxillaris externa facial (external maxillary) artery
- ~ maxillaris interna s. ~ maxillaris
- ~ mediana median artery
- ~ meningea anterior anterior meningeal artery
- ~ meningea media middle meningeal artery
- ~ meningea posterior posterior meningeal artery
- ~ mentalis mental artery
- ~ mesenterica mesenteric artery
- ~ mesenterica inferior inferior mesenteric artery
- ~ mesenterica superior superior mesenteric artery
- ~ metacarpea dorsalis dorsal metacarpal artery
- ~ metacarpea palmaris palmar (ventral) metacarpal artery
- ~ metatarsea dorsalis dorsal metatarsal artery
- ~ metatarsea plantaris plantar metatarsal artery
- ~ musculophrenica musculophrenic artery
- ~ nasalis posterior lateralis posterior lateral nasal artery
- ~ nasalis posterior septi posterior septal nasal artery
- ~ nutricia nutrient artery
- ~ nutricia femoris inferior inferior nutrient artery of the femur
- ~ nutricia femoris superior superior nutrient artery of the femur
- ~ nutricia fibulae nutrient artery of the fibula
- ~ nutricia humeri nutrient artery of the humerus
- ~ nutricia pelvis renalis nutrient artery of the renal pelvis
- ~ nutricia tibiae nutrient artery of the tibia
- ~ obturatoria obturator artery
- ~ occipitalis occipital artery
- ~ oesophagea oesophageal artery
- ~ omphalomesenterica omphalomesenteric (vitelline) artery
- ~ ophthalmica opthalmic artery
- ~ ovarica ovarian (ovaric) artery
- ~ palatina ascendens ascending palatine artery
- ~ palatina descendens descending palatine artery
- ~ palatina major major (greater) palatine artery
- ~ palatina minor minor (lesser) palatine artery
- ~ palpebralis lateralis lateral palpebral artery
- ~ palpebralis medialis medial palpebral artery
- ~ pancreatica dorsalis dorsal pancreatic artery
- ~ pancreatica inferior inferior pancreatic artery
- ~ pancreatica major greater pancreatic artery
- ~ pancreaticoduodenalis inferior inferior pancreaticoduodenal artery
- ~ pancreaticoduodenalis superior superior pancreaticoduodenal artery
- ~ penis artery of the penis
- ~ perforans prima first perforating artery
- ~ perforans secunda second perforating artery
- ~ perforans tertia third perforating artery
- ~ pericardiacophrenica pericardiacophrenic artery
- ~ perinealis (perinei) perineal artery
- ~ peronea peroneal artery
- ~ pharyngea ascendens ascending pharyngeal artery
- ~ phrenica inferior inferior phrenic artery
- ~ phrenica superior superior phrenic artery
- ~ plantaris lateralis lateral plantar artery
- ~ plantaris medialis medial plantar artery
- ~ poplitea popliteal artery
- ~ princeps pollicis principal artery of the thumb, princeps pollicis artery
- ~ profunda brachii profunda brachii artery, deep brachial artery
- ~ profunda clitoridis profunda clitoridis artery
- ~ profunda femoris profunda femoris artery, deep femoral artery
- ~ profunda linguae profunda linguae artery, deep lingual artery
- ~ profunda penis profunda penis artery
- ~ pudenda externa external pudendal artery
- ~ pudenda interna internal pudendal artery
- ~ pulmonalis pulmonary artery
- ~ pulmonalis dextra right pulmonary artery, R.P.A.
- ~ pulmonalis sinistra left pulmonary artery, L.P.A.
- ~ radialis radial artery
- ~ radialis indicis radial artery of the index finger
- ~ rectalis inferior inferior rectal (haemorrhoidal) artery
- ~ rectalis media middle rectal (haemorrhoidal) artery
- ~ rectalis superior superior rectal (haemorrhoidal) artery
- ~ recurrens radialis radial recurrent artery
- ~ recurrens tibialis anterior anterior recurrent tibial artery
- ~ recurrens tibialis posterior posterior recurrent tibial artery
- ~ recurrens ulnaris recurrent ulnar artery
- ~ renalis (renis) renal artery
- ~ retroauricularis posterior auricular artery
- ~ retroduodenalis retroduodenal artery
- ~ sacralis lateralis lateral sacral artery
- ~ sacralis media[na] medial (median, middle) sacral artery
- ~ scapularis dorsalis descending (dorsal) scapular artery
- ~ scrotalis anterior anterior scrotal artery
- ~ scrotalis posterior posterior scrotal artery
- ~ segmentalis (segmenti) segmental artery
- ~ sigmoidea sigmoid artery
- ~ spermatica externa cremasteric (external spermatic) artery
- ~ spermatica interna testicular (internal spermatic) artery

Arterienplastik

- ~ sphenopalatina sphenopalatine artery
- ~ spinalis spinal artery
- ~ spinalis anterior anterior spinal artery
- ~ spinalis posterior posterior spinal artery
- ~ spinalis ventralis anterior spinal artery
- ~ sternocleidomastoidea sternocleidomastoid artery
- ~ stylomastoidea stylomastoid artery
- ~ subarcuata subarcuate artery
- ~ subclavia subclavian artery
- ~ subclavia dextra right subclavian artery, R.S.A.
- ~ subclavia sinistra left subclavian artery, L.S.A.
- ~ subcostalis subcostal artery
- ~ sublingualis sublingual artery
- ~ submentalis submental artery
- ~ subscapularis subscapular artery
- ~ supraorbitalis supra-orbital artery
- ~ suprarenalis inferior inferior suprarenal artery
- ~ suprarenalis media middle suprarenal artery
- ~ suprarenalis superior superior suprarenal artery
- ~ suprascapularis suprascapular artery, transverse scapular artery
- ~ supratrochlearis supratrochlear artery
- ~ suralis sural artery
- ~ tarsea lateralis lateral tarsal artery
- ~ tarsea medialis medial tarsal artery
- ~ temporalis media middle temporal artery
- ~ temporalis profunda [anterior] deep temporal artery
- ~ temporalis profunda posterior deep posterior temporal artery
- ~ temporalis superficialis superficial temporal artery
- ~ testicularis s. ~ spermatica interna
- ~ thoracica interna internal thoracic artery
- ~ thoracica lateralis lateral thoracic artery
- ~ thoracica suprema highest thoracic artery
- ~ thoracoacromialis thoracoacromial (acromiothoracic) artery
- ~ thoracodorsalis thoracodorsal artery
- ~ thymica thymic artery
- ~ thyreoidea ima lowest thyroid artery, thyreoidea ima artery
- ~ thyreoidea inferior inferior thyroid artery
- ~ thyreoidea superior superior thyroid artery
- ~ tibialis anterior anterior tibial artery
- ~ tibialis posterior posterior tibial artery
- ~ transversa colli transverse cervical artery
- ~ transversa faciei transverse facial artery
- ~ tympanica anterior anterior tympanic artery
- ~ tympanica inferior inferior tympanic artery
- ~ tympanica posterior posterior tympanic artery
- ~ tympanica superior superior tympanic artery
- ~ ulnaris ulnar artery
- ~ umbilicalis umbilical artery
- ~ uterina uterine artery
- ~ vaginalis vaginal artery
- ~ vertebralis vertebral artery
- ~ vesicalis vesical artery
- ~ vesicalis inferior inferior vesical artery
- ~ vesicalis superior superior vesical artery
- ~ zygomaticoorbitalis zygomatico-orbital artery

Arteriae *fpl* arcuatae renis arcuate arteries
- ~ perforantes perforating arteries

arterialisieren to arterialize
Arterialisierung *f* arterialization
Arteria-mammaria-Implantation *f* Vineberg operation, mammary artery implantation
Arterie *f* artery, arteria *(Zusammensetzungen s. unter Arteria)* ● in einer ~ liegend intra-arterial
~/Kugelsche Kugel's artery
Arteriektasie *f* arteriectasia, arteriectasis
Arteriektomie *f* arteriectomy, excision of the artery
Arteriektopie *f* arteriectopia
arteriell arterial
Arterien... *s. a.* Schlagader...
Arterienagenesie *f* arterial agenesis
Arterienanastomose *f* arterial anastomosis
Arterienaneurysma *n* arterial aneurysm
Arterienarkade *f* arterial arcade
Arterienbildung *f* arteriogenesis
Arterienbogen *m* der Fußsohle plantar arterial arch
- ~ der Hohlhand/oberflächlicher superficial palmar (volar) arch
- ~ der Hohlhand/tiefer deep palmar arch

Arteriendegeneration *f* arteriasis, degeneration of an artery
Arteriendissektor *m* artery dissector
Arteriendruck *m* arterial [blood] pressure
Arterienendothel *n* arterial endothelium
Arterienentfernung *f*[/operative] *s.* Arteriektomie
Arterienentzündung *f s.* Arteriitis
Arterienerkrankung *f s.* Arteriopathie
Arterieneröffnung *f*[/operative] *s.* Arteriotomie
Arterienersatz *m* 1. artery replacement *(Vorgang)*; 2. arterial substitute
Arterienerweichung *f* arteriomalacia
Arterienerweiterung *f* 1. arteriectasia, arterial dilatation; 2. aneurysm *(Zusammensetzungen s. unter Aneurysma)*
Arterienfaßzange *f* artery traction forceps
Arteriengeräusch *n* arterial murmur
Arterieninnenwandentzündung *f* endarteritis
Arterienkatheterung *f* artery catheterization
Arterienklemme *f* artery forceps, haemostat, haemostatic forceps
- ~ nach Kocher Kocher's [mosquito] forceps *(zum Fassen kleiner Blutgefäße)*

Arterienkrampf *m* arteriospasm, arterial spasm
Arterienligatur *f* arterial ligation
Arterienlokalisation *f*/abnorme arteriectopia
Arterienmesser *n* arteriotome
Arteriennaht *f* arteriorrhaphy, suture of the artery
Arterienobstruktion *f* arterial obstruction, obstruction of an artery
Arterienplastik *f* arterioplasty, arterial reconstruction

Arterienprothese

Arterienprothese f arterial prosthesis
Arterienprothesentransplantation f pro[s]thetic arterial grafting
Arterienpuls m arterial pulse
Arterienpulsschreiber m sphygmograph, sphygmometer
Arterienpulsschreibung f sphygmography
Arterienpunktion f arteriopuncture, puncture of an artery, arterial puncture
Arterienrekonstruktion f arterial reconstruction, arterioplasty
Arterienröntgen[kontrast]bild n radioarteriogram
Arterienröntgen[kontrast]darstellung f radioarteriography
Arterienruptur f arteriorrhexis, rupture of an artery
Arterienstamm m arterial trunk
Arterienstein m arteriolith, arterial calculus
Arterienstruktur f arteriostenosis, arterial stricture (stenosis)
Arterientransplantat n artery graft
Arterientrauma n arterial trauma (injury)
Arterienunterbindung f arterial ligation
arterienverkalkend s. arteriosklerotisch
Arterienverkalkung f s. Arteriosklerose
Arterienverschluß m arterial occlusion, occlusion of an artery
Arterienverschlußkrankheit f occlusive arterial disease
Arterienwand f artery wall
Arterienwanddegeneration f arteriasis
Arterienwiderstand m arterial resistance
Arteriitis f arteritis
~ **brachiocephalica** brachiocephalic arteritis, Takayasu syndrome
~ **gigantocellularis** gigantocellular arteritis
~/**nekrotisierende** necrotizing arteritis
~/**rheumatische** rheumatic arteritis
~ **temporalis** temporal arteritis
Arteriofibrose f arteriofibrosis
Arteriogramm n [radio]arteriogram
~/**renales** renal arteriogram
Arteriograph m arteriograph
Arteriographie f arteriography
~/**brachiozephale** brachiocephalic arteriography
~/**panzerebrale** pancerebral arteriography
~/**selektive abdominale** selective abdominal arteriography
Arteriographiebefund m arteriographic findings
arteriographisch [radio]arteriographic
Arteriola f arteriola, arteriole, twig *(präkapillare Arterie)*
~ **recta renis** straight arteriole [of the kidney]
arteriolär arteriolar
Arteriole f s. Arteriola
Arteriolendegeneration f arteriolonecrosis, arteriolar degeneration
Arteriolenendothel n arteriolar endothelium
Arteriolenentzündung f arteriolitis, inflammation of an arteriole
Arteriolenerweiterung f arteriolar vasodilation

Arteriolenhyalinisierung f arteriolosclerosis, arteriolar hyalinization
Arteriolenlumen n arteriolar lumen
Arteriolenwiderstand m arteriolar resistance
Arteriolith m arteriolith, arterial calculus
arteriolithisch arteriolithic
Arteriolitis f arteriolitis, inflammation of an arteriole
Arteriolonekrose f arteriolonecrosis, arteriolar necrosis
Arteriolosklerose f arteriolosclerosis
arteriolosklerotisch arteriolosclerotic
Arteriomalazie f arteriomalacia, softening of the arterial wall
Arterionekrose f arterionecrosis
Arteriopathie f arteriopathy, arterial disease
~/**chronisch obliterierende** s. Arteriosclerosis obliterans
Arteriorrhaphie f arteriorrhaphy, suture of the artery
Arteriorrhexis f arteriorrhexis, rupture of the artery
Arteriosclerosis f s. Arteriosklerose
~ **obliterans** obliterant (peripheral occlusive) arteriosclerosis, chronic obliterating arteriopathy
Arteriosklerose f arteriosclerosis, atherosclerosis, arterial sclerosis; [intimal] arteriosclerosis
~/**senile** senile arteriosclerosis
~/**zerebrale** cerebral arteriosclerosis
arteriosklerosebildend atherogenic
Arterioskleroseentstehung f atherogenesis
Arterioskleroseherd m [arteriosclerotic] plaque
arteriosklerosierend atherogenic
arteriosklerotisch arteriosclerotic
Arteriospasmus m arteriospasm, arterial spasm
arteriospastisch arteriospastic
Arteriostenose f arteriostenosis, arterial stenosis
Arteriotom n arteriotome
Arteriotomie f arteriotomy, incision into an artery
Arteriotrachealfistel f arteriotracheal fistula
arteriovenös arteriovenous
Arteritis f s. Arteriitis
artfremd xenogenic, xenogenous, heterogeneous, foreign
artgleich homogeneous
Arthralgie f arthralgia, arthrodynia, pain in the joint
Arthrektomie f arthrectomy, excision of a joint
Arthritiker m arthritic
Arthritis f arthritis
~/**allergische** allergic arthritis
~/**Charcotsche** Charcot's arthritis (arthrosis), neurotrophic arthritis, neuropathic (neurogenic) arthropathy
~/**chronische** chronic arthritis
~/**degenerative** degenerative arthritis
~/**eitrige** s. ~ purulenta
~ **fungosa** fungoid arthritis
~ **gonorrhoica** gonorrhoeal (gonococcal) arthritis, urethral synovitis
~/**hypertrophe** hypertrophic arthritis
~/**infektiöse** infectious arthritis

Articulatio

~/neurogene s. ~/Charcotsche
~/proliferierende proliferating arthritis
~ purulenta suppurative arthritis, acute suppurative synovitis
~ rheumatica rheumatic (rheumatoid) arthritis
~/septische infectious arthritis
~ tuberculosa tuberculous arthritis (rheumatism)
arthritisch arthritic
Arthritismus *m* arthritism
Arthrochondritis *f* arthrochondritis, inflammation of the joint cartilage
Arthrodese *f* arthrodesis, operative (artificial) ankylosis, surgical joint fusion
Arthrodia *f* arthrodia, gliding joint
Arthrodynie *f* arthrodynia, joint pain, arthralgia
Arthroempyesis *f* arthroempyesis, suppuration of the joint
Arthroendoskopie *f* arthroendoscopy
Arthrogramm *n* arthrogram
Arthrographie *f* arthrography
arthrographisch arthrographic
Arthrogypose *f* arthrogryposis
Arthrogryposis *f* multiplex congenita congenital multiple arthrogryposis, arthrogryposis syndrome
Arthrokatadysis *f* arthrokatadysis; Otto's pelvis
Arthroklasie *f* arthroclasia, arthroclasis
Arthrolith *m* arthrolith
Arthrologie *f* arthrology
Arthrolyse *f* arthrolysis
Arthrometer *n* arthrometer
Arthrometrie *f* arthrometry
Arthromyodysplasia *f* congenita s. Arthrogryposis multiplex congenita
Arthronkus *m* arthroncus, joint tumour
Arthronose *f* arthrosis
Arthropathia *f* deformans spontanea osteoarthritis of the hip joint *(des alternden Menschen)*
Arthropathie *f* arthropathy, joint (articular) disease
~/klimakterische climacteric arthropathy, menopausal arthritis
~/neurogene (neuropathische, tabische) s. Arthritis/Charcotsche
arthropathisch arthropathic
Arthrophyt *m* arthrophyte; joint mouse
Arthroplastik *f* arthroplasty
arthroplastisch arthroplastic
Arthropneumographie *f* arthropneumo[roentgeno]graphy
Arthrorhise *f* arthroereisis, arthrorisis
Arthrorrhagie *f* arthrorrhagia
Arthrose *f* arthrosis
Arthrosis *f* deformans arthrosis (osteoarthritis) deformans
Arthrosklerose *f* arthrosclerosis
Arthroskop *n* arthroscope
Arthroskopie *f* arthroscopy
arthroskopisch arthroscopic
Arthrostomie *f* arthrostomy
Arthrosynovitis *f* arthrosynovitis

Arthrotom *n* arthrotome
Arthrotomie *f* arthrotomy
Arthrozentese *f* arthrocentesis, puncture of a joint
Arthus-Phänomen *n* Arthus' phenomenon, phenomenon of Arthus, local anaphylaxis *(allergische Überempfindlichkeitsreaktion)*
Articulatio *f* articulation, articulatio, joint, junction, junctura *(s. a. unter Gelenk)*
~ acromioclavicularis acromioclavicular joint
~ atlantoaxialis lateralis lateral atlantoaxial (epistropheal) joint
~ atlantoaxialis mediana median atlantoaxial (epistropheal) joint
~ atlantooccipitalis atlantooccipital joint, occipitoatlantoid articulation
~ calcaneocuboidea calcaneocuboid joint
~ carpometacarpea carpometacarpal joint
~ composita compound joint
~ condylaris condylar joint, condylarthrosis, condyloid articulation
~ costotransversaria costotransverse joint
~ cotylica spheroid joint
~ coxae hip joint
~ cricoarytenoidea cricoarytenoid joint
~ cricothyreoidea cricothyroid joint
~ cubiti elbow joint
~ cuneonavicularis cuneonavicular joint
~ ellipsoidea s. ~ condylaris
~ genu[s] knee joint, femorotibial (tibiofemoral) articulation
~ humeri shoulder joint
~ humeroradialis humeroradial joint, radiohumeral articulation
~ humeroulnaris humeroulnar joint
~ incudomallearis incudomalleal joint
~ incudostapedia incudostapedial joint
~ intercarpea intercarpal joint
~ interphalangea interphalangeal joint
~ mediocarpea midcarpal joint
~ metacarpophalangea metacarpophalangeal joint
~ metatarsophalangea metatarsophalangeal joint
~ plana plane (gliding) joint
~ radiocarpea radiocarpal joint, wrist joint [proper]
~ radioulnaris distalis distal radioulnar joint
~ radioulnaris proximalis proximal radioulnar joint
~ sacro-iliaca sacroiliac joint (synchondrosis)
~ sellaris saddle joint
~ sphaeroidea spheroid articulation, ball-and-socket joint
~ sternoclavicularis sternoclavicular joint
~ sternocostalis sternocostal joint
~ subtalaris subtalar joint, talocalcanean articulation
~ synovialis synovial joint, diarthrodial articulation
~ talocalcanearis s. ~ subtalaris
~ talocalcaneonavicularis talocalcaneonavicular joint, subastragaloid articulation

Articulatio

~ **talocruralis** talocrural (ankle) joint
~ **tarsi transversa** transverse tarsal joint
~ **tarsometatarsea** tarsometatarsal joint
~ **temporomandibularis** temporomandibular joint
~ **tibiofibularis inferior** inferior (distal) tibiofibular joint, tibiofibular syndesmosis
~ **tibiofibularis superior** superior (proximal) tibiofibular joint
~ **trochoidea** trochoid (pivot) joint
artikulär articular
Artikulation f 1. articulation *(Stomatologie)*; 2. s. Articulatio
Artikulationsbewegung f articular (articulation) movement
Artikulationsfläche f articular (articulation) surface *(Stomatologie)*
Artikulationspapier n articulating (articulation) paper *(Stomatologie)*
Artikulationsstörung f articulation disturbance
Artikulator m articulator *(dentalmedizinisches Instrument)*
artikulieren 1. to articulate, to be jointed; to become jointed; 2. to articulate, to pronounce distinctly
~/**miteinander** to articulate (z. B. die Zahnreihen)
aryepiglottisch ary[teno]epiglottic, aryepiglottidean
Aryknorpel m arytenoid (triquetrous) cartilage
Aryknorpelentzündung f arytenoiditis
Aryknorpelexstirpation f arytenoidectomy
Aryknorpelfixierung f [/**chirurgische**] arytenoidopexy
Aryknorpelrückseite f dorsal surface of the arytenoid cartilage
Aryknorpelspitze f upper extremity of the arytenoid cartilage
arytenoepiglottisch s. aryepiglottisch
arytenoid arytenoid
Arytenoidektomie f arytenoidectomy
Arytenoiditis f arytenoiditis
Arytenoidopexie f arytenoidopexy
Arznei f s. Arzneimittel
Arznei... s. a. Arzneimittel...
Arzneibuch n pharmacop[o]eia, dispensatory
● **im ~ geführt** official
~/**Internationales** International Pharmacopoeia
Arzneifläschchen n phial, vial
Arzneigabe f 1. medication, dosage *(Verabreichung)*; 2. dose, dosis *(Menge)*
Arzneigemisch n/**flüssiges** mixture
Arzneiglas n medicine bottle
Arzneikapsel f capsule
Arzneikasten m medicine cabinet; first-aid kit
Arzneikräuter npl medical (officinal) herbs
arzneilich medicinal, officinal
Arzneimittel n pharmaceutic[al], pharmaceutical agent (preparation), pharmacon, remedy, medicament, medicine, drug *(s. a. unter* Medikament *und* Mittel*)* ● **als ~ anerkannt** officinal
● **~ anwendend** medicamentous ● **durch ~ bedingt** drug-induced

~/**die Nierenfunktion beeinflussendes** nephrotropic [agent]
~/**flüssiges** liquor
~/**lösendes** resolvent [agent]
~/**opiumhaltiges** opiate
~/**stärkendes** tonic, roborant [agent], restorative remedy
~/**symptomatisches** palliative [agent]
~/**tonisierendes** tonic
Arzneimittel... s. a. Arznei... und Medikamenten...
Arzneimittelabhängiger m drug addict
Arzneimittelabhängigkeit f drug addiction (dependence)
Arzneimittelallergie f drug allergy (hypersensitivity)
Arzneimittelanwendung f medication
Arzneimittelausschlag m drug eruption, medicinal rash
Arzneimittelbehandlung f pharmacotherapy, remedial therapy, pharmaceutical treatment
Arzneimittelchemie f pharmaceutical chemistry
Arzneimitteldermatitis f s. Arzneimittelexanthem
Arzneimittelexanthem n drug eruption, medicinal rash
Arzneimittelfieber n drug fever
Arzneimittelflasche f medicine bottle
Arzneimittelfurcht f pharmacophobia
Arzneimittelgeschmack m medicinal taste
Arzneimittelgewöhnung f 1. drug tolerance; 2. s. Arzneimittelabhängigkeit
Arzneimittelgiftigkeit f drug toxicity
Arzneimittelikterus m drug icterus (jaundice)
arzneimittelinduziert drug-induced
Arzneimittelkombinationstherapie f multidrug therapy
Arzneimittelkunde f 1. pharmaceutics, pharmacy *(Zubereitung)*; 2. s. Arzneimittellehre
Arzneimittelkundiger m pharmac[eut]ist
Arzneimittellehre f pharmacology, pharmaceutics; pharmacopaedics
Arzneimittelmenge f dose, dosis
Arzneimittelmißbrauch m drug abuse
Arzneimittelnesselsucht f medicamentous urticaria
Arzneimittelpsychose f pharmacopsychosis, drug psychosis
Arzneimittelreaktion f drug reaction
Arzneimittelsucht f pharmacomania, pharmacophilia; drug dependence (addiction, habit)
Arzneimittelsuppression f drug suppression
arzneimittelunempfindlich drug-resistant
Arzneimittelvergiftung f drug intoxication (poisoning)
Arzneimittelverordnung f prescription, medication; recipe
Arzneimittelverzeichnis n s. Arzneibuch
Arzneimittelwirkung f drug action
Arzneipapier n charta
Arzneischachtel f chartula *(Dosierungsform)*
Arzneischränkchen n medicine cabinet (cupboard)

Arzneistoff *m* medicinal substance *(s. a.* Arzneimittel*)*
Arzneitrank *m* potion, draught
Arzneiverordnungslehre *f s.* Arzneimittellehre
Arzneiverzeichnis *n s.* Arzneibuch
Arzneivorschrift *f* prescription
Arzneizubereitung *f* 1. dispensing, making-up prescriptions; 2. formulation
Arzt *m* physician, doctor; medical officer *(Militärarzt)* ● **bei Eintreffen des Arztes** on the arrival of the physician ● **bis zum Eintreffen des Arztes** until the arrival of the physician ● **den ~ rufen** to send for the doctor ● **den ~ zu Rate ziehen** to consult the doctor ● **der Aufmerksamkeit des Arztes entgehen** to escape the attention of the physician ● **durch den ~ bewirkt** iatrogenic ● **zum ~ gehen** to see (go to) the doctor
~/approbierter licentiate
~/behandelnder attending physician
~/beratender consultant [physician]
~/die Leichenschau durchführender medical examiner
~/diensttuender doctor on duty
~/konsultierender attending physician
~/Leichenzerlegungen durchführender (überwachender) prosector
~/perfundierender perfusionist
~/perkutierender percussor
~/praktischer [general] practitioner, G. P., medical practitioner, physician
~/überweisender referring physician
Arztbericht *m* medical report
Arztbesuch *m* 1. physician (doctor's) visit; 2. consultation, visit to the doctor
Arzthelfer *m* doctor's assistant; paramedic
Arzthonorar *n* doctor's fee
Ärztin *f* lady doctor (physician)
ärztlich medical
Arzt-Patient-Verhältnis *n* physician-patient relationship
Arztpraxis *f* medical (general) practice
Arzttasche *f* doctor's bag (case), instrument case
Arztwahl *f/freie* free choice of a doctor
Asbestfasern *fpl* asbestos fibres
Asbestfaserung *f* asbestos transformation *(von Knorpeln)*
Asbestkörperchen *n* asbestos body *(bei Asbeststaublunge)*
Asbestose *f* asbestosis, amianthosis, steam-fitter's asthma
Asbeststaublunge[nerkrankung] *f s.* Asbestose
Asbesttransformation *f* asbestos transformation *(von Knorpeln)*
Ascaris *f* ascarid, ascaris
ascendens ascending, ascendent, rising
Aschenbild *n* spodogram
Aschheim-Zondek-Schwangerschaftstest *m* Aschheim-Zondek [pregnancy] test, AZT
Aschner-Phänomen *n* Aschner's phenomenon (oculocardiac reflex)

Aschoff-Geipel-Knötchen *n*, **Aschoff-Talajew-Knötchen** *n* Aschoff's body (nodule) *(im Herzmuskel)*
Aschoff-Tawara-Knoten *m* Tawara's (atrioventricular, auriculoventricular) node *(Reizleitung)*
ASD II secundum [type] atrial septal defect
Asemie *f* asemia, asymboly
~/expressive expressive asemia
~/rezeptive perceptive asemia
Asepsis *f* asepsis
Aseptik *f* aseptic treatment; aseptic surgery
aseptisch aseptic ● **~ machen** to render aseptic, to sterilize ● **vor der aseptischen Ära** preaseptic
asexuell asexual
Asherman-Syndrom *n* Asherman's syndrome (traumatic amenorrhoea), traumatic intrauterine synechiae
Ashman-Phänomen *n* Ashman's phenomenon *(bei Vorhofflimmern)*
Asialie *f* asialia, aptyalism
Asiderose *f* asiderosis
asiderotisch asiderotic
Askariasis *f* ascariasis, ascari[d]osis
Askaridenmittel *n* ascaride [agent]
Askaridiasis *f*, **Askarisbefall** *m s.* Askariasis
askarizid ascaricide
Askorbinsäure *f* ascorbic acid, vitamin C
Askorbinsäuremangel *m* avitaminosis C
Askorbinsäureoxydase *f* ascorbic acid oxidase *(Enzym)*
Askorbinsäuresynthese *f* ascorbic acid synthesis
Äskulapstab *m* staff of Aesculapius, caduceus
Asomnie *f* insomnia, sleeplessness
Asozialität *f* asociality
Asparagin *n* asparagine
Asparaginase *f* asparaginase *(Enzym)*
Asparaginsäure *f* aspartic (asparaginic) acid
Aspartase *f* aspartase *(Enzym)*
Aspartataminotransferase *f* aspartate aminotransferase, glutamic-oxalacetic transaminase
Aspartatdehydrogenase *f* aspartate dehydrogenase *(Enzym)*
Aspartattranskarbamylase *f* aspartate transcarbamylase (carbamyltransferase) *(Enzym)*
Aspartylglukosaminurie *f* aspartylycosaminuria (angeborene Stoffwechselkrankheit)
aspastisch aspastic
Aspergillom *n* aspergilloma
Aspergillose *f* aspergillosis
Aspergillus *m* aspergillus
Aspergillusinfektion *f* aspergillosis
Aspergillusmyzetom *n* aspergilloma
aspermatisch asperm[at]ic, aspermous
Aspermatismus *m* aspermia, aspermatism
Aspermatogenese *f* aspermatogenesis
aspermatös asperm[at]ic, aspermous
Aspermie *f* aspermia, aspermatism
asphyktisch asphyxial
Asphyxie *f* asphyxia, anoxia, suffocation ● **~ bewirkend** asphyxiant

Asphyxie

~/**blaue** blue asphyxia, asphyxia livida
~/**bleiche** pale (white) asphyxia, asphyxia pallida
~/**lokale** local asphyxia
~/**traumatische** traumatic asphyxia (apnoea), asphyxia cyanotica, pressure stasis; ecchymotic mask
Asphyxieatelektase f/**postnatale** postnatal asphyxia atelectasis
Aspiration f aspiration, inhalation
~ **von Erbrochenem** aspiration (inhalation) of vomit
Aspirationsapparat m s. Aspirator
Aspirationsbiopsie f aspiration biopsy
Aspirationsnadel f aspirating needle
Aspirationspneumonie f aspiration pneumonia
Aspirationspsychrometer n aspiration psychrometer
Aspirationsspritze f aspiration syringe
Aspirationszytologie f aspiration cytology
Aspirator m aspirator
aspirieren to aspirate, to inhale
Aspirin n aspirin, acetylsalicylic acid *(Antirheumatikum, Analgetikum)*
Asplenie f asplenia, absence of the spleen
Assam-Fieber n Assam fever *(tropische Infektionskrankheit durch Leishmanien)*
Assimilation f assimilation
~/**schlechte** malassimilation
Assimilationsbecken n assimilation pelvis
Assimilationshypophalangie f assimilation hypophalangia
Assimilationsstörung f malassimilation
Assimilationswirbel m assimilation vertebra
assimilierbar assimilable
~/**nicht** inassimilable, unassimilable
Assimilierbarkeit f assimilability
assimilieren to assimilate
Assistentin f/**medizinisch-technische** medical laboratory assistant
Assistenz f assistance
Assistenzarzt m assistant physician, medical assistant, resident [physician]
Assmann-Frühherd m Assmann's infiltrate (focus)
Assoziation f association
Assoziationsareal n association area
Assoziationsbahn f association tract
Assoziationsdenken n association (associative) thinking
Assoziationsfaser f association fibre
Assoziationsfeld n association field
Assoziationsgedächtnis n association (associative) memory
Assoziationskern m association nucleus
Assoziationslernen n association (associative) learning
Assoziationsparalyse f association paralysis
Assoziationspsychologie f association (associative) psychology
Assoziationsreaktion f association (associative) reaction
Assoziationsversuch m association test (experiment)

Assoziationswort n association word
Assoziationszeit f association time
Assoziationszelle f association cell
Assoziationszentrum n association area
Assoziativerinnerung f association (associative) memory
Assoziativhemmung f associative inhibition (interference)
assoziieren to associate
AST s. Antistreptolysintiter
Ast m ramus, branch
Astasie f astasia *(infolge motorischer Koordinationsstörung)*
Astasie-Abasie-Syndrom n astasia-abasia [syndrome]
astatisch astatic
Asteatosis f asteatosis
Aster m aster *(Mitosefigur)*
Astereognosie f astereocognosy, astereognosis, stereoagnosis, stereoanaesthesia, tactile agnosia
Asterion n asterion *(anthropologischer Meßpunkt)*
asternal asternal
Asternie f asternia
Asthenia f s. Asthenie
~ **universalis congenita** Stiller's disease
Asthenie f asthenia, debility, deficient vitality
~/**anhidrotische** tropical anhidrotic (dyshidrotic) asthenia
~/**neurozirkulatorische** neurocirculatory asthenia, N.C.A., effort syndrome; soldier's heart
~/**unterschwellige** hypasthenia
Astheniker m asthenic [type, person]
asthenisch asthenic
Asthenokorie f asthenocoria *(bei Nebennierenunterfunktion)*
asthenop asthenopic
Asthenoper m asthenope
Asthenophobie f asthenophobia *(krankhafte Angst vor Schwäche)*
Asthenopie f asthenopia, ophthalmocopia
~/**akkommodative** accommodative asthenopia
~/**muskuläre** muscular asthenopia
~/**nervöse** nervous asthenopia
~/**retinale** retinal asthenopia
Asthenospermie f asthenospermia
Asthenozoospermie f asthenozoospermia *(Bewegungslosigkeit der Spermien)*
Ästhesiologie f aesthesiology
Ästhesiometer n aesthesiometer
Ästhesioneuroblastom n aesthesioneuroblastoma
Ästhesioneuroepitheliom n aesthesioneuroepithelioma
Ästhesioneurom n aesthesioneuroma *(in der Nasenhöhle)*
Ästhesiophysiologie f aesthesiophysiology
Asthma n asthma *(anfallartig auftretende Kurzatmigkeit)*
~ **bronchiale** bronchial (allergic) asthma
~ **cardiale** cardiac asthma (dyspnoea), car-

dioasthma, pulmonary oedema, backward [heart] failure
~ **emphysematicum** emphysematous asthma
~/endogenes endogenous (intrinsic) asthma
~/symptomatisches symptomatic asthma
~ **thymicum** thymic asthma
Asthmaanfall m asthmatic attack
asthmaartig asthma-like, asthmoid
asthmaauslösend asthmogenic
Asthmadaueranfall m asthmatic shock (state)
Asthmakranker m asthmatic
Asthmakristalle mpl asthma crystals
~/Charcot-Leydensche Charcot-Leyden crystals
Asthmatiker m asthmatic
asthmatisch asthmatic
Asthmatod m asthma death
asthmatoid asthmatoid, asthma-like
asthmogen asthmogenic
asthmoid asthmoid
Asthmolytikum n antiasthmatic [agent]
Astigmatiker m astigmatic
astigmatisch astigmatic
Astigmatismus m astigmatism, astigmatic aberration, astigmia *(durch Hornhautverkrümmung)*
~/angeborener congenital astigmatism
~/direkter direct astigmatism, astigmatism with the rule
~/erworbener acquired astigmatism
~ **gegen die Regel** s. ~/inverser
~/gemischter mixed astigmatism
~/gerader s. ~/direkter
~/hypermetroper hypermetropic astigmatism
~/hyperoper hyperopic astigmatism
~/inverser inverse astigmatism, astigmatism against the rule
~/irregulärer irregular astigmatism
~ **lenticularis** lenticular astigmatism
~/myoper myopic astigmatism
~ **nach der Regel** s. ~/direkter
~/physiologischer physiologic astigmatism
~/regulärer regular astigmatism
~/schräger oblique astigmatism
~/zusammengesetzter compound astigmatism
Astigmatismusbestimmung f astigm[at]ometry; astigm[at]oscopy
Astigmatometer n astigmometer
Astigmatoskop n astigmoscope
Astigmometer n astigmometer
Astigmometrie f astigmometry
Astigmoskopie f astigmoscopy
Astomie f astomia, absence of the mouth
Astragalektomie f astragalectomy, talectomy
astragalofibular astragalofibular, talofibular
astragalokalkaneal astragalocalcanean, talocalcaneal, talocalcanean
astragalokrural astragalocrural, talocrural
astragalotibial astragalotibial, talotibial
Astragalus m astragalus, talus, ankle-bone
astral astral
Astroblast m astroblast *(Vorstufe eines Astrozyten)*
Astroblastoma n astroblastoma, grade 2 astrocytoma *(Hirngeschwulst)*

Astroglia f astroglia *(Neuroglia aus Astrozyten)*
Astrogliose f astrogliosis
Astrophobie f astrophobia *(krankhafte Angst vor Sternen)*
Astrosphäre f astrosphere *(Mitosefigur)*
Astrozyt m astrocyte, Cajal's (spider) cell *(Nervenzelle in der Großhirnrinde)*
Astrozyten mpl/**Bergmannsche** Bergmann's astrocytes
Astrozytenvermehrung f s. Astrozytose
astrozytisch astrocytic
Astrozytom n [grade 1] astrocytoma *(Hirngeschwulst)*
Astrozytose f astrocytosis, astrogliosis
Astrup m s. Astrup-Bestimmung
Astrup-Bestimmung f [capillary] blood gas analysis
Asymbolie f s. Asemie
Asymmetrie f asymmetry *(z. B. beider Körperhälften)*
asymmetrisch asymmetric[al]
Asymmetropie f asymmetropia, asymmetrical vision
asymptomatisch asymptomatic, symptomless
Asynchronie f/**biliopankreozibale** biliopancreocibal asynchronism
Asynergie f asynergy, lack of coordination *(z. B. von Muskeln)*
asynergisch asynergic
asynklitisch asynclitic
Asynklitismus m asynclitism *(Abweichung der Pfeilnaht aus der Beckenführungslinie bei der Geburt)*
~/hinterer posterior asynclitism, Litzmann's obliquity *(Abweichung nach vorn)*
~/vorderer anterior asynclitism, biparietal (Naegele's) obliquity *(Abweichung nach hinten)*
Asystole f, **Asystolie** f asystole, asystolia, cardiac arrest *(z. B. bei Herzblock)*
asystolisch asystolic
aszendierend ascending, ascendent
Aszites m ascites, hydroperitoneum, dropsy of the belly
~/blutiger bloody (haemorrhagic) ascites, diarrhaemia
~/chylöser chylous (chyliform) ascites
~/mechanischer passive ascites
Aszitesflüssigkeit f ascites (ascitic) fluid
aszitesfrei anascitic
Aszitesinjektion f ascites injection, hydropotherapy
Aszitespunktionskanüle f ascites cannula, anasarca trocar
Aszitezytologie f ascites fluid cytology
aszitisch ascitic
AT s. Alttuberkulin
Ataktilie f atactilia, loss of tactile sense
ataktisch atactic, ataxic
Ataraktikum n ataractic [agent], tranquil[l]izer
ataraktisch ataractic
Ataralgesie f ataralgesia *(Anästhesieform)*
Ataraxie f ataraxia, ataraxy, mental homoeostasis, peace (calm) of mind

Atavismus

Atavismus *m* atavism, throwback, reversion
atavistisch atavistic
Ataxia *f s.* Ataxie
~ **teleangiectatica** ataxia-telangiectasia
Ataxiaphasie *f* ataxiaphasia, syntactic aphasia
Ataxie *f* ataxia, incoordination *(Muskeldysharmonie)*
~/**akute** acute ataxia
~/**alkoholische** alcoholic ataxia
~/**äquilibratorische** equilibratory ataxia
~/**Brocasche** *s.* ~/hysterische
~/**frontale** frontal ataxia
~/**hereditäre** hereditary ataxia
~/**hereditäre zerebelläre** hereditary cerebellar ataxia
~/**hysterische** hysteric (Broca's) ataxia
~/**intrapsychische** intrapsychic ataxia
~/**kinetische** kinetic ataxia
~/**literale** literal ataxia
~/**lokomotorische** locomotor ataxia
~/**motorische** motor ataxia
~/**muskuläre** amyotaxia
~/**optische** optic ataxia
~/**partielle** dystaxia
~/**sensorische** sensory ataxia
~/**spinale** spinal ataxia
~/**spinozerebelläre** spinocerebellar (Sanger-Brown's) ataxia
~/**vasomotorische** vasomotor ataxia
~/**vestibuläre** vestibular (labyrinthine) ataxia
~/**zerebelläre** cerebellar ataxia
~/**zerebrale** cerebral ataxia
ataxieartig atactiform
Ataxiemeßgerät *n* ataxiameter
ataxisch ataxic
Ataxophemie *f* atax[i]ophemia, incoherence, faulty coordination of speech muscles
Atelektase *f* atelectasis
~/**angeborene** congenital atelectasis
~/**erworbene** acquired atelectasis
~/**lobuläre** lobular atelectasis
Atelektaseknistern *n* atelectatic rale
atelektatisch atelectatic
Atelie *f* atelia, lack (deficiency) in development, underdevelopment
Atelocheilie *f* atelocheilia
Atelocheiria *f* atelocheiria
Ateloenzephalie *f* ateloencephalia
Ateloglossie *f* ateloglossia
Atelognathie *f* atelognathia
Atelokardie *f* atelocardia
Atelokinesie *f* atelokinesia
Atelomyelie *f* atelomyelia
Atelopodie *f* atelopodia
Ateloprosopie *f* ateloprosopia
Atelorrhachidie *f* atelorrhachidia
Atelostomie *f* atelostomia
Atem *m* breath ● **außer ~** out of breath, breathless ● **den ~ anhalten** to hold (catch) the breath ● **~ holen** to draw (take) a breath ● **langsam und tief ~ holen** to draw a long deep breath ● **nach ~ ringen** to struggle for breath ● **tief ~ holen** to suspire

~/**übelriechender** foetid breath, bromopnoea
Atem... *s.a.* Atmungs... *und* Respirations...
Atembalg *m* pulmotor
atembar respirable
Atembehinderung *f* respiratory embarrassment (obstruction)
Atembeklemmung *f* difficult breathing, difficulty in breathing; shortness of breath
Atembeschleunigung *f* increase of respiratory rate
Atembeschwerden *pl s.* Atembeklemmung
Atembeutel *m* respiratory bag
Atembewegung *f* respiratory (ventilatory) movement
~/**intrauterine** intrauterine respiratory movement
Atembewegungskurve *f* pneumatogram
Atemdepression *f* respiratory depression
atemdepressiv respiratory depressant
Atemdynamik *f* pneumodynamics
Atemexkursion *f* respiratory excursion
Atemfilter *n(m)* respirator
Atemfrequenz *f* respiratory rate
~/**erhöhte** polypnoea
~/**verminderte** oligopnoea
Atemfunktion *f* respiratory function
Atemgasanalyse *f* respiratory gas analysis
Atemgerät *n* respirator, inspirator *(Zusammensetzungen s. unter Respirator)*
Atemgeräusch *n* respiratory murmur (sound), breath[ing] sounds, pulmonary murmur
~/**bronchiales** bronchial respiration
~/**bronchovesikuläres** bronchovesicular respiration
~/**klingendes** consonating rale
~/**pfeifendes** stridor, wheeze
~/**verschärftes** harsh respiration
Atemgift *n* respiratory poison
Atemgrenzwert *m* maximum breathing capacity
Atemgymnast *m* inhalation therapist
Atemgymnastik *f* respiratory care (exercises)
Atemhauch *m* halitus
atemhemmend respiratory depressant
Atemhilfe *f* respiratory assistance
Ateminsuffizienz *f* respiratory insufficiency (inadequacy)
Atemkapazität *f*/**maximale** maximum breathing capacity
Atemkette *f* respiratory chain
Atemkoeffizient *m* respiratory coefficient
Atemkrise *f* respiratory crisis
Atemkurve *f* pneum[at]ogram; spirogram
Atemkurvenaufzeichnung *f* pneumatography; spirography
Atemkurvenschreiber *m* pneumatograph; spirograph
Atemlähmung *f* respiratory paralysis
atemlos breathless
Atemlosigkeit *f* breathlessness
Atemluft *f* respiratory (tidal) air
Atemmaske *f* respiratory (breathing) mask
Atemmechanik *f* breathing mechanics
Atemminutenvolumen *n* respiratory minute volume

Atemmuskel m respiratory muscle
Atemmuskulatur f/**akzessorische** accessory respiratory muscles
Atemmuster n breathing patterns
Atemnot f dyspnoea, breathlessness, respiratory distress, shortness of breath (s.a. Asthma)
~/kardiale cardiac dyspnoea
Atemnotanfall m dyspnoeic attack
Atemnotsyndrom n respiratory distress syndrome, RDS
~/akutes acute respiratory distress syndrome
~ des Neugeborenen respiratory distress syndrome of the newborn, hyaline membrane disease
Atempause f/**inspiratorische** inspiratory standstill
Atemphase f respiratory phase
Atemquotient m respiratory quotient
Atemreflex m respiratory reflex
Atemregulation f respiratory regulation
Atemreserve f respiratory reserve
Atemreservevolumen n/**exspiratorisches** expiratory reserve volume
~/inspiratorisches inspiratory reserve volume
Atemrhythmusstörung f respiratory dysrhythmia
Atemschläuche mpl resuscitation tubes
Atemschmerz m respiratory pain
Atemschwierigkeit f respiratory difficulty (emergency)
Atemsekundenkapazität f one-second forced expiratory volume
Atemspende f artificial respiration, resuscitation
Atemstillstand m respiratory (ventilatory) arrest, respiratory standstill, breath holding; asphyxia
~/exspiratorischer expiratory standstill
~/inspiratorischer inspiratory standstill
Atemstimulation f respiratory stimulation
Atemstoffwechsel m respiratory exchange
Atemstörung f breathing disturbance, respiratory embarrassment
Atemstoß m forced expiration
Atemstoßtest m **nach Tiffeneau** one-second forced expiratory volume
Atemsuffizienz f respiratory adequacy
Atemtätigkeit f respiratory activity
Atemtherapie f respiratory therapy
Atemtiefe f depth of breathing
Atemton m s. Atemgeräusch
Atemübung f respiratory (breathing) exercise
Atemvolumen n tidal air (ventilation, volume)
Atemwegbeteiligung f respiratory tract involvement
Atemwege mpl respiratory tract (ducts, system), air (respiratory) passages
~/obere upper airways (respiratory tract)
~/untere lower airways (respiratory tract)
Atemwegerkrankung f respiratory tract disease (illness)
Atemweginfektion f respiratory [tract] infection, acute respiratory disease
Atemwegschleimhaut f respiratory mucous membrane
Atemwegverbrennung f respiratory tract burn
Atemwegverlegung f respiratory (airway) obstruction
Atemwiderstand m airway resistance
Atemzeit f breathing time, respiratory period
Atemzeitquotient m breathing time quotient
Atemzentrum n respiratory centre
Atemzug m respiration, inspiration, breath
Atemzugintensivierung f bathypnoea
Atemzugvolumen n tidal air (ventilation, volume)
Äthanol n ethanol, ethyl alcohol
~/wasserfreies dehydrated alcohol
Athelie f athelia, absence of the nipples
Äther m ether
Ätherbetäubung f etherization
Ätherempfindlichkeit f ether sensitivity (z. B. von Mikroorganismen)
ätherfest ether-stable
Ätherfestigkeit f ether stability (z. B. von Mikroorganismen)
Ätherinhalation f ether inhalation
Äthermaske f ether mask
Äthernarkose f ether anaesthesia, etherization
atherogen atherogenic
Atherogenese f atherogenesis
Atherom n atheroma, steatoma, sebaceous cyst
Atheromabszeß m atheromatous abscess
atheromatös atheromatous
Atheromatose f atheromatosis
Atheromeinschmelzung f atheromatous abscess
Atherosklerose f s. Arteriosklerose
ätherresistent ether-stable
Ätherresistenz f ether stability (z. B. von Mikroorganismen)
Ätherumlaufzeit f arm-lung time [test], ether circulation time test
Äthervergiftung f ether intoxication (poisoning)
athetoid athetoid
Athetose f athetosis (unwillkürliche umständliche Bewegungen bei Hirnläsion)
~ eines Körperteils monathetosis
~/kongenitale Hammond's disease
Athetotiker m athetoid
athetotisch athetoid
Athletenherz n athlete's (athletic) heart
Athletiker m athletic type
Äthoxyanilin n ethoxyaniline, phenetidine (Grundstoff verschiedener Antipyretika)
Athrepsie f 1. athrepsia, malnutrition; 2. athrepsia, marasmus; 3. athrepsia, athreptic immunity
Äthylalkohol m ethyl alcohol, ethanol
Äthyläther m s. Diäthyläther
Äthylbarbital n diethylbarbituric acid
Äthylendiamintetraessigsäure f ethylenediaminetetraacetic acid, EDTA
athym 1. athymic, without thymus; 2. athymic, without feeling
Athymie f 1. athymia, absence of thymus; 2. athymia, lack of feeling
athyreoid athyreotic
Athyreose f athyreosis, athyroidism, absence of the thyroid

athyreot athyreotic
Ätiologie f aetiology *(Lehre von den Krankheitsursachen)*
ätiologisch aetiologic
Ätiopathogenese f aetiopathogenesis
atlantoaxial atlantoaxial, atlantoepistrophic, atloaxoid
Atlantoaxialgelenk n atlantoaxial joint
atlantookzipital atlantooccipital
Atlantookzipitalgelenk n atlantooccipital joint
Atlantookzipitalmembran f atlantooccipital membrane
Atlas m atlas, first cervical vertebra
Atlasassimilation f atlas assimilation
Atlasbogenresektion f resection of the arch of the atlas
atmen to breathe, to respire
~/**schwer** to gasp, to breathe heavily
~/**tief** to suspire
Atmen n respiration, breathing *(s.a. unter Atmung)*
~/**amphorisches** amphoric respiration (breathing); bottle sound
~/**pueriles** puerile respiration *(verschärftes Vesikuläratmen bei Kindern)*
~/**sakkadiertes** interrupted breathing, jerky (cogwheel) respiration
atmend/schnell tachypnoeic
Atmung f respiration, breathing, pneusis *(s.a. unter Atmen)*
~/**abdominale** abdominal respiration
~/**aerobe** aerobic respiration
~/**anaerobe** anaerobic respiration
~/**angestrengte** laboured respiration, forced breathing
~/**assistierte** assisted (mechanical) respiration
~/**asthmaartige (asthmatoide)** asthmoid respiration
~/**ausreichende** adequate respiration; respiratory adequacy
~/**äußere** external respiration
~/**beschleunigte** accelerated respiration, tachypnoea, polypnoea
~/**Biotsche** Biot's respiration (breathing)
~/**bronchiale** bronchial respiration, tubular breathing
~/**bronchovesikuläre** bronchovesicular respiration (breathing)
~/**Cheyne-Stokessche** Cheyne-Stokes respiration, periodic breathing
~/**erschwerte** impeded (laboured) respiration, difficult (hampered) breathing
~/**fetale** foetal (placental) respiration
~/**flache** hypopnoea, shallow respiration
~/**gesteigerte** hyperpnoea
~/**große** s.~/Kussmaulsche
~/**innere** internal respiration
~/**keuchende** gasping (wheezing) respiration
~/**kontrollierte** controlled respiration
~/**künstliche** artificial respiration (ventilation)
~/**Kussmaulsche** Kussmaul's respiration; air hunger

~/**langsame** slow respiration
~/**oberflächliche** shallow respiration
~/**paradoxe** paradoxical (pendelluft) respiration
~/**periodische** s.~/Cheyne-Stokessche
~/**pfeifende** hissing breathing, wheezing respiration
~/**puerile** puerile respiration *(verschärftes Vesikuläratmen bei Kindern)*
~/**pulmonale** pulmonary respiration
~/**röchelnde** stertorous respiration
~/**schnappende** spasmodic respiration
~/**schnelle** tachypnoea, rapid respiration
~/**schwere** gasping respiration
~/**seufzende** sighing respiration
~/**Silvestersche** Silvester's method
~/**thorakale** thoracic breathing, costal respiration
~/**tiefe** deep respiration
~/**unregelmäßige** irregular respiration
~/**verlangsamte** slow respiration, bradypnoea
~/**vesikuläre** vesicular respiration
~/**ziehende** sighing respiration
Atmungs... s.a. Atem... und Respirations...
Atmungsart f breathing patterns
Atmungsassistenz f respiratory assistance
Atmungsbehinderung f respiratory embarrassment (obstruction)
Atmungsbeschleunigung f polypnoea, tachypnoea
~ **durch Fieber** thermopolypnoea
Atmungsdynamik f pneumodynamics
Atmungsenzym n respiratory enzyme
~/**Warburgsches** cytochrome oxidase
Atmungsepithel n respiratory epithelium
atmungsfähig respirable, transpirable
Atmungsfähigkeit f respirability, transpirability
Atmungsfläche f respiratory surface
Atmungskurve f spirogram; pneum[at]ogram
Atmungslehre f pneum[at]ology
Atmungsoberfläche f respiratory surface
Atmungsorgan n respiratory organ
Atmungsschreiber m spirograph *(Gerät zur Aufzeichnung der Atembewegungen)*
Atmungsschwierigkeit f breathing difficulty (emergency)
Atmungsstörung f breathing disturbance, respiratory embarrassment
Atmungssystem n respiratory system
Atmungstetanie f respiratory tetany
Atmungstyp m breathing (respiratory) patterns
~/**Biotscher** Biot's breathing (respiration)
atmungsunterdrückend respiratory depressant
Atmungsverlangsamung f bradypnoea
Atmungsverminderung f hypoventilation
Atmungsversagen n respiratory failure
Atmungsverstärkung f hyperaeration, hyperventilation
Atmungsvertiefung f bathypnoea
Atmungsvorgang m breathing, respiration, respiratory process
Atonie f atonia, absence of tonus
atonisch atonic
Atonizität f atonicity

Atopie f atopy
Atopik-Dermatitis f atopic dermatitis (eczema), neuroderm[at]itis
atopisch atopic
atoxisch atoxic, not poisonous (toxic); not venomous
ATP s. Adenosintriphosphorsäure
ATPase f s. Adenosintriphosphatase
atraumatisch atraumatic
Atresia f atresia, imperforation
~ **ani** anal atresia
~ **folliculi** atretic follicle
~ **vulvae** vulvar (vulval) atresia, vulvar (vulval) fusion
Atresie f s. Atresia
atretisch atretic, imperforate (z. B. natürliche Körperöffnungen)
Atretogastrie f atretogastria
Atretometrie f atretometria
Atretopsie f atretopsia
Atretorrhinie f atretorrhinia
Atretostomie f atretostomia
Atretozystie f atretocystia
Atreturethrie f atreturethria
Atrichie f, **Atrichose** f atrichia, alopecia
Atrioseptopexie f atrioseptopexy
Atriotomie f atriotomy
atrioventrikulär atrioventricular
Atrioventrikular... s.a. AV-...
Atrioventrikularblock m [heart] atrioventricular block
~ **I. Grades** first-degree atrioventricular (heart) block
~ **II. Grades** second-degree atrioventricular (heart) block
~ **III. Grades** s.~/kompletter
~/**inkompletter** incomplete atrioventricular (heart) block
~/**kompletter (totaler)** complete heart block, total atrioventricular block, third-degree atrioventricular (heart) block
Atrioventrikularbündel n atrioventricular bundle, [conduction] bundle of His (Herzreizleitung)
Atrioventrikularkanal m atrioventricular canal
~/**gemeinsamer** common atrioventricular canal, atrioventricularis communis
~/**persistierender gemeinsamer** persistent common atrioventricular canal
Atrioventrikularklappe f atrioventricular valve
~/**insuffiziente** incompetent AV valve
Atrioventrikularklappeninsuffizienz f atrioventricular valve insufficiency
Atrioventrikularklappenring m atrioventricular valve ring
Atrioventrikularknoten m atrioventricular (Tawara's) node, His-Tawara node (Herzreizleitungssystem)
Atrioventrikularknotenarterie f atrioventricular node artery, Kugel's artery
Atrioventrikularknotenrhythmus m atrioventricular (nodal) rhythm
Atrioventrikularknotenrhythmusstörung f nodal arrhythmia

Atropintropfen

Atrioventrikularknotentachykardie f nodal (junctional) tachycardia
Atrioventrikularrhythmus m atrioventricular rhythm
Atrioventrikularseptum n atrioventricular septum
Atrioventrikulartachykardie f atrioventricular (junctional) tachycardia
Atrium n 1. atrium, vestibule, vestibulum; 2. s. ~ cordis
~ **cordis** atrium [of the heart], vestibule
~ **cordis dextrum** right atrium of the heart
~ **cordis sinistrum** left atrium of the heart
Atropa f **belladonna** belladonna
Atrophia f s. Atrophie
~ **uteri** uterine atrophy, metatrophia
Atrophie f atrophy, emaciation, shrinking
~/**akute gelbe** acute yellow atrophy [of the liver]
~/**arthritische** arthritic atrophy
~/**blaue** blue atrophy
~/**braune** brown atrophy
~/**chronische spinale muskuläre** chronic spinal muscular atrophy
~/**fazioskapulohumerale** facioscapulohumeral atrophy, Landouzy-Déjerine dystrophy
~/**graue** grey atrophy
~/**hemifaziale** hemifacial atrophy
~/**hemilinguale** hemilingual atrophy
~/**idiopathische muskuläre** idiopathic muscular atrophy
~/**interstitielle** interstitial atrophy
~/**ischämische muskuläre** ischaemic muscular atrophy, Volkman's contracture
~/**juvenile muskuläre** juvenile muscular atrophy, pseudohypertrophic muscular paralysis
~/**muskuläre** muscular atrophy
~/**neuropathische** neural (neuropathic) atrophy
~/**neurotrophische** neurotrophic (trophoneurotic) atrophy
~/**olivopontozerebellare** olivopontocerebellar atrophy
~/**pathologische** pathologic atrophy
~/**physiologische** physiological atrophy
~/**progressive muskuläre** Cruveilhier's (progressive muscular) atrophy
~/**progressive spinale muskuläre** progressive spinal muscular atrophy, Aran-Duchenne muscular atrophy, Duchenne-Aran myelopathic atrophy
~/**pseudohypertrophe muskuläre** pseudohypertrophic muscular atrophy (dystrophy)
~/**rote** red atrophy [of the liver]
~/**Sudecksche** Sudeck's atrophy
atrophieren to atrophy
atrophisch atrophic, emaciating; shrinking
Atrophoderma n atrophoderma, atrophy of the skin
Atropin n atropine, hyoscyamine (Alkaloid)
Atropinbehandlung f atropinization
atropinisieren to atropinize
Atropinsulfat n atropine sulphate
Atropintropfen mpl atropine drops

Atropinüberdosierung

Atropinüberdosierung f overatropinization
Atropinum n **sulfuricum** atropine sulphate
Atropinvergiftung f atropine poisoning (intoxication), atropinism
Atropinzufuhr f atropinization
Attacke f attack, paroxysm
Attest n/**ärztliches** medical (doctor's) certificate
Atticus m attic, epitympanum *(Teil der Paukenhöhle)*
Attikotomie f atticotomy
Attizitis f atticitis, inflammation of the attic
Attonität f attonity *(Regungslosigkeit bei katatoner Schizophrenie)*
Atypie f atypia
~/zytologische cytological atypia
Ätzbehandlung f caustic treatment (therapy) *(z. B. von Wunden)*
ätzen to cauterize, to burn out
ätzend cauterant, cauterizing; corrosive *(z. B. Säuren)*
Ätzmittel n caustic [agent], cauterant; escharotic [agent]
Ätzmittelträger m caustic holder
Ätzschorf m eschar, slough
Ätzstift m caustic stick (stylus, pencil)
Ätzung f [chemical] cauterization, cautery
~ mit chemischen Mitteln chemicocautery
Ätzungsbehandlung f chemical cauterization (cautery)
Audimutitas f audimutism *(Stummheit bei erhaltenem Hörvermögen)*
audiogen audiogenic
Audiogramm n audiogram, audiometric curve
Audiologe m audiologist
Audiologie f audiology *(Lehre vom Hören)*
audiologisch audiologic[al]
Audiometer n audiometer
~ nach Békésy Békésy audiometer
Audiometerkalibrierungsschema n audiometer calibration scheme
Audiometrie f audiometry
~ nach Békésy Békésy audiometry
~/objektive evoked response audiometry
Audiometriespezialist m audiometrist
audiometrisch audiometric
Audiookularreflex m audio-ocular reflex, auditooculogyric reflex *(reflektorische Blickwendung zu einer Schallquelle)*
Audiospektrometer n audiospectrometer
audiovisuell audiovisual, visoauditory
Audiphon n audiphone
Audition f audition, [power of] hearing; hearing
auditiv, auditorisch auditory, auditive
auditosensorisch auditosensory
Auerbach-Plexus m Auerbach's (myenteric) plexus
Auer-Körperchen npl Auer bodies *(z. B. bei Leukämie)*
Aufbau m 1. synthesis *(z. B. von körpereigenem Eiweiß)*; 2. composition, structure *(z. B. von Gewebe)*; organization *(z. B. der Chromosomen)*

aufbauen to synthesize; to build up
Aufbaustoffwechsel m anabolism
aufbereiten/den Zahnwurzelkanal to prepare the dental root canal
Aufbewahrung f conservation
Aufbiß m occlusal overlay *(Stomatologie)*
aufblähend flatulent
Aufblähung f 1. inflation, distension, swelling, ballooning; 2. emphysema *(z. B. der Lunge)*; 3. meteorism, tympanism, tympanites *(z. B. des Bauchs)*; flatulence *(z. B. des Darms)*
aufblitzen to scintillate
Aufbohren n terebration *(von Knochen)*; drilling *(von Zähnen)*
aufbrechen to burst, to break [through], to rupture *(z. B. eine Abszeßhöhle)*
aufbrühen to decoct, to infuse
Aufdehnung f bougienage
auffangen to collect, to catch *(z. B. Körperflüssigkeiten)*
Auffassungsgabe f perceptive faculty, perceptiveness, perceptivity; intelligence
Auffassungsschwäche f hypoprosexia *(z. B. bei Psychosen)*
aufflackern/wieder to restart *(z. B. eine Krankheit)*
auffrischen to regenerate *(z. B. Gewebe)*; to restore *(z. B. Körperkräfte)*; to freshen up, to refresh *(z. B. Wunde)*
auffrischend regenerative; restoring; refreshing
Auffrischung f regeneration; restoration; [re-]freshening
Auffrischungsimpfung f booster inoculation
auffüllen to refill, to replenish, to replete
aufgedunsen puffy, bloated, swollen, turgid *(z. B. Gesicht)*
aufgehen to become unstitched *(z. B. chirurgische Naht)*
aufgenommen werden/in das Krankenhaus to be taken to the hospital
aufgepfropft superimposed *(z. B. eine Infektion)*
aufgequollen tumefied *(z. B. Haut)*
aufgeschwemmt pasty, puffy, bloated
aufgeweicht macerative
aufgezweigt bifurcate
Aufguß m infusion
Aufgußtierchen npl infusoria *(Mikroorganismen)*
Aufhängeapparat m suspension apparatus
Aufhängeband n suspensory [ligament]
Aufhängenaht f suspensory suture
Aufhängung f suspension
Aufhellung f translucence *(Radiologie)*
~ des Bewußtseins lucid interval *(z. B. bei Schädel-Hirn-Trauma)*
aufklaffen to gape *(Wunde)*
Aufklärung f/**sexuelle** sexual education
aufkochen to decoct
aufkratzen to excoriate, to scratch open
auflagern to juxtapose *(z. B. bei Steinbildung)*; to apposit *(z. B. am Knochen)*; to layer, to stratify *(z. B. in Schichten)*

Auflagerung f juxtaposition (z. B. bei Steinbildung); apposition (z. B. am Knochen); stratification (z. B. in Schichten)
auflockern 1. to soften, to disintegrate (z. B. Gewebestruktur); 2. to loosen (limber) up (durch gymnastische Übungen)
Auflockerung f 1. softening, disintegration (z. B. von Gewebestrukturen); 2. loosening [up] (z. B. durch Gymnastik)
auflösen 1. to dissolve, to put into solution; 2. to dissolve, to resolve, to decompose
~/sich 1. to dissolve, to pass into solution (z. B. Substanzen); 2. to disintegrate (z. B. Knochen); to decay, to decompose (z. B. Gewebe); to break down (z. B. Phagozyten); to lyse (z. B. Gewebe); to dissolve (z. B. Gallensteine)
auflösend [dis]solvent; resolvent
~/gleichartige Erythrozyten isohaemolytic
Auflösung f 1. dissolution; 2. disintegration, decomposition, decay; lysis
~ artgleicher Erythrozyten isohaemolysis
~ roter Blutkörperchen erythrocytolysis
Auflösungsvermögen n 1. dissolving (solvent) power; 2. resolving power, resolution (eines optischen Systems)
~ des Auges visual discrimination, aligning discrimination (power) of the eye
aufmeißeln to chisel open (z. B. eine Knochenhöhle); to trephine (z. B. den Schädel)
Aufmeißelung f **des Schädels** trephination, trepanation, trephinement
Aufmerksamkeit f attention, attentiveness; concentration
~/fehlende aprosexia
~/geistige concentration
~/gesteigerte hyperprosexia, egersis
~/herabgesetzte hypoprosexia, aprosexia
Aufmerksamkeitsreflex m attention reflex
Aufnahme f 1. absorption (z. B. von Flüssigkeit); resorption, intake, ingestion (z. B. der Nahrung); uptake (z. B. in das Gewebe); 2. reception [office] (eines Krankenhauses); admission [to the hospital], hospitalization; 3. photograph[ing]; record[ing]; 4. radiograph, X-ray film (picture) (Radiologie); shot; record
Aufnahmeabteilung f reception department (ward)
Aufnahmearzt m duty doctor
Aufnahmebefund m findings on admission
aufnahmefähig absorbable, absorptive, absorbent (z. B. für Stoffe); receptive (z. B. für Reize); susceptible (z. B. für Keime)
Aufnahmenummer f registration number
Aufnahmepersonal n reception staff
Aufnahmeschwester f reception nurse
Aufnahmestation f s. Aufnahmeabteilung
Aufnahmetechnik f/**gezielte** directed radiographic technique
~/Stenverssche Stenvers' projection (view)
Aufnahmetubus m radiographic cone (Radiologie)

Aufnahmeuntersuchung f examination on admission, initial examination
Aufnahmezeit f exposure time (Radiologie)
aufnehmbar/nicht non-absorbable
aufnehmen 1. to absorb (z. B. Flüssigkeit); to resorb, to take in (z. B. Nahrungsmittel); to take up (z. B. in das Gewebe); 2. to admit [to the hospital], to hospitalize; 3. to radiograph, to X-ray; to take a photograph; to record
aufnehmend absorbent, resorbent
Aufpfropfung f **einer Krankheit** superimposition
aufplatzen to break [open], to burst [open], to crack, to split (z. B. Wunden)
Aufprallverletzung f impaction injury; dashboard injury
aufpumpen to inflate, to pump up (z. B. Blutdruckmanschette)
aufputschen to dope
Aufputschmittel n [strong] stimulant, excitant, dope
aufquellen to swell (z. B. Gewebe)
aufrauhen to roughen (z. B. den Knochen)
aufrecht upright, erect
Aufrechterhaltung f retention (z. B. einer korrigierten Zahnstellung)
Aufregung f excitement, agitation
~/krankhafte exaltation
aufrichtbar erectile
aufrichten 1. to disimpact (Knochenimpression); 2. to raise, to lift, to sit up (Kranke im Bett); 3. to straighten [up] (Oberkörper); 4. to erect, to become erect (z. B. erektiles Gewebe)
Aufrichten n 1. disimpaction (z. B. des Knochens); 2. sitting up (z. B. von Kranken im Bett); 3. erection (z. B. des Penis)
Aufrichter[muskel] m erector [muscle]; arrector [muscle] (der Haare)
Aufrichtung f erection (z. B. des Penis); orthosis (einer Deformierung)
Aufrichtungsreflex m righting reflex
Aufrichtungszange f disimpaction forceps (z. B. für Nasenbeinfraktur)
aufsättigen to saturate (z. B. Hämoglobin)
Aufsättigung f saturation
aufsaugen to absorb, to resorb, to take up
Aufsaugen n absorption, resorption
aufsaugend absorbent, resorbent
aufschießen to appear, to spring up (z. B. Exanthem); to effloresce (z. B. Hauteflorenzen)
Aufschlagverletzung f s. Aufprallverletzung
aufschließen to digest, to break up (down), to split, to decompose (z. B. Nahrung); to disintegrate, to solubilize (z. B. Stoffe)
Aufschließung f digestion, breaking up (down), splitting, decomposition (z. B. der Nahrung); disintegration (z. B. von Stoffen)
aufschneiden to cut open (z. B. eine Körperhöhle); to dissect (z. B. Leichen); to incise, to lance (z. B. einen Eiterherd); to laparotomize (den Bauch)
Aufschneiderei f[/**krankhafte**] mythomania
Aufschrecken n/**nächtliches** night terrors

Aufschreien 74

Aufschreien n/**nächtliches** night cry
aufschürfen to abrade, to chafe (z. B. die Haut)
~/sich die Haut to graze the skin, to excoriate
Aufschwemmung f suspension
aufsplittern to splinter (z. B. bei Knochenbruch)
Aufsplittern n **der Nägel** onychorrhexis
aufsprießen to appear, to break out (z. B. Hautausschlag)
aufspringen to fissure, to burst, to crack (z. B. die Haut); to become dehiscent, to dehisce, to burst (z. B. eine Wunde)
aufstechen to lance, to incise, to pierce, to break
aufsteigend rising; ascendent, ascending (z. B. eine Arterie); afferent (z. B. zu einem Organ); centripetal (zum Zentrum)
aufstoßen to eruct, to belch
Aufstoßen n eructation, belching, ructus
~/hysterisches hysterical belching
aufstreichen to spread, to smear (z. B. eine Salbe)
aufsuchen/einen Arzt to see (consult) a physician
auftragen to spread, to apply (z. B. eine Salbe)
auftreiben to inflate, to balloon (z. B. durch Gase); to distend
Auftreibung f 1. inflation, ballooning (z. B. durch Gase); distension; 2. meteorism, tympanism, tympanites (z. B. des Bauchs); flatulence (z. B. des Darms)
auftreten to occur, to appear, to arise (z. B. eine Krankheit); to appear, to break out (z. B. ein Exanthem); to be present (z. B. Gallensteine)
Auftreten n occurrence, appearance (z. B. einer Krankheit); outbreak, onset (z. B. eines Exanthems); presence (z. B. von Gallensteinen)
~/doppeltes duplicity
~ eines Hautausschlags onset of the rash (z. B. bei Syphilis)
~/erneutes recurrence (einer Krankheit)
~ sekundärer Geschlechtsmerkmale/vorzeitiges adrenogenital syndrome
auftretend:
~/an vielen Stellen multiple
~/nach dem Gewebetod postnecrotic
~/nach dem Husten posttussive
~/nach dem Tode postmortal
~/nach dem Wochenbett postpuerperal
~/nach der Anästhesie postanaesthetic
~/nach der Entbindung postpartum, postpartal
~/nach der Geburt postnatal
~/nach der Menarche postmenarche
~/nach der Menopause postmenopausal
~/nach der Pubertät postpuber[t]al
~/nach einem Anfall postictal
~/nach einem Herpes postherpetic
~/nach einem Infarkt postinfarction
~/nach einem Scharlach postscarlatinal
~/nach einem Schlaganfall postapoplectic
~/nach einem Unfall posttraumatic
~/nach einer Bestrahlung postradiation
~/nach einer Blutung posthaemorrhagic
~/nach einer Gelbsucht posticteric
~/nach einer Grippe postinfluenzal
~/nach einer Halbseitenlähmung posthemiplegic
~/nach einer Hypnose posthypnotic
~/nach einer Impfung postvaccinal
~/nach einer Infektion postinfectious
~/nach einer Lähmung postparalytic
~/nach einer Leberentzündung posthepatitic
~/nach einer Lungenentzündung postpneumonic
~/nach einer Malaria postmalarial, postpaludal
~/nach einer Nervenentzündung postneuritic
~/nach einer Operation postoperative, postsurgical
~/nach einer operativen Brustentfernung postmastectomy
~/nach einer operativen Milzentfernung postsplenectomy
~/nach einer Streptokokkeninfektion poststreptococcal
~/nach einer Syphilis postsyphilitic
~/nach einer Thrombose postthrombotic
~/nach einer Venenentzündung postphlebitic
~/nach Typhus posttyphoid
~/plötzlich acute
~/selbständig autopathic, protopathic, essential (Krankheiten)
~/verlangsamt tardive
~/vor dem Ausbruch einer Psychose prepsychotic
~/vor dem Geschlechtsverkehr precoital
~/vor dem Tode premortal
~/vor der Agonie preagonal
~/vor der Anästhesie preanaesthetic
~/vor der Entbindung prepartal, prepartum
~/vor der Geburt prenatal
~/vor der Geschwulstentwicklung preneoplastic
~/vor der Knorpelbildung prochondral
~/vor der Menopause premenopausal
~/vor der Pulswelle presphygmic
~/vor der Systole presystolic
~/vor der Tuberkelbildung pretuberculous
~/vor der Tuberkulose pretuberculous
~/vor der Tumorentstehung preneoplastic
~/vor einem Anfall preictal
~/vor einem epileptischen Anfall preconvulsive
~/vor einem Infarkt preinfarction
~/vor einem Karzinom precarcinomatous
~/vor einem Krampf prespastic
~/vor einem Schlaganfall preapoplectic
~/vor einer Albuminurie prealbuminuric
~/vor einer Gelbsucht preicteric
~/vor einer Halbseitenlähmung prehemiplegic
~/vor einer Krebskrankheit precancerous
~/vor einer Lähmung preparalytic
~/vor einer Manie premaniacal
~/vor einer Operation preoperative
~/vor einer Schizophrenie preschizophrenic
~/vorzeitig precocious, precox
Aufwacheffekt m arousal reaction (im Hirnrinden-EEG)
Aufwachepilepsie f matutinal epilepsy
Aufwachhalluzination f hypnagogic (hypnopompic) hallucination

Augenbindehaut

Aufwachraum *m* [post]anaesthetic recovery room
Aufwachübelkeit *f* matutinal nausea
Aufwallung *f* flush; outburst *(psychisch)*
Aufwärtsbewegung *f* sursumvergence, sursumversion, sursumduction *(z. B. der Augen)*
Aufwärtsschielen *n* sursumvergent strabism, upward strabismus, anoopsia [strabismus], hypertropia
aufweichen to macerate, to soften
Aufweichung *f* maceration
Aufweichungsmittel *n* emollient [agent]
Aufweitung *f* bougienage
Aufzeichnung *f* **der Atembewegungen des Brustkorbes** pneum[at]ography
Aufzeichnung *f* **der Darmbewegung** enterography
aufziehen/ eine Spritze to draw up a syringe
aufzweigen to distribute; to bifurcate
Aufzweigung *f* distribution *(z. B. der Nerven)*; bifurcation *(z. B. der Luftröhre)*
Augapfel *m* eyeball, [ocular] globe, bulb of the eye, bulbus oculi
~ **im Bindehautsack/mißgebildeter** cryptophthalmos
~/**[in die Augenhöhle] zurückgesunkener** enophthalmos
Augapfelanschwellung *f* ophthalmophyma, swelling of the eyeball
Augapfelatrophie *f* eye[ball] atrophy, ophthalmatrophy
Augapfelausschälung *f* eye[ball] enucleation
Augapfelbindehaut *f* bulbar conjunctiva
Augapfelbinnendruck *m s.* Augendruck
Augapfelblutung *f* ophthalmorrhagia
Augapfeleinwärtsdrehung *f* intorsion of the globe
Augapfelenukleation *f* ophthalmectomy, enucleation of the eyeball
Augapfelerweichung *f* ophthalmomalacia
Augapfelexzision *f* ophthalmectomy, excision of the eyeball
Augapfelfixation *f* ophthalmostasis, fixation of the eye
Augapfelinzision *f* ophthalmotomy, incision of the eyeball
Augapfelkapsel *f* Tenon's capsula, capsule of Tenon
Augapfelkleinheit *f* microphthalmia; microphthalmos
Augapfelmassage *f* eyeball massage
Augapfelmuskel *m* bulbar muscle
Augapfelperforation *f* eye[ball] perforation
Augapfelpunktion *f* ophthalmocentesis, puncture of the eyeball
Augapfelruptur *f* ophthalmorrhexis, rupture of the eyeball
Augapfelschrumpfung *f s.* Augapfelschwund
Augapfelschwellung *f* ophthalmophyma, swelling of the eyeball
Augapfelschwund *m* ophthalmophthisis, shrinking (shrivelling) of the eyeball, ocular phthisis
Augapfelstarre *f* eye[ball] rigidity
Augapfelumfang *m* equator of the eye
Augapfelvergrößerung *f* macrophthalmia, ophthal[mo]macrosis; macrophthalmos
Augapfelvorfall *m* eye[ball] luxation
Augapfelzittern *n* nystagmus *(Zusammensetzungen s. unter* Nystagmus*)*
Auge *n* eye, oculus, ophthalmus, o. *(s. a. unter* Oculus*)* ● **durch das** ~ transocular ● **innerhalb des Auges liegend** intraocular ● **über den Augen** supra-ocular
~/**blaues** black eye
~/**bloßes** naked (unaided) eye
~/**fehlsichtiges** ametropic eye
~/**führendes** master eye
~/**glänzendes** shining eye
~/**künstliches** artificial eye, ocular (visual) prosthesis, glass eye
~/**linkes** left eye, L. E., l., oculus sinister, O. S.
~/**rechtes** right eye, R. E., r., oculus dexter, O. D.
~/**schielendes** strabismic eye
Augen... *s.a.* Ophthalm...
Augenabstand *m* interocular (interpupillary) distance
Augenabteilung *f* ophthalmology department
Augenabweichung *f* deviation of the eyeballs
~ **nach unten** infraversion
Augenachse *f* optic (visual) axis
Augenachsenabweichung *f* conjugate deviation
Augenanhangsgebilde *npl* ocular adnexa, appendage of the eye, accessory organs of the eye
Augenanschwellung *f* ophthalmophyma, swelling of the eye
Augenäquator *m* equator of the eye
Augenarterie *f* ophthalmic artery
Augenarterien[nerven]geflecht *n* ophthalmic plexus
Augenarzt *m* ophthalmologist, oculist
Augenatrophie *f* ophthalmatrophia, atrophy of the eye
Augenauswärtsrollen *n* excyclophoria, positive (plus) cyclophoria
Augenbad *n* 1. bathing of the eyes, eye douche; 2. eyebath, eyecup
Augenballottement *n* ballottement of the eye
Augenbecher *m* optic cup
Augenbecherspalte *f* fissure of the optic cup
Augenbecherstielspalte *f* fissure of the optic stalk
Augenbeschwerden *pl* ocular discomfort (disorder)
augenbewegend oculogyric, oculomotor
Augenbewegung *f* eye (ocular) movement, oculogyration
~/**ruckartige (sakkadierte)** saccadic eye movement
~/**schnelle** rapid eye movement, REM
Augenbewegungsdarstellung *f* electronystagmography
Augenbinde *f* patch, eye bandage
Augenbindehaut *f* conjunctiva *(Zusammensetzungen s. unter* Conjunctiva*)*

Augenbindehaut...

Augenbindehaut... s. Bindehaut...
Augenbinnendruck m s. Augendruck
Augenbinnenmuskel m intraocular muscle
Augenbläschen n ophthalmic (optic) vesicle *(Embryologie)*
Augenblase f/doppelwandige sekundäre optic cup
Augenblasenstiel m optic stalk
Augenblennorrhoe f ophthalmoblennorrhoea, gonorrhoeal (purulent) blennorrhoea
Augenblick m/heller (lichter) lucidity, lucid interval
Augenblinzeln n blinking
Augenblutung f ophthalmorrhagia, haemorrhage from the eye
Augenbraue f [eye]brow, supercilium, ophrys
Augenbrauenbogen m superciliary (eyebrow) arch, supra-orbital ridge
Augenbrauenentzündung f ophryitis, inflammation of the eyebrow
Augenbrauenkrampf m ophryosis, spasm of the eyebrow
Augenbrauenrekonstruktion f eyebrow reconstruction
Augenbrauenrunzler m corrugator supercilii [muscle]
Augenbrauensenker m depressor supercilii [muscle]
Augenbutter f lema *(Sekret der Meibomschen Drüsen)*
Augenchirurgie f ophthalmic surgery
Augendarre f xerophthalmia, [conjunctival] xerosis, ophthalmoxerosis
Augendeckel m s. Augenlid
Augendiagnose f ophthalmodiagnosis; iri[do]diagnosis
Augendominanz f eye (ocular) dominance
augendrehend oculogyric, oculogyral, ophthalmogyric
Augendrehung f oculogyration, ocular duction (torsion)
Augendruck m [intra]ocular pressure, ocular tension, ophthalmotonus
~/**erhöhter** ocular hypertension
Augendruckerhöhung f ocular hypertension
Augendruckmeßgerät n [ophthalmo]tonometer, tenonometer
~ **nach Schiötz** Schiötz tonometer
Augendruckmessung f ophthalmotonometry
~/**digitale** digital tonometry [of the eyeball]
~/**elektrische** electrotonography [of the eyeball]
Augendruckreflex m eyeball compression reflex
Augendusche f s. Augenbad 1.
Augeneigenspiegelung f auto-ophthalmoscopy
Augeneigenverletzung f oedipism, self-inflicted eye injury
Augeneinschnitt m ophthalmotomy
Augenentfernung f/operative s. Ophthalmektomie
Augenentzündung f ophthalmia, ophthalmitis, inflammation of the eye *(s.a. unter Ophthalmia)*
~ **durch Pilze** mycophthalmia
~ **durch Raupenhaarverletzung** caterpillar [hair] ophthalmia
~/**eitrige** pyophthalmia, ophthalmorrhoea
Augenenukleation f eye enucleation
Augenermüdung f ocular fatigue, fatigue of the eye[s]
Augenerweichung f ophthalmomalacia, softening of the eye
Augenfehlbildung f eye malformation
Augenfehler m ocular defect, defect of the eye[s]
Augenfixierung f ophthalmostasis
Augenfleck m eyespot *(Embryologie)*
Augenfundus m ocular (eye) fundus, fundus [oculi]
Augenfundusgefäßdarstellung f mit Fluoreszein eye fundus fluorescein angiography
Augenfunduskamera f eye fundus camera
Augenfundusmikroskopie f eye fundus microscopy
Augenfundusreflextest m eye fundus reflex test
Augenfundusspiegel m fundoscope
Augenfundusspiegelung f [ophthalmo]fundoscopy, ophthalmoscopy
Augenglas n [eye]glass
Augenhalter m ophthalmostat
Augenhaut f tunic (membrane) of the eyeball
● **in der weißen** ~ **liegend** intrascleral
~/**mittlere** uveal tract *(umfaßt Aderhaut, Ziliarkörper und Regenbogenhaut)*
Augenheilkunde f ophthalmology, ophthalmiatrics, oculistics
Augenherpes m ocular herpes [simplex]
Augenhintergrund m s. Augenfundus
Augenhöhle f orbit[a], orbital cavity, eye socket, hypsiconch ● **durch die** ~ transorbital ● **in der** ~ [liegend] intraorbital ● **über der** ~ supraorbital ● **unter der** ~ [gelegen] infraorbital, suborbital
Augenhöhlen... s. a. Orbita...
Augenhöhlenangiom n orbital angioma
Augenhöhlenblutung f orbital haemorrhage
Augenhöhlenboden m orbital floor, floor (inferior wall) of the orbit
Augenhöhlenbodenfraktur f orbital floor fracture
Augenhöhlendach n orbital roof, orbital plate of the frontal bone, roof (superior wall) of the orbit
Augenhöhlendekompression f orbital decompression
Augenhöhleneingang m margin of the orbit
Augenhöhleneinschnitt m orbitotomy
Augenhöhleneröffnung f/operative orbitotomy
Augenhöhlenfettkörper m fat body of the orbital cavity
Augenhöhlenfettkörperhernie f orbital fat hernia
Augenhöhlengeschwulst f orbital tumour
Augenhöhleninnendruckmesser m orbitonometer
Augenhöhleninnendruckmessung f orbitonometry

Augenhöhlenmuskel m orbital muscle, orbitalis [muscle]
Augenhöhlenperiost n periorbit[a], orbital periosteum
Augenhöhlenperiostentzündung f periorbi[ti]tis
Augenhöhlenrand m orbital margin, margin of the orbit
Augenhöhlenröntgendarstellung f orbitography
Augenhöhlenröntgenschichtbild n orbital tomogram
Augenhöhlenschnitt m orbitotomy
Augenhöhlenvene f/obere superior ophthalmic vein
~/**untere** inferior ophthalmic vein
Augenhöhlenvereiterung f orbital abscess
Augenhöhlenzellgewebsentzündung f orbital cellulitis
Augenhornhaut f s. Hornhaut des Auges
Augenhypertension f ocular hypertension
Augeninfektion f/bakterielle ocular bacterial infection
Augeninnenentzündung f endophthalmitis
Augeninnenmuskel m intraocular muscle
Augeninnenstruktur f intraocular structure
Augenkammer f [aqueous] chamber of the eye, vitreous chamber
~/**hintere** posterior [eye] chamber
~/**vordere** anterior [eye] chamber
Augenkammereinblutung f hyphaema
Augenkammererguß m ophthalmosynchysis
Augenkammertiefe f/vordere anterior chamber depth
Augenkammervereiterung f hypopyon
Augenkammerwasser n ocular (aqueous, vitreous) humour
Augenkammerwinkel m chamber angle
~/**vorderer** anterior chamber angle, angle of the iris (anterior chamber), filtration angle
Augenkammerwinkelfehlbildung f goniodysgenesis
Augenkammerwinkelschnitt m goniotomy
Augenkammerwinkelspiegel m gonioscope
Augenkammerwinkelspiegelung f gonioscopy
Augenkammerwinkelstichelung f goniopuncture (bei Glaukom)
Augenkammerwinkelverwachsung f goniosynechia
Augenkapsel f capsule of the eye, fascia of the bulb
Augenkarzinom n ophthalmocarcinoma
Augenklappe f eye patch
Augenklinik f eye (ophthalmic) hospital
Augenkontusion f eye contusion; black eye
Augenkraftmesser m ophthalmodynamometer
Augenkraftmessung f ophthalmodynamometry (Konvergenzkraftbestimmung)
Augenkrankheit f eye (ophthalmic) disease, ophthalmopathy, oculopathy, ophthalmocace, opsionosis
~/**ägyptische** Egyptian ophthalmia, trachoma, trachomatous (trachoma inclusion) conjunctivitis, granular conjunctivitis (ophthalmia); granular lids

Augenkrise f ocular crisis
Augenlähmung f ocular palsy (paralysis)
Augenleishmaniase f ocular leishmaniasis
Augenlid n [eye]lid, palpebra, blepharon (s.a. unter Palpebra) ● **zwischen den Augenlidern liegend** interpalpebral
~/**kleines** microblepharon
~/**verdicktes** pachyblepharon, thickened eyelid
Augenlid... s.a. Lid...
Augenlidanomalie f eyelid anomaly
Augenlidausstülpung f eversion of the eyelid, squeezing of the lids; ectropion
Augenlidbewegung f eyelid movement
augenlidbildend blepharoplastic
Augenlidbildung f blepharoplasty
Augenlidbindehaut f palpebral conjunctiva
Augenlideinstülpung f blepharelosis, ingrowing of the eyelashes; entropion
Augenlideiterung f blepharopyorrhoea, purulent ophthalmia
Augenlidentzündung f blepharitis, inflammation of the eyelid
Augenlidexzision f blepharectomy, eyelid excision
Augenlidfaszie f palpebral fascia
Augenlidfissur f schizoblepharia, eyelid fissure
Augenlidgeschwulst f blepharoncus, eyelid tumour
Augenlidinzision f blepharotomy, incision of the eyelid
Augenlidkante f margin of the eyelid
Augenlidkolobom n eyelid coloboma
Augenlidkrampf m blepharism, spasm of the eyelid; continuous blinking
~/**klonischer** blepharoclonus
Augenlidlähmung f blepharoplegia, paralysis of the eyelid; blepharoptosis
Augenlidnaht f blepharorrhaphy
Augenlidödem n eyelid oedema, blepharoedema; hydroblepharon
Augenlidplastik f blepharoplasty
Augenlidreflex m [eye]lid reflex
Augenlidrekonstruktion f eyelid reconstruction
Augenlidschrumpfung f [eye]lid retraction
Augenlidschweißsekretion f blepharochromhidrosis
Augenlid- und Bindehautentzündung f blepharoconjunctivitis
Augenlidvarize f varicoblepharon
Augenlidverdickung f pachyblepharosis; pachyblepharon
Augenlidvereng[er]ung f blepharostenosis
Augenlidzeichen n/**Graefesches** Graefe's sign
Augenlidzittern n cillosis, quivering of the eyelid
Augenlidzyanose f blepharocyanosis
Augenlinse f 1. crystalline lens [of the eye], lens; 2. eye lens (eines Okulars)
~/**mobile** phacoplanesis
Augenlinsenäquator m equator of the lens
Augenlinsenerweichung f phacomalacia
Augenlinsenexstirpation f lensectomy, excision of the lens

Augenlinsengeschwulst

Augenlinsengeschwulst f phacoma, phakoma
Augenlinsenkapsel f periphacus, capsule of the lens
Augenlinsenkapselentzündung f periphacitis
Augenlinsenkern m nucleus of the lens
Augenlinsenspiegel m phacoscope
Augenlinsenspiegelung f phacoscopy
Augenlinsenvorfall m phac[ent]ocele, dislocation of the lens, phacometachoresis
Augenluxation f eye luxation
Augenmadenfraß m ophthalmomyiasis
Augenmanifestation f ophthalmic manifestation *(einer Krankheit)*
Augenmelanozytose f ocular melanocytosis
Augenmeridian m meridian of the eye
Augenmetastase f eye metastasis
Augenmigräne f ophthalmic (ocular) migraine *(flimmernde Lichtempfindungen mit Kopfschmerzen bei Gefäßspasmen des Auges oder des Gehirns)*
Augenmißbildung f eye malformation
Augenmodell n ophthalmophantom
Augenmuskel m eye (ocular, bulbar) muscle
~/**äußerer gerader** rectus lateralis bulbi muscle, lateral rectus [muscle]
~/**innerer gerader** internal rectus [muscle], internus [muscle], rectus medialis bulbi muscle
~/**medialer (nasaler) gerader** s.~/**innerer gerader**
~/**oberer gerader** superior rectus [muscle], rectus superior bulbi muscle, intorter
~/**oberer schräger** trochlearis [muscle], superior oblique muscle of the eye
~/**temporaler gerader** s.~/**äußerer gerader**
~/**unterer gerader** rectus inferior bulbi muscle
Augenmuskeldurchtrennung f[/**operative**] ophthalmomyotomy, division of an eye muscle
Augenmuskelentzündung f ophthalmomy[os]itis, inflammation of the eye muscles
Augenmuskelerkrankung f ocular (eye) myopathy
Augenmuskelgleichgewicht n orthophoria
Augenmuskelkraftmesser m optomyometer
augenmuskellähmend ophthalmoplegic
Augenmuskellähmung f ophthalmoplegia, ocular palsy, oculomotor paralysis *(s.a. unter Ophthalmoplegia)*
~/**konjugierte** conjugate gaze palsy (paralysis) *(Koordinationsstörung der Augen)*
Augenmuskelschnitt m ophthalmomyotomy
Augenmuskelsehnenschnitt m tenomyotomy
Augenmyiasis f ophthalmomyiasis
Augenmykose f ophthalmomycosis, oculomycosis
Augennadel f eye needle
Augennerv m ophthalmic nerve *(erster Ast des Nervus trigeminus)*
Augennervenschmerz m ophthalmalgia
Augennetzhaut f s. Netzhaut
Augenneuralgie f ophthalmalgia
Augennystagmus m ocular nystagmus
Augenonchocerciasis f ocular onchocerciasis
Augenoperation f eye operation

Augenoptik f ophthalmic (eye's) optics
Augenoptiker m [ophthalmic] optician, optometrist
Augenperforation f eye perforation
Augenphantom n ophthalmotrope *(Augapfelmodell zur Untersuchung der Augenmuskelbewegung)*
Augenpigmentstörung f ocular pigmentary disturbance
Augenplastik f ophthalmoplasty
Augenplexus m ophthalmic plexus
Augenpocken pl ocular vaccinia
Augenpol m/**hinterer** posterior pole of the eye[ball]
~/**vorderer** anterior pole of the eye[ball]
Augenprothese f ocular prosthesis, artificial eye
Augenpunktion f ophthalmocentesis, paracentesis of the eye
Augenrefraktion f refraction of the eye
Augenreiben n eyeball massage
Augenreizstoff m lacrimator [agent] *(chemischer Kampfstoff)*
Augenrigidität f eye rigidity
Augenringmuskel m orbicularis oculi [muscle]
Augenringmuskelkrampf m blepharospasm
Augenringmuskellähmung f orbicularis oculi muscle paralysis
Augenringmuskelreflex m orbicularis oculi reflex
Augenrollmuskel m s. Augenmuskel/oberer schräger
Augenruhelage f mesoropter
Augensalbe f ophthalmic (eye) ointment, oculentum
Augenschälchen n eyecup
Augenschielstellung f ocular skew deviation
Augenschlagen n nach oben up-beat nystagmus
Augenschlußunfähigkeit f lagophthalmia; hare's eye
Augenschmerz m ophthalmalgia, ophthalmodynia, eye pain
~/**plötzlicher** ophthalmagra
Augenschnitt m ophthalmotomy
Augenschrumpfung f ophthalmophthisis, ocular phthisis
Augenschutz m 1. eye protection; 2. eye protector (shield)
Augenschwäche f weakness of the eyes, asthenopia
Augenschwellung f ophthalmophyma
Augenselbst[be]schädigung f oedipism, self-inflicted eye injury
Augensiderose f eye siderosis
Augensparganose f ophthalmosparganosis
Augenspezialist m ocular (eye) specialist, ophthalmologist
Augenspiegel m ophthalmoscope, [ophthalmo]fundoscope, eye speculum
augenspiegelnd ophthalmoscopic, entoptoscopic, fundoscopic
Augenspiegelung f ophthalmoscopy, [ophthalmo]fundoscopy, entoptoscopy
~/**direkte** direct ophthalmoscopy

Augenspritze f eye syringe
Augenspülglas n undine, eyecup
Augenspülung f ocular irrigation, eye douche
Augenstellung f position of the eyes
Augensymptom n ocular symptom
Augensyndrom n/**nasoethmoidales** nasociliary neuralgia, Charlin's syndrome
Augensyphilis f ocular syphilis
Augenszintigraphie f eye scintigraphy
Augenthermometer n ophthalmothermometer
Augentränen n running of the eyes, epiphora
Augentripper m gonoblennorrhoea, gonococcal conjunctivitis, gonorrhoeal ophthalmia
Augentropfen mpl eyedrops, eyewash, collyrium
Augentropfentest m pharmacodynamic test
Augentumor m eye (ophthalmic) tumour
Augenüberanstrengung f eyestrain, copiop[s]ia
Augenuntersuchung f eye examination
~/orthoskopische orthoscopy
Augenuranlage f optic primordium
Augenverätzung f acid burn of the eyes *(durch Säure)*
Augenverband m eye dressing
Augenverblitzen n flash burn [of the eye], welding flash
Augenverbrennung f eye burn
Augenvereiterung f/**totale** panophthalmia, panophthalmitis
Augenvergrößerung f ophthal[mo]macrosis
Augenverletzung f/**perforierende** perforating eye injury, ocular perforating injury
Augenverschmelzung f [/**angeborene**] symphysopsia
Augenwasser n eye lotion, collyrium, eyewash
Augenwassersucht f hydrophthalmia, buphthalmia, infantile glaucoma; hydrophthalmos, buphthalmos
Augenwimper f [eye]lash, cilium
Augenwinkel m corner of the eye, canthus
~/innerer inner canthus, angle of the eye
Augenwinkelabstandsvergrößerung f [eye] hypertelorism, ocular hypertelorism
Augenwinkelabstandsverringerung f [eye] hypotelorism, ocular hypotelorism
Augenwinkelentzündung f canthitis
Augenwinkellösung f cantholysis
Augenwinkelschnitt m canthotomy
Augenwurm m eye worm
Augenwurmbefall m s. Filariasis
Augenzahn m s. Eckzahn
Augenzerreißung f ophthalmorrhexis, rupture of the eye
Augenzittern n nystagmus, ophthalmodonesis *(Zusammensetzungen s. unter Nystagmus)*
Augenzoster m ocular zoster
Aujeszky-Krankheit f Aujeszky's disease, pseudolyssa, pseudorabies, infectious bulbar paralysis
Aura f aura, prodrome, signal symptom, premonitory sensation *(z. B. vor epileptischen Anfällen)*
~/akustische auditory aura
~/epigastrische epigastric aura
~/epileptische epileptic aura
~/hysterische hysteric aura
~/olfaktorische olfactory aura
~/visuelle visual aura
aural aural
Aurantiasis f aurantiasis, carotinoid pigmentation
Auricula f auricle
~ cordis auricle, auricular appendix, atrial appendage
~ dextra [cordis] right auricular appendage, auricle of the right atrium of the heart
~ sinistra [cordis] left auricular appendage, auricle of the left atrium of the heart
Aurikelklemme f auricle clamp
Aurikulopalpebralreflex m auriculopalpebral reflex
Aurikulotemporalnerv m auriculotemporal nerve
Aurikulotemporalsyndrom n auriculotemporal syndrome
Aurikulozervikalreflex m auriculocervical reflex
Auris f s. Ohr
Auropalpebralreflex m auropalpebral reflex
ausatmen to breathe out, to exhale, to expire
ausatmend expiratory
Ausatmung f breathing out, expiration, exhalation; exsufflation *(mittels Apparates)*
Ausatmungsluft f expiratory (expired) air
Ausatmungsphase f expirium
Ausatmungsstridor m expiratory wheeze
Ausbildungsklinik f teaching (training) hospital
ausbleiben to be absent *(z. B. Muskelkontraktion)*
ausbluten to exsanguinate, to drain of blood, to make bloodless
Ausblutung f exsanguinity, bloodlessness
ausbrechen to break out, to appear, to arise, to start *(z. B. eine Krankheit)*; to erupt, to appear, to break (come) out *(z. B. Exanthem)*
Ausbrecherkarzinom n Pancoast's tumour
ausbreiten[/sich] to propagate, to extend *(z. B. Krankheitserreger)*; to spread *(z. B. Krankheit)*
ausbreitend/sich spreading, propagating, extending; serpiginous *(z. B. Hornhautgeschwür)*
Ausbreitung f propagation, extension, dissemination *(z. B. von Krankheitserregern)*; spread[ing] *(z. B. einer Krankheit)*
~/generalisierte generalization *(z. B. einer Infektion)*
~/hämatogene haematogenous spread
Ausbreitungsfaktor m spreading factor
Ausbreitungsgebiet n area of spreading, spreading area
Ausbreitungsgeschwindigkeit f rate of spreading, spreading rate
Ausbruch m eruption, appearance *(z. B. eines Exanthems)*; outbreak, onset, appearance, start *(z. B. einer Krankheit)*; out[burst], raptus *(z. B. von Empfindungen)*
Ausbrütung f incubation *(Bakteriologie)*
ausbuchten to bulge; to pouch; to protrude; to notch
Ausbuchtung f recess[us], sinus, pouch *(Anatomie)*; notch[ing], incisure *(Radiologie)*

ausdehnen

ausdehnen to extend, to elongate; to distend; to dilate; to expand; to spread; to stretch
~/wieder to reexpand
Ausdehnung f extension, elongation; distension; dilation; expansion; spread[ing]; stretching
Ausdehnungsemphysem n ectatic emphysema
ausdifferenziert mature, ripe; well-differentiated
Ausdifferenzierung f maturation *(von Keimzellen)*
ausdrücken to press (squeeze) out; to strip
ausdruckslos vacant, vacuous, expressionless, inexpressive
ausdrucksvoll expressive, significant
Ausdrucksweise f [mode of] expression, style
~/ungrammatische agramphasia, agrammatism
ausdünsten to evaporate; to perspire, to sweat out; to transpire; to exhale
Ausdünstung f evaporation; perspiration; sweating out; transpiration; exhalation ● **die ~ fördernd** perspiratory
auseinandergehen to diverge, to separate, to divaricate *(z. B. Gefäße)*; to bifurcate *(aufzweigen)*
auseinandergehend divergent *(z. B. Augen beim Schielen)*
auseinanderhalten to keep apart
auseinanderlaufen to diverge, to separate, to divaricate *(z. B. Gefäße)*
Auseinanderschneiden n dissection
Auseinanderweichen n divergence, divarication *(z. B. der Muskeln)*; distraction *(z. B. von Knochenbrüchen)*; dehiscence *(z. B. von Wundrändern)*
Ausfall m 1. falling out, thinning *(z. B. der Haare)*; loss *(z. B. der Zähne)*; 2. fall-out *(von radioaktiven Teilchen)*
ausfallen 1. to fall (come) out, to thin *(z. B. Haare)*; 2. to drop *(z. B. Herzschlag)*; to be absent *(z. B. Muskelreflexe)*; 3. to precipitate, to sediment[ate] *(z. B. Stoffe)*; to fall out *(radioaktive Teilchen)*
ausfällen to precipitate, to sediment[ate]
Ausfallerscheinung f defunctionalization (deficiency) symptom; disturbed function
Ausfällung f precipitation, sedimentation
~ von Antigenen durch Präzipitine precipitation reaction
Ausfließen n effluence, outflow, [ef]flux *(z. B. der Galle)*
Ausflockung f flocculation; coagulation, clotting
Ausflockungsreaktion f flocculation reaction
Ausflockungstest m flocculation test
Ausfluß m 1. effluent, [ef]flux, profluvium; fluor, vaginal discharge; 2. s. Ausfließen; 3. s. Ausflußöffnung
~/blutiger bloody (haemorrhagic) discharge
~/eitriger purulent discharge
~/schleimig-eitriger mucopurulent discharge, mucopus
~/seröser serous discharge, orrhorrhoea
~/weißlicher whites, leucorrhoea

Ausflußbahn f outflow tract
~/linksventrikuläre left ventricular outflow tract, outflow tract of the left ventricle
~/pulmonale pulmonary outflow tract
~/rechtsventrikuläre right ventricular outflow tract, outflow tract of the right ventricle
Ausflußbahnstenose f/linksventrikuläre subvalvular aortic stenosis
~/rechtsventrikuläre stenosis of the right ventricular outflow tract
Ausflußöffnung f orifice, outlet, mouth, discharge, exit[us]
Ausführungsgang m efferent (excretory) duct, [deferent] duct; pore *(z. B. von Schweißdrüsen)* ● **ohne ~** ductless ● **über einem ~** suprameatal
~ der Bartolinischen Drüsen Bartholin's cyst duct
~ der Glandula bulbourethralis duct of the bulbourethral gland
~ der Ohrspeicheldrüse duct of Stensen, Stensen's duct
~ des Samenbläschens duct of the seminal vesicle
Ausführungsgangöffnung f duct orifice
Ausfüllen n **von Erinnerungslücken** confabulation *(bei Gedächtnisstörung)*
Ausgang m exit[us], opening, outlet; pore
~ des kleinen Beckens lower opening of the true pelvis
~ des Magens pylorus
Ausgangsherd m initial focus *(z. B. einer Seuche)*
Ausgangskultur f initial culture *(Mikrobiologie)*
Ausgangsperson f proband
Ausgangsstadium n initial stage *(z. B. einer Infektion)*
ausgeblutet exsanguinated, exsanguine, bloodless
Ausgebrochenes n vomit
ausgefranst lacerated *(z. B. Wunde)*
ausgehend/vom Nervensystem neurogen[et]ic
~/von der Milz splenogenic, splenogenous
~/von der Vene phlebogenous
ausgekrempelt everted *(z. B. Darmabschnitte)*
ausgepolstert padded, bolstered *(z. B. Gipsverband)*
ausgereift mature, fully developed, ripe
ausgerenkt dislocated, luxated *(z. B. Gelenk)*
ausgestülpt everted, ectropionized, exstrophic, evaginated
ausgetrocknet dry, exsiccated
ausgewachsen/voll full-grown, adult; fully developed, mature, ripe
Ausgleich m compensation, balance
ausgleichen to compensate *(z. B. Organfunktion)*; to correct *(z. B. Körperfehler)*; to balance, to equalize
Ausguß m/zylinderförmiger cast *(z. B. in Nierenkanälchen)*
Ausgußstein m staghorn calculus
aushebern/den Magen to pump (siphon) out, to empty [the stomach]

Ausscheidung

ausheilen to heal [completely] *(Wunden)*; to cure [thoroughly] *(Krankheiten)*
Ausheilung f healing [up], healing process; [complete] cure, restoration ● **vollständige ~ haben** to experience complete recovery
Aushöhlung f recess[us], excavation, cavity, hollow
aushusten to expectorate, to cough up *(Sputum)*
Aushusten n expectoration, coughing up
auskeimen to germinate
Auskleidung f 1. lining *(Vorgang)*; 2. lining [membrane], coat, tapetum *(z. B. in Zellen)*
auskochen/Instrumente to sterilize, to boil [out]
auskratzen to curet[te], to abrade *(z. B. die Gebärmutter)*; to scoop (scrape) out *(mit dem scharfen Löffel)*; to excochleate *(z. B. Knochen)*
Auskratzer m excavator
Auskratzung f curettage, abrasion *(z. B. der Gebärmutter)*; scooping (scraping) out *(mit dem scharfen Löffel)*; excochleation *(z. B. von Knochen)*
Auskugeln n s. Ausrenkung
Auskultation f auscultation, stethoscopy
~/indirekte mediate auscultation *(mittels Stethoskops)*
Auskultationsbefund m auscultatory findings
Auskultationsgeräusch n auscultatory sound (murmur)
auskultatorisch auscultatory
auskultieren to auscult[ate]
Auslaugung f lixiviation, leaching, extraction; digestion *(der Nahrung)*
Auslese f selection
Auslöschphänomen n nach **Schultz** Schultz-Charlton blanching phenomenon, scarlet fever test
Auslöschung f extinction *(z. B. eines bedingten Reflexes)*; obliteration *(z. B. von Erinnerungen)*; deletion *(z. B. von Chromosomensegmenten)*
Auslösemechanismus m trigger mechanism *(z. B. eines Herzschrittmachers)*
auslösen to cause, to trigger, to start, to bring on *(z. B. einen Hustenanfall)*; to provoke, to induce *(z. B. Asthma)*; to elicit, to produce *(z. B. eine Muskelkontraktion)*
~/eine Tetanie to tetanize
~/stumpf to free without cutting
ausmeißeln to chisel out *(z. B. Knochen)*
Ausmelk[ungs]prozeß m squeezing back process *(z. B. bei Darminvagination)*
auspinseln to paint *(z. B. den Rachen)*
auspolstern to pad, to stuff, to bolster, to wad *(z. B. Gipsverband)*
Ausprägung f intensity *(z. B. einer Krankheit)*
~/endemische endemicity
auspumpen to pump out, to siphon off, to evacuate
ausquetschen to press (squeeze) out
ausräumen to remove *(z. B. Knochenbruchstücke)*; to curet[te] *(z. B. eine Fehlgeburt)*; to abrade *(z. B. die Gebärmutter)*; to eviscerate *(z. B. die Eingeweide)*
ausreichend sufficient, quantum satis (sufficit), q.s.
ausreißen to tear (pull, pluck) out *(z. B. Haare)*; to avulse, to extract *(z. B. die Nägel)*; to avulse *(z. B. die Sehnen)*
ausrenken to luxate, to dislocate, to put out of joint
Ausrenkung f luxation, dislocation
~/inkomplette subluxation
Ausrichtung f adjustment, alignment; setting, rectification *(z. B. eines Knochenbruchs)*; straightening, orthosis *(z. B. einer Deformierung)*
Ausrottung f/**operative** extirpation, eradication *(z. B. einer Geschwulst)*
Aussaat f spread, dissemination *(z. B. von Keimen)*
~/bronchogene bronchogenic spread
~/hämatogene haematogenous spread
Aussackung f sacculation
Aussatz m leprosy, lepra
~/lombardischer pellagra, aniacinosis
aussätzig leprous
Aussätziger m leper, lazar
Aussatzknoten m leproma
ausschaben to curet[te], to scrape; to abrade
Ausschabung f curettage, abrasion *(z. B. der Gebärmutter)*; excochleation *(z. B. von Knochen)*
ausschälbar/nicht inenucleable, not enucleable
ausschälen to enucleate *(z. B. eine Zyste)*; to shell out *(z. B. eine Geschwulst)*; to decorticate *(z. B. eine Pleuraschwarte)*; to decapsulate *(z. B. ein Organ)*
ausschalten/die Schilddrüse durch Radiojod to radiothyroidectomize
Ausschaltung f exclusion; elimination
Ausschälung f enucleation *(z. B. einer Zyste)*; decapsulation *(z. B. eines Organs)*; decortication *(z. B. einer Pleuraschwarte)*
ausscheiden to eliminate, to excrete; to discharge *(z. B. Urin)*; to discharge, to pass *(z. B. Stuhl)*; to secrete, to excrete *(aus Drüsen)*; to exude *(Schweiß)*; to eject *(z. B. Stoffe)*
ausscheidend excretory; secretory; exudative
~/Eiweiß im Urin proteinuric
Ausscheidung f 1. elimination, excretion; discharge *(z. B. von Eiter)*; diuresis *(von Urin)*; discharge, passage *(z. B. von Stuhl)*; secretion, excretion *(z. B. von Drüsensekreten)*; exudation *(z. B. von Schweiß)*; ejection, dejection *(z. B. von Stoffen)*; 2. excrement, excreted substance (matter), egesta; exudate *(z. B. Schweiß)*; secretion *(z. B. einer Drüse)*; output *(der Niere)*
~ eines hochkonzentrierten Urins oligohydruria
~ rotgefärbten Urins rubriuria
~ von abnorm verdünntem Urin polyhydruria
~ von blauem Schweiß cyanephridosis, excretion of bluish sweat

Ausscheidung

~ von fluoreszierendem Urin photuria
Ausscheidungsdrüse f excretory gland
Ausscheidungsgang m excretory duct
Ausscheidungsgeschwindigkeit f excretory rate; secretory rate
Ausscheidungskapazität f excretory (elimination) capacity
Ausscheidungsorgan n excretory organ, emunctory
Ausscheidungsprodukt n 1. s. Ausscheidung 2.; 2. waste product
Ausscheidungsprozeß m excretory (elimination) process
Ausscheidungspyelogramm n excretion (excretory) pyelogram
Ausscheidungspyelographie f excretion (excretory) pyelography, pyelography by elimination
Ausscheidungsschwelle f excretory threshold
Ausscheidungssystem n excretory system
Ausscheidungsurogramm n excretory urogram
Ausscheidungsurographie f exretory urography
Ausscheidungsvorgang m excretory mechanism
Ausschlag m eruption, rash, exanthem[a]
~/blasiger bullous eruption
~/fleckiger macular rash
~/gesprenkelter mottled rash
~/petechialer petechial rash
ausschleichen to reduce the dose slowly (von hochwirksamen Medikamenten)
ausschließen/eine Krankheit to rule out a disease
Ausschlußdiagnose f diagnosis by exclusion
Ausschlußdiagnostik f diagnosis by exclusion
ausschneiden to cut out, to excise (z. B. eine Wunde); to extirpate, to remove (z. B. Organe)
Ausschneidung f extirpation; excision, exsection
~ eines Augenbindehautstreifens syndectomy
~/keilförmige conization (z. B. der Zervix zur histologischen Untersuchung)
Ausschußwunde f exit wound
ausschütten to secrete, to excrete (aus exokrinen Drüsen); to increte (aus endokrinen Drüsen)
Ausschüttung f secretion, excretion (z. B. von Drüsensekreten); incretion, release (z. B. von Hormonen)
ausschwemmen to flood out, to mobilize (z. B. Ödeme)
Ausschwemmung f von Knochenmarkteilchen myelaemia
ausschwitzen to exude; to sweat out, to transpire; to transudate
Ausschwitzen n exudation; transpiration, sweating; transudation, weeping
ausschwitzend exudative; sweating; transudative, weeping
außen external, outside, outer, exterior, extrinsic
~/von extrinsic
aussenden/Strahlen to emit radiation, to radiate
Außengift n exotoxin
Außenknöchel m lateral (external) malleolus
Außenknöchelzeichen n external malleolar sign, Chaddok's reflex

Außenmeniskus m external meniscus (semilunar fibrocartilage), lateral meniscus
Außenplasma m ectoplasm
Außenrotation f external rotation (z. B. eines Gelenks)
Außenschielen n divergent strabism[us]
Außenschmarotzer m ectoparasite, ectozoon
Außeratemsein n breathlessness
äußerlich external; superficial; topical
Außersichsein n ecstasy (vor Freude); frenzy (vor Zorn)
aussetzen 1. to stop (z. B. der Herzschlag); to interrupt, to stop, to discontinue (z. B. eine Therapie); 2. to expose to (z. B. einer Strahlung)
aussichtslos infaust (Krankheitsverlauf)
ausspannen to relax; to take a rest
aussparen to notch, to form an incisure, to form a recess[us] (z. B. auf Röntgenkontrastbild)
ausspeien s. ausspucken
Aussprache f pronunciation, articulation, catharsis
Aussprachestörung f malarticulation
Aussprechen n des R-Lautes/fehlerhaftes rhotacism
ausspritzen 1. to ejaculate (den Samen); 2. s. ausspülen
ausspucken to expectorate, to spit out
ausspülen to irrigate (z. B. den Darm); to rinse (z. B. den Mund); to wash, to irrigate (z. B. eine Wunde); to douche (z. B. die Scheide); to wash [out], to flush [out] (z. B. Gläser)
ausstellen/ein Rezept to prescribe
~/einen Totenschein to issue the death certificate
ausstopfen to plug, to pack, to pad (z. B. eine Körperhöhle)
~/mit einem Tampon to tampon[ade]
~/mit Watte to wad (z. B. Gipsverband)
Ausstopfung f plugging, packing, padding; wadding
~ mit einem Tampon tamponing, tamponment
ausstoßen to push (force) out, to extrude; to expel, to drive (force) out (z. B. den Fetus); to ejaculate (z. B. den Samen); to expulse, to dislodge, to discharge (z. B. Steine); to knock out a tooth
Ausstoßung f extrusion, pushing out; delivery, expulsion (z. B. des Fetus); ejaculation (z. B. des Samens); discharge, expulsion (z. B. von Steinen)
ausstrahlen to radiate (z. B. Schmerzen); to emit, to radiate (z. B. Strahlung)
Ausstrahlung f radiation (z. B. von Schmerzen); emission, radiation (z. B. von Strahlung)
ausstrecken to stretch out, to extend
ausstreichen 1. to smooth (z. B. Falten); 2. to strip (z. B. die Harnröhre); to milk (z. B. die Extremitäten)
Ausstreichungsmanöver n squeezing back process (z. B. bei Darminvagination)
ausstreuen to sporulate (Sporen); to spread, to disseminate, to scatter (z. B. Keime)

Ausstrich *m* smear ● **einen ~ machen** to take a smear
~/fixierter fixed smear
~/Tzanckscher Tzanck smear (test) *(für Pemphigus vulgaris)*
Ausstrichdiagnose *f* smear diagnosis
Ausstrichpräparat *n* smear preparation
Ausstrombahn *f s.* Ausflußbahn
ausstülpen to turn out; to evaginate *(z. B. den Darm)*; to extrovert *(z. B. ein Hohlorgan)*; to ectropionize *(z. B. das Augenlid)*
Ausstülpung *f* 1. turning outward; evagination *(z. B. des Darms)*; eversion *(z. B. des Gebärmutterhalses)*; ectropionization *(des Augenlids)*; 2. diverticulum *(z. B. des Darms)*; exstrophy *(z. B. der Blase)*; extroversion *(z. B. der Gebärmutter)*; ectropion *(des Augenlids)*
austamponieren to tampon[ade], to pack, to plug
austasten to palpate; to explore
Austausch *m* exchange; replacement, substitution
austauschen/Blut to exchange blood
Austauschharz *n* exchange resin
Austauschtransfusion *f* exchange [blood] transfusion, replacement (substitution) transfusion
austragen/den Fetus to carry to full term
Australia-Antigen *n* Australian antigen, hepatitis virus B antigen
Austreibung *f* expulsion, driving out
Austreibungsgeräusch *n* ejection murmur *(Herz)*
Austreibungskraft *f* expulsive force *(der Gebärmutter)*
Austreibungsperiode *f s.* Austreibungsphase 1.
Austreibungsphase *f* 1. expulsive period, second stage of labour; 2. ejection phase *(des Herzens)*
Austreibungsschmerz *m* expulsive pain *(bei der Geburt)*
Austreibungswehen *fpl* expulsive pains
Austreibungszeit *f* 1. expulsion time *(bei der Geburt)*; 2. ejection time *(des Herzens)*
austreten to extravasate *(z. B. Blut aus den Gefäßen)*; to protrude *(Organe)*; to be secreted *(Schweiß)*; to emigrate *(z. B. Leukozyten aus dem Blut)*; to disengage *(z. B. der Kindskopf)*
Austrittsblock *m* exit block *(Reizleitung)*
Austrittspforte *f* exit orifice
Austrittswunde *f* exit wound
austrocknen to exsiccate, to dry [out]; to dehydrate
austrocknend [ex]siccative, drying, desiccant, desiccative, xerantic
Austrocknung *f* exsiccation, desiccation, drying, xeransis; dehydration ● **die ~ verhindernd** antixerotic ● **empfindlich gegen ~** siccolabile ● **unempfindlich gegen ~** siccostable
~ der Kehlkopfschleimhaut laryngoxerosis
Austrocknungsschmerz *m* xerosalgia
auswachsend/geschwulstig neoplastic *(zu einem Tumor)*
auswandern to emigrate *(z. B. Leukozyten aus dem Blut)*
auswärtsbewegen to abduce, to turn outward *(z. B. die Extremitäten)*

auswärtsdrehen to supinate, to turn out *(z. B. die Hand)*
Auswärtsdrehen *n* supination, turning out *(z. B. der Hand)*
Auswärtsdreher *m* supinator [muscle]
Auswärtsdrehung *f* supination, extorsion *(z. B. Armbewegung) (s. a.* Auswärtskehrung 1.*)*
auswärtskehren to evert, to ectropionize *(Augenlid)*
Auswärtskehrung *f* 1. extropionization, eversion *(des Augenlids)*; 2. ectropion *(ausgestülptes Augenlid)*
Auswärtsschielen *n* exotropia, external strabismus, divergent squint, divergence
~/latentes exophoria *(bei geschlossenen Augen)*
~ nach oben/latentes hyperexophoria
~ nach unten/latentes hypoexophoria
auswärtsschielend exotropic
auswaschen to wash [out], to flush out, to rinse *(z. B. Gläser)*; to irrigate, to wash, to bath, to sponge *(z. B. Wunden)*; to leach (wash) out, to lixiviate *(z. B. Stoffe)*
Auswaschung *f* washing [out], lavage, rinsing; elution *(mittels Lösungsmittel)*
Auswaschungsflüssigkeit *f* flush-out solution *(z. B. bei Nierentransplantation)*
ausweiden to exenterate, to eviscerate *(z. B. die Bauchhöhle)*
Ausweidung *f* evisceration, eventration *(z. B. der Bauchhöhle)*
Ausweitung *f* dila[ta]tion
auswerfen to eject *(z. B. Blutvolumen)*; to expectorate *(z. B. Sputum)*
Auswuchs *m* excrescence, outgrowth, protuberance, protuberantia
Auswurf *m* 1. sputum, expectoration *(Zusammensetzungen s. unter* Sputum*)*; 2. ejection, output *(z. B. des Blutes)*
auswurffördernd expectorant
Auswurffraktion *f* ejection fraction *(des Herzens)*
auszehren to emaciate, to consume, to waste away *(z. B. eine Krankheit)*
auszehrend consumptive, tabescent
Auszehrung *f* consumption, emaciation; tabes[cence], tabefaction; skeletization
ausziehen 1. to extract, to lixiviate *(z. B. Stoffe)*; 2. to draw out, to extract, to pull out *(z. B. Zähne)*; 3. to avulse *(z. B. Haare)*
Ausziehen *n* 1. extraction, lixiviation, digestion *(z. B. von Stoffen)*; 2. extraction *(z. B. von Zähnen)*; 3. avulsion *(z. B. der Haare)*
Ausziehnaht *f* pull-out-suture *(z. B. Sehnennaht)*
Auszug *m* extract, extractive substance; lixivium; percolate *(durch Perkolation gewonnen)*; distillate *(durch Destillation gewonnen)*; essence
Auszupfen *n* **der Haare** trichotillomania
Autismus *m* autism, autistic thinking
autistisch autistic
Auto... *s. a.* Eigen... *und* Selbst...
Autoagglutination *f* autoagglutination *(der Blutkörperchen durch körpereigenes Serum)*

Autoagglutinin

Autoagglutinin n autoagglutinin *(Serumantikörper)*
Autoaggression f autoaggression
Autoaggressionskrankheit f autoaggressive disease
Autoallergie f autoallergy
Autoantikörper m autoantibody
Autochromosom n autosome
autochthon autochthonous, indigenous, endemic *(z. B. Malaria)*; aboriginal, native *(z. B. Gerinnsel)*
Autodigestion f autodigestion, self-digestion
Autoecholalie f autoecholalia
Autoemaskulation f autoemasculation
Autoerastie f s. Autoerotismus
autoerotisch autoerotic
Autoerotismus m autoerotism, ego erotism, autosexualism, narcis[sis]m
Autofluoroskop n autofluoroscope
autogam autogamous, self-fertilizing
Autogamie f autogamy, self-fertilization
autogen autogen[et]ic, autogenous
Autognosis f autognosis, self-knowledge
Autographismus m autographism *(vasomotorisches Nachröten der Haut nach dem Bestreichen)*
Autohämagglutination f autohaemagglutination
Autohämagglutinin n autohaemagglutinin
Autohämolyse f autohaemolysis
Autohämolysin n autohaemolysin *(Serumkörper)*
Autohämotherapie f autohaemotherapy
Autohistoradiographie f autohistoradiography
Autohydrolyse f autohydrolysis, spontaneous hydrolysis
Autohypnose f autohypnosis, autohypnotism, self-hypnosis, self-induced hypnosis, statuvolence
autohypnotisch autohypnotic
Autohypophysektomie f autohypophysectomy
Autoimmunfaktor m autoimmune factor
Autoimmungranulozytopenie f autoimmune granulocytopenia
Autoimmunisierung f autoimmunization
Autoimmunität f autoimmunity
Autoimmunkrankheit f autoimmune disease, autoimmunopathy
Autoimmunnephritis f autoimmune nephritis
Autoimmunnephrose f autoimmune nephrosis
Autoimmunneutropenie f autoimmune neutropenia
Autoimmunorchitis f autoimmune orchitis
Autoimmunpanzytopenie f autoimmune pancytopenia
Autoimmunreaktion f autoimmune reaction
Autoimmunthyreoiditis f autoimmune (Hashimoto's) thyroiditis
Autoinfarzierung f autoinfarction
Autointoxikation f autointoxication, endo-intoxication; endogenous toxicosis
~/enterogene enterotoxication, enterotoxism
Autoisolysin n autoisolysin *(Serumkörper)*
Autokatharsis f autocatharsis *(psychotherapeutische Methode)*

Autokinese f autokinesis
Autoklav m [steam] autoclave, sterilizer
autoklavieren to autoclave
Autokrankheit f car sickness *(Kinetose)*
autolog autologous
Autolyse f autolysis, self-fermentation
Autolysin n auto[cyto]lysin *(Serumkörper)*
Autolysosom n autolysosom
autolytisch autolytic
Automatie f s. Automatismus
Automatismus m automatism *(Vollzug mechanischer Handlungen ohne innere Beteiligung)*
Autonephrektomie f autonephrectomy
autonom autonomic, autonomous, self-governing; vegetative *(ZNS)*
Autonomiezentrum n autonomic centre
Autoophthalmoskop n auto-ophthalmoscope *(zur Augeneigenuntersuchung)*
Autoophthalmoskopie f auto-ophthalmoscopy
Autopathie f autopathy
Autophagie f autophagy
Autophilie f autophilia, pathologic self-esteem
Autophobie f autophobia *(krankhafte Angst vor sich selbst)*
Autophonie f autophonia, tympanophonia
Autoplastik f 1. autograft, autogenous graft, autoplast; 2. autoplasty, autoplastic grafting
autoplastisch autoplastic
Autopneumonektomie f autopneumonectomy *(funktionslose Lunge infolge Hauptbronchusverschluß)*
Autopräzipitin n autoprecipitin
Autoprotektion f autoprotection
Autoproteolyse f autoproteolysis
Autoprothrombin n autoprothrombin
Autopsie f autopsy, obduction, necropsy, postmortem [examination] ● **durch ~ bestätigt** autopsy-confirmed
Autopsiebefund m autopsy findings
Autopsiemesser n autopsy knife
Autopsiesäge f autopsy saw
Autopsyche f autopsyche
autopsychisch autopsychic
Autopsychose f autopsychosis *(krankhafte Störung des Bewußtseins der Persönlichkeit)*
autopsychotisch autopsychotic
Autoradiogramm n autoradiogram
Autoradiographie f autoradiography
autoradiographisch autoradiographic
Autoradiolyse f autoradiolysis *(von Radiopharmaka)*
Autoreduplikation f autoreduplication *(der DNS)*
Autoregulation f autoregulation, self-regulation *(z. B. der Gehirndurchblutung)*
Autoreinfusion f s. Autotransfusion 1.
Autorhythmizität f autorhythmicity *(denervierter Muskeln)*
Autosensibilisierung f autosensitization, autoimmunization
Autosit m autosite *(im Gegensatz zum Parasiten das lebensfähige Individuum einer Doppelmißgeburt)*

Autosom n autosome *(übereinstimmendes Chromosom beider Geschlechter)*
autosomal-dominant dominant autosomal
autosomal-rezessiv recessive autosomal
Autosomatognosie f autosomatognosis
Autosplenektomie f autosplenectomy
Autosterilisation f autosterilization
Autosuggestibilität f autosuggestibility, self-suggestibility
Autosuggestion f autosuggestion, self-suggestion
Autotoleranz f autoimmune tolerance
Autotomie f autotomy
Autotopagnosie f 1. autotopagnosia, body agnosia
Autotransfusion f 1. auto[re]transfusion *(körpereigenen Blutes)*; 2. autoinfusion, autotransfusion *(Blutumverteilung durch Extremitätenkompression)*
Autotransplantat n autotransplant, autograft, autogenous graft, autoplast
Autotransplantation f autotransplantation, autografting, autoplasty
autotroph autotrophic
Autoxydation f autoxidation, auto-oxidation
a. v., a.-v. s. arteriovenös
AV-... s. a. Atrioventrikular...
avalvulär avalvular
avaskulär avascular
Avaskularisation f avascularization
AV-Dissoziation f atrioventricular dissociation
Aversionstherapie f aversion therapy
AV-Fistel f arteriovenous fistula (aneurysm)
Avidität f avidity *(Inaktivierungsrate von Antigenen)*
AV-Intervall n AV (atrioventricular) interval
avirulent avirulent, non-virulent
Avitaminose f avitaminosis, vitamin deficiency disease
AV-Überleitung f atrioventricular conduction
Avulsio f **fasciculi optici** avulsion of the bulb
Avulsion f avulsion *(z. B. von Sehnen)*
Avulsionsfraktur f avulsion fracture
Axanthopsie f axanthopsia, yellow blindness
Axerophthol n s. Vitamin A
axial axial
Axialaufnahme f axial projection *(Radiologie)*
Axilla f axilla, armpit, axillary fossa ● **über der ~ supra-axillary** ● **unter der ~ subaxillary** ● **zur ~ gehörend** axillary
Axillaausräumung f axillary nodal removal
axillär axillary
Axillarbogen m axillary arch
Axillarfalte f axillary plica
Axillaris[nerven]lähmung f axillary (circumflex) paralysis
Axillarlinie f axillary line
~/hintere posterior axillary line
~/mittlere midaxillary line
~/vordere anterior axillary line
Axillarlymphknoten mpl axillary [lymph] glands
Axillarplexus m axillary plexus

Axillarregion f axillary region
Axillarvenenthrombose f axillary vein thrombosis
axiobukkogingival axiobuccogingival
axiobukkolingual axiobuccolingual
Axis m 1. axis, epistropheus, odontoid vertebra; 2. axis, centre line *(s. a. unter Achse)*
~ cordis cardiac axis
~ lentis axis of the lens
~ pupillaris pupillary axis
~ visus visual axis
axofugal axofugal
axogen axogenous
Axolemm[a] n axolemma
Axometer n axometer *(Ophthalmologie)*
Axon n [neur]axon, axis cylinder [process], axial (nerve) fibre, neurite
axonal [neuro]axonal
Axonhügel m axonal hillock
Axonometer n axonometer *(Instrument zur Bestimmung der Astigmatismusachse)*
Axonotmesis f axonotmesis
Axonreflex m axon reflex
Axonschwellung f axonal swelling
axopetal axopetal, axipetal
Axoplasma n axoplasm
Axoplasmafluß m axoplasm flow
Ayerza-Syndrom n Ayerza's syndrome, pulmonary arteriosclerosis
Ayre-Oberflächenbiopsie f Ayre's biopsy *(Gynäkologie)*
Ayre-Spatel m Ayre's spatula
Ayre-T-Stück n Ayre's tube
AZ s. Allgemeinzustand
azellulär acellular
azentrisch acentric
azephal acephalic, acephalous
Azephalie f acephalia
Azephalobrachie f acephalobrachia, abrachiocephalia
Azephalobrachius m acephalobrachius
Azephalocheirie f acephaloch[e]iria
Azephaloch[e]irus m acephaloch[e]irus
Azephalogaster m acephalogaster
Azephalokardie f acephalocardia
Azephalokardius m acephalocardius
Azephalopodie f acephalopodia
Azephalopodius m acephalopodius
Azephalorrhachie f acephalorrhachia
Azephalorrhachus m acephalorrhachus
Azephalothorax m acephalothorax
Azephalozyste f acephalocyst, sterile hydatid [cyst]
Azephalus m acephalus
azetabular acetabular
Azetabulektomie f acetabulectomy
Azetabuloplastik f acetabuloplasty
Azetabulum n acetabulum, cotyloid cavity, vinegar cup ● **unter dem ~ subacetabular**
Azetabulumentfernung f[/operative] acetabulectomy
Azetabulumfräser m acetabulum reamer

Azetabulumrekonstruktion

Azetabulumrekonstruktion f acetabuloplasty
Azetaldehyd m acetaldehyde, ethanal
Azetaldehyddehydrogenase f acetaldehyde dehydrogenase *(Enzym)*
Azetanilid n acetanilid *(Antipyretikum)*
Azetat n/**aktives** s. Azetyl-CoA
Azetazolamid n acetazolamide *(Karboanhydrasehemmstoff)*
Azetessigsäure f acetoacetic acid, beta-ketohydroxybutyric acid
Azetonämie f acetonaemia, diacetaemia
azetonämisch acetonaemic
Azetonasthma n acetonasthma
Azetongeruch m acetone odour
Azetonkörper m acetone (ketone) body
Azetonkörperausscheidung f im Urin s. Azetonurie
Azetonurie f acetonuria, diacet[on]uria
Azetphenetidin n acetophenetidin, phenacetin *(Analgetikum, Antipyretikum)*
Azetylase f acetylase *(Enzym)*
Azetylcholin n acetylcholine *(Überträgersubstanz cholinerger Nervenimpulse)*
Azetylcholinesterase f acetylcholinesterase *(Enzym)*
Azetylcholinesterasehemmer m anticholinesterase inhibitor
Azetylcholinhemmer m cholinergic blocking agent
Azetylcholinhydrolase f acetylcholinesterase *(Enzym)*
Azetyl-CoA acetyl CoA (coenzyme A), active acetate
Azetyl-CoA-Karboxylase-Mangel m acetyl coenzyme A carboxylase deficiency
Azetyldigitoxin n acetyldigitoxin *(Herzglykosid)*
Azetylglukosamin n acetylglucosamine
Azetylierung f acetyl[iz]ation
Azetyl-Koenzym A n acetyl CoA (coenzyme A), active acetate
Azetylmuraminsäure f acetylmuramic acid
Azetylsalizylsäure f acetylsalicylic acid, aspirin *(Antirheumatikum, Analgetikum)*
Azetylsulfonamid n acetylsulphonamide *(Konjugationsprodukt der Leber)*
Azetylzystein n acetylcysteine
azid acidic
Azidämie f acidaemia, acidosis
Azidifikation f acidification
azidifizieren to acidify
Azidimeter n acidimeter, acidometer
Azidimetrie f acidimetry
azidimetrisch acidimetric
Azidismus m heartburn *(des Magens)*
Azidität f acidity
Aziditätsgrad m degree of acidity *(des Magensaftes)*
Azidobakterienmilch f acidophilus milk
Azidobakterium n Lactobacillus acidophilus
azidogen acidogenic, acid-forming
azidophil acidophilic, acidophil[e]
Azidophilie f acidophilia *(Färbung mit sauren Farbstoffen)*

Azidose f acidosis, acidaemia
~/dekompensierte uncompensated acidosis
~/diabetische diabetic acidosis
~/hyperchlorämische hyperchloraemic acidosis
~/kompensierte compensated acidosis
~/metabolische metabolic acidosis
~/renal tubuläre renal tubular acidosis
~/renale renal acidosis
~/respiratorische respiratory (carbon dioxide) acidosis
azidotisch acidotic
Azidurie f aciduria
azidurisch aciduric
aziniform aciniform
azinös acinous, acinal, acinose, acinic *(Drüsen)*
azinotubulär acinotubular *(z. B. Drüse)*
Azinus m acinus
Azinusdrüse f acinous gland
azinusförmig aciniform
Azinuszelle f acinous (acinar, acinic) cell
Azinuszelltumor m acinous cell tumour
Azoospermatismus m, **Azoospermie** f azoospermatism, azoospermia
Azotämie f azotaemia
~/alimentäre alimentary azotaemia
~/extrarenale extrarenal azotaemia
azotämisch azotaemic
Azotorrhoe f azotorrhoea *(im Stuhl oder Urin)*
Azoturie f azoturia
azoturisch azoturic
AZT s. Aschheim-Zondek-Schwangerschaftstest
Azur-Eosin-Lösung f azure II eosin
azurophil azurophilic, azurophil[e]
Azurophilie f azurophilia
AZV s. Atemzugvolumen
Azyanoblepsie f, **Azyanopsie** f acy[an]oblepsia, acyanopsia
azyanotisch acyanotic
azygisch, azygos azygous, azygos, impar, unpaired
azyklisch-taktil acyclic tactile *(z. B. Keimübertragung)*
Azystie f acystia, absence of the urinary bladder

B

B I s. Billroth-I-Anastomose
B II s. Billroth-II-Anastomose
Baastrup-Syndrom n Baastrup's syndrome (disease), kissing spine syndrome, interspinal osteoarthrosis (pseudarthrosis); kissing spines
Babcock-Operation f Babcock's operation *(zur Varizenentfernung)*
Babes-Ernst-Polkörperchen npl Babes-Ernst bodies (corpuscles), metachromatic granules *(in Bakterien)*
Babesiasis f babesiasis, babesiosis, piroplasmosis *(hämolytische Infektionskrankheit)*
Babesieninfektion f, **Babesiose** f s. Babesiasis
Babinski m s. Babinski-Reflex
Babinski-Fröhlich-Syndrom n Babinski-Froehlich syndrome (disease), adiposogenital dystrophy

Babinski-Nageotte-Syndrom n Babinski-Nageotte syndrome, dorsolateral oblongata syndrome, contralateral hemiplegia
Babinski-Reflex m Babinski reflex (phenomenon, sign), fanning sign of Babinski, extensor plantar response
~/**negativer** negative Babinski [response]
~/**positiver** positive Babinski [response] *(Pyramidenbahnzeichen)*
Babinski-Vaquez-Syndrom n Babinski-Vaquez syndrome *(bei Neurosyphilis)*
Baby n/**zyanotisches** blue (cyanotic) baby
Bacelli-Zeichen n Bacelli's sign *(bei Pleuraergüssen)*
Bachmann-Hauttest m, **Bachmann-Intrakutanreaktion** f Bachmann test (reaction) *(zum Trichinosenachweis)*
Bacillus m bacillus *(sporentragendes aerobes Stäbchen)* *(s. a. unter Bazillus und Bakterium)*
~ **anthracis** anthrax bacillus
~ **diphtheriae** diphtheria (Klebs-Löffler) bacillus, Corynebacterium diphtheriae
~ **influenzae** influenza bacillus, Haemophilus influenzae
~ **leprae** lepra (Hansen's) bacillus, Mycobacterium leprae
~ **perfringens** Clostridium perfringens
~ **pestis** Pasteurella pestis
~ **pyocyaneus** Pseudomonas aeruginosa
~ **tetani** tetanus bacillus (clostridium), Clostridium tetani
~ **tuberculosis** Koch's bacillus, Mycobacterium tuberculosis
Backe f cheek, bucca, gena, jowl
Backen... s. a. Wangen...
Backenarterie f buccal artery
Backenfalte f buccal fold
Backenknochen m cheekbone, jawbone, zygomatic (malar) bone
Backenmuskel m buccinator [muscle], cheek muscle
Backennerv m buccal nerve
Backenzahn m buccal (cheek, back) tooth; premolar [tooth] *(vorderer);* molar [tooth] *(hinterer)*
backenzahnförmig molariform, shaped like a molar
Bäckerasthma n bakers' asthma
Bäckerekzem n bakers' eczema
Bäckerkaries f bakers' caries
Bäckerkrätze f bakers' itch
Backwash-Ileitis f backwash ileitis *(bei Colitis ulcerosa)*
Backzahn m s. Backenzahn
Baclesse-Huc-Syndrom n Baclesse-Huc syndrome *(Osteolysen bei myeloplastischen Knochentumoren)*
Bacteriocinogenie f bacteriocinogenia
Bacteriocinogenotypie f bacteriocinogenotypia
Bacteriocinotypie f bacteriocinotypia
Bacteriocintyp m bacteriocin type
Bacterium n bacterium, germ *(s. a. unter Bakterium und Bacillus)*

~ **coli** colon bacterium (bacillus), Escherichia coli
~ **enteritidis** s. Salmonella enteritidis
~ **fusiforme** fusiform bacillus (bacterium), fusobacterium, Fusobacterium fusiforme
~ **mallei** glanders bacillus
~ **parathyphosum A** s. Salmonella paratyphi A
~ **parathyphosum B** s. Salmonella Schottmülleri
~ **paratyphosum C** s. Salmonella Hirschfeldii
~ **pneumoniae** Klebsiella pneumoniae
~ **typhosum** s. Salmonella typhi
Bad n 1. bath; 2. spa, health resort, wateringplace *(Kurort)* ● **ein** ~ **nehmen** to take (have) a bath
~/**absteigendes** graduated bath
~/**adstringierendes** astringent bath
~/**brausendes** effervescent bath
~/**fiebersenkendes** fever-reducing bath
~/**hydroelektrisches** hydroelectric bath
~/**lauwarmes** tepid bath
~/**medizinisches** medicinal bath
~/**türkisches** Turkish bath
Badedermatitis f swimmer's (swamp) itch, cercarial (schistosome) dermatitis
~/**bullöse** dermatitis pratensis, grass dermatitis
Badehosennävus m bathing-trunk naevus
Badeinfektion f swimming-pool infection
Badekonjunktivitis f swimming-pool conjunctivitis
Badekur f s. Bäderbehandlung
Badeotitis f swimming-pool otitis; swimmer's (tank) ear
Bäderabteilung f balneary
Bäderanwendung f s. Bäderbehandlung
Bäderarzt m balneologist; physician at a spa
Bäderbehandlung f balneation, balneotherapeutics, balneotherapy, balnear therapy, balneological treatment
Bäder[heil]kunde f, **Bäderlehre** f balneology, science of baths; crenology
Bädertechnik f balneotechnics
Bädertherapieabteilung f balneary
Baermann-Methode f Baermann's method *(zur Isolierung von Nematodenlarven)*
Baer-Methode f Baer's treatment (method) *(Adhäsionsprophylaxe bei Ankylosen)*
Bagassestaublunge[nkerkrankung] f s. Bagassose
Bagassose f bagasse disease, bagass[c]osis
Bagatellfall m trivial case
Bagatellkrankheit f trivial disease
Bagdadanämie f Baghdad spring anaemia
Bagdadbeule f, **Bagdadgeschwür** n Baghdad boil (sore, ulcer)
Bahia-Beule f Bahia ulcer
Bahima-Krankheit f Bahima disease *(Eisenmangelanämie in Uganda)*
Bahn f tract, tractus, path[way] *(Nervenbahn)*
~/**Edingersche** spinothalamic tract
~/**Flechsigsche** s. Bündel/Flechsigsches
~/**Gowerssche** s. Bündel/Gowerssches
~/**rubrospinale** s. Bündel/Monakowsches
~/**Türcksche** s. Bündel/Türcksches

bahnen

bahnen to facilitate, to canalize
Bahnkreuzung f decussation *(von Nervenbahnen)*
Bahnung f *der Nervenleitung* facilitation, canalization *(z. B. für Reflexabläufe)*
Bahre f 1. bier *(für Tote)*; 2. s. Trage
Baillarger-Streifen mpl Baillarger's bands (stripes, lines, layers), striae of Baillarger
Baillarger-Zeichen n Baillarger's sign, inequality of the pupils
Bainbridge-Reflex m Bainbridge (right heart) reflex
Bajonettfinger m bayonet finger *(bei Subluxation der Fingergelenke)*
Bajonettierknochen m riders' (cavalry) bone
Bajonettzange f bayonet (angled) forceps *(Stomatologie)*
Bakandya n bakandjia, Congo[lese] red fever, red fever of Congo
Baker-Zyste f Baker's cyst *(Arthrocele der Kniekehle)*
Bakteriämie f bacter[i]aemia, bacillaemia
bakteriämisch bacter[i]aemic
Bakterid n bacterid
Bakterie f s. Bakterium
bakteriell bacterial
Bakterien... s. a. Bakterio...
Bakterienagglutination f bacterial agglutination
bakterienähnlich bacter[i]oid
Bakterienaktivität f bacterial activity
Bakterienallergen n bacterial allergen
Bakterienallergie f bacterial allergy
Bakterienangst f bacteriophobia, bacillophobia
Bakterienansiedlung f bacterial settling
Bakterienantagonismus m bacterial antagonism
Bakterienantitoxin n bacterial antitoxin
Bakterienart f bacterial species (group)
bakterienartig bacter[i]oid
bakterienauflösend bacteriolytic
Bakterienauflösung f bacteriolysis
Bakterienausbreitung f spreading of bacteria, bacterial spreading
Bakterienausfluß m bacteriorrhoea
Bakterienaussaat f bacterial seeding (dissemination)
Bakterienausscheider m bacterial carrier, vector
Bakterienausscheidung f *im Urin* bacter[i]uria
Bakterienbefall m bacterial invasion
Bakterienbehandlung f bacteriotherapy
Bakterienchlorophyll n bacteriochlorophyll
bakteriendicht bacteria-proof
Bakteriendissoziation f bacterial dissociation
Bakterieneinschleppung f bacterial contamination
Bakterienektotoxin n bacterial ectotoxin
Bakterienembolie f bacterial (infective) embolism
Bakterienendokarditis f [subacute] bacterial endocarditis
Bakterienendotoxin n bacterial endotoxin
Bakterienenzym n bacterial enzyme
Bakterienerythrin n bacterioerythrin *(roter Bakterienfarbstoff)*

Bakterienfaden m bacterial thread
Bakterienfärbeverfahren n *nach Gram* Gram's staining method (technique), Gram's stain
Bakterienfärbung f bacterial staining
Bakterienfilter n bacterial filter
Bakterienflora f bacterial flora
~/**oropharyngeale** oropharyngeal bacterial flora
Bakterienfluoreszein n bacteriofluorescein
bakterienförmig bacteriform
Bakterienforscher m bacteriologist
bakterienfrei bacteria-free
bakterienfressend bacteriophagic
Bakteriengehalt m bacterial content
Bakteriengeißel f bacterial flagellum
Bakteriengift n bacterial toxin, bacteriotoxin
bakteriengiftig bacteriotoxic
bakterienhaltig bacteria-containing, carrying bacteria
Bakterienhämagglutinin n bacterial h[a]emagglutinin, bacterioh[a]emagglutinin
bakterienhemmend bacteriostatic, antibacterial
Bakterienhemmstoff m bacteriostat; bacteriotoxin
Bakterienhemmung f bacteriostasis
Bakterienhemmungsbereich m bacteriostatic (bacterial) spectrum
Bakterieninfektion f bacterial infection
Bakterieninvasion f bacterial invasion
Bakterienkapsel f bacterial capsule
Bakterienkette f bacterial chain
Bakterienkolonie f/**kleine** microcolony, small bacterial colony
Bakterienkolonienauflösung f bacterioclasis
Bakterienkonjugation f bacterial conjugation
Bakterienkontamination f bacterial contamination
Bakterienkonversion f s. Bakterientransformation
Bakterienkonvolut n bacterial convolution, clump of bacteria
Bakterienkrankheit f bacterial disease
Bakterienkultur f bacterial (microbic) culture
~ **im hängenden Tropfen** hanging drop culture
Bakterienkunde f, **Bakterienlehre** f bacteriology
bakterienlos abacterial
Bakterienplaque f(m) bacterial plaque
Bakterienpolysaccharid n bacterial polysaccharide
Bakterienprotein n bacterial protein, bacterioprotein
Bakterienpyrogen n bacterial pyrogen
bakterienreich bacteria-rich, rich in bacteria
Bakterienresistenz f bacterial resistance
Bakterienribosom n bacterial ribosome
Bakterienruhr f bacillary (asylum) dysentery, shigellosis
Bakterienschädigung f bacterial injury
Bakteriensepsis f bacterial sepsis
Bakterienserotyp m bacterial serotype
Bakterienspektrum n bacterial spectrum
Bakterienstamm m strain of bacteria
Bakterienstreuung f bacterial seeding (dissemination)

bakterientötend bacteri[o]cidal, bacteria-killing, bacteria-destroying, antibacterial; bacteriolytic, bacteriotoxic
Bakterientötung f bacterial destruction; bacteriolysis; bacteriophagia
Bakterientransformation f bacterial transformation
Bakterienüberimpfung f bacterial inoculation
bakterienuntersuchend bacterioscopic
Bakterienvakzination f bacterial vaccination, bacterination
Bakterienvakzine f bacterial vaccine; bacterin
Bakterienvariation f bacterial variation
Bakterienvermehrung f bacterial multiplication
bakterienvertreibend germifuge
Bakterienwachstum n bacterial growth
bakterienwachstum[s]hemmend bacteriostatic, antibacterial
Bakterienwachstum[s]hemmung f bacteriostasis
bakterienwirksam bacteriotropic
Bakterienwirkung f bacterial action
Bakterienzahl f parasite index
Bakterienzählung f bacterial counting
Bakterienzelle f bacterial cell
Bakterienzellplasma n bacterial cytoplasma
Bakterienzellwand f bacterial cell wall
Bakterienzylinder m bacterial cast *(pathologischer Harnbestandteil)*
Bakterin n bacterin; bacterial vaccine
Bakterio... s. a. Bakterien...
Bakteriocholie f bacteriocholia *(Vorhandensein von Bakterien in der Galle)*
bakteriogen bacteriogenic, bacteriogenous
Bakteriohämolysin n bacterioh[a]emolysin
Bakterioklasie f bacterioclasis
Bakteriologe m bacteriologist
Bakteriologenöse f bacteriologic loop *(zur Bakterienkulturverimpfung)*
Bakteriologie f bacteriology
bakteriologisch bacteriologic[al]
Bakteriolyse f bacteriolysis ● ~ **bewirken** to bacteriolyze
Bakteriolysin n bacteriolysin *(bakterienauflösender Antikörper)*
Bakteriolytikum n bacteriolysant
bakteriolytisch bacteriolytic
Bakterioopsonin n bacterio-opsonin
bakteriophag bacteriophagic
Bakteriophag[e] m [bacterio]phage *(bakterientötendes Virus)*
Bakteriophagenindukion f [bacterio]phage induction
Bakteriophagenlehre f bacteriophagology
Bakteriophagenmutanten fpl host range mutants
Bakteriophagentherapie f bacteriophage therapy
Bakteriophagentypisierung f [bacterio]phage typing
Bakteriophagie f bacteriophagia
Bakteriophagologie f bacteriophagology

Bakteriophobie f bacteriophobia *(krankhafte Angst vor Bakterien)*
Bakteriorrhoe f bacteriorrhoea
Bakteriose f bacteriosis
bakterioskopisch bacterioscopic
Bakteriostase f bacteriostasis, arrest (hindrance) of bacterial growth
Bakteriostasespektrum n bacteriostatic (bacterial, antibiotic) spectrum
Bakteriostatikum n bacteriostat; bacteriotoxin
bakteriostatisch bacteriostatic; bacteriotoxic
bakteriotherapeutisch bacteriotherapeutic[al]
Bakteriotherapie f bacteriotherapy
Bakteriotoxämie f bacteriotoxaemia
Bakteriotoxin n bacteriotoxin
bakteriotoxisch bacteriotoxic
bakteriotrop bacteriotropic
Bakteriotropin n bacteriotropin, opsonin *(Serumkörper)*
Bakterium n bacterium, germ *(s. a. unter* Bacterium *und* Bacillus*)* ● **durch Bakterien bewirkt** bacteriogenic, bacteriogenous
~/**aerobes** aerobic bacterium
~/**autotrophes** autotrophic bacterium
~/**Bordet-Gengousches** Bordet-Gengou bacillus (bacterium), Bordatella pertussis
~/**großes** macrobacterium, megabacterium
~/**hämophiles** haemophilic bacterium
~/**hämothermes** haemothermic bacterium
~/**heterotrophes** heterotrophic bacterium
~/**kleines** microbacterium
~/**mesophiles** mesophilic bacterium
~/**pathogenes** pathogenic bacterium
~/**phosphoreszierendes** phosphorescent (photogenic) bacterium, photobacterium
~/**psychrophiles** psychrophilic bacterium
~/**pyogenes** pyogenic bacterium
~/**säurestabiles** acid-fast (acid-resistant) bacterium
~/**thermophiles** thermophilic bacterium
Bakterium-Calmette-Guérin-Impfstoff m BCG (Calmette's) vaccine
bakterizid s. bakterientötend
Bakterizid n bactericide
bakteroid bacter[i]oid
BAL = British antilewisite
Balance f/**glomerulo-tubuläre** glomerulotubular balance
Balanceseite f balancing side
Balanitis f balanitis, inflammation of the glans
~ **clitoridis** balanochlamyditis *(Entzündung von Präputium und Glans der Klitoris)*
~/**eitrige** balanorrhoea, purulent balanitis
Balanoblennorrhoe f balanoblennorrhoea
Balanoplastik f balanoplasty
Balanoposthitis f balanoposthitis
balano-präputial balanopreputial
Balanorrhagie f balanorrhagia, haemorrhage from the glans
Balanorrhoe f balanorrhoea, purulent balanitis
Balantidiasis f balantidiasis, balantidosis, balantidial dysentery *(Darminfektion durch Balantidium coli)*

Balantidienruhr 90

Balantidienruhr f, **Balantidiose** f s. Balantidiasis
Balbiani-Ringe mpl Balbiani rings (in Riesenchromosomen)
Baldrian m valerian
Baldriansäure f valer[ian]ic acid
Baldrianwurzel f valerian root
Balfour-Krankheit f Balfour's disease, chloroleukaemia
Balgabszeß m follicular abscess
Balgdrüse f follicular gland
Balggeschwulst f atheroma, atheromatous (sebaceous) cyst
Balint-Syndrom n Balint's syndrome (Form der visuellen Agnosie)
Balkangrippe f Q. fever (durch Coxiella Burnetti)
Balkannephritis f, **Balkannephropathie** f Balkan nephritis (nephropathy)
Bälkchen n trabecula
Bälkchenbildung f trabeculation
Balken m 1. trabecula; 2. [corpus] callosum (ZNS)
Balkenarterie f 1. trabecular artery (der Milz); 2. anterior artery of the corpus callosum
Balkenbauch m pad of the corpus callosum
Balkenblase f sacculated bladder
Balkendegeneration f corpus callosum degeneration, Marchiafava-Bignami disease (syndrome)
Balkenformierung f trabeculation (in einem Organ)
Balkenfurche f callosal sulcus
Balkenschnabel m rostrum of the corpus callosum
Balkenstrahlung f corpus callosum radiation, radiation of the corpus callosum (Nervenfasern zwischen dem Corpus callosum und den Hemisphären)
Balkenstruktur f trabecularism
Balkenvene f trabecular vein (der Milz)
Ballance-Zeichen n Ballance's sign (bei Milzruptur)
Ballaststoff m roughage, bulk material, bulkage (in der Nahrung)
Ballen m ball [of the thumb]; ball [of the foot]
Ballet-Zeichen n Ballet's sign, palsy of extraocular muscles
Ballingall-Krankheit f Ballingall's disease, maduromycosis; madura foot
Ballismus m ballism[us], jerky movements of the arms
Ballistokardiogramm n ballistocardiogram
Ballistokardiograph n ballistocardiograph
Ballistokardiographie f ballistocardiography
ballistokardiographisch ballistocardiographic
Ballondarmrohr n balloon rectal tube
Ballondegeneration f ballooning degeneration (z. B. bei Speicherkrankheiten)
Ballondilatation f des Uterus ballooning (bagging) of the uterus, metreurysis
Ballonement n ballooning
Ballongegenpulsation f/intraaortale intra-aortic balloon counterpulsation (pumping), IABP

Ballonierung f der Lungen ballooning of the lungs, acute pulmonary emphysema (z. B. bei Erstickung)
Ballonkatheter m balloon catheter
~ **nach Fogarty** Fogarty catheter
Ballonkatheteraufdehnung f balloon catheter dilatation
Ballonokklusion f balloon occlusion
Ballonsella f balloon sella
Ballonseptostomie f/atriale atrial balloon septostomy
Ballonsonde f balloon sound
Ballonspritze f ball (rubber) syringe
Ballontamponade f balloon tamponade
Ballooning-Phänomen n ballooning phenomenon (bei weitem inneren Nasenloch)
Ballotieren n s. Ballottement
Ballottement n ballottement (z. B. der Kniescheibe)
~ **des kindlichen Kopfes** cephalic ballottement
~/**renales** renal ballottement
~/**vaginales** vaginal ballottement
Ballungsreaktion f conglobation reaction (zur Syphilisdiagnostik)
Balneobiologie f balneobiology
Balneogeologie f balneogeology
Balneologe m balneologist
Balneologie f balneology, science of baths
Balneotechnik f balneotechnics
balneotherapeutisch balneotherapeutic[al]
Balneotherapie f balneotherapy, balneation, therapeutic use of bath; arenation
Balneum n **arenae** sand bath
~ **coenosum** mud bath
~ **pneumaticum** air bath
Baló-Krankheit f, **Baló-Sklerose** f Baló's disease (syndrome, concentric sclerosis)
Balsam m balsam, balm
balsamieren to embalm
Balsamum n **canadense** Canada balsam (turpentine)
~ **copaivae** copaiba balsam
~ **peruvianum** Peru[vian] balsam
Balser-Fettgewebsnekrose f Balser's fat necrosis (bei aktuter Pankreatitis)
Bamberger-Albuminurie f Bamberger's [haematogenic] albuminuria
Bambushaare npl bamboo hairs
Bambus[stab]wirbelsäule f bamboo spine; rheumatoid spondylitis
Bancroft-Filarienkrankheit f Bancroft's filariasis, wucheriasis
Band n band, vinculum (z. B. der Fingersehnen); ligament (z. B. der Gelenke); taenia (z. B. des Plexus choroideus); cord (z. B. der Segelklappen); frenum (z. B. der Glans penis); bridle (z. B. einer Narbe); fascicle (z. B. der Gefäße); collar (z. B. der Zähne) (s. a. unter Ligamentum und Fasciculus)
~/**Collessches** Colles' ligament
~/**Coopersches** Cooper's (pubic) ligament
~/**Henlesches** Henle's ligament, inguinal falx

~/**Hesselbachsches** Hesselbach's (interfoveolar) ligament
~/**Poupartsches** Poupart's (inguinal) ligament
~/**Vesaliussches** Vesalius' ligament
Bandage f bandage; dressing *(Verband)* ● eine ~ anlegen s. bandagieren
~/**postoperative** postoperative bandage (support)
bandagieren to bandage, to apply a bandage, to bind
Bandanheftung f[/**operative**] ligamentopexy
Bandansatz m ligament attachment *(z. B. am Knochen)*
Bandapparat m ligamentous apparatus
bandartig band-like, ribbon-like, ligamentous
Bandaufhängung f ligamentous support
Bändchen n frenulum, small ligament
~ **der Bauhinschen Klappe** frenulum of the ileocaecal valve
Banddurchtrennung f[/**operative**] [syn]desmotomy
Bändelung f **der Lungenschlagader** banding of the pulmonary artery
Bandentfernung f[/**operative**] [syn]desmectomy
Bandentzündung f inflammation of a ligament, [syn]desmitis
Bänder npl/**Simonartsche** Simonart's threads, amniotic bands *(Verwachsungsbänder zwischen Eihäuten und Feten)*
Bänderdehnung f stretching of a ligament, desmectasis
Bandererkrankung f disease of a ligament, desmopathy
Bänderlehre f anatomy of the ligaments, [syn]desmology
Bändernaht f suture of a ligament, syndesmorrhaphy
Bänderriß m rupture of a ligament, desmorrhexis
Bänderschmerz m pain in a ligament, desmalgia, desmodynia
Bänderschnitt m cutting (division) of a ligament, [syn]desmotomy
Bändertrauma n ligamentous injury
Bänderüberdehnung f stretching of a ligament
Bänderzerrung f tearing of a ligament
Bandexstirpation f excision of a ligament, [syn]desmectomy
Bandfixierung f syndesmopexy, desmopexia
Bandhaft f syndesmosis, ligamentous symphysis, fibrous joint
Bandhülsenkrone f shell (cap) crown
Banding-Operation f banding operation
Bandkeratitis f band keratitis (keratopathy)
Bandl-Kontraktionsring f Bandl's [retraction] ring
Bandsäge f chain saw
Bandscheibe f intervertebral disk (disc), IVD, intervertebral cartilage
Bandscheibendegeneration f intervertebral disk degeneration
Bandscheibenentfernung f[/**operative**] discoidectomy

Bandscheibenentzündung f discitis, inflammation of an intervertebral disk
Bandscheibenerkrankung f discopathy, disease of an intervertebral disk
Bandscheibenläsion f intervertebral disk lesion
Bandscheibenprolaps m prolapse (dislocation) of an intervertebral disk, herniation of the nucleus pulposus; herniated [intervertebral] disk, ruptured [intervertebral] disk, slipped (protruded) disk
Bandscheibenröntgen[kontrast]bild n discogram
Bandscheibenröntgen[kontrast]darstellung f discography
Bandscheibenschaden m intervertebral disk lesion
Bandscheibenstanze f intervertebral disk rongeur *(Instrument)*
Bandspeicherelektrokardiogramm n electrocardiographic tape monitoring
Bandstriktur f bridle stricture *(z. B. Harnröhre)*
Bandunterlagerung f[/**operative**] syndesmectopia
Bandverbindung f s. Bandhaft
Bandwurm m tapeworm, taenia; flatworm, cestode
~/**ausgewachsener** strobilus, strobila, strobile, adult tapeworm
~/**breiter** broad tapeworm
bandwurmartig taenioid, taeniform; cestoid, cestode
Bandwurmbefall m taeniasis, tapeworm infestation; cestodiasis, cestode infestation
Bandwurmeier npl tapeworm eggs; cestode eggs
Bandwurmfinne f cysticercus *(beim Schweinebandwurm)*; hydatid *(beim Hundebandwurm)*; plerocercoid *(bei Zestoden)*
Bandwurmglied n proglottid, proglottis, tapeworm segment
Bandwurmkopf m scolex, head of the tapeworm
bandwurmkopfartig, bandwurmkopfförmig scoleciform, scolecoid
Bandwurmkrankheit f s. Bandwurmbefall
Bandwurmlarve f larval tapeworm; onc[h]osphere; proscolex
Bandwurmmittel n taeniacide [agent]
bandwurmtötend taeniacide
Bandwurmträger m host of a tapeworm
bandwurmvertreibend taeniafuge, taeniafugal
Bang-Bakterien-Aufschwemmung f s. Bangin
Bang-Granulom n Bang granuloma
Bangin n bangin, abortin
Bang-Rheumatoid n Bang rheumatoid
Banti-Syndrom n Banti's disease (syndrome), portal [bed] block, congestive splenomegaly
Barach-Index m Barach's index *(Kreislaufindex)*
Baranowski-Enzym n s. Glyzerophosphatdehydrogenase
Bárány-Drehstuhlversuch m Bárány's chair test
Bárány-Lärmtrommel f s. Bárány-Trommel
Bárány-Prüfung f/**kalorische** Bárány's [caloric] test

Bárány-Syndrom 92

Bárány-Syndrom n Bárány's syndrome, cerebellar hemicrania
Bárány-Trommel f Bárány's noise box
Bárány-Zeigeversuch m Bárány's pointing test
Barästhesie f 1. baraesthesia, pressure sense; 2. baraesthesia, pressure (weight) perception
Barästhesiometer n baraesthesiometer
Barbital n barbitone, *(Am)* barbital
Barbitalismus m barbitu[r]ism, barbiturate poisoning, barbitalism *(Schlafmittelvergiftung)*
Barbiturat n barbiturate
Barbituratvergiftung f, **Barbiturismus** m s. Barbitalismus
Barbitursäure f barbituric acid, malonyl urea
Barbitursäurepräparat n barbituric acid preparation
Barbotage f barbotage *(Spinalanästhesiemethode)*
Barcoo-Krankheit f Barcoo rot (disease), veld sore
Bardenheuer-Bogenschnitt m Bardenheuer's incision
Bardenheuer-Extension f Bardenheuer's extension [bandage]
Bardet-Biedl-Syndrom n Bardet-Biedl syndrome, Laurence-Moon-Biedl syndrome
Bard-Pic-Syndrom n Bard-Pic syndrome *(bei Pankreaskopfkarzinom)*
Bärensprung-Krankheit f Bärensprung's disease, eczema marginatum
Baritose f baritosis
Bariumbrei m barium meal *(Röntgenkontrastmittel)*
Bariumbreischluck m barium swallow
Bariumeinlauf m barium enema
Bariumgranulom n barium granuloma
Barium-Kineösophagographie f cine-barium oesophagography *(Filmdarstellung der Speiseröhre nach Bariumbreischluck)*
Bariumkontraströntgendarstellung f barium contrast roentgenography
Bariumkontraströntgenogramm n barium contrast X-ray [photograph]
Bariumperitonitis f barium peritonitis
Bariumschluck m barium swallow
Bariumsulfat, reinst n barium meal *(Röntgenkontrastmittel)*
Barker-Operation f 1. Barker's operation, excision of the talus; 2. Barker's operation, excision of the hip
Barlow-Krankheit f s. Krankheit/Möller-Barlowsche
Barlow-Syndrom n Barlow's (electrocardiographic-auscultatory) syndrome
Barnard-Operation f Barnard's operation *(Herztransplantation)*
Barodontalgie f barodontalgia
Barognosis f barognosis, weight perception, weight knowledge
Baromakrometer n baromacrometer *(zur Säuglingsvermessung)*
Barorezeptor m baroreceptor, pressure receptor

Barosinusitis f barosinusitis, aerosinusitis
Barotalgie f barotalgia
Barotitis f baro[o]titis, aerootitis
Barotrauma n barotrauma, air-blast injury, atmospheric blast injury
Barraquer-Operation f Barraquer's operation, phacoerysis *(Ophthalmologie)*
Barraquer-Simons-Krankheit f Barraquer's (Barraquer-Simons) disease, progressive lipodystrophy
Barr-Chromatin-Körperchen n Barr (sex chromatin) body, sex chromatin mass
Barré-Beinhalteversuch m Barré's [pyramidal] sign *(Pyramidenbahnzeichen)*
Barré-Liéou-Syndrom n Barré-Liéou syndrome, [posterior] cervical sympathetic syndrome, cervical migraine
Barr-Epstein-Virus n Barr-Epstein virus
Barriere f bar[rier]
Barr-Zellkörper m s. Barr-Chromatin-Körperchen
Barsony-Pseudodivertikel n Barsony's diverticulum *(bei vegetativer Dysfunktion)*
Bartenwerfer-Syndrom n Bartenwerfer's syndrome, metaphyseal dysostosis enchondralis
Bartfinne f, **Bartflechte** f barber's itch (rash), ringworm of the beard, hyphogenic sycosis, sycosis [of the beard], mentagra, tinea barbae
bartflechtenartig sycosiform
Barthelheimer-Sonde f Barthelheimer's sound
Bartholini-Abszeß m Bartholin's abscess
Bartholini-Drüsen fpl Bartholin's (major vestibular) glands
Bartholinitis f bartholinitis
Bartholini-Zyste f Bartholin's cyst
Bartonella f, **Bartonelle** f bartonella *(Erreger der Peruanischen Warzenkrankheit)*
Bartonelleninfektion f des Nervensystems neurobartonellosis
Bartonelliasis f, **Bartonellosis** f bartonelliasis, bartonellosis, Carrion's disease *(durch Bartonella bacilliformis)*
Bartter-Syndrom n Bartter's syndrome, renal hypoelectrolytaemia
Baryphonie f baryphonia, heavy quality of voice
Barythymie f barythymia, melancholia
Barytose f barytosis, baryta (barium oxide) pneumoconiosis
Barytstaublunge[nerkrankung] f s. Barytose
basal basal, basilar, basic
~ **und seitlich** basilateral
Basalanästhesie f basal (basic) anaesthesia
Basalanästhetikum n basal anaesthetic
Basalbogen m basal arch
Basalfibroid n basal fibroid
Basalfortsatz m basal processus
Basalfrequenz f basal frequency
Basalganglion n basal ganglion
Basalganglionlähmung f basal ganglionic paralysis
Basalioma n basalioma, basiloma, basal-cell cancer (carcinoma) *(bösartige Hautgeschwulst)*
Basalkörnchen n basal granule

Basalkörperchen n basal body *(im Zytoplasma)*
Basalkörpertemperatur f basal temperature
Basalmembran f basal lamina (membrane), basement layer, boundary membrane
Basalmeningitis f basilar meningitis
Basalplatte f basal plate *(Embryologie)*
Basalpneumonie f basal pneumonia
Basalschicht f basal stratum (layer)
Basalsegment n basal segment *(der Lunge)*
Basalsekretion f basal acid output *(von Magensäure)*
Basalstoffwechsel m basal metabolism
Basalstoffwechselbestimmung f metabolimetry
Basalstoffwechselrate f basal metabolic rate
Basaltemperatur f basal temperature
Basalumsatz m basal metabolic rate
Basalvene f basal vein
Basalverschattung f basilar radiodensity *(bei Lungenentzündung)*
Basalwindung f basal turn *(Innenohr)*
Basalzelle f basal cell
Basalzellenadenom n basal-cell adenoma
Basalzellenepitheliom n s. Basalioma
Basalzellengeschwulst f basal-cell tumour
Basalzellenhyperplasie f basal-cell hyperplasia
Basalzellenkarzinom n s. Basalioma
Basalzellenschicht f basal[-cell] layer
Basalzellfüßchen n root foot
Basalzellnävussyndrom n basal-cell naevus syndrome
basedowartig basedoid
basedowförmig basedowiform
Basedow-Herz n thyroid heart; cardiothyrotoxicosis
basedowifizieren to basedowify *(Schilddrüse)*
Basedow-Krankheit f Basedow's (Graves') disease, toxic goitre syndrome; exophthalmic goitre
Basendefizit n base deficit
Baseneinsparung f base economy *(des Organismus)*
basenfreundlich basophil[ocyt]ic
Basengehalt m basicity
~ **im Blut/erhöhter** alkalosis, alkalaemia
Basenmangel m base deficit
Basenüberschuß m base excess, BE
Basenverhältnis n base ratio
Basilararachnoiditis f basilar arachnoiditis
Basilararterie f s. Basilaris
Basilarimpression f basilar impression *(Anatomie)*
Basilaris f basilar artery
Basilarisinsuffizienz f basilar artery insufficiency
Basilarisinsuffizienzsyndrom n [vertebral-]basilar artery insufficiency syndrome
Basilarisverschluß m basilar artery obstruction
Basilarmembran f basilar membrane
Basilarmeningitis f basilar meningitis
Basion n basion *(anthropologischer Meßpunkt)*
Basion-Bregma-Höhe f basibregmatic height
Basion-Bregma-Linie f basibregmatic line (axis)
basiookzipital basioccipital

Basiotrib m s. Basiotripter
Basiotripsie f basiotripsy
Basiotripter m basiotribe, basiotriptor *(Instrument für Totgeburten)*
Basis f basis, base
~ **cerebri** base of the brain (cerebrum)
~ **cordis** base of the heart
~ **cranii** base of the skull (cranium)
~ **mandibulae** base of the mandible
~ **modioli** base of the modiolus
~ **nasi** base of the nose
~ **ossis metacarpalis** base of the metacarpal bone
~ **ossis metatarsalis** base of the metatarsal bone
~ **ossis sacri** base of the sacrum
~ **patellae** base of the patella
~ **prostatae** base of the prostate (prostatic gland)
~ **pulmonis** base of the lung
~ **pyramidis renalis** base of the renal pyramid
~ **stapedis** base of the stapes, stapedial base (footplate), footplate of the stapes
Basisdefekt m basic defect
Basisdiagnostik f basic diagnostics
Basisdokumentation f basic documentation *(von Patientendaten)*
Basisfraktur f fracture of the base of the skull
Basismedikation f basic medication
Basismotivation f basic motivation *(Psychologie)*
Basisnarkose f basal (basis) anaesthesia
Basisplatte f baseplate *(Stomatologie)*
Basistherapie f basic therapy
Basistonus m basic tone (tonus) *(der glatten Muskulatur)*
basitemporal basitemporal
basivertebral basivertebral
Basizität f basicity, alkalinity
basophil basophil[ocyt]ic, basophilous
Basophilenadenom n basophilic adenoma
Basophilenanstieg m basophilia, basophilism
Basophilenleukämie f basophilic leukaemia
Basophilenvermehrung f im Blut basophilia, basophilism
Basophilenverminderung f im Blut basocytopenia
Basophiler m basophil[e], basophilic leucocyte
Basophilie f basophilia, basophilism *(1. Basophilenvermehrung im Blut; 2. bevorzugte Zellfärbung mit basischen Stoffen)*
Basophobie f basophobia *(krankhafte Angst, nicht laufen zu können)*
Bassen-Kornzweig-Syndrom n Bassen-Kornzweig syndrome, abetalipoproteinaemia
Bassini-Nähte fpl Bassini sutures
Bassini-Operation f Bassini's operation (hernioplasty, herniotomy)
Bastard m heterozygote, hybrid
Bastardhund m mongrel dog
Bastardisierung f bastardization, hybridization
Bastardluxurierung f heterosis, hybrid vigor
Bastian-Bruns-Regel f, **Bastian-Symptom** n Bastian's law, Bastian-Bruns sign *(bei Querschnittssyndrom)*

Bathmophobie

Bathmophobie f bathmophobia *(krankhafte Angst vor Treppen)*
bathmotrop bathmotropic
~/negativ negative bathmotropic
~/positiv positive bathmotropic
Bathmotropie f, **Bathmotropismus** m bathmotropism
Bathrozephalie f bathrocephalia
Bathyanästhesie f bath[y]anaesthesia, loss of deep sensibility
Bathyästhesie f bath[y]aesthesia, deep sensibility (sensation)
Bathygastrie f bathygastria
Bathykardie f bathycardia
Bathypnoe f bathypnoea, deep breathing
Batophobie f batophobia, acrophobia *(krankhafte Angst vor Höhen)*
Battarismus m battarism, stammering *(überstürzte, polternde Sprechweise)*
Batteriehörgerät n electric (battery-driven) hearing aid
Battey-Krankheit f Battey's disease *(tuberkuloseähnliche Lungenkrankheit)*
Bau m/**anatomischer** structure; texture
~ des Körpers build, frame, form
Bauch m abdomen, belly, venter ● **durch den ~** transabdominal ● **unter dem ~** subabdominal
~/akuter acute abdomen
~/brettharter wooden belly
Bauch... s. a. Abdominal...
Bauchabtastung f abdominal touch
Bauchaorta f abdominal aorta
Bauchaortakoarktation f abdominal aorta coarctation
Bauchaortanervengeflecht n plexus of the abdominal aorta
Bauchaortenaneurysma n abdominal aortic aneurysm, aortic abdominal aneurysm
Bauchaortenaneurysmaresektion f abdominal aortic aneurysmectomy
Bauchaortenverschluß m abdominal aorta occlusion
Bauchaponeurose f abdominal aponeurosis
Bauchatmer m diaphragmatic breather
Bauchatmung f abdominal breathing, diaphragmatic respiration
Bauchbegleitverletzung f concomitant abdominal injury
Bauchbeschwerden pl abdominal discomfort
Bauchbetastung f abdominal touch
Bauchbinde f abdominal bandage (binder, belt)
~/postnatale postnatal support
~/pränatale prenatal support
Bauchbinnendruck m intra-abdominal pressure
Bauchblähung f abdominal distension
Bauchchirurgie f abdominal surgery
Bauchdecke f abdominal wall
Bauchdecken fpl/**brettharte** abdominal rigidity
Bauchdeckenabwehrspannung f abdominal tenderness (tension)
~/brettharte boardlike [abdominal] rigidity
Bauchdeckenanheftung f der Gebärmutter ventrohysteropexy

Bauchdeckenarterie f/**obere** superior epigastric artery
~/oberflächliche superficial epigastric artery
~/untere deep (inferior) epigastric artery
Bauchdeckenbruch m mit Darm- und Netzinhalt epiploenterocele
~/Spieghelscher Spigelian hernia
Bauchdeckenfixierung f der Gebärmutter ventrohysteropexy
Bauchdeckenhaken m, **Bauchdeckenhalter** m abdominal retractor
Bauchdeckenhärte f abdominal rigidity
Bauchdeckennaht f suture of the abdominal wall, laparorrhaphy
Bauchdeckenreflex m abdominal wall reflex
Bauchdeckenschere f abdominal scissors
Bauchdeckenspannung f abdominal tenderness (tension); rigidity of the abdominal wall
Bauchdeckenvene f/**obere** superior epigastric vein
~/oberflächliche superficial epigastric vein
~/untere deep (inferior) epigastric vein
Bauchdeckenverhärtung f abdominal rigidity
Bauchdeckenverschluß m abdominal wall closure
Bauchdehnung f abdominal distension
Baucheinziehung f/**kahnförmige** scaphoid abdomen
Bauchendoskop n peritoneoscope, laparoscope, coel[i]oscope
Bauchendoskopie f peritoneoscopy, laparoscopy, coel[i]oscopy
Bauchentzündung f abdominal inflammation, coelitis
Bauchepilepsie f abdominal epilepsy
Bauchfell n peritoneum, peritonaeum ● **durch das ~** transperitoneal ● **mit ~ überdecken (übernähen)** to periton[eal]ize ● **neben dem ~** paraperitoneal ● **unter dem ~** subperitoneal
~/parietales parietal peritoneum
~/viszerales visceral peritoneum
Bauchfell... s. a. Peritoneal...
Bauchfellanhang m epiploic appendage
Bauchfellduplikatur f peritoneal fold, caecal plica
~ des Eileiters mesosalpinx
~ des Sigmas mesosigmoid
Bauchfelldurchtrennung f[/**operative**] peritoneotomy
Bauchfellentzündung f peritonitis, inflammation of the peritoneum *(s. a. unter Peritonitis)*
~/eitrige suppurative peritonitis, pyoperitonitis
~/gallige bile (biliary) peritonitis
~/kotige faecal peritonitis
~ mit Luftansammlung pneumoperitonitis
Bauchfellkrankheit f peritoneopathy
Bauchfellplastik f peritoneoplasty
Bauchfellpunktion f peritoneocentesis, abdominal paracentesis
Bauchfellreizung f peritoneal irritation, peritonism
Bauchfellschnitt m peritoneotomy

Bauchfellsegment n peritoneotome
Bauchfelltasche f peritoneal pouch (recess)
Bauchfellverdickung f/**entzündliche** pachyperitonitis
Bauchfellwassersucht f ascites, hydroperitoneum, hydroabdomen, abdominal dropsy
Bauchganglienkette f ventral chain of ganglia
Bauchganglion n abdominal (coeliac) ganglion
Bauchgegend f abdominal region
Bauchgeschwulst f 1. coelioma, coeliothelioma, mesothelioma; 2. s. Bauchtumor
Bauchglatze f abdominal baldness *(um den Nabel)*
Bauchgrippe f abdominal influenza
Bauchhaken m abdominal retractor
Bauchhaut f abdominal skin
Bauchhautreflex m abdominal [skin] reflex
Bauchhernie f abdominal (ventral) hernia, laparocele
Bauchhirn n s. Bauchhöhlengeflecht
Bauchhoden m undescended (retained) testicle; cryptorch[id]ism
Bauchhöhle f abdominal cavity, enterocele
Bauchhöhlenaffektion f intraabdominal affection
Bauchhöhlenarterie f coeliac artery (axis, trunk)
Bauchhöhlenaufblähung f coeliectasia
Bauchhöhlenauskleidung f lining of the peritoneal cavity
Bauchhöhlenbeteiligung f intraabdominal involvement *(bei einer Krankheit)*
Bauchhöhlenbluterguß m haem[at]operitoneum, intraperitoneal haemorrhage
Bauchhöhleneingeweidesenkung f abdominal ptosis
Bauchhöhlenentzündung f coelitis
Bauchhöhleneröffnung f/**nochmalige** relaparotomy
~/**operative** [abdominal] laparotomy, abdominal incision, coeliotomy
~/**transvaginale** coeliocolpotomy
Bauchhöhlenerweiterung f coeliectasia
Bauchhöhlenexsudat n peritoneal exudate
Bauchhöhlenganglion n coeliac (abdominal) ganglion
Bauchhöhlengeflecht n abdominal brain, coeliac (solar) plexus
Bauchhöhlengeschwulst f abdominal tumour, coel[othel]ioma
Bauchhöhlenhydrops m abdominal dropsy, hydroperitoneum, hydroabdomen, ascites
Bauchhöhleninfusion f peritoneoclysis, intraperitoneal infusion
Bauchhöhlenpunktion f abdominal paracentesis, abdominocentesis, paracentesis of the abdomen, peritoneocentesis, coelio[para]centesis, tapping (puncture) of the abdominal cavity
Bauchhöhlensaugrohr n abdominal suction tube
Bauchhöhlenschwangerschaft f abdominal (ectopic) gestation, extrauterine pregnancy (gravidity)

Bauchhöhlenspiegel m laparoscope, peritoneoscope, coel[i]oscope, ventroscope
bauchhöhlenspiegelnd laparoscopic
Bauchhöhlenspiegelung f laparoscopy, peritoneoscopy, coel[i]oscopy, abdominoscopy, ventroscopy
Bauchhöhlenspülung f abdominal (peritoneal) lavage
Bauchhöhlentamponade f abdominal tamponade
Bauchhöhlentuberkulose f abdominal phthisis
Bauchhöhlen- und Brusthöhlenspiegelung f laparothoracoscopy
Bauchhöhlenvereiterung f pyoperitoneum
Bauchhöhlenzyste f abdominal cyst
Bauchinhalt m abdominal contents
Bauchinnendruck m intra-abdominal pressure
Bauchkneifen n gripes
Bauchkolik f abdominal (intestinal) colic
Bauchkompresse f abdominal pack
Bauchkompression f abdominal compression
Bauchkrampf m abdominal cramping
Bauchkrämpfe mpl tormina, griping pains in the bowel
Bauchkrankheit f/**akute** acute abdomen
Bauchlage f abdominal (prone) position ● **in** ~ in prone position
Bauchlängsschnitt m vertical abdominal incision
Bauchlinie f abdominal line
Bauchlunge f abdominal lung; extralobar pulmonary sequestration
Bauchmitte f mesogaster
Bauchmuskel m abdominal muscle
~/**äußerer schräger** external oblique muscle [of the abdomen]
~/**gerader** rectus abdominis [muscle]
~/**innerer schräger** internal oblique muscle [of the abdomen]
~/**querer** transverse abdominal muscle
Bauchmuskelabwehrspannung f/**bretthar te** board-like [abdominal] rigidity, rigidity (protective tension) of the abdominal wall; wooden belly
Bauchmuskeldefekt m/**kongenitaler** prune belly syndrome, abdominal muscle deficiency syndrome
Bauchmuskulatur f abdominal muscles
Bauchnabel m navel, umbilicus, belly button
Bauchnaht f abdominal wall suture, laparorrhaphy, coeliorrhaphy
Bauchnarbenbruch m [postoperative] abdominal hernia
Bauchnervengeflecht n s. Bauchhöhlengeflecht
Bauchoperation f abdominal operation
Bauchorgane npl abdominal viscera, intraabdominal organs
Bauchpresse f abdominal muscular pressure, abdominal press (prelum)
Bauchpunktion f s. Bauchhöhlenpunktion
Bauchquerschnitt m transverse abdominal incision
Bauchraum m s. Bauchhöhle

Bauchreden

Bauchreden *n* ventriloquism
Bauchreflex *m* abdominal reflex
Bauchregion *f* abdominal region ● **zur seitlichen ~ gehörend** latero-abdominal
~/seitliche lateral region of the abdomen
Bauchsauger *m* abdominal suction tube
Bauch-Scheiden-Schnitt *m* laparocolpotomy
Bauchschlagader *f* abdominal artery
Bauchschmerz *m* bellyache, abdominal pain, abdominalgia
Bauchschmerzen *mpl* tormina, griping pains in the bowel
Bauchschnitt *m* abdominal incision, [abdominal] laparotomy, coeliotomy
~ **mit Eileiter- und Eierstockentfernung** laparosalpingo-oophorectomy
~ **mit Gebärmutter-, Eileiter- und Eierstockentfernung** laparohysterosalpingo-oophorectomy
~ **mit Gebärmutter- und Eierstockentfernung** laparohystero-oophorectomy
~/medianer median abdominal incision
~/paramedianer paramedian abdominal incision
~/querer transverse abdominal incision
~/subkostaler subcostal abdominal incision
~/transversaler transverse abdominal incision
~ **und Blaseneröffnung** *f* laparocystidotomy
~ **und Blinddarmeröffnung** *f* laparotyphlotomy
~ **und Darmeröffnung** *f* laparo-enterotomy
~ **und Darmfistelung** *f* laparo-enterostomy
~ **und Dickdarmentfernung** *f* laparocolectomy
~ **und Dickdarmeröffnung** *f* laparocolotomy
~ **und Dickdarmfistelung** *f* laparocolostomy
~ **und Eileiterentfernung** *f* laparosalpingectomy
~ **und Eileitereröffnung** *f* laparosalpingotomy
~ **und Gallenblaseneröffnung** *f* laparocholecystotomy
~ **und Gebärmutteranheftung** *f* laparohysteropexy
~ **und Gebärmutterentfernung** *f* laparohysterectomy
~ **und Gebärmuttereröffnung** *f* laparohysterotomy
~ **und Gebärmutterhalsschnitt** *m* laparo-elytrotomy
~ **und Krummdarmeröffnung** *f* laparo-ileotomy
~ **und Leberschnitt** *m* laparohepatotomy
~ **und Mageneröffnung** *f* laparogastrotomy
~ **und Magenfistelung** *f* laparogastrostomy
~ **und Milzentfernung** *f* laparosplenectomy
~ **und Milzeröffnung** *f* laparosplenotomy
~ **und Myomentfernung** *f* laparomyomectomy
~ **und Nierenentfernung** *f* laparonephrectomy
~ **und Uteruseröffnung** *f* laparo-uterotomy
~ **und Zysteneröffnung** *f* laparocystotomy
Bauchschuß *m* abdominal shot
Bauchseitenlage *f* lateroabdominal (Sim's) position
bauchseitig, bauchseits ventral
Bauchspalte *f* abdominal fissure, gastroschisis, schistosomia, schistocoelia
~/laterale lateral abdominal fissure, pleurosomatoschisis

Bauchspeicheldrüse *f s.* Pankreas
Bauchspeicheldrüsen... *s.a.* Pankreas...
Bauchspeicheldrüsenarterie *f/hintere* dorsal pancreatic artery
~/untere inferior pancreatic artery
Bauchspeicheldrüsenausführungsgang *m* pancreatic duct, Wirsung's canal
Bauchspeicheldrüsenblutung *f* pancreatic haemorrhage
Bauchspeicheldrüsen-Darm-Anastomose *f* pancreaticoenterostomy
Bauchspeicheldrüseneinschnitt *m* pancreatotomy
Bauchspeicheldrüsenentfernung *f* [/operative] pancre[at]ectomy
Bauchspeicheldrüsenerkrankung *f* pancre[at]opathy, disease of the pancreas
Bauchspeicheldrüsenfettnekrose *f* Balser's fat necrosis *(bei akuter Pankreatitis)*
Bauchspeicheldrüsenfistel *f* pancreatic fistula
Bauchspeicheldrüsenfistel-Darm-Anastomose *f* pancreaticoenterostomy
Bauchspeicheldrüsenfistel-Gallenblasen-Anastomose *f* pancreaticocholecystostomy
Bauchspeicheldrüsenfistel-Zwölffingerdarm-Anastomose *f* pancreaticoduodenostomy
Bauchspeicheldrüsenfunktionsstörung *f* dyspancreatism
Bauchspeicheldrüsengeschwürbildung *f* pancreathelcosis
Bauchspeicheldrüsenhals *m* neck of the pancreas
Bauchspeicheldrüsen-Hauptausführungsgang *m* major pancreatic duct, Hoffmann's duct
Bauchspeicheldrüsenhormon *n* pancreatic hormone
Bauchspeicheldrüsenkrebs *m* pancreatic cancer, carcinoma of the pancreas
Bauchspeicheldrüsen-Magen-Anastomose *f* pancreaticogastrostomy
Bauchspeicheldrüsenrand *m/unterer* inferior margin of the pancreas
~/vorderer anterior margin of the pancreas
Bauchspeicheldrüsenresektion *f* pancreatectomy, pancreectomy
Bauchspeicheldrüsenschmerz *m* pancre[at]algia, pain in the pancreas
Bauchspeicheldrüsenschnitt *m* pancreatotomy, incision into the pancreas
Bauchspeicheldrüsenstein *m* pancreatolith, pancreatic calculus
Bauchspeicheldrüsensteinentfernung *f* [/operative] pancreatolithectomy, pancreatolithotomy
Bauchspeicheldrüsen-und Zwölffingerdarmentfernung *f* [/operative] pancreaticoduodenectomy
Bauchspeicheldrüsenunterfunktion *f* hypopancreatism
Bauchspeicheldrüsenvene *f* pancreatic vein
Bauchspeicheldrüsenvergrößerung *f* **durch Sekretstauung** pancreatemphraxis *(bei Gangverschluß)*

Bauchspeicheldrüsen-Zwölffingerdarm-Anastomose f pancreaticoduodenostomy
Bauchspeicheldrüsen-Zwölffingerdarm-Arterie f/**obere** superior pancreaticoduodenal artery
~/**untere** inferior pancreaticoduodenal artery
Bauchspeicheldrüsen-Zwölffingerdarm-Vene f pancreaticoduodenal vein
Bauchsperrer m abdominal retractor
Bauchspiegelung f s. Bauchhöhlenspiegelung
Bauchsymptomatik f abdominal [reference of] symptoms
Bauchtrauma n abdominal trauma (tap, injury)
~/**stumpfes** blunt abdominal trauma, closed abdominal injury
Bauchtrokar m abdominal trocar, [anasacra] trocar
Bauchtuberkulose f abdominal phthisis
Bauchtuch n abdominal pack
Bauchtumor m abdominal tumour
~/**pulsierender** pulsatile abdominal mass
Bauchtupfer m abdominal pad
Bauchtyphus m [abdominal] typhus, typhoid [fever], lent (hospital) fever
Bauchultraschall[schicht]untersuchung f abdominal echotomography
Bauchumfang m abdominal girth
Bauchuntersuchung f/**digitale** abdominal touch
Bauchverband m abdominal bandage
Bauchwand f abdominal wall
Bauchwandabtastung f abdominal touch
Bauchwandarterie f/**obere** superior epigastric artery
~/**untere** inferior epigastric artery
Bauchwandbruch m abdominal (ventral) hernia, laparocele
Bauchwandfistel f abdominal fistula
Bauchwandnaht f laparorrhaphy, coeliorrhaphy
Bauchwandreduktionsplastik f laparectomy
Bauchwandspalte f s. Bauchspalte
Bauchwandteilexzision f[/**operative**] laparectomy
Bauchwandverschluß m abdominal wall closure
bauchwärts ventral
Bauchwunde f abdominal wound
Bauchwundenverschluß m abdominal wound closure
Baudelocque-Diameter m Baudelocque's (external conjugate) diameter
Baudelocque-Tastzirkel m Baudelocque's pelvimeter
Bauernwetzel m s. Mumps
Bauernwurstmilz f s. Porphyrmilz
Bauhin-Klappe f Bauhin's (ileocaecal) valve
baumartig arboreal, arborescent, arboroid, arbor[ac]eous
Baumgarten-Syndrom n Baumgarten's syndrome, Cruveilhier-Baumgarten cirrhosis
Baumwollbinde f cotton [wool] bandage
Baumwollfieber n s. Baumwollpneumokoniose
Baumwollfleck m cotton wool patch (spot) (Augenhintergrund)

Baumwollpneumokoniose f byssinosis, byssophthisis, monday morning fever
Baumwollspinnerkrebs m mule-spinner's cancer
Baumwollstaublunge[nerkrankung] f s. Baumwollpneumokoniose
Baumwollwatte f cotton wool (wadding)
Bauru-Ulkus n Bauru ulcer (Hautleishmaniose)
Bausch m swab; wad, pad (Watte); pledget; pack
Bäuschchennaht f button (bolster) suture, quill[ed] suture
Bauschmuskel m **des Halses** splenius cervicis [muscle]
~ **des Kopfes** splenius capitis [muscle]
Bauxitstaublunge[nerkrankung] f bauxite fume pneumoconiosis
B-Avitaminose f vitamin B avitaminosis (deficiency disease)
Bazillämie f bacillaemia, bacteriaemia
bazillär bacillary
bazillenartig bacilliform
Bazillenausscheider m [bacillus] carrier
Bazillenausscheidung f **im Urin** bacilluria
bazillenbeladen bacilli-laden
bazillenbildend bacilliparous
Bazillendysenterie f bacillary dysentery
Bazillenfärbung f staining of bacilli
bazillenförmig bacilliform
bazillenfrei free from bacilli
Bazilleninfektion f bacillosis
Bazillenkultur f bacilliculture, bacillary culture
Bazillenruhr f s. Bakterienruhr
bazillentötend bacillicidal
Bazillenträger m [bacillus] carrier
bazillogen bacillogenic, bacillogenous
Bazillophobie f bacillophobia (krankhafte Angst vor Bazillen)
Bazillurie f bacilluria
Bazillus m bacillus (sporentragendes aerobes Stäbchen) (s.a. unter Bacillus und Bacterium)
● **durch Bazillen bewirkt** bacillogenic, bacillogenous
~ **Calmette-Guérin** bacillus Calmette-Guérin, BCG
~/**Döderleinscher** Döderlein's bacillus
~/**Hansenscher** Hansen's (lepra) bacillus, Mycobacterium leprae
~/**Johnescher** Johne's bacillus, Mycobacterium paratuberculosis
~/**Klebs-Löfflerscher** Klebs-Löffler (diphtheria) bacillus, Corynebacterium diphtheriae
~/**Kochscher** Koch's bacillus, Mycobacterium tuberculosis, tubercle bacillus, t.b.
Bazillus... s.a. Bazillen...
Bazilluselimination f bacillus elimination
Bazin-Krankheit f Bazin's disease, erythema induratum
BCG s. Bazillus Calmette-Guérin
BCG-Immuntherapie f BCG immunotherapy
BCG-Impfstoff m BCG (Calmette's) vaccine
BCG-Impfung f BCG inoculation (vaccination)
BCG-Test m BCG test

BDR *s.* Bauchdeckenreflex
BE *s.* 1. Basenüberschuß; 2. Beckenendlage
Beachtungswahn *m* delusion of reference
Beard-Syndrom *n* Beard's syndrome, neurasthenia
Bean-Reil-Querfurchen *fpl* Bean's lines (transverse rings) *(der Fingernägel)*
Bean-Syndrom *n* Bean's syndrome, blue rubber bleb naevus syndrome
beatmen to respirate, to ventilate
Beatmung *f* respiration, ventilation
~/**assistiert-kontrollierte** assist-control respiration
~/**kontrollierte** controlled respiration
~/**künstliche** artificial respiration
~/**manuelle** manual respiration
~ nach Silvester/**künstliche** Silvester's method
Beatmungsbeutel *m* anaesthesia bag
Beatmungsentwöhnung *f* weaning from respiration
Beatmungsfrequenz *f* frequency of respiration
Beatmungsgerät *n* breathing apparatus, respirator, inspirator, ventilator, pulmotor, resuscitator
~/**volumengesteuertes** volume respirator, volume-cycled ventilator
Beatmungsnomogramm *n* respiratory nomogram
Beatmungsschlauch *m* resuscitation tube
Beatmungszentrum *n* resuscitation centre, centre of artificial respiration
beben to shiver *(z. B. vor Kälte)*; to tremble *(z. B. vor Erregung)*; to shudder *(erschauern)*; to vibrate
bebend tremulous, trepidant, shivering
bebrüten to incubate *(z. B. Bakterien)*
Bebrütung *f* incubation, cultivation
~/**aerobe** aerobic incubation
~/**anaerobe** anaerobic incubation
Becher *m* 1. calyx *(der Niere)*; 2. beaker, cup *(Laborgerät)*
becherförmig goblet-shaped
Becherkeim *m* gastrula, invaginate planula *(Keimentwicklungsstadium)*
Becherkeimbildung *f* gastrulation
Becherohr *n s.* Katzenohr
Becherzelle *f* goblet cell
Becherzellmetaplasie *f* goblet-cell metaplasia *(bei chronischer Bronchitis)*
Bechterew-Arthrose *f s.* Bechterew-Krankheit
Bechterew-Ischiaszeichen *n* Bechterew's sign (test)
Bechterew-Kern *m* Bechterew's nucleus
Bechterew-Krankheit *f* Bechterew's arthrosis, Bechterew's (Strümpell-Marie) disease, rheumatoid (ancylosing) spondylitis, ancylopoietic spondylarthrosis
Becken *n* 1. pelvis, basin, basin-shaped cavity; 2. pelvis, bony pelvic ring *(s. a. unter* Pelvis*)*; 3. pelvic cavity ● **über dem ~** suprapelvic
~/**allgemein erweitertes** pelvis aequabiliter justo major, generally enlarged pelvis
~/**allgemein verengtes** pelvis aequabiliter justo minor, generally contracted pelvis
~/**enges** narrowed pelvis
~/**flaches** flat pelvis
~/**gespaltenes** split pelvis
~/**großes** major (large, false) pelvis, pavilion of the pelvis
~/**infantiles** infantile pelvis
~/**kleines** minor (lesser, small, true) pelvis
~/**kyphoskoliotisches** kyphoscoliotic pelvis
~/**kyphotisches** kyphotic pelvis
~/**lordotisches** lordotic pelvis
~/**Naegelesches** Naegele (oblique) pelvis, obliquely contracted pelvis *(schrägverengtes, mißgebildetes Becken mit Fehlen eines Kreuzbeinflügels)*
~/**osteomalazisches** osteomalacic (India rubber) pelvis
~/**Otto-Chrobacksches** Otto's pelvis; arthrokatadysis
~/**querverengtes** transversely contracted pelvis
~/**rachitisches** rachitic pelvis
~/**Robertsches** Robert pelvis *(querverengte Beckenmißbildung mit fehlenden Kreuzbeinflügeln)*
~/**skoliotisches** scoliotic pelvis
~/**verengtes** contracted (narrowed) pelvis
Beckenabszeß *m* pelvic abscess
Beckenachse *f* pelvic axis, axis of the pelvis
Beckenanheftung *f* **eines Organs** pelvifixation
Beckenapertur *f* pelvic aperture
Beckenausgang *m* pelvic outlet, outlet of the pelvis, inferior pelvic strait, inferior aperture (opening) of the pelvis minor
Beckenausgangsebene *f* plane of the outlet of the pelvis
Beckenausgangslängsdurchmesser *m* coccygeopubic diameter, anteroposterior diameter of the pelvic outlet
Beckenausgangsquerdurchmesser *m* biischial (intertuberal) diameter, transverse diameter of the pelvic outlet
Beckenausgangszange *f* low forceps
Beckenaußenmessung *f* external pelvimetry
Beckenbauchfellentzündung *f* pelveoperitonitis, pelvioperitonitis, pelvic peritonitis
Becken-Bein-Fuß-Gips *m* plaster cast pelvis-leg-foot
Beckenbindegewebe *n* pelvic fibrous tissue; parametrium
Beckenbindegewebeentzündung *f* pelvic cellulitis; parametritis, exometritis
Beckenbindegewebekrankheit *f* parametropathy
Beckenboden *m* pelvic floor (diaphragm), floor of the pelvis
Beckenbodenmuskel *m* pelvic floor muscle
Beckenbodenplastik *f* colpoperineoplasty
Beckenchirurgie *f* pelvic surgery
Beckendeformität *f* pelvic deformity
Beckendrehung *f* pelvic version *(des Fetus)*
Beckendurchmesser *m* pelvic diameter

~/**äußerer** external diameter
~/**Baudelocquescher** Baudelocque's (external conjugate) diameter
~/**biparietaler** biparietal diameter
~/**gerader (medianer)** median (conjugate) diameter
~/**querer** transverse diameter
~/**schräger** oblique (diagonal conjugate) diameter
Beckendurchtrennung f[/**operative**] pelviotomy, pelvisection
Beckenebene f pelvic plane
Beckeneingang m pelvic inlet, inlet (pavilion) of the pelvis, superior aperture (opening) of the pelvis minor
Beckeneingangsdurchmesser m/**querer** transverse diameter of the pelvic inlet
~/**schräger** oblique diameter of the pelvic inlet
Beckeneingangsebene f plane of the inlet of the pelvis
Beckeneingangszange f high forceps
Beckeneingeweide npl pelvic viscera
Beckeneingeweidefaszie f endopelvic fascia
Beckeneinklemmung f pelvic arrest (des Fetus)
Beckeneinstellung f pelvic presentation (des Fetus)
Beckenendlage f pelvic presentation, breech presentation (lie); foot presentation (bei der Geburt)
~/**dorsoanteriore** s. ~/vordere
~/**dorsoposteriore** s. ~/hintere
~/**dorsotransversale** sacrotransverse breech presentation
~/**hintere** sacroposterior position of the foetus, dorsoposterior breech presentation
~/**I. hintere** s. ~/linke hintere
~/**II. hintere** s. ~/rechte hintere
~/**linke hintere** left sacroposterior position of the foetus, L.S.P.
~/**linke vordere** left sacroanterior position of the foetus, L.S.A.
~/**rechte hintere** right sacroposterior position of the foetus, R.S.P.
~/**rechte vordere** right sacroanterior position of the foetus, R.S.A.
~/**vordere** sacroanterior position of the foetus, dorsoanterior breech presentation
~/**I. vordere** s. ~/linke vordere
~/**II. vordere** s. ~/rechte vordere
Beckenendlagengeburt f breech delivery
Beckenendoskop n pelviscope
Beckenendzange f low forceps
Beckenenge f pelvic strait
~/**obere** superior pelvic strait, superior strait of the pelvis
Beckenentfernung f/**halbseitige** hemipelvectomy
Beckenentzündung f pelvis inflammation
Beckenerkrankung f/**entzündliche** pelvic inflammatory disease
Beckenerweiterungsplastik f pelvioplasty
Beckenexenteration f pelvis exenteration, pelvic evisceration

Beckenfaszie f pelvic fascia
Beckenfraktur f pelvic fracture, fracture of the pelvis; fractured pelvis
Beckenfrakturschlinge f pelvic sling
Beckenführungslinie f axis of the pelvis
Beckenganglion n pelvic ganglion
Beckengeflecht n pelvic plexus
Beckengeschwulst f pelvic neoplasm (tumour)
Beckengips[verband] m plaster hip spica
Beckengürtel m pelvic girdle
Beckengürteldystrophie f pelvic girdle dystrophy
Beckenhaltegürtel m pelvic belt (bei Beinprothesen)
Beckenhämatom n pelvic haematoma
Beckenhernie f pelvic hernia
Beckenhochlage[rung] f pelvic high position, Trendelenburg's (high pelvic) position
Beckenhöhle f pelvic cavity, cavity of the pelvis
Beckenindex m pelvic index
Beckeninnenmessung f internal pelvimetry
Beckenkamm m iliac crest
Beckenkammbiopsie f iliac crest biopsy
Beckenkanal m pelvic canal
Beckenknochen m pelvic bone, hipbone
Beckenknochenbruch m s. Beckenfraktur
Beckenmaße npl pelvic measurements
Beckenmesser m pelvimeter, pelicometer
Beckenmessung f pelvimetry
Beckenneigung f pelvic inclination, obliquity of the pelvis
Beckenneigungsmesser m pelvicliseometer, kliseometer
Beckenneigungswinkel m angle of inclination of the pelvis, pelvivertebral angle
Beckenneoplasma n pelvic neoplasm
Beckennervengeflecht n pelvic plexus
Beckenniere f pelvic kidney
Beckenoperation f pelvic operation
Beckenorgan n pelvic organ
Beckenosteomalazie f pelvic osteomalacia; osteomalacic pelvis
Beckenosteotomie f pelvic osteotomy
Beckenperitoneum n pelvic peritoneum
Beckenplastik f pelvioplasty
Beckenrand m pelvic brim, brim of the pelvis
Beckenrandbruch m fracture of the pelvic brim
Beckenregion f pelvic region
Beckenring m s. Beckengürtel
Beckenringbruch m fracture of the pelvic girdle
Beckenröntgen[kontrast]darstellung f nach Lufteinblasung pneumopelvigraphy
Beckenröntgenuntersuchung f pelvi[oradio]graphy
Beckenschaufel f ala of the ilium
Beckenschiefstand m scoliotic pelvis
Beckenschlinge f pelvic sling (hammock)
Beckenschmerz m pelvic pain
Beckenschräge f s. Beckenneigung
Beckenspaltung f pelvisection, pelviotomy, hebe[osteo]tomy, pubiotomy
Beckenspiegel m pelviscope

Beckenspiegelung

Beckenspiegelung f pelvi[o]scopy
Beckenstütze f pelvic support
Beckenteilresektion f partial pelvectomy; hemipelvectomy
Beckenübersichtsaufnahme f pelvi[oradio]graphy
Beckenuntersuchung f pelvic examination
Beckenvene f pelvic (hypogastric) vein
Beckenvenenthrombose f pelvic venous thrombosis
Beckenverdrehung f pelvic [dis]torsion
Beckenvereng[er]ung f pelvic narrowing (contraction)
Beckenverletzung f pelvic laceration
Beckenvermessung f s. Beckenmessung
Beckenwand f pelvic wall
Beckenzellgewebsentzündung f pelvic cellulitis, parametritis, exometritis
Beckenzirkel m pelvimeter
Becker-Melanose f Becker's melanosis
Beclard-Knochenkern m Beclard's nucleus
bedecken/sich mit Blasen to vesicate
~/wieder mit Epithel (Haut) to reepithelialize
bedeckt/mit Bläschen vesiculate
~/mit Eiterbläschen (Pusteln) pustular
bedingt conditioned (z. B. Reflex)
~/durch Blei saturnine
~/durch Ruptur rhegmatogenous
~/erblich genetic
~/kardial cardiogenic
~/körperlich somatogen[et]ic
~/seelisch psychogen[et]ic
~/triebmäßig psychomotor
Bednar-Aphthen fpl Bednar's aphthae
Bedside-Diagnostik f bedside diagnostics (diagnosis)
Bedside-Methode f, **Bedside-Test** m bedside method (test) (bei Bluttransfusion)
beeinflußbar impressionable, affectable; suggestible
~/nicht refractory, torpid (z. B. eine Krankheit)
Beeinflußbarkeit f **durch Suggestion** suggestibility
~/gesteigerte pithiatism
beeinflussen to influence, to affect
~/hypnotisch to suggest
beeinflussend/das Nervensystem neurotrop[h]ic, neurotrope; neurophilic
~/die Melaninablagerung melanotropic
~/die Muskelkontraktion inotropic
~/seelisch psychotherapeutic
beeinflußt/durch Strahlen radiotropic
Beeinflussung f/**psychische** suggestion (z. B. durch Hypnose)
Beerenaneurysma n saccular aneurysm
Beerengeschwulst f staphyloma (Hervorwölbung an der Kornea oder Sklera)
Befall m involvement, affection, attack; infestation, infection, invasion (durch Ungeziefer) (s. a. unter Infestation)
~ durch mehrere Parasiten polyparasitism
~/pulmonaler pulmonary invasion (affection)

befallen to affect, to attack, to involve; to infest, to infect, to invade
~ werden/von einer Krankheit to be attacked by a disease, to catch a disease, to be taken ill
~ werden/von Parasiten to be parasitized, to be infested with parasites, to be attacked by parasites
befallen von affected with
~ von/nicht unaffected [with]
befallend/ein einzelnes Gelenk mon[o]articular, monarthric
~/mehrere Gelenke multiarticular
~/mehrere Wirtsorganismen heteroxenous (Parasiten)
~/nur ein Nasenloch monorhinic
Befallensein n affection, affliction
Befallsextensität f extensity of invasion
Befallsfähigkeit f invasiveness
Befallsintensität f intensity of invasion
Befangenheit f self-consciousness, shyness; embarrassment
Befehlsautomatie f compulsive (command) automatism
befeuchtend humectant, moistening
Befeuchtung f humidification, moistening
Befeuchtungsapparat m humidifier
Befeuchtungsmittel n humectant [agent]
befördernd/die Ausdünstung perspiratory
befragen/einen Arzt to consult a doctor
Befreiung f 1. liberation [of the arms] (z. B. bei der Geburt); 2. emancipation
Befreiungsgriff m releasing (liberating) trick (beim Rettungsschwimmen)
befriedigen/sich selbst to masturbate
befruchten to inseminate, to introduce semen, to fertilize, to fecundate, to impregnate
~/künstlich to inseminate artificially
Befruchtung f insemination, fertilization, fecundation, impregnation; conception
~/heterologe heterologous (donor) insemination
~/homologe homologous insemination
~/künstliche artificial insemination
Befruchtungsalter n fertilization age (Embryo)
Befruchtungsfähigkeit f **der Frau** fertilization (impregnation) capability
~ des Mannes [fertilization] potency
Befruchtungskoeffizient m coefficient of fecundity
Befruchtungsoptimum n fertilization (impregnation) optimum
Befruchtungspessimum n fertilization (impregnation) minimum
Befruchtungsunfähigkeit f **der Frau** female sterility, incapability of being fertilized
~ des Mannes male sterility, [fertilization] impotency, impotence
Befruchtungsvorgang m fertilization process
befühlen to feel, to touch; to palpate
Befühlen n feeling, touching; palpation, dipping
Befund m findings ● **ohne ~** normal, no abnormality discovered, no appreciable disease, NAD

behandelnd

~/computertomographischer computer tomographic findings
~/endoskopischer endoscopic findings
~/histologischer histological findings (evidence)
~/krankhafter pathological findings
~/mikroskopischer microscopic findings; microscopy picture
~/paraklinischer accessory clinical findings
Befundbericht *m* [medical] report
Befundblatt *n* medical examination form
Befunddokumentation *f*/medizinische medical documentation
Befundträger *mpl*/gesunde patients with fibrotic lesions *(bei Tuberkulose)*
Befundübermittlung *f* recording of findings
Befundung *f* evaluation *(z. B. von Röntgenbildern)*
Begabung *f* 1. aptitude, talent; 2. talent *(Person)*
begatten to copulate, to cohabit, to mate
Begattung *f* copulation, coitus, coition, cohabitation, pareunia
Begattungsfähigkeit *f* copulatory ability
Begehrungsneurose *f* compensation neurosis
begeißelt flagellated
~/beidseitig (bipolar) amphitrichous
~/büschelförmig lophotrichous
Begierde *f* desire, longing; appetite
~/sexuelle libido, sexual desire, lust
Begleitanämie *f* symptomatic (secondary) anaemia
Begleitappendizitis *f* concomitant appendicitis
Begleitarterie *f* accompanying artery
Begleitbeschwerden *pl* accompanying (concomitant) complaints
Begleitbewegung *f* associated [automatic] movement, synkinesia, synkinesis, syncinesis
Begleitblickfeld *n* concomitant field of vision
begleitend concomitant, accompanying, secondary, associated *(z. B. Krankheiten)*; accessory *(z. B. Muskeln)*; collateral *(z. B. Bänder)*
Begleiterkrankung *f* associated disease, accompanying illness, concomitant affection
Begleitglukosurie *f* concomitant (secondary) glycosuria
Begleitmuskel *m* accessory muscle
Begleitmyopathie *f* concomitant myopathy
Begleitnerv *m* accessory nerve
Begleitödem *n* collateral oedema
Begleitpankreatitis *f* concomitant (reactive) pancreatitis
Begleitpsychose *f* associated psychosis
Begleitschielen *n* concomitant squint (strabismus)
Begleitschwitzen *n* concurrent sweating, syn[h]idrosis
Begleitsymptom *n* accessory symptom (sign), concomitant symptom
Begleitvene *f* accompanying vein
Begleitverletzung *f* concomitant (associated) injury
Begnadigungswahn *m* delusion of mercy
Begradigung *f* rectification *(z. B. eines Knochenbruchs)*

begrenzen to limit, to restrict
~/örtlich to localize, to limit
begrenzt/auf ein enges Gebiet endemic *(geographisch oder in Bevölkerungsgruppen)*
~/örtlich local, topic[al] *(z. B. Medikamentenwirkung)*
~/räumlich regional
Begrenzung *f*/örtliche localization *(z. B. von Krankheitsherden)*
Begriffsvermögen *n* intellect, comprehension
begründet rational *(z. B. Therapie)*
begutachten to give an expert opinion
Begutachtung *f*/ärztliche expert evidence (opinion)
behaart hairy, pilary, pilose, pil[e]ous
~/sehr hypertrichotic, hirsute
~/über die ganze Oberfläche flagellated, peritrichous *(z. B. Mikroorganismen)*
~/übermäßig hypertrichotic, hirsute
Behaarung *f* hair, hairiness, pelage
~/abnorm starke hirsutism, hirsuteness, hirsuties
~/übermäßige polytrichia, polytrichosis, hypertrichosis, hypertrichiasis, pilosis
Behaarungsanomalie *f* paratrichosis
behaftet affected *(z. B. mit Krankheiten)*; infected, infested *(z. B. mit Keimen)*; contaminated *(z. B. mit Radioaktivität)*
Behaglichkeitstemperatur *f* comfort temperature
Behaglichkeitstemperaturzone *f* comfort temperature zone
behandelbar[/erfolgreich] treatable; medicable *(mit Medikamenten)*; curable
behandeln 1. to treat; 2. s. ~/erfolgreich
~/abwartend to treat expectantly
~/ärztlich to treat, to doctor, to practice medicine
~/eine Wunde to dress [a wound]
~/erfolgreich to cure, to heal
~/expektativ to treat expectantly
~ lassen/sich [ärztlich] to be attended, to take (get) medical treatment
~/medizinisch to medicate
~/mit Atropin to atropinize
~/mit Chinin to cinchonize, to quininize
~/mit Digitalis to digitalize
~/mit einem Bruchband to treat with a truss
~/mit faradischen Strömen to faradize
~/mit Formaldehyd to formalize
~/mit galvanischem Strom to galvanize
~/mit heißem Dampf to vaporize
~/mit Herzglykosiden to digitalize
~/mit Immunosuppressiva to immunosuppress
~/mit Jodoform to iodoformize
~/mit Medikamenten to medicate
~/mit Röntgenstrahlen to roentgenize
~/mit Sonnenstrahlen (ultravioletten Strahlen) to solarize
~/mit Zitrat to citrate
~/provisorisch to temporize
~/psychoanalytisch to psychoanalyze
~/vorbeugend to treat prophylactically
behandelnd/Krankheiten therapeutic
~/seelisch psychotherapeutic

Behandelnder

Behandelnder m therap[eut]ist
Behandlung f therapy, treatment *(s.a. unter Therapie)* ● eine ~ erfordern (notwendig machen) to require treatment ● in ärztlicher ~ sein to be under medical care ● in zahnärztlicher ~ sein to be under a dentist, to be under dentist's care
~/**abwartende** expectant therapy
~/**ambulante** ambulatory therapy, outpatient treatment
~/**antibiotische** antibiotic therapy
~/**ärztliche** medical care (attendance)
~/**empirische** empiric therapy
~/**expektative** expectant therapy
~/**fiebersenkende** pyretotherapy
~/**gezielte** specific therapy
~/**hydroelektrische** hydroelectric therapy
~/**hydropathische** hydropathy *(innerlich und äußerlich)*
~/**kausale** causal therapy
~/**kieferorthopädische** orthodontic treatment
~/**magnetische** magnetotherapy
~/**medikamentöse** medication, drug (remedial) therapy
~/**medizinische** medical therapy
~ **mit Chinchonaalkaloiden** cinchonization
~/**operative** surgical therapy
~/**orale** oral therapy
~/**palliative** palliative therapy
~/**protrahierte** protracted therapy
~/**provisorische** temporization, provisional therapy, temporary treatment
~/**spezifische** specific therapy
~/**stationäre** stationary therapy, hospital treatment
~/**symptomatische** symptomatic therapy
~/**unspezifische** non-specific therapy
~ **von Geisteskrankheiten** alienism, treatment of mental disorders
~/**vorbeugende** prophylactic therapy
Behandlungs... *s.a. Therapie...*
Behandlungsbedürfnis n desire for therapy
behandlungsbedürftig in need of therapy
Behandlungsbeginn m start of therapy
Behandlungsdauer f duration of therapy
Behandlungsdiagnose f working diagnosis
Behandlungseinstufung f therapeutical classification
Behandlungserfolg m therapeutical success, success of therapy
Behandlungsmethode f therapeutical method, method of treatment
Behandlungsmißerfolg m therapeutical failure, failure of therapy
Behandlungsraum m consulting (treatment) room; surgery
Behandlungsstelle f/**ambulante** ambulance
Behandlungsversuch m therapeutical trial, trial of therapy
Behandlungszyklus m therapeutical cycle
Behçet-Syndrom n Behçet's disease (syndrome), mucocutaneous ocular syndrome

Behelfsprothese f temporary prosthesis
beherbergen/einen Infektionserreger to harbour an infectious agent
beherrschen/eine Infektion to control an infection
~/**eine Operation** to master an operation
Beherrschung f self-control, temperance
Behinderung f/**körperliche** physical handicaps (disability)
beidäugig binocular
beidbrüstig bimastic
beiderseits bilateral
beidfüßig bipedal
Beidhänder m ambidexter
beidhändig ambidextrous
Beidhändigkeit f ambidexterity
beidohrig biauricular, binaural, binotic, diotic
beidseitig bilateral, ambilateral
Beidseitigkeit f bilateralism
Beieierstock m paroophoron
Beigeschmack m smack, extraneous taste; aftertaste
Beihoden m paradidymis, parepididymis, Giraldes' organ
Beimpfen n, **Beimpfung** f inoculation *(einer Bakterienkultur)*
Bein n 1. leg; 2. bone, os
~/**gebrochenes** broken (fractured) leg
Beinamputation f leg amputation
Beinchen n petiole, petiolus
Beinerv m s. Nervus accessorius
Beinextension f leg (lower limb) extension
Beingeflecht n lumbosacral plexus
Beingeschwür n leg (varicose) ulcer
Beingips[verband] m leg plaster
Beingurt m leg strap
Beinhaut f periost[eum]
Beinhautentzündung f periostitis
Beinknochen m bone of the lower limb
Beinkraftmesser m pedodynamometer
Beinlagerungsschiene f leg splint
Beinlähmung f crural paralysis
beinlos legless, acnemous
Beinloser m apus
Beinmuskulatur f leg muscles
Beinorthese f leg orthesis, orthopaedic brace (device) of the leg
Beinprothese f leg prosthesis, artificial leg
Beinschiene f leg splint; leg brace
Beinschmerz m leg pain, skelalgia
Beintieflage f head-up position
Beinvenenthrombose f leg vein thrombosis
Beinverkrümmung f curved leg
Beinverkürzung f shortened leg
Beinverschmelzung f[/**angeborene**] sympodia
Beinvorfall m footling presentation *(bei der Geburt)*
Beischilddrüse f parathyroid gland (body)
Beischlaf m cohabitation, coitus, coition, [sexual] intercourse, pareunia
Beischlafangst f coitophobia
beischlafen to cohabit[ate], to have intercourse

Beischlaffähigkeit f sexual potency; pareunia
Beischlafunfähigkeit f sexual impotency; apareunia
Beißkeil m bite block, mouth wedge
beiwohnen s. beischlafen
Bejel f bejel, endemic syphilis of the Bedouins, [endemic] non-venereal syphilis, Arabian treponematosis
bekämpfen/den Schock to combat the shock
~/die Infektion to combat the infection
Bekanntschaftstäuschung f déjà-vu[e] phenomenon, déjà-pensé phenomenon, illusionary feeling of familiarity *(Psychiatrie)*
Békésy-Audiometer n Békésy audiometer
Békésy-Audiometrie f Békésy audiometry
Beklemmungsgefühl n oppressive feeling, cincture sensation, sensation of constriction
beklommen oppressed; anxious
beklopfen to percuss; to tap
Beklopfen n percussion *(Zusammensetzungen s. unter Perkussion)*; tapping
bekömmlich digestible *(Nahrung)*; salubrious *(z. B. Klima)*
beladen/mit Kohlendioxid to carbonate
Belag m coat[ing], lining, covering; plaque, film *(der Zähne)*; tartar, scale *(Zahnstein)*; coat[ing], fur[ring] *(der Zunge)*; fur, coat, film *(der Tonsillen)*
Beläge mpl/**diphtherische** diphtheritic membranes
Belastbarkeit f/**körperliche** maximum stress; exercise tolerance
belastet/erblich suffering from a hereditary disease
Belastung f load, strain, charge, burden; demand, stress *(der Organe)*; strain *(psychisch)*; exertion, exercise *(bei Funktionsprüfungen)*; affliction *(durch Vererbung)*; exposure *(durch Strahlen)*; weight *(durch Gewicht)*
~/körperliche physical strain, exercise, exertion
~/psychische psychological stress, discomfort, strain
Belastungsasthma n exertion-induced asthma
Belastungsatemnot f s. Belastungsdyspnoe
Belastungs-Claudicatio f exertional claudication
Belastungsdosis f loading dose *(von Strahlen)*
Belastungsdyspnoe f effort (exertional) dyspnoea, dyspnoea on effort (exertion)
Belastungs-EKG n exercise electrocardiogram
Belastungsfähigkeit f resistance to stress
Belastungsinfektion f challenge infection
Belastungsinsuffizienz f exercise (exertional) insufficiency
Belastungsmesser m ergometer
Belastungsmessung f ergometry
Belastungsoxytensiometrie f ergooxytensiometry
Belastungsprobe f tolerance (functional) test *(z. B. des Herzens)*; loading test *(z. B. der Knochen)*
Belastungsschaden m stress damage; loading damage *(z. B. der Knochen)*

Belastungssyndrom n stress syndrome
Belastungstachykardie f exertional (exercise) tachycardia
Belastungstest m exercise tolerance test
Belastungstoleranz f exercise tolerance
Belastungstoleranztest m exercise tolerance test
beleben to animate, to vivify, to vitalize
belebend animating, stimulating
belebt animate[d]
Belebung f animation, vivification
Belegkrankenhaus n general practitioners hospital
Belegzellantikörper m parietal cell antibody
Belegzelle f parietal (acid, border) cell, oxyntic (oxyphilic, delomorphous) cell *(der Magenschleimhaut)*
beleibt obese, corpulent
Beleibtheit f obesity, corpulency
Beleuchtung f/**direkte** direct (vertical) illumination
Belichtungsautomat m phototimer *(Radiologie)*
Belichtungsumfang m [exposure] latitude *(Radiologie)*
Belichtungszeit f exposure time *(für Röntgenfilme)*
Belieben/nach ad libitum, ad lib, quantum libet (placet), quantum vis, QV
Belladonnaalkaloid n belladonna alkaloid
Belladonnavergiftung f atropi[ni]sm
Belladonnin n belladonnine *(ein Belladonnaalkaloid)*
Bell-Delirium n Bell's [acute delirious] mania
bellend barking
Bell-Lähmung f Bell's palsy, peripheral facial paralysis
Belloq-Röhre f Belloq's tube (cannula)
Belloq-Tamponade f Belloq's tamponade *(Nasentamponade)*
Bell-Phänomen n Bell's phenomenon (sign) *(bei peripherer Fazialislähmung)*
belüften to ventilate, to aerate
Belüftung f ventilation, aeration
Belüftungs-Durchblutungs-Verhältnis n ventilation-perfusion ratio
benachbart adjacent, adjoining, limitrophe *(z. B. Organe)*
Bence-Jones-Eiweißkörper m Bence Jones protein
Bence-Jones-Körper-Ausscheidung f **im Urin** Bence Jones proteinuria
Bence-Jones-Protein-Präzipitationstest m Bence Jones protein test
Bence-Jones-Proteinurie f Bence Jones proteinuria
Bence-Jones-Urinzylinder mpl Bence Jones cylinders
Benedict-Probe f Benedict's method (test) *(Glukosenachweis)*
Benedict-Theis-Methode f Benedict and Theis's method *(Phenolkörpernachweis)*

Benedikt-Syndrom

Benedikt-Syndrom *n* Benedikt's (tegmental) syndrome *(herdseitige Okulomotoriuslähmung mit herdgekreuzter Hyperkinese)*
benetzbar wettable, hydrophilic, hydrophile
~/nicht non-wettable, hydrophobic, hydrophobe
Bengalrosa *n* rose bengal *(zur Leberfunktionstestung)*
benigne *s.* gutartig
Bennett-Fraktur *f* Bennett's fracture *(des ersten Mittelhandknochens)*
Bennett-Winkel *m* Bennett angle *(Stomatologie)*
Bennhold-Probe *f* Bennhold's (Congo red) test *(Amyloidosenachweis)*
benommen dizzy, giddy, light-headed; somnolent, drowsy; numb; dazed, confused
~/stark soporose; stuporous, stuporose
Benommenheit *f* dizziness, giddiness, lightheadedness; somnolence, somnolentia, drowsiness; numbness
~/starke sopor; stupor
Benton-Test *m* Benton's test *(visuelle Merkfähigkeitsprüfung)*
Benzanthrazen *n* benzanthracene *(Kanzerogen)*
Benzathin-Penizillin *n* G benzathine penicilline G
Benzidinprobe *f* benzidine test *(Blutfarbstoffnachweis)*
Benzodioxantest *m* benzodioxane test *(Phäochromozytomnachweis)*
Benzoesäure *f* benzoic acid *(Antiseptikum)*
Benzolkarbonsäure *f* benzoic acid *(Antiseptikum)*
2,3-Benzopyrrol *n* indole *(Tryptophanabbauprodukt)*
Benzoylglykokoll *n* benzoylglycine, hippuric acid
Beobachtung *f* **des Patienten** observation of the patient
Beobachtungsfehler *m* error of observation
Beobachtungsstation *f* observation ward
Beobachtungswahn *m* delusion of observation
bepinseln to paint *(z. B. den Rachen)*
Bepti = bionomics, environment, plasmodium, treatment, immunity *(Malariaepidemiologie)*
beraten lassen/sich to get an advice, to seek a counsel
~/sich to consult
Beratung *f* consultation; advice, counsel *(Rat)*
Beratungsstelle *f* advisory centre *(z. B. für Schwangere)*
berauschen to intoxicate; to inebriate
berauschend intoxicant, narcotic
Bereich *m* region, area *(örtlich)*; range *(Meßbereich)*
~ der Aortenbifurkation aortic bifurcation area
~/dermatologischer dermatologist's province
~/immunologisch privilegierter immunologic privileged site
bereiten/Schmerzen to ache
bereitet/nach Vorschrift des Arztes magistral *(Arzneimittel)*
Bereitschaftsbehälter *m* ever-ready container

Bereitschaftsdienst *m* emergency (stand-by) duty ● **~ haben** to be on service (duty)
Bereitschaftspotential *n* expectancy wave *(Neurophysiologie)*
Bereitung *f* preparation *(von Arzneimitteln)*
Bergara-Wartenberg-Syndrom *n* Bergara-Wartenberg's sign *(bei Fazialislähmung)*
Berger-Rhythmus *m* Berger rhythm (wave), alpha rhythm *(EEG)*
Bergflachslunge[nerkrankung] *f s.* Asbestose
Bergkrankheit *f* mountain (altitude) sickness, Acosta's (high mountain) disease, hypobaropathy
Bergmann-Gliafasern *fpl* Bergmann's glia fibres
Bergmannsellenbogen *m* miner's elbow
Bergmannskrankheit *f* miner's disease (sickness), ancylostomiasis
Bergmannslunge *f* miner's phthisis (asthma), anthracosilicosis
Bergmannsnystagmus *m* miner's (pendular) nystagmus
Bergmann-Syndrom *n* Bergmann's (epiphrenal) syndrome
Bergonie-Maske *f* Bergonie's mask *(zur Elektrotherapie)*
Bergstrand-Leberzirrhose *f* Bergstrand's cirrhosis
Bergstrand-Syndrom *n* Bergstrand's osteoblastic disease; osteoid osteoma
Bergung *f* recovery; rescue
Beriberi *f* beriberi, athiaminosis, Ceylon sickness, rice-eaters' disease, kakke, endemic neuritis *(Vitamin-B_1-Mangelkrankheit)*
Beriberi-Herz *n* beriberi heart disease
Berieselung *f* affusion *(z. B. bei Augenspülung)*
Berkefeld-Filter *n* Berkefeld filter
Berlin-Trübung *f* Berlin's disease, Berlin's traumatic oedema of the retina
Berloque-Dermatitis *f*, **Berloque-Krankheit** *f* berlock (berloque) dermatitis
Bernard-Horner-Syndrom *n* Bernard-Horner syndrome, Horner's (oculopupillary) syndrome, cervical sympathetic paralysis syndrome
Berndorfer-Syndrom *n* Berndorfer's syndrome, electrodactyly-ectodermal clefting syndrome, EEC syndrome
Bernhardt-[Roth-]Syndrom *n* Bernhardt-Roth syndrome, Bernhardt's paraesthesia, paraesthetic meralgia
Bernheim-Syndrom *n* Bernheim's syndrome *(Rechtsherzversagen infolge Obstruktion der rechtsventrikulären Ausflußbahn)*
Bernsteinsäure *f* succinic acid
Bernsteinsäuredehydrogenase *f* succinic [acid] dehydrogenase
Berstungsfraktur *f* bursting (split, tuft) fracture
Berten-Hebel *m* Berten's elevatorium *(Stomatologie)*
Bertin-Band *n* iliofemoral ligament
Berufsakne *f* occupational acne
berufsbedingt professional, occupational

Berufsdermatitis f, **Berufsdermatose** f occupational (industrial) dermatosis
Berufsekzem n occupational eczema
Berufshyperkeratose f occupational hyperkeratosis
Berufskrankheit f occupational disease
Berufskrebs m occupational cancer
Berufslähmung f occupational palsy (paralysis)
Berufsneurose f occupational neurosis
Berufsnystagmus m occupational nystagmus
Berufsschaden m occupational (industrial) injury
Berufsspasmus m occupational spasm
Berufstaubheit f occupational deafness
Berufstumor m occupational tumour
Berufsverletzung f occupational (industrial) injury
beruhigen to calm, to tranquilize, to sedate
beruhigend calming, calmative, tranquilizing, sedative, ataraxic, ataractic
Beruhigung f calming, tranquilization, sedation
Beruhigungsbad n sedative [agent] bath
Beruhigungsmittel n calmative [agent], sedative [agent], tranquilizer, depressant, depressor
Berührungsangst f haphephobia, haptephobia
Berührungsempfindlichkeit f thigm[o]aesthesia, sensitiveness to touch
Berührungsempfindung f tactile sensation, sensation of touch
Berührungslokalisation f topaesthesia
Berührungsreflex m tactile reflex
Berührungsreiz m thigmotropism, tactile stimulus
Berührungsschmerz m haphalgesia, sensation of pain
berührungsschmerzhaft tender
Berührungsschmerzhaftigkeit f tenderness
Berührungssinn m sense of touch
Berührungssinnverlust m atactilia
berührungsüberempfindlich hyperaesthetic
Berührungsüberempfindlichkeit f hyperaesthesia, oxyaesthesia, hyperaphia
~ **der Gebärmutter** metryperaesthesia
Berührungsunempfindlichkeit f thigmanaesthesia
berührungsunterempfindlich hypaesthesic, hypaesthetic
Berührungsunterempfindlichkeit f hypaesthesia
Berylliose f berylliosis
Berylliumstaublunge[nerkrankung] f s. Berylliose
besamen to inseminate
~/**künstlich** to inseminate artificially
Besamung f [in]semination
~/**heterologe** heterologous (donor) insemination
~/**homologe** homologous insemination
~/**künstliche** artificial insemination
Besatz m border
beschädigen to injure
Beschädigung f injury
Beschaffenheit f/**venöse** venosity (des Blutes)
Beschäftigung f/**hypochondrische** hypochondriacal preoccupation (Zwangshandlung)

Beschäftigungskrampf m occupational (professional) cramp
Beschäftigungsneuritis f occupational (professional) neuritis
Beschäftigungsneurose f occupational (craft) neurosis, professional hyperkinesia
Beschäftigungstherapie f occupational therapy
Beschäftigungswahn m occupational delirium
bescheinigen to certify, to issue a certificate, to attest
beschleunigen to accelerate (z. B. den Puls)
~/**die Nervenleitfähigkeit** s. bahnen
Beschleunigung f acceleration (z. B. Puls)
Beschleunigungsnerv m accelerator [nerve]
Beschleunigungszentrum n accelerating centre (des Herzens)
Beschmutzungsfurcht f mysophobia
Beschmutzungslust f mysophilia
beschneiden to circumcise
Beschneidung f circumcision, peritomy, posthetomy, removal of the foreskin
Beschneidungsklemme f circumcision clamp
beschränkt dull, narrow-minded, stupid; simple
Beschränktheit f dullness, stupidity
Beschwerden pl complaints, trouble, discomfort, molimina; symptoms
~/**aktuelle** current complaints
~/**orthostatische** orthostatic complaints
~/**zunehmende** progressive symptoms
beseitigen to remove (z. B. Fremdkörper); to dislodge (einen Stein); to clear up (z. B. einen Eiterherd); to disinvaginate (eine Invagination); to eliminate, to eradicate (z. B. Keime)
Beseitigung f **einer Invagination** disinvagination
besessen obsessive, obsessional, obsessed
~/**von einer fixen Idee** monomaniacal
Besessenheit f obsession
besichtigen to inspect, to examine
besiedeln to populate (z. B. Bakterien)
~/**den Dickdarm** to colonize the large intestine (Bakterien)
~/**die Nase** to inhabit the nose
besiedelt sein/von Schmarotzern to be parasitized
Besinnung f consciousness ● **bei ~ sein** to be conscious ● **die ~ verlieren** to lose consciousness ● **ohne ~ sein** to be unconscious ● **zur ~ kommen** to recover consciousness
besinnungslos unconscious, without consciousness ● **~ sein** to be unconscious
Besinnungslosigkeit f unconsciousness
Besnier-Boeck-Schaumann-Krankheit f Besnier-Boeck[-Schaumann's] disease (syndrome), sarcoidosis; Boeck's sarcoid
Besonnenheit f discretion, prudence; collectedness
Besredka-Antigen n Besredka's antigen (Tuberkulosenachweis)
Besserung f improvement, remission, recovery
Besserungsphase f/**diabetische** diabetic remission phase
beständig resistant, stable (z. B. Bakterien); durable (z. B. Sporen)

beständig

~ gegen Pasteurisierung thermoduric, thermotolerant
bestätigt/durch Autopsie autopsy-confirmed
~/durch Laparotomie laparotomy-confirmed
Bestattung f funeral, interment, burial; cremation
Besteck n[/chirurgisches] set of [surgical] instruments
bestehend:
~/aus Fasern fibroid
~/aus Fibrin fibrinous
~/aus Häutchen membranous
~/aus Knochen osseous, osteal
~/aus Muskelgewebe sarcous
~/zur Hälfte aus Sehne semimembranous
bestellen/einen Arzt to send for the doctor
Bestialität f bestiality *(1. tierische Rohheit; 2. Sexualbeziehung mit Tieren)*
bestimmen to determine; to measure; to estimate, to identify
~/die Blutgruppe to type, to group
~/örtlich to localize
bestimmend/eine Krankheit pathognostic
Bestimmung f der Blutgruppe s. Blutgruppenbestimmung
~ der Morbiditätsrate nosomania
~ der phagozytischen Zahl opsonometry
~ der Zuckerkonzentration saccharimetry
bestrahlen to [ir]radiate; to X-ray
Bestrahlung f [ir]radiation; radiotherapy, ray therapy
~/multifraktionierte multifraction irradiation
~/postoperative postoperative radiation
Bestrahlungsblasenentzündung f irradiation cystitis
Bestrahlungschimäre f [ir]radiation chimera
Bestrahlungsdosis f irradiation dose; exposure dose
Bestrahlungsfeld n irradiation field (port)
Bestrahlungsfolge f, Bestrahlungskomplikation f radiation sequela
Bestrahlungskrankheit f radiation sickness (poisoning)
Bestrahlungslampe f [ir]radiation lamp
Bestrahlungsmutation f radiomutation, [ir]radiation mutation
Bestrahlungsplan m irradiation treatment plan
Bestrahlungsplanung f radiotherapy planning
Bestrahlungsprotokoll n irradiation record
Bestrahlungsraum m room for ray therapy
Bestrahlungsserie f [ir]radiation series
Bestrahlungssyndrom n [ir]radiation syndrome
Bestrahlungstechnik f irradiation techniques
Bestrahlungstherapie f [ir]radiation therapy; radiotherapy, ray therapy
bestrahlungsunempfindlich radioresistant
Bestrahlungsunempfindlichkeit f radioresistance
Bestrahlungszeit f exposure time
bestreichen/mit Jod[lösung] to iodize, to paint with iodine
~/mit Salbe to apply ointment to

bestreuen to sprinkle, to strew, to powder
Besuchszeit f visiting time (hours)
Betaglobulin n beta globulin
Betaglukuronidase f beta glucuronidase *(Enzym)*
Betahämolyse f beta h[a]emolysis
Betahämolysin n beta h[a]emolysin
Betalipoprotein n beta lipoprotein
Betalysin n beta lysin
Betaoxydation f beta oxidation *(Fettsäurestoffwechsel)*
Betarezeptor m beta-adrenergic receptor
Betarezeptorenblockade f beta-adrenergic receptor blocking (blockage)
Betarezeptorenblocker m beta-adrenergic blocker, beta-adrenergic [receptor] blocking agent
Betarhythmus m beta rhythm (wave) *(EEG)*
betasten to palpate, to dip, to touch
Betasten n palpation, dipping, touch
betastend palpatory
Betastimulation f beta-adrenergic stimulation
Betastrahlen mpl beta rays
Betastrahler m beta emitter
Betastreptokokken mpl beta streptococci
betäuben to benumb, to soporate; to put to sleep, to render drowsy *(durch Medikamente)*
~/durch Narkose to anaesthetize, to narcotize
~/lokal to anaesthetize locally, to administer a local anaesthetic
~/mit Äther to etherize
~/mit Chloral to chloralize
~/mit Drogen to dope
~/mit Kokain to cocainize
~/Schmerzen to dull, to deaden
Betäuben n s. Betäubung 1.
betäubend anaesthetic, narcotic; soporiferous, soporific, stupefacient
betäubt numb; narcotic, anaesthetized
Betäubung f 1. anaesthetization; stupefaction; dulling *(von Schmerzen);* 2. an[a]esthesia, narcosis; numbness; unconsciousness; stupor
~/örtliche local anaesthesia (analgesia), regional [block] anaesthesia
Betäubungsmittel n anaesthetic, narcotic [agent]; stupefacient [agent]
~/lokales local anaesthetic
Betazellen fpl beta cells
Betazerfall m beta decay *(Radiologie)*
Betelnußkarzinom n betel-nut carcinoma
Betelnußkauen n betel chewing
Beteltumor m betel-nut tumour
betreuen/ärztlich to medicate
~/Kranke to care, to nurse
Betreuung f/ärztliche (medizinische) medical care
~/umfassende comprehensive care
Betriebsarzt m factory doctor, works medical officer
betroffen 1. affected, involved *(z. B. Organe);* 2. embarrassed; shocked *(psychisch)*
~/von Schlafanfällen narcoleptic
Bett n/hydrostatisches hydrostatic bed

Bewegungsfähigkeit

Bettbügel *m* bed cradle
betten/in Paraffin to embed in[to] paraffin
Bettendorff-Probe *f* Bettendorff's test
Bettenkapazität *f* patient capacity
bettlägerig bedridden, bedfast, confined to bed
● ~ **werden** to become bedridden
Bettnässen *n* enuresis, bed-wetting
~/**nächtliches** nocturnal enuresis, nocturia
bettnässend enuretic
Bettruhe *f* bed rest
Bettschüssel *f* bedpan
Bettwaage *f* weighing-bed
betupfen to dab *(z. B. Stirn);* to swab *(z. B. Wunden);* to paint *(z. B. mit Jod)*
Betz-Riesenpyramidenzellen *fpl* Betz's giant pyramidal cells
Beuge *f* bend *(z. B. Ellenbogen)*
Beugebewegung *f* flexion
Beugefurche *f* flexion crease
Beugekontraktur *f* flexion contracture
Beugemuskel *m* flexor [muscle]
Beugemuskelreflex *m* flexor reflex
beugen to bend, to flex
~/**nach vorn** to anteflex, to ventriflex, to antevert *(z. B. Gebärmutter)*
~/**rückwärts** to dorsiflex, to reclinate
Beuger *m* flexor [muscle]
Beugereflex *m* flexion reflex
Beugerhalteband *n* flexor retinaculum of the wrist
Beugesehne *f* flexor tendon (sinew)
Beugesehnentransplantation *f* flexor tendon grafting
Beugung *f* 1. version, flexion, incurvation; 2. diffraction *(des Lichts)*
~ **des Fußes nach der Fußsohle** plantar flexion
Beugungshof *m* diffraction area *(Mikroskopie)*
Beugungsindex *m* index of diffraction, diffraction index
Beugungsmesser *m s.* Beugungswinkelmesser
Beugungsparaplegie *f* paraplegia in flexion
Beugungswinkel *m* 1. angle of inclination *(des Beckens);* 2. angle of diffraction *(Optik)*
Beugungswinkelmesser *m* fleximeter, arthrometer *(für Gelenke)*
Beule *f* lump, swelling; boil *(Furunkel);* tumour; bruise
Beulenkrankheit *f*/**ägyptische** oriental sore
Beulenpest *f* 1. bubonic (glandular) plague; 2. Black Death, black plague
beunruhigt disturbed, troubled, alarmed, maladjusted
Beutel *m* bursa *(Anatomie);* pouch, sac, bag
Beutelblase *f* sacculated bladder
beutelförmig pouched, sacculated, saccular, purse-shaped
Bévan-Operation *f* Bévan's operation *(bei Hodenfehllagerung)*
BE-Virus *n* Barr-Epstein virus
Bevölkerungsabnahme *f* decrease in population
Bevölkerungsdichte *f* density of population
Bevölkerungsimmunität *f* population immunity
Bevölkerungspolitik *f* population policy
Bevölkerungsstatistik *f* population statistics; demography
Bevölkerungsstruktur *f* population structure
Bevölkerungszunahme *f* increase in population
bewegbar movable; flexible *(z. B. Gelenk)*
bewegend [loco]motor, moving
~/**sich in einer Achse** uniaxial
beweglich 1. mobile; movable, motile *(z. B. Spermien);* wandering *(z. B. Bakterien);* migrating *(z. B. Leukozyten);* flexible *(z. B. Gelenk);* 2. mobile, active *(geistig);* 3. *s.* ambulant
● ~ **machen** to mobilize *(Gelenk)*
~/**nicht** non-motile
Beweglichkeit *f* mobility; activity; movability; motility *(z. B. von Spermien);* flexibility *(z. B. der Gelenke)*
~/**eingeschränkte** limited mobility
Beweglichmachung *f*/**chirurgische** mobilization *(z. B. von Gelenken)*
Bewegung *f* 1. motion, movement, locomotion; exercise; 2. *s.* Beweglichkeit; 3. *s.* Emotion
● **sich aus der ~ ergebend** kinematic
~/**auf Wärmereiz gerichtete** thermotaxis
~ **des Fetus/erste** quickening
~/**durch chemische Reize ausgelöste** chemotaxis
~/**geführte** passive exercise
~/**körperliche** physical (bodily) exercise
~/**kreisende** circumduction exercise *(z. B. der Extremitäten)*
~/**organgerichtete** organotaxis
~/**passive** passive exercise
~/**peristaltische** peristalsis, peristole, peristaltic movement *(von Hohlorganen)*
~/**unwillkürliche** involuntary movement
~/**verminderte** hypomotility *(z. B. des Darms)*
~/**verstärkte** hypermotility *(z. B. des Darms)*
~/**wurmähnliche** *s.* ~/peristaltische
Bewegungsablauf *m* [coordinated] movement
Bewegungsablaufstörung *f* movement disorder, dyskinesia *(der Muskeln)*
Bewegungsangst *f* kinesophobia, ergasiophobia
Bewegungsapparat *m* locomotor system
Bewegungsapraxie *f* kinetic apraxia
bewegungsarm hypokinetic; akinesic, akinetic
Bewegungsarmut *f* hypokinesia; akinesia
Bewegungsataxie *f* kinetic ataxia
bewegungsauslösend kinetogenic
Bewegungsausmaß *n* range of movement; joint range *(eines Gelenks)*
Bewegungsbad *n* kinotherapeutic bath
Bewegungsbestrahlung *f* rotation therapy, cineroentgenotherapy
Bewegungsdrang *m* hyperkinesia, hyperpraxia, hyperactivity
Bewegungseinschränkung *f* restricted movement
Bewegungsempfindung *f s.* Bewegungsgefühl
bewegungsfähig motile, mobile
Bewegungsfähigkeit *f* motility *(z. B. der Muskeln),* mobility

Bewegungsgefühl

Bewegungsgefühl n kinaesthesia, sensation of motion
Bewegungsgefühlverlust m kinanaesthesia
Bewegungskern m kinetonucleus, kinetoplast (z. B. bei Flagellaten)
Bewegungskoordination f movement (muscular) coordination
Bewegungskoordinationsstörung f ataxia, incoordination, coordination disturbance, dystaxia
~/**beidseitige** diataxia, bilateral incoordination (ataxia)
~/**einseitige** hemiataxia, monolateral incoordination (ataxia)
~/**extrapyramidale** paraballism
~/**partielle** dyspraxia
Bewegungslehre f kinesiology
bewegungslos akinesic, akinetic, immobile, immovable, non-motile, motionless
Bewegungslosigkeit f akinesia, immobility, motionlessness
Bewegungsmuster n kinetic (movement) pattern (der Muskulatur)
Bewegungsnerv m motor nerve
Bewegungsneuron n motor neuron
Bewegungsneurose f kinesioneurosis
Bewegungsnystagmus m kinetic nystagmus
Bewegungsplasma n kinetoplasm
Bewegungsreflex m motion (kinetic) reflex
Bewegungsreiz m motor stimulus
Bewegungsschmerz m kines[i]algia
Bewegungsschwäche f hypokinesia, hypomotility
Bewegungssinn m kinaesthesia, movement sense
Bewegungssteigerung f hyperkinesia, hypermotility
Bewegungsstörung f movement disorder, dyskinesia; motor disturbance
Bewegungssystem n locomotor system (organs)
Bewegungstherapie f kinesiatrics, kinesiotherapy, kinetotherapy, movement cure (treatment), exercises
Bewegungstremor m kinetic tremor
bewegungsunfähig immotile, immobilized
Bewegungsunsicherheit f bei Muskelparesen pseudoataxia
Bewegungsverlangsamung f/**allgemeine** bradykinesia, bradypragia
Bewegungsverminderung f hypokinesia, hypomotility
Bewegungswahrnehmung f motion perception
bewimpert ciliate[d]
bewirken/allergische Reaktionen to produce allergic reactions
~/**ein Trauma** to traumatize
~/**eine Beruhigung** to sedate
~/**eine Immunisierung** to immunize
~/**eine Infektion** to infect
~/**eine Krankheit** to cause a disease
~/**eine psychische Dämpfung** to sedate
~/**einen tetanischen Muskelkrampf** to tetanize
~/**Hämolyse** to haemolyze, to lake
~/**Immunität** to produce immunity
~/**indirekt (mittelbar)** to mediate
~/**Plasmolyse** to plasmolyze
~/**Übelkeit** to nauseate
bewirkt:
~/**durch Bakterien** bacteriogenic, bacteriogenous
~/**durch den Arzt** iatrogenic
~/**durch Insulin** insulinogenic
~/**durch Komplement** complement-mediated
~/**durch Luftdruck** pneumatic
~/**durch Medikamente** medicamentous
~/**durch Trauma (Unfall)** traumatogenic
bewußt conscious, aware
~/**nicht** unconscious
Bewußtes n conscious
Bewußtheit f consciousness, awareness
bewußtlos unconscious, insensible, faint (ohnmächtig); comatose, comatous ● ~ **werden** to lose consciousness, to become unconscious
Bewußtloser m unconscious person
Bewußtlosigkeit f unconsciousness, insensibility, apsychia, faintness, blackout; coma
~/**anhaltende** lethargic lethargy
~ **beim Aufrechtstehen/kurze** orthostatic syncope
~/**kurze** absence
~/**tiefe** profound unconsciousness; coma
Bewußtsein n consciousness; awareness ● **bei** ~ conscious, in a state of consciousness ● **das** ~ **verlieren** to lose consciousness ● **das** ~ **wiedererlangen** to recover (regain) consciousness ● **ohne** ~ unconscious ● **wieder zu** ~ **kommen** to recover consciousness
~/**[ein]getrübtes** clouded mind (consciousness)
Bewußtseinsaufhellung f/**vorübergehende** lucid interval (bei Schädel-Hirn-Trauma)
Bewußtseinseinengung f hypnotization, hypnoidization, hypnogenesis; narrowed consciousness
bewußtseinsklar conscious
Bewußtseinsklarheit f consciousness, clarity (lucidity) of consciousness
Bewußtseinsschwelle f threshold of consciousness
Bewußtseinsspaltung f splitting (dissociation) of consciousness; schizophrenia
Bewußtseinsstörung f disturbance of consciousness
Bewußtseinstrübung f clouding of the consciousness, disorientation
~/**kurz dauernde** gap, blackout; petit mal
Bewußtseinsverlust m loss of consciousness
bezahnt/gleichartig isodont[ic]
~/**ungleichartig** anisodont
bezeichnend symptomatic, characteristic, semeiotic
Beziehungsideen fpl ideas of reference
Beziehungssyndrom n, **Beziehungswahn** m delusion of reference
Bezirk m zona, region, area

~/kleiner zonule, zonula
~/umschriebener zona, circumscription, circumscribed area
Bezirksepidemiologe *m* district epidemiologist
Bezirkskrankenhaus *n* district hospital
Bezoar[stein] *m* bezoar *(geschwulstartiges Knäuel aus aufgenommener Nahrung)*
Bezold-Abszeß *m* Bezold abscess (mastoiditis) *(Eiterung im Schläfenbein)*
Bezold-Jarisch-Reflex *m* Bezold[-Jarisch] reflex *(blutdrucksenkender Reflex)*
Bezugswahn *m* delusion of reference
B-Galle *f* B (cystic) bile
BHR *s.* Bauchhautreflex
Bianchi-Syndrom *n* Bianchi's syndrome, sensory aphasia with alexia and apraxia *(bei Parietallappenschädigung)*
Biastigmatismus *m* biastigmatism
Biberschwanzleber *f* beaver-tail liver
Biblioklast *m* biblioclast
Bibliokleptomanie *f* bibliokleptomania *(krankhaftes Bücherstehlen)*
Bibliomanie *f* bibliomania
Bibliophobie *f* bibliophobia *(krankhafte Abneigung gegen Bücher)*
Bibliotherapie *f* bibliotherapy
Bichat-Fettpfropf *m* Bichat's fatty ball, corpus adiposum buccae, suctorial pad
Bicuspidalis *f* mitral (bicuspid) valve, left atrioventricular valve
Bidaktylie *f* bidactyly
Bidermom *n* bidermoma *(zweikeimblättrige Geschwulst)*
Bidet *n* bidet
biegbar flexible, pliable; supple
~/nicht stiff
Biegefestigkeit *f* bending strength *(z. B. der Knochen)*
biegen to incurvate; to bend
biegsam flexible, pliable
Biegsamkeit *f/***wächserne** waxy flexibility
Biegung *f* 1. bending, flexion, incurvation; 2. flexure, curvature, bend *(Zusammensetzungen s. unter Flexura)*
Biegungsdiffizillimum *n* flexion difficillimum
Biegungsfazillimum *n* flexion facillimum
Biegungsknochenbruch *m* flexion fracture
Bielschowsky-Syndrom *n* Bielschowsky's syndrome, Bielschowsky-Jansky disease, late infantile amaurotic familial idiocy
Bienengiftbehandlung *f* apiotherapy, melissotherapy
Bienenwabenmakula *f* **von Doyne** honeycomb choroiditis of Doyne
Bier-Anästhesie *f* Bier's local anaesthesia
Bierherz *n* beer heart; beer-drinker's cardiomyopathy
Biermer-Anämie *f* Biermer's anaemia (disease), pernicious (addisonian) anaemia
Biermer-Schallwechsel *m* Biermer's sign *(z. B. bei Pneumothorax mit Erguß)*
Bierprobe *f* beer test *(bei Gonorrhoe)*

Bier-Stauung *f* constriction (Bier's passive) hyperaemia
Biertrinkerkardiomyopathie *f* beer-drinker's cardiomyopathy
Bifidusfaktor *m* [Lactobacillus] bifidus factor
Bifidusflora *f* bifidus flora
Bifokalbrille *f* bifocal spectacles
Bifokallinse *f* bifocal (pantoscopic) lens
bifrontal bifrontal
Bifurcatio *f* bifurcation
~ aortae aortic bifurcation, bifurcation of the aorta
~ tracheae tracheal bifurcation, bifurcation of the trachea
Bifurkation *f* 1. bifurcation *(Anatomie) (Zusammensetzungen s. unter Bifurcatio)*; 2. dichotomy, dichotomous division *(Vorgang)*
Bifurkationsprothese *f* bifurcation graft
Bifurkationssyndrom *n s.* Leriche-Syndrom
Bigeminie *f* bigeminy, bigeminal rhythm *(Auftreten gekoppelter Extrasystolen)*
Bigeminus *m* bigeminal pulse, coupled beat (pulse)
Bigeminusrhythmus *m s.* Bigeminie
Bigler-Hsia-Syndrom *n* Bigler-Hsia's syndrome *(Lipidose)*
Biglieri-Syndrom *n* Biglieri's syndrome *(Defekt der Nebennierensteroidsynthese)*
Big-particle-Biopsie *f* big-particle biopsy *(z. B. aus der Magenschleimhaut)*
Bikarbonat *n* bicarbonate *(Blutpufferion)*
bikonkav biconcave, double concave, concavoconcave
Bikonkavlinse *f* biconcave lens
bikonvex biconvex, double convex, convexo-convex
Bikonvexlinse *f* biconvex lens
bikuspid[al] bicuspid
Bikuspidalklappe *f s.* Bicuspidalis
Bikuspidat *m* bicuspid [dens], premolar [tooth]
Bilateraladrenalektomie *f* bilateral adrenalectomy
Bilateralismus *m* bilateralism
Bild *n/***akustisches** acoustic image
~/klinisches clinical picture
~/röntgenologisches [X-ray] film
bilden:
~/Bindegewebe to fibrose
~/Blasen to vesicate
~/das Endothel to endothelialize
~/den Gelbkörper to luteinize
~/die Innenhaut to endothelialize
~/ein Geschwür to ulcerate
~/ein Konglomerat to conglomerate
~/ein Scheingelenk to ankylose *(Knochen)*
~/eine Fistel to fistulize
~/eine Hernie to herniate
~/eine Kaverne to cavitate
~/eine Narbe to cicatrize
~/einen Thrombus to thrombose
~/Epithel to epithelialize
~/Fettwachs to saponify

bilden

~/Gefäße to vascularize
~/Gerinnsel to embolize
~/Horn to keratinize
~/Kanälchen (Kanäle) to canalize
~/Keratin to keratinize
~/Knorpel to chondrify
~/luftgefüllte Hohlräume to pneumatize (z. B. in einzelnen Schädelknochen)
~/Melanin to melanize
~/Metastasen to metastasize
~/neu to regenerate
~/neue Gefäße to neovascularize, to canalize
~/Nitrat to nitrify
~/Quaddeln to urticate (Haut)
~/Salpeter to nitrify
~/Schorf to scab
~/Sporen to sporulate
~/Stimme to phonate
~/Wundschorf to scab

bildend:
~/die Dauerniere metanephrogenic
~/die Mitte medial
~/einen Blutpfropf thrombotic
~/Fettgewebe lipoplastic
~/Gelenkschmiere synoviparous
~/Gewebelücken lacunar
~/Samenzellen spermatogenic, spermatogenous
~/Serum serous

Bilder npl/**entoptische** entoptic imagery
Bildschirmgerät n video display (Radiologie)
Bildung f formation; development; growth, construction; production
~ einer Doppelmißbildung diplogenesis
~ weißer Blutzellen leucopoiesis
Bildungsfehler m malformation
Bildungsgewebe n/**undifferenziertes** blastema
Bildungshemmung f arrest of development (Embryologie)
Bildungsschicht f matrix (z. B. für Organe)
Bildverstärkerfluoroskopie f image intensification fluoroscopy
Bildwandler m image converter (Radiologie)
Bilharzieninfektion f, **Bilharziose** f s. Schistosomiasis
biliar, biliär biliary
Biliflavin n biliflavin (Gallenfarbstoff)
Bilifuszin n bilifuscin (Gallenfarbstoff)
Bilileukan n bilileukan (Bilirubinabbauprodukt)
Bilinogen n bilinogen (Galleabbauprodukt)
biliös bilious, biliary
Biliprasin n biliprasin, choleprasin (Gallepigment)
Bilirubin n bilirubin (Gallenfarbstoff)
~/direktes conjugated (direct-reacting) bilirubin
~/indirektes unconjugated (indirect-reacting) bilirubin
~/konjugiertes s. ~/direktes
~/nichtkonjugiertes s. ~/indirektes
Bilirubinämie f bilirubinaemia
Bilirubinausscheidung f im Urin bilirubinuria
~ im Urin/erhöhte hyperbilirubinuria
Bilirubinbelastungsprobe f bilirubin [clearance] test

Bilirubinenzephalopathie f s. Kernikterus
Bilirubinglukuronid n bilirubin glucuronide (ausscheidungsfähige Form)
Bilirubinkonjugation f bilirubin conjugation
Bilirubinkonjugationsdefekt m defect in bilirubin conjugation
Bilirubinnachweis m im Blut/**Berghscher** Bergh's test, Van den Bergh's reaction
Bilirubinprobe f/**Gmelinsche** Gmelin's test
Bilirubinreaktion f bilirubin reaction
Bilirubinserumspiegel m bilirubin serum level
Bilirubinspeicherkrankheit f bilirubin thesaurismosis
Bilirubinspiegelerhöhung f im Blut hyperbilirubinaemia
Bilirubinspiegelverminderung f im Blut hypobilirubinaemia
Bilirubin-UDP-glukuronyltransferase f bilirubin UDP-glucuronyl transferase (Enzym)
Bilis f gall, bile, fel (Zusammensetzungen s. unter Galle)
Biliurie f biliuria
Biliverdin n biliverdin, choleverdin (Gallenfarbstoff)
Bilizyanin n bilicyanin (Gallenfarbstoff)
Billroth-I-Anastomose f Billroth I anastomosis (operation)
Billroth-II-Anastomose f Billroth II anastomosis (operation)
bilobulär bilobular, bilobate
bilokulär bilocular, biloculate
Bimalleolarfraktur f bimalleolar fracture, Pott's [eversion] fracture
bimanuell bimanual
binaural binaural, binotic
Binde f 1. bandage; arm band (sling), armlet; 2. sanitary towel (napkin) (bei Menstruation)
~/elastische elastic bandage
~/Esmarchsche Esmarch's bandage
~/T-förmige T bandage
Bindearm m s. Kleinhirnstiel
Bindearmkreuzung f decussation of the superior cerebellar peduncles, decussation of the brachia conjunctiva
Bindegewebe n connective tissue ● ~ **bilden** to form connective tissue, to fibrose
~/die Scheide umgebendes paracolpium
~/elastisches elastic tissue
~/embryonales mesenchyme, embryonic connective tissue, mesenchymal (mucoid) tissue
~/fibröses fibrous tissue
~/gallertiges mucoid connective tissue, Wharton's jelly (Nabelschnur)
~/retikuläres reticular tissue
~/subkutanes subcutaneous [connective] tissue
Bindegewebe... s. **Bindegewebs...**
bindegewebig/derb fibrous, fibrose
Bindegewebsbestandteil m connective tissue element
Bindegewebsbildung f formation (production) of connective tissue, inogenesis, desmoplasia, fibroplasia

~/embryonale mesenchymopoiesis
Bindegewebsentzündung *f* inflammation of the connective tissue, fibrositis
~ **neben dem Kolon** paracolitis
Bindegewebserkrankung *f* connective tissue disease, collagenosis
Bindegewebsersatz *m* connective tissue repair
Bindegewebserweichung *f* softening of the connective tissue
Bindegewebsfaser *f* [connective tissue] fibre
~/**elastische** elastic (yellow) fibre
Bindegewebsfaserbildung *f* fibrogenesis
Bindegewebsfreßzelle *f* endothelial phagocyte, endotheliocyte
Bindegewebsgerüst *n* 1. stroma *(z. B. in Organen)*; 2. cardiac skeleton *(des Herzens)*
Bindegewebsgeschwulst *f* connective tissue tumour, fibroma
~/**harte** desmoid [tumour]
Bindegewebsgrundsubstanz *f* fibroglia
Bindegewebshistiozyt *m* [connective tissue] histiocyte
Bindegewebshülle *f* connective tissue sheath (membrane), adventitia
Bindegewebshypertrophie *f* der Haut pachydermia; pachyderma
Bindegewebskapsel *f* fibrous capsule
~ **der Niere** renal capsule
Bindegewebsmassage *f* connective tissue massage
Bindegewebsmatrix *f* connective tissue matrix
Bindegewebsnävus *m* connective tissue naevus
Bindegewebsschädel *m* desmocranium, membranocranium
Bindegewebsscheide *f* connective tissue sheath
Bindegewebsstörung *f* connective tissue disorder
Bindegewebstumor *m* connective tissue tumour
Bindegewebs- und Fettgewebsgeschwulst *f*[/**gutartige**] fibrolipoma
Bindegewebs- und Muskelfasergeschwulst *f*[/**gutartige**] fibro[leio]myoma
Bindegewebsvermehrung *f* fibrosis
~/**knotige** fibromatosis
Bindegewebsverquellung *f*/**fibrinoide** fibrinoid
Bindegewebswachstum *n* fibroplasia
Bindegewebswanderzelle *f s.* Bindegewebshistiozyt
Bindegewebszelle *f* connective tissue cell, desmocyte
~/**embryonale** mesenchymocyte, mesenchymal cell
~/**stark verzweigte** reticular cell
Bindehaut *f* conjunctiva *(Zusammensetzungen s. unter Conjunctiva)*
Bindehaut... *s. a.* Konjunktiva...
Bindehautabstrich *m* conjunctival swabbing
Bindehautanschoppung *f* conjunctival congestion
Bindehautapplikation *f* conjunctival application
Bindehautaustrocknung *f* conjunctival xerosis; xeroma

Bindehautblutung *f* conjunctival haemorrhage, ophthalmecchymosis
Bindehautdeckung *f* conjunctivoplasty
Bindehautdegeneration *f* conjunctival degeneration
Bindehautentzündung *f* conjunctivitis, [blenn]ophthalmia *(s. a. unter Conjunctivitis)*
~/**allergische** allergic conjunctivitis
~ **durch Strahlen** actinic conjunctivitis
~/**eitrige** purulent conjunctivitis, pyoblennorrhoea
Bindehautepithel *n* conjunctival epithelium
Bindehauterythem *n* conjunctival erythema
Bindehautflecken *mpl*/**Bitotsche** Bitot's patches
Bindehautkalzifizierung *f* conjunctival calcification
Bindehautkatarrh *m* conjunctival catarrh, catarrhal conjunctivitis
~/**akuter** acute contagious conjunctivitis
Bindehautkrampfader *f* varicula
Bindehautlymphom *n* conjunctival lymphoma
Bindehautmelanom *n* conjunctival melanoma
Bindehautnävus *m* conjunctival naevus
Bindehautpetechien *pl* conjunctival petechiae
Bindehautpinzette *f* conjunctival forceps
Bindehautplastik *f* conjunctivoplasty
Bindehautreflex *m* conjunctival (lid) reflex, blink reflex (response)
Bindehautsack *m* conjunctival sac
Bindehautsaum *m* margin of the conjunctiva, margo conjunctivae
Bindehautscheitel *m* fornix of the conjunctiva
Bindehautschwellung *f* chemosis
Bindehauttrockenheit *f* xeroma; xerosis
Bindehautunterblutung *f* **des Auges** subconjunctival ecchymosis (haemorrhage)
Bindehautverletzung *f* conjunctival injury
Bindehautverpflanzung *f* conjunctival transplantation (grafting)
Bindehautzyste *f* conjunctival cyst
Bindendrucklähmung *f* tourniquet paralysis
Bindenklammer *f* bandage clamp
Bindenverband *m* bandage dressing
~ **für ein Auge** monoculus
Bindungsunfähigkeit *f* inability to establish contact *(Psychologie)*
Binet-Simon-Intelligenztest *m* Binet-Simon intelligence test
Bing-Horton-Neuralgie *f* Bing-Horton syndrome, Bing's erythroprosopalgia
Bing-Reflex *m* Bing's reflex *(bei gesteigertem Achillessehnenreflex)*
Bing-von-Neel-Syndrom *n* Bing-Neel syndrome *(Form der Makroglobulinämie)*
Binnenbündel *n* intersegmental tract *(des Rückenmarks)*
Binokelverband *m* binocle bandage *(für beide Augen)*
binokular binocular
Binokularakkommodation *f* binocular accommodation
Binokulardiplopie *f* binocular diplopia

Binokularität

Binokularität *f* binocularity
Binokularmikroskop *n* binocular microscope
Binokularsehen *n* binocular perception (vision)
Binswanger-Syndrom *n* Binswanger's disease (dementia, encephalopathy)
Bioblock *m* biostack *(zum Nachweis von Teilchenstrahlung)*
Biochemie *f* biochemistry, physiological chemistry
biochemisch biochemical, physiochemical
Biodynamik *f* biodynamics *(Lehre von der Lebenstätigkeit)*
Bioelektrizität *f* bioelectricity
Biofeedback *n* biofeedback
Bioflavonoid *n* bioflavonoid, vitamin P complex, citrus flavonoid compound
biogen biogenous
Biogenese *f* biogenesis *(Entwicklung der Organismen, umfaßt Ontogenese und Phylogenese)*
biogenetisch biogenetic
Biohelminthen *fpl* biohelminthes
Bioinsektizid *n* bioinsecticide [agent]
Biokatalysator *m* biocatalyst
Biokinetik *f* biokinetics
Bioklimatologie *f* bioclimatics *(Lehre der Beziehungen zwischen Klima und Organismus)*
biokompatibel biocompatible
Biokompatibilität *f* biocompatibility
Biolumineszens *f* bioluminescence
Biomathematik *f* biomathematics
Biomechanik *f* biomechanics
Biomedizin *f* biomedicine
Biometrie *f*, **Biometrik** *f* biometrics, biostatistics
Biomikroskop *n* biomicroscope
Biomikroskopie *f* biomicroscopy
biomikroskopisch biomicroscopic
Biomorphose *f* biomorphosis
Bionik *f* bionics *(Wissenschaftszweig für technische Verwertbarkeit biologischer Strukturen und Prozesse)*
Biophagie *f* biophagy
Biophor *m* biophore, bioplast
Biophotometer *n* biophotometer *(zur Messung der Dunkeladaptation des Auges)*
Biophysik *f* biophysics
Biophysiologie *f* biophysiology
Bioplasma *n* bioplasm
Biopotential *n* biopotential
Bioprothese *f* bioprosthesis
Biopsie *f* biopsy *(Entnahme von Gewebsproben)*
Biopsieaufsatz *m* biopsy tip
Biopsieküretter *f* biopsy curette
Biopsiematerial *n* biopsy material
Biopsienadel *f* biopsy needle
Biopsieprobe *f* biopsy specimen (piece, sample)
Biopsiestanze *f* biopsy punch
Biopsiezange *f* biopsy forceps
Biorheologie *f* biorheology
Biorhythmus *m* biorhythm
Bios *m* **I** bios I, inositol
~ **IIa** bios IIa, pantothenic acid
~ **IIb** bios IIb, biotin *(Vitamin H)*

Biose *f* biose
Biostatistik *f* biostatistics
Biosynthese *f* biosynthesis
biosynthetisch biosynthetic
Biot-Atemtyp *m* Biot's breathing (respiration) type, Biot's sign
Biotelemetrie *f* biotelemetry *(Meßwertübertragung von Lebensvorgängen)*
Biotest *m* bioassay
Biotin *n* biotin, bios IIb *(Vitamin H)*
Biotransformation *f* biotransformation
Biotropismus *m* biotropism
Biotyp *m* biotype
Bioverfügbarkeit *f* bioavailability
biovular biovular
Biowissenschaft *f* life science
Biozid *n* biocide [agent]
bipar biparous
Bipara *f* bipara
Bipolardruck *m* bipolar pressure
Bipolarität *f* bipolarity
birnenförmig piriform, pyriform, pear-shaped
Bisexualität *f* bisexuality, ambisexuality; hermaphroditism
bisexuell bisexual, ambisexual, ambosexual; hermaphroditic
Biskrabeule *f* Biskra button, cutaneous leishmaniasis [of the Old World], Delhi boil, China (Kandahar, oriental) sore *(Hautleishmaniose)*
Bismuthismus *m* bismuthism, bismuthosis
Bisonnacken *m* bison neck *(bei Morbus Cushing)*
Biß *m*/**geschlossener** closed bite *(der Zähne)*
~/**offener** open bite, open-bite malocclusion, non-occlusion, infra-occlusion
~/**tiefer** supra-occlusion, supraclusion
~/**vorstehender** anterior bite (occlusion)
Bißanomalie *f* abnormal occlusion, malocclusion, occlusion abnormality
Bißebene *f* occlusal (bite) plane
Bißfläche *f* occlusal (bite) surface
Bißflügelaufnahme *f* bite-wing [X-ray]
Bißinfektion *f* bite infection
Bißnahme *f* odontoscopy
Bißring *m* bite ring
Bißstellung *f* dental occlusion
Bißverletzung *f* bite injury
Bißwall *m* occlusal guide
Bißwunde *f* bite [wound], morsus
Bistouri *m* bistoury *(Operationsmesser)*
Bitemporaldurchmesser *m* bitemporal diameter
Bitot-Flecke *mpl* Bitot's spots; xerosis conjunctivae
Bittner-Milchfaktor *m* Bittner milk factor
Biuret *n* biuret, allophanamide, carbamyl urea *(Harnstoffderivat)*
Biuret-Reaktion *f* biuret reaction
biventer, biventral biventer, biventral, digastric
biventrikulär biventricular
Bizeps *m* biceps [muscle], bicipital muscle
Bizepsaponeurose *f* bicipital aponeurosis
Bizeps-Femoris-Reflex *m* hamstring (biceps femoris) reflex

Bizepsfurche f/**seitliche** lateral bicipital sulcus
Bizepsreflex m biceps jerk (reflex)
Bizepssehnenruptur f rupture of the biceps [tendon], biceps [brachii muscle] tendon rupture
Bjerrum-Skotom n Bjerrum's scotoma
BKS s. Blutkörperchensenkungsgeschwindigkeit
Blähbauch m meteorism
blähen to cause flatulence, to inflate; to distend
blähend flatulent, gas-forming
Blähsucht f tympania, tympanism, tympanites, tympanosis; flatulence
Blähung f flatulence, flatus, wind
blähungsmindernd carminative
Blähungsmittel n carminative [agent]
Blalock-Hanlon-Atrioseptektomie f Blalock-Hanlon atrioseptectomy *(Herzchirurgie)*
Blalock-Taussig-Anastomose f Blalock-Taussig anastomosis *(Herzchirurgie)*
Blalock-Taussig-Operation f Blalock-Taussig operation *(Herzchirurgie)*
bland bland, light, mild *(z. B. Kost);* bland, sterile, aseptic *(z. B. Entzündung);* bland, not infected *(z. B. Infarkt)*
Blandin-Nuhn-Drüsen fpl Blandin's (anterior lingual) glands
Bland-White-Garland-Syndrom n Bland-White-Garland syndrome *(Ursprung der linken Koronararterie aus der Lungenarterie)*
Bläschen n vesicle, vesicula, blister; phlctenule, phlyctenula *(der Bindehaut);* phlycten[a] *(bei Verbrennung);* aphtha *(in der Mundschleimhaut)*
~/**synaptisches** synaptic vesicle
bläschenartig vesicular, vesiculate, blister-like; phlyctenular
Bläschenausschlag m herpes phlyctenulosis, dartre; pox
Bläschenbildung f vesiculation
Bläschendrüse f seminal vesicle
Bläschenekzem n vesicular eczema
Bläschenemphysem n vesicular emphysema
Bläschenentwicklung f vesiculation
Bläschenexanthem n vesicular rash
Bläschenflechte f herpes
Bläschenfollikel m vesicular (Graafian) follicle
bläschenförmig vesiculiform, vesicular; phlyctenular
Bläschenkeim m s. Blastula
Bläschenkeratitis f vesicular keratitis
Bläschenkrankheit f epidemic virus exanthema *(durch Coxsackie- oder ECHO-Viren)*
~ **der Hand** cheiropompholyx
Bläschenserum n blister serum
Blase f 1. bladder, vesica *(s. a. unter Harnblase);* 2. bulla, vesica, vesicle, blister, bleb *(z. B. der Haut);* cyst ● **Blasen bilden (ziehen)** to blister, to raise ● **über der** ~ supravesical
~/**atonische** atonic bladder
~/**große** macrocyst
~/**hypotone** hypotonic bladder
~/**irritable** irritable bladder
~/**kleine** microcyst
~/**neurogene** neurogenic (cord) bladder *(z. B. bei Querschnittslähmung)*

~/**paralytische** paralytic bladder
~/**tabische** tabetic bladder
~/**trabekuläre** trabecular bladder
Blasebalggeräusch n bellows murmur (sound) *(Herz)*
Blasen... s. a. Harnblasen...
Blasenanheftung f[/**operative**] vesicofixation
Blasenarterie f s. 1. Harnblasenarterie; 2. Gallenblasenarterie
blasenartig vesicular; cystic, cystoid; bladder-like
Blasenatonie f bladder atonia; atonic (string) bladder
Blasenatresie f atretocystia, bladder atresia; atretic bladder
Blasenausschlag m pemphigus, blister tetter; vesicular (bullous) eruption
Blasenausstülpung f exstrophy of the bladder; inversion of the bladder *(z. B. in die weibliche Harnröhre)*
blasenbildend vesicatory, vesicant, blistering, epispastic
Blasenbildung f vesication, blistering
~ **an der Hand** cheiropompholyx
Blasenbilharziose f bladder (vesical, urinary) schistosomiasis, endemic haematuria
Blasenbinnendruckkurve f cystometrogram
Blasenbinnendruckmesser m cystometer
Blasenbinnendruckmessung f cystometry
Blasendauerkatheter m indwelling urinary catheter
Blasendermatose f bullous dermatosis
Blasendivertikel n bladder (vesical) diverticulum
Blasendreieck n vesical trigone (triangle), trigone of the [urinary] bladder
Blasendreieckentzündung f trigonitis, collitis
Blasenektopie f vesical ectopia
Blasenemphysem n bullous emphysema
Blasenendometriose f endometriosis of the bladder
Blasenentleerung f micturition, voiding of the bladder, urination
Blasenentleerungsmuskel m detrusor vesicae [muscle], detrusor urinae
Blasenentleerungsstörung f voiding disorder of the bladder
Blasenentleerungstraining n bladder training
Blasenentwicklung f vesication
Blasenentzündung f [uro]cystitis, inflammation of the [urinary] bladder
~/**allergische** allergic cystitis
~ **durch Pärchenegel** schistosome cystitis
~/**eitrige** pyocystitis
~/**strahlenbedingte** radiocystitis
Blasenerkältung f chill on the bladder
Blaseneröffnung f cystotomy, vesicotomy
~ **durch Bauchschnitt** laparocystidotomy
Blasenerweiterung f cystectasia, dilatation of the bladder
Blasenerysipel n bullous erysipelas
Blasenexstirpation f 1. cystectomy; 2. bullectomy
Blasenfistel f vesical fistula, cystostomy

Blasenfistelung

Blasenfistelung f[/operative] vesicostomy, cystostomy
Blasenfixierung f[/operative] vesicofixation, cystopexy
blasenförmig vesicular; bullous
Blasenfunktionsstörung f bladder dysfunction
Blasengalle f B (cystic) bile
Blasengegend f vesical region
Blasengeschwulst f bladder tumour
Blasengeschwür n vesical ulcer
Blasengrieß m urinary gravel
Blasengrund m base (fundus) of the urinary bladder
Blasenhernie f bladder (cystic, vesical) hernia, vesicocele, hernia of the bladder
Blasenhypoplasie f bladder hypoplasia; dwarf bladder
Blaseninkontinenz f [urinary] incontinence
Blaseninnendruckmessung f s. Blasenbinnendruckmessung
Blaseninzision f bladder incision, vesicotomy
Blasenkatarrh m [endo]cystitis, catarrh (inflammation) of the bladder
Blasenkeim m s. Blastula
Blasenkontinenz f [urinary] continence
Blasenkörper m body of the urinary bladder
Blasenkrampf m cystospasm, vesical spasm, spasm of the bladder
Blasenkrankheit f 1. pemphigus, blister tetter *(Dermatologie)*; 2. bladder disease
~/ägyptische urogenital schistosomiasis
Blasenkrebs m bladder cancer (malignancy)
Blasenkrise f vesical crisis
Blasenlähmung f cystoplegia, cystoparalysis; paralytic bladder
Blasenleiden n bladder disease (trouble)
Blasen-Mastdarm-Fistel f vesicorectal fistula
Blasen-Mastdarm-Scheiden-Fistel f vesicorectovaginal fistula
Blasenmole f hydatid (cystic, vesicular) mole, hydati[di]form mole, dropsical ovum
~/destruierende destructive [placental] mole, malignant mole [of the placenta], invasive mole
Blasenmolenschwangerschaft f hydatid pregnancy
Blasenneuralgie f cystoneuralgia
Blasenpärchenegel m schistosomum haematobium, blood fluke *(Erreger der Blasenbilharziose)*
Blasenpunktion f vesical puncture, paracentesis of the bladder [wall]
Blasenreizung f irritation of the urinary bladder
Blasenrekonstruktion f cystoplasty
Blasenruptur f bladder rupture (injury), vesical laceration
Blasenschließmuskel m vesical sphincter, sphincter vesicae
~/innerer internal vesical sphincter
Blasenschließmuskelöffnungsmessung f cystosphincterometry
Blasenschließmuskeltraining n bladder training
Blasenschmerz m cystalgia, cystodynia, pain in the bladder

Blasenschnitt m cystotomy, vesicotomy
Blasenschwäche f s. Blasenatonie
Blasenserum n blister serum
Blasenspalte f fissure of the urinary bladder, cystoschisis; schistocystis
Blasenspatel m bladder spatula
Blasenspiegel m cystoscope, lithoscope
~ mit Steinzertrümmerungszange lithotriptoscope
Blasenspiegelung f cystoscopy
~ nach Lufteinblasung aerocystoscopy *(zur Aufdehnung)*
~ und Steinzertrümmerung f lithotriptoscopy
Blasensprenger m membrane puncturing forceps
Blasensprengung f artificial rupture of the membranes
Blasenspritze f bladder (urethral) syringe
Blasensprung m rupture of the amnion (foetal membranes)
~/vorzeitiger premature rupture of the amnion
Blasenspülung f bladder irrigation (rinse, washout)
Blasenstein m vesical (cystic) calculus, bladder stone, cystolith
Blasensteinentfernung f[/operative] cystolithectomy, cystolithotomy, lithocystotomy, vesicolithotomy
Blasensteinleiden n cystolithiasis
Blasenstichtrokar m cystotomy trocar
Blasenstottern n urinary stammering (stuttering), urinary intermittency; stummering bladder
Blasenteilresektion f hemicystectomy, partial cystectomy
Blasentrokar m bladder trocar
Blasenumstülpung f inversion of the bladder (z. B. in die weibliche Harnröhre)
Blasen- und Harnröhrenentzündung f cystourethritis
Blasenverletzung f bladder injury (laceration)
Blasenverschluß m bladder obstruction
Blasenvorfall m bladder hernia, cystocele
Blasenwand f 1. bladder wall *(der Harnblase)*; 2. vesicular wall *(Pathologie)*
Blasenwandentzündung f endocystitis
Blasenwandverkalkung f bladder wall calcification
Blasenwundspreizer m bladder retractor
Blasenwurm m echinococcus, caseworm, bladder worm, cysticercus
Blasenwurmfinne f hydatid
Blasenwurmkrankheit f echinococcosis, cysticercosis, hydatidosis, hydatid disease
Blasenzange f bladder forceps
blasig bullous, vesicular, vesiculate, blistered; phlyctenar, phlyctenous; cystic
blaß pale, pallid, wan ● **~ werden** to turn pale
Blässe f pallor, paleness
~/anämische anaemic pallor
~/periorale perioral pallor
Blastem[a] n blastema
Blastematose f blastematosis, blastopathy

Blastenschub *m* blastic crisis
Blastoderm *n* blastoderm, blastodermic (germ) membrane ● **unter dem** ~ subgerminal
blastodermal blastodermal, blastodermic
Blastodermzerfall *m* blastolysis
blastogen blastogen[et]ic, blastogenous
Blastogenese *f* blastogenesis
blastogenetisch blastogenetic
Blastokinin *n* blastokinin
Blastolyse *f* blastolysis
Blastom *n* blastoma
Blastoma *n* **ependymale** ependymo[cyto]ma *(vom Ependym abgeleitete Ventrikelgeschwulst)*
blastomatös blastomatous
Blastomatose *f* blastomatosis
Blastomer *n* blastomere, cleavage (segmentation) cell *(eines Eies)*
Blastomykose *f* blastomycosis, verrucous mycotic dermatitis
~/**europäische** European blastomycosis, cryptococcosis, Busse-Buschke's disease, torulosis *(durch Cryptococcus neoformans)*
~/**nordamerikanische** North American blastomycosis, Gilchrist's disease (mycosis) *(durch Blastomyces dermatitidis)*
~/**pulmonale** pulmonary blastomycosis
~/**südamerikanische** South American blastomycosis, paracoccidioidomycosis *(durch Blastomyces brasiliensis)*
Blastomyzet *m* blastomycete
Blastomyzetendermatitis *f* blastomycetic dermatitis
Blastomyzin *n* blastomycin
Blastomyzin-Hauttest *m* blastomycin skin test
Blastoneuropore *f* blastoneuropore
Blastopore *f*, **Blastoporus** *m* blastopore, protostoma, archistome, primitive mouth
Blastozöl *n* blastocoele, archicoele, cleavage (segmentation) cavity
Blastozyste *f* blastocyst, blastodermic vesicle
Blasttransformation *f* blastic transformation
Blastula *f* blastula, blastosphere, germ vesicle, vesicular morula, cleavage cavity *(Keimentwicklungsstadium)*
Blastulahaut *f s.* Blastoderm
Blastulation *f* blastulation
Blatt *n* 1. leaf, layer, membrane, lamina, table *(Anatomie)*; 2. blade *(einer Klinge)*
~/**parietales** parietal leaf *(z. B. des Bauchfells)*
~/**viszerales** visceral leaf *(z. B. des Bauchfells)*
Blatter *f* pock, pustule *(Symptom der Pockenkrankheit)*
Blattern *pl* blattern, variola, smallpox *(Zusammensetzungen s. unter Pocken)*
blatternförmig varioliform, vaccinoid, vacciniform
Blauausscheidung *f s.* Blauprobe
Blaublinder *m* tritanope
Blaublindheit *f* tritanop[s]ia, blue blindness
Blaue-Windeln-Syndrom *n* tryptophane malabsorption syndrome
Blaufärbung *f* **der Gliedmaßenenden** acrocyanosis
~ **der Haut** cyanosis; cyanoderma
~ **des Harns** urocyanosis
Blaugelbblindheit *f* blue-yellow blindness, tritanop[s]ia
Blauhusten *m s.* Keuchhusten
Blaulichtbehandlung *f* blue-light treatment
Blaupapier *n* articulating paper *(Stomatologie)*
Blauprobe *f* indigo carmine excretion test *(zur Nierenfunktionsprüfung)*
Blausäurevergiftung *f* hydrocyanism, hydrocyanic acid poisoning
Blauschwäche *f* tritanomaly
Blauschwachsichtigkeit *f* tritanomaly
Blausehen *n*, **Blausichtigkeit** *f* cyanop[s]ia, kyanopsia
Blausucht *f* cyanosis, cyanopathy
~ **des Neugeborenen** cyanosis of the newborn, morbus caeruleus neonatorum; blue baby
Blegvad-Haxthausen-Syndrom *n* Blegvad-Haxthausen syndrome *(zum Syndrom der blauen Skleren gehörend)*
Blei *n* lead ● **durch** ~ **bedingt** saturnine
Bleiabdeckung *f* lead shielding *(Strahlenschutz)*
Bleiamblyopie *f* lead amblyopia
Bleianämie *f* lead anaemia
bleiben:
~/**durchgängig** *s.* ~/offen
~/**karent (nüchtern)** to starve
~/**offen** to remain patent *(z. B. Ductus Botalli)*
bleich pale, pallid
Bleichsucht *f* chlorosis, chloraemia, chlor[o]anaemia, green sickness *(bei Mädchen)*
Bleienzephalitis *f* lead (saturnine) encephalitis
Bleienzephalopathie *f* lead (saturnine) encephalopathy
bleifarben livid
Bleigleichwert *m* lead equivalent
Bleigummihandschuhe *mpl* lead rubber gloves
Bleihand *f* lead hand
Bleikolik *f* lead (painter's) colic *(infolge von Bleivergiftung)*
Bleikrampf *m* lead spasm, painter's cramp, saturnine convulsion
Bleikrankheit *f s.* Bleivergiftung
Bleilähmung *f* lead paralysis, painter's palsy *(Lähmung der Streckermuskulatur nach Bleivergiftung)*
Bleineuritis *f* lead neuritis
Bleiplattennaht *f* button (shotted) suture
Bleipolyneuropathie *f* lead polyneuropathy
Bleirohrrigidität *f* lead-pipe rigidity *(der Muskeln)*
Bleisaum *m* lead (blue) line *(am Zahnfleisch)*
Bleischutz *m* lead protection *(Radiologie)*
Bleistiftstuhl *m* ribbon (lead-pencil) stool *(Zeichen für Dickdarmverengung z. B. bei Krebs)*
Bleivergiftung *f* lead poisoning, saturnism, plumbism ● **durch** ~ **hervorgerufen** saturnine
Blende *f* diaphragm *(Optik, Röntgentechnik)*
blenden to blind, to dazzle

Blendenöffnung

Blendenöffnung f diaphragm opening (aperture)
Blennorrhagie f s. Blennorrhoe
Blennorrhoe f blennorrhagia, blennorrhoea
~ **neonatorum** neonatal blennorhoea, neonatal ophthalmic gonorrhoeal infection
blennorrhoisch blennorrhoeal, blennorrhagic
Blepharadenitis f blepharadenitis
Blepharektomie f blepharectomy
Blepharitis f blepharitis, palpebritis, tarsitis
~ **angularis** angular blepharitis
~ **gangraenosa** gangrenous blepharitis
~ **marginalis** ciliary (marginal) blepharitis, psorophthalmia
~ **parasitica** parasitic blepharitis
~ **simplex** simple blepharitis
~ **squamosa** squamous blepharitis
~ **ulcerosa** ulcerative blepharitis
Blepharoadenitis f blepharoadenitis *(Entzündung der Meibomschen Drüsen)*
Blepharoadenom n blepharoadenoma
Blepharoatherom n blepharoatheroma
Blepharoblennorrhoe f blepharoblennorrhoea
Blepharochalasis f blepharochalasis
Blepharochromhidrose f blepharochromhidrosis
Blepharoklonus m blepharoclonus
Blepharokonjunktivitis f blepharoconjunctivitis
Blepharomelasma n blepharomelasma
Blepharon n blepharon, [eye]lid, palpebra *(Zusammensetzungen s. unter Augenlid und Palpebra)*
Blepharonkus m blepharoncus
Blepharoödem n blepharoedema, eyelid oedema
Blepharophimose f blepharophimosis
Blepharophym[a] n blepharophyma
Blepharoplastik f blepharoplasty
blepharoplastisch blepharoplastic
Blepharoplegie f blepharoplegia
Blepharoptose f [lash] blepharoptosis *(Herabhängen des Oberlids)*
Blepharopyorrhoe f blepharopyorrhoea
Blepharorrhaphie f blepharorrhaphy
Blepharospasmus m blepharospasm, blepharism
Blepharostase f blepharostasis
Blepharostat m blepharostat
Blepharostenose f blepharostenosis
Blepharosynechie f blepharosynechia, blepharosymphysis
Blepharotomie f blepharotomy
Blepharozyanose f blepharocyanosis
Blick m/**starrer** gaze, stare
Blickfeld n field of view (fixation), visual (fixation) field
Blicklinie f visual (fixation) line
Blicknystagmus m gaze nystagmus
Blickparese f gaze palsy
blind blind, amaurotic ● ~ **machen** to blind ● ~ **werden** to grow (become) blind
Blindbehandlung f blind treatment *(ohne exakte Erregerdiagnose)*
Blinddarm m blind gut, caecum, typhlon *(s. a. Wurmfortsatz)* ● **neben dem** ~ paracaecal
Blinddarm... s. a. Zökal... und Zökum...
Blinddarmanheftung f[/**operative**] typhlopexy, caecofixation
Blinddarmdivertikelentzündung f caecum diverticulitis
Blinddarmempyem n typhloempyema
Blinddarmentfernung f durch Unterbauchwechselschnitt McBurney's operation
~/**operative** typhlectomy, caecectomy
Blinddarmentzündung f s. 1. Appendizitis; 2. Zökumentzündung
Blinddarmeröffnung f durch Bauchschnitt laparotyphlotomy
~/**operative** typhlotomy, caecotomy
Blinddarmerschlaffung f typhlatonia
Blinddarmerweiterung f typhlectasia; megacaecum
Blinddarmfistel f 1. typhlostomy *(durch Operation)*; 2. caecal fistula
Blinddarmfistelung f[/**operative**] typhlostomy, caecostomy
Blinddarmgeschwür n caecum ulcer
Blinddarmhernie f caecocele
Blinddarmkrampf m typhlospasm
Blinddarmkrebs m caecum cancer (carcinoma)
Blinddarmnaht f typhlorrhaphy, caecorrhaphy
Blinddarmoperation f append[ic]ectomy
Blinddarmsenkung f typhloptosis, caecoptosis
Blinddarm- und Wurmfortsatzentzündung f typhlitis
Blinddarmverengung f typhlostenosis
Blindenfürsorge f typhlophilia, blind welfare, social service for the blind
Blindenheim n blind asylum
Blindenhund m guide (blind man's) dog
Blindenlehre f typhlology
Blinden[punkt]schrift f braille
Blinder m blind, amaurotic
Blindgang m blind pouch *(Anatomie)*
Blindheit f blindness, amaurosis, ablepsia, cecity, caecitas, typhlosis *(s. a. unter Caecitas)*
~/**psychische** mind blindness
~/**psychogene** hysterical blindness
~/**totale** total blindness, amaurosis
~/**transitorische** transitional blindness
~/**vorübergehende** blackout [of vision]
~/**zentrale** central blindness
~/**zerebrale** cerebral blindness
Blind-loop-Syndrom n blind-loop- syndrome, afferent loop syndrome
Blindsack m blind pouch (sac), pocket, cul-de-sac
Blindsacksyndrom n side-to-side-syndrome *(nach Darmanastomosenoperation)*
Blindschlingensyndrom n s. Blind-loop-Syndrom
Blindstudie f/**einfache** single blind experiment (test)
Blindversuch m blind experiment (test)
~/**einfacher** single blind experiment
~/**doppelter** double blind experiment
Blinzelkrampf m winking (nictitating) spasm
blinzeln to blink, to wink, to nic[ti]tate, to palpebrate

Blinzeln n nict[it]ation, palpebration
Blinzelreflex m blink reflex (response), winking reflex
Blitzangst f keraunophobia
blitzartig foudroyant, fulgurant, fulminous, fulminant *(z. B. Krankheitsverlauf)*
Blitzfigur f lightning figure
Blitzkrampf m lightning convulsion *(bei Epilepsie)*
Blitzlähmung f keraunoparalysis
Blitzstar m lightning (electric) cataract
Blitzverbrennung f lightning burn
Bloch-Sulzberger-Syndrom n Bloch-Sulzberger syndrome, incontinentia pigmenti
Block m 1. block[age], blocking, blockade *(Nervenleitungsunterbrechung)*; 2. s. Herzblock
~/alveolo-kapillärer alveolocapillary block
Blockade f block[age], blocking, blockade
~/fortlaufende extradurale sakrale continuous extradural sacral anaesthesia
~/fortlaufende kaudale continuous caudal anaesthesia
~/fortlaufende spinale continuous spinal anaesthesia
~/lymphatische lymphatic blockade, lymphostasis
blocken s. blockieren
blockieren to block *(z. B. den Endotrachealtubus)*
~/den Schmerz to block the pain
Blockierung f s. Blockade
Blockierungsanästhesie f block anaesthesia
Blockosteotomie f block osteotomy
Blockwirbel m block vertebra
blöd[e] imbecile, weak-minded, idiotic; dement *(im Alter)*
Blöder m imbecile, idiot; dement
Blödsinn m imbecility, weak-mindedness, idiocy; dementia
Bloom-Klippel-Trenaunay-Syndrom n s. Klippel-Trenaunay-Syndrom
Bloom-Syndrom n Bloom's syndrome, congenital teleangiectatic erythema
Blount-Syndrom n Blount-Barber syndrome, osteochondrosis deformans tibiae; non-rachitic bowlegs
Blow-out-Fracture f blow-out fracture *(des Augenhöhlenbodens)*
Blue baby n s. Baby/zyanotisches
Blue-bloater-Typ m blue bloater type *(Emphysematikertyp)*
Blue-diaper-Syndrom n blue-diaper syndrome, familial hypercalcaemia in infants *(bei gestörtem Tryptophanstoffwechsel)*
Blumberg-Zeichen n Blumberg's sign *(Appendizitiszeichen)*
Blumenkohlgewächs n cauliflower-shaped tumour
Blumenkohlohr n cauliflower (boxer's) ear
Blut n blood, sanguis ● **aus ~ bestehend** sanguine ● **~ enthaltend** haematic ● **im ~ lebend** sanguicolous, living in the blood *(z. B. Malariaparasiten)* ● **in das ~ abgegeben werden** to be released into the blood ● **jemandem ~ abzapfen** to bleed a person ● **mit ~ gefärbt** sanguinolent ● **~ spenden** to donate blood ● **~ stillen** to sta[u]nch blood ● **~ übertragen** to transfuse blood, to make a blood transfusion
~/arterialisiertes oxygenated blood
~/arterielles arterial blood
~/gekreuztes cross matched blood
~/gerinnungsunfähiges incoagulable blood; anticoagulated blood
~/geronnenes coagulated (clotted) blood
~/hämolysiertes (hämolytisches) laked blood
~/in das Gewebe ausgetretenes extravasate, extravasation
~/inkompatibles incompatible blood
~/kompatibles compatible blood
~/konserviertes stored blood
~/okkultes occult blood *(z. B. im Stuhl)*
~/oxygeniertes oxygenated blood
~/peripheres peripheral blood
~/rh-negatives Rh-negative blood
~/Rh-positives Rh-positive blood
~/sauerstoffarmes s. ~/venöses
~/sauerstoffreiches s. ~/arterielles
~/ungerinnbares s. ~/gerinnungsunfähiges
~/venöses venous blood
~/verhaltenes pent-up blood
Blutabscheu m haemophobia
Blutagar m(n) blood agar
Blutagglutination f haem[o]agglutination
Blutalbumin n blood albumin
Blutalbuminmangel m hypoalbuminaemia, hypalbuminosis
Blutalkalimeßgerät n haemoalkalimeter
Blutalkalimessung f haemoalkalimetry
Blutalkohol m blood alcohol
Blutalkoholbestimmung f blood alcohol determination
Blutalkoholprobe f blood alcohol test
Blutanalyse f haemanalysis, blood analysis
blutanalytisch haemanalytic
Blutandrang m congestion [of blood]
~ nach dem Kopf cerebral congestion
Blutansammlung f haematoma
Blutanschoppung f congestion [of blood]
blutarm anaemic; bloodless
Blutarmut f anaemia, haemophthisis *(s. a. unter Anämie)*
~/aplastische aplastic (atrophic) anaemia
~ nach Blutverlust posthaemorrhagic anaemia
~/sideroprive iron deficiency anaemia
blutartig haematoid
Blutaspiration f aspiration of blood
Blutauffüllung f blood replacement
blutauflösend haemolytic
blutauflösungsverhindernd antihaemolytic
Blutauge n haemophthalmos
Blutausfluß m haemorrhage
Blutausstrich m blood film (smear)
Blutaustausch m blood exchange, exchange [blood] transfusion
Blutaustritt m extravasation *(aus einem Blutgefäß)*; sanguinous infiltration *(in das Gewebe)*

Blutbahn 118

Blutbahn f bloodstream; circulating blood, circulation
Blutbahnaussaat f, **Blutbahnstreuung** f bloodstream dissemination *(z. B. von Keimen)*
Blutbank f blood bank
Blutbeimengung f admixture of blood
Blutbestandteil m blood constituent (fraction)
Blutbestrahlung f/**extrakorporale** extracorporeal blood irradiation
blutbevorzugend haemotropic *(z. B. Parasiten)*
Blutbikarbonat n blood (plasma) bicarbonate
Blutbild n haemogram, blood picture (count)
~/**großes** complete blood count
~/**weißes** leuco[cyto]gram, white blood count, WBC
blutbildend blood-forming, haemopoietic, haematogenous, haemoplastic, sanguinopoietic, sanguifacient
Blutbildkontrolle f examination of the blood picture
Blutbildung f haema[to]poiesis, formation of blood, haemocytogenesis, haemo[cyto]poiesis, haem[at]ogenesis, haematosis, sanguification
~/**extramedulläre** extramedullary haemopoiesis
Blutbildungsgewebe n haemopoietic tissue
Blutbildungs[knochen]mark n haemopoietic marrow
Blutbildungsstammzelle f haemopoietic stem cell
Blutbildungsstörung f dyshaem[at]opoiesis, anhaemopoiesis, anhaemato[poie]sis
Blutbildungssystem n haemopoietic system
Blutbildungssystemkrankheit f haemopoietic system disease
Blutblase f blood blister
Blutbruch m haematocele
Blutbrust f haemothorax, haemopleura
Blutchlormangel m hypochlor[id]aemia
Blutdepot n blood bank
Blutdiagnose f haematological diagnosis, haemodiagnosis
Blutdialyse f haemodialysis
Blutdiastase f haemodiastase
Blutdruck m blood pressure; afterload ● **den [arteriellen]** ~ **senken** to lower the arterial blood pressure ● **den** ~ **messen** to take the blood pressure ● **mit normalem** ~ normotensive
~/**abfallender** falling blood pressure
~/**arterieller** arterial [blood] pressure
~/**diastolischer** diastolic [blood] pressure
~/**erhöhter** increased blood pressure
~/**erniedrigter** decreased blood pressure
~/**hoher** high blood pressure, hypertension, hyperpiesia *(Zusammensetzungen s. unter Hypertonus)*
~/**mittlerer** mean blood pressure
~/**niedriger** low blood pressure, hypotension, hypopiesia
~/**systolischer** systolic [blood] pressure
Blutdruckabfall m fall (drop, decrease) in blood pressure; hypotension, hypopiesia ● **einen** ~ **bewirken** to cause a fall of blood pressure

~/**orthostatischer** orthostatic (postural) hypotension
Blutdruckabweichung f dysarteriotony
Blutdruckanstieg m rise (increase) in blood pressure; hypertension, hyperpiesia
Blutdruckapparat m s. Blutdruckmeßgerät
Blutdruckaufzeichnung f tonoscillography
Blutdruckaufzeichnungsgerät n tonoscillograph
blutdruckerhöhend hypertensive, [arterio]pressor
Blutdruckerhöhung f s. Blutdruckanstieg
Blutdruckerniedrigung f s. Blutdruckabfall
blutdruckhebend s. blutdruckerhöhend
Blutdruckkurve f blood pressure curve, tonogram
Blutdruckmanschette f sphygmomanometer cuff, blood pressure cuff
Blutdruckmesser m s. Blutdruckmeßgerät
Blutdruckmessergebläse n sphygmomanometer bulb
Blutdruckmeßgerät n sphygmomanometer, blood pressure manometer, haemodynamometer, haemomanometer, tonometer
Blutdruckmessung f sphygmomanometry, blood pressure measurement, haemodynamometry, tonometry
Blutdruckreaktion f [blood] pressure response
Blutdruckreflex m blood pressor reflex
Blutdruckregistriergerät n tonoscillograph
Blutdruckregistrierung f tonoscillography
Blutdruckregulation f blood pressure regulation
Blutdruckschwankung f heterotonia, variation in blood pressure
blutdrucksenkend antihypertensive, hypotensive, vasodepressor, depressant
Blutdrucksenkung f reduction in blood pressure
blutdrucksteigernd hypertensive, [vaso]pressor
~ **durch Vagus[nerven]reizung** vagopressor
Blutdruckstörung f dysarteriotony
Blutdrucktabelle f blood pressure chart
Blutdruckwert m blood pressure value
Blutdruckzügler m pressoreceptor *(in der Aorta)*
blutdurchsetzt blood-stained, blood-streaked *(z. B. Sputum)*
Blutdurchströmung f blood flow
blutdurchtränkt blood-soaked
Blutdyskrasie f blood dyscrasia, haematodyscrasia
Blutegel m leech, hirudo, blood sucker ● ~ **[an-]setzen** to leech, to apply leeches
~/**medizinischer** medicinal leech
Blutegelbefall m hirudiniasis, infestation with leeches
~/**äußerer** external hirudiniasis
~/**innerer** internal hirudiniasis
Blutegelbehandlung f hirudinization, leeching
bluteindickend blood sludging, thickening the blood, pachyhaematous
Bluteindickung f 1. haemoconcentration, pachyhaemia, anhydraemia, blood sludge; 2. blood sludging, thickening of the blood
Bluteinkreuzen n, **Bluteinkreuzung** f cross matching

Bluteisen n blood iron
Bluteisengehalt m/**verminderter** oligosideraemia
Bluteisenmangel m hypoferraemia
Bluteiweiß n blood (plasma) protein
Bluteiweißgehalt m proteinaemia ● **mit normalem** ~ normoproteinaemic
~/**normaler** normoproteinaemia
Bluteiweißmangel m hypoproteinaemia
Blutekel m haemophobia
Blutempfänger m blood recipient, donee
bluten to bleed, to haemorrhage
~/**unter die Haut** to suffuse
blutenthaltend blood-containing
Blutentnahme f withdrawal of blood [samples], blood collection, blood-taking
Blutentnahmenadel f blood lancet
Bluter m bleeder, haemophili[a]c
Bluterbrechen n haematemesis, bloody vomit[ing], vomiting of blood, melanemesis; black vomit
Blutergelenk n haemophilic (bleeders') joint, haemarthros
Bluterguß m haematoma, blood effusion (tumour, lake); ecchymosis
~/**epiduraler** epidural haematoma
~/**flächenhafter** suffusion, sugillation
~ **im Pleuraraum** haemothorax, haemopleura
~ **unter der Haut/flächenhafter** suffusion, sugillation
Bluterkrankheit f haemorrhagic (bleeders') disease, haemophilia
Bluterkrankung f s. Blutkrankheit
Blutersatz m 1. blood replacement; 2. s. Blutersatzmittel
Blutersatzlösung f physiological saline solution
Blutersatzmittel n blood substitute
Bluterythrozytenzahl f/**normale** normocytosis
Blutfärbeindex m [blood] colour index
blutfarbig blood-coloured
Blutfarbstoff m haemoglobin, blood pigment, haemochrome, haemachrome (Zusammensetzungen s. unter Hämoglobin)
blutfarbstoffbestimmend haemoglobinometric
Blutfarbstoffgehaltmesser m s. Blutfarbstoffmesser
Blutfarbstoffgehaltsbestimmung f s. Blutfarbstoffmessung
blutfarbstoffmessend haemoglobinometric
Blutfarbstoffmesser m haemoglobinometer, haemochromometer, haematinometer, tintometer
Blutfarbstoffmessung f haemoglobinometry, haemometry, tintometry
Blutfehlbildung f dyshaem[at]opoiesis
Blutfilarie f blood filaria, Filaria (Wucheria) bancrofti
Blutfilm m/**dicker** thick blood film (beim Blutausstrich)
~/**dünner** thin blood film (beim Blutausstrich)
Blutfleck m blood spot (stain), petechia

Blutfleckenkrankheit f [thrombopenic] purpura, peliosis, purple, Werlhof's disease (Zusammensetzungen s. unter Purpura)
Blutfluß m blood flow
Blutflußmeßgerät n haemodromometer, haemotachometer, tachygraph
Blutflußmessung f haemodromometry, haemotachometry
Blutflußratenmesser m s. Blutflußmeßgerät
Blutflußschreiber m haemodromograph
Blutfraktion f blood fraction
blutfrei blood-free
blutführend sanguiferous, haemophoric, conveying blood
Blutfülle f hyperaemia, hypervolaemia, engorgement; poly[a]emia; congestion; plethora
~/**allgemeine** panhyperaemia
~/**venöse** venous congestion
Blutgas n blood gas
Blutgasanalyse f blood gas analysis
Blutgasanalyseapparat m blood gas analyzer
Blutgefäß n [blood] vessel, vas (s. a. unter Vas)
● **neben einem** ~ paravascular
Blutgefäß... s. a. Gefäß...
Blutgefäßabdrückung f angiopressure, forcipressure
Blutgefäßentwicklung f vessel development, angiogenesis
Blutgefäßinnervation f blood-vessel innervation
Blutgefäßklammer f blood-vessel clip
Blutgefäßmangel m hypovascularity
blutgefäßrekonstruierend angioplastic
Blutgefäßrekonstruktion f angioplasty
Blutgefäßzweig m arteriole, twig
blutgefüllt hyperaemic, haematose, haematic; turgid
Blutgehalt m blood content
~ **der Gebärmutter/vermehrter** metraemia
Blutgerinnsel n thrombus, blood clot, clot [of blood], coagulum (Zusammensetzungen s. unter Thrombus)
Blutgerinnsel... s. a. Gerinnsel... und Thrombus...
Blutgerinnselablagerung f **auf den Herzklappen** thromboendocarditis
blutgerinnselauflösend thrombolytic; thromboclastic
Blutgerinnselauflösung f thrombolysis; thromboclasis
~/**gesteigerte** hyperfibrinolysis
Blutgerinnselentfernung f [/**operative**] thromb[oembol]ectomy, excision of a thrombus
blutgerinnselentwickelnd thrombogenic
Blutgerinnselentwicklung f thrombogenesis
Blutgerinnselpfropf m thromboembolus
Blutgerinnung f blood clotting (coagulation), clotting of blood, haemocoagulation, thrombokinesis
blutgerinnungsauslösend thromboplastic
blutgerinnungsbeschleunigend thromboplastic
Blutgerinnungsdefekt m blood clotting defect

Blutgerinnungsfähigkeit

Blutgerinnungsfähigkeit f/spontane inopexia
Blutgerinnungsfaktor m [blood-clotting] factor
~ **I** [blood-clotting] factor I, fibrinogen
~ **II** [blood-clotting] factor II, prothrombin
~ **III** [blood-clotting] factor III, thromboplastin
~ **IV** [blood-clotting] factor IV, calcium
~ **V** [blood-clotting] factor V, [pro]accelerin, labile factor, serum accelerator globulin, cothromboplastin
~ **VI** [blood-clotting] factor VI, accelerin, accelerator globulin
~ **VII** [blood-clotting] factor VII, [pro]convertin, stable factor, serum accelerator factor, SAF, serum prothrombin conversion factor
~ **VIII** [blood-clotting] factor VIII, thromboplastinogen, antihaemophilic factor (globulin), AHF, AHG, plasma thromboplastic factor A, platelet cofactor I
~ **IX** [blood-clotting] factor IX, Christmas factor, [anti]haemophilic factor B (IX), plasma thromboplastic factor B, plasma thromboplastin component, PTC, platelet cofactor II
~ **X** [blood-clotting] factor X, Stuart-Prower factor
~ **XI** [blood-clotting] factor XI, [anti]haemophilic factor C (XI), [plasma] thromboplastin antecedent, PTA
~ **XII** [blood-clotting] factor XII, Hageman factor, HF, glass (contact) factor
~ **XIII** [blood-clotting] factor XIII, fibrin stabilizing factor, FSF, fibrinase
Blutgerinnungsfaktormangel m [blood-clotting] factor deficiency
Blutgerinnungsfaktor-VIII-Mangel m factor VIII deficiency, haemophilia A, antihaemophilic globulin syndrome
Blutgerinnungsfaktor-IX-Mangel m factor IX deficiency, haemophilia B, Christmas disease (factor deficiency)
Blutgerinnungsfaktor-XI-Mangel m factor XI deficiency, haemophilia C, Rosenthal syndrome
Blutgerinnungsfaktor-V-Mangel-Syndrom n [/angeborenes] parahaemophilia, Owren's disease *(Blutgerinnungsstörung)*
blutgerinnungshemmend anticoagulant
Blutgerinnungshemmung f anticoagulation
Blutgerinnungskrankheit f [blood] coagulation disease
Blutgerinnungsmechanismus m blood-clotting mechanism
Blutgerinnungsneigung f blood coagulability
Blutgerinnungsstörung f blood-clotting disorder
Blutgerinnungssystem n coagulation (blood clotting) system
Blutgerinnungszeit f coagulation time, [blood] clotting time
Blutgeschwulst f s. Hämatom
blutgetränkt blood-soaked
Blutgift n haemotoxin, blood toxin
blutgiftig haemotoxic
Blutgiftigkeit f haemotoxicity
Blutglukosespiegel m blood sugar level

Blutgranulozyten-Clearance f blood granulocyte clearance
Blutgruppe f blood group (type) ● **die ~ bestimmen** to blood-group, to determine (type) the blood group
Blutgruppen-AB0-Isoimmunisierung f blood group AB0 isoimmunization
Blutgruppen-AB0-System n blood group AB0 system
Blutgruppenantigen n blood group antigen
Blutgruppenbestimmung f typing of the blood, [blood] grouping, blood group determination
Blutgruppen-Duffy-System m Duffy blood group system
Blutgruppeneinteilung f blood group classification
Blutgruppenkreuzversuch m, **Blutgruppenprüfung** f cross match test, blood [cross] matching
blutgruppenspezifisch group-specific
Blutgruppen-Testserum n blood grouping serum
Blutgruppentypisierung f s. Blutgruppenbestimmung
Blutgruppenunverträglichkeit f blood group [AB0] incompatibility
Blutgruppenverhalten n blood type
Blutgruppenverträglichkeit f blood group compatibility
bluthaltig blood-containing, sanguineous, sanguiferous, haematic
Bluthämoglobingehalt m/**normaler** normochromia
Blutharnen n haematuria, haematuresis
Blutharnstoff m blood urea
Blutharnstoffbestimmung f blood urea estimation
Blutharnstoffspiegel m blood urea level
Blutharnstoffstickstoff m blood urea nitrogen
Blut-Hirn-Schranke f blood-brain barrier, blood-cerebral barrier, blood-cerebrospinal fluid barrier, blood-cortical barrier, haematoencephalic (haematic encephalic) barrier
Bluthochdruck m hypertension, hyperpiesia, high blood pressure *(Zusammensetzungen s. unter Hypertonus)*
Bluthochdruckkopfschmerz m pressor headache
Bluthusten m haemoptysis, emptysis
Bluthusten n expectoration of blood, spitting of blood-stained sputum
blutig bloody, sanguinolent, sanguine, sanguinous, haematose, haematic; blood-stained, blood-tinged
blutig-eitrig sanguinopurulent
blutig-schleimig sanguinomucous, mucosanguinous
blutig-serös sanguinoserous, serosanguineous
Blut-Innenohr-Schranke f blood-inner ear barrier
Blutinseln fpl blood islands (islets)
Blutkaliumgehalt m/**normaler** normokalaemia
Blutkaliummangel m hypokalaemia, hypopotassaemia

Blutkaliumspiegel/mit normalem normokalaemic
Blutkalziumgehalt m/**normaler** normocalcaemia
Blutkalziumspiegel/mit normalem normocalcaemic
Blut-Kammerwasser-Schranke f blood-aqueous [humour] barrier
Blutkapillare f capillary, micrangium
Blutkoagel n thrombus, coagulum, blood clot
Blutkoagulabilität f blood coagulability
Blutkonkrement n blood calculus, haemolith
Blutkonserve f banked (stored) blood
Blutkonservierung f blood conservation
Blutkörperchen n blood cell (corpuscle) haem[at]ocyte
~/**rotes** red [blood] cell, red [blood] corpuscle, RBC, rbc, blood disk, erythrocyte, haematid (Zusammensetzungen s. unter Erythrozyt)
~/**weißes** white [blood] cell, white [blood] corpuscle, WBC, wbc, leucocyte (Zusammensetzungen s. unter Leukozyt)
Blutkörperchenagglutination f erythrocyte agglutination, haem[o]agglutination
Blutkörperchenauflösung f haemo[cyto]lysis, globulysis
~ **durch körpereigenes Serum** autohaemolysis
Blutkörperchenkrankheit f erythropathy
Blutkörperchenmangel m erythro[cyto]penia, deficiency in erythrocytes
Blutkörperchenmessung f erythrocytometry
Blutkörperchensenkung f erythrocyte (blood) sedimentation, erythrosedimentation
Blutkörperchensenkungsgeschwindigkeit f erythrocyte (blood) sedimentation rate, ESR, BSR
Blutkörperchensenkungsreaktion f erythrocyte (blood) sedimentation test
~ **nach Westergren** Westergren method
Blutkörperchensenkungsröhrchen n sedimentometer
Blutkörperchenzählapparat m haemocytometer; erythro[cyto]meter
Blutkörperchenzählkammer f counting cell (chamber), haema[to]cytometer, haemo[cyto]meter, haematimeter; erythrocytometer
Blutkörperchenzählung f blood count, haema[to]cytometry, haemo[cyto]metry; erythrocytometry
blutkörperchenzerstörend blood cell destroying, haemo[cyto]lytic, globulicidal
Blutkrankheit f blood disease, haemopathy, dysaemia, haematodyscrasia, nosohaemia
~/**Biermersche** Biermer's anaemia (disease), pernicious anaemia
Blutkrankheitslehre f haemopathology, haematologic pathology
Blutkreislauf m [blood] circulation (Zusammensetzungen s. unter Kreislauf)
Blutkreuzprobe f, **Blutkreuzung** f blood cross matching, matching of blood
Blutkuchen m blood clot

Blutkuchenschrumpfung f clot retraction
Blutkultur f blood culture
Blutlakune f blood lacuna
Blut-Leber-Schranke f blood-liver barrier
blutleer bloodless, exsanguin[at]e, pale; anaemic; ischaemic
Blutleere f bloodlessness, exsanguinity, paleness; anaemia; ischaemia
~/**Esmarchsche** Esmarch's exsanguination
~/**örtliche** local anaemia
Blutlehre f haematology
Blutleiter m [cavernous] sinus
Blutleiterblutung f sinus haemorrhage
blutliebend haemophilic, haemotropic (z. B. Parasiten)
Blutlipidmangel m hypolip[id]aemia
Blut-Liquor-Schranke f s. Blut-Hirn-Schranke
blutlos bloodless, exsanguine, exsanguinate
Blutlosigkeit f bloodlessness, exsanguinity
Blutlymphe f haemolymph
Blutlymphknoten m haemolymph node
Blutlymphozyt m blood lymphocyte
Blutmal n birth mark, naevus, spiloma (umschriebene, anlagebedingte oder erbliche Fehlbildung der Haut)
Blutmangel m deficiency (lack) of blood; anaemia
~ **im Herzen** acardiohaemia
Blutmassentransfusion f massive [blood] transfusion
Blutmenge f s. Blutvolumen
Blutmole f blood (haematoma) mole, haematomole (Plazentamißbildung)
Blutmuster n/**Bolensches** Bolen test
Blutnachweis m blood test
Blutnährboden m blood agar
Blut-Netzhaut-Schranke f blood-retina barrier
Blutoxygenation f blood oxygenation, haematosis
Blutparasit m blood (haematozoic) parasite, haem[at]ozoon
Blutpfropf m thrombus, coagulum, blood clot
● **einen ~ bildend** thrombotic
Blutpfropfbildung f thrombosis
Blutpfropfembolie f thromboembolism
Blut-pH-Wert m blood ph [value] ● **den ~ erhöhend** alkalescent
Blut-pH-Wert-Erhöhung f alkalosis, alkalaemia
Blut-pH-Wert-Senkung f acidosis
Blutpigment n s. Blutfarbstoff
Blutplasma n [blood] plasma (Zusammensetzungen s. unter Plasma)
Blutplasma... s. a. Plasma...
Blutplasmabehandlung f plasmatherapy, plasmotherapy
Blutplasmamangel m apoplasmia, oligoplasmia, mioplasma
Blutplasmaüberschuß m polyplasmia
Blutplasmaverdünnung f hydroplasmia
Blutplättchen n s. Thrombozyt
Blutplättchen... s. a. Thrombozyten...
Blutplättchenanomalie f thrombo[cyto]pathy

blutplättchenauflösend

blutplättchenauflösend thrombocytolytic
Blutplättchenauflösung f thrombocytolysis, dissolution of blood platelets
blutplättchenbildend thrombo[cyto]poietic
Blutplättchenbildung f thrombo[cyto]poiesis, formation of blood platelets
Blutplättchenfunktionsstörung f thrombo[cyto]pathy
Blutplättchenthrombus m platelet thrombus
Blutplättchenzählgerät n thrombocytocrit
Blut-pool-Szintigraphie f blood-pool scintigraphy
Blutpräparat n blood preparation
Blutpräzipitin n haemoprecipitin
Blutprobe f 1. blood sample (specimen); 2. s. Blutuntersuchung
Blutprotozoon n blood protozoon
Blutpumpe f blood pump
Blutpunkt m bleeding point *(z. B. der Diphtheriemembran)*
blutreich plethoric, hyperaemic; congestive, turgid
Blutreichtum m plethora, hyperaemia; congestion, turgescence
Blutreinigung f blood purification
Blut-Retina-Schranke f blood-retina barrier
Blutrezirkulation f recirculation of blood
Blutrückstrom m regurgitation; regurgitant stream of blood *(z. B. bei insuffizienten Herzklappen)*
Blutsauerstoff m blood (circulating) oxygen
Blutsauerstoffdissoziationskurve f blood oxygen dissociation curve
Blutsauerstoffgehalt m blood oxygen content
Blutsauerstoffverminderung f hypoxaemia
Blutsaugen n blood-sucking, sanguisuction, haem[at]ophagy
blutsaugend blood-sucking, haem[at]ophagous, haemophagic, blood-feeding, sanguivorous
Blutsäule f blood column
Blutschande f incest
Blutschatten m blood shadow, shadow corpuscle, phantom cell
Blutschizont m blood schizont *(Malariazyklus)*
Blutschwamm m [haem]angioma
Blutschwitzen n blood sweating, haem[ath]idrosis, sweating of blood
Blutsenkung f s. Blutkörperchensenkung
Blutserum n [blood] serum
~/lackfarbenes laky blood serum *(nach Hämolyse)*
Blutserumalbumin n blood albumin
Blutserumbikarbonat n blood bicarbonate *(Blutpufferion)*
Blutserumkultur f seroculture
Blutserumprobe f seroreaction, serological blood test
Blut-Shunten n shunting of blood
Blutsickern n oozing [of blood]
Blutspeicher m blood reservoir
Blutspende f blood donation
Blutspendedienst m blood transfusion service
Blutspender m blood donor
Blutspenderauswahl f blood-donor selection
Blutspendewesen n blood transfusion service
Blutspendezentrale f blood donor centre
Blutspezialist m haematologist, blood specialist
Blutspiegel m blood level
Blutspiegelbestimmung f blood level determination
Blutspiegel[verlaufs]kurve f blood level curve
Blutspucken n haemoptysis, spitting of blood, blood-spitting, emptysis
Blutstammzelle f blood (haemopoietic) stem cell, haemocytoblast
Blutstammzellenleukämie f haemo[cyto]blastic leukaemia
Blutstatus m blood picture
Blutstäubchen n haemoconia, blood dust
Blutstauung f blood stasis (stagnation), haemostasis, stagnation of blood; congestion
~/venöse venostasis, phlebostasis
Blutstein m haem[at]olith
blutstillend haemostatic, [haemo]styptic, ant[i]haemorrhagic, blood-stanching
Blutstillung f haemostasis, [haemo]stypsis, stopping (control) of haemorrhage, stanching of bleeding
~ durch Elektrokoagulation electrohaemostasis
Blutstillungsmeißel m haemostatic chisel
Blutstraße f trace of blood
Blutstrom m bloodstream, flowing blood
Blutstromgeschwindigkeitsmesser m rheometer
Blutströmung f bloodstream, blood flow
Blutströmungsgeräusch n haemic murmur
Blutströmungslehre f haemodynamics, haemorrheology
Blutstuhl m black faeces, haemorrhagic stools; mel[a]ena, melanorrhoea, haemochezia *(Schwarzfärbung durch Blutbeimengung)*
Blutsturz m haemorrhage, haematorrhoea; haemoptoe, haemoptysis, pulmonary haemorrhage; haematemesis
Blutsubstitution f blood substitution
blutsverwandt consanguineous, related by blood, kin
Blutsverwandter m blood relative, next of kin
Blutsverwandtschaft f consanguinity, blood relationship, kinship
Bluttherapie f haematherapy, haem[at]otherapy, haemotherapeutics
Blutthrombokinase f blood thrombokinase
Bluttiter m blood titre
Bluttransfusion f blood transfusion *(s. a. unter Transfusion)*
~/direkte direct (immediate) transfusion
~/indirekte indirect transfusion
~/langsame slow (drip) transfusion
Bluttransfusions... s. a. Transfusions...
Bluttransfusionsdienst m blood transfusion service
Bluttransfusionsgerät n blood transfusion apparatus

Bluttransfusionstechnik f blood transfusion technique
Bluttropfenmuster n/**Bolensches** Bolen test
blutüberfüllt hyperaemic, plethoric; congested
Blutüberfüllung f hyperaemia, plethora; congestion
Blutübersäuerung f hyperoxaemia, oxypathy
Blutübertragung f s. Bluttransfusion
Blut- und Chylusausscheidung f im Urin haematochyluria
Blut- und Luftansammlung f im Pleuraspalt haemopneumothorax
Blut- und Lymphausscheidung f im Urin haematolymphuria
Blutung f bleeding, haemorrhage, staxis, extravasation ● eine ~ **stillen** to stay a haemorrhage, to stanch (stop) a haemorrhage ● eine ~ **verhindern** to prevent haemorrhage
~/**arterielle** arterial (artery) haemorrhage
~/**äußere** external haemorrhage
~/**epidurale** epidural haemorrhage
~/**expulsive** expulsive haemorrhage
~/**extradurale** extradural haemorrhage
~/**heftige** s. ~/massive
~/**innere** internal (concealed) haemorrhage
~ **ins Rückenmark** spinal apoplexy
~/**intestinale** intestinal haemorrhage
~/**intraabdominale** intraabdominal haemorrhage
~/**intrakranielle** intracranial haemorrhage
~/**intrapartale** intrapartum haemorrhage
~/**intraperitoneale** intraperitoneal haemorrhage
~/**intrazerebrale** intracerebral haemorrhage
~/**juvenile** juvenile haemorrhage
~/**konjunktivale** conjunctival haemorrhage
~/**massive** massive (abundant, copious) haemorrhage
~/**monatliche** s. Menstruation
~ **nach Zahnextraktion** odontorrhagia
~/**neuropathische** neuropathic haemorrhage
~/**okkulte** occult haemorrhage
~/**parenchymatöse** parenchymatous haemorrhage
~/**petechiale** petechial (punctate) haemorrhage
~/**postoperative** postoperative bleeding (haemorrhage)
~/**postpartale** postpartum haemorrhage
~/**präklimakterische** menopausal haemorrhage
~/**profuse** profuse haemorrhage
~/**pulmonale** pulmonary haemorrhage
~/**pulsierende** pulsating haemorrhage
~/**renale** renal haemorrhage
~/**retroplazentäre** retroplacental haemorrhage
~/**retrovitreale** retrovitreal haemorrhage
~/**spritzende** spurting haemorrhage
~/**starke** profuse haemorrhage
~/**subarachnoidale** subarachnoidal haemorrhage
~/**subdurale** subdural haemorrhage
~/**subkonjunktivale** subconjunctival haemorrhage (ecchymosis)
~/**traumatische** traumatic haemorrhage
~/**venöse** venous haemorrhage, phleborrhagia
~/**vikariierende** vicarious haemorrhage, supplementary menstruation, xenomenia

Blutungsabszeß m haemorrhagic abscess
Blutungsanämie f [post]haemorrhagic anaemia
Blutungsbereitschaft f haemorrhagic diathesis, bleeding tendency, haematophilia
blutungsfördernd haemagogic, haemagogue
blutungsfrei dry, bloodless
Blutungsinfarkt m haemorrhagic infarct
Blutungskalender m menstruation chart
Blutungskrankheit f haemorrhagic disease (s. a. Bluterkrankheit)
Blutungsneigung f haemorrhagic diathesis, bleeding tendency, haematophilia; hypocoagulability, blood coagulation deficiency
Blutungsrezidiv n rebleeding
Blutungsschock m haemorrhagic (haematogenic) shock, blood-loss shock
blutungsstillend s. blutstillend
Blutungsstillstand m haematischesis
Blutungsübel n s. Blutungsneigung
blutungsverhindernd antihaemorrhagic
Blutungszeit f bleeding time
Blutungszeitbestimmung f/**Dukesche** Duke test
Blutunterdruck m hypotension, hypopiesia
blutunterlaufen suffused with blood, ecchymosed; blood-shot (Auge)
Blutunterlaufung f suffusion of blood, sugillation, extravasation; petechia, ecchymosis, haematoma
Blutuntersuchung f blood examination (test, study)
Blutverdünnung f haemodilution, hydraemia, hydroplasmia
Blutvergiftung f blood poisoning, sept[ic]aemia, py[oh]aemia, tox[in]aemia, toxicaemia, ichorrhaemia, [endo]sepsis (Zusammensetzungen s. unter Sepsis)
Blutverlust m blood loss, loss of blood ● ohne ~ bloodless
Blutverlustschock m haemorrhagic (blood-loss) shock
Blutversorgung f blood supply, supply of (with) blood
Blutverteilung f blood distribution, distribution of blood
Blutverteilungsstörung f disturbance of the blood distribution
Blutviskosität f blood viscosity, viscosity of blood
blutvoll plethoric, rich in blood, turgid
Blutvolumen n blood volume ● **mit normalem** ~ normovolaemic
~/**normales** normovolaemia
~/**zentrales** central blood volume
Blutvolumenauffüllung f blood-volume replacement, replenishment of blood volume
Blutvolumenbestimmung f blood-volume determination
Blutvolumenexpander m blood-volume expander
Blutvolumenmangel m hypovolaemia, blood-volume deficit, deficiency of blood volume
Blutvolumenmangelschock m hypovolaemic (haematogenic) shock

Blutvolumenvermehrung 124

Blutvolumenvermehrung f hypervolaemia
Blutvolumenverminderung f hypovolaemia, hyphaemia, oligaemia, blood-volume reduction
Blutwarze f angiokeratoma, teleangiectatic wart, keratoangioma
Blutwasser n s. Blutserum
blutwasserartig ichorous, ichoroid
Blutwassergehalt m/**verminderter** anhydraemia
Blutwassergeschwulst f seroma
Blutzählkammer f haemacytometer, haematimeter
Blutzelle f s. Blutkörperchen
Blutzellenauflösung f cythaemolysis
blutzellenbildend haemocytoblastic, haemocytogen[et]ic
Blutzellenbildung f haemocytopoiesis, haemocytogenesis
Blutzellenerhöhung f hypercythaemia
Blutzellenverminderung f hypocythaemia
Blutzellenzerfall m haemocytolysis, plasmoschisis
blutzellenzerstörend haemocidal, globulicidal
Blutzirkulation f blood circulation; circulating blood (volume)
Blutzucker m blood sugar (glucose)
Blutzuckerbelastungsprobe f blood-sugar tolerance test
Blutzuckerbestimmung f blood-sugar determination
blutzuckererhöhend blood-sugar increasing, hyperglycaemic
Blutzuckererhöhung f blood-sugar increase; hyperglycaemia, glycaemia, glucohaemia
blutzuckerfrei aglycaemic
Blutzuckergehalt m blood-sugar content
~/**normaler** normoglycaemia
Blutzuckerkontrolle f blood-sugar control (check)
Blutzuckerkonzentration f blood-sugar concentration
blutzuckerlos aglycaemic
Blutzuckermangel m hypoglycaemia
Blutzuckerprofil n blood-sugar profile
blutzuckersenkend blood-sugar decreasing, hypoglycaemic
Blutzuckerspiegel m blood-sugar level ● **mit normalem** ~ normoglycaemic
~/**erhöhter** hyperglycaemia
~/**niedriger** hypoglycaemia, glycopenia
~/**normaler** normoglycaemia
Blutzuckertoleranz f blood-sugar tolerance
Blutzuckerverhalten n blood-sugar reaction
Blutzuckerverminderung f blood-sugar decreasing; hypoglycaemia, glycopenia
Blutzufuhr f blood supply
Blutzusammensetzung f blood composition
Blutzyste f haematocyst, blood (sanguineous) cyst
B-Lymphozyt m B (bone-marrow, bursa-equivalent) lymphocyte
Boas-Druckpunkt m Boas' point *(bei Magengeschwür)*

Bochdalek-Dreieck n [Bochdalek's] lumbocostal triangle, vertebrocostal triangle
Bochdalek-Lücke f foramen of Bochdalek, pleuroperitoneal hiatus
Bockhart-Follikulitis f Bockhart's (follicular) impetigo
Bocksprungpuls m bounding (goat leap) pulse
Bodansky-Einheit f Bodansky unit
Boden m fundus, floor *(z. B. eines Organs)*; base
~ **des vierten (IV.) Ventrikels** floor of the fourth ventricle
Bodenhygiene f soil hygiene
Bodeninsektizid n soil insecticide
Bodensatz m sediment, precipitate, deposit, [bottom] settlings
Bodenverunreinigung f soil pollution
Boeck-Sarkoid n s. Besnier-Boeck-Schaumann-Krankheit
Boerhaave-Syndrom n Boerhaave's syndrome *(submuköse Ruptur der Speiseröhre)*
Boerner-Lukens-Syphilistest m Boerner-Lukens test
Bogen m arch, arcus, bow; curve; flexion *(Zusammensetzungen s. unter Arcus)*
Bogenband n/**mittleres** medial arcuate ligament
~/**seitliches** lateral arcuate ligament [of the diaphragm], lateral lumbocostal arch *(zwischen 2. Lendenwirbelquerfortsatz und 12. Rippe)*
~ **unter der Symphyse** subpubic ligament
Bogenfaser f arcuate fibre
Bogenfasern fpl **des Rautenhirns/äußere** external arcuate fibres
~ **des Rautenhirns/innere** internal arcuate fibres
bogenförmig arched, arcuate, arciform
Bogengang m semicircular canal (duct) *(Innenohr)*
~/**frontaler** superior semicircular canal
~/**häutiger** membranous semicircular canal (duct)
~/**hinterer** posterior semicircular canal [of the bony labyrinth of the inner ear]
~/**hinterer häutiger** posterior semicircular duct of the inner ear
~/**horizontaler** lateral semicircular canal [of the bony labyrinth of the inner ear]
~/**knöcherner** osseous semicircular canal
~/**lateraler** lateral semicircular canal [of the bony labyrinth of the inner ear], horizontal semicircular canal
~/**oberer häutiger** anterior semicircular duct of the inner ear
~/**vorderer häutiger** anterior semicircular duct of the inner ear
Bogengangsampulle f membranous ampulla
~/**hintere** posterior membranous ampulla
~/**vordere** anterior membranous ampulla
Bogenperimeter n arc perimeter
Bogenskotom n/**Bjerrumsches** Bjerrum's scotoma
Bohrdraht m drill wire
Bohrdrahtosteosynthese f drill-wire osteosynthesis

bohren to bore, to trepanize *(z. B. einen Schädel)*; to drill *(z. B. einen Zahn)*
Bohren *n* 1. boring, terebration, trepanation *(z. B. des Schädels)*; drilling *(Stomatologie)*; 2. boring, terebration *(z. B. von Schmerzen)*
bohrend boring, terebrating *(z. B. Schmerzen)*
Bohrer *m* trephine, trepan; perforator *(für Schädeleröffnung)*; drill, burr *(Stomatologie)*
~/zahnärztlicher dental engine, dentist's drill *(Apparat)*
Bohrerführungszange *f* drill guide forceps *(Stomatologie)*
Bohrloch *n* burr (bore) hole
Bohrlochostitis *f* burr-hole ostitis
Bohrlochschutzzange *f* bore-hole protection forceps *(für Knochen)*
Boloskop *n* boloscope *(Röntgenuntersuchungsgerät)*
Bolus *m* bolus
~ alba bolus alba, kaolin *(Adsorptionsmittel bei Darmkatarrhen)*
Bolusinjektion *f* bolus injection
Bolustod *m* bolus death
Bombenverletzung *f* bomb injury
Bonnet-Syndrom *n* Bonnet's syndrome *(Durchblutungsanomalie der Netzhaut)*
Bonnevie-Ullrich-Syndrom *n* Bonnevie-Ullrich syndrome, gonadal dysgenesis (aplasia, hypoplasia)
Booster-Dosis *f* booster dose
Booster-Effekt *m* booster effect
Booster-Impfung *f* booster inoculation
Boostern *n*, **Boosterung** *f s.* Booster-Impfung
Borborygmus *m* borborygmus *(kollerndes gurrendes Darmgeräusch)*
Bordapotheke *f* ship's dispensary
Bordetella *f* **pertussis** Bordetella *f* (Haemophilus *m*) pertussis, Bordet-Gengou bacillus *(Keuchhustenerreger)*
Bordet-Gengou-Agar *m* Bordet-Gengou agar (culture medium) *(zum Nachweis von Bordetella pertussis)*
Borke *f* crust, scab *(z. B. auf einer Wunde)*
~/austernschalenartige rupia
Borkenabtragung *f[/operative]* decrustation
Borkenflechte *f* impetigo [contagiosa]
Borkenkrätze *f/***Boecksche** Boeck's scabies, Norwegian itch, scabies crustosa
borkig crusted, scabby; impetiginoid, impetiginous
Borrelia *f* **recurrentis** Borrelia recurrentis, Spirochaeta obermeieri
Borreliose *f s.* Rückfallfieber
Borrowing-Lending-Phänomen *n* borrowing-lending phenomenon *(Blutverteilungsstörung)*
borstenbesetzt setiferous
bösartig malignant *(z. B. Geschwülste)*; pernicious *(z. B. Krankheiten)*; virulent *(z. B. Viren)*
Bösartigkeit *f* malignancy *(z. B. von Geschwülsten oder Krankheiten)*; virulence *(z. B. von Viren)*
Boston-Exanthem *n* Boston exanthem *(bei ECHO-Virusinfektion)*

Botenribonukleinsäure *f* messenger ribonucleic acid, messenger RNA, mRNA *(dient als Matrize für die Eiweißsynthese)*
Bothriozephalusanämie *f* bothriocephalus (tapeworm) anaemia
Bothriozephalusbefall *m* bothriocephaliasis, diphyllobothriasis
Botryomykose *f* botryomycosis
botryomykotisch botryomycotic
Botulin *n s.* Botulinustoxin
Botulinumantitoxin *n s.* Botulismusantitoxin
Botulinusbazillus *m*, **Botulinusclostridium** *n* botulism bacillus, Clostridium botulinum
Botulinusintoxikation *f s.* Botulismus
Botulinustoxin *n* botulinal (botulism) toxin, botulin
Botulismus *m* botulism, botulinus (clostridial food) poisoning
Botulismusantitoxin *n* botulinum (botulinal, botulism) antitoxin
botulismusartig botulinal
Botulismusserum *n s.* Botulismusantitoxin
Botulismustoxin *n* botulinal (botulism) toxin, botulin
Botulismusvergiftung *f s.* Botulismus
Bouba *f* bouba, Leishmaniasis ulcerosa cutis et mucosae
Bouchard-Knoten *m* Bouchard's node
Boucher-Gsell-Krankheit *f s.* Schweinehirtenkrankheit
Bougainville-Rheumatismus *m* Bougainville rheumatism, epidemic tropical acute polyarthritis
Bougie *f* [dilating] bougie
~/filiforme filiform bougie
~/olivenförmige olive-tipped bougie
Bougierung *f* bougienage
Bournville-Syndrom *n* Bournville's disease, [hypertrophic] tuberous sclerosis
Boutonneuse-Fieber *n* boutonneuse fever, [Mediterranean] exanthematous fever, Mediterranean tick fever
Bouveret-Krankheit *f* Bouveret's syndrome, paroxysmal atrial tachycardia
Boveri-Reaktion *f* Boveri's test *(zum Globulinnachweis im Liquor cerebrospinalis)*
bovin bovine
Bovotuberkulin *n* bovine tuberculin
Bovovakzine *f* bovine vaccine
Bowman-Drüsen *fpl* Bowman's glands
Bowman-Kapsel *f* Bowman's capsule
Bowman-Membran *f* Bowman's membrane, lamina limitans externa corneae, anterior elastic lamina
Boxerdemenz *f* boxer's dementia
Boxerenzephalopathie *f*, **Boxerkrankheit** *f* boxer's encephalopathy, traumatic encephalitis
Boxerohr *n* boxer's (cauliflower) ear
Boxerstellung *f* left anterior oblique [position] *(die linke Schulter ist dem Leuchtschirm bei Durchleuchtung genähert)*
brachial brachial

Brachialgie

Brachialgie f brachialgia *(neuritischen oder vasomotorischen Ursprungs)*
Brachialislähmung f brachial paralysis
Brachialneuralgie f brachial [plexus] neuralgia
Brachialneuritis f brachial neuritis
Brachialparalyse f brachial paralysis
Brachialplexus m brachial plexus
Brachialplexuslähmung f brachial plexus paralysis
~/obere upper brachial plexus paralysis, Erb-Duchenne's paralysis, Erb's palsy (paralysis)
Brachialplexusneuralgie f brachial plexus neuralgia
Brachialplexustrauma n brachial plexus trauma
Brachioradialis m brachioradialis [muscle]
Brachioradialreflex m brachioradialis (supinator longus) reflex
Brachiotomie f brachiotomy
brachiozephal brachiocephalic
Brachium n brachium, [upper] arm ● **unter dem ~ subbrachial** *(Gehirnanatomie)*
~ colliculi inferioris inferior quadrigeminal brachium [of the mid-brain], brachium of the inferior colliculus
~ colliculi superioris superior quadrigeminal brachium [of the mid-brain], brachium of the superior colliculus
~ conjunctivum superior cerebellar peduncle
~ pontis middle cerebellar peduncle, pontocerebellar tract
Brachybasie f brachybasia; shuffling gait
Brachybasophalangie f brachybasophalangia
Brachycheilie f brachych[e]ily
Brachychirie f brachych[e]iria, brachych[e]irism
brachydaktyl brachydactylic, brachydactylous
Brachydaktylie f brachydactyly
Brachyglossie f brachyglossia; short tongue
Brachygnathie f brachygnathia, opisthognathia, opistogeny
Brachymesophalangie f brachymesophalangia
Brachymetakarpalie f brachymetacarpalia
Brachymetapodie f brachymetapody
Brachymorphie f brachymorphy
brachyphalangeal brachyphalangous
Brachyphalangie f brachyphalangia
Brachyrhinie f brachyrhinia
Brachystase f brachystasis, brachystatic contraction
Brachytelephalangie f brachytelephalangia
Brachyzephalie f brachycephalia
Bradyarrhythmie f bradyarrthythmia
Bradyarthrie f s. Bradylalia
Bradydiadochokinese f bradydiadochokinesis
Bradydiastole f bradydiastole
Bradydiastolie f bradydiastolia
Bradyglossie f bradyglossia
bradykard bradycardiac
Bradykardie f bradycardia, brachycardia, bradyrhythmia
Bradykinesie f bradykinesia
bradykinetisch bradykinetic
Bradykinin n bradykinin *(Nonapeptid)*

Bradykininogen n bradykininogen
Bradykorie f bradycoria, pupillary inertia
Bradylalia f bradylalia, bradyarthria *(Kleinhirnsymptomatik)*
Bradylexie f bradylexia
Bradyph[r]asie f bradyph[r]asia
Bradyphrenie f bradyphrenia *(bei Postenzephalitis)*
Bradypnoe f bradypnoea
bradypnoisch bradypnoeic
Bradypragie f bradypragia, bradypraxia
Bradyrhythmie f s. Bradykardie
Bradyspermatismus m, **Bradyspermie** f bradyspermatism, bradyspermia
Bradysphygmie f bradysphygmia
Bradyteleokinese f bradyteleokinesis *(Haltmachen der Bewegung vor dem Ziel, eine Kleinhirnsymptomatik)*
Bradytrophie f bradytrophia
Bradyurie f bradyuria
Bragard-Zeichen n Bragard's sign *(Ischiaszeichen)*
Braille-Schrift f braille
Brain-fag-Syndrom n brain fag syndrome *(bei sozialer Adaptationsstörung)*
branchial, branchiogen branchial, branchiogenic, branchiogenous
Branchiomerie f brachiomerism
Brand m s. Gangrän
Brandbläschen n phlyctenule
Brandblase f burn blister (vesicle)
brandig gangrenous, necrotic, sphaceous ● **~ werden** to become gangrenous, to sphacelate, to necrotize, to necrose, to mummify
Brandliniment n burn liniment
Brandsalbe f burn ointment, ointment for burns (scalds)
Brandschorf m eschar
Brandstifter m/**triebhafter** pyromaniac
Brandstiftungstrieb m pyromania, incendiarism
Brandverletzung f burn injury
Brandwunde f burn *(Verbrennung)*; scald *(Verbrühung)*
Brandwundenbehandlung f treatment of burn wounds
~/offene air-dressing of burn wounds
Brandwundeninfektion f burn wound infection
Brandwundenverband m burn dressing (bandage)
Branham-Effekt m Branham's sign *(bei arteriovenösen Fisteln)*
Braue f s. Augenbraue
Braun-Anastomose f Braun's anastomosis *(zwischen zu- und abführender Darmschlinge)*
Bräune f 1. s. Tonsillitis; 2. s. Pharyngitis; 3. [sun]tan
~/echte s. Diphtherie
bräunen/mittels UV-Strahlen to tan
Braunfleckigkeit f **der Haut** chloasma, melasma
Brausebad n shower bath
brausend effervescent, effervescing, bubbling; sparkling

Braxton-Hicks-Wendung f Braxton-Hicks version (turning) *(geburtshilflicher Handgriff)*
Break-off-Gefühl n break-off feeling *(beim Flug in großen Höhen)*
Brechampulle f perle, friable ampoule
Brechbeutel m vomitory
Brechdurchfall m/**einheimischer** salmonellosis
Brechdurchfallkrankheit f s. Cholera
brechen 1. to fracture, to break *(z. B. Knochen)*; 2. s. erbrechen; 3. to refract *(Optik)*
brechend/nicht 1. aclastic; 2. non-refractive
Brechgefäß n vomitory
Brechkraft f refractive (refracting) power, power of refraction *(z. B. des Auges)*
Brechkraftbestimmung f dioptometry
Brechkrafteinheit f dioptre
Brechkraftgleichheit f **beider Augen** isometropia
Brechkraftmesser m diopt[r]ometer *(z. B. für Brillen)*
~ **des Auges** ophthalmophacometer
Brechkraftmessung f **des Auges** ophthalmophacometry
Brechkraftunterschied m **beider Augen** aniso[metro]pia
Brechmittel n emetic [agent], nauseant, vomitory
Brechneigung f tendency to vomit[ing]
Brechreflex m vomiting (gag) reflex
Brechreiz m nausea, sicchasia, retching, vomiturition ● ~ **erregend** nauseant, nauseous, nauseating
brechreizhemmend antinauseant
Brechschale f vomitory; vomiting basin
Brechung f refraction
Brechungsexponent m s. Brechungsindex
Brechungsfehler m refractive error (anomaly), error of refraction, ametropia
Brechungsindex m refractive index, index of refraction
Brechungsmessung f s. Brechzahlmessung
Brechungsverhältnis n s. Brechungsindex
Brechungsvermögen n refractivity, refractive power
Brechungswinkel m refraction angle, angle of refraction
Brechwert m s. Brechungsindex
Brechwurzel f ipecac[uanha] *(Bronchialsekretolytikum)*
Brechzahlmesser m refractometer
Brechzahlmessung f refractometry, measurement of refraction index
Brechzentrum n vomiting centre
Bregma n bregma *(Kreuzungspunkt der Kranz- und Pfeilnaht)*
bregmatisch bregmatic
Breitbandantibiotikum n s. Breitspektrumantibiotikum
breitbeckig platypellic, platypelloid, platypelvic
breitfüßig broad-footed
breitgaumig platystaphyline

breitgesichtig broad-faced, platyopic, euryprocephalus, chamaeprosopic, mesopic
Breitgesichtigkeit f platyopia, euryprocephalia, chamaeprosopia
breithüftig broad-hipped
breitkiefrig eurygnathic
Breitkiefrigkeit f eurygnathism
breitköpfig platycephalic, platycephalous
breitnasig platyrrhine, broad-nosed
breitschädelig eurycephalic
Breitspektrumantibiotikum n broad-spectrum antibiotic, wide-spectrum antibiotic
breitzungig platyglossal
Breiumschlag m/**heißer** cataplasm[a]
Bremsstrahlung f bremsstrahlung
brennbar combustible, inflammable
brennen 1. to burn, to smart *(z. B. Wundschmerz)*; 2. to burn, to cauterize *(ätzen mit Instrumenten)*
Brennen n **beim Wasserlassen** burning, scalding
~ **der Augen** smarting
~ **des Magens** heartburn
~ **mit einem Kauter** cauterization
Brenner-Tumor m Brenner tumour, brenneroma *(Eierstockgeschwulst)*
Brennfleck m focal spot (point) *(der Röntgenröhre)*
Benninstrument n cautery [knife]
Brennpunkt m focus, focal point
Brennpunktabstand m focus (focal) distance
brennpunktlos astigmatic
Brennschlinge f cautery loop *(Instrument)*
Brennwert m s. Wert/kalorischer
Brenztraubensäure f pyruvic acid
Brenztraubensäureschwachsinn m s. Phenylketonurie 2.
bretthart board-like *(z. B. die Bauchdecken)*
Bride f bridle, adhesion
Bridenstriktur f bridle stricture
Brillantgrün n brilliant green *(Vitalfarbstoff)*
Brillantkresylblau n brilliant cresyl blue *(Vitalfarbstoff)*
Brillantkresylblaufärbung f brilliant cresyl blue stain *(Supravitalfärbung)*
Brille f spectacles, [eye] glasses ● **eine ~ tragen** to wear glasses
~/**stenopäische** stenopaeic spectacles
Brillenfassung f, **Brillengestell** n spectacle frame
Brillenglas n spectacle lens, eyeglass
Brillenglasbestimmung f refractometry
Brillengläserprobiergestell n trial-frame
Brillenhämatom n spectacle haematoma
Brillenverschreibung f prescription for glasses
Brissaud-Syndrom n 1. Brissaud's (alternating hemiplegia) syndrome; 2. Brissaud's disease, infantile hypothyroidism
bRNS s. Botenribonukleinsäure
Broca-Aphasie f Broca's [efferent motor] aphasia
Broca-Sprachzentrum n Broca's speech centre

Brodie-Abszeß

Brodie-Abszeß *m* Brodie's abscess *(Knochenabszeß)*
Brodmann-Felder *npl* Brodmann's areas *(Gehirn)*
Brodmann-Hirnkarte *f* Brodmann's map
Bromakne *f* bromine acne; bromoderma
Bromausschlag *m*, **Bromexanthem** *n s.* Bromakne
Bromhidrosis *f* bromhidrosis, bromidrosis, osmidrosis, foetid perspiration; foetid sweat *(infolge von Zersetzungsvorgängen)*
Bromhyperhidrose *f* bromhyperhidrosis *(verstärkte Sekretion übelriechenden Schweißes)*
Bromismus *m* bromide (bromine) poisoning, bromi[ni]sm
Bromkachexie *f* bromide cachexia
Bromkresolpurpur *m* bromocresol purple
Bromoderma *n* bromoderma
Bromomanie *f* bromomania
Brompemphigus *m* bromide pemphigus
Brompräparat *n* bromide (bromine) preparation
Brompsychose *f* bromomania
Bromsulphthalein-Belastungsprobe *f* bromosulphophthalein test
Bromsulphthalein-Clearance *f* bromosulphophthalein clearance
Bromvergiftung *f s.* Bromismus
bronchial bronchial
Bronchial... *s.a.* Bronchus...
Bronchialabsaugung *f* bronchial aspiration
Bronchialarterien *fpl* bronchial arteries
Bronchialasthma *n* bronchial (allergic) asthma
Bronchialatemgeräusch *n* bronchial breath sound
Bronchialatmung *f* bronchial breathing, tubular respiration
Bronchialaufzweigung *f* bronchial arborization
Bronchialbaum *m* bronchial (bronchus, respiratory) tree
Bronchialblutung *f* bronchorrhagia
Bronchialdrüse *f* bronchial gland
Bronchialdrüsenentzündung *f* bronchadenitis
Bronchialdrüsentuberkulose *f* bronchial phthisis, bronchogenic tuberculosis
Bronchialentzündung *f s.* Bronchitis
Bronchialerschlaffung *f*[/**chronische**] *s.* Bronchialerweiterung
Bronchialerweichung *f* bronchomalacia
Bronchialerweiterung *f* bronchiectasia, bronchodilatation
Bronchialexpektorans *n* bronchial stimulant
Bronchialexsudat *n* bronchial exudate
Bronchialfistel *f* bronchial fistula
~/operative bronchostomy
Bronchialfremdkörper *m* intrabronchial foreign body
Bronchialfremitus *m* bronchial fremitus
Bronchialgeräusch *n* bronchial sounds
Bronchialkarzinom *n* bronchial cancer, bronchiolar carcinoma, bronchogenic (bronchoalveolar) carcinoma
Bronchialkatarrh *m* bronchial catarrh, bronchitis

Bronchialknorpel *m* bronchial cartilage
Bronchialknospe *f* bronchial bud
Bronchialkrampf *m* bronchial spasm, bronch[i]ospasm
Bronchiallähmung *f* bronchoplegia
Bronchialleiden *n* bronchopathy
Bronchiallymphknoten *m* bronchial gland
Bronchiallymphknotenentzündung *f* bronchadenitis
Bronchiallymphknotentuberkulose *f s.* Bronchialtuberkulose
Bronchialmuskelkrampf *m s.* Bronchialkrampf
Bronchialmuskellähmung *f* bronchoplegia
Bronchialmuskulatur *f* bronchial muscles
Bronchialmykose *f* bronchomycosis
Bronchialödem *n* bronchoedema
Bronchialplastik *f* bronchoplasty
Bronchialpneumonie *f s.* Bronchopneumonie
Bronchialpolyp *m* bronchial polyp
Bronchialschleim *m* bronchial mucus
Bronchialschleimdrüse *f* bronchial gland
Bronchialschleimhaut *f* bronchial mucosa
Bronchialschleimhautentzündung *f* endobronchitis
Bronchialschleimhautmembran *f* bronchial mucous membrane
Bronchialschleimhautödem *n* bronchoedema
Bronchialschleimhautreizung *f* bronchial irritation
Bronchialschleimhautschwellung *f* bronchoedema
Bronchialsekret *n* bronchial mucus (secretion)
Bronchialsekretion *f* bronchial secretion
Bronchialseptum *n* bronchial septum
Bronchialspangenerweichung *f* bronchomalacia
Bronchialstein *m* broncholith, bronchial calculus
Bronchialsteinleiden *n* bronchOlithiasis
Bronchialstimme *f* bronchiloquy, bronchophony
Bronchialstumpf *m* bronchial stump
Bronchialstumpfnähapparat *m* bronchial stump suture appliance
Bronchialsystem *n* respiratory tree
Bronchialtoilette *f* bronchial toilet
Bronchialtuberkulose *f* bronchogenic tuberculosis, bronchial phthisis
Bronchialtumor *m* bronchial tumour (neoplasm)
Bronchialvene *f* bronchial vein
Bronchialvereng[er]ung *f* bronchostenosis, bronchial stenosis
Bronchialverlegung *f* bronchial obstruction
Bronchialverletzung *f* bronchial injury
Bronchialverschluß *m* bronchial occlusion
Bronchialverzweigung *f* bronchial arborization
Bronchialwandbruch *m* bronchocele
Bronchialzyste *f* bronchial (bronchogenic) cyst
Bronchie *f* bronchus, bronchial (air) tube *(Zusammensetzungen s. unter Bronchus)* ● **die Bronchien spiegeln** to bronchoscope ● **von den Bronchien ausgehend** bronchogenic, bronchogenous
Bronchiektase *f s.* Bronchiektasie
Bronchiektasen *fpl*/**sackförmige** sacculated bronchiectasis

Bronchiektasenhöhle f bronchiectatic cavity
Bronchiektasie f bronchiectasis, bronchiectasia
bronchiektatisch bronchiectatic
bronchienerweiternd bronchodilator, bronchodilating
Bronchien- und Speiseröhrenspiegelung f broncho-oesophagoscopy
bronchiogen bronchiogenic
bronchiolar bronchiolar
Bronchiolarepithel n bronchiolar epithelium
Bronchiolarkarzinom n bronchiolar (diffuse lung) carcinoma
Bronchiolarobstruktion f bronchiolar obstruction
Bronchiole f bronchiole, bronchiolus
Bronchiolektasie f bronchiolectasia, bronchiolectasis
Bronchiolenentzündung f bronchiolitis, capillary bronchitis
Bronchiolenepithel n bronchiolar epithelium
Bronchiolenerschlaffung f bronchiolectasia
Bronchiolenerweiterung f[/chronische] bronchiolectasia
Bronchiolenschleimhaut f bronchiolar mucosa, mucous membrane of the bronchioles
Bronchiolenverlegung f bronchiolar obstruction
Bronchiolenverschluß m bronchiolar occlusion
Bronchiolitis f bronchiolitis, capillary bronchitis
~ **obliterans** obliterating bronchiolitis, silo-filler's disease
Bronchiolus m bronchiole, bronchiolus
Bronchitiker m bronchitic
Bronchitis f bronchitis, bronchial catarrh
~/**akute** acute bronchitis
~/**asthmoide** asthmoid bronchitis
~ **capillaris** capillary bronchitis, bronchiolitis
~/**chronische** chronic bronchitis
~/**eitrige** putrid bronchitis
~/**fibrinöse** fibrinous bronchitis
~/**kruppöse** croupous (plastic) bronchitis
~ **pituitosa** bronchitis pituitosa *(Hustenanfälle mit Auswurf großer Schleimmengen)*
bronchitisch bronchitic
Bronchitiskessel m bronchitis (croup) kettle
Bronchitissputum n bronchitic sputum
bronchoalveolar bronchoalveolar
Bronchoalveolitis f bronchoalveolitis
Bronchoblennorrhoe f bronchoblennorrhoea
Bronchodilatation f bronchodilatation, bronchiectasis
Bronchodilatator m bronchodilator, bronchodilating agent
bronchogen bronchogenic, bronchogenous
Bronchogramm n bronchogram
Bronchographie f bronchography
Bronchographiekatheter m catheter for bronchography
bronchographisch bronchographic
Bronchokandidiasis f bronchocandidiasis
bronchokavernös bronchocavernous
Bronchokonstriktion f bronchoconstriction
bronchokonstriktorisch bronchoconstrictor
Broncholith m broncholith, bronchial calculus
Brocholithiasis f broncholithiasis
Bronchologie f bronchology
Broncholytikum n bronchodilator, bronchodilating agent
Bronchomalazie f bronchomalacia
Bronchomoniliasis f bronchomoniliasis
bronchomotorisch bronchomotor
bronchoösophageal broncho-oesophageal
Bronchoösophagealfistel f broncho-oesophageal fistula
Bronchoösophagologie f broncho-oesophagology
Bronchoösophagoskopie f broncho-oesophagoscopy
Bronchopathie f bronchopathy
Bronchophonie f bronchophony, pectorophony *(verstärkte Stimmenleitung bei infiltrativen Lungenprozessen)*
Bronchoplastik f bronchoplasty
Bronchoplegie f bronchoplegia
bronchopleural bronchopleural
Bronchopleuralfistel f bronchopleural fistula
Bronchopleuropneumonie f bronchopleuropneumonia
Bronchopneumonie f bronchopneumonia, bronchial (catarrhal, lobular) pneumonia
bronchopneumonisch bronchopneumonic
Bronchopneumopathie f bronchopneumopathy
bronchopulmonal bronchopulmonary
Bronchopulmonalsegment n bronchopulmonary segment
Bronchorrhagie f bronchorrhagia
Bronchorrhaphie f bronchorrhaphy
Bronchorrhoe f bronchorrhoea *(Hustenanfälle mit Auswurf großer Schleimmengen)*
Bronchosekretolytikum n bronchial mucolytic
Bronchoskop n bronchoscope
~/**flexibles** bronchofibrescope
Bronchoskopie f bronchoscopy
bronchoskopieren to bronchoscope
Bronchoskopiezange f bronchoscopic forceps
bronchoskopisch bronchoscopic
Bronchospasmus m bronch[i]ospasm, bronchial spasm
Bronchospirochätose f bronchospirochaetosis, Castellani's bronchitis (disease)
Bronchospirographie f bronchospirography *(Lungenfunktionsprüfung)*
Bronchospirometer n bronchospirometer
Bronchospirometrie f bronchospirometry *(Lungenfunktionsprüfung)*
Bronchostomie f bronchostomy
Bronchotetanie f bronchotetany *(Bronchialmuskelkrämpfe mit asthmoiden Anfällen)*
Bronchotomie f bronchotomy, incision into the bronchus
bronchotracheal bronchotracheal
bronchovesikulär bronchovesicular, vesiculobronchial
Bronchovesikuläratmen n bronchovesicular breathing, rude (harsh) respiration
Bronchozele f bronchocele

Bronchulus

Bronchulus *m* bronchiole, bronchiolus
Bronchus *m* bronchus, bronchial (air) tube
● **durch den ~ transbronchial**
~ intermedius stem bronchus
Bronchus... *s. a.* Bronchial...
Bronchusabriß *m* bronchus rupture (tear)
Bronchusadenom *n* bronchoadenoma, bronchial adenoma
Bronchusaufdehnung *f* bronchodilatation
Bronchusblocker *m* bronchus occluder
Bronchusblutung *f* bronchorrhagia
Bronchuschondrom *n* bronchus chondroma
Bronchuseröffnung *f*/**operative** bronchotomy
Bronchuserweichung *f* bronchomalacia
Bronchuserweiterung *f*[/**chronische**] bronchiectasia, bronchodilatation
Bronchusfaßzange *f* bronchial [grasping] forceps
Bronchus-Gallengang-Fistel *f* bronchobiliary fistula
Bronchus-Haut-Fistel *f*/**operative** bronchostomy
Bronchusinzision *f* bronchotomy
Bronchuskarzinoid *n* bronchus carcinoid
Bronchusklemme *f* bronchus forceps
Bronchusknorpelring *m* bronchial ring
Bronchusnähapparat *m* bronchus suture appliance
Bronchusnaht *f* bronchorrhaphy, bronchial suture
Bronchuspilzerkrankung *f* bronchomycosis
Bronchus-Pleura-Fistel *f* bronchopleural fistula
Bronchusrekonstruktion *f* bronchoplasty
Bronchusring *m* bronchial ring
Bronchusruptur *f* bronchus rupture
Bronchus-Speiseröhren-Fistel *f* broncho-oesophageal fistula
Bronchusspiegelung *f s.* Bronchoskopie
Bronchusspülung *f* bronchial washing (lavage)
Bronchustamponade *f*/**bronchoskopische** bronchoscopic bronchus tamponade (tamponage)
Bronchustuberkulose *f* bronchial phthisis, bronchogenic tuberculosis
Bronchus- und Lungenerkrankung *f* bronchopneumopathy
Bronchusvereng[er]ung *f* bronchostenosis, bronchial stenosis
Bronchuszange *f* bronchial forceps
Bronchuszusammenziehung *f* bronchoconstriction
Bronzediabetes *m* bronze diabetes, haemachromatosis, Troissier-Hanot-Chauffard syndrome
Bronzehaut *f* bronzed skin *(bei Nebennierensuffizienz)*
Bronzekrankheit *f* bronzed disease (skin), Addison's disease
Bronzeleber *f* bronze liver
Brooke-Krankheit *f* 1. Brooke's disease, contagious follicular keratosis; 2. Brooke's tumour (epithelioma)
Brown-Séquard-Syndrom *n* Brown-Séquard paralysis *(bei halbseitiger Rückenmarkverletzung)*

Brucella *f* **abortus** abortus bacillus
Brucellosis *f s.* Bruzellose
Bruch *m* 1. hernia *(der Eingeweide)*; 2. [bone] fracture *(s. a. unter* Fraktur *und* Knochenbruch*)* ● **einen ~ einrichten** to set (reduce) a fracture ● **einen ~ schienen** to splint a fracture
~/äußerer external hernia
~/direkter direct hernia
~/echter true hernia
~/einfacher simple (closed) fracture
~/eingekeilter impacted fracture
~/eingeklemmter incarcerated (strangulated) hernia
~/epigastrischer epigastric hernia
~/extrakapsulärer extracapsular (extraarticular) fracture
~/indirekter indirect (lateral, oblique) hernia
~/inkarzerierter *s.* ~/eingeklemmter
~/innerer internal hernia
~/irreponibler irreducible hernia
~/komplizierter complicated (open, compound) fracture
~/pathologischer pathological fracture
~/postoperativer postoperative (cicatricial) hernia
~/reponibler reducible hernia
~/unkomplizierter simple (closed) fracture
Bruch... *s.a.* Fraktur...
Bruchband *n* hernia bandage (truss), rupture support
Bruchbehandlung *f* 1. hernia treatment; 2. fracture treatment
Bruchbildung *f* herniation, hernia formation
Brucheinklemmung *f* hernia incarceration, strangulation of the hernia
Brucheinrenkung *f* reduction of a fracture
brüchig fragile, friable *(z. B.* Knochen*)*
Brüchigkeit *f* fragility *(z. B. der* Knochen*)*; brittleness *(z. B. der* Haare*)*; onychorrhexis *(z. B. der* Nägel*)*
Bruchkanal *m* hernial canal
Bruchklemme *f* hernia forceps
Bruchlehre *f* herniology
Bruchmesser *n* herniotome, hernia knife (bistoury)
Bruchnaht *f* herniorrhaphy
Bruchoperation *f* hernioplasty; herniotomy, herniorrhaphy
Bruchpforte *f* hernial orifice (opening)
Bruchpunktion *f* herniopuncture
Bruchreposition *f* 1. hernia reduction; 2. reduction of a fracture
Bruchsack *m* hernial sac
Bruchsackhals *m* neck of the hernial sac
Bruchschienung *f* fracture splinting
Bruchstück *n* 1. fracture fragment *(z. B. des* Knochens*)*; 2. chromosome segment
Bruchstückhebung *f* disimpaction *(Knochen)*
Bruchstückverschiebung *f* fragment dislocation (displacement) *(des Knochens)*
Bruchverschiebung *f* fracture dislocation (displacement *(des Knochens)*

Brücke f 1. pons *(des Gehirns)*; 2. [dental] bridge ● **unter der ~** subpontine ● **zur ~ gehörend** pontine, pontile
~/achromatische achromatic bridge *(bei Zellteilung)*
~/kieferorthopädische retainer
Brückenarm m s. Kleinhirnstiel
Brückenbahn f/**frontale** frontopontine tract
~/temporale temporopontine tract, Türck's bundle
Brückenblutung f pontine haemorrhage (apoplexy)
Brückengips[verband] m bridge plaster bandage
Brückengliom m pontine glioma
Brückenkallus m bridge (bridging) callus *(des Knochens)*
Brückenkern m pontine nucleus
Brückenkolobom n bridge coloboma *(der Iris oder Aderhaut)*
Brückenlappen m bridge (bridging) flap *(bei Hauttransplantation)*
Brückenlappenplastik f tube (tunnel, double-end) graft
Brückensymptom n pontine symptom
Brückentransplantat n bridge (bridging) graft
Brückenwinkel m pontile (cerebellopontine) angle
Brugia-malayi-Befall m Malayan filariasis
Brunhilde-Typ m, **Brunhilde-Virus** n Brunhilde virus
Brust f 1. breast, mamma *(s.a. Brustdrüse)*; 2. pectus, thorax *(s.a. Brustkorb)* ● **die ~ operativ entfernen** to mastectomize ● **einem Säugling die ~ geben** to give the breast, to nurse, to breast-feed ● **einen Säugling von der ~ entwöhnen** to wean a suckling ● **mit der ~ ernähren** to nurse at the breast
~/aberrierende aberrant mamma
~/akzessorische accessory (supernumerary) mamma
Brust... s. a. Mamma...
Brustableitung f chest lead *(EKG)*
Brustabschnitt m mammary region
Brustabsonderung f breast discharge
Brustabszeß m breast (mammary) abscess
Brustamputation f breast (mammary) amputation, mammectomy, mastectomy
~ nach Halsted/radikale Halsted's radical mastectomy
Brustaorta f 1. thoracic aorta; 2. primitive (dorsal) aorta
Brustaortanervengeflecht n plexus of the thoracic aorta
Brustarterie f/**innere** internal thoracic (mammary) artery
~/oberste highest thoracic artery
~/seitliche lateral thoracic artery
Brustatmung f thoracic breathing, costal respiration
Brustatrophie f breast (mammary) atrophy, mastatrophy
Brustaufbau m breast reconstruction

Brust-Bauch[höhlen]-Spalte f thoracocoeloschisis, thoracogastroschisis
Brustbein n sternum, breastbone ● **durch das ~ transsternal** ● **neben dem ~** parasternal ● **über dem ~ suprasternal**, episternal ● **unter dem ~ substernal** ● **zum ~ gerichtet** adsternal
Brustbein... s.a. Sternal...
Brustbeinansatz m sternal insertion
Brustbeinbereich m sternal region
Brustbein[hand]griff m [sternal] manubrium *(oberster Teil des Brustbeins)*
Brustbeinhandgriff-Brustbeinkorpus-Gelenk n gladiomanubrial joint
Brustbeinknorpelhaft f sternal synchondrosis
Brustbeinkörper m gladiolus, body of the sternum
brustbeinlos asternal
Brustbeinmesser n sternotome
Brustbeinmuskel m sternalis [muscle]
Brustbein-Rippen-Gelenk n sternocostal articulation (joint)
Brustbein-Schildknorpel-Muskel m sternothyroid [muscle]
Brustbein-Schlüsselbein-Gelenk n sternoclavicular articulation (joint), manubrioclavicular junction
Brustbeinspalte f sternoschisis, schistosternia; bifid (cleft) sternum
Brustbeinspaltung f[/**operative**] sternotomy
brustbeinwärts adsternal
Brustbeinwinkel m angle of the sternum, angle of Louis (Ludwig)
Brustbein-Zungenbein-Muskel m sternohyoid [muscle]
Brustbeklemmung f stenocardia
Brustbereich m mammary region
Brustbiopsie f breast biopsy
Brustbluterguß m mastecchymosis
Brustblutung f mastorrhagia
Brustdornmuskel m spinalis thoracis [muscle]
Brustdrüse f mamma, mammary gland, breast ● **auf die ~ wirkend** mammotropic ● **über der ~** supramammary ● **unter der ~** submammary
Brustdrüsenabsonderung f breast discharge
Brustdrüsenabszeß m breast (mammary) abscess
Brustdrüsenadenom n mastadenoma
Brustdrüsenblutung f mastorrhagia, mastomenia
Brustdrüsenektopie f breast-gland ectopia
Brustdrüsenentzündung f mastitis, mastadenitis, mammitis *(Zusammensetzungen s. unter Mastitis)*
Brustdrüsenganggeschwulst f ductal tumour
Brustdrüsengangkarzinom n ductal carcinoma
Brustdrüsengangpapillom n ductal papilloma
Brustdrüsengewebe n breast tissue
Brustdrüsenkarzinom n s. Brustkrebs
Brustdrüsenkörper m corpus mammae, mammary corpus
Brustdrüsenläppchen n lobule of the mammary gland

Brustdrüsenlymphgeflecht

Brustdrüsenlymphgeflecht *n* mammary lymphatic plexus
Brustdrüsenschmerz *m* mammalgia, mastalgia, mastodynia, mazalgia
Brustdrüsenschwellung *f* breast (mammary) engorgement
Brustdrüsenstein *m* mammary calculus
brustdrüsenstimulierend mammotropic
Brustdrüsenszirrhus *m* mammary scirrhus, mastoscirrhus
Brustdrüsenvenengeflecht *n* mammary venous plexus
Brustdrüsenvergrößerung *f* mastoplasia, mastauxy
Brusteinblutung *f* mastecchymosis
Brusteiterung *f* breast (mammary) abscess
Brustenge *f* stenocardia
Brustentfernung *f*[/**operative**] mastectomy, mammectomy, mammary amputation
~/**radikale** radical mastectomy
Brustentwicklung *f* **bei Männern** gynaecomastia
Brustentzündung *f* mastitis, mammitis, mastadenitis *(Zusammensetzungen s. unter* Mastitis*)*
Brusterkrankung *f* 1. mastopathy, mazopathy; 2. thoracopathy
Brusternährung *f* breast feeding
Brustfalte *f* mammary fold
Brustfell *n* pleura *(Zusammensetzungen s. unter* Pleura*)*
Brustfell... *s.a.* Pleura...
Brustfellentfernung *f*[/**operative**] pleurectomy
Brustfellentzündung *f* pleurisy, pleuritis, inflammation of the pleura *(s.a. unter* Pleuritis*)*
~ **bei Typhus** pleurotyphoid
~/**beidseitige** double pleuritis
~/**eitrige** purulent pleurisy
~/**feuchte** humid (wet) pleurisy
~ **im Bereich eines Zwischenlappenspalts** interlobitis
~/**rheumatische** rheumatic pleurisy
~/**trockene** dry pleurisy
Brustfellinzision *f* pleurotomy
Brustfellkrampf *m* pleurospasm
Brustfellresektion *f* pleurectomy
Brustfellsarkom *n* pleural sarcoma
Brustfellschmerz *m* pleuralgia, pleurodynia
Brustfibroadenom *n* breast fibroadenoma
brustförmig mammiform, mastoid, breast-shaped
Brustgang *m* thoracic duct
Brustganglion *n* thoracic ganglion
Brustgangröntgen[kontrast]bild *n* ductogram
Brustgangröntgen[kontrast]darstellung *f* ductography
Brustgegend *f* 1. mammary region; 2. thoracic region
Brustgeschwür *n* mammary ulcer, ulcer of the breast
Brustgeschwürbildung *f* masthelcosis
Brustgewebe *n* breast tissue
Brustgürtel *m* pectoral girdle
Brusthöhle *f* chest cavity, thoracis space, respiratory cavity
Brusthöhlenerkrankung *f* thoracopathy
Brusthöhlenfistelung *f*[/**operative**] thoracostomy
Brusthöhlenpunktion *f* thora[co]centesis, pleurocentesis
Brusthöhlenspiegel *m* thoracoscope
Brusthöhlenspiegelung *f* thoracoscopy
Brusthöhlenvereiterung *f* pyothorax
Brustinzision *f* mastotomy
Brustkorb *m* thorax, rib (thoracic) cage, chest, pectus ● **durch den** ~ transthoracic
~/**enger** stenothorax
~/**instabiler** flail chest
Brustkorb... *s.a.* Thorax...
Brustkorbarterie *f*/**innere** internal thoracic (mammary) artery
Brustkorbatmung *f* chest (thoracic) breathing, costal respiration
Brustkorb-Bauch[höhlen]-Spalte *f* thoracocoeloschisis, thoracogastroschisis
Brustkorberöffnung *f*/**operative** thoracotomy, pleuracotomy
Brustkorberweiterung *f* extension of the thorax
Brustkorbfistel[ung] *f*/**operative** thoracostomy
Brustkorbhälfte *f* hemithorax
Brustkorbhebung *f* rise of the thorax
Brustkorbindex *m* thoracic index
Brustkorblängsvene *f*/**linke** hemiazygous vein
~/**zusätzliche** accessory hemiazygous vein
Brustkorböffnung *f*/**obere** superior aperture of the thoracic cavity
~/**untere** inferior boundary of the thoracic cavity
Brustkorbpflasterverband *m* rib strapping
Brustkorbplastik *f* thoracoplasty
Brustkorbschmerz *m* chest pain, thoracodynia, thoracalgia, pectoralgia
Brustkorbspalte *f* thoracoschisis; schistothorax, fissured chest
Brustkorb- und Baucheröffnung *f*[/**operative**] thoracocoeliotomy, thoracolaparotomy
Brustkorbvene *f*/**innere** internal thoracic (mammary) vein
~/**seitliche** lateral thoracic vein
Brustkorbverband *m* chest strap[ping]
Brustkorbvereng[er]ung *f* thoracostenosis; stenothorax
Brustkorbverletzung *f*/**offene** sucking chest wound
Brustkorbvermessung *f* thoracometry
Brustkorbwiedereröffnung *f*[/**operative**] rethoracotomy
Brustkrebs *m* mastocarcinoma, breast cancer, carcinoma of the breast
Brustkrebsbehandlung *f* breast cancer treatment
Brustlage *f* breast presentation *(bei der Geburt)*
Brustleiste *f* milk ridge
Brustmilch *f* breast milk
Brustmilchgang *m* thoracic duct, galactophorous canal (duct), galactophore
Brustmilchpumpe *f s.* Brustpumpe

Brustmuskel *m* pectoralis [muscle], pectoral muscle ● **unter den Brustmuskeln** subpectoral
~/großer pectoralis major [muscle]
~/kleiner pectoralis minor [muscle]
~/querer transversalis sterni [muscle], transverse thoracic muscle
Brustmuskelfaszie *f* pectoral (pectoralis) fascia
Brustmuskelreflex *m* pectoral reflex
Brustmuskelschmerz *m* thoracomyodynia
Brustmuskulatur *f* pectoral muscles
Brustnahrung *f* breast feeding
Brustnerv *m* thoracic nerve
Brustplastik *f s.* 1. Mammaplastik; 2. Brustkorbplastik
Brustprothese *f* breast prosthesis
Brustpumpe *f* breast pump, lactisugium
Brustregion *f*/**seitliche** lateral pectoral region
Brustrekonstruktion *f* breast reconstruction
Brustrückbildung *f* breast reduction *(z. B. nach Stillperiode)*
Brust-Rücken-Arterie *f* thoracodorsal artery
Brustsarkom *n* breast (mammary) sarcoma
Brustschallbild *n* stethogram
Brustschallschreibung *f* stethography
Brust-Schlüsselbein-Gelenk *n* stenoclavicular articulation (joint)
Brustschmerz *m* 1. thoracalgia, thoracodynia, chest (pectoral) pain, pectoralgia; 2. *s.* Mastalgie
Brust-Schulter-Arterie *f* acromiothoracic (thoracoacromial) artery
Brust-Schulter-Vene *f* acromiothoracic (thoracoacromial) vein
Brustselbstuntersuchung *f* breast self-examination
Brustspalt *m* thoracoschisis
Bruststein *m* mammary calculus
Bruststillung *f* breast feeding
Bruststimme *f* pectoriloquy *(bei Lungenkrankheiten)*
Bruststimmenhören *n* pectorophony *(bei Lungenauskultation)*
Brustszirrhus *m* mastoscirrhus *(Brustkrebs)*
Brustunterblutung *f* mastecchymosis
Brustunterentwicklung *f* breast hypoplasia, hypomastia, hypomazia
Brustvene *f*/**innere** internal thoracic (mammary) vein
Brustvereiterung *f* 1. breast (mammary) abscess; 2. pyothorax
Brustvergrößerung *f* breast hyperplasia (hypertrophy), hypermastia, hypermazia, mastoplasia, mastauxy
~/abnorme macromastia, macromazia
~/operative breast augmentation
Brustvergrößerungsoperation *f* breast augmentation operation, augmentation mammoplasty
Brustverkleinerung *f* 1. *s.* Brustunterentwicklung; 2. breast reduction *(z. B. nach Stillperiode)*
~/abnorme micromastia, micromazia
~/operative breast reduction

Brustwand *f* chest (thoracic) wall
Brustwandableitung *f* precordial (chest) lead *(EKG)*
Brustwanddeformierung *f* chest wall deformity
Brustwand-EKG *n* precordial (chest) electrocardiogram
Brustwandentzündung *f* parapleuritis
Brustwandfistel *f* thoracic fistula
Brustwandhamartom *n* hamartoma of the chest wall
Brustwandhautverschiebelappen *m* sliding chest wall flap
Brustwandphlegmone *f* phlegmon of the chest wall
Brustwandschienung *f* splinting of the chest
Brustwandschlürfen *n* traumatopnoea
Brustwandstabilisierung *f* fixation of the chest wall
Brustwandverletzung *f* chest wound (injury)
Brustwarze *f* mamilla, [mammary] papilla, [breast] nipple, thelium, teat ● **über der ~** supramamillary
~/akzessorische accessory nipple
~/eingezogene crater nipple
~/retrahierte retracted nipple
~/überzählige supernumerary nipple
Brustwarzen... *s.a.* Mamillen...
brustwarzenähnlich mamillary, mastoid[al]
Brustwarzenblutung *f* thelorrhagia
Brustwarzenentzündung *f* mamillitis, thelitis, nipple inflammation
Brustwarzenerektion *f* theleretism, thelotism
brustwarzenförmig mamilliform, mammary
Brustwarzengeschwulst *f* theloncus
Brustwarzenhof *m* mammary areola, areola [of the breast]
Brustwarzenhypoplasie *f* microthelia, hypoplasia of the nipple
Brustwarzenkrebs *m* breast nipple carcinoma
Brustwarzenrekonstruktion *f* mamilliplasty, theleplasty
Brustwarzenschmerz *m* thelalgia
Brustwarzenüberzahl *f* hyperthelia
Brustwarzenvenenzeichnung *f* thelophlebostemma
Brustwassersucht *f* hydrothorax, hydropleura, exudative pleuritis
Brustwirbel *m* thoracic vertebra
Brustwirbelsäule *f* thoracic spine
Brustwunde *f* chest wound
Brustzyste *f* mammary (breast) cyst
Brutapparat *m*, **Brutkasten** *m* incubator
Bruton-Krankheit *f* Bruton's (congenital sex-linked) agammaglobulinaemia
Brutschrank *m* **für Neugeborene** couveuse
Bruxismus *m* bruxism, grinding (gnashing) of the teeth, brygmus *(nächtliches Zähneknirschen)*
Bruxomanie *f* bruxomania
Bruzellen-Agglutinationstest *m* brucella agglutination test
Bruzellen-Antikörper *m* antibrucella antibody
Bruzellenarthritis *f* brucellar arthritis

Bruzellenarthropathie

Bruzellenarthropathie *f* brucellar arthropathy
Bruzellendermatitis *f* brucellar dermatitis
Bruzellenendokarditis *f* brucellar endocarditis
Bruzellenimpfstoff *m* brucella vaccine
Bruzelleninfektion *f* **des Nervensystems** neurobrucellosis
Bruzellenphage *m* brucella phage
Bruzellose *f* brucellosis, brucelliasis, Bang's disease, Mountain fever, Mediterranean phthisis *(Infektionskrankheit durch Brucella melitensis)*
Brygmus *m s.* Bruxismus
BSG *s.* Blutkörperchensenkungsgeschwindigkeit
Bubble-Sack *m* dispersion oxygenator
Bubo *m* bubo, inguinal panus
~**/syphilitischer** syphilitic bubo
~**/tropischer** tropical adenitis, venereal lymphogranulomatosis; venereal lymphogranuloma
~**/venerischer** venereal bubo
Buboadenitis *f* buboadenitis
Bubonalgie *f* bubonalgia, inguinal pain
Bubonenpest *f* bubonic (glandular) plague, malignant polyadenitis
Bubonulus *m* bubonulus *(Abszeß des Penisrückens)*
Bucca *f s.* Backe
Buccinator *m* buccinator [muscle]
Buchdruckerlähmung *f* printer's palsy
Bücherabneigung *f* bibliophobia
Büchersammeltrieb *m*[**/krankhafter**] bibliomania
Bücherschänder *m* biblioclast
Bücherstehltrieb *m*[**/krankhafter**] bibliokleptomania
Buchstabe *m*/**kleinster lesbarer** minimal of reading
Buchstabenagraphie *f* literal agraphia
Buchstabenblindheit *f*[**/zentrale**] alexia, typholexia, wordblindness
Buchstabenkeratitis *f* striate keratitis
Buchstabenschreibunfähigkeit *f* literal agraphia
Bucht *f* sinus; niche, recess; fossa
buchtig sinuous
Buckel *m* gibbus, hunchback, hump[back], kyphos
~**/Pottscher** Pott's disease (gibbus), angular curvature (kyphosis) of the spine; spinal caries
Buckelbildung *f* **mit Wirbelsäulenseitenverkrümmung** kyphoskoliosis
bucklig gibbous, kyphotic
Buckliger *m* hunchback, humpback
Buckligkeit *f* gibbosity, kyphosis, humpbackedness
Bucky-Blende *f* [Potter-]Bucky diaphragm *(Radiologie)*
Budd-Chiari-Syndrom *n* Chiari's (Budd-Chiari) syndrome, hepatic vein occlusion (thrombosis)
Büffelnacken *m* bison neck *(bei Morbus Cushing)*
Bufotoxin *n* bufotoxin *(Glykosid)*
bukkal buccal
bukkodental buccodental
bukkogingival buccogingival
bukkolabial buccolabial
bukkolingual buccolingual
Bulbäranästhesie *f* bulbar anaesthesia
Bulbärapoplexie *f* bulbar apoplexy
Bulbärataxie *f* bulbar ataxia
Bulbärhirnschaden *m* bulbar brain lesion
Bulbärhirnschädigung *f* bulbar brain lesion
Bulbärparalyse *f* bulbar palsy (paralysis)
~**/infektiöse** infectious bulbar paralysis
~**/progressive** progressive bulbar paralysis, Duchenne's disease (palsy)
Bulbärpoliomyelitits *f* bulbar poliomyelitis
Bulbärsklerose *f* bulbar sclerosis
Bulbärsprache *f* bulbar speech
Bulbärzeichen *n* bulbar sign
Bulbokavernosus *m* bulbocavernosus [muscle]
bulbospinal bulbospinal
Bulbospongiosus *m* bulbospongiosus [muscle]
Bulbospongiosusreflex *m* bulbospongiosus reflex
Bulbourethraldrüse *f* bulbourethral (Cowper's) gland
Bulbus *m* bulb
~ **aortae (arteriosus, cordis)** aortic (arterial) bulb, bulb of the heart
~ **cornus posterioris** bulb of the posterior horn
~ **corporis cavernosi urethrae** bulb of the corpus cavernosum [urethrae]
~ **corporis spongiosi penis** bulb of the corpus cavernosum [urethrae]
~ **duodeni** duodenal bulb (cap)
~ **jugularis** jugular bulb
~ **oculi** bulb of the eye, eyeball, [ocular] globe *(Zusammensetzungen s. unter Augapfel)*
~ **olfactorius** olfactory bulb, mamillary apophysis *(Teil des Riechhirns)*
~ **penis** bulb of the penis
~ **pili** bulb of the hair, hair bulb
~ **urethrae** bulb of the urethra, urethral bulb
~ **vaginae** vaginal bulb
~ **venae jugularis inferior** lower (inferior) bulb of the internal jugular vein
~ **venae jugularis superior** upper (superior) bulb of the internal jugular vein
~ **vestibuli vaginae** bulb of the vestibule [of the vagina], vestibular bulb of the vagina
Bulbusatrophie *f* atrophy of the globe
Bulbusbindehaut *f* bulbar conjunctiva
Bulbusdeformierung *f* bulbar deformity *(des Duodenums)*
Bulbusdruckreflex *m* oculocardiac reflex *(Absinken der Herzfrequenz durch Druck auf die Augäpfel)*
Bulbusfaszie *f* bulbar fascia
Bulbusintorsion *f* intorsion of the globe
Bulbusprellung *f* contusion of the globe
Bulbusreflex *m s.* Bulbusdruckreflex
Bulbusschenkel *m* bulbar limb
Bulimie *f* b[o]ulimia, hyperorexia, ad[d]ephagia, sitomania
Bulla *f* bulla, blister, vesica *(s. a. unter* Blase*)*
~ **emphysematosa** emphysematous bulla

~ **epithelialis** epithelial bleb
~ **ethmoidalis** ethmoid bulla
Bulldogklemme f bulldog clamp (forceps)
bullös bullous, blistered, vesiculate
Bündel n bundle, tract[us], fascicle
~/**Flechsigsches** Flechsig's tract, [posterior] spinocerebellar tract, dorsal spinocerebellar fasciculus of Flechsig
~/**Gowerssches** Gowers tract (column), [anterior] spinocerebellar tract, anterolateral fasciculus of Gowers
~/**Heldsches** vestibulospinal (spinal vestibular) tract, descending vestibular root
~/**Hissches** [conduction] bundle of His, atrioventricular bundle, sinoventricular band *(Herzreizleitung)*
~/**Meynertsches** Meynert's bundle, habenulopeduncular tract
~/**Monakowsches** Monakov's bundle (fasciculus, fibres), rubrospinal tract
~/**papillomakuläres** papillomacular bundle
~/**Remaksches** Remak's band
~/**Türcksches** Türck's bundle, temporopontine tract
~/**Vicq d'Azyrsches** Vicq d'Azyr's bundle (fasciculus), mamillothalamic tract
Bündelbildung f fasciculation
Bündelungseffekt m bunching effect *(Krankheitshäufung nach Schutzimpfungen)*
Buntsehen n chrom[at]opsia, chromatic vision
Buphthalmie f buphthalmia, hydrophthalmia, infantile glaucoma
buphthalmisch buphthalmic
Buphthalmus m buphthalmos, hydrophthalmos
Burdwan-Fieber n Burdwan fever *(s. a. Kala-Azar)*
Burkitt-Lymphom n s. Burkitt-Tumor
Burkitt-Tumor m Burkitt's lymphoma (tumour), African lymphoma
Burnett-Syndrom n Burnett's (milk-alkali, milk-drinkers') syndrome
Burning-feet-Syndrom n burning feet syndrome
Bursa f bursa, sac
Bursektomie f bursectomy
Bursitis f bursitis, bursal synovitis
~ **der Achillessehne** achillobursitis
~ **praepatellaris** prepatellar bursitis; housemaid's knee
~ **radioulnaris** radio-ulnar bursitis
Bursolith m bursolith
Bursopathie f bursopathy
Bursotomie f bursotomy
Bürstenmassage f brush massage
Bürstensaum m brush (ciliated) border *(von Epithelzellen)*
Bürstensaummembran f brush-border membrane
büschelförmig fasciculate[d] *(Anatomie)*; penicilliform *(z. B. Bakterien)*
Buschgelbfieber n sylvan (jungle) yellow fever, scrub typhus

Buschke-Ollendorf-Syndrom n Buschke-Ollendorf syndrome, disseminated lenticular dermatofibrosis
Buttersäure f butyric (butanoic) acid
BWS s. Brustwirbelsäule
Bypass m/**aortoiliakaler** aortoiliac bypass
~/**aortokoronarer** aortocoronary bypass
~/**axillofemoraler** axillofemoral bypass
~/**femoropoplitealer** femoropopliteal bypass
~/**kardiopulmonaler** cardiopulmonary bypass
~/**überkreuzter** overcross bypass
Bypass-Chirurgie f bypass surgery
~/**aortokoronare** aortocoronary bypass surgery
Bypass-Operation f bypass operation
~/**aortokoronare** aortocoronary bypass operation
Bypass-Verfahren n bypass procedure
Byssinose f byssinosis, byssophthisis, monday morning fever
Bywaters-Syndrom n 1. Bywaters' syndrome (disease), crush syndrome; 2. Bywaters' disease, lower nephron syndrome
B-Zellen fpl beta cells *(der Bauchspeicheldrüse)*

C

C. s. Clearance
C' complement *(Wirkgruppe im Blutserum)*
C 1, C$_1$ costa I, first rib
Cabot-Ringe mpl Cabot's rings (ring bodies)
Cachexia f cachexia *(s. a. unter Kachexie)*
~ **exophthalmica** exophthalmic goitre
~ **splenica** splenic cachexia
~ **strumipriva (thyreopriva)** strumiprival (thyreoprival) cachexia
Cadaverin n cadaverine *(Leichengift)*
Caecitas f cecity, caecitas, blindness, ablepsia, amaurosis, typhlosis *(s. a. unter Blindheit)*
~ **diurna** day blindness, hemeralopia
~ **spatialis** spatial blindness
~ **verbalis** word blindness, alexia
Caecum n s. Blinddarm
Café-au-lait-Flecken mpl café au lait spots
Caffey-de-Toni-Syndrom n Caffey's disease (syndrome), infantile cortical hyperostosis
Caffey-Silvermann-Syndrom n Caffey's disease (syndrome), infantile cortical hyperostosis
Caissonkrankheit f caisson disease, decompression sickness, diver's paralysis
Cajal-Horizontalzellen fpl Cajal's horizontal cells
Cajal-Silberimprägnation f Cajal's silver [impregnation] method *(zur Nervenzellfärbung)*
Calabarbeulen fpl, **Calabarschwellung** f Calabar swellings
Calcaneus m s. Fersenbein
Calcar m calcar, spur
Calcificatio f s. Kalzifikation
Calcinosis f calcinosis, calcium thesaurismosis (gout)
~ **circumscripta** calcinosis circumscripta, Profichet's syndrome *(umschriebene Kalkablagerungen in der Haut der Extremitäten)*

Calcinosis

- ~ **cutis circumscripta** calcinosis cutis circumscripta, hypodermolithiasis
- ~ **progrediens** calcinosis progrediens, lipocalcinogranulomatosis *(Cholesterinspeicherkrankheit)*
- ~ **universalis** universal (interstitial) calcinosis
- ~ **universalis interstitialis** calcinosis universalis interstitialis, lipocalcinogranulomatosis *(Cholesterinspeicherkrankheit)*

Calcitonin n calcitonin, thyrocalcitonin *(Nebenschilddrüsenhormon)*
Calcium n **gluconicum** calcium gluconate
Calcium... s. Kalzium...
Calculus m calculus, stone, concrement, concretion
- ~ **felleus** biliary calculus, bile-stone, gall-stone, cholelith
- ~ **renalis** renal calculus, kidney stone, nephrolith
- ~ **salivalis** salivary calculus, sialolith, ptya[lo]lith
- ~ **vesicae** vesical calculus, bladder stone, vesicolith, cystolith

Caldwell-Luc-Operation f Caldwell-Luc operation *(Radikaloperation der Kieferhöhle)*
Caliculus m caliculus, calyculus
- ~ **gustatorius** gustatory bud (bulb), taste corpuscle
- ~ **ophthalmicus** optic cup

California-encephalitis-Virus n California encephalitis virus
California-Enzephalitis f California encephalitis
California-Virus-Komplex m California virus complex
Calix m s. Calyx
Callositas f callosity
Calmette-Guérin-Bazillus m bacillus Calmette-Guérin, BCG
Calmodulin n calmodulin *(Kalziumionen bindendes Regulatorprotein)*
Calor m calor, heat; fever *(Entzündungszeichen)*
Calot-Dreieck n Calot's triangle, triangle of Calot
Calvaria f calvaria, calva[rium], skull cap, [cranial] vault, calotte
Calvé-Legg-Perthes-Erkrankung f s. Perthes-Erkrankung
Calvé-Syndrom n Calvé's disease, osteochondritis deformans juvenilis
Calvé-Wirbel m Calvé's vertebra plana
Calyces fpl **renales** renal calyces (calyxes)
- ~ **renales majores** major calyces of the kidney
- ~ **renales minores** minor calyces of the kidney

Calymmatobacterium n **granulomatis** Calymmatobacterium (Donovania, Klebsiella) granulomatis, Donovan body *(Erreger des Granuloma inguinale)*
Calyx m calyx, calix, cup
Camera f camera, chamber
- ~ **anterior bulbi** s. ~ oculi anterior
- ~ **oculi** aqueous chamber of the eye[ball], vitreous chamber
- ~ **oculi anterior** anterior [eye] chamber, anterior chamber of the eye[ball]
- ~ **oculi posterior** posterior [eye] chamber, posterior chamber of the eye[ball]
- ~ **posterior bulbi** s. ~ oculi posterior
- ~ **vitrea bulbi** s. ~ oculi

cAMP s. Adenosinmonophosphat/zyklisches
Camper-Linie f Camper's (facial, auriculo-nasal) line
Camurati-Engelmann-Syndrom n Engelmann's (Camurati-Engelmann) disease, progressive diaphysial dysplasia
Canaliculitis f canaliculitis *(Entzündung der Tränenkanäle)*
Canaliculus m canaliculus
- ~ **biliferus** bile canaliculus
- ~ **caroticotympanicus** caroticotympanic canal
- ~ **chordae tympani** canal of the chorda tympani
- ~ **cochleae** cochlear canaliculus
- ~ **dentalis** dentinal tubule, dental canaliculus
- ~ **lacrimalis** lacrimal canaliculus (duct)
- ~ **mastoideus** mastoid canaliculus
- ~ **tympanicus** tympanic canaliculus, Jacobson's canal

Canalis m canal[is], channel, duct *(s. a. unter Kanal)*
- ~ **adductorius [Hunteri]** adductor canal [of Hunter], subsartorial (Hunter's) canal
- ~ **alimentarius** alimentary canal (tract, tube)
- ~ **alveolaris** alveolar (dental) canal
- ~ **alveolaris inferior** inferior alveolar canal
- ~ **alveolaris maxillae (superior)** maxillary (superior alveolar) canal
- ~ **analis** anal canal
- ~ **atrioventricularis communis** common atrioventricular canal
- ~ **caroticus** carotid canal
- ~ **carpi** carpal canal (tunnel)
- ~ **centralis [medullae spinalis]** central canal [of the spinal cord], Stilling's (spinal medullary) canal, neurocanal, ventricle of the cord, syringocoele
- ~ **cervicis [uteri]** cervical (uterocervical) canal
- ~ **condylaris** condylar (condyloid) canal
- ~ **craniopharyngeus** craniopharyngeal canal
- ~ **facialis** facial canal, Fallopian aquaeductus (canal)
- ~ **femoralis** femoral (crural) canal, Cloquet's canal
- ~ **hyaloideus** hyaloid (Cloquet's) canal
- ~ **incisivus** incisive canal
- ~ **infraorbitalis** infraorbital (suborbital) canal
- ~ **inguinalis** inguinal canal
- ~ **intestinalis** intestinal canal
- ~ **mandibulae** mandibular canal, inferior dental canal
- ~ **musculotubarius** musculotubal (musculotuberal) canal *(im Schläfenbein)*
- ~ **nasolacrimalis** nasolacrimal canal
- ~ **nervi facialis** canal for the facial nerve
- ~ **nervi hypoglossi** hypoglossal canal
- ~ **nervi petrosi majoris** canal of the greater petrosal nerve
- ~ **nervi petrosi minoris** canal of the lesser petrosal nerve

- ~ **Nucki** Nuck's canal (diverticulum) *(Bauchfellausstülpung beim weiblichen Geschlecht)*
- ~ **nutricius** nutrient (nutritive, Haversian) canal
- ~ **obturatorius** obturator canal
- ~ **olfactorius** olfactory canal
- ~ **omphalomesentericus** omphalomesenteric canal *(Embryologie)*
- ~ **opticus** optic canal
- ~ **palatinus major** greater palatine canal
- ~ **palatinus minor** smaller palatine canal
- ~ **palatovaginalis (pharyngeus)** palatovaginal (pharyngeal) canal
- ~ **pterygoideus** pterygoid canal
- ~ **pterygopalatinus** pterygopalatine (sphenopalatine) canal
- ~ **pudendalis** pudendal (Alcocks's) canal
- ~ **pyloricus** pyloric canal (channel), pylorus
- ~ **radicis dentis** root canal
- ~ **sacralis** sacral (sacrococcygeal) canal
- ~ **semicircularis** semicircular canal (duct) *(Innenohr)*
- ~ **semicircularis anterior** anterior semicircular canal
- ~ **semicircularis horizontalis** horizontal semicircular canal *(Innenohr)*
- ~ **semicircularis lateralis** lateral semicircular canal
- ~ **semicircularis osseus** osseous semicircular canal *(Innenohr)*
- ~ **semicircularis posterior** posterior semicircular canal [of the bony labyrinth of the inner ear]
- ~ **semicircularis superior** superior semicircular canal *(Innenohr)*
- ~ **sphenopalatinus** sphenopalatine canal
- ~ **spinalis** spinal (craniovertebral) canal
- ~ **spiralis cochleae** spiral canal of the cochlea
- ~ **spiralis modioli** spiral canal of the modiolus
- ~ **utriculosaccularis** sacculo-utricular canal *(Innenohr)*
- ~ **vaginae** vaginal canal
- ~ **ventriculi** gastric canal
- ~ **vertebralis** vertebral (spinal, neural) canal
- ~ **vomerovaginalis** vomerovaginal (basipharyngeal) canal

Cancer *m s.* Carcinoma
- ~ **en cuirasse** corset cancer, cancer en cuirasse

Cancrum *n* **oris** noma, oral gangrene
Candicidin *n* candicidin *(Antimykotikum)*
Candida *f* **albicans** Candida (Monilia) albicans, thrush fungus
Candida-Exanthem *n* candida exanthema
Candida-Infektion *f* candidal infection
- ~ **der Niere** renal candidal infection

Candida-Meningitis *f* candidal meningitis
Candidämie *f* candidaemia
Candida-Mykid *n* candidid
Candida-Mykose *f s.* Candidiasis
Candida-Sepsis *f* candidal sepsis
Candidiasis *f* candidiasis, candidosis
Candidid *n* candidid
Canicola-Fieber *n* canicola fever, canine leptospirosis

Caninus *m* canine [tooth], eye tooth
Cannabis *f* **indica** Indian hemp
Cannon-Davis-Syndrom *n* Cannon-Davis syndrome *(funktionelle Dysmenorrhoe)*
Cannon-Notfallsyndrom *n* Cannon's syndrome *(Teil des Adaptationssyndroms)*
Cannula *f* cannula, tube
Canthariden *fpl s.* Kanthariden
Cantharidinintoxikation *f s.* Kantharidismus
Canthoplastik *f s.* Kanthoplastik
Canthus *m s.* Kanthus
Capitatum *n* capitate bone, capitatum
Capitellum *n* capitellum
Capitulum *n* capitulum, head *(Zusammensetzungen s. unter Caput)*
Caplan-[Colinet-]Syndrom *n* Caplan's syndrome *(Anthrakosilikose der Lunge)*
Capsula *f* capsula, capsule *(s. a. unter Kapsel)*
- ~ **adiposa renis** fatty capsule of the kidney
- ~ **articularis** articular (joint) capsule
- ~ **articularis acromioclavicularis** capsule of the acromioclavicular joint
- ~ **articularis articulationis radiocarpeae** capsule of the wrist joint
- ~ **articularis articulationis tarsi transversae** capsule of the transverse tarsal joint
- ~ **articularis articulationis temporomandibularis** capsule of the temporomandibular joint
- ~ **articularis calcaneocuboideae** capsule of the calcaneocuboid joint
- ~ **articularis carpometacarpea pollicis** capsule of the carpometacarpal joint of the thumb
- ~ **articularis coxae** capsule of the hip joint
- ~ **articularis cubiti** capsule of the elbow joint
- ~ **articularis genus** capsule of the knee joint
- ~ **articularis humeri** capsule of the shoulder joint
- ~ **articularis mandibulae** capsule of the temporomandibular joint
- ~ **articularis radioulnaris distalis** capsule of the distal radioulnar joint
- ~ **articularis sternoclavicularis** capsule of the sternoclavicular joint
- ~ **articularis talocruralis** capsule of the talocrural (ankle) joint
- ~ **articularis tibiofibularis** capsule of the tibiofibular joint
- ~ **bulbi** Tenon's capsule, capsule of Tenon, fascia of the bulb
- ~ **externa** external capsule
- ~ **fibrosa perivascularis** hepatobiliary capsule
- ~ **fibrosa renis** renal capsule, fibrous capsule of the kidney
- ~ **glomeruli** glomerular (Bowman's, Malpigian) capsule
- ~ **hepatis** Glisson's capsule, capsule of the liver
- ~ **interna** internal capsule
- ~ **lentis** lens (crystalline) capsule, capsule of the lens
- ~ **ossea labyrinthi** osseous labyrinth *(des Ohres)*
- ~ **prostatis** prostatic capsule, capsule of the prostate

Caput *n* caput, head

Caput

- ~ **breve musculi bicipitis brachii** short head of the biceps muscle of the arm
- ~ **breve musculi bicipitis femoris** short head of the biceps muscle of the leg
- ~ **epididymidis** head of the epididymis
- ~ **femoris** femoral head
- ~ **fibulae** fibular head
- ~ **humerale musculi extensoris carpi ulnaris** humeral head of the extensor carpi ulnaris muscle
- ~ **humerale musculi flexoris carpi ulnaris** humeral head of the flexor carpi ulnaris muscle
- ~ **humerale musculi pronatoris teretis** humeral head of the pronator teres muscle
- ~ **humeri** humeral head, capitulum of the humerus
- ~ **laterale musculi gastrocnemii** lateral head of the gastrocnemius muscle
- ~ **laterale musculi tricipitis brachii** lateral head of the triceps brachii muscle
- ~ **longum musculi tricipitis brachii** long head of the triceps [brachii] muscle
- ~ **mallei** head of the malleus
- ~ **mandibulae** head of the mandible
- ~ **mediale musculi gastrocnemii** medial head of the gastrocnemius muscle
- ~ **mediale musculi tricipitis brachii** medial head of the triceps brachii muscle
- ~ **medusae** medusa head, cirsomphalos
- ~ **nuclei caudati** head of the caudate nucleus
- ~ **obliquum musculi adductoris hallucis** oblique head of the adductor hallucis muscle
- ~ **obliquum musculi adductoris pollicis** oblique head of the adductor pollicis muscle
- ~ **obstipum** wry-neck, torticollis
- ~ **obstipum acquisitum** acquired torticollis
- ~ **obstipum musculare** muscular torticollis
- ~ **ossis metacarpalis** head of the metacarpal bone
- ~ **ossis metatarsalis** head of the metatarsal bone
- ~ **pancreatis** head of the pancreas
- ~ **profundum musculi flexoris pollicis brevis** deep head of the flexor pollicis brevis muscle
- ~ **radii** head of the radius
- ~ **stapedii (stapedis)** head of the stapes, stapedial head
- ~ **superficiale musculi flexoris pollicis brevis** superficial head of the flexor pollicis brevis muscle
- ~ **tali** head of the talus
- ~ **transversum musculi adductoris hallucis** transverse head of the adductor hallucis muscle
- ~ **transversum musculi adductoris pollicis** transverse head of the adductor pollicis muscle
- ~ **ulnae** head of the ulna
- ~ **ulnare musculi extensoris carpi ulnaris** ulnar head of the extensor carpi ulnaris muscle

Carate f carate, pinta, azul *(Hautkrankheit durch Treponema carateum)*
Carbo m **activatus** activated charcoal
- ~ **medicinalis** medicinal charcoal

Carbonisatio f carbonization, burn of fourth degree, fourth-degree burn
Carboxyhämoglobin n carboxyhaemoglobin
Carboxyhämoglobinämie f carboxyhaemoglobinaemia
Carboxymethylzellulose f carboxymethylcellulose *(Laxans)*
Carcinoma n carcinoma, cancer *(bösartige Geschwulst) (s. a. unter Karzinom)*
- ~ **adenomatosum** adenocarcinoma
- ~ **basocellulare** basal-cell cancer (carcinoma) *(der Haut)*
- ~ **cutaneum** epithelioma, epidermal cancer (carcinoma)
- ~ **durum** hard carcinoma
- ~ **lenticulare** lenticular carcinoma
- ~ **spinocellulare** spinocellular (prickle-cell) carcinoma *(epitheliale Haut- und Schleimhautgeschwulst)*
- ~ **spongiosum** medullary cancer
- ~ **ventriculi** gastric carcinoma
- ~ **vesicae** vesical carcinoma, bladder cancer
- ~ **villosum** villous carcinoma

Cardiazolkrampf m cardiazol spasm
Cardio... s. a. Kardio...
Cardiomegalia f **glycogenica** Pompe's disease, generalized glycogenosis, acid maltase deficiency, cardiac glycogen storage disease *(kardiomegale Form der Glykogenspeicherkrankheit)*
Cardiopathia f cardiopathy, heart disease
- ~ **chagasia** Chagas' myocarditis

Carditis f carditis, inflammation of the heart
- ~ **rheumatica** rheumatic carditis

Caries f 1. caries, bone decay; 2. s. ~ dentium
- ~ **acuta** acute caries
- ~ **alba** white caries
- ~ **columnae vertebralis** s. ~ spinalis
- ~ **dentium** [dental] caries, dental decay, saprodontia
- ~ **florida** florid caries
- ~ **humida** wet (humid) caries
- ~ **nigra** black caries
- ~ **penetrans** penetrating caries
- ~ **profunda** deep caries
- ~ **sicca** dry caries
- ~ **spinalis** spinal caries, caries of the spine, Pott's disease

Caries... s. Karies...
Carina f carina
- ~ **tracheae** carina [tracheae], bronchial septum
- ~ **urethralis vaginae** urethral carina (ridge of the vagina)

Carman-Meniskuszeichen n Carman's [meniscus] sign
Carminativum n remedium carminative [agent]
Carnitin n carnitine, vitamin B_T
Caroli-Syndrom n Caroli's syndrome *(Dilatation der intrahepatischen Gallengänge)*
Carotis f s. Halsschlagader
Carotis-externa-Aneurysma n external carotid artery aneurysm

Carotis-externa-Arteriogramm n external carotid arteriogram
Carotis-interna-Aneurysma n internal carotid artery aneurysm
Carotis-interna-Arteriogramm n internal carotid arteriogram
Carpale n carpal bone
Carpenter-Syndrom n Carpenter's syndrome, acrocephalopolysyndactyly
Carpule f carpule, cartridge ampoule
Carpus m carpus, wrist
~ **curvus** carpokyphosis, carpus curvus, Madelung's deformity
Carrel-Flasche f Carell's flask *(für Gewebekulturen)*
Carrier m carrier *(1. Keimträger; 2. Dauerausscheider)*
Carrier-Kultur f carrier culture *(Zellkultur)*
Carrier-Mechanismus m carrier mechanism
Carrier-Protein n carrier protein
Carr-Price-Reaktion f Carr-Price test *(zum Nachweis von Vitamin A und D)*
Carswell-Trauben fpl Carswell's grapes, pulmonary tubercles
Cartilagines fpl **laryngeales** laryngeal cartilages
Cartilago f cartilage, cartilaginous (chondral) tissue *(s. a. unter* Knorpel*)*
~ **alaris** alar cartilage
~ **alaris major** greater (major) alar cartilage
~ **alaris minor** lesser (minor) alar cartilage
~ **articularis** articular (arthrodial) cartilage
~ **arytenoidea** arytenoid (triquetrous) cartilage
~ **auriculae** auricular cartilage
~ **basialis** basilar cartilage
~ **conchalis** conchal cartilage
~ **corniculata** corniculate cartilage [of Santorini], Santorini's cartilage *(Kehlkopf)*
~ **costalis** costal cartilage, costicartilage, costocartilage
~ **cricoidea** cricoid [cartilage], annular (innominate) cartilage
~ **cuneiformis [Wrisbergi]** cuneiform cartilage [of Wrisberg], Wrisberg's cartilage, cartilage of Wrisberg
~ **epiglottica** epiglottic cartilage
~ **epiphysialis** epiphyseal cartilage
~ **meatus acustici** cartilage of the external acoustic meatus
~ **nasalis accessoria** accessory nasal cartilage, sesamoid (epactal) cartilage
~ **nasi lateralis** lateral (upper) nasal cartilage
~ **septi nasi** septal cartilage [of the nose], cartilaginous septum [of the nose]
~ **sesamoidea** sesamoid cartilage
~ **sternoclavicularis** omosternum
~ **thyreoidea** thyroid cartilage, scutum
~ **trachealis** tracheal cartilage (ring)
~ **tubae auditivae** cartilage (cartilaginous part) of the auditory tube, Eustachian cartilage
~ **vomeronasalis** vomeronasal (subvomerine) cartilage, Huschke's (Jacobson's) cartilage
Caruncula f caruncula, caruncle *(aus lockerem Bindegewebe und Gefäßen)*
~ **hymenalis** hymenal caruncle
~ **sublingualis** sublingual caruncle (papilla)
~ **urethrae** urethral caruncle
Carus m carus, profound lethargy, deep coma, stupor
Casal-Halsband n Casal's collar (necklace) *(bei Pellagra)*
Casoni-Test m Casoni [skin] test, Casoni reaction *(zum Echinokokkennachweis)*
Cassava-Vergiftung f Cassava poisoning *(durch Manihot aipi oder Manihot utilissima)*
Casser-Fontanelle f Casser's (Casserio's) fontanel, posterolateral fontanel
Cassirer-Syndrom n Cassirer's [acroasphyxia] syndrome
Castañeda-Färbung f Castañeda's stain *(zum Rickettsiennachweis)*
Castañeda-Impfstoff m Castañeda vaccine *(gegen Typhus)*
Castellani-Bronchitis f s. Castellani-Krankheit
Castellani-Farblösung f Castellani's paint (carbol-fuchsine solution)
Castellani-Krankheit f Castellani's disease, bronchospirochaetosis
Castle-intrinsic-Faktor m s. Intrinsic-Faktor/Castlescher
Cataracta f cataract *(s. a. unter* Katarakt *und* Star*)*
~ **anularis** annular (ring) cataract
~ **centralis congenita** s. ~ nuclearis
~ **cerulea** cerulean (punctiform) cataract
~ **complicata** complicated cataract
~ **congenita membranacea** congenital membranaceous cataract
~ **coronaria** coronary cataract
~ **corticalis** cortical cataract
~ **diabetica** diabetic cataract
~ **electrica** electric (lightning) cataract
~ **fusiformis** fusiform cataract
~ **incipiens** incipient cataract
~ **intumescens** intumescent (swollen) cataract
~ **membranacea** membranous cataract, pseudoaphakia
~ **nigra** black cataract
~ **nuclearis** nuclear cataract *(auf den Alterskern der Linse beschränkte Trübung)*
~ **polaris anterior** anterior polar cataract
~ **polaris posterior** posterior polar cataract
~ **punctata** punctate (blue dot) cataract
~ **pyramidalis** pyramidal cataract
~ **rosiformis** rosette cataract
~ **senilis** senile cataract
~ **stellaris** stellate (sutural) cataract
~ **subcapsularis** subcapsular cataract
~ **suturalis** sutural (stellate) cataract
~ **tetanica** tetanic cataract
~ **traumatica** traumatic cataract
~ **zonularis** zonular (lamellar) cataract
Cauda f tail, cauda
~ **epididymidis** tail of the epididymis
~ **equina** cauda equina *(unterster Rückenmarkabschnitt)*

Cauda

~ **pancreatis** tail of the pancreas, pancreatic tail
Cauda-equina-Syndrom n cauda [equina] syndrome
Cava f s. Vena cava
Cavernoma n lymphaticum cavernous lymphangioma
C-Avitaminose f avitaminosis C, scurvy, scorbutus
Cavitas f s. Cavum
~ **glenoidalis** glenoid cavity
Cavum n cavity, cavern, cavum, space
~ **abdominis** abdominal cavity
~ **articulare** joint cavity
~ **conchae** cavity of the concha
~ **coronale** pulp chamber
~ **corporis uteri** s. ~ uteri
~ **dentis** pulp cavity [of the tooth]
~ **epidurale (extradurale)** epidural space, extradural cavity (space)
~ **infraglotticum** infraglottic cavity
~ **laryngis** laryngeal cavity, cavity of the larynx
~ **leptomeningicum** subarachnoid space
~ **Meckeli** cave of Meckel
~ **mediastinale anterius** anterior mediastinum (mediastinal area)
~ **mediastinale posterius** posterior mediastinum (mediastinal area)
~ **medullare** medullary (bone-marrow) cavity, medullary space [of the bone]
~ **nasi** nasal cavity (fossa)
~ **oris** oral cavity
~ **pelvis** pelvic cavity, cavity of the pelvis
~ **pericardii** pericardial cavity (space)
~ **peritonei** peritoneal cavity
~ **pharyngis** cavity of the pharynx
~ **pleurae** pleural cavity (space)
~ **pleuropericardiacoperitoneale** pleuroperitoneal cavity, embryonic coelom
~ **Retzii** cave (space) of Retzius
~ **septi pellucidi** cavity of the septum pellucidum
~ **subarachnoidale** subarachnoid space
~ **subdurale** subdural space
~ **thoracis** thoracic cavity (space)
~ **trigeminale** trigeminal cave
~ **tympani** s. Paukenhöhle
~ **uteri** cavity of the uterus (fundus), endometrial cavity, uterine canal
CB-[EKG-]Ableitung f CB lead
Ceelen-Gellerstedt-Syndrom n Ceelen-Gellerstedt syndrome, idiopathic pulmonary haemosiderosis
Cellulae fpl **ethmoidales** ethmoid [air] cells, ethmoid antrum (sinus), ethmoid labyrinth [of cells]
~ **ethmoidales anteriores** anterior ethmyoid [air] cells
~ **ethmoidales mediales** middle ethmoid [air] cells
~ **ethmoidales posteriores** posterior ethmoid [air] cells
~ **mastoideae** mastoid [air] cells, mastoid sinus
~ **pneumaticae** [tubal] air cells

~ **tympanicae** tympanic [air] cells
Cellulitis f/**anaerobe** anaerobic cellulitis (myositis)
~ **orbitae** orbital cellulitis
Centrum n **medianum** median centre *(Thalamus)*
~ **tendineum [diaphragmatis]** central (trefoil) tendon of the diaphragm
~ **tendineum perinei** perineal body
Cephal... s. a. Kephal... *und* Zephal...
Cephalopagus m **occipitalis** occipital cephalopagus (craniopagus)
Cera f cera, wax
Cercaria f s. Zerkarie
Cerclage f cerclage
Cerebellum n s. Kleinhirn
Cerebrum n cerebrum, brain *(s. a. unter Gehirn)*
~ **abdominale** solar (coeliac) plexus, abdominal brain
Cerumen n cerumen, earwax
Cervix f cervix, neck
~ **uteri** uterine cervix (neck), cervix of the uterus, neck of the womb
~ **vesicae** neck of the [urinary] bladder
Cestan-Chenais-Syndrom n Cestan's (Cestan-Chenais) syndrome *(Hemiplegia alternans)*
Cestode m s. Zestode
CF-[EKG-]Ableitung f CF lead
C-Galle f C bile
Chagas-Herz n s. Chagas-Myokarditis
Chagas-Krankheit f Chagas' (Cruz') disease, American (Brazilian) trypanosomiasis, schizotrypano[somia]sis, barbeiro fever *(Tropenkrankheit durch Trypanosoma cruzi)*
Chagas-Myokarditis f Chagas' myocarditis
Chagom n chagoma *(Primärherd der Chagas-Krankheit)*
Chalasie f chalasia
Chalazion n chalazion, Meibomian cyst
Chalazionklemme f chalazion clamp
Chalazodermie f chalazodermia, dermatochalasis, dermatolysis
Chalikose f chalicosis; stonecutter's lung
Chalkose f chalcosis
Chalon n chalone *(Mitoseinhibitor)*
chamäkonchal chamaeconchous
Chamäkonchie f chamaeconchia
chamäkranial chamaecranial
chamäprosop chamaeprosopic
Chamäprosopie f chamaeprosopia
chamäzephal chamaecephalic, chamaecephalous
Chamäzephalie f chamaecephalia
Chamäzephalus m chamaecephalus
Chamomilla f c[h]amomile
Charakter m character
Charakterabnormität f character abnormality
Charakteranalyse f character analysis
Charakterbildung f character formation
Charakterlehre f characterology
Charakterneurose f character neurosis
Charakterpanzerung f character defence
Charakterstörung f character disorder; behaviour disturbance

Chiasma-[opticum-]Läsion

Charakterstruktur f character structure
Charas n charas, bhang, cannabis indica *(Rauschgift)*
Charcot-Gelenk n Charcot's joint; Charcot's arthritis (arthropathy, arthrosis)
Charcot-Krankheit f 1. Charcot's disease, amyotrophic lateral sclerosis; 2. s. Krankheit/Charcot-Mariesche; 3. s. Charcot-Gelenk
Charcot-Leyden-Kristalle mpl Charcot-Leyden crystals
Charcot-Syndrom n I Charcot's syndrome, intermittent claudication
~ II Charcot's syndrome, amyotrophic lateral sclerosis
Charcot-Trias f Charcot triad *(Nystagmus, Intentionstremor und skandierende Sprache)*
Charcot-Weiss-Baker-Syndrom n Charcot-Weiss-Baker syndrome, collapse (carotid sinus) syndrome
Charcot-Zirrhose f Charcot's (biliary) cirrhosis
Charcot-Zone f Charcot's (hysterogenic) zone
Charente-Fieber n Charente fever *(Leptospirose)*
Charlin-Syndrom n Charlin's syndrome, nasociliary neuralgia
Charta f charta
Chasteck-Paralyse f Chastek paralysis *(Vitamin B_1-Avitaminose)*
Chauffard-Still-Syndrom n Chauffard-Still syndrome, Still's disease *(juvenile Rheumatoidarthritis)*
ChE s. Cholinesterase
Check-valve-Mechanismus m check valve mechanism *(Atemphysiologie)*
Chediak-Higashi-Syndrom n Chediak-Higashi anomaly (syndrome)
Chefarzt m medical superintendent, chief (head) physician
Chefchirurg m chief (senior) surgeon, surgeon-in-chief
Cheilalgie f cheilalgia
Cheilektomie f cheilectomy
Cheilitis f ch[e]ilitis, inflammation of the lips
~ **glandularis** glandular cheilitis
Cheiloangioskop n cheiloangioscope
Cheiloangioskopie f cheiloangioscopy
Cheilognathopalatoschisis f cheilognathopalatoschisis; cleft lip face palate, wolfjaw
Cheilognathoprosoposchisis f cheilognathoprosoposchisis
Cheilognathouranoschisis f cheilognathouranoschisis
Cheiloplastik f cheiloplasty, labioplasty
Cheilorrhaphie f cheilorrhaphy, labiorrhaphy
Cheiloschisis f cheiloschisis; cleft lip, harelip
Cheilosis f cheilosis
Cheilostomatoplastik f cheilostomatoplasty
Cheilotomie f cheilotomy
Cheiralgia f **paraesthetica** paraesthetic cheiralgia, Wartenberg's disease
Cheiralgie f cheiralgia, pain in the hand
Cheirarthritis f ch[e]irarthritis
Cheiromegalie f ch[e]iromegaly

Cheiroplastik f ch[e]iroplasty
Cheiropompholyx f ch[e]iropompholyx *(Bläschenbildung an den Händen)*
Cheiroskop n cheiroscope *(Instrument zur Schielbehandlung)*
Cheirospasmus m ch[e]irospasm, writers' cramp
Chelatbildner m chelating agent
Chelatbildung f chelation, chelate formation
Chelidonin n chelidonine *(Alkaloid)*
Chemie f/**analytische** analytical chemistry
~/**forensische** forensic (legal) chemistry
~/**pharmazeutische** pharmaceutical chemistry
~/**physiologische** physiological chemistry
Chemilumineszenz f chemiluminescence
Chemochirurgie f chemosurgery *(Entfernung von Krebsgewebe nach chemischer Fixierung)*
chemochirurgisch chemosurgical
Chemodektom n chemodectoma, non-chromaffine paraganglioma
Chemodifferenzierung f chemodifferentiation
Chemoembolisation f chemoembolization
chemoimmunotherapeutisch chemoimmunotherapeutic
Chemoimmunotherapie f chemoimmunotherapy
Chemokaustik f chemicocautery
Chemokoagulation f chemocoagulation
Chemomorphose f chemomorphosis
Chemonukleolyse f chemonucleolysis
Chemoprophylaxe f chemoprophylaxis
Chemoreflex n chemoreflex
chemoresistent chemoresistant
Chemoresistenz f chemoresistance
Chemorezeptor m chemo[re]ceptor
Chemosis f chemosis
Chemosynthese f chemosynthesis
chemosynthetisch chemosynthetic
chemotaktisch chemotactic
Chemotaxis f chemotaxis
Chemothalamotomie f chemothalamotomy
chemotherapeutisch chemotherapeutic
Chemotherapie f chemotherapy
~ **der Harnwege** urochemotherapy
~/**endermale** endermosis
~/**palliative** palliative chemotherapy
chemotisch chemotic
Chemotropismus m chemotropism
Chenodesoxycholsäure f chenode[s]oxycholic acid *(Gallensäure)*
Chenopodiumöl n chenopodium oil
Cherubinismus-Syndrom n cherubinism [syndrome]
Chiari-Frommel-Syndrom n Chiari-Frommel syndrome *(Persistenz der Laktation nach der Geburt)*
Chiasma n chiasm[a], decussation *(s. a. unter Decussatio)*
~ **nervorum opticorum** s. ~ **opticum**
~ **opticum** optic chiasma (commissure), decussation of the optic nerve
Chiasmakompression f chiasmal compression
chiasmal chiasmal
Chiasma-[opticum-]Läsion f optic chiasma lesion

Chiasmasyndrom

Chiasmasyndrom *n* chiasmatic syndrome, [optic] chiasma syndrome
Chiasmatumor *m* optic chiasma tumour
Chiclerogeschwür *n* chicle[ro] ulcer, chiclero's ear, bay sore, chewing gum ulcer
Chilaiditi-Syndrom *n* Chilaiditi's syndrome *(Lageanomalie des Dick- und Dünndarms)*
Chilitis *f s.* Cheilitis
Chimäre *f* chimera
Chimärismus *m* chimerism
China[baum]rinde *f s.* Cinchona
Chinchona *f s.* Cinchona
Chinidin *n* quinidine, chinidine *(Cinchonaalkaloid)*
Chinidinintoxikation *f* cinchonism
Chinidinsulfat *n* quinidine sulphate
Chinin *n* quinine *(Cinchonaalkaloid)* ● **mit ~ behandeln** to quininize
β-Chinin *n s.* Chinidin
Chininamblyopie *f* quinine amblyopia
Chininfieber *n* quinine fever
Chininrausch *m* quininism, cinchonism
Chininsulfat *n* quinine sulphate
Chinintherapie *f* quinine therapy, cinchonization, quinchonization
Chininvergiftung *f* quininism, cinchonism
Chinolin *n* quinoline, chinoline
Chinon *n* quinone, chinone
Chir... *s. a.* Cheir...
Chiragra *n* ch[e]iragra
Chiropraktik *f* chiropractic, chiropraxis
Chiropraktiker *m* chiropractor
Chirurg *m* surgeon, chirurgeon
~ für plastische Chirurgie plastic surgeon
~/operierender operator
Chirurgie *f* surgery, chirurgery
~/allgemeine general surgery
~/aseptische aseptic surgery
~/dermatoplastische dermatoplastic surgery
~/kardiovaskuläre cardiovascular surgery
~/kleine minor surgery
~/kosmetische cosmetic surgery
~/mastoidotympanoplastische mastoidotympanoplastic surgery
~ mit dem elektrischen Messer electrosurgery
~/orthopädische orthopaedic surgery
~/pelvine pelvic surgery
~/plastische plastic (reparative) surgery; anaplasty
~/vaskuläre vascular surgery
chirurgisch surgical, chirurgic[al] ● **auf chirurgischem Wege** operative, operational
~/nicht non-surgical
Chitosamin *n* chitosamine *(ein Glukosamin)*
Chitralfieber *n* Chitral fever, phlebotomus (three-day) fever
Chlamydien *npl* clamydia *(Trachomerreger)*
Chlamydieninfektion *f* chlamydial infection
Chloasma *n* chloasma, liver spot
Chlorakne *f* chloracne, chloric (chlorine) acne
Chloral *n* chloral, trichloracetaldehyde
Chloralhydrat *n* chloral hydrate

Chloralose *f* chloralose *(Narkotikum)*
Chlorambuzil *n* chlorambucil *(Zytostatikum)*
Chlorämie *f s.* Chloranämie
Chloramin *n* T chloramine-T *(Antiseptikum)*
Chloramphenikol *n* chloramphenicol *(Antibiotikum)*
Chloramphenikolintoxikation *f* chloramphenicol intoxication, grey syndrome
Chloramphenikolsukzinat *n* chloramphenicol succinate
Chloranämie *f* chlor[o]anaemia, chlorotic, anaemia, [hyper]chloraemia, chlorosis, green sickness
~/achylische achylic chloranaemia *(Eisenmangelanämie durch Salzsäuremangel im Magen)*
Chloratum *n* hydratum chloral hydrate
Chlorausschlag *m s.* Chlorakne
chloren to chlorinate, to chlorinize
Chloren *n* chlorination
Chlorfinnen *fpl s.* Chlorakne
Chlorhydrie *f* chlorhydria
Chloridausscheidung *f* chloride excretion (elimination)
~ im Urin chloriduria
~ im Urin/erhöhte hyperchloruria
~ im Urin/verminderte hypochloruria
Chloridverschiebung *f* chloride shift *(zwischen Erythrozyten und Plasma)*
chlorieren to chlorinate
Chlorkalk *m* chloride of lime, chlorinated lime *(Desinfektionsmittel)*
Chlormadinon *n* chlormadinone *(Kontrazeptivum)*
Chlormadinonazetat *n* chlormadinone acetate
Chlorochin *n* chloroquine *(Malariamittel)*
chlorochinresistent chloroquine-resistant
Chlorochinresistenz *f* chloroquine resistance
Chlorochinretinopathie *f* chloroquine retinopathy
Chloroform *n* chloroform, trichloromethane *(Narkotikum)*
Chloroformabusus *m* chloroformism
Chloroformbetäubung *f* chloroformization
chloroformieren to chloroform
Chloroleukämie *f* chloroleukaemia, Balfour's disease, Aran's cancer
Chlorolymphom *n*, **Chlorom** *n* chloromyeloma, chlorosarcoma, green cancer, chloro[lympho]ma *(Geschwulst bei Chloroleukämie)*
Chlorom-Chloroleukämie *f s.* Chloroleukämie
Chloromyelom *n s.* Chlorolymphom
Chloropsie *f* chlorop[s]ia, green vision
Chloroquin *n* chloroquine *(Malariamittel)*
Chlorosarkom *n s.* Chlorolymphom
Chlorosarkomatosis *f* chlorosarcomatosis
Chlorose *f* chlorosis, chlorotic anaemia, [hyper]chloraemia, chlor[o]anaemia, green sickness
~/ägyptische Egyptian chlorosis, ancylostomiasis *(Bergmannskrankheit)*
Chlorspiegelerhöhung *f* **im Blut** hyperchlor[id]aemia

Chlorspiegelverminderung f im Blut hypochlor[id]aemia
Chlortetrazyklin n chlortetracycline *(Antibiotikum)*
Chlorung f chlorination
Chlorwasserstoffsäure f hydrochloric acid
Choana f s. Choane
Choanalatresie f choanal atresia
Choane f internal (posterior) naris, posterior nasal orifice
~/**primäre (primitive)** primary choana
Cholagogum n cholagogue [agent]
Cholämie f cholaemia
cholämisch cholaemic
Cholangiektasie f cholangiectasis
Cholangioadenom n cholangioadenoma
Cholangioenterostomie f cholangioenterostomy
Cholangiogastrostomie f cholangiogastrostomy
Cholangiogramm n cholangiogram
Cholangiographie f cholangiography
~/**intraoperative** [per]operative cholangiography
~/**intravenöse** intravenous cholangiography
~/**perkutane transhepatische** percutaneous transhepatic cholangiography, PTC
Cholangiographiekanüle f cholangiography cannula
Cholangiographiezange f cholangiography forceps
cholangiographisch cholangiographic
Cholangiohepatitis f cholangiohepatitis
Cholangiohepatoadenom n cholangiohepatoadenoma
Cholangiohepatom n cholangiohepatoma
Cholangiokarzinom n cholangiocarcinoma, bile-duct carcinoma
cholangiolär cholangiolar
Cholangiolitis f cholangiolitis
cholangiolitisch cholangiolitic
Cholangiom n cholangioma
Cholangiometrie f cholangiometry
cholangiometrisch cholangiometric
Cholangiopankreatikographie f/**retrograde endoskopische** endoscopic retrograde cholangiopancreatography, E. R. C. P.
Cholangiostomie f cholangiostomy, bile-duct drainage
Cholangiotomie f cholangiotomy
Cholangitis f cholangitis, angiocholitis
cholangitisch cholangitic
Cholansäure f cholanic acid *(Gallensäure)*
Cholaskos m cholascos, choleperitoneum
Cholebilirubin n cholebilirubin
Cholechromopoese f cholechromopoiesis
Choledochektasie f choledochectasia
Choledochektomie f choledochectomy
Choledochitis f choledochitis
Choledochoenterostomie f choledochoenterostomy
Choledochogramm n choledochogram
Choledochographie f choledochography
choledochokutan choledochocutaneous
Choledocholith m choledocholith, common bile-duct stone

Choledocholithiasis f choledocholithiasis, common bile-duct stone disease
Choledocholithotomie f choledocholithotomy
Choledocholithotripsie f choledocholithotripsy
Choledochoplastik f choledochoplasty
Choledochorrhaphie f choledochorrhaphy
Choledochoskop n choledochoscope
Choledochoskopie f choledochoscopy
Choledochostomie f choledochostomy
Choledochotomie f choledochotomy
Choledochozele f choledochocele
Choledochozystektomie f choledochocystectomy
Choledocho-Zystojejunostomie f choledochocystojejunostomy
Choledochozystostomie f choledochocystostomy
Choledochus m choledochus, common [bile] duct
Choledochusanastomose f choledochus (common bile-duct) anastomosis
Choledochuschirurgie f choledochus (common bile-duct) surgery
Choledochus-Choledochus-Anastomose f choledochocholedochostomy
Choledochus-Choledochus-Naht f choledochocholedochorrhaphy
Choledochusdilatation f choledochus dilatation, dilatation of the common bile duct
Choledochusdilatator m choledochus (common bile-duct) dilator
Choledochusdrainage f choledochus (common bile-duct) drainage
Choledochus-Dünndarm-Anastomose f choledochoenterostomy
Choledochusentzündung f choledochitis, inflammation of the choledochus
Choledochusfistel f choledochus fistula
Choledochusfistelung f[/**operative**] choledochostomy
Choledochus-Gallenblasen-Anastomose f choledochocystostomy
Choledochusinzision f choledochotomy
Choledochusklemme f choledochus (common bile-duct) forceps
Choledochuskrebs m choledochus (common bile-duct) cancer
Choledochus-Krummdarm-Anastomose f choledochoileostomy
Choledochus-Leerdarm-Anastomose f choledochojejunostomy
Choledochusleiden n choledochus (common bile-duct) disease
Choledochus-Magen-Anastomose f choledochogastrostomy
Choledochusplastik f choledochoplasty
Choledochusrekonstruktion f choledochus (common bile-duct) reconstruction
Choledochusresektion f choledochectomy
Choledochussphinkter m choledochal sphincter
Choledochusstein m common bile-duct stone, choledocholith

Choledochussteinleiden

Choledochussteinleiden n common bile-duct stone disease, choledocholithiasis
Choledochusstenose f choledochus stenosis, stenosis of the common bile duct
Choledochusuntersuchung f choledochus (common bile-duct) exploration
Choledochusverletzung f choledochus injury, common bile-duct trauma
Choledochuszange f choledochus (biliary) forceps
Choledochus-Zwölffingerdarm-Anastomose f choledochoduodenostomy
Choledochus-Zwölffingerdarm-Fistel f choledochoduodenal fistula
Choledochuszyste f choledochus (choledochal) cyst, common bile-duct cyst
Choledochuszyste-Leerdarm-Anastomose f choledochocystojejunostomy
Choledochuszystenexstirpation f choledochocystectomy
Choleglobin n choleglobin *(Gallepigment)*
Cholekalziferol n cholecalciferol, vitamin D_3
cholekinetisch cholagog[ue], choleretic
Cholelith m cholelith, chololith, gall-stone, gallstone *(Zusammensetzungen s. unter Gallenstein)*
Cholelithiasis f cholelithiasis, biliary lithiasis
cholelithisch cholelithic
Cholelithotomie f cholelithotomy
Cholelithotripsie f cholelithotripsy, cholelithotrity
Cholemesis f cholemesis, vomiting of bile
Choleperitoneum n choleperitoneum, biliary peritonitis; cholascos
cholepoetisch cholepoietic
Choleprasin n choleprasin *(Gallepigment)*
Cholepyrrhin n cholepyrrhin
Cholera f cholera
~ **aestiva** summer cholera (diarrhoea), cholera morbus
~ **algida** algid cholera
~/**asiatische** Asiatic cholera
~/**endemische** endemic cholera
~ **nostras** salmonellosis, cholera nostras
~/**pandemische** pandemic cholera
~ **sicca (siderans)** dry cholera
choleraähnlich s. choleraartig
Choleraantiserum n anticholera serum
choleraartig cholera-like, choleriform, choleroid, choleraic
Choleradiagnostik f cholera diagnosis
Choleradiarrhoe f cholerine
Choleraenterotoxin n cholera enterotoxin
Choleraerreger m s. Choleravibrion
Choleraimpfstoff m cholera vaccine
cholerakrank suffering from cholera
Choleramanie f choleromania
Choleraschutzimpfung f cholera vaccination (inoculation)
Choleraserum n anticholera serum
Choleravibrio[n] m cholera vibrio, comma bacillus
Cholerese f choleresis

Choleretikum n choleretic [agent]
choleretisch choleretic
cholerisch choleric
Cholerophobie f cholerophobia *(krankhafte Angst vor Cholera)*
Cholerrhagie f cholerrhagia, biliary (bile) flow
Cholestan n cholestane
Cholestanol n cholestanol, dihydrocholesterol
Cholestase f cholestasis, biliary stasis
Cholestasehepatitis f cholestatic (cholangiolitic) hepatitis
Cholestaseikterus m cholestatic jaundice
Cholestaseleber[funktions]störung f cholestatic hepatic disorder
Cholestasezirrhose f cholestatic cirrhosis
Cholesteatom n cholesteatoma, pearl[y] tumour
cholesteatomatös cholesteatomatous
Cholesteatommatrix f cholesteatoma matrix
Cholesteatomzyste f cholesteatoma cyst
Cholesteatose f cholesteatosis
Cholesterase f cholesterase *(Enzym)*
Cholesterin n cholesterol, cholesterin *(Lipoidbestandteil)*
Cholesterinablagerung f cholester[ol]osis
Cholesterinämie f cholester[ol]aemia
Cholesterinausscheidung f im Urin cholesterinuria
Cholesterinbildung f cholesterolopoiesis
Cholesterinblutspiegel m cholesterol [blood] level, serum cholesterol
Cholesteringranulomatose f, **Cholesterinlipoidose** f s. Hand-Schüller-Christian-Syndrom
Cholesterinperikarditis f cholesterol pericarditis
Cholesterinperitonitis f cholesterol peritonitis
Cholesterinpolyp m cholesterol polypus
Cholesterinspeicherkrankheit f cholesterol thesaurismosis (storage disease)
Cholesterinspiegelerhöhung f im Blut hypercholesterolaemia, hypercholester[in]aemia
Cholesterinspiegelverminderung f im Blut hypocholesterolaemia, hypocholester[in]aemia
Cholesterinstein m cholesterol calculus
Cholesterinsynthese f cholesterolopoiesis
Cholesterol n s. Cholesterin
Cholesterosis f cholester[ol]osis
Choleszintigramm n cholescintigram
Choleszintigraphie f cholescintigraphy
choleszintigraphisch cholescintigraphic
Cholezystagogum n cholecystagogue [agent]
Cholezystalgie f cholecystalgia; gall-bladder colic
Cholezystektasie f cholecystectasia
Cholezystektomie f cholecystectomy
~ **mit Gallenwegsuntersuchung** cholecystectomy with common-duct exploration
~/**orthograde** orthograde cholecystectomy
~/**retrograde** retrograde cholecystectomy
Cholezystenterorrhaphie f cholecystenterorrhaphy
Cholezystenterostomie f cholecystenterostomy
Cholezystitis f cholecystitis, inflammation of the gall-bladder

Cholezystitiszeichen n/**Boassches** Boas' sign
Cholezystocholangiographie f cholecystocholangiography
cholezystoduodenal cholecystoduodenal
Cholezystoduodenostomie f cholecystoduodenostomy, duodeno[chole]cystostomy
Cholezystoenterostomie f cholecystoenterostomy
cholezystogastrisch cholecystogastric
Cholezystogastrostomie f cholecystogastrostomy
Cholezystogramm n cholecystogram
Cholezystographie f cholecystography
cholezystographisch cholecystographic
Cholezystoileostomie f cholecystoileostomy
Cholezystojejunostomie f cholecystojejunostomy
cholezystokinetisch cholecystokinetic
Cholezystokinin n cholecystokinin
Cholezystokinin-Pankreozymin n cholecystokinin-pancreozymin
Cholezystokolostomie f cholecystocolostomy
cholezystokutan cholecystocutaneous
Cholezystolith m chole[cysto]lith, cystic calculus, gall-stone *(Zusammensetzungen s. unter Gallenstein)*
Cholezystolithiasis f cholecystolithiasis
Cholezystolithotomie f cholecystolithotomy
Cholezystopathie f cholecystopathy, cholecystic (gall-bladder) disease
Cholezystopexie f cholecystopexy
Cholezystorrhaphie f cholecystorrhaphy, suture of the gall-bladder
Cholezystose f/**hyperplastische** hyperplastic cholecystosis
Cholezystostomie f cholecystostomy
Cholezystotomie f cholecystotomy
Cholin n choline, bilineurine
Cholinazetylase f choline acetylase *(Enzym)*
cholinergisch cholinergic, cholinogenic; parasympathicotonic
Cholinesterase f cholinesterase *(Enzym)*
Cholinesterasehemmer m cholinesterase inhibitor (blocking agent)
cholinomimetisch cholinomimetic
Cholinoxydase f choline oxidase *(Enzym)*
Chololith m s. Cholelith
Cholorrhoe f cholorrhoea, biliary (bile) flow
Cholothorax m cholothorax
Cholsäure f cholic acid *(Gallensäure)*
Cholurie f choluria
chondral chondral, cartilagin[e]ous
Chondralgie f chondralgia, chondrodynia, pain in the cartilage
Chondrektomie f chondrectomy, excision of the cartilage
Chondrifikation f chondrification, cartilaginification
Chondrin n chondrin
Chondriokont m s. Mitochondrium
Chondriom n chondriome *(Gesamtheit der Mitochondrien)*

Chondriosom n s. Mitochondrium
Chondriosphäre f chondriosphere
Chondritis f chondritis, inflammation of the cartilage
Chondroalbuminoid n chondroalbuminoid
Chondroangiopathie f chondroangiopathy
Chondroblast m chondroblast, chondroplast
Chondroblastom n chondroblastoma
Chondrodermatitis f chondrodermatitis
Chondrodysplasie f chondrodysplasia, dyschondroplasia
chondrodystroph chondrodystrophic
Chondrodystrophia f **calcificans congenita** congenital calcareous chondrodystrophy; congenital stippled epiphyses
Chondrodystrophie f chondrodystrophy, achondroplasty, achondroplasia
~/**hyperplastische** hyperplastic chondrodystrophy
~/**hypoplastische** hypoplastic chondrodystrophy
chondrodystrophisch chondrodystrophic
chondroektodermal chondroectodermal
Chondrofibrom n chondrofibroma
Chondrofibrosarkom n chondrofibrosarcoma
chondrogen chondrogen[et]ic
Chondrogenese f chondrogenesis, chondrosis
chondrogenetisch chondrogen[et]ic
chondroid chondroid, cartilaginoid
Chondroitin n chondroitin *(Mukopolysaccharid)*
Chondroitinschwefelsäure f chondroitinsulphuric (chondroitic) acid
Chondrokalzinose f chondrocalcinosis, pseudogout
Chondrokarzinom n chondrocarcinoma
Chondroklast m chondroclast
chondrokostal chondrocostal
chondrokranial chondrocranial
Chondrokranium n chondrocranium
Chondrolipom n chondrolipoma
Chondroliposarkom n chondroliposarcoma *(bösartiger Tumor)*
Chondrom n chondroma
Chondromalacia f **patellae** patellar chondromalacia
Chondromalazie f chondromalacia, softening of the cartilage
chondromatös chondromatous, cartilagin[e]ous, chondral, chondric
Chondromatose f chondromatosis
Chondrombildung f/**multiple** chondromatosis
Chondromer n chondromere
Chondrometaplasie f chondrometaplasia
Chondromukoid n chondromucoid
Chondromyxom n chondromyxoma
Chondromyxosarkom n chondromyxosarcoma *(bösartiger Tumor)*
Chondroosteosarkom n chondroosteosarcoma
Chondropathia f **tuberosa** Tietze's disease (syndrome)
Chondropathie f chondropathy
Chondroplastik f chondroplasty
Chondroporose f chondroporosis

Chondroprotein 146

Chondroprotein *n* chondroprotein
Chondrosarcoma *n* **myxomatodes** myxochondrosarcoma
Chondrosarkom *n* chondrosarcoma, enchondrosarcoma
chondrosarkomatös chondrosarcomatous
Chondrosarkomatose *f* chondrosarcomatosis
Chondrose *f* chondrosis, chondrogenesis
chondrosternal chondrosternal
Chondrotom *n* [ec]chondrotome; arthrotome
Chondrotomie *f* chondrotomy, dissection of the cartilage
chondrotroph chondrotrophic
Chondrozyt *m* chondrocyte, cartilage corpuscle (cell)
Chopart-Amputation *f* Chopart's amputation
Chopart-Amputationsstumpf *m* Chopart's [amputation] stump
Chopart-Gelenk *n* Chopart's joint (mediotarsal articulation)
Chorda *f* 1. chord[a], cord *(z. B. Sehnen und Nerven)*; 2. *s.* ~ dorsalis
~ **dorsalis** notochord
~ **tendinea** tendinous cord, tendon of the papillary muscle *(der Herzklappen)*
~ **uteroovarica** utero-ovarian ligament
Chordageschwulst *f* chordoma, chordoid tumour
Chordamesoblast *m* chordamesoblast *(Embryologie)*
Chordamesoderm *n* chordamesoderm *(Embryologie)*
Chordaspeichel *m* chorda saliva
Chordektomie *f* cordectomy
Chordenzephalon *n* chordencephalon
Chorditis *f* chorditis, inflammation of a vocal fold
~ **nodosa (tuberosa)** singer's nodes (nodules)
Chordoblastom *n* chordoblastoma
Chordoepitheliom *n* chordoepithelioma
Chordokarzinom *n* chordocarcinoma
Chordom *n* chordoma, chordoid tumour
Chordotomie *f* chordotomy, spinal tractotomy *(Rückenmark)*
~/**Foerstersche** Foerster's operation
Chorea *f* chorea
~ **bei aufrechter Körperhaltung** orthochorea
~/**chronisch progressive hereditäre** *s.* ~/Huntingtonsche
~ **gravidarum** chorea gravidarum, chorea of pregnancy
~/**Huntingtonsche** Huntington's chorea (disease), chronic progressive hereditary chorea, degenerative (adult hereditary) chorea
~/**infektiöse (infektiös-toxische)** *s.* ~/Sydenhamsche
~ **minor [infectiosa]** *s.* ~/Sydenhamsche
~/**rheumatische** rheumatic chorea
~/**senile** senile chorea, chronic progressive nonhereditary chorea
~/**Sydenhamsche** Sydenham's (dancing) chorea, Saint Vitus' dance, Saint Anthony's dance, infectious chorea (myoclonia)

choreaartig, choreatisch choreatic, choreal, choreic, choreiform, choreoid
choreoathetoid choreoathetoid
Choreoathetose *f* choreoathetosis
~/**paroxysmale** paroxysmal choreoathetosis
Choreomanie *f* choreomania
chorial chorionic
Chorioadenom *n* chorioadenoma, destructive [placental] mole, invasive mole
Chorioadenoma *n* **destruens** *s.* Chorioadenom
Chorioallantois *f* chorioallantois
Chorioallantoismembran *f* chorioallantoic membrane
Chorioamnionitis *f* chorioamnionitis
Chorioangiom *n* chorioangioma
Chorioangiopagus *m* chorioangiopagus
Chorioblastom *n* chorioblastoma
Chorioblastose *f* chorioblastosis
choriogen choriogenic
Choriogenese *f* choriogenesis
chorioid choroid[al]
Chorioidea *f* choroid, chorioid[ea], choroid coat (membrane) ● **zwischen ~ und Sklera liegend** perichoroid[al]
Chorioidea… *s. a.* Aderhaut…
Chorioideaangiom *n* choroid angioma
Chorioideaexstirpation *f* choroid plexectomy
Chorioideakarzinom *n* choroid cancer (carcinoma)
Chorioideakatarakt *f* choroid cataract
Chorioideamelanom *n* choroid melanoma
Chorioideamelanomzelle *f* choroid melanoma cell
Chorioideapapillom *n* choroid papilloma
Chorioidearuptur *f* choroid rupture
Chorioideaspalte *f* choroid fissure
Chorioidea- und Retinaerkrankung *f* chorioretinopathy
Chorioideavaskularisation *f* choroid vascularization
Chorioides *f s.* Chorioidea
Chorioiditis *f* choroiditis, chorioiditis
~/**diffuse** diffuse (disseminated) choroiditis
~/**Doynesche** honeycomb choroiditis of Doyne, Doyne's familial honeycombed choroiditis
~/**eitrige** suppurative choroiditis
~/**exsudative** exudative choroiditis
~/**Förstersche** Förster's (areolar central) choroiditis
~ **juxtapapillaris** juxtapapillary choroiditis, Jensen's disease (retinopathy)
~/**seröse** serous choroiditis
~/**zentrale** central choroiditis
choriokapillar choriocapillary
Choriokarzinom *n* choriocarcinoma, trophoblastoma, syncytioma
Choriom *n* chorioma, chorio[n]epithelioma
Choriomeningitis *f* choriomeningitis
~/**lymphozytäre** benign lymphocytic [chorio]meningitis
Chorion *n* chorion
~ **allantoideum** allantochorion

Chorionentwicklung f choriogenesis
Chorionentzündung f chorionitis, inflammation of the placenta
Chorionepitheliom n chorio[n]epithelioma
Choriongonadotropin n chorionic gonadotrophin
~/humanes human chorionic gonadotrophin
Chorionhormon n chorionic hormone
Chorionkarzinom n chorionic carcinoma
Chorionmembran f chorionic plate
Chorionplatte f chorionic plate
Chorionplattenarterie f chorionic plate artery
Chorionthyreotropin n/**humanes** human chorionic thyrotropin
Chorionzelle f chorionic cell
Chorionzellproliferation f chorioblastosis
Chorionzotte f chorionic villus
Chorionzottenbüschel n cotyledon
Chorionzyste f chorionic cyst
Chorioretinitis f choroidoretinitis, retinochoroiditis
Chorioretinoiridozyklektomie f chorioretino-iridocyclectomy (Entfernung der Ader- und Netzhaut, der Iris und des Ziliarkörpers)
Chorioretinopathie f chorioretinopathy
Choriozele f choriocele
Choristoblastom n, **Choristom** n choristoma, choristoblastoma (Tumor aus embryonaler Gewebeversprengung)
Choroidoiritis f choroidoiritis
Choroidozyklitis f choroidocyclitis
Christmas-Faktor m s. Blutgerinnungsfaktor IX
chromaffin chromaffine, phaeochrome
Chromaffinkörper m chromaffine body
Chromaffinoblastom n chromaffinoblastoma
Chromaffinom n chromaffinoma
Chromaffinopathie f chromaffinopathy (Erkrankung des chromaffinen Gewebes)
Chromatelopsie f chromatelopsia
Chromatgeschwür n chrome ulcer
Chromatid n, **Chromatide** f chromatid
Chromatin n chromatin
chromatinartig chromatoid
chromatinauflösend chromatolytic
Chromatinauflösung f chromatolysis
Chromatinfaden m chromatin thread
Chromatingerüst n chromatin network, karyomitome, karyoreticulum (Zellkern)
Chromatinkern m chromatin nucleus
Chromatinkörper m chromatin body
chromatin-negativ chromatin-negative
chromatin-positiv chromatin-positive
Chromatinstaub m chromatin dust
chromatisch chromatic
Chromatismus m chromatism
Chromatodermatose f chromatodermatosis
Chromatodysopsie f chromatodysopia
chromatogen chromatogenous
Chromatogramm n chromatogram
Chromatograph m chromatograph
Chromatographie f chromatography, chromatographic analysis (Verfahren zur Trennung von Stoffgemischen)

chromatographieren to chromatograph
chromatographisch chromatographic
Chromatolyse f chromatolysis (z. B. in Nervenzellen)
chromatolytisch chromatolytic
Chromatometrie f chromatometry
Chromatopathie f chromatopathy
chromatophil s. chromophil
chromatophob s. chromophob
chromatophor chromatophoric, chromatophorous
Chromatophor n chromatophore
Chromatoplasma n chromatoplasm
Chromatoplast m chromatoplast
Chromatopsie f chrom[at]opsia, chromatic (coloured) vision
Chromatoptometer n chromatoptometer
Chromatoptometrie f chrom[at]optometry
Chromatosis f chromatosis
Chromaturie f chromaturia
Chromgeschwür n chrome ulcer
Chromhidrosis f chromhidrosis, secretion of coloured sweat
Chromidiumnetz n chromidial net
Chromkatgut n chromized catgut
Chromkatgutnaht f chromic catgut suture
Chromoblast m chromoblast
Chromoblastomykose f chromoblastomycosis, chromo[hypho]mycosis (tropische Hautpilzinfektion); mossy foot
Chromodermatose f chromodermatosis
chromogen chromogenic
Chromolipoid n chromolip[o]id, lipochrome
Chromomer n chromomere
Chromomykose f s. Chromoblastomykose
Chromonema n chromonema
Chromonychie f chromonychia
chromophil chromophil[e], chromatophil
Chromophiler m chromophile [cell]
Chromophilie f chromophilia
chromophob chromophobe, chromophobic
Chromophober m chromophobe
Chromophobie f chromophobia
chromophor chromophoric, chromophorous
Chromophor m chromophore
Chromoplasma n chromoplasm
Chromoplast m chromoplast
Chromoprotein n chromoprotein
Chromoproteinniere f crush (chromoprotein) kidney; lower nephron nephrosis
Chromosom n chromosome, chromatin body
~/akzessorisches accessory chromosome, heterosome
~/homologes homologous chromosome
chromosomal chromosomal
Chromosomenaberration f chromosomal aberration
Chromosomenabnormität f chromosome abnormality
Chromosomenabschnitt m chromosomal segment; karyomere
Chromosomenabweichung f chromosome abnormality; chromosomal deletion

Chromosomenanalyse

Chromosomenanalyse f chromosome analysis
Chromosomenanzahl f chromosome number
Chromosomenbruch m chromosome break[age]
Chromosomenbrücke f chromosome bridge
Chromosomendefizienz f chromosome deficiency
Chromosomenfigur f chromosome figure
Chromosomenfragmentation f fragmentation of chromosomes, chromosome fragmentation
Chromosomengröße f chromosome size
Chromosomengruppe f chromosome group
Chromosomenkarte f chromosome (genetic) map
Chromosomenkomplement n chromosome complement
Chromosomenkonjugation f conjugation of chromosomes, chromosome conjunction, parasynapsis
Chromosomenlokalisation f chromosome location, genetic mapping
Chromosomenmarker m chromosomal marker
Chromosomenmutation f mutation of chromosomes, chromosome mutation
Chromosomenreduktion f reduction of chromosomes, chromosome reduction
Chromosomensatz m set of chromosomes, chromosome set
~/**diploider** diploid set of chromosomes
~/**euploider** euploid set of chromosomes
~/**haploider** haploid set of chromosomes
~/**polyploider** polyploid set of chromosomes
Chromosomenschaden m chromosomal damage
Chromosomenschädigung f chromosomal damaging
Chromosomensegment n chromosome segment; karyomere
Chromosomenspirale f chromosome coil
Chromosomenstruktur[ver]änderung f chromosomal aberration
Chromosomentranslokation f translocation of chromosomes, chromosome translocation
Chromosomenverdopplung f reduplication of chromosomes, chromosome reduplication
Chromosomenverschmelzung f fusion of chromosomes
Chromosomenzahl f chromosome number
Chromotrichomykose f chromotrichomycosis
Chromozystoskopie f chromocystoscopy *(Funktionsprüfung der Nieren durch intravenöse Farbstoffinjektion mit Blasenspiegelung)*
chromozystoskopisch chromocystoscopic
Chromozyt m chromocyte
Chromulkus n chrome ulcer
Chronaxie f chronaxy *(Reizauslösungszeit des doppelten Reizschwellenstroms)*
Chronaximeter n chronaximeter
chronisch chronic
chronisch-kalzifizierend chronic calcific[ant]
Chronizität f chronicity
chronotrop chronotropic
Chrysiasis f chrysiasis, chrysosis *(Hautverfärbung nach Goldbehandlung)*

Chrysoderma f chrysoderma
Chrysops m **discalis** chrysops discalis, [western] deer fly *(Überträger der Tularämie)*
Chrysosis f s. Chrysiasis
Chrysotherapie f chrysotherapy, gold treatment
Chvostek-Zeichen n Chvostek's sign *(Mundwinkelzuckung beim Beklopfen der Wange)*
Chylämie f chylaemia
Chylangiom n chylangioma
Chylaskos m chylascos, chyloperitoneum
Chyloderma n chyloderma
Chylomediastinum n chylomediastinum
Chylomikron n chylomicron *(Fettpartikel im Blut)*
Chyloperikard[ium] n chylopericardium
Chylopoese f chylopoiesis
Chylorrhoe f chylorrhoea
chylös chylous
Chylothorax m chylothorax
Chylozele f chylocele *(bei Elephantiasis)*
Chylurie f chyluria, albinuria, albiduria, galacturia
Chylus m chyle, chylus ● **keinen ~ absondernd** achylic
Chylusansammlung f **im Brustfellraum** chylothorax
~ **im Herzbeutel** chylopericardium
~ **im Mittelfellraum** chylomediastinum
chylusartig chyliform, chyloid, chylous
Chylusaszites m chylous ascites
chylusbildend chylopoietic, chylifacient
Chylusbildung f chylopoiesis, chylification
Chyluserhöhung f **im Blut** chylaemia
Chylusfluß m chylorrhoea
chylusführend chylophorous, chyliferous
Chylusmangel m deficiency of chyle; oligochylia, achylia, absence of chyle
Chylusüberproduktion f polychylia, excessive formation of chyle
Chylusvarize f chyle varix
Chyluszyste f chylous cyst, chylocele
Chymorrhoe f chymorrhoea, discharge of chyme *(z. B. aus dem Magen)*
Chymosin n chymosin, chymase, rennin
Chymosinogen n chymosinogen, renninogen, prorennin *(Chymosinvorstufe)*
Chymotrypsin n chymotrypsin *(Enzym)*
α-Chymotrypsin n alpha-chymotrypsin *(Enzym)*
α$_1$-Chymotrypsin n α$_1$-chymotrypsin *(Proteinaseinhibitor)*
Chymotrypsinogen n chymotrypsinogen *(inaktive Chymotrypsinvorstufe)*
Chymus m chyme, chymus
chymusartig chymous
Chymusbildung f formation of chyme, chymopoiesis, chymification
Chymusentleerung f s. Chymorrhoe
chymuslos achymous
Chymusmangel m oligochymia, deficiency of chyme; achymia, absence of chyme
Cicatrix f cicatrix, scar *(s. a. unter Narbe)*
~ **filtrans** filtering scar
Cicutoxin n cicutoxin *(Alkaloid des Wasserschierlings)*

Cilium *n s.* Wimper
Cimex *m* **hemipterus** Cimex hemipterus, oriental bedbug
~ **lectularius** Cimex lectularius, common bedbug
Cimino-Brescia-Fistel *f* Cimino-Brescia shunt *(zur Dialyse)*
Cinchona *f* cinchona [bark], quina
Cinchonaalkaloid *n* cinchonic alkaloid
Cinchona[alkaloid]vergiftung *f* cinchonism
Cineangiokardiographie *f s.* Kineangiokardiographie
Cingulum *n* 1. cingulum *(Anatomie)*; 2. herpes zoster; 3. basal ridge *(eines Zahns)*; 4. cingulum *(gürtelförmiger Heftpflasterverband)*
~ **membri inferioris** pelvic girdle
~ **membri superioris** shoulder girdle
Circulus *m* circulus, circle
~ **arteriosus cerebri [Willisi]** arterial cerebral circle, arterial circle of the cerebrum, [arterial] circle of Willis
~ **arteriosus iridis major** greater arterial circle of the iris
~ **arteriosus iridis minor** lesser arterial circle of the iris
~ **arteriosus (vasculosus) nervi optici** arterial (vascular) circle of the optic nerve, Zinn's circle
Circumferentia *f* **articularis radii** articular circumference of the head of the radius
~ **articularis ulnae** articular circumference of the head of the ulna
Cirrhosis *f* **hepatis** liver cirrhosis, cirrhosis of the liver *(Zusammensetzungen s. unter Leberzirrhose)*
Cisterna *f* **cerebellomedullaris** cerebellomedullary cistern
~ **chiasmatis** cistern of the chiasma, chiasmatic cistern
~ **chyli** cisterna chyli, Pecquet's cistern
~ **corporis callosi** cistern of the corpus callosum
~ **fossae lateralis cerebri** cistern of the lateral cerebral fossa, cistern of the Sylvian fissure
~ **interpeduncularis** interpeduncular cistern
~ **pontis** pontine cistern
~ **venae magnae cerebri** cistern of the great cerebral vein, superior cistern
Citrat *n s.* Zitrat
Citrovorum-Faktor *m* citrovorum factor, leucovorin, folinic acid
Citrullin *n s.* Zitrullin
Civatte-Krankheit *f* Civatte's (reticulated pigmented) poikiloderma
CL-Ableitung *f* CL lead *(EKG)*
Cladosporiose *f* cladosporiosis *(durch Cladosporium trichoides)*
Clarke-Headfield-Syndrom *n* Clarke-Headfield syndrome, pancreatic infantilism
Clarke-Säule *f* Clarke's column, thoracic nucleus
Clastothrix *f* clastothrix, trichorrhexis nodosa
Claudicatio *f* claudication, limping
~ **intermittens** intermittent claudication
Claustrum *n* claustrum *(Gehirnabschnitt)*
Clava *f* clava

Clavicula *f s.* Klavikula
Clavus *m* clavus, corn
Clearance *f* clearance *(Maß für die Stoffausscheidung aus dem Blut)*
Clearance-Test *m* clearance test
CL-EKG-Ableitung *f* CL lead
Click *m*/**systolischer** systolic [ejection] click *(des Herzens)*
Clivus *m* clivus *(der Schädelbasis)*
Cloaca *f* cloaca *(Embryologie)*
~ **urogenitalis** urogenital cloaca
~ **vesicorectovaginalis** vesicorectovaginal cloaca
Clonorchiasis *f* clonorchiasis, clonorchosis, Chinese liver fluke disease
Clonorchis *m* **sinensis** Clonorchis sinensis, liver (hepatic) fluke
Clonorchosis *s.* Clonorchiasis
Clonus *m* **uteri** uterine clonus
Clostridium *n* clostridium *(Bakteriengattung)*
~ **botulinum** Clostridium botulinum, bacillus of allantiasis, van Ermengen's bacillus
~ **septicum** vibrion septique
~ **tetani** Clostridium tetani
~ **Welchi[i]** Welch (gas gangrene) bacillus
Clostridium... *s.* Klostridien...
Clot-observation-Test *m* clot observation test *(bei Blutgerinnung)*
Clownismus *m* clownism
Clue cells clue cells *(bei Infektion mit Hämophilus vaginalis)*
Clunes *f* clunes, buttocks
Cluster-Kopfschmerz *m* 1. cluster headache, migraine; 2. cluster headache, histamine cephalalgia, erythroprosopalgia, Bing-Horton neuralgia
Clutton-Syndrom *n* Clutton's joints (syndrome), symmetrical bilateral hydrarthrosis *(bei Syphilis)*
CoA coenzyme A
Coagulum *n s.* Koagulum
Coarctatio *f* coarctation
~ **aortae** aortic coarctation, coarctation of the aorta
~ **aortae abdominalis** abdominal aorta coarctation
Coat *n* coat *(spezifische Proteinhülle von Viren)*
Coccidie *f* coccidium *(Sporozoon)*
Coccidio... *s. a.* Kokzidio...
Coccidioidomycosis *f* coccidio[ido]mycosis, California disease, valley fever, desert fever (rheumatism), San Joaquin [valley] fever, Posada's disease *(durch Coccidioides immitis)*
~ **progressiva** progressive coccidioidomycosis; coccidioidal granuloma
Coccus *m s.* Kokke
Coccyx *f s.* Steißbein
Cochlea *f s.* Schnecke
Coecum *m s.* Blinddarm
~ **mobile** wandering caecum
Coelom *n s.* Zölom
Coeur *m* **en sabot** sabot (wooden-shoe) heart *(Radiologie)*

Coffey-Mayo-Operation

Coffey-Mayo-Operation f Coffey's operation *(Harnleiterimplantation in den Darm)*
Coil-Niere f coil kidney (dialyzer) *(bei Dialyse)*
Coitus m s. Koitus
Colica f s. Kolik
Colitis f colitis, inflammation of the colon
- ~ **granulomatosa** granulomatous (regional) colitis, Crohn's disease of the colon
- ~ **mucosa** mucous colitis (colic), intestinal (colic) myxoneurosis, myxomembranous mucocolitis, membranous enteritis; spastic irritable colon
- ~ **polyposa** polypous colitis; colonic pseudopolyps
- ~ **spastica** spastic colitis
- ~ **ulcerativa (ulcerosa)** ulcerative colitis
- ~ **ulcerosa chronica** chronic ulcerative colitis

Colliculitis f **seminalis** [seminal] colliculitis, verumontanitis
Colliculus m s. ~ seminalis
- ~ **facialis** facial colliculus (eminence)
- ~ **inferior** inferior colliculus (quadrigeminal body)
- ~ **seminalis** seminal colliculus, [seminal] hillock, urethral colliculus, verumontanum
- ~ **superior** superior colliculus (quadrigeminal body)
- ~ **superior mesencephali** superior colliculus of the mesencephalon, preopticus

Collum n 1. collum, neck; 2. s. Cervix uteri
- ~ **anatomicum humeri** anatomic neck [of the humerus]
- ~ **chirurgicum humeri** surgical neck [of the humerus]
- ~ **costae** neck of the rib
- ~ **dentis** neck of the tooth
- ~ **femoris** femoral neck, neck of the femur
- ~ **folliculi pili** neck of the hair follicle
- ~ **glandis penis** neck of the penis
- ~ **mandibulae** neck of the mandible
- ~ **radii** neck of the radius
- ~ **scapulae** neck of the scapula
- ~ **tali** neck of the talus
- ~ **vesicae felleae** neck of the gall bladder

Colon n colon, large bowel (intestine) *(s. a. unter Dickdarm und Kolon)* ● unter dem ~ **sigmoideum** subsigmoid
- ~ **ascendens** ascending colon
- ~ **descendens** descending colon
- ~ **sigmoideum** sigmoid [colon], sigma, sigmoid flexure, pelvic colon *(S-förmiger Dickdarmabschnitt)*
- ~ **transversum** transverse colon

Colon-Sigmoideum-Resektion f sigmoid colon resection
Colorado-Zeckenfieber f Colorado tick fever, [American] mountain fever *(durch Dermacentor andersoni)*
Columbia-SK-Virus n Columbia-SK virus
Columna f column[a]
- ~ **anterior medullae spinalis** anterior column of the spinal medulla, anterior grey column
- ~ **fornicis** column of the fornix
- ~ **lateralis medullae spinalis** lateral column of the spinal medulla, lateral grey column
- ~ **posterior medullae spinalis** posterior column of the spinal medulla, posterior grey column
- ~ **rugarum** column of the vagina, vaginal column
- ~ **rugarum anterior** anterior column of the vagina
- ~ **rugarum posterior** posterior column of the vagina
- ~ **vertebralis** vertebral (spinal) column, spine, backbone, rachis

Columnae fpl **anales** anal columns, columns of Morgagni
- ~ **carneae** carneous trabeculae (columns)
- ~ **rectales** rectal columns *(längs verlaufende Schleimhautfalten im Mastdarm)*
- ~ **renales** renal columns

Coma n coma, comatose state, carus *(s. a. unter Koma)*
- ~ **apoplecticum** apoplectic coma
- ~ **basedowicum** Basedowian (hyperthyroid) coma
- ~ **diabeticum** diabetic coma
- ~ **eclampticum** eclamptic coma
- ~ **hepaticum** hepatic coma
- ~ **hypochloraemicum** hypocloraemic coma
- ~ **hypoglycaemicum** hypoglycaemic coma
- ~ **uraemicum** uraemic coma

Combustio f **bullosa** burn of second degree, second-degree burn
- ~ **erythematosa** burn of first degree, first-degree burn
- ~ **escharotica (gangraenosa)** burn of third degree, third-degree burn

Comedo m comedo, blackhead
Comedo... s. Komedo...
Commissura f commissura, commissure *(Anatomie)*
- ~ **anterior alba medullae spinalis** anterior white commissure of the spinal cord
- ~ **anterior cerebri** anterior commissure [of the cerebrum]
- ~ **anterior grisea medullae spinalis** anterior grey commissure of the spinal cord
- ~ **fornicis [hippocampi]** commissure of the fornix, fornical (hippocampal) commissure, psalterium
- ~ **habenularum** habenular commissure
- ~ **labiorum anterior** anterior commissure of the labia majora
- ~ **labiorum oris** commissure of the upper and lower lip
- ~ **labiorum posterior** posterior commissure of the labia majora
- ~ **palpebralis** palpebral commissure
- ~ **palpebrarum lateralis** lateral commissure of the upper and lower eyelid
- ~ **palpebrarum medialis** medial commissure of the upper and lower eyelid
- ~ **posterior alba medullae spinalis** posterior white commissure of the spinal cord
- ~ **posterior cerebri** posterior commissure [of the cerebrum]

~ **posterior grisea medullae spinalis** posterior grey commissure of the spinal cord
~ **rostralis cerebri** anterior commissure [of the cerebrum]
~ **supraoptica** supra-optic commissure
Commissurotomie f s. Kommissurendurchtrennung
Commotio f concussion, commotion
~ **cerebri** concussion of the brain, brain concussion, cerebral commotion
~ **medullae spinalis** spinal cord concussion, concussion of the spinal cord
~ **retinae** concussion of the retina, Berlin's disease *(Sehschwäche nach Augenprellung)*
~ **spinalis** s. ~ medullae spinalis
Compliance f [der Lunge] compliance [of the lung] *(Maß für die Lungendehnbarkeit in Abhängigkeit von der Volumenänderung)*
Compressio f compression
~ **cerebri** cerebral compression, compression of the brain
~ **medullae spinalis** spinal cord compression, compression of the spinal cord
Computerdiagnose f computer[-assisted] diagnosis
Computerdiagnostik f computer[-assisted] diagnosis
Computertomogramm n computer[-assisted] tomogram, computer tomography scan
Computertomograph m computer[-assisted] tomograph, computer tomography scanner, CT scanner
Computertomographie f computer[-assisted] tomography, computerized (computed) tomography, CT, computer tomographic scanning
Computertomographie-... s. CT-...
computertomographisch computer tomographic
Concha f concha
~ **nasalis** nasal concha, turbinate [bone]
~ **nasalis inferior** inferior nasal concha, inferior [nasal] turbinate, maxilloturbinal
~ **nasalis media** middle nasal concha, middle [nasal] turbinate
~ **nasalis superior** superior nasal concha, superior [nasal] turbinate
~ **[ossis] sphenoidalis** sphenoid[al] concha, sphenoid turbinated process, sphenoturbinal bone, bone of Bertin
Concretio f 1. s. Verwachsung ; 2. concretion, calculus, stone; 3. concretion, dental deposit
~ **cordis** concretion of the heart
~ **lacrimalis** tear stone
~ **pericardii** concretion of the heart
~ **praeputii** praeputial concretion
Concussio f concussion, commotion
Condyloma n s. Kondylom
Condylus m condylus, condyle
~ **femoris lateralis** s. ~ lateralis femoris
~ **femoris medialis** medial condyle of the femur
~ **humeri** condyle of the humerus
~ **lateralis femoris** lateral condyle of the femur, lateral femoral condyle

~ **lateralis tibiae** lateral condyle of the tibia
~ **medialis humeri** medial condyle of the humerus
~ **medialis tibiae** medial condyle of the tibia
~ **occipitalis** occipital condyle
Confluens m **sinuum** confluence of the sinuses, torcular [Herophili]
Congestion-Fibrosis-Syndrom n pelvic congestion *(Fibrose des Beckenbindegewebes)*
Conjugata f conjugata, conjugate diameter
~ **diagonalis** diagonal conjugate diameter
~ **externa** external conjugate diameter, Baudeloque's diameter *(Geburtshilfe)*
~ **vera** true (anatomic) conjugate diameter *(bei der Beckenvermessung)*
Conjunctiva f conjunctiva ● **unter der** ~ subconjunctival
~ **bulbaris** bulbar conjunctiva
~ **limbaris** limbal conjunctiva
~ **palpebralis** palpebral conjunctiva
~ **scleralis** scleral conjunctiva
~ **tarsalis** tarsal conjunctiva
Conjunctiva... s. Bindehaut...
Conjunctivitis f conjunctivitis, [blenn]ophthalmia, inflammation of the conjunctiva *(s. a. unter* Bindehautentzündung *und* Konjunktivitis*)*
~ **aestivalis** summer catarrh
~ **catarrhalis** catarrhal conjunctivitis, epidemic (acute contagious) conjunctivitis; pink-eye
~ **catarrhalis aestiva** vernal conjunctivitis (keratoconjunctivitis), spring catarrh
~ **electrica** actinic (arc-flash) conjunctivitis
~ **follicularis** follicular conjunctivitis
~ **gonorrhoica** gonorrhoeal (blennorrhoeal) conjunctivitis, gonococcal ophthalmia, gonoblennorrhoea
~ **granulosa** granular conjunctivitis (ophthalmia), trachomatous (trachoma inclusion) conjunctivitis, trachoma, Egyptian conjunctivitis (ophthalmia); granular lids
~ **nodularis** nodular conjunctivitis
~ **phlyctaenulosa** phlyctenular conjunctivitis (ophthalmia)
~ **scrophulosa** scrofulous conjunctivitis (ophthalmia)
~ **trachomatosa** s. ~ granulosa
Conn-Syndrom n Conn's syndrome, [primary] hyperaldosteronism
Constrictor m constrictor [muscle]
Contrecoup m contrecoup, counterstroke
Contrecoup-Fraktur f contrecoup fracture, fracture by contrecoup
Contrecoup-Schädelfraktur f contrafissura, counterfissure
Contrecoup-Verletzung f countrecoup injury
Contusio f contusion, bruise
~ **bulbi** eye contusion
~ **cerebri** cerebral contusion
~ **cordis** heart contusion
~ **medullae spinalis** spinal cord contusion
~ **thoracis** thoracic contusion
Conus m conus, cone

Conus

- ~ **arteriosus [infundibulum]** infundibulum [of the heart]
- ~ **elasticus [laryngis]** cricothyroid membrane
- ~ **lenticularis** lens cone
- ~ **medullaris (terminalis)** terminal cone, conus medullaris

Cooley-Anämie f Cooley's anaemia (disease), thalassaemia major

Coolidge-Hochvakuum-Röntgenröhre f, **Coolidge-Röhre** f Coolidge tube

Coombs-Serum n Coombs (antiglobulin) serum

Coombs-Test m [Race-]Coombs test, antiglobulin test, antihuman globulin (serum) test
- ~/**direkter** direct Coombs test
- ~/**indirekter** indirect Coombs test, Rh blocking test

Cooper-Band n Cooper's (pubic) ligament

Cooper-Faszie f Cooper's (cremasteric) fascia

Cooper-Hernie f Cooper's hernia

Cooper-Streifen m Cooper's ligament *(am Ellenbogengelenk)*

CO₂-Partialdruckerhöhung f hypercapnia, hypercarbia

CO₂-Partialdruckverminderung f hypocapnia, hypocarbia

Copula f **linguae** copula *(embryonale Zungenwurzel)*

Cor n cor, heart *(s. a. unter Herz)*
- ~ **adiposum** fatty heart
- ~ **biloculare** bilocular heart
- ~ **biventriculare** biventricular heart
- ~ **bovinum** bovine (ox) heart
- ~ **dextrum** right heart
- ~ **hirsutum** s. ~ villosum
- ~ **mobile** mobile (wandering) heart
- ~ **pulmonale** pulmonary heart [disease]
- ~ **sinistrum** left heart
- ~ **triatriatum** triatrial heart
- ~ **triloculare [biatriatum]** trilocular (three-chambered) heart; single ventricle [of the heart]
- ~ **villosum** villous (hairy, shaggy) heart, trichocardia

Cord-bladder f cord (neurogenic) bladder *(z. B. bei Querschnittslähmung)*

Cori-Ester m Cori ester, glucose-1-phosphate

Cori-Syndrom n s. Glykogenose Typ III

Corium n corium, dermis, derm[a], [true] skin, cutis

Cornea f cornea

Cornea... s. Kornea... und Hornhaut...

Corner-Allen-Test m Corner-Allen test *(zum Gelbkörperhormonnachweis)*

Corniculum n **iridis** pillar of the iris
- ~ **laryngis** corniculate cartilage

Cornu n cornu, horn
- ~ **Ammonis** Ammon's horn, hippocampus
- ~ **anterius** anterior horn, ventral cornu
- ~ **anterius medullae spinalis** anterior horn [of the spinal medulla]
- ~ **anterius substantiae griseae** grey (anterior) horn of the spinal cord
- ~ **anterius ventriculi lateralis** anterior horn of the lateral ventricle *(Gehirn)*
- ~ **coccygea (coccygeum)** cornu of the coccyx, coccygeal cornu *(Gelenkfortsatz)*
- ~ **inferius cartilaginis thyreoideae** inferior horn of the thyroid cartilage
- ~ **inferius marginis falciformis** inferior horn of the falciform margin
- ~ **inferius ventriculi lateralis** inferior (temporal) horn of the lateral ventricle, underhorn
- ~ **laterale medullae spinalis** lateral horn [of the spinal medulla]
- ~ **laterale substantiae griseae** lateral horn of the spinal cord
- ~ **majus ossis hyoidei** greater cornu of the hyoid bone, thyrohyal
- ~ **minus ossis hyoidei** lesser cornu of the hyoid bone
- ~ **posterius** posterior horn, dorsal cornu
- ~ **posterius medullae spinalis** posterior horn [of the spinal medulla]
- ~ **posterius substantiae griseae** posterior horn of the spinal cord
- ~ **posterius ventriculi lateralis** posterior horn of the lateral ventricle *(Gehirn)*
- ~ **sacrale** cornu of the sacrum, sacral cornu *(Gelenkfortsatz)*
- ~ **superius cartilaginis thyreoideae** superior horn of the thyroid cartilage
- ~ **superius marginis falciformis** superior horn of the falciform margin
- ~ **uteri** cornu of the uterus, uterus horn

Corona f corona, crown
- ~ **capitis** crown of the head
- ~ **clinica** clinical crown *(Stomatologie)*
- ~ **dentis** crown of the tooth

Coronavirus n corona virus

Corpora npl bodies, granules *(s. a. unter Körper)*
- ~ **amylacea prostatae** prostatic concretions
- ~ **Arantii** bodies of Arantius, nodules of the semilunar valves
- ~ **arenacea** sand bodies, brainsand granules
- ~ **oryzoidea** rice bodies

Corpus n corpus, body *(s. a. unter Körper)* ● über dem ~ **callosum** supracallosal
- ~ **adiposum buccae** sucking pad
- ~ **adiposum orbitae** fat body of the orbital cavity
- ~ **alienum** foreign body
- ~ **amygdaloideum** amygdaloid body (nucleus), amygdala
- ~ **amylaceum** amyloid body
- ~ **articulare mobile** s. ~ liberum
- ~ **atreticum** atretic follicle
- ~ **calcanei** body of the calcaneus
- ~ **callosum [corpus]** callosum
- ~ **cavernosum** cavernous body, cavernosum
- ~ **cavernosum clitoridis** s. ~ clitoridis
- ~ **ciliare** ciliary body
- ~ **clitoridis** clitoridal body, body of the clitoris
- ~ **costae** body of the rib
- ~ **epididymidis** body of the epididymus
- ~ **femoris** shaft of the femur
- ~ **fibulae** shaft of the fibula
- ~ **fornicis** body of the fornix

~ **geniculatum laterale** lateral geniculate body *(Schaltstelle der Sehbahn)*
~ **geniculatum mediale** medial geniculate body
~ **glandulae bulbourethralis** body of the bulbourethral gland
~ **humeri** shaft of the humerus
~ **liberum** joint body (mouse), articular calculus
~ **luteum** yellow body, luteal corpus, corpus luteum *(Zusammensetzungen s. unter Gelbkörper)*
~ **luteum graviditatis** corpus luteum of pregnancy, true corpus luteum
~ **luteum menstruationis** corpus luteum of menstruation, false corpus luteum
~ **mamillare** mamillary body *(erbsengroße weiße Erhabenheit an der Hirnbasis)*
~ **mandibulae** body of the mandible
~ **maxillae** body of the maxilla
~ **ossis hyoidei** body of the hyoid [bone]
~ **ossis metacarpalis** shaft of the metacarpal bone
~ **ossis metatarsalis** shaft of the metatarsal bone
~ **penis** shaft of the penis
~ **pineale** pineal body (appendage, gland), cerebral (false) apophysis, epiphysis, epiphyseal process, conarium
~ **quadrigeminum** quadrigeminum, quadrigeminal body
~ **radii** shaft of the radius
~ **restiforme** inferior cerebellar peduncle
~ **spongiosum penis** spongy body [of the penis]
~ **spongiosum urethrae muliebris** corpus spongiosum of the female urethra
~ **sterni** body of the sternum, gladiolus
~ **striatum** striatum
~ **subthalamicus [Luysi]** Corpus Luysii, body of Luys, subthalamic nucleus
~ **suprarenale** suprarenal (adrenal) gland, epinephros
~ **tali** body of the talus
~ **tibiae** shaft of the tibia
~ **trapezoideum** trapezoid body
~ **ulnae** shaft of the ulna
~ **uteri** body of the uterus, uterine body
~ **ventriculi** body of the stomach
~ **vertebrae** body of the vertebra
~ **vesicae felleae** body of the gall-bladder
~ **vesicae urinariae** body of the urinary bladder
~ **vesiculae seminalis** body of the seminal vesicle
~ **vitreum** vitreous body (humour)
~ **Wolffi** Wolffian body, mesonephros
Corpuscula *npl* corpuscles, bodies *(s. a. unter Körperchen)*
~ **nervosa articularia** articular corpuscles
~ **nervosa genitalis** genital corpuscles
Corpusculum *n* corpusculum, corpuscle, body; granule *(s. a. unter Körperchen)*
~ **bulboideum [Krause's]** end bulb, bulbous corpuscle
~ **lamellosum** lamellar (Pacini's, Vater-Pacini) corpuscle

~ **renis [Malpighi]** renal corpuscle, Malpighian body
~ **tactum** tactile (touch, oval) corpuscle, Meissner's corpuscle
Corpus-luteum-Bildung *f* luteinization
Corpus-luteum-Hormon *n* luteal hormone
Corpus-luteum-Insuffizienz *f* luteal corpus insufficiency
Corpus-luteum-Phase *f* **[des Ovarialzyklus]** progestation stage [of the ovarian cycle]
Corpus-luteum-Zyste *f* lutein (corpus luteum) cyst
Corrigan-Krankheit *f* Corrigan's disease, aortic incompetence [syndrome]
Corrigan-Puls *m* Corrigan's pulse, cannon ball pulse *(bei Aorteninsuffizienz)*
Corrigens *n* corrigent agent, corrective [agent] *(zur Geschmacksverbesserung)*
Corrugator *m* corrugator [muscle]
Cortex *m* cortex *(s. a. unter Kortex)*
~ **cerebelli** cortex of the cerebellum, cerebellar cortex
~ **cerebri** cortex of the cerebrum (brain), cerebral cortex
~ **glandulae suprarenalis** cortex of the suprarenal gland
~ **lenticularis** lens cortex
~ **nodi lymphatici** cortex of the lymph node
~ **renis** cortex of the kidney
~ **visivus** visual centre (cortex, area)
Cortisol *n s.* Kortisol
Corvisart-Gesicht *n* Corvisart's face
Corynebacterium *n* acnes acne bacillus
~ **diphtheriae** Corynebacterium diphtheriae, diphtheria (Klebs-Löffler) bacillus
~ **pseudodiphtheriticum** Corynebacterium pseudodiphthericum, Hofmann's bacillus
Corynebacterium-diphtheriae-Septikämie *f* Corynebacterium diphtheriae septicaemia
Coryza *f* coryza, common cold, rhinitis, nasitis, nasal catarrh, pharyngoconjunctival fever
~/**allergische** allergic coryza (rhinitis), hey fever
Costa *f* costa, costal bone, rib
~ **fluctuans** floating rib
~ **spuria** false (asternal) rib
~ **vera** true (sternal) rib
Costen-Syndrom *n* Costen's syndrome, Costen's temporo-mandibular arthrosis
Costo... *s.* Kosto...
Councilman-Körperchen *npl* Councilman bodies (cells) *(bei Koagulationsnekrose der Leber)*
Couveuse *f* couveuse, incubator
CO-Vergiftung *f* carbon monoxide poisoning
Cowper-Drüsen *fpl* Cowper's (bulbocavernous, bulbourethral) glands
Cowperitis *f* cowperitis, inflammation of the Cowper's glands
Cowper-Zyste *f* Cowper's cyst
Cow-pox *s.* Kuhpocken
Coxa *f* coxa, hip *(s. a. unter Hüfte)*
~ **plana** coxa plana, osteochondritis deformans juvenilis

Coxalgie

Coxalgie f s. Koxalgie
Cox-Dottersackvakzine f s. Cox-Vakzine
Coxsackie-Virus n Coxsackie virus
Cox-Vakzine f Cox vaccine, [epidemic] typhus vaccine
CR s. Kremasterreflex
Cramer-Schiene f Cramer's (wire) splint
Cranio... s. a. Kranio...
Craniopagus m **frontalis** frontal craniopagus (cephalopagus)
~ **occipitalis** occipital craniopagus (cephalopagus)
~ **parietalis** parietal craniopagus (cephalopagus), acrocephalopagus
Cranium n [cerebral] cranium, skull, brain-pan, brain case (s. a. unter Schädel)
~ **bifidum** bifid skull
~ **cerebrale** neurocranium
~ **viscerale** visceral cranium
CR-EKG-Ableitung f CR lead
Cremaster m s. Kremastermuskel
Crena f crena, furrow, notch, cleft
~ **ani (clunicum)** glutaeal furrow
Crescendo-Geräusch n crescendo murmur (des Herzens)
Creutzfeld-Jakob-Krankheit f Creutzfeld-Jacob disease (syndrome) (degenerative Hirnerkrankung)
Crigler-Najjar-Syndrom n Crigler-Najjar syndrome, congenital hyperbilirubinaemia, congenital familial non-haemolytic jaundice
Crinis m s. Haar
Crista f crista, crest; ridge, rim
~ **anterior fibulae** crest of the fibula
~ **anterior tibiae** crest of the tibia, shin
~ **buccinatoria** buccinator crest
~ **bulboventricularis** bulboventricular crest
~ **capitis costae** crest of the head of the rib
~ **colli costae** crest of the neck of the rib
~ **conchalis** conchal (turbinate) crest, inferior turbinal crest
~ **conchalis maxillae** conchal crest of the maxilla
~ **ethmoidalis maxillae** ethmoid crest [of the maxilla]
~ **ethmoidalis ossis palatini** ethmoid crest [of the palatine bone]
~ **falciformis** falciform crest
~ **femoris** linea aspera
~ **frontalis** frontal crest
~ **iliaca** crest of the ilium, iliac crest
~ **infratemporalis** infratemporal crest
~ **intertrochanterica** intertrochanteric crest
~ **lacrimalis** lacrimal crest
~ **lacrimalis anterior** anterior lacrimal crest
~ **lacrimalis posterior** posterior lacrimal crest
~ **medialis fibulae** oblique line of the fibula
~ **musculi supinatorius** supinator crest
~ **nasalis maxillae** nasal crest [of the maxilla]
~ **nasalis ossis palatini** nasal crest [of the palatine bone]
~ **obturatoria** obturator crest
~ **occipitalis externa** external occipital crest
~ **occipitalis interna** internal occipital crest
~ **palatina** palatine crest
~ **pubica** pubic crest
~ **pyramidis** petrous ridge [of the temporal bone]
~ **sacralis** sacral crest
~ **sphenoidalis** sphenoid crest
~ **supraventricularis** supraventricular (infundibuloventricular) crest
~ **terminalis atrii dextri** terminal crest
~ **tuberculi majoris** posterior bicipital ridge
~ **tuberculi minoris** anterior bicipital ridge
~ **urethralis [urethrae masculinae]** urethral crest
Crocidismus m crocidism (unruhige Gesten z. B. bei Typhus)
Cronkhite-Canada-Syndrom n Cronkhite-Canada syndrome, gastrointestinal polyposis
Cross match s. Kreuzprobe
Crossing-over crossing-over (Genaustausch in der Meiose)
Crotalusantitoxin n crotalus antitoxin (antivenin), polyvalent crotaline antivenin
Cro[talus]toxin n crotoxin (Gift der Klapperschlange)
Croup m s. Krupp
Crouzon-Krankheit f Crouzon's disease (syndrome), craniofacial dystosis
CRP s. Protein/C-reaktives
CRST-Syndrom n CRST syndrome, calcinosis [cutis], Raymand's phenomenon, sclerodactyly, and teleangiectasis
Crus n 1. crus, shank, lower leg; 2. crus, peduncle, stalk, limb
~ **anterius capsulae internae** anterior limb of the internal capsule
~ **anterius stapedis** anterior process (crus) of the stapes (am Steigbügel des Ohres)
~ **breve incudis** short crus (process) of the incus
~ **cerebelli** crus of the cerebellum
~ **cerebri** crus of the cerebrum
~ **clitoridis** crus of the clitoris
~ **commune** common crus (Innenohr)
~ **dextrum diaphragmatis** right crus of the diaphragm
~ **diaphragmatis** diaphragmatic crus
~ **fasciculi atrioventricularis dextrum** right branch of the atrioventricular bundle
~ **fasciculi atrioventricularis sinistrum** left branch of the atrioventricular bundle
~ **fornicis** crus (posterior pillar) of the fornix
~ **helicis** crus of the helix
~ **longum incudis** long crus (process) of the incus
~ **osseum commune** common crus (Innenohr)
~ **pedunculi** crus of the cerebrum
~ **penis** crus of the penis
~ **penis dextrum** right crus of the penis
~ **penis sinistrum** left crus of the penis
~ **pontocerebellare** pontocerebellar tract
~ **posterius capsulae internae** posterior limb of the internal capsule
~ **posterius stapedis** posterior process (crus) of the stapes (am Steigbügel des Ohres)

~ **sinistrum diaphragmatis** left crus of the diaphragm
Crush-Niere f crush kidney
Crush-Syndrom n crush (compression) syndrome, Bywaters' (ischaemic muscular necrosis) syndrome
Crush-Syndrom-Niere f crush kidney
Crusta f crusta, crust, eschar, slough, scab
~ **inflammatoria** s. ~ phlogistica
~ **lactea** milky tetter, milk crust, cradle cap *(Ekzem der Kinder)*
~ **phlogistica** buffy crust (coat), crusta phlogistica *(auf geronnenem Blut)*
Crutchfield-Klammer f Crutchfield tongs, skull calliper of Crutchfield
Crux f **mortis** crux mortis *(der Temperatur- und Pulskurve)*
Cruz-Krankheit f s. Chagas-Krankheit
Crypta f crypta, crypt
~ **iridis** iris crypt
Cryptae fpl **tonsillares tonsillae palatinae** tonsillar crypts of the palatine tonsils
~ **tonsillares tonsillae pharyngeae** tonsillar crypts of the lingual tonsils
Cryptococcosis f s. Kryptokokkose
Cryptococcus m s. Kryptokokke
CT s. Computertomographie
CT-Angiographie f computer [tomographic] angiography
CT-Befund m computer tomographic findings
CT-Bild n s. Computertomogramm
CT-Schädelbild n computerized cranial tomogram
Cubitus m 1. cubitus, forearm; 2. cubitus, ulna; 3. cubitus, elbow
~ **varus** gunstock deformity
Culdoskopie f s. Kuldoskopie
Cullen-Zeichen n Cullen's sign *(bei Extrauteringravidität)*
Culmen m **monticuli** culmen [monticuli]
Cumulus m **oophorus (ovigerus)** ovarian cumulus, germ hillock, ovigerous (vitelline) disk
Cuneus m cuneus, cuneate lobule
Cuniculus m cuniculus, burrow
Cupula f **[cochleae]** cupula [of the cochlea]
~ **dextra diaphragmatis** right dome of the diaphragm
~ **diaphragmatis** cupula of the diaphragm
~ **pleurae** cupula (dome) of the pleura
~ **sinistra diaphragmatis** left dome of the diaphragm
Curling-Ulkus n Curling's ulcer *(Magengeschwür bei Verbrennungen)*
Curschmann-Spiralen fpl Curschmann's spirals *(bei Asthma bronchiale)*
Curschmann-Steinert-Syndrom n Curschmann-Steinert syndrome, myotonic (muscular) dystrophy
Curvatura f curvatura, curvature
~ **ventriculi major** greater curvature [of the stomach]
~ **ventriculi minor** lesser curvature [of the stomach]

cushingähnlich, cushingartig cushingoid
Cushing-Syndrom n Cushing's disease (syndrome)
Cuspis f cuspis, cusp *(an Herzklappen)*
~ **anterior** anterior cusp
~ **anterior valvae atrioventricularis dextrae** s. ~ anterior valvulae tricuspidalis
~ **anterior valvae atrioventricularis sinistrae** s. ~ anterior valvulae bicuspidalis
~ **anterior valvulae bicuspidalis** anterior leaflet of the mitral valve, anterior cusp of the left atrioventricular valve
~ **anterior valvulae tricuspidalis** anterior tricuspid leaflet, anterior cusp of the right atrioventricular valve
~ **dorsalis** s. ~ posterior
~ **medialis valvulae tricuspidalis** septal tricuspid leaflet, septal cusp of the right atrioventricular valve
~ **posterior** posterior (dorsal) cusp
~ **posterior valvae atrioventricularis dextrae** s. ~ posterior valvulae tricuspidalis
~ **posterior valvae atrioventricularis sinistrae** s. ~ posterior valvulae bicuspidalis
~ **posterior valvulae bicuspidalis** posterior leaflet of the mitral valve, posterior cusp of the left atrioventricular valve
~ **posterior valvulae tricuspidalis** posterior tricuspid leaflet, posterior cusp of the right atrioventricular valve
~ **septalis** septal cusp (leaflet)
~ **septalis valvae atrioventricularis dextrae** septal tricuspid leaflet, septal cusp of the right atrioventricular valve
~ **valvae (valvulae)** cusp of the valve
~ **ventralis** s. ~ anterior
Cuticula f cuticula, cuticle
~ **capsularis** capsular lamella
~ **dentis** dental (enamel) cuticle
Cutis f cutis, [true] skin, derm[a], dermis *(s. a. unter Haut)*
~ **anserina** anserine skin, goose-skin, gooseflesh, horripilation
~ **hyperelastica** [hyper]elastic skin, India rubber skin; [Ehlers-]Danlos syndrome
~ **laxa** 1. dermatorrhexis; 2. dermatolysis
~ **marmorata** marble (mottled) skin, erythrocyanosis *(vasomotorische Zirkulationsstörung der Haut)*
~ **vera** true skin
Cutler-Test m Cutler-Power-Wilder test *(Nebennierenrindenfunktionsprobe)*
Cyan... s. Zyan...
Cyst... s. a. Kyst... und Zyst...
Cystadenoma n cystadenoma, adenocystoma
~ **adamantinum** [cystic] adamantinoma
~ **cylindrocellulare colloides ovarii** pseudomucinous cystadenoma
~ **lymphomatosum papillare** cystadenolymphoma, Warthin's tumour
Cystein n cysteine
Cystosarcoma n cystosarcoma

Cystosarcoma

~ phylloides phylloid sarcoma, periductal (intracanalicular, serocystic) sarcoma, proliferous (teleangiectatic) cystosarcoma, pearly cystosarcoma phylloides, mixed (tuberous cystic) tumour of the breast, pseudosarcoma of the breast
Cytomegalia f **infantum** cytomegalia inclusion body disease, cytomegalovirus inclusion disease (syndrome), salivary gland virus disease, cytomegalovirus syndrome
C-Zellen fpl C cells (in Langerhansschen Inseln)

D

d s. 1. dexter; 2. Rh-negativ
D s. 1. detur; 2. divide; 3. Rh-positiv
D. s. 1. Dosis; 2. Ductus
D_1 D_1, first dorsal vertebra
Dach n tegmen, tectum, roof, cap (Zusammensetzungen s. unter Tegmen und Tectum)
dachförmig tectiform, roof-like
Dachziegelverband m rib strapping
d'Acosta-Syndrom n Acosta's disease, mountain (altitude) sickness
Da Costa-Syndrom n Da Costa's syndrome, effort syndrome, angina of effort
Dactylitis f **syphilitica** syphilitic phalangitis (dactylitis)
Dactylolysis f **spontanea** spontaneous dactylolysis
Dakryagogum n dacryagogue [agent]
Dakryoadenalgie f dacryoadenalgia
Dakryoadenektomie f dacryoadenectomy, excision of the lacrimal gland
Dakryoadenitis f dacryoadenitis, lacrimal adenitis, inflammation of the lacrimal gland
Dakryoadenoszirrhus m dacryadenoscirrhus
Dakryoblennorrhoe f dacryoblennorrhoea
Dakryokanalikulitis f dacryocanaliculitis, inflammation of the lacrimal canal
Dakryolith m dacryolith, lacrimal (tear) stone
Dakryolithiasis f dacryolithiasis
Dakryom n dacryoma, lacrimal tumour
Dakryon n dacryon (vordere obere Tränenbeinspitze)
Dakryophlegmone f dacryophlegmon
Dakryops m dacryops
Dakryorhinostomie f s. Dakryozystorhinostomie
Dakryorrhoe f dacryorrhoea, lacrimation, lachrymation, flow of tears
Dakryosinusitis f dacryosinusitis
Dakryostenose f dacryo[cystorhino]stenosis, nasolacrimal duct stenosis
Dakryozystektomie f dacryocystectomy, tear-sac extirpation
Dakryozystis f dacryocyst[is], lacrimal (tear) sac
Dakryozystitis f dacryocystitis, inflammation of the lacrimal sac
Dakryozystoblennorrhoe f dacryocystoblennorrhoea
Dakryozystogramm n dacryocystogram
Dakryozystographie f dacryocystography
Dakryozystoptose f dacryo[cysto]ptosis
Dakryozystorhinostenose f dacryo[cystorhino]stenosis
Dakryozystorhinostomie f dacryocystorhinostomy, dacryorhinocystostomy
Dakryozystostenose f dacryocystostenosis
Dakryozystostomie f dacryocystostomy
Dakryozystotomie f dacryocystotomy, incision into the lacrimal sac
Dakryozystozele f dacryo[cysto]cele
Daktylion n dactylion
Daktylitis f dactylitis
Daktylogramm n dactylogram, fingerprint
Daktylographie f dactylography
Daktylogrypose f dactylogryposis
Daktylologie f dactylology
Daktylolyse f dactylolysis
Daktylomegalie f dactylomegaly
Daktylophasie f dactylophasia
Daktyloskopie f dactyloscopy
Daktylospasmus m dactylospasm
Daktylosymphyse f dactylosymphysis; syndactylism
Daktylus m dactylus, dactyl, finger; toe (s. a. unter Digitus)
Daltonismus m daltonism, colour blindness
Damenbinde f sanitary towel (napkin)
Damm m perineum
Damm... s. a. Perineal...
Dammarterie f perineal artery
Dammbruch m perineal (ischeorectal) hernia, perineocele
Dämmerattacke f twilight (dream) state
Dämmerungsschwachsichtigkeit f day blindness
Dämmerungssehen n scotopia, scotopic (twilight, night) vision
Dämmerzustand m semi-consciousness, trance; twilight (dream) state
Dammfaszie f fascia diaphragmatis urogenitalis inferior, perineal membrane
Dammfistel f perineal fistula
Dammhämatom n perineal haematoma
Dammhoden m perineal testis
Dammnaht f 1. perineal raphe, raphe perinei (Anatomie); 2. perineal suture, perineorrhaphy, episiorrhaphy (Chirurgie)
Dammnerven mpl perineal nerves
Dammoperation f/**plastische** s. Dammplastik
Dammplastik f perineoplasty, episioplasty
Dammregion f perineal region
Dammrekonstruktion f[/**operative**] perineosynthesis
Dammriß m laceration of the perineum, perineal tear
~ I. Grades first-degree laceration of the perineum (nur Dammhaut betroffen)
~ II. Grades second-degree laceration of the perineum (Dammuskulatur betroffen)
~ III. Grades third-degree laceration of the perineum (Afterschließmuskel beteiligt)

Darmblutung

~/inkompletter incomplete laceration of the perineum
~/kompletter complete laceration of the perineum
~/zentraler central laceration of the perineum
Damm-Scheiden-Fistel f perineovaginal fistula
Damm-Scheiden-Naht f s. Kolpoperineorrhaphie
Damm-Scheiden-Plastik f s. Kolpoperineoplastik
Dammschere f episiotomy scissors
Dammschmerz m perineal pain
Dammschnitt m perineotomy, episiotomy, perineal incision
Dammschutz m perineal support, support of the perineum
Dammstütze f perineal crutch
Dammuskel m perineal muscle, muscle of the perineum
~/oberflächlicher querer superficial transverse perineal muscle
~/querer transversus perinei muscle
~/tiefer querer deep transverse perineal muscle
Dammuskelkrampf m perineal spasm
Dammuskulatur f muscles of the perineum
Dammverlängerung f[/operative] perineauxesis
Damoiseau-Ellis-Linie f Damoiseau's (Ellis') curve (bei Pleuraergüssen)
Dämonomaner m demonomaniac
Dämonomanie f, **Dämonopathie** f demonomania, demonopathy
Dämonophobie f demonophobia (krankhafte Angst vor Dämonen)
Dampfanwendung f vaporization
Dampfbad n 1. vapour bath, steambath; 2. vaporarium, estuarium
Dampfbehandlung f vapotherapy
Dampfdusche f vapour douche
dämpfen 1. to sedate, to calm (z. B. eine Erregung); to sedate, to calm, to reduce, to dull (z. B.Schmerzen); to damp[en] (z. B. Stimmung); to damp[en], to deaden (z. B. Schall); 2. to steam (z. B. Verbandstoff)
dämpfend sedative, calming, reducing, damping
Dampfsterilisation f steam sterilization
Dampfsterilisator m [steam] autoclave, steam sterilizer
Dämpfung f 1. sedation, calming (z. B. einer Erregung); calming (z. B. von Schmerzen); damping (z. B. des Schalls); 2. dullness (z. B. bei Perkussion der Lunge)
~/absolute absolute dullness (des Herzens)
~/medikamentöse medicinal restraint (bei erregten Patienten)
Dämpfungsbezirk m area (region) of dullness
Dämpfungsmittel n sedative [agent]
Dampfverkochung f vapocauterization, vaporization (von Gewebe)
Danbolt-Closs-Syndrom n Danbolt-Closs-syndrome, acrodermatitis enteropathica
Dandyfever n s. Denguefieber
Dandy-Walker-Syndrom n Dandy-Walker syndrome (angeborene Atresie des Foramen Magendi)

Danebenreden n paralalia (Sprachstörung)
Danlos-Syndrom n [Ehlers-]Danlos syndrome; hyperelastic cutis, India-rubber man
Darm m bowel[s], intestine[s], intestinum, gut, enteron ● **den ~ reinigend** purgative ● **vom ~ ausgehend** enterogenous
~/gerader rectum
~/vergrößerter megaloenteron, enlarged intestine
Darm... s. a. Intestinal...
Darmabführung f purgation, catharsis, evacuation of the bowel[s] (durch Abführmittel)
Darmaffektion f intestinal affection
Darmanastomose f intestinal anastomosis, enteroanastomosis
Darmatonie f intestinal atony
Darmatresie f intestinal atresia
Darmaufblähung f, **Darmauftreibung** f s. Darmblähung
Darmbad n/**subaquales** enterocleaner
Darmbakterien npl s. Darmflora
Darmbefall m intestinal invasion (durch Keime)
Darmbein n ilium [bone], iliac bone ● **unter dem ~** subiliac ● **zwischen den Darmbeinen** transiliac
Darmbeinabszeß m iliac abscess
Darmbeinfaszie f iliac fascia
Darmbeingegend f iliac region
Darmbeingrube f iliac fossa
Darmbeinkamm m iliac crest, crest of the ilium
Darmbeinkörper m body of the ilium
Darmbeinlymphknoten m iliac lymph node
Darmbeinmuskel m iliacus [muscle], iliac muscle
~/kleiner iliacus minor [muscle], iliocapsularis [muscle]
Darmbeinrauhigkeit f iliac tuberosity
Darmbeinrippenmuskel m iliocostalis [muscle]
Darmbeinschaufel f ala (wing) of the ilium
Darmbeinstachel m iliac spine, spinous process of the ilium
~/hinterer oberer posterior superior iliac spine, posterosuperior spine of the ilium
~/hinterer unterer posterior inferior iliac spine, posteroinferior spine of the ilium
~/vorderer oberer anterior superior iliac spine, anterosuperior spine of the ilium
~/vorderer unterer anterior inferior iliac spine, anteroinferior spine of the ilium
Darmbeinstacheldistanz f interspinal diameter
Darmbein-Steißbein-Muskel m iliococcygeus [muscle]
Darmbeschwerden fpl intestinal complaint[s]
Darmbewegung f peristalsis, bowel movement, peristaltic motion
~/fehlende aperistalsis
~/gegenläufige antiperistalsis
Darmbiopsie f intestinal biopsy
Darmblähung f meteorism, aerenterectasia, tympanities, flatulence
Darmblatt n endoderm, entoderm, entoblast
Darmblutung f intestinal haemorrhage (bleeding), enterorrhagia, enterohaemorrhage

Darmbrand

Darmbrand *m* darmbrand, necrotizing enteritis, enteritis necroticans
Darmbruch *m* intestinal hernia, enterocele
Darmdauerausscheider *m* chronic enteric (intestinal) carrier
Darmdekontamination *f* intestinal (gut) decontamination
Darmdilatation *f* enterectasis, intestinal dilatation
Darmdistomiasis *f* intestinal distomiasis
Darmdivertikel *n* intestinal diverticulum
Darmdottergang *m* omphalomesenteric (omphalo-intestinal) duct *(embryonale Verbindung von Darm und Dottersack)*
Darmdrüsen *fpl* intestinal glands *(s. a.* Drüsen/Brunnersche *und* Drüsen/Lieberkühnsche*)*
Darmdrüsenblatt *n* endoderm, entoderm, entoblast
Darmdrüsenentzündung *f* enteradenitis
Darmdurchbruch *m* intestinal perforation
Darmdysbakterie *f s.* Darmflora/gestörte
Darmdyspepsie *f* intestinal dyspepsia
Darmegel *m* intestinal fluke *(Leber- und Darmparasit des Menschen)*
Darmegelbefall *m* intestinal distomiasis
Darmeinklemmung *f* intestinal incarceration (strangulation)
Darmeinlauf *m* enema, enteroclysis
Darmeinstülpung *f* invagination, intestinal (enteric) intussusception
Darmektasie *f* enterectasis
Darmentfernung *f[/operative]* enterectomy, intestinal resection
Darmentkeimung *f* intestinal decontamination
Darmentleerung *f[/natürliche]* defaecation, motion
Darmentzündung *f* inflammation of the bowels; enteritis *(des Dünndarms)*; colitis *(des Dickdarms) (s. a.* Enteritis *und* Colitis*)*
Darmepithel[ium] *n* intestinal epithelium
Darmepithelzelle *f* intestinal epithelial cell
Darmerkrankung *f* intestinal disease, enteropathy
Darmeröffnung *f[/operative]* enterotomy
Darmerweiterung *f* enterectasis
Darmfaltung *[/operative]* intestinal plication, enteroplication
Darmfaserblatt *n* splanchnopleure
Darmfaßpinzette *f*, **Darmfaßzange** *f* intestinal grasping (tissue) forceps
Darmfistel *f* intestinal fistula
Darmfistelung *f[/operative]* enterostomy
Darmfixierung *f* enteropexy, fixation of the intestine
Darmflora *f* intestinal flora
~/gestörte disturbed intestinal flora
Darmfollikel *m* intestinal follicle
Darmfunktion *f* bowel function
Darmgang *m s.* Darmdottergang
Darmgas *n* flatus, intestinal gas, flatulence
darmgasbildend flatulent
Darmgasbildung *f* flatulence

Darmgefäßdysplasie *f* intestinal angiodysplasia
Darmgeräusch *n* bowel sound, peristaltic sounds; borborygmus
Darmgeschwür *n* intestinal ulcer, enterelcosis, ulcer[ation] of the intestine
Darmgrimmen *n s.* Darmkolik
Darmgrippe *f* abdominoenteric influenza, intestinal (abdominal) flu, viral gastroenteritis
Darmhormone *npl* intestinal hormones *(Sekretin und Cholezystokinin)*
Darminfarkt *m* intestinal (enteromesenteric) infarct
Darminfarzierung *f* intestinal (enteromesenteric) infarction
Darminfektion *f* intestinal infection
~ mit Acanthocephala acanthocephaliasis
Darminhalt *m* intestinal contents
Darminhaltsstauung *f* enterostasis
Darminkontinenz *f* intestinal incontinence
Darmkanal *m* intestinal canal (tract) • **außerhalb des Darmkanals** abenteric
Darmkatarrh *m* enteritis
Darmkeimgleichgewicht *n* intestinal microbial balance
Darmklemme *f* intestinal forceps (clamp)
~/Payrsche Payr's [intestinal crushing] clamp
~/weichfassende *s.* ~/Payrsche
Darmkolik *f* enterospasm, intestinal (abdominal) colic
Darmkompressorium *n/Payrsches s.* Darmklemme/Payrsche
Darmkontinenz *f* intestinal continence
Darmkontinuität *f* intestinal (bowel) continuity
Darmkrampf *m* enterospasm, intestinal cramp
Darmkrebs *m* intestinal carcinoma, cancer of the bowels
Darmkrise *f* intestinal crisis
darmlähmend enteroplegic, enteroparalytic; antiperistaltic
Darmlähmung *f* enteroplegia, enteroparalysis; ileus
Darm-Leber-Rezirkulation *f* enterohepatic cycling
Darmleiden *n* enteropathy, intestinal trouble
Darmlösung *f[/operative]* enterolysis
Darmlymphe *f* chylus, chyle
Darmlymphemangel *m* oligochylia
Darmlymphgefäß *n* intestinal lymph vessel
Darmlymphgefäßerweiterung *f* intestinal lymphangiectasia
Darmmesser *n* enterotome
Darmmilzbrand *m* intestinal anthrax
Darmmuskulatur *f* myenteron, intestinal muscles
Darmmykose *f* enteromycosis, intestinal mycosis
Darmnadel *f* intestinal needle
Darmnähapparat *m* intestine suture appliance
Darmnaht *f* enterorrhaphy, intestinal suture
Darmnerven *mpl* intestinal nerves
Darmnetz *n* epiploon, [greater] omentum
Darmnetzbruch *m* epiploenterocele, enterepiplocele
Darmobstruktion *f* intestinal (bowel) obstruction

Darmoperation *f* intestinal (bowel) operation
~/plastische enteroplasty
Darmparasit *m* intestinal (enterozoic) parasite, enterozoon
Darmperforation *f* intestinal perforation, enterobrosis
Darmperistaltik *f* peristalsis, bowel movement, peristaltic motion
Darmpilzerkrankung *f* enteromycosis, intestinal mycosis
Darmpinzette *f* intestinal forceps
Darmplastik *f* enteroplasty
Darmpolyp *m* intestinal polyp
Darmprotozoen *npl* intestinal protozoa
Darmpunktion *f* intestinal puncture, enterocentesis
Darmquetsche *f* intestinal crushing clamp
Darmreinigung *f* purgation, catharsis, intestinal cleansing
Darmresektion *f* intestinal resection, enterectomy
Darmresorption *f* intestinal resorption (absorption)
Darmrohr *n* rectal (flatus) tube
Darmruptur *f* enterorrhexis, rupture of the intestine
Darmsaft *m* intestinal (enteric) juice
Darmschere *f* enterotomy (bowel) scissors
Darmschistosomiasis *f* intestinal schistosomiasis
Darmschleim *m* intestinal mucus
Darmschleimhaut *f* intestinal mucosa (mucous membrane), enteric mucosa
Darmschleimhautentzündung *f* mucoenteritis, endoenteritis
Darmschleimhautkatarrh *m* s. Darmschleimhautentzündung
Darmschleimhautoberfläche *f* intestinal wall mucosal surface
Darmschlinge *f* intestinal loop
Darmschmerz *m* enterodynia, enteralgia, pain in the intestine
Darmschnitt *m* enterotomy
Darmsekret *n* intestinal secretion
Darmsenkung *f* enteroptosis, Glénard's disease, visceroptosis
Darmsepsis *f* enterosepsis
Darmserosa *f* intestinal serosa
Darmspatel *m* intestinal spatula
Darmspiegel *m* enteroscope
darmspiegelnd enteroscopic
Darmspiegelung *f* enteroscopy
Darmspülung *f* intestinal lavage, irrigation of the bowels, enteroclysis, clyster
Darmstauung *f* intestinal stasis, enterostasis
Darmstein *m* intestinal calculus, enterolith, alvinolith
Darmsteinleiden *n* enterolithiasis
Darmstenose *f* enterostenosis, intestinal stenosis (stricture)
Darmstörung *f* intestinal trouble
Darmstriktur *f* s. Darmstenose

Darmtätigkeit *f* bowel function, peristalsis
Darm-Tbk *f* intestinal tuberculosis
Darmträgheit *f* obstipation, constipation
Darmtraining *n* bowel training
Darmtrakt *m* intestinal canal (tract)
Darmtrichine *f* intestinal trichinella, Trichinella spiralis
Darm- und Lebervorfall *m* enterohepatocele
Darmverdauung *f* intestinal digestion
Darmverdauungsstörung *f* intestinal dyspepsia
Darmverdrehung *f* volvulus, twisting of the bowels
Darmvereinigung *f* enteroanastomosis, enteroenterostomy
Darmvergrößerung *f* enteromegaly; megaloenteron
Darmverlegung *f* s. Darmverschluß
Darmverschlingung *f* volvulus, twisting of the bowels
Darmverschluß *m* ileus, intestinal obstruction, bowel occlusion
~/adynamischer adynamic (inhibitory, paralytic) ileus, pseudoileus
~/arteriomesenterialer arteriomesenteric ileus
~ durch Kindspech meconium ileus
~/hyperdynamischer [hyper]dynamic ileus, spastic ileus
~/mechanischer mechanical (occlusive) ileus, mechanical bowel occlusion
~/paralytischer s. ~/adynamischer
Darmvorbereitung *f* bowel preparation
Darmwand *f* intestinal (bowel) wall
Darmwandbruch *m* partial enterocele, Richter's hernia
Darmwandemphysem *n* intestinal pneumatosis
Darmwind *m* flatus, wind
Darmwindung *f* intestinal convolution
Darmzotten *fpl* intestinal villi
Darm-zu-Darm-Anastomose *f* s. Darmvereinigung
Darmzyste *f* enterocyst, enteric cyst
darstellen to demonstrate, to visualize *(Radiologie)*
~/eine Kontraindikation to contraindicate
~/in Schichten to tomograph
~/rein to isolate, to prepare
darstellend/mittels Ultraschalls ultrasonographic
Darwin-Höcker *m* Darwin's (auricular) tubercle
Daseinsanalyse *f* existential analysis
Dasselbeule *f* warble tumour
Dasselfliegenmadenbefall *m* dermatobiasis
Daturismus *m* daturism, poisoning by stramonium
Dauerabsaugung *f* continuous aspiration (suction)
Daueranästhesie *f*/**kaudale** fractional caudal anaesthesia
~/spinale fractional spinal anaesthesia
Dauerausscheider *m* chronic (permanent) carrier
Dauerausscheidung *f* chronic (permanent) carriage

Dauerbehandlung 160

Dauerbehandlung f long-term therapy, continuous (prolonged) treatment
Dauerbelastung f continuous load *(z. B. von Organen)*; continuous stress *(z. B. der Psyche)*
Dauerbeobachtung f continuous observation
Dauerberieselung f continuous irrigation *(z. B. einer Wunde)*
Dauerdrainage f continuous drainage
Dauereinlauf m continuous enema
Dauererektion f des männlichen Glieds priapism, persistent erection of the penis
Dauererfolg m lasting success *(z. B. einer Therapie)*
Dauerfüllung f permanent filling *(Stomatologie)*
Dauergabe f long-term administration *(z. B. von Medikamenten)*
Dauergeräusch n continuous murmur
Dauerheilung f permanent cure (healing), persistent recovery
Dauerimmunität f permanent (long-lasting) immunity
Dauerinfusion f continuous infusion (injection), intravenous drip
Dauerkallus m permanent (definitive) callus
Dauerkatheter m indwelling (permanent, continuous) catheter, self-retaining catheter
~/intravenöser continuous intravenous access (catheter)
Dauerkaudalanästhesie f continuous caudal anaesthesia
Dauerknorpel m permanent cartilage
Dauerkontraktion f/uterine continued (tetanic) contraction of the uterus
Dauerkrampf m continuous spasm
Dauermedikation f continuous (long-term) medication
Dauernarkose f continuous (prolonged) anaesthesia
Dauerniere f metanephros, definitive kidney *(entwicklungsgeschichtlich zuletzt gebildete Niere)*
● **die ~ bildend** metanephrogenic
Dauerparasit m permanent parasite
Dauerperfusion f continuous perfusion *(z. B. von Organen)*
Dauerpräparat n 1. long-term preparation *(Medikament)*; 2. permanent preparation *(Mikrobiologie)*
Dauersaugdrainage f continuous suction drainage
~/geschlossene continuous closed drainage
Dauersaugung f continuous suction [drainage]
Dauerschaden m permanent damage
Dauerschlafbehandlung f prolonged sleep therapy
Dauerschmerz m continuous (permanent) pain
Dauerspülkatheter m catheter for continuous irrigation
Dauertetanus m continuous (duration, prolonged) tetanus
Dauertracheostoma n permanent tracheostomy
Dauertremor m continuous tremor
Dauertropf m/intravenöser continuous intravenous drip

Dauertropfinfusion f/intravenöse continuous intravenous drip
Dauerversuch m long-term experiment
Dauerzugang m/intravenöser continuous intravenous access
Dauerzugbehandlung f continuous traction [treatment] *(bei Knochenbrüchen)*
Dauerzustand m permanent condition
Daumen m pollex, thumb
~/dreigliedriger triphalangism, triphalangy
Daumenabzieher m abductor pollicis [muscle]
~/kurzer abductor pollicis brevis [muscle]
~/langer abductor pollicis longus [muscle]
Daumenanzieher m adductor pollicis [muscle]
Daumenaufbau m pollicization *(plastische Chirurgie)*
Daumenballen m thenar [eminence], ball of the thumb
Daumenballenatrophie f/genuine genuine atrophy of the thenar muscles; carpal tunnel syndrome
Daumenballenmuskel m thenar [muscle]
Daumenballenregion f thenar area
Daumenbeuger m flexor pollicis [muscle]
~/kurzer flexor pollicis brevis [muscle]
~/langer flexor pollicis longus [muscle]
Daumenbeuge[r]sehne f thumb flexor tendon
Daumenfach n thenar space
Daumengegensteller[muskel] m opponens pollicis [muscle], flexor ossis metacarpi pollicis [muscle]
Daumenglied n phalanx of the thumb
Daumenhauptarterie f principal artery of the thumb
Daumenkuppe f tip of the thumb
Daumenneubildung f[/plastische] pollicization
Daumenreflex m thumb reflex
Daumenstrecker m extensor pollicis [muscle]
~/kurzer extensor pollicis brevis [muscle]
~/langer extensor pollicis longus [muscle]
dazukommend intercurrent *(Krankheit)*
dazwischenlagern/sich to interpose *(z. B. Muskelteile zwischen Knochenbrüche)*
Dazwischenlagerung f interposition
dazwischenliegend intermediary, intermediate, interstitial
dazwischenstellen to interpose
DB s. Dienstbeschädigung
DC-Defibrillierung f s. DC-Schock
DC-Schock m direct-current shock, capacitance-discharge defibrillation *(Herzrhythmisierung)*
DD s. Differentialdiagnose
DDT n dichlorodiphenyltrichloroethane, DDT
Deafferentierung f deafferentation *(Durchtrennung der hinteren Nervenwurzeln zur Schmerzausschaltung)*
Deamidase f s. Desamidase
Deaminase f s. Desaminase
debil 1. debile, feeble, weak; 2. debile, feeble-minded, mentally deficient
Debiler m debilitant, moron
Debilität f 1. debility, feebleness, weakness; 2. debility, feeble-mindedness, moronity

Degeneration

Debré-de Toni-Fanconi-Syndrom n [Debré-de Toni-]Fanconi syndrome, de Toni-Fanconi[-Debré] syndrome, amino diabetes, renal amino acid diabetes
Debré-Semelaigne-Syndrom n Debré-Semelaigne syndrome *(Form des Myxödems)*
Debridement n debridement [of wound], wound toilet
Debris m debris, devitalized tissue; foreign material
Decidua f decidua *(Gebärmutterschleimhaut während einer Schwangerschaft)*
~ **basalis** basal decidua
~ **capsularis** capsular decidua, epichorion
~ **marginalis** marginal decidua
~ **menstrualis** menstrual decidua, pseudodecidua
~ **parietalis** parietal decidua
~ **reflexa** s. ~ capsularis
~ **serotina** basal decidua
~ **vera** parietal decidua
Deckbiß m closed bite
Decke f integument[um], tegment; tegmen, tectum, roof, cap *(s. a. unter Tegmen und Tectum)*
Deckel m operculum
Deckepithel n surface epithelium
Deckglas n cover glass (slip)
Deckglas[faß]pinzette f cover glass forceps
Deckhaut f integument[um], tegment
Deckhülle f cover[ing], coat[ing]
Deckmembran f covering (tectorial) membrane
Deckplättchen n cover glass (slip)
Deckplatte f deck plate *(Embryologie)*; cover plate *(eines Wirbels)*
Deckung f/**plastische** plastic covering, grafting *(Chirurgie)*
Deckzelle f surface (cover) cell
Deckzellenepithel n mesothelium
Deckzellengeschwulst f mesothelioma
Deckzellensarkom n mesothelial sarcoma *(bösartig)*
Decussatio f decussation *(s. a. unter Chiasma)*
~ **lemniscorum** decussation of the lemnisci, sensory decussation
~ **pedunculorum cerebellarium superiorum** decussation of the superior cerebellar peduncles, decussation of the brachia conjunctiva
~ **pyramidum** pyramidal decussation, decussation of the pyramids
~ **supramamillaris** supramamillary decussation, commissure of Forel
~ **tegmenti dorsale** dorsal tegmental decussation
~ **tegmenti ventralis** ventral tegmental decussation, [tegmental] decussation of Forel
Dedifferenzierung f dedifferentiation
Defäkation f defaecation, discharge of faeces, evacuation, dejection, movement (motion) of the stools
Defäkationsprostatorrhoe f defaecation prostatorrhoea
Defäkationsreflex m defaecation reflex
Defäkationsreflexzentrum n defaecation reflex centre
Defäkationsspermatorrhoe f defaecation spermatorrhoea
Defäkationsstimulus m defaecation stimulus
Defäkationsstörung f defaecation disturbance
Defäkationstraining n bowel training
Defäkationszentrum n defaecation centre
Defatigatio f s. Ermüdung
defäzieren to defaecate
Defekt m defect, deficiency, failure
~/**immunologischer** immunodeficiency
Defektbildung f/**angeborene** [congenital] malformation
Defektdysproteinämie f s. Defektproteinämie
Defektheilung f partial recovery
Defektimmunopathie f immunodeficiency syndrome (disease)
Defektkoagulopathie f deficiency coagulopathy
Defektproteinämie f deficiency proteinaemia
Defektpseudarthrose f defective pseudarthrosis
Defektzustand m defective state
Defeminierung f defemination, defeminization
deferent deferent
Deferentitis f deferentitis, inflammation of the vas defferens
Deferveszenz f defervescence, lysis, paracme
Deferveszenzstadium n defervescent stage
Defibrillation f defibrillation, cardioversion *(des Herzens)*
~/**äußere (geschlossene)** closed-chest defibrillation
~/**intrathorakale** open-chest defibrillation
Defibrillator m defibrillator *(Apparat zur Elektroschocktherapie des Kammerflimmerns)*
defibrillieren to defibrillate
defibrinieren to defibrinate
Defibrinierung f defibrination
Defibrinierungssyndrom n defibrination syndrome
Definitivbehandlung f definitive treatment
Definitivwirt m definitive (end) host
Deflexionslage f deflection presentation *(des Fetus)*
Defloration f defloration
Deflorationspyelitis f defloration pyelitis
Deflorationszystitis f defloration cystitis
deflorieren to deflower, to deflorate
Deformierung f deformation, malformation
Deformität f deformity, dysmorphia, abnorm[al]ity
~/**Klippel-Feilsche** Klippel-Feil deformity (syndrome) *(angeborener Kurzhals)*
~/**Sprengelsche** Sprengel's deformity
Defrontalisation f s. Leukotomie
Defurfuration f defurfuration, desquamatio furfuracea *(bei Masern)*
Degeneration f 1. degeneration, devolution *(z. B. von Gewebe)*; involution *(z. B. des Gehirns)*; 2. degeneracy; dystrophia; retroplasia, retrograde metaplasia *(z. B. von Zellen) (s. a. unter Entartung)*

Degeneration

~/**absteigende** descending degeneration
~/**albuminoide** albuminoid (albuminous) degeneration, cloudy swelling *(Pathohistologie)*
~/**amyloidartige** amyloid (bacony) degeneration, glassy swelling
~/**atheromatöse** atheromatous degeneration
~/**aufsteigende** ascending degeneration
~ **der grauen Substanz** degeneration of grey matter, poliodystrophia
~/**fettige** fatty degeneration, steatosis
~/**fibrinöse** fibrinous degeneration
~/**fibröse** fibrous degeneration
~/**gallertige** gelatiniform (colloid) degeneration
~/**glasige** glassy degeneration
~/**hepatolentikuläre** hepatolenticular degeneration, Westphal-Strümpell pseudosclerosis, Wilson's disease
~/**hyaline** hyaline (vitreous) degeneration; hyalinosis, hyalinization
~/**kalkige** calcareous degeneration
~/**käsige** caseous (cheezy) degeneration, tyrosis, caseation
~/**mukoide** mucous (mucinous) degeneration
~/**parenchymatöse** parenchymatous degeneration
~/**pigmentartige** pigmentary (pigmental) degeneration
~/**polypöse** polypoid degeneration
~/**retikulare** reticular degeneration
~/**sekundäre** s. ~/Wallersche
~/**tapetochorioideale** tapetochoroidal degeneration
~/**tapetoretinale** tapetoretinal degeneration
~/**vakuoläre** vacuolar degeneration
~/**wachsartige** waxy degeneration
~/**Wallersche** Wallerian (secondary) degeneration
~/**Zenkersche** Zenker's degeneration
~/**zerebrale** cerebral degeneration
~/**zerebromakuläre (zerebroretinale)** cerebromacular (cerebroretinal) degeneration
~/**zystische** cystic degeneration
Degenerationsart *f* degenerative (involution) form
Degenerationsarthritis *f* degenerative arthritis
Degenerationsatrophie *f* degenerative atrophy
Degenerationskrankheit *f* degenerative disease
Degenerationspannus *m* degenerative pannus
Degenerationspsychose *f* degenerative psychosis
Degenerationsreaktion *f* reaction of degeneration
Degenerationsschaden *m* degenerative lesion
degenerativ degenerative
degenerieren to degenerate; to deteriorate
~/**käsig** to caseate
degenerierend degenerating; retrogressive
degeneriert degenerate; dystrophic, paratrophic
Degenerierung *f* s. Degeneration 1.
Deglutition *f* s. Schlucken
Dehelminthisation *f* dehelminthization
Dehiszenz *f* dehiscence

dehnbar elastic, flexible; dilatable, distensible
~/**nicht** inelastic, inflexible
Dehnbarkeit *f* elasticity, flexibility; dilatability, distensibility
dehnen to stretch, to distend; to dilate; to extend; to expand
Dehnmuskel *m* dilator [muscle]
Dehnsonde *f* [dilating] bougie
Dehnung *f* distension; dila[ta]tion *(z. B. im Kaliber)*; extension *(gerichtet)*; expansion *(ungerichtet)*; elongation *(z. B. des Gebärmutterhalses)*; tensure *(z. B. eines Organs)*
~/**übermäßige** parectasia *(z. B. eines Organs)*
Dehnungsbougie *f* [dilating] bougie
Dehnungsinstrument *n* dilator, divulsor
Dehnungsreflex *m* stretch reflex
Dehnungsrezeptor *m* stretch receptor; pressoreceptor *(in der Aorta)*
Dehnungsschmerz *m* dilating pain *(Geburt)*
Dehydrase *f* s. Dehydrogenase
Dehydratation *f* dehydration, anhydration, water lack
dehydratisieren to dehydrate
dehydrieren 1. to dehydrate; 2. to dehydrogenate, to dehydrogenize
Dehydrierung *f* 1. dehydration; 2. dehydrogen[iz]ation
Dehydrierungserschöpfung *f* dehydration (water-depletion heat) exhaustion
Dehydrierungstherapie *f* dehydration therapy
Dehydro-7-cholesterin *n* 7-dehydrocholesterol *(Provitamin D_3)*
Dehydrocholsäure *f* dehydrocholic acid *(galletreibendes Mittel)*
Dehydrogenase *f* dehydrogenase *(Enzym)*
Dehydro-Hydrokortison *n* s. Prednisolon
Dehydrokortikosteron *n* dehydrocorticosterone
Dehydrokortison *n* s. Prednison
Dehydromorphin *n* dehydromorphine, oxymorphine *(Analgetikum)*
Deiter-Kern *m* Deiter's (lateral vestibular) nucleus
Deiter-Zellen *fpl* Deiter's cells
Dejektion *f* s. Defäkation
Déjerine-Klumpke-Lähmung *f* Déjerine-Klumpke's paralysis (syndrome), lower brachial plexus paralysis
Déjerine-Landouzy-Dystrophie *f* Déjerine-Landouzy dystrophy (myopathy), fascioscapulohumeral muscular dystrophy
Déjerine-Roussy-Syndrom *n* Déjerine-Roussy syndrome, thalamic syndrome
Déjerine-Sottas-Syndrom *n* Déjerine-Sottas disease (neuropathy), hypertrophic interstitial neuropathy *(Form der neuralen Muskelatrophie)*
dejodieren to deiodinate
dekalzifizieren to decalcify
dekalzinieren to decalcify
dekantieren to decant
Dekanülierung *f* decannulation
Dekapitation *f* decapitation, detruncation

Dekapitationshaken *m* decapitating hook
Dekapitator *m* decapitator, decollator *(Instrument)*
dekapitieren to decapitate
Dekapsulation *f* 1. decapsulation, removal of a capsule *(allgemein)*; 2. Edebohls' operation, nephrocapsulectomy, renal decortication
dekapsulieren to decapsulate, to remove a capsule [from]; to decorticate
dekaptieren *s.* dekapitieren
Dekarboxylase *f* decarboxylase *(Enzym)*
dekarboxylieren to decarboxylate
Dekarboxylierungsenzym *n* decarboxylating enzyme
Dekompensation *f* decompensation *(eines Organs)*
~/kardiale cardiac decompensation
dekompensieren to decompensate, to undergo decompensation
Dekomposition *f* 1. decomposition *(allgemein)*; putrefaction *(der Proteine)*; fermentation *(der Kohlehydrate)*; 2. marasmus *(der Säuglinge)*
Dekompression *f* decompression, removal of compression (pressure)
~/gastrointestinale gastrointestinal decompression
Dekompressionskammer *f* decompression chamber
Dekompressionskrankheit *f* decompression sickness, caisson disease, compressed-air illness (sickness), aeroemphysema, chokes, dysbarism
Dekompressionsschmerzen *mpl* bends *(z. B. an Knochen)*
Dekonjugation *f* deconjugation *(z. B. von Gallensäuren)*
dekonjugieren to deconjugate
Dekontamination *f* decontamination
~/radioaktive radioactive decontamination
dekontaminieren to decontaminate
Dekorporation *f* decorporation *(z. B. radioaktiver Substanzen)*
Dekortikation *f* decortication, removal of a cortex
Dekortikationshaltung *f* decorticate position (posture)
Dekortikationsstarre *f* decorticate rigidity
dekortizieren to decorticate
Dekrement *n* decrement, decrease *(z. B. einer Krankheit)*
Dekrementleitung *f* decremental conduction *(Physiologie)*
Dekrementlinien *fpl* decremental lines *(Strahlentherapie)*
Dekrepitation *f* decrepitation, crackling noise
dekrepitieren to decrepitate, to explode with a crackling noise
Dekreszendo *n* decrescendo *(z. B. von Herzgeräuschen)*
Dekrustation *f* decrustation, detachment of a crust
Dekubitalgeschwür *n s.* Dekubitus

Dekubitalnekrose *f* decubital gangrene
Dekubitalphlegmone *f* decubital phlegmon
Dekubitalsepsis *f* decubital sepsis
Dekubitus *m* decubitus, decubital (pressure) ulcer, bedsore, decubitus (pressure) sore
Dekubitusmatratze *f* oscillating (rocking) bed
Dekurarisierung *f* decurarization
Delaktation *f* 1. delactation, cessation of lactation; 2. weaning *(eines Säuglings)*
Delamination *f* delamination, separation of the blastoderm
Del Castillo-Syndrom *n* Del Castillo's syndrome, testicular dysgenesis syndrome
deletär deleterious, noxious, destructive, hurtful, harmful, injurious
Deletion *f* deletion *(Chromosomenmutation)*
~ des Chromosoms Nr. 5 deletion-5 syndrome, cri-du-chat syndrome
Deletionssyndrom *n* deletion syndrome
Delhibeule *f* Delhi boil (sore), cutaneous leishmaniasis [of the Old World]
De Lima-Operation *f* De Lima's operation, transmaxillary ethmoidectomy
Delipoidose *f* delipoidosis
Delir *n s.* Delirium
delirant 1. delirious; 2. *s.* delirbewirkend
delirbewirkend delirifacient, deliriant
deliriant, deliriös delirious
Delirium *n* delirium *(Bewußtseinstrübung mit Verwirrtheit, Desorientierung und Verkennung der Umgebung)* ● **~ erzeugend** delirifacient, deliriant ● **im ~ befindlich** delirious
~/afebriles afebrile delirium
~/akutes acute delirium
~/alkoholisches *s.* ~ tremens
~/chronisch-alkoholisches chronic alcoholic delirium (psychosis), Korsakoff's psychosis
~ febrile febrile delirium, pyretotyphosis
~/leichtes mild (partial) delirium, subdelirium
~/mussitierendes quiet (low muttering) delirium
~/schweres grave (severe) delirium
~/seniles senile delirium, dotage, imbecility of old age
~ tremens alcohol delirium, delirium tremens (alcoholicum), oinomania, potomania, enomania, tremor of drinkers
Delle *f* impression, pit, fovea; fosette; lacuna, lake ● **eine ~ bilden** to pit
Dellenbildung *f* pitting, dimpling *(z. B. in der Haut)*
Dellwarze *f* contagious (epithelial) molluscum *(erbsengroße wachsgelbe Hautgeschwulst mit zentraler Eindellung)*
dellwarzenartig molluscoid
delomorph delomorphous, delomorphic *(z. B. Parietalzelle)*
Delorme-Operation *f* 1. Delorme's operation (decortication), pericardiectomy, decortication of the heart; 2. *s.* Rehn-Delorme-Operation
Deltaaktivität *f* delta-activity *(EEG)*
deltaförmig deltoid
Deltamuskel *m* deltoid [muscle] ● **unter dem ~** subdeltoid

Deltamuskelentzündung 164

Deltamuskelentzündung f deltoiditis, inflammation of the deltoid muscle
Deltamuskelreflex m deltoid reflex
Deltarhythmus m delta rhythm *(EEG)*
Deltastrahlen mpl delta rays
Deltawelle f delta wave *(EEG)*
Deltazelle f delta cell *(in der Hypophyse)*
deltopektoral deltopectoral
Delusion f delusion
delusorisch delusory, deceptive
Demarkation f demarcation, separation, establishing of limits, marking (ascertainment) of boundaries *(z. B. abgestorbener Gewebsteile)*
Demarkationslinie f demarcation line, line of demarcation *(zwischen totem und lebendem Gewebe)*
Demarkationspotential n demarcation (injury) potential
Demarkationsring m demarcation ring
Demarkationsstrom m demarcation (injury) current
demarkieren to demarcate
dement demented
Dementer m dement, demented person
Dementia f dementia, aphrenia, aphronesia, anoia *(s. a. unter Demenz)*
~ **agitata** agitated dementia
~ **epileptica** epileptic dementia (psychosis)
~ **paralytica** paralytic (paretic) dementia, general paralysis of the insane, general paresis
~ **paranoides** paranoid dementia
~ **tabetica** tabetic dementia
Demenz f dementia, aphrenia, aphronesia, anoia *(s. a. unter Dementia)*
~/**alkoholische** alcoholic dementia (insanity)
~/**apoplektische** apoplectic dementia
~/**arteriosklerotische** arteriosclerotic psychosis
~/**posttraumatische** traumatic dementia
~/**präsenile** presenile dementia (psychosis), Alzheimer's disease
~/**schizophrene** schizophrenic dementia
~/**sekundäre** secondary dementia
~/**semantische** semantic dementia
~/**senile** senile dementia (psychosis), presbyophrenia
~/**terminale** terminal dementia
~/**toxische** toxic dementia
~/**traumatische** traumatic dementia
demethylieren to demethylate
Demethylierung f demethylation
Demineralisation f demineralization, loss of mineral salts
~/**kariöse** carious demineralization; dental caries
demineralisieren to demineralize
Demodexbefall m demodicidosis, infestation with demodex
Demodexmilbe f hair follicle mite, follicular (face) mite, Demodex folliculorum
Demoralisation f demoralization
Demyelinisation f demyelin[iz]ation, myelinoclasis *(des Zentralnervensystems)*
Demyelinisationskrankheit f demyelinating disease

denaturieren to denatur[at]e, to denaturize *(Eiweiß)*
Denaturierung f denatur[iz]ation
Dendrit m [neuro]dendrite, [neuro]dendron
dendritenlos adendritic
dendritisch dendritic, dendroid
Dendrophilie f dendrophilia *(Vorliebe für Bäume)*
denervieren to denervate, to cut off the nerve supply
Denervierung f 1. denervation, resection (removal) of the nerves, interruption of the nerve supply; 2. enervation, weakness, lassitude; reduction of strength *(seelischer Zustand)*
Denervierungspotential n denervation potential
Dengue n s. Denguefieber
dengue-artig dengue-like
Denguefieber n dengue, dengue [haemorrhagic] fever, dandy (solar) fever, breakbone fever
Denidation f denidation
denitrifizieren to denitrify
Denken n thinking; mental activity; cerebration
~/**archaisches** archaic-paralogical thinking
~/**assoziatives** associative thinking
~/**autistisches** autistic thinking, autism
~/**dereistisches** dereistic thinking, dereism
~/**magisches** magical thinking
~/**schizophrenes** schizophrenic thinking
~/**wirklichkeitsfernes** s. ~/dereistisches
Denkfaulheit f mental laziness
Denkinhalt m thought contents
Denkmechanismus m mental mechanism (dynamism)
Denkprozeß m mental process
Denkschwäche f logasthenia
Denkvermögen n intellect, intellectual (thinking) power
Denkvorgang m mental (thinking) process
Denkweise f way of thinking; mentality
Dens m 1. dens, tooth *(s.a. unter Zahn)*; 2. s. Dens axis
~ **acutus** incisor tooth
~ **axis** dens of the axis, odontoid process
~ **bicuspidatus** bicuspid [dens]
~ **caninus** canine [tooth]
~ **epistrophei** s. ~ axis
~ **incisivus** incisor [tooth]
~ **molaris** molar [tooth]
~ **praemolaris** premolar [tooth]
~ **serotinus (sophroneticus)** wisdom tooth
Densfraktur f dens (odontoid) fracture
Densimeter n densi[to]meter
Densimetrie f densi[to]metry
densimetrisch densi[to]metric
Densografie f densography
dental dental
Dental... s.a. Zahn...
Dentalanästhesie f dental anaesthesia
Dentaldysplasie f dental dysplasia
Dentaleinheit f dental unit
Dentalepithel n dental epithelium
Dentalfluorose f dental fluorosis
~/**chronische endemische** chronic dental fluorosis, poikilodentosis; mottled enamel

Dentalfollikel *m* dental follicle (sac)
Dentalfortsatz *m* dental process
Dentalgie *f* dentalgia, toothache
Dentalinfektion *f* dental infection
Dentalkaries *f s.* Karies
Dentalkeramik *f* dental ceramics
Dentalnekrose *f* dental necrosis
Dentaloberhäutchen *n* dental cuticle
Dentalorgan *n* dental organ
Dentalosteom *n* dental osteoma
Dentalperiostitis *f* dental periostitis
Dentalpinzette *f* dental (tooth) forceps
Dentalporzellan *n* dental porcelain
Dentalpräparat *n* dental preparation
Dentalprophylaxe *f* dental prophylaxis, prophylactodontia
Dentalpunkte *mpl* dental points
Dentalschiene *f* interdental splint
Dentatektomie *f* dentatectomy *(operative Ausschaltung des Nucleus dentatus)*
Dentes *mpl* decidui milk (deciduous) teeth
~ **permanentes** permanent teeth (dentition)
Dentifikation *f s.* Dentinbildung
dentiform dentiform, tooth-shaped, odont[in]oid
Dentifricium *n* dentifrice, tooth-paste
Dentikel *m* denticle, pulp stone
~/**adhärenter** adherent denticle
~/**echter** true denticle
~/**falscher** false denticle
~/**freier** free denticle
~/**interstitieller** interstitial denticle
Dentin *n* dentin[e], ivory
~/**intermediäres** intermediate dentin
~/**irreguläres** irregular dentin
~/**primäres** primary dentin
~/**sekundäres** secondary dentin
~/**transparentes** transparent dentin
dentinartig dentinoid
dentinbildend dentinogenic, dentinogenous
Dentinbildner *m* dentinoblast
Dentinbildung *f* dentinification, formation of dentin, dentinogenesis, odonto[gene]sis
Dentinbildungszelle *f* odontoblast, dentinal cell
Dentinfibrille *f* dentinal fibril
Dentinhypoplasie *f* dentinal hypoplasia
Dentinifikation *f s.* Dentinbildung
Dentinkanälchen *n* dentinal tubule
Dentinoblast *m* dentinoblast
Dentinoblastom *n* dentinoblastoma
dentinogen *s.* dentinbildend
Dentinogenesis *f* imperfecta dentinogenesis imperfecta; hereditary opalescent dentin
Dentinoid *n* dentinoid
Dentinom *n* dentinoma
Dentinosteoid *n* dentinosteoid
Dentinresorption *f* dentin resorption, odontoclasis, odontolysis
Dentist *m* dentist
Dentition *f* dentition, teething, dentification, odontiasis
~/**primäre** primary (deciduous) dentition
~/**sekundäre** secondary (permanent) dentition
~/**verzögerte** delayed dentition
dentoalveolär dentoalveolar
dentogingival dentogingival
dentoid dentoid, tooth-like
Denudation *f* denudation *(z. B. des Zahnhalses)*
Deossifikation *f* deossification
Depersonalisation *f* depersonalization *(Störung des Ich-Erlebens bei Schizophrenie)*
Depersonalisationssyndrom *n* depersonalization syndrome
depigmentieren to depigment
Depigmentierung *f* depigmentation, loss (removal) of pigment
Depigmentierungsanomalie *f* depigmentation anomaly
Depilation *f* depilation, epilation
Depilatorum *n* depilatory [agent]
depilieren to depilate, to remove hair, to epilate
Depletionssyndrom *n* depletion syndrome
Depletionstest *m* depletion test
Depolarisation *f* depolarization
depolarisieren to depolarize
Depolymerase *f* depolymerase *(Enzym)*
Depolymerisation *f* depolymerization
depolymerisieren to depolymerize
Depot *n* deposit, depot
Depotbehandlung *f* depot treatment
Depoteisen *n* depot iron
Depotfett *n* depot fat
Depotimpfstoff *m* depot (repository) vaccine
Depotinjektion *f* depot (repository) injection
Depotkortikosteroid *n* depot corticosteroid
Depotpenizillin *n* depot (repository) penicillin
Depotpräparat *n* depot preparation, repository
Depotwirkung *f* depot effect *(eines Medikaments)*
Depression *f* 1. depression, dejection *(psychische Störung)*; 2. depression, dimple
~/**agitierte** agitated depression
~/**anankastische** anancastic depression
~/**ängstlich-agitierte** anxious agitated depression
~/**ängstliche** anxious depression
~/**endogene** endogenous depression
~/**exogene** exogenous depression
~/**hypochondrische** hypochondriacal depression
~/**initiale** initial depression
~/**klimakterische** climacteric depression
~/**konstitutionelle** constitutional depressive disposition
~/**periodische** periodic depression
~/**reaktive** reactive (situational) depression, depressive neurosis (reaction)
~/**symptomatische** symptomatic depression
~/**vegetative** vegetative depression
Depressionsfraktur *f* depressed fracture
depressionshemmend antidepressant
Depressionsimmunität *f* depressive immunity
Depressionszustand *m* depressive state (condition)
depressiv depressive; causing depression
Depressivum *n* depressant [agent]

Depressor

Depressor *m* 1. depressor [muscle]; 2. depressor [nerve]; 3. *s.* Depressorium
Depressorenzentrum *n* depressor area *(ZNS)*
depressorisch depressor, inhibitory
Depressorium *n* depressor[ium] *(Instrument)*
Depressorreflex *m* depressor reflex
Depressorsubstanz *f* depressor substance
deprimiert depressed *(Psyche)*
Deprivation *f* deprivation *(Verlust lebenswichtiger Bedingungen für den Organismus)*
~/**emotionale** emotional deprivation
~/**motorische** motor deprivation
~/**sensorische** sensory deprivation
Deprivationssyndrom *n* deprivation syndrome
Deradelphus *m* deradelphus *(Doppelmißgeburt mit Verschmelzung der oberen Körperhälfte und Extremitätenverdopplung)*
Derattisation *f* deratization, extermination of rats
derb hard, compact, resistant, firm *(z. B. Gewebe)*
Dercum-Krankheit *f* Dercum's disease, adipositas (adiposis) dolorosa, neurolipomatosis
dereierend dereistic
Dereismus *m* der[e]ism
dereistisch dereistic
derenzephal derencephalous
Derenzephalie *f* derencephalia
Derenzephalus *m* derencephalus *(Mißgeburt)*
Derivation *f s.* Ableitung 2.
Derma *f* derm[a], dermis, cutis, skin *(Zusammensetzungen s. unter Cutis und Haut)*
Dermacentor *m* **andersoni** Dermacentor andersoni, wood tick
dermal dermal, dermic, cutaneous
Dermalgie *f s.* Dermatalgie
Dermanyssus *m* **avium (gallinae)** bird[-face] mite, poultry mite, chicken louse
Dermatalgie *f* derm[at]algia, dermatodynia, dermatagra, pain in the skin
Dermatikum *n* dermatic
dermatisch dermatic, dermal, cutaneous
Dermatitis *f* derm[at]itis, scytitis, inflammation of the skin *(s. a. unter Hautentzündung)*
~ **actinica** actinic dermatitis
~/**allergische** allergic dermatitis
~ **ammoniacalis** diaper (napkin area) dermatitis
~ **atopica** atopic dermatitis
~ **atrophicans** atrophic (Oppenheim's) dermatitis, diffuse atrophy of the skin
~/**bösartige papilläre** malignant papillary dermatitis, Paget's disease
~ **bullosa** bullous dermatitis
~ **carcinomatosa** carcinomatous dermatitis
~ **chronica atrophicans maculosa** anetoderma
~ **coccidioides (coccidiosa)** coccidioidal granuloma
~ **congelationis** frostbite
~ **cosmetica** cosmetic dermatitis
~ **dysmenorrhoeica** dysmenorrhoeic dermatitis
~ **epidemica** epidemic dermatitis, Savill's disease
~ **erythematosa** erythema
~ **escharotica** escharotic dermatitis
~ **excoriativa infantum** inflammatory excoriation of the skin in infants
~ **exfoliativa generalisata [Wilson-Brocq]** generalized exfoliative dermatitis
~ **exfoliativa infantum** Ritter's disease
~ **exfoliativa Leiner** exfoliative dermatitis
~ **exsudativa** weeping (exudative) dermatitis
~ **gangraenosa** sphaceloderma
~ **gangraenosa infantum** gangrenous varicella
~ **glandularis erythematosa** lupus erythematosus
~ **haemostatica** haemostatic dermatitis
~ **herpetiformis [Duhring]** herpetiform dermatitis, Duhring's disease
~ **hypostatica** hypostatic dermatitis
~ **lichenoides chronica atrophicans** chronic atrophic lichenoid dermatitis
~ **lichenoides chronica pruriens** neuroderm[at]itis
~ **lichenoides purpurea et pigmentata** pigmented purpuric lichenoid dermatitis, Gougerot-Blum disease
~ **medicamentosa** drug dermatitis
~ **multiformis** *s.* ~ herpetiformis
~ **mycotica** mycotic dermatitis
~/**nässende** weeping dermatitis
~ **nodularis necrotica** necrotizing nodular dermatitis
~ **nummularis** nummular dermatitis
~ **papillaris capillitii** keloid acne, keloidal folliculitis, framboesiform sycosis
~ **papulosquamosa atrophicans** Degos' disease
~ **pediculoides ventricosus** straw itch
~ **photoelectrica** solar dermatitis
~ **phototoxica** berlock (berloque) dermatitis
~ **psoriasiformis nodularis** chronic lichenoid pityriasis
~ **seborrhoeica (seborrhoeides)** seborrhoeic dermatitis (eczema), seborrhoea
~ **simplex** erythema
~ **solaris** solar dermatitis, sun burn
~ **toxica** toxic dermatitis, toxidermitis
~ **traumatica** traumatic dermatitis
~ **variegata** maculopapular erythroderma
~ **vegetans** vegetative dermatitis
~ **venenata** contact dermatitis
~ **verrucosa** chromoblastomycosis, chromo[hypho]mycosis; mossy foot
Dermatoautoplastik *f* dermatoautoplasty
Dermatobiasis *f* dermatobiasis
Dermatochalasis *f* dermatochalasis; cutis laxa
Dermatodynie *f s.* Dermatalgie
Dermatofibrom *n s.* Dermatofibroma lenticulare
Dermatofibroma *n* **lenticulare** dermatofibroma, simple fibroma; nodular subepidermal fibrosis *(gutartige, zellreiche Geschwulstform der Haut)*
Dermatofibrosarkom *n* dermatofibrosarcoma
dermatogen dermatogenic, dermatogenous
Dermatoheteroplastik *f* dermatoheteroplasty
Dermatokoniose *f* dermatoconiosis

Dermatologe *m* dermatologist
Dermatologie *f* dermatology
dermatologisch dermatologic[al]
Dermatolyse *f* dermatolysis; dermatochalasis; loose skin, cutis laxa
dermatolytisch dermatolytic
Dermatom *n* 1. dermatome, dermatomic area (Hautabschnitt); 2. derma[to]tome, cutisector; 3. dermatome, cutis plate
~/**elektrisches** electrodermatome
Dermatomegalie *f* dermatomegaly
Dermatomreduziergetriebe *n* reduction gear unit for dermatome
Dermatomyiasis *f* dermatomyiasis
Dermatomykose *f* [epi]dermatomycosis
Dermatomyom *n* dermatomyoma
Dermatomyositis *f* dermatomyositis, multiple myositis, pseudotrichinosis
Dermatoneurologie *f* dermatoneurology
Dermatoneurose *f* dermatoneurosis, skin neurosis, neurosis of the skin
Dermatopathie *f* dermatopathy, skin disease, disease of the skin
dermatopathisch dermatopathic
Dermatopathologie *f* dermatopathology, pathology of the skin
Dermatopathophobie *f* dermato[patho]phobia (krankhafte Angst vor Hautkrankheiten)
Dermatophiliasis *f* dermatophiliasis, dermatophilosis
Dermatophlebitis *f* derm[at]ophlebitis
Dermatophobie *f s.* Dermatopathophobie
Dermatophyt *m* dermatophyte, dermatomyces, dermatomycete
Dermatophytid *n* dermatophytid (Hautausschlag bei Pilzerkrankung)
Dermatophytie *f,* **Dermatophytose** *f* dermatophytosis, epidermophytosis, ringworm of the feet; athlete's foot
Dermatoplastik *f* dermatoplasty
dermatoplastisch dermatoplastic
Dermatopolyneuritis *f* dermatopolyneuritis, erythroedema polyneuropathy, Feer's disease, acrodynia
Dermatoprophylaxe *f* derm[at]ophylaxis, protection against skin infection
Dermatorrhagie *f* dermatorrhagia, bleeding from the skin
Dermatorrhexis *f* 1. dermatorrhexis, rupture of the skin capillaries; 2. *s.* Ehlers-Danlos-Syndrom
Dermatose *f* dermatosis, skin disease
~/**aktinische** actinic dermatosis
~/**allergische** allergic dermatosis
~/**angioneurotische** angioneurotic dermatosis
~/**lichenoide** lichenoid dermatosis
~/**pigmentierte** pigmented dermatosis, Schönberg's disease
~/**postvakzinale** postvaccinal dermatosis
~/**präkanzeröse** [Bowen's] precancerous dermatosis, Bowen's disease

~/**progressive pigmentäre** progressive pigmentary dermatosis, Schamberg's disease (dermatosis)
~/**Unnasche** Unna's dermatosis, seborrhoeic eczema
Dermatosklerose *f* dermatosclerosis; scleroderma
Dermatoskopie *f* dermatoscopy, examination of the skin
Dermatostomatitis *f* dermatostomatitis
Dermatotherapie *f* dermatotherapy, treatment of skin disease
Dermatotomie *f* dermatotomy, dissection of the skin
dermatotrop dermatotropic
Dermatozellulitis *f* dermatocellulitis
Dermatozoon *n* dermatozoon
Dermatozoonose *f* dermatozoonosis
Dermatozyste *f* dermatocyst
Dermatrophie *f* dermatrophy, atrophy of the skin
Dermitis *f s.* Dermatitis
Dermoblast *m* dermoblast
Dermofluometrie *f* dermofluometry
Dermogramm *n* derm[at]ogram
Dermograph *m* 1. dermatograph (Instrument zur Hautmarkierung); 2. dermograph (Hautzeichen bei Dermographie)
Dermographie *f* derm[at]ographia, dermographism, autographism, factitious urticaria (vasomotorisches Nachröten der Haut nach dem Bestreichen)
~/**rote** red dermographism
~/**weiße** white dermographism
dermographisch dermographic
Dermographismus *m s.* Dermographie
dermoid dermoid
Dermoid *n* dermoid [cyst]
~/**wanderndes** wandering dermoid
Dermoidentfernung *f*[/**operative**] dermoidectomy
Dermoidgeschwulst *f* dermoid tumour
Dermoidkystom *n* dermoid [cyst]
Dermoidzyste *f* dermoid [cyst]
Dermoidzystenausschälung *f* dermoidectomy
Dermolipom *n* dermolipoma
Dermolysin *n* dermolysin
Dermophyt *m* derm[at]ophyte
Dermosynoviitis *f* dermosynovitis
dermotrop dermotropic
Dermotropismus *m* dermotropism
Desadaptation *f* maladjustment (an die Umwelt)
Desamidase *f* deamidase, desamidase (Enzym)
desamidieren to deamidate, to desamidate, to deamidize
Desaminase *f* deaminase, desaminase (Enzym)
desaminieren to deaminate, to desaminate, to deaminize
Desaminierung *f* deamination, desamination
Desaminierungsenzym *n* deaminating enzyme
Desault-Verband *m* Desault's bandage (apparatus), sling and swathe (z. B. bei Oberarmfraktur)

Descemetitis

Descemetitis f descemetitis, inflammation of Descemet's membrane, keratitis punctata
Descemet-Membran f Descemet's membrane, posterior elastic lamina, internal basal lamina
Descemetozele f descemetocele
descendens descending
Descensus m descensus, descent; prolapse *(eines Organs)*
~ **testis** descent of the testicle (testis), orchiocatabasis *(aus der Bauchhöhle in das Skrotum)*
~ **uteri** uterine descensus
~ **ventriculi** gastroptosis
Deschamps m, **Deschamps-Unterführungsnadel** f Deschamps' needle *(für Gefäßligaturen)*
desensibilisieren to desensitize, to hyposensitize, to deallergize *(z. B. gegenüber Antigenen)*
Desensibilisierung f desensitization, hyposensitization, deallergization
Desensibilisierungsbehandlung f desensitization (allergen-desensitizing) treatment
Desensibilisierungsmethode f desensitization method
Desensibilisierungstest m desensitization test
Desinfektion f disinfection
Desinfektionsanstalt f disinfecting station
Desinfektionsapparat m disinfector
Desinfektionslösung f disinfecting solution (fluid)
Desinfektionsmittel n, **Desinfiziens** n disinfectant [agent]
desinfizieren to disinfect; to sterilize
desinfizierend disinfectant; sterilizing
Desinfizierung f disinfection
Desinsektion f disinsection, disinsectization, deinsectization
Desinvagination f disinvagination *(z. B. einer Darmeinstülpung)*
Desmalgie f desmalgia, desmodynia, pain in a ligament
Desmarres-Lidhalter m Desmarres' lid retractor
Desmin n desmin *(kontraktiles Eiweiß)*
Desminfilament n desmin filament
Desmitis f desmitis, inflammation of a ligament
desmogen desmogenous
desmoid desmoid, fibrous, fibroid
Desmoid n desmoid [tumour]
Desmoidfibrom n desmoid fibroma
Desmoidgeschwulst f s. Desmoid
Desmokranium n desmocranium
Desmolase f desmolase *(Enzym)*
Desmolyse f desmolysis
Desmopathie f desmopathy, disease of a ligament
Desmopexie f desmopexia, fixation of a ligament
desmoplastisch desmoplastic
Desmorrhexis f desmorrhexis, rupture of a ligament
Desmosom n desmosome
Desmotomie f desmotomy, cutting (incision) of a ligament
Desmozyt m desmocyte
Desmurgie f desmurgia
Desobliteration f desobliteration, endarter[i]ectomy, intimectomy
desobliterieren to desobliterate, to endarterectomize *(Gefäßinnenhaut)*
Desodorans n deodorant, deodorizer
desodorieren to deodorize
desodorierend deodorant
Desorganisation f disorganization, dedifferentiation
desorientiert disoriented
Desorientierung f disorientation *(bei Bewußtseinsstörung)*
Desoxyadenosin n deoxyadenosine
Desoxycholsäure f deoxycholic acid *(Gallensäure)*
Desoxydation f deoxygenation *(z. B. des Bluts)*; deoxidation
2-Desoxy-D-ribose f deoxyribose
Desoxyephedrin n deoxyephedrine
Desoxyguanosin n deoxyguanine
Desoxykortikosteron n deoxycorticosterone *(Nebennierenrindenhormon)*
Desoxypentose f deoxypentose
Desoxyribonuklease f deoxyribonuclease, DNase *(Enzym)*
Desoxyribonukleinsäure f deoxyribonucleic acid, DNA, thymonucleic (thymus nucleic) acid
Desoxyribonukleinsäurepolymerase f deoxyribonucleic acid polymerase *(Enzym)*
Desoxyribonukleinsäurereplikation f deoxyribonucleic acid replication
Desoxyribonukleinsäuresynthese f deoxyribonucleic acid synthesis
Desoxyribonukleinsäurevirus n deoxyribonucleic acid virus
Desoxyribonukleotid n deoxyribonucleotide
Desoxyribose f deoxyribose
Desoxyuridin n deoxyuridine
Desoxyzytidin n deoxycytidine
Desquamatio f **furfuracea** defurfuration *(z. B. bei Masern)*
Desquamation f desquamation, peeling, exfoliation, shedding, casting off, ecdysis
Desquamationsphase f desquamation phase
desquamativ desquamative
Desquamativgingivitis f [chronic] desquamative gingivitis
Desquamativkatarrh m desquamative catarrh
destillieren to distill
destruieren to destruct
Destruktion f destruction
Destruktionsluxation f destructive luxation
Desynchronisation f desynchronization
Deszemetozele f descemetocele
deszendierend descending
deszendiert descended
Deszensus m s. Descensus
Detelektase f detelectasis, collapse
Detorsion f detorsion
Detoxikation f detoxi[fi]cation
Detrition f detrition *(z. B. der Zähne)*

Detritus *m* detritus
Detrusor *m* **vesicae** detrusor vesicae [muscle], detrusor urinae
Detrusorkontraktion *f* detrusor contraction
Detrusorschwäche *f* detrusor weakness
Detrusorspasmus *m* detrusor spasm
Detumeszenz *f* detumescence, subsidence of swelling
detur let it be given, detur
deuteranomal deuteranomalous
Deuteranomalie *f* deuteranomaly, deuteranomalop[s]ia
deuteranop deuteranopic
Deuteranoper *m* deuteranope
Deuteranopie *f* deuteranop[s]ia, green blindness
Deuteroalbumose *f* deuteroalbumose, deuteroproteose
Deuterohämatin *n* deuterohaematin
Deuterohämin *n* deuterohaemin
Deuteropathie *f* deuteropathy, secondary disease
deuteropathisch deuteropathic
Deuteroplasma *n* deut[er]oplasm
Deutsches Rotes Kreuz *n* German Red Cross
Deutschländer-Syndrom *n* Deutschländer's disease (syndrome), march foot *(Ermüdungsbruch von Mittelfußknochen)*
Devagination *f s.* Desinvagination
Devaskularisation *f* devascularization, devasation
Deviation *f* deviation *(z. B. der Augenachsen)*
~/gleichsinnige (konjugierte) conjugate deviation
Deviationsmesser *m* deviometer *(Instrument zur Schielmessung)*
devital devital
Devitalisation *f* devitalization [of the pulp]
devitalisieren to devitalize, to destroy vitality
Dexamethason *n* dexamethasone
Dexamethason-Hemmtest *m* dexamethasone suppression test *(Nebennierenrindenfunktion)*
Dexiokardie *f s.* Dextrokardie
dexter dexter, right, on the right side
Dextran *n* dextran *(Polysaccharid)*
dextraural dextraural, right-eared
Dextrin *n* dextrin *(Stärkeabbauprodukt)*
Dextrinausscheidung *f* **im Urin** dextrinuria
Dextrinose *f* dextrinosis
Dextrodeviation *f* dextrodeviation, deviation to the right
Dextrogramm *n* dextro[cardio]gram, right-side cardiogram
dextrogyr dextrogyral, dextrogyrate, dextrogyre, dextrorotatory
dextrokardial dextrocardial
Dextrokardie *f* dextrocardia, dexiocardia, dextroposition of the heart
Dextrokardie... *s.* Rechtsherz...
Dextrokardiogramm *n s.* Dextrogramm
dextrokular dextrocular, right-eyed
dextromanual dextromanual, right-handed
dextropedal dextropedal, right-footed
Dextroposition *f* dextroposition, displacement to the right
Dextrose *f* dextrose, D-glucose, glycose, grape (starch) sugar
Dextroseausscheidung *f* **im Urin** dextrosuria
Dextrotorsion *f* dextrotorsion; dextroclination, twisting to the right
Dextroversion *f* dextroversion, version (turning) to the right
dextrovertiert dextroverted, turned to the right
dextrozerebral dextrocerebral
Dezerebration *f* decerebration, brain ablation, removal of the brain
Dezerebrationshaltung *f* decerebrate position
Dezerebrationsrigidität *f* decerebrate rigidity
dezerebrieren to decerebrate, to decerebrize, to remove the brain
Dezerebrierung *f* 1. *s.* Dezerebration; 2. decerebration, encephalotomy *(des Fetus bei Totgeburt)*
Dezidua *f* decidua *(Gebärmutterschleimhaut während der Schwangerschaft) (Zusammensetzungen s. unter* Decidua*)*
Deziduaendometritis *f* decidual endometritis, deciduitis
Deziduafissur *f* decidual fissure
Deziduagewebe *n* decidual tissue
Deziduamembran *f* decidual membrane
Deziduaschleimhautentzündung *f* decidual endometritis
Deziduazelle *f* decidual cell
Deziduom *n* deciduoma
Diabetes *m s.* 1. ~ mellitus; 2. ~ insipidus ● **vorbeugend gegen** ~ antidiabetogenic
~ **albuminurinicus** lipoid nephrosis
~/**alimentärer** alimentary diabetes (glucosuria)
~/**biliärer** biliary diabetes, Hanot's disease
~/**fettbedingter** fat diabetes
~ **insipidus** insipid diabetes
~/**insulinpflichtiger** insulin deficiency diabetes
~ **intermittens** intermittent diabetes
~/**juveniler** juvenile (growth onset) diabetes
~/**latenter** latent diabetes
~/**manifester** manifest diabetes
~ **mellitus** [pancreatic] diabetes
~/**neurogener** neurogenous diabetes
~ **renalis** renal diabetes (glucosuria)
~/**toxischer** toxic diabetes
~/**zerebraler** cerebral diabetes
Diabetesangiopathie *f* diabetic angiopathy
Diabetesangst *f* diabetophobia
diabetesartig diabetic-like
Diabetesätiologie *f* diabetic aetiology
Diabetesbehandlung *f* diabetotherapy
Diabetesdiät *f* diabetic diet
Diabeteseinstellung *f s.* Diabetesbehandlung
diabeteserzeugend diabetogenic, diabetogenous
Diabetesfaktor *m* diabetogenic factor
Diabetesgangrän *f* diabetic gangrene
Diabeteskatarakt *f* diabetic cataract
Diabeteskoma *n* diabetic coma
Diabeteskranker *m s.* Diabetiker

Diabetes[poly]neuritis

Diabetes[poly]neuritis f diabetic [poly]neuritis
diabetesverhütend antidiabetogenic
Diabetiker m diabetic
~/juveniler juvenile-onset diabetic
Diabetikerdiät f diabetic diet
Diabetikermarmelade f diabetic jam
Diabetikermilch f diabetic milk
Diabetikerneuritis f diabetic neuritis
Diabetikerneuropathie f diabetic neuropathy
Diabetikerretinitis f diabetic retinitis
Diabetikerretinopathie f diabetic retinopathy
Diabetikerschokolade f diabetic chocolate
diabetisch diabetic
diabetogen diabetogenic, diabetogenous
Diabetophobie f diabetophobia *(krankhafte Angst vor Zuckerkrankheit)*
Diabrosis f diabrosis, perforating ulceration
Diadochokinese f diadochokinesis *(Fähigkeit zu schnellen antagonistischen Bewegungen)*
Diagnose f diagnosis ● **die ~ kennen** to know the diagnosis; to hold the key for diagnosis ● **die richtige ~ stellen** to make the correct diagnosis ● **eine ~ bestätigen** to confirm a diagnosis ● **eine ~ stellen** to diagnose, to make a diagnosis
~/abweichende divergent diagnosis
~ am Bett bedside diagnosis
~ aus dem weißen Blutbild leucodiagnosis
~/bakterielle bacteriodiagnosis
~/biologische biological diagnosis
~/computergestützte computer-assisted diagnosis
~ einer Nervenerkrankung neurodiagnosis
~ ex juvantibus diagnosis ex juvantibus, diagnosis based on the result of therapy
~/falsche false diagnosis, misdiagnosis
~/histologische histodiagnosis, histological diagnosis
~/klinische clinical diagnosis
~/mikroskopische microscopic diagnosis
~ per exclusionem diagnosis by exclusion
~/serologische immunodiagnosis, serodiagnosis, serum (serological) diagnosis
~/vorläufige provisional (tentative) diagnosis
Diagnoseklassifikation f diagnostic classification
Diagnosemittel npl means of diagnosis
Diagnosestellung f making (establishing) a diagnosis
~ aus dem Zungenzustand glossomantia
Diagnosestrategie f diagnostic strategy
Diagnosezeichen n diagnostic sign
Diagnostik f diagnostics, diagnosis
Diagnostiker m diagnostician
Diagnostikinstrument n means of diagnosis
diagnostisch diagnostic, diacritic[al]
diagnostizierbar diagnosable, diagnoseable
diagnostizieren to diagnose, to diagnosticate, to make (establish) a diagnosis
Diagonaldurchmesser m diagonal conjugate diameter *(des Beckens)*
Diakinese f diakinesis *(Zellteilungsstadium)*

Diaklase f diaclasis, fracture
Diaklast m diaclast *(Instrument)*
diaklastisch diaclastic
Diakrise f diacrisis
diakritisch diacritic[al], diagnostic
Dialysance f dialysance *(Maß für Stoffaustausch zwischen Blut und Dialysierflüssigkeit)*
Dialysat n dialyzate, dialysate, dialyzing fluid; dialyzate, diffusate, dialyzed substance
Dialysator m s. Dialysegerät
Dialyse f dialysis; haemodialysis *(Verfahren zur Trennung von gelösten Stoffen)* ● **eine ~ durchführen** to dialyze; to haemodialyze ● **sich einer ~ unterziehen** to be dialyzed
Dialyseabteilung f dialysis unit
Dialysebehandlung f dialysis therapy (treatment)
Dialysedienst m dialysis service
Dialysegerät n dialyzer, dialysis machine, artificial kidney; haemodialyzer
Dialysepatient m dialysis (artificial kidney) patient
Dialyseraum m dialysis room
Dialysezeit f dialyzing period
dialysierbar dialyzable, diffusible
Dialysierbarkeit f dialyzability, diffusibility
dialysieren to dialyze; to haemodialyze
Dialysierlösung f dialyzate, dialysate, dialyzing fluid
Dialysier[lös]ungskompartiment n dialysate compartment
Dialysis f pupillaris pupillary dialysis
dialytisch dialytic
Diameter m diameter *(s.a. unter Durchmesser)*
~ anterotransversa anterotransverse (temporal) diameter
~/Baudeloquescher Baudeloque's diameter, external conjugate diameter *(Geburtshilfe)*
~ biischiadica biischial diameter
~ biparietalis biparietal diameter
~ diagonalis diagonal conjugate diameter
~ frontooccipitalis fronto-occipital (occipitofrontal) diameter
~ mediana median (conjugate) diameter
~ mentooccipitalis mento-occipital (occipitomental) diameter
~ obliqua pelvis oblique diameter of the pelvis inlet
~ obliqua prima first oblique diameter
~ obliqua secunda second oblique diameter
~ pelvis pelvic diameter
~ posterotransversa posterotransverse (parietal) diameter
~ sagittalis sagittal diameter
~ transversa pelvis transverse diameter of the pelvic outlet, transverse (biischial) diameter
Diamid n diamide
Diamin n diamine
Diaminausscheidung f im Urin diaminuria
2,6-Diaminohexansäure f 2,6-diaminohexanoic acid, lysine
Diaminooxydase f diamine oxidase *(Enzym)*

2,4-Diamino-5-p-chlorphenyl-6-äthylpyrimidin *n* pyrimethamine *(Antimalariamittel)*
α, δ-Diaminovaleriansäure *f* 2,5-diamino-n-valeric acid, ornithine *(Aminosäure)*
Diamond-Blackfan-Syndrom *n* Diamond-Blackfan syndrome, erythrogenesis imperfecta, chronic idiopathic erythroblastopenia, chronic aregenerative anaemia
Diamorphin *n* diamorphine, diacetylmorphine, acetomorphine, heroin *(Rauschgift)*
Diapedese *f* diapedesis, emigration *(z. B. von Blutzellen)*
diaphan diaphanous, transparent
Diaphanometer *n* diaphanometer
Diaphanometrie *f* diaphanometry
Diaphanoskop *n* diaphanoscope, electrodiaphane
Diaphanoskopie *f* diaphanoscopy, electrodiaphany, transillumination
diaphanoskopisch diaphanoscopic
Diaphorase *f* diaphorase *(Enzym)*
Diaphorese *f* diaphoresis, profuse perspiration
Diaphoretikum *n* diaphoretic [agent], sudorific [agent]
diaphoretisch diaphoretic, sud[or]iferous, sudatory
Diaphragma *n* 1. diaphragm[a], midriff *(Anatomie)*; 2. diaphragm, membrane *(Dialyse, Elektrolyse)*
~ **irido-lenticulare** iris lens diaphragm
~ **oris** oral diaphragm
~ **pelvis** pelvic diaphragm, floor of the pelvis
~ **sellae** diaphragm of the sella, tentorium of the hypophysis
~ **urogenitale** urogenital diaphragm, triangular ligament
Diaphragma... *s.a.* Zwerchfell...
Diaphragmaaponeurose *f* central tendon
Diaphragmahernie *f* diaphragmatic hernia, diaphragmatocele
diaphragmal diaphragmatic
Diaphragmalgie *f* diaphragmalgia, phrenalgia, pain in the diaphragm
Diaphragmapessar *n* diaphragm pessary
diaphragmatisch diaphragmatic
Diaphragmatozele *f* diaphragmatocele, diaphragmatic hernia
Diaphragmitis *f* diaphragm[at]itis, inflammation of the diaphragm, phrenitis
diaphysär diaphysary, diaphyseal, diaphysial
Diaphyse *f* diaphysis, shaft
Diaphysendysplasie *f* diaphyseal dysplasia
~/**progressive** progressive diaphyseal dysplasia, Engelmann's disease
Diaphysenentfernung *f[/operative]* diaphysectomy
Diaphysensklerose *f* diaphyseal sclerosis
Diaphysensklerosierung *f/progressive s.* Diaphysendysplasie/progressive
Diaplasis *f* diaplasis, reposition *(z. B. eines Gelenkes)*
diaplazentar diaplacental

Diarrhoe *f,* **Diarrhö[e]** *f* diarrhoea, enterorrhoea, looseness
~/**milde** paradysentery, mild diarrhoea
~/**tuberkulöse** tuberculous diarrhoea
diarrhöisch diarrhoeal, diarrhoeic
diarthrisch diarthric, diarticular, diarthrodial
Diarthrose *f* diarthrosis, thoroughjoint, diarthrodial (synovial) joint
Diaschisis *f* diaschisis *(Tätigkeitsausfall eines Nervenabschnitts infolge Stimulationsausfalls)*
Diaskop *n* diascope *(Glasspatel)*
Diaskopie *f* diascopy *(Hautuntersuchungsmethode)*
Diastalsis *f* diastalsis *(Form der Darmbewegung)*
Diastase *f* 1. *s.* Amylase; 2. diastasis *(Loslösung z. B. von Knochen)*; 3. *s.* Diastasis cordis
Diastasis *f* **cordis** diastasis, final phase of diastole
diastatisch diastatic
Diastema *n* diastema, cleft, fissure
Diastematokranie *f* diastematocrania, cranioschisis
Diastematomyelie *f* diastematomyelia
Diaster *m* diaster, amphiaster *(Mitosefigur)*
Diastole *f* diastole ● **am Anfang der ~ [liegend]** protodiastolic ● **am Ende der ~ [liegend]** telediastolic ● **nach der ~ [liegend]** postdiastolic ● **vor der ~ [liegend]** prediastolic
~/**arterielle** arterial diastole
~/**fehlende** adiastole, absence of diastole
~/**verkürzte** bradydiastole
Diastolenanfang *m* protodiastole
Diastolenende *n* telediastole
Diastolengeräusch *n* diastolic murmur
Diastolenmitte *f* mesodiastole
Diastolenverkürzung *f* bradydiastole
Diastolikum *n* diastolic [murmur]
diastolisch diastolic
Diät *f* diet, regimen ● **auf ~ setzen** to put on a diet ● **~ halten** to keep (adhere to) a diet, to diet ● **strenge ~ halten** to observe a strict diet, to keep to a strict diet, to diet
~/**angemessene** adequate diet
~/**ausgeglichene** balanced diet
~/**blande** bland diet
~/**diabetische** diabetic diet
~/**eiweißarme** low-protein diet
~/**eiweißreiche** high-protein diet
~/**fettarme** low-fat diet
~/**fettreiche** high-fat (fat-rich) diet
~/**flüssigkeitsbeschränkte** restricted fluid diet
~/**hochkalorische** high-caloric diet
~/**ketogene** ketogenic diet
~/**kochsalzarme** hypochlorization
~/**kochsalzreiche** hyperchloridation
~/**natriumarme** low-sodium diet
~/**optimale** optimal diet
~/**oxalatárme** low-oxalate diet
~/**purinfreie** purine-free diet
~/**salzarme** low-salt diet
~/**salzfreie** salt-free diet
~/**schlackenarme** low-residue diet

Diät

~/strenge strict (rigorous) diet
~/unterkalorische low-caloric diet
~/vitaminreiche high-vitamin diet
Diätassistentin f assistant dietician
Diataxie f diataxia
Diätbehandlung f dietetic (dietary) treatment, dietotherapy, alimentotherapy, trophotherapy
Diäteinhaltung f adherence to a diet
Diätetik f dietetics
Diätetiker m dietician, dietitian
diätetisch dietetic
Diätfehler m dietary lapse
diatherm 1. diathermic; 2. s. diatherman
diatherman diathermanous, diathermic
Diathermie f diathermy; (short-wave) diathermy, electrothermy
~/chirurgische surgical diathermy, diathermocoagulation, diathermy coagulation, electrosurgery
~/medizinische medical diathermy, thermopenetration
Diathermiebehandlung f diathermic therapy
Diathermieblutstillung f electrohaemostasis
Diathermiegerät n diathermy [unit], electrotherm
Diathermiemesser n diathermy (electrosurgical) knife, cautery [knife], electrotome, acusector
Diathermieschnitt m acusection
Diathermiestrom m diathermy current
diathermisch 1. diathermic; 2. electrosurgical
Diathermokoagulation f diathermy coagulation, diathermocoagulation, surgical diathermy
Diathese f diathesis (z. B. für Krankheiten); constitution ● **ohne ~** adiathetic
~/allergische allergic diathesis
~/hämorrhagische haemorrhagic diathesis, bleeding tendency
~/neuropathische psychopathic (neuropathic) diathesis
~/rheumatische rheumatic diathesis
~/variköse varicose diathesis
2-(Diäthylamino)-2',6'-azetoxylidid n lidocaine, lignocaine (Lokalanästhetikum)
Diäthyläther m diethyl ether (Narkoseäther)
Diäthylbarbitursäure f diethylbarbituric acid (Schlafmittel)
Diäthylmalonylharnstoff m diethylmalonylurea
Diäthylstilböstrol n diethylstilboestrol (Östrogenwirkstoff)
Diätkontrolle f dietary supervision
Diätküche f diet kitchen
Diätmaßnahme f dietary measure
Diätplan m diet[ary] plan
Diätregime n dietary regimen, dietetic rule
Diätschema n dietary
Diätschwester f diet nurse
Diätvorschrift f diet prescription
Diazepam n diazepam (Beruhigungsmittel)
Diazetämie f diacetaemia
Diazeturie f diacet[on]uria
Diazetylmorphin n diacetylmorphine, diamorphine, acetomorphine, heroin (Rauschgift)
1,3-Diazin n 1,3-diazine, pyrimidine

Diazo[nium]reaktion f diazo reaction
Dibothriozephaliasis f s. Diphyllobothriasis
Dicheilus m dicheilus, double lip (Mißbildung)
Dicheirus m dicheirus (Mißbildung)
Dichlordiäthylsulfid n dichlorodiethyl sulphide, yellow cross, mustard gas, yperite (hautschädigender Kampfstoff)
Dichlordiphenyltrichloräthan n dichlordiphenyltrichlororethane, DDT
2',5-Dichloro-4'-nitrosalizylanilid n niclosamide (Antiwurmmittel)
dichotom dichotomic
Dichotomie f dichotomy, dichotomous division
dichroisch s. dichromatisch
Dichroismus m dichroism (von Kristallen)
dichroit[isch] dichroic
Dichromasie f dichromatism, dichroma[top]sia
Dichromat[er] m dichromat[e]
dichromatisch dichromatic, dichroic
Dichromatopsie f s. Dichromasie
dichromophil dichromophil
Dichromophilie f dichromophilism
dichtemessend densimetric
Dichtemesser m densimeter, densitometer
Dichtemessung f densimetry, densitometry
dick 1. corpulent, stout, fat, obese (Person); chubby (Wangen); 2. thick, clotted, coagulated (Blut); 3. s. dickflüssig; 4. swollen (z. B. Gelenk)
dickblütig thick-blooded, pachyhaematous
Dickblütigkeit f pachyhaemia
Dickdarm m colon, large bowel (intestine) (s. a. unter Kolon) ● **um den ~ liegend** pericol[on]ic
~/absteigender descending colon
~/aufsteigender ascending colon
~/querer transverse colon
~/überlanger dolichocolon
Dickdarm... s. a. Kolon...
Dickdarmarterie f colic artery, colica
~/linke left colic artery
~/mittlere middle colic artery
~/rechte right colic artery
Dickdarmarterienaneurysma n colic artery aneurysm
Dickdarmbazillus m colon bacillus
Dickdarmbeweglichkeit f colon motility
Dickdarmblähung f pneumocolon
Dickdarm-Blinddarm-Anastomose f colocaecostomy
Dickdarmblutung f colonorrhagia
Dickdarmchirurgie f colon surgery
Dickdarm-Dickdarm-Anastomose f colocolostomy
Dickdarmeinengung f colon stenosis
Dickdarmentfernung f[/operative] colectomy
Dickdarmentzündung f colitis, inflammation of the colon
Dickdarmeröffnung f[/operative] colotomy
Dickdarmerweiterung f colon dilatation
Dickdarmfistel f colostomy; colonic fistula
Dickdarmfistelung f colostomy
~ durch Lendenschnitt lumbocolostomy

Dickdarmfixation f an der Leber colohepatopexy
~/**operative** colopexy, fixation of the colon
Dickdarmgekröse n mesocolon *(an der hinteren Bauchwand als Bauchfellduplikatur)*
~/**absteigendes** descending mesocolon
~/**aufsteigendes** ascending mesocolon
Dickdarmgekröseansatz m mesocolic band (taenia)
Dickdarmgeschwür n colon ulcer
Dickdarmgeschwürbildung f colon ulceration
Dickdarm-Harnblasen-Fistel f colovesical fistula
Dickdarmkatarrh m catarrhal colitis
Dickdarmleiden n colonopathy, colonic disease
Dickdarmminderdurchblutung f colon ischaemia
Dickdarmschenkel m/**absteigender** descending colon
~/**aufsteigender** ascending colon
~/**querer** transverse colon
Dickdarmschleimhaut f colon mucosa, mucous membrane of the colon
Dickdarmschleimhautentzündung f endocolitis
Dickdarmschmerz m colonalgia, pain in the colon
Dickdarmspiegelung f colo[no]scopy
Dickdarmtänie f colon taenia
Dickdarmteilentfernung f[/**operative**] hemicolectomy
Dickdarmtumor m colonic tumour (neoplasm)
Dickdarmverdrehung f colon volvulus
Dickdarmvereng[er]ung f colon stenosis
Dickdarmverlängerung f colon elongation
Dickdarmverlegung f s. Dickdarmverschluß
Dickdarmverschluß m colon (large bowel) obstruction
Dickdarmzerreißung f colon rupture
Dickdarmzwischenschaltung f colon interposition
Dickenmesser m pachymeter, pachometer, thickness gauge
Dickfilm m thick blood film *(Hämatologie)*
Dickfingerigkeit f pachydactyly
dickflüssig viscous, viscid, viscose, ropy; thick
dickfüßig pachypodous
dickhaarig pachytrichous
dickhäutig thick-skinned, pachydermatous, pachydermial, pachydermic, pachyhymenic
Dickhäutigkeit f pachydermia; pachyderma
dickköpfig pachycephalic, pachycephalous
Dickköpfigkeit f pachycephalia *(abnorm kurzer Schädel)*
dickleibig corpulent, obese, stout, thick
Dickleibigkeit f corpulence, obesity, stoutness
dicklippig macrocheilous, thick-lipped
Dicklippigkeit f macrocheilia
dickmachend obesogenous
dicknasig pachyrhine, pachyrhinic, thick-nosed
Dickschädeligkeit f s. Dickköpfigkeit
Dick-Serum n Dick toxin, scarlet fever streptococcus toxin
Dick-Test m Dick test, scarlet fever test
Didaktylie f bidactyly, didactylism

Didelphus m didelphia, dimetria, double uterus
didelphys didelphic
Didymalgie f didymalgia, didymodynia, orchi[d]algia; orchiodynia, orchioneuralgia, testalgia, testicular pain
Didymitis f didymitis, orchi[di]tis, orcheitis, testitis, inflammation of the testis
Didymus m didymus, orchis, testis, testicle, male gonad *(Zusammensetzungen s. unter Hoden)*
Diebstahlfurcht f kleptophobia
Dienst m duty, attendance *(s.a. Bereitschaftsdienst)*
~/**medizinischer** medical service
~ **ohne Besonderheiten** uneventful service
Dienstbeschädigung f disability
diensthabend on duty
dienzephal diencephalous, diencephalic
Dienzephalon n diencephalon, interbrain, betweenbrain
Diesterase f diesterase *(Enzym)*
Differentialagglutination f differential agglutination
Differentialblutbild n differential blood picture, differential [blood] count
~/**weißes** differential leucocyte (white cell) count
Differentialdiagnose f differential diagnosis, diacrisis
Differentialdiagnostik f differential diagnosis
differentialdiagnostisch differential diagnostic, diacritic[al]
differentialfärbend differential staining
Differentialfärbung f differential staining *(von Bakterien)*
Differentialzellbild n differential cell picture
Differentialzytologie f differential cytology
differenzieren/sich to differentiate, to be differentiated
differenziert differentiated, ripe *(z. B. Geschwulst)*
~/**höher** prosoplastic, higher differentiated
~/**nicht** undifferentiated *(z. B. Gewebe)*
Differenzierung f differentiation *(z. B. von Geweben)*
~/**höhere** higher differentiation, prosoplasia
Differenzierungsantigen n differentiation antigen
Differenzierungsgrad m stage (degree) of differentiation
Differenzierungshemmung f inhibition of differentiation
Differenzierungsnährboden m differentiation agar
Differenzierungsphase f differentiation stadium
Differenzierungsreiz m differentiating stimulus
Diffraktionsbereich m diffraction area *(Mikroskopie)*
Diffraktometer n diffractometer
diffundierbar diffusible
diffundieren to diffuse
Diffusion f diffusion
~/**erleichterte** facilitated diffusion
Diffusionsbarriere f diffusion barrier

diffusionsfähig

diffusionsfähig diffusible
Diffusionsfähigkeit f diffusibility
Diffusionsfaktor m diffusion factor
Diffusionsgeschwindigkeit f rate of diffusion
Diffusionskapazität f/**pulmonale** pulmonary diffusing capacity
Diffusionskonstante f diffusion constant
Diffusionsschranke f s. Diffusionsbarriere
Diffusionsstörung f diffusion abnormality; impaired diffusion
digastrisch digastric
Digenesis f digenesis, alteration of generation
Di George-Syndrom n Di George's syndrome, thymic aplasia
digestibel s. verdaulich
Digestion f s. Verdauung
Digestivum n digestive [agent], digester, digestant
Digilanid n lanatoside *(Herzglykosid)*
digital digital, digitate
Digitalein n digitalein *(Herzglykosid)*
Digitalfurche f digital furrow
Digitalin n digitalin *(Herzglykosid)*
Digitalis f [**purpurea**] digitalis, foxglove
digitalisartig digitaloid
Digitalisbehandlung f digitalization
Digitaliseffekt m digitalis effect
Digitaliseinheit f digitalis unit
Digitaliseinstellung f digitalization
Digitalisglykosid n digitalis glycoside
digitalisieren to digitalize
Digitalisierung f digitalization
Digitalismus m s. Digitalisvergiftung
Digitalispause f interruption of digitalis treatment
Digitalispräparat n digitalis preparation
Digitalispulver n powdered digitalis
Digitalisunverträglichkeit f digitalis intolerance
Digitalisvergiftung f digitalism, digitalis intoxication (poisoning)
Digitalkompression f digital compression
Digitalose f digitalose *(sechswertiger Zucker)*
Digitalreflex m digital reflex
digitiform finger-shaped, digitiform
Digitogenin n digitogenin *(Glykosidbestandteil)*
Digitoxigenin n digitoxigenin *(Glykosidbestandteil)*
Digitoxin n digitoxin *(Herzglykosid)*
Digitus m 1. digit[us], finger, dactyl[us] *(s. a. unter* Finger*)*; 2. digitus, toe *(s. a. unter* Zehe*)*
~ **anularis** ring finger
~ **hippocraticus** clubbed finger
~ **malleus** hammer finger
~ **medius** middle finger
~ **minimus** little finger
~ **mortuus** dead finger
~ **primus** thumb, pollex
~ **primus pedis** great toe, hallux
~ **quartus** ring finger
~ **quartus pedis** fourth toe
~ **quintus** little finger
~ **quintus pedis** little toe
~ **secundus** index finger, forefinger
~ **secundus pedis** second toe
~ **tertius** middle finger
~ **tertius pedis** third toe
Diglossie f diglossia; bifid (double) tongue
Diglossus m diglossus *(Mißbildung)*
Diglyzerid n diglyceride *(Fettstoffwechsel)*
Dignathus m dignathus *(Mißbildung)*
Digoxigenin n digoxigenin *(Glykosidbestandteil)*
Digoxin n digoxin *(Herzglykosid)*
Dihydrochinidin n dihydroquinine *(herzrhythmisierendes Mittel)*
Dihydrocholesterin n dihydrocholesterol
Dihydroergosterin n dihydroergosterine *(Provitamin D_4)*
Dihydroergotamin n dihydroergotamine *(Mutterkornalkaloid)*
Dihydrokodein n dihydrocodeinone *(Hustenmittel)*
Dihydrostreptomyzin n dihydrostreptomycin *(Antibiotikum)*
Dihydrotachysterol n dihydrotachysterol *(bewirkt Blutkalziumspiegelerhöhung)*
1,2-Dihydroxyanthrachinon n 1,2-dihydroxyanthraquinone, alizarin *(Farbstoff)*
1,3-Dihydroxybenzol n 1,3-dihydroxybenzene, resorcin[ol]
3,3'-Dihydroxy-α-karotin n 3,3'-dihydroxy-α-carotene, lutein *(gelber Farbstoff)*
3,4-Dihydroxyphenylalanin n 3-4-dihydroxyphenylalanine, dopa, DOPA *(Zwischenprodukt der Melaninbildung)*
3-(3,4-Dihydroxyphenyl)-L-Alanin n 3-(3,4-dihydroxyphenyl)-L-alanine, [laevo]dopa *(Antiparkinsonmittel)*
2,6-Dihydroxypurin n 2,6-dioxopurine, xanthine *(Purinstoffwechsel)*
Dijodthyronin n [3,5-]diiodothyronine *(in der Schilddrüse)*
Dijodtyrosin n [3,5-]diiodotyrosine, iodogorgoic acid *(in der Schilddrüse)*
Diklidotomie f diclidotomy
Dikorie f s. Diplokorie
dikrot dicrotic, dicrotous *(Puls)*
Dikrotie f, **Dikrotismus** m dicrotism *(Puls)*
Diktyitis f dictyitis
Diktyokinese f dictyokinesis
Diktyoma n dictyoma
Diktyosom n dictyosome *(Teil des Golgi-Apparats in Spermatozyten)*
Dikumarin n, **Dikumarol** n dicoumarin, dicoumarol, bishydroxycoumarin, 3,3-methylenebis(4-hydroxycoumarin) *(gerinnungshemmender Stoff)*
Dilatatio f **cordis** dilatation of the heart
Dilatation f dila[ta]tion, enlargement, distension *(Zustand oder Vorgang)*
Dilatationsbougie f s. Dilatator 1.
Dilatator m 1. dilator, divulsor, [dilating] bougie; 2. dilator [muscle], dilating muscle
dilatatorisch dilating
dilatierbar dilatable

dilatieren to dilate, to expand, to enlarge, to widen
dilatiert dilated, ectatic
Dilatometer n dilatometer
dilu[t]ieren to dilute, to make less concentrated
dilutiert dilute
Dilution f dilution
Dilutionstest m dilution test
Dimerkaprol n dimercaprol, [British] antilewisite
2,3-Dimerkaptopropan-1-ol n s. Dimerkaprol
Dimethylaminoazobenzol n dimethylaminoazobenzene, methyl (butter) yellow, Töpfer's reagent
Dimethylaminobenzaldehyd m dimethylaminobenzaldehyde, Ehrlich's reagent
Dimethylbenzol n dimethylbenzene, xylene, xylol
1,3-Dimethylxanthin n 1,3-dimethylxanthine, theophylline *(Alkaloid)*
3,7-Dimethylxanthin n 3,7-dimethylxanthine, theobromine *(Alkaloid)*
dimorph dimorphic, dimorphous
Dimorphie f dimorphism *(z. B. von Lepra)*
Dinukleotid n dinucleotide
Dioptometer n diopt[r]ometer
Dioptometrie f dioptometry
Dioptrie f diopter, dioptre *(Einheit der Brechkraft)*
dioptrisch dioptric
3,4-Dioxyphenylalanin n s. 3,4-Dihydroxyphenylalanin
Dipetalonemiasis f dipetalonemiasis, acanthocheilonemiasis
diphallisch diphallic
Diphallus m diphallus
Diphenylhydantoin n diphenylhydantoin, 5,5-Diphenyl-2,4-imidazolidinedione *(Antikrampfmittel)*
Diphonie f diphonia, diphthongia, double voice
1,3-Diphospho-Glyzerinsäure f 1,3-diphosphoglyceric acid *(Fettstoffwechselprodukt)*
Diphosphopyridinnukleotid n s. Nikotinamid-adenin-dinukleotid
Diphosphothiamin n diphosphothiamine, cocarboxylase
Diphtheria f cutanea cutaneous diphtheria
~ gravis malignant diphtheria
Diphtherie f diphtheria *(Infektionskrankheit durch Corynebacterium diphtheriae)*
Diphtherieadsorbatimpfstoff m adsorbed diphtheria vaccine
Diphtherieantitoxin n diphtheria antitoxin
diphtherieartig diphtheroid, diphtheria-like
Diphtheriebakterienseptikämie f diphtheria bacillus septicaemia, Corynebacterium diphtheriae septicaemia
Diphtheriebakterium n, **Diphtheriebazillus** m Corynebacterium diphtheriae, diphtheria (Klebs-Löffler) bacillus
Diphtheriegeschwür n diphtheric ulcer
Diphtherieimpfstoff m diphtheria vaccine
Diphtheriekrupp m croupous pharyngitis
Diphtherielaryngitis f diphtheritic laryngitis

Diphtheriemembran f diphtheritic membrane
Diphtherienekrose f diphtheritic necrosis
Diphtherieneuritis f diphtheritic neuritis
Diphtheriepharyngitis f diphtheritic pharyngitis
Diphtheriepseudomembran f diphtheritic membrane, croupous false membrane
Diphtherieserum n antidiphtheritic serum
Diphtherietoxin n diphtheria toxin, diphtherotoxin
~/formalinentgiftetes formalin-detoxified diphtherial toxin
Diphtherietoxoid n diphtheria toxoid
Diphtheriolysin n diphtheriolysin
diphtherisch diphtheritic, diphtherial, diphtheric
diphtheroid diphtheroid
Diphtheroid n diphtheroid *(1. diphtherieartiges Bakterium; 2. diphtherieartige Krankheit)*
Diphthongie f s. Diphonie
Diphyllobothriasis f diphyllobothriasis, dibothriocephaliasis
Diphyllobothrium n **latum** fish (broad) tapeworm, Diphyllobothrium latum
Diphyllobothrium-latum-Befall m s. Diphyllobothriasis
diphyodont diphyodont, having two dentitions
Diphyodontie f diphyodontia
Diplakusis f diplacusis, double hearing
Diplegia f facialis bilateral peripheral facial palsy
Diplegie f diplegia, bilateral paralysis
Diplobazillus m diplobacillus
Diplobazilluskonjunktivitis f diplobacillary (Morax-Axenfeld's) conjunctivitis
Diplococcus m diplococcus *(paarweise zusammenliegende Kokken)*
~ gonorrhoeae gonococcus, diplococcus of Neisser
~ pneumoniae [Fränkel's] pneumococcus
Diploe f diploe, diploic bone
Diploevenen fpl diploic veins
Diplogenesis f diplogenesis
diploid diploid *(Chromosomensatz)*
Diplokorie f diplocoria, dicoria, doubleness of the pupil; double pupil
Diplomyelie f diplomyelia
Diplonema n diplonema *(Mitosestadium)*
Diplopagus m diplopagus
Diplophonie f s. Diphonie
Diplopie f diplopia, double vision, ambiopia
~/beidseitige ampho[tero]diplopia
~/binokuläre binocular diplopia
~/einäugige monodiplopia, monocular diplopia
~/heteronyme heteronymous (crossed, heteronomous) diplopia
~/homonyme homonymous (direct, homonomous) diplopia
~/monokulare monocular diplopia, monodiplopia
~/physiologische physiological diplopia
Diplopiemesser m, **Diplopiometer** n diplopiometer
Diploskop n diploscope *(ophthalmologisches Instrument)*
Diplosom[at]ie f diplosom[at]ia

Diplozephalie

Diplozephalie f diplocephalia
Diplozephalus m diplocephalus *(Mißgeburt)*
Diprosopie f diprosopia
Diprosopus m diprosopus *(Mißgeburt)*
dipsoman dipsomaniac
Dipsomaner m dipsomaniac
Dipsomanie f dipsomania, posiomania *(periodisch auftretender Alkoholismus)*
Dipsophobie f dipsophobia
Dipsotherapie f dipsotherapy, thirst cure
Dipygus m dipygus *(Mißgeburt)*
Dipylidiasis f dipylidiasis
Dipylidium n **caninum** dog tapeworm
Dipylidium-caninum-Befall m s. Dipylidiasis
Dipyridamol n dipyridamole *(gefäßerweiterndes Mittel)*
Direktauskultation f immediate auscultation
Direktbeleuchtung direct illumination *(Mikroskopie)*
Direkterregung f direct excitation
Direktlaryngoskopie f direct laryngoscopy
Direktophthalmoskopie f direct ophthalmoscopy
Direktperkussion f direct percussion
Direktreizung f direct excitation
Direktsuggestion f direct suggestion
Direkttransfusion f direct (immediate) transfusion
Dirofilarienbefall m dirofilariasis
Dirrhinus m dirrhinus *(Mißbildung)*
Disaccharid n disaccharide
Disaccharidase f disaccharidase *(Enzym)*
Disaccharidbelastungstest m disaccharide tolerance test
Disaccharidintoleranz f disaccharide intolerance
Disaccharidmalabsorption f dissacharide malabsorption
Discus m diskus, disk, disc
~ **articularis** articular disk
~ **articularis articulationis acromioclavicularis** articular disk of the acromioclavicular joint
~ **articularis articulationis radioulnaris distalis** articular disk of the distal radioulnar joint
~ **articularis articulationis sternoclavicularis** articular disk of the sternoclavicular joint
~ **articularis articulationis temporomandibularis** articular disk of the temporomandibular joint
~ **interpubicus** fibrocartilage of the pubic symphysis
~ **intervertebralis** intervertebral cartilage (disk)
~ **nervi optici** optic disk (papilla), pitting of the optic nerve
Disgerminom n dysgerminoma, disgerminoma *(bösartige Eierstock- oder Hodengeschwulst)*
Disinsektion f disinsection, disinsectization, extermination of insects
Disinsertion f disinsertion
Diskklappe f s. Diskusherzklappe
Diskogramm n discogram
Diskographie f discography
Diskopathie f discopathy
Diskriminanzanalyse f discriminant analysis
Diskrimination f discrimination, distinguishing *(z. B. des Tastsinns)*
~/**taktile** tactile discrimination
Diskus m diskus, disk, disc *(Zusammensetzungen s. unter Discus)*
Diskusentfernung f[/operative] discoidectomy
Diskusentzündung f discitis, inflammation of a disk
Diskushernie f herniated (slipped) disk, ruptured intervertebral disk
Diskusherzklappe f caged-lens prosthesis (valve)
Diskusniere f disk kidney
Diskusplazenta f discoid placenta, discoplacenta
Diskuswerferhaltung f discobolus attitude *(bei einseitiger Labyrinthreizung)*
Dislocatio f dislocation, displacement; luxation *(s. a. unter Dislokation)*
~ **ad axim cum contractione** overriding *(Knochenbruch)*
~ **atlantoaxialis** atlantoaxial dislocation
~ **subcoracoidea capitis humeri** subcoracoid dislocation of the head of the humerus
Dislokation f dislocation, displacement; luxation *(s.a. unter Dislocatio)*
~/**alte** old dislocation
~/**einfache** simple dislocation
~/**habituelle** habitual dislocation
~/**inkomplette** incomplete (partial) dislocation; subluxation
~/**komplette** complete dislocation
~/**komplizierte** complicated (compound) dislocation
~/**pathologische** pathological dislocation
~/**traumatische** traumatic dislocation
~/**unkomplizierte** simple dislocation
~/**veraltete** old dislocation
dislozieren to dislocate, to displace, to disjoint; to disarticulate
Dislozierung f s. Dislokation
Dispermie f dispermia
Dispersionsoxygenator m bubble oxygenator
Dispersionsvermögen n dispersive power
Dispersionswinkel m angle of dispersion
Disposition f 1. disposition, predisposition *(z. B. für eine Krankheit)*; 2. disposition, temperament
Dissektion f dissection
~/**scharfe** sharp dissection
Dissektionsadenektomie f dissection adenoidectomy
Dissektionsklemme f s. Dissektor
Dissektionsschere f dissecting scissors
Dissektionstonsillektomie f dissection tonsillectomy
Dissektor m dissector, dissecting forceps
Dissemination f dissemination, dispersion of a disease; dispersion of disease germs
Dissimilation f dissimilation, disassimilation, catabolism, catabiosis
dissimilieren to dissimilate, to catabolize
Dissimulant m dissimulator, feigner

Dissimulation f dissimulation, feigning, disguising
dissimulieren to dissimulate, to conceal symptoms of disease, to feign, to disguise *(Krankheiten)*
Dissolution f 1. dissolution, separation; 2. dissolution, solution; 3. dissolution, decomposition; death, decease
Dissoziation f dissociation
~/**albumino-zytologische** albuminocytologic dissociation
~/**atrioventrikuläre** atrioventricular dissociation
Dissoziationskonstante f dissociation constant
distal distal, D.
Distalbiß m distoclusion, posterio-occlusion
Distensionsluxation f distension luxation
Distensionszyste f distension cyst
Distichiasis f distichia[sis] *(Lidanomalie)*
Distickstoffmonoxid n nitrous oxide *(Narkosegas)*
Distomiasis f distomiasis, distomatosis, fascioliasis, liver rot
Distomie f distomia, duplication of the mouth
Distomum n **haematobium** Distomum haematobium *(Erreger der Urogenitalbilharziose)*
~ **hepaticum** liver (hepatic) fluke *(Erreger der Faszioliasis)*
~ **pulmonis** Paragonimus westermani
Distomus m distomus *(Mißbildung)*
Distorsion f distortion
Distorsionsfraktur f sprain fracture
Distraktion f distraction *(z. B. von Knochenbrüchen)*
Distraktionsklammer f traction bar
Distribution f distribution *(z. B. von Nerven)*
Districhiasis f districhiasis
Diszision f discission, needling
Diszisionsnadel f discission needle
Diszitis f discitis, inflammation of an interarticular cartilage
Diurese f diuresis
~/**forcierte** forced diuresis
diuresefördernd diuretic
diuresehemmend antidiuretic, inhibiting diuresis
Diuretikum n diuretic [agent], urinative [agent], uragogue [agent], emictory [agent]
diuretisch diuretic, uragogue, emictory
Divagation f divagation, rambling
Divergenz f divergence
Divergenzbreite f amplitude of divergence
Divergenzwinkel m divergence angle, angle of divergence
divergieren to diverge
Diverticulum n **sigmoideum** sigmoid diverticulum
Divertikel n diverticulum, outpouching, pocket, sac
~/**allantoenterisches** allantoenteric diverticulum
~/**angeborenes** congenital diverticulum
~/**echtes** true diverticulum
~/**falsches** false diverticulum
~/**Meckelsches** Meckel's diverticulum *(Rest des embryonalen Dottergangs)*

~/**Nucksches** Nuck's diverticulum *(meist obliterierter Processus vaginalis peritonei)*
~/**supradiaphragmatisches** supradiaphragmatic diverticulum
~/**Zenkersches** Zenker's diverticulum (pouch), pharyngeal (pharyngo-oesophageal) diverticulum
Divertikelabtragung f[/**operative**] diverticulectomy
Divertikelanheftung f diverticulopexy
Divertikelbildung f diverticularization, formation of diverticula
Divertikelentzündung f diverticulitis, inflammation of a diverticulum
Divertikelhäufung f diverticulosis
Divertikelhernie f diverticulum hernia
Divertikelröntgen[kontrast]bild n diverticulogram
Divertikelröntgen[kontrast]darstellung f diverticulography
Divertikulektomie f diverticulectomy
Divertikulogramm n diverticulogram
Divertikulographie f diverticulography
Divertikulopexie f diverticulopexy
Divertikulose f diverticulosis
divide divide *(Rezeptformular)*
Divinyläther m divinyl ether *(Narkoseäther)*
Divulsion f divulsion, tearing apart
dizephal dicephalous, bicephalous, bicapitate
Dizephalie f dicephalia
Dizephalus m dicephalus *(Mißgeburt)*
DMH s. Hilfe/Dringliche Medizinische
DNS s. Desoxyribonukleinsäure
DNS-Polymerase f DNS (deoxyribonucleic acid) polymerase *(Enzym)*
DNS-Replikation f DNS (deoxyribonucleic acid) replication
DNS-Synthese f DNS (deoxyribonucleic acid) synthesis
DNS-Virus n DNS (deoxyribonucleic acid) virus
Doggennase f cleft (bifid) nose; median nasal fissure
Doggerbankjucken n Dogger bank itch *(allergische Dermatitis)*
Dogiel-Körperchen n Dogiel's [genital] corpuscle
Döhle-Körper m Doehle body *(bei der May-Hegglin-Anomalie)*
Doktor m s. Arzt
~ **der Medizin** Doctor of Medicine, M.D.
Dolchstichschmerz m boring pain
dolichofazial dolichofacial, dolichoprosopic
Dolichokolon n dolichocolon
dolichopelvin dolichopelvic, dolichopellic
dolichoprosop s. dolichofazial
Dolichostenomelie f s. Arachnodaktylie
dolichozephal long-headed, dolichocephalic, dolichocephalous
Dolichozephalie f dolichocephalia
Dolichozephalus m dolichocephalus
Dollinger-Bielschowsky-Syndrom n Dollinger-Bielschowsky syndrome, Bielschowsky [-Jansky's] disease, late infantile amaurotic familial idiocy

Dolor

Dolor *m* dolor, pain, ache *(s.a. unter Schmerz)*
~ **coxae** sciatica
Domatophobie *f* domatophobia *(krankhafte Angst vor Aufenthalt in Häusern)*
dominant dominant
Dominanz *f* dominance; predominance
~ **einer Hirnhälfte** cerebral dominance
dominieren to predominate
dominierend dominant
Donath-Landsteiner-Antikörper *m* Donath-Landsteiner antibody
Donath-Landsteiner-Phänomen *n* Donath-Landsteiner phenomenon
Donath-Landsteiner-Test *m* Donath-Landsteiner test *(zum Kältehämolysinnachweis)*
Donaufieber *n* Danube fever
Donor *m* donor
Donovania *f* **granulomatis** Donovan body *(Erreger des Granuloma inguinale)*
Donovaniasis *f* donovaniasis, venereal (ulcerating) granuloma
Dopa *n*, **DOPA** *s.* 3,4-Dihydroxyphenylalanin
Dopamin *n* dopamine
Dopa-Oxydase *f* dopa oxidase, dopase *(Enzym)*
Dopa-Oxydase-Aktivität *f* dopa-oxidase activity
Dopase *f s.* Dopa-Oxydase
dopen to dope
Dopingmittel *n* dope
Doppelachsengelenk *n* biaxial joint
doppelachsig biaxial
Doppelanlage *f* diplogenesis
Doppelaorta *f* double aorta
Doppelastigmatismus *m* biastigmatism
Doppelballon-Sonde *f*/**Blakemoresche** Blakemore's tube
Doppelbefruchtung *f* dispermy
Doppelbild *n* double image
Doppelbildersehen *n s.* Diplopie
Doppelbildung *f* duplicature *(z. B. der Bauchfellfalte)*
Doppelblase *f* bilocular bladder
Doppelblindversuch *m* double blind trial (experiment, test, study)
~/**gekreuzter** double-blind crossover trial
~/**klinischer** double-blind clinical trial
Doppelblindversuchsgruppe *f* double-blind group
doppelbrechend birefringent, birefractive, double-refracting
Doppelbrechung *f* birefringence, double refraction
Doppelbruch *m* double fracture
doppelbrüstig bimastic
Doppelchromosom *n* double chromosome
Doppeldenken *n* duplicated thinking
Doppelektropium *n* [**des Augenlids**] double eversion of the eyelid
Doppelfärbbarkeit *f* dichromophilism
doppelfärbend dichromophil
Doppelfarbigkeit *f* dichroism *(z. B. von Kristallen)*
Doppelfärbung *f* double staining

Doppelfokusglas *n* bifocal lens
Doppelgebärmutter *f* double (duplex) uterus
doppelgelenkig biarticular
Doppelgelenkmuskel *m* two-joint muscle
Doppelgeräusch *n* reduplicated murmur
~/**Duroziezsches** Duroziez' murmur (sign) *(bei Aorteninsuffizienz)*
doppelgeschlechtlich bisexual, ambisexual, ambosexual; hermaphroditic
Doppelgeschlechtlichkeit *f* bisexuality, ambisexuality, sexual ambiguity; hermaphroditism
Doppelgeschwür *n* kissing ulcer
Doppelgesicht *n* diprosopus
Doppelgesichtigkeit *f* diprosopia
doppelgestaltig dimorphic, dimorphous
Doppelgestaltigkeit *f* dimorphism *(z. B. von Lepra)*
doppelgipfelig dicrotic, dicrotous *(Pulskurve)*
Doppelgipfligkeit *f* dicrotism *(Pulskurve)*
Doppelhand *f* dicheirus *(Mißgeburt)*
doppelhändig ambidextrous
Doppelhändigkeit *f* ambidexterity, ambidextrism
Doppelhören *n* double hearing, diplacusis
Doppelinfektion *f* double infection
doppelkapselig bicapsular
doppelkeimblättrig diploblastic
doppelkeimig bigerminal
Doppelkinn *n* double-chin
Doppelknoten *m* double knot
Doppelkontrastdarstellung *f* double contrast radiography
Doppelkontrasteinlauf *m* double contrast enema
Doppelkontraströntgendarstellung *f* double contrast radiography
Doppelkontrasttechnik *f* double contrast technique
Doppelkontrastuntersuchung *f* double contrast examination
Doppelkontrastverfahren *n* double contrast technique
doppelköpfig dicephalous
Doppelköpfiger *m* dicephalus
Doppelköpfigkeit *f* dicephalia
Doppellappenamputation *f* double-flap amputation
doppelläufig double-lumen, double-barrelled *(z. B. Anus praeternaturalis)*
Doppelligatur *f* double ligation (ligature)
Doppellippe *f* douple lip; dicheilia
Doppellöffel *m*/**scharfer** double-ended [bone] curette
Doppelmißbildung *f* 1. diplosom[at]ia, monstrosity; 2. *s.* Doppelmißgeburt
~ **mit Brustbeinverschmelzung** sternopagia, sternodymia
~ **mit einem Kopf** syncephaly
~ **mit seitlicher Beckenverschmelzung** ischiopagia
~ **mit Wirbelsäulenverschmelzung** spondylodidymia
~ **mit Wirbelverschmelzung** vertebrodidymia

Doppelmißgeburt f disomus, twin monster
~/**komplette** diplopagus
~ mit **Brustbeinverschmelzung** sternopagus, xiphopagus
~ mit **Brustkorb- und Bauchverwachsung** gastrothoracopagus
~ mit **Brust- und Gesichtsverschmelzung** prosopothoracopagus, prosoposternodidymus
~ mit **doppelter unterer Körperhälfte** dipygus
~ mit **einem Kopf** synencephalus, monocephalus, monocranius
~ mit **einem Nabel** omphalomonodidymus
~ mit **gemeinsamer Wirbelsäule** rachipagus
~ mit **Gesichtsverwachsung** proso[po]pagus
~ mit **Kieferverwachsung** polygnathus
~ mit **Nabelverwachsung** monomphalus, omphalopagus, omphalodidymus
~ mit **nur einem Abdomen** gastrodidymus
~ mit **Rumpfverschmelzung** somatodidymus, somatopagus
~ mit **Schädelverwachsung** syncephalus, symphyocephalus
~ mit **seitlicher Beckenverschmelzung** ischiopagus, ischiodidymus
~ mit **seitlicher Verwachsung am Thorax** ectopagus
~ mit **Stirnverwachsung** frontal craniopagus
~ mit **verwachsenem Brustkorb** thoracodidymus
~ mit **Verwachsung am Kreuzbein** pygopagus, pygodidymus
~ mit **Verwachsung am Thorax** thoracopagus
~ mit **Wirbelsäulenverschmelzung** spondylodymus
~ mit **Wirbelverschmelzung** vertebrodidymus
doppeln to imbricate *(z. B. eine Faszie)*
Doppelnase f double nose; dirrhinia
Doppelniere f double kidney; renal duplication
doppelohrig binaural, bi[n]auricular
Doppelpatella f bipartite patella
Doppelpenis m diphallus
Doppelplazenta f duplex (bilobed, bipartite) placenta
Doppelpromontorium n double promontory
Doppelpupille f double pupil; di[plo]coria
Doppelrefraktion f birefringence, double refraction
Doppelrhythmus m double rhythm
Doppelscheide f double vagina
doppelschlägig dicrotic, dicrotous
Doppelschlägigkeit f dicrotism *(Puls)*
Doppelschwangerschaft f double gestation
doppelsichtig diplopic
Doppelsichtigkeit f diplopia, double vision, ambiopia *(Zusammensetzungen s. unter Diplopie)*
Doppelsichtigkeitsmesser m diplopiometer
doppelsinnig ambiguous
Doppelstern m diaster, amphiaster *(Mitosefigur)*
Doppelstiellappen m double-pedicle flap
Doppelstimme f double voice, diphonia, diphthongia
doppelt double; diploid *(z. B. Chromosomensatz)*
Doppelton m reduplicated sound

~/**Traubescher** Traube's sign, Duroziez' murmur, pistol-shot phenomenon (sound) *(bei Aorteninsuffizienz)*
Doppeltsehen n s. Doppelsichtigkeit
Doppelung f 1. duplicature *(z. B. der Bauchfellfalte)*; 2. doubling, imbrication *(z. B. der Fasziennaht)*
doppelzellig bicellular
Doppelzervix f double cervix
Doppelzunge f bifid (double) tongue; diglossia
Doppler-Echokardiographie f Doppler echocardiography
Doppler-Ultraschall-Flowmeter n Doppler ultrasonic flowmeter
Dorn m spine, spina *(Zusammensetzungen s. unter Spina)*
dornartig spinal
Dornfortsatz m spinous process [of the vertebra], vertebral (neural) spine, spina ● **unter dem** ~ subspinous
dornig spinal, spinulose, spinous, spinate, spiny
Dornmuskel m spinalis [muscle]
Doromanie f doromania *(abnorme Schenksucht)*
dorsalflektieren to dorsiflex
Dorsalflexion f dorsiflexion
Dorsalflexionsmuskel m dorsiflexor [muscle]
Dorsalgie f dorsalgia
Dorsalkrümmung f dorsal curve (curvature) *(der Wirbelsäule)*
Dorsalplatte f dorsal (root, deck) plate *(Embryologie)*
Dorsalsklerose f dorsal sclerosis
dorsalwärts dorsad
dorsoanterior dorsoanterior
Dorsolumbarregion f dorsolumbar region
dorsosakral dorsosacral
Dorsum n 1. dorsum, upper surface *(eines Körperteils)*; ridge; 2. s. Rücken
~ **linguae** dorsum of the tongue
~ **manus** dorsum of the hand
~ **pedis** dorsum of the foot
~ **penis** dorsum of the penis
Dosieraerosol n controlled dosage aerosol
dosieren to dose *(z. B. Arzneien)*
Dosierung f dosage, dosing
dosierungsabhängig dose-related
Dosierungsintervall n dosage interval
Dosierungsregel f dosage rule
Dosierungsschema n dosage schedule
Dosierungsvorschrift f dosage instruction
Dosimeter n dosimeter, dosemeter
Dosimetrie f dosimetry
dosimetrisch dosimetric
Dosis f dose, dosage ● **in geteilten Dosen** in divided doses, refracta dosi
~/**absolut tödliche** invariably lethal dose, LD 100, LD_{100}
~/**aufgenommene** absorbed dose
~/**definierte tägliche** defined daily dose
~/**effektive** effective dose
~/**einschleichende** low initial dose
~/**geeignete** appropriate dose

Dosis

~/geringste letale minimum lethal dose
~/geringste wirksame minimum effective dose
~/höchstzulässige maximum permissible dose
~/homöopathische homoeopathic dose
~/letale lethal dose, LD, fatal dose
~/maximal tolerierte maximum tolerated dose
~/mittlere letale median lethal dose, LD 50, LD_{50}
~/subdiabetogene subdiabetogenic dose *(des Insulins)*
~/subletale sublethal dose
~/suprapyhsiologische suprapyhsiologic dose
~/therapeutische therapeutic (curative) dose
~ tolerata tolerance dose *(z. B. von Röntgenstrahlen)*
dosisabhängig dose-related, dose-dependent
Dosiserhöhung f dose build-up
Dosishöhe f dosage level
Dosisleistung f dose rate
Dosisleistungsmesser m dose rate meter
Dosisleistungsmessung f dose rate measurement
Dosismesser m s. Dosimeter
Dosisrate f s. Dosisleistung
Dosis-Wirkungs-Analyse f dose-action analysis
Dosis-Wirkungs-Beziehung f dose-action relationship
Dosis-Wirkungs-Kurve f dose-effect curve
Dosis-Zeit-Beziehung f dose-time relationship
Dotter n yolk, vitellus
dotterarm oligolecithal, miolecithal, alecithal *(Eizelle)*
Dotterbildung f vitellogenesis
Dottergang m vitelline (vitellointestinal, umbilical) duct, yolk stalk
Dotterhaut f vitelline membrane
Dotterhöhle f vitelline (yolk) cavity
Dottersack m vitelline (yolk) sac, vitellicle, umbilical vesicle
Dottersackarterie f vitelline (omphalomesenteric) artery
Dottersackentoderm n yolk-sac entoderm
Dottersackentwicklung f omphalogenesis
Dottersackkreislauf m vitelline (omphalomesenteric) circulation
Dottersackkultur f yolk-sac culture
Dottersackvene f vitelline (omphalomesenteric) vein
Dottersackzyste f vitelline cyst
Douglas m 1. Douglas pouch, rectouterine fossa (excavation, space), rectouterine cul-de-sac [of Douglas]; 2. Douglas pouch, rectovesical fossa (excavation, space), rectovesical cul-de-sac [of Douglas]
Douglasabszeß m 1. Douglas [pouch] abscess, rectouterine cul-de-sac abscess; 2. Douglas [pouch] abscess, rectovesical cul-de-sac abscess
Douglaseröffnung f [durch die Scheide] culdotomy
Douglaspunktion f Douglas pouch puncture
~ durch die Scheide culdocentesis
Douglasraum m s. Douglas

Douglas[raum]spiegelung f [durch die Scheide] culdoscopy
Doyen m Doyen's [rib] raspatory
DPN = Diphosphopyridinnukleotid
Dracunculus m medinensis dragon worm
Dracunculus-medinensis-Befall m dracontiasis, dracunculiasis, guinea worm infection (infestation)
Dragée n dragée, coated tablet
~/magensaftresistentes keratinoid
Drahtbiegezange f wire bending pliers
Drahtbügel m cradle *(für Extremitäten)*
Drahtcerclage f [wire] cerclage; intermaxillary wiring *(bei Kieferbrüchen)*
Drahtextension f wire (pin) extension *(bei Knochenbruch)*
~/Böhlersche Böhler's splint
Drahtextensionsbügel m wire traction bow
Drahtfixation f wiring, wire fixation *(z. B. bei Knochenbrüchen)*
~/äußere external wire (skeletal) fixation
~/intramedulläre intramedullary wire fixation
Drahtnaht f wire suture
Drahtpuls m wiry pulse
Drahtsäge f wire (Gigli's) saw
Drahtsägeneinführungsinstrument n conductor for wire saws
Drahtschere f wire cutting scissors
Drahtschienung f wiring
Drahtspanner m [bone] wire tightener
Drahtspannzange f [bone] wire tightening forceps
Drahtspickung f wiring *(bei Knochenbrüchen)*
Drahtumschlingung f [wire] cerclage
Drahtzug m s. Drahtextension
Drain n(m) drain, drainage, [drainage] tube
Drainage f/geschlossene closed drainage
Drainageöffnung f drainage issue
Drainageröhrchen n s. Drain
drainieren to drain
Drakontiasis f, Drakunkulose f dracontiasis, dracunculiasis, guinea worm infection (infestation)
Drän n(m) s. Drain
Drang m desire, nisus, molimen, effort
Drangedal-Krankheit f s. Krankheit/Bornholmer
Drapetomanie f drapetomania *(krankhafter Wandertrieb)*
Drastikum n drastic [agent]
drehen to rotate, to revolve; to turn *(z. B. bei der Geburt)*
drehend [/sich] rotatory, rotational
Dreher m s. Drehmuskel
Drehfraktur f torsion fracture
Drehgelenk n rotation (pivot) joint
Drehkrampf m rotatory spasm, gyrospasm
Drehlappen m rotation (swinging) flap
Drehmuskel m rotator [muscle], rotatory muscle
Drehnystagmus m rotatory nystagmus
Drehosteotomie f rotation (rotatory) osteotomy
Drehschwindel m rotatory vertigo
~/Menièrescher Menière's vertigo
Drehtick m rotatory tic

Drehung f rotation; revolution; turning, torsion (z. B. bei der Geburt)
~/abnorme malrotation, twist
~ entgegen dem Uhrzeigersinn counterclockwise rotation
~ im Uhrzeigersinn clockwise rotation
Drehungsnystagmus m rotation (rotatory) nystagmus
Dreh[ungs]vermögen n/**optisches** optical activity (z. B. von Lösungen)
Drehversuch m /**Baranyscher** Barany's rotation (turning) test (zur Prüfung des Gleichgewichts)
Drehwirbel m rotation vertebra
dreiarmig tribrachius
dreibäuchig trigastric (z. B. Muskel)
dreibranchig trivalve (z. B. Spekulum)
Dreieck n triangle, trigone, trigonum (s.a. unter Trigonum)
~/Bochdaleksches Bochdalek's foramen, lumbocostal (vertebrocostal) triangle
~/Bryantsches Bryant's (iliofemoral) triangle
~/Calotsches Calot's triangle, cystic triangle [of Calot] (zwischen Leber- und Gallenblasengang)
~/Einthovensches Einthoven's triangle (EKG)
~/Garlandsches Garland's triangle (bei Pleuraerguß)
~/Grocco-Rauchfußsches Grocco's (paravertebral) triangle
~/Hesselbachsches Hesselbach's triangle, triangular area of Hesselbach
~/Lieutaudsches trigone of the [urinary] bladder, Lieutaud's triangle
~/Petitsches Petit's (lumbar) triangle
~/Scarpasches Scarpa's (femoral) triangle
Dreieckbein n triquetrum, triangularis, cuneiform [bone of the carpus]
dreieckig triangular; triquetral, triquetrous
Dreieckklemme f triangular forceps
Dreieckkopf m trigonocephalus
dreieckköpfig trigonocephalous
Dreieckköpfigkeit f trigonocephalia
Dreieckstuch n triangular arm-sling
Dreiecksverband m triangular bandage
Dreiecktuchverband m cravat [bandage]
Dreieraufspaltung f trifurcation
Dreierrhythmus m [des Herzens] triple (gallop) rhythm
dreifach triple, threefold, triplex; trigeminal; triploid (Chromosomensatz)
Dreifach-Bypass m triple (threefold) bypass (Herzkranzgefäßchirurgie)
dreifächerig trilocular, tripartite
Dreifachfärbung f triple stain (Histologie)
Dreifachimpfstoff m triple vaccine
Dreifachimpfung f triple vaccination
Dreifachkombinationstherapie f triple drug therapy
Dreifachlähmung f triplegia
Dreifachsehen n, **Dreifachsichtigkeit** f triplopia
Dreifachstethoskop n triple change stethoscope
Dreifachverzweigung f trifurcation
dreifarbensichtig trichrom[at]ic, trichroic

Dreifarbensichtiger m trichromat[e]
Dreifarbensichtigkeit f trichromatopsia, trichromatism
Dreifarbigkeit f trichro[mat]ism (z. B. von Kristallen)
Dreifingerfurche f distal transverse crease (der Hand)
dreifingrig tridactyl
Dreifuß m tripus
Dreigebärende f tripara
Dreigesichtigkeit f triprosopia
dreigestaltig trimorphic, trimorphous
dreigeteilt trifid, trichotomous
dreigipfelig tricrotic (Puls)
Dreigipfligkeit f tricrotism (Puls)
Dreigläserprobe f three-glass test
dreihändig trimanual
dreihöckrig tritubercular
Dreikammerherz n trilocular heart
dreikammerig trilocular
dreikeimblättrig triploblastic, tridermic
dreikernig trinucleate
dreiklappig trivalvular
dreiknotig tritubercular
dreiköpfig tricipital, triceps, three-headed
Dreikopfmuskel m triceps [muscle], tricipital muscle
Dreilamellennagel m triflanged (cloverleaf) nail (zur Knochenbruchbehandlung)
dreilappig trilobate, trilobular
dreimal pro Tag, ~ täglich three times a day, ter in die, t.i.d.
dreischichtig trilaminar
dreischlägig tricrotic (Puls)
Dreischlägigkeit f tricrotism (Puls)
dreispaltig trifid
Dreistärkenbrille f trifocal spectacles
Dreistärkenglas n trifocal lens
dreistrahlig triradial, triradiate
Dreitagefieber n three-day fever, Chitral (Phlebotomus) fever
Dreitagefieberexanthem n rose rash of infants, exanthema subitum, sixth disease, [Filatov-] Duke's disease (masernähnlicher Hautausschlag im Kindesalter)
dreitägig tertian (z. B. Fieberintervall bei Malaria)
dreivalvulär trivalvular
Dreiweg[e]hahn m three-way stopcock (tap)
dreizellig tricellular
dreizipflig tricuspid[ate]
Drepanozyt m s. Sichelzelle
drepanozytär drepanocytic
Drepanozytenanämie f, **Drepanozytose** f s. Sichelzellenanämie
Drescherlunge[nerkrankung] f farmer's lung (Getreidestaublungenerkrankung)
Dressler-Syndrom n I Dressler's (postmyocardial infarction) syndrome
~ II Dressler's disease, paroxysmal (intermittent, recurrent) haemoglobinuria (durch Kälteagglutinine)
Drift f/**genetische** genetic drift

Drigalski-Conradi-Nährboden

Drigalski-Conradi-Nährboden m Drigalski-Conradi culture medium *(zum Nachweis von Enterobakterien)*
Drilling m triplet
Drillingsgeburt f triplet birth
Drillingsschwangerschaft f triplet pregnancy
Drittelrohrplatte f one third tubular plate *(Osteosynthese)*
Drittgebärende f tertipara
Drittschwangere f tertigravida
DRK s. Deutsches Rotes Kreuz
Droge f drug
~/natürliche crude drug
Drogenabhängiger m drug addict
Drogenabhängigkeit f drug addiction (habit, dependence)
Drogenauszug m [/alkoholischer] tincture, tinct., tr.
Drogenikterus m drug jaundice (icterus)
Drogenkunde f pharmacognostics, pharmacognosy *(Bestimmungs- und Erkennungslehre der Drogen)*
drogenkundlich pharmacognostic
Drogenmißbrauch m misuse of drugs, drug abuse
Drogenpsychose f drug psychosis
Drogenspezialist m pharmacognosist
drogensüchtig drug-addicted, drug-dependent
Dromedar[fieber]kurve f camel curve
Dromomanie f dromomania, drapetomania *(motorische Unruhe bei Epileptikern)*
Dromophobie f dromophobia *(krankhafte Angst vor dem Laufen)*
dromotrop dromotropic *(Herz)*
Droperidol n droperidol *(Tranquilizer)*
Droperidol-Fentanyl-Kombination f droperidol fentanyl compound, thalamonal
Drosselgrube f jugular fossa
Drosselvene f jugular vein
~/äußere external jugular vein
~/innere internal jugular vein
~/vordere oberflächliche anterior jugular vein
Drosselvenenkompression f jugular compression
Druck m pressure *(Zusammensetzungen s. a. unter Blutdruck)* ● **mit gleichem onkotischem ~** iso-oncotic ● **mit gleichem osmotischem ~** iso-osmotic
~/fester firm pressure
~/gleicher osmotischer isotonia
~/intraabdomineller intra-abdominal pressure
~/intrakapillärer intracapillary pressure
~/intrakranieller intracranial pressure
~/intraokularer intra-ocular pressure (tension)
~/intrapleuraler intrapleural pressure
~/intrathorakaler intrathoracic pressure
~/intraventrikulärer intraventricular pressure
~/kolloidosmotischer colloid osmotic pressure
~/linksventrikulärer enddiastolischer left ventricular end-diastolic pressure
~/negativer negative pressure
~/onkotischer oncotic pressure
~/osmotischer osmotic pressure
~/rechtsventrikulärer right ventricular pressure
~/unterschiedlicher osmotischer anisotonia
~/venöser venous pressure
Druckabfall m decompression, reduction of pressure, decrease in pressure
Druckanästhesie f compression anaesthesia *(Nervenleitungsstörung infolge Druckschädigung)*
Druckanpassungsstörung f dysbarism *(z. B. bei Dekompressionskrankheit)*
Druckanstieg m increase of pressure, rise in pressure, compression
Druckarbeit f work against pressure
Druckatrophie f pressure (compression) atrophy
druckaufnehmend pressoreceptive *(z. B. Nerven)*
Druckaufzeichnung f tonography
Druckbeatmung f/**positive** positive pressure respiration
Druckblock m pressure block *(z. B. der Nervenleitung)*
druckempfindlich pressosensitive, sensitive to pressure
Druckempfindlichkeit f sensitivity to pressure
Druckempfindung f barognosis, pressure perception
Druckempfindungsvermögen n baraesthesia, pressure sense
drücken to press, to compress; to strain *(beim Stuhlgang)*
Druckentlastung f decompression
~ des Darms intestinal decompression
Druckentlastungsoperation f **bei Glaukom/Elliotsche** Elliot's operation
druckerhöhend pressor *(Blutdruck)*; oncotic *(Gewebedruck)*
druckerhöht hypertonic *(z. B. osmotischer Druck)*
Druckerhöhung f 1. compression; 2. s. Druckanstieg; 3. s. Hypertonus
Druckerniedrigung f 1. decompression; 2. s. Druckabfall; 3. s. Hypotonus
Druckgeschwür n pressure sore (ulceration), decubital (decubitus) ulcer, bedsore
Druckgradient m pressure gradient *(z. B. beim Herzkatheterismus)*
Druckinfusion f pressure infusion, infusion under pressure
Druckkammer f compression (pressure) chamber
Druckklemme f pressure clamp
Druckkompresse f pressure compress
Druckkonus m pressure cone
Druckkreis m [pressure] phosphene *(Lichterscheinung bei Druck auf die Augen)*
Druckkurve f pressure curve, tonogram
Druckkurvenschreiber m tonograph
Druckkurvenschreibung f tonography
Drucklähmung f pressure palsy, compression paralysis *(z. B. eines Nervs)*
~ des Nervus radialis drunkard's arm paralysis
Druckluftkrankheit f decompression sickness, caisson disease, bends, aeroembolism

Drüsenabsonderung

Druckmanschette f cuff, pneumatic tourniquet
Druckmesser m tonometer, manometer
Druckmessung f tonometry
Drucknekrose f pressure necrosis
Drucknerv m pressor nerve
Druckneuritis f pressure (compression) neuritis
Drucknystagmus m compression nystagmus
Druckosteosyntheseplatte f compression bone plate
Druckosteosyntheseschraube f compression bone screw
Druckplattenherz n pusher-plate heart *(künstliches Herz)*
Druckplatteninstrumentarium n bone plate compression instrument set
Druckplattenosteosynthese f compression plating
Druckpuls m pressure pulse
Druckpunkt m 1. pressure spot *(Hauteindellung)*; 2. pressure point *(Hautpunkt mit einem Drucksinnesempfänger)*
~/**Boasscher** Boas' point *(bei Magengeschwür)*
Druckrezeptor m pressoreceptor *(in der Aorta)*
Druckschmerz m tenderness on pressure
druckschmerzhaft tender on pressure, painful on palpation, painful to touch
Druckschmerzhaftigkeit f tenderness
Druckschreiber m tonograph
Druckschreibung f tonography
drucksenkend hypotonic
Drucksenkung f s. Druckabfall
drucksensibel pressosensitive
Drucksinn m pressure sense, baraesthesia
Druck-Sog-Beatmung f alternating positive-negative pressure breathing
Druckspatel m depressor
Drucksprung m pressure gradient *(z. B. beim Herzkatheterismus)*
Druckstelle f pressure sore, bedsore
Drucksymptom n pressure symptom; compression sign
Drucküberwachung f pressure monitoring
Druckunempfindlichkeit f compression anaesthesia *(Nervenleitungsstörung infolge Druckschädigung)*
Druckverband m pressure bandage, compression dressing
druckvermindert hypotonic *(z. B. osmotischer Druck)*
Druckverminderung f 1. decompression; 2. s. Druckabfall; 3. s. Hypotonus
Druckverplattung f compression plating *(von Knochen)*
druckwahrnehmend pressoreceptive
Druckwahrnehmung f barognosis, perception of pressure
Druse f druse *(bei Aktinomykose)*
Drüse f gland, glandula
~/**akzessorische** accessory gland
~/**alveoläre** alveolar gland
~/**anakrine** anacrine gland
~/**apokrine** apocrine gland
~/**azinöse** acinous gland
~/**azinotubuläre** acino-tubular gland
~/**Bartholinische** Bartholin's gland, greater vestibular gland
~/**Blandinsche** Blandin's (anterior lingual) gland
~/**Bonnotsche** Bonnot's (interscapular) gland
~/**ekkrine** eccrine gland
~/**endoepitheliale** endo-epithelial gland
~/**endokrine** endocrine gland, ductless (closed, false) gland
~/**enterochromaffine** enterochromaffine gland
~/**exkretorische** excretory gland
~/**exokrine** exocrine gland
~/**gemischte** s. ~/seromuköse
~/**holokrine** holocrine gland
~/**inkretorische** incretory gland
~/**merokrine** merocrine gland
~/**miliäre** miliary gland
~ **mit äußerer Sekretion** s. ~/exkretorische
~ **mit innerer Sekretion** s. ~/endokrine
~/**Nabothsche** Nabothian gland, Naboth's follicle, gland of the cervix of the uterus
~/**peptische** peptic gland
~/**periproktische** circumanal gland
~/**Rosenmüllersche** Rosenmüller's gland (node)
~/**säurebildende** acid gland
~/**seromuköse** seromucous (mixed) gland
~/**seröse** serous (albuminous) gland
~/**tubulöse** tubular gland
~/**Virchowsche** Virchow's (signal) node, gland of Virchow-Troisier *(supraklavikuläre Lymphknotenmetastase)*
~/**vulvovaginale** vulvovaginal gland
Drüsen fpl glands, glandulae ● **mehrere ~ betreffend** multiglandular
~/**Bowmansche** Bowman's glands
~/**Brunnersche** Brunner's (duodenal) glands
~/**Cowpersche** Cowper's glands, bulbourethral (bulbocavernous, anteprostatic) glands
~/**Krausesche** Krause's glands, accessory lacrimal glands
~/**Lieberkühnsche** Lieberkühn's (intestinal) glands, crypts of Lieberkühn
~/**Littrésche** Littré's (urethral) glands *(beim Mann)*
~/**Meibomsche** Meibomian glands, palpebral follicles, tarsal (tarsoconjunctival) glands
~/**Mollsche** Moll's (ciliary) glands *(münden in die Haarbälge der Augenwimpern)*
~/**Montgomerysche** Montgomery's glands, areolar glands of Montgomery
~/**Morgagnische** Morgagni's (urethral) glands
~/**Nuhnsche** Nuhn's (anterior lingual) glands
~/**Peyersche** Peyer's glands (patches) *(im unteren Dünndarm)*
~/**Skenesche** Skene's (para-urethral) glands *(bei der Frau)*
~/**Tysonsche** Tyson's glands, preputial (odoriferous) glands
~/**Zeissche** Zeis's glands, [sebaceous] glands of Zeis
Drüsenabsonderung f secretion, secernment

Drüsenabszeß

Drüsenabszeß *m* glandular abscess
drusenartig drusenoid
drüsenartig glandular, gland-like, adenoid, adenose
Drüsenausführungsgang *m* efferent (glandular, excretory) duct
Drüsenbalg *m* follicle
drüsenbedingt glandular, adenogenous
Drüsenbeere *f* acinus
Drüsenendstück *n*/**beerenförmiges** acinus
Drüsenentfernung *f*[/operative] adenectomy
Drüsenentwicklung *f* adenogenesis, gland development
Drüsenentzündung *f* adenitis, glandular inflammation, inflammation of a gland
~/**multiple** polyadenitis
Drüsenepithel *n* glandular epithelium
Drüsenepitheltumor *m* glandular epithelial tumour
Drüsenepithelzelle *f* glandular epithelial cell
Drüsenerkrankung *f* adenopathy, glandular disease
Drüsenerweichung *f* adenomalacia, softening of a gland
Drüsenextrakt *m* glandular extract
Drüsenfasergeschwulst *f* adenofibroma
Drüsenfieber *n* glandular fever
~/**lymphämoides** *s.* ~/Pfeiffersches
~/**Pfeiffersches** Pfeiffer's disease (glandular fever), [infectious] mononucleosis, [acute] infectious adenitis, lymphocytic (monocytic) angina, acute benign adenitis (lymphoblastosis), kissing disease
drüsenförmig adeniform, adenoid, glandiform
Drüsenfunktion *f*/**mangelnde** anadenia, deficiency of glandular activity
Drüsenfunktionsschwäche *f* adenasthenia
Drüsengang *m* glandular duct
Drüsengangsgeschwulst *f* ductal tumour
Drüsengangskarzinom *n* ductal carcinoma
Drüsengangspapillom *n* ductal papilloma
Drüsengeschwulst *f* glandular tumour, adenoncus
~/**gutartige** adenoma
Drüsengewebe *n* glandular tissue
Drüseninsuffizienz *f* anadenia, glandular insufficiency
Drüseninzision *f* adenotomy
Drüsenkapsel *f* glandular capsule
Drüsenkrebs *m* glandular carcinoma, adenocarcinoma
Drüsenlappen *m* glandular lobe (lobule)
drüsenlos aglandular, eglandular
Drüsenlosigkeit *f*/**angeborene** anadenia
Drüsenlumen *n* glandular lumen
Drüsenöffnung *f* glandular orifice
Drüsenpest *f* glandular (bubonic) plague, minor pestis *(leicht verlaufende Pestform)*
Drüsenphlegmone *f* adenophlegmon, glandular phlegmon, phlegmonous adenitis
Drüsenpolyp *m* adenomatous polyp
Drüsensarkom *n* adenosarcoma, glandular sarcoma

Drüsenschlauch *m* glandular tube
drüsenschlauchartig syringoid
Drüsenschmerz *m* adenalgia, adenodynia
Drüsenschnitt *m* adenotomy
Drüsenschwäche *f* adenasthenia
Drüsenschwellung *f* glandular swelling (enlargement)
Drüsenschwund *m* anadenia
Drüsensekret *n* glandular secretion
Drüsensekretion *f* glandular secretion, secernment
Drüsenstörung *f* glandular disturbance
Drüsensystem *n*/**endokrines** endocrinium, endocrine [glandular] system
Drüsentätigkeit *f* glandular activity
Drüsentuberkulose *f* glandular tuberculosis (phthisis)
Drüsenüberfunktion *f* adenohypersthenia, glandular hyperactivity, excessive glandular activity
Drüsen- und Fasergewebsgeschwulst *f* adenofibroma, fibroadenoma
Drüsen- und Zellgewebsentzündung *f* adenocellulitis
Drüsenunterfunktion *f* adenasthenia, hypoadenia, glandular insufficiency, deficient glandular activity
Drüsenvergrößerung *f* glandular enlargement, hyperadenosis
Drüsenverhärtung *f* adenosclerosis, hardening of a gland
Drüsenverlagerung *f* adenectopia, displacement (malposition) of a gland
Drüsenzelle *f* glandular cell
drüsig adenoid, glandular
drüsig-blasig adenocystic
Dschungelframbösie *f* bush yaws
Dschungelgelbfieber *n* sylvan (jungle) yellow fever
Dubin-Johnson-Syndrom *n* Dubin-Johnson syndrome, Dubin-Sprinz syndrome, chronic idiopathic jaundice *(gestörte Bilirubinausscheidung aus der Leberzelle)*
Duchenne-Erb-Lähmung *f* Duchenne-Erb palsy (syndrome), upper brachial plexus paralysis, upper cervical radicular syndrome
Duchenne-Griesinger-Syndrom *n* Duchenne-Griesinger disease, Duchenne's muscular dystrophy, pseudohypertrophic infantile muscular dystrophy, pseudohypertrophic muscular paralysis
Duchenne-Syndrom *n* I Duchenne's disease, tabes dorsalis, locomotor ataxia
~ II Duchenne's paralysis (disease), progressive bulbar paralysis
Ductuli *mpl* **aberrantes** aberrant ductules
~ **efferentes testis** efferent ductules [of the testis]
Ductulus *m* ductule, ductulus, canaliculus; duct
~ **alveolaris** alveolar duct
~ **biliferus** cholangiole, bile ductule (capillary)
~ **biliferus intercellularis** *s.* ~ biliferus intralobularis

~ **biliferus interlobularis** biliary [interlobular] ductule, interlobular bile duct
~ **biliferus intralobularis** bile capillary (canaliculus), biliary intralobular ductule
Ductus *m* duct, ductus, canal, channel, canalis *(s. a. unter* Meatus *und* Gang*)*
~ **accessorius** accessory duct
~ **arteriosus [Botalli]** ductus arteriosus, Botallo's duct
~ **arteriosus Botalli/offener** patent ductus arteriosus, patent Botallo's duct
~ **biliferus** biliary (gall) duct, bile vessel
~ **biliferus intralobularis** biliary intralobular canal
~ **Botalli** *s.* ~ arteriosus
~ **choledochus** choledochus, common [bile] duct
~ **cochlearis** cochlear duct, membranous cochlear canal, spiral canal of the cochlea
~ **cysticus** cystic duct
~ **deferens** deferent canal (duct), seminal (spermatic) duct, duct of the testicle
~ **ejaculatorius** ejaculatory canal (duct)
~ **endolymphaticus** endolymphatic (otic) duct
~ **epididymidis** epididymal duct, duct of the epididymis
~ **epoophori longitudinalis [Gartneri]** longitudinal epoophoron duct, longitudinal duct of the epoophoron, Gartner's duct
~ **glandulae bulbourethralis** duct of the bulbourethral gland
~ **hepaticus** hepatic duct
~ **hepaticus communis** common hepatic duct
~ **hepaticus dexter** right hepatic duct
~ **hepaticus sinister** left hepatic duct
~ **hepatopancreaticus** hepatopancreatic duct
~ **lacrimalis** lacrimal duct (canaliculus)
~ **lactiferus** lactiferus (lacteal, milk) duct, galactophorous duct (canal), galactophore
~ **lobi caudati dexter** right duct of the caudate lobe of the liver
~ **lobi caudati sinister** left duct of the caudate lobe of the liver
~ **lymphaticus dexter** right lymphatic duct
~ **mesonephricus [Wolffi]** mesonephric (Wolffian) duct
~ **nasofrontalis** nasofrontal duct, infundibulum of the frontal sinus
~ **nasolacrimalis** lacrimonasal (lacrimal) duct
~ **omphalo[mes]entericus** omphalomesenteric (omphalo-intestinal) duct, vitelline (vitello-intestinal, umbilical) duct, yolk stalk *(embryonale Verbindung von Darm und Dottersack)*
~ **pancreaticus** pancreatic duct, Wirsung's canal, duct of Wirsung, Hoffmann's duct
~ **pancreaticus accessorius [Santorinii]** accessory pancreatic duct, duct of Santorini, Bernard's canal (duct)
~ **pancreaticus major** major pancreatic duct
~ **papillaris renis** papillary duct
~ **paramesonephricus** paramesonephric duct *(Embryologie)*
~ **paraurethralis** para-urethral duct, Skene's duct
~ **parotideus** parotid duct, Stensen's (Stenonian) duct
~ **perilymphaticus** perilymphatic (periotic) duct, aquaeduct of the cochlea
~ **pharyngobrachialis** pharyngobrachial duct
~ **reuniens** Hensen's canal
~ **semicircularis** semicircular duct [of the inner ear], membranous semicircular canal
~ **semicircularis anterior** anterior semicircular duct
~ **semicircularis lateralis** lateral semicircular duct
~ **semicircularis posterior** posterior semicircular duct
~ **semicircularis superior** anterior semicircular duct
~ **seminalis** seminal duct
~ **spermaticus** spermatic duct
~ **sublingualis** sublingual duct
~ **submandibularis** submandibular (Wharton's) duct
~ **thoracicus** thoracic duct
~ **thoracicus dexter** right lymphatic (thoracic) duct
~ **thymopharyngeus** thymopharyngeal duct
~ **thyreocervicalis** thyreocervical duct
~ **thyreoglossus** thyroglossal duct
~ **thyreopharyngeus** thyropharyngeal duct
~ **utriculosaccularis** utriculosaccular duct
~ **venosus** duct of Arantius *(Embryologie)*
~ **Wolffi** *s.* ~ mesonephricus
Ductus-choledochus-Anastomose *f* common bile duct anastomosis
Ductus-choledochus-Chirurgie *f* common bile duct surgery
Ductus-choledochus-Drainage *f* common bile duct drainage
Ductus-choledochus-Erkrankung *f* common bile duct disease
Ductus-choledochus-Exploration *f* common bile duct exploration
Ductus-choledochus-Karzinom *n* common bile duct cancer
Ductus-choledochus-Läsion *f* common bile duct trauma
Ductus-choledochus-Rekonstruktion *f* common bile duct reconstruction
Ductus-choledochus-Zyste *f* common bile duct cyst
Duffy-System *n* Duffy blood group system
Duft *m* odour, scent, fragrance
duftend oderant, odoriferous, fragrant
Duhring-Krankheit *f* Duhring's disease, dermatitis herpetiformis [Duhring]
Duke-Probe *f* Duke test *(zur Bestimmung der Blutungszeit)*
Duktus *m s.* Ductus
Duktuskarzinom *n* ductal carcinoma
duktuslos ductless
Duktusmündung *f* mouth of the ductus *(z. B. des Ductus Botalli)*
Duktuspapillom *n* ductal papilloma
Duktustumor *m* ductal tumour

Dum-Dum-Fieber

Dum-Dum-Fieber n dumdum fever, febrile tropical splenomegaly *(tropische Infektionskrankheit durch Leishmanien)*
dumm dull, stupid, asynetic, unintelligent; foolish, stupid *(töricht)*
Dummheit f dullness, stupidity, asynesia; foolishness, stupidity
dumpf dull, blunt, obtuse *(Schmerz)*; flat, dull *(bei Perkussion)*
Dumping-Syndrom n dumping (postgastrectomy) syndrome; dumping stomach
dunkel dark; dark-coloured *(Haut)*; high-coloured *(Urin)*; venous *(Blut)*
Dunkeladaptation f dark adaptation
Dunkeladaptationsmessung f dark adaptometry
dunkeladaptiert dark-adapted
Dunkelfeld n dark field
~/physiologisches physiologic scotoma, blind spot
Dunkelfeldmikroskopie f dark-field microscopy
dunkelfeld-negativ dark-field-negative *(mikroskopischer Treponemennachweis)*
dunkelfeld-positiv dark-field-positive *(mikroskopischer Treponemennachweis)*
dunkelhäutig dark-skinned, melanous, melanodermic
Dunkelhäutigkeit f darkness of skin, melanoderm[i]a
Dunkelphasenkontrast m dark-phase contrast *(Mikroskopie)*
dunkelpigmentiert melanotic, melanoid
dünn thin, tenuous, lean, meagre *(Person)*; thin, serous, poor *(Blut)*; thin, fluid *(Flüssigkeit)*; thin, loose *(z. B. Stuhl)*
Dünndarm m small bowel (intestine)
Dünndarmbiopsie f small bowel biopsy
Dünndarmblutung f bleeding from the small bowel
Dünndarm-Dickdarm-Anastomose f enterocolostomy
Dünndarm-Dickdarm-Einscheidung f enterocolic intussusception
Dünndarmdrüse f intestinal gland
Dünndarmeinscheidung f enteric intussusception
Dünndarmentzündung f small bowel enteritis
Dünndarmfistel f small bowel fistula
Dünndarmgekröse n jejuno-ileal mesentery, mesentery [proper]
Dünndarmileus m/**hoher** high intestinal obstruction
Dünndarmkatarrh m enteritis, intestinal catarrh
Dünndarmknäuel n coil of small intestine
Dünndarmpassageuntersuchung f small bowel follow-through X-ray examination
Dünndarmperforation f intestinal perforation
Dünndarmperistaltik f small bowel peristalsis
Dünndarmresektion f intestinal (small bowel) resection
Dünndarmröntgenaufnahme f X-ray of the small bowel
Dünndarmschleimhaut f intestinal mucosa, mucous membrane of the small bowel
Dünndarmschlinge f intestinal loop
Dünndarmvene f intestinal vein
Dünndarmverschluß m small bowel obstruction
~/hoher high intestinal obstruction
Dünndarmvolvulus m intestinal volvulus, volvulus of the small bowel
Dünnfilm m thin blood film *(Hämatologie)*
dünnhäutig thin-skinned, leptodermic, leptoderm[at]ous
Dünnschichtchromatographie f thin-layer chromatography
Dünnschichtenausstrich m thin-film method *(Hämatologie)*
Dünnschichttomographie f thin-section tomography
Dünnschnitt m /**mikroskopischer** microsection *(eines Gewebepräparats)*
Dünn- und Dickdarmentfernung f[/**operative**] enterocolectomy
Dünn- und Dickdarmentzündung f s. Enterokolitis
duodenal duodenal
Duodenal... s. a. Zwölffingerdarm...
Duodenalaspirat n duodenal aspirate
Duodenalatresie f duodenal atresia
Duodenalbulbus m duodenal bulb (cap)
Duodenaldivertikel n duodenal diverticulum
Duodenaldivertikelentfernung f[/**operative**] duodenal diverticulectomy
Duodenaldrüse f duodenal gland
Duodenalektasie f duodenectasia
Duodenalfistel f duodenal fistula; duodenostomy
Duodenalfistelung f[/**operative**] duodenostomy
Duodenalgekröse n mesoduodenum
Duodenalileus m/**akuter** acute duodenal ileus, arteriomesenteric (gastromesenteric) ileus
Duodenalmukosa f duodenal mucosa
Duodenalpapille f duodenal papilla
Duodenalpassage f duodenal passage
Duodenalperforation f duodenal perforation
Duodenalplastik f duodenoplasty
Duodenalregurgitation f duodenal regurgitation
Duodenalsaft m duodenal juice
Duodenalsonde f duodenal tube
Duodenalspiegelung f duodenoscopy
Duodenalspülung f duodenal lavage (irrigation)
Duodenalstenose f duodenal stenosis
Duodenalstumpfdehiszenz f duodenal stump dehiscence
Duodenalstumpfinsuffizienz f duodenal stump dehiscence
Duodenalstumpfperforation f duodenal stump perforation
Duodenalulkus n duodenal ulcer
Duodenalulkuspatient m duodenal ulcer patient
Duodenalvene f duodenal vein
Duodenalwand f duodenal wall
Duodenalzotte f duodenal villus
Duodenektomie f duodenectomy
Duodenitis f duodenitis, inflammation of the duodenum
Duodenocholangitis f duodenocholangitis

Duodenoduodenostomie f duodenoduodenostomy
Duodenoenterostomie f duodenoenterostomy
Duodenogramm n duodenogram
Duodenographie f duodenography
Duodenoileostomie f duodenoileostomy
Duodenojejunalfalte f duodenojejunal fold (plica)
Duodenojejunalhernie f duodenojejunal hernia
Duodenojejunostomie f duodenojejunostomy
Duodenopankreatektomie f duodenopancreatectomy, pancreaticoduodenectomy, Whipple resection
Duodenopylorektomie f duodenopylorectomy
Duodenorrhaphie f duodenorrhaphy
Duodenoskopie f duodenoscopy
Duodenostomie f duodenostomy
Duodenotomie f duodenotomy
Duodenum n duodenum, dodecadactylon
~/ausgewalztes megaduodenum
Duodenum... s. a. Zwölffingerdarm...
Duodenumeröffnung f[/operative] duodenotomy
Duodenum-Gallenblasen-Anastomose f duodeno[chole]cystostomy
Duodenummobilisierung f**/Kochersche** Kocher's manoeuvre
Duodenumresektion f duodenectomy
Duplikation f duplication, doubling
Duplikatur f duplicature (z. B. der Bauchfellfalte)
Duplizitätstheorie f **des Sehens** duplicity theory [of vision]
Dupuytren-Kontraktur f Dupuytren's contracture
Dura f [mater] dura [mater], pachymeninx, scleromeninx
~ mater encephali dura mater of the brain
~ mater spinalis dura mater of the spinal cord
Duraarterie f dural artery
Duraast m dural branch
Duraausstülpung f dural sleeve
Duraendotheliom n dural endothelioma
Durahäkchen n dura retractor
Duraklammer f, **Duraklip** m dura (brain) clip
Duramesser n dura knife
Duraplastik f duraplasty
Durarekonstruktion f duraplasty
Durarinne f grooved director
Durasack m dural sac (tube)
Durascheide f dural sheath
Duraschere f dura scissors
Durasinus m dural [venous] sinus
Duraverschluß m dural closure
durchatmen/tief to breathe deeply
Durchblasung f perflation (z. B der Eileiter)
Durchblutung f blood flow, [blood] circulation
Durchblutungserhöhung f hyperaemization
durchblutungsfördernd favouring the blood flow
durchblutungshemmend inhibiting the blood flow
Durchblutungsmessung f blood flow measurement
Durchblutungsstörungen fpl circulatory disturbances, disturbed circulation

durchbohren to perforate, to pierce; to transfix
~/den Fetusschädel to transforate
durchbohrend perforans, perforating; penetrating
Durchbohrung f 1. perforation, piercing; 2. transfixion
durchbrechen 1. to burst, to erupt (z. B. Abszeß); to perforate (z. B. Magengeschwür); to erupt, to come through (z. B. Zahn); to perforate, to rupture (z. B. Organ); 2. to become manifest, to appear (z. B. eine Krankheit)
Durchbruch m 1. breakthrough; bursting (z. B. eines Abszesses); perforation (z. B. eines Magengeschwürs); eruption (z. B. eines Zahns); perforation, rupture (z. B. eines Organs); 2. manifestation, appearance (z. B. einer Krankheit)
Durchbruchblutung f breakthrough [uterine] bleeding
Durchbruchstelle f fracture location (side) (z. B. eines Knochens); bursting point (z. B. eines Abszesses)
durchdringend penetrating
Durchdringung f penetration, permeation
Durchdringungsfähigkeit f penetration power (z. B. von Strahlen)
Durchfall m s. Diarrhoe
durchfallbekämpfend antidiarrhoeal
Durchfallneigung f looseness
durchfallskrank suffering from diarrhoea; diarrhoeic
durchfallverhütend antidiarrhoeal
durchflechten/eine Sehne to splice a tendon
Durchflußgeschwindigkeit f flow rate (z. B. des Blutes)
Durchflußmesser m flowmeter
durchführen/die Blutkreuzung to match
~/ein Experiment to make (carry out) an experiment
~/eine Äthernarkose to etherize
~/eine Dekapitation to decapitate
~/eine Dialyse to dialyze; to haemodialyze
~/eine Endarteriektomie to endarterectomize
~/eine Hämodialyse to haemodialyze
~/eine Implantation to implant
~/eine Inzision to cut into, to incise, to make an incision
~/eine Konisation to cone
~/eine Kürettage to curet, to abrade
~/eine Laparotomie to laparotomize
~/eine Leicheneröffnung to section
~/eine Leichenzerlegung to prosect
~/eine Maßanalyse to titrate
~/eine Milzexstirpation to splenectomize, to perform a splenectomy
~/eine Narkose to anaesthetize
~/eine Operation to operate, to perform an operation
~/eine Parathyreoidektomie to parathyroidectomize
~/eine Parazentese to puncture, to make a paracentesis

durchführen

~/eine Peritomie to peritomize
~/eine Prämedikation to premedicate
~/eine Radiojodbehandlung der Schilddrüse to radiothyroidectomize
~/eine Schilddrüsenentfernung to thyroidectomize
~/eine Tamponade to tampon[ade], to plug with a tampon
~/eine Tenotomie to tenotomize
~/eine Transfusion to transfuse, to make a transfusion
~/eine Trepanation to trepanize, to trephine
~/eine Wundtoilette to debride the skin edges
~/einen Luftröhrenschnitt to tracheotomize, to perform a tracheostomy
~/einen Tierversuch to vivisect
~/schnell eine Operation to hurry forward an operation
~/wegen einer bösartigen Erkrankung to do for malignancy (z. B. Radikaloperation)
durchgängig patent, open ● ~ **bleiben** to remain patent (z. B. Ductus botalli) ● ~ **sein** to be patent (z. B. Gefäß)
Durchgangssyndrom n transitional syndrome
durchgebrochen perforated (z. B. Geschwür); ruptured (z. B. Organ)
durchgelegen sore
Durchimpfung f mass vaccination (inoculation)
durchlässig porotic, porous; permeable; pervious
~/für Wärmestrahlen diathermic, diathermanous
Durchlässigkeit f porosity; permeability; perviousness
Durchlaßstrahlung f leakage radiation
durchleuchtbar transilluminable
durchleuchten 1. to fluoroscope, to screen; 2. s. röntgen; 3. to transilluminate (mit Licht)
~ **lassen/sich** to have a fluoroscopic examination
durchleuchtend fluoroscopic, radioscopic, roentgenoscopic
Durchleuchtung f 1. fluoroscopy, fluoroscopic examination, screening; 2. s. Röntgen; 3. transillumination (mit Licht)
Durchleuchtungsbild n fluoroscopic image
Durchleuchtungsgerät n 1. fluoroscope, roentgenoscope; 2. diaphanoscope, electrodiaphane (mit Licht)
Durchleuchtungskontrolle f fluoroscopic control
Durchleuchtungsschirm m fluoroscopic (fluorescent) screen
Durchleuchtungsuntersuchung f mit Licht diaphanoscopy
durchlöchert perforated, pierced; cribriform (siebartig)
Durchlöcherung f perforation, piercing
durchmachen/die Inkubationszeit to incubate
Durchmarsch m s. Diarrhoe
Durchmesser m diameter (s.a. unter Diameter)
~/bitemporaler bitemporal diameter
~/okzipitofrontaler occipitofrontal diameter
~/okzipitomentaler occipitomental diameter
~/l. schräger right anterior oblique [position] (die rechte Schulter ist dem Leuchtschirm bei Durchleuchtung genähert)

188

~/ll. schräger left anterior oblique [position] (die linke Schulter ist dem Leuchtschirm bei Durchleuchtung genähert)
durchscheinend pellucid, translucent, translucid, not opaque (z. B. beim Durchleuchten); glassy, vitreous; hyaline (Knorpel)
~/nicht adiaphanous, non-transparent
durchschlafen to sleep through
durchschneiden 1. to transect, to intersect, to cut across (through) (mittels Instrument); 2. to cut out (Nahtmaterial in der Wunde); 2. to appear (Kindskopf bei der Geburt)
~/den Vagusnerv to vagotomize
Durchschneidung f der Trommelfellfalte plicotomy
Durchschnittsalter n average age
Durchschnittsdosis f average dose
Durchschnittsgewicht n average weight
Durchschnittsgröße f average height (des Körpers); average seize (z. B. eines Organs)
Durchschußwunde f through-and-through bullet wound
durchseihen to percolate, to strain, to filter
durchsetzen to infiltrate; to permeate
Durchsetzung f infiltration; permeation
durchseucht contaminated
durchsichtig pellucid; transparent, translucent
durchsickern to ooze through (z. B. Blut)
Durchspülung f lavage, irrigation, washing out (z. B. des Darms)
durchstechen to puncture (z. B. eine Körperhöhle); to pierce [through], to perforate, to prick (z. B. ein Organ); to transfix (z. B. mittels Naht)
Durchstechung f paracentesis (z. B. des Trommelfells)
Durchstichamputation f amputation by transfixion
Durchstichligatur f suture (transfixion) ligature
Durchstichnaht f transfixion suture
durchströmen to perfuse, to flow (run, stream) through
~/wellenförmig ein Blutgefäß to pulsate
Durchströmung f perfusion, flow through
durchtränken to imbibe, to impregnate; to saturate
Durchtränkung f imbibition, impregnation; saturation
durchtrennen to transect, to cut, to divide, to sever; to separate
~/Adhäsionen to cut (sever) adhesions
~/den Vagusnerv to vagotomize
~/eine Sehne to tenotomize
Durchtrennung f transection, section, sectio, cutting, division, severance; separation
– **der Galea aponeurotica** epicraniotomy
– **der hinteren Rückenmarkwurzeln** posterior rhizotomy
– **der vorderen Rückenmarkwurzeln** anterior rhizotomy
– **der Vorderseitenstrangbahn** chordotomy (Rückenmark)

~ **der Zonula ciliaris** zonulotomy
~ **des Ligamentum cricothyreoideum** thyrocricotomy *(Luftröhrenschnitt)*
~/**scharfe** sharp dissection
durchtreten to appear *(Kindskopf bei der Geburt)*
Durchtreten *n* **des Kopfes** appearance of the head
Durchtrittsebene *f* planum *(des kindlichen Schädels bei der Geburt)*
Durchtrittsloch *n* emissary, passage
durchuntersuchen[/gründlich] to examine thoroughly
Durchuntersuchung *f/***gründliche** thorough-examination
durchwachsen to grow through, to infiltrate, to penetrate *(z. B. Geschwulst)*
durchwandern to pass through, to transmigrate *(z. B. Zellen)*
Durchwanderung *f* transmigration *(z. B. von Zellen)*; diapedesis *(z. B. der Leukozyten)*
Durchzuglaken *n* draw-sheet
Durchzugoperation *f* pull-through operation *(z. B. bei Rektumexstirpation)*
Durst *m* thirst
~/**krankhaft gesteigerter** polydipsia, anadipsia, diposis
~/**übermäßiger** hydromania
~/**unstillbarer** anadipsia
Durstbehandlung *f* thirst cure
Durstfieber *n* thirst fever
Durstgefühl *n/***vermindertes** oligodipsia
Durstlosigkeit *f* adipsy, adipsia, absence of thirst
Durstverminderung *f* oligodipsia
Durstversuch *m* thirst (concentration) test
Dusche *f* 1. douche *(Gerät)*; 2. shower [bath], douche; affusion *(z. B. zur Augenspülung)*
Düseninjektion *f* jet injection *(mittels Impfpistole)*
Dyade *f* dyad
Dynamograph *m* dynamograph
Dynamometer *n* dynamometer
Dynamometrie *f* dynamometry
Dysadaptation *f* dys[ad]aptation *(z. B. der Netzhaut)*
Dysakusis *f* dysacousia, dysacousma, dysecoia
Dysämie *f* dysaemia
Dysäquilibrium *n* disequilibrium, instability *(z. B. Elektrolythaushalt)*
Dysarthrie *f* dysarthria *(Sprachstörung infolge Sprechmuskelstörung)*
dysarthrisch dysarthric
Dysarthrosis *f* dysarthrosis
Dysästhesie *f* dysaesthesia, abnormality of the sense of touch
Dysbakterie *f* disturbed bacterial flora
Dysbasie *f* dysbasia, difficulty in walking
Dysbulie *f* dysboulia, impairment of will power
Dyschezie *f* dyschezia, painful defaecation
Dyschirie *f* dyscheiria
Dyscholie *f* dyscholia
Dyschondroplasie *f* dyschondroplasia
Dyschromasie *f s.* 1. Dyschromie; 2. Dyschromatopsie

Dyschromatopsie *f* dyschromatopsia, partial colour blindness
Dyschromie *f* dyschromia, discoloration *(der Haut z. B. nach Syphilis)*
Dysdiadochokinese *f* dysdiadochokinesia *(Unfähigkeit zu schnellen entgegengesetzten Bewegungen, z. B. Pronation und Supination)*
Dysembryom *n* dysembryoma, teratoma, teratoid tumour
Dysemesis *f* dysemesis, painful vomiting; retching
dysendokrin dysendocrine
Dysendokrinismus *m* dysendocrinism
Dysenterie *f* dysentery
~/**bakterielle** bacillary dysentery, shigellosis
Dysenteriebazillus *m* dysentery (Shiga) bacillus
dysenteriebeseitigend antidysenteric
Dysenterieserum *n* antidysenteric serum
dysenterisch dysenteric
Dysergasie *f* dysergasia *(Geistesstörung infolge Giftwirkung)*
Dyserythropoese *f* dyserythropoiesis
Dysfibrinogenämie *f* dysfibrinogenaemia
Dysfunktion *f* dysfunction, abnormal function
Dysgammaglobulinämie *f* dysgammaglobulinaemia
Dysgenesie *f* dysgenesis, abnormal development
Dysgerminom *n* dysgerminoma, disgerminoma *(bösartige Eierstock- oder Hodengeschwulst)*
Dysgeusie *f* dysgeusia, abnormality of the sense of touch
Dysglobulinämie *f* dysglobulinaemia
dysgnath dysgnathic
Dysgnathie *f* dysgnathia
Dysgnosie *f* dysgnosia, disorder of intellectual function
dysgonisch dysgonic, seeding badly *(Bakterien)*
Dysgrammatismus *m* dysgrammatism, partial agrammatism
Dysgraphie *f* dysgraphia
Dyshäm[at]opoese *f* dyshaem[at]opoiesis
Dyshidrosis *f* 1. dyshidria, dyshidrosis; pompholyx; 2. cheiropompholyx *(Bläschenbildung an den Händen)*; podopompholyx *(Bläschenbildung an den Füßen)*
Dyshorie *f* dyshoria
dyshormonal dyshormonal, dyshormonic
Dyshormonose *f* dyshormonism
Dyskaryose *f* dyskaryosis
Dyskeratose *f* dyskeratosis
Dyskeratosis *f* **follicularis vegetans** follicular keratosis (psorospermosis), Darier's disease
dyskeratotisch dyskeratotic
Dyskinesie *f* dyskinesia *(der Muskeln)*
dyskinetisch dyskinetic
Dyskorie *f* dyscoria
Dyskrasie *f* dyscrasia
Dyslalie *f* dyslalia *(Sprachstörung)*
Dyslexie *f* dyslexia
Dyslipoproteinämie *f* dyslipoproteinaemia
Dyslochie *f* dyslochia, disordered lochial discharge

Dyslogie

Dyslogie f dyslogia *(Sprachstörung bei fehlerhafter Gedankenbildung)*
Dysmasesie f dysmasesis, difficult mastication, difficulty in chewing
Dysmaturität f dysmaturity
Dysmegalopsie f dysmegalopsia *(Sehstörung mit falscher Größenvorstellung)*
Dysmenorrhoe f dysmenorrhoea, difficult (painful) menstruation; menstrual colic
~/**angeborene** congenital dysmenorrhoea
~/**erworbene** acquired dysmenorrhoea
~/**primäre** primary (essential) dysmenorrhoea
~/**psychogene** psychogenic dysmenorrhoea
~/**sekundäre** secondary dysmenorrhoea
Dysmenorrhoea f **membranacea** membranous dysmenorrhoea *(schmerzhafter Abgang von Gebärmutterschleimhaut während der Regelblutung)*
dysmenorrhoisch dysmenorrhoeic
Dysmetrie f dysmetria *(Störung des Ausmaßes einer Zielbewegung)*
Dysmimie f dysmimia, inability to imitate
Dysmnesie f dysmnesia; impaired (defective) memory
dysmorph dysmorphic, malformed, ill-shaped
Dysmorphie f dysmorphia, deformity
Dysmyotonie f dysmyotonia
dysontogenetisch dysontogenetic
Dysontogenie f dysontogenesis *(z. B. des Gewebes)*
Dysopie f dysop[s]ia, defective vision
Dysorexie f dysorexia; impaired (deranged) appetite
Dysosmie f dysosmia; defect (impaired) sense of smell
Dysostosis f dysostosis, defective ossification
~ **cleidocranialis** cleidocranial dysostosis (dysplasia), anosteoplasia
~ **craniofacialis** craniofacial dysostosis, Crouzon's disease
~ **enchondralis metaepiphysaria Typ Morquio** Morquio's syndrome, mucopolysaccharidosis [type] IV, keratosulphaturia, familial osteochondrodystrophy, eccentro-chondroosteodystrophy
~ **mandibulofacialis** mandibulofacial dysostosis
~ **mandibulofacialis unilateralis** unilateral mandibular facial dysostosis
~ **multiplex** Hurler's disease (syndrome), mucopolysaccharidosis [type] I, Pfaundler-Hurler syndrome *(erbliche Phosphatidstoffwechselstörung)*
Dysparathyreoidismus m dysparathyroidism, disorder of parathyroid function
Dyspareunie f dyspareunia, difficult coitus
Dyspepsie f dyspepsia, indigestion, disturbed digestion
dyspeptisch dyspeptic
Dysperistaltik f dysperistalsis, painful (abnormal) peristalsis
dysphag dysphagic
Dysphagie f dysphagia, difficulty in swallowing
~/**sideropenische** sideropenic dysphagia
Dysphasie f dysphasia *(Sprachverlust infolge Hirnstörung)*
Dysphemie f dysphemia, stammering
Dysphonia f **spastica** phonic spasm
Dysphonie f dysphonia, impairment of voice
Dysphorie f 1. dysphoria, morbid restlessness; 2. physical discomfort, malaise
dysphorisch dysphoric
Dysphrasie f dysphrasia *(Sprachstörung infolge Intelligenzdefekts)*
Dyspituitarismus m dyspituitarism, disorder of pituitary function
Dysplasia f **epiphysialis multiplex** multiple osteochondritis
Dysplasie f dysplasia, abnormal development
~/**chondroektodermale** chondroectodermal dysplasia, Ellis-van Creveld syndrome
~/**chondromatöse** chondromatosis, multiple chondrome
~/**ektodermale** ectodermal dysplasia
~/**fibröse monostotische** monostotic fibrous dysplasia, Jaffé-Lichtenstein disease (syndrome)
~/**Lamy-Maroteauxsche** Maroteaux-Lamy syndrome, mucopolysaccharidosis [type] VI
dysplastisch dysplastic
Dysplenie f dyssplenism
Dyspnoe f dyspnoea, difficult respiration, laboured breathing; breathlessness
~ **bei Azetonämie** acetonasthma
dyspnoisch dyspnoeic, dyspnoeal
Dysporia f **broncho-entero-pancreatica [congenita familiaris]** cystic (fibrocystic) disease of the pancreas, cystic fibrosis [of the pancreas], mucoviscidosis, mucosis, familial (congenital) pancreatic steatorrhoea, chronic interstitial pancreatitis of infancy, Anderson's disease (syndrome) *(Sekretionsstörung mit Auswirkungen an Bauchspeicheldrüse, Bronchial- und Darmdrüsen)*
Dyspraxie f dyspraxia
Dysproteinämie f dysproteinaemia
Dysraphie f dysraphism, araphia
Dysrhythmie f dysrhythmia, disturbance of rhythm *(z. B. des Herzens)*
~/**respiratorische** respiratory dysrhythmia
dysrhythmisch dysrhythmic
Dyssekretion f dyssecretosis
Dyssomnie f dyssomnia, disorder of sleep
Dysspermie f dysspermia, dysspermatism
Dyssynergia f dyssynergia, asynergy, disturbance of muscular coordination
~ **cerebellaris myoclonia** myoclonus epilepsy, Hunt's disease
~ **cerebellaris progressiva** progressive cerebellar dyssynergy, dentate cerebellar ataxia
Dystasie f dysstasia, difficulty in standing
Dystaxie f dystaxia
Dysthanasie f dysthanasia, painful death
dysthym dysthymic
Dysthymie f 1. dysthymia, mental depression; 2. dysthymia, disorder of thymus function

Dysthyreose f dysthyroidism, thyroid disorder
Dystithie f dystithia, difficulty in breast-feeding, difficulty of nursing
dystok dystocic
Dystokie f dystocia, difficult labour (parturition), parodynia; slow birth
Dystonia f musculorum deformans Oppenheim's disease
Dystonie f dystonia, disorder of tonicity (z. B. von Muskeln und Gefäßen)
~/neurozirkulatorische neurocirculatory asthenia (syndrome); soldier's heart
~/vegetative neurodystonia
dystonisch dystonic
dystop dystopic, malpositional, displaced
Dystopie f dystopia, malposition, aberration, faulty placement of an organ
dystroph dystrophic, paratrophic
Dystrophia f s. Dystrophie
~ **adiposogenitalis** adiposogenital dystrophy (syndrome), neuropituitary syndrome, adiposogenitalism, Froehlich's syndrome, Babinski-Froehlich disease
~ **mesodermalis hyperplastica** Marchesani syndrome
~ **myotonica** myotonic [muscular] atrophy, myotonic dystrophy, atrophic myotonia
Dystrophie f dystrophy, defective (faulty) nutrition (s. a. unter Dystrophia)
~/Déjerine-Landouzysche Déjerine-Landouzy dystrophy (myopathy), fascioscapulohumeral muscular dystrophy
~/zerebromakuläre cerebromacular (cerebroretinal) degeneration
dystrophisch dystrophic, paratrophic
Dysurie f dysuria, difficult (painful) urination
Dyszephalie f dyscephalia
Dyszooamylie f dyszooamylia (Unfähigkeit der Glykogenspeicherung)
Dyszoospermie f dyszoospermia, disordered spermatozoon formation
D-Zelle f delta cell

E

E s. Emmetropie
Eales-Syndrom n Eales' disease, retinal periphlebitis (vasculitis), juvenile repeated retinal and vitreous haemorrhage
Eaton-Lambert-Syndrom n Eaton-Lambert syndrome, paraneoplastic (pseudomyasthenic) syndrome (bei kleinzelligem Bronchialkarzinom)
Eaton-Virus n Eaton virus (agent)
Ebbe-Flut-Drainage f tidal drainage
Eberthella f typhi (typhosa) Salmonella typhi (typhosa), typhoid bacillus
Ebner-Dentinfibrillen fpl Ebner's dentinal fibrils
Ebner-Drüsen fpl Ebner's glands (seröse Spüldrüsen der Zunge)
Ebola-Fieber n Ebola fever (hämorrhagisches Fieber in Zaïre)

Ebola-Virus n Ebola virus
Ebstein-Syndrom n Ebstein's anomaly (malformation, disease)
Eburnifikation f eburnation, eburnification, condensing (productive) osteitis
eburnifizieren to eburnate
Eburnisation f s. Eburnifikation
Echinokokke f echinococcus, caseworm
Echinokokkenbefall m s. Echinokokkose
Echinokokkenblase f hydatid
~/skolexfreie sterile [echinococcus] cyst, acephalocyst
Echinokokkenblasengeschwulst f hydatidoma
Echinokokkenfremitus m echinococcus fremitus, hydatid fremitus (thrill)
Echinokokkenkrankheit f s. Echinokokkose
Echinokokkose f echinococcosis, echinococciasis, hydatidosis, hydatid disease
Echinokokkushauttest m [nach Casoni] echinococcal skin test, echinococcus test, Casoni [skin] test, Casoni reaction
Echinokokkusleberzyste f echinococcal hepatic cyst
Echinokokkusnierenzyste f echinococcal cyst of kidney
Echinokokkustest m s. Echinokokkushauttest
Echinokokkustumor m hydatidoma
Echinokokkuszyste f hydatid (echinococcus) cyst
Echinokokkuszystenentfernung f[/operative] echinococcotomy
Echinokokkuszysteneröffnung f[/operative] hydatidostomy
Echinostoma n ilocanum Echinostoma ilocanum (Darmparasit auf Java)
~ **lindoënsis** Echinostoma lindoensis (Darmparasit auf Celebes)
Echinostomainfestation f echinostomiasis
Echoakusie f echoacousia, echoacousis, subjective experience of hearing echoes
Echoaortographie f echoaortography
Echoenzephalogramm n echo[sono]encephalogram, sonoencephalogram
Echoenzephalograph m echoencephalograph, sonoencephalograph
Echoenzephalographie f echoencephalography, sonoencephalography
echoenzephalographisch echoencephalographic
Echoerscheinungen fpl echo phenomena
Echogramm n echo[sono]gram, [ultra]sonogram
Echographie f 1. echography, [ultra]sonography, ultrasonication; 2. echographia (Form der Aphasie oder Agraphie)
echographisch echographic, [ultra]sonographic
Echohören n s. Echoakusie
Echokardiogramm n echocardiogram
Echokardiographie f echocardiography
echokardiographisch echocardiographic
Echokardiotomographie f ultrasonic cardiotomography, ultrasono-cardiotomography
echokardiotomographisch ultrasonic-cardiotomographic

Echokinese

Echokinese f echokinesia, echokinesis, echomatism, echopraxia
echokinetisch echokinesic
echolal echolalic
Echolalie f echolalia, echophrasia, echo speech
echolalisch echolalic
Echomimie f echomimia, imitation of movements
Echookulogramm n echooculogram
Echookulographie f echooculography
echookulographisch echooculographic
Echoorbitogramm n echoorbitogram
Echoorbitographie f echoorbitography
echoorbitographisch echoorbitographic
Echopathie f echopathy
echopathisch echopathic
Echophonie f echophony
Echophrasie f s. Echolalie
Echopraxie f s. Echokinese
Echorenogramm n echorenogram
Echorenographie f echorenography
echorenographisch echorenographic
Echotomogramm n echotomogram
Echotomographie f echotomography
echotomographisch echotomographic
Echouterogramm n echouterogram
Echouterographie f echouterography
echouterographisch echouterographic
ECHO-Virus n ECHO virus, enteric cytopathogenic human orphan virus
ECHO-Virusinfektion f ECHO virus infection
Echtheit f **der Gefühlsäußerung** genuineness *(bei Psychotherapie)*
Eckzahn m canine [tooth], eye tooth
Eckzahngrube f canine fossa
Eckzahnmuskel m caninus [muscle]
Ecstrophia f ex[s]trophy
~ **vesicae** extrophy of the bladder, fissure of the urinary bladder
Ecthyma n ecthyma, pustular eruption
~ **syphiliticum** ecthymatous syphilid
Ectopia f ectopia *(s. a. unter Ektopie)*
~ **cordis** ectocardia, exocardia, displacement of the heart
~ **lentis** ectopia lentis, displacement of the crystalline lens
~ **pupillae congenita** ectopia pupillae congenita, congenital displacement of the pupil
Ectropium n s. Ektropium
ED s. 1. Erythemdosis; 2. Erhaltungsdosis
Eddowes-Syndrom n Eddowes' disease (syndrome), osteogenesis imperfecta
Edinger-Westphal-Kern m Edinger-Westphal nucleus of the oculomotor nerve
EDTA EDTA, ethylenediamine tetraacetic acid
Edwards-Syndrom n Edwards' (trisomy 18) syndrome, trisomy E syndrome
EEG s. Elektroenzephalogramm
EEG-Ableitung f electroencephalographic lead
EEG-Aufzeichnung f electroencephalography
EEG-Schreiber m electroencephalograph
Effekt m/**virulenzsteigernder** virulence-enhancing effect
~/**zytostatischer** cytostatic action
Effektivdosis f effective dose, ED 50
Effektivtemperatur f effective temperature
Effektor m effector *(Physiologie)*
Effektornerv m effector (efferent) nerve
Effektorzelle f effector cell
Effeminierung f effemination
efferent efferent, carrying (conducting) away
Efferenz f efference *(Nervenphysiologie)*
Efferveszenz f effervescence, onset (invasion) of a disease *(z. B. bei Infektionskrankheiten)*
Efflation f eructation, belching
Effloreszenz f efflorescence, skin eruption (rash)
Effloreszenzenrückbildung f deflorescence
effloreszieren to effloresce *(z. B. Hautausschlag)*
effloreszierend efflorescent
Effluvium n 1. effluvium, efflux, outflow *(s. a. Erguß)*; 2. effluvium, exhalation; emanation
Effort-Syndrom n effort (Da Costa's) syndrome, angina of effort
Effusion f effusion *(Zusammensetzungen s. unter Erguß)*
Egesta npl egesta, ejecta, excrements, excreted matter
Egoismus m egoism
Egoist m egoist
egoistisch egoistic
Egozentrie f egocentricity, egocentrism
egozentrisch egocentric, self-centered
Eheabneigung f, **Ehehaß** m s. Eheverachtung
ehelich conjugal, marital; legitimate *(Kind)*
ehelos unmarried, agamous
Eheverächter m misogamist
Eheverachtung f misogamy, aversion to marriage
Ehlers-Danlos-Syndrom n [Ehlers-]Danlos syndrome, congenital mesodermal dystrophy, generalized elastic fibrodysplasia, dermatorrhexis; india-rubber man
Ehrenritter-Ganglion n Ehrenritter's ganglion, superior ganglion of the glossopharyngeal nerve
Ehrlich-Karzinom n Ehrlich carcinoma (tumour) *(transplantables Karzinom)*
Ei n egg, ovum
~/**befruchtetes** fecundated ovum, spermatovum
Eialbumin n ovalbumin, egg albumin
eiartig ovoid, egg-shaped
Eiaustritt m s. Eisprung
Eibefruchtung f fertilization, fecundation, insemination of the egg ● **vor der** ~ progamic, progamous
eibildend oogenetic, ovigen[et]ic, ovigenous, ovulogenous
Eibildung f oogenesis, ovigenesis, ovogenesis
Eichel f glans, balanus
Eichelbändchen n frenulum (frenum) of the prepuce
Eichelblutung f balanorrhagia
Eichelentzündung f balanitis, inflammation of the glans penis
~/**eitrige** balanorrhoea, purulent balanitis
Eichelgonorrhoe f balanoblenorrhoea, gonorrhoeal inflammation of the glans penis

Eichelhypospadie f balanic hypospadias
Eichelplastik f balanoplasty, plastic surgery of the glans penis
Eicheltripper m s. Eichelgonorrhoe
Eichel- und Vorhautentzündung f balanoposthitis
Eichelvorhautkatarrh m balanoposthitis
Eid m des Hippokrates oath of Hippokrates, hippokratic oath
Eidotter n vitellus, yolk, deut[er]oplasm
Eieinnistung f nidation, implantation of the ovum (in der Gebärmutterschleimhaut)
eienthaltend oviferous
Eientwicklung f oogenesis, ovigenesis, ovogenesis
Eierschalenknistern n parchment (Dupuytren's eggshell) crackling
Eierschalennagel m egg-shell nail
Eierstock m ovary, o[v]arium, oophoron, female gonad ● **aus dem ~ stammend** oophorogenous, ovariogenic ● **durch den ~ bedingt** oophorogenous (z. B. Krankheit)
~/vereiterter pyo-ovarium
Eierstock... s. a. Ovarial... und Oophor...
Eierstockabszeß m ovarian (ovary) abscess; pyoovarium
Eierstockanheftung f oophoro[pelio]pexy; oopho[ro]rrhaphy
Eierstockanlage f primary ovary
Eierstockaplasie f ovarian aplasia
Eierstockarterie f ovarian artery
Eierstockband n ovarian ligament
Eierstockblutung f oophorrhagia, haemorrhage from the ovary
Eierstockdermoidzyste f ovarian dermoid cyst
Eierstockdysgenesie f ovarian dysgenesis
Eierstockeiterung f ovarian (ovary) abscess; pyoovarium
Eierstockentfernung f[/operative] excision of an ovary, ovariectomy, ovariosteresis, oophorectomy, oothecectomy; female castration
Eierstockentzündung f ovaritis, oophoritis, inflammation of an ovary
Eierstockerkrankung f ovariopathy, oophoropathy, ovarian disease
Eierstockerweichung f oophoromalacia, softening of an ovary
Eierstockfistelung f ovariostomy, oophorostomy
Eierstockfixierung f oophoro[pelio]pexy, ovariopexia, fixation of an ovary; oopho[ro]rrhaphy
Eierstockfollikel m ovarian follicle, ovisac
~/degenerierter atretic follicle
Eierstockfunktionsschwäche f hypoovar[ian]ism
Eierstockfunktionsstörung f dysovarism
Eierstockgekröse n mesovarium
Eierstockgeschwulst f oophoroma, ovarian tumour, ovarioncus
Eierstockhilus m hilum of the ovarium
Eierstockhormon n ovarian hormone
Eierstockhyperplasie f ovarian hyperplasia
Eierstockhypertrophie f ovarian hypertrophy

Eierstockhypoplasie f ovarian hypoplasia
Eierstockinsuffizienz f ovarian insufficiency
Eierstockkrebs m ovarian cancer (carcinoma)
Eierstockleiden n ovariopathy, oophoropathy, ovarian disease
Eierstockmorphologie f ovarian morphology
Eierstocknaht f oophorrhaphy
Eierstocknervengeflecht n ovarian plexus
Eierstockneuralgie f ovarian neuralgia, ovariodysneuria
Eierstockplastik f oophoroplasty, plastic operation of the ovary
Eierstockpol m/unterer lower pole of the ovary
Eierstockpseudomyxom n ovarian pseudomyxoma
Eierstockpunktion f ovariocentesis, puncture of an ovary
Eierstockruptur f ovariorrhexis, rupture of an ovary
Eierstockschmerz m ovarialgia, oophoralgia, oothecalgia
Eierstockschnitt m ovariotomy, oophorotomy
Eierstockschwangerschaft f ovarian pregnancy, ovariocyesis, oocyesis
Eierstocktasche f ovarian bursa
Eierstockteratom n ovarian teratoma, compound ovarian tumour
Eierstocktransplantat n ovarian graft
Eierstocktransplantation f ovarian transplantation
Eierstocküberfunktion f hyperovar[ian]ism
Eierstock- und Eileiterbruch m salpingo-oophorocele, salpingo-oothecocele
Eierstock- und Eileiterentzündung f oophorosalpingitis
Eierstock- und Eileiterexstirpation f ovariosalpingectomy, oophorosalpingectomy
Eierstockunterfunktion f hypoovar[ian]ism
Eierstockvene f ovarian vein
~/linke left ovarian vein
~/rechte right ovarian vein
Eierstockverdrehung f ovarian torsion
Eierstockvereiterung f ovarian abscess; pyoovarium
Eierstockvergrößerung f oophorauxe, enlargement of the ovary
Eierstockverhärtung f sclero-oophoritis, sclero-oothecitis
Eierstockvorfall m ovariocele, ovarian hernia (Senkung des Eierstocks in einen Leistenbruch)
Eierstockwucherung f oophorauxe
eierstockzerstörend ovariolytic
Eierstockzyste f ovarian (oophoritic) cyst
Eierstockzystenbildung f oophorocystosis
Eierstockzystenentfernung f[/operative] oophorocystectomy
Eierstockzystenfistelung f oophorocystostomy
eiertragend ovigerous
Eifersuchtswahn m delusion of infidelity
eiförmig ovoid, oviform, egg-shaped
Eifreisetzung f s. Eisprung
Eifurchung f cleavage (segmentation) of the ovum

eigelbarm 194

eigelbarm oligolecithal *(Eizelle)*
Eigelenk *n* condylar joint, condyloid (ellipsoid) articulation, condylarthrosis
Eigen... *s. a.* Selbst... *und* Auto...
Eigenamputation *f* autoamputation
Eigenanamnese *f* autoanamnesis
Eigenbewegung *f* spontaneous movement
Eigenbewußtsein *n* autopsyche
Eigenblutbehandlung *f* autohaemotherapy
Eigenblutinjektion *f* autohaemotherapy
Eigenbluttransfusion *f* auto[re]transfusion
Eigendiagnose *f* autodiagnosis
Eigenfluoreszenz *f* autofluorescence
Eigenfunktion *f* characteristic function
Eigengeruch *m* characteristic odour
Eigengewebetransplantat *n* autograft, autotransplant, autogenous graft, autoplast
Eigengewebetransplantation *f* autografting, autotransplantation, autoplasty
eigengewebeverpflanzend autoplastic
Eigenhauttransplantation *f* dermato-autoplasty
Eigenhören *n* autophonia, tympanophonia
Eigeninfusion *f* autoinfusion, autotransfusion *(Blutumverteilung durch Extremitätenkompression)*
Eigeninokulation *f* autoinoculation, self-inoculation, self-injection
Eigenliebe *f* egoism
Eigenreflex *m* proprioceptive reflex
Eigenreflexe *mpl*/**fehlende** areflexia
Eigenrezeptor *m* proprioceptor
Eigenrhythmus *m*/**ventrikulärer** idioventricular rhythm
Eigenschaft *f*/**angeborene** innateness
Eigenserum *n* autoserum
Eigenserumbehandlung *f* autoserotherapy
Eigenserumdiagnostik *f* autoserodiagnosis
Eigenstimulation *f* self-stimulation
Eigenstrahlung *f* characteristic (natural) radiation
Eigentoxin *n* autotoxin
Eigenvakzination *f* autovaccination, self-inoculation
Eigenvakzine *f* autovaccine, autogenous vaccine
Eigenvakzinebehandlung *f* autogenous vaccine theraphy
Eigenverletzung *f* autolesion, self-inflicted lesion *(s. a.* Selbstverstümmelung*)*
Eignungsprüfung *f* aptitude test
Eihaut *f* 1. amnion, amnios, foetal membrane *(Embryologie)*; 2. oolemma
Eihautbildung *f* amniogenesis
Eihäute *fpl* birth membranes
Eihautentzündung *f* amnionitis, amniotitis, inflammation of the amnion
Eihautkultur *f* chorioallantoic (chicken embryo) culture *(Mikrobiologie)*
Eihautsack *m* amniotic sac
Eihautschnitt *m* amniotomy
Eihautzerreißung *f* amniorrhexis, foetus membrane rupture, amniotic sac rupture
Eihügel *m* ovarian cumulus, vitelline (ovigerous) disk

Eiimplantation *f* nidation, implantation of the ovary
Eikeimzelle *f* ovigerm
Eikonometer *n* eikonometer, aniseikometer *(ophthalmologisches Gerät)*
Eileiter *m* [uterine] tube, tuba, Fallopian tube, salpinx [uterina], oviduct ● **neben dem** ~ paratubal, parasalpingeal
~/vereiterter pyosalpinx, pus tube
Eileiter... *s. a.* Tuben...
Eileiterablösung *f* salpingolysis
Eileiterabort *m* tubal abortion
Eileiterabszeß *m* uterine tube abscess, pyosalpinx
Eileiteradenomyom *n* endosalpingioma
Eileiterampulle *f* ampulla of the uterine tube
Eileiterampullenabort *m* ampullar abortion
Eileiteranheftung *f*[/**operative**] salpingopexy
Eileiter-Bauchhöhlen-Schwangerschaft *f* tuboabdominal pregnancy
Eileiterbeweglichkeit *f* uterine tube motility
Eileiterblutung *f* haem[at]osalpinx; haemorrhagic salpingitis
Eileiterdarstellung *f* salpingography
Eileiter-Eierstock-Abszeß *m* tubo-ovarian abscess
Eileiter-Eierstock-Schwangerschaft *f* tubo-ovarian pregnancy
Eileiter-Eierstock-Zyste *f* tubo-ovarian cyst
Eileiter-Eileiter-Anastomose *f* salpingosalpingostomy, salpingostomatomy
Eileitereinpflanzung *f* **in die Gebärmutter** hysterosalpingostomy
Eileiterendometriose *f* endosalpingiosis, tubal endometriosis (adenomyosis), isthmic nodular salpingitis
Eileiterenge *f* isthmus of the Fallopian (uterine) tube
Eileiterentfernung *f* **durch Bauchschnitt** laparosalpingectomy
~/operative salpingectomy, tubectomy
Eileiterentzündung *f* salpingitis, inflammation of the oviduct (Fallopian tube)
~/eitrige pyosalpingitis, purulent (pyogenic) salpingitis
Eileitereröffnung *f* **durch Bauchschnitt** laparosalpingotomy
~/operative salpingotomy, incision of the oviduct
Eileiterfalte *f* tubal plica
Eileiterfistel *f* salpingostomy; tubal fistula
Eileiterfistelung *f*[/**operative**] salpingostomy
Eileitergekröse *n* mesosalpinx
Eileitergonorrhoe *f* gonococcal salpingitis
Eileiterhernie *f* salpingocele
Eileiterhydrops *m* hydrosalpinx
Eileiterlösung *f* salpingolysis
Eileitermole *f* tubal (uterine tube) mole
Eileiternaht *f* salpingorrhaphy
Eileiteröffnung *f* **in die Bauchhöhle** fimbriated end of the oviduct
Eileiterplastik *f* salpingoplasty, [uterine] tuboplasty

Eileiterresektion f salpingectomy, resection (excision) of an oviduct
Eileiterriß m tubal (uterine tube) rupture
Eileiterröntgen[kontrast]bild n salpingogram
Eileiterröntgen[kontrast]darstellung f salpingography
Eileiterschleimhaut f uterine tube mucosa, endosalpinx, mucous membrane of the uterine tube
Eileiterschleimhautentzündung f endosalpingitis
Eileiterschleimhautfalte f tubal plica
Eileiterschwangerschaft f tubal pregnancy, oviductal (Fallopian, uterine tube) pregnancy, salpingocyesis
Eileitertrichter m infundibulum of the uterine tube
Eileitertuberkulose f tuberculous salpingitis
Eileiter- und Bauchfellentzündung f salpingoperitonitis
Eileiter- und Eierstockbruch m salpingo-oophorocele
Eileiter- und Eierstockentfernung f durch Bauchschnitt laparosalpingo-oophorectomy
~/operative salpingo-oophorectomy, salpingo-ovariectomy, salpingo-ovariotomy, tubo-ovariotomy
Eileiter- und Eierstockentzündung f salpingo-oophoritis, salpingo-oothecitis, tubo-ovaritis
~/eitrige pyosalpingo-oophoritis
Eileiter- und Eierstockhernie f salpingo-oophorocele
Eileiterunterbindung f uterine tube ligation
Eileiterverdickung f/entzündliche pachysalpingitis, parenchymatous salpingitis
Eileitervereinigung f[/operative] salpingosalpingostomy, salpingostomatomy
Eileitervereiterung f pyosalpingitis; pus tube, pyosalpinx
Eileiterverengung f uterine tube obstruction
Eileiterverklebung f uterine tube occlusion, tubal block
Eileiterverkochung f uterine tube coagulation
Eileiterverlegung f salpingemphraxis
Eileiterverpflanzung f uterine tube transplantation
Eileiterverschleimung f mucosalpinx
Eileiterverschluß m uterine tube occlusion, tubal block
Eileiterverstopfung f salpingemphraxis
Eileiterwiedereinpflanzung f uterine tube reimplantation
eilos anovular, anovulatory
Eilösung f s. Eisprung
einarmig monobrachial, one-armed
einäschern to cremate, to incinerate
Einäscherung f cremation, incineration
Einäscherungshalle f crematory
einatmen to inspire, to breathe in; to inhale
~/Dämpfe to inhale
~/tief to take a deep breath
Einatmen n inspiration, breathing-in; inhalation (z. B. von Dämpfen)
Einatmungsluft f inspired air

einäugig 1. monocular, uniocular, one-eyed, monophthalmic (ein Auge betreffend); 2. cyclopic, cyclopean (z. B. Mißbildung)
Einäugigkeit f 1. monophthalmia, unilateral anophthalmia; 2. cyclopia, synophthalmia (z. B. Mißbildung)
einbalsamieren to embalm, to mummify
Einbalsamierung f embalmment
einbeinig monoscelous, one-legged
einbetten 1. to embed, to include (z. B. histologische Schnitte); 2. s. einnisten/sich; 3. s. einpflanzen
~/in Paraffin to embed in paraffin
Einbetten n 1. embedding, mounting, inclusion (histologischer Schnitte); 2. s. Einnistung; 3. s. Einpflanzung
Einbettungsmittel n mountant, mounting medium, embedding compound
einbiegen to incurvate
Einbiegung f incurvation
Einbildung f imagination; illusion; hallucination
Einbildungskraft f power of imagination; fantasy, phantasy
einblasen to insufflate, to blow into
Einblasen n insufflation (z. B. von Medikamentenpulvern oder Gasen)
Einbläser m insufflator
einbrechend invasive (z. B. bösartige Geschwulst)
Einbruch m invasion (z. B. einer bösartigen Geschwulst)
Einbuchtung f recess[us]; incisure, incisura; fissure; groove; vallecula; crypt
eindämmen to control (z. B. eine Infektion)
eindampfen to evaporate, to inspissate
Eindampfen n evaporation, inspissation
Eindellung f dell, dimple, slight depression, impression, gutter
eindicken to thicken, to inspissate
Eindickung f thickening, inspissation
eindringen to infiltrate (z. B. Geschwulst); to penetrate (z. B. Fremdkörper); to invade (z. B. Krankheitskeime); to diffuse (z. B. Gase)
Eindringen n infiltration (z. B. einer Geschwulst); penetration (z. B. eines Fremdkörpers); invasion (z. B. von Krankheitskeimen); diffusion (von Gasen)
eindringend invasive
~/nicht [in den Körper] non-invasive
Eindringungsfähigkeit f invasiveness (z. B. von Krankheitskeimen, Tumorzellen)
eindrüsig uniglandular
Einehe f monogamy
eineiig univoval, uniovular, monovular, monozygotic, enzygotic
einengen to constrain, to constrict; to contract; to coarctate
Einengung f 1. stricture (z. B. des Darms); coarctation (z. B. der Aorta); stenosis (z. B. eines Gefäßes); 2. constriction; contraction (Vorgang)
~ des Schädelinnenraums craniostenosis

einfach

einfach simple, uncomplicated (z. B. Knochenbruch); primitive (z. B. Denken); haploid (Chromosomensatz)
Einfachblindstudie f single-blind study
einfächerig monolocular, unilocular
einfachgebärend monotocous
Einfachschwangerschaft f monocyesis
Einfachsehen n, **Einfachsichtigkeit** f haplopia
einfachzähnig haploidentical
Einfachzucker m simple sugar, monosaccharide
einfädig monofilament[ous], unifilar
einfallend invasive (z. B. Bakterien); incident (Strahlen)
einfältig simple[-minded]
Einfarbensehen n monochromatopsia, monochromasia, monochromatism (Farbenblindheit mit einfarbigem Zapfensehen und guter zentraler Sehschärfe)
einfarbig monochrom[at]ic, monochroic
einfingrig monodactylous
Einfingrigkeit f monodactyly
Einfließen n infusion, inflow
einflößen to instil[l], to infuse
Einflößen n instillation, infusion
Einflußbahn f inflow tract (Herz)
Einflußstauung f neck vein distension
Einfühlungsvermögen n empathy
einführen/ein Instrument to insert (introduce) an instrument
~/einen Katheter to catheterize, to introduce a catheter
~/einen Tubus to intubate (in die Luftröhre)
Einfuhr- und Ausfuhrkurve f intake and output chart (z. B. bei Infusionstherapie)
Einführung f insertion, introduction; intromission
Einführungssonde f für Giglisägen Gigli's saw guide
einfüßig monoscelous, one-footed
Einfüßiger m monopus
Einfüßigkeit f monopodia
Eingang m orifice, orificium, ostium, aperture, mouth, aditus, entrance, introitus (zu einer Körperhöhle)
eingeben to administer, to give (z. B. Medikamente)
~/durch den Mund to give by mouth
eingebildet imaginary, fictitious; illusory, illusional
eingeboren 1. native, indigenous; 2. s. angeboren
eingedickt thickened, pachytic
eingefallen pinched (z. B. Gesicht); sunken, hollow (z. B. Augen)
eingeißelig monotrichous
eingekeilt impacted (z. B. Fraktur)
eingeklemmt incarcerated, strangulated (z. B. Hernie); impacted (z. B. Meniskus) ● ~ **werden** to become impacted (z. B. Meniskus)
eingelenkig mon[o]articular, monarthric, uniarticular
eingeliefert werden/in das Krankenhaus to be hospitalized, to be taken to the hospital
eingerenkt/nicht unreduced (Gelenk)
eingerichtet/nicht unreduced (Knochenbruch)
eingerissen lacerated (z. B. ein Muskel)
eingescheidet invaginated (z. B. der Darm)
eingeschlafen numb (z. B. eine Extremität)
eingeschlechtig monosexual, unisexual
eingeschmolzen/eitrig mature (z. B. Abszeß)
eingeschnürt incarcerated, strangulated, constricted (z. B. der Darm)
eingestaltig monomorphic, monomorphous
Eingestaltigkeit f monomorphism
eingestülpt invaginated (z. B. der Darm)
Eingestülptes n intussusceptum (z. B. ein Darmabschnitt)
eingetrocknet dry, xerotic
Eingeweide n[pl] bowels, intestines, guts; enteron; viscera ● **auf die Eingeweide gerichtet** viscerotropic (z. B. Bakterien)
Eingeweideabschnitt m viscerotome
Eingeweidebruch m [intestinal] hernia, splanchnocele, enterocele
~/Richterscher Richter's hernia
Eingeweideempfindung f splanchnaesthesia
Eingeweideerkrankung f splanchnopathy
Eingeweideeröffnung f/**transabdominale** coelioenterotomy
Eingeweideganglion n visceral ganglion
Eingeweidegeflecht n enteric (visceral) plexus
Eingeweidegefühl n splanchnaesthesia
eingeweidehemmend visceroinhibitory
Eingeweidehormon n intestinal hormone
Eingeweideinduration f splanchnosclerosis
Eingeweidekrampf m enterospasm, spasm of the intestine
Eingeweidelehre f splanchnology
Eingeweidemesser n viscerotome
Eingeweidemißbildung f perosplanchnia, malformation of the viscera
Eingeweidemuskel m visceral (involuntary) muscle (s. a. Muskel/glatter)
Eingeweidemuskulatur f involuntary (non-striated) musculature, visceral muscles
Eingeweidenerv m splanchnic (visceral) nerve
~/kleiner lesser splanchnic nerve
Eingeweidenervendurchtrennung f[/**operative**] splanchnicotomy
Eingeweidenervenrezeptor m visceroceptor
Eingeweidenervensystem n visceral nervous system
Eingeweideobstruktion f splanchnemphraxis
Eingeweideorgan n viscus.
Eingeweideparasit m enterozoon, visceral parasite
Eingeweideprolaps m splanchnocele, visceral prolapse
Eingeweidereflex m visceral reflex
Eingeweiderheumatismus m visceral rheumatism
Eingeweideröntgen[kontrast]bild n viscerogram
Eingeweideröntgen[kontrast]darstellung f viscerography
Eingeweideruptur f visceral rupture

Eingeweideschmerz m visceralgia, splanchnodynia, enteralgia
Eingeweideschnitt m viscerotomy
Eingeweidesenkung f splanchnoptosis, enteroptosis, visceroptosis, Glénard's disease, abdominal ptosis
Eingeweidespiegelung f splanchnoscopy
Eingeweidestein m splanchnolith, enterolith
Eingeweidesteinerkrankung f splanchnolithiasis, enterolithiasis
eingeweidestimulierend visceromotor
Eingeweidetransposition f transposition of the viscera
Eingeweidevergrößerung f[/abnorme] splanchnomegaly, visceromegaly, enteromegaly
Eingeweideverhärtung f splanchnosclerosis
Eingeweideverkleinerung f[/abnorme] splanchnomicria
Eingeweideverlagerung f splanchnectopia
Eingeweidevorfall m 1. s. Eingeweideprolaps; 2. evisceration, eventration *(z. B. aus einer Bauchwunde)*
Eingeweidevorlagerung f eventration *(z. B. bei Operation)*
Eingeweidewurm m [intestinal] helminth, enthelminth
Eingeweidezerlegung f splanchnotomy
Eingeweidezerreißung f visceral disruption
eingewiesen werden/in das Krankenhaus to be taken to the hospital
eingipfelig monocrotic *(Pulskurve)*
Eingipfeligkeit f monocrotism *(der Pulskurve)*
eingipsen to put (fix) in plaster *(z. B. eine Gliedmaße)*
Eingliederung f rehabilitation
Eingriff m 1. measure, procedure; treatment; intervention; 2. s. ~/operativer ● **durch ärztlichen** ~ medical; operative, operational, surgical
~/**chirurgischer** [surgical] operation
~/**explorativer** exploratory operation
~/**koronarchirurgischer** coronary surgery
~/**operativer** operation, operational treatment, operative procedure, surgical intervention
einheimisch 1. endemic, nostrate *(z. B. Krankheiten)*; 2. native, indigenous *(z. B. Personen)*
Einheit f unit
~/**biologische** biological unit
~/**enzymatische** enzymatic (enzyme) unit
~/**fetoplazentale** foetoplacental unit
~/**Internationale** international unit, I. U. *(für Wirkstoffe)*
~/**motorische** motor unit
einhergehen [mit] to be accompanied [by] *(z. B. eine Krankheit)*
einhodig monorchid
Einhodigkeit f monorchi[di]sm
einhornig unicornous
einimpfen to inoculate *(z. B. Impfstoff)*; to [in]vaccinate *(z. B. Pockenlymphe)*; to inject *(z. B. mit einer Spritze)*

Einimpfung f inoculation *(z. B. von Serum)*; [in]vaccination *(z. B. von Pockenlymphe)*; injection *(z. B. mit einer Spritze)*
einkammrig unicamerate, single-chambered
einkapseln to encapsulate; to encyst; to embed
~/**sich** to become encapsulated
Einkapselung f encapsulation; encystation, encystment
Einkeilung f impaction *(z. B. eines Knochenbruchs)*; gomphosis *(z. B. der Zähne)*
einkeimig monogerminal, unigerminal
einkernig mononuclear, uninuclear
Ein-Kind-Sterilität f one-child sterility
einklemmen to incarcerate, to strangulate *(z. B. Darmschlingen)*; to impact *(z. B. einen Knochenbruch)*
Einklemmung f 1. incarceration, strangulation *(z. B. eines Eingeweidebruchs)*; 2. impaction *(z. B. eines Knochenbruchs)*
Einklemmungsbruch m 1. incarcerated hernia; 2. impacted fracture
einköpfig uniceps *(Muskel)*
Einkoten n encopresis
Einlage f 1. temporary filling; 2. inlay *(Stomatologie)*; 3. instep raiser, arch-support *(Orthopädie)*
Einlagefüllung f inlay *(Stomatologie)*
einlagern to deposit, to store *(z. B. Substanzen)*; to impregnate *(z. B. Farbstoffe)*; to embed *(Gewebeschnitte)*; to infiltrate *(Flüssigkeit)*
~/**Hyalin** to hyalinize
~/**Mineralien** to mineralize
Einlagerung f deposition, storage *(z. B. von Substanzen)*; infiltration *(z. B. von Flüssigkeit)*; impregnation *(z. B. von Farbstoffen)*; mounting, embedding *(von Gewebeschnitten)*
einlappig monolobular, unilob[ul]ar
Einlauf m enema, clyster, rectal injection ● **einen** ~ **machen** to administer an enema
~/**hoher** high enema
Einlaufmittel n enema
einlegen to embed *(z. B. Gewebeschnitte)*
~/**einen Tamponadestreifen** to tampon[ade]
Einlegestab m obturator, mandrin *(einer Hohlkanüle)*
einleiten 1. to induce, to initiate *(z. B. eine Behandlung)*; 2. to introduce, to fill in *(z. B. Flüssigkeiten)*
~/**eine Anästhesie** to anaesthetize
einliefern/in ein Krankenhaus to admit (take) to the hospital
Einlieferung f admission *(in ein Krankenhaus)*
● **vor der** ~ **geboren** born before arrival
Einmalgebrauchsblutlanzette f disposable blood lancet
Einmalgebrauchskanüle f disposable hypodermic cannula (needle)
Einmalgebrauchsplastiksonde f disposable plastic tube
Einmalgebrauchsspritze f disposable syringe
Einmal-pro-Tag-Dosierung f once-a-day-dosage
Einmaltransfusionsbesteck n disposable transfusion pack, disposable plastic transfusion set

Einnässen

Einnässen n **am Tag** diurnal enuresis
~/nächtliches nocturnal enuresis, nocturia
einnässend enuretic
einnehmen/Arzneimittel to take a medicament, to dose
~/Kokain to cocainize
Einnehmen n ingestion *(z. B. von Nahrung)*, taking *(z. B. von Medizin)* ● **nicht zum ~** for external application *(Medikament)*
einnervig mononeural
einnierig mononephrous
einnisten/sich to become implanted *(z. B. befruchtetes Ei)*
Einnistung f nidation, implantation, embedding *(z. B. der befruchteten Eizelle in die Gebärmutterschleimhaut)*
einohrig monotic, uniaural
einpacken to pack
einpassen to fit; to position; to adjust; to adapt
einpflanzen to implant, to graft *(z. B. Gewebe)*
Einpflanzung f implantation, plantation, grafting *(z. B. von Gewebe)*
einpinseln to paint *(z. B. den Rachen)*
Ein-Punkt-Diskriminierung f one-point discrimination *(Tastsinn)*
Einreibemittel n embrocation; liniment *(flüssig)*
einreiben to rub [in], to embrocate
einreibend iatraliptic
Einreibung f 1. embrocation, [in]friction, rubbing in, [in]unction; 2. s. Einreibemittel
einreißen to lacerate, to tear *(z. B. Organe)*; to split *(z. B. einen Nagel)*
Einreißen n laceration
einrenken to set, to reduce *(z. B. eine Fraktur)*; to set *(z. B. eine Luxation)*
Einrenkung f **von Gelenken** reposition, reduction, diaplasis
einrichten to set, to reduce *(einen Knochenbruch)*; to coapt *(z. B. Wundränder)*
Einrichtung f/**ambulante** ambulant clinic
Einrichtungen fpl/**sanitäre** sanitation
Einrichtungsinstrument n repositor
Einriß m laceration, tear *(z. B. in einem Organ)*; rhagade, crack, fissure *(z. B. in der Haut)*
einritzen/die Haut to scarify, to scratch
Einsalbung f [in]unction *(s. a. Einreibung 1.)*
Einsamkeitsdrang m [/**krankhafter**] agromania, insane passion for solitude
Einsamkeitspsychose f isolation psychosis
einsaugen to resorb, to suck in, to absorb, to imbibe
einscheiden to invaginate
Einscheidung f invagination, intussusception, introsusception
Einschichtenanastomose f single-layer anastomosis
Einschichtenepithel n simple (single-layered) epithelium
Einschichtengewebekultur f monolayer tissue culture
einschichtig single-layered, unilaminar, monostratified

einschieben to insert *(z. B. ein Instrument)*
~/einen Tubus to intubate *(in die Luftröhre)*
einschießen 1. to lancinate *(Schmerzen)*; 2. to rush in *(Milch)*
Einschlafdosis f narcotic dose
einschlafen 1. to fall (drop) asleep; 2. to get (go) to sleep, to become numb *(Gliedmaßen)*
einschläfern to put to sleep; to narcotize, to anaesthetize; to hypnotize
einschläfernd narcotic, somnifacient, somnific, soporiferous, soporific; hypnogen[et]ic, hypnogenous, hypnagogic
Einschläferung f narcotization, anaesthetization; hypnotization, hypnoidization, hypno[si]genesis
Einschlaffurcht f hypnophobia
Einschlafhalluzination f hypnagogic hallucination
Einschlafmittel n narcotic, somnifacient agent, soporific, hypnagogue
Einschlafstörung f difficulty in falling asleep
einschlägig 1. monocrotic *(Puls)*; 2. appropriate *(z. B. Medikament)*
Einschlägigkeit f monocrotism *(des Pulses)*
Einschlagtuch n pack-sheet, wet sheet
Einschleichen n creeping *(z. B. eines Reizes)*
einschleppen to introduce *(z. B. eine Infektion)*; to import *(z. B. eine Krankheit)*
einschließen to include, to enclose
Einschlußblennorrhoe f inclusion blennorrhoea
Einschlußkonjunktivitis f inclusion (swimming-pool, diver's) conjunctivitis, paratrachoma
Einschlußkörperchen n 1. inclusion body; 2. cytomegalic inclusion body
Einschlußkörperchen npl/**Guarniersche** Guarnieri bodies, eosinophilic cytoplasmic inclusions *(bei Pockenvirusinfektion)*
~/Halberstädter-Prowazeksche trachoma bodies (granulations) *(bei Trachom)*
~/Negrische Negri bodies *(im Zentralnervensystem)*
Einschlußkörperchenenzephalitis f inclusion body encephalitis [of Dawson]
Einschlußkörperchenkrankheit f cytomegalic [inclusion body] disease, cytomegalovirus inclusion disease (syndrome)
Einschlußzyste f inclusion cyst
einschmelzen to liquefy; to break down, to maturate *(z. B. ein Abszeß)*; to colliquate *(z. B. Gewebe)*
einschmelzend liquefactive, colliquative *(z. B. Gewebe)*
Einschmelzung f liquefaction; softening, maturation *(z. B. eines Abszesses)*; colliquation, colliquative softening *(von Geweben)*
~/eitrige s. Abszeß
einschneiden to cut in, to incise; to lance *(mit einer Lanzette)*
~/scharf to lancinate *(Schmerzen)*
Einschneiden n cut, incision
einschneidend incisional
Einschnitt m 1. incisure, incisura, notch; fissure; groove; 2. s. Einschneiden

einschnüren to strangulate *(z. B. den Darm)*
einschrumpfen to atrophy, to shrink
Einschußwunde f wound of entry
Einschwemmkatheter m flow-directed balloon-tipped catheter
einseitig unilateral; semilateral
einsickern to infiltrate, to soak, to seep [in], to ooze, to leak
Einsonderung f incretion, internal secretion
einspeicheln to [in]salivate *(die Nahrung beim Kauen)*
Einspeichelung f insalivation, invscation *(der Nahrung)*
Einspeisungsgefäß n feeder [vessel], feeding vessel
einspritzbar injectable
einspritzen to inject, to give an injection *(in den Körper)*
~/das Gift to envenom *(bei Schlangenbiß)*
Einspritzung f injection
~/subkutane subcutaneous injection
einsprossen to vascularize *(Blutgefäße)*
Einstauchung f impaction *(z. B. eines Knochenbruchs)*
einstellen 1. to discontinue, to stop *(z. B. eine Therapie)*; 2. to stabilize [on] *(z. B. auf Medikamente)*; 3. to adjust, to set *(z. B. Apparaturen)*; to focus *(z. B. ein Mikroskop)*
~/auf Digitalis to digitalize
~/sich 1. to present, to engage *(z. B. der Kindskopf bei der Geburt)*; 2. to set in *(z. B. Fieber, Schmerzen)*; to appear *(z. B. ein Exanthem)*
Einstellung f 1. presentation, engagement *(z. B. des Kindskopfs bei der Geburt)*; 2. appearance *(z. B. eines Exanthems)*; 3. stabilization [on] *(z. B. auf Medikamente)*; 4. discontinuation, stopping *(z. B. einer Therapie)*; 5. adjustment *(z. B. von Apparaturen)*; focussing *(z. B. eines Mikroskops)*
Einstellungsnystagmus m end-point nystagmus, [end-]positional nystagmus
Einstellungsreflex m orienting reflex *(reizempfindlicher Organe)*
Einstichelektrode f puncture electrode
Einstrombahn f inflow tract *(im Herzen)*
einströmen to stream (flow) in
Einströmen n inflow; rush *(schnell)*
einstufen to grade, to classify *(z. B. einen Körperschaden)*; to sort *(Militärmedizin)*
Einstufung f[/medizinische] triage, sorting sick and wounded *(Militärmedizin)*
Einstufungsabteilung f casualty department
Einstufungsfeldscher m casualty officer
Einstufungsoffizier m casualty officer
Einstufungsplatz m casualty clearing station
einstülpen to invaginate; to introvert
Einstülpung f invagination, intussusception, indigitation, introsusception *(z. B. des Darms)*; introversion *(z. B. eines Organs)*; entropion *(des Augenlids)*
Eintagsfieber n ephemera, ephemeral fever
eintauchen to immerse, to dip

Einteilungsschema n der Leukozyten/Arneth-sches Arneth' classification (count formula, index)
einträufeln to instil[l], to drop in, to pour into in drops
Einträufler m instillator
eintretend/spät (verzögert) tardy, tardive
~/vorzeitig in die Pubertät premature
~/zufällig accidental
Eintritt m der Geschlechtsreife s. Pubertät
Eintrittspforte f hilus, hilum *(an Organen)*
~ des Erregers portal of entry [of the agent]
Eintrittswunde f entry wound *(für Keime)*
eintrocknen to dry up; to desiccate; to mummify
eintröpfeln s. einträufeln
eintrüben/sich to opacify, to cloud
Eintrübung f 1. opacification, clouding *(z. B. der Augenhornhaut)*; 2. opacity *(Trübungszustand)*
Ein- und Ausfuhrbilanz f intake and output record *(z. B. bei Infusionstherapie)*
einverleiben to incorporate
Einverleibung f incorporation
Einverständnis n eines Patienten informed consent *(z. B. für eine Operation)*
einwachsen 1. to vascularize *(Gefäße)*; 2. to grow in *(z. B. Nägel)*
einwärts inward, entad; toward the centre
Einwärtsbeugung f in[tro]flexion, inward flexion; pronation *(der Hand)*
einwärtsdrehen to pronate *(z. B. Arm)*; to intort *(Auge)*
Einwärtsdreher m pronator [muscle]
~/runder pronator radii teres [muscle]
~/viereckiger pronator quadratus [muscle]
Einwärtsdrehung f intorsion, intortion
~ beider Augen/unwillkürliche conclination, adtorsion
~ der Hand pronation, mesial rotation of the forearm
einwärtskehren to entropionize *(das Augenlid)*
Einwärtskehrung f des Augenlids entropion
Einwärtsrollen n der Augen incyclophoria
Einwärtsschielen n esotropia, internal strabismus, convergent squint, cross-eye, esophoria
~/intermittierendes intermittent convergent strabismus
~/latentes esophoria; endophoria *(bei geschlossenen Augen)*
~ nach oben/latentes hyperesophoria
~ nach unten/latentes hypoesophoria
Einwegkanüle f disposable needle
Einwegspritze f disposable syringe
einweisen/erneut in das Krankenhaus to readmit to the hospital
~/in ein Krankenhaus to admit (refer) to the hospital, to hospitalize
~/in eine Anstalt to commit
Einweisungsdiagnose f admission diagnosis, diagnosis on admission
einwirken to act, to take effect, to influence
einwirkend/auf den Vagus[nerven] vagotrope, vagotropic

Einwirkung

Einwirkung f action *(z. B. von Kraft)*; effect, influence, operation *(z. B. von Medikamenten)*
● **ohne fremde ~** spontaneous
Einwirtzyklus m monoxenia
Einzapfung f gomphosis *(z. B. der Zähne)*
einzehig monodactylous
Einzehigkeit f monodactyly
Einzelathetose f monathetosis
Einzeldosis f single dose
Einzelfall m special (individual) case
Einzelknopfnaht f interrupted suture
Einzellähmung f monoparesis
Einzeller m protozoon, protozoan
einzellig unicellular, monocellular
Einzelmaximaldosis f maximum single dose
Einzelmuskelkrampf m monospasm
Einzelphänomen n isolated phenomenon
Einzelspenderplasma n single-donor plasma
Einzelstern m monaster *(Chromosomenfigur in der Kernteilungsphase)*
Einzelstichnaht f interrupted suture
Einzelsymptom n single sign, isolated symptom
Einzeltherapie f individual treatment *(bei Psychotherapie)*
Einzelzellnekrosen fpl isolated cell necrosis
einziehen to draw back; to retract *(z. B. Mamille)*
Einziehung f retraction *(z. B. der Mamille)*; dimpling *(z. B. bei subkutanem Krebs)*
~/interkostale intercostal retraction
~/subkostale subcostal retraction
Einzinkerhaken m tenaculum
Einzugsbereich m catchment area *(eines Krankenhauses)*
Eipaket n ootheca
Eiplasma n o[v]oplasm, cytoplasm of the egg
Eisbeutel m ice-bag
Eisenablagerung f [im Gewebe] siderosis, ferrugination
~ in der Haut sideroderma
eisenarm poor in iron *(z. B. Hämoglobin)*
Eisenbahnkrankheit f railway disease, train sickness
Eisenbahnnystagmus m railway (train) nystagmus
Eisenbedarf m iron requirement
Eisenbehandlung f ferrotherapy
eisenbindend iron-binding, siderophilous, sideropectic
Eisenbindungskapazität f iron-binding capacity *(von Hämoglobin)*
Eisenblutspiegel m iron blood level
Eisenblutspiegelverminderung f hypoferraemia
Eisendepot n iron depot
eisenfreundlich siderophil[e]
Eisengabe f administration of iron
eisenhaltig siderous, ferrous, ferriferous, containing iron
Eisen(II)-hämoglobin n haemoglobin, ferrohaemoglobin *(Blutfarbstoff)*
Eisen(III)-hämoglobin n methaemoglobin, ferrihaemoglobin *(Blutfarbstoff)*
Eisenmangel m iron deficiency, sideropenia, asiderosis

Eisenmangelanämie f [iron-]deficiency anaemia, asiderotic anaemia, nutritional (chronic) hypochromic anaemia
~ bei Chlorose chlorotic anaemia
Eisenmenger-Komplex m, **Eisenmenger-Syndrom** n Eisenmenger's complex (tetralogy, syndrome)
Eisenporphyrinprotein n iron porphyrin protein *(z. B. Hämoglobin)*
Eisenpräparat n chalybeate, iron preparation, haematic
Eisen(II)-protoporphyrin n ferroprotoporphyrin, haem, [proto]heme
Eisen(III)-protoporphyrin n ferriprotoporphyrin
Eisen(III)-protoporphyrinchlorid n haemin, [proto]hemin
Eisen(III)-protoporphyrinhydroxid n haematin, methaeme
eisenreich rich in iron *(z. B. Hämoglobin)*
eisenresistent iron-resistant *(z. B. Anämie)*
Eisenstaublunge[nerkrankung] f siderosis, siderotic pneumoconiosis, arc-welder's disease (nodulation)
Eisenstoffwechsel m iron metabolism
Eisen- und Fettablagerung f im Gewebe lipoidsiderosis
Eisenverminderung f hypoferraemia
Eisenzufuhr f iron supply
eiskalt algid, chill[y], cold
Eiskrawatte f ice bag for throat, ice collar
Eispackung f ice pack
Eisprung m ovulation ● **den ~ haben** to ovulate
● **ohne ~** non-ovulatory, anovular, anovulatory
Eisprung... s. Ovulations...
Eiter m pus, matter, purulence, purulency
~/blauer blue pus
~/blutiger bloody (sanious) pus
~/jauchiger ichorous pus
~/käsiger cheesy pus
~/schleimiger mucopus
Eiterablagerung f in der Augenvorderkammer hypopyon, lunella, onyx
Eiterabsonderung f pyecchysis, effusion of pus, mattery discharge
Eiteransammlung f abscess *(s. a. unter Abszeß)*
~ hinter der Brustdrüse retromammary abscess
~ hinter der Harnblase retrovesical abscess
~ im Becken pelvic abscess
~ im Beckenbindegewebe parametric abscess
~ im Eileiter pyosalpinx, pus tube
~ im Gehirn pyencephalus
~ im Harnleiter pyoureter
~ im Herzbeutel pyopericardium
~ im Hodensack pyocele
~ im Kehlkopfluftsack laryngopyocele
~ in den Hirnkammern pyocephalus
~ in der Bauchfellhöhle pyoperitoneum, pyaskos
~ in der Gebärmutterhöhle pyometra
~ in der Peritonealhöhle pyoperitoneum
~ in der Scheide pyocolpos
~ in vorgebildeten Höhlen empyema
~ um die Harnröhre periurethral abscess

eiterartig pus-like, puriform, puruloid, pyoid
Eiterausscheidung f **im Urin** pyuria
Eiterausschlag m pyodermia; pyoderma
Eiterbehandlung f pyotherapy
Eiterbeule f abscess, boil; furuncle
eiterbildend pyogenous, pyogen[et]ic, pyopoietic, pus-forming, pus-producing
~/nicht non-pyogenic
Eiterbildung f pyogenesis, pyo[poie]sis, suppuration, formation of pus
~ im Gehirn encephalopyosis
Eiterbläschen n pustule, pus (purulent) blister, pimple, vesiculo-pustule ● **mit Eiterbläschen bedeckt** pustular
eiterbläschenähnlich pustuliform
eiterbläschenbildend pustulant
Eiterbläschenbildung f pustulation, empyesis; pustulosis (an der Haut)
Eiterblase f pus (purulent) blister (s. a. Eiterbläschen)
Eiterbucht f sinus
Eiterentstehung f s. Eiterbildung
Eitererbrechen n pyemesis
Eitererreger m pus[-forming] organism, pyogen[et]ic microorganism
Eiterexsudat n purulent exudate
Eiterflechte f impetigo, crusted tetter, pustular dermatitis; pyodermia, pyoderma
eiterflechtenartig impetiginoid, impetiginous
Eiterfluß m pyorrhoea, blennorrhoea, blennorrhagia, discharge of pus
eiterfrei non-purulent, non-suppurative, clean (z. B. eine Wunde)
Eitergrind m impetigo, crusted tetter
eiterhemmend pyostatic, antipy[ogen]ic
Eiterherd m suppurative (pus) focus
~ im Lendenbereich lumbar abscess
Eiterhöhle f purulent (pus) cavity
Eitermetastase f pyaemic abscess
eitern to suppurate, to discharge matter (pus)
eiternd suppurant, suppurative, purulent
Eiterpfropf m core
Eitertasche f pocket of pus, pyorrhoea pocket (am Zahnfleisch)
Eiter- und Blutansammlung f **in der Brustfellhöhle** pyohaemothorax
Eiter- und Luftansammlung f **im Brustfellraum** pyopneumothorax
~ im Herzbeutel pyopneumopericardium
~ in der Bauchfellhöhle pyopneumoperitoneum
~ in der Gallenblase pyopneumocholecystitis
~ in der Gebärmutterhöhle pyophysometra
Eiterung f 1. pyesis, suppuration, festering, pus formation, empyesis; 2. pyosis, purulence, purulency
Eiterverhaltung f purulent retention, retention of pus
Eiterverschlucken n pyophagia
Eiterzelle f pus cell, pyocyte
Eiterzyste f pyocyst
eitragend ovigerous, oviferous
Eitransport m egg transport

eitrig purulent, pyic, pyoid; pus-like
eitrig-serös seropurulent
Eiwanderung f migration of the ovum
Eiweiß n protein; proteid (s. a. unter Protein) ● ~ **im Urin ausscheidend** proteinuric
Eiweiß... s. a. Protein...
Eiweißabbau m proteolysis, protein degradation (breakdown)
eiweißabbauend proteolytic, proteoclastic
Eiweißabbaustoffwechsel m protein catabolism
Eiweißablagerung f proteinosis (im Gewebe)
eiweißähnlich proteinaceous, proteinic, albuminoid
eiweißarm low (poor) in protein
Eiweißaufbau m protein synthesis
Eiweißausscheidung f **im Urin** prote[in]uria
~ im Urin bei Fieber febrile proteinuria
~/nächtliche noctalbuminuria, nyctalbuminuria
Eiweißbedarf m protein requirement
Eiweißbehandlung f protein therapy (treatment), proteotherapy
eiweißbindend protein-binding, proteopectic, proteopexic
Eiweißblutspiegel m protein blood level
Eiweißdiät f protein diet
Eiweißeinsparung f protein economy
Eiweißernährung f protein nutrition, proteotherapy, protein therapy (treatment)
eiweißgebunden protein-bound (z. B. Elemente)
Eiweißgehalt m protein content
Eiweißgerinnung f denatur[iz]ation; protein coagulation
eiweißhaltig protein-containing, albuminous
Eiweißhülle f protein coat (membrane) (der Bakterien)
Eiweißkonzentration f protein concentration
Eiweiß-Lipopolysaccharid-Komplex m protein lipopolysaccharide complex
Eiweißmangel m protein deficiency, lack of protein; hypoproteinosis
Eiweißmangelernährung f protein malnutrition
Eiweißmangelödem n hunger oedema (swelling), famine (nutritional) oedema
Eiweißmangelsituation f protein deficiency condition
Eiweißmaximum n protein maximum
Eiweißminimum n protein minimum
Eiweißoptimum n protein optimum
Eiweißprobe f protein test
~/Spieglersche Spiegler's test
Eiweißquotient m protein quotient
eiweißreich protein-rich, albuminous, rich in protein
eiweißspaltend proteolytic, proteoclastic; proteopeptic
Eiweißspaltung f proteolysis, protein decomposition, splitting of protein; proteopepsis
Eiweißspeicherung f proteinosis (im Gewebe)
Eiweißstoffwechsel m protein metabolism, proteometabolism
Eiweißsynthese f protein synthesis
Eiweißuntersuchung f/**Esbachsche** Esbach's method

eiweißverdauend proteopeptic, proteolytic, proteoclastic
Eiweißverdauung f proteopepsis, proteolysis
Eiweißverlust m protein loss
Eiweißverwertung f protein utilization
Eiweißzersetzung f protein decomposition
Eiweißzufuhr f protein intake
Eizelle f ovum, ovule, ovulum, o[v]ocyte, ovotid
~/**befruchtete** oosperm, zygote, fertilized ovum
~/**primäre** primary oocyte
Eizellenkern m oocyte nucleus
Eizytoplasma n ooplasm
Ejaculatio f **praecox** premature ejaculation, prospermia
Ejakulat n ejaculate, semen
~/**blutiges** haem[at]ospermia; discharge of bloody semen
Ejakulation f ejaculation, ejection of semen; emission
Ejakulationsreflex m ejaculatory (ejaculation) reflex
Ejakulationsschmerz m dysspermatism, dysspermia, painful ejaculation
Ejakulationsverlangsamung f bradyspermatism, bradyspermia
Ejakulationszentrum n ejaculation centre
ejakulatorisch ejaculatory
ejakulieren to ejaculate
Ejektion f ejection, expulsion
Ejektionsfraktion f ejection fraction (des Herzens)
Ejektionsklick m ejection click (des Herzens)
Ejektionsphase f ejection phase (des Herzens)
~/**schnelle** rapid ejection phase
Ekchondrom n ecchondroma (vom Knorpel ausgehende Geschwulst)
Ekchondrose f ecchondrosis, cartilaginous outgrowth
Ekchymose f ecchymosis, extravasation of blood, suggillation
~/**subkonjunktivale** subconjunctival ecchymosis (haemorrhage)
Ekchymosen fpl/**Tardieusche** Tardieu's ecchymoses (spots)
ekchymotisch ecchymotic
EKG, Ekg s. Elektrokardiogramm
EKG-Ableitung f electrocardiographic lead
~ **des linken Herzens** laevo[cardio]gram
~/**Goldbergersche** Goldberger (augmented unipolar) limb lead
EKG-Aufzeichnung f electrocardiography, ECG
EKG-Befund m electrocardiographic findings
EKG-Extremitätenableitung f bipolar limb lead
EKG-Gerät n [electro]cardiograph, ECG
EKG-Intervall n electrocardiographic interval
EKG-Kontrolle f electrocardiographic control
EKG-Monitor m electrocardiographic monitor
EKG-Oszillograph m electrocardioscope
EKG-Schreiber m [electro]cardiograph, ECG
EKG-Sichtgerät n electrocardioscope
EKG-Standardableitung f bipolar limb lead
EKG-Überwachung f electrocardiographic monitoring
EKG-Überwachungsgerät n electrocardiographic monitor
EKG-Veränderung f electrocardiographic change
EKG-Zacke f electrocardiographic wave
Eklampsie f eclampsia, eclamptogenic toxaemia
eklampsieauslösend eclamptogenic
Eklampsiekrampf m eclamptic convulsion
Eklampsieneigung f s. Eklampsismus
Eklampsismus m eclampsism, pre-eclampsia, pre-eclamptic toxaemia (mit Organschäden)
eklamptisch eclamptic
eklamptogen eclamptogenic
Ekmnesie f ecmnesia (Vorstellung, in einem früheren Lebensabschnitt zu leben)
Ekomanie f ecomania, oikomania (Psychologie)
Ekostatismus m ecostatism, apleuria
Ekphorie f ecphoria
Ekstase f ecstasy ● **in** ~ **[befindlich]** ecstatic
ekstatisch ecstatic
Ekstrophie f s. Ecstrophia
Ektasie f ectasia, dil[at]ation, enlargement, distension, expansion
ektatisch ectatic, dilated, stretched
Ekthyma n ecthyma
Ektoblast m 1. ectoblast, epiblast, primitive (primary) ectoderm (Embryologie); 2. s. Ektoderm
Ektoderm n ectoderm ● **aus dem** ~ **stammen** to be ectodermal in origin
ektodermal ectodermal, ectodermic, deric
Ektodermentwicklung f ectodermal development
Ektodermose f ectodermosis (Erkrankung ektodermaler Hautgebilde)
ektogenetisch ectogen[et]ic, ectogenous
Ektokardie f s. Ectopia cordis
Ektokornea f ectocornea
ektokranial ectocranial
Ektopagus m ectopagus (Mißgeburt)
Ektoparasit m ectoparasite
ektoparasitisch ectoparasitic
Ektophyt m ectophyte
ektophytisch ectophytic
Ektopie f ectopia (s. a. unter Ectopia)
~/**perineale** perineal ectopia (z. B. des Hodens)
~/**renale** renal ectopia; ectopic kidney
ektopisch ectopic
Ektoplasma n ectoplasm, exoplasm
ektoplasmatisch ectoplasmic
Ektoplazenta f ectoplacenta, placental trophoblast, trophoderm
ektoplazental ectoplacental
Ektosit m ectosite
Ektotoxin n ectotoxin, exotoxin, exogenous toxin
Ektozoon n ectozoon
Ektrodaktylie f ectrodactyly, extrodactylism, oligodactyly
Ektromelie f ectromelia, congenital absence of a limb (Gliedmaßenverstümmelung)
Ektromelus m ectromelus (Mißgeburt)
Ektropie f s. Ektropium
ektropionieren to ectropionize (Augenlider)
Ektropionieren n ectropionization

Ektropium n ectropion, ectropium, eversion (z. B. des Augenlids)
Ektropodismus m ectropodism
Ektrosyndaktylie f ectrosyndactyly
Ekzem n eczema (allergische Hautkrankheit mit Ausschlag)
~/**akutes** acute eczema
~/**allergisches** allergic eczema (dermatitis)
~/**atopisches** atopic eczema (dermatitis)
~/**endogenes** endogenous eczema
~/**feuchtes** moist eczema, humid tetter
~/**nässendes** exudative (weeping) eczema
~/**schuppendes** squamous eczema
~/**seborrhoisches** seborrhoeic eczema (dermatitis)
~/**trockenes** dry eczema (tetter)
ekzemähnlich, ekzemartig eczematoid, resembling eczema
Ekzematid n eczematid
~/**seborrhoisches** seborrhoeic dermatitis (eczematid)
ekzematisch eczematic, eczematous
ekzematisierend eczematogenic
Ekzematisierung f eczematization
ekzematogen eczematogenic
Ekzematoidreaktion f eczematoid reaction (dermatitis)
ekzematös eczematous
Ekzematose f eczematosis
ekzemauslöseı eczematogenic
Ekzembildung ı eczematization
Elaiom n eleoma, oleogranuloma, oleoma (Fremdkörpergeschwulst nach Injektion von Ölen)
Elastance f elastance of the lung, elastic recoil [of the lung] (Maß für die Lungendehnbarkeit in Abhängigkeit von der Druckänderung)
Elastase f elastase (Enzym)
Elastica f elastica (elastische Bindegewebsmembran der Blutgefäße)
~ **externa** external elastic lamina (membrane)
~ **interna** internal elastic lamina (membrane)
Elastin n elastin (Skleroprotein)
elastisch elastic; flexible
Elastizität f elasticity
Elastofibrom n elastofibroma
Elastom[a] n elastoma
Elastometrie f s. Tonometrie
Eleidin n eleidin (lichtbrechende Substanz im Stratum lucidum der Haut)
Elektivoperation f elective operation, operation of election
elektrisieren to electrify
Elektrisierung f electrization, electrification
elektroakustisch electroacoustic
Elektroanästhesie f electroanaesthesia, electric anaesthesia
Elektroblitzbehandlung f fulguration (z. B. von Geschwülsten)
Elektrochirurgie f electrosurgery, galvanosurgery
Elektrochirurgie-Antriebseinheit f/hochtourige high-speed electrosurgical unit

Elektrochirurgiegerät n electrosurgical unit
elektrochirurgisch electrosurgical
Elektrode f electrode
~/**differente** different electrode
~/**flache** plate [electrode]
~/**indifferente** indifferent electrode
Elektrodenableitung f/**intrakardiale** intracardial electrode lead (EKG)
Elektrodenpaste f electrode (conducting) jelly (z. B. für Elektroschocktherapie)
Elektrodenpotential n electrode potential
Elektrodensalbe f s. Elektrodenpaste
Elektrodermatogramm n electrodermatogram
Elektrodermatom n electrodermatome
Elektrodiagnostik f electrodiagnosis
Elektrodurographie f electrodurography
Elektroejakulation f electroejaculation
Elektroendosmose f electro[end]osmosis
Elektroenzephalogramm n electroencephalogram, EEG (Zusammensetzungen s. unter EEG)
Elektroenzephalograph m electroencephalograph, EEG
Elektroenzephalographie f electroencephalography, EEG
elektroenzephalographisch electroencephalographic
Elektrofieberbehandlung f electropyrexia, fever therapy
Elektrofototherapie f electrophototherapy
Elektrogastrogramm n electrogastrogram
Elektrogastrograph m electrogastrograph
Elektrogastrographie f electrogastrography
Elektrogustometrie f electrogustometry
Elektrohämostase f electrohaemostasis
Elektrohysterographie f electrohysterography
Elektrokardiogramm n [electro]cardiogram, ECG, EKG
~/**endokardiales** endocardial (intracavitary) electrocardiogram
~/**fetales** cardiotocogram
Elektrokardiogramm... s. EKG-...
Elektrokardiograph m [electro]cardiograph, ECG
Elektrokardiographie f [electro]cardiography, ECG, EKG
~/**fetale** cardiotocography
elektrokardiographisch electrocardiographic
Elektrokardioskop n electrocardioscope
Elektrokardioskopie f electrocardioscopy
Elektrokatarakt f electric cataract
Elektrokaustik f electrocautery
Elektrokauter m cautery [knife], electrosurgical knife
Elektrokauterisation f electrocautery
Elektrokoagulation f electrocoagulation
elektrokoagulieren to electrocoagulate
Elektrokochleographie f electrocochleography
Elektrokoma n electrocoma
Elektrokonvulsion f electric convulsion
elektrokonvulsiv electroconvulsive
Elektrokortikogramm n electrocorticogram
Elektrokortikographie f electrocorticography
Elektrokrampf m electric convulsion, electrofit

Elektrokrampfbehandlung

Elektrokrampfbehandlung f electroconvulsive treatment, electric convulsive therapy, ECT
Elektrokution f electrocution
Elektrokymograph m electrokymograph
Elektrokymographie f electrokymography *(Darstellung der mechanischen Herzrandbewegungen mittels Durchleuchtung)*
Elektrolithotripsie f electrolithotrity
Elektrolytentgleisung f electrolyte imbalance
Elektrolytersatz m electrolyte replacement
Elektrolythaushalt m electrolyte metabolism
elektrolytisch electrolytic
Elektrolytkonzentration f electrolyte concentration
Elektrolytlösung f/bilanzierte balanced electrolyte solution
Elektrolytstörung f electrolyte disturbance
Elektrolytsubstitution f electrolyte replacement [therapy]
Elektrolyttransport m electrolyte transport
Elektrolytuntersuchung f electrolyte study
Elektrolytverlust m electrolyte loss
Elektrolytverschiebung f electrolyte shift
Elektromassage f electromassage
elektromedizinisch electromedical
elektromotorisch electromotor
Elektromyogramm n electromyogram
Elektromyographie f electromyography, EMG
elektromyographisch electromyographic
Elektronarkose f electronarcosis *(milde Form der Elektroschocktherapie)*
elektronegativ electronegative
Elektronenabtastmikroskop n scanning [beam] electron microscope
Elektronenabtastmikroskopie f scanning [beam] electron microscopy
Elektronenmikroskop n electron microscope
Elektronenmikroskopaufnahme f electron [photo]micrograph
Elektronenmikroskopie f electron microscopy
elektronenmikroskopisch electron microscopic
Elektronenmikroskopuntersuchung f electron microscope study, electron microscopy investigation
Elektronystagmogramm n electronystagmogram
Elektronystagmograph m electronystagmograph
Elektronystagmographie f electronystagmography
elektronystagmographisch electronystagmographic
Elektrookulogramm n electrooculogram, EOG
Elektrookulographie f electrooculography
elektrookulographisch electrooculographic
Elektroolfaktogramm n electroolfactogram
Elektroolfaktographie f electroolfactography
Elektropathologie f electropathology
elektropharmakologisch electropharmacologic
Elektrophobie f electrophobia *(krankhafte Angst vor elektrischem Strom)*
Elektrophorese f electrophoresis
Elektrophoresemobilitätstest m electrophoresis motility test

Elektrophoresewanderung f electrophoretic migration *(z. B. von Proteinen)*
elektrophoretisch electrophoretic
Elektrophysiologie f electrophysiology
elektrophysiologisch electrophysiologic[al]
elektropositiv electropositive
Elektropunktur f electropuncture *(Zerstörung krankhaften Gewebes durch eine Nadelelektrode)*
Elektroresektion f electroresection
Elektroresektoskop n electroresectoscope
Elektroretinogramm n electroretinogram, ERG
Elektroretinographie f electroretinography
elektroretinographisch electroretinographic
Elektrosauger m electric suction pump
Elektroschlaf m electrotherapeutic sleep
Elektroschock m electroshock, electric (electroconvulsive) shock, ECS
Elektroschockbehandlung f electroshock (electroconvulsive) therapy, electric shock treatment, EST
~ **des Herzens** cardioversion
Elektroschockkoma n electrocoma
Elektrostimulation f electrostimulation
Elektrotherapie f electrotherapeutics, electrotherapy, electrization
~ **bei Nervenerkrankungen** neuroelectrotherapy
Elektrotomie f electrotomy, electroscission, electrosection
elektrotonisch electrotonic
Elektrotonographie f electrotonography
elektrotonographisch electrotonographic
Elektrotonus m electrotonus
Elektrovibrationsmassage f electrovibratory massage
Elektrozystoskop n electrocystoscope
Elektrozystoskopie f electrocystoscopy
Elementarkörnchen n elementary body
Elementarkörperchen n elementary body
Elementarsubstanz f elementary substance
Elephantiasis f elephantiasis, fefe, myelolymphangioma, pachydermia, elephant leg *(Hautverdickung durch Lymphstauung bei Filarieninfektion)*
~ **graecorum** lepra, leprosy
~/**idiopathische** idiopathic elephantiasis, Milroy's disease
~ **neuromatosa** pachydermatocele
~ **palpebralis** palpebral elephantiasis
~ **scrotalis (scroti)** lymph scrotum, oschelephantiasis
elephantiasisartig elephantoid
Elephantiasisfieber n elephantoid fever
Elephantiasiskranker m elephantiac
Elevatio f **scapulae congenitalis** Sprengel's deformity, [congenital] elevation of the scapula
Elevation f elevation *(z. B. einer Zahnwurzel)*
Elevatorium n elevator, levator *(Instrument)*
Elfenbein n s. Dentin
elfenbeinartig eburneous *(z. B. Knochen nach Osteomyelitis)*
Eliminationskinetik f elimination kinetics *(z. B. von Substanzen)*

Ellbogen m s. Ellenbogen
Elle f ulna, cubitus
Ellenarterie f ulnar artery
~/rückläufige recurrent ulnar artery
~/vordere rückläufige anterior ulnar recurrent artery
Ellenbogen m elbow, cubitus
Ellenbogengelenk n elbow joint
Ellenbogengelenkentzündung f olecranarthritis, olenitis, inflammation of the elbow joint
Ellenbogengelenkerkrankung f olecranarthropathy
Ellenbogengelenktuberkulose f olecranarthrocace
Ellenbogengrube f [ante]cubital fossa
Ellenbogenreflex m elbow reflex (jerk)
Ellenbogenstrecker m extensor of the elbow
Ellenhinterrand m posterior border of the ulna
Ellenkopf m head of the ulna
Ellenleiste f/vordere anterior margin of the ulna
Ellennerv m ulnar (cubital) nerve
Ellen-Speichen-Gelenk n/distales distal radioulnar joint
Ellenvene f ulnar vein
ellenwärts ulnad
Ellipsoidgelenk n ellipsoid articulation, condylar (condyloid) joint, condylarthrosis
Elliptozyt m elliptocyte, ovalocyte
Elliptozytenanämie f elliptocytosis, ovalocytosis, oval-cell anaemia
~ Typ Fanconi/konstitutionelle hyperchrome Fanconi's anaemia (disease), congenital hypoplastic anaemia
Elliptozytose f s. Elliptozytenanämie
Ellis-van-Creveld-Syndrom n Ellis-van Creveld syndrome, chondroectodermal dysplasia
Elongation f elongation, lengthening (z. B. des Gebärmutterhalses)
Elschnig-Körperchen npl Elschnig's pearls (in der Pupille)
Elternbild n parent image
Elternfigur f parent figure
Elterngeneration f parental generation
Elternteil n parent
El-Tor-Vibrion n eltor (El Tor) vibrion
eluieren to elute, to wash out; to extract
Elution f elution, washing out; extraction
Elutionsrate f rate of elution
Emanationstherapie f emanotherapy, radiotherapy
Emaskulation f emasculation, castration, eviration
Embolämie f embolaemia
Embolektomie f embolectomy (aus einer Schlagader)
~/pulmonale pulmonary embolectomy
Embolektomiekatheter m embolectomy catheter
Embolie f embolism
~/arterielle artery embolism
~/blande bland embolism, microembolism
~/hämatogene haematogenous embolism

~/massive macroembolism
~/paradoxe paradoxical (crossed) embolism
Emboliegefahr f danger of embolism
Embolierisiko n risk of embolism
Embolietod m death from embolism
Embolisation f embolization
embolisch embolic
embolisieren to embolize
Embololalie f, **Embolophrasie** f embo[lo]lalia, embolophrasia (Gebrauch sinnloser Flickwörter oder Silben)
Embolus m embolus
~/paradoxer paradoxical (crossed) embolus
~/reitender riding embolus, straddling (saddle) embolus
Embolusentfernung f[/operative] s. Embolektomie
Embolusfaßzange f embolus grasping forceps
embolusförmig emboliform
Embryektomie f embryectomy, removal of an extrauterine embryo
Embryo m embryo[n] (s. a. unter Fetus)
~/künstlicher manikin (zum Erlernen geburtshilflicher Handgriffe)
Embryo... s. a. Fetus... und Fetal...
Embryoabtötung f embryoctony, killing of a foetus
embryoähnlich embryoid
Embryoblast m embryoblast (Teil der Keimscheibe)
Embryoentfernung f[/operative] embryectomy (z. B. bei Extrauteringravidität)
Embryoernährung f embryotrophy
embryoförmig embryoniform
embryogen embryogen[et]ic
Embryogenese f embryogeny, embryogenesis, embryological development
embryogenetisch embryogen[et]ic
Embryokardie f embryocardia
Embryologe m embryologist
Embryologie f embryology
~/vergleichende comparative embryology
embryologisch embryologic
Embryom[a] n embryoma
Embryomesser n embryotome
embryomorph embryomorphous
embryonal embryonal, embryonic
Embryonalanlage f embryonic area (disk, shield)
Embryonalbindegewebe n embryonic connective tissue
Embryonalentwicklung f embryogeny, embryogenesis, embryological development
Embryonalgewebe n embryonic tissue
Embryonalhülle f embryonic sheath; amnion, amnios
Embryonalknorpel m embryonal cartilage
Embryonalkreislauf m foetal circulation
Embryonalmark n embryonic marrow
Embryonalstar m embryonal cataract
Embryonaltumor m embryonal tumour
Embryonalzelle f embryonic cell
Embryonalzölom n embryonic coelom

Embryopathie

Embryopathie f embryopathy
embryopathisch embryopathic
Embryopathologie f embryopathology
embryoplastisch embryoplastic
embryoschädigend embryocidal
Embryospezialist m embryologist
Embryotom n embryotome
Embryotomie f embryotomy *(unter der Geburt)*
embryotötend embryocidal
embryotoxisch embryotoxic
Embryotoxon n embryotoxon
~ **anterior** anterior embryotoxon, anterior dysplasia of the cornea
~ **posterior** posterior embryotoxon, posterior marginal dysplasia of the cornea
embryotroph embryotrophic
Embryotrophie f embryotrophy
EMC-Syndrom n s. Enzephalomyokarditis
Emenagogum n emmenagogue [agent]
Emesis f emesis, vomiting, vomit[us], vomiturition *(Zusammensetzungen s. unter Erbrechen)*
Emetikum n emetic [agent], vomitive
Emetophobie f emetophobia *(Angst vor Erbrechen)*
Eminentia f eminence, eminentia, prominence, protuberance, projection *(s. a. unter Tuber)*
~ **alveolaris** alveolar eminence
~ **arcuata** arcuate eminence
~ **carpi radialis** radial (ulnar) eminence of the wrist
~ **collateralis** collateral eminence
~ **conchae** eminence of the concha
~ **cruciformis** cruciate eminence
~ **fossae triangularis** triangular eminence, eminence of the triangular fossa
~ **iliopubica** iliopubic (iliopectineal) eminence
~ **intercondylaris** intercondylar eminence
~ **intercondylaris tibiae** spine of the tibia
~ **jugularis** jugular eminence
~ **pyramidalis** pyramidal eminence, pyramid of the tympanum
~ **scaphae** eminence of the scapha (scaphoid fossa)
Emission f emission; seminal discharge, ejaculation *(des Samens)*
Emissionshistospektroskopie f emission histospectroscopy
Emissionsspektrum n emission spectrum *(Radiologie)*
Emmenologie f emmenology *(Lehre von der Menstruation)*
emmetrop emmetropic
Emmetroper m emmetrope
Emmetropie f emmetropia, E., normal (perfect) vision
Emotion f emotion, feeling, sentiment; affect
emotional, emotionell emotional, emotive
Emotionspsychose f emotional (affective) psychosis
emotionsschwach athymic
Emotionsschwäche f hypothymia
Emotivität f emotivity, capacity for emotion

empfangen 1. to conceive, to be (become) pregnant; 2. to receive *(z. B. Reize)*
empfangend 1. conceptive; 2. receptive
Empfänger m recipient, donee *(z. B. von Transplantaten)*
Empfängerplasma n recipient plasma
Empfängerserum n recipient serum
empfänglich 1. susceptible, impressionable, sensitive *(psychisch)*; 2. predisposed; susceptible, prone (liable) to *(z. B. für Krankheiten)*
Empfänglichkeit f 1. susceptibility, impressionability; 2. predisposition, susceptibility
Empfängnis f conception, syllepsis, impregnation ● **nach der** ~ postconceptual
empfängnisfähig conceptive, capable of conception (impregnation)
empfängnisfördernd proconceptive
empfängnisunfähig not capable of conception (impregnation)
empfängnisverhütend contraceptive, anticonceptive
Empfängnisverhütung f contraception, conception control, prevenception; birth control
Empfängnisverhütungsmethode f contraceptive method
Empfängnisverhütungsmittel n contraceptive [agent]
Empfängniszeit f time of conception
empfindlich sensible, sensitive; tender, sore *(z. B. gegenüber Schmerzen)*; susceptible, sensitive *(z. B. gegenüber Medikamenten)*; excitable, irritable *(z. B. gegenüber Reizen)*; delicate *(Instrumente, Tests)*
~/**gegenüber Antigenen wenig** hypoergic
Empfindlichkeit f sensibility, sensitivity, sensitiveness; sensitiveness, tenderness *(z. B. gegenüber Schmerzen)*; susceptibility *(z. B. gegenüber Medikamenten)*; excitability, irritability *(z. B. gegenüber Reizen)*
~/**gesteigerte** hypersensitivity, hypersensitiveness
~/**verminderte** hyposensitivity, hyposensitiveness
Empfindlichkeitsmesser m aesthesiometer
Empfindlichkeitsschwelle f sensitivity threshold
Empfindlichkeitstest m sensitivity (susceptibility) test
Empfindsamkeit f sensibility; sentimentality
Empfindung f 1. sensation *(Sinnesempfindung)*; 2. perception; 3. feeling, sentiment ● **ohne sexuelle** ~ asexual
empfindungsfähig sensitive
Empfindungsfähigkeit f sensitivity, sensitiveness
Empfindungskälte f frigidity
Empfindungslehre f aesthesiology
empfindungslos insensible; insensitive, anaesthetic; analgesic *(z. B. gegenüber Schmerzen)*; numb, dead *(z. B. Gliedmaßen)*
Empfindungslosigkeit f insensibility, insensitiveness, anaesthesia, analgesia; numbness *(von Gliedmaßen)*
~ **der Gliedmaßenenden** acroanaesthesia

Empfindungsphysiologie f aesthesiophysiology
Empfindungsstörung f paraesthesia, dysaesthesia, paralgesia
~ **an Gliedmaßenenden** acroparaesthesia
~/**dissoziierte** dissociated anaesthesia, sensory dissociation
~/**lokale** topoparaesthesia, localized paraesthesia
Empfindungsvermögen n sensibility; capacity of sensation
emphraktisch emphractic
Emphysem n emphysema
~/**alveolares** alveolar emphysema
~/**atrophisches** atrophic (small-lunged) emphysema
~/**bullöses** bullous emphysema
~/**großblasiges** giant bullous emphysema
~/**interstitielles** interstitial emphysema
~/**kompensatorisches** compensatory (compensating, ectatic) emphysema
~/**kutanes** cutaneous emphysema
~/**obstruktives** obstructive emphysema
~/**pulmonales** pulmonary emphysema
~/**subkutanes** subcutaneous emphysema; pneumohypoderma
~/**vesikuläres** vesicular emphysema
emphysematös emphysematous
Emphysemblase f emphysematous bulla, air cyst
Emphysemblasenentfernung f[/operative] bullectomy
Emphysemdyspnoe f pneumatodyspnoea
Emphysemknistern n emphysema crackling
Emphysemthorax m emphysematous chest, barrel[-shaped] chest
Emplastrum n plaster, emplastrum
Emprosthotonus m emprosthotonus *(Körperkrampf in vornübergebeugter Stellung)*
Empyem n empyema
Empyemflüssigkeit f empyema fluid
Empyemhöhle f empyema space
Emulgator m 1. emulsifier, emulsifying agent; 2. emulsifier, emulsification machine
emulgierbar emulsifiable
Emulgieren n emulsification
Emulgier[ungs]mittel n s. Emulgator 1.
Emulgiervermögen n emulsifying power
Emulsion f 1. emulsion; 2. emulsion ointment
Emulsionsverfahren n emulsion process
Enamel n s. Zahnschmelz
Enamelfaser f enamel fibre (column)
Enameloblast m enameloblast
Enamelom n enameloma
Enanthem n enanthem[a]
Enarthrose f enarthrosis, enarthrodial (multiaxial) articulation, ball-and-socket joint
Enarthrosis f **sphaeroidea** spheroid articulation (joint)
Encephal... s. a. Enzephal...
Encephalitis f [en]cephalitis, cerebritis, neuraxitis; brain fever *(s. a. unter Enzephalitis)*
~ **corticalis** cortical encephalitis
~ **epidemica (lethargica)** lethargic (epidemic) encephalitis, [von] Economo's disease, sleeping sickness, herpes [simplex] encephalitis, influenzal (herpetic) encephalitis
~ **periaxialis diffusa** diffuse periaxial encephalitis, Schilder's disease, diffuse sclerosis
~ **subcorticalis chronica** chronic subcortical encephalitis
Encephalomyelitis f encephalomyelitis, myelencephalitis *(s. a. unter Enzephalomyelitis)*
~ **haemorrhagica necrotisans** [acute] necrotizing haemorrhagic encephalomyelitis, brain purpura
~ **periaxialis concentrica** concentric periaxial encephalomyelitis, [sudanophilic] concentric sclerosis, Baló's [concentric] disease *(Form der multiplen Sklerose)*
enchondral en[do]chondral, intracartilaginous
Enchondrom n enchondroma
~ **fibrosum** fibroenchondroma
enchondromatös enchondromatous
Enchondromatose f enchondromatosis, Ollier's disease
Enchondrose f enchondrosis
Endangi[i]tis f en[do]angiitis, endovasculitis, intimitis
~ **obliterans** s. Endarteriitis obliterans
Endaortitis f end[o]aortitis
Endapparat m/**taktiler** tactile end organ
Endarborisation f end arborization *(z. B. von Gefäßen)*
Endarterie f end (terminal) artery
Endarteriektomie f endarter[i]ectomy, intimectomy, desobliteration
Endarteriektomiestripper m endarterectomy stripper
Endarteriitis f end[o]arteritis
~ **der Hirngefäße/syphilitische** syphilitic endarteritis of cerebral vessels, Heubner's disease (endarteritis)
~ **obliterans** obliterating endarteritis (endangitis), Buerger's disease, arteriofibrosis *(Gefäßverschlußkrankheit)*
Endaufzweigung f end (terminal) arborization *(z. B. von Nervenfasern)*
endaural endaural
Endbäumchen n telodendr[i]on, telodendrite *(z. B. bei Nerven)*
Enddarm m s. Rektum
enddiastolisch end-diastolic
Endemie f endemia; endemic disease
~/**über Länder ausgedehnte** pandemia
Endemielehre f endemiology
Endemieneigung f endemicity
Endemieregion f endemic region (area)
Endemiologie f endemiology
endemisch endemic, nostrate *(Krankheiten)*
~/**nicht** non-endemic
Endfüßchen n end foot (bulb), terminal bouton, synaptic knob, neuropodium *(Synapsenendigung der Nervenfasern)*
Endglied n terminal (distal) phalanx, end (ungual) phalanx
Endhirn n endbrain, telencephalon

Endhirnbläschen

Endhirnbläschen n telocele
Endigung f/**axonale** axonal termination
Endkallus m definitive callus
Endkern m end-nucleus, terminal nucleus, nucleus of termination
Endkolben m/**Krausescher** Krause's corpuscle (end bulb) *(Kälterezeptor der Haut)*
Endkörperchen n/**Ruffinisches (wärmesensibles)** Ruffini's cell (corpuscle, end organ)
Endo-Amylase f endo-amylase
Endoaneurysmorrhaphie f endoaneurysmorrhaphy
endobronchial endobronchial, intrabronchial
Endobronchitis f endobronchitis
Endocarditis f en[do]carditis *(s. a. unter Endokarditis)*
~ **gonorrhoica** gonococcal endocarditis
~ **lenta** viridans (subacute bacterial) endocarditis
~ **Libman-Sacks** Libman-Sacks endocarditis (disease, syndrome), atypical verrucous endocarditis *(bei Lupus erythematodes)*
endodermal endodermal, entodermal
Endodermatozoonose f endodermatozoonosis
Endoenzym n endoenzyme, intracellular enzyme
Endogamie f endogamy
endogen endogenous, endogen[et]ic
endoglobulär endoglob[ul]ar
Endokard n endocardium ● **unter dem** ~ subendocardial
Endokardelektrode f endocardial electrode
Endokardentzündung f/**bakterielle** bacterial endocarditis
Endokardfibroelastose f [endocardial] fibroelastosis
Endokardfibrose f endocardial fibrosis
endokardial endocardial, endocardiac, intracardial, intracordal, intracardiac, i. c.
Endokardialgeräusch n endocardial murmur
Endokarditis f en[do]carditis *(s. a. unter Endocarditis)*
~/**abszedierende** pustulous endocarditis
~/**akute bakterielle** acute bacterial endocarditis
~/**fetale** foetal (right-side) endocarditis
~/**fibröse** fibrous endocarditis
~/**infektiöse** infectious endocarditis
~/**kalzifizierende** calcific endocarditis
~/**murale** mural endocarditis
~/**mykotische** mycotic endocarditis
~/**nichtbakterielle** non-bacterial endocarditis
~/**nichtbakterielle thrombotische** non-bacterial thrombotic endocarditis
~/**polypöse** polypous endocarditis
~/**rheumatische** rheumatic endocarditis
~/**septische** septic (malignant) endocarditis
~/**ulzeröse** ulcerative endocarditis
~/**verruköse** verrucous (vegetative) endocarditis
endokarditisch endocarditic
Endokardkissen n endocardial cushion
Endokardkissendefekt m endocardial cushion defect, ECD
Endokardleiste f endocardial ridge
Endokard-Perikard-Myokardentzündung f endoperimyocarditis, pancarditis

Endokardsklerose f endocardial sclerosis
Endokard- und Myokardentzündung f endomyocarditis
Endokard- und Myokardfibrose f endomyocardial fibrosis
Endokard- und Perikardentzündung f endopericarditis
Endokardverdickung f endocardial thickening
Endokolitis f endocolitis
endokranial endocranial, intracranial
Endokraniitis f endocranitis, external pachymeningitis
Endokranium n endocranium, dura mater of the brain
endokrin endocrine, endocrinic, endocrinous, incretory, secreting internally
Endokrindrüse f endocrine gland, ductless (closed, false) gland
Endokrinium n endocrinium, endocrine system (organs)
Endokrinologe m endocrinologist
Endokrinologie f endocrinology *(Lehre von der inneren Sekretion)*
endokrinologisch endocrinological
Endokrinopath m endocrinopath, endocrinopathic [person]
Endokrinopathie f endocrinopathy, endocrine disease, endocrinosis *(durch Ausfall einer endokrinen Drüse)*
Endokrinose f s. Endokrinopathie
Endokrinotherapie f endocrinotherapy, endocrine therapy
Endolabyrinthitis f endolabyrinthitis
endolaryngeal endolaryngeal
Endolarynx m endolarynx, interior (cavity) of the larynx
endolumbal endolumbar
endolymphangial endolymphangeal, endolymphangial
endolymphatisch endolymph[at]ic
Endolymphdrainage f endolymphatic drainage
Endolymphe f endolymph, otic fluid
Endolymphentlastung f endolymphatic shunt
Endolymphgang m endolymphatic (otic) duct
Endolymphsack m endolymphatic sac, ELS, otic sac
Endolymphströmung f lymphokinesis *(in den häutigen Bogengängen)*
Endolyse f endolysis
Endolysin n endolysin
Endomesoderm n endomesoderm *(Embryologie)*
Endometrektomie f endometrectomy
Endometrialzyklus m endometrial cycle
endometrioid endometrioid, resembling endometrium
Endometriom n endometrioma
Endometriose f endometriosis
endometriotisch endometriotic
Endometritis f endometritis
~/**bakteriotoxische** bacteriotoxic endometritis
~ **exfoliativa** exfoliative (membranous) dysmenorrhoea *(schmerzhafter Abgang von Gebärmutterschleimhaut während der Regelblutung)*

~ **gonorrhoica (specifica)** gonorrhoeal endometritis
endometritisch endometritic
Endometrium n endometrium, uterine mucosa
Endometrium... s. a. Gebärmutterschleimhaut...
Endometriumabstrichkürette f endometrial biopsy curette
endometriumartig endometrioid
Endometriumatrophie f endometrium atrophy
Endometriumbiopsie f endometrial biopsy
Endometriumbiopsiekürette f endometrial biopsy curette
Endometriumdrüse f endometrium gland
Endometriumdrüsenhyperplasie f endometrium glandular hyperplasia
Endometriumhyperplasie f endometrium hyperplasia
~/**glanduläre** endometrium glandular hyperplasia
Endometriumkarzinom n endometrial cancer (carcinoma)
Endometriummetaplasie f endometrium metaplasia
Endometriumpolyp m endometrium polyp
Endometriumproliferationsphase f endometrium proliferation
Endometriumsaugbiopsie f endometrium aspiration, endometrial suction biopsy
Endometriumsepsis f endometrial sepsis
Endometriumwachstum n endometrium proliferation
Endometriumzyklus m endometrial cycle
Endometriumzyste f endometrium cyst
Endometriumzytologie f endometrium cytology
Endomitose f endomitosis
Endomyokardfibrose f endomyocardial fibrosis
Endomyokarditis f endomyocarditis
Endomyoperikarditis f endomyopericarditis, pancarditis
Endomysium n endomysium
Endoneuralanästhesie f endoneural anaesthesia
Endoneuralraum m endoneural space
Endoneuralscheide f endoneural sheath, sheath of Henle
Endoneuralscheidenentzündung f endoneuritis
Endoneuritis f endoneuritis
Endoneurium n endoneurium
Endoneuriumentzündung f endoneuritis
Endoparasit m endoparasite
endoparasitisch endoparasitic
Endopeptidase f endopeptidase
endoperikardial endopericardial, intrapericardial
Endoperikarditis f endopericarditis
Endoperimyokarditis f endoperimyocarditis
Endophlebitis f endophlebitis
Endophorie f s. Esophorie
Endophthalmitis f endophthalmitis
~ **phacoanaphylactica** phacoanaphylactic endophthalmitis
~ **septica** septic endophthalmitis
Endophyt m endophyte
endophytisch endophytic
Endoplasma n endoplasm, entoplasma

endoplasmatisch endoplasmic
Endoprothese f intraluminal tube (z. B. bei Speiseröhrenkrebs)
Endorgan n end (terminal) organ
~/**taktiles** tactile end organ
Endosalpingiom n endosalpingioma
Endosalpingiosis f endosalpingiosis, isthmic nodular salpingitis
Endosalpingitis f endosalpingitis
Endoskelett n endoskeleton
Endoskop n endoscope
Endoskopie f endoscopy
Endoskopiebefund m endoscopic findings
Endoskopiker m endoscopist
endoskopisch endoscopic
Endoskoppolypektomie f endoscopic polypectomy
Endost n endosteum, medullary membrane
endostal endostal, intraosseous
Endosteitis f endost[e]itis, central osteitis
Endosteom n endost[e]oma
Endosteum n endosteum, medullary membrane
Endostitis f endost[e]itis, central osteitis
Endostosis f endostosis, inflammation of the endosteum
Endotendineum n endotendineum
Endothel n endothelium ● **das ~ bilden** to endothelialize ● **durch das ~ transendothelial** ● **unter dem ~** subendothelial
endothelartig endothelioid
Endothelauskleidung f endothelial lining
Endothelbildung f endothelialization
Endotheldystrophie f endothelial dystrophy
Endothelgeschmeidigkeit f endothelial pliability
Endothelgeschwulst f endothelioma
Endothelgewebe n endothelial tissue
Endothelgift n endotheliotoxin
endothelial endothelial
endothelialisieren to endothelialize
Endothelialisierung f endothelialization
Endothelioangiitis f endothelioangiitis
Endothelioblastom n endothelioblastoma
Endotheliom n endothelioma
Endotheliomatose f endotheliomatosis (Endotheliomanhäufung)
Endotheliose f endotheliosis
Endotheliozyt m endotheliocyte, endothelial phagocyte
Endothelium n s. Endothel
Endothelkarzinom n endothelial cancer (carcinoma)
Endothelleukozyt m endothelial leucocyte, histiocyte
Endothelproliferation f endothelial proliferation
Endothelsarkom n endothelial sarcoma
Endothelwachstum n endothelial proliferation
Endothelwanderzelle f endothelial leucocyte, histiocyte
Endothelzelle f endothelial cell
Endothelzellenkrebs m endothelial cancer (carcinoma)
Endothrix f endothrix (Fadenpilz der Trichophytonarten)

Endotoxikose

Endotoxikose f endotoxicosis
Endotoxin n endotoxin
~/bakterielles bacterial endotoxin
Endotoxinämie f endotoxaemia
Endotoxineinschwemmung f endotoxin infusion
Endotoxinschock m endotoxin (bacteriaemic) shock
Endotoxinvergiftung f endotoxicosis
Endotoxoidinfusion f endotoxoid infusion
Endotrachealnarkose f endotracheal anaesthesia
Endotrachealtubus m endotracheal tube
endourethral endourethral
Endovaskulitis f endovasculitis
Endozervitis f endocervitis, endotrachelitis
Endozervix f endocervix
Endozervixbiopsiekürette f endocervical biopsy curette
Endozytose f endocytosis
Endphalanx f terminal (distal) phalanx, end (ungual) phalanx
Endplatte f end plate *(Nervenendapparat für die Erregungsübertragung)*
~/motorische motor end plate, neuromuscular junction, soleplate
Endplattenmembran f telolemma
Endplattenpotential n end plate potential, e. p. p.
Endschlagader f end (terminal) artery
Endschwankung f final ventricular deflection *(im EKG)*
Endsilbenwiederholung f/**taktartige** logoclonia
Endstadium n final (terminal) stage *(z. B. einer Krankheit)*
Endstellennystagmus m [end-]positional nystagmus, end-point nystagmus
Endstrombahn f terminal vascular bed; capillary system
Endwirt m definitive host
End-zu-End-Anastomose f end-to-end anastomosis
End-zu-End-Gastroduodenostomie f end-to-end gastroduodenostomy
End-zu-Seit-Anastomose f end-to-side anastomosis
End-zu-Seit-Gastroduodenostomie f end-to-side gastroduodenostomy
Enema n s. Einlauf
energetisch gleichwertig isodynamic
Energie f/**kinetische** kinetic energy
~/psychische psychic energy
~/thermische thermic energy
energiearm energy-poor, low-energy
Energiebilanz f energy balance
Energiehaushalt m energy metabolism; energy exchange
Energiequelle f source of energy
energiereich energy-rich, high-energy
Energiespeicherung f energy storage
Energiestoffwechsel m energy metabolism
Energieträger m energy carrier
Energieübertragung f energy transfer

Energieumsatz m energy turnover
Energieverbrauch m energy consumption
Energiezufuhr f energy supply
Enervation f 1. enervation, weakness, lassitude; reduction of strength *(seelischer Zustand)*; 2. s. Enervierung
Enervierung f enervation, removal (resection) of a nerve
ENG s. Elektronystagmographie
Enge f narrowness; stenosis, stegnosis *(z. B. einer Körperöffnung)*; stricture *(z. B. eines Hohlorgans)*; strait *(z. B. des Beckens)*; isthmus *(z. B. der Schilddrüse)*
Engramm n engram, neurogram, mnemonic (memory) trace
Engwinkelglaukom n narrow-angle glaucoma, closed-angle glaucoma, acute angle-closure glaucoma, obstructive (iris-block, congestive) glaucoma
engzahnig stenodont
Enkolpitis f encolpitis
Enkopresis f encopresis *(psychisch bedingte ungewollte Stuhlentleerung)*
Enolase f enolase *(Enzym)*
Enophthalmie f s. Enophthalmus
Enophthalmiker m enophthalmic
enophthalmisch enophthalmic
Enophthalmus m enophthalmos, enophthalmus
Enostose f en[t]ostosis
entaktivieren to decontaminate *(z. B. bei Radioaktivität)*; to deactivate *(z. B. chemische Verbindungen)*
Entaktivierung f decontamination *(z. B. bei Radioaktivität)*; deactivation *(z. B. chemischer Verbindungen)*
entamidieren to de[s]amidate, to deamidize
entaminieren to de[s]aminate, to deaminize
Entamöbenbefall m endamoebiasis, entamoebiasis
entarten to degenerate
Entartung f 1. degeneration, devolution; 2. degeneracy *(s. a. unter* Degeneration*)*
~/bindegewebige fibroid degeneration *(Pathohistologie)*
~/blasige cystic degeneration
~/erbliche hereditary degeneration, heredodegeneration
~/körnige albuminous degeneration
Entase f entasia, entasis
entbinden to deliver
entbindend parturient
~/mehrfach polytocous
~/normal eutocic
Entbindung f labour, delivery, parturition, confinement, [child]birth, accouchement, lying-in *(s. a.* Geburt*)* ● **vor der ~** antepartal
~ durch Gebärmutterhalsschnitt low cervical caesarean section
~ durch Leistenschnitt laparelytrotomy
~/erschwerte dystocia, parodynia, difficult parturition (labour)
~/instrumentelle instrumental labour, embryulcia

~/natürliche s. ~/vaginale
~/normale normal (safe) delivery
~/prämature premature delivery
~/vaginale vaginal delivery
Entbindungsklinik f maternity (lying-in) hospital
Entbindungskunst f obstetrics, O. B., midwifery
Entbindungsraum m delivery (birth) room
Entbindungsschock m postpartum shock
Entbindungsstation f maternity ward
entblocken to unblock (z. B. einen Tubus)
entblößen to expose
Entblößung f exposure, denudation
entbunden werden to be delivered, to be confined
Entdifferenzierung f dedifferentiation
Ente f urinal, urine bottle (für Bettlägerige)
enteisenen to desiderize, to deprive of iron
Enteiweißung f deproteinization
entenfüßig pigeon-toed
Entengang m duck (myopathic) gait
entepithelialisieren to de-epithelialize
Entepithelialisierung f de-epithelialization
enteral enteral, enteric, intestinal
Enteralgie f enteralgia, enterodynia, pain in the intestine
Enteramin n enteramine (Katecholamin)
Enterektomie f enterectomy, intestinal resection
Enterelkosis f enterelcosis, ulceration of the intestine
Enteric-Cytopathogenic-Human-Orphan-Virus n ECHO virus
enterisch enteral, enteric, intestinal
Enteritis f enteritis, inflammation of the intestinal tract
~/aktute fibrinöse acute fibrinous enteritis
~ anaphylactica anaphylactic enteritis
~/chronisch vernarbende chronic cicatrizing enteritis
~/gallige feline enteritis
~/membranöse membranous (acute fibrinous) enteritis
~/mukomembranöse (muköse) mucous (mucomembranous) enteritis
~ necroticans enteritis necroticans, necrotizing enteritis, darmbrand
~/phlegmonöse phlegmonous enteritis
~/polypöse polypous enteritis
~/pseudomembranöse pseudomembranous enteritis
~ regionalis [Crohn] regional enteritis (enterocolitis, ileitis), segmental enteritis, Crohn's disease
Entero... s. a. Darm...
Enteroadenitis f enteradenitis
Enteroanastomose f enteroanastomosis; enteroenterostomy
Enterobiasis f enterobiasis, oxyuriasis, pinworm infection
Enterobius m vermicularis (vermiformis) Enterobius vermicularis, pinworm, seatworm, oxyurid
Enterobiusinfektion f s. Enterobiasis
Enterodynie f enterodynia, enteralgia, pain in the intestine

Enteroenterostomie f enteroenterostomy
Enteroepiplozele f enterepiplocele, epiploenterocele
Enterogastron n enterogastrone (Hormon)
enterogen enterogenous, enterogen[et]ic
Enteroglukagon n enteroglucagon (Hormon)
Enterogramm n enterogram
Enterograph m enterograph
Enterographie f enterography (Aufzeichnung der Darmbewegung)
enterographisch enterographic
enterohepatisch enterohepatic
Enterohepatitis f enterohepatitis, inflammation of the bowel and liver
Enterohepatozele f enterohepatocele
Enterokinase f enterokinase (Enzym)
Enterokokkenendokarditis f enterococcal endocarditis
Enterokokkus m enterococcus
Enterokolektomie f enterocolectomy
Enterokolitis f enterocolitis
~/pseudomembranöse pseudomembranous enterocolitis
Enterokolitissyndrom n enterocolitis syndrome
Enterokolostomie f enterocolostomy
Enterokrinin n enterocrinin (Hormon)
Enterokystom[a] n enterocystoma (Rest des Ductus omphalomesentericus)
Enterolith m enterolith, intestinal calculus, alvinolith
Enterolithiasis f enterolithiasis
Enterolyse f enterolysis
Enteromegalie f enteromegaly
Enteromyiasis f enteromyiasis, intestinal myiasis
Enteromykose f enteromycosis, intestinal mycosis
Enteron n enteron, intestine[s], intestinum, bowel[s], alimentary canal (Zusammensetzungen s. unter Darm)
Enteroparalyse f enteroparalysis, enteroplegia; ileus
Enteropathie f enteropathy, disease of the intestine
enteropathisch enteropathic
enteropathogen enteropathogenic
Enteropexie f enteropexy, fixation of the intestine
Enteroplastik f enteroplasty
enteroplastisch enteroplastic
Enteroplegie f enteroplegia, enteroparalysis
enteroplegisch enteroplegic
Enteroptose f enteroptosis, visceroptosis, Glénard's disease
enteroptotisch enteroptotic
enterorektal enterorectal
enterorenal enterorenal
Enterorrhagie f enterorrhagia, intestinal haemorrhage (bleeding)
Enterorrhaphie f enterorrhaphy, intestinal suture
Enterorrhexis f enterorrhexis, rupture of the intestine
Enterosiderin n enterosiderin

Enteroskop 212

Enteroskop *n* enteroscope
Enteroskopie *f* enteroscopy
enteroskopisch enteroscopic
Enterospasmus *m* enterospasm, intestinal cramp
Enterostase *f* enterostasis, intestinal stasis
Enterostenose *f* enterostenosis, intestinal stenosis
Enterostoma *n* enterostomy, intestinal fistula
Enterostomie *f* enterostomy
Enterotom *n* enterotome
Enterotomie *f* enterotomy
Enterotoxin *n* enterotoxin
Enterotoxinämie *f* enterotoxaemia
enterotoxinbildend enterotoxi[no]genic, enterotoxin-producing
Enterotoxinvergiftung *f* enterotoxication, enterotoxism
Enterotyphus *m* enterotyphus, typhoid fever
enterovesikal enterovesical
Enterovirenexanthem *n* enteroviral rash
Enterovirus *n* enterovirus *(zur Gruppe der Poliomyelitis-, Coxsackie- und ECHO-Viren gehörend)*
Enterozele *f* enterocele, intestine hernia
Enterozentese *f* enterocentesis, intestinal puncture
Enterozöle *f* enterocoele
Enterozoon *n* enterozoon, intestinal (entozoic) parasite
Enterozyste *f* enterocyst, enteric cyst
Enterozystoplastik *f* enterocystoplasty
Enterozystozele *f* enterocystocele
entfalten/das Rektum to balloon out the rectum *(durch Lufteinblasung)*
Entfaltungsknistern *n* crepitant rale *(Lunge)*
Entfärbung *f* **der Haut** depigmentation
entfernen to remove, to eliminate; to resect, to extirpate, to ablate
~/**das Epithel** to de-epithelialize
~/**das Gehirn** to decerebrate, to decerebrize
~/**das Hämoglobin** to dehaemoglobinize
~/**den Samenleiter** to vasectomize
~/**den Thymus** to thymectomize
~/**die Brust** to mastectomize
~/**die Haare** to epilate
~/**die Hypophyse** to hypophysectomize
~/**die Milz** to splenectomize
~/**die Nebenniere** to adrenalectomize
~/**die Nebenschilddrüse** to parathyroidectomize
~/**die Nieren** to nephrectomize
~/**ein Ganglion** to deganglionate
~/**Fettgewebe** to defat
~/**Fibrin** to defibrinate
~/**mineralische Substanzen** to demineralize
~/**Organe [teilweise]** to resect
~/**Stickstoff** to denitrify
~/**totes Gewebe** to necrectomize
entfernt distal, distant
Entfernung *f* 1. removal, elimination; clearance; 2. *s.* ~/operative
~ **der Bauch- und Thoraxorgane** evisceration, exenteration
~ **der Rachenwucherungen und der Mandeln/operative** adenotonsillectomy
~ **des gesamten Dickdarms/operative** pancolectomy
~ **des inneren Augenwinkels/operative** rhinocanthectomy
~ **des Lungenoberlappens/operative** upper lobectomy (lobe resection)
~ **des Nervus phrenicus/operative** phren[i]ectomy
~ **des Omentum majus** bursectomy
~/**operative** removal, resection, extirpation, ablation, obliteration
~ **toten Gewebes[/operative]** necrectomy
entfetten 1. to defat, to remove the fat; 2. to reduce the corpulence
~/**die Haut** to degrease the skin
Entfettung *f* defatting, degreasing
Entfettungskost *f* low-caloric diet
Entfettungskur *f* treatment for obesity
entfiebern to defervesce, to become afebrile
entfiebernd defervescent, lyterian, paracmic
entfiebert defervescent
Entfieberung *f* defervescence, lysis, paracme
entflammen to inflame
entflimmern to defibrillate
Entflimmerung *f* defibrillation *(der Herzkammern) (Zusammensetzungen s. unter Defibrillation)*
Entfremdung *f* alienation; estrangement
entgiften 1. to detoxicate, to detoxify; 2. *s.* entseuchen
entgiftend detoxicant
Entgiftung *f* 1. detoxi[fi]cation, disintoxication; 2. *s.* Entseuchung
Entgiftungsmittel *n* detoxicant [agent]
Entgiftungsvorgang *m* detoxification process
enthaaren to depilate, to epilate, to remove hair
enthaarend depilatory, decalvant
Enthaarung *f* depilation, epilation
Enthaarungsmittel *n* depilatory [agent]
Enthaarungspinzette *f* epilating forceps
enthalten/im Arzneimittelbuch officinal, pharmacopoeial
enthaltsam abstinent, temperate, continent
Enthaltsamkeit *f*, **Enthaltung** *f* abstinence, temperance *(z. B. gegenüber Alkohol)*; abstinence, continence *(geschlechtlich)*
enthaupten *s.* dekapitieren
Enthemmung *f* exaltation, disinhibition
enthirnen to decerebrate
Enthirnung *f* decerebration
~ **des Fetus** encephalotomy *(bei Totgeburt)*
Enthirnungsstarre *f* decerebrate rigidity
enthypnotisieren to dehypnotize
entjungfern *s.* deflorieren
entkalken to decalcify
Entkalkung *f*, **Entkalzifizierung** *f* decalcification
entkapseln to decorticate, to decapsulate
Entkapselung *f* decortication, decapsulation
entkeimen to sterilize, to degerm; to disinfect; to pasteurize *(vorübergehend)*

entkeimend disinfectant
Entkeimung f sterilization, degermation; disinfection; pasteurization
Entkeimungsmittel n disinfectant [agent], germicide
entkernen to enucleate
Entkernung f enucleation
entkoppeln to deconjugate
Entkopplung f deconjugation *(z. B. von Gallensäuren)*
entkräftet prostrate[d]; exhausted, debilitated; stricken down
Entkräftung f[/hochgradige] prostration; extreme exhaustion, debilitation
Entladungseffekt m detonator effect *(Synapse)*
Entladungsläsion f discharging lesion *(Physiologie)*
Entlassungsbericht m record on discharge
Entlastungsnaht f relaxation (tension) suture
Entlastungsoperation f relieving operation
Entlastungsschnitt m relaxation (releaving, relaxing) incision
entlausen to delouse
Entlausung f delousing
Entlausungsmittel n lousicide, pediculicide
entleeren to discharge, to evacuate, to empty; to defaecate, to purge *(den Darm)*; to void *(z. B. die Blase)*
Entleerungsmuskel m detrusor muscle
Entleerungsmuskelkontraktion f detrusor contraction
Entleerungszeit f emptying time *(z. B. der Blase)*
entlüften to deaerate, to vent, to ventilate
Entlüftungskatheter m venting catheter
entmannen to castrate, to emasculate
Entmannung f castration, emasculation
Entmannungskomplex m castration complex
entmarken to demyelinate, to demyelinize
Entmarkung f demyelin[iz]ation, myelinoclasis *(des ZNS)*
Entmarkungskrankheit f demyelinating disease
entmineralisieren to demineralize
Entmündigung f interdiction
Entnahme f collection *(z. B. von Blutproben)*
entnarkotisieren to denarcotize
entnehmen/Blut to draw blood *(z. B. aus einer Vene)*
~/eine Probe to sample *(z. B. Gewebe)*
entnerven s. denervieren
Entoblast m entoblast, primitive entoderm
Entoderm n endoderm, entoderm
entodermal endodermal, entodermal
Entodermausstülpung f endodermal pouch
entomogen entomogenous
Entomophobie f entomophobia *(krankhafte Angst vor Insekten)*
Entomosis f entomosis
entoptisch entoptic
Entoptoskop n entoptoscope *(ophthalmologisches Instrument)*
Entoptoskopie f entoptoscopy
entoptoskopisch entoptoscopic

Entozoon n entozoon
entrinden to decorticate *(z. B. ein Organ)*
entropionieren to entropionize
Entropium n entropion, blepharelosis
entrunden to unround *(z. B. die Pupillen)*
Entschädigungsneurose f compensation neurosis
Entschlackung f purification; catharsis; purging
Entschlackungsdiät f obesity diet
entseuchen 1. to disinfect; 2. to decontaminate *(Nuklearmedizin)*
entseuchend 1. disinfectant; 2. decontaminating
Entseuchung f 1. disinfection; 2. decontamination
~/radioaktive [radioactive] decontamination
Entseuchungsmittel n disinfectant; decontaminating substance
entspannen [/sich] to relax
entspannend relaxant
entspannt/völlig relaxed, atonic *(z. B. ein Muskel)*
Entspannung f relaxation
Entspeicherung f release; mobilization
entspiralisieren to despiralize, to decoil *(z. B. die Chromosomen)*
entsprechend/einander reciprocal
entstammen to be descended from *(abstammen)*; to come from, to originate in
entstammend:
~/dem After proctogenic
~/dem Mastdarm proctogenic
~/dem Samen spermatogenic
~/nicht der Leber anhepatogenic
entstanden:
~/auf dem Lymphweg lymphogenous, lymphogenic, lymph-borne *(z. B. Metastasen)*
~/außen exogenous, exogen[et]ic
~/durch anomale Entwicklung dysontogenetic *(z. B. Tumoren)*
~/durch Gift toxicogenic
~/durch radioaktiven Zerfall radiogenic
~/durch Spaltung schizogenic
~/innen endogenous, endogen[et]ic
entstehend/gerade nascent
Entstehung f genesis, formation; origination; nascency
entstellen to deform, to disfigure *(z. B. das Gesicht)*
Enttäuschung f disillusionment; frustration
entwässern to dry, to desiccate *(z. B. Drogen)*; to dehydrate *(z. B. den Körper)*; to exsiccate *(z. B. die Haut)*
entwässernd drying, desiccant; dehydrating; exsiccant
entwässert desiccated, dry
Entwässerung f drying, desiccation *(z. B. von Drogen)*; dehydration, anhydration *(z. B. des Körpers)*; exsiccation *(z. B. der Haut)*
Entwässerungsbehandlung f dehydration therapy
entweiblichen to defeminize
Entweiblichung f defemin[iz]ation

entwesen

entwesen to disinfest
Entwesung f disinfestation; deinsectization
entwickeln 1. to develop, to evolve; 2. to liberate *(Geburtshilfe)*
~/Blasen to vesicate
~/sich to evolve, to be evolved
Entwickeln n liberation *(z. B. die Arme bei der Geburt)*
entwickelnd/sich außen exogenous, exogen[et]ic
~/sich innen endogenous, endogen[et]ic
entwickelt/nicht voll immature *(unreif)*
~/unvollkommen aplastic *(z. B. ein Organ)*
~/vollkommen definitive *(z. B. ein Organ)*
~/vollständig mature *(reif)*
Entwicklung f 1. development; genesis; growth; 2. s. Entwickeln ● **durch anomale ~ entstanden** dysontogenetic *(z. B. Tumoren)* ● **zur vollständigen ~ gelangen** to mature
~/andersartige heterogenesis *(z. B. durch Virusinfektion)*
~/gestörte arrested development
~/gleichartige homogenesis
~/gleiche isogenesis
~/mehrerer Mikrogliome microgliomatosis
~/pränatale prenatal development
~/psychische psychogenesis
Entwicklungsalter n developmental age *(s. a. Pubertät)*
Entwicklungsanomalie f developmental anomaly
Entwicklungsbad n developing bath *(z. B. für Röntgenfilme)*
Entwicklungsbeschleunigung f [developmental] acceleration
Entwicklungsfehler m developmental defect
Entwicklungsgeschichte f ontogenesis; embryology; phylogenesis
~ des Menschen anthropogenesis
Entwicklungsgleichheit f isogenesis
Entwicklungskrise f developmental crisis
Entwicklungslösung f developing solution, developer *(für Röntgenfilme)*
Entwicklungsphase f developmental phase
Entwicklungsphysiologie f developmental physiology
Entwicklungspsychologie f developmental psychology
Entwicklungsquotient m developmental quotient
Entwicklungsrückschlag m atavism
Entwicklungsschaden m/**embryonaler** embryopathy
Entwicklungsstadium n developmental stadium
Entwicklungsstörung f developmental disturbance (disease), dysontogenesis *(z. B. des Gewebes)*
Entwicklungsstufe f developmental stage
Entwicklungsverfrühung f acceleration
Entwicklungszeit f 1. developmental time *(Embryologie)*; 2. incubation [period] *(z. B. für Keime)*; 3. development time *(für Röntgenfilme)*

Entwicklungszustand m developmental state
entwöhnen to wean *(z. B. einen Säugling)*
Entwöhnen n weaning *(z. B. eines Säuglings)*
entziehen to withdraw *(z. B. Drogen)*
~/Wasser s. entwässern
Entziehung f withdrawal *(z. B. von Drogen)*
Entziehungsheim n sanatorium for alcoholics
Entziehungskur f withdrawal treatment, detoxication therapy
Entzückung f ecstasy
Entzugsblutung f withdrawal bleeding
Entzugsdelirium n withdrawal (abstinence) delirium
Entzugserscheinung f withdrawal (abstinence) phenomenon
Entzugssymptom n withdrawal symptom
Entzugssyndrom n withdrawal syndrome, acute delirium
~/aortoiliakales aortoiliac steal syndrome
entzünden to inflame
~/sich to become (get) inflamed
entzündet inflamed; inflammatory *(z. B. Gewebe)*; sore *(z. B. Haut)*; tender
~/etwas (gering) subinflammatory
entzündlich inflammatory, phlogistic
Entzündung f inflammation *(z. B. des Gewebes)*; sore *(z. B. der Haut)*
~ aller Herzwandschichten pancarditis
~ der Horn- und Bindehaut keratoconjunctivitis
~ der Orbitaperiostauskleidung periconchitis
~ der Pia mater und der Arachnoidea piarachnitis, piitis
~ der Rückenmarkhäute perimyelitis
~ der Scheidenumgebung paracolpitis
~ des Dickdarmbauchfellüberzugs pericol[on]itis
~ des männlichen Glieds penitis
~ des Os naviculare scaphoiditis
~/diphtherische diphtheritic inflammation, pseudomembranous mucositis
~/eitrige suppurative inflammation
~/exsudative exudative inflammation
~/interstitielle interstitial inflammation
~/produktive productive (plastic) inflammation *(mit Gewebsneubildung)*
~/proliferative proliferative inflammation
~/pseudomembranöse pseudomembranous inflammation (mucositis)
~/seröse serous inflammation
~/subdiaphragmale subdiaphragmal inflammation, subphrenitis
entzündungserregend phlogogenic, phlogogenous
Entzündungsexsudat n inflammatory exudate
Entzündungsgewebe n inflammatory tissue
entzündungshemmend anti-inflammatory, antiphlogistic
Entzündungsherd m focus of inflammation
Entzündungsmakrophage m inflammatory macrophage
Entzündungsödem n inflammatory oedema
Entzündungsprozeß m inflammatory process

Entzündungsreaktion f inflammatory reaction (response)
Entzündungszeichen n inflammatory sign (symptom)
Entzündungszelle f inflammatory cell
Entzündungszustand m inflammatory condition
Enukleation f enucleation
enukleieren to enucleate
Enuresis f enuresis, urorrhoea, uracratia
~ **diurna** diurnal enuresis
~ **nocturna** nocturnal enuresis, nocturia
Enuretiker m enuretic [person]
enuretisch enuretic
Envenomation f envenom[iz]ation
Enzephal... s. a. Encephal...
Enzephalasthenie f encephalasthenia
Enzephalatrophie f [en]cephalatrophy, atrophy of the brain
Enzephalitis f [en]cephalitis, cerebritis, neuraxitis; brain fever (s. a. unter Encephalitis)
~/**akute disseminierte** acute disseminated encephalitis
~ **B** s. ~/**japanische**
~/**durch Arboviren** arbovirus encephalitis
~/**hämorrhagische** haemorrhagic encephalitis
~/**japanische** Japanese B encephalitis, summer encephalitis
~ **mit Höhlenbildung** porencephalitis
~/**otogene** otogenic encephalitis, otoencephalitis
~/**postinfektiöse** postinfection encephalitis
~/**postvakzinale** postvaccinal encephalitis
~/**von Bogaertsche** panencephalitis
enzephalitisbewirkend encephalitogenic
enzephalitisch encephalitic
Enzephalitisvirus n encephalitis virus, encephalovirus, arbovirus, arthropod-borne virus
Enzephaloarteriographie f encephaloarteriography
Enzephalodysplasie f encephalodysplasia
Enzephalogie f encephalogy
Enzephalogramm n encephalogram
Enzephalographie f encephalography
enzephalographisch encephalographic
Enzephalolith m encephalolith, calculus of the brain
Enzephalom[a] n encephaloma, tumour of the brain
Enzephalomalazie f encephalomalacia, encephalodialysis, cerebral softening, softening of the brain
enzephalomalazisch encephalomalacic
Enzephalomeningitis f encephalomeningitis
Enzephalomeningopathie f encephalomeningopathy, meningo-encephalopathy
Enzephalomeningozele f encephalomeningocele, meningo-encephalocele
Enzephalometer n encephalometer
Enzephalomyelitis f encephalomyelitis, myelencephalitis (s. a. unter Encephalomyelitis)
~/**myalgische** myalgic encephalomyelitis
~/**postvakzinale** postvaccinal encephalomyelitis
Enzephalomyeloneuropathie f encephalomyeloneuropathy

Enzephalomyelopathie f encephalomyelopathy
Enzephalomyeloradikulitis f encephalomyeloradiculitis
Enzephalomyeloradikulopathie f encephalomyeloradiculopathy
Enzephalomyelosis f encephalomyelosis
Enzephalomyokarditis f encephalomyocarditis
Enzephalomyokarditisvirus n encephalomyocarditis virus, Columbia-SK-virus
Enzephalon n encephalon, brain, cerebrum (Zusammensetzungen s. unter Gehirn)
Enzephalopathie f encephalopathy, cephalopathy, cerebropathy, cerebral disease, disease of the brain
~/**portosystemische** portosystemic encephalopathy
~/**rheumatische** rheumatic encephalopathy, cerebral rheumatism
enzephalopathisch encephalopathic
Enzephalopsychose f encephalopsychosis
Enzephalorrhagie f encephalorrhagia, haemorrhage in the brain, cerebral [pericapillary] haemorrhage
Enzephalose f encephalosis, organic (degenerative) brain disease
Enzephalosklerose f encephalosclerosis, hardening (sclerosis) of the brain
Enzephaloskop n encephaloscope
Enzephaloskopie f encephaloscopy
enzephaloskopisch encephaloscopic
enzephalospinal encephalospinal
Enzephalotom n encephalotome
Enzephalotomie f encephalotomy
Enzephalozele f encephalocele, cerebral hernia, craniocele, hernia of the brain
Enzephalozystozele f encephalocystocele
Enzianviolett n gentian violet
Enzym n enzyme, zyme, ferment
~/**autolytisches** autolytic enzyme
~/**eiweißspaltendes** proteoloytic enzyme, protease
~/**extrazelluläres** extracellular enzyme, exoenzyme, ectoenzyme
~/**fettspaltendes** lipolytic enzyme
~/**gelbes** yellow (flavin) enzyme, flavoprotein
~/**glykolytisches** glycolytic enzyme
~/**intrazelluläres** intracellular enzyme, endoenzyme, organized ferment
~/**kapsuliertes** [en]capsulated enzyme
~/**Schardingersches** xanthine oxidase
~/**stärkespaltendes** amylolytic (starch-reducing) enzyme, amylase
~/**zellständiges** s. ~/**intrazelluläres**
Enzymaktivator m enzyme activator
Enzymaktivierung f enzyme activation, activation of enzymes
Enzymaktivität f enzyme activity
enzymatisch enzym[at]ic, zymotic, fermentative, fermental
Enzymauflösung f enzymolysis
Enzymausscheidung f im Urin enzymuria
enzymbildend zymogenic, zymoplastic, enzyme-producing

Enzymbildung

Enzymbildung f zymogenesis, enzyme production
Enzymeinheit f enzyme unit
Enzymentgleisung f enzymatic disorder
Enzymfreisetzung f enzyme release
Enzymhemmung f enzyme inhibition
Enzyminduktion f enzyme induction
enzyminduzierend enzyme-inducing
Enzymkinetik f enzyme kinetics
Enzymlehre f enzymology
Enzymmangel m enzyme deficiency, enzymopenia, azymia
Enzymologie f enzymology
Enzymolyse f enzymolysis
enzymolytisch enzymolytic
Enzymopathie f enzymopathy
Enzymopenie f s. Enzymmangel
Enzympräparat n enzyme preparation
Enzymprotein n zymoprotein
Enzymsubstitution f enzyme substitution
Enzymsynthese f enzyme synthesis
Enzymvorstufe f proenzyme
~/**inaktive** inactive enzyme precursor; zymogen
Enzymwirkung f enzymic (enzymatic) action
EOG s. Elektrookulographie
Eonismus m eonism, transves[ti]tism, transsexualism
Eosin n eosin
Eosinfärbbarkeit f eosinophilia
eosinfärbend eosinophil[e]
Eosin-Methylenblau-Färbung f eosin-methylene blue stain
Eosinopenie f eosinopenia; acido[cyto]penia
eosinopenisch eosinopenic
eosinophil eosinophil[e], eosinophilic
Eosinophilengranulom n eosinophilic [xanthomatous] granuloma
Eosinophilenleukämie f eosinophilic (eosinophilocytic) leukaemia
Eosinophilensturz m s. Eosinopenie
Eosinophilenvermehrung f s. Eosinophilie
Eosinophilenverminderung f s. Eosinopenie
Eosinophiler m eosinophil[e], eosinophilic leucocyte; acidocyte, acidophile leucocyte
Eosinophilie f eosinophilia, acidophilia, acidocytosis
~/**tropische** [pulmonary] tropical eosinophilia; eosinophilic lung
~/**verstärkte** hypereosinophilia
Eosinophilie-Hepatomegalie-Syndrom n eosinophilia-hepatomegaly syndrome (allergische Krankheit bei Nematodenbefall der Leber)
Eosinotaxis f eosinotaxis
Ependym n ependyma, ependymal layer (zone) (Gliazellschicht des Rückenmarkkanals und der Hirnventrikel) ● unter dem ~ subependymal
ependymal ependymal
Ependymentzündung f s. Ependymitis
Ependymerkrankung f s. Ependymopathie
Ependymgeschwulst f, **Ependymgliom** n s. Ependymom
Ependymitis f ependymitis, inflammation of the ependyma
Ependymoblast m ependymoblast
Ependymoblastom n ependymoblastoma
Ependymom n ependymoma, ependymocytoma (vom Ependym abgeleitete Ventrikelgeschwulst)
Ependymopathie f ependymopathy, disease of the ependyma
Ependymozyt m s. Empendymzelle
Ependymschicht f s. Ependym
Ependymspongioblastom n ependymal spongioblastoma
Ependymzelle f ependymal cell, ependymocyte
Ependymzyste f ependymal cyst
Ephedrin n ephedrine (spasmolytisches und antiallergisches Sympathikomimetikum)
~/**razemisches** dl-ephedrine, racephedrine
Ephelis f ephelis, freckle, sunspot
ephemer ephemeral, temporary, transient (z. B. Fieber)
Ephemera pl ephemera, ephemeral fever
~ **maligna** English sweating fever
Ephidrosis f ephidrosis, hyperhidrosis, excessive sweating
Epiandrosteron n epiandrosterone, 3-β-hydroxy-17-androstanone (androgenes Steroid)
Epiblast m 1. epidermal ectoderm; 2. primitive ectoderm (der Blastula)
Epiblepharon n epiblepharon
epibulbär epibulbar
epichordal epichordal
epichorial epichorial
Epichorion n epichorion
Epicondylus m epicondyle, epicondylus, supracondylar eminence
~ **lateralis femoris** lateral epicondyle of the femur
~ **lateralis humeri** lateral epicondyle of the humerus
~ **medialis femoris** medial epicondyle of the femur
~ **medialis humeri** medial epicondyle of the humerus
Epidemie f epidemic
~/**beherrschbare** controllable epidemic
~/**über Länder ausgedehnte** pandemia
Epidemieanamnese f epidemiological history
epidemieartig epidemic
Epidemiefähigkeit f epidemicity (z. B. von Bakterien)
epidemiefrei non-epidemic
Epidemiegeschehen n epidemic occurrence
Epidemieneigung f epidemicity
Epidemiespezialist m epidemiologist
Epidemieverlauf m epidemic curve
Epidemiologe m epidemiologist
Epidemiologie f epidemiology (Lehre von der Entstehung, Verbreitung und Bekämpfung von Infektionskrankheiten)
~/**aerobiologische** aerobiological epidemiology
epidemiologisch epidemiologic
epidemisch epidemic; zymotic
epidermal epidermal, epider[mat]ic, epidermatous

Epidermatozoonose f epi[dermato]zoonosis
Epidermis f epiderm[is], tegumentary epithelium, scarf skin ● **unter der** ~ subepidermal, subepidermic, subcuticular
Epidermis... s. a. Oberhaut...
Epidermisablösung f epidermolysis
Epidermisaffektion f epiderm[id]osis
Epidermisanhanggebilde n epidermal appendage
Epidermisanomalie f epiderm[id]osis
epidermisartig epidermoid
Epidermisauflösung f epidermolysis
Epidermisdysplasie f epidermodysplasia
Epidermisierung f epidermi[dali]zation, epithel[ial]ization
Epidermiskrebs m epidermal cancer
Epidermisplastik f epidermoplasty
Epidermistransplantation f epidermis transplantation
Epidermiszelle f epidermal cell
Epidermiszerfall m epidermolysis
Epidermiszyste f epidermis cyst
Epidermitis f epidermitis, inflammation of the epidermis
Epidermoid n epidermoid
Epidermoidcholesteatom n epidermoid cholesteatoma
Epidermoidom[a] n epidermoidoma
Epidermoidzelle f epidermoid cell
Epidermoidzyste f epidermoid cyst
Epidermolysis f epidermolysis
~ **bullosa** bullous epidermolysis, Köbner's disease, Goldscheider's disease
~ **bullosa dystrophica** dystrophic bullous epidermolysis
~ **bullosa hereditaria letalis** lethal hereditary bullous epidermolysis
~ **bullosa simplex** simple bullous epidermolysis
Epidermom n epidermoma
Epidermomykose f epidermomycosis
Epidermophytid n epidermophytid *(allergisches Hautexanthem bei Epidermomykosen)*
Epidermophytie f epidermophytosis
~/tropische tropical tinea circinata
Epidermosis f epidermosis
epididymal epididymal
Epididymektomie f epididymectomy
Epididymis f epididymis, parorchis
Epididymis... s. Nebenhoden...
Epididymitis f epididymitis, inflammation of the epididymis
Epididymodeferentektomie f epididymodeferentectomy
Epididymoorchidektomie f epididymo-orchi[d]ectomy
Epididymoorchitis f epididymo-orchitis, inflammation of the epididymis and the testis
Epididymotomie f epididymotomy
Epididymovasostomie f epididymovasostomy
Epiduralabszeß m epidural abscess
Epiduralanästhesie f epidural anaesthesia
Epiduralblutung f epidural haemorrhage

Epiduralempyem n extradural empyema
Epiduralhämatom n epidural haematoma
Epiduralraum m epidural space, extradural cavity
~/spinaler spinal epidural space
epifaszial epifascial
Epifollikulitis f epifolliculitis, inflammation of the hair follicles
epigam epigamous, occurring after conception
Epigastralgie f epigastralgia, pain in the epigastrium
epigastrisch epigastric
Epigastrium n s. Oberbauch
Epigastrius m epigastrius *(Doppelmißbildung)*
Epigastrozele f epigastrocele, epigastric hernia
Epiglottidektomie f epiglott[id]ectomy
Epiglottis f epiglottis ● **unter der** ~ subepiglottic ● **vor der** ~ pre-epiglottic
epiglottisch epiglottal, epiglottic, epiglottidean
Epiglottischondrom n chondroma of epiglottis
Epiglottisexstirpation f epiglott[id]ectomy
Epiglottisheber m levator epiglottidis [muscle]
Epiglottisknorpel m epiglottic cartilage
Epiglottissenker m depressor epiglottidis [muscle]
Epiglottitis f epiglottitis, inflammation of the epiglottis
Epignathus m epignathus *(Doppelmißbildung)*
Epikanthus m epicanthus, epicanthic (eye, Mongolian) fold
Epikard n epicardium, visceral pericardium ● **unter dem** ~ subepicardial
Epikardelektrode f epicardial electrode
Epikardia f epicardia *(unteres Ösophagusende zwischen Zwerchfell und Magen)*
epikardial epicardial
Epikardresektion f epicardiectomy
Epikondylalgie f epicondylalgia
epikondylär epicondylar, epicondylian, epicondylic
Epikondylenschmerz m epicondylalgia
Epikondylitis f epicondylitis, inflammation of the epicondyle; tennis elbow
Epikondylus m s. Epicondylus
Epikondylusentzündung f s. Epikondylitis
Epikondylusfraktur f epicondylar fracture
epikranial epicranial
Epikraniotomie f epicraniotomy
Epikranium n epicranium
Epikranius m epicranius [muscle]
Epikrise f epicrisis
Epikutantest m patch test *(zur Feststellung von Allergien)*
Epilation f s. Enthaarung
Epilationsdosis f epilating dose *(Radiologie)*
Epilepsia f s. Epilepsie
~ **larvata** masked (latent) epilepsy
~ **partialis continua** continuous epilepsy
~ **procursiva** procursive (accelerative, temporal lobe) epilepsy
~ **tarda** tardy (delayed) epilepsy
~ **traumatica** traumatic epilepsy
Epilepsie f epilepsy, falling sickness, Saint Valentine's (Avertin's) disease *(s. a. unter Epilepsia)*

Epilepsie

~/akinetische akinetic epilepsy
~/autonome autonomic epilepsy
~/durch Licht erzeugte photic epilepsy
~/extrapyramidale extrapyramidal (striatal) epilepsy
~/hypothalamische hypothalamic epilepsy
~/idiopathische idiopathic epilepsy
~/kryptogene cryptogenic epilepsy
~/photogene photic epilepsy
~/psychische psychic epilepsy
~/psychomotorische psychomotor epilepsy, dawning attack
~/reaktive reactive epilepsy
~/sensorische sensory epilepsy
~/symptomatische symptomatic epilepsy
~/zerebellare cerebellar epilepsy (fit)
Epilepsieanfall m seizure
~/abortiver absence attack
~/großer generalized seizure, grand mal epilepsy
~/gustatorischer gustatory seizure (fit)
epilepsieartig epileptiform, epileptoid
epilepsieauslösend epileptogenic, epileptogenous
Epilepsiedaueranfall m epileptic (convulsive) state
Epilepsiefokus m epileptogenic focus
Epilepsieform f/milde paraepilepsy
Epilepsiekranker m epileptic
Epilepsielehre f epileptology
Epilepsiemittel n antiepileptic [agent]
Epilepsiespezialist m epileptologist
Epileptiker m epileptic
epileptisch epileptic
epilieren s. enthaaren
Epimyokard[ium] n epimyocardium (Embryologie)
Epimysium n epimysium; muscular fascia
Epinephrektomie f epinephrectomy, adrenalectomy, excision of the adrenals
Epinephrin n s. Adrenalin
Epinephritis f epinephritis, adrenalitis, inflammation of an adrenal gland
Epinephron n epinephros, adrenal (suprarenal) gland
epineural epineural, epineurial
Epineurium n epineurium, cellular sheath
Epiorchium n epiorchium
Epipalatum n epipalatum (Doppelmißbildung)
epiperikardial epipericardial
epipharyngeal epipharyngeal, nasopharyngeal
Epipharynx m epipharynx, nasopharynx, pharyngonasal cavity, rhinopharynx, postnasal space
Epiphora f epiphora; watery eye
epiphrenisch epiphrenal, epiphrenic
epiphysär 1. epiphyseal, epiphysial; 2. pineal
Epiphyse f 1. epiphysis, epiphyseal process; 2. epiphysis, pineal body (gland, appendage), conarium, false (cerebral) apophysis ● neben den Epiphysen [liegend] juxta-epiphysial
Epiphysen... s. a. Zirbeldrüsen...
epiphysenartig epiphysoid
Epiphysendysplasie f epiphyseal dysplasia

Epiphysenentzündung f s. Epiphysitis
Epiphysenerkrankung f 1. epiphysiopathy; 2. epiphysiopathy, pinealopathy
Epiphysenexstirpation f pinealectomy, excision of the pineal body
Epiphysenfraktur f epiphyseal fracture
Epiphysenfuge f epiphyseal (growth) cartilage
Epiphysenfugenschluß m s. Epiphysenschluß
Epiphysengleiten n epiphysiolisthesis
Epiphysenknochenvaskularisation f bone epiphyseal vascularization
Epiphysenknorpel m epiphyseal cartilage (plate)
Epiphysenlinie f epiphyseal line
Epiphysenlösung f epiphysiolysis, epiphyseolysis, epiphyseal separation
epiphysennah juxta-epiphysial
Epiphysennekrose f epiphysionecrosis
~ des Capitulum humeri osteochondrosis of the capitulum humeri (im Kindesalter)
Epiphysenossifikationszentrum n epiphyseal centre of ossification
Epiphysenplatte f epiphyseal plate (disk) (Wirbelkörper)
Epiphysenregion f epiphyseal region (area)
Epiphysenscheibe f s. Epiphysenplatte
Epiphysenschluß m epiphyseal closure (union)
Epiphysenschlußauslösung f[/operative] epiphysiodesis
Epiphysensprengung f epiphyseal separation
Epiphysenverlagerung f epiphysiolisthesis
Epiphysenwachstum n epiphyseal growth
Epiphysenwachstumszentrum n epiphyseal growth centre
Epiphyseodese f epiphysiodesis
Epiphysiolisthesis f epiphysiolisthesis
Epiphysiolyse f epiphysiolysis, epiphyseolysis
Epiphysiopathie f epiphysiopathy
Epiphysis f cerebri s. Epiphyse 2.
Epiphysitis f epiphysitis, inflammation of the epiphysis
epipleural epipleural
Epiploenterozele f epiploenterocele, enteroepiplocele
epiploisch epiploic
Epiploitis f epiploitis, inflammation of the epiploon (omentum)
Epiploon n epiploon, [greater] omentum (Zusammensetzungen s. unter Omentum)
Epiplopexie f epiplopexy, omentofixation
Epiplorrhaphie f epiplorrhaphy, omentorrhaphy, suture of the omentum
Epiploscheozele f epiploscheocele
Epiplozele f epiplocele, omentocele
Epipygus m epipygus (Mißgeburt)
Episioklisie f episioclisia, closure of the vulva
Episioperineoplastik f episioperineoplasty
Episioperineorrhaphie f episioperineorrhaphy
Episioplastik f episioplasty
Episiorrhagie f episiorrhagia, haemorrhage from the vulva
Episiorrhapie f episiorrhaphy
Episiostenose f episiostenosis

Episiotomie f episiotomy
Episiotomieschere f episiotomy scissors
Episklera f episclera *(Bindegewebe zwischen Binde- und Lederhaut des Auges)*
Episkleraentzündung f episcleritis
Episkleralraum m episcleral space
Episom n episome *(genetisches Element in Bakterien)*
epispadial epispadial
Epispadie f epispadia[s]
Epispadieträger m epispadiac
Epispastikum n epispastic [agent]
Epistase f epistasis
Epistaxis f epistaxis, rhinorrhagia, nosebleed, nasal bleeding (haemorrhage)
Episthotonus m episthotonus, episthotonos, emprosthotonos
Epistropheus m axis, epistropheus, odontoid vertebra
Epitarsus m epitarsus, congenital pterygium *(anomale Bindehautfalte am Auge)*
Epitendineum n epitendineum, epitenon, fibrous sheath of a tendon
Epithalamus m epithalamus *(umfaßt Stria medullaris, Trigonum habenulae, Habenula und Epiphyse)*
Epithel n epithelium, epithelial tissue *(s. a. unter Epithelium)* ● **unter dem ~** subepithelial ● **wieder mit ~ bedecken** to reepithelialize
~/**interpapilläres** interpapillary epithelium, rete peg
~/**kubisches** cuboidal epithelium
~/**mehrschichtiges** laminated (stratified) epithelium
~/**mesenchymales** mesenchymal epithelium
~/**pyramidenförmiges** pyramidal epithelium
~/**respiratorisches** respiratory epithelium
~/**sensorisches** sensory (nerve) epithelium
Epithelablösung f s. Epidermolysis
epithelartig epithel[i]oid
Epithelauflösung f epitheliolysis
Epithelauskleidung f epithelial lining
epithelbildend epitheliogen[et]ic
Epithelbildung f epithel[ial]ization
Epithelblase f epithelial bleb
Epitheldifferenzierung f epithelial differentiation
Epitheldrüse f epithelial gland
Epitheldysplasie f epithelial dysplasia
Epitheleinschlüsse mpl epithelial inclusion bodies *(s. a. Körperchen/Halberstädter-Prowazeksche)*
Epithelentfernung f de-epithelialization
Epithelentzündung f epitheliitis
Epithelgeschwulst f epithelioma
Epithelgewebe n epithelial tissue, epithelium
Epithelhyperplasie f epithelial hyperplasia
epithelial epithelial
Epithelialisierung f epithel[ial]ization, epidermization
Epitheliitis f epitheliitis
Epitheliolyse f epitheliolysis
Epithelioma n epithelioma
~ **adamantinum** adamantinoma
~ **adenoides cysticum** multiple benign cystic epithelioma, Brooke's tumour, trichoepithelioma [papulosum multiplex]
~ **adenomatosum** adenoma
~ **basocellulare** basal-cell carcinoma
~ **chorioepidermale** choriocarcinoma
~ **contagiosum** fowl pox, sorehead
epitheliomartig epitheliomatous
Epitheliomatose f epitheliomatosis, multiple squamous-cell carcinomas
Epitheliomyosis f epitheliomyosis, isthmic nodular salpingitis
epithelisieren to epithel[ial]ize
Epithelium n epithelium, epithelial tissue *(s. a. unter Epithel)*
~ **ciliare** ciliary epithelium
Epithelkörperchen n parathyroid, parathyroid body (gland)
Epithelkörperchenadenom n parathyroid adenoma
Epithelkörperchenhormon n s. Parathormon
Epithelkörperchenüberfunktion f s. Hyperparathyreoidismus
Epithelkörperchenunterfunktion f s. Hypoparathyreoidismus
Epithelmigration f epithelial migration
Epithelnävus m epithelial naevus
Epithelnekrose f epithelial necrosis
Epithelneubildung f reepithelialization
Epitheloidzelle f epithelioid (alveolated) cell
Epitheloidzellgranulom n epithelioid cell granuloma
epithelomesenchymal epithelomesenchymal
Epithelperle f epithelial pearl, cell cone
Epithelrest m epithelial remnant (rest, debris) of Malassez
Epithelscheide f/**Hertwigsche** Hertwig's epithelial root sheath
Epithelschicht f epithelial layer
Epithelverfall m epitheliolysis
Epithelzelle f epithelial cell, epicyte
Epithelzellengeschwulst f epithelioma
Epithelzellenkultur f epithelial cell culture
epithelzellenschädigend antiepithelial
Epithelzellkrebs m epithelial carcinoma
Epithelzylinder m epithelial cast *(im Urin)*
Epithelzyste f epithelial cyst
Epituberkulose f 1. epituberculosis, epituberculous infiltration; 2. epituberculosis *(bei Kindern)*
epitympanal epitympanic
Epitympanon n epitympanum, epitympanic recess (space), superior tympanic cavity, attic [of the middle ear]
Epityphlitis f s. Appendizitis
Epityphlon n s. Appendix vermiformis
Epizoon n epizoon
Epizoonose f epi[dermato]zoonosis
Epizystotomie f epicystotomy
Epizyt m 1. epicyte, cell wall; 2. s. Epithelzelle
Eponychium n eponychium, nail fold (mantle)
Epoophorektomie f epoophorectomy

Epoophoron

Epoophoron n epoophoron, parovarium, Rosenmüller's organ, body of Rosenmüller, ovarian appendage
Epoophoronentzündung f paroophoritis
Epoophoronzyste f epoophoral cyst
Epstein-Barr-Virus n Epstein-Barr virus, EB virus, EBV
Epstein-Barr-Virus-Antikörper m Epstein-Barr virus antibody
Epstein-Syndrom n Epstein's (nephrotic) syndrome
Epulis f epulis *(Kiefergeschwulst)*
~ **congenita** congenital epulis
~ **fibrosa** fibrous epulis
~ **gigantocellularis** gigantocellular epulis
~ **granulomatosa** granulomatous epulis
~ **sarcomatodes** sarcomatous epulis
epulisartig epuloid
Epulofibrom n epulofibroma
Equinokavus m equinocavus [deformity]
Equinovalgus m equinovalgus [deformity]
Equinovarus m equinovarus [deformity]
Equinus m equinus [deformity]
Erbabweichung f mutation, idiovariation
Erbanlage f gene, hereditary (genetic) factor
● **mit gleichen Erbanlagen** isogenic, isogenous, isologous
Erbbild n [eines Lebewesens] genotype, idiotype
Erbeigenschaft f inherited characteristic
Erbeinheit f s. Erbanlage
erben to inherit
Erbfaktor m s. Erbanlage
Erbfehler m hereditary defect
erbgleich syngeneic, syngenesious
~ **transplantiert** syngenesioplastic
Erbgrind m favus, honeycomb ringworm (tetter)
Erbgut n genotype; heritage, heredity, inheritance
Erbhygiene f eugenics
Erbkonstitution f hereditary constitution
Erbkrankheit f hereditary (inherited) disease
Erblehre f genetics, genesiology
erblich hereditary, inheritable
~/**nicht** non-hereditary, adventitious
Erblichkeit f heredity, heritability
erblinden to become (grow) blind, to lose one's sight
Erblindung f 1. loss of sight, visual deprivation; 2. s. Blindheit
Erblinie f bloodline
Erbmasse f genom[e], heritage, heredity
Erbmassenvereinigung f amphimixis, crossbreeding, heterozygosis, interbreeding
Erbmaterial n hereditary material
erbrechen[/sich] to vomit, to retch
Erbrechen n vomit[ing], retching, emesis, vomiturition ● ~ **auslösend** vomitive, emetic
~/**eitriges** pyemesis
~/**epidemisches** epidemic vomiting; water-vomiting disease
~/**fäkales** faecal (stercoraceous) vomiting
~/**idiopathisches** idiopathic (functional) vomiting
~/**käsiges** caseous vomiting, tyremesis
~/**kotiges** copremesis
~/**morgendliches** morning nausea (sickness) *(bei Schwangerschaft)*
~/**schmerzhaftes** painful vomiting, dysemesis
~/**schwarzes** black vomit[ing], coffee-ground vomiting, melanemesis
~/**übermäßiges** excessive vomiting, hyperemesis
~/**unstillbares** pernicious vomiting
erbrechenauslösend vomitive, emetic
erbrechend emetic
Erbrochenes n vomit[us]
Erbsenbein n pisiform [bone] *(Handwurzelknochen)*
erbsenförmig pisiform *(z. B. Knochen)*
Erbsensuppenstuhl m pea-soup stool *(bei Typhus)*
Erbspezialist m geneticist
Erbsprung m mutation
Erbsyphilis f heredosyphilis, prenatal syphilis
ERCP, E.R.C.P. s. Cholangiopankreatikographie/endoskopische retrograde
Erdbeergallenblase f strawberry gallbladder
Erdbeernase f rhinophym[a], toper's (whisky) nose
Erdbeerpocken pl framboesia, yaws, pian, coco, bouba *(durch Treponema pertenue)*
Erdbeerzunge f strawberry tongue *(bei Scharlach)*
Erdessen n geophagy, geophagism, earth eating
erdessend geophagous
Erdheim-Tumor m craniopharyngioma, hypophyseal (craniopharyngeal) duct tumour, suprasellar cyst
erdrosseln to strangulate, to strangle
Erdrosseln n strangulation
erektil erectile
Erektion f erection
Erektionsfähigkeit f erectility
Erektionsstörung f erection disturbance; impaired erection
Erektionszentrum n erection centre
Erektor m erector [muscle]
ererbbar inheritable
ererbt hereditary, congenital
erethisch erethi[s]tic, erethismic
Erethismus m erethism
erfassend perceptive, perceptual
~/**instinktiv** intuitional, intuitive
Erfolgsorgan n effector organ *(Physiologie)*; end (target) organ *(z. B. von Hormonen)*
erforderlich essential *(z. B. Vitamine, Minerale)*
Erfordernishochdruck m compensatory hypertension
Erfordernishypertrophie f adaptive hypertrophy
Erfrierung f congelation, frost injury, frostbite *(z. B. an Extremitäten)*
ERG s. Elektroretinogramm
Ergastoplasma n 1. ergastoplasm *(basophiler Zytoplasmabezirk)*; 2. rough-surfaced endoplasmic reticulum

Ergastoplasmamembran f ergastoplasmic membrane
ergießen/sich to empty, to discharge itself; to flush; to pour; to flow [into]
Ergobasin n ergobasine *(Mutterkornalkaloid)*
Ergodermatose f ergodermatosis, occupational (industrial) dermatosis
Ergogramm n ergogram
Ergograph m ergograph
ergographisch ergographic
Ergokalziferol n ergocalciferol, vitamin D_2
Ergokornin n ergocornine *(Mutterkornalkaloid)*
Ergokristin n ergocristine *(Mutterkornalkaloid)*
Ergokryptin n ergocryptine *(Mutterkornalkaloid)*
Ergometer n ergometer, dynamometer
Ergometerfahrrad n ergometer bicycle
Ergometrie f ergometry
Ergometrin n ergometrine *(Mutterkornalkaloid)*
ergometrisch ergometric
Ergonovin n ergonovine *(Mutterkornalkaloid)*
Ergosin n ergosine *(Mutterkornalkaloid)*
Ergosom n ergosome, polyribosome
Ergosterin n, **Ergosterol** n ergosterin, ergosterol
Ergotamin n ergotamine *(Mutterkornalkaloid)*
Ergothionein n ergothioneine *(Histidinderivat)*
Ergotismus m ergotism, ergot poisoning; creeping sickness
Ergotoxin n ergotoxine *(Mutterkornalkaloid)*
ergotrop ergotropic
ergreifend affective, affecting
Ergriffenheit f emotion
Erguß m effusion, effluvium; discharge; exudation; ejaculation
~/subduraler subdural effusion
~/symptomatischer sympathetic effusion
erhalten/am Leben to keep alive
~/sich gesund to keep well (in good health), to conserve the health
Erhaltung f 1. conservation; 2. maintenance
Erhaltungsdosis f maintenance dose
Erhaltungsstoffwechsel m conservation metabolism
Erhaltungstherapie f maintenance treatment
erhärten to harden, to solidify
~/eine Diagnose to corroborate a diagnosis
erheben/die Anamnese to compile (take off) the history
erhöhen to raise *(z. B. die Temperatur)*; to intensify *(z. B. einen Reiz)*
~/den kolloidosmotischen Druck to increase the colloidal oncotic pressure
erhöhend/die Reizschwelle des Herzens negative bathmotropic
Erhöhung f **der Muskelspannung** hypermyotonia
erholen/sich to recover; to convalesce; to rest; to improve; to recuperate *(s. a. entspannen/sich)*
erholend[/sich] convalescent; recovering; anastatic
Erholung f convalescence; recovery; anastasis *(s. a. Entspannung)*
Erholungsaufenthalt m convalescence stay
Erholungsheim n convalescent (recreation) home, sanatorium

Erholungskur f recreation cure
Erholungsphase f recovery phase
Erholungsreise f recreation trip
erigierbar erectile
erigieren to erect
Erinnerung f 1. recollection, remembrance; 2. s. Gedächtnis
Erinnerungsaphasie f amnestic aphasia
Erinnerungsdosis f booster dose *(bei Impfung)*
Erinnerungsfälschung f delusive remembrance; pseudomnesia; confabulation; paramnesia
Erinnerungshalluzination f remembrance hallucination
Erinnerungsillusion f memory illusion
Erinnerungslücke f amnesia, memory loss, lethe
Erinnerungsschwäche f hypomnesia
Erinnerungsspur f engram, neurogram, memory trace
Erinnerungstäuschung f mnemic delusion
Erinnerungsverlust m amnesia, loss of memory
~ für bekannte Gegenstände pragmatamnesia
Erinnerungsvermögen n memory, power of recollection
~/gesteigertes hyper[a]mnesia
Erinnerungsvorgang m ecphoria
erkälten/sich to catch a cold, to take a chill
Erkältung f [common] cold, chill ● **an einer ~ leiden** to suffer from colds ● **sich eine ~ holen** to catch a cold ● **sich vor ~ schützen** to keep a cold out
~ der Atemwege catarrh
~/schwere (starke) severe (heavy) cold
Erkältungsinfekt m [common] cold
Erkältungskrankheit f catarrhal fever, common cold
Erkältungs[krankheits]syndrom n common cold syndrome
erkennbar perceptible *(mit Sinnesorganen)*; identifiable *(z. B. Symptom)*; diagnosable *(z. B. Krankheit)*
~/nur mit dem Mikroskop microscopic
erkranken [an] to fall ill [with], to contract a disease
erkrankt affected, diseased; ill, sick
~/an einer Manie manic, maniacal
Erkrankung f illness, sickness *(s. a. unter Krankheit und Morbus)*
~/bakterielle bacteriosis, bacterial disease
~ der grauen Hirnsubstanz polioencephalopathy
~ der grauen Rückenmarksubstanz poliomyelopathy
~ der harten Hirnhaut pachymeningopathy
~ der weichen Hirnhaut leptomeningopathy
~ der weißen Hirnsubstanz leucoencephalopathy
~ der weißen Rückenmarksubstanz leucomyelopathy
~ des Kniegelenkfettkörpers Hoffa's disease; traumatic solitary lipoma of the knee joint
~/fieberhafte febrile disease
~/gemischte miscellaneous disease
~/heredodegenerative heredodegenerative disease

Erkrankung

~ infolge Sympathikusstörung sympathicopathy
~/innersekretorische endocrine disease (disorder)
~ mehrerer Drüsen polyadenopathia
~ mehrerer Gelenke polyarthropathy
~ mehrerer Muskeln polymyopathy
~/respiratorische respiratory disease
~/rheumatische rheumatic disease
~/urogenitale urogenital disease
~/venerische venereal disease, VD
~/zerebrale cerebral disease (affection)
Erkrankungs... s. a. Krankheits...
Erkrankungshäufigkeit f morbidity [rate], sickness rate
Erkrankungsziffer f morbidity rate; incidence rate
erleichtern to relieve, to ease, to alleviate, to palliate (z. B. Schmerzen)
erleichternd palliative
Erleichterung f relief, easing, alleviation, palliation (z. B. von Schmerzen)
erleiden to suffer, to endure
erleidend/einen Rückfall relapsing, palindromic
erliegen to die [from] (z. B. einer Krankheit)
Ermattung f exhaustion, weariness; fatigue
Ermüdbarkeit f fatig[u]ability
ermüden to tire, to fatigue, to wear [down]; to tire, to become exhausted, to weary
ermüdend fatiguing, tiring, wearisome
Ermüdung f fatigue, tiredness, defatigation
Ermüdungsaspiration f fatigue aspiration
Ermüdungserscheinung f fatigue symptom
Ermüdungsfraktur f fatigue fracture
Ermüdungskontraktur f fatigue contracture
Ermüdungsneurose f fatigue neurosis
Ermüdungsnystagmus m fatigue nystagmus; occupational nystagmus
Ermüdungsspasmus m fatigue spasm; functional spasm; movement spasm, business (professional, occupational) spasm; telegrapher's cramp (spasm)
ermuntern to stimulate, to encourage; to rouse, to stir up
ernähren to nourish, to feed
~/mit der Brust to nurse, to suck[le], to breastfeed
~/schlecht to malnourish
~ von/sich to live (feed) on
ernährend nourishing, nutritive, nutritious, nutritory, nutrient; alimentary; trophic
~/nicht not nourishing, inalimental
~/sich von anorganischen Stoffen autotrophic
~/sich von Milch lactivorous
~/sich von organischen Stoffen heterotrophic
ernährt/schlecht malnourished, ill-fed
Ernährung f 1. nourishing, nourishment, feeding, nutrition, alimentation; trophism; 2. food, nourishment, nutriment ● die ~ ändernd modifying nutrition; metatrophic
~/hochkalorische parenterale intravenous hyperalimentation
~/künstliche artificial feeding
~/parenterale parenteral (intravenous) feeding
~/rektale rectal alimentation
~/schlechte malnutrition
~/vorgeschriebene diet[ary]
Ernährungsarterie f [des Knochens] nutrient artery
Ernährungsbalance f nutritive balance (bei optimaler Ernährung)
Ernährungsdynamik f trophodynamics
Ernährungsfaktor m nutritional factor
Ernährungsfehler m false diet
Ernährungsfettsucht f alimentary obesity
Ernährungsgastrostomie f feeding (alimentary) gastrostomy
ernährungsgestört dystrophic; trophesial, trophesic (z. B. Gewebe)
Ernährungsgewohnheit f nutritional habit
Ernährungsgleichgewicht n nutritive equilibrium
Ernährungsimbalance f nutritive imbalance
Ernährungsjejunostomie f feeding jejunostomy
Ernährungskanal m [des Knochens] nutrient (nutritive) canal
Ernährungskern m trophonucleus
Ernährungslehre f dietetics; trophology, threpsology
Ernährungsnerv m trophic nerve
Ernährungsphysiologie f physiology of nutrition
Ernährungsplasma n trophoplasm
Ernährungsproblematik f feeding difficulty
Ernährungssonde f feeding tube
Ernährungsstörung f dystrophy, nutritional disturbance
~ der Extremitäten acrotrophoneurosis
Ernährungstherapie f dietotherapy, alimentary therapeutics, trophotherapy
Ernährungswechsel m change of nutrition
Ernährungsweise f way of feeding ● die ~ ändernd metatrophic
Ernährungswissenschaft f dietetics; sitology, trophology, threpsology, science of nutrition
Ernährungszelle f trophocyte
Ernährungszustand m nutritional state (status)
erneuern to renew; to regenerate (Körpersubstanz)
erneuernd/sich regenerative
Erneuerung f renewal; regeneration (von Körpersubstanz)
erneuerungsfähig regenerable
Erntefieber n harvest (field) fever, swamp (mud, slime) fever (Infektionskrankheit durch Leptospira grippotyphosa)
Erntekrätze f trombidiosis, trombiculosis, trombiculiasis
eröffnen/den Bauch to laparotomize
~/den Schädel to trepanize, to trephine
~/eine Leiche to section
~/mit einer Lanzette to lance
eröffnet/nicht atretic, atresic, imperforate (z. B. natürliche Körperöffnungen)
Eröffnungsperiode f period of dilatation (bei der Geburt)
Eröffnungsschmerzen fpl dilating pains

erogen erogenous, ero[to]genic
Erosio f **falsa (glandularis, papillaris) der Portio** false erosion of the cervix uteri
Erosion f erosion; aphtha *(in der Mundschleimhaut)*
~ der Zähne dental erosion
Erosionsaneurysma n erosive aneurysm
Erotik f erotic[ism], erotism
erotisch erotic
erotogen erogenous, ero[to]genic
Erotographomanie f erotographomania
Erotomaner m erotomaniac
Erotomanie f erotomania, eromania; aphrodisiomania; lagneia
Erotopath m erotopath
Erotopathie f erotopathy
erotopathisch erotopathic
Erotophobie f erotophobia *(krankhafte Angst vor sexueller Erregung)*
erregbar excitable, irritable, erethistic, erethismic
~/leicht choleric
~/schwach hypoaffective
~/stark hyperaffective
Erregbarkeit f excitability, irritability; emotivity
~/übermäßige hyperexcitability, hyperirritability; hyperaffectivity
~/verminderte hypoexcitability, hypoirritability; hypoaffectivity
erregen to excite, to irritate; to agitate; to stimulate; to sharpen *(Appetit)*
~/Brechreiz to nauseate
~/sich to agitate
erregend exciting, excitant, irritant; stimulant
~/Brechreiz nauseant, nauseous
~/geschlechtlich (sexuell) ero[to]genic, erogenous, erotic
Erreger m germ; pathogen, pathogenic organism *(z. B. Bakterium)*
erregerhaltig germ-containing; containing pathogens
Erregernachweis m demonstration of pathogenic organisms; germ identification
Erregerspektrum n antibiotic spectrum, bacterial (bacteriostatic) spectrum, antibacterial (antimicrobial) spectrum
Erregerstamm m strain *(z. B. Bakterien)*
erregt excited; stimulated; agitated *(psychisch)*
~/durch Mißhandlungen geschlechtlich masochistic
~/manisch hyperthymic
Erregung f 1. excitation, irritation, stimulation; 2. excitement; agitation; emotion *(s. a. Erregungszustand)*
~/kurzzeitige heftige affect
~/geschlechtliche sexual excitation
~/manische hyperthymia
Erregungsimpuls m excitatory impulse
Erregungskurve f excitation curve
Erregungsleitung f conduction *(z. B. des Herzens)*
~/saltatorische (sprunghafte) saltatory conduction

Erregungsleitungbahn f conduction pathway
Erregungsleitungssystem n conduction system *(z. B. des Herzens)*
Erregungsleitungsunterbrechung f/**vorübergehende** parabiosis *(eines Nerven)*
Erregungsphase f excitation phase, excitement stage
Erregungsrückbildung f repolarisation *(Physiologie)*
Erregungsübertragung f neural transmission *(Nervenphysiologie)*; transit of impulse *(z. B. bei Muskelkontraktion)*
Erregungswelle f excitation wave
Erregungszone f erogenous zone
Erregungszustand m stage of excitation; erethism; state of agitation, emotional state
erröten to blush, to flush, to grow red
Erröten n 1. flush[ing]; 2. rubescence
~/zwangshaftes erythromania
errötend flushing, blushing, rubescent
Errötungsfurcht f erythrophobia, [morbid] fear of blushing
Ersatz m 1. regeneration *(natürlicher Vorgang)*; replacement *(Austausch z. B. von Organen)*; repair; 2. substitute; prosthesis; transplant
~/bindegewebiger connective tissue repair
~/orthopädischer pro[s]thesis, orthesis
Ersatzbildung f substitute formation
Ersatzfibrose f replacement fibrosis
Ersatzflüssigkeit f replacement fluid
Ersatzmembran f spare diaphragm *(des Stethoskops)*
Ersatzpräparat n substitute [preparation]
Ersatzschlag m, **Ersatzsystole** f escaped beat
erscheinen to appear *(z. B. ein Symptom)*
Erscheinung f 1. appearance; manifestation; 2. sign, symptom *(einer Krankheit)*; 3. phenomenon; 4. vision *(Traum)* ● **mit gleicher äußerer ~** isophenic
~/äußere habit[us]
Erscheinungsbild n appearance, course; clinical picture *(z. B. einer Krankheit)*
~ [eines Lebewesens]/äußeres phenotype, external characteristics
erschlaffen to relax, to slacken
erschlaffend relaxant
erschlafft relaxed; atonic
Erschlaffung f relaxation; atonia, atonicity; detumescence, diminution of swelling
Erschlaffungsunfähigkeit f eines Schließmuskels achalasia
erschöpfen to exhaust, to tire, to fatigue, to prostrate
~/sich to become exhausted; to become weary *(z. B. Muskeln)*
Erschöpfung f exhaustion, tiredness, fatigue, lassitude; depletion *(z. B. bei Blutverlust)*; defatigation *(z. B. der Nerven oder Muskeln)*
~ der Körperkräfte prostration
~/geistige mental exhaustion; brain-fag
~/nervöse fatigue state
Erschöpfungsatrophie f exhaustion atrophy

Erschöpfungsdelir[ium]

Erschöpfungsdelir[ium] *n s.* Erschöpfungspsychose
Erschöpfungskrankheit *f* exhaustion disease
Erschöpfungslähmung *f* exhaustion paralysis
Erschöpfungsneurose *f* fatigue neurosis
Erschöpfungspsychose *f* exhaustion psychosis (delirium), exhaustive delir
Erschöpfungsreaktion *f* reaction of exhaustion
Erschöpfungszustand *m* state of exhaustion
Erschütterung *f* 1. concussion; vibration; 2. concussion, commotion *(z. B. des Gehirns)*; shock *(z. B. eines Nerven)*; 3. trauma; emotional upset; strong emotion; shock; inner turmoil *(z. B. der Psyche)*
Erschütterungsschwerhörigkeit *f* concussion deafness
ersetzen to repair, to regenerate *(natürlich)*; to replace *(z. B. durch eine Prothese)*
ersetzend/die Tätigkeit eines ausgefallenen Organs vicarious
erstarren 1. to become numb (stiff), to get benumbed *(Glieder)*; to be chilled *(vor Kälte)*; 2. to congeal, to solidify; to gel[ate]
Erstarrung *f* 1. numbness, obdormition, stiffening *(z. B. der Glieder)*; torpidity, torpor *(Psychiatrie)*; 2. congelation *(z. B. von Flüssigkeiten)*
Erste-Hilfe-Ausbildung *f* first-aid instruction
Erste-Hilfe-Kasten *m* first-aid box (kit)
Erste-Hilfe-Maßnahme *f* first-aid measure
Erste-Hilfe-Tasche *f* first-aid bag
Ersterscheinung *f* initial manifestation *(z. B. einer Krankheit)*
erstgebärend primiparous
Erstgebärende *f* primipara
Erstgeburt *f* primiparity, first delivery (birth)
Ersthelfer *m* first-aider
Ersthilfe *f* first-aid, first-aid treatment
ersticken 1. to suffocate, to asphyxiate, to choke *(z. B. durch Gase)*; 2. to stifle *(z. B. Gefühle)*
~/am Lungenödem to drown
Ersticken *n* suffocation, asphyxia, asphyxiation; choking *(z. B. durch Verlegung der Luftwege)* ● **dem ~ nahe** asphyxial
~/traumatisches traumatic asphyxia
erstickend asphyxiant, asphyxial
Erstickung *f s.* Ersticken
Erstickungsanfall *m* chokes, choking fit, attack of suffocation
Erstickungsgefahr *f* danger of suffocation
Erstickungstod *m* death by asphyxia
Erstimmunisierung *f* primary immunization
Erstimpfung *f* primary vaccination, first inoculation
Erstreaktion *f* primary immune response
Erstschwangere *f* primigravida, unigravida
ertastbar tactile
ertauben to become deaf
Ertaubung *f/plötzliche* sudden deafness
Ertränkungssucht *f* hydromania
ertrinken to drown
Eruktation *f* eructation, belching

Eruption *f* 1. eruption, brash *(z. B. bei Hautausschlag)*; 2. eruption *(z. B. Zahndurchbruch)*
Eruptionsphase *f* eruptive phase
Eruptionsstadium *n* eruptive stage
eruptiv eruptive
erwachen/aus der Narkose to wake from (after) the anaesthesia, to come out of the anaesthesia, to recover
~/aus der Ohnmacht to revive, to return to consciousness (strength), to recover
erwachend awakening, hypnopompic
erwachsen adult, grown-up, full-grown ● **~ sein** to be grown-up
Erwachsenenalter *n* adulthood
Erwachsenendiabetes *m* adult onset diabetes, late-onset diabetes
Erwachsenengebiß *n* secondary dentition, permanent dentition (teeth)
Erwachsenenprogerie *f* adult progeria
Erwachsenenzöliakie *f* adult coeliac disease (syndrome)
Erwachsener *m* adult, grown-up
Erwachsensein *n* adulthood
Erwärmungsschmerz *m* therm[o]algesia
Erwartungsangst *f* expectation anxiety
Erwartungsneurose *f* expectation neurosis
erwecken/wieder zum Leben to reanimate
erweichen to soften *(z. B. Gewebe)*; to macerate *(z. B. Knochen)*
Erweichen *n* softening *(z. B. von Geweben)*; malacia, maceration *(z. B. von Knochen)*
erweichend softening, malacic *(z. B.Gewebe)*; emollient *(z. B. Dermatikum)*
Erweichung *f* 1. malacia, softening; 2. mollities, softness
~ der Knochen osteomalacia
~ der Mundorgane stomatomalacia
~ der Trachealringe tracheomalacia
~/rote red softening
Erweichungsherd *m* softening focus (area) *(z. B. im Gehirn)*
Erweiterer *m* dilator [muscle]
erweitern to dilate *(dehnen)*; to enlarge *(vergrößern)*; to distend *(spreizen)*
~/das Rektum to balloon out the rectum
erweitert ectatic
Erweiterung *f* ectasia, dilatation, dilation *(Dehnung)*; enlargement *(Vergrößerung)*; distension *(Spreizung)*
~ des linken Ventrikels left ventricular dilatation
~ des rechten Ventrikels right ventricular dilatation
~/synaptische synaptic knob
erweiterungsfähig dilatable
Erwerbsfähigkeit *f* earning capacity, capability of earning
Erwerbsunfähigkeit *f* earning incapacity, inability to earn, disability
erworben acquired
~/im Krankenhaus hospital-acquired
~/zufällig adventitious
erwürgen to strangle, to throttle

Erwürgen n strangulation, strangling
Ery s. Erythrozyt
Erysipel n s. Erysipelas
Erysipelantitoxin n erysipelas antitoxin
erysipelartig erysipelatous
Erysipelas n erysipelas, St. Anthony's fire
~ ambulans ambulant erysipelas
~ bullosum bullous erysipelas
~ gangraenosum gangrenous erysipelas
~ migrans migrant (wandering) erysipelas
~ phlegmonosum phlegmonous erysipelas
~ vesiculosum vesicular erysipelas
Erysipeloid n erysipeloid, zoonotic erysipelas; fish-handler's disease (Infektionskrankheit durch Erysipelothrix insidiosa)
Erysipeloid[anti]serum n antierysipeloid serum
Erysiphak m erysiphake, erisiphake
Erythema n erythema
~ anulare annular erythema
~ arthriticum epidemicum epidemic arthritic erythema; streptobacillary (Haverhill) fever
~ atrophicans lupus erythematosus
~ autumnale trombiculiasis, trombiculosis, trombidiosis
~ brucellum brucella dermatitis
~ chronicum migrans annulus migrans
~ exsudativum exudative erythema
~ exsudativum multiforme [majus] dermatostomatitis, Stevens-Johnson syndrome
~ fugax spiloplania, transient skin erythema
~ gluteae gluteal (napkin) erythema
~ hyperaemicum hyperaemic erythema
~ induratum [Bazin] Bazin's disease
~ infectiosum [acutum] [acute] infectious erythema, megalerythema; Sticker's (fifth) disease
~ iris erythema iris
~ malignum malignant erysipelas
~ neonatorum erythema of the newborn
~ nodosum nodal (nodular) fever
~ nodosum syphiliticum Mauriac's disease
~ palmarum palmar erythema; liver palms
~ pernio chilblain
~ perstans persistent (permanent) erythema
~ pudicitiae morbid flushing
~ punctatum s. ~ scarlatiniforme
~ scarlatiniforme (scarlatinoides) scarlatiniform erythema, desquamative exfoliative erythema
~ simplex simple erythema
~ solare sun burn
~ toxicum toxic erythema
~ traumaticum traumatic erythema
~ variolosum variolous erythema
~ venenatum s. ~ toxicum
erythemartig erythem[at]oid
Erythematodes m lupus [erythematosus], L.E. (Hautkrankheit mit verschiedensten Krankheitsbildern)
~. disseminatus butterfly lupus
Erythematodes-Zelltest m lupus erythematosus [cell] test
erythematös erythematous

Erythemaufflackern n erythematous reaction
erythembewirkend erythemogenic
Erythemdosis f erythema dose (Radiologie)
~/minimale minimal erythema dose, M.E.D.
Erythemreaktion f erythematous reaction
Erythemschwellendosis f threshold erythema dose (Radiologie)
Erythralgie f erythralgia, erythromelalgia, pain and redness of the skin
Erythrämie f 1. erythraemia, erythrocythaemia; 2. erythraemia, myelopathic (primary, splenomegalic) polycythaemia, polycythaemia rubra (vera), Osler's (Vaquez's) disease, Vaquez-Osler disease
~/akute erythroleukaemia, acute erythraemic myelosis, di Guglielmo's disease (syndrome)
~/chronische chronic erythraemic myelosis (disease), Heilmeyer-Schöner disease
Erythrasma n erythrasma (Hauterkrankung durch Corynebacterium minutissimum)
Erythrit[ol] n erythritol (Zuckeralkohol)
Erythroblast m erythroblast, erythrocytoblast (kernhaltige Erythrozytenvorstufe)
~/basophiler basophilic erythroblast
~/orthochromatischer orthochromatic erythroblast
Erythroblastämie f erythroblastaemia
Erythroblastenanämie f erythroblastic anaemia, Cooley's anaemia (disease)
erythroblastenartig erythroblastic
Erythroblastengeschwulst f des Knochenmarks erythroblastoma
Erythroblastenvermehrung f im Blut erythroblastosis
Erythroblastenverminderung f im Blut erythroblastopenia
erythroblastisch erythroblastic
Erythroblastom n erythroblastoma
Erythroblastomatose f erythroblastomatosis
Erythroblastopenie f erythroblastopenia
Erythroblastopenie-Syndrom n erythroblastopenia syndrome, Josephs-Diamond-Blackfan anaemia, erythrogenesis imperfecta, congenital aplastic anaemia
Erythroblastophthise f erythroblastophthisis
Erythroblastose f erythroblastosis (s. a. unter Erythroblastosis)
~/akute s. Erythrämie/akute
Erythroblastosis f erythroblastosis
~ fetalis (neonatorum) foetal erythroblastosis, newborn haemolytic disease, haemolytic disease of the newborn
erythroblastotisch erythroblastotic
Erythrochloropsie f erythrochlorop[s]ia, erythrochloropy
Erythrocuprein n erythrocupreine
Erythrödem n erythroedema [polyneuropathy], acrodynia
Erythroderma n erythroderma, erythrodermia (s. a. Erythema)
~ desquamativum [Leiner] desquamative erythrodermia, Leiner's disease (syndrome)

Erythroderma

~ ichthyosiforme congenitum congenital ichthyosiform erythroderma
Erythrodermatitis f erythrodermatitis
Erythrodermia f **desquamativa** s. Erythroderma desquamativum
Erythrodermie f s. Erythroderma
Erythrodextrin n erythrodextrin
Erythrodiapedese f erythrodiapedesis
Erythrodontie f erythrodontia, reddish pigmentation of the teeth
erythrogen 1. erythrogenic, inducing skin rash; 2. erythrogenic, erythrocytopoietic
Erythrogenese f erythrogenesis, formation of erythrocytes
Erythrogonium n erythrogonium, erythrogone; stem cell
Erythroklasis f erythroclasis
erythroklastisch erythroclastic
Erythrokont m erythroconte *(bei perniziöser Anämie)*
Erythroleukämie f erythroleukaemia, acute erythraemic disease (myelosis), di Guglielmo's disease (syndrome)
Erythroleukoblastose f erythroleucoblastosis
Erythroleukomyelose f s. Erythroleukämie
Erythrolyse f erythro[cyto]lysis
Erythrolysin n erythro[cyto]lysin *(die Erythrozyten auflösender Serumkörper)*
Erythromanie f erythromania
Erythromelalgie f erythromelalgia, red neuralgia, acromelalgia, Mitchell's disease *(anfallsweises schmerzhaftes Anschwellen der Haut an den Gliedern)*
Erythromelie f erythromelia *(Hautatrophie mit blauroter Verfärbung an Beinen und Armen)*
Erythromyelose f erythromyelosis
erythromyeloblastisch erythromyeloblastic
Erythromyzin n erythromycin *(Antibiotikum)*
Erythron n erythron
Erythroneozytose f erythroneocytosis
Erythroparasit m erythroparasite
Erythropathie f erythropathy
Erythropenie f s. Erythrozytenverminderung im Blut
Erythropenin n erythropenin
Erythrophag[e] m erythrophage
Erythrophagozytose f erythrophagocytosis, erythrophagia
~/monozytäre monocytic erythrophagocytosis
erythrophil erythrophil[ous]
Erythrophobie f erythrophobia *(krankhafte Angst vor Schamröte)*
Erythro-4-phosphat n erythro-4-phosphate, erythrose
Erythrophthise f erythroblastophthisis
Erythroplasie f **[Queyrat]** erythroplasia of Queyrat, Queyrat's erythroplasia
Erythropoetin n erythropoietin *(Hormon)*
erythropoetisch s. erythrozytenbildend
Erythroprosopalgie f erythroprosopalgia, redness and pain in the face
Erythropsie f erythrop[s]ia, red vision
Erythropsin n erythropsin, visual purple, rhodopsin, retinal pigment
Erythrorrhexis f erythro[cyto]rrhexis
Erythroschisis f erythrocytoschisis
Erythrose f, **Erythro-Tetrose** f erythrose
Erythrourie f erythr[ocyt]uria
Erythrozyanose f erythrocyanosis *(vasomotorische Zirkulationsstörung der Haut)*
Erythrozyt m erythrocyte, red [blood] cell, RBC, rbc, red corpuscle, blood disk
~/entfärbter achromatocyte
~/hämoglobinloser anerythrocyte
~/kernhaltiger nucleated erythrocyte
~/kernloser akaryocyte
~/kugeliger spherocyte
~/normalgroßer normo[erythro]cyte
~/polychromatischer polychromatic erythrocyte
~/polychromatophiler polychromatophilic erythrocyte
~/sichelförmiger s. Sichelzelle
~/übermäßig großer macro[normo]cyte
~/übermäßig kleiner microcyte
erythrozytär erythrocytic
Erythrozytenaggregation f sludging of the blood, blood sludge, intravascular agglutination
Erythrozytenantikörper m erythrocyte antibody
Erythrozytenantikörpernachweis m erythrocytic antibody detection
Erythrozytenarmut f anaemia, erythro[cyto]penia, oligo[erythro]cythaemia
erythrozytenauflösend erythrocytolytic
Erythrozytenauflösung f erythrocytolysis, erythro[cyto]rrhexis
Erythrozytenaufnahme f **durch Phagozyten** erythrophagocytosis
Erythrozytenaufspaltung f erythrocytoschisis
Erythrozytenausscheidung f **im Urin** erythr[ocyt]uria
erythrozytenbildend erythro[cyto]poietic, erythrogenic
Erythrozytenbildung f erythropoiesis, erythro[cyto]genesis
~/fehlende (unzureichende) anerythroplasia
Erythrozytenbildungsstörung f dyserythropoiesis
Erythrozytendegeneration f erythrocyte degeneration
Erythrozytenenzym n erythrocyte enzyme
Erythrozytenfärbung f **nach Giemsa** Giemsa's stain
Erythrozytenfragilitätsprobe f erythrocyte fragility test
Erythrozytenfragmentation f erythro[cyto]rrhexis
erythrozytenfressend erythrophagous
Erythrozytenfreßzelle f haemophage
erythrozytenfreundlich erythrophilous
Erythrozytenglutathionreduktase f erythrocyte glutathione reductase *(Enzym)*
Erythrozyten-Hämoglobin-Quotient m cell-colour ratio
Erythrozytenkonzentrat n packed erythrocytes (red blood cells)

Erythrozytenkonzentrattransfusion f transtusion of packed cells
Erythrozytenmangel m erythro[cyto]penia, oligo[erythro]cythaemia
Erythrozytenmembran f erythrocyte membrane
Erythrozytenmembraneiweiß n erythrocyte membrane protein
Erythrozytenparasit m erythroparasite
erythrozytenphagozytierend erythrophagous
Erythrozytenphagozytose f erythrophagocytosis, erythrophagia
Erythrozytenphase f erythrocytic phase *(der Malariaerreger)*
Erythrozytenphosphoglukomutase f erythrocyte phosphoglucomutase *(Enzym)*
Erythrozytenreifung f/**mangelnde** anhaem[at]opoiesis, anhaematosis
Erythrozytenreifungsfaktor m erythrocyte maturation factor, erythrocyte-maturing factor; vitamin B_{12}, Castle's factor
Erythrozytenresistenz f erythrocyte resistance
Erythrozytenschatten m erythrocyte (blood) shadow, shadow [cell], ghost corpuscle, phantom cell, achromatocyte
Erythrozytenschizogonie f erythrocytic schizogony *(der Malariaerreger)*
Erythrozytensedimentation f erythrocyte sedimentation, erythrosedimentation
Erythrozytensedimentationsgeschwindigkeit f erythrocyte sedimentation rate, ESR
Erythrozytensenkung f s. Erythrozytensedimentation
Erythrozytenüberlebenszeit f erythrocyte survival [time], red cell life span
Erythrozyten- und Leukozytenauflösung f cythaemolysis
Erythrozytenverklumpung f haem[o]agglutination
Erythrozytenvermehrung f [im Blut] erythrocytosis, erythr[ocyth]aemia, hyperglobulia, hypercythaemia
~ **in Höhen** high-altitude erythraemia
Erythrozytenverminderung f [im Blut] erythro[cyto]penia, hypoglobulia, oligo[erythro]cythaemia, hypocythaemia
Erythrozytenvolumen n packed cell volume
Erythrozytenvorstufe f erythrocyte precursor
Erythrozytenzahl f erythrocyte count, RBC, rbc
erythrozytenzählend erythrocytometric
Erythrozytenzählung f erythrocytometry
Erythrozytenzerfall m erythro[cyto]lysis, splitting of erythrocytes, erythrocytorrhexis, haemolysis; haemoclasis
erythrozytenzerstörend destructing erythrocytes, erythroclastic, haemoclastic; haemophagic, haemophagous
Erythrozytenzerstörung f erythrocyte destruction, erythroclasis, haemoclasis
Erythrozytoblast m s. Erythroblast
erythrozytodegenerativ erythrodegenerative
Erythrozytogenese f erythrogenesis, formation of erythrocytes

Erythrozytolyse f erythro[cyto]lysis
Erythrozytolysin n erythro[cyto]lysin *(die Erythrozyten auflösender Serumkörper)*
Erythrozytometer n erythro[cyto]meter
Erythrozytometrie f erythrocytometry
erythrozytometrisch erythrocytometric
Erythrozytopenie f s. Erythrozytenverminderung [im Blut]
Erythrozytopoese f erythro[cyto]poiesis, erythrocytogenesis
erythrozytopoetisch erythro[cyto]poietic
Erythrozytorrhexis f erythro[cyto]rrhexis
Erythrozytose f s. Erythrozytenvermehrung [im Blut]
erzeugt/im Darm enterogenous
~/**im Kehlkopf** laryngeal *(z. B. ein Ton)*
Erziehung f/**psychologische** psychagogy
ES s. Extrasystole
Escherichia f **coli** colon bacillus, colibacillus *(Dickdarmflora)*
~ **coli/enteropathogene** enteropathogenic Escherichia coli
Eserin n eserine, physostigmine *(Alkaloid der Kalabarbohne)*
Esmarch-Schlauch m Esmarch's bandage
Esmarch-Staubinde f Esmarch's tourniquet
Esophorie f esophoria, endophoria *(Einwärtsschielen bei geschlossenen Augen)*
Esotropie f esotropia, convergent squint (strabismus); cross-eye
Espundia f espundia, bouba, mucocutaneous (South American) leishmaniasis, Breda's disease, Bahia ulcer
Essen n 1. eating; 2. meal, repast; 3. s. Nahrung
● **nach dem** ~ after meals (food), post cibum, p. c. ● **vor dem** ~ before meals, ante cibum, a. c.
~/**hastiges (schnelles)** rapid eating, tachyphagia
essentiell essential *(z. B. Vitamine, Minerale)*; genuine, idiopathic *(z. B. Krankheit)*
Essigsäure f acetic acid
Eßlöffelmenge f tablespoonful, tbsp.
Eßlust f appetite
~/**übersteigerte** orexomania
Eßsucht f phagomania, sitomania
Esterase f esterase *(Enzym)*
Esteraseaktivität f esterase activity
Esthiomene n esthiomene *(Vulvageschwür)*
Ethambutol n ethambutol *(Tuberkulostatikum)*
Ethanol n s. Äthanol
Ether m s. Äther
Ethmoid n s. Siebbein
ethmoidal ethmoid[al]
Ethmoidektomie f ethmoidectomy
Ethmoiditis f s. Siebbeinzellenentzündung
Ethmoidotomie f ethmoidotomy, incision into an ethmoid sinus
ethmosphenoidal ethmosphenoid[al]
Ethmozephalie f ethmocephalia *(Mißbildung)*
Ethmozephalus m ethmocephalus *(Mißgeburt)*
Ethologie f ethology
Ethyl... s. Äthyl...

etikettieren

etikettieren to label
E. U. s. Extrauteringravidität
Eucholie f eucholia
Euchromatin n euchromatin *(Chromosomenbestandteil)*
euchromatisch euchromatic
Euchromatopsie f euchromatopsia, normal colour vision
Euchromosom n euchromosome, autosome
Euchylie f euchylia
Eugenik f eugenics
eugenisch eugenic
Euglobulin n euglobulin
eugnath eugnathic
Eugnathie f eugnathy
eugonisch eugonic *(Bakterien)*
eukaryot eukaryotic
Eumenorrhoe f eumenorrhoea, normal menstruation
eumorph eumorphic
Eunuch m eunuch
eunuchenartig eunuchoid
Eunuchenstimme f eunuchoid voice
Eunuchismus m eunuchism
Eunuchoidismus m eunuchoidism *(Körperzustand infolge mangelhafter Keimdrüsenentwicklung)*
~/hypophysärer pituitary eunuchoidism
Eupepsie f eupepsia, normal digestion
eupeptisch eupeptic
Euphonie f euphonia
Euphorie f euphoria, hypercoenaesthesia
euphorieauslösend euphoretic
Euphoriezustand m euphoric state
Euphorikum n euphoriant [agent]
euphorisch euphoric
euploid euploid *(Chromosomensatz)*
Euploidie f euploidy
Eupnoe f eupnoea, normal respiration
Eupraxie f eupraxia
eurygnath eurygnathic, eurygnathous
Eurygnathismus m eurygnathism
euryprosop eurycephalous
Euryprozephalie f euryprocephalia
Eusystole f eusystole
Euthanasie f euthanasia
Euthyreoidismus m euthyroidism, normal thyroid function
euthyreot euthyroid
Eutokie f eutocia, normal labour
eutokisch eutocic
eutop eutopic, situated normally
Evagination f evagination, outpouching, protrusion of an organ
evakuieren to evacuate, to exhaust; to empty; to remove
evaporieren to evaporate
Eventration f eventration
Eversion f eversion, turning outward (inside out)
Eversionsfraktur f eversion fracture
Eviratio f 1. eviration *(Verlust der männlichen Geschlechtseigenschaften und Austausch durch weibliche)*; 2. eviration, castration; emasculation; 3. loss of potency
Eviszeration f evisceration; exenteration
eviszerieren to eviscerate; to exenterate, to disembowel
Evulsio f fasciculi (nervi) optici avulsion of the bulb
Evulsion f evulsion, tearing out *(z. B. von Polypen)*
Ewing-Sarkom n Ewing's sarcoma (tumour) *(bösartige Knochenmarkgeschwulst)*
Exairese f exeresis, exairesis, avulsion
Exaltation f exaltation, ecstatic spiritual elevation
Exanthem n exanthem[a], anthema; rash
Exanthema n **subitum** [Filatov-]Duke's disease, rose rash of infants, fourth (sixth) disease, scarlatinella, parascarlatina, parascarlet, pseudorubella
exanthematisch exanthematous, exanthematic
Exanthemfieber n exanthematous (eruptive) fever
Exartikulation f exarticulation, disarticulation
exartikulieren to exarticulate, to disarticulate
Exazerbation f exacerbation, augmentation, increase in severity *(z. B. einer Krankheit)*
exazerbieren to exacerbate
Excavatio f excavation, cavity
~ **disci (papillae nervi optici)** excavation of the optic disk, optic disk hole, cupped disk
~ **rectouterina** Douglas pouch, rectouterine fossa (excavation, pouch, space), rectouterine cul-de-sac [of Douglas]
~ **rectovesicalis** Douglas pouch, rectovesical fossa (excavation, pouch, space), rectovesical cul-de-sac [of Douglas]
~ **vesicouterina** vesicouterine excavation (pouch), uterovesical pouch
Exenteration f exenteration, evisceration ● **eine ~ durchführen** to exenterate, to eviscerate
exenzephal exencephalic, exencephalous
Exenzephalie f exencephalia
Exenzephalus m exencephalus
Exfoliatio f areata linguae benign migratory glossitis, wandering rash; geographic[al] tongue
Exfoliation f exfoliation, falling off in scales
Exfoliativvaginitis f exfoliative vaginitis
Exfoliativzytologie f exfoliative cytology
Exhairese f s. Exairese
Exhalation f exhalation
Exhärese f s. Exairese
Exhaustion f exhaustion
exhibitionieren to practice indecent exposure
Exhibitionismus m exhibitionism, indecent exposure of a person
Exhibitionist m exhibitionist
exhumieren to exhume
Exhumierung f exhumation; disinternment
Exitus m exitus, death
Exkavation f excavation, cavity *(s. a. unter Excavatio)*
~/glaukomatöse randständige glaucomatous cup

Exkavator m excavator
Exklusion f exclusion
~/allelische allelic exclusion *(Genetik)*
Exkochleation f excochleation, scooping out a cavity
Exkoriation f excoriation, abrasion of the skin
Exkrement n excrement, dejection; faeces
Exkret n excretion, excreted substance (matter)
Exkretion f excretion, discharge of waste products
Exkretionsgang m excretory duct
Exkretionshemmung f excretion inhibition
Exkretionsmechanismus m excretory mechanism
Exkretionsorgan n excretory organ
Exkretionsschwelle f excretory threshold
Exkretionsstörung f excretory disturbance
exkretorisch excretory
Exoamylase f amylase
Exoenzym n exoenzyme, extracellular enzyme
exoerythrozytär exoerythrocytic
exogam exogamous
Exogamie f exogamy
Exogastrula f exogastrula
exogen exogen[et]ic, exogenous
Exohysteropexie f exohysteropexy
Exokardie f exocardia
exokrin exocrine
Exokrindrüse f exocrine gland
Exometritis f exometritis, parametritis, pelvic cellulitis
Exomphalos m, **Exomphalus** m exomphalos
Exopeptidase f exopeptidase *(Enzym)*
Exophorie f exophoria *(Auswärtsschielen bei geschlossenen Augen)*
Exophthalmometer n exophthalmometer, proptometer, orthometer, statometer
Exophthalmometrie f exophthalmometry
exophthalmometrisch exophthalmometric
Exophthalmos m s. Exophthalmus
Exophthalmus m exophthalmus, exophthalmos; ophthalmoptosis
~/pulsierender pulsating exophthalmus
exophthalmusmessend exophthalmometric
Exophthalmusmesser m s. Exophthalmometer
exophytisch exophytic
Exoplasma n exoplasm, ectoplasm
Exostose f exostosis, hyperostosis, hyperosteogeny
Exostosenabtragung f exostosectomy
Exostosenentfernung f[/operative] exostosectomy
exotherm[isch] exothermic, exothermal
Exotoxin n exotoxin, exogenous toxin
exotrop exotropic
Exotropia f exotropia
Exozervix f exocervix
Exozöl n exocoelom
Exozölmembran f exocoelomic membrane
Exozölom n exocoelom
Exozyklophorie f exocyclophoria
Exozytose f exocytosis

Expektorans n expectorant [agent]; solvent [agent]
Expektoration f expectoration
expektorieren to expectorate *(Sputum)*
expektorierend expectorant
Experimentalmedizin f experimental medicine
Explantation f explantation *(z. B. von Gewebe)*
explantieren to explant
Exploration f exploration, examination, investigation
Explorationselektrode f exploring electrode
Explorationsoperation f exploratory operation
Explorationssonde f explorer, tine *(Stomatologie)*
Explorativlaparotomie f exploratory laparotomy
Explorativthorakotomie f exploratory thoracotomy
exploratorisch exploratory
Explosionsschock m shell shock
Explosionstrauma n blast injury (syndrome)
Exposition f exposure
Expositionsanamnese f history of exposure
Expositionskeratitis f exposure keratitis
Expression f expression
Expulsion f expulsion; extrusion
Exsanguination f exsanguination
Exsikkator m exsiccator, desiccator
exsikkieren to exsiccate
exsikkierend exsiccative, exsiccant
exsikkiert exsiccated, dry
Exsikkose f exsiccosis, exsiccation
Exspiration f expiration, exhalation
Exspirationsgeräusch n expiratory sound
Exspirationsluft f expired air
exspiratorisch expiratory
exspirieren to expire, to exhale, to breathe out
Exstirpation f extirpation
~ des Nucleus dentatus dentatectomy
exstirpieren to extirpate, to excise
~/den Samenleiter to vasectomize
~/den Thymus to thymectomize
~/die Nebenniere to adrenalectomize
~/ein Ganglion to deganglionate
Exstrophia f s. Ecstrophia
Exsudat n exudate
~/blutiges sanguineous exudate
~/entzündliches inflammatory exudate
~/hämorrhagisches haemorrhagic exudate
~/purulentes purulent exudate
~/seröses serous exudate
Exsudation f exudation; weeping *(einer Wunde)*
Exsudationsphase f exudative phase
exsudativ exudative
exsudieren to exude
exsudierend exudative, weeping
Exsufflation f exsufflation *(mittels Apparats)*
Exsufflator m exsufflator
Extension f 1. extension, stretching *(z. B. von Muskeln)*; 2. skeletal traction
Extensionsapparat m extension apparatus, hyperextension frame, traction appliance
Extensionsbügel m extension bar (stirrup)

Extensionsdraht

Extensionsdraht *m* extension wire
Extensionsfraktur *f* extension fracture
Extensionsparaplegie *f* paraplegia in extension
Extensionsschiene *f* extension (traction) splint
Extensor *m* extensor [muscle]
Extensorenretinakulum *n* extensor retinaculum [of the wrist], dorsal carpal ligament
Extensormuskel *m* extensor [muscle]
Extensorsehne *f* extensor tendon
Exterorezeptor *m* exteroceptor
exterozeptiv exteroceptive
Extinktion *f* extinction *(z. B. eines bedingten Reflexes)*
Extorsion *f* extorsion, turning outward; outward rotation
extraartikulär extraarticular; abarticular
Extractio f lentis extraction of cataract
extrahieren to extract, to leach, to lixiviate
~/**einen Zahn** to extract a tooth
~/**Venen** to strip
Extrahieren *n* extraction, leaching
extraintestinal abenteric
extrakapsulär extracapsular
extrakardial extracardiac, extracardial, exocardial, exocardiac
Extrakardialgeräusch *n* extracardial (exocardial) murmur
extrakorporal extracorporeal
Extrakorporalkreislauf *m* extracorporeal circuit (circulation)
extrakranial, extrakraniell extracranial
Extrakt *m* extract[ive]; percolate *(durch Perkolation gewonnen)*
Extraktion *f* 1. extraction, leach[ing]; lixiviation *(von Stoffen);* 2. extraction, embryulcia *(des Fetus)*
~ **einer Beckenendlage** breech extraction
Extraktionsgeburt *f* instrumental labour
Extraktionszange *f*, **Extraktor** *m* extractor *(z. B. für Zähne)*
extramedullär extramedullary *(1. Knochenmark; 2. Rückenmark)*
extramural extramural
extranukleär extranuclear, exonuclear
extraoral extraoral, extrabuccal
extraossal, extraossär extraosseous
Extraperitonealgewebe *n* extraperitoneal tissue
Extraperitonealisierung *f* extraperitonealization
extraplazental, extraplazentar extraplacental
Extrapyramidalsystem *n* extrapyramidal system
extrasphinkterisch extrasphincteric
Extrasystole *f* extrasystole, premature contraction, ectopic (premature) beat
~/**interpolierte** interpolated beat (extrasystole)
Extrasystolie *f* ectopic cardiac rhythm
extrasystolisch extrasystolic
extrathorakal extrathoracic
Extrauteringravidität *f* extrauterine gestation (pregnancy), paracyesis, eccyesis, exfoetation, metacyesis
extravasal extravascular
Extravasat *n* extravasate, extravasation

Extravasation *f* extravasation
Extravasatzyste *f* extravasation cyst
Extravaskularraum *m* extravascular space
extrazellulär extracellular
Extrazellulärflüssigkeit *f* extracellular fluid, E.C.F.
Extrazellulärraum *m* extracellular space
extrazerebral extracerebral
Extremitas *f* extremity, extremitas, farthest point, terminal portion *(eines Organs)*
~ **acromialis [claviculae]** acromial (lateral) end of the clavicle
~ **anterior (inferior) lienis** lower pole of the spleen, lateral end of the spleen
~ **inferior renis** lower pole of the kidney
~ **inferior testis** lower end of the testis
~ **posterior lienis** upper pole of the spleen, medial end of the spleen
~ **sternalis claviculae** sternal (medial) end of the clavicle
~ **superior lienis** upper pole of the spleen
~ **superior renis** superior pole of the kidney
~ **superior testis** upper end of the testis
~ **tubaria [ovarii]** tubal extremity of the ovary, upper pole of the ovary
~ **uterina [ovarii]** uterine extremity of the ovary, lower pole of the ovary
Extremität *f* 1. extremity, limb, member, membrum; 2. *s.* Extremitas
~/**obere** arm, pectoral (thoracic) limb, upper extremity
~/**untere** leg, pelvic limb, lower extremity
Extremitätenableitung *f* limb (extremity) lead *(EKG)*
~/**bipolare** bipolar limb lead
~/**unipolare** unipolar limb lead
Extremitätenbewegung *f*/**verstärkte** acrokinesia, acrokinesis
Extremitätenerkrankung *f* acropathy
Extremitätenknochenschmerz *m* acrostealgia
Extremitätenknospe *f* limb bud *(Embryologie)*
Extremitätenlähmung *f*/**einseitige** monoplegia
Extremitätennervenerkrankung *f* acroneuropathy
Extremitätenneurose *f* acroneurosis
Extremitätenödem *n* oedema of the extremities
Extremitätenparalyse *f* acroparalysis
Extremitätenprothese *f* amputation appliance
Extremitätenschwellung *f* oedema of the extremities
Extremitätensinn *m* acrognosis
Extremitätenverstümmelung *f*/**angeborene** hemimelia
Extremitätenvorfall *m* compound presentation *(Geburtslage)*
Extrinsic-Faktor *m* extrinsic factor
~/**Castlescher** Castle's extrinsic factor
Extroversion *f* extroversion, extraversion *(1. Drehbewegung; 2. psychischer Zustand)*
extrovertieren to extrovert
extrovertiert extroverted
Extrovertierter *m* extrovert, extroverted personality

Extubation f extubation
Exulceratio f **umbilici** omphalelcosis
Exzenterkompressionsplatte f eccentric compression bone plate
Exzentriker m eccentric
exzentrisch eccentric
Exzerebration f excerebration, cephalotomy
exzidieren to excise *(z. B. Wunden)*
Exzision f excision, exsection
~/keilförmige wedge excision (resection)
Exzitans n analeptic [agent]
Exzitation f excitation *(Erregungszustand)*
Exzitationselektrode f exciting electrode
Exzitationskurve f excitation curve
Exzitationsstadium n excitement stage, excitation phase
Exzitationswelle f excitation curve
EZR s. Extrazellulärraum

F

Fabella f fabella *(Sesambein des Musculus gastrocnemius)*
Fabismus m favism, fabism[us] *(hämolytische Anämie infolge Enzymmangels)*
Fabry-Syndrom n Fabry's disease, angiokeratoma corporis diffusum universale
Facharzt m specialist
~ für Allgemeinmedizin medical (general) practitioner
~ für Anästhesie (Anästhesiologie) anaesthetist, anaesthesiologist
~ für Anatomie anatomist
~ für Augenheilkunde ophthalmologist, oculist
~ für Bäderheilkunde balneologist
~ für Biochemie biochemist
~ für Chirurgie surgeon
~ für Frauenheilkunde gynaecologist
~ für Geburtshilfe obstetrician
~ für Geschlechtskrankheiten venereologist
~ für Hals-, Nasen- und Ohrenheilkunde oto[rhino]laryngologist, rhinologist
~ für Hautkrankheiten dermatologist
~ für Innere Medizin internist
~ für Kieferorthopädie orthodontist
~ für Kinderheilkunde paediatrician, paediatrist
~ für Kinderstomatologie paediadontist, paedodontist
~ für Mikrobiologie microbiologist
~ für Nerven- und Geisteskrankheiten neuropsychiatrist
~ für Neurochirurgie neurosurgeon
~ für Neurologie neurologist
~ für Ophthalmologie ophthalmologist
~ für Orthopädie orthopaedist
~ für Pathologie pathologist
~ für Pharmakologie pharmacologist
~ für Physiologie physiologist
~ für Psychiatrie psychiatrist, psychiater
~ für Radiologie radiologist, roentgenologist
~ für Urologie urologist, urinologist

~ für Zahnheilkunde dentist
fachärztlich specialist; by specialist's
Fachkrankenhaus n special hospital (clinic)
Fachschwester f nurse specialist, special nurse
Facies f 1. face, facies, appearance of the face; 2. facies, surface *(z. B. von Organen)*
~ antonina s. **~ leontina**
~ gastrica gastric surface
~ hippocratica hippocratic face
~ leon[t]ina lion's face; leontiasis
~ lingualis lingual surface
~ myopathica (myotonica) myopathic facies, hatchet face
~ poplitea popliteal plane
~ temporalis temporal plane
FAD s. Flavinadenindinukleotid
Fädchenkeratitis f filamentary (filamentous) keratitis
Faden m thread; filum, filament *(Histologie)*; fibre *(Anatomie)*; thread *(im Urin)*
Fadenbakterien npl filamentary (filamentous) bacteria
Fadenentfernung f suture removal
Fadenfänger m suture hook
fadenförmig filiform, thread-like, thready, nemaline
Fadenführer m ligature carrier
Fadenführungszange f ligature guide forceps
Fadengabel f suture pusher
Fadenhaltezange f ligature holding forceps, knot tying forceps
Fadenpinzette f ligature forceps
Fadenulkus n suture line ulcer
Fadenwurm m nematode, intestinal roundworm (nematode)
Fadenwurmbefall m, **Fadenwurminfektion** f nematodiasis, nemat[h]osis, nematization
fadenwurmtötend nematocide, nematicide
Fädenziehen n suture removal
Faeces fpl s. Fäzes
Fähigkeit f 1. aptitude, ability; faculty, talent; 2. capacity
~/phagozytische phagocytic ability
fahl livid, sallow, ashy
Fahlheit f lividity, livor
Fahrradergometer n bicycle ergometer; ergometer bicycle
fäkal faecal, stercor[ace]ous, stercoral, stercorary
Fäkalabszeß m faecal (stercoral) abscess
Fäkalfistel f faecal fistula
Fäkalflora f faecal flora
Fäkalien pl s. Fäzes
Fäkalom n faecaloma, stercoroma, coproma, scatoma
Fäkalstase f faecal (intestinal) stasis, coprostasis
Fäkalstauung f faecal impaction
Fäkalstein m faecalith, stercolith, coprolith
Fäkalstrom m faecal stream
Fäkalurie f faecaluria
Faktor m 1. factor; 2. s. Blutgerinnungsfaktor
~/antinuklearer antinuclear factor, ANF

Faktor

~/exophthalmusproduzierender exophthalmus-producing substance (factor), EPS
~/migrationshemmender migration-inhibiting factor
Faktorenserum *n* factor serum
Faktormangel *m s.* Blutgerinnungsfaktormangel
Faktorsubstitution *f* factor replacement
fakultativ facultative; voluntary; potential
Fall *m* case *(eines Patienten)*
~/leichter mild case
~/schwerer problem case
~/tödlich verlaufender fatal case
Fallbericht *m* case report, casuistics
Fallbeschreibung *f* description of a case
fällen to precipitate, to sediment[ate]
Fallhand *f* drop hand, wristdrop, carpoptosis
Fallot-Pentalogie *f* Fallot's pentalogy, pentalogy of Fallot *(Herzfehler mit Pulmonalstenose, Rechtsherzhypertrophie, Vorhofseptumdefekt, reitender Aorta und Ventrikelseptumdefekt)*
Fallsucht *f s.* Epilepsie
Fällung *f/chemische* chemical precipitation; chemocoagulation
Fällungsmittel *n* precipitant, precipitating agent
falsch false, spurious *(z. B. Aneurysma)*
fälschen to adulterate *(z. B. Mixturen)*
Falte *f* 1. plica, fold *(Anatomie) (Zusammensetzungen s. unter* Plica*)*; 2. *s.* Hautfalte
Fältelung *f* convolution *(z. B. des Darms)*
falten to fold, to plicate; to wrinkle
Falten *fpl/Kerckringsche* Kerckring's folds, valves of Kerckring *(Querfalten im Dünndarm)*
Faltenbildung *f* plication; rhytidosis *(der Hornhaut)*
Faltengesicht *n* wrinkly face
Faltenzunge *f* scrotal (fissured) tongue, furrowed (grooved) tongue
faltig plicated, rugose, rugous; wrinkled *(z. B. Haut)*
Faltigkeit *f* rugosity
Faltungsoperation *f* plication [operation] *(z. B. des Magens)*; cinching operation *(des Augenmuskels)*
~/Noblesche Noble's plication operation
Falx *f* falx
~ aponeurotica *s.* **~ inguinalis**
~ cerebelli cerebellar falx, falcula
~ cerebri cerebral falx
~ chorioideae choroid crescent
~ inguinalis inguinal falx, Henle's ligament
~ myopica myopic crescent
falziform falciform, sickle-shaped, falcular
Falziparum-Malaria *f* falciparum malaria, algid (estivo-autumnal, pernicious) malaria, malignant [tertian] malaria *(durch Plasmodium falciparum)*
Familienanamnese *f* family [case] history
Familienkrankheit *f* familial (heredodegenerative) disease
Familienplanung *f* family planning *(s.a.* Geburtenregelung*)*

Fanconi-Anämie *f* Fanconi's anaemia (disease, syndrome), congenital hypoplastic anaemia
Fanconi-Syndrom *n s.* 1. Fanconi-Anämie; 2. Abderhalden-Kaufmann-Lignac-Syndrom; 3. Debré-de Toni-Fanconi-Syndrom
Fango *m* fango, mud *(Mineralschlamm)*
Fangotherapie *f* fango therapy
faradisieren to faradize
Faradisierung *f*, **Faradotherapie** *f* faradization, faradism, faradotherapy
farbabweisend chromophobe, chromophobic
Farbanpassung *f* chromatic (colour) adaptation *(des Auges)*
färbbar/doppelt dichromophil[e], amphophilic
~/leicht chromophil[e], chromophilic, chromatophil
~/leicht mit Azurfarbstoffen azurophil[e]
~/mit basischen und sauren Farbstoffen amphophil[ic], polychromatophilic
~/mit Chromsalzen chromaffin
~/mit Eosin eosinophil[e], eosinophilic
~/mit mehreren Farbstoffen polychromatophilic, polychromophil[e], polychromatic
~/mit Metallsalzen metallophil[e]
~/mit Osmium osmiophilic
~/mit Pyronin pyroninophilic
~/mit Safranin safranophil[e]
~/mit sauren Farbstoffen acidophilic, oxyphil[e], oxyphilic
~/mit Silber argyrophil[e], argyrophilic
~/mit Sudan sudanophil[ic]
~/nicht achromatophil[e]
~/normal orthochrom[at]ic
~/nur mit einer Farbe monochromatophil[ic]
~/schlecht chromophobe, chromophobic
Färbbarkeit *f/gesteigerte* hyperchromatism, hyperchromatosis *(z. B. des Zellkerns)*; hyperchromia *(z. B. der Erythrozyten)*
~/leichte chromophily, chromatophilia
farbbildend chromogenic, chromatogenous
Farbbildung *f* chromogenesis
Farbe *f* colour; pigment; dye; stain ● **nicht ~ annehmend** achromatophil
Färbeindex *m* colour index *(Hämoglobingehalt des Einzelerythrozyten)*
Farbempfindung *f* colour perception, sensation of colour
färben to colour, to dye; to stain *(z. B. mikroskopische Präparate)*
Farbenagnosie *f* colour (chromatic) agnosia
Farbenanpassung *f* colour (chromatic) adaptation
Farbenbezeichnungsstörung *f* colour (chromatic) aphasia; amnesic colour blindness
farbenblind colour-blind
Farbenblinder *m* monochromat[e], achromat
~/partiell dichromat[e]
Farbenblindheit *f* colour blindness, chromatodysopia, chromatelopsia, chromatopseudopsis, daltonism
~/amnestische amnesic colour blindness, colour name aphasia; colour agnosia

~/**halbseitige** hemi[a]chromatopsia
~/**partielle** partial colour blindness, colour amblyopia, dyschromatopsia; dichromasia, dichromatopsia, dichromatism
~/**totale** total colour blindness, achromatopsia
~/**zentrale** central colour blindness, colour aphasia
Farbenblindheitstest *m* **nach Ishihara** Ishihara test *(mit Farbtafeln)*
färbend mit ... *s.* **färbbar mit ...**
Farbenerkennungsstörung *f* colour agnosia
Farbenhalluzination *f* colour hallucination
Farbenhören *n* colour hearing, psychochromaesthesia, phonopsia *(Synästhesieform)*
Farbenprüfung *f* chrom[at]ometry, colorimetry
Farben[reiz]schwelle *f* colour threshold
Farbenschwellentest *m* colour threshold test
Farbensehen *n* colour (chromatic) vision, chrom[at]opsia
~/**gestörtes** parachromato[ble]psia, parachromatism
~/**normales** euchromatopsia
Farbensehmesser *m* chromatoptometer
Farbensehmessung *f* chrom[at]optometry
Farbensehschärfemesser *m* chromatoptometer
Farbensehschärfemessung *f* chrom[at]optometry
Farbensehstörung *f* colour vision defect, parachromato[ble]psia, parachromatism
Farbensehtafel *f* pseudoisochromatic plate *(zur Farbsinnprüfung)*
Farbensehtest *m* colour vision test
~ **nach Ishihara** Ishihara test *(mit Farbtafeln)*
Farbensichtigkeit *f*/**übersteigerte** hyperchromatopsia
Farbensinn *m* colour sense
Farbenunterscheidungsvermögen *n* colour discrimination
Farbenwahrnehmung *f* colour perception
~ **mit Geschmackszuordnung** pseudogeusaesthesia
Färbeverhalten *n* staining characteristic
farbfreundlich chromophil[e], chromophilic, chromatophil, chromophilous
Farbfreundlichkeit *f* chromophily, chromatophilia
Farbkonzentrationsmesser *m* colorimeter
farblos colourless; achrom[at]ic, achromatous
Farblosigkeit *f* achromia, achromatism
Farblösung *f* staining solution *(für histologische Präparate)*
~/**Castellanische** Castellani's mixture (paint) *(zur Behandlung von Hautkrankheiten)*
Farbmesser *m* colorimeter, chrom[at]ometer
Farbmessung *f* colorimetry, chrom[at]ometry
Farbsinn *m* colour sense
Farbsinnbestimmung *f* chrom[at]optometry
Farbsinnmesser *m* chromatoptometer
Farbsinnprüfung *f* colour vision test
Farbsinnstörung *f* colour vision defect, defective colour vision
Farbskotom *n* colour scotoma

Farbstoff *m* colour, colouring matter, colourant; dye[stuff] *(löslich)*; pigment *(unlöslich)*; stain *(Histologie)* ● **nach Lichteinwirkung** ~ **bildend** photochromogenic
~/**fettlöslicher** fat-soluble (oil-soluble) dye
~/**fluoreszierender** fluorochrome
farbstoffbildend chromogenic
Farbstoffbildung *f* chromogenesis
Farbstoffbindung *f* stain affinity
Farbstoff[konzentrations]messung *f* colorimetry
farbstofftragend chromophoric, chromophorous
Farbstoffträger *m* chromatophore *(s.a. Farbzelle)*
Farbstoffverdünnungskurve *f* dye dilution curve
Farbstoffverdünnungsmethode *f* dye dilution method (technique)
Farbstoffzugabe *f* tinction *(Rezeptur)*
Farbszintigramm *n* colour scan (scintigram)
Farbszintigraphie *f* colour scanning (scintigraphy)
Farbtafel *f* colour chart; confusion colours *(zur Farbsinnprüfung)*
farbtüchtig thrichromatic
Färbung 1. colouring, dyeing; staining *(von mikroskopischen Präparaten)*; tinction *(laut Rezeptur)*; 2. colour[ation]; pigmentation *(Erscheinung)*; 3. stain; tinge *(farbiger Zustand)*
~/**histologische** histological staining
~/**May-Grünwaldsche** May-Grünwald staining *(für Blutkörper)*
~/**Nisslsche** Nissl staining *(zur Darstellung der Nisslschen Schollen)*
~/**pigmentäre** pigmentation
~/**verstärkte** hyperchrom[as]ia, hyperchromatosis *(z. B. von Zellen)*
Färbungseigenschaft *f* staining characteristic
Färbungsmethode *f* staining method
Färbungsreaktion *f* staining reaction
Farbwahrnehmung *f* colour perception
Farbzelle *f* chromocyte, chromatophore, chrom[at]oplast
Farmerhaut *f* farmer's skin (disease)
Farmerlunge *f* farmer's lung
Farnkrautbild *n* fern pattern *(Gynäkologie)*
Farnkrautklassifizierung *f* ferning classification *(Gynäkologie)*
Farnkrauttest *m* fern test *(Gynäkologie)*
Farnkrautzunge *f* fern leaf tongue
Fascia *f* fascia *(s. a. unter* Faszie*)*
~ **buccopharyngea** buccopharyngeal fascia
~ **bulbaris (bulbi)** bulbar fascia, fascia of the eyeball, capsule of Tenon (the bulb)
~ **cervicalis [profunda]** [deep] cervical fascia
~ **cervicalis superficialis** superficial cervical fascia
~ **clavipectoralis** clavipectoral (coracoclavicular) fascia
~ **cremasterica** cremasteric (Cooper's) fascia
~ **cribrosa** cribriform fascia
~ **cruris** crural fascia
~ **dentata** dentate fascia

Fascia

- ~ **diaphragmatis pelvis inferior** ischiorectal fascia
- ~ **diaphragmatis pelvis superior** rectovesical fascia
- ~ **endopelvina** endopelvic fascia
- ~ **iliaca** iliac fascia
- ~ **ischiorectalis** ischiorectal fascia
- ~ **lacrimalis** lacrimal fascia
- ~ **lumbodorsalis** lumbodorsal (dorsolumbar, thoracolumbar) fascia
- ~ **obturatoria** obturator fascia
- ~ **orbitalis** orbital fascia
- ~ **palpebralis** palpebral fascia
- ~ **pectinea** pectineal fascia
- ~ **pectoralis** pectoral[is] fascia
- ~ **pelvis** pelvic fascia
- ~ **pelvis parietalis** parietal pelvic fascia
- ~ **pelvis visceralis** visceral pelvic fascia, endopelvic fascia
- ~ **praetrachealis** pretracheal fascia
- ~ **praevertebralis** prevertebral fascia
- ~ **renalis** renal (Gerota's) fascia
- ~ **spermatica externa** external spermatic fascia
- ~ **spermatica interna** internal spermatic fascia, infundibuliform fascia
- ~ **superficialis** superficial fascia
- ~ **thoracolumbalis** s. ~ lumbodorsalis
- ~ **transversalis** transversalis fascia

Fasciculi *mpl* **proprii medullae spinalis** spinospinal tracts, ground bundles

Fasciculus *m* 1. fascicle, fasciculus *(Histologie);* 2. fascicle, fasciculus, fiber, bundle, cord, column *(Neurologie) (s. a. unter* Bündel *und* Tractus*)*

- ~ **anterolateralis superficialis [Gowersi]** Gowers' (anterior spinocerebellar) tract
- ~ **atrioventricularis** atrioventricular bundle, sinoventricular band, bundle of His *(Herzreizleitung)*
- ~ **cerebellospinalis** spinocerebellar tract
- ~ **cerebrospinalis** Flechsig's (direct cerebellar) tract, dorsal (posterior) spinocerebral tract
- ~ **cerebrospinalis anterior** anterior cerebrospinal fasciculus, ventral (anterior) corticospinal tract, column of Türck, direct pyramidal tract
- ~ **cerebrospinalis lateralis** lateral cerebrospinal fasciculus, lateral corticospinal tract, lateral (crossed) pyramidal tract
- ~ **cuneatus medullae spinalis** cuneate (Burdach's) fasciculus, column of Burdach
- ~ **dorsolateralis** dorsolateral fasciculus, marginal bundle, Lissauer's tract
- ~ **gracilis** Goll's column (tract), fasciculus (column) of Goll *(mittlerer Teil der sensiblen Hinterstrangbahn)*
- ~ **lateralis plexus brachialis** lateral cord of the brachial plexus
- ~ **lenticularis** lenticular fasciculus
- ~ **longitudinalis dorsalis** posterior longitudinal fasciculus, dorsal longitudinal bundle
- ~ **longitudinalis dorsalis medullae oblongatae** dorsal longitudinal fibre tract of the medulla oblongata
- ~ **longitudinalis dorsalis mesencephali** dorsal longitudinal fibre tract of the mesencephalon
- ~ **longitudinalis dorsalis pontis** dorsal longitudinal fibre tract of the pons
- ~ **longitudinalis inferior cerebri** inferior longitudinal fasciculus
- ~ **longitudinalis medialis** medial longitudinal bundle (fasciculus)
- ~ **longitudinalis superior cerebri** superior longitudinal fasciculus
- ~ **mamillotegmentalis** mamillotegmental tract (fasciculus)
- ~ **mamillothalamicus** mamillothalamic tract (fasciculus)
- ~ **medialis plexus brachialis** medial cord of the brachial plexus
- ~ **occipitothalamicus** occipitothalamic fasciculus
- ~ **opticus** optic nerve (fasciculus)
- ~ **posterior plexus brachialis** posterior cord of the brachial plexus
- ~ **retroflexus** habenulopeduncular tract, Meynert's fasciculus
- ~ **solitarius** solitary fasciculus
- ~ **subcallosus** subcallosal fasciculus
- ~ **Türcki** s. ~ cerebrospinalis anterior
- ~ **uncinatus** uncinate (unciform) fasciculus, hook bundle

Fasciola *f* **hepatica** liver (hepatic) fluke
Fascioliasis *f* fascioliasis, distomiasis, distomatosis, liver rot
Fasciolopsiasis *f* fasciolopsiasis
Fasciolopsis *m* **buski** intestinal fluke *(Leber- und Darmparasit des Menschen)*
Fasciolopsis-buski-Infestation *f* fasciolopsiasis
Faser *f* fibre, filum, filament *(Zusammensetzungen s. a. unter* Fibrae*)* ● **aus Fasern bestehend** fibrous, fibrose, fibroid
- ~/**argentaffine** argentaffine fibre
- ~/**argentophile** argentophil[e] fibre
- ~/**argyrophile** argyrophile fibre
- ~/**elastische** elastic (yellow) fibre
- ~/**kollagene** collagen fibre
- ~/**Purkinjesche** Purkinje fibre
- ~/**Remaksche** Remak's fibre
- ~/**retikuläre** reticular fibre

faserartig fibroid, fibrous, fibrose; fibrilliform, filiform
faseraufösend fibrolytic
Faserbindegewebe *n* fibrous [connective] tissue, white fibrous tissue
faserbindegewebsbildend fibroblastic
Fäserchen *n* fibril
Faserfehlbildung *f* fibrodysplasia, fibrous dysplasia
faserförmig fibriform, fibrilliform, filamentous
Fasergeschwulst *f* s. Fibroma
Fasergewebe *n* fibrous tissue
fasergewebsauflösend fibrolytic
Fasergewebsauflösung *f* fibrolysis
fasergewebsbildend fibromatogenic
Fasergewebshyperplasie *f* fibrous hyperplasia

Fasergewebsproliferation *f* fibrous tissue proliferation; fibroelastosis
faserig fibrous, fibrose; fibrillar[y], filamentary, filamentous; fibrotic
Faserigkeit *f* fibrousness *(des Gewebes)*
faserig-knöchern fibro-osseous
Faserkallus *m* fibrous callus
Faserknorpel *m* fibrous cartilage, fibrocartilage *(Zusammensetzungen s. unter* Fibrocartilago*)*
faserknorpelartig fibrocartilaginous
Faserknorpelentzündung *f* fibrochondritis, inochondritis
Faserknorpelgeschwulst *f* chondrofibroma
Faserknorpelring *m* 1. falciform (semilunar) cartilage, interarticular fibrocartilage; 2. meniscus *(im Kniegelenk)*
~/äußerer lateral (external) meniscus, external semilunar fibrocartilage *(im Kniegelenk)*
~/innerer medial (internal) meniscus, internal semilunar fibrocartilage *(im Kniegelenk)*
Faserkrebs *m* fibrocarcinoma
Faseroptikbronchoskop *n* fibre-optic bronchoscope
Faseroptikbronchoskopie *f* fibre-optic bronchoscopy
Faseroptikendoskop *n* fibre-optic endoscope
~/flexibles flexible fibre-optic endoscope
Faseroptikendoskopie *f* fibre-optic endoscopy
Faseroptikgastroduodenoskopie *f* fibre-optic gastroduodenoscopy
Faseroptikinstrument *n* fibrescope
Faseroptikkolonoskopie *f* fibre-optic colonoscopy
Faseroptiksigmoidoskopie *f* fibresigmoidoscopy
faserreich fibrotic *(z. B. Gewebe)*
Faserring *m* fibrous ring
Faserscheide *f* fibrous sheath
Faserschicht *f* fibrous layer
Faserstoff *m* fibrin *(Eiweißprodukt der Blutgerinnung)*
Faserstrang *m* fibrous bundle
Faserstreifen *mpl*/**Hunter-Schregersche** Hunter-Schreger bands *(Hell-Dunkel-Streifung auf Zahnschmelzschliffen)*
Faserung *f* fibrillation; texture
Faserzelle *f* fibre cell
faserzellenbildend fibroblastic
Faßbauch *m* pot belly
Faßthorax *m* barrel[-shaped] thorax; emphysematous chest
Fassung *f* composure, self-control
Fassungsvermögen *n* capacity
Faßzange *f* [pick-up] forceps, volsella, volsellum [forceps], alligator forceps
fasten to fast, to starve, to abstain from food
Fasten *n* fast[ing], starvation, abrosia, nesteia; abstinence
Fastentherapie *f* starvation cure, treatment by fasting, nestiatria, nestitherapy, nestotherapy
Fastigium *n* 1. fastigium *(Anatomie)*; 2. fastigium, acme *(z. B. des Fiebers)*
faszial fascial

Faszial... *s.* Faszien...
Faszie *f* fascia *(s. a. unter* Fascia*)* ● **unter der ~** subfascial
~/Bucksche Buck's fascia, deep fascia of the penis
~/Coopersche Cooper's (cremasteric) fascia
Faszienentfernung *f*[/**operative**] fasciectomy, aponeurectomy *(Muskel)*
Faszienentzündung *f* fasciitis, inflammation of a fascia
Faszienfixierung *f* fasciodesis, suturing a fascia to skeletal attachment
Faszienhülle *f* fascial envelope
Faszienkanal *m*/**Alcockscher** Alcock's canal, fascial canal of Alcock
Faszienlappen *m* flap of fascia *(zur Transplantation)*
Faszienmesser *n* fasciotome
Fasziennaht *f* fasciorrhaphy, aponeurorrhaphy
Faszienplastik *f* fascioplasty
Faszienraum *m* fascial space
Faszienreflex *m* fascial reflex
Faszienrekonstruktion *f* fascioplasty
Faszienresektion *f* fasciectomy
Faszienschnitt *m* fasciotomy, incision of a fascia
Faszienstreifen *m* fascial strip
Faszienstripper *m*/**röhrenförmiger** tubular fascial stripper
Faszientransplantat *n* fascial graft (transplant)
Faszikel *m* 1. fasciculus, fascicle *(Histologie)*; 2. fasciculus, fascicle, bundle, tract, cord, column *(Neurologie) (Zusammensetzungen s. unter* Fasciculus*)*
Faszikelbildung *f* fasciculation
Faszikelhülle *f* perineurium, lamellar sheath *(der Nerven)*
faszikulär fascicular, fasciculate[d]
Faszikulation *f* fasciculation, fascicular twitching *(Muskel)*
Faszikulationspotential *n* fasciculation potential
Fasziodese *f* fasciodesis
Fasziorrhaphie *f* fasciorrhaphy
Fasziotom *n* fasciotome, fasciatorne
Fasziotomie *f* fasciotomy, incision of a fascia
Fauces *npl* [isthmus of the] fauces
Faulbrand *m s.* Gangrän
Faulecke *f* perleche, migrating cheilitis
faulen to putrefy, to rot, to decay, to decompose
Faulen *n* putrefaction ● **zum ~ bringen** to putrefy
faulend putrescent, rotting
faulig putrid, putrefactive, rotten, decayed
Fäulnis *f* putrefaction, putrescence, rot, rottenness, decomposition ● **durch ~ entstanden** saprogenic, saprogenous ● **in ~ übergehen** *s.* faulen ● **in ~ übergehend** putrescent
Fäulnisbewohner *m* saprophyte
fäulniserregend putrefactive, putrefacient, saprogenic, saprogenous; septic
Fäulniserreger *m* saprogen, saprophyte, putrefactive microorganism (bacterium)
fäulnisliebend saprophilous
fäulnisverhindernd, fäulniswidrig antiputrefactive

Faustgelenk

Faustgelenk n carpus
Favismus m favism, fabism[us] *(hämolytische Anämie infolge Enzymmangels)*
Favus m favus, honeycomb tetter, crusted ringworm
Favusschuppe f favus cup, scutulum
Fäzes pl faeces; excrement; stool, dejection, stercus, ordure *(Zusammensetzungen s. unter Stuhl)*
Fazialis m facial (seventh cranial) nerve
Fazialisbeteiligung f affection of the facial nerve
Fazialisdekompression f facial nerve decompression *(bei Einklemmung)*
Fazialisdiplegie f facial diplegia, bilateral peripheral facial palsy
Fazialisentzündung f facial neuritis
Fazialiskanal m facial canal, Fallopian aquaeduct (canal)
Fazialiskanalöffnung f hiatus of the facial canal
Fazialiskern m facial nucleus
Fazialisknie n/**äußeres** external genu facialis (of the facialis nerve)
~/**inneres** internal genu facialis
Fazialiskrampf m facial (mimic) spasm, convulsive (facial) tic, mimetic convulsion
Fazialislähmung f facial (seventh) nerve paralysis, facial palsy, facioplegia
~/**beidseitige** bilateral [peripheral] facial paralysis, facial diplegia, prosopodiplegia
~/**halbseitige** unilateral [peripheral] facial palsy, facial monoplegia
~/**periphere** peripheral facial palsy, Bell's disease (paralysis)
Fazialisneuralgie f facial neuralgia
Fazialisneurinom n neurinoma of facial nerve
Fazialisparese f s. Fazialislähmung
Fazialisphänomen n nach **Chvostek** facialis (face) phenomenon, Chvostek's sign
Fazialisplexus m facial plexus
Fazialisschwäche f facial weakness
Fazialistick m s. Fazialiskrampf
Fazialiszeichen n/**Chvosteksches** facialis (face) phenomenon, Chvostek's sign
Fazialiszucken n s. Fazialiskrampf
Fazialvene f facial vein
~/**gemeinsame** common facial vein
~/**vordere** anterior facial vein
febril febrile, feverish
febril-allergisch febrile-allergic
Febris f fever, pyrexia *(s.a. unter Fieber)*
~ **aphthosa** aphthous fever, foot and mouth disease
~ **biliosa** s. Gelbfieber
~ **bullosa** bullous fever *(bei Pemphigus)*
~ **continua** continued fever
~ **gastrica** gastric fever
~ **herpetica** herpetic fever
~ **quartana** quartan fever (malaria) *(durch Plasmodium malariae)*
~ **quintana** quintan[a] fever, trench (five-day, shinbone) fever; Wolhynia (Volhynia) fever, Werner-His disease *(durch Rickettsia quintana)*
~ **quotidiana** 1. quotidian fever; 2. quotidian fever (malaria) *(durch Plasmodium vivax)*
~ **recurrens** recurrent (relapsing) fever
~ **scarlatina** scarlet fever, scarlatina
~ **undulans** undulant fever
~ **undulans abortus** Bang's disease *(durch Brucella abortus)*
~ **undulans melitensis** Mediterranean fever (phthisis), Malta (Gibraltar) fever *(durch Brucella melitensis)*
~ **undulans suis** brucellosis, brucelliasis *(durch Brucella suis)*
~ **uveoparotidea** uveoparotid fever, uveoparotitis, Heerfordt's disease (syndrome)
Fechterstellung f right anterior oblique [position] *(die rechte Schulter ist dem Leuchtschirm bei Durchleuchtung genähert)*
federförmig feather-like, feather-shaped, penniform, pennate *(z. B. ein Muskel)*
Federlanzette f spring lancet
Federöhr n spring eye *(der chirurgischen Nadel)*
Feedback-Hemmung f feedback inhibition
fehlabbildend astigmatic
Fehlabbildung f erroneous projection
Fehladaptation f dysadaptation *(z. B. der Netzhaut)*
Fehlbehandlung f false treatment, malpractice
Fehlbewegung f parakinesia
Fehlbildung f malformation, abnormality, dysgenesis, peroplasia; teratism, teratosis
~/**embryonale** caenogenesis
Fehldiagnose f false diagnosis, misdiagnosis
Fehlentwicklung f maldevelopment, defective development
Fehler m defect *(körperlich)*; vitium *(z. B. des Herzens)*; deficiency *(Mangelhaftigkeit)*; imperfection *(Unvollkommenheit)*; failure *(Versagen)*; error *(statistisch)*
~/**kardiovaskulärer** cardiovascular defect
fehlernähren to malnourish
fehlernährt malnourished, dystrophic, paratrophic
Fehlernährung f malnutrition, false (defective) nutrition, underfeeding, athrepsia; dystrophia
Fehlfunktion f malfunction, dysfunction, defective function
Fehlgeburt f 1. abortion, miscarriage, immature (premature) delivery, foetus loss *(s.a. unter Abort und Abortus)*; 2. abortion, abort[us], aborted foetus ● **eine ~ auslösen** to induce an abortion ● **eine ~ haben** to abort, to miscarry, to have an abortion ● **nach einer ~** postabortal
~/**akzidentelle** accidental abortion
~/**ausgelöste** induced abortion
~/**beginnende** incipient (beginning) abortion
~/**drohende** imminent (impending, threatened) abortion
~/**eingeleitete** induced abortion
~/**habituelle** habitual abortion
~/**späte** late abortion
~/**unvollständige** incomplete abortion

~/verhaltene missed abortion *(Verbleiben einer unreifen abgestorbenen Frucht in der Gebärmutter)*
~/vollständige complete abortion
Fehlgeburtsneigung *f*/**krankhafte** habitual abortion, recurrent abortion
fehlgedreht malturned
fehlgelagert dystopic
Fehlgelenk *n* pseudarthrosis, supplementary articulation, nearthrosis
Fehllage *f* dystopia, aberration *(z. B. von Organen)*
~ **des Kindes bei der Geburt** abnormal presentation, malpresentation
Fehlprognose *f* false prognosis
Fehlregulation *f* false regulation, dysregulation *(Physiologie)*
Fehlreposition *f* malreduction
Fehlrotation *f* malrotation
Fehlschluß *m* false conclusion, paralogism
fehlsichtig ametropic
Fehlsichtiger *m* ametrope
Fehlsichtigkeit *f* ametropia, defective vision (sight); refractive error
Fehlsinnmutation *f* missense mutation
Fehlstellung *f* malposition, abnormal position
~ **von Knochenbruchstücken** malreduction
Fehlverdauung *f* maldigestion, disordered (imperfect) digestion
Fehlvereinigung *f* malunion *(z. B. von Knochenbrüchen)*
Fehlverwachsung *f* malunion *(z. B. von Knochenbrüchen)*
Feigwarze *f s.* Kondylom
Feigwarzen *fpl* **der Harnröhre** urethral condylomata
feigwarzenartig condylomatous
Feil[en]hauerlunge *f* pneumosiderosis, arc-welder's disease (nodulation), siderosis [pulmonum] *(Lungenverhärtung durch eisenhaltigen Staub)*
feinfühlig sensible, sensitive
Feinfühligkeit *f* sensibility
Feingefühl *n* sensitivity, sensitiveness
feinhörig micracoustic
Feinnadelpunktion *f* fine needle puncture (biopsy) *(z. B. der Leber)*
Feinrasterblende *f*/**Lysholmsche** Lysholm grid *(Röntgenologie)*
Feinstimmigkeit *f* microphonia
Feinstruktur *f* fine structure, ultrastructure
feist corpulent, obese
Feiung *f* immunity, resistance
~/**stille** latent (naturally acquired) immunity
Fekundation *f* fecundation, fertilization, impregnation
Fel *n s.* Galle
Feld *n* field, area
Feldanästhesiologie *f* military anaesthesiology
Feldblockade *f* field block [anaesthesia] *(örtliche Betäubung)*
Feldblockanästhesie *f* field block [anaesthesia]

Feldchirurgie *f* military surgery
Feldepidemiologie *f* field epidemiology
Felder *npl*/**Brodmannsche** Brodmann's areas *(Gehirn)*
Feldfieber *n* field fever, harvest (water, swamp, slime, mud) fever *(Infektionskrankheit durch Leptospira grippotyphosa)*
Feldlazarett *n* field [surgical] hospital
Feldscher *m* feldsher; army (field) surgeon
Feldversuch *m* field trial, field investigation of epidemics
Fellatio *f* fellatio
Felsenbein *n* petrosa, petrous [temporal] bone, petrous pyramid, petrous part (portion) of the temporal bone; otocranium
Felsenbeinaufnahme *f*/**Stenverssche** Stenvers' projection
Felsenbeinentzündung *f* petrositis
~/**fortgeleitete** paramastoiditis
Felsenbeinfortsatz *m* **des Keilbeins** petrosal process
Felsenbeinleiste *f* petrous ridge [of the temporal bone]
Felsenbeinnerv *m* petrosal nerve
Felsenbeinpyramide *f s.* Felsenbein
Felsenbeinsinus *m*/**oberer** superior petrosal sinus
~/**unterer** inferior petrosal sinus
Felsenbeinspitze *f* petrous apex
Felsengebirgsfieber *n* Rocky Mountain spotted fever, R.M.S.F., tick fever (typhus)
~/**südamerikanisches** Brazilian (South American) spotted fever
Felsengebirgsfieberimpfstoff *m* Mountain spotted fever vaccine
Felty-Syndrom *n* Felty's syndrome, adult Still disease
feminin 1. feminine, female; 2. effeminate, unmanly
feminisieren to feminize
Feminisierung *f* feminization
~/**testikuläre** testicular feminization
Feminismus *m* feminism
femoral femoral
Femoral... *s. a.* Femur... *und* Oberschenkel...
Femoraldreieck *n* femoral triangle
Femoralektopie *f* femoral ectopia
Femoralhernie *f* femoral (crural, Cooper's) hernia, femorocele
~ **mit Darminhalt** enteromerocele
Femoralhernienaht *f* femoral herniorrhaphy
Femoralhernienoperation *f* femoral hernioplasty
Femoralhernienregion *f* femoral hernial region
Femoralhernienverschluß *m* [/**operativer**] femoral herniorrhaphy
Femoralherniotomie *f* femoral herniotomy (hernioplasty)
Femoralis... *s.* Femoral...
Femoralkanal *m* femoral (crural) canal
Femoralnervenanästhesie *f* femoral nerve block
Femoralpuls *m* femoral pulse
Femoralreflex *m* femoral reflex

Femoralring

Femoralring *m* femoral (crural) ring
Femoralscheide *f* femoral sheath
femoro-iliakal femoro-iliac
femoropopliteal femoropopliteal
femorotibial femorotibial
Femur *n* femur, thigh-bone
Femur... *s. a.* Femoral... *und* Oberschenkel...
Femurfraktur *f* femoral fracture
Femurknorren *m*/**seitlicher** lateral femoral condyle
Femurkopf *m* femoral head, head of the femur
  • **unter dem ~** subcapital
Femurkopfprothese *f* femoral head prosthesis
Femurkopfstößel *m* femoral head driver
Femurschaft *m* femoral shaft, shaft of the femur
Femurschaftfraktur *f* femoral shaft fracture
Fenestra *f* fenestra, window *(Anatomie)*
  ~ **cochleae** cochlear fenestra (window), round window *(Ohr)*
  ~ **ovalis** vestibular fenestra (window), oval window *(Ohr)*
  ~ **rotunda** *s.* ~ cochleae
  ~ **vestibuli [ovalis]** *s.* ~ ovalis
Fenestration *f s.* Fensterungsoperation
Fenster *n* fenestra, window *(1. anatomische Öffnung; 2. Öffnung im Gipsverband)*
~/**aortopulmonales** aorticopulmonary fenestration (fistula, window)
~/**ovales** *s.* Fenestra ovalis
~/**Stensensches** Stensen's foramen
~/**Winslowsches** Winslow's foramen
Fensterung[soperation] *f* fenestration [operation], windowing operation
Fentanyl *n* fentanyl *(Schmerzmittel)*
Ferment *n s.* Enzym
Fermentationschemie *f* fermentation chemistry
Fermentationslehre *f* zymology
Fermentationssaccharimeter *n* fermentation saccharimeter
fermentierend zymogenic, zymogenous
Fermentierung *f* fermentation, zymo[ly]sis
~/**käsige** caseous fermentation
Fernbehandlung *f* teletherapy, teleotherapeutics
Fernbestrahlung *f* teleradiotherapy, teleradiology
Fernbrille *f* spectacles for distant vision, distance glasses
Ferndiagnose *f* telognosis
Ferndurchleuchtung *f* telefluoroscopy
Fernmessung *f* telemetry
Fernmetastase *f* distant metastasis
Fernpunkt *m* far point, punctum remotum *(des Auges)*
Fernpunktbestimmung *f* optometry
Fernrezeptor *m* tele[re]ceptor, teloreceptor
fernsichtig farsighted, long-sighted, hyperopic
Fernsichtigkeit *f* farsightedness, long-sightedness, hyperopia
Fernübertragung *f* des Elektrokardiogramms telecardiography
  ~ **von Meßdaten** telemetry
Ferriprotoporphyrin *n* ferriprotoporphyrin

Ferritin *n* ferritin *(Speicherform des Eisens im Organismus)*
Ferrohäm *n* ferrohaem, [reduced] haem[e]
Ferroprotoporphyrin *n* ferroprotoporphyrin
Ferse *f* heel
Fersenbein *n* calcaneus, calcaneum, heel bone
Fersenbeinapophyse *f* calcaneal apophysis
Fersenbeinapophysenentzündung *f* calcaneal apophysitis, Sever's disease
Fersenbeinarteriengeflecht *n* calcaneal rete
Fersenbeinbruch *m* calcaneal fracture
Fersenbeinentzündung *f* calcaneitis, inflammation of the calcaneus
Fersenbeingrube *f* calcaneal sulcus
Fersenbeinkörper *m* body of the calcaneus
Fersenbeinrolle *f* peroneal trochlea (tubercle) of the calcaneus, trochlear process of the calcaneus
Fersenbeinschmerz *m s.* Fersenschmerz
Fersenbeinsporn *m* calcaneal (heel) spur
Fersenbeinvergrößerung *f*/**abnorme** tarsomegaly, enlargement of the tarsal bone
Fersenhöcker *m* calcaneal tuber[osity]
Fersenneuralgie *f* talalgia, calcan[e]odynia
Fersenring *m* heel ring cushion
Fersenrolle *f s.* Fersenbeinrolle
Fersenschmerz *m* calcan[e]odynia, talalgia
Fertigschläger *m* nail impactor *(Traumatologie)*
fertil fertile, uberous; prolific; fruitful
Fertilisationsalter *n* fertilization (foetal) age
Fertilität *f* fertility, fecundity, uberty; productiveness
Fertilitätsfaktor *m* fertility (F) factor, sex factor
Fertilitätsvitamin *n* fertility vitamin, tocopherol, vitamin E, antisterility factor
Fessel *f* vinculum
~/**kurze** short vinculum
~/**lange** long vinculum
festhaftend adherent, attached; sessile
festigen to strengthen; to stabilize; to consolidate
festigend strengthening; stabilizing; consolidant
Festigung *f* strengthening; stabilization; consolidation *(z. B. von Knochen)*
Festination *f* festination, festinating gait *(z. B. bei Parkinsonismus)*
festklemmen to impact *(z. B. Knochen)*; to clamp
Festklemmung *f* impaction *(z. B. Knochen)*
festschnallen to strap *(z. B. auf dem Operationstisch)*
festsitzend sessile *(z. B. eine Geschwulst)*; tight *(z. B. ein Verband)*
feststellen 1. to determine; to state; to diagnose, to find *(eine Krankheit)*; to type *(eine Blutgruppe)*; 2. to perceive, to observe *(wahrnehmen)*
festwachsen to take *(z. B. Transplantate)*; to adhere, to attach *(z. B. Organe)*
Festwerden *n* congelation, consolidation, hardening, solidification; clotting *(z. B. des Blutes)*; knitting *(z. B. einer Fraktur)*; setting *(z. B. eines Gipsverbandes)*

Fet *m* s. Fetus
fetal foetal
Fetal... s. a. Fetus... *und* Embryonal...
Fetalalter *n* foetal age
Fetalanhänge *mpl* foetal appendages
Fetalasphyxie *f* foetal asphyxia
Fetalatmung *f* foetal (prenatal) respiration
Fetaldistress *m* foetal distress
Fetalentwicklung *f* foetation, foetal (prenatal) development
Fetalgeräusch *n* foetal souffle
Fetalhämoglobin *n* foetal haemoglobin, haemoglobin F
Fetalismus *m* foetalism *(Persistenz fetaler Zeichen nach der Geburt)*
Fetalknorpel *m* foetal cartilage
Fetalkrankheit *f* foetopathy, intrauterine disease
Fetalkreislauf *m* foetal circulation
Fetalleben *n* foetal (intrauterine) life
Fetalmembran *f* foetal membrane
Fetalstadium *n* foetal stage
Fetalstoffwechsel *m* foetal metabolism
Fetaltod *m* foetal death
fetid foetid
Fetischismus *m* fetishism
Fetoglobulin *n* foetoglobulin
Fetographie *f* foetography, foetal radiography
Fetologie *f* foetology
fetometrisch foetometric
Fetopathie *f/***diabetische** diabetic foetopathy; big baby
Fetoplazentareinheit *f* foetoplacental unit
α-Fetoprotein *n* alpha foetoprotein
Fetose *f/***hämolytische** newborn haemolytic disease
Fetoskopie *f* foetoscopy
fetoskopisch foetoscopic
fett *s.* 1. fetthaltig; 2. fettleibig
Fett *n* fat, adeps
Fettabbau *m* lipolysis
Fettablagerung *f* fat deposit (infiltration), lipo[mato]sis
Fettaffinität *f* fat affinity, lipophilia, lipotropism
Fettanhäufung *f/***umschriebene** lipo[mato]sis, lipopexia, adipopexis
fettanlagernd adipopectic, adipopexic
Fettanreicherung *f* lipo[mato]sis
~ im Blut lipaemia, lip[o]idaemia, lipohaemia, pionaemia
Fettansatzphase *f* lipotrophic (fat gain) phase
Fettansetzen *n* lipotrophy
fettansetzend lipotrop[h]ic, obesogenous
fettartig fat-like, lipoid[ic], liparoid
Fettauflösung *f* lipolysis
Fettaufnahme *f* lipophagia *(durch Zellen)*
fettaufnehmend lipophagic
Fettausscheidung *f* **im Urin** lipuria, adiposuria, pimeluria
Fettbildung *f* lipogenesis, adipogenesis
Fettbruch *m* lip[ar]ocele, adipocele, steatocele
Fettdurchfall *m* stea[to]rrhoea, fatty diarrhoea
Fettdurchtränkung *f* s. Fettentartung

Fettdurchwachsung *f* lipo[mato]sis
fetteinlagernd lipotrophic, steatogenous
Fetteinlagerung *f* lipotrophy
Fettembolie *f* fat embolism
Fettentartung *f* fatty metamorphosis, fat infiltration *(z. B. des Gewebes)*
Fettentfernung *f*[**/operative**] lipectomy, adipectomy
fettfrei non-lipid, non-fat[ty]
fettfressend lipophagic *(z. B. Phagozyten)*
Fettgeschwulst *f* lipoma, adipoma, steatoma, pimeloma, adipose tumour
Fettgewebe *n* adipose tissue, fat[ty] tissue ● **~ bildend** lipoplastic
~/subseröses fatty subserous tissue
Fettgewebsanhäufung *f/***umschriebene** lipo[mato]sis
fettgewebsbildend lipoplastic
Fettgewebsbruch *m* lipocele, adipocele, fat hernia
Fettgewebsdurchwachsung *f* lipo[mato]sis, fat infiltration *(z. B. des Gewebes)*
Fettgewebsentfernung *f*[**/operative**] adipectomy, lipectomy
Fettgewebsentzündung *f* adipositis, adipose tissue inflammation, steatitis, pimelitis
Fettgewebsgeschwulst *f* lipoma, adipoma, steatoma, pimeloma, adipose tumour
Fettgewebsnekrose *f* fat necrosis, adiponecrosis, steatonecrosis
~/Balsersche Balser's fat necrosis
Fettgewebsresektion *f* lipectomy, adipectomy
Fetthaarigkeit *f* liparotrichia
fetthaltig fat-containing, fatty, adipose, lipoferous
Fettherz *n* fatty heart; cardiomyolipsis
fettig 1. adipose, lipoid[ic], liparoid; sebaceous *(z. B. Drüsen)*; greasy *(z. B. Haut)*; 2. s. fetthaltig
Fettinfiltration *f* fat infiltration, fatty metamorphosis; steatosis
Fettintoleranz *f* fatty food intolerance
Fettkapsel *f* **der Niere** adipose capsule [of the kidney]
Fettknochenmark *n* fat marrow
Fettkörper *m/***Hoffascher** Hoffa's fat pad
~/infrapatellärer infrapatellar fat pad
Fettleber *f* fatty liver; fatty degeneration (infiltration) of the liver
fettleibig obese, adipose, corpulent, fat, liparous
Fettleibigkeit *f* obesity, obeseness, adiposity, adiposis, corpulence, fatness, polypionia
fettliebend lipophile
fettlösend lipolytic
fettlöslich fat-soluble, liposoluble
Fettlöslichkeit *f* solubility in fat, liposolubility
Fettmangel *m* **im Gewebe** lipopenia, hypoliposis
Fettmark *n* fat marrow, yellow [bone] marrow
Fettnekrose *f* fat necrosis, adiponecrosis, steatonecrosis
Fettniere *f* fatty kidney; fatty degeneration (infiltration) of the ren

Fettpolster

Fettpolster *n* [fat] pad
fettproduzierend lipogenic, lipogenous, adipogenous, steatogenous, lipoblastic, lipoplastic
fettreich lipomatous; high-fat *(z. B. Ernährung)*
Fettsäure *f* fatty acid
~/essentielle essential fatty acid, EFA
Fettsäureausscheidung *f* im Urin lipaciduria
Fettsäureerhöhung *f* im Blut lipacidaemia
Fettsäuresynthese *f* fatty acid synthesis
Fettschicht *f* fatty layer
Fettschwund *m* fat[ty] atrophy *(z. B. des Gewebes)*
fettspaltend fat-splitting, lipolytic, adipolytic, lipodieretic
Fettspaltung *f* fat splitting, lip[id]olysis, lipoclasis, adipolysis, lipodieresis
~/enzymatische enzymatic lipolysis
fettspeichernd adipopectic, adipopexic
Fettspeicherung *f* lipopexia, adipopexis
Fettspeicherungskrankheit *f* lip[o]idosis, lipid storage disease, lipoid thesaurismosis
Fettspiegelerhöhung *f* im Blut hyperlip[id]aemia
Fett[spiegel]verminderung *f* im Blut hypolip[id]aemia
Fettsteiß *m* steatopygia
Fettstoffwechsel *m* fat metabolism, lipometabolism
Fettstuhl *m* fatty stool[s]; stea[to]rrhoea, pimelorrhoea
Fettsucht *f* obesity, adiposity, adiposis, fatness; lipo[mato]sis ● **~ bewirkend** obesogenous
~/adrenokortikale adrenal cortical obesity *(bei Morbus Cushing)*
~/alimentäre alimentary obesity
~/dienzephale diencephalic obesity
~/hypophysäre hypophyseal (pituitary) obesity
~/hypothalamische hypothalamic obesity
~/übermäßige hyperadiposis
~/zerebrale cerebral obesity
fettsüchtig obese, adipose, liparous
Fett- und Blutansammlung *f* im Gelenk lipohaemarthrosis
Fettunverträglichkeit *f* fatty food intolerance
Fettvakuole *f* fat vacuole
Fettwachs *n* adipocere
Fettwachsbildung *f* saponification *(bei Leichenzersetzung)*
Fettzelle *f* fat (adipose) cell, lipocyte, adipocyte
~/jugendliche lipoblast
fettzellenbildend lipoblastic
Fettzellenkarzinom *n* lipomatous carcinoma
fettzersetzend lipolytic
Fettzersetzung *f* lipolysis
fettzerstörend lipodieretic
Fettzerstörung *f* lipodieresis
Fettzylinder *m* fatty cast *(im Urin)*
Fetuin *n* foetoin
Fetus *m* foetus, interogestate *(ab 3. Schwangerschaftsmonat)* ● **einen lebensunfähigen ~ entbinden** to bring forth a non-viable foetus ● **ohne ~** afoetal
~/amorpher amorphous foetus, amorphus, anideus
~ papyraceus papyraceous foetus
~/verknöcherter ossified foetus, ostembryon
Fetus... *s. a.* Fetal... *und* Embryo...
Fetusauspressung *f* expression of the foetus
Fetusbetrachtung *f* foetoscopy
Fetusbewegung *f* foetal movement
Fetusdarstellung *f* foetography
Fetusendokarditis *f* foetal endocarditis
Fetuserstickung *f* foetal asphyxia
Fetusherzstromkurve *f* cardiotocogram
Fetuslage *f* position of the foetus
Fetuslehre *f* foetology
Fetusmaturität *f* foetus maturity
Fetusschädelperforation *f* foetal skull perforation, transforation
Fetusschädigung *f* foetal damage
Fetustod *m* foetal death
fetustötend foeticide
Fetustötung *f* embryoctony
Fetusüberwachung *f* foetus monitoring
fetusvermessend foetometric
Fetusvermessung *f* foetometry
Fetuswachstum *n* foetal growth
feucht wet, humid, moist *(z. B. Gangrän)*
Feuchtgewicht *n* wet weight
Feuchthaltemittel *n* humectant [agent]
Feuchtigkeitsmesser *m* psychrometer
Feuchtmachen *n* humidification
Feuerbestattung *f* cremation, incineration
Feuerleger *m*/**triebhafter** pyromaniac
Feuermal *n* port-wine mark (naevus, stain)
Feuerstar *m* glassblower's (glassworker's) cataract
Feuersteinleber *f* brimstone (fire-stone) liver
F_1-Generation *f* filial generation, F1
FH *s.* Follikelhormon
Fiber *f s.* Faser
Fiberskop *n* fibrescope
Fibrae *fpl* fibres
~ arcuatae cerebri association fibres [of the cerebrum]
~ arcuatae externae external arcuate fibres, Rolando's fibres
~ arcuatae externae dorsales dorsal external arcuate fibres
~ arcuatae externae medullae oblongatae *s.* ~ arcuatae externae
~ arcuatae externae ventrales ventral external arcuate fibres
~ arcuatae internae internal arcuate fibres
~ corticospinales corticospinal tracts
~ lentis lens fibres
~ meridionales musculi ciliaris meridional fibres of the ciliary muscle, tensor muscle of the choroid, Brücke's muscle
~ pyramidales [medullae oblongatae] pyramidal fibres, corticospinal tract
~ zonulares zonular fibres
fibrillär fibrillar[y], fibrillate
Fibrillationspotential *n* fibrillation potential
Fibrille *f* fibril[la]

Fibrillenarchitektur f fibrillary architecture
Fibrillenauflösung f fibrillolysis
Fibrillenbildung f fibrillogenesis
Fibrillenscheide f fibril sheath
Fibrillenzittern n fibrillary tremor
fibrillieren to fibrillate *(Muskel)*
Fibrillieren n fibrillation *(von Muskeln)*
Fibrillogenese f fibrillogenesis
Fibrillolyse f fibrillolysis
Fibrin n fibrin *(Eiweißprodukt der Blutgerinnung)*
● **aus ~ bestehend** fibrinous
Fibrinabbauprodukt n fibrin degradation product
Fibrinablagerung f fibrin deposition
Fibrinadhäsion f fibrin adhesion
Fibrinanhäufung f [im Blut] fibrinosis
fibrinartig fibrinoid
Fibrinase f fibrinase, fibrin stabilizing factor, FSF, [blood-clotting] factor XIII
Fibrinauflagerung f fibrin deposit (adhesion)
fibrinauflösend fibrinolytic
Fibrinauflösung f s. Fibrinolyse
Fibrinausscheidung f im Urin fibrinuria
fibrinbildend fibrinogenous, fibrinogenic
Fibrinbildung f fibrinogenesis
Fibrinentfernung f aus dem Blut defibrination
Fibrinexsudat n fibrinous exudate
Fibrinfaser f fibrin strand
Fibrinfilm m fibrin film
Fibringerinnsel n fibrin clot
fibrinhaltig fibrinous
fibrinlösend fibrinolytic
Fibrinmangel m fibrinopenia
Fibrinmonomer n fibrin monomere
Fibrinniederschlag m fibrin film
fibrinogen fibrinogenous, fibrinogenic
Fibrinogen n fibrinogen, [blood-clotting] factor I
Fibrinogenanomalie f fibrinogen anomaly
Fibrinogenauflösung f fibrinogenolysis
Fibrinogenderivat n fibrinogen derivative
Fibrinogenmangel m fibrinogen (factor I) deficiency, fibrinogenopenia
~ im Blut afibrinogenaemia; hypofibrinogenaemia
Fibrinogenolyse f fibrinogenolysis
Fibrinogenopenie f s. Fibrinogenmangel
Fibrinogenspiegelerhöhung f im Blut hyperfibrinogenaemia
Fibrinogen[spiegel]verminderung f im Blut hypofibrinogenaemia
fibrinoid fibrinoid
Fibrinoid n fibrinoid
Fibrinokinase f fibrinokinase *(Enzym)*
Fibrinolyse f fibrinolysis
Fibrinolyseaktivator m fibrinolysis activator
Fibrinolysefaktor m fibrinolysis factor
fibrinolysehemmend antifibrinolytic
Fibrinolyseinhibitor m fibrinolysis inhibitor
Fibrinolyseproaktivator m fibrinolysis proactivator
Fibrinolysetest m fibrinolysis test
Fibrinolysin n fibrinolysin, plasmin
Fibrinolysinaktivierung f fibrinolysin activation

Fibrinolysinmangel m plasminogenopenia
Fibrinolytikum n fibrinolytic [agent]
fibrinolytisch fibrinolytic
Fibrinopeptid n fibrinopeptide
fibrinös fibrinous
Fibrinose f fibrinosis
fibrinös-eitrig fibr[in]opurulent
fibrinös-serös fibroserous
fibrinozellulär fibrinocellular
Fibrinpolyp m fibrinous polyp
Fibrinschaum m fibrin foam
Fibrinschwamm m fibrin sponge
Fibrinspaltprodukt n fibrin split (degradation) product
Fibrinspaltung f fibrin splitting
Fibrinspiegel m fibrin level
Fibrinspiegelerhöhung f im Blut hyperfibrinaemia, [hyper]inosaemia, hyperinosis
Fibrinspiegelverminderung f im Blut hypofibrinaemia, hypoinosaemia, hypoinosis
Fibrinstein m fibrin (fibrinous) calculus
Fibrinstern m fibrin star (aster)
Fibrinthrombus m fibrin (white) thrombus
Fibrin- und Blutansammlung f im Pleuraspalt fibrohaematothorax
Fibrinzylinder m fibrin (fibrinous) cast *(im Urin)*
Fibroadenom n fibroadenoma, adenofibroma
~/intrakanalikuläres intracanalicular fibroadenoma (myxoma) *(gutartiger Brusttumor)*
Fibroameloblastom n fibroameloblastoma
Fibroangiolipom n fibroangiolipoma *(Gewächs aus Binde-, Gefäß- und Fettgewebe)*
Fibroangiom n fibroangioma *(Gewächs aus Blut- und Lymphgefäßen sowie Bindegewebe)*
Fibroblast m fibroblast, inoblast *(undifferenzierte Mesenchymzelle)*
Fibroblastengewebekultur f fibroblast tissue culture
Fibroblastom n fibroblastoma *(Bindegewebstumor)*
Fibrocartilago f fibrocartilage, fibrous cartilage
~ basilaris basilar [fibro]cartilage
~ intervertebralis intervertebral fibrocartilage (disk)
Fibrochondritis f fibrochondritis, inochondritis, inflammation of a fibrocartilage
Fibrochondrom n fibrochondroma, inochondroma *(gutartiges Gewächs aus Binde- und Knorpelgewebe)*
Fibrochondroosteom n fibrochondroosteoma
Fibrodysplasie f fibrodysplasia, fibrous dysplasia
fibroelastisch fibroelastic
Fibroelastose f 1. fibroelastosis, fibrous tissue proliferation; 2. [endocardial] fibroelastosis
Fibroendotheliom n fibroendothelioma
Fibroepitheliom n fibroepithelioma
Fibrogliom n fibroglioma
Fibrogranulomatose f fibrogranulomatosis
Fibrohämatothorax m fibrohaematothorax
Fibrohistiozytom n fibrohistiocytoma
fibrokartilaginös fibrocartilaginous
Fibrokarzinom n fibrocarcinoma

fibrokavernös

fibrokavernös fibrocavernous
fibrokollagenös fibrocollagenous
Fibrolipom n fibrolipoma
fibrolipomatös fibrolipomatous
Fibroliposarkom n fibroliposarcoma
Fibrolyse f fibrolysis
fibrolytisch fibrolytic
Fibrom n fibroma *(s.a. unter Fibroma)*
~/**perineurales** perineural fibroma
Fibroma n fibroma *(gutartige Bindegewebsgeschwulst)*
~ **durum** hard fibroma
~ **lipoidicum (lipomatodes)** s. Xanthoma
~ **molle** soft fibroma
~ **pendulum** pendulous fibroma, cutaneous tag
~ **sarcomatosum** s. Fibrosarkom
~ **simplex** simple fibroma, dermatofibroma; nodular subepidermal fibrosis
~ **xanthoma** fibroxanthoma
fibromartig fibromatoid
fibromatös fibromatous
Fibromatose f fibromatosis *(s.a. unter Fibromatosis)*
~/**angeborene** hereditary fibromatosis
Fibromatosis f fibromatosis *(s.a. unter Fibromatose)*
~ **gingivae** diffuse (familial) fibromatosis
~ **ventriculi** leather bottle stomach
fibrombildend fibromatogenic
fibromembranös fibromembranous
Fibromentfernung f/**operative** fibromectomy, fibroidectomy
fibromuskulär fibromuscular
Fibromyangiom n fibromyangioma
Fibromyom n fibromyoma
Fibromyomentfernung f/**operative** fibromyomectomy
Fibromyositis f fibromyositis
Fibromyxolipom n fibromyxolipoma *(gutartige Geschwulst)*
Fibromyxom n fibromyxoma *(gutartige Geschwulst)*
Fibromyxosarkom n fibromyxosarcoma *(bösartige Geschwulst)*
Fibroneurom n fibroneuroma, neurofibroma *(gutartige Geschwulst)*
Fibroosteochondrom n fibroosteochondroma *(gutartige Geschwulst)*
Fibroosteoklasie f fibroosteoclasis
Fibroosteom n fibroosteoma, osteofibroma
Fibroosteosarkom n fibroosteosarcoma, osteofibrosarcoma
Fibropapillom n fibropapilloma
Fibroperikarditis f fibropericarditis
Fibroplasie f fibroplasia
~/**retrolentale** retrolental fibroplasia, retinopathy of prematurity
Fibroplast m fibroplast, fibroblast
fibroplastisch fibroplastic, fibroblastic
Fibropsammom n fibropsammoma *(Mischgeschwulst)*
fibrös fibrous, fibrose, desmoid

Fibrosarcoma n **ovarii mucocellulare carcinomatodes** Krukenberg's tumour
Fibrosarkom n fibrosarcoma *(bösartige Geschwulst)*
fibrosarkomatös fibrosarcomatous
Fibrose f fibrosis
fibrös-fettig fibrofatty
fibrosieren to fibrose
Fibrositis f fibrositis, muscular rheumatismus
Fibrositissyndrom n fibrositis (non-articular rheumatism) syndrome, soft tissue rheumatism
Fibrothorax m fibrothorax
fibrotisch fibrotic
Fibroxanthom n fibroxanthoma *(gutartige Geschwulst)*
Fibroxanthosarkom n fibroxanthosarcoma, malignant fibrous histiocytoma *(bösartige Geschwulst)*
Fibrozyt m fibrocyte, inocyte
Fibula f fibula, calf bone
Fibulahals m fibular neck
fibulär fibular
Fibulaschaft m shaft of the fibula
Fieber n fever, pyrexia *(s.a. unter Febris)* ● **bei einem Kranken ~ messen** to take a patient's temperature ● **~ haben** to be febrile (in fever), to have (run) a temperature ● **im ~** intrafebrile ● **nach dem ~** postfebrile ● **ohne ~** s. fieberfrei ● **vor dem ~** antefebrile ● **während des Fiebers** intrafebrile
~/**adynamisches** adynamic (asthenic) fever
~/**akutes rheumatisches** acute rheumatic fever, Bouillaud's disease (syndrome)
~/**argentinisches hämorrhagisches** Argentine haemorrhagic fever
~/**australisches** [Australian] Q fever
~ **bei Lepra** leprotic fever
~/**biphasisches** saddle-back fever
~/**bolivianisches hämorrhagisches** Bolivian haemorrhagic fever, BHF
~/**bösartiges** malignant fever
~/**epidemisches hämorrhagisches** [epidemic] haemorrhagic fever, Far Eastern haemorrhagic fever, haemorrhagic nephroso-nephritis
~/**eruptives** eruptive (exanthematous) fever
~/**gelbes** s. Gelbfieber
~/**geringes** low fever, slight temperature
~/**hohes** hyperthermia, hyperpyrexia, high temperature
~/**intermenstruelles** intermenstrual fever
~/**intermittierendes** intermittent fever
~/**kolumbianisches** Columbian tick fever
~/**kongolesisches** Congolian red fever, purine typhus
~/**künstliches** artificial fever
~ **mit Bläschenausschlag** vesicular fever
~ **mit Exanthem** exanthematous (eruptive) fever
~ **mit Hämaturie** haematuric fever
~ **mit Hämoglobinausscheidung** haemoglobinuric fever
~/**Omsker hämorrhagisches** Omsk haemorrhagic fever *(durch Arbovirus Gruppe B)*

~/periodisches periodic fever
~/remittierendes remittent fever
~/rezidivierendes recurrent (relapsing) fever
~/rheumatisches rheumatic fever, rheumapyra; inflammatory rheumatism
~/rhodesisches Rhodesian (African coast) fever, East Coast fever
~/septisches septic fever, sept[ic]aemia, ichorrhaemia
~/südafrikanisches South African fever
~/therapeutisches therapeutic fever; pyretotherapy
~/undulierendes undulant fever
~/unklares fever of undetermined origin
~/wechselndes intermittent fever
~/wolhynisches s. Febris quintana
~/zerebrospinales cerebrospinal fever; epidemic cerebrospinal meningitis
Fieberabfall m defervescence, declining of fever, defervescent stage, pyretolysis, remission
~/allmählicher [febrile] lysis
~/schneller [febrile] crisis
~/vorübergehender plötzlicher pseudocrisis
Fieberanfall m febrile attack, pyrexia
Fieberangst f febriphobia, pyrexiophobia
Fieberanstieg m rise (increase) of temperature
Fieberatmung f thermopolypnoea
Fieberattacke f febrile attack, pyrexia
Fieberausbruch m onset of fever
Fieberbehandlung f s. 1. Fiebertherapie; 2. Fieberbekämpfung
Fieberbekämpfung f antipyresis, treatment of fever
fieberbewirkend s. fiebererzeugend
Fieberblase f febrile (fever) blister
Fieberdelir[ium] n febrile delirium, pyretotyphosis
fiebererzeugend pyrogen[et]ic, pyre[c]tic, febrifacient, febrific, febricant
fieberfrei afebrile, apyretic, defervescent, free from fever
Fieberfrost m feverish chill; ague (bei Malaria)
Fiebergipfel m fastigium, febrile acme
fieberhaft s. fiebernd
Fieberhitze f [febrile] heat, feverish heat
Fieberkrampf m febrile convulsion
Fieberkrise f febrile crisis
Fieberkur f s. Fiebertherapie
Fieberkurve f temperature curve
Fieberlehre f pyretology
fieberlos afebrile, apyretic
Fiebermessung f thermometry, temperature measurement
Fiebermittel n antipyretic [agent], febrifuge [agent]
Fiebermücke f anopheles
fiebern to be febrile (feverish, in fever), to have (run) a temperature
fiebernd febrile, pyre[c]tic
~/hoch hyperpyretic
Fieberperiode f febrile period
Fieberphantasieren n pyretotyphosis

Fieberphase f febrile (pyrogenic) stage
Fieberproteinurie f febrile proteinuria
Fieberpuls m febrile pulse
Fieberpurpura f febrile purpura
Fieberreaktion f febrile reaction
Fieberschauer m [febrile] shivers, shivering-fit
Fieberschub m febrile attack; hot stage (bei Malaria)
fiebersenkend antifebrile, antipyretic, febrifugal, defervescent, antithermic
Fiebersenkung f pyretolysis; antipyresis
~/medikamentöse s. Fieberbekämpfung
Fieberspezialist m pyretologist
Fieberstadium n febrile stage
Fiebertabelle f temperature chart
Fiebertherapie f pyretotherapy, fever therapy (treatment)
Fieberthermometer n fever thermometer, [clinical] thermometer
fiebertreibend s. fiebererzeugend
Fiebertyp m febrile type
~/Pel-Ebsteinscher Pel-Ebstein fever (disease, syndrome) (charakteristisch für Lymphogranulomatose)
Fieberwahn m febrile delirium, pyretotyphosis
● mit ~ behaftet light-headed
Fieberzacke f pyrexial spike
fiebrig feverish, febrile, pyretic
~/sehr hyperpyretic
Fiedler-Myokarditis f Fiedler's myocarditis
Figur f/achromatische achromatic figure (spindle)
Fikosis f ficosis
Filament n filament ● ein ~ besitzend unifilar
filamentär filamentary
filamentös filamentous
Filaria f bancrofti Filaria (Wuchereria) bancrofti, blood filaria (Erreger der Elephantiasis)
~ loa Filaria loa, Loa [loa], eye worm (Erreger der Kalabarbeule)
Filariasis f filariasis, filariosis
~/Bancroftsche [lymphoretikuläre] Bancroftian (Bancroft's) filariasis
~ malayi Malayan filariasis
~ ozzardi Ozzard's filariasis, mansonelliasis
Filarie f filaria
filarienartig filariform
Filarienbefall m s. Filariasis
Filarienfieber n filarial (elephantoid) fever
filarienförmig filariform
Filarien-Komplement-Fixationsantikörper m filarial complement-fixing antibody
Filarien-Komplement-Fixationstest m filarial complement fixation test
Filarienkrankheit f s. Filariasis
Filarienmittel n filaricide [agent]
Filariennephropathie f filarial nephropathy
filarientötend filaricidal, filaricide
Filariose f s. Filariasis
Filialgeneration f/erste F1 (filial) generation, F_1
Filiformbougie f filiform bougie
Filmdosimeter n film badge (dosimeter), badge meter

Filmdosimetrie

Filmdosimetrie f film (photographic) dosimetry
Filmoxygenator m film oxygenator
Filter n(m) filter
Filterkerze f filter candle
~ **nach Berkefeld/bakteriendichte** Berkefeld filter
filtern s. filtrieren
Filternarbe f filtering scar
Filterwirkung f filtration efficiency
Filtrat n filtrate
~/**glomeruläres** glomerular filtrate *(der Nieren)*
Filtratfaktor m filtrate factor
Filtration f filtration
~/**glomeruläre** glomerular filtration *(der Nieren)*
Filtrationswinkel m filtration angle, iridian (iris, iridocorneal) angle
filtrieren to filter, to filtrate, to strain
Filum n filum, filament, thread
~ **olfactorium** olfactory nerve
~ **terminale** terminal filament
Filzlaus f crab (pubic) louse, Phthirius pubis, morpio[n]
Filzlausbefall m phthiriasis
~ **der Wimpern und Augenbrauen** lousiness of the eyelashes
Fimbriae fpl **iridis** iris frill
Fimbrie f fimbria
Fimbrienresektion f fimbriectomy
Finalstadium n final stage *(z. B. einer Krankheit)*
Findelkind n foundling
Finger m finger [of the hand], digit[us], dactyl[us] *(s. a. unter* Digitus*)* ● **mit verwachsenen Fingern** syndactyl[ous]
~/**abgestorbener** dead finger
~/**perkutierender** plexor, plessor
~/**schnellender (springender)** spring (trigger) finger *(bei Sehnenscheidenentzündung)*
Fingerabdruck m fingerprint, dactylogram, dermatogram, dermatoglyphic sign
Fingerabdruckuntersuchung f dactyloscopy, dermatoglyphics
Fingeragnosie f finger agnosia
fingerähnlich digitiform
Fingeramputation f finger (digital) amputation, dactylolysis
Fingeraphasie f finger aphasia
Fingerarterie f/**gemeinsame palmare** common palmar digital artery
~/**gemeinsame volare** common volar digital artery
Fingerbeere f finger pad, digital pulp
Fingerbeerenpunktion f finger (digital) prick
Fingerbeuger m flexor digitorum [muscle]
~/**oberflächlicher** flexor digitorum superficialis [muscle]
~/**tiefer** flexor digitorum profundus [muscle]
Fingerbeugerreflex m finger flexor reflex
Fingerbeugersehnenscheide f ulnar bursa
Fingerbrand m digital gangrene
Fingerdruck m digital compression
Fingerendglied n ungual phalanx, end-phalanx, distal phalanx of the finger

Fingerentfernung f[/**operative]** dactylolysis
Fingerentzündung f dactylitis, inflammation of a finger
Finger-Finger-Versuch m finger-finger test
fingerförmig digitiform, finger-shaped, digital, digitate
Fingerfortsatz m digitation
Finger-fracture-Technik f finger fracture technique (method) *(bei Leberresektion)*
Fingerfurche f digital furrow
Fingergelenk n finger (interphalangeal) joint; knuckle
Fingergelenkprothese f finger joint prosthesis
Fingergelenkversteifung f symphalangism
~/**operative** capsulodesis *(durch Bohrdrahtfixation)*
Fingerglied n phalanx
Fingergliederzwischengelenk n interphalangeal joint
Fingergrundgelenk n metacarpophalangeal joint
Fingergrundglied n proximal phalanx of the finger
Fingerhut m/**roter** foxglove, digitalis
Fingerhutvergiftung f digitalism, digitalis poisoning
Fingerknöchel m knuckle
Fingerknöchelpolster n knuckle pad
Fingerknochen m phalanx, finger bone
Fingerknochenentzündung f phalangitis, inflammation of a phalanx
Fingerkompression f digital compression
Fingerkontraktur f/**schmerzhafte** dactylocampsodynia
Fingerkrampf m dactylospasm
Fingerkuppe f pulp
Fingerlappen m/**gekreuzter** cross[ed] finger flap *(Traumatologie)*
Fingerling m fingerstall, [finger] cot
fingerlos adactyl[ous]
Fingerlosigkeit f adactyly
~ **mit Fingerverschmelzung** ectrosyndactyly
Fingerminderzahl f hypodactyly
Fingermittelglied n middle phalanx of the finger
Fingernagel m finger-nail, onyx
Fingernagelpuls m nail (Quinke's) pulse
Fingernagelzerstörung f/**triebartige** onychotillomania *(Verhaltensstörung)*
Finger-Nasen-Versuch m finger-nose test
Fingerperkussion f finger percussion
Fingerplethysmograph m finger plethysmograph
Fingerpulpa f finger pulpa, pulp of the finger
Fingerpunktion f finger puncture
Fingerreflex m digital reflex
Fingerrepositionszange f finger reposition forceps
Fingerringsäge f finger ring saw
Fingerrückenarterie f dorsal digital artery of the hand
Fingersäge f metacarpal saw
Fingerschmerz m digitalgia
Fingerschraube f finger screw
Fingerspickdraht m boring wire for fingers

Fingerspitze f finger tip
Fingerspitzenpulpa f finger pulp, pulp of the finger
Fingersprache f maniloquism, dactylology, conversation by means of signs
Fingersprengung f [der Mitralklappe] finger fracture [operation of the mitral valve]
Fingersteifigkeit f symphalangism
Fingerstrecker m extensor digitorum [muscle]
~/**gemeinsamer** extensor digitorum communis [muscle], extensor communis digitorum [muscle], common extensor [muscle] of the fingers
Fingertonometrie f digital tonometry
Fingerüberzahl f hyperdactylia, polydactyly
Fingerumlauf m panaritium, whitlow
Finger- und Zehenknochenauftreibung f/**tuberkulöse** tuberculous dactylitis
Fingerverdickung f/**angeborene** pachydactyly
Fingervergrößerung f dactylomegaly
Fingerverkrümmung f dactylogryposis
Fingerverkümmerung f perodactyly
Fingerverwachsung f syndactyly, symphysodactyly, dactylosymphysis, ankylodactyly
Finne f cysticercus, bladder worm *(Bandwurmentwicklungsstadium)*
Finnenausschlag m acne *(Hauterkrankung mit Knötchen- und Pustelbildung)*
First m ridge *(Anatomie)*
fischähnlich fish-like, ichthyoid
Fischbandwurm m fish (broad) tapeworm, Diphyllobothrium latum
Fischbandwurmbefall m diphyllobothriasis, dibothriocephaliasis
Fischernährung f ichthyophagia
fischessend ichthyophagous
Fischgift n fish toxin, ichthyotoxin
Fischschuppenkrankheit f ichthyosis, fishskin (aligator-skin, fish-scale) disease, sauriasis
Fischvergiftung f fish poisoning, ichthyotoxism, ichthyism[us]
Fischwirbelkrankheit f juvenile osteoporosis
Fissur f 1. fissure, fissura; groove *(Anatomie)*; cleft *(Embryologie)*; rhagade *(z. B. der Schleimhaut)*; 2. s. Fissurenknochenbruch
~/**primäre** primary fissure
fissurenförmig fissured; rhagadiform *(Haut)*
Fissurenknochenbruch m fissured fracture
Fissurenlinie f fissure line
Fistel f fistula, syrinx *(s.a. unter Fistula)* ● eine ~ **bilden** to fistulize
~/**anale** anal fistula, fistula in ano
~/**anorektale** anorectal fistula
~/**aortointestinale** aortointestinal fistula
~/**appendikovesikokolische** appendicovesicocolic fistula
~/**arteriotracheale** arteriotracheal fistula
~/**arteriovenöse** arteriovenous fistula
~/**branchiogene** branchial [cyst] fistula, lateral fistula of the neck *(Rest des Ductus thymopharyngicus)*
~/**bronchobiliäre** bronchobiliary fistula
~/**choleszystocholedochale** cholecystocholedochal fistula
~/**cholezystoduodenale** cholecystoduodenal fistula
~/**cholezystogastrische** cholecystogastric fistula
~/**cholezystokolische** cholecystocolonic fistula
~/**Ecksche** Eck's fistula, portacaval anastomosis
~/**enterokutane** enterocutaneous fistula
~/**enterovaginale** enterovaginal fistula
~/**enterovesikale** enterovesical fistula
~/**extrasphinkterische** extrasphincteric fistula
~/**gastroduodenale** gastroduodenal fistula
~/**gastrointestinale** gastrointestinal fistula
~/**gastrokolische** gastrocolic fistula
~/**gastrokutane** gastrocutaneous fistula
~/**hepatopleurale** hepatopleural fistula
~/**kolovesikale** vesicocolonic fistula
~/**oroantrale** oroantral fistula
~/**perineovaginale** perineovaginal fistula
~/**perinephrobronchiale** perinephrobronchial fistula
~/**rektale** rectal fistula, rectofistula
~/**sakrokokzygeale** sacrococcygeal fistula
~/**tracheokutane** tracheocutaneous fistula
~/**tracheoösophagokutane** tracheo-oesophageal-skin fistula
~/**umbiliko-enterale** umbilical enteric fistula
~/**ureterovaginale** ureterovaginal fistula
~/**vesikointestinale** vesico-intestinal fistula
~/**vesikovaginale** vesicovaginal fistula
Fistelbildung f fistula formation, fistul[iz]ation
Fistelentfernung f[/**operative**] fistulectomy, syringectomy
Fistelgang m fistula [duct], syrinx
Fistelgangausschneidung f syringectomy
Fistelgeräusch n whistling sound *(der Lunge)*
Fistelhaken m fistula hook
Fistelinzision f fistulotomy
Fistelmesser n fistula knife, fistulatome, syringotome
fisteln to fistulize *(operativ)*
Fisteloperation f s. Fistelspaltung
Fistelspaltung f fistulotomy, fistulatomy, syringotomy
Fistelstimme f falsetto [voice], head-voice
Fisteltasche f fistula bag
Fistelungsoperation f filtering operation *(Glaukom)*
Fistelvene f fistula vein *(zur Dialyse)*
Fistula f fistula, syrinx *(s.a. unter Fistel)*
~ **externa** external fistula
~ **interna** internal fistula
~ **rectovaginalis** rectovaginal fistula
~ **rectovesicalis** rectovesical fistula
Fistulogramm n fistulogram
Fistulographie f fistulography
Fixation f 1. fixation, pexis, anchorage *(z. B. eines Organs)*; 2. fixation *(histologischer Schnitte)*
~/**intramedulläre** intramedullary fixation *(von Knochenbrüchen)*
Fixationsachse f fixation axis
Fixationsfeld n fixation field, field of fixation
Fixationslähmung f fixation palsy

Fixationslinie

Fixationslinie f fixation line
Fixationslösung f fixative [fluid]
Fixationsnystagmus m fixation nystagmus
Fixationsprozeß m fixation process *(z. B. histologischer Präparate)*
Fixationspunkt m fixation point
Fixationsreflex m fixation reflex
Fixationsverband m immovable bandage *(z. B. bei einer Fraktur)*
fixieren 1. to fix, to keep in place *(Chirurgie)*; 2. to fix, to mordant *(histologische Präparate)*; 3. to focus; to stare at *(mit dem Auge)*
Fixier[färbe]mittel n mordant
fixiert fixed *(z. B. histologische Präparate)*; immobile *(z. B. Knochen)*; adherent *(z. B. Organe)*
Fixierung f s. Fixation
Fixierungsmittel n 1. fixative [agent], fixing agent; 2. s. Fixierfärbemittel
flach flat, plane, plain, planar
Flachbecken n flat (platypelloid) pelvis
Fläche f 1. area; plane, planum; 2. facies, surface, face *(z. B. von Organen)*
Flachfräser m flat trephine *(Traumatologie)*
flachgaumig platystaphyline
Flachkopf m platycephalus, chamaecephalus, homalocephalus
flachköpfig platycephalic, chamaecephalic, chamaecephalous, planiceps
Flachköpfigkeit f platycephalia, chamaecephalia
flachliegend recumbent *(z. B. ein Patient)*
Flachmeißel m spud, flat chisel *(Traumatologie)*
flachnasig platyrrhine
Flachrücken m flat back
flachschädelig s. flachköpfig
Flachsstaublunge[nerkrankung] f flax dressers' phthisis
flachzellig flat-celled, planocellular
flachzungig platyglossal
Flagellat m flagellate
Flagellateninfektion f flagellosis
Flagellation f flagellation
Flagellenantigen n flagellar antigen
Flagellenbildung f exflagellation
Flagellum n flagellum
Flammennävus m port-wine mark (naevus, stain)
Flammenphotometer n flame [spectro]photometer
Flammenphotometrie f flame [spectro]photometry
flammenphotometrisch flame [spectro]photometric
Flanke f flank, side, latus
Flankenschmerz m flank pain, pain in the side
Flapping-Tremor m flapping tremor, asterixis
Fläschchen n small bottle; vial, phial *(für Arzneien)*
Flasche f nursing (feeding) bottle
Flaschenkind n weanling, bottle[-fed] child
Flaschennase f bottle nose
Flaschenpilz m Pityrosporum ovale
Flattern n flutter *(z. B. des Herzens)*
Flattertremor m flapping tremor, asterixis

Flatterwelle f flutter (F) wave *(EKG)*
flatulent flatulent
Flatulenz f flatulence, tympanites
Flatus m flatus, wind
~ **vaginalis** garrulity of the vulva
Flaum m s. Flaumhaar
flaumartig lanuginous
Flaumhaar n vellus, lanugo *(des Fetus)*
Flavin n flavin *(1. gelber Farbstoff, Antiseptikum; 2. wasserlösliches gelbes Pigment, Flavinenzym)*
Flavinadenindinukleotid n flavin[e] adenine dinucleotide, FAD, riboflavin (isoalloxazine) dinucleotide
Flavinenzym n flavin (yellow) enzyme, flavoprotein
Flavinmononukleotid n flavin[e] mononucleotide, FMN, riboflavin 5'-phosphate, isoalloxazine mononucleotide
Flavoproteid n s. Flavinenzym
Flechte f lichen; herpes; eczema; tetter, ringworm *(z. B. bei Kindern)*; tinea *(z. B. des Barts)* *(s. a. unter Tinea und Lichen)*
~/**fressende** lupus
~/**kriechende** serpigo
flechtenartig, flechtenförmig lichenoid, lichenous; herpetic; eczematous; sycosiform; lupiform, lupoid
Fleck m spot, patch, macule, macula
~/**blauer** bruise
~/**blinder** [Mariotte's] blind spot, optic (cupped) disk, optic papilla *(Eintrittsstelle des Sehnervs am Augenhintergrund)*
~/**erhabener** plaque
~/**gelber** yellow spot [of the retina], macula [lutea], area of most distinct vision *(der Netzhaut)*
~/**Mariottescher** s. ~/blinder
~/**umschriebener** plaque
Flecken mpl/**Bitotsche** Bitot's patches; xerosis conjunctivae *(der Bindehaut bei Vitamin-A-Mangel)*
~/**Forchheimersche** Forchheimer spots *(bei Röteln am Gaumen)*
~/**Koplikkche** Koplik's spots (sign) *(bei Masern)*
~/**Tardieusche** Tardieu's ecchymoses (spots) *(petechiale Blutungen seröser Häute)*
Fleckfieber n fleckfieber, [fleck] typhus, typhus (prison) fever, spotted disease, petechial (exanthematous, sporadic) typhus
~/**amerikanisches** Rocky Mountain spotted fever, RMSF, tick fever (typhus)
~/**brasilianisches** Brazilian spotted fever, Sao Paulo typhus
~/**endemisches** endemic (murine) typhus, rat[-borne] typhus, uraturia (shop, flea-borne) typhus *(durch Rickettsia mooseri)*
~/**epidemisches (klassisches)** epidemic (European, louse-borne) typhus, jail (ship) fever *(durch Rickettsia prowazeki)*
~/**kolumbianisches** Columbian spotted fever
~/**murines** s. ~/endemisches
~/**neotropisches** neotropic spotted fever

Fleckfiebererkrankung f rickettsiosis, rickettsial disease
Fleckfieberimpfstoff m [epidemic] typhus vaccine, Cox vaccine
Fleckfieberknoten m typhus nodule
Fleckfieberrezidiv n recrudescent typhus, Brill's disease
Fleckfieberrickettsie f spotted fever rickettsia, Rickettsia prowazeki
fleckig patchy, macular, maculate; spotty; dotted
Fleckschatten m spotty shadow *(Radiologie)*
Flecktyphus m s. Fleckfieber
Fleisch n flesh; pulp[a] *(Organparenchym)*
~/**wildes** proud flesh
fleischähnlich, fleischartig carneous, sarcoid, sarcous
Fleischbälkchen *npl* im Herzen carneous trabeculae (columns)
fleischessend carnivorous, zoophagous
Fleischfaserstuhl m creatorrhoea
Fleischgeschwulst f s. Sarkom
Fleischhaut f des Hodensacks [tunica] dartos
fleischig fleshy, carneous; sarcoid, sarcous *(z. B. ein Muskel)*
fleischlos fleshless *(Anatomie)*; meatless *(Ernährung)*
Fleischmole f carneous (fleshy) mole
Fleischvergiftung f meat poisoning
Fleischwärzchen n fleshy wart, caruncula *(aus lockerem Bindegewebe und Gefäßen)*
Fleischwunde f flesh wound
flexibel 1. flexible; 2. adaptable *(anpassungsfähig)*
~/**nicht steif,** inflexible
Flexibilitas f **cerea** waxy flexibility
Fleximeter n fleximeter
Flexio f **uteri** uterine flexion, metrocampsis
Flexion f flexion, incurvation, bending
Flexionsfraktur f flexion fracture
Flexionsparaplegie f flexion paraplegia, paraplegia in flexion
Flexor m flexor [muscle]
Flexorenkanal m flexor canal (tunnel)
Flexorreflex m flexor reflex
Flexorsehne f flexor tendon
Flexura f flexure, flexura, bend, curvature
~ **coli[ca] dextra** right colic flexure, hepatic (right) flexure of the colon
~ **coli sinistra** left colic flexure, splenic (left) flexure of the colon
~ **duodeni inferior** inferior duodenal flexure
~ **duodenojejunalis** duodenojejunal flexure (angle, junction)
~ **lienalis** splenic flexure
~ **perinealis recti** perineal flexure [of the rectum]
~ **sacralis recti** sacral flexure
Fliege f fly ● **durch Fliegen übertragen** fly-borne
Fliegenlarvenbefall m **der Haut** derm[at]omyiasis
Fliegensehen n myiode[s]opsia
Fliegeratelektase f aeroatelectasis *(bei reiner Sauerstoffatmung in großen Höhen)*

Fliegerneurose f aeroneurosis, air pilot's disease
Fliegerohr n aviator's ear; aero-otitis, otic barotrauma, barotitis media
Fliegersinusitis f aerosinusitis
Flimmerbewegung f ciliary action, fibrillary movement
Flimmerepithel n ciliated (vibrating) epithelium
Flimmerhaar n cilium
flimmern 1. to flicker *(z. B. Licht)*; 2. to fibrillate *(Herz)*; 3. to scintillate *(z. B. Augenskotom)*; 4. to flagellate *(Mikroorganismen)*
Flimmern n 1. flickering *(z. B. des Lichts)*; 2. fibrillation *(z. B. des Herzens)*; 3. scintillation, sensation of sparks *(z. B. ein Augenskotom)*; 4. flagellation *(von Mikroorganismen)*
~ **vor den Augen** coruscation, sensation of light flashes
Flimmerpotential n fibrillation potential
Flimmerschwelle f fibrillation threshold
Flimmerskotom n flimmer (scintillating) scotoma, ocular migraine *(flimmernde Lichtempfindungen mit Kopfschmerzen bei Gefäßspasmen des Auges oder des Gehirns)*
Flimmerwelle f fibrillation (f) wave *(EKG)*
Flimmerzelle f ciliated (flagellated) cell
Flocculus m flocculus, floccule *(Teil der Kleinhirnhemisphäre)*
flocken to flocculate, to coagulate, to clot
Flockenbildung f flocculation
Flockensehen n myiode[s]opsia
Flockungsreaktion f flocculation reaction (test)
~/**Meinickesche** Meinicke's test *(serologischer Syphilisnachweis)*
Floh m flea, pulex
Flohbefall m pulicatio, flea infestation
Flohbiß m, **Flohstich** m flea-bite
flohstichartig pulicaris
flohtötend pulicidal
florid[e] 1. florid *(Gesundheit)*; 2. florid, active *(z. B. Krankheit)*
Flucht f **in eine Krankheit** nosophilia
flüchtig 1. inconstant *(z. B. Symptom)*; transient *(z. B. Hautausschlag)*; ephemeral *(z. B. Fieber)*; 2. volatile *(Substanzen)*
Fluchtreaktion f escape mechanism
Fluchtreflex m escape reflex
Flügel m wing, ala
~ **des Pflugscharbeins** ala of the vomer
flügelartig wing-like, alar, aliform, pterygoid
Flügelband n alar odontoid ligament
Flügelfalte f alar plica
Flügelfell n 1. webbed neck, sphinx-neck, pterygium colli, patagium *(am Hals)*; 2. pterygium *(Wucherung der Augapfelbindehaut auf die Augenhornhaut)*
flügelförmig wing-shaped, alar, aliform, pterygoid
Flügelfortsatz m alar (pterygoid) process, ala
● **zwischen dem ~ und dem Gaumenknochen liegend** pterygopalatine
Flügelgaumengrube f pterygopalatine (sphenomaxillary) fossa

Flügelgrube

Flügelgrube f pterygoid fossa
Flügelhaut f s. Flügelfell
Flügelkanüle f butterfly[-mounted] needle
Flügelknorpel m alar cartilage
~/**großer** major alar cartilage
~/**kleiner** minor alar cartilage
Flügelmuskel m/**äußerer** lateral pterygoid muscle
~/**innerer** medial pterygoid muscle
Flügelplatte f 1. alar plate (lamina), wing (dorsolateral) plate *(Embryologie)*; 2. pterygoid plate *(des Keilbeins)*
Flügelschlagen n flapping tremor
Flügelskapula f alar (winged) scapula, angel's scapula (wing)
Flugmedizin f aeromedicine, aviation medicine
flugmedizinisch aeromedical
Flugzeugkrankheit f air (flying) sickness *(Kinetose)*
Fluktuation f fluctuation *(z. B. bei Perkussion)*
Fluor m albus whites, white flow, leucorrhoea, leucorrhagia
~ **vaginalis** vaginal discharge (flux)
~/**weißlicher** s. Fluor albus
Fluoreszein n fluorescein, resorcinolphthalein
Fluoreszeinangiogramm n fluorescein angiogram
Fluoreszeinangiographie f fluorescein angiography
Fluoreszeinangioretinographie f fluorescein angioretinography (retina angiography)
Fluoreszeindensimetrie f fluorescein densimetry
Fluoreszeindensimetriekurve f fluorescein densimetry curve
Fluoreszeinfarbstoff m fluorescein dye
fluoreszeinmarkiert fluorescein-labelled, fluorescein-tagged *(z. B. Antikörper)*
Fluoreszeintest m fluorescein test
Fluoreszeinvitalfärbung f fluorescein vital staining (dye)
Fluoreszenz-Antikomplement-Konjugat n fluorescent anticomplement conjugate
Fluoreszenz-Antikörper m fluorescent antibody
Fluoreszenz-Antikörper-Lösung f fluorescent antibody solution
Fluoreszenz-Antikörper-Reaktion f fluorescent antibody reaction
Fluoreszenz-Antikörper-Technik f fluorescent antibody technique
Fluoreszenz-Antikörper-Test m fluorescent antibody test
Fluoreszenz-Antikörper-Untersuchung f fluorescent antibody examination
Fluoreszenzfarbstoff m fluorescent dye, fluorochrome
Fluoreszenzmessung f s. Fluorometrie
Fluoreszenzmikroskop n fluorescence microscope
Fluoreszenzmikroskopie f fluorescence microscopy
fluoreszenzmikroskopisch fluorescence microscopic
Fluoreszenz-Rabies-Antikörper-Test m fluorescent rabies antibody test
Fluoreszenzschirm m fluorescent screen
Fluoreszenzschirmbild n fluoroscopic image *(von Organen)*
Fluoreszenzstrahlung f fluorescent radiation
Fluoreszenz-Treponema-Antikörper-Absorptionstest m fluorescent treponemal antibody absorption test, FAA-ABS test
Fluoreszenz-Treponema-Antikörpertest m fluorescent treponemal antibody test, FTA test
Fluoreszenzzytophotometrie f fluorescence cytophotometry
fluoreszieren to fluoresce
fluoreszierend fluorescent
fluoridieren to fluoridate, to fluoridize *(Trinkwasser)*
Fluoridierung f fluoridation
fluorisieren s. fluoridieren
Fluoroangiofotografie f fluoroangiophotography
Fluorochrom n fluorochrome
Fluorochromfärbung f fluorochrome staining
Fluorographie f fluorography, fluoro-radiography
fluorographisch fluorographic
Fluorometer n fluorometer, fluorimeter, fluorophotometer, fluorescence meter
Fluorometrie f fluorometry, fluorimetry, fluorophotometry
fluorometrisch fluorometric, fluorimetric
Fluororöntgenographie f photofluorography, photofluoroscopy
Fluorose f fluorosis
Fluoroskop n fluoroscope
Fluoroskopie f fluoroscopy
fluoroskopisch fluoroscopic
5-Fluorourazil n 5-fluorouracil *(Chemotherapeutikum bei Tumoren)*
Fluorprophylaxe f fluorine prophylaxis *(gegen Karies)*
Fluorschädigung f der Zähne/**chronische** chronic dental fluorosis, poikilodentosis; mottled enamel
Fluorvergiftung f/**chronische** fluorosis
Flush m flush, blush *(Hautrötung im Gesicht)*
Fluß m flow, flux *(z. B. der Galle)*
Flußfieber n/**Japanisches** Japanese flood (river) fever, tsutsugamushi fever (disease), tropical (rural, mite-borne) typhus, Malayan [scrub] typhus, Queensland coastal fever
flüssig liquid, fluid
Flüssig-Gas-Chromatographie f liquid-gas chromatography
Flüssigkeit f liquid, fluid; liquor; humour *(des Auges)*
~/**extrazelluläre** extracellular fluid
~/**intrazelluläre** intracellular fluid
~/**seröse** serous fluid
Flüssigkeitsablassen n tapping *(z. B. bei Aszites)*
Flüssigkeitsabsonderung f exudation; transudation
Flüssigkeitsansammlung f accumulation of fluid; oedema *(z. B. im Gewebe)*

~ im **Eierstock** hydrovarium
~ im **Eileiter** hydrosalpinx
~ im **Mittelohr** hydrotympanum, hydromyrinx
~ im **Rückenmark** hydrorrhachis
Flüssigkeitsaufnahme f fluid intake *(in den Körper)*; pinocytosis *(durch Zellen)*
Flüssigkeitsausschwitzung f transudation
Flüssigkeitsbeschränkung f/**therapeutische** dipsotherapy
Flüssigkeitsersatz m fluid replacement
Flüssigkeitsgleichgewicht n fluid equilibrium, water balance *(des Körpers)*
Flüssigkeitslunge f fluid (wet) lung
Flüssigkeitsretention f fluid retention *(im Körper)*
Flüssigkeitsspiegel m fluid level *(Ileusdiagnostik)*
Flüssigkeitstransport m/**transendothelialer** cytopempsis, transendothelial fluid transport
Flüssigkeitsverlust m fluid loss
Flüssigkeitszufuhr f fluid supply
Flüssigwerden n liquefaction, deliquescence
Flußrate f flow (transfer) rate
Fluß-Volumen-Kurve f flow-volume curve
Flüstersprache f 1. whispering, hypophonia; 2. whispered (whispering) pectoriloquy *(bei der Lungenauskultation)*
Flüsterstimme f whispering voice
Flüsterstimmenfortleitung f whispered (whispering) pectoriloquy *(bei Lungenkrankheiten)*
FMN s. Flavinmononukleotid
Foetor m foetor, stench *(s. a. unter Fötor)*
~ **hepaticus** hepatic foetor, liver breath
Fokalanfall m focal attack
Fokalinfektion f s. Fokus 1.
Fokus m 1. focus, focal infection, source of infection *(Zusammensetzungen s. unter Herd)*; 2. focus, focal point *(Optik)*; 3. focus *(abnormes Zentrum der Reizbildung)*
Fokus-Film-Abstand m focus-film distance *(Radiologie)*
Fokus-Haut-Distanz f focus-skin distance *(Radiologie)*
Fokussanierung f focal assanation
Foley-Katheter m Foley [balloon] catheter
Folgeerkrankung f secondary disease, deuteropathy
Folgeerscheinung f sequela, sequence *(z. B. einer Krankheit)*; aftereffect *(z. B. von Drogen)*
Folgeschaden m secondary damage *(z. B. einer Verletzung)*
Folgezustand m resulting condition, sequela, sequence *(z. B. einer Krankheit)*
Folie à deux communicated (double) insanity
Folinsäure f folinic acid, citrovorum (lactobacillus casei) factor
Folliculi mpl **lymphatici aggregati appendicis vermiformis** aggregate follicles of the vermiform appendix
~ **lymphatici aggregati intestini tenuis** aggregate follicles (glands), aggregate nodules [of the small intestine]

~ **lymphatici gastrici** lymph nodules of the stomach
~ **lymphatici laryngei** lymph nodules of the larynx
~ **lymphatici lienales** lymph nodules of the spleen
~ **lymphatici recti** lymph nodules of the rectum
~ **ovarici vesiculosi** vesicular ovarian follicles
Folliculitis f folliculitis, inflammation of a follicle
~ **barbae** sycosis [of the beard], barber's itch, deep folliculitis, hyphogenic sycosis
~ **keloidalis** keloidal folliculitis, keloid acne
~ **nuchae** nuchal folliculitis, framboesiform sycosis
~ **simplex** superficial folliculitis
Folliculus m s. Follikel
~ **lingualis** lingual follicle, lymph node of the lingual tonsil
~ **lymphaticus** lymph follicle (nodule)
~ **oophorus vesiculosus** vesicular (Graafian) follicle
Follikel m 1. follicle, folliculus *(Anatomie)* *(s.a. unter Folliculus)*; 2. follicle, lymph node; 3. ovarian follicle ● **neben einem** ~ parafollicular
~/**Graafscher** Graafian (vesicular) follicle
~/**kolloidhaltiger** colloid follicle
~/**persistierender** persistent follicle
Follikelabszeß m follicular abscess
follikelartig folliculoid
Follikelatresie f atretic follicle
Follikelentwicklung f follicular development
Follikelentzündung f s. Folliculitis
Follikelepithelzelle f/**Graafsche** granulosa (follicular epithelial) cell
Follikelflüssigkeit f follicular fluid
Follikelgeschwür n follicular ulcer
Follikelhormon n follicular hormone
Follikelhormonmangelproduktion f hypofolliculinaemia
Follikelhormonüberproduktion f hyperfolliculinaemia
Follikelhyperkeratose f follicular hyperkeratosis
Follikelreifung f follicular maturation
Follikelreifungshormon n follicle-ripening hormone, follicle-stimulating hormone, FSH
Follikelschmerz m intermenstrual (middle) pain
Follikelsprung m ovulation, rupture of the follicle
Follikelstigma n follicular stigma
Follikeltrachom n follicular trachoma
Follikelzeichen n follicular stigma
Follikelzelle f follicular cell
Follikelzyste f follicular cyst
Folliklis f folliclis; tuberculous papules
follikulär follicular
Follikularkatarrh m follicular conjunctivitis
Follikulom n folliculoma
Folsäure f folic acid, lactobacillus casei factor
Folsäureantagonist m folic acid antagonist, antifolic [agent]
folsäureantagonistisch antifolic
Folsäurebiosynthese f folic acid biosynthesis
Folsäuremangel m folic acid deficiency

Folsäuremangelanämie

Folsäuremangelanämie f folic acid deficiency anaemia
Folsäurestoffwechsel m folic acid metabolism
Fontanella f fontanel[la]
~ **anterior** anterior (frontal, great) fontanel, bregmatic space
~ **nasofrontalis** nasofrontal fontanel
~ **posterior** posterior (occipital, small) fontanel
~ **posterolateralis** posterolateral (mastoid) fontanel
Fontanelle f s. Fontanella
Fontanellenvorwölbung f bulging of the fontanel
Fontanellenzeichen n fontanel sign
Fonticulus m s. Fontanella
Foramen n foramen, orifice, aperture *(Anatomie) (s.a. Fenster)*
Forameneintritt m foraminous entry
Foramenerweiterung f foraminotomy
Foramenhernie f foraminal hernia
Foramen-jugulare-Syndrom n jugular foramen syndrome *(bei Schädelbasisfraktur)*
Foraminotomie f foraminotomy
forensisch forensic
Form/von feststehender delomorphous
formabweichend variform
Formaldehyd m formaldehyde, methanal *(Desinfektionsmittel)*
Formalin n formalin, aqueous solution of formaldehyde *(Desinfektionsmittel, Fixierungsmittel für histologische und anatomische Präparate)*
formalingetötet formalin-killed
Formalinspülung f formolage *(von Echinokokkuszysten)*
Formatio f **reticularis** reticular formation (substance)
~ **reticularis medullae oblongatae** reticular formation of the medulla oblongata
~ **reticularis medullae spinalis** reticular formation of the spinal cord
~ **reticularis mesencephali** reticular formation of the mesencephalon
~ **reticularis pedunculi cerebri** reticular formation of the cerebral peduncles
~ **reticularis pontis** reticular formation of the pons
formbar plastic, mouldable, pliable; deformable
~/**durch Wärme** thermoplastic
Formbarkeit f plasticity
formen to form, to model, to mould; to die *(Zahnabdruck)*
~/**Laute** to phonate
formenbildend morphogen[et]ic
Formenbildung f morphogenesis, morphogeny
Formenbildungslehre f morphology
formengleich plesiomorphous
Formengleichheit f plesiomorphism
Formensinn m form (stereognostic) sense
Formentwicklung f s. Formenbildung
Formikation f formication
formlos formless, amorphous, amorphic
Formol n s. Formalin
Formol-Gel-Reaktion f formol gel reaction

Fornix m fornix, vault
~ **conjunctivae** conjunctival fornix, fornix of the conjunctiva, palpebral fold
~ **pharyngis** vault of the pharynx
~ **vaginae** vaginal fornix, vault of the vagina
~ **vaginae lateralis** lateral vaginal fornix
Fornixkommissur f fornical commissure
Fornixschenkel m crus (posterior column) of the fornix
fortbewegen/sich to move
fortbewegend/sich locomotive, locomotor
Fortbewegung f movement, motion, locomotion
Fortbewegungssystem n locomotor system
fortgeschritten advanced *(z. B. Krebsleiden)*
fortpflanzen/sich to reproduce, to propagate
Fortpflanzung f reproduction, propagation, generation
~/**geschlechtliche** sexual generation (reproduction), gamogenesis
~/**ungeschlechtliche** asexual reproduction, agamogenesis
~/**zweigeschlechtliche** amphigony
Fortpflanzungsalter n age of reproduction; child-bearing age (period)
fortpflanzungsfähig reproductive, generative, capable of reproduction
~/**nicht** s. fortpflanzungsunfähig
Fortpflanzungsfähigkeit f reproductiveness, generative faculty
Fortpflanzungsorgan n generative (reproductive) organ, organ of generation
Fortpflanzungsperiode f reproductive period, genesial cycle; child-bearing period
Fortpflanzungsrate f reproduction rate
Fortpflanzungssystem n reproductive system, generative (genital) tract
Fortpflanzungstrieb m generative instinct, instinct of propagation
fortpflanzungsunfähig incapable of reproduction, infertile ● ~ **machen** to render incapable of reproduction
Fortpflanzungsunfähigkeit f infecundity, infertility
Fortsatz m process[us] *(s. a. Processus und Appendix)*
~/**griffförmiger** manubrium
~/**schnabelförmiger** rostrum
~/**Tomesscher** Tomes's (ameloblastic) process
fortschreiten to progress *(z. B. eine Krankheit)*
Fortschreiten n progression *(z. B. einer Krankheit)*
fortschreitend progressive *(Krankheit)*; phagedaenic *(Geschwür)*
Forzeps m(f) [obstetrical] forceps, tongs
Fossa f fossa, pit, depression
Fossula f **optica** optic pit
fötal s. fetal
Fotochemie f photochemistry
fotochemisch photchemical
Fotokatalyse f photocatalysis
Fötor m foetor, stench *(s. a. unter Foetor)*
~ **ex ore** bad breath, halitosis, bromopnoea

Fotosensibilität f photosensitivity
Fötus m s. Fetus
foudroyant foudroyant, fulminant *(z. B. Krankheitsverlauf)*
Fovea f fovea, pit, groove, depression
foveal foveal, pitted
Foveareflex m foveolar reflex
Foveola f foveola, small pit (groove)
~ **coccygea** coccygeal foveola
~ **gastrica** gastric foveola (pit)
Foveolae fpl **granulares** granular foveolas
foveomakulär foveomacular
Fragezeichenfieber n Q fever *(durch Coxiella Burnetti)*
Fragilitas f **crinium** trichoptilosis, trichoschisis
~ **ossium** osteopsathyrosis, osteogenesis imperfecta
Fragmentation f framentation
Fragmentationsmyokarditis f fragmentation myocarditis
Fragmentdislokation f fragment dislocation (displacement)
Fraktionierung f/**Cohnsche** Cohn fractionation *(Gerinnungsfaktorenisolierung)*
Fraktur f fracture *(s. a. unter Bruch und Knochenbruch)*
~/**beabsichtigte** diaclasis
~/**Bennettsche** Bennett's fracture, stave of the thumb
~/**Collesche** Colle's (silver-fork) fracture
~/**Cottonsche** Cotton's (trimalleolar) fracture
~/**eingestauchte** impacted fracture
~/**geschlossene** closed (simple) fracture
~/**inkomplette** incomplete fracture
~/**intrakapsuläre** intracapsular fracture
~/**intrauterine** intrauterine (congenital) fracture
~/**Jeffersonsche** Jefferson's fracture
~/**komplette** complete fracture
~/**kongenitale** s. ~/intrauterine
~/**nichtgeheilte** ununited fracture
~/**offene** open (complicated, compound) fracture
~/**osteochondrale** osteochondral fracture
~/**parietookzipitale** parieto-occipital fracture
~/**pertrochantere** pertrochanteric fracture
~/**Pottsche** Pott's [eversion] fracture
~/**suprakondyläre** supracondylar fracture
~/**transkondyläre** transcondylar (diacondylar) fracture
Fraktur... s. a. Bruch...
Frakturaufrichtung f disimpaction
Frakturausrichtung f alignment [of the fracture]
Frakturbett n fracture bed
Frakturdislokation f fracture dislocation (displacement)
Frakturfieber n fracture fever
Frakturform f fracture outline
Frakturfragment n fracture fragment
Frakturkallus m fracture callus
Frakturkonsolidierung f consolidation of bone fracture
Frakturlinie f fracture line
Frakturmechanismus m mechanism of fracture

Frakturnagel m fracture nail
Frakturreposition f reduction of a fracture
Frakturstelle f fracture site
Framboesia f **tropica** s. Frambösie
Frambösie f framboesia, yaws, bouba, pian, coco, Breda's disease *(durch Treponema pertenue)*
~/**kindliche** childhood yaws
~/**tertiäre** tertiary yaws, gangosa
frambösieartig framboesiform
Frambösieerreger m Treponema pertenue
Frambösie-Initialaffekt m framboesioma
Frambösiekranker m yawey
Franse f fringe, fimbria, villus
Frau f/**eine Mißgeburt gebärende** monstripara
~/**lesbische** lesbian
~/**mannstolle** nymphomaniac
~/**mehrfach schwangere** plurigravida
~/**menstruierende** menstruant
~ **während der Geburt** parturient
~/**wiederholt schwangere** multigravida
Frauenarzt m gynaecologist
Frauenheilkunde f gynaecology, gyniatrics
Frauenklinik f gynaecological hospital
Frauenleiden n gynaecopathy, women's disease
Frauenstation f female ward
Fraulichkeit f muliebrity, feminine nature
Freiheitsgrad m degree of freedom *(Statistik)*
freilegen to expose, to lay open *(durch Operation)*; to uncover *(z. B. eine Wunde)*; to denude *(z. B. Zahnwurzel)*
Freiluftbehandlung f open-air treatment
Freiluftkur f open-air cure
freimachen to uncover; to free [from] *(z. B. von Schmerzen)*; to clear *(z. B. die Atemwege)*
~/**den Oberkörper** to strip to the waist
~/**sich** to undress, to take off the clothes
Freimachen n **der Atemwege** clearing of the respiratory passages
freipräparieren to mobilize, to expose *(Organe)*
Freipräparation f mobilization, exposure *(z. B. von Organen)*
Freisaugen n suctioning *(z. B. der Luftröhre)*
freisetzen to release, to set free, to liberate *(z. B. Energie)*; to mobilize *(Stoffwechselprodukten)*
Freisetzung f release, liberation *(z. B. von Energie)*; mobilization *(z. B. von Stoffwechselprodukten)*
Freisetzungsfaktor m **für Luteinisierungshormon** luteinizing hormone releasing factor
Freiübungen fpl physical (gymnastic) exercises, gymnastics
Fremd... s. a. Hetero...
Fremdbahnung f heterofacilitation
Fremdbeeinflußbarkeit f heterosuggestibility
Fremdbeeinflussung f heterosuggestion
Fremddiagnostik f xenodiagnosis
Fremdeiweiß n foreign protein
Fremdeiweißfieber n/**künstliches** [foreign] protein fever
Fremdenabneigung f xenophobia
Fremdgeruch m heterosmia
Fremdgeschmack m heterogeusia

Fremdgewebetransplantation

Fremdgewebetransplantation *f* heteroplasty
fremdgewebeverpflanzend heteroplastic
Fremdhauttransplantation *f* dermatoheteroplasty
Fremdhypnose *f* heterohypnosis
Fremdimpfstoff *m* heterovaccine
Fremdinfektion *f* heteroinfection
Fremdkörper *m* foreign body
Fremdkörperappendizitis *f* foreign-body appendicitis
Fremdkörperaspiration *f* foreign-body aspiration
Fremdkörperentfernung *f* foreign-body removal
Fremdkörperentzündung *f* perialienitis, perixenitis
Fremdkörperextraktionszange *f* foreign-body extraction forceps
Fremdkörperfaßzange *f* foreign-body forceps
Fremdkörpergefühl *n* foreign-body sensation
Fremdkörpergranulom *n* foreign-body granuloma
Fremdkörperlokalisation *f* foreign-body localization
Fremdkörperreaktion *f* foreign-body reaction; perixenitis, perialienitis
Fremdkörperreiz *m* foreign-body irritation
Fremdkörperriesenzelle *f* foreign-body giant cell
Fremdkörperriesenzellenreaktion *f* foreign-body giant cell reaction
Fremdkörpervaskulitis *f* foreign-body vasculitis
Fremdkörperzange *f* foreign-body forceps
Fremdplasma *n* alloplasm
Fremdserumbehandlung *f* heteroserotherapy
Fremdsuggestion *f* heterosuggestion
Fremdtransplantat *n* heterotransplant, heterograft, heterologous graft
Fremdtransplantatabstoßung *f* heterotransplant rejection
Fremdtransplantation *f* heterotransplantation, heteroplastic grafting, heteroplasty
Fremdtransplantatrejektion *f* heterotransplant rejection
Fremitus *m* fremitus; thrill, vibration
Frenektomie *f* frenectomy
Fren[ul]otomie *f* frenotomy
Frenulum *n* frenulum
~ **clitoridis** frenulum of the clitoris
~ **labii** frenulum of the lip
~ **labiorum pudendi** frenulum of the pudendum, fourchet[te]
~ **linguae** frenulum of the tongue
~ **preputii penis** frenulum of the prepuce
~ **valvulae coli (ileocaecalis)** frenulum of the ileocaecal valve
Frenum *n* frenum, bridle
Frequenzsenkung *f* frequency decrease, slowing of frequency *(z. B. des Pulses)*
fressend rodent, phagedenic *(z. B. Ulkus)*; corrosive *(z. B. Säure)*
~/**faulende Stoffe** saprophagous
Freßzelle *f* phagocyte
~/**große** macrophage, scavenger [cell]
~/**kleine** microphage

Friedländer-Bakterium *n* Friedländer's bacillus
Friedländer-Pneumonie *f* Friedländer's pneumonia
Frieselausschlag *m* miliaria, prickly heat, sudamina, summer eruption, heat (tropical sweat) rash
Frigidität *f* frigidity, sexual coldness
Frigotherapie *f* frigotherapy
Friktion *f* friction, rubbing, attrition
Frischblut *n* fresh [whole] blood
Frischplasma *n* fresh plasma
Frisör[kontakt]dermatitis *f* hairdresser's dermatitis
Froin-Syndrom *n* Froin's (spinal block) syndrome
Frons *f* s. Stirn
Frontalebene *f* frontal plane
Frontallappen *m* s. Stirnlappen
Frontalnaht *f* frontal suture
Frontalrinde *f* frontal cerebral cortex
frontoethmoidal frontoethmoid
frontookzipital frontooccipital
frontoparietal frontoparietal
Frontoparietotemporallappen *m* frontoparietotemporal flap
Frontotomie *f* frontal lobotomy
frontozerebellar frontocerebellar
Frontzahn *m* front (anterior) tooth
Froschbauch *m* frog belly
Froschkopf *m* toad head
Fröschleingeschwulst *f* s. Ranula
Frostbeule *f* chilblain, frost-bite, pernio, pagoplexia
Frostblase *f* frost blister
Frösteln *n* shiver[ing]; chill
Frucht *f* s. Fetus
Fruchtaustreibung *f* expression of the foetus
fruchtbar fertile, fecund, uberous
Fruchtbarkeit *f* fertility, fecundity, uberty
Fruchtbarkeitsindex *m* coefficient of fecundity
Fruchtblase *f* amniotic sac, bag of waters
Fruchtblasenhakenzange *f* amnion hook
Fruchtblasensprengungsinstrument *n* membrane puncturing forceps
Fruchthüllenverkalkung *f* lithokelyphos
Fruchtkuchen *m* secundines
Fruchtschmiere *f* **des Neugeborenen** cheesy varnish, vernix caseosa
Fruchtwasser *n* amniotic fluid (liquor), waters
Fruchtwasserabgang *m*/**vorzeitiger** amniorrhoea
Fruchtwasseraspiration *f* amniotic fluid aspiration
Fruchtwasserembolie *f* amniotic [fluid] embolism
Fruchtwasserfluß *m* amniorrhoea
Fruchtwassermangel *m* oligo[hydr]amnios
Fruchtwasserprobe *f* amniotic fluid sample
Fruchtwasserpunktion *f* amniotic puncture, amniocentesis
Fruchtwassersack *m* s. Fruchtblase
fruchtwasserspiegelnd amnioscopic
Fruchtwasserspiegelung *f* amnioscopy

Fruchtwasservermehrung f[/übermäßige] hydramnios, [poly]hydramnion
Fruchtwasserzelle f amniotic fluid cell
Fruchtwasserzytologie f amniotic fluid cytology
Fruchtzucker m, **Fructose** f s. Fruktose
Frühabort m early abortion
Frühantigen n early antigen
Frühbehandlung f early treatment
Frühepilepsie f early posttraumatic epilepsy
Früherkennung f early detection (recognition)
frühgeboren premature
Frühgeborenenpflege f premature nursery
Frühgeborenenretinopathie f retinopathy of prematurity
Frühgeborenes n premature infant
Frühgeburt f 1. premature delivery (birth, labour), preterm birth (parturition); 2. s. Frühgeborenes
● eine ~ haben to deliver prematurely
Frühglaukom n early glaucoma
Frühinvalidität f early invalidism
Frühjahrskonjunktivitis f spring catarrh (conjunctivitis, ophthalmia), summer catarrh, vernal keratoconjunctivitis
Frühjahrstetanie f spring tetany
Frühkarzinom n early cancer
Frühkaverne f early cavity (Tuberkulose)
Frühprotein n early protein
Frühreaktion f early reaction
~/**immunologische** immediate hypersensitivity
frühreif premature; precocious
Frühreife f [/körperliche und geistige] prematurity, precocity, premature (precocious) puberty, pubertas praecox
~/**sexuelle** sexual precocity
Frührezidiv n early relapse
Frühschwangerschaft f early pregnancy
Frühsommer-Enzephalitis f/**russische** Russian spring-summer encephalitis
Frühstadium n early stage
Frühsymptom n early (premonitory) symptom
Frühsyphilis f early syphilis
Frühtodesfall m early death
Frühvergreisung f der Haut geromorphism
Frühwochenbett n puerperium
Fruktofuranosidase f saccharase (Enzym)
Fruktokinase f fructokinase (Enzym)
Fruktose f fructose, fruit sugar, laevulose
Fruktose-1,6-diphosphat n fructose-1,6-diphosphate, Harden-Young ester
Fruktosediphosphataldolase f fructose diphosphate aldolase (Enzym)
D-Fruktose-1,6-diphosphorsäureester m s. Fruktose-1,6-diphosphat
Fruktoseintoleranz f fructose intolerance (Fruktoseverwertungsstörung infolge Enzymdefekts)
Fruktose-1-phosphat n fructose-1-phosphate
Fruktose-6-phosphat n fructose-6-phosphate
Fruktosidase f fructosidase, invertase, invertin, sucrase (Enzym)
Fruktosurie f fructosuria, laevulosuria
Frustration f frustration
FSH s. Hormon/follikelstimulierendes

Fuchsin n/**saures** acid fuchsin (Gewebefarbstoff)
füge hinzu! add, adde (Rezeptur)
fühlbar palpable, tactile
~/**nicht** impalpable
fühlen 1. to feel, to sense; to experience; 2. to palpate, to touch (z. B. den Bauch)
führend/nach außen efferent
~/**zu Konvulsionen** convulsive
~/**zur Antikörperbildung** immunologic
Führungsdraht m guide wire
Führungshohlsonde f guiding probe
Führungsinstrument n guiding instrument, director; intubating guide (bei Intubation)
Führungskatheter m guiding catheter
Führungssonde f guiding probe
Führungsspieß m guide pin (z. B. bei Knochennagelung)
Führungsstab m mandrin (für Katheter); stylet
α-Fukosidase f α-fucosidase (Enzym)
β-Fukosidase f β-fucosidase (Enzym)
füllen to replete (z. B. ein Hohlorgan); to fill, to stop (z. B. einen Zahn)
Füllstoff m 1. excipient (in Arzneien); 2. roughage, bulkage (in der Nahrung); 3. filling [material], filler (Stomatologie)
Füllung f inlay, filling (Stomatologie)
Füllungsdefekt m filling defect (z. B. auf Röntgenaufnahmen)
Füllungsphase f/**schnelle** rapid filling phase (in der Herzkammerdiastole)
fulminant fulminant, fulminating, foudroyant
Fumarase f fumarase (Enzym)
Fumarsäure f fumaric acid
Fumarsäurehydrogenase fumaric hydrogenase (Enzym)
Functio f **laesa** loss of function
Fundektomie f fund[us]ectomy
Fundoplastik f fundoplasty
Fundoplicatio f fundoplication (z. B. des Magens)
~ **nach Nissen** Nissen fundoplication
Fundoskopie f funduscopy, fundoscopy
fundoskopisch funduscopic, fundoscopic
Fundus m fundus, bottom
~ **oculi** eye (ocular) fundus, eyeground
~ **uteri** uterine fundus (base), fundus of the uterus
~ **ventriculi** [gastric] fundus, fornix of the stomach; oxyntic gland area
~ **vesicae** fundus of the urinary bladder
~ **vesicae felleae** fundus of the gall-bladder
~ **vesicae urinariae** s. ~ vesicae
Fundusamputation f fund[us]ectomy
Fundusdrüse f fundic (fundus) gland
Fundusdystrophie f fundus dystrophy, macular degeneration
Fundusfluoreszeinangiographie f fundus fluorescein angiography
Fundusfotografie f fundus photography
Fundusmikroskopie f fundus microscopy
Fundusplastik f fundoplasty
Fundusreflex m fundus reflex

Fundusspiegelung 254

Fundusspiegelung f s. Fundoskopie
fünffingerig pentadactyl[ous]
Fünfgläserprobe f five-glass test
Fünfjahresüberlebensrate f five-year survival rate
Fünflinge mpl quintuplets
Fünftage[wechsel]fieber n s. Febris quintana
Fünftgebärende f quintipara
fünfzehig pentadactyl[ous]
Fungämie f fungaemia
Fungistase f fungistasis
Fungistatikum n fungistat, fungistatic [agent]
fungistatisch fungistatic
fungizid fungicidal, antifungal, antimycotic
fungoid fungoid, myc[et]oid
Fungosität f fungosity
Fungus m fungus, mycete (s. a. unter Pilz)
~ **articuli** fungous arthritis (synovitis)
Funguspneumonie f fungal pneumonia
Funiculitis f 1. funiculitis, spermatitis; 2. funiculitis, spinal nerve root inflammation
Funiculus m 1. funicle, funiculus, cord; 2. s. Samenstrang
~ **anterior medullae spinalis** anterior column of white matter of the spinal cord
~ **lateralis medullae spinalis** lateral column of white matter of the spinal cord
~ **posterior medullae spinalis** posterior column of white matter of the spinal cord
~ **posterolateralis** posterolateral (dorsolateral) fasciculus
~ **spermaticus** spermatic cord, funiculus
~ **umbilicalis** umbilical cord, belly stalk, funis
Funikelhydrozele f funicular hydrocele
funikulär funicular
Funikulus m s. Funiculus
Funkensehen n photopsia, spintherism; scintillation
funkensehend photoptic
Funktionsausfall m functional loss (z. B. eines Organs)
Funktionsbehinderung f functional impairment; impaired function
Funktionshypertrophie f functional hypertrophy
Funktionsminderung f decreased function
Funktionsprüfung f functional test (z. B. eines Organs)
Funktionsreserve f functional reserve
Funktionssteigerung f hyperfunction (z. B. eines Organs)
Funktionsstörung f malfunction, dysfunction; functional disturbance (disorder, impairment)
Funktionsverlust m defunctionalization, functional loss
Funktionsverminderung f hypofunction (z. B. eines Organs)
Furanose f furanose (Zuckermodifikation)
Furche f furrow, groove; fissure; sulcus (Anatomie); crease; rhagade (z. B. der Haut); semicanal (z. B. im Knochen); crena (z. B. im After); vallecula; cerebral sulcus, anfractuosity (zwischen den Gehirnwindungen)

~/**Harrisonsche** Harrison's groove (bei Rachitis)
~/**Rolandosche** s. Sulcus centralis
~/**Sylviussche** s. Sulcus cerebri lateralis
furchend/sich teilweise meroblastic (bei der Eiteilung)
~/**sich vollständig** holoblastic
Furchenzunge f furrowed (scrotal) tongue
Furcht f anxiety, fear, dread; fright; horror; terror; pavor (s. a. unter Pavor)
~/**krankhafte** phobia
Furchtlosigkeit f/**völlige** pantaphobia, total absence of fear
Furchung f segmentation, cleavage (der Eizelle)
Furchungskern m segmentation (conjugation) nucleus
Furchungsteilung f s. Furchung
Furchungszelle f segmentation (cleavage) cell, blastomere (eines Eies)
furibund furibund, raging; maniacal
Furor m 1. furor, fury, madness, rage; 2. furor, maniacal attack
Furosemid n furosemide, frusemide (Diuretikum)
Fürsorgerin f social (welfare) worker; almoner (im Krankenhaus)
Fürsorgestelle f dispensary
Furunculus m **orientalis** Jeddah ulcer, oriental sore, cutaneous leishmaniasis
Furunkel m furuncle, furunculus, boil ● **einen ~ reifen lassen** to bring a furuncle to a head
furunkelartig furunculoid
Furunkelhäufung f furunculosis
furunkulär, furunkulös furuncular, furunculous
Furunkulose f furunculosis
fusiform fusiform
Fusionsbreite f amplitude of fusion
Fusionsfähigkeit f [des Auges] fusion faculty, fusional vergence power
Fusionsniere f fused kidney
Fusobakterium n fusobacterium
Fusospirillose f fusospirillosis (Infektion mit Fusobakterien und Spirillen)
fusospirochätal fusospirochaetal
Fusospirochätose f fusospirochaetosis, fusospirochaetal disease (Infektion mit Fusobakterien und Spirochäten)
Fuß m foot, pes (Zusammensetzungen s. unter Pes) ● **ohne Füße** apodal, apodous
Fußabdruck m, **Fußabguß** m footprint, podogram, pelmatogram, ichnogram
Fußanschwellung f pedal oedema, podoedema
Fußaußenrand m lateral border of the foot
Fußbad n foot bath, pediluvium
Fußballen m ball [of the foot]
Fußball[er]knie n football knee
Fußbeschwerden fpl foot trouble
Füßchen n peduncle, pedunculus, petiole, petiolus
Füßchenfortsatz m foot process
Füßchenzelle f foot cell
Fußdeformität f foot deformity
Fußeinwärtsdrehung f inversion of the foot
Fußfehlbildung f atelopodia, foot deformation

Fußflechte f dermatophytosis pedis; athlete's foot
Fußgelenk n joint of the foot; ankle [joint]
Fußgelenkentzündung f podarthritis, inflammation of the ankle
Fußgelenkluxation f ankle [joint] luxation
Fußgewölbe n plantar arch, vault of the foot
Fußgicht f podagra
Fußinnenrand m medial border of the foot
Fußknöchel m malleolus
Fußkraftmesser m pododynamometer
Fußlage f foot presentation, footling [presentation] *(bei der Geburt)*
Fußlängsgewölbe n longitudinal vault of the foot
Fußlehre f podology
Fußleiden n pedopathy, foot disease
fußlos footless, apodal, apodous, apous
Fußloser m apus
Fußlosigkeit f [/angeborene] apodia, ectropodism
Fußmykose f pedal mycosis, mycosis pedis
Fußmyzetom n pedal mycetoma
Fußnagelpflege f pedicure
Fußödem n pedal oedema, podoedema
Fußorthopäde m podiatrist
Fußorthopädie f podiatry
Fußpflege f 1. pedicure, chiropody; 2. s. Fußorthopädie
Fußpfleger m 1. chiropodist; 2. podiatrist
Fußpilzerkrankung f s. Fußmykose
Fußplatte f footplate *(des Steigbügels im Ohr)*
Fußpuls m foot pulse
Fußrand m/**innerer** medial border of the foot
~/**seitlicher** lateral border of the foot
Fußreflex m/**Bingscher** Bing's sign
Fußrolle f bolster for the foot
Fußrücken m back (dorsum) of the foot
Fußrückenarterie f dorsalis pedis [artery], dorsal pedal artery
Fußrückenbogenarterie f arcuate artery of the foot
Fußrückenreflex m dorsal reflex of the foot
Fußschmerz m pedal pain, podalgia, pedialgia, pododynia
Fußschweißbildung f/**übelriechende** podobromhidrosis
Fußschwellung f s. Fußödem
Fußsohle f sole [of the foot], planta, vola
Fußsohlenarterie f/**äußere** lateral plantar artery
~/**innere** medial plantar artery
Fußsohlenfaszie f plantar fascia (aponeurosis)
Fußsohlenfaszienentzündung f plantar fascitis
Fußsohlenläsionen fpl **bei Frambösie** crab yaws
Fußsohlennerv m/**äußerer** lateral plantar nerve
~/**innerer** medial plantar nerve
Fußsohlenreflex m plantar reflex (response)
Fußsohlenschmerz m plantalgia
Fußsohlenverhornung f/**verstärkte** plantar hyperkeratosis (callosity)
fußsohlenwärts plantar
Fußsohlenwarze f plantar wart (verruca), planter's wart

Fußspann m instep
Fußspulmuskeln mpl lumbrical muscles of the toe
Fußunterentwicklung f atelopodia
Fußverstauchung f sprained ankle
Fußvorlagerung f s. Fußlage
Fußwurzel f tarsus
Fußwurzelarterie f/**mittlere** medial tarsal artery
~/**seitliche** lateral tarsal artery
Fußwurzelband n transverse ligament [of the foot]
Fußwurzelentzündung f tarsitis, inflammation of the tarsal bone
Fußwurzelgelenk n tarsal joint
Fußwurzelinzision f tarsotomy, incision into the tarsal bone
Fußwurzelknochen m tarsal bone
Fußwurzelknochenentfernung f [/**operative**] tarsectomy, excision of a tarsal bone
Fußwurzelknochensenkung f tarsoptosia, tarsoptosis; flat foot
Fußwurzel-Mittelfuß-Gelenk n tarsometatarsal joint
Fußwurzelschmerz m tarsalgia, pain in the tarsus
Fußwurzelzerbrechen n tarsoclasis *(bei Klumpfuß)*
Fußzellen fpl foot cells, Sertoli cells
Fuszin n fuscin *(braunes Pigment der Augennetzhaut)*
Füttern n feeding
F-Verteilung f F distribution *(Statistik)*
f-Welle f f (fibrillation) wave *(EKG)*
F-Welle f F (flutter) wave *(EKG)*

G

GABA s. Gammaaminobuttersäure
Gabe f 1. dose *(Menge)*; 2. administration *(Zufuhr)*
Gabeldeformität f silver-fork deformity *(bei Speichenfraktur)*
gabeln [/**sich**] to bifurcate, to fork, to branch, to dichotomize
Gabelung f 1. bifurcation, forking; 2. dichotomy, dichotomous division
gähnen v to yawn, to oscitate
Gähnen n yawning
Gähnkrampf m oscitancy, oscitation, oscedo, yawning fit; convulsive yawning
Gaisböck-Syndrom n Gaisböck's syndrome (disease), polycythaemia [rubra] hypertonica
Galaktagogum n galactagogue [agent]
Galaktämie f galactaemia
Galaktase f galactase *(Enzym)*
Galakthidrosis f galacthidrosis, sweating of a milk-like fluid
galaktisch galactic
galaktogen galactogenous
Galaktogramm n galactogram, ductogram
Galaktographie f galactography, ductography

galaktographisch

galaktographisch galactographic
galaktoid galactoid
Galaktokinase f galaktokinase *(Enzym)*
Galaktokinasemangel m galaktokinase deficiency
Galaktometer n galactometer
galaktophag galactophagous, subsisting on milk
galaktophor galactophorous
Galaktophoritis f galactophoritis, inflammation of a lactiferous duct
Galaktopoese f galactopoiesis, production of milk
galaktopoetisch galactopoietic
galaktopyretisch galactopyretic
Galaktorrhoe f [ga]lactorrhoea, excessive flow of milk
Galaktosämie f galactosaemia, galactose diabetes
Galaktosamin n galactosamine, chondrosamine *(Aminoderivat der Galaktose)*
Galaktose f galactose, brain sugar *(Aldohexose)*
Galaktoseausscheidung f im Urin galactosuria
Galaktosebelastungstest m galactose tolerance test
Galaktosediabetes m s. Galaktosämie
Galaktoseintoleranz-Syndrom n galactose intolerance syndrome
Galaktose-1-phosphat-uridyl-transferase f galactose-1-phosphate uridyl transferase, phosphogalactose uridyl transferase
Galaktosestoffwechsel m galactose metabolism
Galaktosetoleranztest m galactose tolerance test
Galaktoseverwertungsstörung f galactose intolerance; galactosaemia, galactose diabetes
Galaktosid n galactoside *(Glykosid)*
Galaktosidase f galactosidase *(Enzym)*
α-Galaktosidase f α-galactosidase
β-Galaktosidase f β-galactosidase
Galaktoskop n galactoscope
Galaktosphingosid n galactosphingoside *(Zerebrosid)*
Galaktostase f galactostasis, galactoschesis, suppression of milk secretion
Galaktotherapie f [ga]lactotherapy
Galaktozele f galactocele, galactoma, lactocele
Galakturie f galacturia, discharge of milk-like urine; chyluria
Galant-Reflex m Galant's reflex (response) *(beim Säugling)*
Galea f s. ~ aponeurotica ● unter der ~ subgaleal
~ **aponeurotica** galea, galeal (epicranial) aponeurosis, aponeurotic portion of the occipitofrontalis muscle
Galealappen m galea flap
Galeazange f galea forceps
Galenikum n galenical [agent]
galenisch galenic[al]
Galeophilie f galeophilia
Galeophobie f galeophobia *(krankhafte Angst vor Katzen)*
Gallamintrijodid n gallamine triiodide *(Muskelrelaxans)*

Galle f gall, bile, fel
~ **aus dem Ductus choledochus** A bile
~ **aus dem Ductus hepaticus** C bile
~ **aus der Gallenblase** B (cystic) bile
~/**weiße** white bile
Galle... s. a. Gallen...
galleabsondernd cholagog[ue], choleretic
Galle-Agar m bile salt agar
Galleausscheidung f im Urin choluria
gallebildend cholepoietic, biligen[et]ic
Gallebildung f cholepoiesis, biligenesis, bile production (secretion)
~/**vermehrte** hypercholia
~/**verminderte** hypocholia
galleentleerend cholagog[ue], choleretic
Galleerbrechen n vomiting of bile, bilious vomiting, cholemesis
gallefrei acholic
Gallemangel m oligocholia, hypocholia, lack of bile; acholia
Gallen... s. a. Galle...
Gallenabfluß m biliary (bile) flow
Gallenabflußbehinderung f biliary (bile) stasis
Gallenabflußstörung f biliary dyskinesia (engorgement)
Gallenableitung f biliary (bile) drainage
Gallenabsonderung f biliation, choleresis, biliary (bile) secretion
Gallenansammlung f in der Brusthöhle cholothorax
Gallenausscheidung f biliation, choleresis
~ **im Urin** biliuria
Gallenbeschaffenheit f/**normale** eucholia
Gallenblase f gall-bladder, gallbladder, cholecyst[is], vesica fellea
~/**gestaute** stasis gall-bladder; gall-bladder engorgement
Gallenblasenampulle f ampulla of the gall-bladder
Gallenblasenanheftung f[/**operative**] cholecystopexy; cholecystorrhaphy
Gallenblasenarterie f cystic artery
Gallenblasenatonie f atonia of the gall-bladder, cholecystatonia
Gallenblasenausführungsgang m cystic duct
Gallenblasenbeschwerden pl gall-bladder complaint
Gallenblasenbett n gall-bladder bed, cystic fossa
Gallenblasen-Choledochus-Fistel f cholecystocholedochal fistula
Gallenblasendarstellung f cholecystography
Gallenblasendauerausscheidung f gall-bladder carrier state
Gallenblasen-Dickdarm-Fistel f cholecystocolonic fistula
Gallenblasen-Dickdarm-Fistelung f[/**operative**] cholecystocolostomy
Gallenblasendrainage f cholecystostomy
Gallenblasendreieck n cystic triangle [of Calot]
Gallenblasen-Dünndarm-Anastomose f cholecyst[o]enterostomy
Gallenblasen-Dünndarm-Fistelung f[/**operative**] cholecyst[o]enterostomy

Gallengang-...

Gallenblasen-Dünndarm-Naht f cholecyst[o]enterorrhaphy
Gallenblasen-Duodenum-Fistelung f[/operative] cholecystoduodenostomy
Gallenblasenentfernung f[/operative] cholecystectomy, excision of the gall-bladder, gall-bladder resection
gallenblasenentleerend cholecystagogic, cholecystokinetic
Gallenblasenentleerung f gall-bladder evacuation
Gallenblasenentzündung f cholecystitis, inflammation of the gall-bladder
~ mit Luftansammlung pneumocholecystitis
Gallenblasenerkrankung f cholecystopathy, cholecystic (gall-bladder) disease
Gallenblaseneröffnung f[/operative] cholecystotomy
Gallenblasenerweiterung f cholecystectasia
Gallenblasenexstirpation f s. Gallenblasenentfernung/operative
Gallenblasenfaßzange f gall-bladder forceps
Gallenblasenfistel f gall-bladder fistula *(spontan entstanden)*; cholecystostomy *(durch Operation)*
Gallenblasenfistelung f[/operative] cholecystostomy
Gallenblasenfixierung f[/operative] cholecystopexy
Gallenblasenfundus m gall-bladder fundus, fundus of the gall-bladder
Gallenblasenfunktionstest m gall-bladder function test
Gallenblasengalle f B (cystic) bile
Gallenblasen-Gallengang-Röntgen[kontrast]darstellung f cholecystocholangiography
Gallenblasengrube f incisure of the gall-bladder
Gallenblasenhals m neck of the gall-bladder
Gallenblasenhalssphinkter m collum-cysticus sphincter
Gallenblasenhydrops m hydrops of the gall-bladder, hydrocholecystis
Gallenblasen-Ileum-Fistelung f[/operative] cholecystoileostomy
Gallenblasen-Jejunum-Fistelung f[/operative] cholecystojejunostomy
Gallenblasenkeimdauerausscheidung f gall-bladder carrier state
Gallenblasenkolik f biliary (gall-bladder) colic; cholecystalgia
Gallenblasen-Kolon-Anastomose f cholecystocolostomy
Gallenblasenkontraktion f gall-bladder contraction
Gallenblasenkörper m body of the gall-bladder
Gallenblasenkrebs m gall-bladder cancer (carcinoma)
Gallenblasen-Krummdarm-Anastomose f cholecystoileostomy
Gallenblasen-Leerdarm-Anastomose f [chole-]cystojejunostomy
Gallenblasenleiden n cholecystopathy, gall-bladder disease

Gallenblasen-Magen-Anastomose f cholecystogastrostomy
Gallenblasen-Magen-Fistel f cholecystogastric fistula
Gallenblasen-Magen-Fistelung f[/operative] cholecystogastrostomy
Gallenblasennaht f cholecystorrhaphy, suture of the gall-bladder
Gallenblasenoperation f gall-bladder operation
Gallenblasenperforation f gall-bladder perforation
Gallenblasenreflex m cholecystic reflex
Gallenblasenreservoir n 1. gall-bladder reservoir; 2. gall-bladder carrier state
Gallenblasenröntgen[kontrast]bild n cholecystogram
Gallenblasenröntgen[kontrast]darstellung f cholecystography
Gallenblasenschleimhaut f gall-bladder mucosa, mucous membrane of the gall-bladder
Gallenblasenschmerz m cholecystalgia
Gallenblasenstein m gall-bladder stone, cystic calculus *(s.a. Gallenstein)*
Gallenblasentrokar m gall-bladder trocar
Gallenblasenvene f cystic vein
Gallenblasenverletzung f gall-bladder injury
Gallenblasenvolvulus m gall-bladder volvulus
Gallenblasenwand f gall-bladder wall
Gallenblasenzange f gall-bladder forceps
Gallenblasenzeichen n/**Courvoisiersches** Courvoisier's sign
Gallenblasen-Zwölffingerdarm-Anastomose f [chole]cystoduodenostomy
Gallenblasen-Zwölffingerdarm-Fistel f cholecystoduodenal fistula
Gallendrainage f biliary (bile) drainage
Galleneindickung f pachycholia
gallenfarbig bile-stained
Gallenfarbstoff m biliary (bile) pigment
Gallenfarbstoffreaktion f/**Rosenbachsche** Rosenbach's test
Gallenfistel f biliary fistula, bile leakage
Gallenfluß m biliary (bile) flow, cholorrhoea, cholerrhagia
~/verdünnter hydrocholeresis
gallenflußhemmend anticholagogue
Gallenflußstauung f biliary (bile) stasis
Gallengang m bile (biliary, gall) duct, bile vessel; hepatic duct *(aus der Leber)*; cystic duct *(aus der Gallenblase)*
~/gemeinsamer common [bile] duct
~/interlobulärer biliary ductule
~/intralobulärer biliary intralobular canal
~/kleiner cholangiole
Gallengang... s.a. Gallengangs...
Gallengang-Darm-Anastomose f hepaticoenterostomy, cholangioenterostomy
Gallengangdarstellung f/**intraoperative** [intra]operative cholangiography
Gallengang-Dünndarm-Fistelung f[/operative] choledochoenterostomy
Gallengang-Gallenblasen-Fistelung f[/operative] choledochocystostomy

17 Nöhring dtsch./engl.

Gallengang-...

Gallengang-Gallenblasen-Jejunum-Fistelung f[/operative] choledochocystojejunostomy
Gallengang-Ileum-Fistelung f[/operative] choledochoileostomy
Gallenganginzision f hepaticotomy
Gallengang-Jejunum-Anastomose f hepaticojejunostomy
Gallengang-Jejunum-Fistelung f[/operative] choledochojejunostomy
Gallengangklemme f gall-duct forceps
Gallengang-Magen-Anastomose f hepaticogastrostomy, cholangiogastrostomy
Gallengang-Magen-Fistelung f [/operative] choledochogastrostomy
Gallengangs... s.a. Gallengang...
Gallengangsabszeß m cholangitic (bile-duct) abscess
Gallengangsadenom n bile-duct adenoma, cholangioadenoma
Gallengangsanomalie f bile-duct anomaly
Gallengangsaskariasis f biliary (bile-duct) ascariasis
Gallengangsatresie f bile-duct atresia
Gallengangsbeschädigung f bile-duct trauma
Gallengangsbinnendruck m bile-duct pressure
Gallengangsbinnendruckmessung f cholangiometry
Gallengangschirurgie f bile-duct surgery
gallengangsdarstellend cholangiographic
Gallengangsdarstellung f cholangiography; choledochography
Gallengangsdilatation f bile-duct dilatation
Gallengangsdilatationsolive f common bile duct dilator
Gallengangsdilatator m gall-duct dilator
Gallengangsdrainage f bile-duct drainage, cholangiostomy
Gallengangsdruck m bile-duct pressure
Gallengangsdruckmessung f cholangiometry
Gallengangsdyskinese f biliary dyskinesia
Gallengangseinpflanzung f implantation of the bile duct
Gallengangsentfernung f[/operative] choledochectomy
Gallengangsentzündung f cholangitis, angiocholitis; choledochitis
~ **in der Leber** cholangiolitis
Gallengangserkrankung f bile-duct disease
Gallengangseröffnung f[/operative] choledochotomy; hepaticotomy; cholangiotomy
Gallengangserweiterung f choledochectasia; cholangiectasis
Gallengangsfistel f bile-duct fistula
Gallengangsfistelung f[/operative] hepaticostomy; choledochostomy; cholangiostomy
Gallengangsimplantation f implantation of the bile duct
Gallengangsinfektion f bile-duct infection
Gallengangskarzinom n bile-duct cancer, cholangiocarcinoma
Gallengangsligatur f bile-duct ligation

Gallengangsnaht f hepaticorrhaphy; choledochorrhaphy
Gallengangsonde f gall-duct probe
Gallengangsoperation f gall-duct operation
Gallengangspassage f gall-duct passage
Gallengangsperforation f bile-duct perforation
Gallengangsrekonstruktion f biliary tract reconstruction, choledochoplasty
Gallengangsröntgen[kontrast]bild n cholangiogram
Gallengangsröntgen[kontrast]darstellung f cholangiography
Gallengangsschädigung f bile-duct trauma
Gallengangsspiegel m choledochoscope
Gallengangsspiegelung f choledochoscopy
Gallengangsstein m choledocholith, bile-duct calculus (s.a. Gallenstein)
Gallengangssteinentfernung f[/operative] choledocholithotomy
Gallengangssteinleiden n choledocholithiasis
Gallengangssteinzerquetschung f choledocholithotripsy
Gallengangssystem n biliary tract (tree), bile-duct system; hepatic duct system
Gallengangsteilentfernung f[/operative] partial choledochectomy
Gallengangstrauma n bile-duct trauma
Gallengangstumor m bile-duct tumour
Gallengangsunterbindung f bile-duct ligation
Gallengangsvereng[er]ung f biliary (bile-duct) stricture
Gallengangsverlegung f biliary (bile-duct) obstruction
Gallengangswiederherstellung f[/operative] choledochoplasty
Gallengangswiedervereinigung f[/operative] choledochocholedochostomy
Gallengangszystadenom n bile-duct cystadenoma
Gallengangszyste f choledochal (bile) cyst
Gallengangszystenentfernung f[/operative] choledochocystectomy
Gallengang-Zwölffingerdarm-Fistelung f [/operative] choledochoduodenostomy
Gallenkanälchen n bile canaliculus
Gallenkapillare f biliary (bile) capillary
~**/intralobuläre** biliary intralobular canal (capillary)
Gallenkolik f biliary colic; cholecystalgia
Gallenkontrastmittel n biliary contrast medium
Gallenleck n biliary (bile) leakage
Gallenleiden n bilious complaint, bile-trouble; cholepathy; gall-bladder disease
gallenlos acholic
Gallenlösungsversuch m bile solubility test
Gallennephrose f biliary (bile) nephrosis
Gallenpfropfsyndrom n bile-plug syndrome, inspissated-bile syndrome
Gallenretention f biliary retention
Gallenröntgenaufnahme f biliary radiogram
Gallenrückfluß m biliary (bile) reflux
Gallensalz n bile salt

Gallensalzausscheidung f im Urin biliuria
Gallensalzdekonjugation f bile salt deconjugation
Gallensäure f bile acid
~/ausscheidungsfähige s. ~/konjugierte
~/dekonjugierte unconjugated bile acid
~/konjugierte conjugated bile acid
Gallensäureentkopplung f bile salt deconjugation
Gallensäurekopplung f bile acid conjugation
Gallenschlamm m biliary mud
Gallensekretion f bile secretion, biliation, choleresis
~/übermäßige polycholia
~/unterbrochene acholia
Gallenstauung f biliary stasis, cholestasis
Gallenstauungsikterus m cholestatic (hepatocanalicular) jaundice
Gallenstauungszirrhose f cholestatic (biliary) cirrhosis
Gallenstein m bile-stone, gall-stone, gallstone, biliary calculus, cholelith, chololith
~/kalkhaltiger chalk gall-stone
~/pigmenthaltiger pigment gall-stone
Gallensteinauflösung f dissolution of gall-stones
Gallensteineinklemmung f impaction of gall-stone
Gallensteinentfernung f[/operative] cholelithotomy, hepatolithectomy, hepaticolithotomy
Gallensteinextraktor m gall-stone dislodger
Gallensteinfaßzange f gall-stone forceps
Gallensteinileus m gall-stone ileus
Gallensteininkarzeration f impaction of gall-stone
Gallensteinkolik f biliary (gall-stone) colic; cholecystalgia
Gallensteinleiden n chole[cysto]lithiasis, biliary lithiasis, gall-stone trouble
Gallensteinlöffel m gall-stone scoop (spoon)
Gallensteinpankreatitis f gall-stone pancreatitis
Gallensteinsonde f gall-stone probe
Gallensteinzange f gall-stone forceps
Gallensteinzertrümmerung f cholelithotripsy; hepaticolithotripsy
Gallensystem-Verdauungstrakt-Anastomose f biliodigestive anastomosis
Gallenweg-Darm-Fistel f[/operative] cholangioenterostomy
Gallenwege mpl bile passages (ducts) (s. a. Gallengang)
Gallenweg-Magen-Fistel f[/operative] cholangiogastrostomy
Gallenwegs... s. a. Gallengangs...
Gallenwegschirurgie f bile-duct surgery, biliary stone surgery
Gallenwegsdarstellung f/szintigraphische cholescintigraphy, scintigraphic cholangiography
Gallenwegsdrainage f bile-duct drainage, cholangiostomy
Gallenwegsdyskinesie f biliary dyskinesia
Gallenwegserweiterung f bile-duct dilatation, cholangiectasis

Gallenwegsfehlbildung f bile-duct anomaly
Gallenwegsgeschwulst f bile-duct tumour
Gallenwegsinnendruck m bile-duct pressure
Gallenwegskrankheit f bile-duct disease
Gallenwegskrebs m cholangiocarcinoma, bile-duct cancer
Gallenwegsröntgenaufnahme f biliary radiogram
Gallenwegsröntgendarstellung f über einen T-Drain T-tube cholangiography
Gallenwegsröntgenkontrastdarstellung f biliary radiography
Gallenwegsverschluß m biliary (bile-duct) obstruction
~/anikterischer anicteric biliary obstruction
Gallenwegswiederherstellung f biliary tract reconstruction
Gallepigment n biliary (bile, hepatogenous) pigment, cholochrome
Gallepigmentbildung f cholechromopoiesis
gallertartig jelly-like, gelatinous; colloid[al]; mucinous
Gallertbauch m jelly-belly
Gallertbildung f gelation, jellification
Gallertbindegewebe n mucoid connective tissue
Gallertgeschwulst f myxoma, mucous (colloid) tumour
Gallertgewebe n mucoid (mucous) tissue
~/embryonales embryonic (mucoid) connective tissue
gallertig s. gallertartig
Gallertkrebs m mucinous (colloid) carcinoma (z. B. Brustkrebs)
Gallertkropf m colloid goitre
Galleschlamm m biliary mud
Gallestauung f cholestasis
Gallethrombus m biliary (bile) thrombus
galletreibend cholagog[ue], choleretic
Galleüberproduktion f hypercholia
Galleübertritt m in die Blutkapillaren parapedesis
Gallezusammensetzung f/veränderte dyscholia
Gallezylinder m biliary (bile) cast
gallig biliary, bilious
Galli-Mainini-Reaktion f Galli Mainini reaction, frog test (Schwangerschaftstest)
Gallusgerbsäure f [gallo]tannic acid (Hautgerbungsmittel)
Galopp m/präsystolischer presystolic (atrial) gallop
~/protodiastolischer protodiastolic (ventricular, S₃ filling) gallop
Galoppgeräusch n gallop sound
Galopprhythmus m gallop (cantering) rhythm
Galvanisation f galvanization, galvanotherapy
galvanisieren to galvanize
Galvanochirurgie f galvanosurgery
Galvanokaustik f galvanocautery, galvanocauterization
Galvanokauter m galvanocauter, galvanic cauter
Galvanonarkose f galvanonarcosis (Längsdurchströmung des Rückenmarks mit konstantem Gleichstrom)

Galvanopalpation

Galvanopalpation f galvanopalpation
Galvanopunktur f galvanopuncture
Galvanotaxis f, **Galvanotropismus** m galvanotaxis, galvanotropism *(Ausrichtung der Bewegung von Zellen im Gleichstromfeld)*
Galvanotherapie f s. Galvanisation
Galvanotonus m galvanotonus, tonic response to galvanism
Gamasidiosis f gamasidiosis
Gambienseinfektion f s. Trypanosomiasis/zentralafrikanische
Gamet m 1. gamete, sexual (germ) cell; ovum; sperm; 2. gamete *(Malaria) (s. a. Mikrogamet und Makrogamet)*
gametenabtötend gametocide
gametenbildend gametogenic
Gametenbildung f gametogenesis
Gametenträger m gametocyte carrier *(bei Malaria)*
Gametenvereinigung f union (copulation) of gametes, syngamy
gametenzerstörend gametocide
Gametoblast m gametoblast, sporozoite *(Malaria)*
gametogen gametogenic
Gametogenese f gametogenesis
Gametogonie f gametogony, gamogony
Gametozyt m 1. gametocyte, spermatocyte; oocyte *(vor der Reduktionsteilung)*; 2. gametocyte; microgametocyte *(männlich)*; macrogametocyte *(weiblich) (Malaria)*
Gametozythämie f gametocythaemia
Gammaaminobuttersäure f gamma-amino butyric acid, GABA
Gammafetoprotein n gamma foetoprotein
Gammaglobulin n gamma globulin, γ-globulin
Gammaglobulinmangel m im Blut agammaglobulinaemia
Gammaglobulinmangelkrankheit f gammopathy
Gammaglobulinprophylaxe f gammaglobulin prophylaxis
Gammaglobulinspiegelerhöhung f im Blut hypergammaglobulinaemia
Gammaglobulin[spiegel]verminderung f im Blut hypogammaglobulinaemia
Gamma-Hämolyse f gamma haemolysis
Gamma-Hämolysin n gamma haemolysin
Gammakamera f gamma camera *(Nuklearmedizin)*
Gammakörnchen n gamma granule *(in der Hypophyse)*
Gamma-Rhythmus m gamma rhythm *(EEG)*
Gammastrahlung f gamma rays (radiation)
Gammazismus m gammacism *(Sprachstörung)*
Gammopathie f/**monoklonale** monoclonal gammopathy
Gamna-Gandy-Knötchen npl Gamna-Gandy nodules (bodies) *(in der Milz)*
Gamogonie f gamogony, gametogony
Gamomanie f gamomania, morbid desire to marry
Gamophobie f gamophobia *(krankhafte Angst vor Heirat)*

260

Gampsodaktylie f gampsodactyly
Gampstorp-Syndrom n Gampstorp's disease *(Lähmungen bei Hyperkaliämie)*
Gang m 1. duct, canal[is]; passage; meatus *(s. a. unter Ductus und Meatus)*; 2. gait, walk
~/**Arantiusscher** duct of Arantius *(Embryologie)*
~/**ataktischer** ataxic gait
~/**Bartholinischer** Bartholin's duct
~/**Cuvierscher** duct of Cuvier *(Embryologie)*
~/**Gartnerscher** Gartner's duct *(Embryologie)*
~/**hemiplegischer** hemiplegic gait
~/**Müllerscher** Müller's (paramesonephric) duct *(Embryologie)*
~/**paralytischer** paralytic gait
~/**paretischer** paretic gait
~/**Santorinischer** duct of Santorini, accessory pancreatic duct, Bernard's canal
~/**schwankender** staggering (swaying, reeling) gait, titubation *(z. B. bei Kleinhirnerkrankung)*
~/**Skenescher** Skene's (para-urethral) duct
~/**Stensenscher** Stenson's (Stenonian) duct, parotid duct
~/**tabetischer** tabetic gait
~/**taumelnder** temulence, temulentia
~/**Whartonscher** Wharton's (submandibular) duct *(Ausführungsgang der Unterkieferspeicheldrüse)*
~/**Wirsungscher** Wirsung's duct (canal), duct of Wirsung, pancreatic duct
~/**Wolffscher** Wolffian (mesonephric) duct
~/**zerebellärer** cerebellar gait
Gangabszeß m canalicular abscess
Gangabweichung f deviation of gait
Gangart f gait, walk *(Zusammensetzungen s. unter Gang)*
Gangauskleidungsepithel n duct cell epithelium
Gangbeschleunigung f[/**unwillkürliche**] propulsion, festination *(z. B. bei Parkinsonismus)*
Gänge mpl/**Luschkasche** Luschka's ducts *(verlagerte Gallengänge in der Gallenblasenwand)*
Ganglia npl **plexuum autonomicorum** ganglions of the autonomic nervous system
ganglienartig ganglioid
Ganglienblockade f ganglionic block
Ganglienblocker m ganglionic blocking agent, ganglionoplegic [agent], adrenergic blocker
ganglienblockierend ganglio[no]plegic, ganglia-blocking
Ganglienentfernung f[/**operative**] gangli[on]ectomy, excision of a ganglion
Ganglienentzündung f s. Ganglionentzündung
ganglienförmig gangli[o]form
ganglienlähmend ganglio[no]plegic
Ganglienleiste f ganglionic crest, ganglion ridge
ganglienlos aganglionic
Ganglienmangel m aganglionosis
Ganglienzelle f ganglion cell, gangliocyte
Ganglienzellgliom n ganglion cell glioma (neuroma)
Ganglienzellneurilemm n ganglion cell neurilemma
Ganglienzellschicht f internal pyramidal layer, ganglionic layer of the optic nerve *(Netzhaut)*

Ganglioblast m ganglioblast *(Embryologie)*
Gangliogliom n ganglioglioma
Gangliom n ganglioma *(bösartige Nervengeschwulst)*
Ganglion n 1. ganglion *(Anhäufung von Nervenzellen)*; 2. [synovial] ganglion, weeping sinew, cystic tumour, thecal cyst *(in einer Sehnenscheide)*; cyst *(in einer Gelenkkapsel)* ● **ein ~ entfernen** to deganglionate ● **neben einem ~** paraganglionic
ganglionär ganglionic, ganglial, gangliar
Ganglionektomie f s. Ganglienentfernung/operative
Ganglionentzündung f ganglion inflammation, ganglionitis, neurogangli[on]itis
Ganglioneuroblastom n ganglioneuroblastoma *(Nervengeschwulst)*
Ganglioneurom n ganglioneuroma, gangliocytoma, ganglionic neuroma *(Nervengeschwulst)*
Ganglioneurozytom n ganglioneurocytoma *(Nervengeschwulst)*
Ganglionexstirpation f gangli[on]ectomy
Ganglionitis f s. Ganglionentzündung
Ganglion-stellatum-Blockade f stellate ganglion block
Gangloplegikum n s. Ganglienblocker
ganglioplegisch s. ganglienblockierend
Gangliosid n ganglioside *(Glykolipid)*
Gangliosidose f gangliosidosis *(degenerative ZNS-Erkrankung)*
Gangliozytom n gangliocytoma *(Nervengeschwulst)*
ganglos ductless
Gangöffnung f duct orifice
Gangrän f gangrene, sloughing phagedena; necrosis *(s.a. unter Nekrose)*
~/arteriosklerotische arteriosclerotic gangrene
~/diabetische diabetic gangrene
~/feuchte wet (moist, humid) gangrene, sphacelation *(durch bakterielle Zersetzung)*
~/foudroyante foudroyant (fulminant, infectious, spreading) gangrene
~/senile senile gangrene
~/trockene dry (arteriosclerotic) gangrene, mummification
~/trophische trophic gangrene
Gangränbildung f gangrenosis, sphacelation
gangränös gangrenous, necrotic, sphacelous
Gangstörung f gait disturbance, dysbasia
Gangwandentzündung f meatitis
Ganoblast m ganoblast, ameloblast, adamantoblast
Gänsefuß m goose's foot
Gänsegurgelradialarterie f goose-neck radial [artery]
Gänsehaut f goose-flesh, goose-skin, anserine skin; horripilation
Gänsehautreflex m pilomotor reflex
Ganzkörperaufnahme f whole-body radiography
Ganzkörperbehandlung f systemic therapy
Ganzkörperbestrahlung f total-body irradiation, whole-body exposure

Ganzkörper-Computertomographie f whole-body computed tomography, total-body CT scanning
Ganzkörperkühlung f total-body cooling
Ganzkörperplethysmographie f total-body plethysmography
Ganzkörperretentionstest m whole-body retention test
Ganzkörperröntgenbestrahlung f whole-body X-irradiation
Ganzkörperschwingung f whole-body vibration
Ganzkörperszintigramm n total-body scan
Ganzkörperszintigraphie f total-body scanning
Ganzkörperunterkühlung f total-body cooling
Ganzkörperzähler m whole-body counter, whole-body CT scanner *(Radiologie)*
gären to ferment
gärend fermentative, fermenting, zymotic
Gargoylismus m gargoylism *(s.a. Pfaundler-Hurler-Syndrom)*
Garrulitas f talkativeness, garrulity, hyperphasia
~ vulvae garrulity of the vulva; flatus vaginalis
Gärung f fermentation, zymosis ● **~ bewirkend** zymogenic, zymogenous
~/alkoholische alcoholic fermentation
~/ammoniakalische ammoniacal fermentation
~/bakterielle bacterial fermentation
gärungsauslösend fermentative, zymotic
Gärungsdyspepsie f fermentative dyspepsia
gärungsfördernd zymogenous
gärungshemmend antifermentative, antizymotic
Gasabszeß m gas (tympanitic) abscess, emphysematous abscess
Gasansammlung f meteorism, tympanites
~ in den Dünndarmwänden cystoid intestinal pneumatosis
~ in der Gebärmutter physometra
~ in einem Gelenk pneumarthrosis
Gasauftreibung f pneumatosis
Gasaustausch m gas exchange
~/äußerer external respiration
~/innerer internal respiration
gasbildend gas-forming; flatulent; aerogenic, aerogenous *(z. B. Bakterien)*
~/nicht anaerogenic
Gasbläschenbildung f im Blut aeraemia *(z. B. bei Taucherkrankheit)*
Gasbrand m gas gangrene (phlegmon), gaseous (malignant) oedema, clostridial myonecrosis (infection)
Gasbrandantitoxin n gas gangrene antitoxin
Gasbranderreger m gas gangrene bacillus
Gasbrandklostridium n Welch bacillus, Clostridium perfringens
Gasbrandmyositis f gas gangrene myositis
Gasbrandsepsis f gas sepsis
Gasbrandserum n anti-gas-gangrene serum
Gasbrandtoxin n gas gangrene toxin
Gaseinblasung f insufflation, ballooning *(z. B. in die Bauchhöhle)*
Gasembolie f gas embolism

Gas-Flüssigkeits-...

Gas-Flüssigkeits-Chromatographie f gas-liquid chromatography
gasförmig gaseous, aeriform
gasgefüllt tympanous, gas-filled
Gas-Kontrast-Angiokardiographie f gas contrast angiocardiography
Gasmyelographie f gas myelography
Gaster m gaster, stomach *(Zusammensetzungen s. unter Magen)*
Gastralgie f gastralgia, pain in the stomach, gastrodynia
Gastralgokenose f gastralgokenosis
Gastratrophie f gastratrophia, atrophy of the stomach
Gastrektasie f gastrectasia, dilatation of the stomach
Gastrektomie f gastrectomy
Gastrin n gastrin *(Hormon)*
Gastrinantagonist m gastrin antagonist, antigastrin agent
Gastrinom n gastrinoma
Gastrinspiegelerhöhung f im Blut hypergastrinaemia
gastrisch gastric
Gastritis f gastritis, inflammation of the stomach
~/**atrophische** atrophic gastritis
~ **cirrhoticans** leather bottle stomach
~/**eosinophile** eosinophil gastritis
~/**exfoliative** exfoliative gastritis
~/**granulomatöse** granulomatous gastritis
~/**hypertrophe** hypertrophic gastritis
~/**phlegmonöse** phlegmonous gastritis
gastritisch gastritic
Gastroanastomose f gastroanastomosis
Gastrocnemius m gastrocnemius [muscle]
Gastrodiaphanoskopie f gastrodiaphanoscopy
Gastrodidymus m gastrodidymus
Gastroduodenalsonde f gastroduodenal tube
Gastroduodenalulkus n gastroduodenal ulcer
Gastroduodenitis f gastroduodenitis
Gastroduodenoskopie f gastroduodenoscopy
Gastroduodenostomie f gastroduodenostomy
~ **nach B I** Billroth I anastomosis
Gastrodynie f s. Gastralgie
gastroenteral gastroenteric
Gastroenteralgie f gastroenteralgia
gastroenterisch gastroenteric
Gastroenteritis f gastroenteritis, enterogastritis
Gastroenterokolitis f gastroenterocolitis
Gastroenterokolitis-Syndrom n gastroenterocolitis syndrome
Gastroenterologe m [gastro]enterologist
Gastroenterologie f [gastro]enterology *(Lehre von den Magen- und Darmkrankheiten)*
Gastroenteropathie f gastroenteropathy
Gastroenteroptose f gastroenteroptosis
Gastroenterostomie f gastroenterostomy, gastroenteroanastomosis; Wölfler's operation
Gastroferrin n gastroferrin
Gastrogastrostomie f gastrogastrostomy, gastroanastomosis
gastrogen gastrogenic *(Krankheiten)*

gastrohypertonisch gastrohypertonic
Gastroileostomie f gastroileostomy
gastrointestinal gastro-intestinal, GI
Gastrointestinalabsaugung f gastro-intestinal suction
Gastrointestinalblutung f gastro-intestinal bleeding (haemorrhage)
~/**untere** lower gastro-intestinal bleeding
Gastrointestinalerkrankung f gastro-intestinal illness
Gastrointestinaltrakt m gastro-intestinal tract, alimentary canal
Gastrojejunalfistel f gastrojejunal fistula
Gastrojejunitis f gastrojejunitis
Gastrojejunostomie f gastrojejunostomy
~ **nach B II** Billroth II anastomosis
Gastrokamera f gastrocamera
gastrokardial gastrocardiac
gastrokolisch gastrocolic
Gastrokolitis f gastrocolitis
Gastrokolostomie f gastrocolostomy
gastrolienal gastrolienal, gastrosplenic
Gastrolith m gastrolith, gastric calculus
Gastrolithiasis f gastrolithiasis
Gastrologe m gastrologist
Gastrologie f gastrology *(Lehre von den Magenkrankheiten)*
Gastrolyse f gastrolysis
Gastromalazie f gastromalacia, softening of the gastric walls
Gastromegalie f gastromegaly
gastromesenterial gastromesenteric
Gastromykose f gastromycosis
Gastromyotomie f gastromyotomy
Gastromyxorrhoe f gastromyxorrhoea
gastroösophageal gastro-oesophageal
Gastroösophagitis f gastro-oesophagitis
Gastroösophagoplastik f gastro-oesophagoplasty
Gastroösophagostomie f gastro-oesophagostomy
gastropankreatisch gastropancreatic
Gastropathie f gastropathy, disease of the stomach
Gastropexie f gastropexy, fixation of the stomach
gastrophrenisch gastrophrenic
Gastroplastik f gastroplasty
Gastroplicatio f gastroplication
Gastroptose f gastroptosis
Gastropylorektomie f gastropylorectomy
Gastrorrhagie f gastrorrhagia, gastric bleeding
Gastrorrhaphie f gastrorrhaphy, suture of the stomach
Gastrorrhexis f gastrorrhexis, rupture of the stomach
Gastrorrhoe f gastrorrhoea
Gastroschisis f gastroschisis, coeloschisis *(angeborene Spaltbildung der vorderen Bauchwand)*
Gastroskop n gastroscope
Gastroskopie f gastroscopy, stomachoscopy

gastroskopisch gastroscopic
Gastrospasmus *m* gastrospasm
Gastrostaxis *f* gastrostaxis
Gastrostenose *f* gastrostenosis
Gastrostoma *n* gastrostoma
Gastrostoma-Katheter *m* gastrostomy catheter (tube)
Gastrostomie *f* gastrostomy; laparogastrostomy
~ **nach Kader** Kader's operation
Gastrostomierohr *n* gastrostomy tube (catheter)
Gastrosukkorrhoe *f* gastrosuccorrhoea, Reichmann's disease *(dauernder Magensaftfluß mit Sodbrennen und Erbrechen bei Ulcus duodeni)*
Gastrothorakopagus *m* gastrothoracopagus *(Mißgeburt)*
Gastrotomie *f* gastrotomy
Gastrotonometrie *f* gastrotonometry
gastrotoxisch gastrotoxic
Gastrozele *f* gastrocele, hernia of the stomach
Gastrula *f* gastrula *(Keimentwicklungsstadium)*
Gastrulation *f* gastrulation
Gaumen *m* palate, palatum, roof of the mouth
~/**definitiver** definitive (secondary) palate
~/**gespaltener** cleft palate
~/**gotischer** gothic (high arched) palate
~/**harter** hard palate
~/**knöcherner** osseous palate
~/**primärer** primary palate
~/**sekundärer** secondary (definitive) palate
~/**weicher** soft palate, staphyle
gaumenähnlich palatiform
Gaumenaponeurose *f* palatine aponeurosis
Gaumenarterie *f*/**absteigende** descending palatine artery
~/**aufsteigende** ascending palatine artery
~/**große** greater (major) palatine artery
~/**kleine** lesser (minor) palatine artery
gaumenartig palatiform
Gaumenbein *n* palatine [bone]
Gaumenbeinnaht *f* palatine suture
Gaumenbogen *m* palatine (tonsillar) arch, [palato]maxillary arch, pillar of the fauces
~/**hinterer** palatopharyngeal arch, posterior pillar of the fauces
~/**vorderer** palatoglossal (glossopalatine) arch, anterior pillar of the fauces
Gaumenbrücke *f* palatine bar
Gaumenentzündung *f* palatitis, uranisconitis
Gaumenfenster *n* palatine foramen
Gaumenfistel *f* palatine fistula
gaumenförmig palatiform
Gaumenfortsatz *m* **des Oberkiefers** palatine process [of the maxilla]
Gaumengewölbe *n s.* Gaumenbogen
Gaumenhäkchen *n* palate hook (retractor)
Gaumeninsuffizienz *f* palatine incompetence
Gaumen-Kiefer-Spalte *f* gnathopalatoschisis, uranoschisis, uranoschisma
Gaumenknochennaht *f* interpalatine suture
Gaumenlähmung *f* palatine paralyis, palatoplegia, uranoplegia
Gaumenlappen *m* palatine flap

Gaumenlautbildungsstörung *f* idioglossia
Gaumenlautstammeln *n* gammacism
Gaumenleukoplakie *f* leucoplakia of the palate
Gaumenmandel *f* [palatine] tonsil, faucial tonsil
Gaumenmandelgrube *f* palatine tonsil fossa
Gaumenmandelkappung *f* tonsillotomy
Gaumenmandelkrypten *fpl* tonsillar crypts of the palatine tonsils
Gaumenmandelregion *f* palatine (faucial) tonsillar region
Gaumenmyograph *m* palato[myo]graph, palate myograph *(zur Aufzeichnung der Gaumensegelbewegung)*
Gaumenmyoklonus *m* palatine myoclonus (nystagmus)
Gaumennadel *f* palatine needle
Gaumennaht *f* 1. palate suture, palatorrhaphy, staphylorrhaphy, uran[isc]orrhaphy *(operativ)*; 2. palatine raphe *(in der Mukosa)*; palatine suture *(am Knochen)*
~/**quere** transverse palatine suture
Gaumenplastik *f* palatoplasty, staphyloplasty, urano[staphylo]plasty
Gaumenplatte *f* palate plate
Gaumen-Rachen-Plastik *f* staphylopharyngorrhaphy
Gaumenreflex *m* palatine reflex
Gaumenrekonstruktion *f*[/**operative**] *s.* Gaumenplastik
Gaumenretraktor *m*/**selbsthaltender** self-retaining soft palatal retractor
Gaumenschleimhaut *f* palatine mucosa
Gaumenschlußunfähigkeit *f* palatine incompetence
Gaumensegel *n* palatine velum, soft palate, veil, vellum
Gaumensegelentfernung *f* [/**operative**] staphylectomy
Gaumensegelheber *m* levator veli palatini [muscle], levator palati muscle, staphylinus internus [muscle]
Gaumensegelkrampf *m* palatine spasm
Gaumensegellähmung *f* palatine paralysis, palatoplegia, uranoplegia
Gaumensegelresektion *f* staphylectomy
Gaumensegelspanner *m* tensor veli palatini [muscle], staphylinus externus [muscle], sphenosalpingostaphylinus [muscle]
Gaumenspalte *f* cleft palate, palatoschisis, uranoschisis, uranoschism[a], uranocoloboma
Gaumenspaltenchirurgie *f* cleft palate surgery
Gaumenspaltennaht *f s.* Gaumennaht 1.
Gaumenspaltenplastik *f s.* Gaumenplastik
Gaumenteilresektion *f* hemipalatectomy
Gaumenvene *f* external palatine vein
Gaumenverschlußplatte *f* obturator
Gaumenwiederherstellung *f*/**operative** *s.* Gaumenplastik
Gaumenzäpfchen *n s.* Uvula
Gaumenzäpfchen... *s.a.* Uvula...
Gaumenzäpfchenbluterguß *m* staphylohaematoma

Gaumenzäpfchenentfernung

Gaumenzäpfchenentfernung f[/operative] uvulectomy, staphylectomy, kiotomy
Gaumenzäpfchenentzündung f s. Uvulitis
Gaumenzäpfchenmesser n uvulotome, uvulatome
Gaumenzäpfchenmuskel m muscle of the uvula
Gaumenzäpfchenschnitt m uvulotomy, staphylotomy
Gaumenzäpfchenschwellung f uvular oedema, staphyloedema, staphylygroma
Gaumenzäpfchensenkung f uvuloptosis, staphyloptosis
Gaumenzäpfchenspalte f staphyloschisis; bifid (cleft) uvula
Gaumenzäpfchenzange f staphylagra
Gaumen-Zungen-Muskel m palatoglossus [muscle], palatoglossal muscle, glossopalatinus [muscle]
Gaxen n angophrasia *(Auftreten unartikulierter Laute beim Sprechen)*
Gaze f gauze, carbasus
Gazebausch m gauze pad; tampon
Gazestreifen m gauze wick (strip), wicking
Gazetupfer m gauze sponge (swab)
GE s. Gastroenterostomie
Gebärdennachahmung f mimesis, mimosis
gebären to bear, to give birth to, to bring forth, to be in labour
~/einen lebensunfähigen Fetus to bring forth a non-viable foetus
~/vor dem Termin to give birth prematurely
gebärend parturient, being in labour
~/ein Kind monotocous *(bei einer Geburt)*; uniparous *(Statistik)*
~/zum vierten Mal quadriparous
Gebärende f parturient, para, woman in labour
Gebärkanal m parturient (birth, obstetrical) canal
Gebärmutter f uterus, womb, metra *(Zusammensetzungen s. unter Uterus)*
Gebärmutter... s.a. Uterus...
Gebärmutteraktionspotentialaufzeichnung f electrohysterography
Gebärmutteraktivität f/spontane spontaneous uterine activity
Gebärmutteranhangsgebilde npl uterine adnexe (appendages)
Gebärmutteranheftung f[/operative] hysteropexia, uteropexia, uterofixation *(an die Bauchdecken)*
Gebärmutteranteflexion f anteflexion of the uterus
Gebärmutteraplasie f uterine aplasia
Gebärmutterarterie f uterine artery
Gebärmutteratonie f uterine atonia, metratonia
Gebärmutteratresie f atretometria
Gebärmutteratrophie f uterine atrophy, metratrophia
Gebärmutterauskratzung f curettage, curettement
Gebärmutterbauchfellüberzug m perimetrium
Gebärmutterbeweglichkeit f uterine motility
Gebärmutterbinnendruck m intra-uterine pressure
Gebärmutterbiopsiezange f uterine biopsy forceps
Gebärmutter-Blasen-Fistel f vesicouterine fistula
Gebärmutter-Blasen-Fixation f[/operative] hysterocystopexy
Gebärmutterblutarmut f metranaemia
Gebärmutterblutfülle f metr[a]emia
Gebärmutterblutung f uterine bleeding, metro[meno]rrhagia; menorrhagia *(während der Menstruation)*
Gebärmutterbruch m metrocele, hysterocele, uterine hernia
Gebärmutterdauerkontraktion f tetanic contraction of the uterus
Gebärmutterdrüse f uterine [endometrium] gland
Gebärmutterdusche f metroclyst
Gebärmutter-, Eierstock- und Eileiterentfernung f[/operative] hysterosalpingo-oophorectomy, hysterosalpingo-oothecectomy
~/totale panhysterosalpingo-oophorectomy
Gebärmutter-Eileiter-Anastomose f hysterosalpingostomy
Gebärmutter-Eileiter-Röntgen[kontrast]bild n uterosalpingogram
Gebärmutter-Eileiter-Röntgen[kontrast]darstellung f uterosalpingography
Gebärmuttereinblutung f haematometra, haematometrium
Gebärmutterentfernung f s. Hysterektomie
Gebärmutterentzündung f hysteritis, uteritis, metritis, inflammation of the uterus
~/septische septimetritis
Gebärmuttereröffnung f s. ~/operative
~ durch Bauchschnitt hysterolaparotomy, laparohysterotomy, laparo-uterotomy, gasterhysterotomy, gastrohysterotomy
~ nach Bauchschnitt und Scheidenschnitt laparocolpohysterotomy
~/operative hysterotomy, uterotomy, metrotomy
Gebärmuttererweiterung f metrectasia
Gebärmutterextraktionszange f hysterectomy forceps
Gebärmutterexzision f/vollständige panhysterectomy
Gebärmutterfibrom n uterine fibroma, metrofibroma
Gebärmutterfibromyom n uterine fibromyoma
Gebärmutterfixation f am Bauchfell peritoneopexy
Gebärmutterfixierung f an der Bauchdecke ventrohysteropexy, exohysteropexy
Gebärmutterfundus m uterine base (fundus), fundus of the uterus
Gebärmuttergeräusch n uterine souffle; placental murmur
Gebärmuttergeschwulst f uterine tumour, tumour of the womb
Gebärmuttergonorrhoe f metrogonorrhoea
Gebärmutterhals m cervix [of the uterus], uterine neck, neck of the womb ● **über dem ~** supracervical

Gebärmutterhals... s. a. Zervix... und Zervikal...
Gebärmutterhalsabort m cervical abortion
Gebärmutterhalsadenokarzinom n uterine cervix adenocarcinoma
Gebärmutterhalsamputation f uterine cervix amputation
Gebärmutterhalsausschneidung f/**keilförmige** uterine cervix conization
Gebärmutterhalsausstülpung f eversion of the cervix
Gebärmutterhalsbiopsie f uterine cervix biopsy
Gebärmutterhalsdehnung f uterine cervix dilatation
Gebärmutterhalsdrüse f gland of the cervix of the uterus, Nabothian gland
Gebärmutterhalsentfernung f[/**operative**] cervicectomy, [hystero]trachelectomy
Gebärmutterhalsentzündung f [uterine] cervicitis, endocervicitis, trachelitis
Gebärmutterhalsepithel n uterine cervix epithelium
Gebärmutterhalserosion f uterine cervix erosion
Gebärmutterhalserweiterer m hystereurynter, metreurynter
Gebärmutterhalserweiterung f metreurysis
Gebärmutterhalsfaßzange f cervical grasping forceps
Gebärmutterhalsfistel f cervical fistula
Gebärmutterhalsfixation f trachelopexia
Gebärmutterhalskanal m [endo]cervical canal, uterocervical (cervicouterine) canal, canal of the cervix of the uterus
Gebärmutterhalskanalabstrich m cervical smear
Gebärmutterhalskrebs m uterine cervix carcinoma, cervical cancer
Gebärmutterhalsküreттage f uterine cervix curettage
Gebärmutterhalsnaht f [hystero]trachelorrhaphy
Gebärmutterhalsplastik f [hystero]tracheloplasty
Gebärmutterhalsröntgen[kontrast]aufnahme f cervicogram
Gebärmutterhalsröntgen[kontrast]darstellung f cervicography
Gebärmutterhals-Scheiden-Naht f trachelosyringorrhaphy
Gebärmutterhalsschleimhaut f endocervix
Gebärmutterhalsschleimhautentzündung f endocervicitis
Gebärmutterhalsschnitt m [hystero]trachelotomy
Gebärmutterhalsschwangerschaft f cervical (uterine cervix) pregnancy
Gebärmutterhalssperrer m metranoikter
Gebärmutterhals- und Scheidenentzündung f cervicocolpitis, cervicovaginitis
Gebärmutterhalsvorfall m uterine cervix prolapse
Gebärmutterhalszytologie f uterine cervix cytology
Gebärmutter-Harnblasen-Anastomose f uterocystostomy

Gebärmutterhöhle f uterine (endometrial) cavity, uterine canal, cavity of the uterus
Gebärmutterhöhlenschwangerschaft f uterine pregnancy (gestation), uterogestation
Gebärmutterhöhlenverengung f metrostenosis, uterine cavity stenosis
Gebärmutterhorn n uterine horn, cornu of the uterus
Gebärmutterhornschwangerschaft f cornual pregnancy (gestation)
Gebärmutterischämie f uterine ischaemia
Gebärmutteristhmus m uterine isthmus, isthmus of the uterus (zwischen Körper und Hals)
Gebärmutterkanal m s. Gebärmutterhalskanal
Gebärmutterkontraktilität f uterine contractility
Gebärmutterkontraktion f uterine contraction
~/**mangelnde** metratonia
Gebärmutterkontraktionsschmerzen mpl uterine contraction pains; labour pains
Gebärmutterkörper m uterine body, body of the uterus
Gebärmutterkörperkarzinom n [uterine] corpus carcinoma
Gebärmutterkrampf m uterine spasm, hysterospasm, hysterotrism[us]
Gebärmutterkrankheit f uterine disease, hysteropathy, metropathy
Gebärmutterkrebs m uterine cancer, hysterocarcinoma, metrocarcinoma
Gebärmutterkreislauf m uterine circulation
Gebärmutterkürettage f **nach Zervixdehnung** hysterotrachelectasia
Gebärmutterkürette f uterine curette
Gebärmutterlähmung f uterine paralysis, metroparalysis
Gebärmutterleiomyom n uterine leiomyoma (gutartige Geschwulst)
gebärmutterlos ametrous
Gebärmutterlosigkeit f ametria, [congenital] absence of the uterus
Gebärmutterlösung f hysterolysis
Gebärmutterlymphgefäßentzündung f metrolymphangitis
Gebärmuttermangeldurchblutung f ametrohaemia
Gebärmuttermesenchymom n uterine mesenchymoma
Gebärmuttermesser n uterotome, hysterotome, metrotome
Gebärmuttermund m [/**äußerer**] ectocervix, exocervix
Gebärmuttermundinzision f stoma[to]tomy, cervical incision
Gebärmuttermuskelschnitt m hysteromyotomy
Gebärmuttermuskulatur f myometrium
Gebärmuttermuskulaturentzündung f [myo]metritis, inflammation of the uterine muscular tissue
Gebärmuttermyom n [uterine] myoma, hysteromyoma
Gebärmuttermyomentfernung f[/**operative**] hysteromyomectomy
~/**transabdominale** coeliomyomectomy

Gebärmutternaht

Gebärmutternaht f hysterorrhaphy
Gebärmutternarbe f uterine scar
Gebärmutterneigung f uterine version
Gebärmutternervengeflecht n uterine plexus
Gebärmutternervenversorgung f uterine innervation
Gebärmutterperforation f uterine perforation
Gebärmutterpessar n pessary, uterine veil
Gebärmutterplastik f uteroplasty, hysteroplasty, metroplasty
Gebärmutterriß m uterine rupture, hysterorrhexis, metrorrhexis
Gebärmutterröntgen[kontrast]bild n uterogram, hysterogram
Gebärmutterröntgen[kontrast]darstellung f uterography, hysterography
Gebärmutterrückbildung f involution of the uterus (z. B. nach einer Geburt)
Gebärmutterrückwärtsbeugung f retroversion of the uterus
Gebärmuttersarkom n uterine sarcoma
Gebärmutter-Scheiden-Spiegel m hysterocolposcope
Gebärmutter-Scheiden-Spiegelung f hysterocolposcopy
Gebärmutterschleimhaut f uterine mucosa, endometrium
Gebärmutterschleimhaut... s. a. Endometrium...
Gebärmutterschleimhautabstoßung f denidation
Gebärmutterschleimhautadenoakanthom n endometrium adenoacanthoma
Gebärmutterschleimhautaspiration f endometrium aspiration
Gebärmutterschleimhautauskratzung f curettage, curettement
Gebärmutterschleimhautentfernung f[/operative] endometrectomy
Gebärmutterschleimhautentzündung f s. Endometritis
Gebärmutterschleimhautgeschwulst f endometrioma
Gebärmutterschleimhauthyperplasie f endometrium hyperplasia
Gebärmutterschleimhautkrebs m endometrial cancer, endometrium carcinoma
Gebärmutterschleimhautmetaplasie f endometrium metaplasia
Gebärmutterschleimhautpolyp m endometrium polyp
Gebärmutterschleimhautproliferation f endometrium proliferation
Gebärmutterschleimhautrückbildung f endometrium atrophy
Gebärmutterschleimhautsepsis f endometrium sepsis
Gebärmutterschleimhautversprengung f endometriosis
Gebärmutterschleimhautzelluntersuchung f endometrium cytology
Gebärmutterschleimhautzyklus m endometrium cycle
Gebärmutterschleimhautzyste f endometrium cyst
Gebärmutterschmerz m uterine pain, hysteralgia, hysterodynia, uteralgia, uterism[us], metralgia
Gebärmutterschmierblutung f metrostaxis
Gebärmutterschwangerschaft f uterine pregnancy (gestation), uterogestation
Gebärmuttersenkung f s. Gebärmuttervorfall
Gebärmuttersonde f uterine probe (sound)
Gebärmutterspiegel m hysteroscope, uteroscope, metroscope
gebärmutterspiegelnd hysteroscopic, uteroscopic
Gebärmutterspiegelung f hysteroscopy, uteroscopy
Gebärmutterspülinstrument n metroclyst
Gebärmutterspülkatheter m uterine flushing tube
Gebärmutterstein m uterine calculus, hysterolith, uterolith
Gebärmuttersteinleiden n hysterolithiasis
Gebärmutterstörung f uterine disorder
Gebärmutterszirrhus m metroscirrhus (bösartige Geschwulst)
Gebärmutterteilexstirpation f partial hysterectomy
gebärmuttertonisierend uterotonic
Gebärmuttertripper m uterine gonorrhoea, metrogonorrhoea; gonorrhoeal endometritis
Gebärmutterumstülpung f uterine inversion, inversion of the uterus
Gebärmutter- und Bauchfellentzündung f metroperitonitis
Gebärmutter- und Eierstockentfernung f[/operative] hystero-oophorectomy, hystero-ovariotomy, oophorohysterectomy, ovariohysterectomy
~/**totale** panhystero-oophorectomy
Gebärmutter- und Eileiterentfernung f[/operative] hysterosalpingectomy
~/**totale** panhysterosalpingectomy
Gebärmutter- und Eileiterentzündung f metrosalpingitis
Gebärmutter- und Eileiterröntgen[kontrast]darstellung f hysterosalpingography, hysterotubography, metrosalpingography, metrotubography
Gebärmutter- und Gebärmutterhals[ein]schnitt m hysterocervicotomy
Gebärmutter- und Gebärmutterschleimhautentzündung f metroendometritis
Gebärmutter- und Scheidenentfernung f/totale panhysterocolpectomy, pancolpohysterectomy
Gebärmutter- und Scheidenvorfall m metrocolpocele
Gebärmutterunterentwicklung f uterine hypoplasia
Gebärmuttervene f uterine vein
Gebärmuttervenenentzündung f phlebometritis, metrophlebitis
Gebärmuttervenengeflecht n uterine [venous] plexus

Gebärmuttervereiterung f pyometra
Gebärmuttervergrößerung f metrauxe, metrypertrophia
Gebärmutterverhärtung f uterosclerosis
Gebärmutterverlagerung f metrectopia
gebärmuttervermessend hysterometric, uterometric
Gebärmuttervermessung f hysterometry, uterometry
Gebärmuttervermessungsinstrument n hysterometer, uterometer
Gebärmutterverschleimung f mucometria
Gebärmutterverschluß m hysteratresia
~/operativer hysterocleisis
Gebärmutterverwachsung f uterine synechia
Gebärmuttervorfall m uterine prolapse, prolapse of the uterus, falling of the womb, hysteroptosis, metroptosis
Gebärmutterwandgeschwulst f/**gefäßreiche** angiomyoma
Gebärmutterzange f hysterectomy forceps
Gebärmutterzystenbildung f metrocystosis
Gebein n bones
geben/durch den Mund to administer orally
~/eine Injektion to give an injection
~/Kurare to curarize *(zur Muskelerschlaffung)*
Gebiß n denture, dentition, set of teeth
~/bleibendes permanent denture (teeth)
~/künstliches [artificial] denture, set of false (artificial) teeth, dental prosthesis; dental plate
Gebißabdruck m, **Gebißabguß** m checkbite
Gebißausrichtung f orthodontia, orthodontics, orthodontology, odontorthosis
Gebißcerclage f continuous loop wiring *(bei Kieferfraktur)*
Gebißformel f dental formula
Gebißidentifizierungskarte f dental identification record
Gebißkunde f odontology
Gebißmißbildung f odontoparallaxis, odontoloxia
Gebißschaden m dental defect
Gebißschluß m occlusion *(der Zähne)*
Gebißschlußkraft f occlusion force
Gebißschlußstörung f occlusion disharmony (dystrophy)
gebläht distended, tympanous *(z. B. der Bauch)*
Gebläsedruckball m inflation bulb *(Anästhesie)*
gebogen curved, bent, arcuate, circumflex
~/abnorm valgus
geboren/vor der Einlieferung born before arrival
Gebrechen n physical (bodily) defect; infirmity *(Schwäche)*
gebrechlich frail, invalid, weak *(schwächlich)*; infirm, decrepit *(altersschwach)*
Gebrechlicher m invalid
Gebrechlichkeit f frailty, invalidism; infirmity, decrepitude *(Altersschwäche)*
Geburt f [child]birth, parturition, delivery, labour, lying-in, accoucheraent, confinement, childbearing *(s. a. unter Entbindung)*; birth, presentation, delivery *(des Kindes)* ● **die ~ erleichtern** to facilitate delivery ● **ohne ~** nulliparous, nonparous *(Statistik)* ● **unter der ~** intrapartal, intranatal ● **vor der ~** antenatal ● **während der ~** intrapartal, intranatal
~ einer Mißbildung monstriparity
~ in Beckenendlage breech presentation
~ in Längslage longitudinal presentation
~ in Querlage transverse presentation, cross birth
~ in Schräglage oblique presentation
~ nach dem Termin post-term birth
~ nach vorzeitigem Fruchtwasserabgang dry labour, xerotocia
~/protrahierte protracted labour
~/schnelle rapid childbirth, oxytocia
~/schwierige difficult (complicated) labour
~/überstürzte precipitate labour, oxytocia
~/verzögerte protracted labour; prolonged pregnancy
~ zum Termin term life birth, term parturition
Geburtenabstand m interval between births
Geburtenanstieg m rising birth-rate
Geburtenhäufigkeit f s. Geburtenrate
Geburtenkontrolle f birth control
geburtenlos non-parous, nulliparous
Geburtenplanung f birth planning *(s. a. Geburtenregelung)*
Geburtenrate f birth-rate, natality
~/spezifische specific birth-rate
Geburtenregelung f birth control, contraception, conception control; family planning
Geburtenrückgang m declining (falling) birth-rate
geburtenschwach having a low birth-rate *(Jahrgang)*
geburtenstark having a high birth-rate *(Jahrgang)*
Geburtenüberschuß m birth-rate excess
Geburtenziffer f s. Geburtenrate
geburtsbeschleunigend ecbolic, accelerating labour, oxytocic, ocyodinic
geburtseinleitend parturifacient
Geburtseinleitung f labour induction; first stage of labour
Geburtsfehler m congenital defect
Geburtsgeschwulst f cephalhaematoma *(des Neugeborenen)*
Geburtsgewicht n birth weight, weight at birth
Geburtshelfer m obstetrician, accoucheur, tocologist
Geburtshelferhand f obstetrician's (accoucheur's) hand
Geburtshelferin f midwife, accoucheuse
Geburtshelferstellung f *der Hand* s. Geburtshelferhand
Geburtshemmung f labour inhibition
Geburtshilfe f obstetrics, O. B., midwifery, tocology, tictology
geburtshilflich obstetric[al]
Geburtskalender m periodoscope
Geburtskanal m birth (parturient, obstetrical) canal
Geburtslage f presentation

Geburtslähmung

Geburtslähmung *f* birth palsy, obstetrical paralysis
Geburtslänge *f* birth length
Geburtslöffel *m* obstetrical lever, elevating spoon
Geburtsmal *n* n[a]evus *(umschriebene, anlagebedingte oder erbliche Fehlbildung der Haut)*
Geburtsmechanismus *m* mechanism of labour
Geburtsmembranen *fpl* birth membranes
Geburtsschmerz *m* labour pain, pains
Geburtsstadium *n* labour stage, stage of labour
Geburtsstörung *f* dystocia, paradynia; difficult labour (parturition)
Geburtsurkunde *f* birth certificate
Geburtsverletzung *f* birth injury (trauma)
Geburtsverzögerung *f* bradytocia, slow parturition
~/**aktive** labour inhibition
Geburtsvorgang *m* birth process, parturition
Geburtsweg *m s.* Geburtskanal
Geburtszange *f* [obstetrical] forceps
~/**Bartonsche** Barton's forceps
~/**Simpsonsche** Simpson's forceps
~/**Smelliesche** Smellie's forceps
Geburtszangendrehung *f* forceps rotation
Gedächtnis *n* memory, remembrance, mind, mens, mneme ● **das ~ unterstützend** mnemonic
~/**assoziatives** automatic memory
~/**gutes** retentive memory
~/**immunologisches** immunological memory
~/**schlechtes** bad (poor, weak) memory
~/**visuelles** visual (eye) memory
Gedächtnisfehler *m* paramnesia, lapsus memoriae, slip of memory
Gedächtnishilfe *f s.* Gedächtnisstütze
Gedächtnisleistung *f*/**gesteigerte** hypermnesia
~/**verminderte** hypomnesia
Gedächtnislücke *f* memory gap, obliteration, partial amnesia
Gedächtnisschwäche *f* mnemasthenia, weakness of memory; dysmnesia
Gedächtnisschwund *m s.* Gedächtnisverlust
Gedächtnisspur *f* mnemonic (memory) trace, engram, neurogram
Gedächtnisstärke *f*/**abnorme** hypermnesia
Gedächtnisstörung *f* dysmnesia, impaired memory
Gedächtnisstütze *f* mnemonic (memory) aid
Gedächtnistraining *n* mnemonics, mnemotechnics, mnemotechny *(Lerntechnik)*; memory training, mnemonic exercises
Gedächtnisverlust *m* memory loss, amnesia
Gedankenabriß *m* thought blocking
Gedankenflucht *f* mental aberration
Gedankenlesen *n* thought reading, telemnemonike *(s. a.* Gedankenübertragung*)*
Gedankenleser *m* thought reader
gedankenübertragend telepathic
Gedankenübertragung *f* telepathy, thought transference
Gedärm *n* bowels, entrails, intestines *(s. a.* Eingeweide *und* Darm*)*

Gedeihstörung *f* failure to grow *(z. B. der Säuglinge)*
gedrungen pyknic, stout, stickset
gedunsen pasty, bloated, puffed-up
geerbt/**vom Vater** patroclinous
~/**von der Mutter** matroclinous
gefächert septate
gefährlich foudroyant, fulminant *(z. B. Krankheitsverlauf)*; critical, serious *(z. B. Zustand)*
Gefängnispsychose *f* prison psychosis
gefärbt:
~/**mit Blut** sanguinolent
~/**normal** orthochrom[at]ic
~/**ungleichmäßig** anisochrom[at]ic
Gefäß *n* [blood] vessel, vas *(s. a. unter* Vas*)*
● **neue Gefäße bilden** to neovascularize
~/**kleines** vasculum
Gefäß... *s. a.* Blutgefäß...
Gefäßabbindung *f* ligature
Gefäßabknickung *f* kinking of a vessel
Gefäßanastomose *f* vascular anastomosis
Gefäßanordnung *f* vasculature
Gefäßarchitektur *f* angioarchitecture
gefäßarm poorly vascularized
gefäßartig angioid, vasiform
Gefäßast *m* twig
Gefäßbandschatten *m* cardiovascular shadow *(Radiologie)*
Gefäßbeteiligung *f* vascular involvement
Gefäßbett *n* vascular bed
gefäßbildend angiopoietic, angiogenic, angioblastic, vasifactive
Gefäßbildung *f* angiopoiesis, angiogenesis, vascularization, vasculogenesis
Gefäßbildungszelle *f* angioblast
Gefäßbündel *n* vascular bundle
Gefäßchirurg *m* vascular surgeon
Gefäßchirurgie *f* vascular surgery
Gefäßdarstellung *f s.* Gefäßröntgen[kontrast]darstellung
Gefäßdilatation *f* vascular dilatation, vasodilatation
Gefäßdrossel *f* snare
Gefäßdurchgängigkeit *f* vascular (vessel) patency
Gefäßdurchlässigkeit *f* vascular permeability
Gefäße *npl*/**neugebildete** neovasculature
Gefäßeintrittspforte *f* hilus, hilum *(an Organen)*
Gefäßektasie *f* angiectasia
Gefäßendothelauskleidung *f* vascular endothelial lining
Gefäßendothelzelle *f* vascular endothelial cell
Gefäßentfernung *f*[/**operative**] angiectomy
Gefäßentzündung *f* angi[i]tis, vasculitis, vascular inflammation
gefäßernährend angiotrophic, vasotrophic
Gefäßeröffnung *f*[/**operative**] angiotomy
Gefäßerschlaffung *f s.* Gefäßerweiterung
Gefäßerweichung *f* angiomalacia
gefäßerweiternd vasodilator, vasodilative; vasohypotonic; haemangiectatic
gefäßerweitert [tele]angiectatic, angiotelectatic, haemangiectatic

Gefäßerweiterung f vascular dilatation, vasodilatation, [haem]angioectasia, angiohypotonia
Gefäßexzision f angiectomy
gefäßfehlbildend angiodysplastic; anangioplastic
Gefäßfehlbildung f angiodysplasia, vascular malformation
Gefäßfibrom n angiofibroma
gefäßförmig vasiform, vessel-like
Gefäßgeschwulst f vascular tumour; angioma; angioneoplasm
Gefäßgift n vascular poison
Gefäßgliom n angioglioma
Gefäßhäkchen n vessel hook
Gefäßhaut f vascular membrane
gefäßhemmend vasoinhibitory
Gefäßhüllenentzündung f exarteri[i]tis
Gefäßinnenhaut f intima, [vascular] endothelium
 ● **unter der ~** subintimal
Gefäßinnenhaut... s. Intima...
Gefäßinsuffizienz f vascular insufficiency
Gefäßinzision f vascular incision, angiotomy
Gefäßklemme f vascular clamp, artery (haemostatic) forceps, haemostat, vasotribe
~/atraumatische atraumatic (non-crushing) vascular clamp
~/Pottsche Beck-Potts clamp
Gefäßknäuel n vascular tuft (ball), glomus
Gefäßkompression f angiopressure, vascular compression
gefäßkontrahierend vasoconstrictor
Gefäßkrampf m angiospasm, vascular spasm, vasospasm
Gefäßkrankheit f angiopathy, angiosis, vasculopathy, vascular disease
~/diabetische diabetic angiopathy
Gefäßkranz m **der Hirnbasis** circle of Willis
~/Zinnscher arterial (vascular) circle of the optic nerve, Zinn's circle
gefäßlähmend angioparalytic
Gefäßlähmung f angioparesis, angioparalysis, vasoparalysis
gefäßlos avascular, anangioid
Gefäßlücke f lacuna vasorum (unter dem Leistenband)
Gefäßlumen n vascular lumen
gefäßlumeneinengend angiostenotic
Gefäßlumeneinengung f angiostenosis
Gefäßmangelernährung f angiodystrophia
Gefäßmembran f/**äußere elastische** external elastic lamina (membrane)
~/innere elastische internal elastic lamina (membrane)
Gefäßmesser n vascular (vessel) knife
Gefäßmikroskop n angioscope
Gefäßmikroskopie f angioscopy
Gefäßminderversorgung f angiodystrophia
Gefäßmißbildung f vascular malformation (deformation), angiodysplasia; abnormality of vessels
Gefäßmittelhautdegeneration f medial degeneration
Gefäßmittelschicht f media, middle coat
Gefäßmittelschichtuntergang m medial muscle necrosis
Gefäßmittelschichtverdickung f medial hypertrophy (thickening)
Gefäßnaht f vascular suture, angiorrhaphy
Gefäßnekrose f vascular necrosis, angionecrosis
Gefäßnerv m vasomotor nerve
gefäßnervengelähmt angioparalytic
gefäßnervenhemmend vasoinhibitory
Gefäß-Nerven-Kanal m **im Unterkiefer** mandibular (inferior dental) canal
gefäßnervenlähmend angioparalytic
Gefäßnervenlähmung f/**inkomplette** angioparesis
~/komplette angioparalysis
Gefäßnervenreflex m vasomotor reflex
Gefäßnervenschmerz m angioneuralgia
Gefäßnervensystem n vasomotor system
Gefäßnervenversorgung f blood-vessel innervation
Gefäßnervenzentrum n vasomotor centre
Gefäßnetz n vascular net[work]
Gefäßneuanordnung f neovasculature
Gefäßneubildung f [neo]vascularization, angiopoiesis, vasculogenesis, vasifaction, vasoformation
Gefäßneurose f angioneurosis, vasoneurosis, vasomotor neurosis, neurangiosis
gefäßneurotisch angioneurotic
Gefäßneuversorgung f neovasculature
Gefäßneuverteilung f neovasculature
Gefäßnoma n angionoma
Gefäßobliteration f vascular (vessel) obliteration, angiolysis
Gefäßpathologie f angiopathology
Gefäßperfusion f vascular perfusion
Gefäßperipherie f peripheral vascular region
Gefäßpermeabilität f vascular permeability
Gefäßpermeabilitätsstörung f dyshoria
Gefäßpfropf m embolus, plug (Zusammensetzungen s. unter Embolus)
Gefäßpinzette f vascular forceps
Gefäßplastik f angioplasty
Gefäßpolyp m vascular polyp
Gefäßpulsation f vasomotion
Gefäßreflex m vascular reflex, vasoreflex
gefäßreich vascular, rich in blood vessels
Gefäßreichtum m vascularity
~/pulmonaler pulmonary vascularity
Gefäßring m vascular ring
Gefäßröntgenbild n angiogram
Gefäßröntgen[kontrast]darstellung f angiography
~/intrakranielle intracranial angiography
~ nach Pharmakagabe pharmacoangiography
Gefäßröntgenkontrastschichtbild n angiotomogram
Gefäßröntgen[kontrast]schichtdarstellung f angiotomography
Gefäßröntgenologe f angiographer
Gefäßruptur f vascular rupture, angiorrhexis
Gefäßsarkom n vascular sarcoma, angiosarcoma

gefäßschädigend

gefäßschädigend vasculotoxic
Gefäßschatten m vascular shadow, ghost vessel
Gefäßscheide f [vascular] sheath
Gefäßschere f vascular (vessel) scissors
Gefäßschicht f vascular layer
gefäßschichtend angiotomographic
Gefäßschlinge f vascular loop
Gefäßschmerz m angialgia, angiodynia, vascular pain
Gefäßschwäche f angiasthenia
Gefäßschwamm m angioma
Gefäßschwund m vascular atrophy
Gefäßsklerose f angiosclerosis, vascular sclerosis
gefäßsklerotisch angiosclerotic
Gefäßskotom n angioscotoma *(Sehstörung durch Blutgefäßschatten)*
Gefäß-Spatel-Dissektor m vascular spatula-dissector
Gefäßspülkanüle f vessel irrigating cannula
Gefäßstamm m vascular trunk
Gefäßstauung f vascular congestion (stasis)
Gefäßstein m angiolith
Gefäßstiel m vascular pedicle
Gefäßstiellappen m vascular flap
gefäßstimulierend vasostimulant
Gefäßstörung f vascular disturbance
Gefäßstumpf m vascular stump
Gefäßsystem n vascular system
~/**kapazitives** s. System/venöses
gefäßtonisierend angiotonic
Gefäßtonus m vascular tonus, tone of the vessels
Gefäßtonusverlust m angiasthenia
Gefäßtransplantation f vascular transplantation
Gefäßulkus n, **Gefäßulzeration** f angionoma
Gefäß- und Fasergeschwulst f angiofibroma
Gefäß- und Fettgeschwulst f angiolipoma
Gefäß- und Nervendurchtrennung f[/operative] angioneurotomy
Gefäßunterbindung f vascular ligature, vasoligation, vasoligature
Gefäßverarmung f devascularization, devasation
Gefäßverengerer m vasoconstrictor [agent], vasopressor
gefäßverengernd vasoconstrictor, vasoconstrictive, vasohypertonic; angiostenotic
Gefäßvereng[er]ung f vasoconstriction, angiohypertonia; angiostenosis
Gefäßvergrößerung f angiomegaly
gefäßverhärtend s. gefäßwandverhärtend
Gefäßverkalkung f angiosclerosis, vascular sclerosis
Gefäßverkochung f angiodiathermy
Gefäßverlagerung f angiectopia
Gefäßverlauf m/**abnormer** angiectopia
Gefäßverletzung f vascular lesion (injury), [blood-]vessel trauma
Gefäßverschluß m vascular occlusion, obstruction (blockage, plugging) of a vessel
~/**embolischer** embolism

Gefäßversorgung f vascular supply, vascularization, vasculature
~/**pulmonale** pulmonary vasculature
Gefäßverteilung f vascular distribution, vasculature
Gefäßwand f [blood-]vessel wall
Gefäßwanddurchtritt m **der Blutzellen** diapedesis, emigration
Gefäßwandnekrose f angionecrosis
Gefäßwandschicht f coat, layer, tunica
~/**mittlere** media, middle coat
gefäßwandverhärtet angiosclerotic
Gefäßwandverhärtet angiosclerotic
Gefäßwandverhärtung f angiosclerosis
Gefäßwiderstand m vascular (blood-vessel) resistance
~/**peripherer** peripheral vascular resistance, afterload
gefäßwiederherstellend angioplastic
Gefäßwiederherstellung f angioplasty
gefäßwirksam vasoactive, angiotropic
Gefäßzerfall m angiolysis
Gefäßzusammenziehung f vasoconstriction
gefeit sein to be immune (resistant)
gefingert digitate
Geflecht n reticulum; plexus *(z. B. von Nerven)*; network
~/**Remaksches** Remak's plexus
Geflechtknochen m network bone
gefleckt spotted, speckled, blotched, marbled; naevose
Geflügelpest f/**atypische** avian pseudoplague (pneumoencephalitis), Newcastle disease
geflügelt winged, alate
geformt/normal eumorphic
gefräßig greedy, voracious
Gefräßigkeit f greediness, voracity, polyphagia, acoria
gefrieren to freeze, to congeal
Gefrierfrischplasma n fresh frozen plasma
gefriergetrocknet freeze-dried
Gefrierpunktbestimmung f cryoscopy
Gefrierpunktmesser m cryoscope
Gefrierschnitt m frozen section *(Histologie)*
Gefrierschnittdiagnose f frozen section diagnosis
Gefrierschnittechnik f frozen section technique
Gefrierschnittmikrotom n freezing (freeze) microtome, cryotome
Gefrierschnittuntersuchung f frozen section study (examination)
Gefrierstopptechnik f freeze-stop[ping] technique
gefriertrocknen to freeze-dry, to lyophilize
Gefriertrockner m freeze dryer
Gefriertrocknung f freeze drying, dry freezing, lyophilization
Gefühl n feeling, sensation *(Sinneswahrnehmung)*; feeling, sentiment *(Empfindung)*; emotion
gefühllos insensible, insensitive, senseless, apathetic, indifferent *(z. B. Psyche)*; anaesthetized *(betäubt)*; numb, dead *(z. B. Gliedmaße)*

Gefühllosigkeit f insensibility, unfeelingness, insensitivity, apathy, indifference *(z. B. der Psyche)*; anaesthesia *(Betäubung)*; numbness *(z. B. der Gliedmaßen)*
~ der Gliedmaßenenden acroanaesthesia
gefühlsbedingt affective
Gefühlsbewegung f emotion
Gefühlserregung f emotional excitement
Gefühlsherabminderung f obtusion
Gefühlskälte f/**weibliche** frigidity
Gefühlslähmung f paranaesthesia, sensory paralysis
Gefühlsleben n emotional life
Gefühlslehre f aesthesiology
gefühlsmäßig 1. emotional, emotive, affective; 2. instinctive, instinctual
Gefühlsreaktion f emotional reaction
Gefühlsregung f emotion
Gefühlsstörung f dysaesthesia, paraphia
~/halbseitige hemihypaesthesia
Gefühlsverarmung f emotional flattening
Gefühlsverkehrung f parathymia
Gefühlsverlust m loss of sensation
Gefühlsverminderung f paranaesthesia
geführt/im Arzneibuch official
gegabelt bifurcate[d], branched, forked
Gegenanzeige f contraindication, counterindication *(z. B. bei Therapie)*
Gegend f region *(z. B. des Körpers)*; area *(z. B. der Haut)*
Gegendruck m counterpressure
Gegenenzym n antienzyme
gegenfärben to counterstain
Gegenfärbung f counterstain, differential staining *(Histologie)*
Gegenferment n antiferment *(gärungshemmendes Mittel)*
Gegengift n antidote; antitoxin, counterpoison, toxolysin, toxinicide
Gegengiftbehandlung f toxitherapy
gegenindiziert sein to be contraindicated
Gegeninzision f counterincision, counteropening, counterpuncture
gegenläufig antidromic *(z. B. ein Nerv)*
Gegenmittel n antidote *(s. a. Gegengift)*
Gegenperistaltik f antiperistalsis
Gegenpulsation f counterpulsation *(durch intraaortale Ballonpumpe)*
Gegenreflex m antagonistic reflex
Gegenreiz m contrastimulus, counter-irritant impulse
Gegenschlag m contrecoup, counterstroke
Gegenschock m countershock
Gegenschockbehandlung f countershock therapy (treatment)
Gegenspieler[muskel] m antagonist, antagonistic muscle
Gegenstandsrelation f object relationship
Gegenstoß m counterstroke, counterblow, contrecoup
Gegenstoß[schädel]knochenbruch m contrecoup fracture, contrafissura, counterfissure

gegenüberstellend opponens
Gegenüberstellung f comparison *(z. B. von Symptomen)*
Gegenwirker m antagonist
Gegenwirkung f counteraction, antagonism, antagonistic action
Gegenzug m counterextension, countertraction *(Knochenextension unter Zug in entgegengesetzten Richtungen)*
geheilt werden to be cured
gehemmt backward, mentally retarded; inhibited; frustrated *(Psychologie)*; restrained *(Physiologie)*
gehen/an Krücken to go on crutches, to crutch
~/in Lösung to go into solution, to dissolve; to lyse *(z. B. Bakterien)*
Gehgestell n horse *(Chirurgie)*
Gehgips m walking cast
Gehirn n brain, cerebrum, encephalon ● **mit großem ~** macrencephalous, macrencephalic ● **mit kleinem ~** micrencephalous, micrencephalic ● **mit windungslosem ~** lissencephalous, lissencephalic ● **unter dem ~** subcerebral
~/abnorm großes macrencephalon, megalencephalon
~/kleines micrencephalon
Gehirn... s. a. **Hirn...** und **Zerebral...**
Gehirnangiogramm n cerebral (brain) angiogram
Gehirnangiographie f cerebral (brain) angiography
gehirnartig encephaloid
gehirnbeschädigt brain-damaged, brain-injured
Gehirnbrücke f [Varolian] pons *(Hirnteil oberhalb des verlängerten Rückenmarks)* ● **über der ~** suprapontine
Gehirnentwicklung f cephalogenesis
Gehirnerschütterung f cerebral commotion, brain concussion, concussion of the brain
Gehirnfehlbildung f encephalodysplasia
Gehirngrippe f herpes [simplex] encephalitis, herpetic encephalitis, von Economo's disease
Gehirnhaut f s. Hirnhaut
Gehirnhautentzündung f meningitis, inflammation of the meninges, brain fever *(s. a. unter Meningitis)*; duritis, pachymeningitis
~/abakterielle (aseptische) abacterial (aseptic) meningitis, sterile (simple, virus, epidemic serous) meningitis
~ durch Meningokokken meningococcal meningitis
~/eitrige purulent (pyogenic, suppurative) meningitis
~/idiopathische s. ~/abakterielle
Gehirnhauterkrankung f meningopathy
Gehirnhemisphäre f [cerebral] hemisphere
Gehirnhemisphärendominanz f cerebral dominance
Gehirnhernie f cephalocele
Gehirnhypertrophie f macr[o]encephalia, cerebral (brain) hypertrophy
Gehirnhypotrophie f micr[o]encephalia, cerebral (brain) hypotrophy

Gehirnhypoxie

Gehirnhypoxie f cerebral (brain) anoxia
Gehirninfarzierung f cerebral infarct[ion], cerebrovascular (cerebral vascular) accident, [cerebral] apoplexy, [apoplectic] stroke
Gehirnischämie f cerebral (brain) ischemia
Gehirnkalkulus m encephalolith
Gehirnkompression f cerebral (brain) compression
Gehirnkontusion f cerebral (brain) contusion
Gehirnkrankheit f [en]cephalopathy, cerebropathy, cerebral (brain) disease
~ **der Boxer** boxer's encephalopathy
gehirnlos brainless, anencephalous, [pant]anencephalic
Gehirnlosigkeit f anencephalia
Gehirnmetabolismus m cerebral (brain) metabolism
Gehirnmetastase f cerebral (brain) metastasis
Gehirnminutenblutvolumen n cerebral blood flow
Gehirnperfusion f cerebral (brain) perfusion
Gehirnphysiologie f cerebrophysiology, cerebral physiology
Gehirnröntgen[kontrast]bild n encephalogram
Gehirnröntgen[kontrast]darstellung f encephalography
Gehirn-Rückenmark-Flüssigkeit f cerebro[spinal] fluid, CSF, subarachnoid fluid
Gehirn-Rückenmark-Nervenwurzelentzündung f encephalomyeloradiculitis
Gehirn-Rückenmark-Nervenwurzelerkrankung f encephalomyeloradiculopathy
Gehirnsand m brain sand, acervulus, sabulum
Gehirnschädel m cerebral cranium, neurocranium, brain case, brainpan
Gehirnschaden m brain damage
Gehirnschädigung f s. 1. Gehirnverletzung; 2. Gehirnschaden
Gehirnschwund m encephalatrophy, cerebral (brain) atrophy
Gehirnspiegel m encephaloscope
Gehirnspiegelung f encephaloscopy
Gehirnspinnwebenhaut f arachnoid [of the brain]
Gehirnszintigramm n cerebral scintigram, brain scintiscan
Gehirnszintigraphie f cerebral scintigraphy, brain scanning
Gehirntumor m cerebral (brain) tumour
Gehirn- und Herzmuskelentzündung f encephalomyocarditis
Gehirn- und Hirnhautbruch m encephalomeningocele, meningo-encephalocele
Gehirn- und Hirnhautentzündung f encephalomeningitis, meningo-encephalitis, cerebromeningitis
Gehirn- und Hirnhauterkrankung f encephalomeningopathy, meningo-encephalopathy
Gehirn- und Rückenmarkentzündung f encephalomyelitis, myel[o]encephalitis
Gehirn- und Rückenmarkerweichung f encephalomyelosis

Gehirn- und Rückenmarkkrankheit f encephalomyelopathy
Gehirnunterentwicklung f atel[o]encephalia, imperfect brain development
Gehirnunterseite f lower surface of the cerebrum
Gehirnventrikel m s. Hirnkammer
Gehirnventrikulogramm n cerebral (brain) ventriculogram
Gehirnventrikulographie f cerebral (brain) ventriculography
Gehirnvergrößerung f/**abnorme** macr[o]encephalia, megalencephalia
Gehirnverletzung f cerebral lesion (trauma), brain injury
Gehirnwasserbruch m hydro[en]cephalocele
Gehirnwassersucht f hydrocephalia
Gehirnzerlegung f encephalotomy
Gehör n hearing, audition
Gehöranalyse f auditory analysis
Gehörassoziation f auditory association
Gehörempfindlichkeit f acouaesthesia
Gehörfehler m auditory defect; defective hearing
Gehörgang m acoustic meatus (duct), auditory canal (foramen)
~/**äußerer** external acoustic meatus, external ear canal, external auditory foramen, auricular tube, auditory passage
~/**innerer** internal acoustic meatus, internal ear canal, internal auditory foramen
Gehörgangsentzündung f external otitis
Gehörgangsepidermis f ear canal epidermis
Gehörgangsexostose f ear canal exostosis; surfer's ear
Gehörgangshaar n tragus
Gehörgangsknorpel m cartilage of the external acoustic meatus
Gehörgangsnerv m/**äußerer** external acoustic meatal nerve
Gehörgangsspülung f ear-syringing
Gehörgangswattepfropfen m earplug
Gehörgangvene f labyrinthine (internal auditory) vein
Gehörhalluzination f acoasm[a], acousma, auditory hallucination
Gehörknöchelchen n [auditory] ossicle, ossiculum
Gehörknöchelchenaudiometrie f ossicular chain audiometry
Gehörknöchelchenentfernung f[/**operative**] ossiculectomy
Gehörknöchelchenkette f ossicular chain
gehörlos deaf, unable to hear
Gehörloser m deaf person
Gehörlosigkeit f s. Taubheit 1.
Gehörnerv m auditory (acoustic) nerve
Gehörprobe f hearing test
gehörprüfend audiometric
Gehörprüfer m audiometrist
Gehörprüfung f audiometry
Gehörsand m ear dust, otoconia, statoconia, statoliths

Gehörschutzmasse f earplug
Gehörsinn m acouaesthesia, audition
Gehörskunde f audiology
gehörskundlich audiologic[al]
Gehörspezialist m audiologist
Gehörtäuschung f acoasma, auditory (acoustic) halluzination, phoneme
Gehör- und Gleichgewichtsorgan n statoacoustic organ
Gehörverlust m loss of hearing; deafness
Gehstörung f dysbasia, gait disturbance
Gehstrecke f walking range
Gehstütze f [walking] crutch
gehunfähig abasic, abatic, unable to walk
Gehunfähigkeit f abasia
~ **durch Zwangsvorstellungen** stasibasiphobia
geil salacious, lustful, lecherous, lascivious; fast; hot
Geilheit f salacity, lustfulness, lechery, lasciviousness
Geißel f 1. flagellum, cilium; 2. plague, scourge *(Krankheit)*
Geißelantigen n flagellar antigen
Geißelbewegung f flagellation
Geißelbildung f exflagellation
geißelförmig flagelliform
Geißelschlag m flagellation
Geißeltierchenbefall m flagellosis
Geißelzelle f flagellate (ciliated) cell
Geist m 1. mind, intellect, mens *(Verstand)*; 2. spirit, imagination *(Einbildung)*
Geisterfurcht f ph[ant]asmophobia, demonophobia
Geistersehen n phantasmoscopia
Geistesabnormität f mental aberration
geistesabwesend absent-minded
Geistesabwesenheit f absent-mindedness, absence of mind
Geistesanpassung f mental adjustment
Geisteserschöpfung f mental fatigue
geistesgegenwärtig quick-witted
geistesgestört mentally disturbed (deranged, deterioated), abalienated; paranoi[a]c, paranoid
Geistesgestörter m insane, mentally deranged person, lunatic, defective
Geistesgestörtheit f insanity, mental derangement (alienation), lunacy
Geistesgesundheit f sanity
Geistesklarheit f lucidity
geisteskrank insane, of unsound mind, lunatic, suffering from a mental disorder, brain-sick, vesanic; psychotic
Geisteskranker m insane, lunatic mental patient (case); psychotic
Geisteskrankheit f insanity, lunacy, mental disease (illness), folie, alienism; vesania; psychiatric illness, phrenopathy
~/**schwere** idiocy
geistesschwach feeble-minded, oligophrenic, hypophrenic, mentally deficient
~/**mittelgradig** imbecile

Geistesschwäche f feeble-mindedness, craziness, oligophrenia, hypophrenia, oligopsychia, mental deficiency, amentia, anoia, psychoparesis
~/**mittelgradige** imbecility
Geistesschwacher m/**mittelgradig** imbecile
Geistesstörung f mental derangement (aberration, disorder, deterioration); abalienation, alienism, psychiatric illness, psychonosema
~/**affektive** affective disorder (insanity)
~ **bei Kindern** neophrenia
~/**leichte** paraphora
~ **mit Wahnvorstellungen** paranoia
Geistestätigkeit f/**gesteigerte** hyperphrenia
Geistesträgheit f mental dullness (indolence)
Geistestrübung f mental clouding, obnubilation
Geistesüberaktivität f hyperphrenia
Geistesverfassung f mental state (condition)·
geistesverwirrt abalienated; paranoi[a]c, paranoid
Geistesverwirrung f mental confusion (disorder, aberration), abalienation
Geisteszustand m mental state (condition); mentality
~/**klarer** lucidity
~/**krankhafter** [neuro]psychosis
geistig mental, intellectual; psychic
~ **zurückgeblieben** mentally defective
gekapselt/nicht non-encapsulated
geknickt bent; kinked *(z. B. Gefäß)*
gekörnt granular, granulated
gekreuzt crossed, decussate; cruciform
Gekröse n mesentery, mesenterium *(s. a. unter Mesenterium)*
~ **des geraden Darms** mesorectum
~/**kleines** mesenteriolum, small mesentery
Gekröseanheftung f mes[enteri]opexy
Gekröseansatz m mesenteric attachment
Gekrösearterie f mesenteric artery
~/**kaudale** inferior mesenteric artery
~/**kraniale (obere)** superior mesenteric artery
~/**untere** inferior mesenteric artery
Gekrösearterienröntgen[kontrast]darstellung f mesenteric arteriography
Gekrösedivertikel n mesodiverticulum, mesenteric diverticulum
Gekröseentfernung f[/**operative**] mesenterectomy
Gekröseentzündung f s. Mesenteritis
Gekrösefalte f **der inneren Hodenhüllen** mesorchium
Gekrösefaltung f[/**operative**] mesenteriplication
Gekrösefixierung f mesopexy, mesenteriopexy
Gekrösenervengeflecht n mesenteric plexus
Gekröseraffung f mesent[eri]orrhaphy, mesorrhaphy
Gekrösevene f mesenteric vein
~/**kaudale** inferior mesenteric vein
~/**kraniale (obere)** superior mesenteric vein
~/**untere** inferior mesenteric vein
Gekrösevorfall m mesenteric hernia
Gekrösezyste f mesenteric cyst

gekrümmt

gekrümmt curved, bent, gyrate, circumflex; kyphotic *(Rückgrat)*
Gel *n*/**Flüssigkeit enthaltendes** lyogel *(z. B. Gallerte)*
gelähmt paralytic, palsied, paralyzed
~/**an beiden Beinen vollständig** paraplegic, paraplectic
~/**an beiden Beinen unvollständig** paraparetic
~/**teilweise** paretic
Gelähmter *m* paralytic
~/**an beiden Beinen vollständig** paraplegic, paraplectic
gelangen/zur Reife to matur[at]e *(z. B. Keimzellen)*
gelappt lobate[d], lobed, lobular
Gelasma *n* gelasmus
Gelatine *f* gelatin[e]
Gelatineagar *m* gelatin agar
gelatineartig gelatinous, gelatinoid
Gelatinefilm *m* gelatin film *(Wundabdeckung)*
gelatinehaltig gelatinous
Gelatinekapsel *f* gelatin capsule, perle *(Arzneimittelform)*
Gelatineschwamm *m* gelatin sponge (foam)
Gelatinierung *f* gelatin[iz]ation, gelation
gelatinös gelatinous, tremelloid, tremellose
Gelb-Blau-Sehen *n* xanthocyanop[s]ia, xanthokyanopy
Gelbblindheit *f* yellow blindness, axanthopsia
Gelbbraunfärbung *f* xanthochromia *(z. B. der Gehirnflüssigkeit)*
gelbfarbig xanthochrom[at]ic
Gelbfärbung *f* xanthochro[m]ia *(z. B. der Gehirnflüssigkeit)*; auraniasis *(z. B. der Haut)*
Gelbfettkrankheit *f* yellow fat disease, ceroid lipofuscinosis, neurolipidosis
Gelbfieber *n* yellow fever (jack), amarillic typhus
Gelbfieberepidemie *f* yellow fever epidemic
Gelbfieberimpfstoff *m* yellow fever vaccine
Gelbfieberimpfung *f* yellow fever vaccination
Gelbfiebermücke *f* yellow fever mosquito, Aëdes aegypti
Gelbfieberserum *n* antiamarillic serum
Gelbfluß *m* xanthorrhoea, yellow discharge
gelbgefärbt yellow-coloured, xanthochrom[at]ic
Gelbgießerkrankheit *f* brass-founders' fever (disease)
gelbhäutig yellow-skinned, xanthochroous
Gelbhäutiger *m* xanthoderm
Gelbknoten *m* xanthoma
Gelbkörper *m* corpus luteum, luteal corpus, yellow body
~/**hämorrhagischer** haemorrhagic corpus luteum
~/**prägravider** progestional corpus luteum
~/**zystischer** cystic corpus luteum
Gelbkörperabszeß *m* corpus luteum abscess
Gelbkörperbildung *f* luteinization
Gelbkörperfunktion *f* corpus luteum function
Gelbkörperhämatom *n* corpus luteum haematoma
Gelbkörperhormon *n* corpus luteum hormone, luteine hormone

Gelbkörperinsuffizienz *f* corpus luteum insufficiency, luteal corpus insufficiency
Gelbkörpermangelzustand *m* corpus luteum deficiency, luteal corpus deficiency
Gelbkörperphase *f* luteal phase, progestation stage [of the ovarian cycle]
Gelbkörperreifungshormon *n* luteinizing hormone, LH, interstitial-cell-stimulating hormone
Gelbkörperwirkung *f* luteinizing (corpus luteum) effect
Gelbkörperzyste *f* corpus luteum cyst, luteal [corpus] cyst, lutein cyst
Gelbkreuz *n s.* Yperit
Gelbsehen *n* yellow vision, xanthop[s]ia
Gelbsucht *f* 1. icterus, jaundice *(s. a. unter* Ikterus*)*; 2. [hyper]bilirubinaemia ● ~ **bewirkend** icterogenic, icterogenous
~/**epidemische** infectious hepatitis, epidemic jaundice
~/**postvakzinale** postvaccinal jaundice (icterus), serum hepatitis
gelbsuchtartig icteroid
gelbsüchtig icteric, jaundiced
~/**nicht** non-icteric, non-jaundiced
gelbzahnig xanthodontous
Geldiffusionsprobe *f* gel diffusion test
Geldiffusionstechnik *f* gel diffusion technique
Geldrollenbildung *f* nummulation, rouleaux formation, sludging of the blood, intravascular agglutination *(der roten Blutkörperchen)*; blood sludge
Gelegenheitsappendektomie *f* occasional (eventual, incidental) appendectomy
Gelegenheitsparasit *m* occasional (incidental, periodic) parasite
Gelelektrophorese *f* gel electrophoresis
Gelenk *n* articulatio[n], junction, junctura, joint *(s. a. unter* Articulatio*)* ● **ein ~ betreffend** uniarticular, mon[o]articular, monarthric ● **mehrere Gelenke betreffend** multiarticular, polyarticular ● **neben dem ~** juxta-articular ● **über einem ~** supra-articular
~/**Charcotsches** Charcot's joint [disease], Charcot's arthritis (arthropathy), neuropathic joint disease, neurotrophic arthritis, neurogenic arthropathy
~/**Chopartsches** Chopart's joint, midtarsal joint [of Chopart]
~/**ebenes** gliding joint
~/**einachsiges** uniaxial (rotation, pivot) joint
~/**einfaches** simple joint
~/**falsches** false joint, pseudarthrosis, nearthrosis, supplementary articulation
~/**fehlerhaftes** dysarthrosis
~/**mehrachsiges** multiaxial joint (articulation); enarthrosis
~/**zusammengesetztes** compound articulation
~/**zweiachsiges** biaxial (saddle) joint
Gelenkamputation *f* exarticulation, disarticulation
Gelenkaufnahme *f* arthrogram
Gelenkband *n* articular (joint) ligament

Gelenkbeteiligung f articular (joint) involvement
Gelenkbeweglichkeit f articular (joint) mobility
Gelenkbewegung f/**kreisende** circumduction, helicopodia *(z. B. eines gelähmten Beines)*
gelenkbildend arthroplastic, joint-forming
Gelenkbluterguß m haemarthrosis
Gelenkblutung f arthrorrhagia
Gelenkchondrokalzinose f joint (articular) chondrocalcinosis
gelenkdarstellend arthrographic
Gelenkdarstellung f arthrography
Gelenkdeformation f[/**angeborene**] arthrodysplasia
Gelenkdeformität f joint (articular) deformity, dysarthrosis
Gelenkdysplasie f arthrodysplasia
Gelenkeinblutung f arthrorrhagia; haemarthrosis
Gelenkeinrenkung f redressement
Gelenkempfindung f joint (articular) sensation, arthraesthesia
Gelenkempyem n joint (articular) empyema, arthroempyesis
Gelenkentfernung f[/**operative**] arthrectomy
Gelenkentzündung f arthritis *(s. a. unter Arthritis)*
~/**akute eitrige** acute suppurative arthritis
~ **bei Kindern/tuberkulöse** paedarthrocace
~/**eitrige** pyarthrosis, pyogenic (suppurative) arthritis, pyoarthritis
gelenkentzündungshemmend ant[i]arthritic
Gelenkerguß m joint (articular) effusion, hydrarthrosis
~/**blutiger** s. Hämarthros
~/**eitriger** joint (articular) empyema
~/**intermittierender** intermittent hydrarthrosis
Gelenkerkrankung f joint (articular) disease, arthropathy
~/**degenerative** degenerative joint disease, osteoarthrosis
Gelenkeröffnung f[/**operative**] arthrotomy
Gelenkersatz m articular (joint) replacement
Gelenkfehlbildung f arthrodysplasia
Gelenkfehlstellung f malarticulation
gelenkfern abarticular
Gelenkfett[körper]entzündung f lipo-arthritis
Gelenkfistelung f[/**operative**] arthrostomy
Gelenkfläche f joint (articular) surface
Gelenkflüssigkeit f synovial fluid, synovia
Gelenkfortsatz m joint (articular) process
~/**oberer** superior articular process
~/**unterer** inferior articular process
Gelenkfraktur f joint (articular) fracture, intracapsular fracture
Gelenkfungus m joint (articular) fungus; fungous arthritis (synovitis)
Gelenkfusion f s. Gelenkversteifung/operative
Gelenkgefühl n joint (articular) sensation
Gelenkgicht f gouty arthritis
Gelenkhaut f synovial membrane (capsule), synovialis, synovium
Gelenkhautentzündung f [arthro]synovitis *(Zusammensetzungen s. unter Synovitis)*

Gelenkhöcker m epicondyle, epicondylus, supracondylar eminence
Gelenkhöhle f articular cavity, joint space
Gelenkinnenhautentzündung f s. Gelenkhautentzündung
Gelenkinnenhautzotte f synovial villus
Gelenkinzision f arthrocentesis
Gelenkkapsel f joint (articular) capsule, capsular ligament
Gelenkkapselrekonstruktion f capsuloplasty
Gelenkknorpel m articular (investing) cartilage, [di]arthrodial cartilage
Gelenkknorpelentzündung f arthrochondritis
Gelenkknorpelverkalkung f joint (articular) chondrocalcinosis
Gelenkknorren m condyle
Gelenkknorrenschnitt m condylotomy
Gelenkkopf m condyle, condylus, caput
Gelenkkörper m arthrophyte *(durch Wachstum entstanden)*
~/**freier** joint body (mouse), articular calculus
~/**knorpeliger** floating cartilage
gelenkkrank arthropathic
Gelenklehre f arthrology
Gelenklippe f **am Hüftgelenk** acetabular labrum
~ **am Oberarmgelenk** glenoid labrum (lip)
Gelenkmaus f s. Gelenkkörper/freier
Gelenkmeniskus m joint (articular) meniscus
Gelenkmesser n arthrotome
Gelenkmobilisation f[/**operative**] arthrolysis, arthroclasia, arthroclasis
Gelenkmuskel m articular (joint) muscle
gelenknah juxta-articular
Gelenknerv m articular (joint) nerve
Gelenknervenkörperchen npl articular (joint) corpuscles
Gelenkneubildung f ne[o]arthrosis, pseudarthrosis, supplementary articulation
~/**operative** arthroplasty
Gelenkpfanne f articular fossa, socket
Gelenkplastik f arthroplasty
Gelenkpunktion f arthrocentesis, puncture of a joint
Gelenkraum m articular (joint) space
Gelenkreißen n s. Gelenkrheumatismus
Gelenkrekonstruktion f arthroplasty
Gelenkresektion f arthrectomy
Gelenkrezeptor m joint receptor
Gelenkrheumatismus m articular (joint) rheumatism, rheumatic arthritis, rheumarthritis
~/**akuter** acute articular rheumatism
~/**tuberkulöser** s. Gelenktuberkulose
Gelenkriegel m arthroereisis, arthrorisis
Gelenkriegelbildung f/**operative** arthroereisis, arthrorisis
Gelenkröntgen[kontrast]bild n nach Lufteinblasung pneum[o]arthrogram
Gelenkröntgen[kontrast]darstellung f nach Lufteinblasung pneum[o]arthrography
Gelenkscheibe f 1. joint (articular) disk; 2. s. Meniscus
Gelenkschleimhaut f s. Gelenkhaut

Gelenkschmerz

Gelenkschmerz *m* articular (joint) pain, arthralgia, arthrodynia
Gelenkschmiere *f* synovia, synovial fluid ● ~ **bildend** synoviparous
Gelenkschwellung *f* articular (joint) swelling
Gelenkspalt *m* articular (joint) cavity
Gelenkspiegel *m* arthroscope
gelenkspiegelnd arthroscopic
Gelenkspiegelung *f* arthro[endo]scopy
Gelenkspiel *n* joint play
Gelenksteifigkeit *f* articular (joint) stiffness, arthrosclerosis
Gelenkstein *m* arthrolith
Gelenkstruktur *f* articular (joint) structure
Gelenkszintigraphie *f* articular (joint) scintigraphy
Gelenkteilresektion *f* arthrectomy
Gelenktuberkulose *f* tuberculous arthritis (rheumatism)
Gelenktumor *m* articular (joint) tumour, arthroncus
Gelenküberbeugung *f* [articular] overflexion, [joint] hyperflexion
Gelenkvereiterung *f* articular (joint) suppuration, pyogenic (suppurative) arthritis, arthroempyesis, py[o]arthrosis
Gelenkverkrümmung *f* loxarthrosis
Gelenkverletzung *f* joint lesion (injury), articular trauma
Gelenkverrenkung *f* articular (joint) dislocation, abarticulation
~/**habituelle** habitual dislocation
~/**sich häufig wiederholende** recurrent (relapsing) dislocation
Gelenkversteifung *f* ankylosis, arthrofibrosis, arthrosclerosis
~ **infolge Muskelkontraktur** arthrogryposis
~/**knöcherne** bony ankylosis
~/**künstliche** syndesis
~/**operative** [joint] arthrodesis, articular (joint) fusion, [operative] ankylosis
~/**partielle** partial ankylosis
Gelenkwassersucht *f* hydrarthrosis, articular dropsy
Gelenkwinkelmesser *m* arthrometer
Gelenkwinkelmessung *f* arthrometry
Gelenkzottenentfernung *f*[/**operative**] villusectomy
Gelenkzugang *m*/**hinterer** posterior approach to the joint
~/**vorderer** anterior approach to the joint
Gelenkzwischenknorpel *m s.* Meniscus
Gel-Filtration-Separationstechnik *f* gel filtration separation technique
Gelierung *f* gelation, gelatin[iz]ation
Gelkontaktlinse *f*/**hydrophile** hydrophilic gel contact lens
Gelose *f* gelose, gelosis
Gel-Sol-Umwandlung *f* peptization
Gelverflüssigung *f* gel liquefaction, peptization
Gemeindeschwester *f* community [health] nurse, public health nurse, district (visiting) nurse
Gemeinsinn *m*/**mangelnder** asociality
gemischterbig heterozygous
Gemischterbigkeit *f* heterozygosity
Gemüt *n* 1. mind; emotion, feeling *(Gefühl)*; 2. *s.* Gemütsart
gemütsarm hypoaffective, hypoemotional
Gemütsart *f* nature, cast of mind, temperament
Gemütsbewegung *f* emotion
~/**kurzzeitige heftige** affect
gemütskrank mentally (emotionally) disordered; melancholic; depressed
Gemütskranker *m* emotionally disturbed person
Gemütskrankheit *f* mental disorder, disorder of the mind, emotional disturbance; melancholia; depression; thymopathy
Gemütslage *f* mood, mental condition, emotional stage
~/**depressive** mood depression
Gemütsschwankung *f* emotional lability
Gemütsverfassung *f s.* Gemütslage
Gen *n* gene
~/**an das X-Chromosom gebundenes** X-linked gene
Gena *f* gena, mala, cheek, jowl, bucca
Genänderung *f* mutation *(sprunghafte erbliche Merkmalsänderung)*
Genbestand *m* genom[e]
Genduplikation *f* gene duplication
geneigt inclined, tilted; lox[ot]ic
Generation *f* generation ● **mehrere Generationen einer Familie betreffend** multifamilial
Generationswechsel *m* alternation of generations, heterogenesis, metagenesis
Generationszeit *f* generation time
generativ generative
Generatorpotential *n* generator (receptor) potential
Genese *f* genesis ● **unbekannter** ~ of undetermined origin
genesen to convalesce, to recover, to recuperate
genesend convalescent, recuperative
Genesender *m* convalescent [patient]
Genesung *f* convalescence, recovery, recuperation, healing, cure, restoration; decubation *(von einer Infektionskrankheit)*
Genesungsheim *n* sanatorium, convalescent home
Genesungskur *f* convalescent cure
Genesungsstadium *n* convalescent stage
Genesungsstation *f* recovery ward
Genetik *f* genetics, genesiology
Genetiker *m* geneticist
genetisch genetic
Genick *n* nucha, nape [of the neck]
Genickstarre *f* neck rigidity; stiffening of the neck
Geniculum *n* geniculum
~ **nervi facialis** external genu facialis (of the facialis nerve)
Genie *n* genius
Genin *n* genin, aglycon[e]
Genion *n* genion *(anthropologischer Meßpunkt)*

Gerinnbarkeit

Genisolierung f gene isolation
genital genital
Genitalband n genital cord
Genitale n genital
Genitalfalte f genital (gonadal, sexual) fold
Genitalfurche f genital furrow
Genitalgrube f genital fossa
Genitalherpes m genital herpes
Genitalhöcker m genital eminence, cloacal tubercle (hillock)
Genitalien npl genitalia, genitals, genital (reproductive, sex) organs *(Zusammensetzungen s. unter Geschlechtsorgane)*
Genitalkörperchen npl genital corpuscles
Genitalleiste f genital ridge
Genitalmuskel m/äußerer ischiocavernosus [muscle]
Genitalnerv m genital nerve
Genitalpapille f genital papilla
Genitalreflex m genital (sexual, coital) reflex
Genitalschmerz m genital pain, pudendagra
Genitalschwellung f genital swelling
Genitalsystem n genital system
Genitalsysteminfektion f genital system infection
Genitaltrakt m genital tract
Genitalüberentwicklung f hypergenitalism, macrogenitalism
Genitalunterentwicklung f hypogenitalism, microgenitalism
Genitalverschluß m infibulation
Genitalwulst m genital torus
Genitokruralfalte f genitocrural fold
Genkarte f genetic map
Genkopplung f gene[etic] coupling
Genlokalisation f genetic mapping
Genmanipulation f genetic manipulation
Genmutation f gene mutation
Genmutationsrate f gene mutation rate
Genoblast m genoblast
Genodermatose f genodermatosis
Genom n genom[e]
Genommutation f genome mutation
Genopathie f genopathy
Genotyp m genotype
genotypisch genotypical
Genpaar n allel[e]
Gen-Pool m gene pool
Genrepression f gene repression
Gensatz m genome
Genstruktur f gene structure
Gensynthese f gene synthesis
Gentianaviolett n gentian violet
Gentianaviolett-Färbung f gentian violet stain
Genträger m gene carrier
Gentransfer m gene transfer
Gentransplantation f gene transplantation
Genu n knee, genu *(s. a. unter Knie)*
~ capsulae internae knee of the internal capsule
~ nervi facialis internal genu facialis (of the facialis nerve)
~ recurvatum back knee
~ valgum knock-knee, in-knee, baker leg; gonycrotesis
~ varum bowleg, out-knee, bandy leg; gonyectyposis
Genübertragung f [genetic] transmission, genetic transfer
~/autosomal-dominante autosomal dominant transmission
~/autosomal-rezessive autosomal recessive transmission
genunterdrückend epistatic
Genunterdrückung f gene suppression, epistasis
Geographie f/medizinische noso[chthono]graphy *(Lehre von der geographischen und klimatischen Verbreitung der Krankheiten)*
Geomedizin f geomedicine
Geophagie f geophagy, geophagism
Geraderichten n orthosis *(einer Deformierung)*
geradfingrig orthodactylous
geradlinig 1. [recti]linear, lineal; 2. lineal *(Abstammung)*
Geräusch n noise, sound; murmur *(Nebengeräusch z. B. am Herzen)*; souffle *(z. B. bei der Auskultation)*; rale, rattle *(Atemgeräusch)*
~/akzidentelles accidental murmur
~/arterielles arterial murmur
~/blasendes souffle
~/diastolisches diastolic murmur
~/diastolisch-systolisches continous (systolic-diastolic) murmur
~/funktionelles functional murmur, inorganic (physiological, innocent) murmur *(z. B. Herzgeräusch)*
~/Graham-Steelsches Graham-Steel murmur
~/keuchendes wheezing sound
~/murmelndes murmur
~/objektives objective tinnitus
~/organisches organic murmur
~/pfeifendes whistling murmur
~/rauhes systolisches coarse systolic murmur
~/respiratorisches respiratory murmur (sound)
~/systolisches systolic murmur (bruit)
Geräuschschwelle f noise threshold
Geräuschwahn m acousma, acoasma, auditory halluzination
Gerbsäure f tannic acid *(Hautgerbungsmittel)*
gereizt irritated *(psychisch)*; stimulated *(z. B. Muskel)*
Gereiztheit f irritation; irritability
Geriatrie f geriatrics, geriatric medicine, presby[ti]atrics
Geriatrikum n geriatric [agent]
geriatrisch geriatric
Geriatrist m geriatrician, geriatrist
Gerichtsmedizin f forensic (legal, state) medicine, medical jurisprudence
gerichtsmedizinisch forensic, medicolegal
gerinnbar coagulable, congealable
~/leicht hypercoagulable
~/nicht incoagulable
~/schlecht hypocoagulable
Gerinnbarkeit f coagulability
~/erhöhte hypercoagulability *(z. B. des Blutes)*
~/verminderte hypocoagulability *(z. B. des Blutes)*

gerinnen 278

gerinnen to coagulate, to clot
~ lassen to denaturate *(Eiweiß)*
gerinnend coagulative
Gerinnsel *n* coagulum, clot, thrombus *(Zusammensetzungen s. unter Thrombus)*
Gerinnsel... *s. a.* Thrombus... *und* Blutgerinnsel...
gerinnselartig clot-like, thrombus-like, thromboid
Gerinnselausschwemmung *f* embolaemia
Gerinnselbeobachtung *f* clot observation test
gerinnselbildend thrombogenic
Gerinnselbildung *f* clot formation, coagulum production; embolaemia; thrombosis
Gerinnselretraktion *f* clot retraction
Gerinnselretraktionszeit *f* clot retraction time
Gerinnung *f* coagulation, congelation; coagulation, blood clotting, clotting of blood; pectization *(Kolloidchemie)* ● **~ bewirkend** coagulant
~/disseminierte intravaskuläre disseminated intravascular coagulation
Gerinnungsablaufkurve *f* thrombelastogram *(des Bluts)*
gerinnungsaktiv coagulation-promoting
Gerinnungsdefekt *m* coagulation defect; defective coagulation
gerinnungsfähig coagulable, congealable, able to clot
Gerinnungsfähigkeit *f* coagulability, congealability
Gerinnungsfaktor *m s.* Blutgerinnungsfaktor
Gerinnungshäutchen *n* buffy coat
gerinnungshemmend anticoagulant, anticoagulative
Gerinnungshemmung *f* anticoagulation
Gerinnungskaskade *f* coagulation cascade
Gerinnungskrankheit *f* coagulopathy
Gerinnungslabor[atorium] *n* coagulation laboratory
Gerinnungsmangel *m* [blood] coagulation deficiency
Gerinnungsmechanismus *m* coagulation mechanism
Gerinnungsmittel *n* coagulant [agent]
Gerinnungsneigung *f/*erhöhte hypercoagulability
Gerinnungsnekrose *f* coagulation necrosis
Gerinnungsschwäche *f* hypocoagulability
Gerinnungsstörung *f* coagulation disorder, clotting disturbance
~ bei Giftschlangenbiß envenomation coagulopathy
Gerinnungssystem *n* coagulation system
Gerinnungsthrombus *m* agglutinative thrombus
Gerinnungsuntersuchung *f* coagulation (clotting) study
Gerinnungsverlängerung *f* coagulation delay
Gerinnungsvitamin *n* coagulation vitamin
Gerinnungszeit *f* coagulation (clotting) time
Gerippe *n* skeleton
Germektomie *f* germectomy
Germinom *n* germinoma
Germizid *n* germicide [agent]

Geröchel *n* rattle *(Atemgeräusch)*
Geroderma *n* geroderma; gerodermia
Gerodontie *f*, **Gerodontologie** *f* gerodontia
Geromorphismus *m* geromorphism
geröntgt werden to be X-rayed
Gerontogenese *f* gerontogenesis
Gerontologe *m* gerontologist
Gerontologie *f* gerontology, nostology
gerontologisch gerontological
Gerontopsychiatrie *f* gerontopsychiatry
Gerontoxon *n* gerontoxon, senile (lipoid) arcus
Gerstenkorn *n* hordeolum, sty[e]
~/äußeres external hordeolum *(Eiterbildung in den Zeissschen Liddrüsen)*
~/inneres internal hordeolum, Meibomian stye *(Eiterbildung in den Meibomschen Liddrüsen)*
Geruch *m* smell, odour; scent *(Duft)*
~/übler foetor; bad breath *(Mundgeruch)*
geruchlos odourless, scentless
Geruchsabneigung *f* osmodysphoria, osphresiophobia
~/krankhafte olfactophobia
Geruchsangst *f* osmophobia
Geruchsaura *f* olfactory aura *(z. B. Geruchssensation bei epileptischem Anfall)*
Geruchsbeschreibung *f* odorography
geruchsbeseitigend deodorant
Geruchsblindheit *f* [central] anosmia, olfactory anaesthesia
Geruchsdefekt *m* hyposmia, hyposphresia
Geruchsdysfunktion *f* olfactory (smell) dysfunction
Geruchsempfindlichkeit *f* olfactory sensibility, osmaesthesia
Geruchsempfindung *f*/schlechte cacosmia
Geruchsfälschung *f* parosmia, parosphresis
Geruchshalluzination *f* olfactory hallucination; parosmia, parosphresis
Geruchsknospe *f* olfactory bud
Geruchsmukosa *f* olfactory mucosa (mucous membrane)
Geruchsnerv *m* olfactory nerve
Geruchsorgan *n* olfactory organ
Geruchsschleimhautregion *f* olfactory mucosal region
Geruchsschwäche *f* hyposmia, hyposphresia
Geruchssinn *m* olfaction, smell, sense of smelling, osphresis, rhinaesthesia ● **ohne ~** anosm[at]ic
Geruchssinndysfunktion *f* olfactory dysfunction
Geruchssinnepithel *n* olfactory epithelium
Geruchssinn[hirn]lappen *m* olfactory lobe
Geruchssinnmesser *m* olfactometer, osmometer, osphresiometer
Geruchssinnprüfung *f* olfactometry
Geruchssinnschärfe *f* olfactory (smell) acuity
Geruchssinnwindung *f* olfactory gyrus
Geruchssinnzelle *f* olfactory cell
Geruchsstärkemesser *m* odorimeter
Geruchsstärkemessung *f* odorimetry *(einer Substanz)*

Geruchsstörung f olfactory disturbance, disorder of smell, dysosmia; parosmia, parosphresis
Geruchssystem n olfactory system (apparatus)
Geruchstäuschung f olfactory hallucination; parosmia, parosphresis
Geruchsüberempfindlichkeit f hyperosmia, oxyosmia, oxyosphresia
Geruchsunterempfindlichkeit f hyposmia, hyposphresia
Geruchsunvermögen n anosmia, olfactory anaesthesia
geruchsverhindernd deodorant
Geruchsverlust m anosmia, anosphrasia, anosphresia
~/**teilweiser** merosmia
Geruchsvermögen n/**gesteigertes** hyperosmia
~/**herabgesetztes** hyposmia, hyposphresia
Geruchsvorbote m s. Geruchsaura
Geruchszelle f olfactory cell
gerunzelt rugose, rugous, wrinkled
Gerüsteiweiß n scleroprotein, albuminoid
Gerüstsubstanz f paraplastic substance
Gesamtazidität f total acidity
Gesamtbefinden n general state of health
Gesamtbilirubin n total bilirubin
Gesamtdosis f total dose; total dosage, integrated dose *(Radiologie)*
Gesamteindruck m general aspect *(eines Kranken)*
Gesamteiweiß n total [serum] protein
Gesamtenergiebedarf m total energy requirement
Gesamtflüssigkeitsaufnahme f total fluid intake
Gesamtflüssigkeitsausscheidung f total fluid output
Gesamtheit f **der Körperzellen** soma
Gesamtkörperwasser n total body water
Gesamtleukozyten mpl, **Gesamtleukozytenzahl** f total leucocyte (white) count
Gesamtsauerstoffbedarf m total oxygen demand
Gesamtserumcholesterin n total serum cholesterol
Gesamtstrahlenbelastung f cumulative radiation dose *(Radiologie)*
Gesamturinmenge f total urine volume (output)
Gesäß n buttocks, rump, breech, posterior[s]
Gesäßarterie f/**obere** superior gluteal artery
~/**untere** inferior gluteal artery
Gesäßbacken fpl clunes, nates; buttocks, breech
Gesäßfalte f, **Gesäßfurche** f 1. gluteal sulcus (fold), sulcus gluteus; 2. gluteal furrow, gluteal (internatal) cleft, anal crena
Gesäßhernie f ischiadic (sciatic) hernia
Gesäßmuskel m gluteus [muscle], gluteal muscle
~/**großer** gluteus maximus [muscle]
~/**kleiner** gluteus minimus [muscle]
~/**mittlerer** gluteus medius [muscle]
Gesäßmuskelleiste f gluteal ridge
Gesäßmuskelreflex m gluteal reflex
Gesäßmuskulatur f gluteal musculature (muscles)

Gesäßreflex m gluteal reflex
Gesäßschmerz m pygalgia, pain in the buttocks
Gesäßspalte f s. Gesäßfalte 2.
Gesäßvene f/**obere** superior gluteal vein
~/**untere** inferior gluteal vein
geschäftig hyperpragic, busy, active
geschichtet laminar, laminated, layered, stratified
geschlängelt cirsoid, gyrate, sinuous, convoluted, tortuous
Geschlecht n 1. sex; 2. race, species ● **männlichen Geschlechts** masculine, male ● **sich zum anderen ~ hinwendend** heterosexual ● **sich zum gleichen ~ hinwendend** homosexual; invert ● **weiblichen Geschlechts** feminine, female
geschlechtlich 1. sexual; generic, gamic; 2. venereal
Geschlechtlichkeit f sexuality
Geschlechts... s. a. Sexual...
Geschlechtsakt m sexual act (intercourse), coition, coitus
Geschlechtsambiguität f sexual ambiguity
Geschlechtsausbildung f sex[ual] differentiation
Geschlechtsband n genital cord
geschlechtsbestimmend sex-determining *(Chromosom)*
Geschlechtsbestimmung f sexual determination, sex differentiation
Geschlechtsbevorzugung f sex[ual] preference
Geschlechtschromatin n sex chromatin, Barr body
Geschlechtschromosom n sex chromosome, heterochromosome, allosome
Geschlechtschromosomenaberration f sex chromosome aberration
Geschlechtsdifferenzierung f sex[ual] differentiation, gonochorism
Geschlechtsdrüse f gonad, sexual gland ● **ohne Geschlechtsdrüsen** agonadal
Geschlechtsfalte f genital fold (ridge, plica)
geschlechtsgebunden sex-linked, sex-limited *(z. B. Erbkrankheiten)*
Geschlechtsgrube f genital fossa
Geschlechtshöcker m genital eminence (tubercle)
Geschlechtsinstinkt m genesic sense
Geschlechtskälte f sexual indifference; frigidity
Geschlechtskern m reproductive nucleus, micronucleus
Geschlechtskrankheit f venereal disease, VD ● **an einer ~ leiden** to suffer from a venereal disease ● **gegen eine ~ gerichtet** antivenereal
~/**vierte** fourth venereal disease, venereal lymphogranulomatosis, venereal adenitis, Nicolas-Favre disease; venereal lymphogranuloma
geschlechtskrankheitsfrei non-venereal
geschlechtslos sexless, asexual *(z. B. Fortpflanzung von Bakterien)*
Geschlechtsmerkmal n sex character (characteristic)
~/**primäres** primary sex character

Geschlechtsmerkmal

~/sekundäres secondary sex character
Geschlechtsnerv *m* genital nerve
Geschlechtsorgane *npl* genital (sex) organs, genitals, genitalia, organs of generation ● neben den Geschlechtsorganen paragenital ● ohne äußere ~ anaedeous
~/äußere external genitalia
~/innere internal genitalia
~/männliche male genital organs
~/weibliche female genital organs, muliebria
Geschlechtspapille *f* genital papilla
Geschlechtsperiode *f* genesial cycle, period of sexual activity
geschlechtsreif puber[t]al, sexually mature
~ werdend pubescent
Geschlechtsreife *f* sexual maturity; puberty
Geschlechtsteile *mpl s.* Geschlechtsorgane
Geschlechtstrennung *f* gonochorism
Geschlechtstrieb *m* libido, sexual instinct (drive, desire)
~/gesteigerter aphrodisia, aphrodisiomania, salacity
~/gesteigerter männlicher satyriasis, satyromania
~/verminderter anaphrodisia, sexual anaesthesia
geschlechtstrieberhöhend aphrodisiac
geschlechtstriebsenkend anaphrodisiac
geschlechtstriebsteigernd aphrodisiac
geschlechtstriebvermindernd anaphrodisiac
Geschlechtsumwandlung *f*/operative sex reversal operation
Geschlechtsunterschied *m* sex difference, sexual distinction
Geschlechtsverkehr *m* sexual intercourse (act), [sexual] congress, coitus
Geschlechtszelle *f* gamete, sexual (generative) cell
~/männliche sperm [cell], spermatozoon
~/morphologisch gleiche isogamete
~/morphologisch ungleiche anisogamete
~/weibliche egg, ovum
geschlechtszellenartig gametoid
geschlitzt stenopaeic
Geschmack *m* 1. taste, flavour, gustation *(eines Stoffs)*; 2. *s.* Geschmackssinn; 3. *s.* Geschmacksempfindung
~/übler cacogeusia
Geschmacksanomalie *f* dysgeusia, taste anomaly (abnormality)
Geschmacksblindheit *f* taste blindness; central ageusia
Geschmacksempfindung *f* sensation of taste, gustation, taste
~/gesteigerte hypergeusia
~/üble cacogeusia
~/veränderte parageusia
~/verminderte hypogeusia
Geschmacksfälschung *f*/subjektive parageusia
geschmacksgestört parageusic
Geschmackshalluzination *f* gustatory hallucination
Geschmacksknospe *f* gustatory bud (bulb), taste corpuscle

Geschmacksnerv *m* gustatory nerve
Geschmacksorgan *n* gustatory organ, organ of taste
Geschmackspapille *f* gustatory papilla, taste ridge
Geschmacksporus *m* gustatory (taste) pore
Geschmacksprüfung *f* gustometry
Geschmacksqualität *f* taste quality
Geschmacksregion *f* gustatory region
Geschmacksrezeptor *m* gustatory receptor
Geschmacksrichtung *f*/abnorme parorexia, perverted appetite *(z. B. bei Schwangeren)*
Geschmacksschärfe *f* gustatory acuity
Geschmackssinn *m* [sense of] taste, gustation, gustatory sense ● ohne ~ ageusic
~/gesteigerter oxygeusia
Geschmackssinnesschärfe *f* gustatory acuity
Geschmackssinnstörung *f* gustatory (taste) disorder, dysgeusia, parageusia
Geschmackssinnzentrum *n* gustatory (taste) centre
Geschmacksstörung *f s.* Geschmackssinnstörung
Geschmackstäuschung *f* allotriogeusia
Geschmacksüberempfindlichkeit *f* hypergeusia
Geschmacksunterempfindlichkeit *f* hypogeusia
geschmacksverändert, geschmacksverfälscht parageusic
Geschmacksverlust *m*/halbseitiger hemiageusia
Geschmackszelle *f* gustatory (taste) cell
Geschmackszentrum *n* gustatory (taste) centre
Geschoß[splitter]verletzung *f* shell injury, missile (shell) wound
geschuppt scaly, squamous
geschwängert fecundated, impregnated
geschwänzt caudate, tailed
Geschwätzigkeit *f* talkativeness, loquacity, hyperphasia, polyphrasia; moria *(Orbitalhirnsymptom)*
~/krankhafte logorrhoea
geschweift caudate, tailed
Geschwister *n* sibling
geschwollen swollen, tumid, turgid, tumefacient; inflated *(z. B. durch Luft)*; oedematous *(z. B. durch Wasser)*; tumefacient
Geschwulst *f* 1. growth, tumour, blastoma *(s. a. unter Tumor)*; excrescence; phyma; 2. *s.* Anschwellung ● Geschwülste auflösend oncolytic
~ der weichen Hirnhaut leptomeningioma
~ des mittleren Keimblatts mesodermal tumour
~/gutartige benign tumour (growth)
~/hypernephroide hypernephroid tumour, hypernephroma, epinephroma, Grawitz's tumour
~/infiltrierende infiltrating tumour
~ neben dem Auge parophthalmoncus
~/perityphlitische perityphlitic tumour, conglomerate medley *(bei Appendizitis)*
~/Schminckesche Schmincke's tumour
~/teratoide teratoma, teratoid tumour, tridermoma, dysembryoma
Geschwulstableger *m* metastasis, metastatic tumour

geschwulstartig tumoural, tumour-like
geschwulstauflösend oncolytic
Geschwulstauflösung f oncolysis
geschwulstauslösend oncogen[et]ic
Geschwulstbehandlung f oncotherapy
geschwulstbildend oncogen[et]ic, neoplastic, prosoplastic, tumefacient
Geschwulstbildung f oncogenesis, neoplasia
geschwulsthemmend oncostatic
Geschwulstlehre f oncology, cancerology
Geschwulstspezialist m oncologist
Geschwulstverbreitung f/**embolische** embolization of tumour emboli
geschwulstwirksam tumouraffin
Geschwulstzelle f tumour cell
Geschwulstzellenaussaat f dissemination of tumour cells
Geschwür n ulcer, ulcus *(s. a. unter Ulcus)*; abscess; furuncle, boil; sore *(Druckgeschwür der Haut)* ● **aus einem ~ entstanden** helcogenic
~/**aphthöses** aphthous ulcer
~/**ausgestanztes** punched-out ulcer
~/**blutendes** haemorrhagic ulcer
~/**eiterndes** running ulcer
~/**fressendes** rodent cancer (ulcer), phagedaena *(Basalzellenkarzinom der Haut)*
~/**fungöses** fungous (weak) ulcer
~/**kallöses** callous (indolent) ulcer
~/**neurotrophes** neurotrophic ulcer
Geschwür... *s. a.* Ulkus...
geschwürartig ulcerous, helcoid
geschwürbildend ulcerogenic
Geschwürbildung f ulceration, ulcerogenesis, formation of an ulcer
geschwürig ulcerous, ulcerated, ulcerative
Geschwürlehre f helcology
Geschwürplastik f helcoplasty
Geschwürs... *s.* Geschwür...
Gesetz n/**Bergonié-Tribondeausches** Bergonié-Tribondeau law *(der Strahlenempfindlichkeit von Zellen)*
~/**biogenetisches** biogenetic law
~/**Weber-Fechnersches** Weber's law *(Reizphysiologie)*
gesichert established *(z. B. Diagnose)*
~/**autoptisch** autopsy-confirmed
~/**durch Laparotomie** laparotomy-confirmed
Gesicht n face, facies ● **mit flachem und breitem ~** mesopic
~/**drüsiges** adenoid face
~/**myopathisches** myopathic face
~/**peritoneales** abdominal face
~/**starres** mask[-like] face, masked facies
Gesichtsarterie f facial (external maxillary) artery
~/**quere** transverse facial artery
Gesichtsausdruck m facial expression; physiognomy, face
Gesichtsausschlag m facial rash
~/**schmetterlingsförmiger** butterfly rash
Gesichtsbrand m noma, gangrenous stomatitis
Gesichtsdiagnose f physiognosis
Gesichtseinstellung f *s.* Gesichtslage

Gesichtserstarrung f facial numbness
Gesichtserythem n facial erythema (rash)
Gesichtsfarbe f complexion, colour
Gesichtsfehlbildung f facial malformation, ateloprosopia
Gesichtsfeld n visual field, field of vision (view)
~/**röhrenförmiges** tubular (tube, tunnel) vision
~/**temporales** temporal field
Gesichtsfeldausfall m *s.* Gesichtsfelddefekt
Gesichtsfeldbestimmung f *s.* Gesichtsfeldmessung
Gesichtsfelddefekt m scotoma, scotosis, [visual] field defect, visual field loss
Gesichtsfelddefekte mpl/**Bjerrumsche** Bjerrum's scotoma
Gesichtsfeldeinengung f contraction of the visual field
gesichtsfeldmessend campimetric, perimetric
Gesichtsfeldmesser m campimeter, perimeter
Gesichtsfeldmessung f campimetry, peri[opto]metry, visual perimetry (field examination)
Gesichtsfraktur f facial (face) fracture
~ **nach Le Fort** Le Fort's fracture
Gesichtshautatrophie f facial trophoneurosis
Gesichtshautstraffung f *s.* Gesichtsstraffung
Gesichtshemiplegie f facial hemiplegia
Gesichtsherpes m facial herpes, cold sore
Gesichtsindex m facial index
Gesichtskephalgie f faciocephalgia
Gesichtsknochen m facial bone, bone of the face
Gesichtsknochenbruch m facial bone fracture, face fracture
Gesichtskolobom n facial coloboma
Gesichtskontur f facial contour
Gesichtskonturwiederherstellung f facial contour restoration
Gesichtskopfschmerz m faciocephalgia
Gesichtskrampf m facial spasm (tic); prosopospasm
~/**mastikatorischer** masticatory spasm of the face
~/**mimischer** mimetic spasm (convulsion)
Gesichtslage f facial presentation, face-presentation, prosopotocia *(bei der Geburt)*
~/**hintere** mentoposterior position of the foetus
~/**I. hintere** *s.* ~/**linke hintere**
~/**II. hintere** *s.* ~/**rechte hintere**
~/**linke hintere** left mentoposterior position of the foetus, L. M. P.
~/**linke vordere** left mentoanterior position of the foetus, L. M. A.
~/**rechte hintere** right mentoposterior position of the foetus, R. M. P.
~/**rechte vordere** right mentoanterior position of the foetus, R. M. A.
~/**vordere** mentoanterior position of the foetus
~/**I. vordere** *s.* ~/**linke vordere**
~/**II. vordere** *s.* ~/**rechte vordere**
Gesichtslähmung f facial palsy (paralysis), facioplegia; prosopoplegia
~/**beidseitige** prosopodiplegia

Gesichtslinie

Gesichtslinie *f* facial line, visual axis
gesichtslos aprosopous
Gesichtslosigkeit *f* aprosopia
Gesichtsmaske *f* 1. facial (face) mask; 2. protective mask; 3. face pack
Gesichtsmassage *f* facial massage
Gesichtsmißbildung *f* facial malformation
Gesichtsmuskel *m* facial muscle; mimetic muscle
Gesichtsmuskelkrampf *m* prosopospasm
Gesichtsmuskellähmung *f* facial paralysis; mimetic paralysis
Gesichtsnerv *m* facial (seventh cranial) nerve, facialis, cranial nerve VII
Gesichtsnerven[druck]entlastung *f* facial nerve decompression *(bei Einklemmung)*
Gesichtsnervenentzündung *f* facial neuritis
Gesichtsnervengeflecht *n* in der Ohrspeicheldrüse parotid plexus
Gesichtsnervenlähmung *f* facialis paralysis, facial nerve palsy (paralysis), prosopoplegia
Gesichtsnervenschwäche *f* facial weakness
Gesichtsneuralgie *f* facial (trigeminal) neuralgia
Gesichtsödem *n*/**allergisches** Quincke's disease, angioneurotic oedema, giant urticaria
Gesichtsplastik *f* facioplasty
Gesichtsrose *f* facial erysipelas
Gesichtsröte *f*, **Gesichtsrötung** *f* facial blush (flush)
Gesichtsschädel *m* visceral cranium, viscerocranium
Gesichtsschädelachse *f* craniofacial axis
Gesichtsschädelverletzung *f* craniofacial injury (lesion)
Gesichtsschmerz *m* facial (trigeminal) neuralgia; prosopalgia, prosopodynia
Gesichtssinn *m* visual sense, visus, vision
Gesichtsskoliose *f* facial scoliosis
Gesichtsspalte *f* facial cleft; prosoposchisis, schistoprosopia
~/**mediane** median facial cleft
~/**quere** transverse facial cleft, genal cleft (coloboma, fissure); goniocheiloschisis
~/**schräge** oblique facial cleft; meloschisis, prosopoanoschisis *(embryonale Spaltbildung)*
Gesichtsstarre *f* facial numbness
Gesichtsstraffung *f* face lift[ing], rhytidoplasty
Gesichtsunterentwicklung *f* ateloprosopia, incomplete facial development
Gesichtsvene *f* facial vein
~/**gemeinsame** common facial vein
~/**hintere** posterior facial vein
~/**quere** transverse facial vein
~/**tiefe** deep facial vein
~/**vordere** anterior facial vein
Gesichtsvergrößerung *f* macroprosopia
Gesichtsverletzung *f* facial injury (laceration)
Gesichtswinkel *m* facial angle, visual (optic) angle
Gesichtswunde *f* facial wound
Gesichtszucken *n* convulsive tic, mimetic convulsion (spasm)

Gesichtszüge *mpl*[/**persönliche**] physiognomy
gespalten/dreifach trifid
~/**vielfach** multifid
gespannt stretched; tense, tensive; rigid; distended
gespornt calcarine, calcarate
Gestalt *f* figure, stature *(einer Person)*; configuration *(eines Organs)* ● **die ~ wandelnd** metamorphic ● **von männlicher ~** andromorphous
Gestaltänderung *f* metamorphosis
gestaltbildend morphogen[et]ic
Gestaltbildung *f* morphogenesis, morphogeny
gestaltlich morphologic[al]
gestaltverändernd metamorph[ot]ic
Gestaltveränderung *f* metamorphosis
Gestaltwechsel *m* pleomorphism
Gestammel *n* stammer[ing]
Gestank *m* stench, stink; foetor; mephitis
Gestation *f* gestation, pregnancy, maternity, cyophoria
Gestationsalter *n* gestational age
Gestationstoxikose *f s.* Gestose
gestielt stalked; pedunculate[d], pediculate, pedicellate[d] *(z. B. ein Polyp)*; flapped, petiolated, ribbon-flapped *(z. B. ein Hauttransplantat)*
Gestose *f* gestosis, gestational toxicosis, toxaemia of pregnancy
gestreift striate[d] *(z. B. ein Muskel)*; streaked, streaky, striped *(z. B. Sputum)*
~/**nicht** non-striated
gesund sound, healthy, unaffected, normal *(z. B. Organe)*; salubrious, wholesome *(z. B. Nahrung)*; laudable ● **~ schreiben** to sign off [the sick list] ● **wieder ~ werden** to reconvalesce, to recover, to recuperate
~/**geistig** sane
~/**nicht** ill, sick, unwell; affected *(z. B. ein Organ)*; unhealthy *(z. B. Ernährung)*
Gesunderhaltung *f* preservation of health
Gesundheit *f* 1. health *(Körperzustand)*; saneness, sanity *(geistig)*; 2. wholesomeness, salubrity *(Zuträglichkeit)* ● **die ~ wiedererlangen** to reconvalesce, to recover, to recuperate ● **die ~ wiederherstellend** sanitary
~/**geistige** sanity, saneness, mental health
Gesundheitsamt *n* public health agency, board of health
Gesundheitsattest *n* health certificate
Gesundheitserhaltung *f* preservation of health
Gesundheitserziehung *f* health education
gesundheitsfördernd salutary, sanatory; salubrious
Gesundheitsfürsorge *f* health care; preventive medicine
gesundheitsgefährdend dangerous (injurious, prejudicial) to health
Gesundheitslehre *f* hygiene, hygienics, science of health
Gesundheitsministerium *n* Ministry (Department) of Health
Gesundheitspflege *f* hygiene, sanitation

gesundheitsschädigend, gesundheitsschädlich unhealthy; prejudicial (injurious) to health; insanitary *(z. B. hygienische Verhältnisse)*; insalubrious *(z. B. Klima)*; deleterious *(z. B. Strahlung)*
Gesundheitsschutz *m* health care (protection); industrial hygiene
~/umfassender comprehensive health care
Gesundheitsstörung *f* disturbance of health, unsoundness
Gesundheitswesen *n*/**öffentliches** public health, state medicine
~/Staatliches Public Health Service, National Health Service
Gesundheitszeugnis *n* certificate of health
Gesundheitszustand *m* state of health, physical condition *(z. B. eines Patienten)*; sanitary conditions *(z. B. hygienischer Einrichtungen)*
Gesundung *f* recovery, reconvalescence, cure, recuperation, healing, restoration
geteilt/mehrfach (vielfach) multipartite
getötet/mit Formalin formalin-killed
Getränk *n*/**berauschendes** intoxicant
Getreidemilbe *f* grain itch mite
Getreidemilbenkrätze *f* grain itch, mattress (millers', barley) itch
getrennt halten to isolate
Getriebenheit *f* agitated melancholia, compulsion
getrübt 1. clouded *(Bewußtsein)*; 2. turbid, cloudy *(z. B. Flüssigkeiten)*; clouded, cataractous *(Augenlinse)*
getüpfelt spotted, naevose *(z. B. Haut)*; punctate, dotted, stippled *(z. B. Erythrozyten)*
Gewächs *n s.* Geschwulst 1.
Gewalteinwirkung *f* trauma
Gewebe *n* tissue, tela, web *(s. a. unter Tela)*
● **artgleiches ~ verpflanzend** homoplastic ● **vom ~ abstammend** histogenous ● **von totem ~ abstammend** necrogenic, necrogenous
~/adenoides adenoid tissue
~/dystopes dystopic tissue, enclave
~/eine Zyste umgebendes pericystium
~/elastisches elastic tissue
~/entzündliches inflammatory tissue
~/erektiles erectile (cavernous) tissue
~/fibröses fibrous tissue
~/interstitielles interstitial tissue, interstitium *(z. B. der bindegewebige Raum um Gefäße)*
~/kollagenes collagenous tissue
~/lymphatisches lymphatic tissue
~/nekrotisches necrotic tissue, debris
~/osteoides osteoid [tissue]
~/pharyngotonsilläres pharyngotonsillar tissue
~/retikuläres reticular tissue
~/retroperitoneales retroperitoneal tissue
~/spongiöses cancellous (spongy) bone tissue
~/undifferenziertes indifferent tissue
~/verpflanztes transplanted tissue, transplant, graft
Gewebe... *s. a.* Gewebs...
Gewebeabstrich *m* tissue smear

Gewebeaktivator *m* tissue activator
Gewebeanoxie *f* tissue anoxia
Gewebeantigen *n* tissue antigen
gewebeartig hist[i]oid, tissue-like
gewebeauflösend histolytic; necrotic
Gewebeauflösung *f* histolysis; necrolysis
Gewebeausstrich *m* tissue smear
Gewebebank *f* [tissue] bank
gewebebildend histogen[et]ic; productive; neoblastic
Gewebebildung *f* histogenesis
Gewebechemie *f* histochemistry
Gewebedegeneration *f* tissue degeneration
Gewebedifferenzierung *f* histodifferentiation
~/abnorme prosoplasia *(z. B. Geschwulstbildung)*
Gewebedosis *f* tissue dose *(Radiologie)*
Gewebeeintrocknung *f* mummification
Gewebeeosinophilie *f* tissue eosinophilia
Gewebeersatz *m*/**fibrotischer** replacement fibrosis
~/kollagener collagenization
gewebeersetzend reparative
Gewebeerweichung *f* tissue softening, maceration
Gewebeextrakt *m* tissue extract
Gewebefaßzange *f* tissue grasping forceps
Gewebeflicken *m* patch
Gewebefluoreszenz *f* histofluorescence
Gewebefluoreszenzintensität *f* tissue fluorescence intensity
Gewebeflüssigkeit *f* 1. tissue fluid (juice); 2. *s.* Lymphe
Gewebeimmunität *f* tissue (local) immunity
Gewebeimplantation *f* tissue implantation
Gewebeirritation *f* tissue irritation
Gewebekleber *m* tissue adhesive
Gewebekultur *f* tissue culture
Gewebekulturneutralisationstest *m* tissue culture neutralization test
Gewebekulturzelle *f* tissue culture cell
Gewebelehre *f* histology, minute anatomy
Gewebemorphologie *f* histomorphology
Gewebemykose *f* histomycosis
Gewebenekrose *f* tissue necrosis (debris); gangrene
~/käsige caseous tissue degeneration
Gewebenekrosin *n* tissue necrosin
Gewebepathologie *f* histopathology
Gewebephysiologie *f* histophysiology
gewebephysiologisch histophysiologic[al]
Gewebeprotozoon *n* tissue protozoon
Gewebequetsche *f* histotribe
Gewebequetschung *f* histotripsy
Gewebeschaden *m*, **Gewebeschädigung** *f* tissue damage
Gewebeschicht *f* tissue layer, stratum, tunica, panniculus
Gewebeschutzhülse *f* tissue protector sheath
Gewebeschwund *m* rarefraction
Gewebespaltflüssigkeit *f s.* Lymphe
Gewebespannung *f* turgor, tissue tone (tension)
Gewebespezialist *m* histologist

Gewebespiegel

Gewebespiegel m tissue level
Gewebestreifen m taenia *(Anatomie) (Zusammensetzungen s. unter Taenia)*
Gewebetestung f tissue typing
Gewebetherapie f tissue (tissular) therapy, histotherapy
Gewebetypisierung f tissue typing
gewebeumbildend metaplastic
Gewebeumbildung f 1. metaplasia, tissue transformation; 2. organization *(durch Zelleinwanderung)*
gewebeunverträglich histoincompatible
Gewebeunverträglichkeit f histoincompatibility
Gewebeverkalkung f calcareous degeneration (infiltration) of tissue
Gewebevermessung f histomorphometry
Gewebeverpflanzung f tissue transplantation (grafting)
Gewebeverschiebung f shifting of tissue
gewebeverträglich histocompatible
Gewebeverträglichkeit f histocompatibility
Gewebezerfall m hystolysis; necrosis
Gewebezerfallsmaterial n detritus
Gewebezerreißung f historrhexis
gewebezerstörend tissue-destroying, histoclastic; corrosive *(z. B. Säuren)*
Gewebezerstörung f tissue destruction; corrosion *(z. B. durch Ätzen)*
~ durch Strahlen[ein]wirkung radionecrosis
Gewebs... s. a. Gewebe...
Gewebsabtragung f mit dem elektrischen Messer electroresection
Gewebsatmung f internal (tissue) respiration
Gewebsbrücke f tissue bridge
Gewebsdemarkierung f tissue demarcation, sloughing
Gewebsdiagnose f histodiagnosis
Gewebsdiagnostik f histodiagnosis
Gewebseinschmelzung f histolysis, dissolution of tissue; abscess formation ● **die ~ begünstigen (fördern)** to favour liquefaction
~/käsige caseous abscess
Gewebseiweiß n tissue protein
Gewebsembolie f tissue embolism
Gewebsentwicklung f/**abnorme** heteroplasia
gewebsernährend trophic
gewebsgiftig histotoxic
Gewebsgiftigkeit f histotoxicity
Gewebshormon n tissue hormone
gewebsneubildend neogenetic, productive
Gewebsneubildung f 1. neoplasia; neoplasma; 2. s. Gewebsregeneration
Gewebsparasit m tissue parasite
Gewebsparasitose f tissue parasitosis
Gewebsprotease f tissue protease
Gewebsreaktion f tissue reaction (response)
Gewebsregeneration f tissue regeneration, neogenesis, reorganization
gewebsregenerierend neogenetic
Gewebsreizung f tissue irritation
Gewebssaftbehandlung f histotherapy, opotherapy

Gewebssauerstoffmangel m tissue hypoxia
Gewebsschnitt m tissue section
~ mit dem elektrischen Messer electroscission, electroresection
Gewebsschnittfixation f fixation of tissue section
Gewebsschnittmesser n histotome
Gewebsthrombin n histothrombin
Gewebsthrombokinase f tissue thrombokinase
Gewebsthromboplastin n tissue thromboplastin
Gewebstod m tissue death, necrosis
gewebstot necrotic
Gewebstropismus m tissue tropism
Gewebstrümmer pl debris
gewebsumwandelnd metaplastic
Gewebsuntergang m s. Gewebenekrose
Gewebsvermehrung f tissue proliferation
Gewebsversprengung f [tissue] heteroplasia
Gewebswassersucht f oedema
Gewebswucherung f tissue proliferation ● **mit ~ einhergehend** proliferative, proliferous
Gewichtsextension f weight traction *(Knochenbruchbehandlung)*
Gewichtssinn m barognosis, baraesthesia, pressure sense
Gewichtsverlust m loss of weight, weight reduction
Gewichtszunahme f increase in weight, weight gain
gewinnen to extract, to isolate, to collect *(z. B. Wirkstoffe aus Pflanzen)*
~/durch Perkolation to percolate
Gewitterangst f keraunophobia, fear of lightning
gewöhnen/sich to accustom, to get accustomed, to habit; to acclimatize
Gewohnheit f habit
gewohnheitsmäßig habitual, customary; routine
Gewohnheitstrinker m habitual drunkard
Gewöhnung f habituation, accustoming; addiction; tolerance *(Zustand)*
~ an neue Umweltbedingungen acclimatization
Gewölbe n vault, fornix, arch
Gewölbebogen m posterior column of the fornix *(ZNS)*
Gewölbebogenschenkel m crus of the fornix *(ZNS)*
gewölbt arched, vaulted, arcuate
gewunden twisted, torsive, tortuous *(verdreht)*; flexuose, sinuous *(z. B. Blutgefäße)*; gyrate *(z. B. Hirnwindungen)*; convolute[d] *(z. B. Nierentubuli)*; turbinate, turbinal *(z. B. Innenohrschnecke)*; coiled *(z. B. Drüsengänge)*
gezackt serrate[d] *(z. B. Geschwür)*; notched *(z. B. Knochen)*
gezahnt toothed, dentate[d]; serrate[d] *(z. B. Muskel)*
~/mehrfach multidentate
Giardiasis f giardiasis, lambliasis, lambliose
gib da, d. *(Rezeptur)*
Gibbosität f gibbosity *(s. a. Kyphose)*
Gibbus m gibbus, hump *(s. a. Buckel)*
Gibraltarfieber n Gibraltar fever

Gicht f gout, arthrolithiasis ● **an ~ leidend** gouty, suffering from gout ● **~ verursachend** gouty ● **zur ~ neigend** gouty
~ am Knie gonagra, gout in the knee
~ der Großzehe podagra
~ im Schultergelenk omagra
~/tophöse tophaceous gout
Gichtarthritis f gouty arthritis
Gichtattacke f attack of gout
Gichtdiät f gout diet
gichtig gouty, podagric, podagrous
Gichtknoten m tophus, gouty node (knot), chalkstone, uratoma
gichtkrank gouty, suffering from gout
Gichtkranker m gouty patient
Gichtnephropathie f gouty nephropathy
Gichtniere f gouty (granular) kidney
Gichtperle f gouty pearl
Gichtschmerz m gouty pain
Gichtulkus n gouty ulcer
Giemen n rhonchus, sonorous rale
Giemsa-Färbung f Giemsa's stain
gierig greedy, eager, voracious
gießbeckenartig arytenoid
Gießbeckenknorpel m arytenoid (triquetrous) cartilage
Gießbeckenknorpel... s. Aryknorpel...
Gießerfieber n metal fume fever, metal (brassfounder's) ague, monday (foundryman's) fever
Gießkannenschimmel m aspergillus
Gießkannenschimmel[pilz]krankheit f aspergillosis
Gift n poison, toxin[um], [in]toxicant; venom, venenum *(besonders von Schlangen und Insekten) (Zusammensetzungen s. unter Toxin)*
Gift... s. a. Toxin...
Giftangst f toxi[co]phobia
giftartig toxicoid, toxic
Giftaufnahme f toxin absorption
giftbildend toxin-producing, toxicogenic, toxigenous *(z. B. Bakterien)*; venenific *(z. B. Schlangen)*
Giftbildung f toxin production, formation of toxin
Giftbildungsfähigkeit f toxigenicity
giftbindend toxicopectic, toxopexic
Giftbindung f toxicopexis
giftcharakteristisch toxignomic
Gifteinspritzung f envenomation, venenation *(z. B. durch Schlangen)*
giftempfänglich toxophil[e]
giftenthaltend toxiferous; veneniferous
Giftfestigkeit f immunity against toxin, immunity to poison
Giftgewöhnung f mithridatism *(durch steigende Dosierung)*
gifthaltig toxic, toxiferous, venomous, poisonous
giftig poisonous, toxic, toxicant *(z. B. Substanzen)*; venenous, venomous *(z. B. Tiere)*; virulent *(Bakterien)*; nocuous
Giftigkeit f poisonousness, toxicity *(von Substanzen)*; venomousness *(z. B. von Schlangen)*; virulence *(von Bakterien)*; nocuousness

Giftkrankheit f tox[ic]osis, toxicopathy, toxinosis, toxonosis
Giftkunde f toxicology
Giftkundiger m toxicologist
giftliebend toxophil[e]
Giftneutralisation f toxin neutralization, toxicopexis
giftneutralisierend toxicopectic, toxopexic
Giftpflanze f poisonous plant
Giftpilz m poisonous fungus, toadstool
Giftschlange f venomous snake
Giftschrank m poison cupboard (cabinet)
Giftstoff m toxicant, poisonous matter (substance) *(s. a. Gift)*
Giftsucht f toxicomania
Giftsüchtiger m toxicomaniac
Gifttoleranz f habituation; [poison] tolerance
gifttragend toxophorous, toxiphoric; veneniferous
gifttypisch toxignomic
Giftwirkung f toxic action, toxicity, poisonous effect; virulence
Gigant m giant
Gigantismus m gi[g]antism, somatomegaly, macrosomia, great bodily size
Gigantoblast m gigantoblast
Gigantomanie f gigantomania
Gigantosomie f s. Gigantismus
Gigli-Säge f Gigli's [wire] saw, wire saw
Gilbert-Syndrom n Gilbert's disease (syndrome), hereditary non-haemolytic hyperbilirubinaemia, constitutional hyperbilirubinaemia (hepatic dysfunction), Meulengracht's syndrome
Gingiva f gingiva, gums, [o]ula
Gingiva... s. a. Zahnfleisch...
Gingivafluid n gingival fluid
Gingivahyperplasie f gingival hyperplasia
Gingivakarzinom n gingival carcinoma, ulocarcinoma
Gingivalatrophie f gingival atrophy
Gingivalfibromatosis f gingival fibromatosis
Gingivalretraktion f gingival recession
Gingivalschleimhaut f gingival mucosa
Gingivalspalte f gingival cleft
Gingivalsulkus m gingival sulcus
Gingivaplasmazytom n gingival plasmacytoma
Gingivapolyp m gingival polyp
Gingivaseptum n gingival septum
Gingivektomie f gingivectomy, ulectomy
Gingivitis f gingivitis, ulitis, inflammation of the gums
~ ulcerativa necrotizing ulcerative gingivitis; trench mouth
Gingivoplastik f gingivoplasty
Gingivostomatitis f gingivostomatitis
Ginglymus m ginglymus, hinge joint (articulation)
Gips m 1. plaster [of Paris], calcined (anhydrous) gypsum; 2. s. Gipsverband
Gipsabdruck m plaster cast
Gipsabreißzange f plaster breaker
Gipsbinde f plaster bandage

Gipshülse

Gipshülse f cylinder cast
Gipskorsett n plaster [of Paris] jacket, jacket
Gipskrawatte f plaster collar
Gipslonguette f plaster [of Paris back] slab
Gipsmesser n plaster knife
Gipsraum m plaster room
Gipssäge f plaster saw, cast cutter
Gipsschale f plaster shell, moulded plaster cast
Gipsschere f plaster scissors (shears)
Gipsschiene f plaster splint, plaster [of Paris back] slab
Gipsspreizer m plaster [cast] spreader
Gipstutor m s. Gipshülse
Gipsverband m plaster [of Paris] cast, cast, plaster (immobilizing, immovable) bandage, plaster dressing
Gipsverband-Syndrom n cast syndrome *(bei Gipsverbänden des Rumpfes)*
Gipszange f plaster breaker
Gitalin n gitalin *(Herzglykosid)*
Gitogenin n gitogenin *(Glykosidbestandteil)*
Gitonin n gitonin *(Glykosidbestandteil)*
Gitoxigenin n gitoxigenin *(Glykosidbestandteil)*
Gitoxin n gitoxin *(Herzglykosid)*
Gitter n lattice, grate, railing; reticulum *(Anatomie)*
Gitterfaser f lattice fibre, reticular (reticulin) fibre *(Histologie)*
Gitteroxygenator m screen oxygenator *(Herz-Lungen-Maschine)*
Gitterwerk n lattice [work], network *(Histologie)*
Gitterzelle f gitter (lattice) cell *(Histologie)*
Glabella f 1. glabella, intercilium, frontal baldness (alopecia); 2. glabella *(anthropologischer Meßpunkt)*
Glandula f s. Drüse
glandulär glandular
Glandulographie f s. Galaktographie
Glans f **clitoridis** [clitoridal] glans, balanus
~ penis (phalli) glans, balanus
Glanzauge n glossy eye
Glanzhaut f glossy skin; leiodermia
glanzhäutig leiodermatous
glasartig s. glasig
Glasauge n glass eye, ocular (visual) prosthesis
Glasbläseremphysem n glassblower's emphysema
Glasbläserkrankheit f glassblower's disease (mouth) *(Ohrspeicheldrüsenentzündung)*
Glasbläserstar m glassblower's (glass-worker's) cataract
Gläserprobe f glass test
Glasessen n hyalophagia
Glasfiberbronchoskop n bronchofibrescope
Glashaut f 1. hyaloid membrane (capsule); 2. basal lamina [of the choroid], basal membrane (layer) *(der Aderhaut)* ● unter der ~ subhyaloid
glasig glassy, vitreous; hyalin[e], hyaloid
Glaskörper m vitreous body, vitreous (crystalline) humour *(des Auges)*
Glaskörperablösung f vitreous [body] detachment, detachment of the vitreous body

Glaskörperabszeß m vitreous body abscess
Glaskörperarterie f hyaloid artery
Glaskörperbiopsie f vitreous biopsy
Glaskörper[ein]blutung f vitreous body haemorrhage, haemophthalmia
Glaskörpereinziehung f vitreous retraction
Glaskörperentfernung f[**/operative**] vitrectomy, vitreous body resection
Glaskörperentzündung f hyal[oid]itis, inflammation of the vitreous body
Glaskörperfluorophotometrie f vitreous fluorophotometry
Glaskörperflüssigkeit f vitreous humour
Glaskörpergerüst n vitreous framework (scaffold)
Glaskörperinjektion f intravitreous injection
Glaskörperkanal m hyaloid canal
Glaskörpermembran f vitreous membrane ● unter der ~ subhyaloid
Glaskörpermukoid n hyalomucoid
Glaskörper-Netzhaut-Hyperplasie f vitreoretinal hyperplasia
Glaskörperperle f vitreous pearl
Glaskörperprolaps m vitreous prolapse, prolapse of the vitreous body
Glaskörperpunktion f hyalonyxis, puncture of the vitreous body
Glaskörperretraktion f vitreous retraction
Glaskörpertrübung f vitreous opacity
Glaskörper- und Netzhauterkrankung f vitreoretinal disease, vitreoretinopathy
Glaskörperveränderung f vitreous change
Glaskörpervereiterung f vitreous body abscess; suppurative hyalitis
Glaskörperverflüssigung f liquefaction of the vitreous body, synchysis, synchosis
Glaskörperzentralkanal m hyaloid canal
Glasmundstück n glass mouth piece
Glasspatel m glass spatula, diascope
Glasspateldruck m vitropression, glass [spatula] pressure
Glasspateldruckmethode f vitropression, diascopy
Glasspritze f [all-]glass syringe
glatt 1. smooth *(z. B. Haut)*; 2. uncomplicated, simple *(Knochenbruch)*; 3. non-striated, unstriped *(z. B. Muskeln)*
glätten to rasp *(z. B. den Amputationsstumpf)*
glattflächig smooth-faced; haplodont *(z. B. Zahnkrone)*
glatthaarig leiotrichous, lissotrichous
glatthäutig leiodermatous
Glatthäutigkeit f leiodermia
glatthirnig lissencephalic, lissencephalous
Glatze f bald head (pate), baldness, calvities; alopecia
Glatzenbildung f glabrification; alopecia
Glatzenfurcht f peladophobia
Glatzköpfigkeit f baldness
Glaucoma n glaucoma *(s. a. unter Glaukom)*
~ congenitum (infantile) congenital (infantile) glaucoma, buphthalmia, hydrophthalmia

~ simplex simple glaucoma
Glaukom n glaucoma (s. a. unter Glaucoma)
~/angeborenes s. Glaucoma congenitum
~/hämosiderotisches haemosiderotic glaucoma
~/neovaskuläres neovascular glaucoma
~/primär kindliches s. Glaucoma congenitum
~/totales absolute glaucoma
Glaukomanfall m glaucomatous attack; congestive glaucoma
glaukomatös glaucomatous
Glaukombehandlung f glaucoma treatment, antiglaucomatous therapy
Glaukomblindheit f glaucoma field defect, glaucosis
Glaukomkatarakt f glaucomatous cataract
Glaukommikrochirurgie f glaucoma microsurgery
GLDH s. Glutamatdehydrogenase
gleichartig homogeneous
Gleichartigkeit f homogeneity, homogenousness
gleicherbig homozygous
Gleicherbigkeit f homozygosity
gleichfärbend isochromatophil[e]
gleichfingrig isodactylous
gleichgefärbt isochromatic
gleichgeschlechtlich homosexual (z. B. Zwillinge)
gleichgestaltig isomorphic, isomorphous
Gleichgestaltigkeit f isomorphism (z. B. von Zellen im normalen Blut)
Gleichgewicht n balance, equilibrium
~/hormonales hormonal balance
~ im Flüssigkeitshaushalt fluid equilibrium, water balance (des Körpers)
~/physiologisches physiological equilibrium (balance)
~/seelisches psychic (mental, emotional) balance
Gleichgewichtsapparat m vestibular apparatus (system)
Gleichgewichtsorgan n vestibular (static) organ, organ of equilibrium
Gleichgewichtssinn m vestibular (labyrinthine) sense
Gleichgewichtsstörung f 1. vestibular (labyrinthine) disorder; 2. imbalance, balance disturbance (biologischer Systeme)
gleichgültig indifferent, indolent; apath[et]ic; lethargic; phlegmatic
Gleichgültigkeit f indifference, indolence; apathy; phlegm
~ der Frau/geschlechtliche frigidity
~/tiefste lethargic lethargy
Gleichheit f **der Fingerlängen** isodactylism
~ der Zehenlängen isodactylism
Gleichheitsteilung f [der Chromosomen] equational division, equal cleavage
Gleichmachung f identification (psychologische Identifizierung mit anderen Personen)
gleichmäßig symmetric[al]; constant, uniform
Gleichmäßigkeit f symmetry (z. B. beider Körperhälften)

Gleichmut m ataraxia, calmness
gleichmütig ataractic
gleichnamig homonymous
gleichseitig ipsilateral, epilateral
gleichsinnig synergistic, syner[get]ic
Gleichstrombehandlung f galvanotherapy, galvanization
Gleichstromdefibrillation f [capacitance-discharge] defibrillation (Herzrhythmisierung)
Gleichstromschock m direct current shock
gleichweit of equal width (z. B. Pupillen)
gleichwertig/energetisch isodynamic
Gleichwertigkeit f/**energetische** isodynamia
gleichzehig isodactylous
gleichzeitig simultaneous; isochronal, isochronous
Gleitbewegung f gliding movement
Gleitbruch m sliding hernia, slip[ped] hernia
Gleitgelenk n gliding joint (articulation)
Gleithernie f s. Gleitbruch
Gleitwirbelsäule f spondylolisthetic spine
Glia f [neuro]glia
gliabildend gliogenous
Gliadin n gliadin, gluten (Prolamin in Weizen und Roggen)
Gliadinallergie f gliadin (gluten) sensitivity (s.a. Zöliakie)
Gliadinantikörper m gliadin antibody
Gliafasern fpl/**Bergmannsche** Bergmann's glia (astrocytes)
Gliahyperplasie f gliosis
gliamatös gliomatous
Gliazelle f neuroglia cell
Glied n 1. s. Gliedmaße; 2. s.~/**männliches**; 3. member, part (eines Organs)
~/kleines männliches micropenis, microphallus
~/männliches penis, phallus, coles, member (Zusammensetzungen s. unter Penis)
Gliedarterie f/**tiefe** deep artery of the penis
gliedartig phalloid, phalliform
Gliedaufrichtemuskel m erector penis [muscle]
Gliedendenschmerz m acrodynia
Gliedentfernung f[/**operative**] s. Phallektomie
Gliederhypertrophie f macromelia
Gliederhypotrophie f micromelia
Gliederplastik f meloplasty
Gliederrecken n pandiculation, stretching of the limbs
Gliederschmerz m limb pain, melalgia
Gliederstarre f paraspasm, stiffness of the limbs (doppelseitige spastische Hypertonie der Gliedmaßen)
Gliederstrecken n pandiculation, stretching of the limbs
Gliederwerfen n jac[ti]tation
Gliederzittern n limb tremor
Gliederzucken n jac[ti]tation
Gliedinzision f s. Phallotomie
Gliedkörper m shaft of the penis
Gliedmaße f limb, member, membrum, extremity, extremitas ● **eine ~ betreffend** monomelic
Gliedmaßenableitung f limb lead (beim EKG)

Gliedmaßenamputation

Gliedmaßenamputation f limb amputation, dismemberment
Gliedmaßendystrophie f/**Sudecksche** Sudeck's atrophy (dystrophy), posttraumatic reflex sympathetic dystrophy
Gliedmaßenendenneurose f acroneurosis
Gliedmaßenendenpigmentierung f acropigmentation
Gliedmaßengefühl n acrognosis
Gliedmaßenlähmung f acroparalysis
Gliedmaßenschmerz m acrodynia
Gliedmaßenverstümmelung f[/**angeborene**] ectromelia
Gliedplastik f phalloplasty
Gliedreflex m penile (bulbospongiosus) reflex
Gliedschmerz m phallalgia, phallodynia, pain in the penis
Gliedspalte f penischisis
Gliedvene f/**tiefe** deep vein of the penis
Glioblastom n glioblastoma *(bösartige Großhirngeschwulst)*
~/**großzelliges** macrocellular glioblastoma
~ **multiforme** glioblastoma multiforme, gliocarcinoma
Glioblastose f gliomatosis
Gliofibrosarkom n gliofibrosarcoma *(Nervengeschwulst)*
Gliom n glioma *(Nervengeschwulst)*
~/**nasales** nasal glioma
~/**perineurales** perineural glioma
Glioma n **retinae** glioma of the retina, retinoblastoma *(bösartige Netzhautgeschwulst)*
Gliomatose f gliomatosis
Glioneuroblastom n glioneuroblastoma, glioneuroma *(Nervengeschwulst)*
Gliosarkom n gliosarcoma *(Nervengeschwulst)*
Gliose f gliosis; neuroglia proliferation
Gliotoxin n gliotoxin
Glissonitis f glissonitis *(Entzündung der Glisson-Kapsel)*
Glisson-Kapsel f Glisson's (hepatobiliary) capsule, capsule of the liver
Glisson-Schlinge f Glisson's sling (suspension apparatus)
Globin n globin *(Hämoglobinprotein)*
Globinkettensynthese f globin chain synthesis
Globulin n globulin
~ **A/antihämophiles** antihaemophilic globulin A, AHG, haemophilic factor A
~/**antihämophiles** antihaemophilic globulin
~ **B/antihämophiles** antihaemophilic globulin B, haemophilic factor B, plasma thromboplastic factor B, plasma thromboplastin component, platelet cofactor II, Christmas factor
~ **des Blutserums** serum globulin
α-**Globulin** n α-globulin, alpha globulin
β-**Globulin** n β-globulin, beta globulin
γ-**Globulin** n γ-globulin, gamma globulin
Globulin-Albumin-Index m, **Globulin-Albumin-Quotient** m protein (globulin-albumin) quotient
Globulinämie f globulinaemia
Globulinausscheidung f **im Urin** globulinuria
Globulinerhöhung f **im Blut** hyperglobulinaemia
Globulinfraktion f globulin fraction
α_1-**Globulinfraktion** f α_1-globulin fraction (region)
Globulinpermeabilitätsfaktor m globulin permeability factor
Globulinreaktion f globulin (Nonne-Apelt) reaction
Globus m **oculi** ocular globe
~ **pallidus** globus pallidus, palaeostriatum
glomerulär glomerular, glomerulose
Glomerulitis f glomerulitis, inflammation of the glomeruli
Glomerulonephritis f glomerulonephritis, glomerular nephritis
glomerulonephritisch glomerulonephritic
Glomerulosklerose f glomerulosclerosis
~/**diabetische** diabetic glomerulosclerosis
~/**interkapilläre** intercapillary glomerulosclerosis, Kimmelstiel-Wilson disease (syndrome)
Glomerulum n glomerule, glomerulus ● **neben dem ~ [liegend]** juxtaglomerular
Glomerulumbasalmembran f glomerular [basement] membrane
Glomerulumfiltrat n glomerular filtrate
Glomerulumfiltration f glomerular filtration
Glomerulumfiltrationsrate f glomerular filtration rate, GFR
Glomerulum-Immun-Komplex m glomerular immune complex
Glomerulumkapsel f glomerular (Bowman's, Malpighian) capsule
glomerulumlos aglomerular *(Niere)*
Glomerulumpermeabilität f glomerular permeability
Glomerulumschädigung f glomerular injury
Glomerulus m s. Glomerulum
Glomus n glomus
~ **aorticum** [para]aortic body
~ **caroticum** carotid body (gland)
Glomus-aorticum-Tumor m aortic-body tumour
Glomus-caroticum-Exstirpation f carotid glomectomy
Glomus-caroticum-Tumor m carotid-body tumour
Glomus-jugulare-Tumor m glomus jugulare tumour
Glomustumor m 1. glomus tumour, glomangioma, angiomyoneuroma, angioneuromyoma; 2. carotid-body tumour
Glomustumorentfernung f[/**operative**] carotid glomectomy
Glossa f s. Zunge
glossal glossal, lingual
Glossalgie f glossalgia, pain in the tongue
Glossanthrax m glossanthrax, tongue anthrax
Glossektomie f glossectomy, glossosteresis
Glossitis f glossitis, inflammation of the tongue
~ **areata exfoliativa** benign migratory glossitis, wanderig rash; geographic tongue
~/**atrophische** atrophic (Hunter's) glossitis
~ **dissecans** dissecting glossitis
~/**Huntersche** s. ~/atrophische

~/ideopathische idiopathic glossitis
~ parasitica parasitic glossitis
Glossodynie f glossodynia; burning tongue
glossoepiglottisch glossoepiglottic, glossoepiglottidean
glossohyoid glossohyal, glossohyoid
Glossolalie f glossolalia
Glossomantie f glossomantia
Glossopharyngeusneuralgie f glossopharyngeal neuralgia
Glossopharyngeusparalyse f glossopharyngeal paralysis
Glossoplegie f glossoplegia, glossolysis, paralysis of the tongue
Glossoptosis f glossoptosis
Glossopyrie f glossopyrosis, burning sensation of the tongue
Glossorrhaphie f glossorrhaphy, suturing of the tongue
Glossoschisis f glossoschisis, schistoglossia; cleft tongue
Glossospasmus m glossospasm, spasm of the tongue
Glossotomie f glossotomy, incision of the tongue
Glossotrichie f glossotrichia, glossophytia; hairy tongue
Glossozele f glossocele
Glottis f glottis, glottic slit ● **durch die ~** transglottic ● **über der ~** supraglottic ● **unter der ~** subglottic, subchordal
Glottiskarzinom n glottic cancer (carcinoma)
Glottiskrampf m laryngospasm, glottic (laryngeal) spasm, laryngismus
~ bei Kindern spasmodic croup (laryngitis), tetanic croup, spasm of the glottis
~/phonischer phonic spasm
Glottisödem n glottic oedema, serous angina
Glottisöffner m posterior cricoarytenoid muscle
Glottisschluß m glottic closure
Glotzauge n exophthalmus, exophthalmos
Glotzaugenkrankheit f Graves' disease (ophthalmopathy), exophthalmic goitre
Glucose f s. Glukose
Glukagon n glucagon[e], glycogenolytic hormone, hyperglycaemic[-glycogenolytic] factor *(Bauchspeicheldrüsenhormon)*
Glukagonom n glucagonoma *(Geschwulst)*
Glukagonspiegelerhöhung f im Blut hyperglucagonaemia
Glukagon[spiegel]verminderung f im Blut hypoglucagonaemia
Glukofuranose f glucofuranose
Glukokinase f glucokinase *(Enzym)*
Glukokortikoid n glucocorticoid *(Nebennierenrindenhormon)*
Glukokortikoidbehandlung f glucocorticoid therapy (treatment)
Glukokortikoidrezeptor m glucocorticoid receptor
Glukokortikoidsubstitution f glucocorticoid replacement (substitution)

Glukoneogenese f gluconeogenesis, glyconeogenesis, neoglycogenesis *(Glukosebildung aus Fett oder Eiweiß)*
glukoneogenetisch gluconeogenetic
Glukoproteid n glucoprotein, glycoprotein
Glukosamin n glucosamin, glycosamine, aminoglucose
Glukosaminoglykan n glycosaminoglycan
Glukose f glucose, glycose; D-glucose, dextrose
Glukoseabbau m glucolysis, glycolysis
glukoseabbauend glucolytic, glycolytic
Glukoseausscheidung f im Urin s. Glukosurie
~ im Urin/erhöhte hyperglycosuria
Glukosebelastung f glucose loading
Glukosebelastungsprobe f glucose tolerance test
glukosebildend glucogenic
Glukosedehydrogenase f glucose dehydrogenase *(Enzym)*
Glukoselösung f glucose solution
Glukosenachweis m/**Benediktscher** Benedict's test
Glukose-1-phosphat n glucose 1-phosphate, Cori ester
Glukose-6-phosphat n glucose 6-phosphate, Robison ester
Glukose-6-phosphat-Dehydrogenase f glucose 6-phosphate dehydrogenase *(Enzym)*
Glukose-6-phosphat-Dehydrogenasemangel m glucose 6-phosphate dehydrogenase deficiency
Glukose-1-phosphorsäure f glucose 1-phosphoric acid
Glukose-6-phosphorsäure f glucose 6-phosphoric acid
glukosespaltend glucolytic, glycolytic
Glukosespaltung f glucolysis, glycolysis
Glukosestoffwechsel m glucose metabolism, glycometabolism
Glukosetoleranztest m glucose tolerance test
Glukoseunverträglichkeit f glucose intolerance
Glukoseverwertung f glucose utilization
Glukosid n glucoside *(Glykosid der Glukose)*
Glukosidase f glucosidase *(Enzym)*
glukosidisch glucosidic, glucosidal
Glukosteroidtherapie f glucosteroid therapy (treatment)
Glukosurie f glucosuria, glycosuria, dextrosuria, saccharorrhoea; carbohydraturia
~/alimentäre alimentary (digestive) glucosuria
~/diabetische diabetic glucosuria
~/hyperglykämische hyperglycaemic glucosuria
~/hypophysäre pituitary glucosuria
~/renale renal glucosuria (diabetes), diabetes
glukosurisch glycosuric
Glukuronat n glucuronate
Glukuronid n glucuronide, glucuronoside
Glukuronidase f glucuronidase *(Enzym)*
Glukuronosyl-Transferase f glucuronosyltransferase *(Enzym)*
Glukuronsäure f glucuronic acid
Glutaeus m gluteus

Glutamat

Glutamat *n* glutamate
Glutamatdehydrogenase *f* glutamic acid dehydrogenase *(Enzym)*
Glutamat-Oxalazetat-Transaminase *f* glutamate-oxalacetate transaminase, glutamic-oxalacetic transaminase, GOT, glutamic-aspartatic transferase, aspartate aminotransferase *(Enzym)*
Glutamat-Pyruvat-Transaminase *f* glutamate-pyruvate transaminase, glutamic-pyruvic transaminase, GPT, glutamic-alanine transaminase, alanine aminotransferase *(Enzym)*
Glutamin *n* glutamine
Glutaminase *f* glutaminase *(Enzym)*
Glutaminsäure *f* glutam[in]ic acid
Glutaminsäuredehydrogenase *f* glutamic acid dehydrogenase
Glutaminsäuremonoamid *n* glutamine, glutamylcysteinylglycine
Glutathion *n* glutathione
Glutathionämie *f* glutathionaemia
Glutathionausscheidung *f* im Urin glutathionuria
Glutathionmangel *m* glutathione deficiency
Glutathionreduktase *f* glutathione reductase *(Enzym)*
Glutathionstoffwechsel *m* glutathione metabolism
Glutäus *m* gluteus
gluteal gluteal, natal
Gluteal... *s.* Gesäß...
Gluten *n* gluten, gliadin *(Prolamin in Weizen und Roggen)*
Glutenallergie *f* gluten (gliadin) sensitivity
Glutenunverträglichkeit *f* gluten (gliadin) intolerance
Glycerol *n s.* Glyzerin
Glycocalix *f* fuzzy coat
Glycose *f s.* Glukose
Glykämie *f* glycaemia
Glykocholsäure *f* glycocholic acid *(Gallensäure)*
Glykogen *n* glycogen, animal starch (dextrin)
~/wasserlösliches lyoglycogen *(z. B. im Gewebe)*
Glykogenabbau *m* glycogenolysis
glykogenabbauend glycogenolytic
Glykogenase *f* glycogenase *(Enzym)*
Glykogenbildung *f s.* Glykogenese
Glykogenerschöpfung *f* glycogen depletion
Glykogenese *f* glycogenesis, glycogeny
glykogenetisch glycogenetic, glycogenous
Glykogenolyse *f* glycogenolysis
Glykogenolysehemmung *f* glycogenolysis inhibition; hypoglycogenolysis
Glykogenolysesteigerung *f* hyperglycogenolysis
glykogenolytisch glycogenolytic
Glykogenose *f* glycogenosis, glycogen thesaurismosis (storage disease)
~ **Typ I** Gierke's (glycogen storage) disease, glycogenosis type I of Cori, hepatic (hepatorenal) glycogenosis
~ **Typ II** Pompe's disease, glycogenosis type II of Cori, maltase deficiency, idiopathic generalized glycogenosis, diffuse glycogenic cardiomegalia
~ **Typ III** cardiac glycogen storage disease, glycogenosis type III of Cori, generalized glycogenosis, late infantile acid maltase deficiency, limit dextrinosis, Forbes' disease
~ **Typ IV** amylopectinosis, glycogenosis type IV of Cori, brancher deficiency glycogenosis, Andersen's disease
~ **Typ V** McArdle's disease, glycogenosis type V of Cori, myophosphorylase deficiency glycogenosis
~ **Typ VI** Hers' disease, glycogenosis type VI of Cori, phosphofructokinase deficiency
~ **Typ VII** Tarni's disease, glycogenosis type VII of Cori
~ **Typ VIII** Haijing's disease, glycogenosis type VIII of Cori, phosphorylase kinase deficiency
glykogenspaltend glycogenolytic
Glykogenspaltung *f* glycogenolysis
~/gesteigerte hyperglycogenolysis
~/verminderte hypoglycogenolysis
Glykogenspeicherkrankheit *f s.* Glykogenose
glykogenspeichernd glycopexic
Glykogenspeicherung *f* glycopexis
Glykogensynthese *f* glycogen synthesis
Glykogensynthetase *f* glycogen synthetase *(Enzym)*
Glykogensynthetasemangel *m* glycogen synthetase deficiency
Glykogenverarmung *f* glycogen depletion
Glykokalyx *f* glycocalyx, fuzz coat
Glykokoll *n* glycocoll, glycine, aminoacetic acid
Glykol *n* glycol, diol, dihydric alcohol
Glykolharnstoff *m* glycollylurea, hydantoin *(Antiepileptikum)*
Glykolipid *n* glycolipid[e], glycolipin *(Zerebrosid)*
Glykolylharnstoff *m s.* Glykolharnstoff
Glykolyse *f* glycolysis, glucolysis
Glykolyseenzym *n* glycolytic enzyme
glykolytisch glycolytic
Glykoproteid *n* glycoprotein, glucoprotein
Glykorrhachie *f* glycorrhachia
Glykose *f s.* Glukose
Glykosid *n* glycoside
~/herzwirksames cardiac glycoside
Glykosidase *f* glycosidase *(Enzym)*
glykosidisch glycosidic, glycosidal
Glykosphingolipid *n* glycosphingolipid
Glykosphingosid *n* glycosphingoside *(Zerebrosid)*
Glykosurie *f s.* Glukosurie
Glyzerin *n* glycerol, glycerin
Glyzerinphosphorsäure *f* glycerophosphoric acid
Glyzerintrinitrat *n* glycerol trinitrate, nitroglycerin *(koronargefäßerweiterndes Mittel)*
Glyzerinzäpfchen *n* glycerin suppository
Glyzerophosphatase *f* glycerophosphatase *(Enzym)*
Glyzerophosphatdehydrogenase *f* glycerophosphate dehydrogenase *(Enzym)*
Glyzerophosphatid *n* glycerophosphatide
α-Glyzerophosphatstoffwechselweg *m* α-glycerophosphate pathway

Glyzerophospholipid n glycerophospholipid
Glyzin n glycine, glycocoll, aminoacetic acid
Glyzinausscheidung f **im Urin** glycinuria
~ im Urin/vermehrte hyperglycinuria
Glyzin[spiegel]erhöhung f **im Blut** hyperglycinaemia
Gnathalgie f gnathalgia, gnathodynia, pain of the jaw
Gnathion n gnathion, mental point *(anthropologischer Meßpunkt)*
Gnathitis f gnathitis, inflammation of the jaw
Gnathodynamometer n gnathodynamometer, occlusometer
Gnathodynie f *s.* Gnathalgie
Gnathologie f gnathology
Gnathopalatoschisis f gnathopalatoschisis, uranoschisis, uranoschism[a]
Gnathoplastik f gnathoplasty
Gnathoschisis f gnathoschisis; cleft jaw; cleft alveolar process
Gnathostoma-spinigerum-Infektion f gnathostomiasis
Gnathostomiasis f gnathostomiasis
Gnosis f gnosis
~/taktile stereognosis, stereognostic sense
gnostisch gnostic
GO *s.* Gonorrhoe
Gobletzelle f goblet cell
Goldausschlag m chrysiasis *(Hautverfärbung nach Goldbehandlung)*; chrysoderma
Goldbehandlung f chrysotherapy, aurotherapy
Goldfüllung f gold filling *(Stomatologie)*
Goldinlay n gold inlay *(Stomatologie)*
Goldsolreaktion f colloidal gold test
Golgi-Apparat m Golgi apparatus, canalicular (internal reticular) apparatus
Golgi-Zellen fpl Golgi cells *(Körnerzellen im Stratum granulosum der Kleinhirnrinde)*
Gomphiasis f gomphiasis
Gomphose f gomphosis *(z. B. der Zähne)*
Gonade f gonad, reproductive (sexual) gland *(s. a.* Hoden *und* Eierstock*)* ● **ohne ~** agonadal
Gonadektomie f gonadectomy, removal of the gonad
Gonaden... *s. a.* Keimdrüsen...
Gonadenaplasie f gonadal aplasia
Gonadendysgenesie f gonadal dysgenesis, Bonnevie-Ullrich syndrome, XO (Turner's) syndrome
Gonadenfalte f gonadal fold
Gonadenhypoplasie f gonadal hypoplasia
Gonadenleiste f gonadal (genital) ridge
Gonadenschutz m gonad[al] shield *(Radiologie)*
Gonadentumor m gonadal tumour
Gonadoblastom n gonadoblastoma *(Geschwulst)*
gonadotrop gonadotrophic
Gonadotropin n gonadotrop[h]in, gonadotropic (gonad-stimulating) hormone
Gonadotropinausscheidung f gonadotrop[h]in excretion
~ im Urin/erhöhte hypergonadotropinuria

~ im Urin/verminderte hypogonadotropinuria
Gonadotropinausschüttung f gonadotrop[h]in excretion
gonadotropinhemmend antigonadotrop[h]ic
Gonagra n gonagra, gout in the knee
Gonalgie f gonalgia, pain in the knee
Gonarthritis f gonarthritis, gonitis, inflammation of the knee joint
Gonarthrokaze f gonarthrocace, white swelling
Gonarthrose f gonarthrosis
Gonarthrotomie f gonarthrotomy, incision of the knee joint
Gongylonemainfektion f gongylonemiasis
Goniocheiloschisis f goniocheiloschisis
Goniodysgenese f goniodysgenesis, angle malformation
Goniofotografie f goniophotography
Goniokraniometrie f goniocraniometry
Goniometer n goniometer
Gonion n gonion *(anthropologischer Meßpunkt)*
Goniopunktion f goniopuncture, goniotrephination *(bei Glaukom)*
Gonioskop n gonioscope
Gonioskopie f gonioscopy
gonioskopisch gonioscopic
Goniosynechie f goniosynechia
Goniotomie f goniotomy
Goniotomiemesser n goniotomy knife
Goniotrabekulotomie f goniotrabeculotomy
Gonitis f gonitis, gonarthritis, inflammation of the knee joint
Gonoblennorrhoe f gonoblennorrhoea, gonorrhoeal conjunctivitis, gonococcal ophthalmia
Gonochorismus m gonochorism
Gonokokkämie f gonococcaemia
Gonokokke f gonococcus
Gonokokkenantigen n gonococcal antigen
Gonokokkenarthritis f gonococcal arthritis
Gonokokkenendokarditis f gonococcal endocarditis
Gonokokkenendometritis f gonococcal endometritis
Gonokokkengelenkinfektion f gonococcal joint infection
Gonokokkeninfektion f gonococcal infection, neisserosis
Gonokokkenkapsel f gonococcal capsule
Gonokokken-Komplement-Fixationstest m gonococcal complement fixation test
Gonokokkensalpingitis f gonococcal salpingitis
Gonokokkensepsis f gonococcaemia
gonokokkentötend gonococcide, gonococcicidal
Gonokokkenurethritis f gonococcal (specific) urethritis
Gonokokkenvaginitis f gonococcal vaginitis
Gonokokkenvesikulitis f gonococcal vesiculitis
gonokokkisch gonococcal, gonococcic
~/nicht non-gonococcal
Gonoreaktion f gonodeviation
Gonorrhoe f gonorrhoea, gonococcal (specific, venereal) urethritis, neisserosis, clap, blennorrhoea, blennorrhagia *(Infektion durch Neisseria gonorrhoeae)*

Gonorrhoe

~/**männliche** phallorrhoea
Gonorrhoeerreger *m* gonococcus, Neisseria gonorrhoea
gonorrhoewirksam antigonorrhoeic
gonorrhoisch gonorrhoeal, blennorrhoeal
Gonozele *f* gonocele
Gonyokampsis *f* gonycampsis, knee deformity
Gonyonkus *m* gonyoncus, knee tumour (swelling)
Goodpasture-Syndrom *n* Goodpasture's syndrome, pulmonary-renal syndrome of Goodpasture
GOT *s.* Glutamat-Oxalazetat-Transaminase
Gougerot-Carteaud-Krankheit *f* Gougerot's disease; nodular dermal allergid
Gougerot-Houwer-Sjögren-Syndrom *n s.* Sjögren-Syndrom
Gowers-Bahn *f* Gower's tract (column, fasciculus), anterior spinocerebellar tract
GPT *s.* Glutamat-Pyruvat-Transaminase
Graaf-Follikel *m* graafian (vesicular ovarian) follicle
Graefe-Syndrom *n* Graefe's syndrome, chronic progressive ophthalmoplegia
Graefe-Zeichen *n* Graefe's sign, lid lag *(bei Hyperthyreose)*
Graham-Steel-Geräusch *n* Graham-Steel murmur *(bei Pulmonalisinsuffizienz)*
Graham-Tumor *m* Graham's tumour, non-encapsulated sclerosing tumour
Gramfärbung *f* 1. Gram's staining method (technique), Gram's stain; 2. Gram's stain ● **durch ~ unterscheiden** to establish by gram stain
gramgefärbt gram-stained
gramnegativ gram-negative
grampositiv gram-positive
Granatsplitterwunde *f* shell injury (wound)
Grand mal *n* grand mal, generalized seizure
Grand-mal-Epilepsie *f* grand mal epilepsy, recurrent generalized seizures
Granula *npl*:
~/**azidophile** acidophilic granules
~/**azurophile** azurophilic granules
~/**basophile** basophilic granules
~/**eosinophile** eosinophilic granules
~/**neutrophile** neutrophilic granules
~/**oxyphile** oxyphilic granules
~/**toxische** toxic granules
granulär granular, granulous
~/**nicht** non-granular
Granularzellenmyoblastom *n* granular-cell myoblastoma
Granularzellentumor *m* granular-cell tumour
Granulation *f* granulation
~/**toxische** toxic granulation
~/**überschießende** exuberant (fungous) granulation, proud flesh *(bei der Wundheilung)*
Granulationen *fpl*/**Pacchionische** Pacchionian bodies, arachnoid granulations
Granulationsanomalie *f*/**Aldersche** Alder's anomaly (phenomenon)
Granulationsgeschwulst *f s.* Granuloma
Granulationsgewebe *n* granulation tissue
Granulationsgewebebildung *f* granulation
Granulationsgewebetumor *m* granulation tumour
granuliert granular, granulated
~/**nicht** non-granular
Granuloblast *m* granuloblast *(Leukozytenvorstufe)*
Granulom *n* granuloma *(s.a. unter Granuloma)*
~/**eosinophiles** eosinophilic granuloma
~/**infektiöses** infectious granuloma
~/**lipophages** lipophagic granuloma *(Speicherform endogener und exogener Fettstoffe in Bindegewebszellen)*
~/**periapikales** periapical granuloma
~/**syphilitisches** syphiloma
Granuloma *n* granuloma *(s.a. unter Granulom)*
~ **fungoides** fungoid mycosis, inflammatory fungoid neoplasm, ulcerative scrofuloderma, Auspitz' dermatosis
~ **gangraenescens** Wegener's granulomatosis
~ **inguinale** ulcerating granuloma of the pudenda, pudendal ulcer, donovaniasis
~ **malignum** malignant granuloma
~ **rheumaticum** rheumatic granuloma
~ **trichophyticum** hypertrophic ringworm
~ **venereum** venereal granuloma
granulomatös granulomatous
Granulomatose *f* granulomatosis
~/**progressive septische** chronic granulomatous disease
~/**Wegenersche** Wegener's granulomatosis
Granulophthise *f* granulophthisis *(durch Knochenmarkstörung)*
Granulopoese *f* granulo[cyto]poiesis
Granulopoetin *n* granulopoietin
granulös granular
Granulosamembran *f* granulosa membrane *(Eierstockfollikel)*
Granulosazelle *f* granulosa (follicular) cell
Granulosazellkarzinom *n* granulosa-cell carcinoma
Granulosazelltumor *m* granulosa-cell tumour
Granulozyt *m* granulocyte, granular leucocyte *(mit Zytoplasmakörnern)*
~/**basophiler** basophil[e], basophilic leucocyte
~/**eosinophiler** eosinophil[e], eosinophilic leucocyte
~/**neutrophiler** neutrophil[e], neutrophilic leucocyte, neutrocyte
~/**polymorphkerniger** polymorphonuclear leucocyte, polymorphocyte
~/**segmentkerniger** segmented cell, lobocyte
~/**stabkerniger** band cell (form)
granulozytenbildend granulocytopoietic
Granulozytenbildung *f* granulo[cyto]poiesis
Granulozytendifferenzierung *f* granulocytic differentiation; granulocytopoiesis
Granulozytenhypoplasie *f* granulocytic hypoplasia
Granulozytenleukämie *f* granulocytic leukaemia, myelaemia

granulozytenlos agranulocytic
Granulozytenmangel *m* granulo[cyto]penia; granulophthisis *(durch Knochenmarkstörung)*
Granulozytenverminderung *f* im Blut hypogranulocytosis; agranulocytosis *(z. B. durch Medikamentenwirkung)*
Granulozytenwanderung *f* granulocytic migration
Granulozytopenie *f* granulo[cyto]penia
Granulozytopoese *f* granulo[cyto]poiesis
granulozytopoetisch granulocytopoietic
Granulum *n* granule *(Zusammensetzungen s. unter Granula)*
Graphanästhesie *f* graphanaesthesia
Graphästhesie *f* graphaesthesia
Graphologie *f* graphology
graphologisch graphologic[al]
Graphomaner *m* graphomaniac
Graphomanie *f* graphomania
Graphophobie *f* graphophobia *(krankhafte Angst vor dem Schreiben)*
Graphospasmus *m* graphospasm, writer's cramp
Gräte *f* spine, spina, spinous process
Gratiolet-Strahlung *f* [Gratiolet's] optic radiation
grausam cruel, brutal
~/**wollüstig** sadistic
Grauwerden *n* der Haare [tricho]poliosis, poliothrix
gravid gravid, pregnant
Gravida *f* gravida
Graviditas *f* gravidity, pregnancy, maternity, gestation, cyophoria, cyesis *(s.a. unter Schwangerschaft)*
~ **multiplex** polycyesis
~ **tubaria** tubal (uterine tube) pregnancy, salpingocyesis
Gravidität *f* s. Graviditas
Grawitz-Tumor *m* Grawitz's tumour, epinephroma, hypernephroma, suprarenoma, hypernephroid renal carcinoma, renal-cell (solid-cell) carcinoma *(bösartige Nierengeschwulst)*
Gray-Syndrom *n* grey [baby] syndrome
greifbar palpable; seizable
Greiffunktion *f* griping (prehensile) function
Greifreflex *m* grasp[ing] reflex
~/**tonischer** tonic grasp reflex
Greig-Syndrom *n* Greig's (ocular) hypertelorism, familial excessive hypertelorism
Greisenalter *n* senium, senectitude, old age
~/**verfrühtes** senilism
Greisenbogen *m* s. Greisenring
greisenhaft senile
Greisenhaftigkeit *f* senility
Greisenhaut *f* geroderma; gerodermia
Greisenheilkunde *f* gerontotherapy
Greisenring *m* gerontoxon, senile (lipoid) arcus
Greisenstar *m* senile cataract
Greisenwarze *f* senile wart
Greisenzittern *n* senile tremor
Grenzfall *m* borderline case
Grenzfalläsion *f* border line lesion *(pathologische Gewebeveränderungen)*
Grenzflächenphänomen *n* boundary layer phenomenon
Grenzmembran *f* boundary (limiting) membrane; interface
~ **der Hornhaut/äußere** Reichert's membrane *(des Auges)*
~ **der Netzhaut** limiting membrane [of the retina]
~ **der Netzhaut/äußere** external limiting membrane [of the retina]
~ **der Netzhaut/innere** internal limiting membrane [of the retina]
Grenzschicht *f*/**Bowmannsche** basal lamina, basement membrane of the corneal epithelium
Grenzstrahlen *mpl* grenz (borderline) rays *(weiche Röntgenstrahlen)*
Grenzstrang *m* sympathetic [nerve] trunk, thoracolumbar autonomic nervous system
Grenzstrangganglion *n* sympathetic [trunk] ganglion
Grenzstrangresektion *f* sympath[ic]ectomy
Grenzzelle *f* border cell *(z. B. im Hörorgan)*
Grey-Syndrom *n* grey [baby] syndrome
Grey-Turner-Zeichen *n* [Grey-]Turner's sign
GRID-Syndrom *n* gay related immunodeficiency syndrome
Griff *m* 1. manubrium; handle; 2. manoeuvre
griffelförmig styliform, styloid
Griffelfortsatz *m* der Elle styloid process of the ulna
~ **der Speiche** styloid process of the radius
~ **des Schläfenbeins** styloid process of the temporal bone
Griffelfortsatzentzündung *f* styloiditis
Griffelfortsatz-Schlund-Kopfmuskel *m* stylopharyngeus [muscle]
Griffelfortsatz-Zungenbein-Muskel *m* stylohyoid muscle
Griffelfortsatz-Zungen-Muskel *m* styloglossus [muscle]
Grimmdarm *m* colon
~/**großer** macrocolon
~/**kleiner** microcolon
Grimmdarmarterie *f*/**linke** s. Arteria colica sinistra
Grimmdarmvene *f*/**linke** s. Vena colica sinistra
Grind *m* 1. scab, crust *(z. B. auf Wunden)*; 2. favus, crusted (honeycomb) ringworm; 3. milk (cradle) cap; 4. s. Grindflechte
Grindflechte *f* impetigo, crusted tetter, favus
Grindgeschwür *n* ecthyma
grippal grippal, influenzal, flulike
Grippe *f* influenza, grip[pe], epidemic catarrhal fever
Grippe... s. a. Influenza...
grippeartig influenzal, flulike
Grippeepidemie *f* influenza epidemic
Grippeimpfstoff *m* influenza vaccine
Grippeinfektion *f* influenza infection
Grippepneumonie *f* influenzal pneumonia *(durch Haemophilus influenzae)*
Grippeschutzimpfung *f* influenza vaccination, anti-influenza inoculation

Grippevirus

Grippevirus n influenza virus
Grippevirusimpfstoff m influenza virus vaccine
Groenblad-Strandberg-Syndrom n Groenblad-Strandberg syndrome, pseudoxanthoma elasticum with angioid streaks
Großarmigkeit f macrobrachia, megalobrachia
großäugig macrophthalmic, macrophthalmous, large-eyed
Großäugiger m macrophthalmus
großbäuchig abdominous
großblasig bullous
großbrüstig mammose, mastous, large-breasted
großdrüsig macradenous
Größenwahn m megalomania, macromania, delusion of grandeur
größenwahnsinnig megalomanic
Größenwahnsinniger m megalomaniac
Größersehen n macropsia, megalopia
großfingerig macrodactylous
Großfingrigkeit f macrodactyly
Großfleckenkrankheit f megalerythema, fifth (Sticker's) disease, infectious erythema
großfollikulär macrofollicular
Großfüßigkeit f macropodia, megalopodia
großgesichtig megaprosopous
Großgliedrigkeit f macromegalia, megalomelia
großhändig megalocheirous, large-handed
Großhändigkeit f macroch[e]iria, cheiromegaly
Großhirn n cerebrum, brain
Großhirnfeld n/**Brodmannsches** Brodmann's area
Großhirnhemisphäre f cerebral hemisphere
Großhirnhemisphärenkapsel f/**äußere** external capsule
~/**innere** internal capsule
Großhirnhemisphärenresektion f hemispherectomy
großhirnig macrencephalous, macrencephalic
Großhirnrinde f [cerebral] cortex, cortex of the cerebrum, pallium
Großhirnschenkel m crus of the cerebrum
Großhirnschwäche f cerebrasthenia
Großhirnsichel f falx cerebri
Großhirnwindung f cerebral convolution
großkiefrig megagnathous, pachygnathous, large-jawed
großknotig macronodular
großköpfig macrocephalic, macrocephalous, mega[lo]cephalic, megacephalous
Großköpfiger m macrocephalus
Großköpfigkeit f macrocephalia, megalocephalia
Großlippigkeit f macrocheilia, macrolabia
Großnasigkeit f macrorrhinia
großschädelig s. großköpfig
großzahnig macrodont, megadont[ic]
Großzehe f hallux, hallex, great toe
Großzehenabzieher m abductor hallucis [muscle]
~/**langer** abductor hallucis longus [muscle]
Großzehenanzieher m adductor hallucis [muscle]
Großzehenbeuger m/**kurzer** flexor hallucis brevis [muscle]
~/**langer** flexor hallucis longus [muscle]
Großzehendorsalflexion f Babinski phenomenon (reflex), fanning sign of Babinski
~/**Edelmannsche** s. Großzehensyndrom/Edelmannsches
Großzehenreflex m great-toe reflex (phenomenon)
Großzehenstrecker m/**kurzer** extensor hallucis brevis [muscle]
~/**langer** extensor hallucis longus [muscle]
Großzehensyndrom n/**Edelmannsches** Edelmann's great toe phenomenon (sign) *(Pyramidenbahnzeichen)*
Großzehenzeichen n great-toe phenomenon (reflex)
großzehig macrodactylous
Großzehigkeit f macrodactyly
großzellig macrocellular, large-cell
Großzungigkeit f macroglossia, megaloglossia
Grübchen n fossette, fossula; dimple, scrobiculus; foveola
~/**ethmoido-lakrimales** ethmolacrimal recess
Grübchenbildung f dimpling, pitting, foveation
Grube f fossa, groove, fovea, pit, crypt; cavity, hollow *(Aushöhlung)*; hole; niche; recess[us]
~/**epigastrische** epigastric fossa
~/**Mohrenheimsche** deltopectoral (Mohrenheim's) groove, infraclavicular fossa
~/**Rosenmüllersche** Rosenmüller's fossa, pharyngeal recess, lateral pharyngeal fossa *(hinter dem Tubenwulst)*
Grubenkopfbandwurm m broad tapeworm, Diphyllobotrium latum
Grubenkrankheit f s. Ankylostomiasis
Grubennystagmus m miner's nystagmus
grünblind deuteranopic, green-blind
Grünblinder m deuteranope
Grünblindheit f deuteranop[s]ia, green blindness, achloro[ble]psia
Grund m s. Fundus
Grundfläche f base ● **an der** ~ basal
Grundgewebe n stroma
Grundglied n proximal phalanx
Grundhäutchen n basal lamina (membrane), basement layer
Grundimmunisierung f basic immunization
Grundkrankheit f basic (underlying) disease
gründlich intensive, intense, radical *(z. B. Behandlung)*; careful *(sorgfältig)*
Grundplasma n hyaloplasm, cell sap, enchylema, paraplasm
Grundregel f/**biogenetische** biogenetic law
Grundschicht f dermic layer *(Trommelfell)*
Grundstoffwechsel m basal metabolism
Grundstoffwechselrate f basal metabolic rate
Grundsubstanz f ground (interstitial) substance *(Histologie)*
Grundumsatz m basal metabolic rate
Grundumsatzbestimmung f metabolimetry
Grünholzfraktur f greenstick (subperiosteal) fracture
grünschwach deuteranomalous

Grünschwäche f deuteranomalia
Grünsehen n s. **Grünsichtigkeit**
grünsichtig green-sighted; protanopic
Grünsichtiger m green-sighted person; protanope
Grünsichtigkeit f green-sightedness, green vision, chlorop[s]ia, protanopia, red blindness, anerythroblep[s]ia, anerythropsia
Gruppe f 1. group (z. B. von Atomen); 2. set, assembly; 3. cluster
~/agglutinophore agglutinophore
~/haptophore haptophore, haptophoric group (Haftgruppe der Toxine)
~/prosthetische prosthetic (active) group, agon (nichteiweißartiger Proteidbestandteil)
~/toxophore toxophore, toxophoric group
~/zymophore zymophore (aktiver Enzymabschnitt)
Gruppenagglutination f group agglutination (Serologie)
Gruppenagglutinin n group agglutinin, minor (cross, partial) agglutinin (Serologie)
Gruppenanalyse f group analysis
Gruppenerkrankung f group disease
gruppenfremd incompatible (Blut)
Gruppenpsychotherapie f group psychotherapy (therapy)
gruppenspezifisch group specific
Gruppentherapie f group therapy; group psychotherapy
Grützbeutel m atheroma, steatoma, sebaceous cyst
grützbeutelartig atheromatous
Gryposis f gryposis, abnormal curvature (z. B. der Nägel)
G-Stammeln n gammacism
g-Strophantin n G-Strophantin, ouabain (Herzglykosid)
Guajak-Test m guaiac test (auf Blut im Stuhl)
Guanidin n guanidine, iminourea, carbamidine, aminomethanamidine
Guanin n guanine (Bestandteil der Nukleinsäure)
Guanosin n guanosine (Nukleosid, Baustein der Nukleoproteide)
Gubernaculum n gubernaculum
~ testis gubernacular cord
Guedel-Tubus m standard airway, oropharyngeal airway (tube)
Guérin-Stern-Syndrom n arthrogryposis (Guérin-Stern) syndrome
Guerreiro-Machado-Komplement-Fixationstest m Guerreiro-Machado complement fixation test (bei Chagas-Krankheit)
Guineawurm m guinea (dragon) worm
Guineawurminfestation f guinea worm infection, dracontiasis, dracunculiasis
Gumma n gumma, syphiloma
gummatös gummatous
Gummibandage f rubber bandage
Gummihandschuh m rubber glove
Gummihaut f India rubber skin; dermatorrhexis, [Ehlers-]Danlos syndrome

Gummikatheter m rubber catheter
Gummipolierer m [rubber] polishing wheel (zur Zahnbehandlung)
Gummistrumpf m elastic stocking (z. B. bei Krampfadern)
Gummiüberschuh m galosh, [rubber] overshoe
gummös gummatous, gummy
Gurgel f throat
gurgeln to gargle (mit einem Mundwasser)
Gurkenkernbandwurminfestation f dipylidiasis
Gürtel m 1. cingulum, girdle; zona, zone (Anatomie); 2. belt
Gürtelanästhesie f girdle anaesthesia
Gürtelflechte f s. Herpes zoster
gürtelförmig zonal, zonary
Gürtelgefühl n cincture sensation, girdle pain, zonaesthesia
Gürtelplazenta f zonary (annular) placenta
Gürtelrose f s. Herpes zoster
gürtelrosenförmig zosteriform, zosteroid
Gürtelschmerz m s. **Gürtelgefühl**
Guß m affusion (physiotherapeutische Methode)
gustatorisch gustatory
Gutachten n/ärztliches medical evidence (opinion)
gutartig benign, non-malignant (s. a. unschädlich)
Guttae fpl guttae, drops (Rezeptur)
Guttapercha f(n) gutta percha (z. B. für provisorische Zahnfüllungen)
guttural guttural
GVH-Reaktion f graft versus host reaction
Gymnast m gymnast (Physiotherapeut)
Gymnastik f gymnastics; gymnastic (physical) exercises
gymnastisch gymnastic
Gynäkographie f gynaecography
Gynäkologe m gynaecologist
Gynäkologie f 1. gynaecology, gyniatrics; 2. gynaecology ward
gynäkologisch gynaecologic[al]
Gynäkomastie f gynaecomastia
Gynäkomastie-Aspermiogenese-Syndrom n gynaecomastia-aspermatogenesis syndrome, Klinefelter's syndrome, Klinefelter-Reifenstein-Albright syndrome (Insuffizienz der Hodenkanälchen)
Gynäkophobie f gynae[co]phobia (krankhafte Angst vor Frauen)
Gynäkoplastik f gynoplasty
Gynander m gynander
Gynandrie f s. **Gynandrismus**
Gynandrismus m gynandry, gynandria, gynandrism, female pseudohermaphroditism
~/adipöser adipose gynandrism, gynandrism (Simpson's) syndrome (bei Jungen) (s. a. Gynismus/adipöser)
Gynandroblastom n gynandroblastoma (Eierstockgeschwulst)
Gynandroider m gynandroid
Gynandromorphismus m gynandromorphism, gynandromorphy

Gynatresie

Gynatresie f gynatresia *(angeborener Verschluß der weiblichen Genitalorgane)*
Gynismus m/**adipöser** adipose gynism, gynism (Simpson's) syndrome *(bei Mädchen) (s. a. Gynandrismus/adipöser)*
Gynogenese f gynogenesis *(Entwicklung ohne väterlichen Kernanteil)*
Gyrektomie f gyrectomy, excision of a cerebral gyrus
~/**frontale** frontal gyrectomy
Gyri mpl **annectentes** annectent gyri
Gyrus m gyrus, convolution *(des Gehirns)*
~ **angularis** angular gyrus
~ **centralis posterior** posterior central gyrus
~ **cinguli** cingulate (callosal) gyrus
~ **dentatus** dentate gyrus
~ **fornicatus** limbic cortex (lobe, system)
~ **frontalis** frontal gyrus
~ **frontalis inferior** inferior frontal gyrus
~ **frontalis inferior sinistra** left inferior frontal gyrus
~ **frontalis medius** middle frontal gyrus
~ **frontalis superior** superior frontal gyrus
~ **fusiformis** fusiform gyrus
~ **lingualis** lingual gyrus
~ **occipitalis** occipital gyrus
~ **occipitalis lateralis** lateral occipital gyrus
~ **occipitalis superior** superior occipital gyrus
~ **occipitotemporalis** occipitotemporal gyrus
~ **olfactorius** olfactory gyrus
~ **orbitalis** orbital gyrus
~ **parahippocampalis** hippocampal (uncinate, marginal) gyrus
~ **paraterminalis** paraterminal (subcallosal, subcollateral) gyrus, Zuckerkandl's convolution
~ **parietalis** parietal gyrus
~ **postcentralis** postcentral (posterior central) gyrus, ascending parietal gyrus
~ **precentralis** precentral (anterior central) gyrus, ascending frontal gyrus
~ **rectus** straight gyrus
~ **subcallosus** s. ~ paraterminalis
~ **supracallosus** supracallosal gyrus
~ **supramarginalis** supramarginal gyrus
~ **temporalis inferior** inferior temporal gyrus
~ **temporalis medius** middle temporal gyrus
~ **temporalis superior** superior temporal gyrus
~ **temporalis transversus** transverse temporal gyrus
~ **uncinatus** s. ~ parahippocampalis
Gyrusexzision f gyrectomy

H

Haar n hair, crinis, pile, pilus
Haaranomalie f hair anomaly
haarartig trichoid, hair-like, piliform
Haaratrophie f trichatrophia
Haarauffaserung f trichoptilosis, trichoschisis
haaraufrichtend pilomotor
Haaraufrichter m pilomotor muscle, arrector pilorum [muscle]
Haaraufrichternerv m pilomotor nerve
Haaraufrichtung f piloerection, erection of the hairs, horripilation
Haaraufspaltung f trichoptilosis, trichoschisis, schizotrichia
Haarausfall m psilosis, falling out of hair, trichorrhoea, trichomadesis; alopecia, loss of hair, baldness
~/**bandförmiger** ophiasis *(meist am Hinterkopf und bei Kindern)*
~/**kreisförmiger** pelada, pelade
Haarausreißen n [/**krankhaftes**] tricho[tillo]mania
Haaraustrocknung f xerasia, drying of the hair
Haarbalg m hair follicle
Haarbalg... s.a. Haarfollikel...
Haarbalgentzündung f trichitis, inflammation of the hair bulbs (follicles)
Haarbalgkrankheit f trichocryptosis, disease of the hair follicles
Haarbalgmilbe f follicular (face) mite, Demodex folliculorum
Haarbalgmilbenbefall m demodicidosis, infestation with Demodex
Haarbalgmuskel m arrector pilorum [muscle], pilomotor muscle
Haarberührungsschmerz m trichalgia
haarbewegend pilomotor
haarbildend hair-forming, trichogenous
Haarbildung f piliation
Haarbrüchigkeit f trichoclasia, trichorrhexis
Haarbulbus m hair bulb
Haare npl/**eingewachsene** ingrown hairs
~/**gedrehte** twisted hairs *(Haarabnormität)*
Haarempfindlichkeit f trich[o]aesthesia, hair sensibility
Haarempfindlichkeitsmeßinstrument n trichoaesthesiometer
Haarempfindlichkeitsverlust m trichoanaesthesia
haarentfernend depilatory, removing the hair
Haarentfernung f depilation, epilation, removal of hairs
Haarentfernungsmittel n depilatory [agent], epilator, hair remover
Haarergrauen n [**tricho**]poliosis, canities, greyness of the hair; poliothrix, greying of the hair
Haarernährung f trichotrophy, nutrition of the hair
Haaressen n [/**krankhaftes**] trichophagia, hair-eating
Haarfarbe f 1. hair colour, colour of the hair; 2. hair dye *(Färbemittel)*
Haarfaser f hair fibre
Haarfollikel m hair follicle
Haarfollikel... s.a. Haarbalg...
Haarfollikelhyperkeratose f follicular hyperkeratosis
Haarfollikelverhornung f [/**abnorme**] monilethrix; moniliform (beaded) hair
Haargefäß n capillary [vessel]; micrangium, telangion

Haargefäßentzündung f capillaritis, telangitis, inflammation of the capillaries
Haargefäßerkrankung f telangiosis, disease of the capillary vessels
Haargefäßtumor m telangioma
Haargefühl n trich[o]aesthesia, hair sensibility
Haargefühlverlust m trichoanaesthesia
Haargeschwulst f trichobezoar, pilibezoar, hair ball, egagropilus *(im Magen)*
Haarhyalin n trichohyalin, hyalin of the hair
haarig pil[e]ous, pilose, hairy, covered with hair
haarig-zystisch pilocystic
Haarkanal m f hair canal
Haarkeim m hair matrix (germ)
Haarknäuel n s. Haargeschwulst
Haarknötchenkrankheit f piedra, Beigel's disease *(tropisches Haarpilzleiden)*
Haarkrankheit f trichopathy, tricho[no]sis, disease of the hair
Haarlängsspaltung f trichoptilosis, trichoschisis, splitting of the hairs
Haarlehre f trichology, pilology
Haarlinienknochenbruch m capillary (fissured) fracture
haarlos hairless, atrichous, depilous; bald, glabrous
Haarlosigkeit f hairlessness, psilosis, absence of hair, acomia; baldness, alopecia
Haarnävus m hairy (pilose) naevus
Haarpapille f hair papilla
Haarpigment n hair pigment
Haarpilz m trichomyces
Haarpilzkrankheit f trichomyc[et]osis; trichosporosis, piedra
Haarröhrchen n capillary [tube]
Haarschaft m hair shaft, scapus
Haarscheide f hair sheath
Haarschuppe f scurf, dandruff
Haarschwund m oligotrichia, oligotrichosis, thinness of hairs
Haarsensibilität f trich[o]aesthesia, hair sensibility
Haarsprödigkeit f trichoclasia, trichorrhexis, brittleness of the hair
Haarstein m tricholith
Haarstörung f paratrichosis
Haartalgdrüse f sebaceous (hair) gland
Haartransplantation f hair transplantation
Haartrockenheit f xerosis, dryness of the hair
Haar- und Pflanzenknäuel n trichophytobezoar *(im Magen)*
Haarverfilzung f trichomatosis
Haarverknotung f trichonodosis; knotting hair
Haarverlust m s. Haarausfall
Haarverschlucken n trichophagia
Haarwimpernschlag m ciliary movement *(von Mikroorganismen)*
Haarwirbel m vertex, hair whorl
Haarwuchs m growth of hair
~ **bei Frauen/männlicher** hirsutism, hirsuties *(bei Nebennierenüberfunktion)*
~/**verminderter** hypotrichosis, hypotrichiasis, oligotrichia

~/**verstärkter** hypertrichosis, hypertrichiasis
haarwuchsfördernd trichogenous
Haarwurzel f hair root, root of a hair
Haarwurzelkanal m hair canal
Haarwurzelscheide f root sheath
Haarwurzelscheidenhyalin n trichohyalin
Haarwurzelschmerz m hairache
Haarzelle f hair cell
Haarzunge f hair (hairy) tongue; glossotrichia, glossophytia, trichoglossia
~/**schwarze** black [hairy] tongue, lingua nigra; melanoglossia, nigrites linguae
Haarzupfsucht f tricho[tillo]mania
Haarzwiebel f hair bulb, bulb of the hair
Habena f habena
Habenula f habenula, stalk of the pineal body
Habituation f habituation
habituell habitual
Habitus m habitus, habit [of body], general (physical) appearance
~/**adenoider** adenoidism
~/**leptosomer** leptosomatic habit
~/**pyknischer** pyknic habit
Hacke f, **Hacken** m heel
Hackenfuß m [talipes] calcaneus, calcaneum *(Klumpfuß)*
Hackenversuch m heel-knee test, heel-to-knee-to-toe test
Hadernkrankheit f ragsorters' (woolsorter's) disease, malignant (pulmonary) anthrax
Haem... s.a. Häm...
Haemangioma n s. Hämangiom
~ **capillare** capillary haemangioma
~ **simplex** strawberry haemangioma, rasperry mark
Haemoccult-Test m guaiac test
Hafenarzt m health (port medical) officer
Hafenhygieneinspektion f port sanitary inspection
Haffkine-Vakzine f Haffkine vaccine *(gegen Pest)*
Haffkrankheit f haff disease, bay sickness
haften to adhere, to stick
~/**an der Zelloberfläche** to attach to cell surface
Haftglas n contact (adherent) lens
Haftgruppe f **der Toxine** s. Haptophor
Haftpsychose f prison (jail) psychosis
Hagelkorn n chalazion, Meibomian cyst
Hageman-Faktor m Hageman factor, HF, contact (glass) factor, [blood-]clotting factor XII
Hagemann-Faktor-Mangel m Hageman factor deficiency, factor XII deficiency
hager lean, lanky *(Gestalt)*; emaciated *(abgemagert)*
Hagestolz m misogamist, bachelor
H-Agglutination f H agglutination *(Ausflockung von Bakteriengeißeln)*
H-Agglutinin n H (flagellar) agglutinin
Hahnenkamm-Einheit f capon-comb unit *(bei der Androgenbestimmung)*
Hairless-women-Syndrom n hairless women syndrome, testicular feminization syndrome

Häkchen

Häkchen n 1. hamulus (am Knochen); 2. tenaculum (Instrument)
Haken m hook, uncus
~/scharfer sharp hook
Hakenarmmuskel m coracobrachialis [muscle]
Hakenbein n hamate [bone], hamatum, unciform[e], unciform bone, uncinatum
Hakenbündel n uncinate (hook) bundle, uncinate fasciculus of the cerebrum (hemisphere)
hakenförmig hook-shaped, unciform, hamate, uncinate
Hakenfortsatz m hook-shaped process, hamulus (s.a. unter Hamulus)
~ der Elle olecranon [process]
hakenfortsatzartig 1. olecranoid; 2. unciform, hamate
Hakenfortsatzgrube f olecranon fossa
Hakenkranz m rostellum (des Bandwurms)
Hakenmanschette f hook cuff
Hakennase f hook nose
Hakenwurm m hookworm, Ancylostoma duodenale
Hakenwurmanämie f s. Hakenwurmkrankheit
Hakenwurmei n hookworm egg
Hakenwurmkrankheit f ancylostomiasis, hookworm (brickmaker's) anaemia, Egyptian chlorosis, malcoeur, miner's anaemia (sickness), Saint Gothard's disease, tunnel anaemia (disease), hookworm infestation, necatoriasis
Hakenzange f hooked (tenaculum) forceps, tissue forceps, valsellum
Halb... s.a. Semi...
Halbantigen n s. Hapten
halbblind 1. half-blind, hemiamaurotic, starblind; 2. hemianopic
Halbblindheit f 1. half-blindness, hemiamaurosis; 2. hemianop[s]ia
Halbdornmuskel m semispinalis [muscle]
Halbgeschwister n half sib[ling]
halbhäutig semimembranous
Halbkoma n semicoma
halbkomatös semicomatose
halbkreisförmig semicircular
Halbkugel f hemisphere
Halbmond m/**Ebnerscher** s.~/Gianuzzischer
~/Gianuzzischer (seröser) Gianuzzi's demilune (cell, crescent)
halbmondförmig semilunar
Halbrohrplatte f semitubular plate
Halbschädel m hemicranius, hemicephalus (Mißgeburt)
Halbschädeligkeit f hemicrania, hemicephalia
Halbschlaf m semisomnus, drowse, doze; twilight sleep (nach Medikamentengaben); hypnagogic state (beim Einschlafen); hypnopompic state (beim Erwachen)
halbschlafend half-sleeping, half-waking, semisomnous; hypnagogic; hypnopompic
Halbsehnenmuskel m semitendinosus [muscle]
Halbseiten... s.a. Hemi...
Halbseitenanalgesie f hemianalgesia, unilateral analgesia
Halbseitenblindheit f hemianop[s]ia, hemiamblyopia, hemiablepsia, hemiopia, hemiscotosis
Halbseitenentrindung f hemidecortication
Halbseitenepilepsie f hemiconvulsion
Halbseitengehirn n hemianencephalia
halbseitengelähmt s. hemiplegisch
Halbseitengynandromorph m s. Gynander
Halbseitenherz n hemicardia
Halbseitenhochdruck m hemihypertonus
Halbseitenkopfschmerz m s. Migräne
Halbseitenkrampf m hemispasm
Halbseitenlähmung f s. Hemiplegie
Halbseitenschwitzen n hemihyperhidrosis
Halbseitentaubheit f hemianacousia
Halbseitenunempfindlichkeit f **des Körpers** s. Hemianästhesie
Halbseitenzungenentzündung f hemiglossitis
halbseitig semilateral; unilateral
halbsichtig hemianopic
Halbsichtigkeit f hemianop[s]ia, hemiamblyopia, hemiablepsia, hemiopia, hemiscotosis
halbtaub partially deaf
Halbtaubheit f hemianacousia
Halbwertzeit f half-life [period]
~/biologische biological half-life
~/radioaktive radioactive half-life
Halbwirbel m hemivertebra
Halbzellulose f hemicellulose
Half-change-Methode f half change method (zur Prüfung von Depotpräparaten)
Halisterese f halisteresis, osteohalisteresis, halisteretic atrophy
Halitosis f halitosis, offensive breath, bromopnoea
Halitus m halitus
Hallermann-Syndrom n Hallermann-Streiff[-Francois] syndrome
Hallopeau-Syndrom n Hallopeau's disease, acrodermatitis continua
Hallux m hallux, hallex, great toe
~ malleus hammer-toe
~ valgus intoe
Halluzination f hallucination ● **Halluzinationen hervorrufend** hallucinogenic, hallucinogenous
~/akustische acoasma, auditory hallucination, acousma, phoneme
~/depressive depressive hallucination
~/gustatorische gustatory hallucination
~/hypnagogische hypnagogic hallucination
~/hypnopompische hypnopompic hallucination
~/olfaktorische olfactory hallucination
~/optische s.~/visuelle
~/psychische psychic hallucination
~/psychogene induced (psychogenic) hallucination
~/psychomotorische psychomotor hallucination
~/visuelle visual hallucination, psychovisual sensation, pseudoblepsia, photome
halluzinatorisch hallucinatory, hallucinative, hallucinotic
halluzinieren to hallucinate
halluzinogen hallucinogenic, hallucinogenous

Halluzinogen *n* hallucinogen
Halluzinolytikum *n* hallucinolytic [agent]
Halluzinose *f* hallucinosis
halluzinotisch hallucinotic
Halo *m* halo, areola *(des Auges)*
Halogenakne *f* halogen acne
Halothan *n* halothane *(Inhalationsnarkotikum)*
Halothanhepatitis *f* halothane hepatitis
Halothannarkose *f* halothane anaesthesia
Hals *m* 1. neck; cervix *(z. B. der Gebärmutter)*; collum *(z. B. an Knochen)*; 2. *s.* Rachen ● **unter dem ~** subcervical
~/chirurgischer surgical neck [of the humerus]
~ des Oberarmknochens/anatomischer anatomic neck [of the humerus]
~/steifer stiff neck; nuchal rigidity, crick in the neck
Halsarterie *f s.* Halsschlagader
Halsband *n*/**Casálsches** Casál's collar (necklace) *(bei Pellagra)*
Halsdivertikel *n* cervical diverticulum
Halsdornmuskel *m* spinalis cervicis [muscle]
Halsdreieck *n* neck (cervical) triangle, triangle of the neck
~/hinteres posterior neck triangle, posterior triangle of the neck
~/vorderes anterior neck triangle, anterior triangle of the neck
Halsdrüse *f s.* Halslymphknoten
Halseinblutung *f* trachelematoma
Halseingeweide *npl* cervical viscera
Halseisbeutel *m* ice bag for throat
Halsentzündung *f* sore throat, inflammation of the throat, quinsy, angina
Halsfaszie *f* cervical fascia
~/tiefe deep cervical fascia
Halsfistel *f* cervical fistula
~/laterale lateral cervical fistula, lateral fistula of the neck, branchial [cyst] fistula *(Rest des Ductus thymopharyngicus)*
~/mediane midline cervical fistula, median fistula of the neck, thyroglossal duct fistula
Halsgefäß *n* cervical vessel
Halsgeflecht *n* cervical plexus
Halsgicht *f* trachelagra
Halsgipsverband *m* cervical collar
Halshämatom *n* trachelematoma
Halshydrozele *f* cervical hydrocele
Halslymphknoten *m* cervical (neck) lymph node, cervical gland
~/tiefer deep cervical lymph node
Halslymphknotenausräumung *f* neck [gland] dissection
Halslymphknotenbiopsie *f* cervical lymph node biopsy
Halslymphknotenentzündung *f* cervical adenitis (lymphadenitis), deradenitis
Halslymphknotenerkrankung *f* cervical lymphadenopathy
Halslymphknotenmetastase *f* cervical lymph node metastasis

Halslymphknotentuberkulose *f* cervical tuberculous adenitis, scrofulosis, scrofula, strumous cachexia, king's evil
Halsmandel *f* tonsil
Halsmandelentzündung *f* angina
Halsmarkanschwellung *f s.* Halsrückenmarkanschwellung
Halsmarkröntgen[kontrast]aufnahme *f* cervical myelogram
Halsmarkröntgen[kontrast]darstellung *f* cervical myelography
Halsmuskel *m* cervical (collar) muscle
~/langer longus colli muscle, longus cervicis [muscle]
~/querer transverse nuchal muscle, transversus nuchae [muscle], occipitalis minor [muscle]
Halsmuskelentzündung *f* trachelomyitis
Halsmuskelkrampf *m*/**tonischer** trachelism[us], spasmodic head retraction *(bei Epilepsie)*
Halsmuskelschmerz *m* trachelodynia
Hals-Nasen-Ohren-Besteck *n* ear-nose-throat set, E-N-T set
Hals-Nasen-Ohren-Klinik *f* ear, nose, and throat clinic
Hals-, Nasen- und Ohrenheilkunde *f* oto[rhino]laryngology
Halsnerv *m* cervical nerve
~/äußerer external carotid nerve
~/innerer internal carotid nerve
Halsösophagus[bereich] *m*/**muskulomembranöser** musculomembranous cervical oesophagus
Halsregion *f* cervical region
~/seitliche lateral cervical region, lateral region of the neck
Halsrippe *f* cervical rib
Halsrippensyndrom *n* cervical rib syndrome, Naffziger's syndrome
Halsrückenmark *n* cervical spinal cord
Halsrückenmarkanschwellung *f* cervical intumescence (enlargement), intumescentia *(Anatomie)*
Halsschlagader *f* carotid [artery], carotis, cervical artery
~/aufsteigende ascending cervical artery
~/linke gemeinsame left common carotid artery, L.C.C.
~/oberflächliche superficial cervical artery
~/quere transverse cervical artery
~/rechte gemeinsame right common carotid artery, R.C.C.
Halsschlagader... *s. a.* Karotis...
Halsschlagaderaneurysma *n* carotid [artery] aneurysm
Halsschlagaderchirurgie *f* carotid [artery] surgery
Halsschlagadernervengeflecht *n* carotid plexus
Halsschlagaderunterbindung *f* carotid [artery] ligation
Halsschlagaderveren[er]ung *f* carotid stenosis, carotid artery narrowing
Halsschlinge *f* sling

Halsspalte

Halsspalte f tracheloschisis, cervical fissure, fissure of the neck
Halssteifigkeit f nuchal rigidity; stiff neck, crick in the neck
Halssympathikuslähmung f cervical sympathetic paralysis
Hals- und Gesichtsaktinomykose f cervicofacial actinomycosis
Halsvagus m cervical vagus
Halsvene f cervical vein; jugular vein
~/**äußere** external jugular vein
~/**innere** internal jugular vein
~/**quere** transverse cervical vein, transverse vein of the neck
~/**vordere** anterior jugular vein
Halsvenenstauung f neck vein distention
Halswirbel m cervical vertebra
~/**erster** atlas
~/**siebenter** seventh cervical vertebra
~/**zweiter** axis, epistropheus
Halswirbelkörper m cervical vertebral body
Halswirbelkörperfortsatz m cervical spinal process
Halswirbelkörperverschmelzung f cervical spinal fusion
Halswirbelsäule f cervical spine (vertebral column)
Halswirbelsäulenanomalie f cervical spine anomaly
Halswirbelsäulenbandscheibe f cervical disk
Halswirbelsäulendegeneration f cervical spondylosis
Halswirbelsäulenkyphose f trachelokyphosis
Halswirbelsäulenspaltbildung f mit fehlendem Gehirn derencephalia
Halswirbelsäulensyndrom n cervical spine syndrome
Halswirbelsäulentuberkulose f cervical tuberculous osteomyelitis
Halszyste f cervical cyst
haltbar machen to conserve; to fix *(histologische Präparate)*
Haltbarmachung f conservation; fixation *(z. B. histologischer Präparate)*
Halteband n fixing strap; retinaculum *(Anatomie) (Zusammensetzungen s. unter* Retinaculum*)*
Halteinstrument n carrier
Halteklemme f fixation forceps
halten/getrennt to isolate
~/**im Brutschrank** to incubate
Haltenaht f holding (stay, retaining) suture
Halter m carrier
Haltezange f fixation forceps
Haltung f position, posture, carriage *(Körperhaltung)*; pose
Haltungsfehler m false posture
Haltungsreflex m postural (static) reflex
Haltungsschwindel m positional vertigo
Haltungssinn m posture sense
Haltungsskoliose f postural (habit) scoliosis
Haltungstherapie f orthotherapy
Haltungstonusverlust m cataplexis

Haltungsübung f postural exercise
Haltungsverharren n waxy flexibility *(z. B. bei Gehirnkrankheiten)*
Häm n haem, hem[e], ferroprotoporphyrin 9
Hämabsorptionsvirus n haemabsorption virus
Hämachrom n haemachrome
Hämachromatose f haemachromatosis
Hämagglutination f haemagglutination, haemoagglutination
Hämagglutinationshemmung f haemagglutination inhibition
Hämagglutinationshemmungsantikörper m haemagglutination-inhibition antibody
Hämagglutinationshemmungstest m haemagglutination inhibition test
Hämagglutinationstest m haemagglutination test
Hämagglutinationsvirus n haemagglutination virus
Hämagglutinin n haemagglutinin, haemoagglutinin
Hämalaun n haemalum *(Zellkernfarbstoff)*
Hämangiektasie f haemangiectasia
hämangiektatisch haemangiectatic
Hämangioameloblastom n haemangioameloblastoma
Hämangioblastom n haemangioblastoma; angioreticuloma *(Hirngeschwulst)*
Hämangioblastomatose f haemangioblastomatosis
Haemangioectasia f hypertrophica angioosteohypertrophy, Klippel-Trénaunay-Weber syndrome
Hämangioektasie f haemangiectasia
Hämangioelastomyxom n haemangioelastomyxoma
Hämangioendotheliom n/**bösartiges** malignant haemangioendothelioma, angiosarcoma
~/**gutartiges** benign haemangioendothelioma
Hämangioendotheliosarkom n haemangioendotheliosarcoma
Hämangiolipom n haemangiolipoma
Hämangiom n haemangioma, vascular naevus *(s. a. unter* Haemangioma*)*
~/**bösartiges** malignant haemangioma
~/**kavernöses** cavernous haemangioma, cavernoma
hämangiomatös haemangiomatous
Hämangiomatose f haemangiomatosis
Hämangiomyolipom n haemangiomyolipoma
Hämangioperizytom n [haemangio]pericytoma
Hämangiosarkom n haemangiosarcoma
Hämarthros m haemarthrosis, haemorrhage into a joint
hämarthrotisch haemarthrotic
Hamartie f hamartia *(lokale Gewebsfehlbildung durch atypische Keimmaterialdifferenzierung)*
Hamartoblastom n hamartoblastoma *(Geschwulst)*
Hamartom n hamartoma *(Geschwulst)*
hamartomartig hamartomatous
Hämaskos m haem[at]operitoneum, intraperitoneal haemorrhage

Hämatemesis f haematemesis, vomiting of blood; bloody vomit[ing]
Hämathidrosis f haem[ath]idrosis, sweating of blood; bloody sweat
hämathophagisch haemophagic
Hämatidrosis f s. Hämathidrosis
Hämatin n haematin, methaema, ferrihaeme hydroxide
Hämatinämie f haematinaemia
Hämatinausscheidung f im Urin haematinuria
Hämatinerbrechen n melanemesis, black (coffee-ground) vomiting
Hämato... s. a. Hämo...
Hämatoaerometer n haematoaerometer
Hämatoblast m haematoblast
Hämatocholezystis f haemocholecyst *(Blutansammlung in der Gallenblase)*
Hämatochylozele f haematochylocele
Hämatochylurie f haematochyluria
Hämatodyskrasie f haematodyscrasia
hämatogen haematogenic, haematogenous, blood-borne
Hämatogenese f haem[at]ogenesis, haematopoiesis, formation of blood
Hämatogonie f haematogone, haematogonia
hämatoid haematoid, resembling blood
Hämatoidin n haematoidin *(Hämoglobinbestandteil)*
Hämatokatharsis f haematocatharsis, blood lavage
Hämatokolpometra f haematocolpometra *(Blutansammlung im Uterus und in der Scheide)*
Hämatokolpometrasalpinx f haematocolpometrasalpinx *(Blutansammlung im Uterus, in der Scheide und im Eileiter)*
Hämatokolpos m haematocolpos *(Blutansammlung in der Scheide)*
hämatokolposartig haematocolpos-like
Hämatokrit m 1. haematocrit, haematocrit reading (value), crit, packed-cell volume, volume of packed erythrocytes *(Verhältnis zwischen Erythrozyten- und Plasmavolumen)*; 2. haematocrit *(Laborgerät)*
Hämatokritbestimmung f haematocrit measurement
Hämatokritwert m s. Hämatokrit 1.
Hämatologe m haematologist
Hämatologie f haematology
hämatologisch haematologic
Hämatolymphurie f haematolymphuria
Hämatom n haematoma, blood (lake) tumour, ecchymosis
~/**chronisches subdurales** chronic subdural haematoma, haemorrhagic [internal] pachymeningitis
~/**epidurales** epidural haematoma
~/**retroperitoneales** retroperitoneal haematoma
~/**subarachnoidales** subarachnoid haematoma
~/**subdurales** subdural haematoma
~/**subgaleales** subgaleal haematoma
Hämatometra f haematometra, haematometrium *(Blutansammlung im Uterus)*

Hämatom[m]ole f haematomole, haematoma mole
~/**Breussche** Breus's mole, subchorial tuberous haematoma of the placenta
Hämatomyelie f haematomyelia, spinal apoplexy
Hämatomyelitis f haematomyelitis
Hämatopathologie f haemopathology, haematologic pathology
Hämatoperikard n haem[at]opericardium, intrapericardial haemorrhage
Hämatoperitoneum n haem[at]operitoneum, intraperitoneal haemorrhage
Hämatopoese f haem[at]opoiesis, haemapoiesis, haemacytopoiesis
Hämatopoetin n haem[at]opoietin
hämatopoetisch haem[at]opoietic
Hämatoporphyrie f haematoporphyria *(angeborene Stoffwechselkrankheit)*
Hämatoporphyrin n haematoporphyrin *(Blutfarbstoff)*
Hämatoporphyrinämie f haematoporphyrinaemia
Hämatoporphyrinderivat n haematoporphyrin derivative
Hämatoporphyrinurie f haematoporphyrinuria
Hämatopräzipitin n haematoprecipitin
Hämatorrhachis f haematorrhachis
Hämatorrhoe f haematorrhoea
Hämatosalpinx f haem[at]osalpinx; haemorrhagic salpingitis
Hämatose f haematosis
Hämatoskop n haem[at]oscope *(Instrument zur Blutuntersuchung)*
Hämatospektroskop n haem[at]ospectroscope
Hämatospektroskopie f haem[at]ospectroscopy
hämatospektroskopisch haematospectroscopic
Hämatospermatozele f haematospermatocele
Hämatospermie f haem[at]ospermia
Hämatotoxikose f haem[at]otoxicosis *(Schädigung des Blutbildungssystems durch Gifte)*
hämatotoxisch haem[at]otoxic
Hämatotympanum n haem[at]otympanum; blue drum
Hämatoxylin n haematoxylin *(Farbstoff)*
Hämatoxylin-Eosin-Färbung f haematoxylineosin stain
Hämatozele f haematocele
Hämatozoon n haematozoon
Hämatozyste f haematocyst
Hämatozyt m haem[at]ocyte
Hämatozytolyse f haematocytolysis, dissolution of blood corpuscles
Hamatum n hamate [bone], hamatum, unciform[e], unciform bone, uncinatum
Hämaturie f haematuria; erythr[ocyt]uria
Hämazoin n haemazoin *(Malariapigment)*
Hämin n haemin, ferriprotoporphyrin
Häminkristalle mpl haemin crystals
Hamman-Rich-Syndrom n Hamman-Rich syndrome, diffuse interstitial pulmonary fibrosis, alveolar capillary block syndrome
Hammer m malleus, hammer *(Gehörknöchelchen)*

Hammer-Amboß-Gelenk

Hammer-Amboß-Gelenk n incudomalleal articulation (joint)
Hammerband n/**vorderes** anterior malleal ligament, anterior ligament of the malleus
Hammerbewegung f **bei Chorea** malleation
Hämmerchen n malleolus
Hammerfalte f/**hintere** posterior malleolar (tympanic) fold
~/**vordere** anterior malleolar (tympanic) fold
Hammerfinger m hammer (mallet) finger
Hammerfixierung f[/**operative**] malleus fixation (im Ohr)
Hammerfortsatz m/**dicker seitlicher** lateral process of the malleus (Gehörknöchelchen)
~/**kurzer** short process of the malleus
Hammerhandgriff m handle (manubrium) of the malleus
Hammerinzision f malleotomy
Hammerkopf m head of the malleus
Hammermuskel m salpingomalleus [muscle]
Hammer-Trommelfell-Plastik f malleomyringoplasty
Hammerzehe f hammer-toe
Hammond-Syndrom n Hammond's disease, congenital athetosis
Hämo... s. a. Hämato...
Hämoagglutination f haem[o]agglutination
Hämoalkalimeter n haemoalkalimeter
Hämoalkalimetrie f haemoalkalimetry
Hämoanalyse f haemanalysis
hämoanalytisch haemanalytic
Hämobilie f haemobilia
Hämobilirubin n haemobilirubin
Hämoblast m haemo[cyto]blast
Hämoblastenleukämie f haemo[cyto]blastic leukaemia
Hämoblastose f haemoblastosis (Proliferation des blutbildenden Gewebes)
Hämochezia f haem[at]ochezia
Hämochrom n haemochrome
Hämochromatose f haemochromatosis, bronze diabetes, iron storage disease (Eisenstoffwechselstörung mit Eisenablagerung in den Organen)
Hämochromogen n haemochromogen (Blutfarbstoffabbauprodukt)
Hämochromometer n haemochromometer, haemoglobinometer, haematinometer
Hämodiagnose f haemodiagnosis
Hämodialyse f haemodialysis ● **eine ~ durchführen** to haemodialyse
Hämodialysepatient m haemodialysis patient
Hämodilution f haemodilution
Hämodromograph m haemodromograph
Hämodromometer n haemodromometer
Hämodromometrie f haemodromometry
Hämodynamik f haemodynamics
~/**renale** renal haemodynamics
hämodynamisch haemodynamic
Hämodynamometer n haemodynamometer
Hämodynamometrie f haemo[dynamo]metry
hämoendothelial haemoendothelial

Hämofiltration f haemofiltration
Hämoflagellaten mpl haemoflagellates (Trypanosomen und Leishmanien)
Hämofuszin n haemofuscin (Hämatinabbauprodukt)
Hämoglobin n haemoglobin, Hb (Blutfarbstoff)
~ **A** haemoglobin A
~ **C** haemoglobin C
~ **E** haemoglobin E
~ **F** haemoglobin F, fetal haemoglobin
~/**fetales** s. ~ F
~ **H** haemoglobin H (bei Thalassämie)
~ **M** haemoglobin M (bei Methämoglobinämie)
~ **S** haemoglobin S[C], sickle-cell haemoglobin
Hämoglobinämie f haemoglobinaemia
Hämoglobinauflösung f haemoglobinolysis
Hämoglobinaustritt m aus den Erythrozyten haemolysis
Hämoglobinbestimmung f haemo[globino]metry
hämoglobinbildend haemoglobinogenous, haemoglobic
Hämoglobinelektrophorese f haemoglobin electrophoresis
hämoglobinenthaltend haemoglobinous, haemoglobiniferous
Hämoglobingehalt m haemoglobin level (content) (der Erythrozyten) ● **mit normalem ~** normochromic
~/**erhöhter** hyperchrom[as]ia, hyperchromatosis, increased haemoglobin content
~/**mittlerer korpuskulärer** mean corpuscular haemoglobin, MCH
~/**normaler** orthochromia, normal haemoglobin content
~/**verminderter** hypochrom[as]ia, hypochromatosis, decreased haemoglobin content
hämoglobinhaltig haemoglobinous
Hämoglobinkonzentration f haemoglobin concentration
~/**mittlere korpuskuläre** mean corpuscular haemoglobin concentration, MCHC
Hämoglobinkrankheit f haemoglobinopathy
hämoglobinliefernd haemoglobiniferous, yielding haemoglobin
Hämoglobinmangel m **im Erythrozyten** hypochrom[as]ia, oligochromasia, oligochromaemia, oligoerythrocythaemia
Hämoglobinolyse f haemoglobinolysis, splitting up of haemoglobin
Hämoglobinometer n haemoglobinometer, haemochromometer, haematinometer
Hämoglobinometrie f haemo[globino]metry
hämoglobinometrisch haemoglobinometric
hämoglobinproduzierend haemoglobinogenous
Hämoglobin-S-Krankheit f s. Sichelzellenanämie
Hämoglobinspaltung f s. Hämoglobinolyse
Hämoglobinspiegel m haemoglobin level (content)
hämoglobintragend haemoglobiniferous, carrying haemoglobin
Hämoglobinurie f haemoglobinuria

~/epidemische epidemic haemoglobinuria, black jaundice, Winckel's disease
~/paroxysmale paroxysmal haemoglobinuria
~/toxische toxic haemoglobinuria
hämoglobinurisch haemoglobinuric
Hämogramm n haemogram
Hämohidrose f s. Hämathidrosis
Hämohistioblast m haemohistioblast
Hämohydrosalpinx f haemohydrosalpinx *(Ansammlung blutiger Flüssigkeit im Eileiter)*
Hämoklasie f haemoclasis
hämoklastisch haemoclastic
Hämokoagulation f haemocoagulation
Hämokonie f haemoconia
Hämokonien fpl Müller's dust bodies, [blood] dust of Müller
Hämokoniose f haemoconiosis *(Hämokonienhäufung im Blut)*
Hämokonzentration f haemoconcentration
Hämokultur f haemoculture
Hämokuprein n haemocuprein
Hämolith m haemolith
Hämolymphangiom n haemolymphangioma *(Geschwulst aus Blut- und Lymphgefäßen)*
Hämolymphe f haemolymph, blood and lymph
Hämolymphknoten m haemolymph node
Hämolysat n haemolysate
Hämolyse f haemo[cyto]lysis ● **~ bewirken** to haemolyze, to lake ● **der ~ unterliegen** to undergo haemolysis
~ durch körpereigenes Serum autohaemolysis
~ durch Tetanusbakterientoxin tetanolysis
α-Hämolyse f α-haemolysis
β-Hämolyse f β-haemolysis
Hämolyseaktivität f haemolytic activity
Hämolyseanämie f haemolytic anaemia
Hämolyseauslösung f haemolyzation
Hämolysegelbsucht f haemolytic jaundice
Hämolyseglaukom n haemolytic glaucoma
hämolysehemmend antihaemolytic
Hämolyseindex m haemolytic index
hämolysieren to haemolyze, to lake
hämolysierend haemolytic
~/nicht anhaemolytic
Hämolysierung f haemolyzation
Hämolysin n haemolysin *(Blutkörperchenzerfall bewirkender Serumkörper)*
α-Hämolysin n α-haemolysin
β-Hämolysin n β-haemolysin
γ-Hämolysin n γ-haemolysin *(von Staphylococcus aureus)*
hämolytisch haemolytic
~/nicht anhaemolytic
Hämomanometer n haemomanometer
Hämomediastinum n haemomediastinum *(Blutansammlung im Mittelfellraum)*
Hämometra f haem[at]ometra, haematometrium
Hämomyelogramm n haemomyelogram
Hämopathie f haemopathy, blood disease
Hämopathologie f haem[at]opathology, haematologic pathology
Hämoperfusion f haemoperfusion

Hämoperfusionsbehandlung f haemoperfusion treatment
Hämoperfusionskapsel f haemoperfusion cartridge
Hämophage m haemophage
Hämophagie f haem[at]ophagia
hämophagisch haemophagic, haematophagous
hämophil haemophilic, haemophil[e]
Hämophiler m haemophiliac, bleeder
Hämophilie f haem[at]ophilia, bleeders' disease
~ A haemophilia A, factor VIII deficiency, antihaemophilic globulin syndrome
~ B haemophilia B, factor IX deficiency, Christmas disease (syndrome)
~ C haemophilia C, factor XI deficiency, Rosenthal syndrome
~/vaskuläre vascular haemophilia, angiohaemophilia
Hämophilie-Genträger m carrier of haemophilia, haemophiliac carrier
Hämophobie f haemophobia *(krankhafte Angst vor Blut)*
Hämophthalmie f haemophthalmia
Hämophthalmitis f haemophthalmitis
Hämophthalmus m haemophthalmos
Hämophthise f haemophthisis
Hämopneumothorax m haemopneumothorax
Hämopoetin n haemopoietin, intrinsic factor *(Blutbildungswirkstoff)*
Hämopräzipitin n haemoprecipitin
Hämoprotozoon n haemoprotozoon
Hämoptoe f s. Hämoptyse
Hämoptyse f haemoptysis, spitting of blood (blood-stained sputum), emptysis
~/ostasiatische endemische endemic (parasitic) haemoptysis, paragonimiasis
Hämorrhagie f haemorrhage, bleeding
Hämorrhagin n haemorrhagin, endotheliotoxin
hämorrhagisch haemorrhagic
Hämorrheologie f haemorrheology
Hämorrhoidalplexus m haemorrhoidal plexus
Hämorrhoidalthrombose f haemorrhoidal thrombosis
Hämorrhoidektomie f haemorrhoidectomy, excision of haemorrhoids
Hämorrhoiden fpl haemorrhoids, piles
~/äußere external haemorrhoids (piles)
~/innere internal haemorrhoids (piles)
~/prolabierte prolapsed haemorrhoids (piles)
Hämorrhoidenentfernung f[/operative] haemorrhoidectomy, excision of haemorrhoids
Hämorrhoidenfaßzange f haemorrhoidal forceps, pile clamp
hämorrhoidenhemmend antihaemorrhoidal
Hämorrhoidenklemme f haemorrhoidal forceps, pile clamp
Hämorrhoidenknoten m haemorrhoid, pile
Hämorrhoidenoperation f/Whiteheadsche Whitehead's operation
Hämorrhoidenring m haemorrhoidal ring (zone)
~/äußerer external haemorrhoidal ring
~/innerer internal haemorrhoidal ring

Hämorrhoidensalbe

Hämorrhoidensalbe f haemorrhoidal (pile) ointment
Hämorrhoidenunterbindungsinstrument n haemorrhoidal ligator
Hämorrhoidenvorfall m haemorrhoidal prolapse
Hämosiderin n haemosiderin *(Hämoglobinabbauprodukt)*
Hämosiderinablagerung f im Gewebe s. Hämosiderose
Hämosiderinausscheidung f im Urin haemosiderinuria
Hämosideringlaukom n haemosiderotic glaucoma
Hämosiderose f haemosiderosis
~/**pulmonale** pulmonary haemosiderosis
~/**renale** renal haemosiderosis, nephrosiderosis; blue kidney
hämosiderotisch haemosiderotic
Hämospermie f haemospermia
Hämostase f haemostasis, arrest of bleeding
Hämostatikum n s. Hämostyptikum
hämostatisch s. hämostyptisch
Hämostyptikum n haemostatic [agent], antihaemorrhagic [agent], styptic
hämostyptisch haemostatic, antihaemorrhagic, [haemo]styptic
Hämotachometer n haemotachometer
Hämotachometrie f haemotachometry
Hämotherapie f haemotherapy, haema[to]therapy
Hämothorax m haem[at]othorax, haemopleura
Hämotoxikose f haem[at]otoxicosis *(Schädigung des Blutbildungssystems durch Giftstoffe)*
Hämotoxin n haemotoxin
hämotoxisch haemotoxic
Hämotoxizität f haemotoxicity
hämotrop haemotropic *(z. B. Parasiten)*
Hämotympanum n haem[at]otympanum *(Blutansammlung in der Paukenhöhle)*; blue drum
Hämozyt m haemocyte
Hämozytoblast m haemo[cyto]blast, haematogone *(Blutstammzelle)*
Hämozytoblastenleukämie f haemo[cyto]blastic leukaemia
hämozytoblastisch haemocytoblastic
Hämozytoblastom n haemocytoblastoma
Hämozytogenese f haemocytogenesis, haemocytopoiesis, formation of blood cells
Hämozytolyse f haemocytolysis
Hämozytometer n haemacytometer, haematimeter, erythro[cyto]meter
Hämozytometrie f haema[to]cytometry, haemo[cyto]metry
Hämozytopoese f haemocytogenesis, haemocytopoiesis, formation of blood cells
Hämozytozoon n haemocytozoon
Hämpigment n haem pigment
Hamulus m hamulus *(s. a. unter Hakenfortsatz)*
~ **ossis hamati** hamate (hamular, unciform) process, hook (hamulus) of the hamate bone
~ **pterygoideus** pterygoid hamulus

Hand f hand, manus *(s. a. unter Manus)* ● **die ~ pflegen** to manicure ● **mit der ~ manual** ● **ohne Hände** acheirous
Handaufbau m durch Operation cheiroplasty
Handbad n hand bath
Handballen m ball of the thumb, thenar [eminence]
Handbeugefalte f flexion crease of the wrist, rasceta
Handbeuger m flexor carpi (of the hand)
~/**kurzer radialer** flexor carpi radialis brevis [muscle]
~/**kurzer ulnarer** flexor carpi ulnaris brevis [muscle], ulnocarpus muscle
~/**radialer** flexor carpi radialis [muscle]
~/**ulnarer** flexor carpi ulnaris [muscle]
Handbeugereflex m hand flexor reflex
Handbeugerhalteband n flexor retinaculum [of the wrist]
Handchirurgie f hand surgery
Handeinwärtsdrehung f pronation, mesial rotation of the forearm
Handfehlbildung f atelocheiria
Handfläche f palm [of the hand], vola
Handflächenabszeß m palmar abscess
Handflächenreflex m palmar reflex *(Fingerbeugung bei Reizung der Hohlhand)*
Handflächenschuppenflechte f palmar psoriasis
Handgelenk n wrist [joint], carpus, carpal articulation; joint of the hand
~/**distales** intercarpal articulation, midcarpal joint
~/**proximales** radiocarpal articulation (joint), wrist joint [proper]
Handgelenkband n metacarpal ligament
Handgelenkbandage f demigauntlet bandage
Handgelenkbeugefalte f flexion crease of the wrist
Handgelenkentzündung f cheirarthritis
Handgelenkfurche f wrist crease
Handgelenkgicht f cheiragra, gout in the hand
Handgelenkknochen m wrist (carpal) bone
Handgelenklähmung f wrist drop
Handgelenkprothese f wrist joint prosthesis
Handgelenksverband m demigauntlet bandage
Handgelenkverrenkung f wrist dislocation; dislocated wrist
Handgelenkverstauchung f wrist sprain; sprained wrist
Handgriff m manipulation, manoeuvre
~ **des Hammers** s. Hammerhandgriff
~/**Jendrassikscher** Jendrassik's manoeuvre *(Neurologie)*
~/**Mauriceau-Levretscher** Mauriceau's method *(Geburtshilfe)*
~ **nach Veit-Smellie** s. ~/Smelliescher
~/**Pinardscher** Pinard's manoeuvre *(Geburtshilfe)*
~/**Prager** Prague manoeuvre *(Geburtshilfe)*
~/**Ritgenscher** Ritgen's manoeuvre *(Geburtshilfe)*
~/**Smelliescher** Smellie's method
~/**Wigand-Martin-Winckelscher** Wigand's manoeuvre *(Geburtshilfe)*

Handhypertrophie f macrocheiria, hypertrophy of the hand
Handhypotrophie f microcheiria, hypotrophy of the hand
Handlinie f palm line, line in the palm; crease
Handlungsunfähigkeit f apraxia
Handplastik f cheiroplasty
Handrekonstruktion f cheiroplasty
Handrücken m back (dorsal surface) of the hand, opisthenar
Handrückenarteriennetz n dorsal carpal rete
Handrückenreflex m carpometacarpal (carpophalangeal) reflex
Handrückenvene f vein of the dorsum of the hand
Handschiene f hand splint
Handschmerz m cheiralgia
Handschriftenlehre f graphology
Handschuhbüchse f glove container
Handschuhdermatitis f glove dermatitis
Handschuhparese f gauntlet (glove) anaesthesia
Handschuhpudergranulom n surgical-glove talc granuloma
Handschuhtrommel f glove container (drum)
Hand-Schüller-Christian-Syndrom n Hand-Schüller-Christian disease, Christian syndrome, xanthogranulomatosis, lipoid (cholesterol) granulomatosis
Hand-Schulter-Syndrom n hand-shoulder syndrome
Handstrecker m extensor carpi (of the hand)
~/kurzer radialer extensor carpi radialis brevis [muscle]
~/langer radialer extensor carpi radialis longus [muscle]
~/ulnarer extensor carpi ulnaris [muscle]
~/zusätzlicher radialer extensor carpi radialis accessorius [muscle]
Handstreckerhalteband n extensor retinaculum [of the wrist]
Handstück n **für Zahnbohrer** handpiece for the drill
Handteller m s. Handfläche
Handtuchverband m pelvic hammock *(bei Bekkenfraktur)*
Handüberstreckung f backward deviation of the hand
Hand- und Fußkrampf m carpopedal spasm
Handunterentwicklung f atelocheiria
Handverband m/**handschuhartiger** gauntlet [bandage]
Handvergrößerung f cheiromegaly
~/abnorme macrocheiria
Handverkleinerung f/**abnorme** microcheiria
Handwiederherstellung f[/operative] cheiroplasty
Handwurzel f carpus, wrist
Handwurzelband n transverse carpal ligament
Handwurzel-Finger-Reflex m carpophalangeal reflex
Handwurzelgelenk n s. Handgelenk
Handwurzelkanal m carpal tunnel (canal)

Handwurzelknochen m carpal (wrist) bone
Handwurzelknochenentfernung f[/operative] carpectomy
Handwurzel-Mittelhand-Gelenk n carpometacarpal joint
Handwurzel-Mittelhand-Gelenkverrenkung f carpometacarpal joint dislocation
Handwurzel-Mittelhand-Reflex m carpometacarpal reflex
Hanf m/**indischer** Indian hemp, cannabis indica, bhang
Hängebauch m pendulous abdomen, pendant belly
Hängebrust f mastoptosis, pendulous breast, dropped (sagging) mamma
Hängebrustfixierung f[/operative] mastopexy
Hängegips m hanging cast
Hängehüfte f dropped (hanging) hip
Hängelage f hanging (head-down) position
~/Walchersche Walcher's position *(bei der Geburt)*
Hängemattenverband m hammok bandage
Hanger-Test m s. Kephalin-Cholesterin-Flockungsreaktion
Hängeschulter f dropped shoulder
Hanot-Leberzirrhose f Hanot's cirrhosis (disease), biliary (splenomegalic) cirrhosis
Hansen-Bazillus m Hansen's bacillus, Mycobacterium leprae
Hansenid n hansenid, tuberculoid leprosy
Hansen-Krankheit f s. Lepra
Hanteltumor m dumbbell tumour
H-Antigen n H (flagellar) antigen, histocompatibility antigen *(thermolabiles Antigen geißeltragender Bakterien)*
Hapalonychie f hapalonychia *(abnorme Weichheit der Nägel)*
Haphalgesie f haphalgesia
Haphephobie f haphephobia, haptephobia *(krankhafte Angst vor Berührung)*
haplodont haplodont, haploidentical
haploid haploid *(Chromosomensatz)*
Haplopie f haplopia, single vision
Haploskop n haploscope *(Instrument zur Messung der Tiefenwahrnehmung)*
Haplotyp m haplotype *(Chromosomensatz)*
Hapten n hapten, partial (incomplete) antigen
Haptenhemmung f haptene inhibition
haptisch haptic, tactile
Haptoglobin n haptoglobin *(Serumeiweiß)*
Haptophor m, **Haptophorengruppe** f haptophore, haptophoric group *(Haftgruppe der Toxine)*
haptophorisch haptophoric, haptophorous
Harada-Syndrom n Harada's syndrome, uveo[meningo]encephalitis, idiopathic uveoneuraxitis
Harden-Young-Ester m Harden-Young ester, hexose diphosphate
harmlos harmless, innocuous, innoxious, innocent *(z. B. Medikamente)*

Harn

Harn *m* urine, water *(s. a. unter* Urin*)* ● **im ~ lebend** urinophil[e] *(z. B. Bakterien)* ● **~ lassen** to urinate, to pass water ● **vom ~ stammend** ur[in]ogenous
Harn... *s. a.* Urin...
Harnabfluß *m* urinary outflow
Harnabflußstörung *f* urinary obstruction
Harnabgang *m* urinary discharge, passing of urine
~/unbewußter (ungewollter) uroclepsia, urinary incontinence, involuntary (unconscious) urination
harnähnlich urinous, urinose
Harnalkalose *f* urinary alkalosis
Harnanalyse *f* urinalysis, uranalysis
Harnangst *f* urophobia
Harnantiseptikum *n* urinary antiseptic
harnbereitend *s.* harnbildend
Harnbereitung *f s.* Harnbildung
Harnbeschwerden *pl* dysuria, urinary disorder
harnbildend uropoietic, ur[in]ogenous, uriniparous, urinific
Harnbildung *f* uropoiesis, formation of urine
~/fehlende anuresis, anuria
Harnbildungssystem *n* uropoietic (urinary) system
Harnblase *f* [urinary] bladder, urocyst, vesica *(s. a. unter* Blase*)* ● **durch die ~** transvesical ● **neben der ~** paravesical, paracystic
~/atonische atonic bladder
~/ausgeweitete megabladder, megalocystis
~/autonome automatic (reflex, cord) bladder
~/hypotone hypotonic bladder
Harnblasen... *s. a.* Blasen...
Harnblasenanheftung *f* **an die Bauchwand** ventrocystorrhaphy
Harnblasenarterie *f* vesical artery
~/obere superior vesical artery
~/untere inferior vesical artery
Harnblasenblutung *f* cystorrhagia, bladder haemorrhage, vesical haematuria
Harnblasenbruch *m* vesicocele, hernia of the bladder
Harnblasen-Darm-Anastomose *f* enterocystoplasty
Harnblasen-Dickdarm-Fistel *f* vesicocolonic fistula
Harnblasendilatation *f* bladder dilatation, cystectasia
Harnblasendrainage *f* bladder drainage
Harnblasendysfunktion *f* bladder dysfunction
Harnblasenentfernung *f***/operative** cystectomy
Harnblasenexstrophie *f* bladder exstrophy, exstrophy of the bladder, vesical ectopia
Harnblasenfassungsvermögen *n* bladder capacity
Harnblasenfundus *m* fundus (base) of the urinary bladder
Harnblasenhals *m* vesical neck (cervix), neck of the [urinary] bladder
Harnblasenhalsentzündung *f* trachelocystitis
Harnblasenhalsobstruktion *f* bladder-neck obstruction, vesical neck obstruction
Harnblasenhalsresektion *f* bladder-neck resection
Harnblasenhalsspreizer *m* bladder-neck spreader
Harnblasen-Harnleiter-Prolaps *m* **in die Scheide** cystoureterocele
Harnblasen-Harnröhren-Prolaps *m* **in die Scheide** cystourethrocele
Harnblasen-Harnröhren-Röntgen[kontrast]bild *n* cystourethrogram
Harnblasen-Harnröhren-Röntgen[kontrast]darstellung *f* cystourethrography
Harnblasen-Harnröhren-Spiegel *m* cystourethroscope
Harnblasen-Harnröhren-Spiegelung *f* cystourethroscopy
Harnblasenkapazität *f* bladder capacity
Harnblasenkarzinom *n* bladder cancer (carcinoma)
Harnblasenkatheter *m* bladder catheter; [indwelling] urinary catheter
Harnblasenkatheterung *f* bladder catheterization
Harnblasenkonkrement *n* vesical calculus
Harnblasenkorpus *m* body of the urinary bladder
Harnblasenkrankheit *f* bladder disease
~/bösartige bladder malignancy
Harnblasenmuskulatur *f* bladder musculature, muscles of the bladder
Harnblasen-Nabel-Gang *m* urachus
Harnblasennaht *f* cystorrhaphy
Harnblasennervengeflecht *n* vesical plexus
Harnblasen-Nierenbecken-Nierenparenchym-Entzündung *f* cystopyelonephritis
Harnblasen-Nierenbecken-Röntgen[kontrast]bild *n* cystopyelogram
Harnblasen-Nierenbecken-Röntgen[kontrast]darstellung *f* cystopyelography
Harnblasenobstruktion *f* bladder obstruction
Harnblasenpapillom *n* bladder papilloma
Harnblasenparaylse *f* cystoplegia, bladder paralysis
Harnblasenperforation *f* bladder perforation
Harnblasenplastik *f* cystoplasty
Harnblasenprolaps *m* **in die Leiste** cystobubonocele
Harnblasenreflex *m* bladder (urinary) reflex, vesicourethral reflex
Harnblasen-Rektum-Anastomose *f* cystorectostomy
Harnblasen-Rektum-Prolaps *m* **in die Scheide** cystorectocele
Harnblasenretraktor *m* bladder retractor
Harnblasenröntgen[kontrast]bild *n* cystogram
~ nach Lufteinblasung pneumocystogram
Harnblasenröntgen[kontrast]darstellung *f* cystography
~ nach Lufteinblasung pneumocystography
Harnblasen-Scheiden-Bruch *m* colpocystocele
Harnblasen-Scheiden-Fistel *f* cystovaginal (vesicovaginal) fistula
Harnblasen-Scheiden-Plastik *f* colpocystoplasty

Harnblasen-Scheiden-Schnitt m colpocystotomy
Harnblasen-Scheiden-Septum n vesicovaginal septum
Harnblasenscheitel m apex of the bladder
Harnblasenschleimhaut f bladder mucosa
Harnblasen-Sigma-Fistelung f vesicosigmoidostomy
Harnblasentenesmus m bladder tenesmus, tenesmus of the bladder *(schmerzhafter Harndrang bei Blasensphinkterkrampf)*
Harnblasentraining n bladder training
Harnblasentrauma n bladder trauma
Harnblasentuberkulose f cystophthisis
Harnblasentumor m bladder tumour
Harnblasen- und Darmvorfall m enterocystocele
Harnblasen- und Harnröhrenfixation f cystourethropexy
Harnblasen- und Nierenbeckenentzündung f cystopyelitis
Harnblasen- und Vorsteherdrüsenentfernung f[/operative] cystoprostatectomy
Harnblasenurin m bladder urine
Harnblasenvene f vesical vein
Harnblasenvenengeflecht n vesical plexus
Harnblasenverweilkatheter m indwelling urinary catheter
Harnbrennen n scalding, burning sensation during micturition
Harndesinfizienz n urinary antiseptic
Harndichtebestimmung f urinometry
Harndichtemesser m ur[in]ometer, urogravimeter
Harndichtemessung f ur[in]ometry
Harndrang m uresiaesthesia, urinary urgency, desire (urge) to urinate
~/**häufiger** pollakisuria
~/**schmerzhafter** stranguria, tenesmus
Harn-Eiter-Stauungsniere f uropyonephrosis
Harnelektrolyte npl urine electrolytes
harnen to urinate, to micturate, to pass urine (water)
Harnen n s. Harnlassen
Harnentleerung f[**der Blase**] urinary evacuation, voiding of urine
~/**unwillkürliche** aconuresis, involuntary passage of urine
~/**verlangsamte** bradyuria
Harnfaden m urethral (urinary) thread
Harnfarbstoff m urinary pigment
Harnfieber n/**septisches** urosepsis
Harnfistel f urinary fistula
Harnfluß m urinary [out]flow, diabetes
~/**gleicher** isuria
~/**vermehrter** polyuria
~/**verminderter** oliguria
~/**wechselnder** anisuria *(Wechsel von Polyurie und Oligurie)*
Harnflußmessung f uroflowmetry
Harnflut f polyuria, urorrhagia, hydruria
harnführend uriniferous, conveying urine
Harngang m s. Urachus

harngängig eliminated by the urine *(z. B. Substanzen)*
Harngefühl n uresiaesthesia
Harngift n urotoxin
harngiftig urotoxic
Harngiftigkeit f urotoxicity
Harnglas n urinal
Harngrieß m urocheras, uropsammus, urinary sand (gravel)
Harngrießausscheidung f lithuresis, passage of gravel
harnhemmend antidiuretic
Harninkontinenz f urinary incontinence, incontinence of urine, enuresis, urorrhoea, aconuresis, uracratia
Harnkanälchen n uriniferous (nephric) tubule
Harnkontinenz f urinary continence
Harnkonzentration f urinary concentration
Harnkonzentrierungsschwäche f hyposthenuria *(der Nieren)*
Harnkristall m urinary crystal
Harnlassen n urination, uresis, mic[turi]tion, emiction
~/**gestörtes** dysuria
~/**häufiges** pollakisuria
~/**schmerzhaftes** urodynia
~/**seltenes** oligakisuria
harnleitend uriniferous, conveying urine
Harnleiter m ureter, urinary (metanephric) duct *(s.a. unter Ureter)* ● **neben dem** ~ para-ureteric
~/**erweiterter** mega[lo]ureter
~/**fehlmündender** aberrant ureter
~/**vereiterter** pyoureter
Harnleiter... s.a. Ureter...
Harnleiterabknickung f ureteral kink[ing]
Harnleiterabszeß m ureteral abscess, ureteropyosis; pyoureter
Harnleiteranlage f ureteral bud *(Embryologie)*
Harnleiterauslösung f ureterolysis *(aus Verwachsungen)*
Harnleiter-Blasen-Fistelung f ureterocystostomy
Harnleiter-Blasen-Spiegel m ureterocystoscope
Harnleiter-Blasen-Spiegelung f ureter[o]cystoscopy
Harnleiterblutung f ureterorrhagia, haemorrhage from the ureter
Harnleiterbruch m ureterocele
Harnleiterbruchentfernung f[/**operative**] ureterocelectomy
Harnleiter-Darm-Fistelung f ureteroenterostomy; ureterointestinal anastomosis
Harnleiter-Dickdarm-Fistelung f ureterocolostomy; ureterocolic anastomosis
Harnleitereinpflanzung f ureter implantation, implantation of the ureter
Harnleiterentfernung f[/**operative**] ureterectomy, excision of the ureter
Harnleiterentzündung f ureteritis, inflammation of the ureter
Harnleitererkrankung f ureteropathy, disease of the ureter

Harnleitereröffnung

Harnleitereröffnung *f* [*/operative*] ureterotomy
Harnleitererweiterung *f* ureterectasia
~ durch Harnstauung hydroureter; hydroureterosis
Harnleiterfistel *f* ureterostoma, ureteral fistula
Harnleiterfistelung *f* [*/operative*] ureterostomy
Harnleiterfreilegung *f* ureterolysis *(aus Verwachsungen)*
Harnleiter-Harnblasen-Anastomose *f* ureterocystostomy
Harnleiter-Harnleiter-Anastomose *f* ureteroureterostomy
Harnleiterkatheter *m* ureteral catheter
Harnleiterkatheterisation *f* ureteral catheterization
Harnleiterkrampf *m* ureteral spasm
Harnleitermündung *f* ureteral orifice (meatus)
Harnleitermündungserweiterung *f* [*/operative*] ureteral meatotomy
Harnleiternaht *f* ureterorrhaphy, suture of the ureter
Harnleiternerv *m* ureteral nerve
Harnleiterneueinpflanzung *f* **in das Nierenbecken** ureteropelvineostomy, ureteropyeloneostomy, uretero[neo]pyelostomy
~ in die Blase ureterocystoneostomy, ureteroneocystostomy
Harnleiter-Nierenbecken-Anastomose *f* ureteropyelonephrostomy
Harnleiter-Nierenbecken-Nieren-Entzündung *f* ureteropyelonephritis
Harnleiter-Nierenbecken-Rekonstruktion *f* ureteropelvioplasty
Harnleiter-Nierenbecken-Röntgen[kontrast]aufnahme *f* ureteropyelogram
Harnleiter-Nierenbecken-Röntgen[kontrast]darstellung *f* ureteropyelography
Harnleiter-Nieren-Harnstauung *f* ureterohydronephrosis
Harnleitereröffnung *f* ureteral orifice (ostium)
Harnleiterplastik *f* ureteroplasty
Harnleiterpolyp *m* ureteral polyp
Harnleiterreflux *m* ureteral reflux
Harnleiterrekonstruktion *f* [*/operative*] ureteroplasty
Harnleiter-Rektum-Fistelung *f* ureterorectostomy
Harnleiterröntgen[kontrast]bild *n* ureterogram
Harnleiterröntgen[kontrast]darstellung *f* ureterography
Harnleiter-Scheiden-Fistel *f* ureterovaginal fistula
Harnleiterschienungskatheter *m* ureter splint
Harnleiterschleimhaut *f* mucous membrane of the ureter
Harnleiterschmerz *m* ureteralgia, pain in the ureter
Harnleiter-Sigma-Anastomose *f* ureterosigmoidostomy
Harnleiterspülung *f* ureteral irrigation
Harnleiterstein *m* ureterolith, ureteral calculus
Harnleitersteinentfernung *f* [*/operative*] ureterolithotomy

Harnleitersteinextraktor *m* stone dislodger
Harnleitersteinleiden *n* ureterolithiasis
Harnleiterstriktur *f* ureteral stricture
Harnleiter- und Nierenbeckenentzündung *f* ureteropyelitis
Harnleiter- und Nierenbeckenplastik *f* ureteropyeloplasty
Harnleiter- und Nierenentfernung *f* [*/operative*] ureteronephrectomy
Harnleitervereiterung *f* ureteropyosis; pyoureter
Harnleitervereng[er]ung *f* ureteral stenosis, ureterostenosis
Harnleitervergrößerung *f* ureteromegaly
Harnleiterverletzung *f* ureteral injury
Harnleiterverschluß *m* ureteral obstruction
Harnleiterwiederherstellung *f*/**plastische** ureteral reconstruction
harnlos anuretic
Harnlosigkeit *f* anuria, anuresis
Harnmenge *f* urine amount (volume), urinary output
Harnniederschlag *m* urinary sediment
harnpflichtig usually eliminated with urine *(Stoffwechselprodukte)*
Harn-pH-Wert-Meßgerät *n* urinacidometer, uroacidimeter
Harnprobe *f* urinary specimen *(für Analysen)*
Harnproduktion *f* uropoiesis, production of urine
harnproduzierend uropoietic, urogenous, uriniparous, urinific
Harnretention *f* urinary retention, uroschesis, retention of urine
Harnröhre *f* urethra *(s.a. unter Urethra)* ● **durch die ~** transurethral ● **neben der ~** para-urethral ● **unter der ~** suburethral
~/männliche male urethra
~/weibliche female urethra
Harnröhren... *s.a.* Urethra...
Harnröhrenabstrich *m* urethral smear
Harnröhrenarterie *f* urethral artery
Harnröhrenatresie *f* atreturethria, urethral atresia, atresia of the urethra
Harnröhrenausfluß *m* 1. urethrorrhoea, urethral discharge; gleet *(chronisch)*; 2. urethral exudate
~/eitriger urethroblennorrhoe
Harnröhrenblutung *f* urethrorrhagia, urethral haemorrhage (bleeding)
Harnröhrenbougie *f* urethral bougie
Harnröhrenbruch *m* urethrocele, urethral hernia
Harnröhrendivertikel *n* urethral diverticulum
Harnröhrenenge *f* urethral isthmus
Harnröhrenentfernung *f* [*/operative*] urethrectomy, excision of the urethra
Harnröhrenentzündung *f* urethritis, urethral inflammation *(Zusammensetzungen s. unter Urethritis)*
Harnröhreneröffnung *f* [*/operative*] urethrotomy, incision into the urethra
Harnröhrenerweiterung *f* urethral dilatation
Harnröhrenfistel *f* urethrostoma
Harnröhrenfistelung *f* [*/operative*] urethrostomy

Harnröhrengeschwulst f urethrophyma, urethral tumour
Harnröhrengonorrhoe f s. Urethritis/spezifische
Harnröhren-Harnblasen-Bruch m urethrocystocele
Harnröhren-Harnblasen-Röntgen[kontrast]bild n urethrocystogram
Harnröhren-Harnblasen-Röntgen[kontrast]darstellung f urethrocystography
Harnröhreninfekt m **/aufsteigender** ascending urethral infection
Harnröhrenkatheter m urethral catheter
Harnröhrenkatheterung f urethral catheterization
Harnröhrenkrampf m urethrospasm
Harnröhrenmesser n urethrotome
Harnröhrennaht f urethrorrhaphy, suturation of the urethra, meatorrhaphy
Harnröhrenöffnung f urethral orifice (ostium)
~ **an der Eichelunterseite** balanic hypospadias
~/**äußere** external urethral orifice, external orifice of the urethra
~/**innere** internal urethral orifice, internal orifice of the urethra
Harnröhrenöffnungserweiterung f meatotomy
Harnröhrenöffnungsvereng[er]ung f urethral meatal stenosis
Harnröhrenplastik f urethroplasty
Harnröhrenreizung f urethral irritation
Harnröhrenröntgen[kontrast]bild n urethrogram
Harnröhrenröntgen[kontrast]darstellung f urethrography
Harnröhrenschleimdrüsen fpl urethral glands, Littré's glands
Harnröhrenschleimhaut f urethral mucosa
Harnröhrenschließmuskel m urethral sphincter, external urinary sphincter, sphincter urethrae [membranaceae]
Harnröhrenschmerz m urethralgia, urethrodynia, pain in the urethra
Harnröhrenschwellkörper m **des Penis** spongy body of the penis
Harnröhrenschwellkörperarterie f artery of the bulb of the penis
Harnröhrenschwellkörperentzündung f spongi[os]itis
Harnröhrensonde f urethral sound
Harnröhrenspalte f/**obere** epispadia (angeborene Mißbildung)
~/**seitliche** paraspadias (angeborene Mißbildung)
~/**untere** hypospadias (angeborene Mißbildung)
Harnröhrenspaltträger m epispadiac
Harnröhrenspiegel m urethroscope, meatoscope; aerourethroscope
Harnröhrenspiegelung f urethroscopy, urethrascopy, meatoscopy
~ **mit Luftinsufflation** aerourethroscopy
Harnröhrenstenose f urethral stenosis, urethrostenosis
Harnröhrenstriktur f urethral stricture
Harnröhrenstrikturenoperation f meatotomy
Harnröhrentripper m gonococcal (gonorrhoeal) urethritis

Harnröhren- und Blasendreieckentzündung f urethrotrigonitis
Harnröhren- und Blasenentzündung f urethrocystitis, inflammation of the urethra and the urinary bladder
Harnröhrenvereng[er]ung f urethrostenosis, urethral stenosis
Harnröhrenverletzung f urethral injury
Harnröhrenzange f urethral forceps
Harnruhr f diabetes
~/**einfache** insipid diabetes
Harnsack m/**embryonaler** allantois
Harnsammelröhrchensystem n **der Niere** renal collecting system
Harnsäure f uric (lithic) acid
harnsäureauflösend urisolvent, uricolytic
Harnsäureauflösung f uricolysis, disintegration of uric acid
harnsäureausscheidend uricosuric
Harnsäureausscheidung f **im Urin** uricaciduria, lithuria
~ **im Urin/vermehrte** hyperuric[os]uria, hyperuricaciduria, hyperlithuria
~ **im Urin/verminderte** hypouric[os]uria, hypouricaciduria
harnsäurebildend uricopoietic
Harnsäurebildung f uricopoiesis
Harnsäure[blutspiegel]erhöhung f uric[acid]aemia, hyperuric[acid]aemia, lithaemia
Harnsäuregeschwulst f uratoma
Harnsäurekristall m uric-acid crystal
harnsäurelösend urisolvent, uricolytic
harnsäureproduzierend uricopoietic
Harnsäurespiegel m uric acid level *(im Blut)*
Harnsäurespiegelverminderung f **im Blut** hypouricaemia
Harnsäurestein m uric acid calculus, urate calculus
Harnsediment n urinary sediment
Harnsekretionshemmung f antidiuresis
Harnsepsis f urosepsis
Harnsperre f renal shutdown
Harnstarre f isosthenuria *(mangelnde Konzentrations- und Verdünnungsfähigkeit der Nieren)*
Harnstau m urinary stasis
Harnstauungsniere f hydro[uretero]nephrosis, nephrohydrosis, uronephrosis
Harnstauungsureter m hydroureter, uroureter; hydroureterosis
Harnstein m urolith, urinary calculus
Harnsteinentfernung f[/**operative**] urolithotomy
Harnsteinerkrankung f urolithiasis, urinary lithiasis
Harnsteinlehre f urolithology
Harnstickstoffmeßgerät n uroazotometer
Harnstoff m urea, carbamide
harnstoffausscheidend ureosecretory
Harnstoffausscheidung f **im Schweiß** ur[h]idrosis
~ **im Urin/fehlende** anazoturia
harnstoffbestimmend ureometric

Harnstoffbestimmung 310

Harnstoffbestimmung f ureometry, ureametry
harnstoffbildend ureapoietic, ureagenetic
Harnstoffbildung f ureapoiesis, ureagenesis, formation of urea
Harnstoffblutspiegel m blood urea level
Harnstoff-Clearance f urea clearance
harnstoffmessend ureometric, ureametric
Harnstoffmeßgerät n ureometer, ureameter
Harnstoffmessung f ureometry, ureametry
harnstoffproduzierend ureapoietic, ureagenetic
Harnstoffstickstoff m urea nitrogen
~ **im Blutserum** blood urea nitrogen, BUN
Harnstoffzyklus m urea cycle
Harnstottern n urinary stammering (stuttering, intermittency); stammering bladder
Harnstrahl m/**schwacher** weak urinary stream (z. B. bei Prostataadenom)
Harnsystem n urinary system
Harnsystemröntgen[kontrast]aufnahme f urogram
Harnsystemröntgen[kontrast]darstellung f urography
Harntrakt m urinary tract
Harnträufeln n dribbling of urine; enuresis, urorrhoea, urinary incontinence
harntreibend diuretic, uragogue, emictory, uretic
Harn- und Blutstauungsniere f urohaematonephrosis
Harn- und Geschlechtsorgane npl s. Urogenitalsystem
harnuntersuchend uroscopic
Harnuntersucher m uroscopist
Harnuntersuchung f 1. ur[in]oscopy; 2. urinalysis, uranalysis
Harnvergiftung f uraemia
harnverhaltend ischuretic
Harnverhaltung f ischuria, urinary retention (hesitancy), uroschesis
Harnwaage f ur[in]ometer, urogravimeter
Harnwege mpl urinary tract (passages)
~/**obere** upper urinary tract
~/**untere** lower urinary tract
Harnwegendoskopie f urinary tract endoscopy
Harnwegepithel n urothelium
Harnwegerkrankung f uropathy, urinary tract disease
Harnweginfektion f urinary tract infection
Harnwegkonkrement n urinary calculus
Harnwegleiden n urinary tract affliction
~/**bösartiges** urinary tract malignancy
Harnwegsspiegelung f urinary tract endoscopy
Harnwegverletzung f urinary tract injury
Harnzucker m urinary glucose
Harnzuckerausscheidung f diabetic glycosuria
harnzuckerfrei aglycosuric
Harnzuckertest m urine sugar test
~/**Benediktscher** Benedict's test
Harnzwang m 1. stranguria; 2. s. Harndrang
Harnzylinder m urinary cylinder, cylindroid, urinary (renal) cast (bei Nierenerkrankung im Urin)

Harnzylinder mpl/**Bence-Jonessche** Bence-Jones cylinders
Harnzyste f urinoma
hart hard; solid (fest); hard, sclerotic (z. B. Gewebe); hard, tough (z. B. ein Infiltrat); hard, penetrating (z. B. Strahlung); ● ~ **werden** to harden, to solidify; to indurate, to sclerose (z. B. Gewebe)
harthäutig pachydermatous, scleroderm[at]ous, thick-skinned
Harthäutigkeit f pachyderm[i]a, sclerodermia
hartnäckig refractory, obstinate, inveterate (z. B. eine Krankheit); persistent (z. B. Schmerzen)
Hartspann m [myo]gelosis
Harz n resin
Haschisch m(n) hashish, marihuana, marijuana, bhang, cannabis indica (Rauschgift)
Haschischsucht f cannabism
Haschischvergiftung f cannabism, hashish poisoning
Hasenauge n lagophthalmos, lagophthalmus, hare's eye
Hasenpest f tularaemia, rabbit (deer fly) fever, Ohara's disease
Hasenscharte f cheiloschisis, stom[at]oschisis, lip fissure; harelip, cleft lip
Hashimoto-Syndrom n Hashimoto's disease (struma, thyroiditis), lymphadenoid goitre
Haube f 1. tegmentum (des Mittelhirns); 2. galea, head bandage
Haubenbahn f/**zentrale** central tegmental tract (fasciculus)
Haubenkreuzung f decussatio[n], tegmental (fountain) decussation
~/**Forelsche** [tegmental] decussation of Forel, fountain (ventral tegmental) decussation
~/**Meynertsche** [tegmental] decussation of Meynert, fountain (dorsal tegmental) decussation
Haubenregion f tegmentum (des Mittelhirns)
Hauch m breath, halitus
Haufen mpl/**Peyersche** Peyer's glands (patches) (im unteren Dünndarm)
Häufigkeitsrate f incidence rate (z. B. einer Krankheit)
Hauptagglutinin n major (chief) agglutinin
Hauptarterie f main artery
Hauptbronchus m main (primary) bronchus
~/**linker** left main [stem] bronchus
~/**rechter** right main [stem] bronchus
Hauptgallengang m common [bile] duct, choledochus
Hauptschlagader f s. Aorta
Hauptsymptom n main symptom, cardinal sign
Hauptzelle f 1. chief (peptic) cell (der Magenschleimhaut); 2. chief (principal, central) cell (endokriner Drüsen)
Hauptzellenhyperplasie f chief-cell hyperplasia
Hausapotheke f medicine cupboard
Hausarzt m family doctor (physician)
Hausbehandlung f home (domiciliary) treatment
Hausbesuch m home (domiciliary) visit
Hausentbindung f home delivery

Häuserangst f domatophobia, oikophobia
Hauskeim m hospital germ
Haustralfalte f haustral fold
Haustrenbildung f, **Haustrierung** f haustration, sacculation of colon, haustral churning (segmentation)
Haustrum n haustrum
Haut f 1. skin, cutis, derm[a], dermis *(s. a. unter Cutis)*; 2. coat, tunic; membrane ● **durch die ~** transcutaneous, through the skin ● **durch die ~ hindurch** percutaneous ● **mit verknöcherter ~** osteodermatous ● **unter der ~** subcutaneous, s. c., subdermal, subdermic, hypoderm[at]ic, subintegumental ● **unter die ~ bluten** to suffuse ● **unter die ~ erfolgend** hypoderm[at]ic
~/**aufgesprungene** chapped (cracked) skin
~/**äußere** integument[um], tegument
~/**farblose** achromoderma
~/**gelbe** ochroderma; ochrodermia
~/**harte** callosity
~/**intakte** intact (unbroken) skin
~/**marmorierte** marble skin
~/**pigmentarme** achromoderma
~/**reizbare** irritable skin
~/**rissige** cracked (broken) skin
~/**rötlich entzündete** erythroderma; erythrodermia
~/**seröse** serosa, serous membrane (coat)
~/**trockene** xeroderma; xerodermia
~/**verhornte** horny skin; keratosis
~/**verknöcherte** osteoderma; osteodermia
Hautabschleifung f skin abrasion, dermabrasion
Hautabschnitt m dermatome, cutis plate
Hautabschürfung f excoriation; abrasion
Hautabsonderung f skin (cutaneous) excretion
Hautaffektion f skin affection (trouble), dermatosis
Hautaffinität f dermotropism
hautähnlich skin-like, derm[at]oid
Hautakne f cutaneous (skin) acne
Hautallergie f cutaneous (skin) allergy
Hautamöbiasis f cutaneous amoebiasis
Hautanhangsgebilde npl cutaneous appendages
Hautareal n cutaneous (skin) area
hautartig derm[at]oid
Hautarzt m dermatologist
Hautatmung f [cutaneous] perspiration, transpiration
Hautatrophie f cutaneous atrophy, dermatrophia; atrophoderma
~/**neurotische** trophodermatoneurosis
Hautausschlag m exanthem[a], efflorescence, skin rash (eruption), anthema
~ **an den Extremitäten** acrodermatosis
~/**durch Medikamente hervorgerufener** drug eruption, medicinal rash
~/**eitriger** pyodermatosis; pyoderma
~/**flüchtiger** rash
~/**juckender** urticaria, hives
~/**paravakzinaler** paravaccinia
~/**syphilitischer** syphilid[e]; syphiloderm[a]
Hautausschlagrückgang m deflorescence

Hautaustrocknung f xerodermia
Hautauswuchs m excrescence
Hautbehandlung f dermatotherapy, treatment of the skin
Hautberührungsschmerz m haphalgesia
Hautbestrahlung f irradiation of the skin
Hautbeugefalte f skin flexion crease
Hautbeulenkrankheit f cutaneous myiasis
hautbildend dermatogenous
Hautbildung f cutization, cutification; dermogenesis
~/**fehlende** adermogenesis
Hautbiopsieprobe f skin biopsy specimen
Hautbläschen n phlyctenule, phlyctenula
Hautblase f blister, bulla, bleb
hautblasenbildend blistering, epispastic
Hautblasenbildung f blistering
Hautblasenerkrankung f bullous dermatosis
Hautblastomykose f cutaneous blastomycosis, dermatomycosis
Hautblaufärbung f cyanochroia
Hautblutfülle f dermahaemia, dermohaemia
Hautblutung f cutaneous haemorrhage, skin bleeding, ecchymosis, dermatorrhagia
~ **bei Rheumatismus** rheumatic peliosis
~/**petechiale** cutaneous petechial haemorrhage
Hautblutungen fpl/**punktförmige** petechiae
~/**streifenförmige** vibices
Hautchemotherapie f endermosis, cutaneous chemotherapy
Häutchen n cuticle, tunic[a]; membrane; pellicle *(der Protozoen)* ● **aus ~ bestehend** membranous ● **mit einem ~ überzogen** pelliculate
häutchenartig pellicular
häutchenreich membranous
Hautdefektdeckung f skin grafting
Hautdehnungsstreifen mpl lineae albicantes (gravidarum) *(Hautatrophien durch Zerreißung der elastischen Fasern)*
Hautdepigmentierung f cutaneous depigmentation
Hautdiphtherie f cutaneous diphtheria
Hautdosis f skin dose *(Radiologie)*
Hautdrüse f cutaneous (skin) gland
Hautdurchblutung f cutaneous circulation, skin blood flow
Hauteffloreszenz f cutaneous (skin) efflorescence
Hauteintrocknung f pachylosis
Hauteinziehung f dimple
Hautempfindung f cutaneous (dermal) sensation
Hautemphysem n [sub]cutaneous emphysema, surgical emphysema, pneumo[hypo]derma, aerodermectasia
Hautendigung f cutaneous ending
Hautentartung f cutaneous degeneration
Hautentzündung f derm[at]itis, inflammation of the skin, scytitis *(s. a. unter Dermatitis)*
~ **durch Giftwirkung** toxicodermatitis, toxidermitis
~/**durch Milben verursachte** acarodermatitis
~ **durch radioaktive Strahlen** radiodermatitis

Hautentzündung

~/eitrige pyodermatitis
~ mit Narbenbildung ulodermatitis
~ mit Pigmentbildung melanodermatitis
~ mit Rötung erythrodermatitis
Hauterfrierung f perniosis; chilblains
Hauterkrankung f skin disease
~/eitrige pyodermatosis; pyoderma
~/syphilitische dermosyphilopathy; syphiloderm[a]
Hauternährungsstörung f infolge Nervenschädigung trophodermatoneurosis
Hautersatz m/plastischer dermatoplasty
Hauterschlaffung f dermatochalasis
Hauterythemdosis f [skin] erythema dose, SED (Radiologie)
Hautexkoriation f cutaneous (skin) excoriation
Hautfacharzt m dermatologist
Hautfalte f 1. cutaneous fold, plica, skin crease (große); wrinkle (kleine); 2. patagium, winglike membrane (z. B. das Flügelfell)
Hautfaltenentfernung f[/operative] rhytidectomy
Hautfarbe f skin colour; complexion (im Gesicht)
Hautfett n dermafat, cutaneous fat; sebaceous matter
Hautfettlappen m/gestielter dermic-fat pedicle flap
Hautfibrom n dermatofibroma
Hautfibromatose f dermatofibrosis, nodular subepidermal fibrosis
Hautfilariasis f cutaneous filariasis
Hautflechte f/juckende prurigo
~/kriechende serpigo
~/schuppende psoriasis, psora
~/tuberkulöse lupus [vulgaris]
Hautfleck m patch; spot, blotch, lentigo, freckle
~/brauner liver spot
~/pigmentfreier leucoderma
Hautflecken mpl/weiße vitiligines
Hautflora f cutaneous (skin) flora
Hautfollikel m cutaneous (skin) follicle
Hautfollikelentzündung f epifolliculitis
Hautgangrän f cutaneous (skin) gangrene
Hautgefäß n cutaneous (skin) vessel
Hautgefäßanordnung f cutaneous (skin) vasculature
Hautgefäßentzündung f angiodermatitis
hautgefäßerweiternd telangiectatic, angiotelectatic
Hautgefäßerweiterung f tel[e]angiectasia, telangiectasis, angiotelectasia
Hautgefäßkonstriktion f cutaneous vasoconstriction
Hautgefäßverteilung f cutaneous (skin) vasculature
Hautgefühl n dermal sensation, cutaneous sensibility
Hautgelbfärbung f ochrodermatosis
Hautgeruch m/starker (übler) ozochrotia, strong odour of the skin
Hautgeschwulst f cutaneous (skin) tumour
~/weiche molluscum, soft cutaneous tumour

Hautgift n cutaneous (skin) poison
Hautgrieß m grutum, milium
Hautgrübchen n cutaneous (skin) dimple
Hauthäkchen n cutaneous (skin) retractor
Hauthyperämie f dermahaemia, dermathemia, dermohaemia
Hauthyperämisierung f rubefaction, reddening of the skin; redness of the skin
häutig 1. skinny, derm[at]oid, cutaneous; 2. membranous
Hautimpfstoff m dermovaccine
Hautinfektion f cutaneous (dermal) infection
Hautinnervation f cutaneous (skin) innervation
Hautinzision f cutaneous (skin) incision
Hautjucken n pruritus; itch[ing of the skin]
Hautkapillare f cutaneous capillary
Hautkapillarerweiterung f tel[e]angiectasia, telangiectasis, angiotelectasia, capillary ectasia
Hautkapillarmikroskopie f dermatoscopy
Hautkapillarzerreißung f dermatorrhexis
Hautkeime mpl/ständige resident flora
Hautklammer f skin (wound) clip
Hautknötchen n cutaneous tubercle, skin nodule
~ bei kutaner Leishmaniose leishmanid
~/kleines weißes milium
Hautkontakttest m contact test
Hautkörnerzellenschicht f granular-cell layer of the epidermis
Hautkrankheit f skin disease, dermatosis, dermatopathy
~/angeborene genodermatosis
~ durch Giftwirkung toxicodermatosis, toxicoderm[i]a
~/ekzematische eczematosis
~ mit seröser Exsudation serodermatitis, serodermatosis
~/stark juckende prurigo
Hautkrankheitslehre f dermato[patho]logy
Hautkrebs m skin cancer, cutaneous carcinoma, cancroid
Hautlappen m [cutaneous] flap, flap of the skin
~/gestielter dermal pedicle flap, pedicle graft
Hautläsion f cutaneous lesion, skin (dermal) injury
Hautleishmaniase f Aleppo (Baghdad, Delhi) boil, Biskra (oriental) button, China (Kandahar) sore, Jeddah (tropical) ulcer (durch Leishmania tropica)
~/südamerikanische Brazilian (South American) leishmaniasis, mucocutaneous (nasopharyngeal) leishmaniasis, Bahia (chewing gum) ulcer, chiclero's ear, forest jaws, bay sore, Breda's disease (durch Leishmania braziliensis)
Hautleishmanoid n [post-kala-azar] dermal leishmanoid
Hautlepra f cutaneous (nodular) leprosy
Hautlinien fpl cuticular sulci
Hautlosigkeit f adermia
Hautmadenfraß m dermamyiasis, cutaneous (creeping) myiasis
Hautmanifestation f cutaneous (skin) manifestation

Hautsymptom

~ einer Krankheit dermadrome
Hautmesser n derma[to]tome, cutisector
~/**elektrisches** electrodermatome
Hautmetastase f cutaneous (skin) metastasis
Hautmikroskopie f dermatoscopy
Hautmikrozirkulation f cutaneous (skin) microcirculation
Hautmilzbrand m cutaneous anthrax, anthrax boil, malignant pustule
Hautmittel n dermatic, skin preparation
~/**hyperämisierendes** rubefacient [agent]
Hautmuskel m cutaneous (dermal) muscle
~ **des Halses** platysma [myoides]
Haut-Muskel-Insellappen m myocutaneous insular (island) flap
~/**pektoraler** pectoral myocutaneous insular flap
Haut-Muskel-Lappen m myocutaneous flap
Haut-Muskel-Verschiebelappen m myocutaneous advancement flap
Hautmyiasis f dermamyiasis, cutaneous (skin) myiasis
Hautmykose f dermatomycosis, epidermatomycosis, cutaneous (skin) mycosis
Hautmyom n dermatomyoma
Hautnaht f cutaneous (skin) suture, dermal stitch
Hautnävus m cutaneous naevus
Hautnerv m cutaneous nerve
Hautnervenendigung f cutaneous ending
Hautnervenlehre f dermatoneurology
Hautnervenschmerz m derm[at]algia, dermatagra
Hautneubildung f cutization
Hautneurose f dermatoneurosis
Hautödem n cutaneous oedema
Hautonchocerciasis f onchodermatitis, cutaneous onchocerciasis
Hautpapillarmuster n dermatoglyphics, skin pattern
Hautpapillarmusterbild n dermatogram, dactylogram
Hautpapille f dermal papilla
Hautparasit m dermatozoon, epizoon, cutaneous (skin) parasite
Hautparasitenbefall m epi[dermato]zoonosis, [endo]dermatozoonosis
Hautpigmentierung f cutaneous pigmentation
Hautpigment[ierungs]krankheit f chrom[at]odermatosis, chromatopathy
Hautpigmentstörung f chrom[at]odermatosis, dyschromia
Hautpilz m dermatophyte, dermatomyces, dermatomycete, cutaneous (skin) fungus
~/**oberflächlicher** ectophyte
~/**tiefer** endophyte
Hautpilzerkrankung f dermatophytosis, [epi]dermatomycosis, epidermophytosis, cutaneous mycosis; athlete's foot
Hautplastik f [epi]dermatoplasty, cutaneous (skin) grafting
Haut-Platysma-Schicht f skin-platysma layer
Hautpore f skin pore

Hautprobe f/**Casonische** Casoni (echinococcal) skin test; Casoni reaction
~ **nach Burnet** abortin test
Hautpunktion f skin puncture
Haut-Pupillen-Reflex m cutaneous pupillary reflex
Hautquerschnitt m transverse skin incision
Hautrand m skin edge
Hautreaktion f dermoreaction, cutireaction, cutaneous (skin) reaction
Hautreflex m cutaneous (skin) reflex
~/**psychogalvanischer** psychogalvanic reflex, galvanic skin reaction, GSR
Hautreflexzentrum n cutaneous reflex centre
hautreizend skin irritating, skin-irritant; rubefacient (hyperämisierend); epispastic (blasenziehend)
Hautreizmittel n/**hyperämisierendes** rubefacient [agent]
Hautreizung f cutaneous (skin) irritation
Hautritzung f scarification
hautrötend rubefacient, erythrogenic
Hautrötung f 1. rubefaction, reddening of the skin; 2. erythrodermia, erythrosis, rubeosis, rubedo, redness of the skin, erythema
~/**entzündliche** rubor, inflammatory redness of the skin
~/**kleinfleckige** roseola
Hautsalbe f skin ointment
Hautsarkoidose f cutaneous sarcoidosis
Hautschicht f dermal layer
Hautschlaffheit f dermatochalasis, dermatolysis
Hautschmerz m dermatodynia, derm[at]algia
Hautschnitt m dermatotomy, skin incision
Hautschrift f derm[at]ographia, dermographism, autographism, skin writing (vasomotorisches Nachröten der Haut nach dem Bestreichen)
Hautschuppe f squama, squame, [cutaneous] scale, skin scale
Hautschwiele f callosity
Hautsegment n dermatome, dermatomic area; cutis plate, dermatomere (Embryologie)
Hautsensibilisierung f cutaneous (skin) sensitization
Hautsensibilität f cutaneous sensibility, skin sensitivity
Hautsinn m cutaneous sensation, dermal sense
Hautsklerose f sclerodermia, cutaneous (skin) sclerosis
Hautspaltlinie f tension line [of Langer], cleavage (skin wrinkle) line, line of skin cleavage
Hautspannplatte f skin straightening plate
Hautspannung f cutaneous (skin) tension
Hautstanze f skin (dermal) punch
Hautstellen fpl/**weiße** vitiligines
Hautstich m skin stitch
Hautstichelung f scarification
Hautstiellappen m dermal pedicle flap
Hautstift m derma[to]graph
hautstraffend erugatory
Hautstraffung f erugation
Hautsymptom n dermadrome, cutaneous symptom, skin sign

Hautsyphilis

Hautsyphilis f cutaneous syphilis, dermosyphilopathy; syphiloderm[a]
Hauttalg m cutaneous sebum, sebaceous matter
Hauttest m cutaneous (skin) test
Hauttestantigen n skin test antigen
Hauttestung f skin testing
Hauttransplantat n skin (surface) graft
~/gestieltes pedicled skin graft
~/homologes skin homograft
~/Reverdinsches Reverdin (pinch) graft
Hauttransplantation f skin grafting (transplantation), dermanaplasty, epidermization
Hauttransplantationsmesser n skin graft knife, cutisector
Hauttrockenheit f xerodermia; pachylosis
Haut-Tuberkulin-Probe f skin tuberculin test
Haut-Tuberkulin-Reaktion f dermotuberculin reaction
Hauttuberkulose f cutaneous (skin) tuberculosis, lupus [vulgaris]; scrofuloderma
Hauttuberkuloseknoten m tuberculid[e]
Hautturgor m cutaneous (skin) turgor
Hautüberdeckung f cuti[ni]zation
Hautüberempfindlichkeit f/**halbseitige** hemihyperaesthesia
Haut- und Hautanhangssystem n integumentary system
Haut- und Muskelentzündung f dermatomyositis
Haut- und Periostverdickung f pachydermoperiostosis
Haut- und Schleimbeutelentzündung f dermosynovitis
Haut- und Schleimhautleishmaniase f/**lateinamerikanische** American cutaneous-mucocutaneous leishmaniasis
Hautunterblutung f ecchymosis
Hautuntersuchung f examination of the skin; dermatoscopy
Hautvene f cutaneous vein
Hautvenenentzündung f dermophlebitis
Hautverbrennung f skin burn
Hautverdickung f pachydermia, thickening of the skin; pachyderma
~ und -verhärtung f scleroderm[at]itis
Hautverfärbung f dyschromia (z. B. bei Syphilis)
~/umschriebene macule, macula
Hauthärtung f dermatosclerosis, chorionitis, scleriasis; scleroderma, scleroma, sclerema
~ der Finger sclerodactyly
~ der Finger und des Gesichts acrosclerosis
~ der Gliedmaßenenden acroscleroderma
Hautverhornung f [para]keratosis
~/übermäßige hyperkeratosis
Hautverhornungsanomalie f dyskeratosis
hautverknöchert osteodermatous
Hautverknöcherung f osteodermia, dermostosis
Hautverletzung f cutaneous (skin) lesion, dermal injury; broken skin
Hautverschleimung f mucinosis
Hautverunreinigungen fpl skin contaminants
Hautvoralterung f geromorphism

Hautwassersucht f anasarca; cutaneous (skin) oedema
hautwassersüchtig anasarcous
Hautwunde f cutaneous lesion, skin wound
Hautwurm m malleus, maliasmus (Infektionskrankheit durch Malleomyces mallei)
Hautzerreißung f dermatorrhexis
Hautzoonose f dermatozoonosis
Hautzyanose f cyanoderma
Hautzyste f dermatocyst, cutaneous (skin) cyst
Haverhill-Fieber n Haverhill (streptobacillary) fever, epidemic arthritic erythema
HA-Virus n haemabsorption virus
Hb s. Hämoglobin
HCG s. Choriongonadotropin/humanes
HCVD hypertensive cardiovascular disease
HDL high density lipoprotein
Head-Zonen fpl Head's zones (areas) (Reflexzonen der Haut)
Hebamme f midwife, accoucheuse, maternity nurse
Hebeinstrument n [e]levator
Hebel m/**zahnärztlicher** elevator
Hebemuskel m levator [muscle]
hebephren hebephrenic
Hebephrener m hebephreniac
Hebephrenie f hebephrenia, hebephrenic type of schizophrenia, pubescent insanity
hebephrenisch hebephrenic
Heberden-Arthrose f Heberden's disease (arthritis)
Heberden-Knoten m Heberden's (Heberden-Rosenbach) node
Heberdrainage f suction (siphon) drainage
Hebetomie f heb[oste]otomy, pubiotomy
Hebetudo f hebetude
Heboidophrenie f heboidophrenia (Abortivform der Hebephrenie)
Heb[oste]otomie f heb[oste]otomy, pubiotomy
Hechelatmung f rapid shallow respiration
HED s. Hauterythemdosis
Heerfordt-Mylius-Krankheit f Heerfordt's disease (syndrome), uveoparotid fever, uveoparotitis
Hefe f yeast
Hefepilz m yeast [fungus], saccharomycete
Hefepilzkrankheit f saccharomycosis
Hefepilzseptikämie f yeast septicaemia
heftig severe, violent, sharp, acute (z. B. Schmerzen); bad (Erkältung); intense, intensive (z. B. Reaktion auf Medikamente)
Heftpflaster n adhesive (sticking) plaster, strap
Heftpflasterallergie f hypersensibility to adhesive plaster
Heftpflasterverband m adhesive tape dressing, adhesive bandage (strapping)
Hegar-Stift m Hegar's dilator
Heilanstalt f psychiatric (mental) hospital
Heilanzeige f [therapeutic] indication
Heilbad n therapeutic (medicinal) bath; spa, health resort

heilbar healable, curable, remediable
~/durch Bestrahlung radiocurable
~/medizinisch medicable
~/nicht incurable, irremediable
Heilbarkeit f curability
Heilbehandlung f therapy, therapeutic treatment, [curative] treatment
heilen to treat, to cure *(z. B. Kranke)*; to close, to heal *(z. B. Wunden)*; to consolidate *(z. B. Knochen)*; to sanitize
~/durch Granulierung to heal by granulation
~/per primam intentionem s. ~/primär
~/per secundam intentionem s. ~/sekundär
~/primär to heal by first intention
~/sekundär to heal by granulation (second intention)
heilend curative, remedial; therapeutic, medicinal; consolidant; sanitary; salutary, sanatory
Heilerde f healing earth
Heilerfolg m remedial success, curative effect, therapeutic result
Heilerziehung f **von Sprachgestörten** logopaedia, logopaedics *(z. B. von Stotterern)*
Heilfieber n artificial (therapeutic) fever
Heilgymnastik f medical gymnastics, physiotherapy, kinesiotherapy, kinetotherapy, kinesiatrics
Heilkraft f healing (curative) power; medicinal property *(z. B. einer Arzneipflanze)*
Heilkrampfbehandlung f electroshock therapy
Heilkunde f medicine, medical science; therapeutics
~/physikalische physical therapy, physiotherapy, physiatrics
Heilmittel n drug, remedy, [curative] preparation *(s. a. Medikament)*
~/galenisches galenical
~/lösendes resolvent [agent]
~/spezifisches specific [agent] *(gegen bestimmte Krankheiten)*
Heilmittellehre f pharmacology
Heilnahrung f diet
Heilphase f healing period
Heilprozeß m healing process
heilsam salutary, salubrious, sanatory; curative, remedial, medicinal *(z. B. Medikament)*
Heilsamkeit f salutariness, salubrity; curative effect
Heilschlaf m healing sleep
Heilschlafbehandlung f sleep (narcosis) therapy
Heilschlamm m peloid, fango
Heilschlammbehandlung f peloid treatment, fango therapy
Heilserum n [antitoxic] serum, antitoxin, antiserum
Heilstätte f sanatorium, home, hospital
Heilung f healing, recovery; treatment, therapy, cure *(z. B. einer Krankheit)*; healing, closure, union *(z. B. einer Wunde)*; consolidation *(z. B. eines Knochenbruchs)* ● **eine Krankheit zur ~ bringen** to bring about the cure of a disease ● **vollständige ~ haben** to experience complete recovery
~ per primam first intention healing
~ per secundam second intention healing
Heilungsaussicht f chance of recovery
Heilungsphase f recovery phase *(z. B. einer Krankheit)*; healing phase *(z. B. einer Wunde)*
Heilungsprozeß m healing process
Heilungsverlauf m cure, recovery, curing *(z. B. einer Krankheit)*; healing *(z. B. einer Wunde)*
Heilverfahren n therapy, [medical] treatment, cure
Heilwirkung f curative (therapeutic) effect, healing action
Heimdialyse f home dialysis
Heimdialyseeinheit f home dialysis unit
heimisch endemic, nostrate *(z. B. Krankheiten)*
Heimsuchung f infestation *(durch Ungeziefer)*; affliction *(durch Krankheiten)*
heimtückisch insidious *(z. B. eine Krankheit)*
Heimweh n home-sickness, nostalgia
~/krankhaftes nostomania
heimwehkrank nostalgic
Heiratsangst f gamophobia
Heiratsdrang m/**krankhafter** gamomania
heiratsfähig marriageable, nubile
Heiratsfähigkeit f marriageability, nubility; marriageable age
Heiratsscheu f misogamy
heiser throaty, hoarse; husky *(belegt)*
Heiserkeit f hoarseness, trachyphonia
heiß hot *(z. B. Strumaknoten)*
Heißhunger m b[o]ulimia, morbid appetite, hyperorexia, hyperphagia, ad[d]ephagia, cynorexia
heißhungrig boulimiac, bulimic; voracious, ravenous
Heißluftbad n hot-air bath, sudatory bath, sudatorium; Turkish bath
Heißluftbehandlung f hot-air treatment, aerothermotherapy
Heißluftdesinfektion f hot-air disinfection
Heißluftsterilisation f hot-air sterilization
Heißluftsterilisator m hot-air sterilizer
Heißnadelpunktion f ignipuncture, pyropuncture
Heizkissen n heating pad, electric cushion
Helferin f/**zahnärztliche** dentist's assistant
Helfervirus n helper virus
Helferzelle f helper cell
Helikopodie f helicopodia, helicopod gait, circumduction *(z. B. eines gelähmten Beines)*
Helikotrema n helicotrema *(Verbindung zwischen Pauken- und Vorhoftreppe der Schnecke)*
Helioenzephalitis f helioencephalitis
Heliopathie f heliopathy, pathological disturbance caused by sunlight
Heliophobie f heliophobia *(krankhafte Angst vor Sonnenstrahlung)*
Heliose f heliosis, sun stroke, insolation, thermic fever, siriasis
heliotherapeutisch heliotherapeutic[al]
Heliotherapie f heliotherapy, solar therapy, solarization
heliotrop[isch] heliotropic, phototropic

Heliotropismus 316

Heliotropismus *m* heliotropism, heliotaxis, phototropism
Helix *f* helix
helkogen helcogenic, arising from an ulcer
Helkoma *n* helcoma, corneal ulcer
Helkoplastik *f* helcoplasty
hell lucid *(Augenblick bei Bewußtlosigkeit)*
Hellanpassung *f* light adaptation, photopia *(des Auges)*
Hell-Dunkel-Anpassung *f* accommodation to light and darkness
hellfarbig light-coloured, xanthochrom[at]ic
Hellfeldmikroskopie *f* bright-field microscopy
hellgefärbt amelanotic *(z. B. Haut)*; pale *(z. B. Stuhlgang)*
Helligkeitsanpassung *f s.* Hellanpassung
Helminthe *f* [intestinal] helminth
Helminthemesis *f* helminthemesis
Helminthenabszeß *m* helminthic abscess
helminthenartig helminthoid
Helminthenbefall *m s.* Helminthiasis
helminthentötend helminthicide
Helminthiasis *f* helminthiasis, helminthism
Helminthologie *f* helminthology *(Lehre von den Eingeweidewürmern)*
Helminthophobie *f* helminthophobia *(krankhafte Angst vor Darmwurmbefall)*
Helminthose *f s.* Helminthiasis
Helmzelle *f* helmet cell *(Schizozytenform)*
Helweg-Dreikantenbahn *f* Helweg's tract (bundle), olivospinal tract
Hemeraloper *m* hemeralope
Hemeralopie *f* 1. hemeralopia, day blindness; 2. *s.* Nyktalopie
Hemi... *s.a.* Halbseiten...
Hemiablepsie *f s.* Hemianopsie
Hemiachromatopsie *f* hemi[a]chromatopsia
Hemiageusie *f* hemiageusia
Hemiakardier *m* hemiacardius
Hemialgia *f s.* Migräne
Hemiamaurose *f* hemiamaurosis
Hemiamblyopie *f* hemiamblyopia
Hemianakusis *f* hemianacousia
Hemianalgesie *f* hemianalgesia, unilateral analgesia
Hemianästhesie *f* hemianaesthesia, unilateral anaesthesia
~/**zerebrale** cerebral hemianaesthesia
Hemianenzephalie *f s.* Hemizephalie
hemianop[isch] hemianopic
Hemianopsie *f* hemianop[s]ia, hemi[ambly]opia, hemiablepsia, hemiscotosis
~/**beidseitige** bilateral hemianopsia, central blindness
~/**binasale heteronyme** binasal hemianopsia
~/**bitemporale heteronyme** bitemporal hemianopsia
~/**heteronyme** heteronymous hemianopsia
~/**homonyme** homonymous hemianopsia
~/**laterale** lateral hemianopsia
~/**nasale** nasal hemianopsia
Hemianosmie *f* hemianosmia

Hemiasynergie *f* hemiasynergia
Hemiataxie *f* hemiataxia
Hemiathetose *f* hemiathetosis
Hemiatrophia *f* hemiatrophy
~ **faciei progressiva** progressive facial hemiatrophy, Romberg's disease, facial trophoneurosis, prosopodysmorphia
hemiazygos hemiazygous
Hemiballismus *m* hemiballism[us]
Hemiblock *m*/**linksanteriorer** left anterior hemiblock
Hemichorea *f* hemichorea
Hemichromatopsie *f* hemi[a]chromatopsia
Hemidekortikation *f* hemidecortication
Hemidiaphragma *n* hemidiaphragm
Hemidysästhesie *f* hemidysaesthesia
Hemidystrophie *f* hemidystrophia
Hemienzephalie *f* hemiencephalia
Hemigastrektomie *f* hemigastrectomy
Hemiglossektomie *f* hemiglossectomy
Hemiglossitis *f* hemiglossitis
Hemiglossoplegie *f* hemiglossoplegia
Hemignathie *f* hemignathia
Hemihypalgesie *f* hemihypalgesia
Hemihypästhesie *f* hemihypaesthesia
Hemihyperästhesie *f* hemihyperaesthesia
Hemihyperhidrosis *f* hemihyperhidrosis
Hemihypertonus *m* hemihypertonus
Hemihypertrophie *f* hemihypertrophy
Hemikardie *f* hemicardia
Hemikolektomie *f* hemicolectomy
Hemikranie *f s.* 1. Migräne; 2. Hemienzephalie
Hemilaminektomie *f* hemilaminectomy
Hemilaminektomiespreizer *m* hemilaminectomy retractor
Hemilaryngektomie *f* hemilaryngectomy
Hemimandibulektomie *f* hemimandibulectomy
Hemimaxillektomie *f* hemimaxillectomy
Hemimelie *f* hemimelia; peromelia
Heminephrektomie *f* heminephrectomy
Hemipalatektomie *f* hemipalatectomy
Hemiparalyse *f* hemiparalysis
Hemiparästhesie *f* hemiparaesthesia
Hemiparese *f* hemiparesis
hemiparetisch hemiparetic
Hemiparkinsonismus *m* hemiparkinsonism
Hemipelvektomie *f* hemipelvectomy, interpelvioabdominal amputation
Hemipharyngektomie *f* hemipharyngectomy
Hemiplegia *f s.* Hemiplegie
~ **alterna** alternate (alternating) hemiplegia, Brissaud's disease (syndrome)
~ **alterna facialis** facial hemiplegia alternans, Millard-Gubler syndrome
~ **alterna hypoglossica** Jackson's syndrome
~ **alterna oculomotorica** superior alternating hemiplegia, Weber's syndrome
~ **cruciata** crossed hemiplegia
Hemiplegie *f* hemiplegia, hemiparalysis, semiplegia, semisideration *(s.a. unter* Hemiplegia*)*
~ **des Körpers** cerebral hemiplegia
~/**kontralaterale** contralateral hemiplegia

Hepatitis

~/spastische spastic hemiplegia (paralysis)
~/unvollständige hemiparesis
Hemiplegiker *m* hemiplegic
hemiplegisch hemiplegic, hemiparetic
Hemiprostatektomie *f* hemiprostatectomy
Hemipylorektomie *f* hemipylorectomy
Hemirachischisis *f* hemirachischisis
Hemisakralisation *f* hemisacralization
Hemispasmus *m* hemispasm
Hemisphäre *f* hemisphere; cerebral hemisphere *(des Großhirns)*; cerebellar hemisphere *(des Kleinhirns)*
Hemisphärektomie *f* hemispherectomy
Hemisphärendominanz *f* hemispheric (cerebral) dominance
Hemisphärensyndrom *n* hemispheric syndrome
Hemisphärenunterseite *f* inferior surface of the cerebral hemisphere
Hemistrumektomie *f.* hemistrumectomy
Hemisystole *f* hemisystole
Hemithorax *m* hemithorax
Hemithyreoidektomie *f* hemithyroidectomy
Hemitremor *m* hemitremor
Hemivertebra *f* hemivertebra
Hemivulvektomie *f* hemivulvectomy
Hemizellulose *f* hemicellulose
Hemizephalie *f* hemi[anen]cephalia, hemicrania, partial anencephalia
Hemizephalus *m* hemicephalus *(Mißgeburt)*
hemizygot hemizygous
Hemizystektomie *f* hemicystectomy
hemmen to inhibit, to retard; to block; to obstruct; to occlude
hemmend inhibitory, inhibitive; blocking; obstructive
Hemmkonzentration *f* inhibitory concentration *(z. B. von Antibiotika)*
Hemmkörper *m* inhibitor
Hemmnerv *m* inhibitory nerve
Hemmneuron *n* inhibitory neuron
Hemmreflex *m* inhibitory reflex
Hemmstoff *m* inhibiting substance (agent), inhibitor, retarder
Hemmung *f* inhibition, retardation; backwardness *(geistiger und körperlicher Entwicklung)*; arrest
~/bedingte conditioned inhibition
~ der Ketonkörperbildung antiketogenesis
~/kataplektische cataplexis
~/kompetitive competitive inhibition
~/rückläufige Renshaw (recurrent) inhibition
Hemmungsmechanismus *m* inhibitory mechanism
Hemmungsmißbildung *f* inhibition malformation
Hemophilus *m* parainfluenzae parainfluenza bacillus
Henry-Reaktion *f* Henry's melano-flocculation test *(bei Malaria)*
Hepar *n* hepar, liver *(s. a. unter* Leber*)*
~ adiposum fatty (adipose) liver
~ lobatum syphiliticum packet liver *(im dritten Stadium der Syphilis)*

~ migrans (mobile) wandering (floating) liver, movable liver; hepatoptosis
~ moschatiforme nutmeg liver *(bei chronischer Blutstauung)*
Heparin *n* heparin *(gerinnungshemmender Stoff)*
~/niedrig dosiertes low-dose heparin
Heparinämie *f* heparinaemia
Heparinbehandlung *f* heparin therapy (treatment)
Heparininfusionspumpe *f* heparin infusion pump
heparinisieren to heparinize
Heparinisierung *f* heparinization
Heparinozyt *m* heparinocyte *(z. B. Gewebsmastzelle)*
Heparinspiegelerhöhung *f* im Blut hyperheparinaemia
Hepatalgie *f* hepatalgia, hepatodynia, pain in the liver
Hepatargie *f* hepatargia, hepatic autointoxication; hepatic insufficiency *(durch gestörte Leberfunktion)*
Hepatektomie *f* hepatectomy, excision of the liver
Hepatikagraphie *f* hepatic arteriography
Hepatikoduodenostomie *f* hepaticoduodenostomy
Hepatikoenterostomie *f* hepaticoenterostomy
Hepatikogastrostomie *f* hepaticogastrostomy
Hepatikojejunostomie *f* hepaticojejunostomy
Hepatikolithotomie *f* hepat[ic]olithotomy
Hepatikolithotripsie *f* hepaticolithotripsy
Hepatikorrhaphie *f* hepaticorrhaphy, suturing of the hepatic duct
Hepatikostomie *f* hepaticostomy
Hepatikotomie *f* hepaticotomy
Hepatisation *f* [der Lunge] [pulmonary] hepatization, pneumonic consolidation *(bei Lungenentzündung)*
~/gelbe yellow hepatization
~/graue grey hepatization
~/rote red hepatization, engorgement of the lung
hepatisch hepatic
Hepatitis *f* hepatitis, inflammation of the liver
~ A hepatitis A
~/aggressive aggressive hepatitis
~/akute parenchymatöse acute parenchymatous hepatitis, acute yellow atrophy of the liver
~ B hepatitis B
~/cholestatische cholestatic (cholangiolitic) hepatitis
~/chronische interstitielle chronic interstitial hepatitis
~ epidemica infectious (epidemic, virus) hepatitis, acute infectious icterus, catarrhal (acute febrile) jaundice
~/fulminante fulminant hepatitis
~/infektiöse *s.* ~ epidemica
~/interstitielle interstitial (non-specific) hepatitis, acute non-suppurative hepatitis
~/persistierende persistent hepatitis
~/toxische toxic hepatitis
~/unspezifische *s.* ~/interstitielle

Hepatitisantigen

Hepatitisantigen *n* hepatitis antigen
Hepatitis-A-Virus *n* hepatitis virus A
Hepatitis-A-Virus-Antikörper *m* hepatitis A virus antibody
Hepatitis-B-Antigen *n* hepatitis B antigen
Hepatitis-B-Surface-Antigen *n* hepatitis virus B antigen, hepatitis B surface antigen
Hepatitis-B-Surface-Antikörper *m* hepatitis virus B antibody, hepatitis B surface antibody
Hepatitis-B-Virus *n* hepatitis virus B
Hepatitis-infectiosa-Virus *n* s. Hepatitis-A-Virus
Hepatitis-Virus *n* hepatitis virus
Hepatoadenom *n* hepatoadenoma, liver adenoma
hepatobiliär hepatobiliary
Hepatoblastom *n* hepatoblastoma *(embryonale Lebermischgeschwulst)*
Hepatoduodenostomie *f* hepatoduodenostomy
Hepatoflavin *n* hepatoflavin
hepatogen hepatogenic, hepatogenous
Hepatogramm *n* hepatogram
Hepatographie *f* hepatography
Hepatokarzinogen *n* hepatocarcinogen
Hepatokuprein *n* hepatocuprein *(Kupferproteid der Leber)*
hepatolienal hepatolienal
Hepatolienographie *f* hepatolienography
Hepatolith *m* hepatolith, hepatic calculus
Hepatholithektomie *f* hepatolithectomy
Hepatolithiasis *f* hepatolithiasis
Hepatologe *m* hepatologist
Hepatom *n* hepatoma, liver cell carcinoma
Hepatomalazie *f* hepatomalacia, softening of the liver
Hepatomegalie *f* hepatomegaly, megalohepatia, enlargement of the liver
Hepatonephromegalia *f* **glycogenica** glycogenic hepatonephrosis, Gierke's (glycogen storage) disease, glycogenosis type I of Cori, hepatic (hepatorenal) glycogenosis
Hepatopathie *f* hepatopathy, disease of the liver
Hepatopexie *f* hepatopexy, fixation of the liver
Hepatophlebitis *f* hepatophlebitis, phlebhepatitis
hepatoportal hepatoportal
Hepatoptose *f* hepatoptosis, dislocation of the liver; wandering (floating) liver, movable liver
hepatorenal hepatorenal, hepatonephritic
Hepatorrhagie *f* hepatorrhagia, haemorrhage from the liver
Hepatorrhaphie *f* hepatorrhaphy, suturing of the liver
Hepatorrhexis *f* hepatorrhexis, rupture of the liver
Hepatose *f* hepatosis
Hepatoskopie *f* hepatoscopy
Hepatosplenographie *f* hepatosplenography
Hepatosplenomegalie *f* hepatosplenomegaly, hepatolienomegaly, enlargement of the liver and the spleen
~/ägyptische Egyptian [hepato]splenomegaly, hepatosplenic schistosomiasis

Hepatosplenopathie *f* hepatosplenopathy, disease of the liver and the spleen
Hepatostomie *f* hepatostomy
Hepatotherapie *f* hepatotherapy
Hepatotomie *f* hepatotomy, incision into the liver
Hepatotoxin *n* hepatotoxin
hepatotoxisch hepatotoxic
Hepatotoxizität *f* hepatotoxicity
hepatotrop hepatotropic *(z. B. Parasiten)*
hepatozellulär hepatocellular
hepatozystisch hepatocystic
Hepatozyt *m* hepatocyte, hepatic cell
Herabhängen *n* **des Oberlids** dropping of the lid, ptosis, lid drop
Herabzieher *m* depressor [muscle]
Heranführen *n* adduction *(zur Medianebene des Körpers)*
heranziehen to adduct *(z. B. an den Körper)*
Heranziehen *n* adduction *(zur Medianebene des Körpers)*
Heranzieher *m* adductor [muscle]
herausbilden/Immunität to develop immunity
~/Überempfindlichkeit to develop hypersensitivity
herausführend efferent
herauslösen 1. to lixiviate, to leach, to extract *(Stoffe)*; 2. s. herausschneiden
Herauslösen *n* lixiviation, leaching, extraction *(von Stoffen)*
herausnehmen to remove, to resect *(z. B. Organe)*
herauspressen to force out, to squeeze out
herausragen to project *(z. B. aus der Körperoberfläche)*
herausschneiden to excise; to dissect; to resect
~/die Nieren to nephrectomize
~/die Regenbogenhaut to iridectomize
~/die Thymusdrüse to thymectomize
~/nochmals (wieder) to reexcise
herausspülen to rinse out; to eluate
heraustreten to extravasate *(z. B. Blut aus Gefäßen)*; to protrude *(z. B. der Darm)*
herausziehen 1. to extract; to digest *(Nährstoffe)*; 2. to remove, to retract *(z. B. einen Katheter)*; to withdraw, to draw (pull) out *(z. B. einen Splitter)*; to extract *(z. B. einen Zahn)*
herbeiführen to bring about, to provoke *(z. B. eine Blutung)*; to induce *(z. B. Stuhlgang)*
~/einen Abort to abort
Herbstenzephalitis *f/***russische** Russian autumnal encephalitis
Herbstfieber *n/***japanisches** Japanese autumnal fever
Herd *m* focus, centre, seat
~/Assmannscher Assmann focus
~/epilepsieauslösender epileptogenic focus
~/otosklerotischer otosclerotic focus
Herdanfall *m* focal seizure, local convulsion *(bei Epilepsie)*
~/Jacksonscher focal Jacksonian epileptic attack

~/motorischer focal motor seizure
Herdausräumung f removal of a focus
Herdbestrahlung f crossfire treatment
Herdblutung f focal haemorrhage
Herddosis f depth dose
Herdenzephalomalazie f/**embolische** focal embolic encephalomalacia
Herdepilepsie f focal epilepsy
~/motorische focal motor seizure
Herderkrankung f focal disease
Herdglomerulonephritis f focal glomerulonephritis
Herdinfektion f focal infection
Herdläsion f focal lesion (z. B. des Gehirns)
Herdnekrose f focal necrosis
Herdnephritis f focal nephritis
Herdpathologie f focal pathology
Herdpneumonie f focal pneumonia
Herdsanierung f removal of a septic focus
Herdschädigung f focal lesion (z. B. des Gehirns)
Herdsklerose f focal sclerosis
Herdsymptom n focal symptom (sign)
~/neurologisches focal neurologic sign
hereditär hereditary
Heredität f heredity
Heredoataxia f/**spinale** spinal heredoataxia, hereditary ataxia
Heredodegeneration f heredodegeneration
Heredodegenerationskrankheit f heredodegenerative disease
Heredopathia f **atactica polyneuritiformis** Refsum's disease (syndrome)
Heredosyphilis f heredosyphilis, congenital syphilis
Heritabilität f heritability
Herkunft f origin, birth ● **unterschiedlicher ~** polygenic ● **von pflanzlicher ~** phytogenous
Hermaphrodit m hermaphrodite
~/weiblicher androgyne, androgynus
hermaphroditisch hermaphroditic
Hermaphroditismus m hermaphrodi[ti]sm
~/bilateraler bilateral hermaphroditism
Hernia f hernia; rupture (s. a. unter Hernie)
~ **abdominalis** abdominal (ventral) hernia
~ **adiposa** fatty hernia, adipocele, lipocele
~ **cerebri** cerebral hernia (fungus), encephalocele, fungus of the brain
~ **cicatricata** cicatricial (incisional) hernia
~ **cordis** exocardia
~ **diaphragmatica** diaphragmatic hernia, diaphragmatocele
~ **epigastrica** epigastric hernia, epigastrocele
~ **femoralis** femoral (crural) hernia, femorocele
~ **funicularis** 1. funicular hernia (Samenstrang); 2. s. ~ funiculi umbilicalis
~ **funiculi umbilicalis** funicular hernia, omphalocele (Nabelschnur)
~ **inguinalis** inguinal (groin) hernia
~ **ischiadica** ischiadic (sciatic) hernia
~ **labialis** labial (posterior pudendal) hernia
~ **lumbalis** lumbar hernia
~ **mesenterica** mesenteric hernia
~ **obturatoria** obturator (subpubic) hernia
~ **paraumbilicalis** para-umbilical hernia
~ **pelvis** pelvic hernia
~ **perinealis** perineocele, perineal hernia
~ **recessus duodenojejunalis** Treitz's hernia
~ **retrocaecalis** retrocaecal hernia
~ **scrotalis** scrotal hernia, scrotocele, orchiocele, oscheocele
~ **umbilicalis** umbilical (annular) hernia
~ **ventralis** s. ~ abdominalis
Hernie f hernia; rupture (s. a. unter Hernie) ● **eine ~ bilden** to herniate
~/äußere external hernia, exocele
~/Coopersche Cooper's hernia
~/direkte direct hernia
~/echte true hernia
~/falsche false hernia
~/indirekte indirect (lateral, oblique) hernia
~/inkarzerierte incarcerated hernia
~/innere internal hernia, entocele
~/interstitielle interstitial (intermuscular, interparietal) hernia
~/irreponible irreducible hernia
~/paraösophageale paraoesophageal hernia (Magenvorfall in die Brusthöhle); upside-down stomach
~/rektale rectal hernia
~/reponible reducible hernia
~/retroperitoneale retroperitoneal hernia
~/Richtersche Richter's hernia
~/Spieghelsche Spigelian (Spiegel's) hernia
~/strangulierte strangulated hernia
~/Treitzsche Treitz's hernia
Hernienbildung f herniation
Hernienlehre f herniology
Hernienplastik f hernioplasty
~/inguinale inguinal hernioplasty
Hernienpunktion f herniopuncture
Hernienradikaloperation f radical herniotomy
Herniologie f herniology
Herniorrhaphie f herniorrhaphy
Herniotom n herniotome
Herniotomie f herniotomy
Heroin n heroin, diacetylmorphine, diamorphine, acetomorphine (Rauschgift)
Heroingewöhnung f heroin addiction (habit)
Heroinismus m heroinism
Heroinsucht f heroin addiction (habit), heroinomania
Heroinsüchtiger m heroin addict
Herpangina f herpangina (Virusinfektion)
Herpes m(f) herpes, dartre ● **nach einem ~ auftretend** metaherpetic
~ **corneae** herpes [zoster] of the cornea, herpetic corneal disease
~ **facialis** cold sore
~ **labialis** lip herpes
~ **simplex** herpes simplex
~ **simplex oculi** ocular herpes [simplex]
~ **vegetans** Hebra's disease
~ **zoster** [herpes] zoster, zona, shingles
~ **zoster auricularis** herpes zoster of the ear

Herpes

~ **zoster oculi** ocular zoster
~ **zoster ophthalmicus** s. ~ corneae
~ **zoster oticus** genicular herpes zoster, Hunt's neuralgia, Ramsey-Hunt syndrome
herpesartig herpetiform, dartrous
Herpesenzephalitis f herpes [simplex] encephalitis, herpetic encephalitis
herpesförmig herpetiform
Herpesgruppe f herpes group
Herpesinfektion f herpetic infection
Herpeskeratitis f herpetic keratitis
Herpeskeratokonjunktivitis f herpetic keratoconjunctivitis
Herpeskeratouveitis f herpetic keratouveitis
Herpesneuralgie f herpetic neuralgia
Herpespanuveitis f/**bilaterale** herpetic bilateral panuveitis
Herpes-simplex-Keratitis f herpes simplex keratitis
Herpes-simplex-Virus n herpes simplex virus
Herpesstomatitis f herpetic stomatitis
Herpestonsillitis f herpetic tonsillitis
Herpesulcus n **dendriticum** herpetic dendritic ulcer
Herpesvirus n herpesvirus
~ **varicellae** varicella[-zoster] virus, V-Z virus
Herpesvirusantikörper m herpesvirus antibody
Herpesvirusgruppe f herpes group
Herpes-zoster-Keratitis f herpes zoster keratitis
Hertwig-Epithelscheide f Hertwig's epithelial root sheath
hervorbringend/Mißbildungen teratogen[et]ic
hervorluxieren/den Wurmfortsatz to hook out the appendix
hervorragen to protrude, to project (z. B. Knochen)
hervorrufen/Quaddelbildung to urticate (z. B. Raupen)
hervorstehen to protrude (z. B. die Augen)
hervorstehend protruding
hervorstülpend protrusive, protruding
hervorwölbend protrusive, protruding
hervorwürgen/wieder to regurgitate
hervorwürgend/wieder regurgitant
hervorziehen to protract
Herz n heart, cor (s. a. unter Cor) ● **außerhalb des Herzens** exocardial, exocardiac ● **hinter dem Herzen liegend** retrocardial, retrocardiac ● **neben dem Herzen** paracardial ● **ohne ~** acardiac ● **um das ~ liegend** pericardial, pericardiac
~/**abnorm großes** macrocardia
~/**aortenkonfiguriertes** aortic (wooden-shoe, sabot) heart, boat-shaped heart
~/**hypertrophiertes** hypertrophic heart
~/**künstliches** artificial heart
~/**linkes** left heart
~/**lungenkonfiguriertes** pulmonary heart
~/**nervöses** nervous (irritable) heart
~/**rechtes** right heart
~/**tropfenförmiges** drop (pendulous, hanging) heart

Herzachse f cardiac axis
~/**elektrische** electrical axis of the heart, lead axis
Herzaffektion f heart affection, cardiac involvement
Herzaktion f cardiac action
Herzaktionskurve f/**mechanische** cardiokymogram
Herzaktionspotential n cardiac action potential
Herzamyloidose f cardiac amyloidosis
Herzaneurysma n cardiac aneurysm, cardiocele
Herzanfall m heart attack, cardiac fit, cardiovascular accident
Herzanomalie f cardiac anomaly
Herzanstrengung f strain of the heart
Herzarbeit f cardiac work
Herzarrhythmie f cardiac arrhythmia
herzartig cardioid
Herzasthma n cardiac asthma, cardi[o]asthma
Herzatrophie f cardiac atrophy, acardiotrophia
Herzauslösung f cardiolysis (z. B. aus Perikardverwachsungen)
Herzaußenhaut f epicardium
Herzäußere[s] n exterior of the heart
Herzauswalzung f cardiac enlargement, dilatation of the heart
Herzautomatismus m cardiac self-regulation
Herzbasis f base of the heart
herzbedingt cardiogenic
Herzbefund m cardiac finding[s]
Herzbehandlung f cardiotherapy, cardiac treatment
Herzbeklemmung f nervous cardiac trouble
Herzbelastung f cardiac stress
herzbeschleunigend cardioaccelerator
Herzbeschleunigung f tachycardia, tachyrhythmia, tachysystole, synchopexia
Herzbeschwerden pl cardiac trouble, heart complaint
Herzbeteiligung f cardiac involvement, heart affection
Herzbeutel m pericardium, pericardial (heart) sac (Zusammensetzungen s. unter Perikard)
Herzbeutel... s. a. Perikard...
Herzbeutelbluterguß m haemopericardium
Herzbeutel[druck]entlastung f decompression of the pericardium (heart)
Herzbeutelentzündung f pericarditis, inflammation of the pericardium (Zusammensetzungen s. unter Pericarditis)
Herzbeutelerguß m pericardial effusion; hydropericardium, hydrocardia, dropsy of the pericardium
Herzbeutelfistelung f[/**operative**] pericardiostomy
Herzbeutelpunktion f pericardi[o]centesis, paracentesis of the pericardial sac
Herzbeutelröntgen[kontrast]bild n nach Lufteinblasung pneumopericardiogram
Herzbeutelröntgen[kontrast]darstellung f nach Lufteinblasung pneumopericardiography
Herzbeuteltamponade f pericardial tamponade

Herzbeutelvene f pericardial vein
Herzbeutelvereiterung f pyopericardium
Herzbeutel-Zwerchfell-Arterie f pericardiacophrenic artery
Herzbeutel-Zwerchfell-Vene f pericardiacophrenic vein
Herzbeutelzyste f pericardial [coelomic] cyst
Herzbeweglichkeit f cardiomotility, motility of the heart
Herzbindegewebe n cardiac skeleton
Herzbindegewebsentzündung f ethmocarditis
Herzblock m heart block
~/**atrioventrikulärer** atrioventricular heart block, AV block
~ **dritten Grades** third-degree heart block, total atrioventricular block
~ **ersten Grades** first-degree heart (atrioventricular) block
~/**inkompletter** incomplete heart block
~/**intraventrikulärer** intraventricular heart block, intraventricular conduction delay, incomplete bundle branch block
~/**kompletter** complete heart block
~/**partieller** partial heart block
~/**sinoatrialer** sinoatrial heart block
~/**sinoaurikulärer** sinoauricular heart block
~ **zweiten Grades** second-degree heart (atrioventricular) block
Herzbruch m cardiocele
Herzbuckel m protrusion of the cardiac region
Herzchirurg m cardiac (heart) surgeon, cardiosurgeon
Herzchirurgie f cardiac (heart) surgery, cardiosurgery
Herzdämpfung f cardiac (heart) dullness *(Perkussion)*
~/**absolute** absolute cardiac dullness
~/**relative** relative cardiac dullness
Herzdefibrillation f/**direkte** open-chest defibrillation
~/**geschlossene** closed-chest defibrillation
Herzdegeneration f/**fettige** Quain's fatty degeneration of the heart
Herzdekompensation f cardiac decompensation
Herzdurchleuchtung f cardiac fluoroscopy
Herzdynamik f cardiac dynamics
Herzdysfunktion f cardiac dysfunction
Herzeinschnürung f cardiostenosis
Herzenge f stenocardia, angina
Herzentfernung f[/**operative**] cardiectomy
Herzentlastung f cardiac support
Herzentwicklung f[/**embryonale**] cardiogenesis, development of the heart
Herzentzündung f carditis, inflammation of the heart
~/**rheumatische** rheumatic carditis
Herzeröffnung f[/**operative**] cardiotomy
Herzerschlaffung[sphase] f diastole
Herzerweichung f cardiomalacia
Herzerweiterung f cardiac dilatation, dilatation of the heart, cardiectasis
Herzexploration f cardiac exploration

Herzextraton m [cardiac] click
Herzfehlentwicklung f atelocardia
Herzfehler m cardiac defect
~/**angeborener zyanotischer** cyanotic congenital heart disease
Herzfehlerzelle f septal (heart-failure) cell
Herzfigur f heart form
Herzflattern n ventricular flutter, fluttering of the heart
Herzflimmern n ventricular fibrillation, fibrillation of the heart
Herzfluoroskopie f cardiac fluoroscopy
Herzförderleistung f **je Minute** cardiac output
herzförmig cardioid, cordiform, cordate, heart-shaped
Herzfrequenz f heart rate ● **die ~ senken** to slow the heart [rate]
~/**erhöhte** tachycardia
~/**herabgesetzte** bradycardia, oligocardia
herzfrequenzbeschleunigend cardioaccelerator, cardiokinetic
herzfrequenzsenkend cardioinhibitory
herzfrequenzsteigernd cardioaccelerator, cardiokinetic
herzfrequenzwirksam chronotropic
Herzfrequenzzählgerät n cardiotachometer
Herzfunktion f cardiac (heart) function
Herzfunktionsstörung f cardiac dysfunction
Herzgegend f cardiac region; precordial region, precordium
Herzgekröse n mesocardium
Herzgeräusch n cardiac murmur, heart souffle
~/**akzidentelles (anorganisches)** accidental murmur
~/**diastolisches** diastolic [murmur]
~/**organisches** organic murmur
~/**systolisches** systolic [murmur]
Herzgeschwulst f cardiac tumour
Herzgesetz n/**Starlingsches** Starling's law of the heart
Herzgewebe n cardiac tissue
Herzgewicht n cardiac (heart) weight
Herzglykosid n cardiac glycoside
Herzglykosidtherapie f glycoside treatment; digitalization
Herzgröße f cardiac (heart) size
Herzgrößenmessung f cardiometry
herzhemmend cardioinhibitory
Herzhöhle f cavity of the heart
Herzhypertrophie f cardiac hypertrophy, mega[lo]cardia
Herzindex m cardiac index, CI
Herzinfarkt m myocardial infarct, cardiac (heart) infarct[ion] ● **nach einem ~** postmyocardial infarction
Herzinfundibulum n cardiac infundibulum
Herzinnenhaut f endocardium
Herzinnenhautentzündung f en[do]carditis, inflammation of the endocardium
~/**bakterielle** bacterial endocarditis
~/**rheumatische** rheumatic endocarditis

Herzinnenhaut-Herzaußenhaut-...

Herzinnenhaut-Herzaußenhaut-Herzmuskel-Entzündung f endoperimyocarditis
Herzinnenhaut- und Herzaußenhautentzündung f endopericarditis
Herzinnenhaut- und Herzmuskelentzündung f endomyocarditis
Herzinnenhautverdickung f endocardial sclerosis
Herzinsuffizienz f cardiac insufficiency (power failure)
~/dekompensierte congestive heart failure
Herzinsuffizienzödem n cardiac dropsy (oedema)
Herzisotopenuntersuchung f cardiac radioisotope scanning
Herzjagen n/**anfallartiges** paroxysmal tachycardia
Herzkammer f ventricle [of the heart], heart (cardiac) chambre
~/linke left ventricle [of the heart], L. V.
~/rechte right ventricle [of the heart], R. V.
Herzkammer... s. a. Kammer...
Herzkammerbinnendruck m intraventricular pressure
Herzkammerdepolarisation f ventricular depolarization
herzkammereigen idioventricular
Herzkammererschlaffung f ventricular relaxation
Herzkammerfüllung f ventricular filling
Herzkammerfüllungsdruck m ventricular filling pressure
Herzkammerfüllungsgeräusch n ventricular filling sound
Herzkammerhypertrophie f ventricular hypertrophy
Herzkammerjagen n ventricular tachycardia
Herzkammerkomplex m ventricular [depolarization] complex, QRS complex (EKG)
Herzkammerkontraktion f ventricular contraction
~/vorzeitige ventricular premature beat
Herzkammerpunktion f cardi[o]centesis, cardiopuncture, ventricular puncture, puncture of the heart
Herzkammerscheidewand f [inter]ventricular septum
Herzkammerscheidewanddefekt m ventricular septal defect, Roger's disease
Herzkammervolumen n/**enddiastolisches** ventricular end-diastolic volume
Herzkammerwandspannung f ventricular wall tension
Herzkatheter m [intra]cardiac catheter
Herzkatheterabteilung f cardiac catheterization unit
Herzkathetereinheit f cardiac catheterization unit
Herzkatheterlabor[atorium] n cardiac catheterization laboratory
Herzkatheterschrittmacher m catheter pacemaker
Herzkathetertechnik f cardiac catheterization technique

Herzkatheterung f cardiac catheterization
Herzkatheteruntersuchung f cardiac catheterization
Herzklappe f [cardiac] valve, valve of the heart, valva, valvula ● **oberhalb der ~** supravalvular ● **unterhalb der ~** subvalvular
~/künstliche prosthetic [heart] valve, valvular (heart valve) prosthesis
Herzklappeneinschnitt m valvular incision, diclidotomy
Herzklappenentfernung f[/**operative**] valvulectomy
Herzklappenentzündung f cardi[o]valvulitis, diclidotomy
Herzklappenerkrankung f valvular [heart] disease, cardiac valve disease
~/rheumatische rheumatic valvular disease
Herzklappenersatz m [cardiac] valve replacement (durch Operation)
Herzklappenfehler m cardiac valvular defect, valvular [heart] disease
Herzklappenfläche f cardiac valve area
Herzklappenfunktionsstörung f valvular dysfunction
Herzklappengewebe n cardiac valve tissue
Herzklappeninsuffizienz f valvular incompetence (insufficiency)
Herzklappenmesser n [cardio]valvulotome
Herzklappenöffnungsfläche f cardiac valve area
Herzklappenprothese f valvular (heart valve) prosthesis, prosthetic [heart] valve
~ nach Björk-Shiley tilting disk prosthesis; caged-lens prosthesis (valve)
~ nach Starr-Edwards caged-ball prosthesis (valve)
Herzklappenrekonstruktion f valvuloplasty
Herzklappenring m valvular ring, annulus
Herzklappenringdurchtrennung f[/**operative**] annulotomy
Herzklappenringplastik f annuloplasty
Herzklappenringraffung f annulorrhaphy
Herzklappenschließungston m flapping sound
Herzklappenschluß m closing of the cardiac valves
Herzklappenschlußunfähigkeit f incompetence of the cardiac valves
Herzklappensegel n valvular (valve) cusp, leaflet of the valve
Herzklappensprengung f/**digitale** digital valvulotomy, Brock operation
~/operative [cardio]valvulotomy, valvotomy
Herzklappenton m valvular (valve) sound
Herzklappenvereng[er]ung f valvular stenosis
Herzklappenverletzung f valvular lesion
Herzklopfen n cardiopalmus, [cardiac] palpitation
Herzkomplikation f cardiac complication
Herzkompression f cardiac compression
Herzkonkrement n cardiolith, cardiac calculus
Herzkonstriktion f cardiostenosis, constriction of the heart
Herzkontraktilität f myocardial contractility

Herzkontraktion f myocardial contraction
~/unvollständige aborted systole
~/vorzeitige extrasystole, premature contraction (beat)
Herzkontraktionsfähigkeit f myocardial contractility
Herzkontraktionsphase f systole; miocardia
Herzkontur f cardiac (heart) contour
Herzkraftmesser m cardiometer
Herzkraftmessung f cardiometry
herzkraftsteigernd cardiotonic
Herzkraftversagen n cardiac [power] failure, cardiac pump failure
herzkrank cardiopathic, suffering from heart disease
Herzkranker m cardiac, cardiopath, heart disease patient
Herzkrankheit f cardiopathy, cardiac (heart) disease
~/angeborene congenital heart disease
~/ischämische ischaemic heart disease, IHD
~/koronare coronary heart disease
Herzkrankheitslehre f cardiopathology
Herzkranzgefäß n coronary vessel
Herzkranzgefäß... s. a. Koronar...
Herzkranzgefäßanomalie f coronary anomaly
Herzkranzgefäßröntgenbild n coronary arteriogram
Herzkranzgefäßröntgendarstellung f coronary arteriography
Herzkranzgefäßsystem n coronary system
Herzkranzgefäßverkalkung f coronary [arterio]sclerosis
Herz-Kreislauf-Erkrankung f cardiovascular disease
Herz-Kreislauf-Fehler m cardiovascular defect
Herz-Kreislauf-Insuffizienz f mit Fettsucht cardiopulmonary-obesity syndrome
Herz-Kreislauf-Kollaps m cardiovascular collapse
Herz-Kreislauf-Manifestation f der Syphilis cardiovascular syphilis
Herz-Kreislauf-System n cardiovascular system
Herz-Kreislauf-Versagen n cardiovascular failure
Herz-Kreislauf-Zusammenbruch m cardiovascular collapse
Herzkrise f cardiac (heart) crisis
herzlähmend cardioplegic
Herzlähmung f cardioplegia
Herz-Leber-Winkel m cardiohepatic angle
Herzleistungstraining n cardiac rehabilitation (z. B. nach Herzinfarkt)
Herzlöslösung f[/operative] cardiolysis
Herz-Lungen-Geräusch n cardiopulmonary murmur
Herz-Lungen-Maschine f heart-lung apparatus (machine), HLM, cardiopulmonary bypass
Herz-Lungen-Präparat n heart-lung preparation
Herzmassage f cardiac massage
~/äußere external (closed-chest) cardiac compression, closed cardiac massage, closed-chest heart massage
~/direkte internal (open-chest) cardiac compression, open cardiac massage, open-chest heart massage
~/extrathorakale s. ~/äußere
~/intrathorakale s. ~/direkte
Herzminutenvolumen n cardiac output
Herzmittel n cardiac [agent], cardiac stimulant, cordial [agent]
Herzmittelständigkeit f im Thorax mesocardia
Herzmuskel m myocardium, cardiac (heart) muscle
Herzmuskel... s. a. Myokard...
Herzmuskelbälkchen npl carneous trabeculae (columns)
Herzmuskeldegeneration f myocardial degeneration, myodegeneration
Herzmuskelentzündung f myocarditis, inflammation of the myocardium (Zusammensetzungen s. unter Myokarditis)
Herzmuskelerkrankung f cardiomyopathy, myocardiopathy, myocardial disease; myocardosis
Herzmuskelerschlaffung f cardianeuria, myocardial atonia
Herzmuskelerweichung f cardiomalacia, myomalacia of the heart
Herzmuskelfaser f myocardial (cardiac muscle) fibre
Herzmuskelgewebe n myocardial tissue
Herzmuskelhinterwandinfarkt m posterior myocardial infarction
Herzmuskelinsuffizienz f myocardial insufficiency
Herzmuskelkontraktion f s. Herzkontraktion
Herzmuskelnaht f myocardiorrhaphy, cardiorrhaphy
Herzmuskelnekrose f myocardial necrosis
Herzmuskel-O$_2$-Verbrauch m myocardial oxygen consumption
Herzmuskelschicht f s. Myokard
Herzmuskelschreiber m myocardiograph
Herzmuskelschwäche f s. Herzmuskelinsuffizienz
Herzmuskelspannung f myocardial tone
Herzmuskel- und Herzbeutelentzündung f cardi[o]pericarditis
Herzmuskelversagen n myocardial insufficiency (failure), cardiac [power] failure
Herzmuskelvorderwandinfarkt m anterior myocardial infarction
Herzmuskelzelle f myocardial cell
Herzmuskulatur f cardiac musculature
Herzmyxom n cardiac myxoma
Herznerv m cardiac nerve
Herznervengeflecht n cardiac plexus
Herzneurose f cardioneurosis, cardiac neurasthenia (neurosis), cardiasthenia; irritable heart
Herzoberfläche f surface (exterior) of the heart
Herzödem n cardiac oedema
Herzohr n auricle, auricular appendix, atrial appendage
~/linkes left auricular appendage
~/rechtes right auricular appendage

Herzohrentfernung

Herzohrentfernung f [/operative] atrial appendectomy
Herzohrklemme f auricle clamp
Herzohrresektion f atrial appendectomy
Herzoperation f cardiac (heart) operation; open-heart surgery
Herzpatient m cardiac patient (case)
Herzphysiologie f physiology of the heart
Herzpulskurve f cardiosphygmogram
Herzpulsschreibung f cardiosphygmography
Herzpumpversagen n cardiac decompensation
Herzpunktion f cardi[o]centesis, paracentesis of the heart, cardiopuncture
Herzrand m cardiac margin (border)
~/linker left border of the heart
~/rechter right border of the heart
Herzrasen n heart hurry; ventricular tachycardia
Herzrate f heart rate
Herzreinfarkt m cardiac (myocardial) reinfarction
Herzreizleitungssystem n cardionector; conduction system
Herzreserve f cardiac (myocardial) reserve
herzrhythmisierend antiarrhythmic
Herzrhythmisierung f cardioversion
Herzrhythmus m cardiac rhythm ● **mit doppeltem ~** pararrhythmic
Herzrhythmusstörung f [cardiac] arrhythmia (dysrhythmia)
~/vollständige absolute arrhythmia
Herzröntgenbild n radiocardiogram
Herzröntgendarstellung f radiocardiography
Herzröntgendurchleuchtung f cardiac fluoroscopy
Herzröntgenkontrastdarstellung f radiocardiography
Herzruptur f cardiorrhexis, rupture of the heart, cardioclasia, cardioclasis
Herzschaden m cardiac damage; damaged heart
Herzschallaufzeichnung f [electro]cardiophonography, phonocardiography
Herzschalldämpfung f cardiac dullness (Perkussion)
Herzschallschreiber m phonocardiograph
Herzschallschreibung f [electro]cardiophonography, phonocardiography
Herzschatten m cardiac contour (shadow) (Röntgen)
Herzschattenverbreiterung f cardiac enlargement
Herzscheitel m vertex of the heart
Herzschlag m 1. heartbeat, ictus; palmus, [heart] palpitation (subjektiv empfunden); 2. s. Myokardinfarkt
~/unregelmäßiger ar[r]hythmia
Herzschlagbeschleunigung f tachycardia, tachysystole, tachyrhythmia
Herzschlagfolge f heart rate
~/atmungsbedingte unregelmäßige respiratory arrhythmia
~/unregelmäßige ar[r]hythmia
Herzschlagverlangsamung f bradycardia, brachycardia, brachyrhythmia

Herzschlagvolumen n [cardiac] stroke volume
Herzschlauch m cardiac tube (Embryologie)
Herzschmerz m cardiac pain, cardialgia, cardiodynia
Herzschrägdurchmesser m oblique diameter of the heart
Herzschreiber m cardiograph
Herzschrittmacher m [cardiac] pacemaker
~/künstlicher artificial [cardiac] pacemaker
~/wandernder wandering pacemaker
Herzschrittmacherelektrode f pacemaker (pacing) electrode
Herzschrittmacherjagen n runaway pacemaker failure
Herzschrittmacherpotential n pacemaker stimulus potential
Herzschrittmacherversagen n [cardiac] pacemaker failure
Herzschrittmacherzentrum n focus
Herzschwäche f cardiasthenia, cardiac insufficiency
herzselektiv cardioselective
Herzsenkung f cardioptosis, bathycardia
Herzsilhouette f cardiac silhouette
Herzskelett n cardiac skeleton, skeleton of the heart
Herzsklerose f cardiosclerosis
Herzspender m heart donor
Herzspezialist m cardiologist, heart specialist; cardiac surgeon
Herzspiegel m cardioscope
Herzspiegelung f cardioscopy
Herzspitze f cardiac apex, apex of the heart
Herzspitzengeräusch n apex (apical) murmur
Herzspitzenkardiogramm n apex cardiogram
Herzspitzenstoß m ictus [cordis], apex beat [of the heart], cardiac impulse, left ventricular thrust
herzstärkend cardiotonic, cordial
Herzstärkungsmittel n cardiotonic, cordial [agent]
Herzstechen n cardiodynia, cardialgia, breast pang
Herzstillstand m asystole, cardiac arrest, ventricular standstill
herzstimulierend cardiokinetic
Herzstoß m s. Herzspitzenstoß
Herzstromkurvenzacke f electrocardiographic wave
Herzsymptom n cardiac symptom
Herzsyndrom n/**hyperkinetisches** hyperkinetic heart syndrome
Herztaille f/**verstrichene** effaced heart waist (Radiologie)
Herztamponade f [cardiac] tamponade, heart tamponade
Herzthrombus m heart clot, intracardiac thrombus
Herztiefstand m cardioptosis, bathycardia
Herztod m cardiac (heart) death
Herzton m cardiac sound, heart tone
~/betonter erster cannon sound (bei komplettem Herzblock)

~/dritter third heart sound, ventricular filling sound, filling gallop
~/vierter fourth heart sound
~/zweiter second heart sound
Herztöne *mpl*/gedoppelte reduplicated heart sounds
Herztonikum *n* cardiac tonic
Herztonmikrophon *n* cardiophone
Herztransplantat *n* heart transplant
Herztransplantation *f* heart transplantation
Herztransposition *f* transposition of the heart
Herzüberwachung *f* cardiac monitoring
Herzumriß *m* cardiac contour
Herz- und Atemstillstand *m* cardiopulmonary (cardiorespiratory) arrest
Herz- und Gefäßchirurgie *f* cardiovascular surgery
Herz- und Gefäßklemme *f* cardiovascular forceps
Herz- und Gefäßkrankheit *f* angiocardiopathy, cardiovascular disease
Herz- und Gefäßröntgen[kontrast]darstellung *f* angiocardiography, cardioangiography
Herz- und Gefäßsyphilis *f* cardiovascular syphilis
Herz- und Lebervergrößerung *f* cardiohepatomegaly
Herz- und Perikardentzündung *f* cardi[o]pericarditis
Herzunruhe *f* nervous [heart] palpitations
Herzunterentwicklung *f* atelocardia
Herzuntersuchung *f* heart examination, cardiac exploration
Herzvaskularisation *f* durch Netzgefäße cardiomentopexy
~ durch Perikardanheftung cardiopericardiopexy
Herzvektor *m* cardiac vector
Herzvektoraufzeichnung *f* vectorcardiography, cardiovectography
Herzvektorbild *n* vectorcardiogram, V. C. G.
Herzvektorschreiber *m* vectorcardiograph
Herzvene *f* cardiac vein, vein of the heart
~/große great cardiac vein
~/kleine small cardiac vein
~/mittlere middle cardiac vein
~/vordere anterior cardiac vein
Herzverbreiterung *f* cardiac enlargement
Herzverfettung *f* cardiomyoliposis, fatty degeneration of the heart
Herzvergrößerung *f* cardiomegaly, mega[lo]cardia, cardiac enlargement
Herzverlangsamung *f s.* Herzschlagverlangsamung
Herzversagen *n* cardiac [power] failure, heart failure (insufficiency)
Herzvolumen *n* cardiac volume
Herzvorfall *m* ectocardia
Herzvorhof *m* atrium [of the heart], vestibule, vestibulum *(Zusammensetzungen s. unter* Vorhof*)*
Herzvorhof ... *s. a.* Vorhof...
Herzvorhofmyxom *n* heart atrium myxoma
Herzvorhofscheidewand *f* interatrial (heart atrium) septum
Herzvorhofscheidewanddefekt *m* interatrial septum defect
Herzwand *f* cardiac wall, coat of the heart
Herzwandaneurysma *n* cardiac (mural) aneurysm
Herzwiederbelebung *f* cardiac resuscitation
Herzwirbel *m* vortex of the heart
herzwirksam cardiac-active, cardioactive
Herzzeitvolumen *n* cardiac output
Herzzentrum *n* heart centre *(Klinik für Herzkranke)*
Herz-Zwerchfell-Winkel *m* cardiophrenic angle
Herzzyklus *m* cardiac cycle
Heschl-Querwindungen *fpl* Heschl's (transverse temporal) gyri
Heterästhesie *f* heter[o]aesthesia
heterochrom heterochrom[at]ic, heterochromous
Hetero... *s. a.* Fremd...
Heterochromatin *n* heterochromatin *(Chromosomenbestandteil)*
Heterochromie *f* heterochromia, anisochromia, chromheterotropia *(der Iris)*
Heterochromiestar *m* heterochromic cataract
Heterochromiezyklitis *f* heterochromic cyclitis
Heterochromosom *n* heterochromosome, allosome, heterotypical (sex) chromosome
Heterochronie *f* heterochronia *(Gewebsentstehung zu ungewöhnlicher Zeit)*
heterodont heterodont, anisodont[ic]
Heteroerotismus *m* heteroeroti[ci]sm
heterogametisch heterogametic *(Geschlechtschromosom)*
heterogen heterogenous, inhomogeneous
Heterogenese *f* heterogenesis *(z. B. durch Virusinfektion)*
Heterogenität *f* heterogeneity
Heterogeusie *f* heterogeusia
Heterohämolysin *n* heterohaemolysin *(Serumkörper)*
Heterolalie *f s.* Heterophasie
heterolog heterologous, xenogenic, xenogenous
Heterologie *f* heterology *(morphologisch oder funktionell)*
Heterolysin *n* heterolysin *(Serumkörper)*
Heterometropie *f* heterometropia *(unterschiedliche Refraktion beider Augen)*
heteromorph heteromorphic, heteromorphous
Heteroosteoplastik *f* heteroosteoplasty
Heterophasie *f* heterophasia, heterolalia, heterophemy
Heterophorie *f* heterophoria, latent strabismus
Heteroplasie *f* heteroplasia
Heteroplastik *f* heteroplasty, heterotransplantation, heteroplastic transplantation
heteroplastisch heteroplastic
heteroploid heteroploid *(Chromosomensatz)*
Heteropsie *f* heteropsia
Heterosexualität *f* heterosexuality
heterosexuell heterosexual
Heterosis *f* heterosis, hybrid vigor
Heterosmie *f* heterosmia

Heterosom 326

Heterosom n heterosome
Heterosuggestibilität f heterosuggestibility
Heterosuggestion f heterosuggestion
Heterotaxie f heterotaxia, heterotaxis
Heterotonie f heterotonia
Heterotopie f heterotopia
heterotroph heterotrophic
Heterotropie f heterotropia, strabism[us], squint, cast
Heterovakzine f heterovaccine
heteroxen heteroxenous *(Parasiten)*
heterozygot heterozygous
Heterozygoter m heterozygote
Heterozygotie f heterozygosity
Heufieber n hay fever (asthma), pollenosis, pollen asthma, summer catarrh
Heufieberkonjunktivitis f hay-fever conjunctivitis
Heukrätze f trombiculiasis, trombiculosis, trombidiosis
Heuschnupfen m allergic rhinitis (coryza), rhinallergosis *(s. a. Heufieber)*
Hexadaktylie f hexadactylism
Hexamethylpararosanilin n crystal violet *(Wurmmittel)*
Hexenmilch f witch's milk
Hexenschuß m lumbago, lumbalgia
Hexobarbital n hexobarbital *(Narkosemittel)*
Hexokinase f hexokinase *(Enzym)*
Hexose f hexose
HF s. Herzfrequenz
HHL s. 1. Hypophysenhinterlappen; 2. Hinterhauptslage
HHT s. Hämagglutinationshemmungstest
HI s. Herzindex
Hiatus m hiatus, fissure, gap ● neben dem ~ parahiatal
~ **adductorius** adductor hiatus
~ **aorticus** aortic hiatus
~ **canalis facialis** facial hiatus, hiatus of the facial canal
~ **Falloppii** hiatus of Fallopius, hiatus for greater superficial petrosal nerve
~ **maxillaris** maxillary hiatus (ostium) *(zur Nasenhöhle)*
~ **oesophageus** oesophageal hiatus (foramen), oesophageal orifice of the diaphragm *(Zwerchfellücke)*
~ **sacralis** sacral (sacrococcygeal) hiatus
~ **saphenus** subinguinal fossa
~ **semilunaris** semilunar hiatus
~ **tendineus** adductor hiatus
~ **venae cavae** vena caval hiatus
Hiatushernie f hiatus (hiatal) hernia
Hibernation f hibernation *(Stoffwechselverringerung durch Unterkühlung des Körpers)*
Hidradenitis f hidr[os]adenitis, hydr[os]adenitis, inflammation of a sweat gland, spiradenitis
Hidradenokarzinom n hidradenocarcinoma, hidradenoid carcinoma
Hidroa npl 1. hidroa, sudamina, heat pustules; 2. s. Hidroa aestivale

Hidroa f **aestivale** hydroa aestivale (vacciniforme), recurrent summer eruption, summer prurigo
Hidrorrhoe f hidrorrhoea, profuse perspiration
Hidroschesis f hidroschesis, suppression of the perspiration
High-Density-Lipoprotein n high density lipoprotein
Highmore-Höhle f s. Kieferhöhle
hilär hilar
Hilfe f assistance, help, aid; rescue *(Rettung)* ● ärztliche ~ in Anspruch nehmen to call in medical assistance ● erste ~ leisten to render first aid
~/**Dringliche Medizinische** emergency medical system
~/**Erste** first aid, first-aid treatment
~/**medizinische** medical assistance
Hilfsmittel n adjuvant *(Pharmazie)*
Hilfsmuskulatur f auxiliary muscles (musculature)
Hilfspersonal n/**ärztliches** auxiliary medical personal
Hilfsschwester f assistant (junior) nurse, auxiliary (practical) nurse
Hilus m hilum, hilus *(Gefäßeingang an Organen)*
~ **lienalis** hilum of the spleen
~ **ovarii** hilum of the ovarium
~ **pulmonis** hilum of the lung
~ **renalis** hilum of the kidney
Hilusadenopathie f hilar [lymph] adenopathy
Hilusbeteiligung f hilar involvement
Hilusdrüse f hilar gland
Hilusgefäß n hilar vessel
Hilusgefäßschatten m vascular hilar shadow *(Radiologie)*
Hiluslymphknoten m hilar lymph node
Hiluslymphknotenerkrankung f hilar [lymph] adenopathy
Hiluspneumonie f hilar (central) pneumonia
Hiluspulsation f hilar pulsation
Hilustanzen n hilar dance
Hilustuberkulose f hilar tuberculosis
Hiluszeichnung f hilar marking (image) *(der Lunge)*
~/**verwaschene** diminished hilar marking
Hiluszelle f hilar cell
Hiluszell[en]tumor m hilar-cell tumour
Hiluszyste f hilar cyst
Himbeerpocken pl, **Himbeerwarzensucht** f s. Framboesie
Himbeerzunge f strawberry tongue
hinabführend deferent
hinausführend deferent
hinderlich embarrassing, obstructive; cumbersome
hindern to hinder, to prevent; to inhibit; to obstruct
hindernd inhibitory, inhibitive
Hineindrücken n impression
hineinwachsen to grow in (into); to vascularize *(Gefäße)*

hinfällig infirm, weak; frail, decrepit
Hinfälligkeit f infirmity, weakness; frailty, decrepitude
hinführend afferent *(z. B. zu einem Organ)*
~/zum Gehirn cerebripetal
~/zum Kleinhirn cerebellipetal
~/zur Zelle cellulipetal
hinken to limp, to lame; to hobble *(humpeln)*
Hinken n limping, claudication
~/intermittierendes [intermittent] claudication
hinten posterior
~ und oben posterosuperior
~ und seitlich posterolateral
~ und vorn postero-anterior
Hinterbacke f buttock, glutaeus
Hinterbacken fpl buttocks, nates, breech
Hinterdammgriff m Ritgen's manoeuvre *(Geburtshilfe)*
hinterer posterior, posticous
Hintergrund m fundus *(z. B. des Auges)*
Hinterhaupt n occiput, O., napex ● **neben dem ~** paraoccipital ● **unter dem ~** suboccipital
Hinterhaupt... s. a. Okzipital...
Hinterhauptarterie f occipital artery
Hinterhauptbein n occipital [bone] ● **mit dem ~ verschmelzen** to occipitalize ● **über dem ~** supra-occipital
Hinterhauptbeinfortsatz m paramastoid process
Hinterhauptbein-Scheitelbein-Naht f occipitoparietal suture
Hinterhauptbein-Warzenfortsatz-Naht f occipitomastoid suture
Hinterhauptblutleiter m occipital sinus
Hinterhaupt-Kinn-Durchmesser m occipitomental diameter
Hinterhauptlappen m occipital lobe
Hinterhauptpol m occipital pole
Hinterhauptschuppe f occipital squama
Hinterhauptschuppenwulst m transverse occipital torus
Hinterhauptshöcker m/**äußerer** external occipital protuberance
~/innerer internal occipital protuberance
Hinterhauptsknochen m s. Hinterhauptbein
Hinterhauptslage f vertex presentation (position) *(bei der Geburt)*
~/hintere occipitoposterior position [of the foetus]
~/I. hintere occipitolaevoposterior position [of the foetus], left occipitoposterior position of the foetus, L. O. P.
~/II. hintere right occipitoposterior position of the foetus, R. O. P.
~/linke hintere s. **~/I. hintere**
~/linke vordere s. **~/I. vordere**
~/rechte hintere s. **~/II. hintere**
~/rechte vordere s. **~/II. vordere**
~/vordere occipitoanterior position of the foetus
~/I. vordere occipitolaevoanterior position [of the foetus], left occipitoanterior position of the foetus, L. O. A.
~/II. vordere right occipitoanterior position of the foetus, R. O. A.

Hinterhauptsleiste f/**äußere** external occipital crest
~/innere internal occipital crest
Hinterhaupt-Stirn-Durchmesser m occipitofrontal diameter
Hinterhaupt-Stirn-Umfang m occipitofrontal circumference, OFC
Hinterhauptvene f occipital vein
Hinterhauptwindungen fpl occipital gyri *(des Gehirns)*
~/obere superior occipital gyri
~/seitliche lateral occipital gyri
Hinterhirn n metencephalon, hindbrain *(aus Kleinhirn und Brücke bestehender Teil des Rautenhirns)*
Hinterhirnbruch m, **Hinterhirnvorfall** m notencephalocele
Hinterhorn n posterior horn [of the spinal medulla], dorsal cornu
Hinterhornzelle f posterior [horn] cell *(Rückenmark)*
Hintersäule f dorsal column, posterior grey column
~ des Rückenmarks posterior column of the spinal medulla, posterior longitudinal column of grey matter of the spinal cord
Hinterscheitelbeineinstellung f posterior asynclitism, Litzmann's obliquity *(Abweichung der Pfeilnaht aus der Beckenführungslinie nach vorn bei der Geburt)*
Hinterscheitelbeinlage f posterior parietal presentation
Hinterseitenstrang m dorsolateral fasciculus
Hinterseitenstrangbahn f dorsolateral tract
Hinterwandinfarkt m posterior myocardial infarct[ion]
Hinterwurzel f dorsal root
Hinterwurzelganglion n dorsal root ganglion
Hin- und Hertanzen n ballottement
Hinwendung f **zum anderen Geschlecht** heterosexuality
~ zum gleichen Geschlecht homosexuality
hinziehend/zum Rückenmark myelopetal
hinzukommen to supervene *(z. B. eine zweite Krankheit)*
hinzukommend/zufällig accidental
hinzutretend accessory
Hippokampus m hippocampus, Ammon's horn
Hippokratesgesicht n hippocratic face *(beim Eintritt des Todes)*
Hippurie f hippuria
Hippursäure f hippuric acid, benzoylaminoacetic (urobenzoic) acid, benzoylglycine
Hippursäureausscheidung f **im Urin** hippuria
Hippursäuretest m hippuric acid test *(Leberfunktionsprobe)*
Hippus m [**pupillae**] hippus, tremulous iris, iridodonesis, alternating mydriasis, pupillary athetosis
Hirci mpl hirci, axillary hair
Hirn n brain, cerebrum, encephalon *(Zusammensetzungen s. unter Gehirn)*

Hirn...

Hirn... *s. a.* Gehirn... *und* Zerebral...
Hirnabszeß *m* cerebral (brain) abscess, encephalopyosis, pyencephalus
~/otitischer otic cerebral abscess *(nach Mittelohreiterung)*
Hirnaneurysma *n* cerebral (brain) aneurysm
Hirnanhang *m*, **Hirnanhangdrüse** *f s.* Hypophyse
Hirnanoxie *f* cerebral anoxia
Hirnaquädukt *m* cerebral aquaeduct
Hirnarterie *f* cerebral artery
~/hintere posterior cerebral artery
~/mittlere middle cerebral artery
~/vordere anterior cerebral artery
Hirnarterienröntgen[kontrast]bild *n* cerebral arteriogram
Hirnarterienröntgen[kontrast]darstellung *f* cerebral arteriography
Hirnarteriogramm *n* cerebral arteriogram
Hirnarteriographie *f* cerebral arteriography
Hirnarteriosklerose *f* cerebral (brain) atherosclerosis
~/Binswangersche Binswanger's dementia (encephalopathy)
hirnartig cerebriform
Hirnatrophie *f* cerebral atrophy, encephalatrophy, phrenatrophy
~/Picksche Pick's disease, convolutional cerebral atrophy
~/umschriebene circumscribed cerebral atrophy
Hirnaufnahme *f* cerebral (brain) uptake *(z. B. von Medikamenten)*
Hirnbalken *m* [corpus] callosum ● **über dem ~** supracallosal
Hirnbasis *f* base of the brain
Hirnbasisgefäßkranz *m s.* Hirnbasiskreislauf
Hirnbasishirnhautentzündung *f* basilar meningitis
Hirnbasiskreislauf *m* arterial cerebral circle, arterial circle of Willis (the cerebrum)
Hirnbeteiligung *f* cerebral (brain) involvement
Hirnbiopsiegewebe *n* cerebral (brain) biopsy tissue
Hirnbläschen *n* cerebral (brain) vesicle
Hirnblutfluß *m* cerebral blood flow
Hirnblutkreislauf *m* cerebral (brain) circulation
Hirnblutleiter *m* dural sinus, cranial venous sinus, sinus [of the dura mater]
~/gerader straight (tentorial) sinus
Hirnblutleiterentzündung *f* sinu[s]itis, sinus phlebitis
Hirnblutleiterverschluß *m*/**thrombotischer** sinus thrombosis, thrombosinusitis
Hirnblutung *f* cerebral (brain) haemorrhage, encephalorrhagia
Hirnchirurgie *f* cerebral (brain) surgery
Hirndegeneration *f* cerebral (brain) degeneration, encephalosis
Hirndekompression *f* cranial decompression
Hirndruck *m* cerebral compression, brain pressure
Hirndruckentlastung *f* cranial decompression
Hirndruckerhöhung *f* cerebral compression

Hirndruckmessung *f* ventriculometry
Hirndurchblutung *f* cerebral (brain) circulation, cerebral perfusion (blood flow), CBF
Hirndysfunktion *f* cerebral (brain) dysfunction
Hirneklampsie *f* cerebral eclampsia
Hirnembolie *f* cerebral (brain) embolism
Hirnentlastung *f* cranial decompression
Hirnentzündung *f* [en]cephalitis, cerebritis, cerebral inflammation, brain fever, neuraxitis *(Zusammensetzungen s. unter* Enzephalitis*)*
hirnentzündungsauslösend encephalitogenic
Hirnerkrankung *f* [en]cephalopathy, cerebropathy, encephalosis, cerebral (brain) disease
~/degenerative encephalosis, degenerative brain disease
Hirnerweichung *f* encephalomalacia, encephalodialysis, cerebromalacia, softening [of the brain], cerebral softening
~/rote red softening
Hirnfehlentwicklung *f* encephalodysplasia
Hirnflüssigkeit *f* cerebrospinal fluid (liquor)
Hirnfunktion *f* cerebral (brain) function
Hirnfunktionsstörung *f* cerebral (brain) dysfunction
Hirngefäß *n* cerebral blood vessel
Hirngefäßinsuffizienz *f* cerebrovascular (cerebral vascular) insufficiency
Hirngefäßkrankheit *f* cerebrovascular disease
Hirngefäßmißbildung *f* cerebrovascular (cerebral vascular) malformation
Hirngefäßröntgen[kontrast]bild *n* cerebral angiogram
Hirngefäßröntgen[kontrast]darstellung *f* cerebral angiography
Hirngefäßspasmus *m* cerebral vasospasm
Hirngefäßthrombose *f* cerebral thrombosis
Hirngefäßverkalkung *f* cerebral arteriosclerosis
Hirngefäßverschluß *m* cerebrovascular (cerebral vascular) occlusion
Hirngeräusch *n* cerebral (brain) murmur *(beim Säugling)*
hirngeschädigt brain-damaged, brain-injured
Hirngeschwulst *f* cerebral (brain) tumour, encephaloma
Hirngewebe *n* brain tissue
Hirngewicht *n* brain weight
Hirnglukoseutilisation *f* cerebral glucose utilization
Hirngrube *f* cerebral fossa
Hirnhaut *f* [cranial] meninx, cerebral membrane ● **über der harten ~** supradural ● **unter der ~** submeningeal ● **unter der harten ~** subdural
~/harte dura mater [of the brain], dura, pachymeninx, scleromeninx
~/weiche pia mater [of the brain], pia, leptomeninx *(besteht aus Gefäßhaut und Spinnwebshaut)*
Hirnhautarterie *f*/**hintere** posterior meningeal artery
~/mittlere middle meningeal artery
~/vordere anterior meningeal artery
Hirnhautarterienentzündung *f* meningoarteritis

Hirnhautblutung f meningeal haemorrhage, meningorrhagia, meningorrhoea
Hirnhautbruch m meningocele
Hirnhautgeschwulst f meningeal tumour
Hirnhautgewebe n meningeal tissue
Hirnhautkarzinomatose f meningeal carcinomatosis
Hirnhautkrankheit f meningopathy
Hirnhautmantel m meningeal coat
Hirnhautmilzbrand m meningeal anthrax, anthrax meningitis
Hirnhautnaht f meningeorrhaphy
Hirnhautreizung f meningism, cerebral irritation
Hirnhautseparator m **nach Horseley** Horseley's dura mater separator
Hirnhauttuberkulose f tuberculous meningitis
Hirnhaut- und Gehirnentzündung f meningo-encephalitis, meningocerebritis, meningocephalitis, encephalitic meningitis, encephalomeningitis
Hirnhaut- und Rückenmarkentzündung f myelomeningitis, meningomyelitis
Hirnhautvene f meningeal vein
~/**mittlere** middle meningeal vein
Hirnherd m cerebral focus
Hirnherdzeichen n focal neurologic sign
Hirninfarkt m s. Hirnschlag
Hirnkammer f ventricle [of the brain], cerebral ventricle, brain cavity ● **neben der III.** ~ paraventricular
~/**dritte** third (middle) ventricle
~/**laterale** lateral ventricle
~/**vierte** fourth ventricle
Hirnkammerdrainage f ventriculostomy
Hirnkammerdruckmessung f ventriculometry
Hirnkammerendoskop n ventriculoscope
Hirnkammerendoskopie f ventriculoscopy
Hirnkammerentzündung f ventriculitis
Hirnkammerfistelung f[/**operative**] ventriculostomy
Hirnkammerflüssigkeit f ventricular fluid
Hirnkammer-Herzvorhof-Drainage f ventriculoatriostomy *(bei Hydrozephalus)*
Hirnkammerkanüle f ventricular cannula
Hirnkammer-Peritonealhöhlen-Drainage f ventriculoperitoneal shunt *(bei Hydrozephalus)*
Hirnkammer-Peritoneum-Shunt m brain ventricle peritoneum shunt
Hirnkammerpunktion f ventriculopuncture, ventricular (cranial) puncture
Hirnkammerpunktionskanüle f ventricular cannula
Hirnkammerröntgenbild n ventriculogram
Hirnkammerröntgen[kontrast]darstellung f [brain] ventriculography
Hirnkammerspiegel m ventriculoscope
Hirnkammerspiegelung f ventriculoscopy
Hirnkammersystem n ventricular system
Hirnkammer-Zisternen-Drainage f ventriculocisternostomy, ventriculospinal-subarachnoid shunt *(bei Hydrozephalus)*
Hirnkanüle f cerebral (brain) cannula
Hirnkarte f/**Brodmannsche** Brodmann's map
Hirnklip m brain clip
Hirnkonzentration f brain concentration
Hirnkreislauf m cerebral (brain) circulation
Hirnlähmung f cerebral palsy, brain paralysis
Hirnlehre f encephalogy
Hirnluftembolie f cerebral air embolism
Hirnmalaria f cerebral malaria
Hirnmantel m pallium
Hirnmasse f cerebral mass, brain substance
Hirnmassenblutung f cerebral (brain) haemorrhage, spontaneous intracerebral haemorrhage
Hirnmassenläsion f [cerebral] mass lesion
Hirnmesser n encephalotome, brain knife
Hirnmeßinstrument n encephalometer
Hirnminderdurchblutung f cerebral (brain) ischemia
Hirnminutenblutfluß m, **Hirnminutendurchblutung** f cerebral blood flow
Hirnnerv m cranial (cerebral) nerve
~/**I.** olfactory (first cranial) nerve, cranial nerve I
~/**II.** optic (second cranial) nerve, cranial nerve II
~/**III.** oculomotor (third cranial) nerve, cranial nerve III
~/**IV.** trochlear (fourth cranial) nerve, patheticus, cranial nerve IV
~/**V.** trigeminal (fifth cranial, trifacial) nerve, trigeminus, cranial nerve V
~/**VI.** abducent (sixth cranial) nerve, abducens, cranial nerve VI
~/**VII.** facial (seventh cranial) nerve, facialis, cranial nerve VII
~/**VIII.** vestibulocochlear nerve, acusticus [nerve], auditory (eighth cranial) nerve, cranial nerve VIII
~/**IX.** glossopharyngeal (ninth cranial) nerve, cranial nerve IX
~/**X.** pneumogastric (tenth cranial) nerve, cardiac inhibitory nerve, vagus [nerve], cranial nerve X
~/**XI.** spinal accessory nerve, eleventh cranial nerve, cranial nerve XI
~/**XII.** hypoglossal (twelfth cranial) nerve, hypoglossus, cranial nerve XII
Hirnnervenausfall m/**motorischer** cranial nerve motor loss
Hirnnervenendigung f cranial nerve terminal
Hirnnervenerkrankung f cranial neuropathy
Hirnnervenfunktion f cranial nerve function
Hirnnervenlähmung f cranial nerve palsy (paralysis)
Hirnnervenleiden n cranial neuropathy
Hirnnervenverletzung f cranial nerve lesion
Hirnödem n cerebral oedema, brain swelling; wet (swollen) brain
Hirnparaplegie f cerebral paraplegia
Hirnphykomykose f cerebral phycomycosis
Hirnpotential n/**elektrisches** electrocortical potential
Hirnprolaps m cerebral prolapse, brain herniation, prolapse of the cerebrum; cerebral hernia, brain fungus, encephalocele, craniocele
~ **mit Ventrikelzysten** encephalocystocele

Hirnpunktion

Hirnpunktion f encephalopuncture, cephalocentesis
Hirnpunktionskanüle f brain[-exploring] cannula
Hirnpunktionsnadel f brain[-exploring] needle
Hirnquetschung f cerebral contusion, contusion of the brain
Hirnreflex m cerebral (brain, cranial) reflex
Hirnrinde f cerebral cortex, [brain] cortex ● **neben der ~** paracortical ● **unter der ~** subcortical
Hirnrindenentzündung f periencephalitis, periencephalomeningitis
Hirnrindenexzision f/**umschriebene** topectomy
Hirnrindenpotential n [electro]cortical potential
Hirnrindenpotentialableitung f electrocorticography
Hirnrindenreflex m cortical (cerebral cortex) reflex
~/Haabscher Haab's (cerebral cortex) reflex
Hirnrindensensibilität f cortical sensibility
Hirnrindenstromaufzeichnung f electrocorticography
Hirnrindenstrombild n electrocorticogram
Hirnrindenvene f cortical cerebral vein, cerebral cortical vein
Hirnsauerstoffmangel m cerebral (brain) anoxia
Hirnscanning n brain scanning (scintigraphy)
Hirnschenkeldurchtrennung f[/**operative**] crusotomy
Hirnschlag m cerebral infarct[ion], cerebrovascular (cerebral vascular) accident, [cerebral] apoplexy, [apoplectic] stroke ● **nach einem ~** postapoplectic
Hirnschlagader f cerebral artery
Hirnschnitt m encephalotomy
Hirnschwäche f encephalasthenia
Hirnschwellung f s. Hirnödem
Hirnschwindel m cerebral vertigo
Hirnseitenventrikel m lateral ventricle of the brain, paracoele
Hirnsepsis f encephalosepsis
Hirnsichel f cerebral (brain) falx ● **unter der ~** subfalcial
Hirnsinus m s. Hirnblutleiter
Hirnsklerose f cerebral sclerosis, cerebrosclerosis, encephalosclerosis
Hirnspatel m brain spatula
Hirnstamm m s. Stammhirn
Hirnstein m encephalolith
Hirnstiel m cerebral peduncle
Hirnstieldurchtrennung f[/**operative**] pedunculotomy
Hirnstoffwechsel m cerebral metabolism
Hirnstoffwechselrate f cerebral metabolic rate
Hirnstromaufzeichnung f electroencephalography
Hirnstromkurve f electroencephalogram, EEG
Hirnstromwellen fpl brain waves
Hirnsubstanz f brain substance
~/graue grey brain substance, grey matter of the brain (cerebrum)
~/weiße white brain substance, white matter of the brain (cerebrum)
hirnsubstanzartig cerebriform
Hirnsyndrom n/**organisches** organic brain syndrome (disorder)
Hirntod m cerebral (brain) death; irreversible coma
Hirntrauma n cerebral trauma, brain injury (lesion)
Hirn- und Rückenmarkflüssigkeit f cerebrospinal fluid, CSF; neurolymph
Hirnvene f cerebral vein
~/große great cerebral vein
~/innere internal cerebral vein
~/obere superior cerebral vein
~/untere inferior cerebral vein
~/vordere anterior cerebral vein
Hirnvenenthrombose f cerebral venous thrombosis
Hirnvenenverschluß m cerebral vein occlusion
Hirnventrikel m s. Hirnkammer
Hirnverbindungsarterie f/**hintere** posterior communicating artery of the cerebrum
~/vordere anterior communicating artery of the cerebrum
Hirnvereiterung f pyencephalus, cerebral (brain) abscess; encephalopyosis
hirnverkalkend cerebrosclerotic
Hirnverkalkung f cerebral calcification (s. a. Hirnsklerose)
hirnwärts cerebripetal
Hirnwindung f [cerebral] gyrus, [brain] convolution
Hirnwindungsabdruck m convolutional impression
Hirnwindungsentfernung f[/**operative**] gyrectomy
Hirnzucker m brain sugar, cerebrose
hirsekornartig miliary
hirsekorngroß miliary
Hirsutismus m hirsutism (bei Nebennierenüberfunktion)
Hirudin n hirudin (Gerinnungshemmstoff des Blutegels)
Hirudiniasis f hirudiniasis, infestation by (with) leeches
~ externa external hirudiniasis
~ interna internal hirudiniasis
Hirudo m hirudo, leech, blood sucker
~ medicinalis [medicinal] leech
Hirzismus m hircismus, strong odour of the axilla
HISG s. Immunserumglobulin/humanes
Histamin n histamine, β-imidazole-ethylamine (Gewebshormon)
Histaminantagonist m antihistaminic [agent], antihistamine [drug]
histaminantagonistisch antihistaminic
Histaminase f histaminase, diamine oxidase (Enzym)
Histamindesensibilisierung f histamine desensitization
Histaminfreisetzung f release of histamine

Histamingehalt m/**erhöhter** hyperhistaminaemia *(im Blut)*
Histaminkopfschmerz m s. Horton-Bing-Syndrom
Histaminspiegel m histamine level
Histaminspiegelerhöhung f **im Blut** hyperhistaminaemia
Histamintest m histamine test
His-Tawara-Knoten m His-Tawara node, atrioventricular node *(Herzreizleitungssystem)*
Histidase f histidase *(Enzym)*
Histidin n histidine, β-imidazole-α-alanine
Histidinämie f histidinaemia
Histidinausscheidung f **im Urin** histidinuria
Histidindekarboxylase f histidine decarboxylase *(Enzym)*
Histidin[spiegel]erhöhung f **im Blut** histidinaemia
Histidintest m histidine test
Histioblast m histioblast
Histioleukämie f histiocytic leukaemia
Histiozyt m histiocyte, rhagiocrine (resting wandering) cell *(im Bindegewebe)*
histiozytär, histiozytenartig histiocytoid
Histiozytenvermehrung f histiocytosis
Histiozytom[a] n histiocytoma *(gutartige, zellreiche Geschwulstform der Haut)*
Histiozytose f histiocytosis
~ **X** histiocytosis X, reticuloendotheliosis
Histochemie f histochemistry
Histodiagnose f histodiagnosis
Histodifferenzierung f histodifferentiation
Histofluoreszenz f histofluorescence
histogen histogenous
Histogenese f histogenesis, formation of tissue
histogenetisch histogenetic
Histogramm n histogram *(Statistik)*
Histohäm[at]in n histohaematin
histoinkompatibel histoincompatible
Histoinkompatibilität f histoincompatibility
histokompatibel histocompatible
Histokompatibilität f histocompatibility
Histokompatibilitätsantigen n histocompatibility antigen
Histologe m histologist, microanatomist
Histologie f histology, microanatomy, microscopic (minute) anatomy
~/**mikroskopische** microhistology
~/**pathologische** pathologic histology
histologisch histologic[al]
Histolyse f histolysis, dissolution (breaking down) of tissue
histometaplastisch histometaplastic
Histomorphologie f histomorphology, morphology of the tissue
Histomorphometrie f histomorphometry
histomorphometrisch histomorphometric
Histomykose f histomycosis
Histon n histone *(Protein)*
Histoneurologie f histoneurology, neurohistology
Histopathologie f histopathology

histopathologisch histopathologic
Histophysiologie f histophysiology, histological physiology
Histoplasmin n histoplasmin *(Antigen)*
Histoplasmintest m histoplasmin [skin] test
Histoplasmom n histoplasmoma
Histoplasmose f histoplasmosis, Darling's disease, [reticuloendothelial] cytomycosis
~/**afrikanische** African histoplasmosis *(durch Histoplasma duboisii)*
Historadiographie f, **Historöntgenographie** f historadiography, microradiography
Historrhexis f historrhexis, breaking up of tissue
Histospektroskopie f histospectroscopy
histospektroskopisch histospectroscopic
Histotherapie f histotherapy
Histothrombin n histothrombin
Histotom n histotome
Histotomie f histotomy
histotoxisch histotoxic
Histotoxizität f histotoxicity
Histotripsie f histotripsy, crushing of tissue
Hitze f heat; febrile heat; calor *(Entzündungszeichen)*
~/**aufsteigende** hot (menopausal) flush[es]
~/**klimakterische** climacteric hot flush[es]
Hitzeangst f thermophobia
Hitzeausschlag m heat rash
hitzebeständig heat-resistant, thermostable; thermoduric, thermotolerant *(Mikroorganismen)*
Hitzebeständigkeit f heat resistance, thermostability; thermotolerance *(von Mikroorganismen)*
hitzeempfindlich heat-sensitive
Hitzeempfindung f heat sensation; heat discomfort
Hitzeerschöpfung f heat exhaustion (prostration)
~/**hydroprive** water-depletion heat exhaustion, water-deficiency heat exhaustion
~/**saloprive** salt-depletion heat exhaustion, salt-deficiency heat exhaustion
~/**tropische anhidrotische** tropical anhidrotic (dishidrotic) asthenia
Hitzeerythem n heat rash, heat-induced erythema
Hitzefieber n heat pyrexia, thermic fever
Hitzegefühl n s. Hitzeempfindung
hitzeinaktiviert heat-inactivated *(z. B. Toxine)*
Hitzekollaps m heat collapse
Hitzekrampf m heat cramp
Hitzepackung f hot pack
hitzeresistent s. hitzebeständig
Hitzerötung f hot flash
Hitzeschaden m heat injury
Hitzestar m heat-ray (glassblowers') cataract
Hitzestauung f heat accumulation *(z. B. im Körper)*
Hitzesterilisation f heat sterilization
hitzeüberdauernd thermoduric, thermotolerant *(Mikroorganismen)*
Hitzeüberempfindlichkeit f hyperthermalgesia, hyperthermo-aesthesia

hitzeunbeständig

hitzeunbeständig thermolabile
Hitzewallung f hot flash; hot flush
~/klimakterische [climacteric] hot flush[es]
hitzezersetzend pyrolytic
Hitzezersetzung f pyrolysis
hitzig hot-headed, hot-tempered; violent, intemperate
Hitzschlag m heatstroke, heat apoplexy (prostration)
H-Kettenkrankheit f heavy chain disease
HLA s. Leukozytenantigen/humanes
HLM s. Herz-Lungen-Maschine
HMG s. Menopausegonadotropin/humanes
HMV s. Herzminutenvolumen
HNO s. Hals-Nasen- und Ohrenheilkunde
HNO-ärztlich otorhinolaryngologic
HNO-Besteck n ear-nose-throat set, E-N-T set
HNO-chirurgisch otosurgical
HNO-Facharzt m oto[rhino]laryngologist
HNO-Klinik f ear, nose, and throat clinic
hochakut hyperacute, peracute, superacute
hochdosiert large-dose (z. B. Medikament)
Hochdruck m s. Hypertonus
Hochdruckpuls m cordy (high-tension) pulse
Hochdruckretinopathie f hypertensive retinopathy
hochgestellt [highly] concentrated (Urin)
hochkalorisch high-caloric
hochköpfig acrocephalic, metriocephalic
Hochkurzschädeligkeit f acrobrachycephalia (Mißbildung des Kopfes)
hochlagern to elevate (z. B. Extremität)
hochschwanger far advanced in pregnancy
Hochspannungs[strahlen]therapie f high-voltage radiation (roentgen) therapy
Höchstbelastung f maximal stress, peak load (z. B. des Körpers)
Höchstdosis f maximum permissible dose
hochsteril ultrasterile
höchstzulässig maximum permissible (z. B. Strahlung)
hochvirulent supervirulent, highly virulent
Hochvoltbestrahlung[sbehandlung] f supervoltage irradiation
hochwirksam highly efficacious, potent (z. B. Medikament)
Höcker m tuber, protuberance, protuberantia; knob
Höckerchen n tubercle, tuberculum
~/Darwinsches Darwin's (ear) tubercle
höckerig tuberous; tubercular
Hockeyschlägerschnitt m hockey-stick incision, lateral-J-shaped incision [of Kocher] (bei Sprunggelenkoperation)
Hockstellung f squatting position (bei Morbus Fallot)
Hoden m testis, testicle, orchis, seminal gland, didymus, male gonad ● **mit drei** ~ triorchid ● **mit nur einem** ~ monorchid
~/ektoper ectopic testis

332

~/nicht deszendierter undescended testis
~/um seine Achse verdrehter inverted testis
Hodenabstieg m descent of the testicle (testis), orchiocatabasis (aus der Bauchhöhle in das Skrotum)
~/fehlender cryptorchi[di]sm
Hodenadenom n testicular adenoma
Hodenanhang m appendix testis, stalked hydatid, hydatid [of Morgagni]
Hodenanheftung f[/operative] s. Hodenfixation
Hodenarterie f testicular (spermatic) artery
~/innere internal spermatic artery
Hodenatrophie f testicular atrophy
Hodenausführungsgänge mpl efferent ductules [of the testis]
Hodenbiopsie f testicular biopsy
Hodenblutung f testicular bleeding (haemorrhage)
Hodenbruch m scrotal hernia, scrotocele, [epipl]oscheocele
Hodendysgenesiesyndrom n testicular dysgenesis syndrome
Hodenentfernung f orchidectomy, excision of the testicle
~ bei Hodenhochstand/operative cryptorchidectomy
Hodenentzündung f orch[id]itis, orcheitis, testitis, didymitis, inflammation of the testis
~ bei Mumps mumps orchitis
Hodenerkrankung f orchidopathy, testicular disease, disease of the testis
Hodenextraktbehandlung f orchidotherapy, treatment with testicular extracts
Hodenfixation f orchi[d]opexy (im Hodensack); cryptorchidopexy (bei nicht deszendiertem Hoden)
Hodenfunktionsstörung f hypo-orchidia, male hypogonadism
Hodengeschwulst f testicular tumour; scrotal tumour
Hodengewebe n/**spezifisches** testicular parenchyma (tissue)
Hodenhämatom n testicular haematoma
Hodenheber m cremaster [muscle]
Hodenheberreflex m cremasteric reflex
Hodenhochstand m cryptorchi[di]sm (ein- oder beidseitig)
Hodenhormon n testicular hormone
Hodeninduration f hardening of the testicle, orchioscirrhus
Hodeninzision f orch[id]otomy
Hodenkanälchen n seminiferous tubule
~/gewundenes contorted tubule of the testis, convoluted seminiferous tubule
Hodenkarzinom n testicular carcinoma (cancer)
~/embryonales testicular embryonal carcinoma
Hodenkeimzellentumor m testicular germ cell tumour
Hodenkompressionsreflex m testicular compression reflex
Hodenlage f/**falsche** parorchidium
Hodenläppchen n lobule of the testis

Hodenleitband n gubernacular cord
hodenlos anorchous
Hodenmaldeszensus m maldescent of the testis
Hodennaht f orchi[d]orrhaphy, suturing (stitching) of the testis
Hodennetz n rete testis
Hodenneuralgie f s. Hodenschmerz
Hodenoperation f/**plastische** orchidoplasty
Hodenparenchym n testicular parenchyma
Hodenplastik f orchi[d]oplasty
Hodenpol m/**unterer** lower end of the testis
Hodenprellung f contusion of the testis
Hodenrand m/**freier (vorderer)** free border of the testis
Hodensack m scrotum, oschea, bag
Hodensack... s. a. Skrotal... und Skrotum...
Hodensackentfernung f[/**operative**] scrotectomy, excision of the scrotum
Hodensackentzündung f scrotitis, oscheitis, inflammation of the scrotum
Hodensackgeschwulst f scrotal tumour
Hodensackhydrozele f scrotal hydrocele, oscheohydrocele
Hodensacknaht f 1. scrotal suture; 2. scrotal raphe, raphe of the scrotum *(Anatomie)*
Hodensackreflex m scrotal reflex
Hodensackscheidewand f scrotal septum
Hodensackstein m oscheolith
Hodensackwasserbruch m scrotal hydrocele, oscheohydrocele
Hodenscheidenentzündung f periorchitis
Hodenschmerz m testicular pain, testalgia, orchi[d]algia, orchiodynia, orchioneuralgia, didymalgia
Hodenschwäche f hypoorchidia
Hodenschwellung f testicular swelling, orchidoncus
Hodensenkung f orchidoptosis, falling of the testicle
Hodensuspensorium n scrotal suspensory (supporter), jockey strap
Hodenteratom n testicular teratoma
Hodentiefstand m orchidoptosis
Hodentorsion f testicular torsion, torsion of the testis
Hodentransplantat n testicular graft
Hodentransplantation f testicular transplantation
Hoden- und Nebenhodenentfernung f[/**operative**] orchido-epididymectomy
Hoden- und Nebenhodenentzündung f s. Orchiepididymitis
Hodenunterfunktion f hypoorchidia
Hodenvene f/**linke** left testicular (spermatic) vein
~/**rechte** right testicular (spermatic) vein
Hodenverhärtung f orchioscirrhus; hardening of the testicle
Hodenverschmelzung f synorchi[di]sm; fusion of the testes
Hodenverwachsung f/**angeborene** synorchi[di]sm

Hodenwasserbruch m **mit chylösem Inhalt** chylocele *(bei Elephantiasis)*
Hodenzwischenzelle f Leydig (interstitial) cell
Hodenzwischenzelleninsuffizienz f hypoleydigism
Hodgkin-Granulom n Hodgkin's granuloma
Hodgkin-Lymphom n Hodgkin's lymphoma
Hodgkin-Sarkom n Hodgkin's sarcoma
Hodophobie f hodophobia *(krankhafte Angst vor dem Reisen)*
Hof m areola, halo
hofartig areolar
Hoffa-Fettkörper m Hoffa's fat pad
Hoffmann-Reflex m Hoffmann's finger reflex
Hoffmann-Syndrom n Hoffmann's syndrome *(Verlangsamung der Muskelrelaxation bei Myxödem)*
Hofmann-Wellenhof-Bakterium n Hofmann's bacillus, Corynebacterium pseudodiphtheriticum
Höhenalkalose f altitude alkalosis *(infolge Luftverdünnung)*
Höhenangst f hypsophobia, acrophobia, batophobia
Höhenanpassung f altitude acclimatization
Höhenhemianopsie f altitudinal hemianopsia
Höhenkrankheit f altitude (mountain) sickness, Acosta's (high mountain) disease, hypobaropathy, oronosus; altitude anoxia *(der Flieger)*
Höhenkur f hypsotherapy
Höhenkurort m high-altitude health resort
Höhenpolyglobulie f high-altitude erythraemia
Höhenschielen n vertical squint, sursumvergent strabism[us], anoopsia [strabismus]
~/**latentes** hyperphoria, anaphoria
Höhenschwindel m vertical (height) vertigo
Höhensonne f quartz (ultra-violet) lamp
Höhentherapie f hypsotherapy
Höhepunkt m climax, acme, crisis *(z. B. in einem Krankheitsverlauf)*
Höhle f cavity, cavern, cavum; ventricle; sinus; pit, fossa; antrum; pocket *(Eiter)*; socket *(z. B. eines Gelenks)*
~/**tuberkulöse** tuberculous cavity
Höhlenbildung f cavity formation, cavitation *(in Geweben und Organen nach Krankheiten)*; pitting *(z. B. in Fingernägeln oder bei Hautödem)*; porosis *(besonders in Knochen)*
~ **im Rückenmark** syringomyelia, myelosyringosis
Höhlengrau n/**zentrales** central grey substance
Hohlfuß m hollow (contracted) foot, [talipes] cavus, arcuate talipes
Hohlhand f palm [of the hand], vola
Hohlhandaponeurose f palmar aponeurosis
Hohlhand[arterien]arkade f, **Hohlhandarterienbogen** m palmar (volar, carpal) arch
Hohlhandarteriennetz n carpal rete
Hohlhandfaszie f palmar fascia
Hohlhandmuskel m/**kurzer** palmaris brevis [muscle]
~/**langer** palmaris longus [muscle]

Hohlhandraum

Hohlhandraum *m* palmar space
Hohlhandreflex *m* palmar reflex *(Fingerbeugung bei Reizung der Hohlhand)*
Hohlkreuz *n* hollow back *(s. a.* Lordose*)*
Hohlmeißel *m* gouge, hollow chisel
Hohlmeißelzange *f* bone rongeur; rib rongeur
Hohlnagel *m* spoon nail; koilonychia
Hohlorgan *n* hollow viscus (organ)
Hohlraum *m* cavity, cavern, cavum, hollow space; lacuna
hohlraumartig cavernous; lacunar
Hohlrücken *m* hollow back *(s. a.* Lordose*)*
Hohlsonde *f* hollow sound, grooved director
Hohlspiegel *m* concave mirror
Höhlung *f s.* Hohlraum *und* Höhle
Hohlvene *f* caval vein, [vena] cava
~/**obere** superior caval vein, superior vena cava, precava
~/**untere** inferior caval vein, inferior vena cava, postcava
Hohlvenen... *s. a.* Kava...
Hohlvenenanomalie *f* caval [vein] anomaly
Hohlvenenblutfluß *m* caval [vein] flow
Hohlvenenentzündung *f* cavitis
Hohlvenenfilter *n(m)* vena cava filter
Hohlvenenkanüle *f* caval (vena cava) cannula
Hohlvenenkanülieren *n* caval (vena cava) cannulation
Hohlvenenkompressionszyanose *f* [vena cava] compression cyanosis
Hohlvenenröntgen[kontrast]bild *n* cavogram
Hohlvenenröntgen[kontrast]darstellung *f* cavography
Hohlvenensystem *n* caval system
Hohlvenenunterbindung *f* caval ligation
Hohlvenenverschluß *m* caval obstruction
holandrisch holandric *(Erbgang)*
Hollander-Test *m* Hollander test, insulin hypoglycaemia test
Höllenstein *m* lunar caustic, lapis infernalis, silver nitrate
Höllensteinpinzette *f* caustic forceps
Holoacardius *m* holoacardius *(Mißgeburt ohne Herz)*
~ **acephalus** holoacardius acephalus
~ **acormus** holoacardius acormus
~ **amorphus** *s.* Anideus
Holoakranie *f* holoacrania
holoblastisch holoblastic *(bei der Eiteilung)*
holodiastolisch holodiastolic
Holoenzym *n* holoenzyme *(bestehend aus Apoenzym und Koenzym)*
holokrin holocrine, holocrinous *(Sekretionsform mit Umwandlung der Drüse zum Sekret)*
Holorachischisis *f* holorachischisis, fissure of the entire spinal cord
holosystolisch holosystolic
Holt-Oram-Syndrom *n* Holt-Oram syndrome, atriodigital dysplasia syndrome *(Vorhofseptumdefekt und Verlust der Daumenopposition)*
Holzphlegmone *f* woody (ligneous) phlegmon

Holzschuhherz *n* sabot (wooden-shoe) heart *(auf Röntgenaufnahmen)*
Holzspatel *m* wooden spatula
Holzstethoskop *n* foetal stethoscope
Homalozephalus *m* homalocephalus, platycephalus, chamaecephalus
Homatropin *n* homatropine *(Alkaloid)*
Homo *m* **sapiens** Homo sapiens, human species, man
homodont homodont, isodont[ic]
Homoerotismus *m* homoeroti[ci]sm
homogen homogeneous, homogenic
Homogenese *f* homogenesis
homogenisieren to homogenize
Homogenisierung *f* homogenization, homogenizing
Homogenität *f* homogeneity
Homogentisinausscheidung *f* im Urin homogentisuria
Homogentisinsäure *f* homogentisic acid, alcapton, 2,5-dihydroxyphenylacetic acid
Homograft *n* homograft, homologous graft, allograft
Homokeratoplastik *f* homokeratoplasty
homolog homologous, homologic, allogeneic *(bei Transplantation zwischen Individuen gleicher Art)*
Homologie *f* homology *(Anatomie)*
homonym homonymous
Homöopath *m* homoeopath[ist]
Homöopathie *f* homoeopathy, hahnemannism *(Gegensatz: Allopathie)*
homöopathisch homoeopathic
Homöoplasie *f* homoeoplasia
Homöostase *f* homoeostasis, steady state, physiological equilibrium
homöostatisch homoeostatic
homöotherm homeothermal, homeothermic
Homoplastik *f* homoplasty
homoplastisch homoplastic
Homosexualität *f* homosexuality, homoeroti[ci]sm, uranism
~/**männliche** sodomy, uranism
~ **mit Knaben/männliche** paederasty, buggery
~/**weibliche** lesbianism, sapphism
homosexuell homosexual; homoerotic
Homosexuelle *f* [female] homosexual, lesbian, urninde
Homosexueller *m* [male] homosexual, uranist, urning; paederast
Homotransplantat *n* homotransplant, homograft
Homotransplantatabstoßung *f* homograft rejection
Homotransplantation *f* hom[e]otransplantation, homoplasty
Homotransplantatrejektion *f* homograft rejection
homozygot homozygous
Homozygoter *m* homozygote
Homozygotie *f* homozygosity
Homozystein *n* homocysteine, 2-amino-4-mercaptobutyric acid

Hormonlehre

Homozystin *n* homocystine
Homozystinausscheidung *f* **im Urin** homocystinuria
Honigwabenlunge *f* honeycomb lung; endstaged lung
Hopfendermatitis *f* hop dermatitis
Hörapparat *m s.* Hörgerät
hörbar audible
Hörbarkeitsgrenze *f* audibility limit
hörbeeinträchtigt hearing impaired
Hörbeeinträchtigung *f* hearing impairment
Hörbereich *m* range of audibility, auditory field (area)
Hörbild *n* acoustic image
Hördefekt *m s.* Hörfehler
Hordeolum *n s.* Gerstenkorn
Hördistanz *f* earshot, hearing [distance]
Hörempfindung *f* hearing, auditory sensation
Hörempfindungsstörung *f* dysacousia, dysecoia, dysacousma
hören to hear
Hören *n* hearing, audition
~ **der eigenen Stimme/verstärktes** autophonia, tympanophonia
~/**schmerzhaftes** odynoacousis
hörend auditory, auditive
Hörentfernung *f* earshot, hearing range
Hörfähigkeit *f* acouaesthesia, hearing ability, ability to hear
Hörfehler *m* hearing disorder, auditory defect; defective hearing, amblyacousia
Hörfunktion *f* auditory function
hörgemindert hearing impaired
Hörgerät *n* audiphone, [air conduction] hearing aid
~/**elektrisches** electric hearing aid
~/**mechanisches** mechanical hearing aid *(s. a.* Hörrohr 2.*)*
hörgeschädigt, hörgestört hearing impaired
Hörgleichgewichtsnerv *m* vestibulocochlear (eighth cranial) nerve
Hörgrenze *f* audibility limit
~/**obere** maximum audible field
~/**untere** minimum audible field
Hörhalluzination *f* auditory hallucination, phoneme
Hörhilfe *f s.* Hörgerät
Horizontalebene *f* horizontal plane
Horizontalhemianopsie *f* horizontal (altitudinal) hemianopsia
Horizontallage *f* horizontal position *(z. B. bei Operation)*
Horizontalnystagmus *m* horizontal (lateral) nystagmus
Horizontalschnitt *m* horizontal incision
Horizontalschwindel *m* horizontal vertigo
Horizontalzelle *f* horizontal cell *(z. B. in der Netzhaut)*
Hörknöchelchen *n* auditory ossicle
Hörkurve *f* audiogram, audiometric curve
Hörmesser *m* acou[o]meter, audiometer
Hörminderung *f* hypoacousia, hearing impairment

Hormion *n* hormion *(anthropologischer Meßpunkt)*
Hormon *n* hormone *(körpereigener Wirkstoff)*
● **mehrere Hormone betreffend** multihormonal
~/**adrenokortikotropes** adrenocorticotrophic (corticotrophic) hormone, ACTH, adrenocorticotrop[h]in
~/**antidiabetisches** antidiabetic hormone
~/**antidiuretisches** antidiuretic hormone
~/**antineuritisches** antineuritic vitamin, vitamin B_1
~/**follikelstimulierendes** follicle-stimulating hormone, FSH, gametogenic (follicle-ripening) hormone
~/**glykogenspaltendes** glycogenolytic hormone
~/**interstitielle Zellen stimulierendes** interstitial-cell-stimulating hormone, ICSH, luteinizing hormone, L. H.
~/**keimdrüsenstimulierendes** gonadotropic (gonad-stimulating) hormone, gonadotrop[h]in
~/**kortikotropes** *s.* ~/adrenokortikotropes
~/**laktotrophes** lactation (lactogenic) hormone, lactogen, galactin, prolactin, mammotrophin, mammogenic (mammary-stimulating) hormone
~/**luteotrophes** luteotrophic hormone, LTH, luteotrophin
~/**melanozytenstimulierendes** melanocyte-stimulating hormone, MSH, intermedin
~/**östrogenes** oestrogenous hormone
~/**parathyreotropes** parathyrotropic hormone
~/**plazentares** placental hormone
~/**schilddrüsenstimulierendes** *s.* ~/thyreotropes
~/**somatotropes** somatotropic (growth) hormone, STH, somatotrop[h]in
~/**thyreotropes** thyrotropic (thyroid-stimulating) hormone, TSH, thyrotrop[h]in
~/**zwischenzellenstimulierendes** *s.* ~/interstitielle Zellen stimulierendes
hormonal hormonal, hormonic
Hormonantagonist *m* antihormone
Hormonausfall[s]krankheit *f* endocrinopathy *(durch Ausfall einer endokrinen Drüse)*
Hormonbehandlung *f* hormonotherapy, endocrinotherapy, hormonal (endocrine) therapy, hormone medication
hormonbildend hormonopoietic, hormonogenic
Hormonbildung *f* hormonopoiesis, hormonogenesis
hormonbindend hormonopexic
Hormondrüse *f* endocrine (incretory) gland
Hormoneinfluß *m* hormonal influence
hormonfixierend hormonopexic
Hormongeschwulstkrankheit *f* endocrine adenomatosis
Hormongleichgewicht *n* hormonal balance
Hormonhaushalt *m* hormonal balance
Hormonhaushaltsstörung *f* dyshormonism
Hormoninsuffizienz *f* hormonal insufficiency
Hormonkrankheit *f* endocrinopathy *(durch Ausfall einer endokrinen Drüse)*
Hormonlehre *f* endocrinology, hormonology

Hormonpräparat

Hormonpräparat n hormone preparation
Hormonstoffwechsel m hormonal metabolism
Hormonstörung f dyshormonism
Hormonsubstitutionstherapie f hormone replacement therapy (treatment)
Hormonungleichgewicht n hormonal imbalance
Hormonwirkung f hormonal action
Horn n 1. horn, keratin; 2. horn, cornu *(Zusammensetzungen s. unter Cornu)* ● ~ **bilden** to keratinize
hornartig s. 1. hornförmig; 2. hornig
hornbildend keratogenetic, keratogenous
Hornbildung f 1. keratogenesis; 2. hornification, cornification *(Verhornung)*
Hörnchenknorpel m corniculate cartilage [of Santorini], Santorini's cartilage *(Kehlkopf)*
Horner-Syndrom n Horner's [oculopupillary] syndrome
Hörnerv m auditory (eighth cranial) nerve, acusticus [nerve]
Hörnerventaubheit f eighth-nerve deafness
Hörnerventoxizität f auditory neurotoxicity
Hornfibrille f keratofibril
hornförmig cornual, corniculate, horn-shaped
Horngeschwulst f keratoma
Hornhaut f 1. horny skin, callus; callosity; 2. ~ **des Auges** ● **unter der** ~ subcorneal
~ **des Auges** cornea
~/**konische** conical cornea
Hornhaut... *s.a.* Kornea... *und* Kerato...
Hornhautabflachung f flattening of the cornea; flat cornea
hornhautablösend keratolytic
Hornhautablösung f keratolysis
Hornhautabschuppung f ecdysis, desquamation
Hornhautamyloidose f corneal amyloidosis
hornhautartig keroid, corneal
Hornhautastigmatismus m corneal astigmatism
hornhautauflösend keratolytic
Hornhautauflösung f keratolysis
Hornhautbildchen n mire *(Ophthalmometrie)*
Hornhautbildung f 1. callosity formation, hornification, cornification; 2. keratogenesis
Hornhaut-Bindehaut-Entzündung f keratoconjunctivitis
Hornhautblutgefäß n corneal blood vessel
Hornhautblutung f corneal bleeding, keratohaemia
Hornhautdarstellung f keratographia
Hornhautdegeneration f corneal degeneration
Hornhautdehydrierung f corneal dehydration
Hornhautdicke f corneal thickness
Hornhautdickenmesser m pachymeter, pachometer *(Ophthalmologie)*
Hornhautdurchlässigkeit f corneal permeability
Hornhautdystrophie f corneal dystrophy
~/**Haab-Dimmersche** Biber-Haab-Dimmer syndrome, corneal lattice dystrophy
~/**knotige** corneal nodular dystrophy
~/**makuläre** macular corneal dystrophy
~/**mikrozystische** corneal microcystic dystrophy
~/**noduläre** corneal nodular dystrophy

336

Hornhautempfindung f corneal sensation
Hornhautendothel n corneal endothelium
Hornhautendotheldekompensation f corneal endothelial decompensation
Hornhautendotheldystrophie f corneal endothelial dystrophy
Hornhautendothelzelle f corneal endothelial cell
Hornhautentfernung f[/**operative**] ker[at]ectomy
Hornhautentzündung f keratitis, keratoiditis, inflammation of the cornea *(s.a. unter Keratitis)*
~/**bandförmige** band keratitis (keratopathy)
~ **durch fehlenden Lidschluß** lagophthalmic keratitis
~ **durch Pilze** mycotic keratitis
~/**eitrige** purulent keratitis
~/**neuroparalytische** neuroparalytic (neurotrophic) keratitis *(infolge fehlender Hornhautsensibilität)*
~/**tiefe** deep keratitis
Hornhautepithel n corneal epithelium
Hornhauterkrankung f keratopathy, corneal disease
Hornhauterosion f corneal erosion
Hornhautersatzplastik f transplantation of the cornea
Hornhauterweichung f keratomalacia, softening of the cornea
Hornhautexzision f ker[at]ectomy
Hornhautfibrom n corneal fibroma
Hornhautfistel f corneal fistula
Hornhautfleck m corneal macula
~/**weißer** white corneal opacity, keratoleucoma, albugo
Hornhautgefäßversorgung f corneal vascularization
Hornhautgeschwür n corneal ulcer, helcoma
Hornhautgewebe n corneal tissue
Hornhautgrenzschicht f/**hintere** posterior elastic lamina of the cornea, Descemet's membrane
Hornhauthernie f kerato[dermato]cele
Hornhauthypospadie f corneal hypospadias
Hornhautinfiltrat n corneal infiltrate
Hornhautinfiltration f corneal infiltration
Hornhautirritation f corneal irritation
Hornhautkegel m keratoconus; conical cornea
Hornhautkeloid n corneal keloid
Hornhautkrümmung f corneal curvature
Hornhautkrümmungshyperopie f curvature hyperopia
Hornhautleukom n leucoma of the cornea, walleye
Hornhautlimbus m corneal limbus
Hornhautlipoidose f corneal lipoidosis
Hornhautmeridian m meridian of the cornea
Hornhautmesser m keratometer
Hornhautmesser n kera[to]tome, corneal knife *(Augenchirurgie)*
~/**kleines** microkeratome
Hornhautmikroskop n corneal microscope
Hornhautnarbe f corneal scar (cicatrix)
~/**feine** corneal macula

Hornhautnebelfleck *m* nebula
Hornhautoberfläche *f*/**äußere** ectocornea
Hornhautödem *n* corneal oedema
Hornhautpannus *m* [corneal] pannus
~ **bei Trachom** trachomatous pannus (keratitis)
Hornhautpapillom *n* corneal papilloma
Hornhautparenchym *n* corneal parenchyma
Hornhautpenetration *f* corneal penetration
Hornhautperforation *f* corneal perforation
Hornhautpilzerkrankung *f* keratomycosis
Hornhautpinzette *f* corneal forceps
Hornhautplexus *m* corneal plexus
Hornhautpräzipitat *n* keratic precipitate
Hornhautpunktion *f* keratocentesis, puncturation of the cornea
Hornhautrand *m* [corneal] limbus, corneal margin
Hornhautrandtrübung *f*/**angeborene** posterior embryotoxon; posterior marginal dysplasia of the cornea
Hornhautreepithelisierung *f* corneal reepithelialization
Hornhautregeneration *f* corneal regeneration
Hornhautreizung *f* corneal irritation
Hornhautring *m* corneal arcus
Hornhautruptur *f* keratorrhexis, rupture of the cornea
Hornhautscheitel *m* vertex of the cornea
Hornhautschmerz *m* keratalgia, pain in the cornea
Hornhautschnitt *m* keratotomy, keratocentesis, incision into the cornea
Hornhautschrumpfung *f*/**narbige** cicatricial shrinking of the cornea
Hornhautschwellung *f* corneal swelling
Hornhautsensibilität *f* corneal sensibility
Hornhautskalpell *n* corneal scalpel *(Augenchirurgie)*
~/**kleines** microkeratome
Hornhautsklerose *f* corneal sclerosis; sclerosing keratitis
Hornhautspalte *f* corneal cleft
Hornhautspaltung *f* keratotomy
Hornhautstaphylom *n* corneal staphyloma
Hornhautstich *m* keratonyxis, puncture of the cornea *(Staroperation)*
Hornhautstroma *n* corneal stroma
Hornhauttransplantat *n* corneal graft (transplant)
Hornhauttransplantation *f* corneal grafting, transplantation of the cornea; keratoplasty
Hornhauttrübung *f* corneal opacification (clouding); corneal opacity, cloudiness of the cornea
Hornhautulkus *n* keratohelcosis
Hornhautulzeration *f* corneal ulceration
Hornhaut- und Bindehauteintrocknung *f* xerophthalmia, [ophthalmo]xerosis; scheroma
Hornhaut- und Lederhautentzündung *f* keratoscleritis, scleroperikeratitis
Hornhaut- und Regenbogenhautentzündung *f* kerato-iritis
Hornhaut- und Traubenhautentzündung *f* kerato-uveitis

Hornhautunempfindlichkeit *f* corneal anaesthesia
Hornhaut-Unterkiefer-Reflex *m* corneomandibular reflex
Hornhautvaskularisation *f* corneal vascularization
Hornhautverdickung *f* **der Hände und Füße** acanthokeratodermia
Hornhautverfettung *f* corneal adiposis
Hornhautvergrößerung *f* keratomegaly
Hornhautverletzung *f* corneal injury (lesion)
Hornhautvernarbung *f* corneal scarring (cicatrication)
Hornhautvorderseite *f* anterior surface of the cornea
Hornhautvorwölbung *f* keratectasia, protrusion of the cornea
~/**kugelige** keratoglobus, anterior staphyloma
Hornhautxerosis *f* corneal xerosis
Hornhautzyste *f* corneal cyst
hornig 1. cornoid, corneous, horny, horn-like; 2. keratotic, keratose, keratinous
hornlösend keratolytic
Hornperle *f* epithelial pearl
Hornschicht *f* **der Haut** horny [cell] layer, [stratum] corneum
Hornschichtverdickung *f* keratoma
Hornschuppe *f* horny scale
Hornsubstanz *f* horny substance, horn, keratin *(Gerüsteiweiß)*
hornsubstanzbildend keratogenetic
Hornsubstanzbildung *f* keratogenesis
Hornzelle *f* horn cell *(1. des Epithels; 2. im Rückenmark)*
Hornzellenschicht *f* horny [cell] layer
Horopter *m* horopter *(visuelle Projektionsebene)*
Hörorgan *n* hearing organ, spiral organ of Corti, organ of hearing
Hörprobe *f* hearing test, auditory analysis, audiometry
Hörprüfgerät *n* audiometer, acoumeter
~/**elektroakustisches** audiometer
Hörreflex *m* acoustic (auditory, aural) reflex
Hörreflexschwellenmessung *f* acoustic reflex threshold measurement
Hörrinde *f* auditory cortex *(im ZNS)*
Hörrohr *n* 1. stethoscope; 2. ear trumpet, otophone
Hörsaal *m*/**anatomischer** theatre
Hörschädigung *f* hearing impairment
Hörschärfe *f* hearing (auditory) acuity
Hörschärfebestimmung *f*/**audiometrische** audiometry
Hörschärfemeßgerät *n* audiometer, ac[o]umeter; sonometer
Hörschärfeprobe *f* audiometric (auditory acuity) test
Hörschwelle *f* auditory (hearing) threshold
Hörschwellenaudiogramm *n* threshold audiogram
Hörschwellentest *m* audiometric (auditory acuity) test

Hörschwund

Hörschwund *m* hearing loss
Hörsteigerung *f* hyperacousia, oxyakoia
Hörstein *m* otolith, statolith; ear dust
Hörstörung *f* parac[o]usis, paracousia, auditory dysfunction, hearing disorder, defective hearing
Hörstrahlung *f* acoustic (auditory) radiation, geniculotemporal tract *(im ZNS)*
Hörstummheit *f* audimutism, hearing mutism *(Stummheit bei erhaltenem Hörvermögen)*
Hörsturz *m* sudden deafness (loss of hearing)
Hörsystem *n* auditory system
Hörtest *m* auditory (hearing) test
~/Politzerscher Politzer's test
Horton-Bing-Syndrom *n* Horton's syndrome (headache), histamine cephalalgia, histaminic (cluster) headache, erythromelalgia of the head
Hörtraining *n* auditory (auricular) training
Hörtrauma *n* auditory (acoustic) trauma
Hör- und Gleichgewichtsnerv *m* vestibulocochlear (eighth cranial) nerve
Hör- und Gleichgewichtsorgan *n* vestibulocochlear organ
Hörverlust *m* hearing loss
~/akuter *s.* Hörsturz
Hörvermögen *n* [power of] hearing, audition
Hörverschlechterung *f* hearing impairment
Hörweite *f* earshot, hearing [distance], hearing range ● **außer ~** out of hearing ● **in ~** within hearing
Hörweitenmesser *m* acoumeter, audiometer
Hörzentrum *n* auditory (acoustic) centre
Hospital *n* hospital, infirmary
Hospitalbrand *m* hospital gangrene
hospitalisieren to hospitalize
Hospitalisierung *f* hospitalization, admission to the hospital
Hospitalisierungszeit *f* hospitalization time (period)
Hospitalismus *m* hospitalism
Host-versus-graft-Reaktion *f* host-versus-graft reaction *(Immunologie)*
Houssay-Syndrom *n* Houssay phenomenon *(bei Diabetes mellitus)*
Howell-Jolly-Körper *m* Howell-Jolly body *(bei Erythrozytenzellkernzerfall)*
Howship-Lakunen *fpl* Howship lacunas *(Nischen bei Knochenentwicklung)*
Howship-Romberg-Syndrom *n* Howship-Romberg syndrome (sign), neuralgia obturatoria
HSS *s.* Herzspitzenstoß
HT *s.* Herzton
HTLV3-Virus *n* HTLV3 virus *(Erreger von AIDS)*
Hufeisenfistel *f* horseshoe fistula
Hufeisenniere *f* horseshoe (unguliform) kidney, fused (confluent) kidney
Hufeisenplazenta *f* horseshoe placenta
Hufeisenriß *m* horseshoe tear
Hüft... *s. a.* Hüftgelenk...
Hüftarterie *f/*äußere external iliac artery
~/gemeinsame common iliac artery
~/innere internal iliac artery, hypogastric artery

Hüftbein *n* hipbone, innominate bone
Hüftbeinkamm *m* iliac crest
Hüftbeinloch *n* obturator foramen
Hüftbeinlocharterie *f* obturator artery
Hüftbeinlochvene *f* obturator vein
Hüftbeinstachel *m* iliac spine
Hüfte *f* hip, coxa *(s. a. unter Coxa)*; haunch
~/schnappende snapping hip
Hüftgelenk *n* hip joint
Hüftgelenk... *s. a.* Hüftgelenks...
Hüftgelenkchirurgie *f* hip joint surgery
Hüftgelenkdysplasie *f* dysplasia coxae luxans
Hüftgelenkentzündung *f* coxarthritis, coxitis, inflammation of the hip joint, osphyarthritis
Hüftgelenkeröffnung *f*[/operative] coxotomy
Hüftgelenkersatz *m* hip replacement
~/totaler total hip replacement
Hüftgelenkkopf *m s.* Hüftkopf
Hüftgelenkkopfprothese *f* hip prosthesis
Hüftgelenkleiden *n* coxarthropathy, hip joint disease
~/deformierendes osteoarthritis of the hip joint *(des alternden Menschen)*
Hüftgelenkluxation *f/*angeborene congenital hip displacement, congenital dislocation of the hip, luxatio coxae congenita
~/erworbene hip disarticulation (dislocation)
Hüftgelenkoperation *f* hip joint surgery
Hüftgelenkprothese *f* hip prosthesis
~/totale total hip joint prosthesis
Hüftgelenks... *s. a.* Hüftgelenk...
Hüftgelenkschmerz *m* coxalgia, coxodynia, pain in the hip joint
Hüftgelenkspfanne *f* acetabular fossa, acetabulum
Hüftgelenkspfannenbruch *m* acetabular fracture
Hüftgelenkspfannenexstirpation *f* acetabulectomy
Hüftgelenkspfannengrube *f* acetabular fossa
Hüftgelenkspfannenprothese *f* hip (acetabulum) cup
Hüftgelenkspfannenrekonstruktion *f* acetabuloplasty
Hüftgelenktuberkulose *f* hip joint tuberculosis, coxotuberculosis
Hüftgicht *f* ischiagra
Hüftkappe *f* hip cup
Hüftkopf *m* head of the femur
Hüftkopfgleiten *n* epiphysiolysis capitis femoris
hüftlahm lame in the hip, hip-shot
Hüftlendenarterie *f* iliolumbar artery
Hüftlendenmuskel *m* iliopsoas [muscle]
Hüftlendenvene *f* iliolumbar vein
Hüftlochmuskel *m/*äußerer obturator externus [muscle]
~/innerer obturator internus [muscle]
Hüftluxation *f/*angeborene *s.* Hüftgelenkluxation/angeborene
Hüftmuskel *m* sciatic muscle
Hüftnerv *m* ischiadic (sciatic) nerve
Hüftnervenblockade *f* sciatic nerve block
Hüftnervenentzündung *f* ischiatitis

Hüftpfanne f s. Hüftgelenkspfanne
Hüftregion f hip region, region of the hip
Hüftschmerz m s. Hüftgelenkschmerz
Hüftvene f/**äußere** external iliac vein
~/**gemeinsame** common iliac vein
~/**innere** internal iliac vein, hypogastric vein
Hüftverband m hip bandage
Hüftverrenkung f hip disarticulation (dislocation)
Hügel m hillock, mons, mount, colliculus, clivus
~/**kleiner** hillock
~/**oberer** superior colliculus (quadrigeminal body) *(der Vierhügelplatte des Mittelhirns)*
~/**unterer** inferior colliculus (quadrigeminal body) *(der Vierhügelplatte des Mittelhirns)*
Hügelchen n hillock, colliculus
Hühnerauge n clavus, corn
Hühnerbrust f carinate (chicken) breast, pigeon chest
Hühnersarkom n/**übertragbares** Rous' sarcoma *(bösartige Geschwulst)*
Hülle f coat; tunica *(Überzug)*; membrane, velament[um]; tegument *(Deckhaut)*; sheath *(Sehnenscheide)*; theca *(Bindegewebskapsel)*
Hülsenbandwurm m s. Hundebandwurm
Humanalbumin n human serum albumin
Humangenetik f human genetics
Humanmedizin f human medicine
humanpathogen pathogenic for man
Humanserum n human serum
Humerus m humerus
Humeruskopf m head of the humerus, humeral head
Humerusrolle f trochlea of the humerus
Humerusschaft m shaft of the humerus
Humor m humour
~ **aqueus** aqueous humour
~ **vitreus** vitreous humour
humoral humoral
humpeln to hobble, to limp
Hund m/**roter** s. Lichen tropicus
Hundebandwurm m dog tapeworm; hydatid tapeworm, echinococcus hydatidosis
Hundebandwurmbefall m s. Hundebandwurmerkrankung
Hundebandwurmerkrankung f echinococcosis, hydatidosis, hydatid disease
~/**pulmonale** pulmonary echinococcosis
Hundebandwurmfinne f echinococcus, hydatid, caseworm
Hundebandwurmfinneninfestation f s. Hundebandwurmerkrankung
Hundefieber n/**Stuttgarter** s. Hundeseuche/Stuttgarter
Hundefloh m dog flea, Ctenocephalides canis
Hundeseuche f/**Stuttgarter, Hundetyphus** m Stuttgart disease, canicola fever, canine leptospirosis
Hundsfieber n, **Hundskrankheit** f phlebotomus (pappataci) fever, Chitral (three-day) fever *(durch die Pappatacimücke übertragene Arboviruserkrankung der Tropen)*
Hundswut f s. Tollwut

Hunger m hunger, fames
Hungerazidose f starvation acidosis
Hungerentkräftung f inanition, marasmus
Hungergefühl n sensation of hunger
Hungerkachexie f inanition, marasmus
Hungerkontraktion f hunger contraction *(des Magens)*
Hungerkur f hunger (fasting) cure, starvation cure
hungern to hunger, to go hungry *(Hunger leiden)*, to starve; to fast *(nüchtern bleiben)*
Hungern n starvation, abrosia
Hungerödem n nutritional (famine) oedema, hunger swelling
Hungerschwäche f s. Hungerentkräftung
Hungertherapie f starvation cure (treatment), nestiatria, nestitherapy, nestotherapy
Hungertod m starvation, death from starvation
Hungertyphus m s. Fleckfieber
Hungerzustand m fasting state; inanition
Hunter-Glossitis f Hunter's (atrophic) glossitis
Hunter-Schreger-Streifen mpl Hunter-Schreger bands *(Zahnschmelz)*
Hunter-Syndrom n Hunter's syndrome, mucopolysaccharidosis [type] II, gargoylism
Huntington-Chorea f Huntington's chorea (disease)
Hunt-Syndrom n Hunt's (geniculate) neuralgia
Hürthle-Zelladenom n Huerthle cell adenoma
Hürthle-Zellkarzinom n **der Schilddrüse** Huerthle cell carcinoma of the thyroid
Hürthle-Zelltumor m Huerthle cell tumour, oncocytoma
hüsteln to cough slightly
Hüsteln n tussiculation
husten to cough [up]
~/**Blut** to cough up blood, to spit
Husten m cough, tussis
~/**bellender** hacking (barking) cough
~/**blutiger** bloody cough
~/**krampfartiger** convulsive cough
~/**produktiver** productive cough
~/**reflektorischer** reflex cough
~/**trockener** dry (unproductive) cough
Hustenanfall m fit (attack) of coughing, coughing paroxysm
Hustenbonbon m [cough-]lozenge, pectoral lozenge
hustenlindernd antitussive
hustenlösend solvent, expectorant
Hustenmittel n antitussive [agent], cough remedy (preparation)
Hustenplatte f cough plate *(Bakterienkulturplatte)*
Hustenreflex m cough reflex
hustenreizlindernd antitussive
Hustensaft m cough-mixture
hustenstillend cough-easing, pectoral, antitussive
Hustensynkope f cough syncope
Hustenzentrum n coughing centre
Hütchen n conical pipe

Hutchinson-Gilford-Syndrom 340

Hutchinson-Gilford-Syndrom *n* Hutchinson-Gilford disease (syndrome), premature senility syndrome, childhood progeria
Hutchinson-Tonnenzähne *mpl*, **Hutchinson-Zähne** *mpl* Hutchinson's teeth
HV *s.* Herzvolumen
HVG-Reaktion *f s.* Host-versus-graft-Reaktion
HVL *s.* Hypophysenvorderlappen
HWS *s.* Halswirbelsäule
HWZ *s.* Halbwertzeit
hyalin 1. hyalin[e]; 2. vitreous
Hyalin *n* hyaline *(glasiger kolloidaler Eiweißkörper)*
Hyalinausscheidung *f* im Urin hyalinuria
Hyalineinlagerung *f* hyalinization
hyalinisieren to hyalinize
Hyalinisierung *f* hyalinization
Hyalinknorpel *m* hyaline cartilage
Hyalinknorpelzelle *f* hyalocyte
Hyalinmembran *f* hyaline membrane *(1. in Gewebeschichten; 2. beim Neugeborenen)*
Hyalinmembran-Krankheit *f* hyaline membrane disease, respiratory distress syndrome of the newborn
Hyalinokalzinose *f* hyalinocalcinosis
Hyalinose *f* hyalinosis; hyaline degeneration
Hyalinosis *f* cutis et mucosae lipoid proteinosis
Hyalinverkalkung *f* hyalinocalcinosis
Hyalinzylinder *m* hyaline cast
Hyalinzylinderausscheidung *f* cylindruria
Hyalinzylindergeschwulst *f* cylindroma
Hyalitis *f* 1. hyal[oid]itis, inflammation of a hyaline membrane; 2. hyal[oid]itis, inflammation of the vitreous humour
hyaloidokapsulär hyaloideo-capsular
Hyalomukoid *n* hyalomucoid
Hyalophagie *f* hyalophagia, eating of glass
Hyalophobie *f* hyalophobia *(krankhafte Angst vor Glas)*
Hyaloplasma *n* hyaloplasm, cell sap, enchylema, interfilar mass, paraplasm, paramitome
Hyaloserositis *f* hyaloserositis, hyalocapsulitis
Hyalosom *n* hyalosome *(Zellstruktur)*
Hyalozyt *m* hyalocyte
Hyaluronat *n* hyaluronate
Hyaluronidase *f* hyaluronidase, spreading agent (factor), hyaluronate lyase *(Enzym)*
Hyaluronsäure *f* hyaluronic acid
Hybrid[e] *m*, **Hybride** *f* hybrid; heterozygote
Hydantoin *n* hydantoin *(Antiepileptikum)*
Hydantoinhyperplasie *f* hydantoin hyperplasia
Hydatide *f* 1. hydatid, acephalocyst; 2. *s.*~/Morgagnische
~/Morgagnische 1. hydatid of Morgagni, stalked hydatid, appendix vesiculosus *(am Eileiter)*; 2. hydatid of Morgagni, pedunculated hydatid, appendix epididymidis
Hydatidenflüssigkeit *f* hydatid fluid
Hydatidensand *m* hydatid sand
Hydatidenschwirren *n* hydatid fremitus (thrill), hydatid resonance
Hydatidenzyste *f* hydatid cyst

Hydatidom[a] *n* hydatidoma
Hydatidostomie *f* hydatidostomy
Hydatidozele *f* hydatidocele
hydradenoid hidradenoid, hydradenoid
Hydradenom *n* 1. hidradenoma, hydradenoma; 2. hidradenoma papilliferum; 3. syringoma; 4. cylindroma
Hydrämie *f* hydraemia
hydrämisch hydraemic
Hydramnion *n* [poly]hydramnion, hydramnios
Hydranenzephalie *f* hydranencephaly
Hydrargyrophobie *f* hydrargyrophobia *(krankhafte Angst vor Quecksilber)*
Hydrargyrosis *f* hydrargyria[sis], hydrargyrism, hydrargyrosis, chronic mercurial poisoning, mercurialism, mercurialization
Hydrargyrum *n* bichloratum mercuric chloride, mercury dichloride *(Antiseptikum)*
~ chloratum mercurous chloride *(Laxativum, Diuretikum, Antisyphilitikum)*
Hydrarthros *m* hydrarthros; hydrarthrosis
Hydrase *f*, **Hydratase** *f* hydrase *(Enzym)*
Hydratation *f*, **Hydratisierung** *f* hydration
Hydrenzephalomeningozele *f* hydrencephalomeningocele
Hydriatrie *f s.* Hydrotherapie
Hydroa *npl s.* Hidroa
Hydroadenom *n* hydradenoma, hidradenoma
Hydroaeroperitoneum *n* hydraeroperitoneum
Hydrobilirubin *n* hydrobilirubin
Hydroblepharon *n* hydroblepharon, oedema of the eyelids
Hydrocephalus *m* **communicans** communicating hydrocephalus
~ herniosus hydro[en]cephalocele
Hydrocholeresis *f* hydrocholeresis
hydrocholeretisch hydrocholeretic
Hydrodipsomanie *f* hydrodipsomania
Hydroenzephalozele *f* hydro[en]cephalocele
Hydrogymnastik *f* hydrogymnastics
Hydrohämatonephrose *f* hydrohaematonephrosis *(Ansammlung von blutigem Urin im Nierenbecken)*
Hydrohämatosalpinx *f* hydrohaematosalpinx, haemohydrosalpinx *(Ansammlung von blutiger Flüssigkeit im Eileiter)*
Hydrohepatose *f* hydrohepatosis
Hydrokinesiotherapie *f* hydrokinesitherapy
Hydrokolpos *m* hydrocolpos
Hydrokortison *n* hydrocortisone, cortisol, 17-α-hydroxycorticosterone *(Nebennierenrindenhormon)*
Hydrokystom *n* hidrocystoma, hydrocystoma
Hydrolabilität *f* hydrolability
Hydrolabyrinth *n* hydrolabyrinth
Hydrolase *f* hydrolase *(Enzym)*
~/lysosomale lysosomal hydrolase
Hydrolyse *f* hydrolysis
~/enzymatische enzymatic hydrolysis, zymohydrolysis
hydrolysierbar hydrolyzable
hydrolysieren to hydrolyze

Hymen

Hydromanie f hydromania
Hydromassage f hydromassage
Hydromeningitis f hydromeningitis
Hydromeningozele f hydromeningocele
Hydrometra f hydrometra, uterine dropsy
Hydrometrokolpos m hydrometrocolpos
Hydromikrozephalie f hydromicrocephalia
Hydromphalus m hydromphalos
Hydromyelie f hydromyelia
Hydromyelozele f hydromyelocele
Hydromyom n hydromyoma
Hydronephrose f hydronephrosis
hydronephrotisch hydronephrotic
Hydropelvis f hydropelvis
Hydropenie f s. Hypohydratation
Hydroperikard[ium] n hydropericardium, hydrocardia, dropsy of the pericardium
Hydroperitoneum n hydroperitoneum, hydroabdomen, ascites, dropsy of the belly
hydrophil hydrophilic, hydrophil[e], hydrophilous
Hydrophilie f hydrophilia, hydrophilism
hydrophob hydrophobic, hydrophobe
Hydrophobie f 1. hydrophobia, aquaphobia; 2. s. Tollwut
hydrophthalmisch buphthalmic
Hydrophthalmus m hydrophthalmos, buphthalmos
~ **congenitus** congenital hydrophthalmos (buphthalmos); congenital (infantile) glaucoma
Hydropneumoperikard[ium] n hydropneumopericardium
Hydropneumoperitoneum n hydropneumoperitoneum
Hydropneumothorax m hydropneumothorax
Hydropotherapie f hydropotherapy
Hydrops m hydrops, dropsy
~ **articuli (articulorum)** hydrarthros; hydrarthrosis
Hydropyelon n hydropyelon
Hydropyonephrose f hydropyonephrosis
Hydrorrhachis f hydrorrhachis
Hydrorrhoe f hydrorrhoea, [copious] watery discharge
Hydrorrhoea f **gravidarum** hydrorrhoea gravidarum, forewaters
Hydrosalpinx f hydrosalpinx; salpingian (tubal) dropsy
Hydrospermatozele f hydrospermatocele
Hydrospermatozyste f hydrospermatocyst
Hydrospirometer n hydrospirometer
Hydrosudotherapie f hydrosudotherapy
Hydrosyringomyelie f hydrosyringomyelia
Hydrotherapie f water cure, hydrotherapy *(äußerlich)*; hydropathy *(äußerlich und innerlich)*
Hydrothorax m hydrothorax, hydropleura, dropsy of the chest
Hydrotis f hydrotis *(Flüssigkeitsansammlung im Mittelohr)*
Hydrotympanum n hydrotympanum, hydromyrinx, fluid in the middle ear, middle ear effusion
Hydroureter m hydroureter; hydroureterosis

Hydroureteronephrose f hydroureteronephrosis
Hydrovarium n hydrovarium; ovarian dropsy
2-Hydroxybenzoesäure f 2-hydroxybenzoic acid, salicylic acid
Hydroxybenzol n hydroxybenzene, phenol, carbolic acid
Hydroxybenzylpenizillin n hydroxybenzylpenicillin
Hydroxybernsteinsäure f hydroxysuccinic (malic) acid
β-Hydroxybuttersäure f β-hydroxybutyric acid
β-Hydroxybutyrat-Dehydrogenase f β-hydroxybutyric dehydrogenase *(Enzym)*
17-Hydroxydesoxykortikosteron n 17-hydroxydesoxycorticosterone
11-Hydroxykortikosteroid n 11-hydroxycorticosteroid
17-α-Hydroxykortikosteron n 17-α-hydroxycorticosterone
Hydroxynervon n oxynervon *(Zerebrosid)*
Hydroxyprolin n hydroxyproline *(Eiweißbaustein)*
6-Hydroxypurin n s. Hypoxanthin
18-Hydroxysteroiddehydrogenase f 18-hydroxysteroid dehydrogenase *(Enzym)*
5-Hydroxytryptamin n 5-hydroxytryptamine *(ein Katecholamin)*
Hydrozele f hydrocele
~/**Nucksche** Nuck's hydrocele *(bei offenem Processus vaginalis peritonei)*
~/**skrotale** oscheohydrocele
~/**vereiterte** pyocele
Hydrozelenoperation f hydrocelectomy
hydrozephal hydrocephalic, hydrocephaloid
Hydrozephalie f hydrocephalia; dropsy of the brain, water on the brain
Hydrozephalus m hydrocephalus
~/**toxischer** toxic hydrozephalus
Hydrozephaluskind n hydrocephalic child
Hydrozystadenom n hydrocystadenoma, syringoma, adenoma of the sweat glands
Hygiene f 1. hygiene, hygienics; 2. hygiene, sanitation
~/**mangelnde** insanitation, insanitary conditions
~/**psychische** mental hygiene
Hygienearzt m hygienist, sanitarian
Hygienedurchsetzung f hygienization
Hygienemaßnahme f sanitation, sanitary measure
Hygieniker m hygienist, sanitarian
hygienisch hygienic, sanitary; healthful
Hygroma n hygrom[a], hydrom[a]; weeping sinew, ganglion
~ **cysticum colli congenitum** hygroma cysticum colli, cystic (multiloculated) hygroma, cavernous lymphangioma
hygromatös hygromatous
hygroskopisch hygroscopic
Hymen m(n) hymen, maidenhead
~ **anularis (circularis)** annular (circular) hymen
~ **cribriformis** cribriform hymen
~ **falciformis** falciform (sickle-shaped) hymen
~ **imperforatus** imperforate hymen

Hymenalatresie

Hymenalatresie f hymenal atresia
Hymendurchtrennung f [/operative] hymenotomy
Hymenentfernung f [/operative] hymenectomy
Hymenentzündung f hymenitis, inflammation of the hymen
Hymenexzision f hymenectomy
Hymenitis f s. Hymenentzündung
Hymennaht f hymenorrhaphy
Hymenolepisinfestation f hymenolepiasis
Hymenorrhaphie f hymenorrhaphy
Hymenotom n hymenotome
Hymenspaltung f hymenotomy
Hymenverschluß m [/angeborener] hymenal atresia
hyoepiglottisch hyoepiglottic, hyoepiglottidean
hyoglossal hyoglossal
hyoid hyoid
Hyoszin n hyoscine (Alkaloid)
Hyoszyamin n hyoscyamine (Alkaloid)
Hypakusis f hypacousia
Hypalbuminämie f hypoalbuminaemia, hypalbuminosis
Hypalgesie f hypalgesia, hypalgia
hypalgesisch, hypalgetisch hypalgesic, hypalgetic
Hypamnion n hypamnion (bei Fruchtwassermangelzustand)
Hypästhesie f hypaesthesia
hypästhetisch hypaesthesic, hypaesthetic
Hyper... s. a. Super...
Hyperabduktion f hyperabduction, superabduction
Hyperabduktionssyndrom n hyperabduction (Wright's) syndrome
Hyperabduktionstest m hyperabduction test
Hyperadipositas f hyperadiposis
hyperadrenal hyperadrenal
Hyperadrenalinämie f hyperadrenal[in]aemia
Hyperadrenalismus m hyperadrenalism, hyperadrenia, hyper[adreno]corticism
hyperaffektiv hyperaffective
Hyperaffektivität f hyperaffectivity
hyperaktiv hyperactive
Hyperaktivität f hyperactivity, superactivity, excessive activity
Hyperakusis f hyperacousia, oxyakoia
Hyperaldosteronismus m [hyper]aldosteronism
Hyperalgesie f hyperalgesia, hyperalgia
hyperalgesisch, hyperalgetisch hyperalgesic, hyperalgetic
Hyperalgie f s. Hyperalgesie
Hyperalimentation f hyperalimentation, superalimentation, overfeeding, forced alimentation (feeding)
~/**intravenöse** intravenous hyperalimentation
Hyperalimentose f hyperalimentosis
hyperallergen hyperallergenic
Hyperämie f hyperaemia, engorgement
~/**passive** passive (Bier's) hyperaemia
~/**peristatische** peristatic hyperaemia, peristasis
~/**pulmonale** pulmonary hyperaemia (plethora)

Hyperaminoazidämie f hyperaminoacidaemia, hyperacidaminaemia
Hyperaminoazidurie f hyperaminoaciduria, hyperacidaminuria
hyperämisch hyperaemic; turgid
hyperämisierend rubefacient, causing hyperaemia
Hyperämisierung f hyperaemization
Hyperammonämie f hyperammonaemia
Hyperamnesie f hyper[a]mnesia
Hyperamylasämie f hyperamylasaemia
Hyperandrogenismus m hyperandrogenism
Hyperaphie f hyperaphia
Hyperästhesie f hyperaesthesia, oxyaesthesia
hyperästhetisch hyperaesthetic, hyperaesthesic
hyperazid hyperacid, superacid
Hyperazidität f hyperacidity, superacidity, excessive acidity
Hyperazotämie f [hyper]azotaemia
Hyperazoturie f [hyper]azoturia
Hyperbilirubinämie f [hyper]bilirubinaemia
~/**angeborene familiäre** congenital hyperbilirubinaemia, congenital familial non-haemolytic jaundice, Crigler-Najjar-syndrome
~/**hereditäre konstitutionelle [idiopathische]** constitutional hyperbilirubinaemia (hepatic dysfunction), Gilbert's disease (syndrome), chronic intermittent juvenile jaundice, hereditary non-haemolytic hyperbilirubinaemia, familial non-haemolytic jaundice
~/**physiologische** physiological hyperbilirubinaemia
Hyperbilirubinurie f hyperbilirubinuria
Hyperbulie f hyperbulia, exaggerated willfulness
Hyperchlorämie f hyperchlor[id]aemia
hyperchlorämisch hyperchloraemic
Hyperchlorhydrie f hyperchlorhydria, gastroxynsis, gastric hyperacidity
Hyperchlorurie f hyperchloruria
hypercholesterämisch hypercholesterolaemic
Hypercholesterinämie f hypercholesterolaemia, hypercholester[in]aemia, cholesteraemia
hypercholesterolämisch hypercholesterolaemic
Hypercholie f hypercholia, excessive bile secretion
Hyperchondroplasie f hyperchondroplasia
hyperchrom hyperchromic
Hyperchromämie f hyperchromaemia (Blutfärbeindex über 1)
Hyperchromasie f hyperchrom[as]ia, hyperchromatosis (z. B. von Zellen)
Hyperchromatismus m hyperchromatism, hyperchromatosis, hyperchromia (z. B. des Zellkerns)
Hyperchromatopsie f hyperchromatopsia
Hyperchromatose f, **Hyperchromie** s. Hyperchromatismus
Hyperchylie f hyperchylia
Hyperchylomikronämie f hyperchylomicronemia, fat-induced familial hypertriglyceridaemia
Hyperdaktylie f hyperdactyly, polydactyly
Hyperdiploidie f hyperdiploidy

Hyperdistension f hyperdistention, superdistension
Hyperdiurese f hyperdiuresis
Hyperdontie f hyperdontia
Hyperdynamie f hyperdynamia
Hyperemesis f hyperemesis, excessive vomiting
hyperemetisch hyperemetic
Hypereosinophilie f hypereosinophilia
hypererg hyperergic
Hyperergie f hyperergia, hyperergasia
Hypererosie f erotomania, eromania, lagneia
Hyperesophorie f hyperesophoria
hyperexkretorisch hyperexcretory
Hyperexophorie f hyperexophoria
hyperextendieren to hyperextend
Hyperextension f hyperextension, superextension
Hyperfibrinämie f [hyper]inosaemia, hyperinosis
Hyperfibrinogenämie f hyperfibrinogenaemia
Hyperfibrinolyse f hyperfibrinolysis
Hyperflexion f hyperflexion, overflexion
Hyperfluoreszenz f hyperfluorescence *(des Auges)*
Hyperfollikulinämie f, **Hyperfollikulinie** f hyperfolliculinaemia
Hyperfunktion f hyperfunction *(z. B. eines Organs)*
Hypergalaktie f hypergalactia, hypergalactosis
Hypergammaglobulinämie f hypergammaglobulinaemia
Hypergastrinämie f hypergastrinaemia
Hypergenitalismus m hypergenitalism
Hypergeusie f hypergeusia
Hyperglobulie f hyperglobulia
Hyperglobulinämie f hyperglobulinaemia
Hyperglukagonämie f hyperglucagonaemia
Hyperglykämie f [hyper]glycaemia, glucohaemia
Hyperglykämieneigung f glycophilia
hyperglykämisch hyperglycaemic
Hyperglykogenolyse f hyperglycogenolysis
Hyperglykorrhachie f hyperglycorrhachia
Hyperglykosurie f hyperglycosuria
Hyperglyzinämie f hyperglycinaemia
Hyperglyzinurie f hyperglycinuria
Hypergonadismus m hypergonadism
hypergonadotrop hypergonadotropic
Hypergonadotropinurie f hypergonadotropinuria
Hyperheparinämie f hyperheparinaemia
Hyperhidrose f hyperhidrosis, hyper[h]idrosis, polyhidrosis, ephidrosis, sudatoria, excessive sweating
Hyperhistaminämie f hyperhistaminaemia
Hyperhydratation f hyperhydration, overhydration *(z. B. bei Infusionstherapie)*
Hyperhydratationssyndrom n hyperhydration (overinfusion) syndrome
hyperimmun hyperimmune
Hyperimmunisation f hyperimmunization
hyperimmunisieren to hyperimmunize
Hyperimmunität f hyperimmunity
Hyperimmunoglobulinämie f hyperimmunoglobulinaemia

Hyperimmunserum n hyperimmune serum
Hyperinosämie f, **Hyperinose** f [hyper]inosaemia, hyperinosis
Hyperinsulinämie f hyperinsulinaemia
Hyperinsulinismus m [hyper]insulinism
Hyperinvolution f hyperinvolution
Hyperirritabilität f hyperirritability
Hyperkaliämie f hyperkalaemia, [hyper]potassaemia
hyperkaliämisch hyperkalaemic
Hyperkalziämie f [hyper]calcaemia, hypercalcinaemia
hyperkalziämisch hypercalcaemic
Hyperkalzifikation f hypercalcification
Hyperkalziurie f hypercalciuria
Hyperkapnie f hypercapnia, hypercarbia
Hyperkatharsis f hypercatharsis
Hyperkeratinisierung f hyperkeratinization
Hyperkeratosis f hyperkeratosis
~ **excentrica** hyperkeratosis excentrica, porokeratosis
~ **linguae** hyperkeratosis linguae, nigrities linguae; black hairy tongue
hyperkeratotisch hyperkeratotic
Hyperketonämie f hyperketonaemia
Hyperketonurie f hyperketonuria
Hyperkinese f hyperkinesia
~/**choreatische und athetotische** choreoathetosis
Hyperkoagulabilität f hypercoagulability
Hyperkortisolismus m, **Hyperkortizismus** m hyper[adreno]corticism, hypercortisolism, hyperadrenalism, hyperadrenal corticalism, hyperadrenia
Hyperkryästhesie f hypercryalgesia, hypercryaesthesia
Hyperlaktation f hyperlactation, superlactation
Hyperleukozytose f hyperleucocytosis
Hyperlipämie f hyperlip[id]aemia
hyperlipämisch hyperlipaemic
Hyperlipasämie f hyperlipasaemia
Hyperlipoproteinämie f hyperlipoproteinaemia
~/**familiäre** familial hyperlipoproteinaemia, essential familial hyperlipaemia
Hyperlithurie f hyperlithuria
Hyperlordose f hyperlordosis
Hyperluteinisierung f hyperluteinization
Hypermagnesiämie f hypermagnesaemia
Hypermaner m hypermaniac
Hypermanie f hypermania *(schwere Form der Manie)*
Hypermaniekranker m hypermaniac
hypermanisch hypermanic
Hypermastie f hypermastia, hypermazia
Hypermelanose f hypermelanosis
Hypermenorrhoe f hypermenorrhoea
Hypermetabolismus m hypermetabolism
hypermetrop hyperopic, farsighted, long-sighted, hypermetropic
Hypermetroper m hyperope, hypermetrope
Hypermetropie f hyper[metr]opia, farsightedness, long-sightedness

Hypermimie

Hypermimie f hypermimia
Hypermineralisation f hypermineralization
Hypermineralokortizismus m hypermineralocorticoidism
Hypermnesie f hypermnesia
Hypermotilität f hypermotility (z. B. des Darms)
Hypermyotonie f hypermyotonia
Hypernatriämie f hypernatraemia
Hypernatriämiesyndrom n hypernatraemic syndrome
hypernatriämisch hypernatraemic
Hypernephritis f hypernephritis
hypernephroid hypernephroid
Hypernephrom n hypernephroma, hypernephroid renal carcinoma, epinephroma, Grawitz's tumour, renal-cell (solid-cell) carcinoma (bösartige Nierengeschwulst)
Hyperodontie f hyperodontia
Hyperonychie f hyperonychia
hyperop hyperopic, farsighted, long-sighted, hypermetropic
Hyperoper m hyperope, hypermetrope
Hyperopie f hyper[metr]opia, farsightedness, long-sightedness
Hyperorexie f hyperorexia, b[o]ulimia, ad[d]ephagia, sitomania
Hyperornithinämie f hyperornithaemia, ornithinaemia
Hyperosmie f hyperosmia, oxyosmia, oxyosphresia
Hyperosmolarität f hyperosmolarity (des Serums)
Hyperostosis f hyperostosis, hyperosteogeny
~ **corticalis infantilis** infantile cortical hyperostosis, Caffey's disease (syndrome)
~ **frontalis interna** calvarial (internal frontal) hyperostosis, enostosis of calvaria
Hyperöstrogenämie f hyperoestrogenaemia, hyperoestrinaemia
Hyperöstrogenismus m hyperoestrogenism
Hyperoxalurie f hyperoxaluria
Hyperparathyreoidismus m hyperparathyroidism, hyperparathyreosis
hyperparathyreot hyperparathyroid
Hyperpathie f hyperpathia
Hyperperfusion f hyperperfusion
Hyperperistaltik f hyperperistalsis, hyperprochoresis
Hyperphagie f hyperphagia
Hyperphalangie f, **Hyperphalangismus** m hyperphalangia, hyperphalangism
Hyperphenylalaninämie f hyperphenylalaninaemia
Hyperphonie f hyperphonia
Hyperphorie f hyperphoria, anaphoria
Hyperphosphatämie f hyperphosphataemia
~/**familiäre** familial hyperphosphataemia, phosphate diabetes
hyperphosphatämisch hyperphosphataemic
Hyperphosphaturie f hyperphosphaturia
Hyperphrenie f hyperphrenia
hyperphrenisch hyperphrenic

Hyperpigmentation f hyperpigmentation
hyperpigmentiert hyperpigmented
Hyperpinealismus m hyperpinealism
Hyperpituitarismus m hyperpituitarism
Hyperplasie f hyperplasia, overgrowth (von Organen und Geweben)
~/**polypöse** polypoid hyperplasia
~/**pseudoepitheliomatöse** pseudoepitheliomatous hyperplasia
hyperplastisch hyperplastic
Hyperpnoe f hyperpnoea
Hyperpolarisationsblock m hyperpolarization (anode) block (Nervenleitung)
Hyperporose f hyperporosis
Hyperpraxie f hyperpraxia
Hyperpresbyopie f hyperpresbyopia
Hyperprolaktinämie f hyperprolactinaemia
Hyperprolanämie f hyperprolactinaemia
Hyperprolinämie f [hyper]prolinaemia
Hyperprosexie f hyperprosexia
Hyperproteinämie f hyperproteinaemia
hyperproteinämisch hyperproteinaemic
Hyperprothrombinämie f [hyper]prothrombinaemia
Hyperpselaphesie f hyperpselaphesia
Hyperptyalismus m hyperptyalism
hyperpyretisch hyperpyretic, hyperpyrexial
Hyperpyrexie f hyperpyrexia
hyperreflektorisch hyperreflexic
Hyperreflexie f hyperreflexia
Hyperresonanz f hyperresonance (z. B. bei Pneumothorax)
Hypersalivation f hypersalivation
Hypersegmentierung f hypersegmentation (z. B. von Organen)
Hypersekretion f hypersecretion, oversecretion
hypersekretorisch hypersecretory
hypersensibel hypersensitive (s.a. überempfindlich)
hypersensibilisieren to hypersensitize
Hypersensibilisierung f hypersensitization
Hypersensibilität f s. Überempfindlichkeit
Hypersensitivitätsangiitis f hypersensitivity angiitis
Hyperserotoninämie f hyperserotoninaemia
Hypersomnie f hypersomnia
Hypersomnie-Bulimie-Syndrom n hypersomnia-boulimia-syndrome, Kleine-Levin syndrome
Hypersomnolenz f hypersomnolence
Hyperspadie f hyperspadia, epispadia (angeborene Mißbildung)
Hyperspermie f hyperspermia
Hypersplenie f, **Hypersplenismus** m hypersplenism, hypersplenia
Hypersteatosis f hypersteatosis
Hypersthenie f hypersthenia
Hypersthenurie f hypersthenuria
Hypersuprarenalismus m hypersuprarenalism
Hypersympathikotonus m hypersympathicotonus
Hypersystolie f hypersystole
Hypertelorismus m [eye] hypertelorism, ocular hypertelorism

Hypertensin *n s.* Angiotensin
Hypertensinogen *n s.* Angiotensinogen
Hypertension *f s.* Hypertonus
hypertensiv hypertensive
Hypertensivum *n* hypertensor
Hyperthelie *f* hyperthelia
Hyperthermie *f* hyperthermia
Hyperthrombinämie *f* hyperthrombinaemia
Hyperthrombozytämie *f* hyperthrombocytaemia
hyperthym hyperthymic
Hyperthymie *f* hyperthymia
Hyperthymismus *m* hyperthymism
Hyperthyreoidismus *m s.* Hyperthyreose
Hyperthyreose *f* [hyper]thyroidism, hyperthyreosis, hyperthyroidosis; Basedow's disease
~/**jodinduzierte** jodbasedow
Hyperthyreoseauslösung *f* hyperthyroidation
hyperthyreot hyperthyroid
Hyperthyreotropinämie *f* hyperthyrotropinaemia
Hyperthyreotropinismus *m* hyperthyrotropinism
Hyperthyroxinämie *f* hyperthyroxinaemia
hyperton 1. hypertensive, hypertonic *(z. B. Blutdruck)*; 2. hypertonic *(z. B. Muskel)*
Hypertonie *f* 1. *s.* Hypertonus; 2. hypertonia, hypertonus *(z. B. des Muskels)*; 3. hypertonicity *(z. B. des osmotischen Drucks)*
hypertonisch hypertonic *(z. B. osmotischer Druck)*
Hypertonus *m* hypertension, hyperpiesia, high blood pressure ● **durch ~ bedingt** hypertensive
~/**arterieller** arterial hypertension, Huchard's disease
~/**essentieller** essential hypertension
~/**juveniler** juvenile hypertension
~/**maligner** malignant hypertension
~/**neurogener** neurogenic hypertension
~/**neuromuskulärer** neuromuscular hypertension; anxiety tension state
~/**portaler** portal hypertension
~/**primärer** primary hypertension
~/**pulmonaler** pulmonary [arterial] hypertension
~/**renaler** renal [vascular] hypertension
Hypertonusenzephalopathie *f* hypertensive encephalopathy
hypertonuserzeugend hypertensive
Hypertonuskopfschmerz *m* pressor headache
Hypertonusniere *f* hypertensive nephritis
Hypertonuspatient *m* hypertensive patient
hypertonussenkend antihypertensive
Hypertrichose *f* hypertrichosis, hypertrichiasis
Hypertriglyzeridämie *f* hypertriglyceridaemia
hypertroph hypertrophic
Hypertrophie *f* hypertrophy, overgrowth *(Organvergrößerung durch Kernverdopplungswachstum)*
~ **des linken Ventrikels** left ventricular hypertrophy, LVH
~ **des rechten Ventrikels** right ventricular hypertrophy, RVH
~/**physiologische** physiological hypertrophy
hypertrophieren to hypertrophy
Hypertropie *f* hypertropia

Hypertyrosinämie *f* hypertyrosinaemia
Hyperurikämie *f* hyperuric[acid]aemia
hyperurikämisch hyperuricaemic
Hyperurik[os]urie *f* hyperuric[os]uria, hyperuricaciduria
hypervaskulär hypervascular
Hypervaskularität *f* hypervascularity
Hyperventilation *f* hyperventilation, overventilation, hyperaeration
Hyperventilationsalkalose *f* hyperventilation alkalosis
Hyperventilationssyndrom *n* hyperventilation syndrome
Hyperventilationstetanie *f* hyperventilation tetany
hyperventilieren to hyperventilate
Hypervigilität *f* hypervigility
Hyperviskositätssyndrom *n* hyperviscosity syndrome
Hypervitaminose *f* hypervitaminosis
~ **A** hypervitaminosis A
Hypervolämie *f* hypervolaemia
hypervolämisch hypervolaemic
Hyperzementose *f* hypercementosis
Hyperzeruloplasminämie *f* hyperceruloplasminaemia
Hyperzythämie *f* hypercythaemia
Hyperzytochromie *f* hypercytochromia
Hyperzytose *f* hypercytosis
Hyphäma *n* hyphaem[i]a
Hypinose *f* hypinosis
Hypnagogum *n* [remedium] hypnagogue [agent]
Hypnalgie *f* hypnalgia
Hypnoanalyse *f* hypnoanalysis *(Psychotherapie)*
Hypnogenese *f* hypnogenesis
hypnogenetisch hypnogen[et]ic, hypnogenous
Hypnolepsie *f* hypnolepsy
Hypnologie *f* hypnology *(Lehre vom Schlaf)*
Hypnonarkoanalyse *f* hypnonarcoanalysis *(Psychotherapie)*
Hypnonarkose *f* hypnonarcosis
Hypnophobie *f* hypnophobia *(krankhafte Angst vor dem Schlafen)*
Hypnophrenose *f* hypnophrenosis
Hypnose *f* hypnosis, hypnotism ● **eine ~ auslösen** to hypnotize ● **für ~ empfänglich** hypnotic
hypnoseähnlich hypnoid[al]
Hypnoseauslösung *f* hypnotism, hypnogenesis
Hypnosebehandlung *f* hypnotherapy
hypnoseerzeugend hypnogen[et]ic, hypnogenous
Hypnoseerzeugung *f* hypnotism, hypnogenesis
Hypnosespezialist *m* hypnotist
Hypnosetherapie *f*/**Bernheimsche** Bernheim's therapy (hypnotherapy)
Hypnosezustand *m* hypnosis
Hypnotikum *n* [remedium] hypnotic, somnifacient [agent], soporific
hypnotisch hypnotic, hypnagogic, hypnic ● **~ beeinflussen** to hypnotize; to suggest
Hypnotiseur *m* hypnotist, pathetist

hypnotisierbar 346

hypnotisierbar hypnotizable
hypnotisieren to hypnotize
Hypnotisierter m hypnotic
Hypnotisierung f hypnotization, hypnoidization, hypnosigenesis
Hypoadenie f hypoadenia
Hypoadrenalinämie f hypoadrenal[in]aemia
Hypoadrenalismus m hypoadrenalism, hypoadrenia, hypo[adreno]corticism
Hypoaffektivität f hypoaffectivity
Hypoaktivität f hypoactivity
Hypoakusis f hyp[o]acousia
Hypoalbuminämie f s. Hypalbuminämie
Hypoaldosteronismus m hypoaldosteronism
Hypoalimentation f hypoalimentation, insufficient nourishment
Hypoaminoazidämie f hypoaminoacidaemia, hypoacidaminaemia
Hypoamylasämie f hypoamylasaemia
Hypoandrogenismus m hypoandrogenism
Hypoasthenie f hypasthenia
Hypoazidität f hypoacidity
Hypoazoturie f hypoazoturia
Hypobilirubinämie f hypobilirubinaemia
Hypobulie f hypobulia
Hypochlorämie f hypochlor[id]aemia
hypochlorämisch hypochloraemic
Hypochlorhydrie f hypochlorhydria, gastric hypoacidity
Hypochlorurie f hypochloruria
Hypocholesterinämie f hypocholesterolaemia, hypocholester[in]aemia
Hypocholie f hypocholia
Hypochonder m hypochondriac
Hypochondrie f hypochondriasis, hypochondria, neuriasis
hypochondrisch hypochondriacal
Hypochondrium n hypochondrium, hypochondriac region
Hypochondriumreflex m hypochondrial reflex
hypochrom hypochromic
Hypochromämie f hypochromaemia (Blutfärbeindex unter 1)
Hypochromasie f hypochrom[as]ia, hypochromatosis (z .B. von Zellen)
hypochromatisch hypochromatic
Hypochromatismus m hypochromatism, hypochromatosis, hypochromia (z. B. des Zellkerns)
Hypochromatose f, **Hypochromie** f s. Hypochromatismus
Hypochylie f hypochylia
Hypodaktylie f hypodactyly
Hypodermoklyse f hypoderm[at]oclysis
Hypodermolithiasis f hypodermolithiasis
Hypodontie f hypodontia
Hypodynamie f hypodynamia
Hypoelektrolytämie f/renale renal hypoelectrolytaemia
Hypoergie f hypoergia, hypoergasia
Hypoesophorie f hypoesophoria
Hypoexophorie f hypoexophoria
Hypoferrinämie f hypoferraemia

Hypofibrinogenämie f hypofibrinogenaemia
Hypofollikulin[äm]ie f hypofolliculinaemia
Hypofunktion f hypofunction (z. B. eines Organs)
Hypogalaktie f hypogalactia, hypogalactosis, oligogalactia
Hypogammaglobulinämie f hypogammaglobulinaemia
Hypogastrium n s. Unterbauch
Hypogenitalismus m hypogenitalism
Hypogeusie f hypogeusia
Hypoglobulie f hypoglobulia
Hypoglossitis f hypoglossitis, inflammation of the sublingual tissue
Hypoglossus m hypoglossus, hypoglossal nerve
Hypoglossusatrophie f hypoglossal atrophy
Hypoglossuskanal m hypoglossal canal
Hypoglossuslähmung f hypoglossal paralysis; glossoplegia, glossolysis
Hypoglottis f hypoglottis
hypoglottisch hypoglossal, sublingual
Hypoglukagonämie f hypoglucagonaemia
Hypoglykämie f hypoglycaemia, glycopenia
Hypoglykämieschock m hypoglycaemic shock
hypoglykämisch hypoglycaemic
Hypoglykogenolyse f hypoglycogenolysis
Hypoglykorrhachie f hypoglycorrhachia
Hypognathus m hypognathus (Mißgeburt)
Hypogonadismus m hypogonadism
~/hypophysärer pituitary hypogonadism
hypogonadotrop hypogonadotropic
Hypogonadotropinurie f hypogonadotropinuria
Hypogranulozytose f hypogranulocytosis
Hypohidrose f hypohidrosis, hyphidrosis, ischidrosis
hypohidrotisch hypohidrotic, ischidrotic
hypohormonal hypohormonal, hypohormonic
Hypohydratation f hypohydration, hypopenia, water deprivation
Hypoimmunität f hypoimmunity
Hypoinsulinismus m hypoinsulinism
Hypoirritabilität f hypoirritability
Hypokaliämie f hypokalaemia, hypopotassaemia
Hypokalziämie f hypocalc[in]aemia
Hypokalzifikation f hypocalcification
Hypokalziurie f hypocalciuria
Hypokapnie f hypocapnia, hypocarbia
Hypokeratosis f hypokeratosis
Hypokinese f hypokinesia
Hypokoagulabilität f hypocoagulability
Hypokortisolismus m, **Hypokortizismus** m hypo[adreno]corticism, hypocortisolism, hypoadrenalism, hypoadrenal corticalism, hypoadrenia
Hypolaktation f hypolactation
Hypoleukozytose f hypoleucocytosis
Hypolipämie f hypolip[id]aemia
Hypomagnesiämie f hypomagnesaemia
Hypomaner m hypomaniac
Hypomanie f hypomania (leichte Form der Manie)
Hypomaniekranker m hypomaniac
hypomanisch hypomaniac

Hypomastie f hypomastia, hypomazia
Hypomelanose f hypomelanosis
Hypomenorrhoe f hypomenorrhoea
Hypometabolismus m hypometabolism
Hypometropie f s. Myopie
Hypomimie f hypomimia
Hypomineralisation f hypomineralization
Hypomineralokortizismus m hypomineralocorticoidism
Hypomnesie f hypomnesia
Hypomotilität f hypomotility *(z. B. des Darms)*
Hypomyotonie f hypomyotonia
Hyponatriämie f hyponatraemia
Hyponatriämiesyndrom n hyponatraemic syndrome
Hyponychium n hyponychium
Hypoorchidismus m hypoorchidia
Hypoosmolarität f hypoosmolarity *(des Serums)*
Hypoostosis f hypoostosis, hypoosteogeny
Hypoöstrogenismus m hypooestrogenism
Hypoparathyreoidismus m, **Hypoparathyreose** f hypoparathyroidism, hypoparathyreosis
Hypoperfusion f hypoperfusion
Hypoperistaltik f hypoperistalsis
Hypophalangie f, **Hypophalangismus** m hypophalangia, hypophalangism
Hypopharyngoskop n hypopharyngoscope
Hypopharyngoskopie f hypopharyngoscopy
Hypopharynx m hypopharynx, laryngopharynx, laryngeal pharynx
Hypopharynxkarzinom n hypopharyngeal carcinoma
Hypopharynxmoniliasis f moniliasis of hypopharynx
Hypopharynxspiegelung f hypopharyngoscopy
Hypophonie f hypophonia
Hypophorie f hypophoria, cataphoria
Hypophosphatämie f hypophosphataemia
hypophosphatämisch hypophosphataemic
Hypophosphatasie f hypophosphatasia
Hypophosphaturie f hypophosphaturia
hypophren hypophrenic, feeble-minded
Hypophrenie f hypophrenia, feeble-mindedness
Hypophrenium n hypophrenium
hypophysär hypophyseal, hypophysial, pituitary
Hypophyse f hypophysis [cerebri], pituitary [gland], pituitary appendage (body)
Hypophysektomie f hypophysectomy, pituitectomy
~/transsphenoidale transsphenoidal hypophysectomy
Hypophysenadenom n hypophyseal (pituitary) adenoma
~/basophiles basophilic adenoma (tumour) of the pituitary
~/eosinophiles eosinophilic adenoma (tumour) of the pituitary
Hypophysenapoplexie f hypophyseal (pituitary) apoplexy, acute pituitary vascular accident
Hypophysenausschaltung f hypophysectomy, pituitectomy

~ durch Röntgenbestrahlung radiohypophysectomy
~ durch Ultraschall ultrasonic hypophysectomy
Hypophysenentfernung f[/operative] s. Hypophysektomie
Hypophysenentzündung f hypophysitis, inflammation of the hypophysis cerebri
Hypophysenerkrankung f pituitarism
Hypophysenfunktion f hypophyseal (pituitary) function
Hypophysenfunktionsstörung f dyspituitarism, dyshypophysia
Hypophysenfunktionstest m hypophyseal function test
Hypophysengangsgeschwulst f hypophyseal duct tumour
Hypophysengesamtextrakt m whole pituitary
Hypophysengonadotropin n/**humanes** human hypophysis gonadotropin
Hypophysengrube f hypophyseal (pituitary) fossa
Hypophysenhinterlappen m neurohypophysis, posterior lobe of the hypophysis, infundibular process
Hypophysenhinterlappenextrakt m posterior pituitary [extract]
Hypophysenhinterlappenhormon n posterior pituitary hormone
Hypophysenhormonausfall f/**totaler** panhypopituitarism
Hypophyseninsuffizienz f pituitary insufficiency, [pan]hypopituitarism, hypobasophilism
~/postpartale postpartum acute (haemorrhagic) hypopituitarism
Hypophysenkreislauf m hypophyseal circulation
Hypophysenkürette f hypophyseal (pituitary) curette
Hypophysennekrose f/**postpartale** postpartum pituitary necrosis, Sheehan's syndrome
Hypophysenpinzette f hypophyseal (pituitary) forceps
Hypophysenstiel m hypophyseal (pituitary) stalk, infundibular stem, infundibulum [of the hypophysis], stalk of the neurohypophysis
Hypophysenstieldurchtrennung f[/operative] hypophyseal (pituitary) stalk section
Hypophysenstielzyste f hypophyseal (pituitary) stalk cyst
Hypophysenstörung f dyspituitarism, dyshypophysia
Hypophysensystem n hypophyseal (pituitary) system
Hypophysentasche f Rathke's (craniobuccal) pouch *(Aussackung der primären Mundhöhle)*
Hypophysentumor m hypophyseal (pituitary) tumour
Hypophysenüberfunktion f hyperpituitarism
Hypophysenunterfunktion f hypopituitarism, hypobasophilism
Hypophysenvorderlappen m adenohypophysis, anterior lobe of the hypophysis, antehypophysis, prehypophysis

Hypophysenvorderlappenadenom n/basophiles basophilic adenoma of the anterior lobe, Cushing's disease (syndrome); pituitary basophilism
~/chromophobes chromophobe adenoma (tumour) of the anterior lobe
Hypophysenvorderlappenextrakt m anterior pituitary [extract]
Hypophysenvorderlappengonadotropin n anterior pituitary gonadotropin
Hypophysenvorderlappenhormon n anterior pituitary hormone
Hypophysenvorderlappeninsuffizienz f hypophyseal cachexia, [hypo]pituitary cachexia, Simmond's cachexia (disease)
Hypophysenvorderlappenüberfunktion f antuitarism
Hypophysenzelle f/chromophobe chromophobe cell of the hypophysis
Hypophysenzwerg m hypophyseal (pituitary) dwarf
Hypophysenzwischenhirnsystem n hypophyseal portal system, hypophyseoportal circulation, hypothalamus hypophysis system
Hypophysenzwischenlappen m intermediate lobe of the hypophysis, zona intermedia
Hypophysenzyste f hypophyseal (pituitary) cyst
Hypophysis f cerebri s. Hypophyse
Hypophysitis f hypophysitis
Hypopinealismus m hypopinealism
Hypopituitarismus m hypopituitarism, hypobasophilism
Hypoplasia f hypoplasia *(von Organen und Geweben)*
~ **cutis congenita** focal dermal hypoplasia syndrome
~ **medullae spinalis** hypoplasia medullae spinalis, myelatelia
hypoplastisch hypoplastic
Hypopnoe f hypopnoea
Hypoporose f hypoporosis
Hypopraxie f hypopraxia
Hypoprolaktinämie f hypoprolactinaemia
Hypoprolanämie f hypoprolactinaemia
Hypoprosexie f hypoprosexia
Hypoproteinämie f hypoproteinaemia
Hypoproteinosis f hypoproteinosis
Hypoprothrombinämie f hypoprothrombinaemia
Hypopselaphesie f hypopselaphesia
Hypoptyalismus m hypoptyalism
Hypopyon n hypopyon, lunella, onyx
Hypopyonkeratitis f hypopyon keratitis
Hyporeflexie f hyporeflexia
Hyposalivation f hyposalivation
Hyposekretion f hyposecretion
hyposekretorisch hyposecretory
hyposensibilisieren to hyposensitize
Hyposensibilisierung f hyposensitization
Hyposensibilität f hyposensitivity *(z. B. auf äußere Reize)*
Hyposexualität f hyposexuality
Hyposmie f hyposmia, hyposphresia
Hyposomnie f hyposomnia

Hypospadia f hypospadias *(angeborene Mißbildung)*
~ **glandis** balanic hypospadias
~ **penis** penile hypospadias
~ **perinealis** perineal hypospadias
~ **scrotalis** scrotal hypospadias
Hypospadie f s. Hypospadia
Hypospadieträger m hypospadiac
Hypospermatogenese f hypospermatogenesis
Hyposplenie f, **Hyposplenismus** m hyposplenism, hyposplenia
Hypostase f hypostasis
Hypostasepneumonie f hypostatic pneumonia
hypostatisch hypostatic; genetically suppressed
Hyposteatosis f hyposteatosis
Hyposthenie f hyposthenia
Hyposthenurie f hyposthenuria
Hyposuprarenalismus m hyposuprarenalism
Hyposympathikotonus m hyposympathicotonus
Hyposynergie f hyposynergia
Hyposystolie f hyposystole
Hypotaxie f hypotaxia
Hypotelorismus m [eye] hypotelorism, ocular hypotelorism
Hypotension f hypotension, hypopiesia
hypotensiv hypotensive
Hypotensivum n hypotensor
hypothalamisch hypothalamic
Hypothalamus m hypothalamus *(Teil des Zwischenhirns)*
Hypothalamus-Hypophysen-Eierstock-System n hypothalamic-pituitary-ovarian system
Hypothalamus-Hypophysen-System n hypothalamus-hypophysis system
Hypothenar n hypothenar
Hypothenarareal n hypothenar area
Hypothenarelektrode f hypothenar electrode
Hypothenarmuskel m hypothenar muscle
Hypothenarreflex m hypothenar reflex
Hypothermie f hypothermia
hypothym hypothymic, athymic
Hypothymie f hypothymia
Hypothymismus m hypothymism
hypothyreoid hypothyroid
Hypothyreoidismus m s. Hypothyreose
Hypothyreose f hypothyroidism, hypothyr[e]osis, thyroid insufficiency, subthyroidism
Hypothyreoseauslösung f hypothyroidation
hypothyreot hypothyroid
hypoton 1. hypotensive, hypotonic *(z. B. Blutdruck)*; 2. hypotonic *(z. B. Muskel)*
Hypotonie f 1. s. Hypotonus; 2. hypotonia, hypotonus *(z. B. des Muskels)*; 3. hypotonicity *(z. B. des osmotischen Drucks)*
hypotonisch hypotonic *(z. B. osmotischer Druck)*
Hypotonizität f hypotonicity *(z. B. des osmotischen Drucks)*
Hypotonus m hypotension, hypopiesia, low blood pressure
~/orthostatischer orthostatic (postural) hypotension
Hypotrichose f hypotrichosis, hypotrichiasis

Hysterosalpingographie

Hypotrijodthyroninämie f hypotriiodothyroninaemia
Hypotrophie f hypotrophy, hypogenesis
Hypotropie f hypotropia
Hypotympanon n hypotympanum
Hypourikämie f hypouric[acid]aemia
Hypourik[os]urie f hypouric[os]uria, hypouricaciduria
Hypovaskularität f hypovascularity
Hypovasopressinämie f hypovasopressinaemia
Hypoventilation f hypoventilation, hypoaeration
~/alveoläre alveolar hypoventilation
Hypoventilationssyndrom n [alveolar] hypoventilation syndrome
hypoventilieren to hypoventilate
Hypoviskositätssyndrom n hypoviscosity syndrome
Hypovitaminose f hypovitaminosis, subvitaminosis
~ A hypovitaminosis A
Hypovolämie f hypovolaemia
hypovolämisch hypovolaemic
Hypoxämie f hypoxaemia
Hypoxämietest m hypoxaemia test
hypoxämisch hypoxaemic
Hypoxanthin n hypoxanthine, 6-hydroxypurine *(Zwischenstoffwechselprodukt der Nukleoproteide)*
Hypoxie f hypoxia
hypoxisch hypoxic
Hypozythämie f hypocythaemia
Hypozytose hypocytosis
Hypsarrhythmie f hypsarrhythmia *(im EEG z. B. bei Propulsiv-petit-mal)*
hypsarrhythmisch hypsarrhythmoid
Hypsikonchie f hypsiconchy
Hypsistaphylie f hypsistaphylia
hypsizephal hypsicephalic, hypsocephalous
Hypsizephalie f hypsicephalia
Hypsizephalus m hypsicephalus
Hypsophobie f hypsophobia *(krankhafte Angst vor Höhen)*
Hysteralgie f hysteralgia, hysterodynia, uteralgia, uterodynia, uterism[us], uterine pain
Hysteratresie f hysteratresia
Hysterectomia f **abdominalis** s. Hysterektomie/abdominale
Hysterektomie f hysterectomy, uterectomy, metrectomy, excision of the uterus
~/abdominale abdominal (caesarean) hysterectomy, Wertheim's hysterectomy (operation), hysterolaparotomy, laparohysterectomy, gastrohysterectomy
~/partielle partial hysterectomy
~/radikale radical hysterectomy
~/totale total hysterectomy, panhysterectomy
~/vaginale vaginal hysterectomy, Schauta-Wertheim operation
Hysterektomieklemme f hysterectomy forceps
Hystereurynter m hystereurynter, metreurynter
Hysterie f hysteria, hysterics *(Psychoneurose)*
● **von ~ befallen** hysterical

hysterieartig hysteroid[al], hysteriform
hysteriebewirkend hysterogenic, hysterogenous
Hysterieneigung f hysterical tendency
Hysterieneurose f hysterical neurosis
Hysteriepsychose f hysterical psychosis
Hysterieskala f hysteria scale
Hysteriker m, **Hysterikerin** f hysteriac
hysterisch hysteric[al]
Hysteritis f s. Metritis
Hystero... s. a. Utero... und Gebärmutter...
Hysterodynie f s. Hysteralgie
Hysteroepilepsie f hysteroepilepsy, hysterical convulsion (epilepsy, seizure)
hysterofren[atorisch] hysterofrenic, hysterofrenatory
Hysterogramm n hysterogram, uterogram, metrogram
Hysterographie f hysterography, uterography, metrography
hysterographisch hysterographic, uterographic
Hysterokatalepsie f hysterocatalepsy
Hysterokleisis f hysterocleisis
Hysterokolposkop n hysterocolposcope
Hysterokolposkopie f hysterocolposcopy
Hysterolaparotomie f hysterolaparotomy
Hysterolith m hysterolith, uterolith, uterine calculus
Hysterolithiasis f hysterolithiasis
Hysterologie f hysterology
Hysterolyse f hysterolysis
Hysteromalazie f hysteromalacia, softening of the uterus
Hysteromanie f hysteromania, nymphomania, andromania, metromania
Hysterometer n hysterometer, uterometer
Hysterometrie f hysterometry, uterometry
hysterometrisch hysterometric, uterometric
Hysteromyom n hysteromyoma
Hysteromyomektomie f hysteromyomectomy
Hysteromyotomie f hysteromyotomy
Hysterooovariektomie f hystero-oophorectomy, hystero-ovariotomy, oophorohysterectomy, ovariohysterectomy
Hysteropathie f hysteropathy, metropathy, uterine disease (disorder)
hysteropathisch hysteropathic, metropathic
Hysteropexie f hysteropexia, uteropexia, uterofixation *(an die Bauchdecken)*
Hysteroplastik f hysteroplasty, uteroplasty, metroplasty
Hysteroptose f hysteroptosis, metroptosis, uterine prolapse
Hysterorrhaphie f hysterorrhaphy
Hysterorrhexis f hysterorrhexis, metrorrhexis, rupture of the uterus
Hysterosalpingektomie f hysterosalpingectomy
Hysterosalpingogramm n hysterosalpingogram, uterosalpingogram
Hysterosalpingographie f hysterosalpingography, uterosalpingography, hysterotubography, metrosalpingography, metrotubography

Hysterosalpingo-Oophorektomie

Hysterosalpingo-Oophorektomie f hysterosalpingo-oophorectomy, hysterosalpingo-oothecectomy
Hysterosalpingostomie f hysterosalpingostomy
Hysteroskop n hysteroscope, uteroscope
Hysteroskopie f hysteroscopy, uteroscopy
Hysteroskopisch hysteroscopic, uteroscopic
Hysterospasmus m hysterospasm, hysterotrism[us]
Hysterotom n hysterotome, uterotome, metrotome
Hysterotomia f abdominalis s. Hysterotomie/abdominale
Hysterotomie f hysterotomy, uterotomy, metrotomy
~/**abdominale** abdominal hysterotomy, gasterhysterotomy, gastrohysterotomy
Hysterotrachelektasie f hysterotrachelectasia
Hysterotrachelektomie f [hystero]trachelectomy, cervicectomy
Hysterotracheloplastik f [hystero]tracheloplasty
Hysterotrachelorrhaphie f hysterotrachelorrhaphy
Hysterotrachelotomie f hysterotrachelotomy
Hysterotubographie f s. Hysterosalpingographie
Hysterozele f hysterocele, metrocele, uterine hernia
Hysterozervikotomie f hysterocervicotomy
hysterozystisch hysterocystic
Hysterozystopexie f hysterocystopexy

I

I s. Schneidezahn
i.a. s. intraarteriell
Ianthinopsie f ianthinopsia, violet vision
Iatrik f iateria, therapeutics, medicine
iatrisch iatric[al]
iatrogen iatrogenic
Iatrogendiabetes m iatrogenic diabetes
Iatrogenie f iatrogenesis
I-Band n I-band (Histologie)
I-Blutgruppe f I blood group
i.c. s. 1. intrakutan; 2. intrakardial
Ich-Betonung f egotism
ichbezogen autistic, egocentric; egoistic
Ichnogramm n ichnogram, footprint, podogram, pelmatogram
Ichor m ichor, sanies
ichoroid ichorous, ichoroid, thin, watery, serous, sanious
Ichorrhoe f ichorrhoea
Ichthyismus m ichthyism[us], poisoning from fish, ichthyotoxism
Ichthyoakanthotoxin n ichthyoacanthotoxin (Fischgift)
ichthyophag ichthyophagous
Ichthyophagie f ichthyophagia
Ichthyophobie f ichthyophobia (krankhafte Angst vor Fischen)
Ichthyosis f ichthyosis, fishskin (fish-scale, alligator-skin) disease, sauriasis
~ **congenita** congenital ichthyosis, ichthyosis congenita (foetalis); harlequin foetus
~ **linguae (oris)** psoriasis of the tongue, psoriasis buccalis, leucoplakia [buccalis], leucoplasia, leucokeratosis; smoker's tongue (patches)
ichthyosisartig ichthyosiform
Ichthyotoxin n ichthyotoxin
ichthyotoxisch ichthyotoxic
Ichthyotoxismus m s. Ichthyismus
ICR s. Interkostalraum
ICSH s. Hormon/interstitielle Zellen stimulierendes
Icterus m icterus, jaundice (s.a. unter Ikterus und Gelbsucht)
~ **gravis** icterus gravis, acute yellow atrophy of the liver, acute parenchymatous hepatitis
~ **gravis neonatorum** icterus gravis neonatorum, gravis neonatorum jaundice, erythroblastosis foetalis (neonatorum) (bei Rh-Inkompatibilität)
~ **infectiosus** s. Ikterus/Weilscher
~ **intermittens juvenilis Meulengracht** constitutional hyperbilirubinaemia (hepatic dysfunction), Gilbert's disease (syndrome), Meulengracht's syndrome (infolge Funktionsstörung der Lebergewebszellen bei Jugendlichen)
~ **neonatorum** newborn jaundice, jaundice of the newborn, paedicterus
Ictus m ictus, stroke
~ **apoplecticus** apoplectic fit
~ **cordis** ictus, apex beat [of the heart], cardiac (apex) impulse, left ventricular thrust
ID s. 1. Infektionsdosis; 2. Initialdosis
Id s. Idioplasma
Id n id (1. Unterbewußtsein; 2. Chromosomenbestandteil; 3. allergischer Hautausschlag)
Idee f/fixe fixed idea, monoideism (Psychiatrie)
Ideenbildung f ideation
Ideenflucht f idea chase, flight of ideas
Ideenverbindung f association of ideas
Identifikation f[/psychoanalytische] identification (mit anderen Personen)
identifizieren to identify; to type (z. B. Bakterienkultur)
Identifizierungsreaktion f identification reaction
Identifizierungsschwelle f identification threshold
Identität f identity
Identitätskrise f identity crisis
ideogenetisch ideogenetic, ideogenous
ideomotorisch ideomotor, ideomuscular
Idioglossie f idioglossia
Idiogramm n idiogram (Genetik)
idiomuskulär idiomuscular
Idioneurose f idioneurosis
idiopathisch idiopath[et]ic, genuine, essential (z. B. Krankheiten)
Idioplasma n idioplasm, germ plasm
Idiosom n idiosome (1. Geschlechtschromosom; 2. Spermienteil; 3. Zytoplasmabereich)
Idiospasmus m idiospasm
idiospastisch idiospastic
Idiosynkrasie f idiosyncrasy

Idiot *m* idiot, ament; cretin
Idiotie *f* idiocy, amentia
~ **bei Xerodermie** xerodermic idiocy, de Sanctis-Cacchione syndrome
~/**familiäre amaurotische** amaurotic familial (family) idiocy, cerebral sphingolipidosis
~/**infantile amaurotische** infantile amaurotic familial idiocy, Tay-Sachs disease
~/**juvenile amaurotische familiäre** juvenile amaurotic familial idiocy, Batten's (Batten-Mayou's, Spielmeyer-Vogt) disease, cerebromacular degeneration
~/**mongoloide** Mongolian (mongoloid) idiocy, mongolism, Down's (trisomy 21) syndrome
~/**spätinfantile amaurotische** late infantile amaurotic familial idiocy, Bielschowsky's (Bielschowsky-Jansky) disease
~ **vom Typ Kufs/familiäre Kufs'** disease, late juvenile amaurotic familial idiocy
IE, I.E. *s.* Einheit/!nternationale
Ig *s.* Immunglobulin
Ig M-Antikörper *m s.* Immunglobulin-M-Antikörper
Ignipunktur *f* ignipuncture *(bei Zystennieren)*
IHK *s.* Herzkrankheit/ischämische
IH-Virus *n* hepatitis virus A
ikterisch icteric, icteroid, jaundiced ● ~ **sein** to be icteric (jaundiced)
ikterogen icterogenic, icterogenous
Ikterus *m* icterus, jaundice *(s.a. unter* Icterus *und* Gelbsucht*)* ● **ohne** ~ anicteric
~/**acholurischer** acholuric jaundice
~/**cholestatischer** cholestatic hepatitis, hepatocanalicular jaundice
~/**chronisch acholurischer** *s.* ~/**familiärer hämolytischer**
~/**chronischer idiopathischer** chronic idiopathic jaundice, Dubin-Johnson syndrome, Dubin-Sprinz syndrome
~/**falscher** false icterus, pseudojaundice
~/**familiärer hämolytischer** familial haemolytic icterus (anaemia), chronic acholuric (familial) jaundice, congenital family icterus, congenital haemolytic anaemia (icterus), haemolytic splenomegaly, hereditary spherocytosis, spherocytic anaemia, Minkowski-Chaufford syndrome
~/**familiärer nichthämolytischer** familial nonhaemolytic icterus (jaundice), Gilbert-Lereboullet syndrome
~/**hämolytischer** haemolytic jaundice, haematogenous splenomegaly
~/**hepatozellulärer (hepatozytärer)** hepatocellular jaundice, hepatogenic icterus
~/**hyperhämolytischer** hyperhaemolytic jaundice
~/**mechanischer** mechanical icterus
~/**parenchymatöser** parenchymatous icterus
~/**physiologischer** physiologic jaundice
~/**posthepatischer** posthepatic (obstructive) jaundice
~/**prähepatischer** prehepatic jaundice
~/**Weilscher** Weil's (Fiedler's) disease, leptospiral (haemorrhagic, infectious spirochaetal) jaundice, icterogenic spirochaetosis, icterohaemorrhagic fever
Ikterus-Index *m* icterus index
Ikterusrezidiv *n* recurrence of icterus
Iktus *m s.* Ictus
Ikwafieber *n* Ikwa (trench) fever
Ileitis *f* ileitis, inflammation of the ileum
~ **regionalis (terminalis)** [ileum] regional enteritis, regional (terminal, distal) ileitis, granuloma of the intestine
Ileoaszendostomie *f* ileoascendostomy
Ileoileostomie *f* ileoileostomy
Ileokolitis *f* ileocolitis
Ileokolostomie *f* ileocolostomy
Ileokutanfistel *f* ileocutaneous fistula
Ileoproktostomie *f,* **Ileorektostomie** *f* ileorectostomy, ileoproctostomy
Ileorrhaphie *f* ileorrhaphy
Ileosigmoidostomie *f* ileosigmoidostomy
Ileostoma *n* ileostomy, ileal stoma
Ileostomie *f* ileostomy
Ileostomiebeutel *m* ileostomy bag
Ileothorakopagus *m* ileothoracopagus *(Mißgeburt)*
Ileotomie *f* ileotomy
Ileotransversostomie *f* ileotransversostomy
Ileotyphlitis *f* ileotyphlitis
Ileovaginalfistel *f* ileovaginal fistula
Ileovesikalfistel *f* ileovesical fistula
ileozökal ileocaecal, ileocecal, ileocaecalic
Ileozökalaktinomykose *f* ileocaecal actinomycosis
Ileozökaleinstülpung *f* ileocaecal (enterocolic) intussusception
Ileozökalfalte *f* ileocaecal fold
Ileozökalfistel *f* ileocaecostomy
Ileozökalgeräusch *n* ileocaecal gurgle
Ileozökalgrube *f* ileocaecal fossa
Ileozökalklappe *f* ileocaecal (colic, ileocolic, Bauhin's) valve, ileal operculum
Ileozökallipomatose *f* ileocaecal lipomatosis
Ileozökalregion *f* ileocaecal region
Ileozökalresektion *f* ileocaecectomy
Ileozökaltuberkulose *f* ileocaecal tuberculosis
Ileozökostomie *f* ileocaecostomy
Ileozökum *n* ileocaecum
Ileozökumfistelung *f*[/**operative**] ileocaecostomy
Ileozystoplastik *f* ileocystoplasty
Ileum *n* ileum
Ileum... *s. a.* Krummdarm...
Ileumarterie *f* ileal artery
Ileumeröffnung *f* ileotomy
~ **durch Bauchschnitt** laparo-ileotomy
Ileumexstirpation *f* ileectomy
Ileumintussuszeption *f* ileal intussusception
Ileummesenterium *n* ileal mesentery
Ileumnaht *f* ileorrhaphy; suturing of the ileum
Ileum-Rektum-Anastomose *f* ileorectostomy, ileoproctostomy

Ileumresektion

Ileumresektion f ileectomy
Ileumschnitt m ileotomy
Ileumstoma n ileal stoma
Ileumtransplantat n ileal graft (transplant)
Ileum-Vagina-Fistel f ileovaginal fistula
Ileumvene f ileal vein
Ileus m ileus, bowel (intestinal) obstruction
~/**adynamischer** adynamic (inhibitory) pseudoileus
~/**arteriomesenterialer** arteriomesenteric ileus
~/**dynamischer** [hyper]dynamic ileus
~/**mechanischer** mechanical ileus
~/**paralytischer** paralytic ileus
~/**reflektorischer** reflex [inhibition] ileus
~/**spastischer** spastic ileus
Ileusdekompensation f ileus decompensation; decompensational ileus
iliakal iliac
Iliakalabszeß m iliac abscess
Iliakallymphknoten m iliac lymph node
iliakolumbal lumboiliac
Iliofemoralband n iliofemoral ligament
Iliofemoraldreieck n iliofemoral (Bryant's) triangle
Iliofemoralvene f iliofemoral vein
Ilioinguinalis-Syndrom n ilioinguinalis [nerve] syndrome
Iliolumbalband n iliolumbar ligament
Iliopektineallinie f iliopectineal line
Iliopsoasfaszie f iliopsoas fascia
Iliopsoastest m iliopsoas test
Iliosakralarthritis f iliosacral arthritis
Ilioumbilikallinie f umbilico-iliac line
Ilium n ilium [bone], iliac bone
Ilium... s. Darmbein...
Illusion f illusion, delusion; waking dream, phantasm ● **in der ~ bestehend** illusory, illusional
illusorisch illusory, illusional
i.m. s. intramuskulär
IM s. Mononucleosis infectiosa
Imagination f imagination
Imago n imago *(Psychoanalyse)*
Imagozid n imagocide *(Insektizid)*
imbezil[l] imbecile
Imbeziller m imbecile
Imbezillität f imbecility
Imbibition f imbibition
β-Imidazolylalanin n β-imidazole-α-alanine, histidine
Iminoharnstoff m iminourea, carbamidine, guanidine, aminomethanamidine
Imitation f imitation
imitieren to imitate
Imitieren n **von Gebärden[/krankhaftes]** echomimia
immatur immature, unripe
Immersionslinse f s. Immersionsobjektiv
Immersionsmikroskop n immersion microscope
Immersionsmikroskopie f immersion microscopy
Immersionsobjektiv n immersion objective (lens) *(eines Mikroskops)*
Immersionsöl n immersion oil
Immission f immission *(z. B. von Schadstoffen)*
Immissionskonzentration f immission concentration
Immobilisation f immobilization
Immobilisationsosteoporose f immobilization (inactivity) osteoporosis
Immobilisationsverband m immobilizing (immovable) bandage
immobilisieren to immobilize
immun immune ● **~ machen** s. immunisieren ● **~ sein gegen** to be immune to
Immun... s. a. Immuno...
Immunabwehrhemmung f [durch Arzneimittel] immunosuppression
Immunabweichung f immune deviation
Immunadhärenz f immune adherence
Immunadsorption f immunoadsorption
Immunagglutinin n immune agglutinin
Immunantikörper m immune antibody
Immunantwort f immune response
~/**fehlende** immunological unresponsiveness
~/**zellübertragene** cell-mediated immune response
Immunauswahl f immunoselection
Immunbiologie f immunobiology
Immunchemie f immunochemistry
immunchemisch immunochemical
Immundefekt m immune deficiency, immunodeficiency
Immundefizienzsyndrom n immunodeficiency syndrome
Immundepression f immunodepression
Immundermatologie f immunodermatology
Immundiagnose f immundiagnosis
Immundiagnostik f immundiagnosis
Immunelektronenmikroskopie f immunoelectron microscopy
Immunelektroosmophorese f immunoelectroosmophoresis
Immunelektrophorese f immunoelectrophoresis
Immunendokrinologie f immunoendocrinology
Immunenzymtechnik f immuno-enzymatic technique
Immunepidemiologie f immunoepidemiology
Immunfaktor m immune factor
Immunferritintechnik f immune ferritin technique
Immunfluoreszenz f immunofluorescence
Immunfluoreszenzantikörper m immunofluorescence antibody
Immunfluoreszenzdirektfärbung f direct immunofluorescence staining
Immunfluoreszenzfärbung f immunofluorescence staining
Immunfluoreszenztest m immunofluorescence test
Immungammaglobulin n immunogammaglobulin
Immungenetik f immunogenetics
Immunglobulin n immunoglobulin, immune [serum] globulin, IG, Ig, gamma globulin

Immunoassay

~ **A** immunoglobulin A, Ig A, gamma-A globulin, γA
~ **D** immunoglobulin D, Ig D, gamma-D globulin, γD
~ **E** immunoglobulin E, Ig E, gamma-E globulin, γE
~ **G** immunoglobulin G, Ig G, gamma-G globulin, γG
~ **M** immunoglobulin M, Ig M, gamma-M globulin, γM
Immunglobulinämie f immunoglobulinaemia
Immunglobulinbindungsfaktor m immunoglobulin binding factor, IBF
Immunglobulinbruchstück n immunoglobulin fragment
Immunglobulindefekt m immunoglobulin disorder
Immunglobulinkette f immunoglobulin chain
~/**schwere** heavy immunoglobulin chain, H chain
Immunglobulinmangel m immunoglobulin deficiency
Immunglobulinmangelkrankheit f immunoglobulin (immunologic) deficiency disease
~/**primäre** primary immunoglobulin deficiency disease
Immunglobulin-M-Antikörper m immunoglobulin M antibody
Immunglobulinmedikation f immunoglobulin medication
Immunglobulinprofil n immunoglobulin profile
Immunglobulinspiegelerhöhung f [im Blut] [hyper]immunoglobulinaemia
Immunglobulinstörung f immunoglobulin disorder
Immunhämatologie f immunohaematology
Immunhämolyse f immunohaemolysis
Immunhämolysin n immune haemolysin
Immunhistochemie f immunohistochemistry
immunhistologisch immunohistologic
immunisieren to immunize, to make (render) immune
immunisierend immunifacient, immunogenic, immunizing
immunisiert immunized, immune
Immunisierung f immunization ● **eine ~ durchführen** s. immunisieren
~/**adoptive** adoptive immunization
~/**aktive** active immunization
~/**aktive und passive** serovaccination, active and passive immunization
~/**passive** passive immunization
~/**stille** occult (natural) immunization
Immunisierungsbehandlung f immunization therapy
Immunisierungseinheit f immunizing unit, IU
Immunisierungsstärke f immunogenicity (eines Antigens)
Immunisierungsverfahren n immunization procedure
Immunität f immunity ● **~ bewirkend** immunifacient, immunogenic ● **~ erzeugen** to produce immunity
~/**aktive** active immunity

~/**angeborene** native (innate) immunity, congenital (natural) resistance
~/**antibakterielle** antibacterial immunity
~/**antitoxische** antitoxic immunity
~/**antivirale** antiviral immunity
~/**bleibende** permanent immunity
~/**erhöhte** hyperimmunity
~/**erworbene** acquired immunity
~/**herabgesetzte** hypoimmunity
~/**humorale** humoral immunity
~/**individuelle** individual immunity
~/**konstitutionelle** constitutional immunity
~/**künstliche** artificial immunity
~/**lokale** local immunity
~/**natürliche** s. ~/angeborene
~/**partielle** partial immunity
~/**passive** passive immunity, sero-immunity, orrho-immunity
~/**spezifische** specific immunity
~/**typenspezifische** type-specific immunity
~/**unspezifische** non-specific immunity
~/**zellständige (zellübertragene)** cell-mediated immunity
~/**zelluläre** cell[ular] immunity
Immunitätsdefekt m immune deficiency, immunodeficiency
immunitätshemmend immunosuppressive; antiimmune
Immunitätslage f state of immunity
Immunitätsmangel m immunodeficiency; hypoimmunity
Immunitätsmangelsyndrom n immunodeficiency syndrome
~/**erworbenes** acquired immunodeficiency syndrome, AIDS (s. a. GRID-Syndrom)
~/**kombiniertes** combined immunodeficiency syndrome
Immunitätsmangelzustand m immune deficiency state
Immunitätsstörung f dysimmunity
Immunitätsverlust m loss of immunity, disimmunity
immunkompetent immunocompetent
Immunkompetenz f immunocompetence, immunological (immune) competence
~/**zellständige (zellübertragene)** cell-mediated immunocompetence
Immunkomplex m immune (antigen-antibody) complex
Immunkörper m immune body, antibody (Zusammensetzungen s. unter Antikörper)
Immunmangel m immune deficiency, immunodeficiency
Immunmangelkrankheit f/**primäre** primary immunoglobulin (immunologic) deficiency disease
Immunmangelsyndrom n immunodeficiency syndrome
Immunmechanismus m immune (immunologic) mechanism
Immuno... s.a. Immun...
Immunoassay m immunoassay

Immunoblast

Immunoblast *m* immunoblast
Immunodiffusion *f* immunodiffusion
Immunofluoreszenztechnik *f* immunofluorescence technique
immunogen immunogenic, immunizing, immunifacient
Immunogen *n* immunogen
Immunoglobulin *n s.* Immunglobulin
Immunologe *m* immunologist
Immunologie *f* immunology *(Lehre von den immunbiologischen Reaktionen)*
immunologisch immunologic[al]
Immunoperoxidase-Färbung *f* immunoperoxidase staining
Immunophorese *f* immunophoresis
Immunoselektion *f* immunoselection
Immunosuppression *f s.* Immunsuppression
immunosupprimieren to immunosuppress
Immunotherapie *f* immunotherapy, serotherapy
Immunotransfusion *f* immunotransfusion
Immunozyt *m* immunocyte
immunozytochemisch immunocytochemical
Immunparalyse *f* immunologic paralysis
Immunpathogenese *f* immunopathogenesis
Immunpathologie *f* immunopathology
Immunphagozytose *f* immunophagocytosis
Immunphänomen *n* immunity phenomenon
Immunprophylaxe *f* immunoprophylaxis
Immunprotein *n* immunprotein, immune protein
Immunprozeß *m* immune process
Immunreaktion *f* immunoreaction, immune reaction (response)
~/**fehlende** immunologic paralysis
~/**zellständige (zellübertragene)** cell-mediated immune response
immunreaktiv immunoreactive
Immunreaktivität *f* immunoreactivity
immunregulatorisch immunregulatory
Immunreproduktion *f* immunological reproduction
immunresistent immunoresistant
immunserologisch immunoserologic
Immunserum *n* immunoserum, immune serum, antiserum
Immunserumbehandlung *f* antiserum treatment
Immunserumglobulin *n* immune serum globulin *(s.a. unter Immunglobulin)*
~/**humanes** human immune serum globulin
Immunstatus *m* immune status, immunological state
Immunstimulation *f* immune stimulation, immunostimulation
Immunsuppression *f* immunosuppression
~/**hochdosierte** high-dosage immunosuppression
Immunsuppressionsbehandlung *f* immunosuppressive treatment, immunosuppression therapy; antirejection therapy *(bei Transplantatabstoßung)*
immunsuppressiv immunosuppressive, immunosuppressant

Immunsuppressivum *n* immunosuppressive [agent], immunodepressant [agent], immunodepressive [agent]
Immunsystem *n* immune (immunological) system
Immunsystemreaktion *f* immune system reaction
Immuntest *m* immunoassay
Immunthrombozytopenie *f* immunological thrombocytopenia
immuntolerant hyposensitive ● ~ **machen** to hyposensitize
Immuntoleranz *f* immune (immunologic) tolerance, hyposensitivity, hyposensitiveness
Immuntoleranzerzeugung *f* hyposensitization *(gegenüber Antigenen)*
Immunvaskulitis *f* immunological vasculitis
Immunvorgang *m* immune (immunological) process
impaktiert impacted *(z. B. Knochenbruch)*
Impaktion *f* impaction
Impedanzaudiometrie *f* impedance audiometry
Impedanzplethysmographie *f* impedance plethysmography
Impedanzpneumographie *f* impedance pneumography
Imperforatio *f* **ani** aproctia; imperforate anus
imperforiert imperforate
impermeabel impermeable, impervious
Impetiginisation *f* impetiginization *(Aufpfropfung einer Eiterflechte auf andere Hautkrankheiten)*
impetiginös *s.* impetigoartig
Impetigo *f* impetigo, crusted tetter
~ **follicularis** Bockhart's impetigo, superficial pustular perifolliculitis
~ **herpetiformis [Hebra]** Hebra's disease, pustular psoriasis
~ **neonatorum** neonatal impetigo, pemphigoid
impetigoartig impetiginoid, impetiginous
Impfangst *f* vaccinophobia
Impfarzt *m* vaccinator, vaccinating physician, vaccinist, inoculator
Impfausschlag *m* vaccination (vaccine) rash
Impfausweis *m* immunization register, certificate of vaccination
impfbar inoculable; vaccinable
Impfbesteck *n* vaccination set
Impfbläschen *n* vaccinid
Impfblatter *f* vaccina
Impfdermatitis *f* postvaccinal dermatosis
impfen to inoculate; to vaccinate
~/**gegen Pocken** to vaccinate, to variolate
Impfen *n s.* Impfung
Impfenzephalitis *f* postvaccinal (vaccination) encephalitis
Impfenzephalomyelitis *f* postvaccinal (vaccination) encephalomyelitis
Impfexanthem *n* vaccination (vaccine) rash
Impffeder *f s.* Impflanzette
Impffederhalter *m* pen holder
Impffieber *n* vaccinal fever

Impfgerät *n* inoculator, vaccinator
Impfinstrumentarium *n*, **Impfinstrumente** *npl* vaccination instruments
Impfkalender *m* calendar of vaccination
Impflanzette *f* [vaccination] lancet, vaccinostyle, vaccinator
Impfling *m* vaccinee, person to be vaccinated; vaccinate, vaccinated person
Impflymphe *f* vaccine, lymph
Impfmalaria *f* impfmalaria, induced malaria
Impfmesserchen *n s.* Impflanzette
Impfmethode *f* vaccination procedure
Impfmyelitis *f* postvaccinal myelitis
Impfnadel *f* vaccination needle
Impfnarbe *f* vaccination scar (mark)
Impfpaß *m*/**internationaler** international certificate of vaccination
Impfpflicht *f* compulsory vaccination
impfpflichtig liable to vaccination
Impfpistole *f* jet vaccinator, jet injector
Impfpocke *f* vaccina
Impfpocken *pl* inoculation smallpox
Impfpockenvirus *n* vaccinia (vaccine) virus
Impfprogramm *n* vaccination program[me]; vaccination campaign
Impfreaktion *f* vaccination (postvaccinal) reaction
Impfschein *m* certificate of vaccination
Impfschema *n* vaccination scheme
Impfschutz *m* vaccine protection
Impfstatus *m* vaccination status
Impfstoff *m* vaccine, lymph
~/**durch Formalin und Äthylenoxid inaktivierter** formalin-ethylene oxide inactivated vaccine
impfstoffbildend vacci[no]genous
Impfstoffcharge *f*, **Impfstoffpartie** *f* lot of vaccine
Impfstoffproduktion *f* vaccine production
Impftechnik *f* vaccination technique
Impfung *f* inoculation; vaccination, vaccinotherapy, vaccine therapy (immunoprophylaxis)
~/**bakterielle** bacterination
~ **im Kindesalter** childhood vaccination
~ **mit Rotzbakterienextrakt** malleinization
~/**prophylaktische** preventive (protective) inoculation
~ **und Serumbehandlung** *f*/**aktive** serovaccination
Impfvarizellen *fpl* vaccination varicella
Impfverfahren *n* vaccination procedure
Impfzubehör *n* vaccination instruments
Implantat *n* implant; [implantation] graft
Implantatabstoßung *f* graft rejection, rejection of the implant
Implantatausstoßung *f* extrusion of the implant
Implantatbruch *m* fracture of the implant
Implantatentfernung *f* removal of the implant
Implantation *f* implantation *(z. B. einer Gelenkprothese)*; nidation, implantation *(z. B. der befruchteten Eizelle in die Gebärmutterschleimhaut)*
~ **des Bauchspeicheldrüsengangs in das Jejunum** pancreaticojejunostomy

Implantationsepidermoid *n* implantation epidermoid
Implantationsgabel *f* implant forceps *(Instrument)*
Implantationsmaterial *n* implant[ation] material
Implantationsmetastase *f* implantation metastasis
Implantationszyste *f* implantation cyst
Implantatkorrosion *f* corrosion of the implant
Implantatlockerung *f* loosening of the implant
implantieren to implant; to embed; to nidate, to set in
impotent impotent
Impotentia *f s.* Impotenz
Impotenz *f* impotence, incapacity, invirility, eviration, acratia
~/**organische** organic impotence
Imprägnation *f* 1. *s.* Befruchtung; 2. impregnation, infusion, saturation *(Histologie)*
Impressio *f* impression
~ **digitata** digital (convolutional) impression
~ **ligamenti costoclavicularis** costal tuberosity *(Schlüsselbein)*
~ **trigemini [ossis temporalis]** trigeminal impression [of the temporal bone]
Impression *f* impression *(Zusammensetzungen s. unter* Impressio*)*
Impressionsfraktur *f* impression (gutter, depressed) fracture
Impressionstonometer *n* impression tonometer
Impressionstonometrie *f* impression (indentation) tonometry *(Augendruckmessung)*
Impuls[iv]handlung *f* impulsive action
Impulszytophotometrie *f* impulse cytophotometry
Imputabilität *f* imputability
in dies in dies, in d.
in situ in situ, in place, in the natural location
in vitro in vitro (glass), outside the living body
in vivo in vivo, in the living organism
inagglutinabel inagglutinable
inaktiv inactive, quiescent, latent, dormant *(z. B. Tuberkulose)*; inactive, inert *(z. B. Pharmaka)*; inactive, torpid *(Psyche)* ● ~ **machen** to inactivate, to render inactive
Inaktivierung *f* inactivation *(z. B. eines Serums)*
Inaktivität *f* inactivity, quiescence, latency *(z. B. der Tuberkulose)*; inactivity, inertia *(z. B. von Pharmaka)*; inactivity, torpidity, torpor *(psychische)*
Inaktivitätsarteriosklerose *f* disuse (involutional) arteriosclerosis
Inaktivitätsatrophie *f* disuse (inactivity, involutional) atrophy
Inaktivitätsosteoporose *f* disuse (inactivity) osteoporosis
Inanition *f* inanition, starvation, limophthisis
Inappetenz *f* inappetence, loss of appetite
Incisura *f* incisure, notch, fissure, groove
Inclinatio *f* **pelvis** inclination (obliquity) of the pelvis
Incontinentia *f* incontinence, acathexia *(s. a. unter* Inkontinenz*)*

Incontinentia

~ alvi incontinence of the faeces
~ pigmenti incontinentia pigmenti, melanosis cutis degenerativa, Bloch-Sulzberger syndrome
~ urinae incontinence of urine
Incubus *m* incubus, nightmare
Incus *m* incus, anvil *(Gehörknöchelchen)*
Incus-Homotransplantat *n* incus homograft
Index *m* 1. index finger, forefinger; 2. index, value
~/chemotherapeutischer chemotherapeutic index
~/nasaler nasal index
α-Index *m* alpha index
indigestibel indigestible
Indigestion *f* indigestion, digestive disturbance, dyspepsia, disturbed digestion
Indigoblau *n*, **Indigotin** *n* indigo [blue]
Indikan *n* indican *(Tryptophanabbauprodukt)*
Indikanämie *f* indicanaemia
Indikanausscheidung *f* im Urin indicanuria
Indikation *f* indication *(für bestimmtes Heilverfahren)* ● **eine ~ haben** to be indicated
~/vitale vital indication
Indikatorbakterien *npl* indicator bacteria
Indikatordilutionstechnik *f* indicator-dilution technique
Indikatorenzym *n* indicator enzyme
Indikatorisotop *n* tracer [element]
Indikatorpapier *n* indicator (test) paper
Indikatorverdünnungsmethode *f* indicator-dilution method
Indisposition *f* indisposition, malaise
Individualantigen *n* individual antigen
Individualdisposition *f* individual disposition
Individualentwicklung *f* ontogeny, ontogenesis
individualisieren to individualize
Individualpsychologie *f* individual psychology
Individualresistenz *f* individual immunity
indiziert sein to be indicated
~ sein/nicht to be contraindicated
Indol *n* indole, 2,3-benzopyrrole *(Tryptophanabbauprodukt)*
Indolausscheidung *f* im Urin indoluria
Indolazeturie *f* indolaceturia
indolent 1. indolent, non-painful, causing little pain *(z. B. eine Geschwulst)*; 2. indolent, slow in healing, sluggish *(z. B. ein Geschwür)*
Indolenz *f* indolence, insensibility to pain
Indol-3-essigsäure *f* indoleacetic (indole-3-acetic) acid
Indolessigsäureausscheidung *f* im Urin indolaceturia
Indoxyl *n* indoxyl, 3-hydroxyindole *(Tryptophanabbauprodukt)*
Indoxylämie *f* indoxylaemia
Indoxylausscheidung *f* im Urin indoxyluria
Induktionsapparat *m* inductor[ium] *(Physiologie)*
Induktionsirresein *n* induced insanity
Induktionspsychose *f* induced psychosis
Induktor *m* inductor[ium] *(Physiologie)*
Induratio *f* s. Induration

~ penis plastica fibrous cavernitis, Peyronie's disease, penile strabismus
Induration *f* induration, hardening, sclerosis *(z. B. von Organen) (s. a. unter Induratio)*
~/braune brown induration *(der Lunge)*
~/schiefrige grey induration *(der Lunge)*
Indurationsmyokarditis *f* indurative myocarditis
indurativ indurative, indurating, hardening
indurieren to indurate, to get hard (sclerotic), to harden
induriert indurate[d], hardened, sclerotic, sclerosed
Indusium *n* griseum supracallosal gyrus
Industrieanthropometrie *f* industrial anthropometry
Industrieneurologie *f* industrial neurology
Industriepsychologie *f* industrial psychology
Industrietoxikologie *f* industrial toxicology
inert inert, inactive
Inertia *f* uteri uterine inertia
infantil infantile
Infantilismus *m* infantilism
~/intestinaler intestinal infantilism, [infantile] coeliac disease, idiopathic infantile steatorrhoea, Heubner-Herter disease, gluten-induced enteropathy
~/psychischer psychoinfantilism
~/sexueller sex infantilism
Infarctus *m* s. Infarkt
~ cerebri s. Hirnschlag
~ cordis s. Herzinfarkt
Infarkt *m* infarct[ion] *(1. Absterben von Organen oder Organteilen nach lang dauernder Blutleere; 2. Ablagerung von Kalksalzen in der Nierenpapille)*
~/anämischer anaemic (white) infarct
~/blander bland infarct
~/enteromesenterialer enteromesenteric infarction
~/hämorrhagischer haemorrhagic (red) infarct
~/roter s. ~/hämorrhagischer
~/vernarbter cicatrized infarct
~/weißer s. ~/anämischer
Infarktbildung *f* s. Infarzierung
Infarktektomie *f* infarctectomy
Infarktentfernung *f*[/operative] infarctectomy
Infarktgröße *f* infarct size
Infarktkaverne *f* infarct cavern
Infarktnarbe *f* infarct[ion] scar; cicatrized infarct
Infarzierung *f* infarction, emphraxis
~/hämorrhagische haemorrhagic infarction
infaust infaust, infavourable, unpropitious *(z. B. Prognose einer Krankheit)*
Infekt *m* infection, infectious disease ● **einen grippalen ~ haben** to suffer from common colds
~/akuter respiratorischer acute respiratory disease
~/begleitender intercurrent infect
~ der oberen Luftwege common cold
~/grippaler influenzal infect, common cold, catarrhal fever

Influenzavirus

Infektarthritis f infectious arthritis
Infektion f infection ● einer ~ **Widerstand bieten** to resist infection ● **gegenüber einer ~ hochempfindlich machen** to render hypervulnerable to infection
~/**abortive** abortive infection
~/**aufsteigende** ascending infection
~/**äußere** heteroinfection
~/**bakterielle** bacterial infection
~/**Bangsche** Bang's disease, brucellosis, brucelliasis
~/**direkte** direct (contact) infection
~/**endogene** endogenous infection
~/**erneute** reinfection, secondary infection
~/**hämatogene** haematogenic (blood-borne) infection
~/**kryptogene** cryptogenous infection
~/**latente** latent infection
~/**lymphogene** lymphatic (lymph-borne) infection
~/**milde** mild infection, subinfection
~ **mit Ascaris lumbricoides** ascariasis
~/**parasitäre** parasitic infection
~/**primäre** primary infection
~/**pulmonale** pulmonary infection
~/**pyogene** pyogenic infection
~/**schleichende** slow infection
~/**sekundäre** secondary infection
~/**septische** septic infection
~/**stumme** s. ~/latente
~/**tödliche** lethal infection
~/**verborgene** hidden infection; cryptoinfection
~/**zusätzliche** secondary infection
Infektionsabteilung f isolation (infectious) ward
Infektionsallergie f infectious allergy
Infektionsanfälligkeit f susceptibility to infection
Infektionsdosis f infective dose, ID
Infektionseintrittspforte f atrium of infection
Infektionserreger m infective (infectious) agent
Infektionsgefahr f danger of infection
Infektionsherd m [infective] focus, nidus; focal infection
Infektionsimmunität f infection immunity, premunition
Infektionskeim m infective (infectious) agent
Infektionskrankheit f infectious (communicable) disease, infection
~/**anzeigepflichtige** notifiable (certifiable) infectious disease
~/**durch Trinkwasser übertragene** water-borne infectious disease
Infektionskrankheitsbeginn m invasion
Infektionskrankheitsbekämpfung f control of infectious diseases
Infektionsprophylaxe f/**chirurgische** surgical prophylaxis against infection
Infektionsprozeß m infectious process
Infektionspsychose f infectious psychosis
Infektionsrate f infection rate
Infektionsreservoir n reservoir of infection
Infektionsresistenz f resistance of infection
Infektionsschutz m protection against infections
● ~ **bewirkend** phylactic
Infektionsspital n lazaret[te]
Infektionsstadium n stage of infection
Infektionsstation f isolation ward
infektionsverhindernd anti-infective, anti-infectious
Infektionsverhütung f prevention of infection
Infektionsvorgang m infectious process
Infektionsweg m route of infection
Infektionszeitpunkt m time of infection
infektiös infectious, infective; contagious
~/**nicht** non-infectious; non-contagious
Infektiosität f infectivity, infectiosity; infectiousness; contagiousness (z. B. eines Krankheitserregers)
inferior inferior, lower
Inferiorität f inferiority
infertil infertile, sterile
Infertilität f infertility, sterility, infecundity
Infestation f infestation, infection, invasion (durch Ungeziefer) (s. a. unter Befall)
~ **mit dem chinesischen Leberegel** Chinese liver fluke disease
~ **mit Glyciphagus domesticus** grocer's itch
Infibulation f infibulation
Infiltrat n infiltrate, infiltration
~/**entzündliches** inflammatory infiltration
~/**perityphlitisches** perityphlitic (periappendicular) infiltration
~/**pulmonales** pulmonary infiltration
~/**seröses** serous infiltration
Infiltration f infiltration, permeation
~/**leukozytäre** leucocytic infiltration
~/**lymphozytäre** lymphocytic infiltration
~/**plasmazelluläre** plasma cell infiltration
~/**pulmonale** pulmonary infiltration
~/**zelluläre** cellular infiltration
Infiltrationsanästhesie f infiltration anaesthesia (analgesia)
infiltrieren to infiltrate
infizierbar infectable; infestable
infizieren to infect; to infest; to poison
~/**erneut** to reinfect
~/**mit Malaria** to malarialize
~/**sich** to infect; to get infected
infizierend/nicht non-infectious; non-contagious
Inflammation f inflammation (Zusammensetzungen s. unter Entzündung)
inflammatorisch inflammatory
inflatieren to inflate
Inflation f inflation
Inflexion f inflexion, inward bending (curving)
Influenza f influenza, flu, grip[pe]; epidemic catarrhal fever
Influenza... s. a. Grippe...
Influenzainfektion f influenza infection
Influenzameningitis f influenzal meningitis (durch Haemophilus influenzae)
Influenzavakzine f influenza vaccine
Influenzavirus n influenza virus
~ **A2** A_2 influenza virus, Asian influenza virus
~ **Typ A** type A influenza virus
~ **Typ A Hongkong** Hong Kong influenza A virus

Influenzavirusvakzine

Influenzavirusvakzine f influenza virus vaccine
infraalveolär infra-alveolar
infraaurikulär infra-auricular
Infraaxillarregion f infra-axillary region
infradiaphragmatisch infradiaphragmatic
infraglenoidal infraglenoid
infraglottisch infraglottic
Infraklavikulargrube f infraclavicular fossa
Infraklavikularregion f infraclavicular region
Infrakostallinie f infracostal line
Infraktion f infraction, incomplete fracture
inframamillär inframamillary
Inframammärregion f inframammary region
inframandibulär inframandibular
inframaxillär inframaxillary
Infraokklusion f infra-occlusion, infraclusion, infraversion *(Stomatologie)*
Infraorbitalanästhesie f infra-orbital block anaesthesia
Infraorbitalarterie f infra-orbital artery
Infraorbitalkanal m infra-orbital canal
Infraorbitalleiste f infra-orbital ridge (rim)
Infraorbitalnaht f infra-orbital suture
Infraorbitalnerv m infra-orbital nerve
Infraorbitalregion f infra-orbital region
Infraorbitalsulkus m infra-orbital sulcus (groove)
Infrarotbehandlung f infrared therapy
Infrarotlampe f infrared lamp
Infrarotmikroskopie f infrared microscopy
Infrarotstrahlung f infrared radiation
Infraskapularregion f infrascapular (subscapular) region
Infraspinatusreflex m infraspinatus reflex
infrasternal infrasternal
Infratemporalleiste f infratemporal crest
Infratemporalregion f infratemporal region
infratentoriell infratentorial
infratonsillär infratonsillar
Infraversion f infraversion *(des Auges)*
infravesikal infravesical
infrazygomatisch infrazygomatic
Infriktion f [in]friction *(s. a. Einreibung 1.)*
Infundibularfortsatz m infundibular process
infundibuliform infundibuliform
Infundibulom n infundibuloma *(Geschwulst des Infundibulum hypothalami)*
Infundibulum n 1. infundibulum; 2. s. ~ hypothalami
~ **ethmoidale** ethmoid infundibulum
~ **hypothalami** infundibulum [of the hypophysis], infundibular stem, stalk of the neurohypophysis
~ **tubae uterinae** infundibulum of the uterine tube
Infundibulumstenose f infundibular [pulmonic] stenosis *(der rechten Herzkammer)*
infundieren to infuse
~**/unter Druck** to hasten infusion
Infusion f 1. infusion *(Vorgang)*; 2. [drip] infusion, phleboclysis
~**/intravenöse** intravenous infusion, phleboclysis
Infusionsbesteck n infusion equipment (set), intravenous giving set

Infusionscholangiogramm n infusion cholangiogram
Infusionscholangiographie f infusion cholangiography
Infusionsflasche f infusion bottle
Infusionsgeschwindigkeit f flow rate, rate of infusion
Infusionskanüle f infusion cannula
Infusionskatheter m/**venöser** indwelling intravenous catheter
Infusionsklemme f gate-clip
Infusionslösung f infusion [solution]
~**/Darrowsche** Darrow's solution
Infusionsreaktion f infusion reaction
Infusionsständer m infusion stand
Infusionstherapie f infusion therapy, drip treatment, parenteral fluid therapy
Infusionsurogramm n excretory urogram
Infusionsurographie f excretory urography
Infusorien npl Infusoria *(Mikroorganismen)*
ING s. Isotopennephrogramm
Ingesta npl ingesta
Ingestion f ingestion, food intake
Ingredienz f ingredient, constituent
Inguen n s. Inguinalregion
Inguinal... s. a. Leisten...
Inguinaldreieck n inguinal triangle (trigone)
Inguinalfalte f inguinal fold
Inguinalhernie f inguinal hernia
~**/inkomplette** bubonocele, incomplete inguinal hernia
Inguinalhernienregion f inguinal hernial region
Inguinalkanal m inguinal canal
Inguinalligament n inguinal (Poupart's) ligament
Inguinalregion f inguinal region, groin, inguen
inguinoabdominal inguino-abdominal
Inguinodynie f inguinodynia, pain in the groin (inguinal region)
inguinoskrotal inguinoscrotal
Inhalation f inhalation *(z. B. von Dämpfen)*
Inhalationsbehandlung f inhalation treatment (therapy)
Inhalationsgerät n inhalator, inhaler, inhaling apparatus; inspirator
Inhalationsnarkose f inhalation anaesthesia (analgesia) *(zentrale Analgesie durch gas- oder dampfförmige Narkosemittel)*
Inhalationsnarkotikum n inhalation anaesthetic agent
Inhalationspneumonie f inhalation pneumonia
Inhalator m inhalator, inhalor; inspirator
Inhalatorium n inhalatorium, inhalation room *(Therapieabteilung)*
inhalieren to inhale, to breathe in
inhärent inherent
inhibieren to inhibit, to retard; to block; to obstruct; to occlude
Inhibin n inhibin *(Hodenhormon)*
Inhibition f inhibition, retardation; backwardness; arrest *(geistiger und körperlicher Entwicklung)*
Inhibitor m inhibitor

inhibitorisch inhibitory, inhibitive
Inhibitorpeptid *n* inhibitor peptide
Inhibitorproteid *n* inhibitor proteid
Inion *n* inion, external occipital protuberance
Initialdelir *n* initial delir[ium]
Initialdosis *f* initial dosis
Initialkaverne *f* initial cavern
Initialperfusion *f* initial perfusion
Initialschrei *m* initial cry *(bei Epilepsie)*
Initialsklerose *f* initial sclerosis
Initialsymptom *n* initial symptom, onset, first sign
Initialtherapeutikum *n* initial therapeutic agent
Initialtherapie *f* initial therapy
Injektion *f* injection; infusion ● **eine ~ geben** *s.* injizieren ● **zur ~ geeignet** injectable
~/blutige injection *(z. B. der Schleimhäute)*
~ in das Cavum subarachnoidale lumbar subarachnoid injection
~/intrakardiale intracardiac injection
~/intramuskuläre intramuscular injection
~/intrathekale intrathecal injection
~/intravenöse intravenous injection
~/subkonjunktivale subconjunctival injection
~/subkutane subcutaneous injection, hypodermic [injection]
Injektionslösung *f* injection solution
Injektionsnadel *f* cannula, hypodermic needle
~ Nr. 14 14-gauge needle
Injektionsnarkose *f* intravenous anaesthesia
Injektionspräparat *n* injection preparation
Injektionsspritze *f* [hypodermic] syringe
~/Lüersche Luer[-lock] syringe *(Ganzglasspritze mit eingeschliffenem Kolben)*
Injektionsstelle *f* injection site, site of injection
injizierbar injectable
injizieren to inject; to give (make) an injection
Inka-Bein *n*, **Inka-Knochen** *m* Inca (interparietal) bone
Inkarzeration *f* incarceration, strangulation *(z. B. eines Eingeweidebruchs)*
inkarzerieren to incarcerate, to strangulate *(z. B. Darmschlingen)*; to impact *(z. B. einen Knochenbruch)*
inkarzeriert incarcerated, strangulated ● **~ werden** to become impacted *(z. B. Meniskus)*
Inklination *f* inclination
inklinieren to incline
Inklinometer *n* inclinometer *(zur Augendurchmesserbestimmung)*
Inklusion *f*/**fetale** foetal inclusion
inkohärent incoherent, disconnected; illogical; inconsistent
Inkohärenz *f* incoherence, absence of connection of ideas; incongruity (inconsequence) of speech
inkompatibel incompatible
Inkompatibilität *f* incompatibility *(z. B. im Rh-System)*
Inkompensation *f* incompensation *(Zustand zwischen Kompensation und Dekompensation)*

inkompetent incompetent, insufficient, inadequate
Inkompetenz *f* 1. incompetence, insufficiency, inadequacy of natural function; 2. incompetence, incapacity, want of legal fitness
inkomplett 1. incomplete; 2. hemiparetic
inkontinent incontinent, acathectic
Inkontinenz *f* incontinence, acathexia *(s. a. unter Incontinentia)*
~/anorektale anorectal incontinence
Inkoordination *f* incoordination
Inkorporation *f* incorporation *(z. B. von radioaktivem Material)*
Inkorporationsdosimetrie *f* incorporation dosimetry
inkorporieren to incorporate
Inkret *n* incretion
Inkretdrüse *f* incretory (endocrine) gland
Inkretion *f* incretion, internal secretion
Inkretionsorgan *n* incretory (endocrine) organ
inkretorisch incretory, endocrine
Inkrustation *f* incrustation
inkrustieren to incrust
Inkubation *f* 1. incubation, breeding *(Mikrobiolo-*
Inkubation *f* 1. incubation, breeding *(Mikrobiologie)*; 2. *s.* Inkubationszeit
Inkubationshämolyse *f* incubation haemolysis
Inkubationsimpfung *f* incubation vaccination
Inkubationsresistenz *f* incubation resistance
Inkubationsstadium *n* incubation stage
Inkubationszeit *f* incubation period (time)
Inkubator *m* incubator *(1. Mikrobiologie; 2. Gerät für Frühgeborenenaufzucht)*
Inkubatorpflege *f* incubator care
inkubieren to incubate
Inkudektomie *f* incudectomy
inkudomalleal incudomalleal
inkudostapedial incudostapedial
inkurabel incurable, immedicable
Inkurabilität *f* incurability
Inkurvation *f* incurvation
Inlay *n* inlay *(Stomatologie)*
Innenfläche *f* 1. inner surface; 2. palm [of the hand] ● **mit der ~ nach oben** supine *(z. B. Hand)*
Innenhaut *f* endothelium, internal lining membrane *(z. B. von Körperhöhlen)*; endosteum *(von Knochen)*; intima *(von Gefäßen)*; endocardium *(des Herzens)*
Innenknöchel *m* **[des Schienbeins]** *s.* Malleolus medialis
Innenkörper *m*/**Ehrlichscher (Heinzscher)** Ehrlich-Heinz granule, Heinz body
innenliegend intrinsic
Innenlymphe *f* endolymph
Innenmeniskus *m* internal meniscus (semilunar fibrocartilage), medial meniscus *(im Kniegelenk)*
Innenohr *n* inner (internal) ear, labyrinth[us], statoacoustic organ
Innenohraplasie *f* inner ear aplasia
Innenohrdegeneration *f* inner ear degeneration

Innenohreingang

Innenohreingang *m* vestibule of the inner ear
Innenohrentzündung *f* internal otitis, inflammation of the internal ear
Innenohrfibrose *f* vestibulofibrosis
Innenohrhydrops *m* hydrops of the labyrinth, dropsy of the internal ear
Innenohroperation *f* endaural operation
Innenohrschwerhörigkeit *f* perceptive deafness (hearing loss), labyrinthine deafness
Innenohrsklerose *f* otosclerosis of inner ear
innenohrtoxisch vestibulotoxic
Innenohrtoxizität *f* vestibulotoxicity *(z. B. von Streptomyzin)*
Innenplasma *n* endoplasm
Innenrotation *f* internal rotation *(z. B. eines Gelenks)*
Innenschmarotzer *m* endoparasite, entozoon
innerlich internal
innersekretorisch endocrine, endocrinous, endocrinic
Innervation *f* innervation, nerve supply *(z. B. eines Organs)*
~/reziproke reciprocal innervation
Innervationspause *f* silent period
innervieren to innervate
innewohnend inherent
Inochondritis *f s.* Fibrochondritis
Inochondrom *n s.* Fibrochondrom
Inokulation *f* inoculation; vaccination *(Zusammensetzungen s. unter Impfung)*
Inokulations... *s. a.* Impf...
Inokulationsfähigkeit *f* inoculability
Inokulationshepatitis *f* inoculation jaundice, serum (virus) hepatitis
Inokulationsmalaria *f* impfmalaria, induced malaria
Inokulator *m* inoculator, vaccinator
inokulierbar inoculable, vaccinable
inokulieren to inoculate; to vaccinate
Inokulum *n* inoculum, inoculable material
inoperabel inoperable
Inoperabilität *f* inoperability
Inopexie *f* inopexia
Inosämie *f* inosaemia
Inosin *n* inosine, hypoxanthine riboside
Inosit *m*, **Inositol** *n* inosite, inositol; bios I
Inositolausscheidung *f* im Urin inosit[ol]uria, inosuria
Inositolhexaphosphorsäure *f* phytic (inositolhexaphosphoric) acid
Inoskulation *f* inosculation *(z. B. von Blutgefäßen)*
Inosurie *f* inosuria, inosit[ol]uria
inotrop inotropic
Inotropie *f* inotropism
inpalpabel impalpable
Insalivation *f* insalivation *(der Nahrung)*
Insania *f* insanity, mental derangement
Inscriptio *f* inscriptio[n] *(1. Bestandteil eines Rezepts; 2. sehnige Unterbrechung der Muskelkontinuität)*
Inscriptiones *fpl* **tendineae** tendinous inscriptions (intersections)

Insektenabschreckungsmittel *n* insectifuge, insect repellent
Insektenangst *f* entomophobia
insektenbedingt insect-borne
Insektenbefall *m* entomosis, insect infestation
insektentötend insecticidal
Insektenvernichtung *f* disinsection, disinsectization
Insektenvernichtungsmittel *n* insecticide
Insektenvertreibungsmittel *n* insectifuge, insect repellent
Insektizid *n* insecticide
Insektizidvergiftung *f* insecticide poisoning
Insel *f* 1. island; 2. *s.* Insula Reili; 3. islet, island, granule *(der Bauchspeicheldrüse)*
Inseladenom *n* insul[in]oma, islet[-cell] adenoma *(der Bauchspeicheldrüse)*
Inselhormon *n s.* Insulin
Insellappen *m* island flap *(Hauttransplantation)*
Inseln *fpl/***Langerhanssche** islets of Langerhans (the pancreas), Langerhans' cells (islands), pancreatic islets (islands, glomerules) *(Insulin produzierende Zellinseln der Bauchspeicheldrüse)*
Inselschwelle *f des Gehirns* limen insulae
Inseltransplantat *n* island graft
Inselzelladenom *n s.* Inseladenom
Inselzellantikörper *m* islet-cell antibody
Inselzellen *fpl/***Langerhanssche** islets of Langerhans (the pancreas), cells of the islet, islet (beta) cells
Inselzellenkarzinom *n* islet-cell cancer (carcinoma)
Inselzelltransplantation *f* [pancreatic] islet cell transplantation
Inselzelltumor *m* [pancreatic] islet-cell tumour, Langerhansian adenoma, nesidioblastoma *(gutartig)*
Insemination *f* [in]semination *(1. Besamung; 2. Eizellenbefruchtung)*
~/donogene *s.* ~/heterologe
~/heterologe heterologous (donor) insemination, A.I.D.
~/homologe homologous insemination, A.I.H.
~/künstliche artificial insemination (fecundation)
~/maritogene *s.* ~/homologe
inseminieren to inseminate
insensibel insensible, insensitive
Insensibilität *f* insensibility, insensitiveness
Insertio *f* insertion *(Ansatz z. B. eines Muskels am Knochen)*
~ velamentosa velamentous insertion
Insertionsaponeurose *f* aponeurosis of insertion
In-sich-selbst-Verliebtsein *n* narc[iss]ism, autophilia
insidiös insidious *(z. B. eine Krankheit)*
insipidus insipid, tasteless
Inskription *f s.* Inscriptio
Insolation *f* 1. insolation, solarization; 2. insolation, heatstroke, heliosis, thermoplegia
Insolationsdermatitis *f* sun burn
Insolationskollaps *m* heat prostration

Insomnie f insomnia, sleeplessness, [abnormal] wakefulness, vigilance, agrypnia, anhypnosis
Inspersion f inspersion *(z. B. mit Puder)*
Inspiration f inspiration, inhaling, breathing in
Inspirationskapazität f inspiratory capacity, IC
Inspirationskrampf m inspiratory spasm
Inspirationsmitte f midinspiration
Inspirationsmuskel m inspiratory muscle
Inspirationsphase f inspirium, inspiration
inspiratorisch inspiratory
inspirieren to inspire, to inhale, to breathe in
Inspirometer n inspirometer
Inspissation f inspissation
Instillation f instillation, instilment, dropping a liquid into a cavity
Instillator m instillator
instillieren to instil[l], to introduce (pour) in drops
Instinkt m instinct ● **durch den ~ bestimmt** instinctive, instinctual
instinktiv instinctive, instinctual
Instrument n 1. [surgical] instrument; 2. [measuring] instrument; apparatus
~ zur elektrischen Gewebsabtragung electroresectoscope
~ zur Messung der Gebärmutterkontraktionen metrodynamometer
~ zur Neugeborenenvermessung paedometer
Instrumentarium n instrumentarium, instrumentation, [equipment of] instruments
~/urologisches genitourinary instrumentation
Instrumentenanreichung f instrumentation
Instrumentenbesteck n instrumentarium, pack
Instrumentenkocher m [instrument] sterilizer
Instrumentensatz m instrumentarium, pack
Instrumentenschrank m instrument cupboard (cabinet)
Instrumententisch m instrument table, table for (with) the instruments
Instrumentieren n instrumentation
Instrumentierschwester f scrub (instrument) nurse
Insudat n insudate
Insudation f insudation
insudieren to insudate
insuffizient insufficient, incompetent, inadequate
Insuffizienz f insufficiency, incompetence, inadequacy *(eines Organs)*
~/ovarielle ovarian insufficiency
~/pulmonale respiratory insufficiency (inadequacy, failure)
~/renale renal insufficiency (shutdown)
~/respiratorische respiratory insufficiency (inadequacy)
~/vaskuläre vascular insufficiency
~/venöse venous insufficiency
~/zirkulatorische circulatory failure
Insufflation f insufflation *(z. B. von Medikamentenpulvern oder Gasen)*
Insufflationskatheter m insufflation catheter
Insufflationsnarkose f insufflation narcosis (anaesthesia)
Insufflator m insufflator

Integumentum

Insula f **[Reili]** insula, island of Reil *(verdeckter Teil der Großhirnrinde)*
Insulae fpl pancreatis s. Inseln/Langerhansssche
insulär insular
Insulin n insulin, antidiabetic hormone *(der Bauchspeicheldrüse)* ● **durch ~ bewirkt** insulinogenic ● **mit ~ behandeln** to insulinize
~/immunreaktives immunologically detectable insulin
Insulinallergie f insulin allergy
Insulinämie f insul[in]aemia
Insulinase f insulinase *(Enzym)*
Insulinatrophie f insulin atrophy
Insulinbedarf m insulin requirement
Insulinbildung f insulinogenesis
Insulinblutspiegelerhöhung f[/exzessive] hyperinsulinaemia
Insulineinstellung f insulinization
Insulinfreisetzungspeptid n insulin-releasing peptid, IRP
Insulinhypertrophie f insulin hypertrophy
Insulinhypoglykämie f insulin hypoglycaemia
Insulinhypoglykämietest m insulin hypoglycaemia test
Insulininfusion f insulin infusion
Insulininfusionspumpe f insulin infusion pump
Insulinkoma n insulin coma (shock), hypoglycaemic shock
Insulinkomatherapie f insulin coma therapy, ICT, insulin shock therapy (treatment), IST, hypoglycaemic shock therapy
Insulinlipodystrophie f insulin lipodystrophy
Insulinmangel m hypoinsulinism
Insulinmangelproduktion f hypoinsulinism
insulinogen insulinogenic
Insulinom n s. Insulom
insulinpflichtig insulin-dependent
Insulinproduktion f insulinogenesis
Insulinresistenz f insulin resistance
Insulinrezeptor m insulin receptor
Insulinschock m s. Insulinkoma
Insulinspritze f insulin syringe
Insulintherapie f insulinization
Insulintoleranztest m insulin tolerance test
Insulinüberproduktion f [hyper]insulinism
Insulinüberschuß m [hyper]insulinism
Insulom n insul[in]oma, islet[-cell] adenoma *(der Bauchspeicheldrüse)*
Insult m insult, stroke *(s. a. unter* Anfall*)* ● **nach einem apoplektischen ~** postapoplectic
~/apoplektischer apoplectic stroke, cerebral [vascular] accident, [cerebral] apoplexy, cerebrovascular accident, cerebral infarct[ion]
~/hämorrhagischer sanguineous apoplexy, brain haemorrhage
~/zerebrovaskulärer s. ~/apoplektischer
Insultpatient m stroke patient
Insuszeptibilität f insusceptibility
Integraldosis f integral (volume) dose, integral absorbed dose *(Radiologie)*
Integument[um] n integument[um], tegument
~ commune tegumentary epithelium

Intellekt

Intellekt m intellect
intelligent intelligent
Intelligenz f intelligence, intellect; noopsyche
Intelligenzdefekt m intellectual defect; defective intelligence
Intelligenzmangel m intellectual (mental) deficiency
Intelligenzquotient m intelligence quotient, IQ, I. Q. *(Maß für Verstandesstärke)*
Intelligenzstörung f intellectual disorder, dysgnosia
Intelligenztest m intelligence test
~/**analytischer** analytic intelligence test
Intensimeter n intensitometer *(Radiologie)*
Intensität f intensity *(z. B. einer Bestrahlung)*
intensiv intensive, intense *(z. B. Gefühle)*
intensivieren to intensify
Intensivmedizin f intensive care [medicine]
Intensivpflege f intensive care
Intensivpflegeeinheit f intensive care unit, ICU
Intensivpflegeschwester f intensive care nurse
Intensivpflegestation f s. Intensivstation
Intensivpsychotherapie f intensive psychotherapy
Intensivstation f intensive care unit, ICU *(s. a. unter Intensivtherapieeinheit)*
~/**koronare** coronary care unit
Intensivtherapie f intensive care
~/**kardiologische** emergency cardiac care
Intensivtherapieeinheit f intensive care unit, ICU
~/**chirurgische** surgical intensive (acute) care unit
~/**kardiologische** emergency cardiac care unit
Intention f 1. intention, aim, purpose; 2. intention, process (manner) of healing
Intentionskrampf m intention spasm
Intentionspsychose f intention psychosis
Intentionsrigidität f intention rigidity
Intentionstremor m intention (action) tremor, volitional (kinetic, effort) tremor
Intentionsübungen fpl intention exercises
Interalveolarseptum n 1. interalveolar septum *(zwischen den Lungenbläschen)*; 2. s. Interdentalseptum
Interanularsegment n interannular segment *(Nervenfaserabschnitt zwischen zwei Ranvierschen Schnürringen)*
interartikulär interarticular
interarytenoid interarytenoid
interatrial, interaurikulär interatrial, interauricular
Interaurikularbündel n/**Bachmannsches** Bachmann's bundle, interatrial myocardial band *(Reizleitung)*
interaxonal interaxonal
interazinös interacinar, interacinous
Interchromatingranula npl interchromatin granules
Interdentalpapille f interdental papilla
Interdentalraum m interdental space
Interdentalschiene f interdental splint

Interdentalschienung f interdental splinting
Interdentalseptum n interdental (interalveolar) septum *(Stomatologie)*
Interdentium n interdentium
Interdigitalgelenk n interdigital joint (articulation), knuckle *(der Hand)*
Interdigitalraum m interdigit, web space
Interdiktion f interdiction *(bei einer Geisteskrankheit)*
interesselos indifferent; lethargic
interfaszikulär interfascicular
Interferenzdissoziation f interference dissociation, double rhythm (tachycardia) *(Überleitungsstörung bei Herzblock)*
Interferenzmikroskop n interference microscope
Interferenzphänomen n interference (cell-blockade) phenomenon *(Virologie)*
Interferometer n interferometer
Interferometrie f interferometry
Interferon n interferon *(Virologie)*
Interferongenese f interferogenesis
Interferonogen n interferonogen
Interferonproduktion f interferon production
Interferonstimulation f interferon stimulation
interfibrillär interfibrillar
interfilamentär interfilamentous
Interfilarmasse f interfilar mass
interfollikulär interfollicular
Interfoveolarligament n interfoveolar ligament
Interglobulardentin n interglobular dentin
Interglobularraum m interglobular space
interglutäal intergluteal
intergyral intergyral
Interhemisphärenfurche f interhemispheric (intercerebral) fissure
interhemisphärisch interhemispheric, inter[hemi]cerebral
Interkalarstaphylom n intercalary staphyloma
interkapillär intercapillary
interkarotid intercarotic, intercarotid
interkartilaginär intercartilaginous
Interkinese f s. Interphase
interklavikulär interclavicular
interkondylär intercondylar, intercondyloid, intercondylous
Interkondylargrube f intercondylar fossa (notch)
Interkondylarlinie f intercondylar line
Interkondylarvorsprung m intercondylar eminence *(Kniegelenk)*
Interkostalarterie f intercostal artery
~/**hintere** posterior intercostal artery
Interkostalband n intercostal membrane
Interkostalblock m intercostal nerve block[ade]
Interkostaldrain m intercostal drain (chest tube)
Interkostaleinziehung f intercostal retraction
Interkostalgefäß n intercostal vessel
Interkostalmembran f intercostal membrane
Interkostalmuskeln mpl intercostal muscles
~/**äußere** external intercostal muscles
~/**innere** internal intercostal muscles
~/**innerste** innermost intercostal muscles
Interkostalnerv m intercostal nerve

Interkostalnervenblockade f intercostal nerve block[ade]
Interkostalneuralgie f intercostal neuralgia, costalgia
Interkostalraum m intercostal space, interspace, spatium intercostale
~/fünfter linker fifth left interspace
Interkostalretraktion f intercostal retraction
Interkostalspatium n s. Interkostalraum
Interkostalvene f intercostal vein
~/hintere posterior intercostal vein
~/linke obere left intercostal superior vein
~/rechte obere right intercostal superior vein
~/vordere anterior intercostal vein
Interkrikothyreotomie f intercricothyreotomy
interkurrent intercurrent *(z. B. Krankheit)*
Interkuspidation f intercusping, intercuspation *(der Zähne)*
interligamentär interligamentary, interligamentous
Interlobärerguß m interlobar effusion
Interlobärfissur f interlobar fissure
Interlobärpleuritis f, **Interlobitis** f interlobitis, interlobar pleuritis
interlobulär interlobular
intermalleolar intermalleolar
intermamillär intermamillary
Intermaxillarknochen m incisive bone, intermaxillary [bone], intermaxilla, premaxilla
Intermaxillarknochennaht f intermaxillary suture
intermediär intermediary, intermediate
Intermediärfilament n intermediate filament
Intermediärkallus m intermediate callus
Intermediärknorpel m intermediary cartilage
Intermediärkörper m intermediate body of Flemming *(bei der Zellteilung)*
Intermediärlamelle f intermediate lamella *(des Knochens)*
Intermediärlinie f intermediate line
Intermediärplexus m intermediate plexus
Intermediärstoffwechsel m intermediary metabolism
Intermediärzellkarzinom n intermediary (intermediate-cell) carcinoma
Intermediat n intermediate *(Stoffwechselzwischenprodukt)*
Intermedin n intermedin, melanocyte-stimulating hormone, MSH
intermenstrual intermenstrual
intermetakarpal intermetacarpal
intermetatarsal intermetatarsal
Intermission f intermission *(fieberfreies Intervall)*
intermitotisch intermitotic
intermittierend intermittent
intermural intermural *(z. B. Organe)*
Intermuskularseptum n intermuscular septum
intern internal
~ und chirurgisch medicosurgical
Internationales Arzneibuch n International Pharmacopoeia
Interneuron n interneuron, internuncial cell (neuron), intercalated neuron
interneuronal interneuronal
Internist m internist, internal specialist, specialist in internal medicine
interokklusiv interocclusal
interolivär interolivary
interorbital interorbital
Interossalleiste f interosseous margin (crest, ridge)
Interozeption f interoception, proprioception, muscle sense
interozeptiv interoceptive
Interozeptor m interoceptor, proprioceptor *(z. B. an inneren Organen)*
interpalatin[al] interpalatine
interpapillär interpapillary
interparoxysmal interparoxysmal
Interpedunkularraum m interpeduncular space
interphalangeal interphalangeal, phalangophalangeal
Interphase f interphase, interstage, interkinesis *(Ruhephase z. B. bei Zellteilung)*
Interphasenkern m interphase (resting) nucleus
Interphasenzelle f resting cell
interphasisch interphasic
interpleural interpleural
Interponat n bridging graft
interponieren to interpose
Interposition f interposition *(z. B. von Muskelfetzen zwischen Knochenbruchenden)*
Interpositionsoperation f interposition operation *(Lagerung des Gebärmutterkörpers zwischen Scheide und Blase)*
interproximal interproximal, interproximate
interpubisch interpubic
interpupillär interpupillary
Interradikularseptum n interradicular septum
Interruptio f s. Schwangerschaftsunterbrechung
Intersectiones fpl tendineae tendinous inscriptions (intersections)
Intersegmentalreflex m intersegmental reflex
Intersektion f intersection, inscriptio[n]
interseptovalvulär interseptovalvular
Intersex m intersex
Intersexualität f intersexuality
intersexuell intersexual
Intersexueller m intersex
Intersigmoidalhernie f intersigmoid hernia
Interskapularreflex m interscapular reflex
Interskapularregion f interscapular region
interskapulothorakal interscapulothoracic
Interspinaldurchmesser m interspinal diameter
Interspinallinie f interspinal line
Interstitialraum m s. Interstitium
Interstitialzelle f interstitial (Leydig) cell
interstitiell interstitial
Interstitiom n interstitioma, interstitial-cell tumour, Leydig-cell tumour
Interstitium n interstitium, interstice, interstitial tissue *(z. B. der bindegewebige Raum um Gefäße)*
Intersystole f intersystole
intersystolisch intersystolic

interthorakoskapulär 364

interthorakoskapulär interthoracicoscapular
intertragisch intertragic
intertriginös intertriginous
Intertrigium *n* web space
Intertrigo *f* intertrigo
intertrochantär intertrochanteric
Intertubularsubstanz *f* intertubular substance
interuretär interureteric, interureteral
Intervall *n*/**atrioventrikuläres** atrioventricular interval
~/**elektrokardiographisches** electrocardiographic interval
~/**freies** lucid interval *(Bewußtseinslage z. B. nach Schädel-Hirn-Trauma)*
Intervallappendektomie *f* interval appendectomy
Intervallcholezystektomie *f* interval cholecystectomy
Intervallfieber *n* periodic fever
Intervalloperation *f* interval operation
Intervalltonsillektomie *f* interval tonsillectomy
intervalvulär intervalvular
intervaskulär intervascular
interventrikulär interventricular *(z. B. des Herzens)*
Intervertebralscheibe *f* intervertebral disk
Intervillärraum *m* intervillous space
Intervillärthrombose *f* intervillous thrombosis
Intervillärzirkulation *f* intervillous circulation
intervillös intervillous
Interzellularbrücke *f* intercellular bridge, desmosome
Interzellularödem *n* intercellular oedema, spongiosis
Interzellularplexus *m* intercellular plexus
Interzellularraum *m* intercellular space
Interzellularspalten *fpl* intercellular spaces
Interzellularsubstanz *f* intercellular substance
Interzellularzement *m* intercellular cement
intestinal intestinal, enteric, enteral
Intestinal... *s. a.* Darm...
Intestinalangina *f* intestinal angina
Intestinalanthrax *m* intestinal anthrax
Intestinalarterie *f* intestinal artery
Intestinalbilharziose *f* intestinal schistosomiasis, Egyptian splenomegaly
Intestinaldekompression *f* intestinal decompression
Intestinaldigestion *f* intestinal digestion
Intestinalfaszioliasis *f* intestinal distomiasis
Intestinalhernie *f* intestinal hernia
Intestinalinkarzeration *f* intestinal incarceration
Intestinalmukosa *f* intestinal mucosa (mucous membrane), enteric mucosa
Intestinalmyiasis *f* intestinal myiasis
Intestinalreflex *m* intestinal (myenteric) reflex
Intestinalschistosomiasis *f*/**Ägyptische** *s.* Intestinalbilharziose
Intestinalstase *f* intestinal stasis, enterostasis
Intestinalstrangulation *f* intestinal strangulation
Intestinalteleangiektasie *f* intestinal teleangiectasia

Intestinaltuberkulose *f* intestinal tuberculosis
Intestinalvene *f* intestinal vein
Intestinum *n* intestine, intestinum, bowel *(s. a. unter* Darm*)*
~ **caecum** *s.* Blinddarm
~ **crassum** *s.* Dickdarm
~ **duodenum** *s.* Duodenum
~ **ileum** *s.* Ileum
~ **jejunum** *s.* Jejunum
~ **rectum** *s.* Rektum
~ **tenue** *s.* Dünndarm
Intima *f* [tunica] intima, [vascular] endothelium
Intimaarteriosklerose *f* intimal arteriosclerosis
Intimaausschälung *f* intimectomy, desobliteration, endarter[i]ectomy
Intimaentzündung *f* intimitis, [endo]angiitis, endovasculitis
Intimafibrose *f* intimal fibrosis
Intimahyperplasie *f* intimal hyperplasia
Intimaproliferation *f* intimal proliferation
Intimaruptur *f* intimal rupture
Intimasklerose *f* intimal sclerosis
Intimatuberkel *m* intimal tubercle
Intimaveränderung *f* intimal change
Intimaverdickung *f* intimal thickening
Intimektomie *f* intimectomy, desobliteration, endarter[i]ectomy
intorquieren to intort
Intorsion *f* intorsion, intortion
Intoxikation *f* [in]toxication, poisoning; venenation *(durch tierisches Gift)*
~/**putride** putrid (septic) intoxication, sapraemia
Intoxikationsamaurose *f* toxic amaurosis
Intoxikationsamblyopie *f* toxic amblyopia
Intoxikationsparkinsonismus *m* intoxication parkinsonism
Intoxikationspsychose *f* toxic psychosis
Intoxikationszeichen *n* intoxication sign (symptom)
intra vitam intravital
Intraabdominalblutung *f* endoabdominal (intraabdominal) haemorrhage
Intraabdominaldruck *m* intra-abdominal pressure
intraalveolär intra-alveolar
intraarteriell intra-arterial
intraartikulär intra-articular
intraatrial intra-atrial, intra-auricular
intraazinös intra-acinar, intra-acinous
intrabronchial intrabronchial, endobronchial
intracholedochal intracholedochal, endocholedochal
intradermal intradermal, intradermic, endodermal, intracutaneous
intraembryonal intra-embryonic
intraepidermal intra-epidermal
intraepiphyseal intra-epiphysial
intraepithelial intra-epithelial
intraerythrozytär intra-erythrocytic
intrafaszikulär intrafascicular
intrafistular intrafistular
intrafollikulär intrafollicular

Intrafusalfaser f intrafusal fibre *(quergestreifte Muskelfaser)*
intragastral intragastric
intraglandulär intraglandular
intraglutäal intragluteal
intrahepatisch intrahepatic
Intrahepatoduktojejunostomie f intrahepatoductojejunostomy
intrakapillär intracapillary
intrakapsulär intracapsular
intrakardial intracardial, intracordal, intracardiac, i.c., endocardial, endocardiac
intrakartilaginär intracartilaginous
intrakavernös intracavernous
intrakavitär intracavitary
intrakondylär intracondylar, intracondyloid, intracondylous
intrakorneal intracorneal
intrakorpuskulär intracorpuscular
intrakranial, intrakraniell intracranial, endocranial
intrakutan intracutaneous, intradermal
Intrakutanimpfung f intradermal vaccination
Intrakutaninjektion f intradermal injection
~ **mit der Impfpistole** intradermal jet injection
Intrakutannaht f intradermal (subcuticular) suture, buried (continuous) suture
Intrakutanreaktion f intradermal reaction
Intrakutantest m intradermal test
Intrakutantestung f intradermal testing
intralabyrinthär intralabyrinthine
intralaryngeal intralaryngeal, endolaryngeal
intraleukozytär intraleucocytic
intraligamentär intraligamentary, intraligamentous
intralobär intralobar
Intralobulararterie f intralobular artery
intramammär intramammary
intramedullär intramedullary *(z. B. Rückenmark)*
intramenstrual intramenstrual
intramural intramural, intraparietal *(z. B. eines Organs)*
intramuskulär intramuscular, i.m.
intramyokardial intramyocardial
intramyometrial intramyometrial
intranasal intranasal, endonasal
intraneural intraneural, endoneural
intranukleär intranuclear, endonuclear
Intraokulardruck m intra-ocular pressure (tension)
intraoperativ intraoperative
Intraoralschiene f intra-oral splint
intraorbital intra-orbital
intraossal intra-ossal, intra-osseous
intraösophageal intra-oesophageal
intraparietal intraparietal
intrapartal intrapartum
intrapelvin intrapelvic, endopelvic
Intraperikardialraum m intrapericardial space
intraperitoneal intraperitoneal, endoperitoneal
intrapharyngeal intrapharyngeal, endopharyngeal

intraplazentar intraplacental
Intrapleuraldruck m intrapleural pressure
intraprostatisch intraprostatic
intrapsychisch intrapsychic[al]
intrapulmonal intrapulmonary
intrasellar intrasellar
Intraspinalblock m intraspinal block
Intrathorakaldruck m intrathoracic pressure
intratracheal intratracheal, endotracheal
Intratrachealnarkose f endotracheal anaesthesia
intraumbilikal intra-umbilical
Intrauterinamputation f congenital (intra-uterine) amputation
Intrauterinasphyxie f foetal (intra-uterine) asphyxia
Intrauterindruck m intra-uterine pressure
Intrauteringravidität f intra-uterine gravidity, uterogestation, uterine pregnancy, entopic gestation
Intrauterinleben n intra-uterine life
Intrauterinpessar n, **Intrauterinspange** f intrauterine [contraceptive] device, IUD
Intrauterintod m intra-uterine death
intravasal intravascular
Intravasat n intravasate
Intravasation f intravasation
intravaskulär intravascular
intravenös intravenous, I.V., i.v.
intraventrikulär intraventricular, endoventricular
Intravitalfärbung f intravital staining; intravital stain
intravitreal intravitreous, intravitreal
intrazellulär intracellular, endocellular
Intrazellularflüssigkeit f intracellular fluid
Intrazellularraum m intracellular space
intrazerebellar intracerebellar
Intrazerebralblutung f intracerebral haemorrhage
Intrazerebralhämatom n intracerebral haematoma
intrazervikal intracervical, endocervical
intrazytoplasmatisch intracytoplasmic
Intrinsic-Albuminurie f intrinsic albuminuria
Intrinsic-Allergie f intrinsic allergy
Intrinsic-Asthma n intrinsic asthma
Intrinsic-Faktor m/**Castlescher** [Castle's] intrinsic factor, haemopoietin, apoerythrein *(fehlt bei perniziöser Anämie)*
Introflexion f introflexion
Introitus m introitus, aditus, aperture, entrance, orifice, ostium *(zu einer Körperhöhle)*
~ **vaginae** vaginal introitus (orifice, ostium)
Introjektion f introjection
Intromission f intromission
Introspektion f introspection
introspektiv introspective
introvertieren to introvert
introvertiert introvert *(Persönlichkeit)*; introverted, introversive, invaginated *(z. B. Gebärmutter)*
Introvertierter m introvert
intrudieren to intrude, to move apically *(einen Zahn)*

Intrusion

Intrusion *f* intrusion
Intubation *f* intubation, tubage, laryngeal catheterization *(z. B. in die Luftröhre)*
~/endotracheale endotracheal intubation
~/tracheale tracheal intubation
Intubationsinstrument *n* intubator
Intubationsnarkose *f* endotracheal anaesthesia
Intubationstubus *m* intubation tube
Intubationszange *f* endotracheal tube introducing forceps
Intubator *m* intubator
intubieren to intubate *(in die Luftröhre)*
Intubierender *m* intubationist
Intuition *f* intuition, intuitiveness ● **auf ~ beruhend** *s.* **intuitiv**
intuitiv intuitional, intuitive
Intumescentia *f* intumescence, intumescentia, swelling, enlargement
~ cervicalis cervical intumescence (enlargement)
~ lumbalis lumbar intumescence (enlargement)
~ nodorum lymphaticorum lymphadenectasis
intumeszent intumescent
Intumeszenz *f s.* **Intumescentia**
Inturgeszenz *f* inturgescence
Intussuszeption *f* intussusception, introsusception, invagination, indigitation
Intussuszeptum *n* intussusceptum
Intussuszipiens *n* intussuscipiens
Inulase *f* inulase, inulinase *(Enzym)*
Inulin *n* inulin
Inulin-Clearance *f* inulin clearance
Inulinraum *m* inulin space
Inunktion *f* 1. inunction, anointing; 2. ointment
Invaginat *n* intussusceptum
Invaginatausstreichung *f* milking back of intussusceptum
Invaginatausstülpung *f* disinvagination
Invagination *f* invagination, intussusception, introsusception, indigitation
Invaginationsvakuole *f* invagination vacuole
invaginieren to invaginate, to intussuscept
invalid[e] invalid, disabled, valetudinarian *(z. B. durch Krankheit)*
Invalide *m* invalid, valetudinarian
Invalidität *f* invalidity, invalidism, valetudinarianism
Invasion *f* invasion *(z. B. von Krankheitserregern)*
Invasionsfähigkeit *f* invasiveness
invasiv invasive
Invasivität *f* invasiveness
invers inverse
Inversio *f* inversion, reversion
~ uteri uterus inversion, inversion of the uterus
~ vaginae vaginal inversion, inversion of the vagina
Inversion *f s.* **Inversio**
Inversionsfraktur *f* inversion fracture
~ des Sprunggelenks reversed Pott's fracture
Inversionshoden *m* inverted testis
Invertase *f* invertase, invertin, saccharase, sucrase *(Enzym)*

invertieren to invert, to turn inside out; to turn outside in; to turn upside down; to reverse in position (relationship); to subject to inversion
Invertin *n s.* **Invertase**
Invertose *f*, **Invertzucker** *m* invertose, invert sugar
inveteriert inveterate, long established; recurrent, chronic, resisting treatment *(z. B. eine Entzündung)*; long-lasting, persistent *(z. B. Krankenhausgeruch)*
In-vitro-Befruchtung *f* in-vitro fertilization
In-vitro-Test *m* in-vitro test
In-vitro-Untersuchung *f* in-vitro study
Involukrum *n* involucre, involucrum *(bei Osteomyelitis)*
involuntär involuntary, unintentional; independent
Involution *f* involution, devolution *(z. B. eines Organs)*
~/senile senile involution
involutionierend involutional
Involutionsarteriosklerose *f* involutional (disuse) arteriosclerosis
Involutionsatrophie *f* involutional (disuse, inactivity) atrophy
Involutionsdepression *f* involutional depression, involution melancholia
Involutionsentropion *n* involutional entropion
Involutionsform *f* involution form *(z. B. bei Mikroorganismen)*
Involutionsosteoporose *f* involutional (disuse, inactivity) osteoporosis
~/präsenile presenile involutional osteoporosis
Involutionsparaphrenie *f* involutional paraphrenia (paranoid state)
Involutionsperiode *f* involutional period
Involutionspsychose *f* involutional psychosis *(des alternden Menschen)*
Involutionszyste *f* involutional cyst
Inzest *m* incest
Inzidenzrate *f* incidence rate *(z. B. einer Krankheit)*
inzidieren to incise, to cut [into], to lance
inzidierend incisional
Inzision *f* incision, cut
~ der kleinen Schamlippen nymphotomy
~/schräge oblique incision
Inzisionsschere *f* incision scissors
inzisiv incisive
Inzisiv *m s.* **Schneidezahn**
inzisolabial incisolabial
inzisolingual incisolingual
Inzisur *f s.* **Incisura**
Inzucht *f* in[ter]marriage, inbreeding, endogamy; incest
Inzyklophorie *f* incyclophoria
Inzyklotropie *f* incyclotropia
Iodoform *n s.* **Jodoform**
Iodopsin *n s.* **Jodopsin**
Ionenaustausch *m* ion exchange
Ionenaustauschchromatographie *f* ion-exchange chromatography

Ionenaustauscher *m* ion exchanger
Ionenaustauscherharz *n* ion-exchange resin
ionenbildend ionogenic
Ionenmesser *m* ionometer *(für Strahlenbelastung)*
Ionenmessung *f* ionometry
Ionenpumpe *f* ionic pump
Ionenstärke *f* ionic strength
Ionenzähler *m* ionometer *(Strahlenbelastungsmessung)*
Ionenzählung *f* ionometry
Ionisationsdosimeter *n* ionization dosimeter
Ionisationskammer *f* ionization chamber *(Ionenzählrohr)*
Ionisationspotential *n* ionization potential
ionogen ionogenic
Ionometer *n* ionometer
Ionometrie *f* ionometry *(Strahlenbelastungsmessung)*
Iontophorese *f* iontophoresis, ionotherapy *(Medikamenteneinführung in den menschlichen Körper mittels elektrischer Ströme)*
Iontophoreseanästhesie *f* iontophoretic anaesthesia
Iontophoresezeit *f* iontophoresis time
Iophobie *f* iophobia *(krankhafte Angst vor Giften)*
Ipekakuanha *f* ipecac[uanha] *(Bronchialsekretolytikum)*
IPPB *s.* Überdruckbeatmung/intermittierende
Ipsation *f s.* Masturbation
IQ *s.* Intelligenzquotient
Iridalgie *f* ir[id]algia, pain in the iris
Iridauxesis *f* iridauxesis, thickening of the iris
Iridektom *n* iridectome
Iridektomie *f* iridectomy, corectomy ● **eine ~ ausführen** to iridectomize
iridektomieren to iridectomize
Iridektomieschere *f* iridectomy (iris) scissors
Iridenkleisis *f* iridencleisis, iris inclusion [operation] *(zur Behandlung des grünen Stars)*
Irideremie *f* irideremia, aniridia, congenital absence of the iris
Iridesis *f* iri[do]desis, forming of a new pupil
Iridoavulsion *f* irido-avulsion, avulsion of the iris
Iridochorioiditis *f* iridochorioiditis *(Entzündung der Regenbogen- und Aderhaut)*
Iridodialysis *f* 1. iridodialysis, loosening (separation) of the iris from its attachment; 2. iridodialysis, splitting (division) of the iris; 3. iridodialysis, separation of the iris from the ciliary body
Iridodiastase *f* iridodiastasis, marginal defect of the iris
Iridodonesis *f* iridodonesis, hippus, pupil unrest; tremulous iris
Iridokapsulitis *f* iridocapsulitis, inflammation of the iris and the lens capsule
Iridokapsulotomie *f* iridocapsulotomy
Iridokeratitis *f* iridokeratitis, keratoiritis, inflammation of the iris and the cornea
Iridokinese *f* iridokinesia, contraction and expansion of the iris
iridokinetisch iridokinetic

Iridokolobom *n* iridocoloboma, iris coloboma, congenital fissure of the iris
Iridokornealwinkel *m* iridocorneal (filtration) angle
Iridokorneosklerektomie *f* iridocorneosclerectomy *(bei Glaukom)*
Iridomalazie *f* iridomalacia, softening of the iris
Iridonkosis *f* iridoncosis, thickening of the iris
Iridonkus *m* iridoncus, tumour (swelling) of the iris
Iridoparalysis *f* iridoparalysis, iridoplegia, paralysis of the sphincter of the pupil; rigidity of the pupil
Iridopathie *f* iridopathy, disease of the iris
Iridoplegie *f s.* Iridoparalysis
Iridoptosis *f s.* Irisprolaps
iridopupillär iridopupillary
Iridorrhexis *f* iridorrhexis, rupture of the iris
Iridoschisis *f* iridoschisis, iridoschisma, coloboma of the iris
Iridosklerosis *f* iridosclerosis
Iridosklerotomie *f* iridosclerotomy *(bei Glaukom)*
Iridoskop *n* iridoscope
Iridoskopie *f* iridoscopy
Iridosteresis *f* iridosteresis, irideraemia, congenital absence of the iris
Iridotasis *f s.* Irisstreckung
Iridotom *n* iridotome
Iridotomie *f* iri[do]tomy, irotomy
Iridozele *f* iridocele *(durch eine Augenwunde)*
Iridozyklektomie *f* iridocyclectomy
Iridozyklitis *f* iridocyclitis, inflammation of the iris and the ciliary body
Iridozyklochorioiditis *f* iridocyclochorioiditis
Iris *f* 1. iris; 2. *s.* Irisblende ● **die ~ herausschneiden** to iridectomize
~ bombé iris bombé, umbrella iris
~/fehlende aniridia
~/pupillenlose acorea
~ tremulans tremulous iris; hippus, iridodonesis
Iris... *s. a.* Regenbogenhaut...
Irisabreißung *f* irido-avulsion, avulsion of the iris
Irisangiographie *f* iris angiography
Irisanomalie *f* iris anomaly
Irisatrophie *f* iris atrophy
Irisbefestigung *f* iri[do]desis
Irisblende *f* iris diaphragm *(Mikroskopie)*
Irisdiastase *f s.* Iridodiastase
Irisdilatator *m* iridodilator
Iriseinschneidung *f* iri[do]tomy, irotomy
Irisektropium *n* iridectropium, eversion of the iris
Irisentfernung *f[/operative]* iridectomy
Irisentropium *n* iridentropium, inversion of the iris
Irisexairese *f* iridavulsion
Irisfixation *f* iri[do]desis
Irisgefäßendothel *n* iridial vascular endothelium
Irishämorrhagie *f* iridaemia
Irisinkarzeration *f* iris incarceration
Irisinversion *f* iridentropium, inversion of the iris
Iriskonstriktor *m* iridoconstrictor

Iriskontraktionsreflex 368

Iriskontraktionsreflex *m* iris contraction reflex *(Pupillenverengung auf Licht)*
Iris-Kornea-Sklera-Fensterungsoperation *f* iridocorneosclerectomy *(bei Glaukom)*
Iriskrankheit *f* iridopathy, disease of the iris
Iriskrause *f* iris frill
Iriskrypte *f* iris crypt
Irislinsendiaphragma *n* iris lens diaphragm
Irismuskulaturlähmung *f s.* Iridoparalysis
Irispigment *n* iris pigment
Irispigmentation *f* iris pigmentation
Irispigmentschicht *f* iris pigmented layer
Irispinzette *f* iris forceps
Irisprolaps *m* prolapse of the iris, iridoptosis; iris hernia, iridocele
Irisrepositorium *n* iris repositor
Irisretraktion *f* iris retraction
Irisretraktor *m* iris retractor
Irisrückseite *f* posterior surface of the iris
Irisruptur *f* rupture of the iris, iridorrhexis
Irisschenkel *m* pillar of the iris
Irisschlottern *n* iridodonesis, hippus; tremulous iris
Irisschmerz *m* ir[id]algia, pain in the iris
Irisskalpell *n* iridotome
Irisspalte *f* iridoschisis, iridoschisma
~/angeborene iridocoloboma, congenital coloboma of the iris
Irisspiegel *m* iridoscope
Irisspiegelung *f* iridoscopy
Irisstreckung *f* stretching of the iris, iridotasis, iris inclusion [operation]
Irissynechie *f* iris synechia
Iristeilexzision *f* iritoectomy
Iristransillumination *f* iris transillumination
Iris- und Sklerapunktion *f* iridosclerotomy *(bei Glaukom)*
Irisverwachsung *f/ringförmige* seclusion of the pupil
Irisvorderseite *f* anterior surface of the iris
Iriszittern *n* pupillary athetosis, hippus; pupil unrest
Iritis *f* iritis, inflammation of the iris
Irradiation *f* irradiation
irre *s.* irrsinnig
irreponibel irreducible *(z. B. Bruch)*
Irrer *m* insane person, madman, lunatic; psychopath
~/manisch-depressiv cyclothyme, cyclothymi[a]c
Irresein *n* insanity, mental derangement; dementia
~/induziertes induced (communicated) insanity
~/manisch-depressives manic-depressive illness (psychosis, reaction), intermittent (recurrent, cyclic) insanity, circular dementia, cyclothymia, cyclophrenia *(Psychose)*
~/periodisches periodic insanity (mania)
irreversibel irreversible, non-reversible
Irrigation *f* irrigation
Irrigator *m* irrigator
irritabel irritable; excitable
Irritabilität *f* irritability; excitability

Irritation *f* irritation; excitation
Irrsinn *m* insanity, mental derangement; dementia
irrsinnig insane, mentally deranged; dement; delirious
Ischämie *f* ischaemia
ischämisch ischaemic
Ischiagra *f* ischiagra, gout of the hip joint
Ischialgie *f* ischialgia, ischiodynia, ischioneuralgia, sciatica, sciatic neuralgia (neuritis)
ischialgisch ischialgic
Ischias *f s.* Ischialgie
Ischiasnerv *m* sciatic nerve
ischiatisch ischiadic, ischial, ischiatic, sciatic
Ischidrosis *f* ischidrosis
Ischiektomie *f* ischiectomy
ischiofemoral ischiofemoral
ischiokavernös ischiocavernous
ischiokokzygeal ischiococcygeal
Ischiomyelitis *f* ischiomyelitis, lumbar myelitis
Ischiopagie *f* ischiopagia
Ischiopagus *m* ischiopagus, ischiodidymus *(Mißgeburt)*
Ischiopubikum *n* ischiopubis
Ischiopubiotomie *f* ischiopubiotomy *(zur Erweiterung des engen Beckens unter der Geburt)*
ischiopubisch ischiopubic
Ischiorektalabszeß *m* ischiorectal abscess
Ischiorektalfaszie *f* ischiorectal fascia
Ischiorektalgrube *f* ischiorectal fossa *(Raum zwischen Diaphragma pelvis und Fascia obturatoria)*
Ischiorektalhernie *f* ischiorectal hernia
Ischiorektalregion *f* ischiorectal region
ischiosakral ischiosacral, sacrosciatic
ischiovertebral ischiovertebral
Ischium *n* ischium, os ischii
Ischocholie *f* ischocholia
Ischogalaktie *f* ischogalactia
Ischomenie *f* ischomenia
ischuretisch ischuretic
Ischuria *f* ischuria
Islandkrankheit *f* Iceland disease, benign myalgic encephalomyelitis
Isoagglutination *f* iso[haemo]agglutination
Isoagglutinin *n* iso[haem]agglutinin *(gegen artgleiche Erythrozyten gerichteter Antikörper)*
Isoagglutinogen *n* iso-agglutinogen
Isoajmalin *n* isoajmaline *(Alkaloid)*
Isoalloxazin *n* isoalloxazine *(Bestandteil des Vitamins B_2)*
Isoamylalkohol *m* isoamyl alcohol
Isoantigen *n* iso-antigen
Isoantikörper *m* iso-antibody *(im Blut)*
isochrom[atisch] isochromatic
isochromatophil isochromatophil[e]
Isochromosom *n* isochromosome
isochron isochronal, isochronous
Isodaktylismus *m* isodactylism
Isodosenkurve *f* isodose curve
Isodosis *f* isodose *(Strahlentherapie)*
isodynam isodynamic *(gleiche Energiemengen liefernd)*

Isodynamie f isodynamia
Isodynamiegesetz n isodynamic law
Isoenzym n iso[en]zyme
Isoenzymmuster n isoenzyme pattern
isogam isogamous, isogamic
Isogamet m isogamete
Isogamie f isogamy
Isogenese f isogenesis
isognath isognathous *(Gebiß)*
Isohämagglutination f s. Isoagglutination
Isohäm[o]agglutinin n s. Isoagglutinin
Isohämolyse f isohaemolysis
Isohämolysin n iso[haemo]lysin *(gegen artgleiche Erythrozyten gerichteter blutauflösender Stoff)*
Isohydrie f isohydria, water equilibrium
Isoikonie f isoiconia
Isoimmunisierung f isoimmunization
Isokomplement n isocomplement
Isokorie f isocoria
Isokortex m isocortex *(Teil der Großhirnrinde mit Sechsschichtenfolge der Zellarchitektur)*
Isolaktose f isolactose
Isolation f s. Isolierung
Isoleuzin n isoleucine *(essentielle Aminosäure)*
isolieren to isolate, to sequester; to quarantine
Isolierstation f isolation ward
isoliert werden/im Laboratorium to be isolated in the laboratory
Isolierung f isolation, sequestration; quarantine
isolog isologous, syngeneic, syngenesious
Isomerase f isomerase *(Enzym)*
isometrisch isometric
isometrop isometropic
Isometroper m isometrope
Isometropie f isometropia
isomorph isomorphic, isomorphous
Isomorphie f isomorphism *(z. B. von Zellen im normalen Blut)*
Isoniazid n, **Isonikotinsäurehydrazid** n isoniazid, isonicotinic acid hydrazide *(Tuberkulostatikum)*
Isonormoleukozytose f isonormocytosis
isoosmotisch iso-osmotic
isoperistaltisch isoperistaltic
isophän isophenous, isophenic
Isophorie f isophoria
Isopie f isopia
Isopräzipitin n isoprecipitin *(gegen artgleiches Serum gerichteter, Ausflockung bewirkender Antikörper)*
Isoprenalin n isoproterenol, isoprenaline, isopropylarterenol *(Broncholytikum)*
Isopropanol n 2-propanol, isopropyl alcohol *(Desinfektionsmittel)*
Isopteren fpl isopters
Isoserotherapie f isoserotherapy
Isoserum n isoserum
Isoserumbehandlung f isoserotherapy
Isospora f **hominis** Isospora hominis *(eine Darmerkrankung hervorrufende Kokzidienart)*
Isosporabefall m isosporosis
Isosthenurie f isosthenuria *(mangelnde Konzentrations- und Verdünnungsfähigkeit der Nieren)*
isosthenurisch isosthenuric
Isotonie f isotonia, isotonicity
isotonisch 1. isotonic *(z. B. Blutdruck)*; 2. iso-osmotic
Isotop n/**radioaktives** radioactive isotope, radioisotope
Isotopenabtastung f radioisotope scanning
Isotopenangiogramm n radionuclide angiocardiogram
Isotopenangiographie f radionuclide angiography
Isotopenaufnahme f, **Isotopenbild** n radioisotope scan
Isotopendarstellung f radioisotope scanning
Isotopenindikator m isotopic tracer (indicator)
Isotopenkamera f radioisotope camera
isotopenmarkiert radioisotope-labelled, radiolabelled, isotopically labelled
Isotopenmarkierung f isotopic labelling
Isotopennephrogramm n radioisotope renogram, radioactive renal scintiscan
Isotopennephrographie f radioisotope (isotopic, radionuclide) renography
Isotopentechnik f radioisotope technique
Isotopentest m radionuclide test
Isotopentracer m isotopic tracer (indicator)
Isotopenzisternographie f isotope cisternography
Isotransplantat n isotransplant, isograft
Isotransplantation f isotransplantation
isotrop isotropic *(Muskelfasern)*
Isotropie f isotropy
Isovolämie f isovolaemia
isovolumetrisch isovolumetric
Isozitratdehydrogenase f isocitric acid dehydrogenase *(Enzym)*
Isozitronensäure f isocitric acid
Isozytolysin n isocytolysin
Isozytotoxin n isocytotoxin
Isthmektomie f isthmectomy, excision of an isthmus
Isthmitis f isthmits, inflammation of the isthmus of the fauces
Isthmus m isthmus ● **durch den ~** transisthmian
~ **aortae** aortic isthmus, isthmus of aorta
~ **faucium** isthmus of the fauces *(Übergang von der Mund- zur Rachenhöhle)*
~ **glandulae thyroideae** isthmus of the thyroid gland *(Verbindungsstück der beiden Schilddrüsenlappen)*
~ **gyri cinguli (fornicati)** isthmus of the cingulate gyrus, isthmus of the limbic lobe, isthmus of gyrus fornicatus
~ **hippocampi** s. ~ gyri cinguli
~ **tubae auditivae** isthmus of auditory (Eustachian) tube *(Grenze von knöchernem und knorpeligem Teil der Ohrtrompete)*
~ **tubae uterinae** isthmus of the uterine tube, isthmus of Fallopian tube
~ **uteri** uterine isthmus, isthmus of the uterus *(zwischen Körper und Hals)*

Isthmusendometrium n isthmic endometrium
Isthmusentfernung f[/operative] isthmectomy, excision of an isthmus
Isurie f isuria
Iteration f iteration, repetition [of movements]
Ithylordose f ithylordosis
ITS s. Intensivstation
IUD s. Intrauterinpessar
i. v. intravenous, I. V., i. v.
i. v.-Cholangiogramm n intravenous cholangiogram
i. v.-Cholangiographie f intravenous cholangiography
Ivemark-Syndrom n Ivemark's syndrome *(multipler Organfehlbildungen)*
Ixodiasis f ixodiasis, ixodism *(Befall durch Ixodesarten)*
ixodisch ixodic

J

J s. Joule
Jaccoud-Arthritis f Jaccoud's arthritis, chronic postrheumatic fever arthritis
Jacket-Krone f jacket crown *(für zerstörte Frontzähne)*
Jackson-Anfall m Jacksonian seizure (convulsion), Jacksonian epileptic fit (attack)
Jackson-Epilepsie f Jacksonian epilepsy
Jacod-Syndrom n Jacod's syndrome (triad)
Jacquet-Erythem n Jacquet's erythema, diaper rash
Jactatio f capitis jac[ti]tation
Jadassohn-Krankheit f 1. Jadassohn's disease, anetoderma; 2. Jadassohn's disease, granulosis rubra nasi; 3. Jadassohn's disease, pityriasis rubra
Jaffé-Lichtenstein-Syndrom n Jaffé-Lichtenstein disease (syndrome)
Jahresbeule f cutaneous leishmaniasis [of the Old World], oriental (Delhi) boil, Kandahore (China) sore
5-Jahresheilungsrate f five-year survival rate
Jähzorn m irascibility
jähzornig irascible, hot-tempered; choleric
Jakob-Creutzfeld-Syndrom n Creutzfeld-Jakob disease (syndrome), spastic pseudosclerosis
Jaktation f jac[ti]tation
Janizeps m janiceps *(symmetrische Doppelmißbildung mit Verschmelzung der Köpfe)*
Jansen-Syndrom n Jansen's syndrome, metaphyseal dysostosis
Januskopf m s. Janizeps
Japan-B-Enzephalitis f Japanese B encephalitis
Japan-B-Enzephalitis-Vakzine f Japan B encephalitis vaccine
Japan-B-Enzephalitis-Virus n Japanese B encephalitis virus *(Arbovirus)*
Japan-B-Enzephalomyelitis f Japan B encephalomyelitis
Jargonaphasie f jargon aphasia

jauchig ichorous, ichoroid
Jeddah-Ulkus n Jeddah ulcer
Jeep-Krankheit f s. Pilonidalkrankheit
Jeghers-Peutz-Syndrom n s. Peutz-Jeghers-Syndrom
Jejunalarterie f jejunal artery
Jejunalatresie f jejunal atresia
Jejunaldivertikel n jejunal diverticulum
Jejunalulkus n jejunal ulcer
Jejunalvene f jejunal vein
Jejunektomie f jejunectomy, removal (excision) of the jejunum
Jejunitis f jejunitis, inflammation of the jejunum
jejunogastral jejunogastric
jejunoileal jejuno-ileal
Jejunoileitis f jejuno-ileitis
Jejunoileostomie f jejuno-ileostomy
Jejunoileum n jejuno-ileum
Jejunojejunostomie f jejunojejunostomy
Jejunokolostomie f jejunocolostomy
Jejunoplastik f jejunoplasty
Jejunorrhaphie f jejunorrhaphy
Jejunostomie f s. 1. Jejunumfistelung/operative; 2. Jejunumfistel
Jejunotomie f jejunotomy, incision into the jejunum
Jejunozökostomie f jejunocaecostomy
Jejunum n jejunum
Jejunum... s. a. Leerdarm...
Jejunumepithel n jejunal epithelium
Jejunumfistel f jejunostomy
Jejunumfistelung f[/operative] jejunostomy
Jejunum-Ileum-Anastomose f jejuno-ileostomy
Jejunum-Ileum-Mesenterium n jejuno-ileal mesentery
Jejunum-Ileum-Verbindung f[/operative] jejuno-ileostomy
Jejunum-Jejunum-Anastomose f jejunojejunostomy
Jejunum-Kolon-Anastomose f jejunocolostomy
Jejunummesenterium n jejunal mesentery, mesojejunum
Jejunumnaht f jejunorrhaphy; suturing of the jejunum
Jejunumplastik f jejunoplasty
Jejunumresektion f s. Jejunektomie
Jejunumschlinge f loop of jejunum
Jejunum- und Ileumentzündung f jejuno-ileitis
Jejunum-Zökum-Anastomose f jejunocaecostomy
Jenaer Nomenklatur f Jena Nomina Anatomica, JNA
Jendrassik-Handgriff m Jendrassik's manoeuvre
Jensen-Retinopathie f Jensen's retinopathy (disease), juxtapapillary choroiditis
Jensen-Sarkom n Jensen's sarcoma (tumour) *(transplantierbares Sarkom)*
Jerichobeule f Jerico boil
Jervell-Lange-Nielson-Syndrom n Jervell and Lange-Nielson's syndrome, cardioauditory syndrome
Jet-Injektion f jet injection

Jet-Injektor *m* jet injector
JNA *s.* Jenaer Nomenklatur
Joch *n s.* Jugum
Jochbein*n* zygomatic bone, zygoma, cheekbone, yoke-bone, malar
Jochbein-Augenhöhlen-Arterie *f* zygomatic artery
Jochbeinentzündung *f* zygomatitis, inflammation of the zygomatic bone
Jochbeinfraktur *f* zygomatic fracture
Jochbeinmuskel *m* zygomatic muscle, zygomaticus [muscle]
~/**großer** major zygomatic muscle
~/**kleiner** minor zygomatic muscle
Jochbein-Oberkiefer-Naht *f* zygomaticomaxillary suture
Jochbeinregion *f* zygomatic region
Jochbein-Stirnbein-Naht *f* zygomaticofrontal suture
Jochbogen *m* zygomatic arch, inferior temporal arcade ● **durch den ~** transzygomatic
Jochpilze *mpl* zygomycetes
Jochpilzspore *f* zygospore
Jod *n* iodine
~/**proteingebundenes** protein bound iodine, PBI
~/**radioaktives** radioiodine, iodine-131, radioactive iodine
Jodaffinität *f* iodophilia *(der weißen Blutkörperchen)*
Jodakne *f* iodine acne
Jodausschlag *m* iodine acne
Jodbasedow *m* jodbasedow
Jodbehandlung *f* iodotherapy
~/**Plummersche** Plummer's treatment *(Vorbehandlung bei Strumaoperationen)*
Jodbestimmung *f*/**quantitative** *s.* Jodometrie
Jodempfindlichkeit *f* iodine sensibility
jodfärbbar iodophil, iodinophil[e]
Jodfärbbarkeit *f* iodophilia
jodieren to iodinate, to iodize, to treat with iodine (iodide)
Jodierung *f* iodination
Jodisationsdefekt *m* iodization defect
Jodismus *m s.* Jodvergiftung
Jod-Jodkalium-Lösung *f* iodine-potassium iodide solution
Jodlösung *f* iodine solution
~/**alkoholische** iodine tincture
~/**antiseptische** iodine antiseptic solution
Jodmangel *m* iodine deficiency
Jodmangelkretinismus *m* endemic cretinism
Jodmangelkropf *m* endemic (iodine deficiency) goitre
Jododerm *n* iododerma *(flache Knotenbildung an den Gliedern nach langem Jodgebrauch)*
Jodoform *n* iodoform, tri-iodomethane *(Wundantiseptikum)*
jodoformieren to iodoformize
Jodoformvergiftung *f* iodoformism
Jodometrie *f* iodometry, iodimetry
jodometrisch iodometric, iodimetric
jodophil iodophil, iodinophil[e]

Jodophilie *f* iodophilia
Jodopsin *n* iodopsin, visual violet *(Sehpigment der Netzhautzapfenzellen)*
Jodothyreoglobulin *n* iodothyroglobulin
Jodpemphigus *m* iodine pemphigus
Jodpinzette *f* iodine forceps
Jodprobe *f* 1. iodine test *(z. B. für Gallenfarbstoffe)*; 2. *s.* Jodstärkeprobe
~/**Schillersche** iodine (Schiller's) test *(zur Frühdiagnostik von Muttermundkrebs)*
Jodprophylaxe *f* iodine prophylaxis
Jodsensibilität *f* iodine sensibility
Jodstärkeprobe *f*, **Jodstärkereaktion** *f* iodine test for starch
Jodtinktur *f* iodine tincture, tincture of iodine
Jodvergiftung *f* iodism, iodine poisoning (intoxication)
Johnin *n* johnin, paratuberculin
Jolly-Ermüdungsreaktion *f* Jolly's reaction *(bei Muskelerkrankung)*
Jolly-Körper *mpl* Jolly bodies *(Kernzerfallsreste der Erythrozyten)*
Jones-Kriterien *npl* Jones criteria *(Rheuma)*
Joule *n* joule *(SI-Einheit für Arbeit, Energie und Wärmemenge)*
Juckempfindung *f*, **Jucken** *n* itching, pruritus *(Zusammensetzungen s. unter Pruritus)*
juckend itching, pruriginous; urticant
Juckreiz *m* itching, pruritus
juckreizauslösend pruritic, pruriginous; urticant
juckreizlindernd, juckreizstillend antipruritic, antipruriginous
Jugenddiabetes *m* juvenile-onset (early-onset) diabetes
Jugendirresein *n* hebephrenia, hebephrenic insanity *(Schizophrenieform)*
jugendlich juvenile
Jugendpsychiatrie *f* juvenile psychiatry
Jugendpsychologie *f* juvenile psychology
Jugendsexualität *f* juvenile sexuality
Jugendzahnarzt *m* paedodontist
Jugendzahnpflege *f* paedodontia, paedodontology, paedodontics
Jugofrontalindex *m* jugofrontal index
Jugomandibularindex *m* jugomandibular index
jugomaxillär jugomaxillary
Jugularkompression *f* jugular compression
Jugularvenendruck *m* jugular venous pressure
Jugularvenenpuls *m* jugular [venous] pulse
Jugulum *n* jugulum
Jugum *n* jugum, yoke, bridge
Junctura *f* junction, junctura
~ **cartilaginea** synchondrosis, cartilaginous joint (symphysis)
~ **fibrosa** syndesmosis, fibrous joint
~ **lumbosacralis** lumbosacral articulation (joint, junction)
~ **ossium** joint, articulation *(Zusammensetzungen s. unter Gelenk)*
~ **sacrococcygea** sacrococcygeal joint (junctura, symphysis)
~ **synovialis** synovial joint

Jungfernhäutchen 372

Jungfernhäutchen *n* hymen, maidenhead *(Zusammensetzungen s. unter* Hymen*)*
Jungfrau *f* virgin
jungfräulich virginal, maiden
Jungfräulichkeit *f* virginity, maidenhood
Jünglingsalter *n* adolescence
Junius-Kuhnt-Krankheit *f* Junius-Kuhnt disease, disciform macular degeneration
juvenil juvenile, young; immature
Juvenilenstruma *f* juvenile goitre
juxtaartikulär juxta-articular
juxtaglomerulär juxtaglomerular
juxtapapillär juxtapapillary
juxtaponieren to juxtapose
Juxtaposition *f* juxtaposition *(z. B. bei Steinbildung)*

K

Kabeltransplantat *n* cable graft
Kabure *n* kabure [itch] *(Hauterkrankung durch Schistosoma japonicum)*
kachektisch cachectic
Kachexie *f* cachexia *(s. a. unter* Cachexia*)*
~/hypophysäre (hypophyseoprive) *s.* ~/Simmondsche
~/ovariprive ovariprival cachexia
~/Simmondsche Simmond's cachexia (disease), hypophyseal cachexia, [hypo]pituitary cachexia
~/suprarenale suprarenal cachexia, Addison's disease
~/thymoprive thymoprival cachexia
~/thyreoprive thyreoprival cachexia
~/tuberkulöse tuberculous cachexia
Kachexieaphthen *fpl* cachectic (Bednar's) aphthae
Kachexieödem *n* cachectic oedema
Kadaverin *n* cadaverine *(Leichengift)*
Kadaverniere *f* cadaver kidney
Kadaverreaktion *f* cadaveric reaction *(der Muskeln)*
Kadavertransplantat *n* cadaver transplant, cadaveric graft
Kader-Fistel *f* Kader's (Kader-Senn) operation
kaffeesatzartig coffee-ground-like
Kaffeesatzerbrechen *n* melanemesis, black vomit[ing], coffee-ground vomiting
Kaffeesucht *f* coffee addiction (habituation)
Kaffein *n* caffeine, coffeine *(Alkaloid)*
Kagaminestsu-Fieber *n* Kagaminestsu fever
kahl bald[-headed], glabrous
Kahlheit *f* baldness, alopecia, calvities, acomia
~/angeborene congenital alopecia (baldness)
kahlköpfig bald[-headed], glabrous
kahlmachend decalvant
Kahnbauch *m* scaphoid (boat-shaped) abdomen, navicular (carinate, carinal) abdomen *(eingezogener Bauch bei Gehirnhautentzündung)*
Kahnbein *n* scaphoid [bone], navicular bone *(1. Handwurzelknochen; 2. Fußwurzelknochen)*
Kahnbeinbruch *m* scaphoid fracture

~ der Hand carpal scaphoid fracture
Kahnbeinentzündung *f* scaphoiditis, osteochondrosis of the navicular bone
Kahnbein-Mondbein-Gelenk *n* scaphoid-lunate articulation
Kahnbeinnekrose *f* des Fußes/aseptische Köhler's disease (tarsal scaphoiditis), epiphysitis of the tarsal scaphoid
Kahnbein-Trapezium-Gelenk *n* scaphoid-trapezium joint
Kahn-Flockungsreaktion *f* Kahn [flocculation] test *(Serumprobe auf Syphilis)*
kahnförmig scaphoid, navicular
Kahngesicht *n* scaphoid face
Kahnschädel *m* scaphocephalus, cymbocephalus
kahnschädelig scaphocephalous, scaphocephalic
Kahnschäd[e]ligkeit *f* scaphocephalia, cymbocephaly
Kahn-Test *m s.* Kahn-Flockungsreaktion
Kahnthorax *m* scaphoid thorax
Kainophobie *f* kainophobia *(krankhafte Angst vor dem Neuen)*
Kaiserschnitt *m* caesarean section, caesarotomy; abdominal delivery, delivery by caesarean section; laparohysterotomy, hysterolaparotomy ● **durch ~ entbunden werden** to be delivered by caesarian section ● **einen ~ durchführen** to do (perform) a caesarian section ● **einen ~ haben** to have a caesarian section
~/unterer zervikaler low cervical caesarean section, laparotrachelotomy
Kaiserschnittentbindung *f* delivery by caesarean section, abdominal delivery
Kakke *f s.* Polyneuritis/endemische
Kakogeusie *f* cacogeusia, bad taste
Kakorraphiophobie *f* kakorraphiophobia *(krankhafte Angst vor Fehlern)*
Kakosmie *f* cacosmia, bad odour
Kakostomie *f* cacostomia
Kala-Azar *f* kala-azar, febrile tropical splenomegaly, Burdwan fever *(tropische Infektionskrankheit durch Leishmania donovani)*
Kalabarbeule *f* Calabar boil
Kalabarbohne *f* Calabar bean, physostigma
Kalabarödem *n s.* Kalabarschwellung
Kalabarschwellung *f* Calabar swelling *(bei Loa-loa-Infektion)*
Kaliämie *f* kalaemia
Kaliektasis *f* caliectasis
Kalifornia-Virus *n s.* California-encephalitis-Virus
Kalikopapillitis *f* calycopapillitis
Kalischer-Krankheit *f* Kalischer's disease, naevoid amentia, Sturge-Weber disease
Kaliumausscheidung *f* kaliuresis
Kaliumeinschränkung *f* potassium restriction
Kaliumjodid *n* potassium iodide
Kaliummangel *m* potassium depletion
Kaliumrestriktion *f* potassium restriction
Kaliumspiegel *m* potassium level

Kaliumspiegelerhöhung f **im Blut** hyperkalaemia, hyperpotassaemia
Kaliumspiegelverminderung f **im Blut** hypokalaemia hypopotassaemia
Kaliumverarmung f potassium depletion
Kaliumvergiftung f potassium intoxication
Kalkablagerung f 1. calcareous (calcium) deposit *(z. B. im Gewebe)*; 2. s. Kalkeinlagerung
~ **im Knorpel** chondrocalcinosis, pseudogout
kalkaneal calcaneal, calcanean
Kalkaneodynie f calcan[e]odynia, pain in the heel
kalkaneonavikulär calcaneonavicular, calcaneoscaphoid
Kalkaneus m s. Fersenbein
Kalkariurie f calcariuria
kalkarm calcipenic, deficient in calcium
Kalkarmut f s. Kalkmangel
kalkbindend calcipexic, calcipectic, fixing calcium
Kalkeinlagerung f calcification, calcium deposition, calcareous infiltration (degeneration) *(z. B. in das Gewebe)*
~/**erhöhte** hypercalcification
~/**verminderte** hypocalcification
Kalkgicht f calcium gout, [interstitial] calcinosis, hypodermatolithiasis
kalkhaltig calciferous, calcareous, calcigerous
Kalkmangel m calcipenia, calcium deficiency, hypocalcia; acalcinosis
Kalkniere f cement (calcified) kidney
Kalkosphärit m calcosphaerite *(Protein-Kalzium-Komplex im Gewebe)*
Kalkpräparat n calcium (chalk) preparation
Kalksalzablagerung f incrustation, calcification *(s. a. Kalkeinlagerung)*
kalksalzhaltig calciferous
Kalksalzverlust m **der Knochen** halisteresis
kalkspeichernd calcipexic, calcipectic
Kalkstaublunge[nerkrankung] f calcicosis, chalicosis, flint disease
Kalkstoffwechsel m calcium metabolism
Kalkulose f s. Steinleiden
Kalkverlust m calciprivia; halisteresis *(z. B. von Knochen)*
Kalkzylinder m calcified cast *(z. B. in Harnkanälchen)*
Kallidin n kallidin *(Dekapeptid)*
Kallidinogen n kallidinogen *(Vorstufe von Kallidin)*
Kallikrein n kallikrein *(Enzym)*
Kallikrein-Kinin-System n kallikrein-kinin system
kallös callous, callus-like
Kallus m callus
~/**bleibender** permanent callus
~/**definitiver** definitive callus
Kallusbildung f callus formation
Kallusbrücke f callous (callus) bridge *(z. B. bei Knochenbruchheilung)*
Kallusmangelproduktion f hypoporosis, deficient formation of callus
Kallusüberproduktion f hyperporosis, excessive formation of callus

Kalomel n calomel, mild mercurous chloride *(Laxativum, Diuretikum, Antisyphilitikum)*
Kalomelelektrode f calomel electrode
Kalomelsalbe f calomel ointment
Kalorie f calorie *(SI-fremde Einheit der Wärmemenge) (s. a. Joule)*
kalorienarm low-caloric
Kalorienbedarf m caloric requirement
Kalorienbeschränkung f caloric restriction
Kaloriengehalt m caloric content
kalorienreich high-caloric
Kalorisation f calorization *(zur Labyrinthprüfung)*
kalorisch caloric
Kalotte f calotte, calva[rium], calvaria, skull cap, [cranial] vault
Kalottenartikulation f calvarial articulation
Kalottenhöhe f calvarial height
Kalottenschmerz m helmet headache
Kälte f/**sexuelle** frigidity
Kälteagglutination f cold [haem]agglutination
Kälteagglutinationsphänomen n cold agglutination phenomenon
Kälteagglutinationstest m cold agglutination test
Kälteagglutinin n cold agglutinin
Kälteagglutininämie f cold agglutininaemia
Kälteagglutininkrankheit f cold agglutinin disease
Kälteallergie f cold allergy
Kälteanästhesie f cry[o]anaesthesia, crymoanaesthesia, refrigeration anaesthesia
Kälteantikörper m cold antibody
Kälteanwendung f cryoapplication
kältebeständig cold-resistant, cryotolerant, frigostable
Kältebeständigkeit f cold resistance, cryotolerance, frigostability
Kältechirurgie f cryosurgery, cryogenic surgery
Kälte-Druck-Test m cold pressure (pressor) test *(Blutdruckanstieg bei Kältereiz)*
kälteempfindlich cold-sensitive, frigolabile; psychrophobic
Kälteempfindlichkeit f cold sensitivity (susceptibility); cryaesthesia
~/**abnorme** psychrophobia
Kälteempfindung f cryaesthesia, psychroaesthesia
Kälteerschöpfung f cold exhaustion
Kältefixierung f cryopexy, cryofixation
Kältefurcht f psychrophobia
kältefürchtend psychrophobic
Kältegefühl n sensation of coldness; algor, chill
~/**schmerzhaftes** psychroalgia
~/**subjektives** psychroaesthesia
Kältehämagglutination f cold [haem]agglutination
Kältehämagglutinin n cold [haem]agglutinin
Kältehämoglobinurie f/**paroxysmale** paroxysmal cold haemoglobinuria, Donath-Landsteiner phenomenon
Kältehämolyse f cold haemolysis
Kältehämolysin n cold haemolysin

Kältekonservierung

Kältekonservierung f cryopreservation
kälteliebend psychrophilic, cry[m]ophilic *(z. B. Mikroorganismen)*
Kältemarmorierung f der Haut blue mottling of the skin; marble skin, cutis marmorata
Kältemesser m cryometer *(Thermometer)*
Kältepackung f cold pack
Kältepräzipitat n cryoprecipitate
Kältepunkt m cold spot, Krause's corpuscle (end bulb)
Kälteschaden m, Kälteschädigung f cold injury (trauma)
Kälteschmerz m cryalgesia, crymodynia
Kältesensibilität f cryaesthesia
Kältesinn m cryaesthesia
Kältetherapie f cry[m]otherapy, psychrotherapy, frigotherapy
Kältetod m cold death
Kältetoleranz f tolerance to cold, frigostability
Kältetotenflecke mpl post-mortem lividity by cold
Kälteüberempfindlichkeit f hypercryaesthesia, hypercryalgesia
kälteunempfindlich cryotolerant, frigostable
Kälteunempfindlichkeit f cryoanaesthesia, frigostability
Kälteurtikaria f cold (congelation) urticaria
Kältewiderstandsfähikeit f cold resistance, tolerance to cold
Kältezittern n trembling by cold
Kaltsterilisation f cold sterilization
Kaltwasserbehandlung f cold-water treatment
Kalvariasarkoidose f calvarial sarcoidosis
Kalyx m calyx, calix
Kalziämie f calcaemia
Kalzibilie f calcibilia
Kalziferol n calciferol, sunshine vitamin, irradiated ergosterol
Kalzifikation f calcification
Kalzifikationslinie f calcification line
kalzifizieren to calcify
Kalzikose f calcicosis
Kalzinose f calcinosis, calcium gout (thesaurismosis) *(Zusammensetzungen s. unter Calcinosis)*
Kalziotherapeutikum n calcium therapeutic [agent]
Kalzipenie f calcipenia
Kalziphylaxie f calciphylaxis
Kalzitonin n calcitonin, thyrocalcitonin *(Nebenschilddrüsenhormon)*
Kalziumablagerung f calcium deposition; calcinosis, calcium gout (thesaurismosis)
~ in der Niere renal calcium deposit
Kalziumantagonist m calcium antagonist [drug]
Kalziumausscheidung f im Urin calciuria
~/erhöhte hypercalciuria
~/verminderte hypocalciuria
Kalziumblutspiegel m calcium blood level
Kalziumerschöpfung f calcium depletion
Kalziumgleichgewicht n calcium balance
kalziumhaltig calciferous

Kalziumhunger m calcium hunger
Kalziumimprägnation f calcium impregnation, calcareous degeneration *(z. B. des Gewebes)*
Kalziumkarbonat n calcium carbonate
Kalziummangel m calcium deficiency; calcipenia, acalcinosis, hypocalc[in]aemia *(im Blut)*
Kalziumoxalatstein m calcium oxalate calculus *(Nierenstein)*
Kalziumspeicherung f calcium thesaurismosis, calcinosis
Kalziumspiegel m calcium level
Kalziumspiegelerhöhung f [im Blut] hypercalc[in]aemia
Kalziumspiegelverminderung f [im Blut] hypocalc[in]aemia
Kalziumstoffwechsel m calcium metabolism
Kalziumsulfat n calcium sulphate
Kalziumtherapie f calcium therapy
Kalziumthiosulfat n calcium thiosulphate *(z. B. zur Zellmembranstabilisierung)*
Kalziumverarmung f calcium depletion
Kalziumzeit f calcium time *(Blutgerinnung)*
Kambiumschicht f cambium layer *(des Periosteums)*
Kamerunbeule f Cameroon boil *(s. a. Kalabarschwellung)*
Kamerunfieber n Cameroon (malarial) fever
Kamille f/echte chamomile
Kamillenbad n chamomile bath
Kaminfegerkrebs m chimney-sweeps' cancer
Kamm m crest, crista, ridge, pecten *(Zusammensetzungen s. unter Crista)*
kammartig pectinate, pectineal
Kammer f 1. chamber, camera *(s. a. unter Camera)*; 2. ventricle, ventriculus *(Zusammensetzungen s. unter Herzkammer)*
~/feuchte moist chamber *(Bakteriologie)*
Kammer... s. a. Herzkammer... und Ventrikel...
Kammerarrhythmie f ventricular arrhythmia
Kammerautomatismus m ventricular automatism
Kammerdepolarisationskomplex m ventricular depolarization complex, QRS complex
Kammerdiastole f ventricular diastole
Kammerdruck m [intra]ventricular pressure
Kammerdruckkurve f ventricular pressure curve
Kammereigenrhythmus m idioventricular rhythm
Kammerendteil m S-T interval *(EKG)*
Kammererregung f ventricular excitation
Kammerersatzsystole f escape beat
Kammerextrasystole f ventricular extrasystole (premature beat), premature ventricular contraction
Kammerflattern n ventricular flutter
Kammerflimmern n ventricular fibrillation
Kammerfrequenz f ventricular frequency
Kammerjäger m vermin-destroyer, rat killer, pest infestation officer
Kammerkontraktion f ventricular contraction (systole)

Kammerrepolarisationskomplex *m* ventricular repolarization complex, T wave
Kammerrhythmus *m* ventricular rhythm
Kammerseptum *s.* Herzkammerscheidewand
Kammerstillstand *m* ventricular standstill
Kammersystole *f* ventricular systole
Kammertachyarrhythmie *f* ventricular tachyarrhythmia
Kammertachykardie *f* ventricular tachycardia
Kammerteil *m* ventricular deflection *(EKG)*
Kammervolumen *n* ventricular volume (capacity)
Kammerwand *f* ventricular wall
Kammerwasser *n* aqueous humour *(Auge)*
Kammerwasserabfluß *m* aqueous humour outflow
Kammerwinkel *m* chamber (iridocorneal) angle
Kammerwinkelfotografie *f* goniophotography
kammförmig pectiniform, pectinate, pectineal
Kammlinie *f* pectineal line *(des Oberschenkelknochens)*
Kammuskel *m* pectineus [muscle]
Kampfer *m* camphor
kampferartig camphoraceous
Kampferspiritus *m* camphor spirit
Kampfersucht *f* camphoromania
Kampfervergiftung *f* camphorism, camphor intoxication (poisoning)
Kampfgas *n* war (casualty) gas
Kampfstoff *m* [chemical] warfare agent
~/augenreizender lacrimator [agent]
~/biologischer biological warfare agent
~/blasenbildender vesicant [agent]
~/chemischer chemical warfare agent; war gas
~/lungenreizender lung irritant [agent], choking gas
~/nasenreizender sternutator [agent]
Kampfstoffanzeiger *m* war gas indicator
Kampfstoffschädigung *f* war gas injury
Kampimeter *n* campimeter
~/stereoskopisches stereocampimeter
Kampimetrie *f* campimetry, peri[opto]metry
kampimetrisch campimetric, perimetric
Kamptodaktylie *f* camptodactyly
Kamptokormie *f* camptocormia *(nach vorn gebeugte Zwangshaltung des Körpers)*
Kamptopsie *f* camptopsia
Kanadabalsam *m* Canada balsam (turpentine)
Kanal *m* channel, canal[is], duct, meatus *(s. a. unter Canalis)*
~/Alcockscher *s.* Canalis pudendalis
~/Cloquetscher *s.* Canalis hyaloideus
~/Haversscher *s.* Canalis nutricius
~/Hunterscher *s.* Canalis adductorius
~/Jacobsonscher Jacobson's tympanic canal
~/Schlemmscher Schlemm's canal, venous sinus of the sclera *(Abflußkanal der vorderen Augenkammer)*
~/Stillingscher 1. *s.* Canalis centralis [medullae spinalis]; 2. Stilling's canal, hyaloid canal of the vitreous body
~/Volkmannscher Volkmann's (nutrient artery) canal

Kanalbildung *f* canalization
Kanälchen *n s.* Canaliculus
Kanälchenbildung *f* canalicul[iz]ation
kanalförmig canalicular, canal-shaped
Kanalgasvergiftung *f* sewer gas poisoning, mephitis
kanalikulär canalicular
Kanalikulitis *f* canaliculitis
Kanalikuloplastik *f* canaliculoplasty
Kanalikulorhinostomie *f* canaliculorhinostomy
Kanalikulotomie *f* canaliculotomy
Kanalikulus *m s.* Canaliculus
kanalisieren to canalize
Kanalisierung *f* canalization *(1. Blutgefäßeinsprossung; 2. Nervenleitungsverbesserung)*
Kangri-Krebs *m* Kangri burn (basket cancer)
Kanikola-Fieber *n* canicola fever, Stuttgart disease
Kanincheneinheit *f* rabbit unit
Kaninchenhornhauttest *m* rabbit-cornea test
Kaninchenpest *f* myxomatosis
Kaninchenspirochätose *f* rabbit spirochaetosis
Kankroid *n* cancroid
Kankroidperle *f* cancroid pearl (corpuscle)
Kankrophobie *f s.* Karzinophobie
Kannabis *n* cannabis [indica], bhang
Kannabismus *m* cannabism, cannabis intoxication
Kanner-Syndrom *n* Kanner's syndrome, infantile autism
Kannibalismus *m* cannibalism, anthropophagy *(sexuelle Abnormität)*
Kanonenschlag[ton] *m* cannon sound *(bei komplettem Herzblock)*
Kante *f* edge, ridge, ledge; border, margin; limbus
Kanthariden *fpl* cantharides
Kantharidenblasentest *m* cantharidic blister test
Kantharideninfektion *f* canthariasis
Kantharidin *n* cantharidin
Kantharidismus *m* cantharidism, cantharidin intoxication, cantharidal poisoning
Kanthektomie *f* canthectomy
Kanthitis *f* canthitis
Kantholyse *f* cantholysis
Kanthoplastik *f* canthoplasty
Kanthorrhaphie *f* canthorrhaphy
Kanthotomie *f* canthotomy
Kanthus *m* canthus, palpebral angle
kanulär cannular, cannulate
Kanüle *f* cannula, needle, tubule; [hypodermic] needle *(einer Spritze)* ● **eine ~ einführen** to insert a cannula
~ Nr. 14 14-gauge needle
~/subkutane hypodermic needle
~/weitlumige large-bore cannula
Kanülenabknickung *f* kinking of the cannula
kanülenartig cannular, cannulate
Kanülenbläser *m* cannula dryer
Kanüleneinführung *f s.* Kanülierung
Kanülenentfernung *f* decannulation
kanülenförmig cannular

kanülieren

kanülieren to cannulize, to cannulate
Kanülierung f cannul[iz]ation, insertion of a cannula
kanzerogen cancerogenic, carcinogen[et]ic, cancerigenic, causing cancer
Kanzerogen n cancerogen, carcinogen, oncogenetic [agent]
Kanzerogenese f carcinogenesis
Kanzerogenität f carcinogenicity
Kanzerologie f cancerology, cancer research
Kanzerophilie f carcinophilia *(des Gewebes)*
Kanzerophobie f s. Karzinophobie
kanzerös cancerous, carcinous, carcinomatous
kanzerozid cancericidal
Kaolin n kaolin *(Adsorptionsmittel bei Darmkatarrhen)*
Kaolinkataplasma n kaolin cataplasm
Kaolinose f kaolinosis
Kapazitanz f capacitance *(Lungenfunktionsprüfung)*
Kapazität f capacity
~/**inspiratorische** inspiratory capacity
~/**phagozytische** phagocytic capacity
~/**respiratorische** respiratory capacity
~/**vitale** vital capacity
kapillar capillary
Kapillaraktivität f capillary activity
Kapillarangiom n capillary angioma
Kapillaranziehung f capillary attraction
Kapillarbett n capillary bed ● **vor dem** ~ junctional-capillary
Kapillarbildungszelle f angioblast
Kapillarbinnendruck m intracapillary pressure
Kapillarblut n capillary blood
Kapillarblutanalyse f capillary blood gas analysis
Kapillarblutung f capillary bleeding (haemorrhage)
Kapillarbronchitis f capillary bronchitis, bronchiolitis
Kapillarbrüchigkeit f capillary brittleness
Kapillardilatation f capillary dilatation
Kapillardrain m(n) capillary drain
Kapillardrainage f capillary drainage
Kapillardruck m capillary pressure
Kapillardurchlässigkeit f capillary permeability
Kapillare f s. 1. Kapillargefäß; 2. Kapillarröhrchen
~/**arterielle** arterial capillary
~/**arterioläre** arteriolar capillary
Kapillareinsprossung f capillary budding, vascularization, organization
Kapillarektasie f capillary ectasia, capillarectasia
Kapillarembolie f capillary embolism
Kapillarendothel n capillary endothelium
Kapillarendothelzelle f capillary endothelial cell
Kapillarendurchblutung f capillary flow (circulation)
Kapillarerweiterung f capillary dilatation, capillarectasia
Kapillarfragilität f capillary fragility
Kapillarfraktur f capillary fracture
Kapillargebiet n capillary region
Kapillargefäß n capillary [vessel]

376

Kapillargefäßerweiterung f capillary vasodilatation
Kapillargift n capillary poison
Kapillarhämangiom n capillary haemangioma, teleangiectatic angioma
Kapillarhülle f capillary sheath
Kapillarinnenhaut f capillary endothelium
Kapillaritätsanziehung f capillary attraction, capillarity
Kapillaritis f capillaritis, inflammation of the capillaries, telangitis
Kapillarknospenbildung f capillary budding
Kapillarkrankheit f capillaropathy
Kapillarmikroelektrode f capillary microelectrode
Kapillarmikroskopie f capillar[i]oscopy
Kapillarnetzschicht f choriocapillary lamina (layer), choriocapillaris *(der Regenbogenhaut)*
Kapillarniere f s. Dialysegerät
Kapillarokklusion f capillary occlusion
Kapillaropathie f capillaropathy
Kapillaroskopie f capillar[i]oscopy
Kapillarpermeabilität f capillary permeability
Kapillarplexus m capillary plexus
Kapillarpuls m capillary pulse
~/**Quinckescher** Quincke's pulse
Kapillarpulsation f capillary pulsation
Kapillarpunktion f capillary puncture
Kapillarresistenz f capillary resistance
Kapillarresistenzprobe f capillary resistance test
Kapillarröhrchen n, **Kapillarröhre** f capillary [tube]
Kapillarscheide f capillary sheath
Kapillarschranke f capillary barrier
Kapillarsprossung f capillary budding
Kapillarstase f capillary stasis
Kapillarsystem n capillary system
Kapillarteleangiektasie f capillary teleangiectasia
Kapillarthrombose f capillary thrombosis
Kapillarverschluß m capillary closure
Kapillarverschlußdruck m/**pulmonaler** pulmonary capillary pressure, [pulmonary artery] wedge pressure
Kapillarviskosimeter n capillary-tube viscosimeter
Kapillarwand f capillary wall
Kapillarwiderstand m capillary resistance
Kapillarwirkung f capillary action, capillarity
Kapistration f capistration
Kapitulum n capitulum, head *(s. a. unter Caput)*
Kaposi-Krankheit f 1. Kaposi's disease (sarcoma, syndrome), multiple idiopathic haemorrhagic sarcoma; 2. Kaposi's disease (varicelliform eruption)
Kappe f cap
~/**phrygische** phrygian cap *(Gallenblasenröntgendiagnostik)*
Kappenmuskel m trapezius [muscle] ● **unter dem** ~ subtrapezial
Kappenplastik f cap arthroplasty *(Orthopädie)*

Kapsel *f* capsule, capsula *(s. a. unter Capsula)*
● **ohne ~** acapsular ● **unter der ~** subcapsular
~/äußere external capsule
~/Bowmansche Bowman's (Malpighian, glomerular) capsule
~/Glissonsche Glisson's capsule
~/innere internal capsule
~/Tenonsche Tenon's capsule, fascia of the bulb
Kapselankylose *f* capsular ankylosis
Kapselantigen *n* capsular antigen
kapselartig capsular
Kapselbakterien *npl* capsulated bacteria
Kapselband *n* capsular ligament
Kapselbildung *f* capsular formation
Kapselblutung *f* capsular bleeding (haemorrhage)
Kapseldezidua *f* capsular decidua
Kapseleinschluß *m* capsulation *(z. B. Medikament)*
Kapseleinschnitt *m* capsulotomy
Kapselentfernung *f*[*/operative*] capsulectomy, decapsulation
Kapselentzündung *f* capsulitis, inflammation of a capsule *(z. B. der Linsenkapsel)*
Kapseleröffnung *f*[*/operative*] caps[ul]otomy
Kapselfalte *f* capsular fold
Kapselfärbung *f* capsular staining
Kapselfaßzange *f* capsule (lobe) grasping forceps
kapselförmig capsular
Kapselhäutchen *n* capsular lamella
Kapselhyalinisierung *f* capsular hyalinization, hyalocapsulitis
Kapselisthmus *m* capsular isthmus
kapsellos acapsular, non-encapsulated *(z. B. Bakterien)*
Kapselmesser *n* capsulotome
Kapselnaht *f* capsulorrhaphy, suture of a capsule *(z. B. der Linsenkapsel)*
Kapselphlegmone *f* capsular phlegmon
Kapselpinzette *f* capsule forceps
Kapselplastik *f* capsuloplasty
Kapselpolysaccharid *n* capsular polysaccharide
Kapselpseudozirrhose *f* capsular pseudocirrhosis
Kapselquellungsreaktion *f* capsular quellung reaction *(Pneumokokkenserologie)*
Kapselraffung *f* capsulorrhaphy, suture of a capsule *(z. B. der Linsenkapsel)*
Kapselschnitt *m* capsulotomy
Kapselschwellung *f* capsular swelling (quellung)
Kapselstar *m* capsular cataract
Kapselzirrhose *f* capsular (Glisson's) cirrhosis
Kapsid *n* capsid
Kapsomer *n* capsomere
Kapsulektomie *f* capsulectomy, excision of a capsule *(z. B. der Linsenkapsel)*
Kapsulitis *f* capsulitis, inflammation of a capsula *(z. B. der Linsenkapsel)*
Kapsulodese *f* capsulodesis
kapsulolentikulär capsulolenticular

Kapsulorrhaphie *f* capsulorrhaphy, suture of a capsule *(z. B. der Linsenkapsel)*
kapsulothalamisch capsulothalamic
Kapsulotom *n* capsulotome
Kapsulotomie *f* capsulotomy, incision of a capsule
Kaptation *f* captation
Kapuzenmuskel *m s.* Kappenmuskel
Karbachol *n* carbachol *(Parasympathikomimetikum)*
Karbamazepin *n* carbamazepine *(Antikonvulsivum)*
Karbamid *n* carbamide, urea
Karbaminohämoglobin *n* carb[amin]ohaemoglobin
Karbazidometer *n* carbacidometer
Karbinol *n* carbinol *(Methanolderivat)*
Karboanhydrase *f* carbonic anhydrase *(Enzym)*
~ der Niere renal carbonic anhydrase
Karboanhydrasehemmer *m* carbonic anhydrase inhibitor
Karbohydrase *f* carbohydrase
Karbohydrat *n* carbohydrate
Karbolanilinfuchsinfärbung *f* carbol-aniline fuchsin[e] stain[ing]
Karbolfuchsinfärbung *f* carbol-fuchsin[e] stain[ing]
Karbolfuchsinlösung *f* carbol-fuchsin[e] solution, Castellani's paint
Karbolgentianaviolettlösung *f* carbol-gentian-violet solution
Karbolsäure *f* carbolic acid, phenol
Karbolsäurevergiftung *f* carbolism, phenol (carbolic acid) poisoning
Karbolurie *f* carboluria
Karbonisation *f* 1. carbonation, impregnation with carbon dioxide; 2. carbonization, charring *(von Gewebe)*
karbonisieren to carbonate, to impregnate with carbon dioxide
Karbonometer *n* carbonometer
Karboxyhämoglobin *n* carboxyhaemoglobin
Karboxyhämoglobinämie *f* carboxyhaemoglobinaemia
Karboxylase *f* 1. carboxylase, α-keto acid [de]carboxylase, α-ketodecarboxylase; 2. [amino acid] carboxylase, amino acid decarboxylase
Karboxymyoglobin *n* carboxymyoglobin
Karboxypeptidase *f* carboxypeptidase *(Enzym)*
Karboxypolypeptidase *f* carboxypolypeptidase *(Enzym)*
Karbunkel *m* carbuncle
karbunkulös carbuncular
Karbunkulose *f* carbunculosis
Kardia *f* cardia, cardiac orifice, oesophagogastric junction
~/klaffende chalasia
Kardiaachalasie *f* achalasia [of the cardia], cardiospasm
Kardiadilatation *f* cardiodiosis *(durch Instrumente)*

Kardiadilatator

Kardiadilatator *m* cardia dilator, cardiodilator
Kardiadrüse *f* cardiac gland *(Magen)*
Kardiaeröffnung *f*[/operative] cardiotomy
Kardiainsuffizienz *f* cardia insufficiency
Kardiakum *n* cardiac [agent], cardiac stimulant
kardial cardiac ● ~ **bedingt** cardiogenic
Kardialgie *f* cardialgia, cardiodynia
Kardiamyotomie *f s.* Kardiomyotomie
Kardiareflex *m* cardia reflex
Kardiarekonstruktion *f* cardia reconstruction
Kardiaresektion *f* cardiectomy
Kardiasphinkter *m* cardiac sphincter
Kardiasphinkterinsuffizienz *f* cardiac sphincter insufficiency
Kardiasprengung *f*[/operative] *s.* Kardiomyotomie
Kardiektasie *f* cardiectasis
Kardiektomie *f* cardiectomy
Kardinalpunkt *m*/**biologischer** biological cardinal point
Kardinalsymptom *n* cardinal symptom
kardioakzeleratorisch cardioaccelerator
Kardioangiographie *f s.* Angiokardiographie
Kardioangiologie *f* cardioangiology
kardioangiologisch cardioangiological
kardioangiospastisch cardioangiospastic
kardioaortal cardioaortic
kardioarteriell cardioarterial
Kardiochirurg *m* cardiac (heart) surgeon, cardiosurgeon
Kardiochirurgie *f* cardiac (heart) surgery, cardiosurgery
kardiodepressiv, kardiodepressorisch cardiodepressive
kardiodynamisch cardiodynamic
Kardiodynamometrie *f* cardiodynamometry
kardiofazial cardiofacial
kardiogen cardiogenic
Kardiogenese *f* cardiogenesis
Kardiogramm *n* cardiogram
Kardiograph *m* cardiograph
Kardiographie *f* cardiography
kardiographisch cardiographic
kardiohepatisch cardiohepatic
Kardiohepatomegalie *f* cardiohepatomegaly
kardioinhibitorisch cardioinhibitory
kardiokutan cardiocutaneous
Kardiokymogramm *n* cardiokymogram
Kardiokymographie *f* cardiokymography
kardiokymographisch cardiokymographic
Kardiolipin *n* cardiolipin *(Syphilisserologie)*
Kardiolipin-Mikroflockungstest *m* cardiolipin microflocculation test, CMT
Kardiolipintest *m* cardiolipin test
Kardiolith *m* cardiolith, cardiac calculus
Kardiologe *m* cardiologist
Kardiologie *f* cardiology *(Lehre vom Herzen und seinen Funktionen)*
Kardiolysis *f* cardiolysis
Kardiomalazie *f* cardiomalacia
Kardiomegalie *f* cardiomegaly, cardiac hypertrophy

Kardiomelanosis *f* cardiomelanosis, melanosis of the heart
Kardiomentopexie *f* cardiomentopexy *(Netzanheftung zur Verbesserung der Herzdurchblutung)*
Kardiometer *n* cardiometer
Kardiometrie *f* cardiometry
kardiometrisch cardiometric
Kardiomotilität *f* cardiomotility, motility of the heart
Kardiomyopathie *f* cardiomyopathy, myocardiopathy, myocardosis
~/**hypertrophe obstruktive** hypertrophic obstructive cardiomyopathy, HOCM, muscular (idiopathic hypertrophic) subaortic stenosis, IHSS
~/**kongestive** congested (dilated) cardiomyopathy
~/**nichtobstruktive hypertrophe** non-obstructive hypertrophic cardiomyopathy
~/**restriktive** restricitive cardiomyopathy
Kardiomyopexie *f* cardiomyopexy *(Muskelanheftung zur Verbesserung der Herzdurchblutung)*
Kardiomyotomie *f* cardiomyotomy, cardiooesophagomyotomy, cardiodiosis
Kardioneurose *f* cardioneurosis, cardiac neurosis (neurasthenia), cardiasthenia; irritable heart
kardioösophageal cardio-oesophageal
Kardiopalmus *m* cardiopalmus
Kardiopath *m* cardiopath
Kardiopathie *f* cardiopathy, heart disease
Kardiopathologie *f* cardiopathology
Kardioperikarditis *f* cardi[o]pericarditis
Kardiopexie *f* cardio[pericardio]pexy
Kardiophobie *f* cardiophobia *(krankhafte Angst vor Herzkrankheiten)*
Kardiophon *n* cardiophone
Kardioplastik *f* cardioplasty
Kardioplegie *f* cardioplegia, paralysis of the heart
kardioplegisch cardioplegic
Kardiopneumographie *f* cardiopneumography
Kardioptose *f* cardioptosis, bathycardia
kardiopulmonal cardiopulmonary, cardiopulmonic, cardiopneumatic
Kardioradiologie *f* cardioradiology
kardioradiologisch cardioradiologic
kardiorenal cardiorenal, cardionephric
kardiorespiratorisch cardiorespiratory
Kardiorrhaphie *f* cardiorrhaphy
Kardiorrhexis *f* cardiorrhexis, rupture of the heart
Kardiosklerose *f* cardiosclerosis
Kardioskop *n* cardioscope
Kardioskopie *f* cardioscopy
Kardiospasmus *m* cardiospasm, achalasia [of the cardia]
Kardiosphygmogramm *n* cardiosphygmogram
Kardiosphygmographie *f* cardiosphygmography
kardiosphygmographisch cardiosphygmographic
Kardiostenose *f* cardiostenosis
Kardioszintigraphie *f* cardioscintigraphy
Kardiotachograph *m* cardiotachograph

Kardiotachometer *n* cardiotachometer
Kardiotokogramm *n* cardiotocogram
Kardiotokograph *m* cardiotocograph
Kardiotokographie *f* cardiotocography
Kardiotomie *f* cardiotomy, incision of the heart
Kardiotonikum *n* cardiotonic [agent], cardiac stimulant
kardiotoxisch cardiotoxic
Kardiovalvulitis *f* cardi[o]valvulitis
Kardiovalvulotom *n* cardiovalvulotome
Kardiovalvulotomie *f* cardiovalvulotomy
kardiovaskulär cardiovascular, CV
Kardiovaskularklemme *f* cardiovascular forceps
Kardiovektographie *f* vectorcardiography, cardiovectography
Kardioversion *f* cardioversion, capacitance-discharge defibrillation *(Herzrhythmisierung)*
Kardiozele *f* cardiocele
Kardiozentese *f* cardi[o]centesis, cardiopuncture
Karditis *f* carditis, inflammation of the heart
~/rheumatische rheumatic carditis
karditisch carditic
Karenchyma *n* karenchyma
karent bleiben to starve
Karenz *f* deficiency, starvation
Karenzzeit *f* waiting (restriction) period
Karies *f* [dental] caries, dental decay, saprodontia
Kariesanfälligkeit *f* caries susceptibility (disposition)
Kariesbefall *m* affection by caries
karieserzeugend cariogenic
kariesfördernd promoting caries
Kariesfrequenz *f* frequency of caries
karieshemmend anticariogenic, anticarious
Karies-Index *m* caries index
Karieskontrolle *f* caries control
Kariesmarke *f* caries mark
Kariesprophylaxe *f* caries prophylaxis
Kariesresistenz *f* caries resistance
Kariesrezidiv *n* recurring caries
Karieszone *f* caries zone
Karina *f* carina *(Zusammensetzungen s. unter Carina)* ● **neben der ~** paracarinal
Karinapunktion *f* carinal puncture
kariogen cariogenic
kariös carious
kariostatisch cariostatic
Karmin *n* carmine [dye]
Karminativum *n* carminative [agent]
Karminzelle *f* carmine cell *(Adenohypophyse)*
Karnaubawachs *n* carnauba wax
Karnifikation *f* carnification *(Lungengewebeverdichtung)*
karnös carneous
Karnosin *n* carnosine, β-alanylhistidine
Karnosinämie *f* carnosinaemia
Karotidenhüpfen *n* dance (dancing) of the carotid arteries
Karotidenknötchen *n* carotid body (gland)
karotikotympanal caroticotympanic
Karotin *n* carotene, carotin

Karotisthrombose

Karotinablagerung *f* carotenosis *(im Gewebe)*
Karotinämie *f* carotenaemia
Karotinoid *n* carotenoid
Karotinose *f* carotenosis
Karotinspiegelerhöhung *f* carotenaemia *(im Blut)*
Karotis *f s.* Arteria carotis
Karotis... *s. a.* Halsschlagader...
Karotisangiographie *f* carotid angiography (arteriography)
Karotisbulbus *m* carotid bulb
Karotisdreieck *n* carotid triangle
~/oberes superior carotid triangle
~/unteres muscular (inferior carotid) triangle
Karotisdrüse *f* carotid body (gland)
Karotiseinengung *f s.* Karotisstenose
Karotisendarteriektomie *f* carotid endarterectomy
Karotis-externa-Ligatur *f* ligation of external carotid artery
Karotisgabel *f* carotid bifurcation
Karotisgabeltumor *m* carotid-body tumour
Karotisganglion *n* carotid ganglion
Karotishülle *f* carotid sheath
Karotisinsuffizienz *f* carotid artery insufficiency
Karotisinsuffizienzsyndrom *n* carotid artery [insufficiency] syndrome, carotid [arterial] occlusive disease
Karotiskanal *m* carotid canal
Karotisklemme *f* carotid clamp
Karotisknötchen *n s.* Karotiskörper
Karotiskörper *m* carotid body (gland)
Karotiskörpergeschwulst *f* carotid-body tumour
Karotiskörperreflex *m* carotid-body reflex
Karotisligatur *f* carotid [artery] ligation
Karotisnerv *m* carotid nerve
~/äußerer external carotid nerve
~/innerer internal carotid nerve
Karotisphonoangiographie *f* carotid phonoangiography
Karotisplexus *m* carotid plexus
Karotispuls *m* carotid pulse
Karotispulskurve *f* carotid pulse curve
Karotisscheide *f* carotid sheath
Karotisschlinge *f* carotid loop
Karotissinus *m* carotid sinus
Karotis-Sinus-Cavernosus-Fistel *f* carotid-sinus-cavernosus fistula
Karotissinusdruck *m* carotid sinus pressure
Karotissinusmassage *f* carotid sinus massage
Karotissinusnerv *m* carotid sinus nerve
Karotissinusreflex *m* carotid sinus reflex
Karotissinusstimulation *f* carotid sinus stimulation
Karotissinussyndrom *n* carotid sinus syndrome, Charcot-Weiss-Baker syndrome
~/hypersensitives carotid sinus hypersensitivity
Karotissinussynkope *f* carotid sinus syncope
Karotissiphon *m* carotid siphon
Karotisstenose *f* carotid stenosis (artery narrowing)
Karotisthrombose *f* carotid artery thrombosis

Karotisverschluß

Karotisverschluß *m* carotid [arterial] occlusion, carotid artery obstruction
Karotisverschlußkrankheit *f* carotid [arterial] occlusive disease, carotid artery insufficiency syndrome
Karpalarteriennetz *n* carpal rete
Karpalgegend *f* carpal region
Karpalgelenk *n* intercarpal (mediocarpal) joint
Karpaltunnel *m* carpal tunnel (canal)
Karpaltunnelsyndrom *n* carpal tunnel syndrome, tardy median palsy
Karpektomie *f* carpectomy
Karpogramm *n* carpogram
Karpometakarpalgelenk *n* carpometacarpal joint
Karpometakarpalreflex *m* carpometacarpal reflex
Karpopedalspasmus *m* carpopedal spasm
Karpophalangealreflex *m* carpophalangeal reflex
Karpoptose *f* carpoptosis, wristdrop
Karpus *m* carpus, wrist
Kartagener-Syndrom *n* Kartagener's syndrome (triad) *(angeborene Bronchiektasen mit Mißbildungen der Lungenarterie, Wabenlunge, Eiterungen der Nasennebenhöhlen, fehlenden Stirnhöhlen und anderen Mißbildungen)*
kartilaginär, kartilaginös cartilagin[e]ous
Kartoffelkur *f* potato diet
Kartoffelleber *f* potato liver
Kartoffelnase *f* potato nose
Karunkel *f* caruncle, caruncula *(aus lockerem Bindegewebe und Gefäßen) (Zusammensetzungen s. unter* Caruncula*)*
Karyoblast *m* karyoblast
karyochrom karyochrome
karyochromatophil karyochromatophilic
karyogam karyogamic
Karyogamie *f* karyogamy *(bei geschlechtlicher Fortpflanzung)*
karyogen karyogenic
Karyogenese *f* karyogenesis
Karyogramm *n* karyogram
Karyokinese *f* karyokinesis, [karyo]mitosis, mitotic division *(mit Chromosomenausbildung)*
karyokinetisch karyokinetic, [karyo]mitotic *(bei Zellteilungen)*
Karyoklasie *f s.* Karyorrhexis
karyoklastisch karyoclastic
karyolobär karyolobic *(Zellkern)*
Karyologie *f* karyology *(Lehre vom Zellkern)*
Karyolymphe *f* karyolymph, nuclear lymph, enchylema
Karyolyse *f* karyolysis
karyolytisch karyolytic
Karyomegalie *f* karyomegaly
Karyomer *n* karyomere
Karyometrie *f* karyometry
Karyomikrosom *n* karyomicrosome *(im Zellkern)*
Karyomitom *n* karyomitome, karyoreticulum *(des Zellkerns)*
Karyomitose *f s.* Karyokinese
Karyon *n s.* Zellkern
Karyonkose *f* karyoncosis
Karyophage *m* karyophage
Karyoplasma *n* karyoplasm, nucleoplasm
karyoplasmatisch karyoplasmatic
Karyopyknose *f* karyopyknosis
Karyopyknoseindex *m* karyopyknotic index
karyorrhektisch karyorrhectic *(Zellkern nach dem Zelltod)*
Karyorrhexis *f* karyorrhexis, karyoclasis, karyoklasis, splitting of the nucleus
Karyoschisis *f* karyoschisis
Karyosom *n* karyosome, false nucleolus
Karyostase *f* karyostasis
Karyotheka *f* karyotheca, nuclear membrane
Karyotyp *m* karytype
karyotypisieren to karyotype
karzinogen carcinogen[et]ic, cancerogenic, cancerigenic, causing cancer
Karzinogen *n* carcinogen, cancerogen, oncogenetic [agent]
Karzinogenese *f* carcinogenesis
Karzinogenizität *f* carcinogenicity
Karzinoid *n* carcinoid [tumour], spheroidal-cell carcinoma, argentaffinoma, argentaffine carcinoma (tumour)
karzinoidartig carcinoid-like
Karzinoidmetastase *f* carcinoid metastasis
Karzinoidsyndrom *n* carcinoid (argentaffinoma) syndrome, carcinoidosis, functioning [carcinoid] syndrome
Karzinolyse *f* carcinolysis
Karzinom *n* carcinoma, cancer *(bösartige Geschwulst) (s. a. unter* Carcinoma*)*
~ **/alveoläres** alveolar carcinoma
~ **/azinöses** acinous carcinoma
~ **/branchiogenes** branchial (gill cleft) carcinoma, branchioma
~ **/bronchiogenes** bronchogenic carcinoma
~ **der Bartholinischen Drüsen** Bartholin's gland carcinoma
~ **/entzündliches** inflammatory carcinoma
~ **/hepatozelluläres** hepatocellular (liver cell) carcinoma
~ **/hypernephroides** hypernephroid renal carcinoma, hypernephroma, renal-cell carcinoma, Grawitz's tumour, clear-cell carcinoma
~ **/kleinzelliges** small-cell carcinoma [of the lung], oat-cell carcinoma, reserve-cell carcinoma *(bösartigste Form des Bronchialkarzinoms)*
~ **/lobuläres** lobular carcinoma *(z. B. der Brustdrüse)*
~ **/medulläres** medullary carcinoma
~ **/melanotisches** melanotic carcinoma
~ **/muzinöses** mucinous carcinoma
~ **/periportales** periportal carcinoma
~ **/polypöses** polypoid carcinoma
~ **/szirrhöses** scirrhous (hard) carcinoma, scirrhus [carcinoma]
~ **/tuberöses** tuberous carcinoma
Karzinom... *s. a.* Krebs...
karzinomähnlich carcinomatoid
karzinomatös carcinomatous, cancerous
Karzinomatose *f* carcino[mato]sis

Karzinomaussaat f **der Leptomeninx** meningeal carcinomatosis
Karzinomchirurgie f cancer surgery
karzinomempfänglich carcinophilic
Karzinomempfänglichkeit f carcinophilia *(des Gewebes)*
Karzinomexstirpation f carcin[om]ectomy, carcinosectomy
karzinomförmig carcinomatoid
Karzinommetastase f carcinoma metastasis
~/osteoklastische osteoclastic cancer metastasis
~/osteoplastische osteoplastic cancer metastasis
Karzinommetastasenabsiedlung f carcino[mato]sis
Karzinomnest n cancer nest
Karzinompatient m cancer patient
Karzinompopulation f cancer population
Karzinomprophylaxe f cancer prophylaxis
Karzinomschmerz m cancer pain
karzinophil carcinophilic
Karzinophilie f carcinophilia *(des Gewebes)*
Karzinophobie f carcino[mato]phobia, cancerophobia *(krankhafte Angst vor einer Krebserkrankung)*
karzinös carcinous, cancerous, carcinomatous, cancroid, cancriform
Karzinosarkom n carcinosarcoma, sarcocarcinoma
Karzinose f carcino[mato]sis
karzinostatisch carcinostatic, cancerostatic
Kasabach-Merritt-Syndrom n Kasabach-Merritt syndrome *(thrombozytopenische Purpura mit tuberonodösen Angiomen bei Kindern)*
Kaschin-Beck-Krankheit f Urov (Kashin-Beck) disease *(Knochenkrankheit durch Fusarium sporotrichiella)*
Kaschmirkrebs m s. Kangri-Krebs
käseartig cheesy, cheese-like, caseous, tyroid
Kasease f casease *(Enzym)*
Käsefliege f cheese fly, Piophila casei
Kasein n casein
Kaseinogen n caseinogen
Käseschmiere f cheesy varnish, vernix caseosa
Käsevergiftung f cheese poisoning
käsig caseous, tyroid, cheesy, cheese-like
Kaskadenmagen m cascade (waterfall) stomach
Kastrat m castrate, eunuch
Kastration f castration, emasculation *(beim Mann)*; oophorectomy, sterilization *(bei der Frau)*
Kastrationsangst f castration anxiety
Kastrationskomplex m castration complex
kastrieren to castrate, to emasculate *(Männer)*; to oophorectomize, to sterilize *(Frauen)*
Kast-Syndrom n Kast's syndrome *(Häufung von kavernösen Hämangiomen und Chondromen)*
Kasuistik f casuistics, case report
Kasus m case
katabol[isch] catabolic, catabiotic
katabolisieren to catabolize, to dis[as]similate

Katabolismus m catabolism, catabiosis, dis[as]similation
Katabolismusrate f catabolic rate
Katabolit m catabolite
Katadidyma n, **Katadidymus** m catadidymus, superior duplictity *(Doppelmißgeburt mit Verschmelzung im unteren Körperbereich)*
katadikrot catadicrotic
Katadikrotismus m catadicrotism *(doppelte Erhebung im abfallenden Teil der Pulswelle)*
Katakrotismus m catacrotism *(Erhebung im abfallenden Teil der Pulswelle)*
Katalase f catalase *(Enzym)*
Katalaseaktivität f catalase activity
Katalasehemmer m catalase inhibitor
Katalasemangel m[/**angeborener**] acatalasia
~ im Blut acatalasaemia
Katalepsie f catalepsia, katalepsia, ecstasy
kataleptisch cataleptic
Katalyse f catalysis
katalysieren to catalyze
Katamenien npl s. Menstruation
Katamnese f catamnesis
katamnestisch catamnestic
Kataphasie f cataphasia *(Sprachstörung)*
Kataphorese f cataphoresis *(Elektrophorese)*
Kataphorie f cataphoria
kataphorisch cataphoric
Kataplasie f cataplasia, kataplasia
Kataplasma n cataplasm[a], poultice
kataplektisch cataplectic
Kataplexie f cataplexis
Katarakt f cataract *(s. a. unter Cataracta und Star)*
~/angeborene congenital cataract
~/blaue blue (cerulean) cataract
~/glaukomatöse glaucomatous cataract
~/juvenile juvenile cataract
~/käsige cheesy (caseous) cataract
~/lentikuläre lenticular cataract
~/periphere peripheral cataract
~/reife mature (ripe) cataract
~/überreife hypermature (overripe) cataract
~/unreife immature (unripe) cataract
Katarakt... s. a. Star...
Kataraktauge n cataract eye
Kataraktchirurgie f cataract surgery
Kataraktextraktion f cataract extraction
Kataraktlöffel m cataract spoon
Kataraktmesser n cataract knife
Kataraktnadel f cataract needle
kataraktogen cataractogenic
Kataraktogenese f cataractogenesis
Katarrh m catarrh, cold
~/chronischer chronic catarrh
~ der oberen Luftwege catarrhal fever, catarrh of the respiratory tract
~/eitriger purulent catarrh
~/postgonorrhoischer postgonorrhoeic catarrh
katarrhal[isch] catarrhal
katarrhlösend anticatarrhal
Katarrhstadium n catarrhal stage

Katastrophenreaktion

Katastrophenreaktion f catastrophic reaction
Katathermometer n katathermometer, catathermometer *(zur Bestimmung der Abkühlungsgröße)*
Katathymer m catathymic
Katathymie f catathymia, catathymic type of schizophrenia
Katatoner m catatonic
Katatonie f catatonia, katatonia, catatonic type of schizophrenia *(muskelstarre Form)*
Katatoniker m catatonic
Katatrikrotismus m catatricrotism *(dreifache Erhebung im abfallenden Teil der Pulswelle)*
Katayamafieber n s. Katayamakrankheit
Katayamakrankheit f Katayama disease (fever, syndrome), Asiatic (hepatosplenic) schistosomiasis, oriental [intestinal] schistosomiasis
Katayamasyndrom n[/japanisches] s. Katayamakrankheit
Katecholamin n catecholamine
Katecholaminausschüttung f catecholamine excretion
Katecholaminstoffwechsel m catecholamine metabolism
Katelektrotonus m catelectrotonus *(Physiologie)*
Katgut n [cat]gut *(Nahtmaterial aus Schafsdarm)*
~/chromiertes chromi[ci]zed catgut
Katgutfaden m catgut thread
Katgutnaht f catgut suture
Katgutunterbindung f catgut ligature
Katharsis f catharsis, purgation, cleansing
Kathartikum n cathartic [agent], purgative [agent]
Kathepsin n cathepsin, kathepsin *(Enzym)*
Katheter m catheter ● einen ~ einführen to introduce a catheter, to catheterize
~ Charr[ière] 9 nine Charrière catheter
~/doppelläufiger double-channelled catheter
~/elastischer flexible catheter
~/gebogener elbowed catheter
~/männlicher male catheter
~/weiblicher female catheter
~/weicher soft catheter
Katheterangiographie f catheter angiography
Katheteranwendung f catheterism
Katheterbiopsie f catheter biopsy
Katheterdilatation f catheter dilatation
Kathetereinführung f catheterization, tubage
~/perkutane percutaneous catheterization
Kathetereinführungszange f catheter introduction forceps
Katheterembolie f, **Katheterembolisation** f catheter embolism, transcatheter embolization
Katheterfieber n catheter fever
Katheterinfektion f catheter[-induced] infection
Katheterinfusion f/**intravenöse** cut-down infusion
katheterisieren to catheterize
Katheterismus m catheterism
kathetern to catheterize
Katheteroperation f catheter operation
Katheterpunktion f catheter puncture

Katheterskala f catheter gauge (scale)
Katheterspanner m catheter introducer
Katheterspitze f catheter tip
Kathetertechnik f catheter technique
Katheterung f catheterization, catheterism
Katheterurin m catheter urine
Kathisophobie f kathisophobia *(krankhafte Angst vor dem Hinsetzen)*
Kationenaustauscher m cation exchanger
Kationenaustausch[er]harz n cation-exchange resin
Katodenöffnungsklonus m cathodal opening clonus *(Physiologie)*
Katodenöffnungstetanus m cathodal opening tetanus *(Physiologie)*
Katodenöffnungszuckung f cathodal opening contraction *(Physiologie)*
Katodenschließungsklonus m cathodal closure clonus *(Physiologie)*
Katodenschließungstetanus m cathodal closure (closing) tetanus *(Physiologie)*
Katodenschließungszuckung f cathodal closure contraction *(Physiologie)*
Katodenstrahloszillograph m cathode-ray oscillograph
Katodenstrahloszilloskop n cathode-ray oscilloscope
Katzenauge n/**amaurotisches** amaurotic cat's eye; cat's-eye amaurosis
Katzenaugenpupille f cat's-eye pupil
Katzenaugensyndrom n cat's-eye syndrome
Katzeneinheit f cat unit *(Pharmakologie)*
Katzenkratzkrankheit f cat-scratch disease (syndrome), CSD, cat-bite fever, sterile (non-bacterial) regional lymphadenitis, benign reticulosis
Katzenohr n cat (cat's) ear
Katzenpupille f cat's-eye pupil
Katzenschreisyndrom n cat cry (Lejeune's) syndrome
Kauakt m mastication, [act of] chewing
Kauapparat m masticatory apparatus
Kaudaanästhesie f[/**extradurale**] [extradural] caudal anaesthesia
~/fraktionierte fractional caudal anaesthesia
Kaudadaueranästhesie f continous caudal anaesthesia
Kauebene f occlusal plane *(der Zähne)*
kauen to masticate, to chew, to manducate
Kauen n mastication, chewing, manducation
~/erschwertes dysmasesia
kauend masticatory, chewing, manducatory
Kaufläche f masticatory surface *(Zahn)*
Kauflächenhöckerchen n dental tubercle
Kaufmann-Abderhalden-De Lignac-Syndrom n s. Abderhalden-Kaufmann-Lignac-Syndrom
Kauftrieb m/**krankhafter** oniomania
Kaukraft f masticatory force
Kaukraftmesser m gnathodynamometer, occlusometer
Kaumuskel m masticatory muscle, muscle of mastication; masseter [muscle]
Kaumuskelarterie f masseteric artery

Kaumuskelkrampf *m* masticatory spasm, trismus, lockjaw
Kaumuskellähmung *f* masticatory paralysis
Kaumuskelreflex *m* masseter reflex, jaw jerk
Kaumuskel-Unterkiefer-Schläfen-Region *f* masseter-mandibular-temporal region
Kaumuskelvene *f* masseteric vein
Kaumuskulatur *f* masticatory muscles
Kauorgan *n* masticatory organ
Kausalgie *f* causalgia, synaesthesialgia
Kausalgiesyndrom *n* causalgia syndrome
Kausalität *f* causality
Kausaltherapie *f* causal therapy (treatment)
Kaustik *f s.* Kauterisation
Kaustikum *n* caustic [agent]
Kaustörung *f* dysmasesia
Kauter *m* cautery [knife], cauter, electrosurgical knife
Kauterchirurgie *f* cautery surgery
Kauterisation *f* cauterization, cautery, ustion
kauterisieren to cauterize
Kautschukpflaster *n s.* Heftpflaster
Kauunfähigkeit *f* amasesis, inability to chew
Kava *f* caval vein, [vena] cava
Kava... *s. a.* Hohlvenen...
Kavablutstrom *m* caval [vein] flow
Kavakatheter *m* caval [vein] catheter
Kava-Kompressions-Syndrom *n* caval [vein] compression syndrome
Kavaligatur *f* caval [vein] ligation
Kavaobstruktion *f* caval [vein] obstruction
Kava-Obstruktions-Syndrom *n* caval [vein] obstruction syndrome
Kaverne *f* 1. cavern, cavity; 2. cavern, tuberculous cavity
Kavernenbildung *f* cavity formation, cavitation *(z. B. an der Lunge)*
Kavernenblutung *f* cavernous bleeding (haemorrhage)
Kavernendrainage *f* cavernous drainage, cavernostomy
Kaverneneröffnung *f/operative* cavernotomy
Kavernenkarzinom *n* cavernous carcinoma
Kavernenperforation *f* cavernous perforation
Kavernenplombierung *f* cavernous plombage
Kavernenpunktion *f* cavernous puncture
Kavernenrasseln *n* cavernous rale
Kavernensaugdrainage *f* cavernous suction drainage, Monaldi's drainage
Kavernenstimme *f* cavernous voice, pectoriloquy *(bei Lungenkrankheiten)*
Kavernensymptom *n* cavernous symptom
Kavernentamponade *f* cavernous tamponade
Kavernenton *m* caverniloquy *(bei Lungenkavernen)*
Kavernitis *f* cavern[os]itis
~/fibröse fibrous cavernitis, Peyronie's disease
Kavernom *n* 1. cavernoma, cavernous tumour; 2. cavernous haemangioma
kavernomatös cavernomatous
kavernös cavernous
Kavernoskopie *f* cavernoscopy

kavernoskopisch cavernoscopic
Kavernosogramm *n* cavernosogram
Kavernosographie *f* cavernosography *(Schwellkörperdarstellung des Penis)*
Kavernostomie *f* cavernostomy
Kavernotomie *f* cavernotomy
Kaviarkörperchen *npl* kaviar spots *(Venektasien der Zunge)*
Kavität *f* cavity *(Stomatologie)*
Kavogramm *n* [vena]cavogram
Kavographie *f* [vena]cavography
Kavum *n* cavum, cavity
Kayser-Fleischer-Pigmentring *m* Kayser-Fleischer ring
KBR *s.* Komplementbindungsreaktion
kebozephal cebocephalic, cebocephalous
Kebozephalie *f* cebocephalia *(Mißbildung)*
Kebozaphalus *m* cebocephalus
Kedanikrankheit *f* Kedani disease (fever), tsutsugamushi disease
Kedanimilbe *f* Trombicula akamushi *(Überträger der Tsutsugamushikrankheit)*
kegelförmig cone-shaped, coniform, conical
Kegelknorpel *m* Wrisberg's (cuneiform) cartilago
Kegelschnitt *m* conization, conical section
Kehldeckel *m* epiglottis
Kehldeckelentfernung *f/operative* epiglottidectomy
Kehldeckelentzündung *f* epiglottitis, inflammation of the epiglottis
Kehldeckelhöckerchen *n* epiglottic tubercle
Kehldeckelknorpel *m* epiglottic cartilage
Kehldeckelmuskel *m* aryepiglottic muscle
Kehldeckelstiel *m* epiglottic pedicle
Kehle *f* throat
Kehlkopf *m* larynx
~/künstlicher artificial larynx
~ und Luftröhre *f* laryngotrachea
Kehlkopf... *s. a.* Larynx...
Kehlkopfamyloidose *f* laryngeal amyloidosis
Kehlkopfanschwellung *f* laryngeal oedema
Kehlkopfarterie *f/obere* superior laryngeal artery
~/untere inferior laryngeal artery
Kehlkopfatresie *f* laryngeal atresia
Kehlkopfausmessung *f* laryngometry, measurement of the larynx
Kehlkopfband *n* laryngeal ligament
Kehlkopfblutung *f* laryngorrhagia, laryngeal bleeding, haemorrhage from the larynx
Kehlkopfchorea *f* laryngeal chorea
Kehlkopfdiaphragma *n* laryngeal diaphragm
Kehlkopfdiphtherie *f* laryngeal diphtheria, laryngostasis, diphtheritic (croupous) laryngitis, diphtheric (true) croup
Kehlkopfdivertikel *n* laryngeal diverticulum
Kehlkopfeingang *m* laryngeal inlet, entrance to the larynx, vestibule of the larynx
Kehlkopfentzündung *f* laryngitis, inflammation of the larynx
Kehlkopferöffnung *f/mediane* median laryngotomy; laryngofissure
~/operative laryngotomy, incision of the larynx

Kehlkopferweichung

Kehlkopferweichung f laryngomalacia
Kehlkopfetage f/**untere** cavity of the larynx
Kehlkopfexstirpation f laryngectomy, extirpation (excision) of the larynx
Kehlkopfexstirpierter m laryngectomee
Kehlkopffistel f laryngostoma
Kehlkopffistelung f[/**operative**] laryngostomy
Kehlkopfgeschwulst f laryngeal tumour
Kehlkopfhöhle f laryngeal cavity
Kehlkopfinduration f laryngoscleroma
Kehlkopfkanüle f tracheotomy cannula (tube)
Kehlkopfkatarrh m laryngeal catarrh
Kehlkopfknorpel mpl laryngeal cartilages
Kehlkopfknötchen n singer's node
Kehlkopfkrampf m laryngeal spasm, laryngospasm, laryngismus
Kehlkopfkrankheit f laryngopathy, disease of the larynx
Kehlkopfkrebs m laryngeal cancer, carcinoma of the larynx
Kehlkopfkrise f laryngeal crisis
Kehlkopfkrupp m s. Kehlkopfdiphtherie
Kehlkopflähmung f laryngoplegia, laryngoparalysis, laryngeal paralyis, paralysis of the larynx
Kehlkopflanzette f laryngeal lancet
Kehlkopf-Luftröhren-Entzündung f s. Laryngotracheitis
Kehlkopf-Luftröhren-Inspektion f s. Laryngotracheoskopie
Kehlkopf-Luftröhren-Schnitt m s. Laryngotracheotomie
Kehlkopf-Luftröhren-Speiseröhren-Spalte f laryngotracheo-oesophageal cleft
Kehlkopfluftsack m laryngocele
Kehlkopfmanifestation f laryngeal manifestation
Kehlkopfmesser n s. Laryngotom
Kehlkopfmessung f laryngometry
Kehlkopfmodell n s. Laryngophantom
Kehlkopfmuskel m/**querer** transverse arytenoid muscle
~/schräger oblique arytenoid muscle
Kehlkopfmuskellähmung f s. Kehlkopflähmung
Kehlkopfnaht f laryngorrhaphy; suturing of the larynx
Kehlkopfneoplasma n laryngeal neoplasm
Kehlkopfnerv m/**unterer** inferior laryngeal nerve
Kehlkopfneuralgie f laryngalgia, pain in the larynx
Kehlkopfödem n laryngeal oedema
Kehlkopfplastik f laryngoplasty
Kehlkopfpolyp m laryngeal polyp
Kehlkopfpunktion f s. Laryngozentese
Kehlkopfrachen m laryngeal pharynx, laryngopharynx, hypopharynx
Kehlkopfrachenspiegel m hypopharyngoscope
Kehlkopfrasseln n laryngeal rale
Kehlkopfreflex m laryngeal reflex
Kehlkopfregion f region of the larynx
Kehlkopfresektion f/**halbseitige** hemilaryngectomy
Kehlkopfringknorpel m annular cartilage [of the larynx]

Kehlkopfröntgenbild n laryngogram
Kehlkopfröntgen[kontrast]darstellung f laryngography, roentgen [contrast] examination of the larynx
Kehlkopfschädigung f laryngeal trauma
Kehlkopfschleimhaut f laryngeal mucosa, mucous membrane of the larynx
Kehlkopfschmerz m laryngalgia, pain in the larynx
Kehlkopfschwellung f laryngeal oedema
Kehlkopfsenkung f laryngoptosis
Kehlkopfskelett n laryngeal skeleton
Kehlkopfsonde f laryngeal probe
Kehlkopfspalte f laryngeal cleft (fissure), laryngofissure; cleft larynx
Kehlkopfspaltung f 1. laryngotomy; 2. laryngofissure
Kehlkopfspezialist m laryngologist
Kehlkopfspiegel m laryng[end]oscope, laryngeal mirror
Kehlkopfspiegeltest m laryngeal mirror test
Kehlkopfspiegelung f laryngoscopy (Zusammensetzungen s. unter Laryngoskopie)
Kehlkopfsprache f laryngeal speech
Kehlkopfspritze f laryngeal syringe
Kehlkopfstellknorpel m arytenoid (triquetrous) cartilage
Kehlkopfstimme f laryngophony
Kehlkopfstridor m laryngeal stridor
Kehlkopftasche f laryngeal ventricle (sinus); laryngeal saccule
Kehlkopftrockenheit f laryngoxerosis, dryness of the throat
Kehlkopftuberkulose f laryngeal tuberculosis (phthisis), laryngophthisis; tuberculous laryngitis
Kehlkopftyphus m laryngotyphoid
Kehlkopf- und Luftröhreneröffnung f[/**operative**] laryngotracheotomy
Kehlkopf- und Rachenentfernung f[/**operative**] laryngopharyngectomy
Kehlkopf- und Rachenentzündung f laryngopharyngitis, hypopharyngitis
Kehlkopfvene f/**obere** superior laryngeal vein
~/untere inferior laryngeal vein
Kehlkopfvereng[er]ung f laryngeal stenosis, laryngostenosis, laryngemphraxis
Kehlkopfverhärtung f laryngoscleroma
Kehlkopfverhornung f laryngeal keratosis, keratosis of the larynx
Kehlkopfverlegung f laryngeal obstruction
Kehlkopfverletzung f laryngeal trauma
Kehlkopfverschluß s. Kehlkopfverlegung
Kehlkopfzyste f laryngeal cyst
Kehr-Zeichen n Kehr's sign (bei Milzruptur)
Keil m 1. cuneus, cuneate lobule (der Großhirnhemisphären); 2. gag (Mundsperrer)
Keilbein n 1. sphenoid [bone] (Schädelbasisknochen); 2. cuneiform (Fußwurzelknochen)
● **durch das ~** transsphenoidal
Keilbeinflügel m/**großer** greater sphenoidal wing, great wing of the sphenoid [bone]

~/kleiner lesser wing of the sphenoid, small wing of the sphenoid [bone]
Keilbeinflügelknochen *m* alisphenoid [bone]
Keilbeinfontanelle *f* sphenoid (anterolateral) fontanel
Keilbeinfortsatz *m* sphenoid process
Keilbeinhöhle *f* sphenoid [air] sinus
Keilbeinhöhlenentzündung *f* sphenoiditis, sphenoid sinusitis
Keilbeinhöhleneröffnung *f*[/operative] sphenoidotomy
Keilbeinhöhlenkatarrh *m* sphenoid sinusitis, sphenoiditis
Keilbeinhöhlenöffnung *f* opening of the sphenoid sinus *(Anatomie)*
Keilbeinleiste *f* sphenoid crest
Keilbeinnaht *f* sphenoid suture
Keilbein-Schläfenbein-Naht *f* squamosphenoid suture
Keilbein-Unterkiefer-Band *n* sphenomandibular ligament
Keilexzision *f* wedge excision (resection)
keilförmig cuneiform, cuneate, wedge-shaped, sphenoid[al]
Keilhöckerchen *n* cuneiform tubercle *(Kehlkopf)*
Keilknorpel *m* Wrisberg's (cuneiform) cartilage
Keilosteotomie *f* cuneiform osteotomy
Keilschädel *m* sphenocephalus
Keilschädeligkeit *f* sphenocephalia
Keilwirbel *m* wedged vertebra
Keim *m* 1. germ; 2. embryo
~/auslösender causative germ (microorganism)
~/krankheitserregender (pathogener) pathogenic germ, pathogen
Keimabsiedlung *f* bacterial metastasis
Keimanlage *f* blastoderm
Keimbekämpfung *f* antisepsis
Keimbekämpfungsmittel *n* antiseptic [agent]
Keimbesiedlung *f* bacterial flora *(z. B. des Dickdarms)*; bacterial invasion *(z. B. bei einer Infektion)*
Keimbläschen *n* blastocyst, blastodermic vesicle
Keimblase *f* blastula, germ vesicle
Keimblatt *n* blastodermic (germ) layer
~/äußeres ectoderm, ectoblast, epiblast
~/inneres endoderm, entoderm, entoblast
~/mittleres mesoderm, mesoblast
Keimblätterbildung *f* formation of germ layers
Keimdislokation *f* germ dislocation
Keimdrüse *f* gonad, reproductive (sexual) gland
~/männliche male gonad, testis, testicle, orchis
~/weibliche female gonad, ovary, oophoron
Keimdrüsen... *s. a.* Gonaden...
Keimdrüsenblutgefäß *n* gonadal vessel
Keimdrüsenentfernung *f*/operative gonadectomy, castration; oophorectomy
Keimdrüsenepithel *n* germ (germinal) epithelium
Keimdrüsenextraktbehandlung *f* gonadotherapy
Keimdrüsengeschwulst *f* gonadal tumour
Keimdrüsengewebe *n* gonadal tissue
Keimdrüsenhormon *n* gonadal (sexual) hormone
Keimdrüseninsuffizienz *f* gonadal insufficiency

Keimdrüsenleiste *f* gonadal ridge
keimdrüsenstimulierend gonadotropic
Keimdrüsenüberfunktion *f* hypergonadism
Keimdrüsenunterfunktion *f* hypogonadism
Keimeintrittspforte *f* portal of entry [of the germ]
Keimeintrittswunde *f* entry wound [of the germ]
keimen to germinate
Keimentwicklung *f s.* Keimlingsentwicklung
Keimentwicklungslehre *f* embryology
Keimepithel[ium] *n* germ (germinal) epithelium
Keimfalte *f* germ (genital) ridge
Keimfilter *n* bacterial filter
Keimfleck *m* germinal spot, germinative macula
keimfrei germ-free, sterile, aseptic, abacterial, amicrobic
Keimfreiheit *f* sterility, asepsis
Keimfreimachung *f* sterilization
keimhaltig germ-containing, septic, non-sterile
Keimhaut *f* blastoderm, germinal membrane
Keimhöhle *f* germinal cavity
Keimhügel *m* germ hillock
Keimknospe *f* germ bud
Keimling *m* embryo[n], foetus
Keimlingsentwicklung *f* embryogeny, embryogenesis, embryological development
Keimlingsernährung *f* embryotrophy
keimlingsnährend embryotrophic
keimlingsschädigend embryopathic, embryotoxic
Keimlingstötungsmittel *n* embryotoxic [agent]
Keimlingstoxizität *f* embryotoxicity
Keimplasma *n* germ (germinal) plasm
Keimpol *m* germ (germinal, animal) pole
keimschädigend 1. embryopathic, embryotoxic; 2. germicide
Keimschädigung *f* 1. embryopathy; 2. damage to germs
Keimschädlichkeit *f* embryotoxicity
Keimscheibe *f* germ (germinal) disk, blastodisk, embryonic area (blastoderm, shield), gastrodisk
Keimschicht *f* 1. germ (germinal) layer *(z. B. für Organe)*; 2. germinative (Malpighian) layer *(der Oberhaut)* ● **unter der ~** subgerminal
Keimschlauch *m* sporocyst *(Entwicklungsstadium der Leberegel)*
Keimselektion *f* germinal selection
keimtötend 1. germicidal, antiseptic, bactericidal; 2. embryotoxic
Keimtötungsmittel *n* embryotoxic [agent]
Keimtoxizität *f* embryotoxicity
Keim[über]träger *m* carrier
Keimung *f* germination
Keimverlagerung *f* aberration, dystopia
keimvernichtend *s.* keimtötend
Keimverschleppung *f* germ conveyance, vection
Keimversprengung *f*, **Keimverstreuung** *f* germinal spreading, germ dispersion (scattering), dissemination of germs
Keimwachstum *n*/**vulvovaginales** vulvovaginal flora

Keimwulst

Keimwulst *m* germinal swelling
Keimzahl *f* bacterial (germ) count *(z. B. im Urin)*
Keimzahlbestimmung *f* germ (bacterial) count
Keimzelle *f* germ (germinal) cell, gamete, gametozyte, gonoblast, gonocyte
~/männliche male gamete, sperm
~/weibliche female gamete, ovum, egg
keimzellenartig gametoid
keimzellenbildend gametogenic
Keimzellenbildung *f* gametogenesis
Keimzellengeschwulst *f* germinoma, germ cell tumour
Keimzentrum *n* germ (germinal) centre *(Lymphknoten)*
Keirospasmus *m* keirospasm, xyrospasm, shaving cramp
Keith-Flack-Knoten *m* Keith-Flack node, Keith's (sinoatrial) node *(Herzreizleitung)*
Keith-Wagner-Barker-Stadienklassifikation *f* Keith-Wagner-Barker classification (staging) of hypertensive fundus
Kelch *m* calyx, cup
kelchartig calycine, cup-like
Kelchausgußstein *m* staghorn calculus *(in der Niere)*
Kelchdivertikel *n* calyceal diverticulum
kelchförmig calyciform, cup-shaped
Kelchstein *m* calyceal calculus
Kell-Blutgruppensystem *n* Kell blood group system
Kellnerkrampf *m* waiter's cramp
Keloid *n* keloid, kelis, cheloid, keloma
Keloidakne *f* keloid acne, keloidal folliculitis
Keloidareal *n* keloid area
keloidartig keloidal, pseudokeloid
Keloidbildung *f* keloid formation
Keloidbildungsneigung *f* keloidosis
Keloid-Blastomykose *f* keloid blastomycosis
Keloidnarbe *f* keloid scar
Keloidose *f* keloidosis
Keloidsykose *f* keloid sycosis *(unter Narbenbildung abheilende follikuläre Eiterbläschen der Wangen- und Bartgegend)*
Keloplastik *f* keloplasty
Kelotomie *f* kelotomy
Keniafieber *n* Kenya fever (tick typhus)
Kennedy-Syndrom *n* [Foster-]Kennedy syndrome *(z. B. bei Frontalhirntumoren)*
Kennzeichen *n* sign, characteristic; symptom; mark; stigma
kennzeichnen to mark, to label, to tag; to designate, to characterize; to distinguish
kennzeichnend characteristic, specific; symptomatic
~/eine Krankheit pathognostic
~/für die Todesart thanatognostic
Kennzeit *f* chronaxy *(Reizauslösungszeit des doppelten Reizschwellenstroms)*
Kenophobie *f* kenophobia *(krankhafte Angst vor großen Räumen)*
Kephal... *s. a.* Zephal...
Kephalagra *f* cephalagra

Kephalhämatom *n* cephal[o]haematoma
Kephalhydrozele *f* cephalhydrocele
Kephalin *n* cephalin, kephalin
Kephalin-Cholesterin-Flockungsreaktion *f* cephalin[-cholesterol] flocculation test
Kephalin-Cholesterin-Flockungswert *m* cephalin[-cholesterol] flocculation value
Kephalin-Cholesterin-Probe *f* cephalin[-cholesterol] flocculation test
Kephalindex *m* cephalic index
Kephalisation *f* cephalization
Kephalodynie *f s.* Kopfschmerz
Kephalofazialindex *m* cephalofacial index
Kephalogenese *f* cephalogenesis
Kephalogramm *n* cephalogram
Kephalograph *m* cephalograph
Kephalographie *f* cephalography
kephalographisch cephalographic
Kephalohydrozele *f* cephalohydrocele
Kephalometer *n* cephalometer
Kephalometrie *f* cephalometry
kephalometrisch cephalometric
Kephalonie *f* cephalonia
Kephalopagus *m s.* Kraniopagus
kephalopelvin cephalopelvic
Kephaloplegie *f* cephaloplegia
Kephaloskopie *f* cephaloscopy
Kephalosporin *n* cephalosporin *(Antibiotikum)*
Kephalosporiose *f* cephalosporiosis *(Pilzinfektion)*
Kephalotetanus *m* cephalotetanus, cephalic tetanus
kephalothorakal cephalothoracic
Kephalothorakoileopagus *m* cephalothoracoiliopagus
Kephalothorakopagus *m* cephalothoracopagus *(Zwillingsmißgeburt mit Kopf- und Brustkorbverwachsung)*
Kephalotom *n* cephalotome *(Instrument)*
Kephalotomie *f* cephalotomy
Kephalotomieschere *f* cephalotomy (decapitating) scissors
Kephalotraktor *m* cephalotractor *(Geburtszange)*
Kephalotrib *m* cephalotribe
Kephalotripsie *f* cephalotripsy, cranioclasty, cranioclasis, basiotripsy *(bei einer Totgeburt)*
Kephalotripter *m* cephalotribe
Kephalozele *f* cephalocele
Kephalversion *f* cephalic version *(bei der Geburt)*
Kerasin *n* kerasin *(Zerebrosid)*
Kerasinspeicherkrankheit *f* kerasin thesaurismosis (storage disease), familial splenic anaemia
Keratalgie *f* keratalgia, pain in the cornea
Keratektasie *f* keratectasia, protrusion of the cornea
Keratektomie *f* ker[at]ectomy, excision of the cornea
Keratiasis *f* keratiasis
Keratin *n* keratin *(Gerüsteiweiß)* ● **~ bilden** to keratinize ● **sich zu ~ umwandeln** to keratinize
~/falsches pseudokeratin
keratinbildend keratogenetic

Keratinbildung f keratogenesis
Keratinisation f keratinization [process]
keratinisieren to keratinize
keratinophil keratinophilic
Keratinozyt m keratinocyte
keratinreich keratin-rich
Keratinüberproduktion f hyperkeratinization
Keratitis f keratitis, keratoiditis, inflammation of the cornea (s. a. unter Hornhautentzündung)
~ **anularis** s. ~ marginalis
~ **arborescens** arborescent (dendritic) keratitis
~ **bendiformis** band keratitis (keratopathy)
~ **bullosa** bullous keratitis
~ **disciformis** disciform keratitis
~ **e lagophthalmo** lagophthalmic (exposure) keratitis
~ **fascicularis** fascicular keratitis
~ **filamentosa** filamentary keratitis
~ **herpetica** herpetic keratitis
~ **interstitialis** interstitial keratitis
~ **marginalis** marginal (annular) keratitis
~ **parenchymatosa** parenchymatous keratitis
~ **parenchymatosa anaphylactica** parenchymatous anaphylactic keratitis
~ **phlyctaenulosa** phlyctenular keratitis (ophthalmia), phlyctenular [kerato]conjunctivitis
~ **punctata** punctate keratitis, descemetitis
~ **punctata leprosa** punctate keratitis of leprous origin
~ **purulenta** purulent keratitis; keratitis hypopyon
~ **rosacea** rosacea keratitis
~ **striata** striate keratitis
~ **superficialis** superficial keratitis
~ **vesicularis** vesicular keratitis
Kerato... s. a. Hornhaut...
Keratoakanthom n keratoacanthoma, acanthokeratoma, self-healing epithelioma (gutartige Hautwucherung)
Keratoblast m keratoblast
Keratochromatose f keratochromatosis
Keratoconjunctivitis f **punctata** punctate keratoconjunctivitis
Keratoderma n **climacterium** climacteric (endocrine) keratoderma
Keratodermatose f keratodermia; keratoderma
Keratoektasie f keratoectasia
Keratoelastose f keratoelastosis
Keratofibrille f keratofibril
Keratofotografie f keratophotography
Keratogenese f keratogenesis
Keratoglobus m keratoglobus
Keratographie f keratographia
Keratohämie f keratohaemia
Keratohelkose f keratohelcosis, ulceration of the cornea
Keratohyalin n keratohyalin (Hornsubstanzvorstufe der Oberhaut)
Keratoiridoskop n keratoiridoscope
Keratoiridozyklitis f keratoiridocyclitis (Entzündung der Hornhaut, der Regenbogenhaut und des Strahlenkörpers)
Keratoiritis f keratoiritis, iridokeratitis

Keratokonjunktivitis f keratoconjunctivitis
~/**aktinische** actinic keratoconjunctivitis
Keratokonus m keratokonus; conical cornea
Keratolyse f keratolysis
Keratolysis f **bullosa hereditaria** hereditary bullous keratolysis
Keratolytikum n keratolytic [agent]
Keratom n s. 1. Keratoma; 2. Keratotom
Keratoma n keratoma
~ **benignum congenitale** congenital benign keratoma
Keratomalazie f keratomalacia, softening of the cornea
Keratomegalie f keratomegaly
Keratometer n keratometer
Keratometrie f keratometry (Messung des Hornhautdurchmessers und der Hornhautkrümmung)
Keratomykose f keratomycosis
Keratonyxis f keratonyxis, puncture of the cornea; couching [for cataract]
Keratopathie f keratopathy
Keratoplastik f keratoplasty (Operation zum Ersatz der Hornhaut)
keratoplastisch keratoplastic
Keratoprotein n keratoprotein
Keratoprothese f keratoprosthesis
Keratorrhexis f keratorrhexis, rupture of the cornea
Keratosis f keratosis
~ **blennorrhagica** blennorrhagic keratosis, gonorrhoeal parakeratosis
~ **follicularis** follicular keratosis (psorospermosis)
~ **follicularis vegetans** Darier's disease
~ **palmoplantaris (palmaris et plantaris)** palmar and plantar keratosis, congenital palmoplantar hyperkeratosis (Epidermiswucherungen mit starker Verhornung)
~ **palmoplantaris circumscripta** Unna-Thost syndrome
~ **seborrhoeica** seborrhoeic keratosis
Keratoskleritis f keratoscleritis
Keratoskop n keratoscope
Keratoskopie f keratoscopy (Methode zur Bestimmung der Hornhautkrümmung)
keratotisch keratotic
Keratotom n kera[to]tome (Instrument)
Keratotomie f keratotomy
Keratouveitis f kerato-uveitis
Keratozele f kerato[dermato]cele, descemetocele
Keratozentese f keratocentesis, puncturation of the cornea
Keratozyt m keratocyte
Keraunoneurose f keraunoneurosis (durch Blitzschlag oder Starkstrom)
Keraunoparalyse f keraunoparalysis (Lähmung durch Blitzschlag oder Starkstrom)
Keraunophobie f keraunophobia (krankhafte Angst vor Blitzschlag oder Starkstrom)
Kerckring-Falten fpl Kerckring (circular) folds
Kerektomie f ker[at]ectomy

Kerion

Kerion n Celsi Celsus' kerion *(Pilzerkrankung mit Geschwürsbildung und Eiterbläschen)*
Keritherapie f keritherapy *(Paraffinölbehandlung)*
Kerley-Linien fpl Kerley (septal) lines
Kern m nucleus; karyon, karyoplast, endoplast *(s. a. unter Nucleus und Zellkern)* ● neben einem ~ paranuclear, paranucleate ● ohne ~ non-nucleated ● über einem ~ supranuclear ● vielgestaltige Kerne besitzend polymorphonuclear
~/**Bechterewscher** Bekhterev's (superior vestibular) nucleus
~/**Burdachscher** Burdach's (cuneate) nucleus *(im verlängerten Rückenmark)*
~/**Deitersscher** Deiters' (lateral vestibular) nucleus
~/**Gollscher** Goll's (gracilis) nucleus
~/**Monakowscher** Monakov's (accessory cuneate) nucleus *(Hirnstamm)*
~/**Schwalbescher** Schwalbe's nucleus, principal (medial) vestibular nucleus
~/**Westphal-Edingerscher** [Edinger-]Westphal nucleus, autonomic nucleus of the oculomotor nerve
Kernagenesie f nuclear agenesis
Kernanhang m nuclear appendage
Kernanomalie f nuclear anomaly
Kernaplasie f nuclear aplasia *(Fehlentwicklung der Hirnnervenkerne)*
kernauflösend karyolytic
Kernauflösung f karyolysis
Kernausstoßung f nuclear expulsion
Kernbruchstück n nuclear fragment
Kernchromatin n nuclear chromatin, chromoplasm
Kerndurchmesser m nuclear diameter
Kerne mpl/**Jaworskische** Jaworski's corpuscles *(freie Leukozytenkerne im Magensaft)*
Kernechtrot n kernechtrot, nuclear fast red
Kerneinschluß m intranuclear inclusion
Kerneinschlußkörper m intranuclear inclusion body
Kernentwicklung f karyogenesis
Kernfaden m nuclear thread
kernfärbend karyochrome
Kernfärbung f nuclear staining
Kernfigur f nuclear figure *(Kernteilung)*
kernförmig nucleiform
Kernfurchung f segmentation of the nucleus
Kerngerüst n chromatin, nuclear network (reticulum)
Kerngeschlecht n nuclear sex
Kerngeschlechtsbestimmung f nuclear sex determination
Kerngift n nucleotoxin
kerngiftig nucleotoxic
kernhaltig nucleated
Kernhülle f nuclear membrane, karyotheca
Kernhyaloplasma m nucleohyaloplasm
Kernikterus m kernicterus, nuclear icterus (jaundice) *(Bilirubinpigmentation des ZNS)*

388

Kernkörperchen n nucleole, nucleolus
kernkörperchenartig nucleoliform
Kernkugeln fpl [Howell-]Jolly bodies *(bei Erythrozytenzellkernzerfall)*
Kernlähmung f nuclear paralysis
Kernläsion f nuclear lesion (injury)
kernlos non-nucleated, anuclear, akaryote, acaryote
Kernmasse f nuclear mass
Kernmaterial n nuclear material
Kernmembran f nuclear membrane, karyotheca
Kernneurose f organic neurosis
Kernophthalmoplegie f nuclear ophthalmoplegia
Kernphase f nuclear phase
Kernplasma n karyoplasm, nucleoplasm, plasm[a]
Kern-Plasma-Relation f nucleocytoplasmic ratio
Kernpolymorphie f nuclear polymorphism
Kernporen fpl nuclear pores
Kernproliferation f nuclear proliferation
Kernprotein n nucleoprotein
Kernpyknose f karyopyknosis
Kernpyknose-Index m karyopyknotic (nucleopyknotic) index
Kernregion f nuclear region
Kernretikulum n nucleoreticulum, nuclear reticulum
Kernrotation f nuclear rotation
Kernruhe f karyostasis
Kernsaft m nuclear juice (sap), karyolymph
Kernschleife f chromosome, chromatin body
Kernschwellung f nuclear swelling
Kernschwund m kernschwund
Kernsegment n nuclear segment
Kernsegmentierung f nuclear segmentation (fragmentation)
Kernspindel f nuclear spindle, nucleospindle
Kernspinresonanz-Verfahren n nuclear magnetic resonance [technique]
Kernstar m nuclear cataract *(auf den Alterskern der Linse beschränkte Trübung)*
Kernstrahlung f nuclear radiation
Kernsubstanz f chromatin
Kernteilung f nuclear division
~/**direkte** amitosis
~/**indirekte** s. Karyokinese
Kernteilungsendphase f telophase, teleomitosis
Kernteilungsfigur f mitotic figure
Kernteilungsphase f/**erste** prophase
Kerntrümmer pl nuclear debris
Kerntyp m karyotype
Kernvakuole f nuclear vacuole
Kernvergrößerung f karyomegaly
Kernvermessung f karyometry
kernverschmelzend karyogamic
Kernverschmelzung f karyogamy, conjugation *(bei geschlechtlicher Fortpflanzung)*
kernzerbrechend karyoclastic
Kernzerfall m karyorrhexis, karyolysis *(nach dem Zelltod)*
kernzertrümmernd karyoclastic
Kernzertrümmerung f karyoclasis, karyoklasis

Kerzenfleckphänomen n candle spot phenomenon
Ketamin n ketamine (Anästhetikum)
Ketoazidose f ketoacidosis
Ketoazidurie f ketoaciduria, ketonuria
Ketogenese f s. Ketonkörperbildung
Ketoglutarsäure f ketoglutaric acid (Zwischenprodukt beim Abbau der Zitronensäure zu Bernsteinsäure)
Ketoheptose f ketoheptose
Ketohexose f ketohexose
β-Ketohydroxybuttersäure f beta-ketohydroxybutyric acid
Ketokarbonsäure f keto acid
Ketolyse f ketolysis
Ketonämie f ketonaemia
ketonämisch ketonaemic
ketonbildend ketogen[et]ic, ketoplastic
Ketonkörper m ketone (acetone) body
Ketonkörperabbau m [/metabolischer] ketolysis
ketonkörperabbauend ketolytic
Ketonkörperausscheidung f im Urin ketonuria, ketoaziduria, diacet[on]uria
Ketonkörperazidose f ketoacidosis, diabetic acidosis
ketonkörperbildend ketogen[et]ic, ketoplastic
Ketonkörperbildung f ketogenesis, ketoplasia (z. B. bei Diabetes mellitus)
Ketonkörper[spiegel]erhöhung f im Blut hyperketonaemia
ketonkörpervermehrend ketotic
Ketoplasie f ketoplasia
α-Ketopropionsäure f ketopropionic acid
Ketoreduktase f ketoreductase (Enzym)
Ketosäure f keto (ketonic) acid
Ketose f 1. ketose, ketonic sugar; 2. ketosis (Ketonkörpervermehrung bei schwerem Diabetes mellitus)
Ketoseausscheidung f im Urin ketosuria
Ketose-1-phosphat-Aldolase f ketose-1-phosphate aldolase (Enzym)
Ketosteroid n ketosteroid
Ketozucker m ketose, ketonic sugar
Kette f/leichte light chain (z. B. der Immunglobuline)
~/schwere heavy chain (z. B. der Immunglobuline)
Kettenligatur f chain (interlocking) ligature
Kettennaht f chain suture
Kettenreflex m chain reflex
Kettensäge f chain saw
keuchen to gasp [for breath]
Keuchen n gasp[ing]; wheezing
Keuchhusten m whooping (chin) cough, pertussis
Keuchhustenantiserum n antipertussis serum
keuchhustenartig pertussal, pertussoid
Keuchhustenbakterium n Bordetella (Haemophilus) pertussis, Bordet-Gengou bacillus
Keuchhustenimpfstoff m pertussis vaccine
Keuchhusten[schutz]impfung f pertussis vaccination

Kieferluxation

Keuchhustenserum n antipertussis serum
Keule f club; pestle (Mörser)
Keulenfinger m clubbed finger
keulenförmig clubbed, club-shaped, claviform
Keuschheit f chastity
Kidd-Blutgruppensystem n Kidd blood group system
Kiefer m jaw[-bone]
~/schnappender snapping jaw
Kieferanomalie f anomaly of the jaws, dysgnathia
Kieferarterie f maxillary artery
Kieferbogen m [palato]maxillary arch; mandibular arch
Kieferchirurg m dental (oral) surgeon
Kieferchirurgie f dental (oral) surgery
kieferchirurgisch orosurgical
Kieferentzündung f gnathitis, inflammation of the jaws
Kieferfehlbildung f atelognathia
Kieferfortsatz m maxillary process
Kieferfraktur f jaw fracture, fracture of the jaw
Kieferfrakturstabilisator m jaw fracture appliance
Kiefer-Gaumen-Spalte f gnathopalatoschisis; cleft hard palate
Kiefergelenk n [temporo]mandibular joint
Kiefergelenkarthrose f/Costens Costen's temporomandibular arthrosis, Costen's (temporomandibular joint) syndrome
Kiefergelenkvene f vein of the temporomandibular joint
Kiefergelenkwinkel m mandibular (gonial) angle
Kieferhöhle f maxillary [air] sinus, Highmore's (maxillary) antrum, antrum of Highmore
Kieferhöhlenempyem n maxillary empyema
Kieferhöhlenentzündung f maxillary sinusitis, antritis
Kieferhöhlenerkrankung f maxillary sinus disease
Kieferhöhlenhaken m antrum retractor
Kieferhöhlenöffnung f maxillary hiatus (ostium) (zur Nasenhöhle)
Kieferhöhlenperforation f maxillary perforation
Kieferhöhlenradikaloperation f Caldwell-Luc operation
Kieferhöhlenspiegel m antroscope
Kieferhöhlenspiegelung f antroscopy
Kieferhöhlenstanze f antrum punch
Kieferhöhlentrokar m antrum trocar
Kieferhypertrophie f macrognathia
Kieferhypotrophie f micrognathia
Kieferklemme f lockjaw, trismus
Kieferknochen m jaw[-bone]
Kieferkrebs m jaw carcinoma
Kieferlehre f gnathology
Kieferlippenspalte f cheilognathoschisis
kieferlos agnathous, jawless
Kieferloser m agnathus
Kieferlosigkeit f agnathia
Kieferluxation f luxation of the mandible (lower jaw)

Kiefermuskel

Kiefermuskel *m* masseter [muscle]
~/zweibäuchiger digastric muscle
Kiefernekrose *f* durch **Phosphor** phospho[r]necrosis; phossy jaw
Kieferneuralgie *f* gnathalgia, gnathodynia
Kieferorthopäde *m* orthodontist
Kieferorthopädie *f* orthodontia, orthodontics, dental orthopaedics, orthodontology, odontorthosis
kieferorthopädisch orthodontic
Kieferosteomyelitis *f* jaw osteomyelitis
Kieferplastik *f* gnathoplasty
Kieferprothetik *f* prosthetic dentistry
Kieferreflex *m* jaw reflex (jerk)
kieferrekonstruierend gnathoplastic
Kieferrekonstruktion *f/operative* gnathoplasty
Kiefersäge *f* mandibular saw
Kieferschmerz *m* gnathalgia, gnathodynia, pain in the jaw
Kieferspaltbildung *f* schizognathism
Kieferspalte *f* gnathoschisis; cleft maxilla (jaw)
Kiefersperre *f s.* Kieferklemme
Kiefersteifigkeit *f* stiffness of the jaw
Kieferstellung *f/gerade* orthognathia, orthognathism
Kiefertrauma *n* jaw injury (trauma)
Kieferunterentwicklung *f* atelognathia
Kieferverlust *m/halbseitiger* hemignathia
Kieferwinkel *m* mandibular (gonial) angle
Kieferwinkelfraktur *f* mandibular angle fracture
Kieferwinkellymphom *n* lymphoma of the mandibular angle
Kieferzungenbeinmuskel *m* mylohyoid muscle
Kieferzyste *f* jaw cyst
Kiel *m* carina *(Zusammensetzungen s. unter Carina)*
Kielbauch *m* carinate abdomen
Kielbrust *f* carinate (chicken) breast, pigeon chest, scaphoid thorax
Kielkopf *m* scaphocephalus
kielköpfig scaphocephalous, scaphocephalic
Kielköpfigkeit *f* scaphocephalia
Kiemenbogen *m* branchial arch, visceral (pharyngeal) arch
~/erster mandibular (first) arch
Kiemenbogensyndrom *n* branchial (visceral) arch syndrome
Kiemenbogensystem *n* branchial (visceral) arch system
Kiemenfurche *f* branchial cleft, visceral (pharyngeal) groove
Kiemengang *m* branchial cleft (duct), visceral cleft (fissure)
Kiemengangfistel *f* branchial [cyst] fistula, branchiogenic fistula
Kiemengangkarzinom *n* branchial (branchiogenic) carcinoma, branchioma
Kiemengangzyste *f* branchial [cleft] cyst, branchial inclusion cyst
Kiemenspalte *f s.* Kiemengang
Kiementasche *f* branchial pouch, visceral (pharyngeal) pouch

Kienböck-Atrophie *f* Kienböck's atrophy *(beim Sudeck-Syndrom)*
Kienböck-Erkrankung *f* Kienböck's disease, lunatomalacia, osteochondrosis of the lunate bone
Kiesel[gur]lunge *f* kieselgur lung, silic[ath]osis, Potter's asthma (consumption, rot)
Killerlymphozyt *m* killer lymphocyte *(Immunologie)*
Kimmelstiel-Wilson-Syndrom *n* Kimmelstiel-Wilson disease (syndrome), intercapillary nephrosclerosis, diabetic glomerulosclerosis
Kinäde *m* passive paederast
Kinanästhesie *f* kinanaesthesia
Kinase *f* kinase *(Enzym)*
Kinästhesie *f* kinaesthesia, kinaesthetic memory
Kinästhesietraining *n* kinaesthetic training
Kinästhesiometer *n* kinaesthesiometer, kinesiaesthesiometer *(Instrument zur Prüfung des Muskelsinns)*
Kind *n* child, infant
~/ausgesetztes foundling
~/ausgetragenes full-term child
~/ausgezehrtes (marantisches) waster
~/neugeborenes newborn, neonate
~/totgeborenes still-born child
~/ungeborenes unborn child
Kindbett *n* childbed, puerperium, lying-in [period]
Kindbett... *s. a.* Puerperal... *und* Wochenbett...
Kindbettfieber *n* childbed fever, puerperal sepsis, lech[i]opyra
Kindbettmastitis *f* puerperal mastitis; caked breast
Kindentwicklung *f* child development
Kinderabneigung *f* paedophobia, misopaedia
Kinderanästhesie *f* paediatric anaesthesia
Kinderarzt *m* paediatrician, paediatrist, children's specialist
kinderärztlich paediatric
Kinderbronchoskop *n* infant bronchoscope
Kinderchirurg *m* paediatric surgeon
Kinderchirurgie *f* paediatric surgery
Kinderdosis *f* children's dosage
kinderfreundlich paedophilic
Kindergarten *m* kindergarten, infant-school
Kindergärtnerin *f* kindergarten teacher
Kinderheilkunde *f* paediatrics, paediatry
kinderheilkundlich paediatric
Kinderhort *m* day-nursery
Kinderintensivpflege *f* paediatric intensive care
Kinderkardiologie *f* paediatric cardiology
Kinderklinik *f* children's (paediatric) hospital
Kinderkrankenschwester *f* children's (paediatric) nurse
Kinderkrankenstation *f* paediatric ward
Kinderkrankheit *f* paediatric (childhood) disease, children's complaint
Kinderlähmung *f/spinale* [paralytic] spinal poliomyelitis, infantile paralysis, polio[myelitis], Heine-Medin disease *(Entzündung der grauen Rückenmarksubstanz)*
Kinderlähmungs... *s.* Poliomyelitis...

Kinderleishmaniose f infantile leishmaniasis
kinderlieb paedophilic
Kinderliebe f paedophilia
kinderlos childless
Kinderlosigkeit f childlessness
Kindermädchen n [dry-]nurse, nurse-maid
Kindermord m infanticide
Kindermörder m infanticide
Kinderpsychiater m child psychiatrist, paedopsychiatrist
Kinderpsychiatrie f child psychiatry, paedopsychiatry
Kinderpsychologe m child (paediatric) psychologist
Kinderpsychologie f child (paediatric) psychology
Kinderpsychotherapie f child (paediatric) psychotherapy
Kindersanatorium n sanatorium for children
Kinderstation f children's (paediatric) ward
Kindersterblichkeit f infant mortality
Kindersterblichkeitsrate f infantile mortality rate
Kindervermessung f paedometry
Kinderwurm m Enterobius vermicularis, pinworm
Kinderwurmbefall m enterobiasis, pinworm infection
Kinderzahnarzt m paediadontist
Kinderzahnheilkunde f paediadontology, paed[i]odontia, paedodontics, paedodontology
Kinderzäpfchen n suppository for children
Kindesabzehrung f paedatrophia
Kindesalter n [/frühes] [early] infancy
~/**spätes** late infancy, childhood
Kindesannahme f affiliation
Kindesaussetzung f exposure of infants
Kindesauszehrung f paedatrophia
Kindesentbindung f s. Entbindung
Kindesentwicklung f child development
Kindeslage f s. Kindslage
Kindesmißhandlung f cruelty to children, child abuse, ill-treatment of a child
Kindesmißhandlungssyndrom n battered child syndrome
Kindesschrei m vagitus, cry of the infant
Kindestötung f infanticide (nach der Geburt); aborticide (in der Gebärmutter)
Kindeszerstückelung f/**operative** embryotomy (unter der Geburt)
Kindheitsexanthem n childhood exanthem[a]
Kindheitspsychose f neophrenia
kindisch infantile, childish, puerile
Kindischsein n puerilism
kindlich infantile, puerile
Kindsabtreibung f [illegal] abortion
Kindsbewegung f foetal movement (in der Gebärmutter)
~/**erste** quickening
Kindskopf m foetal head
Kindskopfeinkeilung f im Geburtskanal paragomphosis
Kindslage f presentation (bei der Geburt)
~/**anomale** malpresentation

~/**longitudinale** longitudinal presentation
~/**quere** transverse presentation
Kindspech n meconium (Neugeborenenstuhl)
Kindspechausscheidung f meconiorrhoea
Kindspechileus m meconium ileus
Kindsteil m foetal part
~/**vorausgehender** presenting foetal part
~/**vorgefallener** prolapsed foetal part
Kineangiogramm n cineangiogram
Kineangiographie f cineangiography (Darstellung von Gefäßen)
Kineangiokardiogramm n cineangiocardiogram
Kineangiokardiographie f cineangiocardiography (Darstellung des Herzens und der herznahen Gefäße)
kineangiokardiographisch cineangiocardiographic
Kinecholangiographie f cinecholangiography (Darstellung der Gallenwege)
Kinedensitometrie f cinedensitometry
Kinefluorographie f cinefluorography
Kinefluoroskopie f cinefluoroscopy
Kinekoronararteriogramm n cinecoronary arteriogram
Kinekoronarogramm n cinecoronary arteriogram
Kinekoronarographie f cinecoronary arteriography (Darstellung der Herzkranzgefäße)
Kinematik f kinematics (Lehre von den Bewegungen)
Kineösophagogramm n cineoesophagogram
Kineösophagographie f cineoesophagography (Darstellung der Speiseröhre)
kineösophagographisch cineoesophagographic
Kinephlebographie f cinephlebography (Darstellung der Venen)
Kineplastik f kineplasty, kineplastic (kinematic) amputation (Weichteilplastik an Amputationsstümpfen, bei der die Muskelkräfte zur Bewegung ausgenutzt werden)
Kineradiogramm n cineradiogram
Kineradiographie f cineradiography, cineroentgenography, X-ray motion picture photography
kineradiographisch cineradiographic
Kineradiotherapie f kineradiotherapy, kineroentgenotherapy
Kinesalgie f kinesalgia, pain on muscular exertion
Kinesimeter n kinesi[o]meter
Kinesiologie f kinesiology (Lehre von den mechanischen und anatomischen Grundlagen der Bewegung)
Kinesioneurose f kinesioneurosis
Kinesitherapie f kinesiatrics, kinesiotherapy, kinetotherapy, movement cure
Kineskop n kinescope (Instrument zur Refraktionsprüfung des Auges)
Kinesophobie f kinesophobia (krankhafte Angst vor Bewegungen)
Kinetokardiogramm n kinetocardiogram (z. B. Ballistokardiogramm)
Kinetonukleus m kinetonucleus, kinetoplast, parabasal body (z. B. bei Flagellaten)

Kinetoplasma

Kinetoplasma n kinetoplasm
Kinetoplast m s. Kinetonukleus
Kinetose f kinetosis, kinesia, motion sickness *(z. B. Flugzeugkrankheit)*
Kinetotherapie f s. Kinesitherapie
Kineventrikulogramm n cineventriculogram
Kineventrikulographie f cineventriculography *(Darstellung der Herzventrikel)*
Kinin n kinin *(pharmakologisch aktives Polypeptid)*
Kininogen n kininogen
Kininogenase f kininogenase, kinin forming enzyme
Kinn n chin, mentum ● **mit dem ~ nach hinten liegend** mentoposterior *(Fetus bei der Geburt)* ● **mit dem ~ nach vorn liegend** mentoanterior *(Fetus bei der Geburt)* ● **über dem ~** supramental ● **unter dem ~** submental
Kinnarterie f mental artery
Kinnaufbau m chin reconstruction, mentoplasty
Kinnaufbauplastik f augmentation mentoplasty
Kinnbackenkrampf m lockjaw, trismus
Kinndreieck n mental protuberance (process)
Kinnerv m mental nerve
Kinnfistel f mental (chin) fistula
Kinnflechte f mentagra
Kinnlage f mental (chin) presentation *(des Fetus bei der Geburt)*
~/hintere mentoposterior position
~/linke hintere left mentoposterior position
~/linke vordere left mentoanterior position
~/rechte hintere right mentoposterior position
~/rechte vordere right mentoanterior position
~/vordere mentoanterior position
Kinnloch n mental foramen
Kinnmuskel m mentalis [muscle], levator menti [muscle]
Kinnplastik f genioplasty
Kinnpunkt m mental point
Kinnreflex m chin reflex
Kinnregion f mental region
Kinnrekonstruktion f chin reconstruction, mentoplasty
Kinnvorsprung m mental protuberance (process)
Kinn-Zungenbein-Muskel m geniohyoid [muscle]
Kinn-Zungen-Muskel m genio[hyo]glossus [muscle]
Kinometer n kinometer *(gynäkologisches Instrument)*
Kinoplasma n kinoplasm *(Zytoplasmaabschnitt)*
Kionitis f kionitis
Kiotomie f kiotomy, uvulectomy, amputation of the uvula
Kippgelenk n amphiarthrosis
Kirschner-Draht m Kirschner [threaded] wire *(für Osteosynthese)*
Kirschner-Drahtextension f Kirschner's traction
Kirschner-Drahtfixation f Kirschner wire fixation
Kittel m [physician's white] coat; gown *(des Chirurgen)*
Kittniere f caseous pyonephrosis

Kittsubstanz f cement substance *(für Zellverbindungen)*
Kitzelgefühl n titillation, tickling
kitzeln to titillate, to tickle
Kitzler m s. Klitoris
Kjehldal-Analyse f Kjehldal method *(zur Stickstoffbestimmung in organischen Substanzen)*
klaffen to gape, to yawn
Klaffen n dehiscence *(z. B. einer Wunde)*
Klammer f clamp, clip
~/Michelsche Michel clip *(Hautklammer)*
Klammerentfernungszange f clip removing forceps
Klammerhaltezange f bone staple holding forceps, clipholder
Klammernahtgerät n stapling device (machine)
Klammersetzzange f clip applying forceps
Klammertechnik f clamp technic
Klammerzange f clip forceps
Klang m tone, sound; clang; tone
~/amphorischer metallischer amphoric resonance
Klanganalyse f clang analysis
Klangassoziation f clang association
Klanghalluzination f musical hallucination
Klangmesser m phonometer
Klangmessung f phonometry *(Hörprüfung)*
Klangtaubheit f clang deafness
Klappe f valve, valva, valvule, valvula *(s. a. Herzklappe)*
~/Bauhinsche Bauhin's valve, ileocaecal (ileocolic) valve
~ der unteren Hohlvene Eustachian valve
~/Gerlachsche Gerlach's valve *(am Wurmfortsatz)*
~/Hasnersche Hasner's (lacrimal) valve *(Schleimhautfalte an der Tränengangsmündung)*
~/Heistersche Heister's valve, spiral valve [of Heister] *(Gallenblasenschleimhautfalte)*
~/kleine valvula
~/Thebesiussche Thebesian valve
Klappen fpl/**Houstonsche** Houston's valves, horizontal folds of the rectum
Klappen... s. a. Herzklappen...
Klappenaffektion f valvular disease
Klappenaneurysma n valvular aneurysm
Klappenansatz m valvular attachment
Klappenapparat m valvular apparatus
klappenartig valvular
Klappenchirurgie f valve surgery
Klappendurchtrennung f[/operative] valv[ul]otomy
Klappendysfunktion f valvular dysfunction
Klappenebene/auf at valve level
Klappenendokarditis f valvular endocarditis
Klappenexstirpation f valvulectomy
klappenförmig valviform
Klappengeräusch n heart (valvular) murmur
Klappenhämatom n valvular haematoma
Klappenläsion f valvular lesion
klappenlos avalvular, valveless
Klappenoperation f valve surgery

Klappenperforation f valvular perforation
Klappenplastik f valvuloplasty
Klappenschlußfähigkeit f [valvular] competence, competence of the valve
Klappenschlußton m flapping sound
Klappenstenose f valvular stenosis
Klappenzipfel m valvular (valve) cusp
~/**hinterer** posterior cusp
~/**vorderer** anterior cusp
Klapperschlangengift n rattlesnake (crotalus) venom, crotoxin
Klapperschlangenserum n anticrotalus serum, crotalus antitoxin
Klapp-Kriechen n Klapp's creeping treatment *(zur Skoliosebehandlung)*
Klappmesserphänomen n clasp-knife phenomenon (rigidity, spasticity)
klar 1. evident, obvious, manifest, distinct *(z. B. Symptomatik)*; 2. lucid, conscious *(z. B. Bewußtsein)*; 3. clear *(z. B. Urin)*
Klärfaktor m clearing factor *(z. B. im Plasma)*
Klärungsreaktion f/**Meinickesche** Meinicke's [clearing] test *(serologischer Syphilisnachweis)*
Klarzellsarkom n clear cell sarcoma *(bösartige Geschwulst)*
Klasmatozyt m clasmatocyte *(Monozyt)*
Klassifikation f **der Neugeborenen** classification of newborns
klassifizieren to classify; to type *(z. B. Blutgruppe)*
Klassifizierung f classification
klassisch classical *(z. B. Symptomatik)*
klastisch clastic
Klastothrix f clastothrix
Klatschpräparat n impression preparation
Klatschung f slapping, tapotement *(Massage)*
Klauenfuß m claw foot
Klauenhand f claw hand
Klaustrophilie f claustrophilia *(krankhafte Neigung, sich einzuschließen)*
Klaustrophobie f claustrophobia *(krankhafte Angst vor geschlossenen Räumen)*
Klavikel f s. Klavikula
Klavikotomie f clavicotomy
Klavikula f clavicle, clavicula, collarbone
Klavikula... s. a. Schlüsselbein...
Klavikulaexstirpation f claviculectomy
Klavikulafraktur f clavicle fracture
Klavikulapseudarthrose f clavicle pseudarthrosis
klavikular clavicular
Klavikulargrube f clavicular fossa
Klavikularlinie f clavicular line
Klavikularregion f clavicular region
Klavikulektomie f claviculectomy
klavikulohumeral cleidohumeral
klavikulokostal cleidocostal
klavikuloskapulär cleidoscapular
klavikulosternal cleidosternal
Klavus m clavus, corn
kleben to adhere; to agglutinate
klebend adhesive *(z. B. Pflaster)*; agglutinative *(z. B. Blutgerinnsel)*

Klebepflaster n adhesive [plaster]
Klebereiweiß n gluten *(in Weizen und Roggen)*
Klebestreifen m adhesive strip
Klebeverband m adhesive dressing (bandage)
klebrig sticky, viscous, viscid, viscose *(z. B. Flüssigkeiten)*; clammy *(z. B. Haut)*; glutinous *(z. B. Auswurf)*
Klebsiella f Klebsiella *(gramnegatives Stäbchen)*
~ **pneumoniae** pneumobacillus, Friedländer's bacillus
Klebsiellenpneumonie f klebsiellal (Friedländer's) pneumonia
Kleeblattdeformität f cloverleaf deformity *(Röntgenzeichen bei Zwölffingerdarmgeschwür)*
Kleeblattschädel m cloverleaf skull
Kleeblattschädeldeformität f cloverleaf skull deformity *(Fetusmißbildung)*
Kleiderlaus f body (clothes) louse
Kleiderlausbefall m lousiness of the body
Kleidotomie f cleidotomy, clavic[ul]otomy
kleieartig furfuraceous, pityroid, branny
Kleieflechte f pityriasis versicolor, chromophytosis
Kleiepilz m Malassezia furfur *(Erreger der Pityriasis versicolor)*
Kleieschuppung f furfuraceous desquamation
Kleinarmigkeit f microbrachia
kleinäugig microphthalmic, microphthalmous
Kleinäugiger m microphthalmus
Kleinäugigkeit f microphthalmia, nanophthalmia
Kleinautoklav m baby autoclave
Kleinbrüstigkeit f micromastia
kleindrüsig micradenous
Kleine-Levin-Syndrom n Kleine-Levin syndrome *(periodische Somnolenz mit Heißhungerzuständen)*
Kleinersehen n micropsia
Kleinfinger m little finger
Kleinfingerabzieher m abductor digiti minimi manus [muscle]
Kleinfingerballen m hypothenar [prominence], hypothenar eminence
Kleinfingerbeugekontraktur f camptodactyly
Kleinfingerbeuger m/**kurzer** flexor digiti minimi (quinti) brevis [muscle] of the hand
Kleinfingergegensteller m opponens digiti minimi manus [muscle], opponens digiti quinti [muscle] of the hand
kleinfingerig microdactylous
Kleinfingerigkeit f microdactyly
Kleinfingerstrecker m extensor digiti minimi [muscle], extensor digiti quinti proprius [muscle]
~/**ulnarer** extensor carpi ulnaris digiti minimi [muscle]
kleinfollikulär microfollicular
Kleinfüßigkeit f micropodia
Kleingliedrigkeit f micromelia
Kleinhändigkeit f microcheiria
Kleinheitswahn m micromania *(krankhafte Unterschätzung der eigenen Leistungen und der eigenen Persönlichkeit)*

Kleinhirn

Kleinhirn *n* cerebellum, parencephalon, little brain, microencephalon, opisthencephalon ● **neben dem** ~ paracerebellar ● **über dem** ~ supracerebellar ● **unter dem** ~ subcerebellar
Kleinhirnabszeß *m* cerebellar abscess
Kleinhirnagenesie *f* cerebellar agenesis
Kleinhirnanfall *m* cerebellar fit
Kleinhirnaplasie *f* cerebellar aplasia
Kleinhirnapoplexie *f* cerebellar apoplexy
Kleinhirnarterie *f*/**obere** superior cerebellar artery
~/**untere hintere** posterior inferior cerebellar artery
~/**untere vordere** anterior inferior cerebellar artery
Kleinhirnastrozytom *n* cerebellar astrocytoma
Kleinhirnataxie *f* cerebellar ataxia
Kleinhirnatrophie *f* cerebellar atrophy
Kleinhirnbrückenregion *f* cerebellopontine region
Kleinhirnbrückenwinkel *m* cerebellopontine (pontocerebellar) angle
Kleinhirnbrückenwinkelmyelographie *f* cerebellopontine angle myelography
Kleinhirnbrückenwinkeltumor *m* cerebellopontine angle tumour
Kleinhirnbrückenwinkeltumorsyndrom *n* cerebellopontine angle tumour syndrome
Kleinhirndegeneration *f* cerebellar degeneration
Kleinhirndruckkonus *m* cerebellar pressure cone *(Kleinhirneinklemmung im Tentoriumschlitz)*
Kleinhirndysraphie *f* cerebellar dysraphia
Kleinhirneinklemmung *f* cerebellar herniation; pressure cone
Kleinhirnentfernung *f*[/**operative**] decerebellation
Kleinhirnentzündung *f* cerebellitis, parencephalitis, inflammation of the cerebellum
Kleinhirnepilepsie *f* cerebellar epilepsy
Kleinhirnfunktionsstörung *f* cerebellar dysfunction
Kleinhirngang *m* cerebellar gait
Kleinhirngeschwulst *f* cerebellar tumour
Kleinhirngrube *f* cerebellar fossa
Kleinhirnhämangioblastom *n* cerebellar haemangioblastoma
Kleinhirnhemisphäre *f* cerebellar hemisphere
Kleinhirnheterotopie *f* cerebellar heterotopia
Kleinhirnhinterlappen *m* posterior lobe of the cerebellum
Kleinhirnhyperplasie *f* cerebellar hyperplasia
Kleinhirnhypoplasie *f* cerebellar hypoplasia
kleinhirnig micrencephalous, micrencephalic
Kleinhirnigkeit *f* microencephalia
Kleinhirninfarkt *m* cerebellar apoplexy
Kleinhirnkörnerzellenschicht *f* granular-cell layer of the cerebellum, cerebellar granular layer
Kleinhirnlappen *m* cerebellar lobe
~/**hinterer** posterior cerebellar lobe
Kleinhirnlingula *f* cerebellar lingula
Kleinhirnmarksegel *n*/**hinteres** posterior medullary velum
~/**oberes** superior medullary velum
~/**unteres** inferior medullary velum
~/**vorderes** anterior medullary velum
Kleinhirnmarksubstanz *f*/**innere weiße** inner white matter of the cerebellum
Kleinhirnpfropfkern *m* emboliform nucleus
Kleinhirnrigidität *f* cerebellar rigidity
Kleinhirnrinde *f* cerebellar cortex, cortex of the cerebellum
Kleinhirnschenkel *m* cerebellar peduncle, crus of the cerebellum
Kleinhirnschwindel *m* cerebellar vertigo
Kleinhirnseitenstrangbahn *f*/**dorsale (hintere)** Flechsig's (direct cerebellar) tract, posterior (dorsal) spinocerebellar tract, dorsal spinocerebellar fasciculus [of Flechsig]
~/**vordere** Gowers' column (fasciculus, tract), anterior (ventral) spinocerebellar tract, ventral spinocerebellar fasciculus [of Gowers], anterolateral fasciculus of Gowers
Kleinhirnsichel *f* cerebellar falx, falx cerebelli, falcula
Kleinhirnsklerose *f* cerebellar sclerosis
Kleinhirnstiel *m* cerebellar peduncle (stalk), crus of the cerebellum ● **unter den Kleinhirnstielen** subpeduncular
~/**mittlerer** middle cerebellar peduncle, pontocerebellar tract
~/**oberer** superior cerebellar peduncle
~/**unterer** inferior cerebellar peduncle, restiform body
Kleinhirnsyndrom *n* cerebellar syndrome
Kleinhirntonsille *f* cerebellar tonsil, tonsil of the cerebellum, amygdala
Kleinhirntonsilleneinklemmung *f* tonsillar herniation
Kleinhirntonsillenvorfall *m* tonsillar herniation
Kleinhirnunterseite *f* inferior surface of the cerebellar hemisphere
Kleinhirnvene *f*/**obere** superior cerebellar vein
~/**untere** inferior cerebellar vein
Kleinhirnvorderlappen *m* anterior lobe of the cerebellum
Kleinhirnvorfall *m* cerebellar herniation; parencephalocele
Kleinhirnwindung *f* cerebellar gyrus (convolution)
Kleinhirnwurm *m* cerebellar vermis, worm of the cerebellum
Kleinhirnwurmsyndrom *n* flocculonodular syndrome
Kleinhirnwurmzünglein *n* cerebellar lingula
Kleinhirnzeichen *n* cerebellar sign
Kleinhirnzelt *n s.* Tentorium cerebelli
Kleinhirnzyste *f* cerebellar cyst
Kleinkieferwuchs *m* brachygnathia
kleinkiefrig micrognathic, micrognathous
Kleinkind *n* infant
Kleinkindalter *n* infancy
kleinknotig micronodular, nodulous
kleinköpfig microcephalic, microcephalous, nanocephalous

Kleinköpfiger *m* microcephalus, nanocephalus
Kleinköpfigkeit *f* microcephalia, nanocephalia
Kleinlebewesen *n* microorganism, microzoon, microbe
Kleinnasigkeit *f* microrrhinia, brachyrhinia
Kleinsehen *n* microp[s]ia
kleinsehend microptic
Kleinstkind *n* baby *(bis zum ersten Lebensjahr)*
Kleinwuchs *m* hyposomia
~ **der Füße** micropodia
kleinzahnig microdont[ic]
Kleinzehe *f* little toe
Kleinzehenabzieher *m* abductor digiti minimi pedis [muscle]
Kleinzehenbeuger *m*/**kurzer** flexor digiti minimi (quinti) brevis [muscle] of the foot
Kleinzehengegensteller *m* opponens digiti minimi pedis [muscle], opponens digiti quinti [muscle] of the foot
kleinzehig microdactylous
Kleinzehigkeit *f* microdactyly
kleinzellig parvicellular, small-cell
Kleinzungigkeit *f* microglossia
Klemme *f* clamp, forceps; clip
~/**Halstedsche** Halsted's forceps
~/**Péansche** Péan's forceps *(stumpfe Blutgefäßklemme)*
~/**Pottsche** Beck-Potts clamp
klemmen to clamp, to clip; to squeeze
Klemmenhalter *m* clamp holder
Klemmentechnik *f* clamp technique
Klemmzange *f* compression forceps
Kleptomaner *m* kleptomaniac, cleptomaniac
Kleptomanie *f* kleptomania, cleptomania
Kleptophobie *f* kleptophobia, cleptophobia *(krankhafte Angst vor Diebstahl)*
Klick *m*/**perikardialer** pericardial click (knock)
~/**systolischer** systolic [ejection] click
Klimaanpassung *f* acclimatization
Klimabehandlung *f* climatotherapy
Klimafaktor *m* climatic factor
Klimahitzestress *m* climatic heat stress
Klimakophobie *f* climacophobia *(krankhafte Angst vor Treppen)*
klimakterisch climacteric, menopausal
Klimakterium *n* climacterium, climacteric [period], climax, menopause, pausimenia ● **nach dem** ~ postclimacteric, postmenopausal ● **vor dem** ~ preclimacteric, premenopausal
~ **virile** male climacterium
Klimakur *f* climatic cure
Klimaphysiologie *f* climatophysiology
Klimax *f* 1. climax *(z. B. Höhepunkt einer Krankheit)*; 2. s. Klimakterium
Klinefelter-[Reifenstein-Albright-]Syndrom *n* Klinefelter's syndrome, Klinefelter-Reifenstein-Albright syndrome, gynaecomastia-aspermatogenesis syndrome *(Insuffizienz der Hodenkanälchen)*
Kline-Reaktion *f*, **Kline-Test** *m* Kline [flocculation] test *(Schnellmethode zum Nachweis von Syphilis)*

Klinge *f* blade *(z. B. eines Skalpells)*
Klingen *n* tinkle, timbre *(z. B. bei der Auskultation)*; tingle, tingling *(z. B. im Ohr)*; tympania *(z. B. des Bauches)*
~/**metallisches** metallic tinkle *(z. B. bei der Lungenauskultation)*
klingend ringing, consonating *(z. B. bei der Perkussion)*; tympanic, tympanal, tympanitic
~/**hohl und metallisch** amphoric
Klinik *f* clinic, hospital
~/**chirurgische** surgical clinic
~ **für Hals-, Nasen- und Ohrenkrankheiten** ear, nose, and throat clinic
~/**geburtshilfliche** obstetrical clinic, maternity (lying-in) hospital
~/**medizinische** clinic for internal diseases
Klinikaufenthalt *m* stay in hospital
Klinikaufnahme *f* admission to the hospital
Klinikbehandlung *f* hospital treatment
Klinikentbindung *f* hospital delivery
Kliniker *m* clinician
Kliniklabor *n* clinical laboratory
Klinikopathologie *f* clinical pathology
Klinikpackung *f* clinic-size pack *(z. B. eines Medikaments)*
Klinikum *n* teaching hospital; clinical centre (complex)
klinisch clinical ● ~ **manifest werden** to become clinically apparent ● ~ **nicht manifest** silent ● **sich** ~ **unterscheiden von** to differ clinically from
klinisch-epidemiologisch clinicoepidemiologic
klinisch-pathologisch clinicopathologic
klinisch-radiologisch clinicoradiological
klinisch-röntgenologisch clinicoroentgenological
klinodaktyl clinodactylous, clinodactylic
Klinodaktylie *f* clinodactyly *(Stellungsanomalie der Finger)*
Klinoskop *n* clinoscope *(ophthalmologisches Instrument)*
Klinozephalie *f* clinocephalia
Klinozephalus *m* clinocephalus
Klipp *m* clip *(zur Wundnaht)* *(s. a. Klemme)*
Klippel-Feil-Syndrom *n* Klippel-Feil deformity (syndrome) *(angeborener Kurzhals)*
Klippel-Trénaunay-Syndrom *n* Klippel-Trénaunay-Weber syndrome, angioosteohypertrophy
Kliseometer *n* kliseometer
Klistier *n* enema, enteroclysis, clyster, rectal injection ● **ein** ~ **machen** to give an enema
~/**hohes** high enema
Klistierspritze *f* enema (rectal) syringe
Klitoralgie *f* clitoralgia, pain in the clitoris
klitoridal clitor[id]al, clitoridean
Klitoridektomie *f* clitor[id]ectomy, excision of the clitoris
Klitoridotomie *f* clitor[id]otomy, incision of the clitoris, female circumcision
Klitoris *f* clitoris, coles femininus
Klitorisarterie *f* clitoridal artery
~/**tiefe** deep artery of the clitoris, profunda clitoridis artery

Klitorisaufrichtemuskel

Klitorisaufrichtemuskel *m* erector clitoridis [muscle] *(der Frau)*
Klitorisbändchen *n* frenulum of the clitoris
Klitorisblutung *f* clitorrhagia, haemorrhage from the clitoris
Klitoriseichel *f* clitoridal glans
Klitorisentfernung *f*[/operative] *s.* Klitoridektomie
Klitorisentzündung *f* clitori[di]tis, inflammation of the clitoris
Klitorishypertrophie *f* hypertrophy (enlargement) of the clitoris, clitoridauxe, clitorism
Klitorisinzision *f s.* Klitoridotomie
Klitoriskörper *m* clitoridal body, body of the clitoris
Klitoriskrise *f* clitoris crisis
Klitorismus *m* 1. clitorism, spasmodic erection of the clitoris; 2. *s.* Klitorishypertrophie; 3. tribadism
Klitorispräputium *n* clitoridal (female) prepuce
Klitorisrückenarterie *f* dorsal artery of the clitoris
Klitorisschenkel *m* crus of the clitoris
Klitorisschmerz *m* clitoralgia, pain in the clitoris
Klitorisschwellkörpernerven *mpl* cavernous nerves of the clitoris
Klitorisschwellung *f/schmerzhafte s.* Klitorismus 1.
Klitorisvene *f/dorsale* dorsal vein of the clitoris
~/tiefe deep vein of the clitoris
Klitorisvergrößerung *f* clitoromegaly
Klitorrhagie *f s.* Klitorisblutung
Klivus *m* clivus *(der Schädelbasis)*
Kloake *f* cloaca *(Zusammensetzungen s. unter* Cloaca*)*
Kloakenkanal *m* cloacal duct
Kloakenmembran *f* cloacal membrane (plate)
Kloakenscheidewand *f* urorectal septum *(Embryologie)*
Klon *m* clone *(1. erbgleiche Nachkommenschaft; 2. sich gleichartig verhaltende Immunzellen)*
● **mehrere Klone betreffend** multiclonal, polyclonal ● **zu einem ~ gehörend** monoclonal
Klonierung *f* cloning
klonisch [neuro]clonic
klonisch-tonisch clonic-tonic, clonicotonic
Klonismus *m* clonism
Klonizität *f* clonicity
Klonorchiasis *f* clonorchiasis, clonorchiosis, Chinese liver fluke disease
Klonospasmus *m* clonospasm, clonic spasm
Klonospasmuszustand *m* clonism
Klonproliferation *f* clonal proliferation
Klonselektionstheorie *f* clonal selection theory
Klonus *m* clonus
Klonuszustand *m* clonicity
klopfen to beat *(normal)*; to throb, to palpitate *(verstärkt)*; to pulse, to pulsate *(z. B. Pulswelle)*
Klopfen *n* 1. throbbing, palpitation *(z. B. des Herzens)*; pulsation *(z. B. der Pulswelle)*; 2. *s.* Klopfmassage
klopfend beating, throbbing; pulsatile

Klopffinger *m* plessor, plexor
Klopfmassage *f* hacking, hachement, tapping, tapotement
Klopfplättchen *n* plessimeter, pleximeter
Klopfschall *m* percussion sound (note)
~/klingender tympania
klopfschmerzhaft sensitive to percussion
Klopfung *f s.* Klopfmassage
Klostridienmyonekrose *f* clostridial myonecrosis, true gas gangrene
Klostridienonkolyse *f* clostridial oncolysis
Klostridiopeptidase *f* **A** clostridiopeptidase A
Klostridium *n s.* Clostridium
klug intelligent
Klugheit *f* intelligence
klumpen to clot, to clump, to agglutinate, to agglomerate
Klumpen *m* clot, lump; bolus; cluster
Klumpen *n* clotting, aggregation *(z. B. von Blut) (s. a.* Klumpenbildung*)*
Klumpenbildung *f* clotting, clumping, conglomeration, agglutination
Klumpenniere *f* clump kidney
Klumpfuß *m* club-foot, talipes [varus], pes varus *(Zusammensetzungen s. unter* Talipes*)*
klumpfüßig club-footed, talipedic
Klumpfüßiger *m* taliped
Klumphand *f* club-hand, talipomanus, manus vara
klumphändig club-handed
klumpig werden *s.* klumpen
Klysma *n s.* Klistier
KM *s.* Kontrastmittel
Knabberzange *f* nibbling forceps *(bei Knochenoperation)*
knabenhaft puerile
Knabenliebe *f* paederasty, buggery
Knalltrauma *n* blast injury (syndrome)
Knäuel *n* glomerule, glomerulus, glomus
Knäueldrüse *f* glomiform gland, glomus body
Knäuelfilarie *f* onchocerca volvulus *(Übertragung durch die Kriebelmücke)*
Knebelpresse *f* tourniquet
Kneippkur *f* Kneipp [water] cure, hydropathic treatment
Knetmassage *f* kneading massage, petrissage
knickbeinig knock-kneed
Knickbildung *f* kinking *(z. B. der Aorta)*
Knickbruch *m* infraction, incomplete (partial, bent) fracture
Knickfuß *m* pes valgus
Knickhohlfuß *m* talipes cavovalgus
Knickplattfuß *m* pes planovalgus
Knicksenkfuß *m s.* Knickplattfuß
Knie *n* knee, genu *(s. a. unter* Genu*)*
~/blockiertes locked knee *(bei eingeklemmtem Meniskus)*
~/kleines geniculum
~/schnappendes (schnellendes) snapping knee
~/überstrecktes back knee
Kniearterie *f/mittlere s.* Kniegelenkarterie/mittlere

Kniearthrographie f knee arthrography
Kniebeuge f 1. s. Kniekehle; 2. knee bend[ing]
Knie-Brust-Lage f genupectoral (knee-breast) position, knee-chest position *(für Operationen)*
Knie-Ellenbogen-Lage f genucubital (knee-elbow) position *(für Operationen)*
Kniegelenk n knee joint, femorotibial (tibiofemoral) articulation
Kniegelenkamputation f/**Callandersche** Callander's amputation
Kniegelenkarterie f/**absteigende** descending genicular artery
~/**mittlere** middle genicular artery
~/**obere mittlere** medial superior genicular artery
~/**obere seitliche** lateral superior genicular artery
~/**untere mittlere** medial inferior genicular artery
~/**untere seitliche** lateral inferior genicular artery
Kniegelenkarthrose f gonarthrosis
Kniegelenkband n genicular (knee-joint) ligament
Kniegelenkdeformierung f gonycampsis, knee deformity
Kniegelenkentzündung f gonarthritis, gonitis, inflammation of the knee
Kniegelenkerguß m knee-joint effusion, effusion in the knee joint, water on the knee
Kniegelenkeröffnung f[/**operative**] gonarthrotomy, incision of the knee joint
Kniegelenkluxation f luxation of the knee
Kniegelenkmaus f knee-joint mouse
Kniegelenkmuskel m subcrureus [muscle]
Kniegelenkresektion f gonarthrectomy
Kniegelenkröntgen[kontrast]darstellung f knee arthrography
Kniegelenkschwellung f gonyoncus
Kniegelenksperre f s. Knie/blockiertes
Kniegelenktuberkulose f gonarthrocace, white swelling
Kniegelenkvene f genicular vein
Kniegelenkverkrümmung f gonycampsis, knee deformity
Kniegelenkverstauchung f knee-joint strain
Kniegicht f gonagra, gout in the knee
Knie-Hacken-Versuch m heel-knee test, heel-to-knee-to-toe test
Kniehöcker m/**äußerer** lateral geniculate body *(Schaltstelle der Sehbahn)*
~ **des Thalamus/innerer** medial geniculate body
~/**seitlicher und mittlerer** metathalamus *(hinter dem Sehhügel gelegene Gehirnanteile)*
Kniekehle f popliteal region (space, fossa), poples, hollow of the knee
Kniekehlenarterie f popliteal artery
Kniekehlenband n popliteal ligament
Kniekehlenmuskel m popliteus [muscle]
Kniekehlenvene f popliteal vein
Kniekreuzband n/**hinteres** posterior cruciate ligament of the knee
~/**vorderes** anterior cruciate ligament of the knee
Knielage f knee (incomplete breech) presentation *(des Fetus)*

Kniescheibe f knee-cap, patella, rotula, kneepan, whirlbone *(s. a. unter Patella)* ● **neben der** ~ parapatellar ● **über der** ~ suprapatellar ● **unter der** ~ subpatellar
~/**tanzende** floating patella
~/**zweigeteilte** bipartite patella
Kniescheiben... s. a. Patella... und Patellar...
Kniescheibenband n patellar ligament (tendon)
Kniescheibenbasis f base of the patella
Kniescheibenbruch m patellar fracture
Kniescheibenentfernung f[/**operative**] patellectomy, excision of the patella
kniescheibenförmig patelliform
Kniescheibenhalteband n patellar retinaculum
~/**äußeres** lateral patellar retinaculum
Kniescheibennervengeflecht n patellar plexus
Kniescheibenoberkante f base of the patella
Kniescheibenphänomen n patellar clonus *(bei Pyramidenbahnläsion)*
Kniescheibenreflex m s. Patellarsehnenreflex
Kniescheibenresektion f patellectomy, excision of the patella
Kniescheibenrückseite f posterior surface of the patella
Kniescheibenschleimbeutel m [pre]patellar bursa
Kniescheibensehne f patellar ligament (tendon)
Kniescheibenspiel n motility of the patella
Kniescheibenspitze f inferior blunt tip of the patella
Kniescheibenverrenkung f displacement of the patella
Kniescheibenvorderseite f anterior surface of the patella
Kniescheibenzuckung f patellar clonus *(bei Pyramidenbahnläsion)*
Knieschleimbeutel m [pre]patellar bursa
Knieschmerz m gonalgia, pain in the knee
Knieschwellung f gonyoncus
Kniesehnenreflex m s. Patellarsehnenreflex
Knievene f popliteal vein
Knieverband m knee strapping
Knieweichwerden n cataplexis
knirschen to grate *(z. B. ein Gelenk)*
~/**mit den Zähnen** to grind (gnash) the teeth
Knistern n **der Lunge** crepitation; crepitus
~/**subkutanes** subcutaneous crepitance
knisternd crepitant
Knisterrasseln n s. Krepitieren 1.
Knöchel m ankle[bone], malleolus *(am Fuß)*; knuckle *(an der Hand)* ● **über dem** ~ supramalleolar ● **unter dem** ~ submalleolar
~/**äußerer** external malleolus
~/**innerer** internal malleolus
Knöchelarterie f/**hintere äußere** posterior lateral malleolar artery
~/**hintere innere** posterior medial malleolar artery
~/**vordere äußere** anterior lateral malleolar artery
~/**vordere innere** anterior medial malleolar artery
Knöchelaußenband n lateral malleal ligament, lateral ligament of the malleus

Knöchelbruch

Knöchelbruch *m* malleolar fracture
~/trimalleolärer trimalleolar (Cotton's) fracture
Knöchelchen *n* bonelet, ossicle, ossiculum
Knöchelgegend *f* malleolar region
Knöchelgelenk *n* ankle joint
Knöchelpolster *npl* knuckle pads *(bindegewebige Wucherungen)*
Knöchelregion *f* malleolar region
Knöchelsulkus *m* malleolar sulcus
Knöchelverletzung *f* ankle lesion
Knochen *m* bone, os *(s. a. unter Os)* ● **aus ~ [bestehend]** osseous, osteal ● **~ bildend** osteogenic ● **durch den ~** transosseous ● **mehrere Knochen betreffend** polyostotic ● **nicht ~ bildend** non-osteogenic ● **nur einen ~ betreffend** monostotic ● **verstärkt ~ bildend** osteohypertrophic ● **vom ~ gebildet** osteogen[et]ic, osteogenous
~/Bertinscher bone of Bertin
~/brüchiger brittle bone
~/interradikulärer interradicular bone
~/kurzer short bone
~/langer long bone
~/lufthaltiger pneumatic bone
~/platter flat (tabular) bone
~/primärer primary bone
~/Riolanscher Riolan's bone (ossicle) *(Schaltknochen zwischen Hinterhauptsbein und Felsenbein)*
~/schuppenartiger squama, squame
~/sekundärer secondary bone
~/spongiöser spongy bone
Knochen... *s. a.* Osteo...
Knochenabbau *m* osteoclasis, absorption (destruction) of bone
Knochenabbaurate *f* rate of bone absorption
Knochenablagerung *f* bone deposition
Knochenabsorption *f* bone absorption
Knochenabszeß *m* bone abscess
~/Brodiescher Brodie's abscess
Knochenachsenkompression *f* bipolar [bone] pressure
Knochenaffektion *f* affection of bone
Knochenalbuminoid *n* osseo-albuminoid
Knochenalter *n* bone age
Knochenalterung *f* bone ag[e]ing
Knochenaneurysma *n* osteoaneurysm
Knochenankylose *f* bony ankylosis *(Zustand des Knochens)*
Knochenankylosierung *f* bony ankylosis *(durch Operation)*
knochenartig bone-like, osseous, osteal, ossiform, osteoid
Knochenatrophie *f* bone atrophy
~/Sudecksche Sudeck's atrophy (dystrophy), posttraumatic reflex sympathetic dystrophy, traumatic osteoporosis
Knochenaufbau *m s.* Knochenbildung
knochenaufbauend *s.* knochenbildend
knochenauflösend osteolytic
Knochenauflösung *f* osteolysis, ossifluence

Knochenausmuldung *f[/operative]* saucerization *(durch Nekrosenausräumung)*
Knochenauswuchs *m* exostosis, bony outgrowth, hyperostosis, hyperosteogeny, osteophyte
Knochenbälkchen *n* trabecula
Knochenbank *f* bone bank
Knochenbefall *m* affection of bone
Knochenbeteiligung *f* bone (bony) involvement
knochenbildend osteogen[et]ic, osteogenous, bone-forming, osteoblastic, osteoplastic, ossific
Knochenbildung *f* osteogenesis, ost[e]osis, bone formation, ossification
~/enchondrale enchondral bone formation, enchondral ossification (osteogenesis)
Knochenbildungshemmung *f* anost[e]osis, anosteoplasia
Knochenbildungszelle *f* osteogenic cell, osteoblast, osteoplast
Knochenbindegewebsgeschwulst *f* osteofibroma, fibroosteoma
Knochenbinnengeschwulst *f* en[t]ostosis
Knochenbiopsie *f* bone biopsy
Knochenbiopsieinstrument *n* bone biopsy trephine
Knochenblutung *f* osteorrhagia, haemorrhage from the bone
Knochenbohrer *m* bone drill (perforator)
Knochenbrand *m* caries of the bone
knochenbrechend osteoclastic
Knochenbruch *m* [bone] fracture *(s. a. unter Fraktur und Bruch)* ● **einen ~ einstellen** to reduce a fracture
~/epikondylärer epicondylar fracture
~/gesplitterter comminuted fracture
~/nicht durchgebauter ununited fracture
~/nicht reponierter old dislocation
~/spontaner pathologic fracture
~/unvollständiger infraction
~/verkeilter impacted fracture
Knochenbruchankylosierung *f* bony ankylosis
Knochenbruchbehandlung *f* treatment of a bone fracture
Knochenbrucheinrichtung *f* reduction of a fracture, redressement
~/operative open reduction
Knochenbrüchigkeit *f[/abnorme]* osteopsathyrosis, brittleness of the bone
~/erbliche Vrolik's disease
Knochenbruchstück *n* fracture fragment
Knochenbruchverfestigung *f* consolidation of bone fracture
Knochenchirurgie *f* bone surgery
Knochendeformität *f* bone (osseous) deformity
Knochendemineralisierung *f* osteohalisteresis
Knochendrahtnaht *f* wire suture of the bone; bone wiring
Knochendrahtspanner *m* bone wire tightener
Knochendurchblutung *f* bone blood flow
Knochendurchmeißelung *f* osteotomoclasia, osteotomy

Knochendurchtrennung f osteotomy, bone cut
~/gerade linear osteotomy
Knochendysplasie f/fibröse monostotische Jaffé-Lichtenstein disease, monostotic fibrous dysplasia
Knocheneinlagerung f bone deposition
Knocheneiterung f ostempyesis, suppuration within the bone; bone abscess
Knochenektopie f ostectopia
Knochenendotheliom n bone endothelioma
Knochenentfernung f[/operative] ost[e]ectomy
knochenenthaltend ossiferous
knochenentkalkend osteolytic
Knochenentkalkung f osteolysis, osteohalisteresis, ossifluence
Knochenentwicklung f osteogenesis, ossification, ost[e]osis
Knochenentwicklungsstörung f dysostosis, dysosteogenesis
Knochenentzündung f ost[e]itis, inflammation of a bone (s. a. unter Osteitis)
~/totale panosteitis
Knochenepiphyse f osteoepiphysis, bony epiphysis
Knochenepiphysenkrankheit f epiphysiopathy
Knochenepiphysennekrose f epiphysionecrosis
~/aseptische aseptic epiphysionecrosis
Knochenepiphysenvaskularisation f bone epiphyseal vascularization
Knochenernährung f osteotrophy, nutrition of the bone
knochenerweichend osteomalacial
Knochenerweichung f s. Osteomalazie
Knochenextension f bone traction
Knochenfaßzange f bone-holding forceps
Knochenfehlbildung f osteodystrophia
Knochenfeile f bone file, rasparatory, osteotribe, osteotrite
Knochenfett n bone fat
Knochenfissur f fissured fracture; pilation
Knochenfortsatz m bony (bone) process, process[us], apophysis
Knochenframbösie f gummatous periostitis
Knochenfraß m caries (necrosis) of the bone
Knochen-Galea-Lappen m osteoplastic (bone-galea) flap
Knochengelenkfläche f articular surface of the bone
Knochengerüst n skeleton, osseous system
Knochengewebe n osseous (bony) tissue, bone
~/spongiöses cancellous bone tissue
~/unverkalktes osteoid [tissue]
Knochengewebebildung f bone formation, osteosis, osteogenesis
Knochengewebeschwund m rarefaction of bone
Knochengewebeübertragung f bone transplantation (grafting)
Knochengewebeuntergang m osteonecrosis
Knochengewebewachstumsstörung f osteodysplasia
Knochengewebs... s. a. Knochengewebe...
Knochengewebsmangel m imperfect osteogenesis

Knochengewebstod m osteonecrosis
Knochengranulom n/eosinophiles bone eosinophilic granuloma, eosinophilic granuloma of bone
Knochengrundsubstanz f matrix of the bone
Knochenhaft f synost[e]osis
Knochenhaken m bone retractor (hook)
Knochenhalteklammer f bone[-holding] clamp
Knochenhaltezange f bone-holding forceps
Knochenhaut f periost[eum] ● **unter der ~** subperiosteal
Knochenhaut... s. a. Periost...
Knochenhautabheber m periosteal elevator, separator
Knochenhautabhebung f periosteal elevation
Knochenhautabszeß m subperiosteal abscess
Knochenhautauswuchs m periosteophyte
Knochenhautdurchtrennung f[/operative] periosteotomy
Knochenhautelevator m periosteal elevator, separator
Knochenhautentzündung f periost[e]itis, cortical osteitis
Knochenhautlappen m periosteal flap
Knochen-Haut-Lappen m osteocutaneous flap
knochenhautlos aperiosteal
Knochenhautödem n periosteo-oedema
Knochenhautreflex m periosteal reflex
Knochenhautretraktor m periosteal retractor
Knochenhautspaltung f[/operative] periosteotomy
Knochenhauttransplantat n periosteal graft
Knochenhauttumor m periost[e]oma, periosteal tumour
Knochenhebel m bone lever
Knochenheilung f bone healing
Knochenhöhle f 1. bone (marrow) cavity (z. B. der Röhrenknochen); 2. sinus, bony cavity
Knochenhypertrophie f hyperostosis, hyperosteogeny
Knochenhypoplasie f hypoostosis
Knochenimpression f depression of the bone
Knocheninfektion f bone infection
Knocheninnengeschwulst f en[t]ostosis
Knocheninnenhaut f medullary membrane, endosteum
Knocheninnenhautentzündung f perimyelitis
Knocheninnenraumentzündung f endost[e]itis, central osteitis
Knochenisotopenaufnahme f radioisotopic bone scan
Knochenkachexie f osteocachexia
Knochenkanal m bony canal
~/Haversscher Haversian canal
Knochenkeimgewebe n s. Kallus
Knochenkern m ossification centre
Knochenkind n osteopaedion
Knochenklammer f bone clamp (spike), fracture staple
Knochenknabberzange f bone nibblers (nippers)
Knochenknorpel m bone cartilage
Knochen-Knorpel-Bruch m osteochondral fracture

Knochen-Knorpel-Sarkom 400

Knochen-Knorpel-Sarkom *n* osteochondrosarcoma
Knochenkompakta *f s.* Kompakta
Knochenkompressionsplatte *f* compression bone plate
Knochenkrankheit *f* osteopathy, bone disease *(Zusammensetzungen s. unter Osteopathia)*
Knochenkrebs *m* osteocarcinoma, bone cancer
Knochenkrümmung *f* osteocampsia
Knochenlamelle *f* osseous lamella, lamella of bone
~/Haverssche Haversian lamella
Knochenlehre *f* osteology
Knochenleiste *f* crest, crista, ridge *(Zusammensetzungen s. unter Crista)*
Knochenleitung *f s.* Knochenschalleitung
Knochenleitungshörhilfe *f* bone-conduction hearing aid
Knochenleitungstest *m* bone-conduction test
Knochenlokalisation *f* bone localization
Knochenlymphangiom *n* bone lymphangioma
Knochenmangel *m* osteopenia
Knochenmanifestation *f* osseous manifestation
Knochenmark *n* [bone] marrow, medulla ● **durch das ~ bedingt** myelogenic, myelogenous, medullary ● **vom ~ abstammend** bone-marrow derived ● **vom ~ ausgehend** myelogenic, myelogenous
~/embryonales primary marrow
~/gelbes yellow [bone] marrow, fat marrow
~/hämopoetisches haemopoietic marrow
~/primäres primary marrow
~/rotes red [bone] marrow
Knochenmarkaktivität *f* marrow activity
Knochenmarkaplasie *f* bone-marrow aplasia
Knochenmarkaspirat *n* bone-marrow aspirate
Knochenmarkaspiration *f* bone-marrow aspiration
Knochenmarkbehandlung *f* myelotherapy
Knochenmarkbildung *f* myelopoiesis
~ durch Knochenumbau medullization
Knochenmarkbildungsstörung *f* myeloproliferative disorder *(der Blutzellen)*
Knochenmarkdepression *f* bone-marrow depression
Knochenmarkdifferentialblutbild *n* haemomyelogram
Knochenmarkdysplasie *f* bone-marrow dysplasia
Knochenmarkeinfrieren *n* bone-marrow freezing
Knochenmarkeinlagerung *f* bone-marrow storage
Knochenmarkempfänger *m* bone-marrow recipient
Knochenmarkentzündung *f s.* Osteomyelitis
Knochenmarkerschöpfung *f* bone-marrow depletion
Knochenmarkfibrose *f* myelofibrosis
knochenmarkfrei amyelonic
Knochenmarkfunktion *f* bone-marrow function
Knochenmarkgift *n* myelotoxin
Knochenmarkhöhle *f* bone-marrow cavity, marrow space [of the bone], medullary canal (space, cavity)
Knochenmarkhypoplasie *f* bone-marrow hypoplasia
Knochenmarkinsuffizienz *f* panmyelopathy, dysfunction of the bone marrow
Knochenmarkkanal *m* medullary canal
Knochenmarkkeimzelle *f* granuloblast, free rounded cell *(Leukozytenvorstufe)*
knochenmarkkrank myelopathic
Knochenmarkkrankheit *f* myelopathy
Knochenmarklagerung *f* bone-marrow storage
Knochenmarkleukämie *f* myeloid leukaemia
Knochenmarkleukozyt *m* myeloplast
knochenmarklos amyelonic
Knochenmarklymphozyt *m* myelolymphocyte, lymphoblast
Knochenmarkmonozyt *m* myelomonocyte
Knochenmarkmyelome *npl*/**generalisierte** general lymphadenomatosis of bones
Knochenmarknagel *m* medullary (bone-marrow) nail
Knochenmarknagelung *f* medullary (bone-marrow) nailing
Knochenmarkplombierung *f* bone-marrow plombage
Knochenmarkprobe *f* bone-marrow sample
Knochenmarkproliferation *f* panmyelosis
Knochenmarkpunktion *f* bone-marrow puncture
Knochenmarkreserve *f* bone-marrow reserve
Knochenmarkriesenzelle *f* mega[lo]karyocyte
~/vielkernige myeloplax
Knochenmarksarkom *n* myelosarcoma, myelogenic sarcoma
knochenmarkschädigend myelotoxic
Knochenmarkschädigung *f*/**toxische** [pan]myelotoxicosis
Knochenmarkschwindsucht *f* myelophthisis
Knochenmarkschwund *m* panmyelophthisis
Knochenmarksideroblast *m* marrow sideroblast
Knochenmarksklerose *f* myelosclerosis
Knochenmarkspeicher *m* bone-marrow store
Knochenmarkspeicherung *f* bone-marrow storage
Knochenmarksuppression *f* myelosuppression
knochenmarksupprimierend myelosuppressive
Knochenmarktransfusion *f* bone-marrow transfusion
Knochenmarktransplantation *f* bone-marrow transplantation (grafting)
Knochenmarktumor *m* endosteoma, medullary tumour
~/bösartiger bone-marrow malignancy
knochenmarkunterdrückend myelosupressive
Knochenmarkuntersuchung *f* bone-marrow study, examination of bone marrow
Knochenmarkverarmung *f* bone-marrow depletion *(an Zellen)*
Knochenmarkzelle *f* marrow (myeloid) cell, myelocyte
Knochenmatrix *f* bone (osteoid) matrix, matrix of the bone

Knochensystem

Knochenmeißel *m* osteotome, bone chisel
Knochenmesser *n* osteotome, bone knife
Knochenmetastase *f* bone (bony, osseous) metastasis
Knochenmineralgehalt *m* bone mineral content
Knochenmineralisation *f* bone mineralization
Knochenmittelstück *n* diaphysis
Knochen-Muskel-Haut-Lappen *m* osteomyocutaneous flap *(zur Transplantation)*
Knochen-Muskel-Transplantat *n*/**gestieltes** bone-muscle pedicle graft
Knochenmutterzelle *f* osteoblast, osteoplast
Knochennagel *m* fracture pin (nail)
Knochennagelung *f* bone nailing
Knochennaht *f* 1. osteosuture, osteorrhaphy *(z. B. bei einem Knochenbruch)*; 2. suture, sutura, junction *(Anatomie)*
Knochennekrose *f* osteonecrosis, necrosis of bone
Knochenneubildung *f* oste[o]anagenesis, osteanaphysis; bone regeneration
Knochenperiostreflex *m* bone periosteal reflex
Knochen-Periost-Span *m* osteoperiosteal strip
Knochen-Periost-Transplantat *n* osteoperiosteal graft
Knochenplastik *f* osteoplasty, plastic surgery of the bone
Knochenplatte *f* 1. bone plate *(für Osteosynthesen)*; 2. osteoplaque, osseous plate, table *(s. a. Tabula)*
Knochenplattenbiegegerät *n* bone plate wrench (bending device)
Knochenplattenhaltezange *f* bone plate holding forceps
Knochenplattenschränkgerät *n* bone plate contouring device
Knochenprotuberanz *f* bony prominence
Knochenpunktion *f* osteostixis, puncture of the bone; bone biopsy
Knochenraspel *f* raspatory, bone rasp, osteotribe, osteotrite
Knochenreflex *m* bone reflex
Knochenregeneration *f* bone regeneration; oste[o]anagenesis, osteanaphysis
Knochenreiben *n* crepitation, [bony] crepitance *(bei Fraktur)*
Knochenreifung *f* bone (osseous) maturation, osteomaturation
Knochenreißen *n* osteocope, osteocopic pain *(z. B. bei Syphilis)*
Knochenresektion *f* ost[e]ectomy
Knochenresektionszange *f* bone cutting forceps
Knochenresonanz *f* osseous resonance
knochenresorbierend osteolytic
Knochenresorption *f* bone resorption (absorption), osteolysis, ossifluence
Knochenretraktor *m* bone retractor
Knochenriesenwuchs *m* osseous leontiasis
Knochenriesenzelle *f* bone giant cell
Knochenriesenzellentumor *m* bone giant cell tumour
Knochensäge *f* bone saw

Knochensarkom *n* osteosarcoma, osteogenic (bone) sarcoma; sarcomatous ostitis
Knochenschaft *m* diaphysis, shaft
Knochenschaftentfernung *f*[/**operative**] diaphysectomy
Knochenschalleitung *f* bone conduction, osteophony
Knochenschalleitungsaudiometrie *f* bone-conduction audiometry
Knochenschalleitungshören *n* bone-conduction hearing
Knochenschalleitungshörgerät *n* bone-conduction hearing aid
Knochenschalleitungsprobe *f* bone-conduction test
Knochenschalleitungsschärfe *f* bone-conduction acuity
Knochenschalleitungsschwelle *f* bone-conduction threshold
Knochenschicht *f* osteoplaque, bony (osseous) layer
Knochenschmerz *m* ost[e]algia, osteoneuralgia, osteodynia; osteocope, osteocopic pain *(bei Syphilis)*
Knochenschnitt *m* bone cut
Knochenschraube *f* bone screw
Knochenschuppe *f* [bony] scale
Knochenschwammsubstanz *f* spongiosa, cancellous bone
Knochenschwund *m* rarefaction of bone, bone loss, anostosis, osteoporosis, rarefying osteitis, osteophthisis
Knochensensibilität *f* bone (osseous) sensibility, pallaesthesia *(Empfindungsqualität der Tiefensensibilität)*
Knochensequester *m* dead bone
Knochenspan *m* bone onlay (chip)
Knochenspanstößel *m* bone graft impactor
Knochenspantransplantat *n* chip graft of bone
Knochenspitze *f*/**kleine** spicule
Knochensplitter *m* splinter of bone, bone fragment
Knochensplitterzange *f* bone-cutting forceps
Knochenspongiosa *f* cancellous bone
~/heterologe heterologous cancellous bone
Knochensporn *m* osteophyte
knochensporntragend osteophytic
Knochenstabilisierung *f* **mit dem Fixateur/externe** external skeletal fixation
Knochenstammzelle *f* osteoblast, osteoplast
Knochenstoffwechsel *m* bone metabolism
Knochenstörung *f* dysostosis
Knochenstruktur *f* bone structure
Knochenstück *n* bone fragment
~/abgestorbenes (sequestriertes) sequestrum, sequester
Knochensubstanz *f* osseous tissue, bony substance
Knochensucher *m* bone seeker *(knochenmarkierendes Isotop)*
Knochensyphilis *f* gummatous osteitis
Knochensystem *n* osseous system

Knochensystem

~/**Haversches** Haversian system
Knochenszintigramm n bone scintigram (scan)
Knochenszintigraphie f bone scintigraphy (scanning)
Knochentod m osteonecrosis
Knochenton m osseous sound
Knochentransplantat n bone transplant (graft)
Knochentransplantation f bone transplantation (grafting)
Knochentuberkulose f tuberculous (caseous) osteitis, tuberculosis of the bone, tuberculous caries of the bone
Knochentumor m bone tumour
~/**gutartiger** osteoma
~/**pulsierender** osteoid aneurysm
~/**zystischer** osteocystoma
Knochen- und Gelenkentfernung f[/operative] osteoarthrectomy, oste[o]arthrotomy
Knochen- und Gelenkentzündung f osteoarthritis
Knochen- und Gelenkerkrankung f osteoarthropathy
Knochen- und Gelenkexzision f osteoarthrectomy, oste[o]arthrotomy
Knochen- und Gelenkleiden n/**degeneratives** arthrosis
Knochen- und Gelenkresektion f osteoarthrectomy, oste[o]arthrotomy
knochen- und hautbildend osteodermatoplastic
Knochen- und Knochenhautentzündung f osteoperiostitis
Knochen- und Knorpeldegeneration f s. Osteochondrosis
Knochen- und Knorpeldysplasie f osteochondrodysplasia
Knochen- und Knorpelentzündung f osteochondritis
Knochen- und Knorpelskelett n endoskeleton
Knochenunempfindlichkeit f osteoanaesthesia, insensitiveness of the bone
Knochenunterentwicklung f hypoostosis
Knochenvenenentzündung f osteophlebitis
Knochenvenenthrombose f osteothrombosis
Knochenverbiegung f osteocampsia
Knochenverbindung f/**bindegewebige** syndesmosis
~/**unbewegliche** synarthrosis, synarthrodia (ohne Gelenkspalt)
Knochenverdickung f/**lokale** periostosis
Knochenvereiterung f bone abscess
Knochenverhärtung f s. Osteosklerose
Knochenverkrümmung f osteocampsia
Knochenverletzung f bone lesion
Knochenverlust m bone loss
knochenvermessend osteometric
Knochenverpflanzung f bone transplantation (grafting)
Knochenvorsprung m bony prominence
~/**kleiner** tubercle, tuberculum
Knochenwachs n bone wax
Knochenwachstum n bone growth
~/**lineares** linear bone growth

Knochenwachstumsstörung f osteodysplasia
Knochenwachstumszone f metaphysis
Knochenwachstumszonenentzündung f metaphysitis
Knochenwuchs m bone growth
Knochenzange f bone[-cutting] forceps, rongeur, bone-holding forceps
Knochenzelle f osteocyte, bone cell (corpuscle)
Knochenzement m osteocementum
Knochenzerbrechen n/**chirurgisches** osteoclasis (bei schlechter Frakturstellung)
knochenzerbrechend osteoclastic
knochenzerstörend osteolytic; osteoclastic
Knochenzerstörung f osteolysis, ossifluence; osteoclasis; caries of the bone
Knochenzerstörungszelle f osteoclast
Knochenzug m bone (skeletal) traction (bei Knochenbruchbehandlung)
Knochenzyste f bone cyst
knöchern bony, osseous, osteal, ossiform, ossiferous
Knolle f bulb, tuber, phyma
knollenartig bulbiform, bulboid, bulbous, tuberous, phymatoid
Knollenblätterpilzvergiftung f death-head intoxication, death-cup poisoning
Knollennase f rhinophym[a], potato (bottle) nose
Knopflochabszeß m collar-button abscess, shirt-stud abscess
Knopflochdeformität f boutonniere deformity, button-hole dislocation
Knopflochfraktur f button-hole fracture
Knopflochinzision f button-hole incision
Knopflochmitralstenose f mitral button-hole
Knopflochnaht f button-hole suture
Knopflochpanaritium n collar-button abscess
Knopflochstenose f mitral button-hole
Knopfsonde f [bulbous] probe, probang
Knorpel m cartilage, cartilagineous (chondral) tissue (s. a. unter Cartilago) ● **unter dem ~** subcartilaginous, subchondral ● **zu ~ werden** to chondrify
~/**elastischer** elastic cartilage
~/**fibröser** fibrocartilage
~/**Huschkescher** Huschke's cartilage
~/**hyaliner** hyaline cartilage
~/**Jacobsonscher** Jacobson's cartilage
~/**Reichertscher** Reichert's cartilage
~/**Santorinischer** corniculate cartilage [of Santorini], Santorini's cartilage (Kehlkopf)
~/**temporärer** primordial cartilage
~/**Wrisbergscher** Wrisberg's cartilage
Knorpelabbau m chondroporosis; chondroclasis
Knorpelabschnitt m cartilaginous part
knorpelartig chondroid, cartilaginiform, cartilaginoid
Knorpelauflockerung f chondroporosis
Knorpelauswuchs m [en]chondrosis; enchondroma
knorpelbeeinflussend chondrotrophic
knorpelbildend chondrogen[et]ic
Knorpelbildung f chondrogenesis, chondrosis
~/**übersteigerte** hyperchondroplasia

Knorpelbildungsschicht f chondrogenic zone
Knorpelbildungsstörung f chondrodystrophia, achondroplasty, achondroplasia *(Zusammensetzungen s. unter* Chondrodystrophie*)*
Knorpelbildungszelle f chondroblast, chondroplast
Knorpeldurchschneidung f chondrotomy, dissection of the cartilage
Knorpelentfernung f[/operative] chondrectomy, excision of the cartilage
Knorpelentzündung f chondritis, inflammation of the cartilage
Knorpelerweichung f chondromalacia, softening of the cartilage
Knorpelfasergeschwulst f chondrofibroma
Knorpelfehlbildung f chondrodysplasia, dyschondroplasia
knorpelförmig cartilaginiform
Knorpelfragment n cartilage fragment
Knorpelfreßzelle f chondroclast
Knorpelfuge f synchondrosis
Knorpelgelenk n s. Knorpelhaft
Knorpelgelenkkörper m/**freier** floating (loose) cartilage
Knorpelgeschwulst f [en]chondroma
~/**fibröse** fibroenchondroma
Knorpelgewebe n cartilaginous (chondral) tissue, cartilage *(Zusammensetzungen s. unter* Knorpel*)*
Knorpelgewebegrundsubstanz f matrix of the cartilage
Knorpelhaft f synchondrosis, cartilaginous joint (symphysis)
Knorpelhaftdurchtrennung f[/operative] synchondrotomy
Knorpelhaut f perichondrium
Knorpelhautentzündung f perichondritis
knorpelig cartilagin[e]ous, chondromatous, chondral, chondric
knorpelig-knöchern chondro-osseous
Knorpelkapsel f cartilage capsule
Knorpelknochen m cartilage bone
Knorpel-Knochen-Geschwulst f chondroosteoma
Knorpelknötchen npl/**Schmorlsche** Schmorl's nodules
Knorpelkrankheit f chondropathy
Knorpelleim m chondrin; collagen
Knorpelmesser n [ec]chondrotome; arthrotome
Knorpelmischgeschwulst f chondromyxoma, myxochondroma
Knorpelnekrose f chondronecrosis, necrosis of cartilage
Knorpelplastik f chondroplasty
Knorpelporose f chondroporosis
Knorpelprotein n chondroprotein
Knorpelregeneration f cartilage regeneration, regeneration of cartilage
Knorpelresorption f chondroclasis
Knorpelring m cartilaginous ring
Knorpelsarkom n [en]chondrosarcoma
Knorpelschädel m chondrocranium

Knorpelschere f cartilage scissors
Knorpelschmerz m chondrodynia, chondralgia, pain in the cartilage
Knorpelschnitt m chondrotomy, dissection of the cartilage
Knorpelschwund m chondroporosis
Knorpelskelett n cartilaginous skeleton
Knorpelspange f cartilaginous bridge
Knorpelteil m cartilaginous part
Knorpeltransplantat n cartilage transplant (graft)
Knorpeltransplantation f cartilage transplantation (grafting)
Knorpel- und Hautentzündung f chondrodermatitis
Knorpelverknöcherung f endostosis, cartilaginous ossification
knorpelwirksam chondrotrophic
Knorpelwucherung f ecchondrosis, enchondromatosis, Ollier's disease
Knorpelzelle f chondrocyte, cartilage cell (corpuscle)
Knorpelzerstörung f chondroclasis
Knorpelzungenmuskel m chondroglossus [muscle]
Knorrenmuskel m anconeus [muscle]
Knospe f bud, bulb, caliculus, calyculus
Knospung f 1. budding, gemmation *(Virologie)*; 2. blastogenesis *(Embryologie)*
Knötchen n tubercle, tuberculum, nodule, nodulus; papule, papula *(Primäreffloreszenz auf der Haut)*
~/**Aschoff-Geipelsches** Aschoff's nodule
~/**Dürcksches** Dürck's node
Knötchen npl/**Babéssche** Babés nodules (tubercles)
knötchenartig tuberculoid, tubercular, nodular; papuloid; lichenoid, lichenous
Knötchenaussaat f miliary spread
knötchenbedeckt tuberculated, tubercular, nodulate[d], nodose
Knötchenbildung f tubercul[iz]ation, nodulation
Knötchenflechte f s. Lichen
knötchenförmig tuberculoid, tubercular, tuberous, nodular, nodose
Knötchenkrankheit f s. Tuberkulose
Knötchenreaktion f nodular response
knötchentragend papuliferous
Knötchentuberkulose f miliary (disseminated) tuberculosis
Knoten m node, nodus *(s. a. unter* Nodus*)*; nodule; tubercle; granuloma
~/**Aschoff-Tawarascher** Tawara's (His-Tawara) node, atrioventricular (Aschoff's) node *(Herzreizleitung)*
~/**Bouchardscher** Bouchard's node
~/**chirurgischer** surgical (surgeon's) knot, double knot
~/**Cloquetscher** Cloquet's gland (node)
~/**entzündlicher** tophus *(bei Gicht)*
~/**kalter** cold nodule *(der Schilddrüse)*
Knotenarrhythmie f [atrioventricular] nodal arrhythmia

Knotenaussatz

Knotenaussatz *m* lepra, nodular leprosy
Knotenbildung *f* nodulation; nodosity
knotenförmig nodal, nodose, nodular, tubercular
Knotenleber *f* hobnail liver
Knotenrhythmus *m* [atrioventricular] nodal rhythm
Knotenstruma *f* nodular goitre, multinodular (adenomatous) struma
Knotentachykardie *f* [atrioventricular] nodal tachycardia
knotig nodal, nodose, nodular, nodulate, tubercular, tuberous
Knotigkeit *f* nodosity
Knüpfzange *f* knot tying forceps
Koadaptation *f* coadaptation
Koagulabilität *f* coagulability
Koagulans *n s.* Koagulationsmittel
Koagulase *f* coagulase *(Enzym)*
koagulase-negativ coagulase-negative
koagulase-positiv coagulase-positive
Koagulaseprobe *f* coagulase test
Koagulat *n* coagulum, coagulate clot
Koagulation *f* coagulation, clotting; pectization
Koagulationsband *n* coagulation band
~/Weltmannsches Weltmann's coagulation column
koagulationsfördernd coagulative
koagulationshemmend anticoagulative, anticoagulant
Koagulationsmittel *n* coagulant [agent], coagulator
Koagulationsnekrose *f* coagulation necrosis
Koagulationspinzette *f* coagulation forceps
Koagulationsthrombus *m* coagulation thrombus
Koagulationsvitamin *n* coagulation (antihaemorrhagic) vitamin, vitamin K
Koagulationszeit *f*/**aktivierte** activated coagulation time
koagulierbar coagulable
Koagulierbarkeit *f* coagulability
koagulieren to coagulate, to clot
~/mittels Hitze to thermocoagulate
koagulierend coagulant, coagulative
Koagulopathie *f* coagulopathy, blood-clotting disorder, blood coagulation deficiency
~ bei Giftschlangenbiß envenomation coagulopathy
Koagulum *n* coagulum, coagulate, clot
Koaptation *f* coaptation *(von Knochenbrüchen)*
Koarktation *f* coarctation *(Zusammensetzungen s. unter Coarctatio)* • **die ~ überbrücken (umgehen)** to bypass the coarctation
Koarktationsklemme *f* coarctation forceps
Koarktotomie *f* coarctotomy
Kobalamin *n* cobalamin, vitamin B_{12}, Castle's extrinsic factor
Kobaltbestrahlung *f* cobalt[-beam] therapy
Kobalt-60-Einheit *f* cobalt-60 unit *(für Kobaltbestrahlung)*
Kobalttherapie *f* [radio]cobalt therapy
Köbner-Phänomen *n* Köbner's phenomenon *(Dermatologie)*

Kocher-Klemme *f* Kocher forceps
Kocher-Schnitt *m* Kocher incision *(Gallenchirurgie)*
Kochlearisreflex *m* cochlear reflex
kochleostapedial cochleostapedial
kochleovestibulär cochleovestibular
Kochsalzeinschränkung *f* salt (sodium chloride) restriction
Kochsalzinfusion *f* saline (sodium chloride) infusion
Kochsalzlösung *f* salt (sodium chloride) solution
~/hypertone hypertonic sodium chloride solution
~/isotone isotonic sodium chloride solution
~/physiologische physiological saline (sodium chloride) solution, Ringer's solution
Kochsalzmangelerschöpfung *f* heat exhaustion (prostration)
Kochsalzmangelsyndrom *n* low-salt syndrome, salt depletion syndrome
Kochsalzverarmung *f* salt depletion
Kochsterilisator *m* water sterilizer
Kodehydrase *f* codehydrase, coenzyme
~ I *s.* Koenzym I
~ II *s.* Koenzym II
Kodehydrogenase *f* codehydrogenase *(Enzym)*
Kodein *n* codeine, methylmorphine *(Antitussivum)*
Kodeinphosphat *n* codeine phosphate *(Antitussivum)*
Kodekarboxylase *f* codecarboxylase *(Enzym)*
kodieren to code *(z. B. Gene)*
kodiert sein to be encoded in *(Gene)*
Kodon *n* codon *(genetische Informationseinheit)*
Koenzym *n* coenzyme, coferment, prosthetic group *(Enzymanteil)*
~ I coenzyme I, nicotinamide-adenine dinucleotide, NAD, diphosphopyridine nucleotide, DPN
~ II coenzyme II, triphosphopyridine nucleotide, TPN
~ A coenzyme A
Kofaktor *m* cofactor
Koffein *n* caffeine, coffeine, 1,3,7-trimethylxanthine
Koffeinentzugmigräne *f* caffeine-withdrawal headache
Koffeinvergiftung *f* caffeinism, coffeinism, coffein intoxication
Kohabitation *f* cohabitation, intercourse, coitus, coition, pareunia
Kohabitationsfurcht *f* coitophobia
Kohabitationsschmerzen *mpl* dyspareunia
Kohabitationsschock *m* sexual shock
Kohabitationsunfähigkeit *f* apareunia
kohabitieren to cohabitate, to have intercourse
Kohlehydrat *n s.* Kohlenhydrat
Kohlendioxidabsorber *m* carbon dioxide absorption canister
Kohlendioxid-Absorptionsanästhesie *f* carbon dioxide absorption anaesthesia *(geschlossenes Narkosesystem)*
Kohlendioxidanzeiger *m* carbonometer
Kohlendioxidbad *n s.* Kohlensäurebad

Kohlendioxidbehandlung f carbon dioxide therapy
Kohlendioxiderhöhung f im Blut hypercapnia, hypercarbia
Kohlendioxidgehalt m carbon dioxide content ● mit erhöhtem ~ hypercapnic ● mit normalem ~ normocapnic ● mit verringertem ~ hypocapnic
Kohlendioxidmangel m im Blut hypocapnia, hypocarbia, acapnia
Kohlendioxidmesser m carbonometer
Kohlendioxidpartialdruck m partial pressure of carbon dioxide
Kohlendioxidschnee m carbon dioxide snow
Kohlendioxidspannung f carbon dioxide tension
Kohlenhydrat n carbohydrate, saccharide
Kohlenhydratabbau m carbohydrate catabolism
Kohlenhydratausscheidung f im Urin carbohydraturia
kohlenhydratinduziert carbohydrate-induced
Kohlenhydratresorption f carbohydrate resorption (absorption)
Kohlenhydratstoffwechsel m carbohydrate metabolism
Kohlenhydratverdauung f carbohydrate digestion
Kohlenhydratverwertung f carbohydrate utilization
Kohlenmonoxidvergiftung f carbon monoxide poisoning
Kohlenoxidchlorid n carbonyl chloride, phosgene *(lungenschädigender Kampfstoff)*
Kohlenoxidhämoglobin n carboxyhaemoglobin, carbon monoxyhaemoglobin, carbonylhaemoglobin
Kohlenoxidmyoglobin n carboxymyoglobin
Kohlensäurebad n carbon dioxide bath, effervescent bath
Kohlensäuremangel m im Blut hypocapnia, hypocarbia, acapnia
Kohlenstaublunge[nerkrankung] f anthracosis, coal-miner's lung, black phthisis, anthracosilicosis
Kohlenwasserstoff m/**kanzerogener** cancerogenic hydrocarbon compound
Köhler m l s. Krankheit/Köhlersche 1.
~/II s. Krankheit/Köhlersche 2.
Kohletablette f charcoal tablet *(gegen Diarrhöe)*
Kohorte f cohort *(Statistik)*
Kohydr[ogen]ase f II s. Koenzym II
Koilonychie f koilonychia; spoon nail
koilorrhachisch koilorrhachic *(Lendenwirbelsäule)*
Koilozytose f koilocytosis *(Zellveränderung infolge perinukleärer Vakuolen)*
Koitophobie f coitophobia *(krankhafte Angst vor dem Geschlechtsverkehr)*
Koitus m coitus, coition, [sexual] intercourse, sexual act, congress, cohabitation, pareunia
Kojewnikow-Syndrom n Kojevnikov's syndrome (epilepsy)

Kokain n cocaine *(Alkaloid)* ● mit ~ unempfindlich machen to cocainize
Kokainhydrochlorid n cocaine hydrochloride
Kokainintoxikation f cocaine poisoning, cocainism
Kokainisierung f cocainization
Kokainist m s. Kokainsüchtiger
Kokainlösung f cocaine solution *(z. B. zur Hornhautanästhesie)*
Kokainsucht f cocainomania, cocainism
kokainsüchtig cocaine-addicted
Kokainsüchtiger m cocainomaniac, cocainist, cocaine addict
„Kokaintierchen" npl cocaine bug *(Hautparästhesien bei Kokainvergiftung)*
Kokainvergiftung f cocaine poisoning, cocainism
Kokarboxylase f cocarboxylase, thiamine pyrophosphate *(Koenzym)*
Kokardenzelle f target (hat) cell, pessary corpuscle, leptocyte *(Erythrozytenform)*
Kokarzinogen n cocarcinogen *(begünstigt Krebsentstehung)*
Kokarzinogenese f cocarcinogenesis
Kokke f coccus, coccobacillus
kokkenartig coccoid, coccobacilliform
kokkenbedingt s. kokkogen
Kokkenform f coccal configuration
kokkenförmig coccoid, coccobacilliform
Kokkobazillus m coccobacillus, coccus
kokkogen coccogenic, coccogenous
Kokkus m s. Kokke
Kokzidie f coccidium *(Sporozoon)* ● durch Kokzidien hervorgerufen coccidial
Kokzidienbefall m s. Kokzidiose
kokzidienhemmend coccidiostatic
Kokzidienkrankheit f s. Kokzidiose
Kokzidioidengranulom n coccidioidal granuloma
Kokzidioideninfektion f coccidioidal infection
Kokzidioidenmeningitis f coccidioidal meningitis
Kokzidioidenventrikulitis f coccidioidal ventriculitis
Kokzidioidin n coccidioidin *(Antigen)*
Kokzidioidin-Hauttest m coccidioidin skin test
Kokzidioidoma n coccidioidoma
Kokzidioidomykose f coccidio[ido]mycosis, coccidioidosis, California disease, desert fever (rheumatism), San Joaquin [valley] fever, Dosada's disease *(durch Coccidioides immitis)*
Kokzidioidomyköseknötchen n coccidioidoma
Kokzidiose f coccidiosis *(Infektion mit Isospora hominis)*
Kokzidiostatikum n coccidiostatic [agent]
Kokzyalgie f coccyalgia, coccy[go]dynia, pain in the coccyx
Kokzygealneuralgie f coccygeal neuralgia
Kokzygektomie f coccygectomy, excision of the coccyx
Kokzygodynie f s. Kokzyalgie
kokzygozephal coccygocephalous
Kolben m plunger, piston *(z. B. einer Spritze)*
Kolbenfinger m clubbed finger; acropachy
Kolbenschimmel m aspergillus

Kolbenschimmelerkrankung

Kolbenschimmelerkrankung f aspergillosis
~/pulmonale pulmonary aspergillosis
Kolbenschimmelpilz m aspergillus
Kolchizin n colchicine *(Mitosegift)*
Kolchizinbehandlung f colchicinization
Kolektomie f colectomy, colon resection
koliartig coliform
Kolibakteriämie f colibacillaemia *(Auftreten von Escherichia coli im Blut)*
kolibakterienartig coliform
Kolibakterienausscheidung f im Urin coli[bacill]uria
Kolibakteriengruppe f coli group
Kolibakterium n colibacillus, bacterium coli, colon bacillus
koliförmig coliform
Koligruppe f coli group
Koliinfektion f colibacillosis, coli infection
Kolik f colic, bellyache, gripes ● ~ verursachend griping
kolikartig colic-like, colicky
kolikauslösend colic, colicky
Kolikschmerz m colicky (coliquy) pain
Kolinephritis f colinephritis
Kolipyelitis f colipyelitis
Kolipyurie f colipyuria
Kolisepsis f colisepsis
Kolitis f colitis, inflammation of the colon *(Zusammensetzungen s. unter Colitis)*
Koliurie f coli[bacill]uria
Kolizystitis f colicystitis
Kolizystopyelitis f colicystopyelitis
kollabieren to collapse
Kollabieren n collapse; deflation *(z. B. der Lunge)*
kollagen collagenous, collagenic
Kollagen n collagen *(Gerüsteiweiß)*
Kollagenablagerung f collagen deposition
Kollagenase f collagenase *(Enzym)*
kollagenauflösend collagenolytic
Kollagenauflösung f collagenolysis
Kollagenbildung f collagen formation
Kollagenersatz m collagen replacement
Kollagenfaser f collagen (white) fibre, collagenous fibre
Kollagenfibrille f collagen fibril
Kollagengefäßkrankheit f collagen vascular disease
Kollagengel n collagen gel
Kollagengewebe n collagen tissue
Kollagenisierung f collagenization
Kollagenkrankheit f collagen disease *(s. a. Kollagenose)*
Kollagenolyse f collagenolysis
kollagenolytisch collagenolytic
Kollagenose f collagenosis, Becker's disease
kollagenreich collagen-rich, rich in collagen
Kollagenreifung f maturation of collagen
Kollagenspeicherkrankheit f collagen thesaurismosis
Kollagenstoffwechsel m collagen metabolism
Kollagentransplantat n collagen graft

Kollagenumsatz m collagen turnover
Kollagenvernetzung f collagen cross-linking *(z. B. bei Wundheilung)*
Kollaps m collapse
~/kardiovaskulärer cardiovascular (circulatory) collapse
~/reflektorischer reflex collapse
kollapsanfällig collapsible
Kollapsbehandlung f collapse therapy, collapsotherapy
kollapsfähig collapsible
Kollateralarterie f collateral artery
Kollateralatmung f collateral respiration
Kollateralbahn f collateral pathway
Kollateralband n collateral ligament
~/äußeres (fibuläres) fibular (external) collateral ligament of the knee
~/inneres (tibiales) tibial (internal) collateral ligament of the knee
Kollateralbandruptur f collateral ligament rupture
Kollateralfaser f collateral fibre
Kollateralganglion n collateral ganglion
Kollateralgefäß n collateral vessel
Kollateralgefäßbett n collateral vascular bed
Kollateralhyperämie f collateral hyperaemia
Kollateralisation f collateral vascular bed
Kollateralkreislauf m collateral circulation
Kollateralversorgung f supply by collateral vessels *(z. B. eines Organs)*
Kollektivdosis f collective dose *(Radiologie)*
Koller m tantrum; rage
kollern to rumble
Kollern n rumbling *(in den Eingeweiden)*
Koller-Test m Koller's (vitamin-K) test
Kollimator m collimator *(Radiologie)*
Kolliquation f colliquation, colliquative softening *(von Geweben)*
Kolliquationsnekrose f colliquative necrosis
Kollisionstumor m collision tumour, carcinosarcoma, sarcocarcinoma
Kollmann-Bougie f Kollmann's bougie *(zur Harnröhrendehnung)*
Kollmann-Dilatator m Kollmann's dilator *(zur Harnröhrendehnung)*
Kollmann-Urethrotom n Kollmann's urethrotome *(zur Harnröhrenspaltung)*
Kolloid n colloid
~/lösungsmittelabweisendes lyophobic colloid
~/lösungsmittelfreundliches lyophilic colloid
~/protektives protective colloid
Kolloidauflösung f colloidoclasia
Kolloidbildung f colloid formation
Kolloidentartung f colloid degeneration
Kolloidfällung f colloid precipitation
Kolloidfixation f colloidopexy
Kolloidgoldprobe f colloidal gold test
Kolloidkrebs m colloid carcinoma *(z. B. Brustkrebs)*
Kolloidlösung f colloidal solution
Kolloidmilium n colloid milium
Kolloidoklasie f colloidoclasia

kolloidoklastisch colloidoclastic
Kolloidopexie f colloidopexy
Kolloidphagozytose f colloidophagy
Kolloidreaktion f colloid reaction *(im Liquor cerebrospinalis)*
Kolloidstruma f colloid goitre
Kolloidzyste f colloid cyst
Kollonema n collonema
Kollumkarzinom n cervical cancer (carcinoma) *(der Gebärmutter)*
Kollunarium n collunarium, nasal douche
Kollutorium n collutory, collutorium, mouth wash, gargle
Kollyrium n collyrium, eyewash; eye salve, lotion for the eyes
Kolobom n coloboma
kolobomatös colobomatous
Kolohepatopexie f colohepatopexy
Kolokolostomie f colocolostomy
Kolon n colon, large bowel (intestine) *(s. a. unter Colon und Dickdarm)*
~/ausgewalztes megacolon
~/irritables (spastisches) irritable (unstable) colon; irritable bowel syndrome, mucocolitis, spastic (mucous, adaptive) colitis
Kolon... s. a. Dickdarm...
Kolonadenom n colon adenoma
Kolonafter m colostomy
~/doppelläufiger double-barrelled colostomy
~/einläufiger single-barrelled colostomy
Kolonafterbeutel m colostomy bag
Kolonaktinomykose f colon actinomycosis
Kolonanastomose f colon anastomosis
Kolonanheftung f[/operative] colo[no]pexy, colofixation, fixation of the colon
Kolonatresie f colon atresia
Kolondilatation f colon dilatation
Kolondivertikulitis f colon[ic] diverticulitis
Kolondivertikulose f colonic diverticulosis
Kolon-Duodenum-Fistel f coloduodenal fistula
Koloneinlauf m coloclyster
Kolonelongation f colon elongation
Kolonerkrankung f colo[no]pathy, colonic disease
Kolonersatz m colon replacement
Kolonexstirpation f colectomy
Kolonfaltung f coloplication
Kolonfibrolipom n colon fibrolipoma
Kolonfixierung f s. Kolonanheftung/operative
Kolonflexur f/linke left flexure of the colon, left colic flexure, splenic flexure [of the colon]
~/rechte right flexure of the colon, right colic flexure, hepatic flexure [of the colon]
Kolongangrän f colon gangrene
Kolongranulom n colon granuloma
Kolongranulomatose f colon granulomatosis
Kolon-Haut-Fistel f colocutaneous fistula
Kolonhistiozytose f colon histiocytosis
Kolonie f colony *(z. B. von Bakterien)*
Kolonienmorphologie f colonial morphology *(Bakterien)*
Koloninterposition f colon interposition

Kolonintussuszeption f colon intussusception
Kolonischämie f colon ischaemia
Kolonkarzinom n colonic cancer, colon carcinoma
Kolonlufteinblasung f colon air insufflation
Kolonmelanom n colon melanoma
Kolonmesenterium n colon mesentery
Kolonmeteorismus m aerocoly
Kolonmotilität f colon motility
Kolonmukosa f colon mucosa, mucous membrane of the colon
Kolonnaht f colorrhaphy, suture of the colon
Kolonobstruktion f colon obstruction
Kolonperforation f colon perforation
Kolonpolyp m colon polyp
Kolonpolypose f colon polyposis
Kolonpseudopolyp m colon pseudopolyp
Kolonpunktion f colocentesis, colopuncture, puncture of the colon
Kolonreinigung f colon cleaning
Kolon-Rektum-Anastomose f colorectostomy, coloproctostomy, colorectal anastomosis
Kolonresektion f colon resection, colectomy
Kolonruptur f colon rupture
Kolonsenkung f coloptosis, prolapse (falling) of the colon
Kolon-Sigma-Anastomose f colosigmoidostomy
Kolonsklerose f colon sclerosis
Kolonspülung f coloclysis, irrigation of the colon
Kolonstenose f colon stenosis, stenosis of the colon
Kolonstriktur f colonic stricture, stricture of the colon
Kolonteilresektion f hemicolectomy
Kolontransplantat n colon graft (transplant)
Kolontransplantation f colon grafting (transplantation)
Kolonulkus n colon ulcer
Kolonulzeration f colon ulceration
Kolonverletzung f colon injury (trauma), colonic lesion
Kolonvolvulus m colon volvulus
Kolonwinkel m colic angle
Kolopexie f s. Kolonanheftung/operative
Koloproktostomie f coloproctostomy
Koloptose f s. Kolonsenkung
kolorektal colorectal
Kolorektostomie f colorectostomy
Kolorimeter n colorimeter
Kolorimetrie f colorimetry
kolorimetrisch colorimetric
Kolorrhaphie f colorrhaphy, suture of the colon
Kolosigmoidostomie f colosigmoidostomy
Koloskopie f colo[no]scopy
Kolostoma n colostomy
Kolostomapflege f colostomy care
Kolostomie f 1. colostomy; 2. s. Kunstafter
Kolostomiebeutel m colostomy bag
Kolostomieöffnung f colostomy [opening] *(s. a. Kunstafter)*
Kolostralmilch f s. Kolostrum
Kolostrorrhoe f colostrorrhoea

Kolostrum

Kolostrum *n* colostrum, foremilk, first milk, neogala, protogala
Kolostrumdiarrhöe *f*, **Kolostrumfluß** *m* colostrorrhoea
Kolostrumtest *m* colostrum test
Kolotomie *f* colotomy
Kolpalgie *f* colpalgia, colpodynia, pain in the vagina, vaginalgia, vaginodynia
Kolpektasie *f* colpectasia, distension (dilation) of the vagina
Kolpektomie *f* colpectomy, excision of the vagina, vagin[al]ectomy
Kolpeurynter *m* colpeurynter
Kolpeuryse *f* colpeurysis, dilatation of the vagina
Kolpitis *f* [endo]colpitis, vaginitis, elytritis
Kolpodynie *f s.* Kolpalgie
Kolpoepisiorrhapie *f* colpoepisiorrhaphy
Kolpofotografie *f* colpophotography, vaginal photography
Kolpohysterektomie *f* colpohysterectomy
Kolpohysteropexie *f* colpohysteropexy, vaginal hysteropexy
Kolpohysterorrhaphie *f* colpohysterorrhaphy
Kolpohysterotomie *f* colpohysterotomy
Kolpokleisis *f* colpocleisis, Simon's operation, surgical closure of the vaginal canal
Kolpolaparotomie *f* colpolaparotomy
Kolpomikroskopie *f* colpomicroscopy
kolpomikroskopisch colpomicroscopic
Kolpopathie *f* colpopathy, vaginal disease, vaginopathy
Kolpoperineoplastik *f* colpoperineoplasty *(bei Scheidensenkung)*
Kolpoperineorrhaphie *f* colpoperineorrhaphy, vaginoperineorrhaphy, perineauxis
Kolpopexie *f* colpopexy, vaginal fixation, vaginapexy
Kolpoplastik *f* colpoplasty, vaginoplasty
Kolporrhagie *f* colporrhagia, vaginal haemorrhage
Kolporrhaphie *f* colporrhaphy, suture of the vagina
Kolporrhexis *f* colporrhexis, laceration of the vagina
Kolposkop *n* colposcope, vaginoscope
Kolposkopie *f* colposcopy, vaginoscopy
kolposkopisch colposcopic, vaginoscopic
Kolpospasmus *m* colpospasm, vaginal spasm
Kolpostenose *f* colpostenosis, vaginal stenosis, narrowing of the vagina
Kolpotom *n* colpotome, vaginotome
Kolpotomie *f* colpotomy, coleotomy, vaginotomy
Kolpoxerose *f* colpoxerosis, abnormal dryness of the vagina
Kolpozele *f* colpocele, vaginocele
Kolpozystitis *f* colpocystitis
Kolpozystographie *f* colpocystography
Kolpozystoplastik *f* colpocystoplasty
Kolpozystozele *f* colpocystocele
Koma *n* coma, comatose state, carus *(s. a. unter Coma)* ● **nach dem ~** postcomatose ● **vor dem ~** precomatose
~/alkoholisches alcoholic coma
~/endogenes endogenous coma
~/exogenes exogenous coma
~/irreversibles irreversible coma
~/reversibles reversible coma
~/tiefes deep coma
Komabehandlung *f* coma therapy
Komaharnzylinder *m* coma cast *(bei Diabetes mellitus)*
komatös comatose, comatous, carotic
Komavorstadium *n* precoma
Kombinationsaphasie *f* combined aphasia
Kombinationsastigmatismus *m* mixed astigmatism
Kombinationsbehandlung *f* combination therapy
Kombinationsimpfstoff *m* mixed vaccine
Kombinationsimpfung *f* combined vaccination
Kombinationsnarkose *f* mixed (combined, balanced) anaesthesia
Kombinationspräparat *n* compound (combination) preparation
Kombinationsstethoskop *n* combination (triple change) stethoscope
Komedo *m* comedo, blackhead
Komedokarzinom *n* comedocarcinoma, comedo [adeno]carcinoma
Komedomastitis *f* comedomastitis
Komedonenentferner *m* comedones extractor
Komedonenquetscher *m* comedones squeezer
Kommabazillus *m* comma bacillus, cholera vibrio
Kommissur *f* commissure, commissura *(Zusammensetzungen s. unter Comissura)*
Kommissurenaphasie *f* commissural aphasia
Kommissurendurchtrennung *f[/operative]* commissurotomy
Kommissurenfaser *f* commissural fibre
Kommissurenkern *m* commissural nucleus
Kommissurenspaltung *f[/operative]* commissurotomy
Kommissurenzelle *f* commissural cell
kommissurospinal commissurospinal
Kommissurotomie *f* commissurotomy
Kommotion *f* concussion, commotion *(Zusammensetzungen s. unter Commotio)*
Kommotionspsychose *f* concussion psychosis; shell-shock psychosis
kommunizieren to communicate *(auf chirurgischem Wege)*
kompakt compact, consolidated *(z. B. Knochen)*
Kompakta *f* compacta, compact tissue (substance), cortical bone
kompatibel compatible *(z. B. Blutgruppen)*
Kompatibilität *f* compatibility
Kompensationshypertrophie *f* compensatory hypertrophy
Kompensationsmangel *m* incompensation *(Zustand zwischen Kompensation und Dekompensation eines Organs)*
Kompensationsphänomen *n* compensation phenomenon
Kompensationsversagen *n* decompensation *(eines Organs)*

Kompensationsvorgang *m* compensation process
kompensatorisch compensatory
kompensieren to compensate
Komplement *n* complement *(Wirkgruppe im Blutserum)* ● **durch ~ bewirkt** complement-mediated
komplementär complementary, complemental
Komplementäremphysem *n* complementary emphysema
Komplementärfarbe *f* complementary colour
Komplementärluft *f* complemental air, inspiratory reserve volume
Komplementärraum *m* complemental space, pleural sinus (recess)
Komplementation *f* complementation *(Virusreplikation)*
komplementbindend complement-fixing
Komplementbindung *f* complement fixation, fixation of complement
Komplementbindungshemmung *f* complement[-fixation] inhibition
Komplementbindungsreaktion *f* complement-fixation reaction (test)
Komplementdefekt *m* complement defect
Komplementfaktor *m* complement factor
Komplementfixation *f* complement fixation, fixation of complement
Komplement-Fixationsantikörper *m* complement-fixation antibody, CF antibody
Komplement-Fixationstest *m* complement-fixation reaction (test)
komplementfixierend complement-fixing
komplementhemmend anticomplementary
Komplementhemmung *f* complement inhibition
Komplementinhibitor *m* complement inhibitor
Komplementmangel *m* complement deficiency
Komplementoid *n* complementoid
Komplexherd *m* complex focus
Komplexpersönlichkeit *f* complex personality
Komplikation *f* complication, sequela *(z. B. einer Krankheit)*
~/postoperative postoperative complication
komplikationslos uncomplicated, without complications, uneventful
kompliziert complicated, difficult *(z. B. Krankheitsverlauf)*; compound, open *(z. B. Knochenbruch)*
Komponente *f*/**gruppenspezifische** group-specific component
~/zelluläre cellular component
Kompresse *f* compress, dressing, splenium *(Umschlag)*; compress, pad, sponge *(z. B. bei Operationen)*
~/kleine pledget
Kompression *f* compression *(Zusammensetzungen s. unter* Compressio*)*
Kompressionsanurie *f* compression anuria *(beim Crush-Syndrom)*
Kompressionsasphyxie *f* traumatic asphyxia
Kompressionsatelektase *f* compression atelectasis

Kompressionsatrophie *f* compression atrophy
Kompressionsdruck *m* bipolar (compression) pressure
Kompressionsfraktur *f* compression [bone] fracture, crush fracture
Kompressionslähmung *f* compression (tourniquet) paralysis *(z. B. eines Nerven)*
Kompressionsmuskel *m* compressor [muscle]
Kompressionsmyelitis *f* compression myelitis
Kompressionsneuritis *f* compression (pressure) neuritis, entrapment neuropathy
Kompressionsnystagmus *m* compression nystagmus
Kompressionsplatte *f* bone [compression] plate *(für Osteosynthesen)*
Kompressionsplattenspanner *m* bone plate compression device
Kompressionsschlauch *m* compression tube
Kompressionsschraube *f* compression bone screw
Kompressionsstauung *f* traumatic asphyxia, pressure stasis *(z. B. bei Verschüttung)*
Kompressionssyndrom *n* compression syndrome
~/neurovaskuläres neurovascular compression syndrome (symptom)
Kompressionsthrombose *f* compression thrombosis
Kompressionsverband *m* compression dressing (bandage)
Kompressionszyanose *f* compression (traumatic) cyanosis
Kompressorium *n* compressor, tourniquet *(chirurgisches Instrument)*
komprimieren to compress *(z. B. Gase)*; to press together *(z. B. eine blutende Wunde)*
Kompulsivirresein *n* compulsive insanity
Koncha *f* concha *(Zusammensetzungen s. unter* Concha*)*
Konchitis *f* conchitis, inflammation of the concha
Konchoskop *n* conchoscope
Konchotom *n* conchotome
Konchotomie *f* conchotomy
kondensieren to condense *(z. B. Gase)*, to inspissate *(z. B. Flüssigkeiten)*
Kondition *f* condition, state [of health]
Konditionierung *f* conditioning
Konditionierungsreiz *m* conditioning stimulus
Kondom *m(n)* condom, preservative
Konduktion *f* conduction
Konduktor *m* 1. conductor *(Führungsinstrument)*; 2. conductor, carrier *(gesunder Genträger)*
Kondylarfortsatz *m* condylar process
Kondylarkanal *m* condylar (condyloid) canal
Kondylarthrosis *f* condylarthrosis, condyloid joint, condylar articulation
Kondylektomie *f* condylectomy, excision of a condyle
Kondylenachse *f* condylar axis
kondylenähnlich condyloid
Kondylenentfernung *f*[/**operative**] condylectomy

Kondylenfraktur

Kondylenfraktur f condylar fracture
Kondylennagel m condyle nail
Kondylenosteochondrom n condylar osteochondroma
Kondylenplatte f condylar plate
Kondylenschraube f tibial bolt
Kondylom n condyloma, figwart, thymion
~/breites flat (broad, syphilitic) condyloma, mucous patch
~/feuchtes moist papule
~/flaches s. ~/breites
~/spitzes acuminate condyloma, pointed [fig] wart, venereal verruca (wart), moist wart *(Virusinfektion)*
kondylomatös condylomatous
Kondylomatose f condylomatosis
Kondylotomie f condylotomy
Kondylus m condyle, condylus *(Zusammensetzungen s. unter* Condylus*)* ● **durch die Kondylen** transcondylar, transcondyloid ● **über einem ~** supracondylar
kondylusartig condyloid
Kondylusdurchtrennung f[/operative] condylotomy
Konfabulation f [con]fabulation *(bei Gedächtnisstörung)*
Konfidenzintervall n interval of confidence, confidence limits
Konfiguration f configuration *(eines Organs)*
Konfliktreaktion f conflict reaction
Konfliktsituation f conflict situation
Konfliktspannung f conflict tension
konfluieren to flow together
konfluierend confluent
konfus confused, muddle-headed
Konfusion f confusion
Kongelation f congelation
kongenital congenital, inborn, innate, genetous, connate, connatal, inherent, protal, intrinsic
Kongestion f congestion, abnormal accumulation of blood; hyperaemia
Kongestionsabszeß m congestive (wandering) abscess
kongestiv congestive
Konglomerat n conglomerate, conglomeration
Konglomeration f conglomeration
Konglomerattuberkel m conglomerate tubercle
Konglomerattumor m conglomerate medley *(bei Appendizitis)*
konglomerieren to conglomerate
Konglutin n conglutin
Konglutination f conglutination
Konglutinationsphänomen n conglutination phenomenon
Konglutinationstest m conglutination test
konglutinieren to conglutinate, to clot
konglutinierend conglutinant, conglutinate, clotting
Konglutinin n conglutinin
Kongofieber n Congo (Congolese red) fever
Kongorot-Probe f Congo-red test, Bennhold's test *(Amyloidosenachweis)*

Kongressus m s. Koitus
Konidie f s. Konidium
Konidienträger m conidiophore
Konidiophor n conidiophore
Konidium n conidium, conidiospore *(Pilzspore)*
Koniin n coniine *(Alkaloid)*
Konimeter n konimeter, coniometer
Konimetrie f konimetry, coniometry
koni[o]metrisch konimetric
Koniose f coniosis, koniosis, dust disease
Koniotomie f coniotomy, cricothyr[e]otomy, inferior laryngotomy, intercricothyreotomy, thyrocricotomy
Konisation conization *(z. B. der Zervix zur histologischen Untersuchung)*
Konisationsmesser n cone knife
konisieren to cone
konjugal conjugal, marital; ligitimate *(Kind)*
Konjugase f conjugase *(Enzym)*
Konjugation f 1. conjugation *(Genetik)*; 2. s. Konjugierung
Konjugationsikterus m conjugation icterus
Konjugationskern m conjugation nucleus
Konjugationsreaktion f conjugation reaction
konjugieren to conjugate *(z. B. Gallensäuren)*
Konjugierung f conjugation *(z. B. von Gallensäuren)*
Konjunktiva f conjunctiva *(Zusammensetzungen s. unter* Conjunctiva*)*
Konjunktiva… s. a. Bindehaut…
Konjunktivaldrüse f conjunctival gland
Konjunktival-Kältetest m conjunctival cold test
Konjunktivalödem n chemosis, conjunctival oedema
Konjunktivalreaktion f s. Konjunktivaltest
Konjunktivalring m conjunctival ring
Konjunktivaltest m conjunctival reaction, ophthalmic test *(Allergietestung)*
Konjunktivalvarize f varicula
Konjunktivatransplantation f conjunctival transplantation
Konjunktivaumschlagfalte f palpebral fold
Konjunktivitis f conjunctivitis, inflammation of the conjunctiva, [blenn] ophthalmia *(s. a. unter* Conjunctivitis *und* Bindehautentzündung*)*
~/diphtherische diphtheric conjunctivitis
~/Parinaudsche leptotrichal conjunctivitis
Konjunktivodakryozystorhinostomie f conjunctivodacryocystorhinostomy
Konjunktivodakryozystostomie f conjunctivodacryocystostomy
konkav concave *(z. B. Linse)*
~/nach vorn koilorrhachic *(Lendenwirbelsäule)*
konkav-konvex concavo-convex *(z. B. Linse)*
Konkavlinse f concave (dispersing) lens
Konkavspiegel m concave mirror
Konklination f conclination
konkomitierend concomitant
Konkrement n s. Stein
Konkussion f concussion, commotion
Konkussionsstar m concussion cataract
konnatal connatal, connate, inborn, innate, congenital

konsanguin consanguineous
Konsanguinität f consanguinity, blood relationship
konsensuell consensual
Konsensus m consent *(Arzt–Patient)*
konservativ conservative, not operative *(z. B. Therapie)*
Konservenblut n banked blood
Konservenvergiftung f can poisoning
konservieren to preserve, to conserve
Konservierung f preservation, conservation
Konsiliararzt m, **Konsiliarius** m consultant, consultant physician
konsolidieren to consolidate *(z. B. Knochenbruch)*
konsolidierend consolidant
Konsolidierung f consolidation *(z. B. eines Knochenbruchs)*
Konsolidierungstherapie f consolidation therapy, consolidant treatment
Konstipation f constipation, obstipation, costiveness
~/**spastische** spastic constipation
konstipieren to constipate, to obstipate
konstipiert constipated, obstipated, costive
Konstitution f [body] constitution; habit[us]
~/**allergische** allergic constitution
~/**genetische** genetic constitution
~/**lymphatische** lymphatism, lymphatic state, lymphotoxaemia *(Neigung zu Entzündung und Hyperplasie des lymphatischen Gewebes)*
Konstitutionskrankheit f constitutional disease
Konstitutionspsychologie f constitutional psychology
Konstitutionsschwäche f constitutional weakness
Konstitutionssymptom n constitutional (systemic) symptom
Konstitutionstyp m constitutional type
Konstriktion f constriction, contraction, narrowing
konstriktiv constrictive
Konstriktor[muskel] m constrictor [muscle]
konstringieren to constringe, to constrict
Konsultation f consultation
konsultieren to consult, to ask (seek) an advice
~/**einen Arzt** to consult a physician
konsumierend consumptive
Konsumption f consumption
Konsumptionskrankheit f consumptive (wasting, over-use) disease
Konsumtion f s. Konsumption
Kontagion f(n) 1. contagion, communication of disease, infection; contamination; 2. contagious (infectious) disease; 3. s. Kontagium
Kontagiosität f contagiousness, contagiosity *(z. B. einer Krankheit)*
Kontagium n contagium, causative (infective) agent
Kontaktallergen n contactant, contact allergen
Kontaktallergie f contact allergy, contact [hyper]sensitivity

kontaktarm contactless; schizoid
Kontaktaufnahme f contact radiography
Kontaktaugenlinse f s. Kontaktlinse
Kontaktdermatitis f contact dermatitis
~/**allergische** allergic contact dermatitis
Kontaktekzem n s. Kontaktdermatitis
kontaktfreudig sociable
Kontaktgeschwür n contact ulcer
Kontaktgift n contact poison
Kontaktglas n s. Kontaktlinse
Kontakthemmung f contact inhibition *(z. B. von Zellen)*
Kontakthypersensibilität f contact [hyper]sensitivity
Kontaktinfektion f contact infection
Kontaktkrebs m contact cancer
Kontaktlaxans n contact laxative
Kontaktlinse f contact (adherent) lens
Kontaktlinsenträger m contact lens wearer
Kontaktmetastase f contact (klatsch) metastasis
Kontaktperson f contact person
Kontaktpräparat n impression preparation
Kontaktrezeptor m contact receptor
Kontaktring m contact ring *(Schußwunde)*
Kontaktstörung f contact disturbance; disturbed contact
Kontaktstrahlenbehandlung f contact radiation treatment, X-ray contact therapy
Kontakttest m contact test
Kontakttherapie f s. Kontaktstrahlenbehandlung
Kontaktübertragung f contact transmission, transmission by contact
Kontaktverarmung f loss of contacts
Kontamination f 1. contamination; 2. pollution
~/**bakterielle** bacterial contamination
~/**radioaktive** radioactive contamination
Kontaminationsangst f fear of contamination, mysophobia, molysmophobia
kontaminieren to contaminate
kontinent continent, restraining, holding back
~/**nicht** incontinent
Kontinenz f 1. continence, control of organ function; 2. self-restraint
Kontinua f continua, continued fever
Kontraextension f counterextension *(Knochenextension unter Zug in entgegengesetzten Richtungen)*
kontrahieren to contract
Kontraindikation f contraindication, counterindication ● **eine ~ darstellen** to contraindicate
kontraindizieren to contraindicate
kontraindiziert sein to be contraindicated (inadvisable)
Kontrainzision f contraincision, counterincision
kontraktil contractile
Kontraktilität f contractility
Kontraktion f contraction
~/**idiomuskuläre** idiomuscular contraction
~/**isometrische** isometric contraction
~/**isotonische** isotonic contraction
~/**sanduhrförmige** hourglass contraction
~/**tonische** tonic contraction

Kontraktionsatelektase

Kontraktionsatelektase f contraction atelectasis *(der Lunge)*
Kontraktionsfähigkeit f contractility
Kontraktionskraft f contractility
Kontraktionskraftmessung f des Herzens cardiometry
kontraktionslos acontractile
Kontraktionsring m contraction ring *(der Gebärmutter)*
Kontraktionsschwäche f contraction weakness *(von Muskeln)*; subinvolution, incomplete involution *(der Gebärmutter)*
Kontraktionswelle f contraction wave *(von Muskeln)*
Kontraktur f contracture
~ **der Hand- und Fußgelenke** acrocontracture
~/**Duplaysche** Duplay's disease
~/**Dupuytrensche** Dupuytren's contracture, palmar fibromatosis *(an der Hand)*
~/**idiomuskuläre** idiomuscular contracture
~/**ischämische** ischaemic contracture, Volkmann's muscular atrophy
~ **mit Induratio penis plastica/Dupuytrensche** Peyronie's disease
~/**Volkmannsche** s. ~/ischämische
Kontralateralhemiplegie f contralateral hemiplegia
Kontrast m contrast • **nicht ~ gebend** nonopaque, radiopaque, radio-opaque, radiodense
Kontrastaufnahme f contrast radiogram (roentgenogram)
~ **der hinteren Schädelgrube** contrast posterior fossagram
Kontrastaufnahmetechnik f contrast radiography (roentgenography)
Kontrastbrei m contrast (opaque) meal; barium meal
Kontrastdarstellung f s. Kontrastmittel[röntgen]darstellung
Kontrastechokardiographie f contrast echocardiography
Kontrasteinlauf m contrast enema; barium enema
Kontrastfärbung f contrast staining, counterstaining
Kontrastgeben n opacification
kontrastgebend opaque
Kontrastkehlkopfdarstellung f contrast laryngography
Kontrastmahlzeit f contrast (opaque) meal
Kontrastmittel n [X-ray] contrast medium, [radi]opaque medium, contrast material
Kontrastmittelallergie f allergy to the contrast medium
Kontrastmittel[röntgen]aufnahme f contrastmedia radiogram (roentgenogram)
Kontrastmittel[röntgen]darstellung f contrastmedia radiography (roentgenography)
Kontrastmitteluntersuchung f s. Kontrastmittel[röntgen]darstellung
Kontrastmyelographie f contrast myelography
Kontrazeption f contraception, conception control

kontrazeptiv contraceptive, anticonceptive
Kontrazeptivum n contraceptive [agent]
~/**orales** oral contraceptive
Kontrecoup m s. Contrecoup
Kontrektationstrieb m contrectation
Kontrollaufnahme f check-up radiography *(z. B. bei Knochenbruch)*
Kontrollbiß m checkbite
Kontrollcholangiographie f repeat (control) cholangiography
Kontrollgen n control gene
Kontrollgruppe f control group *(Statistik)*
kontrollieren to control, to check; to supervise; to regulate
~/**über einen Bildschirm** to monitor
Kontrollserum n control serum
Kontrollsichtgerät n monitor *(z. B. für EKG)*
Kontrolltier n control animal
Kontrolluntersuchung f medical check-up
Kontrollversuch m control experiment (test)
Kontur f contour, outline *(z. B. auf Röntgenaufnahmen)*
konturiert contoured, outlined
Kontusion f contusion, bruise *(Zusammensetzungen s. unter* Contusio*)*
Kontusionskatarakt f contusion (traumatic) cataract
Kontusionspneumonie f contusion pneumonia
Konus m cone, conus *(Zusammensetzungen s. unter* Conus*)*
Konusbiopsie f cone biopsy
Konussyndrom n conus medullaris syndrome
Konvaleszent m convalescent
Konvaleszenz f convalescence, recovery
konvaleszierend convalescent
Konvergenzbestrahlung f convergence radiation
Konvergenzbreite f amplitude of convergence
Konvergenzlähmung f convergence paralysis
Konvergenzlinse f converging lens
Konvergenznahpunkt m convergence near point
Konvergenzpunkt m convergence point, point of convergence *(des Auges)*
Konvergenzreaktion f convergence reaction
Konvergenzreflex m convergence reflex
Konvergenzschielen n/**intermittierendes** intermittent convergent strabism
Konvergenzschwäche f convergence insufficiency (deficiency), lack of convergence
Konvergenzwinkel m convergence angle, angle of convergence
Konvergenzzentrum n centre of convergence
Konversion f conversion *(bei der Geburt)*
Konversionssymptom n conversion symptom
Konvertin n convertin, stable (serum accelerator) factor, SAF, serum prothrombin conversion factor, blood-clotting factor VII
konvex convex *(z. B. Linse)*
konvex-konkav convexo-concave *(z. B. Linse)*
Konvexlinse f convex (diverging) lens
Konvexspiegel m convex mirror
Konvolut n convolution *(z. B. von Krampfadern)*
Konvolutionsatrophie f convolutional atrophy

Konvolutionshirnatrophie f convolutional cerebral atrophy
Konvolutionsschädelknochenatrophie f convolutional atrophy
Konvulsion f convulsion, spasm[us], trembling *(Zusammensetzungen s. unter Krampf)*
Konvulsionstherapie f s. Krampfbehandlung
Konvulsionszentrum n convulsion centre *(im verlängerten Rückenmark)*
konvulsiv convulsive
Konvulsivum n convulsive [agent]
Konzentration f concentration *(z. B. von Lösungen)*
~/**geistige** concentration
~/**minimale tödliche** minimal lethal concentration
Konzentrationsfähigkeit f 1. concentration power *(psychisch)*; 2. s. Konzentrierungsfähigkeit
~/**mangelnde** paralogia
Konzentrationsmangel m lack of concentration
Konzentrationsschwäche f weakness of concentration; hypocathexis
Konzentrationsstärke f power of concentration; hypercathexis
Konzentrationsversuch m/**Volhardscher** Volhard's [concentration] test
konzentrieren to concentrate
Konzentrierung f concentration
Konzentrierungsfähigkeit f concentrating ability *(z. B. der Niere)*
~/**maximale** maximal concentrating ability
Konzentrierungsleistung f **der Nieren/erhöhte** hypersthenuria
~/**verminderte** hyposthenuria
Konzeption f conception, fecundation of the ovum
konzeptionsfördernd proconceptive
Konzeptionstermin m time of conception
konzeptionsverhütend contraceptive
Konzeptionsverhütung f contraception
Konzeptionsverhütungsmittel n contraceptive [agent]
Konzeptionsversagen n failure of conception
konzeptiv conceptive
Koordination f coordination
Koordinationsschwäche f hyposynergia
Koordinationsstörung f impaired coordination, asynchronism, disturbed synergia
Kopaivabalsam m copaiba balsam
Kopf m 1. head; 2. head, caput *(z. B. eines Knochens)*; condyle *(z. B. eines Gelenks)* ● **ohne** ~ acephalous, acephalic
~/**kahnförmiger** scaphocephalus
~/**nachfolgender** aftercoming head *(bei der Geburt)*
Kopfarterie f s. Halsschlagader
kopfartig cephaloid
Kopfbein n capitate bone, capitatum
Kopfbiß m occlusion (edge-to-edge) bite
Kopf-Brust-Gipsverband m Minerva cast, Minerva [plaster] jacket

Köpfchen n capitulum, capitellum
Kopfdornmuskel m spinalis capitis [muscle]
Kopfeinstellung f/**Roederersche** Roederer's obliquity *(bei der Geburt)*
Kopfekzem n cradle cap
köpfen to decapitate
Kopfextension f head traction *(bei Halswirbelfraktur)*
Kopffallprobe f head dropping test *(bei Meningitis)*
Kopfflechte f ringworm of the scalp
kopfförmig capitate, cephaloid, head-shaped
Kopffortsatz m notochordal process
Kopfgelenk n/**oberes** atlanto-occipital joint
~/**unteres** epistrophial joint
Kopfgicht f cephalagra
Kopfgrind m dandruff; favus, crusted ringworm
Kopfgrippe f herpes [simplex] encephalitis, herpetic encephalitis, von Economo's disease
Kopfhaar n hair of the head, capillus, head hair
Kopfhämatom n cephal[o]haematoma
Kopfhaut f scalp
Kopfhautklammer f scalp clamp (haemostasis clip)
Kopfhautklemme f scalp flap forceps
Kopfhautwunde f scalp wound
Kopfhochlage f head-up position
Kopflage f head (cephalic) presentation; head birth *(bei der Geburt)*
Kopflampe f forehead lamp
Kopflaus f head louse, body (cootie) louse
Kopfläusebefall m lousiness of the hair of the head
Kopflichtbad n electric-light head bath
kopflos headless, acephalic, acephalous
Kopfmesser m cephalometer
Kopfmitte f midhead
Kopfmuskel m head muscle
~/**großer hinterer gerader** rectus capitis posterior major muscle
~/**kleiner hinterer gerader** rectus capitis posterior minor muscle
~/**langer** longus capitis [muscle]
~/**oberer schräger** superior oblique muscle of the head
~/**seitlicher gerader** rectus capitis lateralis muscle
~/**unterer schräger** inferior oblique muscle of the head
~/**vorderer gerader** rectus capitis anterior muscle
Kopfmuskellähmung f cephaloplegia
Kopfneigetest m head-tilting test
Kopfneuralgie f cranial neuralgia
Kopfnicker m s. Kopfwender
Kopfrollen n head rolling
Kopfschlagader f s. Halsschlagader
Kopfschmerz m headache, [en]cephalalgia, cephalodynia
~/**einseitiger** megrim
~/**hartnäckiger** cephalea
~/**heftiger** splitting headache
~ **in beiden Kopfhälften** amphicrania

Kopfschmerz

~ nach Lumbalpunktion leakage (puncture) headache
~/organischer organic headache
~/pochender pounding headache
~/posttraumatischer posttraumatic headache
~/psychogener psychogenic headache
~/vasomotorischer vasomotor headache
Kopfschmerzmittel *n* anticephalalgic [agent], headache remedy
Kopfschmerztablette *f* anticephalalgic (headache) tablet
Kopfschuppe *f* dandruff, scurf
Kopfschüttelnystagmus *m* head shaking nystagmus
Kopfschwarte *f* galea, epicranium; scalp *(mit Haaren)*
Kopfschwartenabriß *m* scalp laceration
Kopfschwartenabszeß *m* scalp abscess
Kopfschwarteninfektion *f* scalp infection
Kopfschwartenwunde *f* scalp wound
Kopfschwartenzange *f* scalp flap forceps
Kopfschweiß *m* head sweat
Kopfspange *f* metal head band
Kopfspiegel *m* [fore]head mirror
Kopfstimme *f* head (falsetto) voice
Kopfstütze *f* head-rest, head support
Kopftetanus *m* cephalotetanus, head tetanus
Kopftieflage *f* head-low position, head-down position (tilt) *(z. B. bei der Geburt)*
Kopfträger *m* atlas
Kopfumfang *m* head circumference, circumference of the head
Köpfung *f* decapitation, detruncation
Kopfverband *m* head bandage (dressing)
Kopfvergrößerung *f*/abnorme megalocephalia
Kopfverletzung *f* head injury
Kopfwackeln *n* nutation
kopfwärts cranial; craniad
Kopfwender *m* sternocleidomastoid [muscle], sternomastoid muscle
Kopfwenderarterie *f* sternocleidomastoid artery
Kopfwendervene *f* sternocleidomastoid vein
Kopfwendung *f* cephalic version *(bei der Geburt)*
Kopfwunde *f* head wound
Kopfzange *f* cephalotractor *(Geburtszange)*
Kopfzug *m* head traction
Kopierungsfehler *m* copy error *(Gen-DNS)*
Kopiopie *f* copiopia, asthenopia, visual fatigue, ophthalmocopia, ophthalmokopia
Koplik-Flecken *mpl* Koplik's spots, oral exanthema of measles
Kopophobie *f* kopophobia *(krankhafte Angst vor Erschöpfung)*
koppeln to conjugate *(z. B. Gallensäuren)*
Kopplung *f* conjugation *(z. B. Gallensäuren)*
~/elektromechanische electromechanical coupling *(Physiologie)*
Kopremesis *f* copremesis, vomiting of faeces, faecal (stercoraceous) vomiting
Koprokultur *f* coproculture
Koprolagnie *f* coprolagnia
Koprolalie *f* coprolalia, coprophrasia, utterance of filthy words

Koprolith *m* coprolith, faecal concretion, faecalith, stercolith
Koprologie *f* coprology *(Lehre von der Stuhlbeschaffenheit)*
Koprom *n* coproma, stercoroma, faecaloma, scatoma
koprophag coprophagous, scatophagous
Koprophagie *f* coprophagia, eating of dung, scatophagia, rhypophagy
koprophil coprophil[e], coprophilic, coprophilous
Koprophilie *f* coprophilia
Koprophobie *f* coprophobia, repugnance to faeces
Koprophrasie *f s.* Koprolalie
Koproporphyrin *n* coproporphyrin
Koproporphyrinausscheidung *f* im Urin coproporphyrinuria
Koprostan *n* coprostane, pseudocholestane
Koprostanol *n* coprostanol, coprosterol, koprostearin
Koprostase *f* coprostasis, faecal stasis, impaction of the faeces
Koprosterin *n*, **Koprosterol** *n s.* Koprostanol
Kopula *f* copula *(embryonale Zungenwurzel)*
Kopulation *f* copulation, sexual congress, mating
kopulieren to copulate, to mate
korakoakromial coracoacromial
korakohumeral coracohumeral
korakoid coracoid
Korakoid *n* coracoid [process]
korakoklavikulär coracoclavicular
Korallenstar *m* coralliform cataract
Korallenstein *m* coral (dendritic) calculus *(Nierenstein)*
Korallenstockthrombus *m* platelet thrombus
Korbfaser *f* basket fibre
Korbhenkelriß *m* loop (bucket-handle) fracture *(Meniskus)*
Korbzelle *f* basket cell
Koredialysis *f* pupillary dialysis
Koreklisis *f* coreclisis, iridencleisis
Korektasis *f* corectasis, dilatation of the pupil
Korektomie *f* corectomy
Korektopie *f* corectopia *(Mißbildung der Pupille)*
Korelyse *f* corelysis, operative destruction of the pupil
Koreometer *n* cor[e]ometer
Koreometrie *f* coreometry, measurement of the pupil
Koreoplastik *f* coreoplasty, plastic operation on the iris
Korium *n* corium, dermis, derm[a], cutis, true skin
Koriumkarzinom *n* basal cell carcinoma
Korkenzieherarterie *f* corkscrew artery
Korkenzieherösophagus *m* corkscrew oesophagus
Korkenzieherureter *m* corkscrew ureter
Kornährenverband *m* spica [bandage], spiral reverse bandage
Körnchen *n* granule, granulum
~/chromophiles chromophile granule

~/**metachromatisches** metachromatic granule
~/**oxyphiles** oxyphilic granule
Körnchen *npl*/**Altmannsche** Altmann's granules
körnchenartig granular, granuliform
Körnchenzellen *fpl*/**oxyphile** cells of Paneth
Kornea *f* cornea
Kornea... *s. a.* Hornhaut...
korneaähnlich corneal, keroid
Korneaanästhesie *f* corneal anaesthesia
Korneahalter *m* corneal holder
Korneaklemme *f* corneal forceps
Korneakrankheit *f* keratopathy, corneal disease
Kornealreflex *m* corneal (blink) reflex, eyelid [closure] reflex, blink response
Korneaprotrusion *f* kerato-ectasia
Korneareflektionsfigur *f* mire *(Ophthalmometrie)*
Korneastärke *f* corneal thickness
Körnelung *f* granulation; granulosis
~/**Maurersche** Maurer's dots *(der roten Blutkörperchen bei Malaria tropica)*
Körnerkrankheit *f*/**Ägyptische** trachoma, trachomatous (trachoma inclusion) conjunctivitis, Egyptian ophthalmia, granular conjunctivitis (ophthalmia); granular lids
körnerlos agranular
Körnerschicht *f* granular layer ● **über der äußeren ~ des Gehirns** supragranular
~/**äußere** outer nuclear layer *(der Netzhaut)*
~ **der Großhirnrinde/äußere** external granular layer of the cerebrum, layer of small pyramidal cells
~ **der Großhirnrinde/innere** internal granular layer of the cerebrum
~ **der Kleinhirnrinde/äußere** external granular layer of the cerebellum
~ **der Kleinhirnrinde/innere** internal granular layer of the cerebellum
~/**Tomessche** Tomes's granular layer, interglobular dentin (space)
Körnerzelle *f* granular (granule) cell
Körnerzellen *fpl*/**Panethsche** cells of Paneth *(in den Lieberkühnschen Krypten)*
körnerzellenfrei agranulocytic
Körnerzellenkarzinom *n* granular-cell carcinoma
Körnerzellenmyosarkom *n* granular-cell myosarcoma
Körnerzellenneurofibrom *n* granular-cell neurofibroma
Körnerzellenschicht *f* granular[-cell] layer
Körnerzellenzystadenom *n* granular-cell cystadenoma
Körnerzellschicht *f* granular[-cell] layer
Körnerzytoplasma *n* granular cytoplasm
Kornflechte *f* grain (miller's, mattress) itch
körnig granular, granulous
~/**nicht** non-granular
Kornzange *f* sponge forceps
Koronar... *s. a.* Herzkranzgefäß...
Koronarangiogramm *n* coronary angiogram
Koronarangiographie *f* coronary angiography

Koronarangioplastik *f*/**perkutane transluminale** percutaneous transluminal coronary angioplasty, PTCA
Koronaranomalie *f* coronary anomaly
Koronararterie *f* coronary artery *(s. a. unter Kranzarterie)*
~/**linke** left coronary artery
~/**rechte** right coronary artery
Koronararterienblutfluß *m* coronary blood flow
Koronararterien-Bypass *m* coronary artery bypass
Koronararterienchirurgie *f* coronary artery surgery
Koronararteriendilatator *m* coronary artery dilator
Koronararterienerkrankung *f* coronary disease
Koronararterienfistel *f* coronary artery fistula
Koronararterienligatur *f* coronary artery ligation
Koronararterienostium *n* coronary arterial ostium (orifice)
Koronararterienperfusion *f* coronary artery perfusion
Koronararterienstenose *f* coronary stenosis
Koronararterienthrombose *f* coronary thrombosis
Koronararterienthrombus *m* coronary [artery] thrombus
Koronararterienverschluß *m* coronary artery occlusion
Koronararterienverschlußkrankheit *f* occlusive coronary artery disease
Koronararteriosklerose *f* coronary [arterio]sclerosis, coronary atheromatosis
Koronarblut *n* coronary blood
Koronar-Bypass-Patient *m* post-bypass patient
Koronarchirurgie *f* coronary [artery] surgery
Koronardurchblutung *f* coronary [blood] flow
Koronareinheit *f* coronary care unit, emergency cardiac care unit
Koronarembolie *f* coronary embolism
Koronargefäß *n* coronary vessel
Koronargefäßbett *n* coronary vascular bed
Koronargefäßerweiterung *f* coronary dilation
Koronarie *f s.* Koronararterie
Koronarienvereng[er]ung *f* coronary stenosis
Koronarinsuffizienz *f* coronary insufficiency, coronary failure [syndrome], intermediate coronary syndrome
Koronarklappe *f* coronary valve
Koronarkrampf *m* coronary spasm
Koronarkrankheit *f* coronary [heart] disease
Koronarkreislauf *m* coronary circulation
Koronarogramm *n* coronary angiogram
Koronarostium *n* coronary orifice (ostium)
Koronarplexus *m* coronary plexus
Koronarreflex *m* coronary reflex
Koronarreserve *f* coronary [flow] reserve
Koronarsinus *m* coronary sinus
Koronarsinuskatheter *m* coronary sinus catheter
Koronarsklerose *f* coronary [arterio]sclerosis
Koronarstenose *f* coronary stenosis
Koronarsulkus *m* coronary sulcus

Koronarthrombose

Koronarthrombose f coronary thrombosis
Koronarvene f coronary vein
Koronarverschluß m coronary occlusion
Körper m 1. [human] body, corpus, soma; trunk; 2. corpus, body *(Anatomie) (Zusammensetzungen s. unter* Corpus*)* ● **nicht in den ~ eindringend** non-invasive ● **vom eigenen ~** autologous
~/lebender organism
Körper mpl bodies, granules *(Zusammensetzungen s. a. unter* Corpora*)*
~/[Howell-]Jollysche Jolly bodies *(z. B. nach Milzentfernung in Erythrozyten)*
Körperabwehr f bodily (body) defense
~ gegen Infektionen/natürliche phylaxis, natural protection against infection
Körperagnosie f body agnosia
Körperaufrichtungsreflex m body-righting reflex
Körperausscheidungen fpl egesta, excreta, ejecta; exudate *(Schweiß)*
Körperauszehrung f phthisis
Körperbau m 1. constitution, build, body structure (form, frame); 2. anatomy
Körperbehaarung f pelage
Körperbehinderung f physical handicap (disability)
Körperbereich m body region ● **einen bestimmten ~ betreffend** regional
Körperbeschaffenheit f habit[us], constitution
Körperbeschreibung f/**morphologische** somatoscopy
Körperbesichtigung f inspection *(bei Untersuchung)*
Körperbewegung f [body] movement
Körperbewegungsmesser m kinesi[o]meter
Körperchen n corpuscle, body; granule *(s. a. unter* Corpusculum*)*
~ der Milz/Malpighisches Malpighian body *(Lymphzellenansammlungen)*
~/[Leishman-]Donovansches Donovan body, Leishman-Donovan parasite *(Erreger des Granuloma inguinale)*
~/Malpighisches Malpighian body, renal corpuscle
~/Pacinisches s. **~/Vater-Pacinisches**
~/Ruffinisches Ruffini's cell (corpuscle, end organ)
~/Vater-Pacinisches Pacinian (Vater-Pacini) corpuscle, lamellar corpuscle
Körperchen npl corpuscles, bodies *(s. a. unter* Corpuscula*)*
~/Babés-Ernstsche Babés-Ernst bodies, polar bodies *(in Diphtheriebakterien)*
~/Guarniersche Guarnieri bodies, eosinophilic cytoplasmic inclusions *(bei Pockenvirusinfektion)*
~/Halberstädter-Prowazeksche [Prowazek-]Halberstaedter bodies *(im Zytoplasma fixiertes Trachomvirus)*
~/Mallorysche Mallory bodies *(Einschlußkörperchen in Leberzellen bei portaler Zirrhose)*
~/Negrische Negri bodies *(im ZNS bei Tollwut)*
~/Paschensche Paschen bodies
~/Russellsche Russell bodies *(der Plasmazellen)*
körpereigen endogenic, endogenous
Körpereiweiß n body protein
Körpereiweißbestand m body protein store
Körpereiweißspeicher m body protein store
Körperempfindung f som[at]aesthesia
Körpererschöpfung f somatasthenia
Körperfalte f body fold
Körperfarbstoff m pigment
Körperfehler m physical defect
körperfern distal, D.
Körperfett n body fat
Körperflanke f flank
Körperflechte f ringworm of the body
Körperflüssigkeit f body fluid, bodily juice, humour, liquor ● **durch Körperflüssigkeiten übertragen** humoral
Körperflüssigkeitskompartment n body fluid compartment
Körperflüssigkeitsmangel m olig[o]hydria
Körperflüssigkeitsverlust m fluid loss
körperfremd exogenic, exogenous
Körperfülle f corpulency
Körpergefühl n som[at]aesthesia
Körpergegend f [body] region
Körpergewicht n [body] weight
Körpergleichgewicht n body balance
~/inneres homoeostasis, steady state
Körpergliederung f segmentation
Körpergröße f [body] height, bodily size
Körperhälfte f half of the body
Körperhaltung f [body] posture, position, attitude
Körperhaltungsbehandlung f orthotherapy
Körperhaltungstraining n postural exercise
Körperhöhle f body cavity ● **durch eine ~** transcavitary
Körperhöhlenspiegel m endoscope
Körperhöhlenspiegelung f endoscopy
Körperhygiene f body (personal) hygiene, physical culture
Körperinneres n interior of the body
Körperkerntemperatur f core temperature of the body
Körperkonstitution f [body] constitution, habit[us]
Körperkraft f physical (bodily) strength
Körperkreislauf m systemic (greater) circulation
Körperlähmung f/**totale** panplegia
Körperlänge f body length
Körperlängen-Gewichts-Index m body-weight ratio
Körperlaus f body (cootie) louse
Körperlehre f somatology
Körperleiden n somatopathy, body disease, bodily disorder
körperlich corpor[e]al, somatic, physical
körperlich-seelisch psychophysic[al]
Körpermaße npl measurements [of the body]
Körpermedianlinie f midline (median line) of the body ● **in der ~ gelegen** median

~/hintere posterior midline of the body
~/vordere anterior midline of the body
Körpermessung f somatometry, anthropometry
Körpermilieu n body environment
Körpermitte f centre (midst) of the body ● **zur ~ gelegen** medial ● **zur ~ gerichtet** medial; mediad
Körpermittellinie f s. Körpermedianlinie
Körpermodell n phantom, manikin
körpernah proximal; proximad
Körperoberfläche f body surface [area]
Körperöffnung f/**natürliche** orifice
Körperparasit m body parasite
Körperpflege f personal grooming, body (personal) hygiene, physical culture
Körperregion f region [of the body]
Körperregionsbeschreibung f topography
Körpersaft m s. Körperflüssigkeit
Körperschaden m bodily (physical) defect
Körperschema n body schema (image)
Körperschichtaufnahme f body tomogram
Körperschichtdarstellung f body tomography
Körperschlagader f s. Aorta
Körperschmerz m somatalgia
~/**allgemeiner** pantalgia, periodynia
Körperschwäche f/**allgemeine** hyposthenia, [som]asthenia, body weakness
Körpersegment n body segment
Körperseite f side of the body ● **auf derselben ~** collateral
Körpersinn m body sense
körperstarr cataleptic, cataleptiform, cataleptoid
Körperstellreflex m body-righting reflex
Körperstellung f [body] posture, attitude, position
~/**aufrechte** orthostatism
Körperteil m part (member) of the body
Körperteile mpl/**vorstehende** acra
Körpertemperatur f [body] temperature ● **oberhalb der ~** lukewarm
Körpertemperatureinstellung f thermotaxis
Körpertemperaturerhöhung f hyperthermia (s. a. Fieber)
Körpertemperaturverringerung f/**physikalische** hypothermia
Körpertod m somatic death
Körpertyp m somatype, body type
Körpertypisierung f somatotyping
Körperunterkühlung f/**kontrollierte** controlled hypothermia
Körperuntersuchung f physical examination, somatoscopy
Körpervene f systemic vein
Körperverfall m som[at]asthenia
Körperverfassung f [body] constitution
körpervermessend somatometric
Körpervermessung f somatometry
Körperwahrnehmung f som[at]aesthesia
Körperwand f body wall ● **zur ~ hin** parietal
Körperwärme f body heat (temperature)
Körperwasseräquilibrium n isohydria
Körperzelle f somatic (body) cell

Körperzergliederung f, **Körperzerlegung** f somatotomy
Körperzustand m [body] constitution, physical condition
korpulent corpulent, stout; obese
Korpulenz f corpulency, stoutness; obesity
Korpus m s. Körper
Korpuskarzinom n s. Gebärmutterkrebs
Korpuskel n s. Körperchen
Korpuskularstrahlung f corpuscular radiation
Korrektionslinse f corrective lens
Korrektur f/**optische** correction
Korrekturosteotomie f corrective osteotomy, osteotomoclasia, osteotomoclasis
Korrelationsanalyse f correlation analysis (Statistik)
Korrelationskoeffizient m coefficient of correlation
Korrigens m corrigent, corrective [agent]
korrodieren to corrode
Korrosion f corrosion (von Gewebe z. B. durch Ätzen)
Korrosionsanatomie f corrosion anatomy
Korrosionsgastritis f corrosive gastritis
Korrosionsmittel n corrosive [agent]
Korrosionspräparat n corrosion preparation
Korrosivum n corrosive [agent]
Korrugator m corrugator [muscle]
Korsakow-Syndrom n Korsakov's [anamnestic] syndrome
Korsett n corset, jacket
Korsettleber f corset liver
Kortex m cortex (s. a. unter Cortex)
~/**heterogenetischer** heterogenetic cortex
~/**motorischer** motor cortex
Kortex... s. a. Rinden...
Kortexadenom n cortical adenoma
kortikal cortical
Kortikalhyperostose f/**kindliche** infantile cortical hyperostosis, Caffey's disease (syndrome)
Kortikalis f corticalis, hard outer layer of the bone
Kortikalisschraube f cortical (cortex) screw
kortikofugal corticifugal, cortico-efferent
Kortikoid n corticoid
Kortikoidbehandlung f corticosteroid therapy
kortikopetal corticipetal, cortico-afferent
Kortikorubralfaser f corticorubral fibre
kortikospinal spinocortical
Kortikosteroid n corticosteroid
Kortikosteroidtherapie f corticosteroid therapy
Kortikosteron n corticosterone (Nebennierenrindenhormon)
kortikotrop corticotrop[h]ic
Kortikotropin n corticotrop[h]in, adrenocorticotrophic hormone, ACTH
kortikozerebral cerebrocortical
Kortin n cortin
Kortisol n cortisol, hydrocortisone, 17α-hydroxycorticosterone (Nebennierenrindenhormon)
Kortisolglaukom n cortisol glaucoma
Kortisolkatarakt f cortisol cataract

Kortisolmyopathie 418

Kortisolmyopathie *f* cortisol myopathy
Kortisolspiegelerhöhung *f* **im Blut** hypercortisolism
Kortisolspiegelerniedrigung *f* **im Blut** hypocortisolism
Kortison *n* cortisone, 17-hydroxydesoxycorticosterone *(Nebennierenrindenhormon)*
Kortisonentzugssyndrom *n* Slocumb syndrome
Korundschmelzerlunge[nerkrankung] *f* Shaver's disease, bauxite fume pneumoconiosis
Koryza *f* coryza, rhinitis, nasitis, nasal catarrh, pharyngoconjunctival fever
Kosmonautenosteoporose *f* cosmonaut's osteoporosis
Kost *f* food; diet *(s. a. unter* Diät*)*
~/flüssige liquid diet
~/kalorienreduzierte low-caloric diet
~/kalorienreiche high-caloric diet
~/vitaminarme low-vitamin diet
~/vitaminreiche high-vitamin diet
Kostalatmung *f* costal respiration
Kostalgie *f* costalgia
Kostektomie *f* costectomy, rib resection
Kosto... *s. a.* Rippen...
Kostochondritis *f* costochondritis
Kostoklavikularligament *n* costoclavicular ligament
Kostoklavikularlinie *f* costoclavicular line
Kostoklavikularsyndrom *n* costoclavicular [compression] syndrome
kostoskapulär costoscapular, scapulocostal
Kostotom *n* costotome
Kostotomie *f* costotomy, cutting of the rib
Kostotransversektomie *f* costotransversectomy
Kostovertebralgelenk *n* costovertebral joint (articulation)
kostozervikal costocervical
Kot *m* faeces; excrement; stool, stercus, ordure, dejection *(Zusammensetzungen s. unter* Stuhl*)*
Kot... *s. a.* Stuhl...
Kotabszeß *m* faecal (stercoral) abscess
kotartig faecal, faecaloid, stercor[ace]ous
Kotausräumung *f*/**digitale** digital morcellation
Kotballen *m*/**harter** scybalum
Koteinklemmung *f* coprostasis, impaction of the faeces
Koterbrechen *n* copremesis, vomiting of faeces, faecal (stercoraceous) vomiting
Kotessen *n* coprophagia, eating of dung, scatophagia, rhypophagy
kotessend coprophagous, scatophagous
Kotfistel *f* faecal (stercoral) fistula
Kotgeruch *m* faecal (stercoral) odour
Kotgeschwulst *f* coproma, stercoroma, faecal tumour, faecaloma, scatoma
Kothalter *m* colostomy bag
kothaltig stercor[ace]ous, stercoral, stercorary, faecal
kotig faecal, faecaloid, faeculent
Kotkeime *mpl* faecal flora
Kotperitonitis *f* faecal peritonitis
Kotrest *m* faecal residue

KO-Tropfen *mpl* knockout drops *(z. B.* Chloralhydratlösung*)*
Kotstauung *f* faecal stasis, coprostasis, impaction of the faeces
~ des Mastdarms proctostasis
Kotstein *m* coprolith, stercolith, faecalith, faecal concretion
Kotstrom *m* faecal stream
Kotverstopfung *f s.* Kotstauung
Kotyledon *f* cotyledon, placental lobe, subdivision of the placenta
Kox... *s. a.* Hüft...
Koxa *f* coxa, hip
Koxalgie *f* coxalgia, coxodynia, pain in the hip joint
Koxarthritis *f* coxarthritis, coxitis, inflammation of the hip joint, osphyarthritis
Koxarthrolisthesisbecken *n* arthrokatadysis
Koxarthropathie *f* coxarthropathy, hip joint disease
Koxitis *f s.* Koxarthritis
Koxodynie *f s.* Koxalgie
Koxotomie *f* coxotomy
Kozymase *f* cozymase
Krabbe-Syndrom *n* I Krabbe's disease, globoid leukodystrophy
~ II hypoplasia musculorum generalisata congenita
Kraft *f* strength, sthenia; force, power
~/körperliche physical strength
~/männliche virility
~/psychische psychic force
Kräfteverfall *m* marasmus, wasting, hyposthenia, exhaustion of strength, cachexia
Kraftfülle *f* [fulness of] strength, sthenia
kräftig 1. strong, sthenic; 2. nourishing *(Mahlzeit)*
kräftigen to strengthen, to invigorate, to roborate, to vitalize; to reinforce, to build up *(z. B. Gesundheit)*
kräftigend strengthening, roborant, invigorating, tonic; reinforcing, building up; nourishing *(z. B. Mahlzeit)*
Kräftigung *f* strengthening; reinforcement
Kräftigungsmittel *n* roborant [agent], tonic
kraftlos asthenic, hyposthenic, weak; adynamic, light-headed; exhausted *(erschöpft)*
Kraftlosigkeit *f* asthenia, hyposthenia, weakness; adynamia, light-headedness; exhaustion *(Erschöpfung)*
kraftvoll sthenic, powerful, strong, full of strength; vital; energetic
Kragen *m*/**Casálscher** Casál's collar (necklace) *(bei Pellagra)*
~/spanischer Spanish collar, paraphimosis
Kragenknopfpanaritium *n* collar-button abscess, collar-stud (shirt-stud) abscess
Krallenfuß *m* claw foot
Krallenhand *f* claw hand
Krallennagelbildung *f* onychogryp[h]osis
Kramer-Schiene *f* Kramer's wire splint
Krampf *m* spasm[us], cramp, crick, jerk, trembling *(z. B. eines Muskels) (s. a. unter* Spas-

mus) ● **hysterische Krämpfe unterbrechend** hysterofrenic, hysterofrenatory ● **nach einem ~** postconvulsive
~ einer Muskelgruppe monospasm
~/halbseitiger hemispasm
~/klonischer clonospasm, clonic spasm, convulsion
~/lokal begrenzter idiospasm
~/motorischer motor seizure
~/schmerzhafter algospasm
~/spastischer spastic muscle contraction
~/tetanischer tetanic spasm
~/tonischer tonic spasm
Krampfader f varix, varicose vein; phlebectasia
Krampfader... s. a. Varizen...
Krampfaderblutung f varix haemorrhage
Krampfaderbruch m varicocele, pampinocele
Krampfaderbruchentfernung f[/operative] varicocelectomy
Krampfaderdiathese f varicose diathesis
Krampfaderentfernung f[/operative] varicectomy, varicotomy, phlebectomy, cirsectomy
Krampfaderentstehung f varication
Krampfaderentzündung f varicophlebitis
Krampfaderexzision f s. Krampfaderentfernung/operative
Krampfadergeschwür n varicose ulcer
Krampfaderknoten m varix
Krampfaderleiden n varicosis, varicosity
Krampfaderoperation f/**Babcocksche** Babcock's operation
Krampfaderröntgen[kontrast]bild n varicogram
Krampfaderröntgen[kontrast]darstellung f varicography
Krampfadersonde f sound for varicose veins
Krampfaderstrumpf m elastic (varicose vein) stocking
Krampfaderverödung f varicosclerosation
Krampfadervorfall m varicocele, pampinocele
krampfadrig variciform
Krampfaktivität f seizure activity
Krampfanfall m convulsive seizure (fit), convulsion, seizure
~/epileptischer epileptic seizure (fit)
~/motorischer motor seizure
Krampfanfälle mpl **des Neugeborenen/tetanische** neonatal tetany
krampfartig convulsive, convulsionary; spasmodic, spasmous, paroxysmal
krampfauslösend spasmogenous, spasmogenic; convulsant
Krampfbehandlung f convulsive shock treatment; anticonvulsive therapy
krampfbereit spasmophilic, spasmodic; convulsive
Krampfbereitschaft f spasmophilia, convulsibility; tetany
krampfen to be convulsive
krampfend spastic, spasmodic; convulsive, convulsant
Krampfender m convulsionary
krampferzeugend spasmogenous, spasmogenic; convulsant, convulsionary

Krampfgift n convulsant
krampfhaft spastic, spasmodic; convulsive; sardonic
krampfhemmend antispastic, antispasmodic; anticonvulsant, anticonvulsive
Krampfhusten m 1. s. Keuchhusten; 2. paroxysmal cough
Krampflehre f spasmology
Krampfleiden n convulsive disorder
krampflos aspastic
krampflösend spasmolytic; antispasmodic, antispastic; anticonvulsant, anticonvulsive
Krampflösung f spasmolysis
Krampfmittel n anticonvulsant [agent], anticonvulsive; antispasmodic, spasmolytic [agent]
Krampfmuster n seizure pattern
Krampfneigung f spasmophilia
Krampfneurose f spasmodic neurosis
Krampfschmerz m algospasm
Krampfstarre f spasmodic rigidity
Krampfsyndrom n tetany
Krampfwehen fpl tetanic contraction of the uterus, uterine tetanus; spasmodic labour
Krampfzustand m spasmodic state
Kranialnerv m cranial nerve
Kranialreflex m cranial reflex
Kraniektomie f craniectomy
Kranio... s. a. Schädel...
Kraniodidymus m craniodidymus
kraniofazial craniofacial
Kraniograph m craniograph
Kraniographie f craniography
Kranioklast m cranioclast, diaclast, basiotribe, basiotriptor
~/Braunscher Braun's cranioclast
Kranioklastie f cranioclasty, cranioclasis
Kraniologie f craniology
Kraniomalazie f craniomalacia, craniotabes
Kraniometer n craniometer
Kraniometrie f craniometry
kraniometrisch craniometric
Kraniopagie f craniopagia, cephalodynia, cephalopagia
Kraniopagus m craniopagus, cephalopagus
Kraniopathie f craniopathy
Kraniopharyngeom n craniopharyngioma, craniopharyngeal (hypophyseal) duct tumour, suprasellar cyst
Kraniophor m craniophore, craniostat
Kranioplastik f cranioplasty
Kraniorhachischisis f cranior[rh]achischisis
kraniosakral craniosacral
Kranioschisis f cranioschisis, diastematocrania, open-roofed skull
Kraniosklerose f craniosclerosis
Kraniostat m craniostat
Kraniostenose f craniostenosis
Kraniostosis f craniostosis, craniosynostosis
Kraniotabes f craniotabes, craniomalacia
Kraniotom n craniotome, cephalotome, trepan, trephine, diaclast
Kraniotomie f craniotomy, cephalotomy, trephining, trepanation

Kraniotomieschere

Kraniotomieschere *f* craniotomy scissors
Kraniotomiezange *f* craniotomy forceps
Kraniotraktor *m* craniotractor *(Geburtshilfeinstrument)*
Kraniozele *f* craniocele, encephalocele
kraniozerebral craniocerebral
kraniozervikal craniocervical
Kranium *n* [cerebral] cranium, skull, brain-pan, brain case *(Zusammensetzungen s. unter Cranium)*
krank sick, ill; diseased, morbid *(z. B. Organe)*; bad, sore *(Zahn)*; invalid, infirm *(gebrechlich)*; powerless, feeble *(s. a.* kränklich*)* ● **sich ~ fühlen** to feel ill (indisposed) ● **sich ~ melden** to report sick ● **~ schreiben** to put a patient on the panel (sick-list) ● **~ sein** to be ill ● **unheilbar ~ sein** to be incurable ill, to be past recovery ● **~ werden** to fall ill, to be taken ill ● **wieder ~ werden** to have a relapse
~/chronisch chronically ill
kränkeln to sicken, to be sickly (ailing), to be of indifferent health, to be in poor health
kränkelnd ailing; valetudinarian, invalid, feeble; in poor health, not robust
Krankenabteilung *f* infirmary, hospital ward
Krankenbehandlung *f* therapy, medical treatment
Krankenbericht *m* case (medical) report
Krankenbesuch *m* [medical] visit *(des Arztes)*; call on an invalid
Krankenbett *n* sick-bed; hospital bed ● **am ~ bedside**
Krankenblatt *n* hospital (ward) chart, clinical record, history of the patient
Krankenfahrstuhl *m* bath (wheel) chair
Krankengeld *n* sick-benefit, sickness benefit
Krankengeschichte *f* 1. anamnesis, clinical history, [case] history; 2. *s.* Krankenblatt
Krankengymnastik *f* physiotherapy, remedial gymnastics
Krankengymnastin *f* physiotherapist
Krankenhaus *n* hospital, clinic, infirmary; lazaret[te] ● **aus dem ~ entlassen** to discharge from hospital ● **im ~ entstehend** nosocomial ● **im ~ erworben** hospital-acquired ● **im ~ liegen** to lie (be) in hospital ● **in das ~ aufgenommen werden** to be taken (admitted) to the hospital, to be hospitalized ● **in das ~ einweisen** to hospitalize
~/allgemeines general hospital
~/städtisches municipal hospital
Krankenhausabteilung *f* department
Krankenhausaufenthalt *m* hospital stay, stay in hospital
Krankenhausaufnahme *f* hospital admission, hospitalization, admission to the hospital
Krankenhausbehandlung *f* hospital treatment, clinical therapy
Krankenhausbett *n* hospital bed
Krankenhauseinlieferung *f* hospital admission
Krankenhauseinweisung *f* hospital admission, admission to the hospital, hospitalization
Krankenhausentlassung *f* hospital discharge, discharge from the hospital
Krankenhausepidemiologie *f* hospital epidemiology
Krankenhaushygiene *f* hospital hygiene
Krankenhausinfektion *f* hospital[-acquired] infection
Krankenhauspatient *m* hospital patient, in-patient
Krankenhausverweildauer *f* hospitalization time, period of hospitalization
Krankenhauswiederaufnahme *f* rehospitalization
Krankenjournal *n s.* Krankenblatt
Krankenkasse *f* National Health Insurance (Service), N.H.I., N.H.S.
Krankenkissen *n* air cushion
Krankenkost *f* [special] diet, invalid diet
Krankenkurve *f* ward (temperature) chart
Krankenluftkissen *n* air cushion
Krankenpflege *f* nursing, attendance, nosotrophy
Krankenpfleger *m* male nurse, orderly, dresser
Krankenrevier *n* sick bay
Krankensaal *m* ward
Krankenschein *m* doctor's (health insurance) certificate, voucher for medical treatment, N.H.S. form
Krankenschwester *f* [hospital-]nurse
~/examinierte graduate nurse, state registered nurse
~/nichtexaminierte practical (trained) nurse
Krankenstand *m* morbidity, number of sick persons
Krankenstation *f* [medical] ward
Krankentrage *f* stretcher, litter
~/fahrbare wheel stretcher, rolling litter
Krankenträger *m* stretcher-bearer, litter carrier, ambulance-man
Krankentransport *m* 1. ambulance-service; 2. carrying (moving) of a sick person
Krankentransportwagen *m* ambulance [car]
Krankenuntersuchung *f* examination, clinical analysis
Krankenversicherung *f* health insurance
Krankenversorgung *f* nosotrophy, attendance, nursing
Krankenwagen *m* ambulance [car]
Krankenwärter *m s.* Krankenpfleger
Krankenzimmer *n* sick-room
Kranker *m* patient, sick person; invalid
~/psychisch mental patient
~/unheilbar incurable
krankhaft morbid, pathologic[al], diseased; abnormal; insane *(psychisch)*
Krankheit *f* disease, illness, sickness, malady, morbus; complaint, trouble, affection *(Leiden)*; indisposition *(Unpäßlichkeit)* *(s. a. unter* Erkrankung *und* Morbus*)* ● **an einer ~ leiden** to suffer from a disease ● **an einer ~ sterben** to die of an illness ● **eine ~ bestimmend** pathognostic ● **eine ~ zur Ausheilung bringen** to bring

about the cure of a disease ● **gegen eine bestimmte ~ wirksam** specific ● **sich eine ~ zuziehen** to contract a disease

~/**Abramische** Abrami's disease, acquired haemolytic icterus

~/**Abt-Letterer-Siwesche** Letterer-Siwe disease, non-lipid histiocytosis (reticuloendotheliosis)

~/**Addisonsche** Addison's disease (syndrome), adrenal cortical insufficiency, suprarenal melanoma (melasma); bronzed skin

~/**akute** acute disease

~/**Albers-Schönbergsche** Albers-Schönberg disease, osteopetrosis, sclerotic osteitis; marble (ivory) bones

~/**allergische** allergosis, allergic disease

~/**Alzheimersche** Alzheimer's disease, presenile sclerosis

~/**Anderssche** Anders' disease, adiposis tuberosa simplex

~/**anfallsartige** paroxysmal disease

~/**anorektale** anorectal disease

~/**ansteckende** contagious (communicable) disease, infectious disease

~/**Aransche (Aran-Duchennesche)** Aran-Duchenne dystrophy (syndrome), myelopathic (progressive spinal) muscular atrophy

~/**aufgepfropfte** superimposed disease

~/**auszehrende** wasting (consumptive) disease

~/**Baastrupsche** Baastrup's disease, interspinal osteoarthrosis, kissing osteophytes (spine syndrome)

~/**Bäfverstedtsche** Bäfverstedt's disease, benign lymphadenosis

~/**Balfoursche** Balfour's disease, Aran's cancer (chloroma, chlorosarcoma), chloroleukaemia

~/**Balósche** Baló's disease (concentric sclerosis) *(Form der multiplen Sklerose)*

~/**Bambergersche** Bamberger-Marie disease, hypertrophic pulmonary osteoarthropathy

~/**Bangsche** Bang's disease, brucellosis, brucelliasis, Mediterranean (Malta, undulant) fever *(durch Brucella abortus)*

~/**Bantische** Banti's disease (syndrome), splenic anaemia, congestive splenomegaly, portal [bed] block

~/**Barlowsche** s. ~/**Möller-Barlowsche**

~/**Basedowsche** Basedow's disease, Grave's disease (ophthalmopathy), exophthalmic goitre

~/**Batten-Mayousche** s. ~/**Spielmeyer-Vogtsche**

~/**Baylesche** Bayle's disease, progressive general paralysis

~/**Bechterew-Pierre-Marie-Strümpellsche** Bechterew's (Strümpell-Marie) disease, Bechterew's arthrosis, rheumatoid (ancylosing) spondylitis, ancylopoietic spondylarthrosis

~/**Beckersche** Becker's disease (endomyocardibrosis)

~/**Behçetsche** Behçet's disease *(Multisystemkrankheit)*

~/**Beigelsche** Beigel's disease, piedra

~/**Bellsche** Bell's disease (mania)

~/**Bennettsche** Bennett's disease (leukaemia)

~/**Bensonsche** Benson's disease, asteroid hyalitis

~/**Bergeronsche** Bergeron's disease, hysterical chorea

~/**Berlinsche** Berlin's disease, traumatic oedema of the retina

~/**Bestsche** Best's disease, congenital macular degeneration

~/**Beurmannsche** Beurmann's disease, disseminated gummatous sporotrichosis

~/**Biedlsche** Biedl's disease, Biedl-Bardet syndrome, Laurence-Moon-Biedl syndrome

~/**Biermersche** Biermer's anaemia (disease), pernicious anaemia

~/**Biettsche** Biett's disease, lupus erythematodes

~/**Bilharzsche** bilharziasis, bilharzial lesion

~/**Binswangersche** Binswanger's dementia (encephalopathy)

~/**Birdsche** Bird's disease, oxaluria, oxalic diathesis

~/**blaue** 1. blue disease, congenital heart disease; 2. Rocky Mountain spotted fever

~/**Bloch-Sulzbergersche** Bloch-Sulzberger syndrome, incontinentia pigmenti

~/**Blountsche** Blount-Barber syndrome, osteochondrosis deformans tibiae; non-rachitic bowlegs

~/**Boeck-Besnier-Schaumannsche** Besnier-Boeck[-Schaumann's] disease, sarcoidosis, benign lymphogranulomatosis; Boeck's sarcoid

~/**Boecksche** 1. s. ~/**Boeck-Besnier-Schaumannsche**; 2. Boeck's scabies, scabies crustosa

~/**Bornholmer** Bornholm disease, epidemic myalgia (pleurodynia), devil's grip

~/**bösartige** malignant disease

~/**Bouchet-Gsellsche** Bouchet-Gsell disease, swineherds' disease

~/**Bouillaudsche** Bouillaud's disease (syndrome), infective endocarditis, rheumatic fever

~/**Bournevillesche** Bourneville's disease, tuberous sclerosis of the brain

~/**Bouveretsche** Bouveret's syndrome, paroxysmal [atrial] tachycardia

~/**Bowensche** Bowen's disease (epithelioma)

~/**Brillsche** Brill's disease, recrudescent louseborne typhus

~/**Brill-Symmerssche** Brill-Symmers disease, giant follicular lymphadenopathy, benign (nodular) lymphoma

~/**Brill-Zinssersche** s. ~/**Brillsche**

~/**Brocqsche** 1. Brocq's disease, parapsoriasis en plaques, parakeratosis psoriasiformis; 2. Brocq's disease, alopecia areata

~/**Brown-Symmerssche** Brown-Symmers disease, acute serous encephalitis in children

~/**Brugschsche** Brugsch's syndrome, acropachyderma; acromicria

~/**Bürgersche** Buerger's disease, thromboangiitis obliterans

~/**Buschkesche** Buschke's disease, scleroedema adultorum

Krankheit

~/**Busse-Buschkesche** Busse-Buschke's disease, cryptococcosis
~/**Calvé-Legg-Perthessche** Calvé's disease, deforming osteochondritis of the hip
~/**Camurati-Engelmannsche** Engelmann's disease, Camurati-Engelmann disease, progressive diaphysial dysplasia
~/**Carrionsche** Carrion's disease, Oroya fever *(durch Bartonella bacilliformis)*
~/**Castellanische** Castellani's bronchitis (disease), spirochaetal haemorrhagic bronchitis
~/**Chagassche (Chagas-Cruzsche)** Chagas' (Cruz') disease, Chagas-Cruz disease, Brazilian (American) trypanosomiasis, schizotrypano[somia]sis, careotrypanosis *(Tropenkrankheit durch Trypanosoma cruzi)*
~/**Charcot-Mariesche** Charcot-Marie-Tooth disease, peroneal (progressive neuropathic) muscular atrophy
~/**Charcotsche** 1. Charcot's disease, amyotrophic lateral sclerosis; 2. *s.* ~/Charcot-Mariesche; 3. Charcot's arthritis (arthropathy, arthrosis), neuropathic joint disease, neurogenic arthropathy, neurotrophic arthritis
~/**Cheadle-Möllersche** Cheadle's disease, infantile scurvy
~/**Christensen-Krabbesche** Christensen-Krabbe disease, progressive cerebral poliodystrophy
~/**Christian-Webersche** Christian-Weber disease, non-suppurative nodular panniculitis
~/**chronische** chronic disease
~/**Civattesche** Civatte's disease, poikiloderma of Civatte
~/**Corrigansche** Corrigan's disease, aortic insufficiency
~/**Corvisartsche** Corvisart's disease, chronic hypertrophic myocarditis
~/**Coutonsche** Couton's disease, tuberculous spondylosis
~/**Crohnsche** 1. Crohn's disease, [ilium] regional enteritis, regional enterocolitis (ileitis); terminal ileitis; 2. Crohn's disease of the colon, granulomatous colitis
~/**Cruveilhier-Baumgartensche** Cruveilhier-Baumgarten cirrhosis (syndrome) *(Erweiterung der Umbilikalvene bei portaler Hypertonie)*
~/**Cruveilhiersche** Cruveilhier's disease, progressive spinal (myelopathic) muscular atrophy
~/**Dalrymplesche** Dalrymple's disease, cyclokeratitis
~/**Dana-Lichtheimsche** Dana-Putnam syndrome, funicular myelitis (myelosis), subacute combined degeneration (sclerosis, system disease)
~/**Dariersche** Darier's disease, follicular keratosis (psorospermosis)
~/**Darlingsche** Darling's disease (histoplasmosis)
~/**De Beurmann-Gougerotsche** de Beurmann-Gougerot disease, sporotrichosis
~/**Degossche** Degos' disease, atrophic papulosquamous dermatitis
~/**Dercumsche** Dercum's disease, adipositas (adiposis) dolorosa, neurolipomatosis

~/**Deutschländersche** 1. Deutschländer's disease, tumour of the metatarsal bone; 2. march foot (fracture) *(Ermüdungsbruch von Mittelfußknochen)*
~/**Devergiesche** Devergie's disease, pityriasis rubra pilaris
~/**Devicsche** Devic's disease, optic neuromyelitis (neuro-encephalomyelopathy)
~/**di Guglielmosche** di Guglielmo's disease (syndrome), acute erythraemic myelosis, malignant erythrocytosis, erythroleukaemia
~/**Döhlesche** Döhle's disease, syphilitic aortitis
~/**Dresslersche** Dressler's disease, intermittent haemoglobinuria
~/**Duchenne-Aransche** Duchenne's (Duchenne-Aran) disease, Aran-Duchenne dystrophy (syndrome), myelopathic (spinal progressive) muscular atrophy
~/**Duchenne-Griesingersche** Duchenne-Griesinger disease, pseudohypertrophic infantile muscular dystrophy
~/**Duchennesche** 1. Duchenne's disease, bulbar paralysis; 2. *s.* ~/Duchenne-Aransche
~/**Duhringsche** Duhring's disease, dermatitis herpetiformis [Duhring]
~/**Dukes-Filatowsche** *s.* ~/Filatow-Dukessche
~/**Duplaysche** 1. Duplay's disease, subdeltoid (subacrominal) bursitis; 2. Duplay's syndrome (contracture), periarticular fibrositis, periarthritis humeroscupularis; frozen shoulder
~/**Durand-Nicolas-Favresche** Durand-Nicolas-Favre disease, venereal lymphogranuloma
~/**Ealessche** Eales's disease *(Glaskörperblutungen durch Periphlebitis retinae)*
~/**Economosche** von Economo's disease, sleeping sickness, herpes [simplex] encephalitis, lethargic (herpetic, epidemic) encephalitis
~/**Eddowessche** Eddowes' disease (syndrome), osteogenesis imperfecta
~/**endemische** endemic disease
~/**Engelmannsche** Engelmann's disease, progressive diaphyseal dysplasia
~/**Engel-Recklinghausensche** *s.* Morbus Recklinghausen
~/**Englische** English (Glisson's) disease, infantile osteomalacia, rachitis, rickets, rickety
~/**epidemische** epidemic [disease]
~/**Epsteinsche** Epstein's disease, pseudodiphtheria
~/**Erb-Charcotsche** Erb-Charcot disease, Erb's spastic spinal paraplegia, Erb's syphilitic paralysis, spasmodic ataxia, spinal meningovascular syphilis
~/**Erb-Goldflamsche** Erb-Goldflam's disease (symptom complex), Goldflam's disease, myasthenia gravis pseudoparalytica *(mit gesteigerter Ermüdbarkeit der quergestreiften Muskulatur)*
~/**erbliche** hereditary (heredodegenerative) disease
~/**Eulenburgsche** Eulenburg's disease, congenital paramyotonia

~/**Fabrysche** Fabry's disease, angiokeratoma corporis diffusum universale
~/**familiäre** familial disease
~/**Favre-Durand-Nicolassche** Favre disease, venereal lymphogranuloma
~/**Feersche** Feer's disease, erythroedema polyneuropathy, dermatopolyneuritis, acrodynia
~/**Fiedlersche** Fiedler's disease, leptospiral jaundice *(durch Leptospira icterohaemorrhagiae)*
~/**Filatow-Dukessche** Filatov-Dukes disease, exanthem[a] subitum, fourth (sixth) disease
~/**Föllingsche** Fölling's disease, phenylketonuria, PKU, phenylpyruvic amentia (oligophrenia)
~/**Franklinsche** Franklin's disease, heavy (H) chain disease
~/**Friedländersche** Friedländer's disease, obliterative arteritis
~/**Friedmannsche** Friedmann's disease, relapsing infantile spastic spinal paralysis
~/**Friedreichsche** 1. Friedreich's disease, hereditary ataxia; 2. Friedreich's disease (spasms), paramyoclonus multiplex
~/**Fröhlichsche** Froehlich's syndrome, Babinski-Froehlich disease, adiposogenital dystrophy (syndrome)
~/**fünfte** fifth disease, infectious erythema, megaloerythema
~/**funktionelle** functional disease
~/**Gaisböcksche** Gaisböck's syndrome, polycythaemia hypertonica
~/**Gauchersche** Gaucher's disease, cerebrosidosis, cerebroside lipidosis, familial splenic anaemia, kerasin thesaurismosis
~/**Gee-Heubner-Hertersche** Gee-Herter[-Heubner] disease, adult coeliac disease, coeliac syndrome (infantilism)
~/**Gilbertsche** Gilbert's disease, constitutional hyperbilirubinaemia (hepatic dysfunction), hereditary non-haemolytic hyperbilirubinaemia, familial non-haemolytic jaundice *(gestörte Bilirubinaufnahme in die Leberzelle)*
~/**Gilchristsche** Gilchrist's disease (mycosis), North American blastomycosis
~/**Gilles-de-la-Tourettesche** Gilles de la Tourette disease (syndrome), motor incoordination with echolalia and coprolalia
~/**Glénardsche** Glénard's disease, splanchnoptosis, enteroptosis, visceroptosis
~/**Glissonsche** *s.* ~/**Englische**
~/**Gougerot-Blumsche** Gougerot-Blum disease, pigmented purpuric lichenoid dermatitis
~/**Graefesche** Graefe's disease, progressive ophthalmoplegia
~/**Griesingersche** Griesinger's disease, ancylostomiasis
~/**Gullsche** Gull's disease, atrophy of the thyroid with myxoedema
~/**Haileysche** Hailey's disease, chronic benign familial pemphigus
~/**Hallervorden-Spatzsche** Hallervorden-Spatz disease (syndrome), progressive pallidal degeneration syndrome

~/**Hallopeausche** Hallopeau's disease, lichen sclerosus et atrophicus
~/**Hand-Schüller-Christiansche** Hand-Schüller-Christian disease, [Schüller-]Christian syndrome, cholesterol thesaurismosis (storage disease), lipid granulomatosis
~/**Hanotsche** Hanot's cirrhosis (disease), biliary cirrhosis
~/**Hansensche** Hansen's disease, lepra, leprosy, Danielssen-Boeck disease *(Zusammensetzungen s. unter Lepra)*
~/**Harleysche** Harley's disease, recurrent haemoglobinuria
~/**Heberdensche** 1. Heberden's disease (arthritis); 2. Heberden's disease, angina pectoris
~/**Hebrasche** Hebra's disease, erythema multiforme exudativum
~/**Heerfordtsche** Heerfordt's disease, uveoparotid fever, uveoparotitis
~/**Heine-Medinsche** Heine-Medin disease, [acute anterior] poliomyelitis, polio, paralytic spinal poliomyelitis
~/**Heubner-Hertersche** Heubner-Herter disease, idiopathic infantile steatorrhoea, infantile coeliac disease, coeliac syndrome (infantilism), pancreatic infantilism, gluten-induced enteropathy
~/**Heubnersche** Heubner's disease (endarteritis), syphilitic endarteritis of the cerebral vessels
~/**Hippel-Lindausche** *s.* ~/**Lindausche**
~/**Hirschsprungsche** Hirschsprung's disease; aganglionic (congenital) megacolon
~/**Hodgkinsche** Hodgkin's disease, lymphogranulomatosis; infectious (malignant) granuloma, lymphogranuloma, malignant (granulomatous) lymphoma, lymphadenoma, lymphosarcoma
~/**Hoffasche** Hoffa's disease, [traumatic] solitary lipoma of the knee joint
~/**Hoffmann-Werdnigsche** Hoffmann-Werdnig disease (syndrome), Hoffmann's atrophy, infantile spinal muscular atrophy
~/**homologe** homologous disease
~/**Huchardsche** Huchard's disease, continued arterial hypertension
~/**Hunter-Addisonsche** Addison's anaemia
~/**Hunter-Hurlersche** Hurler's disease (syndrome), mucopolysaccharidosis [type] I, Pfaundler-Hurler syndrome, lipochondrodystrophy *(erbliche Phosphatidstoffwechselstörung)*
~/**Huntersche** Hunter's disease (syndrome), mucopolysaccharidosis [type] II
~/**Hutchinson-Boecksche** Hutchinson-Boeck disease, generalized sarcoidosis
~/**Hutchinson-Gilfordsche** Hutchinson-Gilford disease, childhood progeria, premature, senility syndrome
~/**idiopathische** idiopathic disease
~/**innere** internal disease
~/**interkurrente** intercurrent disease
~/**interstitielle** interstitial disease
~/**Jakob-Creutzfeldtsche** Jacob's (Jakob-Creutzfeldt) disease (syndrome), spastic pseudosclerosis

Krankheit

~/**Jensensche** Jensen's disease (retinopathy), juxtapapillary choroiditis
~/**Jünglingsche** Jüngling's disease, tuberculous osteitis multiplex cystica
~/**Kahlersche** Kahler's disease, general lymphadenomatosis of bones; multiple myeloma, malignant plasmocytoma
~/**Kalischersche** Kalischer's disease, naevoid amentia
~/**kardiovaskuläre** cardiovascular disease
~/**Kimmelstielsche** Kimmelstiel's disease, intercapillary nephrosclerosis
~/**klimatische** climatic disease
~/**Klippel-Feilsche** Klippel-Feil deformity (syndrome) *(angeborener Kurzhals)*
~/**Klippelsche** Klippel's disease, arthritic general pseudoparalysis
~/**Köbnersche** Köbner's disease, epidermolysis bullosa
~/**Köhlersche** 1. Köhler's [first] disease, tarsal scaphoiditis, epiphysitis juvenilis, osteochondrosis of the navicular bone; 2. Köhler's [second] disease, osteochondrosis (Freiberg's infraction) of the second metatarsal head, juvenile deforming metatarsophalangeal osteochondritis
~/**komplizierende** complicating disease
~/**konstitutionelle** constitutional disease
~/**Koyanagische** Vogt-Koyanagi[-Harada] syndrome, uveomeningoencephalitis
~/**Krabbesche** Krabbe's disease, diffuse infantile familial cerebral sclerosis
~/**Kussmaulsche** Kussmaul's disease, periarteritis nodosa, polyarteritis
~/**Laennecsche** 1. Laennec's disease, alcoholic cirrhosis of the liver; 2. dissecting aneurysm
~/**Landrysche** Landry's disease, acute ascending spinal paralysis
~/**Langdon-Downsche** Down's (Langdon-Down) syndrome, mongolism, Mongolian (mongoloid) idiocy, trisomy 21 syndrome
~/**langwierige** lingering (protracted) disease
~/**Lasèguesche** Lasègue's disease, mania of persecution
~/**Laurence-Moon-Biedlsche** Laurence-Moon-Biedl syndrome, Biedl's disease (syndrome) *(dienzephaloretinale Degeneration, adiposohypogenitales Mißbildungssyndrom)*
~/**Lebersche** Leber's disease (optic atrophy)
~/**Legg-Calvé-Perthessche** Legg-Calvé-Perthes disease (syndrome), osteochondrosis of capitular epiphysis
~/**Leinersche** Leiner's disease, [infantile] desquamative erythroderma
~/**Letterer-Siwesche** Letterer-Siwe disease, nonlipid histiocytosis (reticuloendotheliosis)
~/**Libmann-Sackssche** Libman-Sacks' disease, verrucous endocarditis
~/**Lindausche** Lindau's (Lindau-von Hippel) disease, angiophacomatosis, cerebelloretinal (retinal, multiple) angiomatosis, von Hippel-Lindau disease

~/**Lobsteinsche** Lobstein's disease, osteogenesis imperfecta
~/**manisch-depressive** manic-depressive illness (reaction, psychosis), intermitting insanity, alternating psychosis, periodic insanity (mania)
~/**Marchiafava-Bignamische** Marchiafava-Bignami disease, degeneration of corpus callosum
~/**Mariesche (Marie-Bambergersche)** Bamberger-Marie disease, hypertrophic pulmonary osteoarthropathy
~/**Ménétriersche** Ménétrier's disease, giant hypertrophic gastritis
~/**Merzbacher-Pelizaeussche** s. ~/Pelizaeus-Merzbachersche
~/**Möller-Barlowsche** Möller-Barlow disease, infantile scurvy, scurvy rickets
~/**Mondorsche** Mondor's disease, string phlebitis
~/**Morgagnische** Morgagni's disease, endocranial hyperostosis
~/**Moschcowitzsche** Moschcowitz's disease, febrile pleochromic anaemia
~/**Münchmeyersche** Münchmeyer's disease, diffuse progressive ossifying polymyositis, interstitial calcinosis
~/**neurologische** neurological disease
~/**Nicolas-Favresche** Nicolas-Favre disease, venereal lymphogranuloma
~/**Niemann-Picksche** Niemann's (Niemann-Pick) disease, lipoid histiocytosis
~/**Oppenheimsche** 1. Oppenheim's disease, amyotonia congenita; 2. Oppenheim's disease, dystonia musculorum deformans
~/**organische** organic disease
~/**örtlich begrenzte** endemia
~/**Osgoodsche** s. ~/Schlattersche
~/**Oslersche** s. 1. ~/Vaquez-Oslersche; 2. ~/Rendu-Osler-Webersche
~/**Owrensche** Owren's disease, factor V deficiency, parahaemophilia
~/**Pagetsche** 1. Paget's disease [of bone], Paget's bone disease, osteitis deformans; 2. Paget's disease (cancer), Paget's nipple (mammary) disease
~/**Paltauf-Sternbergsche** s. ~/Hodgkinsche
~/**Parinaudsche** Parinaud's disease (oculoglandular syndrome)
~/**Parkinsonsche** parkinsonism, Parkinson's (Parkinsonian) state, agitated paralysis, paralysis agitans *(extrapyramidales Syndrom mit teigiger Muskelsteifigkeit, Zittern von Körperteilen und Bewegungslosigkeit)*
~/**Pelizaeus-Merzbachersche** Merzbacher-Pelizaeus (Pelizaeus-Merzbacher) disease, familial centrolobular sclerosis, progressive hereditary cerebral leukodystrophy
~/**Perrin-Ferratonsche** Perrin-Ferraton's disease; snapping hip
~/**Perthessche** Perthes' disease, osteochondrosis of capitular epiphysis
~/**Peyroniesche** Peyronie's disease, fibrous cavernitis, penile induration, strabismus of the penis

~/**Pfaundler-Hurlersche** s. ~/Hunter-Hurlersche
~/**Pfeifer-Weber-Christiansche** s. ~/Christian-Webersche
~/**Pick-Herzheimersche** Pick-Herzheimer disease, erythromelia *(Hautatrophie mit blauroter Verfärbung an Beinen und Armen)*
~/**Picksche** circumscribed (convolutional) cerebral atrophy
~/**Pompesche** Pompe's disease, acid maltase deficiency, generalized glycogenosis, cardiac glycogen storage disease
~/**Poncetsche** Poncet's disease, tuberculous rheumatism
~/**Pottsche** Pott's disease, angular (curvature) kyphosis of the spine, spinal caries, tuberculous spondylitis, caries (tuberculosis) of the spine
~/**primäre** primary disease, protopathy
~/**Profichetsche** Profichet's syndrome (disease) *(umschriebene Kalkablagerungen in der Haut der Extremitäten)*
~/**psychisch bedingte** psychogenic (functional) disease, neurosis
~/**Quénusche** Quénu's disease, phlebalgia ischiadica
~/**Quervainsche** Quervain's disease, stenosing tendovaginitis
~/**Quinckesche** Quincke's disease (oedema), angioneurotic oedema
~/**Raynaudsche** Raynaud's disease (phenomenon), symmetric gangrene
~/**Reclussche** Reclus' disease *(gehäuftes Auftreten von Zysten in der Brust)*
~/**Refsumsche** Refsum's disease, heredopathia atactica polyneuritiformis
~/**Reichmannsche** Reichmann's disease, gastrosuccorrhoea
~/**Reitersche** Reiter's syndrome (disease), idiopathic blennorrhoeal arthritis, infectious uroarthritis
~/**Rendu-Osler-Webersche** Rendu-Osler-Weber's disease, Osler-Weber-Rendu disease, hereditary haemorrhagic telangiectasia
~/**Rittersche** Ritter's disease, dermatitis exfoliativa infantum
~/**Rogersche** Roger's disease, ventricular septal defect
~/**Rokitanskysche** Rokitansky's disease, acute yellow atrophy of the liver
~/**Rombergsche** Romberg's disease, facial hemiatrophy
~/**Rosenthalsche** Rosenthal's disease, factor XI deficiency
~/**Roth-Bernhardtsche** Roth-Bernhardt's disease, Bernhardt-Roth syndrome, Bernhardt's paraesthesia, meralgia paraesthetica
~/**Rustsche** Rust's disease, tuberculous spondylitis of cervical vertebrae
~/**Schambergsche** Schamberg's disease, progressive pigmentary dermatosis
~/**Schencksche** Schenck's disease, sporotrichosis
~/**Scheuermannsche** Scheuermann's disease, necrosis of the epiphyses of the vertebrae, juvenile kyphosis, osteochondrosis of the vertebrae
~/**Schildersche** Schilder's disease, [sudanophilic] diffuse sclerosis
~/**Schlattersche** [Osgood-]Schlatter disease, osteochondritis of the tibial tuberosity *(bei Jugendlichen)*
~/**schleichende** creeping (insideous) disease
~/**Schönleinsche** Schönlein's disease (purpura), allergic (non-thrombopenic) purpura
~/**Schottmüllersche** Schottmüller's disease, paratyphoid [fever]
~/**Schüller-Christiansche** s. ~/Hand-Schüller-Christiansche
~/**schwarze** black fever (sickness), visceral leishmaniasis, febrile tropical splenomegaly
~/**sechste** 1. sixth [venereal] disease, venereal lymphogranuloma; 2. s. ~/Filatow-Dukessche
~/**Selter-Swift-Feersche** s. ~/Feersche
~/**Seversche** Sever's disease, epiphysitis of the os calcis
~/**Shaversche** Shaver's disease, bauxite fume pneumoconiosis
~/**Simmondsche** Simmond's cachexia (disease), hypophyseal cachexia, [hypo]pituitary cachexia
~/**spezifische** specific disease
~/**Spielmeyer-Vogtsche** Spielmeyer-Vogt disease, Batten-Mayou's disease, Batten's disease, juvenile amaurotic familial idiocy
~/**Spurway-Eddowessche** Eddowes' disease (syndrome), association of blue sclerotics, otosclerosis, and brittle bones
~/**Stargardtsche** Stargardt's disease (macular degeneration)
~/**Stickersche** Sticker's disease, megalerythema
~/**Stillersche** Stiller's disease, universal asthenia
~/**Stillsche** Still's disease, juvenile rheumatoid arthritis
~/**Strümpell-Bechterew-Mariesche** Strümpell-Marie disease, rheumatoid spondylosis (spondylitis)
~/**Sturge-Webersche** Sturge-Weber's disease, encephalotrigeminal (encephalofacial) angiomatosis
~/**Swiftsche** s. ~/Feersche
~/**systematische** systemic disease
~/**Tay-Sachssche** Tay-Sachs disease, infantile amaurotic familial disease (idiocy)
~/**Thomsensche** Thomsen's disease, congenital myotonia
~/**Tietzesche** Tietze's disease (syndrome) *(schmerzhafte Schwellungen der Rippenknorpel)*
~/**übertragbare** communicable disease
~/**Unnasche** Unna's disease, seborrhoeic dermatitis (eczema)
~/**ursprüngliche** primary disease, protopathy
~/**Vaquez-Oslersche** Vaquez's (Vaquez-Osler) disease, erythr[ocyth]aemia, myelopathic (primary, splenomegalic) polycythaemia, polycythaemia rubra (vera)

Krankheit

~/**vierte** 1. fourth (venereal) disease, granuloma inguinale; 2. gangrenous (specific ulcerative) balanoposthitis; 3. s. ~/Filatow-Dukessche
~/**von Gierkesche** [von] Gierke's disease, glycogen thesaurismosis (storage disease), hepatic (hepatorenal) glycogenosis
~/**von-Hippel-Lindausche** s. ~/Lindausche
~/**Vroliksche** Vrolik's disease, osteogenesis imperfecta congenita
~/**Wartenbergsche** Wartenberg's disease, chiralgia paraesthetica
~/**Weilsche** Weil's disease, icterohaemorrhagic fever (leptospirosis), icterogenic spirochaetosis, leptospiral (spirochaetal) jaundice
~/**Weir-Mitchellsche** Weir-Mitchell's disease, erythromelalgia, red neuralgia *(anfallsweises schmerzhaftes Anschwellen der Haut an den Gliedern)*
~/**Werdnig-Hoffmannsche** Werdnig-Hoffmann atrophy (paralysis), Hoffmann-Werdnig disease (syndrome), Hoffmann's atrophy, infantile spinal muscular atrophy
~/**Wernickesche** Wernicke's disease, [acute] superior haemorrhagic polioencephalitis
~/**Westphal-Strümpellsche** Westphal-Strümpell disease (pseudosclerosis)
~/**Whipplesche** Whipple's disease, intestinal lipodystrophy
~/**Wilsonsche** Wilson's disease, hepatolenticular (progressive lenticular) degeneration
~/**Winckelsche** Winckel's disease, black jaundice, epidemic haemoglobinuria
~/**Winiwartersche (Winiwarter-Bürgersche)** Buerger's disease, thromboangiitis obliterans
~/**zerebrovaskuläre** cerebrovascular disease
Krankheitsabschnitt *m* phase (stage) of the disease
Krankheitsanfall *m* seizure, fit, attack, brash
Krankheitsanfälligkeit *f* susceptibility, disposition; taint
Krankheitsangst *f*/abnorme pathophobia, nosophobia
Krankheitsanlage *f* taint; predisposition
Krankheitsattacke *f* s. Krankheitsanfall
Krankheitsausgang *m* final stage
Krankheitsbeginn *m* onset; outbreak
Krankheitsbericht *m* medical (doctor's) report, [medical] bulletin
~/**abschließender** epicrisis
Krankheitsbeschreibung *f* pathography, nosography
Krankheitsbild *n* clinical picture ● nicht zum ~ gehörend accidental
Krankheitsdauer *f* duration of the disease
Krankheitseinordnung *f* nosotaxy
krankheitsempfänglich susceptible
Krankheitsentstehung *f* pathogenesis, aethiopathology
Krankheitsentwicklung *f* pathopoiesis, nosogeny, nosogenesis, aetiopathogenesis
krankheitserregend pathogen[et]ic, nosopoietic, morbific, morbigenous; virulent
~/**nicht** non-pathogenic

Krankheitserreger *m* pathogen, morbific agent, causative organism, infectious germ ● mit Krankheitserregern behaftet infectious, infective
Krankheitserregereintrittsstelle *f* atrium of infection
Krankheitserregerüberträger *m* vector
Krankheitserregerübertragung *f* vection, infection
Krankheitserscheinung *f* symptom, sign
Krankheitsfall *m* [medical] case, case of illness ● im ~ in case (the event) of illness ● in Krankheitsfällen angewendet applied in illness
Krankheitsfallbeschreibung *f* case report, casuistics
Krankheitsfall-Sterblichkeit[srate] *f* case-fatality rate (ratio) *(Todesfälle je 100 gleichartige Erkrankungen)*
Krankheitsgeschehen *n* course of disease, pathological process
krankheitshalber because of illness, through (owing to) illness
Krankheitshäufigkeit *f* incidence [of the disease]
Krankheitsherausbildung *f* pathopoiesis
Krankheitsherd *m* focus, nidus, seat [of a disease]
Krankheitshöhepunkt *m* climax, state, fastigium
Krankheitskeim *m* germ
Krankheitskeimaussaat *f* dissemination
krankheitskennzeichnend pathognom[on]ic
Krankheitsklassifikation *f* nosotaxy
Krankheitskost *f* [special] diet, invalid diet
Krankheitslehre *f*[/**systematische**] pathology, nosology
Krankheitsnachahmung *f* pathomimesis, pathomimia, pathomimicry
Krankheitsphase *f* phase [of the disease]
Krankheitsrückfall *m* recidivation, relapse, epicrisis
Krankheitsrückgang *m* decrement, paracme
Krankheitsschwere *f* severity [of the disease]
Krankheitsstadium *n* stadium, phase
Krankheitssymptom *n* symptom, sign
Krankheitssymptombeobachtung *f* pathognomy
krankheitstypisch pathognom[on]ic
krankheitsübertragend infectious, pathophoric, pathophorous, morbiphor
Krankheitsüberträger *m* carrier, vector
Krankheitsübertragung *f* pathophoresis, infection, transmission, communication, contagion
Krankheitsunterdrückung *f* abortion
Krankheitsuntertreibung *f* dissimulation
Krankheitsursache *f* cause [of a disease]
Krankheitsverbreitung *f* spread [of the disease], dissemination
krankheitsverhütend prophylactic, preventing
Krankheitsverhütung *f* prophylaxis, prevention of disease
Krankheitsverlauf *m* course (progress) of the disease; pathogenesis ● den ~ voraussagen to prognosticate, to prognose
~/**abortiver** abortion

Krankheitsverlaufsbeobachtung f catamnesis
Krankheitsverschlechterung f/**erneute** recrudescence, relapse
Krankheitsvorbeugung f prophylaxis
Krankheitsvorhersage f prognosis
Krankheitsvortäuschung f simulation, malingering *(s.a. Krankheitsnachahmung)*
Krankheitsvorzeichen n prodrome
Krankheitswahn m hypochondria[sis], neuriasis, nosomania
Krankheitszahl f morbidity [rate]
Krankheitszeichen n sign, symptom, manifestation ● **mehrere ~ aufweisend** polysymptomatic ● **nur ein ~ aufweisend** monosymptomatic
Krankheitszustand m state, pathema
~/plötzlich einsetzender insult
kränklich ailing, weak, unhealthy, in poor health, of weak health, valetudinarian; sickly *(z. B. Aussehen)*
Kränklichkeit f poor (weak) health, valetudinarianism
krankmachend pathogen[et]ic, nosogen[et]ic, morbific, morbigenous
Kranksein n/**eingebildetes** nosomania
Kranz m corona, crown
Kranzarterie f coronary [artery] *(s. a.* unter Koronararterie*)*
~ der Hüfte/oberflächliche superficial iliac circumflex artery
~ der Hüfte/tiefe deep iliac circumflex artery
~ des Armes/hintere posterior humeral circumflex artery
~ des Armes/vordere anterior humeral circumflex artery
kranzförmig coronal
Kranznaht f coronal (frontoparietal) suture
Kranzstar m coronary cataract
Krater m crater
kraterartig craterlike, crateriform, crater-shaped
Krätze f scabies, [seven-year] itch, mange, sarcoptidosis *(durch Krätzemilben hervorgerufene Hautkrankheit)* ● **durch ~ hervorgerufen** scabious
~/norwegische Norwegian itch (scabies), Boeck's scabies
Krätzeangst f scabiophobia, acarophobia
krätzeartig sarcoptoid
Krätzemilbe f itch-mite, sarcoptic mite, acarid, Acarus scabiei
krätzemilbenartig sarcoptoid
Krätzemilbenbefall m sarcoptidosis
Krätzemilbenkanal m cuniculus *(in der Haut)*
krätzemilbentötend scabicide
krätzewirksam antiscabetic, antiscabious
krätzig scabious, itchy
Kratzmarke f scratch mark
Kratzreflex m scratch reflex
Kratztest m scratch test
Kratzwut f titillomania
Kraurosis f kraurosis *(Hautkrankheit)*
~ penis kraurosis of the penis, penile kraurosis
~ vulvae kraurosis of the vulva, vulvar kraurosis, leucokraurosis, leucoplakic vulvitis
Krawatte f/**Schanzsche** cervical collar
Kreatin n creatine, kreatin
Kreatinämie f creatinaemia
Kreatinase f creatinase *(Enzym)*
Kreatinausscheidung f **im Urin** creatinuria
Kreatinerhöhung f **im Blut** creatinaemia
Kreatinin n creatinine, kreatinine, dehydrated creatine
Kreatinin-Clearance f creatinine clearance
Kreatinin-Clearance-Test m creatinine clearance test
Kreatininkoeffizient m creatinine coefficient
Kreatininphosphokinase f creatinine phosphokinase *(Enzym)*
Kreatinkinase f creatine kinase *(Enzym)*
Kreatinkinaseisoenzym n creatine kinase isoenzyme
Kreatinphosphat n creatine phosphate, phosphocreatine, phosphagen
Kreatinphosphokinase f creatine phosphokinase *(Enzym)*
Kreatinphosphorsäure f creatine phosphoric acid
Kreatorrhoe f creatorrhoea
Krebs m cancer, carcinoma *(bösartige Krankheit) (Zusammensetzungen s.* unter Karzinom *und* Carcinoma*)* ● **wegen ~ operiert werden** to be operated upon for carcinoma
krebsartig cancerous, carcinous, carcinomatous, cancroid, cancriform
krebsauslösend, krebsbildend cancerogenic, cancerigenic, carcinogen[et]ic, causing cancer
Krebs... s. a. Karzinom...
Krebsbildung f cancer formation, canceration
Krebschemotherapie f cancer chemotherapy
Krebsekzem n **der Brust** Paget's disease (cancer), Paget's nipple (mammary) disease
Krebsentfernung f[/**operative**] carcin[om]ectomy, carcinosectomy
Krebsentstehung f carcinogenesis
Krebsentwicklung f carcinogenesis
krebserregend cancerogenic, carcinogenic, carcinogen[et]ic
Krebsforschung f cancer research (investigation), cancerology
krebsfreundlich carcinophilic
Krebsfreundlichkeit f carcinophilia *(von Gewebe)*
Krebsfrühdiagnostik f early cancer diagnosis
Krebsfurcht f cancerophobia, carcino[mato]phobia
Krebsgeschwür n cancerous ulcer
Krebsgewebe n cancerous tissue
krebshemmend anticarcinogen, carcinostatic
Krebs-Henseleit-Zyklus m ornithine (Krebs-Henseleit) cycle
Krebsherd m cancerous focus
krebsig carcinomatous
Krebskachexie f cancerous cachexia
Krebskranker m cancer patient

Krebskrankheit

Krebskrankheit f cancer, cancerous (malignant) disease, carcinosis, malignancy
Krebskunde f cancerology, carcinology
Krebsmilch f cancer milk
Krebsmorbidität f cancer morbidity
Krebsregister n cancer register
Krebsspezialist m cancerologist
Krebssterblichkeit f cancer mortality
Krebssterblichkeitsrate f cancer mortality rate
Krebsstruma f cancerous goitre
krebsvernichtend cancericidal
Krebsvirus n cancer virus
Krebsvorbeugung f cancer prophylaxis
Krebsvorsorgeuntersuchung f cancer screening examination
Krebswachstum n cancer growth
Krebszelle f cancer cell
Krebszellennest n cancer nest
krebszellentötend cancericidal
krebszellenzerstörend carcinolytic
Krebszellenzerstörung f carcinolysis
Krebszerfall m carcinolysis
Krebszerstörung f carcinolysis
Krebs-Zyklus m Krebs (citric acid) cycle, tricarboxylic-acid cycle
Kreis m circle, circulus *(s. a. unter* Circulus*)*
~/kleiner orbiculus
Kreisbewegung f circulatory motion (movement), circumduction
kreisförmig circinate, circular, orbicular; gyrate
Kreislauf m circulation; circulatory system ● **dem ~ verlorengehen** to be lost to the circulation ● **den ~ anregen** to stimulate (activate) circulation ● **den ~ wiederherstellen** to re-establish circulation ● **mit verlangsamtem ~** marantic, marasmic
~/enterohepatischer enterohepatic cycling
~/fetaler foetal circulation
~/großer greater (systemic, general) circulation
~/kleiner (pulmonaler) lesser (pulmonary) circulation, lesser circulatory system
kreislaufanregend circulation-activating, activating the circulation
Kreislaufattacke f circulatory embarrassment
Kreislaufbelastungstest m circulatory efficiency test
Kreislaufbeschwerden pl circulatory distress
Kreislaufdysregulation f circulatory dysregulation, disturbance of the circulatory regulation
Kreislaufeffekt m circulatory action
Kreislauferkrankung f circulatory (cardiovascular) disease
Kreislauffunktion f circulatory function
Kreislaufkollaps m circulatory collapse
Kreislauflabilität f circulatory lability (instability)
Kreislaufmittel n cardiovascular agent, cardiotonic drug
Kreislaufregulation f circulatory regulation
Kreislaufregulationsstörung f disturbed circulatory regulation
Kreislaufschwäche f circulatory insufficiency (debility)

Kreislaufsituation f circulatory conditions
Kreislaufstörung f circulatory disorder (disturbance)
Kreislaufsymptom n circulatory symptom
Kreislaufsystem n circulatory (cardiovascular) system
Kreislauftraining n training of the circulation, circulatory training
Kreislaufunterbrechung f circulatory standstill
Kreislaufversagen n circulatory failure (breakdown), failure of circulation, shock
~/peripheres peripheral circulatory failure
Kreislaufzeit f circulation time
Kreislaufzusammenbruch m s. Kreislaufversagen
kreisrund circinate, circular, orbicular; nummular, nummiform
kreißen to be in labour
Kreißen n labour, parturition
kreißend parturient
Kreißende f parturient, woman in labour
Kreißsaal m delivery room, labour (birth) room
Kreisviertel n quadrant *(Brustregion)*
Kremaster m s. Kremastermuskel
Kremasterarterie f cremasteric (external spermatic) artery
Kremasterfaszie f cremasteric (Cooper's) fascia
Kremasterkontraktion f cremasteric contraction
Kremastermuskel m cremaster [muscle]
Kremasterreflex m cremasteric reflex
Kremation f cremation
Krematorium n crematorium, crematory
Kreosol n creosol *(Expektorans)*
Kreosotkarbonat n creosote carbonate *(Expektorans)*
Kreotoxin n kreotoxin *(durch Bakterien produziert)*
Kreotoxismus n kreotoxism
Krepitation f crepitation, crepitance *(bei Fraktur)*
krepitieren to crepitate
Krepitieren n 1. crepitation, crepitant rale, crepitance *(z. B. bei Pneumonie)*; 2. s. Krepitation
~/grobblasiges coarse crepitation *(der Lunge)*
~/subkutanes subcutaneous crepitance
krepitierend crepitant
Kresol n cresol, hydroxytoluene *(Desinfektionsmittel)*
Kresylblau n cresyl blue *(zur Blutfärbung)*
Kretin m cretin
kretinartig cretinoid
Kretinismus m cretinism, thyroid dwarfism *(angeborene Idiotie durch Schilddrüsenunterfunktion)*
~/sporadischer myxidiocy
Kreuz n small of the back
Kreuzallergie f cross sensitivity (allergenicity)
Kreuzband n cruciate knee ligament, crucial ligament [of the knee]
~ des Atlas cruciate ligament of the atlas
~/hinteres posterior cruciate ligament of the knee
~/vorderes anterior cruciate ligament of the knee

Kristallviolett

Kreuzbandruptur f cruciate knee ligament rupture
~/**hintere** posterior cruciate knee ligament rupture
~/**vordere** anterior cruciate knee ligament rupture
Kreuzbein n sacrum, rump bone ● **durch das** ~ transsacral ● **neben dem** ~ parasacral
Kreuzbein... s.a. Sakral...
Kreuzbeinarterie f/**mittlere** middle (median, medial) sacral artery
~/**seitliche** lateral sacral artery
Kreuzbein-Darmbein-Gelenk n sacroiliac articulation (synchondrosis)
Kreuzbein-Darmbein-Region f sacroiliac region
Kreuzbeindruckgeschwür n sacral decubitus ulceration
Kreuzbeinentfernung f[/**operative**] sacrectomy
Kreuzbeingegend f sacral region
Kreuzbeingeschwür n sacral decubitus ulceration
Kreuzbeinhorn n cornu of the sacrum (Gelenkfortsatz)
Kreuzbeinrückseite f dorsal surface of the sacrum
Kreuzbeinschaufel f ala of the sacrum
Kreuzbeinschmerz m sacralgia, sacrodynia
Kreuzbeinsegment n sacral segment
Kreuzbeinspitze f apex (caudal end) of the sacrum
Kreuzbein-Steißbein-Fistel f sacrococcygeal fistula
Kreuzbein-Steißbein-Gegend f sacrococcygeal region
Kreuzbein-Steißbein-Muskel m sacrococcygeus [muscle]
~/**dorsaler** sacrococcygeus dorsalis [muscle], sacrococcygeus posterior [muscle]
~/**ventraler** sacrococcygeus anterior muscle
Kreuzbein- und Hüftbeinentzündung f sacrocoxitis, sacroiliitis
Kreuzbein- und Hüftschmerz m sacrocoxalgia
Kreuzbeinvene f/**mittlere** middle sacral vein
~/**seitliche** lateral sacral vein
Kreuzbeinwirbel m sacral vertebra
Kreuzbiß m crossbite (Stomatologie)
kreuzen to cross; to match (z. B. Blutkonserven); to cross, to interbreed (z. B. Gene)
~/**sich** to intersect, to interbreed; to decussate (z. B. Hirnnerven)
kreuzförmig cruciform, cross-shaped
Kreuzimmunität f cross-immunity
Kreuzinfektion f cross infection
Kreuzinzision f crucial incision
Kreuzkopf m clinocephalus
Kreuzköpfigkeit f clinocephalia
Kreuzprobe f cross match test, matching of blood, cross-matching
Kreuzprobenröhrchen n pilot tube
Kreuzreaktivität f cross-reactivity, cross-reaction
Kreuzresistenz f cross-resistance (Bakterien)
Kreuzschädeligkeit f metopism

Kreuzschmerzen mpl lumbago, pains in the [small of the] back, backache, low back pain
Kreuz-Steißbein n sacrococcyx
Kreuzung f crossing; chiasm[a], decussation (z. B. von Nervenbahnen); interbreeding, crossbreeding (z. B. von Genen)
~/**der Kleinhirnschenkel** decussation of the superior cerebeller peduncles, decussation of the brachia conjunctiva
Kreuzungsphänomen n/**Gunnsches** Gunn's phenomenon, arteriovenous crossing sign
Kreuzverband m figure-of-eight bandage
Kribbelgefühl n, **Kribbeln** n formication, tingle, tingling
kribriform cribriform, cribate
kriechen to creep, to crawl
kriechend serpiginous, creeping
Kriechgeschwür n serpiginous ulcer
Kriegführung f/**biologische** biological warfare
Kriegsneurose f battle fatigue, war neurosis
Kriegspsychose f war psychosis
Kriegstyphus m typhus fever, war typhus, petechial (exanthematous) typhus, prison fever
Kriegsverletzung f war injury (wound)
Kriegszittern n s. Kriegsneurose
Krikoarytenoidgelenk n cricoarytenoid joint
krikoid cricoid, ring-shaped
Krikoidektomie f cricoidectomy
Krikoidknorpel m cricoid cartilage
Krikoidmalformation f cricoid malformation
krikoösophageal crico-oesophageal
krikopharyngeal cricopharyngeal
Krikothyreotomie f cricothyr[e]otomy, coniotomy, inferior laryngotomy, thyrocricotomy (Luftröhrenschnitt)
Krikotomie f cricotomy
Krikotracheotomie f cricotracheotomy
Krio... s. Kryo...
Krise f crisis, acme (z. B. in einem Krankheitsverlauf)
~/**aregeneratorische** aregeneratory crisis (bei hämolytischer Anämie)
~/**hyperthyreote** hyperthyroid crisis
~/**myasthenische** myasthenic crisis
~/**okulare** ocular crisis
~/**rektale** rectal crisis (bei Tabes dorsalis)
~/**thyreotoxische** thyrotoxicosis, thyrotoxaemia, thyrotoxic crisis, thyroid storm
Krisis f s. Krise
Kristallausscheidung f im Urin crystalluria
Kristallbildung f crystallization
Kristalle mpl/**Charcot-Leydensche** [Charcot-] Leyden crystals, asthma crystals
~/**Teichmannsche** Teichmann's (haemin) crystals
kristallin crystalline
~/**nicht** non-crystalline, amorphous
Kristallinse f crystalline lens [of the eye], lens
Kristallkatarakt f crystalline cataract
Kristallophobie f crystallophobia (krankhafte Angst vor Glas)
Kristallviolett n crystal violet, hexamethyl-p-rosaniline hydrochloride (Wurmmittel)

Kritzelschrift

Kritzelschrift f scribbling
Kritzelsucht f graphomania, scribomania
Krokodilhaut f crocodile (toad) skin, phrynoderma
Krokodilklemme f alligator forceps (clamp)
Krokodilstränen fpl crocodile tears
Krokodilstränensyndrom n crocodile tears syndrome
Krone f crown, corona (Zusammensetzungen s. unter Corona)
kronenartig coronoid, crown-like, crown-shaped
Kronenbereich m coronal region (der Zähne)
Kronenfortsatz m der Elle coronoid process of the ulna
~ **des Unterkiefers** coronoid process of the mandible
Kronenfortsatzgrube f coronoid fossa
Kronennaht f coronal suture
Kronenzahn m crown tooth
Kronenzange f crown plier (forceps)
Kropf m goitre, struma, thyrocele (s.a. unter Struma)
~/**angeborener** congenital goitre
~/**endemischer** endemic (simple) goitre
~/**gallertartiger** colloid goitre
~/**großfollikulärer** macrofollicular goitre (adenoma)
~/**kleinfollikulärer** microfollicular goitre (adenoma)
~/**multinodulärer** multinodular goitre
Kropf... s.a. Struma...
kropfartig goitrous
kropfauslösend goitrogenic, goitrogenous
kropfbildend goitrogenic, goitrogenous
Kropfentfernung f[/operative] strumectomy
Kropfentzündung f s. Strumitis
Kropfherz n[/toxisches] goitre (thyroid, thyreotoxic) heart; thyrocarditis (Herzentzündung bei Schilddrüsenüberfunktion)
Kropflöffel m spoon shaped depressor
Kropfoperation f strumectomy
kropfwirksam antistrumous
Krötengift n toad poison (venom), bufotoxin (Glykosid)
Krötenhaut f toad (crocodile) skin, phrynoderma
Krötenkopf m toad head, acranius
Krötentest m [male-]toad test, frog test, bufo reaction (Schwangerschaftsschnelltest)
Krotonöl n croton oil
Krotonölvergiftung f crotonism
Krücke f crutch • **an Krücken gehen** to go on crutches, to walk with crutches, to crutch
Krückenlähmung f crutch palsy (paralysis)
Krugatmen n cavernous respiration, amphoric breathing (respiration)
Krukenberg-Axenfeld-Spindel f Krukenberg's spindle (dreieckförmige Pigmentablagerung an der Hornhauthinterfläche bei kurzsichtigem Auge)
Krukenberg-Tumor m Krukenberg's tumour, drop metastasis
krumm crooked, valgus (z. B. Beine)

krummbeinig with crooked legs, valgoid; bow-legged, bandy-legged (O-beinig); knock-kneed (X-beinig)
Krummdarm m ileum
~ **und Blinddarm** m ileocaecum
Krummdarm... s.a. Ileum...
Krummdarmentfernung f[/operative] ileectomy
Krummdarmentzündung f ileitis
~/**regionäre** terminal ileitis
Krummdarmfistel f ileal stoma, ileostomy
Krummdarmfistelung f/operative ileostomy
Krummdarmgekröse n mesoileum
Krummdarm-Grimmdarm-Verbindung f[/operative] ileocolostomy
Krummdarminvagination f ileal intussusception
Krummdarm-Krummdarm-Verbindung f[/operative] ileoileostomy
Krummdarm-Mastdarm-Verbindur.g f[/operative] ileorectostomy, ileoproctostomy
Krummdarm-Querkolon-Verbindung f[/operative] ileotransversostomy
Krummdarm-Scheiden-Fistel f ileovaginal fistula
Krummdarmschlagader f ileal artery
Krummdarm-Sigmoideum-Verbindung f[/operative] ileosigmoidostomy
Krummdarm- und Blinddarmentzündung f ileotyphlitis
Krummdarm- und Blinddarmvene f ileocolic vein
Krummdarm- und Dickdarmarterie f ileocolic artery
Krummdarm- und Grimmdarmentzündung f ileocolitis
krümmen to incurvate, to incurve, to bend
~/**sich** to bend, to become bent
~/**sich vor Schmerzen** to be convulsed, to writhe [with pain]
Krümmung f curvature, curve, bend; flexure (z. B. des Dickdarms); incurvation (nach innen)
~ **des Magens/konkave** lesser curvature of the stomach
~/**kompensatorische** compensatory curvature (z. B. der Wirbelsäule)
Krümmungsflächenmesser m spherometer
Krümmungs[flächen]messung f spherometry, ophthalmometry (der Hornhaut des Auges)
Krup m s. Krupp
Krupp m croup, exudative angina
~/**diphtherischer** laryngeal diphtheria
~/**echter** croupous (diphtheritic) pharyngitis, diphtheria
Kruppbronchitis f croup (plastic) bronchitis
Krüppel m cripple, crippled (defective) person
• **zum ~ werden** to be crippled
Kruppmembran f croupous membrane
kruppös croupous, croupy
Krusotomie f crusotomy
Kruste f crust, crusta, eschar, slough, scab (s.a. unter Crusta)
~/**dicke** rupia
krustenbildend forming crusts, escharotic
Krustenbildung f incrustation, crust formation
Kryalgesie f cryalgesia, crymodynia

Kryanästhesie f cry[o]anaesthesia
Kryästhesie f cry[o]aesthesia, crymoanaesthesia, refrigeration anaesthesia
Kryoapplikation f cryoapplication
Kryochirurgie f cryosurgery, cryogenic surgery
kryochirurgisch cryosurgical
Kryoextraktion f cryoextraction *(Staroperation)*
Kryoextraktor m cryoextractor
Kryoglobulin n cryoglobulin *(durch Kälte ausfallender Eiweißkörper)*
Kryoglobulinerhöhung f im Blut cryoglobulinaemia
Kryohypophysektomie f cryohypophysectomy *(Hypophysenfunktionsausschaltung durch Kälteanwendung)*
Kryokauter m cryocauter
Kryokauterisation f cryocautery
Kryokoagulation f cryocoagulation
Kryomikrotom n cryostat *(für histologische Dünnschnittechnik unter Kälteanwendung)*
Kryomikrotomschnitt m cryostat section
Kryopexie f cryopexy, cryofixation
Kryophak m cryophake *(zur Linsenunterkühlung)*
Kryoplasma n cryoprecipitated plasma
Kryopräservation f cryopreservation
Kryopräzipitat n cryoprecipitate
Kryopräzipitation f cryoprecipitation
Kryoretinopexie f cryoretinopexy
Kryoskop n cryoscope
Kryoskopie f cryoscopy
kryoskopisch cryoscopic
Kryothalamotomie f cryothalamotomy
Kryotherapie f cryotherapy, krymotherapy
Kryotom n cryotome
Krypte f crypt, crypta
Kryptektomie f cryptectomy
Krypten fpl/**Lieberkühnsche** crypts of Lieberkühn *(Darmsaftdrüsen der Dick- und Dünndarmmukosa)*
Kryptenentfernung f[/**operative**] cryptectomy
Kryptenentzündung f cryptitis
Krypteneröffnung f[/**operative**] cryptotomy
Kryptenlinie f dentate line
Kryptenstein m cryptolith
Kryptensteinleiden n cryptolithiasis
Kryptitis f cryptitis
kryptogen cryptogen[et]ic
Kryptokokke f cryptococcus
Kryptokokkenantigen n cryptococcal antigen
Kryptokokkenknoten m toruloma
Kryptokokkenmeningitis f cryptococcal meningitis
Kryptokokkenperitonitis f cryptococcal peritonitis
Kryptokokkose f cryptococcosis, Busse-Buschke's disease, torulosis *(durch Cryptococcus neoformans)*
~/**pulmonale** pulmonary cryptococcosis
Kryptolith m cryptolith
Kryptolithiasis f cryptolithiasis
Kryptomenorrhoe f cryptomenorrhoea *(z. B. bei intaktem Hymen)*

Kryptomitose f cryptomitosis
Kryptophthalmie f cryptophthalmia
Kryptophthalmus m cryptophthalmus
kryptorchid cryptorchid, undescended
Kryptorchidektomie f cryptorchidectomy
Kryptorchider m cryptorchid, cryptorchis
Kryptorchismus m cryptorchi[di]sm *(ein- oder beidseitig)*
Kryptotomie f cryptotomy
Kryptoxanthin n cryptoxanthin *(Provitamin A)*
Kryptozoit m cryptozoite *(Malariaparasitenstadium)*
Kubebe f cubeb
Kubebenvergiftung f cubebism
kubital cubital
Kuboid n cuboid [bone]
Kuboidzelle f cuboidal cell
Kuchenniere f cake[d] kidney, doughnut (lump, clump) kidney, confluent (scutulate) kidney
Kufs-Syndrom n Kufs' syndrome, adult (late juvenile) amaurotic familial idiocy
kugelbakterienförmig coccobacilliform
Kugelbakterium n coccus, coccobacillus
~/**großes** megacoccus
~/**kleines** micrococcus
Kugelgelenk n spheroid articulation, ball[-and-socket] joint; diarthrosis, thorough joint
Kugelherzklappe[nprothese] f caged-ball prosthesis (valve)
Kugellinse f spherophakia; lentiglobus
Kugelmyom n ball myoma
Kugelsonde f ball probang, bulbous bougie
Kugelthrombus m ball (globoid) thrombus
Kugelventileffekt m ball-valve action *(z. B. durch Gallensteine im Hauptgallengang)*
Kugelventilthrombus m ball-valve thrombus
Kugelzange f bullet forceps
Kugelzelle f spherocyte
Kugelzellenanämie f spherocytic anaemia, [hereditary] spherocytosis, haemolytic splenomegaly, chronic (familial) acholuric jaundice, congenital haemolytic anaemia (icterus)
kühlend cooling, refrigerent, refrigerating, antithermic
Kühlung f cooling, refrigeration
Kuhmilchallergie f cow's milk allergy
Kuhpocken pl bovine smallpox, cowpox, vaccinia
Kuhpockenimpfung f smallpox vaccination
Kuhpockenknötchen n an der **Hand** milker's nodule
Kuhpockenlymphe f vaccine lymph, smallpox (Jenner's) vaccine
Kuldoplastik f culdoplasty
Kuldoskop n culdoscope *(Endoskop)*
Kuldoskopie f culdoscopy, inspection of the pelvic organs
Kuldotomie f culdotomy
Kuldozentese f culdocentesis
Kulissenschnitt m rectus (pararectal) incision *(Bauchhöhleneröffnung durch den geraden Beckenmuskel)*

Kulminationspunkt 432

Kulminationspunkt *m* culmination point *(z. B. einer Krankheit)*
kultivieren to culture, to cultivate
Kultur *f* culture *(z. B. von Bakterien)*
Kulturflasche *f* culture flask (bottle)
Kulturflüssigkeit *f* culture fluid
Kulturmedium *n* [culture] medium
Kulturplatte *f* culture plate
Kulturschale *f* culture dish
Kulturverfahren *n* culture method (technique)
Kumarin *n* coumarin, 1,2-benzopyrone
Kumulationsdosis *f* cumulative dose
Kumulationswirkung *f* cumulative action (effect)
Kunstafter *m* artificial (preternatural) anus, colostomy [opening], enterproctia
Kunstafterbeutel *m* colostomy bag
Kunstarm *m* artificial arm
Kunstauge *n* artificial eye
Kunstbein *n* artificial leg
Kunstfehler *m* [/ärztlicher] malpractice
Kunstgriff *m* manipulation, manoeuvre
Kunstherz *n* artificial heart
künstlich artificial; false *(z. B. Zähne)*
Kunstprodukt *n* artificial product; artefact
Küntscher-Nagel *m* Küntscher (intramedullary) nail
Kupferausscheidung *f* im Urin urinary copper excretion
Kupferblutspiegel *m* copper blood level
Kupferdrahtarterie *f* copper-wire artery
Kupferenzym *n* copper enzyme
Kupferfinnen *fpl* rosacea, facial teleangiectasis; brandy face (nose), rosy drop
kupferfinnenartig rosaceiform
Kupfersaum *m* copper line *(bei Kupfervergiftung)*
Kupferstar *m* sunflower cataract, chalcosis lentis
Kupferstoffwechsel *m* copper metabolism
Kupfervergiftung *f* copper poisoning
Kuppel *f* 1. tympanic attic, epitympanic recess *(im Ohr)*; 2. vault *(des Zwerchfells)*
Kupulometrie *f* cupulometry *(Testung des Gleichgewichtssinns im drehenden Stuhl)*
Kur *f* cure ● eine ~ machen to take a cure ● eine ~ verordnen to prescribe (order) a cure ● zur ~ fahren to go to a health resort
Kurare *n* curare *(Muskelrelaxans)*
kurareähnlich curariform
Kurareapplikation *f* curarization
kurareartig curare-like
Kurarin *n* curarine *(Kurarealkaloidgemisch)*
kurarisieren to curarize
Kurarisierung *f* curarization
kurativ curative, remedial; therapeutic, medicinal; consolidant; sanitary; salutary, sanatory
Kürettage *f* curettage, curettement, abrasion
~/**scharfe** sharp curettage
~/**stumpfe** blunt curettage
Kürette *f* curette, scraper, abrasor, surgical spoon
kürettieren to curet[te], to abrade
kurieren to cure, to heal *(z. B. Kranke)*

Kurort *m* health resort; spa, water[ing] place
Kurpfuscher *m* quack[salver], charlatan
Kurpfuscherei *f* quackery, charlatanism, charlatanry ● ~ betreiben to quack
Kurvatur *f* curvature, curvatura
~/**große** greater curvature [of the stomach]
~/**kleine** lesser curvature [of the stomach]
Kurvenanpassung *f* curve fitting *(Biometrie)*
kurzarmig short-armed
kurzatmig dyspnoeic, dyspnoeal, short of breath, short-winded, pursey; asthmatic
Kurzatmigkeit *f* dyspnoea, shortness of breath, pursiness
Kurzauge *n* platymorphia *(in der Sehachse verkürztes Auge mit Weitsichtigkeit)*
kurzbeinig short-legged, brachyskelic; microscelous
Kurzbeinigkeit *f* brachyskelia; microscelia
kurzfingrig brachydactylic, brachydactylous, brachyphalangous
Kurzfingrigkeit *f* brachydactyly, brachyphalangia
kurzfüßig microscelous
Kurzfüßigkeit *f* microscelia
kurzgesichtig brachyprosopic
Kurzhals *m*/**angeborener** Feil-Klippel syndrome
kurzhändig brachych[e]irous
Kurzhändigkeit *f* brachych[e]irism
kurzkieferig brachygnathous
kurzköpfig brachycephalic, brachycephalous
Kurzköpfigkeit *f* brachycephalia
kurzlebig short-lived, microbiotic
Kurzlippigkeit *f* brachych[e]ilia
Kurznarkose *f* short anaesthesia
Kurznasigkeit *f* brachyrhinia
kurzschädelig *s.* kurzköpfig
Kurzschluß *m* shunt
Kurzschlußanastomose *f* short circuit
Kurzschlußblutvolumen *n*/**intrapulmonales** intrapulmonary shunt volume
Kurzschlußhandlung *f* impulsive act, irrational reaction
Kurzschlußoperation *f* short-circuiting operation *(z. B. am Darm)*
Kurzschlußverbindung *f* shunt
kurzsichtig myopic, short-sighted, near-sighted
Kurzsichtiger *m* myope
Kurzsichtigkeit *f s.* Myopie
Kurzwelle *f s.* Kurzwellenbehandlung
Kurzwellenbehandlung *f* short-wave therapy, electrothermy
Kurzwellendiathermie *f* short-wave diathermy, neodiathermy
Kurzwellendurchströmung *f* endothermy
Kurzwellengerät *n* short-wave [therapy] apparatus, electrotherm
Kurzzeitgedächtnis *n* short-term memory, immediate (recent, primary) memory
kurzzungig brachyglossal
Kurzzungigkeit *f* brachyglossia
Kuspis *f* cusp, cuspis *(an Herzklappen) (Zusammensetzungen s. unter* Cuspis)

Küstenfieber *n* Rhodesian fever, African (East coast) fever, theileriasis *(Infektion mit Theileria)*
kutan cutaneous, dermal
Kutangefühl *n* cutaneous sensation
Kutanimpfung *f* cutaneous inoculation
Kutanreaktion *f* cutaneous reaction, cutireaction
Kutanreflex *m* cutaneous reflex
Kutantest *m* skin test
Kutikula *f* cuticle, cuticula *(Zusammensetzungen s. unter Cuticula)*
Kutikularsaum *m* cuticular border
Kutis *f* cutis, [true] skin, dermis, derm[a] *(Zusammensetzungen s. unter Cutis und Haut)*
Küvette *f* cuvet[te]
Kveim-Test *m* Kveim-Siltzbach test, Nickerson-Kveim test *(Hauttest zum Sarkoidosenachweis)*
Kwashiorkor-Syndrom *n* kwashiorkor [syndrome], malignant malnutrition, red boy [syndrome], plurideficiency syndrome, nutritional dystrophy
Kymogramm *n* kymogram
Kymograph *m* kymograph
Kymographie *f* kymography *(Aufzeichnung mechanischer Vorgänge)*
kymographisch kymographic
Kymokardiogramm *n* cardiokymogram
Kymokardiographie *f* cardiokymography
kymokardiographisch cardiokymographic
kyphös kyphotic; gibbous, humpbacked
Kyphose *f* [rachio]kyphosis, anterior curvature, posterior deformity; gibbosity, humpback, hunchback
~/anguläre Pott's disease, angular kyphosis (curvature) of the spine, spinal caries
~/juvenile juvenile kyphosis
~/Scheuermannsche Scheuermann's disease, adolescent kyphosis
Kyphosebecken *n* kyphotic pelvis
Kyphoskoliose *f* kyphoscoliosis, scoliokyphosis
kyphoskoliotisch kyphoscoliotic
kyphotisch kyphotic; gibbous, humpbacked
Kyst... *s.a.* Cyst... *und* Zyst...
Kystadenofibrom *n* cystadenofibroma
Kystadenokarzinom *n* cystadenocarcinoma, cystocarcinoma
~/pseudomuzinöses mucinous cystadenocarcinoma
~/seröses serous cystadenocarcinoma
Kystokarzinom *n* cystocarcinoma

L

Labenzym *n* lab, chymosin, chymase, rennin
Labialbogen *m* labial arch *(Stomatologie)*
Labialfläche *f* labial surface
Labialismus *m* labialism, use of labial sounds *(Sprachstörung)*
Labiallinie *f* labial line
Labialokklusion *f* labial occlusion *(Stomatologie)*
Labialschwellung *f* labial swelling *(Embryologie)*

Labialseite *f* labial side *(Stomatologie)*
Labialsprache *f s.* Labialismus
Labidodontie *f* labidontia *(Stomatologie)*
labil labile, instable, unstable
Labilität *f* lability, instability
~/emotionale emotional instability
~/vegetative vegetative (autonomic) lability, autonomic imbalance
labioalveolär labio-alveolar
Labiochorea *f* labiochorea, choreic stiffening of the lips
Labiomykose *f* labiomycosis, mycosis of the lips; perlèche, thrush
Labioplastik *f* labioplasty, cheiloplasty
Labiorrhaphie *f* labiorrhaphy, cheilorrhaphy
Labioskrotalschwellung *f* genital (labioscrotal) swelling *(Embryologie)*
labiozervikal labiocervical *(1. die Lippen und die Zähne betreffend; 2. zur Lippenseite der Zahnhälse gehörend)*
Labium *n* lip, labium *(s.a. unter Lippe)*
~ anterius [portionis vaginalis uteri] anterior lip of the cervix of the uterus
~ anterius tubae auditivae anterior lip of the auditory tube
~ articulare articulationis humeri glenoid labrum (lip)
~ caudale valvulae ileocaecalis lower lip of the ileocaecal valve
~ craniale valvulae ileocaecalis upper lip of the ileocaecal valve
~ externum cristae iliacae external lip of the iliac crest
~ inferius oris lower lip *(des Mundes)*
~ internum cristae iliacae internal lip of the iliac crest
~ laterale lineae asperae femoris lateral lip of the linea aspera of the femur
~ limbi tympanicum tympanic lip, lower lip of the osseous spiral lamina
~ limbi vestibulare vestibular lip, upper lip of the osseous spiral lamina
~ majus [pudendi] greater (major) lip
~ mediale lineae asperae femoris medial lip of the linea aspera of the femur
~ minus [pudendi] lesser (minor) lip, nympha
~ ostii uteri lip of the cervix of the uterus
~ posterius [portionis vaginalis uteri] posterior lip of the cervix of the uterus
~ posterius tubae auditivae posterior lip of the auditory tube
~ superius oris upper lip *(des Mundes)*
~ vocale vocal cord (fold)
Labor *n* laboratory, lab ● **im ~ isoliert werden** to be isolated in the laboratory
~/klinisches hospital clinical laboratory
Laboratorium *n s.* Labor
Laboratoriumsexperiment *n* laboratory experiment
Laborbefunde *mpl* laboratory findings
Labordiagnose *f* laboratory diagnosis
Labordiagnostik *f* laboratory diagnostics

Laborinfektion

Laborinfektion f laboratory infection
Laboruntersuchung f laboratory examination (investigation)
Labrum n labrum, lip, brim *(s.a. unter Labium)*
~ **articulare [articulationis coxae]** acetabular labrum
~ **glenoidale** glenoid labrum (lip)
Labyrinth n labyrinth [of the ear], labyrinthus
● **vom ~ ausgehend** labyrinthogenic
~/**häutiges** membranous labyrinth
~/**knöchernes** osseous (bony) labyrinth
Labyrintharterie f labyrinthine artery
Labyrinthbinnendruck m intralabyrinthine pressure
Labyrinthdekompression f decompression of the labyrinth
Labyrinthektomie f labyrinthectomy, excision of the labyrinth
Labyrinthentfernung f[/operative] s. Labyrinthektomie
Labyrinthentzündung f s. Labyrinthitis
Labyrintherkrankung f labyrinthopathy
Labyrintheröffnung f[/operative] labyrinthotomy, incision into the labyrinth
Labyrinthfenster n labyrinthine window
Labyrinthflüssigkeit f labyrinthine (periotic) fluid, perilymph, endolymph *(zwischen knöchernem und häutigem Labyrinth)*
Labyrinthhydrops m labyrinthine hydrops, hydrops of the labyrinth
Labyrinthirritation f labyrinthine irritation
Labyrinthitis f labyrinthitis, inflammation of the labyrinth, labyrinthine otitis
~/**eitrige** suppurative labyrinthitis, pyolabyrinthitis
Labyrinthnystagmus m labyrinthine (vestibular) nystagmus
Labyrinthotomie f s. Labyrintheröffnung/operative
Labyrinthplatte f otic placode, auditory plate
Labyrinthplattenstiel m placodal (auditory) stalk *(Embryologie)*
Labyrinthreflex m labyrinthine reflex
Labyrinthreizung f labyrinthine irritation
Labyrinthschwerhörigkeit f labyrinthine (inner-ear) deafness
Labyrinthschwindel m labyrinthine vertigo, aural (auditory) vertigo
Labyrinthstellreflex m bowing reflex
Labyrinthstörung f labyrinthine disorder
Labyrinthsymptom n labyrinthine symptom
Labyrinthuntersuchung f labyrinthine testing
Labyrinthus m s. Labyrinth
~ **ethmoidalis** ethmoid sinus (antrum, cells), ethmoid labyrinth [of cells]
Labyrinthvene f labyrinthine vein
Lac n milk; milky fluid; milk-like medicinal preparation
Lacertus m **fibrosus** lacertus [fibrosus], bicipital aponeurosis
Lachen n laughing; laugh, risus
~/**hebephrenes** hebephrenic laugh, cachinnation *(bei Schizophrenie)*
~/**hysterisches** hysterical laugh
~/**krampfhaftes** compulsive laughing
~/**sardonisches** sardonic laugh (grin), canine spasm *(Gesichtsstarre bei Tetanus)*
Lachgas n laughing gas, nitrous oxide, dinitrogen monoxide
Lachgasanalgesie f nitrous oxide analgesia
Lachgasnarkose f nitrous oxide anaesthesia
Lachgas-Sauerstoff-Narkose f nitrous oxide-oxygen anaesthesia
Lachkrampf m gelasmus, spasmodic laughter
lackfarben laky, laked *(z. B. Blut)*
Lackmuspapier n litmus paper
Lacrima f s. Träne
Lactat n s. Laktat
Lactobacillus m lactobacillus
~ **acidophilus** lactobacillus acidophilus
~ **bifidus** lactobacillus bifidus
~ **casei** lactobacillus casei *(Testorganismus für Vitamin B_2)*
~ **gastrophilus** lactobacillus gastrophilus
~ **lactis Dorner** lactobacillus lactis Dorner
Lactobacillus-casei-Faktor m lactobacillus casei factor
Lactobacillus-lactis-Dorner-Faktor m lactobacillus lactis Dorner factor
Lacuna f lacuna, hole, gap, hollow, cavity, small pit; lake
~ **lateralis** lateral lacuna, parasinoidal sinus *(Ausbuchtung der Hirnblutleiter)*
~ **musculorum** lacuna musculorum *(unter dem Leistenband liegend)*
~ **urethralis** urethral lacuna
~ **vasorum** lacuna vasorum *(unter dem Leistenband liegend)*
Lacus m lake, lacus *(z. B. Blutsee)*
~ **lacrimalis** lacrimal lake
Lage f 1. situs, location *(z. B. eines Organs)*; position *(s.a. unter Stellung)*; presentation *(des Fetus bei der Geburt)*; 2. layer *(Schicht)* ● **in natürlicher ~** in situ
~/**abnorme** abnormal presentation *(des Fetus)*
~/**rechtsseitige** dextrality
~/**spiegelbildliche** situs inversus
Lageanomalie f malposition, abnormal position
Lagerfieber n camp fever
lagern to splint, to place on a splint *(z. B. ein gebrochenes Bein)*; to position *(Patienten)*; to lay, to place *(betten)*
Lagerpsychose f camp psychosis
Lagerung f positioning *(z. B. eines Patienten)*
~/**Trendelenburgsche** Trendelenburg's (high pelvic) position
Lagerungsdrainage f postural drainage *(z. B. zur Lungenabszeßentleerung)*
Lagerungsprobe f Ratschow's test *(zur Gefäßuntersuchung)*
Lagerungs- und Klopfdrainage f postural-percussion drainage
Lagesinn m sense of position, acrognosis
Lagophthalmie f lagophthalmia
Lagophthalmus m lagophthalmos, lagophthalmus, blepharodiastasis; hare's eye

Lag-Periode f lag period (phase) *(anfängliche Wachstumsverzögerung bei Mikroorganismen nach Aussaat in ein Substrat)*
lahm lame; paralyzed
lähmen to paralyze
lähmend paralysant, paralyzing
Lahmheit f lameness
Lähmung f paralysis, palsy *(komplett)*; paresis *(partiell)* *(s.a. unter Paralyse)*
~ **aller vier Gliedmaßen** tetraplegia, tetraparesis
~/**alternierende** alternating paralysis, alternate hemiplegia
~/**atrophische** atrophic paralysis
~/**aufsteigende** ascending paralysis (poliomyelitis, polyneuritis), [Landry]-Guillain-Barré syndrome, Landry's ascending paralysis, infectious [poly]neuritis
~/**Bellsche** Bell's disease (palsy, paralysis)
~/**Bernhardsche** Bernhard-Roth syndrome, Bernhard's paraesthesia
~/**Brown-Séquardsche** Brown-Séquard paralysis
~/**Déjerine-Klumpkesche** Déjerine-Klumpke's paralysis (syndrome), lower brachial plexus paralysis
~ **der Beine in Beugestellung/vollständige** paraplegia in flexion
~ **der Beine in Streckstellung/vollständige** paraplegia in extension
~ **der Beine/teilweise** paraparesis
~ **der Irismuskulatur/teilweise** iridoparesis
~ **der Irren/progressive** general paralysis of the insane
~ **der Kehlkopfmuskeln** laryngoparalysis
~ **der Regenbogenhautmuskulatur** iridoplegia, iridoparalysis
~ **der Regenbogenhautmuskulatur/teilweise** iridoparesis
~ **der vier Extremitäten** quadriplegia
~ **des Afterschließmuskels** proctoparalysis, proctoplegia
~ **des äußeren geraden Augenmuskels** lateral rectus muscle palsy
~/**doppelseitige** diplegia, bilateral paralysis, cerebral paraplegia
~ **dreier Gliedmaßen** triplegia
~/**Duchenne-Aransche** Aran-Duchenne dystrophy (syndrome), progressive spinal muscular atrophy
~/**Duchenne-Erbsche** Duchenne-Erb palsy (syndrome), upper brachial plexus paralysis, Erb's (Erb-Duchenne's) paralysis
~ **eines einzelnen Gliedes** monoplegia
~ **eines Muskels** monomyoplegia
~/**halbseitige** hemiplegia
~/**ischämische** ischaemic paralysis
~/**kapsuläre** capsular hemiplegia (paralysis)
~/**Klumpkesche** Klumpke's palsy (paralysis), lower brachial plexus paralysis, lower arm [type of] paralysis, lower radicular syndrome
~/**kontralaterale** contralateral (cruciate) paralysis
~/**kortikale** cortical paralysis

~/**Millard-Gublersche** Millard-Gubler paralysis (syndrome), facial hemiplegia alternans
~/**motorische** motor paralysis
~/**periphere** peripheral paralysis
~/**progressive** progressive paralysis
~/**psychogene** psychogenic paralysis
~/**schlaffe** flaccid paralysis
~/**sensomotorische** sensomotor paralysis
~/**sensorische** sensory paralysis, sensoparalysis
~/**spastische** spastic paralysis
~/**unvollständige** paresis
~/**vollständige motorische** paralysis
~/**zentrale** central paralysis (palsy), nuclear paralysis
Lähmungsabasie f paralytic abasia
Lähmungsaphonie f paralytic aphonia
lähmungsfrei non-paralytic
Lähmungskrankheit f paralytic disease
Lähmungsmydriasis f paralytic mydriasis
Lähmungsschielen n paralytic strabism[us], paretic squint *(nach Augenmuskellähmung)*
Lähmungsschwindel m paralytic vertigo
Laienhelfer m first-aider
Laienhilfe f first aid, first-aid treatment
Laki-Lorand-Faktor m fibrin stabilizing factor, FSF, fibrinase, [blood-clotting] factor XIII
lakrimal lachrymal, lacrimal
Lakrimale n lacrimale *(anthropologischer Meßpunkt)*
Lakrimotom n lacrimotome
Lakrimotomie f lacrimotomy, incision of the nasolacrimal duct
Lakritze f liquorice
Laktagogum n lactagogue [agent]
Laktalbumin n lactalbumin
Laktase f lactase, galactosidase *(Enzym)*
Laktasemangelsyndrom n lactase deficiency syndrome
Laktat n lactate
Laktatanhäufung f lactate (lactic acid) accumulation
Laktatazidose f lactate (lactic acid) acidosis
Laktatdehydrogenase f lactate (lactic acid) dehydrogenase, LAD *(Enzym)*
Laktation f lactation, galactosis *(aus der Brust)*
Laktationsamenorrhoe f lactation amenorrhoea
Laktationshemmung f lactation inhibition
Laktationshormon n lactation (lactogenic) hormone, lactogen, galactin, prolactin, mammotrophin, mammogenic (mammary-stimulating) hormone
Laktationsmastitis f lactation (puerperal) mastitis
Laktationsperiode f lactation [period]
Laktationspsychose f lactation psychosis
Laktationsstörung f dysgalactia, disordered milk secretion
Laktat-Pyruvat-Quotient m lactate pyruvate ratio
Laktazidämie f lactacidaemia, lacticaemia
Laktazidase f lactacidase *(Enzym)*

Laktazidose

Laktazidose f s. Laktatazidose
Laktazidurie f lactaciduria
Lakteszenz f lactescence (z. B. der Darmlymphe)
laktieren to lactate
Laktifugum n lactifuge [agent]
laktigen lactigenous
Laktigen n lactogen
Laktobakterium n s. Lactobacillus
Laktodensimeter n lactodensimeter (Milchwaage)
Laktoflavin n lactoflavin, riboflavin, vitamin B_2, hepatoflavin
Laktoflavinavitaminose f ariboflavinosis
Laktogen n s. Laktationshormon
Laktoglobulin n lactoglobulin
Laktometer n lactometer, galactometer
Laktoperoxydase f lactoperoxidase (Enzym)
Laktoprotein n lactoprotein
Laktorrhoe f [ga]lactorrhoea, excessive flow of milk
Laktose f lactose, lactin, milk sugar
Laktoseausscheidung f im Urin lactosuria
Laktoseintoleranz f lactose intolerance
Laktoskop n lactoscope, lactocrit (Instrument zur Bestimmung des Fettgehalts der Milch)
Laktotherapie f [ga]lactotherapy, treatment by milk diet
Laktotoxin n lactotoxin
Laktotropin n s. Laktationshormon
Laktovegetarier m lactovegetarian (sich von Milch- und Pflanzenkost ernährende Person)
laktovegetarisch lactovegetarian
Laktulose f lactulose (Kohlenhydrat)
Lakunarzelle f lacunar cell (abortive Sternberg-Zelle)
Lakune f s. Lacuna
Lallen n lallation, lalling; babbling
Lalognosis f lalognosis, understanding of speech
Laloneurose f laloneurosis, nervous speech disorder
Lalopathie f lalopathy, speech disorder
Lalopathologie f lalopathology (Lehre von den Sprachstörungen)
Lalophobie f lalophobia, laliophobia (krankhafte Angst vor dem Sprechen)
Laloplegie f laloplegia, paralysis of the speech organs
Lalorrhoe f lalorrhoea, abnormal flow of words
Lambdanaht f occipital suture
Lambdazismus m lambdacism[us], labdacism (1. Unvermögen der L-Aussprache; 2. häufiger Gebrauch des L-Lautes als Ersatz für den R-Laut)
Lambl-Exkreszenzen fpl Lambl's excrescences (an der Aortenklappe)
Lamblia f intestinalis Lamblia intestinalis (Dünndarmparasit)
Lambliasis f lambliasis, lambliose, giardiasis, infection with Giardia intestinalis
Lamblienbefall m, **Lamblienruhr** f s. Lambliasis
lamellar lamellar, lamellose; lamellated
~/nicht non-lamellar
Lamelle f lamella

~/Haverssche Haversian (concentric) lamella
lamellenartig lamellar
Lamellenkeratoplastik f lamellar keratoplasty
Lamellenknochen m lamellar bone
Lamellenkörperchen n lamellar corpuscle, [Vater-]Pacini corpuscle
Lamellennagel m cloverleaf nail
Lamina f lamina, layer, membrane, thin plate
Laminagramm n laminagram
Laminagraph m laminagraph
Laminagraphie f laminagraphy, laminography, sectional radiography
laminar laminar, laminate[d]
Laminariastift m laminaria tent (zur Erweiterung des Gebärmutterhalskanals)
Laminarströmung f laminar air flow
Laminarströmungssystem n laminar air flow system
Laminektomie f laminectomy (Operation zur Freilegung des Rückenmarks)
~/zervikale cervical laminectomy
Laminektomiefräse f laminectomy osteotome
Laminektomiestanze f laminectomy punch
Laminektomiewundspreizer m self-retaining laminectomy retractor
Laminektomiezange f laminectomy rongeur
Laminotomie f laminotomy
Lampenbürstenchromosom n lampbrush chromosome
Lamprophonia f lamprophonia, clearness of voice
Lanatosid n lanatoside (Herzglykosid)
Landambulatorium n country ambulatorium
Landarzt m country doctor
Landkartenschädel m map-like skull
Landkartenzunge f geographic tongue; benign migratory glossitis
Landmannshaut f farmer's skin; farmer's disease
Landpraxis f country practice
Landry-Guillain-Barré-Syndrom n [Landry-]Guillain-Barré syndrome, [Landry's] ascending paralysis, infectious [poly]neuritis, ascending poliomyelitis, acute idiopathic polyneuritis
Landstreicherekzem n vagabonds' eczema
langarmig long-armed
langbeinig long-legged, macroscelous
Langbeinigkeit f macroscelia
Langdon-Down-Syndrom n Down's syndrome, mongolism, Mongolian (mongoloid) idiocy, trisomy 21 syndrome
Länge f length (z. B. eines Muskels); length, height (des Körpers) ● mit gleicher ~ isometric
Längen-Breiten-Index m length-breadth index
Längen-Höhen-Index m length-height index
Längenwachstum n linear growth, growth in length (des Körpers)
langfingerig long-fingered, megalodactylous, macrodactylous
Langfingerigkeit f megalodactyly, macrodactyly
langfüßig long-footed, longipedate
langgesichtig dolichofacial, dolichoprosopic
langhaarig long-haired

langhalsig long-necked, dolichoderous
langhändig long-handed, longimanous
Langkopf *m* dolichocephalus
langköpfig dolichocephalic, dolichocephalous
Langköpfigkeit *f* dolichocephalia, dolichocephalism
langlebig long-lived, longeval, macrobiotic
Langlebigkeit *f* longevity, macrobiosis
Langlochplatte *f* slotted bone plate *(für Osteosynthese)*
Langmuskel *m* longus [muscle], longitudinal muscle
~ **der Zunge/oberer (oberflächlicher)** longitudinalis superior [muscle], superior longitudinal muscle of the tongue
~ **der Zunge/tiefer (unterer)** longitudinalis inferior [muscle], inferior longitudinal muscle of the tongue
~ **des Halses** trachelomastoid [muscle]
~ **des Rückens** longissimus muscle
langnasig long-nosed, dolichorrhine
Langniere *f* double (tandem) kidney *(mit zwei Nierenbecken)*
Längsabweichung *f* longitudinal aberration
langsam slow; sluggish *(träge)*; heavy *(schwerfällig)*; phlegmatic
Langsamkeit *f*/**geistige und körperliche** phlegm
Längsband *n* longitudinal ligament
Längsbruch *m* longitudinal (vertical) fracture
Längsbündel *n*/**mediales** medial longitudinal bundle (fasciculus) *(des Rückenmarks)*
~/**oberes** superior longitudinal bundle (fasciculus) *(des Rückenmarks)*
langschädelig *s.* langköpfig
Längsdurchmesser *m*/**unterer** inferior longitudinal diameter *(des Schädels)*
Längsfalte *f* longitudinal fold
Längsfaser *f* longitudinal fibre
Längsfissur *f* longitudinal fissure
Längsgang *m* **des Epoophorons** longitudinal duct of the epoophoron, longitudinal epoophoron duct
längsgerichtet longitudinal
Längsgewölbe *n* **des Fußes** longitudinal arch [of the foot]
Längsinzision *f* longitudinal incision
Längslage *f* longitudinal (polar) presentation *(bei der Geburt)*
Längsleiste *f* longitudinal ridge
Längsrichtung/**in [der]** longitudinal
Längsschnitt *m* longitudinal incision (section)
Längsspalte *f* longitudinal cleft
Längsstreifung *f* longitudinal striping
Längsteilung *f* longitudinal division (splitting)
Längswulst *m* **im Zwölffingerdarm** longitudinal duodenal plica
Längszug *m* longitudinal traction *(z. B. bei einer Fraktur)*
Langzeitanwendung *f* long-term use, long-term application *(z. B. von Medikamenten)*
Langzeitbehandlung *f* long-term therapy (treatment)
Langzeitbeobachtung *f* long-term follow-up
Langzeitgedächtnis *n* long-term memory, remote (distant, secondary) memory
Langzeitpräparat *n* long-acting preparation
Langzeitwirkung *f* prolonged (sustained) action
Lanolin *n* lanolin, hydrous wool fat
Lansing-Virus *n* Lansing virus
lanugoartig lanuginous
Lanugohaare *npl* lanugo [hairs] *(des Fetus)*
Lanze *f* lancet
lanzenförmig lance-shaped, lanciform
Lanzenmesser *n* lancet
Lanzette *f* lancet
lanzinierend lancinating *(z. B. Schmerzen)*
Laparektomie *f* laparectomy, excision of the abdominal wall
Laparocholezystotomie *f* laparocholecystotomy
Laparoelytrotomie *f* laparo-elytrotomy
Laparoenterostomie *f* laparo-enterostomy
Laparoenterotomie *f* laparo-enterotomy
Laparogastroskopie *f* laparogastroscopy
Laparogastrostomie *f* laparogastrostomy
Laparogastrotomie *f* laparogastrotomy
Laparohepatotomie *f* laparohepatotomy
Laparohysterektomie *f* laparohysterectomy
Laparohystero-Oophorektomie *f* laparohystero-oophorectomy
Laparohysteropexie *f* laparohysteropexy
Laparohysterosalpingo-Oophorektomie *f* laparohysterosalpingo-oophorectomy
Laparohysterotomie *f* laparohysterotomy
Laparoileotomie *f* laparo-ileotomy
Laparokolektomie *f* laparocolectomy
Laparokolostomie *f* laparocolostomy
Laparokolotomie *f* laparocolotomy
Laparokolpohysterotomie *f* laparocolpohysterotomy
Laparokolpotomie *f* laparocolpotomy
Laparomyomektomie *f* laparomyomectomy
Laparonephrektomie *f* laparonephrectomy
Laparorrhaphie *f* laparorrhaphy
Laparosalpingektomie *f* laparosalpingectomy
Laparosalpingo-Oophorektomie *f* laparosalpingo-oophorectomy
Laparosalpingotomie *f* laparosalpingotomy
Laparoskop *n* laparoscope, coelioscope
Laparoskopie *f* laparoscopy, coelioscopy, coelioscopy, abdominoscopy
laparoskopisch laparoscopic
Laparosplenektomie *f* laparosplenectomy
Laparosplenotomie *f* laparosplenotomy
Laparothorakoskopie *f* laparothoracoscopy
Laparotomie *f* [abdominal] laparotomy, ventrotomy ● **durch ~ bestätigt** laparatomy-confirmed
laparotomieren to laparotomize, to perform a laparotomy
Laparotrachelotomie *f* laparotrachelotomy
Laparotyphlotomie *f* laparotyphlotomy
Laparouterotomie *f* laparo-uterotomy
Laparozele *f* laparocele, abdominal (ventral) hernia
Laparozystidotomie *f* laparocystidotomy

Laparozystotomie

Laparozystotomie f laparocystotomy
Lapis m **infernalis** lunar caustic, lapis infernalis, silver nitrate
Läppchen n lobule, lobulus *(s.a. unter Lobulus)*
● **mehrere Läppchen betreffend** multilobular
● **nur ein ~ betreffend** monolobular
läppchenförmig lobular, lobulated
Läppchenpneumonie f lobular pneumonia
Lappen m 1. lobe, lobulus *(eines Organs)* *(Zusammensetzungen s. unter Lobus)*; 2. flap *(zur Hauttransplantation)* ● **viele Lappen betreffend** multilobar, multilobate
~/doppelt gestielter double-pedicle flap
~/einstieliger unipedicle flap
~/freier split skin flap
~/frontoparietotemporaler frontoparietotemporal flap
~/gedrehter rotation flap
~/gestielter pedicle (gauntlet, pocket) flap
~/Homescher Home's lobe, subtrigonal gland
Lappenarterie f lobar artery
lappenartig flap-like; lobular, lobulated
Lappenatrophie f lobar atrophy *(z. B. des Gehirns)*
Lappenbronchus m lobar bronchus
Lappenentzündung f lobitis, inflammation of a lobe
Lappenexstirpation f s. Lobektomie
Lappengefäß n lobar vessel
Lappenleber f/**syphilitische** packet liver *(im dritten Stadium der Syphilis)*
Lappenpneumonie f lobar pneumonia
Lappenresektion f s. Lobektomie
Lappenriß m horseshoe tear
Lappensklerose f s. Lobärsklerose
lappig lobate[d], lobed, lobular
Lapsus m **pilorum** alopecia
~ unguium lapsus unguium, falling out of the nails
Lärmbekämpfung f noise abatement
Lärmschwerhörigkeit f noise trauma deafness
Larson-Johansson-Syndrom n Larson-Johansson disease, Sinding-Larson disease *(Osteochondrosis der Patella)*
l-Arterenol n levarterenol
Larva f **migrans cutanea** hypodermyasis, sandworm disease, creeping eruption, bather's itch
larvenartig larval
larviert larvate, larval, larvaceous, masked *(z. B. Krankheitssymptom)*
Larvizidum n larvicide [agent]
Laryngalgie f laryngalgia, pain in the larynx
Laryngealfremitus m laryngeal fremitus
Laryngealstenose f laryngeal stenosis
Laryngektomie f laryngectomy, extirpation (excision) of the larynx
laryngektomieren to laryngectomize, to perform a laryngectomy
Laryngektomierter m laryngectomee
Laryngektomietubus m laryngectomy tube
Laryngismus m laryngismus, laryngeal spasm, laryngospasm
~ stridulus spasmodic croup (laryngitis), tetanic croup, spasm of the glottis
Laryngitis f laryngitis, inflammation of the larynx
~ subglottica mit Stimmritzenkrampf acute spasmodic laryngitis
laryngitisch laryngitic
Laryngogramm n laryngogram
Laryngograph m laryngograph *(Gerät zur Kehlkopfdarstellung)*
Laryngographie f laryngography, roentgen [contrast] examination of the larynx
Laryngologe m laryngologist
Laryngologie f laryngology *(Lehre vom Kehlkopf und seinen Krankheiten)*
Laryngomalazie f laryngomalacia
Laryngometrie f laryngometry, measurement of the larynx
Laryngoparalyse f laryngoparalysis, laryngoplegia, paralysis of the larynx, laryngeal paralysis
Laryngopathie f laryngopathy, disease of the larynx
Laryngophantom n laryngophantom, artificial larynx
Laryngopharyngektomie f laryngopharyngectomy, excision of the larynx and pharynx
Laryngopharyngitis f hypopharyngitis, inflammation of the larynx and pharynx
Laryngopharynx m laryngopharynx, laryngeal pharynx, hypopharynx
Laryngophonie f laryngophony
Laryngoplastik f laryngoplasty
Laryngoplegie f s. Laryngoparalyse
Laryngoptose f laryngoptosis
Laryngopyozele f laryngopyocele
Laryngorhinologie f laryngorhinology
Laryngorrhagie f laryngorrhagia, laryngeal bleeding, haemorrhage from the larynx
Laryngorrhaphie f laryngorrhaphy; suturing of the larynx
Laryngorrhoe f laryngorrhoea
Laryngosklerom n laryngoscleroma
Laryngoskop n laryng[end]oscope, laryngeal mirror
Laryngoskopie f laryngoscopy
~/direkte direct laryngoscopy
~/indirekte indirect laryngoscopy
Laryngoskopiker m laryngoscopist
laryngoskopisch laryngoscopic
Laryngospasmus m s. Laryngismus
Laryngostenosis f laryngostenosis, laryngemphraxis, laryngeal stenosis
Laryngostoma n laryngostomy
Laryngostomie f laryngostomy
Laryngostomiekanüle f laryngostomy cannula (tube)
Laryngostroboskop n laryngostroboscope
Laryngostroboskopie f laryngostroboscopy
Laryngotom n laryngotome
Laryngotomia f s. Laryngotomie
~ superior superior (subhyoid) laryngotomy, thyrohyoid laryngotomy
Laryngotomie f laryngotomy, incision of the larynx

~/mediane median laryngotomy; laryngofissure
Laryngotrachea f laryngotrachea
Laryngotracheitis f laryngotracheitis, inflammation of the larynx and trachea
Laryngotracheobronchitis f laryngotracheobronchitis, inflammation of the larynx, trachea, and bronchi
Laryngotracheobronchoskopie f laryngotracheobronchoscopy
Laryngotracheoskopie f laryngotracheoscopy
Laryngotracheotomie f laryngotracheotomy
Laryngoxerose f laryngoxerosis, dryness of the throat
Laryngozele f laryngocele
Laryngozentese f laryngocentesis, puncture of the larynx
Larynx m larynx *(Zusammensetzungen s. unter Kehlkopf)*
Larynx... *s.a.* Kehlkopf...
Larynxendoskop n laryngendoscope
Larynxmesser n *s.* Laryngotom
Larynxpemphigus m pemphigus of the larynx
Larynxsarkoidose f sarcoidosis of the larynx
Larynx- und Tracheaentzündung f *s.* Laryngotracheitis
Laserbehandlung f laser therapy
Laserchirurgie f laser surgery
Laseriridotomie f laser iridotomy
Laserphotokoagulation f laser photocoagulation
Laserverbrennung f laser burn
Läsion f lesion, injury, wound
~/raumfordernde space-occupying lesion *(z. B. des Gehirns)*
Lassafieber n Lassa fever
Lassafiebervirus n Lassa virus
Lassitudo f **visionis** ophthalmocopia, ophthalmokopia
latent latent, hidden, dormant, concealed, not manifest
Latenz f latency, dormancy
Latenzstadium n latent (latency) stage, latency; incubation [period]
Latenzzeit f latent (latency) period
Lateralaberration f lateral aberration
Lateralhernie f lateral (indirect, oblique) hernia
Lateralinfarkt m lateral infarction
Lateralnystagmus m lateral nystagmus
Lateralsinus m lateral sinus
Lateralsinusthrombose f lateral sinus thrombosis
Lateralsklerose f lateral sclerosis
~/amyotrophe amyotrophic lateral sclerosis, Charcot's disease (syndrome)
Lateralthrombus m lateral thrombus
Lateralwurzelabszeß m lateral root abscess *(Zahnwurzel)*
Lateroabdominalposition f latero-abdominal position
Laterodeviation f laterodeviation
Lateroduktion f lateroduction *(Seitwärtsbewegung z. B. des Auges)*
Lateroflexion f lateroflexion *(Seitwärtsbewegung z. B. der Gebärmutter)*
Lateropulsion f lateropulsion *(Symptom bei Parkinsonismus)*
Laterotorsion f laterotorsion
Lateroversion f lateroversion, lateriversion *(Seitwärtsbewegung z. B. der Gebärmutter)*
Latexagglutinationstest m latex agglutination test
Latexfixationstest m latex fixation test
Latexpartikelagglutination f latex particle agglutination
Lathyrismus m lathyrism *(chronische Vergiftung durch die Platterbse Lathyrus)* ● **~ bewirkend** lathyrogenic
laudabel laudable, commendable, healthy
***dl*-Laudanin** n *dl*-laudanine *(Opiumalkaloid)*
***l*-Laudanin** n laudanidine *(Opiumalkaloid)*
Laudanosin n laudanosine *(Opiumalkaloid)*
Laudanum n laudanum *(Opiumtinktur)*
Laufbandergometer n treadmill ergometer
laufen/Amok to run amok
laufend suppurating, discharging, running *(z. B. eitrige Wunde)*
Laufepilepsie f procursive epilepsy
Laufgips m walking cast
Lauftrieb m dromomania, drapetomania, mania for roaming; insane vagabondage *(motorische Unruhe bei Epileptikern)*
Lauge f 1. lye, base, alkaline solution; 2. liquor
Laurence-Moon-Biedl-Bardet-Syndrom n Laurence-Moon-Biedl syndrome *(Erbleiden)*
Laus f louse, pediculus, Phthir[i]us ● **durch Läuse bedingt (hervorgerufen)** louse-borne
Läuseangst f pediculophobia, phthiriophobia
Läusebefall m pediculation, lice infestation, phthiriasis, lousiness
Läuseei n nit
Läuseinfektion f *s.* Läusebefall
läuseinfiziert lousy
Läusekrankheit f pediculosis, lousiness
Läusemittel n lousicide, pediculicide, antiphthiriac [agent]
Läuserückfallfieber n lice relapsing fever
Laut m sound; tone
lautbildend phonatory
Lautbildung f phonation
Lautbildungsstörung f malarticulation, defective production of sounds
lautbildungsunfähig anarthric
Lautbildungsunfähigkeit f anarthria
Lautempfindung f sound perception
Lautlehre f phonetics
lautlich phon[et]ic
Lautmalerei f onomatopoiesis, formation of meaningless words
Lautnachahmung f onomatopoiesis, imitation of sounds
Lautverwechslung f paralalia, pararthria *(Sprachstörung)*
Lautwahrnehmung f sound perception
lauwarm lukewarm

Lavage

Lavage *f* lavage, lavation *(z. B. einer Wunde)*
Lävodopa *n* laevodopa *(Antiparkinsonmittel)*
Lävoduktion *f* laevoduction
Lävokardie *f* laevocardia
Lävokardiogramm *n* laevo[cardio]gram
Lävothyroxin *n* laevothyroxine *(Schilddrüsenhormon)*
Lävotorsion *f* laevotorsion
Lävulin *n* laevulin *(Zwischenprodukt der Inulinspaltung)*
Lävulinsäure *f* laevulinic acid
Lävulosämie *f* laevulosaemia
Lävulose *f* laevulose, fructose, fruit sugar
Lävulosebelastungstest *m* laevulose tolerance test
Lävulosetest *m* laevulose test
Lävulosurie *f* laevulosuria, fructosuria
Laxans *n* laxative [agent], aperient [agent], purgative
~/vegetabiles vegetable laxative
Laxantiengebrauch *m* laxative (purgative) use
Laxantienmißbrauch *m* laxative (purgative) abuse
Laxativ[um] *n s.* Laxans
Laxheit *f* laxity
laxierend laxative
Lazarett *n* lazaret[te], military hospital
Lazarettfieber *n* hospital fever
Lazarettschiff *n* hospital ship
Lazarettzug *m* hospital train
Lazeration *f* 1. laceration, tearing; 2. laceration *(Wunde)*
Lazerationsektropium *n* laceration ectropion *(der Gebärmutter)*
lazerieren to lacerate, to wound by tearing
lazeriert lacerated, torn
LD *s.* Dosis/letale
LD 50 *s.* Dosis/mittlere letale
LD 100 *s.* Dosis/absolut tödliche
L-Dopa *n* laevodopa *(Antiparkinsonmittel)*
L.E. *s.* Lupus erythematodes
leben to live, to be alive
~/nach Diät to diet
~/von etwas to live on something
Leben *n* life ● **am ~ bleiben** to survive ● **am ~ erhalten** to keep alive ● **das ganze ~ andauernd (anhaltend)** lifelong ● **einen Patienten am ~ erhalten** to bring a patient through alive ● **im ~** in vivo *(z. B. Versuch)* ● **sich das ~ nehmen** to commit suicide ● **während des Lebens** intravital ● **wieder zum ~ erwecken** to reanimate ● **~ zerstörend** life-destroying
~/langes longevity
lebend living, live
~/bei hohen Temperaturen thermobiotic
~/bei Sauerstoffmangel microaerophilic
~/im Blut sanguicolous *(z. B. Malariaparasiten)*
~/im Kot coprozoic
~/in Monogamie monogamic, monogamous
~/in Polygamie polygamous
~/in Symbiose symbiotic
~/in totem Gewebe necrophilous *(Bakterien)*
~/von Blut sanguivorous
~/von faulenden Stoffen saprophytic, saprophagous
Lebendfarbstoff *m* vital stain (dye)
Lebendfärbung *f* vital staining
lebendgebärend viviparous
lebendgeboren live-born
Lebendgeburt *f* live (viable) birth
Lebendgeburtenziffer *f* natality
Lebendgewicht *n* live weight
lebendig living; alive
Lebendigkeit *f* vitality, liveliness, vivacity; mobility
Lebendimpfstoff *m* live vaccine
Lebendvirusimpfung *f* live-virus vaccination
Lebendzellenmikroskopie *f* biomicroscopy
Lebendzellkultur *f* biocytoculture
Lebensaktivität *f* vital activity
Lebensbedingungen *fpl* living conditions, conditions of live ● **gesunde ~ schaffen** to sanitize
lebensbedrohend life-threatening
Lebensdauer *f* life[-time], life-span ● **von langer ~** vital
~/lange vitality
Lebenseinheit *f* biophore
Lebensenergie *f* vital energy
lebenserhaltend preserving life; vital
Lebenserhaltungstrieb *m* instinct of self-preservation
Lebenserwartung *f* life expectancy, expectation of life
~/mittlere mean afterlifetime (expectation of life)
lebensfähig viable
~/nicht non-viable
Lebensfähigkeit *f* viability; vitality
Lebensfunktion *f* vital function
lebensgefährlich dangerous [to life], perilous; critical
Lebenskraft *f* vital force (energy), vitality, bioenergy
lebenskräftig viable, vital
lebenslang lifelong
Lebensmittel *npl* food[-stuffs], aliment, nutriment
Lebensmittelvergiftung *f* food poisoning, bromatotoxism, poisoning by food
~ durch Botulismustoxin botulism
~ durch Salmonellen salmonellal food poisoning
~ durch Staphylokokken staphylococcal food poisoning
lebensmüde weary (tired) of life
lebensnotwendig necessary to life
Lebensrhythmus *m* life (biological) rhythm
Lebenstätigkeit *f* vital activity
lebensunfähig non-viable
Lebensunfähigkeit *f* non-viability
Lebensweise *f* way of life (living)
~/geregelte (gesundheitsgemäße) regime[n]
~/ungesunde unhealthy [way of] life
~/vegetarische vegetarianism
lebenswichtig vital, essential
Lebenszyklus *m* life cycle

~ **mit einem Wirt** monoxenia
Leber f liver, hepar *(s.a. unter Hepar)* ● **die** ~ **bevorzugend** hepatotropic *(z. B. Parasiten)* ● **durch die** ~ transhepatic ● **neben der** ~ parahepatic ● **unter der** ~ subhepatic ● **von der** ~ **stammend** hepatogenic, hepatogenous ● **von der** ~ **weg[führend]** hepatopetal
~/**knotige** nodular liver
~/**zirrhotische** cirrhotic liver
Leberabbau[stoffwechsel] m hepatic catabolism
Leberabszeß m liver (hepatic) abscess, hepatophyma; suppurative hepatitis
~/**pyogener** hepatic pyogenic abscess
Leberabtastbild n **nach Isotopenmarkierung** liver scan
Leberabtastung f **nach Isotopenmarkierung** liver scanning
Leberadenom n hepatic (liver) adenoma, hepatoadenoma
Leberaffektion f liver affection
Leberamöbiasis f hepatic amoebiasis
Leberamyloidose f hepatic amyloidosis; sago (waxy, lardaceous) liver
Leberangiosarkom n hepatic angiosarcoma
Leberanheftung f hepatopexy, fixation of the liver
Leberanschoppung f hepatic engorgement, congestion of the liver
Leberapoplexie f hepatic apoplexy
Leberarterie f hepatic artery
~/**gemeinsame** common hepatic artery
~/**zusätzliche** accessory hepatic artery
Leberarteriendarstellung f hepatic arteriography
Leberarterien-Lebervenen-Fistel f hepatic artery-hepatic vein fistula
Leberarterienröntgen[kontrast]darstellung f hepatic arteriography
leberartig hepar-like, hepatoid
Leberaspirationsbiopsie f aspiration liver biopsy
Leberatrophie f hepatic atrophy, hepatatrophy, atrophy of the liver
~/**akute gelbe** acute yellow atrophy of the liver, Budd's cirrhosis, malignant jaundice, icterus gravis, Rokitansky's disease
~/**rote** red atrophy [of the liver]
leberauflösend hepatolytic
Leberausfall m hepatic (liver) failure
Leberbeteiligung f liver involvement
Leberbett n liver bed
~ **der Gallenblase** gall-bladder bed (fossa)
Leberbettnaht f liver bed suture
Leberbindegewebskapsel f s. Leberkapsel
Leberbiopsie f hepatic (liver) biopsy
Leberbiopsieprobe f hepatic biopsy specimen
Leberblindpunktion f blind hepatic biopsy
Leberblutung f hepatorrhagia, haemorrhage from the liver
Leberdämpfung f/**relative** relative hepatic dullness *(bei Perkussion)*
Leberdeazetylisierung f hepatic deacetylation *(von Stoffen)*

Leberdegeneration f/**fettige** fatty degeneration of the liver
Leberdekompensation f hepatic (liver) decompensation
Leber-Dickdarm-Band n hepatocolic ligament
Leberdistomiasis f hepatic distomiasis
Leberdurchblutung f hepatic (liver) blood flow
Leberdystrophie f hepatic (liver) dystrophy
Leberechinokokkose f hepatic hydatid disease
Leberechinokokkuszyste f echinococcal hepatic cyst
Leberegel m hepatic (liver) fluke, clonorchid fluke, Distomum hepaticum
~/**chinesischer** Clonorchis sinensis
Leberegelbefall m clonorchiasis *(durch Clonorchis sinensis)*; opisthorchiasis, opisthorchosis *(durch Opisthorchis felineus)*; fascioliasis, liver rot *(durch Fasciola hepatica)*
Leberegelkrankheit f/**ostasiatische** s. Leberegelbefall
Leberegellarve f cercarian
Leberentzündung f hepatitis, inflammation of the liver *(Zusammensetzungen s. unter Hepatitis)*
Leberenzephalopathie f hepatic (liver) encephalopathy
Leberenzym n hepatic (liver) enzyme
Leberenzyminduktion f hepatic enzyme induction
Leberenzymsynthese f hepatic enzyme synthesis
Lebererkrankung f hepatic (liver) disease, hepatopathy
~/**bösartige** hepatic malignancy
Lebererweichung f hepatomalacia, softening of the liver
Leberextrakt m liver extract
Leberextraktbehandlung f hepatotherapy
Leberfistel f hepatic (liver) fistula
Leberfistelung f[/**operative**] hepatostomy
Leberfixation f hepatopexy, fixation of the liver
Leberfleck m liver spot, naevus
~ **der Haut** lentigo
Leberfunktion f hepatic (liver) function
Leberfunktionsprobe f liver-function test
Leberfunktionsstörung f liver disorder (dysfunction), hepatic function disturbance
Leberfunktionstest m liver-function test
Lebergalle f A bile *(Galle aus dem Gallengang)*
Lebergallenblasengang m choledochus, common (bile) duct
Lebergang m hepatic duct
~/**gemeinsamer** common hepatic duct
~/**linker** left hepatic duct
~/**rechter** right hepatic duct
Lebergangsgalle f C bile
Lebergang-Zwölffingerdarm-Anastomose f hepatoduodenostomy
Lebergang-Zwölffingerdarm-Fistelung f[/**operative**] hepatoduodenostomy
Lebergefäß n hepatic vessel
Lebergeflecht n hepatic plexus

Lebergeruch

Lebergeruch m hepatic foetor, liver breath
Lebergeschwulst f hepatic tumour, hepatoma
Lebergeschwulstzelle f hepatic oncocyte
Lebergewebe n hepatic tissue
lebergewebsauflösend hepatolytic
Lebergift n hepatotoxin, liver toxin
lebergiftig hepatotoxic
Lebergiftigkeit f hepatotoxicity
Leber-Glukuronyl-Transferase-Aktivität f hepatic glucuronyl transferase activity
Leberglykogen n hepatic glycogen, liver sugar
Leberglykogenspiegel m glycogen liver level
Leberhaken m liver retractor
Leberhämosiderose f hepatic haemosiderosis
Leberinsuffizienz f hepatic (liver) insufficiency
Leberinterlobulararterie f interlobular artery of the liver
Leberinterlobularvene f interlobular vein of the liver
Leberinzision f hepatotomy, incision into the liver
Leberisotopendarstellung f radioactive liver scanning
Leberkapsel f Glisson's (hepatobiliary) capsule, capsule of the liver
Leberkapselentzündung f perihepatitis
Leberkapselpseudozirrhose f capsular pseudocirrhosis
Leberkatabolismus m hepatic (liver) catabolism
Leberkoma n hepatic (liver) coma, hepatic encephalopathy
Leberkrankheitsdiagnostik f liver disease diagnosis
Leberkrebs m hepatic cancer, carcinoma of the liver
Leberläppchen n liver lobule, lobule of the liver
 • unter einem ~ sublobular
~/anatomisches anatomic lobule of the liver
Leberläppchengallengang m lobular bile duct
Leberläppchenzentralvene f central hepatic vein, central vein of the liver
Leberlappen m hepatic lobe, lobe of the liver
~/linker left lobe of the liver
~/rechter right lobe of the liver
Leberlappenentfernung f[/operative] hepatic lobectomy
Leberleiden n hepatopathy, hepatic (liver) disease
leberleidend liverish
leberlos anhepatic
Lebermerozoit m hepatic merozoite (Malariaerreger)
Lebermetastase f hepatic (liver) metastasis, hepatic secondary
Lebernadelbiopsie f needle liver biopsy
Lebernaht f hepatorrhaphy; suturing of the liver
Lebernekrose f hepatic necrosis, liver [cell] necrosis (z. B. durch Giftwirkung)
Lebernervengeflecht n hepatic plexus
Leber-Nieren-Band n hepatorenal ligament
Leberonkozyt m hepatic oncocyte
Leber-Pankreas-Gang m hepatopancreatic duct

Leberparenchym n hepatic (liver) parenchyma
Leberparenchymerkrankung f/degenerative hepatosis
Leberparenchymikterus m hepatocellular jaundice
Leberparenchymschädigung f damage of the liver parenchyma
Leberpeliose f hepatic peliosis
Leberpforte f hepatic porta, portal hilum, porta [hepatis]
Leberpforten-Darm-Anastomose f hepatic portoenterostomy
Leberpräkoma n hepatic precoma
Leberpuls m hepatic pulse
Leberpulskurve f hepatogram
Leberpunktataustrich m hepatogram
Leberpunktion f hepatic (liver) biopsy
Leberresektion f hepatectomy, excision of the liver
Leberröntgen[kontrast]bild n hepatogram
Leberröntgen[kontrast]darstellung f hepatography
Leberruptur f hepatorrhexis, liver rupture, rupture of the liver
Lebersaugbiopsie f aspiration liver biopsy
Leber-Scan m liver scan
Leber-Scanning n liver scanning
Leberschaden m hepatic damage, liver lesion
Leberschistosomiasis f hepatic schistosomiasis
Leberschizont m hepatic schizont (Malariaerreger)
Leberschmerz m hepatalgia, hepatodynia, pain in the liver
Leberschnitt m hepatotomy, incision into the liver
Leberschrumpfung f scirrhosis of the liver
Leberschutztherapie f protective liver therapy
Leberschwellung f hepatic engorgement; enlargement of the liver, hepatomegalia, megalohepatia
Lebersenkung f hepatoptosis, dislocation of the liver; dropped (floating, wandering) liver
Lebersiderose f hepatic siderosis; iron liver
Leberspezialist m hepatologist
Leberspiegelung f hepatoscopy
Leberstärke f [hepatic] glycogen, animal starch (dextrin)
leberstärkebildend glycogenetic, glycogenous
Leberstärkebildung f glycogenesis, glycogeny
Leberstauung f hepatic congestion (stasis), congestion in the liver
Leberstein m hepatic calculus, hepatolith
Lebersteinentfernung f[/operative] hepatolithectomy
Lebersteinleiden n hepatolithiasis
Leberstiel m hepatic pedicle
Leberstoffwechsel m hepatic (liver) metabolism
Leberstörung f hepatic dysfunction, liver disorder (disturbance)
Lebersyphilis f syphilis of the liver
Leberszintigramm n liver [scinti]scan
Leberszintigraphie f hepatic scintigraphy, [radioactive] liver scanning

Lebertherapie f hepatotherapy
Lebertiefstand m s. Lebersenkung
Lebertran m cod-liver oil
Lebertransplantation f hepatic transplantation, liver grafting
~/**orthotope** orthotopic liver grafting
Lebertremor m liver flap, hepatic tremor
Lebertuberkulose f hepatic phthisis
Leber- und Milzerkrankung f hepatosplenopathy, disease of the liver and the spleen
Leber- und Milzvergrößerung f hepatosplenomegaly, hepatolienomegaly, enlargement of the liver and the spleen
Leberunterblutung f hepatic peliosis
Leberunterseite f inferior surface of the liver
Lebervene f hepatic vein
~/**linke** left hepatic vein
~/**mittlere** middle hepatic vein
~/**rechte** right hepatic vein
Lebervenenentzündung f hepatophlebitis, phlebhepatitis
Lebervenenröntgen[kontrast]bild n hepatic venogram
Lebervenenröntgen[kontrast]darstellung f hepatic venography
Lebervenenthrombose f hepatic vein thrombosis
Lebervenenverschluß m hepatic vein occlusion
Lebervenenverschlußdruck m wedged hepatic vein pressure
Lebervenenverschlußsyndrom n Budd-Chiari syndrome, hepatic vein occlusion (thrombosis)
Lebervergrößerung f hepatic enlargement, hepatomegaly, megalohepatia
Leberverletzung f liver injury
Leberversagen n hepatic (liver) failure, hepatic decompensation
Leberzelladenom n liver cell adenoma
Leberzellausfall m liver cell failure
Leberzelldysfunktion f hepatocellular dysfunction
Leberzelle f hepatic (liver) cell, hepatocyte
leberzell[en]auflösend hepatolytic
Leberzellenschaden m hepatocellular damage
Leberzellenuntergang m liver [cell] necrosis, hepatolysis (z. B. durch Giftwirkung)
Leberzellerkrankung f hepatocellular disease
Leberzellschädigung f hepatocellular injury
Leberzellschutzsubstanz f hepatocytoprotective substance
Leberzellversagen n liver cell failure
Leberzentralvene f intralobular vein [of the liver]
Leberzirrhose f hepatic (liver) cirrhosis, cirrhosis of the liver
~/**alkoholische** alcoholic cirrhosis
~/**atrophische** atrophic (Laennec's) cirrhosis
~/**biliäre** biliary (Charcot's) cirrhosis
~/**cholestatische** cholestatic cirrhosis
~/**gallige** s. ~/biliäre
~/**kapsuläre** capsular cirrhosis
~/**kardiale** cardiac (central) cirrhosis, cardiocirrhosis
~/**portale** portal cirrhosis, chronic interstitial hepatitis

~/**splenomegale** Hanot's cirrhosis (disease)
Leberzwischenläppchenarterie f interlobular artery of the liver
Leberzwischenläppchenvene f interlobular vein of the liver
Leber-Zwölffingerdarm-Band n hepatoduodenal ligament
Leberzyste f hepatic cyst
lebhaft lively, vivacious, active, quick; sanguine, sanguineous
leblos lifeless; inanimate, dead; unconscious (bewußtlos)
Lecksaft m linctus, lincture
Lederhaut f 1. corium, dermis, derm[a], cutis, [true] skin; 2. sclera, sclerotica, sclerotic coat (des Auges)
Lederhaut... s. a. Sklera...
Lederhautentzündung f scleritis, sclerotitis, scleratitis
Lederhauterweichung f scleromalacia
Lederhautfistel f sclerostomy
Lederhautfistelung f[/operative] sclerostomy (bei Glaukom)
Lederhautinzision f sclero[tico]tomy
Lederhautmesser n sclerotome, sclerotomy knife
Lederhautplastik f scleroplasty
Lederhautschnitt m sclero[tico]tomy
Lederhaut- und Bindehautentzündung f s. Sklerokonjunktivitis
Lederhaut- und Hornhautentzündung f s. Sklerokeratitis
Lederhaut- und Regenbogenhautentzündung f s. Skleroiritis
Leder- und Hornhaut f sclerocornea
Leeraufnahme f survey roentgenograph, plain radiograph
Leerdarm m jejunum
~ **und Krummdarm** m jejuno-ileum
Leerdarm... s. a. Jejunum...
Leerdarmentfernung f[/operative] jejunectomy, removal (excision) of the jejunum
Leerdarmentzündung f jejunitis, inflammation of the jejunum
Leerdarmeröffnung f[/operative] jejunotomy, incision into the jejunum
Leerdarmgekröse n jejunal mesentery, mesojejunum
Le-Fort-Fraktur f Le Fort's fracture (des Oberkiefers)
Lefze f lip
Legasthenie f legasthenia
legen/eine Naht to place (insert) a suture
lehmfarbig clay-coloured (z. B. Stuhl)
Leib m 1. body, corpus; 2. abdomen, belly
Leibbinde f [abdominal] binder
Leibeisbeutel m ice bag for abdominal use
Leibesfrucht f embryo[n]; interogestate, foetus (ab 3. Schwangerschaftsmonat) ● **ohne ~** afoetal
~/**lebensunfähige** abortion
~ **mit abnorm großem Herzen** macrocardius

Leibesfrucht

~ **mit abnorm kleinem Herzen** microcardius
~/**vertrocknete** papyraceous foetus
Leibesfrucht... s. Embryo... und Fetus...
Leibeshöhle f abdominal cavity, enterocoele, coelom
~/**außerembryonale** exocoelom
Leibesübung f gymnastics
Leibesübungen fpl physical (bodily) exercises
leiblich 1. somatic, somal (körperlich); 2. full, own (blutsverwandt)
Leibschmerzen mpl abdominal pain, belly-ache, enteralgia, enterodynia, colic
Leiche f corpse, cadaver • eine ~ eröffnen (zergliedern) to section
Leichenausgrabung f exhumation
Leichenbeschauer m coroner
leichenblaß livid
Leichenblässe f lividity, livor
Leichenblut n cadaver blood
Leicheneröffnung f autopsy, obduction, necropsy, necroscopy; postmortem [examination], coroner's inquest
Leichenfleck m livor mortis
Leichengift n ptomaine
Leichenhalle f morgue, mortuary
Leichenkälte f algor mortis
Leichenkammer f, **Leichenkeller** m postmortem room
Leichenmaterial n cadaver material
Leichenniere f cadaver[ic] kidney
leichenschändend necrophilous, necrophile
Leichenschändung f/**sexuelle** necrophilia, necrophilism
Leichenschau f postmortem [examination]; coroner's inquest, autopsy, obduction, necropsy, necroscopy
Leichenschauhaus n morgue
Leichenstarre f cadaveric rigidity, rigor mortis
Leichentuberkel m dissection tuberkel, pathologist's (prosector's) wart, postmortem wart, necrogenic verruca
Leichenuntersuchung f s. Leichenschau
Leichenverbrennung f cremation, incineration
Leichenwachs n adipocere, lipocere
Leichenwachsbildung f saponification (bei Leichenzersetzung)
Leichenwarze f s. Leichentuberkel
Leichenzergliederung f section
Leichnam m corpse, cadaver
leichtblütig sanguine, sanguineous
leiden to suffer
~/**an einer Erkältung** to suffer from colds
~/**an einer Krankheit** to suffer from a disease
Leiden n 1. affection, affliction, complaint, ailment; 2. illness, disease, malady, malum
~/**bösartiges** malignant disease
~/**familiäres** familial disease
~/**inneres** internal disease
~/**paralytisches** paralytic disease
leidend 1. suffering [from]; 2. ailing, sickly, ill
~/**an Albinismus** albinic
~/**an seniler Demenz** presbyophrenic
~/**an Toxinämie** toxaemic
Leidender m suffering patient
~/**an einer Neurose** neurotic
~/**an Krämpfen** convulsionary
~/**an Rheumatismus** rheumatic
leidenschaftlich passionate, intemperate; enthusiastic
Leimschnüffeln n glue sniffing (zur Rauscherzeugung)
Leinenfaden m linen thread
Leinentuchtasche f canvas roll (für Instrumente)
Leinsamen m linseed
Leinwand f/**zerzupfte** lint (als Verbandstoff verwendet)
Leiodermie f leiodermia
Leiofibromyom n s. Leiomyofibrom
Leiomyoblastom n leiomyoblastoma (gutartige Muskelfasergeschwulst)
Leiomyofibrom n leiomyofibroma (gutartige Bindegewebs- und Muskelfasergeschwulst)
Leiomyom n leiomyoma (gutartige Geschwulst aus glatten Muskelfasern)
Leiomyomatose f leiomyomatosis (Häufung von Leiomyomen)
Leiomyomatosis f **diffusa pulmonum** pulmonary lymphangiomyomatosis
Leiomyosarkom n leiomyosarcoma (bösartige Geschwulst)
leiser werdend decrescent (z. B. Herztöne)
Leiserwerden n **von Herzgeräuschen** decrescendo
Leishman-Donovan-Körperchen n Leishman-Donovan body (parasite)
Leishmania f **brasiliensis** Leishmania brasiliensis (peruviana) (Erreger der Espundia)
~ **donovani** Leishmania donovani (Erreger der Kala-Azar)
~ **infantum** Leishmania infantum (Erreger der Kinderleishmaniose)
~ **tropica** Leishmania tropica (Erreger der Orientbeule)
leishmanial leishmanial
Leishmaniamikroorganismus m leishmanial micro-organism
Leishmaniapseudozyste f leishmanial pseudocyst
Leishmaniasis f leishmaniasis, leishmaniosis, date sore
~ **cutanea (cutis)** cutaneous leishmaniasis, oriental sore, Aleppo boil (button), Jeddah ulcer
~ **furunculosa** tropical sore
~ **infantum** infantile leishmaniasis
~/**südamerikanische** South American leishmaniasis
~ **tropica** tropical sore
Leishmanid n leishmanid
Leishmanieninfektion f s. Leishmaniasis
leishmanientötend leishmanicidal
Leishmanin n leishmanin
Leishmaninallergie f leishmanin sensitivity
Leishmanin-Hauttest m leishmanin [skin] test
Leishmaniose f s. Leishmaniasis

Leishmanoid n leishmanoid *(Hautsymptom bei Leishmaniose)*
Leiste f 1. groin, inguen, inguinal region *(Körperregion)*; 2. s. Crista
Leisten... s. a. Inguinal...
Leistenband n inguinal (Poupart's) ligament
Leistenbeuge f groin
Leistenbruch m inguinal (groin) hernia
~ **bei der Frau** Nuck's hydrocele *(bei offenem Processus vaginalis peritonei)*
~/**direkter** direct hernia
~ **im Samenstrangbereich** funicular hernia
~/**in die großen Schamlippen eingetretener** labial hernia
~/**indirekter** indirect (oblique) hernia
~/**intermuskulärer (interparietaler)** intermuscular (interstitial) hernia, interparietal hernia
Leistenbruchband n hernia bandage (truss)
Leistenbruchgebiet n inguinal hernial region
Leistenbruchoperation f/**Bassinische** Bassini's (hernia) operation, Bassini's herniotomy
Leistenbruchplastik f inguinal hernioplasty
Leistendrüse f inguinal gland
Leistendrüsenentzündung f s. Leistenlymphknotenentzündung
Leistengegend f inguinal region, groin, inguen
● **über der** ~ suprainguinal ● **unter der** ~ subinguinal
Leistengrube f inguinal fossa (fovea, groove)
~/**äußere** external inguinal fossa
~ **des Bauchfells/äußere** lateral inguinal fossa (fovea)
~ **des Bauchfells/innere** medial inguinal fossa (fovea)
~/**innere** internal inguinal fossa
Leistenhoden m inguinal testis, retained (undescended) testis, orchiocele
Leistenlymphknotenentzündung f inguinal [lymph] adenitis, bubonadenitis
Leistenlymphknotenerkrankung f inguinal [lymph] adenopathy
Leistenreflex m inguinal reflex, Geigel's (obliquus) reflex
Leistenring m inguinal (abdominal) ring
~/**äußerer** external inguinal (abdominal) ring, superficial (subcutaneous) inguinal ring
~/**innerer** internal inguinal (abdominal) ring, deep (abdominal) inguinal ring
Leistenschmerz m inguinodynia, pain in the groin, bubonalgia
Leistenschnitt m/**schräger** oblique inguinal incision
Leistensichel f inguinal falx, Henle's ligament, conjoint tendon
leistungsfähig efficient; potent; fit *(körperlich)*
~/**nicht voll** insufficient
Leistungsfähigkeit f efficiency, potency, functional capacity *(eines Organs)*
~/**mangelnde** insufficiency *(eines Organs)*
Leistungsmesser m 1. dynamometer *(für Körperkraft)*; 2. intensimeter *(für Strahlung)*
Leistungsmotivation f achievement motivation

Leistungsreserve f reserve in capacity, reserve force *(z. B. des Herzens)*
leistungsschwach insufficient
Leistungsschwäche f/**funktionelle** insufficiency *(eines Organs)*
leistungsstark efficient, able, fit *(Person)*; sufficient *(z. B. ein Organ)*
Leistungsstimulans n/**psychisches** psychic energizer, psychoactivator
Leistungsverlust m decrease in vitality
Leistungsvermögen n functional capacity
Leitband n gubernaculum
leiten to conduct *(z. B. Nervenreize)*
Leitfähigkeit f conductivity *(z. B. von Nervenbahnen)*
~/**elektrische** electroconductivity
Leitisotop n isotopic tracer (indicator), indicating isotope
Leitpaste f conducting jelly *(Elektroschocktherapie)*
Leitsonde f director
Leitsymptom n direct symptom, indicating sign
Leitung f conduction *(z. B. von Reizen)*
~/**saltatorische** saltatory conduction
Leitungsanästhesie f conduction [block] anaesthesia, nerve block, block anaesthesia
~ **der Sakralnerven** parasacral anaesthesia
Leitungsaphasie f conduction (commissural) aphasia
Leitungsbahn f path[way] *(der Nerven)*
Leitungsbündel n conduction bundle
Leitungsgeschwindigkeit f rate of conduction
Leitungsschwerhörigkeit f conduction deafness
Leitungssonde f catheter
Leitungsstörung f conduction disorder (disturbance, defect)
Leitungssystem n conduction system
Leitungsunterbrechung f block[age], blocking, blockade
Leitungsverzögerung f conduction delay
Lema f lema *(Sekret der Meibomschen Drüsen)*
Lembert-Naht f Lembert's suture *(z. B. am Magen, Darm)*
Lemniscus m lemniscus, band of fibres, fillet, laqueus *(z. B. von Nerven)*
~ **lateralis** lateral lemniscus (fillet), acoustic lemniscus
~ **medialis** medial lemniscus *(Leitungsbahn im verlängerten Mark)*
~ **spinalis** spinal lemniscus
~ **trigeminalis** trigeminal lemniscus, trigeminothalamic tract
Lemoparalysis f lemoparalysis
Lende f loin, flank, lumbus, lumbar region, haunch
Lenden... s. a. Lumbal...
Lendenarterie f lumbar artery
~/**unterste** lowest lumbar artery
Lendenbruch m lumbar hernia
Lendengeflecht n lumbar plexus
Lendengegend f lumbar region ● **über der** ~ supralumbar

Lendenlymphknoten 446

Lendenlymphknoten *m* lumbar lymph node (gland)
Lendenmark *n* lumbar part of the cord
Lendenmarkanschwellung *f* lumbar intumescence (enlargement)
Lendenmarkentzündung *f* ischiomyelitis, lumbar myelitis, osphyomyelitis
Lendenmarkröntgen[kontrast]bild *n* lumbar myelogram
Lendenmarkverdickung *f* lumbar intumescence (enlargement)
Lendenmuskel *m* psoas [muscle]
~/**großer** psoas major muscle, psoas magnus [muscle]
~/**kleiner** psoas minor muscle, psoas parvus [muscle]
~/**viereckiger** quadratus lumborum [muscle]
Lendenmuskelentzündung *f* psoitis
Lendenmuskelkrampf *m* psoas spasm
Lendenrippe *f* lumbar rib
Lendenrückenmarkentzündung *f* ixyomyelitis
Lendenschmerz *m s.* Lumbago
Lendenschnitt *m* **und Dickdarmeröffnung** *f* lumbocolotomy
Lendenwirbel *m* lumbar vertebra
~/**fünfter** basilar vertebra
Lendenwirbelkörper *m* lumbar vertebral body
Lendenwirbelsäule *f* lumbar column, lumbar part of the vertebral column
Leniens *n* lenitive [agent]
lenitiv lenitive, mitigating, soothing, assuasive
Lenkradverletzung *f* steering-wheel injury
Lens *f s.* Linse
Lensektomie *f* lensectomy
Lensometer *n* lensometer
Lentiglobus *m* lentiglobus
Lentigo *f* lentigo, cold freckle
~ **maligna** lentigo maligna
Lentikonus *m s.* Linsenkonus
lentikulär lenticular, lentiform
lentikulostriatal lenticulostriate
lentikulothalamisch lenticulothalamisch
Lentizele *f* lenticele, phac[ent]ocele, phacometachoresis
Leontiasis *f* leontiasis
~ **ossea** osseous leontiasis; megalocephalia
Lepra *f* lepra, leprosy, Danielssen-Boeck disease, Hansen's disease
~ **anaesthetica** anaesthetic (trophoneurotic) lepra, leprous neuritis
~ **arabicum** true lepra
~/**fleckige** macular leprosy
~/**knotige** nodular leprosy
~ **lacarina** lazarine leprosy *(Form der lepromatösen Lepra)*
~ **lepromatosa** lepromatous (malignant) leprosy
~ **maculoanaesthetica** maculoanaesthetic leprosy
~ **manchada** *s.* ~ lacarina
~ **nervosa** neural lepra (leprosy)
~/**tuberkuloide** tuberculoid (benign) leprosy; hansenid, neuroleprid

Lepraantiserum *n* antileprous serum
lepraartig lepromatous
Leprabakterium *n* Mycobacterium leprae, lepra (Hansen's) bacillus
leprabekämpfend antileprotic
Lepraforschung *f* leprology
Lepragesicht *n* lion's face
Lepraimpfstoff *m* antileprosy vaccine
Lepraknoten *m* leproma
Leprakolonie *f* leprosarium, leprosary
leprakrank leprous, leprotic, suffering from leprosy
Leprakrankenhaus *n* leprosarium, leprosary
Leprakranker *m* leper, lazar
Lepralehre *f* leprology
Lepramittel *n* antileprotic [agent], antileprosy drug
Lepraneuritis *f* leprous neuritis
Leprareaktion *f* lepra reaction
Leprarhinitis *f* leprous rhinitis
Lepraserum *n* antileprous serum
Lepraspezialist *m* leprologist
Leprastation *f* leprosarium, leprosary
Leprazelle *f* lepra cell
Leprid *n* leprid[e] *(Lepraausschlag)*
Leprolin *n* leprolin *(Lepravakzine)*
Leprolinprobe *f* leprolin test
Leprologe *m* leprologist
leprologisch leprologic
Leprom *n* leproma
lepromatös lepromatous
Lepromin *n* lepromin *(Lepratestsubstanz)*
Leprominanergie *f* lepromin anergy
Leprominhauttest *m* lepromin [skin] test
Leprophobie *f* leprophobia *(krankhafte Angst vor Lepra)*
leprös leprous, leprotic, lepromatous
Lepröser *m* leper, lazar
Leprosarium *n* leprosarium, leprosary
Leprostatikum *n* leprostatic [agent]
leptochromatisch leptochromatic
Leptomeningiom[a] *n* leptomeningioma
Leptomeningitis *f* leptomeningitis, inflammation of the pia and the arachnoid
Leptomeningopathie *f* leptomeningopathy
Leptomeninx *f* leptomeninx, pia-arachnoid, pi-arachnoid *(besteht aus Gefäßhaut und Spinnwebshaut)*
Leptomonas-Form *f* leptomonas, leptomonad [form] *(extrazelluläres Geißelstadium der Trypanosomen und Leishmanien)*
leptophon leptophonic
Leptophonie *f* leptophonia, weakness (feebleness) of the voice
Leptoprosopie *f* leptoprosopia, narrowness of the face
leptosom leptosomatic
Leptosomer *m* leptosome
Leptospira *f* **haemorrhagiae** Spirochaeta icterogenes
~ **icterohaemorrhagiae** Spirochaeta icterohaemorrhagiae

Leptospirämie f leptospiraemia
leptospirämisch leptospiraemic
Leptospirenausscheidung f im Urin leptospiruria
Leptospirenerkrankung f leptospirosis
leptospirentötend leptospirocidal
Leptospirose f leptospirosis
Leptospirosis f **icterohaemorrhagica** icterohaemorrhagic fever, icterogenic spirochaetosis, leptospiral (spirochaetal) jaundice, Weil's disease, Fiedler's disease
leptospirozid leptospirocidal
Leptothricosis f leptothricosis, leptotrichosis
Leptothrix f leptothrix *(Bakterienart)*
~ **buccalis** Leptothrix buccalis
Leptothrixinfektion f leptothricosis, leptotrichosis
Leptothrixkonjunktivitis f leptotrichal conjunctivitis
Leptotrichia f leptotrichia *(Gattung grampositiver, sporenloser Stäbchen)*
Leptotrichose f leptothricosis, leptotrichosis
Leptotrichosis f **conjunctivae** leptotrichal conjunctivitis
leptozephal leptocephalic, leptocephalous
Leptozephalie f leptocephalia
Leptozephalus m leptocephalus
Leptozyt m leptocyte *(dünner farbarmer Erythrozyt)*
Leptozytose f leptocytosis
Leriche-Syndrom n Leriche's syndrome, aorto-iliac occlusive disease
Léri-Syndrom n Léri type of osteopetrosis, melorheostosis *(Auftreten länglicher Verdichtungsherde in der Knochensubstanz)*
Lernen n/**assoziatives** associative learning
Lernstörung f learning disorder (disturbation)
lerntechnisch mnemonic
Lesbarkeitsminimum n minimal of reading
Lesbierin f lesbian
lesbisch lesbian
Leseblindheit f text blindness
Lesen n/**verlangsamtes** bradylexia
Leseschwäche f s. Leseunfähigkeit
Lesestörung f dyslexia
Lese- und Schreibschwäche f legasthenia
Leseunfähigkeit f reading disability, developmental dyslexia, logagnosia, alexia
Lesezentrum n visual word centre [for reading] *(Gehirn)*
letal lethal, l.
Letaldosis f lethal dose, LD
Letalfaktor m lethal gene
Letalität f lethality, mortality *(Verhältnis der Zahl der Todesfälle zur Erkrankungsfallzahl)*
Letalitätsrate f lethality rate
Lethargie f lethargy
lethargisch lethargic
letztgeboren ultimogenitary
Leuchtbakterium n photobacterium
leuchtend photogenic, phosgenic
Leuchtgasvergiftung f town gas poisoning
Leuchtschirm m fluorescent (fluoroscopic) screen

Leukodystrophie

Leuchtschirmbild n fluoroscopic image
Leuchtschirmfotografie f fluorography, fluororadiography
Leucokeratosis f **linguae** s. Leucoplacia
Leucoma n s. Leukoma
Leucoplacia f leucoplakia, leucokeratosis, leucoplasia; smoker's patches (tongue)
~ **buccalis** buccal psoriasis
~ **penis** kraurosis of the penis
~ **vulvae** leucoplakic vulvitis, kraurosis of the vulva
Leukämid n leukaemid
Leukämie f leukaemia, leuc[a]emia, leucocythaemia
~/**akute** acute leukaemia
~/**aplastische** aplastic leukaemia
~/**chronische** chronic leukaemia
~/**chronische lymphatische** chronic lymphatic leukaemia, lymphadenosis
~/**histiozytäre** histiocytic leukaemia
~/**leukämische** leukaemic (monocytic) leukaemia
~/**lympathische (lymphozytäre)** lymphocytic leukaemia, lymphatic leukaemia, lymphoid (lymphogenous) leukaemia
~ mit **Lymphosarkombildung** sarcoleukaemia
~/**monozytäre** monocytic leukaemia
~/**myeloblastische** myeloblastic leukaemia
~/**myeloische** myeloid leukaemia
~/**unreifzellige** undifferentiated leukaemia
leukämieartig leukaemoid
leukämieauslösend leukaemogenic
Leukämieentstehung f leukaemogenesis
leukämiehemmend antileukaemic
Leukämiemittel n antileukaemic [agent] *(Zystostatikum)*
Leukämiezelle f leukaemic cell
leukämisch leukaemic
leukämogen leukaemogenic
Leukämogenese f leukaemogenesis
leukämoid leukaemoid
Leukanämie f leukanaemia *(Blutkrankheit)*
Leukenzephalitis f leucoencephalitis
Leukergie f leukergy
Leukin n leukin
Leukoagglutination f leucoagglutination
Leukoagglutinin n leucoagglutinin
Leukoblast m leuco[cyto]blast, proleucocyte *(Leukozytenvorstufe)*
~/**kleiner** micro[leuco]blast
leukoblastisch leucoblastic
Leukoblastose f leucoblastosis *(Leukoblastenvermehrung im Blut)*
Leukocidin n leucocidin *(leukozytenzerstörende Substanz)*
leukoderm leucodermic, leucodermatous
Leukoderm n s. Leukoderma
Leukoderma n leucoderma; leucodermia, vitiligo, alphodermia, alphosis
~ **colli syphiliticum** collar of Venus
Leukodermie f s. Leukoderma
Leukodiapedese f leucopedesis
Leukodystrophie f leucodystrophy

Leukoenzephalitis

Leukoenzephalitis f leucoencephalitis
~/subakute sklerosierende subacute sclerosing leucoencephalitis (panencephalitis)
Leukoenzephalopathie f leucoencephalopathy
Leukoerythroblastose f leucoerythroblastosis, myelophthisic anaemia
leukogranulozytär leucogranulocytic
Leukokraurose f leucokraurosis
Leukolymphosarkom n sarcoleukaemia
Leukolyse f s. Leukozytolyse
Leukoma n leucoma, corneal opacity; walleye
~ **adhaerens** adherent leucoma
~ **unguium** leuconychia, onychopacity; gift spots
Leukomethylenblau n leucomethylene blue
Leukomyelitis f leucomyelitis
Leukomyelopathie f leucomyelopathy
Leukomyom n leucomyoma
Leukonychie f s. Leukoma unguium
Leukopathie f leucopathy
Leukopedese f leucopedesis
Leukopenie f leuco[cyto]penia, oligoleucocythaemia, oligoleucocytosis
~/maligne malignant leukopenia, agranulocytosis (z. B. durch Medikamentenwirkung)
~/perniziöse pernicious leucopenia
leukopenisch leuco[cyto]penic
Leukophlegmasie f leucophlegmasia, phlegmasia alba dolens, galactophlebitis (schmerzhafte weiße Beinanschwellung bei Thrombose); milk leg
Leukoplakie f s. Leucoplacia
Leukopoese f leucopoiesis
leukopoetisch leucopoietic
Leukoprotease f leucoprotease (Enzym)
Leukopsin n leucopsin
Leukorrhoe f leucorrhoea, leucorrhagia, whites
Leukosarkom n leucosarcoma
Leukosarkomatose f leucosarcomatosis
Leukose f leucosis (Wucherung des leukozytenbildenden Gewebes)
Leukoskop n leucoscope (Instrument zur Farbsinnuntersuchung)
leukotaktisch leucotactic
Leukotaxin n leucotaxine (erhöht die Kapillarpermeabilität)
Leukotaxis f leucotaxis
Leukotom n leucotome
Leukotomie f leucotomy, lobotomy (operative Durchtrennung der Stirnhirn-Thalamus-Verbindung im Gebiet des Marklagers)
Leukotomiemesser n leucotome
Leukotoxin n leucotoxin
leukotoxisch leucotoxic
Leukotoxizität f leucotoxicity
Leukotrichia f leucotrichia, whiteness of the hair
~ **anularis** ringed hair
Leukotrichose f s. Leukotrichia
Leukovirus n leucovirus
Leukovorin n leucovorin, citrovorum factor, folinic acid
Leukozyt m leucocyte, white [blood] cell, white [blood] corpuscle, WBC, wbc, mobile phagocyte

~/agranulozytärer agranulocyte, non-granular leucocyte
~/azidophiler acidocyte, acidophile leucocyte
~/basophiler basophil[e], basophile leucocyte
~/eosinophiler eosinophil[e], eosinophilic (oxyphilic) leucocyte
~/granulierter granulocyte, granular leucocyte
~/mononukleärer mononuclear leucocyte
~/neutrophiler neutrophil[e], neutrophilic leucocyte, neutrocyte
~/neutrophiler polymorphkerniger neutrophilic polymorphonuclear leucocyte
~/polymorphkerniger polymorph[ocyte], polymorphonuclear leucocyte (reifer neutrophiler Leukozyt)
~/stabkerniger stab leucocyte (cell), staff cell, band cell (form)
Leukozytenalloantikörper m leucocyte alloantibody
Leukozytenanhäufung f leucocytoma
Leukozytenanstieg m leucocytosis; abortive rise (am 6. Tag nach Bestrahlungstherapie)
Leukozytenantigen n/**humanes** human leucocyte antigen
leukozytenanziehend leuco[cyto]tactic
Leukozytenanziehung f leuco[cyto]taxis
Leukozytenarmut f s. Leukozytopenie
leukozytenauflösend leuco[cyto]lytic
Leukozytenauflösung f leuco[cyto]lysis
Leukozytenausscheidung f **im Urin** leucocyturia
Leukozytenausschüttung f **in das Blut** outpouring of leucocytes into the blood
leukozytenbildend leuco[cyto]poietic
Leukozytenbildung f leuco[cyto]poiesis
Leukozytendiagnose f leucodiagnosis
Leukozytendiapedese f leucopedesis
Leukozytenentwicklung f leucocytogenesis
Leukozytenerhöhung f hyperleucocytosis
Leukozytengift n leucocytotoxin
leukozytengiftig leucotoxic
Leukozytengiftigkeit f leucotoxicity
Leukozyteninfiltration f leucocytic (leucocyte) infiltration
Leukozytenlehre f leucocytology
Leukozytenmangel m s. Leukozytopenie
Leukozytenmangelangina f hypoleucocytic angina
Leukozytenmigration f leucocyte migration, migration of the leucocytes
Leukozytenmigrationshemmtest m leucocyte migration inhibition test
Leukozytenmigrationshemmung f leucocyte migration inhibition
Leukozytenmischkultur f mixed leucocyte culture
Leukozytenphosphatase f/**alkalische** leucocyte alkaline phosphatase
leukozytenschädigend leucotoxic
Leukozytenschatten m leucocyte cast
Leukozytenschema n/**Arnethsches** Arneth's classification (count formula, index)
Leukozytenstammzelle f leucocytoblast

Leukozytentherapie f leuco[cyto]therapy
Leukozytentransfusion f leuco[cyto]therapy
Leukozyten- und Thrombozytenmangel m im Blut leucothrombopenia
Leukozytenverklumpung f leukergy
Leukozytenvermehrung f hyperleucocytosis
~/**gutartige** leucocytosis
Leukozytenverminderung f hypoleucocytosis
Leukozytenwall m margination
Leukozytenwanderung f leucocyte migration
~ **durch Gefäßwände** leucopedesis
Leukozytenwanderungshemmung f leucocyte migration inhibition
Leukozytenzahl f white blood cell count, WBC count
~/**normale** isonormocytosis
Leukozytenzahlerhöhung f hyperleucocytosis
Leukozytenzählkammer f leucocytometer
leukozytenzerstörend leucotoxic; leucocytolytic
Leukozytenzusammenballung f leukergy
Leukozytenzylinder m leucocyte (white cell) cast (im Urin)
Leukozythämie f s. Leukämie
leukozytisch leucocytic, leucocytal
Leukozytoblast m leucocytoblast
Leukozytogenese f leucocytogenesis
Leukozytolyse f leuco[cyto]lysis
Leukozytolysin n leuco[cyto]lysin (leukozytenauflösender Stoff)
leukozytolytisch leuco[cyto]lytic
Leukozytom n leucocytoma
Leukozytometer n leucocytometer
Leukozytopenie f leuco[cyto]penia, oligoleucocythaemia, oligoleucocytosis
leukozytopenisch leucocytopenic
Leukozytopoese f leucocytopoiesis
leukozytopoetisch leucocytopoietic
Leukozytose f leucocytosis
leukozytotaktisch leucocytotactic
Leukozytotaxis f leucocytotaxis
Leukozytothrombopenie f leucothrombopenia
Leuzin n leucine, α-aminoisocaproic acid
Leuzinaminopeptidase f leucine aminopeptidase (Enzym)
Leuzinausscheidung f im Urin leucinuria
Leuzintoleranztest m leucine tolerance test
Levarterenol n levarterenol
Levator[muskel] m levator [muscle]
Levatorzeichen n levator sign
Levitation f levitation (Schweben z. B. von Menschen im Traum)
Lewisit n lewisite (hautschädigender Kampfstoff)
Leydig-Zelltumor m Leydig-cell tumour, interstitial-cell tumour, interstitioma
Lezithalbumin n lecithalbumin (Phosphorproteid im Eidotter)
Lezithin n lecithin
lezithinähnlich lecithoid
Lezithinämie f lecithinaemia
Lezithinase f lecithinase (Enzym)
lezithinreich polylecithal, lecithin-rich

Lezithoprotein n lecithoprotein
LH s. Luteinisierungshormon
libidinös libidinal
Libido f libido
Lichen m lichen (s. a. unter Flechte)
~ **albus** lichen albus, chronic atrophic lichenoid dermatitis
~ **chronicus Vidal** lichen simplex chronicus, neuroderm[at]itis
~ **infantum** s. Strophulus
~ **myxoedematosus** papular mucinosis
~ **psoriasis** chronic lichenoid pityriasis (chronische entzündliche Hautkrankheit mit roten Knötchen und Flecken)
~ **ruber accuminatus** pityriasis rubra pilaris, Devergie's disease
~ **scrofulosorum** papular scrofuloderma
~ **tropicus** summer rash, miliaria
Lichenifizierung f, **Lichenisation** f lichenification, lichenization (chagrinlederartige Veränderung der Haut bei Knötchenflechte)
lichenoid lichenoid, lichenous
Licht n light ● **durch** ~ **erzeugt** photogenic; phosgenic ● **durch** ~ **hervorgerufen** photic
~/**auffallendes** incident light
~/**durchfallendes** translucent light
~/**kohärentes** coherent light
~/**künstliches** artificial light
~/**natürliches** natural light
~/**ultraviolettes** ultraviolet light
Licht... s. a. Photo...
lichtabhängig photic
lichtadaptierend photopic
Lichtallergie f photo-allergy
lichtanpassend photopic
Lichtanpassung f photopia, light adaption (des Auges)
Lichtbad n light bath
Lichtbehandlung f phototherapy, treatment with light [rays]
Lichtbogenkonjunktivitis f arc-flash conjunctivitis
Lichtbogenstar m electric cataract
lichtbrechend refractive, refractile, dioptric
~/**doppelt** anisotropic (Muskelfasern)
~/**einfach** isotropic (Muskelfasern)
~/**nicht** non-refractive
Lichtbügel m electric cradle
Lichtdermatose f photodermatosis, photodermatitis, solar dermatitis
lichtdurchlässig translucent; non-opaque (Radiologie)
lichtelektrisch photoelectric
lichtempfindend photoperceptive
lichtempfindlich light-sensitive, photosensitive
Lichtempfindlichkeit f light sensitivity, photosensitivity, photaesthesia
~/**abnorme** phot[augi]ophobia, photodysphoria
Lichtempfindlichkeitssteigerung f der Haut photosensitization
Lichtempfindung f light perception; [iridoretinal] light sensation (z. B. bei Augendruck); phose, photism (bei Reizung anderer Sinnesorgane)

Lichterscheinung 450

Lichterscheinung *f* photopsia; visual aura; phosphene *(beim Druck auf die Augen)*
lichtersehend photoptic
Lichterythem *n* photoerythema
lichterzeugend photogenic, phosgenic, photic
Lichtkarzinogenese *f* photocarcinogenesis
Lichtkasten *m* electric heat cradle, apparatus for light bath treatment
Lichtkeratokonjunktivitis *f* electric ophthalmia, flash blindness (ophthalmia); flasheye
Lichtkrankheit *f* photopathy; actinodermatitis
Lichtleiter *m*/**faseroptischer** fibre-optic light guide
lichtliebend photophilic, photophilous
Lichtmessung *f* photometry
Lichtmikroskopie *f* light microscopy
Lichtpocken *pl* summer prurigo, recurrent summer eruption *(Bläschenbildung bei Sonnenbrand)*
Lichtreflex *m* 1. light (pupillary) reflex; 2. light reflex (spot) *(z. B. am gesunden Trommelfell)*
lichtscheu photophobic, lucifugous
Lichtscheu *f* photophobia, photangiophobia, photodysphoria, photaesthesia, phen[g]ophobia
Lichtschmerz *m* photalgia, photodynia
Lichtschock *m* photoshock
Lichtschutz *m* light protection
Lichtschwellenwert *m* visible minimum
lichtsensibilisieren to photosensitize
Lichtsinn *m* light sense (perception)
Lichtsinnprüfgerät *n* light sense tester
Lichtstärkemesser *m* photometer
Lichtstärkemessung *f* photometry
Lichtstrahlenbad *n* light bath
Lichtstrahlenbehandlung *f s.* Lichtbehandlung
Lichtstrahlenkrankheit *f* photopathy; actinodermatitis
Lichtstrahlenwirkung *f* actinism
Lichtüberempfindlichkeit *f* photophobia, photangiophobia, photodysphoria, photaesthesia
lichtübertragend photoconductive
lichtundurchlässig opaque, impervious to light, light-opaque ● **~ werden** to opacify
Lichtverschorfung *f* photocauterization
Lichtvorliebe *f* photophilia
lichtwahrnehmend photoperceptive, photoreceptive
Lichtwahrnehmung *f* light perception, photoperception
Lid *n* [eye]lid, palpebra, blepharon *(Zusammensetzungen s. unter Augenlid und Palpebra)*
Lid... *s. a.* Augenlid...
Lidabszeß *m* eyelid abscess
Lidanomalie *f* eyelid anomaly
Lidarterie *f*/**mittlere** medial palpebral artery
~/seitliche lateral palpebral artery
Lidaußenwinkel *m* temporal angle
Lidband *n* palpebral ligament
~/laterales lateral palpebral ligament
~/mediales medial (canthal) palpebral ligament
Liddrüsenentzündung *f* blepharadenitis

Lideinwärtskehrung *f* blepharelosis, ingrowing of the eyelid; entropion
Lidelephantiasis *f* palpebral elephantiasis
Lidentfernung *f*[/**operative**] blepharectomy
Lidfaserplatte *f s.* Lidknorpel
Lidflackern *n* cillosis, quivering of the eyelid
Lidfurche *f* palpebral commissure
Lidhalter *m* blepharostat, eyelid holder
~/Desmarresscher Desmarres' [eyelid] retractor
Lidhauterschlaffung *f* blepharochalasis, false ptosis
Lidheber *m*/**oberer** levator palpebrae superioris [muscle]
Lidhypertrophie *f* macroblepharia
Lidhypotrophie *f* microblepharia
Lidknorpel *m* tarsus, tarsal plate, palpebral cartilage ● **unter dem ~** subtarsal
~/oberer tarsal plate of the upper eyelid
~/unterer tarsal plate of the lower eyelid
Lidknorpel... *s. a.* Tarsus...
Lidknorpelentfernung *f*[/**operative**] tarsectomy, excision of the tarsus
Lidknorpelentzündung *f* tarsitis, inflammation of the tarsus
Lidknorpelerweichung *f* tarsomalacia, softening of the tarsus
Lidknorpelgeschwulst *f* tarsophyma, tarsal tumour
Lidknorpelinzision *f* tarsotomy, incision of the tarsus of the eyelid
Lidknorpelnaht *f* tarsorrhaphy; suturing of the tarsus
Lidknorpelrekonstruktion *f* tarsoplasia, tarsoplasty
Lidknorpelschnitt *m* tarsotomy
Lidkonjunktiva *f* palpebral conjunctiva
lidlos ablepharous
Lidlosigkeit *f* **des Auges** ablepharia; ablepharon
Lidmuskelkrampf *m* blepharospasm, winking (nictitating) spasm, nictitation
Lidokain *n* lidocaine, lignocaine *(Lokalanästhetikum)*
Lidptose *f* [eyelid] ptosis, dropping of the lid
Lidrand *m* lid margin, margin of eyelid
Lidrandentzündung *f* [marginal] blepharitis, palpebritis, tarsitis
~ mit Wimpernausfall ptilosis
Lidrandhautfalte *f*/**dicke** epiblepharon
Lidrandplastik *f* marginoplasty, tarsocheiloplasty
Lidrandrekonstruktion *f s.* Lidrandplastik
Lidrandverwachsung *f* ankyloblepharon
Lidretraktion *f* eyelid retraction
~ hinter den Augapfel capistration
Lidretraktor *m* eyelid retractor
Lidritze palpebral fissure (aperture)
Lidschlag *m* blink[ing]
~/seltener eyelid lag, infrequent blink
Lidschlagreflex *m* blinking reflex, blink response
Lidschluß *m* eyelid closure
~ bei Fazialislähmung/fehlender Bell's phenomenon (sign)
Lidschlußreaktion *f* Westphal-Piltz reflex (reaction, phenomenon)

Lidschlußreflex *m* [eye]lid closure reflex
Lidschlußunfähigkeit *f* blepharodiastasis, apraxia of lid closure
Lidschwellung *f* blepharoncus; eyelid oedema, blepharoedema
Lidspalte *f* palpebral fissure (aperture), eyelid fissura
Lidspaltenfleck *m* pinguecula
Lidspaltenrekonstruktion *f*[/operative] canthoplasty
Lidspaltenverkürzung *f* blepharophimosis; cantorrhaphy
Lidspaltenwinkel *m*/**mittlerer** medial angle of the eye
~/**seitlicher** lateral angle of the eye
Lidspalterweiterung *f* lagophthalmia; hare's eye
~/**operative** blepharotomy; canthoplasty
Lidspaltverengung *f* blepharostenosis
~/**operative** tarsorrhaphy
Lidsperrer *m* blepharostat, eyelid retractor
Lidumschlagfalte *f* palpebral fold
Lidumstülpung *f* nach außen ectropion
Lidvene *f* vein of the eyelid, palpebral vein
~/**obere** superior palpebral vein
Lidvergrößerung *f*/**abnorme** macroblepharia
Lidverklebung *f* blepharosynechia, blepharosymphysis
Lidverwachsung *f* blepharosynechia
~ **mit dem Augapfel** symblepharon
Lidwinkel *m* canthus, palpebral angle, angle of the eye
Lidwinkelentfernung *f*[/operative] canthectomy
Lidwinkelentzündung *f* canthitis, angular blepharitis
~/**innere** angular blepharitis
Lidwinkel[frei]lösung *f* cantholysis
Lidwinkelnaht *f* canthorraphy
Lidwinkelspaltung *f*[/operative] canthotomy
Lidwinkelverwachsung *f* syncanthus, ankyloblepharon
Lidzwinkern *n* blepharism
Liebe *f*/**lesbische** lesbianism, tribadism, sapphism
Liebesfurcht *f* erotophobia
Liebeswahnsinniger *m* erotomaniac
Liebeszwang *m* ero[to]mania, aphrodisiomania
liefern/einen Röntgenkontrast to cast an X-ray shadow
Liegekur *f* rest-cure
liegen/in den Wehen to [be in] labour, to be in throes
liegend:
~/**am Hornhautrand des Auges** pericorneal
~/**am Rande** peripheral
~/**am seitlichen Rand** lateromarginal
~/**an der Grundfläche** basal
~/**an der Halsvorderseite** precervical
~/**an der Rippeninnenseite** intracostal
~/**an normaler Stelle** normotopic
~/**auf dem Bauch** ventricumbent
~/**auf dem Perikard** epipericardial
~/**auf dem Rücken** supine

~/**auf der Pleura** epipleural
~/**außen** external, extrinsic
~/**außerhalb des endoplasmatischen Retikulums** interreticular
~/**dicht neben dem Magenpförtner** juxtapyloric
~/**hinten** posterior
~/**hinten und oben** posterosuperior
~/**hinter dem After** postanal
~/**hinter dem Augapfel** retrobulbar
~/**hinter dem Auge** retro-ocular, postocular
~/**hinter dem äußeren Gehörgang** postauditory
~/**hinter dem Bauchfell** retroperitoneal
~/**hinter dem Blinddarm** retrocaecal
~/**hinter dem Bronchus** retrobronchial
~/**hinter dem Brustbein** retrosternal
~/**hinter dem Dickdarm** retrocolic
~/**hinter dem Fersenbein** retrocalcaneal
~/**hinter dem Gaumen** postpalatine
~/**hinter dem Gebärmutterhals** retrocervical
~/**hinter dem Gelenkfortsatz** postcondylar
~/**hinter dem Glaskörper** retrovitreal
~/**hinter dem Herzen** retrocardiac, postcordial
~/**hinter dem Jochbein** retromalar
~/**hinter dem Kapillargebiet** postcapillary
~/**hinter dem Kreuzbein** postsacral
~/**hinter dem Labyrinth** retrolabyrinthine
~/**hinter dem Magen** retrogastric
~/**hinter dem Mastdarm** retrorectal
~/**hinter dem Mund** postoral
~/**hinter dem Mutterkuchen** retroplacental
~/**hinter dem Ohr** retroauricular
~/**hinter dem Olivenkern** postolivary
~/**hinter dem Rachen** retropharyngeal, postpharyngeal
~/**hinter dem Ringknorpel des Kehlkopfes** postcricoid
~/**hinter dem Schlüsselbein** retroclavicular, postclavicular
~/**hinter dem Tarsus** retrotarseal
~/**hinter dem Unterkiefer** retromandibular
~/**hinter dem Warzenfortsatz** retromastoid
~/**hinter dem Zwölffingerdarm** retroduodenal
~/**hinter den Rippen** postcostal
~/**hinter der Augenhöhle** retro-orbital, postorbital
~/**hinter der Augenlinse** retrolental retrolenticular
~/**hinter der Brust** retromammary
~/**hinter der Gebärmutter** retro-uterine, postuterine
~/**hinter der Harnblase** retrovesical, postvesical
~/**hinter der Hohlvene** retrocaval
~/**hinter der Kniescheibe** retropatellar
~/**hinter der Leber** posthepatic
~/**hinter der Luftröhre** retrotracheal
~/**hinter der Maxilla** retromaxillary
~/**hinter der Medulla oblongata** postbulbar
~/**hinter der Milz** postsplenic
~/**hinter der Nase** retronasal, postrhinal
~/**hinter der Nasenhöhle** retronasal
~/**hinter der Netzhaut** retroretinal
~/**hinter der Ohrspeicheldrüse** retroparotid

liegend

~/hinter der **Pupille** retro-iridian
~/hinter der **Pyramide** retropyramidal
~/hinter der **Pyramidenbahn** postpyramidal
~/hinter der **Rachenmandel** retrotonsillar
~/hinter der **Schilddrüse** retrothyroid
~/hinter der **Skapula** postscapular
~/hinter der **Speiseröhre** retro-oesophageal, postoesophageal
~/hinter der **Symphyse** retrosymphyseal, retropubic
~/hinter der **Vorsteherdrüse** retroprostatic, postprostatic
~/hinter der **Zentralfurche** postcentral
~/hinter der **Zunge** retrolingual
~/hinter einem **Ganglion** postganglionic
~/hinter einer **Sehne** retrotendinous
~/hinter einer **Stenose** poststenotic
~/hinter einer **Synapse** postsynaptic
~/im **Amnion** intra-amniotic
~/im **Auge[ninneren]** entoptic
~/im **Bereich der Nase** perirhinal
~/im **Blutserum** intraserous
~/im **Darm[kanal]** intra-intestinal
~/im **Ductus choledochus** endocholedochal
~/im **Embryo** intraembryonic
~/im **Epithel** intra-epithelial
~/im **Gehirn** intracerebral, intracephalic
~/im **Gesäßmuskel** intraglutaeal
~/im **Glaskörper** intravitreous, intravitreal
~/im **Großhirn** intracerebral
~/im **Handgelenk** intracarpal
~/im **Herzmuskel** intramyocardial
~/im **Hoden** intratesticular
~/im **Kehlkopf** intralaryngeal, endolaryngeal
~/im **Kleinhirn** intracerebellar
~/im **Knochen** intra-ossal, intraosseous
~/im **Knorpel** intracartilaginous, intrachondral, en[do]chondral
~/im **Labyrinth** intralabyrinthine
~/im **Magen** intragastric
~/im **Nasenrachen** postnasal
~/im **Nukleus** endonuclear
~/im **Ohr** entotic
~/im **Rachen** endopharyngeal
~/im **Rektum** intrarectal
~/im **Schädel[inneren]** intracranial
~/im **Sterben** moribund
~/im **Türkensattel** intrasellar
~/im **Wirbelsäulenkanal** intraspinal, intraspinous
~/im **Zellkern** intranuclear, endonuclear
~/im **Zungenbein** intrahyoid
~/im **Zwölffingerdarm** intraduodenal
~/im **Zytoplasma** intracytoplasmic
~/in den **Gelenkfortsätzen** intracondylar, intracondyloid, intracondylous
~/in den **Harnwegen** postrenal
~/in den **Kapillaren** intracapillary
~/in den **roten Blutkörperchen** intra-erythrocytic
~/in den **Scheitelbeinen** intraparietal
~/in den **Scheitellappen** intraparietal *(des Gehirns)*
~/in der **Augenhöhle** intra-orbital

452

~/in der **Brust** intramammary
~/in der **Fußwurzel** intratarsal
~/in der **Handwurzel** intracarpal
~/in der **Haut** intradermal, intradermic, intracutaneous, endodermal
~/in der **Hornhaut des Auges** intracorneal
~/in der **Körpermittellinie** median
~/in der **Mitte** intermedius
~/in der **Mundhöhle** intra-oral
~/in der **Muskulatur der Gebärmutterwand** intramyometrial
~/in der **Nähe der Pfortader** periportal, peripylic
~/in der **Nähe des Epigastriums** parepigastric
~/in der **Nähe des Zäpfchens** peristaphyline
~/in der **Nase[nhöhle]** intranasal, endonasal
~/in der **Netzhaut** intraretinal
~/in der **Oberhaut** intra-epidermal, intracuticular
~/in der **Paukenhöhle** intratympanic
~/in der **Peritonealhöhle** intraperitoneal
~/in der **Plazenta** intraplacental
~/in der **Pleurahöhle** intrapleural
~/in der **Ruhepause** interphasic
~/in der **Speiseröhre** intra-oesophageal
~/in der **Vorsteherdrüse** intraprostatic
~/in der **Wand** intraparietal
~/in der **Wange** intrabuccal
~/in der **weißen Augenhaut** intrascleral
~/in der **Zunge** intralingual
~/in einem **Bläschen** intrafollicular
~/in einem **Blutkörperchen** intraglobular
~/in einem **Bronchiolus** intrabronchiolar
~/in einem **Bronchus** intrabronchial, endobronchial
~/in einem **Erythrozyten** intracorpuscular, intraerythrocytic
~/in einem **Faszikel** intrafascicular
~/in einem **Gang** intraductal
~/in einem **Gelenk** intra-articular
~/in einem **Herzvorhof** intra-atrial, intra-auricular
~/in einem **Hohlraum** intracavernous
~/in einem **Kanälchen** intracanalicular
~/in einem **Kelch** intracalyceal
~/in einem **kleinen Bündel** intrafascicular
~/in einem **Läppchen** intralobular
~/in einem **Lappen** intralobar
~/in einem **Leukozyten** intraleucocytic
~/in einem **Lumen** intraluminal
~/in einem **Lungenbläschen** intra-alveolar
~/in einem **Meatus** intrameatal
~/in einem **Nerven** intraneural, endoneural
~/in einem **Nierenkelch** intracalyceal
~/in einem **Ohr** intra-aural
~/in einem **Wirbelkörperfortsatz** intraspinal, intraspinous
~/in einem **Zahnfach** intra-alveolar
~/in einer **Arterie** intra-arterial
~/in einer **Blase** intracystic
~/in einer **Drüse** intraglandular
~/in einer **Drüsenbeere** intra-acinar, intra-acinous
~/in einer **Epiphyse** intra-epiphysial
~/in einer **Fissur** intrafissural

~/in einer Fistel intrafistular
~/in einer Gelenkkapsel intracapsular
~/in einer Herzkammer intraventricular, endoventricular
~/in einer Hirnwindung intragyral
~/in einer Höhle intracavitary
~/in einer Kaverne intracavernous
~/in einer Schleimhaut intramucosal
~/in einer Wand intramural
~/in einer Zelle intracellular, endocellular
~/in einer Zisterne intracisternal
~/in Richtung der Achse axial
~/innen internal, intrinsic
~/innerhalb der Blutgefäße intravascular
~/innerhalb der Brusthöhle intrathoracic
~/innerhalb der Gebärmutter intra-uterine
~/innerhalb der Geschmacksknospen intragemmal
~/innerhalb der Harnblase intravesical
~/innerhalb der Harnröhre intra-urethral
~/innerhalb der harten Hirnhaut intradural
~/innerhalb der Hirnhäute intrameningeal
~/innerhalb der Leber intrahepatic
~/innerhalb der Luftröhre intratracheal, endotracheal
~/innerhalb der Lunge intrapulmonary
~/innerhalb der Milz intrasplenic
~/innerhalb der Nieren intrarenal
~/innerhalb des Auges intra-ocular
~/innerhalb des Bauchfells intraperitoneal
~/innerhalb des Bauchraums intra-abdominal, endoabdominal, endocoeliac
~/innerhalb des Beckens intrapelvic, endopelvic
~/innerhalb des Brustbeins intrasternal
~/innerhalb des Brustfells intrapleural
~/innerhalb des Harnleiters intra-ureteral
~/innerhalb des Herzbeutels intrapericardial
~/innerhalb des Herzens intracardial, intracardiac, intracordal, i. c.
~/innerhalb des Hodensacks intrascrotal
~/innerhalb des Knies intrageneric
~/innerhalb des Liquorraums intrathecal
~/innerhalb des Marks intramedullary
~/innerhalb des Nabels intra-umbilical
~/innerhalb des Nervus facialis intrafacial
~/innerhalb des Schädels intracranial, endocranial
~/innerhalb des Schulterblatts intrascapular
~/innerhalb einer Gelenkschleimhaut intrasynovial
~/innerhalb einer Mandel intratonsillar
~/innerhalb einer Membran intramembranous
~/innerhalb einer Synovialmembran intrasynovial
~/innerhalb eines Eileiters intratubal
~/innerhalb eines Muskels intramuscular, i. m.
~/innerhalb eines Rollhügels intratrochanteric
~/innerhalb eines Segments intrasegmental
~/innerhalb eines Wirbels intravertebral
~/links sinistral
~/mit dem Kinn nach hinten mentoposterior
~/mit dem Kinn nach vorn mentoanterior

~/nach der Regelblutung postmenstrual
~/neben dem Eierstock parovarian
~/neben dem Glomerulum juxtaglomerular
~/neben dem Kinn paramental
~/neben dem Ohr parotic, parotid
~/neben dem Olivenkern parolivary
~/neben den Epiphysen juxta-epiphysial
~/neben der Brust paramammary
~/neben der Papille juxtapapillary
~/neben der Sella turcica parasellar
~/neben der Wirbelsäule juxtaspinal
~/oberhalb eines Wirbelkörpers epineural
~/peripher eines Nervenkerns infranuclear
~/rechts dextral
~/rückseitig dorsal
~/rumpfwärts proximal, proximad
~/seitwärts lateral
~/über dem Brustbein episternal
~/über dem Zwerchfell epiphrenal, epiphrenic
~/über der Kniescheibe epipatellar
~/über der Paukenhöhle epitympanic
~/um das Auge periocular, periophthalmic
~/um das äußere Ohr periauricular
~/um das Claustrum periclaustral
~/um das Ependym periependymal
~/um das Gehirn pericerebral
~/um das Herz pericardial, pericardiac
~/um das Herzohr periauricular
~/um das Ohr periotic
~/um das Rektum perirectal
~/um das Steißbein pericoccygeal
~/um das Zäpfchen periuvular
~/um das Zökum pericaecal
~/um den After perianal
~/um den Aquaeductus cerebri periaqueductal
~/um den Augapfel peribulbar
~/um den Blinddarm perityphlic
~/um den Bronchiolus peribronchiolar
~/um den Bronchus peribronchial
~/um den Dickdarm pericol[on]ic
~/um den Eierstock periovarian
~/um den Eileiter peritubal, perisalpingian
~/um den Geburtstermin perinatal
~/um den gelben Fleck perimacular
~/um den Harnleiter periureteric
~/um den Herzvorhof periatrial
~/um den Kehlkopf perilaryngeal
~/um den Magen perigastric
~/um den Magenpförtner peripyloric
~/um den Mastdarm und den After periproctal, periproctic
~/um den Mund perioral
~/um den Nabel periumbilical, periomphalic, parumbilical
~/um den Nagel periungual
~/um den Rachen peripharyngeal
~/um den Samenstrang perifunicular
~/um den Schädel pericephalic
~/um den Warzenhof periareolar
~/um den Wurmfortsatz periappendicular, periappendiceal
~/um die Adventitia periadventitial

liegend

~/um die **Aorta** periaortic
~/um die **Axilla** periaxillary
~/um die **Bauchspeicheldrüse** peripancreatic
~/um die **Concha** periconchal
~/um die **Corona** pericoronal
~/um die **Dendriten** peridendritic
~/um die **Eingeweide** perienteric
~/um die **Epiglottis** periepiglottic
~/um die **Gallenblase** peri[chole]cystic
~/um die **Gebärmutter** periuterine, perimetric
~/um die **Geschlechtsorgane** perigenital
~/um die **Harnblase** pericystic
~/um die **Harnröhre** periurethral
~/um die **Hirnanhangsdrüse** perihypophyseal
~/um die **Hohlvenen** pericaval
~/um die **Hornhaut** perikeratic
~/um die **Kiefer** perignathic
~/um die **Leber** perihepatic
~/um die **Luftröhre** peritracheal
~/um die **Milz** perisplenic
~/um die **Niere** perirenal, perinephric
~/um die **Pleura** peripleural
~/um die **Scheide** perivaginal
~/um die **Schilddrüse** peristrumous
~/um die **Sehnervenpapille** peripapillary
~/um die **Speiseröhre** perioesophageal
~/um die **Synovia** perisynovial
~/um die **Uvula** peristaphyline
~/um die **Vorsteherdrüse** periprostatic
~/um die **Vulva** perivulvar
~/um die **Wirbelsäule** perispondylic
~/um die **Zahnwurzelspitze** periapical
~/um die **Zelle** pericellular
~/um die **Zunge** periglottic
~/um ein **Blutgefäß** perivascular
~/um ein **Ei** periovular
~/um ein **Ganglion** periganglionic
~/um ein **Gelenk** periarticular
~/um ein **Kanälchen** pericanalicular
~/um ein **Läppchen** perilobular
~/um ein **Ligament** periligamentous
~/um ein **Lymphgefäß** perilymphatic, perilymphangeal, perilymphangial
~/um ein **Neuron** perineuronal
~/um eine **Arteriole** periarteriolar
~/um eine **Bursa** peribursal
~/um eine **Drüse** periglandular
~/um eine **Fistel** perifistular
~/um eine **Geschmacksknospe** perigemmal
~/um eine **Hernie** perihernial
~/um eine **Kapillare** pericapillary
~/um eine **Linse** perilenticular, perilental
~/um eine **Mandel** peritonsillar
~/um eine **Papille** peripapillary
~/um eine **Rippe** pericostal
~/um eine **Schlagader** periarterial
~/um eine **Vene** perivenous
~/um eine **Wurzel** periradicular *(z. B. eines Nerven)*
~/um eine **Zahnwurzel** periradicular
~/um eine **Zelle** pericytial
~/um einen **Achsenzylinder** periaxonal
~/um einen **Azinus** periacinous
~/um einen **Follikel** perifollicular
~/um einen **Gang** periductal
~/um einen **Haarfollikel** peritrichial
~/um einen **Hilus** perihilar
~/um einen **Infektionsherd** perifocal
~/um einen **Kern** perinuclear
~/um einen **Lappen** perilobar
~/um einen **Nävus** perinaevoid
~/um einen **Nerven** perineural
~/um einen **Nierenkelch** pericalyceal
~/um einen **Sinus** perisinusoidal, perisinuous
~/um einen **Trochanter** peritrochanteric
~/unten und hinten inferoposterior
~/unten und in der Mitte inferomedial, inferomedian
~/unten und seitlich inferolateral
~/unten und vorn infero-anterior
~/unter dem **Brustbein** infrasternal
~/unter dem **Herzen** infracardiac
~/unter dem **Jochbein** infrazygomatic
~/unter dem **Kleinhirnzelt** infratentorial
~/unter dem **Nabel** infra-umbilical
~/unter dem **Oberkiefer** inframaxillary
~/unter dem **Ohr** infra-auricular
~/unter dem **Schlüsselbein** infraclavicular
~/unter dem **Schulterblatt** infrascapular
~/unter dem **Sehhügel** hypothalamic
~/unter dem **Unterkiefer** inframandibular
~/unter dem **Zahnfach** infra-alveolar
~/unter dem **Zungenbein** infrahyoid
~/unter dem **Zwerchfell** infradiaphragmatic
~/unter der **Achselhöhle** infra-axillary
~/unter der **Augenhöhle** infra-orbital
~/unter der **Brust** inframammary, postmammary
~/unter der **Brustwarze** inframamillary
~/unter der **Gaumenmandel** infratonsillar
~/unter der **Harnblase** infravesical
~/unter der **Haut** hypodermic, hypodermatic
~/unter der **Kniescheibe** infrapatellar
~/unter der **Luftröhre** infratracheal
~/unter der **Rinde** infracortical
~/unter der **Rippe** infracostal
~/unter der **Rolle** infratrochlear
~/unter der **Scheide** infravaginal
~/unter der **Schläfe** infratemporal
~/unter der **Schulterblattgräte** infraspinous
~/unter der **Stimmritze** infraglottic
~/unter einem **Nervenkern** infranuclear
~/vor dem **After** preanal
~/vor dem **Bauchfell** preperitoneal, properitoneal
~/vor dem **Becken** prepelvic
~/vor dem **Brustbein** presternal
~/vor dem **Gaumen** prepalatal
~/vor dem **Herzen** precordial, precardiac
~/vor dem **Hinterhaupt** preoccipital
~/vor dem **Kapillargebiet** precapillary
~/vor dem **Kehldeckel** pre-epiglottic
~/vor dem **Kehlkopf** prelaryngeal
~/vor dem **Kreuzbein** presacral
~/vor dem **Larynx** prelaryngeal
~/vor dem **Limbus** prelimbic

~/vor dem **Magenpförtner** prepyloric
~/vor dem **Mastdarm** prerectal
~/vor dem **Mittelohr** pretympanic
~/vor dem **Mund** preoral
~/vor dem **Oberkieferknochen** premaxillary
~/vor dem **Ohr** preauricular, pro-otic, anteaural
~/vor dem **Olivenkern** preolivary
~/vor dem **Schienbein** pretibial
~/vor dem **Schildknorpel** prethyroid[eal], prethyroidean
~/vor dem **Schlüsselbein** preclavicular
~/vor dem **Steißbein** precoccygeal
~/vor dem **Tarsus** pretarsal
~/vor dem **Tectum mesencephali** pretectal
~/vor dem **Tragus** pretragal
~/vor dem **Tränensack** prelacrimal
~/vor dem **Trommelfell** pretympanic
~/vor den **Mahlzähnen** premolar
~/vor den **Rippen** precostal
~/vor den **Skalenusmuskeln** prescalene
~/vor der **Ampulla** preampullary
~/vor der **Aorta** preaortic
~/vor der **Eieinnistung** prenidatory
~/vor der **Geschlechtsphase** prereproductive
~/vor der **Harnblase** prevesical
~/vor der **Kniescheibe** prepatellar
~/vor der **Leber** prehepatic
~/vor der **Luftröhre** pretracheal
~/vor der **Netzhaut** preretinal
~/vor der **Niere** prerenal
~/vor der **Pubertät** prepuber[t]al
~/vor der **Pyramide** prepyramidal
~/vor der **Regelblutung** premenstrual
~/vor der **Rückensaite** prechordal
~/vor der **Schilddrüse** prethyroid[eal], prethyroidean
~/vor der **Skapula** prescapular
~/vor der **Urwirbelsäule** prechordal
~/vor der **Zentralfurche** precentral
~/vor einem **Ganglion** preganglionic
~/vor einem **Krankheitsausbruch** premorbid
~/vor einem **Wirbel** prevertebral
~/vor einer **Synapse** presynaptic
~/**voraus** praevia
~/**vorn** anterior, anticus, a.
~/**während der Monatsblutung** intramenstrual
~/**weiter oben** superior
~/**zur Körperwand hin** parietal
~/**zwischen äußerer und innerer Kopfschlagader** intercarotic, intercarotid
~/**zwischen Bändern** interligamentary, interligamentous
~/**zwischen Brustkorb und Schulterblatt** interthoracicoscapular
~/**zwischen Chorioidea und Sklera** perichoroid[al]
~/zwischen den **Augenhöhlen** interorbital
~/zwischen den **Augenlidern** interpalpebral
~/zwischen den **Bläschen** interalveolar
~/zwischen den **Brüsten** intermammary
~/zwischen den **Brustfellen** interpleural
~/zwischen den **Brustwarzen** intermamillary

~/zwischen den **Fingergliedern** interphalangeal
~/zwischen den **Fingern** interdigital
~/zwischen den **Fußwurzelknochen** intertarsal
~/zwischen den **Gaumenknochen** interpalatine
~/zwischen den **Gelenkfortsätzen** intercondylar, intercondyloid, intercondylous
~/zwischen den **Gesäßbacken** internatal
~/zwischen den **Gesäßmuskeln** interglutaeal
~/zwischen den **Geschmacksknospen** intergemmal
~/zwischen den **Gießbeckenknorpeln** interarytenoid
~/zwischen den **Großhirnstielen** interpeduncular
~/zwischen den **Handwurzelknochen** intercarpal
~/zwischen den **Harnleitern** interureteric, interureteral
~/zwischen den **Herzvorhöfen** interatrial, interauricular
~/zwischen den **Hirnhäuten** intermeningeal
~/zwischen den **Hirnhemisphären** interhemispheric, inter[hemi]cerebral
~/zwischen den **Kammern** interventricular
~/zwischen den **Keilbeinflügelfortsätzen** interclinoid
~/zwischen den **Knöcheln** intermalleolar
~/zwischen den **Knochen** interosseous, interosseal
~/zwischen den **Kondylen** intercondylar, intercondyloid, intercondylous
~/zwischen den **Lippen** interlabial
~/zwischen den **Mittelfußknochen** intermetatarsal
~/zwischen den **Mittelhandknochen** intermetacarpal
~/zwischen den **Muskeln** intermuscular
~/zwischen den **Nasenknochen** internasal
~/zwischen den **Nasenlöchern** internarial
~/zwischen den **Nieren** interrenal
~/zwischen den **Oberkieferknochen** intermaxillary
~/zwischen den **Oberschenkeln** interfemoral
~/zwischen den **Olivenkernen** interolivary
~/zwischen den **Pupillen** interpupillary
~/zwischen den **Rippen** intercostal
~/zwischen den **Rollhügeln** intertrochanteric
~/zwischen den **Schambeinen** interpubic
~/zwischen den **Schenkeln des äußeren Leistenrings** intercrural
~/zwischen den **Schlüsselbeinen** interclavicular
~/zwischen den **Schulterblättern** interscapular
~/zwischen den **Wänden** intermural
~/zwischen den **Warzen** interpapillary
~/zwischen den **Zehen** interdigital
~/zwischen den **Zehengliedern** interphalangeal
~/zwischen der **Bauchfellduplikatur des Ligamentum latum** intraligamentary, intraligamentous
~/**zwischen Dornfortsätzen** interspinal, interspinous
~/**zwischen einer Scheidewand und einer Herzklappe** interseptovalvular

liegend 456

- ~/zwischen **Fäden** interfilar
- ~/zwischen **Fäserchen** interfibrillar
- ~/zwischen **Faszikeln** interfascicular
- ~/zwischen **Filamenten** interfilamentous
- ~/zwischen **Gängen** interductal
- ~/zwischen **Ganglien** interganglionic
- ~/zwischen **Gefäßen** intervascular
- ~/zwischen **Gelenkflächen** interarticular
- ~/zwischen **Herzkranzarterien** intercoronary
- ~/zwischen **Herzvorhof- und Herzkammerkontraktion** intersystolic
- ~/zwischen **Hirnwindungen** intergyral
- ~/zwischen **Höckern** intertuberal
- ~/zwischen **Kanälchen** intertubular
- ~/zwischen **Kapillaren** intercapillary
- ~/zwischen **Klappen** intervalvular
- ~/zwischen **kleinen Kanälchen** intercanalicular
- ~/zwischen **Knorpeln** intercartilaginous, interchondral
- ~/zwischen **Knötchen** intertubercular
- ~/zwischen **Körnerzellen** intergranular
- ~/zwischen **Lamellen** interlamellar
- ~/zwischen **Läppchen** interlobular
- ~/zwischen **Lappen** interlobar
- ~/zwischen **Membranen** intermembranous
- ~/zwischen **Nervenzellen** interneuronal
- ~/zwischen **Platten** interlaminar
- ~/zwischen **Röhrchen** intertubular
- ~/zwischen **Scheiden** intervaginal
- ~/zwischen **Schichten** interparietal
- ~/zwischen **Schulterblatt und Brustkorb** interscapulothoracic
- ~/zwischen **Segmenten** intersegmental
- ~/zwischen **Sigmaabschnitten des Grimmdarms** intersigmoid
- ~/zwischen **Tragus und Antitragus** intertragic
- ~/zwischen **Venen** intervenous
- ~/zwischen **Vorsprüngen** intertuberal
- ~/zwischen **Wänden** interparietal
- ~/zwischen **Wirbeln** intervertebral
- ~/zwischen **Zellen** intercellular
- ~/zwischen **Zotten** intervillous
- ~/zwischen **zwei Achsenzylinderfortsätzen** interaxonal
- ~/zwischen **zwei Ganglien** interganglionic
- ~/zwischen **zwei Herzklappenringen** interannular
- ~/zwischen **zwei Hohlräumen** intercavernous
- ~/zwischen **zwei Knoten** internodal
- ~/zwischen **zwei Ranvierschen Schnürringen** interannular
- ~/zwischen **zwei Zähnen** interdental

Lien *m* lien, spleen
- ~ **accessorius** accessory (supernumerary) spleen, lien[un]culus, splen[unc]ulus
- ~ **migrans (mobilis)** wandering (prolapsed, floating) spleen

Lien... *s. a. Milz... und Splen...*
lienal lienal, splen[et]ic
Lienculus *m* lien[un]culus, splen[unc]ulus
Lienomalazie *f* lienomalacia, splenomalacia, softening of the spleen
Lienomyelomalazie *f* lienomyelomalacia, splenomyelomalacia
lienorenal lienorenal, splenorenal, splenonephritic
Lienotoxin *n* lienotoxin, splenotoxin
Lienozele *f* lienocele, splenocele, hernia of the spleen
Lienterie *f* lientery, lienteric diarrhoea *(Durchfall mit Abgang unverdauter Nahrungsteile)*
Lienunculus *m* lien[un]culus, splen[unc]ulus
Ligament *n s.* Ligamentum
- ~/**Poupartsches** *s.* Ligamentum inguinale

Ligamenta *npl* **auricularia** auricular ligaments
ligamentartig ligamentary, ligamentous
Ligamentopexie *f* ligamentopexy *(Gebärmutterfixierung durch Kürzung des Ligamentum rotundum)*
Ligamentum *n* ligament, band; cord, chord[a] *(s. a. unter Band)*
- ~ **acromioclaviculare** acromioclavicular ligament
- ~ **acromioclaviculare inferius** inferior acromioclavicular ligament
- ~ **alare [articulationis atlantoaxialis]** alar odontoid ligament
- ~ **alare dentis (epistrophei)** *s.* ~ alare
- ~ **anococcygeum** anococcygeal ligament
- ~ **anulare radii** annular ligament of the proximal radioulnar joint
- ~ **anulare stapedis** annular ligament of the stapedial base
- ~ **apicis dentis** apical dental (odontoid) ligament, odontoid (suspensory) ligament
- ~ **Arantii** Arantius' ligament *(Überrest des Ductus venosus)*
- ~ **arcuatum laterale** lateral arcuate ligament [of the diaphragm], lateral lumbocostal arch *(zwischen 2. Lendenwirbelquerfortsatz und 12. Rippe)*
- ~ **arcuatum mediale** medial arcuate ligament
- ~ **arcuatum mediana** median arcuate ligament
- ~ **arcuatum pubis** inferior (arcuate) pubic ligament, subpubic ligament
- ~ **arteriosum** arterial ligament
- ~ **articulare** joint ligament
- ~ **auriculare anterius** anterior auricular ligament
- ~ **auriculare posterius** posterior auricular ligament
- ~ **auriculare superius** superior auricular ligament
- ~ **calcaneocuboideum plantare** plantar calcaneocuboid ligament
- ~ **calcaneofibulare** calcaneofibular ligament
- ~ **calcaneonaviculare** calcaneonavicular ligament
- ~ **calcaneotibiale** calcaneotibial ligament
- ~ **capitis costae radiatum** radiate (stellate) ligament
- ~ **capitis femoris** round ligament of the femur
- ~ **cardinale** cardinal ligament
- ~ **carpi dorsale** dorsal carpal ligament, extensor retinaculum [of the wrist]
- ~ **carpi radiatum** radiate ligament of the wrist
- ~ **carpi transversum** transverse carpal ligament, flexor retinaculum of the wrist

Ligamentum

- ~ **carpi volare** volar carpal ligament
- ~ **collaterale** collateral ligament
- ~ **collaterale carpi radiale** radial collateral ligament of the wrist [joint]
- ~ **collaterale carpi ulnare** ulnar collateral ligament of the wrist [joint]
- ~ **collaterale fibulare** fibular collateral ligament [of the knee], external lateral ligament of the knee [joint]
- ~ **collaterale radiale** external lateral ligament of the elbow [joint], radial collateral ligament of the elbow
- ~ **collaterale tibiale** tibial collateral ligament [of the knee], internal lateral ligament of the knee [joint]
- ~ **collaterale ulnare** internal lateral ligament of the elbow [joint], ulnar collateral ligament of the elbow
- ~ **conoideum** conoid ligament
- ~ **coracoacromiale** coracoacromial ligament
- ~ **coracoclaviculare** coracoclavicular ligament
- ~ **coracohumerale** coracohumeral ligament
- ~ **coronarium hepatis** coronary ligament of the liver
- ~ **costoclaviculare** costoclavicular (rhomboid) ligament
- ~ **costoxiphoideum** costoxiphoid (xiphocostal) ligament
- ~ **cricothyreoideum** cricothyroid ligament, cricocaval membrane, elastic cone
- ~ **cricothyreoideum medium** median cricothyroid ligament *(Band zwischen Ringknorpelbogen und unterem Schildknorpelrand)*
- ~ **cricotracheale** cricotracheal ligament
- ~ **cruciatum anterius** anterior cruciate ligament [of the knee]
- ~ **cruciatum genus** cruciate knee ligament
- ~ **cruciatum genus anterior** s. ~ cruciatum anterius
- ~ **cruciatum genus posterior** s. ~ cruciatum posterius
- ~ **cruciatum posterius** posterior cruciate ligament [of the knee]
- ~ **cruciforme** cruciate ligament of the ankle
- ~ **cruciforme atlantis** cruciate ligament of the atlas
- ~ **deltoideum** deltoid (internal lateral) ligament
- ~ **denticulatum** dentate ligament
- ~ **falciforme hepatis** falciform ligament of the liver
- ~ **fundiforme penis** fundiform ligament of the penis
- ~ **gastrocolicum** gastrocolic ligament
- ~ **gastrohepaticum** gastrohepatic ligament
- ~ **gastrolienale** gastrolienal ligament
- ~ **Gimbernati** s. ~ lacunare
- ~ **glenohumerale** glenohumeral ligament
- ~ **hepatocolicum** hepatocolic ligament
- ~ **hepatoduodenale** hepatoduodenal ligament
- ~ **hepatogastricum** hepatogastric (gastrohepatic) ligament
- ~ **hepatorenale** hepatorenal ligament
- ~ **iliofemorale** iliofemoral ligament, Y ligament [of Bigelow]
- ~ **iliolumbale** iliolumbar ligament
- ~ **incudis posterius** posterior incudal ligament
- ~ **incudis superius** superior incudal ligament
- ~ **inguinale** Poupart's (inguinal) ligament, Vesalius' ligament
- ~ **interclaviculare** interclavicular ligament
- ~ **interfoveolare** interfoveolar ligament, Hesselbach's ligament
- ~ **interspinale** interspinal ligament
- ~ **ischiocapsulare** ischiocapsular ligament
- ~ **ischiofemorale** ischiofemoral ligament
- ~ **laciniatum** flexor retinaculum of the ankle
- ~ **lacunare** lacunar ligament [of Gimbernat], Gimbernat's ligament *(vom Leistenband zum Pecten ossis pubis ziehend)*
- ~ **latum uteri** uterus broad ligament, mesodesma
- ~ **lienorenale** lienorenal ligament
- ~ **longitudinale anterius columnae vertebralis** anterior longitudinal ligament of the spine (vertebral column)
- ~ **longitudinale posterius columnae vertebralis** posterior longitudinal ligament of the spine (vertebral column)
- ~ **mallei anterius** anterior malleal ligament, anterior ligament of the malleus
- ~ **mallei laterale** lateral malleal ligament
- ~ **mallei superius** superior malleal ligament
- ~ **metacarpeum transversum profundum** deep transverse metacarpal ligament
- ~ **metatarseum transversum profundum** deep transverse metatarsal ligament
- ~ **metatarseum transversum superficiale** superficial transverse metatarsal ligament
- ~ **nephrocolicum** nephrocolic ligament
- ~ **nuchae** nuchal ligament
- ~ **ovarii proprium** [proper] ovarian ligament, utero-ovarian ligament
- ~ **palpebrale** palpebral (canthal) ligament
- ~ **palpebrale laterale** lateral palpebral ligament
- ~ **palpebrale mediale** medial palpebral ligament
- ~ **patellae** patellar ligament (tendon)
- ~ **pectinatum anguli iridocornealis** pectinate ligament
- ~ **phrenicocolicum** phrenicocolic ligament, costocolic fold
- ~ **phrenicolienale** phrenicolienal (lienorenal, splenophrenic) ligament
- ~ **pisohamatum** pisohamate ligament
- ~ **pisometacarpeum** pisometacarpal ligament
- ~ **plantare longum** long plantar ligament
- ~ **popliteum arcuatum** popliteal arcuate ligament
- ~ **popliteum obliquum** oblique popliteal ligament
- ~ **pterygospinale** pterygospinous ligament
- ~ **pubicum** pubic (Cooper's) ligament
- ~ **pubicum posterius** posterior pubic ligament
- ~ **pubofemorale** pubofemoral (pubocapsular) ligament
- ~ **puboprostaticum** puboprostatic ligament
- ~ **puboprostaticum laterale** lateral puboprostatic ligament

Ligamentum 458

- **puboprostaticum medium** medial puboprostatic ligament
- **pubovesicale** pubovesical ligament
- **pulmonale** pulmonary ligament
- **quadratum** quadrate ligament
- **radiocarpeum dorsale** dorsal radiocarpal ligament
- **radiocarpeum palmare** palmar radiocarpal ligament
- **reflexum** reflected (Colles') ligament
- **rotundum** round ligament
- **sacrococcygeum dorsale profundum** deep dorsal sacrococcygeal ligament
- **sacrococcygeum laterale** lateral sacrococcygeal ligament
- **sacrococcygeum posterius superficiale** superficial dorsal sacrococcygeal ligament
- **sacrococcygeum ventrale** anterior (ventral) sacrococcygeal ligament
- **sacroiliacum posterius breve** short dorsal sacroiliac ligament
- **sacroiliacum posterius longum** long dorsal sacroiliac ligament
- **sacrospinale** sacrospinous ligament
- **sacrotuberale** sacrotuberous ligament
- **sacrouterinum** uterosacral ligament
- **sphenomandibulare** sphenomandibular (sphenomaxillary) ligament
- **spirale cochleae** spiral ligament [of the cochlea]
- **sternoclaviculare anterius** anterior sternoclavicular ligament
- **sternoclaviculare posterius** posterior sternoclavicular ligament
- **sternocostale anterius** anterior sternocostal ligament
- **sternocostale posterius** posterior sternocostal ligament
- **stylohyoideum** stylohyoid ligament
- **stylomandibulare** stylomandibular ligament
- **supraspinale** supraspinal ligament
- **suspensorium** suspensory ligament, suspensory
- **suspensorium clitoridis** suspensory ligament of the clitoris
- **suspensorium mammae** suspensory ligament of the breast
- **suspensorium ovarii** suspensory ligament of the ovary, infundibulopelvic ligament
- **suspensorium penis** suspensory ligament of the penis
- **talocalcaneum anterius** anterior talocalcaneal ligament
- **talocalcaneum interosseum** interosseous talocalcaneal ligament
- **talocalcaneum laterale** lateral talocalcaneal ligament
- **talocalcaneum mediale** medial talocalcaneal ligament
- **talocalcaneum posterius** posterior talocalcaneal ligament
- **talofibulare** fibulotalar ligament
- **talofibulare anterius** anterior talofibular ligament
- **talofibulare posterius** posterior talofibular ligament
- **talonaviculare** talonavicular ligament
- **talotibiale anterius** anterior talotibial ligament
- **talotibiale posterius** posterior talotibial ligament
- **teres hepatis** round ligament of the liver
- **teres uteri** uterus round ligament, Fallopian arch
- **thyreohyoideum** lateral thyrohyoid ligament, hyothyroid ligament
- **thyreohyoideum medianum** middle (median) thyrohyoid ligament
- **tibiofibulare anterius** anterior tibiofibular ligament
- **tibiofibulare posterius** posterior tibiofibular ligament
- **tibionaviculare** tibionavicular ligament
- **transversum acetabuli** transverse ligament of the acetabulum
- **transversum atlantis** transverse ligament of the atlas
- **transversum cruris** transverse crural ligament, superior extensor retinaculum
- **transversum genus** transverse ligament of the knee [joint]
- **transversum perinei (praeurethrale)** transverse pelvic (perineal) ligament
- **transversum scapulae inferius** inferior transverse ligament of the scapula
- **transversum scapulae superius** superior transverse ligament of the scapula
- **trapezoideum** trapezoid ligament
- **triangulare dextrum [hepatis]** right triangular ligament [of the liver]
- **triangulare sinistrum [hepatis]** left triangular ligament [of the liver]
- **ulnocarpeum palmare** palmar ulnocarpal ligament
- **umbilicale laterale** lateral umbilical ligament
- **umbilicale mediale** medial (middle) umbilical ligament
- **umbilicale medianum** median umbilical ligament, vesicoumbilical ligament
- **venosum** Arantius' ligament *(Überrest des Ductus venosus)*
- **vestibulare** vestibular ligament
- **vocale** vocal ligament

Ligamentum-conicum-Spaltung f thyrocricotomy *(Luftröhrenschnitt)*
Ligamentum-latum-Schwangerschaft f intraligamentary pregnancy
Ligamentum-latum-Zyste f intraligamentary cyst, junctional cyst
Ligase f ligase *(Enzym)*
Ligatur f ligature, ligation *(z. B. eines Blutgefäßes)*
~/**absorbierbare** absorbable ligature
Ligaturfaden m ligature
Ligaturführer m ligature carrier

Ligaturklemme f ligature forceps
Ligaturnadel f ligature needle
Ligaturschere f ligature scissors
Ligaturträger m ligature guide forceps
Ligaturzange f ligature pliers
ligieren to ligate
limbisch limbal, limbic
Limbus m limbus, border, edge, margin
~ **corneae** corneal limbus (margin), corneoscleral limbus
~ **laminae spiralis osseae** limbus of the spiral lamina
Limbusbindehaut f limbal conjunctiva
Limbusfollikel m limbal follicle *(bei Trachom)*
Limen n limen, boundary; threshold
~ **insulae** limen insulae
~ **nasi** limen nasi *(Grenze zwischen Vorhof und eigentlicher Nasenhöhle)*
Linctus m linctus
lindern to alleviate, to relieve, to assuage *(z. B. Schmerzen)*, to palliate, to mitigate, to obtund, to soothe
lindernd alleviating, relieving, palliative, mitigating, lenitive
Linderung f alleviation, relief, palliation, mitigation, obtundation
Linderungsmittel n palliative [agent], lenitive [agent]
Linea f line *(z. B. an Knochen) (s. a. unter Linie)*
~ **alba** linea alba, white line
~ **alveobasilaris** alveobasilar line
~ **alveolaris** alveolar line
~ **alveonasalis** alveonasal line
~ **anocutanea** anocutaneous line
~ **arcuata ossis ilii** arcuate line [of the ilium]
~ **arcuata vaginae musculi recti abdominis** semicircular line [of Douglas]
~ **aspera femoris** linea aspera
~ **axillaris** axillary line
~ **axillaris posterior** posterior axillary line
~ **clavicularis** clavicular line
~ **costoarticularis** costoarticular line
~ **costoclavicularis** costoclavicular line
~ **dentata** dentate line
~ **epiphysialis** epiphyseal line
~ **facialis** facial (Camper's) line
~ **glutaea anterior** anterior gluteal line
~ **glutaea inferior** inferior gluteal line
~ **glutaea posterior** posterior gluteal line
~ **iliopectinea** iliopectineal line
~ **infracostalis** infracostal line
~ **infrascapularis** infrascapular line
~ **intercondylaris** intercondylar line
~ **intermedia [cristae iliacae]** intermediate line
~ **interspinalis** interspinal line
~ **intertrochanterica** intertrochanteric line
~ **intertuberalis** intertuberal line
~ **labialis** labial line
~ **mamillaris** mamillary line
~ **mediana anterior** anterior median line, anterior midline of the body
~ **mediana posterior** posterior median line, posterior midline of the body
~ **medioaxillaris** midaxillary line
~ **medioclavicularis** medioclavicular (midclavicular) line
~ **mediosternalis** midsternal line
~ **musculi solei** soleal (popliteal) line, line of the soleus muscle
~ **mylohyoidea** mylohyoid line (ridge)
~ **nasolabialis** nasolabial (nasal) line
~ **nuchae inferior** inferior nuchal line
~ **nuchae superior** superior nuchal line
~ **nuchalis terminalis** s. ~ nuchae superior
~ **obliqua cartilaginis thyreoideae** oblique line of the thyroid cartilage
~ **obturatoria** obturator line
~ **parasternalis** parasternal line
~ **pectinea** pectineal line *(des Oberschenkelknochens)*
~ **poplitea** popliteal (soleal) line, line of the soleus [muscle]
~ **scapularis** scapular line
~ **semicircularis [Douglasi]** semicircular line [of Douglas]
~ **semilunaris** semilunar line [of Spieghel], Spigelian line
~ **sinuosa analis** dentate (anorectal) junction
~ **sternalis** sternal line
~ **subcostalis** subcostal line
~ **temporalis inferior [ossis parietalis]** inferior temporal line [of the parietal bone]
~ **temporalis ossis frontalis** temporal line
~ **temporalis superior [ossis parietalis]** superior temporal line [of the parietal bone]
~ **terminalis [pelvis]** terminal (iliopectineal) line
~ **trapezoidea** trapezoid line (ridge) *(am Schlüsselbein)*
~ **umbilicoiliacalis** umbilico-iliac line
Lingua f tongue, glossa, lingua *(s. a. unter Zunge)*
~ **geographica** geographic tongue, wandering rash; benign migratory glossitis
~ **nigra** black tongue, lingua nigra
~ **plicata** plicated (fissured) tongue
~ **scrotalis** scrotal tongue
~ **villosa** hair[y] tongue; trichoglossia, glossotrichia, glossophytia
~ **villosa nigra** black [hairy] tongue
lingual lingual, glossal
Lingual... s. a. Zungen...
Lingualbiß m lingual occlusion *(Stomatologie)*
Lingualplexus m lingual plexus
Linguatulabefall m linguatuliasis, linguatulosis
Lingula f lingula
~ **cerebelli** cerebellar lingula, lingula of the cerebellum
~ **mandibulae** lingula of the mandible
~ **pulmonis** lingula of the lung
~ **sphenoidalis** lingula of the sphenoid
Lingulaentfernung f[/operative] lingulectomy
lingular lingular
Lingularesektion f lingulectomy
linguodental linguodental
linguogingival linguogingival, glossopalatine

Linguopapillitis

Linguopapillitis f linguopapillitis
Linie f line *(z. B. an Knochen) (s. a. unter Linea)*
~/anorektale anorectal line
~/Campersche Camper's line
~/isoelektrische isoelectric level [line]
~/Roser-Nélatonsche Nélaton's line *(Verbindungslinie zwischen dem vorderen oberen Darmbeinstachel und dem Sitzbeinhöcker)*
~/Spieghelsche Spigelian line, semilunar line [of Spieghel]
Linien *fpl* **gleicher Sehschärfe** isopters
Liniment n liniment, embrocation *(Arzneiform)*
Linin n linin *(Teil des Kerngerüsts)*
Linitis f **plastica** linitis plastica; leather bottle stomach
links left, on the left side, sinister, sinistral
Linksabweichung f laevoduction
linksäugig sinistrocular, left-eyed
Linksäugigkeit f sinistrocularity, left-eyedness
linksaurikulär sinistraural, left-eared
Linksdekompensation f backward [heart] failure
Linksdrehung f sinistrorotation, sinistrotorsion
linksfüßig sinistropedal, left-footed
Linksfüßigkeit f left-footedness
Linkshänder m sinistral, left hander
linkshändig sinistral, left-handed, sinistromanual
Linkshändigkeit f sinistrality, left-handedness, mancinism
Linksherz n left heart
Linksherzaneurysma n left ventricular aneurysm
Linksherzbelastung f left ventricle load (strain)
Linksherzdekompensation f left ventricular failure; backward [heart] failure
Linksherzdilatation f left ventricular dilatation
Linksherzdominanz f dominant left ventricle
Linksherz-EKG n sinistro[cardio]gram
Linksherzhypertrophie f left ventricular hypertrophy, hypertrophy of the left ventricle
~ mit Dilatation luxus heart
Linksherzinsuffizienz f left ventricular failure; backward [heart] failure
Linksherzkammerdruck m left ventricular pressure
Linksherzkardiogramm n laevo[cardio]gram *(Radiologie)*
Linksherzkatheterung f left heart catheterization
Linksherzröntgen[kontrast]bild n sinistrogram
Linksherzstauung f s. Linksherzinsuffizienz
Linksherzsyndrom n/**hypoplastisches** hypoplastic left heart syndrome
Linksherzventrikulogramm n left ventriculogram
Linksherzventrikulographie f left ventriculography
Linksherzversagen n left ventricular [heart] failure, left heart failure
Linkskammerdruck m left ventricular pressure
Linkskolostoma n left colostomy
Linkskunstafter m left colostomy
Linkslage f **des Herzens** laevocardia, sinistrocardia *(z. B. bei Situs inversus)*
Links-Rechts-Shunt m left-to-right-shunt
Linksschenkelblock m left bundle-branch block, LBBB
Linksseitenlage f left lateral [position] *(z. B. beim Röntgen)*
linksseitig left[-sided], sinister, sinistral
Linkstyp m left axis deviation (shift), LAD, left dominance *(des EKG)*
Linksverdrehung f sinistrotorsion
Linksverschiebung f left shift, deviation to the left *(im Blutbild)*
Linse f 1. [eye] lens, crystalline lens [of the eye]; 2. lens; eyepiece *(des Mikroskops)*
~/bifokale bifocal lens
~/bikonkave biconcave lens
~/bikonvexe biconvex lens
~/implantierte implanted lens, lens implant
~/konkave concave lens
~/konvexe convex lens
Linsenachse f axis of lens
linsenartig lenticular
Linsenastigmatismus m lens (lenticular) astigmatism
Linsenaufhängeapparat m suspensory ligament of the lens, Zinn's zonule
Linsenaufhängebanddurchtrennung f[/**operative**] zonulotomy
Linsenauflösung f phacolysis
Linsenauspressung f expression of the lens
Linsenbläschen n lens vesicle
Linsendislokation f dislocation of the lens
Linsendurchlässigkeit f lens permeability
Linsenentfernung f[/**operative**] lensectomy
Linsenentzündung f phac[oid]itis, lentitis, inflammation of the eye lens
Linsenextraktion f extraction of the lens; phacoerisis, phacoerysis *(mit einem Saugapparat)*; cryoextraction *(nach Kälteanwendung z. B. bei Staroperation)*
Linsenfasern fpl lens fibres
Linsenfleck m cold freckle, lentigo
~/weißer leucoma
linsenförmig lenticular, lentiform, phacoid
Linsengröße f lens size
Linsengrube f lens pit
Linsenherauslösung f[/**operative**] phacolysis
Linsenhernie f lenticele, phac[ent]ocele, phacometachoresis
Linsenimplantat n lens implant, implanted lens
Linsenkapsel f capsule of the lens, crystalline (lens) capsule, phacocyst
Linsenkapselentfernung f[/**operative**] phacocystectomy
Linsenkapselentzündung f phacocystitis, caps[ul]itis, inflammation of the lens capsule
Linsenkapseleröffnung f[/**operative**] cystitomy
Linsenkapselhäutchenglaukom n capsular glaucoma
Linsenkapselmesser n cystitome
Linsenkern m 1. nucleus of the [eye] lens; 2. lenticular nucleus *(im Gehirn)*
Linsenkernentartung f lenticular degeneration
Linsenkernschlinge f **im Hirnstamm** lenticular loop

Lipoidgranulomatose

Linsenkonus *m* lens cone, lenticonus *(kugelförmige Mißbildung der Linsenvorder- bzw. -hinterfläche)*
Linsenkortex *m* lens cortex
Linsenkrümmung *f* lens curvature
linsenlos aphakial, aphakic
Linsenlosigkeit *f* aphakia, absence of the lens *(Zusammensetzungen s. unter Aphakie)*
Linsenluxation *f* lens luxation, dislocation of the lens, phacometachoresis
Linsenmeßgerät *n* lensometer
Linsennaht *f* 1. lens star *(Anatomie)*; 2. lens suture *(durch Operation)*
Linsenpermeabilität *f* lens permeability
Linsenplakode *f* lens placode
Linsenpol *m*/**hinterer** posterior pole of the lens
~/**vorderer** anterior pole of the lens
Linsenrinde *f* lens cortex
Linsenrückseite *f* posterior surface of the lens
Linsensäckchen *n* lens vesicle (sac)
Linsensauginstrument *n* erysiphake, erisophake
Linsensklerose *f* phacosclerosis
Linsenstern *m* lens star
Linsentrübung *f* lens opacification, opacification of the lens; cataract, lens opacity, phacoscotasmus
Linsentumor *m* phacoma, phakoma
Linsen- und Hornhautastigmatismus *m* biastigmatism
Linsenunterkühler *m* cryophake
Linsenverflüssigung *f* phacoemulsification; fluid cataract
Linsenverhärtung *f* phacosclerosis; hard cataract
Linsenvorderseite *f* anterior surface of the lens
Linsenvorfall *m* lens prolapse, prolapse of the lens, lentoptosis
Linsenwirbel *m* lens vortex, vortex of the lens
Linton-Nachlas-Sonde *f* Linton-Nachlas tube *(für Ösophagusvarizenblutung)*
Lipaemia *f* retinalis retina lipaemia
Lipämie *f* lip[id]aemia, lipoidaemia, lipohaemia, pionaemia
~/**alimentäre** alimentary lipaemia
lipämisch lipaemic
Liparotrichie *f* liparotrichia
Lipase *f* lipase *(Enzym)*
Lipaseausscheidung *f* im Urin lipasuria
Lipase[spiegel]erhöhung *f* im Blut hyperlipasaemia
Lipazidämie *f* lipacidaemia
Lipazidurie *f* lipaciduria
Lipektomie *f* lipectomy, excision of fatty tissue
Lipid *n* lipide, lipin, lipoid *(Sammelbezeichnung für Fette und Lipoide)*
Lipidablagerung *f* im Lungengewebe pneumolipidosis
~ in der **Niere** liponephrosis, lipoid (lipaemic) nephrosis
lipidartig lipidic
Lipidblutspiegel *m* lipid blood level
Lipidentfernung *f* delipidation
Lipidfärbung *f* lipid stain
Lipidgranulomatose *f s.* Lipoidgranulomatose
Lipidhistiozytose *f* lipid histiocytosis, Niemann-Pick disease
lipidisch lipidic
lipidlöslich lipid-soluble, fat-soluble
Lipidlöslichkeit *f* lipid (fat) solubility
Lipidnephrose *f* liponephrosis, lipoid (lipaemic) nephrosis
Lipidose *f s.* Lipidspeicherkrankheit
Lipidozyt *m* lipocyte
Lipidpneumonie *f* lipid pneumonia, oil-aspiration pneumonia
Lipidproteinose *f* lipoid proteinosis, lipoidproteinosis
Lipidsiderose *f* lipoidsiderosis
Lipidspeicherkrankheit *f* lip[o]idosis, lipoid thesaurismosis (storage disease)
Lipidstoffwechsel *m* lipid metabolism
Lipidvermehrung *f* im Blut hyperlip[id]aemia
Lipidzellgeschwulst *f* lipid-cell tumour
Lipoarthritis *f* lipo-arthritis
Lipoblast *m* lipoblast
lipoblastisch lipoblastic
Lipoblastose *f* lipoblastosis
Lipochondrodystrophie *f* lipochondrodystrophy, lipochondroplasia, Hurler's disease, mucopolysaccharidosis [type] I, Pfaundler-Hurler syndrome *(erbliche Phosphatidstoffwechselstörung)*
Lipochondrom *n* lipochondroma
Lipochrom *n* lipochrome, chromolip[o]id *(Farbstoff)*
Lipodystrophia *f* **progressiva** progressive lipodystrophy, Barraquer's (Barraquer-Simons) disease
Lipodystrophie *f* lipodystrophy
~/**intestinale** intestinal lipodystrophy, Whipple's disease
Lipofibrom *n* lipofibroma, adipofibroma
Lipofibromyxom *n* lipofibromyxoma
Lipofibrosarkom *n* lipofibrosarcoma
Lipoflavonoid *n* lipoflavonoid
Lipofuszin *n* lipofuscin, ageing pigment
lipogen lipogen[et]ic, lipogenous
Lipogenese *f* lipogenesis, adipogenesis
Lipogranulom *n* lipogranuloma; lipophagic granuloma *(Speicherform endogener und exogener Fettstoffe in Bindegewebszellen)*
Lipogranulomatose *f* lipogranulomatosis *(Häufung von Lipogranulomen)*
Lipohämarthrosis *f* lipohaemarthrosis
lipoid lipoid[ic]
Lipoid *n* lip[o]id *(fettähnliche Substanz)*
Lipoidbogen *m* der **Hornhaut** lipoid arcus
Lipoidgicht *f* xanthoma tuberosum
Lipoidgranulomatose *f* lipoid (cholesterol) granulomatosis, Hand-Schüller-Christian disease (syndrome), Christian disease (syndrome), xanthogranulomatosis, chronic idiopathic xanthomatosis

Lipoidnachweismethode

Lipoidnachweismethode f/Smith-Dietrichsche Smith-Dietrich method
Lipoidosis f cutis et mucosae lipoid proteinosis
Lipoidpigment n lipochrome *(Farbstoff)*
Lipoidspeicherkrankheit f s. Lipoidgranulomatose
Lipoinsäure f lipoic acid
Lipokalzinogranulomatose f lipocalcinogranulomatosis, cholesterol thesaurismosis (storage disease), Teutschländer's syndrome
Lipolyse f lip[id]olysis, lipoclasis, adipolysis
lipolytisch lipolytic, adipolytic
Lipom[a] n lipoma, pimeloma, steatoma, adipoma, adipose tumour
lipomatös lipomatous
Lipomatose f lipo[mat]osis
lipomelanotisch lipomelanotic
Lipomeningozele f lipomeningocele
lipometabolisch lipometabolic
Lipomyelomeningozele f lipomyelomeningocele
Lipomyohämangiom n lipomyohaemangioma
Lipomyom n lipomyoma
Lipomyosarkom n lipomyosarcoma
Lipomyxosarkom n lipomyxosarcoma
Liponsäure f lipoic acid
Lipopenie f lipopenia
Lipopeptid n lipopeptide
Lipopexia f lipopexia
lipophag lipophagic *(z. B. Zellen)*
Lipophage m lipophage
Lipophagie f lipophagia
lipophil lipophile
Lipophilie f lipophilia, affinity for fat
Lipopolysaccharid n lipopolysaccharide
Lipoprotein n lipoprotein
β-Lipoprotein n beta lipoprotein
Lipoproteinhülle f lipoprotein envelope
β-Lipoproteinmangel m im Blut abetalipoproteinaemia
Lipoproteinmembran f lipoprotein membrane
Lipoproteinspiegelerhöhung f im Blut hyperlipoproteinaemia
Liposarkom n liposarcoma, infiltrating lipoma, primitive-cell (embryonal-cell) lipoma *(bösartige Bindegewebsgeschwulst)*
liposarkomatös liposarcomatous
Liposteatose f liposteatosis
Lipostomie f lipostomy
Lipothymie f lipothymia
Lipotrophie f lipotrophy
Lipovakzine f lipovaccine
Lipoxanthin n lipoxanthin
Lipoxenie f lipoxeny *(Verlassen des Wirts durch den Schmarotzer)*
Lipoxydase f lipoxidase *(Enzym)*
Lipozele f lipocele, adipocele
Lipozyt m lipocyte, adipocyte, fat (adipose) cell
Lippe f lip, labium; labrum *(s. a. unter Labium und Labrum)* ● **ohne ~** acheilous
Lippen fpl labia oris
~/ausgedörrte (ausgetrocknete) parched lips
Lippenausstülpung f cheilectropion, eclabium
Lippenaustrocknung f xerocheilia
Lippenbändchen n frenulum of the lip
Lippenbiß m odaxesmus *(z. B. bei Epilepsie)*; cheilophagia, biting of the lips
Lippenchorea f labiochorea
Lippendrüsen fpl labial glands
Lippeneinschnitt m cheilotomy
Lippenentzündung f ch[e]ilitis, inflammation of the lips
Lippenexzision f cheilectomy
Lippenfehlentwicklung f atelocheilia
Lippenfissur f cheilosis
Lippenfurche f labial groove
Lippenfurchenband n lip furrow band
Lippenhaken m labiotenaculum
Lippenhalter m lip retractor
Lippenherpes m lip herpes, herpes labialis, cold sore
Lippeninzision f cheilotomy
Lippenkapillarmikroskop n cheiloangioscope
Lippenkapillarmikroskopie f cheiloangioscopy
Lippenkarzinom n cheilocarcinoma, lip (smoker's) cancer, carcinoma of the lip
Lippen-Kiefer-Gaumen-Spalte f cheilognathopalatoschisis; cleft lip face palate, wolfjaw
Lippen-Kiefer-Gesichts[schräg]spalte f cheilognathoprosoposchisis
Lippenlesen n lip (speech) reading, labiomancy
lippenlos acheilous
Lippenloser m acheilus
Lippenlosigkeit f acheilia, absence of the lips
Lippenmuskel m orbicularis oris [muscle]
Lippenmuskelreflex m orbicularis oris reflex
Lippenmykose f labiomycosis
Lippennaht f labiorrhaphy, cheilorrhaphy
Lippenplastik f labioplasty, cheiloplasty
Lippenreflex m lip reflex
Lippenrekonstruktion f labioplasty, cheiloplasty
Lippenrhagade f cheilosis
Lippenschleimdrüsenentzündung f glandular cheilitis
Lippenschleimhaut f labial mucosa
Lippenschleimhautrhagade f cheilosis
Lippenschmerz m cheilalgia
Lippenschnitt m cheilotomy
Lippenspalte f cheiloschisis; cleft lip, harelip
Lippensperrer m für Hasenschartenoperation harelip traction bow
Lippenteilentfernung f[/operative] cheilectomy
Lippentrockenheit f xerocheilia
Lippen- und Mundrekonstruktion f cheilostomatoplasty
Lippen- und Wangenplastik f genycheiloplasty
Lippenunterentwicklung f atelocheilia
Lippenverdickung f/abnorme pachych[e]ilia
Lippenvergrößerung f/abnorme macrocheilia, macrolabia
Lippenverkleinerung f/abnorme microcheilia, microlabia
Lippenverwachsung f synch[e]ilia, ankylocheilia
Lippenzittern n labiochorea
Lippenzyanose f cyanosis of lips

Lippitudo f lippitude, lippitudo, blear eye
Lipurie f lipuria, adiposuria, pimeluria
Liquefactio f **corporis vitrei** liquefaction of the vitreous body
Liquefaktionsnekrose f liquefaction (liquefying) necrosis, liquefactive degeneration
liquid liquid, fluid
Liquor m 1. liquor; fluid; 2. s. ~ cerebrospinalis
~ **amnii** amniotic fluid (liquor), waters
~ **amnii spurius** allantoic fluid
~ **cerebrospinalis** [cerebro]spinal fluid, CSF, neurolymph, subarachnoid fluid
~ **folliculi** follicular fluid
~ **pericardii** pericardial fluid
~ **sanguinis** blood plasma
~ **seminis** semen, seminal fluid, sperm
Liquoraustritt m liquorrhoea, cerebrospinal fluid leak
~ **aus dem Ohr** cerebrospinal [fluid] otorrhoea
~ **aus der Nase** cerebrospinal [fluid] rhinorrhoea
~/**fehlender** aliquorrhoea
Liquorbefund m spinal-fluid findings
Liquorblockade f spinal block
~/**subarachnoidale** subarachnoid block
Liquordruck m cerebrospinal [fluid] pressure
Liquorerguß m cephalhydrocele
Liquorfistel f liquor (cerebrospinal fluid) fistula
Liquorfluß m s. Liquoraustritt
Liquorglukose f liquor (cerebrospinal fluid) glucose, glycorrhachia
Liquormangel m aliquorrhoea
Liquormangelkopfschmerz m drainage headache
Liquorpleozytose f liquor (cerebrospinal fluid) pleocytosis
Liquorprotein n cerebrospinal fluid protein
Liquorpunktionskopfschmerz m leakage headache
Liquorraum m subarachnoid space
Liquorrhoe f s. Liquoraustritt
Liquorsperre f spinal block
Liquorzellvermehrung f cerebrospinal fluid pleocytosis
Liquorzucker m cerebrospinal fluid glucose
Liquorzuckererhöhung f hyperglycorrhachia
Liquorzuckerverminderung f hypoglycorrhachia
lispeln to lisp
Lispeln n lisp, sigmatism
Lissenzephalie f lissencephalia
Lissenzephalus m lissencephalus *(Mißgeburt)*
Listeria f **monocytogenes** Listeria monocytogenes *(grampositives, sporenloses Stäbchen)*
Listeriämie f listeraemia
Listeriose f lister[i]osis, listereliosis *(Infektionskrankheit)*
Lithagogum n lithagogue [agent]
Lithämie f lithaemia
Lithektomie f lithectomy
Lithiasis f lithiasis, calculosis, calculous disease
Litholcholsäure f lithocholic acid *(Gallensäure)*
Lithogenese f lithogenesis, calculogenesis, formation of stones

Lithokelyphopädion n litho[kelypho]paedion *(verkalkter Fetus)*
Lithokelyphos n lithokelyphos *(verkalkte Fetalmembran)*
Lithoklast m s. Lithotriptor
Lithologie f lithology *(Lehre von den Steinerkrankungen)*
Litholyse f litho[dia]lysis, solution of calculi
Lithonephritis f lithonephritis
Lithonephrotomie f lithonephrotomy
Lithopädion n lithopaedion, calcified foetus
Lithophon n lithophone
Lithotom n lithotome
Lithotomie f lithotomy
Lithotripsie f lithotrity, lithotripsy, litholapaxy
~ **mittels Ultraschall** ultrasonic litholapaxy
Lithotripter m s. Lithotriptor
lithotriptisch lithotritic
Lithotriptor m lithotrite, lithoclast, lithotriptor
Lithotriptoskop n lithotriptoscope
Lithotriptoskopie f lithotriptoscopy
Lithozystotomie f lithocystotomy
Lithurese f lithuresis
Lithurie f lithuria
Littré-Drüsen fpl Littré's (urethral) glands
Littreitis f littritis, inflammation of the urethral glands
Livedo f livedo *(bläuliche Verfärbung der Haut)*
livedoartig livedoid
livid[e] livid, black and blue
Lividität f lividity, livor
Livor m **mortis** cadaveric lividity
Loa f **Loa** Loa, eye worm *(Erreger der Kalabarbeule)*
Lobäratrophie f lobar atrophy
Lobärpneumonie f lobar pneumonia
Lobärsklerose f lobar sclerosis
~/**chronische infantile** chronic infantile lobar sclerosis *(erbliches Leiden mit spastischen Lähmungen)*
Lobektomie f lobectomy, excision of a lobe *(eines Organs)*
~/**temporale** temporal lobectomy
~/**untere** lower lobectomy
Lobelin n lobeline *(Alkaloid)*
Lobi mpl **renales** renal lobes
Lobitis f lobitis, inflammation of a lobe
Lobotomie f 1. lobotomy, incision into a lobe; 2. s. Leukotomie
lobulär lobular, lobulated
Lobulärpneumonie f bronchopneumonia
Lobulus m lobule, lobulus
~ **auriculae** lobule of the auricle, earlobe
~ **biventer** biventral lobule *(Kleinhirn)*
~ **centralis** central lobule *(Kleinhirn)*
~ **corticalis renis** lobule of the cortex of the kidney
~ **epididymidis** lobule of the epididymis
~ **glandulae mammariae** lobule of the mammary gland
~ **glandulae thyreoideae** lobule of the thyroid gland

Lobulus

~ **hepatis** lobule of the liver, liver lobule
~ **paracentralis** paracentral lobule
~ **parietalis** parietal lobule
~ **parietalis inferior** inferior parietal lobule
~ **parietalis superior** superior parietal lobule
~ **pulmonalis** pulmonary lobule
~ **quadrangularis** quadrangular lobule
~ **semilunaris** semilunar lobule *(Kleinhirn)*
~ **semilunaris inferior** inferior semilunar lobule
~ **semilunaris superior** superior semilunar lobule
~ **simplex** simple (ansiform) lobule
~ **testis** lobule of the testis
~ **thymi** lobule of the thymus
Lobus *m* lobe, lobus *(eines Organs)*
~ **accessorius glandulae lacrimalis** accessory lobe of the lacrimal gland
~ **anterior cerebelli** anterior lobe of the cerebellum
~ **anterior hypophyseos** anterior lobe of the hypophysis, antehypophysis
~ **caudatus [hepatis]** caudate lobe [of the liver]
~ **frontalis** frontal lobe of the brain
~ **glandulae thyreoideae** lobe of the thyroid gland
~ **hepaticus** hepatic lobe
~ **hepatis dexter** right lobe of the liver
~ **hepatis sinister** left lobe of the liver
~ **inferior pulmonis** inferior lobe of the lung
~ **inferior pulmonis dextri** inferior lobe of the right lung
~ **inferior pulmonis sinistri** inferior lobe of the left lung
~ **lateralis thyroideae** lateral thyroid lobe
~ **medius prostatae** median lobe of the prostate
~ **medius pulmonis dextri** middle lobe of the right lung
~ **occipitalis** occipital lobe
~ **olfactorius** olfactory lobe
~ **parietalis** parietal lobe
~ **posterior cerebelli** posterior cerebellar lobe, posterior lobe of the cerebellum
~ **posterior hypophyseos** posterior lobe of the hypophysis
~ **prostatae** lobe of the prostate
~ **pulmonalis** pulmonary lobe
~ **pyramidalis [glandulae thyroideae]** pyramidal lobe
~ **quadratus** quadrate lobe
~ **superior pulmonis** superior lobe of the lung
~ **superior pulmonis dextri** superior lobe of the right lung
~ **superior pulmonis sinistri** superior lobe of the left lung
~ **temporalis** temporal lobe
~ **thymi** lobe of the thymus
Loch *n* foramen; aperture, orifice
~/Winslowisches Winslow's foramen
Lochia *fpl* lochia *(nach der Entbindung)*
~ **alba** lochia alba
~ **rubra** lochia cruenta (rubra)
~ **serosa** lochia serosa
Lochialstauung *f* lochioschesis, lochiostasis, lochial stagnation (retention)

~ **in der Gebärmutter** lochiometra
~ **in der Scheide** lochiocolpos
Lochialzelle *f* lochiocyte
Lochien *fpl s.* Lochia
Lochienzelle *f* lochiocyte
Lochiokolpos *m* lochiocolpos
Lochiometra *f* lochiometra
Lochiometritis *f* loch[i]ometritis, puerperal metritis
Lochioperitonitis *f* lochioperitonitis, puerperal peritonitis
Lochiopyra *f* lochiopyra
Lochiorrhagie *f*, **Lochiorrhoe** *f* lochiorrhagia, lochiorrhoea, lochial discharge
Lochioschesis *f*, **Lochiostase** *f s.* Lochialstauung
Locho... *s.* Lochio...
Lochzange *f* punch forceps
Locus *m* **Kiesselbachi** Kiesselbach's area (space, triangle) *(gefäßreicher Bezirk der Nasenscheidewand)*
Löffel *m*/**chirurgischer** [surgical] spoon, scoop
~/scharfer sharp spoon, scraper; bone curette
Löffelextraktion *f* scoop extraction
Löffelhand *f* spoon hand; total syndactyly
Löffelnagel *m* spoon nail; koilonychia
Logagnosie *f* logagnosia, central word defect; aphasia, alogia
Logamnesie *f* logamnesia, sensory aphasia; word deafness, auditory aphasia; word blindness, visual aphasia
Logaphasie *f* logaphasia, motor aphasia
Logasthenie *f* logasthenia, disturbance of speech comprehension
Logoklonie *f* logoclonia, spasmodic repetition of word syllables
Logokophosis *f* logokophosis, inability to comprehend spoken language
Logomanie *f* 1. logomania, overtalkativeness; 2. *s.* Aphasie
Logoneurose *f* logoneurosis *(Sprachstörung bei fehlerhafter Gedankenbildung)*
Logopädie *f* logopaedia, logopaedics *(Wissenschaft von der Behandlung von Stimm- und Sprachstörungen)*
Logopathie *f* logopathy, disorder of the speech
Logophasie *f* logophasia, dysarthria
Logoplegie *f* 1. logoplegia, paralysis of the speech organs; 2. logoplegia, inability to speak
Logorrhoe *f* logorrhoea, abnormal talkativeness, excessive loquacity
Logospasmus *m* logospasm, spasmodic utterance of words
logotherapeutisch logotherapeutic
Logotherapie *f* logotherapy
Loiasis *f* lo[a]iasis, eye-worm disease, Calabar swellings *(Infektionskrankheit durch Loa loa)*
Loimologie *f* loimology, lemology *(Lehre von den übertragbaren und epidemischen Krankheiten)*
lokal local, topical
Lokalanästhesie *f* local anaesthesia (analgesia), regional [block] anaesthesia
Lokalanästhetikum *n* local anaesthetic

Lokalbehandlung f local therapy (treatment), topical application
Lokalbestrahlung f local irradiation
Lokalerkrankung f local disease
Lokalimmunität f local immunity
Lokalinfektion f local (walled-up) infection
Lokalisation f localization (z. B. von Krankheitsherden)
~/stereotaktische stereotaxia (von Hirnarealen)
lokalisieren to localize
Lokalreaktion f local reaction
Lokalrezidiv n local recurrence
Lokalschmerz m local pain
Lokaltod m local death
Lokalwirkung f local (topical) action
Lokomotion f s. Bewegung 1.
Lokomotivgeräusch n to-and-fro murmur
lokomotorisch locomotor, locomotive
Lokulationssyndrom n loculation (Froin's) syndrome
longitudinal longitudinal, lengthwise
Longitudinalfraktur f longitudinal fracture
lophotrich lophotrichous (Bakterien)
Loquacitas f loquacity, volubility of speech; talkativeness (z. B. bei Hypomanie)
Lordose f lordosis, posterior curvature, anterior deformity; hollow back, saddleback
~ ohne Seitenkrümmung ithylordosis
Lordoskoliose f scoliolordosis, lordoscoliosis, lordosis and scoliosis
lordotisch lordotic
lösen 1. to release (z. B. eine Stauung); to relax (z. B. einen Krampf); to loosen, to mobilize (z. B. verwachsene Organe); 2. to dissolve (z. B. Medikamente)
~/sich 1. to dissolve, to go into solution (z. B. Substanzen); to undergo lysis, to lyse (z. B. Zellen); 2. to loosen (z. B. der Schleim); to resolve (z. B. eine Lungenentzündung)
~/Adhäsionen to loosen adhesions, to detach (free) adhesions
lösend [re]solvent
~/sich nicht unresolved (Lungenentzündung)
Losesein n der Zähne odontoseisis, looseness of the teeth
Losewerden n der Zähne gomphiasis, loosening of the teeth
losgehen to break loose (z. B. ein Thrombus)
Losłaßschmerz m Blumberg's sign (Appendizitiszeichen)
löslich soluble
~/in Fett lipophile
~/leicht freely soluble
~/nicht insoluble
~/schwer slightly soluble
loslösen/sich to break loose (z. B. Thrombus); to detach, to separate (z. B. Netzhaut)
Loslösen n detachment (z. B. der Netzhaut); diastasis (z. B. von Knochen); dislodgement (z. B. von Steinen)
Lost m mustard gas (hautschädigender Kampfstoff)

Lösung f 1. solution, dissolution; 2. resolution (z. B. einer Krankheit); adhesiolysis (z. B. von Verwachsungen); lysis (z. B. von Thromben)
● **in ~ gehen** to go into solution, to dissolve; to lyse (z. B. Bakterien)
~/Benediktsche Benedict's solution (zum Glukosenachweis)
~ der Arme liberation of the arms (bei der Geburt)
~ der Lunge von der Brustkorbwand/operative pneumo[no]lysis, thoracolysis (zur Ruhigstellung)
~/isotonische isoosmotic solution
~/kolloid[al]e colloidal solution
~/Lugolsche Lugol's solution (wäßrige Jodlösung)
~/molare molar solution
~/Ringersche Ringer's solution
~ von Perikardverwachsungen pericardiolysis
~ von Pleuraverwachsungen pleurolysis
~ von Verwachsungen am Eileiter salpingolysis
~/zu untersuchende test solution, T. S.
Lösungsdruck m solution pressure
Lösungsmittel n solvent [agent]
~ für Schleim expectorant [agent]
lösungsmittelabstoßend lyophobe
lösungsmittelanziehend lyophil[e]
Lösungsstadium n stage of resolution (einer Lungenentzündung)
Lösungsvermittler m solubilizer; disintegrator
Lotion f lotion, wash, liquid medicinal preparation
Louis-Bar-Syndrom n Louis-Bar syndrome, ataxia-telangiectasia
Löwengesicht n leonine face, facies leontina; leontiasis
Loxarthrose f loxarthrosis
Loxophthalmus m loxophthalmus
Loxoscelesnekrose f, **Loxoscelismus** m loxoscelism (durch Giftspinnenbiß)
LSD n s. Lysergsäurediäthylamid
L-Stottern n paralambdacism
LTH s. Hormon/luteotrophes
L-Thyroxin n laevothyroxine (Schilddrüsenhormon)
L-Tryptophan n α-amino-3-indolepropionic acid
Lücke f lacuna, lake (s. a. unter Lacuna)
~/anatomische diastasis
~/Bochdaleksche Bochdalek's foramen (lumbocostal triangle)
~/zeitliche interval
lückenhaft lacunar
Lückenschädel m craniolacunia
Lues f lues, syphilis, Spanish pox (Zusammensetzungen s. unter Syphilis)
Lues... s. Syphilis...
Luetin n luetin (Syphilisspirochätenextrakt)
luetisch luetic, syphilitic
Luft f 1. air; 2. breath ● **durch ~ bewirkt** pneumatic ● **nach ~ ringen** to suffocate
Luftabgang m aus der Scheide garrulity of the vulva

luftabhängig

luftabhängig aerobic
Luftansammlung *f* **im Brustfellraum** pneum[at]othorax, aeropleura
~ **im Dickdarm** pneumocolon; aerocoly
~ **im Gewebe** pneum[at]ocele, pneumonocele *(z. B. im Skrotum)*
~ **im Herzbeutel** pneumopericardium
~ **im Herzen** pneumatocardia
~ **im Hirnventrikel** pneumoventricle
~ **im Magen** aerogastria
~ **im Mediastinum** pneumomediastinum; mediastinal emphysema
~ **im Mittelohr** pneumotympanum
~ **im Retroperitonealraum** pneumoretroperitoneum
~ **im Rückenmarkkanal** pneum[at]orrhachis
~ **im Schädel** pneumocranium
~ **in den Hirnkammern** pneumoencephalocele; pneumatocephalia
~ **in der Peritonealhöhle** pneumoperitoneum, pneumascos, aeroperitoneum
~ **in der Scheide** aerocolpos
~ **in einem Gelenk** pneumarthrosis
~/**subdiaphragmale** subdiaphragmatic air *(z. B. bei Magenperforation)*
~ **unter der Haut** pneumoderma
Luftansaugung *f* **an Brustwandwunden** traumatopnoea
Luftbad *n* air bath
Luftbehandlung *f* aerotherapy, pneum[at]otherapy
Luftbett *n* air bed
Luftbläser *m* [warm] air syringe, chip syringe *(Stomatologie)*
Luftdruckkrankheit *f s*. 1. Caissonkrankheit; 2. Höhenkrankheit
Luftdruckverletzung *f* air-blast injury
Luftdusche *f* air syringe
~/**Politzersche** 1. Politzer bag *(Instrument)*; 2. politzerization, tympanic (Eustachian) inflation
Luftembolie *f* air embolism (embolization), aeroembolism; pneumathaemia
~/**zerebrale** cerebral air embolism
lüften to ventilate, to air
luftenthaltend aeriferous
Luftfahrtmedizin *f* aeromedicine, aviation (air) medicine; aero space medicine
luftgefüllt air-filled, pneumatic
Luftgeschwulst *f* aerocele
lufthaltig aeriferous, pneumatic
Lufthunger *m s*. Luftnot
lufthungrig short of breath, dyspnoeic
Luftinfektion *f* air-borne infection
Luftinsufflation *f* insufflation, ballooning *(z. B. in die Bauchhöhle)*
Luftkeim *m* air-borne germ
Luftkissen *n* air cushion
Luftkrankheit *f* 1. air sickness *(Kinetose)*; 2. aeropathy, aviator's disease *(infolge Luftdruckänderung)*
Luftleitung *f* air (aerotympanal) conduction, AC *(beim Hörvorgang)*

Luftleitungsaudiogramm *n* air conduction audiogram
Luftleitungsaudiometrie *f* air conduction audiometry
Luftleitungshörprobe *f* air conduction test
Luftleitungsschwelle *f* air conduction threshold
luftliebend aerophil[e]
Luftnot *f* shortness of breath, dyspnoea, air hunger
Luftring *m* [ring-shaped] air cushion
Luftröhre *f* trachea, windpipe ● **durch die** ~ transtracheal ● **neben der** ~ paratracheal
Luftröhren... *s. a.* Trachea...
Luftröhrenarterie *f* bronchial artery
Luftröhrenaspiration *f* tracheal aspiration
Luftröhrenast *m* bronchial (air) tube, bronchus *(Zusammensetzungen s. unter Bronchus)*
Luftröhrenaufzweigung *f* tracheal bifurcation
Luftröhrenblutung *f* tracheorrhagia, haemorrhage from the trachea
Luftröhren-Bronchien-Spiegel *m* tracheobronchoscope
Luftröhren-Bronchien-Spiegelung *f* tracheobronchoscopy
Luftröhrenbruch *m* trache[l]ocele
Luftröhreneinengung *f* tracheostenosis, contraction (narrowing) of the trachea
Luftröhrenentzündung *f* trach[e]itis, inflammation of the trachea
~/**eitrige** purulent tracheitis; tracheopyosis
Luftröhrenerkrankung *f* tracheopathy, disease of the trachea
Luftröhreneröffnung *f*[/**operative**] *s*. Tracheotomie
Luftröhrenerweichung *f* tracheomalacia, softening of the tracheal cartilages
Luftröhrenerweiterung *f* tracheaectasy, dilatation of the trachea
Luftröhrenfistel *f* tracheostoma
Luftröhrenfistelung *f*[/**operative**] tracheostomy
Luftröhrengabelung *f* bifurcation of the trachea
Luftröhrengeschwür *n* tracheal ulcer, trachielcus
Luftröhrengeschwürbildung *f* trachielcosis, ulceration of the trachea
Luftröhren-Haut-Fistel *f* tracheocutaneous fistula
Luftröhrenkatheter *m* tracheo[s]tomy tube, tracheal catheter
Luftröhrenknorpelring *m* tracheal ring (cartilage)
Luftröhrennaht *f* tracheorrhaphy; suturing of the trachea
Luftröhrenplastik *f* tracheoplasty
Luftröhrenröntgen[kontrast]bild *n* tracheogram
Luftröhrenröntgen[kontrast]darstellung *f* tracheography
Luftröhrenröntgenschichtaufnahme *f* laminagram of the trachea
Luftröhrenschmerz *m* trachealgia, pain in the trachea
Luftröhrenschnitt *m s*. Tracheotomie
Luftröhrenspalte *f* tracheofissure; tracheoschisis
Luftröhren-Speiseröhren-Fistel *f* tracheo-oesophageal fistula

Luftröhren-Speiseröhren-Haut-Fistel f tracheo-oesophageal-skin fistula
Luftröhrenspiegel m tracheoscope
Luftröhrenspiegelung f tracheoscopy
Luftröhrenton m tracheophony
Luftröhren- und Bronchienentzündung f tracheobronchitis, inflammation of the trachea and the bronchi
Luftröhren- und Kehlkopferöffnung f[/operative] tracheolaryngotomy, incision into the larynx and the trachea
Luftröhrenvene f tracheal vein
Luftröhrenvereng[er]ung f tracheal stenosis, tracheostenosis
~ **nach einer Tracheotomie** posttracheotomy stenosis *(im Bereich des Luftröhrenschnitts)*
Luftröhrenverschluß m tracheal obstruction
Luftschalleitungsschwelle f air conduction threshold
Luftschlauch m air tube
Luftschlucken n air swallowing, aerophagy, pneumophagy
Luftsichel f/subdiaphragmale subdiaphragmatic air *(z. B. bei Magenperforation)*
luftübertragen air-borne
luftunabhängig anaerobic, anaerobiotic
Luft- und Blutansammlung f **im Herzbeutel** pneumohaemopericardium
~ **in der Brusthöhle** pneumohaemothorax
Luft- und Eiteransammlung f **im Herzbeutel** pneumopyopericardium
~ **in der Brusthöhle** pneumopyothorax
Luft- und Flüssigkeitsansammlung f **im Brustfellraum** hydropneumothorax
~ **im Herzbeutel** hydropneumopericardium, pneumohydropericardium
~ **in der Bauchhöhle** hydropneumoperitoneum
~ **in der Brusthöhle** pneumohydrothorax
~ **in der Gebärmutter** pneumohydrometra
Luft- und Raumfahrtmedizin f aerospace medicine
Luft- und Speichelschlucken n aerosialophagy
Luft- und Wassertherapie f aerohydrotherapy
Luftverschmutzung f air pollution
Luftwege mpl air passages, airways, respiratory tract
~/**obere** upper airways (respiratory tract)
Luftweginfektion f respiratory infection
Luftwegverschluß m airway obstruction
Luftwegwiderstand m airway resistance
Luftzuführungsschlauch m inflating tube *(Anästhesie)*
Luftzyste f air cyst
Lügen n/**krankhaftes** pathologic mendacity
Lügendetektor m lie detector
Lumbago f lumbago, lumbodynia, lumbalgia, lumbar pain, backache in the lumbar region
Lumbal... s. a. Lenden...
Lumbalabschnitt m lumbar segment
Lumbalabszeß m lumbar abscess
Lumbalanästhesie f spinal (caudal) anaesthesia, rachianaesthesia, rachianalgesia

~/**Biersche** Bier's anaesthesia
Lumbalbandscheibenvorfall m lumbar disk protrusion
Lumbaldreieck n lumbar (Petit's) triangle
Lumbalganglion n lumbar ganglion
Lumbalgie f s. Lumbago
Lumbalhernie f lumbar hernia
Lumbalisation f lumbarization *(ausbleibende Verschmelzung des ersten Kreuzbeinwirbels mit dem Kreuzbein)*
Lumbalnadel f s. Lumbalpunktionskanüle
Lumbalnerv m lumbar nerve
Lumbalplexus m lumbar plexus
Lumbalpunktion f lumbar puncture, spinal puncture (tap), rachi[a]centesis
Lumbalpunktionsbesteck n lumbar puncture set
Lumbalpunktionskanüle f spinal (lumbar puncture) needle
Lumbalpunktionskopfschmerz m [lumbar] puncture headache, drainage (spinal-fluid loss) headache
Lumbalreflex m lumbar reflex
Lumbalregion f lumbar region
Lumbalrinne f lumbar gutter
Lumbalschmerz m s. Lumbago
Lumbalsegment n lumbar segment
lumbodorsal lumbodorsal, dorsolumbar
Lumbokolostomie f lumbocolostomy
Lumbokolotomie f lumbocolotomy
lumbokostal lumbocostal, costolumbar
Lumbokostalbogen m lumbocostal arch
Lumbokostaldreieck n lumbocostal triangle [of Bochdalek], vertebrocostal triangle
lumbosakral lumbosacral, sacrolumbar
Lumbosakralgelenk n lumbosacral articulation (joint, junction)
Lumbosakralkorsett n lumbosacral corset *(Traumatologie)*
Lumbosakralplexus m lumbosacral plexus
Lumbosakralraum m lumbosacral space
Lumbosakralschmerz m lumbosacral pain, backache, backalgia
Lumbosakralwinkel m lumbosacral angle
Lumbus m s. Lende
Lumineszenz f luminescence
Lumisterin n lumisterol *(Zwischenprodukt der Vitamin-D_2-Bildung infolge UV-Bestrahlung)*
Lunambulismus m, **Lunatismus** m lunatism, lunacy
Lunatum n lunate bone
Lunatummalazie f lunatomalacia, Kienböck's disease
Lunge f lung, pulmo ● **die** ~ **bevorzugend** pneumotropic
~/**eiserne** iron lung
~/**linke** left lung
~/**rechte** right lung
Lungen... s. a. Pulmonal...
Lungenabnormität f pulmonary abnormality
Lungenabschnitt m pulmonary segment
Lungenabschnittkollaps m atelectasis, apneumatosis *(Zusammensetzungen s. unter Atelektase)*

Lungenabszeß

Lungenabszeß *m* pulmonary (lung) abscess
Lungenabszeßdrainage *f* cavernostomy
Lungenabtastung *f* **nach radioaktiver Markierung** lung [scinti]scanning
Lungenadenomatose *f* pulmonary adenomatosis
Lungenaktinomykosis *f* pulmonary actinomycosis
Lungenalveole *f* pulmonary (lung) alveolus, air sac
Lungenalveolenmikrolithiasis *f* pulmonary alveolar microlithiasis
Lungenalveolenproteinose *f* pulmonary alveolar proteinosis
Lungenalveolensurfaktant *m* lung alveolus surfactant
Lungenanheftung *f* **an der Thoraxwand** pneumopexy
Lungenanschoppung *f* pulmonary congestion *(bei Pneumonie)*
Lungenareal *n* pulmonary area
Lungenarterie *f* pulmonary artery (trunk)
~/**linke** left pulmonary artery, L. P. A.
~/**rechte** right pulmonary artery, R. P. A.
Lungenarterienaneurysma *n* aneurysm of pulmonary artery
Lungenarterienast *m* pulmonary artery branch
Lungenarterienbändelung *f* banding of the pulmonary artery, pulmonary arterial banding *(bei Herzfehlern)*
Lungenarteriendruck *m* pulmonary arterial (trunk) pressure
Lungenarterienentzündung *f* pulmonary arteritis
Lungenarterienfüllung *f* filling of the pulmonary artery
Lungenarterienhypertonus *m* pulmonary arterial hypertension
Lungenarterienmitteldruck *m* mean pulmonary artery pressure
Lungenarterienpuls *m* pulmonary pulse
Lungenarterienpulsation *f* pulmonary arterial pulsation
Lungenarterienstamm *m* pulmonary trunk, [main] pulmonary artery
Lungenarterienstammdruck *m* pulmonary trunk pressure
Lungenarterientransposition *f* transposition of the pulmonary artery
Lungenarterienveränderung *f* pulmonary arterial change
Lungenarterienvereng[er]ung *f* pulmonary arterial stenosis
Lungenarterienverkalkung *f* Ayerza's disease (syndrome), pulmonary arterial sclerosis, sclerosis of the pulmonary vascular bed
Lungenaspergillose *f* pulmonary aspergillosis
Lungenatelektase *f* pulmonary atelectasis
Lungenatmung *f* pulmonary respiration
Lungenausflußbahn *f* pulmonary outflow tract
Lungenauskultation *f* pulmonary auscultation
Lungenauskultationsabnormität *f* pulmonary auscultatory abnormality
Lungenbefall *m* pulmonary invasion
Lungenbefund *m*/**positiver** pulmonary (lung) involvement
Lungenbiopsie *f* lung biopsy
Lungenbläschen *n* lung (pulmonary) alveolus, air sac
Lungenbläschenbefall *m* alveolar involvement *(bei einer Pneumonie)*
Lungenbläschenerweiterung *f* alveolar ectasia
Lungenbläschenscheidewand *f* interalveolar septum
Lungenblastomykose *f* pulmonary blastomycosis
Lungenblutfülle *f* pulmonary plethora
Lungenblutsturz *m s.* Lungenblutung
Lungenblutung *f* pulmonary haemorrhage, pneumorrhagia; haemoptysis
~ **mit Glomerulonephritis** pulmonary-renal syndrome of Goodpasture
Lungenchirurgie *f* pulmonary (lung) surgery
Lungencompliance *f* pulmonary (lung) compliance
Lungendekortikation *f* pulmonary (lung) decortication
Lungendichte *f* pulmonary (lung) density
Lungendiffusionskapazität *f* pulmonary diffusing capacity
Lungendistomiasis *f s.* Lungenegelbefall
Lungendrainage *f* cavernostomy
Lungendurchblutung *f* pulmonary blood flow
Lungendystrophie *f*/**progressive** vanishing lungs
Lungenechinokokkose *f* pulmonary echinococcosis
Lungenegel *m* lung fluke, Paragonimus westermani
Lungenegelbefall *m* paragonimiasis, parasitic (endemic) haemoptysis
~ **des Gehirns** cerebral paragonimiasis
Lungenembolektomie *f* pulmonary embolectomy, Trendelenburg's operation
Lungenembolie *f* pulmonary embolism
Lungenembolisierung *f* pulmonary embolization
Lungenembolus *m* pulmonary embolus
Lungenembolusversprengung *f* pulmonary embolization
Lungenemphysem *n* pulmonary emphysema, pneumonectasis, pneumonectasia, emphysema of the lungs
Lungenentfaltung *f*/**fehlende** apneumatosis, atelectasis *(nach der Geburt) (Zusammensetzungen s. unter* Atelektase*)*
Lungenentfernung *f*[/**operative**] pneum[on]ectomy, pulmonectomy
Lungenentzündung *f* pneumonia, pulmonitis, inflammation of the lungs *(s. a. unter* Pneumonie*)* ● **nach einer ~ auftretend** metapneumonic
~/**atypische** atypical pneumonia
~ **durch Klebsiella pneumoniae** Friedländer's pneumonia
~ **durch Pilze** fungal pneumonia
~/**hypostatische** hypostatic pneumonia
~/**katarrhalische** catarrhal pneumonia

~/**lobuläre** bronchial (lobular) pneumonia, bronchopneumonia
~ **nach Bariuminhalation** baritosis
~/**tuberkulöse** caseous pneumonia, pulmonary tuberculous infection
~/**zentrale** central pneumonia
Lungenerkrankung f pulmonary disease, pneumonopathy, lung affection
~/**bösartige** pulmonary malignancy
~/**obstruktive** obstructive pulmonary disease
Lungenfaßpinzette f lung dissecting (tissue) forceps
Lungenfaßzange f lung grasping forceps
Lungenfeld n pulmonary field *(Röntgenologie)*
Lungenfell n pulmonary (visceral) pleura
Lungenfellentzündung f pleurisy, pleuritis, inflammation of the pleura
Lungenfibrose f pulmonary fibrosis, pneumosclerosis
~ **bei Anthrakose** black induration
~/**diffuse interstitielle** diffuse interstitial pulmonary fibrosis, Hamman-Rich syndrome
~/**interstitielle** interstitial pulmonary fibrosis, pulmonary scleroderma
Lungenfistel f pulmonary fistula
~/**arterio-venöse** pulmonary arteriovenous fistula
Lungenfixierung f **an der Brustwand[/operative]** pneumonopexy
Lungenflüssigkeit f lung fluid (water)
Lungenfrühinfiltrat n s. Lungenherd/Assmannscher
Lungenfunktion f pulmonary function
Lungenfunktionsstörung f pulmonary disorder (function impairment)
Lungenfunktionstest m pulmonary function study (test)
Lungenfunktionsüberwachung f pulmonary monitoring
Lungengangrän f gangrene of the lung, necropneumonia
Lungengefäßanordnung f pulmonary vasculature
Lungengefäßbett n pulmonary vascular bed
lungengefäßdarstellend angiopneumographic
Lungengefäßröntgen[kontrast]bild n pneumoangiogram
Lungengefäßröntgen[kontrast]darstellung f pneumoangiography
Lungengefäßverteilung f pulmonary vasculature
Lungengefäßwiderstand m pulmonary vascular resistance
Lungengefäßzeichnung f pulmonary vascularity (vascular markings)
Lungengeräusch n pulmonary murmur
Lungengewebe n pulmonary tissue
Lungengewebeerweichung f pneumomalacia, softening of the lung tissue
Lungengewebepunktion f pneumocentesis, puncture of the lung
Lungengewebeschnitt m pneumonotomy
Lungengewebeverdichtung f carnification
Lungengewebeverfestigung f pulmonary (pneumonic) consolidation

~/**milzartige** splenization
Lungengrenze f lung border
Lungenhämosiderose f pulmonary haemosiderosis; red induration [of the lung]
Lungenherd m/**Assmannscher** Assmann focus, early pulmonary infiltrate
Lungenhernie f pneum[at]ocele, pneumonocele *(durch einen Brustwandspalt)*
Lungenhilus m pulmonary hilum, hilum of the lung
Lungenhilusnähapparat m lung hilus suture appliance
Lungenhiluszyste f hilar cyst
Lungenhyperämie f hyperaemia of the lungs, pulmonary plethora
Lungeninduration f/**rote** red induration [of the lung]
Lungeninfarkt m pulmonary infarct
Lungeninfarzierung f pulmonary infarction (apoplexy)
Lungeninfektion f pulmonary infection
Lungeninfiltrat n pulmonary infiltrate
~/**eosinophiles** eosinophilic pneumonitis, Loeffler's syndrome
Lungeninfiltration f pulmonary (pneumonic) infiltration
Lungeninsuffizienz f respiratory insufficiency (inadequacy)
~/**posttraumatische** posttraumatic pulmonary insufficiency; adult respiratory distress syndrome; shock lung
Lungeninvasion f pulmonary invasion
Lungenkapazität f/**totale** total lung capacity
Lungenkapillarbett n pulmonary capillary bed
Lungenkapillare f pulmonary capillary
Lungenkapillarnetz n pulmonary capillary network
Lungenkapillarthrombose f pulmonary capillary thrombosis
Lungenkapillarverschlußdruck m pulmonary capillary wedge pressure, PCWP, pulmonary [artery] wedge pressure
Lungenkarzinom n lung cancer (carcinoma)
~/**diffuses** diffuse lung carcinoma
Lungenkaverne f pulmonary cavity (cavern)
Lungenkavernenfistelung f pulmonary cavernostomy
Lungenknospe f lung bud
Lungenkollaps m pulmonary collapse, collapse of the lung; atelectasis, apneumatosis
Lungenkollapsgeräusch n collapse rale
Lungenkrampf m/**inspiratorischer** apneusis
Lungenkrankheit f s. Lungenerkrankung
Lungenkrankheitsbehandlung f pneumonotherapy
Lungenkrebs m lung cancer (carcinoma)
Lungenkryptokokkose f pulmonary cryptococcosis
Lungenläppchen n pulmonary lobule
Lungenläppchenatelektase f lobular atelectasis
Lungenlappen m pulmonary lobe
Lungenlappenentfernung f[/**operative**] pulmonary lobectomy

Lungenlappenentzündung

Lungenlappenentzündung f lobitis, inflammation of a lobe
Lungenmanifestation f pulmonary (lung) manifestation
Lungenmetastase f pulmonary (lung) metastasis
Lungenmikroabszeß m pulmonary (lung) microabscess
Lungenmilzbrand m pulmonary (malignant) anthrax, woolsorter's (ragsorters') disease
Lungenmittellappen m/**rechter** middle lobe of the right lung
Lungenmittellappenresektion f/**rechtsseitige** resection of the middle lobe of the right lung
Lungenmoniliasis f pneumonomoniliasis, pulmonary moniliasis
Lungenmykose f pneumomycosis, pulmonary mycosis
Lungenmyzetom n pulmonary mycetoma
Lungennaht f pneumonorrhaphy, suture of the lung
Lungenoberlappen m superior lobe of the lung
~/**linker** superior lobe of the left lung
~/**rechter** superior lobe of the right lung
Lungenödem n pulmonary oedema, pneumonoedema; wet lung
Lungenparagonimiasis f pulmonary paragonimiasis
Lungenparenchym n pulmonary (lung) parenchyma
Lungenperfusion f pulmonary (lung) perfusion
Lungenpest f pneumonic (lung) plague; plague pneumonia
Lungenphykomykose f pulmonary phycomycosis
Lungenpilzinfektion f pulmonary fungal infection
Lungenproteinose f/**alveoläre** pulmonary alveolar proteinosis
Lungenpunktion f pulmonary (lung) puncture, pneumocentesis
Lungenrand m/**unterer** inferior border of the lung
Lungenreflex m pulmonary (lung) reflex
Lungenreife f pulmonary (lung) maturity
~/**fetale** foetal pulmonary maturity
Lungenreizstoff m lung irritant [agent] *(chemischer Kampfstoff)*
Lungenresektion f pneumoresection, pulmonary (lung) resection
Lungenrezirkulation f pulmonary recirculation *(bei Herzfehlern)*
Lungenröntgendarstellung f pneum[at]ography
Lungensarkoidose f pulmonary sarcoidosis
Lungenschall m pulmonary (lung) sound
lungenschwindsüchtig phthisic[al], phthinoid
Lungensegmentatelektase f segmental atelectasis
Lungensegmententfernung f[/**operative**] segmentectomy
Lungensilikose f pneumosilicosis
Lungenspatel m lung spatula
Lungenspezialist m pulmonologist, pulmonary (lung) specialist, chest physician

Lungenspitze f apex (tip) of the lung
Lungenspitzenentzündung f apex pneumonia
Lungensporotrichose f pulmonary sporotrichosis
Lungenstammarterie f main pulmonary artery (trunk)
Lungenstauung f 1. pulmonary congestion, congestion of the lung; 2. backward [heart] failure
Lungenstein m s. Pneumolith
Lungenstörung f pulmonary disorder (function impairment)
Lungensymptom n pulmonary symptom
Lungenszintigraphie f lung [scinti]scanning, pulmonary scanning, pulmonary (lung) scintigraphy
Lungenteilentfernung f pneumoresection
Lungentranspiration f pulmonary transpiration
Lungentransplantat n lung transplant
Lungentuberkulose f lung tuberculosis, [pulmonary] phthisis, pneumonophthisis, tuberculosis of the lung *(Zusammensetzungen s. unter Tuberkulose)*
Lungentuberkuloseinfiltrat n/**infraklavikuläres** s. Lungenherd/Assmannscher
Lungentularämie f pneumonic tularaemia
Lungenüberlüftung f hyperventilation, overventilation [of the lung]
Lungenüberwachung f pulmonary monitoring
Lungen- und Brustfellentzündung f pneumopleuritis
Lungen- und Darmentzündung f pneumoenteritis
Lungenunterbelüftung f hypoventilation
Lungenunterlappen m inferior lobe of the lung
~/**linker** inferior lobe of the left lung
~/**rechter** inferior lobe of the right lung
Lungenunterlappenarterie f/**linke** left lower lobar pulmonary artery
~/**rechte** right lower lobar pulmonary artery
Lungenunterlappenentfernung f[/**operative**] lower lobectomy
Lungenunterlappeninfiltrat n lower-lobe pulmonary infiltrate
Lungenunterrand m inferior border of the lung
Lungenvene f pulmonary vein
~/**fehlmündende** anomalous draining pulmonary vein
~/**linke** left pulmonary vein
~/**linke obere** superior left pulmonary vein
~/**linke untere** inferior left pulmonary vein
~/**rechte** right pulmonary vein
~/**rechte obere** superior right pulmonary vein
~/**rechte untere** inferior right pulmonary vein
Lungenvenenabfluß m pulmonary venous drainage
Lungenvenenblut n pulmonary venous blood
Lungenvenenfehlmündung f anomalous pulmonary venous drainage, transposition of the pulmonary veins
Lungenverfestigung f pulmonary (lung, pneumonic) consolidation
~/**leberartige** red hepatization *(bei Lungenentzündung)*

Lymphadenopathie

Lungenverschattung f pulmonary opacification *(Röntgenologie)*
Lungenvolumen n pulmonary (lung) volume
Lungenvorderrand m anterior margin of the lung
Lungenvorfall m pneum[at]ocele, pneumonocele *(durch einen Brustwandspalt)*
Lungenwiderstand m pulmonary (lung) resistance
Lungenwurzel f root of the lung
Lungenzange f lung forceps
Lungenzeichnung f pulmonary (lung) markings *(Radiologie)*
Lungenzwerchfellfläche f base of the lung
Lungenzyste f pulmonary cyst
Lunula f lunula *(am Fingernagel)*
Lupinidin n lupinidine, sparteine *(Alkaloid)*
Lupus m 1. lupus, chronic progressive ulcerative skin lesion; 2. s. ~ erythematodes; 3. s. ~ vulgaris
~ **erythematodes** lupus [erythematosus], L. E. *(Hautkrankheit mit verschiedensten Krankheitsbildern)*
~ **erythematodes cerebri** cerebral lupus erythematosus
~ **erythematodes discoides** discoid lupus erythematosus
~ **erythematodes disseminatus** butterfly lupus
~ **vulgaris** lupus vulgaris, true tuberculosis of the skin
lupusartig lupiform, lupoid
Lupus-erythematodes-Faktor m lupus erythematosus factor, lupus erythematosus plasma (serum) factor
Lupus-erythematodes-Körperchen n lupus erythematosus body
Lupus-erythematodes-Zelle f lupus erythematosus cell
Lupus-erythematodes-Zelltest m lupus erythematosus [cell] test
Lupusglomerulonephritis f lupus glomerulonephritis
Lupuskeloid n lupus keloid
Lupusnephritis f lupus nephritis
Lustgas n s. Lachgas
Lustseuche f s. Lues
Lusus m naturae lusus naturae
Lutealphase f luteal phase
Lutein n lutein *(gelber Farbstoff)*
luteinisieren to luteinize
Luteinisierung f luteinization
Luteinisierungshormon n luteinizing (interstitial-cell-stimulating) hormone, LH
Luteinisierungshormonfreisetzung f luteinizing hormone release
Luteinom n s. Luteom
Luteinzelle f lutein cell
Luteinzyste f lutein cyst, luteal [corpus] cyst
Lutembacher-Syndrom n Lutembacher's syndrome *(Herzfehler)*
Luteohormon n luteal (corpus luteum) hormone
Luteolysin n luteolysin

Luteom n lute[in]oma, luteoblastoma, luteinized granulosa-cell carcinoma, lipid-cell tumour of the ovary
Luteotrophin n s. Laktationshormon
Luxatio f **coxae congenita** congenital hip displacement
Luxation f dislocation, luxation, abarticulation
~/**alte** old dislocation
~/**angeborene** congenital dislocation
~/**frische** recent dislocation
~/**habituelle** habitual dislocation, recurrent (relapsing) dislocation
~/**inkomplette** incomplete (partial) dislocation, subluxation
~/**komplette** complete dislocation
~/**komplizierte** complicated dislocation
~/**offene** compound dislocation *(z. B. eines Gelenks)*
~/**subglenoidale** subglenoid dislocation *(des Humeruskopfes)*
Luxationshüfte f luxatio coxae congenita, hip displacement, congenital dislocation of the hip
luxieren to dislocate, to luxate, to disjoint
~/**inkomplett** to sublux
luxiert dislocated, disjoint *(Gelenk)*
Luxusherz n luxus heart
Luziferase f luciferase *(Enzym)*
Luziferin n luciferine
LVEDP s. Druck/linksventrikulärer enddiastolischer
Lyase f lyase *(Enzym)*
Lykorexie f lycorexia, ravenous (Wolfish) appetite
Lymphabfluß m lymphatic drainage, outflow of lymph
Lymphabflußgefäß n efferent lymphatic
Lymphadenektomie f lymphadenectomy
Lymphadenie f lymphadenia, hypertrophy of lymphatic tissue
Lymphadenitis f lymphadenitis, adenolymphitis, inflammation of lymph nodes
~ **bronchialis** bronchadenitis
~ **cervicalis** cervical adenitis
~ **granulomatosa venerea** venereal lymphogranuloma[tosis], venereal adenitis, fourth venereal disease
~ **inguinalis** inguinal lymphadenitis
~ **inguinalis subacuta** esthiomene, Nicolas-Favre disease
~ **mesenterica** mesenteric lymphadenitis
Lymphadenogramm n lymphadenogram, roentgenogram of lymph nodes
Lymphadenographie f lymphadenography, roentgenography of lymph nodes
Lymphadenohypertrophie f lymphadenohypertrophy
lymphadenoid lymphadenoid, resembling lymphatic tissue
Lymphadenom n lymphadenoma
Lymphadenopathie f 1. lymphadenopathy, disease of the lymph nodes; 2. lymph node enlargement

Lymphadenopathie

~/großfollikuläre giant follicular lymphadenopathy
~/subokzipitale suboccipital lymphadenopathy
~/zervikale cervical lymphadenopathy
lymphadenopathisch lymphadenopathic
Lymphadenose f lymphadenosis, hyperplasia of lymphatic tissue
Lymphadenosis f **benigna cutis** benign lymphadenosis, Bäfverstedt's disease
Lymphadenotomie f lymphadenotomy, incision of a lymph node
Lymphagogum n **[remedium]** lymphagogue [agent]
Lymphangiektasie f lymphangiectasia, dilatation of the lymphatic vessels
~/intestinale intestinal lymphangiectasia
lymphangiektatisch lymphangiectatic
Lymphangiektomie f lymphangiectomy, excision of a lymphatic vessel
Lymphangioendotheliom n lymphangio-endothelioma
Lymphangiofibrom n lymphangiofibroma
Lymphangiogramm n lymphangiogram
Lymphangiographie f lymph[angi]ography
Lymphangioleiomyomatose f lymphangioleiomyomatosis
Lymphangiologie f lymphangiology
Lymphangiom n lymphangioma, angiolymphoma *(gutartige Lymphgefäßgeschwulst) (s. a. unter Lymphangioma)*
~/angeborenes zystisches cystic hygroma (lymphangioma)
~ des Darms und Mesenteriums chylangioma
~/kavernöses cavernous lymphangioma
Lymphangioma n s. Lymphangiom
~ circumscriptum congenitale lymphangiectodes
~ tuberosum multiplex hydrocystadenoma, lymphangioma tuberosum multiplex *(Schweißdrüsengeschwulst)*
Lymphangiomatose f lymphangiomatosis
Lymphangiophlebitis f lymphangiophlebitis, inflammation of the lymph vessels and veins
Lymphangioplastik f lymphangioplasty
Lymphangiosarkom n lymphangiosarcoma *(bösartige Lymphgefäßgeschwulst)*
Lymphangiotomie f lymphangiotomy
Lymphangitis f s. Lymphgefäßentzündung
lymphangitisch lymphangitic
lymphartig lymphoid
Lymphatikostomie f lymphaticostomy
lymphatisch lymphatic
Lymphatismus m lymphatism, lymphotoxaemia, lymphatic state (constitution) *(Neigung zu Entzündung und Hyperplasie des lymphatischen Gewebes)*
Lymphausbreitung f lymphatic spread *(Metastasen)*
Lymphausfluß m lymphorrhoea, lymphorrhage, lymphorrhagia
Lymphausscheidung f **im Urin** lymphuria
lymphbildend lymphopoietic, lymphogenous

Lymphbildung f lymphopoiesis, lymphogenesis, formation of lymph
Lymphdrüse f s. Lymphknoten
Lymphe f lymph[a] *(eiweißhaltige Körperflüssigkeit)*
Lymphemangel m alymphia
Lymphendotheliom n lymphangio-endothelioma
Lymphflüssigkeit f s. Lymphe
Lymphfollikel m lymph follicle (nodule)
Lymphgefäß n lymphatic [vessel], lymph channel
● **um ein ~ liegend** perilymphangeal, perilymphangial, perilymphatic
~/entzündetes leader
Lymphgefäßausschneidung f lymphangiectomy
Lymphgefäßdurchtrennung f[/operative] lymphangiotomy
Lymphgefäßentzündung f lymphangi[i]tis, inflammation of a lymphatic vessel
~/durch ein Gerinnsel verursachte thrombolymphangitis
Lymphgefäßersatz m lymphangioplasty
lymphgefäßerweiternd lymphangiectatic
Lymphgefäßerweiterung f lymphangiectasia, lymphatic teleangiectasis; lymphatic varix
Lymphgefäßexstirpation f lymphangiectomy
Lymphgefäßfistelung f[/operative] lymphaticostomy
Lymphgefäßknospe f lymph bud
Lymphgefäßlehre f lymphangiology
Lymphgefäßplastik f lymphangioplasty
Lymphgefäßschnitt m lymphangiotomy
Lymphgefäß- und Venenentzündung f lymphangiophlebitis
Lymphgefäßverschluß m lymphatic obstruction
Lymphgeschwulst f lymphocyst, lymphocele
Lymphgewebe n lymphatic (lymphoid) tissue; adenoid tissue
lymphgewebeauflösend lymphatolytic
Lymphgewebeauflösung f lymphatolysis
lymphgewebebildend lymphoproliferative
Lymphgewebebildung f lymphoproliferation
lymphgewebezerstörend lymphatolytic
Lymphgewebezerstörung f lymphatolysis
Lymphkanal m s. Lymphgefäß
Lymphkapillare f lymph capillary
Lymphknospe f lymph bud
Lymphknötchen n lymph nodule (follicle)
Lymphknoten m lymph[atic] node, lymphatic gland, lymphonodus, lymphoglandula
~/axillärer axillary [lymphatic] gland
~/Cloquetscher Cloquet's gland, node of Cloquet
~/entzündlich vergrößerter panus, inflamed lymph node
~/Rosenmüllerscher Rosenmüller's gland, node of Rosenmüller
~/subklavikulärer subclavian lymph gland
~/supraklavikulärer supraclavicular signal node
~/Virchowscher Virchow's node, gland of Virchow-Troisier *(supraklavikuläre Lymphknotenmetastase)*
lymphknotenartig [lymph]adenoid

Lymphknotenbeteiligung f lymph node involvement
Lymphknotenbiopsie f lymph node biopsy
Lymphknotenbioptat n lymph node biopsy specimen
Lymphknotendissektion f lymph node dissection
Lymphknotenentfernung f[/operative] lymphadenectomy
Lymphknotenentzündung f s. Lymphadenitis
Lymphknotenerkrankung f s. Lymphadenopathie
Lymphknotengeschwulst f lymphadenoma
~/**bösartige** lymphoma
~/**käsige** tyroma
Lymphknotenhyperplasie f lymph node hyperplasia
Lymphknotenhypertrophie f lymphadenhypertrophy
Lymphknotenhypoplasie f lymph node hypoplasia
Lymphknoteninzision f lymphadenotomy
Lymphknotenkortex m cortex of the lymph node
Lymphknotenmark n medulla of the lymph node
Lymphknotenmetastase f lymph node metastasis
Lymphknotenpunktion f lymph node puncture
Lymphknotenschwellung f swelling (enlargement) of a lymph node
Lymphknotensinus m lymph sinus [space]
Lymphknotentuberkulose f tuberculosis of the lymphatic glands, glandular tuberculosis
Lymphknotenvergrößerung f lymph node enlargement, hyperadenosis
~/**zystische** adenolymphocele
Lymphknotenzyste f lymphadenocyst
Lymphkörperchen n s. Lymphozyt
Lymphkrankheit f lymphopathy
Lymphoblast m lympho[cyto]blast *(Lymphozytenstammzelle)*
lymphoblastenartig lymphoblastoid, lymphoblast-like
Lymphoblastengeschwulst f lymphoblastoma
Lymphoblastenleukämie f lymphoblastic leukaemia
lymphoblastisch lymphoblastic
Lymphoblastom n lymphoblastoma
Lymphoblastose f lymphoblastosis *(Lymphoblastenvermehrung im peripheren Blut)*
Lymphocytoma n **cutis** Spiegler-Fendt-sarcoid
Lymphocytosis f **infectiosa acuta** Smith's syndrome
Lymphödem n lymphatic oedema, lymphoedema
~ **des Armes** arm lymphoedema
~/**familiäres chronisches** hereditary (congenital) lymphoedema, idiopathic elephantiasis, Milroy's disease
~ **nach Brustamputation** postmastectomy lymphoedema
lymphödematös lymphoedematous
Lymphodermie f lymphodermia

Lymphoepitheliom n lympho-epithelioma, Schmincke's tumour
lymphogen lymphogenous, lymphogenic, lymphborne
Lymphogenese f lymphogenesis
Lymphogonie f lymphogonium *(Lymphozytenstammzelle)*
Lymphogranuloma n **inguinale** inguinal lymphogranuloma, tropical (climatic) bubo, fourth venereal disease, [Durand-]Nicolas-Favre disease
~ **venerea** venereal lymphogranuloma (adenitis), fifth venereal disease, Donovan's disease
Lymphogranulomatose f Hodgkin's disease; malignant granuloma, granulomatous lymphoma
Lymphographie f lymph[angi]ography
lymphohämatogen lymphohaematogenous
lymphohistiozytär lymphohistiocytic
Lymphohistiozytose f lymphohistiocytosis *(Lymphozyten- und Histiozytenvermehrung im Blut)*
lymphoid lymphoid, adenoid
Lymphoidzelle f lymphoid cell
Lymphoidzellenangina f infectious mononucleosis, lymphocytic angina, Pfeiffer's disease (glandular fever), acute benign lymphoblastosis, [acute] infectious adenitis
Lymphokinese f lymphokinesis
Lymphom n lymphoma *(meist bösartig)*
~/**immunoblastisches** immunoblastic lymphoma
~/**lymphozytäres** lymphocytic lymphoma
lymphomartig lymphomatoid, lymphomatous
Lymphomatose f lymph[aden]omatosis
Lymphomonozyt m lymphomonocyte
Lymphomonozytose f lymphomonocytosis *(Lymphozyten- und Monozytenvermehrung im Blut)*
Lymphomyelozyt m lymphomyelocyte
Lymphonodulus m lymph nodule (follicle)
~ **lienalis Malpighi** Malpighian body, splenic nodule (corpuscle) *(Lymphzellenansammlungen)*
~ **solitarius** solitary follicle
Lymphonodus m s. Lymphknoten
Lymphopathie f lymphopathy
Lymphopenie f s. Lymphozytopenie
Lymphopoese f lympho[cyto]poiesis
Lymphoproliferation f lymphoproliferation
lymphoproliferativ lymphoproliferative
Lymphoprotease f lymphoprotease *(Enzym)*
Lymphoretikulosis f 1. lymphoreticulosis; nodular (benign) lymphoma; 2. lymphoreticulosis, reticuloendothelial hyperplasia
Lymphorrhagie f, **Lymphorrhoe** f lymphorrhoea, lymphorrhage, lymphorrhagia
Lymphosarkom n lymphosarcoma, lymphatic sarcoma *(bösartige Geschwulst)*
~/**Burkittsches** Burkitt's lymphoma (tumour)
Lymphosarkomatose f lymphosarcomatosis *(bösartige Geschwulsterkrankung)*
Lymphostase f lymphostasis, lymphatic blockade, stoppage of the lymph flow
Lymphotaxis f lymphotaxis
Lymphotoxin n lymphotoxin
Lymphozyste f lymphocyst, lymphocele

Lymphozyt

Lymphozyt *m* lymphocyte, lymph cell (corpuscle), achroacyte
~/großer macrolymphocyte
lymphozytär lymphocytic
lymphozytenähnlich lymphocytoid
Lymphozytenangina *f* lymphocytic angina *(Halsentzündung mit überwiegend lymphatischem Blutbild)*
Lymphozytenantikörper *m* lymphocyte antibody
Lymphozytenbewegung *f* lymphotaxis *(z. B. auf chemische Reize)*
lymphozytenbildend lympho[cyto]poietic
Lymphozytenbildung *f* lympho[cyto]poiesis
Lymphozytenchoriomeningitis *f* lymphocytic choriomeningitis, acute aseptic meningitis
Lymphozytenchoriomeningitisvirus *n* lymphocytic choriomeningitis virus
Lymphozytenentwicklung *f* lympho[cyto]poiesis
Lymphozytengift *n* lymphotoxin
Lymphozytengiftigkeit *f* lymphocytotoxicity
Lymphozyteninfiltration *f* lymphocytic infiltration
Lymphozytenklon *m* lymphocyte clone
Lymphozytenkultur *f* lymphocyte culture
Lymphozytenleukämie *f* lymphocytic leukaemia
Lymphozytenlymphom *n* lymphocytic lymphoma
Lymphozytenmangel *m* lymphocytopenia
~/angeborener congenital lymphocytopenia, Nezelof's syndrome
Lymphozytenmeningitis *f* lymphocytic meningitis
Lymphozytenmikrozytotoxizitätstest *m* lymphocyte microcytotoxicity test
Lymphozytenmischkultur *f* mixed lymphocyte culture
Lymphozytenpleozytose *f* lymphocytic pleocytosis
Lymphozyten[reifungs]reihe *f* lymphocytic (lymphoid) series
Lymphozytensarkom *n* lymphocytic sarcoma
Lymphozytenschwund *m* lympho[cyto]penia
Lymphozytenstammzelle *f* lymphoid stem cell
Lymphozytentoxizitätstest *m* lymphocytotoxicity test
Lymphozytentransformation *f* lymphocyte transformation
Lymphozytentransformationstest *m* lymphocyte transformation test
lymphozytentransformierend lymphocyte-transforming
Lymphozytentransfusion *f* lymphocyte transfusion
Lymphozyten-Tuberkulin-Reaktion *f* lymphocyte-tuberculin reaction
lymphozytenvermittelt lymphocyte-mediated
Lymphozythämie *f* lymphocythaemia, achroacytosis
Lymphozytom *n* lymphocytoma *(bösartige Lymphzellengeschwulst)*
Lymphozytomanhäufung *f* lymphocytomatosis
Lymphozytomatose *f* lymphocytomatosis

Lymphozytopenie *f* lympho[cyto]penia *(Lymphozytenverminderung im peripheren Blut)*
Lymphozytopoese *f* lympho[cyto]poiesis
Lymphozytose *f* lymphocytosis *(Lymphozytenvermehrung im peripheren Blut)*
~/infektiöse infectious lymphocytosis, Carl Smith's disease
~/relative relative lymphocytosis
Lymphozytotoxin *n* lymphocytotoxin
Lymphozytotoxizität *f* lymphocytotoxicity
Lymphsinus *m* lymph sinus [space]
Lymphstau *m*, **Lymphstauung** *f s.* Lymphostase
Lymphstreuung *f* lymphatic spread *(von Metastasen)*
Lymphstrom *m* lymph flow
Lymphsystem *n* lymphatic system
lymphtreibend lymphagogue
Lymphverschluß *m* lymphatic obstruction
Lymphzelle *f s.* Lymphozyt
lymphzellenbildend lympho[cyto]poietic
Lyogel *n* lyogel *(z. B. Gallerte)*
Lyoglykogen *n* lyoglycogen *(z. B. im Gewebe)*
lyophil lyophil[e], lyophilic
Lyophilisierung *f* lyophilization
lyophob lyophobe, lyophobic
Lypemanie *f* lypemania, insanity with depression
Lyse *f s.* Lysis
Lysergsäure *f* lysergic acid *(Grundbaustein der Mutterkornalkaloide)*
Lysergsäurediäthylamid *n* lysergic acid diethylamide, LSD *(Psychosegift)*
Lysholm-Blende *f* Lysholm grid *(Röntgenologie)*
Lysin *n* 1. lysin *(Antikörper)*; 2. lysine, diamino caproic acid
~/intrazelluläres endolysin
lysinbildend lysogenic
Lysinbildung *f* lysogenesis
Lysinzerstörung *f* antilysis
Lysis *f* 1. lysis, action of a lysin; 2. lysis, gradual abatement of symptoms; 3. decline of fever
Lysochrom *n* lysochrome, oil-soluble dye
Lysogenese *f* lysogenesis
Lysokephalin *n* lysocephalin *(Hämolysegift)*
Lysokinase *f* lysokinase *(Enzym)*
Lysolezithin *n* lysolecithin *(Hämolysegift)*
Lysosom *n* lysosome *(Zellplasmakörper)*
Lysosomenhydrolase *f* lysosomal hydrolase *(Enzym)*
Lysosomenhydrolaseaktivität *f* lysosomal hydrolase activity
Lysozym *n* lysozyme, lysosomal enzyme, muramidase *(bakteriolytisches Enzym)*
Lysozymausscheidung *f im Urin* lysozymuria
Lyssa *f s.* Tollwut
Lyssophobie *f* lyssophobia, hydrophobophobia *(krankhafte Angst vor Tollwut)*
lytisch lytic

M

M. s. 1. Musculus; 2. Morbus
Machado-Guerreiro-Reaktion f Machado-Guerreiro reaction *(Komplement-Bindungsreaktion zum Nachweis der Chagas-Krankheit und der Leishmaniasis)*
machen:
~/**adsorptionsfähig** to activate
~/**alkalisch** to alkalinize
~/**anergisch** to hyposensitize
~/**aseptisch** to render aseptic, to sterilize
~/**betrunken** to inebriate
~/**beweglich** to mobilize *(ein Gelenk)*
~/**blind** to blind
~/**blutleer** to avascularize, to render bloodless
~/**durch Erhitzen keimarm** to pasteurize
~/**eine Behandlung notwendig** to require treatment
~/**eine Naht** to suture
~/**eine Röntgenaufnahme** to radiograph, to roentgenograph, to roentgenize
~/**eine Spülung** to irrigate
~/**einen Abstrich** to take a swab
~/**empfindlich** to sensitize
~/**fortpflanzungsunfähig** to sterilize, to render incapable of reproduction
~/**für eine Krankheit empfänglich** to predispose
~/**geruchlos** to deodorize
~/**gesund** to sanitize
~/**haltbar** to fix *(histologische Präparate)*; to conserve
~/**immun** to immunize, to render immune
~/**jemanden für eine Infektion empfänglich** to render a person susceptible to infection
~/**keimfrei** to sterilize, to render sterile (free from micro-organisms); to sanitize, to autoclave *(im Autoklaven)*
~/**lichtempfindlich** to photosensitize
~/**mit Kokain unempfindlich** to cocainize
~/**neutral** to neutralize
~/**radioaktiv** to activate
~/**sauer** to acidify, to acidulate
~/**schläfrig** to soporate
~/**schmerzlos** to anaesthetize, to analgize
~/**sichtbar** to visualize *(dem Auge)*
~/**taub** to deafen
~/**überempfindlich** to hypersensitize
~/**unbeweglich** to immobilize *(z. B. ein Gelenk)*
~/**unempfindlich** to render insensitive, to desensitize, to hyposensitize; to anaesthetize; to immunize, to render resistant (immune)
~/**unfruchtbar** to sterilize, to render sterile; to castrate
~/**ungerinnbar** to anticoagulate, to make incoagulable; to heparinize
~/**unwirksam** to inactivate, to render inactive; to neutralize; to paralyse
~/**wieder wirksam** to reactivate; to regenerate
~/**zum Krüppel** to mutilate, to main
machend:
~/**immun** immunifacient

~/**trunken** intoxicant
~/**viskös** pachytic
Macleod-Syndrom n MacLeod's syndrome, unilateral radiolucency of the lung; unilateral translucent lung
Macula f 1. macula, spot; 2. macula, pigmented macule, melanotic freckle *(der Haut)*; 3. s. ~ cornea; 4. s. ~ lutea
~ **acustica utriculi** s. ~ utriculi
~ **adhaerens** macula adhaerens, desmosome
~ **caerulea** macula cerulea, blue spot
~ **cornea** [corneal] macula, corneal opacity (scar) *(des Auges)*
~ **densa** macula densa *(kernreicher Bezirk im Mittelstück des Tubulus renalis)*
~ **flava** macula flava, yellow spot; yellow nodule
~ **germinativa** germinative macula, germinal area, nucleolus of the ovum
~ **lutea** macula [lutea], yellow spot [of the retina] *(Stelle des schärfsten Sehens)*
~ **sacculi** saccular macula *(Rezeptor für die Gleichgewichtsempfindung)*
~ **solaris** macula solaris, freckle; lentigo
~ **utriculi** utricular macula *(Rezeptor für die Gleichgewichtsempfindung)*
Macula... s. Makula...
Madagaskargeschwür n Madagascar (oriental) sore
Madarose f madarosis, loss of the eyelashes or eyebrows
Madenbefall m, **Madenfraß** m s. Madenkrankheit
Madenkrankheit f myiasis, myiosis
~ **des Auges** ophthalmomyiasis
~ **des Darms** enteromyiasis, intestinal myiasis
Madenwurm m Enterobius (Oxyuris) vermicularis, oxyurid, pinworm, thread-worm
madenwurmartig oxyurid
Madenwurmerkrankung f enterobiasis, oxyuriasis *(durch Enterobius vermicularis)*
Madonnenfinger mpl s. Marfan-Syndrom
Madurafraß m maduromycosis
Madurafuß m Madura (fungus) foot; mycetoma
Maduromykose f maduromycosis
Magen m stomach, gaster ● **auf nüchternen** ~ on an empty stomach ● **den** ~ **auspumpen** to empty (pump out) the stomach ● **durch den** ~ **transgastric** ● **mit einem** ~ monogastric ● **mit mehreren Mägen** polygastric ● **vom** ~ **ausgehend** gastrogenic
~/**angelhakenförmiger** fishhook stomach
~/**langgestreckter** J stomach
Magenabsaugung f gastric aspiration, suction drainage of the stomach
Magenachlorhydrie f gastric achlorhydria
Magenadenomyom n gastric adenomyoma
Magenaktionsstromaufzeichnung f electrogastrography
Magenaktionsstromkurve f electrogastrogram
Magenanazidität f gastric anacidity
Magenantrum n gastric antrum
Magenantrumresektion f antrectomy

Magenarterie

Magenarterie f gastric artery
~/kurze short gastric artery
~/linke left gastric artery, left stomach coronary artery
~/rechte right gastric artery, right stomach coronary artery
Magenaspirat n gastric aspirate
Magenatonie f gastro-atonia, atony of the stomach, gastroparesis, gastroparalysis, gastrasthenia, gastric insufficiency
Magenatrophie f gastratrophia, atrophy of the stomach, gastric atrophy
Magenausgang m s. Magenpförtner
Magenaushebung f, **Magenauspumpen** n gastric aspiration, siphonage, evacuation (pumping out) of the stomach
Magenausspülung f washing out of the stomach
Magenausweitung f megalogastria
Magenbeschwerden fpl gastric complaints (trouble), stomach disorder
Magenbezoar m s. Magenstein 2.
Magenbinnendruckmessung f gastrotonometry
Magenblähung f gastrotympanites, gastric flatulence; gaseous distention of the stomach
Magenblase f gastric bubble
Magenblutung f gastrorrhagia, gastric bleeding, haemorrhage from the stomach; gastrostaxis
Magenbrennen n heartburn, pyrosis
Magenbruch m gastrocele
Magenchromoskopie f gastric chromoscopy
Magen-Darm-Absaugung f gastro-intestinal suction
Magen-Darm-Aktinomykose f gastro-intestinal actinomycosis
Magen-Darm-Anastomose f gastroenteroanastomosis, gastroenterostomy
Magen-Darm-Blutung f gastro-intestinal haemorrhage (bleeding)
~/untere lower gastro-intestinal bleeding
Magen-Darm-Entzündung f enterogastritis, gastroenteritis
Magen-Darm-Fistel f gastro-intestinal fistula
Magen-Darm-Grippe f abdominal influenza
Magen-Darm-Infektion f gastro-intestinal infection
Magen-Darm-Kanal m gastro-intestinal tract, digestive canal (tube)
Magen-Darm-Krankheit f gastroenteropathy, gastro-intestinal disease (illness)
Magen-Darm-Manifestation f gastro-intestinal manifestation
Magen-Darm-Milzbrand m gastro-intestinal anthrax
Magen-Darm-Passage f gastro-intestinal passage
Magen-Darm-Reizung f gastro-intestinal irritation
Magen-Darm-Schmerz m gastroenteralgia
Magen-Darm-Sekret n gastro-intestinal secretion
Magen-Darm-Senkung f gastroenteroptosis, prolapse of the stomach and intestines

Magen-Darm-Spezialist m [gastro]enterologist
Magen-Darm-Störung f gastro-intestinal disturbance
Magen-Darm-Verbindung f[/operative] gastroenterostomy, gastroenteroanastomosis
Magen-Darm-Verdauung f gastro-intestinal digestion
Magendauerabsaugung f continuous gastric suction
Magendekompression f gastric decompression
Magen-Dickdarm-Anastomose f gastrocolostomy
Magen-Dickdarm-Ligament n gastrocolic ligament
Magen-Dickdarm-Reflex m gastrocolic reflex
Magen-Dickdarm-Verbindung f[/operative] gastrocolostomy
Magendissektion f dissection of the stomach
Magendivertikel n gastric diverticulum
Magendrainageoperation f/**Finneysche** Finney's pyloroplasty
Magendruckentlastung f gastric decompression
Magendrüse f gastric (stomach) gland
Magendrüsenentzündung f gastradenitis, inflammation of the stomach glands
Magen-Dünndarm-Dickdarm-Entzündung f gastroenterocolitis
Magen-Dünndarm-Fistelung f[/operative] Wölfler's operation
Magendurchleuchtung f screening of the stomach
Mageneinbuchtung f angular incisure (notch, sulcus)
Mageneingang m s. Magenmund
Magenektasie f gastrectasia, dilatation of the stomach
Magenentfernung f[/operative] gastrectomy
Magenentleerung f gastric emptying; gastric evacuation
Magenentleerungszeit f gastric emptying time
Magenentzündung f s. Magenschleimhautentzündung
Magenernährungssonde f [gastric] feeding tube
Mageneröffnung f **durch Bauchschnitt** laparogastrotomy
~/operative gastrotomy
~/transabdominale transabdominal gastrotomy, coeliogastrotomy
Magenerosion f gastric erosion
Magenerweichung f gastromalacia, softening of the gastric walls
Magenerweiterung f stomach dilatation, dilatation of the stomach, gastrectasia
~/abnorme megalogastria
Magenfaktor m/**endogener** intrinsic factor, haemopoietin (Blutbildungswirkstoff)
Magenfaltung f gastroplication
Magenfistel f gastrostoma; gastric fistula ● **eine ~ anlegen** to gastrostomize, to perform a gastrostomy
~ nach Kader Kader's gastrostomy
Magenfistelschlauch m gastrostomy tube

Magenfistelung f/**operative** gastrostomy
~/Witzelsche Witzel's operation
Magenfixation f gastropexy, fixation of the stomach
Magenfotografie f gastrophotography
Magenfrühkarzinom n early gastric cancer
Magenfundus m gastric fundus, fundus (fornix) of the stomach
Magenfundusentfernung f [/**operative**] fund[us]ectomy
Magenfundusfaltung[soperation] f fundoplication
Magengegend f epigastrium
Magengekröse n mesogaster, mesogastrium
Magengeschwulst f/**bösartige** gastric malignancy
Magengeschwür n gastric (peptic) ulcer, gastrohelcoma
~/Curlingsches Curling's ulcer *(bei Verbrennungen)*
Magengeschwürentstehung f gastric (stomach) ulceration
Magengeschwürkrebs m ulcerocancer
Magengeschwürleiden n gastrohelcosis
magengiftig gastrotoxic
Magengrübchen n gastric foveola (pit) *(der Magenschleimhaut)*
Magengrube f epigastrium, epigastric region, pit of the stomach, midriff
Magenherauslösung f gastrolysis
Magenhernie f gastrocele, hernia of the stomach
Magenhinterwand f posterior (dorsal) wall of the stomach
Magenhöhle f gastric cavity
Magenhormon n gastric hormone *(z. B. Gastrin)*
Mageninhalt m 1. gastric contents; 2. stomach volume
~/abgesaugter gastric aspirate
Magenkamera f gastrocamera
Magenkardiaentfernung f/**operative** cardiectomy
Magenkatarrh m s. Magenschleimhautentzündung
Magenklemme f stomach clamp (forceps)
Magenkörper m body of the stomach
Magenkrampf m gastrospasm, gastric spasm (contraction), stomach cramp; gastralgia; cardialgia
Magenkrankheit f gastropathy, gastric disease, disease of the stomach
Magenkranzvene f coronary vein of the stomach
Magenkrebs m gastric carcinoma, stomach cancer
Magenkrebsmetastase f stomach cancer metastasis
Magenkrise f gastric crisis, paroxysmal pain in the abdomen
Magen-Krummdarm-Anastomose f gastroileostomy
Magen-Krummdarm-Verbindung f/**operative** gastroileostomy
Magenkurvatur f/**große** greater curvature of the stomach

~/kleine lesser curvature of the stomach
Magenlähmung f s. Magenatonie
Magenlavage f gastric lavage; gastrolavage
Magen-Leber-Ligament n gastrohepatic ligament
Magen-Leerdarm-Fistel f gastrojejunal fistula
Magen-Leerdarm-Verbindung f/**operative** gastrojejunostomy
Magenleiden n gastropathy, gastric disease
Magenleidender m patient with gastric disease (complaints)
magenlos agastric
Magenlosigkeit f agastria
Magenlösung f gastrolysis
Magen-Magen-Anastomose f gastrogastroanastomosis, gastrogastrostomy
Magen-Magen-Verbindung f/**operative** gastrogastrostomy
Magen-Milz-Ligament n gastrolienal ligament
Magenmotilität f gastric motility
Magenmotorik f/**gesteigerte** hyperprochoresis, excessive motor function of the stomach
Magenmund m cardia, cardiac orifice, oesophagogastric junction, inlet of the stomach
Magenmunddrüse f cardiac gland
Magenmunderöffnung f[/**operative**] cardiotomy
Magenmunderweiterer m cardiodilator
Magenmunderweiterung f[/**operative**] cardiodiosis
Magenmundkrampf m cardiospasm; achalasia of the cardia
Magenmundschließer m cardiac sphincter
Magenmundsphinkterdurchtrennung f cardiomyotomy, cardio-oesophagomyotomy
Magennaht f 1. gastrorrhaphy, suture of the stomach; 2. gastroplication
Magenneoplasma n/**bösartiges** gastric malignancy
Magennerv m gastric nerve
Magenneurose f gastric neurosis (neurasthenia), psychic indigestion, nervous dyspepsia
Magenoberfläche f gastric surface
Magenöffnerplastik f cardioplasty
Magenoperation f gastric operation
~/plastische gastroplasty
Magenperforation f gastric perforation, perforation of the stomach
Magenpförtner m pylorus ● **dicht neben dem ~ [liegend]** juxtapyloric ● **durch den ~** transpyloric
Magenpförtner... s. a. Pylorus...
Magenpförtnerdehnungsinstrument n pylorodilator
Magenpförtnerdurchtrennung f[/**operative**] gastromyotomy, pylorotomy
Magenpförtnerentfernung f[/**operative**] [gastro]pylorectomy, excision of the pylorus
Magenpförtnererweiterung f/**Heineke-Mikuliczsche** Heineke-Mikulicz operation
~/operative pyloroplasty
Magenpförtnerplastik f pyloroplasty
Magenpförtnersenkung f pyloroptosia

Magenpförtnerspasmus 478

Magenpförtnerspasmus *m* pylorospasm, spasm of the pylorus
Magenpförtnerspiegelung *f* pyloroscopy
Magenpförtnertiefstand *m* pyloroptosis
Magenpförtnervereng[er]ung *f* pylorostenosis, pyloric stenosis, stricture of the pylorus
Magenpförtnerverschluß *m* obstruction of the pylorus, pyloroschesis
Magenpilzerkrankung *f* gastromycosis
Magenplastik *f* gastroplasty
Magenplexus *m* gastric plexus
Magenpolyp *m* gastric polyp
Magenpolypose *f* gastric polyposis
Magenptose *f* ventroptosis
Magenpumpe *f* stomach pump
Magenquetschklemme *f* pylorus clamp
Magenraffung *f*[/operative] gastroplication
Magenreizung *f* gastric distress (irritation)
Magenresektion *f* gastric resection, partial gastrectomy
Magenriß *m* gastrorrhexis, rupture of the stomach
Magenröntgenaufnahme *f* X-ray of the stomach
Magenröntgenkontrastaufnahme *f* contrast X-ray of the stomach
Magenruptur *f* gastrorrhexis, rupture of the stomach
Magensaft *m* gastric juice (fluid)
Magensaftanalyse *f* gastric analysis
Magensaftfluß *m* gastrorrhoea, secretion of gastric juice
~/dauernder Reichmann's disease, continuous secretion of gastric juice
Magensaftsekretion *f*/übermäßige polygastria, excessive secretion of gastric juice, hyperchylia
~/verminderte hypochylia
Magensaftsekretionsanalyse *f* gastric secretory test
Magensaftüberproduktion *f* hyperchylia
Magensaftunterproduktion *f* hypochylia
Magensäure *f* gastric acid
Magensäuregehalt *m*/normaler euchlorhydria
Magensäuremangel *m* gastric achlorhydria
Magensäuresekretion *f* gastric acid secretion
~/erhöhte hyperchlorhydria, gastroxynsis, gastric hyperacidity
~/verminderte hypochlorhydria
Magenschädigung *f* gastric distress
Magenschatten *m* shadow of the stomach, gastric shadow *(Radiologie)*
Magenschlaffheit *f* s. Magenatonie
Magenschlauch *m* [stomach] tube, gastric aspiration tube
Magenschleim *m* gastric mucus
Magenschleimfluß *m* gastromyxorrhoea, gastric secretion of mucus; gastrorrhoea
Magenschleimhaut *f* gastric mucosa, mucous membrane of the stomach
Magenschleimhautareal *n* gastric [mucosal] area
Magenschleimhautausschälung *f* endogastrectomy

Magenschleimhautbarriere *f* gastric mucosal barrier
Magenschleimhautbezirk *m* gastric [mucosal] area
Magenschleimhautblutung *f* gastrostaxis, oozing from the mucous membrane of the stomach
Magenschleimhautdrüsenentzündung *f* gastradenitis, inflammation of the stomach glands
Magenschleimhautentfernung *f*[/operative] endogastrectomy
Magenschleimhautentzündung *f* gastritis, inflammation of the stomach *(Zusammensetzungen s. unter* Gastritis*)*
Magenschleimhautfalte *f* ruga of the stomach
Magenschleimhauthyperplasie *f*/foveoläre giant hypertrophic gastritis, Ménétrier's disease
Magenschleimhautschutz *m* gastric cytoprotection
Magenschmerz *m* gastralgia, pain in the stomach, gastrodynia, stomachodynia; cardialgia
Magenschnitt *m* gastrotomy
Magenschrumpfung *f* gastrostenosis, shrinking of the stomach
Magenschwindel *m* gastric (stomachal) vertigo
Magensekretion *f* gastric secretion
Magensenkung *f* gastroptosis, gastrokatexia, ventroptosis, ptosis of the stomach; dropped stomach
Magensonde *f* 1. [stomach] tube, gastric aspiration tube; 2. [gastric] feeding tube
~ nach Rehfuß Rehfuss tube
~/[trans]nasale nasogastric [feeding] tube
Magensondenernährung *f* gastrogavage, artificial feeding through a gastrostoma
~/[trans]nasale nasogastric [tube] feeding
Magensondierung *f* intubation of the stomach
Magenspeichelreflex *m* gastrosalivary reflex
Magen-Speiseröhren-Katarrh *m* gastro-oesophagitis
Magen-Speiseröhren-Plastik *f* gastro-oesophagoplasty
Magen-Speiseröhren-Verbindung *f*[/operative] gastro-oesophagostomy
Magenspezialist *m* gastrologist
Magensphinkter *m* pyloric sphincter
Magensphinkterrekonstruktion *f*[/operative] cardioplasty
Magenspiegel *m* gastroscope
Magenspiegelung *f* gastroscopy, stomachoscopy
~ nach Bauchschnitt und Mageneröffnung laparogastroscopy
Magenspülung *f* gastric lavage (irrigation), gastrolavage, lavage (washing out) of the stomach, siphonage
Magenstauung *f* gastric stasis
Magenstein *m* 1. gastrolith, gastric calculus; 2. [gastric] bezoar *(geschwulstartiges Knäuel aus aufgenommener Nahrung)*
Magensteinleiden *n* gastrolithiasis
Magenstraße *f* gastric canal (pathway), magenstrasse

Magenstumpf *m* gastric stump
Magenstumpfkarzinom *n* gastric stump carcinoma
Magenstumpfnähapparat *m* gastric stump suture appliance
Magensturzentleerung *f* dumping stomach (syndrome)
Magenszintigraphie *f* gastric scintiscanning, scanning of the stomach
Magenteilresektion *f* hemigastrectomy, partial gastrectomy
Magentonus *m* gastric tonus (tone)
Magenübersäuerung *f* gastric hyperacidity, gastroxynsis, hyperchlorhydria
Magenulzeration *f* stomach ulceration
Magen- und Darmentzündung *f* gastroenteritis
Magen- und Darmnähapparat *m* intestinal-and-stomach-suturing apparatus
Magen- und Dickdarmentzündung *f* gastrocolitis
Magen- und Leerdarmentzündung *f* gastrojejunitis
Magen- und Netzarterie *f/linke* left gastroepiploic artery
~/**rechte** right gastroepiploic artery
Magen- und Netzvene *f/linke* left gastroepiploic vein
~/**rechte** right gastroepiploic vein
Magen- und Speiseröhrenentzündung *f* gastrooesophagitis
Magen- und Zwölffingerdarmentzündung *f* gastroduodenitis
Magen- und Zwölffingerdarmspiegelung *f* gastroduodenoscopy
Magenunterkühlung *f* gastric cooling
Magenuntersuchung *f* gastric examination
~ **im durchscheinenden Licht** gastrodiaphanoscopy
Magenunverträglichkeit *f* gastric intolerance
Magenvene *f* gastric vein
~/**kurze** short gastric vein
~/**linke** left gastric vein, left stomach coronary vein
~/**rechte** right gastric vein, right stomach coronary vein
Magenverdauung *f* gastric digestion
Magenvereng[er]ung *f* gastrostenosis
Magenvergrößerung *f* gastromegaly
Magenverweilsonde *f* gastrogavage
Magenvolumen *n* gastric volume
Magenvolvulus *m* gastric volvulus, upside-down stomach
Magenvorderwand *f* anterior (ventral) wall of the stomach
Magenvorfall *m* **in den Brustkorb** thoracic stomach
Magenwanderweichung *f* gastromalacia, softening of the stomach walls
Magenwiedervereinigung *f/operative* gastrogastrostomy
Magenzirrhose *f/hypertrophische* linitis plastica

Magen-Zwölffingerdarm-Arterie *f* gastroduodenal artery
Magen-Zwölffingerdarm-Plexus *m* gastroduodenal plexus
Magen-Zwölffingerdarm-Schlauch *m* gastroduodenal tube
Magen-Zwölffingerdarm-Verbindung *f/operative* gastroduodenostomy
Magenzyste *f* gastric cyst
mager meagre, thin, slender; emaciated
Magersucht *f* emaciation, loss of weight
magistral magistral, prepared on prescription *(Arzneimittel)*
Magma *f* **reticulare** reticular magma *(zum Schutz der Embryonalanlage)*
Magnesiämie *f* magnesaemia
Magnesiumhydroxid *n* magnesium hydrate (hydroxide) *(Antazidum, Laxans)*
Magnesiumkarbonat *n* magnesium carbonate *(Antazidum, Laxans)*
Magnesiumoxid *n* magnesium oxide *(Antazidum, Laxans)*
Magnesiumspiegelerhöhung *f* **im Blut** hypermagnesaemia
Magnesiumspiegelverringerung *f* **im Blut** hypomagnesaemia
Magnesiumsulfat *n* magnesium sulphate *(Laxans)*
Magnetextraktion *f* magnet operation
Magnetfeldtherapie *f* magnetotherapy
Magnetokardiographie *f* magnetocardiography *(Messung des Herzmagnetfelds)*
Magnetotherapie *f* magnetotherapy
Magnetreaktion *f* magnet reaction *(des Neugeborenen)*
Magnetreflex *m* magnet reflex *(des Neugeborenen)*
magnozellulär magnocellular
mahlend molar
Mahlzahn *m s.* Molar
Mahlzeit *f* meal, repast ● **nach den Mahlzeiten** postcibal, post cibum, p.c., after meals ● **nach einer** ~ postprandial ● **vor den Mahlzeiten** antecibal, ante cibum, a.c., before meals
Maidismus *m* maidism, poisoning by damaged maize; pellagra
Main *f* **en griffe** claw hand
Maisvergiftung *f s.* Maidismus
Majortest *m* major cross match *(bei der Blutgruppenkreuzprobe)*
MAK *s.* Arbeitsplatzkonzentration/maximale
Makrenzephalie *f s.* Makroenzephalie
Makro... *s.a.* Megalo...
makroadenös macradenous
Makroamylasämie *f* macroamylasaemia
Makroamylase *f* macroamylase *(Enzym)*
Makroamylaseerhöhung *f* **im Blut** macroamylasaemia
Makroangiopathie *f/diabetische* diabetic macroangiopathy
Makroästhesie *f* macroaesthesia *(Empfindungsstörung)*

Makrobakterium

Makrobakterium n macrobacterium
Makrobiose f macrobiosis
Makroblast m macroblast, proerythroblast *(Erythrozytenvorstufe)*
Makroblepharie f macroblepharia, abnormal largeness of the eyelids
Makroblepharon n macroblepharon
Makrobrachie f macrobrachia, abnormal largeness of the arms
Makrocheilie f macroch[e]ilia, macrolabia, abnormal largeness of the lips
Makrocheirie f macroch[e]iria, abnormal largeness of the hands
Makrodaktylie f macrodactyly, abnormal largeness of fingers and toes, dactylomegaly, megalodactyly, megalodactylism
Makrodaktylus m macrodactylus
makrodont macrodont, having large teeth
Makrodontie f macrodontia, megalodontia, abnormal largeness of the teeth
Makroembolie f macroembolism
makroenzephal macrencephalous, macrencephalic
Makroenzephalie f macr[o]encephalia, megalencephalia, abnormal largeness of the brain
Makroenzephalon n macrencephalon, megalencephalon
Makroerythrozyt m macroerythrocyte
makrofollikulär macrofollicular, having large follicles
Makrogamet m macrogamete, megagamete *(Malariaentwicklungsstadium)*
Makrogametozyt m macrogametocyte *(Malariaentwicklungsstadium)*
Makrogamie f macrogamy
Makrogastrie f macrogastria, megalogastria, abnormal largeness of the stomach
Makrogenitosomie f macrogenitosomia [praecox], precocious development
Makroglia f macroglia *(Nervenstützgewebe)*
makroglial, makrogliär macroglial
Makroglobulin n macroglobulin
Makroglobulinämie f macroglobulinaemia
~/Waldenströmsche Waldenström's syndrome (macroglobulinaemia)
Makroglossie f macroglossia, megaloglossia, abnormal largeness of the tongue
makrognath macrognathic, macrognathous
Makrognathie f macrognathia, abnormal largeness of the jaws
Makrographie f macrographia *(krankhafte Neigung zu abnorm großer Schrift)*
Makrogyrie f macrogyria, abnormal largeness of the brain convolutions
Makrohämaturie f erythr[ocyt]uria
Makrokardie f macrocardia, abnormal largeness of the heart
Makrokonidium n macroconidium
Makrolymphozyt m macrolymphocyte, large lymphocyte
Makrolymphozytose f macrolymphocytosis

480

Makromastie f macromastia, macromazia, abnormal largeness of the breasts
Makromelie f macromelia, megalomelia, abnormal largeness of the limbs
Makromelus m macromelus
Makromerozoit m macromerozoite
Makromonozyt m macromonocyte
Makromyeloblast m macromyeloblast
makronodulär macronodular
Makronormoblast m macronormoblast
Makronukleus m macronucleus
Makronychie f macronychia, megalonychosis, abnormal largeness of the nails
Makroorchidie f macroorchidia, abnormal largeness of the testicle
Makroorch[id]ismus m macroorchi[di]sm
Makropathologie f macropathology
Makrophag[e] m macrophage, scavenger [cell], endotheliocyte, endothelial phagócyte *(für körperfremdes Material)*
~/erythrozytenbeladener erythrophage
Makrophagenagglutinationstest m macrophage agglutination test
Makrophagenaktivität f activity of macrophages, macrophagy
Makrophagen-Elektrophorese-Mobilitätstest m macrophage electrophoresis mobility test
Makrophagen-Migrations-Hemmtest m macrophage migration inhibition test
Makrophagozyt m macrophagocyte
Makrophthalmie f macrophthalmia, abnormal largeness of the eyeball
makrophthalmisch macrophthalmic, macrophthalmous
Makrophthalmus m macrophthalmus, megalophthalmus
Makropinozytose f macropinocytosis
Makropodie f macropodia, megalopodia, abnormal largeness of the feet
Makropolyzyt m macropolycyte *(neutrophile Leukozytenform)*
Makropromyelozyt m macropromyelocyte
Makroprosopie f macroprosopia, abnormal largeness of the face
Makroprosopus m macroprosopus
Makropsie f macrop[s]ia, megalopia
Makrorhinie f macrorrhinia, abnormal largeness of the nose
Makroskelie f macroscelia, abnormal length of the legs
Makroskopie f macroscopy, macrographia
makroskopisch macroscopic[al]
Makrosom n macrosome *(Protoplasmastruktur)*
makrosomatisch macrosomatic, giant
Makrosomie f macrosom[at]ia, great bodily size, gi[g]antism, somatomegaly
Makrospore f macrospore
Makrostomie f macrostomia, abnormal largeness of the mouth
Makrothrombozyt m macrothrombocyte, giant platelet
Makrothrombozytose f macrothrombocytosis

Makrotie f macrotia, abnormal largeness of the ears
makrozephal macrocephalic, macrocephalous
Makrozephalie f macrocephalia
Makrozephalus m macrocephalus
Makrozyste f macrocyst
Makrozyt m macro[normo]cyte
Makrozytenanämie f macrocytic anaemia
Makrozythämie f s. Makrozytose
Makrozytose f macrocytosis, macrocythaemia
Makula f s. Macula
Makulaaussparung f sparing of the macula
Makulablutung f **der Netzhaut** retinal macula haemorrhage
Makuladegeneration f macular degeneration, fundus dystrophy
~ **der Netzhaut** retinal macula degeneration
~/**infantile** infantile macular degeneration, Best's disease
~/**juvenile** juvenile macular degeneration, Stargardt's disease
~/**scheibenförmige** disciform macular degeneration
~/**senile** retinal macula senile degeneration
~/**vitelliforme** retinal macula vitelliform degeneration
~/**zystische** retinal macula cystic degeneration
Makuladysplasie f macular dysplasia
Makuladystrophie f macular dystrophy
Makulaeinblutung f **der Netzhaut** retinal macula haemorrhage
Makulaerkrankung f s. Makulopathie
Makulagelb n yellow pigment of the macula
Makulahypoplasie f **der Netzhaut** retinal macula hypoplasia
Makulaneuroretinopathie f macular neuroepitheliopathy (neuroretinopathy)
Makulaödem n macular oedema, retinal macula oedema
Makulapigmentepithel n macular pigment epithelium
makulär macular, spotted; freckled
Makulasehen n macular vision, direct (central) vision
Makulasternfigur f macular star figure
makuloanästhetisch maculoanaesthetic
Makulopapula f maculopapule
makulopapulär maculopapular
Makulopathie f maculopathy, macular disease *(des Auges)*
makulozerebral maculocerebral
Mal n mark; naevus *(umschriebene, anlagebedingte oder erbliche Fehlbildung der Haut)*
~ **de Pinto** pinta, pintoid yaws, carate, piquite, azul *(Hautkrankheit durch Treponema carateum)*
Mala f cheek, mala, gena
Malabsorption f malabsorption, defective absorption *(von Nährstoffen aus dem Magen-Darm-Kanal)*
Malabsorptionssyndrom n malabsorption syndrome

Malacoplacia f **vesicae urinariae** malacoplakia
Malaria f malaria, paludism, ague, paludal (malarial, intermittent) fever ● ~ **erzeugen** to malarialize ● **gegen** ~ **wirkend** malariacidal, destructive to malarial plasmodia ● **mit** ~ **infizieren** to infect with malaria, to malarialize
~ **algida** algid malaria (pernicious fever), cold malaria
~/**allochthone** allochthonous malaria
~/**autochthone** autochthonous malaria
~ **der Marschengegenden** marsh fever
~/**endemische** endemic malaria
~ **falciparum** falciparum (subtertian) malaria, malignant [tertian] malaria, tropical (aestivo-autumnal) malaria
~/**hyperpyretische** hyperpyretic malaria
~/**kardiale** cardiopaludism
~/**perniziöse** pernicious malaria
~ **quartana** quartan fever (malaria) *(durch Plasmodium malariae)*
~ **quotidiana** quotidian malaria
~ **tertiana** [benign] tertian malaria, tertian fever, vivax malaria *(durch Plasmodium vivax);* ovale malaria *(durch Plasmodium ovale)*
~ **tropica** s. ~ falciparum
~ **vivax** s. ~ tertiana
~/**zerebrale** cerebral malaria
Malariaanfall m malarial attack
Malariaantigen n malarial antigen
Malariaausrottung f malaria eradication
Malariaausrottungsprogramm n malaria eradication programme
malariabefallen malariated
malariabekämpfend antimalarial, antipaludian
Malariabekämpfung f antimalarial campaign, fight against malaria; malaria control
Malariabekämpfungsmittel n antimalarial [agent]
Malariaenzephalitis f malarial encephalitis
Malariafieber n s. Malaria
Malariafieberbehandlung f malarialization, malariotherapy, malarial therapy
Malariafiebererzeugung f/**künstliche** s. Malariafieberbehandlung
Malaria-Fluoreszenz-Antikörper-Test m malarial fluorescent antibody test
Malariagebiet n malarious area (region)
Malariagefährdung f malarial risk
Malariageschlechtszelle f gametocyte
Malariagranulom n malarial granuloma
~ **des Gehirns** Dürck's node
Malariahalbmond m malarial crescent
Malariahämoglobinurie f malarial haemoglobinuria
malariahemmend antimalarial, antipaludian
Malariaimmunfluoreszenztest m malarial fluorescent antibody test
Malariaimmunität f malarial immunity
malariainfiziert malariated, malarial, infected with malaria
Malariakachexie f malarial cachexia, limnaemia

Malariakardiomyopathie

Malariakardiomyopathie f malarial cardiomyopathy, cardiopaludism
Malariakontrolle f malaria control
malariakrank malariated, affected with malaria, suffering from malaria
Malariakur f s. Malariafieberbehandlung
malarial malarial, malarious, paludal, palustral
Malariameningitis f malarial meningitis
Malariamilz f malarial (ague cake) spleen
Malariamittel n antimalarial [agent]
Malarianeuritis f malarial neuritis
Malariaparasit m malaria parasite
Malariaperiodizität f malarial periodicity
Malariaperisplenitis f malarial perisplenitis
Malariapigment n malaria pigment
malariaplasmodientötend malariacidal, plasmodicide
Malariaplasmodientötungsmittel n plasmodicide
Malariaprophylaxe f malarial prophylaxis
Malaria-quartana-Fieberanfall m quartan ague *(im 72-Stunden-Intervall)*
Malaria-quintana-Fieberanfall m quintan ague *(im 96-Stunden-Intervall)*
Malariaspezialist m malariologist
Malaria-tertiana-Fieberanfall m tertian ague *(im 48-Stunden-Intervall)*
Malariatherapie f malarial treatment
Malaria-tropica-Fieberanfall m quotidian ague *(im 24-Stunden-Intervall)*
Malariatüpfelung f malarial stippling
malariaverbreitend malaria-carrying
malariaverseucht malarious
Malariologie f malariology *(Lehre von der Malaria)*
malartig naevoid, naeviform
Malartikulation f 1. malarticulation, defective production of speech; 2. malarticulation, defective positioning of joint surfaces
Malassezia f furfur Malassezia furfur *(Erreger der Pityriasis versicolor)*
Malassimilation f malassimilation, defective assimilation
Malatdehydrogenase f malate (malic acid) dehydrogenase *(Enzym)*
Malazie f malacia, abnormal softening *(z. B. von Knochen)*
malazisch malacic, malacial
Maldescensus m testis maldescent of the testis; undescended testicle
Maldigestion f maldigestion, disordered (imperfect) digestion
Malerkolik f, **Malerkrankheit** f painter's colic, lead disease, plumbism *(Verdauungsbeschwerden mit krampfartigen Schmerzen infolge von Bleivergiftung)*
Malereruption f maleruption *(eines Zahns)*
Malformation f malformation, peroplasia, abnormality, dysgenesis, abnormal development (formation); deformity
malförmig naevoid, naeviform

Maliasmus m maliasmus, glanders, malleus, farcy *(Infektionskrankheit durch Malleomyces mallei)*
maligne malignant *(z. B. Geschwülste)*
Malignität f malignancy *(z. B. von Geschwülsten)*
Malignitätsgrad m degree (stage) of malignancy
Malignom n malignant tumour (growth); cancer, carcinoma *(bösartige Epithelgeschwulst)*
Malinsäure f malic acid
Mallein m mallein *(für Hauttest zum Rotznachweis)*
Malleininfektion f malleinization
Malleininjektion f malleinization
malleolar malleolar *(1. einen Knöchel betreffend; 2. den Hammer im Ohr betreffend)*
Malleolarfraktur f malleolar fracture
Malleolengabel f ankle mortise
Malleolus m 1. malleolus, ankle; 2. malleolus *(eines Gehörknöchelchens)*
~ **fibulae (lateralis)** external malleolus, lateral (outer) malleolus *(des oberen Sprunggelenks)*
~ **medialis** internal malleolus, medial (inner) malleolus *(des oberen Sprunggelenks)*
Malleomyces n **mallei** glanders bacillus, Malleomyces mallei
Malleomyringoplastik f malleomyringoplasty *(Operation zur Verbesserung der Schalleitung im Ohr)*
Malleotomie f malleotomy
Malleus m 1. malleus, hammer *(Gehörknöchelchen)*; 2. s. Maliasmus
Malleusfixation f malleus fixation
Mallory-Körperchen npl Mallory bodies *(Einschlußkörperchen in Leberzellen bei portaler Zirrhose)*
Mallory-Weiss-Syndrom n Mallory-Weiss syndrome, oesophagogastric mucosal laceration
Malnutrition f malnutrition, underfeeding, false (defective) nutrition, athrepsia
Malokklusion f malocclusion, abnormal occlusion
Malonylharnstoff m malonyl urea, barbituric acid
Malposition f malposition, abnormal position
Malrotation f malrotation, abnormal (pathological) rotation
Maltafieber n Malta fever, Mediterranean phthisis, Gibraltar (Mountain) fever, brucellosis, brucelliasis *(Infektionskrankheit durch Brucella melitensis)*
Maltase f maltase *(Enzym)*
Maltasemangel m maltase deficiency, Pompe's disease
Maltose f malto[bio]se, malt sugar *(Disaccharid)*
Maltosurie f maltosuria
Malum n malum, disease *(s.a. unter Krankheit)*
~ **coxae senilis** osteoarthritis (hypertrophic arthritis) of the hip joint *(des alternden Menschen)*
~ **perforans pedis** perforating ulcer of the foot *(schmerzlose Geschwürbildung an der Fußsohle)*
Malzzucker m s. Maltose

mamillar mamillary
Mamillarkörper m mamillary body
Mamillarlinie f mamillary line *(durch die Brustwarze gelegte Senkrechte)*
Mamille f mamilla, [breast] nipple, [mammary] papilla, thelium, teat *(Zusammensetzungen s. unter Brustwarze)*
Mamillen... s. a. Brustwarzen...
Mamillenkarzinom n breast nipple carcinoma
Mamillenmuskel m mamillary muscle
Mamillenplastik f mamilliplasty, plastic operation of the nipple, theleplasty
Mamillentumor m theloncus, tumour of the nipple
mamilliform nipple-shaped, mamilliform, mamillary
Mamillitis f mamillitis, thelitis, nipple inflammation
mamilloinfundibular mamilloinfundibular
mamillothalamisch mamillothalamic
Mamma f mamma, breast, mammary gland *(s. a. unter Brust)*
~ **aberrans (erratica)** aberrant mamma
~ **pendulans** pendulous breast; mastoptosis
Mamma... s. a. Brust...
Mammaamputation f/**radikale** radical mastectomy
Mammaaufbauplastik f augmentation mammoplasty, breast augmentation operation
Mammabestrahlung f mamma (breast) radiation
Mammadysplasie f mammary dysplasia
~/**fibröse** fibrous dysplasia of the mamma
Mammahyperplasie f mammary (breast) hyperplasia
Mammahypertrophie f mammary (breast) hypertrophy, macromastia, macromazia, hypermastia, hypermazia
Mammahypoplasie f mammary (breast) hypoplasia
Mammahypotrophie f mammary (breast) hypotrophy, micromastia, micromazia, hypomastia, hypomazia
Mammakalkulus m mammary (breast) calculus
Mammakarzinom n mammary carcinoma, breast cancer, carcinoma of the breast
~/**duktuläres** milk-duct-carcinoma
~/**entzündliches** inflammatory carcinoma of the mamma
Mammakarzinomtherapie f breast cancer treatment
Mammalgie f s. Mastalgie
Mammaplastik f mammoplasty, mammaplasty, mastoplasty
Mammaprothese f breast prosthesis, prosthesis of the mamma
mammär mammary
Mammareduktion f mammary (breast) reduction *(z. B. nach der Stillperiode)*
Mammareduktionsplastik f reduction mammoplasty
Mammarekonstruktion f mammary (breast) reconstruction

Mammaria-interna-Implantation f internal mammary artery implantation
Mammatumor m mammary tumour, breast neoplasm
Mammektomie f s. Mastektomie
Mammogramm n mammogram
Mammographie f mammography
Mammotomie f mammotomy
mammotrop mammotropic
Mandel f tonsil[la], amygdala, paristhmion ● **neben einer** ~ paratonsillar ● **über der** ~ supratonsillar
~/**belegte** coated (furred) tonsil
~/**Luschkasche** Luschka's tonsil
Mandel... s. a. Tonsillen...
Mandelabszeß m quinsy, tonsillar abscess
Mandelatrophie f tonsillar (amygdaline) atrophy
Mandelentfernung f[/**operative**] tonsillectomy, amygdaloidectomy, excision of the tonsils
Mandelentzündung f tonsillitis, tonsillar inflammation, amygdalitis, paristhmitis *(Zusammensetzungen s. unter Tonsillitis)*
Mandelerkrankung f tonsillopathy, disease of the tonsils
Mandelfissur f tonsillar (amygdaline) fissure
Mandelinzision f tonsillotomy, amygdalotomy, incision into the tonsils
Mandelkappung f partial (incomplete) tonsillectomy
Mandelkrypte f tonsillar (amygdaline) crypt
Mandellakune f tonsillar (amygdaline) lacuna
Mandeloberfläche f tonsillar (amygdaline) surface
Mandelpfropf m tonsillar (amygdaline) plug
Mandelpilzinfektion f tonsillomycosis
Mandelstein m tonsillolith, tonsillar calculus, amygdalolith
Mandel- und Rachenentzündung f tonsillopharyngitis
Mandelvergrößerung f tonsillar (amygdaline) hypertrophy
Mandibel f, **Mandibula** f mandible, inferior maxilla, submaxilla, [lower] jaw-bone
Mandibula... s. a. Unterkiefer...
Mandibulahals m neck of the mandible
Mandibulaköpfchen n head of the mandible
Mandibulaluxation f dislocation of the mandible
Mandibulaprothese f mandibular reconstructive device
Mandibularbogen m mandibular (oral) arch
Mandibularesektion f mandibulectomy
Mandibularfortsatz m mandibular process
Mandibularfraktur f fracture of the mandible, mandibular fracture
Mandibulargelenk n temporomandibular articulation, mandibular joint
Mandibulargelenkfortsatz m mandibular condyle
Mandibulargelenkfortsatztumor m mandibular condyle tumour
Mandibulargrube f mandibular (glenoid) fossa *(am Schläfenbein zur Aufnahme des Mandibularköpfchens)*

Mandibularkanal

Mandibularkanal *m* mandibular (inferior dental) canal
Mandibularreflex *m* mandibular reflex, jaw jerk
Mandibularwulst *m* mandibular torus
Mandibulektomie *f* mandibulectomy
Mandibulopharyngealraum *m* mandibulopharyngeal space
Mandrin *m* mandrin, stylet, stilette, obturator *(z. B. einer Hohlkanüle)*
Manganvergiftung *f* manganism, mangan poisoning (intoxication)
Mangel *m* deficiency; deficit
Mangeldurchblutung *f* inadequate circulation
~ **des Uterus** ametrohaemia
Mangelentwicklung *f* atelia
Mangelernährung *f s.* Malnutrition
Mangelernährungskrankheit *f s.* Mangelkrankheit
mangelhaft insufficient
Mangelkrankheit *f* deficiency disease, trophopathy, trophonosis
Mangelödem *n* famine oedema
Mangelperfusion *f* hypoperfusion, underperfusion *(z. B. mit Blut)*
Mangelsymptom *n* deficiency symptom
Manie *f* mania ● **an einer ~ erkrankt** manic, maniacal
~/**akinetische** akinetic mania
~/**akute** acute mania, psychoeclampsia
~/**akute halluzinatorische** acute hallucinatory mania
~/**ängstliche** anxious mania
~/**depressive** depressive mania
~/**endogene** endogenous mania
~/**epileptische** epileptic mania
~/**gehemmte** inhibited mania
~/**hysterische** hysterical mania
~/**leichte** hypomania
~/**periodische** periodical mania
~/**religiöse** religious mania, theomania
~/**remittierende** recurrent mania
~/**suizidale** suicidal mania, thanatomania, autophonomania
~/**transitorische** transitory (severe frenzied) mania
~/**unproduktive** unproductive mania
Manieren *pl*/**clownhafte** clownism
manifest/**klinisch nicht** silent
~ **werden**/**klinisch** to become clinically apparent
Manipulation *f* manipulation, manoeuvre
manisch manic, maniacal
manisch-depressiv manic-depressive, cyclothymic, cyclophrenic
Manisch-Depressiver *m* manic-depressive patient, cyclothyme, cyclothymi[a]c, cycloid personality
Manna *n(f)* manna *(getrockneter Rindensaft der Manna-Esche als Abführmittel)*
Mannbarkeit *f* virility
Männerabneigung *f* androphobia
Männerfurcht *f* androphobia
Männerhaß *m* misandria

Männerheilkunde *f* andriatrics
Männerkrankheit *f* andropathy
Mannesschwäche *f* impotence, invirility
Mannit[ol] *n* mannitol, mannite *(Diuretikum)*
Mannitoltest *m* trial of mannitol
männlich masculine, male, virile, android
Männlichkeit *f* masculinity
Mannose *f* mannose *(Monosaccharid)*
ß-Mannosidase *f* ß-mannosidase *(Enzym)*
Mannstollheit *f* nymphomania, tentigo venerea, metromania, hysteromania, clitoromania, andromania
Mannweib *n* gynander
Manometer *n* manometer
manometrisch manometric
Manöver *n* manoeuvre
~/**Kochersches** Kocher's manoeuvre
~/**Scanzonisches** Scanzoni's manoeuvre *(bei hinterer Hinterhauptslage)*
Manschette *f* cuff *(z. B. am Blutdruckapparat)*
~/**muskulotendinöse** musculotendinous cuff
Manschettenabszeß *m* cuff abscess
Manschettentubus *m* cuffed [tracheal] tubus
Mansonella-ozzardi-Befall *m* mansonelliasis, Ozzard's filariasis
Mansonia *f* Mansonia *(Stechmückenart)*
Mantel *m* mantle *(Anatomie)*; coat[ing] *(spezifische Proteinhülle von Viren)*
Manteldentin *n* mantle dentin
Mantelfaser *f* mantle fibre
Mantelkrone *f* jacket crown *(für zerstörte Frontzähne)*
Mantelschicht *f* mantle layer
Mantelzelle *f* satellite [cell]
Mantoux-Reaktion *f* Mantoux test, intracutaneous tuberculin reaction
Manualhilfe *f* manual expression *(bei der Geburt)*
Manualtherapie *f* chiropractic
Manubrium *n* manubrium
~ **mallei** manubrium (handle) of the malleus
~ **sterni** [sternal] manubrium, episternum, manubrium of the sternum
manuell manual, by the hand
Manus *f* hand, manus *(s.a. unter Hand)*
~ **curta** clubhand
~ **extensa** backward deviation of the hand
~ **flexa** forward deviation of the hand
MAO *s.* Monoaminooxidase
marantisch marantic, marasm[at]ic
Marasmus *m* marasmus, progressive wasting, emaciation, athrepsia, general atrophy
~ **senilis** geromarasmus, senile marasmus
marastisch *s.* marantisch
Marchand-Waterhouse-Friderichsen-Syndrom *n* Waterhouse-Friderichsen syndrome, acute fulminating meningococcaemia, meningococcic adrenal syndrome, fulminating adrenal meningitis
Marchesani-Syndrom *n* Marchesani syndrome *(erbliche Bindegewebskrankheit)*

Marchiafava-Bignami-Syndrom n Marchiafava's disease, Marchiafava-Bignami syndrome, corpus callosum degeneration
Marchiafava-Micheli-Syndrom n Marchiafava-Micheli syndrome, paroxysmal nocturnal haemoglobinuria
Marcus-Gunn-Phänomen n Gunn's phenomenon *(Mitbewegung des Oberlids beim Kauen)*
Marfan-Syndrom n Marfan's syndrome, arachnodactyly, dolichostenomelia
marginal marginal
Marginalkeratitis f marginal (annular) keratitis
Marginalkern m [postero]marginal nucleus
Marginalrasseln n marginal (crepitant) rale
Marginalschicht f marginal layer
Marginalulkus n marginal ulcer
Marginalzelle f marginal cell
Marginoplastik f marginoplasty
Margo m margin, margo, border, boundary
Marie-Bamberger-Syndrom n Marie-Bamberger syndrome (disease), hypertrophic pulmonary osteoarthropathy
Marie-Bechterew-Strümpell-Arthritis f Marie-Strümpell arthritis (disease), rheumatoid spondylitis
Marie-Léri-Syndrom n Marie-Léri syndrome, mutilant arthritis
Marie-Scheuthauer-Sainton-Syndrom n Marie-Scheuthauer-Sainton syndrome, cleidocranial dysostosis
Marie-Strümpell-Enzephalitis f Marie-Strümpell encephalitis, acute infantile hemiplegia
Marie-Syndrom n I Marie's syndrome (disease), acromegaly
~ II Marie's ataxia, cerebellar heredoataxia, hereditary cerebellar ataxia
Marie-Tooth-Syndrom n Marie-Tooth syndrome (disease), peroneal muscular atrophy
Marihuana n marihuana, marijuana, hashish, cannabis indica, bhang *(Rauschgift von Cannabis indica)*
Marihuanasucht f cannabism
Marin-Amat-Syndrom n Marin-Amat syndrome, inverse Marcus Gunn phenomenon *(automatischer Lidschluß bei Öffnung des Mundes)*
Mark n marrow *(z. B. des Knochens)*; medulla *(z. B. des Nervensystems)*; pulp[a] *(z. B. eines Zahns)*
~/**verlängertes** s. Medulla oblongata
Markaktivität f marrow activity
markartig marrow-like; medullary, medulloid; pulpy, pulpiform
Markausräumung f medullectomy; pulpectomy
Markbildung f medullation, myelinization, myelination
Markbündel n medullary bundle (fascicle)
Markentfernung f/**operative** medullectomy; pulpectomy
Markentzündung f s. 1. Myelitis; 2. Osteomyelitis; 3. Pulpitis
Marker-Chromosom n marker chromosome
markhaltig medullary *(z. B. ein Knochen)*; myelinated, medullated *(z. B. ein Nerv)*

Markhemmung f s. Hypersplenie
Markhöhle f marrow space [of the bone], medullary cavity
markieren to mark; to tag, to label *(mit radioaktiven Isotopen)*
markiert tagged, labelled
~/**mit radioaktiven Isotopen** radioisotope-labelled
~/**mit Radiojod** radioiodine-labelled
~/**radioaktiv** radiolabelled
Markierungselement n tracer [element]
Markkallus m central callus
Markkanal m medullary canal
Markknochen m medullary bone
Marklöffel m marrow spoon
marklos non-medullated, marrowless *(z. B. ein Knochen)*; unmedullated, amyeline *(z. B. ein Nerv)*
Markmembran f medullary membrane
Marknagel m intramedullary nail (pin) *(zur Knochenbruchfixierung)*
~ **nach Küntscher** Küntscher nail
Marknagelfixation f intramedullary fixation *(von Knochenbrüchen)*
Marknagelung f [intra]medullary nailing, marrow nailing
Markraum m medullary space [of the bone], marrow cavity
Markraumaufbohrung f intramedullary (medullary canal) reaming
Markraumbohrer m intramedullary (medullary canal) reamer
Markraumbohrerhandstück n medullary reaming hand piece
Markraumnagel m s. Marknagel
Markscheide f medullary (myelin) sheath *(eines Nerven)* ● **mit Markscheiden [versehen]** medullated, myelinic ● **ohne Markscheiden** non-medullated, amyelinic
Markscheidenbildung f myelin[iz]ation, medullation, myelogenesis
Markscheidendegeneration f myelin degeneration
Markscheidenfärbung f/**Weigertsche** Weigert's method
markscheidenhaltig myelinated
markscheidenlos non-medullated, amyelinic
Markscheidenreifung f myelogenesis
Markschwamm m carcinoma solidum medullare, medullary carcinoma
Markschwammniere f medullary spongy kidney
Markschwund m 1. myelophthisis, loss of bone marrow; 2. myelophthisis, wasting of the spinal cord, spinal cord atrophy
Marksegel n velum medullare, medullary velum
Marksinus m **eines Lymphknotens** medullary sinus
Markstrahlen mpl medullary rays
Marksubstanz f medullary substance *(des Gehirns)*
Markzelle f medullary cell, medullocell, myelocyte *(z. B. im Knochenmark)*; pulp cell *(z. B. der Zahnpulpa)*

Marmorfärbung

Marmorfärbung f s. Marmorierung
Marmorhaut f marble (mottled) skin
Marmorierung f marbleization, marmorization *(z. B. der Haut)*
Marmorknochen m marble (ivory) bone
Marmorknochenkrankheit f s. Osteopetrosis
Maroteaux-Lamy-Syndrom n Maroteaux-Lamy syndrome, mucopolysaccharidosis [type] VI
Marschalbuminurie f march albuminuria
Marschenfieber n marsh (swamp) fever
Marschfraktur f march fracture, fatigue (stress) fracture, Deutschländer's disease *(Ermüdungsbruch von Mittelfußknochen)*
Marschhämoglobinurie f march haemoglobinuria
Marschperiostitis f matatarsalgia
Marseillefieber n Marseille fever, Mediterranean exanthematous (tick) fever, boutonneuse fever
Marsupialisation f marsupialization *(z. B. das Einnähen von Zystenrändern in die Bauchwunde)*
marsupialisieren to marsupialize
Maschinengeräusch n machinery[-like] murmur *(Herzgeräusch bei Ductus arteriosus Botalli apertus)*
Masern pl measles, morbilli, epidemic roseola
~/hämorrhagische (schwarze) haemorrhagic (black) measles
Masernantikörper m measles antibody
masernartig morbilliform
Masernausschlag m s. Masernexanthem
Masernenanthem n enanthem[a] of measles
Masernenzephalitis f measles encephalitis
Masernexanthem n exanthem[a] of measles, measles rash
~ der Wangenschleimhaut Koplik's sign, Filatov's spots
Masernhyperimmunserum n measles hyperimmune serum
Masernimmunglobulin n measles immunoglobulin
Masernimmunserum n/humanes human measles immune serum
Masernimpfstoff m measles vaccine
masernkrank measly
Masernrekonvaleszentenserum n measles convalescent serum
Masernriesenzelle f measles giant cell, Warthin-Finkeldey [giant] cell
Masernschleimhautausschlag m enanthem[a] of measles
Masernvirion n measles virion
Masernvirus n measles virus
Masernvirusimpfstoff m measles virus vaccine
~/formalininaktivierter formalin-inactivated measles virus vaccine
Maske f mask
maskenartig mask-like
Maskengesicht n mask[-like] face, masked facies
maskiert masked, concealed, hidden, latent, covert *(z. B. ein Symptom)*

Maskierung f/genetische hypostasis
maskulin s. männlich
maskulinisieren to masculinize, to produce male characteristics
maskulinisierend masculinizing, virilizing, virilligenic
Maskulinisierung f masculinization, masculation, virilization
Masochismus m masochism, passive algolagnia, pain joy
Masochist m masochist
masochistisch masochistic
Massa f lateralis atlantis lateral mass of the atlas
Massage f massage, petrissage
~ mit Wärmeanwendung thermomassage
Massagebehandlung f massotherapy, massage treatment
Massagegerät n masseur, massage device
Massagespezialist m masseur
Maßanalyse f titrimetry, titration
Massenbehandlung f mass treatment
Massenentlausung f mass delousing
Massenerkrankung f epidemic
Massenfluß m mass flow
Massenimmunisierung f mass immunization
Massenimpfung f mass vaccination
Massenpsychose f mass psychosis
Massenvergiftung f mass intoxication
Masseter m masseter [muscle]
Masseterhypertrophie f masseteric hypertrophy
Masseterklonus m masseter (mandibular, jerk) clonus
Massetermuskel m s. Masseter
Masseterreflex m masseter reflex, jaw jerk
Masseur m masseur, rubber
massiv massive, heavy, severe
Massivblutung f in ein Organ s. Apoplexie
Massivtransfusion f mass transfusion
Masson-Tumor m glomus tumour, glomangioma, angiomyoneuroma, angioneuromyoma
Mastadenitis f s. Mastitis
Mastalgie f mastalgia, mastodynia, mazalgia, pain in the mammary gland
Mastatrophie f mastatrophy, atrophy of the mammary gland
Mastdarm m rectum, straight bowel ● **durch den ~** rectal, per rectum
Mastdarm... s. a. Rektum... und Rektal...
Mastdarmampulle f rectal ampulla, ampulla of the rectum
Mastdarmarterie f/mittlere middle rectal artery
~/obere superior rectal artery
~/untere inferior rectal (haemorrhoidal) artery
Mastdarmbiopsie f rectal biopsy
Mastdarm-Blasen-Fistel f rectovesical fistula
Mastdarmbruch m proctocele, rectal hernia, rectocele
Mastdarmdehner m procteurynter
Mastdarmdehnung f procteurysis
Mastdarmentfernung f/operative proctectomy, rectectomy, rectum resection

Mastdarmentzündung f proctitis, rectitis, inflammation of the rectum
Mastdarmeröffnung f/**operative** proctotomy, rectotomy
Mastdarmerweiterung f proctectasia; megarectum
Mastdarmfalten fpl/**quere** transverse folds of the rectum, transverse rectal folds
Mastdarmfistel f rectofistula, rectal fistula
Mastdarmfistelung f/**operative** proctostomy, rectostomy
Mastdarmfixation f proctopexy, rectopexy, fixation of the rectum
~ **am Steißbein** proctococcypexy
Mastdarmhernie f rectal hernia, rectocele, proctocele
Mastdarmkrampf m proctospasm, rectospasm, spasm of the rectum
Mastdarmkrebs m rectal cancer, rectum carcinoma
Mastdarmkrise f rectal crisis (bei Tabes dorsalis)
Mastdarmlähmung f proctoparalysis, proctoplegia
Mastdarm-Mastdarm-Anastomose f rectorectostomy
Mastdarmnaht f proctorrhaphy, rectorrhaphy, suture of the rectum
Mastdarmplastik f proctoplasty, rectoplasty
Mastdarmpolyp m proctopolypus, polypus of the rectum
Mastdarmreflex m rectal (rectum) reflex
Mastdarm-Rektum-Spekulum n rectal specula
Mastdarmresektion f rectum resection, proctectomy, rectectomy
Mastdarm-Scheiden-Fistel f rectovaginal fistula
Mastdarmschleimhaut f rectal mucosa, mucous membrane of the rectum
Mastdarmschmerz m proctalgia, proctodynia, rectalgia, pain in the rectum
Mastdarmschrunde f rectal (rectum) fissure
Mastdarmspiegel m proctoscope, rectoscope, rectal speculum
Mastdarmspiegelung f proctoscopy, rectoscopy
Mastdarmstenose f s. Mastdarmstriktur
Mastdarmstriktur f rectal (rectum) stricture, proctostenosis, rectostenosis, stricture (stenosis) of the rectum, proctencleisis
Mastdarmtripper m gonorrhoeal proctitis
Mastdarm- und Blasenrekonstruktion f proctocystoplasty
Mastdarm- und Blasenschnitt m rectocystotomy
Mastdarm- und Scheidenrekonstruktion f proctocolpoplasty
Mastdarmvene f/**mittlere** middle rectal vein
~/**obere** superior rectal vein
~/**untere** inferior rectal (haemorrhoidal) vein
Mastdarmverschluß m aproctia, proctatresia, rectal atresia, imperforation of the anus
Mastdarmvorfall m rectum prolapse, prolapse of the rectum, rectal procidentia; proctoptosia, proctoptosis
Mastekchymose f mastecchymosis

Mastektomie f mastectomy, excision of the breast, mammectomy
~ **nach [Rotter-]Halsted** Halsted's radical mastectomy
~/**radikale** radical mastectomy
mastektomieren to mastectomize
Masthelkosis f masthelcosis, ulceration of the breast
Mastikation f mastication, manducation
Mastikationsmuskel m muscle of mastication
Mastitis f mastitis, mammitis, inflammation of the breast (mammary gland)
~/**chronisch zystische** mammary dysplasia, chronic cystic mastitis; cystic breast
~/**eitrige** suppurative mastitis, pyogenic infection of the breast
~/**interstitielle** interstitial mastitis
~/**parenchymatöse** parenchymatous (glandular) mastitis
~/**phlegmonöse** phlegmonous mastitis; abscess of the breast
~ **puerperalis** puerperal mastitis; caked breast
~/**retro-mammäre** retromammary (submammary) mastitis, paramastitis
Mastodynie f s. Mastalgie
Mastographie f s. Galaktographie
mastoid 1. mastoid[al]; 2. mastoid[al], nipple-shaped
Mastoid n mastoid [bone], mastoid process
Mastoid... s. a. Warzenfortsatz...
Mastoidalgie f mastoidalgia, pain in the mastoid process
Mastoidektomie f mastoidectomy
~/**radikale** radical mastoidectomy, mastoidotympanectomy
Mastoideozentese f mastoideocentesis, paracentesis of the mastoid cells
Mastoideröffnung f/**operative** s. Mastoidotomie
Mastoiditis f mastoiditis, otantritis, inflammation of the mastoid antrum and air cells
~/**Bezoldsche** Bezold type of mastoiditis
Mastoidotomie f masto[ido]tomy, incision of the mastoid process
Mastoidotympanektomie f s. Mastoidektomie/radikale
Mastoidretraktor m mastoid retractor
Mastokarzinom n mastocarcinoma
Mastopathie f mastopathy, mazopathy, disease of the breast (mammary gland)
~/**fibrozystische** [fibro]cystic disease of the breast
Mastopexie f mastopexy, fixation of a pendulous breast
Mastoplasie f mastoplas[t]ia, mastauxy, hyperplasia of breast tissue
Mastoplastik f mastoplasty, plastic operation on the breast
Mastoptose f mastoptosis; pendulous breasts
Mastorrhagie f mastorrhagia, haemorrhage from the breast (mammary gland)
Mastoscirrhus m mastoscirrhus, scirrhus of the breast (mammary gland)

Mastostomie

Mastostomie f mastostomy, incision and drainage of the breast
Mastotomie f mastotomy, incision of the breast
Mastozytom n mastocytoma
Mastozytose f mastocytosis, mast-cell disease
Masturbation f masturbation, manustupration, onanism, ipsation; voluntary pollution, self-pollution
masturbieren to masturbate
Mastzelle f mastocyte, mast cell
Mastzellengeschwulst f mastocytoma
Mastzellenkultivierung f mast-cell cultivation
Mastzellenleukämie f mast-cell leukaemia
Mastzellenretikulose f mast-cell reticulosis
Mastzellenultrastruktur f mast-cell ultrastructure
Mastzellenvermehrung f s. Mastozytose
matern maternal
Maternität f maternity, motherhood
Matratzennaht f mattress (quilted) suture
Matricaria f chamomilla chamomile
Matrix f matrix (z. B. für Organe)
~ **unguis** nail bed, hyponychium
matt exhausted, tired, faint, weak, feeble; languid, languorous; dull, dim (z. B. Augen)
Mattigkeit f exhaustion, faintness, weakness, fatigue, feebleness; languidness, languor; dullness, dimness (z. B. der Augen)
matur mature, ripe, fully developed; full grown
Maturität f maturity
Maulbeerkeim m s. Morula
Maulbeerstein m mulberry calculus (schwarzer höckeriger Stein des Nierenbeckens oder der Blase)
Maul- und Klauenseuche f [hand-]foot-and-mouth disease, hoof-and-mouth-disease, aphthous fever
Maurer-Fleckung f, **Maurer-Körnelung** f Maurer's dots (clefts) (der roten Blutkörperchen bei Malaria tropica)
Mauriac-Syndrom n Mauriac syndrome (kindlicher Diabetis mellitus mit Milz- und Lebervergrößerung sowie Zwergwuchs)
Mäuseeinheit f mouse unit, M.U.
Maxilla f [superior] maxilla, [superior] maxillary bone, supermaxilla, supramaxilla, upper jaw[bone]
Maxilla... s. a. Oberkiefer...
Maxillafraktur f maxilla fracture
Maxillahypoplasie f maxilla hypoplasia
Maxillaknospe f maxillary bud (Embryologie)
Maxillaosteotomie f maxillary osteotomy
Maxillarnerv m maxillary nerve
Maxillarplexus m/**äußerer** external maxillary plexus
~/**innerer** internal maxillary plexus
Maxillarschmerz m **bei Gicht** siagonagra, gouty pain in the maxilla
maxillawärts admaxillary
Maxillektomie f maxillectomy, excision of the maxilla

Maxillitis f 1. maxillitis, inflammation of the maxilla; 2. maxillitis, inflammation of the submaxillary salivary gland
Maximaldosis f maximum dose
Maximalreiz m maximal stimulus
Maximum-Minimum-Thermometer n maximum and minimum thermometer
May-Grünwald-Färbung f May-Grünwald stain (für Blutkörper)
May-Hegglin-Anomalie f May-Hegglin anomaly (Granulozytenanomalie)
Mazeration f maceration
mazerieren to macerate (z. B. Gewebe)
mazeriert macerative
MCH s. Hämoglobingehalt/mittlerer korpuskulärer
MCHC s. Hämoglobinkonzentration/mittlere korpuskuläre
MCV s. Zellvolumen/mittleres
MDP s. Magen-Darm-Passage
M.E. s. Mäuseeinheit
MEA-Syndrom n MEA syndrome, multiple endocrine adenomatosis syndrome
Meatitis f meatitis, inflammation of the wall of a meatus
Meatorrhaphie f meatorrhaphy
Meatoskop n meatoscope
Meatoskopie f meatoscopy
Meatotomie f meatotomy, incision of a meatus
Meatus m meatus, opening, passage (s. a. unter Ductus und Gang)
~ **acusticus** auditory meatus (canal)
~ **acusticus externus** external acoustic meatus, external ear canal, external auditory foramen
~ **acusticus internus** internal acoustic meatus, internal ear canal, internal auditory foramen
~ **auditorius externus** s. ~ acusticus externus
~ **nasi communis** common meatus of the nose
~ **nasi inferior** inferior nasal meatus, inferior meatus of the nose
~ **nasi medius** middle nasal meatus, middle meatus of the nasal cavity
~ **nasi superior** superior nasal meatus, superior meatus of the nose
~ **nasopharyngeus** nasopharyngeal meatus
~ **urethrae** urethral meatus (opening)
Meatuserweiterung f/**operative** meatotomy
Mechanismus m/**immunologischer** immunologic mechanism
Mechanorezeptor m mechanoreceptor
Mechanotherapeut m mechanotherapist
Mechanotherapie f mechanotherapy
Meckerstimme f egophony, tragophony
Media f media, middle coat
Mediadegeneration f medial degeneration
Mediahypertrophie f medial hypertrophy (thickening), hypertrophy of the media
Medianekrose f medianecrosis, medial muscle necrosis
Medianschnitt m median (midline) incision
Medianus m median nerve
Medianuslähmung f median-nerve palsy

Medizin

Mediasklerose f/**Mönckebergsche** Mönckeberg's (medial) arteriosclerosis, medial calcinosis *(spangenförmige Kalkeinlagerungen in der mittleren Wandschicht von Arterien)*
Mediastinalemphysem n mediastinal emphysema; pneumomediastinum
Mediastinalfibrose f mediastinal fibrosis
Mediastinalflattern n mediastinal flutter
Mediastinalhämatom n mediastinal haematoma
Mediastinallymphknoten m mediastinal lymph node
Mediastinalprozeß m mediastinal process
Mediastinalraum m s. Mediastinum
Mediastinalschatten m mediastinal shadow
Mediastinalverbreiterung f mediastinal extension, widening of the mediastinum *(Radiologie)*
Mediastinalverschiebung f mediastinal shift (displacement)
Mediastinitis f mediastinitis, inflammation of the mediastinum
Mediastinogramm n mediastinogram
Mediastinographie f mediastinography
Mediastinoperikarditis f mediastinopericarditis
Mediastinoperikarditiszeichen n/**Broadbentsches** Broadbent's sign
Mediastinoskop n mediastinoscope
Mediastinoskopie f mediastinoscopy
Mediastinotomie f mediastinotomy, incision into the mediastinum
Mediastinum n mediastinum, mediastinal area, interpleural space
~/**hinteres** posterior mediastinal area, mediastinum posterius
~/**mittleres** middle mediastinal area, mediastinum medium
~/**oberes** superior mediastinal area, mediastinum superius
~ **testis** antrum of the testis, body of Highmore
~/**vorderes** anterior mediastinal area, mediastinum anterius
Mediastinumbluterguß m haemomediastinum
Mediastinumeröffnung f/**operative** s. Mediastinotomie
Mediator m mediator
Mediaverdickung f hypertrophy of the media
Mediaverkalkung f **der Arterien** senile arteriosclerosis
Medikament n drug, remedy, medicament, medicant, medication, medicine *(s. a. unter Arzneimittel und Mittel)* ● **durch Medikamente bewirkt** medicamentous ● **mit Medikamenten behandeln** to medicate
~/**auf Parasiten wirkendes** parasitotropic [agent]
~ **auf Sulfonamidbasis** sulpha drug *(Chemotherapeutikum)*
~/**austrocknendes** desiccant [agent]
~/**blutdruckerhöhendes** [vaso]pressor, hypertensor
~/**blutdrucksenkendes** antihypertensive [agent], hypotensor, depressant [agent], depressor [substance], vasodepressor [agent]
~ **der Wahl** drug of choice
~/**eingespritztes** injection
~/[**herz**]**frequenzerhöhendes** cardioaccelerator [agent], cardiokinetic [agent]
~/**herzfrequenzsenkendes** cardioinhibitory [agent]
~/**herzkraftstärkendes** cardiac tonic, cardiotonic [agent]; cardiac diuretic
~/**herzwirksames** cardiac [agent]
~/**krampflösendes** spasmolytic [agent], antispasmodic [agent], anticonvulsant [agent]
~/**stimmungshebendes** thymoleptic [agent], mood-elevating drug
~/**verschreibungspflichtiges** prescription drug
~ **zur Prämedikation** premedicant
Medikamenten... s. a. Arzneimittel...
Medikamentenabneigung f pharmacophobia
Medikamentenanwendung f/**kritiklose** polypharmacy, polypragmasy
Medikamentenapplikation f s. Applikation
Medikamentenapplikator m medicator, applicator
Medikamentengewebespiegel m tissue drug level
Medikamentenintoxikation f drug intoxication (poisoning)
medikamentenresistent drug-resistant
Medikamentenschrank m medicine cupboard (cabinet)
Medikamentensuppression f drug suppression
Medikamententherapie f medication
Medikamententoxizität f drug toxicity
Medikamentenüberempfindlichkeit f drug hypersensitivity
Medikamentenurtikaria f medicamentous urticaria
medikamentös medicamentous
Medikator m medicator
Medinawurm m Medina worm, dragon (guinea) worm, Dracunculus medinensis
Medinawurminfektion f guinea worm infection, dracontiasis, dracunculiasis
Medioaxillarlinie f midaxillary line *(senkrechte Linie von der Achselhöhlenmitte nach unten)*
mediofrontal mediofrontal, midfrontal
mediokarpal mediocarpal, midcarpal
Medioklavikularlinie f midclavicular (medioclavicular) line *(senkrechte Linie von der Schlüsselbeinmitte nach unten)*
Medionecrosis f **aortae idiopathica cystica** medial necrosis of aorta
mediookzipital medio-occipital, midoccipital
medioplantar medioplantar, midplantar
Mediosternallinie f midsternal (mediosternal) line
Mediotarsalamputation f midtarsal (mediotarsal) amputation
Mediterrananämie f Mediterranean anaemia, familial erythroblastic anaemia, thalass[an]aemia
Medium n medium
Medizin f 1. medicine; 2. s. Medikament
~/**experimentelle** experimental medicine

Medizin

~/**forensische** forensic (legal) medicine, medical jurisprudence
~/**innere (internistische)** [internal] medicine
~/**physikalische** physiatrics, physical medicine
~/**psychosomatische** psychosomatic medicine
~/**suggestive** suggestive medicine
~/**vorbeugende** preventive medicine
Medizinalstatistik f medicostatistics
medizinalstatistisch medicostatistic[al]
Mediziner m physician, medical, doctor (s. a. Arzt)
Medizinfläschchen n vial
Medizinflasche f medicine bottle
medizinisch 1. medical, medicinal; 2. medicinal (arzneilich)
medizinpsychologisch medicopsychological
medizinstatistisch medicostatistic[al]
Medulla f medulla; marrow
~ **glandulae suprarenalis** adrenal (suprarenal) medulla
~ **nephrica** renal medulla
~ **nodi lymphatici** medulla of the lymph node
~ **oblongata** medulla [oblongata]; afterbrain, hindbrain, myelencephalon, marrowbrain, bulb[us]
~ **ossium** bone marrow, medulla
~ **ossium flava** yellow [bone] marrow, fat marrow
~ **ossium rubra** red [bone] marrow
~ **renis** renal medulla
~ **spinalis** spinal cord, spinal marrow, medulla, myelon
medullär medullary
Medullaranästhesie f rachianaesthesia, rachianalgesia
Medullarplatte f medullary (neural) plate (Embryologie)
Medullarrinne f medullary (neural) groove
Medullarwulst m embryonic medullary fold (Neuralrohr)
Medullation f medullation
Medullektomie f medullectomy, excision of the medulla
Medulloblast m medulloblast (primitive Hirnzelle)
Medulloblastom n medulloblastoma (bösartige Kleinhirngeschwulst)
Medulloepitheliom n medulloepithelioma, ependymoma, ependymocytoma (vom Ependym abgeleitete Ventrikelgeschwulst)
Medusenhaupt n medusa head, cirsomphalos
Meeresklimabehandlung f thalassotherapy, marinotherapy
Meerzwiebelvergiftung f scillism
Megacholedochus m megacholedochus
Megaduodenum n megaduodenum
Megakaryoblast m mega[lo]karyoblast
Megakaryoblastenleukämie f megakaryoblastic leukaemia (Megakaryoblastenvermehrung im Knochenmark)
Megakaryoblastom n mega[lo]karyoblastoma (bösartiger Tumor)

Megakaryophthisis f megakaryophthisis (Megakaryozytenverminderung im Knochenmark)
Megakaryozyt m mega[lo]karyocyte, thromboblast
megakaryozytär megakaryocytic
Megakaryozytenleukämie f megakaryocytic (giant-cell) leukaemia
Megakaryozytenmangel m megakaryocytopenia
Megakaryozytenproliferation f megakaryocyte proliferation
Megakaryozytopenie f megakaryocytopenia
Megakaryozytose f megakaryocytosis
Megakokkus m megacoccus
Megakolon n megacolon; enteromegaly
~/**aganglionäres** aganglionic megacolon
~/**funktionelles (idiopathisches)** idiopathic (acquired functional) megacolon
~/**kongenitales** congenital megacolon, giant colon, Hirschsprung's disease
Megalerythema f megalerythema, Sticker's disease
Megalgie f megalgia, severe pain
Megalo... s. a. Makro...
Megaloblast m megaloblast (bei Folsäuremangel)
Megaloblastenanämie f megaloblastic anaemia
megaloblastenartig megaloblastoid
Megaloblastose f megaloblastosis
Megalocystis f s. Megalozystis
Megalokaryoblast m s. Megakaryoblast
Megalokaryozyt m s. Megakaryozyt
Megalokornea f megalocornea, anterior staphyloma, keratoglobus
megaloman megalomanic
Megalomaner m megalomaniac
Megalomanie f megalomania, delusion of grandeur
Megalopapille f megalopapilla
Megalopenis m megalopenis
Megalopththalmos m s. Makrophthalmus
Megalosplenie f megalosplenia
Megalothymus m megalothymus
Megalozystis f megalocystis, megabladder, enlargement of the bladder
Megalozyt m megalocyte (Erythrozytenform)
Megalozytose f megalocytosis
Megamerozoit m megamerozoite
Megaösophagus m megaoesophagus
Megarektosigmoid n megarectosigmoid
Megarektum n megarectum
Megasigma n megasigmoid, macrosigma, megasigma
~/**kongenitales** s. Megakolon/kongenitales
Megaureter m mega[lo]ureter
megazephal mega[lo]cephalic, megacephalous
Megazökum n megacaecum
Mehlmilbe f meal mite
Mehlpneumokoniose f miller's asthma
Mehlstaublunge[nerkrankung] f miller's asthma
mehrdrüsig pluriglandular, multiglandular
Mehrehe f polygamy
Mehrfachallergie f multisensitivity

Mehrfachempfindung f polyaesthesia
Mehrfachfraktur f multiple fracture
Mehrfachfurcht f polyphobia
Mehrfachgeburt f multiple (plural) birth
Mehrfachinfektion f multiple (complex) infection, multiinfection, polyinfection
Mehrfachkernteilung f multiple fission
Mehrfachlähmung f polyplegia
Mehrfachmangelkrankheit f plurideficiency [disease]
Mehrfachmißbildung f polysomus
Mehrfachparese f polyparesis
Mehrfachpupille f multiple pupil
Mehrfachschichtung[sdarstellung] f polytomography
Mehrfachschwangere f multigravida
Mehrfachschwangerschaft f s. Mehrlingsschwangerschaft
Mehrfachschwängerung f multifoetation
Mehrfachsehen n polyop[s]ia *(eines Gegenstandes) (s. a. Diplopie)*
Mehrfachsensibilität f multisensitivity
Mehrfachverletzung f multiple injury
mehrfarbig polychrom[at]ic, polychrome; pleochro[mat]ic
Mehrfarbigkeit f pleochroism *(bei wechselnder Betrachtungsrichtung)*
mehrfingerig multidigitate
mehrganglionär multiganglionate
mehrgebärend multiparous, pluriparous
Mehrgebärende f multipara, pluripara
mehrgeißelig multiflagellate, polymastigate
mehrgelenkig multiarticular, polyarticular
mehrgestaltig pleomorphic, pleomorphous, multiform
mehrhändig polycheirous
mehrherdig multifocal, plurifocal
mehrhöckerig multicuspid[al] *(Mahlzahn)*
mehrhodig polyorchid
mehrkammerig multilocular
mehrkapselig multicapsular
mehrkernig multinuclear, multinucleate, polynuclear, polynucleate
mehrklonal multiclonal
mehrknotig multinodular
mehrköpfig multicipital *(z. B. Muskel)*
mehrlappig multilobar, multilobate, polylobular
Mehrlingsschwangerschaft f multigravidity, multiple pregnancy, polycyesis
mehrnervig polyneural, polyneuric
Mehrphasenpersönlichkeitstest m multiphasic personality inventory
mehrpolig multipolar
mehrpolypig multipolypoid
mehrrippig multicostate
mehrschichtig multilayered, stratified, polyptychial *(z. B. Epithelzellen)*
mehrwirtig heteroxenous
mehrwurzelig multirooted
mehrzahnig multidentate
mehrzehig multidigitate
mehrzellig multicellular, polycellular

mehrzentrisch multicentric, polycentric
mehrzipfelig multicuspid[al] *(Herzklappe)*
Mehrzweckklemme f multipurpose clamp
mehrzystisch multicystic, polycystic
Meibomitis f meibomi[ani]tis, blepharoadenitis *(Entzündung der Meibomschen Drüsen)*
Meiose f meiosis, meiotic division (reduction)
Mekometer n mecometer
Mekonalgie f meconalgia *(Schmerzzustand bei Opiumentzug)*
Mekonat n meconate
Mekoneuropathie f meconeuropathia
Mekoniorrhoe f meconiorrhoea, excessive discharge of meconium
Mekonismus m meconism, opium habit; [chronic] opium poisoning
Mekonium n meconium *(Neugeborenenstuhl)*
Mekoniumabgang m s. Mekoniorrhoe
Mekoniumileus m meconium ileus
Mekoniummembran f meconium membrane
Mekoniumperitonitis f meconium peritonitis
Mekonsäure f meconic acid
Melaena f mel[a]ena, melanorrhoea *(Schwarzfärbung des Stuhls durch Blutbeimengung)*
~ **neonatorum** melaena of the newborn
~ **vera** true melaena
melaenaartig melaenic, m[a]elenic
Melalgie f melalgia, pain in the extremities
Melanämie f melanaemia, presence of melanin in the blood
Melancholia f s. Melancholie
~ **agitans (agitata)** agitated melancholia (depression)
~ **attonita** immobile stage of catatonia
~ **simplex** simple melancholia (depression)
Melancholie f melancholia, severe depression, gloominess, tristimania, dysthimia *(s. a. unter Melancholia)*
~**/hypochondrische** extreme hypochondriasis
~**/klimakterische** climacteric melancholia
~**/paranoide** paranoid melancholia
~**/rezidivierende** recurrent melancholia
~**/stuporöse** stuporous melancholia
Melancholiker m melancholiac
melancholisch melancholic, dysthymic
Melanemesis f melanemesis, black vomit[ing], coffee-ground vomiting
Melanidrosis f melanephidrosis, discharge of black sweat
Melanikterus m melanicterus
Melanin n melanin, melanotic pigment *(stickstoffhaltiges dunkles Pigment)* ● ~ **ablagern** to melanize ● ~ **bilden** to melanize
Melaninablagerung f melanization *(z. B. in Geweben)* ● **die** ~ **beeinflussend** melanotropic
~ **in den Hirnhäuten/diffuse** melanomatosis
melaninartig melanotic, melanoid, resembling melanin
Melaninbildung f melanogenesis, production of melanin, melanization
melaninfrei amelanotic
Melaninfreßzelle f melanophage

melaninhaltig 492

melaninhaltig melaniferous, melanotic
Melaninkörnchen *n* melanin granule
Melaninmangel *m* hypomelanosis
Melaninthesaurismose *f* melanin thesaurismosis
melaninüberpigmentiert hypermelanotic
Melaninüberpigmentierung *f* hypermelanosis
Melaninurie *f s.* Melanurie
Melaninzelle *f s.* Melanozyt
Melaninzellengeschwulst *f s.* Melanozytom
Melanismus *m* melanism, melanosis
Melanoameloblastom *n* melanoameloblastoma
Melanoblast *m* melanoblast *(Melanozytenvorstufe)*
Melanoblastenvermehrung *f* melanoblastosis
Melanoblastom *n* melanoblastoma *(bösartige Geschwulst)*
Melanoblastose *f* melanoblastosis
~/neurokutane neurocutaneous melanoblastosis
melanodermal melanodermic
Melanodermatitis *f* melanodermatitis
Melanodermia *f* **phthiriasica** vagabond's disease (pigmentation)
Melanodermie *f* melanodermia; melanoderma
Melanodermitis *f* melanodermatitis
~ toxica toxic melanodermatitis
Melanoepitheliom *n* melano-epithelioma
Melanoflokkulation *f* melanoflocculation, Henry's melano-flocculation test *(Malarianachweis)*
Melanogen *n* melanogen *(Melaninvorstufe)*
Melanogenase *f* melanogenase *(Enzym)*
Melanogenese *f* melanogenesis, production of melanin
Melanoglossie *f* melanoglossia; black tongue
Melanokarzinom *n* melanocarcinoma *(bösartige Geschwulst)*
Melanoleukoderma *n* **colli** melanoleucoderma colli, collar of Venus
Melanom *n* melanom[a], chromatophoroma
~/bösartiges malignant melanoma, black cancer, naevomelanoma, melanomalignancy
~ des Nagelbetts/bösartiges subungual melanoma, melanotic whitlow
~/suprarenales suprarenal melanoma, Addison's disease (syndrome)
Melanomatose *f* melanomatosis *(1. gehäuftes Auftreten von Melanomen; 2. melanotische Pigmentierung der Hirnhäute)*
Melanome *npl/***multiple** melanomatosis
Melanonychie *f* melanonychia, blackening of the finger-nails; blackening of the toe-nails
Melanopathie *f* melanopathy
Melanophage *m* melanophage
Melanophore *f* melanophore
Melanophorenhormon *n* melanophoric hormone
Melanoplakie *f* melanoplakia
Melanopräzipitation *f* melanoprecipitation *(zum Malarianachweis)*
Melanosarkom *n* melanosarcoma, melanotic sarcoma *(bösartige pigmentierte Geschwulst)*
Melanosis *f* melanosis, melanism
~ coli melanosis of the colon

~ lenticularis progressiva xeroderma pigmentosum
~ oculi ocular melanocytosis
Melanosom *n* melanosome
melanotisch melanotic
Melanotrichia *f* **linguae** melanoglossia, nigrities linguae; black [hairy] tongue
melanotrichös melanotrichous, melanocomous, black-haired
melanotrop melanotropic
Melanotropin *n* melanotropin, melanocyte-stimulating hormone
Melanozyt *m* melanocyte, melanoblast, naevus cell
Melanozytentumor *m* melanocytoma *(gutartige pigmentierte Geschwulst)*
Melanozytenvermehrung *f* melanocytosis
Melanozytom *n* melanocytoma *(gutartige pigmentierte Geschwulst)*
Melanozytose *f* melanocytosis *(Vermehrung der Melanozyten)*
Melanurie *f* melanuria *(Braunfärbung des Urins an der Luft bei melanotischen Geschwülsten)*
Melasma *n* melasma
~ suprarenale melasma suprarenale; bronzed skin *(bei Nebenniereninsuffizienz)*
meldepflichtig notifiable
Melioidose *f* melioidosis *(Infektionskrankheit durch Malleomyces pseudomallei)*
Melitis *f* melitis, inflammation of the cheeck
Melitriose *f* melitriose, raffinose
Meliturie *f* mel[l]ituria
Melkergranulom *n* milker's granuloma
Melkerknoten *m* milker's nodule
Melkerkrampf *m* milker's spasm
Melomaner *m* melomaniac
Melomanie *f* melomania, obsessive fondness for music
Meloplastik *f* meloplasty, plastic surgery of the cheeck
Melorheostose *f* melorheostosis *(Auftreten länglicher Verdichtungsherde in der Knochensubstanz)*
Meloschisis *f* meloschisis; cleft cheek
Melotie *f* melotia *(Ohrmuschelmißbildung)*
Membran *f* 1. membrane, membrana; velamen[tum] *(Anatomie)*; *(s. a. unter* Membrana*)*; 2. diaphragm *(Dialyse, Elektrolyse)*
~/alveolodentale alveolodental (periodontal) membrane
~/alveolokapilläre alveolocapillary membrane
~/Bowmansche Bowman's membrane, lamina limitans externa corneae, anterior (external) elastic lamina of the cornea
~/Bruchsche Bruch's [basal] membrane, basal lamina (layer) of the choroid
~/Descemetsche Descemet's membrane, lamina limitans interna corneae, posterior (internal) elastic lamina of the cornea
~/diphtherische diphtheritic membrane
~/fetale foetal membrane
~/fibröse fibrous membrane

~/**Heusersche** Heuser's (exocoelomic) membrane
~/**homogene** homogenous membrane
~/**hyaline** hyaline membrane *(des Neugeborenen)*
~/**muköse** mucous membrane
~/**permeable** permeable membrane
~/**pharyngeale** pharyngeal membrane
~/**postsynaptische** postsynaptic (postjunctional) membrane, subsynaptic (dendritic) membrane
~/**Reichertsche** Reichert's membrane, lamina elastica anterior
~/**Reissnersche** Reissner's membrane, vestibular membrane of Reissner
~/**semipermeable** semipermeable membrane
~/**Shrapnellsche** Shrapnell's membrane, flaccid membrane of Shrapnell, flaccid portion of the drum membrane
~/**synaptische** synapse (synaptic) membrane, synaptolemma
Membrana f membrane, membrana; velament[um], covering membrane *(s. a. unter Membran)*
~ **atlantooccipitalis** atlantooccipital membrane
~ **atlantooccipitalis anterior** anterior atlantooccipital membrane
~ **atlantooccipitalis posterior** posterior atlantooccipital membrane
~ **basalis ductus semicircularis** basal membrane of the semicircular duct *(des Innenohrs)*
~ **decidua** decidual membrane, basal decidua
~ **elastica** elastic membrane
~ **elastica anterior** anterior elastic membrane
~ **[fibro]elastica laryngis** elastic membrane of the larynx
~ **granulosa** granulosa membrane *(Eierstockfollikel)*
~ **intercostalis** intercostal membrane
~ **intercostalis externa** external intercostal membrane
~ **intercostalis interna** internal intercostal membrane
~ **interossea antebrachii** interosseous membrane of the forearm
~ **interossea cruris** interosseous membrane of the leg
~ **limitans** limiting membrane [of the retina]
~ **limitans externa retinae** external limiting membrane [of the retina]
~ **limitans interna retinae** internal limiting membrane [of the retina]
~ **obturatoria** obturator membrane
~ **perinei** perineal membrane
~ **pupillaris** pupillary membrane
~ **pupillaris persistens** atretopsia
~ **quadrangularis** quadrangular membrane
~ **reticularis** reticular membrane *(des Innenohrs)*
~ **stapedis** obturator membrane of the stapes
~ **sterni** sternal membrane
~ **suprapleuralis** suprapleural membrane
~ **synovialis** synovial membrane

~ **tectoria** 1. tectorial membrane of the ductus cochlearis *(des Innenohrs)*; 2. tectorial membrane *(der Halswirbelsäule)*
~ **thyreohyoidea** thyrohyoid (hyothyroid) membrane
~ **tympani** tympanic membrane, tympanum, myrinx, eardrum, drum [membrane], drumhead
~ **tympani secundaria** secondary tympanic membrane, round-window membrane
~ **vestibularis** vestibular membrane of Reissner, Reissner's membrane
~ **vitrea** vitreous membrane, hyaloid membrane (capsule), limiting membrane *(des Auges)*
membranartig membranous, membranoid, resembling a membrane; velamentous
Membranbildung f membrane formation
Membrandepolarisation f depolarization of membranes
Membranfluoreszenz f membrane fluorescence
membrangebunden membrane-bound
Membranknochen m membrane bone
membranös s. membranartig
Membranoxygenator m membrane oxygenator
Membranpotential n membrane (bioelectrical) potential
Membran-Protein-Antigen n membrane protein antigen
membranreich membranous, membrane-rich
membranständig membrane-bound
Membranstethoskop n diaphragm stethoscope, stethoscope with diaphragm, phonendoscope
Membran- und Trichterstethoskop n/**kombiniertes** combination stethoscope with diaphragm and bell
Membranverschluß m **des Afters** aproctia
Membrum n **inferius** lower extremity
~ **muliebre** clitoris
~ **superius** upper extremity
~ **virile** penis
Menadion n menadione, vitamin K_3
Menagogum n menagogue [agent]
Menakme f menacme
Menalgie f menalgia, menorrhalgia, menstrual pain
Menarche f menarche, menophania, initiation (beginning) of the menstrual function
Menge/in ausreichender quantum satis (sufficit)
Menidrosis f men[h]idrosis *(Schweißausbruch anstelle der Monatsblutung)*
Ménière-Syndrom n Ménière's disease (syndrome), endolymphatic hydrops, hydrops of the labyrinth, auditory vertigo
Meningealanthrax m meningeal anthrax
Meningealblutung f meningorrhagia, haemorrhage from the cerebral membranes
Meningealfibroblastom n meningeal fibroblastoma
Meningealgliomatose f meningeal gliomatosis (sarcomatosis)
Meningealhülle f meningeal coat
Meningealkarzinomatose f meningeal carcinomatosis

Meningealraum

Meningealraum *m* meningeal space
Meningealreizung *f* meningeal irritation
Meningealrhabdomyomatose *f* meningeal rhabdomyomatosis
Meningealvene *f*/**mittlere** middle meningeal vein
Meningealzeichen *n* meningeal sign
Meningeom *n s.* Meningiom
Meningeorrhaphie *f* meningeorrhaphy
Meningioblastom *n* meningioblastoma
Meningiofibroblastom *n* meningiofibroblastoma
Meningiom *n* meningioma, meningeal sarcoma, durosarcoma, dural endothelioma
Meningiomatose *f* meningiomatosis
Meningiosarkom *n* meningiosarcoma
Meningiotheliom *n* meningiothelioma
Meningismus *m* meningism[us], pseudomeningitis
Meningitis *f* meningitis, inflammation of the meninges; brain fever; duritis, pachymeningitis *(s. a. unter Gehirnhautentzündung)*
~ **cerebrospinalis** cerebrospinal meningitis; petechial fever
~/**epidemische** epidemic cerebrospinal meningitis; stiff-neck fever
~ **lymphocytaria** lymphocytic meningitis
~ **lymphocytaria benigna** [acute] benign lymphocytic meningitis
~ **serosa** serous (virus) meningitis
~ **tuberculosa** tuberculous meningitis
meningitisch meningitic
Meningitisserum *n* meningitis (antimeningococcic) serum
Meningitophobie *f* meningitophobia *(krankhafte Angst vor Meningitis)*
Meningoarteriitis *f* meningoarteritis
Meningoblastom *n* meningoblastoma
Meningococcus *m* Weichselbaum Weichselbaum's coccus
Meningoenzephalitis *f* meningo-encephalitis, [en]cephalomeningitis, meningocerebritis, meningocephalitis, encephalitic meningitis
meningoenzephalitisch meningo-encephalitic
Meningoenzephalomyelitis *f* meningo-encephalomyelitis
Meningoenzephalopathie *f* meningo-encephalopathy, encephalo-meningopathy
Meningoenzephalozele *f* meningo-encephalocele, encephalomeningocele
Meningokokkämie *f* meningococcaemia
Meningokokke *f* meningococcus
Meningokokkenarthritis *f* meningococcal arthritis
Meningokokkenerkrankung *f* meningococcosis
Meningokokkenmeningitis *f* meningococcal meningitis
Meningokokkenserum *n* meningococcus serum
meningokokkentötend meningococcidal
Meningokokkenvakzine *f* meningococcus vaccine
meningokortikal meningocortical
Meningomyelitis *f* meningomyelitis

Meningomyelozele *f* meningomyelocele *(Vorfall von Rückenmark und Rückenmarkhäuten durch einen Wirbelspalt)*
Meningopathie *f* meningopathy, disease of the meninges
meningoradikulär meningoradicular
Meningorrhagie *f* meningorrhagia, haemorrhage from the cerebral membranes
Meningorrhoe *f* meningorrhoea
Meningosis *f* meningosis
Meningothel *n* meningothelium
Meningotheliom *n* meningothelioma
Meningotyphus *m* meningotyphoid
meningovaskulär meningovascular
Meningozele *f* meningocele
meningozerebral meningocerebral
Meningozyt *m* meningocyte
Meninx *f* [cranial] meninx, cerebral membrane *(Zusammensetzungen s. unter Hirnhaut)*
Meniscus *m* meniscus, falciform cartilage, interarticular [fibro]cartilage, semilunar fibrocartilage *(im Kniegelenk)*
~ **articularis** joint meniscus
~ **lateralis** lateral meniscus, external meniscus (semilunar fibrocartilage)
~ **medialis** medial meniscus, internal meniscus (semilunar fibrocartilage)
~ **tactus** tactile meniscus (disk)
Meniskektomie *f* meniscectomy, excision of a meniscus
Meniskotom *n* meniscotome, meniscus (meniscotomy) knife
Meniskotomie *f* meniscotomy
Meniskozyt *m s.* Sichelzelle
Meniskozytose *f s.* Sichelzellenanämie
Meniskus *m*/**äußerer** *s.* Meniscus lateralis
~/**innerer** *s.* Meniscus medialis
Meniskusentfernung *f*/**operative** meniscectomy, excision of a meniscus
Meniskusentzündung *f* meniscitis, discitis, inflammation of a meniscus
Meniskushaken *m* knee retractor
Meniskusmesser *n s.* Meniskotom
Meniskusschnitt *m* meniscotomy
Meniskuszeichen *n* meniscus sign
Menolipsis *f* menolipsis, cessation of menstruation
Menometrorrhagie *f* menometrorrhagia, functional uterine bleeding
Menopause *f* menopause, pausimenia, climacteric [period], climacterium
Menopausegonadotropin *n* menopausal gonadotropin
~/**humanes** human menopausal gonadotropin
Menopausenarthritis *f* climacteric arthritis
Menopausenpsychose *f* climacteric insanity (psychosis, melancholia)
Menopauseöstrogentherapie *f* menopausal oestrogen therapy
Menorrhagie *f* menorrhagia, excessive menstrual flow
menorrhagisch menorrhagic

Menorrhalgie f menorrhalgia, menalgia, menstrual pain
Menorrhoe f menorrhoea, menstrual outflow, emmenia
Menoschesis f menoschesis, menostasis, suppression of the menses
Menostase f menostasis, cessation of menstruation
Menostaxis f menostaxis
Mensch m man; human [being] *(Individuum)*
Menschenaffe m anthropoid [ape], primate
menschenbevorzugend androphilous *(z. B. Stechmücken)*
Menschenbiß m human bite
Menschenfeind m misanthrope
menschenfeindlich misanthropic
Menschenfeindlichkeit f misanthropia
Menschenfloh m human flea, Pulex irritans
Menschenfresserei f cannibalism *(sexuelle Abnormität)*
Menschenhaß m misanthropia
menschenliebend androphilous *(z. B. Stechmücken)*
menschenpathogen pathogenic for man
menschenscheu shy, unsociable; anthropophobic
Menschenscheu f shyness, unsociableness; anthro[po]phobia
Menschenserum n human serum
Menschentyp m/**athletischer** athletic type
~/**schlanker (schmächtiger)** asthenic type
menschlich human
Mensch-zu-Mensch-Ausbreitung f person-to-person spread *(z. B. von Mikroorganismen)*
Mensch-zu-Mensch-Übertragung f human-to-human transmission, man-to-man transmission, person-to-person transmission *(z. B. einer Krankheit)*
Menses *pl s.* Menstruation.
menstrual menstrual, menstruous
Menstrual... *s. a.* Menstruations...
Menstrualblut n menstrual blood
Menstrualblutung f menorrhoea, menstrual outflow
Menstrualkolik f menstrual colic; dysmenorrhoea *(Zusammensetzungen s. unter Dysmenorrhoe)*
Menstrualperiode f menstrual period
Menstruation f menstruation, emmenia, catamenia, menses, period, terms, monthly sickness ● **die ~ haben** to menstruate ● **zwischen zwei Menstruationen** intermenstrual
~/**anovulatorische** anovular (anovulatory, nonovulational) menstruation
~/**fehlende** amenorrhoea
~/**geringe** scanty menstruation
~/**letzte** last menstrual period
~ **mit zusätzlicher Gebärmutterblutung** menometrorrhagia
~/**periovulatorische** periovulatory menstruation
~/**profuse** profuse menstruation
~/**regurgitierende** regurgitant (retrograde) menstruation
~/**schmerzhafte** painful (difficult) menstruation, dysmenorrhoea
~/**schwache** hypomenorrhoea
~/**seltene** infrequent menstruation, oligomenorrhoea
~/**verborgene** cryptomenorrhoea *(z. B. bei intaktem Hymen)*
~/**verlängerte** menostaxis, prolonged menstruation
~/**verstärkte** hypermenorrhoea, menorrhagia
~/**verzögerte** delayed menstruation
~/**vikariierende** vicarious (supplementary) menstruation, xenomenia
~/**weiße** white menstruation
~/**zu häufige** polymenia, polymenorrhoea
Menstruationsabweichung f [menstrual] irregularity
Menstruationsalter n menstrual age
Menstruationsanamnese f menstrual history
Menstruationsanomalie f menstrual abnormality
menstruationsauslösend emmenagogic
Menstruationsdermatitis f catamenial dermatitis, dermatitis dysmenorrhoeica
Menstruationsepilepsie f catamenial epilepsy
menstruationsfördernd emmenagogic, stimulating the menstrual flow
Menstruationshämoptyse f catamenial haemoptysis
Menstruationsintervall n intermenstruum
Menstruationslehre f emmenology
Menstruationsschmerz m menalgia, menstrual pain, menorrhalgia; dysmenorrhoea, painful (difficult) menstruation
Menstruationsstörung f emmeniopathy, paramenia, menstrual irregularity (disorder)
Menstruationsverhaltung f menoschesis, menostasis, ischomenia, suppression of the menstrual flow
Menstruationszyklus m menstrual cycle ● **zum gleichen ~ gehörend** tautomenial
menstruieren to menstruate
menstruierend menstruant, menstruous
~/**nicht im normalen Zyklus** acyclic
mensual mensual, monthly
Mentagra f mentagra, sycosis
mental 1. mental, pertaining to the chin; 2. mental, pertaining to the mind
Mentalhygiene f mental hygiene
Mentalität f mentality, mental power (activity)
Mentalprotuberanz f mental protuberance, protuberantia mentalis
Mentalpunkt m mental point, gnathion, pogonion
Mentalsuggestion f mental suggestion (healing)
Mentum n *s.* Kinn
Mephitis f mephitis, foul odour
mephitisch mephitic, emitting a foul odour
Meralgia f **paraesthetica** paraesthetic meralgia, Bernhard-Roth syndrome, Bernhard's paraesthesia (disturbance of sensation), Roth-Bernhardt's disease
Meralgie f meralgia, pain in the thigh

Meralopie

Meralopie f meralopia
Meridianus m **bulbi oculi** meridian of the eye
~ **corneae** meridian of the cornea
Merkaptopurin n mercaptopurine *(Zytostatikum)*
Merkmal n symptom, sign, stigma
~/**klinisches** clinical symptom (feature)
Merkschwäche f weakness of memory; amnesic[-confabulatory] syndrome
Merkurialisation f mercurialization
Merkurialismus m s. Quecksilbervergiftung
Merkurialzittern n mercurial tremor *(Vergiftungssymptom)*
Meroakranie f meroacrania
meroblastisch meroblastic
Merogenese f merogenesis, reproduction by segmentation; somite formation
merogenetisch merogen[et]ic
Merogonie f merogony
Meromyosin n meromyosin *(Muskeleiweiß)*
Meropie f meropia, obscuration of vision
Merorachischisis f merorachischisis, partial spina bifida
Merosmie f merosmia, partial loss of the sense of smell
Merozoit m merozoite, enhaem[at]ospore *(Jugendform der Malariaerreger)*
~/**großer** macromerozoite, megamerozoite
Meryzismus m merycism, rumination, regurgitation of food
mesangial mesangial
mesangiokapillär mesangiocapillary
mesangioproliferativ mesangioproliferative
Mesaortitis f mesaortitis, inflammation of the middle coat of the aorta
Mesarteriitis f mesarteritis, inflammation of the middle coat of an artery
Mesaxon n mesaxon *(zwischen Schwannschen Zellen)*
Mesektoderm n mesectoderm
Mesenchym n mesenchyme, mesenchyma, embryonal connective tissue
mesenchymal mesenchymal
Mesenchymgewebe n mesenchymal tissue
Mesenchymom n mesenchymoma
Mesenchymopoese f mesenchymopoiesis
Mesenchymverkalkung f mesenchymal (interstitial) calcinosis
Mesenchymzelle f mesenchymal cell, mesenchymocyte
Mesenchymzell[en]infiltration f mesenchymal cell infiltration
Mesenterektomie f mesenterectomy, excision of a mesentery
Mesenterialansatz m mesenteric insertion (attachment)
Mesenterialarterie f mesenteric artery
Mesenterialarterienembolie f mesenteric artery embolism
Mesenterialarterieninsuffizienz f mesenteric artery insufficiency
Mesenterialarterienvereng[er]ung f mesenteric artery stenosis

Mesenterialentzündung f mesenteritis, inflammation of the mesentery
Mesenterialgefäßthrombose f mesenteric thrombosis
Mesenterialgefäßverschluß m mesenteric vascular occlusion
Mesenterialhernie f mesenteric hernia
Mesenterialinfarkt m mesenteric infarction
Mesenteriallymphknotenentzündung f mesenteric lymphadenitis
Mesenterialnaht f s. Mesenteriorrhaphie
Mesenterialplexus m mesenteric plexus
Mesenterialraffung f s. Mesenteriopexie
Mesenterialthrombose f mesenteric thrombosis
Mesenterialvene f mesenteric vein
Mesenterialvenenthrombose f mesenteric vein (venous) thrombosis
Mesenterialwurzel f root of the mesentery
Mesenterialzyste f mesenteric cyst
Mesenterikagrafie f mesenteric arteriography
Mesenterikastenose f mesenteric artery stenosis
mesenterikomesokolisch mesentericomesocolic
Mesenteriolum n 1. mesenteriolum, small mesentery; 2. s. ~ processus vermiformis
~ **processus vermiformis** mesenteriolum, mesoappendix
Mesenteriopexie f mesopexy, mesenteriopexy, fixation of the mesentery
Mesenteriorrhaphie f mes[ent]orrhaphy, mesenteriorrhaphy, suture of the mesentery
Mesenteriplikation f mesenteriplication
mesenterisch mesenteric
Mesenteritis f mesenteritis, inflammation of the mesentery
Mesenterium n mesentery, mesenterium
~ **coli** colon mesentery
~ **[dorsale] commune** dorsal mesentery
~/**kleines** small mesentery, mesenteriolum
Mesenterium... s. Gekröse...
Mesenteron n mesenteron, midgut
Mesentoderm n mesentoderm *(Embryologie)*
mesenzephal mesencephalic
Mesenzephalitis f mesencephalitis, inflammation of the midbrain
Mesenzephalon n mesencephalon, midbrain
Mesenzephalotomie f mesencephalotomy, incision of the spinothalamic tract in the mesencephalon
mesial mesial
Mesialbiß m mesioclusion, mesio-occlusion
mesiobukkal mesiobuccal
Meskalin n mescaline *(Farbhalluzinationen hervorrufendes Kakteenrauschgift)*
Mesoappendizitis f meso-appendicitis, inflammation of the mesoappendix
Mesobilifuszin n mesobilifuscin *(Spaltprodukt des Bilirubins)*
Mesobilirubin n mesobilirubin *(Reduktionsprodukt des Bilirubins)*
Mesobilirubinogen n mesobilirubinogen *(entsteht durch Reduktion des Mesobilirubins)*

Mesoblast m s. Mesoderm
mesoblastisch s. mesodermal
mesobranchial mesobranchial
Mesocolon n s. Mesokolon
~ **ascendens** ascending mesocolon
~ **descendens** descending mesocolon
~ **sigmoideum** sigmoid mesocolon *(Bauchfellfalte des Sigmas)*
~ **transversum** transverse mesocolon
Mesoderm n mesoderm, mesoblast[ema]
mesodermal mesodermal, mesoblastic
Mesodermgeschwulst f mesodermal tumour
mesodiastolisch mesodiastolic
Mesodivertikulum n mesodiverticulum
Mesoduodenum n mesoduodenum
Mesoepididymis f meso-epididymis
Mesogastrium n mesogastrium, mesogaster, mesogastric region
Mesoglia f mesoglia *(phagozytäre Zelle in der Neuroglia)*
mesognath mesognathous, mesognathic
Mesognathion n mesognathion
Mesohepaticum n **ventrale** falciform ligament of the liver
Mesoileum n mesoileum, mesentery of the ileum
Mesojejunum n mesojejunum, mesentery of the jejunum
Mesokardie f mesocardia
Mesokardium n mesocardium
Mesokolon n mesocolon *(an der hinteren Bauchwand als Bauchfellduplikatur)*
Mesokolonansatz m mesocolic attachment, mesocolic band (taenia)
Mesokolonfaltung f mesocoloplication
Mesokolopexie f mesocoloplication
mesolezithal mesolecithal *(Embryologie)*
Mesometritis f mesometritis
Mesometrium n mesometrium *(Teil der Bauchfellduplikatur beiderseits der Gebärmutter)*
mesomorph[isch] mesomorphic
mesonephrisch mesonephric
Mesonephrom n mesonephroma
Mesonephros m s. Urniere
Mesoösophagus m mesooesophagus *(Embryologie)*
mesopharyngeal mesopharyngeal, oropharyngeal
Mesopharynx m mesopharynx, oropharynx
Mesophlebitis f mesophlebitis
mesopisch mesopic
mesoprosop mesoprosopic
Mesorchium n mesorchium
Mesorektum n mesorectum, mesentery of the rectum
Mesoropter m mesoropter
Mesosalpinx f mesosalpinx
Mesosigma n mesosigmoid, sigmoid mesocolon
Mesosigmoiditis f mesosigmoiditis, inflammation of the mesosigmoid
mesosom mesosomatous
Mesosom n mesosome *(Zytoplasmainvagination)*

Mesotenon m mesotendon *(gefäßführendes Sehnenscheidenbindegewebe)*
Mesothel n mesothelium, mesothelial tissue
Mesothelioma n mesothelioma, coelothelioma, coelioma
Mesothelsarkom n mesothelial sarcoma *(bösartige Geschwulst)*
Mesothelzelle f mesothelial cell
Mesotympanum n mesotympanum
mesovarial mesovarian
Mesovarium n mesovarium
Mesozephaler m mesocephalus *(Mensch mit mittellangem Schädel)*
Mesozephalie f mesocephalia
mesozephalisch mesocephalic
Mesozökum n mesocaecum
messen to measure
~/**den Blutdruck** to measure (take) the blood pressure
~/**die Temperatur** to take the temperature
Messenger-Ribonukleinsäure f messenger ribonucleic acid, messenger-RNA, mRNA *(Matrize für die Eiweißsynthese)*
Messer n knife *(s. a.* ~/chirurgisches*)*
~/**chirurgisches** scalpel
~/**elektrisches** electrosurgical knife, cautery [knife], electrotome, acusector
Messergriff m knife handle
Meßglas n measuring glass, graduated measure
Messingfieber n brass-founder's fever, monday (metal fume) fever, metal ague
Messingpneumokoniose f brass chills
Meßinstrument n measuring instrument; meter
Messung f measurement, mensuration
Mestranol n mestranol *(Kontrazeptivum)*
metabolisch metabolic
metabolisieren to metabolize, to transform by metabolism, to subject to metabolism
Metabolismus m s. Stoffwechsel
Metabolit m metabolite
Metachromasie f metachrom[as]ia, metachromatism
metachromatisch metachromatic
Metagenese f metagenesis, alternation of generations
Metagonimusinfektion f metagonimiasis, infestation with Metagonimus
Metagranulozyt m metagranulocyte
metaherpetisch metaherpetic, occurring after the herpes
metaikterisch meta-icteric, occurring after jaundice
metainfektiös meta-infective, occurring after an infection
Metakarpalknochen m metacarpal bone, bone of the metacarpus
Metakarpalknochenexstirpation f s. Metakarpektomie
Metakarpalköpfchen n head of the metacarpal bone
Metakarpektomie f metacarpectomy, excision of a metacarpal bone

Metakarpophalangealgelenk

Metakarpophalangealgelenk n metacarpophalangeal joint
Metakarpus m metacarpus
Metalbumin n metalbumin, pseudomucin
Metalldampffieber n monday (metal fume) fever, metal ague
Metalleinsprengung f metallization
Metallgeschmack m metallic taste
Metallimprägnation f, **Metallisation** f impregnation with metals, metallization
Metallklang m metallic tinkle, bell sound, noise of brass *(bei Lungenauskultation)*
metallophil metallophil[e] *(z. B. Gewebe)*
Metallophilie f metallophilia *(z. B. von Geweben)*
Metallophobie f metallophobia *(krankhafte Angst vor Metallgegenständen)*
Metalloprotease f metalloprotease *(Enzym)*
Metalloproteid n metalloprotein
Metallose f metallosis
Metallosteosynthese f metal osteosynthesis
Metallpneumokoniose f metallosis
Metallwärmflasche f metal hot water bottle
Metalues f metalues, metasyphilis, parasyphilis
metaluetisch metaluetic, metasyphilitic, occurring after syphilis
metamerisch metameric
metamorph[isch] metamorphic
Metamorphismus m metamorphism
Metamorphopsie f metamorphopsia *(verzerrte Wahrnehmung von Gegenständen durch das Auge)*
Metamorphose f metamorphosis, change of form (structure)
metamorphotisch metamorphotic
Metamyelozyt m metamyelocyte *(Leukozytenentwicklungsstufe)*
Metanephros m metanephros, hind (definitive) kidney *(entwicklungsgeschichtlich zuletzt gebildet)* ● **den ~ bildend** metanephrogenic
Metaphase f metaphase *(Kernteilungsphase)*
Metaphasenchromosom n metaphase chromosome
Metaphasenplatte f metaphase plate
Metaphasenspindel f metaphase spindle
Metaphyse f metaphysis *(Längenwachstumszone der Röhrenknochen)*
metaphyseal metaphyseal, metaphysial
Metaphysenabszeß m/**Brodiescher** Brodie's abscess
Metaphysenchondrodysplasie f metaphyseal chondrodysplasia
Metaphysendekompression f metaphyseal decompression
Metaphysendysostose f metaphyseal dysostosis, Jansen's syndrome
Metaphysendysplasie f metaphyseal dysplasia
Metaphysenentzündung f metaphysitis, inflammation of a metaphysis
Metaphysenosteoporose f metaphyseal osteoporosis
Metaplasie f metaplasia
~/**myeloische** myeloid metaplasia

498

Metaplasis f metaplasis, fulfilled growth and development
Metaplasma n metaplasm
metaplastisch metaplastic
metapneumonisch metapneumonic, occurring after a pneumonia
Metaprotein n metaprotein
Metapsychologie f metapsychology
Metarteriole f metarteriole
Metastase f metastasis, metastatic tumour
● **Metastasen bilden** to metastasize
Metastasenanämie f metastatic anaemia *(infolge Knochenmarkzerstörung durch Tochtergeschwülste)*
Metastasenausbreitung f s. Metastasierung
Metastasierung f metastatic spread, formation of metastases, carcino[mato]sis
~/**gekreuzte** crossed metastasis
~/**paradoxe** paradoxic metastasis
~/**retrograde** retrograde metastasis
Metastasierungsweg m avenue of metastasis
Metatarsalgie f metatarsalgia, pain in the metatarsus, Morton's disease (neuralgia); Morton's foot (toe)
Metatarsalknochen m metatarsal [bone]
Metatarsalknochenexzision f s. Metatarsektomie
Metatarsalköpfchen n head of the metatarsal bone
Metatarsektomie f metatarsectomy, excision of the metatarsus
Metatarsophalangealgelenk n metatarsophalangeal articulation (joint)
Metatarsus m metatarsus
Metathalamus m metathalamus, corpus geniculatum laterale et mediale *(hinter dem Sehhügel gelegene Gehirnanteile)*
Metathrombin n metathrombin
metatroph metatrophic
Metatrophie f metatrophy
Metazerkarien fpl metacercaria *(Trematodengeneration)*
metazoal metazoal, metazoan
Metazoon n metazoan
metazystisch metacystic
metenzephal metencephalic
Metenzephalon n metencephalon, hindbrain *(aus Kleinhirn und Brücke bestehender Teil des Rautenhirns)*
Meteorismus m meteorism, tympanism, tympanites, tympanosis, tympania, aerenterectasia
Meteoropathie f meteoropathy
Meteoropathologie f meteoropathology *(Wissenschaft von den Zusammenhängen zwischen Wetter und Krankheiten)*
Methämalbumin n methaemalbumin, pseudomethaemoglobin *(bei Schwarzwasserfieber)*
Methämalbuminämie f methaemalbuminaemia
Methämoglobin n methaemoglobin, ferrihaemoglobin *(Blutfarbstoff)*
Methämoglobinämie f methaemoglobinaemia, enterogenous cyanosis

Methämoglobinausscheidung f im Urin methaemoglobinuria
Methämoglobin-Reduktase-Mangel m methaemoglobin-reductase deficiency
Methamphetamin n methamphetamine, deoxyephedrine
Methanal n methanal, formaldehyde *(Desinfektionsmittel)*
Methanol n methanol, methyl alcohol
Met Hb s. Methämoglobin
Methionin n methionine *(essentielle Aminosäure)*
Methioninmalabsorptionssyndrom n methionine malabsorption syndrome, oasthouse urine disease
Methode f:
~/**Babcocksche** Babcock's operation
~/**Binet-Simonsche** Binet-Simon intelligence test
~/**chirurgische** surgical procedure
~ **des fallenden Tropfens** falling-drop method
~/**Esbachsche** Esbach's method
~/**Mauriceausche** Mauriceau's method *(in der Geburtshilfe)*
~/**Westergrensche** Westergren method *(Bestimmung der Blutsenkungsgeschwindigkeit)*
Methogastrose f methogastrosis
Methomanie f methomania, methylmania, methylepsia
Methylalkohol m methyl alcohol, methanol
Methylaminoessigsäure f methylamino-acetic acid, sarcosine
Methylbenzol n methylbenzene, toluene, toluol
α-**Methyldopa** n alpha methyldopa *(Anithypertensivum)*
Methylenblau n methylene blue ● **mit ~ färbend** methylenophil[ous]
Methylenblaufärbung f methylene blue staining, staining with methylene blue
Methylenblauinjektion f methylene blue injection
Methylenblauprobe f methylene blue test
methylenophil methylenophil[ous]
Methylenum n **coeruleum** methylene blue
16α-Methyl-9α-fluor-prednisolon n dexamethasone
N-Methylglykokoll n sarcosine
Methylgruppenabspaltung f demethylation
Methylierung f methylation
3-Methylindol n skatol[e], scatole *(Geruchsstoff des Kots)*
N-Methyl-5-methyl-5-zyklohexenylbarbitursäure f hexobarbital *(Narkosemittel)*
Methylmorphin n methylmorphine *(Antitussivum)*
1-Methyl-4-phenylpiperidin-4-karbonsäureäthylester m pethidine *(Narkotikum)*
1-Methyl-2-(3-pyridyl)-pyrrolidin n nicotine *(Alkaloid)*
Methyltestosteron n methyltestosterone *(männliches Sexualhormon)*
N-Methyltetrahydropapaverin n laudanosine *(Opiumalkaloid)*

Methylthiourazil n methylthiouracil *(Thyreostatikum)*
Methyomanie f s. Methomanie
Metopagus m metopagus *(Doppelmißgeburt mit Stirnverwachsung)*
Metopion n metopion *(anthropologischer Meßpunkt)*
Metopium n metopium, metopon, forehead
Metopismus m metopism
Metopopage m s. Metopagus
Metralgie f metralgia, metrodynia, pain in the uterus
Meträmie f metraemia, uterine hyperaemia
Metranämie f metranaemia, uterine anaemia
Metranoikter m metranoikter *(Instrument zur Dehnung der Cervix uteri)*
Metratonie f metratonia, uterine atonia
Metratrophie f metratrophia, uterine atrophy
Metrauxe f metrauxe, uterine hypertrophy
Metrektasie f metrectasia, enlargement of the uterus
Metrektomie f metrectomy, hysterectomy, excision of the uterus
Metrektopie f metrectopia, uterine displacement
Metreurynter m metreurynter, hystereurynter
Metreuryse f metreurysis, dilatation of the uterine cervix
Metritis f metritis, inflammation of the uterus, hysteritis
~ **dissecans** dissecting metritis
~/**septische** septimetritis
metritisch metritic
Metrodynamometer n metrodynamometer
Metrodynie f s. Metralgie
Metroendometritis f metroendometritis
Metrofibrom n metrofibroma, fibroma of the uterus
Metrogonorrhoe f metrogonorrhoea, gonorrhoea of the uterus
Metrogramm n metrogram, hysterogram, uterogram
Metrographie f metrography, hysterography, uterography
Metrokarzinom n metrocarcinoma, carcinoma of the uterus
Metroklyst m metroclyst
Metrokolpozele f metrocolpocele
Metrolymphangitis f metrolymphangitis
Metromalazie f metromalacia, softening of the uterus
Metromanie f metromania, nymphomania, hysteromania, andromania
Metromenorrhagie f metromenorrhagia
Metroneurie f metroneuria, nervous affection of the uterus
Metroparalyse f metroparalysis, uterine paralysis
Metropathie f metropathy, uterine disease (disorder), hysteropathy
metropathisch metropathic, hysteropathic
Metroperitonitis f metroperitonitis, inflammation of the uterus and the peritoneum

Metropexie

Metropexie f metropexy, metropexia, hysteropexy, fixation of the uterus
Metrophlebitis f metrophlebitis
Metroplastik f metroplasty, hysteroplasty, uteroplasty
Metroptose f metroptosis, uterine prolapse
Metrorrhagie f metrorrhagia, uterine haemorrhage
Metrorrhexis f metrorrhexis, rupture of the uterus
Metrorrhoe f metrorrhoea, [abnormal] uterine discharge
Metrosalpingitis f metrosalpingitis
Metrosalpingographie f metrosalpingography, uterosalpingography, metrotubography
Metroskop n metroscope
Metrostaxis f metrostaxis
Metrostenose f metrostenosis
Metroszirrhus m metroscirrhus *(bösartige Geschwulst)*
Metrotom n metrotome, hysterotome, uterotome
Metrotomie f metrotomy, hysterotomy, uterotomy
Metrozele f metrocele, hysterocele
Metrozystose f metrocystosis, formation of uterine cysts
Metryperästhesie f metryperaesthesia, hyperaesthesia of the uterus
Metrypertrophie f metrypertrophia, hypertrophy of the uterus
Meulengracht-Syndrom n Meulengracht's syndrome *(Bilirubinerhöhung im Blut infolge Funktionsstörung der Lebergewebszellen bei Jugendlichen)*
Michelklammer f Michel's clamp, wound (skin) clip
Microfilaria f **nocturna** Onchocerca caecutiens
Microsporon n **furfur** Malassezia furfur *(Erreger der Pityriasis versicolor)*
Mienenspiel n mimesis, mimosis
Miesmuschelgift n mytilotoxin
Miesmuschelvergiftung f mytilotoxism
Migräne f migrain, megrim, hemicrania, brow pang, cluster (arterial) headache, migrainous (sick, blind, bilious) headache ● **durch ~ hervorgerufen** migrainous
~/ophthalmische ophthalmic migraine
~/plötzlich auftretende fulgurating migraine
~/zervikale cervical migraine, Barré-Liéou syndrome
Migräneanfall m migrainous attack
Migränedaueranfall m migrainous state
Migränekopfschmerz m s. Migräne
Migration f migration, movement *(z. B. der Leukozyten)*
Migrationshemmung f migration inhibition
Migrationshemmungsfaktor m migration inhibitory factor *(Tuberkulose)*
migratorisch migratory, migrant
migrieren to migrate, to wander; to shift from one side to another

Mikrenzephalie f s. Mikroenzephalie
Mikroabszeß m microabscess
Mikroadenom n microadenoma
Mikroadenopathie f micro-adenopathy, disease of small lymphatics
mikroaerophil micro-aerophilic, micro-aerophilous
mikroakustisch micracoustic
Mikroanastomose f microanastomosis, microvascular anastomosis
mikroanastomotisch microanastomotic
Mikroanatom m microanatomist
Mikroaneurysma n microaneurysm
Mikroangiopathie f microangiopathy
~/diabetische diabetic microangiopathy
Mikroarteriogramm n microarteriogram
Mikroarteriographie f microarteriography
mikroarteriographisch microarteriographic
Mikrobakterium n microbacterium
mikrobazillär microbacillary
Mikrobe f microbe, micro-organism
Mikrobeninfektion f s. Mikrobiose
mikrobentötend microbicidal, antimicrobic, antimicrobial; antibiotic
Mikrobenvirulenz f microbial virulence
mikrobiell microbial, microbic
Mikrobiologe m microbiologist
Mikrobiologie f microbiology
mikrobiologisch microbiologic[al]
Mikrobion n s. Mikrobe
Mikrobiophobie f micro[bio]phobia *(krankhafte Angst vor Mikroben)*
Mikrobiose f microbiosis, infection by microbes
mikrobiotisch 1. microbiotic, microbic; 2. microbiotic, having a short life
Mikrobismus m s. Mikrobiose
Mikroblast m microblast *(Vorstufe von Mikroerythrozyten)*
Mikroblepharie f microblepharia, abnormal smallness of the eyelids
Mikroblepharon n microblepharon
Mikroblutung f microhaemorrhage
Mikrobrachie f microbrachia, abnormal smallness of the arms
Mikrobrachyzephalie f microbrachycephalia
Mikrocheilie f microcheilia, microlabia, abnormal smallness of the lips
Mikrocheirie f microch[e]iria, abnormal smallness of the hands
Mikrochirurgie f microsurgery, microscopical surgery
mikrochirurgisch microsurgical
mikrodaktyl microdactylous
Mikrodaktylie f microdactyly, abnormal smallness of fingers and toes
Mikrodaktylus m microdactylus
Mikrodissektion f microdissection
mikrodont microdont, having small teeth
Mikrodontie f microdontia, abnormal smallness of the teeth
Mikrodosierung f microdosage, dosage in small quantities

Mikrodrepanozytose f microdrepanocytosis, microdrepanocytic disease, sickle-cell-thalassaemia disease
Mikroembolie f microembolism
mikroenzephal microencephalous, micrencephalic
Mikroenzephalie f micr[o]encephalia, abnormal smallness of the brain
Mikroenzephalon n micrencephalon
Mikroerythrozyt m microerythrocyte
Mikrofibroadenom n microfibroadenoma
Mikrofilament n microfilament *(Zellstruktur)*
Mikrofilariämie f microfilaraemia
Mikrofilarie f microfilaria
mikrofilarientötend microfilaricidal
Mikroflora f microflora
mikrofollikulär microfollicular, having small follicles
Mikrofoto n photomicrograph
Mikrofotografie f 1. microphotography, photomicrography; 2. s. Mikrofoto
Mikrogamet m microgamete *(Malariaentwicklungsstadium)*
Mikrogametenbildung f formation of microgametes *(bei Malaria)*; exflagellation, formation of flagella
Mikrogametozyt m microgametocyte *(Malariaentwicklungsstadium)*
Mikrogamie f microgamy
Mikrogastrie f microgastria, abnormal smallness of the stomach
Mikrogefäßanastomose f microvascular anastomosis
Mikrogefäßchirurgie f microvascular surgery
Mikrogenie f microgenia, abnormal smallness of the chin, brachygnathia
Mikrogenitalismus m microgenitalism, abnormal smallness of the external genitals
Mikroglia f microglia *(Nervenstützgewebe)*
mikroglial, mikrogliär microglial
Mikrogliazelle f microgliocyte *(Nervenstützgewebezelle)*
Mikrogliazellgeschwulst f microglioma
Mikrogliomatose f microgliomatosis
Mikroglobulin n microglobulin
Mikroglobulinspiegel m microglobulin level
Mikroglossie f microglossia, abnormal smallness of the tongue
mikrognath micrognathic, micrognathous
Mikrognathie f micrognathia, abnormal smallness of the jaws
Mikrographie f micrographia *(krankhafte Neigung zu abnorm kleiner Schrift)*
Mikrogyrie f microgyria, abnormal smallness of the brain convolutions
Mikrohämagglutination f microhaemagglutination
Mikrohämagglutinationstest m microhaemagglutination test *(bei Syphilis)*
Mikrohämaturie f erythr[ocyt]uria
Mikrohämorrhagie f microhaemorrhage
Mikroinfarkt m microinfarct

Mikroinfiltration f microinfiltration
Mikroinjektion f microinjection
Mikroinvasion f microinvasion
Mikrokardie f microcardia, abnormal smallness of the heart
Mikrokardiogramm n microcardiogram
Mikrokardiographie f microcardiography
Mikrokarzinom n hyperplastischer Strumen non-encapsulated sclerosing tumour
Mikrokeratom n microkeratome *(Augenchirurgie)*
Mikrokokke f micrococcus
Mikrokolon n microcolon
Mikrokolonie f microcolony
Mikrokomplementfixationsmethode f microcomplement fixing method *(zum Mumpsvirusnachweis)*
Mikrokonidium n microconidium
Mikrokorie f microcoria, abnormal smallness of the pupils
Mikrokornea f microcornea *(des Auges)*
Mikrokultur f/**Prycesche** Pryce slide-culture method *(zur Züchtung von Tuberkulosebakterien)*
Mikroläsion f microlesion
Mikroleukoblast m micro[leuco]blast *(Leukozytenvorstufe)*
Mikrolith m microlith, microscopic calculus
Mikrolithiasis f microlithiasis
Mikromanie f micromania *(krankhafte Unterschätzung der eigenen Leistungen und der eigenen Persönlichkeit)*
Mikromanipulator m micromanipulator *(Teil des Mikroskops)*
Mikromastie f micromastia, micromazia, abnormal smallness of the breasts
Mikromelie f micromelia, abnormal smallness of the limbs
Mikromelus m micromelus
Mikrometastase f micrometastasis
Mikromethode f micromethod
Mikromyelie f micromyelia, abnormal smallness of the spinal cord
Mikromyeloblast m micromyeloblast
Mikronadel f microneedle
mikroneurochirurgisch microneurosurgical
mikronodulär micronodular
Mikronukleus m micronucleus
Mikronychie f micronychia, abnormal smallness of the nails
Mikroorchidie f micro-orchidia, abnormal smallness of the testicle
Mikroorchi[di]smus m micro-orchi[di]sm
Mikroorganelle f micro-organelle
mikroorganisch micro-organic
Mikroorganismenbefall m microbiosis
Mikroorganismus m micro-organism, microbe; germ ● **durch Mikroorganismen verursacht** microbial, microbic
~/hitzebeständiger thermoduric [micro-organism]
~/nitrifizierender nitrifier

Mikroorganismus

~/**pyogener** pyogenic micro-organism
~/**saprogener** saprogen
~/**verursachender** causative micro-organism
~/**wärmeresistenter** thermoduric [micro-organism]
Mikroparasit m microparasite
Mikropathologie f micropathology
Mikropenis m micropenis, microphallus
Mikrophag[e] m microphage *(für körperfremdes Material)*
Mikrophakie f microphakia, Marchesani syndrome, microlentia, abnormal smallness of the crystalline lens
Mikrophobie f microphobia *(1. krankhafte Angst vor Mikroben; 2. krankhafte Angst vor kleinen Dingen)*
Mikrophonie f microphonia, weakness of voice
Mikrophthalmie f microphthalmia, abnormal smallness of the eyeball
mikrophthalmisch microphthalmic, microphthalmous
Mikrophthalmus m microphthalmus
Mikropinosom n micropinosome
Mikropodie f micropodia, abnormal smallness of the feet
Mikropore f microscopic pore *(z. B. in der Dialysemembran)*
Mikroporenfilter n microporous filter
Mikroprosopie f microprosopia, abnormal smallness of the face
Mikroprosopus m microprosopus
Mikropsie f microp[s]ia
Mikropunktion f micropuncture
Mikropus m micropus
Mikropyle f micropyle *(feine Öffnung in der Eihaut)*
Mikrorhinie f microrrhinia, abnormal smallness of the nose
Mikroröntgenographie f feiner Gewebeschnitte historadiography
Mikroskelie f microscelia, abnormal shortness of the legs
Mikroskop n microscope
Mikroskopfotografie f 1. photomicrography; 2. photomicrograph
Mikroskopie f microscopy, micrographia
mikroskopieren to microscope
Mikroskopiker m microscopist, microanatomist
mikroskopisch microscopic[al]
Mikroskopuntersuchung f microscopic examination
Mikrosom n microsome, plasmosome *(Protoplasmastruktur)*
mikrosomatisch microsomatic
Mikrosomenaktivität f microsome activity
Mikrosomie f microsom[at]ia, microplasia, dwarfism
Mikrospektrographie f microspectrography
Mikrospektrophotometrie f microspectrophotometry
Mikrospektroskop n microspectroscope
Mikrosphärozyt m microspherocyte

Mikrosphärozytose f microspherocytosis
Mikrosphygmie f, **Mikrosphyxie** f microsphyxia, microsphygmy
Mikrosplenia f microsplenia, abnormal smallness of the spleen
Mikrospore f microspore
Mikrosporie f microsporosis *(durch Mikrosporon-Arten hervorgerufene Dermatophytie)*
Mikrosporon n microsporum *(Fadenpilz mit kleinen Sporen)*
Mikrosporose f s. Mikrosporie
Mikrostethoskop n microstethoscope
Mikrostomie f microstomia, abnormal smallness of the mouth
Mikrostrabismus m microstrabism[us]
Mikrothelie f microthelia, abnormal smallness of the mamilla
mikrothromboembolisch microthromboembolic
Mikrothrombose f microthrombosis
Mikrothrombus m microthrombus
Mikrotie f microtia, abnormal smallness of the ears
Mikrotom n microtome, section cutter
Mikrotomie f microtomy *(Methode zur Anfertigung von Dünnschnittpräparaten)*
Mikrotomschnitt m microtome section ● **Mikrotomschnitte herstellen** to microtome
Mikrotonometer n microtonometer *(zur Messung des Sauerstoffdrucks im Blut)*
Mikrotrauma n microtrauma
Mikroveraschung f microincineration
Mikrovillus m microvillus *(Zytoplasmafortsatz)*
Mikrowellenspektroskopie f microwave spectroscopy
Mikrowellentherapiegerät n microwave therapy unit
Mikrozentrum n microcentrum, centrosome
Mikrozephalie f microcephalia, oligocephalia
~ **mit Liquorvermehrung** hydromicrocephalia
Mikrozephalus m microcephalus
Mikrozirkulation f microcirculation, microcirculatory system
Mikrozirkulationssystem n s. Mikrozirkulation
Mikrozoon n microzoon
Mikrozoospermie f microzoospermia
Mikrozotte f microvillus *(Zytoplasmafortsatz)*
Mikrozyste f microcyst
Mikrozyt m microcyte
Mikrozytase f microcytase *(mikroorganismenauflösendes Enzym)*
Mikrozytenanämie f microcytic anaemia
Mikrozytenvermehrung f im Blut s. Mikrozytose
Mikrozythämie f s. Mikrozytose
mikrozytisch microcytic
Mikrozytose f microcytosis, microcythaemia
Mikrozytotoxizitätstest m microcytotoxicity test
Miktio[n] f miction, micturition, urination, uresis, emiction
Miktionsbeschwerden pl micturition difficulties, dysuria
Miktionsfurcht f urophobia
Miktionshäufigkeit f micturition (urinary) frequency

Miktionsschmerz *m* urodynia
Miktionsstörung *f* dysuria, voiding disorder of the bladder
Miktionszentrum *n* micturition centre, vesical (vesicospinal) centre
Miktionszystourethrogramm *n* micturating (voiding) cystourethrogram
Miktionszystourethrographie *f* micturating (voiding) cystourethrography
Milbe *f* acarian, acaroid, mite
Milbenbefall *m* acariasis, acari[n]osis
Milbenbekämpfungsmittel *n* acaricide [agent], miticide
Milbendermatitis *f* acarodermatitis
Milbenfleckfieber *n* tsutsugamushi disease (fever), tropical (rural, mite-borne) typhus, Malayan [scrub] typhus, Queensland coastal fever
milbentötend acaricide, acarotoxic, miticidal
Milch *f* milk *(s. a. Muttermilch)*
~/**adaptierte** modified milk *(für Säuglingsernährung)*
~/**eiweißangereicherte** protein-rich milk
~/**mit Vitamin D angereicherte** vitamin D milk *(durch Ultraviolettbestrahlung)*
~/**pasteurisierte** pasteurized milk
~/**sterilisierte** sterilized milk
milchabhängig lactivorous
milchabsondernd lactating, lactigenous, milk-secreting
Milchabsonderung *f* lactation, milk secretion, galactorrhoea, galactosis *(aus der Brust) (s. a. unter* Milchsekretion*)* • **vor der ~** prelacteal
~/**verminderte** hypogalactia, hypogalactosis, oligogalactia
~/**verstärkte** hypergalactia, hypergalactosis, polygalactia, lactorrhoea, superlactation
Milchabszeß *m* milk abscess
milchähnlich lacteal, galactoid, milky
Milchähnlichkeit *f* lactescence *(z. B. der Darmlymphe)*
Milchalbumin *n* lactalbumin
Milch-Alkali-Syndrom *n* milk-alkali syndrome [of hypercalcaemia], Burnett's (milk-drinker's) syndrome
milchartig galactoid, milk-like, milky
Milchbehandlung *f* milk cure, lactotherapy
milchbildend galactopoietic, lactigenous
Milchbildung *f* galactopoiesis, lactation, milk secretion • **die ~ anregend** galactogenous
~/**fehlende** agalactia
Milchborke *f s.* Milchschorf
Milchbruch *m* [ga]lactocele, galactoma
Milchbrustgang *m* thoracic duct
Milchbrustgangdrainage *f* thoracic duct drainage
Milchdiät *f* milk diet
Milchdiätbehandlung *f* [ga]lactotherapy
Milchdrüsen *fpl* lactiferous (mammary) glands • **die ~ aktivierend (anregend)** lactogenic
Milchdrüsenausführungsgang *m* excretory duct of the mammary gland
Milcheiweiß *n* lactalbumin, lactoprotein

Milchsekretion

Milchernährung *f* galactotrophy • **auf ~ basierend** lactivorous
Milchfaktor *m*/**Bittnerscher** milk factor
Milchfieber *n* milk fever, galactopyra *(im Wochenbett zur Zeit des Milcheinschießens)*
Milchfistel *f* lacteal fistula
Milchfleck *m* milk plaque (spot)
Milchfluß *m* [ga]lactorrhoea
~/**fehlender** agalorrhoea
milchflußhemmend antigalactic, galactophygous
milchfördernd [ga]lactogogue
milchführend lactiferous, lactigerous, galactophorous
Milchgang *m* milk (lacteal) duct, lactiferous tubule, galactophore, galactophorous canal
Milchgangabszeß *m* milk (canalicular) abscess
milchgangdarstellend galactographic
Milchgangentzündung *f* galactophoritis
Milchgangkarzinom *n* milk-duct carcinoma
Milchgangröntgen[kontrast]darstellung *f* galactography
Milchgangsinus *m* lactiferous sinus, lacteal ampulla *(spindelförmige Milchgangerweiterung vor der Mündung auf die Brustwarze)*
Milchgangzyste *f* galactocele
Milchgebiß *n* deciduous (primary) dentition; milk teeth, deciduous (temporary) teeth
Milchglobulin *n* lactoglobulin
milchhemmend antigalactic, galactophygous, lactifuge
milchig 1. lacteal, milky; 2. chylous, chyloid, chyliform
Milchigkeit *f* lactescence *(z. B. der Darmlymphe)*
Milchintoleranz *f* milk intolerance
Milchkanälchen *n s.* Milchgang
Milchkruste *f s.* Milchschorf
Milchkur *f* milk cure
Milchleiste *f* milk ridge, mammary line (ridge)
milchlos agalactous
Milchmesser *m* galactometer
Milchpocken *pl* milk pox, minor variola, alastrim, glasspox
Milchpumpe *f* milk (breast) pump, lactisugium
Milchpumpenball *m* breast pump bulb
Milchretention *f s.* Milchverhaltung
Milchsaft *m s.* Chylus
Milchsäure *f* lactic acid
Milchsäureakkumulation *f* lactic acid accumulation
Milchsäureausscheidung *f* **im Urin** lactaciduria
Milchsäureazidose *f* lactic acidosis
Milchsäurebildung *f* lactification *(durch Bakterien)*
Milchsäurestäbchen *n* lactobacillus, lactic acid bacillus
Milchschorf *m* milk crust (scall), cradle cap, milky tetter *(Ekzem bei Kindern)*
Milchschweiß *m* galacthidrosis
Milchsekretion *f* lactation, galactosis, milk secretion *(aus der Brust)*
~ der männlichen Brustdrüse androgalactosaemia

Milchsekretion

~/fehlende agalactia
~ mit erhöhtem Zuckergehalt saccharogalactorrhoea
~/vermehrte hyperlactation, superlactation
~/verminderte hypogalactia, oligogalactia
milchsezernierend lactigenous
Milchstauung f s. Milchverhaltung
Milchstein m lacteal calculus
Milchträufeln n polygalactia
milchtreibend [ga]lactagogue, galactic
Milchtrinkersyndrom n s. Milch-Alkali-Syndrom
Milchunverträglichkeit f milk intolerance
milchverhaltend ischogalactic
Milchverhaltung f ischogalactia, galactostasis, galactoschesis, milk retention
Milchzahnausfall m shedding
Milchzahndurchbruch m deciduous dentition
Milchzähne mpl milk teeth, deciduous (temporary) teeth
Milchzucker m milk sugar, lactose, lactin
Milchzuckerausscheidung f im Urin lactosuria
Milchzuckerunverträglichkeit f lactose intolerance
Milchzyste f [ga]lactocele, lacteal cyst, galactoma
mild mild, bland, lenitive (z. B. Medikamente)
mildern to mitigate; to relieve, to ease, to alleviate (z. B. Schmerzen); to attenuate (z. B. Krankheitssymptome)
Milderung f mitigation; relief, alleviation (z. B. von Schmerzen); attenuation (z. B. von Krankheitssymptomen)
Miliarabszeß m miliary abscess
Miliaraneurysma n miliary aneurysm
Miliaraussaat f miliary spread
Miliarfieber n miliary fever
Miliaria f miliaria, sweat fever, sudamen, prickly heat, summer eruption, heat (tropical sweat) rash, wild fire rash, red gum
~ pustulosa perioritis, miliaria pustulosa
~ rubra s. Miliaria
Miliarknötchenausbreitung f miliary spread
Miliarsklerose f miliary sclerosis
Miliartuberkel m miliary tubercle
Miliartuberkulose f miliary (disseminated) tuberculosis
Milie f s. Milium
Milienmesser n milium knife
Miliennadel f milium needle
Milieu n milieu, environment, peristasis
Milieubehandlung f milieu (situation) therapy
Militärkrankenhaus n military hospital
Militärmedizin f military (war) medicine
Milium n milium, grutum, white head, cutaneous calculus
Millard-Gubler-Lähmung f facial hemiplegia alternans, Millard-Gubler syndrome
Miller-Abbott-Sonde f Miller-Abbott tube (zum Absaugen von Darminhalt aus Magen und Dünndarm)
Milz f spleen, lien ● neben der ~ parasplenic ● über der ~ suprasplenial ● von der ~ ausgehend splenogenic, splenogenous

~/akzessorische accessory (supernumerary) spleen, splen[unc]ulus, lien[un]culus
Milz... s. a. Lien... und Splen...
Milzabszeß m splenic abscess; purulent splenitis
milzähnlich splenoid, spleniform
Milzamyloidose f amyloidosis of the spleen; bacon (waxy, sago) spleen
Milzanämie f splenic anaemia
Milzanheftung f/operative s. Milzfixation
Milzanschoppung f splenemphraxis, congestion of the spleen
Milzapoplexie f splenic apoplexy
Milzarterie f splenic artery
Milzarterienaneurysma n splenic artery aneurysm
Milzarteriennervengeflecht n splenic plexus
Milzarterien-Nierenarterien-Anastomose f/operative splenorenal shunt
Milzarteriographie f splenic arteriography
milzartig splenoid
Milzaspirat n splenic aspirate
Milzatrophie f splenic atrophy, atrophy of the spleen
Milzauflösung f splenolysis
Milzband n splenic ligament
Milzbauchfellentzündung f perisplenitis
Milzbeschwerden fpl splenic complaint
Milzblutung f splenorrhagia, haemorrhage from the spleen
Milzbrand m [malignant] anthrax, Siberian pest, tanner's (ragsorter's, woolsorter's) disease, splenic fever, malignant pustule, milzbrand, charbon (Zusammensetzungen s. unter Anthrax)
milzbrandartig anthracoid
Milzbrandbazillus m anthrax bacillus, Bacillus anthracis
Milzbrandimpfstoff m anthrax vaccine
Milzbrandkarbunkel m anthrax carbuncle
Milzbrandmeningitis f anthrax meningitis
Milzbrandpneumonie f anthrax (woolsorter's) pneumonia
Milzbrandreaktion f/Ascolische Ascoli test [for anthrax]
Milzbrandserum n antianthrax serum, anthrax antiserum
milzbrandtötend anthracidal
Milzbruch m lienocele, splenocele, hernia of the spleen
Milzeinblutung f splenic apoplexy
Milzentfernung f durch Bauchschnitt laparosplenectomy
~/operative splenectomy, lienectomy, excision of the spleen
Milzentzündung f splenitis, lienitis, inflammation of the spleen
Milzerkrankung f splenopathy, lienopathy, disease of the spleen
Milzerweichung f splenomalacia, lienomalacia, softening of the spleen
Milzfixation f splenopexy, lienopexy, fixation of the spleen

Milzfixierungsoperation f/**Bardenheuersche** Bardenheuer's operation
Milzfollikel m s. **Milzkörperchen/Malpighisches**
milzförmig spleniform
Milzfunktionsstörung f dyssplenism
Milzgeräusch n splenic souffle
Milzgeschwulst f splenoma, splenic tumour, tumour of the spleen
Milzgewebeaussaat f splenosis
Milzgift n splenotoxin, lienotoxin
Milzhämangioendotheliom n splenic haemangioendothelioma
Milzhämosiderose f splenic haemosiderosis
Milzhilus m hilum of the spleen, splenic hilum
Milzhypertrophie f splenic hypertrophy, megalosplenia
Milzinfarkt m splenic infarction
Milzinfarzierung f splenic infarction
Milzkalzifikation f splenic calcification
Milzkapselentzündung f episplenitis
Milzkörperchen n/**Malpighisches** splenic nodule, Malpighian corpuscle
Milzlager n splenic bed
Milzloge f splenic bed
milzlos asplenic; splenectomized (nach operativer Entfernung)
Milznaht f splenorrhaphy, suture of the spleen
Milzparenchym n splenic tissue
Milzpol m/**oberer** upper pole of the spleen
~/**unterer** lower pole of the spleen
Milzpulpa f splenic pulp
~/**rote** [splenic] red pulpa, red pulp [cords]
~/**weiße** [splenic] white pulpa
Milzpulpaamyloidose f lardaceous spleen
Milzpunktion f splenic puncture
Milzröntgen[kontrast]bild n splenogram
Milzröntgen[kontrast]darstellung f splenography, lienography
Milzschmerz m splenalgia, splenodynia, pain in the spleen
Milzschnitt m splenotomy, incision into the spleen
~ **nach Baucheröffnung** laparosplenotomy
Milzschwellung f splenic enlargement
Milzselbstabstoßung f autosplenectomy
Milzsenkung f splenoptosis; floating (wandering, prolapsed) spleen
Milzsinus m splenic sinus, sinusoid
Milzstiel m splenic pedicle
Milzstörung f dyssplenism
Milztrabekel fpl splenic trabeculae
Milztrauma n splenic trauma
Milztyphus m splenotyphoid
Milzüberfunktion f hypersplenism, hypersplenia
Milz- und Knochenmarkerweichung f lienomyelomalacia
Milz- und Leberoperation f/**plastische** splenohepatoplasty
Milz- und Lebervergrößerung f splenohepatomegaly
Milzunterfunktion f hyposplenism, hyposplenia
Milzvene f splenic vein

Milzvergrößerung f splenomegaly, megalosplenia, splenauxe
Milzverkalkung f splenic calcification
Milzverkleinerung f microsplenia
Milzverlagerung f splenectopia, displacement of the spleen
Milzzerreißung f splenic rupture
Mimesis f mimesis, mimosis
mimetisch 1. s. **mimisch**; 2. mimetic, imitative
α-mimetisch alpha-mimetic
Mimik f mimesis, mimosis, facial expression
Mimikfälschung f paramimia
Mimikmuskel m mimetic muscle, muscle of facial expression
Mimikmuskellähmung f mimetic paralysis
Mimikmuskulatur f mimetic musculature
Mimiksteigerung f hypermimia
Mimikstörung f dysmimia
Mimikverfälschung f paramimia
Mimikverlust m amimia
Mimikverminderung f hypomimia
mimisch mimetic, mimic
minderaktiv hypoactive
Minderaktivität f hypoactivity
Minderdurchblutung f insufficient blood supply
Minderfärbbarkeit f hypochromatism, hypochromatosis, hypochromia, achromasia (z. B. des Zellkerns)
Minderjähriger m minor
Minderleistung f miopragia
mindern to obtund, to dull, to make dull, to blunt (z. B. die Sensibilität); to diminish, to lessen (verringern)
Minderperfusion f underperfusion (z. B. mit Blut)
Minderperfusionszustand m low perfusion state
minderversorgt trophesial, trophesic (z. B. Gewebe)
Minderwertigkeitsgefühl n feeling of inferiority
Minderwertigkeitskomplex m inferiority complex
Mineralablagerung f, **Mineraleinlagerung** f mineralization
Mineralhaushalt m mineral balance
mineralisieren to mineralize
Mineralisierung f mineralization
Mineralmangel m hypomineralization, mineral deficiency
Mineralokortikoid n mineralocorticoid (den Mineralhaushalt des Körpers beeinflussendes Hormon)
Mineralokortikoid[spiegel]erhöhung f im Blut hypermineralocorticoidism
Mineralokortikoidspiegelverminderung f im Blut hypomineralocorticoidism
Mineralokortikoidsubstitution f mineralocorticoid replacement
Mineralquellenbehandlung f crenotherapy
Mineralstoffwechsel m mineral metabolism
Mineralüberschuß m hypermineralization
Mineralverarmung f demineralization
Miniaturhautelektrode f miniature skin electrode
Minimaldosis f minimum dose

Minimalluft

Minimalluft f minimal air *(restliche Luftmenge in einer kollabierten Lunge)*
Minimal[reiz]schwelle f absolute threshold
Minimalstimulus m minimal stimulus
Minimum n **cognoscibile** threshold of perception
~ **legibile** minimum of reading
~ **separabile** minimal separable acuity, separable minimum *(Ophthalmologie)*
~ **visible** visible minimum
Ministerium n **für Gesundheitswesen** Ministry of Health
Minoragglutinin n minor (partial) agglutinin
Minorepilepsie f minor epilepsy
Minortest m **[der Blutgruppenkreuzprobe]** minor cross match
Minuslinse f minus lens
Minuszyklophorie f incyclophoria
Minutenvolumen n minute ventilation (volume) *(der Lunge)*; minute volume, cardiac output *(des Herzens)*
Miopragie f miopragia, decreased functional activity
Miose f, **Miosis** f miosis, myosis, constriction of the pupil [of the eye], stenocoriasis
Miosphygmia f miosphygmia
Miotikum n **[remedium]** miotic [agent]
miotisch miotic
Misandrie f misandria
Misanthrop m misanthrope
Misanthropie f misanthropia
misanthropisch misanthropic
mischbar miscible, mixable
~/**nicht** immiscible, non-miscible
Mischehe f intermarriage, mixed marriage, miscegenation
Mischgeschwulst f mixed tumour
Mischgeschwür n s. Mischschanker
Mischimpfstoff m mixed vaccine
Mischinfektion f mixed (multiple) infection, multiinfection, polyinfection *(Vorhandensein von mehreren Krankheitserregern)*
Mischkultur f mixed culture
Mischling m half-breed
Mischplasma n pooled [human] plasma
Mischschanker m mixed chancre *(bei gleichzeitiger Infektion mit Treponema pallidum und Haemophilus Ducreyi)*
Mischserum n pooled [human] serum
Mischthrombus m stratified thrombus
Mischtrank m mixture
Mischung f mixture, composition
Mischzelle f mixed cell
Mischzellensarkom n mixed cell sarcoma
Miserere n copremesis, faecal (stercoraceous) vomiting
misogam misogamous
Misogam[er] m misogamist
Misogamie f misogamy
Misogyn m misogynist
Misogynie f misogyny
Misologie f misology

Misoneismus m misoneism, neophobia
Misoneist m misoneist
Misopädie f misopaedia
Mißbildung f 1. deformation, deformity, dysmorphia; paraplasia; malformation, dysontogenesis (z. B. des Fetus); abnormalism, abnormality; teratism, teratosis; 2. s. Mißgeburt ● **Mißbildungen bewirkend** teratogen[et]ic
~/**Arnold-Chiarische** Arnold-Chiari malformation (syndrome) *(Hemmungsmißbildung des Kleinhirns)*
~ **mit Beinverschmelzung** symmelia
~ **mit Extremitätenverstümmelung** peromelia
~ **mit freiliegendem Gehirn** exencephalia
~ **mit Ohrenverwachsung** synotia
~ **mit Ohrverschmelzung** otocephalia
~ **mit zwei Köpfen** diplocephalia
Mißbildungsangst f teratophobia
Mißbildungsspezialist m teratologist
Mißbrauch m misuse, abuse
missed abortion s. Fehlgeburt/verhaltene
missed labour s. Wehen/vergebliche
Mißempfindung f **der Haut** paraesthesia
~/**schmerzhafte** paralg[es]ia
mißgebildet deformed, malformed, abnormal, anomalous; teramorphous, teratic, teratoid
~/**allgemein** pantamorphic
Mißgeburt f monster, monstrosity, teras ● **eine ~ hervorrufend** teratogenous, teratogenic
~/**armlose** abrachius
~/**gehirnlose** pantaencephalus
~ **mit abnorm großen Fingern und Zehen** macrodactylus
~ **mit abnorm kleinen Fingern und Zehen** microdactylus
~ **mit Arm- und Brustverschmelzung** thoracomelus
~ **mit Bauchspalte** schistosomus
~ **mit Beinverschmelzung** symmelus
~ **mit Beinverstümmelung** peropus
~ **mit doppeltem Mund** distomus
~ **mit Doppelzunge** diglossus
~ **mit drei Füßen** tripus
~ **mit drei Köpfen** tricephalus
~ **mit einem Arm** monobrachius
~ **mit einem Auge** synophthalmus, cyclops, monops, monoculus
~ **mit Extremitätenspalte** schistomelus
~ **mit flossenartigen Extremitäten** phocomelus
~ **mit freiliegendem Gehirn** exencephalus
~ **mit Gesichtsspalte** schistoprosopus
~ **mit Gliedmaßenverstümmelung** ectromelus
~ **mit Halswirbelsäulenspalte und fehlendem Gehirn** derencephalus
~ **mit Höhlenbildungen in der Hirnsubstanz** porencephalus
~ **mit Kopfrudiment** paracephalus
~ **mit überzähligen Gliedern** polymelus
~ **mit verkümmerten Armen** perobrachius
~ **mit verkümmerten Extremitäten** peromelus
~ **mit Verkümmerung der Finger und Zehen** perodactylus

- ~ mit verminderter Gliederzahl oligomelus
- ~ mit Verschmelzung der unteren Extremitäten sirenomelus, siren[-limb], sympus
- ~ mit Verstümmelung der Hände peroch[e]irus
- ~ mit verwachsenen Fingern oder Zehen syndactylus
- ~ mit vier Armen tetrabrachius
- ~ mit vier Beinen tetramelus
- ~ mit vier Händen tetrach[e]irus
- ~ mit vier Ohren tetraotus
- ~ mit windungslosem Gehirn lissencephalus
- ~ mit zwei Köpfen craniodidymus, di[plo]cephalus
- ~ mit zwei Unterkiefern dignathus
- ~ ohne Extremitäten amelus
- ~ ohne Finger oder Zehen adactylus
- ~ ohne Gehirn anencephalus
- ~ ohne Gehirn und Rückenmark amyelencephalus
- ~ ohne Gesicht aprosopus
- ~ ohne Hände acheirus
- ~ ohne Herz acardiac[us]
- ~ ohne Hoden anorchus
- ~ ohne Kopf acephalus
- ~ ohne Kopf, Brustkorb und Bauch acephalogaster
- ~ ohne Kopf und Arme acephalobrachius
- ~ ohne Kopf und Brustkorb acephalothorax
- ~ ohne Kopf und Füße acephalopodius
- ~ ohne Kopf und Hände acephaloch[e]irus
- ~ ohne Kopf und Herz acephalocardius
- ~ ohne Kopf und Wirbelsäule acephalorrhachus
- ~ ohne Lippen acheilus
- ~ ohne Rückenmark amyelus
- ~ ohne Rumpf acormus
- ~ ohne Schädel acranius

Mißgestalt f deformity, deformation, dysplasia; abnormalism, abnormality; teratism
mißgestaltet deformed; dysplastic; teramorphous, teratic, teratoid
Mißokklusion f malocclusion, abnormal occlusion
Mißstimmung f malaise
Mitbeteiligung f involvement (z. B. eines Organs)
mitbewegend/sich synkinetic
Mitbewegung f[/unwillkürliche] synkinesia, synkinesis, syncinesis, associated [automatic] movement, accessory movement
Mitella f mitella, arm sling
Mitempfindung f/abnorme synaesthesia (in Sinnesorganen)
~/schmerzhafte synalgia (z. B. in Gliedern)
Mitesser m comedo, blackhead
Mitesser... s. Komedo...
Mithridatismus m mithridatism (Giftgewöhnung durch steigende Dosierung)
Mitochondrien npl mitochondria, Altmann's granules
Mitochondriengenom n mitochondrial genome
Mitochondrienmatrix f mitochondrial matrix
Mitochondrienstruktur f mitochondrial structure
Mitochondrienteilung f chondriokinesis

Mitochondrium n mitochondrium, chondriocont (Zellorganelle)
mitogenetisch mitogen[et]ic
Mitose f mitosis, mitotic division, karyokinesis (mit Chromosomenausbildung) ● ~ bewirkend mitogen[et]ic
~/pathologische pathologic mitosis
Mitoseapparat m mitotic apparatus
Mitoseendphase f telophase, teleomitosis
Mitosefigur f mitotic figure
Mitosegift n mitotic poison; antimitotic [agent]
Mitosehemmstoff m antimitotic [agent], mitotic inhibitor
Mitoseindex m mitotic index
Mitosespindel f achromatic figure (spindle)
Mitosestillstand m mitotic arrest
Mitosom n mitosome
mitotisch mitotic, karyokinetic (bei Zellteilungen)
Mitralanuloplastik f mitral annuloplasty
Mitralatresie f mitral atresia, atresia of mitral orifice
Mitraldiastolikum n mitral diastolic
Mitraldurchfluß m mitral valve flow
Mitralfehler m mitral valvular defect
Mitralgeräusch n mitral murmur
~/diastolisches mitral diastolic
~/systolisches mitral systolic
Mitralgesicht n mitral facies
Mitralinsuffizienz f mitral incompetence (insufficiency), mitral regurgitation
~ mit Mitralsegelprolaps floppy valve syndrome
Mitralis f s. Mitralklappe
Mitralispuls m mitralized pulse
Mitralklappe f mitral (left atrioventricular) valve, bicuspid valve (valvula) (Herzklappe zwischen linkem Herzvorhof und linker Herzkammer)
Mitralklappenanpassung f mitral valve coaptation
Mitralklappenatresie f mitral atresia, atresia of mitral orifice
Mitralklappendeformierung f deformity of the mitral valve
Mitralklappenersatz m mitral valve replacement
Mitralklappengeräusch n mitral murmur
Mitralklappengewebe n mitral valvular tissue
Mitralklappenöffnungsfläche f mitral valve area
Mitralklappenprolaps m mitral valve prolapse
Mitralklappenprothese f mitral valve prosthesis
Mitralklappenrekonstruktion f mitral valve repair
Mitralklappenring m mitral ring
Mitralklappensegel n/hinteres posterior leaflet (cusp) of the mitral valve
~/vorderes anterior leaflet (cusp) of the mitral valve
Mitralklappensprengung f[/operative] mitral commissurotomy (valvotomy)
Mitralklappensystolikum n mitral systolic
Mitralklapptentrichter m mitral funnel
Mitralklappenvereng[er]ung f s. Mitralstenose
Mitralkommissurotomie f mitral commissurotomy (valvotomy)

Mitralkonfiguration

Mitralkonfiguration f mitralization, mitral configuration *(bestimmte Herzform bei Mitralfehlern)*
Mitralöffnung f mitral orifice
Mitralöffnungsfläche f mitral valve area
Mitralöffnungston m opening mitral snap
Mitralringplastik f mitral annuloplasty
Mitralsegelspalte f cleft mitral valve
Mitralstenose f mitral stenosis, MS, mitral obstruction (valve stenosis)
Mitralstenosedilatator m dilator for mitral valve
Mitralstenosegeräusch n murmur of mitral stenosis
Mitralstenoseindex m mitral stenosis index
Mitralstenosesprengung f mitral commissurotomy (valvotomy)
Mitralvitium n mitral valve defect
Mitschwingen n resonance *(z. B. bei der Perkussion)*
mitschwingend resonant
Mitte f middle; midpoint; centre; waist ● **die ~ bildend** medial ● **in der ~ befindlich** medial ● **in der ~ und dazwischenliegend** intermediomedial ● **nach der ~ zu gelegen** mesial ● **nach hinten und zur ~ gerichtet** posteromedial ● **neben der ~** paramedial ● **zur ~ gerichtet** mediad
Mittel n agent; preparation *(s. a. unter Arzneimittel und Medikament)*
~/abkühlendes refrigerant [agent]
~/ableitendes revulsant [agent]
~/abortauslösendes abortifacient [agent], ecbolic [agent]
~/adstringierendes astringent [agent]
~/amöbentötendes amoebicide, antiamoebic [agent]
~/angstlösendes anxiolytic [agent]
~/anregendes stimulant [agent], analeptic
~/ansäuerndes acidulant [agent]
~/antianämisches antianaemic [agent]
~/antiarrhythmisches antiarrhythmic [agent]
~/antidepressives antidepressant [agent]
~/antidiuretisches antidiuretic [agent]
~/antiepileptisches antiepileptic [agent]
~/antifibrinolytisches antifibrinolytic [agent]
~/antihämolytisches antihaemolytic [agent]
~/antihämorrhoidales antihaemorrhoidal [agent]
~/antihypnotisches antihypnotic [agent]
~/antiluetisches antiluetic [agent], antisyphylitic [agent]
~/antimikrobielles antimicrobial [agent]
~/antimitotisches antimitotic [agent]
~/antinarkotisches antinarcotic [agent]
~/antineuritisches antineuritic [agent]
~/antiparasitisches antiparasitic [agent]
~/antiphlogistisches antiphlogistic [agent]
~/antipruritisches antipruritic [agent]
~/antipyretisches antipyretic [agent], febrifuge [agent]
~/antirachitisches antirachitic [agent]
~/antiseptisches antiseptic [agent]
~/antithrombotisches antithrombotic [agent]
~/antithyroides antithyroid [agent]
~/antitrypanosomales antitrypanosomal [agent]
~/antriebssteigerndes thymoleptic [agent]
~/appetitanregendes appetizer, aperitive
~/appetitverringerndes anoretic [agent], anorexiant [agent], antiobesic [agent]
~/askaridentötendes ascaricide [agent]
~/ausfällendes precipitant [agent].
~/auswurfförderndes expectorant [agent]
~/bakterienhemmendes antibacterial (antigerminative) agent
~/bandwurmkopftötendes scolicidal [agent]
~/bandwurmtötendes taeniacide [agent]; scolicidal [agent]
~/bandwurmtreibendes taeniafuge [agent]
~/bazillentötendes bacillicide [agent]
~/blasenziehendes vesicant [agent]
~/Blut ableitendes revulsant [agent]
~/Blut umverteilendes revulsant [agent]
~/blutbildendes haematinic [agent]
~/Blutschizonten tötendes blood schizonticide
~/blutstillendes haemostatic [agent], styptic [agent], antihaemorrhagic [agent]; astringent [agent]
~/blutungsförderndes haemagogue [agent]
~/bronchialschleimlösendes bronchial mucolytic
~/bronchienerweiterndes bronchodilator, bronchodilating agent
~/chemisches chemical agent
~/chlamydienwirksames antichlamydial [agent]
~/das Pilzwachstum hemmendes fungistat
~/den Geschlechtstrieb dämpfendes (herabsetzendes) an[t]aphrodisiac
~/den Geschlechtstrieb steigerndes aphrodisiac [agent], genital stimulant
~/den Speichelfluß anregendes sialagogue [agent], sialogogue
~/depressionsbekämpfendes antidepressant [agent]
~/desinfizierendes disinfectant
~/desodorierendes deodorant
~/die Gallenblase entleerendes cholecystagogue [agent]
~/die Psyche dämpfendes psychoplegic [agent]
~/die Resorption von Exsudaten förderndes resorbent [agent]
~/die Speichelsekretion förderndes ptysmagogue [agent]
~/die Zellkernteilung bewirkendes mitogen
~/eine Erschlaffung bewirkendes relaxant [agent]
~/eiterhemmendes pyostatic [agent]
~/eiterziehendes suppurant [agent]
~/empfängnisverhütendes contraceptive [agent], contraceptivum
~/entzündungshemmendes antiphlogistic [agent], astringent [agent]
~/erfrischendes refrigerant [agent]
~/erstickend wirkendes asphyxiant [agent]
~/erweichendes emollient [agent]
~/euphorisierendes euphoriant [agent]
~/fibrinauflösendes fibrinolytic [agent]
~/fibrinolysehemmendes antifibrinolytic [agent]

Mittel

~/**fiebererzeugendes** pyretogen
~/**fiebersenkendes** antipyretic [agent], febrifuge [agent]
~/**fungizides** fungicide [agent], antifungal [agent], antimycotic [agent]
~/**galletreibendes** cholagogue [agent], choleretic [agent]
~/**gameten[ab]tötendes** gametocide [agent]
~/**gebärmuttertonisierendes** uterotonic [agent]
~/**geburtsauslösendes** ecbolic [agent]; abortion-producing agent
~/**geburtsbeschleunigendes** labour-accelerating agent, ecbolic [agent]
~/**gefäßerweiterndes** vasodilator [agent]
~/**gefäß[nerven]hemmendes** vasoinhibitor [agent]
~/**gefäßstimulierendes** vasostimulant [agent]
~/**gefäßtonisierendes** vasotonic [agent]
~/**gefäßverenge[r]ndes** vasoconstrictor [agent], vasopressor
~ **gegen Angina pectoris** antianginal agent
~ **gegen Asthma** antiasthmatic [agent]
~ **gegen Bilharziose** antischistosomal [agent]
~ **gegen Diabetes** antidiabetic [agent]
~ **gegen Durchfall** costive [agent]
~ **gegen Erbrechen** antiemetic [agent]
~ **gegen Fadenwurmbefall** nematocide [agent]
~ **gegen Filarien** antifilarial [agent]
~ **gegen Gelenkentzündung** antiarthritic [agent]
~ **gegen Histamin** antihistaminic [agent], antihistamine [drug]
~ **gegen Krätze** antiscabetic [agent]
~ **gegen Lepra** antileprotic [agent]
~ **gegen Rheumatismus** antirheumatic [agent]
~ **gegen Schistosomiasis** antischistosomal [agent]
~ **gegen Schuppenflechte** antipsoriatic [agent]
~ **gegen Skorbut** antiscorbutic [agent]
~ **gegen Syphilis** antisyphylitic [agent], antiluetic [agent]
~ **gegen Tetanus** antitetanic [agent]
~ **gegen Tollwut** antirabic [agent]
~ **gegen Übelkeit** antinauseant [agent]
~ **gegen Wundinfektion** antiseptic [agent]
~/**gerinnselauflösendes** thrombolytic [agent]
~/**gerinnungshemmendes** anticoagulant [agent]
~/**geschwulstauflösendes** oncolytic [agent]
~/**gonokokken[ab]tötendes** gonococcide [agent]
~/**granulationsförderndes** incarnative [agent]
~/**harnhemmendes** antidiuretic [agent]
~/**harntreibendes** diuretic [agent], urinative [agent], uragogue [agent], emictory [agent]
~/**hautrötendes** rubefacient [agent]
~/**herzbeschleunigendes** cardioaccelerator [agent]
~/**herzrhythmisierendes** antiarrhythmic [agent]
~/**herzstärkendes** cordial [agent]
~/**herzstimulierendes** cardiac stimulant
~/**hornhaut[ab]lösendes** keratolytic [agent]
~/**hustenlösendes** solvent [agent]
~/**hypnotisches** hypnotic [agent]
~/**immunitätshemmendes** immunosuppressive (immunodepressive) agent, immunodepressant [agent]
~/**insektenvertreibendes** insect repellent
~/**juckreizlinderndes** antipruritic [agent]
~/**kardioinhibitorisches** cardioinhibitory [agent]
~/**kardiokinetisches** cardiokinetic [agent]
~/**keimhemmendes** antigerminative [agent]
~/**keimlingschädigendes** embryotoxic [agent]
~/**keimtötendes** germicide [agent], disinfectant, antiseptic [agent]
~/**kokzidienhemmendes** coccidiostatic [agent]
~/**koronargefäßerweiterndes** coronary vasodilating agent
~/**krankheitsverhütendes** prophylactic [agent]
~/**krätzemilbentötendes** scabicide [agent]
~/**Lähmungen hervorrufendes** paralysant
~/**larventötendes** larvicide [agent]
~/**läusetötendes** pediculicide [agent]
~/**leberschizontentötendes** hepatic schizonticide
~/**leprahemmendes** leprostatic [agent]
~/**lokal schmerzausschaltendes** local anaesthetic
~/**lymphtreibendes** lymphagogue [agent]
~/**magenstärkendes** stomachic, gastric stimulant
~/**menstruationsförderndes** [em]menagogue, menagogue agent
~/**mikrobentötendes** microbicide [agent], antimicrobial [agent]
~/**milbentötendes** miticide [agent]
~/**milchhemmendes** lactifuge [agent]
~/**milchtreibendes** galactagogue [agent], lactogen
~/**Mißbildungen bewirkendes** teratogenic [agent]
~/**mitosehemmendes** antimitotic [agent]
~/**moskitotötendes** mosquitocide [agent]
~/**mückentötendes** culicide [agent]
~/**mückenvertreibendes** culifuge [agent]
~/**muskelerschlaffendes** muscle relaxant [agent]
~/**natriumausscheidendes** natriuretic agent
~/**nematodentötendes** nematocide [agent]
~/**nervenlähmendes** neuroplegic [agent]
~/**nervenschmerzstillendes** antineuralgic [agent]
~/**neuroplegisches** neuroplegic [agent]
~/**nierenwirksames** nephrotropic [agent]
~/**oxyurentötendes** oxyuricide [agent]
~/**oxyurenvertreibendes** oxyurifuge [agent]
~/**parasitentötendes** parasiticide [agent]
~/**parasitotropes** parasitotropic [agent]
~/**pilzhemmendes** fungistat, mycostat
~/**pilztötendes** fungicide [agent], antimycotic [agent], antifungal [agent]
~/**plasmodientötendes** plasmodicide
~/**protektiv wirkendes** protective
~/**protozoentötendes** protozoacide
~/**Psychose erzeugendes** psychotogen
~/**pupillenerweiterndes** mydriatic [agent], cycloplegic [agent]
~/**pupillenverenge[r]ndes** miotic [agent]
~/**radiomimetisches** radiomimetic [agent]

Mittel

~/reizendes stimulant [agent]
~/RR-senkendes antihypertensive [agent]
~/säureneutralisierendes antacid [agent]
~/schilddrüsenhemmendes antithyroid [agent]
~/schistosomentötendes schistosomacide [agent]
~/schizontentötendes schizontocide [agent], schizonticidal drug *(in der Schizontenphase wirksames Malariamittel)*
~/schlafhemmendes antihypnotic [agent]
~/schlafvertreibendes agrypnode
~/schleimlösendes expectorant [agent]
~/schmarotzertötendes parasiticide [agent]
~/schmerzstillendes analgesic, antalgic [agent], anodyne [agent], obtundent [agent]
~/schwangerschaftsverhütendes contraceptive [agent], contraceptivum
~/schweißhemmendes antihidrotic [agent], antisudoral [agent]
~/schweißtreibendes diaphoretic [agent], sudorific [agent]
~/sedierendes sedative [agent]
~/sekretionsförderndes secretagogue [agent]
~/spasmolytisches spasmolytic [agent]
~/speichelhemmendes antisialic [agent]
~/speicheltreibendes sialagogue [agent], sialogogue, ptyalogogue [agent]
~/spermientötendes spermatocide
~/spirillentötendes spirillicide [agent]
~/spirochätentötendes spirochaeticide [agent], antispirochaetic [agent]
~/sporentötendes sporicide [agent]
~/stechmückentötendes anophelicide [agent]
~/stechmückenvertreibendes anophelifuge [agent]
~/steinabtreibendes lithagogue [agent]
~/sympathikushemmendes sympatholytic [agent]
~/sympathikusstimulierendes sympathomimetic [drug]
~/thrombolytisches thrombolytic [agent]
~/thromboseverhinderndes antithrombotic [agent]
~/thymoleptisches thymoleptic [agent]
~/tränentreibendes dacryagogue [agent]
~/trichomonadentötendes trichomonacide [agent], trichomonicide
~/trypanosomentötendes trypanocide [agent], antitrypanosomal [agent]
~/tuberkelbakterienhemmendes tuberculostatic [agent]
~/tuberkelbakterientötendes tuberculocide
~/umverteilendes revulsant [agent]
~/vasodepressorisches vasodepressor [agent]
~/verdauungsförderndes digestive [agent], digestant
~/verflüssigendes liquefacient [agent]
~/vorbeugendes prophylactic [agent]
~/wehenanregendes oxytocic [agent], parturifacient [agent]
~/wurmabtreibendes vermifuge [agent]
~/wurmtötendes vermicide [agent]

~/zykloplegisches cycloplegic [agent]
Mittelbauchgegend f s. Mesogastrium
Mittelbauchquerschnitt m transverse midabdominal incision
Mitteldarm m midgut, mesenteron
Mittelfach n der Hohlhand middle palmar space
Mittelfeld n midzone *(der Lunge) (Radiologie)*
Mittelfell n s. Mediastinum
Mittelfellentzündung f s. Mediastinitis
Mittelfellpleura f mediastinal pleura
Mittelfellraum m s. Mediastinum
Mittelfellspiegelung f mediastinoscopy
Mittelfell- und Herzbeutelentzündung f mediastinopericarditis
Mittelfellvene f/obere anterior mediastinal vein
Mittelfinger m middle finger, medius
Mittelfingerstrecker m extensor digiti medii [muscle]
Mittelfleisch n perineum, perinaeum
Mittelfurche f an der Großhirnkonvexität Rolando's fissure, rolandic fissure (sulcus)
Mittelfuß m metatarsus
Mittelfußamputation f Lisfranc's amputation *(im Fußwurzel-Mittelfuß-Gelenk)*
Mittelfußarterie f/dorsale dorsal metatarsal artery
~/plantare plantar metatarsal artery
Mittelfußband n metatarsal ligament
Mittelfußknochen m metatarsal bone
Mittelfußknochenentfernung f[/operative] metatarsectomy
Mittelfußknochenköpfchen n head of the metatarsal bone
Mittelfußrückenarterie f dorsal metatarsal artery
Mittelfußrückenvene f dorsal metatarsal vein
Mittelfußschmerz m metatarsalgia
Mittelfußvene f/dorsale dorsal metatarsal vein
~/plantare plantar metatarsal vein
Mittelfußverkürzung f/angeborene brachymetapody
Mittelfuß-Zehen-Gelenk n metatarsophalangeal articulation (joint)
mittelgesichtig mesoprosopic
Mittelgesichtsfraktur f middle face fracture
Mittelglied n middle phalanx
mittelgroß mesosomatous
Mittelhand f metacarpus
Mittelhandarterie f/dorsale dorsal metacarpal artery
~/palmare (ventrale) palmar metacarpal artery
Mittelhand-Finger-Gelenk n metacarpophalangeal joint
Mittelhandknochen m metacarpal [bone], bone of the metacarpus
Mittelhandknochenbruch m metacarpal fracture
Mittelhandknochenentfernung f/operative metacarpectomy
Mittelhandknochenköpfchen n head of the metacarpal bone
Mittelhandknochenüberzähligkeit f polymetacarpalism

Mittelhandknochenverkürzung f/angeborene brachymetacarpalia
Mittelhandnerv m median nerve
Mittelhandrekonstruktion f metacarpal reconstruction
Mittelhandrückenarterie f dorsal metacarpal artery
Mittelhandrückenvene f dorsal metacarpal vein
Mittelhandvene f/palmare (volare) palmar (volar) metacarpal vein
Mittelhirn n midbrain, mesencephalon
Mittelhirndach n tectum of the mesencephalon
Mittelhirnentzündung f s. Mesenzephalitis
Mittelhirnepilepsie f midbrain epilepsy (fit)
Mittelhirnhaube f tegmentum
Mittelhirnschnitt m mesencephalotomy
Mittelhirnunterseite f inferior surface of the mesencephalon
mittelköpfig mesocephalic, orthocephalic, orthocephalous
Mittelköpfiger m mesocephalus *(Mensch mit mittellangem Schädel)*
Mittelköpfigkeit f mesocephalia, orthocephalia
Mittellappen m middle lobe
Mittellappenarterie f middle lobe artery
Mittellappenbronchus m middle lobe bronchus
Mittellappenentfernung f[/operative] middle lobectomy
Mittellappenhypertrophie f median lobe hypertrophy *(der Prostata)*
Mittellappenpneumonie f middle lobe pneumonia
Mittellappensyndrom n middle lobe syndrome
~/**Brocksches** Brock's syndrome
Mittellinie f midline, median (middle) line ● neben der ~ paramedian
Mittelmeeranämie f Mediterranean anaemia, thalass[an]aemia, familial erythroblastic (microcytic) anaemia
Mittelmeerfieber n Malta (Gibraltar) fever, Mediterranean fever (phthisis), brucellosis, brucelliasis *(Infektionskrankheit durch Brucella melitensis)*
Mittelohr n middle ear, tympanum
Mittelohraspirator m middle ear aspirator
Mittelohrbelüftung f middle ear ventilation
Mittelohrdach n epitympanum, epitympanic recess (space), superior tympanic cavity, attic [of the middle ear]
Mittelohrdruck m middle ear pressure
Mittelohreiterung f purulent (suppurative) otitis media
~/durch Fliegenlarven hervorgerufene otomyiasis *(in den Tropen)*
Mittelohrentzündung f otitis media, middle ear inflammation, inflammation of the middle ear
~/akute otitis media acuta; acute ear
Mittelohrerguß m middle ear effusion, fluid in the middle ear, hydrotympanum, hydromyrinx
Mittelohrerkrankung f middle ear disease
Mittelohrfunktion f middle ear function
Mittelohrkatarrh m middle ear catarrh

Mittelohrschleimhaut f middle ear mucosa
Mittelohrschmerz m durch Luftdruckunterschiede barotalgia
Mittelohrschwerhörigkeit f middle ear deafness
Mittelohrspalte f middle ear cleft
Mittelohr- und Innenohrentzündung f panotitis
Mittelohrventilation f middle ear ventilation
Mittelohrwiederherstellungschirurgie f middle ear reconstructive surgery
Mittelphalanx f middle phalanx
Mittelschmerz m midpain, middle (intermenstrual) pain
Mittelstrahlprobe f midstream specimen [of urine]
Mittelstrahlurin m midstream urine
Mittelwertabweichung f standard deviation
Mittönen n resonance *(z. B. bei der Perkussion)*
mittönend resonant
Mixtur f mixture
Mizell n, **Mizelle** f micelle, micell[a]
M-Komponent-Hypergammaglobulinämie f M-component hypergammaglobulinaemia, monoclonal gammopathy
Mnemasthenie f mnemasthenia, weakness of memory
Mneme f s. Gedächtnis
mnemisch mnemic
Mnemonik f s. Mnemotechnik
mnemonisch mnemonic
Mnemotechnik f mnemo[tech]nics, mnemotechny *(Lerntechnik)*
mnemotechnisch mnemonic
Mobilisation f mobilization *(z. B. von Gelenken)*
mobilisieren 1. s. ~/to mobilize, to render movable *(z. B. Gelenke)*; 2. to mobilize, to free; to make accessable *(z. B. Organa)*; to mobilize, to release, to liberate *(z. B. Speicherstoffe)*
Mobilisierungsoperation f mobilization operation
Mobilität f mobility
Möbius-Syndrom n Möbius' syndrome, [infantile] nuclear aplasia, congenital oculofacial paralysis, congenital facial diplegia
Modell n 1. s. ~/anatomisches; 2. cast *(z. B. eines Zahns)*
~/anatomisches phantom, anatomical model, manikin
Moderatorband n moderator band *(Reizleitung des Herzens)*
Modiolus m modiolus *(knöcherne Achse des Gehörorgans)*
Modus m der Plazentalösung/Schultzescher Schultze's placenta *(durch retroplazentares Hämatom)*
Mogigraphie f mogigraphia, writer's cramp
Mogilalie f mogilalia, difficulty in speech; stuttering
Mogiphonie f mogiphonia
Mohn m papaver, poppy
Mohnsaft m meconium
Mohnsäure f meconic acid
Mola f **carnosa** carneous mole

Mola

~ **hydatidosa** hydatic (cystic) mole, hydati[di]form mole, dropsical ovum
molar molar
Molar *m* molar [tooth]
~/**dritter** wisdom tooth
Molardrüse *f* molar gland *(in der Wangenschleimhaut)*
molarförmig molariform
Molarzange *f* molar forceps
Mole *f* mole *(Fehlentwicklung des befruchteten Eies)*
Molekularbewegung *f* molecular movement
Molekularbiologie *f* molecular biology
Molekularschicht *f* **des Kleinhirns** molecular layer of the cerebellum
Molenschwangerschaft *f* molar (hydatid) pregnancy
Molimina *npl* molimina, pains
~ **menstrualia** molimina menstrualia
Molitor *m* **verrucae** wart virus
Molluscum *n* **contagiosum** contagious (epithelial) molluscum *(erbsengroße wachsgelbe Hautgeschwulst mit zentraler Eindellung)*
~ **pseudocarcinomatosum (sebaceum)** sebaceous molluscum, keratoacanthoma *(gutartige Hautwucherung)*
Molluscumkörperchen *npl* molluscum bodies *(enthalten den Viruserreger der Dellwarzen)*
molluskoid molluscoid
Molybdänvergiftung *f* molybdenosis, [chronic] molybdenum poisoning
Molysmophobie *f* molysmophobia *(krankhafte Angst vor Infektion)*
Monarthritis *f* monarthritis, inflammation of a single joint *(z. B. bei Tripper)*
monartikulär mon[o]articular, monarthric
Monaster *m* monaster, mother star *(Chromosomenfigur in der Kernteilungsphase)*
Monathetose *f* monathetosis
Monatsbinde *f* sanitary towel (napkin)
Monatsblutung *f s.* Menstruation
Mond *m*[/**kleiner**] lunula, [half-]moon *(am Fingernagel)*
Mondbein *n* lunar bone, lunare, lunate [bone], semilunar *(Handwurzelknochen)*
Mondbeinerweichung *f s.* Mondbeinnekrose/aseptische
Mondbeinnekrose *f*[/**aseptische**] lunatomalacia, softening of the lunatum, Kienböck's disease
Mondgesicht *n* moon face *(bei Nebennierenrindenüberfunktion)*
Mondsüchtiger *m* lunatic, somnambulist, moonwalker
Mondsüchtigkeit *f* lunatism, lunacy, somnambulism, moon-walking
Mongolenfalte *f* Mongolian (eye) fold, epicanthus, epicanthic fold
Mongolenfleck *m* Mongolian (sacral) spot *(im Säuglingsalter auftretender bläulicher Fleck in der Kreuzbein- oder Gesäßgegend)*
Mongolismus *m* mongolism, Mongolian (mongoloid) idiocy, Down's syndrome, trisomy 21 [syndrome]

Monilethrix *f* monilethrix, moniliform (beaded) hair
Monilia *f* Monilia *(Pilzgattung; normale Mund- und Darmbewohner)*
~ **albicans (candida)** thrush fungus, Monilia (Candida) albicans
Moniliainfektion *f* monilial infection
Moniliaösophagitis *f* monilial oesophagitis
Moniliasis *f* moniliasis *(durch Moniliaarten hervorgerufene tropische Darmkrankheit)*
monilienartig moniliform
Monoaminooxydase *f* monoamine oxidase, MAO *(Enzym)*
Monoamin[o]oxydaseinhibitor *m* monoamine oxidase inhibitor, MOAI
Monoblast *m* monoblast *(Monozytenvorstufe)*
Monoblastenleukämie *f* monoblastic leukaemia
Monoblepsie *f* monoblepsia, monocular vision
Monobrachius *m* monobrachius
Monochromasie *f* monochromasia, monochromatism, total colour blindness *(mit einfarbigem Zapfensehen und guter zentraler Sehschärfe)*
Monochromat[er] *m* monochromat[e]
monochromatisch monochrom[at]ic, monochroic
monochromatophil monochromatophil[ic]
Monochromator *m* monochromator *(optisches Instrument zur Herstellung einfarbigen Lichts)*
Monodaktylie *f*, **Monodaktylismus** *m* monodactyly, monodactylism
Monodiplopie *f* monodiplopia
monoflagellär monotrichous
monogam monogamic, monogamous
Monogamie *f* monogamy
3-Monohydroxycholansäure *f* lithocholic acid *(Gallensäure)*
Monojodtyrosin *n* monoiodotyrosine *(Schilddrüsenstoffwechselprodukt)*
monoklonal monoclonal
Monokokke *f* monococcus
monokrot monocrotic *(Pulskurve)*
Monokrotie *f* monocrotism *(z. B. des Pulses)*
Monokulus *m* monoculus
monoman monomaniacal
Monomaner *m* monomaniac
Monomanie *f* monomania, monopsychosis
monomorph monomorphic, monomorphous
Monomorphismus *m* monomorphism
Monomphalus *m* monomphalus, omphalopagus, omphalodidymus
Monomyoplegie *f* monomyoplegia
Mononeuritis *f* mononeuritis, inflammation of a single nerve
Mononucleosis *f* mononucleosis, monocytosis, mononuclear leucocytosis
~ **infectiosa** Pfeiffer's disease (glandular fever), infectious mononucleosis, [acute] infectious adenitis, lymphocytic (monocytic) angina, acute benign adenitis, kissing disease
mononukleär mononuclear
Mononukleose *f s.* Mononucleosis
mononukleoseartig mononucleosis-like

513 Morbus

Mononukleotid *n* mononucleotide
Monoparese *f* monoparesis
Monophasie *f* monophasia *(Beschränkung auf einzelne Wörter oder Sätze)*
monophasisch monophasic
Monophobie *f* monophobia *(krankhafte Angst vor dem Alleinsein)*
Monophthalmie *f* monophthalmia, synophthalmia, synopsia, cyclopia
Monoplegie *f* monoplegia
monoplegisch monoplegic
Monopodie *f* monopodia
Monopus *m* monopus
monorchid monorchid[ic]
Monorchid[er] *m* monorchid
Monorchidismus *m*, **Monorchie** *f* monorchi[di]sm
Monosaccharid *n* monosaccharide, monose, simple sugar
Monose *f s.* Monosaccharid
monosomatisch monosomatic, monosomatous *(Chromosomen)*
Monosomie *f* monosomy *(Chromosomensatz)*
Monospasmus *m* monospasm
Monotherapie *f* monotherapy
Monothermie *f* monothermia
Monoxenie *f* monoxenia
monozellulär monocellular
Monozephalus *m* monocephalus, monocranius
Monozyesis *f* monocyesis
monozystisch monocystic
Monozyt *m* monocyte, transitional cell (leucocyte), splenocyte
~/großer macromonocyte
~ mit Resten von Malariapigment pigmentophage
Monozytenangina *f* monocytic angina
Monozytenanstieg *m s.* Monozytose
Monozytenentwicklung *f* monocytopoiesis
Monozytenleukämie *f* monocytic leukaemia
Monozytenmangel *m* monocytopenia
Monozytenreifung *f* monocytopoiesis
Monozyten[reifungs]reihe *f* monocytic series
Monozytenvermehrung *f* im Blut *s.* Monozytose
Monozytenverminderung *f* im Blut monocytopenia
Monozytenzytotoxizität *f* monocyte cytotoxicity
monozytisch monocytic
Monozytopenie *f* monocytopenia
Monozytopoese *f* monocytopoiesis
Monozytose *f* monocytosis, mononucleosis, mononuclear leucocytosis
Mons *m* mons
~ pubis (veneris) pubic eminence, mount of Venus, mons pubis (veneris)
Monsterbildung *f s.* Mißbildung
Monstripara *f* monstripara
Monstrosität *f s.* 1. Mißgeburt; 2. Mißbildung
Monteggia-Knochenbruch *m* Monteggia's fracture
Moorbad *n* mud bath
Moorkur *f* pelotherapy, mud treatment

Moorpackung *f* mud pack
Moosfasern *fpl* moss[y] fibres *(zum Kleinhirn ziehende Nervenfasern)*
Moraxella *f* **lacunata** Morax-Axenfeld bacillus, Morax's diplobacillus *(Erreger der Lidwinkelkonjunktivitis)*
morbid morbid, unsound, diseased; pathologic *(s. a. krank)*
Morbidität *f* morbidity
Morbiditätsrate *f* morbidity (sick) rate, morbidity
Morbilität *f s.* Morbidität
Morbillen *mpl* morbilli, measles
morbilliform morbilliform, measles-like, resembling measles
Morbus *m* morbus, disease, illness, sickness, malady *(s. a. unter* Krankheit*)*
~ anglicus *s.* Krankheit/Englische
~ apoplectiformis *s.* ~ Ménière
~ asthenicus Stiller's disease, universal asthenia
~ caducus *s.* Epilepsie
~ caeruleus cyanotic congenital heart disease; blue baby
~ cardiacus heart disease
~ castrensis epidemic typhus
~ coeliacus coeliac disease (infantilism)
~ coxae hip joint disease
~ Crouzon Crouzon's disease, craniofacial dysostosis
~ Cushing 1. Cushing's disease (syndrome), pituitary basophilism; 2. Cushing's disease, adrenal cortical hyperfunction
~ divinus *s.* Epilepsie
~ gallicus *s.* Syphilis
~ haemolyticus neonatorum newborn haemolytic disease
~ haemorrhagicus neonatorum newborn haemorrhagic disease, haemorrhagic disease of newborn
~ Henoch-Schönlein Schönlein's disease (purpura), allergic (non-thrombopenic) purpura
~ Jaffe-Lichtenstein Jaffe-Lichtenstein disease, cystic osteofibromatosis
~ maculosus neonatorum *s.* ~ haemorrhagicus neonatorum
~ maculosus Werlhofi *s.* ~ Werlhof
~ Ménière Ménière's disease (syndrome), endolymphatic hydrops *(umfaßt Schwindelerscheinungen, Erbrechen, Nystagmus, Innenohrschwerhörigkeit und Ohrensausen)*
~ Ollier Ollier's disease, dyschondroplasia; multiple chondromas
~ Ormond Ormond's disease, retroperitoneal fibrosis
~ phlyctenoides *s.* Pemphigus
~ Recklinghausen 1. Recklinghausen's (Engel-Recklinghausen) disease, [generalized] osteitis fibrosa cystica; 2. Recklinghausen's disease, neurofibro[phaco]matosis, neuroblastomatosis, neurinomatosis, multiple neurofibroma (neuroma)
~ sacer *s.* Epilepsie
~ saltatorius *s.* Chorea

Morbus

~ **Sudeck** Sudeck's disease (atrophy), traumatic osteoporosis, posttraumatic reflex sympathetic dystrophy
~ **vesicularis** s. Pemphigus
~ **virgineus** s. Chlorose
~ **vulpis** s. Alopezie
~ **Werlhof** Werlhof's disease, idiopathic thrombocytopenic purpura, haemorrhagic (essential) purpura, land scurvy
Morcellation f, **Morcellement** n morcellation (z. B. von Tumoren)
Mordsucht f phonomania, homicidomania
Morgagni-Adams-Stokes-Syndrom n Morgagni-Adams-Stokes syndrome, Adams-Stokes disease, Morgagni's disease (syndrome), complete (total) heart block
Morgagni-Syndrom n Stewart-Morel[-Morgagni] syndrome, metabolic craniopathy
Morgagni-Turner-Albright-Syndrom n Ullrich-Turner syndrome, [male] Turner's syndrome, gonadal dysgenesis syndrome
Morgensteifigkeit f morning stiffness
Morgentemperatur f morning temperature
Moria f moria, joking mania (Orbitalhirnsymptom)
moribund moribund
Morphin n morphine (Hauptalkaloid des Opiums)
Morphinentzugssyndrom n amorphinism (bei Süchtigen)
Morphinismus m morphinism, morphi[n]omania, morphine habit
Morphinismusbehandlung f demorphinization
Morphinist m morphinist, morphine addict
morphinistisch morphinistic
Morphinmiosis f pinpoint (pinhole) pupil (extrem enge und starre Pupille)
Morphinomaner m s. Morphinist
Morphinomanie f s. Morphinismus
Morphinvergiftung f/**chronische** morphinism
Morphium n morphine (Hauptalkaloid des Opiums)
Morphiumentzug m demorphinization
Morphiummethyläther m codeine
Morphiumsucht f s. Morphinismus
Morphiumsüchtiger m s. Morphinist
Morphogenese f morphogenesis, morphogeny
morphogenetisch morphogen[et]ic
Morphologe m morphologist
Morphologie f morphology
~/**pathologische** pathomorphology, pathomorphism
morphologisch morphologic[al]
Morphometrie f morphometry (Verfahren zur Ausmessung von Körperformen)
morphometrisch morphometric
Morpio m morpio, crab louse
Morquio-Syndrom n s. Mukopolysaccharidose Typ IV
Mors f mors, death
~ **putativa** apparent death
~ **subitanea** sudden death
~ **thymica** thymic death

Mörser m mortar
Morsus m 1. morsus, bite; 2. morsus, pain
mortal mortal, fatal, causing death; terminating in death
Mortalamputation f mortal amputation (Stomatologie)
Mortalität f mortality, death rate
~/**perinatale** perinatal mortality, stillbirth rate, natimortality
Mortalitätsrisiko n mortality risk
Mortalitätsziffer f death rate
Morula f morula, mulberry mass, vitelline sphere (frühes Keimentwicklungsstadium)
Morula-Magma f reticular magma (zum Schutz der Embryonalanlage)
Morulastadium n morula (mulberry) state
Morulation f morulation, formation of the morula
Morulazelle f morular cell [of Mott]
Mosaikknochen m mosaic bone
Moskito m mosquito
Moskitogift n mosquitocide [agent]
Moskitoklemme f mosquito forceps (zum Fassen kleiner Blutgefäße)
Moskitomittel n mosquitocide [agent]
moskitoübertragen mosquito-borne
Moskito-Vektor m mosquito vector
motil motile, able to move, moveable
Motilität f motility (z. B. der Spermien)
Motilitätspsychose f motor psychosis
Motilitätsstörung f motiliy disturbance
Motivation f motivation
Motoneuron n motoneuron, motor neuron (cell)
Motoneuronerkrankung f motor neuron disease
motorisch motor[ic], producing motion
Mottenfraßerscheinung f moth-eaten appearance (phenomenon) (an Knochen)
Mouches fpl **volantes** muscae volitantes, floaters (kleine Glaskörpertrübungen des Auges)
Moulage f moulage, cast
mRNA, mRNS s. Messenger-Ribonukleinsäure
MS s. 1. Sklerose/multiple; 2. Mitralstenose
M-Stottern n mytacism, mutacism
MTA s. Assistentin/medizinisch-technische
Mücken fpl/**fliegende** muscae volitantes, floaters (kleine Glaskörpertrübungen des Auges)
Mückensehen n myiode[s]opsia, fixed muscae
mückentötend culicidal
Mückentötungsmittel n culicide [agent]
Mückenvertreibungsmittel n culifuge [agent]
Mucosa f mucosa, mucous membrane (s. a. unter Schleimhaut)
~ **labialis** labial mucosa
~ **pharyngis** pharyngeal mucosa
~ **urethrae** urethral mucosa
müde tired; weary; fatigue, exhausted (erschöpft) ● ~ **werden** to tire, to get tired
Müdigkeit f tiredness, minuthesis; exhaustion, fatigue
Mühlradgeräusch n mill-wheel murmur, water-wheel sound (bei Lungenembolie)
Mukoderm n mucoderm
Mukoenteritis f mucoenteritis

Mukoepidermoidkarzinom n mucoepidermoid cancer (carcinoma) *(mit Schleim- und Hornbildung)*
Mukoepidermoidtumor m mucoepidermoid tumour
Mukogingivalchirurgie f mucogingival surgery
Mukoglobulin n mucoglobulin
mukoid mucoid, mucinoid
Mukoid n mucoid
Mukoidgewebe n mucoid tissue
Mukoidkarzinom n mucoid carcinoma
Mukoidzyste f mucoid cyst
Mukoitinschwefelsäure f mucoitinsulphuric acid
Mukokolitis f mucocolitis, mucous colitis
Mukokolpos m mucocolpos, accumulation of mucus in the vaginal canal
mukokutan mucocutaneous
Mukolyse f mucolysis, dissolution (liquefaction, dispersion) of mucus
mukolytisch mucolytic, dissolving (liquefying, dispersing) mucus
mukomembranös mucomembranous
Mukometrie f mucometria, accumulation of mucus in the uterine cavity
Mukopeptidschicht f mucopeptide layer
Mukoperichondrium n mucoperichondrium
Mukoperiost n mucoperiosteum
Mukopolysac[c]harid n mucopolysaccharide
Mukopolysaccharidausscheidung f im Urin mucopolysacchariduria
Mukopolysaccharidose f mucopolysaccharidosis, MPS *(angeborene Stoffwechselerkrankung)*
~ **Typ I** Hurler's disease, Pfaundler-Hurler syndrome, mucopolysaccharidosis [type] I *(erbliche Phosphatidstoffwechselstörung)*
~ **Typ II** Hunter's syndrome, mucopolysaccharidosis [type] II, gargoylism
~ **Typ III** Sanfillipo's syndrome, mucopolysaccharidosis [type] III
~ **Typ IV** Morquio's syndrome, mucopolysaccharidosis [type] IV, keratosulphaturia, Morquio-Brainsford disease, hereditary (familial) osteochondrodystrophy
~ **Typ V** Scheie's syndrome, mucopolysaccharidosis [type] V
~ **Typ VI** Maroteaux-Lamy syndrome, mucopolysaccharidosis [type] VI
Mukoproteid n, **Mukoprotein** n mucoprotein
mukopurulent mucopurulent, puromucous, containing mucus and pus
Mukopus m mucopus
Mukopyozele f mucopyocele
Mukormykose f mucormycosis
~/**rhinozerebrale** rhinocerebral mucormycosis
Mukorrhoe f mucorrhoea
mukös mucous, slimy
Mukosa f s. Mucosa
Mukosa... s. a. Schleimhaut...
Mukosalpinx f mucosalpinx
mukosanguinös mucosanguineous, containing mucus and blood

Mukosaprolaps m mucosal prolapse
mukoserös mucoserous
Mukoserotympanum n mucoserotympanum
Mukositis f mucositis, inflammation of mucous membrane
mukostatisch mucostatic, arresting the secretion of mucus
Mukoviszidose f mucoviscidosis, [fibro]cystic disease of the pancreas, cystic fibrosis [of the pancreas], mucosis, congenital pancreatic steatorrhoea, chronic interstitial pancreatitis of infancy, Andersons's disease (syndrome)
Mukozele f mucocele
Mukus m s. Schleim
Mulatte m mulatto
Muliebria fpl muliebria, female genital organs
Mull m mull, gauze, carbasus
Mullbinde f mull (gauze) bandage
Müllerasthma n miller's asthma
Mulltupfer m mull (gauze) pad
Multangulum n multangular bone, multangulum
~ **minus** trapezoid [bone], trapezium [bone], minor multangulum
multidental 1. multidentate, having many teeth; 2. multidentate, having many tooth-like processes
Multifetation f multifoetation
multifid multifid, divided into many parts
multiflagellär multiflagellate
multifokal multifocal, plurifocal
multiform multiform, polymorphous
Multigravida f multigravida, plurigravida
Multigravidität f multigravidity
Multiinfektion f multi-infection, mixed infection
multiklonal multiclonal, polyclonal
multikostal multicostate
multikuspid[al] 1. multicuspid[al], having many cusps *(Herzklappe)*; 2. multicuspid[al] *(Mahlzahn)*
multilobulär multilobar, multilobate, polylobular
multilokulär multilocular, multiloculated, plurilocular
multinukleär multinuclear, multinucleate, polynuclear, polynucleate
multipar multiparous
Multipara f multipara, pluripara
multiseptiert multiseptate
Multisysteminfektion f multisystem infection
Multivitamin[präparat] n multivitamin [preparation]
mumifizieren to mummify
Mumifizierung f mummification
Mumps m mumps, [epidemic] parotitis, parotiditis, inflammation of the parotid gland
Mumpshauttest m mumps skin test
Mumpsimpfstoff m mumps virus vaccine
Mumpsmeningitis f mumps meningitis
Mumpsorchitis f mumps orchitis
Mumpspankreatitis f mumps pancreatitis
Mund m 1. mouth, os; stoma; 2. s. Mündung
• **durch den ~** by the mouth, orally, [per] oral
• **durch den ~ geben** to administer orally (by

Mund

the mouth) ● **vom ~ weggerichtet** aboral ● **zum ~ gerichtet** orad
Mund... s. a. Mundhöhlen...
Mundatmung f mouth breathing (respiration)
Mundatresie f atretostomia, oral atresia, imperforation of the mouth
mundbildend stomatoplastic
Mundblutung f stomatorrhagia, haemorrhage from the mouth
Mundboden m oral diaphragm, floor of the mouth
Mundbodenentzündung f paraglossitis
Mundbucht f, **Munddarm** m stomodaeum
Mundeingang m vestibule of the mouth
Mundenge f stenostomia
Mundentzündung f s. Stomatitis
Mundfäule f stomatonecrosis, noma of the mouth, stomacace, stomatocace, ulcerative stomatitis
Mundfehlbildung f atelostomia
mundfern aboral
Mundgeruch m/**aromatischer** aromatic breath
~/**fauler** foul (foetid) breath
~/**übler** halitosis, bad breath; stomatodysodia, ozostomia, cacostomia, bromopnoea
~/**urämischer** uraemic breath
Mundhöhle f oral cavity
~/**definitive** s. ~/**sekundäre**
~/**primäre** primary oral cavity
~/**sekundäre** secondary oral cavity
Mundhöhlen... s. a. Mund...
Mundhöhlenanatomie f oral anatomy
Mundhöhlendach n palate, palatum, roof of the mouth
Mundhöhlenerkrankung f stomatopathy, stomatosis, disease of the mouth
Mundhöhlenphysiologie f oral physiology
Mundhygiene f oral hygiene
Mundkeil m [mouth] gag, mouth wedge
Mund-Kieferhöhlen-Fistel f oroantral fistula
mundlos astom[at]ous, astomic
mundnah adoral
Mundoperation f/**plastische** stomatoplasty
Mundplatte f oral plate (Embryologie)
Mundrachen m oropharynx, mesopharynx
Mundrachenbakterienflora f oropharyngeal bacterial flora
Mundrachenraum m s. Mundrachen
Mundregion f oral region
Mundrekonstruktion f stomatoplasty
Mundringmuskel m orbicularis oris [muscle]
Mundschleimhaut f oral mucosa, mucous membrane of the oral cavity
Mundschleimhautaphthe f canker sore
Mundschleimhautentzündung f stomatitis
Mundschleimhautgeschwür n canker sore
Mundschmerz m stomalgia, stomatodynia, pain in the mouth
Mundsoor m oral moniliasis, soor, thrush
Mundspalte f 1. s. Stomatoschisis; 2. oral fissure, rima oris
Mundspaltenverbreiterung f macrostomia (Hemmungsmißbildung)

Mundspatel m spatula, tongue depressor
Mundspatelhalter m tongue blade holder
Mundsperre f trismus, lock jack
Mundsperrer m [mouth] gag, mouth wedge
Mundspiegel m dental (mouth) mirror, odontoscope, stomatoscope
Mundspiegelung f odontoscopy, stomatoscopy
Mundspirochäte f oral treponema
Mundspritze f dental (mouth) syringe
Mundspülglas n tumbler of rinsing water
Mundspülmittel n mouthwash
Mundspülung f mouth rinsing (bath), rinsing of the mouth
Mundtrockenheit f hypoptyalism, dryness of the mouth, xerostomia; dry mouth
Mundtubus m oral airway
Mundtuch n mask (z. B. des Operateurs)
Mündung f orifice, orificium, opening, ostium, mouth; pore, porus
Mundunterentwicklung f atelostomia
Mundvereng[er]ung f stenostomia, narrowing of the mouth
Mundvorhof m oral vestibule, vestibule of the mouth
mundwärts adoral; orad
Mundwasser n mouthwash, gargle, collutorium
Mundwinkel m labial angle (commissura), angle (corner) of the mouth, angle of the lips
Mundwinkelentzündung f angular stomatitis (cheilosis)
Mundwinkelheber m levator anguli oris [muscle]
Mundwinkelrhagaden fpl perleche; angular cheilosis
Mundwinkelsenker m depressor anguli oris [muscle]
Mundwinkelzucken n/**Chvosteksches** Chvostek's sign
Mund-zu-Mund-Beatmung f mouth-to-mouth breathing (insufflation, resuscitation), transanimation
Mund-zu-Nase-Beatmung f mouth-to-nose breathing (ventilation)
munter lively, active, gay, merry, quick (lebhaft); vigorous; awake (wach)
münzenförmig nummular, nummiform, coin-shaped (z. B. Hautexanthem)
mural mural (z. B. Thrombus)
Muramidase f muramidase (Enzym)
Muraminsäure f muramic acid
Murray-Valley-Gehirnentzündung f Murray Valley encephalitis, Australian X disease (Virusinfektion)
Muschel f nasal concha, turbinate [bone]
Muschelentzündung f conchitis
Muschelknorpel m conchal cartilage
Muschelleiste f conchal crest
Muschelvergiftung f mytilotoxism
Muscularis f **mucosae** muscularis mucosae
Musculi mpl:
~ **intercostales** intercostal muscles
~ **intercostales externi** external intercostal muscles

Musculus

- ~ **intercostales interni** internal intercostal muscles
- ~ **intercostales intimi** innermost intercostal muscles
- ~ **interossei** interossei muscles
- ~ **interossei dorsales manus** dorsal interossei muscles of the hand
- ~ **interossei dorsales pedis** dorsal interossei muscles of the foot
- ~ **interossei palmares** palmar interossei muscles
- ~ **interossei plantares** plantar interossei muscles
- ~ **interspinales cervicis** interspinales muscles of the neck
- ~ **interspinales lumborum** interspinales muscles of the lumbar region
- ~ **interspinales thoracis** interspinales muscles of the thoracic region
- ~ **intertransversarii** intertransverse muscles, intertransversales *(Muskeln der Halswirbelquerfortsätze)*
- ~ **intertransversarii laterales lumborum** lateral lumbar intertransverse muscles
- ~ **intertransversarii mediales lumborum** medial lumbar intertransverse muscles
- ~ **intertransversarii posteriores cervicis** posterior cervical intertransverse muscles
- ~ **intertransversarii thoracis** thoracic intertransverse muscles
- ~ **levatores costarum** levatores costarum [muscles]
- ~ **levatores costarum breves** short levatores costarum muscles
- ~ **levatores costarum longi** long levatores costarum muscles
- ~ **lumbricales** lumbrical muscles, lumbricals
- ~ **lumbricales manus** lumbrical muscles of the hand
- ~ **lumbricales pedis** lumbrical muscles of the foot
- ~ **pectinati** pectinate muscles
- ~ **perinei** muscles of the perineum
- ~ **rotatores breves** rotatores breves muscles
- ~ **rotatores cervicis** rotatores cervicis muscles
- ~ **rotatores longi** rotatores longi muscles
- ~ **rotatores lumborum** rotatores lumborum muscles
- ~ **rotatores spinae** rotatores spinae [muscles]
- ~ **rotatores thoracis** rotatores thoracis [muscle]
- ~ **subcostales** subcostal muscles, subcostals
- ~ **transversocostales breves et longi** levatores costarum muscles

Musculus *m* muscle, musculus *(s.a. unter Musculi und Muskel)*

- ~ **abdominis** abdominal muscle
- ~ **abductor** abductor [muscle]
- ~ **abductor digiti minimi manus** abductor digiti minimi manus [muscle]
- ~ **abductor digiti minimi pedis** abductor digiti minimi pedis [muscle]
- ~ **abductor hallucis** abductor hallucis [muscle]
- ~ **abductor hallucis longus** abductor hallucis longus [muscle]
- ~ **abductor indicis** abductor indicis [muscle]
- ~ **abductor pollicis brevis** abductor pollicis brevis [muscle]
- ~ **abductor pollicis longus** abductor pollicis longus [muscle]
- ~ **accessorius** accessory muscle
- ~ **adductor** adductor [muscle]
- ~ **adductor brevis** adductor brevis [muscle]
- ~ **adductor digiti secundi** adductor digiti secundi [muscle]
- ~ **adductor hallucis** adductor hallucis [muscle]
- ~ **adductor longus** adductor longus [muscle]
- ~ **adductor magnus** adductor magnus [muscle]
- ~ **adductor minimus** adductor minimus [muscle]
- ~ **adductor pollicis** adductor pollicis [muscle]
- ~ **anconeus** anconeus [muscle]
- ~ **antitragicus** antitragicus [muscle]
- ~ **arrector pilorum** arrector pilorum [muscle], pilomotor muscle
- ~ **articularis** articular muscle
- ~ **articularis genus** articularis genus [muscle], subcrureus [muscle]
- ~ **aryepiglotticus** aryepiglotticus [muscle]
- ~ **arytenoideus obliquus** oblique arytenoid [muscle]
- ~ **arytenoideus transversus** transverse arytenoid [muscle]
- ~ **auricularis** auricularis [muscle], auricular muscle
- ~ **auricularis anterior** anterior auricular muscle, attrahens aurem [muscle]
- ~ **auricularis posterior** posterior auricular muscle
- ~ **auricularis superior** superior auricularis muscle, attolens aurem [muscle]
- ~ **auriculofrontalis** auriculofrontalis [muscle]
- ~ **biceps** biceps [muscle]
- ~ **biceps brachii** biceps brachii [muscle]
- ~ **biceps femoris** biceps femoris [muscle]
- ~ **bipennatus** bipennate muscle
- ~ **biventer** biventer [muscle]
- ~ **brachialis** brachialis [muscle]
- ~ **brachioradialis** brachioradialis [muscle]
- ~ **bronchooesophageus** broncho-oesophageal muscle
- ~ **buccinator** buccinator [muscle]
- ~ **bulbi** bulbar muscle
- ~ **bulbocavernosus** *s.* ~ bulbospongiosus
- ~ **bulbospongiosus** bulbospongiosus [muscle], bulbocavernosus, detrusor urinae, ejaculator urinae [muscle], accelerator urinae [muscle]; vaginal sphincter
- ~ **caninus** caninus [muscle]
- ~ **capitis** head muscle
- ~ **carpi ulnaris digiti minimi** extensor carpi ulnaris digiti minimi [muscle]
- ~ **cephalopharyngicus** superior constrictor pharyngis [muscle]
- ~ **chondroglossus** chondroglossus [muscle]
- ~ **ciliaris** ciliary muscle
- ~ **coccygeus** coccygeus [muscle], ischiococcygeus [muscle]
- ~ **colli** collar muscle

Musculus

- **compressor** compressor [muscle]
- **constrictor pharyngis** constrictor muscle of the pharynx
- **constrictor pharyngis inferior** inferior pharyngeal constrictor [muscle], inferior constrictor pharyngis (muscle of the pharynx), infraconstrictor, laryngopharyngeus [muscle]
- **constrictor pharyngis medius** middle pharyngeal constrictor [muscle], medial constrictor pharyngis (muscle of the pharynx), hyopharyngicus muscle
- **constrictor pharyngis superior** superior pharyngeal constrictor [muscle], superior constrictor pharyngis (muscle of the pharynx)
- **coracobrachialis** coracobrachialis [muscle]
- **coracobrachialis brevis (superior)** coracobrachialis brevis [muscle]
- **corrugator glabellae (supercilii)** corrugator supercilii [muscle]
- **cremaster** cremaster [muscle]
- **cricoarytenoideus lateralis** lateral cricoarytenoid muscle
- **cricoarytenoideus posterior** posterior cricoarytenoid muscle
- **cricothyreoideus** cricothyroid muscle
- **cutaneus** cutaneous muscle
- **deltoideus** deltoid muscle
- **depressor** depressor [muscle]
- **depressor alae nasi** alar part of the nasalis muscle
- **depressor anguli oris** depressor anguli oris [muscle], triangularis
- **depressor labii inferioris** depressor labii inferioris [muscle], quadratus labii inferioris [muscle]
- **depressor septi nasi** depressor septi nasi [muscle]
- **depressor supercilii** depressor supercilii [muscle]
- **detrusor** detrusor [muscle]
- **digastricus** digastric muscle
- **dilatator pupillae** dilator pupillae [muscle]
- **dorsi** dorsal muscle
- **epicranius** epicranius [muscle]
- **erector** erector [muscle]
- **erector penis** ischiocavernosus [muscle]
- **erector spinae** erector spinae [muscle], sacrospinalis [muscle]
- **extensor** extensor [muscle]
- **extensor carpi radialis accessorius** extensor carpi radialis accessorius [muscle]
- **extensor carpi radialis brevis** extensor carpi radialis brevis [muscle]
- **extensor carpi radialis longus** extensor carpi radialis longus [muscle]
- **extensor carpi ulnaris** extensor carpi ulnaris [muscle]
- **extensor digiti medii** extensor digiti medii [muscle]
- **extensor digiti minimi** extensor digiti minimi [muscle], extensor digiti quinti proprius [muscle]
- **extensor digitorum** extensor digitorum [muscle]
- **extensor digitorum brevis** extensor digitorum brevis [muscle]
- **extensor digitorum communis** extensor digitorum communis [muscle], extensor communis digitorum [muscle], extensor [muscle] of the fingers
- **extensor digitorum longus** extensor digitorum longus [muscle]
- **extensor hallucis brevis** extensor hallucis brevis [muscle]
- **extensor hallucis longus** extensor hallucis longus [muscle]
- **extensor indicis** extensor indicis [muscle], extensor indicis proprius [muscle]
- **extensor pollicis brevis** extensor pollicis brevis [muscle]
- **extensor pollicis longus** extensor pollicis longus [muscle]
- **flexor** flexor [muscle]
- **flexor carpi radialis** flexor carpi radialis [muscle]
- **flexor carpi radialis brevis** flexor carpi radialis brevis [muscle], radiocarpeus [muscle]
- **flexor carpi ulnaris** flexor carpi ulnaris [muscle]
- **flexor carpi ulnaris brevis** flexor carpi ulnaris brevis [muscle], ulnocarpeus [muscle]
- **flexor digiti minimi brevis manus** flexor digiti minimi (quinti) brevis [muscle] of the hand
- **flexor digiti minimi brevis pedis** flexor digiti minimi (quinti) brevis [muscle] of the foot
- **flexor digitorum accessorius** flexor digitorum accessorius [muscle]
- **flexor digitorum brevis** flexor digitorum brevis [muscle]
- **flexor digitorum longus** flexor digitorum longus [muscle]
- **flexor digitorum profundus** flexor digitorum profundus [muscle]
- **flexor digitorum superficialis** flexor digitorum superficialis [muscle]
- **flexor hallucis brevis** flexor hallucis brevis [muscle]
- **flexor hallucis longus** flexor hallucis longus [muscle]
- **flexor pollicis brevis** flexor pollicis brevis [muscle]
- **flexor pollicis longus** flexor pollicis longus [muscle]
- **flexor profundus digitorum** flexor digitorum profundus [muscle], perforans manus [muscle]
- **frontalis** frontalis muscle, frontal belly
- **gastrocnemius** gastrocnemius [muscle]
- **gemellus inferior** inferior gemellus [muscle]
- **gemellus superior** superior gemellus [muscle]
- **genioglossus** genio[hyo]glossus, genioglossus muscle
- **geniohyoideus** geniohyoid [muscle]
- **glossopalatinus** palatoglossus [muscle], palatoglossal muscle
- **glutaeus** glutaeus [muscle]

Musculus

- ~ **glutaeus maximus** glutaeus maximus [muscle]
- ~ **glutaeus medius** glutaeus medius [muscle]
- ~ **glutaeus minimus** glutaeus minimus [muscle]
- ~ **gracilis** gracilis [muscle]
- ~ **helicis major** helicis major [muscle]
- ~ **helicis minor** helicis minor [muscle]
- ~ **hyoglossus** hyoglossus [muscle]
- ~ **iliacus** iliacus [muscle]
- ~ **iliacus minor** iliocapsularis [muscle]
- ~ **iliococcygeus** iliococcygeus [muscle], iliococcygeal muscle
- ~ **iliocostalis** iliocostalis [muscle], iliocostalis dorsi [muscle]
- ~ **iliocostalis cervicis** iliocostalis cervicis [muscle]
- ~ **iliocostalis lumborum** iliocostalis lumborum [muscle], sacrolumbalis [muscle]
- ~ **iliocostalis thoracis** iliocostalis thoracis [muscle]
- ~ **iliopsoas** iliopsoas [muscle]
- ~ **incisurae helicis** incisurae helicis [muscle]
- ~ **infraspinatus** infraspinatus [muscle], postscapularis [muscle]
- ~ **ischiobulbosus** ischiobulbosus [muscle]
- ~ **ischiocavernosus** ischiocavernosus [muscle]; erector clitoridis [muscle] *(der Frau)*; erector penis [muscle] *(des Mannes)*
- ~ **latissimus dorsi** latissimus dorsi [muscle]
- ~ **levator** levator [muscle]
- ~ **levator anguli oris** levator anguli oris [muscle]
- ~ **levator ani** levator ani [muscle]
- ~ **levator claviculae** levator claviculae [muscle], omocervicalis [muscle]
- ~ **levator epiglottidis** levator epiglottidis [muscle]
- ~ **levator glandulae thyroideae** levator glandulae thyroideae [muscle]
- ~ **levator labii superioris** levator labii superioris [muscle]
- ~ **levator labii superioris alaeque nasi** levator labii superioris alaeque nasi [muscle]
- ~ **levator palpebrae superioris** levator palpebrae superioris [muscle]
- ~ **levator prostatae** levator prostatae [muscle]
- ~ **levator scapulae** levator scapulae [muscle], levator anguli scapulae [muscle]
- ~ **levator veli palatini** levator veli palatini [muscle], levator palati [muscle], staphylinus internus [muscle]
- ~ **linguae** lingualis [muscle]
- ~ **longissimus capitis** longissimus capitis [muscle], trachelomastoid [muscle]
- ~ **longissimus cervicis** longissimus cervicis [muscle]
- ~ **longissimus dorsi** longissimus dorsi [muscle]
- ~ **longissimus thoracis** longissimus thoracis [muscle]
- ~ **longitudinalis inferior** longitudinalis inferior [muscle]
- ~ **longitudinalis inferior linguae** inferior longitudinalis muscle of the tongue
- ~ **longitudinalis superior** longitudinalis superior [muscle]
- ~ **longitudinalis superior linguae** superior longitudinal muscle of the tongue
- ~ **longus** longus [muscle]
- ~ **longus capitis** longus capitis [muscle]
- ~ **longus colli** longus colli muscle, longus cervicis [muscle]
- ~ **masseter** masseter [muscle]
- ~ **mentalis** mentalis [muscle], levator menti [muscle]
- ~ **multifidus** multifidus [muscle], multifidus spinae [muscle]
- ~ **mylohyoideus** mylohyoid muscle
- ~ **nasalis** nasalis [muscle]
- ~ **obliquus** oblique muscle
- ~ **obliquus auriculae** oblique auricular muscle
- ~ **obliquus bulbi inferior** inferior oblique muscle [of the eye]
- ~ **obliquus bulbi superior** superior oblique muscle of the eye, trochlearis [muscle]
- ~ **obliquus capitis inferior** inferior oblique muscle of the head
- ~ **obliquus capitis superior** superior oblique muscle of the head
- ~ **obliquus externus abdominis** external oblique muscle of the abdomen
- ~ **obliquus internus abdominis** internal oblique muscle of the abdomen
- ~ **obturatorius** obturator [muscle]
- ~ **obturatorius externus** obturator externus [muscle]
- ~ **obturatorius internus** obturator internus [muscle]
- ~ **occipitalis** posterior belly of the epicranius muscle
- ~ **occipitofrontalis** occipitofrontalis [muscle]
- ~ **oculi** ocular muscle
- ~ **omohyoideus** omohyoid [muscle]
- ~ **opponens digiti minimi manus** opponens digiti minimi manus [muscle], opponens digiti quinti [muscle] of the hand
- ~ **opponens digiti minimi pedis** opponens digiti minimi pedis [muscle], opponens digiti quinti [muscle] of the foot
- ~ **opponens hallucis** flexor ossis metacarpi pollicis [muscle]
- ~ **opponens pollicis** opponens pollicis [muscle]
- ~ **orbicularis** orbicularis [muscle]
- ~ **orbicularis oculi** orbicularis oculi [muscle], orbicularis palpebrarum [muscle]
- ~ **orbicularis oris** orbicularis oris [muscle]
- ~ **orbitalis** orbitalis [muscle], orbital muscle
- ~ **palatoglossus** palatoglossus [muscle], palatoglossal muscle, glossopalatinus [muscle]
- ~ **palatopharyngeus** palatopharyngeus [muscle], staphyl[in]opharyngeus [muscle]
- ~ **palmaris brevis** palmaris brevis [muscle]
- ~ **palmaris longus** palmaris longus [muscle]
- ~ **papillaris** papillary muscle
- ~ **papillaris anterior** anterior papillary muscle

Musculus

- **papillaris anterior ventriculi dextri** anterior papillary muscle of the right ventricle
- **papillaris anterior ventriculi sinistri** anterior papillary muscle of the left ventricle
- **papillaris posterior** posterior papillary muscle
- **papillaris posterior ventriculi dextri** posterior papillary muscle of the right ventricle
- **papillaris posterior ventriculi sinistri** posterior papillary muscle of the left ventricle
- **papillaris septalis** septal papillary muscle
- **pectineus** pectineus [muscle]
- **pectoralis** pectoralis [muscle]
- **pectoralis major** pectoralis major [muscle]
- **pectoralis minor** pectoralis minor [muscle]
- **pennatus** pennate muscle
- **peroneus accessorius** peroneus accessorius [muscle], accessory peroneal muscle
- **peroneus accessorius digiti minimi** peroneus accessorius digiti minimi [muscle]
- **peroneus accessorius quartus** peroneus accessorius quartus [muscle], peroneocalcaneus externus [muscle]
- **peroneus accessorius tertius** peroneus accessorius tertius [muscle]
- **peroneus brevis** peroneus brevis [muscle]
- **peroneus longus** peroneus longus [muscle]
- **peroneus tertius** peroneus tertius [muscle]
- **piriformis** piriformis [muscle], piriform muscle
- **plantaris** plantaris [muscle]
- **popliteus** popliteus [muscle]
- **procerus** procerus [muscle]
- **pronator** pronator [muscle]
- **pronator quadratus** pronator quadratus [muscle]
- **pronator teres** pronator radii teres [muscle]
- **psoas** psoas [muscle]
- **psoas major** psoas major muscle, psoas magnus [muscle]
- **psoas minor** psoas minor muscle, psoas parvus [muscle]
- **pterygoideus lateralis** lateral (external) pterygoid muscle
- **pterygoideus medialis** medial (internal) pterygoid muscle
- **pubococcygeus** pubococcygeus [muscle]
- **puboprostaticus** puboprostatic muscle
- **puborectalis** puborectalis [muscle]
- **pubovesicalis** pubovesicalis [muscle]
- **pyramidalis** pyramidalis [muscle]
- **pyramidalis auriculae** pyramidal muscle of the ear
- **quadratus femoris** quadratus femoris [muscle]
- **quadratus labii mandibularis** quadratus labii inferioris [muscle]
- **quadratus lumborum** quadratus lumborum [muscle]
- **quadratus plantae** quadratus plantae muscle, flexor digitorum accessorius [muscle]
- **quadriceps femoris** quadriceps femoris [muscle], vastus muscle
- **quadriceps surae** quadriceps surae [muscle]
- **rectococcygeus** rectococcygeus [muscle]
- **rectourethralis** rectourethralis [muscle]
- **rectouterinus** rectouterine muscle
- **rectovesicalis** rectovesicalis [muscle]
- **rectus** rectus [muscle]
- **rectus abdominis** rectus abdominis [muscle]
- **rectus bulbi inferior** rectus inferior bulbi muscle, inferior rectus [muscle]
- **rectus bulbi lateralis** external rectus [muscle], rectus lateralis bulbi [muscle]
- **rectus bulbi medialis** internal rectus [muscle], rectus medialis bulbi [muscle], internus [muscle]
- **rectus bulbi superior** superior rectus [muscle], rectus superior bulbi muscle, intorter
- **rectus capitis anterior** rectus capitis anterior [muscle]
- **rectus capitis lateralis** rectus capitis lateralis [muscle]
- **rectus capitis posterior major** rectus capitis posterior major [muscle]
- **rectus capitis posterior minor** rectus capitis posterior minor [muscle]
- **rectus femoris** rectus femoris [muscle]
- **rhomboideus major** rhomboideus major [muscle]
- **rhomboideus minor** rhomboideus minor [muscle]
- **risorius** risorius [muscle]
- **rotator** rotator [muscle]
- **sacrococcygeus** sacrococcygeus [muscle]
- **scarococcygeus anterior** sacrococcygeus anterior [muscle], [sacro]coccygeus ventralis [muscle], curvator coccygeus [muscle]
- **sacrococcygeus dorsalis (posterior)** sacrococcygeus posterior [muscle], [sacro]coccygeus dorsalis [muscle], extensor coccygeus [muscle]
- **sacrospinalis** sacrospinalis [muscle]
- **salpingopharyngeus** salpingopharyngeus [muscle]
- **sartorius** sartorius [muscle]
- **scalenus anterior** scalenus anterior [muscle], anterior scalene muscle
- **scalenus medius** scalenus medius [muscle], middle scalene muscle, mediscalenus [muscle]
- **scalenus minimus** scalenus minimus [muscle]
- **scalenus posterior** scalenus posterior [muscle], posterior scalene muscle
- **semimembranosus** semimembranosus [muscle]
- **semispinalis** semispinalis [muscle]
- **semispinalis capitis** semispinalis capitis [muscle], complexus [muscle]
- **semispinalis cervicis** semispinalis cervicis [muscle]
- **semispinalis thoracis** semispinalis thoracis [muscle]
- **semitendinosus** semitendinosus [muscle]
- **serratus** serratus [muscle]
- **serratus anterior** serratus anterior muscle, serratus magnus [muscle]
- **serratus posterior inferior** serratus posterior inferior muscle

- serratus posterior superior serratus posterior superior muscle
- soleus soleus [muscle]
- sphincter sphincter [muscle]
- sphincter ampullae hepatopancreaticae sphincter of the hepatopancreatic ampulla, sphincter of Oddi
- sphincter ani anal sphincter
- sphincter ani externus external anal sphincter [muscle], external sphincter of the anus
- sphincter ani internus internal anal sphincter [muscle], internal sphincter of the anus
- sphincter ductus choledochi sphincter of the common bile duct, sphincter of Boyden
- sphincter Oddi s. ~ sphincter ampullae hepatopancreaticae
- sphincter pupillae sphincter pupillae [muscle]
- sphincter pylori pyloric sphincter, sphincter of the pylorus
- sphincter urethrae sphincter urethrae [muscle], urethral sphincter, external urethral (urinary) sphincter
- sphincter urethrae diaphragmaticae sphincter urethrae [membranaceae]
- sphincter vesicae sphincter vesicae [muscle], internal vesical sphincter
- spinalis spinalis [muscle]
- spinalis capitis spinalis capitis [muscle]
- spinalis cervicis spinalis cervicis [muscle]
- spinalis thoracis spinalis thoracis [muscle]
- splenius capitis splenius capitis [muscle]
- splenius cervicis splenius cervicis [muscle]
- stapedius stapedius [muscle]
- sternalis sternalis [muscle]
- sternoclavicularis sternoclavicularis [muscle]
- sternocleidomastoideus sternocleidomastoid [muscle]
- sternocostalis sternocostalis [muscle]
- sternohyoideus sternohyoid [muscle]
- sternothyreoideus sternothyroid [muscle]
- styloglossus styloglossus [muscle]
- stylohyoideus stylohyoid [muscle]
- stylopharyngeus stylopharyngeus [muscle]
- subanconeus subanconeus [muscle]
- subclavius subclavius [muscle]
- subscapularis subscapularis [muscle]
- supinator supinator [muscle]
- suprahyoideus suprahyoid [muscle]
- supraspinatus supraspinatus [muscle]
- suspensorium duodeni suspensory muscle of the duodenum
- tarsalis inferior tarsalis inferior [muscle], inferior tarsal muscle, tarsal muscle of the lower eyelid
- tarsalis superior tarsalis superior [muscle], superior tarsal muscle, tarsal muscle of the upper eyelid
- temporalis temporalis [muscle]
- temporoparietalis temporoparietalis [muscle]
- tensor tensor [muscle]
- tensor chorioideae tensor muscle of the choroid
- tensor fasciae latae tensor fasciae latae [muscle]
- tensor tympani tensor tympani [muscle], tensor muscle of the drum, salpingomalleus [muscle]
- tensor veli palatini tensor veli palatini [muscle], staphylinus externus [muscle], sphenosalpingostaphylinus [muscle], palatosalpingeus [muscle]
- teres major teres major [muscle]
- teres minor teres minor [muscle]
- thyreoarytenoideus thyroarytenoid muscle
- thyreoepiglotticus thyroepiglottic muscle
- thyreohyoideus thyrohyoid muscle
- tibialis anterior tibialis anterior [muscle]
- tibialis posterior tibialis posterior [muscle]
- tragicus tragicus [muscle]
- transversospinalis transversospinalis [muscle]
- transversus abdominis transversus abdominis [muscle], transverse abdominal muscle
- transversus auriculae transversus auriculae [muscle], transverse auricular muscle
- transversus linguae transversus linguae [muscle], transverse lingual muscle
- transversus menti transversus menti [muscle], transverse mental muscle
- transversus nuchae transversus nuchae [muscle], transverse nuchal muscle, occipitalis minor [muscle]
- transversus perinei profundus deep transverse muscle of the perineum
- transversus perinei superficialis superficial transverse muscle of the perineum, superficial transverse perineal muscle
- transversus thoracis transversus thoracis [muscle], transverse thoracic muscle, transversalis sterni [muscle]
- trapezius trapezius [muscle]
- triangularis triangularis [muscle]
- triceps brachii triceps brachii [muscle]
- triceps surae triceps surae [muscle]
- uvulae staphylinus medius [muscle], muscle of the uvula
- vastus intermedius vastus intermedius [muscle], crureus [muscle], femoral muscle
- vastus lateralis vastus lateralis [muscle]
- vastus medialis vastus medialis [muscle]
- verticalis linguae vertical lingual muscle
- vocalis vocalis [muscle]
- zygomaticus zygomaticus [muscle], zygomatic muscle
- zygomaticus major zygomaticus major [muscle], major zygomatic muscle
- zygomaticus minor zygomaticus minor [muscle], minor zygomatic muscle

Musculus-rectus-bulbi-lateralis-Innervation f lateral rectus muscle innervation

Musculus-rectus-bulbi-lateralis-Lähmung f lateral rectus muscle palsy

Musikantenknochen m funny (crazy) bone, medial epicondyle of the humerus

Musikblindheit f music blindness, musical alexia

Musikepilepsie

Musikepilepsie f musicogenic epilepsy
Musikomaner m melomaniac
Musikomanie f musicomania, melomania
Musiktaubheit f 1. musical deafness, sensory amusia; 2. tone deafness
Musiktherapie f musicotherapy, musical therapy
Musiktrieb m s. Musikomanie
Muskarin n muscarine *(Fliegenpilzgift)*
muskarinartig muscarinic
Muskarinvergiftung f muscarinism, mushroom poisoning
Muskarinwirkung f muscarinic action
Muskat[nuß]leber f nutmeg liver *(bei chronischer Blutstauung)*
Muskel m muscle, musculus *(s. a. unter Musculus und Musculi)* ● **auf Muskeln gerichtet** myotropic ● **im ~ entstanden** myogen[et]ic, myogenous ● **vom ~ ausgehend** myogen[et]ic, myogenous
~/antagonistischer antagonistic muscle
~/birnenförmiger piriformis [muscle], piriform muscle
~/doppelbäuchiger double-bellied muscle
~/doppeltgefiederter bipennate muscle
~/dreiköpfiger triceps [muscle], tricipital muscle
~/einfach gefiederter unipennate muscle
~/gefiederter pennate muscle
~/gerader rectus [muscle]
~/gestreifter s. ~/quergestreifter
~/glatter smooth (unstriped) muscle, unstriated (non-striated) muscle *(s. a. ~/unwillkürlicher)*
~/Hornerscher Horner's muscle
~/inspiratorischer inspiratory muscle
~/intraokulärer intraocular muscle
~/langer longus [muscle]
~/mimischer mimetic muscle, muscle of facial expression
~/quergestreifter striped (striated) muscle *(s. a. ~/willkürlicher)*
~/roter red muscle
~/synergistischer synergistic muscle, synergist
~/unwillkürlicher involuntary muscle *(s. a. ~/glatter)*
~/viszeraler visceral (organic) muscle
~/von Brückescher Brücke's muscle, meridional portion of the ciliary muscle, tensor muscle of the choroid
~/willkürlicher voluntary muscle *(s. a. ~/quergestreifter)*
~/zweibäuchiger biventer [muscle]
~/zweiköpfiger biceps [muscle], bicipital muscle
Muskel... s. a. Myo...
Muskelabwehrspannung f muscular defence (guarding) *(z. B. bei Peritonitis)*
Muskeladenylsäure f muscular adenylic acid, adenosinemonophosphoric acid
Muskelagenesie f muscle agenesis
muskelähnlich myoid, muscular
Muskelaktion f muscle action, muscular activity
Muskelaktionskurve f myogram
Muskelaktionspotential n muscular action potential

Muskelaktionspotentialbild n electromyogram
Muskelaktionsstromaufzeichnung f electromyography, EMG
Muskelaktionsstromkurve f electromyogram
Muskelaktivität f/**übermäßige** hyperdynamia
~/verminderte hypodynamia
Muskelanästhesie f muscle (muscular) anaesthesia
Muskelansatz m muscular insertion, muscle attachment
Muskelanstrengung f muscle (muscular) exertion
Muskelantagonist m antagonistic muscle
Muskelapparat m musculature
Muskelarterie f muscular artery
muskelartig myoid, muscular
Muskelatonie f myatonia, amyotonia, lack of muscular tone
Muskelatrophie f muscular atrophy, myatrophy, amyotrophia
~/Duchennesche Duchenne's muscular dystrophy
~/kindliche spinale infantile spinal muscular atrophy, Werdnig-Hoffmann atrophy (paralysis), Hoffmann's atrophy, Hoffmann-Werdnig syndrome
~/neurale progressive progressive neuromuscular (neural muscular) atrophy, progressive neuropathic (peroneal) muscular atrophy, Charcot's (Charcot-Marie-Tooth) disease
~/progressive progressive muscular atrophy, wasting paralysis (palsy), chronic poliomyelitis anterior
~/progressive spinale progressive (chronic) spinal muscular atrophy, myelopathic muscular atrophy, Aran-Duchenne dystrophy (syndrome), Duchenne-Aran disease
~/pseudohypertrophe infantile Duchenne's pseudohypertrophic infantile muscular dystrophy, pseudohypertrophic muscular paralysis, Duchenne-Griesinger disease
Muskelauffaserung f myodiastasis, disintegration (separation) of the muscle
muskelauflösend sarcolytic
Muskelauflösung f myo[cyto]lysis, sarcolysis
Muskelausschneidung f excision of a muscle, myectomy
Muskelbälkchen npl **im Herzen** carneous trabeculae (columns)
Muskelbauch m [muscle] belly, venter [of the muscle] ● **mehrere Muskelbäuche besitzend** polygastric
Muskelbeschwerden pl muscular aching
Muskelbeteiligung f muscular involvement
muskelbewegend myokinetic
Muskelbewegung f myokinesis, muscular movement
~/gesteigerte hyperkinesia
~/verminderte hypokinesia
Muskelbewegungskurve f myokinesiogram
muskelbildend myoblastic, sarcopoietic, sarcogenic

Muskelbildung f/**mangelnde** amyoplasia
Muskelbildungszelle f s. Myoblast
Muskelbinde f muscular fascia, epimysium, fibrous sheath of a muscle
Muskelbindegewebe n endomysium
Muskelbindegewebsentzündung f fibromyositis
Muskelbiopsie f muscle biopsy
Muskelblutleere f myoischaemia
Muskelbündel n muscular fascicle (fasciculus), muscle bundle
Muskeldegeneration f muscle (muscular) degeneration, myodegeneration
~/**Zenkersche** Zenker's [muscular] degeneration, Zenker's hyaline necrosis, waxy degeneration of muscle
Muskeldehnung f muscular stretching (extension), myotasis, myentasis
Muskeldehnungsreflex m muscle (muscular) stretch reflex
Muskeldehnungswiderstand m muscle tone
Muskeldurchtrennung f in Faserrichtung muscle-splinting incision
~/**operative** s. Myotomie
Muskeldystrophie f muscular dystrophy, myodystrophia
~/**infantile spinale progressive** s. Muskelatrophie/kindliche spinale
~/**pseudohypertrophe infantile** s. Muskelatrophie/pseudohypertrophe infantile
~/**skapulo-humerale** Erb's scapulohumeral juvenile muscular dystrophy
Muskeleigenreflex m muscular proprioceptive reflex, deep tendon reflex
Muskeleigenreflexhyperaktivität f deep tendon reflex hyperactivity
Muskeleiweiß n myoprotein, myoalbumin
Muskelendplatte f muscle (neuromuscular) spindle, motor endplate
Muskelentspannung f muscle (muscular) relaxation
Muskelentwicklung f/**mangelhafte** amyoplasia, lack of muscle formation
~/**übermäßige** hypermyotrophy
Muskelentzündung f my[os]itis, sarcitis, inflammation of the muscle (s. a. unter Myositis)
~/**akute multiple** polymyositis, acute multiple myositis
~/**allgemeine** panmyositis
Muskelermüdbarkeit f muscular fatigability
Muskelermüdung f muscular fatigue
~/**schnelle** apocamnosis (z. B. bei Myasthenia gravis)
Muskelernährung f myotrophy, nutrition of the muscle
Muskelerotismus m muscle erotism
Muskelerregbarkeit f muscle irritability, muscular excitability
Muskelerregung f muscle irritation, muscular excitation
Muskelerschlaffung f muscle (muscular) relaxation
Muskelerweichung f softening of a muscle, myomalacia

Muskelexzision f excision of a muscle, myectomy
Muskelfaser f muscle fibre
muskelfaserauflösend myolytic, sarcolytic
Muskelfaserauflösung f myolysis, sarcolysis
muskelfaserbildend myoblastic
Muskelfaserbildungszelle f s. Myoblast
Muskelfaserentzündung f parenchymatous myositis
Muskelfaserhülle f s. Muskelhülle
Muskelfaserprotoplasma n sarcoplasm, muscle plasm, myoplasm
Muskelfaserschicht f der **Darmschleimhaut** muscularis [mucosae]
Muskelfasersegment n sarcomere
Muskelfaserunterbrechung f/**sehnige** inscriptio[n]
Muskelfaszie f [muscular] fascia; aponeurosis
Muskelfaszienentfernung f[/**operative**] aponeurectomy
Muskelfaszienentzündung f myofascitis
Muskelfasziennaht f aponeurorrhaphy
Muskelfibrille f s. Myofibrille
Muskelfibrillenflimmern n fibrillary tremor (contraction)
Muskelfibrillenzuckung f fibrillary twitching
Muskelfibrillieren n fibrillar twitching
Muskelfreßzelle f myophage
Muskelgefühl n muscle (muscular) sense
~/**fehlendes** amyoaesthesia
Muskelgeräusch n muscle sound, muscular murmur
Muskelgeschwulst f muscular tumour, myoma
Muskelgewebe n muscle (muscular) tissue
● **aus** ~ **bestehend** muscular, sarcous
Muskelgewebe... s. a. Muskel...
Muskelgewebeprobe f muscle (muscular) biopsy
Muskelgift n muscle poison
Muskelgleichgewicht n muscle (muscular) balance
~/**gestörtes** muscle (muscular) imbalance
Muskelhämoglobin n s. Myoglobin
Muskelharmonie f/**gestörte** incoordination
Muskelhärte f [myo]gelosis
Muskelhernie f hernia (protrusion) of a muscle, myocele
Muskelhülle f myolemm[a], sarcolemma, muscular sheath
~/**bindegewebige** perimysium
Muskelhüllenentzündung f perimysitis
Muskelhypertonie f hypermyotonia, muscle (muscular) hypertonia
Muskelhypertonus m muscular hypertonicity; tetanism
Muskelhypertrophie f muscle (muscular) hypertrophy, myohypertrophia, hypermyotrophy
Muskelhypotonie f muscle (muscular) hypotonia, hypomyotonia
Muskelinsuffizienz f muscle (muscular) insufficiency
Muskelischämie f muscle (muscular) ischaemia, myoischaemia

Muskelkater

Muskelkater *m* muscular aching, soreness of muscles
Muskelkaterkrankheit *f* pleurodynia, Bornholm disease
Muskelknoten *m* [myo]gelosis
Muskelkontraktilität *f* muscle (muscular) contractility
Muskelkontraktion *f* muscle (muscular) contraction ● **die ~ beeinflussend** inotropic
~/anaerobe anaerobic contraction
~/idiomuskuläre idiomuscular contraction
~/klonische clonic contraction
Muskelkontraktionsschreiber *m* myograph
Muskelkontraktur *f* muscle (muscular) contracture
~/ischämische (Volkmannsche) Volkmann's [ischaemic] contracture
Muskelkoordinationsstörung *f* disturbance of muscular coordination, dyssynergia
Muskelkraft *f* muscle strength, muscular power (force)
Muskelkraftbeeinflussung *f* inotropism
Muskelkraftmesser *m* [myo]dynamometer
Muskelkraftmessung *f* [myo]dynamometry
Muskelkraftphysiologie *f* physiology of muscular action, myodynamics
Muskelkrampf *m* muscular spasm, muscle cramp, myospasm
~ der Extremitäten acromyotonia
~/tonischer tonic muscle spasm, myotonus
~/tonisch-krampfhafter spasm[us], muscular spasm
muskelkrank myopathic
Muskelkrankheit *f s.* Myopathia
Muskelkunde *f* myology
Muskellähmung *f* muscular paralysis, myoparalysis, paralysis of a muscle
~ bei Arsenvergiftung arsenical paralysis
~/ischämische ischaemic (Volkmann's) paralysis
Muskellappen *m* muscular flap, flap of a muscle
Muskellücke *f* 1. muscular diastasis, diastasis of a muscle; 2. lacuna musculorum *(unter dem Leistenband)*
Muskelmasse *f* muscular mass, mass of muscles
Muskelmesser *n* myotome
Muskelminderaktivität *f* hypodynamia
Muskelnaht *f* suture of a muscle, myorrhaphy, myosuture
Muskelnekrose *f* muscular necrosis, necrosis of a muscle, myonecrosis
Muskel-Nerven-Platte *f* myoneural junction
Muskelneueinpflanzung *f* advancement of muscle *(Schieloperation)*
Muskelödem *n* muscular oedema, oedema of a muscle, myoedema
Muskeloperation *f*/**plastische** musculoplasty, plastic surgery on a muscle
Muskelparalyse *f*/**Volkmannsche** Volkmann's (ischaemic) paralysis
Muskelparese *f* myoparesis
Muskel-Periost-Lappen *m* musculoperiosteal flap
Muskelphosphorylase *f* muscle (muscular) phosphorylase
Muskelphosphorylasemangel *m* muscle phosphorylase deficiency
Muskelplasma *n* muscle plasm, myoplasm, sarcoplasm
Muskelplastik *f* musculoplasty, myoplasty
Muskelplatte *f* muscle plate; muscular segment, myotome
Muskelreaktion *f* muscle (muscular) reaction
Muskelreflex *m* muscle (muscular) reflex
Muskelregeneration *f* muscle (muscular) regeneration
Muskelreißen *n* muscular rheumatism
Muskelreiz *m* muscle (muscular) stimulus
Muskelreizbarkeit *f* muscle (muscular) irritability
Muskelrelaxans *n* muscle relaxant [agent]
Muskelrelaxation *f* muscle (muscular) relaxation
Muskelretraktor *m* muscle (muscular) retractor
Muskelrezeptor *m* myoreceptor
Muskelrheumatismus *m* muscular rheumatism
Muskelrigidität *f* muscle (muscular) rigidity
Muskelriß *m* rupture of a muscle, myorrhexis
Muskelscheide *f* sarcolemma, epimysium, muscular sheath
Muskelscheidenentzündung *f* myofascitis
Muskelschicht *f* 1. muscle layer, muscular coat; 2. muscularis *(z. B. in Hohlorganen)*
Muskelschienung *f* muscle splinting
Muskelschlaffheit *f* myatonia, amyotonia, muscular atonia
~/angeborene congenital myatonia
Muskelschmerz *m* muscular pain (aching), myalgia, myodynia, pain in a muscle ● **~ bewirkend** algiomuscular
Muskelschnitt *m* myotomy, cutting of a muscle
muskelschwach myasthenic, dystrophic, paratrophic
Muskelschwäche *f* muscular asthenia (debility), muscle weakness, myasthenia, amyosthenia, muscle insufficiency
~/allgemeine hyposthenia
Muskelschwund *m* muscle wasting *(s. a.* Muskelatrophie*)*
Muskelsegment *n* muscular segment, myomere, sarcomere, myotome
Muskelsehne *f* muscular tendon, tendon of a muscle
Muskelsehnenhülle *f* musculotendinous cuff
Muskelsehnenspindel *f* muscle tendon spindle
Muskelsensibilität *f* muscle sensibility, myaesthesia
Muskelsinn *m* proprioception, muscle sense, myaesthesia, kinaesthesia, kinaesthetic memory
Muskelsinnverlust *m* muscle anaesthesia
Muskel-Skelett-Schmerz *m* musculoskeletal pain
Muskelspannung *f* muscle tension, myotonia, muscular tenderness
~/erhöhte muscular hypertonicity (hypertonia, hypertonus)
~/verminderte muscular hypotonicity (hypotonia, hypotonus)

Muskelspindel *f* muscle (muscular) spindle
Muskelspontanruptur *f* spontaneous rupture of a muscle
Muskelstärke *f*/**allgemeine** hypersthenia
muskelstarr rigid, stiff; catatonic
Muskelstarre *f* muscular rigidity, muscle stiffness
~ **durch Kälteeinwirkung** paramyotonia
Muskelstroma *n* myostroma
Muskelsystem *n* muscular system
Muskeltätigkeit *f* muscle action, muscular activity
Muskeltod *m* muscular death
Muskelton *m* muscle (muscular) sound, phonomyoclonus
Muskeltonaufzeichnung *f* phonomyography
Muskeltonus *m* muscle tone, muscular tonus
● **mit normalem** ~ normotonic
~/**normaler** normotonia
~/**verringerter** myatonia, amyotonia
Muskeltonuserhöhung *f* muscular hypertonicity
Muskeltonusschwäche *f* hypomyotonia
Muskeltonusstörung *f* myodystonia, dysmyotonia
Muskeltonusverminderung *f* myatonia, amyotonia
Muskeltransplantat *n* muscle graft, muscular transplant
~/**freies** free muscle transplant
~/**gestieltes** pedicled muscle graft
~/**lappenförmiges** flapped muscle transplant
Muskeltransplantation *f* muscular transplantation, muscle grafting; myoplasty
Muskeltrichter *m* muscular funnel *(gebildet durch die vier geraden Augenmuskeln)*
Muskelüberaktivität *f* hyperdynamia
Muskelüberdehnung *f* muscle hyperextension
muskel- und nervenkrank neuromyopathic
Muskel- und Sehnenentzündung *f* myotenositis
Muskel- und Sehnenschnitt *m* myotenotomy
Muskelursprung *m* origin of a muscle
Muskelvene *f* muscular vein
Muskelverhärtung *f* [myo]gelosis; myosclerosis
Muskelverhärtungskopfschmerz *m* indurative headache
Muskelverknöcherung *f*[/**umschriebene**] ossifying myositis *(z. B. durch Kalkeinlagerungen als Unfallfolge)*
Muskelverkürzung *f* muscular shortening; muscle contraction
Muskelversprengung *f* displacement of a muscle, myectopy
Muskelvorlagerung *f* advancement of muscles
Muskelwirkung *f* muscle action
Muskelwogen *n* quivering of the muscles, myokymia; live-flesh
Muskelzellauflösung *f* myocytolysis
Muskelzelle *f* muscle cell, myocyte
~/**glatte** smooth muscle cell
Muskelzellengeschwulst *f* myocytoma
Muskelzellennekrose *f* myocyte necrosis
Muskelzerrung *f* muscle (muscular) strain

Muskelzitterkurve *f* tremogram
Muskelzittern *n* muscular tremor (trembling), amyostasia
~/**blitzartiges** myoclonia
~/**krampfartiges** vellication
~ **mehrerer Muskeln** synclonus
Muskelzucken *n* muscle (muscular) twitching, twitch[ing], vellication, fasciculation; live-flesh
~/**blitzartiges** myoclonia
Muskelzuckung *f* [muscle] twitch, palmus
~/**nervöse** tic
Muskelzuckungen *fpl*/**rhythmische** myorhythmia
Muskelzuckungspotential *n* fasciculation potential
Muskelzug *m* muscle pull, muscular traction
muskulär muscular
Muskulatur *f* musculature, muscles, muscular system (apparatus); flesh
~/**glatte** smooth (unstriped, non-striated) musculature, involuntary musculature
~/**mimische** mimetic musculature
~/**quergestreifte** striped (striated) musculature, voluntary musculature
muskulös muscular
~ **und elastisch** musculoelastic
~ **und fibrös** musculofibrous
muskuloskeletal musculoskeletal
Mussitation *f* mussitation
mutagen mutagenic
Mutagen *n* mutagen
mutant mutant *(z. B. ein Gen)*
Mutante *f* mutant, variant *(durch Mutation vom Ausgangstyp abweichendes Individuum)* ● **Mutanten bildend** mutagenic
Mutantenbildung *f* mutagenesis
Mutantenbildungsfähigkeit *f* mutagenicity
Mutantenträger *m* carrier
Mutase *f* mutase *(Enzym)*
Mutation *f* mutation *(sprunghafte erbliche Merkmalsänderung)* ● **durch ~ entstanden** mutant
~/**induzierte** induced mutation
~/**natürliche** natural mutation
~/**somatische** somatic mutation
~/**sprunghafte** saltation, saltatory mutation
Mutationsauslösung *f* mutagenesis, induction of mutation
Mutationsgleichgewicht *n* mutation equilibrium
Mutationshäufigkeit *f* mutation frequency
Mutationsrate *f* mutation rate
Mutationsstörung *f* mutation disorder (disturbance)
mutierend mutant, mutative
Mutilation *f* mutilation, autolesion
mutilieren to mutilate, to maim
Mutismus *m* mutism, dumbness, inability to speak, anepia *(bei intaktem Sprechapparat)*
Mutterband *n* ligament of the uterus (womb)
~/**breites** broad ligament of the uterus, ligamentum latum uteri, mesodesma
~/**rundes** round ligament of the uterus, ligamentum teres uteri

Mütterberatungsstelle

Mütterberatungsstelle f maternity (child-welfare) centre
Mutterkomplex m mother complex (fixation)
Mutterkorn[alkaloid]vergiftung f ergotism, ergot poisoning
Mutterkuchen m s. Placenta
mütterlich maternal
mütterlicherseits matrilineal
Muttermal n s. Naevus
~/braunes s. Naevus pigmentosus
muttermalähnlich naevoid, naeviform
Muttermilch f mother (breast) milk ● **durch ~ ernährt** breast-fed
Muttermilch... s. a. Milch...
Muttermilchentwöhnung f delactation
Muttermilchikterus m breast-milk jaundice
Muttermilchmangel m galactacrasia, oligo[ga]lactia, agalactia
Muttermilchpumpe f breast pump, lactisugium
Muttermord m matricide
Muttermörder m matricide
Muttermund m cervical os, mouth of the uterus (womb)
~/äußerer external cervical (uterine) os, external mouth of the womb, external os, ostium of the uterus
~/innerer internal cervical (uterine) os, internal mouth of the womb, internal os
Muttermund... s. a. Zervix... und Gebärmutterhals...
Muttermunderöffner m metreurynter, hystereurynter
Muttermunderöffnung f metreurysis
Muttermundfaßzange f volsella, volsellum [forceps], uterine volsellum forceps
Muttermundkrebs m cervical cancer (carcinoma)
Muttermundlippe f lip of the cervix of the uterus
~/hintere posterior lip of the cervix of the uterus
~/vordere anterior lip of the cervix of the uterus
Muttermundlippenausstülpung f false erosion of the cervix uteri
Mutterschaft f maternity, motherhood
Müttersterblichkeit f maternal mortality
Müttersterblichkeitsrate f maternal mortality rate
Mutterstern m monaster, mother star *(Chromosomenfigur in der Kernteilungsphase)*
Muttertrompete f s. Salpinx
Mutterzelle f mother (parent) cell
Mütze f/**phrygische** phrygian cap *(Gallenblasenröntgendiagnostik)*
muzigen mucigenous
muzilaginös mucilaginous
Muzilago m mucilage, mucilago
Muzin n mucin *(Glykoproteid)*
muzinartig mucinous, mucinoid
Muzinose f mucinosis
Muzintherapie f mucin therapy
Muzinzyste f mucinous cyst
Myalgie f myalgia, myodynia, muscular pain
~/epidemische epidemic myalgia, devil's grip

MyaR s. Reaktion/myasthenische
Myastasie f amyostasia
Myasthenia f **gravis [pseudoparalytica]** [Erb-]Goldflam's disease, myasthenia, bulbospinal paralysis *(Krankheit mit gesteigerter Ermüdbarkeit der quergestreiften Muskulatur)*
Myasthenie f s. 1. Myasthenia gravis pseudoparalytica; 2. Muskelschwäche
Myastheniekrise f myasthenic crisis
Myastheniesyndrom n myasthenic syndrome
myasthenisch myasthenic
Myästhesie f myaesthesia, muscle sensibility
Myatonia f myatonia, amyotonia, lack of muscular tone
~ congenita congenital myatonia, Oppenheim's disease
Myatrophie f s. Muskelatrophie
Mycetoma n **pedis** mycetoma, maduromycosis; Madura foot
Mycobacterium n:
~ bovis Mycobacterium bovis *(Erreger der Rindertuberkulose)*
~ Johne s. ~ paratuberculosis
~ leprae Mycobacterium leprae, Hansen's (lepra) bacillus
~ paratuberculosis Johne's bacillus
~ tuberculosis Mycobacterium tuberculosis, Koch's (tubercle) bacillus
Mycobacterium-paratuberculosis-Impfstoff m johnin
Mycoplasma n **pneumoniae** Mycoplasma pneumoniae, Eaton agent (virus) *(Erreger der primär atypischen Pneumonie)*
Mycoplasmapneumonie f mycoplasmal pneumonia
Mycosis f **fungoides** mycosis (granuloma) fungoides, fungoid dermatitis, inflammatory fungoid neoplasm, ulcerative scrofuloderma
Mydriasis f mydriasis, platycoria, dilatation of the pupil
~ alternans s. ~/springende
~/paralytische paralytic mydriasis
~/spastische spasmodic mydriasis
~/springende springing (alternating, bounding) mydriasis
Mydriatikum n mydriatic [agent], cycloplegic [agent]
mydriatisch mydriatic
Myektomie f myectomy, excision of a muscle
Myektopie f myectopy, displacement of a muscle
Myelalgie f myelalgia, pain in the spinal cord
Myelapoplexie f myelapoplexy, haemorrhage within the spinal cord
myelenzephal myelencephalic, myelencephalous
Myelenzephalitis f myelencephalitis, inflammation of the brain and the spinal cord
Myelenzephalon n myelencephalon, marrowbrain, hindbrain
Myelhämie f myelaemia, myeloid (splenomedullary, granulocytic) leukaemia
Myelin n myelin[e], white substance of Schwann

myelinauflösend myelinolytic
myelinbildend myelinogenetic, producing myelin
Myelinbildung f myel[in]ogenesis, myelinogeny
Myelindegeneration f myelin degeneration
Myelinfigur f myelin figure (form)
myelinfrei unmyelinated, amyelinic *(Nerv)*
myelinhaltig myelinated *(Nerv)*
Myelinisierung f myelin[iz]ation *(der Nervenfasern)*
Myelinolyse f myelinolysis, myelolysis, myelinoclasis, disintegration of myelin
myelinolytisch myelinolytic, myelinoclastic
Myelinom n myelinoma
Myelinopathie f myelinopathy, disease of myelin
Myelinscheide f myelin (medullary) sheath *(der Nerven)*
myelinscheidenlos amyelinic, non-myelinated, unmyelinated *(Nerv)*
Myelinzerfall m s. Myelinolyse
Myelitis f myelitis, medullitis, inflammation of the spinal cord, notomyelitis *(s. a. unter Rückenmarkentzündung)*
~ **disseminata** disseminated (diffuse) myelitis
~/**postvakzinale** postvaccinal myelitis
myelitisch myelitic
Myeloblast m myeloblast, granuloblast, free rounded cell *(Leukozytenvorstufe)*
~/**großer** macromyeloblast
~/**kleiner** micromyeloblast
Myeloblastenleukämie f myeloblastic leukaemia
Myeloblastenleukose f myeloblastic leucosis
Myeloblasthämie f myeloblastaemia
myeloblastisch myeloblastic
Myeloblastom n myeloblastoma *(bösartige Myeloblastengeschwulst)*
Myeloblastomatose f myeloblastomatosis
Myeloblastose f myeloblastosis
Myelodiastase f myelodiastasis
Myelodysplasie f myelodysplasia
Myeloenzephalitis f myeloencephalitis
Myelofibrose f myelofibrosis, fibrosis of the bone marrow
myelogen myelogenic, myelogenous, produced in the bone marrow
Myelogenese f 1. myelogenesis, development of the nervous system; 2. myelogenesis, deposition of myelin around the axis cylinder
Myelogramm n myelogram *(1. Röntgenbild des Rückenmarks; 2. Differentialausstrich von Knochenmarkzellen)*
Myelographie f myelography, roentgenography of the spinal cord
~/**lumbale** lumbar myelography
~/**zervikale** cervical myelography
myelographisch myelographic
Myeloidmyelom n myeloid myeloma
Myeloidose f myeloidosis
Myeloidsarkom n myeloid sarcoma
myeloisch myeloid
Myelolymphozyt m myelolymphocyte
Myelom n myeloma *(bösartige Geschwulst)*
~/**multiples** multiple myeloma, Kahler's disease

~/**nichtsezernierendes** non-secretory myeloma
Myelomalazie f myelomalacia, softening of the spinal cord
Myelomatose f myelomatosis, sarcomatous osteitis
Myelomeningitis f myelomeningitis, inflammation of the spinal cord and the meninges
Myelomeningozele f myelomeningocele, meningomyelocele *(angeborene Mißbildung mit Vorfall von Rückenmark und Rückenmarkhäuten)*
Myelomglobulin n myeloma globulin
Myelomonozyt m myelomonocyte
myelomonozytisch myelomonocytic
Myelomzelle f myeloma cell
Myelon n myelon, spinal cord (marrow)
Myeloneuritis f myeloneuritis
Myeloparalyse f s. Rückenmarklähmung
Myelopathie f 1. myelopathy, disease of the spinal cord; 2. myelopathy, disease of the myeloid tissue
myelopathisch myelopathic
myelopetal myelopetal, moving toward the spinal cord
Myelophthise f 1. myelophthisis, spinal cord atrophy *(bei Tabes dorsalis)*; 2. myelophthisis, loss of bone marrow
myelophthisisch myelophthisic
Myeloplast m myeloplast, leucocyte of the bone marrow
Myeloplegie f myeloplegia
Myelopoese f myelopoiesis, formation of bone marrow
Myeloradikulitis f myeloradiculitis, inflammation of the spinal cord and spinal nerve roots
Myeloradikulodysplasie f myeloradiculodysplasia
Myeloradikulopathie f myeloradiculopathy, disease of the spinal cord and spinal nerve roots
Myelorrhagie f myelorrhagia, spinal haemorrhage
Myelorrhaphie f myelorrhaphy, suture of a severed spinal cord
Myelosarkom n myelosarcoma
Myeloschisis f myeloschisis
Myelose f 1. myelosis, granulocytic leukaemia; 2. myelocytosis; 3. malignant plasmocytoma
~/**erythroleukämische** erythroleukaemia, erythraemic disease (myelosis), die Guglielmo's disease (syndrome)
Myelosklerose f 1. myelosclerosis, multiple sclerosis of the spinal cord; 2. myelosclerosis, sclerosis of the bone marrow
myelosklerotisch myelosclerotic
Myelospongium n myelospongium *(Embryologie)*
myelosuppressiv myelosuppressive
Myeloszintigramm n myeloscintigram
Myeloszintigraphie f myeloscintigraphy
Myelotherapie f myelotherapy
Myelotom n myelotome
Myelotomie f myelotomy
Myelotoxikose f myelotoxicosis

Myelotoxin

Myelotoxin n myelotoxin
myelotoxisch myelotoxic
Myelozele f myelocele
Myelozyste f myelocyst
Myelozystogramm n myelocystogram
Myelozystographie f myelocystography
myelozystographisch myelocystographic
Myelozystozele f myelocystocele *(Vorwölbung von Rückenmarkteilen mit Flüssigkeitsansammlung in den Rückenmarkhüllen)*
Myelozyt m myelocyte *(Reifungsstufe der weißen Blutzellen)*
Myelozytenleukose f myelocytic leucosis
Myelozythämie f myelocythaemia
myelozytisch myelocytic
Myelozytom n myelocytoma *(bösartige Geschwulst)*
Myelozytose f myelocystosis
Myentasis f s. Myotasis
myenterisch myenteric
Myenteron n myenteron
Myiasis f myiasis, myiosis
~ **linearis migrans** creeping disease
Myiodesop[s]ie f myiode[s]opsia, appearance of muscae volitantes; fixed muscae
Mykid n mycid *(Pilzexanthem)*
mykobakteriell mycobacterial
Mykobakterienerkrankung f mycobacteriosis
Mykobakterienprotein n mycobacterial protein
Mykobakteriose f mycobacteriosis
Mykogastritis f mycogastritis
Mykohämie f mycohaemia
Mykologe m mycologist
Mykologie f mycology
mykologisch mycologic[al]
Mykomyringitis f mycomyringitis
Mykophthalmie f mycophthalmia
Mykopräzipitin n mycoprecipitin
Mykose f mycosis, fungal (mycotic) disease; mycotic infection *(s. a. unter Pilzbefall)*
~ **der Extremitäten** acromycosis
~/**subkutane** subcutaneous mycosis
~/**tiefe** deep mycosis, histomycosis
Mykostase f mycostasis, fungistasis
mykostatisch mycostatic, fungistatic
mykotisch mycotic
Mykotisierung f mycotization, secondary mycosis
Mykotoxikose f mycotoxicosis, mycetism, mushroom poisoning
Mykotoxin n mycotoxin
mylohyoid mylohyoid[ean]
mylopharyngeal mylopharyngeal
myoarchitektonisch myoarchitectonic
Myo... s. a. Muskel...
Myoblast m myoblast, sarcoblast, sarcoplast, sarcogenic cell
Myoblastenmyom n myoblastic myoma
~ **der Unterlippe** Abrikosow's tumour *(granuläres Neurom)*
myoblastisch myoblastic, sarcopoietic, sarcogenic

Myoblastoma n myoblastoma
Myocardium n s. Myokard
Myoclonia f **epileptica** s. Myoklonusepilepsie
Myodiastase f s. Muskelauffaserung
Myodynamik f myodynamics
myodynamisch myodynamic
Myodynamometer n myodynamometer
Myodynamometrie f myodynamometry
Myodynie f s. Myalgie
Myodystonie f myodystonia, disorder of muscular tone
myoelastisch myoelastic
myoelektrisch myoelectric[al]
Myoepithel n myoepithelium
myoepithelial myoepithelial
Myoepitheliom n myoepithelioma *(Schweißdrüsengeschwulst)*
myofaszial myofascial
Myofibrille f myofibril, muscular fibril, muscle rod, sarcostyle *(die Kontraktion bewirkendes Muskelelement)*
Myofibroblast m myofibroblast
Myofibrom n myofibroma
Myofibrosarkom n myofibrosarcoma
Myofibrose f myofibrosis
Myofibrositis f myofibrositis, inflammation of the perimysium
Myofilament n myofilament *(die Kontraktion bewirkendes Muskelelement)*
Myogelose f [myo]gelosis
myogen myogen[et]ic, myogenous
Myogen n myogen *(Muskeleiweiß)*
Myoglobin n myo[haemo]globin, muscle (muscular) haemoglobin *(roter Muskelfarbstoff)*
Myoglobinausscheidung f **im Urin** myoglobinuria
Myogramm n myogram
Myograph m myograph
Myographie f myography *(Aufzeichnung der Muskelkontraktion)*
myographisch myographic
Myohämatin n myohaematin *(Enzym)*
Myohämoglobin n s. Myoglobin
Myohysterektomie f myohysterectomy
Myohysteropexie f myohysteropexy
myoid myoid, muscular
Myokard n myocardium, heart (cardiac) muscle
Myokard... s. a. Herzmuskel...
Myokardaktionspotential n myocardial action potential
Myokardamyloidose f myocardial amyloidosis
Myokardbrücke f myocardial bridge
Myokardelektrode f myocardial electrode
Myokardenergiestoffwechsel m myocardial energy metabolism
Myokardentzündung f s. Myokarditis
Myokardfibrose f myofibrosis
Myokardfunktion f myocardial function
myokardial myocardial
Myokardinfarkt m myocardial infarct[ion]
  ● **nach einem** ~ postmyocardial infarction
~/**inferiorer** inferior myocardial infarction

Myorrhaphie

Myokardinfarzierung f myocardial infarction
Myokardiogramm n myocardiogram
Myokardiograph m myocardiograph
Myokardiographie f myocardiography
Myokardiopathie f myocardiopathy, cardiomyopathy, myocardial disease
Myokardiorrhaphie f myocardiorrhaphy
Myokardischämie f myocardial ischaemia
Myokarditis f myocarditis, inflammation of the myocardium
~/**Fiedlersche** Fiedler's (idiopathic) myocarditis
~/**interstitielle** interstitial myocarditis
~/**rheumatische** rheumatic myocarditis
Myokardkontraktilität f myocardial contractility
Myokardleistungsfähigkeit f myocardial efficiency
Myokardmyozyt m s. Myokardretikulozyt
Myokardose f myocardosis (z. B. bei Kreislauf- und Ernährungsstörungen)
Myokardperfusion f myocardial perfusion
Myokardperfusionsszintigraphie f myocardial perfusion scintigraphy
Myokardprotektion f myocardial protection
Myokardpseudozyste f myocardial pseudocyst
Myokardreserve f myocardial reserve
Myokardretikulozyt m Anitschkow cell (myocyte), cardiac histiocyte, myocardial reticulocyte
Myokardrevaskularisation f myocardial revascularization
Myokardrevaskularisationsverfahren n/operatives myocardial revascularization surgical procedure
Myokardsauerstoffverbrauch m myocardial oxygen consumption
Myokardschaden m myocardial lesion (damage)
~/**alkoholinduzierter** alcoholic myocardiopathy
Myokardstoffwechsel m myocardial metabolism
Myokardszintigramm n myocardial scintigram
Myokardszintigraphie f myocardial scintigraphy
Myokardtonus m myocardial tone
Myokardtropismus m myocardial tropism
Myokard- und Perikardentzündung f myocarditis
Myokardwandspannung f myocardial wall tension
Myokardzelle f myocardial cell
Myokinase f myokinase (Enzym)
Myokinesiogramm n myokinesiogram
Myokinesiographie f myokinesiography (Darstellung des Muskelbewegungsablaufs)
myokinetisch myokinetic
Myoklonie f myoclonia
myoklonisch myoclonic
Myoklonus m myoclonus, clonic spasm of a muscle
Myoklonusepilepsie f myoclonus epilepsy, Unverricht's (association) disease; myoclonic [astatic] seizure
Myoklonusepilepsiedaueranfall m myoclonic status

Myokolpitis f myocolpitis
myokutan myocutaneous
Myokymie f s. Muskelwogen
Myolemm[a] n s. Muskelhülle
Myolipom n myolipoma, lipomyoma
Myologie f myology (Lehre von den Muskeln)
Myolyse f s. Muskelauflösung
Myom[a] n 1. myoma, muscular tumour; 2. [uterus] myoma
Myomalacia f cordis myomalacia of the heart
Myomalazie f myomalacia, softening of muscle tissue
myomartig, myomatös myomatous
Myomatose f myomatosis
Myomausschälung f/operative myomectomy (aus der Gebärmutter)
Myomentfernung f durch Bauchschnitt laparomyomectomy
Myomer n myomere
Myometrektomie f myometrectomy
myometrial myometrial
Myometritis f myometritis, inflammation of the uterine muscular tissue
Myometrium n myometrium
Myometriumdrüse f myometrial gland
Myometriumerschlaffung f myometrium relaxation
Myometriumkontraktilität f myometrium contractility
Myometriumkontraktion f myometrium contraction
Myometriumzelle f myometrium cell
Myomexstirpation f myomectomy
Myomheber m myoma screw (Instrument)
Myommesser n myomatome, myoma knife
Myomotomie f myomectomy
Myonecrosis f gangraenosa gangrenous myonecrosis
myoneural myoneural, neuromuscular, neuromyal, neuromyic
Myoneuralgie f myoneuralgia, muscle neuralgia
myop myopic, short-sighted, near-sighted
Myopathia f myopathy, muscle disease
~ **cordis** myocardosis (z. B. bei Kreislauf- und Ernährungsstörungen)
~ **rachitica** rachitic myopathy
myopathisch myopathic
Myoper m myope
Myoperikarditis f myopericarditis
Myophage m myophage
Myophagie f myophagia
Myopie f myopia, my., short-sightedness, nearsightedness, dysphotia, hypometria
Myopiesichel f myopic crescent
myopisch myopic
myoplastisch myoplastic
MyoR s. Reaktion/myotonische
Myorhythmie f myorhythmia
myorhythmisch myorhythmic
Myorrhaphie f myorrhaphy, myosuture, suture of a muscle

Myorrhexis

Myorrhexis f myorrhexis, rupture of a muscle
Myosarkom n myosarcoma
Myosin n myosin *(Muskeleiweiß)*
Myosinausscheidung f **im Urin** myosinuria
Myositis f myositis, sarcitis, inflammation of a muscle *(s. a. unter Muskelentzündung)*
~ **epidemica** epidemic myositis, [epidemic] pleurodynia, Bornholm disease
~/**interstitielle** interstitial myositis
~/**ischämische** ischaemic myositis
~ **ossificans** ossifying myositis *(z. B. durch Kalkeinlagerungen als Unfallfolge)*
~/**parenchymatöse** parenchymatous myositis
~/**suppurative** suppurative myositis, pyomyositis
myositisch myositic
Myosklerose f myosclerosis, sclerosis (hardening) of a muscle
Myospasmus m s. Muskelkrampf
myostatisch myostatic
myotaktisch myotactic
Myotasis f myotasis, stretching of a muscle, myentasis
myotendinös myotendinous
Myotenositis f myotenositis
Myotenotomie f myotenotomy
Myotom n 1. myotome *(Muskelgruppe mit gleicher Spinalnerveninnervation)*; 2. s. Myotomiemesser
Myotomie f myotomy, dissection of a muscle
Myotomiemesser n myotome
Myotonia f myotonia
~ **atrophica (atrophicans)** myotonic [muscular] atrophy, myotonic atrophy (dystrophy), atrophic myotonia
~ **congenita** congenital myotonia
~ **dystrophica** s. ~ atrophica
myotonisch myotonic
Myotonus m myotonus, tonic muscle spasm
myotrop myotropic
Myotrophie f myotrophy, nutrition of the muscle
myovaskulär myovascular
Myozele f s. Muskelhernie
Myozyt m myocyte, muscle cell
Myozytolyse f myocytolysis
Myozytom n myocytoma
Myringektomie f myring[od]ectomy, tympanectomy
Myringitis f myringitis, inflammation of the tympanic membrane
~ **bullosa** bullous myringitis
Myringomykose f myringomycosis
Myringoplastik f myringoplasty, tympanoplasty
myringoplastisch myringoplastic
Myringoskop n myringoscope
Myringoskopie f myringoscopy
Myringotom n myringotome
Myringotomie f myringotomy, puncture of the eardrum, tympanotomy
Myrtenblattsonde f myrtiform (myrtle-leaf) probe
mysophil mysophilic
Mysophilie f mysophilia

mysophob mysophobic
Mysophobie f mysophobia *(krankhafte Angst vor Schmutz)*
Mytazismus m mytacism, mutacism
Mythomanie f mythomania
Mytilotoxin n mytilotoxin
Mytilotoxismus m mytilotoxism
Myxadenitis f myxadenitis, inflammation of a mucous gland
~ **labialis** glandular cheilitis
Myxadenom n myx[o]adenoma, adenomyxoma
Myxasthenie f myxasthenia
Myxidiotie f myxidiocy
Myxiosis f myxiosis
Myxoadenom n s. Myxadenom
Myxoblastom n myxoblastoma
Myxochondrofibrosarkom n myxochondrofibrosarcoma
Myxochondrom n myxochondroma
Myxochondrosarkom n myxochondrosarcoma
Myxödem n myxoedema, Gull's disease *(bei Schilddrüsenunterfunktion)*
~/**infantiles** infantile myxoedema; Brissaud's infantilism
myxödemartig myxoedematoid
myxödematös myxoedematous
Myxödemherz n myxoedema heart
Myxoedema n **circumscriptum thyrotoxicum** circumscribed myxoedema
Myxoenchondrom n myxoenchondroma
Myxofibrom n myxofibroma *(Mischgeschwulst aus Schleim- und kollagenem Bindegewebe)*
Myxofibrosarkom n myxofibrosarcoma
Myxogliom n myxoglioma
myxoid myxoid
Myxolipom n myxolipoma, lipomyxoma
Myxoliposarkom n myxoliposarcoma
Myxom n myxoma, mucous tumour, collonema *(s. a. unter Myxoma)*
~/**intrakanalikuläres** intracanalicular myxoma (fibroadenoma) *(gutartiger Brusttumor)*
~/**zystisches** cystic myxoma
Myxoma n s. Myxom
~ **cavernosum** cystic myxoma
~ **cordis** cardiac myxoma
~ **medullare (simplex)** myxoma, mucous tumour
myxomartig pseudomyxomatous
myxomatös myxomatous
Myxomatose f myxomatosis
Myxomyom n myxomyoma
Myxomyzeten mpl myxomycetes
Myxoneurom n myxoneuroma
Myxoneurose f myxoneurosis
Myxopoese f myxopoiesis, formation of mucus
Myxorrhoe f myxorrhoea, [copious] mucous discharge
Myxosarkom n myxosarcoma *(bösartige Geschwulst aus Schleimgewebe)*
myxosarkomatös myxosarcomatous
Myxovirus n myxovirus
Myxozyt m myxocyte
Myzel n mycelium

myzelartig mycelioid
Myzelfaden *m* mycelial thread, hypha
Myzelphase *f* mycelial phase
Myzetismus *m s.* Mykotoxikose
myzetogen mycetogenic, mycetogenous
myzetoid mycetoid, mycoid, fungoid
Myzetologie *f* mycology
Myzetom *n* mycetoma, maduromycosis; Madura foot

N

N. *s.* Nervus
Nabel *m* navel, umbilicus, umbo, omphalos, omphalus ● **durch den** ~ transumbilical ● **neben dem** ~ paraumbilical, paraomphalic ● **über dem** ~ supraumbilical ● **um den** ~ **liegend** periumbilical, periomphalic ● **unter dem** ~ subumbilical
~/**hervorstehender** acromphalus
Nabel... *s. a.* Umbilikal...
Nabelabszeß *m* empyocele, umbilical (navel) abscess
Nabelansatz *m*/**häutiger** velamentous insertion of the navel
Nabelarterie *f* umbilical artery
Nabelarterienkatheter *m* umbilical artery catheter
nabelartig umbilicate[d]
Nabelausschneidung *f s.* Nabelentfernung/operative
Nabelband *n* umbilical ligament
~/**laterales** lateral umbilical ligament
~/**mediales** medial umbilical ligament
~/**medianes** median umbilical ligament
Nabelbändchen *n* umbilical tape
Nabelbereich *m* umbilical region
Nabelbinde *f* umbilical binder (bandage)
Nabelbläschen *n* umbilical vesicle, yolk (vitelline) sac, vitellicle
Nabelblennorrhoe *f* umbilical blennorrhoea
Nabelblut *n* cord blood
Nabelblutung *f* omphalorrhagia, haemorrhage from the umbilicus
Nabelbruch *m* umbilical (annular) hernia, omphalocele; exomphalos
~ **mit Netzinhalt** epiplomphalocele
Nabelbruchband *n* umbilical belt (hernia bandage)
Nabeldiphtherie *f* umbilical (navel) diphtheria
Nabeleiterung *f* empyocele; pyoumbilicus
Nabelentfernung *f*[/**operative**] umbilectomy, omphalectomy, excision of the navel
Nabelentzündung *f* omphalitis, inflammation of the navel
Nabelerysipel *n* umbilical (navel) erysipelas
Nabelfalte *f*/**mediane** median umbilical fold
~/**mittlere** medial (middle) umbilical fold
~/**seitliche** lateral umbilical fold
nabelförmig umbilicate[d]
Nabelgangrän *f* umbilical (navel) gangrene

Nabelschnurvorlagerung

Nabelgeschwulst *f* tumour of the umbilicus, omphaloma
Nabelgeschwür *n* umbilical ulcer, ulceration of the umbilicus, omphalelcosis
Nabelgrube *f* umbilical fossa
Nabelinfektion *f* umbilical infection
Nabelkrampfader *f* varicomphalus
Nabellymphfluß *m* lymphatic effusion at the navel, omphalorrhoea
Nabelpapille *f* umbilical papilla
Nabelphlegmone *f* omphalophlegmon, umbilical phlegmon
Nabelreposition *f* omphalotaxis, reposition of the prolapsed umbilicus
Nabelring *m* umbilical (navel) ring
Nabelruptur *f* omphalorrhexis, rupture of the umbilicus
Nabelschnitt *m*/**querer** transverse umbilical incision
Nabelschnur *f* umbilical cord, abdominal (belly) stalk, funis
Nabelschnurabklemmung *f* umbilical cord clamping
Nabelschnurabquetschung *f* omphalotripsy, surgical crushing of the umbilical cord
Nabelschnurband *n* umbilical tape
Nabelschnurbindegewebe *n*/**gallertiges** jelly of Wharton, Wharton's gelatin
Nabelschnurblut *n* umbilical cord blood
Nabelschnurdurchblutung *f* umbilical cord blood flow
Nabelschnurdurchtrennung *f* cutting of the umbilical cord, omphalotomy
Nabelschnurgefäß *n* umbilical vessel ● **durch die Nabelschnurgefäße verbunden** omphaloangiophagous *(Zwillingsmißbildung)*
Nabelschnurgeräusch *n* umbilical souffle, funicular (foetal) souffle
Nabelschnurklemme *f* umbilical cord clamp, umbilical seal
Nabelschnurkompression *f* umbilical cord compression
Nabelschnurkreislauf *m* umbilical circulation
Nabelschnurobstruktion *f* umbilical cord obstruction
Nabelschnurpuls *m* umbilical pulse, funic[ular] pulse
Nabelschnurquetsche *f* omphalotribe
Nabelschnurquetschung *f* crushing of the umbilical cord, omphalotripsy
Nabelschnurrückverlagerung *f* reposition of the prolapsed umbilicus, omphalotaxis
Nabelschnurschere *f* umbilical cord scissors
Nabelschnurschnitt *m* cutting of the umbilical cord, omphalotomy
Nabelschnurverdrehung *f* torsion (twisting) of the umbilical cord; twisted cord
Nabelschnurvorfall *m* omphaloproptosis, umbilical cord prolapse, prolapse of the umbilical cord; funis (cord) presentation *(bei der Geburt)*
Nabelschnurvorlagerung *f* funis (cord) presentation *(bei der Geburt)*

Nabelskalpell

Nabelskalpell n omphalotome
Nabelstrang m s. Nabel
Nabelstumpf m umbilical stump, stump of the cord
Nabelvene f umbilical (allantoic) vein
Nabelvenenentzündung f omphalophlebitis, inflammation of the umbilical veins
Nabelvenenkatheter[isier]ung f umbilical vein catheterization
Nabelvenen-Pfortader-Thrombose f umbilical-portal thrombosis
Nabelvenenportographie f umbilical vein portography
Nabelvenentransplantat n umbilical vein graft
Nabelverband m umbilical belt (dressing, bandage)
Nabelvereiterung f pyoumbilicus
Nabelvorfall m s. Nabelbruch
Nabelwassergeschwulst f hydromphalos
Nabelzeichen n/**Hofstätter-Cullensches** Cullen's sign *(Braunfärbung des Nabels bei Bauchhöhlenschwangerschaft)*
nachahmen 1. to imitate; 2. to mimic
Nachahmen n/**automatenhaftes** echopraxia, echokinesia, echomatism
nachahmend 1. imitative; 2. mimetic, mimic
Nachahmung f imitation; simulation *(z. B. von Krankheitssymptomen)*
Nachamputation f reamputation
Nachaußenschielen n exophoria *(bei geschlossenen Augen)*
Nachaußenstülpen n eversion
Nachbargewebe n neighbouring (adjacent) tissue
Nachbehandlung f aftertreatment, follow-up treatment, aftercare; postoperative therapy
Nachbelastung f [des Herzens] afterload
Nachbeobachtungszeit f follow-up period
Nachbestrahlung f postoperative [ir]radiation
Nachbild n afterimage, accidental image; aftervision
~/**negatives** negative afterimage
~/**positives** positive afterimage
Nachbildtest m afterimage test
Nachbildung f von Körperteilen moulage
Nachblutung f afterbleeding, secondary bleeding, postoperative haemorrhage
Nacheffekt m aftereffect
Nacheindruck m afterimpression
Nachempfindung f aftersensation, afterperception; afterimpression
Nachen m scapha, navicular fossa of the ear *(Grube zwischen Helix und Anthelix der Ohrmuschel)*
Nachentladung f afterdischarge *(des Hirnpotentials)*
Nachfärbung f afterstaining, counterstaining
Nachgeburt f after-birth, placenta, secundines *(Zusammensetzungen s. unter Placenta)*
nachgeburtlich postnatal, postpartum
Nachgeburtsausstoßung f expulsion of the placenta (after-birth)

Nachgeburtsblutung f postpartum haemorrhage (bleeding)
Nachgeburtsperiode f placental stage, postpartum period
Nachgeschmack m aftertaste
~/**krankhafter bitterer** picrogeusia, pathological bitter taste
Nachhirn n s. Myelenzephalon
Nachhören n afterhearing
nachimpfen to revaccinate
Nachinnenschielen n esophoria; endophoria *(bei geschlossenen Augen)*
Nachinnenschlagen n retropulsion *(einer Krankheit)*
Nachkomme f offspring, descendant
Nachkommengeneration f/**erste** filial generation, F1
Nachkommenschaft f progeny; offsprings
Nachkommenzeugung f procreation
Nachkrankheit f sequela, secondary disease
nachlassen to decrease *(z. B. Krankheitserscheinungen)*; to relieve, to subside *(z. B. Schmerzen)*; to fail *(z. B. Herzkraft)*
Nachlassen n decrement *(z. B. von Krankheitserscheinungen)*; remission *(z. B. von Fieber)*; failure, decompensation *(z. B. der Herzkraft)*
~/**unvollständiges** remittence *(z. B. von Symptomen)*
Nachlast f afterload
nachleuchten to phosphoresce *(z. B. nach vorhergehender Bestrahlung)*
nachleuchtend phosphorescent, phosphorous
Nachmilch f after-milk
Nachniere f hind kidney, metanephros
Nachnystagmus m afternystagmus
Nachobenschielen n hypertropia
Nachoperation f reoperation
Nachpotential n afterpotential
Nachschlafhalluzination f hypnopompic hallucination
Nachschlaginstrument n nail impactor
Nachschmerz m afterpain
Nachsehen n aftervision
Nachsorge f aftercare, follow-up, aftertreatment
Nachsprechen n [/**krankhaftes**] echolalia, echophrasia, echo speech
nachsprechend echolalic
Nachsprechkrankheit f echopathy
Nachstar m aftercataract, secondary cataract
Nachtadaptation f scotopia
Nachtangst f 1. night terrors; 2. nyctophobia, noctiphobia
nachtblind night-blind, nyctalopic
Nachtblinder m nyctalope
Nachtblindheit f night blindness, nyctalopia, nyctotyphlosis, nocturnal amblyopia, day sight
Nachtlarvenfilarie f onchocerca caecutiens
Nachton m aftersound
Nachtripper m gleet
Nachtsanatorium n night hospital
Nachtschmerz m night pain, nyctalgia
Nachtschweiß m night sweat *(z. B. bei Lungentuberkulose)*

Nachtschwester f night nurse
nachtsichtig scotopic, nyctalope
Nachtsichtigkeit f night-sightedness, night vision, nyctalopia, hemeralopia, scotopia, day blindness
nachtwandeln to somnambulate, to sleep-walk
Nachtwandeln n somnambulism, sleep-walking, somnambulance, noctambulation, active oneirodynia, hypnobatia
nachtwandelnd somnambulistic, sleep-walking, noctambulic
Nachtwandler m somnambulist, sleep-walker, noctambulist
Nachuntenschielen n hypotropia
~/latentes hypophoria
Nachwehen pl afterpains
nachweisen/durch Gram-Färbung to establish by gram stain
~/eine Schwangerschaft to detect the existence of pregnancy
Nachweismittel n [detection] reagent; indicator
nachwirken to have an aftereffect
Nachwirkung f aftereffect
Nacken m nape, nucha, back of the neck
~/steifer stiff neck; stiffness of the neck *(z. B. bei Hirnhautentzündung)*
Nackenaponeurose f nuchal aponeurosis
Nackenarterie f/tiefe deep cervical artery
Nackenaufrichtungsreflex m neck-righting reflex
Nackenband n nuchal ligament
Nackenbeuge f neck bend
Nackenfurche f neck furrow
Nackengrube f nuchal fossa
Nackenhaar n back-hair
Nacken-Hinterhaupt-Kopfschmerz m cervico-occipital neuralgia
Nackenhöcker m nuchal tubercle
Nackenlinie f nuchal line
Nackenmuskulatur f nuchal muscles
Nackenreflex m neck reflex
Nackenregion f region of the neck, nuchal (cervical) region
Nackenschmerz m neck pain, cervicodynia, trachelodynia
Nackenspalte f tracheloschisis, [congenital] fissure of the neck
Nackensteife f, **Nackensteifigkeit** f neck stiffness, nuchal rigidity, stiffness of the neck; stiff neck
Nacken-Steiß-Länge f nape-breech length
Nackenvene f/tiefe deep cervical vein
Nackenzeichen n/**Brudzinskisches** Brudzinski's neck sign *(bei Meningitis)*
NAD s. Nikotinamid-adenin-dinukleotid
Nadel f needle, acus
~/angeschliffene cutting needle
~/atraumatische atraumatic (eyeless, swedged) needle
~/chirurgische surgical (suture) needle; acus
~/gerade straight needle
~/Reverdinsche Reverdin's needle

~/runde round needle
~/scharfe cutting needle
Nadelangst f belonephobia
nadelartig needle-like
Nadelaspiration f needle aspiration
Nadelaspirationsbiopsie f needle aspiration biopsy
Nadelaspirationszytologie f needle aspiration cytology
Nadelbiopsie f needle biopsy
Nadeldose f needle case *(im chirurgischen Besteck)*
nadelförmig needle-shaped
Nadelgefühl n acanthaesthesia
Nadelhalter m needle holder (carrier), needle forceps, acutenaculum
Nadellehre f acupuncture
Nadelmesser n discission needle
Nadel[spitzen]pupille f pinpoint (pinhole) pupil
Nadelstichelung f acupuncture
Nadelstichgefühl n acanthaesthesia
NADP s. Nikotinamid-adenin-dinukleotidphosphat
Naevus m naevus, spiloma, birth-mark, mother's mark, mole *(umschriebene, anlagebedingte oder erbliche Fehlbildung der Haut)*
~ **arachnoideus (araneus)** arachnoid (spider) naevus, spider [angioma], stellate naevus
~ **comedonicus** follicular naevus
~ **depigmentosus** amelanotic naevus
~ **flammeus** s. ~ vasculosus
~ **lipomatodes superficialis** focal dermal hypoplasia syndrome
~ **lymphaticus** lymphatic naevus
~ **morus** mulberry (strawberry) mark
~ **osteohypertrophicus** Klippel-Trénaunay-Weber syndrome, angioosteohypertrophy
~ **papillomatosus** naevus papillomatosus
~ **pigmentosus** pigmented naevus (mole), liver spot
~ **pilosus** pilose (hairy) naevus
~ **sebaceus** sebaceous naevus
~ **spilus** naevus spilus *(Pigmentvermehrung der Haut)*
~ **spongiosus albus** white sponge naevus of the mucosa, congenital leucokeratosis mucosae oris
~ **stellaris** stellar naevus
~ **vasculosus** strawberry haemangioma (mark), port-wine mark (naevus, stain)
~ **verrucosus** verrucous (epidermal, linear) naevus
Naffziger-Syndrom n Naffziger's (scalenus anterior) syndrome
Nagel m 1. nail, onyx, unguis; 2. nail, pin ● **unter dem ~** hyponychial, subungual
~/brüchiger brittle nail
~/eingewachsener ingrowing nail; onychocryptosis
~/löffelförmiger spoon nail
~/Steinmannscher Steinmann nail (pin)
Nagel... s. a. Onych...

Nagelabfallen

Nagelabfallen *n* onychoptosis, falling off of the nails
Nagelablösung *f* onycholysis, loosening of the nails
nagelähnlich onychoid, resembling a nail
nagelartig onychoid
Nagelaufspaltung *f* onychoschizia, schizonychia
Nagelausfall *m* onychomadesis, loss of the nails, lapsus unguium
Nagelausreißzange *f* nail extraction forceps
Nagelbeißen *n s.* Nägelknabbern
Nagelbett *n* nail bed, hyponychium, matrix, onychostroma
Nagelbettentzündung *f* onychitis, inflammation of the matrix [of a nail], matrixitis, felon
Nagelbettgeschwulst *f* onychoma, tumour of the nail bed
Nagelbettsyphilis *f* syphilis of the nail bed
Nagelbettvereiterung *f* [par]onychia, panaris, runaround
nagelbildend onychogenic
Nagelbildung *f/abnorme* paronychosis
~/übermäßige hyperonychia
Nagelbrechen *n* onychoclasis, breaking of the nails
Nagelbrüchigkeit *f* onychorrhexis, brittleness of the nails
Nageldegeneration *f* onychexallaxis, degeneration of the nails
Nageleinschnitt *m* onychotomy, incision of a nail
Nageleinwachsung *f* onychocryptosis; ingrowing nail
Nagelentfernung *f[/operative]* onychectomy, excision of a nail
Nagelentzündung *f* onychitis, onyxitis, inflammation of the nail matrix, onychia
Nagelernährung *f* onychotrophy, nutrition of the nails
Nagelerweichung *f* onychomalacia, softening of the nails
Nagelextraktion *f* 1. onychectomy, excision of a nail; 2. extraction of a nail, removal of a pin
Nagelextraktionsinstrument *n* nail extraction hook
Nagelextraktionszange *f* nail extraction forceps
Nagelfalz *m* perionychium, paronychium, nail fold (wall)
Nagelfalzentzündung *f* perionychia, paronychia, panaris, runaround, felon
Nagelfalzmykose *f* paronychomycosis
Nagelfalzpanaritium *n s.* Nagelbettvereiterung
Nagelfissurbildung *f* onychorrhexis, splitting of the nails
nagelförmig onychoid, unguiform, nail-shaped
Nagelgeschwulst *f* 1. onychyma; 2. *s.* Nagelbettgeschwulst
Nagelgeschwür *n* panaritium, paronychia, whitlow
~/melanotisches melanotic whitlow
Nagelgeschwürbildung *f* onychohelcosis, ulceration of the nails
Nagelgrube *f* nail groove

Nagelhalteplatte *f* nail holding plate *(Osteosynthese)*
Nagelhartsubstanz *f* onychin
Nagelhautschere *f* cuticle scissors
Nagelhautzange *f* cuticle nippers
Nagelhypertrophie *f* hyperonychia, nail hypertrophy, macronychia, megalonychosis, onychauxis
Nagelhypotrophie *f* nail hypotrophy, hypo-onychia, micronychia
Nagelinduration *f* scleronychia
Nagelinzision *f* onychotomy, incision of a nail
Nägelkauen *n s.* Nägelknabbern
Nagelkauer *m* onychophagist
Nägelknabbern *n* nail biting, biting the nails, onychophagia
Nagelkrankheit *f* onychopathy, onychonosus, disease of the nails
Nagellockerung *f* loosening of the nails, onychorrhiza
Nagellokalisation *f/abnorme* onychoheterotopia
Nagelmatrix *f s.* Nagelbett
Nagelmißbildung *f* onychodystrophy
Nagelmond *m* lunula, selene, moon [of the nails]
Nageloberhäutchen *n* eponychium
Nagelpilzwucherung *f* onychomycosis, ringworm of the nails
Nagelplatte *f* nail plate
Nagelplattenquerfurchen *fpl/*Beau-Reilsche Beau's lines
Nagelpuls *m* nail pulse
Nagelpulsaufzeichnung *f* onychography, recording of the nail pulse
Nagelpulsaufzeichnungsgerät *n* onychograph
Nagelpulskurve *f* onychogram
Nagelrand *m/freier* free edge of the nail
~/seitlicher lateral margin of the nail
Nagelschmerz *m* onychalgia, pain in the nails, onychodynia; painful nails
Nagelschuppung *f* piptonychia, shedding of the nails
Nagelschwund *m* onychatrophia, atrophy of the nails
Nagelspaltbildung *f* onychorrhexis, splitting of the nails
Nagelspaltschere *f* scissors for splitting fingernails, nail-splitting scissors
Nagelsplittern *n* onychoschizia, schizonychia
Nagelung *f* nailing *(eines Knochens)*
~/intramedulläre medullary (marrow) nailing
Nagelverdickung *f* pachyonychia, pachyonyxis
Nagelvergrößerung *f* megalonychosis
Nagelverhärtung *f* scleronychia
Nagelverkrümmung *f* onychogryp[h]osis, gryposis
Nagelwachstum *n/verstärktes* onychauxis
Nagelwall *m s.* Nagelfalz
Nagelweichheit *f/abnorme* hapalonychia
Nagelwucherung *f* onychophyma, onychauxis, megalonychosis
Nagelwurzel *f* nail root, rhizonychia, rhizonychium

Nagelzange f nail cutters
Nagelzieher m nail extractor
nagend rodent *(z. B. Geschwür)*
Nagerpest f sylvatic plague
Nagetiergift n rodenticide [agent]
Nahaufnahme f contact radiogram
Nahbrille f spectacles for near vision, pulpit spectacles
nähen to sew, to suture, to stitch
~/eine Wunde to suture a wound
Nahpunkt m near point *(Ophthalmologie)*
~/relativer relative (convergence) near point
Nährboden m substrate, culture medium
~/Endoscher Endo's medium
nähren to nourish, to nurse; to feed
Nähren n feeding
nährend s. nahrhaft
nahrhaft nutrient, nutritive, nutritious, nutritory
Nährlösung f nutrient solution, liquid culture medium
Nährmedium n culture medium, [nutrient] medium
Nährmittel n foodstuff, nutrient
Nährstoff m nutrient, nutritive (nutritious) substance
Nährstoffabsorption f nutrient absorption
Nährstoffbedarf m nutrient demand
Nährstoffgehalt m nutrient content
Nährstoffmangel m nutrient deficiency
Nährstoffmangelerscheinung f nutrient deficiency symptom
Nährstoffresorption f/verminderte malabsorption *(aus dem Magen-Darm-Kanal)*
Nahrung f food, nourishment, nutriment; diet ● **~ verweigern** to reject (refuse) food
~/gesamte aufgenommene ingesta
Nahrungsaufnahme f eating; ingestion, food intake ● **nach ~** postprandial
Nahrungsaversion f apositia
Nahrungsbedarf m nutritional requirements
Nahrungsbeschränkung f dietetic restriction
Nahrungsbissen m alimentary bolus
Nahrungscholesterol n alimentary cholesterol
Nahrungsentzug m denutrition, withdrawal of food
Nahrungskarenz f abrosia, abstinence from food, fasting
Nahrungsmangel m alimentary deficiency, lack of food
Nahrungsmittel n food[stuff], nourishment, aliment
Nahrungsmittelallergen n nutritional (nutritive) allergen
Nahrungsmittelallergie f nutritional (food) allergy
Nahrungsmittelinfektion f nutritional (food) infection
Nahrungsmitteltabelle f food table
nahrungsmittelübertragen food-borne
Nahrungsmittelüberwachung f food control
Nahrungsmittelvergiftung f food poisoning, alimentary toxicosis
~/akute bakterielle enterocolitis syndrome

nahrungsverweigernd refusing food
Nahrungsverweigerung f [insane] rejection of food, sitieirgia; sitophobia
Nahrungsverwertung f food utilization
Nahrungswege mpl food passages
Nahrungszufuhr f/systematische alimentotherapy
Nährwert m nutritive (nutritional) value
Nahsehen n near vision
Nahsehstörung f near vision disturbance
Naht f 1. seam, suture, sutura, raphe *(Anatomie) (s. a. unter* Raphe *und* Sutura*);* 2. s. **~/chirurgische** ● **eine ~ entfernen** to remove a suture ● **eine ~ legen** to place (insert) a suture
~/chirurgische suture
~/fortlaufende continuous suture, running (uninterrupted) suture, glover's stitch
~ in Schichten suture in layers
~/mit dem Nähapparat genähte chain-stitch suture
~/nichtresorbierbare non-absorbable suture
~/paraneurale paraneural suture
~/primäre primary suture
~/resorbierbare resorbable suture
~/sekundäre secondary suture, resuture
~/sero-seröse Lembert's (sero-serous) suture *(z. B. am Magen, Darm)*
~/versenkte buried suture
~/verzögerte delayed suture
Nahtbildung f/fehlende dysraphism, araphia *(Embryologie)*
Nahtdehiszenz f dehiscence of a suture
Nahtklammer f suture clip
Nahtlinie f suture line
Nahtmaterial n suture material
Nahtreihe f row of sutures
Nahtstar m sutural (stellate) cataract
Nahtstelle f seam
Nahtstichabszeß m stitch abscess
Nahttechnik f suture technique
Nahttisch m table for suturing materials
Nahtverschluß m suture closure *(z. B. eines Gefäßes)*
Nalidixinsäure f nalidixic acid *(Antibiotikum)*
Nalorphin n nalorphine, allylnormorphine *(Morphinantagonist)*
Namensverwechslung f paranomia
Namenszwang m onomatomania
Nanismus m s. Nanosomie
nanoid nanoid, nanous, dwarfish; stunted
Nanomelie f nanomelia
Nanophthalmie f nanophthalmia
Nanophthalmus m nanophthalmos, nanophthalmus
Nanosomie f nanosomia, nanism, dwarfism, microsomia, microplasia
Nanosomus m nanosomus, dwarf
nanozephal nanocephalous
Nanozephalie f nanocephalia, abnormal smallness of the head
Nanozephalus m nanocephalus
Napfkucheniris f umbrella iris, iris bombé

Naphthalin

Naphthalin n naphthalene *(Antiwurmmittel)*
Narbe f scar, cicatrix; mark, pit *(z. B. bei Pocken)* ● **eine ~ bilden** to cicatrice, to scar, to form a scar
~ der Hornhaut/weiße leucoma
~/hypertrophische keloid, kelis, cheloid, keloma
narbenartig cicatricial, scar-like
narbenbedeckt scarred
narbenbildend cicatrizant, scarring, ulotic
Narbenbildung f cicatrization, scarring, scar (cicatricial) formation; epulosis
Narbenbruch m cicatricial hernia, incisional (postoperative) hernia
Narbendurchtrennung f cicatricotomy, ulotomy
Narbenektropion n cicatricial ectropion
Narbenentfernung f[/operative] cicatricectomy, excision of a cicatrix
Narbenentropion n cicatricial entropion
Narbengebiet n cicatricial (scar) area
Narbengewebe n cicatricial (scar) tissue
Narbengewebekontraktion f cicatricial tissue contraction
Narbenhypertrophie f cicatricial (scar) hypertrophy
Narbenkeloid n keloid, kelis, cheloid, keloma
Narbenkontraktur f cicatricial contraction, scar tissue contracture
Narbenkrebs m cicatricial cancer, scar carcinoma
Narbenniere f cicatricial (scarred) kidney
Narbenpemphigoid n cicatricial pemphigoid
Narbenplastik f keloplasty
Narbenpterygium n pseudopterygium, cicatricial pterygium
Narbenschrumpfung f **der Kornea** cicatricial shrinking of the cornea
Narbenskoliose f cicatricial scoliosis
Narbenstenose f cicatricial stenosis
Narbenstrang m bridle
Narbenstriktur f bridle (cicatricial) stricture
Narbenstrikturdurchtrennung f kelotomy
Narbentrachom n cicatricial trachoma; trachomatous entropion
Narbenveränderung f cicatricial change
Narbenvereng[er]ung f cicatricial narrowing
Narbenwucherung f s. Narbenkeloid
Narbenzug m bridle
narbig cicatricial, cicatrized, scarred; pitted, marked
Naris f s. Nasenöffnung
Narkoanalyse f narcoanalysis, narcodiagnosis *(Befragung nach bestimmten Erlebnissen bei Enthemmung durch Schlafmittel)*
Narkohypnose f narcohypnosis, hypnonarcosis, narcosuggestion
Narkokatharsis f narcocatharsis
Narkolepsie f narcolepsy, paroxysmal sleep
narkoleptisch narcoleptic
Narkologie f narcology
Narkomaner m narcomaniac
Narkomanie f narcomania; narcotism
Narkose f 1. narcosis, anaesthesia *(s. a. unter Anästhesie)*; 2. s. Narkotisierung ● **aus der ~ erwachen** to recover ● **durch ~ bedingt** induced by anaesthesia ● **eine ~ durchführen** to narcotize ● **in ~ [befindlich]** under anaesthesia ● **nach der ~** postanaesthetic ● **unter ~ setzen** to narcotize ● **vor der ~** prenarcotic
~/ambulante outpatient anaesthesia
~/halboffene semiopen anaesthesia
~/intratracheale intratracheal (endotracheal) anaesthesia
~/intravenöse intravenous anaesthesia, phlebanaesthesia, phlebonarcosis
~/orotracheale orotracheal anaesthesia
~/rektale rectal anaesthesia
Narkosearzt m anaesthetist, anaesthesiologist
Narkoseäther m anaesthetic aether
Narkoseeinleitung f induction of anaesthesia, anaesthetization
Narkosegas n anaesthetic gas
Narkosegerät n anaesthetic machine (apparatus)
Narkosegift n narcotic poison
narkosehemmend antinarcotic
Narkoseindex m anaesthetic index
Narkosekrampf m narcospasm
Narkoselähmung f anaesthesia (narcosis) paralysis
Narkosemaske f anaesthetic (ether) mask, face mask for anaesthesia
~/Schimmelbuschsche Schimmelbusch's mask
Narkosemittel n s. Narkotikum
Narkoserisiko n anaesthetic risk
Narkoseschlaf m narcoma, narcoti[ci]sm
Narkosespritze f anaesthesia syringe
Narkosestadium n plane of anaesthesia, stage of general anaesthesia
Narkosesucht f narcosomania
Narkosesystem n/**geschlossenes** closed[-circuit] anaesthesia
~/kontinuierliches continuous flow system
~/offenes open[-circuit] anaesthesia
Narkosetechnik f anaesthetic technique
~/geschlossene closed[-circuit] anaesthesia
~/offene open[-circuit] anaesthesia
Narkosetisch m anaesthetic table
Narkosetropfer m [ether and] chloroform dropper
Narkosetubus m [anaesthetic] airway, [anaesthetic] tube, tubus
Narkoseübelkeit f postanaesthetic nausea
Narkoseverfahren n **mit Kohlendioxidabsorption** carbon dioxide absorption anaesthesia *(geschlossenes Narkosesystem)*
Narkosevorbereitung f premedication
Narkosomanie f narcosomania
Narkospasmus m narcospasm
Narkotikum n narcotic [agent], anaesthetic [agent]; stupefacient [agent]; drug
Narkotin n narcotine *(schwach einschläferndes Alkaloid)*
narkotisch narcotic, anaesthetic; soporiferous, soporific; stupefacient
narkotisieren to narcotize, to anaesthetize; to soporate; to stupefy
~/mit Äther to etherize

~/mit Chloral to chloralize
narkotisierend narcotic, anaesthetic
Narkotisierung f narcotization, narcosis, anaesthetization; stupefaction
Narzißmus m narc[iss]ism, autophilia
Narzißt m narcissist
narzißtisch narcissistic
nasal nasal, n., rhinal ● nasalen Ursprungs rhinogenous
Nasal... s. a. Nasen...
Nasalfeld n nasal field
Nasalsprache f rhinophonia, nasal twang
Nase f nose, nasus (s. a. unter Nasus) ● durch die ~ pernasal ● hinter der ~ postnasal ● über der ~ supranasal ● unter der ~ subnasal ● von der ~ ausgehend rhinogenous
~/äußere external nose
~/gebogene aquiline nose
~/schiefe squint nose
Näseln n [nasal] twang (s. a. Nasensprache)
Nasenabstrich m nasal smear (swab)
Nasenanteil m/knöcherner bony [part of the] nose
~/knorpeliger cartilaginous [part of the] nose
Nasenatmer m nasal breather
Nasenatmung f nasal breathing (respiration)
Nasenatresie f atretorrhinia
Nasenaugenarterie f nasociliary artery
Nasenaugennerv m nasociliary nerve
Nasenaugennervneuralgie f nasociliary neuralgia
Nasenausfluß m rhinorrhoea, nasal discharge, discharge of nasal mucus
Nasenbasis f base of the nose
Nasenbein n nasal bone, bridge of the nose
Nasenbeinfraktur f nasal bone fracture, fracture of the nose
nasenbildend rhinoplastic
Nasenbinnendruckmesser m nasomanometer
Nasenbluten n epistaxis, nasal bleeding (haemorrhage), rhinorrhagia, nosebleed
Nasenboden m floor of the nose
Nasenbruch m fracture of the nose
Nasendehner m rhineurynter, nasal dilator
Naseneingang m vestibule of the nose
Naseneinschnitt m rhinotomy
Nasenentzündung f s. Rhinitis
Nasenerkrankung f rhinopathy, disease of the nose
Naseneröffnung f[/operative] rhinotomy, incision into the nose
Nasenfacharzt m rhinologist
Nasenfeld n nasal field (area)
Nasenflügel m wing (ala) of the nose
Nasenflügelatmen n flaring of the nasal ali
Nasenflügelhaken m nostril retractor
Nasenflügelknorpel m/großer greater alar cartilage
Nasenflügelkollaps m nasal alar collapse
Nasenflügeln n flaring of the nasal ali
Nasenfluß m rhinorrhoea, mucous discharge from the nose

Nasenfortsatz m des Stirnbeins nasal process of the frontal bone
~/mittlerer nasomedial (median nasal) process
~/seitlicher nasolateral (lateral nasal) process
Nasenfremdkörper m nasal foreign body
Nasengang m nasal meatus
~/gemeinsamer common meatus of the nose
~/mittlerer middle meatus of the nose (nasal cavity), middle nasal meatus
~/oberer superior meatus of the nose, superior nasal meatus
~/unterer inferior meatus of the nose, inferior nasal meatus
Nasenganglabyrinth n nasal labyrinth
Nasengangverschluß m rhinocleisis, obstruction of the nasal passages
Nasen-Gaumen-Ausschlag m nasopalatine eruption (z. B. bei Herpes zoster)
Nasengerüstzerstörung f nasal collapse (z. B. bei Lepra)
Nasengewölbe n nasal vault
Nasengliom n nasal glioma
Nasenhaar n vibrissa, rhinothrix
Nasenhämatom n rhinhaematoma
Nasenheilkunde f rhinology
Nasenhöhle f nasal cavity (fossa) ● neben der ~ paranasal
~/definitive secondary nasal cavity
~/primäre primary nasal cavity
~/sekundäre secondary nasal cavity
Nasenhöhlenarterie f/hintere seitliche posterior lateral nasal artery
Nasenhöhlenlabyrinth n nasal labyrinth
Nasenhöhlenscheidewandarterie f/hintere posterior septal nasal artery
Nasenhöhlenschleimhaut f mucous membrane of the nasal cavity
Nasenhöhlenverlegung f nasal obstruction
Nasenindex m nasal index
Naseninfektion f nasal infection
Naseninnendruckmesser m nasomanometer
Nasenirrigator m nasal irrigator
Nasenkanüle f nasal cannula, rhinophore
Nasenkapsel f nasal capsule
Nasenkatheter m intranasal catheter
Nasenklammer f nasal (nose) clip
Nasenknochennaht f internasal suture
Nasenknochennekrose f rhinonecrosis, necrosis of the nasal bones
Nasenknorpel m nasal cartilage, cartilage of the nose
~/seitlicher lateral nasal cartilage
Nasenkrankheit f rhinopathy, disease of the nose
Nasenlabyrinth n nasal labyrinth
Nasenleiste f nasal crest (1. am Gaumenbein; 2. am Oberkieferbein)
Nasen-Lippen-Falte f nasolabial fold
Nasen-Lippen-Plastik f rhinocheiloplasty
Nasenloch n nostril, orifice of the nose, naris
● [nur] ein ~ betreffend monorhinic
nasenlos arrhinic

Nasenlosigkeit

Nasenlosigkeit f arrhinia
Nasen-Mundhöhlen-Gang m incisive canal
Nasenmuschel f turbinate [bone], nasal concha
~/mittlere middle nasal concha, middle [nasal] turbinate
~/obere superior nasal concha, superior [nasal] turbinate
~/untere inferior nasal concha, inferior [nasal] turbinate, maxilloturbinal
Nasenmuschelleiste f turbinate crest
Nasenmuschelmesser n conchotome, turbinotome
Nasenmuschelresektion f turbinectomy, excision of the turbinate
Nasenmuschelschnitt m turbinotomy, conchotomy, incision into the turbinate
Nasenmuskel m nasalis [muscle]
Nasennaht f rhinorrhaphy
Nasennebenhöhle f [para]nasal sinus, air (accessory nasal) sinus
Nasennebenhöhleneingang m paranasal sinus ostium
Nasennebenhöhleneiterung f sinus suppuration
Nasennebenhöhlenentzündung f [naso]sinusitis
~ durch Luftdruckunterschiede barosinusitis
Nasennebenhöhlenerkrankung f sinus disease
Nasennebenhöhleneröffnung f[/operative] sinusotomy
Nasennebenhöhlenkarzinom n paranasal sinus carcinoma
Nasennebenhöhlenröntgen[kontrast]aufnahme f sinogram, paranasal sinus X-ray photograph
Nasennebenhöhlenröntgen[kontrast]darstellung f sinography
Nasenekrose f rhinonecrosis
Nasenneurose f rhinoneurosis, neurosis of the nose
Nasen-Oberkiefer-Naht f nasomaxillary suture
Nasenobstruktion f nasal obstruction
Nasenöffnung f nostril, orifice of the nose, naris
~/hintere (innere) choana, internal naris
Nasenoperation f/**plastische** rhinoplasty
Nasenparasit m nosoparasite
Nasenplastik f rhinoplasty
nasenplastisch rhinoplastic
Nasenpolyp m rhinopolyp, nasal polyp (Wucherung der Nasenschleimhaut)
Nasenpolypen mpl adenoids, adenoid vegetations (lymphatisches Gewebe im Nasenrachen)
Nasenpyramide f nasal pyramid
Nasenrachen m rhinopharynx, nasopharynx, epipharynx, nasal portion of the pharynx, postnasal space, pharyngonasal cavity
Nasenrachenabstrich m nasopharyngeal swab
Nasenrachenabstrichkultur f nasopharyngeal swab culture
Nasenrachenchondrom n chondroma of nasopharynx
Nasenrachenentzündung f s. Rhinopharyngitis
Nasenrachenexsudat n nasopharyngeal exudate
Nasenrachenfibroangiom n fibroangioma of the nasopharynx

Nasenrachenfibrom n nasopharyngeal fibroma
Nasenrachenflora f nasopharyngeal flora
Nasenrachenmesser n adenotome, lymphotome
Nasenrachenraum m s. Nasenrachen
Nasenrachenspiegel m nasopharyngoscope, salpingoscope
Nasenrachenspiegelung f nasopharyngoscopy, salpingoscopy, pharyngorhinoscopy, posterior rhinoscopy
Nasenrachenstein m rhinopharyngolith
Nasenrachen-Tamponadekatheter m nasopharyngeal haemostatic catheter
Nasen-Rachen-Tubus m nasotracheal tube
Nasenreflex m nasal reflex
Nasenregion f nasal region
Nasenrekonstruktion f nasal reconstruction
Nasenreservoir n nasal reservoir (der Bakterien)
Nasenrücken m nasal dorsum, bridge of the nose
Nasenrückenarterie f dorsal nasal artery
Nasenrückenlappen m dorsal nasal flap
Nasenrückenrotationslappen m dorsal nasal rotation flap
Nasenrückfluß m nasal regurgitation
Nasensäge f nasal saw
Nasensalbe f nose ointment
Nasenscheidewand f nasal septum ● **neben der** ~ paraseptal
~/knöcherne osteoseptum [of the nose]
~/knorpelige cartilaginous septum [of the nose]
~/membranöse membranous septum [of the nose], membranous part of the nasal septum, nasal membranous septum
Nasenscheidewandabszeß m nasal septal abscess
Nasenscheidewandchirurgie f nasal septal surgery
Nasenscheidewanddeviation f nasal septal deviation
Nasenscheidewanddickenmesser m septometer
Nasenscheidewanddurchtrennung f[/operative] septotomy
Nasenscheidewandentfernung f[/operative] septectomy
Nasenscheidewand-Hautplastik f nasal septal dermoplasty
Nasenscheidewandknorpel m nasal septal cartilage, septal cartilage of the nose, cartilaginous septum [of the nose]
Nasenscheidewandmesser m septometer
Nasenscheidewandmesser n septotome
Nasenscheidewandperforation f nasal septal perforation
Nasenscheidewandplastik f nasoseptoplasty
Nasenscheidewandrekonstruktion f septo[rhino]plasty
Nasenscheidewandschnitt m septotomy
Nasenscheidewandsenker m depressor septi nasi [muscle]
Nasenschleimhaut f nasal mucosa, mucous membrane of the nasal cavity

Nasenschleimhautabschwellung f nasal decongestion
Nasenschleimhautabschwellungsmittel n nasal decongestant [agent]
Nasenschleimhautabstrich m nasal smear
Nasenschleimhautanschwellung f nasal congestion
Nasenschleimhautentzündung f rhinitis, nasitis, coryza, nasal catarrh
Nasenschleimhauttrockenheit f xeromycteria, xerorhinia
Nasenschleimhaut- und Kehlkopf[schleimhaut]entzündung f rhinolaryngitis
Nasenschleimhaut- und Rachenentzündung f s. Rhinopharyngitis
Nasenschmarotzer m nosoparasite
Nasenschnitt m rhinotomy, incision into the nose
Nasensekret n nasal secretion (discharge)
~/eitriges purulent nasal discharge
Nasensekretion f nasal secretion
Nasenseptum n s. Nasenscheidewand
Nasenskelett n nasal skeleton
Nasenskelettprothese f nasoskeletal support
Nasenskelettstruktur f nasal skeletal structure
Nasensonde f nasal tube
Nasenspalte f/angeborene rhinoschisis
Nasenspekulum n s. Nasenspiegel
Nasenspezialist m rhinologist
Nasenspiegel m nasal speculum, nasoscope, rhinoscope, rhinoscopic mirror
Nasenspiegelung f nasoscopy, rhinoscopy
~/hintere pharyngorhinoscopy, posterior rhinoscopy
Nasenspitze f nasal tip, tip (apex) of the nose
Nasensprache f nasal voice, nasolalia, rhinolalia, rhinophonia
~/geschlossene closed nasolalia *(bei Verlegung oder Einengung der Nase)*
~/offene open rhinolalia *(bei mangelndem Verschluß des Nasenrachens)*
Nasenspritze f nasal syringe
Nasenspülung f rhinenchysis, nasal irrigation
Nasenstein m rhinolith, nasal calculus (concretion)
Nasensteinkrankheit f rhinolithiasis
Nasenstimme f nasal voice *(s. a.* Nasensprache*)*
Nasen-Stirnbein-Naht f nasofrontal suture
Nasentampon m rhinobyon, nasal plug
Nasentamponade f nasal tamponade, nasal plugging (packing)
Nasen-Tamponade-Rohr n nasal tamponade tube
Nasentrepan m, **Nasentrokar** m nasal trephine
Nasentropfen mpl nose drops, collunarium
Nasentuberkulom n tuberculoma of the nose
Nasentubus m nasal airway, rhinophore
Nasen- und Kehlkopfentzündung f rhinolaryngitis
Nasen- und Kehlkopflehre f rhinolaryngology
Nasen- und Kehlkopfschleimhautentzündung f rhinolaryngitis

Nasen- und Kehlkopfspezialist m rhinolaryngologist
Nasen- und Nasennebenhöhlenentzündung f rhinosinusitis
Nasen- und Nasennebenhöhlenerkrankung f rhinosinusopathy
Nasenuntersuchung f nose examination
~ mit dem Rhinoskop rhinoscopy
Nasenvereng[er]ung f rhinostenosis, stenomycteria, nasal stenosis
Nasenverkleinerung f/operative rhinomiosis
Nasenverlegung f nasal obstruction
Nasenvorhof m vestibule of the nose
Nasenvorhofshaar n vibrissa, rhinothrix
Nasenwege mpl nasal passages
Nasenwegsverlegung f nasal airway obstruction, rhinocleisis
Nasenwulst m/**lateraler** nasolateral process
~/medialer nasomedial process
Nasenwurzel f root of the nose
Nasenzerstörung f rhinonecrosis
Nasenzusammenbruch m nasal collapse *(z. B. bei Lepra)*
Nasion n nasion, nasal point *(anthropologischer Meßpunkt)*
Nasobasilarlinie f nasobasilar line
Nasofrontalfontanelle f nasofrontal fontanel
Nasofrontalnaht f nasofrontal suture
Nasolabialfalte f nasolabial crease (groove), melolabial crease
Nasolabiallinie f nasolabial (nasal) line
Nasolakrimalfurche f nasolacrimal groove
Nasolalia f s. Nasensprache
Nasomanometer n nasomanometer
nasomaxillär nasomaxillary
nasookzipital naso-occipital
nasopalatinal nasopalatine
Nasopalpebralreflex m nasopalpebral reflex
nasopharyngeal nasopharyngeal, epipharyngeal, rhinopharyngeal
Nasopharyngealflora f nasopharyngeal flora
Nasopharyngealtubus m nasopharyngeal tube
Nasopharyngitis f s. Rhinopharyngitis
Nasopharyngoskop n nasopharyngoscope
Nasopharyngoskopie f nasopharyngoscopy
Nasopharynx m s. Nasenrachen
Nasoskop n nasoscope
Nasoskopie f nasoscopy
Nasotrachealtubus m nasotracheal tube
Nässen n discharge, weeping *(von Wunden)*
nässend weeping, oozing, madescent, madidans; humectant
Naßerfrierung f der Füße immersion feet
Nässungsmittel n humectant [agent]
Nasus m nose, nasus *(s. a. unter* Nase*)*
~ aduncus hook nose
~ cartilagineus cartilaginous part of the nose
~ incurvus saddle[-back] nose, swayback nose
~ osseus bony [part of the] nose
~ simus pug nose
naszierend nascent
natal natal

Natalität

Natalität *f* natality
Nates *fpl* nates, clunes; buttocks, breech
nativ native, natural; inborn
Natriämie *f* natraemia
natriumausscheidend natriuretic
Natriumausscheidung *f* **im Urin** natriuria
natriumausschwemmend natriuretic
Natriumbarbiturat *n* sodium barbital *(Schlafmittel)*
Natriumchloridlösung *f* sodium chloride solution, solution of [common] salt
~/isotone isotonic sodium chloride solution
~/physiologische physiological salt solution
Natriummangelsyndrom *n* hyponatraemic syndrome
Natriumpentobarbital *n* sodium pentobarbital *(Schlafmittel)*
Natriumpumpe *f* sodium pump *(Membrantheorie)*
Natriumsalizylat *n* sodium salicylate
Natriumspiegelerhöhung *f* **im Blut** hypernatraemia
Natriumspiegelverminderung *f* **im Blut** hyponatraemia
~ im Blut/scheinbare pseudohyponatraemia
Natriumüberschußsyndrom *n* hypernatraemic syndrome
Natriumverarmung *f* sodium depletion
Natriuretikum *n* natriuretic agent
natriuretisch natriuretic
Naturheilkunde *f* physiatrics, physical medicine
Naturheilverfahren *n* naturopathy
natürlich native, natural; physical ● **auf natürlichem Wege** by the natural ways
Naturtrieb *m* [natural] instinct
Naturwidrigkeit *f* abnormalism, abnormality
Nausea *f* nausea, sicchasia, malaise
~ gravidarum morning sickness [of pregnancy]
~ marina (navalis) seasickness, naupathia
Nauseosum *n* remedium nauseant
Naviculare *n s.* Kahnbein
navikular navicular
Navikularfraktur *f* carpal scaphoid fracture
Navikular[spongiosa]schraube *f* [carpal] scaphoid screw *(bei Kahnbeinfraktur)*
nävoid naevoid, naeviform
Nävus *m s.* Naevus
nävusartig naevus-like, naevoid, naeviform
Nävusbasalzellenkarzinom *n* naevoid basal cell carcinoma
Nävuskarzinom *n* naevocarcinoma
Nävusmelanom *n* naevomelanoma
Nävuszyste *f* naevoid cyst
Nearthrose *f* ne[o]arthrosis, pseudarthrosis, supplementary articulation
Nebelsehen *n* nephelop[s]ia *(bei Hornhauttrübung)*
Nebenarterie *f* collateral artery
~ des Arms/mittlere medial collateral artery
~ des Arms/speichenseitige radial collateral artery

Nebenausführungsgang *m* **der Bauchspeicheldrüse** accessory pancreatic duct, Bernard's canal, duct of Santorini
Nebenbauchspeicheldrüse *f* accessory pancreas
Nebenbefund *m* secondary (accessory) findings
Nebenblatter *f* vaccinola
Nebendrüse *f* accessory gland
Nebeneierstock *m* parovarium, epoophoron, ovarian appendage
Nebeneierstockentzündung *f* parovaritis, paroophoritis, inflammation of the parovarium
nebeneinanderstellen[/sich] to juxtapose
Nebeneinanderstellung *f* juxtaposition
Nebenhirnanhang *m* parahypophysis, accessory pituitary body
Nebenhoden *m* epididymis, parorchis *(s. a.* Epididymis*)*
Nebenhodenanhängsel *n* epididymal appendage
Nebenhodenentfernung *f*/**operative** epididymectomy
Nebenhodenentzündung *f* epididymitis, inflammation of the epididymis
Nebenhodengang *m* epididymal duct, duct of the epididymis
Nebenhodengekröse *n* mesoepididymis
Nebenhodengrube *f* epididymal fossa
Nebenhoden-Hoden-Resektion *f* epididymo-orchi[d]ectomy
Nebenhodeninzision *f* epididymotomy
Nebenhodenkanal *m* canal of the epididymis
Nebenhodenkopf *m* head of the epididymis
Nebenhodenkörper *m* body of the epididymis
Nebenhodenläppchen *n* lobule of the epididymis
Nebenhodenresektion *f* epididymectomy
Nebenhoden-Samenleiter-Anastomose *f* epididymovasostomy
Nebenhodenschweif *m* tail of the epididymis
Nebenhodentuberkulose *f* tuberculosis of the epididymis
Nebenhoden- und Hodenentfernung *f*[/**operative**] epididymo-orchi[d]ectomy
Nebenhoden- und Hodenentzündung *f* epididymo-orchitis
Nebenhoden- und Samenstrangentfernung *f*[/**operative**] epididymodeferentectomy
Nebenhöhle *f s.* Nasennebenhöhle
Nebenkern *m* paranucleus, accessory nucleus
Nebenkörnchen *n* paranucleolus *(im Zellkern)*
Nebenkropf *m* accessory (aberrant) goitre
Nebenmagen *m* accessory stomach
Nebenmilz *f* accessory (supernumerary) spleen, splen[unc]ulus, lien[un]culus
Nebenniere *f* suprarenal (adrenal) gland, epinephros, paranephros ● **aus den Nebennieren stammend** adrenogenous
Nebennierenadenom *n* adrenal adenoma
Nebennierenaktivität *f* adrenal activity
Nebennierenangiographie *f* adrenal angiography
Nebennierenapoplexie *f* adrenal apoplexy, adrenal haemorrhage [syndrome], fulminating adrenal meningitis, Waterhouse-Fridrichsen syndrome, acute fulminating meningococcaemia, meningococcic adrenal syndrome

Nebennierenarterie f suprarenal artery
~/mittlere middle suprarenal artery
~/obere superior suprarenal artery
~/untere inferior suprarenal artery
Nebennierenblutung f/akute s. Nebennierenapoplexie
Nebennierendysfunktion f hypoadrenalism, adrenal insufficiency
Nebennierenentzündung f adrenalitis, hypernephritis, epinephritis, paranephritis
Nebennierenexstirpation f epinephrectomy, adrenalectomy, suprarenalectomy
nebennierenexstirpiert adrenalectomized
Nebennierenfunktionsstörung f adrenalism, suprarenalism
Nebenniereninsuffizienz f adrenal insufficiency, hyposuprarenalism
Nebennierenkrankheit f adrenalopathy, suprarenalopathy, disease of the adrenal gland
nebennierenlos adrenoprival
Nebennierenmark n adrenal (suprarenal) medulla
Nebennierenmarkhormon n adrenal medullary hormone
Nebennierennekrose f adrenal (suprarenal) necrosis
Nebennierenphlebographie f adrenal (suprarenal) phlebography, epinephro-phlebography
Nebennierenrand m/mittlerer medial margin of the suprarenal gland
Nebennierenrinde f adrenal (suprarenal) cortex, cortex of the suprarenal gland
Nebennierenrindenadenom n [adrenal] cortical adenoma, adrenal hypernephroma
Nebennierenrindenextrakt m adrenocortical (adrenal cortex) extract, cortin
Nebennierenrindengeschwulst f 1. adrenal cortical tumour, corticosupraren[al]oma; 2. Cushing's disease (syndrome)
Nebennierenrindenhormon n [adreno]cortical hormone, adrenal cortical hormone, [adreno]corticoid
Nebennierenrindenhormonausfall m/akuter acute adrenal failure, Addisonian crisis
Nebennierenrindenhyperplasie f adrenal cortical hyperplasia, Conn's syndrome
Nebennierenrindeninsuffizienz f adrenal cortical Insufficiency, Addison's disease (syndrome), hypoadrenalism, hypoadrenia
~/akute acute adrenal failure, Addisonian crisis
~/sekundäre Addisonism
Nebennierenrindenkarzinom n [adreno]cortical carcinoma, adrenal hypernephroma
Nebennierenrindenkrankheit f adrenal cortical disease
Nebennierenrindensteroid n adrenal corticosteroid (cortical steroid)
Nebennierenrindenszintigraphie f adrenal cortical scintigraphy
Nebennierenrindenüberfunktion f hyper[adreno]corticism, hyper[adrenal]corticalism, hypersuprarenalism, hyperadrenalism, hyperadrenia

Nebennierenrindenunterfunktion f hypo-[adreno]corticism, hypo[adrenal] corticalism, hyposuprarenalism, hypoadrenalism, hypoadrenia
nebennierenrindenwirksam adrenocorticotrophic
Nebennierenröntgen[kontrast]bild n adrenogram
Nebennierenröntgen[kontrast]darstellung f adrenography
Nebennierenstörung f adrenalism, suprarenalism
Nebennierentumor m adrenal tumour, paranephroma, supranephroma
Nebennierenüberfunktion f hyperadrenalism, hyperadrenia, hypersuprarenalism
Nebennierenunterfunktion f hypoadrenalism, hypoadrenia, hyposuprarenalism
Nebennierenvene f suprarenal vein
~/linke left suprarenal vein
~/rechte right suprarenal vein
Nebennierenvenenröntgendarstellung f adrenal phlebography, epinephro-phlebography
Nebennierenversagen n adrenal failure
~/akutes s. Nebennierenapoplexie
nebennierenwirksam adrenalotropic
Nebennierenzyste f adrenal cyst
Nebenohrspeicheldrüse f accessory parotid gland, admaxillary gland
Nebenplazenta f accessory (succenturiate) placenta
Nebenpocke f vaccinola
Nebenreaktion f side reaction
Nebenschilddrüse f parathyroid [gland], parathyroid (epithelial) body, Gley's (accessory thyreoid) gland
~/untere inferior parathyroid gland
Nebenschilddrüsenadenom n parathyroid adenoma
Nebenschilddrüsenentfernung f[/operative] parathyroidectomy, Mandl's operation
Nebenschilddrüsenextrakt m parathyroid extract
Nebenschilddrüsenfunktionsstörung f dysparathyroidism
Nebenschilddrüsengeschwulst f parastruma
Nebenschilddrüsengewebe n parathyroid tissue
Nebenschilddrüsenhormon n parathyroid hormone, parathormone
Nebenschilddrüsenhyperplasie f parathyroid hyperplasia
Nebenschilddrüseninsuffizienz f parathyroid insufficiency, hypoparathyroidism, hypoparathyreosis
Nebenschilddrüsenkapsel f parathyroid capsule
Nebenschilddrüsenkrankheit f parathyropathy
nebenschilddrüsenlos parathyroprival
Nebenschilddrüsentetanie f parathyroid tetany
Nebenschilddrüsenüberfunktion f hyperparathyroidism, hyperparathyreosis, parathyrotoxicosis

Nebenschilddrüsenunterfunktion 542

Nebenschilddrüsenunterfunktion f hypoparathyroidism, hypoparathyreosis
Nebenschluß m s. Shunt
Nebentränendrüse f accessory lobe of the lacrimal gland
Nebenweg m s. Shunt
Nebenwirkung f side effect (z. B. von Medikamenten)
Nebenwirt m reservoir host
Necator m **americanus** Necator americanus, American hookworm (Erreger der Ankylostomiasis)
Neck-Dissektion f neck [gland] dissection
Necrobiosis f **lipoidica diabeticorum** lipoid necrobiosis of diabetics
Neenzephalon n neencephalon, neoencephalon
Negativakkommodation f negative accommodation
Negativfärbung f negative staining (histologischer Präparate)
Negativismus m negativism
~/**passiver** passive negativism
nehmen:
~/**die Pille** to take the pill
~/**eine Probe** to sample
~/**Kokain** to cocainize
neigen 1. to incline; to tilt; 2. to lean, to tend, to be inclined; to be prone (susceptible)
~/**sich nach hinten** to retroflex
~/**zur Stuhlverstopfung** to admit to constipation
neigend:
~/**zu Krämpfen** spasmophilic
~/**zur Gicht** gouty
Neiger m pronator [muscle]
Neigung f 1. inclination (Anatomie); obliquity (z. B. eines Organs); version (z. B. der Gebärmutter); 2. tendency (z. B. zu Knochenbrüchen); addiction (Gewöhnung)
~ **zum Blutzuckeranstieg** glycophilia
~ **zum Fettansatz** lipophilia
~ **zum Rückwärtslaufen** retropulsion (z. B. bei Tabes dorsalis)
neigungsentsprechend catathymic
Neigungsmesser m inclinometer
Neigungswinkel m angle of inclination
Neisseria f Neisseria (gramnegative Diplokokke)
~ **gonorrhoea** Neisseria gonorrhoeae
~ **meningitidis** Neisseria meningitidis, meningococcus, Weichselbaum's coccus
Neisserieninfektion f neisserosis
Nekrektomie f necrectomy, escharotomy
nekrektomieren to necrectomize
Nekrobiose f necrobiosis (von einzelnen Zellen in einem Gewebeverband)
nekrobiotisch necrobiotic
nekrogen necrogenic, necrogenous; causing necrosis
Nekrohormon n necrohormone
Nekrolyse f necrolysis
Nekromanie f necromania
nekrophag necrophagic, necrophagous, subsiding on dead bodies

Nekrophagie f necrophagia (der Mikroorganismen)
nekrophil necrophilous
Nekrophilie f necrophilia, necrophilism
nekrophob necrophobe
Nekrophobie f necrophobia (krankhafte Angst vor dem Tod und vor Toten)
Nekropneumonie f necropneumonia, gangrene of the lung
Nekropsie f necropsy, necroscopy, autopsy, postmortem examination
Nekrose f necrosis (Tod von Zellen); mortification (s.a. unter Gangrän) ● **Nekrosen abtragen (ausräumen)** to necrectomize
~/**aseptische** aseptic (simple, quiet) necrosis
~/**blande** bland necrosis
~ **des Wirbelkörperknochenkerns** Calve's disease; Calve's vertebra plana
~/**fettige** steatonecrosis
~/**ischämische** ischaemic necrosis
~/**käsige** caseous (cheesy) necrosis
~/**nichtinfektiöse** non-infectious necrosis
~/**spontane** spontaneous necrosis
~/**trockene** dry necrosis, mummification
~/**zentrale** central necrosis
Nekroseabtragung f s. Nekrosenausräumung
nekrosebildend necrosis-creating
Nekrosebildung f sphacelation
Nekrosehormon n necrohormone
Nekrosenabstoßung f sloughing
Nekrosenausräumung f necrectomy
~ **aus dem Ohr** otonecrectomy
Nekrosepfropf m **des Furunkels** necrotic core of the furuncle
Nekrosin n necrosin (giftige Zellsubstanz)
Nekroskopie f necropsy, necroscopy
Nekrospermie f necro[zoo]spermia
nekrotisch necrotic, sphacelous, dead; gangrenous
nekrotisieren to necrose, to necrotize, to sphacelate
Nekrotisierung f sphacelation
Nekrotisierungsprozeß m necrotizing process
Nekrotoxin n necrotoxin, necrotizing factor
Nekrozoospermie f necro[zoo]spermia
Nekrozytose f necrocytosis
Nekrozytotoxin n necrocytotoxin
Nelson-Test m Nelson's test (serologischer Syphilisnachweis)
Nemathelminthe f nemathelminth, round worm
Nemathelminthiasis f nemathelminthiasis, infestation by round worms
Nematode f [intestinal] roundworm, [intestinal] nematode
Nematodenbefall m nematization, nematosis, nemathelminthiasis, infestation by nematodes
Nematodenendophthalmitis f nematode endophthalmitis
Nematodenmittel n nematocide [agent]
nematodentötend nematocide, nematicide
Nematodiasis f s. Nematodenbefall
Nematospermie f nematospermia

Nematozid nematocide *[agent]*
Neoadventitia *f* neoadventitia
neoarthrotisch nearthrotic
neoblastisch neoblastic
Neogenese *f* neogenesis
neogenetisch neogenetic
Neointima *f* neointima
Neokortex *m* neocortex *(stammesgeschichtlich junger Teil der Großhirnrinde)*
Neologismus *m* neologism *(z. B. bei Schizophrenie)*
Neomembran *f* neomembrane, false membrane
Neomyzin *n* neomycin *(Antibiotikum)*
neonatal neonatal, neonate
Neonatalblennorrhoe *f* neonatal blennorrhoea
Neonatologe *m* neonatologist
Neonatologie *f* neonatology, nepiology, nipiology *(Lehre vom Neugeborenen)*
Neopallium *n* neopallium
Neophilismus *m* neophilism, philoneism
Neophobie *f* neophobia, misoneism *(krankhafte Angst vor dem Neuen)*
Neophrenie *f* neophrenia
Neoplasie *f* neoplasia
Neoplasma *n* neoplasm, [new]growth, tumour *(Zusammensetzungen s. unter Tumor)*
Neoplasmabildung *f* neoplasia
neoplastisch neoplastic
Neostigmin *n* neostigmine *(parasympathikusstimulierendes Mittel)*
Neostriatum *n* neostriatum *(umfaßt Putamen und Nucleus caudatus)*
neovaskulär neovascular
Neovaskularisation *f* neovascularization
neovaskularisieren to neovascularize
Neozerebellum *n* neocerebellum *(stammesgeschichtlich junger Teil des Kleinhirns)*
Neozystostomie *f* neocystostomy
Nephelometer *n* nephelometer
Nephelometrie *f* nephelometry
nephelometrisch nephelometric
nephelop[isch] nephelopic
Nephelopsie *f* nephelopia *(bei Hornhauttrübung)*
Nephralgie *f* nephralgia, pain in the kidney
nephralgisch nephralgic
Nephratonie *f* nephratonia, atony of the kidney
Nephrauxe *f* nephrauxe, enlargement of the kidney
Nephrektasie *f* nephrectasia, dilatation (distention) of the kidney
Nephrektomie *f* nephrectomy, excision of the kidney *(s.a. unter Nierenentfernung)*
~/**bilaterale** bilateral nephrectomy
~/**intrakapsuläre** intracapsular nephrectomy
~/**partielle** partial nephrectomy
nephrektomieren to nephrectomize
Nephritis *f* nephritis, inflammation of the kidney, renal inflammation *(s.a. unter Nierenentzündung)*
~/**chronisch interstitielle** chronic interstitial nephritis
~/**chronisch parenchymatöse** chronic parenchymatous nephritis
~/**degenerative** degenerative nephritis
~/**fibröse** fibrous nephritis
~ **gravidarum** nephritis of pregnancy
~/**idiopathische** idiopathic nephritis
~/**lupoide** lupus nephritis
~/**megalozytäre interstitielle** megalocytic interstitial nephritis
nephritisch nephritic
nephritogen nephritogenic
Nephro... *s.a.* Nieren...
nephroabdominal nephroabdominal
Nephroblastom *n* nephroblastoma, Wilm's tumour, nephroblastic nephroma
Nephrodystrophie *f* nephrodystrophy, nephrosis, nephropathy
nephrogastrisch nephrogastric
nephrogen nephrogenic, nephrogenous
Nephrogenese *f* nephrogenesis
Nephrogramm *n* nephrogram
Nephrographie *f* nephrography
nephrographisch nephrographic
Nephrohydrose *f* nephrohydrosis, hydronephrosis
nephroid nephroid, kidney-shaped, reniform, resembling a kidney
Nephrokalzinose *f* nephrocalcinosis, renal calcinosis
Nephrokaps[ul]ektomie *f* nephrocaps[ul]ectomy, excision of the renal capsule
Nephrokapsulotomie *f* nephrocapsulotomy, incision of the renal capsule, renal capsulotomy
nephrokardial nephrocardiac
Nephrokarzinom *n* nephrocarcinoma, carcinoma of the kidney
nephrokolisch nephrocolic
Nephrokolopexie *f* nephrocolopexy
Nephrokoloptose *f* nephrocoloptosis
Nephrolith *m s.* Nierenstein
Nephrolithiasis *f s.* Nierensteinleiden
Nephrologe *m* nephrologist
Nephrologie *f* nephrology *(Lehre von der Niere und ihren Krankheiten)*
Nephrolyse *f* nephrolysis *(1. Nierenauflösung; 2. Nierenlösung aus Verwachsungen)*
Nephrolysin *n* nephrolysin
nephrolytisch nephrolytic
Nephrom *n* 1. nephroma, kidney tumour; 2. renal-cell carcinoma
~/**embryonales** embryonal nephroma, embryoma of the kidney, embryonal mixed tumour of the kidney
Nephromalazie *f* nephromalacia, softening of the kidney
Nephromegalie *f* nephromegaly, enlargement of the kidney
Nephron *n* nephron *(funktionelle Niereneinheit)*
Nephronbildung *f* nephrogenesis
Nephronophthise *f* nephronophthisis
Nephroparalyse *f* nephroparalysis, paralysis of the kidney

Nephropathie

Nephropathie f nephropathy, disease of the kidney, renal disease
Nephropathie-Taubheits-Syndrom n hereditary (familial haemorrhagic) nephritis, Alport's syndrome
nephropathisch nephropathic
Nephropexie f nephropexy, fixation of the kidney
Nephrophthise f nephrophthisis, nephrotuberculosis, renal tuberculosis
nephropoetisch nephropoietic
Nephropoietin n nephropoietin
Nephroptose f nephroptosis, downward displacement of the kidney; floating (wandering) kidney
Nephropyelitis f nephropyelitis, parenchymatous inflammation of the kidney
nephropyelitisch nephropyelitic
Nephropyelolithotomie f [nephro]pyelolithotomy, pelvilithotomy
Nephropyeloplastik f nephropyeloplasty
Nephrorrhagie f nephrorrhagia, haemorrhage from the kidney, renal haemorrhage
Nephrorrhaphie f nephrorrhaphy (1. Nierenanheftung; 2. Naht einer Nierenwunde)
Nephros m s. Niere
Nephrose f 1. nephrosis, nephropathy, nephrodystrophia, degenerative renal disease; 2. nephrotic syndrome
~/cholämische bile nephrosis
~/hämoglobinurische haemoglobinuric nephrosis
~ mit Nieren[parenchym]entzündung nephrosonephritis
~/myoglobinurische myoglobinuric nephrosis; crush kidney
Nephrosiderose f nephrosiderosis
Nephrosklerose f nephrosclerosis, renal sclerosis
~/arteriolāre (interkapilläre) intercapillary nephrosclerosis
Nephrosonephritis f nephrosonephritis
Nephrosplenopexie f nephrosplenopexy, fixation of the kidney and the spleen
Nephrostoma n nephrostomy
nephrostomal nephrostomal
Nephrostomie f nephrostomy
Nephrostomiedrain n(m) nephrostomy tube
Nephrostomiekatheter m nephrostomy catheter
nephrotisch nephrotic
Nephrotom n nephrotome, nephromere (embryonale Anlage der Harnorgane)
Nephrotomie f nephrotomy, incision into the kidney
~/lumbale lumbar nephrotomy
Nephrotomogramm n nephrotomogram, renal tomogram
Nephrotomographie f nephrotomography, renal tomography
nephrotomographisch nephrotomographic
Nephrotoxin n nephrotoxin
nephrotoxisch nephrotoxic
Nephrotoxizität f nephrotoxicity, renal toxicity

nephrotrop nephrotropic
Nephroureterektomie f nephro-ureterectomy
Nephroureterzystektomie f nephro-uretercystectomy
Nephrozele f nephrocele
Nephrozirrhose f s. Nierenschrumpfung
Nephrozystanastomose f nephrocystanastomosis
Nephrozystitis f nephrocystitis, inflammation of the kidney and the bladder
Nephrozystose f nephrocystosis
Nerv m nerve, nervus (s. a. unter Nervus und Nervi) ● **mehrere Nerven betreffend** polyneural, polyneuric ● **neben einem ~** paraneural ● **vom ~ weg** abnerval ● **von den Nerven ausgehend** neurogen[et]ic, neurogenous
~/afferenter afferent (esodic, centripetal) nerve
~/autonomer autonomic nerve
~/drucksenkender depressor [nerve]
~/efferenter efferent (exodic, centrifugal) nerve
~/gemischter mixed nerve
~/Jacobsonscher Jacobson's (tympanic) nerve
~/markhaltiger medullated nerve
~/markloser non-medullated nerve
~/motorischer motor nerve
~/parasympathischer parasympathetic nerve
~/peripherer peripheral nerve
~/pilomotorischer pilomotor nerve
~/pressorischer pressor nerve
~/sensibler (sensorischer) sensory nerve
~/somatischer somatic nerve
~/sympathischer sympathetic nerve
~/vasomotorischer vasomotor nerve
~/vegetativer autonomic nerve
nerval nerval, nervous
Nerven... s. a. Neuro...
Nervenachsenzylinder/durch den transaxonal
Nervenaffinität f neurotropism
nervenähnlich neuroid
Nervenaktionspotential n nerve action potential
Nervenanastomose f nerve anastomosis, neuroanastomosis
nervenartig neuroid
Nervenarzt m neurologist, neuropathist
Nervenauflösung f neurolysis
Nervenausdrehen n [neur]exeresis, exairesis
Nervenausreißung f neurorrhexis, avulsion (s. a. Nervenausdrehen)
Nervenausschaltung f enervation
Nervenausschneidung f neurectomy
Nervenbahn f nerve tract, neuron pathway, path[way]
~/efferente efferent nerve pathway, descending tract
Nervenbahnanastomose f neuroanastomosis
Nervenbahndurchtrennung f[/operative] tractotomy
Nervenbahnung f facilitation (z. B. für Reflexabläufe)
Nervenbehandlung f neurotherapy
Nervenbeschädigung f neurotrauma, wounding of a nerve

545 Nervenklemme

Nervenbildung f neurogenesis, neurogeny, formation of nerves
Nervenbiopsie f nerve biopsy
Nervenblockade f neural blockade, nerve anaesthesia (block), [infiltration] block anaesthesia
~/**infiltrative** infiltration block anaesthesia
~/**periphere** peripheral nerve blockage
Nervenbogen m neural arc
Nervenbündel n nerve bundle, [nerve] fascicle
Nervenbündelscheide f perineurium, lamellar sheath
nervendämpfend neuroplegic
Nervendegeneration f nerve degeneration
nervendegenerativ neurodegenerative
Nervendehnung f nerve stretching, neurotony neurectasia, neurodiastasis
Nervendekompression f nerve decompression
Nervendruckpunkt m painful (tender) point
Nervendruckreizung f pressure irritation of a nerve, neurothlipsis
Nervendurchtrennung f/**komplette** neurotmesis
~/**operative** neurotomy
Nerveneinpflanzung f[/**operative**] neurotization, implantation of nerves
Nerveneinsprossung f neuronal invasion (bei Wundheilung)
Nerveneintritt m nerve entry
Nervenendapparat m neuromuscular junction, peripheromittor (zur Übertragung der Erregung von der Nerven- auf die Muskelfaser)
Nervenendaufzweigung f end branch, endbrush, telodendr[i]on, teledendrite
Nervenendfaser f s. Nervenendigung
Nervenendigung f nerve ending, nerve terminal (termination), teleneurite
~/**freie** free nerve ending
~/**motorische** motor nerve terminal
~/**reizaufnehmende freie** interoceptor; peripheroceptor (z. B. an inneren Organen)
Nervenendkolben m end bulb
Nervenendorgan n end organ
Nervenentfernung f[/**operative**] s. Neurexhairese
Nervenentzündung f neuritis, inflammation of a nerve, neuraxitis, neurophlegmon (s. a. unter Neuritis) ● auf ~ beruhend neuritic
~/**allgemeine** panneuritis, general (multiple) neuritis
~ **bei Arsenvergiftung** arsenical polyneuropathy
~ **durch Strahlenwirkung** actinoneuritis; radioneuritis
~/**toxische** toxic neuritis
nervenentzündungshemmend antineuritic
Nervenernährung f neurotrophy, nutrition of nervous tissue
Nervenerregbarkeit f nerve excitability
Nervenerregungsleitung f nerve conduction
Nervenerschöpfung f enervation
Nervenerweichung f neuromalacia, softening of nerve tissue
Nervenextraktion f s. Neurexhairese

Nervenfaser f nerve fibre (filament), neurofibril, twing
~/**adrenerge** adrenergic nerve fibre
~/**marklose** Remak's fibre
~/**präganglionäre** preganglionic neuron
~/**sympathische** sympathetic fibre
nervenfaserartig neurofibrillar[y]
Nervenfaseratrophie f nerve fibre atrophy
Nervenfaseraxon n Remak's band
Nervenfaserbündel n fascicle, fasciculus
Nervenfäserchen n nerve filament
Nervenfasereinsprossung f neurotization
Nervenfaserentzündung f neurofibrositis
nervenfaserförmig neurofibrillar[y]
Nervenfasergeflecht n neuropil[e]; neurospongium
Nervenfaserschicht f nerve fibre layer
Nervenfieber n fleckfieber, fleck typhus
nervenförmig neuroid
Nervenfortsatz m [neur]axon, axis cylinder [process], neurite, nerve process, axial fibre
Nervenfortsatzentzündung f neuraxitis
Nervenfreilegung f neurolysis
Nervenfreßzelle f neuronophage
Nervenfunktion f nerve function
Nervenganglion n neuroganglion
Nervenganglionentzündung f neurogangli[on]-itis, inflammation of a neuroganglion
Nervengas n nerve gas
Nervengeflecht n neuroplexus, nerve plexus
~ **der äußeren Kopfarterie** external carotid plexus
~ **der hinteren Herzkranzarterie** posterior coronary plexus of the heart
~ **der inneren Kopfarterie** internal carotid plexus
~/**sympathisches** sympathetic plexus
nervengeflechtartig plexiform
Nervengeflechtexstirpation f plexectomy
Nervengewebe n nerve (nervous, neural) tissue
Nervengewebeauflösung f neurolysis, dissolution of nervous tissue
Nervengeweberegeneration f neuranagenesis, regeneration of nerve tissue
Nervengewebeverkalkung f neurosclerosis
Nervengewebeversprengung f neurectopia, displacement of nervous tissue
Nervengewebezerfall m neurolysis, dissolution of nervous tissue
Nervengewebezyste f neural cyst
Nervengift n neurotoxin
nervengiftig neurotoxic
Nervengiftigkeit f neurotoxicity
Nervenhäkchen n nerve hook (retractor)
Nervenheilkunde f neurology
nervenhemmend neuroinhibitory
Nervenhemmstoff m neuroinhibitor
Nervenhülle f s. Nervenscheide
Nervenimpuls m nerve (nervous, neural) impulse
Nervenkabeltransplantat n cable graft
Nervenkabeltransplantation f nerve grafting
Nervenkernlähmung f nuclear paralysis
Nervenklemme f nerve forceps

Nervenklinik

Nervenklinik f mental hospital
Nervenknoten m ganglion *(Zusammensetzungen s. unter Ganglion)*
nervenkrank neuropathic, neuropathologic[al]; neurothic
Nervenkranker m neuropath; neurotic
Nervenkrankheit f neuropathy, nervous (nerve) disease *(Zusammensetzungen s. unter Neuropathie)*
Nervenkreuzung f crossway; decussatio[n]
nervenlähmend neuroparalytic, neuroplegic
Nervenlähmung f neuroparalysis
Nervenleitgeschwindigkeit f nerve conduction speed (velocity)
Nervenleitung f nerve conduction
Nervenleitungsanosmie f afferent anosmia
Nervenleitungsbahn f s. Nervenbahn
Nervenleitungsstörung f nerve block
Nervenlepra f neural lepra (leprosy), leprous neuritis
Nervenmark n myelin[e]
nervenmarkauflösend myelinolytic
Nervenmarkauflösung f myel[in]olysis
Nervenmarkerkrankung f myelinopathy
Nervenmechanismus m neuromechanism
Nervenmesser n neurotome
Nervennaht f nerve suture, suture of a nerve, neurosuture, neurorrhaphy
~/paraneurale paraneural suture
Nervenplastik f neuroplasty *(zur Überbrückung von Nervendefekten)*
Nervenpotential n nerve potential, neuropotential; nerve energy
Nervenpräparation f neurolysis
Nervenpräparationsschere f nerve dissecting scissors
Nervenpunktion f neuronyxis, puncture of a nerve
Nervenquetschung f neurotripsy, crushing (bruising) of a nerve
Nervenregeneration f nerve regeneration
Nervenregulation f neuroregulation
Nervenreiz m nervous stimulus (impulse); nervous irritation
Nervenreizsyndrom n nerve entrapment syndrome
Nervenschädigung f neurotrauma, wounding of a nerve, axonotmesis
Nervenscheide f nerve (nervous, neural) sheath; epineurium; neurilem[m]a, neurolemma
Nervenscheidenentzündung f neurothecitis, adventital neuritis, perineuritis, inflammation of a nerve sheath
Nervenschmerz m s. Neuralgie
nervenschmerzartig neuralgiform
nervenschmerzstillend antineuralgic
Nervenschnitt m neurotomy
Nervenschock m nerve (nervous) shock
nervenschwach neurasthenic; nervous, aneuric; psychasthenic
Nervenschwäche f s. Neurasthenie
Nervensegment n neuromere, neurotome

Nervensegmentierung f neuromery
Nervenskalpell n neurotome
Nervenspeicher m neural store
Nervenstamm m nerve trunk
nervenstark neurosthenic
Nervenstärke f neurosthenia
nervenstärkend neurotonic, nerve-strengthening
Nervenstatus m state of neural symptoms, neurostatus
Nervenstimulation f nerve stimulation
Nervenstimulator m nerve stimulator
Nervenstörung f nerve (nervous) disturbance
Nervenstrang m nerve twing, nervous tract *(s. a. Nervenbahn)*
Nervenstreckung f neurotony, stretching of a nerve
Nervenstützgewebe n [neuro]glia
Nervensymptom n nerve (nervous) symptom
Nervensystem n nervous system ● *das ~ beeinflussend* neurotrop[h]ic, neurotrope; neurophilic ● *vom ~ ausgehend* neurogen[et]ic, neurogenous, neural
~/adrenerges adrenergic nervous system
~/autonomes autonomic (involuntary) nervous system, visceral (vegetative) nervous system, interofective system
~/parasympathisches parasympathetic nervous system, craniosacral [autonomic nervous] system *(Bestandteil des vegetativen Nervensystems)*
~/peripheres peripheral nervous system
~/somatisches somatic nervous system
~/sympathisches sympathetic nervous system, sympathicus, orthosympathetic system
~/vegetatives s. ~/autonomes
~/zentrales central nervous system, CNS, neuraxis, neural (cerebrospinal) axis
Nerventätigkeit f nerve (nervous) function
Nerventransplantat n nerve graft (transplant)
Nerventransplantation f nerve grafting (transplantation)
Nervenüberanstrengung f nerve (nervous) strain
Nervenüberträgerstoff m neurotransmitter, neurohumour
Nerven- und Augenspezialist m neuro-ophthalmologist
Nerven- und Blutgefäßentfernung f[/operative] angioneurectomy
nerven- und geisteskrank neuropsychopathic; neuropsychiatric
Nerven- und Geisteszustand m neurostatus
Nerven- und Gelenksymptomatik f neuroarthritism
Nerven- und Muskelentzündung f neuromyositis
Nerven- und Nervenwurzelentzündung f radiculoneuritis
Nerven- und Nervenwurzelerkrankung f radiculoneuropathy
Nerven- und Rückenmarkentzündung f s. Neuromyelitis
Nervenverbindung f[/operative] nerve anastomosis

Nervenverlagerung f neurectopia
Nervenverletzung f neurotrauma, axonotmesis, nerve injury (lesion)
Nervenverpflanzung f neuroplasty *(zur Überbrückung von Nervendefekten)*
Nervenversorgung f nerve supply, [nervous] innervation, neurotization *(eines Organs)*
~ **der Gewebe** neurotrophy
nervenwärts neuralward
Nervenwurzel f nerve root
~/**sensorische** sensory root
Nervenwurzelanästhesie f nerve root anaesthesia
Nervenwurzelarterie f radicular artery
Nervenwurzelblockade f nerve root block
Nervenwurzeldurchtrennung f[/operative] radicotomy, rhizotomy
Nervenwurzelentfernung f[/operative] radiculectomy, excision of a [spinal] nerve root
Nervenwurzelentzündung f radiculitis, inflammation of a nerve root
Nervenwurzelerkrankung f radiculopathy, disease of a nerve root
Nervenwurzelneuralgie f radiculalgia, neuralgia of a nerve root, radicular pain
Nervenwurzelreizung f nerve root irritation
Nervenwurzel- und Rückenmarkerkrankung f radiculomyelopathy
Nervenzelldegeneration f neuroabiotrophy
Nervenzelle f s. Neuron
Nervenzellen fpl/Cajalsche cells of Cajal
Nervenzellenauflösung f neurocytolysis
Nervenzellenentzündung f neuronitis, inflammation of neurons
Nervenzellenerkrankung f neuronopathy, disease of neurons
Nervenzellenfortsatz m neurite
Nervenzellenmitochondrium n neurosome
Nervenzellenphagozyt m neuronophage
Nervenzellenphagozytose f neuronophagy, neuronophagocytosis
Nervenzellenzerstörung f nerve cell destruction, neurocytolysis
Nervenzellenzytoplasmafortsatz m [neuro]dendrite, [neuro]dendron
Nervenzellgift n neurocytolysin
Nervenzellplasma n neuroplasm
Nervenzentrum n nerve centre
~/**sensorisches** sensorium, sensory nerve centre
Nervenzerfall m neurolysis, dissolution of nervous tissue
Nervenzusammenbruch m nervous breakdown
Nervi mpl:
~ **alveolares superiores** superior alveolar nerves
~ **cardiaci thoracici** cardiac thoracic nerves
~ **cavernosi clitoridis** cavernous nerves of the clitoris
~ **cavernosi penis** cavernous nerves of the penis
~ **cervicales** cervical nerves
~ **ciliares breves** short ciliary nerves
~ **ciliares longi** long ciliary nerves
~ **clunium inferiores** inferior cluneal nerves
~ **clunium medii** medial cluneal nerves
~ **clunium superiores** superior cluneal nerves
~ **digitales dorsales nervi radialis** dorsal digital nerves of the radial nerve
~ **digitales dorsales nervi ulnaris** dorsal digital nerves of the ulnar nerve
~ **digitales dorsales pedis** dorsal digital nerves of the foot
~ **digitales palmares communes nervi mediani** common palmar digital nerves of the median nerve
~ **digitales palmares communes nervi ulnaris** common palmar digital nerves of the ulnar nerve
~ **digitales palmares proprii nervi mediani** proper palmar digital nerves of the median nerve
~ **digitales palmares proprii nervi ulnaris** proper palmar digital nerves of the ulnar nerve
~ **digitales plantares communes nervi plantaris lateralis** common plantar digital nerves of the lateral plantar nerve
~ **digitales plantares communes nervi plantaris medialis** common plantar digital nerves of the medial plantar nerve
~ **haemorrhoidales medii** middle haemorrhoidal nerves
~ **haemorrhoidales superiores** superior haemorrhoidal nerves
~ **labiales anteriores** anterior labial nerves
~ **labiales posteriores** posterior labial nerves
~ **lumbales** lumbar nerves
~ **perinei** perineal nerves
~ **phrenici accessorii** accessory phrenic nerves
~ **pterygopalatini** pterygopalatine nerves
~ **rectales inferiores** inferior rectal nerves
~ **sacrales** sacral nerves
~ **scrotales anteriores** anterior scrotal nerves
~ **scrotales posteriores** posterior scrotal nerves
~ **splanchnici lumbales** lumbar splanchnic nerves
~ **splanchnici pelvini** pelvic splanchnic nerves
~ **splanchnici sacrales** sacral splanchnic nerves
~ **supraclaviculares laterales** lateral supraclavicular nerves
~ **supraclaviculares mediales** medial supraclavicular nerves
~ **terminales** terminal nerves
~ **thoracales anteriores** anterior thoracic nerves
~ **thoracales posteriores** posterior thoracic nerves
~ **thoracici** thoracic nerves
~ **vaginales** vaginal nerves
nervös 1. nervous, restless; 2. nervous, irritable, excitable
Nervosität f 1. nervousness, nervosity, restlessness; 2. nervousness, irritability, morbid excitability
Nervus m nerve, nervus *(s. a. unter* Nerv *und* Nervi*)*
~ **abducens** abducent nerve, cranial nerve VI, sixth cranial nerve

Nervus

- ~ **accelerans** accelerator nerve
- ~ **accessorius** [spinal] accessory nerve, cranial nerve XI, eleventh cranial nerve
- ~ **acusticus** s. ~ vestibulocochlearis
- ~ **alveolaris inferior (mandibularis)** inferior alveolar (dental) nerve
- ~ **ampullaris anterior** anterior ampullary nerve
- ~ **ampullaris lateralis** lateral ampullary nerve
- ~ **ampullaris posterior** posterior ampullary nerve
- ~ **auricularis magnus** great auricular nerve
- ~ **auricularis posterior** posterior auricular nerve
- ~ **auriculotemporalis** auriculotemporal nerve
- ~ **axillaris** axillary (circumflex) nerve
- ~ **buccalis** buccal nerve
- ~ **canalis pterygoidei** nerve of the pterygoid canal, Vidian nerve
- ~ **cardiacus** cardiac nerve
- ~ **cardiacus cervicalis inferior** inferior cervical cardiac nerve
- ~ **cardiacus cervicalis medius** middle cervical cardiac nerve
- ~ **cardiacus cervicalis superior** superior cervical cardiac nerve
- ~ **caroticotympanicus inferior** inferior caroticotympanic nerve
- ~ **caroticotympanicus superior** superior caroticotympanic nerve
- ~ **caroticus externus** external carotid nerve
- ~ **caroticus internus** internal carotid nerve
- ~ **cavernosus clitoridis major** greater cavernous nerve of the clitoris
- ~ **cavernosus penis major** greater cavernous nerve of the penis
- ~ **cerebralis** cerebral nerve
- ~ **ciliaris** ciliary nerve
- ~ **coccygeus** coccygeal nerve
- ~ **cochleae** cochlear nerve
- ~ **cranialis** cranial nerve
- ~ **cranialis I** s. ~ olfactorius
- ~ **cranialis II** s. ~ opticus
- ~ **cranialis III** s. ~ oculomotorius
- ~ **cranialis IV** s. ~ trochlearis
- ~ **cranialis V** s. ~ trigeminus
- ~ **cranialis VI** s. ~ abducens
- ~ **cranialis VII** s. ~ facialis
- ~ **cranialis VIII** s. ~ vestibulocochlearis
- ~ **cranialis IX** s. ~ glossopharyngeus
- ~ **cranialis X** s. ~ vagus
- ~ **cranialis XI** s. ~ accessorius
- ~ **cranialis XII** s. ~ hypoglossus
- ~ **cutaneus antebrachii lateralis** lateral cutaneous nerve of the forearm, lateral antebrachial cutaneous nerve
- ~ **cutaneus antebrachii medialis** medial cutaneous nerve of the forearm, medial antebrachial cutaneous nerve
- ~ **cutaneus antebrachii posterior** posterior cutaneous nerve of the forearm, posterior antebrachial cutaneous nerve
- ~ **cutaneus antebrachii ulnaris** s. ~ cutaneus antebrachii medialis
- ~ **cutaneus brachii lateralis inferior** inferior lateral brachial cutaneous nerve
- ~ **cutaneus brachii lateralis superior** superior lateral brachial cutaneous nerve
- ~ **cutaneus brachii medialis** medial cutaneous nerve of the arm, medial brachial cutaneous nerve
- ~ **cutaneus brachii posterior** posterior brachial cutaneous nerve
- ~ **cutaneus brachii ulnaris** s. ~ cutaneus brachii medialis
- ~ **cutaneus dorsalis intermedius** intermediate dorsal cutaneous nerve of the foot
- ~ **cutaneus dorsalis lateralis** lateral dorsal cutaneous nerve of the foot
- ~ **cutaneus dorsalis medialis** medial dorsal cutaneous nerve of the foot
- ~ **cutaneus femoris lateralis** lateral cutaneous nerve of the thigh, lateral femoral cutaneous nerve
- ~ **cutaneus femoris medialis** medial cutaneous nerve of the thigh, medial femoral cutaneous nerve
- ~ **cutaneus femoris posterior** posterior cutaneous nerve of the thigh, posterior femoral cutaneous nerve
- **cutaneus surae lateralis** lateral cutaneous nerve of the calf, lateral sural cutaneous nerve
- ~ **cutaneus surae medialis** medial sural cutaneous nerve
- ~ **depressor** depressor [nerve]
- ~ **depressor cordis** depressor [nerve] of the heart
- ~ **dorsalis clitoridis** dorsal nerve of the clitoris
- ~ **dorsalis penis** dorsal nerve of the penis
- ~ **dorsalis scapulae** dorsal scapular nerve
- ~ **ethmoidalis anterior** anterior ethmoid nerve
- ~ **ethmoidalis posterior** posterior ethmoid nerve
- ~ **facialis** facial nerve, cranial nerve VII, seventh cranial nerve
- ~ **femoralis** femoral nerve
- ~ **frontalis** frontal nerve
- ~ **genitofemoralis** genitofemoral nerve
- ~ **glossopalatinus** glossopalatine nerve
- ~ **glossopharyngeus** glossopharyngeal nerve, cranial nerve IX, ninth cranial nerve
- ~ **glutaeus inferior** inferior gluteal nerve
- ~ **glutaeus superior** superior gluteal nerve
- ~ **hypogastricus** hypogastric nerve
- ~ **hypoglossus** hypoglossal nerve, hypoglossus, cranial nerve XII, twelfth cranial nerve
- ~ **iliohypogastricus** iliohypogastric nerve
- ~ **ilioinguinalis** ilioinguinal nerve
- ~ **infraorbitalis** infra-orbital nerve
- ~ **infratrochlearis** infratrochlear nerve
- ~ **intercostalis** intercostal nerve
- ~ **intercostobrachialis** intercostobrachial nerve
- ~ **intermedius** intermedius [nerve], glossopalatine nerve
- ~ **interosseus antebrachii anterior** anterior interosseous nerve of the forearm

- ~ **interosseus antebrachii posterior** posterior interosseous nerve of the forearm
- ~ **interosseus cruris** crural interosseous nerve
- ~ **ischiadicus** ischiadic (sciatic) nerve
- ~ **jugularis** jugular nerve
- ~ **lacrimalis** lacrimal nerve
- ~ **laryngeus inferior** inferior laryngeal nerve
- ~ **laryngeus recurrens** recurrent laryngeal nerve
- ~ **laryngeus superior** superior laryngeal nerve
- ~ **lingualis** lingual nerve
- ~ **lumboinguinalis** lumboinguinal nerve
- ~ **mandibularis** mandibular nerve
- ~ **massetericus** masseteric nerve
- ~ **masticatorius** masticator nerve
- ~ **maxillaris** maxillary nerve
- ~ **meatus acustici (auditorii) externi** external acoustic meatal nerve
- ~ **medianus** median nerve
- ~ **mentalis** mental nerve
- ~ **musculocutaneus** musculocutaneous nerve of the arm, perforans gasseri [nerve]
- ~ **mylohyoideus** mylohyoid nerve
- ~ **nasociliaris** nasociliary nerve
- ~ **nasopalatinus [Scarpae]** nasopalatine nerve
- ~ **obturatorius** obturator nerve
- ~ **occipitalis major** greater (major) occipital nerve
- ~ **occipitalis minor** lesser (minor) occipital nerve, third occipital nerve
- ~ **octavus** s. ~ vestibulocochlearis
- ~ **oculomotorius** oculomotor nerve, cranial nerve III, third cranial nerve
- ~ **olfactorius** olfactory nerve, cranial nerve I, first cranial nerve
- ~ **ophthalmicus** ophthalmic nerve *(erster Ast des Nervus trigeminus)*
- ~ **opticus** optic nerve, cranial nerve II, second cranial nerve
- ~ **palatinus major** greater (major) palatine nerve
- ~ **parasympathicus** s. ~ vagus
- ~ **pectoralis medialis** medial pectoral nerve
- ~ **peronaeus communis** common peroneal nerve, lateral (external) popliteal nerve
- ~ **peronaeus profundus** deep peroneal nerve
- ~ **peronaeus superficialis** superficial peroneal nerve
- ~ **petrosus** petrosal nerve
- ~ **petrosus major** greater [superficial] petrosal nerve
- ~ **petrosus minor** lesser [superficial] petrosal nerve
- ~ **petrosus profundus** deep petrosal nerve
- ~ **petrosus superficialis major** s. ~ petrosus major
- ~ **petrosus superficialis minor** s. ~ petrosus minor
- ~ **phrenicus** phrenic nerve
- ~ **plantaris fibularis (lateralis)** lateral plantar nerve
- ~ **plantaris medialis** medial plantar nerve
- ~ **pneumogastricus** s. ~ vagus
- ~ **pterygoideus externus (lateralis)** lateral pterygoid nerve
- ~ **pterygoideus medialis** medial pterygoid nerve
- ~ **pterygopalatinus** sphenopalatine nerve
- ~ **pudendus** pudendal nerve
- ~ **radialis** radial (musculospiral) nerve
- ~ **saccularis** saccular nerve
- ~ **saphenus** saphenous nerve
- ~ **sphenopalatinus** sphenopalatine nerve
- ~ **spinalis** spinal nerve
- ~ **spinosus** spinosal nerve
- ~ **splanchnicus** splanchnic nerve
- ~ **splanchnicus imus** lowest splanchnic nerve
- ~ **splanchnicus major** greater splanchnic nerve
- ~ **splanchnicus minor** lesser splanchnic nerve
- ~ **stapedius** stapedius nerve
- ~ **statoacusticus** s. ~ vestibulocochlearis
- ~ **subclavius** subclavian nerve
- ~ **subcostalis** subcostal nerve
- ~ **sublingualis** sublingual nerve
- ~ **suboccipitalis** suboccipital nerve
- ~ **subscapularis** subscapular nerve
- ~ **supraclavicularis** supraclavicular nerve
- ~ **supraorbitalis** supra-orbital nerve
- ~ **suprascapularis** suprascapular nerve
- ~ **supratrochlearis** supratrochlear nerve
- ~ **suralis** sural (short saphenous) nerve
- ~ **sympathicus** sympathetic nerve, thoracolumbar autonomic nervous system
- ~ **temporalis profundus** deep temporal nerve
- ~ **thoracicus longus** long thoracic nerve [of Bell]
- ~ **thoracodorsalis** thoracodorsal nerve
- ~ **tibialis** tibial (medial popliteal) nerve
- ~ **transversus colli** transverse nerve of the neck
- ~ **trigeminus** trigeminal (trifacial) nerve, trigeminus, cranial nerve V, fifth cranial nerve
- ~ **trochlearis** trochlear nerve, patheticus, cranial nerve IV, fourth cranial nerve
- ~ **tympanicus** tympanic (Jacobson's) nerve
- ~ **ulnaris** ulnar (cubital) nerve, musician's nerve
- ~ **utricularis** utricular nerve
- ~ **utriculoampullaris** utriculoampullary nerve
- ~ **vagus** vagus [nerve], pneumogastric (parasympathetic) nerve, cardiac inhibitory nerve, cranial nerve X, tenth cranial nerve
- ~ **vertebralis** vertebral nerve
- ~ **vestibularis** vestibular nerve, vestibular branch of the auditory nerve
- ~ **vestibulocochlearis** vestibulocochlear nerve, acoustic (auditory) nerve, cranial nerve VIII, eighth cranial nerve
- ~ **Vidianus** Vidian nerve
- ~ **zygomaticus** zygomatic nerve

Nesselfieber n, **Nesselsucht** f s. Urtikaria
Netz n 1. net, rete *(z. B. von Kapillargefäßen) (Zusammensetzungen s. unter Rete)*; reticulum, fine network *(z. B. des Protoplasmas)*; 2. s. Omentum
Netz... s. a. Omentum...
Netzabdeckung f omental overcoat *(z. B. bei Blinddarmperforation)*
Netzabtragung f oment[um]ectomy, epiploectomy
Netzanheftung f[/operative] omentopexy, omentofixation, epiplopexy

Netzansatz

Netzansatz *m* omental taenia, attachment of the omentum
netzartig reticular, retiform, reticulated, reticulose
Netzbeutel *m* 1. omental bursa, bursa omentalis, bursa of the omentum, lesser peritoneal cavity, lesser sac [of the peritoneum] *(Bauchfelltasche zwischen Leber und Magen)*; 2. omental sac
Netzbeuteleingang *m* epiploic foramen [of Winslow], Winslow's foramen
Netzbeutelentfernung *f*[/operative] bursectomy
Netzbeutelöffnung *f s.* Netzbeuteleingang
Netzbruch *m* omental hernia, omentocele, epiplocele
Netzdeckung *f* omental patching *(bei chirurgischem Eingriff)*
Netzeinklemmung *f* omental incarceration
Netzeinschnitt *m s.* Omentotomie
Netzentfernung *f/operative s.* Omentektomie
Netzentzündung *f* omentitis, inflammation of the omentum, epiploitis
Netzfixierung *f* omentopexy, omentofixation, epiplopexy
netzförmig retiform, reticulated, reticulose
Netzhaut *f* retina, optomeninx ● **unter der** ~ subretinal
Netzhaut... *s. a.* Retina...
Netzhautabbild *n* optogram, retinal image
Netzhautabbildung *f/anomale* abnormal retinal correspondence, binocular false projection
Netzhautabhebung *f s.* Netzhautablösung
Netzhautablösung *f* retinal detachment (non-attachment), detachment (separation) of the retina
~ **durch Netzhauteinriß** rhegmatogenous retinal detachment
~/**periphere** retinodialysis
Netzhautaktionsstromaufzeichnung *f* electroretinography
Netzhautaktionsstromkurve *f* electroretinogram, ERG
Netzhautaneurysma *n* retina aneurysma
Netzhautangiom *n* angioma of the retina
Netzhautangiomatose *f* retinal (cerebelloretinal) angiomatosis, Hippel-Lindau disease
Netzhautanheftung *f* retinopexy; retinal re-attachment
~/**kryochirurgische** retinal cryopexy, cryoretinopexy
Netzhautapoplexie *f* retinal apoplexy
Netzhautarterie *f* [central] retinal artery, central artery of the retina
Netzhautarterienspasmus *m* retinal artery spasm
Netzhautarterienvereng[er]ung *f* retina arteriolar narrowing
Netzhautarteriole *f* retina arteriole
netzhautartig retinoid
Netzhautassoziationszelle *f* retina amacrine cell
Netzhautasthenopie *f* retinal asthenopia
Netzhautatrophie *f* retina (retinal) atrophy, neurodeatrophia
Netzhautauflösungsvermögen *n* resolving power of the retina
Netzhautaufspaltung *f* retinoschisis
Netzhautbefund *m* retinal findings
Netzhautbild *n* 1. optogram, retinal (ocular) image; 2. retinogram
Netzhautblutung *f* retinal haemorrhage
Netzhautdarstellung *f* retinography
Netzhautdegeneration *f* retinal (retina lattice) degeneration
~/**senile** retinal senile degeneration
~/**zystische** retinal cystic degeneration
Netzhautdurchblutung *f* retina blood flow
Netzhautdysplasie *f* retinal dysplasia
Netzhautdystrophie *f*/**pigmentäre** retinal pigmentary dystrophy
Netzhautempfindlichkeitsstörung *f* photoparaesthesia *(durch Licht)*
Netzhautentzündung *f* retinitis, inflammation of the retina *(s. a. unter Retinitis)*
~/**diabetische** diabetic retinitis (retinopathy)
Netzhauterkrankung *f* retinopathy, disease of the retina, retinal disease *(Zusammensetzungen s. unter Retinopathie)*
Netzhautermüdung *f* retinal fatigue
Netzhauterweichung *f* retinomalacia, softening of the retina
Netzhautexsudat *n* retinal exudate
Netzhautfalte *f* retinal fold
Netzhautfaser *f* retinal fibre
Netzhautfibroplasie *f* retinal fibroplasia
Netzhautfixation *f* retinopexy; retinal re-attachment
Netzhautfluoreszeinangiographie *f* retinal fluorescein angiography
Netzhautfotografie *f* retinography
Netzhautganglienzelle *f* retinal ganglion cell
~/**bipolare** retinal bipolar ganglion cell
Netzhautganglienzellschicht *f* retinal ganglion cell layer
Netzhautganglion *n* retinal ganglion
Netzhautgefäß *n* retinal blood vessel
netzhautgefäßdarstellend angioretinographic
Netzhautgefäßentzündung *f* retinal vasculitis
Netzhautgefäßerkrankung *f* retinal vascular disease
Netzhautgefäßröntgen[kontrast]bild *n* angioretinogram
Netzhautgefäßröntgen[kontrast]darstellung *f* angioretinography
Netzhautgefäßsystem *n* retinal vascular system
Netzhautgefäßverschluß *m* retinal blood vessel occlusion
Netzhautgeschwulst *f* retinal tumour
Netzhautgliagewebe *n* retinal glial tissue
Netzhautgliom *n* retinal glioma
Netzhauthorizontal[nerven]zelle *f* retinal horizontal nerve cell
Netzhautischämie *f* retinal ischaemia
Netzhautkapillare *f* retinal capillary
Netzhautkapillarerweiterung *f* retinal capillary dilatation

Netzhautkoagulator *m* retinal coagulator
Netzhautkolobom *n* retinal coloboma, coloboma of the retina
Netzhautkorrespondenz *f* retinal correspondence
~/anomale anomalous retinal correspondence, ARC
~/normale normal retinal correspondence, NRC
Netzhautläsion *f* retinal wound (injury, lesion)
Netzhautnachbild *n* photogene
Netzhautnekrose *f* retinal necrosis
Netzhautneovaskularisierung *f* retinal neovascularization
Netzhautneuroepitheliom *n* retinal neuroepithelioma
Netzhautneuroepithelschicht *f* retinal neuroepithelial layer
Netzhautoberfläche *f* retinal surface
Netzhautödem *n* retinal oedema
Netzhautperforation *f* retinal perforation
Netzhautperiphlebitis *f* retinal periphlebitis
Netzhautperivaskulitis *f* retinal perivasculitis
Netzhautphotorezeptor *m* retinal photoreceptor
Netzhautphysiologie *f* retinal physiology
Netzhautpigment *n* retinal pigment
Netzhautpigmentation *f* retinal pigmentation
Netzhautpigmentepithel *n* retinal pigment epithelium
Netzhautpigmentepithelentzündung *f* retinal pigment epitheliitis
Netzhautpigmentepithelerkrankung *f* retinal pigment epitheliopathy
Netzhautpigmentepithelzelle *f* retinal epithelial cell
Netzhautprojektion *f* retinal projection
Netzhautreflex *m* retinal (red) reflex
Netzhautrezeptor *m* retinal receptor
Netzhautriß *m* retinal break, retinal hole (tear)
Netzhautrivalität *f* retinal rivalry
Netzhautschädigung *f* **durch Chlorochin** chloroquine retinopathy
Netzhautschmerz *m* neurodealgia, pain in the retina
Netzhautschwellung *f* retinal swelling
Netzhautsiderose *f* retinal siderosis
Netzhautstäbchen *n* [retinal] rod
Netzhautstreifen *mpl/***gefäßähnliche** angioid streaks
Netzhautteleangiektasie *f* retinal teleangiectasia
Netzhauttrübung *f/***ödemartige** Berlin's disease *(partiell oder total)*
Netzhaut- und Aderhautentzündung *f* chorioretinitis
Netzhaut- und Aderhauterkrankung *f* chorioretinopathy
Netzhaut- und Aderhautvernarbung *f* chorioretinal scarring
Netzhaut- und Sehnervenpapillenentzündung *f* retinopapillitis, inflammation of the retina and the optic papilla
Netzhautunterblutung *f* subretinal haemorrhage
Netzhautvene *f* [central] retinal vein, central vein of the retina

Netzhautvenenstase *f* retinal venous stasis
Netzhautvenenthrombose *f* retinal vein thrombosis
Netzhautvenenverschluß *m* retinal vein occlusion
Netzhautwiederanlegung *f* re-attachment of the retina
Netzhautzapfen *m* [retinal] cone
Netzhautzapfendegeneration *f* retinal cone degeneration
Netzhautzelle *f* retinal cell
~/amakrine retina amacrine cell
~/bipolare retinal bipolar ganglion cell
Netzhautzentralarterie *f s.* Netzhautarterie
Netzhautzentralvene *f s.* Netzhautvene
Netzhautzerreißung *f* retinal rupture
Netzhautzerstörung *f* retinal destruction
Netzhernie *f* omental hernia, omentocele, epiplocele
Netzkörperchen *n* dictyosome *(Teil des Golgi-Apparats)*
netzlos anepiploic
Netzmittel *n* wetting agent
Netznaht *f* omentorrhaphy, suture of the omentum, epiplorrhaphy
Netzplastik *f* 1. omentoplasty, epiploplasty, omental graft[ing]; 2. meshgraft *(bei Hauttransplantation)*
Netzresektion *f s.* Omentektomie
Netzschnitt *m s.* Omentotomie
Netztransplantat *n* 1. omental graft; 2. meshgraft
Netz- und Milzfixation *f* omentosplenopexy, fixation of the omentum and the spleen
Netzvenole *f* omental venule
Netzverdrehung *f* torsion of the omentum
Netzvolvulus *m* omentovolvulus, volvulus of the omentum
Netzwerk *n* network, reticulum, lattice *(z. B. von Fasern)*
Neuansteckung *f* reinfection
neubildend regenerative
Neubildung *f* 1. regeneration *(z. B. von Organen)*; 2. neoplasm, new growth, tumour
~/organähnliche homoeoplasia
Neudifferenzierung *f* redifferentiation *(z. B. von Gewebe)*
Neufeld-Kapselquellungsreaktion *f* Neufeld quellung test *(Färbungsreaktion für die Pneumokokkentypisierung)*
neugeboren newborn
Neugeborenenanoxie *f* anoxia of the newborn
Neugeborenenapoplexie *f* neonatal apoplexy
Neugeborenenasphyxie *f* asphyxia of the newborn, blue asphyxia
Neugeborenenatelektase *f* congenital atelectasis, atelectasis of the newborn
Neugeborenenatemnotsyndrom *n* idiopathic respiratory distress of the newborn, postnatal asphyxia atelectasis
Neugeborenendiarrhoe *f* diarrhoea of the newborn

Neugeboreneneinschlußkonjunktivitis

Neugeboreneneinschlußkonjunktivitis f neonatal blennorrhoea
Neugeborenenerythroblastose f haemolytic disease of the newborn
Neugeborenengonoblennorrhoe f neonatal ophthalmic gonorrhoeal infection, gonorrhoeal conjunctivitis of the newborn
Neugeborenenhornhauttrübung f embryotoxon
Neugeborenenhyperbilirubinämie f/**idiopathische** congenital familial non-haemolytic jaundice, Crigler-Najjar syndrome
Neugeborenenikterus m newborn jaundice, jaundice of the newborn
~/**physiologischer** physiological jaundice of the newborn, paedicterus
~/**schwerer** icterus gravis neonatorum (bei Rh-Inkompatibilität)
Neugeborenenintensivpflege f neonatal intensive care
Neugeborenenintensivtherapieeinheit f neonatal intensive care unit
Neugeborenenkropf m goitre of the newborn
Neugeborenenmorbidität f newborn morbidity
Neugeborenenmord m neonaticide
Neugeborenenmörder m neonaticide
Neugeborenenmyasthenie f neonatal myasthenia
Neugeborenenödem n oedema of the newborn, congenital oedema
Neugeborenenophthalmie f newborn ophthalmia
Neugeborenenpemphigoid n neonatal pemphigoid
Neugeborenenperiode f neonatal period
Neugeborenenpflege f newborn nursery (care)
Neugeborenenrhinitis f rhinitis of the newborn, stuffy nose syndrome
Neugeborenensepsis f neonatal septicaemia, Winckel's disease
Neugeborenensklerödem n neonatal oedema
Neugeborenenspezialist m neonatologist
Neugeborenensterblichkeit f newborn mortality
Neugeborenensterblichkeitsrate f newborn mortality rate
Neugeborenensubduralhämatom n neonatal subdural haemorrhage
Neugeborenentetanus m neonatal tetanus, tetanus infantum (neonatorum); tetany of the newborn
Neugeborenentod m neonate death
Neugeborenentripper m s. Neugeborenengonoblennorrhoe
Neugeborenenunterhautfettgewebsnekrose f subcutaneous necrosis of the newborn, subcutaneous fat necrosis
Neugeborenenvermessung f paedometry
Neugeborenenwassersucht f s. Neugeborenenödem
Neugeborenes n newborn [child], neonate, neonatus
~/**künstliches** manikin (zum Erlernen geburtshilflicher Handgriffe)
~/**reifes** near-term neonate
~/**übergewichtiges** heavy-for-date newborn
Neuhirn n neencephalon, neoencephalon
Neuner-Regel f [nach Wallace] [Wallace's] rule of nines (zur Bestimmung der Verbrennungsfläche)
Neuntgebärende f nonipara
Neur... s. a. Nerven...
neural neural
Neuralektoderm n neural ectoderm
Neuralfalte f neural fold
Neuralfurche f neural groove (Embryologie)
Neuralgia f s. Neuralgie
~ **nasociliaris** nasociliary neuralgia
~ **nocturna** nyctalgia
~ **tympanica** earache, otodynia, ot[oneur]algia, otagra
Neuralgie f neuralgia, neurodynia, neuralgic (nerve) pain, ague (s. a. unter Neuralgia)
~/**Arnoldsche** Arnold's neuralgia
~ **des Nervus petrosus superficialis major** greater superficial petrosal neuralgia
~/**Huntsche** Hunt's neuralgia
~ **in mehreren Nerven** polyneuralgia
~/**Mortonsche** Morton's neuralgia, metatarsalgia
neuralgiform neuralgiform
neuralgisch neuralgic
Neuralkanal m neural canal, neurocoele (Embryologie)
Neuralleiste f neural (ganglionic) crest, ganglion ridge
Neuralplatte f neural plate, medullary streak (Embryologie)
Neuralrinne f neural groove (Embryologie)
Neuralrohr n neural (medullary) tube (Embryologie)
Neuralrohrbodenplatte f basal plate of the neural tube
neuralwärts neuralward
Neuralwulst m lateral plate (Neuralrohr)
Neuralzyste f neural cyst
Neuraminidase f neuraminidase (Enzym)
Neuraminidasetherapie f neuraminidase treatment
Neuraminsäure f neuraminic acid
Neurangiosis f neurangiosis, neurosis of blood vessels
Neurapraxie f neurapraxia, axonapraxia (Nervenhüllenverletzung mit Wiederherstellung der Nervenleitfähigkeit)
Neurasthenia f s. Neurasthenie
~ **cerebralis** cerebral neurasthenia, encephalasthenia, lack of brain power
~ **cordis** cardiac neurasthenia, cardioneurosis
Neurasthenie f neur[o]asthenia, nervous debility (prostration), nervosism, neurosism, enervation, fatigue state (s. a. unter Neurasthenia)
~/**angiopathische** angiopathic (angioparalytic) neurasthenia
~ **bei seelischen Störungen** psychasthenia, obsessive neurasthenia

~/grippale grippal neurasthenia
~/optische optic neurasthenia
~/traumatische traumatic neurasthenia
Neurasthenieschwindel *m* neurasthenic vertigo
Neurastheniker *m* neurastheniac
neurasthenisch neurasthenic, phrenasthenic
Neuraxon *n* [neur]axon, neurite, axis cylinder [process], axial fibre, nerve process
Neurektasie *f* neurectasia, neurodiastasis, stretching of a nerve
Neurektomie *f* neurectomy, excision of a nerve, neurexeresis, denervation
Neurektopie *f* neurectopia, displacement of a nerve
neurenterisch neur[o]enteric
Neurex[h]airese *f* neurexeresis, nerve avulsion; neurorrhexis
Neurilemm[a] *n* neurilem[m]a, neurolemma, nerve (Schwann's) sheath, sheath of Schwann
neurilemmal neurilemmal
Neurilemmentzündung *f* neurilemmitis, schwannitis, inflammation of the neurilemma
Neurilemmom *n* neurilemmoma, neurinoma, schwannoma, schwannoglioma, nerve-sheath tumour
Neurilemmzelle *f* neurilemmal sheath cell
Neurin *n* neurine *(bei Fäulnis aus Cholin entstehender Leichengiftstoff)*
Neurinom *n s.* Neurilemmom
Neurit *m s.* Neuraxon
Neuritis *f* neuritis, neurophlegmon, inflammation of the nerve, neuraxitis *(s. a. unter Nervenentzündung)*
~/absteigende descending neuritis
~/alkoholbedingte alcoholic neuritis
~/aufsteigende ascending neuritis
~/degenerative degenerative neuritis
~/diabetische diabetic neuritis
~/diphtherische diphtheritic neuritis
~/disseminierte disseminated (parenchymatous) neuritis
~/ernährungsbedingte dietetic neuritis
~/interstitielle hypertrophe interstitial hypertrophic neuritis
~/latente latent neuritis
~/lipomatöse lipomatous neuritis
~ multiplex multiple neuritis, polyneuritis
~ optica optic neuritis
~ optica retrobulbaris retrobulbar neuritis
~/periaxiale periaxial neuritis
~/periphere peripheral neuritis
~/porphyriebedingte porphyric neuritis
~/postinfektiöse postfebrile neuritis
~/retrobulbäre retrobulbar neuritis
~/segmentäre segmental (segmentary) neuritis
~/syphilitische syphilitic neuritis
~/tabische tabetic neuritis
~/traumatische traumatic neuritis
neuritisch neuritic
Neuro... *s. a.* Nerven...
Neuroabiotrophie *f* neuroabiotrophy
Neuroanatom *m* neuroanatomist

Neuroanatomie *f* neuroanatomy, anatomy of the nervous system
neuroanatomisch neuroanatomic[al]
Neuroapophyse *f* neuroapophysis
Neuroarthropathie *f* neuroarthropathy
Neuroastrozytom *n* neuroastrocytoma, ganglioglioma
Neurobartonellose *f* neurobartonellosis
Neurobiologie *f* neurobiology
Neurobiotaxis *f* neurobiotaxis
Neuroblast *m* neuroblast *(embryonale Nervenzelle)*
Neuroblastoma *n* [sympatheticum] neuroblastoma, sympathoma *(bösartige Neuroblastengeschwulst)*
Neuroblastomatose *f* neuroblastomatosis
Neurobruzellosis *f* neurobrucellosis
Neurochemie *f* neurochemistry
Neurochirurg *m* neurosurgeon, neurological surgeon
Neurochirurgie *f* neurosurgery; brain surgery
neurochirurgisch neurosurgical
Neurochorioiditis *f* neurochoroiditis, inflammation of the choroid coat and ciliary nerves
Neurochorioretinitis *f* neurochoroidoretinitis, inflammation of the optic nerve, the choroid, and the retina
Neurodendrit *m* [neuro]dendrite, [neuro]dendron
Neuroderm *n* neuroderm
Neurodermatitis *f* neuroderm[at]itis, chronic circumscribed neurodermatitis, atopic dermatitis (eczema), lichen simplex chronicus
~ disseminata disseminated neurodermatitis
Neurodermatose *f* neurodermatosis, dermatoneurosis
Neurodermatrophie *f* neurodermatrophia
Neurodermitis *f s.* Neurodermatitis
Neurodiagnose *f* neurodiagnosis
Neurodiastase *f* neurodiastasis, neurectasia
Neurodynie *f s.* Neuralgie
Neurodystonie *f* neurodystonia
Neuroektoderm *n* neuroectoderm
neuroektodermal neuroectodermal
Neuroelektrotherapie *f* neuroelectrotherapy, neuroelectrotherapeutics
Neuroepithel *n* neur[o]epithelium *(aus Sinnes- und Stützzellen bestehend)*
neuroepithelial neuroepithelial
Neuroepitheliom *n* neuroepithelioma, aesthesioneuroepithelioma, aesthesioneuroblastoma, olfactory neuroblastoma
Neuroepithelioma *n* retinae neuroepithelioma (neuroblastoma, glioma) of the retina, retinoblastoma, retinocytoma *(bösartig)*
neurofibrillär neurofibrillar[y]
Neurofibrille *f* neurofibril
Neurofibrillennetz *n* neurofibril lattice
Neurofibrom *n* neurofibroma, fibroneuroma, endoneural (perineural) fibroma *(gutartige Geschwulst aus Nerven- und Bindegewebe)*
Neurofibromatose *f s.* Neurofibromatosis generalisata

Neurofibromatosis

Neurofibromatosis *f* [generalisata] neurofibromatosis, neurofibrophacomatosis, neuroblastomatosis, neurinomatosis, Recklingshausen's disease; multiple neurofibroma (neuroma)
Neurofibrome *npl*/**generalisierte (multiple)** *s.* Neurofibromatosis generalisata
Neurofibromyxom *n* neurofibromyxoma
Neurofibrosarkom *n* neurofibrosarcoma, neurilemmosarcoma, neurogenic sarcoma, malignant neurilemmoma (neurinoma, schwannoma), sarcoma of peripheral nerve, schwannosarcoma
Neurofibrositis *f* neurofibrositis
Neurofilament *n* neurofilament
neurogastrisch neurogastric
neurogen neurogen[et]ic, neurogenous
Neurogenese *f* neurogenesis, formation of nerves
Neuroglia *f* [neuro]glia
neurogliabildend gliogenous
Neurogliaproliferation *f* neuroglial proliferation
neurogliär neuroglial
Neurogliawucherung *f* gliomatosis
Neurogliazelle *f* [neuro]gliocyte, spongiocyte
Neurogliom *n* neuroglioma, neurospongioma (gutartige Geschwulst aus Neuroglia)
Neuroglio[mato]se *f* neuroglio[mato]sis
Neurogliozyt *m* neurogliocyte
Neurogliozytom *n* neurogliocytoma
Neurohämatologie *f* neurohaematology
Neurohistologie *f* neurohistology, histoneurology
Neurohormon *n* neurohormone
neurohypophysär neurohypophyseal, neuropituitary
Neurohypophyse *f* neurohypophysis, posterior lobe of the hypophysis
Neuroinhibitor *m* neuroinhibitor
neuroinhibitorisch neuroinhibitory
Neurokalorimeter *n* neurocalorimeter *(zur Messung der Nerventemperatur)*
neurokardial neurocardiac
Neurokeratin *n* neurokeratin *(Eiweißkörper der Nervenmarkscheiden)*
Neurokranium *n* neurocranium, cerebral cranium, brain case, brainpan
neurokrin neurocrine, neurosecretory
Neurokrinie *f* neurocrinia, neurosecretion
neurokutan neurocutaneous
Neurolemm[a] *n s.* Neurilemm[a]
Neuroleprid *n* neuroleprid
Neuroleptanalgesie *f* neuroleptoanalgesia, neuroleptic analgesia (anaesthesia)
neuroleptanalgetisch neuroleptoanalgesic
Neuroleptanästhesie *f s.* Neuroleptanalgesie
Neuroleptikum *n* neuroleptic [agent] *(Psychopharmakon)*
neuroleptisch neuroleptic
Neurolipidspeicherkrankheit *f* neurolipid storage disease
Neurolipomatose *f* neurolipomatosis, Dercum's disease

Neurologe *m* neurologist, neuropathist
Neurologie *f* neurology, neuriatry *(Lehre von der Anatomie, Physiologie und Pathologie des Nervensystems)*
neurologisch neurologic[al]
Neurolymphe *f* neurolymph, cerebrospinal fluid
Neurolymphomatose *f* neurolymphomatosis, lymphoblastic infiltration of a nerve
Neurolyse *f* 1. neurolysis *(operative Nervenfreilegung)*; 2. neurolysis, dissolution of a nerve
Neurolysin *n* neurolysin
neurolytisch neurolytic
Neurom *n* neuroma *(Nervenfasergeschwulst) (s. a. unter Neuroma)*
~/**bösartiges** malignant neuroma
~/**granuläres** granular-cell myoblastoma (schwannoma)
~/**markhaltiges** medullated (myelinic) neuroma, myelinoma
~/**traumatisches** traumatic neuroma
~/**zystisches** cystic (false) neuroma
Neuroma *n s.* Neurom
~ **teleangiectodes** naevoid neuroma
~ **verum** true neuroma
Neuromalazie *f* neuromalacia, softening of the nerves
neuromartig neuromatoid
neuromatös neuromatous
Neuromatose *f* neuromatosis
Neuromer *n* neuromere, neurotome
Neuromerie *f* neuromery
Neuromimese *f* neuromimesis *(hysterische Simulierung einer organischen Erkrankung)*
neuromimetisch neuromimetic
neuromotorisch neuromotor
neuromuskulär neuromuscular, neuromyal, neuromyic
Neuromyasthenie *f* neuromyasthenia, benign myalgic encephalomyelitis
Neuromyelitis *f* neuromyelitis, inflammation of the spinal cord and of nerves
~ **optica** optic neuromyelitis, Devic's disease, optic neuro[encephalo]myelopathy *(mit Erblindung und Querschnittslähmung)*
neuromyoarteriell neuromyoarterial
Neuromyon *n* neuromyon *(funktionelle Einheit von Muskelfaser und Nerv)*
neuromyopathisch neuromyopathic
Neuron *n* neuron[e], neure, neurocyte, nerve cell
~/**ableitendes** efferent neuron
~/**bipolares** bipolar neuron
~/**motorisches** motoneuron, motor neuron (cell)
~/**oberes motorisches** upper motor neuron
~/**peripheres** peripheral [sensory] neuron, protoneuron
~/**polymorphes** polymorphic neuron
~/**postganglionäres** postganglionic (exciter) neuron
~/**präganglionäres** preganglionic neuron
~/**sensorisches** sensory neuron
~/**sympathisches** sympathetic cell
~/**unteres motorisches** lower motor neuron
~/**zuleitendes** afferent neuron

Neuronagenesie f neuronagenesis, lack of neuron development
neuronal neuronal, neuronic
Neuronenbildung f/**fehlende** s. Neuronagenesie
Neuronenentzündung f s. Neuronitis
Neuronenlehre f, **Neuronentheorie** f neuron theory (doctrine)
Neuronitis f neuronitis, inflammation of neurons
Neuronkrankheit f neuronopathy
Neuronographie f neuronography
neuronophag neuronophagic
Neuronophag[e] m neuronophage
Neuronophagie f neuronophagy, neuronophagocytosis
Neuroophthalmologe m neuro-ophthalmologist
Neuroophthalmologie f neuro-ophthalmology
neuroophthalmologisch neuro-ophthalmologic[al]
neurooptisch neuro-optic
Neuropapillitis f neuropapillitis
Neuroparalyse f neuroparalysis *(Lähmung infolge Erkrankung des Nervensystems)*
neuroparalytisch neuroparalytic
Neuropath m neuropath
Neuropathie f neuropathy, nervous (nerve) disease
~/diabetische diabetic neuropathy
~/progressive hypertrophe interstitielle [progressive] hypertrophic interstitial neuropathy (rediculoneuropathy), Déjérine-Sottas disease (syndrome)
neuropathisch neuropathic, neuropathologic[al]
Neuropathogenese f neuropathogenesis, development of nervous diseases
Neuropathologie f neuropathology *(Lehre von den Nervenkrankheiten)*
neuropathologisch neuropathologic[al]
Neurophagie f neuronophagy, neuronophagocytosis
Neuropharmakologie f neuropharmacology *(Lehre von der Arzneimittelwirkung auf das Nervensystem)*
Neurophysiologe m neurophysiologist
Neurophysiologie f neurophysiology *(Lehre von den biologischen und elektrophysikalischen Vorgängen im Nervensystem)*
neurophysiologisch neurophysiologic[al]
Neuropil[em] n neuropil[e], neuropilem, molecular (dotted) substance
Neuroplasma n neuroplasm
~ des Achsenzylinders axoplasm
neuroplasmatisch neuroplasmic
Neuroplegikum n neuroplegic [agent]
neuroplegisch neuroplegic
Neuropodium n neuropodium
Neuroporus m neuropor[e] *(Öffnung am oberen und unteren Ende des embryonalen Neuralrohrs)*
Neuropsychiater m neuropsychiatrist
Neuropsychiatrie f neuropsychiatry *(Lehre von den Nerven- und Geisteskrankheiten)*

neuropsychiatrisch neuropsychiatric
Neuropsychologie f neuropsychology
Neuropsychopathie f neuropsychopathy *(Geistesstörung infolge organischer Nervenkrankheit)*
neuropsychopathisch neuropsychopathic
Neuroptikomyelitis f neuropticomyelitis
Neuroradiologie f neuroradiology, neuroroentgenology
neuroradiologisch neuroradiologic[al]
Neuroretina f neuroretina
Neuroretinitis f neuroretinitis, inflammation of the optic nerve and the retina, papilloretinitis
Neuroretinopathie f neuroretinopathy
Neurorrhaphie f neurorrhaphy, suture of a cut nerve, neurosuture, nerve suture
Neurorrhexis f neurorrhexis, neurexeresis, nerve avulsion
Neurosarkom n neurosarcoma
Neurose f neurosis, parapathia *(funktionelle Störung im Bereich der höheren Nerventätigkeit)* ● **auf einer ~ beruhend** neurotic ● **eine ~ bewirkend** neurotigenic, neurotogenic
~/angstbedingte anxiety neurosis
~/hysterische hysterical neurosis
~/infantile infantile neurosis
~/konfliktbedingte psychoneurosis, psychoneurotic disorder
~/lokale toponeurosis
~/traumatische traumatic neurosis
neuroseartig neurosal
Neurosebehandlung f/**Bernheimsche** Bernheim's therapy
Neurosekranker m neurotic
Neurosekret n neurosecretion
neurosekretorisch neurosecretory
neurosensorisch neurosensorial, neurosensory
Neurosklerose f neurosclerosis
Neurosom n neurosome
Neurospasmus m neurospasm
Neurospongium n neurospongium
Neurostatus m neurostatus, state of neural symptoms
Neurosthenie f neurosthenia
neurosthenisch neurosthenic
Neurosyphilid n neurosyphilid
Neurosyphilis f neurosyphilis, neurolues
Neurosyphilisrezidiv n neurorelapse, neurorecidive, neurorecurrence
Neurotabes f **peripherica** neurotabes
neurotendinös neurotendinal, neurotendinous
Neurotherapie f neurotherapy, treatment of nervous disorders
Neurothlipsis f neurothlipsis, pressure irritation of a nerve
Neurotiker m neurotic
Neurotisation f neurotization *(1. Nervenversorgung; 2. Regeneration durchtrennter Nerven; 3. Nerveneinpflanzung)*
neurotisch neurotic, nervous
Neurotmesis f neurotmesis
neurotogen neurotigenic, neurotogenic

Neurotom

Neurotom n 1. neurotome, needle-like knife; 2. s. Neuromer
Neurotomie f neurotomy
Neurotonie f 1. neurotony, neurotonia, instability of the vegetative nervous system; 2. s. Neurektasie
neurotonisch neurotonic
Neurotoxin n neurotoxin
neurotoxisch neurotoxic
Neurotoxizität f neurotoxicity
Neurotransmitter m neurotransmitter, neurotumour
Neurotrauma n neurotrauma, wounding of a nerve
Neurotripsie f neurotripsy, bruising of a nerve
neurotrop s. neurotropisch
Neurotrophie f neurotrophy, nutrition of nervous tissue
neurotrophisch neurotrophic
Neurotropie f neurotropism
neurotropisch neurotrop[h]ic, neurotrope, neurophilic
Neurovakzine f neurovaccine, nerve tissue vaccine (im Nervengewebe gezüchteter Impfstoff)
Neurovirus n neurovirus
neuroviszeral neurovisceral, neurosplanchnic
neurozirkulatorisch neurocirculatory
Neurozyt m neurocyte (Zusammensetzungen s. unter Neuron)
Neurozytolyse f neurocytolysis
Neurozytolysin n neurocytolysin
Neurozytom n neurocytoma (Geschwulst aus unausgereiften embryonalen Nervenzellen)
Neurula f neurula (Embryologie)
Neurulation f neurulation (Embryonalstadium mit Bildung der Nervenplatte und des Nervenrohrs)
Neutralbiß m s. Neutrokklusion
Neutralfarbe f neutral stain ● sich besonders mit **Neutralfarben färbend** neutrophilic
neutralfärbend neutrophilic
Neutralfärbung f neutral staining (von Geweben)
Neutralfett n neutral lipid
Neutralisation f neutralization (z. B. einer Giftwirkung durch ein Gegenmittel)
Neutralisationsantikörper m neutralizing antibody
Neutralisationstest m neutralization test
neutralisieren to neutralize
~/**das Toxin** to neutralize the toxin
neutralisierend neutralizing; antacid, antiacid
Neutralreaktion f neutral reaction
Neutralrot n neutral red (Azurfarbstoff für Vital- und Supravitalfärbung von Geweben)
Neutralrotkörperchen npl neutral red bodies (in Lymphozyten)
Neutrokklusion f neutral occlusion, neutr[o]occlusion, orthognathia, orthognathism
Neutronenbehandlung f neutron therapy
Neutronenbestrahlung f neutron irradiation
Neutropenie f neutropenia
~/**maligne** malignant neutropenia, agranulocytosis (z. B. durch Medikamentenwirkung)

neutrophil neutrophilic
Neutrophilenleukämie f neutrophilic leukaemia
Neutrophilenmangel m im Blut s. Neutropenie
Neutrophilen[reifungs]reihe f neutrophilic series
Neutrophilenserie f neutrophilic series
Neutrophiler m neutrophil[e], neutrophilic leucocyte, neutrocyte
~/**segmentkerniger** filamented (polymorphonuclear) neutrophile
~/**stabkerniger** non-filamented neutrophile, stab (rod) neutrophile
Neutrophilie f neutrophilia, neutrophilic leucocytosis (Vermehrung der neutrophil granulierten weißen Blutzellen)
Neutrotaxis f neutrotaxis (anlockende und abstoßende Wirkung der neutrophilen Leukozyten)
Neutrozytose f s. Neutrophilie
Newcastle-Krankheit f Newcastle disease, avian pneumoencephalitis
Newcastle-Virus n Newcastle [disease] virus
Nezelof-Syndrom n Nezelof's syndrome, congenital lymphocytopenia
Niazin n niacin (Vitamin)
Niazinamid n niacinamide, nicotinamide (Vitamin)
niazin-negativ niacin-negative (Mycobacterium tuberculosis)
niazin-positiv niacin-positive (Mycobacterium tuberculosis)
Nichtabstoßung f take (von Transplantaten)
nichtadhärent non-adherent
nichtallergisch anallergic
Nichtanfälligkeit f resistance (eines Individuums gegenüber Krankheiten)
Nicht-A-Nicht-B-Hepatitis f non-A non-B hepatitis
nichtansteckend non-infectious
nichtartikulär non-articular
Nichtauseinanderweichen n non-disjunction (von Tochterchromosomen)
Nichtausscheider m non-secretor
nichtbakteriell non-bacterial, abacterial
nichtbrechend non-refractive
nichtchirurgisch non-surgical
nichtchromaffin non-chromaffin
nichtdeszendiert undescended (z. B. Hoden)
nichtdominant non-dominant
Nichteintreten n non-engagement (des Kindskopfes bei der Geburt)
nichteiternd non-suppurative, non forming pus
nichtentzündlich non-inflammatory
nichtfärbbar achromatophil, non-stainable
Nichtfärbbarer m achromatophil (z. B. Mikroorganismus)
Nichtfärbbarkeit f achromatophilia (Histologie)
Nichtfärbung f achromasia (Histologie)
nichtgebärend non-parous
nichtgeimpft non-vaccinated, unvaccinated
nichtgelähmt non-paralytic, unparalysed
nichtgestreift non-striated, unstriated, unstriped
nichthaftend non-adherent
Nicht-Hämoglobin-Eisen n haemosiderin
Nicht-HNO-Facharzt m non-otolaryngologist

Nicht-Hodgkin-Lymphom *n* non-Hodgkin's lymphoma
nichtikterisch non-icteric, non-jaundiced
nichtinvasiv non-invasive
nichtlebensfähig non-viable, not viable; incapable of surviving
nichtlipidisch non-lipid
nichtmyogen non-myogenic
nichtorganspezifisch non-organ-specific
nichtovulatorisch non-ovulatory, not ovulatory
nichtparasitär non-parasitic
nichtpathogen non-pathogenic
nichtpathognomonisch non-pathognomonic
nichtpigmentiert non-pigmented, achromatous
nichtschattengebend non-opaque, radiolucent, not opaque *(Radiologie)*
nichtschwanger non-pregnant, non-gravid
nichtseptiert non-septate
nichtspezifisch non-specific
nichtsporogen non-sporogenous, not sporogenous
nichtsyphilitisch non-syphilitic, non-luetic
nichtthrombozytopenisch non-thrombo[cyto]penic
nichttoxisch non-toxic
nichttraumatisch non-traumatic
nichtvenerisch non-venereal
nichtverhärtet non-indurated
Nichtwahrnehmung *f* agnosia
~ **der eigenen Erkrankung** anosognosia
nichtzirrhotisch non-cirrhotic
nichtzyanotisch non-cyanotic *(z. B. Herzfehler)*
Nickbewegung *f* nutation
Nickerson-Kveim-Test *m* Nickerson-Kveim test *(Hauttest zum Sarkoidosenachweis)*
Nickhaut *f* nictitating membrane *(rudimentär)*
Nickkrampf *m* nodding spasm, salaam convulsion (seizure), gyrospasm
Nidation *f* nidation, implantation *(z. B. der befruchteten Eizelle in die Gebärmutterschleimhaut)*
Nidus *m* nidus, focus of infection
Niederfrequenztherapie *f* low-frequency therapy
niedergeschlagen dejected, depressed *(Psyche)*
Niederkunft *f s.* Geburt
Niederschlag *m* precipitate; sediment; deposit
~/**radioaktiver** [radioactive] fall-out, radioactive dust
niederschlagen/sich to precipitate, to sediment, to deposit
Niederspannungselektrophorese *f* low-tension electrophoresis
Niedervoltage *f* low voltage *(EKG)*
Niedrigdruckglaukom *n* low-tension glaucoma
Niedrigdruckhydrozephalie *f* low-pressure hydrocephalia, occult hydrocephalia
Niere *f* kidney, ren, nephros ● **die Nieren entfernen** to nephrectomize ● **neben der** ~ paranephric ● **nur eine** ~ **betreffend** mononephrous ● **ohne Nieren** renoprival, anephric ● **über der** ~ suprarenal ● **von der** ~ **ausgehend** nephrogenic, nephrogenous

~/**amyloidartige** amyloid (lardaceous, waxy) kidney
~/**arteriosklerotische** arteriosclerotic kidney
~/**atrophische** atrophic kidney
~/**ektope** ectopic kidney
~/**fettig degenerierte** fatty kidney
~/**geschrumpfte** contracted (cirrhotic, granular) kidney
~/**große rote** large red kidney *(bei Glomerulonephritis)*
~/**große weiße** large white kidney *(bei chronisch interstitieller Nephritis)*
~/**kleine rote** small red kidney *(bei Nephrosklerose)*
~/**kleine weiße** small white kidney
~/**künstliche** artificial kidney, dialysis machine
~/**polyzystische** polycystic kidney
~/**sackförmige** sacciform kidney
~/**solitäre** solitary kidney
~/**stumme** inactive kidney
~/**tastbare** palpable kidney
~/**überzählige** supernumerary kidney
~/**zuckerausscheidende** leaky kidney
~/**zystische** cystic kidney
Nieren... *s. a.* Nephro...
Nierenabstoßung *f* kidney rejection
Nierenabszeß *m* renal abscess, nephropyosis
Nierenabtastung *f* kidney scanning *(nach Isotopenmarkierung)*
Nierenadenom *n* nephradenoma
Nierenadenosarkom *n* adenosarcoma (embryoma) of the kidney, embryonal mixed tumour of the kidney, Wilm's tumour, nephrogenic dysembryoma, embryonal (mesoblastic) nephroma
Nierenagenesie *f* renal (kidney) agenesis
nierenähnlich nephroid
Nierenaktinomykose *f* renal actinomycosis
Nierenamöbenabszeß *m* renal amoebic abscess
Nierenamyloidose *f* renal amyloidosis; amyloid (lardaceous, waxy) kidney
Nierenanheftung *f* nephrorrhaphy
Nierenanomalie *f* renal (kidney) anomaly
Nierenapoplexie *f* renal apoplexy
Nierenarkadenvene *f* arcuate vein
Nierenarterie *f* renal artery
~ **zwischen den Nierenpyramiden** interlobar artery of the kidney
Nierenarterienfibrodysplasie *f* renal artery fibrodysplasia
Nierenarterienrekonstruktion *f* renal artery reconstruction
Nierenarterienröntgen[kontrast]bild *n* renal arteriogram
Nierenarterienröntgen[kontrast]darstellung *f* renal arteriography
Nierenarterienstenose *f* renal artery stenosis
Nierenarterienverkalkung *f* [arterial] nephrosclerosis
Nierenarteriolensklerose *f* arteriolar nephrosclerosis
nierenartig nephroid, reniform
Nierenatonie *f* atony of the kidney, nephratonia

Nierenauflösung

Nierenauflösung *f* nephrolysis, dissolution of the kidney
Nierenausscheidung *f* renal excretion; renal output
Nierenausscheidungskapazität *f* renal excretory capacity
Nierenausscheidungsschwelle *f* renal threshold
Nierenballottement *n* renal ballottement
Nierenbecken *n* renal (kidney) pelvis, pelvis of the ureter • vom ~ ausgehend pyelogenic
Nierenbeckenaffektion *f* pyelopathy, disease of the renal pelvis
Nierenbeckenausgußstein *m* staghorn calculus
Nierenbeckendarstellung *f s.* Pyelographie
Nierenbeckendehnung *f* hydropelvis *(durch Urinansammlung)*
Nierenbeckendurchleuchtung *f* pyelofluoroscopy
Nierenbeckenentzündung *f* pyelitis, inflammation of the renal pelvis
Nierenbeckenepithel *n* renal pelvic epithelium
Nierenbeckenerkrankung *f* pyelopathy, disease of the renal pelvis
Nierenbeckenernährungsarterie *f* nutrient artery of the renal pelvis
Nierenbeckeneröffnung *f* [/operative] pyelotomy, pelviotomy
Nierenbeckenerweiterung *f* pyelectasia, dilatation of the renal pelvis
Nierenbeckenfistel *f* nephrostoma, pyelostoma
Nierenbeckenfistelung *f* [/operative] nephrostomy, pyelostomy
Nierenbecken-Harnblasen-Anastomose *f* pelvioneocystostomy
Nierenbecken-Harnleiter-Plastik *f* pyelo-ureteroplasty
Nierenbecken-Harnleiter-Röntgen[kontrast]darstellung *f* pelviureteroradiography
Nierenbeckenkelchsystem *n* pyelocalyceal system
Nierenbeckenplastik *f* [nephro]pyeloplasty
Nierenbeckenröntgen[kontrast]bild *n s.* Pyelogramm
Nierenbeckenröntgen[kontrast]darstellung *f s.* Pyelographie
Nierenbeckenruptur *f* kidney pelvis rupture
Nierenbeckenschnitt *m* pyelotomy, pelviotomy, incision of the renal pelvis
Nierenbeckensteinentfernung *f* [/operative] [nephro]pyelolithotomy, pelviolithotomy
Nierenbeckensteinschnitt *m* [nephro]pyelolithotomy, lithonephrotomy
Nierenbecken- und Harnblasenentzündung *f* pyelocystitis
Nierenbecken- und Harnleitererweiterung *f* pyelo-ureterectasis, dilatation of the renal pelvis and the ureter
Nierenbecken- und Nierengewebeentzündung *f* pyelonephritis, interstitial nephritis, inflammation of the kidney and the pelvis
Nierenbecken- und Nierenkelcherweiterung *f* pelvocalycectasis

Nierenbeckenvenenentzündung *f* pyelophlebitis, inflammation of the veins of the renal pelvis
Nierenbeckenverkleinerung *f* durch Wandfaltung [/operative] pyeloplication
nierenbedingt renal, nephrogenous
nierenbeeinflussend nephrotropic
Nierenbeteiligung *f* renal (kidney) involvement
Nierenbildung *f* nephrogenesis
~/fehlende renal (kidney) agenesis
Nierenbindegewebskapsel *f* fibrous capsule of the kidney
Nierenbiopsie *f* renal (kidney) biopsy
Nierenblutung *f* renal haemorrhage, haemorrhage from the kidney, nephrorrhagia
Nierenbruzellose *f* renal brucellosis
Nieren-Clearance *f* renal clearance
Nierendegeneration *f* renal (kidney) degeneration
~/polyzystische polycystic kidney disease
Nierendekapsulation *f s.* Nephrokaps[ul]ektomie
Nierendekortikation *f* renal decortication
Nierendiabetes *m* renal diabetes (glucosuria)
Nieren-Dickdarm-Band *n* nephrocolic ligament
Nierendilatation *f* dilatation (distention) of the kidney, nephrectasia
Nierendurchblutung *f* renal (kidney) blood flow
Nierendysfunktion *f* renal dysfunction
Nierendysplasie *f*/zystische renal cystic dysplasia; multicystic kidney
Nierenechinokokkuszyste *f* echinococcal cyst of the kidney
Niereneinschnitt *m* nephrotomy
~ über einen Lendenschnitt lumbar nephrotomy
Nierenektopie *f* renal (kidney) ectopia; ectopic kidney
Nierenentfernung *f* excision of the kidney, nephrectomy *(s. a. unter* Nephrektomie*)*
~ durch Bauchschnitt laparonephrectomy, abdominal nephrectomy
~/halbseitige heminephrectomy
~ über einen Lendenschnitt lumbar nephrectomy
Nierenentwicklung *f* nephrogenesis
Nierenentzündung *f* inflammation of the kidney, nephritis, renal inflammation *(s. a. unter* Nephritis*)* • eine ~ bewirkend nephritogenic
~ durch Nierensteine lithonephritis
~/eitrige suppurative nephritis, pyonephritis
~/hereditäre familiäre [familial] hereditary nephritis, Alport's syndrome
~/unspezifische interstitial nephritis
Nierenerkrankung *f* nephropathy, renopathy, renal (kidney) disease
Nierenerweichung *f* nephromalacia, softening of the kidney
Nierenerweiterung *f* nephrectasia, dilatation of the kidney
Nierenfaßzange *f* kidney elevating (holding) forceps •
Nierenfaszie *f* renal (Gerota's) fascia
Nierenfettkapsel *f* fatty capsule of the kidney, adipose capsule [of the kidney]

Nierenfettkapselentzündung f epinephritis
Nierenfistel f renal fistula *(pathologisch)*
~/operative nephrostoma, renal fistula
Nierenfistelkatheter m renal fistula catheter
Nierenfixation f nephropexy, fixation of the kidney
nierenförmig reniform, kidney-shaped
Nierenfreipräparation f nephrolysis
Nierenfunktion f renal (kidney) function
Nierenfunktionsstörung f renal dysfunction
Nierenfunktionstest m renal (kidney) function test
Nierenfunktionsuntersuchung f/seitengetrennte split renal function study
Nierengefäßröntgen[kontrast]bild n renal angiogram
Nierengefäßröntgen[kontrast]darstellung f renal angiography
Nierengefäßstiel m renal vascular pedicle
Nierengeflecht n renal plexus
Nierengeschwulst f kidney tumour, renal neoplasm
Nierengewebe n renal tissue
Nierengewebeentnahme f renal biopsy
Nierengewebe- und Glomerulumentzündung f glomerulonephritis
Nierengewebsauflösung f nephrolysis
nierengewebsbildend nephropoietic
Nierengewebsentartung f nephrosis, nephrodystrophia; nephropathy
Nierengewebsschwund m nephronophthisis
Nierengift n nephrotoxin
nierengiftig nephrotoxic
Nierengiftigkeit f nephrotoxicity, renal toxicity
Nierenglomerulafibrose f glomerulosclerosis
Nierenglomerulum n s. Glomerulum
Nierenhämodynamik f renal haemodynamics
Nieren-Harnblasen-Anastomose f nephrocystanastomosis
Nieren-, Harnleiter- und Blasenentfernung f[/operative] nephrouretercystectomy
Nierenhernie f nephrocele
Nierenhilus m kidney hilum, hilum of the kidney
Nierenhochdruck m arterial hypertension of renal origin
Niereninfarkt m renal (kidney) infarction
Niereninsuffizienz f s. Nierenversagen
Niereninterlobularvene f interlobular vein of the kidney
Nierenisotopenbild n radioactive renal scintiscan
Nierenkanälchen n renal tubule
~/gewundenes convoluted renal tubule
Nierenkanälchenzylinder m renal (urinary) cast *(bei Nierenerkrankung im Urin)*
Nierenkapsel f capsule of the kidney, perinephrium, perinephros, perinephric capsule
Nierenkapselausschneidung f excision of the renal capsule, nephrocaps[ul]ectomy
Nierenkapselentzündung f perinephritis, capsular nephritis, inflammation of the perinephrium *(Zusammensetzungen s. unter Perinephritis)*

Nierenkapseleröffnung f[/operative] renal capsulotomy, nephrocapsulotomy
Nierenkapselinzision f renal capsulotomy, nephrocapsulotomy
Nierenkarbunkel m renal carbuncle
Nierenkelch m renal calix
Nierenkelchabflachung f calyceal blunting
Nierenkelchabnormität f calyceal abnormality
Nierenkelchdivertikel n calyceal diverticulum
Nierenkelche mpl renal calyces
~/große major calyces [of the kidney]
~/kleine minor calyces [of the kidney]
Nierenkelchentfernung f[/operative] calycectomy
Nierenkelchepithel n calyceal epithelium
Nierenkelcherweiterung f calycectasis, calyceal dilatation (widening)
Nierenkelchveränderung f calyceal abnormality
Nierenklemme f kidney clamp
Nierenknäuel n s. Glomerulum
Nierenknäulchenkapsel f Bowman's capsule, Malpighian capsule
Nierenkolik f renal colic
Nierenkonservierungsgerät n kidney preservation unit
Nierenkonzentrierungstest m kidney concentration test
Nierenkörperchen n renal corpuscle
Nierenkortex m s. Nierenrinde
Nierenkrankheit f nephropathy, renopathy, renal (kidney) disease
Nierenkrebs m nephrocarcinoma, renal (kidney) carcinoma
Nierenkreislauf m kidney circulation
Nierenkrise f renal crisis
Nierenlager n renal bed
Nierenläppchen npl renal lobes
Nierenlokalisation f renal localization
nierenlos renoprival, anephric
Nierenlösung f aus Verwachsungen nephrolysis
Nierenmark n renal medulla, medulla of the kidney
Nierennaht f nephrorrhaphy
Nierenneoplasma n renal neoplasm
Nierennervengeflecht n renal plexus
Nierenödem n renal oedema (dropsy)
Nierenonkozytom n renal oncocytoma
Nierenpapille f renal papilla
Nierenpapillennekrose f renal papillary necrosis
Nierenparalyse f nephroparalysis
Nierenparenchym n renal parenchyma
Nierenparenchymphase f nephrographic phase *(Radiologie)*
Nierenparenchym- und Nierenbeckenentzündung f parenchymatous inflammation of the kidney, nephropyelitis
Nierenparenchymzerstörung f renal parenchymal destruction
Nierenperfusion f renal (kidney) perfusion
Nierenperfusionsdruck m renal perfusion pressure
Nierenpforte f s. Nierenhilus

Nierenplasmafluß

Nierenplasmafluß *m* renal plasma flow, RPF
Nierenpol *m*/**oberer** superior pole of the kidney
~/unterer lower pole of the kidney
Nierenpunktion *f* renipuncture, needling of the kidney
Nierenpyramide *f* renal pyramid
Nierenpyramidenbasis *f* base of the renal pyramid
Nierenrand *m*/**seitlicher** convex border of the kidney
Nierenrinde *f* renal cortex, cortex of the kidney
Nierenrindenarterie *f* interlobular artery of the kidney
Nierenrindenläppchen *n* lobule of the cortex of the kidney
Nierenrindenvene *f* interlobular vein of the kidney
Nierenrolle *f* kidney roll
Nierenröntgen[kontrast]bild *n* nephrogram, renogram
Nierenröntgen[kontrast]darstellung *f* nephrography, renography, renal radiography
Nierenröntgenschichtbild *n* nephrotomogram, renal tomogram
Nierenröntgenschichtdarstellung *f* nephrotomography, renal tomography
Nierenrückseite *f* posterior surface of the kidney
Nierenruptur *f* kidney rupture (laceration)
Nierensammelröhrchensystem *n* renal collecting system
nierenschädigend nephrotoxic
Nierenschale *f* kidney basin (tray)
Nierenschatten *m* renal shadow *(Radiologie)*
Nierenschichtaufnahme *f* nephrotomogram
Nierenschichten *n* nephrotomography, renal tomography
nierenschichtend nephrotomographic
Nierenschmerz *m* nephralgia, pain in the kidney
Nierenschnitt *m* nephrotomy, incision into the kidney
Nierenschrumpfung *f* nephrocirrhosis; contracted (cirrhotic, granular) kidney
Nierenschwelle *f* renal [excretion] threshold
Nierenschwund *m* nephronophthisis
Nierenselbststabstoßung *f* autonephrectomy
Nierensenkung *f* s. Nephroptose
Nierensinus *m* renal sinus
Nierenspezialist *m* nephrologist
Nierenspülkatheter *m* renal irrigation catheter
Nierenstein *m* nephrolith, renal calculus, kidney stone
Nierensteinabgang *m* passage of a renal stone
nierensteinartig nephrolithic
Nierensteinauflösung *f* renal stone dissolution
Nierensteinentfernung *f*[/**operative**] nephrolithotomy
Nierensteinleiden *n* nephrolithiasis
~ mit Nierenvereiterung pyonephrolithiasis
Nierensteinschnitt *m* lithonephrotomy
Nierensteinzange *f* kidney stone forceps
Nierenstiel *m* renal pedicle
Nierenstielklemme *f* renal pedicle clamp

Nierenstiellymphknoten *m* renal pedicle lymph node
Nierenstielverletzung *f* renal pedicle injury
Nierenszintigraphie *f* renal scintigraphy, kidney scanning
Nierentätigkeit *f* renal (kidney) function
Nierenteilentfernung *f*[/**operative**] heminephrectomy; partial nephrectomy
Nierentransplantat *n* renal (kidney) transplant
Nierentransplantatabstoßung *f* kidney rejection
Nierentransplantation *f* kidney transplantation, renal transplant operation
Nierentransplantationszentrum *n* renal transplant centre
Nierentuberkulose *f* nephrotuberculosis, renal tuberculosis, nephrophthisis
Nierentubulus *m* renal (nephric, uriniferous) tubule
Nierentubulusabsorption *f* renal tubular absorption
Nierentubulusazidose *f* renal tubular acidosis
Nierentubulusepithel *n* renal tubular epithelium
Nierentubulusfunktion *f* renal tubular function
Nierentubulusnekrose *f* renal tubular necrosis
Nierentubulusreabsorption *f* renal tubular reabsorption
Nieren- und Blasenentzündung *f* nephrocystitis
Nieren- und Dickdarmfixation *f* nephrocolopexy
Nieren- und Dickdarmsenkung *f* nephrocoloptosis
Nieren- und Harnleiterentfernung *f*[/**operative**] nephro-ureterectomy
Nieren- und Milzfixation *f* [/**operative**] fixation of the kidney and the spleen, nephrosplenopexy
Nierenvene *f* renal vein
~ zwischen den Nierenpyramiden interlobar vein of the kidney
Nierenvenenthrombose *f* renal vein thrombosis
Nierenverdünnungstest *m* [renal] dilution test
Nierenvereiterung *f* nephropyosis, pyonephrosis; pyonephrotic kidney
Nierenvergrößerung *f* enlargement of the kidney, nephromegaly, nephrauxe ● **eine ~ bewirkend (fördernd)** renotrop[h]ic
Nierenverkalkung *f* nephrocalcinosis; cement kidney; nephrosclerosis
Nierenverlagerung *f* renal ectopia
Nierenverletzung *f* renal injury, kidney trauma
Nierenversagen *n* renal failure (shutdown), renal (kidney) insufficiency
~/akutes acute renal insufficiency (failure); lower nephron nephrosis (syndrome), acute tubular necrosis, haemoglobinuric nephrosis, ischaemic tubulorrhexis; crush kidney *(nach Trauma)*
~/terminales end-stage renal disease (failure)
Nierenvorderseite *f* anterior surface of the kidney
Nierenvorfall *m* nephrocele
Nierenwassersucht *f* uronephrosis, renal dropsy
nierenwirksam nephrotropic
Nierenzelle *f* renal cell

Nierenzellenkarzinom n renal cell carcinoma, hypernephroid renal carcinoma, hypernephroma, solid-cell carcinoma
Nierenzwischenläppchenvene f interlobular vein of the kidney
Nierenzylinder m renal (urinary) cast *(bei Nierenerkrankung im Urin)*
Nierenzyste f renal (kidney) cyst
Nierenzystenbildung f nephrocystosis
niesen to sneeze
Niesen n sneezing, sneeze, sternutation
Nieskrampf m ptarmus
Niesmittel n sternutator [agent], ptarmic [agent]
Niesreflex m sneezing (nasal) reflex
Nigrities f linguae nigrities linguae
Nihilismus m nihilism
~/therapeutischer nihilism
Niklosamid n niclosamide *(Antiwurmmittel)*
Nikolski-Zeichen n Nikolsky's sign *(bei Pemphigus vulgaris)*
Nikotin n nicotine *(Alkaloid)*
Nikotinamblyopie f tobacco amblyopia
Nikotinamid n nicotinamide, nicotinic acid amide, niacinamide *(Vitamin)*
Nikotinamid-adenin-dinukleotid n nicotinamide-adenine dinucleotide, NAD, coenzyme I, codehydrogenase I, cozymase
Nikotinamid-adenin-dinukleotidphosphat n nicotinamide-adenine dinucleotide phosphate, NADP, diphosphopyridine nucleotide, DPN
Nikotineffekt m nicotinic action
nikotinerg[isch] nicotinergic
Nikotingehalt m nicotine content
Nikotinherz n tobacco (smoker's) heart
Nikotinismus m s. Nikotinvergiftung
Nikotinmißbrauch m nicotine abuse
Nikotinsäure f nicotinic acid, niacin, pellagramin *(Vitamin)*
Nikotinsäureamid n s. Nikotinamid
Nikotinsäureavitaminose f aniacinosis, pellagra, Asturian leprosy
Nikotinvergiftung f nicotinism, tobaccoism, poisoning by nicotine
Nikotinwirkung f nicotinic action
Niktation f nic[ti]tation
Nilbeule f s. Orientbeule
Niphablepsie f niphablepsia, niphotyphlosis, snow blindness, solar photophthalmia
Nische f recess[us] *(Anatomie)*; niche, crater (z. B. der Magenschleimhaut)
Nisse f nit
Nissl-Färbung f Nissl's [staining] method
Nissl-Körperchen n Nissl's body, chromophile granule
Nissl-Substanz f Nissl's (chromophile) substance
Nisus m nisus, strong effort (struggle)
Nitrazepam n nitrazepam *(Antikonvulsivum)*
Nitrifikant m nitrifier, nitrate (nitric) bacterium
nitrifizieren to nitrify
Nitrifizierung f nitrification *(Oxydation des Ammoniaks über Nitrit zu Nitrat durch Bakterien)*
Nitrit n nitrite *(Methämoglobinbildner)*

Nitritausscheidung f im Urin nitrituria
Nitrofurantoin n nitrofurantoin *(Chemotherapeutikum)*
Nitroglyzerin n nitroglycerin, glycerol trinitrate *(koronargefäßerweiterndes Mittel)*
Nitroprussid n nitroprusside *(blutdrucksenkendes Mittel)*
N-Lost m nitrogen mustard *(chemischer Kampfstoff)*
n-Lösung f normal solution
NMR s. Resonanz/kernmagnetische
NNH s. Nasennebenhöhle
NNM s. Nebennierenmark
NNR s. Nebennierenrinde
nodös nodal, nodular, nodose
Nodosität f nodosity
nodulär nodular
Noduli *mpl*:
~ **lymphatici laryngei** laryngeal tonsils
~ **lymphatici tubarii** Eustachian tonsils
~ **valvularum semilunarium** nodules of the semilunar valves
~ **vocales** vocal nodules, singer's nodes, trachoma of the vocal bands
nodulös nodulous
Nodulus m nodule, nodulus
~ **cutaneus** dermatofibroma; nodular subepidermal fibrosis
~ **iridis** iris nodule
Nodus m node, nodus *(s. a. unter Knoten)*
~ **atrioventricularis** atrioventricular (Aschoff's) node, Tawara's node *(Herzreizleitungssystem)*
~ **lymphaticus** lymph node, lymph[atic] gland, lymphonodus, lymphoglandula
~ **lymphaticus axillaris** axillary lymph (lymphatic) node
~ **lymphaticus cervicalis** cervical lymph node
~ **lymphaticus cervicalis profundus** deep cervical lymph node
~ **lymphaticus cervicalis superficialis** superficial cervical lymph node
~ **lymphaticus femoralis profundus** deep femoral lymph node
~ **lymphaticus lumbalis** lumbar lymph gland (node)
~ **sinoauricularis** node of Keith and Flack
~ **sinuatrialis** sinoatrial (sinus) node, pacemaker of the heart *(Herzreizleitung)*
Nokardia f nocardia *(zu den Aktinomyzeten gehörender aerober Mikroorganismus)*
Nokardienbefall m nocardial infection (infestation)
Nokardienzellwand f nocardial cell wall
Nokardiose f nocardiosis *(die Haut und die Lungen befallende Pilzkrankheit)*
Noktalbuminurie f noctalbuminuria, nyctalbuminuria
noktambul noctambulic
Noktambulismus m noctambulism, noctambulation, sleep-walking
Noma n(f) noma, water cancer, gangrenous stomatitis
~ **pudendi** pudendal gangrene

Nomenklatur 562

Nomenklatur f/**Jenaer** Jena Nomina Anatomica, JNA
~/Pariser Paris Nomina Anatomica, PNA
Nomenklaturlehre f onomatology
nomotop nomotopic
Non-Hodgkin-Lymphom n non-Hodgkin lymphoma
Nonigravida f nonigravida
Nonipara f nonipara
Nonne-Apelt-Test m Apelt's (Nonne-Apelt) test *(Nachweis für erhöhten Globulingehalt in der Hirn-Rückenmark-Flüssigkeit)*
Nonne-Meige-Milroy-Syndrom n Nonne-Milroy-Meige syndrome, Milroy's disease, idiopathic elephantiasis
Nonnengeräusch n, **Nonnensausen** n venous hum, humming-top murmur
Nonokklusion f non-occlusion
nonovulatorisch non-ovulatory
Noogenetik f noogenetics
Noonan-Syndrom n Noonan's syndrome
Noopsyche f noopsyche
Noradrenalin n noradrenaline, norepinephrine, arterenol *(Sympathikuswirkstoff)*
l-**Noradrenalin** n levarterenol
Nord-Queensland-Zeckenbißfieber n North Queensland tick typhus [fever] *(durch Rickettsia australis)*
Nörgler m querulent
Normabweichung f variety, abnormality, heterology *(morphologisch oder funktionell)*
Normalakkommodation f normal accommodation, emmetropization
Normalatmung f normal respiration (breathing), eupnoea
Normalbedingungen fpl standard conditions
Normalbewegung f eupraxia
Normalbiß m normal (ideal) occlusion
Normalbrechungszustand m des Auges s. Normalakkommodation
Normalelektrode f standard calomel electrode
Normalentbindung f eutocia, normal parturition
Normalerythrozyt m normo[erythro]cyte
Normalfärbbarkeit f normochromasia
normalfärbend normochrom[at]ic, orthochromophile
normalfarbsichtig trichrom[at]ic, trichroic
Normalfarbsichtiger m trichromat[e]
Normalfarbsichtigkeit f trichromatopsia, trichromatism
Normalfärbung f normochromasia
Normalfrequenz f normal frequency *(des Pulses)*
Normalfunktion f orthergasia
Normalgebiß n eugnathy
Normalgeburt f normal delivery
normalgeschlechtlich heterosexual
Normalgeschlechtlichkeit f heterosexuality
Normalgewicht n standard weight
normalgezahnt orthodont
Normalkiefer m eugnathy

Normallage f normal position, normotopia; eusplanchnia *(der Eingeweide)*; normal presentation *(des Fetus bei der Geburt)*
~ des Herzens laevocardia
Normallösung f normal solution
Normalposition f orthotopia, normal position
● **in ~** orthotopic
Normalreaktion f orthocrasia, normal reaction *(auf Arzneimittel)*
Normalserum n normal serum
normalsichtig emmetropic, orthoptic, orthoscopic
Normalsichtiger m emmetrope
Normalsichtigkeit f emmetropia, E.
Normalstimme f euphonia
Normalsystole f eusystole
Normaltemperatur f normothermia, normal temperature
Normalverdauung f eupepsia
normalzahnig orthodont
normalzellig normocytic
Normalzustand m normal condition, orthergasia
Normoblast m normoblast, eosinophilic erythroblast, [meta]karyocyte
~/basophiler basophilic (early) normoblast, basophilic erythroblast, early erythroblast [of Sabin]
~/großer macronormoblast
~/orthochromatischer orthochromatic normoblast
~/polychromatischer polychromatophilic (intermediate) normoblast
Normoblastenvermehrung f im Knochenmark normoblastosis
normoblastisch normoblastic
Normoblastose f normoblastosis
Normochlorhydrie f euchlorhydria
normochrom normochrom[at]ic
Normochromasie f normochromasia
Normochromie f normochromia
Normoglykämie f normoglycaemia
normoglykämisch normoglycaemic
Normokaliämie f normokalaemia
normokaliämisch normokalaemic
Normokalziämie f normocalcaemia
normokalziämisch normocalcaemic
Normoleukozytose f isonormocytosis
Normoproteinämie f normoproteinaemia
normoproteinämisch normoproteinaemic
Normoreflexie f normoreflexia
Normospermie f normospermia
normotherm normothermic
normoton normotonic *(z. B. Muskeln)*; normotensive *(z. B. der Blutdruck)*
Normotonie f normotonia; normotension
normotop normotopic
Normotopie f normotopia
Normovolämie f normovolaemia
normovolämisch normovolaemic
Normozyt m normo[erythro]cyte
Normozytenanämie f normocytic anaemia
normozytisch normocytic
Normozytose f normocytosis

Normwidrigkeit f abnormalism, abnormality
Nosoagnosie f anosognosia, nosoagnosia *(subjektives Nichterkennen von krankhaften Veränderungen)*
nosogen nosogen[et]ic, nosopoietic
Nosogenese f nosogeny, nosogenesis
Nosogeographie f nosogeography, nosochthonography *(Lehre von der geographischen und klimatischen Verbreitung der Krankheiten)*
Nosographie f nosography
Nosohämie f nosohaemia
nosokomial nosocomial
Nosologie f nosology
nosologisch nosologic[al]
Nosomanie f nosomania
Nosometrie f nosometry
Nosoparasitismus m nosoparasitism
Nosophilie f nosophilia
Nosophobie f nosophobia *(krankhafte Angst vor Krankheit)*
Nosotherapie f nosotherapy *(z. B. Heilfieberbehandlung)*
Nosotrophie f nosotrophy
Nostalgie f nostalgia, nostomania
nostalgisch nostalgic
Nostomanie f nostomania, nostalgia
Notalgie f notalgia
Notamputation f emergency (urgent) amputation
Notanenzephalie f notanencephalia, congenital absence of the cerebellum
Notarzt m emergency physician
Notarztsystem n emergency medical system
Notaufnahme f emergency admission *(in das Krankenhaus)*
Notaufnahmeraum m emergency room
Notbehandlung f emergency treatment
Notenblindheit f note (music) blindness, musical aphasia
Notenzephalie f notancephalia
Notenzephalozele f notencephalocele
Notfall m emergency, case of emergency
Notfallchirurgie f emergency surgery
Notfalldiagnostik f emergency diagnosis
Notfallendoskopie f emergency endoscopy
Notfallmaßnahme f emergency procedure
Notfallmedikament n emergency drug (remedy), resuscitating drug
Notfallmedizin f emergency medicine
Notfallnierenexstirpation f emergency nephrectomy
Notfalloperation f emergency operation
Notfallreaktion f/**Cannonsche** Cannon's [emergency] response, fight-or-flight reaction
Notfallsituation f emergency situation
Notfallthorakotomie f emergency thoracotomy
Notfalltracheotomie f emergency tracheotomy
Notfalltransfusion f emergency transfusion
Notmaßnahme f emergency procedure (measure)
Notnephrektomie f emergency nephrectomy
Notochordalplatte f notochordal plate

Notogenese f notogenesis
Notomelus m notomelus *(asymmetrische Mißgeburt mit akzessorischen Gliedern am Rücken)*
Notomyelitis f notomyelitis
Notoperation f emergency operation
Nottracheotomietrokar m intercricothyreotomy trocar
Nottransfusion f emergency transfusion
Notverband m provisional bandage, emergency (first-aid) dressing
notwendig essential *(z. B. Vitamine, Minerale)*
Notzucht f rape, ravishment
Novokain n novocaine, procaine *(Lokalanästhetikum)*
Noxe f noxa, noxiousness
Nubekula f nubecula
Nucha f nucha, nape [of the neck] *(s. a. Nacken)*
nuchal nuchal
nüchtern fasting, empty *(z. B. Magen)*; sober *(ohne Alkohol)*; not intoxicated ● ~ **bleiben** to go empty, to starve, to fast ● ~ **gelassen werden** to be given nothing by mouth
Nüchternblutzucker m fasting blood sugar
Nüchternprobe f fasting specimen *(z. B. Blutentnahme)*
Nüchternschmerz m hunger pain, gastralgokenosis
Nüchternsekret n fasting gastric contents
Nüchternsekretion f basal secretion *(der Magenschleimhaut)*
~/**nächtliche** continuous night secretion
Nüchternspeichel m resting saliva
Nuckel m pacifier *(für Säuglinge)*
Nuclei mpl **anteriores thalami** anterior nuclei of the thalamus
~ **laterales thalami** internal nuclei of the thalamus
Nucleinsäure f s. Nukleinsäure
Nucleolus m nucleole, nucleolus
Nucleus m nucleus; karyon, karyoplast, endoplast *(s. a. unter Kern)*
~ **accessorius nervi oculomotorii** autonomic nucleus of the oculomotor nerve
~ **ambiguus** ambiguous nucleus
~ **caudatus** caudate nucleus
~ **centralis inferior** inferior central nucleus
~ **centralis thalami** central nucleus of the thalamus
~ **cochlearis dorsalis** dorsal cochlear nucleus
~ **cochlearis ventralis** ventral cochlear nucleus
~ **colliculi inferioris** nucleus of the inferior colliculus
~ **conterminalis** retropyramidal nucleus
~ **corporis geniculati lateralis** nucleus of the lateral geniculate body
~ **corporis geniculati medialis** nucleus of the medial geniculate body
~ **corporis trapezoidei** nucleus of the trapezoid body
~ **cuneatus** cuneate (Burdach's) nucleus *(im verlängerten Rückenmark)*

Nucleus

- ~ **cuneatus accessorius** accessory (external) cuneate nucleus, nucleus of Monakov *(Hirnstamm)*
- ~ **dentatus cerebelli** dentate nucleus, dentatum
- ~ **dorsalis** thoracic nucleus, Clarke's column (dorsal nucleus)
- ~ **dorsalis corporis trapezoidei** superior olivary nucleus
- ~ **dorsalis nervi vagi** dorsal motor nucleus of the vagus [nerve]
- ~ **dorsomedialis hypothalami** dorsomedial hypothalamic nucleus
- ~ **emboliformis cerebelli** emboliform nucleus
- ~ **facialis** branchiomotor nucleus of the visceral nerve
- ~ **fastigii** fastigial nucleus
- ~ **globosus cerebelli** globose nucleus
- ~ **gracilis** gracilis (Goll's) nucleus
- ~ **habenulae** habenular nucleus
- ~ **hypothalamicus** subthalamic nucleus *(grauer Kern des Zwischenhirns)*
- ~ **inferior pontis** inferior nucleus of the pons
- ~ **intercalatus** intercalated nucleus
- ~ **intermediomedialis** intermediomedial nucleus, lateral sympathetic nucleus
- ~ **interpeduncularis** interpeduncular nucleus *(Nervenzellanhäufung im Mittelhirn)*
- ~ **lateralis dorsalis thalami** dorsal lateral nucleus of the thalamus
- ~ **lateralis hypothalami** lateral hypothalamic nucleus
- ~ **lateralis thalami** lateral nucleus of the thalamus
- ~ **lemnisci lateralis** nucleus of the lateral lemniscus
- ~ **lenticularis (lentiformis)** lenticular nucleus *(im Gehirn)*
- ~ **lentis** nucleus of the lens
- ~ **medialis centralis thalami** medial central nucleus of the thalamus
- ~ **medialis dorsalis** dorsomedial nucleus of the thalamus
- ~ **medialis thalami** medial nucleus of the thalamus
- ~ **motorius nervi trigemini** motor nucleus of the trigeminal nerve, masticator nucleus
- ~ **nervi abducens** abducent nucleus
- ~ **nervi facialis** facial nucleus, nucleus of the facial nerve
- ~ **nervi hypoglossi** hypoglossal nucleus
- ~ **nervi oculomotorii** oculomotor nucleus *(Ursprungskern des III. Hirnnerven im Mittelhirn)*
- ~ **nervi trochlearis** trochlear nucleus
- ~ **nervi vagi** vagal nucleus, nucleus of the vagus nerve
- ~ **olivaris** olivary body, [inferior] olivary nucleus, inferior olive
- ~ **olivaris accessorius dorsalis** dorsal accessory olivary nucleus
- ~ **olivaris accessorius medialis** medial accessory olivary nucleus
- ~ **olivaris inferior** s. ~ olivaris
- ~ **olivaris metencephali** superior olivary nucleus
- ~ **originis** nucleus of origin
- ~ **originis nervi oculomotorii** ocular motor nucleus
- ~ **parafascicularis thalami** parafascicular nucleus of the thalamus
- ~ **paraventricularis hypothalami** paraventricular nucleus of the hypothalamus
- ~ **paraventricularis thalami** paraventricular nucleus of the thalamus
- ~ **pontis** pontine nucleus
- ~ **posterior thalami** posterior nucleus of the thalamus, pulvinar [thalami] *(hinteres Ende des Thalamus im Gehirn)*
- ~ **pulposus** pulp of the intervertebral disk
- ~ **reticularis** reticular nucleus
- ~ **reticularis thalami** reticular nucleus of the thalamus
- ~ **ruber** red nucleus
- ~ **salivatorius** salivatory nucleus
- ~ **salivatorius inferior** inferior salivatory nucleus
- ~ **salivatorius superior** superior salivatory nucleus
- ~ **sensorius principalis nervi trigemini** main sensory nucleus of the trigeminal nerve
- ~ **spinalis nervi accessorii** spinal accessory nucleus
- ~ **subthalamicus** subthalamic nucleus *(grauer Kern des Zwischenhirns)*
- ~ **superior pontis** superior nucleus of the pons
- ~ **supraopticus hypothalami** supra-optic nucleus of the hypothalamus
- ~ **tegmenti** tegmental nucleus
- ~ **terminationis** nucleus of termination
- ~ **thalamicus** thalamic nucleus
- ~ **thoracicus** s. ~ dorsalis
- ~ **tractus mesencephali nervi trigemini** nucleus of the mesencephalic tract of the trigeminal nerve
- ~ **tractus solitarii** nucleus of the tractus solitarius
- ~ **tractus spinalis nervi trigemini** nucleus of the spinal tract of the trigeminal nerve
- ~ **ventralis anterior [thalami]** anterior ventral nucleus of the thalamus
- ~ **ventralis lateralis [thalami]** lateral ventral nucleus of the thalamus
- ~ **ventralis posterolateralis thalami** posterior ventral nucleus of the thalamus
- ~ **ventralis posteromedialis thalami** posteromedial ventral nucleus of the thalamus
- ~ **ventralis thalami** ventral nucleus of the thalamus
- ~ **vestibularis** vestibular nucleus
- ~ **vestibularis inferior** inferior (spinal) vestibular nucleus
- ~ **vestibularis lateralis** lateral vestibular nucleus, Deiter's nucleus
- ~ **vestibularis medialis** medial (principal) vestibular nucleus, nucleus of Schwalbe
- ~ **vestibularis superior** superior vestibular nucleus, angular nucleus, nucleus of Bekhterev

Nucleus-pulposus-Auflösung f/chemische chemonucleolysis

Nucleus-pulposus-Prolaps *m* herniation of nucleus pulposus; slipped disk, protruded (herniated) intervertebral disk
Nudismus *m* nudism
Nudomanie *f* nudomania
Nudophobie *f* nudophobia *(krankhafte Angst vor nackten Körpern)*
Nuklearfaden *m* nuclear thread
Nuklearmedizin *f* nuclear medicine
Nuklearmembran *f* nuclear membrane
Nuklearspindel *f* nuclear spindle, nucleospindle
Nuklease *f* nuclease *(Enzym)*
Nukleid *n* nucleide *(Nuklein-Metall-Verbindung)*
nukleiform nucleiform
Nuklein *n* nuclein
Nukleinase *f* nucleinase *(Enzym)*
Nukleinsäure *f* nucle[in]ic acid
Nukleinsäurekern *m* nucleic acid core
Nukleoalbumin *n* nucleoalbumin
Nukleoalbuminurie *f* nucleoalbuminuria
Nukleoglukoproteid *n* nucleoglucoproteid, nucleoglucoprotein
Nukleohyaloplasma *n* nucleohyaloplasm
Nukleokapsid *n* nucleocapsid
Nukleolarsubstanz *f* nucleolar substance
Nukleole *f* nucleole, nucleolus
nukleolenartig nucleolar
nukleolenförmig nucleoliform
nukleolenlos anucleolar
Nukleoplasma *n* nucleoplasm
Nukleoproteid *n* nucleoproteid, nucleoprotein
Nukleoretikulum *n* nucleoreticulum, nuclear reticulum
Nukleosid *n* nucleoside
Nukleosidase *f* nucleosidase *(Enzym)*
Nukleosiddiphosphat *n* nucleoside diphosphate
Nukleosidmonophosphat *n* nucleoside monophosphate
Nukleosidtriphosphat *n* nucleoside triphosphate
Nukleotid *n* nucleotide
Nukleotidase *f* nucleotidase, nucleophosphatase *(Enzym)*
Nukleotoxin *n* nucleotoxin
nukleotoxisch nucleotoxic
Nukleus *m s.* Nucleus
nullipar nulliparous
Nullipara *f* nullipara *(Frau, die nicht geboren hat)*
Nulliparität *f* nulliparity *(Zustand vor der ersten Geburt)*
nummular nummular, nummiform
Nußgelenk *n* enarthrosis, spheroid (multiaxial) articulation, ball-and-socket joint
Nutation *f* nutation
Nutrition *f s.* Ernährung
nutritiv *s.* ernährend
Nyktalgie *f* nyctalgia, night pain
Nyktalopie *f* nyctalopia, night blindness, nyctotyphlosis, hesperanopia
Nyktaphonie *f* nyctaphonia, loss of voice during the night
nyktohemeral nyct[er]ohemeral
Nyktophilie *f* nyctophilia

Nyktophobie *f* nyctophobia, noctiphobia *(krankhafte Angst vor Dunkelheit)*
Nyktophonie *f* nyctophonia, loss of voice during the day
Nykturie *f* nycturia, nocturia
Nympha *f* nympha
Nymphektomie *f* nymphectomy
Nymphitis *f* nymphitis, inflammation of the labia minora
nymphohymenal nymphohymenal
nymphokarunkulär nymphocaruncular
nymphoman nymphomaniac
Nymphomanie *f* nymphomania, clitoromania, andromania, hysteromania, metromania
Nymphomanin *f* nymphomaniac
nymphomanisch nymphomaniac
Nymphonkus *m* nymphoncus
Nymphotomie *f* nymphotomy
nystagmiform nystagmiform, nystagmoid
nystagmisch nystagmic
Nystagmogramm *n* nystagmogram
Nystagmograph *m* nystagmograph; electronystagmograph
Nystagmographie *f* nystagmography, nystagmus recording; electronystagmography *(Aufzeichnung des Augenzitterns)*
Nystagmometrie *f* nystagmometry
Nystagmovisometrie *f* nystagmovisometry
Nystagmus *m* nystagmus
~/**angeborener** congenital nystagmus
~/**dissoziativer** dissociated (disjunctive) nystagmus
~/**erblicher** hereditary nystagmus
~ **gegen die Regel** nystagmus against the rule
~/**kalorischer** caloric nystagmus
~/**labyrinthärer** labyrinthine nystagmus
~/**latenter** latent (occlusion) nystagmus
~/**Ohmscher** miner's nystagmus
~/**optokinetischer** optokinetic (railway) nystagmus
~/**oszillatorischer** oscillatory (oscillating) nystagmus, undulatory (vibratory) nystagmus
~/**physiologischer** physiological nystagmus, endpoint (end-positional) nystagmus
~ **retractorius** retraction nystagmus
~/**rhythmischer** rhythmic (resilient, jerking) nystagmus
~/**rotatorischer** rotatory nystagmus
~/**vestibulärer** vestibular nystagmus
nystagmusartig nystagmiform, nystagmoid
Nystagmusaufzeichnung *f s.* Nystagmographie
Nystagmusbild *n* nystagmogram
Nystagmusintensität *f* nystagmus intensity
Nystagmuskurve *f* nystagmogram
Nystagmusmyoklonie *f* nystagmus-myoclonus
Nystagmusrichtung *f* nystagmus direction
Nystagmusschlag *m* nystagmus beat
Nystagmusschreibung *f s.* Nystagmographie
Nystagmuszeichen *n*/**Bardsches** Bard's sign
Nystatin *n* nystatin *(Antibiotikum)*

O.

O

O. *s.* Oculus
O-Agglutination *f* O agglutination
O-Agglutinin *n* O agglutinin
O-Anästhesie *f* Oberst's method
O-Antigen *n* O antigen *(thermostabiles Antigen des Bakterienkörpers)*
O-Antikörper *m* O antibody
Oat-cell-Karzinom *n* oat-cell carcinoma, reserve-cell carcinoma, small-cell carcinoma [of the lung] *(bösartigste Form des Bronchialkarzinoms)*
O_2-Aufsättigung *f* **des Bluts** arterialization, oxygenation of blood
o.B. *s.* Befund/ohne
Obdormition *f* obdormition *(z. B. von Gliedmaßen)*
Obduktion *f* obduction, autopsy, [medico-legal] post-mortem examination, thanatopsy
Obduktions... *s.a.* Sektions...
Obduktionsbefund *m* post-mortem findings
obduzieren to perform an autopsy
O-Bein *n* bandy leg, bowleg, out-knee, genu varum; gonyectyposis
O-beinig bandy-legged, bow-legged, varus, rhaeboscelic
Obelion *n* obelion *(anthropologischer Meßpunkt)*
● **zum ~ hin [gerichtet]** obeliad
oben [liegend] superior, superincumbent, superjacent
Oberarm *m* brachium, upper arm
Oberarmabduktionsgips *m* airplane splint
Oberarmarterie *f* brachial artery
Oberarmfaszie *f* brachial fascia
Oberarmfraktur *f* humerus fracture; fractured humerus (upper arm)
Oberarmgelenkknorren *m/innerer* medial condyle of the humerus
Oberarmgips[verband] *m* cast brace
Oberarmknochen *m* humerus
Oberarmknochen... *s.a.* Humerus...
Oberarmknochenernährungsarterie *f* nutrient artery of the humerus
Oberarmknochengelenkkörper *m/distaler* condyle of the humerus
Oberarmknochenhals *m/chirurgischer* surgical neck [of the humerus]
Oberarmknochenkopf *m* head of the humerus, humeral head
Oberarmknorren *m* condyle of the humerus
Oberarmnagel *m* humerus nail
Oberarmrückseite *f* posterior surface of the arm
Oberarm-Speichen-Gelenk *n* humeroradial joint (articulation)
Oberarm-Speichen-Muskel *m* brachioradialis [muscle]
Oberarmvene *f* brachial vein
Oberarmvorderseite *f* anterior surface of the arm
Oberarzt *m* senior physician

Oberbauch *m* epigastrium, epigastric region, pit of the stomach, upper abdomen, midriff
Oberbauchabwehrspannung *f* upper abdominal rigidity
Oberbauchbeschwerden *fpl* epigastric complaints (discomfort)
Oberbauchbruch *m* epigastrocele, epigastric hernia
Oberbaucherkrankung *f* epigastric disease
Oberbauchmedianschnitt *m* median upper abdominal incision
Oberbauchnervengeflecht *n* epigastric plexus
Oberbauchregion *f* epigastric region, epigastrium
Oberbauchschmerz *m* epigastric (upper abdominal) pain, epigastralgia
Oberbauchschnitt *m/querer* upper transverse abdominal incision, epigastric transverse incision
Oberfläche *f* surface, superficies, facies *(z. B. von Organen)*
~/respiratorische respiratory surface
oberflächenaktiv surface-active
Oberflächenanalgesie *f s.* Oberflächenanästhesie
Oberflächenanästhesie *f* topical anaesthesia, surface (permeation) analgesia
Oberflächenanästhetikum *n* surface (topical) anaesthetic
Oberflächenanatomie *f* surface anatomy
Oberflächenantibiotikum *n* topical antibiotic
Oberflächenbehandlung *f* topical treatment
Oberflächenbestrahlung *f* surface irradiation (X-ray therapy)
Oberflächenbiopsie *f* surface[-cell] biopsy
Oberflächendosis[leistung] *f* surface dose *(Radiologie)*
Oberflächenepithel *n* surface (superficial) epithelium
Oberflächenepithelzelle *f* surface epithelial cell
Oberflächenfaktor *m* contact (Hageman, glass) factor, blood-clotting factor XII
~ der Lungenalveolen lung alveolus surfactant
Oberflächenfaktormangel *m* factor XII deficiency
Oberflächenfaszie *f* superficial fascia
Oberflächengastritis *f* superficial gastritis
Oberflächenhypothermie *f* surface hypothermy
Oberflächenregion *f* superficial zone
Oberflächensensibilität *f* superficial sensibility
Oberflächenspannung *f* surface tension
Oberflächenzellbiopsie *f* surface[-cell] biopsy
oberflächlich superficial, surface
Obergrätenmuskel *m* supraspinatus [muscle]
Oberhaut *f* epiderm[is], tegument, tegumentary epithelium, scarf skin
Oberhaut... *s. a.* Epidermis...
oberhautähnlich epidermoid
Oberhautbildung *f* epidermization
Oberhautentzündung *f* epidermitis, inflammation of the epidermis
Oberhauterkrankung *f* epidermosis

Oberhautfehlbildung f epidermidosis
Oberhautfehlentwicklung f epidermodysplasia
Oberhautpilzkrankheit f epidermomycosis
Oberhautzellgewebe n epidermic tissue
Oberin f matron
Oberkiefer m upper jaw[-bone], [supra]maxilla, supermaxilla, superior maxilla (maxillary bone) ● **hinter dem** ~ retromaxillary ● **über dem** ~ supramaxillary
Oberkiefer... s. a. Maxilla...
Oberkieferalveolarkanal m maxillary canal
Oberkieferarterie f [internal] maxillary artery, Vidian artery
~/hintere posterior superior alveolar artery
~/vordere anterior superior alveolar artery
Oberkieferchondrosarkom n chondrosarcoma of the maxilla
Oberkieferdesmoidgeschwulst f maxillary desmoid tumour
Oberkieferentfernung f[/operative] maxillectomy, excision of the maxilla
Oberkieferentzündung f maxillitis, inflammation of the maxilla
Oberkiefereröffnung f[/operative] maxillary osteotomy
Oberkieferfortsatz m maxillary process, nasal process of the maxilla
~ der unteren Nasenmuschel maxillary process of the inferior nasal concha
~ des Gaumenbeins maxillary process of the palatine bone
~ des Jochbeins maxillary process of the zygomatic bone
Oberkiefergeschwulst f maxillary tumour
Oberkiefergewölbe n maxillary arch
Oberkieferhöcker m maxillary tuberosity
Oberkieferhöhle f maxillary sinus, antrum of Highmore ● **durch die** ~ transmaxillary
Oberkieferhöhlenentzündung f maxillary sinusitis
Oberkieferhöhlenstein m maxillary antrolith
Oberkieferknochenbruch m maxilla fracture, fracture of the upper jaw
oberkiefernah admaxillary
Oberkiefernervengeflecht n superior dental plexus *(der Zähne)*
Oberkieferschmerz m pain in the maxilla, siagonagra
Oberkieferspalte f maxillary fissure; cleft maxilla
Oberkieferteilresektion f hemimaxillectomy
Oberkiefervene f maxillary vein
Oberkieferzahn m maxillary tooth
Oberkörper m [upper] trunk, upper body; chest
Oberlappen m upper lobe
Oberlappenarterie f upper lobe artery
Oberlappenbronchus m upper lobe bronchus
Oberlappenkollaps m upper lobe collapse
Oberlappenresektion f upper lobectomy (lobe resection)
Oberlid n upper [eye]lid, upper palpebra
Oberlidfalte f epicanthic (eye, Mongolian) fold, epicanthus

Oberlidfollikel m upper tarsal follicle
Oberlidhautfalte f s. Oberlidfalte
Oberlidheber m levator palpebrae superioris [muscle], tarsalis superior [muscle], tarsal muscle of the upper eyelid
Oberlidregion f region of the upper eyelid
Oberlidsenkung f ptosis, dropping of the lid
Oberlidvene f superior palpebral vein, vein of the upper eyelid
Oberlippe f upper lip *(des Mundes)*
Oberlippenarterie f superior labial artery
Oberlippenheber m levator labii superioris [muscle], quadratus labii superioris [muscle]
Oberlippenregion f region of the upper lip
Oberlippenspalte f cheiloschisis; cleft lip, harelip
Oberlippen- und Nasenflügelheber m levator labii superioris alaeque nasi [muscle]
Oberlippenvene f superior labial vein
Oberschenkel m 1. thigh; 2. s. Oberschenkelknochen
Oberschenkel... s. a. Femoral... und Femur...
Oberschenkeladduktor m adductor of the thigh
Oberschenkeladduktoren[eigen]reflex m adductor reflex of the thigh
Oberschenkelamputation f thigh (above-knee) amputation
~/Grittische Gritti-Stokes amputation
~/osteoplastische osteoplastic amputation
~/suprakondyläre supracondylar amputation
Oberschenkelamputierter m thigh (above-knee) amputee
Oberschenkelarterie f femoral artery
~/oberflächliche superficial femoral artery
~/tiefe deep femoral artery, profunda femoris artery
Oberschenkelarteriennervengeflecht n femoral plexus
Oberschenkelbruch m 1. femoral fracture, fracture of the femur; fractured femur; 2. s. Femoralhernie
Oberschenkeldekollement n degloving (decollement) of thigh
Oberschenkel[draht]extension f quadriceps femoris extension *(Traumatologie)*
Oberschenkelfaszie f fascia lata
Oberschenkelfaszienspanner m tensor fasciae latae muscle
Oberschenkelgelenkknorren m/**äußerer** lateral condyle of the femur
~/innerer medial condyle of the femur
Oberschenkelhautablederung f degloving of thigh
Oberschenkelhals m femoral neck, neck of the femur
Oberschenkelhalsbruch m neck of the femur, femoral neck, collum femoris
Oberschenkelhautnerv m/**seitlicher** lateral cutaneous nerve of thigh, lateral femoral cutaneous nerve
Oberschenkelknochen m femur, thigh-bone
Oberschenkelknochenbruch m femoral fracture, fracture of the femur

Oberschenkelknochenhals

Oberschenkelknochenhals *m* s. Oberschenkelhals
Oberschenkel[knochen]kopf *m* s. Femurkopf
Oberschenkelkranzarterie *f* femoral circumflex artery
~/**mittlere** medial femoral circumflex artery
~/**seitliche** lateral femoral circumflex artery
Oberschenkelkranzvene *f* femoral circumflex vein
~/**mittlere** medial femoral circumflex vein
~/**seitliche** lateral femoral circumflex vein
Oberschenkelmuskel *m*/**gerader** rectus femoris [muscle]
~/**vierköpfiger** quadriceps femoris [muscle]
Oberschenkelmuskulatur *f* femoral muscles (musculature)
Oberschenkelnagel *m* femur nail
Oberschenkelnerv *m* femoral nerve
Oberschenkelnervenblockade *f* femoral nerve block
Oberschenkelneuralgie *f* meralgia
Oberschenkelphlebitis *f* femoral phlebitis
Oberschenkelprothese *f* above-knee prosthesis
Oberschenkelregion *f* femoral region
Oberschenkelrückseite *f* posterior surface of the thigh
Oberschenkelschmerz *m* meralgia
Oberschenkelseptum *n* femoral septum
Oberschenkelstreck *m* quadriceps femoris extension *(Traumatologie)*
Oberschenkelvene *f* femoral vein
~/**tiefe** deep femoral vein
Oberschenkelvenenentzündung *f* femoral phlebitis
Oberschenkelvenenkanülierung *f* femoral vein cannulation
Oberschenkelvenenpunktion *f* femoral vein puncture
Oberschenkelvorderseite *f* anterior surface of the thigh
Oberschlüsselbeingrube *f* supraclavicular fossa
Oberschwester *f* head (staff) nurse
Obesität *f* s. Fettsucht
Obex *m(f)* obex *(im 4. Hirnventrikel)*
Objektbeziehung *f* object relationship
Objektträger *m* [microscopic] slide
Objektträgeragglutination *f* slide agglutination
Objektträgerkultur *f* slide culture
Objektträgerkulturverfahren *n* **nach Pryce** Pryce slide-culture method *(zur Züchtung von Tuberkulosebakterien)*
Obliquität *f* obliquity
~/**Litzmannsche** Litzmann's obliquity, posterior asynclitism *(Abweichung der Pfeilnaht aus der Beckenführungslinie nach vorn bei der Geburt)*
~/**Naegelesche** Naegele's (biparietal) obliquity, anterior asynclitism *(Abweichung der Pfeilnaht aus der Beckenführungslinie nach hinten bei der Geburt)*
Obliquusreflex *m* obliquus reflex
Obliteration *f* obliteration *(z. B. von Hohlräumen)*
obliterieren to obliterate, to become obliterated *(z. B. Hohlräume)*
~/**nicht** to remain patent *(z. B. Ductus Botalli)*
obliterierend obliterative
Oblongata-Syndrom *n* oblongata syndrome
Obsession *f* obsession, imperative idea; persisting emotion
obsessiv obsessive, obsessional
obsessiv-kompulsiv obsessive-compulsive
Obstetrik *f* obstetrics, O.B., midwifery, tictology
Obstipation *f* obstipation, constipation, costiveness
obstipieren to obstipate, to constipate
obstipiert obstipated, constipated, costive
obstruieren to obstruct
Obstruktion *f* obstruction, emphraxis *(z. B. des Darms)*
~ **der oberen Luftwege** upper airway obstruction
Obstruktionsatelektase *f* obstructive (absorption) atelectasis *(entsteht durch Luftaufsaugung in den Alveolen nach Bronchusverstopfung)*
Obstruktionshydrozephalus *m* obstructive hydrocephalus
obstruktiv obstructive
Obturation *f* obturation, closing, occluding, blocking-up
Obturationsatelektase *f* s. Obstruktionsatelektase
Obturator *m* 1. obturator [muscle]; 2. obturator, mandrin *(einer Hohlkanüle)*; 3. obturator, artificial palate
Obturatorfaszie *f* obturator fascia
Obturatorhernie *f* obturator (subpubic, pelvic) hernia
Obturatorhernienschnitt *m* obturator herniotomy
Obturatorlinie *f* obturator line
Obturatormembran *f* obturator membrane
Obturatormuskel *m* obturator [muscle]
Obturatorring *m* obturator ring
Obturatorzeichen *n* obturator sign *(Röntgen)*
obturieren to obturate *(z. B. Hohlräume)*
Obtusion *f* obtusion, dullness of sensibility, blunting of perception
Occlusio *f* s. Okklusion 1.
~ **dentium** intercuspation, intercusping
~ **pupillae** pupillary obliteration (occlusion)
Ochrodermatose *f* ochrodermatosis
Ochrodermie *f* ochrodermia
Ochronose *f* ochronosis *(Schwarzfärbung der Knorpel und des straffen Bindegewebes)*
Ochsenauge *n* buphthalmos, hydrophthalmos, megalophthalmus
Ochsenherz *n* bovine (ox) heart, cor bovinum; bubocardia
Oculus *m* oculus, o., eye ophthalmus *(s.a. unter Auge)*
~ **caesius** s. Glaukom
~ **contusus** black eye
~ **dominans** master eye
~ **lacrimans** epiphora
~ **leporinus** hare's eye, lagophthalmos, lagophthalmus
~ **purulentus** hypopyon, lunella, onyx

Od-Blut n [group] O Rh-negative blood
OD-Blut n [group] O Rh-positive blood
Ödem n [o]edema
~/**alimentäres** alimentary (nutritional, famine) oedema
~/**angioneurotisches** angioneurotic oedema, angioedema, giant urticaria, Quincke's disease (oedema), acute circumscribed (essential) oedema
~ **der Gliedmaßenenden** acroedema
~/**entzündliches** inflammatory oedema
~/**hysterisches** hysterical (blue) oedema
~/**kardiales** cardiac oedema (dropsy)
~/**kollaterales** collateral oedema
~/**lymphatisches** lymphatic oedema
~/**malignes** malignant (gaseous) oedema, gas gangrene (phlegmon), progressive emphysematous necrosis
~/**nephrotisches** nephrotic oedema
~/**nichtentzündliches** non-inflammatory oedema
~/**pulmonales** pulmonary oedema; wet lung
~/**Quinckesches** s. ~/angioneurotisches
~/**renales** renal oedema (dropsy)
~/**terminales** terminal oedema *(der Lunge)*
~/**toxisches** toxic oedema
ödematös oedematous, pasty, tumid, turgid
o-**Diphenoloxydase** f s. Tyrosinase
Ödipuskomplex m Oedipus complex ● **mit dem ~ behaftet** oedipal
Odont... s.a. Zahn... *und* Dental...
Odontalgie f odontalgia, odontodynia, toothache
odontalgisch odontalgic
Odontatrophie f odontatrophia, atrophy of the teeth
Odontektomie f odontectomy, surgical removal of a tooth
Odonterismus m odonterism, chattering of the teeth
Odontexesis f odontexesis, cleaning and polishing of the teeth
Odontiatrie f odontiatria, treatment of the teeth
Odontitis f odontitis, inflammation of a tooth
Odontoblast m odontoblast, dentine (dentinal) cell
Odontoblastenfortsatz m odontoblastic process, Tome's (dentinal) fibre
Odontoblastentumor m odontoblastoma
odontoblastisch odontoblastic
Odontoblastom n odontoblastoma
Odontoclasis f odontoclasis, breaking of a tooth
odontogen odontogenic, odontogenous
Odontogenese f 1. odontogenesis, odontosis, development of a tooth; 2. s. Dentinbildung
Odontogenesis f **imperfecta** imperfect odontogenesis
Odontogramm n odontogram
Odontographie f odontography
odontographisch odontographic
Odontohyperästhesie f odontohyperaesthesia, sensitiveness of a tooth
Odontoklast m odontoclast

Odontoknesis f odontocnesis, itching of the gums
Odontolith m odontolith, dental calculus; tartar [on the teeth], [dental] scale, dental deposit
Odontolithiasis f ondontolithiasis
Odontologe f odontology, dentistry
Odontologie f odontology, dentistry
odontologisch odontologic
Odontoloxie f odontoloxia, odontoparallaxis, irregularity (obliquity) of the teeth
Odontolyse f odontolysis, absorption of dental tissue
Odontom n odontoma *(gutartige Zahnkeimgeschwulst)*
Odontonekrose f odontonecrosis, necrosis (massive decay) of a tooth
Odontoparallaxe f s. Odontoloxie
Odontopathie f odontopathy, disease of the teeth
Odontophobie f odontophobia *(krankhafte Angst vor Zähnen)*
Odontoplastik f 1. odontoplasty, reshaping of a tooth; 2. s. Orthodontie; 3. odontoplasty *(Implantation von künstlichen Zähnen)*
Odontorrhagie f odontorrhagia, haemorrhage following tooth extraction
Odontoseisis f odontoseisis, looseness of the teeth
Odontoskop n odontoscope, dental mirror
Odontoskopie f odontoscopy
Odontotherapie f odontotherapy, treatment of diseased teeth
Odontotomie f odontotomy, cutting into a tooth, incision into the dental canal
Odontotripie f odontotrypy, boring (drilling) of a tooth
Odontotripsis f odontotripsis, wearing away of the teeth
Odontozele f odontocele, dentoalveolar cyst
Odor m s. Geruch
Odorimeter n odorimeter
Odorimetrie f odorimetry *(z. B. einer Substanz)*
Odynakusis f odynacousis, painful hearing
Odynometer n odynometer
Odynometrie f odynometry, measuring of pain
Odynophagie f odynophagia, painful swallowing
Odynophobie f odynophobia *(krankhafte Angst vor Schmerzen)*
Odynurie f odynuria, painful urination
Oedema n s. Ödem
~ **neonatorum** s. Neugeborenenödem
Oesophagus m s. Ösophagus
offen 1. open; patent *(z. B. ein Gefäß)*; clear *(Luftwege)*; patulous *(Muttermund)*; 2. extroverted *(Psyche)* ● ~ **sein** to be patent *(z. B. ein Gang)*
offenhalten/die Luftwege to maintain the airways clear
offiziell official
offizinal s. offizinell
offizinell officinal, medicinal *(Arzneimittel)*
~/**nicht** unofficinal, magistral

öffnen

öffnen to open; to cut *(z. B. ein Hohlorgan)*; to lance *(einen Abszeß)*; to autopsy *(eine Leiche)*; to dissect *(z. B. ein anatomisches Präparat)*
Öffnung f opening, orifice, orificium, aperture *(s. a. unter Orificium und Ostium)*; foramen; pore, porus; hiatus *(s. a. unter Hiatus)*
~ **des Canalis palatini/untere** lesser palatine foramen
~ **des Fazialiskanals** facial hiatus
~ **des knöchernen Gehörgangs/äußere** external acoustic pore
~ **des knöchernen Gehörgangs/innere** internal acoustic pore
Öffnungston m opening snap *(der Herzklappen)*
Öffnungszuckung f opening contraction *(Physiologie)*
Ohnmacht f faint[ing], swoon, unconsciousness; light-headedness *(Benommenheit)*; obnubilation, mental clouding ● **aus der ~ erwachen** to revive, to return to consciousness (strength) ● **in ~ fallen** to faint, to swoon
~/**kurze** blackout; syncope, syncopal attack
ohnmächtig faint[ing], unconscious, in a faint; light-headed
Ohnmachtsanfall m fainting fit, syncope, syncopal attack
Ohr n ear, auris ● **ein ~ betreffend** monotic, monaural ● **hinter dem ~** retroauricular, postauricular ● **neben dem ~ liegend** parotic, parotid ● **über dem ~** supra-auricular ● **vom ~ ausgehend** otogenic, otogenous
~/**abstehendes** lop (protruding) ear, prominent (outstanding) auricle
~/**äußeres** external ear *(s.a. Ohrmuschel)*
~/**Darwinsches** macacus ear *(kleiner Vorsprung am Ohrmuschelrand)*
~/**inneres** inner (internal) ear
~/**mittleres** middle ear
Ohr... s.a. Ohren...
Ohrabstehen n ear protrusion
Ohrarterie f/**hintere** posterior auricular artery
~/**innere** internal auditory artery
~/**tiefe** deep auricular artery
~/**vordere** anterior auricular artery
Ohratresie f aural atresia
Ohrausfluß m/**blutiger** s. Othämorrhoe
~/**eitriger** s. Otopyorrhoe
Ohrbeteiligung f ear involvement
Ohrbläschen n otocyst, auditory (otic) vesicle *(Embryologie)*
Ohrblutgeschwulst f s. Othämatom
Ohreiterung f s. Othelcosis
Ohren... s.a. Ohr...
Ohrenarzt m otologist, ear specialist, aurist
Ohrenbeschwerden pl ear complaints
Ohrenblutung f ot[haem]orrhagia, bleeding (haemorrhage) from the ear
Ohrenheilkunde f otology, otiatrics
Ohrenkatarrh m otocatarrh, aural catarrh
Ohrenklappe f ear protector
Ohrenklingen n tinnitus [aurium], ringing in the ear, parac[o]usis, paracusia

Ohrenkrankheit f otopathy, disease of the ear
Ohrenlaufen n s. Otorrhoe
ohrenlos anotous, without [external] ears
Ohrenloser m anotus *(Mißgeburt)*
Ohrenlosigkeit f anotia
Ohrenmichel m s. Mumps
Ohrensausen n tinnitus [aurium], susurrus aurium
Ohrenschmerz m earache, otalgia, otodynia, otagra, pain in the ear; otoneuralgia
Ohrenspiegel m otoscope, auriscope, ear speculum, myringoscope
Ohrenspiegelung f otoscopy, myringoscopy
Ohrenspritze f ear syringe
Ohrentropfen mpl ear drops
Ohrentzündung f otitis, inflammation of the ear; aerootitis *(durch Luftdruckabfall)*; baro[o]titis *(durch Luftdruckunterschiede) (Zusammensetzungen s. unter Otitis)*
Ohren- und Nasenheilkunde f otorhinology
Ohrenzange f aural forceps
Ohrfluß m/**eitrig-schleimiger** otoblenorrhoea
ohrförmig ear-shaped, auriform
Ohrgeräusch n tinnitus [aurium]
Ohrgrube f auditory (otic) pit
Ohrhämatom n s. Othämatom
Ohrhöckerchen n/**Darwinsches** Darwin's [ear] tubercle
Ohrinzision f ototomy, incision into the ear
Ohrkanal m auricular (auditory) canal
Ohrkapsel f otic capsule *(Embryologie)*
Ohrknorpel m ear (auricular) cartilage
Ohrkomplikation f ear (aural) complication
Ohrläppchen n earlobe, lobule of the auricle
Ohrläppchenelektrode f earlobe electrode
Ohrleiste f helix
Ohrmikrochirurgie f aural microsurgery
Ohrmikroskop n otomicroscope
Ohrmißbildung f ear malformation
Ohrmuschel f pinna [of the ear], auricle, pavilion of the ear; external ear
Ohrmuschelgrube f/**untere** inferior part of the concha of the ear
Ohrmuschelhöcker m antitragus
Ohrmuschelhypertrophie f macrotia
Ohrmuschelhypoplasie f microtia
Ohrmuschelknorpelhöcker m helical spine
Ohrmuschelloser m anotus
Ohrmuschelplastik f otoplasty
Ohrmuschelverdickung f pachyotia
Ohrmuschelvergrößerung f/**abnorme** macrotia
Ohrmuschelverkleinerung f/**abnorme** microtia
Ohrmuschelwindung f crus of the helix
Ohrmuskel m auricular muscle, auricularis [muscle]
~/**hinterer** posterior auricular muscle, auricularis posterior muscle
~/**oberer** superior auricular muscle, auricularis superior muscle, attolens aurem [muscle]
~/**vorderer** anterior auricular muscle, auricularis anterior muscle, attrahens aurem [muscle]

Ohrmuskelschwäche f otomyasthenia, weakness of the ear muscles
Ohrolive f earpiece, ear tip *(am Stethoskop)*
Ohrpinzette f ear forceps
Ohrplastik f otoplasty
Ohrplatte f otic placode, auditory plate
Ohrplattenstiel m placodal (auditory) stalk *(Embryologie)*
Ohrpolyp m ear polyp[us], otopolypus
Ohrpolypenzange f ear polypus forceps
ohrschädigend ototoxic
Ohrschmalz n earwax, cerumen
Ohrschmalzdrüse f ceruminous gland
Ohrschmalzpfropf m ceruminoma
Ohrschmalzsekretion f/**verstärkte** ceruminosis
Ohrschwindel m aural (auditory) vertigo
Ohrsonde f ear probe
Öhrsonde f probe with eye
Ohrspeicheldrüse f parotid [gland], parotid salivary gland
Ohrspeicheldrüsenatrophie f parotid gland atrophy
Ohrspeicheldrüsenausführungsgang m parotid (Stensen's) duct
Ohrspeicheldrüsenentzündung f s. Mumps
Ohrspeicheldrüsenexstirpation f s. Parotidektomie
Ohrspeicheldrüsenfaszie f parotid fascia
Ohrspeicheldrüsenfistel f parotid [gland] fistula
Ohrspeicheldrüsengangröntgen[kontrast]bild n parotid sialogram
Ohrspeicheldrüsengangröntgen[kontrast]darstellung f parotid sialography
Ohrspeicheldrüsengebiet n parotid region
Ohrspeicheldrüsengewebe n parotid glandular tissue
Ohrspeicheldrüsenstein m parotid stone (gland calculus)
Ohrspeicheldrüsenvene f parotid vein
Ohrspeicheldrüsenverhärtung f parotidosclerosis, induration (sclerosis) of the parotid gland
Ohrspeicheldrüsenzyste f parotid cyst
Ohrspülung f irrigation of the ear canal
Ohrtrichter m ear speculum
Ohrtrichterhalter m ear speculum holder
Ohrtrompete f Eustachian (otopharyngeal) tube, [oto]salpinx, auditory (pharyngotympanic) tube, tuba, tube
Ohrtrompeten... *s.a.* Tuben...
Ohrtrompetendysfunktion f Eustachian tube dysfunction
Ohrtrompetenentzündung f [Eustachian] salpingitis, eustachitis, syringitis
Ohrtrompetenkatheterismus m salpingocatheterism
Ohrtrompetenknorpel m Eustachian cartilage, cartilage of the auditory tube
Ohrtrompetenschleimhaut f mucous membrane of the auditory tube
Ohrtrompetenstenose f salpingostenochoria, salpingemphraxis
Ohrtupfer m earplug

Ohr- und Warzenfortsatzentzündung f otomastoiditis, otitis with mastoiditis
Ohrvene f ear (auricular) vein
~/hintere posterior auricular vein
~/innere internal auditory vein
~/vordere anterior auricular vein
Ohrverschluß m s. Otokleisis
Ohrwatte f earplug
Oidiomykose f oidiomycosis *(Pilzerkrankung durch Oidium cutaneum)*
oidiomykotisch oidiomycotic
Oidium n **albicans** Oidium albicans, thrush fungus
Oikophobie f oikophobia *(krankhafte Angst vor Häuslichkeit)*
okkludieren to occlude, to close
Okklusion f 1. occlusion, closure, obliteration (s. a. unter Occlusio) 2. occlusion *(Stomatologie)*
~/anomale (fehlerhafte) abnormal occlusion, malocclusion
Okklusionsangiographie f occlusion angiography *(mittels Ballonkatheterblockade)*
Okklusionsebene f occlusion (bite) plane *(Stomatologie)*
Okklusionsikterus m obstructive jaundice, resorptive icterus *(durch Galleabflußstauung)*
Okklusionsileus m occlusive (mechanical) ileus
Okklusionskraft f occlusion force
Okklusionskurve f curve of occlusion *(Stomatologie)*
Okklusionsligatur f occluding ligature
Okklusionsnystagmus m occlusion nystagmus
Okklusionsstörung f occlusion dysharmony (dystrophy) *(Stomatologie)*
Okklusionstrauma n occlusion trauma
Okklusionsverband m occlusive dressing (bandage)
Okklusivpessar n occlusive (check) pessary, diaphragm pessary
okkult occult, hidden; concealed; obscure
Oktagravida f octigravida
Oktipara f octipara
Okular n eyepiece *(des Mikroskops)*
Okularbild n ocular image
Okularnystagmus m ocular nystagmus
Okulentum n oculentum
Okuloelektromyogramm n oculoelectromyogram
okulofazial oculofacial
okulogyr oculogyric, oculogyral
okulokardial oculocardiac
okulokutan oculocutaneous
okulomotorisch oculomotor
Okulomotorius m oculomotor (third cranial) nerve
Okulomotoriuskern m ocular motor nucleus
Okulomotoriuslähmung f oculomotor palsy (paralysis)
Okulomykose f oculomycosis
okulo-otokutan oculo-otocutaneous
Okulopathie f s. Augenkrankheit
okulopathisch oculopathic

Okuloplethysmographie

Okuloplethysmographie f oculoplethysmography
okulopupillär oculopupillary
okulosensorisch oculosensory
okulozephalogyr oculocephalogyric
Okzipital... s.a. Hinterhaupt...
Okzipitalbogen m occipital arc
Okzipitaldreieck n occipital triangle
Okzipitalisation f occipitalization (z. B. des Atlas)
okzipitalisieren to occipitalize
Okzipitalnervenschmerz m occipital neuralgia
Okzipitalplexus m occipital plexus
Okzipitalpunkt m occipital point
Okzipitalsinus m occipital sinus
Okzipitalwinkel m occipital angle
Okzipitalzisterne f cerebellomedullary cisterna
okzipitoanterior occipito-anterior
okzipitoaxial occipito-axial
Okzipitofrontalzirkumferenz f occipitofrontal (head) circumference
okzipitotemporal occipitotemporal
Okziput n s. Hinterhaupt
Öl n oleum, oil
~/ätherisches volatile (essential) oil
Ölbehandlung f oleotherapy
Oleandervergiftung f oleandrism
Oleandomycin n oleandomycin (Antibiotikum)
Olekranon n olecranon [process]
Olekranonfraktur f olecranon fracture
Olekranonreflex m elbow reflex
Olekranonregion f olecranon region
Olekranonspitze f olecranon tip
Olekranonsporn m olecranon spur
Oleogranulom n oleogranuloma, oleoma, eleoma (Fremdkörpergeschwulst nach Ölinfektion)
Oleom n, **Oleosklerom** n s. Oleogranulom
Oleothorax m oleothorax
Olfaktometer n olfactometer; osmometer, osphresiometer
Olfaktometrie f olfactometry
Olfaktophobie f olfactophobia (krankhafte Angst vor Gerüchen)
Ölgeschwulst f s. Oleogranulom
ölhaltig oily, oleaginous
ölig oily, oleaginous; greasy; unctuous
Oligakisurie f oligakisuria (Wasserlassen in großen Intervallen)
Oligämie f oligohaemia, oligaemia, deficiency in blood volume, hyphaemia
Oligergasie f oligergasia, oligergastic disorder
Oligoblast m oligoblast (Oligodendrozytenvorstufe)
Oligoblennie f oligoblennia, deficient secretion of mucus
Oligocholie f oligocholia, deficiency of the bile
Oligochromämie f oligochromaemia, deficiency of haemoglobin in the blood
Oligochromasie f oligochromasia, deficiency of haemoglobin in the erythrocytes
Oligochylie f oligochylia, deficiency of bile
Oligochymie f oligochymia, deficiency of chyme
Oligodaktylie f oligodactyly (angeborenes Fehlen von Fingern und Zehen)
Oligodendroblastom n oligodendroblastoma
Oligodendroglia f oligodendroglia (Nervengewebestützsubstanz)
Oligodendrogliazelle f oligodendrocyte
Oligodendrogliom n oligodendroglioma, oligodendroma (gutartige Hirngeschwulst)
Oligodendrogliomatosis f oligodendrogliomatosis
Oligodendrozyt m oligodendrocyte
Oligodipsie f oligodipsia
Oligodontie f oligodontia
oligodynamisch oligodynamic
Oligoerythrozythämie f oligoerythrocythaemia
Oligogalaktie f oligogalactia, deficient secretion of milk
oligogen oligogenic
Oligogen n oligogene
Oligoglobulie f oligoglobulia
Oligohidrie f olig[o]hidria, deficient perspiration
Oligohydramnie f oligo[hydr]amnios, deficiency of amniotic fluid
Oligohydrie f olig[o]hydria, oligydria, deficiency of body fluids
Oligohydrurie f oligohydruria
Oligokardie f oligocardia
Oligolalie f oligolalia
oligolezithal oligolecithal (z. B. Eizelle)
Oligomanie f oligomania
Oligomelus m oligomelus (Mißgeburt)
Oligomenorrhoe f oligomenorrhoea, scanty (abnormally infrequent) menstruation
Oligonukleotid n oligonucleotide
Oligophosphaturie f oligophosphaturia
oligophren oligophrenic
Oligophrenie f oligophrenia, mental deficiency, micropsychia, defective mental development
Oligoplasmie f oligoplasmia, deficiency of plasma
Oligopnoe f oligopnoea, retarded breathing
Oligoptyalismus m oligoptyalism, oligosialia, diminished secretion of saliva
Oligosialie f s. Oligoptyalismus
Oligosiderämie f oligosideraemia, deficiency of iron in the blood
Oligospermie f oligospermatism, oligo[zoo]spermia, scarcity of spermatozoa
Oligotrichie f oligotrichia
Oligozythämie f oligocythaemia, deficiency of blood cells
Oligurie f oliguresis, oliguria, hypouresis, reduced output of urine
oligurisch oliguric
Öl-Immersionslinse f oil-immersion lens
Öl-Immersions-Mikroskop n oil-immersion light microscope
Öl-Immersions-Objektiv n oil-immersion objective
Oliva f, **Olive** f olive, oliva (Gehirnabschnitt)
olivenförmig olivary
Olivenkern m olivary body (nucleus) ● **vom ~ weg gerichtet** olivifugal ● **zum ~ hin gerichtet** olivipetal
~/unterer inferior olive (olivary nucleus)

Olivensonde f olive-tipped bougie
Oliver-Cardarelli-Zeichen n Oliver's sign *(Kehlkopfpulsationen bei Aortenerweiterung)*
olivospinal olivospinal
Ollier-Syndrom n Ollier's syndrome (disease), dyschondroplasia
Ölplombe f **des Thorax** oleothorax
Öltherapie f oleotherapy
Ölung f unction
Omagra f(n) omagra, gout in the shoulder
Omalgie f omalgia, omodynia, pain in the shoulder
Omarthralgie f omarthralgia, pain in the shoulder joint
Omarthritis f omarthritis, inflammation of the shoulder joint
Ombrophobie f ombrophobia *(krankhafte Angst vor Regen)*
omental omental
Omentektomie f oment[um]ectomy, epiploectomy, excision of the omentum
Omentitis f omentitis, inflammation of the omentum (epiploon), epiploitis
Omentofixation f s. Omentopexie
Omentokardiopexie f cardiomentopexy
Omentopexie f omentopexy, omentofixation, epiplopexy
Omentoplastik f omentoplasty, epiploplasty, omental graft[ing]
Omentorrhaphie f omentorrhaphy, epiplorrhaphy, suture of the omentum
Omentosplenopexie f omentosplenopexy, fixation of the omentum and the spleen
Omentotomie f omentotomy, incision of the omentum
Omentozele f omentocele, omental hernia, epiplocele
Omentum n omentum, epiploon; apron ● ohne ~ anepiploic
~ **majus** greater (gastrocolic) omentum, caul
~ **minus** lesser (gastrohepatic) omentum, omentulum
Omentum... s. a. Netz...
Omentumbedeckung f omental overcoat *(z. B. bei Blinddarmperforation)*
Omentumeinschnitt m s. Omentotomie
Omentumnaht f s. Omentorrhaphie
Omitis f omitis, inflammation of the shoulder
omnivor omnivorous *(z. B. Bakterien)*
omohyoid omohyoid
Omphalektomie f omphalectomy, excision of the navel, umbilectomy
omphalisch omphalic, umbilical
Omphalitis f omphalitis, inflammation of the navel
Omphalochorion n omphalochorion, yolk sac placenta
Omphalogenese f omphalogenesis, development of the yolk sac
Omphaloma n omphaloma, tumour of the umbilicus

omphalomesenterial omphalomesenteric
Omphalomonodidymus m omphalomonodidymus *(Mißgeburt)*
Omphalopagus m omphalopagus, omphalodidymus *(Mißgeburt)*
Omphalophlebitis f s. Nabelvenenentzündung
Omphalophlegmone f omphalophlegmon, umbilical phlegmon
Omphaloproptosis f omphaloproptosis, prolapse of the umbilical cord, umbilical cord prolapse; funis (cord) presentation *(bei der Geburt)*
Omphalorrhagie f omphalorrhagia, haemorrhage from the umbilicus
Omphalorrhexis f omphalorrhexis, rupture of the umbilicus
Omphalorrhoe f omphalorrhoea, lymphatic effusion at the navel
Omphalos m s. Nabel
omphalospinal omphalospinous
Omphalotaxis f omphalotaxis, reposition of the prolapsed umbilicus
Omphalotom n omphalotome
Omphalotomie f omphalotomy, cutting of the umbilical cord
Omphalotripsie f omphalotripsy, crushing of the umbilical cord
Omphalotriptor m omphalotribe
Omphalozele f omphalocele, umbilical hernia
Omphalus m s. Nabel
Onanie f onanism, masturbation, ipsation; self-pollution
Onanist m onanist
Onchocerca f onchocerca *(Nematodengattung; durch Stechmücken übertragene Krankheitserreger der Tropen)*
~ **volvulus** onchocerca volvulus *(Übertragung durch die Kriebelmücke)*
Onchodermatitis f onchodermatitis
Onchozerkenbefall m s. Onchozerkose
Onchozerkom n onchocercoma
Onchozerkose f onchocerciasis, onchocercosis, [tropical] river blindness, volvulosis
Onchozerkoseknoten m onchocercoma
Oneirismus m oneirism
Oneirodynia f oneirodynia, somnambulism and nightmare
~ **activa** active oneirodynia, somnambulism, sleepwalking, somnambulance, hypnobatia
~ **passiva** passive oneirodynia, nightmare
Oneirogmus m s. Pollutio
oneiroid oneiric
Oneirologie f oneirology, science of dreams
Oneiroskopie f oneiroscopy, dream interpretation, analysis of dreams
Oniomanie f oniomania
Oniro... s. Oneiro...
Onkinozele f onkinocele, inflammatory swelling of the tendon sheaths
onkogen oncogen[et]ic
Onkogen n oncogen
Onkogenese f oncogenesis, tumour formation
Onkograph m oncograph

Onkographie

Onkographie f oncography *(Aufzeichnung von Volumenschwankungen der Organe)*
onkographisch oncographic
Onkologe m oncologist, cancerologist
Onkologie f oncology, cancerology
onkologisch oncologic
Onkolyse f oncolysis, lysis (destruction) of tumour cells
Onkolytikum n oncolytic [agent]
onkolytisch oncolytic, destroying tumour cells
Onkometer n oncometer
Onkometrie f oncometry *(Messung von Volumenschwankungen der Organe)*
onkometrisch oncometric
Onkosphäre f onc[h]osphere, proscolex
onkostatisch oncostatic
onkotherapeutic oncotherapeutic
Onkotherapie f oncotherapy, treatment of tumours
onkotisch oncotic
Onkotomie f oncotomy, incision of a tumour
onkotrop oncotropic, tumouraffin
Onkozyt m 1. oncocyte, tumour cell; 2. oncocyte, oxyphilic granular cell
onkozytisch oncocytic
Onkozytom n oncocytoma, oxyphilic granular cell adenoma
~/renales renal oncocytoma
Onomastik f, **Onomatologie** f onomatology
Onomatomanie f onomatomania
Onomatopoese f onomatopoiesis, formation of meaningless words
Ontogenese f ontogeny, ontogenesis, individual development
ontogenetisch ontogen[et]ic
Onych... s.a. Nagel...
Onychalgie f onychalgia, onychodynia, pain in the nails; painful nails
Onychatrophie f onychatrophia, atrophy of the nails
Onychauxis f s. Nagelhypertrophie
Onychektomie f onychectomy, excision of a nail
Onychexallaxis f onychexallaxis, degeneration of the nails
Onychie f onychia, onychitis, inflammation of the nail matrix
Onychin n onychin *(harte Nagelsubstanz)*
Onychitis f s. Onychie
Onychodystrophie f onychodystrophy
Onychogramm n onychogram
Onychograph m onychograph
Onychographie f onychography *(Darstellung des Nagelpulses)*
onychographisch onychographic
Onychogryposis f onychogryp[h]osis; curved (hooked) nails
Onychohelkosis f onychohelcosis, ulceration of the nails
Onychoheterotopia f onychoheterotopia
Onychoklasis f onychoclasis, breaking of the nails
Onychokryptosis f onychocryptosis; ingrowing nails
Onycholysis f onycholysis, loosening of the nails
Onychomadesis f onychomadesis, loss of the nails, lapsus unguium
Onychomalazie f onychomalacia, softening of the nails
Onychomykose f onychomycosis, ringworm of the nails
Onychopathie f onychopathy, disease of the nails, onychonosus; onychoschisis
onychopathisch onychopathic
Onychopathologie f onychopathology *(Lehre von den Nagelkrankheiten)*
Onychophagie f onychophagia, biting of the nails
Onychophym n onychophyma, thickening of the nails
Onychoptose f onychoptosis, falling-off of the nails
Onychorrhexis f onychorrhexis, splitting and brittleness of the nails
Onychoschisis f onychoschizia, schizonychia
Onychostroma n s. Nagelbett
Onychotillomanie f onychotillomania, neurotic picking at the nails *(Verhaltensstörung)*
Onychotomie f onychotomy, incision into a nail
Onychotrophie f onychotrophy, nutrition of the nails
Onyx m s. Nagel 1.
Onyxitis f s. Onychie
Ooblast m ooblast
Oogenese f o[v]ogenesis, ovigenesis
oogenetisch oogenetic, ovigen[et]ic, ovigenous
Oogonium n o[v]ogonium, primordial ovum
Ookinese f ookinesis
Ookinet m ookinete *(Entwicklungsstufe der Malariaerreger)*
ookinetisch ookinetic
Oolemma n oolemma
Oophoralgie f oophoralgia, ovarialgia, oothecalgia, pain in the ovary
Oophorauxe f oophorauxe, enlargement of the ovary
Oophorektomie f oophorectomy, oothectomy, excision of an ovary, ovariectomy, ovariosteresis; female castration
Oophoritis f oophoritis, ovaritis, inflammation of an ovary
Oophoro... s.a. Eierstock... und Ovar...
Oophorohysterektomie f oophorohysterectomy, ovariohysterectomy, hystero-oophorectomy, hystero-ovariotomy
Oophorom n oophoroma, tumour of the ovary
Oophoromalazie f oophoromalacia, softening of an ovary
Oophoromanie f oophoromania *(psychische Störung infolge Eierstockfunktionsstörung)*
Oophoron n oophoron, ovary, o[v]arium *(Zusammensetzungen s. unter Eierstock)*
Oophoropathie f oophoropathy, ovariopathy, ovarian disease
Oophoropexie f oophoropexy, ovariopexia, fixation of an ovary

Oophoroplastik f oophoroplasty, plastic operation of the ovary
Oophorosalpingektomie f oophorosalpingectomy, ovariosalpingectomy
Oophorosalpingitis f oophorosalpingitis, tuboovaritis, salpingo-oophoritis, ovariosalpingitis
Oophorostomie f oophorostomy, ovariostomy
Oophorotomie f oophorotomy, ovariotomy, oophorocystostomy, incision into the ovary
oophorozökal oophorocaecal
Oophorozystektomie f oophorocystectomy, excision of an ovarian cyst
Oophorozystose f oophorocystosis
Oophorozystostomie f oophorocystostomy
Oophorrhagie f oophorrhagia, haemorrhage from an ovary
Oophorrhaphie f oopho[ro]rrhaphy, suture of an ovary
Ooplasma n ooplasm
Ooporphyrin n ooporphyrin
Oospermium n oosperm, fertilized egg, zygote
Oothek f s. Oophoron
Oozyste f oocyst
Oozyt m, **Oozyte** f s. Eizelle
Oozytennukleus m oocyte nucleus
OP m s. Operationssaal
opak opaque, opake, impervious to light
~/nicht non-opaque
Opaleszenz f opalescence (z. B. des Urins)
opaleszieren to opalesce
opaleszierend opalescent
Opeidoskop n opeidoscope (Instrument zur Projektion der Stimmschwingungen)
operabel operable
Operabilität f operability (z. B. einer Geschwulst)
Operateur m operator, operating surgeon
Operation f operation ● **bei der Durchführung einer ~** in doing an operation ● **eine ~ vornehmen** to operate, to perform (carry out) an operation ● **einer ~ folgend** postoperative, postsurgical ● **mittels ~** operative, operational ● **schleunigst eine ~ durchführen** to hurry forward an operation ● **sich einer ~ unterziehen** to undergo (have) an operation, to be operated ● **während einer ~** intraoperative, during the operation
~ am offenen Herzen open-heart surgery (technique), open-intracardiac operation
~/aseptische clean operation; aseptic surgery
~/Baldwinsche Baldwin operation (Vaginalplastik)
~/Baldy-Frankesche Baldy-Webster operation (zur Gebärmutterfixation)
~/Bardenheuersche Bardenheuer's operation (zur Milzfixation)
~/Bassinische Bassini operation (bei Leistenbruch)
~/Bergenhemsche Bergenhem's operation (Harnleiterimplantation in das Rektum)
~/Brocksche Brock operation, pulmonary valvotomy
~/Caldwell-Lucsche Caldwell-Luc operation (bei Kieferhöhlenvereiterung)
~/Coffey-Mayosche Coffey's operation, ureterosigmoidostomy
~/dringliche emergency operation
~/einzeitige one-stage (single-stage) operation
~/elektive elective operation
~/Förstersche Foerster's operation, posterior rhizotomy
~/Fredet-Ramstedtsche Fredet-Ramstedt operation (bei Pylorusstenose)
~/Henle-Albeesche Albee's (Albee-Delbet) operation (bei Schenkelhalsfraktur)
~/kosmetische cosmetic operation
~/lebensgefährliche capital operation
~/Leriche-Brüningsche Leriche's operation, periarterial sympathectomy
~/Mandlsche Mandl's operation (zur Nebenschilddrüsenadenomentfernung)
~/mastoidotympanoplastische mastoidotympanoplastic surgery
~/osteoplastische osteoplasty, osteoplastic operation
~/Pirogowsche Pirogoff's amputation (des Fußes)
~/plastische plastic operation
~/Pottsche Pott's operation, Pott's and Smith's procedure (Verbindung zwischen großer Körperschlagader und Lungenschlagader bei Fallotscher Tetralogie)
~/radikale radical operation
~/Ramstedt-Webersche Ramstedt operation, pyloromyotomy
~/Rehn-Delormesche Rehn's operation (zur Behebung des Mastdarmvorfalls)
~/rekonstruktive reconstructive operation
~/Schauta-Wertheimsche Schauta-Wertheim operation, abdominal hysterectomy; vaginal hysterectomy
~/schwierige difficult (capital) operation
~/Simonsche Simon's operation (bei Blasen-Scheiden-Fistel und Dammriß)
~/Taussig-Blalock-Pottsche Taussig-Blalock operation (Schaffung eines künstlichen Ductus Botalli)
~/Totische Toti's operation, dacryocystorhinostomy
~/Trendelenburgsche Trendelenburg's operation (bei Lungenembolie)
~/Vinebergsche Vineberg operation (zur Herzmuskelrevaskularisierung)
~/vitale emergency operation
~/Wertheimsche Wertheim's hysterectomy (operation), radical (caesarean) hysterectomy
~/Westsche West's operation, dacryocystorhinostomy
~/Whipplesche Whipple's operation, duodenopancreatectomy
~/Wölflersche Wölfler's operation, anterior gastroenterostomy
~ zum Zeitpunkt der Wahl elective operation, operation of election
~/zweizeitige two-stage operation
Operationsassistent m assisting surgeon

Operationsbedingung

Operationsbedingung f operating condition
Operationsbericht m operation record
Operationsgebiet n operating field
Operationshandschuhe mpl surgical gloves
Operationskittel m [surgical] gown, surgeon's (doctor's) overall
Operationskleidung f theatre clothing
Operationslicht n theatre light
Operationsmesser n scalpel, operating knife
Operationsmethode f surgical method
Operationsmikroskop n operating (surgical) croscope
Operationsmortalität f operative mortality
Operationsmortalitätsrate f operative mortality rate
Operationsmütze f operating cap
Operationsnarbe f operation (postoperative) scar
Operationsnarbenbruch m incisional hernia
Operationsrisiko n operative (operation) risk
Operationssaal m [operating] theatre, operating room
Operationssaalausrüstung f operating-theatre equipment
Operationssaalpersonal n operating-room staff
Operationssaaltemperatur f operating-room temperature
Operationsschere f operating (surgical) scissors
Operationsschock m operative (surgical) shock
Operationsschürze f surgeon's (operating) apron
Operationsschwester f surgical (scrub) nurse, instrument (theatre) sister
Operationssitus m site of the operation
Operationsskalpell n scalpel, operating knife
Operationsstuhl m/zahnärztlicher dental [operating] chair
Operationstaktik f operative procedure
Operationsteam n operating (surgical) team
Operationstechnik f operative technique
Operationstisch m operating table
Operationstuch n towel, drape
Operationsverfahren n operative (surgical) procedure
~/**mehrzeitiges** staged operative procedure
Operationswahn m tomomania
Operationswunde f surgical (operation) wound
operativ operative, surgical, operational
~/**nicht** non-surgical, conservative
Operculum n 1. operculum (des Großhirns); 2. operculum, lid, cover; valve; 3. operculum (eines Zahnes) ● ein ~ besitzend operculate[d]
~ **frontale** frontal operculum
~ **frontoparietale (proper)** [fronto]parietal operculum
~ **temporale** temporal operculum
operierbar operable
~/**nicht [mehr]** inoperable
Operierbarkeit f operability (z. B. einer Geschwulst)
operieren to operate [on a patient]
~/**dringend** to hurry forward an operation
~/**ein betäubtes Tier** to vivisect

operiert werden to have an operation, to undergo surgery
~ **werden an** to be operated on (upon)
~ **werden/wegen Krebs** to be operated upon for carcinoma
Opernglashand f opera-glass hand (bei Rheumatoidarthritis)
Operon n operon (Genetik)
Ophiasis f ophiasis (Glatzenbildung am Hinterkopf von Kindern)
Ophidiasis f ophidism, ophidiasis, ophiotoxaemia, poisoning from snake venom
Ophidiophobie f ophidiophobia (krankhafte Angst vor Schlangen)
ophiophob ophiophobe
Ophiotoxämie f s. Ophidiasis
Ophryitis f ophr[y]itis, inflammation (dermatitis) of the eyebrow
Ophryon n ophryon
Ophryosis f ophryosis, spasm of the eyebrow
Ophthalm... s. a. Augen...
Ophthalmalgie f ophthalmalgia, ophthalmodynia, pain in the eye
Ophthalmatrophie f ophthalmatrophia, atrophy of the eye
Ophthalmecchymose f ophthalmecchymosis, blood effusion into the conjunctiva
Ophthalmektomie f ophthalmectomy, excision of an eye; enucleation of the eyeball
Ophthalmenzephalon n ophthalmencephalon, visual nervous mechanism (apparatus)
Ophthalmia f ophthalmia, ophthalmitis, inflammation of the eye (s. a. unter Augenentzündung)
~ **eczematosa** ophthalmia eczematosa, phlyctenulosis
~ **electrica** electric ophthalmia, flash blindness, actinic (ultraviolet) ray ophthalmia; flasheye
~ **migratoria** migratory (sympathetic) ophthalmia
~ **neonatorum** purulent (gonorrhoeal) conjunctivitis of the newborn
~ **nivalis** snow blindness, solar photophthalmia
~ **nodosa** nodose ophthalmia, caterpillar [hair] ophthalmia
~ **sympathica** s. ~ migratoria
Ophthalmie f s. Ophthalmia
Ophthalmiekranker m ophthalmiac
ophthalmisch ophthalmic
Ophthalmitis f s. Ophthalmia
ophthalmitisch ophthalmitic
Ophthalmoblennorrhoe f ophthalmoblennorrhoea, purulent (gonnorrhoeal) ophthalmia
Ophthalmochirurgie f ophthalmic surgery
Ophthalmochromoskopie f ophthalmochromoscopy
Ophthalmodiagnostik f ophthalmodiagnostics
Ophthalmodiaphanoskop n ophthalmodiaphanoscope
Ophthalmodiaphanoskopie f ophthalmodiaphanoscopy
Ophthalmodonese f ophthalmodonesis, tremulous (oscillatory) eye movement

Ophthalmodynamographie f ophthalmodynamography
Ophthalmodynamometer n ophthalmodynamometer
Ophthalmodynamometrie f ophthalmodynamometry *(1. Druckmessung in den Netzhautgefäßen; 2. Konvergenzkraftbestimmung)*
Ophthalmodynie f s. Ophthalmalgie
Ophthalmoeikonometer n ophthalmo-eikonometer
Ophthalmograph m ophthalmograph
Ophthalmographie f ophthalmography, description of the eyes
Ophthalmokarzinom n ophthalmocarcinoma, carcinoma of the eyeball
Ophthalmokopie f ophthalmocopia, ophthalmokopia, eye-strain; fatigue of the eyes
Ophthalmolith m ophthalmolith
Ophthalmologe m ophthalmologist, oculist
Ophthalmologie f ophthalmology, ophthalmiatrics, oculistics
ophthalmologisch ophthalmologic[al]
Ophthalmomalazie f ophthalmomalacia, softening of the eye
Ophthalmometer n ophthalmometer
Ophthalmometrie f ophthalmometry *(Bestimmung des Refraktionsfehlers der Augen)*
Ophthalmomyiasis f ophthalmomyiasis
Ophthalmomykose f ophthalmomycosis
Ophthalmomyositis f ophthalmomy[os]itis, inflammation of the eye muscles
Ophthalmomyotomie f ophthalmomyotomy, division of an eye muscle
Ophthalmoneuritis f ophthalmoneuritis, optic neuritis, inflammation of the ophthalmic nerve
Ophthalmoneuromyelitis f ophthalmoneuromyelitis, optic neuromyelitis, neuro-optic myelitis
Ophthalmopathie f s. Augenkrankheit
Ophthalmophakometer n ophthalmophacometer
Ophthalmophakometrie f ophthalmophacometry
Ophthalmophobie f ophthalmophobia *(krankhafte Angst vor dem Angesehenwerden)*
Ophthalmophthisis f ophthalmophthisis, ocular phthisis, shrinking (shrivelling) of the eyeball
Ophthalmophyma n ophthalmophyma, swelling of the eyeball
Ophthalmoplastik f ophthalmoplasty
ophthalmoplastisch ophthalmoplastic
Ophthalmoplegia f s. Ophthalmoplegie
~ **externa** external ophthalmoplegia, paralysis of the external ocular muscles
~ **interna** internal ophthalmoplegia, paralysis of the iris and ciliary apparatus
~ **plus (progressiva)** progressive external ophthalmoplegia
Ophthalmoplegie f ophthalmoplegia, paralysis of the eye muscles; paralysis of the oculomotor nerve *(s.a. unter Ophthalmoplegia)*
~/**komplette** total ophthalmoplegia
ophthalmoplegisch ophthalmoplegic

Ophthalmoreaktion f ophthalmoreaction, oculoreaction, ophthalmic (conjunctival) reaction, conjunctival test *(zur Allergietestung)*
Ophthalmorrhagie f ophthalmorrhagia, haemorrhage from the eye
Ophthalmorrhexis f ophthalmorrhexis, rupture of the eyeball
Ophthalmorrhoe f ophthalmorrhoea, discharge from the eye
Ophthalmos m ophthalmos, ophthalmus, o., eye, oculus *(Zusammensetzungen s. unter* Auge *und* Oculus*)*
Ophthalmoskop n ophthalmo[fundo]scope
Ophthalmoskopie f ophthalmo[fundo]scopy
Ophthalmoskopiker m ophthalmoscopist
ophthalmoskopisch ophthalmoscopic
Ophthalmosonometrie f ophthalmosonometry
Ophthalmostase f ophthalmostasis, fixation of an eye
Ophthalmostat m ophthalmostat
Ophthalmostatometer n ophthalmostatometer
Ophthalmostatometrie f ophthalmostatometry, measurement of the eye position
Ophthalmosterese f ophthalmosteresis, loss of the eye
Ophthalmosynchisis f ophthalmosynchisis, effusion into the eye
Ophthalmothermometer n ophthalmothermometer
Ophthalmotomie f ophthalmotomy, incision into the eye, dissection of the eye
Ophthalmotonometer n ophthalmotonometer
Ophthalmotonometrie f ophthalmotonometry, measurement of intraocular tension
Ophthalmotonus m ophthalmotonus, intraocular tension
Ophthalmotropometer n ophthalmotropometer
Ophthalmotropometrie f ophthalmotropometry, measurement of the eye movements
Ophthalmozele f ophthalmocele
Ophthalmozentese f ophthalmocentesis, puncture of the eye
Opiat n opiate
Opiophagie f s. Opiumgenuß
Opisthenar m s. Handrücken
Opisthion n opisthion *(anthropologischer Meßpunkt)*
Opisthognathie f opisthognathia, opisthogeny, opisthognatism, recession of the lower jaw
Opisthokranion n opisthocranion *(anthropologischer Meßpunkt)*
Opisthorchiasis f opisthorchiasis, opisthorchosis
Opisthorchis m Opisthorchis
~ **felineus** Siberian liver fluke
~ **noverca** Indian liver fluke
~ **sinensis** s. Clonorchis sinensis
opisthotonisch opisthotonic
Opisthotonus m opisthotonus, opisthotonos
opisthotonusartig opisthotonoid
Opium n opium
Opiumalkaloid n opium alkaloid
Opiumentzugsschmerz m meconalgia

Opiumgenuß *m* opiophagism, opiophagy, eating of opium
Opiummißbrauch *m* opium misuse, abuse of opium
Opiumpsychose *f* meconeuropathia
Opiumsäure *f* meconic acid
Opiumsucht *f* opiomania, opium habit, addiction to opium, opiumism, meconism
opiumsüchtig addicted to opium
Opiumsüchtiger *m* opiomaniac, opiophile
Opiumvergiftung *f* opium poisoning, meconism
Opotherapie *f* 1. opotherapy, organotherapy; histotherapy; 3. opotherapy, treatment by juices
Opozephalus *m* opocephalus *(Mißgeburt)*
Oppenheim-Reflex *m* Oppenheim's reflex *(Pyramidenbahnzeichen)*
oppilativ oppilative, closing the pores; constipating
opponens opponens, opposing
opponieren to oppose *(den Daumen)*
Oppressionsgefühl *n* oppressive feeling
Opsin *n* opsin *(Sehfarbstoff)*
opsinogen opsinogenous, producing opsinogens
Opsinogen *n* ops[in]ogen
Opsionosis *f* opsionosis
Opsiurie *f* opsiuria
Opsoklonus *m* opsoclonus
opsonieren to opsonize, to opsonify, to subject to opsonification *(Bakterien im Blut)*
Opsonierung *f* opsonification, opsonization *(Bakterienveränderung durch Opsonine zur Vernichtung durch Leukozyten)*
Opsonin *n* opsonin, bacteriotropin *(bereitet Vernichtung von Bakterien durch Leukozyten vor)*
opsoninaffin opsonophilic
Opsoninaffinität *f* opsonophilia
opsoninanziehend opsonophilic
Opsoninindex *m* opsonic (phagocytic) index
Opsoninindexbestimmung *f* opsonometry
opsoninproduzierend opsinogenous, producing opsinogens
opsoninstimulierend opsinogenous
Opsoninwirkung *f* opsonic action
Opsonologie *f* opsonology *(Lehre von den Opsoninen)*
Opsonometrie *f* opsonometry
opsonophil opsonophilic
Opsonophilie *f* opsonophilia
Opsonotherapie *f* opsonotherapy *(Krankheitsbehandlung durch Stimulierung der Opsoninbildung)*
opsonozytophagisch opsonocytophagic
Optästhesie *f* optaesthesia, visual sensibility
Optik *f* optics *(eines Geräts)*
Optiker *m* optician
~/brillenbestimmender ophthalmic (sight-testing) optician, optometrist
optikochiasmatisch opticochiasm[at]ic, optochiasmic
optikofazial opticofacial
optikopupillär opticopupillary
optikoziliar opticociliary

Optikozöle *f* opticocoele, cavity of the optic vesicle
Optikus *m* optic nerve, second [cranial] nerve
Optikusatrophie *f* optic atrophy
~/Lebersche Leber's disease (optic atrophy)
Optikusexkavation *f* cupping of the disk
Optikusneuritis *f* optic (retrobulbar) neuritis, optic neuromyelitis (perineuritis)
Optikusneuropathie *f* optic neuropathy, opticoneuropathy
~/retrobulbäre retrobulbar optic neuropathy
Optikusstörung *f* optic nerve disturbance
Optimaldosis *f* optimum dose
optisch optic[al]
Optoblast *m* optoblast *(lange Netzhautganglienzelle)*
Optogramm *n* optogram
optokinetisch opt[ic]okinetic
Optometer *n* optometer, optimeter
Optometrie *f* optometry, optimetry, measurement of the visual powers
Optometrist *m* optometrist
Optomyometer *n* optomyometer
Optomyometrie *f* optomyometry, measurement of the strength of the extrinsic eye muscles
Optotyp *m* optotype *(zur Bestimmung der Sehschärfe)*
Ora *f* ora, margin
oral 1. oral; 2. [per]oral, per os, by mouth, orally given *(z. B. Medikamentenapplikation)*
Orale *n* orale *(anthropologischer Meßpunkt)*
Oralimmunisierung *f* oral immunization
Oralinfektion *f* oral infection
Oralmoniliasis *f* oral moniliasis
Oralstadium *n* oral stage (phase) *(Psychologie)*
oralwärts orad, toward the mouth (oral region)
Orangenileus *m* orange ileus
Orbiculus *m* orbiculus, small disk
~ ciliaris orbiculus ciliaris, ciliary ring *(pigmentierter Abschnitt des Strahlenkörpers am Auge)*
orbikular orbicular
Orbikularis[muskel] *m* orbicularis, orbicular muscle
Orbikularisphänomen *n* Westphal-Pilcz reflex, paradoxical pupillary phenomenon
Orbita *f* orbit[a], orbital cavity, eye socket, hypsiconch
Orbita... s. a. Augenhöhlen...
Orbitaabszeß *m* orbital abscess
Orbitabreite *f* orbital width
Orbitadruckentlastung *f* orbital decompression
Orbitadruckmessung *f* orbitometry
Orbitahämatom *n* orbital haemorrhage
Orbitahöhe *f* orbital height
orbital orbital
Orbitale *n* orbitale *(anthropologischer Meßpunkt)*
Orbitalfaszie *f* orbital fascia
Orbitalgegend *f* orbital region
Orbitalindex *m* orbital index *(Verhältnis von Breite zu Höhe des Augenhöhleneingangs)*
Orbitallappen *m* orbital lobe *(des Stirnhirns)*
Orbitaltumor *m* orbit tumour

Orbitalvenenröntgen[kontrast]darstellung f orbit phlebography, orbital venography
orbitanah adorbital
Orbitaschwellung f orbital swelling
Orbitatomogramm n orbital tomogram
Orbitawand f/**äußere** lateral orbital wall
~/innere medial orbital wall
Orbitazellulitis f orbital cellulitis
Orbitographie f orbitography
Orbitometer n orbitometer
Orbitometrie f orbitometry
Orbitotomie f orbitotomy, incision into the orbit
Orchialgie f orchi[d]algia, orchiodynia, orchioneuralgia, didymalgia, testicular pain
Orchidektomie f orchi[d]ectomy, excision of the testicle
Orchidoepididymektomie f orchido-epididymectomy
Orchidoncus m orchidoncus, tumour of the testicle
Orchidopathie f orchidopathy, disease of the testicle
Orchidopexie f [crypt]orchidopexy, orchiopexy
Orchidoptose f orchi[d]optosis, falling of the testicle
Orchidorrhaphie f orchi[d]orrhaphy; suturing (stitching) of the testis
Orchidotherapie f orchidotherapy, treatment with testicular extracts
Orchidotomie f orch[id]otomy, orchiotomy, incision into the testicle
Orchiepididymitis f orchi-epididymitis, epididymo-orchitis, inflammation of the testicle and the epididymis
Orchio... s. Orchido...
Orchiodynie f s. Orchialgie
Orchis m s. Hoden
Orchitis f s. Hodenentzündung
orchitisch orchitic
Orcho... s. Orchido...
Ordination f prescription, recipe
ordinieren to prescribe
Oreximanie f oreximania
Organ n organ[um], organon (s. a. unter Organum) ● **außerhalb eines Organs** extrinsic ● **innerhalb eines Organs** intrinsic
~/Cortisches [spiral] organ of Corti, Corti apparatus, acoustic organ, basilar papilla
~/endokrines endocrine (incretory) organ
~/Giraldessches organ of Giraldes, paradidymis, parepididymis
~/hormonales s. ~/endokrines
~/künstliches artificial organ
~/parenchymatöses parenchymatous organ
~/rudimentäres rudimentary organ, rudiment[um], vestige, vestigium
~/statisches static organ
~/statoakustisches statoacoustic (vestibulocochlear) organ
~/vestibuläres vestibular organ
Organa npl **genitalia feminina** female genital organs
~ **genitalia masculina** male genital organs
~ **uropoetica** urinary system
Organablagerung f deposition (storage) into an organ; deposit in an organ
organähnlich organoid
Organanheftung f[/**operative**] organopexy, fixation of an organ
Organanlage f primordium, organ anlage
~/normale normal placement of organs, orthophoria
Organbefall m organic affection
Organbeteiligung f organic involvement
Organbetrachtung f organoscopy
organbildend organogen[et]ic
Organbildung f organogenesis, development of organs; growth of organs
Organe npl/**lebenswichtige** vitals, vital organs
Organeinblutung f parenchymatous haemorrhage (bleeding)
Organeinwirkung f organotropism, organotropy
Organelle f organelle
~/melaninenthaltende melanin-containing organella, melanosome
Organempfänger m organ recipient
Organerkrankung f organopathy, organic disease
Organersatz m artificial organ
~/mechanischer orthopraxy
Organfaßzange f organ grasping forceps
Organfehlbildung f 1. extrophy; 2. malformation
Organfixierung f organopexy, fixation of an organ
organfreundlich organophil[e], organophilic
Organgefühl n organ[ic] sensation
Organgeräusch n organic murmur
Organgewebe n/**spezifisches** parenchym[a]
Organgewebsentzündung f parenchymatitis, parenchymatous inflammation
Organhypertrophie f organic hypertrophy
Organisation f organization (durch Zelleinwanderung)
Organisationsphase f organizing phase (bei Entzündung)
organisch organic
organisieren/sich 1. to organize, to induce organization; 2. to form into organs
organisierend/sich organizing, unresolved (z. B. Lungenentzündung)
organisiert werden to organize, to undergo organization (z. B. sich regenerierendes Gewebe)
Organismen mpl/**pleuropneumonieähnliche** pleuropneumonia-like organisms (zur Gattung der Mykoplasmen gehörende Mikroorganismen)
Organismus m organism ● **am lebenden ~** in vivo (z. B. Versuch) ● **nicht am lebenden ~** in vitro (z. B. Versuch)
~/sauerstoffabhängiger aerobe (z. B. Bakterien)
~/sauerstoffunabhängiger anaerobe
Organkonservierung f organ preservation
Organlage f position of the organ
Organlehre f organology

Organneurose 580

Organneurose f organ neurosis
Organogenese f s. Organbildung
Organopathie f organopathy, organic disease
Organopexie f organopexy, fixation of an organ
organophil organophil[e], organophilic
Organoskopie f organoscopy
Organotaxis f organotaxis
Organotherapie f organotherapy, opotherapy; histotherapy
organotrop organotropic
organotroph organotrophic *(die Organernährung betreffend)*
Organotropie f organotropism, organotropy
Organpräparat n organic preparation
Organpsychose f organic psychosis
Organschädigung f organic lesion (injury)
Organsitus m field
Organspende f organ donation (procurement)
Organspender m organ donor
organspezifisch organ-specific
Organspezifität f organ specifity
Organspiegelung f organoscopy
Organstörung f organic disturbance (disorder)
Organstück n/abgestorbenes sequestrum
Organsystem n organ system, system[a]
Organtransplantat n organ transplant
Organtransplantation f organ transplantation
Organum n organ[um], organon *(s. a. unter Organ)*
~ **auditus** organ of hearing, internal ear
~ **generativum** organ of generation
~ **gustus** gustatory organ, organ of taste
~ **olfactus** olfactory organ, organ of smell
~ **spirale** s. Organ/Cortisches
~ **vestibulare** organ of equilibrium
~ **visus** visual organ, organ of vision
~ **vomeronasale** vomeronasal organ
~ **vomeronasale Jacobsoni** Jacobson's organ
Organvergrößerung f organomegaly, splanchnomegaly
~/scheinbare pseudohypertrophy
Organverkleinerung f splanchnomicria
Organverlagerung f heterotopia; ectopia, dystopia, aberration *(infolge Entwicklungsstörung)*
~/angeborene heterotaxia
Organwirkung f organotropism, organotropy
Orgasmus m orgasm
Orgasmusunfähigkeit f dyspareunia
Orientbeule f Aleppo boil (button), oriental (tropical) sore, cutaneous leishmaniasis [of the Old World]
Orientierung f/gestörte impaired orientation
Orientierungsreflex m orienting reflex *(reizempfindlicher Organe)*
Orientierungsverlust m loss of orientation
Orificium n orifice, orificium, aperture *(s. a. unter Ostium)*
~ **atrioventriculare** atrioventricular orifice
~ **externum isthmi** external cervical (uterine) os, external mouth of the womb
~ **internum isthmi** internal cervical (uterine) os, internal mouth of the womb
~ **nasi** nostril, naris
~ **ureteris** ureteral orifice (ostium)
~ **urethrae** urethral orifice (ostium), orifice of the urethra
~ **urethrae externum** external urethral orifice
~ **urethrae femininae externum** external orifice of the female urethra
~ **urethrae femininae internum** internal orifice of the female urethra
~ **urethrae internum** internal urethral orifice
~ **urethrae masculinae externum** external orifice of the male urethra
~ **urethrae masculinae internum** internal orifice of the male urethra
~ **vaginae** vaginal orifice (ostium), vaginal introitus, external orifice of the vagina
Ornithin n ornithine *(Aminosäure)*
Ornithinerhöhung f im Blut [hyper]ornithaemia
Ornithin-Transkarbamylase f ornithine transcarbamylase *(Enzym)*
Ornithin-Transkarboxylase f ornithine transcarboxylase *(Enzym)*
Ornithinzyklus m ornithine cycle
Ornithodoros f Ornithodorus *(Lederzeckengattung)*
Ornithose f ornithosis, psittacosis
Ornithosevirus n ornithosis virus
orofazial orofacial
orolingual orolingual
oronasal oronasal
oropharyngeal oropharyngeal, mesopharyngeal
Oropharyngealtubus m oropharyngeal tube, standard airway
Oropharynx m oropharynx, mesopharynx
Ororrhoe f orrhorrhoea, watery (serous) discharge
Oroya-Fieber n Oroya fever, Carrión's disease, bartonelliasis, bartonellosis *(durch Bartonella bacilliformis)*
Ort m:
~ **der Wahl** point of election *(z. B. bei Operation)*
~/**Kiesselbachscher** Kiesselbach's area (space, triangle) *(gefäßreiche Gegend am vorderen Teil der Nasenscheidewand)*
~ **verringerter Widerstandsfähigkeit** locus minoris resistentiae
Orthese f orthesis, orthopaedic (orthotic) device
Orthochorea f orthochorea
orthochrom[atisch] orthochrom[at]ic
Orthochromie f orthochromia, normal haemoglobin content of the erythrocytes
orthochromophil orthochromophil[e], normally staining
orthodaktyl orthodactylous
Orthodentin n orthodentin
Orthodiagramm n orthodiagram
Orthodiagraphie f orthodiagraphy, orthoroentgenography
Orthodiaskop n orthodiascope
Orthodiaskopie f orthodiascopy
orthodolichozephal orthodolichocephalous
orthodont orthodont

Orthodontie f orthodontia, orthodontics, orthodontology, odontorthosis
Orthoergasie f orthoergasia, state of normal functioning
orthogen orthogen[et]ic
Orthogenese f orthogenesis
orthognath orthognathic
Orthognathie f orthognathia, orthognathism
Orthognathodontie f s. Orthodontie
orthograd orthograde
Orthokrasie f orthocrasia *(Normalreaktion auf Arzneimittel)*
orthomesozephal orthomesocephalous
Orthopäde m 1. orthopaedist, orthopaedic surgeon; 2. prosthetist
Orthopädie f orthopaedics, orthopaedic surgery
orthopädisch orthopaedic
Orthoperkussion f orthopercussion
Orthophonie f orthophony, correct production of sound
orthophor orthophoric
Orthophorie f 1. orthophoria, normal balance of eye muscles; 2. orthophoria, normal placement of organs
Orthophrenie f orthophrenia, normal mental reactivity
Orthopnoe f orthopnoea *(starke Atemnot beim Liegen)*
orthopnoeisch orthopnoeic
Orthopraxie f orthopraxy, mechanical correction of deformities
Orthoptik f orthoptics, treatment of defective binocular vision
orthoptisch orthoptic
Orthoptoskop n orthoptoscope
Orthoröntgenographie f orthodiagraphy, orthoroentgenography
Orthoskop n orthoscope *(Ophthalmologie)*
Orthoskopie f orthoscopy
orthoskopisch orthoscopic
Orthostase f orthostasis, orthostatism
Orthostasealbuminurie f orthostatic albuminuria
Orthostasehypotonus m orthostatic hypotension
Orthostasepurpura f orthostatic purpura
Orthostasesynkope f orthostatic syncope
orthostatisch ortho[sta]tic
Orthotherapie f orthotherapy, treatment of disorders of posture
orthotonisch orthotonic
Orthotonus m orthotonus
Orthotopie f orthotopia, normal position of an organ
orthotopisch orthotopic
orthozephal orthocephalic, orthocephalous
Orthozephalie f orthocephalia
örtlich local, regional, topical
ortsgerecht normotopic, normally located
ortstypisch normotopic
Orzinprobe f nach Bial Bial's test
Os n 1. bone, os *(s. a. unter Knochen)*; 2. mouth, os, stoma
~ **acetabuli** acetabular (cotyloid) bone
~ **calcis** heel bone
~ **capitatum** capitate bone, capitatum, magnum
~ **carpi** carpal bone
~ **coccygis** coccyx
~ **costale** costa, costal bone
~ **coxae** hipbone, innominate bone
~ **cranii** cranial bone
~ **cuboideum** cuboid [bone]
~ **cuneiforme** cuneiform [bone]
~ **cuneiforme intermedium** intermediate cuneiform bone
~ **cuneiforme laterale** lateral cuneiform bone
~ **cuneiforme mediale (primum)** medial cuneiform bone
~ **cuneiforme secundum** intermediate cuneiform bone
~ **cuneiforme tertium** lateral cuneiform bone
~ **ethmoidale** ethmoid [bone]
~ **extremitatis inferioris** bone of the lower limb
~ **extremitatis superioris** bone of the upper limb
~ **faciei** bone of the face
~ **frontale** frontal bone
~ **hamatum** hamate [bone], hamatum, unciform[e], unciform bone
~ **hyoideum** hyoid [bone]
~ **ilium** ilium [bone], iliac bone
~ **Incae** Inca (incarial) bone
~ **incisivum (intermaxillare)** incisive bone, intermaxillary [bone], intermaxilla, premaxilla
~ **interparietale** interparietal bone
~ **ischii** ischium
~ **lacrimale** lacrimal bone
~ **lenticulare** lenticular apophysis, lenticular process [of the incus] *(ovales Köpfchen des Ambosses)*
~ **lunatum** lunar bone, lunare, lunate [bone], semilunar *(Handwurzelknochen)*
~ **membri inferioris** bone of the lower limb
~ **membri superioris** bone of the upper limb
~ **metacarpale** metacarpal [bone], bone of the metacarpus
~ **metatarsale** metatarsal [bone], bone of the metatarsus
~ **multangulum** multangular bone, multangulum
~ **multangulum majus** s. ~ trapezium
~ **multangulum minus** s. ~ trapezoideum
~ **nasale (nasi)** nasal bone
~ **naviculare** navicular bone
~ **occipitale** occipital [bone]
~ **orbiculare** s. ~ lenticulare
~ **orbitale** orbital bone
~ **palatinum** palatine [bone]
~ **parietale** parietal [bone]
~ **pisiforme** pisiform [bone] *(Handwurzelknochen)*
~ **pneumaticum** pneumatic bone
~ **pubis** pubic bone, pubis
~ **sacrum** sacrum
~ **scaphoideum** scaphoid [bone]
~ **sesamoideum** sesamoid bone
~ **sphenoidale** sphenoid [bone]
~ **styloideum** styloid bone of the third metacarpal

~ **tarsi** tarsal bone
~ **temporale** temporal bone
~ **trapezium** trapezium [bone], greater multangular [bone]
~ **trapezoideum** trapezoid [bone], lesser multangular [bone]
~ **triquetrum** triquetral bone, triquetrum, triangularis
~ **uteri externum** external cervical (uterine) os, external mouth of the womb
~ **uteri internum** internal cervical (uterine) os, internal mouth of the womb
~ **zygomaticum** zygomatic bone, zygoma, yokebone, cheekbone, malar
Oscedo f oscedo, oscitancy, oscitation
Oscheitis f oscheitis, scrotitis, inflammation of the scrotum
Oschelephantiasis f oschelephantiasis, elephantiasis of the scrotum *(hochgradige Lymphstauung)*
Oscheohydrozele f oscheohydrocele, scrotal hydrocele
Oscheolith m oscheolith
Oscheoma n oscheoma, tumour of the scrotum
Oscheoplastik f oscheoplasty, scrotoplasty
Oscheozele f oscheocele, scrotal hernia, scrotocele
Oschitis f s. Oscheitis
Osculum n osculum, small aperture, minute opening
Oskulation f osculation, act of yawning
Osmästhesie f osmaesthesia, olfactory sensibility
osmiumfreundlich osmiophilic
Osmodiuretikum n osmotic diuretic
Osmodysphorie f osmodysphoria, intolerance of certain odours
Osmofragilität f osmotic fragility *(der Erythrozyten)*
Osmofragilitätstest m osmotic fragility test
Osmol n osmol *(Einheit der Osmolarität)*
osmolal osmolal
Osmolalität f osmolality
osmolar osmolar
Osmolarität f osmolarity
Osmologie f osmology, osphresiology *(Lehre vom Geruchssinn)*
Osmometer n 1. osmometer, olfactometer, osphresiometer; 2. osmometer
Osmometrie f 1. osmometry, olfactometry, osphresiometry; 2. osmometry, measurement of osmotic pressure
Osmonosologie f osmonosology *(Lehre von den Geruchsstörungen)*
Osmophobie f osmophobia, osphresiophobia *(krankhafte Angst vor Gerüchen)*
Osmorezeptor m osmoreceptor *(im Gehirn)*
Osmose f osmosis
Osmosologie f osmology
Osmotherapie f osmotherapy
ösophageal oesophageal
Ösophagektasie f oesophagectasia, dilatation of the oesophagus

Ösophagektomie f oesophagectomy, excision of the oesophagus
Ösophagismus m oesophagism[us], oesophagospasm, spasmodic contraction of the oesophagus
Ösophagitis f oesophagitis, inflammation of the oesophagus
Ösophagobronchialfistel f oesophagobronchial fistula
Ösophagoduodenostomie f oesophagoduodenostomy
Ösophagodynie f oesophagodynia, oesophagalgia, pain in the oesophagus
Ösophagoduodenostomie f oesophagoduodenostomy
ösophagogastral oesophagogastric
Ösophagogastrektomie f oesophagogastrectomy
Ösophagogastroduodenoskopie f oesophagogastroduodenoscopy
Ösophagogastroplastik f oesophagogastroplasty
Ösophagogastroskop n oesophagogastroscope
Ösophagogastroskopie f oesophagogastroscopy
Ösophagogastrostomie f oesophagogastrostomy
Ösophagogramm n oesophagogram
Ösophagographie f oesophagography
ösophagographisch oesophagographic
Ösophagojejunostomie f oesophagojejunostomy
Ösophagomalazie f oesophagomalacia, softening of the wall of the oesophagus
Ösophagomyotomie f oesophagomyotomy
Ösophagoösophagostomie f oesophagooesophagostomy
Ösophagopathie f oesophagopathy, disease of the oesophagus
ösophagopharyngeal oesophagopharyngeal, pharyngo-oesophageal
Ösophagoplastik f oesophagoplasty
Ösophagoskop n oesophagoscope
Ösophagoskopie f oesophagoscopy
ösophagoskopisch oesophagoscopic
Ösophagospasmus m s. Ösophagismus
Ösophagostomie f oesophagostomy
Ösophagotom n oesophagotome
Ösophagotomie f oesophagotomy, incision of the oesophagus
Ösophagotrachealfistel f oesophagotracheal fistula
Ösophagus m oesophagus, gullet
Ösophagus... s. a. Speiseröhren...
Ösophagusableitung f oesophageal lead *(des EKG)*
Ösophagusachalasie f oesophageal achalasia
Ösophagusarterie f oesophageal artery
Ösophagusballonsonde f oesophageal balloon tube
Ösophagusblutung f oesophageal haemorrhage
Ösophagusbougie f oesophageal bougie
Ösophagus-Candidamykose f oesophageal moniliasis

Osteoarthropathie

Ösophagus-Darm-Anastomose f oesophago-enterostomy
Ösophagusdilatation f oesophagectasia
Ösophaguseingang m oesophageal inlet
Ösophaguselektrode f oesophageal lead
Ösophagusendoprothese f oesophageal endoprosthesis
Ösophagusgekröse n mesooesophagus *(Embryologie)*
Ösophagus-Hämorrhagie-Tamponadesonde f oesophageal haemostatic tube
Ösophagushiatus m oesophageal hiatus (foramen), oesophageal orifice of the diaphragm
Ösophagushiatusgleithernie f sliding oesophageal hiatus hernia
Ösophagushiatushernie f oesophageal hiatus hernia
Ösophagushiatushernienplastik f oesophageal hiatus hernioplasty
Ösophaguskatheter m oesophageal catheter, probang
Ösophaguskompression f oesophageal compression
Ösophagusmanometrie f oesophageal manometry
Ösophagusmesser n oesophagotome
Ösophagusmoniliasis f oesophageal moniliasis
Ösophagusmotilität f oesophageal motility
Ösophagusmotilitätsstörung f oesophageal motility disorder
Ösophagusobstruktion f obstruction of the oesophagus
Ösophagus-Ösophagus-Anastomose f oesophago-oesophagostomy
Ösophagusparalyse f oesophageal paralysis, lemoparalysis
Ösophagusplastik f oesophagoplasty
Ösophagusprolaps m oesophageal prolapse
Ösophagusptose f oesophagoptosis
Ösophaguspulsionsdivertikel n Zenker's diverticulum (pouch)
Ösophagusruptur f oesophageal rupture (tear)
Ösophagusspontanruptur f spontaneous oesophageal rupture, Boerhaave syndrome
Ösophagusstenose f oesophageal stenosis, oesophagostenosis, lemostenosis
Ösophagusstethoskop n oesophagus stethoscope
Ösophagusstriktur f oesophageal stricture
Ösophagustraktionsdivertikel n oesophageal traction diverticulum
Ösophagusulzeration f oesophageal ulceration
Ösophagusvarizen fpl oesophageal varices (piles)
Ösophagusvene f oesophageal vein
Ösophagusverdrängung f oesophagectopy
Ösophaguszange f oesophageal forceps
Ösophalgie f s. Ösophagodynie
Osphresiologie f s. Osmologie
Osphresiophobie f s. Osmophobie
Osphyalgie f osphyalgia, pain in the loins
Osphyarthritis f osphyarthritis, inflammation of the loins
Osphyomyelitis f osphyomyelitis, lumbar myelitis
ossal, ossär bony, osseous, osteal, ossiform
Ossein n ossein[e], ostein[e] *(Gerüsteiweiß der Knochen)*
osseofibrös osseofibrous
osseokartilaginös osseocartilaginous
osseoligamentös osseoligamentous
Ossiculum n ossicle, ossiculum, bonelet
~ **auditus (tympani)** auditory ossicle
Ossifikation f 1. ossification, bone formation *(s.a. unter Osteogenesis)*; 2. ossification, conversion into bone
~/**enchondrale** enchondral ossification (bone formation)
Ossifikationskern m s. Ossifikationszentrum
Ossifikationsstörung f dysostosis
~/**enchondrale** chondrodystrophia
Ossifikationszentrum n ossification centre, centre of ossification
ossifizieren to ossify, to turn into bone
Ossikulektomie f ossiculectomy, excision of the ossicles of the ear
Ossikulotomie f ossiculotomy, incision into the bonelets of the ear
Ossikulum n s. Ossiculum
Ostalgie f ost[e]algia, pain in the bone
Osteitis f ost[e]itis, inflammation of a bone *(s.a. unter Knochenentzündung)*
~ **alveolaris** alveolar osteitis; dry socket
~ **carnosa** carneous osteitis
~ **condensans** condensing (formative, sclerosing) osteitis; eburnation; osteosclerosis
~ **condensans generalisata** osteopoikilosis, osteopecilia; spotted bones
~ **cystica** osteitis tuberculosa cystica (multiplex cystoides), Jüngling's disease
~ **fibrosa cystica** parathyroid osteosis, osteitis fibrosa cystica (osteoplastica), Albright's disease
~ **fibrosa cystica generalisata** parathyroid osteitis (osteodystrophia), Recklinghausen's disease
~ **fibrosa disseminata** fibrous dysplasia
~ **fibrosa generalisata/renale** renal rickets (osteodystrophy)
osteitisch osteitic
Ostektomie f ost[e]ectomy, excision of a bone
Ostektopie f ostectopia, displacement of a bone
Ostembryon m ostembryon, ossified foetus; ossification of a foetus
Osteo... s.a. Knochen...
Osteoakusis f osteoacousia, osteoacusis; osteophony, bone conduction
Osteoanästhesie f osteoanaesthesia, insensitiveness of bone
Osteoarthrektomie f oste[o]arthrotomy
Osteoarthritis f osteoarthritis, degenerative joint disease
osteoarthritisch osteoarthritic
Osteoarthropathie f osteoarthropathy, disease of joints and bones

Osteoarthropathie

~/pulmonale [hypertrophic] pulmonary osteoarthropathy, osteopulmonary arthropathy, toxigenic osteoperiostitis ossificans *(z. B. bei Herzfehlern)*; clubbed fingers
Osteoarthrose *f* osteoarthrosis
osteoartikulär osteoarticular
Osteoblast *m* osteoblast, osteoplast
osteoblastisch osteoblastic, osteoplastic
Osteoblastom *n* osteoblastoma *(vom Knochen ausgehende Geschwulst)*
osteochondral osteochondral, osteochondrous, osteocartilaginous
Osteochondritis *f* 1. osteochondritis, inflammation of bones and cartilage; 2. osteochondrosis
~ **deformans [coxae] juvenilis** deforming osteochondritis of the hip (head of the femur), osteochondrosis of capitular epiphysis
~ **dissecans** osteochondrolysis
~ **dissecans/juvenile** juvenile osteochondritis dissecans
~ **syphilitica** syphilitic osteochondritis
Osteochondrodysplasie *f* osteochondrodysplasia
Osteochondrodystrophie *f* osteochondrodystrophy
Osteochondrom *n* osteochondroma, chondroosteoma
Osteochondromatose *f* osteochondromatosis; multiple hereditary exostoses
Osteochondromyxom *n* osteochondromyxoma
Osteochondromyxosarkom *n* osteochondromyxosarcoma
Osteochondrosarkom *n* osteochondrosarcoma
Osteochondrose *f* osteochondrosis, osteochondritis
Osteochondrosis *f* **deformans tibiae** Blount-Barber syndrome *(aseptische Knochennekrose des medialen Tibiakondylus)*
~ **dissecans** osteochondrolysis
osteodermatoplastisch osteodermatoplastic
Osteodermie *f* osteodermia, bony formation in the skin
Osteodesmose *f* osteodesmosis, ossification of a tendon
Osteodiastase *f* osteodiastasis, separation of a bone
Osteodynie *f s.* Ostalgie
Osteodysplasie *f* osteodysplasia
Osteodystrophia *f* osteodystrophy
~ **deformans [Paget]** deforming osteodystrophia, Paget's disease [of bone]
~ **fibrosa** fibrous dysplasia
~ **fibrosa generalisata [Recklinghausen]** *s.* Morbus Recklinghausen
Osteodystrophie *f* osteodystrophy
~/renale renal osteodystrophy (rickets), pseudorickets
Osteofibrochondrom *n* osteofibrochondroma
Osteofibrochondrosarkom *n* osteofibrochondrosarcoma
Osteofibrolipom *n* osteofibrolipoma
Osteofibrom *n* osteofibroma, fibro-osteoma
Osteofibromatose *f* osteofibromatosis
Osteofibrosarkom *n* osteofibrosarcoma, fibroosteosarcoma
Osteofibrose *f* osteofibrosis
osteogen osteogen[et]ic, osteogenous
~/nicht non-osteogenic
Osteogenesis *f* osteogenesis, osteogeny, ostosis, formation of bone; development of bony tissue
~ **imperfecta** imperfect osteogenesis, Eddowes' disease (syndrome); osteopsathyrosis; brittle bones
~ **imperfecta congenita** congenital imperfect osteogenesis, Vrolik's disease
~ **imperfecta cystica** cystic imperfect osteogenesis
~ **imperfecta tarda** Lobstein's disease *(Knochenkrankheit mit abnormer Knochenbrüchigkeit)*
osteogenetisch osteogen[et]ic, osteogenous
osteohypertroph[isch] osteohypertrophic
osteoid osteoid
Osteoid *n* osteoid [tissue]
Osteoidosteom *n* osteoid osteoma
osteokartilaginös *s.* osteochondral
Osteokarzinom *n* osteocarcinoma, bone cancer
Osteoklasie *f* 1. osteoclasis, destruction of bony tissue; resorption of bone; 2. osteoclasis, surgical refraction of bones *(bei schlechter Frakturstellung)*
Osteoklast *m* osteoclast
Osteoklastentumor *m* osteoclastoma
osteoklastisch osteoclastic
Osteoklastom *n* osteoclastoma
Osteokopie *f* osteocope, osteocopic pain *(z. B. bei Syphilis)*
Osteokranium *n* osteocranium
Osteolipochondrom *n* osteolipochondroma
Osteolipom *n* osteolipoma
Osteologie *f* osteology
Osteolyse *f* osteolysis, ossifluence, dissolution of bone
osteolytisch osteolytic
Osteoma *n* osteoma
~ **cutis** dermostosis, bony metaplasia in the skin
~ **dentale** dental exostosis
~ **durum (eburneum)** eburnated (compact) osteoma *(gutartige Knochengeschwulst aus hartem Knochengewebe)*; ivory osteosis
~ **medullosum** medullary osteoma *(gutartige Knochengeschwulst)*
~ **spongiosum** spongy osteoma *(gutartige Knochengeschwulst mit schwammigen Knochen- und Markräumen)*
osteomähnlich osteomatoid, osteomatous
Osteomalazie *f* osteomalacia, softening of the bones *(durch Kalksalzverarmung)*; adult rickets
~/juvenile juvenile osteomalacia
~/senile senile osteomalacia
osteomalazisch osteomalacial
osteomartig osteomatoid, osteomatous
Osteomatose *f* osteomatosis

Osteometrie f osteometry
osteometrisch osteometric
Osteomyelitis f osteomyelitis, carious (necrotic) osteitis, medullitis, myelitis, pyogenic inflammation of bone marrow
~/chronisch sklerosierende chronic sclerosing osteomyelitis
osteomyelitisch osteomyelitic
Osteomyelographie f osteomyelography *(Röntgendiagnostik)*
osteomyelographisch osteomyelographic
osteomyokutan osteomyocutaneous
Osteomyxochondrom n osteomyxochondroma
Osteon n osteon[e], Haversian system *(lamelläre Knochengrundstruktur)*
Osteonephropathie f osteonephropathy *(Knochenveränderungen infolge Nierenkrankheit)*
Osteoneuralgie f osteoneuralgia, neuralgia of a bone
Osteopädion n osteopaedion, calcified foetus
Osteopathia f osteopathy, bone disease
~ **condensans disseminata** disseminated condensing osteopathy, osteopoikilosis, osteopecilia; spotted bones
~ **hyperostotica [scleroticans] multiplex infantilis** Camurati-Engelmann disease, progressive diaphyseal dysplasia
~ **hypertrophicans toxica** Bamberger-Marie disease
osteopathisch osteopathic
Osteopenie f osteopenia
osteoperiostal osteoperiosteal
Osteoperiostitis f osteoperiostitis, inflammation of the bone and periosteum
~ **ossificans toxica** Bamberger-Marie disease
Osteopetrosis f osteopetrosis, sclerotic osteitis, Albers-Schönberg disease; marble bones
~ **generalisata** general osteopetrosis
Osteophlebitis f osteophlebitis, inflammation of the veins of the bone
Osteophonie f osteophony, osteoacousia, bone conduction
Osteophthise f osteophthisis, wasting of the bones
Osteophyt m osteophyte, bony outgrowth
osteophytisch osteophytic
Osteophytose f osteophytosis
Osteoplastik f osteoplasty, plastic surgery of the bone
osteoplastisch osteoplastic
Osteopoikilie f osteopoikilosis, osteopecilia; spotted bones
Osteoporose f osteoporosis, rarefying osteitis
~/juvenile juvenile osteoporosis
~/postmenopausische presenile involutional osteoporosis *(bei Frauen)*
~/senile senile osteoporosis
~/traumatische traumatic osteoporosis, posttraumatic reflex sympathetic dystrophy, Sudeck's atrophy
osteoporotisch osteoporotic

Osteopsathyrose f osteopsathyrosis, Lobstein's disease *(Knochenkrankheit mit abnormer Knochenbrüchigkeit)*
Osteoradionekrose f osteoradionecrosis
Osteorrhagie f osteorrhagia, haemorrhage from the bones
Osteorrhaphie f osteorrhaphy; suturing (wiring) of bone
Osteosarkom n osteosarcoma, osteogenic (bone) sarcoma
osteosarkomatös osteosarcomatous
Osteosclerosis f **fragilis generalisata** s. Osteopoikilie
Osteoseptum n osteoseptum
Osteosis f osteosis, metaplastic bone formation
Osteosklerose f osteosclerosis, hardening of bones; eburnation
osteosklerotisch osteosclerotic
Osteospongiom n osteospongioma
Osteosteatom n osteosteatoma
Osteostixis f osteostixis, puncturing of a bone
Osteosynovitis f osteosynovitis
Osteosynthese f osteosynthesis *(operative Knochenbruchbehandlung mit Fixation der Bruchenden)*
Osteothrombose f osteothrombosis
Osteotom n osteotome
Osteotomie f osteotomy
Osteotrophie f osteotrophy, nutrition of bones
Osteozystom n osteocystoma
Osteozyt m osteocyte, bone cell (corpuscle)
Ostitis f s. Osteitis
Ostium n ostium, mouth, aperture *(s. a. unter Orificium)* ● **neben einem ~** paraostial
~ **abdominale tubae uterinae** fimbriated end of the oviduct
~ **aortae** aortic orifice *(Ausgang von der linken Herzkammer in die Aorta)*
~ **atrioventriculare** atrioventricular orifice
~ **atrioventriculare dextrum** right atrioventricular ostium, tricuspid orifice, T. O.
~ **atrioventriculare sinistrum** left atrioventricular ostium, mitral orifice
~ **cardiacum** cardia, cardiac orifice, oesophagogastric junction
~ **maxillare** maxillary ostium (hiatus) *(zur Nasenhöhle)*
~ **pharyngeum tubae auditivae** pharyngeal opening of the Eustachian tube
~ **tympanicum tubae auditivae** tympanic opening of the Eustachian tube
~ **ureteris** ureteral orifice (ostium)
~ **urethrae** urethral orifice (ostium), orifice of the urethra
~ **urethrae externum** external urethral orifice
~ **urethrae femininae externum** external orifice of the female urethra
~ **urethrae femininae internum** internal orifice of the female urethra
~ **urethrae internum** internal urethral orifice
~ **urethrae masculinae externum** external orifice of the male urethra

Ostium

~ **urethrae masculinae internum** internal orifice of the male urethra
~ **uteri cervical** os, ostium of the uterus
~ **uteri externum** external cervical (uterine) os, external mouth of the womb
~ **uteri internum** internal cervical (uterine) os, internal mouth of the womb
~ **vaginae** external orifice of the vagina, vaginal (introitus) ostium
Ostium-primum-Defekt *m* ostium primum defect *(Herzfehler)*
Ostium-secundum-Defekt *m* ostium secundum defect *(Herzfehler)*
Östradiol *n* oestradiol, dihydrotheelin, dihydroxyoestrin *(Follikelhormon)*
Östrin *n* oestrin
Östriol *n* oestriol
östrogen oestrogenic
Östrogen *n* oestrogen, oestrogenic hormone *(weibliches Keimdrüsenhormon)*
Östrogenapplikation *f* oestrogenization
Östrogenbehandlung *f* oestrogen treatment
Östrogenmangel *m* oestrogen deficiency
Östrogenmangelproduktion *f* hypooestrogenism
Östrogenphase *f* oestrous stage [of the ovarian cycle]
Östrogenrezeptor *m* oestrogen receptor
Östrogenrezeptorprotein *n* oestrogen receptor protein
Östrogenspiegel *m* oestrogen level
Östrogenspiegelerhöhung *f* **im Blut** hyperoestrinaemia, hyperoestrogenaemia
Östrogensubstitutionstherapie *f* oestrogen replacement therapy
Östrogenüberproduktion *f* hyperoestrogenism
Östromanie *f* metromania, nymphomania, clitoromania, andromania
Östron *n* oestrone, ketohydroxyestrin
Östrus *m* oestrus
oszillatorisch oscillatory
Oszillogramm *n* oscillogram
Oszillograph *m* oscillograph
Oszillographie *f* oscillography
oszillographisch oscillographic
Oszillometer *n* oscillometer
Oszillometrie *f* oscillometry
oszillometrisch oscillometric
Oszillopsie *f* oscillopsia, oscillating vision
Oszilloskop *n* oscilloscope
Oszitation *f* oscitancy, oscitation, act of yawning
Otalgie *f* otalgia, otodynia, otoneuralgia, otagra, earache
otalgisch otalgic
Othämatom *n* othaematoma, haematoma of the external ear; boxer's ear
Othämorrhagie *f s.* Ohrenblutung
Othämorrhoe *f* othaemorrhoea, sanguinous discharge from the ear
Othelcosis *f* othelcosis, suppuration of the ear, otopyosis
Otiatrie *f* otology, otiatrics, therapeutics of ear diseases

otiatrisch otologic[al]
Otikodinie *f* oticodinia, oticodinosis, vertigo from ear disease *(Meniérescher Symptomkomplex)*
Otitis *f* otitis, inflammation of the ear
~ **externa** external otitis, inflammation of the external ear
~ **interna** internal otitis, inflammation of the internal ear
~ **labyrinthica** labyrinthine otitis
~ **mastoidea** mastoiditis, mastoid inflammation
~ **media** middle ear inflammation, inflammation of the middle ear; acute ear
~ **media adhaesiva** adhesive otitis media
~ **media serosa** secretory otitis media; glue ear
~ **sclerotica** otosclerosis *(Schwerhörigkeit durch Verknöcherung der Gehörknöchelchen)*
otitisch otitic
Otoblenorrhoe *f* otoblenorrhoea
Otochirurg *m* aural surgeon
Otochirurgie *f* aural surgery
otochirurgisch otosurgical
Otodynie *f s.* Otalgie
Otoenzephalitis *f* otoencephalitis
otogen otogenic, otogenous
Otokleisis *f* otocleisis, closure of the auditory passages
Otokonien *fpl* otoconia, statoconia, statoliths, ear dust
Otokranium *n* otocranium, otocrane
Otolaryngologe *m* otolaryngologist
Otolaryngologie *f* otolaryngology
Otoliquorrhoe *f* otoliquorrhoea, cerebrospinal [fluid] otorrhoea
Otolithen *mpl s.* Otokonien
Otolithenmembran *f* otolithic membrane
Otologe *m* otologist, aurist, ear specialist
Otologie *f* otology, otiatrics
otologisch otologic[al]
Otomastoiditis *f* otomastoiditis, otitis with mastoiditis
Otomyasthenie *f* 1. otomyasthenia, weakness of the ear muscles; 2. otomyasthenia, defective hearing
Otomyiasis *f* otomyiasis
Otomykose *f* otomycosis
Otonekrektomie *f* otonecrectomy
Otoneurasthenie *f* otoneurasthenia
Otoneurologie *f* otoneurology
otoneurologisch otoneurological
Oto-Ophthalmo-Laryngoskopie-Besteck *n* oto-ophthalmo-laryngoscopy set
Otopathie *f* otopathy, disease of the ear
otopharyngeal otopharyngeal
Otophon *n* otophone
Otoplastik *f* otoplasty
Otopyorrhoe *f* otopyorrhoea, copious purulent discharge from the ear
Otorhinolaryngologe *m* otorhinolaryngologist
Otorhinolaryngologie *f* otorhinolaryngology
otorhinolaryngologisch otorhinolaryngologic
Otorhinologie *f* otorhinology
Otorrhagie *f s.* Ohrenblutung

Otorrhoe f otorrhoea, discharge from the ear
Otosklerose f otosclerosis, otospongiosis *(Schwerhörigkeit durch Verknöcherung der Gehörknöchelchen)*
Otosklerosefokus m otosclerotic focus
otosklerotisch otosclerotic
Otoskop n otoscope
Otoskopie f otoscopy
Otoskopie-Besteck n otoscopy set
otoskopisch otoscopic
Ototomie f ototomy, incision into the ear
ototoxisch ototoxic
Ototoxizität f ototoxicity
Otozephalie f otocephalia, synotia
Otozephalus m otocephalus, synotus *(Mißgeburt)*
Otozyste f otocyst *(Embryologie)*
Ouabain n ouabain, G-strophantin *(Herzglykosid)*
Ovalozyt m ovalocyte, elliptocyte
Ovalozytose f ovalocytosis, oval-cell anaemia, elliptocytosis
Ovar n ovary, o[v]arium, oophoron, female gonad *(s.a. unter Eierstock)*
~/polyzystisches polycystic ovary
Ovar... *s.a.* Oophor... *und* Eierstock...
Ovardysfunktion f dysovarism
Ovardysgerminom n ovarian dysgerminoma, embryoma of the ovary *(bösartige Geschwulst)*
ovarial ovarian, oaric
Ovarial... *s.a.* Oophor... *und* Eierstock...
Ovarialagenesie f ovarian agenesis, Turner's syndrome
Ovarialeinblutung f ovarian apoplexy
Ovarialgravidität f ovarian pregnancy, oocyesis, ovariocyesis
Ovarialhernie f ovariocele, ovarian hernia *(Senkung des Eierstocks in einen Leistenbruch)*
Ovarialhydrops m ovarian dropsy; hydrovarium
Ovarialkarzinom n ovarian cancer (carcinoma)
Ovarialkystadenom n/**mehrkammeriges (multilokuläres)** multilocular cyst of ovary
Ovarialkystom n ovarian cystoma (dermoid cyst)
Ovarialschwäche f hypoovar[ian]ism
Ovarialsekretion f/**gesteigerte** hyperovar[ian]ism
~/verminderte hypoovar[ian]ism
Ovarialsklerose f sclero-oophoritis
Ovarialtorsion f ovarian torsion
Ovarialtumor m ovarioncus, oophoroma, tumour of the ovary
ovariogen ovariogenic
ovariolytisch ovariolytic
Ovariomanie f s. Oophoromanie
Ovariopathie f ovariopathy, oophoropathy, ovarian disease
Ovariorrhexis f ovariorrhexis, rupture of an ovary
Ovariosalpingektomie f oophorosalpingectomy, ovariosalpingectomy
Ovariotomie f s. Oophorotomie
Ovariozele f s. Ovarialhernie
Ovariozentese f ovariocentesis, puncture of an ovary

Ovariumerweichung f s. Oophoromalazie
Ovarplastik f oophoroplasty
Ovidukt m s. Eileiter
oviduktal oviductal, oviducal
ovifer oviferous
oviger ovigerous
Ovogonium n o[v]ogonium, primordial ovum
ovoid ovoid, egg-shaped, oval
Ovomuzin n ovomucin *(Glykoproteid)*
Ovoplasma n ovoplasm
ovotestikulär ov[ari]otesticular
Ovotestis m ov[ar]otestis *(Geschlechtsdrüse eines Zwitters mit sperma- und eierbildenden Abschnitten)*
Ovovitellin n ovovitellin, lecithalbumin *(Phosphorproteid im Eidotter)*
Ovularabort m ovular abortion
Ovulation f ovulation
Ovulationsalter n ovulational age *(des Embryos)*
Ovulationsauslösung f ovulation induction
Ovulationsbestimmung f ovulation timing
Ovulationshemmer m ovulation inhibitor
Ovulationshemmung f ovulation inhibition
ovulationslos non-ovulatory, anovular, anovulatory
Ovulationsschmerz m intermenstrual (middle) pain
ovulatorisch ovulatory
ovulieren to ovulate
ovulogen ovulogenous
Ovulum n ovule, ovulum
~ Nabothi Nabothian gland
Owren-Faktor m cothromboplastin
Oxalämie f oxalaemia
Oxalat n oxalate
Oxalatvergiftung f oxalism
Oxalessigsäure f oxalacetic acid
Oxalose f oxalosis *(Stoffwechselstörung)*
Oxalsäure f oxalic acid
Oxalsäureausscheidung f im Urin oxaluria
Oxalsäuregehalt m des Blutes/**erhöhter** oxalaemia
Oxalsäurevergiftung f oxalism
Oxyblepsie f oxyblepsia
oxychromatisch oxychromatic
Oxydase f oxidase, oxydase, oxidizing enzyme
Oxydation f oxidation, oxidization
β-Oxydation f beta oxidation *(Fettsäurestoffwechsel)*
Oxydationsenzym n oxidizing enzyme
Oxydationswasser n water of combustion
oxydieren to oxidize
~/zu Nitrat to nitrify
Oxydoreduktase f oxidoreductase *(Enzym)*
Oxygenase f oxygenase *(Enzym)*
oxygenieren to oxygenate *(z. B. Hämoglobin)*
Oxygenierung f oxygenation *(des Hämoglobins)*
~/hyperbare hyperbaric oxygenation
Oxygeusie f oxygeusia, acuteness of the sense of taste
Oxyhämatin n oxyhaematin
Oxyhämatoporphyrin n oxyhaematoporphyrin

Oxyhämoglobin

Oxyhämoglobin *n* oxyhaemoglobin
Oxyhämoglobindissoziation *f* oxyhaemoglobin dissociation
Oxyhämoglobindissoziationskurve *f* oxyhaemoglobin dissociation curve
Oxykodon *n* oxycodone *(Analgetikum)*
Oxylalie *f* oxylalia, swiftness of speech
Oxymeter *n* oximeter
Oxymetrie *f* oximetry, oxymetry *(des arteriellen Blutes)*
Oxymorphin *n* oxymorphine *(Analgetikum)*
Oxynervon *n* oxynervon *(Zerebrosid)*
Oxyopie *f* oxyopia, acuteness of vision
Oxyoptrie *f* oxyopter *(Einheit der Sehschärfe)*
Oxyosmie *f* oxyosmia, oxyosphresia, acuteness of the sense of smell
Oxypathie *f* 1. oxypathy, acuteness of sensation; 2. oxypathy, acid poisoning
oxyphil oxyphil[e], oxyphilic, oxyphilous
Oxyphilie *f* oxyphilia, acidophilia *(Färbung mit sauren Farbstoffen)*
Oxyphonie *f* oxyphonia, shrillness (sharpness) of voice
Oxyprolin *n* oxyproline *(Eiweißbaustein)*
Oxytetrazyklin *n* oxytetracycline *(Antibiotikum)*
Oxytokie *f* oxytocia, rapid parturition (childbirth)
Oxytozikum *n* oxytocic [agent]
Oxytozin *n* oxytocin, oxytocic hormone *(verstärkt Gebärmutterkontraktionen)*
oxytozisch oxytocic, ocyodinic
Oxyurenabtreibungsmittel *n* oxyurifuge [agent]
Oxyurenappendizitis *f* oxyuric appendicitis, appendicitis oxyurica
oxyurenartig oxyurid
Oxyurenmittel *n* oxyuricide [agent]
Oxyuriasis *f* oxyuriasis *(durch Oxyuris vermicularis)*
Oxyuris *m* **vermicularis** *s.* Enterobius vermicularis
oxyzephal oxycephalic, oxycephalous, steeple-shaped
Oxyzephalie *f* oxycephalia
Oxyzephalus *m* oxycephalus, steeple head (skull)
Ozaena *f* ozaena, atrophic (dry) rhinitis
Ozochrotie *f* ozochrotia, strong odour of the skin
ozochrotös ozochrotous
Ozonisierung *f* ozonization
Ozostomie *f* ozostomia, foulness of the breath

P

paaren/sich to mate, to pair, to couple
paarig paired, geminate
PAB *s.* Para-Aminobenzoesäure
Pacemaker *m s.* Herzschrittmacher
Pachometer *n* pachymeter, pachometer *(zur Messung der Hornhautdicke des Auges)*
Pachyakrie *f* pachyacria
Pachyblepharon *n* pachyblepharon, thickened eyelid; pachyblepharosis
Pachycheilie *f* pachy[e]ilia, thickness of the lips
Pachycholie *f* pachycholia, thickness of the bile
pachychromatisch pachychromatic *(z. B. der Zellkern)*
Pachydaktylie *f* pachydactyly *(Vergrößerung der Finger und Zehen)*
Pachyderma *n s.* Pachydermia
pachydermatös pachydermatous, pachydermial, pachydermic, thick-skinned; pachyhymenic
Pachydermia *n* pachydermia, abnormal thickness of the skin; pachyderma
~ **laryngis** laryngeal pachydermia *(Plattenepithelwucherung der Stimmbänder bei chronischer Kehlkopfentzündung)*
~ **lymphangiectatica** lymphangiectatic pachydermia
~ **occipitalis** occipital pachydermia
Pachydermoperiostose *f* pachydermoperiostosis
Pachyglossie *f* pachyglossia, thickness of the tongue
pachygnath pachygnathous
Pachygyrie *f* pachygyria *(Abflachung und Verbreiterung der Hirnwindungen)*
Pachyhämie *f* pachy[h]aemia, thickness of the blood
Pachyleptomeningitis *f* pachyleptomeningitis, inflammation of the dura and pia
Pachylosis *f* pachylosis
Pachymeningitis *f* pachymeningitis, perimeningitis, duritis, inflammation of the dura mater
~ **cervicalis hypertrophica** hypertrophic cervical pachymeningitis
~ **circumscripta** circumscribed pachymeningitis
~ **externa** external meningitis, endocranitis; epidural abscess
~ **haemorrhagica interna** haemorrhagic [internal] pachymeningitis
~ **interna** internal meningitis
pachymeningitisch pachymeningitic, perimeningitic
Pachymeningopathie *f* pachymeningopathy, disease of the dura mater
Pachymeninx *f* pachymeninx, dura [mater], scleromeninx, dura mater of the brain
Pachymeninxentzündung *f s.* Pachymeningitis
Pachymukosa *f* pachymucosa
Pachynsis *f* pachynsis; abnormal thickening *(z. B. einer Membran)*
pachyntisch pachyntic
Pachyonychia congenita congenital pachyonychia, Schäfer's syndrome
Pachyonychie *f* pachyonychia, pachyonyxis; thickening of the nails
Pachyotie *f* pachyotia, thickness of the ears
Pachypelviperitonitis *f* pachypelviperitonitis
Pachyperikarditis *f* pachypericarditis
Pachyperiostose *f* pachyperiostosis *(z. B. der langen Röhrenknochen)*
Pachyperitonitis *f* pachyperitonitis
Pachypleuritis *f* pachypleuritis
pachypodös pachypodous, having thick feet
pachyrhin pachyrhine, pachyrhinic

Pachysalpingitis f pachysalpingitis, parenchymatous salpingitis, mural (hypertrophic) salpingitis
Pachysalpingoovaritis f pachysalpingo-ovaritis, pachysalpingo-oothecitis
Pachysomie f pachysomia
pachytrichös pachytrichous, thick-haired
Pachyvaginitis f pachyvaginitis
pachyzephal pachycephalic, pachycephalous
Pachyzephalie f pachycephalia *(abnorme Dicke der Schädelknochen)*
Pachyzephalus m pachycephalus
Packung f pack, packing
~/**feuchtwarme** hot wet pack
~/**heiße** hot pack
Pädarthrokaze f paedarthrocace
Pädatrophie f 1. paedatrophia, wasting disease of children; 2. tabes mesenterica, tuberculous mesenteric lymphadenitis
Päderast m paederast
Päderastie f paederasty, buggery
Pädiater m paediatrician, paediatrist, children's specialist
Pädiatrie f paediatrics, paediatry
pädiatrisch paediatric
Pädologe m paedologist
Pädologie f paedology, paidology *(Lehre von der körperlichen und geistigen Entwicklung der Kinder)*
Pädometer n paedometer
Pädometrie f paedometry
Pädonosologie f paedonosology
pädophil f paedophilic
Pädophilie f 1. paedophilia, fondness for children; 2. paedophilia *(geschlechtliche Befriedigung an Kindern)*
Pädophobie f paedophobia *(krankhafte Angst vor Kindern)*
Page-Syndrom n Page's (adrenosympathetic) syndrome
pagetartig pagetoid
Paget-von-Schrötter-Syndrom n Paget-Schroetter's syndrome, effort (axillary vein) thrombosis, intermittent venous claudication
Paketleber f packet liver *(im dritten Stadium der Syphilis)*
Paläoenzephalon n palaeoencephalon
Paläogenese f palaeogenesis
paläokinetisch palaeokinetic
Paläokortex m palaeocortex
Paläoolive f palaeoolive
Paläontologie f palaeontology
Paläopallium n palaeopallium
Paläopathologie f palaeopathology
Paläopsychologie f palaeopsychology
Paläostriatum n palaeostriatum, globus pallidus
Paläothalamus m palaeothalamus
Paläozerebellum n palaeocerebellum
palatal palatine, palatal, palatic
palatiform palatiform
palatin s. palatal
Palato... s. a. Urano... *und* Gaumen...

palatoglossal palatoglossal
palatomaxillär palatomaxillary
palatonasal palatonasal
Palatopagus m **parasiticus** palatopagus parasiticus, epipalatum *(Doppelmißbildung)*
palatopharyngeal palatopharyngeal, pharyngopalatine
Palatoplegie f palatoplegia, paralysis of the soft palate, palatine paralysis
palatopterygoid palatopterygoid
Palatorrhaphie f palatorrhaphy, staphylorrhaphy, suture of a cleft palate, palate suture, uranorrhaphy, uraniscorrhaphy
Palatoschisis f palatoschisis, fissure of the palate; cleft palate
Palatum n palate, palatum, roof of the mouth *(Zusammensetzungen s. unter Gaumen)*
Palikinesie f palikinesia, palinkinesis, pathologic repetition of movements
Palilalie f palilalia, pathologic repetition of words
Palindromie f palindromia, recurrence of a disease
Palingenese f palingenesis *(Wiederholung stammesgeschichtlicher Vorstufen in der Individualentwicklung)*
Palingraphie f palingraphia, pathologic repetition of letters
Palinmnese f palinmnesis, memory for past events
Palinopsie f palinopsia
Palisadenwurmbefall m strongyloidiasis, strongylosis, intestinal capillariasis, anguilluliasis, anguillulosis
Pallanästhesie f pallanaesthesia, loss of vibration sense
Pallästhesie f pallaesthesia, vibratory sense, sensibility to vibrations, bone sensibility
pallästhetisch pallaesthetic
palliativ palliative
Palliativbehandlung f palliative treatment
Palliativoperation f palliative operation
Palliativum n palliative [agent]
pallidal palli[d]al
pallidohypothalamisch pallidohypothalamic
pallidoretikulär pallidoreticular
pallidothalamisch pallidothalamic
Pallidotomie f pallidotomy
Pallidum n pallidum *(Anteil des strio-pallidären Systems)*
Pallidumatrophie f pallidum atrophy, palaeostriatal syndrome
Pallidumdurchtrennung f[/**operative**] pallidotomy
palliopontin palliopontine
Pallium n pallium, [brain] mantle
Pallor m s. Blässe
Palma f **manus** palm [of the hand], hollow of the hand
Palmarabszeß m palmar abscess
Palmaraponeurose f palmar aponeurosis, deep palmar fascia
Palmarbogen m palmar arch

Palmarerythem

Palmarerythem n palmar erythema; red palms
Palmarfibromatose f palmar fibromatosis
Palmarhyperkeratose f palmar hyperkeratosis
Palmaris-longus-Sehne f palmaris longus tendon
Palmarraum m palmar space
Palmarreflex m palmar reflex *(Fingerbeugung bei Reizung der Hohlhand)*
palpabel palpable
~/nicht impalpable
Palpation f palpation, dipping, touch
~/bimanuelle bimanual palpation
Palpationsbefund m palpatory findings
Palpatoperkussion f palpatory percussion, palpatopercussion
palpatorisch palpatory
Palpebra f palpebra, [eye]lid, blepharon *(s. a. unter Augenlid)*
~ **frontalis** upper [eye]lid
~ **inferior (malaris)** lower [eye]lid
~ **superior** upper [eye]lid
~ **tertia** nictitating membrane *(rudimentär)*
palpebral palpebral
palpieren to palpate, to touch, to feel
Palpitation f palpitation, palmus
palpitieren to palpitate
paludal paludal, palustral, malarial, malarious
Paludismus m paludism, paludal (intermittent) fever, malaria, ague *(Tropenkrankheit mit regelmäßigen Fieberanfällen und Schüttelfrost)*
Pamaquin n pamaquine *(Antimalariamittel)*
Panagglutination f panagglutination
Panagglutinin n panagglutinin
Pananästhesie f pananaesthesia
Panaritium n panaritium, panaris, whitlow, felon
Panarteri[i]tis f panarteritis *(Entzündung aller Arterienwandschichten)*
Panarthritis f panarthritis *(Entzündung aller Gelenkteile)*
Panästhesie f panaesthesia
Panatrophie f panatrophy
panazinös panacinar, panacinous
Pancavern[os]itis f pancavernositis *(Entzündung aller Corpora cavernosa)*
Panchromfärbung f panchrome stain *(für Blutausstriche)*
Pancreas n pancreas *(s. a. unter Pankreas)*
~ **accessorium** accessory pancreas
~ **anulare** annular pancreas
Pandemie f pandemia, pandemy
pandemisch pandemic
Pandy-Reaktion f Pandy's test *(Nachweis für Globuline im Liquor)*
Panelektroskop n panelectroscope
Panendoskop n panendoscope
Panendoskopie f panendoscopy
Panenzephalitis f 1. panencephalitis, generalized inflammation of the brain; 2. subacute sclerosing panencephalitis
Pangenesis f pangenesis *(Entwicklungs- und Vererbungstheorie von Darwin)*
Panglossie f panglossia, excessive (psychotic) garrulity

Panhämozytopenie f panhaematopenia, pancytopenia
Panhidrose f panhidrosis, generalized perspiration
Panhyperämie f panhyperaemia, general plethora
Panhypogonadismus m panhypogonadism
panhypophysär panhypopituitary
Panhypopituitarismus m panhypopituitarism, anterior pituitary insufficiency, Simmond's disease
Panhysterektomie f panhysterectomy, total excision of the uterus
Panhysterokolpektomie f panhysterocolpectomy, pancolpohysterectomy
Panhystero-oophorektomie f panhystero-oophorectomy
Panhysterosalpingektomie f panhysterosalpingectomy
Panhysterosalpingo-oophorektomie f panhysterosalpingo-oophorectomy
Panik f panic, extreme anxiety attack
Panikverhalten n panic (catastrophic) reaction
Panimmunität f panimmunity, general immunity to disease (infection)
Pankarditis f pancarditis, endoperimyocarditis
Pankolektomie f pancolectomy, excision of the entire colon
Pankrealgie f pancre[at]algia, pain in the pancreas
Pankreas n pancreas *(s. a. unter Pancreas)* ● **aus dem ~ stammend** pancreatogenic, pancreatogenous ● **neben dem ~** parapancreatic
~/artefizielles artificial pancreas
Pankreas... s. a. Bauchspeicheldrüsen...
Pankreasamylase f pancreatic amylase, amylopsin *(Enzym)*
Pankreasanlage f pancreatic anlage
Pankreasapoplexie f[/akute] acute haemorrhagic pancreatitis, pancreatic haemorrhage
pankreasauflösend pancreatolytic
Pankreasauflösung f pancreatolysis
Pankreasazinus m pancreatic acinus
Pankreasdiabetes m pancreatic diabetes
Pankreasdiarrhoe f pancreatic diarrhoea
Pankreasdiastase f pancreatic diastase *(Enzym)*
Pankreasdivertikel n pancreatic diverticulum *(Embryologie)*
Pankreasdysfunktion f dyspancreatism
Pankreasendopeptidase f pancreatic endopeptidase *(Enzym)*
Pankreasentzündung f s. Pankreatitis
Pankreasenzym n pancreatic enzyme
Pankreasenzympräparat n pancreatic enzyme preparation
Pankreasexopeptidase f pancreatic exopeptidase *(Enzym)*
Pankreasexstirpation f pancreatectomy, pancreectomy
Pankreasfibrose f pancreatic fibrosis
~/zystische pancreatic cystic fibrosis, [fibro]cystic disease of the pancreas, muco[viscido]sis,

familial (congenital pancreatic) steatorrhoea, chronic interstitial pancreatitis of infancy, Anderson's disease (syndrome) *(Sekretionsstörung mit Auswirkungen an Bauchspeicheldrüse, Bronchial- und Darmdrüsen)*
Pankreasgang *m* pancreatic duct
Pankreasgang-Harnleiter-Anastomose *f* pancreatic duct ureterostomy
Pankreasgang-Jejunum-Anastomose *f* pancreatic duct jejunostomy
Pankreasgangröntgen[kontrast]darstellung *f* pancreatography
Pankreasgang[s]steinentfernung *f[/operative]* pancreaticolithotomy
Pankreasgangsystem *n* pancreatic ductal system
Pankreasgegend *f* pancreatic region
Pankreasgeschwulst *f* pancreatic tumour
Pankreasgewebe *n* pancreatic tissue
Pankreasinseln *fpl* islets of Langerhans (the pancreas)
Pankreasinselzelle *f* beta (pancreatic islet) cell, cell of the islet
Pankreasinselzellkarzinom *n* pancreatic islet cell carcinoma
Pankreasinselzelltransplantation *f* pancreatic islet cell transplantation
Pankreasinsuffizienz *f* pancreatic insufficiency; hypopancreatism
Pankreasinzision *f* pancreatotomy, incision into the pancreas
Pankreaskarzinom *n* pancreatic cancer, carcinoma of the pancreas
Pankreaskopf *m* head of the pancreas
Pankreaskörper *m* body of the pancreas
Pankreaskrankheit *f* pancreatopathy, pancreatic disease
Pankreaslipase *f* pancreatic lipase, pancreatolipase, steapsin *(Enzym)*
pankreaslos apancreatic; pancreatectomized
Pankreasnekrose *f* pancreatic necrosis
~/akute acute necrosis of the pancreas; acute haemorrhagic pancreatitis
Pankreaspeptidase *f* pancreatopeptidase *(Enzym)*
Pankreaspseudozyste *f* pancreatic pseudocyst
Pankreasrückseite *f* posterior surface of the pancreas
Pankreassaft *m* pancreatic juice
Pankreassaftfluß *m*/**verstärkter** pancreatic succorrhoea
Pankreasschwanz *m* tail of the pancreas, pancreatic tail
Pankreasschwanzresektion *f* caudal pancreatectomy
Pankreassekret *n* pancreatic juice
Pankreasstühle *mpl* pancreatic diarrhoea
Pankreasulzerierung *f* pancreathelcosis, ulceration of the pancreas
Pankreasunterseite *f* inferior surface of the pancreas
Pankreasvorderseite *f* anterior surface of the pancreas

pankreaswirksam pancrea[to]tropic
Pankreaszerstörung *f* pancreatolysis
Pankreaszyste *f* pancreatic cyst
Pankreatalgie *f* pancre[at]algia, pain in the pancreas
Pankreatektomie *f* pancreatectomy, pancreectomy
Pankreatemphraxis *f* pancreatemphraxis, congestion of the pancreas *(bei Gangverschluß)*
Pankreatikocholezystostomie *f* pancreaticocholecystostomy
Pankreatikoduodenektomie *f* pancreaticoduodenectomy
Pankreatikoduodenostomie *f* pancreaticoduodenostomy
Pankreatikoenterostomie *f* pancreaticoenterostomy
Pankreatikogastrostomie *f* pancreaticogastrostomy
Pankreatikojejunostomie *f* pancreaticojejunostomy
pankreatikolienal pancreaticosplenic, splen[ic]opancreatic
Pankreatin *n* pancreatin *(Enzym)*
Pankreatitis *f* pancreatitis, pancreatic inflammation, inflammation of the pancreas
~/akute haemorrhagische acute haemorrhagic pancreatitis
~/akute interstitielle acute interstitial pancreatitis
~/chronisch-rezidivierende chronic relapsing pancreatitis
pankreatitisch pancreatitic
Pankreato... *s. a.* Pankreatiko...
Pankreatographie *f* pancreatography
Pankreatolith *m* pancreatolith, pancreatic calculus (stone)
Pankreatolithektomie *f* pancreatolithectomy, pancreatolithotomy, pancreaticolithotomy
Pankreatolyse *f* pancreatolysis, destruction of the pancreatic tissue
Pankreatopathie *f* pancre[at]opathy, disease of the pancreas
Pankreatotomie *f* pancreatotomy, incision into the pancreas
pankrea[to]trop pancrea[to]tropic
pankreopriv pancreoprivic
Pankreozym *n* pancreozyme
Pankreozymin *n* pancreozymin
Panmetritis *f* panmetritis, inflammation of the total uterus
Panmyelopathie *f* panmyelopathy; aplastic anaemia
Panmyelophthise *f* panmyelophthisis, wasting of the bone marrow
Panmyelose *f* panmyelosis
Panmyelotoxikose *f* panmyelotoxicosis
Panmyositis *f* panmyositis, generalized muscular inflammation
Panner-Syndrom *n* osteochondrosis of the capitulum humeri, Panner's disease
Panneuritis *f* panneuritis, general neuritis

Panneuritis

- **~ epidemica** epidemic panneuritis, beriberi, Ceylon sickness, kakke *(Vitamin-B₁-Mangelkrankheit)*
- **Panniculus** *m* panniculus, [tissue] layer, membrane
- **~ adiposus** subcutaneous fat layer
- **Pannikulitis** *f* panniculitis, inflammation of the panniculus adiposus
- **Pannus** *m* pannus, membrane-like vascularization of the cornea
- **~ carnosus (crassus)** carneous pannus
- **~ degenerativus** degenerative pannus
- **~ tenuis** slight pannus
- **~ trachomatosus** trachomatous keratitis (pannus)
- **Panophthalmie** *f s.* Panophthalmitis
- **Panophthalmitis** *f* panophthalmitis, panophthalmia, inflammation of all eye structures
- **~ purulenta** purulent panophthalmitis
- **Panoramastereoskop** *n* stereophantoscope
- **Panostitis** *f* panost[e]itis, inflammation of the total bone
- **Panotitis** *f* panotitis, inflammation of the total ear
- **Panphlebitis** *f* panphlebitis *(Entzündung aller Venenwandschichten)*
- **Panphobie** *f s.* Pantophobie
- **Panplegie** *f* panplegia
- **Pansinusitis** *f* pansinusitis, inflammation of all paranasal sinuses
- **Pansinusitis-Syndrom** *n* pansinusitic syndrome
- **Pansklerose** *f* pansclerosis *(z. B. eines Organs)*
- **Panstrongylus** *m* **megistus** Panstrongylus megistus *(Überträger der Chagas-Krankheit)*
- **pansystolisch** pansystolic, holosystolic
- **Pantalgie** *f* pantalgia, pain over the whole body
- **pantamorph** pantamorphic, formless
- **Pantanenzephalie** *f* pantanencephalia, total congenital absence of the brain
- **Pantanenzephalus** *m* pantanencephalus *(Mißgeburt)*
- **Pantaphobie** *f* pantaphobia, total absence of fear
- **Panthenol** *n* panthenol *(Dermatikum)*
- **Pantophobie** *f* pantophobia, pan[o]phobia *(krankhafte Angst vor allen äußeren Dingen)*
- **Pantothensäure** *f* pantothenic acid, filtrate factor, bios IIa, anti-grey-hair factor *(Vitamin-B-Komplex)*
- **Panus** *m* 1. panus, inflamed non-suppurating lymph node; 2. *s.* Lymphogranuloma venereum
- **~ inguinalis** inguinal panus
- **Panuveitis** *f* panuveitis, inflammation of the entire uveal tract
- **Panzerebralarteriographie** *f* pancerebral arteriography
- **Panzerherz** *n* armoured (bony) heart
- **Panzerkrebs** *m* cuirass (corset, jacket) cancer, cancer en cuirasse
- **Panzerniere** *f* fibrous perinephritis
- **Panzytopenie** *f* pancytopenia, panhaematopenia
- **Papageienkrankheit** *f* psittacosis, parrot disease (fever)
- **Papageienzunge** *f* parrot tongue
- **Papain** *n* papain *(Anwendung bei Magen- und Darmstörungen; Antiwurmmittel)*
- **Papanicolaou-Abstrich** *m* Papanicolaou smear
- **Papanicolaou-Färbung** *f* Papanicolaou stain[ing]
- **Papanicolaou-Karzinomdiagnostik** *f* Papanicolaou's diagnosis; exfoliative cytology
- **Papaverin** *n* papaverine *(Opiumalkaloid)*
- **Papel** *f* papule, papula, pimple *(Primäreffloreszenz auf der Haut)*
- **~/feuchte** moist (mucous) papule, syphilitic condyloma
- **~/flache** flat[tened] papule
- **~/trockene** dry papule, papule of chancre
- **papelartig** papuloid, condylomatous
- **Papelbildung** *f* papulation, papule formation
- **papeltragend** papuliferous
- **Papelstadium** *n* papular stage
- **papierartig** papyraceous, paper-like
- **Papierchromatographie** *f* paper chromatography
- **Papierelektrophorese** *f* paper[-zone] electrophoresis
- **Papilla** *f* papilla, nipple-shaped elevation (eminence) ● **neben der ~ [liegend]** juxtapapillary
- **~ circumvallata** [circum]vallate papilla
- **~ conica** conical papilla
- **~ dentis** dental papilla
- **~ duodeni major [Vateri]** major (greater) duodenal papilla, papilla of Vater
- **~ duodeni minor** minor (smaller) duodenal papilla, papilla of Santorini
- **~ fasciculi optici** optic disk (papilla)
- **~ filiformis** filiform papilla
- **~ foliata** foliate papilla, taste ridge
- **~ fungiforme** fungiform papilla
- **~ incisiva** incisive pad, palatine papilla
- **~ interdentalis** interdental papilla
- **~ lacrimalis** lacrimal papilla (tubercle)
- **~ lenticularis** lenticular papilla
- **~ lingualis** lingual papilla
- **~ mammae** *s.* Mamille
- **~ parotidea** parotid papilla
- **~ pili** hair papilla
- **~ renalis** renal papilla
- **~ urethralia** urethral papilla
- **~ vallata** *s.* ~ circumvallata
- **~ Vateri** *s.* ~ duodeni major
- **Papillarkörper** *m* papillary body
- **Papillarlinie** *f* 1. mamillary (nipple) line; 2. dermal ridge
- **Papillarlinienmuster** *n* dermal ridge pattern
- **Papillarmuskel** *m* papillary muscle
- **~/hinterer** posterior papillary muscle
- **~/septaler** septal papillary muscle
- **~/vorderer** anterior papillary muscle
- **Papillarmuskelsehne** *f* tendinous cord, tendon of the papillary muscle
- **Papille** *f s.* Papilla
- **Papillektomie** *f* papillectomy, excision of a papilla
- **Papillenabblassung** *f* optic [disk] pallor, pallor of the disk *(an der Netzhaut)*

papillenartig papillary, papillate
Papillenblässe f s. Papillenabblassung
Papillenchorioiditis f juxtapapillary choroiditis, Jensen's disease (retinopathy)
Papillenentfernung f[/operative] s. Papillektomie
Papillenentzündung f 1. papillitis, inflammation of a papilla; 2. optic neuritis, inflammation of the optic papilla
Papillenexkavation f excavation (cupping) of the optic disk
papillenförmig papilliform
Papillengefäßtrichter m optic pit
papillennah juxtapapillary
Papillennekrose f papillary necrosis
Papillenödem n papilloedema, oedema of the optic disk (papilla); engorged papilla, choked disk *(des Auges)*
Papillenstauung f papillary stasis *(des Auges)*
papillentragend papilliferous
Papillen- und Netzhautentzündung f neuroretinitis
Papillen- und Netzhauterkrankung f neuroretinopathy
Papillitis f s. Papillenentzündung
Papillom n s. Papilloma
~/fibrosquamöses fibrosquamous papilloma
~/malignes malignant papilloma
Papilloma n papilloma *(gutartige Geschwulst aus gefäßhaltigem Bindegewebe) (s. a. unter* Papillom*)*
~ chorioideum choroid papilloma
~ lineare linear papilloma; linear ichthyosis
~ molle soft papilloma
~ venereum venereal papilloma, condyloma
~ vesicae bladder papilloma
papillomakulär papillomacular
papillomartig papillomatous
Papillomatose f papillomatosis
Papilloretinitis f papilloretinitis
Papillosarkom n papillosarcoma
Pappatacifieber n pappataci (three-day) fever, phlebotomus (Chitral, sand-fly) fever *(Arborviruserkrankung der Tropen)*
Pappmundstück n cardboard mouth piece
Papula f s. Papel
papulär papular
Papulation f s. Papelbildung
papuloerythematös f papuloerythematous
Papulopustula f papulopustule
papulopustulös papulopustular
Papulose f s. Papulosis
Papulosis f papulosis; multiple papules
~ atrophicans maligna malignant atrophic papulosis, atrophic papulosquamous dermatitis, Degos' disease
papulosquamös papulosquamous
papulovesikulär papulovesicular
Para f para, parturient, woman in labour
Para-Aminobenzoesäure f para-aminobenzoic acid
Para-Aminobenzoesäure-β-diäthylaminoäthylester m procaine *(Lokalanästhetikum)*
Para-Aminohippursäure f para-aminohippuric acid, 4-aminobenzoylglycine
Para-Aminohippursäure-Test m para-aminohippuric acid test *(zur Bestimmung der Nierendurchblutung)*
Para-Aminosalizylsäure f para-aminosalicylic acid, PAS *(Mittel gegen Tuberkulose)*
Paraamyloid n para-amyloid
Paraamyloidose f para-amyloidosis, atypical amyloidosis
Paraanalgesie f para-analgesia
Paraanästhesie f para-anaesthesia
paraaortal para-aortic, paraortic
Paraappendizitis f para-appendicitis
Paraballismus m paraballism
Parabasalkörperchen n parabasal body
Parabazillus m parabacillus
Parabiose f parabiosis *(1. Nebeneinanderleben zweier Individuen; 2. transitorische Unterdrückung der Nervenleitfähigkeit)*
Parablepsie f parablepsia, false vision
Parabulie f parabulia, perversion of the will
Paracentesis f paracentesis, [surgical] puncture, tapping
~ abdominis abdominal paracentesis, paracentesis of the abdomen, abdominocentesis
~ bulbi ophthalmocentesis, paracentesis of the eye, puncture of the eyeball
~ cordis paracentesis of the heart
~ oculi s. ~ bulbi
~ pericardii paracentesis of the pericardial sac
~ thoracis thora[co]centesis
~ vesicae paracentesis of the bladder [wall]
Paracholera f paracholera
Paracholie f paracholia *(Gelbsucht durch Leberzellschädigung)*
Parachord n parachordal [cartilage]
Parachordalplatte f parachordal plate
Parachroma n parachroma, abnormal coloured skin; parachromatosis
Parachromatismus m, **Parachromatopsie** f parachromatopsia, parachromatism, parachromatoblepsia
Parachromatose f parachromatosis, abnormal colouration of the skin; parachroma
parachromophor parachromophorous
Paracoccidioides m **brasiliensis** Paracoccidioides (Blastomyces) brasiliensis *(Erreger der südamerikanischen Blastomykose)*
Paracusia f parac[o]usis, paracousia
~ duplicata double hearing, diplacusis
Paracusis f **Willisiana** paracousis Willisii *(Besserhören bei Lärm und Körpererschütterungen)*
Paradenitis f paradenitis
paradental paradental, paradontal
Paradentitis f s. Periodontitis
~ profunda simplex paradental pyorrhoea
Paradentopathia f **dystrophica** s. Parodontose
Paradentose f s. Parodontose
paradidymal paradidymal

Paradidymis

Paradidymis *m* 1. paradidymis, parepididymis, Giraldes' organ; 2. *s.* Paroophoron
paradiphtherisch paradiphtherial, paradiphtheritic
Paradontalabszeß *m* paradontal abscess
Paradontologie *f s.* Periodontologie
Paradontopathie *f* paradontopathy, periodontopathy
Paradoxon *n*/**immunologisches** immunological paradoxon
Paradysenterie *f* paradysentery
Paraepilepsie *f* paraepilepsy, abortive epileptic attack
Paraerythroblast *m* paraerythroblast
Paraffinakne *f* paraffin acne
Paraffineinbettung *f* embedding in paraffin *(Histologie)*
Paraffingaze *f* paraffin gauze
Paraffininjektion *f* paraffin injection
Paraffinölbehandlung *f* keritherapy
Paraffinom *n* paraffinoma *(Geschwulst durch eine Paraffininjektion)*
Paraffinschnitt *m* paraffin section *(Histologie)*
parafollikulär parafollicular
Paraform *n*, **Paraformaldehyd** *m* paraform[aldehyde] *(Desinfektionsmittel)*
Paragammazismus *m* paragammacism *(Ersatz der Verschlußlaute durch Zahnlaute)*
Paragangliom *n* paraganglioma, paraganglioneuroma, chromaffino[blasto]ma
~/nichtchromaffines non-chromaffine paraganglioma, chemodectoma
Paraganglion *n* paraganglion
~ caroticum carotid-body tumour
paraganglionär paraganglionic
Parageusie *f* parageusia, perversion of the taste sense
Paragglutination *f* paragglutination
Paraglobulin *n* paraglobulin, fibr[in]oplastin
Paraglobulinausscheidung *f* **im Urin** paraglobulinuria
Paraglossitis *f* paraglossitis
Paragomphosis *f* paragomphosis, impaction of the foetal head *(während der Geburt)*
Paragonimiasis *f* paragonimiasis, parasitic (endemic) haemoptysis
Paragonimus *m* **westermani** Paragonimus westermani, lung fluke
Paragrammatismus *m* paragrammatism
Paragranuloma *n* paragranuloma
Paragraphie *f* paragraphia *(Verwechseln oder Umstellen von Buchstaben)*
Parahämophilie *f* parahaemophilia *(Blutgerinnungsstörung)*
Parahepatitis *f* parahepatitis
Parahidrosis *f* par[a]hidrosis, paridrosis
Parahypnose *f* parahypnosis
Parahypophyse *f* parahypophysis, accessory pituitary gland
Parainfluenza *f* para-influenza
Parainfluenzabazillus *m* para-influenza bacillus
Parainfluenzavirus *n* para-influenza virus

Parakanthom[a] *n* paracanthoma
Parakeratose *f* parakeratosis
Parakeratosis *f* **scutularis** scutulate parakeratosis
Parakinesie *f* parakinesia
Parakokzidioidomykose *f* paracoccidioidomycosis
Parakolitis *f* paracolitis
Parakolpitis *f* paracolpitis
Parakolpium *n* paracolpium
Parakusis *f s.* Paracusia
Paralalie *f* paralalia *(Sprachstörung)*
Paralambdazismus *m* paralambdacism
Paralbumin *n* paralbumin *(in Eierstockzysten vorkommende Eiweißsubstanz)*
Paraldehyd *m* paraldehyde *(Schlafmittel)*
Paraldehydvergiftung *f* paraldehydism
Paralepra *f* paraleprosy *(abortive Lepraform)*
Paralexie *f* paralexia *(Lesestörung)*
Paralgesie *f* paralgesia, paralgia; paraesthesia
paralgetisch paralgesic
Paralipophobie *f* paralipophobia *(krankhafte Angst vor Pflichtverletzungen)*
Parallaxe *f* parallax ● **durch ~ bestimmt** parallactic
Parallelallergie *f* group allergy
Paralogie *f* paralogia
Paralogismus *m* paralogism
Paraluteinzelle *f* paralutein cell *(im Corpus luteum)*
Paralyse *f* paralysis, palsy *(s. a. unter Lähmung)*
~/amyotrophe amyotrophic paralysis
~ des III. Hirnnerven oculomotor palsy (paralysis)
~/Erb-Duchennesche Erb's (Erb-Duchenne's) paralysis, Duchenne-Erb palsy (syndrome), upper brachial plexus paralysis
~/galoppierende galloping paralysis
~/gekreuzte crossed (cruciate) paralysis
~/gemischte mixed (motor and sensory) paralysis
~/inkomplette incomplete (partial) paralysis
~/mimetische mimetic paralysis
~/myopathische myopathic paralysis
~/periodische periodic (recurrent) paralysis
~/spinale spinal paralysis, myeloparalysis
~/temporäre temporary paralysis
paralysieren to paralyze, to paralyse
paralysierend paralyzant, paralysant
Paralysis *f s.* Paralyse
~ agitans agitated paralysis, shaking palsy
Paralyssa *f* paralyssa *(südamerikanische Tollwutform)*
Paralytiker *m* paralytic
paralytisch paralytic, paralyzed, palsied
~/nicht non-paralytic
~/nicht komplett subparalytic
Paramanie *f* paramania, joy by complaining
Paramastitis *f* paramastitis, submammary (retromammary) mastitis
Paramastoiditis *f* paramastoiditis
Paramedialsulkus *m* paramedial sulcus

Paramedianschnitt *m* paramedian incision
paramedizinisch paramedical
Paramenia *f* paramenia, difficult (disordered) menstruation
Parameningokokkenmeningitis *f* parameningococcus meningitis
Parametrienklemme *f* parametrium clamp
Parametrismus *m* parametrism
Parametritis *f* parametritis, inflammation of the parametrium, exometritis
~ **anterior** anterior parametritis
~ **chronica atrophicans** chronic atrophic parametritis
~ **chronica posterior** chronic posterior parametritis
~ **posterior** posterior parametritis
parametritisch parametritic
Parametrium *n* parametrium
Parametriumabszeß *m* parametric abscess
Parametriumentzündung *f s.* Parametritis
Parametropathia *f* **spastica** pelvic congestion *(Fibrose des Beckenbindegewebes)*
Parametropathie *f* parametropathy, disease of the parametrium
Paramimie *f* paramimia
Paramnesie *f* paramnesia, retrospective falsification
Paramutation *f* paramutation
Paramuzin *n* paramucin
Paramyeloblast *m* paramyeloblast
Paramyeloid *n* paramyeloid, atypical amyloid
Paramyoclonus *m* **multiplex** polyclonia, essential myoclonia; polymyoclonus
Paramyosinogen *n* paramyosinogen *(Muskelplasmaeiweiß)*
Paramyotonia *f* **congenita** congenital paramyotonia, Eulenburg's disease
Paramyotonie *f* paramyotonia
Paramyxovirus *n* paramyxovirus
Paranasalsinus *m* paranasal (air) sinus
Paranästhesie *f* para-anaesthesia
paraneoplastisch paraneoplastic
Paranephritis *f* 1. paranephritis, inflammation of the paranephros (adrenal gland); 2. paranephritis, inflammation of the paranephric tissue
Paranephrom *n* paranephroma
Paraneuralanalgesie *f* paraneural analgesia
Paranoia *f* paranoia
~ **/akute halluzinatorische** acute hallucinatory paranoia
paranoid paranoiac, paranoic, paranoid
Paranoidismus *m* paranoidism
Paranoiker *m* paranoiac
Paranoismus *m* paranoidism
Paranomie *f* paranomia
Paranuklein *n* paranuclein, paranucleoprotein, pseudonuclein, pseudochromatin *(Eiweißkomponente der Nukleinsäure)*
Paranukleolus *m* paranucleolus *(im Zellkern)*
Paranukleoprotein *n s.* Paranuklein
Paranukleus *m* paranucleus
Paraösophagealhernie *f* paraoesophageal (parahiatal) hernia
Paraösophagealzyste *f* paraoesophageal cyst
Paraparese *f* paraparesis
paraparetisch paraparetic
Parapathie *f* parapathia, psychoneurotic disorder
Parapedese *f* parapedesis
Parapertussis *f* parapertussis *(durch Bordatella pertussis)*
Parapharyngealraum *m* parapharyngeal space
Paraphasie *f* paraphasia
Paraphemie *f* paraphemia
Paraphilie *f* paraphilia, sexual perversion
Paraphimose *f* paraphimosis, Spanish collar, capistration
Paraphobie *f* paraphobia, slight degree of phobia
Paraphonia *f* **puberum** paraphonia of the puberty
Paraphonie *f* paraphonia, morbid alteration of the voice
Paraphora *f* paraphora, slight mental disorder
Paraphrasia *f* **vesana** jumbling of words
Paraphrasie *f* paraphrasia
paraphren paraphrenic
Paraphrenie *f* paraphrenia
Paraphrenitis *f* paraphrenitis *(Entzündung des Brustfell- oder Bauchfellüberzugs des Zwerchfells)*
Paraplasie *f* paraplasia
Paraplastin *n* paraplastin
Paraplegie *f* paraplegia
~ **/obere** superior paraplegia, paralysis of both arms
~ **/schlaffe** flaccid paraplegia
~ **/spastische** spastic paraplegia
~ **/untere** inferior paraplegia, paralysis of both legs
paraplegieartig paraplegiform
Paraplegiker *m* paraplegic
paraplegisch paraplegic, paraplectic
Parapleuritis *f* parapleuritis, inflammation of the chest wall
Parapneumonie *f* parapneumonia
Parapoplexie *f* parapoplexy, slight apoplexy, masked cerebrovascular accident
Parapraxie *f* parapraxia, irrational behaviour
Paraproktitis *f* paraproctitis, inflammation of the paraproctium
Paraproktium *n* paraproctium *(den Mastdarm und den After umhüllendes Binde- und Fettgewebe)*
Paraprostatitis *f* paraprostatitis
Paraprotein *n* paraprotein
Paraproteinämie *f* paraproteinaemia
Parapsis *f* parapsis, morbid sense of touch
Parapsoriasis *f* parapsoriasis en plaques, Brocq's disease
~ **en gouttes** chronic lichenoid pityriasis *(chronische entzündliche Hautkrankheit mit roten Knötchen und Flecken)*
Parapsychologie *f* parapsychology
Pararauschbrandbazillus *m* Clostridium septicum, vibrion septique
Pararektalschnitt *m* pararectal (pararectus) incision *(bei Bauchhöhleneröffnung)*

Pararhotazismus

Pararhotazismus *m* pararhotacism
Pararhythmie *f* pararrhytmia *(Nebeneinanderbestehen zweier Reizbildungszentren am Herzen)*
pararhythmisch pararrhythmic
Pararthrie *f* pararthria
Parasakralanästhesie *f* parasacral anaesthesia; presacral block
Parasalpingitis *f* parasalpingitis
Parasekretion *f* parasecretion
Parasexualität *f* parasexuality
Parasinoidalsinus *m* parasinoidal sinus
Parasit *m* parasite *(1. Mikroorganismus; 2. lebensunfähiges Individuum einer Doppelmißgeburt)* ● **von Parasiten befallen** parasitenladen, parasitized
~/**fakultativer** facultative (accidental, occasional) parasite
~/**obligatorischer** obligatory parasite
~/**periodischer** periodic parasite
~/**permanenter** permanent parasite
Parasitämie *f* parasitaemia
parasitär parasitic, parasitogenic
Parasitenbefall *m* parasitization *(s. a. Parasitose)*
parasitenfrei non-parasitic
Parasitenindex *m* parasite index *(der Prozentsatz positiver Blutausstriche einer Bevölkerungsgruppe bei parasitären Erkrankungen)*
Parasiteninfektion *f s.* Parasitose
parasitentötend parasiticidal, parasiticide
Parasitenumlauf *m* **im Blut** parasitaemia
Parasitenwirksamkeit *f* parasitotropism *(z. B. bestimmter Medikamente)*
Parasiten-Wirt-Lehre *f* xenology
Parasitenzyklus *m* parasitic cycle *(z. B. bei Malaria)*
Parasitenzyste *f* parasitic cyst
parasitisch parasitic
~/**nicht** non-parasitic
Parasitismus *m* parasitism
~/**artefizieller** artificial parasitism
parasitizid parasiticidal, parasiticide
Parasitologe *m* parasitologist
Parasitologie *f* parasitology
Parasitophobie *f* parasitophobia *(krankhafte Angst vor Parasiten)*
Parasitose *f* parasitosis, parasitic disease
parasitotrop parasitotrope, parasitotropic
Parasitotropismus *m* parasitotropism *(z. B. bestimmter Medikamente)*
Parasom *n* parasome *(Zytoplasmakörper)*
Paraspadie *f* paraspadia[s]
Paraspasmus *m* paraspasm *(doppelseitige spastische Hypertonie der Gliedmaßen)*
Parasprue *f* parasprue
Parasteatose *f* parasteatosis, disorder of sebaceous secretions
Parasternalgegend *f* parasternal region
Parasternallinie *f* parasternal (costoclavicular) line
Parästhesie *f* paraesthesia, paralgesia

~/**Roth-Bernhardtsche** Roth-Bernhardt's disease, paraesthetic meralgia
Parastruma *f* parastruma
Parasympathikolytikum *n* parasympathicolytic [agent] *(die Wirkung einer Vagusreizung blokkierender Stoff)*
parasympathikolytisch parasympathicolytic
Parasympathikomimetikum *n* parasympathicomimetic [agent] *(die Wirkung einer Vagusreizung auslösender Stoff)*
parasympathikomimetisch parasympathicomimetic
Parasympathikotonie *f* parasympathicotonia, parasympathetic preponderance
parasympathikotonisch parasympathicotonic
Parasympathikus *m* parasympathetic [nerve], pneumogastric nerve *(Bestandteil des vegetativen Nervensystems)*; parasympathetic nervous system
Parasympathikusdenervierung *f* parasympathetic denervation
Parasympathikusfaser *f* parasympathetic fibre
parasympathikuslähmend parasympatholytic
parasympathikusreizend parasympathomimetic
parasympathikustonuserhöhend parasympathicotonic
parasympathikustonussenkend parasympathicolytic
parasympathisch parasympathetic
Parasympatholytikum *n* parasympatholytic [agent]
Parasynapse *f* parasynapsis
Parasynovitis *f* parasynovitis
Parasyphilis *f* parasyphilis, paralues *(Nachkrankheit der Syphilis)*
parasyphilitisch parasyphilitic, paraluetic
Parasystolie *f* parasystole, parasystolic rhythm *(parallele Impulsgebung von zwei Reizbildungszentren des Herzens)*
parasystolisch parasystolic
Paratenon *n* paratenon
paratherapeutisch paratherapeutic
Parathormon *n* parathormone, parathyroid hormone, [thyro]calcitonin *(Nebenschilddrüsenhormon)*
Parathymie *f* parathymia
parathyreoid[al] parathyroid
Parathyreoidea *f s.* Nebenschilddrüse
Parathyreoidektomie *f* parathyroidectomy, excision of the parathyroid
parathyreoidektomieren to parathyroidectomize, to perform a parathyroidectomy, to remove the parathyroid
Parathyreopathie *f* parathyropathy, parathyroid disease
parathyreopriv parathyr[e]oprival, parathyroprivous
Parathyreotoxikose *f* parathyrotoxicosis
parathyreotrop parathyrotrop[h]ic
Parathyreotropin *n* parathyrotropin
Paratonie *f* paratonia *(Unvermögen zur willkürlichen Muskelerschlaffung)*

Paratonsillarabszeß *m* peritonsillar abscess, quinsy
Paratonsillitis *f* paratonsillitis, peritonsillitis, periamygdalitis
Paratrachealadenitis *f* paratracheal adenitis
Paratrachealzyste *f* paratracheal cyst
Paratrachom *n* paratrachoma, inclusion conjunctivitis
Paratrichose *f* paratrichosis
Paratuberkulin *n* paratuberculin, johnin
paratuberkulös paratuberculous
Paratuberkulose *f* paratuberculosis
Paratyphlitis *f* paratyphlitis
Paratyphus *m* paratyphoid [fever], Schottmüller's disease
Paratyphusbazillus *m* Salmonella paratyphi
Paratyphusimpfstoff *m* paratyphoid vaccine
Paratyphusosteomyelitis *f* paratyphoid osteomyelitis
paraumbilikal para-umbilical, para-omphalic, par-umbilical
Paraumbilikalhernie *f* para-umbilical hernia
Paraumbilikalvene *f* para-umbilical vein [of Sappey]
Paraureteritis *f* para-ureteritis
Paraurethraldrüse *f* para-urethral gland
Paraurethraldrüsengang *m* para-urethral duct
Paravaginitis *f* paravaginitis
Paravakzinia *f* paravaccinia
paravenös paravenous
paraventrikulär paraventricular
Paravertebralabszeß *m* paravertebral abscess
Paravertebralanästhesie *f* paravertebral anaesthesia
Paravertebraldreieck *n* paravertebral (Grocco's) triangle
Paravertebralganglion *n* paravertebral ganglion
Paravertebrallinie *f* paravertebral line
Paravitaminose *f* paravitaminosis
Paraxon *n* paraxon
Parazentese *f* 1. *s.* Paracentesis; 2. paracentesis [tympani], myringotomy ● **eine ~ durchführen** to puncture, to perform a paracentesis
Parazentesemesser *n* myringotome
Parazentesenadel *f* paracentesis needle; myringotome
Parazentrallappen *m* paracentral lobule
Parazentralskotom *n* paracentral scotoma
Parazentralsulkus *m* paracentral sulcus
Parazephalus *m* paracephalus *(Mißgeburt)*
Parazervikalblockade *f* paracervical block
Parazystitis *f* paracystitis
Pärchenegel *m s.* Schistosoma
Pärchenegelbefall *m s.* Schistosomiasis
Pärchenegellarve *f* cercarian
Parektasie *f* parectasia, excessive stretching *(z. B. eines Organs)*
Parenchym *n* parenchym[a]
Parenchymblutung *f* parenchymatous bleeding (haemorrhage)
Parenchymentzündung *f* parenchymatitis, inflammation of a parenchyma

Parenchymgewebe *n* parenchymal tissue
Parenchymikterus *m* parenchymatous jaundice
Parenchymlappen *m* parenchymal lobule
Parenchymorgan *n* parenchymatous organ
Parenchymzerstörung *f* parenchymal destruction
Parentalgeneration *f* parental generation *(Genetik)*
parenteral parenteral, para-oral
Parergasie *f* parergasia
Parese *f* paresis, partial paralysis
Paresegang *m* paretic gait
paretisch paretic
Pargylin *n* pargyline *(blutdrucksenkendes Mittel)*
Paridrosis *f* par[h]idrosis, parahidrosis
Parietalblock *m* parietal block
Parietaldurchmesser *m* parietal diameter
Parietaleminenz *f* parietal eminence (boss), parietal protuberance (tubercle)
Parietalläppchen *n* parietal lobule
Parietallappen *m* parietal lobe
Parietalthrombus *m* parietal (lateral) thrombus
Parietalwinkel *m*/**Broscher** Broca's [parietal] angle
Parietalzelle *f* parietal (acid) cell, oxyntic (oxyphilic) cell *(der Magenschleimhaut)*
Parietalzellenareal *n* oxyntic gland area
Parietalzellenvagotomie *f* parietal cell vagotomy
parietoviszeral parietovisceral, parietosplanchnic
Parkinsonismus *m* parkinsonism, Parkinsonian state, Parkinson's disease *(extrapyramidales Syndrom mit teigiger Muskelsteifigkeit, Zittern von Körperteilen und Bewegungslosigkeit)*
Parkinsonkrise *f* Parkinsonian crisis
Parkinson-Syndrom *n s.* Parkinsonismus
parodontal peri[o]dontal, peridental, periodontic
Parodontitis *f s.* Periodontitis
Parodontium *n s.* Periodontium
Parodontose *f* periodontosis, paradentosis, parodentosis, periodental disease, cementopathia
Parodynie *f* parodynia, morbid labour, difficult parturition
Paromomyzin *n* paromomycin *(Breitspektrumantibiotikum)*
Paroniria *f* paroniria, morbid dreaming; nightmare
paronychial paronychial
Paronychie *f* paronychia, panaris, runaround, felon
Paronychium *n* paronychium, perionychium
Paronychomykose *f* paronychomycosis
Paronychose *f* paronychosis
Paroophoritis *f* paroophoritis, inflammation of the paroophoron
Paroophoron *n* paroophoron
Parophthalmie *f* parophthalmia, inflammation about the eye
Parophthalmonkus *m* parophthalmoncus
Paropsie *f* paropsia, paropsis, false (disordered) vision
Parorchidie *f* parorchidium, misplacement of a testicle

Parorexie

Parorexie *f* parorexia, pica, perverted appetite *(z. B. bei Schwangeren)*
Parosmie *f* parosmia, parosphresis, perversion of the sense of smell
Parostitis *f* parost[e]itis
Parostose *f* parost[e]osis *(Knochenbildung an abnormer Stelle)*
parotid parotid[ean]
Parotidektomie *f* parotidectomy, excision of the parotid gland
Parotis *f s.* Ohrspeicheldrüse
Parotisinduration *f s.* Ohrspeicheldrüsenverhärtung
Parotislipomatose *f* parotid lipomatosis
Parotissialogramm *n* parotid sialogram
Parotisspeichel *m* parotid saliva
Parotitis *f* **[epidemica]** *s.* Mumps
parotitisch parotitic
Parovarialzyste *f* parovarian (perisalpingian) cyst
Parovariotomie *f* parovariotomy, excision of a parovarian cyst
Parovaritis *f* parovaritis, inflammation of the parovarium
Parovarium *n* parovarium, ovarian appendage, epoophoron
Parovariumentzündung *f s.* Parovaritis
Paroxysmalstadium *n* paroxysmal stage
Paroxysmus *m* 1. paroxysm, sudden attack; intensification of symptoms; 2. spasm, fit, convulsion, seizure; 3. outburst of emotion
Partial... *s. a.* Teil...
Partialantigen *n* partial (incomplete) antigen, hapten
Partialdruck *m* partial pressure
Partialdruckgradient *m* partial pressure gradient
Parturiometer *n* parturiometer *(Instrument zur Messung der Austreibungskraft des Uterus)*
Partus *m* partus, parturition, [child]birth, delivery *(Entbindung)*; labour, lying-in *(s. a. unter Geburt)*
~ **agrippinus** breech presentation
~ **immaturus** premature birth, preterm parturition
~ **maturus** labour at [full] term, term parturition
~ **praecipitatus** precipitate labour, oxytocia
~ **serotinus** delayed labour; prolonged pregnancy
~ **siccus** dry labour, xerotocia
Parulis *f* parulis, gumboil
Parvovirus *n* parvovirus
PAS *s.* Para-Aminosalizylsäure
Paschachurda *n* paschachurda *(Hautleishmaniase)*
Paschen-Körperchen *npl* Paschen bodies (granules)
PAS-Reaktion *f s.* Perjodsäure-Schiff-Reaktion
Passivismus *m* passivism
Passivist *m* passivist
Paste *f* pasta, paste, ointment-like preparation
~/Lassarsche Lassar's paste, pasta zinci salicylata
pastenartig pasty

Pasteurella *f* **pestis** Pasteurella pestis, plague bacillus
~ **pseudotuberculosis** Pasteurella pseudotuberculosis *(Erreger der Lymphadenitis mesenterialis Masshoff)*
~ **tularensis** Pasteurella tularensis *(Erreger der Tularämie)*
Pasteurellose *f* pasteurellosis, haemorrhagic septicaemia
Pasteurisierapparat *m* pasteurizer
pasteurisieren to pasteurize
Pasteurisierung *f* pasteurization
Pastia-Zeichen *n* Pastia's lines (sign) *(Auftreten von kleinsten Hautblutungen in den Ellenbeugen bei beginnendem Scharlach)*
Pastille *f* pastil[le], lozenge
Pastillenherstellung *f* trochiscation
pastös pasty
Patagium *n* patagium, wing-like membrane
Patch *m* patch *(Chirurgie)*
Patch-Test *m* patch test *(z. B. zur Allergietestung)*
Patella *f* patella, knee-cap, knee-pan, whirlbone, rotula *(s. a. unter Kniescheibe)*
~ **bipartita** bipartite patella
~ **cubiti** elbow cap
Patella... *s. a.* Patellar... *und* Kniescheiben...
Patellachondromalazie *f* patellar chondromalacia
Patellafixierung *f s.* Patellopexie
Patellafraktur *f* patellar fracture
Patellahochstand *m* high position of the patella
Patellaluxation *f* displacement of the patella
Patellar... *s. a.* Patella... *und* Kniescheiben...
Patellarklonus *m* patellar clonus *(bei Pyramidenbahnläsion)*
Patellarplexus *m* patellar plexus
Patellarreflex *m s.* Patellarsehnenreflex
Patellarregion *f* region of the patella
Patellarsehne *f* patellar tendon (ligament)
Patellarsehnenreflex *m* patellar [tendon] reflex, quadriceps reflex, knee jerk, knee reflex [phenomenon] *(Streckung des Unterschenkels nach Schlag gegen die Patellarsehne)*
Patellektomie *f* patellectomy, excision of the patella
patellofemoral patellofemoral
Patellopexie *f* patellapexy, fixation of the patella
Pathergasie *f* pathergasia
Pathergie *f* pathergia, pathergy *(bei Allergie)*
Pathetismus *m* pathetism
Pathetist *m* pathetist
Pathoanatomie *f* patho-anatomy
Pathobiochemie *f* pathobiochemistry
pathogen pathogen[et]ic, morbific, morbigenous
Pathogen *n* pathogen, pathogenic agent
Pathogenese *f* pathogenesis, aetiopathology
pathogenetisch *s.* pathogen
Pathogenität *f* pathogenicity
Pathognomik *f* pathognomy
pathognomonisch pathognom[on]ic
pathognostisch pathognostic

Pathohistologie f pathologic histology
pathohistologisch histopathologic
Pathoklise f pathoclisis
Patholesie f patholesia, hysterical condition
Pathologe m pathologist
Pathologie f pathology
~/**allgemeine** general pathology
~/**bakterielle** bacteriopathology
~/**klinische** clinical pathology, clinicopathology
~/**makroskopische** macropathology
~/**mikroskopische** micropathology
~/**spezielle** f special pathology
pathologisch pathologic[al], morbid
Pathomechanismus m pathogenetic mechanism
Pathomimie f pathomimesis, pathomimia, pathomimicry, imitation of a disease
Pathomorphismus m pathomorphism, pathomorphology, abnormal (perverted) morphology
Pathoneurose f pathoneurosis
pathopher pathopheric, pathophorous
Pathophilie f pathophilia *(emotionale Krankheitsanpassung bei chronischen Leiden)*
Pathophobie f pathophobia *(krankhafte Angst vor Krankheiten)*
Pathophorese f pathophoresis, transmission of disease
Pathophysiologie f pathophysiology, physiopathology, pathologic physiology
pathophysiologisch pathophysiologic, physiopathologic
Pathopsychologie f pathopsychology
pathopsychologisch pathopsychologic[al]
Patient m patient ● **einen Patienten durchbringen** to bring a patient through alive ● **einen Patienten operieren** to operate upon a patient
~/**ambulanter** out-patient
~/**hoch fiebernder** hyperpyrexic patient
~/**krampfender** convulsionary
~ **mit hohem Risiko** high-risk patient
~ **mit Hyperkapnie** hypercapnic patient
~ **mit Hypokapnie** hypocapnic patient
~/**nierentransplantierter** postrenal transplant patient
~/**schrittmacherstimulierter** pacemade patient
~/**stationärer** in-patient
Patientenakte f record
Patientenauswahl f patient selection
Patientenblut n patient's blood
Patientengut n case material
Patientenhaut f patient's skin
Patientenkarteikarte f [record] card
Patientenkurve f temperature chart
Patientenüberwachung f/**computergestützte** computer-assisted (computer-based) patient monitoring
Patientenvorstellung f [case] presentation
Paukenfell n s. Trommelfell
Paukenhöhle f tympanic cavity, barrel of the ear, cavity of the middle ear ● **über der** ~ supratympanic, epitympanic ● **unter der** ~ subtympanic

Paukenhöhlenarterie f tympanic artery
~/**hintere** posterior tympanic artery
~/**obere** superior tympanic artery
~/**untere** inferior tympanic artery
~/**vordere** anterior tympanic artery
Paukenhöhlenboden m floor of the tympanum (tympanic cavity)
Paukenhöhlendach n roof of the tympanum (tympanic cavity)
Paukenhöhlenkuppel f attic, epitympanic recess (space), epitympanum, superior tympanic cavity
Paukenhöhlenkuppeleiterung f attic suppuration
Paukenhöhlenkuppelentzündung f atticitis
Paukenhöhlenkuppelraum m s. Paukenhöhlenkuppel
Paukenhöhlenschleimhaut f mucous membrane of the tympanic cavity
Paukenhöhlensklerose f tympanosclerosis
Paukenhöhlen- und Warzenfortsatzentzündung f tympanomastoiditis
Paukenhöhlenvene f tympanic vein
Paukentreppe f tympanic scala
Pausbackigkeit f cherubism
Pause f/**diastolische** diastolic pause, perisystole
~/**[end]exspiratorische** expiratory standstill
~/**kompensatorische** compensatory pause
~/**postextrasystolische** s. ~/kompensatorische
Pavor m pavor, horror; anxiety, dread, fear; fright *(s. a. unter* Angst*)*
~ **diurnus** day terrors, daytime anxiety
~ **nocturnus** night terrors, nyctophobia, noctiphobia
Payr-Schnitt m Payr's incision *(zur Kniegelenkseröffnung)*
PBJ s. Jod/proteingebundenes
PCO₂ s. Kohlendioxidpartialdruck
PCP s. Polyarthritis/primär chronische
PCWP s. Lungenkapillarverschlußdruck
Péan-Klemme f Péan's forceps *(stumpfe Blutgefäßklemme ohne Krallen)*
Pecten m **ossis pubis** pubic pecten, pecten of the pubic bone, pectineal line
Pectus n pectus, chest, thorax, breast *(s. a. unter* Brustkorb*)*
~ **carinatum** pigeon chest, carinate (chicken) breast
~ **excavatum** funnel (cobbler's) chest; koilosternia
~ **gallinaceum** s. ~ carinatum
pedal podal[ic]
Pedialgie f pedialgia, neuralgic pain in the foot
Pediculoides m **ventricosus** grain itch mite
Pediculosis f pediculosis, lousiness, infestation with lice
~ **capitis** lousiness of the hair of the head
~ **corporis** lousiness of the body
~ **palpebrarum** lousiness of the eyelashes
Pediculus m 1. pediculus, louse, Phthirius; 2. pediculus, pedicle
~ **arcus vertebrae** vertebral pedicle
~ **humanus capitis** head louse
~ **humanus corporis** body (cootie) louse

Pedikulophobie

Pedikulophobie f pediculophobia *(krankhafte Angst vor Läusen)*
Pedikulose f s. Pediculosis
Pediküre f 1. podiatry, pedicure, chiropody; 2. pedicure, podiatrist, chiropodist
Pediluvium n pediluvium, footh bath
Pedodynamometer n pedodynamometer
Pedometer n pedometer
Pedometrie f pedometry
Pedopathie f pedopathy, disease of the foot
Pedunculus m pedunculus, peduncle, stalk
~ **anterior cerebellaris** anterior cerebellar peduncle, prepeduncle
~ **cerebellaris** cerebellar peduncle (stalk)
~ **cerebellaris inferior** inferior cerebellar peduncle, restiform body
~ **cerebellaris medius** middle cerebellar peduncle
~ **cerebellaris superior** superior cerebellar peduncle
~ **cerebri** cerebral peduncle
~ **corporis pinealis** pineal peduncle, peduncle of the pineal body
~ **olfactorius** olfactory peduncle
~ **olivaris** olivary peduncle
Pedunkulotomie f pedunculotomy, dissection of the cerebral peduncles
Peitschenkatheter m whip catheter
Peitschenschlagverletzung f whiplash injury
Peitschenwurm m whipworm, trichuris, Trichocephalus dispar (trichiuris)
Peitschenwurminfektion f trichuriasis, trichocephaliasis, trichocephalosis
pektanginös anginal, anginose
Pektoralfaszie f pectoral[is] fascia
Pektoralfremitus m pectoral (vocal) fremitus
Pektoralgie f pectoralgia, pain in the breast
Pektoralislymphknoten m pectoral lymphatic node
Pektoral[muskel]reflex m pectoral reflex
Pektoralvene f pectoral vein
Pektoriloquie f pectoriloquy *(bei Lungenkrankheiten)*
Pektorophonie f pectorophony *(bei Lungenauskultation)*
Pelade f pelada, pelade, alopecia areata
Peladophobie f peladophobia *(krankhafte Angst vor Haarausfall)*
Pelioma n pelioma, livid spot
~ **typhosum** typhoid pelioma *(fleckige Hautblutungen bei Typhus)*
Peliosis f peliosis, purpura *(s. a. unter Purpura)*
~ **hepatis** hepatic peliosis
Pelizaeus-Merzbacher-Syndrom n Pelizaeus-Merzbacher disease, chronic infantile lobar sclerosis, familial centrolobar sclerosis *(erbliches Leiden mit spastischen Lähmungen)*
Pellagra f pellagra, Asturian (Lombardy) leprosy, aniacinosis, ariboflavinosis
pellagraartig pellagroid, pellagrous
pellagraauslösend pellagragenic
pellagrakrank pellagrous, pellagrose, affected with pellagra
Pellagrakranker m pellagrin
Pellagrapräventivfaktor m antipellagra (pellagrapreventive) factor, pp factor
Pellagraspezialist m pellagrologist
pellagrös pellagrous, pellagrose
Pellikula f pellicle, thin skin (membrane), cuticle *(der Protozoen)*
Pellotin n pellotine *(Alkaloid)*
pelluzid pellucid, transparent; translucent; not opaque
Pelmatogramm n pelmatogram, footprint
Pelologie f pelology *(Lehre vom Heilschlamm)*
Pelose f peloid, mud
Pelotherapie f pelotherapy, treatment with mud
Pelveoperitoneum n pelveoperitoneum; perimetrium
Pelveoperitonitis f s. Pelvioperitonitis
Pelvienzephalographie f pelvicephalography
Pelvienzephalometrie f pelvicephalometry
Pelvifixation f pelvifixation
Pelvikliseometer n pelvicliseometer
Pelvimeter n pelvimeter, pelicometer
Pelvimetrie f pelvimetry, measurement of the pelvis
~/**äußere** external pelvimetry
~/**innere** internal pelvimetry
Pelviographie f s. Pelvioradiographie
Pelviolithotomie f pelviolithotomy, pyelolithotomy
Pelvioneozystostomie f pelvioneocystostomy
Pelvioperitonitis f pelvioperitonitis, pelveoperitonitis, pelvic peritonitis
Pelvioplastik f pelvioplasty
Pelvioradiographie f pelvioradiography, pelvigraphy *(s. a. Pelviradiometrie)*
Pelviotomie f 1. pelviotomy, pyelotomy, incision of the renal pelvis; 2. pelviotomy, pelvisection, cutting of the pelvis
Pelviperitonitis f s. Pelvioperitonitis
Pelviradiometrie f pelviradiometry, X-ray pelvimetry
Pelvis f 1. pelvis, basin, basin-shaped cavity; 2. pelvis, bony pelvic ring *(s. a. unter Becken)*; 3. pelvic cavity
~ **nana** dwarf pelvis
~ **renalis** s. Nierenbecken
~ **spinosa** pelvis spinosa, acanthopelvis
Pelvisakrum n pelvisacrum
Pelviskop n pelviscope
Pelviskopie f pelvi[o]scopy
Pelviureteroradiographie f pelviureteroradiography
Pelvizellulitis f pelvicellulitis, pelvic cellulitis
Pemphigoid n pemphigoid
~ **neonatorum** neonatal impetigo (pemphigus)
Pemphigus m pemphigus, blister tetter
~/**akuter** acute (febrile) pemphigus
~ **chronicus** chronic pemphigus
~ **contagiosus** contagious pemphigus
~ **neonatorum** neonatal impetigo (pemphigus)
~ **tropicus** tropical pemphigus
pemphigusartig pemphigoid

Pemphigus[begleit]fieber n bullous fever
Pendelatmungssystem n to-and-fro method (Anästhesie)
Pendelluftatmung f pendelluft (paradoxical) respiration
Pendelnystagmus m pendular (oscillatory, vibratory) nystagmus
Pendelrhythmus m foetal rhythm, embryocardia
Pendulum n palatini palatine velum
Penektomie f s. Penisamputation
penetrant penetrating
Penetranz f penetrance (Wahrscheinlichkeit der Manifestation eines Gens im Phänotyp)
Penetration f penetration, permeation
Penetrationsverletzung f penetrating injury
Penetrationswunde f penetrating wound
penetrieren to penetrate, to permeate
Penicilli mpl lienis splenic penicilli
Penicillin n s. Penizillin
Penicillium n penicillium
Penicillus m penicillus, brush-like arterial branch
Penis m penis, phallus, coles
~/**abnorm großer** megalopenis, macrophallus
~/**abnorm kleiner** micropenis, microphallus
~ **palmatus** webbed penis
~ **plasticus** penis plasticus; penile strabismus, Payronie's disease
Penis... s. a. Phallus...
Penisamputation f penectomy, phallectomy, amputation of the penis
Penisarterie f artery of the penis
~/**schneckenförmige** coiled artery of the penis
~/**tiefe** profunda penis artery
Penisdauererektion f priapism
Penisentzündung f s. Phallitis
Penisgeschwür n penile ulcer
Penishals m neck of the penis
Penishypospadie f penile hypospadias
Penisinduration f/**plastische** Peyronie's disease, penile strabismus; penis plasticus
Peniskarzinom n penis carcinoma
Penisklemme f penis clamp
Penisplastik f phalloplasty
Penisreflex m penile (bulbospongiosus) reflex
Penisrückenarterie f dorsal artery of the penis
Penisrückenspalte f[/**angeborene**] epispadia[s]
Penisrückenvene f/**oberflächliche** superficial dorsal vein of the penis
~/**tiefe** deep dorsal vein of the penis
Penisschaft m shaft (body) of the penis
Penisschenkel m crus of the penis
~/**rechter** right crus of the penis
~/**linker** left crus of the penis
Penisschmerz m phallalgia, phallodynia, pain in the penis
Penisschwellkörpernerven mpl cavernous nerves of the penis
Penisspalte f penischisis; cleft penis
Penisvorhaut f prepuce of the penis
Penizillamin n penicillamin
Penizillin n penicillin (Antibiotikum) ● **gegenüber ~ empfindlich sein** to be susceptible to penicillin
~/**halbsynthetisches** semisynthetic penicillin
~ **V** penicillin V, phenoxymethylpenicillin (säurefestes Penizillin)
~ **X** hydroxybenzylpenicillin
Penizillinase f penicill[in]ase (penizillinspaltendes Enzym)
penizillinaselabil penicillinase-labile
penizillinasestabil penicillinase-stable
Penizillinbehandlung f penicillin therapy
penizillinempfindlich penicillin-sensitive
penizillinresistent penicillin-resistant
Penizillinsäure f penicillic acid
Penizillinsensibilitätstest m penicillin sensivity test
Penizillin-Streptomyzin-Blutagar m penicillin-streptomycin blood agar (bakterienhemmendes Kulturmedium für Pilze)
penizillinunempfindlich penicillin-insensitive, penicillin-fast
Penoskrotalhypospadie f penoscrotal hypospadias
pentadaktyl pentadactyl
Pentagastrin n pentagastrin (Magensaftstimulator)
Pentalogie f pentalogy
~/**Fallotsche** pentalogy of Fallot (Herzfehler mit Pulmonalstenose, Rechtsherzhypertrophie, Vorhofseptumdefekt, reitender Aorta und Ventrikelseptumdefekt)
Pentapeptid n pentapeptide
Pentaquin n pentaquin[e] (Antimalariamittel)
Pentastomiasis f pentastomiasis
Pentastomiden npl Pentastomida
Pentastomum n pentastome
Pentastomuminfestation f pentastomiasis
Pentatrichomonasinfektion f pentatrichomoniasis
Pentobarbitalnatrium n pentobarbital sodium, sodium pentobarbital (Schlafmittel)
Pentosämie f pentosaemia
Pentose f pentose
Pentoseausscheidung f im Urin pentosuria
Pentosenachweistest m/**Bialscher** Bial's test
Pentosephosphatzyklus m pentose phosphate cycle
Pepsin n pepsin (Enzym des Magensafts)
Pepsinase f pepsinase (Enzym)
Pepsinausscheidung f im Urin pepsinuria
Pepsinbehandlung f pepsinotherapy
pepsinbildend pepsinogenous, peptogenic, peptogenous, pepsiniferous
pepsinhaltig pepsiniferous
pepsinogen pepsinogenous
Pepsinogen n pepsinogen, propepsin (inaktive Pepsinvorstufe)
Pepsinsekretion f pepsin secretion ● **die ~ anregend** pepsigogue
pepsinstimulierend pepsigogue
Pepsinüberproduktion f hyperpepsinia
Peptid n peptide
~/**gastrisches inhibitorisches** gastric inhibitory peptide, GIP

Peptidase

Peptidase f peptidase *(Enzym)*
Peptidbindung f peptide bond
peptidspaltend peptidolytic
Peptisation f peptization
peptisch peptic, pepsic, proteopeptic
peptisieren to peptize
peptogen peptogenic, peptogenous
Pepton n peptone *(Proteinderivat)*
Peptonämie f peptonaemia
Peptonaufspaltung f pepto[no]lysis
Peptonausscheidung f im Urin peptonuria
peptonhaltig peptonic
peptonproduzierend peptogenic, peptogenous
per anum per anum, by the anus, rectal, per rectum
~ **cutem** percutaneous, through the skin
~ **rectum** s. per anum
~ **vias naturales** by the natural ways
perakut peracute, hyperacute, superacute
Perflation f perflation *(z. B. der Eileiter)*
perforant perforating, perforans
Perforation f perforation
Perforationsperitonitis f perforative peritonitis
Perforationswunde f perforating wound
Perforator m perforator *(chirurgisches Instrument)*
Perforatorium n 1. perforatorium, acrosome *(am Kopf des Spermiums)*; 2. s. Perforator
perforieren to perforate; to transforate *(den Fetusschädel)*
perforiert perforate
~/nicht imperforate
perfundieren to perfuse
Perfusat n perfusate
Perfusion f perfusion
~/extrakorporale extracorporeal [circulatory] perfusion
Perfusionslösung f perfusion (flush-out) solution *(z. B. bei Nierentransplantation)*
Perfusionsmangelzustand m low perfusion state
Perfusionsszintigramm n perfusion scintigram (scan)
Perfusionsszintigraphie f perfusion scintigraphy (scanning)
pergamentartig papyraceous, parchment
Pergamentfetus m papyraceous foetus
Pergamenthaut f parchment (paper) skin; xeroderma
Pergamentknistern n parchment crackling *(bei Rachitis)*
Periadenitis f periadenitis
Perialienitis f perialienitis, perixenitis
Perianalabszeß m perianal abscess
Perianalhaut f perianal skin
Periangiitis f periangiitis
Periapikalabszeß m [peri]apical abscess
Periapikalgranulom n periapical (dental) granuloma
Periapikalzyste f periapical cyst
periappendikulär periappendicular, periappendiceal
Periappendizitis f periappendicitis

Periarteriitis f periarteritis
~ **nodosa** nodular periarteritis, polyarteritis *(knötchenartige Verdickungen an kleinen Schlagadern)*
Periarthritis f periarthritis
~ **calcarea** calcareous periarthritis
~ **humeroscapularis (scapulohumeralis)** scapulohumeral periarthritis, Duplay's disease, periarthritis of the shoulder; frozen shoulder
Periblepsie f periblepsia, staring expression *(bei Psychose)*
Peribronchiolitis f peribronchiolitis
Peribronchitis f peribronchitis
Pericardiomediastinitis f **adhaesiva** adhesive pericardiomediastinitis; cardiosymphysis
Pericarditis f pericarditis, inflammation of the pericardium *(s. a. unter Perikarditis)*
~ **adhaesiva** adhesive (adherent) pericarditis
~ **calculosa** bony (armoured) heart
~ **carcinomatosa** carcinomatous pericarditis
~ **constrictiva** constrictive pericarditis; chronic cardiac compression, cicatricial pericardial contraction
~ **exsudativa** exudative pericarditis, hydropericarditis
~ **mediastinalis** mediastinal pericarditis
~ **obliterans** obliterating pericarditis
~ **serofibrinosa** serofibrinous pericarditis
~ **suppurativa** suppurative pericarditis
Pericementum n pericementum, root membrane
pericholangiolitisch pericholangiolitic
Pericholangitis f pericholangitis, periangiocholitis
pericholangitisch pericholangitic
pericholezystisch pericholecystic
Pericholezystitis f peri[chole]cystitis
perichondral perichondr[i]al
Perichondritis f perichondritis, inflammation of the perichondrium
perichondritisch perichondritic
Perichondrium n perichondrium
Perichondrom n perichondroma
Perideferentitis f perideferentitis
Peridektomie f peri[dec]tomy, peritectomy *(streifenförmige Bindehautexstirpation um die Hornhaut des Auges)*
Perididymis f perididymis, tunica vaginalis testis
Perididymitis f perididymitis, inflammation of the perididymis
Peridivertikulitis f periverticulitis
Periduodenitis f periduodenitis
Periduralanästhesie f peridural (epidural) anaesthesia
Periektomie f s. Peridektomie
Perienteritis f perienteritis, inflammation of the peritoneal coat
Perienzephalitis f periencephalitis, periencephalomeningitis
Periepididymitis f periepididymitis
Perifollikulitis f perifolliculitis, inflammation around the hair follicles
Perigangliitis f perigangliitis

Perigastritis f perigastritis
Periglossitis f periglossitis
Perihepatitis f perihepatitis
~ **chronica hyperplastica** chronic hyperplastic perihepatitis; froasted (sugar-icing) liver
perihilär perihilar
Perijejunitis f perijejunitis
perikapillär pericapillary
Perikard n pericardium, heart sac ● **unter dem** ~ subpericardial
~/**fibröses** fibrous pericardium
~/**parietales** parietal pericardium
~/**seröses** serous pericardium
~/**viszerales** visceral (cardiac) pericardium
Perikard... s. a. Herzbeutel...
Perikardablösung f cardiolysis
Perikarddekompression f decompression of the pericardium (heart)
Perikardektomie f pericard[i]ectomy, excision of the pericardium
Perikardempyem n empyema of the pericardium
Perikardentzündung f s. Perikarditis
Perikarderöffnung f[/operative] pericardiotomy, incision of the pericardium
Perikardflüssigkeit f pericardial fluid
Perikardhöhle f pericardial cavity (space)
perikardiakophrenisch pericardi[ac]ophrenic
perikardial pericardial, pericardiac
Perikardiolyse f pericardiolysis
Perikardiomediastinitis f pericardiomediastinitis
perikardiopleural pericardiopleural, pleuropericardial
Perikardiorrhaphie f pericardiorrhaphy, suture of the pericardium
Perikardiostoma n pericardiostomy
Perikardiostomie f pericardiostomy
Perikardiotomie f pericardiotomy, incision of the pericardium
Perikardiozentese f pericardi[o]centesis, paracentesis of the pericardial sac
Perikarditis f pericarditis, inflammation of the pericardium (s. a. unter Pericarditis)
~/**eitrige** purulent pericarditis, pyopericarditis
~/**fibröse** fibrous pericarditis, fibropericarditis
~/**hämorrhagische** haemorrhagic pericarditis
~/**rheumatische** rheumatic pericarditis
~/**tuberkulöse** tuberculous pericarditis
~/**urämische** uraemic pericarditis
perikarditisch pericarditic
Perikardmesotheliom n pericardial mesothelioma
Perikardreibegeräusch n pericardial [friction] rub; attrition (to-and-fro) murmur
Perikardresektion f s. Perikardektomie
Perikardumschlagfalte f reflection of pericardium
Perikard- und Mediastinumentzündung f pericardiomediastinitis
Perikardverdickung f pachypericarditis
Perikardverkalkung f pericardial calcification
Perikaryon n perikaryon (um den Zellkern liegender Zellteil)

Perikolitis f pericoli[ni]tis
Perikolpitis f pericolpitis
Perikonchitis f periconchitis, inflammation of the lining of the orbit
perikorneal pericorneal, perikeratic
Perikoronitis f pericoronitis
Perikostalnaht f pericostal suture
Perikranium n pericranium, cranial periosteum
Perilabyrinth n perilabyrinth
Perilabyrinthitis f perilabyrinthitis
Perilaryngitis f perilaryngitis
Perilymphadenitis f perilymphadenitis
Perilymphangitis f perilymphangitis
perilymphatisch 1. perilymphatic, perilymphangeal, perilymphangial (Lymphgefäße); 2. perilymphatic (Perilymphe)
Perilymphe f perilymph, labyrinthine (periotic) fluid (zwischen knöchernem und häutigem Labyrinth)
Perilymphesystem n perilymphatic system
Perilymphfistel f perilymph fistula
Perilymphraum m perilymphatic (periotic) space
Perimastitis f perimastitis
Perimeningitis f perimeningitis, pachymeningitis
Perimeter n perimeter, campimeter
Perimetermarke f perimetric target
Perimetrie f peri[opto]metry, visual perimetry (field examination), campimetry
perimetrisch perimetric, campimetric
Perimetritis f perimetritis, inflammation of the perimetrium
perimetritisch perimetritic
Perimetrium n perimetrium
Perimetriumentzündung f s. Perimetritis
Perimetrosalpingitis f perimetrosalpingitis
Perimyelitis f 1. perimyelitis, inflammation of the endosteum; 2. perimyelitis, spinal meningitis
Perimyositis f perimyositis
Perimysium n perimysium
~ **externum** epimysium
~ **internum** endomysium
perinasal perirhinal
Perinatalperiode f perinatal period
Perinatalpflege f perinatal care
Perinatalsterblichkeit f perinatal mortality
Perinatologie f perinatology
Perineal... s. a. Damm...
Perinealhernie f perineal (ischiorectal) hernia, perineocele
Perinealhypospadie f perineal hypospadias
Perineauxesis f perineauxesis
Perineometer n perineometer
Perineoplastik f perineoplasty, episioplasty
perineorektal perineorectal
Perineorrhaphie f perineorrhaphy, episiorrhaphy, suture of the perineum
perineoskrotal perineoscrotal
Perineosynthese f perineosynthesis
Perineotomie f perineotomy, episiotomy, perineal incision
perineovaginal perineovaginal
perineovaginorektal perineovaginorectal

perineovulvar

perineovulvar perineovulvar
Perinephritis f perinephritis, capsular nephritis, inflammation of the perinephrium
perinephritisch perinephritic
Perinephrium n perinephrium, perinephros, perinephric capsule, capsule of the kidney
Perineum n perineum
Perineuralanästhesie f perineural anaesthesia (analgesia)
Perineuralraum m perineural space
Perineuritis f perineuritis, inflammation of the perineurium
perineuritisch perineuritic
Perineurium n perineurium, nerve (lamellar) sheath
Periode f 1. period; cycle; 2. s. Menstruation
~/isoelektrische isoelectric period
periodontal peri[o]dontal, peridental, periodontic
Periodontalabszeß m peridontal abscess
Periodontaltasche f peridontal pocket
Periodontitis f periodontitis, pericementitis, paradentitis, parodontitis, alveolodental osteoperiostitis
Periodontium n periodontium, paradentium, periodontal ligament (membrane), odontoperiosteum
Periodontoklasie f periodontoclasia
Periodontologe m periodontist
Periodontologie f periodontology, periodontics (Lehre von der Zahnwurzelhaut)
Periodontose f s. Parodontose
Periodoskop n periodoscope
periokulär periocular, circumocular, circumbulbar
Perionychie f perionychia
Perionychium n perionychium, paronychium
Perioophoritis f perioophoritis, periovaritis, perioothecitis, paroophoritis
Perioophorosalpingitis f perioophorosalpingitis, perisalpingo-ovaritis, perioothecosalpingitis
perioperativ perioperative
Periophthalmitis f periophthalmitis
perioral perioral, circumoral
Periorbita f periorbit[a], periosteum of the eye socket
periorbital periorbital, circumorbital
Periorbitalabszeß m periorbital abscess
Periorbitalödem n periorbital oedema
Periorbi[ti]tis f periorbi[ti]tis, inflammation of the periorbita
Periorchitis f periorchitis
Periösophagitis f perioesophagitis
Periost n periost[eum]
Periost... s. a. Knochenhaut...
Periostdysplasie f periosteal dysplasia
Periostelevatorium n periosteal elevator, separator
Periosteom n periost[e]oma, periosteal tumour
Periosteophyt m periosteophyte
Periosteotomie f periosteotomy, incision of the periosteum
Periostgeschwulst f periosteal tumour, periost[e]oma

Periostitis f periost[e]itis, cortical osteitis, inflammation of the periosteum
Periostlamelle f periosteal lamella
Periostmesser n periosteum knife
Periostose f periostosis
Periost- und Knochenmarkentzündung f periosteomedullitis
Periostverdickung f/entzündliche pachyperiostosis (der langen Röhrenknochen)
periovariell periovarian
periovulär periovular
Peripachymeningitis f peripachymeningitis
Peripankreatitis f peripancreatitis
Periphakitis f periphacitis
Periphakus m periphacus, capsule of the crystalline lens
peripheriewärts axofugal
Periphlebitis f periphlebitis
periphlebitisch periphlebitic
Periphrenitis f periphrenitis
Peripleuritis f peripleuritis
Periporitis f periporitis
periportal periportal, peripylic
Periproktealdrüse f periproctic (circumanal) gland
periproktisch periproctic, circumanal, periproctal
Periproktitis f periproctitis, perirectitis
Periproktium n paraproctium (den Mastdarm und den After umhüllendes Binde- und Fettgewebe)
Periprostatitis f periprostatitis
Peripyelitis f peripyelitis
Peripylephlebitis f peripylephlebitis
Perirektalabszeß m perirectal (anorectal) abscess
perirenal perirenal, perinephric
Perisalpingitis f perisalpingitis
Perisalpinx f perisalpinx
Perisigmoiditis f perisigmoiditis
Perisinusitis f perisinu[s]itis
Perisinusoidalraum m perisinusoidal space, space of Disse, lymphatic space of the liver
Perispermatitis f perispermatitis
Perisplenitis f perisplenitis
~ cartilaginea cartilaginous perisplenitis, hyaline capsulitis
Perispondylitis f perispondylitis
Peristaltik f peristalsis, peristole, vermicular motion, vermiculation, bowel movement
~/gesteigerte hyperperistalsis
~/rückläufige reversed peristalsis, antiperistalsis
~/verlangsamte bradystalsis
~/verminderte hypoperistalsis
Peristaltikschwäche f hypoperistalsis
Peristaltikstörung f dysperistalsis; peristaltic unrest
Peristaltikverlangsamung f bradystalsis
Peristaltikverstärkung f hyperperistalsis
peristaltisch peristaltic (z. B. Magen- und Darmbewegung)
Peristaphylitis f peristaphylitis
Peristase f 1. peristasis, environment; 2. peristasis (der Blutzirkulation)

Peristrumitis f peristrumitis
Perisystole f perisystole
Peritendineum n peritendineum, peritenon
Peritendinitis f peritendinitis, peritenonitis
Peritenon n s. Sehnenscheide
Perithel n s. Perithelium
Perithéliom n perithelioma
Perithelium n perithelium, pericapillary cells *(äußerste Zellschicht kleinster Blut- und Lymphgefäße)*
Perithelzelle f perithelial cell
Perithyreoiditis f perithyroiditis
Peritomie f peri[dec]tomy, peritectomy *(streifenförmige Bindehautexstirpation um die Hornhaut des Auges)*
Peritonaeum n s. Peritoneum
Peritoneal... s. a. Bauchfell...
Peritonealdialyse f [trans]peritoneal dialysis
Peritonealerguß m peritoneal effusion
Peritonealexsudat n peritoneal exudate
Peritonealfibrose f peritoneal fibrosis
Peritonealflüssigkeit f peritoneal fluid
Peritonealflüssigkeitsabsaugung f peritoneal aspiration
Peritonealhöhle f peritoneal cavity
Peritonealhülle f peritoneal covering (lining)
Peritonealirritation f peritoneal irritation, peritonism
Peritonealisation f peritonealization
peritonealisieren to peritonealize, to peritonize, to cover with peritoneum
Peritonealkarzinomatose f peritoneal carcinomatosis
Peritonealmakrophage m peritoneum macrophage
Peritonealmesotheliom n peritoneal mesothelioma
Peritonealpseudomyxom n peritoneum pseudomyxoma, jelly-belly
Peritonealrand m peritoneal margin
Peritonealrezessus m peritoneal recess
Peritonealsack m peritoneal sac
Peritonealschmerz m peritonealgia, peritoneal pain
Peritonealspüllösung f intraperitoneal irrigation solution
Peritonealspülung f [intra]peritoneal lavage
Peritonealsyndrom n abdominal syndrome
Peritonealtransfusion f peritoneal transfusion
Peritonealtuberkulose f peritoneal tuberculosis; tuberculous peritonitis
Peritonealüberzug m peritoneal covering (lining)
Peritonealumschlagfalte f peritoneal reflection
Peritoneoklyse f peritoneoclysis
peritoneomuskulär peritoneomuscular
Peritoneopathie f peritoneopathy, disease of the peritoneum
peritoneoperikardial peritoneopericardial
Peritoneopexie f peritoneopexy
Peritoneoskop n peritoneoscope
Peritoneoskopie f peritoneoscopy, examination of the peritoneum

peritoneosubarachnoidal peritoneosubarachnoid, peritoneothecal
Peritoneotomie f peritoneotomy, incision into the peritoneum
Peritoneozentese f peritoneocentesis, puncture of the peritoneal cavity
Peritoneum n peritoneum, peritonaeum *(Zusammensetzungen s. unter Bauchfell)*
Peritoneumhomotransplantat n peritoneum homograft
Peritoneumklemme f peritoneal forceps
Peritonismus m peritonism, pseudoperitonitis
Peritonitis f peritonitis, inflammation of the peritoneum *(s. a. unter Bauchfellentzündung)*
~ **adhaesiva** adhesive peritonitis
~/**diffuse** diffuse (general) peritonitis
~/**lokale** localized (circumscribed) peritonitis
~/**pyogene** pyoperitonitis, purulent peritonitis
peritonsillär peritonsillar, circumtonsillar
Peritonsillarabszeß m peritonsillar (retrotonsillar) abscess, quinsy
Peritonsillarraum m peritonsillar space
Peritonsillitis f peritonsillitis, periamygdalitis, paratonsillitis
Peritracheitis f peritracheitis
peritrich[ial] peritrichial *(z. B. Mikroorganismen)*
peritrochantär peritrochanteric
Perityphlitis f perityphlitis
perityphlitisch perityphlitic
Periumbilikalkolik f periumbilical colic
Periumbilikalregion f periumbilical region
Periureteritis f periureteritis
Periurethralabszeß m periurethral abscess
Periurethritis f periurethritis
Perivaginitis f perivaginitis
perivaskulär perivascular, circumvascular
Perivaskulitis f perivasculitis
perivenös perivenous, paravenous
Perivesikulitis f perivesiculitis
Perivisceritis f perivisceritis
perizellulär pericellular, pericytial
Perizementoklasie f pericementoclasia
Perizystitis f pericystitis
Perizystium n pericystium
Perizyt m pericyte, adventitial cell
Perizytom n pericytoma
Perjodsäure f periodic acid
Perjodsäurefärbung f s. Perjodsäure-Schiff-Reaktion
Perjodsäure-Schiff-Reaktion f periodic acid Schiff reaction, PAS *(Nachweis für Polysaccharide)*
Perkolat n percolate
Perkolation f percolation • **durch** ~ **gewinnen** to percolate
perkolieren to percolate
Perkussion f percussion
~/**auskultierende** auscultatory (auditory) percussion, acouophonia
~/**direkte** direct (immediate) percussion
~/**indirekte** indirect (mediate) percussion
~/**palpierende** palpatory percussion, palpatopercussion

Perkussionsbefund

Perkussionsbefund m percussion findings
Perkussionsgebiet n percussion area
Perkussionshammer m plexor, plessor, percussion hammer; patella hammer
Perkussionsplättchen n pleximeter, plessimeter
Perkussionsschall m s. Perkussionston
Perkussionstest m percussion test
Perkussionston m percussion note (sound)
Perkussionswelle f percussion wave
Perkussor m percussor
perkussorisch percussory; percussible
perkutan percutaneous, transcutaneous, through the skin
Perkutanpunktion f percutaneous needle puncture
Perkutanreaktion f percutaneous reaction
perkutieren to percuss; to tap
perkutorisch s. perkussorisch
Perle f 1. perle *(Arzneimittelform)*; 2. bead, drop *(z. B. Schweiß)*
Perlèche f perleche
Perlgeschwulst f pearly tumour, cholesteatoma
Perlzyste f pearl cyst
Permeabilität f permeability *(z. B. von Scheidewänden)*
Permeabilitätsvitamin n vitamin P
Permeation f permeation
pernasal pernasal
Pernio m pernio, chilblain, frost-bite
Perniosis f perniosis, presence of chilblains
perniziös pernicious, noxious
perniziosaartig perniciosiform
Perniziosafleckung f Mauer's stippling (dots, clots) *(der roten Blutkörperchen bei Malaria tropica)*
Perobrachius m perobrachius *(Mißgeburt)*
Peroch[e]irus m peroch[e]irus *(Mißgeburt)*
Perodaktylie f perodactyly
Perodaktylus m perodactylus *(Mißgeburt)*
Peromelie f peromelia; hemimelia
Peromelus m peromelus *(Mißgeburt)*
Peroneuslähmung f peroneal palsy (paralysis)
Peroneusmuskel m peroneal muscle
Peroneusnerv m peroneal nerve
Peroneusphänomen n peroneal [nerve] phenomenon
Peroneusreflex m peroneal reflex
Peroneuszeichen n peroneal sign
Peropus m peropus *(Mißgeburt)*
peroral peroral, per os, by the mouth
Perosplanchnie f perosplanchnia
perossal perosseous, transmitted through bone
Peroxisom n peroxisome
Peroxydase f peroxidase *(Enzym)*
Persekutionsdelirium n persecution complex (mania)
Perseveration f perseveration *(Wiederholung von gleichen Handlungen)*
persistieren to persist, to last
Personal n /**ärztliches** medical staff
~/medizinisches medical personnel
~/mittleres medizinisches middle (medium-grade) medical personnel
~/pflegerisches nursing staff
Personifizierung f personification
Persönlichkeit f personality
~/abnorme psychopathic personality
~/aggressive aggressive personality
~/exzentrische eccentric personality
~/gefühlsbetonte emotional personality
~/gespaltene dissociated (split) personality, multiple (schizoid) personality
~/hysterische hysterical personality
~/neurotische neurotic personality
~/psychopathische psychopathic personality
~/schizoide s. ~/gespaltene
~/zyklothyme cyclothymic personality
Persönlichkeitsabbau m personality disorganization; impaired cerebral function
Persönlichkeitsbeschreibung f psychographia
Persönlichkeitsbewußtsein n autopsyche
Persönlichkeitsbild n psychogram, psychic profile
Persönlichkeitsbildung f personality formation
Persönlichkeitsentfaltung f personality development; individualization
Persönlichkeitsfaktorentest m personality inventory
Persönlichkeitsstörung f personality disorder; disturbed personality
Persönlichkeitsstruktur f personality structure
Persönlichkeitstest m personality test
Persönlichkeitsveränderung f personality change
Persorption f persorption *(Direktaufnahme von Stoffen durch die Körperoberfläche)*
Perspiratio f **insensibilis** insensible perspiration (water loss)
~ sensibilis sensible perspiration
Perspiration f perspiration, transpiration, diaphoresis
perspiratorisch perspiratory
perspirieren to perspire, to sweat
Perthes-Erkrankung f Perthes' disease, osteochondrosis of the capitular epiphysis
Pertubation f pertubation, perflation of the oviduct, tubal insufflation
pertussal pertussal, pertussoid
Pertussis f s. Keuchhusten
Perubalsam m Peru[vian] balsam
Peruwarze f Peruvian wart
Peruwarzenkrankheit f Carrion's disease, Oroya fever *(durch Bartonella bacilliformis)*
pervers perverse, perverted, abnormal
Perverser m pervert; erotopath
Perversion f perversion; erotopathy
~/sexuelle sexual perversion (deviation), parasexuality, paraphilia
Pervigilium n s. Schlaflosigkeit
Perzeption f perception, pcpt.
~/autokinetische autokinetic perception; apparent movement
Perzeptionsstörung f perceptive disorder
Perzeptionszeit f perception time
perzeptiv perceptive, perceptual

Pes *m* pes, foot
- ~ **anserinus** pes anserinus, goose's foot
- ~ **cavus** pes cavus, hollow foot
- ~ **contortus** pes contortus, clubfoot
- ~ **equinocavus** equinocavus [deformity]
- ~ **equinovalgus** equinovalgus [deformity]
- ~ **equinovarus** equinovarus [deformity]
- ~ **equinus** [tali]pes equinus, equinus [deformity], drop foot, foot drop
- ~ **excavatus** *s.* ~ cavus
- ~ **hippocampi** pes hippocampi, hippocampus, Ammon's horn
- ~ **malleus valgus** hammer toe
- ~ **planovalgus** [pes] planovalgus
- ~ **planus** [tali]pes planus, flatfoot, splayfoot
- ~ **valgus** [tali]pes valgus
- ~ **varus** pes varus, inward clubfoot

Pessar[ium] *n* pessary, pess[ul]um
Pest *f* plague, pestilence, pest *(Infektionskrankheit durch Pasteurella pestis) (Zusammensetzungen s. unter Pestis)*
Pestadenitis *f* minor pestis *(leicht verlaufende Pestform)*
pestartig pestilential, pestiferous
Pestbazillus *m* plague bacillus, Pasteurella pestis
Pestbeule *f* plague carbuncle, pestilential (malignant) bubo
pestbringend pestilential
Pestbubo *m s.* Pestbeule
Pestfleck *m* plague spot
Pestfloh *m* plague (rat) flea, Xenopsylla cheopis
Pestforschung *f* pestology
Pesthaus *n* pesthouse, lazaret[te]
Pestikämie *f* pesticaemia
Pestilenz *f* pestilence
pestilenzialisch pestilential
Pestimpfstoff *m* plague vaccine
Pestis *f s.* Pest
- ~ **bubonica** bubonic (glandular) plague
- ~ **minor** minor pestis *(leicht verlaufende Pestform)*
- ~ **siderans** septicaemic plague

Pestizid *n* pesticide
pestkrank plague-infected
Pestmeningitis *f* plague meningitis
Pestologie *f* pestology
Pestpneumonie *f* plague pneumonia, lung plague
Pestseptikämie *f* septicaemic plague
pestübertragend pestiferous
Petechialblutung *f* petechial haemorrhage
Petechialfieber *n s.* Fleckfieber
Petechiasis *f* petechiasis
Petechien *pl* petechiae
Petechiometer *n* petechiometer *(zur Messung der Kapillarpermeabilität)*
Pethidin *n* pethidine *(Narkotikum)*.
Petiolus *m* petiole, petiolus
- ~ **epiglottidis** pedicle of the epiglottis.

Petit mal *n* petit mal, absence attack, minor motor seizure

Petrifikation *f* petrifaction *(z. B. eines Gewebes durch Kalkablagerung)*
Petrischale *f* Petri [culture] dish, Petri plate *(für Bakterienkulturen)*
Petrissage *f* petrissage, kneeding massage
petrobasilar petrobasilar
Petroleumgaze *f* petroleum-jelly gauze
petromastoid[al] petromastoid
petrookzipital petro-occipital
Petrositis *f* petrositis, inflammation of the petrous pyramid
petrosphenoidal petrosphenoid
petrosquamös petrosquamous
petrotympanal petrotympanic
Peutz-Jeghers-Syndrom *n* Peutz-Jeghers syndrome, Jeghers-Peutz syndrome, intestinal polyposis-cutaneous pigmentation syndrome; multiple intestinal polyposis
Pexie *f* pexis, fixation, attachment *(z. B. von Organen bei Lageänderung)*
Peyote *m*, **Peyotl** *f* peyote *(Rauschgift)*
Pezzer-Katheter *m* de Pezzer catheter
Pfählungsverletzung *f* impalement injury
Pfanne *f* socket *(eines Gelenks)*
pfannenförmig acetabular
Pfannenfräser *m* acetabulum reamer
Pfannengelenk *n* ball-and-socket joint
Pfannenstiel-Querschnitt *m* Pfannenstiel's incision *(Bauchdeckenschnitt an der oberen Schambehaarungsgrenze)*
Pfannenvorwölbung *f*/**intrapelvine** arthrokatadysis
Pfaundler-Hurler-Syndrom *n* Hurler's disease, Pfaundler-Hurler syndrome, mucopolysaccharidosis [type] I
Pfeffer-und-Salz-Fundus *m* pepper-and-salt fundus *(Augenhintergrund)*
pfeifend sibilant, whistling *(Atemgeräusch)*
Pfeifenraucherkrebs *m* smoker's (claypipe) cancer
Pfeiler *m* pillar, column; abutment *(Stomatologie)*
Pfeilerchorda *f* strut chorda *(Herz)*
Pfeilerzelle *f* pillar cell
Pfeilnaht *f* sagittal (interparietal, longitudinal) suture
Pfeilnahtfontanelle *f* sagittal fontanel
Pferdebremse *f*/**amerikanische** horse (deer) fly *(Überträger der Tularämieerreger)*
Pferdeenzephalitis *f*/**östliche** Eastern equine encephalitis (encephalomyelitis) *(durch Stechmücken übertragene Arbovirusinfektion)*
~/**Venezolanische** Venezuelan equine encephalitis (encephalomyelitis)
~/**westliche** Western equine encephalitis (encephalomyelitis)
Pferdeschweif *m* cauda equina *(unterster Rückenmarkabschnitt)*
Pferdeserum *n* horse serum
PFK *s.* Phosphofruktokinase
pflanzenessend phytophagous
Pflanzenesser *m* vegetarian

Pflanzenfaserknäuel

Pflanzenfaserknäuel n phytobezoar, food ball *(im Magen)*
Pflanzengift n phytotoxin, vegetable poison
Pflanzenkost f vegetarian diet
Pflanzenstaublunge[nerkrankung] f phytopneumoconiosis
pflanzlich vegetable
Pflaster n plaster, emplastrum, splenium; patch
● **ein ~ auflegen** to apply a plaster
Pflasterepithel n pavement (squamous) epithelium
Pflastersteinnävus m paving-stone naevus
Pflasterstreifen m strap
Pflastertest m patch test
Pflasterverband m adhesive bandage (strapping)
Pflasterzugverband m butterfly [bandage]
Pflege f nursing, care
Pflegeheim n nursing home
pflegen to nurse *(z. B. einen Kranken)*
Pflegepersonal n nursing staff
Pfleger m dresser, [male] nurse, orderly
Pflichtassistent m intern[e], clerk
Pflichtassistenz f internship, clerkship
Pflichtimpfung f compulsory vaccination
Pflugscharbein n vomer ● **unter dem ~** subvomerine
Pfortader f portal [vein], porta
Pfortaderangiographie f porto[veno]graphy, portal venography
Pfortaderblut n portal [vein] blood
Pfortaderdarstellung f **über die Nabelvene** umbilical vein portography
Pfortaderdekompression f portal decompression
Pfortaderdilatation f pylephlebectasia
Pfortaderdruck m portal [venous] pressure
Pfortaderdurchblutung f portal blood flow
Pfortaderentzündung f pylephlebitis, portal phlebitis, inflammation of the portal vein
Pfortadererweiterung f pylephlebectasia
Pfortaderhochdruck m portal hypertension
Pfortader-Hohlvenen-Anastomose f portacaval anastomosis, Eck's fistula
Pfortaderkreislauf m portal circulation
Pfortader-Nierenvenen-Anastomose f portorenal shunt
Pfortaderröntgen[kontrast]darstellung f porto[veno]graphy, portal venography
Pfortaderstauung f portal hypertension
Pfortaderstauungsaszites m mechanical ascites
Pfortadersystem n portal system
~/hypophysäres hypophyseal portal system
Pfortaderthrombose f pylethrombosis, portal vein thrombosis
~ und -entzündung f pylethrombophlebitis
Pfortaderverschluß m pylemphraxis, portal [vein] obstruction, occlusion of the portal vein
Pfortaderzirrhose f portal (atrophic) cirrhosis
Pforte f *s.* Hilus
Pfötchenstellung f **der Hand** obstetrician's hand *(Tetaniezeichen)*

Pfropf m 1. plug; core; tampon; 2. embolus; thrombus
Pfropfhebephrenie f grafted hebephrenia
Pfropfschizophrenie f grafted schizophrenia
Pfropfung f grafting, implantation, transplantation
Pfundnase f rhinophym[a], potato (bottle) nose
PG *s.* Prostaglandin
Phage m [bacterio]phage *(bakterientötendes Virus)*
Phagedaena f phagedaena *(besonders bei Syphilis)*
~ tropica tropical [sloughing] phagedaena, tropical ulcer
phagedänisch phagedaenic *(Geschwür)*
Phageninduktion f phage induction
Phagentypisierung f phage typing
Phagolyse f phago[cyto]lysis
Phagoly[so]som n phago[lyso]some, phagocytic (digestive) vacuole
Phagomanie f phagomania
Phagosom n *s.* Phagolysosom
Phagozyt m phagocyte
phagozytär phagocytic, phagocytal
Phagozytenbildungszelle f phagocytoblast
phagozytenhemmend antiphagocytic
Phagozytenzerfall m phago[cyto]lysis
phagozytierbar phagocytable
phagozytieren to phagocytize, to phagocytose *(z. B. Bakterien)*
Phagozytin n phagocytin
phagozytisch phagocytic, phagocytal
Phagozytoblast m phagocytoblast *(Phagozytenvorstufe)*
Phagozytolyse f phago[cyto]lysis
phagozytolytisch phagocytolytic
Phagozytose f phagocytosis, cytophagy, englobement
Phagozytosefähigkeit f phagocytic ability
Phagozytoseindex m phagocytic (opsonic) index
Phagozytosekapazität f phagocytic capacity
Phagozytosevakuole f *s.* Phagolysosom
Phakitis f phacitis, inflammation of the crystalline lens
phakoanaphylaktisch phacoanaphylactic
Phakoanaphylaxie f phacoanaphylaxis
Phakoemulsifikation f phacoemulsification
Phakoeresis f phacoerisis, phacoerysis *(mit einem Saugapparat)*
Phakofragmentator m phacofragmentator
phakoid phacoid
Phakolyse f 1. phacolysis, dissolution of the crystalline lens; 2. phacolysis, discission of the crystalline lens
phakolytisch phacolytic
Phakom n phacoma, phakoma
Phakomalazie f phacomalacia, softening of the crystalline lens; soft cataract
Phakomatose f phacomatosis
Phakometer n phacometer *(Gerät zur Ausmessung optischer Linsen)*
Phakoplanese f phacoplanesis; wandering-lens

Phakoskleroma n phacoscleroma
Phakosklerose f phacosclerosis, hardening of the crystalline lens
Phakoskop n phacoscope
Phakoskopie f phacoscopy
Phakoskotasmus m phacoscotasmus, clouding of the crystalline lens
phakotoxisch phacotoxic
Phakozele f phac[ent]ocele, phacometachoresis
Phakozystektomie f phacocystectomy
Phakozystitis f phacocystitis, inflammation of the lens capsule
Phalangektomie f phalangectomy, excision of a phalanx; amputation of a finger
Phalangenmesser n phalangeal knife
Phalangenüberzahl f polyphalangism, hyperphalangism
Phalangenunterzahl f hypophalangism
Phalangisation f phalangization (Fingerneubildung aus einem Knochenstumpf)
Phalangitis f phalangitis, inflammation of a phalanx
~ **syphilitica** syphilitic phalangitis
Phalanx f phalanx
~ **distalis digitorum manus** distal phalanx of the finger
~ **distalis digitorum pedis** distal phalanx of the toe
~ **media digitorum manus** middle phalanx of the finger
~ **media digitorum pedis** middle phalanx of the toe
~ **proximalis digitorum manus** proximal phalanx of the finger
~ **proximalis digitorum pedis** proximal phalanx of the toe
Phalanxentfernung f[/operative] s. Phalangektomie
Phallalgie f phallalgia, phallodynia, pain in the penis
Phallektomie f phallectomy, penectomy, amputation of the penis
Phallitis f phallitis, penitis, inflammation of the penis, priapitis
Phallokampsis f phallocampsis
Phalloplastik f phalloplasty
Phallorrhagie f phallorrhagia, haemorrhage from the penis
Phallorrhoe f phallorrhoea, gonorrhoea in the male
Phallotomie f phallotomy, incision of the penis
Phallus m phallus, penis, coles (Zusammensetzungen s. unter Penis)
Phallus... s. a. Penis...
phallusartig phalloid, phallic
phallusförmig phalliform
Phallusrekonstruktion f phalloplasty
Phallusretraktion f phallocrypsis, retraction of the penis
Phallusverkrümmung f phallocampsis
phanerogenetisch phanerogen[et]ic
Phanerose f phanerosis

Phänomen n phenomenon
~/**Argyll-Robertsonsches** Argyll Robertson pupil (sign)
~/**Arthussches** Arthus' phenomenon, phenomenon of Arthus, local anaphylaxis (allergische Überempfindlichkeitsreaktion)
~/**Aschnersches** Aschner's phenomenon, oculocardiac reflex
~/**Bellsches** Bell's phenomenon (sign) (Augenbewegung nach oben bei Lidschluß)
~/**Köbnersches** Koebner's phenomenon, isomorphic provocative reaction; isomorphic irritation effect (Dermatologie)
~/**Lasèguesches** Lasègue's sign (bei Bandscheibenprolaps); straight-leg-raising test
~/**Littensches** Litten's (diaphragmatic) sign, diaphragm phenomenon
~/**Nikolskisches** Nikolsky's sign (bei Pemphigus vulgaris)
~/**Raynaudsches** Raynaud's phenomenon, angiospastic syndrome (Blaufärbung der Gliedmaßen infolge Gefäßspasmus)
~/**Rombergsches** Romberg's sign (Fallneigung bei geschlossenen Augen infolge Kleinhirnerkrankung)
~/**Shwartzman-Sanarellisches** Shwartzman phenomenon (reaction) (nach wiederholter Endotoxininjektion)
~/**Wenckebachsches** Wenckebach phenomenon (EKG)
Phänotyp m phenotype ● **vom gleichen ~** isophenic
phänotypisch phenotypic
Phantasie f phantasy, fantasy; imagination
Phantasiebild n phantasm, imaginary picture
phantasieren to have phantasies; to be delirious
Phantasieren n phantasmoscopia, seeing of delirious phantasms; confabulation (bei Gedächtnisstörung)
phantasierend light-headed
Phantasma n phantasm, phantom
Phantasmophobie f phantasmophobia, phasmophobia, fear of ghosts
Phantasmoskopie f phantasmoscopia
Phantom n 1. phantom, model of the body; manikin (zum Erlernen geburtshilflicher Handgriffe); 2. phantom, phantasm
Phantombein n phantom leg
Phantomglied n phantom limb
Phantomhand f phantom hand
Phantomschmerz m phantom [limb] pain, pseudoaesthesia
Phantomzahnschmerz m phantom odontalgia
Phantosmie f phantosmia, pseudosmia
phäochrom phaeochrome
Phäochromoblast m phaeochromoblast (Phäochromozytenvorstufe)
Phäochromoblastom n phaeochromoblastoma, malignant phaeochromocytoma
Phäochromozyt m phaeochromocyte (z. B. im Nebennierenmark)

Phäochromozytom

Phäochromozytom n phaeochromocytoma, chromaffino[blasto]ma, chromophile tumour, paraganglio[neuro]ma
Pharmakatoleranz f habituation
Pharmakoangiographie f pharmacoangiography
Pharmakochemie f pharmaceutical chemistry
Pharmakodiagnose f pharmacodiagnosis
Pharmakodynamik f pharmacodynamics *(Lehre von der Arzneimittelwirkung im Organismus)*
pharmakodynamisch pharmacodynamic
Pharmakogenetik f pharmacogenetics *(Lehre von den erblichen Formen der Arzneimittelreaktionen)*
Pharmakognosie f pharmacognostics, pharmacognosy *(Bestimmungs- und Erkennungslehre der Drogen)*
pharmakognostisch pharmacognostic
pharmakokinetisch pharmacokinetic
Pharmakologie f pharmacology, pharmacopaedics
pharmakologisch pharmacologic[al]
Pharmakomanie f pharmacomania
Pharmakon n pharmacon; drug, medicine, remedy
Pharmakophilie f pharmacophilia
Pharmakophobie f pharmacophobia *(krankhafte Angst vor Pharmaka)*
Pharmakopöe f pharmacop[o]eia
Pharmakopsychose f pharmacopsychosis
Pharmakoradiographie f pharmacoradiography
Pharmakotherapie f pharmacotherapy
Pharmazeut m pharmaceutist, pharmacist, druggist
Pharmazeutikum n pharmaceutical [agent]
pharmazeutisch pharmaceutic[al], pharmacal
Pharmazie f pharmaceutics, pharmacy
Pharyng... s. a. Rachen... *und* Schlund...
Pharyngalgie f pharyngalgia, pharyngodynia, pharyngeal pain (discomfort)
pharyngeal pharyngeal
Pharyngektasie f pharyngectasia
Pharyngektomie f pharyngectomy, excision of the pharynx
Pharyngismus m pharyngism, pharyngospasm
Pharyngitis f pharyngitis, inflammation of the pharynx; sore throat
~/**abakterielle** pharyngoconjunctival fever
~/**akute** acute (catarrhal) pharyngitis, serous angina
~ **durch β-hämolysierende Streptokokken** beta-haemolytic streptococcal pharyngitis
~ **follicularis (glandularis)** follicular (glandular) pharyngitis; clergyman's sore
~/**trockene** dry pharyngitis
~/**ulzeröse** ulcerative pharyngitis
pharyngitisch pharyngitic
pharyngobranchial pharyngobranchial
Pharyngodynie f s. Pharyngalgie
pharyngoepiglottisch pharyngo-epiglottic
pharyngoglossal pharyngoglossal
Pharyngokeratose f pharyngokeratosis, keratosis of the pharynx

Pharyngokonjunktivalfieber n pharyngoconjunctival fever
pharyngolaryngeal pharyngolaryngeal
Pharyngolaryngektomie f pharyngolaryngectomy
Pharyngolaryngitis f pharyngolaryngitis, inflammation of the larynx and the pharynx
Pharyngolith m pharyngolith
Pharyngologie f pharyngology *(Lehre von den Rachenkrankheiten)*
pharyngologisch pharyngologic
pharyngomaxillär pharyngomaxillary
Pharyngomykose f pharyngomycosis
pharyngonasal pharyngonasal
Pharyngoösophagus m pharyngo-oesophagus
Pharyngoparalyse f pharyngoparalysis, pharyngoplegia, pharyngolysis
Pharyngopathie f pharyngopathy, disease of the pharynx
Pharyngoplastik f pharyngoplasty
Pharyngoplegie f s. Pharyngoparalyse
Pharyngorhinitis f pharyngorhinitis, inflammation of the nasopharynx
Pharyngorhinoskopie f pharyngorhinoscopy
Pharyngorrhagie f pharyngorrhagia, haemorrhage from the pharynx
Pharyngorrhoe f pharyngorrhoea, discharge from the pharynx
Pharyngoskop n pharyngoscope
Pharyngoskopie f pharyngoscopy
pharyngospasmodisch pharyngospasmodic
Pharyngospasmus m pharyngospasm
Pharyngostenose f pharyngostenosis, pharyngostenia, pharyngoperistole, narrowing of the pharynx, lemostenosis
Pharyngotherapie f pharyngotherapy
Pharyngotomie f pharyngotomy, incision of the pharynx
Pharyngotonsillitis f pharyngotonsillitis, pharyngo-amygdalitis, adenopharyngitis
pharyngotracheal pharyngotracheal
pharyngotympanal pharyngotympanic
Pharyngoxerose f pharyngoxerosis, dryness of the pharynx
Pharyngozele f pharyngocele
Pharynx m pharynx, throat, throttle, fauces
Pharynx... s. a. Rachen... *und* Schlund...
Pharynxaponeurosis f pharyngeal aponeurosis
Pharynxchirurgie f pharyngeal surgery
Pharynxdivertikel n pharyngeal (pharyngo-oesophageal) diverticulum
Pharynxdysphagie f pharyngeal dysphagia
Pharynxhernie f pharyngocele
Pharynxinzision f s. Pharyngotomie
Pharynxkrise f pharyngeal crisis
Pharynx-, Larynx- und Ösophagusexstirpation f pharyngo-laryngo-oesophagectomy, pharyngo-oesophagolaryngectomy
Pharynxmoniliasis f pharyngeal moniliasis
Pharynxmukosa f mucous membrane of the pharynx, pharyngeal mucosa
Pharynxobstruktion f pharyngemphraxis, obstruction of the pharynx

Pharynx-Ösophagus-Ersatz m pharyngo-oesophageal replacement
Pharynx-Ösophagus-Prothese f pharyngo-oesophageal prosthesis
Pharynxrekonstruktion f pharyngeal reconstruction; pharyngoplasty
Pharynxtonsille f s. Rachenmandel
Pharynxtumor m pharyngeal tumour
Pharynx- und Larynxentfernung f/operative pharyngolaryngectomy
Pharynx- und Larynxentzündung f pharyngolaryngitis
Pharynxwand f pharyngeal wall
Phase f phase, stage, stadium, period
~/refraktäre refractory period
Phasendifferenzhaploskop n phase-difference haploscope
Phasenkontrastmikroskop n phase-contrast microscope
Phasenkontrastmikroskopie f phase-contrast microscopy
Phemister-Span m Phemister bone chip (onlay)
Phenazetin n phenacetin, acetophenetidin *(Analgetikum, Antipyretikum)*
Phenazetinmißbrauch m phenacetin abuse
Phenetidin n phenetidin *(Grundstoff verschiedener Antipyretika)*
Phenetidinausscheidung f im Urin phenetidinuria
Phengophobie f phen[g]ophobia *(krankhafte Angst vor Licht)*
Phenobarbital n phenobarbital *(Hypnotikum)*
Phenobarbitalbehandlung f phenobarbital therapy
Phenol n phenol, carbolic acid
Phenolausscheidung f im Urin phenoluria, carboluria
Phenolphthalein n phenolphthalein *(Indikatorsubstanz; Abführmittel)*
Phenolphthaleintest m phenolphthalein test *(zum Nachweis von okkultem Blut im Stuhl)*
Phenolrot n phenolsulphonephthalein
Phenolrotprobe f phenolsulphonephthalein test *(Nierenfunktionsdiagnostik)*
Phenolsulfonphthalein n phenolsulphonephthalein
Phenolsulfonphthaleintest m phenolsulphonephthalein test *(Nierenfunktionsdiagnostik)*
Phenolvergiftung f carbolism, phenol poisoning
Phenothiazin n phenothiazine *(Wurmmittel)*
Phenoxymethylpenizillin n phenoxymethyl penicillin, penicillin V *(säurefestes Penizillin)*
Phenylalanin n phenylalanine *(essentielle Aminosäure)*
Phenylalaninämie f phenylalaninaemia
Phenylalanin[spiegel]erhöhung f im Blut hyperphenylalaninaemia
Phenylamin n phenylamine, aniline
Phenyläthylbarbitursäure f phenylethylbarbituric acid, phenobarbital *(Hypnotikum)*
Phenylbrenztraubensäureschwachsinn m phenylpyruvic amentia (oligophrenia)

Phenylbutazon n phenylbutazone *(Analgetikum, Antiphlogistikum)*
Phenylhydrazinprobe f phenylhydrazine test *(zum Nachweis für Monosaccharide)*
Phenylketonkörperausscheidung f im Urin phenylketonuria, PKU
Phenylketonurie f 1. phenylketonuria, PKU; 2. phenylpyruvic amentia (oligophrenia)
phenylketonurisch phenylketonuric
Phialophora f **verrucosa** Phialophora verrucosa *(Erreger der Chromoblastomycosis)*
Philadelphiachromosom n Philadelphia chromosome
Philtrum n philtrum *(Rinne in der Oberlippenmitte)*
Phimose f phimosis
phimotisch phimotic
Phiole f phial, vial
Phlebalgia f **ischiadica** Quénu's disease
Phlebalgie f phlebalgia, venalgia, pain in a vein
Phlebasthenie f phlebasthenia
Phlebektasie f phlebectasia, venectasia, dilatation of a vein; varicosity
Phlebektomie f phlebectomy, venectomy, excision of a vein
Phlebektopie f phlebectopia, displacement of a vein
Phlebemphraxis f phlebemphraxis, plugging of a vein *(z. B. durch Blutgerinnsel)*
Phlebex[h]airese f phlebexeresis, excision of a vein
Phlebitis f phlebitis, inflammation of a vein
~ **migrans** migrating phlebitis
phlebitisch phlebitic
Phlebo... s. a. Venen...
phlebogen phlebogenous
Phlebogramm n 1. phlebogram, venogram, roentgenogram of a vein; 2. phlebogram *(des Venenpulses)*
Phlebograph m phlebograph
Phlebographie f 1. phlebography, venography, X-ray photography of a vein; 2. phlebography, recording of venous pulsations
phlebographisch 1. phlebographic, venographic; 2. phlebographic
Phlebokarzinom n phlebocarcinoma
Phleboklysis f phleboclysis, venoclysis
Phlebolith m phlebolith, phlebolite, vein stone
Phlebolithiasis f phlebolithiasis
phlebolithisch phlebolithic
Phlebologie f phlebology
Phlebometritis f phlebometritis, inflammation of the uterine veins
Phlebonarkose f phlebonarcosis, phlebanaesthesia
Phlebophlebostomie f phlebophlebostomy, venovenostomy
Phlebopiezometrie f phlebopiezometry, measurement of the venous pressure
Phleborrhagie f phleborrhagia, venous bleeding, haemorrhage from a vein
Phleborrhaphie f phleborrhaphy, venesuture, suture of a vein, venisuture

Phleborrhexis

Phleborrhexis f phleborrhexis, rupture of a vein
Phlebostase f 1. phlebostasis, venostasis, venous stasis; 2. phlebostasis, bloodless phlebotomy
Phlebostenose f phlebostenosis, constriction of a vein
Phlebotom n phlebotome
Phlebotomie f phlebotomy, venotomy, venesection, venae sectio, venous (surgical) cutdown
Phlebotomus m Phlebotomus *(tropische Mückengattung)*
~ **argentipes** Phlebotomus argentipes *(Kala-Azar-Überträger in Indien)*
~ **chinensis** Phlebotomus chinensis *(Kala-Azar-Überträger in China)*
~ **intermedius** Phlebotomus intermedius *(Überträger der südamerikanischen Leishmaniase)*
~ **papatasii** Phlebotomus papatasii *(Überträger des Pappatacifiebers)*
~ **sergenti** Phlebotomus sergenti *(Überträger der Orientbeule)*
~ **verrucarum** Phlebotomus verrucarum *(Überträger des Oroyafiebers)*
Phlebotomusfieber n s. Pappatacifieber
Phlegma n phlegm
Phlegmasia f phlegmasia, inflammation *(s. a. unter Entzündung)*
~ **alba dolens** phlegmasia alba dolens, leucophlegmasia, thrombotic phlegmasia; white (milk) leg
~ **cerulea dolens** phlegmasia cerulea dolens, blue phlebitis
phlegmatisch phlegmatic
Phlegmona f **colli profunda** Ludwig's angina *(Zellgewebsentzündung des Mundbodens und der oberen Halsgegend)*
Phlegmone f phlegmon
~/**emphysematöse** emphysematous phlegmon
~/**perityphlitische** periappendicular phlegmon, appendix mass
phlegmonös phlegmonous
phlogistisch phlogistic
phlogogen phlogogenic, phlogogenous
Phlogosis f phlogosis, inflammation, erysipelas
Phlyktäne f phlycten, phlyctaena; vesicle
phlyktänulös phlyctenar, phlyctenous
Phobie f phobia, morbid dread (fear), anxiety neurosis (reaction, state)
~/**milde** paraphobia
Phobophobie f phobophobia *(Angst vor Angstanfällen)*
Phokomelie f phocomelia
Phokomelus m phocomelus *(Mißgeburt)*
Phonasthenie f phonasthenia, weakness of the voice
Phonation f phonation, formation of speech sounds
~/**gesteigerte** hyperphonia, superenergetic phonation
Phonationskrampf m phonatory spasm
Phonationsschwäche f hypophonia, subenergetic phonation

Phonationsstörung f dysphonia
Phonationsverlust m aphonia; speechlessness
phonatorisch phonatory
Phoneme npl phoneme
Phonendoskop n phonendoscope
Phonetik f phonetics *(Lehre von der Atmung, Stimme und Lautbildung)*
phonetisch phonetic
Phoniater m phoniatrician
Phoniatrie f phoniatrics, phoniatry *(Lehre von den Erkrankungen des Stimmapparats)*
phonieren to phonate, to produce sounds
phonisch phonic
Phonismus m phonism *(Synästhesieform)*
Phonoangiographie f phonoangiography
Phonofotografie f phonophotography *(fotografische Darstellung der Stimmschwingungen)*
Phonokardiogramm n phonocardiogram, PCG, electrocardiophonogram, stethogram
Phonokardiograph m phonocardiograph, electrocardiophonograph
Phonokardiographie f phonocardiography, electrocardiophonography, stethography
phonokardiographisch phonocardiographic
Phonokinefluorokardiographie f phonocinefluorocardiography
Phonomanie f phonomania, homicidal mania
Phonometer n phonometer
Phonometrie f phonometry
Phonomyographie f phonomyography
Phonomyoklonus m phonomyoclonus
Phonopathie f phonopathy, disease (disorder) of the voice
Phonophobie f phonophobia *(krankhafte Angst vor dem Sprechen)*
Phonopsie f phonopsia *(Synästhesieform)*
phonorezeptiv phonoreceptive
Phonorezeptor m phonoreceptor
Phorologie f phorology *(Lehre von den Krankheitsüberträgern)*
Phorometer n phorometer
Phorometrie f phorometry *(Messung der Augenachsenablenkung)*
Phorooptometer n phorooptometer *(ophthalmologisches Instrument)*
Phoroskop n phoroscope *(Linsengestell zur Sehprüfung)*
Phosgen n phosgene, carbonyl chloride *(lungenschädigender Kampfstoff)*
Phosis f phose
Phosphatämie f phosphataemia
Phosphatase f phosphatase *(Enzym)*
~/**alkalische** alkaline phosphatase
~/**saure** acid phosphatase
Phosphatasebestimmungsmethode f/**Bodanskysche** Bodansky's method
Phosphatasemangelrachitis f hypophosphatasia
Phosphatausscheidung f **im Urin** phosphaturia
~/**vermehrte** hyperphosphaturia
~/**verminderte** hypophosphaturia, oligophosphaturia
Phosphatdiabetes m phosphate (phosphatic) diabetes

Phosphatgruppenaustausch m transphosphorylation
Phosphatid n phosphatide
Phosphatidthesaurismose f phosphatide thesaurismosis
Phosphatometer n phosphatometer *(zur Urinphosphatbestimmung)*
Phosphatspiegelerhöhung f im Blut hyperphosphataemia
Phosphatspiegelverminderung f im Blut hypophosphataemia
Phosphen n phosphene *(subjektive Lichterscheinung bei Druck auf die Augen)*
Phosphoaminolipid n phosphoaminolipid
Phosphodiesterase f phosphodiesterase *(Enzym)*
Phosphoenolbrenztraubensäure f phosphoenolpyruvic acid *(Zwischenprodukt des Kohlenhydratstoffwechsels)*
Phosphofruktokinase f phosphofructokinase, PFK *(Enzym)*
Phosphofruktokinase-Mangelkrankheit f phosphofructokinase deficiency disease
Phosphofruktomutase f phosphofructomutase *(Enzym)*
Phosphoglukomutase f phosphoglucomutase *(Enzym)*
Phosphoglukonsäure f phosphogluconic acid
Phosphoglukoseisomerase f phosphoglucose isomerase *(Enzym)*
Phosphoglyzerinsäure f phosphoglyceric acid
Phosphoglyzerolaldehyd m phosphoglyceraldehyde
Phosphoglyzeromutase f phosphoglyceromutase *(Enzym)*
Phosphohexoisomerase f phosphohexoisomerase *(Enzym)*
Phosphohexokinase f phosphohexokinase *(Enzym)*
Phosphokreatin n phosphocreatine, phosphagen
Phospholipase f phospholipase *(Enzym)*
Phospholipid n phospholipid
Phosphomonoesterase f phosphomonoesterase *(Enzym)*
Phosphopenie f phosphopenia, deficiency of phosphorus
Phosphoprotein n phosphoprotein
Phosphorausscheidung f im Urin phosphoruria
Phosphoreszenz f phosphorescence
phosphoreszieren to phosphoresce
phosphoreszierend phosphorescent, phosphorous
Phosphorhidrose f phosphor[h]idrosis
Phosphoribomutase f phosphoribomutase *(Enzym)*
Phosphorismus m s. Phosphorvergiftung
Phosphormangel m im Körper phosphopenia
Phosphornekrose f phospho[r]necrosis; phossy jaw
Phosphorolyse f phosphorolysis
Phosphorverarmungssyndrom n phosphorus depletion syndrome
Phosphorvergiftung f phosphorism, poisoning by phosphorus
Phosphorverlustsyndrom n phosphorus depletion syndrome
Phosphorylase f phosphorylase *(Enzym)*
phosphorylieren to phosphorylate
Phosphorylierung f phosphorylation
~/oxydative oxidative phosphorylation
Phosphorylierungsenzym n phosphorylation enzyme
Phosvitin n phosvitin *(Phosphoprotein)*
Photalgie f photalgia, photodynia
Photästhesie f s. 1. Lichtempfindlichkeit; 2. Photophobie
Photisma n photism, visual image
Photo... s. a. Licht...
photoaktinisch photoactinic
Photobakterium n photobacterium
photobiotisch photobiotic
Photochemie f photochemistry
photochemisch photochemical
Photochemotherapie f photochemotherapy
photochromatisch photochromatic
photochromogen photochromogenic
Photochromogen n photochromogen *(pigmentbildendes Mykobakterium)*
Photodermatitis f photodermatitis, photodermatosis, solar dermatitis; photosensitization dermatitis
photodynamisch photodynamic
Photodynie f s. Photalgie
photoelektrisch photoelectric
photogen photogenic; phosgenic
Photogen n photogene
Photokatalyse f photocatalysis
Photokauterisation f photocauterization
Photokeratographie f photokeratography
Photokoagulation f photocoagulation
Photokoagulationstherapie f photocoagulation therapy
Photokonjunktivitis f photoconjunctivitis, actinic [kerato]conjunctivitis
Photokymograph m photokymograph
Photolumineszenz f photoluminescence
Photolyse f photolysis
Photomanie f photomania
Photometer n photometer
Photometrie f photometry
photometrisch photometric
photomotorisch photomotor
Photonystagmographie f photonystagmography
Photoparästhesie f photoparaesthesia, defective (perverted) retinal sensitivity
Photopathie f photopathy
photopathologisch photopathologic
photoperzeptiv photoperceptive
photophil photophilic, photophilous, seeking (loving) light
Photophilie f photophilia
photophob photophobic, fearing light
Photophobie f 1. photophobia *(krankhafte Angst vor Licht)*; 2. phot[augi]ophobia, photodysphoria, photaesthesia

Photophthalmia

Photophthalmia f **electrica** electric ophthalmia, flash blindness (ophthalmia); flasheye
Photophthalmie f photophthalmia
Photopsie f photopsia, subjective sensation of light flashes
Photopsin n photopsin, cone opsin *(Sehfarbstoff)*
photoptisch photoptic
Photoretinitis f photoretinitis, sun blindness
photorezeptiv photoreceptive
Photorezeptor m photoreceptor
Photosensibilisierung f photosensitization
Photosensibilität f photosensitivity
photosensitiv photosensitive, light-sensitive
Photosynthese f photosynthesis
photosynthetisch photosynthetic
phototaktisch phototactic
Phototaxis f phototaxis *(aktive Bewegungsänderung eines Organismus durch Lichtwirkung)*
phototherapeutisch phototherapeutic
Phototherapie f phototherapy, treatment with light [rays]
phototonisch phototonic
phototrop phototropic
phototroph phototrophic *(z. B. Bakterium)*
Phototropismus m phototropism
Photurie f photuria, passage of phosphorescent urine
Phren... *s. a.* Zwerchfell...
Phrenalgie f 1. phrenalgia, diaphragmalgia, pain in the diaphragm; 2. phrenalgia, psychalgia; melancholia
Phrenasthenie f phrenasthenia, mental deficiency, feebleness of mind
Phrenastheniker m phrenasthenic
phrenasthenisch phrenasthenic
Phrenatrophie f phrenatrophy, atrophy of the brain; idiocy
Phrenemphraxis f phrenemphraxis, crushing of a phrenic nerve, phrenic emphraxis, phrenicotripsy, phreniclasis
Phrenesie f phrenesis, frenzy; delirium; insanity
phrenetisch phrenetic
phrenikogastrisch phrenicogastric
phrenikokolisch phrenicocolic
phrenikokostal phrenicocostal
phrenikolienal phrenicolienal, phrenicosplenic
phrenikoösophageal phrenico-oesophageal
Phrenikotomie f phrenicotomy, division of the phrenic nerve
Phrenikus m phrenic nerve
Phrenikusdurchtrennung f [/operative] *s.* Phrenikotomie
Phrenikusex[h]airese f phrenicoexeresis *(vom Halse her)*
Phrenikusneuralgie f phrenic neuralgia
Phrenikusparalyse f phrenic nerve paralysis
Phrenikusquetschung f *s.* Phrenemphraxis
Phrenikusresektion f phren[i]ectomy, resection of the phrenic nerve
Phrenitis f 1. phrenitis, inflammation of the diaphragm; 2. acute delirium, frenzy; 3. *s.* Enzephalitis

Phrenodynie f *s.* Phrenalgie
phrenoglottisch phrenicoglottic
phrenohepatisch phrenicohepatic
Phrenokardie f phrenocardia
Phrenolepsie f phrenolepsia
Phrenologie f phrenology
Phrenoparalyse f phrenoparalysis, phrenoplegia, paralysis of the diaphragm
Phrenopathie f phrenopathy, mental disease (disorder)
Phrenoplegie f *s.* Phrenoparalyse
Phrenoptose f phrenoptosis
Phrenosin n phrenosin *(Zerebrosid)*
Phrenospasmus m 1. phrenospasm, spasm of the diaphragm; 2. *s.* Kardiospasmus
Phrynoderm n phrynoderma, toad skin, sharkskin *(bei Vitamin-A-Mangel)*
Phthalsäure f phthalic acid
Phthalylsulfathiazol n phthalylsulphathiazole *(Antibiotikum)*
Phthalylsulfazetamid n phthalylsulphacetamide *(Antibiotikum)*
Phthionsäure f phthioic acid *(durch Mycobacterium tuberculosis gebildet)*
Phthiriasis f phthiriasis, infestation with lice
Phthiriophobie f phthiriophobia *(krankhafte Angst vor Läusen)*
Phthirus m Phthir[i]us
~ **pubis** pubic (crab) louse, morpio
Phthise f *s.* Phthisis
Phthisiologie f phthisiology
Phthisiophobie f phthisiophobia *(krankhafte Angst vor Lungentuberkulose)*
Phthisiotherapie f phthisiotherapy
Phthisis f 1. phthisis, consumption; 2. *s.* Lungentuberkulose
~ **bulbi** ophthalmophthisis, ocular phthisis, shrinking of the eyeball
~ **corneae** cicatricial shrinking of the cornea
~ **florida** florid phthisis, galloping consumption
phthisisch phthisic[al], phthinoid, consumptive
pH-Wert m pH value
~ **des Bluts** blood pH [value]
pH-Wert-Verschiebung f pH shift
Phykomykose f phycomycosis
phykomykotisch phycomycotic
Phylaxis f phylaxis, protection against infection
Phylogenese f phylogeny, phylogenesis
phylogenetisch phylogen[et]ic, phyletic
~ **jung** phylogenetically recent
Phylum n phylum
Phyma n phyma *(Hautgeschwulst)*
phymatoid phymatoid
Phymatose f phymatosis, formation of phymas
Physalide f physaliphorous cell *(große blasige Zelle des Chordoms)*
Physiatrik f *s.* Physiotherapie
physikalisch-chemisch physicochemical
Physikum n preliminary [medical] examination, first medical examination
Physiognomie f 1. physiognomy, countenance, facies; 2. *s.* Physiognosis

Physiognosis f physiognosis *(Krankheitsdiagnostik aus dem Gesichtsausdruck)*
Physiologe m physiologist
Physiologie f physiology *(Lehre von den normalen Lebensvorgängen im Organismus)*
~/**pathologische** pathophysiology, pathologic physiology
~/**zerebrale** cerebrophysiology, cerebral physiology
physiologisch physiologic[al]
~/**nicht** unphysiologic[al]
physiologisch-anatomisch physiologico-anatomic
Physiotherapeut m physiotherapist, physical therapist
physiotherapeutisch physiotherapeutic
Physiotherapie f physical therapy, physiotherapy, physiatrics
physisch physical
Physohämatometra f physohaematometra *(Gas- und Blutansammlung in der Gebärmutter)*
Physohydrometra f physohydrometra *(Gas- und Flüssigkeitsansammlung in der Gebärmutter)*
Physometra f physometra *(Gasansammlung in der Gebärmutter)*
Physopyosalpinx f physopyosalpinx *(Gas- und Eiteransammlung im Eileiter)*
Physostigma n physostigma
Physostigmin n physostigmine, eserine *(Alkaloid)*
Phytinsäure f phytic acid
Phytobezoar m phytobezoar, food ball
phytogen phytogenous, phytogenic
Phytohämagglutinin n phytohaemagglutinin
Phytohämagglutininantigen n phytohaemagglutinin antigen
Phytohämagglutininstimulation f phytohaemagglutinin stimulation
phytophag phytophagous
Phytophotodermatitis f phytophotodermatitis
Phytopneumokoniose f phytopneumoconiosis
Phytopräzipitin n phytoprecipitin
Phytothrombokinase f phytothrombokinase *(Enzym)*
Phytotoxin n phytotoxin
phytotoxisch phytotoxic
Pia f **mater [encephali]** pia mater [of the brain]
~ **mater spinalis** pia mater of the spinal cord
Pia-Arachnoidea f pia-arachnoid, piarachnoid
Pian m s. Frambösie
Pica f pica, desire for strange food *(z. B. bei Schwangerschaft)*
Pica-Krankheit f pica *(krankhaftes Essen nichtphysiologischer Nahrung infolge Appetitstörung)*
Pickel pimple, pustule *(s. a. Pustel)*
pick[e]lig pimpled, pimply, pustular
Pickwick-Syndrom n Pickwickian (cardiopulmonary-obesity) syndrome
Picornavirus n picornavirus *(kleines RNS-haltiges Virus)*
Picrotoxin n picrotoxin

Pigmentschwund

Piedra f piedra, Beigel's disease *(tropisches Haarpilzleiden)*
Pigment n pigment, colouring matter ● **[schon] im Dunkeln** ~ **erzeugend** scotochromogenic
~/**körpereigenes** endogenous (autochthonous) pigment
~/**körperfremdes** exogenous (extraneous) pigment
Pigmentablagerung f pigmentation, pigment deposition
~/**abnorme** chromatism
~ **im Herzmuskel** cardiomelanosis
pigmentarm depigmented, achromic *(z. B. die Haut)*; hypochromic *(z. B. Zellen)*
Pigmentarmut f depigmentation, achromia, achromatosis *(z. B. der Haut)*; hypochromia, hypochromatism *(z. B. von Zellen)*
Pigmentation f pigmentation
pigmentbildend chromogenic
Pigmentbildung f pigmentogenesis, chromogenesis, production of pigments
~/**verstärkte** polychromia
Pigmenteinlagerung f pigmentary infiltration
~/**erhöhte** hyperpigmentation
~/**verminderte** hypopigmentation
Pigmententartung f pigmentary degeneration
pigmententhaltend chromatophorous
Pigmentepithel n pigmentary epithelium
Pigmentepithelmakrophage m pigment epithelial macrophage
Pigmentfehler m pigmentary defect
Pigmentfreßzelle f pigmentophage
Pigmentgeschwulst f pigmented tumour *(s. a. Melanom)*
pigmentiert pigmented, pigmentary; melanotic
~/**schwach** unpigmented; amelanotic
Pigmentierung f pigmentation
~/**abnorme** chromatosis, chromatism
~ **der Mundschleimhaut** melanoplakia
Pigmentinkontinenz f incontinentia pigmenti, Bloch-Sulzberger syndrome
Pigmentkatarakt f pigmented cataract, Vossius cataract (lenticular ring)
Pigmentkörnchen n pigment granule
Pigmentkörperübertragung f cytocrinia
pigmentlos non-pigmented, achromatous, leucodermic, leucodermatous
Pigmentlosigkeit f **der Haare** achromotrichia
~ **der Haut** achromodermia
Pigmentmangel m hypochromia, achromia, achromatosis *(z. B. bei Albinismus)*
~/**angeborener totaler** albinism *(mit Astigmatismus, Nystagmus und Photophobie)*
Pigmentnävus m pigmented mole (naevus)
Pigmentring m/**Kayser-Fleischerscher** Kayser-Fleischer ring *(Farbeinlagerung in der Hornhautperipherie bei Pseudosklerose)*
Pigmentsarkom n melanotic sarcoma
Pigmentsaum m pigment border
Pigmentschicht f pigment layer
Pigmentschwund m depigmentation

Pigmentspindel

Pigmentspindel f/**Krukenbergsche** Krukenberg's spindle *(dreieckförmige Pigmentablagerung an der Hornhauthinterfläche bei kurzsichtigem Auge)*
Pigmentstörung f pigment disorder, dyschromia; melanopathy
~ **der Nägel** chromonychia
pigmenttragend chromophoric, chrom[at]ophorous, pigment-bearing; pigment-carrying
Pigmentträger m chromophore
Pigmentveränderung f pigmentary change
Pigmentverarmung f depigmentation
~ **der Haut** skin depigmentation
Pigmentverlust m depigmentation
Pigmentzelle f pigment cell, chromatophore; naevus cell, melanocyte
Pigmentzellentumor m melanoma
Pigmentzellnävus m pigmented (naevus cell) naevus
Pigmentzirrhose f pigmentary cirrhosis
Pikazismus m s. Pica-Krankheit
Pikrogeusie f picrogeusia, pathologic bitter taste
Pili mpl:
~ **anulati** ringed hair
~ **incarnati** ingrown hairs
~ **moniliformes** monilethrix, moniliform (beaded) hair
~ **tactiles** tactile hairs
~ **torti** twisted hairs *(Haarabnormität)*
Pille f 1. pill, pilula, pilule *(feste Arzneiform)*; 2. oral contraceptive, the pill ● **die ~ nehmen** to be on the pill *(zur Schwangerschaftsverhütung)* ● **Pillen schlucken** to take pills
~/**große** bolus
~/**kleine** parvule
Pillendrehen n pill-rolling [movement], bread crumbing *(bei Parkinsonismus)*
Pillendrehertremor m pill-rolling (bread-crumbing) tremor
pillenförmig pill-shaped, pilular
Pillenschachtel f pill-box
Piloerektion f piloerection, horripilation, erection of the hairs
Pilokarpin n pilocarpine *(Alkaloid)*
Pilokarpin-Augentropfen mpl pilocarpine eye drops
pilomotorisch pilomotor
Pilonidalabszeß m pilonidal abscess
Pilonidalfistel f pilonidal fistula
Pilonidalkrankheit f pilonidal (jeep) disease
Pilonidalsinus m pilonidal (sacrococcygeal dimple) sinus
Pilonidalzyste f pilonidal (sacrococcygeal) cyst
pilozystisch pilocystic
Pilula f s. Pille
Pilus m s. Haar
Pilz m fungus, mycete ● **durch Pilze hervorgerufen** mycetogenic, mycetogenous
Pilzagar m/**Sabouraudscher** Sabouraud's agar *(Kulturmedium)*
Pilzaneurysma n mycotic aneurysm
pilzartig fungoid, fungal, mycetoid, mycoid

Pilzaussaat f fungal seeding
pilzbedingt mycetogen[et]ic, mycetogenous
Pilzbefall m fungal infection, mycosis *(s. a. unter Mykose)*
~ **der Hornhaut** keratomycosis
~ **der Lungen** pneumomycosis, pulmonary fungal infection
~ **der Nägel** onychomycosis
~ **der Nase** rhinomycosis
~ **des Auges** ophthalmomycosis, oculomycosis
~ **des Nagelfalzes** paronychomycosis
~ **des Ohres** otomycosis
~/**sekundärer** mycotization, secondary mycosis
pilzbefallen infested by a fungus
Pilzblutvergiftung f fungaemia
Pilzerkrankung f fungal (mycotic) disease, mycosis
Pilzfaden m hypha, mycelial thread
Pilzflechte f [epi]dermatomycosis
pilzförmig fungiform
Pilzgeflecht n mycelium
Pilzgift n mycotoxin
pilzhemmend fungistatic, mycostatic
Pilzhemmung f fungistasis, mycostasis
Pilzinfektion f fungal (mycotic) infection, mycosis
Pilzkeratitis f mycotic keratitis
Pilzknäuel n fungus ball
Pilzkugel f fungus ball
Pilzkunde f mycology
Pilzmittel n fungicide, antifungal [agent], antimycotic [agent]
Pilzsepsis f fungaemia
Pilzspore f fungal spore
Pilzsporenkrankheit f sporomycosis
Pilzstamm m fungal strain
pilztötend fungicidal; antimycotic, antifungal
Pilzvergiftung f mycotoxicosis, mycetism, mushroom poisoning
Pilzverstreuung f fungal seeding
pilzwachstumshemmend fungistatic, mycostatic
Pilzwachstumshemmung f fungistasis, mycostasis
Pilzzellwand f fungal cell wall
Pimelopterygium n pimelopterygium
pineal pineal
Pinealblastom n pinealblastoma *(bösartige Epiphysengeschwulst)*
Pinealektomie f pinealectomy, excision of the pineal body
Pinealom n pinealoma, pinealcytoma, pineal seminoma (tumour, germinoma)
Pinealozytom n s. Pinealom
Pinguecula f pinguecula, palpebral blotch
pinienzapfenförmig piniform
Pinna f s. Ohrmuschel
Pinosom n pinosome
Pinozyt m pinocyte
Pinozytose f pinocytosis *(Stoffaufnahmemodus in die Zelle)*
Pinozytosevakuole f pinosome
pinozytotisch pinocytotic

Pinselarterie f s. Penicillus
Pinselschimmel n penicillium
Pinta f pinta, pintoid yaws, piquite, quitiqua, spotted sickness, carate, azul *(Hautkrankheit durch Treponema carateum)*
Pintafleck m s. Pintid
Pintakranker m pintillo
Pintid n pintid *(Hauteruption im Sekundärstadium)*
Pinzette f forceps, pincers
~/**anatomische** dissecting (dressing) forceps
~/**chirurgische** surgical (tissue) forceps, fixation (toothed) forceps
Piperazin n piperazine *(Antiwurmmittel)*
Pipette f pipet[te], dropper
pipettieren to pipet[te]
Piptonychie f piptonychia, shedding of the nails
piriform piriform, pyriform, pear-shaped
Piroplasmose f piroplasmosis, babesiasis, babesiosis *(hämolytische Infektionskrankheit)*
pisiform pisiform, pea-shaped
Pistolenschußphänomen n pistol-shot phenomenon (sound) *(bei Aorteninsuffizienz)*
Pistolenschußwunde f pistol-shot wound
Pithiatismus m pithiatism
Pituitarismus m pituitarism, disorder of pituitary function
Pituizyt m pituicyte *(Gliazellform im Hypophysenhinterlappen)*
Pituizytom n pituicytoma
Pityriasis f pityriasis, branny desquamation of the skin
~ **lichenoides** maculopapular erythroderma
~ **lichenoides chronica** chronic lichenoid pityriasis *(chronische entzündliche Hautkrankheit mit roten Knötchen und Flecken)*
~ **nigra** melasma
~ **rubra** exfoliative dermatitis
~ **rubra pilaris** pityriasis rubra pilaris, Devergie's disease
~ **versicolor** chromophytosis, pityriasis versicolor
Pityriasis-Kryptokokke f Pityrosporum ovale
Pityrosporon n **ovale** Pityrosporum ovale
PKG s. Phonokardiogramm
Placenta f placenta, after-birth, secundines ● **durch die** ~ transplacental ● **neben der** ~ paraplacental ● **ohne** ~ aplacental ● **unter der** ~ subplacental
~ **accessoria** accessory placenta
~ **bipartita** bipartite (bilobed, duplex) placenta
~ **circumvallata** circumvallate placenta
~ **cirsoidea** cirsoid placenta
~ **discoidea** discoid placenta, discoplacenta
~ **duplex** s. ~ bipartita
~ **extrachorialis** extrachorial placenta
~ **fenestrata** fenestrated placenta
~ **foetalis** foetal placenta
~ **incarcerata** incarcerated placenta
~ **maternalis** maternal (uterine) placenta
~ **membranacea** membranous placenta
~ **multilobulata** multilobed (multipartite) placenta

~ **nappiformis** s. ~ circumvallata
~ **praevia** placenta praevia; placental presentation
~ **praevia centralis** central placenta praevia
~ **praevia lateralis** lateral placenta praevia
~ **praevia marginalis** marginal placenta praevia
~ **praevia partialis** partial placenta praevia
~ **praevia totalis** total (complete) placenta praevia
~ **reniformis** reniform placenta
~ **spuria** spurious placenta
~ **succenturiata** succenturiate placenta
~ **tripartita** tripartite placenta
~ **uterina** s. ~ maternalis
Placenta... s. Plazenta...
Plage f plague, infestation
plagiozephal plagiocephalic, plagiocephalous
Plagiozephalie f plagiocephalia, plagiocephalism
Plagiozephalus m plagiocephalus, wry-head
Plakode f placode
Plakodenstiel m placodal (auditory) stalk *(Embryologie)*
plan planar, plane
Planigramm n planigram, tomogram
Planigraphie f planigraphy, planography, tomography, stratigraphy
plankonkav planoconcave *(z. B. eine Linse)*
plankonvex planoconvex *(z. B. eine Linse)*
Planta f planta, sole of the foot
Plantalgie f plantalgia
plantar plantar
Plantaraponeurose f plantar aponeurosis (fascia)
Plantarbeugung f plantar flexion
Plantarfaszie f s. Plantaraponeurose
Plantarfaszienentzündung f plantar fascitis
Plantarfibromatose f plantar fibromatosis
plantarflektieren to plantarflex
Plantarflexion f plantar flexion
Plantarhöcker m plantar tubercle
Plantarhyperkeratose f plantar hyperkeratosis
Plantarreflex m plantar reflex
Plantarreflexzentrum n plantar reflex centre
Planum n planum, plane *(des kindlichen Schädels bei der Geburt)*
~ **nuchale** nuchal plane
~ **occipitale** occipital plane
~ **orbitale** orbital plane
~ **popliteum** popliteal plane
~ **sternale** sternal plane
~ **temporale** temporal plane
Plaque m(f) 1. plaque, patch; 2. [dental] plaque
~/**arteriosklerotischer** atherosclerotic plaque
~/**atheromatöser** atheromatous plaque
plaquebildend plaque-forming
Plaques mpl/**Peyersche** Peyer's glands (patches), aggregate follicles *(im unteren Dünndarm)*
Plasma n plasm[a], blood plasma
~/**kryopräzipitiertes** cryoprecipitated plasma
~/**lyophilisiertes** lyophilized plasma
Plasma... s. a. Blutplasma...
Plasmaablösung f plasmolysis *(von der Zellwand infolge Wasserentzugs)*

Plasmaaktivierung

Plasmaaktivierung *f* plasma activation
Plasmaakzeleratorglobulin *n* plasma accelerator globulin
Plasmaalbuminmangel *m* analbuminaemia
Plasmaausschwitzung *f* plasmex[h]idrosis
Plasmaaußenschicht *f* ectoplasm
Plasmabikarbonat *n* plasma bicarbonate
Plasmacholesteringehalt *m* plasma cholesterol content (value)
Plasmaeisen *n* plasma iron
Plasmaersatz *m* 1. plasma replacement; 2. *s.* Plasmaersatzstoff
~ **mit niedrigem Molekulargewicht** low-molecular-weight plasma substitution
Plasmaersatzstoff *m* plasma substitute, [plasma] volume expander
Plasmaexpander *m s.* Plasmaersatzstoff
Plasmafluß *m*/**renaler** renal plasma flow
Plasmafülle *f* polyplasmia
Plasmagabe *f* plasma infusion
Plasmagammaglobulin *n* plasma gamma globulin
Plasmagel *n* plasmagel
Plasmahaut *f s.* Plasmamembran
Plasmahäutchen *n* pellicle *(der Protozoen)*
Plasmainnenschicht *f* endoplasm
Plasmakaliumspiegel *m* plasma potassium level
Plasmakonserve *f* dried human plasma
Plasmalemm *n s.* Plasmamembran
Plasmamembran *f* plasma membrane, plasmalemma
Plasmapherese *f* plasmapheresis, plasmaphoresis, plasma filtration treatment
Plasmaprotein *n* plasma protein
Plasmaproteinaustritt *m* plasma-protein escape *(durch Kapillarwände)*
Plasmaproteinfraktion *f* plasma-protein fraction
Plasmaproteinspiegel *m* plasma-protein level
Plasmaproteinstörung *f* dysproteinaemia
Plasmaprothrombinaktivität *f* plasma prothrombic activity
Plasmareninaktivität *f* plasma renin activity
Plasmasol *n* plasmasol
Plasmastrahlung *f* astrosphere, aster *(bei Mitose)*
Plasmathromboplastin *n* plasma thromboplastin
Plasma-Thromboplastin-Antecedent *n s.* Blutgerinnungsfaktor XI
Plasma-Thromboplastin-Komponente *f s.* Blutgerinnungsfaktor IX
plasmatisch plasm[at]ic
Plasmatogamie *f* plasmatogamy
Plasmatorrhexis *f* plasmatorrhexis
Plasmatransfusion *f* plasma transfusion
Plasma- und Serumeiweißerhöhung *f* hyperproteinaemia
Plasma- und Serumeiweißverminderung *f* hypoproteinaemia
Plasmavolumen *n* plasma volume
Plasmavolumenexpander *m* plasma volume expander
Plasmavolumenschrumpfung *f* plasma volume shrinkage

Plasmazelle *f* plasma cell, plasmacyte, plasmocyte
plasmazellenartig plasmacytoid
Plasmazellendyskrasie *f* plasmatic (plasma cell) dyscrasia
plasmazellenförmig plasmacytoid
Plasmazellengeschwulst *f* plasma-cell tumour; plasmoma
Plasmazellengranulom *n* plasma cell granuloma
Plasmazelleninfiltration *f* plasma cell infiltration
Plasmazellenleukämie *f* plasmacytic (plasma cell) leukaemia
Plasmazellenmastitis *f* plasma cell mastitis
Plasmazellenmyelom *n* plasmacytic (plasma cell) myeloma
Plasmazellenneoplasie *f* plasma cell neoplasia
Plasmazellenproliferat *n* plasma cell proliferate
Plasmazellenreihe *f* plasmacytic series
Plasmazellensarkom *n* plasmacytic sarcoma
Plasmazellenvermehrung *f* **im Blut** plasmacytosis
Plasmazerfall *m* plasmolysis, endolysis
Plasmazersetzung *f* plasmoschisis
Plasmin *n* plasmin, fibrinolysin
~/**inaktives** *s.* Plasminogen
Plasmininhibitor *m* plasmin inhibitor
Plasminogen *n* plasminogen, profibrinolysin *(Plasminvorstufe)*
Plasminogenaktivator *m* plasminogen activator
Plasminogenmangel *m* plasminogenopenia
Plasminogenproaktivator *m* plasminogen proactivator
Plasmodesmen *npl* plasmodesmata *(feinste fädige Plasmaverbindungen zwischen den Zellen)*
Plasmodiblast *m* plasmodi[tropho]blast
plasmodientötend plasmodicidal, antiplasmodial
plasmodisch plasmodial, plasmodic
Plasmodium *n* Plasmodium *(Blutparasit)*
~ **falciparum** Plasmodium falciparum, Oscillaria malariae, aestivo-autumnal parasite *(Erreger der Malaria falciparum)*
~ **immaculatum** *s.* ~ falciparum
~ **malariae** Plasmodium malariae, quartan parasite *(Erreger der Malaria quartana)*
~ **ovale** Plasmodium ovale *(Erreger der Malaria ovale)*
~ **vivax** Plasmodium vivax, tertian parasite *(Erreger der Malaria tertiana)*
Plasmodium-ovale-Infektion *f* ovale infection
Plasmodium-vivax-Infektion *f* vivax infection
plasmodizid plasmodicidal, antiplasmodial
Plasmogamie *f* plasmogamy, plastogamy, cytoplasmic fusion of cells
Plasmolyse *f* plasmolysis *(von der Zellwand infolge Wasserentzugs)* ● **der ~ unterliegen** to plasmolyze
plasmolytisch plasmolytic
Plasmom *n* plasmoma, malignant plasmacytoma
Plasmorrhexis *f* plasmorrhexis
Plasmoschise *f* plasmoschisis, protoplasmatic fragmentation (cleavage)

Plasmosom n 1. plasmosome, true nucleolus; 2. cytoplasmic granule
Plasmotropismus m plasmotropism
Plasmozyt m s. Plasmazelle
Plasmozytom n plasmacytoma, plasmocytoma
~/**malignes** malignant plasmacytoma, plasmacytic myeloma (sarcoma), Kahler's disease
Plasmozytomzelle f myeloma cell
Plasmozytose f plasmacytosis
Plastein n plastein *(proteinähnliche Substanz)*
Plastik f plastic operation; graft[ing] *(z. B. der Haut)*; culdoplasty *(der Excavatio rectouterina)*
plastisch plastic
Plastizität f plasticity
Plateaupuls m plateau pulse
Plathelminthe f s. Plattwurm
Platinöse f platinum (bacteriological) loop *(zur Bakterienkulturverimpfung)*
Platinspatel m platinum spatula
Platonychie f platonychia, dystrophy of the nails
Plätschergeräusch n splashing (plashing) sound; succussion (shaking) sound
platt flat; plane; flattened
Plättchen n lamella; scale; platelet
Plättchenthrombus m platelet thrombus
Platte f plate; lamina; scale
~ **des Flügelfortsatzes/seitliche** lateral pterygoid lamina (plate)
Platten fpl/**Peyersche** s. Plaques/Peyersche
Plattenepithel n squamous epithelium
~/**einfaches (einschichtiges)** pavement (tabular) epithelium, tessellated (simple squamous) epithelium
Plattenepithelkarzinom n squamous[-cell] carcinoma, epidermoid cancer
Plattenepithelzelle f squamous cell
Plattenepithelzellenmetaplasie f squamous[-cell] metaplasia
Plattenknochen m tabular bone
Plattenkultur f plate culture, platiculture
Plattenzellepitheliom n squamous[-cell] epithelioma, epidermoid cancer
Plattfuß m flatfoot, splayfoot, [tali]pes planus
plattfüßig flatfooted, plantigrade
Plattfüßigkeit f platypodia
plattköpfig s. platyzephal
plattnasig broad-nosed
Plattsehnenmuskel m semimembranosus [muscle]
Plattwurm m fluke[-worm], flatworm, platyhelminth
Platybasie f platybasia, atlas assimilation *(bei Pagetscher Krankheit)*
Platyknemie f platycnemia, platycnemism *(der Tibia)*
platyknemisch platycnemic
Platymorphie f platymorphia *(in der Sehachse verkürztes Auge mit Weitsichtigkeit)*
platyop platyopic
Platyoper m platyope
Platyopia f platyopia, broadness of the face
Platypodie f platypodia, flatness of the foot

Platysma f platysma [myoides]
platysmaartig platysma-like
Platysmaphänomen n platysmal phenomenon
Platyspondylie f platyspondylia, platyspondylisis
Platystenzephalie f platystencephalia, platystenocephalism
platyzephal platycephalic, chamaecephalic, chamaecephalous
Platyzephalie f platycephalia, chamaecephalia
Platyzephalus m platycephalus, chamaecephalus, homalocephalus
Platzangst f agoraphobia, kenophobia
Platzbauch m burst abdomen
Plazebo n placebo, dummy *(Scheinmedikament)*
Plazenta f placenta, after-birth, secundines *(Zusammensetzungen s. unter Placenta)*
plazentaähnlich placentoid
Plazentaantigen n placenta antigen
Plazentaapoplexie f placental apoplexy
Plazentaatmung f placental respiration
Plazentaaufbau m placental structure
Plazentaausräumung f placenta removal
~/**manuelle** manual placenta removal
Plazentabarriere f placental barrier, placental membrane
Plazentabehandlung f placentotherapy
Plazentabildung f placentation ● **vor der** ~ preplacental
Plazentablut n placental blood
Plazentablutgefäß n placental blood vessel
Plazentaentzündung f s. Plazentitis
Plazentaerkrankung f placentopathy, disease of the placenta
plazentaförmig placentoid
Plazentageräusch n placental murmur (souffle, bruit)
Plazentageschwulst f placentoma
Plazentagewicht n placental weight
Plazentahormon n placental hormone
Plazentahypoplasie f placental hypoplasia
Plazentainfarkt m placental (infarction) apoplexy
Plazentainsuffizienz f placental insufficiency
Plazentakreislauf m placental circulation
plazental placental, placentar, mazic
Plazentalaktogen n placental lactogen
~/**humanes** human placenta lactogen
Plazentalakune f placental blood space
Plazentaläppchen n placental lobe, cotyledon
Plazentalöffel m placenta scoop
Plazentalokalisation f placental localization
plazentalos aplacental
Plazentalösung f placenta separation, detachment (abruption) of the placenta, mazolysis
~/**vorzeitige** premature detachment (abruption) of the placenta
Plazentamikrosomenfraktion f placental microsomal fraction
Plazentaparasit m placental parasite
Plazentapassage f placental transmission (transfer) *(z. B. von Medikamenten)*
Plazentaperfusion f placenta perfusion
Plazentaperiode f placental stage

Plazentapermeabilität

Plazentapermeabilität f placental permeability
plazentar placentar, placental, mazic
Plazentarest m **nach der Geburt** placental polyp
Plazentaretention f retained placenta
Plazentaröntgen[kontrast]darstellung f placentography
Plazentarpolyp m placental polyp
Plazentarstadium n placental stage
Plazentaschädigung f placenta damage
Plazentaschranke f placental barrier (membrane)
Plazentaseparation f placenta separation
Plazentasitz m placental site
Plazentastruktur f placental structure
Plazentatherapie f placentotherapy
Plazentathrombose f placental thrombosis
Plazentatrophoblast m [placental] trophoblast, trophoderm, ectoplacenta
Plazentaübertritt m placental transmission (transfer) *(z. B. von Medikamenten)*
Plazentavorlagerung f placenta praevia; placental presentation *(vor den Muttermund)*
Plazentazellgift n syncytiotoxin
Plazentazotte f placental villus
Plazentitis f placentitis, inflammation of the placenta, chorionitis
Plazentographie f placentography
Plazentom n placentoma
Plazentopathie f placentopathy
Plazentose f placentosis
Plazidoscheibe f Placido's disk, keratoscope
plazieren/eine Naht to place a suture
pleiochrom[atisch] pleochromatic, pleochroic
pleiotrop pleiotropic
Pleiotropie f, **Pleiotropismus** m pleiotropism *(Zuordnung vieler Merkmale zu einem Gen)*
Pleochroismus m pleochroism *(bei wechselnder Betrachtungsrichtung)*
Pleochromozytom n pleochromocytoma
Pleochromozytose f pleochromocytosis
Pleokaryozyt m pleokaryocyte
pleomorph pleomorphic, pleomorphous
Pleomorphismus m pleomorphism
Pleonasmus m pleonasm
Pleonosteosis f pleonosteosis
Pleoptik f pleoptics *(Therapieverfahren der Schielamblyopie)*
pleoptisch pleoptic
Pleozytose f pleocytosis *(Zellvermehrung in der Gehirn- und Rückenmarkflüssigkeit)*
~/lymphozytäre lymphocytic pleocytosis
Plesiognathus m plesiognathus
Plesiomorphismus m plesiomorphism
Plesiopie f plesiopia *(Kurzsichtigkeit infolge dauernder Akkommodation)*
Plessimeter n plessimeter, pleximeter
Plessimeterfinger m plessimeter [finger], pleximeter
Plessimeterperkussion f pleximeter (pleximetric) percussion, indirect (mediate) percussion
plessimetrisch pleximetric
Plethora f plethora

~/allgemeine panhyperaemia
plethorisch plethoric
Plethysmogramm n plethysmogram
Plethysmograph m plethysmograph
Plethysmographie f plethysmography *(Messung von Volumenänderungen in Extremitäten)*
plethysmographisch plethysmographic
Pleura f pleura ● **durch die** ~ transpleural ● **unter der** ~ subpleural
~ costalis costal pleura
~ diaphragmatica diaphragmatic pleura
~ mediastinalis mediastinal pleura
~ parietalis parietal pleura
~ pericardiaca pericardial pleura
~ pulmonalis pulmonary pleura
~ visceralis visceral pleura
Pleura... s. a. Brustfell...
Pleuraadhäsion f pleural adhesion
Pleuraanheftung f[/operative] pleurodesis
Pleuraapophyse f pleurapophysis
Pleuradrainage f pleural drainage
Pleuraeinschnitt m s. Pleurotomie
Pleuraemphysem n pleural emphysema
Pleuraempyem n pleural (thoracic) empyema; pyothorax
Pleuraentzündung f s. Pleuritis
Pleuraerguß m [intra]pleural effusion; pleurorrhoea
Pleuraergußbegrenzungslinie f Damoiseau's curve
Pleuraexstirpation f s. Pleurektomie
Pleurafixierung f pleurodesis
Pleuraflüssigkeit f pleural fluid
Pleurahöhle f pleural cavity, pleural sac (space)
Pleurahöhleneröffnung f s. Pleurotomie
Pleurahöhlenröntgendarstellung f pleurography
Pleurakuppel f pleural cupula (dome), cupula of the pleura; cervical pleura
Pleuralgie f pleuralgia, pleurodynia, pain in the pleura
Pleuramesotheliom n mesothelioma of the pleura, pleuroma
Pleurapunktion f pleuracentesis, pleurocentesis, paracentesis of the chest, thora[co]centesis
Pleurarasseln n pleural rale
Pleuraraum m s. Pleurahöhle
Pleurareibegeräusch n pleural friction rub (sound)
Pleuraschock m pleural shock
Pleuraschwarte f pleural peel (callosity, thickening); thickened pleura
Pleuraschweifzeichen n pleural tail sign
Pleurasegment n pleuratome
Pleuraspalt m pleural cavity (space)
Pleuraspiegelung f pleuroscopy
Pleuraspülung f pleuroclysis, pleural lavage
Pleurastein m pleurolith
Pleuraumschlagfalte f pleural reflection
Pleuraverwachsung f pleural adhesion; fibrothorax
Pleuravorfall m pleurocele
Pleurazotte f pleural villus

Pleurektomie f pleurectomy, excision of the pleura; pulmonary decortication
Pleuritis f pleuritis, pleurisy, inflammation of the pleura *(s. a. unter Brustfellentzündung)*
~ **adhaesiva** adhesive pleurisy
~ **diaphragmatica** diaphragmatic pleurisy
~ **exsudativa** exudative pleurisy
~ **fibrinosa** fibrinous pleurisy
~/**interlobäre** interlobitis
~ **mediastinalis** mediastinal pleurisy
~ **proliferativa** proliferating (plastic) pleurisy
~ **pulsans** pulsating pleurisy
~ **serofibrinosa** serofibrinous pleurisy
~ **serosa** serous pleurisy
~ **und Bronchitis** f pleurobronchitis
pleuritisch pleuritic
pleuritiserzeugend pleuritogenous
Pleuritisschmerz m pleuritic pain
Pleurobronchitis f pleurobronchitis
Pleurocholezystitis f pleurocholecystitis
Pleurodese f pleurodesis
Pleurodynia f **epidemica** epidemic pleurodynia, devil's grip, Bornholm disease, epidemic myalgia (myositis)
pleurogen pleurogenic, pleurogenous
Pleurographie f pleurography
Pleurohepatitis f pleurohepatitis
Pleuroklyse f pleuroclysis, pleural lavage
pleurokutan pleurocutaneous
Pleurolith m pleurolith
Pleurolyse f pleurolysis, pneumonolysis
Pleurom n pleuroma, mesothelioma of the pleura
Pleuroparietopexie f pleuroparietopexy
pleuroperikardial pleuropericardial, pericardiopleural
Pleuroperikardialgang m pleuropericardial canal (duct) *(Embryologie)*
Pleuroperikardialmembran f pleuropericardial membrane
Pleuroperikarditis f pleuropericarditis *(Entzündung von Brustfell und äußerem Herzbeutelblatt)*
Pleuroperitonealgang m pleuroperitoneal duct
Pleuroperitonealhiatus m pleuroperitoneal hiatus
Pleuroperitonealhöhle f pleuroperitoneal cavity
Pleuroperitonealkanal m pleuroperitoneal duct
Pleuroperitonealmembran f pleuroperitoneal membrane
Pleuropneumolyse f pleuropneumonolysis
Pleuro-pneumonia-like-organisms pleuropneumonia-like organisms *(zur Gattung der Mykoplasmen gehörende Mikroorganismen)*
Pleuropneumonie f pleuropneumonia, pleuritic pneumonia
pleuropneumonieartig pleuropneumonia-like
Pleuropneumonolyse f pleuropneumonolysis
pleuropulmonal pleuropulmonary
Pleuroskopie f pleuroscopy
Pleurosomatoschisis f pleurosomatoschisis, lateral abdominal fissure
Pleurospasmus m pleurospasm

Pleurothotonus m pleurothotonus, pleurothotonos, tetanic bending of the body
Pleurotomie f pleurotomy, incision of the pleura
Pleurotyphus m pleurotyphoid
pleuroviszeral pleurovisceral
Pleurozele f pleurocele
Pleurozentese f s. Pleurapunktion
Plexektomie f plexectomy, excision of a plexus
Plexus m plexus, network
~ **anococcygeus** anococcygeal plexus
~ **aorticus** aortic plexus
~ **aorticus abdominalis** plexus of the abdominal aorta
~ **aorticus thoracicus** plexus of the thoracic aorta
~/**Auerbachscher s.** ~ **myentericus**
~ **axillaris** axillary plexus
~ **basilaris** basilar plexus *(Venengeflecht im Hirnbasisbereich)*
~/**Batsonscher** Batson's plexus *(Venensystem der Wirbelsäule)*
~ **brachialis** brachial plexus
~ **cardiacus** cardiac plexus
~ **caroticus** carotid plexus
~ **caroticus communis** common carotid plexus
~ **caroticus externus** external carotid plexus
~ **caroticus internus** internal carotid plexus
~ **cavernosi concharum** cavernous plexus of the nasal conchae
~ **cavernosus clitoridis** cavernous plexus of the clitoris *(Nervengeflecht)*
~ **cavernosus penis** cavernous plexus of the penis *(Nervengeflecht)*
~ **cervicalis** cervical plexus
~ **chorioideus** choroid plexus [of the brain]
~ **chorioideus ventriculi lateralis** choroid plexus of the lateral ventricle, paraplexus
~ **chorioideus ventriculi quarti** choroid plexus of the fourth ventricle, metaplexus
~ **chorioideus ventriculi tertii** choroid plexus of the third ventricle
~ **coccygeus** coccygeal plexus
~ **coeliacus** coeliac (solar, epigastric) plexus; abdominal brain
~ **coronarius** coronary plexus
~ **coronarius cordis anterior** anterior coronary plexus of the heart
~ **coronarius cordis posterior** posterior coronary plexus of the heart
~ **deferentialis** deferential plexus
~ **dentalis inferior (mandibularis)** inferior dental plexus
~ **dentalis maxillaris (superior)** superior dental plexus
~ **diaphragmatis** diaphragmatic plexus
~ **entericus** enteric plexus
~ **facialis** facial plexus
~ **femoralis** femoral (crural) plexus
~ **gastricus** gastric plexus
~ **gastricus anterior** anterior gastric plexus
~ **gastricus inferior** inferior gastric plexus
~ **gastricus posterior** posterior gastric plexus

Plexus

- ~ **gastricus superior** superior gastric plexus
- ~ **gastroduodenalis** gastroduodenal plexus
- ~ **haemorrhoidalis** haemorrhoidal plexus
- ~ **hepaticus** hepatic plexus
- ~ **hypogastricus** hypogastric plexus
- ~ **hypogastricus inferior** pelvic (inferior hypogastric) plexus
- ~ **hypogastricus praesacralis (superior)** superior hypogastric plexus, presacral nerve
- ~ **iliacus** iliac plexus
- ~/Jacobsonscher s. ~ tympanicus
- ~ **lienalis** splenic plexus
- ~ **lingualis** lingual plexus
- ~ **lumbalis** lumbar plexus
- ~ **lumbosacralis** lumbosacral plexus
- ~ **maxillaris** maxillary plexus
- ~ **maxillaris externus** external maxillary plexus
- ~ **maxillaris internus** internal maxillary plexus
- ~/Meißnerscher s. ~ submucosus
- ~ **mesentericus** mesenteric plexus
- ~ **mesentericus inferior** inferior mesenteric plexus
- ~ **mesentericus superior** superior mesenteric plexus
- ~ **myentericus [gastric]** myenteric plexus, Auerbach's plexus *(für die Darmbewegungen verantwortliches Nervengeflecht)*
- ~ **nervosus** neuroplexus
- ~ **occipitalis** occipital plexus
- ~ **oesophageus** oesophageal plexus
- ~ **ophthalmicus** ophthalmic plexus
- ~ **ovaricus** ovarian plexus
- ~ **pampiniformis** pampiniform plexus *(weinrankenförmiges Venengeflecht im Samenstrang)*
- ~ **pancreaticoduodenalis** pancreaticoduodenal plexus
- ~ **parotideus** parotid plexus
- ~ **pelvinus** pelvic (inferior hypogastric) plexus
- ~ **perivascularis** perivascular plexus
- ~ **pharyngeus** pharyngeal plexus
- ~ **pharyngeus venosus** pharyngeal [venous] plexus
- ~ **phrenicus** phrenic plexus
- ~ **popliteus** popliteal plexus
- ~ **praevertebralis** prevertebral plexus
- ~ **prostaticus** prostatic plexus
- ~ **pterygoideus** pterygoid [venous] plexus
- ~ **pudendus** pudendal plexus *(Nervengeflecht)*
- ~ **pulmonalis** pulmonary plexus
- ~ **pulmonalis anterior** anterior pulmonary plexus
- ~ **pulmonalis posterior** posterior pulmonary plexus
- ~ **rectalis** rectal plexus
- ~ **rectalis inferior** inferior rectal (haemorrhoidal) plexus
- ~ **rectalis superior** superior rectal (haemorrhoidal) plexus
- ~ **renalis** renal plexus
- ~ **sacralis** sacral plexus
- ~ **solaris** s. ~ coeliacus
- ~ **spermaticus** s. ~ testicularis
- ~ **submucosus** submucous (Meissner's) plexus
- ~ **suprarenalis** suprarenal plexus
- ~ **testicularis** testicular (spermatic) plexus
- ~ **thyreoideus** thyroid plexus
- ~ **thyreoideus impar** thyroid impar plexus
- ~ **tympanicus** tympanic (Jacobson's) plexus
- ~ **uterinus** uterine plexus
- ~ **uterovaginalis** uterovaginal plexus
- ~ **vaginalis** vaginal plexus
- ~ **venosus** venous plexus
- ~ **venosus prostaticus** prostatic (pudendal) plexus
- ~ **venosus rectalis** rectal (haemorrhoidal) plexus
- ~ **venosus sacralis** anterior sacral plexus
- ~ **venosus uterinus** uterine [venous] plexus
- ~ **venosus uterovaginalis** uterovaginal plexus
- ~ **venosus vaginalis** vaginal plexus
- ~ **venosus vesicalis** vesical plexus
- ~ **vesicalis** vesical plexus

plexusartig plexiform
Plexusentfernung *f*[/operative] *s.* Plexektomie
plexusförmig plexiform
Plexuspapillom *n* chorio[n]epithelioma, chorioma

Plica *f* plica, fold
- ~ **alaris** alar plica
- ~ **aryepiglottica** aryepiglottic fold
- ~ **axillaris** axillary plica
- ~ **axillaris anterior** anterior axillary fold
- ~ **axillaris posterior** posterior axillary fold
- ~ **caecalis** caecal plica
- ~ **capsularis** capsular fold
- ~ **ciliaris** ciliary plica
- ~ **circularis** circular fold
- ~ **ductus nasolacrimalis** *s.* ~ lacrimalis
- ~ **duodenalis inferior** inferior duodenal fold, duodenomesocolic fold
- ~ **duodenalis superior** duodenojejunal plica
- ~ **duodenomesocolica** duodenomesocolic fold
- ~ **epigastrica** epigastric fold
- ~ **gastropancreatica** gastropancreatic plica
- ~ **glossoepiglottica** glossoepiglottic fold
- ~ **glossoepiglottica lateralis** lateral glossoepiglottic fold
- ~ **glossoepiglottica mediana** median glossoepiglottic fold, medial glossoepiglottic fold *(Schleimhautfalte zwischen Zungengrund und Kehldeckel)*
- ~ **ileocaecalis** ileocaecal fold
- ~ **inguinalis** inguinal fold
- ~ **interureterica** interureteric ridge, bladder bar, bar of the bladder
- ~ **lacrimalis** lacrimal fold, Hasner's valve *(Schleimhautfalte an der Tränengangsmündung)*
- ~ **lata uteri** broad ligament of the uterus
- ~ **longitudinalis duodeni** longitudinal duodenal plica
- ~ **mallearis anterior** anterior malleolar (tympanic) fold
- ~ **mallearis posterior** posterior malleolar fold
- ~ **mongolica** Mongolian fold
- ~ **palatopharyngea** palatopharyngeal fold

Pneumokokke

~ **polonica** trichoma
~ **rectouterina** rectouterine plica, rectouterine fold [of Douglas]
~ **rectovesicalis** rectovesical plica, rectovesical fold [of Douglas]
~ **sacrogenitalis** sacrogenital fold
~ **salpingopalatina** salpingopalatine fold
~ **salpingopharyngea** salpingopharyngeal fold
~ **semilunaris [coli]** semilunar plica, haustral fold
~ **semilunaris conjunctivae** semilunar fold
~ **spiralis** spiral valve [of Heister], Heister's valve *(Gallenblasenschleimhautfalte)*
~ **sublingualis** sublingual plica
~ **suspensoria ovarii** suspensory ligament of the ovary
~ **synovialis** synovial plica
~ **synovialis [infra]patellaris** [infra]patellar synovial fold
~ **triangularis** triangular fold
~ **umbilicalis lateralis** lateral umbilical fold, hypogastric plica
~ **umbilicalis medialis** middle umbilical fold, medial umbilical plica
~ **umbilicalis mediana** median umbilical fold
~ **ventricularis** s. ~ vestibularis
~ **vesicalis transversa** transverse vesical plica
~ **vestibularis** vestibular fold, false vocal cord
~ **vocalis** vocal cord (fold)
Plicae *fpl* plicae, folds
~ **circulares** Kerckring's folds, valves of Kerckring *(Querfalten im Dünndarm)*
~ **palmatae** palmate folds *(Schleimhautfalten im Gebärmutterhalskanal)*
~ **transversales recti** transverse (horizontal) folds of the rectum, transverse rectal folds (plicae), Houston's valves
Plikotomie *f* plicotomy
Plombe *f* plomb, plug; stopping, filling *(Stomatologie)*
Plombierung *f* plombage, plugging; stopping, filling, odontoplerosis
~/extrapleurale plombage thoracoplasty
Plummer-Vinson-Syndrom *n* Plummer-Vinson syndrome, sideropenic dysphagia
plurifokal plurifocal
pluriglandulär pluriglandular, polyglandular
Plurigravida *f* plurigravida, multigravida
Pluripara *f* pluripara, multipara
pluripotent pluripotent[ial]
Plutomanie *f* plutomania
p. m. s. postmortal
P-mitrale *n* P mitrale [wave] *(EKG)*
Pneu *m* s. Pneumothorax
Pneumarthrosis *f* pneumarthrosis
Pneumaskos *m* s. Pneumoperitoneum
Pneumathämie *f* pneumathaemia, pneumohaemia, aeraemia *(z. B. bei Taucherkrankheit)*
Pneumatisation *f* pneumatization *(Bildung luftgefüllter Höhlen in Knochen)*
~/periaquäduktale periaqueductal pneumatization
pneumatisch pneumatic

pneumatisieren to pneumatize *(z. B. in einzelnen Schädelknochen)*
Pneumato... s. a. Pneumo...
Pneumatokardie *f* pneumatocardia
Pneumatometer *n* pneumatometer
Pneumatometrie *f* pneum[at]ometry *(Messung des Unter- bzw. Überdrucks beim Atmen)*
Pneumatose *f* pneumatosis
Pneumatosis *f* **cystoides intestinalis** cystoid intestinal pneumatosis
Pneumatotherapie *f* pneumatotherapy, treatment by rarefied (condensed) air
Pneumatozele *f* pneum[at]ocele, pneumonocele
Pneumatozephalie *f* pneumatocephalia
Pneumatozephalus *m* pneum[at]ocephalus, pneumoencephalocele
pneumatozystisch pneum[at]ocystic
Pneumaturie *f* pneumaturia
Pneumo... s. a. Pneumato... *und* Lungen...
Pneumoangiogramm *n* pneumoangiogram
Pneumoangiographie *f* pneumoangiography
Pneumoarthrogramm *n* pneumoarthrogram
Pneumoarthrographie *f* pneum[o]arthrography
Pneumobazillus *m* pneumobacillus
pneumobulbär pneumobulbar
Pneumocele *f* pneum[at]ocele, pneumonocele
Pneumocholezystitis *f* pneumocholecystitis
Pneumoconiosis *f* **siderotica** [pneumo]siderosis *(Lungenverhärtung durch eisenhaltigen Staub)*
Pneumocystis *f* **carinii** Pneumocystis carinii
Pneumocystis-carinii-Pneumonie *f* Pneumocystis [carinii] pneumonia, interstitial plasma-cell pneumonia *(der Neugeborenen)*
Pneumoderma *n* pneumoderma
Pneumodynamik *f* pneumodynamics
Pneumoempyem *n* pneumoempyema
Pneumoenteritis *f* pneumoenteritis
Pneumoenteroektasie *f* aerenterectasia; meteorism
Pneumoenzephalogramm *n* pneum[o]encephalogram
Pneumoenzephalographie *f* pneum[o]encephalography
Pneumoenzephalozele *f* pneumoencephalocele
pneumogastrisch pneumogastric
Pneumogramm *n* pneum[at]ogram
Pneumograph *m* pneum[at]ograph
Pneumographie *f* pneum[at]ography *(1. Gelenkdarstellung; 2. Aufzeichnung der Atembewegungen des Brustkorbs)*
Pneumohämoperikard *n* pneumohaemopericardium
Pneumohämothorax *m* pneumohaemothorax
Pneumohydrometra *f* pneumohydrometra
Pneumohydroperikard *n* pneumohydropericardium
Pneumohydrothorax *m* pneumohydrothorax
Pneumohypoderma *n* pneumohypoderma, aerodermectasia
Pneumokokkämie *f* pneumococcaemia
Pneumokokke *f* pneumococcus

Pneumokokkenantikörpertest

Pneumokokkenantikörpertest *m* pneumococcus antibody test
Pneumokokkenblutvergiftung *f* pneumococcaemia
pneumokokkenhemmend antipneumococcic
Pneumokokkeninfektion *f* pneumococcal infection
Pneumokokkenkapselpolysaccharid *n* pneumococcal capsular polysaccharide
Pneumokokkennephritis *f* pneumococcus nephritis
Pneumokokkenperitonitis *f* pneumococcal peritonitis
Pneumokokkenpneumonie *f* pneumococcal pneumonia
pneumokokkentötend pneumococcidal
Pneumokokkosurie *f* pneumococcosuria
Pneumokolon *n* pneumocolon
Pneumokoniose *f* pneumokoniosis, pneumo[no]coniosis, lith[ic]osis, dust disease; miner's phthisis
Pneumokranium *n* pneumocranium *(in den Hirnkammern)*
Pneumolipidose *f* pneumolipidosis
Pneumolith *m* lung stone (calculus), pulmonary concretion, pneumolith *(durch Kalkablagerungen bei chronischen Lungenkrankheiten)*
Pneumolithiasis *f* pneumolithiasis
Pneumolyse *f* pneumo[no]lysis, thoracolysis
~/extrapleurale extrapleural pneumonolysis
Pneumomalazie *f* pneumomalacia, softening of the lung tissue
Pneumomediastinogramm *n* pneumomediastinogram
Pneumomediastinographie *f* pneumomediastinography *(Mediastinumröntgendarstellung nach Lufteinblasung)*
Pneumomediastinum *n* 1. pneumomediastinum, mediastinal emphysema; 2. pneumomediastinum *(Diagnostikmethode)*
Pneumomyelographie *f* pneumomyelography, air myelography
Pneumomykose *f* pneumomycosis; farmer's lung
Pneumonektomie *f* pneum[on]ectomy, pulmonectomy
Pneumonia *f s.* Pneumonie
~ **alba** white pneumonia
~ **gangraenosa** gangrenous pneumonia
~ **migrans** migratory (creeping) pneumonia *(mehrere Lungenlappen nacheinander befallende Lungenentzündung)*
Pneumonie *f* pneumonia, pulmonitis, inflammation of the lungs *(s. a. unter Pneumonia und Lungenentzündung)*
~/abszedierende suppurative pneumonia
~/basale basal pneumonia
~/desquamative desquamative (parenchymatous) pneumonia, primary indurative pneumonia
~/doppelseitige double pneumonia
~/eitrige purulent pneumonia
~/embolische embolic pneumonia
~/herdförmige bronchopneumonia, bronchial (lobular) pneumonia
~/interstitielle interstitial pneumonia, pulmonary cirrhosis
~/interstitielle plasmazelluläre acute pneumonitis, interstitial plasma-cell pneumonia
~/käsige caseous (cheesy) pneumonia
~/pleurogene pleurogen[et]ic pneumonia
~/primär atypische mycoplasmal (primary atypical) pneumonia, Eaton agent (virus) pneumonia *(durch Mycoplasma pneumoniae)*
~/tularämische tularaemic pneumonia
~/virusbedingte virus pneumonia
pneumonisch pneumonic
Pneumonitis *f* pneumonitis, benign pneumonia
Pneumonokoniose *f s.* Pneumokoniose
Pneumonopathie *f* pneumonopathy, lung disease
Pneumonopexie *f* pneumonopexy, fixation of the lung
Pneumonorrhaphie *f* pneumonorrhaphy, suture of the lung
Pneumonose *f* pneumonosis *(verursacht Verminderung des Gasaustauschs)*
Pneumonotherapie *f* pneumonotherapy, treatment of lung disease
Pneumonozele *f* pneum[at]ocele, pneumonocele *(durch einen Brustwandspalt)*
Pneumopelvigraphie *f* pneumopelvigraphy
Pneumoperikard *n* pneumopericardium
Pneumoperikardiogramm *n* pneumopericardiogram
Pneumoperikardiographie *f* pneumopericardiography
pneumoperikardiographisch pneumopericardiographic
Pneumoperikarditis *f* pneumopericarditis *(Perikardentzündung mit Luftansammlung im Herzbeutel)*
Pneumoperitoneum *n* pneumoperitoneum, pneumascos, aeroperitoneum
Pneumoperitonitis *f* pneumoperitonitis
Pneumopexie *f* pneumopexy
Pneumopleuritis *f* pneumopleuritis
Pneumopyelogramm *n* pneumopyelogram
Pneumopyelographie *f* pneumopyelography, air pyelography
Pneumopyoperikard *n* pneumopyopericardium
Pneumopyothorax *m* pneumopyothorax
Pneumoradiographie *f s.* Pneumoröntgenographie
Pneumoretroperitoneum *n* pneumoretroperitoneum
Pneumoröntgenogramm *n* pneumoradiogram
Pneumoröntgenographie *f* pneumoradiography, pneumoroentgenography *(z. B. von Organen)*
Pneumorrhachis *f* pneum[at]orrhachis, pneumorachis
Pneumorrhagie *f* pneumorrhagia, haemorrhage from the lung

Pneumoserothorax m pneumoserothorax *(Gas- und Serumansammlung in der Brusthöhle)*
Pneumosiderose f pneumosiderosis *(Lungenverhärtung durch eisenhaltigen Staub)*
Pneumosilikose f pneumosilicosis
Pneumosklerose f pneumosclerosis
Pneumotachogramm n pneumotachogram *(Aufzeichnung der Strömungsgeschwindigkeit der Atemluft)*
Pneumotachograph m pneumotachograph
Pneumothorax m pneum[at]othorax, aeropleura *(zur Diagnostik oder Therapie)*
~/extrapleuraler extrapleural pneumothorax
~/künstlicher artificial (induced) pneumothorax
~ mit serösem Erguß seropneumothorax
~/offener open pneumothorax; blowing wound *(durch Verletzung der Brustwand)*
~/therapeutischer therapeutic pneumothorax
Pneumothoraxkanüle f pneumothorax needle
Pneumotomie f pneumo[no]tomy, incision of the lung
Pneumotoxin n pneumotoxin
Pneumotympanum n pneumotympanum
Pneumotyphus m pneumotyphoid, pneumotyphus, typhopneumonia, typhoid pneumonia
Pneumoventrikel m pneumoventricle
Pneumoventrikulogramm n pneumoventriculogram
Pneumoventrikulographie f pneumoventriculography
Pneumozentese f pneumocentesis
Pneumozystogramm n pneumocystogram
Pneumozystographie f pneumocystography
PNS s. Nervensystem/peripheres
Pocke f pock, vaccina *(Symptom der Pockenkrankheit)*
Pocken pl smallpox, variola, blattern
~/abgeschwächte pseudosmallpox, pseudovariola, milk pox
~/echte true smallpox
~/hämorrhagische (schwarze) haemorrhagic (malignant, black) smallpox
~/spitze varicella
~/weiße minor variola, glasspox, alastrim
pockenartig variolous, variolar, variolic, varioliform, vacciniform, vaccinoid
Pocken-Ausrottungsprogramm n smallpox eradication programme
Pockenblase f smallpox pustule; vaccinid
Pockeneffloreszenz f smallpox rash
Pockenimmunoglobulin n vaccinia immune globulin
Pockenimpfstoff m variolovaccine, [anti]smallpox vaccine, Jennerian vaccine
~/glyzerinkonservierter glycerinated vaccine virus
Pockeninitialexanthem n variolous erythema
Pockeninokulation f smallpox inoculation
Pockenlymphe f vaccine (calf) lymph, smallpox vaccine, variolovaccine; glycerinated vaccine virus
Pockennarbe f pock-mark, vaccination scar, pit

pockennarbig pock-marked, pocked, pitted
Pockenschutzimpfung f variol[iz]ation, smallpox (vaccinia virus, Jennerian) vaccination
Pockenvirus n smallpox (variola) virus, poxvirus
pockig s. pockennarbig
Podagra n podagra, gout
Podalgie f podalgia, pododynia, pain in the foot
Podarthritis f podarthritis, inflammation of a foot joint
Podenzephalus m podencephalus *(Mißgeburt)*
Podobromhidrose f podobromhidrosis, foetid perspiration of the feet
Pododynamometer n pododynamometer
Pododynie f s. Podalgie
Podogramm n podogram, footprint, ichnogram, palmatogram
Podologie f podology
Podophyllin n podophyllin *(Mitosegift)*
Podophyllotoxin n podophyllotoxin *(Mitosegift)*
Podophyllum n podophyllum *(Mitosegift)*
Podozyt m podocyte *(in der Niere)*
podozytisch podocytic
Pogonion n pogonion *(anthropologischer Meßpunkt)*
Poikiloblast m poikiloblast *(Poikilozytenvorstufe)*
Poikilodentosis f poikilodentosis, chronic endemic fluorosis; mottled enamel
Poikiloderma n s. Poikilodermia
~ reticulare reticulated pigmented poikiloderma, poikiloderma [reticulare] of Civatte
Poikilodermatomyositis f poikilodermatomyositis
Poikilodermia f poikiloderma *(vielgestaltige Hautkrankheit)*
~ atrophicans vasculare atrophic vascular poikiloderma
poikilothermisch poikilothermal, poikilothermic
Poikilothrombozyt m poikilothrombocyte *(abnorm geformter Thrombozyt)*
Poikilozoospermie f poikilozoospermia
Poikilozyt m poikilocyte *(abnorm geformter Erythrozyt)*
Poikilozythämie f poikilocytosis *(Folge einer schweren Blutbildungsstörung)*
Pol m s. Polus
Polarimeter n polarimeter, polariscope
Polarimetrie f polarimetry, polariscopy
polarimetrisch polarimetric
Polarisationsmessung f s. Polarimetrie
Polarisationsmikroskop n polarizing microscope
Polarisationswinkel m polarization angle, angle of polarization
Polarterie f pole artery
Polfärbung f polar stain[ing] *(Histologie)*
Poliklinik f outpatient's department (clinic)
Polio f s. Poliomyelitis
Poliodystrophia f cerebri progressiva infantilis progressive cerebral poliodystrophy
Poliodystrophie f poliodystrophy
Polioenzephalitis f polioencephalitis [acuta]
~/hämorrhagische haemorrhagic polioencephalitis

Polioenzephalomeningomyelitis

Polioenzephalomeningomyelitis f polioencephalomeningomyelitis *(Entzündung der grauen Substanz des Gehirns und des Rückenmarks sowie deren Häute)*
Polioenzephalomyelitis f polioencephalomyelitis, poliomyelencephalitis *(Entzündung der grauen Substanz des Gehirns und des Rückenmarks)*
Polioenzephalopathie f polioencephalopathy *(Krankheit der grauen Hirnsubstanz)*
Poliomyelitis f poliomyelitis, spodiomyelitis, inflammation of the grey substance of the spinal cord
~ **acuta anterior** [acute anterior] poliomyelitis, polio, [paralytic] spinal poliomyelitis, Heine-Medin disease, infantile paralysis
~/**hämorrhagische** haemorrhagic poliomyelitis
poliomyelitisartig poliomyelitis-like
poliomyelitisch poliomyelitic
Poliomyelitisimpfstoff m polio[myelitis] vaccine
~/**formalininaktivierter** Salk vaccine *(zur aktiven Immunisierung)*
~/**inaktivierter** inactivated polio[myelitis] vaccine, IPV
Poliomyelitisimpfung f polio[myelitis] inoculation, antipolio inoculation
Poliomyelitislebendimpfstoff m live poliovirus vaccine
Poliomyelitisschluckimpfung f oral poliomyelitis vaccination
Poliomyelitisvirus n poliomyelitis virus, poliovirus
~ **Typ I** Brunhilde virus
~ **Typ II** Lansing virus
~ **Typ III** Leon virus
Poliomyelopathie f poliomyelopathy *(Krankheit der grauen Rückenmarksubstanz)*
Poliosis f [tricho]poliosis, poliothrix, canities
Poliovirusimpfstoff m/**monovalenter oraler** monovalent oral poliovirus vaccine
~/**oraler** oral poliovirus vaccine
Politzer-Ballon m Politzer bag
Politzer-Test m Politzer's test
Polkafieber n s. Denguefieber
Polkatarakt f polar cataract
Polkörperchen npl polar bodies (globules) *(bei der Reifeteilung der Eizelle)*
~/**Babés-Ernstsche** polar (Babés-Ernst) bodies *(bei Diphtheriebakterien)*
Polkörperchenfärbung f/**Neissersche** Neisser's stain *(zur Darstellung der Babés-Ernstschen Körperchen)*
Pollakisurie f pollakisuria, abnormally frequent micturation
Pollenkrankheit f pollenosis, pollen asthma, hay fever
Pollex m s. Daumen
Polligatur f der Schilddrüse pole ligation
Pollinose f s. Pollenkrankheit
Pollutio f pollution, emission, oneirogmus
~ **diurna (nimiae)** diurnal pollution
~ **nocturna** nocturnal pollution (emission); wet dream

Pollution f s. Pollutio
Polozyt m polocyte
Polstar m polar cataract
~/**hinterer** posterior polar cataract
~/**vorderer** anterior polar cataract
Polster n pad[ding]
polstern to pad *(z. B. Gipsverband)*; to wad *(mit Watte)*
Polsterschiene f padded splint
Polsterung f padding; wadding
Polstrahlung f aster *(bei Mitose)*
Polus m pole, polus
~ **anterior bulbi oculi** anterior pole of the eye[ball]
~ **anterior lentis** anterior pole of the lens
~ **frontalis** frontal pole
~ **occipitalis** occipital pole
~ **posterior bulbi oculi** posterior pole of the eye[ball]
~ **posterior lentis** posterior pole of the lens
~ **temporalis** temporal pole
Polyadenitis f polyadenitis
Polyadenopathie f polyadenopathia
Polyämie f polyaemia
Polyandrie f polyandry
Polyangiitis f polyangiitis
Polyarteriitis f polyarteritis
~ **nodosa** polyarteritis nodosa, necrotizing arteritis *(knötchenartige Verdickungen an kleinen Schlagadern)*
Polyarthralgie f polyarthralgia
Polyarthritis f polyarthritis
~ **bei Tuberkulösen** Poncet's disease
~/**primär chronische** primary chronic polyarthritis, chronic rheumatoid arthritis
~ **rheumatica acuta** rheumatic fever, inflammatory rheumatism, rheumapyra
Polyarthropathie f polyarthropathy
Polyästhesie f polyaesthesia
Polyblepharon n polyblepharon
Polycheirie f polycheiria
Polychemotherapie f polychemotherapy
Polycholie f polycholia
Polychondritis f polychondritis
polychrom polychrome
Polychromasie f polychromasia *(von jungen Erythrozyten)*
polychromatisch polychromatic
polychromatophil polychrom[at]ophilic, polychromatic
Polychromatophilie f polychromatophilia, polychromocytosis, polychromatia
Polychromatozyt m polychromatocyte
Polychromie f polychromia
Polychylie f polychylia
Polycythaemia f polycythaemia, polyglobulia, polyglobulism
~ **hypertonica** Gaisböck's syndrome
~ **rubra** s. Polycythaemia
~ **[rubra] vera** erythr[ocyth]aemia, primary (myelopathic) polycythaemia, Vaquez's (Vaquez-Osler) disease *(krankhafte Erythrozytenvermehrung)*

Polydaktylie f polydactyly, hyperdactyly
Polydipsie f polydipsia, anadipsia, excessive thirst
Polydysplasie f polydysplasia
polydystroph polydystrophic
Polygalaktie f polygalactia
polygam polygamous
Polygamie f polygamy
Polygastrie f polygastria
Polyglobulie f s. Polycythaemia
Polygnathus m polygnathus
Polygyrie f polygyria
Polyhydramnion n polyhydramnion
Polyhydrurie f polyhydruria
Polyhypermenorrhoe f polyhypermenorrhoea
Polyhypomenorrhoe f polyhypomenorrhoea
Polyinfektion f polyinfection
Polykarenzsyndrom n plurideficiency syndrome, nutritional dystrophy, malignant malnutrition; kwashiorkor, red boy
Polykaryozyt m polykaryocyte
Polyklonie polyclonia
Polykorie f polycoria *(an einem Auge)*
Polymastie f polymastia
Polymelie f polymelia
Polymelus m polymelus *(Mißgeburt)*
Polymenorrhoe f polymenorrhoea, polymenia
Polymerie f polymeria
Polymetakarpalismus m polymetacarpalism
Polymikrogyrie f polymicrogyria
polymorph polymorphic
Polymorphie f polymorphism
polymorphkernig polymorphonuclear
Polymorphozyt m polymorph[ocyte], polymorphonuclear leucocyte *(reifer neutrophiler Leukozyt)*
polymorphzellig polymorphocellular
Polymyalgie f polymyalgia
~/**rheumatische** rheumatic polymyalgia
Polymyopathie f polymyopathy
Polymyositis f polymyositis
Polymyxin n polymyxin *(Antibiotikum aus Bacillus polymyxa)*
polyneural polyneural, polyneuric
Polyneuralgie f polyneuralgia
Polyneuritis f polyneuritis, multiple neuritis
~/**akute idiopathische** acute idiopathic polyneuritis
~/**endemische** endemic polyneuritis, beriberi, Ceylon sickness, kakke *(Vitamin-B₁-Mangelkrankheit)*
polyneuritisch polyneuritic
Polyneuromyositis f polyneuromyositis
Polyneuropathie f polyneuropathy
Polyneuroradikulitis f polyneuroradiculitis
polynukleär polynuclear, polynucleate
Polynukleotid n polynucleotide
Polynukleotidase f polynucleotidase *(Enzym)*
Polyodontie f poly[o]dontia
Polyonychie f polyonychia
Polyopie f polyop[s]ia *(eines Gegenstands)*

Polyorchider m polyorchid *(Mann mit überzähligen Hoden)*
Polyorchidie f polyorchi[di]sm
Polyotie f polyotia
Polyp m polyp[us] ● mehrere Polypen betreffend multipolypoid
~/**antrochoanaler** antrochoanal polypus
~ **in der Pars prostatica urethrae** prostatic urethral polyp
~/**nasaler** nasal polyp *(Wucherung der Nasenschleimhaut)*
Polypapilloma n tropicum polypapilloma *(s. a. Frambösie)*
Polyparasitismus m polyparasitism
Polyparese f polyparesis
Polypathie f polypathia
Polypenabtragung f polypectomy
polypenartig polypoid, polypous
Polypenentfernung f/**endoskopische** endoscopic polypectomy
~/**operative** polypectomy
polypenförmig polypiform
polypentragend polypiferous
Polypeptid n polypeptide
Polypeptidämie f polypeptidaemia
Polypeptidase f polypeptidase *(Enzym)*
Polyphagie f polyphagia
Polyphalangismus m polyphalangism
Polyphänie f pleiotropism, pleiotropia *(Zuordnung vieler Merkmale zu einem Gen)*
Polyphobie f polyphobia *(krankhafte Angst vor vielen Dingen)*
Polyphrasie f polyphrasia
Polyplasmie f polyplasmia
Polyplegie f polyplegia
Polypnoe f polypnoea, rapid respiration; panting respiration
Polypodie f polypodia
polypös polypoid, polypous
Polypose f polyposis
~ **des Kolons** colon polyposis
~ **des Magens** gastric polyposis
~/**multiple intestinale** multiple intestinal polyposis
Polypragmasie f polypragmasy, polypharmacy
Polyradikulitis f polyradiculitis
Polyradikuloneuritis f polyradiculoneuritis
Polyradikuloneuropathie f polyradiculoneuropathy
Polyribosom n poly[ribo]some, ergosome
Polysa[c]charid n polysaccharide
Polyserositis f polyserositis, multiple serositis, polyorrhymenitis
Polysialie f polysialia
Polysinusitis f polysinusitis
Polysklerose f polysclerosis
polysom polysomic
Polyspermie f polyspermia, polyspermism
Polystichiasis f polystichia
polysymptomatisch polysymptomatic; polymorphic
polysynaptisch polysynaptic

Polysyndaktylismus 628

Polysyndaktylismus *m* polysyndactylism
Polysynovitis *f* polysynovitis
Polythelie *f* polythelia
Polytomoenzephalographie *f* polytomoencephalography
Polytomographie *f* polytomography
Polytrauma *n* multiple injury
Polytrichie *f* polytrichia, polytrichosis, pilosis
Polytrophie *f* polytrophy
Polyurie *f* polyuria, urorrhagia, hydruria, hyperuresis
Polyuriker *m* polyuric
polyurisch polyuric, hydruric
polyvalent polyvalent
Polyzythämie *f s.* Polycythaemia
polyzythämisch polycythaemic
Polzelle *f* polocyte
Pompe-Syndrom *n* Pompe's (cardiac glycogen storage) disease, generalized glycogenosis, acid maltase deficiency
Pompholyhämie *f* pompholyhaemia
Pomphus *m* pomphus, wheal, blister
Pomum *n* **Adami** *s.* Adamsapfel
Pons *m* **cerebri (varolii)** Varolian pons *(Hirnteil oberhalb des verlängerten Rückenmarks)*
pontin pontine, pontile
pontobulbär pontobulbar
pontomedullär pontomedullary
pontozerebellar pontocerebellar
Poolplasma *n* pooled [human] plasma
Poolserum *n* pooled serum
Poplitealgegend *f* popliteal region (space), poples
Population *f* population
Pore *f* pore, porus *(Zusammensetzungen s. unter Porus)*
porenschließend emphractic, closing pores
porenverstopfend oppilative
Porenverstopfung *f* oppilation
porenzephal porencephalic
Porenzephalie *f* porencephalia
Porenzephalitis *f* porencephalitis
Porenzephalus *m* porencephalus *(Mißgeburt)*
porig porotic, porous
Porigkeit *f* porosity
Poriomane *m* poriomaniac
Poriomanie *f* poriomania, wandering madness; ambulatory automatism
Porokeratose *f* porokeratosis, hyperkeratosis excentrica
porös porotic, porous
Porose *f* porosis *(besonders in Knochen)*
Porosität *f* porosity, porousness
Porozephaliasis *f* porocephaliasis *(Infektionskrankheit durch Porocephalus)*
Porphobilin *n* porphobilin *(Abbauprodukt des roten Blutfarbstoffs)*
Porphobilinogen *n* porphobilinogen *(Zwischenprodukt der Porphyrinsynthese)*
Porphyria *f s.* Porphyrie
~ **cutanea tarda hereditaria** mixed hepatic porphyria

~ **erythropoietica (haemopoietica)** erythropoietic (congenital, photosensitive) porphyria
Porphyrie *f* porphyria *(s. a. unter Porphyria)* *(Anomalie des Porphyrinstoffwechsels)*
~/**akute intermittierende** acute intermittent porphyria, acute hepatic porphyria of Watson, Swedish type of porphyria
~/**hepatoerythropoetische** hepatoerythropoietic porphyria
Porphyrin *n* porphyrin
Porphyrinämie *f* porphyrinaemia
Porphyrinausscheidung *f* **im Urin** [haemato]porphyrinuria, porphyruria
Porphyrinneuritis *f* porphyric neuritis
Porphyrmilz *f* porphyry spleen *(bei Lymphogranulomatose)*
Porphyropsin *n* porphyropsin
Porschwielen *fpl* porokeratosis
Porta *f* porta, hilum *(s. a. unter* Hilus*)*
~ **hepatica (hepatis)** hepatic porta
Portio *f* **vaginalis uteri** ectocervix
Portiofaßzange *f* vulsellum forceps
Portogramm *n* portogram
Portographie *f* porto[veno]graphy, portal venography
portokaval portocaval, portacaval
portorenal portorenal
portosystemisch portosystemic
Porus *m* pore, porus
~ **acusticus externus** external acoustic pore
~ **acusticus internus** internal acoustic pore
~ **gustatorius** gustatory (taste) pore
~ **opticus** optic pore
~ **sudoriferus** sweat pore
Porzellanfüllung *f* porcelain filling *(Stomatologie)*
Porzellanstaublunge[nerkrankung] *f* kaolinosis
Porzellanzahn *m* porcelain tooth
positiv/schwach weakly reactive *(z. B. Agglutination)*
post cibum post cibum, p. c., postcibal, after meals; after food
post menstruum *s.* postmenstruell
~ **mortem** *s.* postmortal
~ **partum** *s.* postpartal
postbulbär postbulbar, retrobulbar
Postcholezystektomiesyndrom *n* postcholecystectomy syndrome
postdikrot[isch] postdicrotic
postdiphtherisch postdiphther[it]ic
postepileptisch postepileptic
posterior posterior
poster[i]oanterior postero-anterior
Posterotransversaldurchmesser *m* parietal diameter
Postextubationsstridor *m* postextubation stridor
Postgastrektomiesyndrom *n* postgastrectomy syndrome
Posthioplastik *f* posthioplasty
Posthitis *f* posthitis, inflammation of the prepuce
Postholith *m* postholith, smegmolith, preputial calculus (concretion)

posthum posthumous
Postikus *m* posticus, posterior cricoarytenoid muscle
Postikuslähmung *f* posticus (abductor) paralysis
Post-Kala-Azar-Hautleishmanoid *n* post-kala-azar dermal leishmanoid
Postkardiotomiepsychose *f* postcardiotomy (postcapillary) psychosis
Postklimakterium *n* postclimacteric period
Postkommissurotomie-Syndrom *n* postcommissurotomy syndrome *(Beschwerdekomplex nach Herzoperation)*
Postkontusionssyndrom *n* postconcussion (minor contusion) syndrome
Postlaminektomie-Syndrom *n* postlaminectomy syndrome
Postligaturödem *n* postligation oedema
Postmenopause *f* postmenopause
Postmenopauseblutung *f* postmenopause bleeding
postmortal postmortal, post mortem, after death
Postmyokardinfarktsyndrom *n* postmyocardial infarction syndrome, postinfarction (Dressler's) syndrome
postnatal postnatal, after birth
postoperativ postoperative, postsurgical
postpartal postpartal, post partum, postpartum, following the birth
Postpartalperiode *f* postpartum period
Postperfusionspsychose *f* postperfusion psychosis
Postperfusionssyndrom *n* postperfusion syndrome
Postperikardiotomiesyndrom *n* postpericardiotomy syndrome
postsynaptisch postsynaptic, subsynaptic
Postthrombosesyndrom *n* postthrombotic syndrome
Posttracheotomiestenose *f* posttracheotomy stenosis *(im Bereich des Luftröhrenschnittes)*
Posttransfusionshepatitis *f* posttransfusion hepatitis
Postvakzinationsdermatitis *f* postvaccinal dermatosis
Postvalvulotomiesyndrom *n* postvalvulotomy syndrome
Potator *m s.* Alkoholiker
potent potent
Potential *n*/**bioelektrisches** bioelectric potential
Potenz *f* potency, power, strength; [sexual] potency
Potenzschwäche *f* impaired potency
Potenzverlust *m* loss of potency, eviration
Potio *f* potion
Potomanie *f* potomania
Potter-Bucky-Blende *f* Potter-Bucky diaphragm *(Radiologie)*
Poxvirus *n* **officinale** vaccinia (vaccine) virus
~ **variolae** variola virus
PP-Faktor *m s.* Pellagrapräventivfaktor
PPLO pleuropneumonia-like organisms
P-pulmonale *n* P pulmonale [wave] *(EKG)*

P-Q-Intervall *n* P-Q interval, P-R interval *(EKG)*
präagonal preagonal
Präalbumin *n* prealbumin
präantiseptisch preantiseptic
Prächordalplatte *f* prechordal plate
Prädentin *n* predentin
Prädiabetes *m* prediabetes
prädiabetisch prediabetic
Prädiastole *f* prediastole
prädiastolisch prediastolic, peridiastolic
Prädigestion *f* predigestion
prädikrot[isch] predicrotic
prädisponieren to predispose
Prädisposition *f* predisposition
Praecipitatum *n* **corneale** keratic precipitate
praecox precocious, precox
Präeklampsie *f* pre-eclampsia, pre-eclamptic toxaemia, eclampsism *(mit Organschäden)*
präeklamptisch pre-eclamptic
Praeputium *n* prepuce, praeputium, foreskin
~ **clitoridis** female (clitoridal) prepuce, prepuce of the clitoris
~ **penis** prepuce of the penis
Präeruptivstadium *n* pre-eruptive stage
Praesentatio *f* **impropria** malpresentation *(des Fetus)*
Präexzitationssyndrom *n* pre-excitation syndrome, Wolff-Parkinson-White syndrome *(EKG)*
präfinal agonal
Präformation *f* preformation
präganglionär preganglionic
Pragmatagnosie *f* pragmatagnosia *(Erkennungsverlust für früher bekannte Gegenstände)*
Pragmatamnesie *f* pragmatamnesia
Prähypophyse *f* adenohypophysis, antehypophysis
präikterisch preicteric
Präinfarkt-Angina *f* preinfarction angina
Präinfarkt-Syndrom *n* preinfarction syndrome
präkanzerös precancerous
Präkanzerose *f* precancerosis
präkapillär precapillary, junctional-capillary
Präkapillare *f* precapillary [arteriole], arteriolar (arterial, junctional) capillary, metarteriole
präkardial precardiac, precordial
Präkarzinom *n* precarcinoma
präklimakterisch preclimacteric
Präkollagenfaser *f* precollagenous (reticular, reticulin) fibre
Präkoma *n* precoma
~/**hepatisches** hepatic precoma
präkomatös precomatose
präkonvulsiv preconvulsive
Präkordialableitung *f* precordial (chest) lead *(beim EKG)*
Präkordialangst *f* precordial fright (anxiety, discomfort), stenocardia; angina [pectoris]
Präkordialregion *f* precordial region
Präkordialschmerz *m* precordial pain, precordialgia
Präkordium *n* precordium

Praktiker

Praktiker m general practitioner
praktizieren to practise, to doctor
Präkuneus m precuneus *(Rindenfeld)*
präleukämisch preleukaemic
prämaligne premalignant
Prämaturität f prematurity
Prämedikation f premedication, preanaesthetic medication
Prämedikationsmittel n premedicant
prämedizieren to premedicate
Prämelanosom n premelanosome
Prämenstrualstadium n premenstrual stage
Prämenstruum n premenstruum, premenstrual period
Prämolarer m premolar [tooth], bicuspid [dens]
prämonitorisch premonitory
prämortal premortal, before death
Prämyeloblast m premyeloblast
Pränatalphysiologie f prenatal (antenatal) physiology
Pränatalüberwachung f prenatal (antenatal) monitoring
präneoplastisch preneoplastic
präokzipital preoccipital
präoperativ preoperative
präovulatorisch preovulatory
Präparat n 1. preparation; 2. s. Medikament
~/anatomisches [anatomical] preparation
~/eisenhaltiges chalybeate
Präputial... s. Vorhaut...
Präputiotomie f preputiotomy
Präputium n s. Praeputium
Präputiumentzündung f s. Posthitis
präpylorisch prepyloric
Präreduktionsphase f prereduction phase *(bei der Zellteilung)*
prärenal prerenal
Präparation f preparation *(z. B. auf eine Operation)*
Präparator m dissector *(Anatomie)*
Präparierbesteck n dissecting set (instruments)
Präparierklemme f dissecting forceps, dissector
Präpariermikroskop n dissecting microscope
Präpariernadel f dissecting (microscopic) needle
Präpariersaal m [/anatomischer] dissecting room (laboratory), anatomic theatre
Präparierschere f dissecting scissors
präpartal prepartal, prepartum
präpatellar prepatellar
Präpatenzzeit f prepatent period *(z. B. von Parasiten)*
präperitoneal preperitoneal, properitoneal
präplazental preplacental
Präponderanz f preponderance
präpuberal prepuber[t]al
Präpubertät f prepuberty
Präsakralblockade f presacral block
Präsenilität f presenility
Präsentation f presentation *(des Fetus bei der Geburt)*
präsentieren/sich to present *(der Fetus bei der Geburt)*

Präservativ n 1. preservative; 2. condom, preservative
Präsklerose f presclerosis
Präskription f prescription
Präsystole f presystole
präternatural preternatural
Präthrombose f prethrombosis
präthyreoidal prethyroid[eal], prethyroidean
Prätrachealfaszie f pretracheal fascia
Prausnitz-Küstner-Reaktion f Prausnitz-Küstner reaction *(Immunologie)*
Prävalenz f prevalence *(einer Krankheit)*
Prävalenzrate f prevalence rate
Pravaz-Spritze f Pravaz's (hypodermic) syringe
Präventivmaßnahme f preventive (prophylactic) measure
Präventivmedizin f preventive (prophylactic) medicine
Prävertebralganglion n prevertebral ganglion
Praxis f practice; consulting rooms ● **eine ~ haben** to practise
Präzipitans n precipitant [agent]
Präzipitat n precipitate
Präzipitation f precipitation
~/chemische chemocoagulation
Präzipitationsreaktion f precipitation reaction
Präzipitationstest m precipitation test; Kahn [flocculation] test *(Serumprobe auf Syphilis)*
präzipitieren to precipitate
Präzipitin n precipitin *(Antikörper)*
Präzipitinogen n precipitinogen *(zur Präzipitinbildung führendes Antigen)*
Präzipitinoid n precipitinoid *(Präzipitin mit durch Hitze zerstörter Funktionsgruppe)*
Präzipitinreaktion f precipitin reaction
Predigerhals m clergyman's sore; follicular (glandular) pharyngitis
Predigerstellung f der Hand preacher's hand
Prednisolon n prednisolone *(Steroid)*
Prednison n prednisone *(Steroid)*
Pregnandiol n pregnanediol
Pregnantriol n pregnanetriol
prellen to contuse, to bruise
Prellung f contusion, bruise
Prelum n abdominale abdominal prelum, squeezing of the abdominal viscera
Presbyakusis f presbyac[o]usia, presbycusis, lessening of the acuteness of hearing
Presbyderma n presbyderma
Presbykardie f presbycardia, senile heart disease
presbyop presbyopic, presbytic
Presbyoper m presbyope
presbyophren presbyophrenic
Presbyophrenie f presbyophrenia
Presbyopie f presbyopia, presbytism, old sightedness
pressen to press; to compress; to strain *(beim Stuhlgang)*; to bear down *(bei der Geburt)*
Pressen n pressing, squeezing, prelum; compression; straining; bearing down
~/digitales digital compression
Preßlufthammerkrankheit f pneumatic-hammer disease, stonecutter's disease

Preßluftkrankheit f compressed-air disease (s. a. Caissonkrankheit)
Preßluftwerkzeugsyndrom n traumatic vasospastic syndrome, pneumatic tool injury
pressorezeptiv pressoreceptive
Pressorezeptor m pressoreceptor (z. B. in der Aorta)
pressorisch pressor
pressosensitiv pressosensitive
Preßwehen pl expulsive pains
Presubiculum n presubiculum (Teil des Gyrus hippocampi)
Preußisch-Blau-Reaktion f Prussian blue reaction (zum Hämosiderinnachweis)
Priapismus m priapism
Prickeln n tingle, tingling [sensation] (z. B. der Haut)
Priemeldermatitis f primerose (primula) dermatitis
Prießnitzumschlag m Priessnitz bandage, cold wet compress
Primachin n primaquine (Antimalariamittel)
primär primary, initial; primordial, primitive, embryonal; principal, main; direct, not mediated (derivative)
Primärabszeß m primary abscess
Primäraffekt m 1. s. Primärkomplex; 2. primary syphilitic (venereal) sore, primary lesion (chancre); 3. framboesioma
Primäramputation f primary amputation
Primäramyloidose f primary amyloidosis
Primäraneurysma n primary aneurysm
Primärantwort f primary immune response
Primärblutung f primary haemorrhage
Primärbronchus m primary (extrapulmonary) bronchus
Primärchoane f primary choana
Primärdentin n primary dentin
Primärdentition f primary dentition
Primäreffloreszenz f primary efflorescence
Primäreiterung f primary abscess
Primärfissur f primary fissure
Primärfleck m herald patch (bei Pityriasis rosacea)
Primärfollikel m primary [ovarian] follicle
Primärgaumen m primary (premaxillary) palate
Primärgebiß n deciduous dentition
Primärgeschwulst f primary tumour
Primärgeschwür n s. Primäraffekt 2.
Primärglaukom n primary glaucoma
Primärheilung f primary (first intention) healing, healing by first intention, immediate union (z. B. einer Wunde)
Primärherd m primary focus
Primärinfektion f primary infection
Primärkaries f primary caries
Primärknochen m primary bone
Primärkomplex m primary (initial) complex (Lokalreaktion an der Erregereintrittspforte); primary pulmonary focus (lesion, complex) (bei Lungentuberkulose)

Primärkomplikation f immediate complication
Primärnaht f primary suture, primary [wound] closure
~/verzögerte delayed primary closure, primary delayed suture
Primäroozyte f primary oocyte
Primärreaktion f primary immune response
Primärröntgenstrahlung f primary radiation
Primärsamenzelle f primary spermatocyte
Primärsequester m primary sequestrum
Primärstrahlung f primary radiation
Primärsyphilis f primary syphilis, protosyphilis
Primärtuberkulose f primary tuberculosis
Primärursache f primary cause
Primärverdauung f primary digestion
Primärverklebung f immediate agglutination (einer Wunde)
Primärzahnung f primary (deciduous) dentition
Primärzotte f primary villus
Primigravida f primigravida
primipar primiparous
Primipara f primipara
primitiv primitive, primordial, embryonic, primary
Primitivaorta f primitive aorta
Primitivauge n eyespot
Primitivchoane f primary choana
Primitivdenken n primitive (anthropoid) thinking, archaic-paralogical thinking
Primitivgaumen m primitive palate
Primitivgrube f primitive pit
Primitivherzvorhof m primitive atrium
Primitivkanal m primitive canal
Primitivknoten m primitive node
Primitivplatte f primitive plate
Primitivrinne f primitive groove (furrow)
Primitivstreifen m primitive streak (line), germinal streak
Primitivwirbel m primitive vertebra, protovertebra
primordial primordial, first-formed, primitive, embryonic
Primordialei n primordial ovum, oogonium
Primordialfollikel m primordial follicle
Primordialknorpel m primordial cartilage
Primordialkranium n embryonic cartilaginous cranium, chondrocranium
Primordialzelle f primordial (embryonic) cell
Primordialzwerg m primordial dwarf
Primordialzyste f primordial cyst
Primordium n primordium
P-R-Intervall n P-R-interval (EKG)
prismaartig prismatic
Prismendioptrie f prism diopter
prismenförmig prismatic
Prismoptometer n prismoptometer
Privatbehandlung f private treatment
Privatklinik f private clinic
Privatpatient m private patient
Privatpraxis f private practice
Proagglutinoid n proagglutinoid
proakrosomal proacrosomal
Proaktivator m proactivator

Proakzelerin

Proakzelerin *n* [pro]accelerin, blood-clotting factor V
Proband *m* proband, test person
Probe *f* 1. sample, specimen; test piece; 2. test *(s. a. unter Prüfung und Test)*
~ **auf okkultes Blut** occult blood test
~/**Bennholdsche** Bennhold's (Congo red) test
~/**Bergmann-Elliotsche** Bergmann-Elliot's test, bilirubin clearance test
~/**Boverische** Boveri's test *(Globulinnachweis im Liquor cerebrospinalis)*
~/**Dicksche** Dick test *(Scharlachtest)*
~/**Gmelinsche** Gmelin's test *(zum Bilirubinnachweis)*
~/**Liebensche** Lieben's test *(zum Azetonnachweis im Harn)*
~/**Neßlersche** nesslerization *(zum Ammoniaknachweis)*
~/**Rivaltasche** Rivalta's test *(zur Unterscheidung zwischen Exsudaten und Transsudaten)*
Probebiß *m* check bite *(Stomatologie)*
Probebohrloch *n* exploratory burr hole
Probeexzision *f* biopsy *(Entnahme von Gewebsproben)*
Probeinzision *f* exploratory incision
Probelaparotomie *f* exploratory laparotomy
Probemahlzeit *f* test meal
Probenentnahme *f* specimen collection
Probenlinse *f* trial-lens
Probepunktion *f* exploratory puncture
Probethoraxeröffnung *f* exploratory thoracotomy
Probetrepanationsloch *n* exploratory burr hole
probieren to probe, to test
Probierglas *n* trial-lens
Problemfall *m* problem case
Processus *m* process[us] *(s. a. unter Fortsatz)*
~ **alaris** [ossis frontalis] alar process
~ **alveolaris** alveolar process
~ **anterior mallei** anterior (long) process of the malleus
~ **articularis** articular process
~ **articularis inferior** inferior articular process
~ **articularis inferior vertebrae** inferior articular process of the vertebra
~ **articularis superior** superior articular process
~ **articularis superior vertebrae** superior articular process of the vertebra
~ **brevis mallei** *s.* ~ **lateralis mallei**
~ **caudatus hepatis** caudate process
~ **ciliaris** ciliary process
~ **clinoideus** clinoid process
~ **clinoideus anterior** anterior clinoid process
~ **clinoideus medius** middle clinoid process
~ **clinoideus posterior** posterior clinoid process
~ **conchae nasalis** *s.* ~ **lacrimalis**
~ **condylaris** condylar process
~ **condyloideus mandibulae** condyloid process of the mandible, mandibular condyle
~ **coracoideus** coracoid [process], beak-shaped process of the scapula
~ **coronoideus mandibulae** coronoid process of the mandible
~ **coronoideus ulnae** coronoid process of the ulna
~ **costalis** costal process
~ **costalis des VI. Halswirbels** Chassaignac's tubercle
~ **ensiformis** *s.* ~ **xiphoideus**
~ **ethmoidalis** ethmoid process
~ **falciformis [ligamenti sacrotuberosi]** falciform process
~ **frontalis maxillae** frontal (nasal) process of the maxilla
~ **frontalis ossis zygomatici** frontosphenoidal process
~ **infundibularis hypophysis** neural lobe
~ **intrajugularis ossis occipitalis** intrajugular process [of the occipital bone]
~ **intrajugularis ossis temporalis** intrajugular process [of the temporal bone]
~ **jugularis ossis temporalis** jugular process
~ **lacrimalis** lacrimal process *(zum Tränenbein ziehender Fortsatz der unteren Nasenmuschel)*
~ **lateralis mallei** lateral (short) process of the malleus *(Gehörknöchelchen)*
~ **lateralis tali** lateral process of the talus
~ **lenticularis incudis** lenticular apophysis, Sylvian bone *(ovales Köpfchen des Ambosses)*
~ **mamillaris [vertebrarum] lumbalium** mamillary process *(Höcker am hinteren Rande des Lendenwirbelgelenkfortsatzes)*
~ **mandibularis** mandibular process
~ **mastoideus** mastoid [bone], mastoid process
~ **maxillaris conchae nasalis inferioris** maxillary process of the inferior nasal concha
~ **maxillaris ossis palatini** maxillary process of the palatine bone
~ **maxillaris ossis zygomatici** maxillary process of the zygomatic bone
~ **nasalis ossis frontalis** nasal process of the frontal bone
~ **orbitalis ossis palatini** orbital process of the palatine bone
~ **orbitalis ossis zygomatici** orbital process of the zygomatic bone
~ **palatinus maxillae** palatine process [of the maxilla]
~ **papillaris hepatis** papillary process *(Erhabenheit der Leber am Lobus caudatus)*
~ **paramastoideus [ossis occipitalis]** paramastoid process [of the occipital bone]
~ **posterior sphenoidalis** sphenoid process of the septal cartilage
~ **posterior tali** posterior process of the talus
~ **pterygoideus ossis sphenoidalis** pterygoid process of the sphenoid bone
~ **pterygospinus** pterygospinous process
~ **pyramidalis ossis palatini** palatine tubercle, tuberosity (pyramidal process) of the palatine bone
~ **sellae medius** middle clinoid process
~ **sphenoidalis ossis palatini** sphenoid process of the palatine bone
~ **spinosus** spinous process [of the vertebra], vertebral (neural) spine

~ **sterni** s. ~ xiphoideus
~ **styloideus ossis metacarpalis III** styloid process of the third metacarpal
~ **styloideus ossis temporalis** styloid process of the temporal bone
~ **styloideus radii** radial styloid process
~ **styloideus ulnae** ulnar styloid process
~ **stylomandibularis** stylomandibular process
~ **supracondylaris** supracondylar process
~ **temporalis ossis zygomatici** temporal process of the zygomatic bone
~ **transversus** transverse process
~ **transversus atlantis** transverse process of the atlas
~ **uncinatus** uncinate process of the pancreas
~ **uncinatus ossis ethmoidalis** uncinate process of the ethmoid bone
~ **uncinatus pancreatis (Winslowi)** uncinate process of the pancreas
~ **vaginalis ossis sphenoidalis** vaginal process of the sphenoid bone
~ **vaginalis peritonei** peritoneal canal, canal of Nuck
~ **vertebralis** vertebral process
~ **vocalis** vocal process
~ **xiphoideus** xiphoid [process], xiphoid cartilage, xiphosternum, ensiform cartilage (process)
~ **zygomaticus maxillae** zygomatic process of the maxilla
~ **zygomaticus ossis frontalis** zygomatic process of the frontal bone
~ **zygomaticus ossis temporalis** zygomatic process of the temporal bone
Procheilie f procheilia
Procheilon n procheilon
Prochoresis f prochoresis, propulsion of food
Prochromatin n prochromatin
Prochromosom n prochromosome
Proctalgia f **fugax** nocturnal proctalgia
Prodrom n prodrome, premonitory manifestation
prodromal prodromal, prodromic, prodromous, premonitory
Prodromalerscheinung f prodromal (preliminary) sign, early symptom, premonition
Prodromalstadium n prodromal period (stage)
Prodromalsymptom n prodromal symptom
produzieren/Immunität to produce immunity
~/**Verdauungsfermente** to elaborate digestive enzymes
Proenzephalie f proencephalia
Proenzephalus m proencephalus *(Mißgeburt)*
Proenzym n proenzyme, zymogen
Proerythroblast m proerythroblast, lymphoid haemoblast [of Pappenheim] *(Erythrozytenvorstufe)*
Proerythrozyt m proerythrocyte
Profibrin n profibrin
Profibrinolysin n profibrinolysin, plasminogen *(Plasminvorstufe)*
Profichet-Syndrom n Profichet's syndrome *(umschriebene Kalkablagerungen in der Haut der Extremitäten)*

Proflavin n proflavine
Profluvium n profluvium
Profundaplastik f profundoplasty *(an der Oberschenkelarterie)*
progam progamic, progamous
Progenie f progenia, anterior occlusion
Progerie f 1. [childhood] progeria, Hutchinson-Gilford syndrome, premature senility syndrome, Gilford-Hutchinson disease; 2. progeria of adult, Werner's syndrome
Progesteron n progesterone, progestational hormone
Proglottis f proglottid, proglottis
prognath prognathic, prognathous
Prognathie f prognathism
~/**alveolosubnasale** alveosubnasal prognathism
Prognose f prognostication, prognosis, prediction ● **eine ~ geben** to prognosticate, to prognose
~/**gute** good (favourable) prognosis
~/**schlechte** bad (poor, unfavourable) prognosis
Prognostiker m prognostician
prognostisch prognostic
prognostizieren to prognosticate, to prognose
Progranulozyt m progranulocyte
progredient progressive, advancing, increasing, gradually extending *(Krankheit)*
Progression f progression, progress, extension
Pro-Insulin n proinsulin
Projektionsfaser f projection fibre
Projektionsfeld n projection area (centre) *(in der Hirnrinde)*
Projektionsperimetrie f projection perimetry *(Ophthalmologie)*
Projektionssystem n projection system *(Nervensystem)*
Projektionszentrum n projection area (centre) *(in der Hirnrinde)*
Prokain n procaine *(Lokalanästhetikum)*
Prokainamid n procaine amide *(Lokalanästhetikum)*
Prokainblockade f **des Ganglion stellatum** procaine block of the stellate ganglion
Prokainesterase f procaine esterase *(Enzym)*
Prokallus m procallus
Prokaryozyt m prokaryocyte
Prokinase f prokinase *(Enzym)*
Prokoagulator m procoagulant
Prokollagen n procollagen
Prokonvertin n [pro]convertin, blood-clotting factor VII
Prokonvertinmangel m proconvertin deficiency
Proktagra f proctagra
Proktalgie f proctalgia, proctodynia, pain in the rectum
Proktatresie f proctatresia, aproctia, rectal atresia, imperforation of the anus
Proktektasie f proctectasia, dilatation of the rectum; dilatation of the anus
Proktektomie f proctectomy, rectectomy, excision of the rectum
Proktenkleisis f proctencleisis, constriction (stenosis) of the rectum

Prokteurynter

Prokteurynter *m* procteurynter
Prokteurysis *f* procteurysis
Proktitis *f* proctitis, rectitis, inflammation of the rectum
proktodäal proctodaeal
Proktodäaldrüse *f* proctodaeal (anal) gland
Proktodäum *n* proctodaeum
proktogen proctogenic
Proktoklysis *f* proctoclysis, rectoclysis
Proktokokzypexie *f* proctococcypexy
Proktokolektomie *f* proctocolectomy
Proktokolitis *f* proctocolitis, rectocolitis, inflammation of the rectum and the colon
Proktokolonoskopie *f* proctocolonoscopy
Proktokolpoplastik *f* proctocolpoplasty
Proktologe *m* proctologist
Proktologie *f* proctology
proktologisch proctologic
Proktoparalyse *f* proctoparalysis, proctoplegia
Proktoperineoplastik *f* proctoperineoplasty
Proktoperineorrhaphie *f* proctoperineorrhaphy
Proktopexie *f* proctopexy, fixation of the rectum, rectopexy
Proktoplastik *f* proctoplasty, rectoplasty
Proktoptose *f* proctoptosia, proctoptosis, prolapse of the anus
Proktorrhagie *f* proctorrhagia, bleeding from the anus
Proktorrhaphie *f* proctorrhaphy, rectorrhaphy, suture of the rectum
Proktorrhoe *f* proctorrhoea, discharge from the anus
Proktosigmoidektomie *f* proctosigmoidectomy, rectosigmoidectomy
Proktosigmoiditis *f* proctosigmoiditis, inflammation of the rectum and the sigmoid
Proktosigmoidoskopie *f* proctosigmoidoscopy, rectosigmoidoscopy
Proktoskop *n* proctoscope, rectoscope, rectal specula
Proktoskopie *f* proctoscopy, rectoscopy
proktoskopisch proctoscopic, rectoscopic
Proktospasmus *m* proctospasm, spasm of the rectum
Proktostase *f* proctostasis
Proktostenose *f* proctostenosis, rectostenosis, stricture of the rectum
Proktostomie *f* proctostomy, rectostomy
Proktotom *n* proctotome, rectotome
Proktotomie *f* proctotomy, rectotomy, incision into the rectum
Proktozele *f* proctocele, rectocele
Proktozystoplastik *f* proctocystoplasty
Prokursivepilepsie *f* procursive epilepsy (epileptic seizure)
prolabieren to prolapse *(z. B. Organe)*
prolabierend proptotic
Prolabium *n* prolabium
Prolaktin *n* prolactin, mammatrophin, mammogenic (mammary-stimulating) hormone, lactogenic (lactation) hormone, lactogen
Prolaktin[spiegel]erhöhung *f* im Blut hyperprolactinaemia
Prolaktin[spiegel]verminderung *f* im Blut hypoprolactinaemia
Prolamin *n* prolamin[e]
Prolan *n* prolan
Prolaps *m* prolapse, prolapsus, procidentia *(Zusammensetzungen s. unter Prolapsus)*
Prolapspessar *n* prolapse pessary; prolapse of the pessary
Prolapsus *m* prolapse, prolapsus, procidentia
~ **ani** anal (anus) prolapse
~ **cerebri** prolapse of the cerebrum
~ **iridis** prolapse of the iris
~ **recti** prolapse of the rectum
~ **uteri** prolapse of the uterus
Proleukozyt *m* proleucocyte
Proliferation *f* proliferation
proliferationshemmend antiproliferative
Proliferationsstadium *n* proliferative stage
proliferativ proliferative, proliferous
proliferieren to proliferate
Prolin *n* proline
Prolinämie *f* prolinaemia
Prolinase *f* prolinase *(Enzym)*
Prolinausscheidung *f* im Urin prolinuria
Prolin[spiegel]erhöhung *f* im Blut prolinaemia
Prolipase *f* prolipase *(Lipasevorstufe)*
Prolymphozyt *m* prolymphocyte
Promazin *n* promazine *(Beruhigungsmittel)*
Promegakaryozyt *m* promegakaryocyte, lymphoid megakaryocyte
Promegaloblast *m* promegaloblast
Promethazin *n* promethazine *(Antihistaminikum)*
Prominentia *f* prominence
~ **laryngea** s. Adamsapfel
~ **mallearis (malleolaris)** malleolar prominence
~ **spiralis** spiral prominence
Promitose *f* promitosis
Promonozyt *m* promonocyte, premonocyte, young monocyte
Promontorium *n* promontory, promontorium
~ **cavi tympani** promontory of the tympanum (middle ear)
~ **ossis sacri** sacral promontory, promontory of the sacrum
Promunturium *n* s. Promontorium
Promyelozyt *m* promyelocyte, premyelocyte
~/**großer** macropromyelocyte
promyelozytisch promyelocytic
Pronatio *f* **dolorosa infantum** nursemaid's (pulled) ellbow; subluxation of the radius
Pronation *f* pronation, mesial rotation of the forearm
Pronationsfraktur *f* pronation fracture
Pronationsphänomen *n* pronation phenomenon (sign)
Pronationsstellung *f* pronation position
Pronation-Supination-Test *m* pronation supination test
Pronator *m* pronator [muscle]
Pronatorleiste *f* pronator ridge
Pronephros *m* pronephros, forekidney, primitive (primordial, head) kidney, archinephron

pronieren to pronate
Pronormoblast *m* pronormoblast, lymphoid haemoblast [of Pappenheim] *(Erythrozytenvorstufe)*
Pronormozyt *m* pronormocyte
Pronukleus *m* pronucleus
Proöstrogen *n* pro-oestrogen
Propellerfraktur *f* propeller fracture
Propepsin *n* propepsin, pepsinogen *(inaktive Pepsinvorstufe)*
Propepton *n* propeptone
Propeptonurie *f* propeptonuria, hemialbumosuria
Properdin *n* properdin *(Plasmaglobulin)*
Prophage *m* prophage
Prophase *f* prophase, first stage of mitosis
Prophylaktikum *n* prophylactic [agent]
prophylaktisch prophylactic, preventive; sanitary
Prophylaxe *f* prophylaxis, prevention
~/Credésche Credé's prophylaxis *(Augentripperprophylaxe beim Neugeborenen)*
Propionsäure *f* propionic (propanoic) acid *(z. B. in der Galle)*
Proplasmozyt *m* proplasmacyte
Propriozeption *f* proprioception, muscle sense
propriozeptiv proprioceptive
Propriozeptor *m* proprioceptor
Proptosis *f* 1. proptosis, falling forward; falling downward; 2. *s.* Prolaps; 3. *s.* Exophthalmus
Propulsion *f* propulsion, festination *(z. B. bei Parkinsonismus)*
propulsiv propulsive
Propylalkohol *m* propylalcohol *(Desinfektionsmittel)*
Prosekretin *n* prosecretin *(Sekretinvorstufe)*
Prosekretkörnchen *n* zymogen granule *(z. B. in der Bauchspeicheldrüse)*
Prosektor *m* prosector, dissector
prosenzephal prosencephalic
Prosenzephalon *n* prosencephalon, forebrain, anterior brain vesicle *(aus Dienzephalon und Telenzephalon)*
Proserozym *n* proserozyme *(Gerinnungsfaktor)*
prosezieren to prosect
Prosopagnosie *f* prosopagnosia
Prosopalgie *f* prosopalgia, prosopodynia, facial pain
Prosoplasie *f* prosoplasia, abnormal tissue differentiation
prosoplastisch prosoplastic
Prosopoanoschisis *f* prosopoanoschisis
Prosopodiplegie *f* prosopodiplegia
Prosopodynia *f s.* Prosopalgie
Prosopodysmorphie *f* prosopodysmorphia
Prosoponeuralgie *f* prosoponeuralgia, trigeminal neuralgia
Prosopopagus *m* proso[po]pagus *(Mißgeburt)*
Prosopoplegie *f* prosopoplegia, peripheral facial palsy
prosopoplegisch prosopoplegic
Prosoposchisis *f* prosoposchisis, congenital facial cleft

Prosopospasmus *m* prosopospasm, spasm of the facial muscles
Prosoposternodymie *f* prosoposternodymia
Prosopothorakopagus *m* prosopothoracopagus, prosoposternodidymus *(Mißgeburt)*
Prosopotokie *f s.* Gesichtslage
Prospermatismus *m*, **Prospermie** *f* prospermia, premature ejaculation
Prostaglandin *n* prostaglandin *(Vorsteherdrüsenhormon)*
Prostaglandinsynthetase *f* prostaglandin synthetase *(Enzym)*
Prostata *f* prostate [gland], prostata, prostatic gland
Prostata... *s. a.* Vorsteherdrüsen...
Prostataabszeß *m* prostatic abscess
Prostataadenom *n* prostatic adenoma
Prostataatrophie *f* prostatic atrophy
Prostatabett *n* prostatic bed
Prostatadrüsengewebe *n* glandular tissue of the prostate
Prostataenukleation *f* prostatic enucleation
Prostataepithel *n* prostatic epithelium
Prostataexstirpation *f s.* Prostatektomie
Prostatafaßzange *f* prostatic lobe forceps
Prostatagang *m* prostatic duct
Prostatagewebe *n* prostatic tissue
Prostataheber *m* levator prostatae [muscle]
Prostatahöhle *f* prostatic cavity
Prostatahypertrophie *f* prostatic hypertrophy, hypertrophy of the prostatic gland
Prostataindex *m* prostatic index
Prostataeinzision *f s.* Prostatotomie
Prostatakapsel *f* prostatic capsule, capsule of the prostate
Prostatakarzinom *n* prostatic cancer, carcinoma of the prostata
Prostatakörperchen *npl* prostatic concretions
Prostatalappen *m* lobe of the prostate
Prostataleiden *n* prostatic disease
Prostatalgie *f* prostatalgia, prostatodynia, pain in the prostatic gland
Prostatamassage *f* prostatic massage
Prostatamittellappen *m*/**hypertropher** subtrigonal gland, median lobe of the prostatic gland
Prostatanadelbiopsie *f* prostatic needle biopsy
Prostatanervenversorgung *f* prostatic nerve supply
Prostatasekret *n* prostatic secretion (fluid)
Prostatasinus *m* prostatic sinus
Prostatastein *m* prostatic calculus, prostatolith
Prostatasteinentfernung *f*/**operative** prostatolithotomy
Prostata- und Harnblaseneröffnung *f*[/**operative**] prostatocystotomy
Prostataverletzung *f* prostatic injury
Prostatazyste *f* prostatic cyst
Prostatektomie *f* prostatectomy, prostatic adenectomy
~/halbseitige hemiprostatectomy
~/perineale perineal prostatectomy
~/transurethrale resectoscopy, transurethral resection of the prostate

prostatisch 636

prostatisch prostatic
Prostatismus m prostatism *(Beschwerdenkomplex bei Prostatavergrößerung)*
Prostatitis f prostatitis, inflammation of the prostatic gland
Prostatogramm n prostatogram
Prostatographie f prostatography
Prostatolith m s. Prostatastein
Prostatomegalie f prostatomegaly
Prostatorrhoe f prostatorrhoea, discharge from the prostata
Prostatotomie f prosta[to]tomy, incision into the prostatic gland
Prostatovesikulektomie f prostatovesiculectomy
Prostatovesikulitis f prostatovesiculitis, prostatoseminal vesiculitis
Prostatozystitis f prostatocystitis
Prostatozystotomie f prostatocystotomy
Prosthion n prosthion *(anthropologischer und kieferorthopädischer Meßpunkt)*
Prostigmintest m prostigmine test *(Schwangerschaftstest)*
Prostration f prostration, extreme exhaustion
Prosulfat n s. Protaminsulfat
Proszillaridin n proscillaridin *(Glykosid)*
Protagonist m protagonist *(Muskel)*
Protamin n protamine *(Heparinantagonist)*
Protaminase f protaminase *(Enzym)*
Protaminsulfat n protamine sulphate *(Heparinantagonist)*
Protaminsulfatpräzipitation f protamine sulphate precipitation
Protamin-Zink-Insulin n protamine zinc insulin *(Depotinsulin)*
protanomal protanomalous
Protanomalie f protanomaly, protanomalopia
Protanoper m protanope
Protanopie f protanopia, anerythroblep[s]ia, red blindness
protanopisch protanopic
Protease f protease *(Enzym)*
Proteaseinhibitor m protease inhibitor
Proteid n proteid[e]
Protein n protein ● **aus ~ gebildet** proteinogenous
~/Bence-Jonessches Bence Jones protein *(bei Plasmozytom)*
~/C-reaktives C-reactive protein, CRP
Protein... s. a. Eiweiß...
Proteinämie f proteinaemia
Proteinantigen n protein antigen
proteinartig proteinic, proteinaceous
Proteinase f proteinase *(Enzym)*
Proteinbindung f protein binding; protein bond
Proteinbindungskapazität f protein binding capacity
Proteinfieber n protein fever
Proteinhydrolysat n protein hydrolysate *(Aminosäurengemisch nach Proteinspaltung)*
Proteinkatabolismus m protein catabolism
Protein-Komplement-Fixations-Test m/**Reiterscher** Reiter's protein complement fixation test

Proteinmantel m protein coat *(der Bakterien)*
proteinogen proteinogenous
Proteinose f proteinosis *(im Gewebe)*
Proteinspiegelerhöhung f **im Blut** hyperproteinaemia
Proteinspiegelverminderung f **im Blut** hypoproteinaemia
Proteintherapie f protein therapy (treatment), proteotherapy
Proteinurie f prote[in]uria
proteinurisch proteinuric
protektiv protective
Proteohormon n proteohormone
Proteolyse f proteolysis
proteolytisch proteolytic, proteoclastic
Proteometabolismus m proteometabolism, protein metabolism
proteopeptisch proteopeptic
Proteose f proteose *(Enzym)*
Proteosurie f proteosuria
Proteus m **mirabilis** Proteus mirabilis *(Enterobakterium)*
~ vulgaris Proteus vulgaris *(Enterobakterium)*
Prothese f 1. pro[s]thesis, prosthetic device, orthesis; artificial limb, amputation appliance; 2. dental plate, [artificial] denture
~/pharyngoösophageale pharyngo-oesophageal prosthesis
Prothesenanpassung f prosthetic fitting
Prothesenhersteller m prosthetist
Prothesis f **ocularis** ocular prosthesis
Prothetik f 1. prosthetics, prosthetic (orthopaedic) surgery; 2. prosthodontia, prosthodontics, prosthetic dentistry
Prothetiker m prosthetist
prothetisch prosthetic
Prothrombin n prothrombin, blood-clotting factor II
Prothrombinaktivator m prothrombin activator
Prothrombinämie f prothrombinaemia
Prothrombinantagonist m antiprothrombin
Prothrombinbestimmung f **nach Quick** Quick's [prothrombin] test
prothrombinbildend prothromb[in]ogenic
Prothrombinbildung f prothrombin biosynthesis, prothrombinopoiesis ● **die ~ fördernd** prothromb[in]ogenic
Prothrombinhemmer m antiprothrombin
Prothrombin-Konsumptions-Index m prothrombin consumption index
Prothrombinmangel m prothrombinopenia
prothrombinogen prothromb[in]ogenic
Prothrombinspiegel m prothrombin level
Prothrombinspiegelerhöhung f **im Blut** prothrombinaemia
Prothrombinspiegelverminderung f **im Blut** hypoprothrombinaemia
Prothrombinzeit f prothrombin time
Prothrombokinase f prothrombokinase *(Thrombokinasevorstufe)*
Prothromboplastin n prothromboplastin
Prothromboplastinzeit f prothromboplastin time

Protist m protist *(Mikroorganismus)*
Protoblast m protoblast
protoblastisch protoblastic
protodiastolisch protodiastolic
Protoelastose f protoelastose *(Elastinspaltprodukt)*
Protoerythrozyt m protoerythrocyte
Protofibrille f protofibril, protofilament
Protoglobulose f protoglobulose
Protohäm n haem, hem[e], ferroprotoporphyrin
Protohämatoblast m protohaematoblast
Protohämin n [proto]haemin, ferriprotoporphyrin
Protoleukozyt m protoleucocyte
Protometrozyt m protometrocyte
Protonenmikroskop n proton microscope
Protopathie f protopathy
protopathisch protopathic; idiopathic
Protopepsie f protopepsia
Protoplasma n protoplasm, sarcode, cytoplasm, bioplasm
protoplasmaartig protoplasm[at]ic, protoplasmal
Protoplasmafärbung f protoplasm stain[ing]
Protoplasmafortsatz m protoplasmic process
protoplasmahaltig protoplasm[at]ic, protoplasmal
protoplasmareich rich in protoplasm, plasmic
Protoplast m protoplast *(Zellkörper)*
Protoporphyrie f protoporphyria
Protoporphyrin n protoporphyrin
Protoporphyrinausscheidung f **im Urin** protoporphyrinuria
Protoproteose f protoproteose
Protosiderin n protosiderin
Protospasmus m protospasm
prototroph[isch] prototrophic *(Bakterien)*
Protovertebra f protovertebra
Protoxin n protoxin *(Toxinvorstufe)*
Protozoenenteritis f protozoan enteritis
Protozoengift n protozoacide
Protozoenlehre f protozoology
protozoenvernichtend protozoacide
Protozoologie f protozoology
Protozoon n protozoon, protozoan ● **durch Protozoen hervorgerufen** protozoal, protozoan
Protozoophage m protozoophage
protrahieren to protract *(z. B. die Wirkung von Arzneimitteln)*
Protrusio f **acetabuli** arthrokatadysis
~ **bulbi** protopsis
Protrusion f protrusion
protrusiv protrusive
Protrypsin n protrypsin *(Trypsinvorstufe)*
Protuberantia f protuberance, protuberantia
~ **mentalis** mental protuberance (process)
~ **occipitalis externa** external occipital protuberance
~ **occipitalis interna** internal occipital protuberance, occipital cross
Protyrosinase f protyrosinase
Provitamin n provitamin *(Vitaminvorstufe)*
Provokationsdiagnostik f provocative diagnosis
Provokationstest m provocation test

provozieren to provoke
provozierend provocative
proximal proximal; proximad
prozephal procephalic
Prozerkoide f procercoid
Prozeß m process, development, course of action (events)
~/**entzündlicher** inflammatory process
~/**raumfordernder** expanding lesion *(bei Schädel-Hirn-Trauma)*
Prozeßschizophrenie f process schizophrenia
Prozymogen n prozymogen
P-R-Segment n P-R segment *(EKG)*
prüfen 1. to test; to assay; to examine; to inspect; to probe *(mit Sonden)*; 2. to control, to check
Prüfung f 1. test; trial, experiment; examination; inspection *(Zusammensetzungen s. unter Probe und Test)*; 2. investigation, control, check
pruriginös pruriginous
Prurigo f prurigo
~ **aestivalis** summer prurigo
~ **chronica nodularis** nodular prurigo
~ **dermographica** dermographic prurigo
Prurigoekzem n **Besnier** Besnier's prurigo [syndrome]
pruritisch pruritic
Pruritus m pruritus, [intense] itching, itch
~ **ani** anal pruritus
~ **hiemalis** winter itch, frost-itch
~ **senilis** senile pruritus
~ **vulvae** vulvar pruritus, itching of the vulva
Psammom n psammoma, angiolithic sarcoma
psammomartig psammomatous
Psammomkörperchen n psammoma body *(verkalkte, zwiebelschalenähnlich geschichtete Geschwulstzelle)*
Psammotherapie f psammotherapy
P-Schleife f P loop *(Vektorkardiographie)*
Pselaphesie f pselaphesia, pselaphesis, tactile sense
Psellismus m psellism, stammering, stuttering *(s. a. Stottern)*
~ **mercurialis** mercurial psellism
Pseud... s. a. Schein...
Pseudarthritis f pseudarthritis
Pseudarthrose f pseudarthrosis, ne[o]arthrosis; false joint, supplementary articulation
~/**interspinale** interspinal pseudarthrosis; Baastrup's disease
Pseudoacholie f pseudoacholia
Pseudoaggrammatismus m pseudoagrammatism
Pseudoaktinomykose f pseudoactinomycosis
Pseudoalbuminurie f pseudoalbuminuria
Pseudoallel n pseudoallele
pseudoalveolär pseudoalveolar
pseudoanaphylaktisch pseudoanaphylactic
Pseudoanaphylaxe f pseudoanaphylaxis
Pseudoangina f **[pectoris]** pseudoangina, mock angina
Pseudoangiom n pseudoangioma
Pseudoankylose f pseudoankylosis, false (fibrous) ankylosis

Pseudoaphakie

Pseudoaphakie f pseudoaphakia; membranous cataract
Pseudoappendizitis f pseudoappendicitis
Pseudoästhesie f pseudoaesthesia
Pseudoataxie f pseudoataxia
Pseudoatherom n pseudoatheroma
Pseudoatrophoderm n pseudoatrophoderma
Pseudoazephalus m pseudoacephalus *(Mißgeburt)*
Pseudobakterium n pseudobacterium
Pseudobazillus m pseudobacillus
Pseudoblepsie f pseudoblepsia
Pseudobubo m pseudobubo
Pseudobulbärparalyse f pseudobulbar palsy (paralysis)
Pseudochalazion n pseudochalazion
Pseudocholesteatom n pseudocholesteatoma
Pseudocholezystitis f pseudocholecystitis
Pseudocholinesterase f pseudocholinesterase *(Enzym)*
Pseudochorea f pseudochorea
Pseudochromästhesie f pseudochromaesthesia
Pseudochromatin n pseudochromatin
Pseudochromie f pseudochromia
Pseudochromosom n pseudochromosome
pseudochylös pseudochylous
Pseudocoarctatio f pseudocoarctation
Pseudodiphtherie f pseudodiphtheria
Pseudodiphtheriebakterium n Hofmann's bacillus
pseudodiphtherisch pseudodiphtheritic
Pseudodysenterie f pseudodysentery
Pseudoelephantiasis f pseudoelephantiasis
pseudoembryonal pseudoembryonic
Pseudoemphysem n pseudoemphysema
Pseudoendometritis f pseudoendometritis
pseudoeosinophil pseudoeosinophil
Pseudoephedrin n pseudoephedrine
Pseudoerosion f/**glanduläre** false erosion of the cervix uteri
Pseudoerysipel n pseudoerysipelas
pseudofollikulär pseudofollicular
Pseudogeusästhesie f pseudogeusaesthesia
Pseudogeusie f pseudogeusia
Pseudoglioma f pseudoglioma
Pseudoglobulin n pseudoglobulin
Pseudogonorrhoe f pseudogonorrhoea
Pseudohämagglutination f pseudohaemagglutination
Pseudohämangioperizytom n pseudohaemangiopericytoma
Pseudohämaturie f pseudohaematuria, false haematuria
Pseudohämophilie f pseudohaemophilia, proconvertin deficiency
Pseudohemiakardius m pseudohemiacardius
Pseudohermaphrodit m pseudohermaphrodite
pseudohermaphroditisch pseudohermaphroditic
Pseudohermaphroditismus m pseudohermaphroditism
~/**männlicher** male pseudohermaphroditism
~/**weiblicher** female pseudohermaphroditism, gynandry, androgyny, androgyneity, androgynism
Pseudohernie f pseudohernia
Pseudohydronephrose f pseudohydronephrosis
Pseudohydrophobie f pseudohydrophobia
Pseudohydrozephalie f pseudohydrocephalia
pseudohypertroph pseudohypertrophic
Pseudohypertrophie f pseudohypertrophy, false hypertrophy
Pseudohyponatriämie f pseudohyponatraemia
Pseudohypoparathyreoidismus m pseudohypoparathyroidism, Seabright-Bantam syndrome
Pseudohypopyon n pseudohypopyon
Pseudoikterus m pseudojaundice
Pseudoileus m pseudoileus
pseudoisochromatisch pseudoisochromatic
Pseudokeratin n pseudokeratin
Pseudokeratose f pseudokeratosis
Pseudoknorpel m pseudocartilage
Pseudokolloid n pseudocolloid
Pseudokoxalgie f pseudocoxalgia
Pseudokrise f pseudocrisis
Pseudokrup[p] m pseudocroup, false (catarrhal) croup, acute spasmodic laryngitis, croupine
Pseudokryptorchismus m pseudocryptorchism
Pseudoleberzirrhose f pseudocirrhosis
Pseudoleukämie f pseudoleukaemia, pseudoleukaemic anaemia
~/**kindliche** infantile pseudoleukaemia, von Jacksch's anaemia
Pseudo-LE-Zelle f tart cell *(Leukozyt mit fremder Kernsubstanz)*
Pseudolipom n pseudolipoma
Pseudolithiasis f pseudolithiasis
Pseudolupus m pseudolupus
Pseudolymphom n pseudolymphoma
Pseudomaladie f pseudomalady
Pseudomamma f pseudomamma
Pseudomegakolon n pseudomegacolon
Pseudomelanose f pseudomelanosis
Pseudomembran f pseudomembrane, false (croupous) membrane
pseudomembranös pseudomembranous
Pseudomeningitis f pseudomeningitis, meningitophobia
Pseudomeninx f pseudomeninx
Pseudomenstruation f pseudomenstruation
Pseudomethämoglobin n pseudomethaemoglobin
Pseudomikrozephalie f pseudomicrocephalia
Pseudomnesie f pseudomnesia
Pseudomonas f **aeruginosa (pyocyanea)** Pseudomonas aeruginosa
Pseudomonas-aeruginosa-Eiter m blue pus
Pseudomongolismus m pseudomongolism
pseudomongoloid pseudomongoloid
Pseudomongoloider m pseudomongoloid
Pseudomuzin n pseudomucin, metalbumin, mucoid
pseudomuzinös pseudomucinous
pseudomyasthenisch pseudomyasthenic

Pseudomyopie f pseudomyopia, false myopia, plesiopia *(infolge dauernder Akkommodation)*
Pseudomyxödem n pseudomyxoedema
Pseudomyxom n pseudomyxoma
Pseudomyxoma n **peritonei** gelatinous ascites (peritonitis); Werth's tumour, jelly-belly
pseudomyxomatös pseudomyxomatous
Pseudonarkose f pseudonarcotism
Pseudoneoplasma n pseudoneoplasm
pseudoneoplastisch pseudoneoplastic
Pseudoneuritis f pseudoneuritis
Pseudoneurom n pseudoneuroma
pseudoneurotisch pseudoneurotic
Pseudonuklein n pseudonuclein
Pseudonukleolus m pseudonucleolus, false nucleolus, karysome
Pseudoophthalmoplegie f pseudo-ophthalmoplegia
Pseudoosteomalazie f pseudo-osteomalacia
Pseudopapillödem n pseudopapilloedema
Pseudoparalyse f pseudoparalysis, pseudoparesis, pseudoplegia
Pseudoparaphrasie f pseudoparaphrasia
Pseudoparaplegie f pseudoparaplegia
Pseudopelade f pseudopelade
Pseudoperitonitis f pseudoperitonitis, peritonism
Pseudopneumonie f pseudopneumonia
Pseudopodium n pseudopod[ium] *(Protoplasmafortsatz kriechender Amöben)*
Pseudopolykorie f pseudopolycoria
Pseudopolyposis f pseudopolyposis
Pseudopolyzythämie f pseudopolycythaemia
Pseudoporenzephalie f pseudoporencephalia
Pseudopsie f pseudopsia, visual hallucination
pseudopsychopathisch pseudopsychopathic
Pseudopterygium n pseudopterygium
Pseudoptose f pseudoptosis
Pseudoptyalismus m pseudoptyalism
Pseudorabies f pseudorabies, Aujeszky's disease
Pseudorheumatismus m pseudorheumatism
Pseudorosette f pseudorosette
Pseudoröteln pl pseudorubella
Pseudoschanker m pseudochancre
Pseudoscharlach m pseudoscarlatina
Pseudoschwachsinn m pseudodementia
pseudoserös pseudoserous
Pseudosklerema n pseudosclerema
Pseudosklerose f pseudosclerosis
~/**Jacob-Creutzfeldtsche** Jakob-Creutzfeldt syndrome, Creutzfeldt-Jakob disease, spastic pseudosclerosis
~/**Westphal-Strümpellsche** Westphal-Strümpell pseudosclerosis
Pseudosmie f pseudosmia, phantosmia
Pseudospermatorrhoe f pseudospermatorrhoea, false spermatorrhoea
Pseudostauungspapille f pseudopapilloedema
Pseudostoma n pseudostoma
Pseudosyphilis f pseudosyphilis
Pseudosyringomyelie f pseudosyringomyelia
Pseudotabes f pseudotabes

Pseudotetanus m pseudotetanus
Pseudotinnitus m pseudotinnitus, objective tinnitus
Pseudotrichinosis f pseudotrichinosis
Pseudotruncus m **arteriosus [communis]** pseudotruncus arteriosus
Pseudotuberkulom n pseudotuberculoma
pseudotuberkulös pseudotuberculous
Pseudotuberkulose f pseudotuberculosis
Pseudotumor m pseudotumour, pseudoneoplasm
~ **cerebri** cerebral pseudotumour, [hypertensive] meningeal hydrops, benign intracranial hypertension *(Hirndrucksymptomatik ohne Tumorursache)*
Pseudotyphus m pseudotyphus
Pseudovaginitis f peritendinitis, peritenonitis
Pseudovakuole f pseudovacuole
Pseudoventrikel m pseudoventricle
Pseudovertebra f false vertebra
Pseudoxanthom n pseudoxanthoma
Pseudoxanthoma n **elasticum** elastic pseudoxanthoma
Pseudozele f pseudocele
Pseudozephalozele f pseudocephalocele
Pseudozirrhose f pseudocirrhosis
Pseudozylinder m pseudocast, false cast *(im Urin)*
Pseudozyste f pseudocyst, false cyst, cystoid
~/**intrasplenische** intrasplenic pseudocyst
Psilosis f 1. psilosis, falling out of hair; 2. s. Sprue
Psittakose f psittacosis, parrot fever
Psoas m psoas [muscle]
Psoasabszeß m psoas abscess
Psoashypertrophie f psoas hypertrophy
Psoasloge f psoas compartment
Psoasmuskel m psoas [muscle]
Psoasmuskelhypertrophie f psoas hypertrophy
Psoas[muskel]schatten m psoas shadow
Psoasscheide f psoas sheath
Psoasspasmus m psoas spasm
Psoaszeichen n psoas sign
Psoitis f psoitis, inflammation of the psoas muscle
Psoriasis f psoriasis, psora
~ **anularis** annular psoriasis
~ **arthropathica** arthropathic psoriasis; psoriatic arthropathy
~ **buccalis** buccal psoriasis
~ **circinata** circinate psoriasis
~ **diffusa** diffuse psoriasis
~ **discoidea** discoid psoriasis
~ **exsudativa** exudative psoriasis
~ **figurata** figure psoriasis
~ **follicularis** follicular psoriasis
~/**generalisierte** generalized psoriasis
~/**girlandenförmige** gyrate psoriasis
~ **linguae** lingual psoriasis, psoriasis of the tongue
~ **nummularis** nummular psoriasis
~ **palmaris** palmar psoriasis

Psoriasis 640

~ **serpiginosa** serpiginous psoriasis
~ **universalis** universal psoriasis
~ **verrucosa** verrucous psoriasis
psoriasisartig psoriasis-like, psoriasiform
Psoriasismittel *n* antipsoriatic [agent]
psoriasiswirksam antipsoriatic
Psorophthalmie *f* psorophthalmia
Psorospermie *f* psorospermiasis, psorospermia
Psorospermium *n* psorosperm
Psorospermosis *f* **follicularis [vegetans]** follicular keratosis (psorospermosis), Darier's disease
PSR *s.* Patellarsehnenreflex
Psychagogik *f* psychagogy
psychagogisch psychagogic
Psychalgie *f* psychalgia, phrenalgia, mental distress
Psychanopsie *f* psychanopsia, psychic (mind) blindness
Psychasthenie *f* psychasthenia, obsessive neurasthenia
Psychastheniker *m* psychasthene
psychasthenisch psychasthenic
Psychataxie *f* psychataxia
Psyche *f* psyche, mind, mens, soul *(Gesamtheit aller Prozesse der höheren Nerventätigkeit)*
psychedämpfend psychoplegic
Psychedämpfung *f* psychoplegia
Psycheklampsie *f* psycheclampsia
Psychialgie *f s.* Psychalgie
Psychiater *m* psychiatrist, psychiater, psychopathist, alienist
Psychiatrie *f* psychiatry, psychiatrics, mental medicine *(Lehre von den Geistes- und Gemütskrankheiten)*
psychiatrisch psychiatric
psychisch psychic, mental; psychological, emotional
psychoakustisch psychoacoustic
Psychoanaleptikum *n* psychoanaleptic [agent], psychic energizer, psychoactivator
Psychoanalgesie *f* psychoanalgesia
Psychoanalyse *f* psychoanalysis
Psychoanalytiker *m* psychoanalyst
psychoanalytisch psychoanalytic
Psychochirurgie *f* psychosurgery
Psychochromästhesie *f* psychochromaesthesia
Psychodiagnose *f* psychodiagnosis
Psychodiagnostik *f* psychodiagnostics
Psychodrama *n* psychodrama *(psychotherapeutische Methode)*
Psychodynamik *f* psychodynamics
psychodynamisch psychodynamic
Psychoenergie *f* psychic energy
Psychoepilepsie *f* psycho-epilepsy, psychic epilepsy
Psychogalvanometer *n* psychogalvanometer
psychogen[etisch] psychogen[et]ic
Psychogenie *f* psychogenesis
Psychogesundheit *f* mental sanity
Psychognosie *f* psychognosis *(Erkenntnis der seelischen Vorgänge)*
psychognostisch psychognostic

psychogogisch psychogogic
Psychogramm *n* psychogram, psychic profile
Psychographie *f* psychographia
psychographisch psychographic
Psychohygiene *f* mental hygiene
Psychokinese *f* psychokinesia, psychokinesis
Psychokoma *n* psychocoma
psychokortikal psychocortical
Psycholagnie *f* psycholagny *(geschlechtliche Erregung durch Vorstellung geschlechtlicher Handlungen)*
Psycholeiden *n* mental illness
Psycholepsie *f* psycholepsy, paralepsy
psycholeptisch psycholeptic
Psychologe *m* psychologist
Psychologie *f* psychology *(Wissenschaft von den seelischen Vorgängen und den Verhaltensweisen)*
psychologisch psychological
Psychometrie *f* psycho[do]metry *(Messung von Zeitabläufen der höheren Nerventätigkeit)*
psychometrisch psychometric
Psychomimetikum *n* psychomimetic
psychomotorisch psychomotor, ideomotor
psychoneurologisch psychoneurologic[al]
Psychoneurose *f* psychoneurosis, psychoneurotic disorder, parapathia
psychoneurotisch psychoneurotic
Psychopath *m* psychopath, psychopathic personality
~/**anankastischer** anancastic personality
~/**paranoider** paranoid personality
~/**schizoider** schizoid personality
~/**zykloider** cyclothymic personality
Psychopathia *f* **martialis** shell-shock
Psychopathie *f* psychopathy, dysthymia
~/**sexuelle** sexual psychopathy
psychopathisch psychopathic, dysthymic
Psychopathologe *m* psychopathologist
Psychopathologie *f* psychopathology *(Lehre von den geistigen und seelischen Störungen)*
psychopathologisch psychopathologic[al]
Psychopharmakologie *f* psychopharmacology
psychopharmakologisch psychopharmacologic
Psychopharmakon *n* psychopharmaceutical [agent], psychopharmacologic drug
Psychophonasthenie *f* psychophonasthenia
Psychophysiologie *f* psychophysiology
psychophysiologisch psychophysiologic
psychophysisch psychophysic[al]
Psychoplegie *f* psychoplegia
Psychoplegikum *n* psychoplegic [agent]
psychoplegisch psychoplegic
Psychoreaktion *f* psychoreaction
Psychorhythmus *m* psychorhythmia
Psychorrhagie *f* psychorrhagia
Psychoschmerz *m s.* Psychalgie
Psychoschock *m* psychic shock
Psychose *f* [neuro]psychosis, phrenopathy, psychiatric illness, folie ● **an einer ~ leidend** psychotic ● **ohne ~** non-psychotic
~/**alkoholische** alcoholic psychosis (dementia, insanity)

~/endogene endogenous psychosis
~/halluzinatorische hallucinatory (perceptional) psychosis
~/hysterische hysterical psychosis
~/manisch-depressive manic-depressive psychosis (reaction, illness)
~/organische organic (idiopathic) psychosis
~/postoperative postoperative psychosis
~/reaktive reactive (situational) psychosis
~/senile senile psychosis (insanity)
Psychosedativum n tranquilizer, ataractic [agent], ataraxic
psychoseerzeugend psychotogenic, psychodelic
psychosefrei non-psychotic
Psychosekranker m psychotic
psychosensorisch psychosensory
psychosexuell psychosexual
psychosomatisch psychosomatic
Psychosomimetikum n s. Psychotikum
psychosozial psychosocial
psychostark neurosthenic
Psychostärke f neurosthenia
psychostimulierend psychogogic
Psychosyndrom n psychosyndrome
~/frühkindliches minimal brain dysfunction syndrome, minimal chronic brain syndrome
~ [/hirn]organisches organic brain syndrome
Psychotest m psychological test
Psychotherapeut m psychotherapist
psychotherapeutisch psychotherapeutic
Psychotherapie f psychotherapy, mind cure, mental healing
Psychotiker m psychotic
Psychotikum n psychotogen, psychomimetic
psychotisch psychotic
~/nicht non-psychotic
psychotogen psychotogenic
Psychotonus m psychotonus ● den ~ vermindernd psycholeptic
Psychotonusverlust m/**plötzlicher** psycholepsy, paralepsy
Psychotrauma n psychotrauma, psychic trauma
psychotrop psychotropic *(z. B. Medikament)*
Psychozustand m/**klarer** lucidity
Psychroalgie f psychroalgia
Psychroästhesie f psychroaesthesia
Psychrometer n psychrometer
psychrophil psychrophilic *(z. B. Mikroorganismen)*
Psychrophilie f psychrophilia
psychrophob psychrophobic
Psychrophobie f psychrophobia *(krankhafte Angst vor Kälte)*
Psychrotherapie f psychrotherapy
PTA plasma thromboplastin antecedent
Ptarmikum n ptarmic [agent], sternutatory
Ptarmus m ptarmus, spasmodic sneezing
PTC 1. s. Cholangiographie/perkutane transhepatische; 2. = plasma thromboplastin component
Pteroylglutaminsäure f pteroylglutamic (folic) acid
pterygial pterygial

Puerperalmetritis

Pterygium n pterygium *(Wucherung der Augapfelbindehaut auf die Augenhornhaut)*
~ **colli** collar pterygium, cervical patagium; webbed neck, sphinx-neck
pterygoid pterygoid
Ptilosis f ptilosis, falling out of the eyelashes
PTKA s. Koronarangioplastik/perkutane transluminale
Ptomain n ptomaine
Ptomainämie f ptomainaemia
Ptomainausscheidung f **im Urin** ptomainuria
Ptomainblutvergiftung f ptomainaemia
Ptosis f ptosis, dropping of the lid, lid drop, [lash] blepharoptosis
PTT s. Thromboplastinzeit/partielle
Ptyalektase f ptyalectasis, dilatation of a salivary gland duct
Ptyalin n ptyalin[e] *(Enzym)*
Ptyalismus m ptyalism, excessive salivation, drooling, polysialia
ptyalogen ptyalogenic
Ptyalogogum n ptyalogogue [agent]
Ptyalogramm n ptyalogram
Ptyalographie f ptyalography
Ptyalolith m s. Sialolith
Ptyalolithiasis f ptyalolithiasis, salivolithiasis, sialolithiasis
Ptyalolithotomie f ptyalolithotomy
Ptyalozele f ptyalocele
Pubeotomie f pubiotomy, section of the pubic bone, hebo[steo]tomy
puberal puber[t]al
Pubertant m puber
Pubertät f puberty, pubescence ● **vorzeitig in die ~ eintretend** premature
~/vorzeitige premature (precocious) puberty, precosity
Pubertätskrise f adolescent crisis
Pubertätsstimmwechsel m paraphonia of the puberty
pubertierend pubescent
Pubertierender m puber
Pubes f pubes, pudental (pubic) region
Pubiotomie f s. Pubeotomie
pubisch pubic
pubosakral sacropubic
Pudenda npl **feminina** pudenda [feminina]; vulva, cunnus
Pudendagra f pudendagra
pudendal pudendal, pudic
Pudendalanästhesie f pudendal anaesthesia
pueril puerile, childish, immature
Puerilismus m puerilism
Puerpera f s. Wöchnerin
Puerperal... s. a. Wochenbett...
Puerperaleklampsie f puerperal convulsion (eclampsia)
Puerperalfieber n puerperal (childbed) fever, loch[i]opyra, lechopyra
Puerperalmastitis f puerperal mastitis; caked breast
Puerperalmetritis f puerperal metritis, loch[i]ometritis

Puerperalperitonitis

Puerperalperitonitis f puerperal peritonitis, lochoperitonitis
Puerperalpsychose f puerperal psychosis (insanity, mania), tocomania
Puerperalsepsis f puerperal sepsis
Puerperalseptikämie f puerperal septicaemia
Puerperalsynovitis f puerperal synovitis
Puerperalthelitis f puerperal thelitis
Puerperium n puerperium, childbed, lying-in [period]
Puffer m buffer
Pufferbehandlung f buffer therapy, buffering
Pufferlösung f buffer solution
puffern to buffer
Pufferung f buffering, buffer therapy
Pufferwirkung f buffer action (effect)
Pulex m Pulex
~ **cheopis** Pulex cheopis *(Pestüberträger)*
~ **irritans** Pulex irritans, human flea
Pulicosis f pulicatio, infestation by fleas; flea bites
Pulmo m pulmo, lung *(Zusammensetzungen s. unter Lunge)*
pulmokardial pulmocardiac
Pulmologe m pulmonologist, pulmonary (lung) specialist, chest physician
pulmonal pulmonary, pulmonic
Pulmonal... *s. a.* Lungen...
Pulmonalis f s. 1. Lungenarterie; 2. Lungenvene; 3. Pulmonalklappe
Pulmonalisinsuffizienz f pulmonary insufficiency
Pulmonalisinsuffizienz-Geräusch n Graham-Steel murmur *(bei Mistralstenose)*
Pulmonalisklemme f pulmonary clamp
Pulmonalisschlußton m pulmonary closure sound
Pulmonalissegel n s. Pulmonalklappensegel
Pulmonaliston m s. Pulmonalton
Pulmonalisvalvulotomie f pulmonary valvulotomy
Pulmonalklappe f pulmonary valve ● **unter der ~** subpulmonary, subpulmonic
Pulmonalklappenschlußunfähigkeit f pulmonary insufficiency
Pulmonalklappensegel n pulmonary leaflet (valve cusp)
Pulmonalklappensprengung f[/operative] pulmonary valvulotomy
Pulmonalklappenton m s. Pulmonalton
Pulmonalklappenvereng[er]ung f s. Pulmonalstenose
Pulmonalkreislauf m pulmonary (lesser) circulation, lesser circulatory system
Pulmonalkreislaufwiderstand m pulmonary resistance
Pulmonalstammvergrößerung f enlargement of the pulmonary trunk
Pulmonalstenose f pulmonary [valvular] stenosis, stenosis of the pulmonary valve
~/**infundibuläre** infundibular pulmonary stenosis
~/**valvuläre** valvular pulmonary stenosis
Pulmonalton m pulmonary sound
~/**zweiter** pulmonary second sound, second pulmonic sound
Pulmonalvene f s. Lungenvene
Pulmonalvenentransposition f transposition of the pulmonary veins, anomalous pulmonary venous drainage
Pulmonektomie f pulmonectomy, pneum[on]ectomy
Pulmonologie f pulmonary medicine
Pulmotor m pulmotor, lungmotor
Pulpa f 1. pulp[a] *(Organparenchym)*; 2. s. ~ dentis
~ **coronale** coronal pulp
~ **dentis** dental (tooth) pulp, endodontium
~ **lienalis** splenic pulp (tissue)
~ **radicularis** radicular pulp
~/**rote** red pulp [cords]
Pulpaarterie f pulp artery
pulpaartig pulpy, pulpiform
Pulpadevitalisation f devitalization [of the pulp] *(Pulpaentfernung aus dem Wurzelkanal)*
Pulpaentzündung f s. Pulpitis
Pulpaexstirpation f s. Pulpektomie
pulpafrei pulpless
Pulpahöhle f dental cavity, pulp cavity [of the tooth]
Pulpahöhlenpräparation f cavity preparation
Pulpaknötchen n pulp nodule
pulpal pulpal, pulpar
Pulpalgie f pulpalgia, pain in the dental pulp
Pulpapolyp m pulp polyp
Pulpaschmerz m s. Pulpalgie
Pulpasiegel n pulp seal (cap) *(Stomatologie)*
Pulpastein m pulp stone
Pulpaumwandlung f pulpation
Pulpavene f pulp vein
Pulpazelle f pulp cell
Pulpektomie f pulpectomy, pulpotomy, removal of the dental pulp
Pulpitis f pulpitis, endodontitis, inflammation of the dental pulp
~/**hyperplastische** hyperplastic pulpitis; pulp polyp
Puls m pulse, pulsus, beat, sphygmus *(s. a. unter Pulsus)* ● **den ~ fühlen** to feel the pulse
~/**alternierender** alternating pulse; alternans of the heart
~/**anakroter** anacrotic pulse
~/**aussetzender** intermittent (interrupted) pulse; miosphygmia
~/**beschleunigter** accelerated (quick) pulse
~/**Corriganscher** Corrigan's pulse, cannon ball pulse *(bei Aorteninsuffizienz)*
~/**dikroter** dicrotic pulse
~/**doppelschlägiger** bigeminal pulse, coupled beat (pulse)
~/**drahtartiger** wiry pulse
~/**dreischlägiger** trigeminal pulse
~/**einschlägiger** monocrotic pulse
~/**epigastrischer** epigastric pulse
~/**fadenförmiger** filiform (shabby) pulse
~/**gespannter** tense (cordy) pulse

~/gespannter und harter hard and cordy pulse, high-tension pulse
~/harter hard pulse
~/hüpfender jerky pulse
~/jagender running pulse
~/katadikroter catadicrotic pulse
~/katakroter catacrotic pulse
~/katatrikroter catatricrotic pulse
~/Kussmaulscher paradoxical pulse
~/langsamer slow pulse
~/monokroter monocrotic pulse
~/nicht fühlbarer imperceptible pulse
~/nicht gespannter low-tension pulse
~/paradoxer paradoxical pulse
~/regelmäßiger regular pulse
~/schnellender sharp pulse; jerky pulse
~/schneller quick (rapid) pulse
~/trikroter tricrotic pulse
~/unregelmäßiger irregular pulse
~/vierschlägiger quadrigeminal pulse
~/wechselnder s. ~/alternierender
~/weicher soft (weak) pulse; microsphygmy, microsphyxia; low-tension pulse
~/zweizipfliger bisferious pulse
Pulsader f s. Arterie
pulsartig sphygmoid, sphygmodic
Pulsation f pulsation, beat, sphygmus, throb
~/epigastrische epigastric pulsation; epigastric pulse
Pulsationsexophthalmus m pulsating exophthalmus
Pulsaufzeichner m sphygmograph, kymograph
Pulsaufzeichnung f sphygmography, kymography
Pulsbeschleunigung f pulse acceleration; quick (accelerated) pulse
Pulsdefizit n pulse deficit; deficient pulse
Pulsdruck m pulse pressure
Pulsdruckamplitude f pulse pressure
Pulsfrequenz f pulse rate
pulsieren to pulsate, to beat, to pulse, to throb
pulsierend pulsating, pulsatile, throbbing
Pulsion f pulsion
Pulsionsdivertikel n pulsion (pressure) diverticulum; pharyngeal (pharyngo-oesophageal) diverticulum
Pulskontrolle f examination of the pulse
Pulskraftmesser m pulsimeter, pulsometer, sphygmodynamometer
Pulskraftmessung f sphygmodynamometry
Pulskurve f sphygmo[bolo]gram
Pulskurvenschreiber m sphygmograph, arteriograph, sphygmo[bolo]meter
Pulskurvenschreibung f sphygmography, arteriography, sphygmo[bolo]metry
pulslos pulseless, acrotic
Pulslosigkeit f absence of the pulse, acrotism
Pulsmesser m s. Pulskraftmesser
Pulsrate f pulse rate
Pulsschlag m pulsation, [pulse] beat, sphygmus (s. a. Puls); palpitation, palmus
Pulsunregelmäßigkeit f irregularity of the pulse

Pulsus m pulse, pulsus, beat, sphygmus (s. a. unter Puls)
~ abdominalis abdominal pulse
~ bisferiens [dicrotus] bisferious pulse
~ capricans goat leap pulse
~ celer quick (rapid) pulse
~ celer et altus Corrigan's pulse, connon ball pulse (bei Aorteninsuffizienz)
~ cordis apex beat [of the heart], apex impulse
~ debilis soft (weak) pulse
~ deficiens deficient pulse
~ deletus absence of the pulse
~ formicans formicant pulse
~ frequens frequent pulse
~ irregularis irregular pulse
~ irregularis perpetuus absolute arrhythmia
~ parvus et tardus plateau pulse
~ plenus full pulse
~ rarus slow pulse
~ simplex monocrotic pulse
~ triplex tricrotic pulse
~ undulosus undulating pulse
~ vibrans vibrating pulse
Pulsverhalten n nature of the pulse
pulsverlangsamt bradycrotic
Pulsverlangsamung f slowing of the pulse rate, bradysphygmia
Pulswelle f pulse wave
~/dreizackige anatricrotism
Pulswellenaufzeichnungsgerät n s. Pulswellenschreiber
Pulswellenmessung f oscillometry, sphygmometry
Pulswellenschreiber m oscillometer, sphygmograph
Pulszahl f pulse rate
Pulszyklus m pulse cycle
Pulver n pulvis, pulv., powder (Arzneiform) ● zu ~ zerreiben (zerstoßen) to pulverize
Pulverbläser m insufflator
pulverisieren to pulverize; to triturate (fein)
Pulverisierung f pulverization; trituration, tripsis
~/feine trituration, tripsis
Pulverstar m/zentraler embryonal nuclear cataract
Pulvinar n thalami pulvinar [thalami] (hinteres Ende des Thalamus im Gehirn)
Pulvis m s. Pulver
pumpen to pump
Pumpenoxygenator m pump oxygenator
Punctum n s. Punkt
~ caecum blind spot
~ dolorosum pain[ful] point
~ lacrimale lacrimal point (punctum)
~ maximum point of maximal impulse (Stelle des lautesten Herztons)
~ proximum near point (Ophthalmologie)
~ remotum far point (Ophthalmologie)
Punkt m point, punctum; spot (s. a. unter Punctum)
~/blutender bleeding point (z. B. Diphtheriemembran)

Punkt

~/Erbscher Erb's (supraclavicular) point
~/hysterofrener hysterofrener (hysterogenic) point
~/McBurneyscher McBurney's point *(Druckpunkt im rechten Unterbauch bei Blinddarmentzündung)*
Punktblutung f punctate haemorrhage
punktförmig punctiform
punktieren to puncture, to tap, to perform a paracentesis; to cannulize
~/eine Vene to puncture a vein
punktiert 1. punctured, tapped; 2. punctate, dotted
Punktion f puncture, tapping, [para]centesis, needling; cannulization *(s. a. unter Paracentesis)*
~/explorative exploratory puncture
~ der Excavatio rectouterina Douglas pouch puncture
Punktionsbesteck n aspirating set
Punktionsbiopsie f needle (aspiration) biopsy
Punktionskanüle f aspirating (exploring) cannula; [puncture] needle
Punktionskopfschmerz m puncture headache
Punktionsnadel f [puncture] needle, aspirating (exploring) needle
Punktionsstelle f site of the puncture (cannula insertion)
Punktmutation f point mutation
Punktstar m punctate (punctiform) cataract
Pupille f pupil[la]
~/Adiesche Adie's [tonic] pupil, pseudo Argyll-Robertson pupil, Adie's syndrome
Pupillen fpl/**springende** hippus; pupil unrest, springing (bounding) mydriasis
Pupillenablösung f corelysis
Pupillenachse f pupillary axis
Pupillenanomalie f pupillary anomaly
Pupillenathetose f pupillary athetosis
Pupillenatonie f pupillatonia
Pupillenatresie f atretopsia
Pupillenbewegung f pupil movement; pupillary reaction
~/träge sluggish pupillary reaction
Pupillendialyse f pupillary dialysis
Pupillendifferenz f inequality of the pupils, anisocoria
Pupillendistanz f interpupillary distance
Pupillendurchleuchtung f transillumination of the pupil
Pupillenektopie f corectopia *(Mißbildung)*
Pupillenengstellung f miosis, myosis
Pupillenerweiterer m dilator pupillae [muscle]
pupillenerweiternd pupillodilator, pupil-dilating, mydriatic; cycloplegic
Pupillenerweiterung f dilatation of the pupil; mydriasis, platycoria
~/paralytische paralytic mydriasis
~/pathologische pathological mydriasis; corectasis
Pupillengleichheit f isocoria
Pupillengröße f pupillary size

Pupillenkontraktion f pupillary contraction, amydriasis
Pupillenlosigkeit f acorea
Pupillenmotilität f pupil motility
Pupillenphänomen n/**paradoxes** Westphal's pupillary reflex, Westphal-Pilcz reflex
Pupillenplastik f coreoplasty
Pupillenrand m pupillary border (margin)
Pupillenreaktion f pupillary response; pupillary reflex
~ auf Dunkelheit pupillary darkness reflex
~/konsensuelle s. ~/unwillkürliche
~/paradoxe paradoxical pupillary reaction *(Pupillenerweiterung bei Lichteinfall)*
~/unwillkürliche consensual eye (light) reflex
~/verlangsamte asthenocoria *(bei Nebennierenunterfunktion)*
Pupillenreflex m pupillary reflex; light (iris contraction) reflex *(Pupillenverengung auf Licht)*
Pupillenrekonstruktion f coreoplasty
Pupillenschluß m coreclisis
Pupillenspiel n pupillary play
Pupillenspielamplitude f amplitude of pupillary movements
Pupillenstarre f pupillary rigidity
~/reflektorische Argyll-Robertson pupil (sign)
Pupillenträgheit f pupillary inertia
Pupillenunruhe f pupil unrest
pupillenverengend miotic, pupilloconstrictor
Pupillenverengerer m sphincter pupillae [muscle]
Pupillenvereng[er]ung f constriction of the pupil; miosis, myosis, stenocoriasis
Pupillenverformung f dyscoria
Pupillenverlagerung f corectopia, displacement of the pupil *(Mißbildung)*
Pupillenvermessung f coreometry
Pupillenverschluß m pupillary obliteration (occlusion), coreclisis
Pupillenzeichen n/**Bumkesches** Bumke's pupil
pupillodilatorisch pupillodilator
Pupillographie f pupillography
pupillokonstriktorisch pupilloconstrictor
Pupillometer n pupillometer, cor[e]ometer
Pupillometrie f pupillometry, coreometry *(Bestimmung des Pupillendurchmessers)*
pupillomotorisch pupillomotor
Pupilloskop n pupilloscope
Pupilloskopie f pupilloscopy, skiascopy, skiametry, umbrascopy
Pupillostatometer n pupillostatometer *(Instrument zur Bestimmung des Pupillenabstands nach Ostwald)*
Pupillotonie f pupillotonia, Adie's syndrome
pupillotonisch pupillotonic
Purgans n s. Purgativum
Purgation f purgation, catharsis
purgativ purgative, cathartic, evacuant
Purgativ[um] n purgative, cathartic [agent], evacuant [agent]
purgieren s. abführen
puriform puriform

Purin n purine
Purinämie f purinaemia
Purinausscheidung f im Urin alloxuria
Purinbase f purine base
purinfrei purine-free
Purinkörper m purine body
Purinstoffwechsel m purine metabolism
Purität f purity
Purkinje-Aderfigur f Purkinje image
Purkinje-Faser f Purkinje fibre
Puromyzin n puromycin *(Antibiotikum aus Streptomyces alboniger)*
Purpura f [thrombopenic] purpura, peliosis, purple; Werlhof's disease
~ **abdominalis** Henoch's purpura
~/**allergische** s. ~/rheumatische
~/**anaphylaktoide** anaphylactoid purpura
~ **anularis teleangiectoides** Majocchi's disease *(rosa-lividrote Flecken der Haut durch Kapillarerweiterung)*
~ **fulminans** fulminant purpura
~/**hämorrhagische** haemorrhagic purpura
~/**Henochsche** Henoch's purpura
~ **Henoch-Schönlein** Henoch-Schönlein purpura
~/**idiopathische thrombozytopenische** idiopathic thrombo[cyto]penic purpura, thrombocytolytic purpura, Werlhof's disease; land scurvy
~/**mechanische** mechanical purpura
~ **necrotica** necrotic purpura
~/**rheumatische** rheumatic purpura (peliosis), allergic (Schönlein's) purpura, Schönlein's disease
~/**sekundäre** secondary purpura
~ **senilis** senile purpura
~ **simplex** simple purpura
Purpurin n purpurin
Purpurinausscheidung f im Urin purpurinuria
purpurogen purpurogenous
purulent purulent, pyic, puruloid, suppurative
~/**nicht** non-purulent, non-suppurative
Purulenz f purulence, purulency, suppuration
Pus n s. Eiter
Pustel f pustule, pimple, pus (purulent) blister, vesiculo-pustule ● **mit Pusteln bedeckt** pustular ● **mit Pusteln einhergehend** pustular
pustelartig pustular, pustuliform
Pustelbildung f pustulation, empyesis; pustulosis *(an der Haut)*
pustelförmig pustuliform
Pustula f **maligna** malignant pustule; anthrax, tanner's disease, Siberian pest
Pustuloderma n pustuloderma
Pustulosis f pustulosis, periporitis
Putamen n putamen *(äußerer Teil des Linsenkerns im Endhirn)*
Putrefaktion f, **Putreszenz** f s. Fäulnis
Putreszin n putrescine *(Amin des Ornithins)*
putrid putrid, sapraemic
Pyämie f pyaemia, pyo[sept]haemia, pyosapraemia
pyämisch pyaemic

Pyarthros m s. Pyarthrose
Pyarthrose f py[o]arthrosis, pyogenic arthritis, acute suppurative synovitis
Pyaskos m pyaskos
Pyelektasie f pyelectasia, dilatation of the renal pelvis
Pyelitis f pyelitis, inflammation of the renal pelvis
pyelitisch pyelitic
Pyelofluoroskopie f pyelofluoroscopy
pyelogen pyelogenic
Pyelogramm n pyelogram, pyelo-ureterogram
~/**intravenöses** intravenous pyelogram, IVP
~/**retrogrades** retrograde pyelogram
Pyelographie f pyelography, pyelo-ureterography
~/**intravenöse** intravenous pyelography, pyelography by elimination
~ **nach Lufteinblasung** air pyelography
~/**retrograde** retrograde (ascending) pyelography *(nach Kontrastmittelgabe über Katheter)*
pyelographisch pyelographic
Pyelolithotomie f pyelolithotomy, pelviolithotomy
pyelolymphatisch pyelolymphatic
Pyelonephritis f pyelonephritis, inflammation of the kidney and the pelvis, interstitial nephritis
Pyelonephrose f pyelonephrosis
Pyelopathie f pyelopathy, disease of the renal pelvis
Pyelophlebitis f pyelophlebitis, inflammation of the veins of the renal pelvis
Pyeloplastik f pyeloplasty
Pyeloplikation f pyeloplication
Pyelostomie f pyelostomy, nephrostomy
Pyelotomie f pyelotomy, pelviotomy, incision of the renal pelvis
pyelotubulär pyelotubular
pyeloureteral pyelo-ureteral, pyelo-ureteric
Pyeloureterektasie f pyelo-ureterectasis, dilatation of the renal pelvis and the ureter
Pyeloureteroplastik f pyelo-ureteroplasty
pyelovenös pyelovenous
Pyelozystitis f pyelocystitis
Pyemesis f pyemesis, vomiting of purulent matter
Pyemotes m **ventricosus** grain itch mite
Pyenzephalus m pyencephalus, abscess of the brain
Pygalgie f pygalgia, pain in the buttocks
Pygmalionismus m pygmalionism *(sexuelle Erregung beim Betrachten und Betasten von Standbildern)*
Pygomelus m pygomelus *(Mißgeburt)*
Pygopagus m pygopagus, pygodidymus *(Mißgeburt)*
pyknisch pyknic
Pyknolepsie f pykno[epi]lepsy *(Häufung von kleinen epileptischen Anfällen)*
Pyknometer n pycnometer, densimeter
pyknomorph pyknomorphic, pyknomorphous *(Nervenzellen)*
Pyknose f pyknosis *(beim Absterben von Zellen)*
pyknotisch pyknotic

Pyknozyt

Pyknozyt *m* oncocyte
Pyknodysostosis *f* pyknodysostosis
Pylemphraxis *f* pylemphraxis, portal [vein] obstruction
Pylephlebektasie *f* pylephlebectasia
Pylephlebitis *f* pylephlebitis, inflammation of the portal vein
Pylethrombophlebitis *f* pylethrombophlebitis
Pylethrombose *f* pylethrombosis, thrombosis of the portal vein
Pyloralgie *f* pyloralgia, pain in the pylorus region
Pylorektomie *f* [gastro]pylorectomy, excision of the pylorus
pylorisch pyloric
pyloroduodenal pyloroduodenal
Pyloroduodenitis *f* pyloroduodenitis
pylorokolisch pylorocolic
Pyloromyotomie *f* pyloromyotomy; [Fredet-] Ramstedt operation *(zur Beseitigung eines Magenpförtnerkrampfs)*
Pyloroplastik *f* pyloroplasty
~ **nach Finney** Finney's pyloroplasty
~ **nach Heineke-Mikulicz** Heineke-Mikulicz operation
Pyloroptose *f* pyloroptosia
Pyloroschesis *f* pyloroschesis, obstruction of the pylorus
Pyloroskopie *f* pyloroscopy
Pylorostenose *f s.* Pylorusstenose
Pylorostomie *f* pylorostomy
Pylorotomie *f* pylorotomy, gastromyotomy, incision of the pylorus
Pylorus *m* pylorus
Pylorus... *s. a.* Magenpförtner...
Pylorusdilator *m* pylorodilator
Pylorusdrüsen *fpl* pyloric glands
Pyloruskanaleröffnung *f/operative s.* Pylorotomie
Pyloruskanalfistelung *f* pylorostomy
Pyloruskanalulkus *n* channel ulcer
Pyloruskrampf *m* pylorospasm, spasm of the pylorus
pylorusnah juxtapyloric
Pylorusnervenplexus *m* pyloric plexus
Pylorusobstruktion *f s.* Pyloroschesis
Pylorusplexus *m* pyloric plexus
Pylorusresektion *f s.* Pylorektomie
Pylorusschließmuskel *m* sphincter of the pylorus
Pylorusschmerz *m s.* Pyloralgie
Pylorusspreizer *m* pylorus spreader
Pylorusstenose *f* pyloric stenosis, pylorostenosis, narrowing (stricture) of the pylorus
Pylorusteilresektion *f* hemipylorectomy
Pylorus- und Zwölffingerdarmentzündung *f* pyloroduodenitis
Pyoblennorrhoe *f* pyoblennorrhoea
Pyochezie *f* pyochezia, discharge of pus with the stools
Pyoderma *n* 1. pyoderma; 2. *s.* Pyodermatose
~ **faciale** facial pyoderma

Pyodermatitis *f* pyodermatitis, pustular skin inflammation
pyodermatös pyodermatous
Pyodermatose *f* pyodermatosis, purulent skin disease
Pyodermie *f s.* Pyoderma
pyogen pyogen[et]ic, pyogenous, pyopoietic, pus-forming, pus-producing
~/**nicht** non-pyogenic
Pyogenese *f* pyogenesis, formation of pus, pyopoiesis
Pyohämothorax *m* pyohaemothorax
Pyokokkus *m* pyococcus
Pyokolpos *m* pyocolpos
Pyokolpozele *f* pyocolpocele
Pyolabyrinthitis *f* pyolabyrinthitis
Pyometra *f* pyometra
Pyometritis *f* pyometritis, suppurative inflammation of the uterus
Pyomyositis *f* pyomyositis, suppurative myositis
Pyonephritis *f* pyonephritis, purulent inflammation of the kidney
Pyonephrolithiasis *f* pyonephrolithiasis
Pyonephrose *f* pyonephrosis; pyonephrotic kidney
pyonephrotisch pyonephrotic
Pyoovarium *n* pyo-ovarium
Pyoperikard *n* pyopericardium
Pyoperikarditis *f* pyopericarditis, purulent pericarditis, purulent inflammation of the pericardium
Pyoperitoneum *n* pyoperitoneum
Pyoperitonitis *f* pyoperitonitis, suppurative inflammation of the peritoneum
Pyophagie *f* pyophagia, swallowing of pus
Pyophthalmie *f* pyophthalmia, purulent ophthalmia, purulent inflammation of the eye
pyophylaktisch pyophylactic
Pyophysometra *f* pyophysometra
Pyopneumocholezystitis *f* pyopneumocholecystitis
Pyopneumoperikard *n* pyopneumopericardium
Pyopneumoperikarditis *f* pyopneumopericarditis *(Herzbeutelentzündung mit Eiter- und Luftansammlung im Herzbeutel)*
Pyopneumoperitoneum *n* pyopneumoperitoneum
Pyopneumoperitonitis *f* pyopneumoperitonitis *(Bauchfellentzündung mit Eiter- und Luftansammlung in der Bauchfellhöhle)*
Pyopneumothorax *m* pyopneumothorax
Pyoptysis *f* pyoptysis, expectoration of pus (purulent matter)
Pyorrhoe *f* pyorrhoea, purulent discharge
Pyorrhoea *f* **alveolaris** chronic suppurative pericementitis
Pyosalpingitis *f* pyosalpingitis, purulent salpingitis
Pyosalpingo-Oophoritis *f* pyosalpingo-oophoritis, inflammation of the ovary and oviduct
Pyosalpinx *f* pyosalpinx, pus tube
Pyoseptikämie *f* pyosepticaemia, pyosepthaemia

Pyospermie f pyospermia
Pyostatikum n pyostatic [agent]
Pyotherapie f pyotherapy, treatment with pus
Pyothorax m pyothorax
Pyoumbilikus m pyoumbilicus
Pyourachus m pyourachus
Pyoureter m pyoureter
Pyoxanthin n pyoxanthin
Pyozele f pyocele
Pyozephalus m pyocephalus
Pyozyanase f pyocyanase *(Enzym)*
Pyozyanin n pyocyanin[e] *(Antibiotikum)*
pyozyaninbildend pyocyanogenic
pyozyanisch pyocyanic
Pyozyanolysin n pyocyanolysin *(durch Pseudomonas aeruginosa erzeugtes Hämolysin)*
Pyozyanose f pyocyanosis *(Infektion durch Pseudomonas aeruginosa)*
Pyozystitis f pyocystitis
Pyramidalstar m pyramidal cataract
Pyramide f 1. pyramid, pyramis *(Zusammensetzungen s. unter Pyramis)*; 2. s. Felsenbein
pyramidenartig pyramidal
Pyramidenbahn f pyramidal (corticospinal) tract
Pyramidenbahndurchtrennung f[/operative] s. Pyramidotomie
Pyramidenbahnerkrankung f pyramidal disorder
Pyramidenbahnfaser f pyramidal tract fibre
Pyramidenbahnkreuzung f pyramidal decussation
Pyramidenbahnstörung f pyramidal disorder
Pyramidenbahnsystem n pyramidal system
Pyramidenbahnzeichen n pyramidal tract sign
pyramidenförmig pyramidal
Pyramidenschicht f/**äußere** external pyramidal layer, layer of pyramidal cells *(in der Großhirnrinde)*
Pyramidenseitenstrangbahn f lateral corticospinal tract
Pyramidensystem n pyramidal system
Pyramidenvorderstrangbahn f anterior corticospinal tract, fascicle of Türck
Pyramidenzelle f pyramidal cell (neuron)
Pyramidotomie f pyramidotomy, section of the pyramidal tract
Pyramis f pyramis, pyramid
~ **cerebelli** pyramid of the cerebellum *(Teil des Kleinhirnunterwurms)*
~ **medullae oblongatae** pyramid of the medulla oblongata
~ **renalis** renal pyramid
~ **vermis** pyramid of the vermis *(Teil des Kleinhirnunterwurms)*
~ **vestibuli** pyramid of the vestibule
pyretisch s. pyrogen
Pyretologie f pyretology
Pyretolyse f pyretolysis, reduction of fever
Pyretotherapie f 1. pyretotherapy, treatment by fever; 2. treatment of fever, antipyresis
Pyretothyphosis f pyretothyphosis, febrile delirium
Pyrexie f s. Fieber

Pyrexiophobie f pyrexiophobia *(krankhafte Angst vor Fieber)*
pyrgozephal pyrgocephalic, pyrgocephalous
Pyrgozephalie f pyrgocephalia; tower head (skull)
3-Pyridinkarbonsäure f niacin *(Vitamin)*
3-Pyridinkarbonsäureamid n niacinamide *(Vitamin)*
Pyridostigmin n pyridostigmine *(Cholinesterasehemmer)*
Pyridoxin n vitamin B_6, Y factor, adermin
Pyridoxinmangel m pyridoxine deficiency
Pyrimethamin n pyrimethamine *(Antimalariamittel)*
Pyrimidin n pyrimidine
Pyrogallol n pyrogallol *(Dermatikum)*
Pyrogallussäure f pyrogallic acid *(Dermatikum)*
pyrogen pyrogen[et]ic, pyrogenous, pyretogen[et]ic, pyretogenous
Pyrogen n pyr[et]ogen *(Abbau- und Stoffwechselprodukt von Bakterien)*
~/**bakterielles** bacterial pyrogen
Pyroglobulin n pyroglobulin
Pyroglobulinämie f pyroglobulinaemia
Pyroglossie f pyroglossia
Pyrokatechase f pyrocatechase *(Enzym)*
Pyrokatechinausscheidung f im Urin pyrocatechinuria
Pyrokatechol n pyrocatechol *(Antiseptikum)*
Pyrolyse f pyrolysis
Pyromane m pyromaniac
Pyromanie f pyromania
Pyronin n pyronin[e] *(Gewebsfarbstoff)*
pyroninophil pyroninophilic
Pyrophobie f pyrophobia *(krankhafte Angst vor Feuer)*
Pyrophosphatase f pyrophosphatase *(Enzym)*
Pyropunktur f pyropuncture
Pyrosis f [gastric] pyrosis, heartburn, [water] brash
Pyrotoxin n pyrotoxin
Pyruvat n pyruvate
Pyruvatkinase f pyruvate kinase *(Enzym)*
Pyruvatkinasemangel m pyruvate kinase deficiency
Pyurie f pyuria
pyurisch pyuric
P-Zacke f P wave [of the electrocardiogram], auricular complex
PZ-Insulin n protamine zinc insulin *(Depotinsulin)*

Q

q. d. s. quaque die
Q-Fieber n Query fever, [Australian] Q fever, Queensland (quatrilateral) fever *(durch Coxiella Burnetti)*
q. h. s. quaque hora
q. i. d. s. quarter in die
q. l. s. quantum libet
q. q. h. s. quaque quarta hora

q. p. s. quantum placet
QRS-Intervall n QRS interval *(EKG)*
QRS-Komplex m QRS complex, ventricular [depolarization] complex *(EKG)*
QRS-Schleife f QRS loop *(Vektorkardiographie)*
QRS-T-Winkel m QRS-T angle *(Vektorkardiographie)*
QRS-Vektor m QRS axis *(im Vektorkardiogramm)*
QRS-Zeit f QRS time *(EKG)*
q. s. s. quantum satis
QT-Intervall n Q-T interval *(EKG)*
Quacksalber m quack[salver], charlatan
Quacksalberei f charlatanism, charlatanry
quacksalbern to quack
Quaddel f urtica, wheal, pomphus ● **Quaddeln erzeugen** to urticate, to produce wheals *(z. B. durch Impfung)*
Quaddelbildung f urtication, whealing
Quaddel-Erythem-Reaktion f wheal and flare reaction
Quadrant m quadrant *(in der Brustregion)*
~/hinterer unterer posterior inferior quadrant *(am Trommelfell)*
Quadranten[hemi]anopsie f quadrantanop[s]ia, quadrantic hemianopia
Quadratus m quadratus [muscle]
Quadratusarkade f lateral arcuate ligament *(des Zwerchfells)*
Quadripara f quadripara, quartipara
Quadriparese f quadriparesis, paresis of all four limbs
Quadriplegie f quadriplegia, paralysis of all four limbs, tetraplegia
quadrizeps quadriceps
Quadrizeps[muskel] m quadriceps [muscle], four-headed muscle
Quadrizepsplastik f quadriceps plasty
Quadrizepsreflex m quadriceps reflex
quälend racking, agonizing, excruciating *(z. B. Schmerzen)*; pinching *(Hunger)*
Quantimeter n quantimeter *(Röntgenstrahlenmeßinstrument)*
quantum libet quantum libet, as much as you please, as much as desired
~ placet quantum placet, as much as you please
~ satis (sufficit) quantum satis (sufficit), as much as suffices
~ vis quantum vis, as much as you will (wish)
quaque die quaque die, every day
~ hora quaque hora, every hour
~ quarta hora every four hours
Quarantäne f quarantine ● **aus der ~ entlassen** to discharge (release) from quarantine ● **die ~ aufheben** to raise the quarantine ● **in ~ liegen** to be under (in) quarantine ● **sich der ~ unterwerfen** to submit to quarantine ● **unter ~ stellen** to [place in] quarantine, to appoint quarantine, to put into quarantine
Quarantänebefreiung f release from quarantine
Quarantänebeschränkungen fpl quarantine restrictions
Quarantäneflagge f quarantine flag; yellow jack
Quarantänehafen m quarantine harbour
Quarantänemaßnahme f quarantine measure
Quarantänepflichtsignal n quarantine routine signal
Quarantäneschein m quarantine (entry) declaration
Quarantänestation f quarantine station, probationary ward, lazaret[te]
Quarantänevorschriften fpl quarantine regulations
Quarantänezeit f quarantine period
Quarantänezeugnis n quarantine certificate
Quartana f s. Quartanfieber
Quartanaanfall m quartan ague *(Fieber im 72-Stunden-Intervall)*
Quartanaparasit m quartan parasite, Plasmodium malariae
Quartanfieber n quartan fever (malaria) *(durch Plasmodium malariae)*
quarter in die quarter in die, q.i.d., four times a day
Quebrachin n quebrachine *(Alkaloid)*
Quecksilber(I)-chlorid n mercurous chloride, mercury(I) chloride *(Laxativum, Diuretikum, Antisyphilitikum)*
Quecksilber(II)-chlorid n mercuric chloride, mercury(II) chloride *(Antiseptikum)*
Quecksilberdiuretikum n mercurial diuretic
Quecksilberexanthem n mercurial rash, mercury dermatitis
Quecksilbergeschwür n mercurial ulcer
Quecksilbernekrose f mercurial necrosis
Quecksilbernephrose f mercurial nephrosis
Quecksilberschmierkur f mercurial inunction (treatment)
Quecksilberstomatitis f mercurial stomatitis
Quecksilbervergiftung f mercurialism, mercurial poisoning, hydrargyria[sis], hydrargyrism, hydrargyrosis
Quecksilberzittern n mercurial tremor *(Vergiftungssymptom)*
Queenslandfieber n s. Q-Fieber
Queensland-Zeckenbißfieber n Queensland tick typhus fever *(durch Rickettsia australis)*
Quellstift m laminaria tent *(zur Erweiterung des Gebärmutterhalskanals)*
Quellungsreaktion f quellung reaction *(Pneumokokkenserologie)*
~/Neufeldsche Neufeld quellung test *(Färbungsreaktion für die Pneumokokkentypisierung)*
Quellungsstar m intumescent cataract
Quellwasserzyste f springwater cyst
Querbruch m transverse fracture
Querdarm m transverse colon
Querdurchmesser m transverse diameter *(z. B. des Kindskopfs)*
Querdurchtrennung f transverse section
Querfortsatz m transverse process
Querfortsatzrippenmuskeln mpl levatores costarum [muscles]
~/kurze short levatores costarum muscles

~/lange long levatores costarum muscles
Querfortsatz- und Rippenentfernung f[/operative] costotransvectomy
Querinzision f transverse incision
~ **der Haut** transverse skin incision
Querkolon n transverse colon
Querkoloneröffnung f[/operative] transversotomy
Querkolonfistelung f/operative transversostomy
Querkolonkunstafter m transversostomy
Querkolonmeso n transverse mesocolon
Querlage f transverse presentation (lie), torso (trunk) presentation *(bei der Geburt)*
~/I. **dorsoanteriore** left dorsoanterior position of the foetus *(Kindesrücken zu den mütterlichen Bauchdecken)*
~/II. **dorsoanteriore** right dorsoanterior position of the foetus
~/I. **dorsoinferiore** left dorsoinferior position of the foetus *(Kindesrücken gegen mütterlichen Beckenboden)*
~/II. **dorsoinferiore** right dorsoinferior position of the foetus
~/I. **dorsoposteriore** left dorsoposterior position of the foetus *(Kindesrücken zur mütterlichen Wirbelsäule*
~/II. **dorsoposteriore** right dorsoposterior position of the foetus
~/I. **dorsosuperiore** left dorsosuperior position of the foetus *(Kindesrücken gegen mütterliches Zwerchfell)*
~/II. **dorsosuperiore** right dorsosuperior position of the foetus
~/eingeklemmte impacted transverse lie (presentation)
Querlagengeburt f cross birth; transverse presentation
Quernaht f transverse suture
Querschnitt m 1. cross incision, transverse section; 2. s. Querschnittslähmung
~/**Pfannenstielscher** Pfannenstiel's incision *(Bauchdeckenschnitt an der oberen Schambehaarungsgrenze)*
Querschnittslähmung f paraplegia *(Zusammensetzungen s. unter Paraplegie)*
Querschnittsverletzung f transverse lesion *(des Rückenmarks)*
Querstand m head in transverse position *(bei der Geburt)*
~/**tiefer** transverse arrest
~/I. **tiefer** left occipitotransverse position of the foetus, L.O.T.
~/II. **tiefer** right occipitotransverse position of the foetus, R.O.T.
Querulant m querulant, querulous (litigious) person
Querwindung f transverse gyrus *(des Gehirns)*
Query-Fieber n s. Q-Fieber
quetschen to squeeze, to pinch; to contuse *(z. B. das Gehirn)*; to bruise *(z. B. einen Muskel)*; to crush *(z. B. einen Knochen)*

Quetschung f 1. squeezing, pinching; contusion; bruise, bruising; 2. crush injury
~ **des Nervus phrenicus** phrenemphraxis, phrenic emphraxis, phrenicotripsy, phreniclasis
Quetschungsbruch m crush (contusion) fracture
Quetschungsregion f bruised area
Quetschungssyndrom n crush syndrome
Quetschverletzung f crushing injury
Quetschwunde f contused wound
Quetschzange f crushing forceps (clamp)
Quinin n s. Chinin
Quintana f quintan (trench) fever *(durch Rickettsia quintana)*
Quintipara f quintipara
Quintusneuralgie f trigeminal neuralgia
qu.l. s. quantum libet
quotidian quotidian, daily; recurring every day
Quotidiana f quotidian malaria
Quotient m/**respiratorischer** respiratory quotient (coefficient), R.Q.
qu.p. s. quantum placet
qu.s. s. quantum satis
q.v. s. quantum vis
Q-Zacke f Q wave [of the electrocardiogram]

R

R. s. 1. Röntgeneinheit; 2. Recipe
rabenschnabelförmig coracoid
Rabenschnabelfortsatz m coracoid [process], beak-shaped process of the scapula ● **unter dem** ~ subcoracoid
Rabies f s. Tollwut
Rabieskörperchen npl/**Babéssche** Babés nodules (tubercles)
rabizid rabicidal
Rachen m pharynx, throat, throttle, fauces ●**neben dem** ~ parapharyngeal ● **unter dem** ~ subpharyngeal
Rachen... s. a. Pharynx... *und* Schlund...
Rachenabstrich m throat swab, pharyngeal swabbing
Rachenbehandlung f pharyngotherapy
Rachenblutung f pharyngorrhagia, haemorrhage from the pharynx
Rachenbruch m pharyngocele
Racheneintrocknung f pharyngoxerosis, dryness of the pharynx
Rachenenge f isthmus of the fauces *(Übergang von der Mund- zur Rachenhöhle)*
Rachenentzündung f pharyngitis, inflammation of the pharynx; sore throat *(Zusammensetzungen s. unter Pharyngitis)*
Racheneröffnung f[/operative] pharyngotomy, incision into the pharynx
Rachenerweiterung f pharyngectasia
Rachenexsudat n pharyngeal exudate
Rachenfistel f pharyngeal fistula
Rachengeschwulst f pharyngeal tumour
Rachenkarzinom n cancer of throat

Rachen-, Kehlkopf- ... 650

Rachen-, Kehlkopf- und Speiseröhrenentfernung f[/operative] pharyngo-laryngo-oesophagectomy, pharyngo-oesophagolaryngectomy
Rachenkeratose f pharyngokeratosis, keratosis of the pharynx
Rachenkrankheit f pharyngopathy, disease of the pharynx
Rachenkultur f throat culture
Rachenmandel f pharyngeal tonsil (adenoids), Luschka's tonsil
Rachenmandelentzündung f inflammation of the adenoids, adenoiditis
Rachenmandelgewebe n pharyngotonsillar tissue
Rachenmandelkrypten fpl tonsillar crypts of the lingual tonsils
Rachenmandelwucherungen fpl adenoids *(lymphatisches Gewebe im Nasenrachen)*
Rachenmembran f pharyngeal membrane
Rachenmündung f **der Ohrtrompete** pharyngeal opening of the auditory (Eustachian) tube
Rachenmuskel m pharyngeal muscle
Rachenmuskelkrampf m pharyngospasm, pharyngeal muscular spasm
Rachenmuskellähmung f pharyngoplegia, pharyngoparalysis, pharyngolysis
Rachenmykose f pharyngomycosis
Rachennaht f raphe of the pharynx
Rachenplastik f pharyngoplasty
Rachenreflex m pharyngeal (faucial) reflex
Rachenring m tonsillar ring
~/lymphatischer (Waldeyerscher) Waldeyer's tonsillar ring
Rachenschleimfluß m pharyngorrhoea, mucous discharge from the pharynx
Rachenschleimhaut f pharyngeal mucosa, mucous membrane of the pharynx
Rachenschleimhautentzündung f s. Rachenentzündung
Rachenschmerz m pharyngalgia, pharyngodynia, pharyngeal pain (discomfort)
Rachenschnitt m pharyngotomy, incision into the pharynx
Rachensklerom n pharyngoscleroma, scleroma of the pharynx
Rachensoor m pharyngeal moniliasis
Rachenspiegel m pharyngoscope
Rachenspiegelung f pharyngoscopy
Rachenspülung f throat washing; pharyngeal douche
Rachenstein m pharyngolith
Rachenstenose f pharyngostenia, pharyngoperistole, narrowing of the pharynx, lemostenosis
Rachenteilentfernung f[/operative] hemipharyngectomy
Rachen- und Kehlkopfkatarrh m inflammation of the larynx and the pharynx, pharyngolaryngitis
Rachen- und Mandelentzündung f pharyngotonsillitis, pharyngo-amygdalitis, adenopharyngitis
Rachenvenengeflecht n pharyngeal [venous] plexus

Rachenwiederherstellung f[/operative] pharyngeal reconstruction; pharyngoplasty
Rachialgie f rachialgia, pain in the vertebral column
Rachianästhesie f rachianaesthesia, rachianalgesia; spinal anaesthesia
Rachiometer n rachiometer
Rachiopathie f rachiopathy, disease of the spine
Rachioskoliose f rachioscoliosis
Rachiotom n rachitome, spine wrench
Rachiotomie f rachi[o]tomy, cutting of the vertebral column
Rachipagus m rachipagus *(Mißgeburt)*
Rachisagra f rachisagra, gout in the spine; pain in the spine
Rachischisis f rachischisis, congenital fissure of the spinal column
~/totale holorachischisis, total rachischisis
Rachitis f rachitis, rickety, rickets, infantile (juvenile) osteomalacia
~ renalis renal dwarfism
~/vitamin-D-resistente vitamin D refractory rickets
rachitisartig rachitic
rachitisbewirkend rachitogenic
rachitisch rachitic, rickety
rachitisfördernd rachitogenic
rachitisverhindernd antirachitic
Rachizele f rachizele *(Vorfall von Wirbelsäulenkanalanteilen bei Wirbelspalte)*
Rachizentese f rachi[o]centesis, puncture into the spinal canal
Rad n rad, radiation absorbed dose *(SI-fremde Einheit der Strahlendosis)*
radförmig trochoid
Radgelenk n trochoid (pivot, rotation) joint
radial radial, radiate
Radialarterie f radial artery
Radialis m s. Radialisnerv
Radialislähmung f paralysis of the radial nerve; carpoptosis, wrist drop
Radialisnerv m radial (musculospiral) nerve
Radialispuls m radial pulse
Radialvene f radial vein
radialwärts radiad, toward the radial side
Radiatio f radiation *(Anatomie)*
~ acustica acoustic (auditory) radiation, thalamotemporal radiation, geniculotemporal tract *(Teil der zentralen Hörbahn)*
~ corporis callosi corpus callosum radiation *(Nervenfasern zwischen dem Corpus callosum und den Hemisphären)*
~ corporis striati corticostriate radiation *(Nervenfasern zwischen der Stirn- und Scheitellappenrinde und dem Corpus striatum)*
~ occipitothalamica occipitothalamic radiation
~ optica [Gratiolet's] optic radiation, geniculocarcine tract
~ pyramidalis pyramidal radiation
~ striothalamica striothalamic radiation
Radiektomie f radiectomy, excision of the root of a tooth

Radikalausräumung f radical extirpation *(z. B. einer Geschwulst)*
Radikalbehandlung f radical cure
Radikalmastoidektomie f radical mastoidectomy
Radikaloperation f radical operation
Radikotomie f s. Rhizotomia
radikulär radicular, radical
Radikulektomie f radiculectomy, excision of a rootlet; resection of spinal nerve roots
Radikulitis f radiculitis, inflammation of a spinal nerve root
Radikulomyelopathie f radiculomyelopathy
Radikuloneuritis f radiculoneuritis
Radikuloneuropathie f radiculoneuropathy
Radikulopathie f radiculopathy, disease of nerve roots
Radio... s. a. Röntgen... *und* Strahlen...
radioaktiv radioactive
~ **markiert** radiolabelled
~/**stark** hot
Radio-B$_{12}$-Harnexkretionstest m s. Schilling-Test
Radiobiologie f radiobiology
radiobiologisch radiobiological
Radiochemie f radiochemistry
Radiodiagnose f radiodiagnosis
Radiodiagnostik f radiodiagnostics, radiodiagnosis
radiodigital radiodigital
Radioeisen n radioiron
radiogen radiogenic
Radiogold n radiogold
Radiogramm n radiogram, radiograph
Radiographie f radiography
radiographisch radiographic
Radiohypophysektomie f radiohypophysectomy
Radioimmunoassay m radioimmunoassay, RIA, radioimmunosorbent test
Radioimmunoelektrophorese f radioimmunoelectrophoresis
Radioimmunoglobulin-Dosimetrie f radioimmunoglobulin dosimetry
Radioimmunologie f radioimmunology
Radioisotop n radioisotope
Radioisotopenscanner m radioisotope scanner
Radioisotopentechnik f radioisotope technique
Radiojod n radioiodine ● **mit** ~ **markiert** radioiodine-labelled
Radiojodbehandlung f radioiodine therapy ●**eine** ~ **der Schilddrüse durchführen** to radiothyroidectomize
Radiojodszintigraphie f radioiodine scintiscanning
Radiokardiogramm n radiocardiogram
Radiokardiographie f radiocardiography
Radiokarpalgelenk n radiocarpal articulation (joint)
Radiokobalt n radiocobalt
Radiokolloid n radiocolloid
Radiokurabilität f radiocurability
Radiokymogramm n radiokymogram
Radiokymographie f radiokymography
radiokymographisch radiokymographic

Radiologe m radiologist
Radiologie f radiology
radiologisch radiologic[al]
Radiolumineszenz f radioluminescense
Radiometer n radiometer
Radiometrie f radiometry
radiometrisch radiometric
Radiomimetikum n radiomimetic [agent]
radiomimetisch radiomimetic
Radionuklid n radionuclide
Radionuklidangiographie f radionuclide angiography
Radionuklidangiokardiogramm n radionuclide angiocardiogram
Radionuklidtest m radionuclide test
Radiopelvimetrie f radiopelvimetry
Radiopharmakon n radiopharmaceutical [agent]
radiopharmazeutisch radiopharmaceutic[al]
Radiophosphor m radiophosphorus
Radiophotolumineszenzdosimetrie f radiophotoluminescent dosimetry
Radiopraxis f radiopraxis
Radiosensibilität f radiosensitivity, radiosensibility
radiosensitiv radiosensitive
Radioskopie f radioscopy; roentgenoscopy
radioskopisch radioscopic; roentgenoscopic
Radiostereoskopie f radiostereoscopy
Radiotherapeut m radiotherapist
radiotherapeutisch radiotherapeutic
Radiotherapie f radiotherapy, radiation [therapy], radiation treatment
Radiotherapie-Abteilung f radiotherapy department
Radiotropismus m radiotropism
Radioulnargelenk n/**distales** distal radioulnar joint
~/**proximales** proximal radioulnar joint
Radiumbehandlung f radium therapy, curietherapy
Radiumemanation f radium emanation
Radiumfernbestrahlung f teleradium therapy
Radiumkanone f teleradium unit; radium bomb *(zur Radiumbestrahlung)*
Radiumnadel f radium needle
Radiumresistenz f radium resistance
Radiumspickung f interstitial radium irradiation *(z. B. des Gewebes)*
Radiumstift m radium needle
Radiumstrahlung f radium radiation
Radiumverbrennung f radium burn *(z. B. der Haut)*
Radius m radius *(Unterarmknochen)*
Radius... s. a. Speichen...
Radiusgelenkfläche f/**distale** distal end of the radius
Radius[knochen]hals m neck of the radius
Radiusköpfchen n head of the radius
Radius-Periost-Reflex m radial [periosteal] reflex, periosteoradial reflex
Radiusrückseite f posterior (dorsal) surface of the radius

Radiussubluxation

Radiussubluxation f subluxation of the radius
Radiusvorderseite f anterior (ventral) surface of the radius
Radix f radix, rad., root *(s. a. unter Wurzel)*
~ **aortae** root of the aorta
~ **dentis** [tooth] root, [anatomic] root of a tooth
~ **dorsalis nervorum spinalium** posterior (dorsal) root of the spinal nerves
~ **inferior ansae cervicalis** inferior root of the ansa cervicalis
~ **iridea** iris root
~ **linguae** root of the tongue
~ **mesenterii** root of the mesentery
~ **nasi** root of the nose
~ **pili** hair root
~ **pulmonis** root of the lung
~ **superior ansae cervicalis** superior root of the ansa cervicalis
~ **unguis** root of the nail
~ **ventralis nervorum spinalium** anterior (ventral) root of the spinal nerves
Radon-219 n radon-219, actinon, actinium emanation
Radonkapsel f radon seed
Rad-Scharnier-Gelenk n trochoginglymus
Raffinase f raffinase *(Enzym)*
Raffinose f raffinose
Raffnaht f purse-string suture
Rakettschnitt m racket amputation
Rami *mpl* **gastrici anteriores nervi vagi** anterior gastric plexus
~ **gastrici posteriores nervi vagi** posterior gastric plexus
Ramsay-Hunt-Syndrom n 1. Ramsay Hunt syndrome, genicular herpes zoster; 2. dyssynergia cerebellaris progressiva
Ramstedt-Weber-Operation f Ramstedt operation *(zur Beseitigung eines Magenpförtnerkrampfs)*
Rand m edge, margin, margo; crest, crista, ridge *(Zusammensetzungen s. unter Crista)*; border; contour; labrum, lip ● **am ~ befindlich** marginal ● **über dem ~** supramarginal
~ **der Niere/mittlerer** concave border of the kidney
~ **des Oberarmknochens/mittlerer** medial border of the humerus
~ **des Oberarmknochens/seitlicher** lateral border of the humerus
Randkeratitis f marginal keratitis
Randpool m marginated pool *(der Granulozyten)*
Randschicht f peripheral layer
Randschleier m marginal fog *(Radiologie)*
Randständigkeit f **der Leukozyten** margination
~ **eines Abszesses** pointing
Randzone f marginal area
Rankenaneurysma n cirsoid (racemose) aneurysm
rankenartig cirsoid
Rankengeflecht n pampiniform plexus
Ranula f ranula, sublingual cyst *(bläschenartige Zystenbildung unter der Zunge)*; hydroglossa, frog tongue

Raphe f raphe, sutura, suture, seam *(s. a. unter Sutura)*
~ **medullae oblongatae** raphe of the medulla oblongata
~ **palati** palatine raphe
~ **penis** raphe of the penis
~ **perinei** perineal raphe, anogenital band
~ **pharyngis** raphe of the pharynx
~ **pontis** pontine raphe, raphe of the pons
~ **scroti** scrotal raphe, raphe of the scrotum
Raptus m 1. raptus, sudden attack, seizure, intense emotion; 2. rape
rarefizieren to rarefy
Rarefizierung f rarefaction
rasend raging, raving, mad, furibund; manic, maniacal; agonising, splitting *(Schmerzen)*
Raserei f rage, [raving] madness, frenzy, furor
Rasiererkrampf m xyrospasm, shaving spasm
Rasierflechte f barber's itch, tinea (sycosis) barbae
Raspatorium n raspatory, xyster, bone rasp; osteotribe, osteotrite
~ **nach Doyen** Doyen's [rib] raspatory
Raspel f [bone] rasp, xyster
raspeln to rasp *(z. B. den Amputationsstumpf)*
Rasse f race
Rasselgeräusch n rhonchus, rale, rattle, rattling *(beim Atmen)*; crepitation, crepitance, crepitant rale *(z. B. bei Pneumonie)*; wheezing *(bei Asthma)*
~/**amphorisches** amphoric rale
~/**brummendes** sonorous rale
~/**feuchtes** moist rale *(in der Lunge)*
~/**giemendes** sibilant rale
~/**großblasiges** coarse [bubbling] rale
~/**kleinblasiges** fine [bubbling] rale
~/**klingendes** consonating rale
~/**knisterndes** crepitant rale
~/**mittelblasiges** medium [bubbling] rale
~/**pfeifendes** whistling rale
~/**trockenes** dry rale *(in der Lunge)*
rasseln to rattle, to crackle; to crepitate; to wheeze
rassisch racial
Rasterbestrahlung[stherapie] f grid irradiation
Rasterelektronenmikroskop n scanning [beam] electron microscope, scanning microscope
Rastermammographie f grid mammography
rastlos restless, hyperpragic
Rastlosigkeit f restlessness, hyperpraxia, irascibility
Rattenbißkrankheit f rat-bite fever, spirillary [rat-bite] fever, sodoku
Rattenfleckfieber n rat (murine) typhus
Rattenfloh m rat flea, Pulex cheopis *(Pestüberträger)*
Rattenpest f murine plague
Rattenvernichtung f deratization, extermination of rats
Raubwanze f reduviid
raubwanzenartig reduviid
Raucherbein n smoker's leg

Raucherherz n smoker's (tobacco) heart
Raucherhusten m smoker's cough
Raucherkrebs m smoker's (clay-pipe) cancer
Raucherzunge f smoker's tongue; leukoplakia
Räude f mange
Räudemilbe f mange (itch) mite
rauh rough, rugose, rugous *(z. B. eine Oberfläche)*; hoarse, gruff, husky *(Stimme)*; harsh *(z. B. ein Geräusch)*
Rauhigkeit f roughness, rugosity, scabrities *(z. B. einer Oberfläche)*
Raum m space, spatium *(s. a. unter Spatium)*; cavity
~ **des Respirationssystems/toter** anatomical dead space
~/**Dissescher** space of Disse, perisinusoidal space [of Disse] *(Spaltbildung zwischen Leberzellen und Leberkapillaren)*
~/**Douglasscher** 1. Douglas pouch (space), rectouterine cul-de-sac [of Douglas], rectouterine fossa (excavation) *(bei der Frau)*; 2. Douglas pouch (space), rectovesical cul-de-sac [of Douglas], rectovesical fossa (excavation) *(beim Mann)*
~/**Prussakscher** Prussak's pouch (space) *(Schleimhautbucht im Innenohr)*
~/**retropharyngealer** retropharyngeal space
~/**Retziusscher** cave of Retzius, prevesical space [of Retzius]
~/**subperiostaler** subperiosteal space
~/**Traubescher** Traube's (semilunar) space
~/**Virchow-Robinscher** Virchow-Robin space, perivascular space of Virchow-Robin
Raumbefeuchter m humidifier
raumbildlich stereoscopic
Raumblindheit f spatial (space) blindness
~/**zentrale** spatial (space) agnosia
Raumdosis f volume (integral) dose *(Radiologie)*
Räume mpl/**Fontanasche** Fontana's spaces, iris angle spaces [of Fontana], spaces of the iridocorneal angle
Raumempfindung f spatial (space) perception
Raumfahrtmedizin f aero-space medicine
raumfordernd space-occupying, expanding; compressive *(z. B. Geschwulst)*
Raumgefühl n spatial (space) feeling
räumlich spatial; stereoscopic
~ **begrenzt** regional
Raumsehvermögen n stereoscopic vision
Raumsinn m spatial (space) sense
Raumsinnmeßinstrument n stereopter
Raumwahrnehmung f spatial (space) perception
Raupendermatitis f caterpillar dermatitis (rash, urticaria)
Raupenhaarkonjunktivitis f caterpillar (nodular) conjunctivitis
Raupenhaarophthalmie f caterpillar [hair] ophthalmia
Rausch m drunkenness, inebriation *(z. B. durch Alkohol)*; intoxication; rausch, light anaesthesia
Rauschen n/**weißes** white noise *(Hörprüfung)*

Rauschgetränk n intoxicant
Rauschgift n narcotic [agent], narcotic poison, dope, intoxicant, drug
Rauschgiftsucht f [drug] addiction, drug dependence (habit), narcotic dependence, narcomania
rauschgiftsüchtig drug-addicted
Rauschgiftsüchtiger m [drug] addict, narcotic [addict], narcomaniac, toxicomaniac
Rauschmittel n narcotic [agent]
rautenförmig rhomboid, rhombic
Rautengrube f rhomboid fossa
Rautenhirn n rhombencephalon, hindbrain
Rautenhirnbogenfasern fpl/**äußere** external arcuate fibres
Rautenhirnhöhle f rhombocele
Rautenmuskel m/**großer** rhomboid major [muscle]
~/**kleiner** rhomboid minor [muscle]
Rautenschwellkörperscheidewand f penile septum
Rauwolfiaalkaloid n rauwolfia alkaloid
Rauwolfin n rauwolfine *(Alkaloid)*
Razemase f racemase *(Enzym)*
razemös racemose *(z. B. Drüsen)*
RBW s. Wirksamkeit/relative biologische
Reabsorptionskapazität f reabsorptive capacity
Reagens n reagent
~/**Barfoeds** Barfoed's reagent *(zum Traubenzuckernachweis)*
~/**Bialsches** Bial's reagent *(zum Pentosenachweis)*
~/**Neßlers** Nessler's reagent (solution) *(zum Ammoniaknachweis)*
~/**Töpfers** Töpfer's reagent *(zum Magensäurenachweis)*
~/**Uffelmannsches** Uffelmann's reagent *(zum Milchsäurenachweis im Magensaft)*
Reagenzglas n test tube ● **im** ~ in vitro
reagieren to react; to respond
~/**allergisch** to be hypersentive [to]
~/**auf Tuberkulin** to react to tuberculin
~/**nicht** to remain inert
~/**positiv** to give a positive reaction
Reagin n reagin, reaginic body *(Antikörper)*
Reaktion f 1. reaction; response; 2. s. Reflex
~/**allergische** allergic reaction
~/**anamnestische** anamnestic reaction
~/**anaphylaktische** anaphylactic reaction
~/**Ascolische** Ascoli test [for anthrax]
~/**Bergersche** Berger rhythm (wave) *(im EEG)*
~/**beschleunigte** accelerated reaction *(bei Pockenwiederimpfung)*
~/**Boverische** Boveri's test *(zum Globulinnachweis im Liquor cerebrospinalis)*
~/**entzündliche** inflammatory reaction (response)
~/**erythematöse** erythematous reaction; flare
~/**falsch negative** false negative reaction
~/**falsch positive** false positive reaction
~/**[Jarisch-]Herxheimersche** Jarisch-Herxheimer reaction *(Antigen-Antikörper-Reaktion)*

Reaktion 654

~/**lokale anaphylaktische** Arthus' phenomenon, phenomenon of Arthus, local anaphylaxis *(allergische Überempfindlichkeitsreaktion)*
~/**Mantouxsche** Mantoux [intradermal tuberculin] test
~/**myasthenische** myasthenic reaction *(Abnahme der muskulären Erregbarkeit gegenüber elektrischem Strom bei Myasthenia gravis)*
~/**myotonische** myotonic reaction
~/**nichtanaphylaktische** non-anaphylactoid reaction
~/**Nonne-Apelt-Schummsche** Nonne-Apelt test *(Nachweis für erhöhten Globulingehalt in der Hirn-Rückenmark-Flüssigkeit)*
~/**normale** natural reaction
~/**Pandysche** Pandy's test *(Nachweis für Globuline im Liquor)*
~/**psychogalvanische** psychogalvanic reflex, galvanic skin response
~/**seelische** psychical reaction
~/**Strausssche** Strauss test *(Malleinreaktion zur Rotzdiagnose)*
~/**Wassermannsche** Wassermann reaction (test) *(zum Syphilisnachweis)*
~/**Widalsche** Widal reaction (test) *(zum Typhusnachweis)*
reaktionsarm indolent; latent
Reaktionsbereitschaft f reactivity; diathesis *(des Körpers)*
reaktionsfähig reactive; responsive
Reaktionsfähigkeit f reactivity; responsiveness
Reaktionskinetik f reaction kinetics
reaktionslos auf Antigen anergic
Reaktionslosigkeit f **auf Antigen** anergy
reaktionsträge of slow reaction, inactive
Reaktionszeit f reaction time
Reaktionszentrum n reaction (germinal) centre *(Lymphoblastenanhäufung in lymphatischen Organen)*
reaktivieren to reactivate
Reaktivität f reactivity
Realitätsangst f reality anxiety
Realitätsprinzip n reality principle *(Psychoanalyse)*
Reamputation f reamputation
Reanimation f [cardiac] resuscitation, reanimation, revivification
Reanimationsbesteck n resuscitative equipment
Reanimationsmaßnahme f resuscitative measure
reanimierbar resuscitable, revivable
~/**nicht** irresuscitable
reanimieren to resuscitate, to reanimate, to revive
Rebound-Effekt m rebound effect *(verstärkte Nachwirkung)*
Rebound-Phänomen n rebound phenomenon *(Kleinhirnsymptomatik)*
Receptaculum n **ganglii petrosi** petrosal fossa
Recessus m recess[us]; niche
~ **cochlearis vestibuli** cochlear recess
~ **costodiaphragmaticus [pleurae]** costodiaphragmatic recess (space), phrenicocostal (pleural reserve) sinus
~ **costomediastinalis [pleurae]** costomediastinal recess (sinus, space), pleural [reserve] sinus
~ **duodenalis inferior** inferior duodenal fossa [of Jonnesco]
~ **duodenalis superior** duodenojejunal (superior duodenal) fossa
~ **ellipticus vestibuli** elliptical (utricular) recess *(im Innenohr)*
~ **epitympanicus** epitympanic recess (space), epitympanum, superior tympanic cavity, attic *(Teil der Paukenhöhle)*
~ **ethmolacrimalis** ethmolacrimal recess
~ **hepatorenalis** hepatorenal pouch (recess)
~ **ileocaecalis inferior** inferior ileocaecal recess
~ **ileocaecalis superior** superior ileocaecal recess
~ **inferior bursae omentalis** inferior recess of the omental bursa
~ **infundibuli** infundibular recess *(Ausbuchtung der 3. Hirnkammer in den Hypophysenstiel)*
~ **intersigmoideus** intersigmoid recess, recess of the pelvic mesocolon *(Bauchfelltasche an der linken Fläche des Mesosigmoideums)*
~ **lateralis ventriculi quarti** lateral recess of the fourth ventricle
~ **lienalis** splenic (lienal) recess
~ **opticus** optic (chiasmal) recess *(Ausbuchtung der 3. Hirnkammer)*
~ **paraduodenalis** paraduodenal fossa (recess)
~ **pharyngeus** pharyngeal recess, Rosenmüller's (lateral pharyngeal) fossa *(hinter dem Tubenwulst)*
~ **pinealis** pineal recess *(Ausbuchtung der 3. Hirnkammer in die Zirbeldrüse)*
~ **piriformis** piriform recess (sinus)
~ **pleuralis** complemental space
~ **posterior fossae interpeduncularis** posterior part of the interpeduncular fossa
~ **retrocaecalis** retrocaecal recess
~ **retroduodenalis** retroduodenal fossa (recess)
~ **sacciformis articulationis radioulnaris distalis** sacciform recess of the wrist
~ **sphenoethmoidalis** sphenoethmoid recess
~ **sphericus vestibuli** spherical recess
~ **superior omentalis** superior recess of the omental bursa
~ **suprapinealis** suprapineal recess
~ **supratonsillaris** supratonsillar recess
~ **tympani superior** superior recess of the tympanic membrane, Prussak's pouch (space) *(Schleimhautbucht im Innenohr)*
Rechenstörung f acalculia, dyscalculia *(bei aphasischem Symptomenkomplex)*
rechts right, on the right side, dexter, dextral
rechtsäugig dextrocular, right-eyed
Rechtsäugigkeit f dextrocularity, right-eyedness
rechtsaurikulär dextraural, right-eared
Rechtsbetonung f dextrality
Rechtsdrehung f dextrotorsion; dextroclination, twisting to the right; dextrogyration

rechtsfüßig dextropedal, right-footed
Rechtsfüßigkeit f right-footedness
Rechtshänder m dextral, right-hander
rechtshändig dextral, right-handed, dextromanual
Rechtshändigkeit f dextrality, right-handedness
Rechtsherz n right heart, dextrocardia
Rechtsherzbelastung f right ventricle load (strain)
Rechtsherzdekompensation f right ventricular failure; backward [heart] failure
Rechtsherzdilatation f right ventricular dilatation
Rechtsherz-EKG n dextro[cardio]gram, right-side cardiogram
Rechtsherzhypertrophie f right ventricular hypertrophy, hypertrophy of the right ventricle
Rechtsherzinsuffizienz f right ventricular failure; backward [heart] failure
Rechtsherzkammerdruck m right ventricular pressure
Rechtsherzkatheterung f right heart catheterization
Rechtsherzröntgen[kontrast]bild n dextrogram
Rechtsherzstauung f s. Rechtsherzinsuffizienz
Rechtsherzventrikulogramm n right ventriculogram
Rechtsherzventrikulographie f right ventriculography
Rechtsherzvergrößerung f right ventricular enlargement
Rechtsherzversagen n right [ventricular congestive] heart failure, right ventricular [heart] failure
Rechtskammerdruck m right ventricular pressure
Rechts-Links-Shunt m right-to-left-shunt
Rechtsneigung f version (turning) to the right, dextroversion
Rechtsschenkelblock m right bundle-branch block, RBBB
Rechtsseitenlage f right lateral [position] (z. B. beim Röntgen)
rechtsseitig right[-sided], dexter, dextral
Rechtstyp m right dominance, right axis deviation (shift), RAD (des EKG)
Rechtsverdrehung f dextrotorsion; dextroclination, twisting to the right
Rechtsverlagerung f dextroposition, displacement to the right
~ **des Herzens** dextrocardia, dexiocardia, dextroposition of the heart
Rechtsverschiebung f right shift, deviation to the right (im Blutbild)
Rechtsverspätung f incomplete right bundle-branch block (im EKG)
Recipe recipe, R., take
Reclinatio f **cataractae** reclination, couching [for cataract]
Rededrang m/**krankhafter** polyphrasia
Redefluß m/**pathologischer** logorrhoea, lalorrhoea

Redesucht f logomania, leresis
Redifferenzierung f redifferentiation (von Geweben)
Redislokation f redislocation, reluxation
Redoxase f oxidoreductase (Enzym)
Redoxpotential n redox potential
Reduktase f reductase (Enzym)
Reduktion f reduction, deoxygenation
Reduktionskost f reducing (obesity) diet
Reduktionsteilung f reduction division, meiosis, heterotypic mitosis
Reduplikation f re[du]plication, doubling
Reduplikationszyklus m replication cycle (z. B. von Bakteriophagen)
reduplizieren to replicate
Reed-Sternberg-Zelle f Dorothy Reed cell (bei Morbus Hodgkin)
Reepithelialisation f reepithelialization
reepithelialisieren to reepithelialize
reexpandieren to reexpand
reexzidieren to reexcise
Referenzwahn m delusion of reference
reflektieren to reflect
Reflektor m reflector
reflektorisch reflex; consensual, involuntory
Reflex m reflex, jerk; response
~/**angeborener** s. ~/unbedingter
~/**Aschnerscher** Aschner's phenomenon
~/**audito-okulogyrischer** audito-oculogyric reflex (reflektorische Blickwendung zu einer Schallquelle)
~/**aurikulozervikaler** auriculocervical reflex
~/**auropalpebraler** cochleopalpebral reflex
~/**auslösbarer** obtainable reflex
~/**Babinskischer** Babinski phenomenon (reflex)
~/**bedingter** conditioned reflex (response), acquired (behaviour) reflex
~/**Brudzinskischer kontralateraler** Brudzinski's contralateral leg sign
~/**ergotroper** ergotropic reflex
~/**erworbener** s. ~/bedingter
~/**Gamperscher** [Gamper's] bowing reflex (Labyrinth-Stellreflex)
~/**gastrokolischer** gastrocolic reflex
~/**gesteigerter** hyperactive (exaggerated) reflex
~/**Haabscher** Haab's reflex
~/**herabgesetzter** hypoactive (feeble) reflex
~/**hypogastrischer** hypogastric reflex
~/**ileogastrischer** ileogastric reflex
~/**kardiorespiratorischer** cardiorespiratory reflex
~/**korneomandibulärer** corneomandibular reflex
~/**krankhafter** pathologic reflex
~/**Moroscher** [Moro] embrace reflex
~/**okulokardialer** oculocardiac reflex (Absinken der Herzfrequenz durch Druck auf die Augäpfel)
~/**okulopalpebraler** oculopalpebral reflex
~/**okulopharyngealer** oculopharyngeal reflex
~/**Oppenheimscher** Oppenheim's reflex (Pyramidenbahnzeichen)
~/**propriozeptiver** proprioceptive reflex
~/**psychogalvanischer** psychogalvanic reflex

Reflex

~/**psychokardialer** psychocardiac reflex
~/**roter** red reflex
~/**unbedingter** unconditioned (inherited) reflex, instinctive response, inborn (natural) reflex
~/**unwillkürlicher** s. ~/unbedingter
~/**vaskulärer** vascular reflex
~/**vasomotorischer** vasomotor reflex
~/**vesikoureteraler** vesicoureteral reflex
~/**vesikourethraler** vesicourethral (vesical) reflex
~/**vestibulärer** vestibular reflex
Reflexablauf m [reflex] circuit
Reflexabschwächung f hyporeflexia
Reflexakinesie f reflex akinesia
Reflexaphasie f aphthongia (Sprachstörung infolge Zungenkrampfs)
Reflexaufzeichnungsinstrument n reflexograph
reflexauslösend reflexogenic
Reflexbahn f reflex path[way]
Reflexbehandlung f reflexotherapy
Reflexbewegung f reflex movement
Reflexblase f [spinal] reflex bladder, automatic (cord) bladder
Reflexbogen m reflex arc
Reflexeffekt m automatic action
Reflexepilepsie f reflex epilepsy
reflexgesteigert hyperreflexic
Reflexhammer m reflex hammer; percussion hammer
Reflexhandlung f reflex action
Reflexhusten m reflex cough
Reflexio[n] f 1. reflection (psychisch); 2. reflection, reflexio (z. B. des Bauchfells)
Reflexionsfaktor m reflection coefficient
Reflexleitung f reflex conduction
Reflexlosigkeit f areflexia, absence of reflexes
Reflexmesser m reflexometer
Reflexmuster n reflex pattern
reflexogen reflexogenic
Reflexograph m reflexograph
Reflexometer n reflexometer
reflexschwach hyporeflexic
Reflexschwäche f hyporeflexia
Reflexspiegel m head mirror
Reflexstatus m/normaler normoreflexia
Reflexsteigerung f hyperreflexia
Reflexstörung f reflex disturbance; abnormal reflex
Reflexstreifen m reflex streak (auf der Netzhaut)
Reflextherapie f reflexotherapy
Reflexverlust m loss of a reflex
reflexvermindert hyporeflexic
Reflexverminderung f hyporeflexia
Reflexverstärkung f intensification (reinforcement) of a reflex
Reflexverzögerung[szeit] f lag [time]; latency
Reflexvorgang m reflex action
Reflexweinen n reflex weeping
Reflexwirkung f reflex (automatic) action
Reflexzentrum n reflex centre
Reflexzonenbehandlung f zone therapy
Reflux m reflux, return flow
~/**vesicoureteraler** vesico-ureteral reflux

Refluxgastritis f reflux gastritis
Refluxösophagitis f reflux [acid-peptic] oesophagitis
refracta dosi in divided doses
refraktär refractory; unresponsive (z. B. gegen Reize)
Refraktärperiode f refractory period
~/**absolute** absolute refractory period
~/**relative** relative refractory period
Refraktärstadium n refractory state (des Herzens)
Refraktion f refraction
Refraktionsanomalie f [refractive] ametropia
Refraktionsfehler m refractive error, error of refraction
Refraktionsgleichheit f beider Augen isometropia
Refraktionsindex m refractive index, index of refraction
Refraktionskeratoplastik f refractive keratoplasty
Refraktionskoeffizient m coefficient of refraction
Refraktionskraft f refractivity
Refraktionsmesser m refractometer
Refraktionsmessung f refractometry
Refraktionspunkt m refraction point
Refraktionsunterschied m beider Augen anisometropia, anisopia
Refraktionsvermögen n refractivity
Refraktionswinkel m refraction angle, angle of refraction
Refraktionsstärke f refractive power
refraktiv/nicht non refractive
Refraktometer n refractometer
Refraktometrie f refractometry
Refrakturierung f refracture, rebreaking (z. B. eines Knochens)
Refrigerans n refrigerant [agent]
Refrigeration f refrigeration
Refsum-Syndrom n Refsum's disease (syndrome), polyneuritiform atactic heredopathy
Regel f[/monatliche] s. Menstruation
Regelbiß m neutro[o]cclusion, neutral occlusion
Regelblutung f s. Menorrhoea
~/**monatliche** s. Menstruation
regelnd regulative
Regelung f regulation
Regelwidrigkeit f abnormalism, abnormality
Regenbogenhaut f iris (Zusammensetzungen s. unter Iris)
Regenbogenhaut... s.a. Iris...
Regenbogenhautarterie f long posterior ciliary artery
Regenbogenhautausreißung f irido-avulsion, avulsion of the iris
Regenbogenhautausschälungsmesser n iridectome
Regenbogenhautausschneidung f s. Iridektomie
Regenbogenhautausstülpung f iridectropium, eversion of the iris
Regenbogenhautbewegung f iridokinesia, contraction and expansion of the iris

Regenbogenhautblutung f iridaemia
Regenbogenhautdefekt m iridodiastasis, marginal defect of the iris
Regenbogenhautdehnung f iridotasis, iris inclusion [operation]
Regenbogenhautdiagnose f iri[do]diagnosis
Regenbogenhautdurchleuchtung f iris transillumination
Regenbogenhauteinkippung f iridentropium, inversion of the iris
Regenbogenhauteinklemmung f 1. iris incarceration; 2. iridencleisis, iris inclusion [operation] *(Behandlung des grünen Stars)*
Regenbogenhauteinziehung f iris retraction
Regenbogenhautentzündung f iritis, inflammation of the iris
Regenbogenhauterkrankung f iridopathy, disease of the iris
Regenbogenhauterweichung f iridomalacia, softening of the iris
Regenbogenhauterweiterer m iridodilator
Regenbogenhautfarbe f iris colour
Regenbogenhautfarbstoff m iris pigment
Regenbogenhautfärbung f iris pigmentation
Regenbogenhautgefäßdarstellung f iris angiography
Regenbogenhauthypoplasie f iris hypoplasia
Regenbogenhautinnenrand m inner circular border of the iris
Regenbogenhautknötchen n iris nodule
Regenbogenhautlücke f iridocoloboma, [iris] coloboma
Regenbogenhautmelanom n iris melanoma
Regenbogenhautmesser n iridotome
Regenbogenhautnekrose f iris necrosis
Regenbogenhautrubeose f iris rubeosis
Regenbogenhautschere f iris (iridectomy) scissors
Regenbogenhautschwellung f iridoncus
Regenbogenhautsklerose f iridosclerosis
Regenbogenhautstroma n iris stroma
Regenbogenhaut- und Hornhautentzündung f iridokeratitis, keratoiritis, inflammation of the iris and the cornea
Regenbogenhaut- und Linsenkapselentzündung f iridocapsulitis, inflammation of the iris and the lens capsule
Regenbogenhaut- und Linsenkapselschnitt m iridocapsulotomy
Regenbogenhaut- und Strahlenkörperentfernung f[/operative] iridocyclectomy
Regenbogenhaut- und Strahlenkörperentzündung f iridocyclitis, inflammation of the iris and the ciliary body
Regenbogenhautverdickung f iridauxesis, thickening of the iris
Regenbogenhautverengerer m iridoconstrictor
Regenbogenhautverklebung f iris synechia
Regenbogenhautvorfall m iridoptosis, prolapse of the iris; iris hernia
Regenbogenhautwurzel f iris root, ciliary margin
Regenbogenhautzerreißung f iridorrhexis, rupture of the iris

Regenbogenhautzyste f iris cyst
Regeneration f regeneration; reproduction
~ **durchtrennter Nerven** neurotization
Regenerationsknötchen n regenerative nodule
Regenerationsstoffwechsel m regenerative metabolism
Regenerationsvorgang m regenerative process
regenerierbar regenerable
regenerieren to regenerate; to reproduce
regenerierend regenerative
Regenerierung f s. Regeneration
Regenfurcht f ombrophobia
Regenschirmiris f umbrella iris, iris bombé
Regenwurmmuskeln mpl lumbrical muscles, lumbricals
~ **der Hand** lumbrical muscles of the hand
Regio f region; area
~ **abdominalis (abdominis)** abdominal region
~ **abdominis inferior** s. ~ hypogastrica
~ **abdominis superior** s. ~ epigastrica
~ **antebrachii anterior** anterior area of the forearm
~ **antebrachii posterior** posterior area of the forearm
~ **antebrachii radialis** radial side of the forearm
~ **antebrachii ulnaris** ulnar side of the forearm
~ **axillaris** axillary region
~ **brachii anterior** anterior area of the arm
~ **brachii lateralis** lateral area of the arm
~ **brachii medialis** medial area of the arm
~ **brachii posterior** posterior area of the arm
~ **buccalis** buccal region, area of the cheek
~ **calcanea** calcanean region, calcaneal area of the heel
~ **cervicalis** cervical region
~ **clavicularis** clavicular region, area of the clavicle
~ **colli anterior** anterior cervical region, anterior region of the neck
~ **colli lateralis** lateral cervical region, lateral region of the neck
~ **colli posterior** posterior cervical region, posterior region of the neck
~ **costalis** costal region
~ **coxae** region of the hip
~ **cruris anterior** anterior crural region, anterior region of the leg
~ **cruris lateralis** lateral crural region, lateral region of the leg
~ **cruris medialis** medial crural region, medial region of the leg
~ **cruris posterior** posterior crural region, posterior region of the leg, calf
~ **cubiti anterior** anterior cubital region
~ **cubiti lateralis** lateral cubital region
~ **cubiti medialis** medial cubital region
~ **cubiti posterior** posterior cubital region
~ **deltoidea** deltoid region
~ **dorsolumbalis** dorsolumbar region
~ **epigastrica** epigastrica, epigastric region, pit of the stomach, midriff
~ **femoralis (femoris)** femoral region

Regio

- ~ **femoris anterior** anterior femoral region, anterior region of the thigh
- ~ **femoris lateralis** lateral femoral region, lateral region of the thigh
- ~ **femoris medialis** medial femoral region, medial region of the thigh
- ~ **femoris posterior** posterior femoral region, posterior region of the thigh
- ~ **frontalis** frontal region
- ~ **genus anterior** anterior region of the knee
- ~ **genus posterior** posterior region of the knee
- ~ **glutaea** gluteal region
- ~ **hyoidea** hyoid region
- ~ **hypochondriaca** hypochondriac region, hypochondrium
- ~ **hypogastrica** hypogastric region, hypogastrium
- ~ **iliaca** iliac region
- ~ **infraaxillaris** infra-axillary region
- ~ **infraclavicularis** infraclavicular region
- ~ **inframammaria** inframammary region
- ~ **infraorbitalis** infra-orbital region
- ~ **infrascapularis** infrascapular region
- ~ **infratemporalis** infratemporal region
- ~ **inguinalis** inguinal region, inguen, groin
- ~ **interscapularis** interscapular region
- ~ **ischiorectalis** ischiorectal region
- ~ **labialis inferior** region of the lower lip
- ~ **labialis superior** region of the upper lip
- ~ **laryngea** region of the larynx
- ~ **lateralis abdominis** lateral region of the abdomen
- ~ **lumbalis** lumbar region
- ~ **malleolaris lateralis** lateral malleolar region
- ~ **malleolaris medialis** medial malleolar region
- ~ **mammaria** mammary region
- ~ **mastoidea** mastoid region (area)
- ~ **mentalis** mental region
- ~ **mesogastrica** s. ~ umbilicalis
- ~ **nasalis** nasal region
- ~ **nuchae** region of the neck
- ~ **occipitalis** occipital region
- ~ **olecrani** olecranon region
- ~ **olfactoria [tunicae mucosae nasi]** olfactory region [of the nose]
- ~ **oralis** oral region
- ~ **orbitalis** orbital region
- ~ **palpebralis inferior** region of the lower eyelid
- ~ **palpebralis superior** region of the upper eyelid
- ~ **pancreatica** pancreatic region
- ~ **parietalis** parietal region
- ~ **patellaris** region of the patella
- ~ **pectoralis anterior** anterior pectoral region
- ~ **pectoralis lateralis** lateral pectoral region
- ~ **pelvis** pelvic region
- ~ **perinealis** perineal region
- ~ **pubica** pubic region
- ~ **respiratoria** respiratory region of the nose
- ~ **sacralis** sacral region
- ~ **scapularis** scapular region
- ~ **sternalis** sternal region
- ~ **subhyoidea** subhyoid region
- ~ **sublingualis** sublingual region
- ~ **submandibularis** submandibular region
- ~ **submentalis** submental region
- ~ **suboccipitalis** suboccipital region
- ~ **subscapularis** subscapular region
- ~ **subthalamica** subthalamic region
- ~ **supraclavicularis** supraclavicular region
- ~ **suprahyoidea** suprahyoid region
- ~ **supraorbitalis** supra-orbital region
- ~ **suprascapularis** suprascapular region
- ~ **suprasternalis** suprasternal region
- ~ **suralis** region of the calf of the leg
- ~ **temporalis** temporal region (area)
- ~ **temporoparietalis** temporoparietal region
- ~ **thyreoidea** thyroid region
- ~ **umbilicalis** umbilical region, mesogaster
- ~ **urogenitalis** urogenital region
- ~ **vertebralis** vertebral region
- ~ **zygomatica** zygomatic region

Regionalanästhesie *f* regional [block] anaesthesia

Regression *f* 1. regression, turning back; 2. [filial] regression; 3. regression *(z. B. bei Schizophrenie)*

regressiv regressive

Regulation *f* regulation

~/**dopaminerge** dopaminergic regulation

Regulationsstörung *f* regulatory disturbance (disorder)

Regulatorgen *n* regulator gene

regulierend regulative

regungslos motionless

Regungslosigkeit *f* motionlessness; torpescence, torpor; numbness, deficiency of sensation; attonity *(bei katatoner Schizophrenie)*

Regurgitation *f* regurgitation *(z. B. bei insuffizienten Herzklappen)*

Regurgitationsgeräusch *n* regurgitant murmur

regurgitieren to regurgitate

regurgitierend regurgitant

Rehabilitand *m* rehabilitant

Rehabilitation *f* rehabilitation

~/**kardiale** cardiac rehabilitation *(z. B. nach Herzinfarkt)*

Rehabilitationsmaßnahme *f* rehabilitation measure

Rehabilitationsprogramm *n* rehabilitative program[me]

rehabilitieren to rehabilitate

Rehn-Delorme-Operation *f* Rehn's operation *(zur Behebung des Mastdarmvorfalls)*

Rehospitalisierung *f* rehospitalization

Rehydration *f* rehydration *(bei Verlust von Körperflüssigkeit)*

Reibahle *f* reamer *(chirurgisches Instrument)*

Reibegeräusch *n* attrition murmur, friction sound; friction rub

Reibung *f* friction, rub[bing]

reichlich 1. abundant *(z. B. Nahrung)*; 2. profuse *(z. B. Blutung)*

Reichmann-Syndrom *n* Reichmann's disease (syndrome), continuous secretion of gastric juice, gastrosuccorrhoea

Reichtumspsychose f delusion of great wealth, plutomania, cresomania
reif 1. ripe, mature *(z. B. Abszeß)*; developed; 2. adult, mature *(psychisch)* ● ~ **werden** to mature, to maturate *(z. B. Keimzellen)*; to mature, to come to a head *(ein Abszeß)*
~/männlich viripotent
Reife f 1. maturity; 2. s. Geschlechtsreife ● **zur ~ gelangen** to maturate *(z. B. Keimzellen)*; to mature, to come to a head *(ein Abszeß)*
reifen to mature, to maturate, to become ripe; to attain full development
Reifen *mpl/***Cabotsche** s. Ringe/Cabotsche
Reifezeichen n sign of maturity
Reifgeborenes n full-term neonate, near-term neonate
Reifgeburt f labour at [full] term
Reifung f maturation *(z. B. von Keimzellen)*
Reifungshemmung f maturation arrest
Reifungskrise f puberal (adolescent) crisis; developmental crisis
Reifungsreihe f/**erythrozytäre** erythron
Reifungsstörung f dysmaturity, disturbed maturity
Reifungsteilung f maturation division; meiosis, reduction division *(von Keimzellen)*
Reifungsvorgang m maturing process; maturation
Reihenimpfung f vaccination campaign; mass vaccination
Reihenschnitt m serial section *(Histologie)*
Reihenschutzimpfung f mass vaccination; mass immunization
Reihenuntersuchung f mass (serial) examination; mass roentgenography, mass screening (survey)
Reimplantation f re[im]plantation
reimplantieren to reimplant
rein pure *(z. B. Substanzen)*; clean *(sauber)*; clear *(z. B. Stimme)*
Reindarstellung f isolation *(z. B. von Hormonen)*
reinerbig homozygous, homozygote
Reinerbiger m homozygote
Reinerbigkeit f homozygosity
Reinfarkt m reinfarction, recurrent infarction
Reinfektion f reinfection, recurrent infection; superinfection
Reinfektionstuberkulose f reinfection tuberculosis
reinfizieren to reinfect
Reinfusion f re[in]fusion, autotransfusion *(z. B. von Blut)*
Reinheit f purity
reinigen to clean; to purify, to refine *(z. B. Substanzen)*; to clarify, to defecate *(z. B. Flüssigkeiten)*; to rinse *(z. B. die Mundhöhle)*; to cleanse, to decontaminate *(z. B. eine Wunde)*; to purge, to evacuate *(z. B. den Darm)*; to clear *(z. B. die Haut)*
Reinigung f cleaning; purification, refinement *(z. B. von Substanzen)*; clarification, defecation *(z. B. von Flüssigkeiten)*; rinsing *(z. B. der Mundhöhle)*; cleansing, decontamination *(z. B. einer Wunde)*; purging, evacuation, catharsis *(z. B. des Darms)*; clearing *(z. B. der Haut)*
~/psychische catharsis
Reinigungseinlauf m cleansing enema
Reinkultur f pure culture *(z. B. von Bakterien)*
Reinnervation f reinnervation
Reinokulation f reinoculation, revaccination
Reinsubstanz f pure substance
Reintegration f reintegration *(Psychiatrie)*
Reintonaudiogramm n pure tone audiogram
Reintonaudiometrie f pure tone audiometry
Reintonhörverlust m pure tone hearing loss
Reintubation f reintubation
Reinversion f reinversion *(der Gebärmutter)*
reisartig riziform
Reiseangst f hodophobia
Reisediarrhoe f traveller's diarrhoea
Reisekrankheit f travel sickness *(s.a. Kinetose)*
Reisesserkrankheit f s. Beriberi
Reisfeldfieber n rice-field fever
Reiskörperchen npl rice bodies
Reisschleim m rice gruel
Reißen n 1. s. Rheumatismus; 2. rupture *(z. B. von Sehnen)*
Reissner-Membran f Reissner's membrane, paries vestibularis ductus cochlearis
Reiswasserstuhl m rice-water stool *(bei Cholera)*
Reiswasserstuhlkrankheit f s. Cholera
reiten/über einem Ventrikelseptumdefekt to straddle a ventricular septal defect *(z. B. Trikuspidalklappe)*
Reiten n **der Aorta** overriding of the aorta *(bei Herzfehlern)*
Reiterknochen m rider's (cavalry) bone; cavalryman's osteoma
Reitermuskel m rider's muscle
Reiter-Syndrom n Reiter's syndrome, infectious uroarthritis, gonococcal (idiopathic blennorrhoeal) arthritis
Reithosenanästhesie f saddle anaesthesia, saddle block [anaesthesia]
Reiz m 1. stimulus; impulse; 2. s. Reizung
~/adäquater adequate stimulus
~/homologer homologous stimulus
~/heterologer heterologous stimulus
~/überschwelliger suprathreshold stimulus
~/unterschwelliger subliminal (subminimal) stimulus
~/zentrifugaler efferent impulse
~/zentripetaler afferent impulse
Reizantwort f response
Reizaufnahmefähigkeit f perceptivity; susceptibility, sensitiveness
reizaufnehmend perceptive, perceptual; sensible, susceptible, sensitive
reizbar irritable, excitable; susceptible, sensitive *(empfindlich)*; nervous; erethismic, erethi[s]tic
~/leicht [over]sensitive; irascible; choleric
Reizbarkeit f irritability, excitability; susceptibility, sensitiveness *(Empfindlichkeit)*; nervousness
~/erhöhte hyperirritability, hyperexcitability

Reizbarkeit

~/**krankhafte** erethism
~/**leichte** sensitivity, oversensitiveness
~/**verminderte** hypoirritability, hypoexcitability
Reizblase f irritable (nervous) bladder
Reizeffekt m/**isomorpher** isomorphic irritation effect, Köbner's phenomenon *(Dermatologie)*
Reizelektrode f exciting electrode
reizempfindlich sensible, susceptible [to stimuli]
reizen to stimulate *(anregen)*; to irritate, to excite *(erregen)*; to provoke
reizend stimulant; irritant, irritating, exciting
~/**zum Niesen** sternutatory
Reizerscheinung f/**meningitische** meningism
Reizfrequenz f frequency of stimulation *(z. B. eines Schrittmachers)*
Reizgift n irritant poison
Reizhusten m hacking (dry) cough
Reizklima n stimulating climate
Reizkolon n irritable colon; mucocolitis, mucous colitis, irritable bowel syndrome
Reizkörpertherapie f irritation (protein shock) treatment, stimulating therapy
Reizleitung f conduction
~/**intraventrikuläre** intraventricular [stimulus] conduction *(des Herzens)*
Reizleitungsbahn f path[way]
reizleitungsbeschleunigend dromotropic *(Herz)*
Reizleitungsblockade f conduction block
Reizleitungsbündel n conduction bundle
Reizleitungsgeschwindigkeit f conduction velocity
Reizleitungssystem n conduction system
reizlos 1. non-irritating, non-exciting; 2. bland
Reizmittel n irritant, excitant; stimulant
Reizpotential n evoked potential
Reizprobe f patch test *(auf der Haut)*
Reizschwelle f stimulus threshold
reizschwellenändernd bathmotropic *(Herz)*
reizschwellenerhöhend negative bathmotropic
reizschwellensenkend positive bathmotropic
Reizung f irritation; excitation *(Erregung)*; stimulation *(Anregung)*; provocation
~/**gastrointestinale** gastro-intestinal irritation
Reizungszustand m irritation
Reizverzögerung f stimulus delay
Reizwahrnehmung f perception, pcpt.
Reizwahrnehmungszeit f perception time
Rejektion f rejection *(eines Transplantats)*
rekalzifizieren to recalcify
Rekalzifizierung f recalcification
Rekalzifizierungszeit f recalcification (recalcified clotting) time
Rekapitulationstheorie f recapitulation theory; biogenetic law
Reklination f 1. reclination *(Vorgang)*; recumbency *(Zustand)*; 2. s. Reclinatio cataractae
reklinieren to recline
Rekombination f recombination *(Genetik)*
Rekombinationsanalyse f recombination analysis
Rekompensation f recompensation *(des Herzens)*

Rekomposition f recomposition
Rekompression f recompression *(z. B. bei Taucherkrankheit)*
Rekonstitution f reconstitution
Rekonstruktion f reconstruction *(z. B. von Körperteilen)*
rekonvaleszent convalescent
Rekonvaleszent m convalescent [patient]
Rekonvaleszentenkost f convalescent diet
Rekonvaleszentenserum n convalescent [human] serum
Rekonvaleszenz f convalescence, recovery, recuperation, anastasis
Rekonvaleszenzstadium n convalescent stage
Rekonvaleszenzzeit f convalescent phase (period)
rekonvaleszieren to [re]convalesce, to undergo [re]convalescence, to recover, to recuperate
rekonvaleszierend convalescent, recuperative, anastatic
Rekordspritze f record syringe
Rekreationstherapie f recreation therapy
Rekrement n recrement
rekrudeszent recrudescent, breaking out again
Rekrudeszenz f recrudescence *(Wiederauftreten von Symptomen nach kurzer Unterbrechung)*
rektal rectal, per rectum, by the anus
Rektal... s. a. Rektum... und Mastdarm...
Rektalabstrich m rectal swab
Rektaldreieck n rectal triangle
Rektaleinlauf m rectal injection
Rektalernährung f rectal alimentation
Rektalfistel f rectofistula, rectal fistula
Rektalgie f rectalgia, proctalgia, proctodynia, pain in the rectum
Rektalinfusion f rectal infusion, rectoclysis, proctoclysis
Rektalintussuszeption f rectal intussusception
Rektalmanometrie f rectal manometry
Rektalmessung f rectal measurement *(der Temperatur)*
Rektalnarkose f rectal anaesthesia
Rektalsinus m rectal sinus, anal sinus (crypt)
Rektal- und Abdominaluntersuchung f double touch
Rektaluntersuchung f rectal examination
Rektitis f rectitis, proctitis, inflammation of the rectum
Rektoklysis f rectoclysis, proctoclysis
Rektopexie f rectopexy, proctopexy, fixation of the rectum
Rektoplastik f rectoplasty, proctoplasty
Rektorektostomie f rectorectostomy
Rektoromanoskopie f rectoromanoscopy, inspection of the rectum and sigmoid
Rektorrhaphie f rectorrhaphy, proctorrhaphy, suture of the rectum
Rektosigmoid n rectosigmoid
Rektosigmoidektomie f rectosigmoidectomy, proctosigmoidectomy
Rektosigmoidoskopie f rectosigmoidoscopy, rectoromanoscopy, proctosigmoidoscopy

Rektoskop *n* rectoscope, rectal specula, proctoscope; anoscope, anuscope
Rektoskopie *f* rectoscopy, proctoscopy; anoscopy
Rektostomie *f* rectostomy, proctostomy
Rektotomie *f* rectotomy, proctotomy, incision into the rectum
Rektovaginalfistel *f* rectovaginal fistula
Rektovesikalfistel *f* rectovesical fistula
Rektozele *f* rectocele, rectal hernia, proctocele
Rektozystotomie *f* rectocystotomy
Rektum *n* rectum, straight bowel ● neben dem ~ pararectal
~/**großes** megarectum
Rektum... *s. a.* Rektal... *und* Mastdarm...
Rektumamputation *f* rectal ablation, rectectomy, proctectomy
Rektum-Anastomosenklemme *f* sigmoid anastomosis clamp
Rektumanheftung *f*[/operative] *s.* Rektopexie
Rektum-Blasen-Plastik *f* proctocystoplasty
Rektumblutung *f* rectorrhagia, proctorrhagia, haemorrhage from the rectum
Rektumdilatation *f* proctectasia; megarectum
Rektumeinschnitt *m s.* Rektotomie
Rektumeinstülpung *f* rectal intussusceptic
Rektumflexur *f* sacral flexure
Rektumgekröse *n* mesorectum
Rektumkanüle *f* rectal cannula
Rektumkarzinom *n* rectal carcinoma, cancer of the rectum
Rektumkatarrh *m s.* Rektitis
Rektumkontinuitätsherstellung *f* rectorectostomy
Rektummesser *n* rectotome, proctotome
Rektumnervengeflecht *n* rectal plexus
Rektumprolaps *m* prolapse of the rectum, rectal procidentia; proctoptosia, proctoptosis
Rektum-Scheiden-Plastik *f* proctocolpoplasty
Rektum-Sigma-Anastomose *f* sigmoidorectostomy, sigmoidoproctostomy
Rektumspreizer *m* rectal retractor
Rektumstumpf *m* rectal stump
Rektumtenesmus *m* rectal tenesmus
Rektum- und Kolonentfernung *f*[/operative] proctocolectomy
Rektum- und Kolonentzündung *f* rectocolitis, proctocolitis, inflammation of the rectum and the colon
Rektum- und Kolonspiegelung *f* proctocolonoscopy
Rektum- und Sigmaentfernung *f*[/operative] rectosigmoidectomy, proctosigmoidectomy
Rektum- und Sigmaentzündung *f* proctosigmoiditis
Rektum- und Sigmaerweiterung *f* megarectosigmoid
Rektum- und Sigmaspiegelung *f* rectosigmoidoscopy, rectoromanoscopy, proctosigmoidoscopy
Rektumuntersuchung *f*/digitale rectal touch
Rektumvenengeflecht *n* rectal [venous] plexus

Rektus *m* rectus [muscle]
Rektusdiastase *f* diastasis recti abdominis
Rektusfaszie *f* rectus fascia
Rektusrandschnitt *m* rectus incision *(Bauchhöhleneröffnung durch den geraden Bauchmuskel)*
Rektusscheide *f* rectus sheath, sheath of the rectus abdominis [muscle]
Rektusschnitt *m* rectus incision
Rektussehne *f* rectus tendon
Rekurarisierung *f* recurarization
Rekurrensfieber *n* recurrent (relapsing) fever
Rekurrenslähmung *f* paralysis of the recurrent laryngeal nerve
rekurrent recurrent
Relaparotomie *f* relaparotomy
relaparotomieren to relaparotomize, to perform a relaparotomy
Relaps *m s.* Rezidiv
Relaxans *n* relaxant [agent]
Relaxation *f* relaxation
Relaxationswärme *f* relaxation heat
relaxieren to relax
relaxierend relaxant
Reluxation *f* reluxation, redislocation
Remedium *n* remedy *(s. a. Arzneimittel)*
Remineralisation *f* remineralization *(z. B. der Knochen)*
Remission *f* remission, remittence *(z. B. von Fieber)*
remittierend remittent
REM-Schlaf *m* rapid-eye-movement sleep, REM-sleep
Ren *m* ren, kidney, nephros *(Zusammensetzungen s. unter Niere)*
reniform reniform, kidney-shaped
Renin *n* renin *(Enzym)*
Renin-Angiotensin-Aldosteron-Mechanismus *m* renin-angiotensin-aldosterone mechanism (system)
Renin-Angiotensin-System *n* renin-angiotensin system, renal pressure system
Rennin *n* rennin, chymosin, chymose *(Enzym)*
Renninogen *n* renninogen, prorennin, chymosinogen
Renogramm *n* renogram, nephrogram
Renographie *f* renography, nephrography, renal radiography
Renopathie *f* renopathy, nephropathy, renal (kidney) disease
renotroph renotrop[h]ic
renovaskulär renovascular
Renshaw-Hemmung *f* Renshaw (recurrent, antidromic) inhibition *(Nervenhemmung)*
Renshaw-Zelle *f* Renshaw cell, [inhibitory] interneuron, intercalated neuron
Rentenneurose *f* pension (compensation) neurosis
Reorganisation *f* reorganization
Reovirus *n* reovirus, respiratory enteric orphan virus
Reparationsphase *f* phase of repair
repellent repellant, repellent

Repellent 662

Repellent n repellent [agent], insectlfuge
Reperitonealisierung f reperitonealization
Repigmentierung f repigmentation
Replantation f re[im]plantation
Replikase f replicase *(Enzym)*
Replikation f replication *(Kopierung der genetischen Information z. B. aus DNS)*
Repneumatisation f repneumatization
Repolarisation f repolarization *(z. B. der Nervenmembranen)*
reponierbar reducible *(z. B. Bruch)*
~/nicht irreducible
reponieren to reduce *(z. B. einen Eingeweidebruch)*
~/eine Fraktur to reduce a fracture, to [re]set
reponiert/nicht unreduced *(z. B. ein Bruch)*
Reposition f reduction *(eines Eingeweidebruchs)*; reduction, taxis, diaplasis *(z. B. eines Gelenks)*; reduction of a fracture, [re]setting; reposition *(der Gebärmutter)*; omphalotaxis *(eines Nabelschnurvorfalls)*
~/blutige (offene) open reduction
~/unblutige closed reduction
Repositorium n repositor
Repression f repression
Repressor m, **Repressorsubstanz** f repressor
Reproduktion f reproduction
Reproduktionsorgane npl genital system (tract)
Reproduktionsperiode f reproductive period
Reproduktionsrate f reproduction rate
Reproduktionsstörung f reproduction disturbance, reproductive disorder
Reproduktionssystem n reproductive system
reproduzieren/sich s. fortpflanzen/sich
Repulsion f repulsion
RES s. System/retikuloendotheliales
Resektion f resection, excision; radiculectomy, Foerster's operation *(der Spinalnervenwurzeln)*
~/abdomino-perineale abdominoperineal resection *(des Rektums)*
~/Whipplesche Whipple resection *(der Bauchspeicheldrüse)*
Resektionsfähigkeit f resectability
Resektionsmesser n resection knife
Resektionsstumpf m resection stump
Resektionsverfahren n resective procedure
Resektoskop n resectoscope
Resektoskopie f resectoscopy
Reserpin n reserpine *(Alkaloid)*
Reserpinbehandlung f reserpinization
Reserpineinstellung f reserpinization
Reservekraft f reserve force
Reserveluft f s. Reservevolumen/exspiratorisches
Reservestreckapparat m/**lateraler** lateral accessory patellar ligament *(des Kniegelenks)*
~/medialer medial accessory patellar ligament *(des Kniegelenks)*
Reservevolumen n reserve volume
~/exspiratorisches expiratory reserve volume, ERV, REV, reserve (supplementary) air
~/inspiratorisches inspiratory reserve volume, IRS, complemental air

Reservezelle f reserve cell
Reservoirwirt m reservoir host
resezierbar resectable
Resezierbarkeit f resectability
Resezierbarkeitsrate f resectability rate
resezieren to resect
residual residual *(z. B. als Krankheitsfolge)*
Residual... s. a. Rest...
Residualabszeß m residual abscess
Residualakkommodation f residual accommodation
Residualalbuminurie f residual albuminuria
Residualastigmatismus m residual astigmatism
Residualgehör n residual hearing
Residualkapazität f residual capacity
~/funktionelle functional residual capacity
Residualkörperchen n residual body
Residualluft f residual air
~/funktionelle functional residual air
Residualschizophrenie f residual schizophrenia
Residualtuberkulom n residual tuberculoma
Residualvolumen n residual volume
~/funktionelles functional residual volume, stationary air
resistent resistant ● **~ sein [gegen]** to be resistant [to]
~ gegen eine Behandlung resistant to treatment, recalcitrant
Resistenz f resistance *(eines Individuums)*
~/bakterielle bacterial resistance
~/erworbene acquired resistance; acquired immunity
~/geminderte diminished (lessened) resistance
~/gesteigerte increased resistance
~/natürliche natural resistance; natural immunity
Resistenzbestimmung f resistance determination
Resistenztest m susceptibility test *(z. B. bei Bakterien gegenüber Antibiotika)*
Resolution f resolution *(einer Krankheit)*
Resolvens n resolvent [agent]
resonant resonant, tympan[it]ic, tympanal
Resonanz f resonance, tympania *(z. B. bei der Perkussion)*
~/kernmagnetische nuclear magnetic resonance, NMR
Resorbens n resorbent [agent]
resorbierbar absorbable
~/nicht non-absorbable
resorbieren to absorb, to resorb
resorbierend absorbent, resorbent
resorbiert werden to resorb, to undergo resorption
Resorption f absorption, resorption; incorporation *(radioaktiver Stoffe)*
Resorptionsatelektase f absorption (obstructive) atelectasis *(entsteht durch Luftaufsaugung in den Alveolen nach Bronchusverstopfung)*
Resorptionsikterus m absorptive (resorptive) jaundice, regurgitation jaundice
Resorzin n resorcin, resorcinol
Resorzinprobe f resorcinol test *(auf freie Salzsäure im Mageninhalt)*

Resorzinvergiftung f resorcinism, chronic poisoning by resorcinol
respirabel respirable
Respiration f respiration, breathing, pneusis *(Zusammensetzungen s. unter Atmung)*
Respirations... *s.a.* Atmungs...
Respirationsapparat m *s.* Respirator
Respirationstrakt m respiratory tract
Respirationstraktallergose f respiratory tract allergosis (allergic disease)
Respirationstraktbeteiligung f respiratory tract involvement
Respirationstrakterkrankung f respiratory tract illness
Respirationstraktinfektion f respiratory tract infection
Respirator m respirator, inspirator
~/assistiert-kontrollierter assist-control respirator
~/volumengesteuerter volume[-cycled] ventilator
respiratorisch respiratory
respirieren to respire, to breathe
Respirometer n respirometer
Respirometrie f respirometry
Rest... *s.a.* Residual ...
Restalkohol m residual alcohol
Restblut n residual blood
Restenose f restenosis
Restharn m residual urine ● **ohne ~** without residual urine
Restitutio f **ad integrum** restitutio ad integrum, complete return to health
Restitution f restitution, restoration
Restkaverne f residual cavity
restlich residual
Restlumen n residual lumen
Restoration f restoration
Restproteinurie f residual proteinuria
Reststickstoff m non-protein nitrogen
Restzustand m/**fetaler** foetalism *(Persistenz fetaler Zeichen nach der Geburt)*
Resuszitation f [cardiac] resuscitation, reanimation, revivification
Resuszitator m resuscitator
retardiert retarded, backward
Retardierter m/**geistig** retardate
Retardierung f retardation, delay, hindrance, backwardness *(geistiger und körperlicher Entwicklung)*
~/geistige mental retardation (subnormality)
Retardpräparat n sustained-release preparation, controlled-release drug, prolonged-action drug
Rete n rete, net[work]
~ acromiale acromial rete *(Arteriennetz)*
~ arteriosum arterial network
~ articulare articular rete
~ calcaneum calcaneal rete
~ carpi carpal rete
~ carpi dorsale dorsal carpal rete
~ mucosum epidermal rete
~ patellae patellar rete
~ plantare plantar rete
Retentio f **urinae** retention of urine
Retention f 1. retention, holding back *(z. B. von Körperflüssigkeiten)*; 2. retention *(z. B. einer korrigierten Zahnstellung)*
~ der Plazenta retention of the placenta; retained placenta
Retentionseinlauf m retention enema
Retentionshyperlipämie f retention hyperlipaemia
Retentionsikterus m retention (obstructive) jaundice
Retentionstoxikose f retention toxicosis
Retentionszyste f retention cyst
Rethorakotomie f rethoracotomy
Reticulum n *s.* Retikulum
retikulär reticular, reticulated, reticulose
Retikulin n reticulin
Retikulinfärbung f reticulin stain
Retikulinfaser f reticular (reticulin) fibre, precollagenous (lattice) fibre, argentophile (argentaffine) fibre
Retikuloendothel n reticulo[endo]thelium
retikuloendothelial reticuloendothelial, retothelial, lymphoreticular
Retikuloendotheliom n reticuloendothelioma
Retikuloendotheliose f reticuloendotheliosis, histiocytosis X
~ der Säuglinge/diffuse Letterer-Siwe disease, non-lipid histiocytosis (reticuloendotheliosis)
Retikuloendothelzelle f reticuloendothelial cell
retikulohistiozytär reticulohistiocytary
Retikulom n reticuloma
Retikuloplasmozytom n reticuloplasmocytoma
Retikulosarkom n reticulocytic (retothelial) sarcoma, retothelio[sarco]ma, reticulothelioma, reticulosarcoma, reticuloendothelial (trabecular syncytial) sarcoma
~/lymphoblastisches lymphoblastic reticulosarcoma
Retikulose f reticulosis
~/leukämische [a]leukaemic reticulosis, leukaemic (monocytic) leukaemia
~/medulläre medullary reticulosis
Retikulozyt m reticulocyte, reticulated erythrocyte, proerythrocyte, skein cell
Retikulozytenbildung f reticulocytogenesis ● **die ~ anregend** reticulocytogenic
Retikulozytenvermehrung f **im Blut** reticulocytosis
Retikulozytenverminderung f **im Blut** reticulo[cyto]penia
retikulozytogen reticulocytogenic
Retikulozytopenie f reticulo[cyto]penia
Retikulozytose f reticulocytosis
Retikulum n reticulum, [fine] network
~/endoplasmatisches endoplasmic reticulum
~/rauhes endoplasmatisches rough[-surfaced] endoplasmic reticulum
Retikulumzelle. f reticulum (reticular) cell, reticuloendothelial cell
Retikulumzellensarkom n *s.* Retikulosarkom

Retina

Retina f retina, optomeninx
Retina... s.a. Netzhaut...
Retinaaktionsstrombild n electroretinogram, ERG
Retinaaktionsstromschreibung f electroretinography
Retinaculum n retinaculum *(Anatomie)*
- **extensorum [manus]** extensor retinaculum [of the wrist], dorsal carpal ligament
- **flexorum [manus]** flexor retinaculum [of the wrist], transverse carpal ligament
- **musculorum extensorum pedis inferius** inferior extensor retinaculum, cruciate ligament of the ankle
- **musculorum extensorum [pedis] superius** superior extensor retinaculum, transverse crural ligament
- **musculorum flexorum pedis** flexor retinaculum of the ankle, laciniate (internal annular) ligament
- **musculorum peronaeorum** peroneal (fibular) retinaculum
- **musculorum peronaeorum inferius** inferior peroneal retinaculum
- **musculorum peronaeorum superius** superior peroneal retinaculum
- **patellae** patellar retinaculum
- **patellae laterale** lateral [accessory] patellar ligament
- **patellae mediale** medial [accessory] patellar ligament
- **uteri** parametrium

Retinadestruktion f retinal destruction
Retinaentzündung f s. Retinitis
Retinakryopexie f retinal cryopexy
Retinamalazie f retinomalacia, softening of the retina
Retinaneuralgie f neurodealgia
Retinaruptur f retinal rupture
Retinaverletzung f retinal wound
Retinen n retinene *(prosthetische Gruppe des Sehpurpurs)*
Retinitis f retinitis, inflammation of the retina
- **angiospastica** angiospastic retinitis
- **centralis serosa** central serous retinopathy, central angiospastic retinitis
- **circinata** circinate retinitis (retinopathy)
- **disciformis** disciform macular degeneration, central disk-shaped retinopathy
- **exsudativa** exudative retinitis, Coat's disease
- **haemorrhagica** haemorrhagic retinitis
- **nephritica** renal retinitis, vascular retinopathy
- **proliferans** proliferating retinitis

Retinoblastom n retinoblastoma *(bösartige Netzhautgeschwulst)*
Retinochorioiditis f retinochoroiditis
- **juxtapapillaris** s. Retinopathie/Jensensche

Retinodialyse f retinodialysis, disinsertion of the retina
Retinographie f retinography
Retinol n retinol, vitamin A
Retinol-Dehydrogenase f retinol dehydrogenase *(Enzym)*
Retinolmangel m retinol deficiency
Retinometer n retinometer
Retinopapillitis f retinopapillitis
Retinopathia f s. Retinopathie
- **angiospastica** angiospastic retinitis
- **gravidarum** retinopathy of pregnancy

Retinopathie f retinopathy, disease of the retina *(s. a. unter Retinopathia)*
- **/degenerative** s. Retinosis
- **/diabetische** diabetic retinitis (retinopathy)
- **/Jensensche** Jensen's disease (retinopathy), juxtapapillary choroiditis

Retinopexie f retinopexy, fixation of the retina
Retinoschisis f retinoschisis
- **/senile** senile retinoschisis

Retinosis f retinosis, degenerative disease of the retina
Retinoskop n retinoscope
Retinoskopie f retino[skia]scopy, scotoscopy, skiascopy, skiametry, umbrascopy *(objektive Refraktionsbestimmung des Auges)*; pupilloscopy
Retinozytom n retinocytoma
Retothel n retothelium
retothelial retothelial
Retotheliom n s. Retikulosarkom
Retotheliose f reticulosis
Retothelsarkom n s. Retikulosarkom
retrahieren to retract *(z. B. eine Sehne)*
Retraktion f retraction *(z. B. einer Sehne)*; clot retraction, syneresis
Retraktionsnystagmus m retraction nystagmus
Retraktionsring m retraction (constriction) ring *(der Gebärmutter)*
Retraktionszeit f [clot] retraction time
Retraktor m retractor, rib spreader
- **/gezahnter** sharp retractor

Retransfusion f autotransfusion, [auto]reinfusion *(eigenen Bluts)*
Retrobulbärabszeß m retrobulbar abscess
Retrobulbäranästhesie f retrobulbar anaesthesia
Retrobulbärblutung f retrobulbar haemorrhage
Retrobulbärneuritis f retrobulbar (orbital optic) neuritis
Retrobulbärphlegmone f retrobulbar phlegmon
Retrobulbärraum m retrobulbar space
Retrocheilie f retrocheilia
Retrocollis m spasmodicus retrocollis [spasmodicus], spasmodic wryneck
Retrodeviation f retrodeviation, backward displacement
retroflektieren to retroflex
Retroflexio f uteri uterus retroflexion, retroflexion of the uterus *(Abknickung des Gebärmutterkörpers nach hinten)*
Retroflexion f retroflexion
Retrognathismus m retrognathia, retrognathism
retrograd retrograde
retrokardial retrocardiac, retrocordial
Retrokardialraum m retrocardiac (Holzknecht's) space *(Radiologie)*
Retromammärabszeß m retromammary abscess

Retromandibularabszeß *m* retromandibular abscess
Retroorbitalkopfschmerz *m* retro-orbital headache
Retroperistaltik *f* retrostalsis, reversed peristalsis
Retroperitonealfibrose *f* retroperitoneal fibrosis
Retroperitonealgeschwulst *f* retroperitoneal tumour
Retroperitonealgewebe *n* retroperitoneal tissue
Retroperitonealhämatom *n* retroperitoneal haematoma
Retroperitonealhernie *f* retroperitoneal hernia
Retroperitonealraum *m s.* Retroperitoneum
Retroperitonealraumentzündung *f* retroperitonitis
Retroperitoneum *n* retroperitoneum, retroperitoneal space
Retropharyngealabszeß *m* retropharyngeal abscess
Retropharyngealhämatom *n* retropharyngeal haematoma
Retropharyngealraum *m* retropharyngeal space
Retropharyngitis *f* retropharyngitis
Retropharynx *m* retropharynx
Retroplasie *f* retroplasia
Retroposition *f* retroposition, backward displacement
Retropulsion *f* 1. retropulsion, backward progression *(z. B. bei Tabes dorsalis)*; 2. retropulsion *(Zurücktreiben des Fetuskopfes in den Wehen)*
Retrosternalpuls *m* retrosternal pulse
Retrosternalschmerz *m* retrosternal pain, substernal discomfort
Retrosternalstruma *f* retrosternal goitre
retrosymphysär retrosymphyseal
Retrotonsillarabszeß *m* retrotonsillar abscess
Retroversio *f uteri* retroversion of the uterus
Retroversioflexion *f* retroversioflexion *(z. B. der Gebärmutter)*
Retroversion *f* retroversion
retrovertieren to retrovert
Retrovesikalabszeß *m* retrovesical abscess
Retrozession *f* retrocession *(z. B. der Gebärmutter)*
Retrozökalappendizitis *f* retrocaecal appendicitis
retten to rescue, to save; to recover *(befreien)*; to sanitize
Rettung *f* rescue; recovery
Rettungsschwimmen *n* life-saving swimming
Rettungsschwimmer *m* lifeguard, life-saver
Rettungswagen *m* ambulance [car]
Revagotomie *f* revagotomy
Revakzination *f* revaccination
Revaskularisation *f* revascularization
Revaskularisationssyndrom *n* revascularization syndrome
revaskularisieren to revascularize
Reverdin-Läppchen *n* Reverdin (pinch) graft
Reverdin-Nadel *f* Reverdin's needle
reversibel reversible

Revitalisierung *f* revitalization
Revulsion *f* revulsion *(z. B. von Blut)*
Rezept *n* 1. [medical] prescription, formula, recipe; 2. prescription blank ● **ein ~ ausstellen** to prescribe, to write [out] a prescription
Rezeptausstellung *f* prescription writing
Rezeptblock *m* prescription pad
Rezeptivfeld *n* receptive field *(der Retina)*
Rezeptor *m* receptor
~/adrenerger adrenergic receptor
~ für den osmotischen Druck osmoreceptor *(im Gehirn)*
α-Rezeptor *m* alpha[-adrenergic] receptor
β-Rezeptor *m* beta[-adrenergic] receptor
Rezeptorenblockade *f* receptor blocking
~/adrenerge adrenergic receptor blocking
Rezeptorenblocker *m* receptor blocker (blocking drug)
α-Rezeptorenblocker *m* alpha-adrenergic blocker, alpha-adrenergic receptor blocking agent
β-Rezeptorenblocker *m* beta-adrenergic blocker, beta-adrenergic receptor blocking agent
β-Rezeptoren-Stimulation *f* beta-adrenergic stimulation
Rezeptorfrühpotential *n* early receptor potential
Rezeptorpotential *n* receptor (generator) potential
Rezeptur *f* prescription, formula, recipe, formulation
Rezepturvorschrift *f* inscriptio[n]
Rezession *f* recession *(z. B. des Zahnfleischrands)*
rezessiv recessive *(bei Vererbung)*
Rezidiv *n* relapse, recurrence, recidivation, palindromia *(z. B. einer Krankheit)*
~/neurologisches neurorelapse, neurorecidive, neurorecurrence
Rezidivblutung *f* rebleeding
rezidivfrei relapse-free, recurrence-free, without relapse
rezidivieren to relapse, to recur *(Krankheiten)*
rezidivierend relapsing, recurrent, palindromic
~/nicht non-relapsing, non-recurrent; benign *(z. B. Geschwulst)*
Rezidivoperation *f* relapse operation
Rezidivprophylaxe *f* prevention of recurrency (recidivation)
Rezidivrate *f* recurrence (relapse) rate
Rezidivzeichen *n* sign of recurrence, symptom of recidivation
Rezirkulation *f/pulmonale* pulmonary recirculation *(bei Herzfehlern)*
RG *s.* Rasselgeräusch
rh Rh-negative
Rh Rh-positive
Rh-... *s.* Rhesus...
Rhabdomyoblast *m* rhabdomyoblast
Rhabdomyoblastom *n* rhabdomyoblastoma
Rhabdomyochondrom *n* rhabdomyochondroma
Rhabdomyom *n* rhabdomyoma, striocellular myoma *(gutartige Geschwulst aus quergestreiften Muskelfasern)*

Rhabdomyosarkom

Rhabdomyosarkom n rhabdomyosarcoma *(bösartige Geschwulst aus quergestreiften Muskelfasern)*
Rhabdophobie f rhabdophobia *(krankhafte Angst vor Stockschlägen)*
Rhachi... s. Rachi...
Rhagade f rhagade, fissure (crack) in the skin
rhagadenförmig rhagadiform, fissured, cracked
Rhamnoglykosid n rhamnoglucoside
Rhamnose f rhamnose
Rhamnosid n rhamnoside *(Glykosid)*
0 rh-Blut n [group] 0 Rh-negative blood
0 Rh-Blut n [group] 0 Rh-positive blood
Rh-Blutgruppe f Rh blood group
Rheobase f rheobase *(niedrigstes elektrisches Reizpotential)*
Rheoenzephalogramm n rheoencephalogram
Rheoenzephalographie f rheoencephalography
rheoenzephalographisch rheoencephalographic
Rheokardiogramm n rheocardiogram
Rheokardiographie f rheocardiography
rheokardiographisch rheocardiographic
Rheologie f rheology
rheologisch rheologic
Rheometer n rheometer
Rheotachygramm n rheotachygram
Rheotachygraphie f rheotachygraphy
rheotachygraphisch rheotachygraphic
Rhesusaffe m rhesus monkey
Rhesusagglutinogen n Rh agglutinogen
Rhesus-Antigen n Rh[esus] antigen
Rhesus-Antikörper m Rh[esus] antibody
Rhesus-Desensibilisierung f Rh[esus] desensitization
Rhesusfaktor m Rh[esus] factor
Rhesusfaktor-Antiserum n Rh[esus] antiserum
Rhesusfaktor-Blockierungsserum n Rh[esus] blocking serum
Rhesus-Immunisierung f Rh[esus] immunization
Rhesus-Immunoglobulin n Rh[esus] immune globulin
Rhesus-Inkompatibilität f Rh[esus] incompatibility
Rhesus-Isoimmunisierung f Rh[esus] isoimmunization
Rhesus-Sensibilisierung f Rh[esus] sensitization
Rhesus-Typisierung f Rh[esus] typing
Rheuma n s. Rheumatismus
rheumaartig rheumatoid
Rheumabehandlung f antirheumatic therapy
Rheumabeschwerden pl rheumatic complaints
Rheumafaktor m rheumatoid factor
Rheumaknötchen n rheumatic nodule
Rheumakranker m rheumatic
Rheumakrankheit f rheumatic disease
Rheumalehre f rheumatology
Rheumarthritis f rheumarthritis, rheumatic arthritis
Rheumaschmerz m s. Rheumatalgie
Rheumaspezialist m rheumatologist
Rheumatalgie f rheumatalgia, chronic rheumatic pain
Rheumatiker m rheumatic
rheumatisch rheumatic
Rheumatismus m rheumatism
~/**akuter** rheumatic fever, inflammatory (acute articular) rheumatism, rheumapyra, Bouillaud's disease (syndrome)
~/**chronischer** chronic articular rheumatism; rheumatoid arthritis
~/**viszeraler** visceral rheumatism
Rheumatismusknötchen n/**Aschoff-Geipelsches** Aschoff's nodule
rheumatoid rheumatoid
Rheumatoidarthritis f rheumatoid arthritis, atrophic (proliferative) arthritis, chronic infectious arthritis
~/**juvenile** juvenile rheumatoid arthritis, Still's disease
Rheumatoidepiskleritis f rheumatoid episcleritis
Rheumatoidskleritis f rheumatoid scleritis
Rheumatologe m rheumatologist
Rheumatologie f rheumatology *(Lehre von den rheumatischen Erkrankungen)*
rheumatologisch rheumatologic
Rhexis f s. Ruptur
Rh-Faktor m s. Rhesusfaktor
Rhin... s. a. Nasen...
Rhinalgie f rhinalgia, rhinodynia, pain in the nose
Rhinallergose f rhinallergosis, hay fever
Rhinästhesie f rhinaesthesia, sense of smell
rhinenzephal rhinencephalic
Rhinenzephalon n rhinencephalon, olfactory brain, smell-brain, nosebrain
Rhineurynter m rhineurynter
Rhinion n rhinion *(anthropologischer Meßpunkt)*
Rhinitis f rhinitis, nasitis, coryza, nasal catarrh
~/**allergische** allergic coryza
~ **atrophicans cum foetore** atrophic rhinitis, ozaena
~ **caseosa** caseous rhinitis
~/**eitrige** purulent rhinitis
~/**hypertrophe** hypertrophic rhinitis
~/**membranöse** membranous rhinitis
~/**pseudomembranöse** pseudomembranous rhinitis
~ **sicca** dry rhinitis
~ **vasomotorica** vasomotor rhinitis (catarrh)
Rhinocheiloplastik f rhinocheiloplasty
Rhinodakryolith m rhinodacryolith
Rhinoderma n rhinoderma
Rhinodynie f s. Rhinalgie
rhinogen rhinogenous
Rhinokanthektomie f rhinocanthectomy
Rhinokleisis f rhinocleisis, obstruction of the nasal passages
Rhinokyphose f rhinokyphosis
Rhinolalia aperta open rhinolalia, hypernasality, cleft palate speech *(bei mangelndem Verschluß des Nasenrachens)*
Rhinolalie f rhinolalia
Rhinolaryngitis f rhinolaryngitis
Rhinolaryngologe m rhinolaryngologist
Rhinolaryngologie f rhinolaryngology

Rhinoliquorrhoe f cerebrospinal [fluid] rhinorrhoea
Rhinolith m rhinolith, nasal calculus (stone)
Rhinolithiasis f rhinolithiasis
Rhinologe m rhinologist
Rhinologie f rhinology *(Lehre von den Nasenkrankheiten)*
rhinologisch rhinologic
Rhinomanometer n rhinomanometer
Rhinometer n rhinometer
Rhinomykose f rhinomycosis
Rhinopathie f rhinopathy, disease of the nose
Rhinopharyngitis f rhinopharyngitis, pharyngorhinitis, nasopharyngitis
~ **acuta** pharyngoconjunctival fever
~ **mutilans** gangosa
Rhinopharyngolith m rhinopharyngolith
Rhinopharyngozele f rhinopharyngocele
Rhinopharynx m rhinopharynx, epipharynx, nasopharynx, postnasal space
Rhinophonie f rhinophonia
Rhinophykomykose f rhinophycomycosis
Rhinophym n rhinophym[a], potato (hammer) nose, whisky[-rum] nose, bottle nose; pachydermatosis
Rhinorrhagie f rhinorrhagia, nosebleed[ing], epistaxis, nasal bleeding (haemorrhage)
Rhinorrhaphie f rhinorrhaphy
Rhinorrhoe f 1. rhinorrhoea, discharge of nasal mucus; 2. cerebrospinal [fluid] rhinorrhoea
Rhinoschisis f rhinoschisis
Rhinosinusitis f rhinosinusitis
Rhinosinusopathie f rhinosinusopathy
Rhinosklerom n rhinoscleroma *(Infektionskrankheit durch Klebsiella rhinoscleromatis)*
Rhinoskop n rhinoscope, nasoscope, nasal speculum, rhinoscopic mirror
Rhinoskopie f rhinoscopy, nasoscopy
rhinoskopisch rhinoscopic
Rhinosporidiose f rhinosporidiosis *(Infektionskrankheit durch Rhinosporidium seeberi)*
Rhinostenose f rhinostenosis, stenomycteria
Rhinotomie f rhinotomy, incision into the nose
Rhinotracheitis-Virus n rhinotracheitis virus
Rhinovakzination f rhinovaccination
Rhinovirus n rhinovirus
Rhinozephalie f rhinocephalia
Rhinozephalus m rhinocephalus
rhizoid rhizoid[al], rootlike
Rhizotomia f rhizotomy, radicotomy, division of a nerve root
~ **anterior** anterior rhizotomy
~ **posterior** posterior rhizotomy, Foerster's operation
Rh-negativ Rh[esus]-negative
Rhodesiafieber n Rhodesian (African coast) fever
Rhodnius m Rhodnius [prolixus] *(Trypanosoma cruzi übertragende Raubwanzenart)*
Rhodogenese f rhodogenesis
rhodophylaktisch rhodophylactic
Rhodopsin n rhodopsin, erythropsin, visual purple (substance), retinal pigment

Rhodopsinbleichen n rhodopsin bleaching
rhombenzephal rhombencephalic
Rhombenzephalon n rhombencephalon, hindbrain
rhomboid rhomboid, rhombic
Rhombozöle f rhombocoele
Rhonchus m s. Rasselgeräusch
Rhotazismus m rhotacism
Rh-positiv Rh[esus]-positive
Rh-Sensibilisierung f Rh[esus] sensitization
Rh-Typisierung f Rh[esus] typing
Rh-Unverträglichkeit f Rh[esus] incompatibility
Rhypophagie f rhypophagy, eating of filth
Rhypophobie f rhypophobia, molysmophobia *(krankhafte Angst vor Schmutz)*
rhythmisch rhythmic[al]; regular
rhythmisierend antiarrhythmic
Rhythmus m rhythm; wave
~/**alternierender** alternating rhythm
~ **cordis** cardiac (heart) rhythm
~/**ventrikulärer** ventricular rhythm
α-Rhythmus m alpha rhythm (wave) *(im EEG)*
β-Rhythmus m beta rhythm (wave) *(im EEG)*
γ-Rhythmus m gamma rhythm (wave) *(im EEG)*
rhythmusgestört arrhythmic[al], dysrhythmic
rhythmuslos arrhythmic[al]
Rhythmusstörung f dysrhythmia, rhythm disturbance, arrhythmia *(z. B. des Herzens)*
Rhytidektomie f rhytidectomy, excision of wrinkles
Rhytidoplastik f rhytidoplasty, face-lift[ing]
Rhytidosis f rhytidosis, wrinkling
Riboflavin n riboflavin, vitamin B_2, hepatoflavin, lactoflavin
Riboflavinadenosindinukleotid n riboflavin adenine dinucleotide
Riboflavinavitaminose f ariboflavinosis
Riboflavin-5-phosphat n riboflavin-5'-phosphate, isoalloxazine mononucleotide, flavin mononucleotide, FMN
Ribonuklease f ribonuclease, RNase *(Enzym)*
Ribonukleinprotein n ribonucleoprotein, RNP
Ribonukleinsäure f ribonucleic acid, RNA
Ribonukleinsäure-Polymerase f ribonucleic acid polymerase *(Enzym)*
Ribonukleinsäuresynthese f ribonucleic acid synthesis
Ribonukleinsäurevirus n ribonucleic acid virus
Ribose f ribose
Ribosid n riboside
Ribosom n ribosome *(Zellorganelle)*
Ribosomproteid n ribosomal protein
richten/einen Knochenbruch to reduce a fracture
Rickettsia f rickettsia
~ **akari** Rickettsia akari *(Erreger der Rickettsienpocken)*
~ **australis** Rickettsia australis *(Erreger des Queensland-Zeckenbißfiebers)*
~ **Burneti** Rickettsia burnetii *(Erreger des Q-Fiebers)*
~ **Conori** Rickettsia conorii *(Erreger des Mittelmeerfiebers)*

Rickettsia

- **Mooseri** Rickettsia mooseri *(Erreger des murinen Fleckfiebers)*
- **Prowazeki** Rickettsia prowazekii *(Erreger des klassischen Fleckfiebers)*
- **quintana** Rickettsia quintana (wolhynica) *(Erreger des Wolhynischen Fiebers)*
- **rickettsi** Rickettsia rickettsii *(Erreger des Felsengebirgsfiebers)*
- **siberica** Rickettsia siberica *(Erreger des asiatischen Zeckenbißfiebers)*
- **tsutsugamushi** Rickettsia tsutsugamushi (orientalis), scrub typhus rickettsia *(Erreger der Tsutsugamushikrankheit)*

Rickettsiämie f rickettsaemia
rickettsienartig rickettsial
rickettsienhemmend rickettsiostatic
Rickettsien-Komplement-Fixationsreaktion f rickettsial complement fixation reaction
Rickettsienkrankheit f rickettsiosis, rickettsial disease
Rickettsienlehre f rickettsiology
Rickettsienpocken pl rickettsial pox; vesicular rickettsiosis
Rickettsienvakzine f rickettsial vaccine
Rickettsiose f rickettsiosis, rickettsial disease
Riechampulle f perle
Riechapparat m olfactory apparatus
Riechen n olfaction, osmesis
riechend odorant, odoriferous
Riechepithel n olfactory epithelium
Riechfaden m olfactory nerve
Riechgrube f olfactory pit, nasal fossa *(Embryologie)*
Riechhirn n s. Rhinenzephalon
Riechkanal m olfactory canal *(Embryologie)*
Riechkapsel f olfactory capsule *(Embryologie)*
Riechkolben m olfactory bulb, mamillary apophysis
Riechnerv m olfactory nerve, first cranial nerve
Riechorgan n olfactory organ, organ of smell
Riechplakode f olfactory placode *(Embryologie)*
Riechregion f [der Nase] olfactory region [of the nose]
Riechschärfe f olfaction acuity
Riechschleimhaut f olfactory mucosa (mucous membrane)
Riechschleimhautregion f olfactory mucosal region
Riechsinn m olfactory sense ● **mit ausgeprägtem** ~ oxyrhine
Riechstörung f olfactory dysfunction
Riechsystem n olfactory system
Riechzelle f olfactory cell
Riechzentrum n olfactory centre *(des Gehirns)*
Riemenmuskel m **des Halses** splenius cervicis [muscle]
- **des Kopfes** splenius capitis [muscle]

Riese m giant
Riesenauge n megalophthalmos, megalophthalmus
Riesenchromosom n giant chromosome
Riesendarmegel m/**fernöstlicher** intestinal fluke, fasciolopsis *(Leber- und Darmparasit des Menschen)*
Riesendarmegelbefall m fasciolopsiasis
Rieserythrozyt m giant erythrocyte
Riesenfinger m giant finger
Riesenkolon n giant colon
Riesenkornea f macrocornea *(des Auges)*
Riesenpigmentnävus m giant pigmented naevus
Riesenpyramidenzelle f giant pyramidal cell
~/**Betzsche** Betz giant pyramidal cell, cell of Betz
Riesenthrombozyt m giant platelet
Riesenureter m mega[lo]ureter
Riesenvakuole f giant vacuole
Riesenwuchs m gi[g]antism, macrosomia, somatomegaly
- **der Füße** macropodia
- **der Schädelknochen** megalocephalia
~/**halbseitiger** hemihypertrophy
Riesenzelle f giant cell, gigantocyte
~/**Aschoff-Geipelsche** Aschoff cell
~/**Langhanssche** Langhans' giant cell, giant cell of the Langhans type *(z. B. in tuberkulösem Gewebe)*
~/**Sternbergsche** Sternberg[-Reed] cell
~/**Warthin-Finkeldeysche** Warthin-Finkeldey [giant] cell, measles giant cell
Riesenzellenarteriitis f giant-cell arteritis, temporal (cranial) arteritis, granulomatous angiitis
Riesenzellenepulis f giant-cell epulis
Riesenzellenglioblastom n giant-cell glioblastoma
Riesenzellengranulom n giant-cell granuloma
Riesenzellengranulomatose f giant-cell granulomatosis
Riesenzellenkarzinom n giant-cell carcinoma
Riesenzellenleukämie f megakaryocytic (giant-cell) leukaemia, piastrenaemia
Riesenzellenmangel m megakaryocytopenia
Riesenzellensarkom n giant-cell sarcoma
Riesenzellentumor m giant-cell tumour
Riesenzellenxanthom n giant-cell xanthoma
Rift-Tal-Fieber n Rift Valley fever
Rift-Tal-Fieber-Retinitis f Rift Valley fever retinitis
Rift-Tal-Fieber-Virus n Rift Valley fever virus
rigid[e] rigid, stiff; inflexible; immobile
Rigidität f [muscular] rigidity, rigor, stiffness; inflexibility; immobility
~/**zerebelläre** cerebellar rigidity
Rigor m rigor, [muscular] rigidity, stiffness
- **mortis** postmortem (cadaveric) rigidity
Rima f rima, slit, cleft; fissure, fissura
- **cornealis** corneal cleft
- **glottidis** glottic slit, glottis
- **palpebrarum** eyelid fissura, palpebral fissure (aperture)
- **pudendi** pudendal cleft
Rinde f cortex ● **von der** ~ **weggerichtet** corticifugal
Rinden... s.a. Kortex...
Rindenagraphie f cerebral agraphia

Rindenakinesie f cerebral akinesia
Rindenaphasie f central aphasia
Rindenblindheit f cortical (central, cerebral) blindness
~/psychische psychic (mind) blindness, psychanopsia
Rindendegeneration f cortical degeneration
Rindenepilepsie f cortical epilepsy
Rindenfeld n cortical field (area)
~/motorisches motor cortex, pyramidal (motor cortical) area
Rindenknochen m cortical bone
Rindenleseunfähigkeit f cortical alexia
rindennah juxtacortical
Rindenschicht f cortical layer (substance)
● **durch die ~** transcortical
Rindensinus m cortical sinus *(im Lymphknoten)*
Rindenstar m cortical cataract
Rindentaubheit f cortical deafness, central (cerebral, psychic) deafness
rindenwärts corticipetal
Rindenzentrum n cortical centre; sensory area (cortex); motor area (cortex)
Rinderantiserum n bovine antiserum
Rinderbandwurm m beef tapeworm, Taenia saginata
Rinderserum n bovine serum
Rindertuberkulose f bovine tuberculosis, perlsucht
Ring m ring, an[n]ulus; circle, circulus
ringartig annular, circular, areolar
Ringbiopsie f ring (cone) biopsy
Ringblutung f ring haemorrhage
Ringdurchtrennung f/operative annulotomy
Ringe mpl/**Cabotsche** Cabot's rings, ring bodies *(bei Bleivergiftung oder Blutarmut)*
Ringelhaare npl ringed hair
Ringelröteln pl infectious erythema, fifth disease
ringen/nach Luft to gasp, to suffocate
Ringer-Laktatlösung f lactated Ringer's solution
Ringfinger m ring finger
ringförmig annular, circular, ring-shaped, cricoid, orbicular, areolar
Ringgriffinstrument n ring handle instrument
Ringhymen m(n) annular (circular) hymen
Ringkeratitis f annular keratitis
Ringknorpel m cricoid [cartilage], annular cartilage
Ringknorpel-Aryknorpel-Gelenk n cricoarytenoid joint
Ringknorpel-Aryknorpel-Gelenkentzündung f cricoarytenoid joint arthritis
Ringknorpel-Aryknorpel-Gelenkversteifung f cricoarytenoid ankylosis
Ringknorpeldurchtrennung f[/operative] cricotomy
Ringknorpelentfernung f[/operative] cricoidectomy
Ringknorpelfehlbildung f cricoid malformation
Ringknorpelspaltung f cricotomy
Ringkörperchen npl/**Cabotsche** s. Ringe/Cabotsche

Ringmesser n ring knife, adenotome, adenoid curette, lymphotome
Ringmuskel m 1. orbicularis [muscle], orbicular muscle; 2. sphincter [muscle]
Ringpankreas n annular pancreas
Ringpessar n ring (doughnut) pessary
Ringschildknorpelmuskel m cricothyroid muscle
~/hinterer keratocricoid [muscle]
Ringskotom n ring (annular) scotoma
Ringstar m ring (annular) cataract
Ringstriktur f annular stricture
Ringstripper m endarterectomy stripper, artery cleaner
Ringthrombus m annular thrombus
Ringtrübung f/**Vossiussche** Vossius cataract (lenticular ring), pigmented cataract
Rinne f furrow, groove, [semi]canal, sulcus *(Zusammensetzungen s. unter Sulcus)*
Rinne positiv s. Rinne-Schalleitungsversuch/positiver
Rinne-Schalleitungsversuch m Rinne's test
~/negativer Rinne's test negative
~/positiver Rinne's test positive
Rippe f rib, costa, costal bone ● **durch die Rippen** transcostal ● **über der ~** supracostal ● **unter den Rippen** subcostal
~/echte true (sternal) rib
~/falsche false (asternal) rib
Rippen... s.a. Kosto...
Rippenapproximator m rib approximator
Rippenbett n rib bed
Rippenbogen m costal arch, arch of the rib
Rippenbogenrandschnitt m subcostal incision
~ nach Kocher Kocher incision *(Gallenchirurgie)*
Rippenbruch m rib fracture
Rippenchondrosarkom n costal chondrosarcoma
Rippendurchtrennung f[/operative] costotomy, cutting of the rib
Rippenfaßzange f rib holding forceps
Rippenfell n costal pleura
Rippenfellentzündung f pleurisy, pleuritis, inflammation of the pleura *(Zusammensetzungen s. unter Pleuritis)*
Rippenfell- und Lungenentzündung f pleuropneumonia
Rippenfellverdickung f/entzündliche pachypleuritis
rippenförmig costiform
Rippenfraktur f rib fracture
Rippengelenklinie f costoarticular line
Rippenhals m neck of the rib
Rippenhalter m/**hinterer** scalenus posterior [muscle], posterior scalene muscle
~/kleiner scalenus minimus [muscle]
~/mittlerer scalenus medius [muscle], middle scalene muscle
~/vorderer scalenus anterior [muscle], anterior scalene muscle
Rippenhebemuskeln mpl levatores costarum [muscles]
Rippenknorpel m costal cartilage, costicartilage, costocartilage

Rippenknorpelentzündung

Rippenknorpelentzündung f costochondritis
Rippenknorpelimplantat n costal cartilage implant
Rippenkontraktor m rib contractor
Rippenkörper m body of the rib
rippenlos acostate, ecostate
Rippenlosigkeit f apleuria, absence of the ribs, ecostatism
Rippenperiostreflex m costal periosteal reflex
Rippenpleura f costal pleura
Rippenrand m costal margin
Rippenraspatorium n rib raspatory
Rippenresektion f rib resection, costectomy
~ **mit Brustkorberöffnung** thoracectomy
Rippenretraktor m rib retractor
Rippenschere f rib shears, rib cutting forceps; costotome
Rippenschmerz m costalgia
Rippen-Schwertfortsatz-Band n costoxiphoid ligament
Rippensegment n segment of the rib
Rippensperrer m rib retractor
Rippenusur f rib notching
Rippenusurenbildung f notching of the ribs
Rippenverband m rib strapping
Rippenwinkel m epigastric angle
Rippen-Wirbelsäulen-Winkel m costovertebral angle
Rippenzange f rib cutting forceps; costotome
Rippen-Zwerchfell-Linie f costodiaphragmatic line
Rippen-Zwerchfell-Winkel m costophrenic angle
Risikogeburt f high-risk delivery
Risikoneugeborenes n high-risk neonate
Risikopatient m high-risk patient
~/**koronarer** coronary high-risk patient
Risikoschwangerschaft f high-risk pregnancy
Riß m rupture, rhexis, tear; scissura, scissure
Rißwunde f lacerated wound, laceration
Rist m instep
Risus m risus, laughter
~ **sardonicus** sardonic grin (laugh), canine spasm (Gesichtsstarre bei Tetanus)
Ritze f rima, slit; fissure, fissura (Anatomie) (Zusammensetzungen s. unter Rima)
ritzen to scratch; to scarify (die Haut)
Ritz[ungs]technik f scratch technique (bei Impfung)
Ritzungstest m scratch test
RIVA s. Ramus interventricularis anterior
Rivalta-Test m Rivalta's test (zur Unterscheidung zwischen Exsudaten und Transsudaten)
Riva-Rocci-Blutdruckmessung f Riva-Rocci's method
Rivus m rivus
Rizinusvergiftung f ricinism
RNS s. Ribonukleinsäure
robbengliedrig phocomelic
Robbengliedrigkeit f phocomelia
Roborans n roborant [agent], tonic
roborierend roborant

Röcheln n stertorous breathing; death rattle
röchelnd wheezing, stertorous
Rocky-Mountain-Fieber n Rocky Mountain spotted fever, R. M. S. F., mountain (tick) fever
Rocky-Mountain-Fieber-Impfstoff m Rocky mountain spotted fever vaccine
rodens rodent
Rodentizid n rodenticide [agent]
Roentgen n s. Röntgeneinheit 1.
Rohdroge f crude drug
Röhrchen n tubule, tubulus; tube (z. B. aus Glas)
Röhre f tube; canal[is]; duct; fistula
~/**Eustachische** Eustachian tube, auditory (otopharyngeal) tube, otosalpinx
röhrenförmig tubular, cylindroid, syringoid
Röhrenknochen m tubular (long) bone
Röhrensehen n tubular (tube) vision, tunnel (gun-barrel) vision
Rohrzucker m saccharose
Rollappen m tubed flap (zur Hautverpflanzung)
Rolle f 1. roll; 2. s. Trochlea
Rollenbildung f rouleaux formation (der Erythrozyten)
rollenförmig roll-shaped, pivot-like, pulley-shaped
Rollhügel m s. Trochanter
Rollstuhl m wheel-chair
Romanoskop n [recto]romanoscope, sigmoidoscope
Romanoskopie f romanoscopy, sigmo[ido]scopy
röntgen to radiograph, to roentgenograph, to roentgenize, to X-ray
Röntgen n 1. radiography, roentgenography, X-ray examination, X-ray photography; 2. s. Röntgeneinheit 1.
Röntgen... s. a. Röntgenstrahlen...
Röntgenabsorptionshistospektroskopie f roentgen absorption histospectroscopy
Röntgenabteilung f X-ray department, radiological (radiology) department
Röntgenapparat m X-ray unit
Röntgenarzt m radiographer
Röntgenassistentin f X-ray assistant; radiographer
Röntgenaufnahme f 1. roentgenogram, roentgenograph, X-ray photograph (picture), radiogram, radiograph, skiagram; 2. s. Röntgendarstellung ● **eine ~ machen** to roentgenize, to take an X-ray, to radiograph
~/**aufliegende** decubitus radiography
~/**gehaltene** stress roentgenogram
~ **im I. schrägen Durchmesser** right anterior oblique roentgenogram
~ **im II. schrägen Durchmesser** left anterior oblique roentgenogram
~ **in Boxerstellung** left anterior oblique roentgenogram
~ **in Fechterstellung** right anterior oblique roentgenogram
~ **in Seitenlage** lateral decubitus film
Röntgenaufnahmetechnik f **des Nervensystems** neuroradiology, neuroroentgenology

~/stereoskopische stereoradiography
Röntgenausrüstung f X-ray equipment
Röntgenbefund m radiographic (roentgenographic) findings
Röntgenbestrahlung f X-irradiation; X-ray treatment
Röntgenbild n s. Röntgenaufnahme 1.
Röntgenbildverstärker m X-ray image intensifier
röntgend X-ray photographic; roentgenographic, radiographic
Röntgendarstellung f roentgenography, X-ray photography, radiography, skiagraphy
~ des Urogenitalsystems urogenital tract radiography
~/gezielte spot-film roentgenography
~/stereoskopische stereoradiography
Röntgendiagnose f X-ray diagnosis, radiodiagnosis
Röntgendiagnostik f X-ray diagnosis, radiodiagnostics, diagnostic radiology
~/kardiovaskuläre cardioradiology
röntgendicht roentgenopaque
Röntgendoppelkontrastuntersuchung f air contrast examination
röntgendurchleuchtend radioscopic, roentgenoscopic, fluoroscopic
Röntgendurchleuchtung f radioscopy, roentgenoscopy, fluoroscopy, skiascopy, umbrascopy, orthodiascopy
~ innerer Organe radiostereoscopy
Röntgendurchleuchtungsapparat m roentgenoscope, fluoroscope
Röntgeneinheit f 1. röntgen, roentgen [unit], r [unit] *(SI-fremde Einheit der Exposition)*; 2. s. Röntgenabteilung
Röntgenfernaufnahme f teleroentgenogram
Röntgenfernaufnahmetechnik f tele[o]roentgenography, teleradiography
Röntgenfernbestrahlung f teleroentgen therapy
Röntgenfilm m X-ray film
Röntgenfilmaufnahmetechnik f cineradiography, cineroentgenography, roentgen cinematography, X-ray motion picture photography
Röntgenfisteldarstellung f fistulography
Röntgenfluoroskopie f roentgenoscopy, fluoroscopy, radioscopy
röntgenfluoroskopisch fluoroscopic, roentgenoscopic, radioscopic
röntgenfotografisch X-ray photographic
Röntgenhinweis m radiographic sign
Röntgeninstitut n radiological institute
Röntgenkardiogramm n roentgenocardiogram
Röntgenkardiographie f roentgenocardiography
Röntgenkinematographie f roentgen cinematography
Röntgenkontrast m X-ray shadow ● **einen ~ ergeben** to cast an X-ray shadow
Röntgenkontrastbild n contrast radiogram (roentgenogram)
Röntgenkontrastdarstellung f contrast radiography, contrast[-media] roentgenography
röntgenkontrastgebend [radi]opaque

Röntgenkontrastmittel n radiopaque (X-ray contrast) medium, contrast medium (material)
Röntgenkontrastuntersuchung f contrast [X-ray] study
Röntgenkontrolle f radiological (X-ray) check
Röntgenkymogramm n roentgenokymogram, X-ray kymogram
Röntgenkymograph m roentgenokymograph
Röntgenkymographie f roentgenokymography, X-ray kymography
röntgenkymographisch roentgenokymographic
Röntgenleeraufnahme f survey radiograph (roentgenograph), preliminary film
Röntgenmikroaufnahme f microradiogram
Röntgenmikrodarstellung f microradiography
Röntgennachbestrahlung f postoperative X-ray irradiation
~ nach Brustamputation postmastectomy radiotherapy
Röntgenogramm n s. Röntgenaufnahme 1.
Röntgenographie f s. Röntgendarstellung
röntgenographisch roentgenographic, radiographic
Röntgenologe m radiologist, roentgenologist
Röntgenologie f radiology, roentgenology
röntgenologisch radiologic[al], roentgenologic
Röntgenometer n roentgenometer
Röntgenometrie f roentgenometry
Röntgenoskopie f s. Röntgenfluoroskopie
Röntgenplatte f X-ray plate
Röntgenraum m X-ray room
Röntgenreihenuntersuchung f mass radiography (roentgenography), X-ray mass examination
Röntgenröhre f X-ray (roentgen) tube
Röntgenschatten m X-ray shadow
Röntgenschichtapparat m tomograph, laminagraph
Röntgenschichtaufnahme f tomogram, laminagram, planigram
~ des Körpers body section roentgenogram
Röntgenschichtdarstellung f tomography, planigraphy, planography, stratigraphy, laminagraphy, laminography, sectional radiography
~ des Körpers body section roentgenography
Röntgenschichtung f s. Röntgenschichtdarstellung
Röntgenschichtungsgerät n tomograph, laminagraph
Röntgenschichtverfahren n s. Röntgenschichtdarstellung
Röntgenschirm m fluorescent (X-ray) screen
Röntgenschirmbild n photofluorogram
röntgenschirmbilddarstellend photofluorographic
Röntgenschirmbildfotografie f photofluorography, photofluoroscopy, fluororoentgenography
Röntgenschirmbildverfahren n photofluorography, photofluoroscopy, fluorography
Röntgenseriendarstellung f serial roentgenography

Röntgenstereofernaufnahmetechnik 672

Röntgenstereofernaufnahmetechnik f telestereoroentgenography, teleroentgenography, teleradiography
Röntgenstrahlen mpl X-rays, roentgen rays ● für
~ **undurchlässig sein** to be opaque to X-rays ●
mit ~ behandeln to roentgenize
~/**harte** hard X-rays
~/**weiche** soft X-rays
Röntgenstrahlen... s.a. Röntgen...
Röntgenstrahlenanämie f radiation (roentgen-ray) anaemia
Röntgenstrahlenbehandlung f X-ray therapy, roentgen-ray treatment, roentgenotherapy
Röntgenstrahlendermatitis f roentgen[-ray] dermatitis; actinodermatitis, actinic dermatitis
röntgenstrahlendicht sein to be opaque to X-rays
Röntgenstrahlendosimetrie f photographic dosimetry
röntgenstrahlendurchlässig radiolucent, roentgenolucent, radioparent, non-opaque, radiotransparent, transradiant
Röntgenstrahlendurchlässigkeit f radiolucency, radioparency
röntgenstrahlenempfindlich radiosensitive
Röntgenstrahlenempfindlichkeit f radiosensitivity, radiosensibility
röntgenstrahleninduziert X-ray induced
Röntgenstrahlenintensität f intensity of X-rays
röntgenstrahlenundurchlässig radio[o]paque, roentgenopaque
Röntgenstrahlenundurchlässigkeit f radio[o]pacity
Röntgenstrahlenverbrennung f radiation (X-ray) burn
Röntgenstrahlung f roentgen radiation, X-radiation; X-rays
Röntgenstreustrahlen mpl scattered rays
Röntgentechnik f X-ray technique; X-ray technology
Röntgentechniker m X-ray technician
Röntgentherapie f X-ray therapy, roentgen-ray treatment, roentgenotherapy
Röntgentherapie-Abteilung f radiotherapy department
Röntgentiefenbestrahlung[stherapie] f deep roentgen-ray therapy, high-voltage radiation (roentgen) therapy
Röntgentisch m X-ray table
~/**kippbarer** tilting [screening] stand
Röntgenübersichtsaufnahme f X-ray plain film, plain radiograph, scout (preliminary) film
Röntgenuntersuchung f radiographic (X-ray) examination, radiological study
Röntgenverschattung f radiodensity; X-ray shadow
~/**basale** basilar radiodensity (bei Lungenentzündung)
Röntgenzeichen n radiographic (X-ray) sign
Röntgenzielaufnahme f spot-film roentgenography (radiography)
Rosazea f rosacea, brandy face (nose), rosy drop, facial teleangiectasis

rosazeaförmig rosaceiform
Rose f erysipelas, St. Anthony's fire (Zusammensetzungen s. unter. Erysipelas)
Rosenkranz m/**rachitischer** rachitic rosary, rickety beads; beading [of the ribs]
Rosenthal-Syndrom n Rosenthal syndrome, factor XI deficiency syndrome
Rosenvene f saphena, saphenous vein
~/**große** great saphenous vein
~/**kleine** small (short) saphenous vein
Roseola f roseola, rose[-coloured] rash
~ **infantum** pseudorubella, rose rash of infants (masernähnlicher Hautausschlag)
~ **syphilitica** syphilitic roseola
~ **typhosa** typhoid roseola, rose spots
Rosettenkatarakt f rosette cataract
rostbraun, rostfarben rubiginous, rust-coloured (z. B. Sputum)
rostral rostral
Rostrum n rostrum (Anatomie)
~ **corporis callosi** rostrum of the corpus callosum
~ **sphenoidale** rostrum of the sphenoid
rot werden to flush
Rotameter n rotameter
Rotationsbestrahlung f rotation therapy
Rotationsfraktur f torsion fracture
Rotationsgelenk n rotation joint, pivot (rotatory) articulation
Rotations[haut]lappen m sliding (swinging) flap (Transplantat)
Rotationsmuskel m rotator [muscle]
Rotationsnystagmus m rotation (rotary) nystagmus
Rotationsosteotomie f rotary osteotomy
Rotationsschielen n cyclophoria (bei abgedecktem Auge); cyclotropia (bei nichtabgedecktem Auge)
Rotationsstadium n **der Geburt** rotation stage of labour
Rotationswirbel m rotation vertebra
Rotator m rotator [muscle]
rotatorisch rotatory, rotational
rotblind protanopic, red-blind
Rotblinder m protanope, red-blind
Rotblindheit f protanopia, red blindness, anerythroblep[s]ia, anerythropsia
Rotblütigkeit f polycythaemia, polyglobulia, polyglobulism
Röte f flush (des Gesichts); erythema; redness (der Haut)
Röteln pl rubella, roseola, [epidemic] rubeola, röteln, German (three-day) measles, French measles
Rötelnantikörper m rubella antibody
rötelnartig rubella-like, rubelliform
Rötelnembryopathie f rubella embryopathy, [congenital] rubella syndrome
Rötelnenzephalitis f rubella encephalitis
Rötelnenzephalopathie f rubella encephalopathy
Rötelnimpfstoff m rubella vaccine
Rötelninfektion f rubella infection
Rötelnlebendvirusimpfstoff m live rubella virus vaccine

Rötelnvirion n rubella virion
Rötelnvirus n rubella virus
rötend rubescent
Rotfinnen fpl s. Rosazea
rotfinnenartig rosaceiform
Rot-Grün-Sichtigkeit f erythrochlorop[s]ia
Rotharnen n rubriuria
Roth-Bernhard-Syndrom n Bernhard-Roth syndrome, Bernhard's paraesthesia, meralgia paraesthetica
rotierend rotatory, rotational
Rotlauf m s. Erysipeloid
rotschwach protanomalous, protanopic
Rotschwäche f protanomaly, protanomalopia
rotschwachsichtig protanomalous, protanopic
Rotsichtigkeit f erythrop[s]ia; red vision
Rötung f rubescence, redness; rubor *(Entzündungszeichen)*
~ der Handflächen red palms
Rotwerden n rubescence, reddening
Rotz m malleus, maliasmus, glanders, farcy *(Infektionskrankheit durch Malleomyces mallei)*
Rotzbakterienextrakt m mallein *(für Hauttest zum Rotznachweis)*
Rotzbakterium n glanders bacillus
Rouget-Zelle f Rouget's (adventitial) cell, pericyte
Routineuntersuchung f routine examination
RQ s. Quotient/respiratorischer
RR s. Riva-Rocci-Blutdruckmessung
R-R-Intervall n R-R interval *(im EKG)*
RR-Manschette f blood pressure cuff
RR-senkend antihypertensive
Rubefaziens n rubefacient [agent]
Rubella f s. Röteln
Rübenzucker m beet sugar, saccharose
Rübenzuckerausscheidung f im Urin beeturia
Rubeola f s. Röteln
Rubeose f rubeosis
Rubeosis f iridis [diabetica] rubeosis of the iris
rubiginös rubiginous, rust-coloured *(z. B. Sputum)*
Rubor m rubor *(Entzündungszeichen)*
Rückansicht f back (posterior) view
Rückatmung f rebreathing, rehalation
Rückatmungsbeutel m rebreathing bag
rückbilden to regress, to involute; to degenerate
rückbildend/sich re[tro]gressive, involutional
Rückbildung f re[tro]gression, involution, devolution *(z. B. eines Organs)*; retroplasia, cataplasia, kataplasia *(des Gewebes)*; degeneration
Rückbildungsform f involution form *(z. B. von Mikroorganismen)*
Rückbildungspsychose f involutional psychosis
Rücken m back, dorsum *(s. a. unter Dorsum)*; ridge ● **auf dem ~ liegend** supine, lying on the back ● **mit dem ~ nach vorn** dorsoanterior ● **zum ~ hin gerichtet** dorsoposterior
Rückenansicht f back (posterior) view
Rückenlage f supine (dorsal) position
~ mit erhöhtem Oberkörper dorsal elevated position

Rückenlagerung f dorsal decubitus position *(z. B. zur Operation)*
Rückenmark n spinal cord (marrow), medulla, myelon
~/verlängertes medulla [oblongata], oblongata, afterbrain, bulb[us]
Rückenmarkanästhesie f rachianaesthesia, spinal anaesthesia, rachianalgesia
Rückenmarkarachnoidea f spinal arachnoid
Rückenmarkarterie f spinal artery
~/hintere posterior spinal artery
~/vordere anterior spinal artery
Rückenmarkatrophie f myelatrophy, spinal atrophy, myelophthisis
Rückenmarkaufspaltung f myelodiastasis
Rückenmarkblutung f myelorrhagia, spinal haemorrhage
~/epidurale epidural spinal haemorrhage
Rückenmarkbruch m myelocele
Rückenmarkdarre f s. Tabes dorsalis
Rückenmarkdegeneration f spinal cord degeneration
Rückenmarkdekompression f spinal cord decompression
Rückenmarkdurchtrennung f spinal cord transection (transverse lesion)
Rückenmarkeinblutung f haematomyelia, myelapoplexy, haemorrhage within the spinal cord
Rückenmarkentzündung f [rachio]myelitis, medullitis, inflammation of the spinal cord, notomyelitis *(s. a. unter Myelitis)*
~ mit Einblutung haematomyelitis
~ mit Höhlenbildung syringomyelitis
Rückenmarkepilepsie f spinal epilepsy
Rückenmarkerkrankung f myelopathy, disease of the spinal cord
Rückenmarkeröffnung f[/operative] myelotomy
Rückenmarkerschütterung f spinal cord concussion, concussion of the spinal cord
Rückenmarkerweichung f myelomalacia, softening of the spinal cord
Rückenmarkfehlbildung f myelodysplasia
Rückenmarkgeschwulst f spinal cord tumour
Rückenmarkhämatom n/**epidurales** epidural spinal haematoma
Rückenmarkhaut f [spinal] meninx
~/harte dura mater of the spinal cord
~/weiche pia mater of the spinal cord
Rückenmarkhaut[ein]blutung f haematorrhachis
Rückenmarkhautentzündung f spinal meningitis, perimyelitis
Rückenmarkhemiplegie f spinal hemiplegia
Rückenmarkhinterstrangsklerose f s. Tabes dorsalis
Rückenmarkhypoplasie f micromyelia, myelatelia
Rückenmarkirritation f spinal irritation
Rückenmarkkanal m spinal canal, [cranio]vertebral canal
Rückenmarkkanalpunktion f rachi[o]centesis
Rückenmarkkanüle f spinal needle

Rückenmarkkompression

Rückenmarkkompression f [spinal] cord compression
Rückenmarkkontusion f spinal cord contusion, contusion of the spinal cord
Rückenmarkkonus m cone-like termination of the spinal cord
rückenmarkkrank myelopathic
Rückenmarklähmung f spinal paralysis, rachioplegia, myeloparalysis, myeloplegia
rückenmarklos amyelic, amyelonic
Rückenmarkmesser n myelotome
Rückenmarknaht f myelorrhaphy, suture of a severed spinal cord
Rückenmarknerv m spinal nerve
Rückenmarknervenbahndurchtrennung f spinal tractotomy
Rückenmarknervenwurzel f spinal nerve root
Rückenmarkpachymeningitis f spinal pachymeningitis
Rückenmarkpunktion f rachi[o]centesis
Rückenmarkreflex m spinal reflex
Rückenmarkreizung f spinal irritation
Rückenmarkröntgen[kontrast]bild n myelogram
Rückenmarkröntgen[kontrast]darstellung f myelography, roentgenography of the spinal cord (s. a. unter Myelographie)
~ **nach Lufteinblasung** pneumomyelography, gas (air) myelography
Rückenmarkschmerz m myelalgia, pain in the spinal cord
Rückenmarkschock m spinal shock
Rückenmarkschwindsucht f s. Tabes dorsalis
Rückenmarksklerose f myelosclerosis, multiple sclerosis of the spinal cord
Rückenmarkspaltbildung f myeloschisis
Rückenmarkspalte f myelodiastasis
~/**angeborene** diastematomyelia
Rückenmarkspinnwebenhaut f arachnoid of the spinal cord
Rückenmarksyphilis f myelosyphilis
Rückenmarkszintigramm n myeloscintigram
Rückenmarkszintigraphie f myeloscintigraphy
Rückenmark- und Nervenwurzelentzündung f myeloradiculitis, inflammation of the spinal cord and spinal nerve roots
Rückenmark- und Nervenwurzelerkrankung f myeloradiculopathy, disease of the spinal cord and spinal nerve roots
Rückenmark- und Nervenwurzelfehlbildung f myeloradiculodysplasia
Rückenmarkunterentwicklung f myelatelia
Rückenmarkvene f spinal vein
~/**dorsale äußere** posterior external spinal vein
~/**innere** internal spinal vein
~/**ventrale äußere** anterior external spinal vein
Rückenmarkverdoppelung f diplomyelia
Rückenmarkverhärtung f s. Rückenmarksklerose
Rückenmarkverletzung f spinal cord injury (lesion)
Rückenmarkwurzeldurchschneidung f/**hintere** posterior rhizotomy
~/**vordere** anterior rhizotomy
Rückenmarkwurzeldurchtrennung f[/**operative**] radicotomy
Rückenmarkzentralkanal m spinal medullary canal, ventricle of the cord
Rückenmarkzyste f myelocyst
Rückenmarkzystenröntgen[kontrast]bild n myelocystogram
Rückenmarkzystenröntgen[kontrast]darstellung f myelocystography
Rückenmuskel m dorsal muscle
~/**breiter** latissimus dorsi [muscle]
~/**langer** longissimus dorsi [muscle]
~/**vielgespaltener** multifidus, multifidus [spinae] muscle
Rückenmuskelreflex m dorsal reflex
Rückenmuskelstarrkrampf m opisthotonus, opisthotonos
Rückenreflex m dorsal (back) reflex
Rückenschmerz m backache, backalgia, pain in the back, dorsalgia, rachialgia, notalgia
Rückenstrecker[muskel] m erector spinae [muscle], sacrospinalis [muscle], extensor of the back
Rückenstreckerreflex m erector spinae reflex
Rückenstreckmuskelstarrkrampf m pleurototonus
Rückenverletzung f back injury
rückenwärts dorsad
Rückenwirbel m thoracic vertebra, spondylus
Rückerinnerung f recall (1. Psychologie; 2. Immunologie)
Rückfall m s. Rezidiv
Rückfallfieber n relapsing (recurrent, spirillum) fever
Rückfluß m reflux, backflow, regurgitation
~/**venöser** venous return
Rückflußileitis f backwash ileitis
Rückgang m/**zeitweiliger** temporary remission, remittence (z. B. von Symptomen)
rückgebildet rudimentary
Rückgrat n vertebral (spinal) column, backbone, rachis
Rückgratreflex m spinal reflex; Galant's reflex (response) (beim Säugling)
Rückgratspalte f rachischisis
Rückgratverkrümmung f **nach hinten** [rachio]kyphosis, posterior deformity, anterior curvature, gibbosity; hunchback, humpback
~ **nach vorn** lordosis, anterior deformity, posterior curvature; saddleback
~/**seitliche** scoliosis, skoliosis
Rückinfusion f refusion (z. B. von körpereigenem Blut)
Rückkopplung f feedback (Physiologie)
~/**negative** negative feedback
Rückkopplungssystem n feedback system
rückläufig retrograde, regressive, recurrent
rückpflanzen to reimplant
Rückpflanzung f re[im]plantation
Rucksackverband m figure-of-eight dressing (plaster bandage) (bei Schlüsselbeinfraktur)

Rückschlag *m* 1. atavism, throwback, reversion; 2. *s.* Rezidiv
rückschlagend atavistic
Rückstand *m* residue, residium
Rückstoß *m* back stroke; rebound
Rückstoßphänomen *n* rebound phenomenon *(Kleinhirnsymptomatik)*
Rückstoßverletzung *f* contrecoup injury
Rückstoßwellenkardiogramm *n* ballistocardiogram
Rückstoßwellenkurve *f* **des Herzschlagvolumens** ballistocardiogram
Rückstrom *m s.* Rückfluß
Rückstromgeräusch *n* regurgitant murmur *(z. B. bei Herzklappeninsuffizienz)*
Rückwärtsabknickung *f* retroflexion *(z. B. der Gebärmutter)*
Rückwärtsbeuger *m* dorsiflexor [muscle]
Rückwärtsbeugung *f* retroversion, retroflexion, dorsiflexion; recurvation
~ **und Rückwärtsknickung** *f* retroversioflexion *(z. B. der Gebärmutter)*
Rückwärtsgehen *n*/**unwillkürliches** opisthoporeia
Rückwärtsinsuffizienz *f* **des Herzens** backward failure
Rückwärtslagerung *f* retroposition
Rückwärtsneigung *f* reclination; recumbency *(Zustand)*
Rückwärtsverlagerung *f* retroposition, retrodisplacement *(der Gebärmutter)*
rückwirken to react
rückwirkend reactive, reacting
Rückwirkung *f* reactivity, reaction
Ructus *m* **hystericus** hysterical belching
Rudiment *n* rudiment[um], vestige, vestigium
Rudimentärstadium *n* rudimentary state, vestigial stage
rufen/nach dem Arzt to send for the doctor
Ruga *f* ruga, fold, wrinkle, ridge, furrow
~ **gastrica** ruga of the stomach
~ **vaginalis** ruga of the vagina
Ruheatemnot *f* dyspnoea at rest
Ruheatem[zug]volumen *n* resting tidal volume
Ruheblutdruck *m* resting blood pressure
Ruheelektrokardiographie *f* resting electrocardiography
Ruhekern *m* resting nucleus
Ruhelage *f* resting position
ruhelos restless
Ruheokklusion *f* restbite
Ruhephase *f* resting stage, interphase, interstage, interkinesis *(z. B. bei Zellteilung)*
Ruhepotential *n* resting potential
Ruheschmerz *m* rest pain; night pain
Ruhespeichel *m* resting saliva
Ruhestoffwechsel *m* basal metabolism
Ruhetremor *m* resting (passive) tremor, static (non-intention) tremor
Ruhezelle *f* resting cell
ruhigstellen to immobilize, to fix *(z. B. einen Knochenbruch)*; to relax, to tranquillize *(psychisch)*
Ruhigstellung *f* immobilization, fixation *(z. B. eines Knochenbruchs)*; relaxation *(psychisch)*
~ **im Gipsverband** closed plaster treatment
Ruhigstellungsverband *m* immobilizing (immovable) bandage
Ruhr *f* asylum (bacillary) dysentery, shigellosis
ruhrartig dysenteriform
Rumination *f* rumination, merycism
Rumpel-Leede-Phänomen *n* Rumpel-Leede phenomenon (sign) *(bei erhöhter Blutungsneigung)*
Rumpf *m* torso, trunk
Rumpfhautzone *f*/**hyperästhetisch-hyperalgische** Head's area (zone)
rumpfnah proximal, proximad
Rumpfspalte *f* schistocormia
Rundherd *m* coin lesion *(in der Lunge)*
Rundkopf *m* trochocephalus
rundköpfig trochocephalic
Rundköpfigkeit *f* trochocephalia
Rundmeißelzange *f* rib rongeur
Rundmuskel *m*/**großer** teres major [muscle]
~/**kleiner** teres minor [muscle]
Rundnadel *f* round (curved) needle
Rundrücken *m* round back, hunchback, humpback; kyphosis
~/**jugendlicher** juvenile kyphosis, Scheuermann's disease
Rundstiellappen *m* tunnel (tube) flap, gauntlet (pocket) flap
Rundstiellappentransplantat *n* tunnel (tube) graft, rope graft
Rundwurm *m* roundworm
Rundzelle *f* round cell
Rundzelleninfiltration *f* round-cell infiltration
Rundzellenkarzinom *n* round-cell carcinoma
Rundzellensarkom *n* round-cell sarcoma, globocellular sarcoma
Runzel *f s.* Ruga
Runzelbildung *f* **der Haut** rhytidosis of the skin
Runzelentfernung *f*[/**operative**] *s.* Rhytidektomie
runzelig rugose, rugous; wrinkled
Runzeligkeit *f* rugosity
Runzelung *f* rhytidosis
Runzler *m* corrugator [muscle]
Rupia *f* rupia
rupiaartig rupioid
Ruptur *f* rupture, rhexis, rhegma ● **durch** ~ **bedingt** rhegmatogenous
~/**zweizeitige** delayed rupture
rupturiert ruptured
Rushpin *m* intramedullary Rush type of pin
Rüssellippe *f* macrocheilia, macrolabia
R-Zacke *f* R wave [of the electrocardiogram]

SA
S

SA s. sinoatrial
Sabbern n slavering, drooling; ptyalism
Säbelbein n bandy (bow, boomerang) leg; gonyectyposis
Säbelscheidentibia f sabre tibia (shin)
Säbelscheidentrachea f scabbard trachea
Sabinaölvergiftung f sabinism, savin poisoning
Sabin-Feldmann-Test m Sabin-Feldman dye test *(zum Toxoplasmoseantikörpernachweis)*
Sabin-Tschumakow-Impfstoff m Sabin oral poliomyelitis vaccine
sabulös sabulous, gritty, sandy
Sabulum n sabulum, brain sand, acervulus
Saccharase f saccharase, sucrase, invertase, invertin *(Enzym)*
Saccharephidrose f saccharephidrosis
Saccharid n saccharide, carbohydrate
Saccharifikation f saccharification
Saccharimeter n saccharimeter
Saccharimetrie f saccharimetry
Saccharin n saccharin, benzosulphimide
Saccharobiose f saccharobiose
Saccharogalaktorrhoe f saccharogalactorrhoea
saccharolytisch saccharolytic
Saccharometer n saccharometer *(Senkspindel zur Bestimmung der Dichte von Zuckerlösungen)*
Saccharomykose f saccharomycosis
Saccharomyzet m saccharomycete
Saccharorrhoe f saccharorrhoea
Saccharose f saccharose, sucrose
Saccharoseausscheidung f im Urin saccharosuria
Saccharurie f saccharuria
Sacculus m saccule, sacculus
~ **alveolaris** alveolar sac
~ **laryngis** laryngeal saccule (pouch), saccule of the larynx
Saccus m sac[cus], bag, pouch; sacculation
~ **conjunctivae** conjunctival sac
~ **endolymphaticus** endolymphatic sac, ELS
~ **lacrimalis** lacrimal (tear) sac, dacryocyst
~ **omphaloentericus (vitellinus)** yolk (vitelline) sac, vitellicle, umbilical vesicle
Sachs-Georgi-Reaktion f Sachs-Georgi test *(serologische Flockungsreaktion zur Syphilisdiagnostik)*
Sack m s. Saccus
Sackaneurysma n saccular aneurysm
Sackbildung f sacculation
Sackblase f saccular bladder
Säckchen n s. Sacculus
Sackniere f sacciform kidney; hydronephrosis
~**/vereiterte** pyonephrotic kidney; pyonephrosis
Sadismus m sadism
Sadist m sadist
sadistisch sadistic
Sadomasochismus m sadomasochism
sadomasochistisch sadomasochistic
Safranin n safranin[e] *(gelber Farbstoff zur Bakterienfärbung)* ● **mit ~ färbend** safranophil[e]

Safranleber f saffron-coloured liver
safranophil safranophil[e]
Saft m juice, succus; fluid *(Zusammensetzungen s. unter* Succus*)*
Saftabsonderung f/**übermäßige** succorrhoea
Säge f/**Giglische** Gigli's [wire] saw
sägeartig serrate[d]
Sägemuskel m serratus [muscle]
~**/hinterer oberer** serratus posterior superior muscle
~**/hinterer unterer** serratus posterior inferior muscle
~**/vorderer** serratus anterior muscle, serratus magnus [muscle]
Sagittaldurchmesser m sagittal diameter
Sagittalebene f sagittal plane
Sagittalfontanelle f sagittal fontanel
Sagittalnaht f sagittal (interparietal) suture
Sagittalschnitt m sagittal section
Sagittalsinus m sagittal sinus
Sagoleber f sago liver
Sagomilz f sago spleen
Saint-Louis-Enzephalitis f St. Louis encephalitis
Saisonkrankheit f seasonal disease
Saite f chorda, cord *(Zusammensetzungen s. unter* Chorda*)*
saitenförmig chordal
Saitenwarze f acrochordon *(Hautpolyp an Augenlidern)*
Sakkuluseröffnung f/**operative** sacculotomy
Sakral... s.a. Kreuzbein...
Sakralanästhesie f sacral anaesthesia, [trans]sacral block
Sakraldaueranästhesie f continuous sacral anaesthesia
Sakraldekubitus m sacral decubitus [ulceration]
Sakralgie f sacralgia, sacrodynia
Sakralindex m sacral index
Sakralisation f sacralization *(Verwachsung des fünften Lendenwirbels mit dem Kreuzbein)*
sakralisieren to sacralize
Sakralkanal m sacral (sacrococcygeal) canal
Sakralnerv m sacral nerve
Sakralnervengeflecht n sacral plexus
Sakralregion f sacral region
Sakrodynie f sacralgia, sacrodynia
Sakroiliakalgelenk n sacroiliac articulation (synchondrosis)
Sakroiliakalregion f sacroiliac region
Sakrokokzygealchordom n sacrococcygeal chordoma
Sakrokokzygealfistel f sacrococcygeal fistula
Sakrokokzygealgelenk n sacrococcygeal joint (junctura, symphysis)
Sakrokokzygealraum m sacrococcygeal space
Sakrokokzygealregion f sacrococcygeal region
Sakrokokzygealteratom n sacrococcygeal teratoma
Sakrokokzygealzyste f sacrococcygeal (pilonidal) cyst
Sakrokoxalgie f sacrocoxalgia
Sakrokoxitis f sacrocoxitis, sacroiliitis

Sakrum n s. Kreuzbein
Saktosalpinx f sactosalpinx
Salaamkrampf m salaam convulsion (seizure), nodding spasm
Salbe f ointment, unguentum, ung., salve, unction
~/antibiotische antibiotic ointment
salbenartig ointment-like
Salbenbüchse f jar of ointment
Salbeneinreibung f infriction
Salbengesicht n hatchet face, myopathic facies
Salbengrundlage f ointment base, vehicle, excipient
Salbenspatel m spatula
Salbenverband m ointment dressing
Salbung f unction
salinisch saline, salty
Saliva f s. Speichel
Salivation f s. Speichelsekretion
Salizylattherapie f salicylate therapy
Salizylismus m salicylism
Salizylsäure f salicylic acid
Salizylsäureamid n salicylamide *(Analgetikum, Antipyretikum)*
Salizyl[säure]vergiftung f salicylism
Salk-Formolimpfstoff m s. Salk-Vakzine
Salk-Vakzine f Salk (poliomyelitis) vaccine *(zur aktiven Immunisierung)*
Salmiak m ammonium chloride
Salmonella f salmonella
~ **enteritidis** Salmonella enteritidis
~ **Hirschfeldii** Salmonella hirschfeldii (paratyphosi C), Bacterium paratyphosum C
~ **paratyphi A** Salmonella paratyphi A
~ **paratyphi B** s. ~ Schottmülleri
~ **paratyphi C** s. ~ Hirschfeldii
~ **Schottmülleri** Salmonella schottmülleri, Salmonella paratyphi B, Bacterium paratyphosum B
~ **typhi** Salmonella typhi (typhosa), typhoid bacillus
Salmonellenarthritis f salmonellal arthritis
Salmonellenbakteriämie f salmonellal bacteriaemia
Salmonellenenteritis f salmonellosis
Salmonellenenterokolitis f salmonellal enterocolitis
Salmonelleninfektion f salmonellal infection
Salmonellose f salmonellosis
Salpeterbildung f nitrification *(Oxydation des Ammoniaks über Nitrit zu Nitrat durch Bakterien)*
Salpingektomie f salpingectomy, tubectomy, excision of an oviduct
~/abdominale laparosalpingectomy
Salpingemphraxis f 1. salpingemphraxis, obstruction of an oviduct; 2. salpingemphraxis, obstruction of the Eustachian tube
Salpingitis f 1. salpingitis, inflammation of an oviduct; 2. s. ~ Eustachii
~/chronisch interstitielle mural (chronic interstitial) salpingitis

Salzmangelsyndrom

~ **Eustachii** syringitis, salpingitis, inflammation of the Eustachian tube
~ **gonorrhoica** gonococcal salpingitis
~ **haemorrhagica** haemorrhagic salpingitis; haemosalpinx
~ **parenchymatosa** parenchymatous salpingitis, pachysalpingitis
~/purulente purulent salpingitis
~/pyogene pyogenic salpingitis, pyosalpingitis
salpingitisch salpingitic
salpingoabdominal salpingo-abdominal, tubo-abdominal
Salpingogramm n salpingogram
Salpingograph m salpingograph
Salpingographie f salpingography
Salpingokatheterismus m salpingocatheterism
Salpingolyse f salpingolysis
Salpingo-Oophorektomie f salpingo-oophorectomy, salpingo-ovariectomy, salpingo-ovariotomy, tubo-ovariotomy
Salpingo-Oophoritis f salpingo-oophoritis, salpingo-oothecitis, tubo-ovaritis
Salpingo-Oophorozele f salpingo-oophorocele
Salpingoperitonitis f salpingoperitonitis
Salpingopexie f salpingopexy, fixation of an oviduct
Salpingoplastik f salpingoplasty, tuboplasty
Salpingorrhaphie f salpingorrhaphy, suture of an oviduct
Salpingosalpingostomie f salpingosalpingostomy, salpingostomatomy
Salpingostenochorie f salpingostenochoria, stricture of the auditory tube
Salpingostoma n salpingostomy
Salpingostomatoplastik f salpingostomatoplasty
Salpingostomie f salpingostomy
Salpingotomie f salpingotomy
Salpingozele f salpingocele
Salpinx f salpinx, uterine (Fallopian) tube, tuba, oviduct
Salpinxentzündung f s. Salpingitis
Salpinxexstirpation f s. Salpingektomie
Salpinxfixation f salpingopexy, fixation of an oviduct
Salpinx- und Peritoneumentzündung f salpingoperitonitis
Saltation f 1. saltation, genetic mutation; 2. saltation, dancing, leaping *(bei Chorea)*; 3. saltation, saltatory conduction *(Nervenleitung)*
saltatorisch saltatoric, saltatorial, dancing, leaping
Salubrität f salubrity
Saluretikum n sal[idi]uretic, saline diuretic
Salz n/**[künstliches] Karlsbader** Carlsbad salt
salzarm low-salt
Salzbeschränkung f salt restriction
salzfrei salt-free
Salzlösung f saline solution
~/äquilibrierte isoosmotic solution
Salzmangel m lack of salt
Salzmangeldiät f low-salt diet, hypochlorization
Salzmangelsyndrom n low-salt syndrome, salt-depletion syndrome, salt-deficiency syndrome

Salzsäure

Salzsäure *f* hydrochloric acid
Salzsäureausscheidung *f* **im Magen** chlorhydria
salzsäurefrei *f* achlorhydric
Salzsäuremangel *m* achlorhydria; anacidity *(im Magen)*
Salzüberschußdiät *f* hyperchloridation
Salz- und Flüssigkeitsbeschränkung *f* salt and fluid restriction
Salzverarmung *f* salt depletion
Salzverlustnephritis *f* salt-losing nephritis
Salzverlustniere *f* salt-wasting kidney
Samen *m* semen, sperma; seminal fluid ● **dem ~ entstammend** spermatogenic, spermatogenous ● **~ erzeugend** spermatic
Samen... s.a. Sperma...
Samenabsonderung *f*/**vermehrte** hyperspermia
~/verminderte oligospermia, oligospermatism, oligozoospermia
Samenagglutination *f* semen agglutination
Samenausscheidung *f* **im Urin** *s.* Spermaturie
Samenbank *f* sperm storage bank
samenbildend spermatopoietic, gonepoietic
Samenbildung *f* spermatogenesis, gonepoiesis
~/fehlende aspermia, aspermatism
~/vermehrte hyperspermatogenesis
~/verminderte hypospermatogenesis
Samenbildungsdefekt *m* spermatogenic defect
Samenbildungsschwäche *f* hypospermatogenesis
Samenbildungsstörung *f* dyspermatism, dyspermia; aspermatogenesis
Samenbildungszelle *f* spermatogenic cell
Samenblase *f* seminal vesicle, spermatocyst, gonecyst
samenblasendarstellend vesiculographic
Samenblasenentfernung *f*[/**operative**] *s.* Spermatozystektomie
Samenblasenentzündung *f s.* Spermatozystitis
Samenbaseneröffnung *f*[/**operative**] *s.* Spermatozystotomie
Samenblasengonorrhoe *f* gonococcal vesiculitis
Samenblasenkörper *m* body of the seminal vesicle
Samenblasenröntgen[kontrast]bild *n* vesiculogram
Samenblasenröntgenkontrastdarstellung *f* vesiculography
Samenblasenstein *m* spermatic calculus, spermolith, gonecystolith
Samenbruch *m s.* Spermatozele
Samenentleerung *f* emission of semen
Samenenzym *n* seminal fluid enzyme
Samenerguß *m* ejaculation, effluvium seminis
~/fehlender aspermia, aspermatism
~/nächtlicher nocturnal emission (pollution); wet dream, oneirogmus
~/unwillkürlicher pollution
~/vorzeitiger premature ejaculation, prospermia
Samenfaden *m* spermatozoon, spermatic filament, [zoo]sperm
Samenfluß *m s.* Spermatorrhoe
~ ohne Koitus diurnal pollution

Samenflüssigkeit *f* seminal fluid
~/eitrige pyospermia
samenführend seminiferous
samenhaltig spermatic
Samenhügel *m* seminal colliculus (hillock), urethral colliculus, verumontanum
Samenhügelentzündung *f* [seminal] colliculitis, verumontanitis
Samenkanälchen *n* spermatic (seminal) canal, seminiferous tubule
~/gewundenes convoluted seminiferous tubule, contorted tubule of the testis
Samenkanälchenabszeß *m* spermatic abscess
Samenleiter *m* spermatic (seminal) duct, deferent canal (duct), duct of the testicle
Samenleiterampulle *f* Henle's ampulla, ampulla of the ductus deferens
Samenleiteranastomose *f* vasovasostomy
Samenleiterarterie *f* deferential artery
Samenleiterdurchtrennung *f*[/**operative**] vasotomy, vasosection
Samenleiterentfernung *f*[/**operative**] vasectomy, vasoresection, spermectomy
Samenleiterentzündung *f* vasitis, deferentitis
Samenleiterfistelung *f* vasostomy
Samenleiter-Hoden-Anastomose *f* vasoorchidostomy
Samenleiternaht *f* vasorrhaphy
Samenleiter-Nebenhoden-Anastomose *f* vasoepididymostomy
Samenleiternervengeflecht *n* deferential plexus
Samenleiterpunktion *f* vasopuncture
Samenleiter- und Samenbläschenentfernung *f*[/**operative**] vasovesiculectomy
Samenleiter- und Samenbläschenentzündung *f* vasovesiculitis
Samenleiterunterbindung *f* vasoligature
Samenreifungsstörung *f* aspermatogenesis
Samenstrang *m* spermatic cord, funiculus
Samenstrangbruch *m*/**Blut enthaltender** haematospermatocele
Samenstrangentzündung *f* funiculitis, inflammation of the spermatic cord, c[h]orditis, spermatitis
Samenstrangfaszie *f*/**äußere** external spermatic fascia
~/innere internal spermatic fascia
Samenstranghydrozele *f* funicular hydrocele
Samenstrangneuralgie *f* spermoneuralgia
Samenstrangscheide *f* spermatic sheath
Samenstrangscheidenentzündung *f* perispermatitis
Samenstrangschmerz *m* spermoneuralgia
Samenstrangtorsion *f* spermatic cord torsion
Samenstrangvene *f*/**linke** left spermatic (testicular) vein
~/rechte right spermatic (testicular) vein
samentragend seminiferous
Samenverhaltung *f* spermatoschesis
Samenzelle *f* spermatic (seminal) cell, spermatocyte, sperm ● **Samenzellen bildend** spermatogenic, spermatogenous

Samenzellenauflösung f s. Spermatolyse
Samenzellenbildungsstörung f dysspermatism, dysspermia
Samenzell[en]entwicklung f spermatogenesis
samenzellenförmig spermatoid
Samenzellenkern m sperm nucleus
Samenzellenkrankheit f spermatopathy
Samenzellenmangel m azoospermia, azoospermatism
Samenzellenverminderung f spermatacrasia
Samenzyste f seminal cyst
Sammellinse f convex (condensing, converging) lens
Sammelröhrchen n collecting tubule *(in der Niere)*
Sammelspiegel m concave mirror
Sammelurin m 24-hour urine
Sammelvene f collecting vein *(in der Leber)*
Sanarelli-Shwartzman-Phänomen n Shwartzman phenomenon (reaction) *(Antigen-Antikörper-Reaktion)*
Sanatio f **per primam [intentionem]** healing by first intention, first intention healing, immediate union
~ **per secundam [intentionem]** healing by second intention, second intention healing, delay in primary wound closure
Sanatorium n sanatorium
Sand m sand, sabulum
Sandbad n sand bath, arenation
Sandbadbehandlung f arenation, [ps]ammotherapy
Sandfliege f sand fly, Phlebotomus
Sandfliegenfieber n phlebotomus (sand-fly) fever, Chitral (three-day) fever
Sandfloh m sand flea, chigger, Sarcopsylla (Tunga) penetrans
Sandflohbefall m dermatophiliasis, dermatophilosis, tungiasis, chigger infestation
Sandgeschwulst f sand tumour, psammoma
sandig sandy, gritty, sabulous, psammous
Sandkörperchen npl sand bodies
Sandtherapie f [ps]ammotherapy, arenation
Sanduhrblase f hourglass (bilocular) bladder
Sanduhrgeschwulst f hourglass (dumb bell) tumour
Sanduhrkontraktion f hourglass contraction
Sanduhrmagen m hourglass (bilocular) stomach
~/physiologischer physiological hourglass stomach
Sanfillipo-Syndrom n Sanfillipo's syndrome, mucopolysaccharidosis [type] III
Sängerknötchen npl singer's (teacher's) nodules, vocal nodes
sanguinisch sanguine
sanguinolent sanguinolent
sanguinopurulent sanguinopurulent
sanguinös sanguineous
sanguinoserös sanguinoserous
Sanguis m blood, sanguis *(Zusammensetzungen s. unter Blut)*
sanieren to sanitize, to apply sanitary measures

sanierend sanitary
Sanierung f sanitation
sanitär sanitary, hygienic
Sanitäter m ambulance (first-aid) man; [medical] orderly *(Militär)*
Sanitätsdienst m medical service
Santonin n santonin *(Wurmmittel)*
Santoninvergiftung f santonism
Santorini-Knorpel m Santorini's cartilage
São-Paulo-Fieber n, **São-Paulo-Rickettsiose** f São Paulo fever (typhus)
Saphenaentfernung f[/operative] saphenectomy
Saphena-magna-System n greater saphenousvenous system
Saphenastripping n saphenectomy
Saphenektomie f saphenectomy
Saponifikation f saponification *(bei Leichenzersetzung)*
saponiform saponaceous
Sapphismus m sapphism, lesbianism, female homosexuality
Saprämie f sapraemia, septic (putrid) intoxication
saprämisch sapraemic
saprogen saprogenic, saprogenous
saprophag saprophagous
saprophil saprophilous
Saprophyt m saprophyte
saprophytisch saprophytic
Sarcoma n sarcoma *(bösartige Bindegewebsgeschwulst) (s. a. unter Sarkom)*
~ **botryoides** botryoid sarcoma
~ **cutaneum teleangiectaticum multiplex** multiple idiopathic haemorrhagic sarcoma
~ **myxomatodes** myxomatous sarcoma
Sarcoptes f Sarcoptes
~ **scabiei** Acarus scabiei, sarcoptic (itch) mite
sardonisch sardonic
Sargdeckelkristalle mpl coffin-lid crystals, triple phosphate crystals
Sarin n sarin *(Nervenkampfstoff)*
Sarkoenchondrom n sarcoenchondroma
Sarkoendotheliom n sarcoendothelioma
sarkogen sarcogenic
Sarkohydrozele f sarcohydrocele
Sarkoid n sarcoid
~/Boecksches Boeck's sarcoid *(s. a. Sarkoidose)*
Sarkoidgranuloma n sarcoid granuloma
Sarkoidose f sarcoidosis, benign lymphogranulomatosis, Hutchinson-Boeck disease
Sarkoidosetest m/**Kveimscher** Kveim-Siltzbach test
Sarkoiduveitis f sarcoid uveitis
sarkokarzinomatös sarcocarcinomatous
Sarkolemm n sarcolemma, myolemma
Sarkoleukämie f sarcoleukaemia
Sarkolyse f sarcolysis, disintegration of soft tissues
sarkolytisch sarcolytic
Sarkom n sarcoma *(bösartige Bindegewebsgeschwulst) (s. a. unter Sarcoma)*

Sarkom 680

~/embryonales embryonal nephroma, embryoma (embryonal mixed tumour) of the kidney
~/intrakanalikuläres intracanalicular sarcoma
~/lymphozytäres lymphocytic sarcoma
~/osteogenes osteogenic sarcoma, sarcoma of bone, malignant bone aneurysm (cyst)
~/zylindromatöses cylindromatous sarcoma, cylindrosarcoma
~/zystenhaltiges cystosarcoma
Sarkomantikörpertiter *m* antisarcoma antibody titer
sarkomartig sarcoid, sarcomatoid
sarkomatös sarcomtous
Sarkomatose *f* sarcomatosis
sarkombildend sarcomagenic
Sarkomer *n* sarcomere
Sarkomesotheliom *n* sarcomesothelioma *(bösartiges Mesotheliom)*
Sarkoplasma *n* sarcoplasm, myoplasm
sarkopoetisch sarcopoietic
Sarkoptidose *f* sarcoptidosis
Sarkosin *n* sarcosine
Sarkosinämie *f* sarcosinaemia
Sarkosporidienbefall *m* sarcosporidiasis, sarcosporidiosis
Sarkozele *f* sarcocele *(Hodengeschwulst)*
Sartenkrankheit *f* paschachurda, oriental boil *(Hautleishmaniase)*
Sartorius *m* sartorius [muscle], tailor's muscle
Sarzinen *fpl* Sarcina *(harmlose Magenbakterien)*
Satellit *m* 1. *s.* Satellitenzelle; 2. satellite chromosome
Satellitenzelle *f* satellite [cell], capsular cell
Sattel *m* sella, saddle *(Anatomie)*
Sattelembolus *m* saddle (straddling, riding) embolus
Sattelgelenk *n* saddle joint
Sattelkopf *m* clinocephalus
sattelköpfig clinocephalic
Sattelköpfigkeit *f* clinocephalia
Sattelnase *f* saddle[-back] nose, swayback nose
Sattelthrombus *m* saddle (riding) thrombus
sättigen/mit Kohlendioxid to carbonate
~/mit Sauerstoff to oxygenate, to oxygenize *(z. B. Hämoglobin)*
Sättigung *f* saturation
Sättigungsgefühl *n* sensation of satiety
Sättigungszentrum *n* satiety centre
saturieren to saturate *(z. B. Hämoglobin)*
Saturnismus *m* saturnism, lead (saturnine) poisoning, plumbism
Satyriasis *f* satyriasis, satyromania, gynaecomania *(gesteigerter Geschlechtsdrang beim Mann)*
Satzbildungsvermögen *n*/**fehlendes** aphrasia
säubern to clean; to decontaminate
Säuberung *f* cleaning; decontamination
Saubohnenkrankheit *f* favism *(hämolytische Anämie infolge Enzymmangels)*
Saucerisation *f* saucerization *(durch Nekrosenausräumung)*
sauer acidic; sour

sauerfärbend oxychromatic
säuerlich acescent; sourish
säuern to acidify, to acidulate; to go sour
Sauerstoff *m* oxygen ● **absolut von ~ abhängig** obligately aerobic ● **absolut von ~ unabhängig** obligately anaerobic
Sauerstoffabgabe *f* deoxygenation
sauerstoffabhängig aerobic
sauerstoffangereichert oxygen-enriched
Sauerstoffanreicherung *f* **des Bluts** arterialization, oxygenation of blood
Sauerstoffaufnahme *f* oxygen uptake (absorption)
Sauerstoffaufnahmefähigkeit *f* oxygen capacity *(des Hämoglobins)*
Sauerstoffausschöpfung *f* oxygen extraction
Sauerstoffbad *n* oxygen bath
Sauerstoffbehandlung *f* oxygen treatment (therapy)
~/hyperbare hyperbaric oxygenation
Sauerstoffdefizit *n* oxygen deficit
Sauerstoffdifferenz *f* oxygen difference
~/arteriovenöse arteriovenous oxygen difference, venoarterial oxygen content difference
Sauerstoffdiffusion *f* oxygen diffusion
Sauerstoffdissoziationskurve *f* oxygen dissociation curve
Sauerstoffdruck *m* oxygen pressure
Sauerstoffelektrode *f* oxygen electrode
Sauerstoffflasche *f* oxygen cylinder (bottle)
Sauerstoffgehalt *m* oxygen content
Sauerstoffgerät *n* oxygen apparatus
sauerstoffhaltig oxygenic
Sauerstoffinsufflator *m* oxygen insufflator
Sauerstoffkapazität *f* oxygen capacity *(des Hämoglobins)*
sauerstofflos anoxic
Sauerstoffmangel *m* oxygen deficiency (want) ● **bei ~ lebend** microaerophilic
~ im Blut anoxaemia
~ im Gewebe tissue anoxia
~/völliger anoxia
Sauerstoffmangelbelastungstest *m* anoxaemia test
Sauerstoffmangelemphysem *n* hypoxic emphysema
Sauerstoffmangelenzephalopathie *f* anoxic (hypoxic, hypotensive) encephalopathy
Sauerstoffmangelerythrozytose *f* anoxaemic erythrocytosis
Sauerstoffmangelkopfschmerz *m* anoxic headache
Sauerstoffmangeltest *m* anoxaemia test
Sauerstoffpartialdruck *m* partial pressure of oxygen
Sauerstoffpartialdrucksenkung *f* hypoxaemia
Sauerstoffsättigung *f* oxygen saturation, oxygenation *(des Hämoglobins)*
~/arterielle arterial oxygen saturation
~ des Bluts arterialization, oxygenation of blood
~/mangelnde arterial desaturation
~/prozentuale arterielle arterial blood oxygen percent saturation

~/prozentuale venöse venous blood oxygen percent saturation
Sauerstoffsättigungsmesser m oximeter
Sauerstoffsättigungsmessung f oximetry, oxymetry *(des arteriellen Bluts)*
Sauerstoffschuld f oxygen debt, recovery oxygen
Sauerstoffspannung f oxygen tension
~/arterielle arterial oxygen tension
~ des Bluts blood oxygen tension
Sauerstofftoleranz f oxygen tolerance
Sauerstofftransport m oxygen transport
Sauerstofftransportkapazität f oxygen carrying capacity
Sauerstofftransportmodell n oxygen transport model
Sauerstoffüberdrucktherapie f hyperbaric oxygenation
sauerstoffunabhängig anaerobic, anaerobiotic
Sauerstoffuntersättigung f oxygen desaturation
Sauerstoffutilisation f oxygen utilization
Sauerstoffverbrauch m oxygen consumption
Sauerstoffzelt n oxygen tent
Sauerstoffzufuhr f oxygen supply, administration of oxygen
Säuerung f acidification, acidulation
Säufernase f whisky[-rum] nose, brandy (bottle) nose, toper's nose
Säuferwahnsinn m methomania, methylmania, enomania; alcohol delirium, delirium tremens
Saugbiopsie f aspiration biopsy
Saugdrainage f suction (negative pressure) drainage
~/geschlossene underwater seal drainage
~/Monaldische Monaldi drainage (method) *(tuberkulöser Einzelhöhlen mit einem Katheter durch die Brustwand)*
Saugdrainageflasche f suction-drainage bottle, underwater drainage bottle
Saugdrainagesystem n/geschlossenes underwater-seal system, water-seal drainage system
Saugelektrode f suction electrode
saugen to suck, to suckle
~/an der Brust to suck the breast
säugen to nurse [at the breast], to breast-feed, to lactate, to give the breast
Saugen n suction
Säugen n breast-feeding, lactation
Sauger m pacifier, dummy teat
~/elektrischer electric suction pump
Säugetierpassage f mammalian passage
Saugflasche f 1. nursing (feeding) bottle; 2. suction flask
Saugglocke f erysiphake, erisophake
Saugkanüle f suction cannula (tube)
Saugkürettage f suction curettage
Saugkürette f [intra-uterine] suction curette
Säugling m infant, baby, suckling
Säuglingsalter n early infancy
Säuglingsekzem n infantile eczema
Säuglingsfürsorge f infant welfare
Säuglingsheilkunde f neonatology, neonatal paediatrics

Säuglingsmeßapparat m mecometer
Säuglingsnahrung f baby food
Säuglingsretikulose f/akute Letterer-Siwe disease, non-lipid histiocytosis (reticuloendotheliosis)
Säuglingsschwester f baby (dry) nurse, [trained] children's nurse
Säuglingssepsis f[/Winckelsche] Winckel's disease, epidemic haemoglobinuria; black jaundice
Säuglingsstation f nursery
Säuglingssterblichkeit f neonatal mortality, infant[ile] mortality
Saugnapf m sucking disk, hooklet *(des Bandwurms)*
Saugpumpe f suction pump; breast pump (cup)
Saugreflex m sucking (lip) reflex
Saugrohr n/gläsernes pipet[te], suction tube
Saugspüldrainage f suction irrigation
Saugwurm m trematode
Saugwurmbefall m trematodiasis
Saugzytologie f aspiration cytology
Säule f column, pillar
~/Clarkesche Clarke's column
~/thermoelektrische thermopile
Säulenchromatographie f column chromatography
Säulenepithel n columnar (cylindrical, rod) epithelium
Säulenepithelzelle f columnar (cylindrical) cell
Säulenzellenepitheliom n columnar (cylindrical) epithelioma
Saum m limbus, border; edge
Sauna f sauna; vapour bath, vaporarium
säureausscheidend aciduric; oxyntic
Säureausscheidung f im Urin aciduria
Säure-Basen-Gleichgewicht n acid-base balance, acid-alkali equilibrium
Säure-Basen-Haushalt m acid-base metabolism
Säure-Basen-Status m acid-base status
säurebeständig acid-resistant, acid-proof, acid-fast
Säurebeständigkeit f acidoresistance, acid-fastness
säurebildend acidogenic, acidifying, acid-forming *(z. B. Bakterien)*
säurebindend ant[i]acid
säurefärbend acidophilic, oxyphilic
säurefest s. säurebeständig
säurefreundlich acidophilic
Säuregehalt m acid content; [degree of] acidity
säuregehaltsbestimmend acidimetric
Säuregehaltsmesser m acidimeter, acidometer
Säuregehaltsmessung f acidimetry
Säuregrad m [degree of] acidity
säurelabil acid-labile
säureliebend acidophilic, oxyphilic
Säuremangel m hypoacidity, subacidity
Säurerückschlag m acid rebound *(verstärkte Magensäuresekretion nach Antazidatherapie)*
säuresezernierend oxyntic, acid-secreting
Säureüberschuß m hyperacidity, superacidity

säureunbeständig

säureunbeständig acid-labile
Säurevergiftung f acid intoxication, acidism
s.c. s. subkutan
Scabies f papuliformis (papulosa) rank itch
Scabrities f scabrities
Scala f scala *(Innenohr)*
~ **tympani** tympanic scala
~ **vestibuli** vestibular scala
Scalenus-anterior-Syndrom n cervicobrachial (cervicothoracic outlet) syndrome, compression-traction syndrome
Scanner m [radioisotope] scanner, scintigraph
Scanningelektronenmikroskop n scanning [electron] microscope, scanning beam electron microscope
Scapha f scapha, navicular fossa of the ear *(Grube zwischen Helix und Anthelix der Ohrmuschel)*
Scapula f alata alar (winged) scapula, angel's scapula (wing)
Scapus m scapus, shaft
~ **pili** hair shaft
Scarlatina f s. Scharlach
Schaber m scraper, rasp
Schabmesser n scraper
Schachtel f chartula, charta *(Dosierungsform)*
Schädel m skull, [cerebral] cranium, brain case, brainpan *(s.a. unter* Cranium*)*
~/**knöcherner** osteocranium
Schädel... s.a. Kranio...
Schädelanlage f/bindegewebige desmocranium, membranocranium
Schädelauskultation f cephaloscopy
Schädelaußenseite/auf der supracranial
Schädelbasis f skull base, base of the skull, cranial floor
Schädelbasisabplattung f platybasia, atlas assimilation *(bei Pagetscher Krankheit)*
Schädelbasisbruch m basal (basilar) skull fracture; fractured base
Schädelbasisröntgenaufnahme f base-view roentgenogram of the skull
Schädel-Becken-Mißverhältnis n cephalopelvic disproportion *(bei der Geburt)*
Schädelbinnendruck m intracranial pressure
Schädelbohrer m trepan, trephine, craniotome
Schädel-Computertomographie f cranial computer tomography
Schädeldach n calvaria, calvarium, skull cap, [cranial] vault, roof of the skull
Schädeldachinnenschicht f inner table of the skull
Schädeldachknochenhaut f/äußere pericranium
Schädeldachsarkoidose f calvarial sarcoidosis
Schädeleinstellung f engagement, cranial presentation *(bei der Geburt)*
Schädeleröffnung f[/operative] trepanation, cephalotomy, craniotomy, cephalotrypesis
Schädelerweichung f craniomalacia, craniotabes
Schädelextension f skull (head) traction
Schädelextensionsklammer f skull traction calliper

Schädelfehlbildung f skull malformation
Schädelform f shape of the skull
schädelförmig cephaloid
Schädelfraktur f skull fracture
Schädelgewölbe n cranial vault
Schädelgrube f cranial fossa
~/**hintere** posterior cranial fossa
~/**mittlere** middle cranial fossa
~/**vordere** anterior cranial fossa
Schädelhalter m craniostat, skull holder, traction tongs, head clamp
~ **für Halswirbelextension** cervical traction tongs
~ **für Wirbelextension** skull traction tongs
Schädelhämatom n cephal[o]haematoma
Schädel-Hirn-Trauma n craniocerebral (cerebrocranial) trauma
~ **I. Grades** brain concussion
~ **II. Grades** brain contusion
~ **III. Grades** brain compression
Schädelhöhle f cranial cavity
Schädelindex m cranial (cephalic) index
Schädelinnendruck m intracranial pressure
Schädelinneres n interior of the cranium
Schädelklammer f nach Crutchfield skull calliper of Crutchfield
Schädelknochen m skull (cranial) bone
Schädelknochenentfernung f[/operative] craniectomy
Schädelknochenhaut f pericranium
Schädelknochennaht f cranial suture
Schädelknochenrekonstruktion f cranioplasty
Schädelknochenschalleitung f osteoacousia, osteophony
Schädelknochenschwammsubstanz f diploe, diploic bone
Schädelknochenzange f craniotomy forceps
Schädelkonfiguration f cranial configuration
Schädelkrankheit f craniopathy
Schädellage f cephalic (vertex) presentation *(bei der Geburt)*
Schädellänge f cranial length
Schädellehre f craniology
~/**Gallsche** phrenology
schädellos acranial
Schädelmeßinstrument n craniometer, cephalometer; cephalograph
Schädelmeßpunkt m craniometric point
Schädelnaht f cranial suture
Schädelnahtverknöcherung f/vorzeitige craniostosis, craniosynostosis
Schädelosteomyelitis f osteomyelitis of the skull
Schädelosteoporose f osteoporosis of the skull; fenestrated skull
Schädelperiostauskleidung f endocranium
Schädelplastik f cranioplasty
Schädelquetscher m cranioclast
Schädelröntgenaufnahme f skull radiogram
Schädelröntgendarstellung f skull radiography
Schädelspalte f cranioschisis; bifid skull
Schädeltrauma n cranial (head) trauma
Schädeltrepanation f s. Schädeleröffnung

Schädelübersichts[röntgen]aufnahme f plain skull radiogram
Schädel- und Wirbelsäulenspaltbildung f cranior[rh]achischisis
Schädelvereng[er]ung f craniostenosis
Schädelvergrößerung f/**abnorme** megalocephalia
Schädelverletzung f skull (cranial) injury
Schädelvermessung f craniometry; cephalometry, craniography
Schädelvolumen n cranial capacity
schädelwärts cranial
Schädelwinkelmessung f goniocraniometry
Schädelzange f skull cutting forceps, cranial [rongeur] forceps
Schädelzertrümmerer m cephalotribe, sphenotribe, cranioclast, basiotribe
Schädelzertrümmerung f[/**operative**] cephalotripsy, sphenotripsy, cranioclasty, cranioclasis, basiotripsy *(bei Totgeburten)*
Schädelzug m skull traction
schädigen to harm; to affect, to injure, to be detrimental; to traumatize
Schädigung f affection, impairment; lesion; traumatism, trauma[tosis]
~/**raumfordernde** space-occupying lesion *(z. B. des Gehirns)*
schädlich harmful, detrimental; deleterious, injurious *(verletzend)*; noxious *(giftig)*; pernicious *(zerstörerisch)*; unwholesome *(ungesund)*; insalubrious *(z. B. Klima)*
Schädlichkeit f harmfulness; injuriousness; noxiousness
Schädling m parasite; pest *(z. B. Insekt)*
Schädlingsbekämpfungslehre f pestology
Schädlingsbekämpfungsmittel n pesticide; insecticide
Schafblutagar m(n) sheep blood agar
Schäfer-Syndrom n Schäfer's syndrome, congenital pachyonychia
Schafhaut f s. Amnion
Schafpocken pl s. Varizellen
Schaft m shaft, scapus
Schaftplatte f intertrochanteric bone plate *(Osteosynthese)*
Schafzellenagglutinin n sheep cell agglutinin
Schälblatter f pemphigus, blister tetter
schälen to peel, to exfoliate, to scale; to desquamate
Schälen n peeling, exfoliation; desquamation *(der Haut)*
schälend peeling, exfoliating, scaling; desquamative
Schalenpessar n cup pessary
Schalenständer m basin stand
Schälflechte f Leiner's disease, desquamative erythrodermia
Schall m sound
Schalleitung f sound conduction *(beim Hörvorgang)*
~/**knöcherne** bone conduction
Schalleitungsapparat m sound-conducting apparatus

Schalleitungshörverlust m conductive hearing loss
Schalleitungsschwelle f conduction threshold
Schalleitungsschwerhörigkeit f conduction deafness, conductive hearing loss
Schalleitungstaubheit f transmission deafness
Schallempfindungsapparat m sound-perceiving apparatus
Schallfelder npl/**Krönigsche** Krönig's fields *(Lungenschallfelder über den Lungenspitzen)*
schallinduziert audiogenic
Schallmesser m phonometer
Schallmessung f phonometry
Schallrezeptor m phonoreceptor
Schallstärkemesser m phonometer
Schallstärkemessung f phonometry
Schalltrauma n acoustic trauma
schallwahrnehmend phonoreceptive
Schallwechsel m/**Wintrichscher** Wintrich's sign *(über einer Lungenkaverne)*
Schaltkern m intercalated nucleus
Schaltneuron n intercalated neuron, [inhibitory] interneuron, internuncial cell
Schaltraum m switch room *(Radiologie)*
Schaltstück n intercalated duct *(im Drüsenausführungsgang)*
Schalttisch m control table *(Radiologie)*
Scham f/**weibliche** pudendum [femininum]; pubes; vulva, cunnus
Schamarterie f/**äußere** external pudendal artery
~/**innere** internal pudendal artery
Schambein n pubic bone, pubis ● **über dem** ~ suprapubic
Schambeinentfernung f[/**operative**] symphysiectomy
Schambeinfuge f [pubic] symphysis
Schambeinkamm m pubic pecten, pecten of the pubic bone; pectineal line
Schambeinnaht f symphysiorrhaphy
Schambeinspaltung f pubiotomy, hebosteotomy, hebotomy
Schambeinsymphyse f [pubic] symphysis
Schambeinwinkel m angle of the pubes
Schamberg m mons pubis, mount of Venus, pubic eminence
Schambogen m pubic arch
Schamfuge f [pubic] symphysis
Schamfugendurchtrennung f[/**operative**] symphysiotomy, symphysectomy, synchondrotomy
Schamgegend f pudendal (pubic) region, pubes
● **zur** ~ **gehörend** pubic, pudendal, pudic
Schamhaar n pubic (genital) hair, pubisure
Schamhaarausfall m genital alopecia
Schamhügel m s. Schamberg
Schamlippe f labium
~/**große** greater labium, major lip
~/**kleine** lesser labium, minor lip, nympha
Schamlippen fpl labia pudendi
Schamlippenkommissur f frenulum of the pudendum, fourchet[te]
~/**hintere** posterior junction of the labia majora
~/**vordere** anterior junction of the labia majora

Schamspalte f pudendal cleft
Schamvene f/**äußere** external pudendal vein
~/**innere** internal pudendal vein
Schändung f rape, ravishment
Schanker m chancre
~/**harter** hard chancre, primary sore
~/**Hunterscher** s. ~/syphilitischer
~/**Nisbetscher** bubonulus *(Abszeß des Penisrückens)*
~/**syphilitischer** syphilitic (Hunterian) chancre, syphilelcos, syphilelcus
~/**weicher** soft chancre, chancroid, chancroidal (venereal) ulcer
schankerartig chancroidal, chancrous, chancriform
Scharbock m s. Skorbut
scharf sharp, acute *(Sinneswahrnehmung)*; acrid, pungent, hot *(Geschmack)*; intense *(Schmerz)*
Scharfblick m /**diagnostischer** diagnostic acumen
Scharlach m scarlet fever, scarlatina
Scharlachantiserum n antiscarlatinal serum
Scharlachantitoxin n scarlet fever antitoxin
scharlachartig scarlatiniform, scarlatinoid
Scharlachausschlag m scarlet-fever rash, scarlatiniform (canker) rash
Scharlachexanthem n scarlatinal exanthema
Scharlachfieber n scarlet fever, scarlatina
Scharlachimmunserum n scarlet-fever immune serum
~/**humanes** human scarlet fever immune serum
Scharlachnephritis f scarlatinal (scarlatinous) nephritis
Scharlachrekonvaleszentenserum n scarlet fever convalescent serum
Scharlachrot n scarlet red *(als Scharlachrotsalbe zur Epithelialisierung)*
Scharlachserum n antiscarlatinal serum; scarlet fever antitoxin
Scharlachserum-Reaktion f nach Dick scarlet fever test
Scharlachtoxin n scarlatinal (erythrogenic) toxin, scarlet fever streptococcus toxin
scharlachwirksam antiscarlatinal
Scharlatanerie f charlatanism, charlatanry
Scharniergelenk n ginglymus, hinge joint
Scharpie f lint *(als Verbandstoff verwendet)*
Schattenprobe f retino[skia]scopy, pupilloscopy, scotoscopy, shadow test, retinoscopy *(objektive Refraktionsbestimmung des Auges)*
Schätzung f **des Körperschadens** medical assessment
Schauder m shiver[ing], shivering-fit
schaudern to shudder, to shiver
„**Schaufensterkrankheit**" f intermittent claudication
Schaukelbewegung f see-saw movement
Schaumoxygenator m bubble oxygenator
Schaumzelle f foam (xanthoma) cell
Schaumzelltumor m granular-cell myoblastoma (schwannoma)

Schauta-Wertheim-Operation f bei **Scheidenvorfall** interposition (Schauta-Wertheim) operation
Scheckhaut f vitiligo, white leprosy
Scheibe f disk, disc[us]
scheibenartig discoid, disk-shaped
Scheibenbandwurm m pork tapeworm
Scheibenblastula f discoblastula
Scheibendiffusionstechnik f disk diffusion technique *(Bakteriologie)*
Scheibenelektrophorese f disk electrophoresis
Scheibenentfernung f [/**operative**] discoidectomy
scheibenförmig disciform, discoid, orbicular
Scheibengastrula f discogastrula
Scheibenkeratitis f disciform keratitis
Scheibenniere f disk kidney
Scheibenoxygenator m disk oxygenator
Scheibenplazenta f discoid placenta, discoplacenta
Scheibenrose f discoid lupus erythematosus
Scheide f 1. sheath; theca; 2. s. Vagina 1.
~/**Schwannsche** Schwann's sheath, sheath of Schwann, neurillem[m]a
~/**weibliche** s. Vagina 1.
Scheiden... s. a. Vaginal...
Scheidenabriß m colporrhexis
Scheidenabstrich m vaginal smear
Scheidenabszeß m/**mantelförmiger** vaginal cuff abscess
Scheidenagenesie f vaginal agenesia
Scheidenampulle f ampulla of the vagina
Scheidenaplasie f vaginal aplasia
Scheidenarterie f vaginal artery
Scheidenatresie f colpatresia, vaginal atresia; ankylokolpos
Scheidenausfluß m vaginal discharge, whites
~/**gelber** xanthorrhoea
Scheidenaustastung f vaginal touch
scheidenbildend vaginiferous
Scheidenblutung f vaginal bleeding (haemorrhage), colporrhagia
Scheidendammnaht f episioperineorrhaphy, vaginoperineorrhaphy, colpoperineorrhaphy
Scheidendammplastik f episioperineoplasty, colpoperineoplasty *(bei Scheidensenkung)*
Scheidendammriß m laceration of the perineum, vaginoperineal laceration
Scheidendammschnitt m episiotomy, vaginoperineotomy
Scheidendehner m colpeurynter
Scheidendehnung f[/**operative**] colpeurysis
Scheidendoppelbildung f vaginal duplication
Scheideneingang m vaginal orifice (ostium), vaginal introitus, vestibule (external orifice) of the vagina, vulvar canal
Scheideneingangsnaht f episioclisia
Scheideneingangsplastik f episioplasty
Scheideneingangsvereng[er]ung f episiostenosis
Scheideneingangsverwachsung f ankylokolpos
Scheideneinriß m colporrhexis

Scheidenentfernung f[/operative] colpectomy, vagin[al]ectomy
Scheidenentzündung f [endo]colpitis, encolpitis, vaginitis, elytritis, coleitis, inflammation of the vagina *(Zusammensetzungen s. unter Vaginitis)*
Scheidenepithel n vaginal epithelium
Scheidenerkrankung f colpopathy, vaginopathy, vaginal disease
Scheideneröffnung f[/operative] colpotomy, coleotomy, vaginotomy
Scheidenersatzplastik f/Baldwinsche Baldwin operation
Scheidenerweiterung f colpectasia, vaginal dilatation
Scheidenfistel f vaginal fistula
Scheidenfixation f[/operative] colpopexy, vaginopexy
Scheidenflora f vaginal flora
Scheidengewölbe n vaginal fornix (vault), fornix of the vagina
~/**hinteres** posterior vaginal fornix
~/**seitliches** lateral vaginal fornix
~/**vorderes** anterior vaginal fornix
Scheidengonorrhoe f vaginal gonorrhoea; gonococcal vaginitis
Scheidenhalter m vaginal retractor
Scheidenhämatozele f vaginal haematocele
Scheidenhäutchen n/hinteres frenulum of the pudendum, fourchet[te]
Scheidenhinterwand f posterior wall of the vagina
Scheidenirrigator m vaginal douche
Scheidenkanal m vaginal canal
Scheidenkrampf m colpospasm, vaginism[us], vulvismus, vaginal spasm
Scheidenkrebs m vaginal cancer (carcinoma)
Scheidenmesser n colpotome, vaginotome
Scheidenmikroskopie f colpomicroscopy
Scheidenmuskelentzündung f myocolpitis
Scheidenmykose f vaginomycosis
Scheidennaht f colporrhaphy, suture of the vagina
Scheidennervengeflecht n vaginal plexus
Scheidenöffnung f s. Scheideneingang
Scheidenpessar n vaginal pessary
Scheidenpförtner m vaginal sphincter
Scheidenprolaps m colpoptosis, coleoptosis, vaginal prolapse; colpocele, vaginocele
Scheidenrekonstruktion f colpoplasty, vaginoplasty
Scheidenröntgen[kontrast]bild n vaginogram
Scheidenröntgen[kontrast]darstellung f vaginography
Scheiden-Scheidenvorhof-Bereich m vulvovaginal area
Scheiden-Scheidenvorhof-Flora f vulvovaginal flora
Scheidenschleim m vaginal mucus
Scheidenschleimhaut f vaginal mucosa, mucous membrane of the vagina

Scheidenschleimhautdrüse f vaginal gland
Scheidenschleimhautentzündung f s. Scheidenentzündung
Scheidenschleimhautfalte f/querverlaufende ruga of the vagina
Scheidenschmerz m colpalgia, colpodynia, vaginalgia, vaginodynia, pain in the vagina
Scheidenschwellung f colpoedema
Scheidensenkung f s. Scheidenprolaps
Scheidenspülung f vaginal douche
scheidentragend vaginiferous
Scheidentrichomoniasis f vaginal trichomoniasis
Scheidentumor m/eiterhaltiger pyocolpocele
Scheidenumstülpung f inversion of the vagina
Scheiden- und Gebärmutterentfernung f[/operative] colpohysterectomy
Scheiden- und Gebärmuttereröffnung f[/operative] colpohysterotomy
Scheiden- und Gebärmutterfixation f[/operative] colpohysteropexy
Scheiden- und Gebärmutternaht f colpohysterorrhaphy
Scheiden- und Harnblasenentzündung f colpocystitis
Scheiden- und Scheidenvorhofnaht f colpoepisiorrhaphy
Scheiden- und Zervixkanalentzündung f cervicocolpitis, cervicovaginitis
Scheidenuntersuchung f vaginal examination
~/**digitale** vaginal touch
Scheidenvenengeflecht n vaginal plexus
Scheidenverdopplung f double vagina
Scheidenvereng[er]ung f colpostenosis, narrowing of the vagina
Scheidenverschleimung f mucocolpos
Scheidenverschluß m colpatresia
~/**operativer** colpocleisis, colpoepisiorrhaphy
Scheidenvorderwand f anterior wall of the vagina
Scheidenvorhof m vestibule of the vagina (vulva), vulvar canal
Scheidenvorhofdrüse f vestibular gland
Scheidenvorhofentfernung f/halbseitige hemivulvectomy
Scheidenvorhofentzündung f vulvitis, inflammation of the vulva
Scheidenvorhofschwellkörper m bulb of the vestibule [of the vagina]
Scheidenvorhofschwellkörperarterie f artery of the bulb of the vestibule of the vagina
Scheidenwand f vaginal wall
Scheidenwandverdickung f/entzündliche pachyvaginitis
Scheidenwiederherstellung f/operative colpoplasty, vaginoplasty
Scheidewand f membrane, diaphragm; septum (Anatomie) (s.a. unter Septum) ● durch die ~ transseptal
~ **des Herzens** [cardiac] septum
~/**halbdurchlässige** semipermeable membrane
~/**kleine** septulum
Scheidewandabtrennung f septation

Scheie-Syndrom

Scheie-Syndrom n Scheie's syndrome, mucopolysaccharidosis [type] V
Schein... s.a. Pseud...
Scheinagglutination f pseudoagglutination
Scheinagraphie f pseudoagraphia
Scheinakromegalie f pseudoacromegaly
Scheinamnesie f pseud[o]amnesia
Scheinanämie f pseud[o]anaemia, apparent anaemia
Scheinaneurysma n pseudoaneurysm
Scheinanfall m pseudoseizure
Scheinanorexie f pseudoanorexia
Scheinapoplexie f pseudoapoplexy
Scheinapraxie f pseudoapraxia
Scheinastereognosis f pseudoastereognosis
Scheinaszites m pseudoascites
Scheinathetose f pseudoathetosis
Scheinbehandlung f placebo treatment
Scheinbewegung f apparent movement
Scheinbild n phantasm, phantom; illusion
Scheinbildersehen n phantasmoscopia
Scheinbrust f pseudomamma
~ **beim Mann** pseudogynaecomastia
Scheinbrustdrüse f pseudomamma
Scheindemenz f pseudodementia
Scheindivertikel n pseudodiverticulum, false diverticulum
Scheinepilepsie f pseudoepilepsy
Scheinerbrechen n pseudovomiting
Scheinfieber n pseudofever
Scheinfraktur f pseudofracture
Scheinfütterung f sham feeding
Scheinganglion n pseudoganglion
Scheingelbsucht f pseudojaundice
Scheingelenk n pseud[o]arthrosis; false joint (articulation)
Scheingelenkbildung f bony ankylosis
Scheingelenkversteifung f false ankylosis
Scheingeruch m pseudosmia, phantosmia
Scheingeschmack m pseudogeusia
Scheingeschwulst f pseudotumour, pseudoneoplasm
Scheingicht f pseudogout
Scheinglaukom n pseudoglaucoma
Scheinglottis f pseudoglottis
Scheingynäkomastie f pseudogynaecomastia
Scheinhalluzination f pseudohallucination
Scheinkolobom n pseudocoloboma
Scheinkrankheit f pseudomalady, malingering
Scheinlähmung f pseudoparalysis, pseudoparesis, pseudoplegia
~ **der Extremitäten** pseudoparaplegia
Scheinluxation f pseudoluxation
Scheinmalaria f pseudomalaria
Scheinmanie f pseudomania
Scheinnystagmus m pseudonystagmus
Scheinödem n pseudo-oedema
Scheinparaplegie f pseudoparaplegia
Scheinparasit m pseudoparasite
Scheinphlegmone f pseudophlegmon
Scheinpräparat n placebo, dummy
Scheinreaktion f pseudoreaction

Scheinschwangerschaft f pseudocyesis, pseudopregnancy, false (phantom) pregnancy, hysterical (afoetal) pregnancy
Scheinstimme f pseudovoice
Scheinstrabismus m pseudostrabism[us]
scheintot mortisemblant, anabiotic
Scheintod m apparent death, necromimesis
Scheintympanie f pseudotympany
Scheinwahrnehmung f pseudoaesthesia
Scheinwirbel m pseudovertebra, false vertebra
Scheinzwittertum n s. Pseudohermaphroditismus
Scheitel m s. 1. Vertex; 2. Apex ● **zum ~ gehörend** bregmatic
Scheitelbein n parietal [bone] ● **zwischen den Scheitelbeinen** interparietal
Scheitelbeindurchmesser m biparietal diameter
Scheitelbein-Hinterhauptbein-Fraktur f parieto-occipital fracture
Scheitelbeinlappen m parietal lobe
Scheitelbeinvorderrand m anterior border of the parietal bone
Scheitelbrechwert m vertex power (des Auges)
Scheitelhirnlappen m/**unterer** inferior parietal lobe (lobule)
Scheitelhirnwindung f parietal gyrus
Scheitelhöcker m parietal eminence (boss), parietal protuberance (tubercle)
Scheitellage f vertex (parietal) presentation (bei der Geburt)
Scheitellappen m parietal lobe ● **unter dem ~** subparietal ● **zwischen den Scheitellappen** interparietal
Scheitelregion f parietal region
Schenkel m 1. pedicle, pediculus; peduncle; limb (einer Schleife); crus of the cerebrum; 2. s. Oberschenkel; 3. s. Unterschenkel
~/**absteigender** descending limb (der Henleschen Schleife)
~/**aufsteigender** ascending limb (der Henleschen Schleife)
Schenkelanzieher m/**großer** adductor magnus [muscle]
~/**kleiner** adductor minimus [muscle]
~/**kurzer** adductor brevis [muscle]
~/**langer** adductor longus [muscle]
Schenkelblock m bundle-branch block (EKG)
~/**inkompletter** incomplete bundle branch block
Schenkelbruch m femoral hernia, femorocele, Cooper's hernia
Schenkeldreieck n femoral (Scarpa's) triangle
Schenkelhals m femoral neck, neck of the femur
Schenkelhalsfraktur f femoral neck fracture
Schenkelhalsnagel m hip (femoral neck) nail
Schenkelhalsnagelung f hip nailing
Schenkelhalsplatte f femoral neck plate
Schenkelhalsschraube f hip (femoral neck) screw
Schenkelkopf m femoral head, head of the femur
Schenkelkranzarterie f/**mediale** medial femoral circumflex artery

~/seitliche lateral femoral circumflex artery
Schenkelkranzvene f/mediale medial femoral circumflex vein
Schenkelmuskel m muscle of the thigh, crural muscle
~/äußerer vastus lateralis muscle
~/gerader rectus femoris muscle
~/innerer vastus medialis muscle
~/mittlerer vastus intermedius muscle
~/zweiköpfiger biceps femoris [muscle]
Schenkelnerv m femoral nerve
Schenkelstrecker m/vierköpfiger quadriceps femoris [muscle], vastus [muscle]
Schenktrieb m doromania
Schere f/chirurgische surgical scissors
Scherenbiß m normal occlusion (bite)
~/eugnather neutral occlusion, neutro[o]cclusion
Scherendissektion f scissors dissection
Scherengang m scissors gait, cross-legged progression; leg scissoring
Scherfraktur f shear fracture
Scherpilzflechte f trichophytosis
Scheu f timidity; shyness
Scheuermann m s. Krankheit/Scheuermannsche
Scheuklappenhemianopsie f bitemporal hemianopsia
Schicht f layer, lamina, stratum (s.a. unter Stratum); zone ● in Schichten darstellen to tomograph (Radiologie)
~ der Großhirnrinde/multiforme layer of fusiform cells
Schichtaufnahme f s. 1. Schichtdarstellung; 2. Schichtbild
Schichtbild n tomogram, laminagram
Schichtdarstellung f tomography, laminagraphy, laminography, layer (sectional) radiography
schichten to tomograph (Radiologie)
Schichtenbildung f stratification, formation of layers
Schichtepithel n stratified epithelium
Schichtstar m lamellar (zonular) cataract
Schichtstein m alternating calculus
Schichtthrombus m stratified (mixed) thrombus
Schichtung f stratification, lamination
schichtweise layer by layer
Schiebelappen m sliding flap
Schieber m bedpan
schief oblique; wry
Schiefhals m s. Torticollis
Schiefkopf m plagiocephalus, wry-head
schiefköpfig plagiocephalic, plagiocephalous
Schiefköpfigkeit f plagiocephalia
schiefliegend oblique; transverse
Schielamblyopie f strabismic (strabismal) amblyopia
Schielauge n squinting (strabismic) eye, cross eye, loxophthalmus
Schielbehandlung f durch Muskeltraining orthoptics
Schielbrille f strabismus spectacles
Schielchirurgie f strabismus surgery
schielen to squint

Schielen n squint, strabism[us], cast, heterotropia (s. a. unter Strabismus)
~/beidseitiges bilateral squint, binocular strabismus
~/einseitiges monolateral (unilateral) squint, monocular (unilocular) strabismus
~/latentes latent squint (deviation), dynamic strabismus, heterophoria
~/rotierendes cyclophoria (bei abgedecktem Auge); cyclotropia, permanent (essential) cyclophoria (bei offenem Auge)
schielend squinting, strabismic, strabismal
Schielhaken m squint (strabismus) hook
Schielkapsel f occluder
Schielmesser n strabotome, strabismus knife
Schielmeßgerät n strabometer, strabismometer
Schieloperation f strabotomy, squint (strabismus) operation
Schielverband m occluder
Schielwinkel m strabismus (deviation) angle, angle of squint
Schielwinkelmesser m strab[ism]ometer
Schielwinkelmessung f strab[ism]ometry
Schienbein n shinbone, tibia, cnemis, shank
Schienbein... s. a. Tibia...
Schienbeinarterie f tibial artery
~/hintere posterior tibial artery
~/hintere rückläufige posterior recurrent tibial artery
~/vordere anterior tibial artery
~/vordere rückläufige anterior recurrent tibial artery
Schienbeinfraktur f tibial fracture, fracture of the tibia
Schienbeingelenkknorren m/äußerer lateral condyle of the tibia
~/innerer medial condyle of the tibia
Schienbeinkante f shin, ridge of the tibia
~/mittlere medial border of the tibia
Schienbeinmuskel m tibial muscle, tibialis [muscle]
~/hinterer tibialis posterior [muscle]
~/vorderer tibialis anterior [muscle]
Schienbeinnerv m tibial (medial popliteal) nerve
Schienbeinschaft m tibial shaft, shaft of the tibia
Schienbeinschmerz m tibialgia, pain in the shinbone; painful shin
Schienbeinvene f tibial vein
~/hintere posterior tibial vein
~/vordere anterior tibial vein
Schienbeinvorderkante f shin, tibial crest
Schiene f splint
~/Magnusonsche Magnuson splint (zur Ruhigstellung von Oberarmbrüchen)
~/Volkmannsche Volkmann's splint (zur Knochenbruchlagerung)
schienen to splint, to fix splints, to apply a splint (z. B. einen Bruch)
Schienenhülsenapparat m splint apparatus
Schienung f splinting, splint-fixation, splintage
Schießscheibenzelle f target (hat) cell, pessary corpuscle (Erythrozytenform)

Schießscheibenzellenanämie f Cooley's (target cell) anaemia, Mediterranean anaemia (disease), erythroblastic anaemia
Schiffsarzt m ship surgeon, ship's doctor
Schiffslazarett n ship's hospital, sick bay
schildartig scutulate, scutate
Schilddrüse f thyroid [gland] ● **die ~ entfernen** to thyroidectomize ● **durch die ~** transthyroid ● **ohne ~** s. schilddrüsenlos ● **von der ~ ausgehend** thyr[e]ogenic, thyrogenous
~/getrocknete desiccated thyroid; thyroid [extract]
Schilddrüsen... s. a. Thyreo...
Schilddrüsenabhängigkeit f thyrotropism
Schilddrüsenabszeß m thyroid abscess
Schilddrüsenadenom n/**makrofollikuläres** macrofollicular adenoma
~/mikrofollikuläres microfollicular adenoma
~/toxisches toxic goitre
Schilddrüsenaplasie f thyroaplasia
Schilddrüsenarterie f thyroid artery
~/obere superior thyroid artery
~/untere inferior thyroid artery
~/unterste unpaare lowest thyroid artery
Schilddrüsenchirurgie f thyroid surgery
Schilddrüsendivertikel n thyroid diverticulum
Schilddrüsenentfernung f thyroidectomy
~/halbseitige hemithyroidectomy
~/subtotale subtotal (near-total) thyroidectomy
Schilddrüsenentzündung f thyroiditis, thyroadenitis, inflammation of the thyroid [gland] *(Zusammensetzungen s. unter Thyreoiditis)*
Schilddrüsenerkrankung f thyropathy, disease of the thyroid, thyroid disease; thyrosis
Schilddrüsenfollikel m thyroid follicle
Schilddrüsenfollikellumen n thyroid follicular lumen
Schilddrüsenfunktion f thyroid function (activity)
Schilddrüsenfunktionsstörung f dysthyroidism, thyrosis
Schilddrüsenfunktionstest m thyroid function test
Schilddrüsengift n thyroidotoxin
Schilddrüsenhaken m thyroid [gland] retractor
Schilddrüsenheber m levator glandulae thyroideae [muscle]
schilddrüsenhemmend antithyroid
Schilddrüsenhormon n thyroid hormone
Schilddrüsenhormonbehandlung f thyrotherapy, thyroidization
Schilddrüsenhormonbiosynthese f thyroid hormone biosynthesis
Schilddrüsenhormonmangel m athyreosis, athyroidism
Schilddrüsenhormonstoffwechsel m thyroid hormone metabolism
Schilddrüsenhormonsubstitution f thyroid replacement
Schilddrüsenhypertrophie f hypertrophy of the thyroid
Schilddrüseninzision f thyro[ido]tomy, incision into the thyroid [gland]

Schilddrüsenisthmus m thyroid isthmus, isthmus of the thyroid [gland] *(Verbindungsstück der beiden Schilddrüsenlappen)*
Schilddrüsenisthmusresektion f isthmectomy; median strumectomy
Schilddrüsenkachexie f thyroprivous (strumiprival) cachexia
Schilddrüsenkapsel f thyroid capsule
Schilddrüsenkapselentzündung f perithyroiditis
Schilddrüsenkarzinom n thyroid carcinoma, cancer of the thyroid [body], malignant goitre
~/papilläres papilliferous carcinoma of the thyroid
Schilddrüsenknoten m thyroid nodule
Schilddrüsenkolloid n thyrocolloid
Schilddrüsenkörper m thyroid body, body of the thyroid [gland]
Schilddrüsenkrise f thyroid crisis
Schilddrüsenläppchen n lobule of the thyroid gland
Schilddrüsenlappen m [lateral] thyroid lobe, lobe of the thyroid [gland]
schilddrüsenlos thyroprival, thyroprivic, thyroprivous, athyreotic; thyreoidectomized
Schilddrüsenlosigkeit f athyreosis, athyroidism
Schilddrüsennervengeflecht n thyroid plexus
Schilddrüsennormalfunktion f euthyroidism
Schilddrüsenophthalmopathie f thyroid ophthalmopathy
Schilddrüsenparenchym n thyroid parenchyma
Schilddrüsenpolunterbindung f pole ligation
Schilddrüsenpräparat n thyroid [gland] preparation, thyroid
Schilddrüsenprotein n thyroprotein
Schilddrüsenregion f thyroid region
Schilddrüsensarkom n sarcomatous goitre
Schilddrüsenseitenlappen m lateral thyroid lobe
Schilddrüsensenkung f thyroptosis
schilddrüsenstimulierend thyrotrophic
Schilddrüsenstörung f dysthyroidism, thyroid dysfunction
Schilddrüsensubstitution f thyroid replacement
Schilddrüsensuppression f thyroid suppression
Schilddrüsenszintigramm n thyroid scintigram (scan)
Schilddrüsenszintigraphie f thyroid scintigraphy (scanning)
Schilddrüsentätigkeit f thyroid activity ● **die ~ steuernd** thyrotrophic
Schilddrüsentumor m tumour of the thyroid, thyroncus
Schilddrüsenüberfunktion f hyperthyroidism, hyperthyreosis, hyperthyroidosis, Basedow's disease; thyrotoxicosis, thyrotoxaemia, thyroid storm
Schilddrüsen- und Nebenschilddrüsenentfernung f[/operative] excision of the thyroid and parathyroids, thyroparathyroidectomy
Schilddrüsenunterfunktion f hypothyroidism, hypothyr[e]osis, thyroid insufficiency, subthyroidism
Schilddrüsenvene f thyroid vein

~/**mittlere** middle thyroid vein
~/**obere** superior thyroid vein
~/**untere** inferior thyroid vein
Schilddrüsenvergrößerung f 1. enlargement of the thyroid, thyromegaly; 2. s. Struma
Schilddrüsenzungenfistel f thyroglossal duct fistula
Schilddrüsenzungengang m thyroglossal duct
Schilddrüsenzungengangzyste f thyroglossal [duct] cyst
schildförmig scutulate, scutiform; thyr[e]oid
Schildknorpel m thyroid cartilage, scutum
Schildknorpeldurchtrennung f[/**operative**] thyro[chondro]tomy
Schildknorpelhorn n/**unteres** inferior horn (cornu) of the thyroid cartilage
Schildknorpelinzisur f/**untere** inferior thyroid notch
Schildknorpel-Kehldeckel-Muskel m thyroepiglottic muscle
Schildknorpelmesser n thyrotome
Schildknorpelspaltung f/**operative** thyro[chondro]tomy
Schildknorpel-Zungenbein-Band n thyrohyoid ligament
Schildknorpel-Zungenbein-Muskel m thyrohyoid muscle
Schillern n opalescence (z. B. des Urins)
schillernd opalescent
Schilling-Test m Schilling test (Absorptionstest für Vitamin B_{12})
Schimmel m mould; mildew
schimmelbelegt mucoriferous, mouldy
Schimmelbusch-Maske f Schimmelbusch's mask (für Äthernarkose)
Schimmelpilz m mould [fungus]
Schimmelpilzerkrankung f mucormycosis, hyphomycosis
schimmernd opalescent
schimmlig mouldy, mucoriferous
Schinkenmilz f waxy (lardaceous) spleen
Schiötz-Tonometer n Schiötz tonometer
Schipperfraktur f chip (clay-shoveller's) fracture
Schirmbildaufnahme f photofluorogram
Schirmbilddarstellung f [photo]fluorography, photoroentgenography
Schistenzephalie f schistencephalia, schizencephaly
Schistoglossie f schistoglossia; bifid (cleft) tongue
Schistomelie f schistomelia; cleft extremity
Schistomelus m schistomelus (Mißgeburt)
Schistoprosopie f schistoprosopia, congenital fissure of the face; cleft face
Schistoprosopus m schistoprosopus (Mißgeburt)
Schistosoma n schistosome, blood fluke, bilharzia worm
~ **haematobium** Schistosoma haematobium (Erreger der Blasenbilharziose)
~ **japonicum** Schistosoma japonicum (Erreger der Katayamakrankheit)
~ **Mansoni** Schistosoma mansoni (Erreger der Darmschistosomiasis)
schistosomal schistosomal
Schistosomenbefall m s. Schistosomiasis
Schistosomendermatitis f schistosome dermatitis, cercarian (cercarial) dermatitis, water (swimmer's) itch
Schistosomenmittel n schistosomacide, schistosomacidal agent
schistosomentötend schistosomacidal
schistosomenwirksam antischistosomal
Schistosomenzerkarie f schistosomal cercaria
Schistosomenzystitis f schistosome cystitis
Schistosomiasis f schistosomiasis, haemic distomiasis, bilharziasis, bilharzial lesion
~/**asiatische (hepatolienale)** s. ~ japonica
~/**intestinale** intestinal (Manson's, visceral) schistosomiasis, Egyptian splenomegaly (durch Schistosoma mansoni)
~ **japonica** oriental [intestinal] schistosomiasis, Asiatic (hepatic) schistosomiasis, Katayama disease (durch Schistosoma japonicum)
~ **urogenitalis** vesical (urinary, bladder) schistosomiasis (durch Schistosoma haematobium)
~/**viszerale** s. ~/intestinale
Schistosomie f s. Schistozölie
Schistosomus m schistosomus (Mißgeburt)
Schistothorax m schistothorax, congenital fissure of the chest; cleft chest
schistozephal[isch] schistocephalic
Schistozephalus m schistocephalus (Mißgeburt)
Schistozölie f schistocoelia, coelosoma, congenital fissure of the abdomen; cleft belly, schistosomia
Schistozystis f schistocystis
Schistozyt m schistocyte, schizocyte, burr cell (Erythrozytenfragment)
Schistozytose f schistocytosis (Schistozytenvermehrung im Blut)
schizoaffektiv schizoaffective
Schizoblepharie f schizoblepharia
Schizogenese f schizogenesis, schizogony, reproduction by fission
schizognath schizognathous
Schizognathismus m schizognathism
schizogon schizogonic
Schizogonie f 1. schizogony (z. B. der Malariaerreger); 2. s. Schizogenese
~/**exoerythrozytäre** exoerythrocytic schizogony
schizoid schizoid
Schizoider m schizoid
Schizoidismus m schizoidism, schizoidia
Schizomykose f schizomycosis
Schizomyzet m schizomycete
Schizont m schizont (Entwicklungsstadium der Malariaerreger)
Schizontenmittel n schizontocide [agent], schizonticidal drug (in der Schizontenphase wirksames Malariamittel)
schizontentötend schizontocide
Schizonychie f schizonychia, splitting of the nails
Schizophasie f schizophasia; word salad

schizophren

schizophren schizophrenic
schizophren-affektiv schizoaffective
Schizophrener *m* schizophreniac, split personality
Schizophrenie *f* schizophrenia, schizophrenic reaction
~/**katathyme** catathymia, catathymic type of schizophrenia
~/**katatone** catatonia, katatonia, catatonic type of schizophrenia *(muskelstarre Form)*
~/**kindliche** childhood type of schizophrenia
~/**reaktive** reactive schizophrenia
schizophrenieartig schizophrenia-like
schizothym schizothymic
Schizothymie *f* schizothymia; schizoidism
Schizotrichie *f* schizotrichia, splitting of the hairs
Schlackenstoff *m* waste product (material)
● **durch Schlackenstoffe bedingt** spodogenous
Schlaf *m* sleep, somnus
~/**fester** sound sleep
~/**kurzer** nap
~/**leichter** slumber
~/**paradoxer** rapid-eye-movement sleep, REM sleep
~/**suggestiver** hypnotic sleep
~/**tiefer** deep (heavy) sleep
schlafähnlich sleep-like; hypnoid[al]
Schlafanfall *m* narcolepsy, narcoleptic attack
● **von Schlafanfällen betroffen** narcoleptic
Schlafangst *f* hypnophobia
Schlafapnoe *f* sleep apnoea
Schlafbedürfnis *n* sleep requirement
Schlafbehandlung *f* narcosis therapy, hypnotherapy; therapeutical sleep
schlafbewirkend hypnagogic
schlafbringend hypnogen[et]ic, hypnogenous, somniferous, hypnic
Schläfe *f* temple ● **über der ~** supratemporal
● **unterhalb der ~** subtemporal
Schläfenabstand *m* temporal diameter
Schläfenarterie *f*/**hintere tiefe** deep posterior temporal artery
~/**mittlere** middle temporal artery
~/**oberflächliche** superficial temporal artery
~/**tiefe vordere** deep anterior temporal artery
Schläfenbein *n* temporal bone
Schläfenbeindurchmesser *m* bitemporal diameter
Schläfenbeinfibrosarkom *n* fibrosarcoma of the temporal bone
Schläfenbeinfraktur *f* fracture of the temporal bone
Schläfenbeinpyramide *f* petrous part of the temporal bone
Schläfenbeinschuppe *f* temporal squama
Schläfen-Brücken-Gegend *f* temporopontine region
Schläfengegend *f* temporal region [of the skull], temporal area
Schläfengrube *f* temporal fossa
Schläfenknochen *m s.* Schläfenbein
Schläfenlappen *m* temporal lobe ● **durch den ~** transtemporal

Schläfenlappenepilepsie *f* temporal lobe epilepsy
Schläfenlappenfurche *f*/**mittlere** middle temporal sulcus
~/**untere** inferior temporal sulcus
Schläfenlappenspitze *f* temporal pole
Schläfenlappenvorfall *m* temporal lobe hernia
Schläfenlappenwindung *f*/**mittlere** middle temporal gyrus
Schläfenlinie *f* temporal line
Schläfenmuskel *m* temporalis [muscle]
Schläfen-Scheitel-Muskel *m* temporoparietalis muscle
Schläfensehfeld *n* temporal field
Schläfenvene *f*/**mittlere** middle temporal vein
~/**oberflächliche** superficial temporal vein
~/**tiefe** deep temporal vein
Schläfenwindung *f*/**obere** superior temporal convolution (gyrus)
~/**untere** inferior temporal convolution (gyrus)
Schlafepilepsie *f* sleep epilepsy, narcolepsy
schlaferzeugend hypnogen[et]ic, hypnogenous, hypnotic, soporific, somnifacient, somnific, inducing (causing, promoting) sleep
Schlaferzeugung *f* hypnogenesis
schlaff flaccid, flabby, loose *(z. B. Haut)*; relaxed *(z. B. Muskel)*; atonic *(z. B. Muskeltonus)*; torpid, lax *(träge)*; lethargic, languid *(apathisch)*
● **~ werden** to relax *(z. B. ein Muskel)*
Schlaffhaut *f* loose skin; dermatochalasis, looseness of the skin
Schlaffheit *f* flaccidity, flabbiness, looseness *(z. B. der Haut)*; relaxation *(z. B. eines Muskels)*; atonia, atonicity *(z. B. des Muskeltonus)*; torpidity, laxity *(Trägheit)*; lethargy, languor *(Apathie)*
Schlafgestörter *m* somnopathist; insomniac
schlafhemmend ant[i]hypnotic, hypnapagogic, agrypnotic, antilethargic
Schlafkrankheit *f* sleeping sickness, trypanosomiasis, trypanosom[at]osis, trypanosome fever *(Zusammensetzungen s. unter Trypanosomiasis)*
~/**europäische** *s.* Krankheit/Economosche
Schlafkur *f* sleeping cure, hypnotherapy
Schlaflähmung *f* sleep (predormital) paralysis, night palsy *(infolge Druckschädigung eines Nerven)*
schlaflos sleepless, wakeful; restless
Schlafloser *m* insomniac
Schlaflosigkeit *f* sleeplessness, wakefulness, insomnia, vigilance
Schlafmittel *n* somnifacient [agent], soporific, hypnagogue [agent], hypnotic, narcotic
Schlafmuster *n* sleep pattern
Schlafredner *m* somniloquist
schläfrig sleepy, drowsy; somnolent; soporose, soporific
Schläfrigkeit *f* sleepiness, drowsiness; sopor; somnolence, somnolentia *(leichterer Grad der Bewußtseinsherabsetzung)*
~/**abnorme** hypnolepsy

~/**erhöhte** hypersomnolence
Schlafschmerz *m* hypnalgia
Schlafschwäche *f* hyposomnia
Schlafstörung *f* sleep disturbance, dyssomnia, somnopathy, hypnophrenosis; disturbed sleep
Schlafsucht *f* hypersomnia; lethargic lethargy
~/**anfallsweise** narcolepsy
schlafsüchtig *f* somnolent, narcoleptic, lethargic
Schlaftablette *f* sleeping tablet
Schlaftherapie *f* sleep (narcosis) therapy, hypnotherapy; therapeutical sleep
Schlaftiefe *f* depth of sleep
schlafverhindernd hypnapagogic
schlafvertreibend somnifugous, agrypnotic
Schlaf-Wach-Rhythmus *m* circadian (sleeping-waking) rhythm
schlafwandeln to somnambulate
Schlafwandeln *n s.* Somnambulismus
Schlag *m* 1. beat, pulsion; ictus *(z. B. des Herzens)*; 2. stroke, apoplexy *(s.a.* Schlaganfall*)*; blow
Schlagader *f* artery, arteria, a. *(Zusammensetzungen s. unter* Arteria*)*
Schlagader... *s.a.* Arterien...
Schlagaderblutung *f* artery haemorrhage (bleeding)
Schlagaderfibrose *f* arteriofibrosis
Schlagaderinnenhaut *f* artery endothelium
Schlagadernekrose *f* arterionecrosis
Schlagaderthrombose *f* artery thrombosis
Schlagadervereng[er]ung *f* arteriostenosis, arteriarctia
Schlagaderverlegung *f* artery obstruction
Schlagaderverletzung *f* artery trauma (injury)
Schlagaderverstopfung *f* obstruction of an artery, arterial obstruction
Schlaganfall *m* [cerebral] apoplexy, [apoplectic] stroke, cerebrovascular accident, cerebral [vascular] accident, cerebral infarct[ion]
schlaganfallartig apoplectiform, apoplectoid
schlagen to pulse, to pulsate *(z. B. der Puls)*; to throb *(heftig)*; to beat, to palpitate *(z. B. das Herz)*
Schlagen *n* pulsation *(z. B. des Pulses)*; beating, [heart] palpitation
schlagend pulsatile, pulsating; beating, palpitating
Schlagvolumen *n* [heart] stroke volume, cardiac output, discharge volume
Schlagvolumenhochdruck *m* stroke-volume hypertension
Schlagvolumenmessung *f* ballistocardiography
Schlamm *m* mud, fango
Schlammbad *n* mud bath
Schlammfieber *n* swamp (slime, mud) fever, harvest (field, water) fever *(Infektionskrankheit durch Leptospira grippotyphosa)*
Schlammkur *f* pelotherapy
Schlammpackung *f* mud (fango) pack
Schlammtherapie *f* fango therapy, pelotherapy
Schlangenbiß *m* snake bite
Schlangenbißvergiftung *f* ophidism, ophidiasis, snake-bite poisoning, envenomization

Schlangenfurcht *f* ophidiophobia
schlangenfürchtend ophiophobe
Schlangengegengift *n* antivenin, antivenene
Schlangengift *n* snake venom, venin, venene
Schlangengiftantikörper *m* antivenin, antivenene
Schlangengiftintoxikation *f s.* Schlangenbißvergiftung
Schlangenlinienpsoriasis *f* serpiginous psoriasis
Schlangenserum *n* antisnakebite (antivenomous) serum, antivenene
schlankfingrig leptodactylous
Schlankmuskel *m* gracilis muscle
schlankwüchsig leptosomatic
Schlankwüchsiger *m* leptosome
schlankzehig leptodactylous
Schlauch *m* tube, tubule, tubulus
~/**Müller-Abbottscher** Müller-Abbott tube *(zum Absaugen von Darminhalt aus Magen und Dünndarm)*
~/**muskulomembranöser** musculomembranous tube *(z. B. Pharynx)*
schlauchartig tubular; syringoid
Schlauchdrain *n(m)* rubber-tube drain
Schlauchdrainage *f* [rubber-]tube drainage
schlauchförmig tubular
Schlauchhörrohr *n* phonendoscope
Schlauchklemme *f* tubing clamp (forceps)
Schlauchstethoskop *n* binaural stethoscope
Schlauchwurm *m* nemathelminth
Schlauchwurmbefall *m* nemathelminthiasis
schlechtschmeckend bad-tasting, unpalatable
schlechtsitzend ill-fitting *(z. B. Gipsverband)*
schleichend slow *(Vorgang)*; chronic, insidious *(z. B. eine Krankheit)*; lingering *(z. B. Fieber)*
Schleife *f* loop; ansa, lemniscus *(Anatomie)*
~/**Henlesche** Henle's loop, loop of Henle *(Teil des Hauptstücks der Nierenkanälchen)*
Schleifenbahn *f s.* Lemniscus
schleifenförmig loop-shaped; ansate, ansiform
Schleifenkreuzung *f* decussation of the lemnisci, sensory decussation
Schleifstein *m*/**zahnärztlicher** carborundum wheel stone
Schleim *m* mucus, phlegm, mucilage, mucilago
~/**eitriger** mucopus
~/**zäher** viscid mucus
Schleimabgang *m* mucous discharge; proctorrhoea *(durch den After)*
schleimabsondernd mucous, muciparous, secreting phlegm (mucus)
Schleimabsonderung *f* myxiosis, secretion of mucus; laryngorrhoea *(aus dem Kehlkopf)*
Schleimansammlung *f* **im Uterus** mucometria
~ **in der Vagina** mucocolpos
~ **in einem Hohlraum** mucocele
schleimartig mucous, muc[in]oid, myxoid, muciform, pseudomucinous
schleimauflösend muc[in]olytic
Schleimausfluß *m* **aus der Scheide/weißer** leucorrhoea
schleimausscheidend muciferous

schleimbedeckt

schleimbedeckt mucous, covered with mucus
Schleimbehandlung f mucin therapy
Schleimbelag m mucous coating
Schleimbeutel m [synovial] bursa
Schleimbeutelentfernung f[/operative] bursectomy
Schleimbeutelentzündung f bursitis, bursal synovitis, inflammation of a bursa *(Zusammensetzungen s. unter Bursitis)*
Schleimbeuteleröffnung f[/operative] bursotomy
Schleimbeutelkrankheit f bursopathy
Schleimbeutelstein m bursolith
schleimbildend mucigenous, muciferous, mucous
Schleimbildung f myxopoiesis, formation of mucus
Schleimbildungsschwäche f myxasthenia
Schleimdrüse f mucous (muciparous) gland
Schleimdrüsenentzündung f myxadenitis, inflammation of a mucous gland
Schleimdrüsengeschwulst f myx[o]adenoma, adenomyxoma
Schleimepithel n mucous epithelium
Schleimfäden mpl [mucous] threads, shreds *(z. B. im Urin)*
Schleimfluß m myxorrhoea, mucorrhoea, flow of mucus
Schleimgeschwulst f s. Myxom
Schleimgewebe n mucous tissue
schleimhaltig mucous, muciferous, muculent, mucus-filled
Schleimhaut f mucosa, mucous membrane *(s.a. unter Mucosa)* ● **unter der ~** submucosal, submucous
~/verdickte pachymucosa
Schleimhautanästhesie f surface anaesthesia (analgesia)
Schleimhautauskleidung f mucosal lining
Schleimhautausschlag m enanthem[a], eisanthema, endermosis
Schleimhautausstülpung f mucosal herniation; diverticulum
Schleimhautaustrocknung f myxasthenia
Schleimhautbeteiligung f mucosal involvement
Schleimhautdefekt m erosion
Schleimhauteinblutung f bleeding into mucous membranes
Schleimhautentzündung f mucositis, inflammation of the mucosa, catarrh
Schleimhautfalte f mucosal fold
Schleimhautgeschwulst f myxoedema *(bei Schilddrüsenunterfunktion)*
Schleimhautgrenze f mucocutaneous border
Schleimhaut-Haut-Übergang m mucocutaneous junction
schleimhäutig mucomembranous
Schleimhautleishmaniasis f/**südamerikanische** South American leishmaniasis, mucocutaneous leishmaniasis, espundia, bouba
Schleimhautmelanom n mucosal melanoma
Schleimhautmikrokolonie f mucosal microcolony

Schleimhaut-Muskel-Naht f mucous membrane muscle suture
Schleimhautnekrose f mucosal necrosis
Schleimhautoberfläche f mucosal surface
Schleimhautödem n mucosal oedema
Schleimhautpemphigoid n mucosal pemphigoid
Schleimhautpemphigus m mucous membrane pemphigus
Schleimhautpenetration f mucosal penetration
Schleimhaut-Periost-Lappen m mucoperiosteal flap *(bei plastischer Operation)*
Schleimhautpolyp m mucous polypus
Schleimhautreizung f irritation of the mucosa
Schleimhautreliefröntgen[kontrast]darstellung f mucosal relief roentgenography
Schleimhauttasche f mucosal pocket *(s. a. Divertikel)*
Schleimhauttransplantat n mucosal graft
Schleimhautüberzug m mucosal lining
Schleimhautveränderung f mucosal change
Schleimhautverdickung f pachymucosa
Schleimhautvorfall m mucosal prolapse
schleimhemmend mucostatic
Schleimhülle f mucosity
schleimig mucous, mucid, mucilaginous, phlegmatic
schleimig-blutig mucohaemorrhagic, mucosanguineous
schleimig-eitrig puromucous, mucopurulent
schleimig-fibrös mucofibrous
schleimig-flockig mucoflocculent
schleimig-serös mucoserous
schleimlösend 1. muc[in]olytic; 2. expectorant
Schleimmangel m oligoblennia
Schleimpfropf m mucous (cervical) plug
Schleimpilze mpl myxomycetes
schleimreich muculent
Schleimretentionszyste f mucocele
Schleimsekretion f mucous secretion
~/fehlende amyxorrhoea
schleimsezernierend muciferous, secreting mucus
Schleim- und Eiterzyste f mucopyocele
Schleimzelle f mucous (mucin) cell
Schleimzellenchondrom n myxochondroma *(Mischgeschwulst)*
Schleimzellenfibrom n myxofibroma *(Mischgeschwulst aus Schleim- und kollagenem Bindegewebe)*
Schleimzellenlipom n myxolipoma *(Mischgeschwulst)*
Schleimzylinder m mucous cast *(im Urin)*
Schleimzyste f muc[in]ous cyst
Schlepperprotein n carrier protein
schleudern to centrifuge, to centrifugate
schließen to close *(z. B. eine Wunde)*; to suture *(eine Naht)*; to occlude *(Zähne)*
Schließmuskel m s. Sphincter
Schließmuskel... s. a. Sphinkter...
Schließmuskeldurchtrennung f[/operative] sphincterotomy
Schließmuskelentfernung f[/operative] sphincterectomy

Schließmuskelentzündung f sphincteritis, inflammation of a sphincter
Schließmuskelerschlaffung f sphincteric relaxation
Schließmuskelkrampf m sphincterism, spasm of the sphincter ani
Schließmuskelrekonstruktion f sphincteroplasty
Schließmuskelschluß m sphincteric contraction, sphincter constriction
Schließmuskelschmerz m sphincteralgia, pain in a sphincter
Schließmuskelschwäche f sphincter weakness
Schlinge f 1. snare, loop *(Instrument)*; 2. s. Schleife
~/Glissonsche Glisson's sling (suspension apparatus)
Schlingen n deglutition, [act of] swallowing
Schlingenbildung f kinking *(z. B. des Darms)*
Schlingendreher m knot tier; wire twister
schlingenförmig s. schleifenförmig
Schlingeninstrument n snare
Schlingenkatheter m sling catheter
Schlittenmikrotom n sliding microtome
Schlitz m slit; fissure, cleft
Schlitzbrille f stenopaeic spectacles
Schlitzmesser n lancet
Schlitztuch n split towel *(bei Operationen)*
Schlottergelenk n flail joint
schlottern to tremble
Schluckauf m s. Singultus
Schluckbeschwerden pl [pharyngeal] dysphagia, difficulty in swallowing
schlucken to swallow
Schlucken n [act of] swallowing, deglutition
~/schmerzhaftes odynophagia
Schlucken m s. Singultus
Schluckimpfstoff m oral vaccine
~/Sabinscher Sabin oral poliomyelitis vaccine
Schluckimpfung f oral vaccination
Schluckreflex m swallowing (deglutition) reflex
Schluckschmerz m odynophagia, pain on deglutition; pharyngeal discomfort (pain)
Schluckstörung f dysphagia
Schluckunfähigkeit f aphagia, aglutition
Schlund m pharynx, throat, throttle, fauces; gullet; oesophagus
Schlund... s. a. Pharynx... und Rachen...
Schlundarterie f pharyngeal artery
~/aufsteigende ascending pharyngeal artery
Schlundbogen m pharyngeal arch
~/erster oral arch
Schlundbougie f oesophagus bougie
Schlundbucht f piriform recess (sinus)
Schlunderkrankung f pharyngopathy, disease of the pharynx
Schlundhöhle f cavity of the pharynx
Schlund-Kopf-Gaumen-Muskel m palatopharyngeus [muscle], staphyl[in]opharyngeus [muscle]
Schlundkopftubenmuskel m salpingopharyngeus [muscle]
Schlundkopfvene f pharyngeal vein
Schlundkrampf m pharyngospasm, pharyngism, spasm of the pharyngeal muscles
Schlundkrebs m cancer of throat
Schlundlähmung f pharyngoplegia, pharyngo[para]lysis, paralysis of the pharyngeal muscles, lemoparalysis
Schlundmuskulatur f pharyngeal musculature (muscles)
Schlundnervengeflecht n pharyngeal plexus
Schlundrohr n oesophageal tube
Schlundschnürer m constrictor pharyngis [muscle], constrictor muscle of the pharynx
~/mittlerer middle constrictor pharyngis [muscle]
~/oberer superior constrictor pharyngis [muscle]
~/unterer inferior constrictor pharyngis [muscle], infraconstrictor, laryngopharyngeus [muscle]
Schlundspalte f branchial cleft
Schlundtasche f pharyngeal (branchial, visceral) pouch
~/laterale Rosenmüller's (lateral pharyngeal) fossa *(hinter dem Tubenwulst)*
Schlundtrockenheit f pharyngoxerosis
Schlundveren[er]ung f pharyngostenia, pharyngoperistole
Schluß m closure *(z. B. der Herzklappe)*
Schlußbiß m, **Schlußbißstellung** f intercuspation, intercusping, occlusion *(der Zähne)*
Schlüsselbein n collarbone, clavicle, clavicula
● über dem ~ supraclavicular ● unter dem ~ subclavian, subclavicular
Schlüsselbein... s. a. Klavikula...
Schlüsselbeinarterie f subclavian artery
~/linke left subclavian artery
~/rechte right subclavian artery
Schlüsselbeindurchtrennung f[/operative] clavic[ul]otomy, cleidotomy
Schlüsselbeinentfernung f[/operative] claviculectomy
Schlüsselbeingrube f/obere supraclavicular region
~/untere infraclavicular region
Schlüsselbeinheber m levator claviculae [muscle], omocervicalis [muscle]
Schlüsselbeinosteomyelitis f osteomyelitis of the clavicle
Schlüsselbeinscheingelenk n clavicle pseudarthrosis
Schlüsselbeinunterfläche f inferior surface of the clavicle
Schlüsselbeinvene f subclavian vein
~/linke left subclavian vein
~/rechte right subclavian vein
Schlüsselbeinverrenkung f clavicle dislocation (luxation)
Schlußfähigkeit f competence
Schlußunfähigkeit f incompetence, insufficiency; regurgitation
schmächtig leptosomatic, asthenic *(Körperbau)* *(s. a. schmal)*
schmal slender *(schlank)*; thin *(dünn)*; narrow *(eng)*
schmalbeckig leptopelvic

schmalfingrig

schmalfingrig leptodactylous
Schmalgesicht *n* leptoprosope
schmalgesichtig leptoprosopic, cryptozygous
Schmalgesichtigkeit *f* leptoprosopia, narrowness of the face
Schmalkopf *m* leptocephalus, stenocephalus
schmalköpfig leptocephalic, leptocephalous, stenocephalous
Schmalköpfigkeit *f* leptocephalia, stenocephalia, smallness of the head
Schmallippigkeit *f* microcheilia, microlabia
schmalnasig leptorrhine
schmalwüchsig leptosomatic, asthenic
Schmalwüchsiger *m* leptosome
schmalzahnig leptodontous
schmalzehig leptodactylous
Schmarotzer *m s.* Parasit
Schmauchhof *m* contact ring *(einer Schußwunde)*
schmecken to taste
Schmeckfähigkeit *f* degustation
Schmelz *m* [dental] enamel, adamantine
Schmelz... *s. a.* Zahnschmelz...
Schmelz-Dentin-Grenze *f* amelodental (dentoenamel) junction
Schmelzfaser *f s.* Schmelzprisma
Schmelzgeschwulst *f* enameloma, enamel drop
Schmelzhaube *f* enamel cap
Schmelzhäutchen *n* enamel cuticle
Schmelzhypoplasie *f* hypoplasia of enamel
Schmelzlamelle *f* enamel lamella
Schmelzleiste *f* enamel (dentogingival) lamina, dental ridge
Schmelznische *f* enamel niche (crypt)
Schmelzorgan *n* enamel (dental) organ
Schmelzperle *f* enamel pearl
Schmelzprisma *n* enamel prism (column, fibre)
Schmelzpulpa *f* enamel pulp
Schmelzzelle *f s.* Ameloblast
Schmelzzellengeschwulst *f s.* Ameloblastom
Schmelz-Zement-Grenze *f* cervical line *(des Zahns)*
Schmerz *m* pain, dolor, ache ● **Schmerzen bereiten** to ache, to cause (produce) pain ● **Schmerzen haben** to be in pain, to have [a] pain
~/**anhaltender** continuous pain
~/**blitzartiger** lightning pain
~/**bohrender** boring (terebrating) pain
~/**brennender** burning pain
~/**dumpfer** dull pain
~/**einschießender** shooting (fulgurant) pain
~/**fortgeleiteter** referred (heterotopic) pain
~/**heftiger** severe (violent, sharp) pain, megalgia
~ **in mehreren Gelenken** polyarthralgia
~ **in mehreren Muskeln** polymyalgia
~/**klopfender** throbbing pain
~/**krampfartiger** spasmodic pain; colic
~/**lanzinierender** lancinating pain
~/**psychischer** psychogenic (hysteric) pain, psychalgia, phrenalgia, mental pain
~/**reflektorischer** referred (reflex) pain

~/**scharfer** sharp pain
~/**schneidender** cutting (stabbing) pain
~/**stechender** darting pain, stitch
~/**wandernder** wandering pain
Schmerzangst *f* odynophobia
Schmerzattacke *f* attack of pain
schmerzauslösend dolorogenic, algogenic, algesiogenic
schmerzausschaltend anaesthetic
Schmerzausschaltung *f* elimination of pain; anaesthetization; anaesthesia, narcosis *(s. a. unter* Anästhesie*)*
~ **durch Kälteanwendung** cryoanaesthesia
~/**psychische** psychoanalgesia
Schmerzausschaltungsmittel *n* anaesthetic [agent]
Schmerzausstrahlung *f* radiation of pain
schmerzbereitend odynopean, causing pain, algesiogenic, algogenic
schmerzbringend dolorogenic
schmerzempfindlich sensitive to pain, algesic
Schmerzempfindlichkeit *f* pain sensitivity, algesia, algaesthesia
Schmerzempfindlichkeitsmessung *f* algometry, algesimetry
Schmerzempfindung *f* pain sensation, sensation of pain
~/**brennende** sensation of burning pain; causalgia
~/**örtliche** top[o]algia, localized pain
Schmerzempfindungsrezeptor *m* noci[per]ceptor
Schmerzempfindungsstörung *f* dysaesthesia
schmerzen to ache, to cause (give) pain, to hurt, to smart
Schmerzen *mpl* pain, molimina *(s. a.* Schmerz*)*
~ **bei der Regelblutung** molimina menstrualia
schmerzend *s.* schmerzhaft
Schmerzerlebnis *n* experience of pain; pain sensation
schmerzfrei free from pain, painless, without pain
Schmerzfreiheit *f* analgesia, freedom from pain, anodynia
Schmerzgefühl *n s.* Schmerzempfindung
Schmerzgeilheit *f*/**aktive** active algolagnia, sadism
~/**passive** [passive] algolagnia, masochism
Schmerzgrenze *f* threshold of pain
schmerzhaft painful, sore, algetic, dolorogenic
schmerzlindernd analgetic, analg[es]ic, antalgic, relieving (alleviating) pain, anodyne, anodynous; palliative, obtundent
Schmerzlinderung *f* relief (alleviation) of pain, odynolysis
schmerzlos painless, free from pain, without pain
Schmerzlosigkeit *f* painlessness
Schmerzlust *f* pain joy
Schmerzmessung *f* odynometry
Schmerzmessungsinstrument *n* odynometer
Schmerzmittel *n* analgesic, antalgic [agent], anodyne [agent], obtundent

Schmerzpunkt m pain[ful] point
Schmerzreaktion f pain reaction
~/gesteigerte hyperpathia
Schmerzreflex m pain reflex; nociceptive reflex
Schmerzrezeptor m pain receptor; noci[per]ceptor
Schmerzschwelle f pain threshold
Schmerzsinn m pain sense
schmerzstillend analgetic, analg[es]ic, anodyne, anodynous; antineuralgic; sedative, obtundent
Schmerzstillungsmittel n s. Schmerzmittel
schmerzüberempfindlich hyperalgesic, hyperalgetic, hyperaesthetic
Schmerzüberempfindlichkeit f hyperalg[es]ia, hyperaesthesia, oxyaesthesia
schmerzunempfindlich anaesthetic, insensitive to pain; indolent
Schmerzunempfindlichkeit f alganaesthesia, analgesia, insensitivity to pain; indolence
~/halbseitige hemihypalgesia
~/natürliche anaesthesia
schmerzunterempfindlich hypalgesic, hypalgetic, hypaesthesic, hypaesthetic
Schmerzunterempfindlichkeit f hypalg[es]ia, hypaesthesia
Schmerzverminderung f odynolysis
Schmerzwollust f [passive] algolagnia, masochism
Schmetterlingsfigur f butterfly rash (patch)
Schmetterlingsflechte f butterfly lupus, [discoid] lupus erythematosus
Schmetterlingsfraktur f butterfly fracture
Schmierblutung f [vaginal] spotting
Schmierinfektion f smear infection
Schmierkur f inunction [treatment]
Schmutzessen n rhypophagy
schmutzfürchtend mysophobic
schmutzliebend mysophilic
Schnabel m s. Rostrum
Schnabelbecher m feeding cup
schnabelförmig rostrate, rostral, rostriform; coracoid
Schnabeltasse f feeding cup
Schnappatmung f gasping breathing
schnappen/nach Luft to gasp for breath
Schnapsnase f bottle nose, whisky[-rum] nose
schnarchen to snore
schnaufen to wheeze, to breathe heavily
Schnecke f cochlea *(Labyrinthteil)*
~/häutige spiral canal of the cochlea
Schneckenachse f modiolus
Schneckenachsenbasis f base of the modiolus
Schneckenendolymphe f cochlear endolymph
schneckenförmig cochleariform
Schneckengang m cochlear duct
Schneckengelenk n cochlear articulation
Schneckenkuppel f cupula of the cochlea, apex of the osseous cochlea
Schneckenloch n helicotrema *(Verbindung zwischen Pauken- und Vorhoftreppe der Schnecke)*
Schneckenrohr n spiral canal of the cochlea

Schneeblindheit f snow blindness, chionablepsy, niphablepsia, niphotyphlosis; solar photophthalmia
Schneeflockenstar m snowflake (snowstorm) cataract
Schneide f blade, edge *(des Skalpells)*
schneiden to cut, to section; to incise
Schneiden n **mit dem elektrischen Messer** thermocautery, acusection
Schneiderkrampf m tailor's cramp (spasm)
Schneidermuskel m sartorius [muscle], tailor's muscle ● **unter dem ~** subsartorial
Schneidezahn m incisor [tooth], front tooth
Schneidezähne mpl/**tonnenförmige** notched teeth
Schnelldesensibilisierung f rapid desensitization (hyposensitization) *(bei Allergie)*
Schnelldiagnose f rapid diagnosis
Schnelldiagnose-Test m rapid diagnostic test
Schnelldiagnostik f rapid diagnosis
Schnelldigitalisierung f rapid digitalization
Schnelle Medizinische Hilfe f emergency medical system
schnellend snapping *(z. B. ein Finger)*
Schnellgeburt f oxytocia, rapid childbirth, forced delivery, precipitate labour
Schnellschnittdiagnose f quick section diagnosis *(zur Tumordiagnostik)*
Schnitt m 1. cut, sectio[n]; incision *(Chirurgie)*; 2. s. Schnittwunde; 3. [micro]section *(Mikroskopie)*
~/histologischer histological section
~/McBurneyscher McBurney's incision *(bei Blinddarmentzündung)*
~/mikroskopischer microsection *(eines Gewebepräparats)*
Schnittentbindung f caesarean section, caesarotomy, abdominal delivery, delivery by caesarean section, tomotocia
Schnittführung f type of incision
~ neben der Körpermittellinie paramedian incision
Schnittwunde f cut, incision [wound]
Schnupfen m coryza, rhinitis, common cold, nasal catarrh, nasitis, pharyngoconjunctival fever
Schnupfenvirus n common cold virus
schnurartig funiform, threadlike, restiform
Schnürmarke f constriction mark *(z. B. bei Darmeinklemmung)*
Schnürmuskel m constrictor [muscle]; sphincter [muscle]
Schnürring m constriction ring *(z. B. der Gebärmutter)*
~/Ranvierscher Ranvier's node (constriction) *(zirkuläre Einschnürung der Myelinhüllen der Nervenfasern)*
Schock m shock
~/anaphylaktischer anaphylactic (allergic) shock
~/endokriner endocrine shock
~/hämorrhagischer haemorrhagic (blood-loss) shock
~/hypoglykämischer hypoglycaemic (insulin) shock

Schock

~/**hypovolämischer** hypovolaemic (wound) shock
~/**kardiogener** cardiogenic (cardiac) shock
~/**neurogener** neurogenic shock
~/**protrahierter** delayed shock
~/**psychischer (seelischer)** psychic (mental) shock
~/**septischer** septicaemic (bacteriaemic) shock
~/**traumatischer** traumatic shock
schockartig shock-like
Schockbekämpfung f shock therapy (treatment)
Schockfieber n traumatic fever
Schocklunge f shock lung; adult respiratory distress syndrome, congestive atelectasis, post-traumatic pulmonary insufficiency
Schockniere f shock kidney; lower nephron nephrosis (syndrome)
Schockorgan n shock organ
Schockpatient m patient in shock
Schockraum m emergency room
Schocktherapie f shock therapy (treatment)
Schockzeichen n shock symptom
Schokoladenzyste f chocolate cyst *(der Schilddrüse)*
Schollen fpl/**chromatophile (Nisslsche)** Nissl bodies (granules), tigroid bodies *(in Nervenzellen)*
Schollenmuskel m soleus [muscle]
Schonhaltung f relieving posture *(z. B. bei Knochenbrüchen)*
Schonkost f bland (mild) diet
Schorf m crust, scab, slough, eschar
Schorfabtragung f escharotomy
schorfbedeckt crusted, scabbed
schorfbildend forming a crust, scab-forming, escharotic
schorfig scabby, sloughy, escharotic
Schorfigkeit f scabbiness, scabrities; roughness
Schornsteinfegerkrebs m chimney-sweeps' cancer
schräg oblique, slanting, lox[ot]ic; transverse, transversal
Schrägbruch m oblique fracture
Schrägkultur f slant culture
Schräglage f oblique presentation *(des Fetus)*
Schrägmuskel m oblique muscle • zu einem ~ gehörend obliquus
Schrägschnitt m oblique incision (section)
Schrägstellung f obliquity, oblique position
~ **der Gebärmutter** metrocampsis
Schrägverband m oblique bandage
Schraubenzugextension f Spanish windlass *(bei Knochenbruch)*
Schreck m fright; pavor, horror; terror
Schreckreaktion f startle reaction (reflex, response)
Schreibangst f graphophobia
Schreiben n/**fehlerhaftes** anorthography
schreibgestört paragraphic
Schreibkrampf m graphospasm, writer's cramp (paralysis), telegrapher's cramp, mogigraphia, ch[e]irospasm
Schreibstörung f dysgraphia, paragraphia *(Verwechseln oder Umstellen von Buchstaben)*

Schreibsucht f graphomania, scribomania
Schreibsüchtiger m graphomaniac
schreibunfähig agraphic
Schreibunfähigkeit f [log]agraphia, inability to write
~/**völlige** absolute agraphia
Schreibzentrum n writing centre *(Gehirn)*
Schreiknötchen npl singer's nodes (nodules), vocal nodes
Schrittmacher m s. Herzschrittmacher
Schrittmesser m pedometer
Schrittmessung f pedometry
schröpfen to bleed, to cup, to venesect
Schrumpfblase f contracted bladder
schrumpfen to shrink; to atrophy; to involute; to shrivel, to retract *(z. B. Gewebe)*
Schrumpfen n shrinkage; atrophy; involution; shrivelling, retraction *(z. B. von Gewebe)*
schrumpfend shrinking, stringent; atrophic
Schrumpfgallenblase f scleroatrophic cholecystitis
Schrumpfmagen m/**derber** leather bottle stomach *(mit plumpen, starren Schleimhautfalten)*; linitis plastica
Schrumpfniere f shrunken (contracted) kidney, atrophic (end-stage) kidney; cirrhosis of the kidney
Schrunde f fissure, crack, rhagade
schrundenartig fissured, cracked, rhagadiform
Schub m attack; [intermittent] episode
~/**cholangitischer** intermittent hepatic (biliary) fever
~ **einer chronischen Mastoiditis/akuter** acute-on-chronic mastoiditis
~/**schizophrener** schizophrenic episode
Schubladenphänomen n drawer sign
Schuhform f sabot heart *(des Herzens)*
Schuhzweckenleber f hob-nail liver *(bei Leberzirrhose)*
Schuldgefühle npl guilt feelings
Schulter f shoulder
~/**hängende** dropping shoulder
Schulter-Arm-Schmerz m cervicobrachialgia
Schulter-Arm-Syndrom n shoulder-hand syndrome, cervicobrachialgic (cervical radicular) syndrome, cervicobrachial neuritis
Schulterblatt n scapula, shoulder blade • über dem ~ suprascapular • unter dem ~ subscapular
~/**geflügeltes** alar scapula
Schulterblatt... s.a. Skapula...
Schulterblattanheftung f[/**operative**] scapulopexy
Schulterblattarterie f/**obere** suprascapular artery
Schulterblattbereich m scapular region
Schulterblattentfernung f[/**operative**] scapulectomy, excision of the shoulder blade
Schulterblattgräte f spine of the scapula • über der ~ supraspinous
Schulterblatthaken m scapula retractor
Schulterblatthals m neck of the scapula

Schulterblattheber *m* levator scapulae [muscle]
Schulterblatthochstand *m*/**angeborener** congenital elevation of the scapula, Sprengel's deformity
Schulterblattkranzarterie *f* circumflex scapular artery
Schulterblattmuskel *m* trapezius [muscle]
Schulterblattmuskulatur *f* scapular musculature
Schulterblattpfanne *f* glenoid cavity
Schulterblattrand *m*/**mittlerer** medial border of the scapula
~/oberer superior border of the scapula
Schulterblattreflex *m* [inter]scapular reflex
Schulterblattresektion *f* scapulectomy, excision of the shoulder blade
Schulterblattretraktor *m* scapula retractor
Schulterblattrückseite *f* posterior surface of the scapula
Schulterblattschmerz *m* scapulalgia, scapulodynia, pain in the scapula
Schulterblattvene *f* suprascapular vein
Schulterblattwinkel *m*/**unterer** inferior angle of the scapula
Schultereckgelenk *n* acromioclavicular joint, scapuloclavicular joint
Schulterentzündung *f* omitis, inflammation of the shoulder
Schultergelenk *n* shoulder joint
Schultergelenkarthrodese *f* arthrodesis of the shoulder joint
Schultergelenkeinrenkung *f* reduction of the shoulder joint
~ nach Kocher Kocher's manoeuvre
Schultergelenkentzündung *f* omarthritis, inflammation of the shoulder joint
Schultergelenkkapselband *n* glenohumeral ligament
Schultergelenkschmerz *m* omarthralgia, pain in the shoulder joint
Schultergelenkverrenkung *f* dislocation of the shoulder joint; slipped shoulder
Schultergelenkversteifung *f* arthrodesis of the shoulder
Schultergicht *f* omagra, gout in the shoulder
Schultergürtel *m* shoulder (pectoral) girdle
Schultergürteldystrophie *f* shoulder-girdle dystrophy, upper limb girdle dystrophy
Schultergürtelschmerz *m* brachial neuritis
Schultergürtelsyndrom *n* shoulder-girdle syndrome
Schultergürteltrauma *n* shoulder-girdle trauma
Schulter-Hals-Syndrom *n* shoulder-neck syndrome
Schulter-Hand-Syndrom *n* shoulder-hand syndrome
Schulterhöhe *f* 1. acromion [process] *(Anatomie)*; 2. shoulder level
Schulterhöhenabtragung *f*[/**operative**] acromionectomy
Schulterlage *f* shoulder presentation *(des Fetus)*
schulterlos anomous, without shoulders
Schulterluxation *f* s. Schultergelenkverrenkung

Schultermuskelermüdung *f* shoulder muscular fatigue
Schulter-Schlüsselbein-Band *n* acromioclavicular ligament
Schulterschmerz *m* omalgia, omodynia, shoulder pain
Schulterstütze *f* shoulder support *(zur Operationslagerung)*
Schulterverband *m* shoulder spica
Schultervorfall *m* shoulder presentation *(bei der Geburt)*
Schulter-Zungenbein-Muskel *m* omohyoid muscle
Schultz-Syndrom *n* Schultz's syndrome (paraesthesia) *(Form der Akroparästhesie)*
Schuppe *f* scale *(der Haut)*; dandruff *(des Kopfes)*; scutulum, favus cup; squama, squame *(des Knochens)* *(Zusammensetzungen s. unter Squama)*
schuppen to scale, to peel, to desquamate; to exfoliate
schuppenartig scaly, squamous
schuppend scaling, desquamative, exfoliative
Schuppenflechte *f* s. Psoriasis
schuppenflechtenartig psoriasiform, psoriasis-like
Schuppenkrankheit *f* 1. s. Psoriasis; 2. ichthyosis
schuppig scaly, scale-like, squamous, squamosal; pityroid
schuppig-kleiig furfuraceous
Schuppung *f* scaling, peeling, desquamation, exfoliation, ecdysis
Schürfwunde *f* excoriation, abrasion [of the skin]
Schußfraktur *f* [gun]shot fracture
Schußverletzung *f* [gun]shot injury
Schußwunde *f* [gun]shot wound, bullet wound
Schusterbrust *f* shoemaker's breast (chest), funnel (cobbler's) chest
schüttelempfindlich tremolabile
schüttelfest tremostable
Schüttelfrost *m* [shaking] chill, shivers, shivering-fit, rigor; ague *(bei Malaria)*
Schüttelkrampf *m* clonus; myoclonus, myoclonia
~/halbseitiger hemiballism
Schüttelkrampfdauerzustand *m* myoclonic status
Schüttellähmung *f* shaking palsy, agitated paralysis *(s. a. Parkinsonismus)*
Schüttelmixtur *f* shaking mixture
schütteln to shake
~/sich to shake, to shudder *(z. B. vor Ekel)*; to shiver *(z. B. vor Kälte)*
Schüttelreflex *m* shivering reflex
Schutz *m* protection, defence; immunity
Schutzbrille *f* protective spectacles, safety goggles
Schutzeiweiß *n* protective protein
schützen/[sich] gegen eine Infektion to protect against infection
schützend protective

Schützengrabenfieber 698

Schützengrabenfieber *n* trench (shinbone, Volhynia) fever, Werner-His disease, quintan (five-day) fever *(durch Rickettsia quintana)*
Schutzenzym *n* protective (defensive) enzyme
Schutzhülle *f* protective cover; enteric coating *(einer Tablette)*
schutzgeimpft vaccinated; toxoid-protected
Schutzimpfung *f* protective inoculation, prophylactic immunization
Schutzinstinkt *m* protective instinct
Schutzkolloid *n* protective colloid
Schutzlosigkeit *f* anaphylaxis *(Immunologie)*
Schutzmaske *f* protective mask; gas mask
Schutzmechanismus *m* protective (defence) mechanism
Schutzmittel *n* preservative, preventive; prophylactic; contraceptive
Schutzreaktion *f* defence response
Schutzreflex *m* protective (defence) reflex
Schutzsalbe *f* protective ointment
Schutzschürze *f* protective apron
Schutzverband *m* protective dressing (bandage)
schwach weak; hyposthenic, asthenic *(körperlich)*; infirm *(gebrechlich)*; poor, delicate, weak *(Gesundheit)*
Schwäche *f* weakness, debility, lack of strength; acratia, loss of power; hyposthenia, asthenia *(körperlich)*; infirmity *(Gebrechlichkeit)*; insufficiency *(eines Organs)*; languor, enervation *(Ermattung)*; inertia, lack of activity *(z. B. von Organen)*; adynamia, loss of muscular power, loss of vital power
~ **der vier Extremitäten** quadriparesis
~/**motorische** paresis
schwächen to weaken, to debilitate; to paralyse
schwächlich weak, feeble; hyposthenic; valetudinarian
schwachsichtig amblyopic, asthenopic, weak-sighted
Schwachsichtigkeit *f* amblyopia, asthenopia, weak sight[edness]
~ **durch Bleivergiftung** lead amblyopia
~ **durch Nichtgebrauch** amblyopia of disuse
Schwachsinn *m* oligophrenia, hypophrenia, mental deficiency, feeble-mindedness, debility
~/**erworbener** dementia, aphrenia, aphronesia
~/**hochgradiger** idiocy, anoia, severe mental subnormality
~/**mittelgradiger** imbecility
~/**moralischer** moramentia, moral idiocy (insanity)
~/**vorgetäuschter** pseudodementia
schwachsinnig oligophrenic, mentally defective, feeble-minded, oligophrenic, hypophrenic, debilitant
~/**mittelgradig** imbecile
Schwachsinniger *m* oligophrenic (feeble-minded) person, debilitant, ament, moron, morament, dement
~/**hochgradig** idiot
~/**mittelgradig** imbecile
Schwachsinnigkeit *f s.* Schwachsinn

Schwamm *m* sponge; fungus
schwammartig spongy, spongioform, spongioid, sponge-like; fungoid
Schwämmchen *npl s.* Soor
schwammig spongy, spongiose, spongioid; cancellous, cancellate *(z. B. Knochen)*
Schwammschicht *f* spongy layer
Schwammsubstanz *f* **der Schädelknochen** diploe, diploic bone
Schwanenhalsmeißel *m* swan-necked gouge
schwanger gravid, pregnant ● ~ **sein** to be pregnant ● ~ **werden** to become pregnant, to conceive
~/**nicht** not pregnant, acyetic
Schwangere *f* pregnant woman, gravida
Schwangerenberatungsstelle *f* antenatal clinic, maternity centre
Schwangerenchloasma *n s.* Schwangerschaftsmal
Schwangerengelüste *pl* pica
schwängern to impregnate, to make (render) pregnant, to fecundate
Schwangerschaft *f* pregnancy, gravidity, cyesis, gestation, foetation ● **die ~ unterbrechen** to interrupt (terminate) pregnancy ● **nach der ~** postgravid, postgestational ● **vor der ~** pregravid, pregestational
~ **außerhalb der Gebärmutter** eccyesis, ectopic gestation, extra-uterine pregnancy
~/**eingebildete (hysterische)** pseudopregnancy, pseudocyesis, false pregnancy
~/**interstitielle** interstitial pregnancy (gestation), mural (parietal) gestation
~/**mehrfache** multiple pregnancy
~/**membranöse** membranous pregnancy
~ **mit einem Fetus** monocyesis
~ **mit mehreren Feten** polycyesis
~/**übertragene** prolonged pregnancy
~/**weit fortgeschrittene** far advanced pregnancy
Schwangerschaftsabbruch *m*/**ärztlicher** pregnancy termination, premature termination of pregnancy, [induced] abortion
Schwangerschaftsanämie *f* anaemia of pregnancy
Schwangerschaftsangst *f* pregnophobia
Schwangerschaftscholestase *f* pregnancy cholestasis
Schwangerschaftschorea *f* acute chorea of pregnancy
Schwangerschaftsdauer *f* gestation[al] period, duration of pregnancy
Schwangerschaftsdiabetes *m* gestational diabetes, diabetes of pregnancy
Schwangerschaftsdiagnostik *f* cyesiognosis, diagnosis of pregnancy
Schwangerschaftseklampsie *f* eclampsia of pregnancy
Schwangerschaftserbrechen *n* vomiting of pregnancy
Schwangerschaftserhaltung *f* maintenance of pregnancy
Schwangerschaftsfrühtest *m* early pregnancy test

Schwangerschaftsgingivitis f pregnancy gingivitis
Schwangerschaftskomplikation f pregnancy complication
Schwangerschaftskrampfen n eclampsia, eclamptogenic toxaemia
schwangerschaftslos acyetic
Schwangerschaftslosigkeit f acyesis
Schwangerschaftsmal n cyasma, mask of pregnancy, uterine mask
Schwangerschaftsmegaloblastenanämie f megaloblastic (haemolytic) anaemia of pregnancy
Schwangerschaftsmonat m month of pregnancy
Schwangerschaftsnephritis f nephritis of pregnancy
Schwangerschaftsniere f pregnancy kidney; nephritis of pregnancy
Schwangerschaftsödem n oedema of pregnancy
Schwangerschaftspsychose f gestational psychosis
Schwangerschaftsrate f pregnancy rate
Schwangerschaftsreaktion f/**Aschheim-Zondeksche** Aschheim-Zondek reaction (test), AZR
Schwangerschaftsretinopathie f retinopathy of pregnancy
Schwangerschaftsstreifen mpl lineae albicantes (gravidarum) *(Hautatrophien durch Zerreißung der elastischen Fasern)*
Schwangerschaftssymptome npl gravidism
Schwangerschaftstest m pregnancy test
~/**immunologischer** immunologic test for pregnancy
Schwangerschaftstoxikose f gestational toxicosis, toxaemia of pregnancy, gestosis; pre-eclampsia, pre-eclamptic toxaemia, eclampsism *(mit Organschäden)*
schwangerschaftsunfähig acyetic
Schwangerschaftsunfähigkeit f acyesis
Schwangerschaftsunterbrechung f interruption of pregnancy, interruptio[n]
~/**illegale** illegal abortion
schwangerschaftsverhütend contraceptive
Schwangerschaftsverhütung f prevention of pregnancy, prevenception, contraception, conception control
Schwangerschaftsverlängerung f prolongation of pregnancy; prolonged pregnancy
Schwangerschaftsverlauf m course of pregnancy
Schwangerschaftszeichen n sign of pregnancy
Schwangerschaftszellen fpl pregnancy cells *(des Hypophysenvorderlappens)*
schwanken to stagger; to fluctuate *(z. B. Fieber)*
schwankend staggering; fluctuating, amphibolic *(z. B. Typhusfieber)*; intermittent *(Puls)*; precarious *(Gesundheit)*
Schwannitis f schwannitis, schwannosis
Schwannogliom n s. Schwannom
Schwannom n schwannoma, schwannoglioma
Schwannzellensarkom n schwannosarcoma

Schwanz m tail, cauda *(Zusammensetzungen s. unter Cauda)*
Schwanzfalte f tail fold *(Embryologie)*
schwanzförmig caudal, tail-shaped
schwanzlos acaudal, acaudate
schwanzwärts caudal
Schwärmspore f zoospore, zoosperm
Schwärmzelle f swarm cell; zoospore, zoosperm
Schwarte f thick skin; scalp *(der Kopfhaut)*; callositiy, induration, scar *(der Pleura)*
Schwarzer Tod m Black Death, black plague
Schwarzfärbung f black colouration *(z. B. des Stuhls)*
~ **der Finger- und Zehennägel** melanonychia
Schwarzfleckigkeit f **der Haut** melasma
schwarzhaarig melanotrichous, black-haired
Schwarzharnen n melanuria
schwarzharnend melanuric
Schwarzruhr f melaena, melanorrhoea
Schwarzsucht f [toxic] melanodermatitis, melanism
Schwarzwasserfieber n blackwater (canebrake yellow) fever, haemoglobinuric (West-African) fever, malarial haemoglobinuria (haematuria); melanuria
Schwatzepilepsie f garrulous epilepsy
Schwatzsucht f panglossia, loquacity, garrulity
Schwebegefühl n sensation of floating, levitation *(z. B. von Menschen im Traum)*
Schwebekörpermesser m rotameter
Schwefelbad n sulphur[ated] bath
Schwefelbakterien npl sulphur bacteria, thiobacteria
schwefelfarbig sulphur-coloured
schwefelliebend thiophil[e], thiophilic
Schwefelsalbe f sulphur ointment
Schweifkern m caudate nucleus
Schweifkernkopf m head of the caudate nucleus
Schweigepflicht f professional secrecy
Schweinebandwurm m pork tapeworm, Taenia solium
Schweinebandwurmfinnenbefall m cysticercosis
Schweinehirtenkrankheit f meningitis porcinarii
Schweiß m sweat, sudor, perspiration
~/**blutiger** bloody sweat
~/**kalter** cold sweat
~/**stinkender** foetid perspiration; brom[h]idrosis, osmidrosis *(infolge von Zersetzungsvorgängen)*
schweißabsondernd sudoriparous
Schweißabsonderung f s. Schwitzen 1.
schweißbedeckt covered in sweat
Schweißbildung f s. Schweißproduktion
Schweißbläschen n s. Schweißfriesel
Schweißdrüse f sweat (perspiratory) gland, sudoriferous (sudoriparous, coil) gland
Schweißdrüsenabszeß m sudoriparous abscess
Schweißdrüsenadenom n sweat gland adenoma, spir[aden]oma, hidradenoma, syringadenoma
schweißdrüsenanregend sudomotor
schweißdrüsenartig hidradenoid

Schweißdrüsenentzündung

Schweißdrüsenentzündung f hidr[os]adenitis, hydr[os]adenitis, spiradenitis, inflammation of a sweat gland
~ **an Händen und Füßen** dyshidrosis *(bei Pilzerkrankung)*
schweißdrüsenförmig hidradenoid
Schweißdrüsenhyperplasie f/papilläre hidradenoma
Schweißdrüsenkarzinom n sweat gland carcinoma, hidradenocarcinoma, hidradenoid carcinoma
Schweißdrüsenkeratose f sudorikeratosis, keratosis of the sweat glands
Schweißdrüsennävus m hidradenoma, syringocystadenoma
Schweißdrüsenretentionszyste f hidrocystoma
schweißdrüsenstimulierend sudomotor
Schweißdrüsentumor m sweat gland tumour
~/**gutartiger** hidradenoma
~/**zystischer** syringocystoma
Schweißfluß m hidrorrhoea
schweißfördernd s. schweißtreibend
Schweißfriesel f sudamen, miliaria, prickly heat, summer eruption, tropical sweat rash, red gum
schweißhemmend an[ti]hidrotic, antisudorific, emphractic
schweißig sweaty, sudoral; wet, clammy
Schweißmangel m olig[o]hidria, hypohidrosis
Schweißpore f sweat pore
Schweißproduktion f hidropoiesis, sweat production
~/**fehlende** anhidrosis
~/**übermäßige** hyperhidrosis, ephidrosis, excessive sweating
~/**verminderte** hyp[o]hidrosis, ischidrosis
schweißproduzierend sweating, hidropoietic, sudoriferous, sudorific
Schweißsekretion f diaphoresis, sweat secretion, [h]idrosis, hydrosis
schweißsezernierend sudoriparous
Schweißstauungssyndrom n tropical anhidrotic (dyshidrotic) asthenia
Schweißtest m sweat test
schweißtreibend diaphoretic, sudatory, sudoriferus, sudorific, hidrotic, sweat-producing
Schweißverdunstung f sweat evaporation
Schweißverhaltung f hidroschesis, retention of sweat; suppression of the perspiration
Schwelle f 1. threshold; 2. limen *(Anatomie)*
schwellen to swell, to tumefy, to intumesce
schwellend swelling, tumefacient
Schwellendosis f threshold dose
Schwellenempfindung f threshold sensation
Schwellenenergie f threshold energy
Schwellenperkussion f threshold percussion
Schwellenreiz m threshold (minimal, liminal) stimulus
Schwellensehschärfe f/räumliche displacement threshold acuity
Schwellensubstanz f threshold substance
~ **der Niere** threshold body
Schwellenwert m threshold (liminal) value

Schwellenwertperkussion f threshold percussion, orthopercussion
Schwellgewebe n erectile (cavernous) tissue
Schwellkörper m cavernous body, [corpus] cavernosum
Schwellkörperentzündung f cavern[os]itis, inflammation of the corpus cavernosum
Schwellkörpergewebe n erectile (cavernous) tissue
Schwellkörperharnröhre f cavernous urethra
Schwellung f swelling, tumefaction, tumescence, tumidity, turgescence; engorgement, enlargement; lump
~ **durch Lymphstauung** lymphoedema
~/**glasige** glassy swelling
~/**harte** non-tender swelling *(z. B. einer Drüse)*
~/**trübe** cloudy swelling; albuminous (parenchymatous) degeneration *(Pathohistologie)*
Schwellungszustand m tumidity
Schwenklappen m rotation flap *(zur Transplantation)*
schwer heavy; dangerous, severe *(Verletzung)*; serious, difficult *(Krankheitsfall)*
schwerbeschädigt seriously (severely) disabled
Schweregrad m [degree of] severity *(einer Krankheit)*
Schwerelosigkeit f weightlessness, null gravity, zero gravity, z-G
Schwerfärbbarkeit f chromophobia
Schwerhörigkeit f dysacousia, dysecoia, dysacousma, impairment of hearing
~/**leichte** hypacousia, amblyacousia, defective hearing
Schwerkettenkrankheit f H (heavy) chain disease, Franklin's disease
schwerkrank seriously (dangerously) ill
Schwermetallintoxikationstremor m metallic tremor
Schwermetallsaum m heavy metal line *(des Zahnfleischs)*
Schwermetallvergiftung f heavy metal poisoning
Schwermütigkeit f s. Melancholie
schwertförmig xiphoid, xyphoid, ensiform
Schwertfortsatz m xiphosternum, xiphoid [process], ensiform (xiphoid) cartilage ● **über dem** ~ supraxiphoid
Schwertfortsatzentzündung f xiphoiditis, inflammation of the xiphoid process
Schwertfortsatzschmerz m xiphodynia, pain in the xiphoid process
Schwertfortsatzwinkel m xiphoid angle
schwerverdaulich indigestible, stodgy
schwerverletzt seriously injured; badly (severely) wounded
Schwester f nurse
~/**assistierende** scrub nurse
~/**ausgebildete** trained nurse
~/**examinierte** registered nurse
~/**instrumentierende** scrub nurse
~/**leitende** matron
Schwesternausbildung f training of nurses

Schwesternschule f nurse's training school
Schwesternschülerin f [preclinical] student nurse
Schwiele f callosity, tyloma
schwielenartig callous, tylotic
Schwielenbildung f tylosis
Schwimmbadkonjunktivitis f swimming-pool (acute contagious) conjunctivitis, inclusion blennorrhoea, paratrachoma
Schwimmhaut f web, patagium
Schwimmprobe f floating (hydrostatic) test *(Gerichtsmedizin)*
Schwindel m vertigo, dizziness, giddiness, lightheadedness, lipothymia, dinus *(s. a. unter* Vertigo*)*
~/horizontaler horizontal vertigo
~/neurasthenischer neurasthenic vertigo
~/objektiver objective vertigo
~/paralytischer paralytic vertigo
~/subjektiver subjective vertigo
~/vertikaler vertical vertigo
~/vestibulärer vestibular vertigo
~/zentraler central (cerebral) vertigo
Schwindelanfall m attack of vertigo, vertiginous (giddy) attack
schwindelbeseitigend dinic[al], relieving vertigo
Schwindelgefühl n [sensation of] vertigo, feeling of giddiness (dizziness); staggers
~/neurasthenisches neurasthenic vertigo
~/objektives objective vertigo
schwindelig vertiginous, dizzy, giddy, lightheaded, dinic[al]
schwinden to fade away; to shrink; to atrophy; to wear off
schwindend fading away; shrinking; atrophic; wearing off
Schwindflechte f lupus [vulgaris]
Schwindsucht f s. 1. Phthisis 1.; 2. Lungentuberkulose; 3. Tabes dorsalis
~/galoppierende galloping (florid) phthisis, galloping consumption
Schwindsuchtbehandlung f phthisiotherapy, antituberculous therapy
schwindsüchtig 1. phthisic[al], phthinoid, consumptive, tuberculous; 2. tabescent
schwingen to oscillate; to vibrate
schwingend oscillatory; vibrating
Schwingung f oscillation; vibration
Schwingungsaufzeichnung f oscillography
Schwingungsempfindlichkeit f seismaesthesia
Schwingungskurve f oscillogram
Schwingungsschreiber m oscillograph
Schwingungssehen n oscillopsia
schwirren to thrill
Schwirren n thrill; fremitus
~/diastolisches diastolic thrill
~/präkordiales precordial thrill
~/präsystolisches presystolic thrill
~/systolisches systolic thrill
Schwitzbad n sudatorium, sweat (hot-air) bath
Schwitzbehandlung f sudotherapy
Schwitzbläschen npl hidroa, sudamina, heat pustules
schwitzen to sweat, to perspire, to transpire
Schwitzen n 1. sweating, perspiration, transpiration, sudation; 2. weeping *(einer Wunde)*
~ am gesamten Körper panhidrosis
~/anomales dyshidrosis
~/übermäßiges excessive sweating, sudoresis, hyperhidrosis, hidrorrhoea, [h]idrosis, polyhydrosis, ephidrosis
~/vermindertes hyp[o]hidrosis
~ von Händen und Füßen/verstärktes acrohyperhidrosis
schwitzend sweating; exudative, weeping
~/vermindert hypohidrotic
~/verstärkt hyperhidrotic
Schwitzkur f sweating cure
Schwitzneigung f tendency to sweat
Schwitzraum m sudatorium, sweating (hot-air) room
Schwund m wasting, depletion; rarefaction *(z. B. des Knochengewebes)*; atrophy *(z. B. eines Muskels)*
Schwund- und Haftphänomen n adherence-disappearance phenomenon
Scillaintoxikation f scillism, poisoning by squill
Sclerema n sclerema, sclerosis of the skin
~ neonatorum neonatal oedema, sclerema (oedema) of the newborn
~ oedematosum scleroedema
Scleroedema n scleroedema
~ adultorum Buschke's disease (scleroedema)
Sclerosis f sclerosis *(z. B. von Geweben) (s. a. unter* Sklerose*)*
~ cerebelli cerebellar sclerosis, sclerosis of the cerebellum
~ cerebri cerebral sclerosis, sclerencephalia, sclerosis of the brain tissue
~ corii (dermatis) s. Sklerodermie
~ ossium condensing osteitis
~ ventriculi sclerotic gastritis
Scotoma n 1. scotoma, scotosis, visual field defect; 2. scotoma, mental blind spot *(s. a. unter* Skotom*)*
~ anulare annular (ring) scotoma
~ centralis central scotoma
Scrub-Typhus m scrub typhus
Seabright-Bantam-Syndrom n Seabright-Bantam syndrome *(fehlende Organreaktion auf Hormonwirkung)*
Sebolith m sebolith, sebolite, sebaceous calculus
Seborrhoe f s. Seborrhoea
Seborrhoea f seborrhoea, seborrhagia, steatorrhoea
~ capitis seborrhoea of the scalp
~ congestiva chronic discoid lupus erythematodes
~ corporis seborrhoeic dermatitis of the trunk
~ sicca dry seborrhoea, seborrhoeic dermatitis with scaling
seborrhoisch seborrhoeic, seborrhoeal
Sebozystomatosis f sebocystomatosis, presence of multiple sebaceous cysts; steatocystoma multiplex

Sebum

Sebum *n* sebum, tallow
~ cutaneum cutaneous sebum
~ palpebrale palpebral sebum
Secale *n* cornutum ergot
sechsfingrig sexidigital, sexidigitate
Sechsfingrigkeit *f* hexadactylism
Sechsling *m* sextuplet
Sechstgebärende *f* sextipara
Sechstschwangere *f* sextigravida
Sechszehigkeit *f* hexadactylism
Seclusio *f* pupillae seclusion of the pupil
Sectio *f* sectio[n], cut[ting]
~ caesarea *s.* Kaiserschnitt
sedativ sedative, calmative, soothing, quieting
Sedativ[um] *n* sedative [agent], calmative [agent]; tranquillizer; depressant, depressor
sedieren to sedate, to calm; to tranquillize
sedierend *s.* sedativ
Sedierung *f* sedation, tranquillization
~/medikamentöse medicinal restraint *(bei erregten Patienten)*
Sediment *n* sediment, hypostasis; deposit
Sedimentation *f* sedimentation; deposition
Sedimentationsgeschwindigkeit *f* sedimentation rate
Sedimentationskonstante *f*/Svedbergsche Svedberg sedimentation unit
Sedimentationsprobe *f* sedimentation test
Sedimentationsvolumen *n* packed cell volume *(der Erythrozyten)*
Sedimentationszeit *f* sedimentation time *(der Erythrozyten)*
See *m* lake, lacus *(z. B. Blutsee)*
Seebad *n* seaside resort
Seeklima *n* maritime (sea-coast) climate
Seeklimatherapie *f* marinotherapy
seekrank seasick
Seekrankheit *f* seasickness, pelagism, naupathia *(Kinetose)*
Seele *f* mind, mens, psyche
Seelenbehandlung *f* psychotherapy, mind cure
Seelenblindheit *f* psychic (mind, soul) blindness, psychanopsia, visual agnosia
Seelenheilkunde *f* psychotherapy
seelenkrank mentally ill
Seelenleben *n* mental (psychic) life
Seelenleiden *n* psychopathy, mental disease
Seelenqual *f* mental (mind) agony
Seelenreinigung *f* catharsis, [therapeutic] release of mental tension
Seelenruhe *f* ataraxia, ataraxy, peace of mind, mental homoeostasis
seelenruhig ataractic
Seelenschmerz *m* psychic (mind, soul) pain, psychalgia, phrenalgia
Seelenspaltung *f s.* Schizophrenie
Seelentaubheit *f* psychic (mind, soul) deafness, acousmatagnosis, word deafness, auditory verbal agnosia
seelisch psychic, mental, emotional; psychological
~ bedingt psychogen[et]ic, psychogenous

~ beeinflussend psychotherapeutic
~ behandelnd psychotherapeutic
seelisch-funktionell psychic
seelisch-körperlich psychosomatic, psychophysic[al]
Seemannshaut *f* sailor's skin
Segel *n* veil, velum, cusp[is], leaflet *(z. B. an Herzklappen) (Zusammensetzungen s. unter Cuspis und Velum)*
Segel[flieger]ohr *n* protruding ear
Segment *n* segment[um] ● aus Segmenten [gebildet] segmental, segmentary
Segmentanästhesie *f* segmental anaesthesia
segmentär segmental, segmentary
Segmentarterie *f*/obere superior segmental artery *(der Lunge)*
Segmentatelektase *f* segmental atelectasis
Segmentation *f* segmentation, cleavage; merogenesis, reproduction by segmentation
Segmentationshöhle *f* segmentation cavity, blastocoele
Segmentationskern *m* segmentation nucleus
Segmentationszelle *f* segmentation cell, blastomere
Segmentbildung *f s.* Segmentation
Segmentblockade *f* segmental block
Segmentbronchus *m*/oberer superior segmental bronchus *(der Lunge)*
Segmentdemyelination *f* segmental demyelination
Segmentdiagnose *f* niveau (level) diagnosis *(z. B. bei Rückenmarkverletzung)*
Segmentektomie *f* segmentectomy, segmental resection, excision of a segment
Segmententfernung *f*[/operative] *s.* Segmentektomie
segmentförmig segmental, segmentary
segmentfrei non-segmented
segmentiert segmented
~/nicht non-segmented
Segmentierungsbewegung *f* segmenting movement *(des Darms)*
Segmentnerv *m* segmental nerve
Segmentnervenentzündung *f* segmental neuritis
segregieren to segregate
Sehachse *f*[/optische] visual (optic) axis, sagittal axis of the eye, line of vision *(gedachte Linie zwischen Hornhaut- und Netzhautmittelpunkt des Auges)*
Sehbahn *f* optic pathway (tract), visual pathway ● über der ~ supra-optic
Sehbarkeitsminimum *n* visible minimum
Sehebene *f* visual plane
Sehempfindlichkeit *f* optaesthesia
Sehen *n* vision, sight, visus; visual sense *(s.a. unter Visus)*
~/achromatisches achromatic vision
~/asymmetrisches asymmetrical vision, asymmetropia
~/beidäugiges binocular vision (perception), ambiocularity
~/direktes direct (central, foveal) vision

~/einäugiges monocular vision, monoblepsia
~/farbiges chromatic vision
~/gestörtes defective vision, dysopia
~/indirektes indirect (peripheral) vision
~/oszillierendes oscillating vision, oscillopsia
~/photopisches photopic vision
~/räumliches stereoscopic (solid) vision, stereopsis, depth perception
~/skotopisches scotopic vision
~/stereoskopisches s. ~/räumliches
~/vergrößertes macrop[s]ia, megalopia
~/verkleinertes microp[s]ia
~ von farbigen Ringen halo (rainbow, iridescent) vision
~/zentrales s. ~/direktes
sehend/schnell tachistoscopic
~/vierfarbig tetrachromic
Sehfehler m visual defect
Sehfeld n visual field, field of vision
~/nasales nasal (olfactory) field (der Netzhaut)
Sehfeldausfall m visual field defect
Sehfeldprüfung f visual perimetry (field examination)
Sehgelb n xanthopsin, visual yellow
Sehgrenze f horopter (visuelle Projektionsebene)
Sehhilfe f visual aid (s.a. Brille)
Sehhügel m s. Thalamus
Sehkraft f visual power, vision
Sehkraft- und Sehweitenbestimmung f optometry
Sehkraft- und Sehweitenmesser m optometer
Sehlinie f visual line
Sehlinienablenkung f parallax
Sehmüdigkeit f visual fatigue, copiopia, ophthalmocopia, ophthalmokopia
Sehne f tendo[n], tendineum, sinew, leader; ligament (Zusammensetzungen s. unter Tendo) ● zur Hälfte aus ~ bestehend semimembranous
Sehnenabriß m disinsertion
sehnenartig tendinous
Sehnenausrißfraktur f avulsion fracture
Sehnendurchtrennung f[/operative] tenotomy, desmotomy
Sehnenentfernung f[/operative] ten[on]ectomy, excision of a tendon
Sehnenentzündung f tendinitis, inflammation of a tendon, ten[d]onitis, desmitis
Sehnenfaltungsinstrument n tendon tucker
Sehnenfaser f tendinous fibre
Sehnenfaßzange f tendon seizing forceps
Sehnenfesselung f[/operative] tenodesis, tendon suspension, fixation of a tendon
Sehnenfortsatz m digitation
Sehnenhaken m tendon hook
Sehnenhaube f galeal (epicranial) aponeurosis
Sehnenhaut f aponeurosis
Sehnenhüllgewebe n paratenon
Sehnenhüpfen n subsultus clonus (tendinum), twitching of the tendon
Sehnenkappe f aponeurosis
Sehnenknarren n ten[d]ophony
~/schmerzhaftes crepitant tenalgia

Sehnenknöchelchen n sesamoid bone
Sehnenmesser n tenotome, tenotomy knife
Sehnen-Muskel-Plastik f tenomyoplasty
Sehnenmuzin n tendomucin, tendomucoid
Sehnennaht f tenorrhaphy, ten[din]osuture, suture of a divided tendon; desmopexia
Sehnenplastik f ten[din]oplasty, tendoplasty
Sehnenplatte f aponeurosis
Sehnenreflex m tendon reflex (jerk)
Sehnenrekonstruktion f s. Sehnenplastik
Sehnenscheide f peritenon, tendon (synovial, mucous) sheath ● innerhalb einer ~ intravaginal
~/fibröse epitendineum, epitenon
Sehnenscheidenabszeß m thecal abscess (felon); phlegmonous (purulent) tendovaginitis
Sehnenscheidenentfernung f[/operative] tenosynovectomy, vaginectomy, excision of the tendon sheath
Sehnenscheidenentzündung f ten[d]osynovitis, ten[d]ovaginitis, tendinous (vaginal) synovitis, [tenonto]thecitis (Zusammensetzungen s. unter Tendovaginitis)
Sehnenscheidenexstirpation f tenosynovectomy, vaginectomy
Sehnenscheidenganglion n s. Sehnenscheidenzyste
Sehnenscheidengeschwulst f tenosynovioma
Sehnenscheidenhaken m tendon hook
Sehnenscheideninfektion f tendon-sheath infection
Sehnenscheidenknötchen n tendon-sheath nodule
Sehnenscheidenschrumpfung f thecostegnosis, contraction of a tendon sheath
Sehnenscheidenschwellung f onkinocele
Sehnenscheidentuberkulose f tuberculous ten[d]osynovitis, granular tendovaginitis
Sehnenscheidenvereng[er]ung f thecostegnosis, contraction of a tendon sheath
Sehnenscheidenzyste f thecal cyst, cystic tumour of the tendon sheath, cyst of the joint capsule
Sehnenschere f tendon (tenotomy) scissors
Sehnenschmerz m tenalgia, tenodynia, pain in a tendon, desmalgia, desmodynia
Sehnenschnappen n snap
Sehnenspindel f tendon spindle
Sehnenstripper m tendon stripper
Sehnentransplantat n tendon graft
Sehnentransplantation f tendon grafting (transplantation)
Sehnen- und Muskelschnitt m tenomyotomy
Sehnenverknöcherung f ossification of a tendon; ten[on]ostosis, osteodesmosis
Sehnenverkürzung f tendon shortening, shortening of a tendon
Sehnenverlängerung f tendon lengthening, lengthening of a tendon
Sehnenzerrung f stretching of a tendon, desmectasis; strained tendon
Sehnerv m optic (visual) nerve, second cranial nerve

Sehnervenabriß

Sehnervenabriß *m* avulsion of the bulb
Sehnervenatrophie *f* optic [nerve] atrophy
~ **bei Syphilis** optic tabes
~/**familiär auftretende** Leber's disease (optic atrophy)
Sehnervendegeneration *f* optic [nerve] atrophy
Sehnervenentzündung *f* optic neuritis, ophthalmoneuritis, inflammation of the optic nerve, neuropticomyelitis, neuropapillitis
Sehnervenerkrankung *f* optic neuropathy
Sehnervenfaser *f* optic nerve fibre
Sehnervenfaserbündel *n* papillomacular bundle
Sehnervengliom *n* optic nerve glioma
Sehnervengrube *f* excavation of the optic disk
Sehnervenhypoplasie *f* optic nerve hypoplasia
Sehnervenkolobom *n* optic nerve coloboma
Sehnervenkreuzung *f* optic chiasma (commissure), decussation of the optic nerve
Sehnervenkreuzungsgeschwulst *f* optic chiasma tumour
Sehnervenkreuzungverletzung *f* optic chiasma lesion
Sehnervenloch *n* optic foramen
Sehnervenpapille *f* optic disk (papilla)
Sehnervenscheide *f* sheath of the optic nerve
Sehnervenscheidenentzündung *f* optic perineuritis
Sehnervenstumpf *m* stump of the optic nerve
Sehnerventrichter *m* optic pit
Sehnerven- und Aderhautentzündung *f* neurochoroiditis
Sehorgan *n* visual organ, organ of vision (sight)
Sehpigment *n* visual pigment
Sehprobentafel *f*/**Snellensche** *s*. Snellen-Tafel
Sehprüfung *f* sight-testing, testing of vision, vision (sighting) test
~/**Snellensche** Snellen test
Sehpurpur *m* visual purple (substance), rhodopsin, erythropsin, retinal pigment
sehpurpurbildend purpurogenous
sehpurpurregenerierend rhodophylactic
Sehpurpurregenerierung *f* rhodophylaxis, rhodogenesis
Sehrinde *f s*. Sehzentrum
Sehschärfe *f* visual acuity, acuteness of vision, visus
~ **beider Augen/gleiche** isopia
~/**erhöhte** oxyblepsia, hyperacuity
Sehschärfebestimmung *f* eidoptometry, estimation of the acuity of vision
Sehschärfemesser *m* photoptometer
Sehschärfetafel *f* near vision chart
~ **mit Buchstaben** confusion letters
Sehschulung *f* orthoptics
sehschwach weak-sighted
Sehschwäche *f* weak sight[edness], weakness of vision
Sehschwelle *f* visual threshold
Sehsphäre *f s*. Sehzentrum
Sehstörung *f* visual disturbance (trouble), dysop[s]ia, optic dysfunction
Sehstrahlung *f*[/**Gratioletsche**] [Gratiolet's] optic radiation, geniculocalcarine radiation (tract)

Sehtafel *f s*. Snellen-Tafel
Sehtrübung *f* blurring of vision
Sehventrikel *m* opticocoele
Sehverlust *m* visual deprivation, loss of vision
Sehvermögen *n* sight, [strength of] vision
Sehverschlechterung *f* blurring of vision
Sehweiß *n* leucopsin
Sehwinkel *m* visual (optic) angle
Sehzeichen *n* optotype *(zur Bestimmung der Sehschärfe)*
Sehzelle *f* visual cell
Sehzentrum *n* optic (visual) centre, visual cortex, striate (visual) area
Seife *f*/**medizinische** medicated soap
Seifenstühle *mpl* soapy stools
seifig saponaceous
Seismästhesie *f* seismaesthesia
Seismotherapie *f* seismotherapy
Seite *f* side; flank, latus ● **zwei Seiten betreffend** [am]bilateral
Seitenbahn *f* lateral tract
Seitenband *n* collateral ligament
Seitenbetonung *f* laterality *(einer Körperhälfte)*
Seitendarstellung *f* lateral (side) view *(Radiologie)*
Seitenfontanelle *f* lateral fontanel
Seitenganglion *n* lateral ganglion
Seitenhirnblutleiter *m* lateral sinus
Seitenhorn *n* lateral horn [of the spinal medulla], lateral cornu
Seitenkettentheorie *f*/**Ehrlichsche** Ehrlich's side-chain theory
Seitenkontaktaufnahme *f* lateral decubitus film
Seitenlage *f* lateral position (decubitus)
Seitenlappen *m* lateral lobe
Seitenlappenvergrößerung *f* lateral lobe enlargement
Seitennystagmus *m* lateral nystagmus
Seitenpropulsion *f* lateropulsion *(Symptom bei Parkinsonismus)*
Seitensäule *f* **der grauen Substanz des Rückenmarks** lateral column of grey matter of the spinal cord
Seitenstrang *m* **der weißen Substanz des Rückenmarks** lateral column of white matter of the spinal cord
Seitenstrangganglion *n* lateral chain ganglion
Seitenthrombus *m* lateral thrombus
Seitenventrikel *m* lateral ventricle
Seitenventrikelhorn *n*/**unteres** inferior horn of the lateral ventricle
Seitenverbindung *f* shunt *(z. B. von Gefäßen)*
seitlich lateral; parietal
~ **und dazwischenliegend** intermediolateral
Seitwärtsablenkung *f* laterodeviation
Seitwärtsbewegung *f* lateroduction; abduction *(z. B. des Auges)*
Seitwärtsdrehen *n* laterotorsion
Seitwärtsfallen *n* lateropulsion *(Symptom bei Parkinsonismus)*
Seitwärtsneigung *f* lateroversion, lateriversion *(z. B. der Gebärmutter)*

Seitwärtsverdrehung f laterotorsion
Seitwärtsverlagerung f lateroflexion, lateroposition *(z. B. der Gebärmutter)*
Sejunktion f sejunction *(Psychologie)*
Sekret n secretion *(einer Drüse)*
Sekretagogum n secretagogue [agent]
Sekretentleerung f emission
sekretfördernd productive *(z. B. beim Husten)*
Sekretin n secretin *(Zwölffingerdarmhormon)*
Sekretinsuppressionstest m secretin suppression test
Sekretion f secretion
~/**innere** internal (endocrine) secretion, incretion
~/**vermehrte** hypersecretion, supersecretion
~/**verminderte** hyposecretion, deficient (weak) secretion
sekretionsanregend secretomotor
sekretionsfördernd secretagogue, secretogogue
sekretionshemmend secretoinhibitory, antisecretory
Sekretionskanälchen n secretory canaliculus
Sekretionsmechanismus m secretory mechanism
Sekretionsnerv m secretory nerve
Sekretionsphase f secretory phase
Sekretionsstörung f dyssecretosis, disturbed secretion, parasecretion
Sekretionsverminderung f hyposecretion
Sekretlöffel m secretion curette (scoop)
sekretoinhibitorisch secretoinhibitory
Sekretolytikum n secretolytic [agent]
sekretolytisch secretolytic
sekretorisch secretory
Sektion f 1. sectio[n], dissection; 2. s. Obduktion
Sektions... s.a. Obduktions...
Sektionsbericht m autopsy record
Sektionsbesteck n set of postmortem instruments
Sektionsdiagnose f postmortem diagnosis
Sektionssaal m autopsy (dissecting) room, dissection (post-mortem) laboratory
Sektionstisch m autopsy table
~/**anatomischer** dissection table
Sektionstuberkel m dissection tubercle
Sektorensinusektomie f trabeculectomy *(am Auge)*
sekundär secondary; concomitant; collateral
Sekundärabszeß m secondary abscess
Sekundäraffekt m secondary lesion
Sekundäramenorrhoe f secondary amenorrhoea
Sekundäramputation f secondary amputation
Sekundäramyloidose f secondary amyloidosis
Sekundärdentin n secondary dentin, irregular (adventitious) dentin
Sekundärdentition f secondary dentition
Sekundärdigestion f secondary digestion
Sekundärdysmenorrhoe f secondary (acquired) dysmenorrhoea
Sekundäreffloreszenz f secondary efflorescence; erosion
Sekundärfluoreszenz f secondary fluorescence
Sekundärgeschwulst f metastasis

Sekundärglaukom n secondary glaucoma
Sekundärheilung f second[ary] intention healing, healing by second intention, delay in primary wound closure
Sekundärhydatide f secondary hydatid
Sekundärinfektion f secondary infection
Sekundärkaries f secondary caries
Sekundärkatarakt f secondary cataract, aftercataract
Sekundärknochen m secondary bone
Sekundärkrankheit f secondary (concomitant) disease, deuteropathy, sequela
Sekundärläsion f secondary lesion
Sekundärnaht f secondary (delayed) suture, secondary wound closure, resuture
Sekundärreaktion f secondary immune response
Sekundärsequester m secondary sequestrum
Sekundärstadium n secondary stage
~ **der Syphilis** secondary syphilis
Sekundärstrahlung f secondary radiation
Sekundärverdauung f secondary digestion
Sekundärzotte f secondary villus
Sekundärzyste f secondary cyst
Sekundenherztod m sudden death
Sekundenkapazität f forced expiratory volume *(der Lunge)*
Sekundigravida f secundigravida
sekundipar secundiparous
Sekundipara f secundipara
Sekundum-Defekt m secundum [type] atrial septal defect
Selbst... s.a. Eigen... und Auto...
Selbstanalyse f self-analysis, ego analysis, autoanalysis *(psychotherapeutische Methode)*
selbständig separate; independent; spontaneous; idiopathic, protopathic, autopathic *(Krankheiten)*
Selbstansteckung f self-infection, autoinfection
Selbstauflösung f 1. autolysis, self-digestion; self-fermentation; 2. auto[haemo]lysis
Selbstbeeinflußbarkeit f self-suggestibility, autosuggestibility
Selbstbeeinflussung f self-suggestion, autosuggestion
Selbstbefriedigung f s. Masturbation
selbstbefruchtend autogamous
Selbstbefruchtung f self-fertilization, autogamy
Selbstbehandlung f self-treatment, autotherapy
Selbstbeobachtung f self-observation, introspection
Selbstbeschränkung f restriction of ego, ego restriction
Selbstentmannung f autoemasculation
Selbsterhaltungstrieb m instinct of self-preservation
selbsternährend autotrophic
Selbstheilung f autotherapy; spontaneous healing
Selbstimpfung f self-inoculation, self-injection, autoinoculation, autovaccination
Selbstinfektion f self-infection, autoinfection
Selbstkontrolle f self-control

45 Nöhring dtsch./engl.

Selbstleuchten

Selbstleuchten *n* autofluorescence
Selbstliebe *f*/**geschlechtliche** autosexualism, autoerotism, ego erotism
Selbstmord *m* suicide ● ~ **begehen** to commit suicide, to take one's own life
Selbstmordabsicht *f* suicidal intent
Selbstmorddrang *m* autophonomania, suicidal mania, thanatomania
Selbstmörder *m* suicide, self-murder
selbstmörderisch suicidal
Selbstmordversuch *m* suicide attempt, attempted suicide
Selbstoxydation *f* auto-oxidation
selbstsüchtig egoistic
selbsttätig automatic, spontaneous
Selbsttäuschung *f* illusion; autosuggestion, self-suggestion
Selbsttötung *f s.* Selbstmord
~ **durch Hungern** apocarteresis, suicide by self-starvation
Selbstüberhebung *f* egotism
Selbstüberschätzung *f* egomania
Selbstverdauung *f* self-digestion, autodigestion, autolysis
Selbstverdauungsferment *n* autolytic enzyme
selbstvergiftend autointoxicant
Selbstvergiftung *f* autointoxication
Selbstverstümmelung *f* [self-]mutilation, self-infliction, autolesionism
Selbstwendung *f* spontaneous version *(des Fetus bei der Geburt)*
Selbstzerstörung *f* autodestruction, inward aggression
Selbstzerstückelung *f* autotomy
selbstzufrieden self-satisfied, complacent
Seldinger-Technik *f* Seldinger guide-wire technique *(der Kathetereinführung)*
Selektion *f* selection
Selektionsdruck *m* selection pressure *(Genetik)*
Selektionstheorie *f* selection theory
selektiv selective
Selenvergiftung *f* selenosis, selenium poisoning
Sella *f* sella, saddle *(Anatomie)*
Sellaregion *f* sellar region
Semen *n s.* Samen
Semi... *s.a.* Halb...
Semicanalis *m* semicanal[is]
~ **musculi tensoris tympani** semicanal of the tensor tympani muscle
~ **tubae auditivae** semicanal of the auditory tube
Semiflexion *f* semiflexion
semikartilaginös semicartilaginous
semilateral semilateral
Semilunarklappe *f* semilunar valve
Semilunarknorpel *m* semilunar (falciform) cartilage
Semilunarlinie *f* semilunar line [of Spieghel]
semimaligne semimalignant
semimembranös semimembranous
Seminom *n* seminoma, seminomal (seminal) carcinoma, seminomatous testis cancer, spermatocytoma

seminomartig seminomatous
Seminurie *f* semenuria, seminuria
Semiologie *f*, **Semiotik** *f* semeiology, symptomatology, semiotics, semeiotics
semipermeabel semipermeable
Semipronation *f* semipronation
Semispinalis *m* semispinalis [muscle]
Semisupination *f* semisupination
semitendinös semitendinous
Semitendinosus *m* semitendinosus [muscle]
Seneszenz *f* senescence, old age *(zwischen 61 und 75 Jahren)*
Senfgas *n* mustard gas, yperite *(hautschädigender Kampfstoff)*
Senfgasschädigung *f* mustard-gas burn; mustard-gas intoxication
Senfpflasterbehandlung *f* sinapism, sinapisation, application of a mustard plaster
Sengstaken-[Blakemore-]Sonde *f* Sengstaken-Blakemore [oesophageal] tube, Blakemore's tube
senil senile
Senilismus *m* senilism
Senilität *f* senility
Senium *n* senium, senectitude *(zwischen 75 und 90 Jahren)*
Senke *f*/**frühdiastolische** early diastolic dip *(der Herzdruckkurve)*
senkend decreasing, lowering; depressant
~/**die Körpertemperatur** algogenic
~/**die Reizschwelle des Herzens** positive bathmotropic
Senkfuß *m* [tali]pes planus, flatfoot; tarsoptosia, tarsoptosis
Senkfußeinlage *f* arch-support, instep-raiser
Senkmagen *m* dropped stomach; ventroptosis, gastroptosis, gastrokateixia
Senkniere *f* floating (wandering) kidney; nephroptosis
Senkung *f* descent, descensus *(eines Organs)*; pronation *(des inneren Fußrandes)*
Senkungsabszeß *m* gravitation abscess, hypostatic (wandering) abscess
Senkungsblutfülle *f* hypostasis, hypostatic hyperaemia
Senkungsmuskel *m* depressor [muscle]
Sensation *f s.* Empfindung
sensibel sensible; sensitive, susceptible *(s. a. empfindlich)*
Sensibilisator *m* sensitizer
sensibilisieren to sensitize
Sensibilisierung *f* sensit[iz]ation, sensibilization, allergization
Sensibilisierungsdosis *f* sensitizing dose
Sensibilisierungsreaktion *f* sensitization response
Sensibilität *f* sensibility, sensitivity, sensitiveness; aesthesia *(Sinnesqualität)*
~/**epikritische** epicritic sensibility
~/**gesteigerte taktile** hyperaphia
~/**taktile** tactile sensibility
Sensibilitätsprobe *f* sensibility (susceptibility) test

Sensibilitätsprüfinstrument *n* aesthesiometer
Sensibilitätssteigerung *f* pathergia, pathergy *(bei Allergie)*
Sensibilitätsverlust *m* sensory loss
sensitiv *s.* sensibel
sensoriell sensorial, sensory
sensorimotorisch senso[ri]motor
sensorineural sensorineural
sensorisch sensorial, sensory
Sensorium *n* 1. sensorium, centre for sensations, perceptorium; 2. sensorium, sensory apparatus; 3. sensorium, consciousness
Sensus *m s.* Sinn
Sentiment *n* sentiment
Separator *m* 1. separator; 2. periosteal elevator
separieren to separate
Sepsis *f* sepsis, sept[ic]aemia, blood poisoning, ichorrhaemia, py[oh]aemia, toxicaemia
~/**bakterielle** bacterial sepsis
~/**endogene** endosepsis
~/**intestinale** intestinal sepsis (toxaemia), enterosepsis
~/**kryptogene** cryptogenic pyaemia
~/**metastasierende** septicopyaemia, pyaemia, pyohaemia
~/**nichtmetastasierende** septicaemia, septaemia
Septektomie *f* septectomy
septenfrei non-septate
Septhämie *f s.* Sepsis
septiert septate
~/**mehrfach** multiseptate
~/**nicht** non-septate
Septierung *f* septation
Septigravida *f* septigravida
Septikämie *f s.* Sepsis
septikämisch *s.* septisch
Septikophlebitis *f* septicophlebitis
Septikopyämie *f* septicopyaemia, septic pyaemia
septikopyämisch septicopyaemic
septisch septic[aemic]
Septometer *n* septometer
Septotom *n* septotome
Septotomie *f* septotomy, cutting of the nasal septum
Septulum *n* septulum, small septum
Septum *n* septum, dividing wall, septation
~ **anococcygeum** anococcygeal ligament
~ **aorticopulmonale (aorticum)** aorticopulmonary septum, bulbar (truncoconal) septum
~ **atrioventriculare** atrioventricular septum
~ **bulbae urethrae** bulbourethral septum
~ **canalis musculotubarii** septum of the musculotuberal canal
~ **cervicale intermedium** intermediate cervical septum
~ **corporum cavernosorum** penile septum
~ **femorale [Cloqueti]** femoral septum
~ **glandis penis** septum of the glans penis
~ **interatriale** [inter]atrial septum
~ **interdentale** interdental septum
~ **intermusculare** intermuscular septum

Sequestrektomie

~ **intermusculare anterius cruris** anterior intermuscular septum of the leg
~ **intermusculare brachii laterale** lateral intermuscular septum of the arm
~ **intermusculare brachii mediale** medial intermuscular septum of the arm
~ **intermusculare femoris laterale** lateral intermuscular septum of the thigh
~ **intermusculare femoris mediale** medial intermuscular septum of the thigh
~ **intermusculare posterius cruris** posterior intermuscular septum of the leg
~ **interventriculare** [inter]ventricular septum
~ **interventriculare primum** bulboventricular crest
~ **linguae** lingual septum
~ **medianum posterius** dorsal median septum
~ **[membranaceum] nasi** nasal (membranous) septum
~ **orbitale** orbital septum
~ **pectiniforme corporis cavernosi penis** pectiniform septum
~ **pellucidum** pellucid septum
~ **penis** penile septum
~ **rectovaginale** rectovaginal septum
~ **rectovesicale** rectovesical septum
~ **scroti** scrotal septum
~ **transversum** transverse septum *(Embryologie)*
~ **urethrovaginale** urethrovaginal septum
~ **urorectale** urorectal (Douglas') septum
~ **ventriculorum** *s.* ~ interventriculare
Septumbildung *f* septation
Septumdefekt *m* septal (septum) defect
~/**aortopulmonaler** aorticopulmonary septal defect
Septumdeviation *f* septal deviation
Septumentfernung *f*[/**operative**] septal resection, septectomy
Septumflachmeißel *m* septum chisel
Septumhohlmeißel *m* septum gouge
septumlos non-septate
Septummeißel *m* septum chisel
Septumperforation *f* septal perforation
Septumplastik *f* septoplasty, septorhinoplasty
Septumschwingmesser *n* septum swivel knife
Septumspritze *f* septum syringe
Septumzyste *f* septal cyst
Sequenzszintigraphie *f* serial (sequential) scintigraphy
Sequester *m* sequestrum, sequester, dead bone
● **einen ~ bilden** to sequester
Sequesterausräumung *f*[/**operative**] sequestrectomy
Sequesterbildung *f* sequestration
Sequesterentfernung *f*[/**operative**] sequestrectomy
Sequesterfreilegung *f*[/**operative**] sequestrotomy
Sequesterzange *f* sequestrum forceps
Sequestration *f* sequestration
Sequestrationsdermoid *n* sequestration dermoid
Sequestrektomie *f* sequestrectomy

sequestrieren

sequestrieren to sequester
Sequestrotomie f sequestrotomy
Serienarteriographie f serial arteriography
Serienschnitt m serial section *(Histologie)*
Serin n serine, α-amino-β-hydroxypropionic acid
Sero... s. a. Serum...
seroalbuminös sero-albuminous
Serochrom n serochrome
Serodermatitis f serodermatitis
Serodermatose f serodermatosis
Serodiagnose f serodiagnosis, orrhodiagnosis
Serodiagnostik f serodiagnostics; diagnostic serology
serodiagnostisch serodiagnostic
serofibrinös serofibrinous, fibroserous
serofibrös serofibrous
Seroflokkulation f seroflocculation
Serokonversion f seroconversion
Serokultur f seroculture
Serologe m serologist
Serologie f serology, orrhology *(Lehre von den Eigenschaften des Blutserums)*
~/diagnostische diagnostic serology
serologisch serologic
Serolysin n serolysin
Serom n seroma
seromembranös seromembranous
seromukös seromucous, seromucoid
seromuskulär seromuscular
seromuzinös seromucinous
seronegativ seronegative *(Seroreaktion)*
Seropneumothorax m seropneumothorax
seropositiv seropositive *(Seroreaktion)*
Seroprophylaxe f seroprophylaxis, serum prophylaxis, seroprevention
seropurulent seropurulent
Seroreaktion f seroreaction, serum reaction, orrhoreaction
seroresistent seroresistant
Seroresistenz f seroresistance
serös serous
Serosa f serosa, serous membrane ● unter der ~ subserous
Serosaauskleidung f serous lining
Serosaschicht f serous (serosal) layer
serös-blutig serosanguineous
seroserös seroserous
Serositis f serositis
serosynovial serosynovial
Serosynovitis f serosynovitis
serotherapeutisch serotherapeutic[al]
Serotherapie f s. Serumbehandlung
Serothorax m serothorax *(Serumansammlung im Brustkorb)*
Serotonin n serotonin, enteramine, 5-hydroxytryptamine *(Katecholamin)*
Serotonin[spiegel]erhöhung f im Blut hyperserotoninaemia
Serotoxin n serotoxin, anaphylatoxin
Serotyp m serotype *(z. B. Bakterien)*
Serovakzination f serovaccination
serozymogen serozymogenic

serozystisch serocystic
serpiginös serpiginous
Serpigo f serpigo
Sertoli-Zelle f Sertoli cell, trophocyte *(im Hoden)*
Sertoli-Zell[en]geschwulst f Sertoli cell tumour
Serum n serum, orrhos ● ~ bildend serous
~/antitoxisches antitoxic serum
~/humanes human serum
~/krankheitsgleiches isoserum
~/menschliches human serum
~/zytotoxisches cytotoxic serum
Serum... s. a. Sero...
serumabsondernd serous
Serum-Ac-Globulin n serum accelerator globulin
serumähnlich serous
Serumakzelerator m accelerator globulin
Serumalbumin n serum albumin, seralbumin
~/humanes human serum albumin
~/mit Jod 131 markiertes iodinated I 131 serum albumin
Serumalbuminausscheidung f im Urin sero-albuminuria
Serumalbuminspiegel m serum albumin level
Serumallergie f serum sickness
Serumamylase f serum amylase, haemodiastase
Serumamylasespiegel m serum amylase level
serumartig serous
Serumausflockung f seroflocculation
Serumausschlag m serum (antitoxin) rash
Serumbehandlung f serotherapy, serum therapy, orrhotherapy, [anti]serum treatment, immunoglobulin medication, toxitherapy
~/prophylaktische seroprophylaxis, serum prophylaxis, seroprevention
Serumbikarbonat n blood bicarbonate *(Blutpufferion)*
Serumbilirubin n serum bilirubin
Serumbilirubinspiegel m bilirubin serum level
Serumcholinesterase f/**unspezifische** pseudocholinesterase *(Enzym)*
Serumelektrolyt m serum electrolyte
Serumelektrolytspiegel m serum electrolyte level
Serumelektrophorese f serum electrophoresis
Serumenzym n serum enzyme
Serumfarbstoff m serochrome
Serumferritin n serum ferritin
Serumfibrinogenstörung f dysfibrinogenaemia
Serumgastrin n serogastrin
Serumgastrinspiegel m serogastrin level
Serumglobulin n seroglobulin, serum globulin
Serumglobulinstörung f dys[gamma]globulinaemia
Serum-Glutamat-Oxalazetat-Transaminase f serum glutamic oxaloacetic transaminase, SGOT
Serum-Glutamat-Pyruvat-Transaminase f serum glutamic pyruvic transaminase, SGPT
Serumgonadotropin n serum gonadotropin
Serumgruppe f serogroup
Serumgruppeneinteilung f serogrouping
serumhaltig serous

Serumhepatitis f [homologous] serum hepatitis, inoculation (transfusion) jaundice, postvaccinal jaundice, virus hepatitis
Serumhepatitis-Antigen n s. SH-Antigen
Serumhepatitis-Virus n SH (serum-hepatitis) virus
Serumikterus m [/homologer] s. Serumhepatitis
Serumimmunität f sero-immunity, passive immunity, orrho-immunity
Serumimmunoglobulin n serum immunoglobulin
Serumimmunoglobulinkonzentration f serum immunoglobulin concentration
Seruminjektion f serum injection
Serum-Komplement-Fixationsreaktion f serum complement fixation reaction
Serum-Komplement-Fixationstiter m serum complement fixation titer
Serumkonzentration f serum concentration
Serumkrankheit f serum sickness
Serumkreatininkonzentration f serum creatinine concentration
Serumlabilitätsprobe f serum tolerance test
Serumlipase f serolipase, serum lipase (Enzym)
Serumlipidspiegel m serum lipid level
Serumlipoproteinstörung f dyslipoproteinaemia
Serumneuritis f serum neuritis
Serum-Neutralisationstest m serum neutralization test
Serumparalyse f serum paralysis
Serumphosphatase f/saure serum acid phosphatase
Serumprobe f 1. serum sample; 2. serological test
Serumprotein n serum protein
~/antigenbindendes s. Immunglobulin
Serumschock m serum shock
Serumschutzimpfung f seroprophylaxis, serum prophylaxis, seroprevention
Serumspiegel m serum level
Serumurtikaria f serum urticaria
Serumzwischenfall m serum accident
sesamartig sesamoid
Sesambein n sesamoid bone
Sesambeinentzündung f sesamoiditis, inflammation of the sesamoid bone
Sesamoiditis f s. Sesambeinentzündung
sessil sessile
setzen/auf Diät to diet
~/Quaddeln to raise weals
Seuche f plague, epidemic
~/bösartige pestilence
seuchenartig epidemic
Seuchenbekämpfung f control of epidemics
Seuchenlehre f loimology, pestology
Seuchenverbreitung f spreading of an epidemic
Sex m sex
Sextigravida f sextigravida
Sextipara f sextipara
Sexualdysfunktion f sexual dysfunction
Sexualentwicklung f sexual development
Sexualerregung f sexual excitation

Sexualerziehung f sexual education
Sexualfunktionsstörung f sexual dysfunction
Sexualhormon n sex hormone
Sexualhormonbehandlung f gonadotherapy
Sexualhygiene f sex hygiene
Sexualität f sexuality
Sexualleben n sex[ual] life
Sexuallehre f sexology
Sexuallust f libido
Sexualneurose f sexual neurosis
Sexualogie f sexology
Sexualpotenz f sexual potency, virility
Sexualpsychologie f sexual psychology
Sexualreflex m sexual (genital) reflex
Sexualschwäche f hyposexuality
Sexualstörung f sexual dysfunction
sexualtriebgestört erotopathic
Sexualtriebgestörter m erotopath
Sexualtriebstörung f erotopathy
Sexualverhalten n sexual behaviour
Sexualzyklus m sexual cycle
sexuell sexual; gamic; venereal
sezernieren to secrete, to excrete
~/Speichel to salivate
sezernierend secretory, excretory; exudative
~/Gelenkschmiere synoviparous
Sezierbesteck n set of post mortem instruments, dissecting instruments
sezieren to dissect, to prosect, to section, to perform an autopsy
~/ein betäubtes Tier to vivisect
Seziermesser n autopsy knife
SGOT s. Serum-Glutamat-Oxalazetat-Transaminase
SGPT s. Serum-Glutamat-Pyruvat-Transaminase
SGR s. Sachs-Georgi-Reaktion
SH-Antigen n Australian (hepatitis virus B) antigen, hepatitis B surface antigen
Shaver-Syndrom n Shaver's disease, bauxite fume pneumoconiosis
Sheehan-Syndrom n Sheehan's syndrome, postpartum acute (haemorrhagic) hypopituitarism
Shiga-Kruse-Bazillus m Shiga bacillus
Shigellose f shigellosis, asylum (bacillary) dysentery
SHT s. Schädel-Hirn-Trauma
Shunt m shunt
~/arteriovenöser arteriovenous (venous-arterial) shunt
~/mesenteriko-kavaler mesocaval shunt
~/mesokavaler mesocaval shunt
~/peritoneovenöser peritoneovenous (peritoneal-venous) shunt
~/portokavaler portocaval shunt
~/portorenaler portorenal shunt
~/portosystemischer portosystemic shunt
~/splenorenaler splenorenal shunt
~/ventrikuloperitonealer ventriculoperitoneal (brain ventricle peritoneum) shunt
shunten to shunt (z. B. Blut von einer Herzkammer in die andere bei Herzfehler)
Shunt-Größe f degree (magnitude) of shunt

Shunt-Hyperbilirubinämie 710

Shunt-Hyperbilirubinämie f shunt hyperbilirubinaemia
Shunt-Operation f shunt (short-circuiting) operation
Shunt-Umkehr f shunt reversal *(bei Herzfehlern)*
Shunt-Volumen n shunt volume
SH-Virus n s. Serumhepatitis-Virus
Siagonagra f siagonagra, gouty pain in the maxilla
Sialadenitis f sial[o]adenitis, sialitis, inflammation of a salivary gland
Sialagogum n sialagogue [agent], sialogogue
Sialaporie f s. Speichelmangel
Sialektasie f sialectasia, enlargement of a salivary gland
Sialemesis f sialemesis, [hysteric] vomiting of saliva
sialisch sialic, sialine
Sialoadenektomie f sialoadenectomy, excision of a salivary gland
Sialoadenotomie f sialoadenotomy, incision into a salivary gland
Sialoaerophagie f sialoaerophagy, swallowing of saliva and air
Sialoangiektasie f s. Speichelgangerweiterung
Sialoangiitis f s. Speichelgangentzündung
Sialodocholithiasis f sialodocholithiasis
Sialodochoplastik f sialodochoplasty
Sialogastron n sialogastrone
Sialogramm n sialogram
Sialographie f sial[aden]ography, sialoangiography
Sialolith m sialolith, salivary calculus, ptya[lo]lith
Sialolithiasis f sialolithiasis, salivolithiasis
Sialolithotomie f sia[lo]lithotomy, ptyalolithotomy
Sialologie f sialology
Sialom n sialoma, sialadenoncus, salivary tumour
Sialomuzin n sialomucin
Sialoporie f s. Speichelmangel
Sialoprotein n sialoprotein
Sialorrhoe f s. Speichelfluß
Sialostenose f sialostenosis, narrowing of a salivary duct
Sichel f s. Falx
sichelförmig falciform, falcate, falcular, sickle-shaped
Sichelzelle f sickle cell, sickled erythrocyte, drepanocyte, meniscocyte
Sichelzellenanämie f sickle-cell anaemia, sickl[a]emia, Herrick's anaemia, sickle haemoglobinopathy, drepanocytosis, drepanocythaemia, meniscocytosis, African (crescent cell, drepanocytic) anaemia, Dresbach's syndrome
Sichelzellenanämiemerkmal n sickle-cell trait
sichelzellenförmig [micro]drepanocytic
Sichelzellenhämoglobin n sickle-cell haemoglobin, haemoglobin S[C]
Sichelzellenkrise f sickle-cell crisis
Sichelzellenretinopathie f sickle-cell retinopathy
sichtbar visible ● **röntgenologisch ~ sein** to cast an X-ray shadow

~/kaum adelomorphic, adelomorphous *(z. B. Drüsenzellen des Magens)*
~/mit bloßem Auge macroscopic
~/mit dem Normalmikroskop nicht ultravisible
Sichtbarmachung f visualization; phanerosis
Sichtbarwerden n phanerosis
Sickerblutung f oozing haemorrhage, seeping bleeding
sickern to ooze, to seep *(z. B. Blut)*
Sideroblast m sideroblast *(Erythrozytenvorstufe)*
Sideroblastenanämie f sideroblastic anaemia
Siderodermie f sideroderma
Siderodromophobie f siderodromophobia *(krankhafte Angst vor dem Eisenbahnfahren)*
Siderofibrose f siderofibrosis
Sideropenie f sideropenia
sideropenisch sideropenic
Siderophag[e] m siderophage
siderophil siderophil[e], siderophilous
Siderophile m siderophil[e]; siderophilous cell
Siderophilie f siderophilia
Siderophilin n siderophilin, transferrin
Siderose f 1. siderosis, ferrugination, excess of iron in the blood (body); 2. siderosis, arc-welder's disease (nodulation)
Siderosilikose f siderosilicosis
Siderosis f **bulbi** siderosis of the eye, eye siderosis
~ hepatis hepatic siderosis; iron liver
~ oculi s. Siderosis bulbi
~ pulmonum pneumosiderosis *(Lungenverhärtung durch eisenhaltigen Staub)*
siderotisch siderotic
Siderozyt m siderocyte
Siderozytenvermehrung f **im Blut** siderocytosis
siebartig cribriform, cribrate, cribral
Siebbein n ethmoid [bone]
Siebbeinarterie f ethmoid artery
~/hintere posterior ethmoid artery
~/vordere anterior ethmoid artery
Siebbeinblase f ethmoid bulla
Siebbeineinschnitt m ethmoid notch
Siebbeinentfernung f[/operative] ethmoidectomy
Siebbeinentzündung f s. Siebbeinzellenentzündung
Siebbeinfibroangiom n fibroangioma of the ethmoid sinus
Siebbeinfortsatz m ethmoid process
Siebbeinhöhle f ethmoid sinus (antrum, cells), ethmoid labyrinth [of cells]
Siebbeinhöhlenausräumung f[/operative] ethmoidectomy
Siebbeinhöhlenentzündung f s. Siebbeinzellenentzündung
Siebbeinhöhleneröffnung f[/operative] ethmoidotomy, incision of an ethmoid sinus
Siebbeinhöhlenschleimhaut f ethmoid mucosa
Siebbeinhöhlentumor m ethmoid sinus tumour
Siebbein-Keilbein-Naht f ethmosphenoid suture
Siebbeinkerbe f ethmoid notch
Siebbeinlabyrinth n s. Siebbeinhöhle

Siebbeinleiste f ethmoid crest
Siebbeinloch n ethmoid foramen, ethmoid (orbital) canal
~/hinteres posterior ethmoid foramen
~/vorderes anterior ethmoid foramen
Siebbein-Oberkiefer-Naht f ethmoidomaxillary suture
Siebbeinschleimhaut f ethmoid mucosa
Siebbein-Stirnbein-Naht f ethmo[ido]frontal suture
Siebbein-Tränenbein-Naht f ethmolacrimal suture
Siebbeintrichter m ethmoid infundibulum
Siebbeinvene f ethmoid vein
~/hintere posterior ethmoid vein
~/vordere anterior ethmoid vein
Siebbeinzellen fpl ethmoid [air] cells
~/hintere posterior ethmoid cells
~/obere middle ethmoid cells
~/vordere anterior ethmoid cells
Siebbeinzellenentfernung f[/operative] ethmoidectomy
Siebbeinzellenentzündung f ethmoiditis, inflammation of the ethmoid bone, ethmoid sinusitis
~/hintere posterior ethmoidal sinusitis
~/vordere anterior ethmoidal sinusitis
Siebbeinzellengeschwulst f ethmoid sinus tumour
Siebbeinzellen- und Tränennasengangentzündung f dacryosinusitis
Siebentagefieber n seven-day fever, dengue [fever], dandy (haemorrhagic) fever
siebförmig cribriform, cribrate, cribral, cribrose
Siebplatte f des Siebbeins cribriform plate of the ethmoid
Siebplattenfraktur f cribriform plate fracture
Siechenhaus n infirmary, hospital for incurables, lazaret[te]
Siechtum n infirmity, sickliness; invalidism; marasmus, athrepsia
Siegelringzelle f signet-ring cell
Siegelringzellenkarzinom n signet-ring-cell carcinoma
Sigma n sigmoid [colon], sigmoid flexure, sigma, pelvic colon *(S-förmiger Dickdarmabschnitt)*
~/vergrößertes megasigmoid
Sigmaanheftung f[/operative] sigmoidopexy, romanoscopy
sigmaartig sigmoid
Sigmabereich m sigmoid area
Sigma-Blasen-Fistel f sigmoidovesical fistula
Sigmadivertikel n sigmoid diverticulum
Sigmadivertikulitis f sigmoid diverticulitis
Sigmaentfernung f[/operative] sigmoidectomy
Sigmaentzündung f sigmoiditis, inflammation of the sigmoid [flexure]
Sigmaeröffnung f[/operative] s. Sigmoidotomie
Sigmafistelung f[/operative] s. Sigmoidostomie
Sigmafixierung f[/operative] s. Sigmoidopexie
sigmaförmig sigmoid
Sigmakarzinom n sigmoid cancer (carcinoma)
Sigma-Kunstafter m sigmoidostomy, sigmoid colostomy

Sigmaniere f sigmoid kidney
Sigmaoperation f/**plastische** sigmoidoplasty
Sigmapolyp m sigmoid polyp
Sigma-Scheiden-Fistel f sigmoidovaginal fistula
Sigmaspiegelung f s. Sigmoidoskopie
Sigmatismus m 1. sigmatism *(häufiger Gebrauch des S-Lauts)*; 2. lisp *(falsche Aussprache der Zischlaute)*
Sigmawiedervereinigung f sigmoidosigmoidostomy
Sigmazismus m s. Sigmatismus
Sigmoid n s. Sigma
Sigmoid-Dickdarm-Anastomose f colosigmoidostomy
Sigmoidektomie f sigmoidectomy
Sigmoiditis f sigmoiditis, inflammation of the sigmoid
Sigmoidoanastomose f sigmoidosigmoidostomy
Sigmoidopexie f sigmoidopexy, romanopexy
Sigmoidoplastik f sigmoidoplasty
Sigmoidoproktostomie f sigmoidoproctostomy, sigmoidorectostomy
Sigmoidosigmoidostomie f sigmoidosigmoidostomy
Sigmoidoskop n sigmoidoscope, rectoromanoscope
Sigmoidoskopie f sigmo[ido]scopy, romanoscopy
sigmoidoskopisch sigmoidoscopic
Sigmoidostomie f sigmoidostomy, sigmoid colostomy
Sigmoidotomie f sigmoidotomy, incision into the sigmoid
Sigmoskopie f s. Sigmoidoskopie
Signallymphknoten m signal node
Signalsymptom n signal symptom *(z. B. bei Epilepsie)*
Signum n sign[um]; symptom
Silbenstottern n syllable stumbling (stuttering); literal ataxia
Silberamalgam n silver amalgam *(Stomatologie)*
Silberdrahtarterie f silver-wire artery *(der Netzhaut)*
silbereinlagernd argentaffine
Silbereinlagerung f in der Haut argyrosis, argyria
silberfärbend argentaffine
Silberfärbung f argentation, silver staining *(Histologie)*
~/Fontanasche Fontana's silver stain[ing] *(von Spirochäten)*
silberfreundlich argyrophile, argyrophilic, argentophil[e], argentaffine
Silberfreundlichkeit f argyrophilia
silberhaltig argentic, argentous
Silberimprägnation f argyrosis, argyria *(der Haut)*
Silberimprägnierung f argentation, silver impregnation *(Histologie)*
~/Cajalsche Cajal's silver method (impregnation) *(Darstellungsmethode des Nervengewebes)*
~/Fontanasche Fontana's silver stain[ing] *(von Spirochäten)*
silbern argentic

Silbernitrat

Silbernitrat *n* silver nitrate, lunar caustic, lapis infernalis
Silber- und Eisenstaublunge[nerkrankung] *f* argyrosiderosis
Silbervergiftung *f* argyrism, argyria
Silikatose *f* s. Silikose
Silikat- und Eisenstaublunge[nerkrankung] *f* silicosiderosis
Silikon *n* silicone
Silikose *f* silic[at]osis, Potter's asthma, stonecutter's phthisis, chalicosis, calcicosis
Silikosekranker *m* silicotic
Silikosiderose *f* silicosiderosis
Silikotuberkulose *f* silicotuberculosis, Potter's phthisis (consumption, rot), tuberculosilicosis
siliziumdioxidhaltig siliceous, silicious
Simulant *m* malingerer, simulator
Simulation *f* malingering, simulation *(z. B. von Krankheiten)*
Simulator *m* simulator
simulieren to malinger, to simulate *(z. B. eine Krankheit)*
Simultanakkommodation *f* binocular accommodation
Simultanperzeption *f* simultaneous perception
Simultanschichtdarstellung *f* multi-layer tomography *(Radiologie)*
Simultansehen *n* binocular vision; simultaneous perception
~/**foveales** simultaneous foveal perception
~/**makuläres** simultaneous macular perception
Sinapismus *m* sinapism, sinapisation, application of a mustard plaster
Sinciput *n* sinciput
Sinding-Larson-Johansson-Syndrom *n* Sinding-Larson disease, Larson-Johansson disease *(Osteochondroseform)*
Singultus *m* singultus, singultation, hiccough, hiccup, spasmolygmus; pseudoglottic myoclonia
sinister sinister, left, on the left side
Sinistrogramm *n* sinistro[cardio]gram, left-side cardiogram
sinistrokardial sinistrocardial
Sinistrokardie *f* sinistrocardia, sinistroposition of the heart
Sinistrokardiogramm *n* s. Sinistrogramm
sinistropedal sinistropedal, left-footed
Sinistrotorsion *f* sinistrotorsion; sinistroclination, twisting to the left
sinken to fall, to drop, to go down *(z. B. Temperatur)*; to fall, to decrease *(z. B. Blutdruck)*
Sinn *m* sense, sensus
Sinnesanpassung *f* mental adjustment
Sinnesapparat *m* sensorium
Sinnesbahn *f* sensory tract
Sinnesempfindung *f* sensation, sensory perception, feeling, aesthesia
Sinnesepithel *n* sensory epithelium, neur[o]epithelium *(aus Sinnes- und Stützzellen bestehend)*
Sinnesepithelzelle *f* sensory epithelial cell
Sinneshaar *n* sensory hair
Sinnesnerv *m* sensory nerve
Sinnesnervenbahn *f* sensory tract
Sinnesnervenzelle *f* sensory nerve cell
Sinnesorgan *n* sense (sensory) organ
Sinnesphysiologie *f* aesthesiophysiology
Sinnesreiz *m* sensory stimulus
Sinnesschärfe *f* acuteness of the senses
Sinnesstörung *f* sensory disturbance
Sinnesstumpfheit *f* dullness of the senses, hebetude
Sinnestäuschung *f* illusion; hallucination; phantom
~/**optische** optical illusion, phantasm
Sinneswahrnehmung *f* sensory perception, pcpt; apperception
Sinneszelle *f* sensory cell
Sinneszell[en]schicht *f* sensory cell layer
Sinneszentrum *n* sensory centre, sensory cortex (area)
sinnlich sensual; voluptuous, carnal; animal
Sinnlichkeit *f* sensuality; voluptuousness
sinoatrial, sinoaurikulär sinoatrial, sinoauricular, SA
Sinogramm *n* sinogram
Sinographie *f* sinography
Sinuitis *f* s. Sinusitis
Sinus *m* sinus *(Anatomie)* ● neben einem ~ parasinoidal
~ **alae parvae** sphenoparietal sinus
~ **analis** anal sinus (crypt), rectal sinus
~ **aortae [Valsalvae]** aortic (Valsalva's) sinus, sinus of Valsalva
~ **caroticus** carotid sinus
~ **cavernosus** cavernous sinus
~ **circularis** circular sinus
~ **coronarius** coronary sinus
~ **durae matris** dural [venous] sinus, cranial venous sinus
~ **epididymidis** sinus of the epididymis, digital fossa
~ **frontalis** frontal sinus
~ **intercavernosus** intercavernous sinus
~ **intercavernosus anterior** anterior intercavernous sinus
~ **intercavernosus posterior** posterior intercavernous sinus
~ **lactiferus** lactiferous sinus, lacteal ampulla
~ **lienalis** splenic sinus
~ **lymphaticus** lymph sinus [space]
~ **maxillaris** maxillary [air] sinus, antrum of Highmore
~ **nasalis** paranasal sinus
~ **obliquus pericardii** oblique sinus of the pericardium
~ **occipitalis** occipital sinus
~ **paranasalis** paranasal sinus
~ **petrosus** petrosal sinus
~ **petrosus inferior** inferior petrosal sinus
~ **petrosus superior** superior petrosal sinus
~ **phrenicocostalis [pleurae]** phrenicocostal (costophrenic) sinus, costodiaphragmatic recess (space)

~ **piriformis** piriform recess (sinus)
~ **prostaticus** prostatic sinus
~ **rectalis** s. ~ analis
~ **rectus** tentorial (straight) sinus
~ **renalis** renal sinus
~ **sagittalis** sagittal (longitudinal) sinus
~ **sagittalis inferior** inferior sagittal sinus, falciform (falcial) sinus
~ **sagittalis superior** superior sagittal sinus
~ **sigmoideus** sigmoid sinus
~ **sphenoidalis** sphenoid [air] sinus
~ **sphenoparietalis** sphenoparietal sinus
~ **tonsillaris** tonsillar fossa
~ **transversus durae matris** transverse sinus [of the dura mater]
~ **transversus pericardii** transverse sinus of the pericardium
~ **tympani** tympanic sinus
~ **urogenitalis** urogenital sinus, genitourinary slit
~ **Valsalvae** s. ~ aortae Valsalvae
~ **venosus sclerae** venous sinus of the sclera, ciliary (Schlemm's) canal
Sinusarrhythmie f sinus [node] arrhythmia
Sinusbildung f sinus formation
Sinusbradykardie f sinus [node] bradycardia
Sinus-cavernosus-Entzündung f cavernous sinus phlebitis
Sinus-cavernosus-Fehlbildung f cavernous sinus malformation
Sinus-cavernosus-Fistel f cavernous sinus fistula
Sinus-cavernosus-Geschwulst f cavernous sinus tumour
Sinus-cavernosus-Syndrom n cavernous sinus syndrome
Sinus-cavernosus-Thrombophlebitis f cavernous sinus thrombophlebitis
Sinus-cavernosus-Thrombose f cavernous sinus thrombosis
Sinus-Dura-Winkel m sinodural angle
Sinuseröffnung f[/operative] sinu[s]otomy
Sinusitis f 1. sinu[s]itis, sinus phlebitis; 2. s. Nasennebenhöhlenentzündung
~ **ethmoidalis** ethmoid sinusitis
~ **ethmoidalis anterior** anterior ethmoid sinusitis
~ **ethmoidalis posterior** posterior ethmoid sinusitis
~ **frontalis** frontal sinusitis
~ **maxillaris** maxillary sinusitis, antritis, highmoritis
~ **paranasalis** nasosinusitis
~ **sphenoidalis** sphenoid sinusitis, sphenoiditis
Sinusknoten m[/Keith-Flackscher] sinus (sinoatrial) node, node of Keith and Flack, pacemaker of the heart *(Herzreizleitung)*
Sinusknotenausfall m sinus arrest
Sinusknotenbradykardie f sinus [node] bradycardia
Sinusknotenrhythmus m sinus [node] rhythm
Sinusknotentachykardie f sinus [node] tachycardia
Sinus-lateralis-Thrombose f lateral sinus thrombosis

Sinusoid m sinusoid
Sinusotomie f sinusotomy
~/**frontale** frontal sinusotomy
Sinusphlebitis f sinu[s]itis, sinus phlebitis
Sinusrhythmus m sinus [node] rhythm
Sinustachykardie f sinus tachycardia
Sinusthrombose f sinus thrombosis
Sinus-Valsalva-Aneurysma n aortic sinus aneurysm, aneurysm of sinus Valsalva, aneurysm of aortic sinus
Sirene f symmelus *(Mißgeburt)*
Sirenenbildung f symmelia
sirenenförmig sirenoid
Sirenomelie f sirenomelia
Sirenomelus m sirenomelus; siren[-limb], sympus
Sitieirgie f sitieirgia, anorexia nervosa
Sitiologie f sitology, dietetics
Sitiomanie f sitomania, bulimia; craving for food
Sitophobie f sitophobia *(krankhafte Angst vor dem Essen)*
Situationsangst f situational anxiety (crisis)
Situationspsychose f situational psychosis
Situationsschwermut m situational depression
Situs m situs, site, location; field; position
~ **inversus [viscerum]** situs inversus, transposition of the viscera, heterotaxia
Sitzangst f acathisia
Sitzbad n sitz (hip) bath
Sitzbein n ischium
Sitzbeinapophysenlösung f ischiadic apophyseal separation
Sitzbeinhöcker m ischiadic tuber, sciatic tuberosity, tuberosity of the ischium
Sitzbeinknorren m s. Sitzbeinhöcker
Sitzbeinresektion f ischiectomy
Sitzbeinstachel m ischiadic (sciatic) spine, spine of the ischium
Sitzbein und Schambein n ischiopubis
Sitzbein- und Schambeinschnitt m ischiopubiotomy *(zur Erweiterung des engen Beckens unter der Geburt)*
Sjögren-Syndrom n Sjögren's syndrome, xerodermosteosis, Gougerot-[Houwer-]Sjögren syndrome
SK s. Streptokinase
s. k. s. subkutan
Skabies f scabies, [seven-year] itch, mange *(durch Krätzemilben hervorgerufene Hautkrankheit)*
~ **crustosa (Norwegica)** Norwegian scabies (itch), Boeck's scabies
Skabiophobie f scabiophobia *(krankhafte Angst vor Skabies)*
skabiös scabious
Skabizid n scabicide [agent]
Skalenektomie f scalenectomy, excision of the scalene muscles
Skalenotomie f scalenotomy, severing of a scalene muscle
Skalenus-anterior-Syndrom n scalenus anterior (anticus) syndrome, thoracic outlet syndrome, brachial plexus compression syndrome

Skalenusdurchtrennung

Skalenusdurchtrennung f [/operative] s. Skalenotomie
Skalenusentfernung f [/operative] s. Skalenektomie
Skalenuslücke f scalene fissure
Skalenuslymphknotenbiopsie f scalene lymph node biopsy
Skalenusmuskel m scalenus [muscle]
Skalenusmuskelexstirpation f s. Skalenektomie
Skalenus-Syndrom n s. Skalenus-anterior-Syndrom
Skalp m scalp
Skalpell n scalpel, [surgical] knife
Skalpellgriff m [knife] handle
skalpieren to scalp
Skalpierung f scalping, avulsion of the scalp
Skalpierungsverletzung f scalp laceration
skandieren to scan
Skandieren n scanning [speech]
skaphoid scaphoid, navicular, boat-shaped
Skaphoiditis f scaphoiditis, inflammation (osteochondrosis) of navicular bone
skaphozephal scaphocephalic
Skaphozephalie f scaphocephalia
Skaphozephalus m scaphocephalus
Skapula f s. Schulterblatt
Skapula... s. a. Schulterblatt...
Skapulafixation f s. Skapulopexie
Skapula-Humerus-Reflex m scapulohumeral reflex
Skapulalgie f scapulalgia, scapulodynia, pain in the scapular region
Skapulalinie f scapular line
Skapularegion f scapular region
Skapulektomie f scapulectomy, excision of the shoulder blade
Skapulodynie f s. Skapulalgie
Skapuloperiostreflex m scapulohumeral reflex
Skapulopexie f scapulopexy, fixation of the shoulder blade
Skarabiasis f scarabiasis, beetle disease
Skarifikationsmesser n scarificator, scarifying knife
skarifizieren to scarify
Skarifizierung f scarification
skarlatiniform scarlatiniform, scarlatinoid, resembling scarlet fever
Skatakratia f scatacratia, scoracratia, faecal incontinence
Skatämie f scataemia
Skatol n skatol[e], scatole *(Geruchsstoff des Kots)*
Skatologie f scatology
skatologisch scatologic
Skatom n scatoma
Skatophagie f scatophagia, eating of excrement
skatophagisch scatophagous, excrement-eating
Skatophilie f scatophilia *(Vorliebe für Kot oder Schmutz)*
Skatophobie f scatophobia *(krankhafte Angst vor Kot oder Schmutz)*
Skatoskopie f scatoscopy, inspection of the faeces

Skeleton n s. Skelett
Skelett n skeleton, osseous system
Skelettalter n skeleton age
skelettartig skeletal
Skelettdeformierung f deformity of the skeleton
skelettförmig skeletal
Skelettgebilde n skeletal structure
skelettieren to skeletonize
Skelettierung f skelet[on]ization
Skelettknochenvermessung f osteometry
Skelettmetastase f skeletal metastasis
Skelettmuskel m skeletal (somatic) muscle
Skelettmuskulatur f skeletal muscles (musculature)
Skelettpräparierung f skeletization
Skelettstruktur f skeletal structure
Skelettzug m skeletal traction
Skeneitis f sken[e]itis, inflammation of the paraurethral glands
Skiaskop n skiascope, retinoscope
Skiaskopie f skiascopy, retino[skia]scopy, koroscopy, scotoscopy; shadow test *(objektive Refraktionsbestimmung des Auges)*
Skiaskotom n skiascotoma
Sklera f sclera, sclerotica, sclerotic coat *(des Auges)* ● **über der ~** suprascleral ● **unter der ~** subscleral, hyposcleral
Sklera... s. a. Lederhaut...
Skleraatrophie f scleral atrophy
Sklerabindehaut f scleral conjunctiva
Skleradegeneration f/hyaline scleral hyaline degeneration
Skleradenitis f scleradenitis
Skleraeindellung f scleral depression
~ durch Plombenaufnähung scleral buckling [procedure], scleral buckle operation
skleral scleral
Skleraoberflächenarterie f episcleral artery
Skleraoberflächenvene f episcleral vein
Skleraperforation f scleral perforation
Sklerapunktion f sclero[tico]nyxis, scleroticopuncture, puncture of the sclera
Skleraresektion f scleral resection
Sklerarigidität f scleral rigidity
Skleraspaltung f [/operative] s. Sklerotomie
Sklerasporn m scleral spur
Sklerateilentfernung f [/operative] s. Sklerektomie
Sklera- und Choroideaentzündung f s. Sklerochoroiditis
Sklera- und Iristeilentfernung f [/operative] sclerecto-iridectomy *(bei Glaukom)*
Skleravorwölbung f s. Sklerektasie
Sklerektasie f bulging out of the sclera, scleral ectasia, sclerectasia, sclerectasis
Sklerektomie f sclerectomy, excision of the sclera
Sklerem n s. Sklerema
Skleren fpl/blaue blue sclerotics
sklerisch sclerotic
Skleritis f scleritis, sclerotitis, scleratitis, inflammation of the sclera

skleroadipös scleroadipose
skleroatroph[isch] scleroatrophic
Skleroblastema n scleroblastema
skleroblastemisch sceleroblastemic
Sklerochoroiditis f sclerochoroiditis, inflammation of the sclera and the choroid coat
Sklerodaktylie f sclerodactyly, scleroderma of the fingers and toes
Sklerodermatitis f scleroderm[at]itis, inflammation and hardening of the skin
Sklerodermie f scleroderma, chorionitis, scleriasis, dermatosclerosis, skleriasis
Sklerodermitis f s. Sklerodermatitis
Sklerödem n scleroedema
~/Buschkesches Buschke's disease (scleroedema)
Sklerogyrie f sclerogyria, atrophic scarring of the cerebral convulsions
Skleroiritis f sclero-iritis, inflammation of the sclera and the iris
Sklerokeratitis f sclerokeratitis, inflammation of the sclera and the cornea; sclerosing keratitis
sklerokonjunktival scleroconjunctival
Sklerokonjunktivitis f scleroconjunctivitis, inflammation of the sclera and the conjunctiva
Sklerokornea f sclerocornea
sklerokorneal sclerocorneal
Sklerom n scleroma (knotenförmige Schleimhautinfiltrate der oberen Luftwege)
Skleromalazie f scleromalacia, softening of the sclera
~/senile senile scleromalacia
Skleromyxödem n scleromyxoedema
Skleronychie f scleronychia, induration and thickening of the nails
Skleronyxis f s. Sklerapunktion
Sklero-Oophoritis f sclero-oophoritis, sclerosing inflammation of the ovary
Skleroperikeratitis f scleroperikeratitis
Sklerophthalmie f sclerophthalmia
Skleroplastik f scleroplasty
Skleroprotein n scleroprotein, albuminoid
sklerös sclerous
Sklerose f sclerosis (z. B. von Geweben) (s. a. unter Sclerosis)
~/allgemeine general sclerosis
~ der Haut sclerosis of the skin, scleroma
~ der Hirnwindungen s. Sklerogyrie
~ des Nervengewebes neurosclerosis
~/familiäre zentrolobuläre familial centrolobular sclerosis
~/generalisierte general sclerosis
~/multiple multiple (multilocular) sclerosis, MS, cerebrospinal (insular) sclerosis, diffuse (disseminated) sclerosis, polysclerosis
~/tuberöse hypertrophische Bourneville's disease
sklerosebewirkend sclerogenic, scler[at]ogenous
sklerosieren to sclerose (z. B. Gewebe)
sklerosierend sclerogenic, scler[at]ogenous
Sklerosierungsbehandlung f sclerotherapy
Sklerosierungsmittel n sclerosant [agent]
Sklerostenose f sclerostenosis
~ des Magens linitis plastica
Sklerostomie f sclerostomy (bei Glaukom)
Sklerotherapie f sclerotherapy
sklerotisch 1. sclerotic, indurated, hard; 2. sclerotic, sclerous, sclerosal
Sklerotom n sclerotome, sclerotomy knife
Sklerotomie f sclero[tico]tomy, incision into the sclera
Sklerotomiemesser n s. Sklerotom
Skolex m s. Bandwurmkopf
Skoliose f scoliosis, skoliosis, lateral curvature [of the spine]
Skoliosebecken n scoliotic pelvis
Skoliosemesser m scoliosometer (Instrument)
Skoliosepelvis f scoliotic pelvis
Skoliosevermessung f scoliosometry
Skoliosometer n scoliosometer
Skoliosometrie f scoliosometry
skoliotisch scoliotic
Skopolamin n scopolamine, hyoscine (Alkaloid)
Skorbut m scurvy, scorbutus, avitaminosis C
~/kindlicher infantile scurvy, Barlow's (Cheadle's) disease; scurvy rickets (Vitamin-C-Mangelkrankheit)
skorbutartig scurvy-like
skorbutauslösend scorbutigenic
skorbutisch scorbutic
skorbutverhindernd antiscorbutic
skotochromogen scotochromogenic
Skotom n 1. scotoma, scotosis, visual field defect; 2. scotoma, mental blind spot
~/Bjerrumsches Bjerrum's (sickle-shaped) scotoma
~/peripapilläres peripapillary scotoma
~/physiologisches physiological scotoma; blind spot
Skotomagraph m scotomagraph (Instrument)
Skotomausmessung f scotometry
Skotombestimmung f scotometry
Skotometer n scotometer
Skotometrie f scotometry
Skotomschreiber m scotomagraph
Skotophilie f scotophilia, love of darkness
Skotophobie f scotophobia (krankhafte Angst vor Dunkelheit)
skotopisch scotopic
Skotopsin n scotopsin (Sehstoff)
Skrobikulus m scrobiculus
skrofelartig scrofulous
Skrofeln fpl scrofula
Skrofuloderm[a] n scrofuloderma
skrofulös scrofulous
Skrofulose f scrofulosis, strumous cachexia, tuberculosis of cervical lymph nodes, king's evil
skrofulotuberkulös scrofulotuberculous
Skropheln fpl scrofula
Skrotal... s. a. Hodensack...
Skrotalarterie f scrotal artery
~/hintere posterior scrotal artery
~/vordere anterior scrotal artery

Skrotalfistel

Skrotalfistel f scrotal fistula
Skrotalhaut f scrotal skin
Skrotalhautkrebs m s. Skrotumkarzinom
Skrotalhernie f scrotal hernia, scrotocele, oscheocele
~ **mit Echinokokkuszysten** hydatidocele
Skrotallymphgefäß n scrotal lymphatic [vessel]
Skrotalreaktion f/**Neill-Moosersche** Neill-Mooser reaction *(Tierversuch zum Nachweis von Rickettsia mooseri)*
Skrotalreflex m scrotal (dartos muscle) reflex
Skrotalsack m s. Skrotum
Skrotalvene f scrotal vein
~/**hintere** posterior scrotal vein
~/**vordere** anterior scrotal vein
Skrotektomie f scrotectomy, excision of the scrotum
Skrotum n scrotum, oschea, bag
Skrotumelephantiasis f oschelephantiasis; lymph scrotum *(durch hochgradige Lymphstauung)*
Skrotumkarzinom n carcinoma of the scrotum, chimney-sweeps' cancer (carcinoma)
Skrotumplastik f scrotoplasty, oscheoplasty
Skrotumzystozele f scrotal cystocele
Skybalum n scybalum
Sludge-Phänomen n **der Erythrozyten** sludging of the erythrocytes; rouleaux formation
Smegma n smegma
~ **embryonum** cheesy varnish, vernix caseosa
Smegmolith m smegmolith
SMH s. Schnelle Medizinische Hilfe
Smith-Petersen-Nagel m Smith-Petersen nail
Snellen-Tafel f Snellen's (near vision) chart; Snellen's whole-line optotypes
Sodbrennen n heartburn, [gastric] pyrosis, [water] brash
Sodoku n sodoku, spirillary [rat-bite] fever, rat-bite fever
Sodomie f sodomy, paederasty, buggery
Sodomit m sodomist
Sofortagglutination f immediate agglutination
Sofortallergie f immediate allergy, immediate hypersensitivity [reaction]
Sofortbehandlung f immediate therapy
Sofortgedächtnis n short-term memory
Sofortkomplikation f immediate complication
Sofortnekrose f immediate necrosis
Sofortreaktion f immediate reaction
~/**allergische** s. Sofortallergie
Sohle f sole [of the foot], planta
Sohlenfläche f plantar surface
Sohlenplatte f sole plate
Sohlenspanner m plantaris [muscle]
Sohlenviereckmuskel m quadratus plantae [muscle], flexor digitorum accessorius [muscle]
Sol n 1. sol, colloidal solution; suspensoid; 2. sol, salt
~ **carolinum [factitium]** Carlsbad salt
Solarasphyxie f sunstroke, thermic fever, siriasis
Solarium n solarium, sun parlor

Solarplexus m solar (coeliac) plexus, abdominal brain
Solarretinopathie f solar retinitis (retinopathy)
Solartherapie f solar therapy, solarization
Solitärbündel n solitary fasciculus (tract)
Solitärenchondrom n solitary enchondroma
Solitärexostose f solitary exostosis
Solitärfollikel m solitary follicle
Solitärknoten m solitary (signal) node *(z. B. ein Lymphknoten)*; sentinel pile *(Hämorrhoide)*
Solitärtuberkel m solitary (conglomerate) tubercle
Solitärzyste f solitary cyst
Solum n **tympani** floor of the tympanic cavity
~ **ventriculi quarti** floor of the fourth ventricle
Solutio f **Castellani** Castellani's mixture (paint) *(zur Behandlung von Hautkrankheiten)*
Solvens n 1. solvent [agent]; 2. resolvent [agent]; expectorant [agent]
Soma n 1. soma *(als Gegensatz zur Psyche)*; 2. soma, body tissue; 3. s. Rumpf
Soman n soman *(Nervenkampfstoff)*
Somästhesie f somaesthesia, consciousness of the body; awareness of bodily sensations
somästhetisch somaesthetic
somatikoviszeral somaticovisceral
somatisch somatic
somatochrom somatochrome
Somatodidymus m somatodidymus, somatopagus *(Mißgeburt)*
Somatodymie f somatodymia
somatogen somatogen[et]ic
Somatogramm n somatogram
Somatologie f somatology *(Lehre vom menschlichen Organismus)*
somatologisch somatologic
Somatomedin n somatomedin
Somatometrie f somatometry
somatometrisch somatometric
Somatopagus m s. Somatodidymus
Somatopathie f somatopathy
somatopathisch somatopathic
Somatoplasma n somatoplasm
somatopleural somatopleural
somatosensorisch somatosensory
Somatoskopie f somatoscopy
somatoskopisch somatoscopic
Somatostatin n somatostatin
Somatotherapie f somatotherapy
somatotopisch somatotopic
somatotrop somatotropic
Somatotrop[h]in n somatotrop[h]in, somatotropic (growth) hormone, STH
Somatotyp m somatotype, body type
Somit m somite, metamere, mesoblastic (mesodermal) segment
Sommercholera f s. Sommerdiarrhoe
Sommerdiarrhoe f summer cholera (diarrhoea)
Sommerenzephalitis f summer encephalitis
Sommerjucken n summer prurigo
Sommersprosse f sunspot, freckle, ephelis
sommersprossig freckled

somnambul somnambulistic, noctambulic
Somnambuler *m* somnambulist, sleep-walker
Somnambulimus *m* somnambulism, sleep-walking, somnambulance, hypnobatia, active oneirodynia
Somniloquie *f* somniloquy, somniloquence, somniloquism, talking in sleep
Somniloquist *m* somniloquist
somnolent somnolent, sleepy
Somnolenz *f* somnolence, somnolentia *(leichter Grad der Bewußtseinsherabsetzung)*
somnoleszent somnolescent
Somogyi-Einheit *f* Somogyi unit *(der Amylaseaktivität)*
Sonde *f* probe, sound, probang, tube
~/Blakemoresche Blakemore's tube
~/Starcksche Starck's cardiodilator
Sondenernährung *f* tube feeding, gastrogavage
sondieren to probe, to sound
Sondierkanüle *f* exploring needle
Sondierkatheter *m* exploratory catheter
Sondierung *f* probe, sounding
Sonnenbad *n* sun bath
Sonnenbestrahlung *f* insolation, heliation, solarization
Sonnenblumenstar *m* sunflower cataract
Sonnenbrand *m* sun burn, solar dermatitis; heliosis
Sonnenbräune *f* [sun]tan
Sonnenempfindlichkeit *f* heliosensitivity
Sonnenfinsternisblindheit *f* eclipse-blindness
Sonnengeflecht *n s.* Solarplexus
Sonnenstich *m* sunstroke, heliosis, heat stroke, helioencephalitis, thermoplegia
Sonnenstrahlenbehandlung *f* heliotherapy, solar therapy, solarization, therapeutic insolation
Sonnenstrahlenblindheit *f* sun blindness; eclipse-blindness
Sonnenstrahlenfurcht *f* heliophobia
Sonnenstrahlenretinitis *f* solar retinitis (retinopathy)
Sonnenstrahlenüberempfindlichkeit *f* heliosensitivity
Sonnenuntergangsphänomen *n* setting-sun phenomenon
Sonogramm *n* [ultra]sonogram
Sonographie *f* [ultra]sonography, ultrasonication, pulse-echo diagnosis
sonographisch [ultra]sonographic
Sonometer *n* sonometer
sonor sonorous, resonant; sounding
Soor *m* soor, candidiasis, parasitic (aphthous, mycotic) stomatitis, stomatomycosis, oral moniliasis, thrush *(Mundschleimhautentzündung durch Candida albicans)*
Soorerkrankung *f* **der Bronchien** bronchocandidiasis, bronchomoniliasis
Soorinfektion *f* candidal infection
Soorpilz *m* Candida (Oidium) albicans, thrush fungus

Sopor *m* sopor, profound sleep
soporös soporous, soporose
Sorbit *m* sobite, sorbitol *(Zuckeralkohol)*
Sordes *m* sordes *(Beläge bei Fieber)*
Sozialfürsorge *f* social welfare
Sozialfürsorgerin *f* social worker
Sozialhygiene *f* social hygiene
Sozialmedizin *f* social medicine
sozialmedizinisch sociomedical
Sozialpsychologie *f* social psychology
Sozialversicherung *f* social (health) insurance
Soziologe *m* sociologist
Soziologie *f* sociology
soziologisch sociological
Spalt *m* cleft *(Embryologie)*; fissure, fissura *(z. B. im Knochen)*; scissura, scissure *(z. B. der Haare)*
~/synaptischer synaptic gap
Spaltbecken *n* split pelvis
Spaltbildung *f* 1. *s.* Spalt; 2. dysraphism *(der Wirbelsäule)*; araphia *(z. B. des Neuralrohrs)*; coloboma *(z. B. des Augenlids)*; 3. cleavage *(z. B. bei der Zellteilung)*
Spalte *f* cleft *(Embryologie)*; rhagade *(z. B. der Haut)*; hiatus *(z. B. im Zwerchfell)*; crena *(z. B. am Anus)*; rima *(z. B. am Gesäß) (Zusammensetzungen s. unter Rima)*
spalten to split, to cleave
spaltend splitting; clastic, breaking up [into fragments]
spalterbig heterozygous
Spalterbigkeit *f* heterozygosity
Spaltfraktur *f* split fracture
Spaltfuß *m* cleft foot
Spalthand *f* cleft (lobster-claw) hand
Spalthaut *f* split-thickness skin
Spalthauttransplantat *n* split-thickness [skin] graft, split-[-skin] graft, partial-thickness skin graft
Spalthauttransplantatentnahmestelle *f* split-thickness skin graft donor site
Spalthauttransplantation *f* split-thickness grafting
Spaltkiefer *m* cleft jaw; gnathoschisis, schizognathism
Spaltlampe *f* slit lamp; corneal microscope
Spaltlampenmikroskop *n* slit-lamp microscope
Spaltlampenmikroskopie *f* slit-lamp microscopy
Spaltlampenuntersuchung *f* slit-lamp examination
Spaltlinie *f* cleavage line *(z. B. der Haut)*
Spaltlippe *f* cleft lip, harelip; cheiloschisis
Spaltpenis *m* fissured penis; penischisis
Spaltpilz *m* schizomycete, schizomyces
Spaltpilzerkrankung *f* schizomycosis
Spaltraum *m*/**perivaskulärer** perivascular space [of Virchow-Robin], Virchow-Robin space
Spaltschädel *m* schistocephalus
Spaltschädeligkeit *f* schistencephalia
Spaltthorax *m* schistothorax; fissure of the thorax

Spaltung

Spaltung f 1. splitting, cleavage, fission, discission (z. B. der Linsenkapsel); lancing, incision (z. B. eines Abszesses); distrix (der Haarenden); 2. splitting, dissociation (z. B. der Persönlichkeit) ● **durch ~ entstanden** schizogonic
~ der Herztöne splitting of the heart sounds
~/hydrolytische hydrolytic cleavage
Spaltungsirresein n s. Schizophrenie
Spaltungsteilung f schizogenesis, schizogony
Spaltwirbel m cleft (butterfly) vertebra; bifid spine
~ mit Hautüberdeckung spina bifida occulta; cryptomeror[rh]achischisis
Spaltzäpfchen n cleft uvula; staphyloschisis
Spaltzunge f cleft (fissured, bifid) tongue; schistoglossia, glossoschisis
Span m chip (eines Knochens)
Spananlagerungsoperation f/**Campellsche** Campell's operation
Spann m instep
Spanner m tensor [muscle]
Spannmuskel m **des weichen Gaumens** palatosalpingeus [muscle]
Spannung f tension, excitement (Erregung); stress, strain (psychisch); tone, tonus (z. B. eines Muskel)
~/emotionale emotional tension
Spannungsblase f tension bulla (z. B. der Haut)
Spannungsgrad m intensity (einer Muskelkontraktion)
Spannungsirresein n catatonia, katatonia, catatonic type of schizophrenia (muskelstarre Form)
Spannungspneu[mothorax] m tension (valvular) pneumothorax
Spannungszustand m tone, tonus (z. B. eines Muskels); tonicity, turgor (z. B. des Gewebes)
Sparganuminfektion f sparganosis
Spartein n sparteine (Alkaloid)
Spasmoanalgetikum n spasmoanalgesic [agent]
spasmodisch spasmodic, spasmous, spastic, convulsive
spasmogen spasmogenic, convulsant
Spasmologie f spasmology, epileptology
Spasmolygmus m s. Singultus
Spasmolyse f spasmolysis
Spasmolytikum n spasmolytic [agent], antispasmodic [agent]
spasmolytisch spasmolytic, antispasmodic
Spasmophemie f s. Stottern
spasmophil spasmophil[e], spasmophilic
Spasmophilie f spasmophilia, spasmophilic diathesis
Spasmus m spasm[us], cramp, jerk (s. a. unter Krampf)
~ glottidis glottic (laryngeal) spasm, laryngospasm, laryngismus
~/inspiratorischer inspiratory spasm
~ muscularis muscular spasm, muscle cramp
~ nictitans nictitating (winking) spasm, nictitation

~ nutans gyrospasm
~ palatinus palatine spasm
~ rotatorius rotatory spasm
Spastik f spasticity
Spastiker m spastic
spastisch spastic, spasmodic, convulsive
Spastizität f spasticity
Spätabort m late abortion
Spätallergie f delayed allergy
Spätdiagnose f late diagnosis
Späteinfluß m late influence
Spatel m spatula, blade
spatelförmig spatula-shaped, spatulate[d], spatular
Spätepilepsie f tardy (delayed) epilepsy
Spätergebnis n late result (einer Therapie)
Spätgeburt f delayed labour; retarded birth
Späthämolyse f late haemolysis
Spatia npl **anguli iridis** iris angle spaces [of Fontana], spaces of the iridocorneal angle, Fontana's spaces
~ intervaginalia intervaginal spaces
Spatium n space, spatium (s. a. unter Raum)
~ infracolicum infracolic space
~ intercostale intercostal space
~ perilymphaticum perilymphatic (periotic) space
~ praeputiale preputial sac (space)
~ praevesicale prevesical space [of Retzius], space (cave) of Retzius
~ prostaticum anterior interlevator cleft
~ retroperitoneale retroperitoneal space, retroperitoneum
~ retropubicum retropubic space
Spätkomplikation f late complication
Spätlähmung f late paralysis
Spätmanifestation f late manifestation
Spätparkinsonismus m delayed parkinsonism
Spätrachitis f late rickets
Spätreaktion f delayed-type hypersensitivity (Immunologie)
Spätreflex m delayed reflex
Spätrezidiv n late recurrence (relapse)
Spätschmerz m delayed pain
Spätsymptom n delayed symptom; late sign
Spätsyndrom n/**postalimentäres** post-cibal late syndrome (Dumping-Syndrom)
Spätsyphilis f late (latent, retarded) syphilis
spätsystolisch late systolic
Spättodesfall m late death
Spättyp m delayed-reaction type (Immunologie)
Speckhaut f buffy coat (des Blutes)
speckig lardaceous; amyloid
Speckleber f amyloid liver, waxy (lardaceous) liver
Speckmilz f bacon spleen, waxy (amyloid) spleen
Speckniere f amyloid kidney, waxy (lardaceous) kidney
Speiche f radius (Unterarmknochen)
Speichel m saliva, sialon, ptysma
Speichelamylase f salivary amylase (Enzym)
speichelanregend salivatory, salivant

Speichelantiseptikum n salivary antiseptic
speichelartig sialic, sialine, salivous, sialoid
speichelbedingt ptyalogenous, ptyalogenic
speichelbildend sialogenous
Speicheldiagnostik f sialosemeiology
Speicheldiastase f ptyalin, ptyalase *(Enzym)*
Speicheldrüse f salivary gland
Speicheldrüsenentfernung f[/operative] sialoadenectomy, excision of a salivary gland
Speicheldrüsenentzündung f sial[o]adenitis, sialitis, inflammation of a salivary gland
Speicheldrüsenfunktionsstörung f salivary gland disorder
Speicheldrüsengang m s. Speichelgang
Speicheldrüsengeschwulst f salivary [gland] tumour, sialoadenoncus, sialoma
Speicheldrüsengewebe n salivary gland tissue
Speicheldrüseninzision f sialoadenotomy, incision of a salivary gland
Speicheldrüsenkatheter m salivary gland catheter
Speicheldrüsenröntgen[kontrast]bild n sialogram
Speicheldrüsenröntgenkontrastdarstellung f sialo[angio]graphy, sialadenography
Speicheldrüsenschwellung f sialectasia
Speicheldrüsenvergrößerung f salivary gland enlargement
Speicheldrüsenzyste f ptyalocele
Speichelerbrechen n sialemesis, [hysteric] vomiting of saliva
Speichelfistel f salivary fistula, sialosyrinx
Speichelfluß m salivation, sialosis, sialorrh[o]ea
 ● den ~ **anregend** sialagogic, sialogogic, ptyalogogue
~/**vermehrter** ptyalorrhoea, ptyalism, excessive salivation, drooling, polysialia
~/**verminderter** oligoptyalism, oligosialia
speichelflußhemmend antisialagogue
Speichelgang m salivary duct
Speichelgangdrain m sialosyrinx
Speichelgangentzündung f sialoangitis, sialoductitis
Speichelgangerweiterung f dilatation of the salivary ducts, sialoangiectasis, ptyalectasis
Speichelgangrekonstruktion f sialodochoplasty
Speichelgangspritze f sialosyrinx
Speichelgangsteinleiden n sialodocholithiasis
Speichelgangvereng[er]ung f sialostenosis, narrowing of a salivary duct
Speichelgangzyste f salivary duct cyst
speichelhemmend antisialagogue, antisialic
Speichelkörperchen n salivary corpuscle
Speichelleukozyt m salivary corpuscle
Speichelmangel m hyposalivation, hypoptyalism, sialoporia, sialaporia
speicheln to salivate *(die Nahrung)*
Speichelreflex m salivary reflex
Speichelsauger m saliva ejector, sucker
Speichelsekretion f salivary secretion, salivation
~/**fehlende** aptyalism, aptyalia, asialia
~/**vermehrte** hypersalivation, hyperptyalism
~/**verminderte** hyposalivation, hypoptyalism
Speichelsekretionszentrum n salivary centre
Speichelstein m s. Sialolith
speichelstimulierend salivatory, salivant
Speicheltasche f sputum bag
speicheltreibend salivatory, salivant, sialagogic, sialogogic, ptyalogogue
Speichel- und Luftschlucken n swallowing of saliva and air, sialoaerophagy
Speichelverdauung f salivary digestion
Speichelverhaltung f sialoschesis, retention of saliva
Speichelvorverdauung f salivary digestion
Speichelzentrum n salivary centre
Speichelzyste f sialocele, ptyalocele
Speichen... s.a. Radius...
Speichenarterie f radial artery
~/**rückläufige** radial recurrent artery
Speichenfraktur f/**Collessche (distale)** Colles' fracture [of the radius]
~ **mit Gabelrückenstellung** silver-fork fracture
Speichen-Handwurzel-Gelenk n radiocarpal articulation, wrist joint [proper]
Speichenhinterrand m posterior border of the radius
Speichenkörper m shaft of the radius
Speichenleiste f/**vordere** anterior margin of the radius
Speichennerv m radial nerve
Speichenschaft m shaft of the radius
Speichenvene f radial vein
Speicherelektrokardiogramm n tape-recorded electrocardiogram
Speicherfett n depot fat
Speicherkörnchen n storage granule
Speicherkrankheit f storage disease, thesaurismosis
Speicherorgan n storage organ
speien to spit; to vomit *(erbrechen)*
Speiglas n spitton
Speisebrei m chyme, chymus
Speisebreiverminderung f oligochymia
Speisegefäß n feeder vessel *(z. B. eines Organs)*
Speisenabneigung f apositia
Speiseröhre f oesophagus, gullet ● **durch die ~** transoesophageal ● **neben der ~** paraoesophageal
~/**erweiterte** megaoesophagus
Speiseröhren... s.a. Ösophag...
Speiseröhrenatresie f oesophageal atresia
Speiseröhren-Bronchus-Fistel f oesophagobronchial fistula
Speiseröhrendivertikel n oesophageal diverticulum
Speiseröhrenendothese f oesophageal endoprosthesis
Speiseröhrenentfernung f[/operative] oesophagectomy, excision of the oesophagus
Speiseröhrenentzündung f oesophagitis, inflammation of the oesophagus
~ **durch Monilia** monilial oesophagitis
Speiseröhreneröffnung f[/operative] oesophagotomy, incision into the oesophagus

Speiseröhrenerweichung

Speiseröhrenerwelchung f oesophagomalacia, softening of the wall of the oesophagus
Speiseröhrenerweiterung f oesophagectasia, dilatation of the oesophagus; megaoesophagus
Speiseröhrenfaltungsoperation f oesophagoplication
Speiseröhrenfistel f oesophageal fistula
~/operative oesophagostoma
Speiseröhrenfistelung f[/operative] oesophagostomy
Speiseröhreninnendruckmessung f oesophageal manometry
Speiseröhrenkrampf m oesophagospasm, oesophagism[us], spasmodic contraction of the oesophagus
Speiseröhrenkrebs m oesophageal cancer (carcinoma)
Speiseröhrenlähmung f oesophageal paralysis, lemoparalysis
Speiseröhren-Leerdarm-Anastomose f oesophagojejunostomy
Speiseröhren-Luftröhren-Fistel f oesophagotracheal fistula
Speiseröhren-Magen-Anastomose f oesophagogastrostomy
Speiseröhren-Magen-Zwölffingerdarm-Spiegelung f oesophagogastroduodenoscopy
Speiseröhrenmuskeldurchtrennung f[/operative] oesophagomyotomy
Speiseröhrennervengeflecht n oesophageal plexus
Speiseröhrenöffnung f oesophagostoma, oesophagostomy
Speiseröhrenrekonstruktion f oesophagoplasty
Speiseröhrenröntgen[kontrast]bild n oesophagogram
Speiseröhrenröntgen[kontrast]darstellung f oesophagography
Speiseröhrensonde f oesophageal sound
Speiseröhrensoor m oesophageal moniliasis
Speiseröhren- und Magenentfernung f[/operative] oesophagogastrectomy
Speiseröhren- und Magenplastik f oesophagogastroplasty
Speiseröhren- und Magenspiegelung f oesophagogastroscopy
Speiseröhrenvereng[er]ung f oesophagostenosis, oesophageal stenosis, lemostenosis
Speiseröhrenverlagerung f oesophagectopy
Speiseröhrenverlegung f obstruction of the oesophagus
Speiseröhrenzerreißung f oesophageal rupture (tear)
Speiseröhren-Zwölffingerdarm-Anastomose f oesophagoduodenostomy
Speisewege mpl food passages
Spektrum n/**antibiotisches** antibiotic (bacteriostatic) spectrum, antibacterial spectrum
Spekulum n speculum (Instrument)
Spendeareal n donor area (z. B. für Hauttransplantate)

spenden to donate (z. B. Blut)
Spender m donor (von Blut oder Transplantaten)
Spenderblut n donor blood
Spenderbluteinsparung f saving of donor blood
Spendererythrozyt m donor erythrocyte
Spender-gegen-Empfänger-Reaktion f graft-versus-host reaction
Spendergewebe n donor tissue
Spenderleiche f cadaver donor
Spenderorgan n donor organ
Spenderplasma n donor plasma
Spendersamen m donor semen
Spenderserum n donor serum
Sperma n sperm, semen; seminal fluid
Sperma... s.a. Samen...
Spermasekretion f/**vermehrte** hyperspermia
~/verminderte oligo[zoo]spermia, oligospermatism
Spermatakrasie f spermatacrasia
Spermatide f s. Samenzelle
Spermatitis f spermatitis, inflammation of the vas deferens, deferentitis, funiculitis
Spermatocystitis f **gonorrhoica** gonococcal vesiculitis
Spermatogenese f s. Samenbildung
Spermatogonie f spermatogonium, spermatophore, sperm[at]ospore
Spermatogramm n spermiogram
Spermatologie f spermatology
Spermatolyse f sperm[at]olysis, solution of spermatozoa
Spermatolysin n spermatolysin
spermatolytisch spermatolytic
Spermatopathie f spermatopathy
Spermatorrhoe f sperm[at]orrhoea, gonocratia
Spermatorrhoea f **dormientum** nocturnal emission (pollution)
Spermatoschesis f spermatoschesis
Spermatotoxin n sperma[to]toxin
Spermatozele f spermatocele, gonocele; hydrospermatocele
Spermatozelektomie f spermatocelectomy
Spermatozoenbildung f spermiogenesis
Spermatozoenreifung f spermatogenesis, spermiogenesis
spermatozoentötend spermatocidal, spermicidal
Spermatozoon n s. Samenzelle
Spermatozystektomie f spermatocystectomy, vesiculectomy, excision of the seminal vesicles
Spermatozystitis f spermatocystitis, inflammation of a seminal vesicle, [seminal] vesiculitis, gonadocystitis
Spermatozystotomie f spermatocystotomy, vesiculotomy
Spermatozyt m s. Samenzelle
Spermaturie f spermaturia, semenuria, seminuria
spermienartig spermatoid, spermatic
Spermienbeweglichkeit f sperm motility
Spermienbewegung f sperm migration
Spermiengift n sperma[to]toxin
Spermienkopf m sperm head, head of the spermatozoon

Spermienlebensfähigkeit *f* sperm viability
spermienlos aspermatic, aspermatous
Spermienmißbildung *f* terato[zoo]spermia
Spermiennukleus *m* sperm nucleus
Spermienpenetration *f* sperm penetration
Spermienschwanz *m* sperm tail
spermientötend spermatocidal, spermicidal
Spermienvitalität *f* sperm viability
Spermienzählung *f* sperm count
Spermienzerfall *m s.* Spermatolyse
Spermin *n* spermin[e]
Spermiogenese *f* spermiogenesis, spermatogenesis
Spermiogramm *n* spermiogram
Spermium *f s.* Samenzelle
Spermiumzentrosom *n* sperm centre
spermizid spermatocidal, spermicidal
Spermolith *m* spermolith, calculus in the spermiduct
Sperrer *m* retractor *(Chirurgie)*
Sperrliquor *m* spinal block syndrome
Sperrung *f* block[ing], blockage
~ der Gelenkbeweglichkeit arthroereisis, arthrorisis *(durch Operation)*
Spezialist *m* **für Sprachstörungen** lalophomiatrist, speech pathologist
Spezifikum *n* specific [agent] *(gegen bestimmte Krankheiten)*
spezifisch specific *(z. B. Symptom)*
~/nicht non-specific
Sphärometer *n* spherometer
Sphärophakie *f* spherophakia; bullet lens
Sphäroplast *m* spheroplast *(gramnegatives zellwandarmes Bakterium)*
Sphärozyt *m* spherocyte
Sphärozytenanämie *f* spherocytic anaemia, [hereditary] spherocytosis, haemolytic splenomegaly, chronic (familial) acholuric jaundice, congenital haemolytic icterus
Sphärozytenvermehrung *f* **im Blut** *s.* Sphärozytose
sphärozytisch spherocytic
Sphärozytose *f* spherocytosis, globe-cell anaemia
~/hereditäre hereditary spherocytosis
Sphenion *n* sphenion *(anthropologischer Meßpunkt)*
sphenoethmoidal sphenoethmoid
sphenofrontal sphenofrontal
sphenoidal sphenoid[al]
Sphenoiditis *f* sphenoiditis, inflammation of the sphenoid sinus
Sphenoidostomie *f* sphenoidostomy
Sphenoidotomie *f* sphenoidotomy, incision into the sphenoid sinus
sphenomalar sphenomalar
sphenomandibular sphenomandibular
sphenomaxillar sphenomaxillary
sphenookzipital spheno-oocipital, sphenobasilar
sphenoorbital sphenorbital
sphenopalatinal sphenopalatine
sphenoparietal sphenoparietal

sphenopetrosal sphenopetrosal
sphenosquamös sphenosquamosal
sphenotemporal sphenotemporal
Sphenozephalie *f* sphenocephalia
Sphenozephalus *m* sphenocephalus
sphenozygomatisch sphenozygomatic
Sphincter *m* sphincter [muscle], constrictor [muscle], obturator [muscle]
~ ani anal sphincter
~ choledochus choledochal sphincter
~ urethrae urethral sphincter, external urinary sphincter
Sphingolipid *n* sphingolipid
Sphingolipidose *f* sphingolipidosis, neurolipidosis, neuronal storage disease
Sphingolipidspeicherkrankheit *f s.* Sphingolipidose
Sphingomyelin *n* sphingomyelin, Niemann-Pick lipid *(glyzerinfreies Phosphatid)*
Sphingomyelinase *f* sphingomyelinase *(Enzym)*
Sphingomyelinspeicherkrankheit *f* Niemann-Pick disease
Sphingosin *n* sphingosine
Sphinkter *m s.* Sphincter
Sphinkter... *s.a.* Schließmuskel...
Sphinkterachalasie *f* sphincteric achalasia
Sphinkteralgie *f* sphincteralgia, pain in the sphincter ani
Sphinkterektomie *f* sphincterectomy, excision of a sphincter
Sphinkterfunktion *f* sphincter function
Sphinkterismus *m* sphincterism, spasm of the sphincter ani
Sphinkteritis *f* sphincteritis, inflammation of a sphincter
Sphinkterlähmung *f* sphincter paralysis
Sphinktermechanismus *m* sphincteric mechanism
Sphinktermuskulatur *f* sphincteric musculature
Sphinkterogramm *n* sphincterogram
Sphinkterolyse *f* sphincterolysis *(Lösung von Regenbogenhautverwachsungen an der Hornhaut)*
Sphinkteroskop *n* sphincteroscope
Sphinkteroskopie *f* sphincteroscopy
Sphinkterotomie *f* sphincterotomy, cutting of a sphincter
Sphinkterplastik *f* sphincteroplasty
Sphinkterreflex *m* sphincteric reflex
Sphinktertätigkeit *f* sphincteric action
Sphinktertenesmus *m s.* Sphinkterismus
sphygmisch sphygmic[al]
Sphygmobologramm *n* sphygmobologram
Sphygmobolometer *n* sphygmobolometer
Sphygmobolometrie *f* sphygmobolometry
Sphygmochronograph *m* sphygmochronograph
Sphygmochronographie *f* sphygmochronography
Sphygmodynamometer *n* sphygmodynamometer
Sphygmodynamometrie *f* sphygmodynamometry

sphygmodynamometrisch 722

sphygmodynamometrisch sphygmodynamometric
Sphygmogramm n sphygmogram
Sphygmograph m sphygmograph; sphygmometer; arteriograph
Sphygmographie f sphygmography
sphygmographisch sphygmographic
Sphygmokardiogramm n sphygmocardiogram, cardiosphygmogram
Sphygmokardiographie f sphygmocardiography, cardiosphygmography
sphygmokardiographisch sphygmocardiographic, cardiosphygmographic
Sphygmomanometer n sphygmomanometer
Sphygmomanometerball m sphygmomanometer bulb
Sphygmomanometrie f sphygmomanometry
sphygmomanometrisch sphygmomanometric
Sphygmooszillometer n sphygmooscillometer
Sphygmophon n sphygmophone
Sphygmoplethysmograph m sphygmoplethysmograph
Sphygmoplethysmographie f sphygmoplethysmography
Sphygmoskop n sphygmoscope
Sphygmoskopie f sphygmoscopy
sphygmoskopisch sphygmoscopic
Sphygmosystole f sphygmosystole
Sphygmotonogramm n sphygmotonogram
Sphygmotonograph m sphygmotonograph
Sphygmotonometer n sphygmotonometer
Sphygmus m sphygmus, pulse, pulsus *(Zusammensetzungen s. unter Puls)*
Spica f spica [bandage], spiral reverse bandage; figure-of-eight bandage
Spidernävus m s. Spinnennävus
Spiegel m 1. mirror; reflector; 2. speculum *(Instrument)*
spiegelartig mirror-like *(Bakterien)*
Spiegelbilder npl/**Purkinje-Sansonsche** Purkinje-Sanson's images
Spiegelhaploskop n mirror haploscope *(Ophthalmologie)*
Spiegelsehen n mirror vision
Spiegelsprache f mirror speech *(Verstellung von Silben beim Sprechen)*
Spiegelungsinstrument n s. Endoskop
Spiegler-Fendt-Sarkoid n Spiegler-Fendt sarcoid
Spieltherapie f play therapy
Spilus m spilus *(Pigmentvermehrung der Haut)*
Spina f spine, spina ● über einer ~ supraspinal
~ **angularis** angular spine
~ **bifida** bifid spine; butterfly vertebra
~ **bifida occulta** occult bifid spine; cryptomeror[rh]achischisis, hemirachischisis
~ **bifida occulta/rudimentäre** myelodysplasia
~ **bifida/partielle** merorachischisis
~ **bifida/totale** holorachischisis
~ **helicis** helical spine, spine of the helix
~ **iliaca** iliac spine, spinous process of the ilium
~ **iliaca anterior inferior** anterior inferior iliac spine

~ **iliaca anterior superior** anterior superior iliac spine
~ **iliaca dorsalis caudalis** posterior inferior iliac spine
~ **iliaca posterior inferior** posterior inferior iliac spine
~ **iliaca posterior superior** posterior superior iliac spine, posterosuperior spine of the ilium
~ **ischiadica** ischiadic (sciatic) spine, spine of the ischium
~ **mentalis** mental spine
~ **nasalis anterior [maxillae]** anterior nasal spine
~ **nasalis ossis frontalis** frontal (nasal) spine
~ **nasalis posterior [ossis palatini]** palatine (posterior nasal) spine, nasal spine of the palatine bone
~ **ossis sphenoidalis** sphenoid (angular) spine
~ **scapulae** scapular spine, spine of the scapula
~ **suprameatum** suprameatal (Henle's) spine
~ **trochlearis** trochlear spine
~ **tympanica major** greater tympanic spine
~ **tympanica minor** lesser tympanic spine
~ **ventosa** spina ventosa; tuberculous dactylitis
spinal 1. spinal *(Rückenmark)*; 2. spinal, rachidial, rachidian *(Wirbelsäule)*
Spinalanästhesie f spinal anaesthesia, rachianaesthesia, rachianalgesia, intraspinal block
~/**extradurale** extradural (peridural, epidural) anaesthesia
~/**fraktionierte** fractional spinal anaesthesia
Spinalapoplexie f spinal apoplexy
Spinaldaueranästhesie f continuous spinal anaesthesia
Spinalepilepsie f spinal epilepsy
Spinalganglion n spinal (dorsal root) ganglion
Spinalgie f spinalgia, pain in the spinal region
Spinalhemiplegie f spinal hemiplegia
Spinaliom n prickle-cell carcinoma *(epitheliale Haut- und Schleimhautgeschwulst)*
Spinalkanal m spinal canal
Spinalmark n s. Rückenmark
Spinalmeningitis f spinal meningitis
Spinalmuskellähmung f rachioparalysis
Spinalnadel f spinal needle
Spinalnerv m [cerebro]spinal nerve
Spinalnervenwurzel f spinal nerve root
~/**hintere** posterior root
Spinalnervenwurzelkompression f/**zervikale** cervical spinal root compression
Spinalnervenwurzelkrankheit f radiculopathy
Spinalpachymeningitis f spinal pachymeningitis
Spinalparalyse f spinal paralysis; rachioplegia
~/**spastische** spastic spinal paralysis, Erb's spastic spinal paraplegia, Erb-Charcot's disease *(bei zerebrospinaler Syphilis)*
Spinalpunktion f spinal puncture, rachi[o]centesis
Spinalreflex m spinal reflex
Spinalschock m spinal shock
Spinalwurzel f spinal root
Spinalwurzelkompression f/**zervikale** cervical spinal root compression

Spinalwurzelkrankheit f radiculopathy, disease of nerve roots
Spinalwurzelneuritis f radiculitis, inflammation of a spinal nerve root
Spindel f spindle
~/achromatische achromatic spindle (figure)
~/neuromuskuläre neuromuscular spindle
Spindelbasis f base of the modiolus
Spindelbrücke f intermediate body of Flemming *(bei der Zellteilung)*
Spindelfaser f spindle fibre
Spindelfaseransatzstelle f centromere
spindelförmig fusiform, spindle-shaped; fusocellular
Spindel[haar]krankheit f monilethrix; moniliform (beaded) hair
Spindelstar m spindle (fusiform) cataract
Spindelzelle f spindle (fusiform) cell
spindelzellenförmig fusocellular, fusicellular
Spindelzellenkarzinom n spindle-cell carcinoma
Spindelzellensarkom n fusocellular (spindle-cell) sarcoma
Spinnbarkeit f threadability *(des Zervikalschleims)*
Spinnenbäuchigkeit f arachnogastria *(bei Bauchwassersucht)*
Spinnenbißvergiftung f arachn[o]idism
Spinnenfinger mpl spider fingers
Spinnenfingerigkeit f arachnodactyly, acromacria, Marfan's syndrome, dolichostenomelia; spider fingers
Spinnenfurcht f arachnephobia
Spinnenhautzotten fpl arachnoid villi (granulations)
Spinnenmal n s. Spinnennävus
Spinnennävus m spider (arachnoid, stellate) naevus, spider [angioma]; vascular spider
Spinnenzelle f spider cell
spinnenwebartig arachnoid[al]
Spinnwebenhaut f s. Arachnoidea
Spinnwebenhautentzündung f s. Arachnoiditis
spinös spinous, spinose
spinozellulär spinocellular
Spintherismus m spintherism, sensation of sparks
Spiralen fpl/**Curschmannsche** Curschmann's spirals
Spiralfraktur f spiral (torsion) fracture
Spiralgelenk n cochlear articulation, spiral joint
Spiralisierung f coiling *(der Chromosomen)*
Spiralschlingenkatheter m armoured sling catheter
Spiralverband m spiral bandage
Spirem n spirem[e] *(Knäuelstadium der Prophase)*
Spirillämie f spirillaemia
spirillämisch spirillaemic
Spirille f spirillum *(schraubenförmig gewundenes Bakterium)*
Spirillenabszeß m spirillar abscess
spirillenauflösend spirillolytic
Spirillenauflösung f spirillolysis
Spirillenerkrankung f spirillosis
Spirillenfieber n spirillum fever
Spirilleninfektion f spirillosis
spirillentötend spirillicidal
spirillizid spirillicidal
Spirillose f spirillosis
spirillotoxisch spirillotoxic
spirillotrop spirillotropic
Spirillum n mirius (morsus muris) Spirillum minus *(Erreger der Rattenbißkrankheit)*
Spirochaeta f spiroch[a]ete, treponema *(s. a. unter Treponema)*
~ cuniculi Spirochaeta cuniculi
~ icterogenes Spirochaeta icterogenes
~ icterohaemorrhagiae Spirochaeta icterohaemorrhagiae
~ recurrentis Spirochaeta obermeieri
Spirochaetosis f icterohaemorrhagiae icterohaemorrhagic fever, icterogenic spirochaetosis, Weil's disease, leptospiral (spirochaetal) jaundice
spirochätal spirochaetal, spirochaetic, treponemal
Spirochätämie f spirochaetaemia
Spirochäte f s. Spirochaeta
spirochätenauflösend spirochaetolytic
Spirochätenauflösung f spirochaetolysis
Spirochätenerkrankung f spirochaetosis
Spirochäteninfektion f spirochaetal infection, treponem[at]osis, treponemiasis, treponemal disease
Spirochätenspezialist m treponematologist
spirochätentötend spirochaeticidal, antispirochaetic, treponemicidal
spirochätogen spirochaetogenous
Spirochätolyse f spirochaetolysis
spirochätolytisch spirochaetolytic
Spirochätose f spirochaetosis
Spirochäturie f spirochaeturia
Spirogramm n spirogram
Spirograph m spirograph
Spirographie f spirography *(Darstellung der Atemgrößen)*
spirographisch spirographic
Spirometer n spirometer, pne[umat]ometer, aeroplethysmograph
Spirometrie f spirometry, pneumatometry *(Messung der Atemgrößen)*
spirometrisch spirometric
Spironolakton n spironolactone *(Aldosteronantagonist)*
Spitze f tip (z. B. der Nase); apex (z. B. der Lunge); vertex, top, summit, crown (z. B. des Schädels) • **von der ~ weggerichtet** abapical
~ und Welle f spike and wave *(im EEG)*
Spitzenband n apical dental (odontoid) ligament
Spitzenfeld n apical area (field) *(der Lunge)*
Spitzenherd m apical focus *(der Lunge)*
Spitzenlungenentzündung f apical pneumonia
Spitzenpotential n spike potential
Spitzenstoß m apex beat [of the heart]
spitzenwärts apical

Spitzfuß

Spitzfuß *m* [tali]pes equinus, drop foot, toedrop; equinus [deformity]
Spitzfußstellung *f* foot (ankle) drop
Spitzhohlfuß *m* [tali]pes equinocavus; equinocavus [deformity]
Spitzklumpfuß *m* [tali]pes equinovarus; equivovarus [deformity]
Spitzknickfuß *m* [tali]pes equinovalgus; equinovalgus [deformity]
Spitzkopf *m* steeple head (skull), oxycephalus; hypsicephalus
spitzköpfig steeple-shaped, oxycephalic, oxycephalous; hypsicephalic, hypsocephalous
Spitzköpfigkeit *f* oxycephalia; hypsicephalia
spitznasig oxyrhine
Spitzpocken *pl s*. Varizellen
Spitzzahn *m* canine [tooth], eye tooth, tusk
Splanchnästhesie *f* splanchnaesthesia
splanchnästhetisch splanchnaesthetic
Splanchnektopie *f* splanchnectopia
Splanchnemphraxis *f* splanchnemphraxis, obstruction of a viscus
Splanchniektomie *f* splanchnicectomy
Splanchnikotomie *f* splanchnicotomy, division of a splanchnic nerve
Splanchnikus *m* splanchnic nerve
Splanchnikusdurchtrennung *f*[/operative] *s*. Splanchnikotomie
Splanchnikushaken *m* splanchnic retractor
Splanchnikusresektion *f s*. Splanchnikotomie
splanchnisch splanchnic
Splanchnoderm *n* splanchnoderm
Splanchnodiastase *f* splanchnodiastasis, separation of a viscus; displacement of a viscus
Splanchnodynie *f* splanchnodynia, pain in an abdominal organ
Splanchnographie *f* splanchnography
Splanchnolith *m* splanchnolith, enterolith, intestinal calculus
Splanchnolithiasis *f* splanchnolithiasis, enterolithiasis
Splanchnologie *f* splanchnology
Splanchnomegalie *f* splanchnomegaly, enlargement of the viscera
Splanchnomikrie *f* splanchnomicria, smallness of the viscera
Splanchnopathie *f* splanchnopathy, disease of the viscera
Splanchnopleura *f* splanchnopleure
splanchnopleural splanchnopleural
Splanchnoptose *f* splanchnoptosia, splanchnoptosis, abdominal ptosis, visceroptosis
Splanchnosklerose *f* splanchnosclerosis, induration of the viscera
Splanchnoskopie *f* splanchnoscopy
splanchnoskopisch splanchnoscopic
splanchnosomatisch splanchnosomatic
Splanchnotomie *f* splanchnotomy
Splanchnozele *f* splanchnocele
Splanchnozöle *f* splanchnocoele
Splen *m s*. Milz
Splen... *s*. *a*. Lien... *und* Milz...

Splenalgie *f* splenalgia, splenodynia, pain in the spleen
Splenektomie *f* splenectomy, lienectomy, excision of the spleen
splenektomieren to splenectomize
Splenektopie *f* splenectopia, displacement of the spleen; wandering (floating) spleen
Splenisation *f* splenization *(der Lunge)*
Splenitis *f* splenitis, lienitis, inflammation of the spleen
Splenium *n* 1. splenium, compress, bandage; 2. *s*. ~ corporis callosi
~ corporis callosi splenium, pad of the corpus callosum
Splenodynie *f s*. Splenalgie
splenogen splenogenic, splenogenous
Splenogramm *n* splenogram
Splenogranulomatosis *f* **siderotica** siderotic splenogranulomatosis
Splenographie *f* splenography, lienography
splenographisch splenographic
Splenohepatomegalie *f* splenohepatomegaly
Splenohepatoplastik *f* splenohepatoplasty
Splenolysis *f* splenolysis
Splenom *n* splenoma
splenomedullär splenomedullary, splenomyelogenous, lienomedullary
Splenomegalie *f* splenomegaly, enlargement of the spleen, splenauxe
~/hypercholesterolämische hypercholesterolaemic splenomegaly
~/tropische febrile tropical splenomegaly, kalaazar, visceral leishmaniasis, black fever (sickness), Burdwan (Assam, dumdum) fever
Splenopathie *f* splenopathy, lienopathy, disease of the spleen
splenopathisch splenopathic
Splenopexie *f* splenopexy, lienopexy, fixation of the spleen
Splenoportogramm *n* splenoportogram
Splenoportographie *f* splenoportography
splenoportographisch splenoportographic
Splenorrhagie *f* splenorrhagia, haemorrhage from the spleen
Splenorrhaphie *f* splenorrhaphy, suture of the spleen
Splenose *f* splenosis
Splenotomie *f* splenotomy, incision into the spleen
Splenotyphoid *n* splenotyphoid
Splenozyt *m* splenocyte
Splitterblutung *f* splinter haemorrhage
Splitterbruch *m* splintered fracture, split (comminuted) fracture
Splitterklemme *f* splinter forceps
Splitterpinzette *f* splinter forceps
Spodiomyelitis *f* spodiomyelitis, acute anterior poliomyelitis, paralytic spinal poliomyelitis
Spodogramm *n* spodogram, ash picture
Spodographie *f* spodography
Spondyl... *s*. *a*. Vertebral... *und* Wirbel...
Spondylalgie *f* spondylalgia, spondylodynia, pain in a vertebra

Spondylarthritis f spondylarthritis, arthritis of the spine
~ **ancylopoetica** ankylosing spondylarthritis (spondylitis), Bechterew's arthritis (disease), Strümpell-Marie spondylitis; poker back (spine)
Spondylarthrokaze f spondyl[arthr]ocace, tuberculosis of the vertebrae
Spondylexarthrose f spondylexarthrosis, dislocation of a vertebra
Spondylitis f spondylitis, inflammation of the vertebrae
~ **deformans** deforming spondylitis
~ **tuberculosa** tuberculous spondylitis, tuberculosis of the spine, spinal caries, dorsal phthisis; Pott's disease, angular curvature (kyphosis) of the spine
~ **typhosa** typhoid spine
spondylitisch spondylitic
Spondyloarthropathie f spondyloarthropathy
Spondylodese f spondylo[syn]desis, spinal fusion
Spondylodidymie f spondylodidymia
Spondylodymus m spondylodymus
Spondyloepiphysaria f Maroteaux-Lamy syndrome, mucopolysaccharidosis [type] VI
Spondylolisthesis f spondylolisthesis, forward displacement of a vertebra
Spondylolyse f spondylolysis, dissolution of a vertebra
Spondylomalazie f spondylomalacia, softening of a vertebra
Spondylopathia f **deformans** spondylosis
Spondylopathie f spondylopathy, disease of a vertebra
Spondyloptose f spondyloptosis
Spondylopyosis f spondylopyosis, suppuration of a vertebra
Spondylose f spondylosis, ankylosis of a vertebral joint
Spondylotomie f spondylotomy, section of a vertebra; rachi[o]tomy
Spondylus m s. Wirbel 1.
Spongioblast m spongioblast
Spongioblastoma n spongioblastoma *(Hirntumor)*
~ **multiforme** multiform spongioblastoma
~ **polare** polar spongioblastoma
~ **primitivum** ependymo[cyto]ma *(vom Ependym abgeleitete Ventrikelgeschwulst)*
spongioid spongioform, spongioid
Spongioneuroblastom n spongioneuroblastoma *(Hirntumor)*
Spongioplasma n spongioplasm
spongiös spongiose, spongy, cancellous, cancellate
Spongiosa f spongiosa, spongy substance, diploe, diploic (cancellous) bone
Spongiosaausschabung f decancellation
Spongiosaschraube f spongiosa (lag) screw, cancellous bone screw
Spongiose f spongiosis
Spongiositis f spongi[os]itis, inflammation of the corpus spongiosum

spongiotisch spongiotic
Spongiozyt m spongiocyte
spontan 1. spontaneous; impulsive; 2. automatic
Spontanabort m spontaneous (accidental) abortion
Spontanagglutination f spontaneous agglutination
Spontanallergie f spontanenous allergy
Spontanamputation f spontaneous amputation
Spontananeurysma n spontaneous (primary) aneurysm
Spontanatmung f spontaneous respiration
Spontanbewegung f spontaneous movement
Spontanblutung f spontaneous haemorrhage
Spontandepolarisation f spontaneous depolarization
Spontanentleerung f spontaneous drainage *(eines Abszesses)*
Spontanerysipel n spontaneous erysipelas
Spontanfraktur f spontaneous (pathological) fracture
Spontangeburt f spontaneous labour
Spontanheilung f spontaneous healing (cure, recovery), autotherapy
Spontanluxation f spontaneous (pathological) luxation
Spontanmutation f spontaneous [gene] mutation, natural mutation
Spontannekrose f spontaneous necrosis
Spontannystagmus n spontaneous nystagmus
Spontanperforation f spontaneous perforation *(z. B. eines Organs)*
Spontanpneumothorax m spontaneous pneumothorax
Spontanremission f spontaneous regression (remission)
Spontanruptur f spontaneous rupture
Spontanwehen fpl spontaneous uterine activity
Spontanwendung f spontaneous version *(des Fetus bei der Geburt)*
Sporangium n sporangium
Spore f spore
~/**große** macrospore
~/**kleine** microspore, sporule
Sporenagglutination f sporoagglutination
sporenbildend sporogenous, sporogenic, spore-producing, sporiferous
~/**nicht** non-sporogenous, non-spore-forming, non-sporulating
Sporenbildung f formation of spores, sporulation, sporogenesis
Sporenentwicklung f sporogenesis
Sporenkapsel f spore capsule
Sporentierchen n s. Sporozoon
sporentötend sporicidal
sporentragend sporiferous
Sporenverstreuung f spore dispersal
sporenzerstörend sporicidal
Sporidieninfektion f sporidiosis
Sporidiose f sporidiosis
sporizid sporicidal
Sporn m spur, calcar

Sporoblast

Sporoblast *m* sporoblast
Sporogenese *f s.* Sporenbildung
Sporogonie *f* sporogony
Sporomykose *f* sporomycosis
Sporont *m* sporont
sporontentötend sporontocide
Sporotrichin *n* sporotrichin *(Hauttestantigen zum Sporotrichosenachweis)*
Sporotrichon *n* **Beuermanni (Schenckii)** sporotrichum beuermanni (schenckii) *(Sporotrichoseerreger)*
Sporotrichose *f* sporotrichosis, Schenck's (de Beurmann-Gougerot) disease
~/pulmonale pulmonary sporotrichosis
Sporozoit *m* sporozoite
Sporozoon *n* sporozoon, sporozoan
Sporozoose *f* sporozoosis
Sporozyste *f* sporocyst *(1. Entwicklungsstadium der Plasmodien; 2. Entwicklungsstadium der Leberegel)*
Sporozyt *m* sporocyte
Sportlerherz *n* athlete's heart
Sporula *f* sporule, microspore
Sporulation *f* sporulation
Spracharmut *f* hypologia
Sprachartikulationsstörung *f* anarthria; logophasia
Sprachaudiometrie *f* speech audiometry
Sprachbehandlung *f* logotherapy
Sprache *f* speech
~/abgehackte staccato speech
~/ataktische ataxic speech
~/klosige thick speech
~/näselnde rhinolalia, rhinophonia
~/skandierende scanning speech
~/verwaschene clipped (slurred) speech
~/zerebelläre cerebellar speech *(verwaschene Sprache bei Kleinhirnerkrankung)*
Sprachfehler *m* speech defect
Sprachheilbehandlung *f* logotherapy, speech therapy
Sprachheilerziehung *f* logopaedia, logopaedics; logotherapy *(z. B. von Stotterern)*
Sprachheilkunde *f* logopaedia, logopaedics
Sprachlähmung *f* laloplegia
Sprachlosigkeit *f* logoplegia, aglossia
Sprachneurose *f* laloneurosis
Sprachstörung *f* speech disorder, lalopathy, phonopathy; dysphrasia *(infolge Intelligenzdefekts)*
~/psychische psychophonasthenia
Sprachtherapeut *m* speech therapist
Sprachtherapie *f* speech therapy, logotherapy
Sprachverständnis *n* lalognosis
Sprachverwirrtheit *f* schizophasia, divagation
Sprachzentrum *n* speech (language) centre *(der Hirnrinde)*
~/motorisches motor speech area, Broca's centre (convolution, gyrus), centre for motor speech
Sprechangst *f* lal[i]ophobia
Sprechapparat *m s.* Kehlkopf/künstlicher

Sprechen *n* **im Schlaf** *s.* Somniloquie
~/schnelles oxylalia, tachylalia, tachylogia, tachyphemia, tachyphrasia
Sprechfehler *m* 1. lapsus linguae; 2. *s.* Sprachfehler
Sprechkanüle *f* speaking tube *(bei Tracheotomie)*
Sprechkrampf *m* logospasm
Sprechstundenhilfe *f* consulting-room assistent, receptionist
Sprechstundenzimmer *n* [doctor's] consulting room, physician's office
Sprechunfähigkeit *f* alalia *(Artikulationsstörung)*
Sprechunvermögen *n* anepia, inability to speak, mutism *(bei intaktem Sprechapparat)*
Sprechventil *n* phonation valve *(für Tracheostomiekanülen)*
Sprechweise *f/verlangsamte* bradyarthria, bradylalia *(Kleinhirnsymptomatik)*
Sprechzimmer *n s.* Sprechstundenzimmer
Sprengung *f/digitale* finger fracture [operation of the mitral valve] *(bei Mitralstenose)*
Sprenkelung *f* mottling *(z. B. von Gewebe)*
Sprew *f s.* Sprue
Springwurm *m* Enterobius vermicularis, threadworm, seatworm, oxyurid
Spritze *f* syringe ● **eine ~ aufziehen** to draw up a syringe ● **eine ~ geben** to give an injection, to inject
~/Pravazsche Pravaz's syringe
~/subkutane hypodermic [syringe]
~ zur Speichelgangspülung sialosyrinx
spritzen to inject, to give an injection
Spritzenabszeß *m* syringe abscess
Spritzenansatz *m* nozzle
Spritzenhepatitis *f* syringe jaundice, homologous serum hepatitis
Spritzenkanüle *f* hypodermic needle, cannula
Spritzentisch *m* table for the syringes
sprossen to sprout; to germinate
Sproßpilz *m* blastomycete
Sproßpilzdermatose *f* blastomycetic dermatitis
Sproßpilzerkrankung *f s.* Blastomykose
Sprossung *f* sprouting; germination, budding, blastogenesis
Sprue *f* sprue, psilosis, tropical stomatitis; Ceylon sore mouth
~/einheimische (nichttropische) idiopathic (nontropical) sprue, idiopathic adult steatorrhoea
~/tropische tropical sprue (aphthae)
Sprüher *m* sprayer, atomizer
Sprungbein *n* talus, ankle-bone, astragalus ● **unter dem ~** subtalar, subastragalar
Sprungbeinentfernung *f[/operative]* talectomy, astragalectomy, excision of the talus
Sprungbeinfortsatz *m/seitlich hervorragender* lateral process of the talus
Sprungbeinfraktur *f* ankle fracture; fractured talus
Sprungbeinhals *m* neck of the talus
Sprungbeinkopf *m* head of the talus
Sprungbeinkörper *m* body of the talus

Sprungbeinrolle f trochlea of the astragalus
Sprunggelenk n/**oberes** talocrural (ankle) joint
~/**unteres** talocalcaneonavicular joint
Sprunggelenkarthrodese f ankle arthrodesis
Sprunggelenkfraktur f/**bimalleoläre** Pott's [eversion] fracture, bimalleolar fracture
~/**Cottonsche** Cotton's (trimalleolar) fracture
Sprunggelenkgabel f tibiofibular (ankle) mortise
Sprunggelenkversteifung f ankle arthrodesis
sprunghaft erratic, volatile; saltatoric, jerky
Sprungknie n sprung knee
Spruw f s. Sprue
Spucknapf m spittoon, cuspidor
Spülapparat m irrigator
Spüldrainage f through drainage
spülen to irrigate (ausspülen); to flush (durchspülen); to gargle (den Rachen); to rinse (den Mund)
Spulendialysator m coil kidney (dialyzer)
Spülflüssigkeit f rinsing (lavage) fluid (z. B. für die Bauchhöhle); mouth wash (s. a. Spüllösung)
Spülgefäß n irrigator
Spüllösung f dialysate, dialyzate (für Dialyse); flush-out solution (z. B. bei Nierentransplantation) (s. a. Spülflüssigkeit)
Spüllösungsseite f dialysate compartment
Spülung f irrigation (z. B. einer Wunde); rinsing (z. B. der Mundhöhle); wash (z. B. der Harnblase); lavage, lavation (z. B. der Bauchhöhle); douche (z. B. der Scheide); siphonage (z. B. des Magens) ● eine ~ machen s. spülen
Spulwurm m ascarid, ascaris
Spulwurmbefall m ascariasis, ascari[d]osis
Spulwurminfektion f **der Gallengänge** biliary (bile-duct) ascariasis
Spurenelement n trace element
Sputum n sputum, expectoration
~/**blutiges (blutig tingiertes)** bloody (bloodstreaked) sputum
~/**eitriges** purulent sputum, pyoptysis
~/**rostfarbenes (rubiginöses)** rusty sputum (bei Lungenentzündung)
~/**schleimig-eitriges** mucopurulent sputum
~/**schleimiges** mucous sputum
~/**übelriechendes** malodorous sputum
Sputumabstrich m sputum smear
Sputumausstrich m sputum smear, smear of sputum
Squama f squama, squame
~ **frontalis** frontal squama
~ **occipitalis** occipital squama
~ **temporalis** temporal squama
squamös squamous, squamosal, scaly, scale-like
Stäbchen n 1. s. Stäbchenbakterium; 2. [retinal] rod
~/**Döderleinsches** Döderlein's bacillus
Stäbchenbakterium n rod, rod-shaped bacterium
stäbchenförmig rod-shaped
stäbchenlos rodless
Stäbchensehen n rod (scotopic) vision

stäbchensichtig rod-monochromat
Stäbchen-Zapfen-Schicht f layer of rods and cones (der Netzhaut)
Stäbchenzelle f rod cell
ST-Abgang m/**hoher** high takeoff (im EKG)
stabil/thermisch heat-stable
Stabilisierungsoperation f stabilizing operation (Traumatologie)
Stabkerniger m stab (staff, band) cell, staff (band) form
Stabkultur f stab culture (Mikrobiologie)
stabsichtig astigmatic
Stabsichtigkeit f s. Astigmatismus
Stachel m s. Spina
Stachelbecken n spinous pelvis, acanthopelvis
Stachelflechte f Devergie's disease, pityriasis rubra pilaris
stachelförmig spiniform, spinal, spicular, acanthoid
stachelig spinulose, spiny, spinous, acanthaceous
Stachelzelle f spinous cell, prickle (heckle, stickle) cell; acanthocyte
stachelzellenartig spinocellular
Stachelzellengeschwulst f acanthoma
Stachelzellenkrebs m prickle-cell carcinoma (epitheliale Haut- und Schleimhautgeschwulst)
Stachelzellenschicht f **der Epidermis** prickle[-cell] layer
Stachelzellentumor m acanthoma
Stachelzellenvermehrung f **im Blut** acanthocytosis
Stachelzellschichthypertrophie f acanthosis
Stachelzellschichtzerreißung f acanthorrhexis
stachlig acanthoid
Stadium n stage, stadium, phase
~ **amphiboles** amphibolic stage (Krankheitsstadium zwischen Höhepunkt und Heilung)
~ **augmenti** stadium augmenti
~ **caloris** hot stage of a fever
~ **decrementi** decrement, defervescent stage (z. B. des Fiebers)
~/**endoerythrozytäres** endoerythrocytic phase (stage) (der Malariaparasiten)
~ **eruptionis** eruptive stage
~/**exoerythrozytäres** exoerythrocytic phase (stage) (der Malariaparasiten)
~/**fortgeschrittenes** advanced stage
~/**katarrhalisches** catarrhal stage
~ **prodromorum** prodromal period (stage)
~/**refraktäres** refractory stage
Stadtgelbfieber n urban yellow fever
Stagnation f stagnation, stasis (z. B. des Bluts)
Stagnationsmastitis f stagnation mastitis
stagnieren to stagnate
Stahldrahtnaht f steel wire suture
Stalagmometer n stalagmometer
Stamm m 1. stem; strain (z. B. von Bakterien); 2. trunk (z. B. eines Gefäßes); truncus (Anatomie) (Zusammensetzungen s. unter Truncus)
Stammbronchus m stem (main) bronchus
~/**linker** left main bronchus
~/**rechter** right main bronchus

stammeln

stammeln s. stottern
Stammesgeschichte f phylogeny, phylogenesis
~/menschliche anthropogenesis, anthropogeny
stammesgeschichtlich phylogen[et]ic, phyletic
Stammfettsucht f buffalo (adrenal cortical) obesity (z. B. bei Nebennierenrindenüberfunktion)
Stammhirn n brain stem (axis)
Stammhirnepilepsie f brain-stem epilepsy (fit), brain-stem seizure
Stammhirnfunktion f brain-stem function
Stammhirngeschwulst f brain-stem tumour
Stammhirnläsion f brain-stem lesion
Stammhirnpotential n brain-stem potential
Stammhirnschaden m brain-stem damage
Stammhirnverletzung f brain-stem lesion (trauma)
Stammlappen m insula, central lobe (verdeckter Teil der Großhirnrinde)
Stammlösung f stock solution
Stammvagotomie f truncal vagotomy, Dragstedt's operation
Stammzelle f stem (parent, mother) cell, blast (ancestral) cell
Stammzellenleukämie f stem-cell (blast-cell) leukaemia, haemo[cyto]blastic leukaemia, embryonal (undifferentiated-cell) leukaemia
Standardableitung f nach Einthoven standard extremity (limb) lead
Standardabweichung f standard deviation, SD (Statistik)
Standardbedingungen fpl standard conditions
Standardbikarbonat n standard bicarbonate
Standardextremitätenableitung f standard extremity (limb) lead
Standardfehler m standard error (Statistik)
Standardlösung f standard solution
Standardtodesrate f adjusted death rate
Stanzbiopsie f punch biopsy
Stanze f punch [forceps]
stanzen to punch
Stapedektomie f stapedectomy, excision of the stapes
Stapediotenotomie f stapediotenotomy
Stapedius m stapedius [muscle]
Stapediusreflex m stapedius reflex
Stapediussehne f stapedius tendon
Stapes m s. Steigbügel
Staphyle f s. Uvula
Staphylektomie f staphylectomy, uvulectomy, excision of the uvula
Staphylhämatom n staphylhaematoma; haemorrhage from the uvula
Staphylion n staphylion (anthropologischer Meßpunkt)
Staphylitis f staphylitis, uvulitis, kionitis, inflammation of the uvula
Staphylococcus m staphylococcus
~ **albus** Staphylococcus albus (epidermidis)
~ **aureus** Staphylococcus aureus (pyogenes)
~ **citreus** Staphylococcus citreus
~ **epidermidis** s. ~ albus
~ **pyogenes** s. ~ aureus
Staphylödem n staphyloedema, staphylygroma, uvular oedema
Staphyloderma n staphyloderma
Staphylokinase f staphylokinase (Enzym)
Staphylokokkämie f staphylococcaemia
Staphylokokkenantitoxin n staphylococcus antitoxin
Staphylokokkendermatitis f staphylodermatitis
Staphylokokkenendokarditis f staphylococcal endocarditis
Staphylokokkenenteritis f staphylococcal enteritis
Staphylokokkenenterotoxin n staphylococcal enterotoxin
Staphylokokkenerkrankung f staphylococcal disease
Staphylokokkenfurunkulose f staphylococcal furunculosis
Staphylokokkenhämolysin n staphylo[haemo]lysin
Staphylokokkenhämolysinantikörper m antistaphylo[haemo]lysin
Staphylokokkeninfektion f staphylococcal infection
Staphylokokkenosteomyelitis f staphylococcal osteomyelitis
Staphylokokkenperikarditis f staphylococcal pericarditis
Staphylokokkenpneumonie f staphylococcal pneumonia
Staphylokokkenpyodermie f staphylococcal pyoderma, staphyloderma
Staphylokokkensepsis f staphylococcal sepsis
Staphylokokkenserum n staphylococcus antitoxin
Staphylokokkentoxin n staphylococcus toxin
Staphylokokkentoxoid n staphylococcus toxoid
Staphylokokkenvakzine f staphylococcus vaccine
Staphylokokkose f staphylococcosis, staphylococcia
Staphylolysin n staphylo[haemo]lysin
Staphylom n staphyloma
~ **ciliare** ciliary staphyloma
~ **corneae** corneal staphyloma
~ **uveale** uveal staphyloma
Staphylomeröffnung f[/operative] staphylotomy
Staphylomykose f staphylomycosis
Staphylonkus m staphyloncus
Staphylopharyngorrhaphie f staphylopharyngorrhaphy
Staphyloplastik f staphyloplasty, palatoplasty, urano[staphylo]plasty
Staphyloptose f staphyloptosis, uvuloptosis, elongation of the uvula
Staphylorrhaphie f staphylorrhaphy, palatorrhaphy, suture of a cleft palate, uranorrhaphy, uraniscorrhaphy
Staphyloschisis f staphyloschisis; cleft uvula
Staphylotom n staphylotome, uvulotome

Staphylotomie *f* staphylotomy, uvulotomy
Staphylotoxin *n* staphylotoxin
Star *m* cataract *(s. a.* unter Cataracta *und* Katarakt*)*
~ **durch Röntgenbestrahlung/grauer** irradiation cataract
~/**grauer** grey (lenticular) cataract
~/**grüner** glaucoma
Star... *s. a.* Katarakt...
starbildend cataractogenic
Starbildung *f* cataractogenesis, formation of a cataract
Stargardt-Syndrom *n* Stargardt's disease, Stargardt's (juvenile) macular degeneration
stark intensive, intense *(z. B. Reaktionen auf Medikamente)*; strong, hypersthenic *(körperlich)*
Stärke *f* 1. intensity; strength, force; 2. starch, amylum
~/**antigene** antigenic strength, immunogenicity
~/**psychische** psychic force
~/**tierische** animal starch (dextrin)
stärkeartig amyloid
Stärkeausscheidung *f* im Urin amyluria
stärkeenthaltend amylaceous
Stärke-Gel-Elektrophorese *f* starch-gel electrophoresis
Stärkehydrolyse *f* amylolysis
Stärkekörnchen *n* starch granule
stärkelösend amylolytic
stärken to strengthen, to invigorate; to vitalize
stärkend strengthening, invigorating; tonic, restorative; roborant; analeptic
stärkespaltend amylolytic, amyloclastic
Stärkespaltung *f* amylolysis
Stärkeverdauungsstörung *f* amylodyspepsia
Stärkezucker *m* starch sugar, dextrin
Starlinse *f* cataract lens
Staroperation *f* cataract operation (extraction), couching
starr stiff, rigid *(z. B. ein Muskel)*; numb *(z. B. Glieder)*; cataleptic, cataleptiform, cataleptoid
Starre *f* stiffness, rigidity, rigor *(z. B. von Muskeln)*; numbness *(z. B. der Glieder)*; catalepsy
Starr-Edwards-Klappe[nprothese] *f* Starr-Edwards valve prothesis
Starrkrampf *m s.* Tetanus
~ **bei gestrecktem Körper** orthotonus; opisthotonus
starrkrampfartig tetanic, tetanal
Starstechen *n* reclination, couching [for cataract], needling [of the cataract], cataract extraction
Stase *f,* **Stasis** *f s.* Stauung
Stasobasophobia *f* stasibasiphobia *(krankhafte Angst vor dem Laufen und Stehen)*
Stasophobie *f* stasiphobia *(krankhafte Angst vor dem Aufrechtstehen)*
Station *f* ward
~/**interne** medical ward
~/**psychiatrische** psychopathic ward
Stationsarzt *m* ward physician

Stationsschwester *f* ward sister, charge nurse
Statistik *f*/**medizinische** medical statistics
statokinetisch statokinetic
Statokonien *fpl* statoconia, statoliths, otoconia, ear dust
Statolithen *mpl s.* Statokonien
statuenhaft statuesque, ecstatic, cataleptic
Statur *f* stature
~/**kleine** brachymorphy
Status *m* state, status, condition *(s. a.* unter Zustand*)*
~ **anginosus** anginose state, preinfarction angina, severe attack of angina pectoris
~ **arthriticus** arthritic state *(bei Gicht)*
~ **asthmaticus** asthmatic state (shock)
~ **embryocardicus** embryocardia
~ **epilepticus** epileptic (convulsive) state
~ **lymphaticus** lymphatic state, lymphatism, lymphotoxaemia *(Neigung zu Entzündung und Hyperplasie des lymphatischen Gewebes)*
~ **migrainus** migrainous state
~ **nascendi** nascent state
~ **praesens** present stage (condition, state)
~ **raptus** status raptus, ecstasy
~ **spongiosus** spongy state *(des Gehirns infolge multipler Hohlraumbildung)*
~ **thymicolymphaticus** thymicolymphatic state
Stauballergie *f* dust allergy
Stauberkrankung *f* **der Haut** dermatoconiosis
Staubgehaltmesser *m* konimeter, coniometer
Staubgehaltmessung *f* konimetry, coniometry
Staubinde *f* tourniquet, compression bandage
Staubinfektion *f* dust infection
Staubkrankheit *f* dust disease, coniosis, koniosis
Staublunge[nerkrankung] *f* pneumo[no]coniosis, [pneumo]coniosis, [pneumo]koniosis, lith[ic]osis, dust disease
Staublungentuberkulose *f s.* Silikotuberkulose
Staublungenzelle *f* dust cell
Staub[teilchen]zähler *m s.* Staubgehaltmesser
Stauchungs[knochen]bruch *m* impacted (compression) fracture
Staumanschette *f* pneumatic tourniquet, cuff
Stauschlauch *m* tourniquet, compression tube
~/**Esmarchscher** Esmarch's bandage
Stauung *f* stoppage, stasis, stagnation, congestion
~/**venöse** venous stasis, chronic passive congestion
Stauungsaszites *m* mechanical ascites
Stauungsblutfülle *f* congestive (passive) hyperaemia
Stauungsbronchitis *f* congestive bronchitis
Stauungsbruch *m* crush fracture
Stauungsdermatitis *f* stasis dermatitis
Stauungsdermatose *f* stasis dermatosis
Stauungsdiffusion *f* diffusion stasis
Stauungsgallenblase *f* stasis gall-bladder
Stauungsgastritis *f* congestive gastritis
Stauungsgelbsucht *f* obstructive (mechanical) jaundice *(durch Galleabflußstauung)*
Stauungsgeschwür *n* stasis ulcer

Stauungsharnleiter

Stauungsharnleiter *m* uroureter
Stauungsherz[versagen] *n* congestive heart (cardiac) failure
Stauungsleber *f* stasis (cardiac) liver
Stauungsleberzirrhose *f* congestive cirrhosis, cardiac (central) cirrhosis, cardiocirrhosis
Stauungslunge *f* congested (cardiac) lung; pulmonary congestion
Stauungsmastitis *f* stagnation mastitis
Stauungsödem *n* mechanical dropsy; cardiac oedema
Stauungspapille *f* engorged papilla, choked disk; papilloedema, oedema of the optic disk (papilla)
Stauungspurpura *f* mechanical purpura
Stauungssymptom *n* congestive symptom, stasis phenomenon
Stauungstest *m* [nach Rumpel-Leede] tourniquet test
Steapsin *n* steapsin
Steapsinogen *n* steapsinogen *(Steapsinvorstufe)*
Stearinsäure *f* stearic acid
Steatitis *f* steatitis, inflammation of adipose tissue, adipositis, pimelitis
Steatocystoma *n* **multiplex** steatocystoma multiplex; sebocystomatosis
Steatokryptose *f* steatocryptosis
Steatolyse *f* steatolysis
steatolytisch steatolytic
Steatom *n* 1. steatoma, sebaceous cyst, atheroma; 2. steatoma, lipoma, adipose tumour, adipoma, pimeloma
Steatopygie *f* steatopygia, excessive fatness of the buttocks
Steatorrhoe *f* 1. stea[to]rrhoea; fatty stools; 2. *s.* Seborrhoea
~/idiopathische idiopathic steatorrhoea
Steatose *f* 1. steatosis, fatty degeneration; 2. steatosis, disease of the sebaceous glands
Steatozele *f* steatocele, lip[ar]ocele, adipocele
Stechbecken *n* bed-pan
stechen to sting, to stitch, to pierce; to puncture *(punktieren)*; to couch *(eine Katarakt)*; to lance *(z. B. einen Abszeß)*
~/blitzartig to lancinate, to shoot *(Schmerzen)*
Stechmücke *f* mosquito
Steckbecken *n* bed-pan
stehend/aufrecht orthostatic, orthotic
Stehlangst *f* kleptophobia, cleptophobia
Stehltrieb *m* [/krankhafter] kleptomania, cleptomania
Stehreflex *m* static reflex
Stehstörung *f* dysstasia, difficulty in standing
Stehunfähigkeit *f* astasia *(infolge motorischer Koordinationsstörung)*; stasiphobia *(durch Zwangsvorstellung)*
steif stiff, rigid
Steifigkeit *f* stiffness, rigidity, rigor *(z. B. von Muskeln)*
Steigbügel *m* stapes, stirrup [bone] ● **über dem ~ suprastapedial**
Steigbügelentfernung *f s.* Stapedektomie

Steigbügelköpfchen *n* head of the stapes, stapedial head
Steigbügelmobilisierung *f* stapes mobilization
Steigbügelmuskel *m* stapedius [muscle]
Steigbügelmuskelsehnendurchtrennung *f* stapediotenotomy
Steigbügelplatte *f* footplate of the stapes, stapedial base (footplate)
steigen to rise, to increase *(z. B. Fieber)*
Steigerung *f*/**virale** virus enhancement
Steilgaumen *m* gothic (high-arched) palate; hypsistaphylia
Steiltyp *m* vertical type *(im EKG)*
Stein *m* stone, calculus, concrement, concretion *(s. a. unter* Calculus*)*
~/mikroskopisch kleiner microlith
steinabtreibend lithagogue
steinartig calculous, lithous, lithoid
steinauflösend litholytic
Steinauflösung *f* litholysis
steinbildend lithogenetic, lithogenous, lithiasic
Steinbildung *f* lithogenesis, formation of stones, stone formation, calculogenesis, lithiasis
Steinentfernung *f*/**operative** lithectomy
Steinfaßzange *f* lithotomy (stone grasping) forceps
~ nach Randall Randall's stone forceps
Steinhauerlunge[nerkrankung] *f s.* Silikose
Steinhörsonde *f* lithophone
steinig lithous
Steinkind *n* calcified foetus, lithopaedion *(abgestorbene versteinerte Frucht bei Extrauteringravidität)*
~ in versteinerten Fruchthüllen lithokelyphopaedion
Steinleiden *n* lithiasis, calculosis, calculous disease
~/scheinbares pseudolithiasis
steinleidend calculous
Steinmann-Nagel *m* Steinmann nail (pin)
Steinmole *f* stone (calcified) mole
Steinschnitt *m* lithotomy, vesicolithotomy, cystolithotomy
~/hoher high lithotomy, epicystotomy
Steinschnittlage *f* lithotomy position, dorsosacral (dorsal recumbent) position
Steinschnittmesser *n* lithotome
Steinstaublunge *f s.* Silikose
steintreibend lithagogue
steinzerquetschend lithotritic
Steinzertrümmerer *m* lithotrite, lithoclast, lithotriptor
steinzertrümmernd lithotritic
Steinzertrümmerung *f* lithotrity, lithotripsy, litholapaxy
~/elektrische electrolithotrity
Steiß *m* 1. breech, buttocks, rump; 2. *s.* Steißbein
Steißbein *n* coccyx, rump-bone
Steißbeinentfernung *f*[/**operative**] coccygectomy, excision of the coccyx
Steißbeinfistel *f* [sacro]coccygeal fistula

Steißbeinganglion n coccygeal ganglion
Steißbeinhorn n coccygeal cornu, cornu of the coccyx *(Gelenkfortsatz)*
Steißbeinmuskel m coccygeus [muscle], ischiococcygeus [muscle]
Steißbeinnerv m coccygeal nerve
Steißbeinneuralgie f coccygeal neuralgia
Steißbeinplexus m coccygeal plexus
Steißbeinschmerz m coccyalgia, coccy[go]dynia, pain in the coccyx; anorectal syndrome
Steiß-Fuß-Lage f footling (double breech) presentation *(des Fetus bei der Geburt)*
Steißgeburt[entbindung] f breech delivery
Steißgeburtentwicklung f breech extraction
Steißlage f breech presentation (lie) *(des Fetus bei der Geburt)*
Steißplexus m coccygeal plexus
Steißwirbel m coccygeal vertebra
Stella f lenticularis lens star
Stellatum n stellate (cervicothoracic) ganglion
Stellatumblockade f stellate [ganglion] block, procaine block of the stellate ganglion
Stelle f **der Wahl** point of election *(z. B. bei der Operation)*
~ **des geringsten Widerstands** locus minoris resistentiae
~/**durchgelegene** sore, spot
~/**höckrige** tuberosity
~/**verengte** isthmus
stellen/eine Diagnose to diagnose, to make a diagnosis
Stellknorpel m s. Aryknorpel
Stellreflex m postural (righting) reflex, placing reaction
Stellung f position, posture, attitude *(s. a. unter Lage)*
~ **beider Augen/gleiche** isophoria
Stellungsanomalie f malposition, abnormal (anomalous) position
Stellungsosteotomie f positional osteotomy
Stellwehen fpl rotation stage of labour
Stenion n stenion *(anthropologischer Meßpunkt)*
stenodont stenodont
Stenokardie f s. Angina pectoris
Stenokardiesyndrom n anginal syndrome
stenokardisch anginal
Stenokrotaphie f stenocrotaphy, narrowness of the temporal region
stenopäisch stenopaeic
Stenose f stenosis, stegnosis, stricture
~/**supraaortische** supra-aortic stenosis
Stenosegeräusch n stenosal murmur
Stenoserezidiv n restenosis
stenosieren to stenose, to constrict, to narrow
stenosiert stenotic
Stenostomie f stenostomia, narrowing of the mouth
Stenothorax m stenothorax, narrowness of the thorax
stenotisch stenotic
stenozephal stenocephalous
Stenozephalie f stenocephalia

Stephanion n stephanion *(anthropologischer Meßpunkt)*
Steppergang m steppage (equine, foot-drop) gait
Sterbebett n death-bed
Sterbefall m death, exitus
sterben to die; to necrose, to necrotize *(z. B. Gewebe)*
~/**am Lungenödem** to drown
~/**an einer Krankheit** to die of an illness
~/**an einer Verletzung** to die from a wound (trauma)
~/**an Krebs** to die of cancer
~/**bei der Geburt** to die in childbed
~/**durch einen Schlaganfall** to die from apoplexy
~/**eines gewaltsamen Todes** to die a violent death, to die in one's boots
~/**eines natürlichen Todes** to die a natural death, to die in one's bed
Sterben n dying, death ● **im ~ liegen** to be dying (moribund)
sterbend dying, moribund
sterbenskrank sick to death
Sterbeurkunde f death certificate
sterblich mortal
Sterblichkeit f 1. mortality; 2. mortality rate
Sterblichkeitsziffer f mortality (death) rate
Stereoagnosie f stereoagnosis, astereocognosy, astereognosis, tactile agnosia
Stereoanästhesie f stereoanaesthesia
Stereoarthrolyse f stereoarthrolysis
Stereoenzephalotom n stereoencephalotome
Stereoenzephalotomie f stereoencephalotomy *(stereotaktische Operation)*
Stereognosis f stereognosis, stereognostic sense
stereognostisch stereognostic
Stereokampimeter n stereocampimeter
Stereokampimetrie f stereocampimetry
Stereoophthalmoskop n stereo-ophthalmoscope
Stereophantoskop n stereophantoscope
Stereophoroskop n stereophoroscope *(Ophthalmologie)*
Stereopsis f stereopsis, stereoscopic (solid) vision, depth perception
Stereopter m stereopter
Stereoradiographie f stereoradiography
Stereoröntgenographie f stereoroentgenography; stereoradiography
Stereoskop n stereoscope
Stereoskopie f stereoscopy
stereoskopisch stereoscopic
Stereostroboskop n stereostroboscope
stereotaktisch stereotactic, stereotaxic
Stereotaxie f stereotaxia *(von Hirnarealen)*
Stereotaxis f, **Stereotropismus** m stereotropism, stereotaxia, thigmotaxis, thigmotropism *(gezielte Bewegung auf Berührung)*
Stereotypie f stereotypy
Stereovektorkardiograph m stereovectorcardiograph

Stereovektorkardiographie

Stereovektorkardiographie f stereovectorcardiography
ST-Erhöhung f s. ST-Hebung
steril 1. sterile, aseptic, abacterial; 2. sterile, infertile; barren, acyetic *(Frau)*
Sterilbereich m sterile area
Sterilisation f 1. sterilization; 2. sterilization; castration
~/fraktionierte tyndallization
Sterilisationsanlage f sterilization plant
Sterilisator m sterilizer, sterilizing apparatus
Sterilisierbarkeit f capability of sterilization
sterilisieren 1. to sterilize, to render sterile (free from micro-organisms); to autoclave *(im Autoklaven)*; 2. to sterilize, to render incapable of reproduction; to castrate
Sterilisierrahmen m sterilizing rack
Sterilisierraum m sterilizing room
Sterilisiertrommel f sterilizing drum, drum sterilizer
Sterilisierzange f sterilizing forceps
Sterilität f 1. sterility; 2. sterility, infertility, infecundity
~/weibliche acyesis, atocia, barrenness
Sterkobilin n stercobilin *(Bilirubinabbauprodukt)*
Sterkobilinogen n stercobilinogen
Sterkoporphyrin n stercoporphyrin
sterkoral stercor[ace]ous, stercoral, stercorary
Sternal... s. a. Brustbein...
Sternalbiopsie f sternal biopsy
Sternalgegend f sternal region
Sternalgie f sternalgia, sternodynia, pain in the sternum
Sternallinie f sternal line
Sternalmark n sternal marrow
Sternalmembran f sternal membrane
Sternalpunktat n sternal biopsy specimen
Sternalpunktion f sternal puncture
Sternalpunktionskanüle f sternal puncture needle
Sternalrand m sternal border, margin of the sternum
Sternalrippe f sternal rib
Sternaltransfusion f sternal transfusion
Sternennävus m stellar naevus
sternförmig stellate, stellar, star-shaped
Sternfraktur f stellate fracture
Sternganglion n stellate ganglion
Sternkatarakt f stellate (sutural) cataract
Sternoklavikularband n sternoclavicular ligament
~/hinteres posterior sternoclavicular ligament
~/vorderes anterior sternoclavicular ligament
Sternoklavikulargelenk n sternoclavicular articulation (joint)
Sternoklavikularwinkel m sternoclavicular angle
Sternokleidomastoideus m sternocleidomastoid [muscle]
Sternopagie f sternopagia, sternodymia
Sternopagus m sternopagus *(Mißgeburt)*
Sternoschisis f sternoschisis
Sternotom n sternotome

Sternotomie f sternotomy, cutting through the sternum
Sternum n sternum, breastbone *(s. a. unter Brustbein)*
~ bifidum bifid sternum
Sternummeißel m sternum chisel
sternumnah adsternal
Sternumschere f sternum shears
Sternzelle f stellate (spider, star) cell, astrocyte
Sternzellen fpl/**Kupffersche** Kupffer cells, stellate cells of the liver
Steroid n steroid
steroidbildend steroidogenic
Steroidbildung f steroidogenesis
Steroiddiabetes m steroid diabetes
Steroidgeschwür n steroid ulcer
Steroidglaukom n steroid glaucoma
Steroidhormon n steroid hormone
steroidisch steroidal
Steroidkatarakt f steroid cataract
steroidogen steroidogenic
Steroidosteoporose f steroid osteoporosis
Sterol n sterol
Steron n sterone
Stertor m stertor
Stethogoniometer n stethogoniometer
Stethoskop n stethoscope ● **mit dem ~** stethoscopic
stethoskopisch stethoscopic
Stethoskopschlauch m stethoscope tubing
Steuerung f control; regulation
Stevens-Johnson-Syndrom n Stevens-Johnson syndrome, dermatostomatitis
Stewart-Morel-Morgagni-Syndrom n Stewart-Morel[-Morgagni] syndrome, metabolic craniopathy
STH s. Hormon/somatotropes
ST-Hebung f ST [segment] elevation, ST high takeoff *(im EKG)*
Sthenie f sthenia
sthenisch sthenic
Stich m stitch
Stichelung f scarification
Stichelungsmesser n scarificator, scarifier
Stichinzision f stab (button-hole) incision
Stichverletzung f stab [wound]
Stickgas n choking (suffocating) gas *(chemischer Kampfstoff)*
Stickstoffausscheidung f im Urin/gesteigerte hyperazoturia
~ im Urin/verminderte hypoazoturia
~/mangelnde nitrogen retention
~/vermehrte azotorrhoea *(z. B. im Stuhl)*
Stickstoffeliminierung f denitrogenation, elimination of nitrogen
Stickstofferhöhung f im Blut hyperazotaemia
Stickstoffgleichgewicht n nitrogen balance (equilibrium)
stickstoffhaltig nitrogenous
Stickstofflost m s. Stickstoffyperit
Stickstoff(I)-oxid n nitrous oxide
Stickstoffretention f im Blut nitrogen retention

Stickstoffyperit n nitrogen mustard *(chemischer Kampfstoff)*
Stiefelherz n boot-shaped heart
Stiel m stalk *(Anatomie)*; peduncle, pedunculus *(im Gehirn) (Zusammensetzungen s. unter Pedunculus)*; stem, pedicle, pediculus *(z. B. einer Geschwulst)*; petiole, petiolus *(z. B. der Epiglottis)*; handle *(Handgriff)*
stieläugig stalk-eyed
Stielbildung f pediculation, pedicellation
Stieldrehung f torsion of a pedicle
stielförmig peduncular, pedunculate, pediculate; restiform
Stielgeschwulst f peduncular tumour; polyp[us]
Stielklemme f pedicle clamp
Stiellappen m pedicle flap, pedicled graft
Stiellappentransplantation f pedicle flap grafting
Stielspalte f fissure of the optic stalk
Stierhornmagen m steerhorn (cow-horn) stomach *(nach Kontrastmittelfüllung)*
Stiernacken m bull-neck, bison neck *(z. B. bei Diphtherie)*
stiernackig bull-necked
Stift m 1. pin, peg; peg, pivot *(Stomatologie)*; 2. stylus *(Anatomie)*
Stiftzahn m post-crown, peg tooth, pivot tooth (crown)
Stigma n stigma *(s. a.* Symptom*)*
Stigmabildung f stigmatization
stigmatisieren to stigmatize
stigmatisiert stigmatose
Stigmatisierung f stigmatization
Stilben n stilbene
Stilböstrol n stilboestrol
Stilett n stilett[e], stylet
Stillamenorrhoe f lactation amenorrhoea
stillen 1. to nurse, to [breast-]feed, to suckle; to lactate; 2. to appease, to assuage *(den Hunger)*; to satisfy *(den Appetit)*; to quench, to slake *(den Durst)*; 3. to sta[u]nch, to stop, to arrest *(z. B. eine Blutung)*; to alleviate, to soothe, to kill *(z. B. Schmerzen)*
Stillen n 1. nursing, [breast-]feeding *(eines Säuglings)*; 2. satisfaction, assuage *(des Hungers)*; quenching *(des Durstes)*; 3. stopping, arrest, sta[u]nching *(einer Blutung)*; alleviation, mitigation, soothing, killing *(von Schmerzen)*
Stillicidium n lacrimarum epiphora
~ **urinae** dribbling of urine
Stillperiode f lactation period
Stillprobe f breast-feeding test
Stillraum m nursing-room
Stillstand m standstill, arrest, cessation, stoppage; stasis
Stillstandsatelektase f compression atelectasis
Stillstörung f dystithia
Stillstuhl m nursing chair
Still-Syndrom n Still's disease *(viszerale Form der juvenilen Rheumatoidarthritis)*
Stimmapparat m vocal apparatus

Stimmschwäche

Stimmband n vocal c[h]ord (ligament, fold), phonatory band, phonocorda ● **unter den Stimmbändern** subchordal
~/**falsches** false vocal cord, vestibular fold
Stimmbandentfernung f[/**operative**] cordectomy, excision of a vocal fold
Stimmbandentzündung f chorditis, inflammation of a vocal fold
Stimmbanderholung f vocal cord recovery
Stimmbandfixation f cordopexy, fixation of a vocal fold
Stimmbandkarzinom n carcinoma of the vocal cord
Stimmbandknötchen n vocal node (nodule)
Stimmbandkrampf m vocal (laryngeal) cord spasm
Stimmbandlähmung f vocal cord paralysis, phonetic paralysis
Stimmbandläsion f vocal cord lesion
Stimmbandmuskel m vocalis [muscle]
Stimmbandödem n vocal cord oedema
Stimmbandschwäche f vocal cord weakness
Stimmbandschwellung f vocal cord swelling
Stimmbandüberanstrengung f phonasthenia
stimmbildend phonatory
Stimmbildung f phonation, formation of vocal sound, voice formation; formation of speech sounds
~/**richtige** orthophony
Stimmbildungsstörung f dysphonia, phonopathia
Stimmbruch m change of voice
Stimme f voice, vox
~/**heisere** hoarse (husky) voice
~/**näselnde** rhinophonia, twang
~/**schrille** oxyphonia, shrill voice
Stimmenhören n phoneme, hearing of voices
stimmenrein lamprophonic
Stimmenreinheit f lamprophonia, clearness of voice
Stimmenweichheit f leptophonia
Stimmfalte f s. Stimmband
Stimmfremitus m vocal (pectoral) fremitus, tactile (tussive) fremitus
Stimmgabeltest m tuning-fork test
~/**Politzerscher** Politzer's test
~/**Weberscher** Weber's test
Stimmheilkunde f phoniatrics, phoniatry
Stimmhöhenwechsel m paraphonia
Stimmklang m/**scharfer** oxyphonia
Stimmkrampf m phonatory spasm
stimmlich vocal, phonetic
stimmlos voiceless, aphonic, aphonous
Stimmlosigkeit f voicelessness, aphonia, anaudia
~ **am Tage** nyctophonia
~ **in der Nacht** nyctaphonia
Stimmritze f s. Glottis
stimmschwach leptophonic
Stimmschwäche f leptophonia, phonasthenia, weakness of the voice, microphonia

Stimmung

Stimmung f mood, temper, spirits
~/**behagliche** euphoria
~/**depressive** mood depression
~/**unbehagliche** dysphoria
Stimmverlust m loss of voice
Stimmwechsel m change of voice
Stimulans n stimulant [agent], excitant [agent], dope
Stimulation f stimulation; innervation *(durch Nervenreize)*
β-Stimulation f beta-adrenergic stimulation
Stimulationselektrode f pacing electrode
Stimulator m stimulator
stimulieren to stimulate; to innervate *(mittels Nervenreizen)*; to excite *(reizen)*; to animate, to dope *(anregen)*; to pacemake *(mit einem Schrittmacher)*
stimulierend stimulant
~/**die Milchdrüsen** lactogenic
~/**die Wärmeproduktion** thermoexcitory
~/**α-Rezeptoren** alpha-mimetic
Stimulus m s. Reiz 1.
stinkend malodorous, mephitic, foetid
Stinknase f ozaena; atrophic rhinitis
Stippchen n stipple, dot
Stippchengallenblase f strawberry (sandpaper) gall-bladder; cholesterosis (cholesteatosis) of the gall-bladder
Stirn f forehead, frons, metopion
Stirnarterie f frontal artery
~/**äußere seitliche** supra-orbital artery
Stirnband n head band
Stirnbein n frontal bone
Stirnbeinfortsatz m frontal process
Stirnbeinhöhle f s. Stirnhöhle
Stirnbein-Jochbein-Naht f frontozygomatic suture
Stirnbein-Nasenbein-Naht f frontonasal suture
Stirnbein-Oberkiefer-Naht f frontomaxillary suture
Stirnbein-Schläfenbein-Naht f frontotemporal suture
Stirnbeinschuppe f frontal squama
Stirnbein-Siebbein-Naht f frontoethmoid suture
Stirnbein-Tränenbein-Naht f frontolacrimal suture
Stirnfurche f frontal sulcus
~/**untere** inferior frontal sulcus
Stirnglatze f glabella, frontal baldness (alopecia), intercilium
Stirnglatzenmittelpunkt m ophryon *(anthropologischer Meßpunkt)*
Stirnhautsenker m procerus [muscle]
Stirnhirnabszeß m frontal cerebral abscess
Stirnhirnataxie f frontal ataxia
Stirnhirnschnitt m frontal lobotomy
Stirnhirnwindung f frontal gyrus (convolution)
~/**linke untere** left inferior frontal gyrus
~/**mittlere** middle frontal gyrus
~/**obere** superior frontal gyrus
~/**untere** inferior frontal gyrus
Stirnhöcker m frontal eminence
Stirnhöhle f frontal sinus

Stirnhöhlenentzündung f frontal sinusitis
Stirnhöhlenerkrankung f frontal sinus disease
Stirnhöhleneröffnung f[/**operative**] frontal sinusotomy
Stirnhöhlenfraktur f frontal sinus fracture
Stirnhöhlenkanal m nasofrontal duct
Stirnhöhlenkarzinom n frontal sinus carcinoma
Stirnhöhlenmukozele f frontal sinus mucocele
Stirnhöhlenöffnung f opening of the frontal sinus
Stirnhöhlenosteom n frontal sinus osteoma
Stirnhöhlenradikaloperation f/**Killiansche** Killian's operation
Stirnhöhlen- und Knochenentzündung f frontal sinusitis-osteomyelitis
Stirnhöhlenvereiterung f frontal sinus suppuration
Stirnknochenverdickung f enostosis of calvaria
Stirnkopfschmerz m frontal headache, metopodynia
Stirnlage f brow presentation *(des Fetus bei der Geburt)*
Stirnlampe f forehead lamp, head-light
Stirnlappen m frontal lobe [of the brain], forehead flap
Stirnlappenataxie f frontal ataxia
Stirnlappenentfernung f[/**operative**] frontal lobotomy
Stirnleiste f frontal crest
Stirnnaht f frontal (metopic) suture
Stirnnerv m frontal nerve
Stirnpol m frontal pole
Stirnregion f frontal region
stirnseitig frontal
Stirnspiegel m frontal mirror, [fore]head mirror
Stirnvene f frontal vein, vein of the forehead
stirnwärts frontal
Stirnwindung f s. Stirnhirnwindung
Stirnwindungsentfernung f[/**operative**] frontal gyrectomy
Stockschnupfen m chronic rhinitis, chronic cold in the nose
Stockung f s. Stauung
Stoff m matter, substance; medium *(s.a. unter Substanz)*
~/**absorbierender** absorbent [agent]
~/**absorbierter** absorbate
~/**adrenalineffekthemmender** adrenolytic agent
~/**adsorbierender** adsorbent [agent]
~/**adsorbierter** adsorbate
~/**allergieauslösender** allergen
~/**anaphylaktischer** anaphylactogen
~/**bakterienauflösender** bacteriolysant
~/**bakterientötender** bactericide
~/**erythrozytenverklumpender** haemagglutinin
~/**fiebererzeugender** pyr[et]ogen
~/**giftbildender** toxogen
~/**giftneutralisierender** toxolysin
~/**haarwuchsfördernder** trichogen
~/**halluzinogener** hallucinogen
~/**krebserregender** carcinogen, cancerogen, oncogenetic [agent]

~/leberkrebserregender hepatocarcinogen
~/pilzfällender mycoprecipitin
~/sensibilisierender sensitizer
Stoffabgabe f/zelluläre exocytosis
Stoffaufnahme f/zelluläre endocytosis
Stoffwechsel m metabolism ● im ~ umsetzen (verändern) to metabolize, to transform by metabolism
~/aerober aerobic metabolism, aerobiosis
~/anaerober anaerobic metabolism, anaerobiosis
~/luft[sauerstoff]abhängiger s.~/aerober
~/luftunabhängiger s. ~/anaerober
Stoffwechselabfall m waste [product]
Stoffwechselaktivität f metabolic activity
Stoffwechselalkalose f metabolic alcalosis
Stoffwechselantagonist m antimetabolite
Stoffwechselausscheidungsprodukt n metabolic waste product
Stoffwechselazidose f metabolic acidosis
Stoffwechselendprodukt n metabolite; catabolite
Stoffwechselentgleisung f metabolic imbalance
Stoffwechselgift n metabolic toxin
Stoffwechselgleichgewicht n metabolic equilibrium (balance)
Stoffwechselgrundumsatz m basal metabolic rate
Stoffwechselinsuffizienz f hypometabolism
Stoffwechselkern m trophonucleus
Stoffwechselkrankheit f metabolic disease
Stoffwechsellage f metabolic status (condition)
Stoffwechsellehre f metabology
Stoffwechselpigment n metabolic pigment
Stoffwechselsteigerung f hypermetabolism
Stoffwechselstörung f metabolic disorder (disturbance), dysbolism
Stoffwechselüberfunktion f hypermetabolism
Stoffwechselungleichgewicht n metabolic imbalance
Stoffwechselunterfunktion f hypometabolism
Stoffwechselverlangsamung f bradytrophia
Stoffwechselweg m [metabolic] pathway
Stoffwechselzwischenprodukt n intermediate
Stöhnen n/exspiratorisches gruntings
Stoma n stoma, opening, orifice, minute pore (s.a. Mund)
Stomachikum n stomachic [agent]; stomachic tonic
Stomachodynie f stomachodynia, pain in the stomach
Stomachus m s. Magen
Stomakaze f s. Stomatitis ulceromembranacea
Stomalgie f s. Stomachodynie
Stomatitis f stomatitis, inflammation of the mouth
~ aphthosa aphthous (herpetic) stomatitis
~ epidemica foot-and-mouth disease, hand-foot-and-mouth disease
~ exsudativa exudative (foetid) stomatitis
~ gangraenosa gangrenous stomatitis, stomatonecrosis, noma of the mouth
~ membranacea membranous stomatitis

~ mercurialis mercurial stomatitis
~ syphilitica syphilitic stomatitis
~ ulcerativa Plaut-Vincenti s. ~ ulceromembranacea
~ ulceromembranacea (ulcerosa) stomacace, stomatocace, Vincent's (ulcerative) stomatitis; trench mouth
Stomatoglossitis f stomatoglossitis
Stomatologe m stomatologist
Stomatologie f stomatology; dentistry
~/konservierende conservative (restorative) dentistry, endodontology, endodontics, endodontia
stomatologisch stomatologic[al]
Stomatomalazie f stomatomalacia, softening of the structures of the mouth
Stomatomykose f s. Soor
Stomatopathie f stomatopathy, stomatosis, disease of the mouth
stomatopathisch stomatopathic
Stomatoplastik f stomatoplasty
stomatoplastisch stomatoplastic
Stomatorrhagie f stomatorrhagia, haemorrhage from the mouth
Stomatoschisis f stom[at]oschisis, fissure of the mouth; harelip
Stopfmittel n costive [agent], antidiarrhoeal
Störung f disorder, disturbance; defect
~/gastrointestinale gastro-intestinal disturbance
~/somatopsychische somatopsychic disorder
~/vestibuläre vestibular disorder
Stoßbehandlung f massive dose therapy
Stoßstangenfraktur f bumper fracture
Stotterblase f stammering bladder; urinary stammering (stuttering, intermittency)
Stotterer m stutterer, stammerer
stottern to stutter, to stammer
Stottern n stuttering, stammering, spasmophemia, lingual titubation, mogilalia, dysphemia
Strabismometer n s. Strabometer
Strabismus m strabism[us], squint, cast, heterotropia; anorthopia (s.a. unter Schielen)
~ accommodativus accommodative strabismus (squint)
~ alternans alternating strabismus (squint), binocular (bilateral) strabismus
~ concomitans concomitant strabismus (squint)
~ concomitans verticalis vertical concomitant strabismus
~ convergens convergent strabismus (squint), internal strabismus; esotropia; cross-eye
~ convergens intermittens intermittent convergent strabismus
~ divergens divergent strabismus (squint), divergence, external strabismus, exotropia; wall-eye
~/paralytischer paralytic strabismus, paretic squint (nach Augenmuskellähmung)
~ sursumvergens sursumvergent strabismus, anoopsia [strabismus]
~ verticalis vertical strabismus (squint), hypertropia
Strabismus... s. Schiel...
Strabometer n strab[ism]ometer

Strabometrie

Strabometrie f strab[ism]ometry
Strabotom n strabotome
Strabotomie f strabotomy *(Schieloperation)*
Strahlamputation f ray amputation
strahlen to radiate
β-Strahlen mpl beta rays
Strahlen... s.a. Radio... *und* Strahlungs...
Strahlenanämie f radiation (roentgen-ray) anaemia
strahlenbedingt radiation-induced
strahlenbehandelt [ir]radiation-treated
Strahlenbehandlung f radiotherapy, [ir]radiation therapy, radiation [treatment]; emanotherapy; actinotherapy *(z. B. mittels UV- oder Röntgenstrahlung)*
strahlenbelastet radiation-exposed
Strahlenbelastung f/**höchstzulässige** maximum permissible exposure
strahlenbildend actinogenic
strahlend radiant
Strahlenderm[at]itis f radiation (roentgen) dermatitis, radiodermatitis; roentgenoderma
Strahlendermatose f actinic dermatosis
strahlendicht s. strahlenundurchlässig
~/nicht s. strahlendurchlässig
Strahlendosis f radiation dose, dosage, dose, exposure
Strahlendosismesser m [radiation] dosimeter, dosemeter
Strahlendosismessung f dosimetry
strahlendurchlässig non-opaque, radio[trans]parent, radiolucent
Strahlendurchlässigkeit f radioparency, radiolucency
strahlenempfindlich radiosensitive; radioresponsive
Strahlenempfindlichkeit f radiosensitivity, radiosensibility, radiation sensitivity
Strahlenerythem n radiation erythema
strahlenfest s. strahlenunempfindlich
strahlenförmig 1. radial, radiate; 2. actiniform
strahlengeschädigt radiation-damaged, damaged by radiation
strahleninduziert radiation-induced, induced by radiation
Strahlenintoxikation f radiation poisoning
Strahlenkastration f radiation castration
Strahlenkatarakt f [ir]radiation cataract, cyclotron cataract
Strahlenkater m radiation (X-ray) sickness
Strahlenkeratitis f actinic keratitis
Strahlenkeratokonjunktivitis f actinic keratoconjunctivitis
Strahlenkeratose f actinic keratosis
Strahlenknochennekrose f osteoradionecrosis
Strahlenkonjunktivitis f actinic conjunctivitis
Strahlenkörper m ciliary body
Strahlenkörperentzündung f cyclitis, inflammation of the ciliary body
Strahlenkrankheit f radiation (X-ray) sickness
Strahlenkrebs m radiation carcinoma
Strahlenmutation f radiomutation

Strahlenmyelitis f radiation myelitis
Strahlennekrose f radiation necrosis, radionecrosis
Strahlenneuritis f actinoneuritis; radioneuritis
Strahlenpathologie f radiopathology
strahlenpathologisch radiopathological
Strahlenpilz m ray fungus, actinomycete
Strahlenpilzkrankheit f s. Aktinomykose
Strahlenreaktion f radioreaction
strahlenresistent radioresistant
Strahlenresistenz f radioresistance
Strahlenretinitis f actinic retinitis
Strahlenretinopathie f radiation retinopathy
Strahlenschädigung f radiation injury (lesion); irradiation damage
Strahlenschutz m radiation shielding, X-ray protection
Strahlenschutzplakette f badge meter, film badge *(für medizinisches Personal)*
Strahlenstärkemesser m roentgenometer
Strahlenstärkemessung f roentgenometry
strahlensterilisiert radiation-sterilized
Strahlensyndrom n radiation syndrome
strahlentransparent s. strahlendurchlässig
strahlenundurchlässig radiodense, opaque
Strahlenundurchlässigkeit f radiodensity, radio[o]pacity
strahlenunempfindlich radioresistant
Strahlenunempfindlichkeit f radioresistance
Strahlenverbrennung f radiation (X-ray) burn
Strahlenverletzung f radiation injury (lesion)
Strahlenzone f astrosphere *(bei Mitose)*
Strahlenzystitis f radiocystitis, irradiation cystitis
Strahlenzytologie f radiation cytology
Strahlung f radiation
~/energiearme soft radiation
~/energiereiche hard radiation
~/Gratioletsche Gratiolet's optic radiation *(Anatomie)*
~/harte hard radiation
~/infrarote infrared radiation
~/ionisierende ionizing (ionization) radiation
~/weiche soft radiation
Strahlungs... s.a. Strahlen... *und* Radio...
Strahlungsabschirmung f radiation shielding
Strahlungsabsorption f radiation absorption
Strahlungsdetektor m scintillation counter (detector)
Strahlungsfibrose f radiation fibrosis
Strahlungsintensität f radiation intensity
strahlungsmessend actinometric; radiometric
Strahlungsmesser m actinometer; radiometer
Strahlungsmessung f actinometry; radiometry
Strahlungsstärkemeßgerät n intensitometer
Strang m funicle, funiculus, cord *(s.a. unter Funiculus)*; tract, tractus *(s.a. unter Tractus)*; chorda, cord *(s.a. unter Chorda)*; bridle, frenum
~/Burdachscher Burdach's (cuneate) fasciculus
~/Gollscher Goll's column (tract), column of Goll *(mittlerer Teil der sensiblen Hinterstrangbahn)*

Streptococcus

Stränge *mpl*/**amniotische** Simonart's threads *(Verwachsungsbänder zwischen Eihäuten und Feten)*
strangförmig funicular; chordal; restiform
Strangulation *f* strangulation
Strangulationsileus *m* strangulation ileus
Strangulationsverschluß *m* strangulation obstruction *(z. B. des Darms)*
strangulieren to strangulate
~/sich to strangulate
Strangurie *f* stranguria, painful urination; dribbling of urine
Straßen-Virus *n* street rabies virus
Stratifikation *f* stratification, disposal in layers
Stratigraphie *f s.* Tomographie
Stratum *n* stratum, layer, lamina *(s.a. unter Schicht)* ● **unter dem ~ papillare** subpapillary
~ **bacillorum retinae** layer of rods and cones *(der Netzhaut)*
~ **basale** basal[-cell] layer *(z. B. der Gebärmutterschleimhaut)*
~ **basale epidermidis** basal[-cell] layer *(der Oberhaut)*
~ **circulare membranae tympani** circular fibrous layer of the tympanic membrane
~ **circulare tunicae muscularis coli** inner circular layer of the muscular coat of the colon
~ **circulare tunicae muscularis intestini tenuis** inner circular layer of the muscular coat of the small intestine
~ **circulare tunicae muscularis recti** inner circular layer of the muscular coat of the rectum
~ **circulare tunicae muscularis tubae uterinae** inner circular layer of the muscular coat of the uterine tube
~ **circulare tunicae muscularis ventriculi** circular fibres of the muscular coat of the stomach
~ **compactum** compact layer
~ **corneum** corneum, horny [cell] layer
~ **cylindricum** basal[-cell] layer *(der Oberhaut)*
~ **ganglionare nervi optici** internal pyramidal layer *(der Netzhaut)*
~ **ganglionare retinae** retinal ganglion cell layer
~ **germinativum** germinative (Malpighian) layer
~ **granulosum** granular[-cell] layer
~ **granulosum cerebelli** granular-cell layer of the cerebellum
~ **granulosum epidermidis** granular-cell layer of the epidermis
~ **granulosum folliculi ovarici vesiculosi** granular-cell layer of the vesicular ovarian follicle
~ **Malpighii** *s.* ~ germinativum
~ **moleculare cerebelli** molecular layer of the cerebellum
~ **neuroepitheliale retinae** retinal neuroepithelial layer
~ **papillare corii** papillary layer
~ **pigmenti corporis ciliaris** pigmented cell layer of the ciliary body
~ **pigmenti iridis** pigmented cell layer of the iris
~ **reticulare** reticular layer *(Hautschicht)*
~ **spinosum** prickle[-cell] layer

~ **synoviale** synovial membrane
~ **zonale corporum quadrigeminorum** stratum zonale of the midbrain
~ **zonale thalami** stratum zonale of the thalamus
Streckapparat *m* extension (traction) apparatus, hyperextension frame
~/lateraler akzessorischer lateral accessory patellar ligament *(des Kniegelenks)*
~/medialer akzessorischer medial accessory patellar ligament *(des Kniegelenks)*
Streckbarkeit *f* extensibility *(z. B. eines Muskels)*
Streckbett *n* extension bed
Strecker *m* extensor [muscle]
Streckerhalteband *n* extensor retinaculum [of the wrist]
Streckersehne *f* extensor tendon
Streckmuskel *m* extensor [muscle]
Streckparaplegie *f* paraplegia in extension
Streckschiene *f* splint
Strecksehne *f* extensor tendon
Streckung *f* extension
Streckungsparaplegie *f* paraplegia in extension
Streckverband *m* extension bandage; extension apparatus
Streifen *m* stripe, strike; strap, pack *(Tamponade)*; stria *(der Haut) (s.a. unter Stria)*; band *(z. B. im Gehirn)*; layer *(z. B. von Zellen)*; streak *(z. B. im Schleim)*
~/Cooperscher Cooper's ligament *(am Ellenbogengelenk)*
~/Maissiatscher Maissiat's band, iliotibial band (tract)
Streifen *mpl*/**Baillargersche** Baillarger's bands (layers, lines) *(in der Großhirnrinde)*
Streifeneinlegen *n* packing
streifenförmig striate[d]
Streifenhügel *m s.* Striatum
Streifenkeratitis *f* striate keratitis
Streifenperkussion *f* strip percussion
Streifenretinoskopie *f* streak retinoscopy
Streifentamponade *f* packing, wicking
Streifenverband *m* strapping
Streifung *f* stria, striation
~/bronchovaskuläre bronchovascular markings *(im Lungenröntgenbild)*
Strepitus *m* strepitus, sound, noise
~ **uteri[nus]** uterine souffle
Streptidin *n* streptidine
Streptikämie *f* strepticaemia, streptosepticaemia
Streptobacillosis *f* **venerea** soft chancre, chancroid, chancroidal ulcer
Streptobacillus *m* streptobacillus
~ **moniliformis** Streptobacillus moniliformis *(Erreger des Haverhill-Fiebers)*
streptobazillär streptobacillary
Streptococcus *m* streptococcus *(s.a. unter Streptokokke)*
~ **anhaemolyticus** anhaemolytic streptococcus
~ **haemolyticus** haemolytic streptococcus
~ **pyogenes [der Lancefield-Gruppe A]** Streptococcus pyogenes [of Lancefield's group A]

47 Nöhring dtsch./engl.

Streptococcus

~ **viridans** viridans streptococcus
Streptodermie f streptoderma; streptodermatitis, streptococcal dermatitis
Streptodornase f streptodornase, streptococcal deoxyribonuclease *(Enzym)*
Streptokinase f streptokinase *(Enzym)*
Streptokinaseaktivierung f streptokinase activation
Streptokinase-Streptodornase f streptokinase-streptodornase
Streptokokkämie f streptococcaemia, septic[a]emia
Streptokokke f streptococcus *(s.a. unter Streptococcus)*
~ **der Gruppe A/β-hämolysierende** group A beta-haemolytic streptococcus
~ **der Gruppe B/β-hämolysierende** beta-haemolytic streptococcus group B
α-Streptokokke f alpha streptococcus
β-Streptokokke f beta streptococcus
Streptokokkenangina f streptoangina
Streptokokkenantitoxin n streptococcus antitoxin
Streptokokkendermatitis f s. Streptodermie
Streptokokken-Desoxyribonuklease f streptococcal deoxyribonuclease
Streptokokkenenzym n streptococcal enzyme
Streptokokkenerkrankung f s. Streptokokkeninfektion
Streptokokkenhämolysin n strepto[haemo]lysin
Streptokokkenhämolysinantikörper m antistrepto[haemo]lysin
Streptokokkenhyaluronidase f streptococcal hyaluronidase
Streptokokkeninfektion f streptococcal infection, streptococc[ic]osis
~ **der oberen Luftwege** streptococcal upper respiratory infection
Streptokokkenmeningitis f streptococcus meningitis
Streptokokkenpharyngitis f streptococcal pharyngitis, streptococcal sore throat; septic sore throat
Streptokokkenpneumonie f streptococcus pneumonia
Streptokokkenpyodermie f streptoderma
Streptokokkensepsis f streptococcal sepsis, streptosepticaemia
Streptokokkenserum n streptococcus antitoxin
streptokokkentötend streptococcicide
Streptolysin n s. Streptokokkenhämolysin
Streptomyzin n streptomycin *(Antibiotikum)*
Streptothrizin n streptothricin *(Antibiotikum)*
Streptotrichose f streptotric[h]osis
Streß m stress
Streßgeschwür n stress ulcer
Streßharninkontinenz f stress urinary incontinence
Streßinkontinenz f stress incontinence *(der Psyche)*
Streßphänomen n stress phenomenon
Streßreaktion f stress reaction

streuen to strew, to scatter; to disseminate; to spread *(ausbreiten)*
Streustrahlen mpl scattered rays
Streuung f scattering; dissemination; spread
~/**hämatogene** haematogenous spread
Stria f 1. stria, streak, stripe, narrow band *(s.a. unter Streifen)*; 2. s. Streifung
~ **longitudinalis lateralis corporis callosi** lateral longitudinal stria
~ **longitudinalis medialis corporis callosi** medial longitudinal stria
~ **olfactoria** olfactory root
Striae fpl:
~ **Baillargeri interni et externi** Baillarger's bands (layers, lines) *(in der Großhirnrinde)*
~ **cutis distensae** s. ~ gravidarum
~ **gravidarum** lineae albicantes (gravidarum) *(Hautatrophien durch Zerreißung der elastischen Fasern)*
~ **medullares acusticae (fossae rhomboideae)** s. ~ medullares ventriculi quarti
~ **medullares ventriculi quarti** acoustic (auditory) striae, bands of Piccolomini, Bergmann's cords (fibres) *(Streifen am Boden der Rautengrube)*
Striatum n [corpus] striatum, striatal body ● **unter dem ~** subcallosal
Striatumsyndrom n [Hunt's] striatal syndrome
Strickkörper m s. Kleinhirnstiel
Stridor m stridor, wheeze
~/**exspiratorischer** expiratory stridor
~/**inspiratorischer** inspiratory stridor
stridulös stridulous, strident
Striktur f stricture, ste[g]nosis, narrowing
Strikturbildung f stricture formation
Strikturendurchtrennung f[/**operative**] s. Strikturotomie
Strikturotomie f stricturotomy; coarctotomy
striozellular striocellular
strippen/Venen to strip
Stroma n stroma ● **vom ~ ausgehend** stromatogenous
Stromatin n stromatin *(Protein)*
strömen to stream, to flow; fo flush
Strömungsgeräusch n/**arterielles** arterial murmur
Strömungsgeschwindigkeit f flow velocity
Strongyloides m **intestinalis (stercoralis)** strongyloid threadworm
Strongyloidiasis f, **Strongyloidosis** f strongyloidiasis, strongylosis, intestinal capillariasis, anguilluliasis, anguillulosis
Strophanthin n strophantin *(Glykosid)*
Strophozephalie f strophocephalia
Strophozephalus m strophocephalus *(Mißgeburt)*
Strophulus m strophulus, red gum, lichen infantum
Strudelvene f vortex vein *(am Auge)*
Struktur f structure; texture
~/**knötchenförmige** nodularity
~/**zelluläre** cellularity

strukturell structural; textural
Strukturgen n structural gene
Strukturpsychologie f structural psychology
Struma f struma, goitre, thyrocele (s.a. unter Kropf)
~/**akzessorische** accessory (aberrant) goitre
~/**chromaffine suprarenale** chromaffino[blasto]ma
~ **colloides** colloid goitre
~ **diffusa** diffuse goitre
~/**eisenharte** iron-hard tumour of the thyroid, Riedel's struma, woody (ligneous) thyroiditis (mit Bindegewebswucherung, Atrophie und Follikelschwund)
~ **endothoracica** s. ~/retrosternale
~/**euthyreote** non-toxic goitre
~ **follicularis** parenchymatous goitre
~/**hyperthyreote** hyperthyroid goitre
~/**hypothyreote** hypothyroid goitre
~/**iatrogene** iatrogenic goitre
~/**juvenile** juvenile goitre
~ **lingualis** lingual goitre (thyroid) (Insel von versprengtem Schilddrüsengewebe am Zungengrund)
~ **lymphomatosa [Hashimoto]** lymphadenoid goitre, Hashimoto's disease (struma)
~ **maligna** malignant (cancerous) goitre, cancer of the thyroid [body]
~ **nodosa** nodular (adenomatous) goitre, adenoma of the thyroid gland
~ **nodosa multiplex** multinodular goitre
~ **parenchymatosa** parenchymatous goitre
~/**retrosternale** retrosternal (mediastinal) goitre, substernal thyroid
~/**Riedelsche** s. ~/eisenharte
~ **simplex** simple (endemic) goitre
Struma... s.a. Kropf...
strumaförmig strumiform
Strumakrebs m cancerous (malignant) goitre
strumalindernd antistrumous
Strumaresektion f strumectomy
~/**halbseitige** hemistrumectomy
Strumektomie f strumectomy
strumigen goitrogenic, goitrogenous
strumipriv strumiprival, strumiprivic, strumiprivous, thyroprival
Strumitis f strumitis, thyroiditis, thyroadenitis, inflammation of a goitrous thyroid gland
strumös strumous, strumose, goitrous
Strümpell-Zeichen n Strümpell's sign, tibialis phenomenon
Strychnin n strychnine (Alkaloid)
Strychninapplikation f strychninization
Strychninvergiftung f strychnism, strychnine poisoning
Strychnismus m s. Strychninvergiftung
ST-Senkung f ST [segment] depression (im EKG)
ST-Strecke f ST segment (im EKG)
~/**erhöhte** ST high takeoff
ST-Streckenerhöhung f s. ST-Hebung
ST-Streckensenkung f s. ST-Senkung
Stuart-Power-Faktor m Stuart-Power factor, [blood-clotting] factor X

Stufenschädel m bathrocephaly
Stufenschnitt m step (serial) section (Histologie)
Stuhl m 1. stool, dejection, stercus, ordure, excrement; faeces; 2. s. Stuhlentleerung
~/**acholischer** acholic (clay-coloured) stool
~/**blutiger** haemorrhagic stool
~/**bräunlicher** brownish stool
~/**breiiger** pultaceous (doughy, pasty) stool
~/**dunkler** dark stool
~/**dünner** loose stool
~/**dünnflüssiger** liquid stool; enterorrhoea
~/**eitriger** pyochezia
~/**erbsbreiartiger** pea-soup stool (bei Typhus)
~/**fester** hard stool
~/**geformter** well-formed stool
~/**gelblicher** yellowish stool
~/**lehmfarbener** clay-coloured stool
~/**reiswasserähnlicher** rice-water stool (bei Cholera)
~/**spinatartiger** spinach stool
Stuhl... s.a. Kot...
Stuhldauerausscheider m chronic enteric (intestinal) carrier
Stuhldauerausscheidung f chronic enteric carrier state
Stuhldrang m/**schmerzhafter** tenesmus
Stuhlentleerung f defaecation, dejection, evacuation, motion, movement
Stuhlentleerungsreflex m defaecation reflex
Stuhlentleerungsreiz m defaecation stimulus
stuhlfördernd aperient, laxative, purgative
Stuhlgang m s. 1. Stuhlentleerung; 2. Stuhl ● ~ **haben** to have stools
~/**gesteigerter** hypercatharsis
stuhlinkontinent sein to be incontinent of faeces
Stuhlinkontinenz f faecal (anal, rectal) incontinence, incontinence of the faeces, scatacratia, scoracratia, encopresis
Stuhlkonsistenz f consistency of the stool
Stuhlkontrolle f scatoscopy
Stuhlkultur f stool culture, coproculture
Stuhlprobe f stool (faecal) specimen
Stuhlstopfmittel n costive [agent]
Stuhltraining n bowel training
Stuhluntersuchung f scatoscopy
stuhlverstopft constipated, obstipated, costive
Stuhlverstopfung f constipation, costiveness, obstipation ● **zu ~ führen** to obstipate, to constipate
~/**spastische** spastic constipation
Stuhlzäpfchen n [rectal] suppository, medicated bougie
Stuhlzwang m/**schmerzhafter** straining tenesmus
stumm mute, dumb
Stummer m mute, dumb man
Stummheit f muteness, dumbness, anepia; mutism (bei intaktem Sprechapparat)
stumpf blunt, obtuse; apathetic; dull, insensible
Stumpf m stump
Stumpfheit f languor, dullness, numbness; lethargic lethargy
Stumpfneuralgie f stump neuralgia

Stumpfneurom 740

Stumpfneurom *n* stump (amputation) neuroma
Stumpfplastik *f*/**Symesche** Syme's amputation
Stumpfschmerz *m* [amputation] stump pain
Stumpfsinn *m* stupidity
stündlich every hour, hourly, quaque hora, q. h.
Stupor *m* stupor, stupefaction, hebetude, carus, psychocoma; attonity *(bei katatoner Schizophrenie)*
~/melancholischer melancholic stupor
~ vigilans catalepsia
stuporös stuporous, hebetudinous
Stupsnase *f* snub (pug) nose
Sturge-Weber-Syndrom *n* Sturge-Weber syndrome, naevoid amentia, encephalotrigeminal (meningocutaneous) angiomatosis
Sturzentleerung *f* **[des Magens]** dumping stomach (syndrome)
Sturzgeburt *f* precipitate labour, oxytocia
Stutenserumgonadotropin *n* pregnant mare serum gonadotrophin
Stütze *f* support; sustentaculum *(Anatomie)*
stützend supporting; sustentacular; suspensory
Stützgerüst *n* sustentaculum
Stützverband *m* suspensory [bandage]
Stützzelle *f* sustentacular (supporting) cell
Stützzellen *fpl*/**Deitersche** cells of Deiter *(des Spiralorgans)*
~/Hensensche cells of Hensen *(im Cortischen Organ)*
~/Sertolische Sertoli cells *(im Hoden)*
stylohyoid stylohyoid
Styloiditis *f* styloiditis, inflammation of the styloid process
stylomandibulär stylomandibular, stylomaxillary
stylomastoid[al] stylomastoid
Stylus *m* stylus *(Anatomie)*
Stypsis *f* 1. stypsis, astringency; astringent action *(s. a.* Blutstillung*)*; 2. stypsis, treatment by astringents
Styptikum *n* styptic [agent]; astringent
styptisch [haemo]styptic; astringent
subakut subacute
Subaortenstenose *f*/**idiopathische hypertrophe** [idiopathic] hypertrophic subaortic stenosis
Subarachnoidalblutung *f* subarachnoid haemorrhage
~/spinale spinal subarachnoid haematoma
Subarachnoidalraum *m* subarachnoid (meningeal) space
~ der Lendenwirbelsäule lumbar subarachnoid space
Subazidität *f* subacidity, hypoacidity
Subdelir[ium] *n* subdelirium
subdiaphragmatisch *s.* subphrenisch
Subduralabszeß *m* subdural abcess (empyema)
Subduralblutung *f* subdural haemorrhage
Subduralerguß *m* subdural effusion
Subduralhämatom *n* subdural haematoma
Subduralraum *m* subdural (meningeal) space
Subendokardfibroelastose *f* subendocardial fibroelastosis (sclerosis)
Subendokardsklerose *f* subendocardial sclerosis

Subglossitis *f* subglossitis, inflammation of the lower surface of the tongue
Subiculum *n* **promontorii** support of the promontory
subikterisch subicteric
Subinfektion *f* subinfection
Subinvolution *f* subinvolution, incomplete involution
Subklavia *f s.* 1. Arteria subclavia; 2. Vena subclavia
Subklavia-Aneurysma *n* subclavian aneurysm
Subklavia-Anzapfsyndrom *n* subclavian steal syndrome, brachial-basilar insufficiency syndrome
Subklavia-Punktion *f* subclavian [vein] puncture
Subklavikularregion *f* subclavicular region
subklinisch subclinical
Subkostallinie *f* subcostal line
Subkostalschnitt *m* subcostal incision
Subkostalwinkel *m* subcostal angle
subkutan subcutaneous, s. c., subdermal, subintegumental, hypoderm[at]ic
Subkutanabszeß *m* subcutaneous abscess
Subkutanemphysem *n* subcutaneous emphysema
Subkutangewebe *n* subcutaneous [connective] tissue
Subkutaninfusion *f* hypoderm[at]oclysis
Subkutaninjektion *f* subcutaneous injection, hypodermic [injection]
Subkutankanüle *f* hypodermic needle
Subkutanmedikation *f* hypodermic medication
Subkutanödem *n* subcutaneous oedema
Subkutanspritze *f* hypodermic [syringe]
Subkutis *f* subcutis, hypodermis
Sublimat *n* mercuric (mercury) chloride *(Antiseptikum)*
Sublimatnephrose *f* mercurial nephrosis
Sublimatprobe *f* **nach Spiegler** Spiegler's test *(zum Eiweißnachweis)*
sublingual sublingual, subglossal
Sublingualregion *f* sublingual region
Subluxation *f* subluxation, semiluxation, incomplete dislocation
subluxieren to sublux
Submandibulardrüse *f* submandibular gland
Submentalregion *f* submental region
Submentalschnitt *m* submental incision
submikroskopisch submicroscopic[al]
Submukosa *f* submucosa, submucous membrane
Subokzipitaldreieck *n* suboccipital triangle
Subokzipitalgrube *f* suboccipital fossa
Subokzipitalpunktion *f* suboccipital (cisternal) puncture
Subokzipitalregion *f* suboccipital region
subphrenisch subphrenic, subdiaphragmatic, hypophrenic
Subscriptio *f* subscription *(Rezept)*
Subskapulargrube *f* subscapular fossa
Subskapularregion *f* subscapular region
Substantia *f* 1. substantia, substance *(Morphologie)*; 2. *s.* Substanz 1.

~ **adamantina** adamantine, enamel
~ **alba** white substance (matter) of the brain
~ **alba medullae spinalis** white matter of the [spinal] cord
~ **compacta** compacta, compact bone (tissue), cortical bone
~ **glandularis prostatae** glandular tissue of the prostate
~ **grisea centralis** central grey substance
~ **grisea cerebri** grey substance (matter) of the brain
~ **grisea medullae spinalis** grey matter of the [spinal] cord
~ **lentis** fibrous substance of the lens
~ **nigra** [substantia] nigra *(Gehirnabschnitt)*
~ **perforata** perforated substance
~ **perforata anterior** anterior perforated substance (space), preperforatum
~ **perforata posterior** posterior perforated substance (space)
~ **propria sclerae** connective tissue of the sclera
~ **reticularis alba [Arnoldi]** reticular white substance
~ **reticularis alba medullae oblongatae** white reticular substance of the medulla oblongata
~ **reticularis grisea medullae oblongatae** grey reticular substance of the medulla oblongata
~ **spongiosa** s. Spongiosa
Substanz f 1. substance, matter *(s. a. unter Stoff)*; 2. s. Substantia 1.
~/**antiketogene** antiketogen
~/**chromophile** chromophile substance
~/**den Zerfall bewirkende** disintegrator
~/**langwirkende schilddrüsenstimulierende** long-acting thyroid stimulator, LATS
~/**leberzellenschützende** hepatocytoprotective substance
~/**oberflächenaktive** surface-active substance, surfactant
~/**onkotisch aktive** oncotic agent
~/**spermienauflösende** spermatolysin
~/**strumigene** goitrogen
~/**zellhemmende** cytostatic [agent]
Substitution f substitution, replacement
Substitutionstherapie f substitution therapy
Substrathydrolyse f substrate hydrolysis
Subsultus m tendinum subsultus clonus (tendinum), involuntary twitching of the muscles
Subthalamusregion f subthalamic region
subtotal subtotal, near-total
Subungualabszeß m subungual abscess
Succinat n s. Sukzinat
Succus m succus, juice
~ **entericus** enteric juice
~ **gastricus** gastric juice (fluid)
~ **intestinalis** intestinal juice
~ **pancreaticus** pancreatic juice
~ **prostaticus** prostatic fluid
Sucht f mania; addiction, habit, dependence *(nach Rauschgift)*
süchtig manic, maniacal; addicted ● ~ **sein** to addict, to suffer from addiction

Süchtiger m maniac; [drug] addict
Sucrose f s. Saccharose
Sudabad n enterocleaner
Sudamen n sudamen *(Hautkrankheit)*
Sudanfarbstoff m Sudan dye (stain)
sudanophil sudanophilic
Sudanophilie f sudanophilia, affinity to Sudan dyes
Sudation f s. Schwitzen
Sudatorium n 1. sudatorium, hot-air bath; 2. sudatorium, sweating room
Sudeck m, **Sudeck-Syndrom** n Sudeck's atrophy (dystrophy), posttraumatic reflex sympathetic dystrophy, traumatic osteoporosis
Sudokeratose f sudorikeratosis, keratosis of the sweat glands
Sudor m s. Schweiß
sudorifer sudoriferous, sweat-producing; sudorific, inducing sweating
Sudorifikum n sudorific [agent]
Sudotherapie f sudotherapy
Suffokation f s. Ersticken
suggerieren to suggest
suggestibel suggestible, amenable to suggestion
Suggestibilität f suggestibility
Suggestion f suggestion *(z. B. durch Hypnose)* ● **durch ~ beeinflussen** to suggest
Suggestionsbehandlung f suggestion therapy, suggestive treatment, pithiatism; teletherapy, teleotherapeutics
Suggestivmedizin f suggestive medicine
Suggestivtherapie f s. Suggestionsbehandlung
Sugillation f sugillation, ecchymosis, bruise, suffusion
Suizid m s. Selbstmord
Sukorrhoe f succorhoea, excessive flow of a secretion
Sukzinat n succinate
Sukzinatdehydrogenase f succinic [acid] dehydrogenase
Sukzinsäure f succinic acid
Sukzinylcholinchlorid n succinylcholine (suxamethonium) chloride *(Muskelrelaxans)*
Sulcus m sulcus; groove, furrow; semicanal
~ **alveolabialis** alveolabial sulcus
~ **alveolingualis** alveolingual sulcus
~ **ampullaris** ampullary sulcus
~ **anthelicis transversus** transverse sulcus of the anthelix
~ **aorticus** aortic sulcus
~ **arteriae occipitalis** occipital groove
~ **arteriae subclaviae** subclavian sulcus
~ **atrioventricularis** atrioventricular sulcus
~ **bicipitalis lateralis** lateral bicipital sulcus
~ **bicipitalis medialis** medial bicipital sulcus
~ **calcanei** calcaneal sulcus
~ **caroticus** carotid groove
~ **centralis [cerebri]** central sulcus [of Rolando], central fissure
~ **centralis insulae** circular sulcus
~ **centralis Rolandi** s. ~ centralis cerebri
~ **cerebri lateralis** lateral cerebral sulcus, Sylvian fissure

Sulcus

- ~ **chiasmatis** chiasmatic sulcus, optic groove
- ~ **cinguli** cingulate sulcus (fissure)
- ~ **collateralis** collateral sulcus
- ~ **coronarius** coronary sulcus
- ~ **corporis callosi** callosal sulcus
- ~ **costae** costal sulcus
- ~ **cutis** cuticular sulcus
- ~ **frontalis inferior** inferior frontal sulcus
- ~ **frontalis superior** superior frontal sulcus
- ~ **glutaeus** glutaeal sulcus (fold)
- ~ **hippocampi** hippocampal sulcus, dentate fissure
- ~ **horizontalis cerebelli** horizontal cerebellar fissure
- ~ **hypothalamicus** hypothalamic sulcus, sulcus of Monro
- ~ **infraorbitalis** infraorbital sulcus (groove)
- ~ **interatrialis** interatrial sulcus (groove)
- ~ **intermedius posterior [medullae spinalis]** posterior intermediate sulcus
- ~ **intertubercularis** intertubercular sulcus, bicipital groove
- ~ **interventricularis** interventricular groove
- ~ **interventricularis anterior** anterior longitudinal cardiac sulcus, anterior interventricular furrow (groove)
- ~ **interventricularis posterior** posterior longitudinal cardiac sulcus, posterior interventricular furrow (groove)
- ~ **intraparietalis** intraparietal sulcus
- ~ **lacrimalis maxillae** lacrimal sulcus
- ~ **lateralis anterior medullae spinalis** anterolateral spinal sulcus
- ~ **lateralis posterior medullae spinalis** posterolateral spinal sulcus
- ~ **malleolaris** malleolar sulcus
- ~ **medialis cruris cerebri** oculomotor sulcus
- ~ **medianus linguae** median lingual sulcus, raphe of the tongue
- ~ **mylohyoideus** mylohyoid groove
- ~ **nervi petrosi majoris** canal of the greater petrosal nerve
- ~ **nervi petrosi minoris** canal of the lesser petrosal nerve
- ~ **nervi radialis** radial sulcus, [musculo]spiral groove
- ~ **obturatorius** obturator groove
- ~ **occipitalis lateralis** lateral occipital sulcus
- ~ **occipitalis transversus** transverse occipital sulcus
- ~ **olfactorius lobi frontalis** olfactory sulcus
- ~ **orbitalis** orbital sulcus
- ~ **palatinus major ossis palatini** pterygopalatine groove (sulcus)
- ~ **paracentralis** paracentral sulcus
- ~ **paramedialis** paramedial sulcus
- ~ **parieto-occipitalis** parieto-occipital sulcus (fissure)
- ~ **parolfactorius** parolfactory sulcus
- ~ **parolfactorius posterior** posterior parolfactory sulcus
- ~ **petrosus inferior ossis temporalis** inferior petrosal sulcus of the temporal bone
- ~ **petrosus superior ossis temporalis** superior petrosal sulcus of the temporal bone
- ~ **postcentralis** postcentral sulcus
- ~ **praecentralis** precentral sulcus, presylvian fissure
- ~ **sclerae** scleral sulcus
- ~ **sinus sagittalis superior** sagittal sulcus
- ~ **sinus sigmoidei** sigmoid groove, sulcus of the sigmoid sinus
- ~ **sinus transversi** sulcus of the transverse sinus
- ~ **spiralis externus** external spiral sulcus
- ~ **spiralis internus** internal spiral sulcus
- ~ **subparietalis** subparietal sulcus
- ~ **tali** talar sulcus
- ~ **temporalis** temporal sulcus
- ~ **temporalis inferior** inferior temporal sulcus
- ~ **temporalis medius** middle temporal sulcus
- ~ **temporalis superior** superior temporal sulcus
- ~ **temporalis transversus** transverse temporal sulcus
- ~ **terminalis atrii dextri** terminal cardiac sulcus
- ~ **terminalis linguae** terminal lingual sulcus
- ~ **tubae auditivae** sulcus of the auditority tube
- ~ **tympanicus** tympanic sulcus
- ~ **venae umbilicalis** umbilical fissure

Sulfadiazin *n* sulphadiazine
Sulfaguanidin *n* sulphaguanidine
Sulfamerazin *n* sulphamerazine
Sulfamethazin *n* sulphamethazine
Sulfanilamid *n* sulphanilamide
Sulfanilsäure *f* sulphanilic acid
Sulfapyrazol *n* sulphapyrazole
Sulfapyridin *n* sulphapyridine
Sulfathiazol *n* sulphathiazole
Sulfazetamid *n* sulphacetamide
Sulfhämoglobin *n* sulph[met]haemoglobin
Sulfhämoglobinämie *f* sulphhaemoglobinaemia; enterogenous cyanosis
Sulfonamid *n* sulphonamide
Sulfonamidpräparat *n* sulpha drug *(Chemotherapeutikum)*
Sulfonsäureamid *n* sulphonamide
Sulfosalizylsäure *f* sulphosalicylic acid
Sulfosalizylsäureprobe *f* sulphosalicylic acid test
Sulkowitsch-Probe *f* Sulkowitsch's test *(zum Kalziumnachweis im Urin)*
Sulze *f*/**Whartonsche** Wharton's jelly, jelly of Wharton; embryonic connective tissue
Summationsgalopp *m* summation gallop *(der Herztöne)*
Sumpffieber *n s.* Malaria
Super... *s. a.* Hyper...
Supercilium *n s.* Augenbraue
Superfekundation *f* superfecundation, superimpregnation
Superfetation *f* superfoetation
Superinfektion *f* superinfection
Superparasit *m* superparasite
superparasitisch superparasitic
Superscriptio *f* superscription *(der Rezeptur)*
Supination *f* 1. supination, upward turning of the palm; 2. supination, inversion of the foot

Supinationswinkel *m* supination angle, angle of supination
supinieren to supinate
Suppositorium *n* suppository, medicated bougie
Suppression *f* suppression *(z. B. der Monatsblutung)*
Suppressorband *n* suppressor area (band) *(in der Hirnrinde)*
Suppressorlymphozyt *m* suppressor cell (lymphocyte) *(Immunologie)*
supprimieren to suppress
Suppurans *n* suppurant [agent]
Suppuration *f* suppuration, formation of pus, empyesis, pyogenesis
suppurativ suppurative, pus-producing, pyogenous
suppurieren to suppurate
supradiaphragmatisch supradiaphragmatic, epiphrenic, epiphrenal
Suprahyoidregion *f* suprahyoid region
Suprainguinalregion *f* suprainguinal region
Supraklavikulardreieck *n* supraclavicular triangle
Supraklavikulargrube *f* supraclavicular fossa
Supraklavikularpunkt *m* supraclavicular point
Supraklavikularregion *f* supraclavicular region
Suprakondylarfraktur *f* supracondylar fracture
Suprakondylarleiste *f* supracondylar ridge
Supraokklusion *f* supra-occlusion, supraclusion
Supraorbitalneuralgie *f* supra-orbital neuralgia
Supraorbitalreflex *m* supra-orbital (orbicularis oculi) reflex
Suprapatellarreflex *m* suprapatellar reflex
Suprarenalektomie *f* suprarenalectomy, adrenalectomy, epinephrectomy
Suprarenin *n s.* Adrenalin
Suprasternalregion *f* suprasternal (episternal) region
Supratonsillarabszeß *m* supratonsillar abscess
Supraventrikularleiste *f* supraventricular (infundibuloventricular) crest
Supravitalfärbung *f* [supra]vital staining
Sura *f s.* Wade
sural sural
Surditas *f* surdity, deafness
Surdomutitas *f s.* Taubstummheit
Suspension *f* suspension
Suspensionskolloid *n* suspensoid
Suspensorium *n* suspensorium, suspensory
~ **testis** cremaster [muscle]
Süßholz *n* liquorice
Süßstoff *m* saccharin
Sustentakulum *n* sustentaculum, support
suszeptibel susceptible, sensitive
Suszeptibilität *f* susceptibility, sensitivity
Sutura *f* suture, sutura, raphe, seam *(s. a. unter Raphe)*
~ **coronalis** coronal (frontoparietal) suture
~ **cranialis** cranial suture
~ **dentata** dentate suture
~ **ethmofrontalis** ethmofrontal suture
~ **ethmoideomaxillaris** ethmoidomaxillary suture
~ **ethmolacrimalis** ethmolacrimal suture
~ **ethmosphenoidalis** ethmosphenoid suture
~ **frontalis** frontal (metopic) suture
~ **frontoethmoidalis** frontoethmoid suture
~ **frontolacrimalis** frontolacrimal suture
~ **frontomaxillaris** frontomaxillary suture
~ **frontonasalis** frontonasal suture
~ **frontotemporalis** frontotemporal suture
~ **frontozygomatica** frontozygomatic suture
~ **incisiva** incisive suture
~ **infraorbitalis** infraorbital suture
~ **intermaxillaris** intermaxillary suture
~ **internasalis** internasal suture
~ **interpalatina** interpalatine suture
~ **lacrimoconchalis** lacrimoconchal suture
~ **lacrimomaxillaris** lacrimomaxillary suture
~ **lambdoidea** lambdoid (occipital) suture
~ **maxillolacrimalis** maxillolacrimal suture
~ **nasomaxillaris** nasomaxillary suture
~ **occipitomastoidea** occipitomastoid suture
~ **occipitoparietalis** occipitoparietal suture
~ **palatina mediana** median palatine suture
~ **palatina transversa** transverse palatine suture
~ **palatoethmoidalis** palato-ethmoidal suture
~ **palatomaxillaris** palatomaxillary suture
~ **parietomastoidea** parietomastoid suture
~ **petrooccipitalis** petro-occipital suture
~ **petrosphenoidea** petrosphenoid suture
~ **petrosquamosa** petrosquamous suture
~ **sagittalis** sagittal (longitudinal, interparietal) suture
~ **serrata** serrated suture
~ **sphenoethmoidalis** sphenoethmoid suture
~ **sphenofrontalis** sphenofrontal suture
~ **sphenomaxillaris** sphenomaxillary suture
~ **sphenooccipitalis** spheno-occipital suture
~ **sphenoorbitalis** sphenopalatine suture
~ **sphenoparietalis** sphenoparietal suture
~ **sphenopetrosa** sphenopetrosal suture
~ **sphenosquamosa** sphenosquamosal suture
~ **sphenotemporalis** sphenotemporal suture
~ **sphenozygomatica** sphenozygomatic suture
~ **squamomastoidea** squamomastoid suture
~ **squamosa cranii** squamosal suture
~ **temporozygomatica** zygomaticotemporal suture
~ **zygomaticofrontalis** zygomaticofrontal suture
~ **zygomaticomaxillaris** zygomaticomaxillary suture
~ **zygomaticotemporalis** zygomaticotemporal suture
Sycosis *f* sycosis
~ **barbae** hyphogenic sycosis
~ **framboesiformis Hebra** framboesiform sycosis
~ **parasitica** parasitic (contagious) sycosis
~ **simplex (vulgaris)** sycosis [of the beard], deep folliculitis
sykosiform sycosiform, resembling sycosis
Symbiont *m* symbion[t]
Symbiose *f* symbiosis ● **in ~ zusammenlebend** symbiotic
symbiotisch symbiotic

Symblepharon

Symblepharon n symblepharon
Symblepharose f symblepharosis
Symbolagnosie f symbolic agnosia
Symboldenken n symbolismus
Symbolophobie f symbolophobia *(krankhafte Angst vor symbolischen Handlungen)*
Symmelie f symmelia, fusion of the feet and legs
Symmelus m symmelus *(Mißgeburt)*
Symmetrie f symmetry *(z. B. beider Körperhälften)*
Symparalyse f symparalysis, conjugate gaze palsy (paralysis) *(Koordinationsstörung der Augen)*
Sympathektomie f sympath[ic]ectomy, excision of the sympathetic nerve
~/periarterielle periarterial sympathectomy, Leriche's operation
Sympathikoblast m sympath[ic]oblast
Sympathikoblastom n sympathicoblastoma *(bösartige Geschwulst)*
sympathikochromaffin sympathochromaffin
Sympathikogoniom n sympathicogonioma *(bösartige Geschwulst)*
Sympathikolytikum n sympatholytic [agent], adrenergic blocker (blocking agent)
sympathikolytisch sympatholytic, adrenolytic
Sympathikomimetikum n sympathomimetic [drug]
Sympathikoneuritis f sympathiconeuritis, inflammation of the sympathetic ganglions
sympathikoparalytisch sympathicoparalytic
Sympathikopathie f sympathicopathy, disease of the sympathetic nervous system
Sympathikotonie f sympatheticotonia
sympathikotonisch sympath[et]icotonic
Sympathikotonus m sympatheticotonus
Sympathikotripsie f sympathicotripsy
sympathikotrop sympathicotropic
Sympathikozytom n sympathicocytoma
Sympathikus m sympathicus, sympathetic [nerve] *(Bestandteil des vegetativen Nervensystems)*; orthosympathetic (sympathetic nervous) system, thoracolumbar autonomic nervous system
Sympathikusblockade f sympathetic blockage
Sympathikusentzündung f s. Sympathikoneuritis
Sympathikuserregung f sympatheticotonia
Sympathikusfaser f sympathetic fibre
Sympathikusganglienkette f gangliated sympathetic chain
Sympathikusganglion n sympathetic ganglion
sympathikuslähmend sympatheticoparalytic
Sympathikusnerven... s. Sympathikus...
Sympathikusneuroblastom n sympathicogonioma *(bösartige Geschwulst)*
Sympathikusplexus m sympathetic plexus
Sympathikusquetschung f sympathicotripsy
Sympathikusschwäche f hyposympathicotonus
Sympathikusübererregung f sympatheticotonia
Sympathikusüberfunktion f hypersympathicotonus

sympathikuswirksam sympathomimetic, sympatheticomimetic
Sympathikuszelle f sympathetic cell
Sympathin n sympathin *(Sympathikuswirkstoff)*
sympathisch sympath[et]ic
Sympathoblast m sympathicoblast
Sympathoblastom n sympathicoblastoma *(bösartige Geschwulst)*
Sympathogoniom n sympath[ic]ogonioma *(bösartige Geschwulst)*
Symphalangie f symphalangism
Symphyozephalus m symphyocephalus, syncephalus
Symphyse f s. Symphysis
symphyseal symphyseal, symphysial, symphysic
Symphysenbogenband n arcuate ligament of the pubis, arcuate (inferior) pubic ligament
Symphysenlösung f symphysiolysis, separation of the symphysis pubis
Symphysenmesser n symphysiotome
Symphysenschnitt m symphysiotomy, symphyseotomy, synchondrotomy
Symphysensprengung f fracture-separation of the symphysis pubis
Symphysenzeichen n symphysis sign
~/Brudzinskisches Brudzinski's symphysis sign
Symphysiektomie f symphysiectomy, excision of the symphysis pubis
Symphysiolyse f s. Symphysenlösung
Symphysion n symphysion *(anthropologischer Meßpunkt)*
Symphysiorrhaphie f symphysiorrhaphy, suture of a divided symphysis
Symphysiotom n symphysiotome
Symphysiotomie f symphysiotomy, symphysectomy, synchondrotomy
Symphysis f symphysis *(s. a. Synchondrosis)*
● **durch die ~** transsymphyseal ● **unterhalb der ~** subpubic
~ cartilaginea cartilaginous joint (symphysis)
~ ligamentosa ligamentous symphysis
~ mandibulae mandibular symphysis
~ [ossium] pubis [pubic] symphysis
~ sacrococcygea sacrococcygeal joint (junctura, symphysis)
symphysisch symphyseal, symphysial, symphysic
Symphysopsie f symphysopsia, cyclopia
Symplasma n symplasm
Sympodie f sympodia
Symptom n symptom, sign
~/beherrschendes dominating symptom
~/kardiales cardiac symptom
~/Queckenstedtsches Queckenstedt manoeuvre (sign, test) *(zur Überprüfung der Liquorpassage zwischen Gehirn und Rückenmark)*
symptomatisch symptomatic, semeiotic
Symptomatologie f symptomatology, semeiotics, semeiology, semiotics
symptomatologisch symptomatologic
symptombezogen symptomatic, semeiotic
Symptomenkomplex m s. Syndrom

~/**Ménièrescher** Ménière's disease (syndrome) *(umfaßt Schwindelerscheinungen, Erbrechen, Nystagmus, Innenohrschwerhörigkeit und Ohrensausen)*; endolymphatic hydrops, hydrops of the labyrinth
Symptomenlehre *f s.* Symptomatologie
symptomfrei symptom-free
symptomlos asymptomatic; symptom-free
Synalgie *f* synalgia *(z. B. in Gliedern)*
synalgisch synalgic
Synapse *f* synapse *(Nervenverbindungsstelle)* ● **hinter der ~** subsynaptic ● **mehrere Synapsen betreffend** polysynaptic ● **nur eine ~ betreffend** monosynaptic
Synapsenbildung *f* synaptogenesis
Synapsenbläschen *n* synaptic vesicle
Synapsenentwicklung *f* synaptogenesis
Synapsenknopf *m* synaptic knob
Synapsenlehre *f* synaptology
Synapsenmembran *f* synapse (synaptic) membrane, synaptolemma
Synapsenreifung *f* synaptic maturation
Synapsenspalt *m* synaptic gap
Synapsenübertragung *f* synaptic transmission (conduction)
Synapsenverbindung *f* synaptic junction
synaptisch synaptic
Synaptologie *f* synaptology
Synaptosom *n* synaptosome *(Synapsenstruktur)*
Synarthrose *f* synarthrosis, synarthrodial joint
Synästhesialgie *f* synaesthesialgia
Synästhesie *f* synaesthesia *(in Sinnesorganen)*
Syncephalus m asymmetros asymmetric syncephalus *(Doppelmißgeburt)*
Syncheilie *f* synch[e]ilia, fusion of the lips
Synchondrosis *f* synchondrosis, cartilaginous joint (symphysis)
~ **intersphenoidalis** intersphenoid synchondrosis
~ **manubriosternalis** manubriosternal synchondrosis
~ **petrooccipitalis** petro-occipital synchondrosis
~ **sphenooccipitalis** spheno-occipital synchondrosis
~ **sternalis** sternal synchondrosis, gladiomanubrial joint
~ **xiphosternalis** xiphosternal junction (synchondrosis), xiphosternal articulation (joint)
Synchysis *f* **[corporis vitrei]** synchysis, synchesis, liquefaction of the vitreous body
Syncytioma n malignum syncytioma, choriocarcinoma, trophoblastoma
Syncytiotoxin *n* syncytiotoxin
syndaktyl syndactyl[ous]
Syndaktylie *f* syndactyly, symphysodactyly, dactylosymphysis; webbed fingers; webbed toes
~/**multiple** polysyndactylism
~/**totale** total syndactyly
Syndaktylus *m* syndactylus
Syndektomie *f* syndectomy, circumcision of the eye
Syndese *f* syndesis
Syndesmektomie *f* syndesmectomy, excision of a ligament

Syndesmektopie *f* syndesmectopia, ligamentous displacement
Syndesmitis *f* syndesmitis, inflammation of a ligament
syndesmochorial syndesmochorial
Syndesmologie *f* syndesmology
Syndesmopexie *f* syndesmopexy, attachment of a ligament
Syndesmorrhaphie *f* syndesmorrhaphy, suture of a ligament
Syndesmosis *f* syndesmosis, ligamentous symphysis, fibrous joint
~ **tibiofibularis** tibiofibular syndesmosis
~ **tympanostapedia** tympanostapedial syndesmosis
Syndesmotomie *f* syndesmotomy, division (cutting) of a ligament
Syndrom *n* syndrome, symptom complex, group of symptoms
~/**adiposogenitales** adiposogenital (Fröhlich's) syndrome
~/**adrenogenitales** adrenogenital syndrome, adrenal cortical hyperplasia, congenital adrenal hyperplasia
~/**amnestisches** amnestic syndrome, amnestic[-confabulatory] syndrome
~/**amyostatisches** amyostatic syndrome
~/**angioosteohypertrophisches** angioosteohypertrophy, Klippel-Trénaunay-Weber-syndrome
~/**anorektales** anorectal syndrome
~/**apallisches** apallic syndrome
~/**aurikulotemporales** auriculotemporal (Frey's) syndrome
~ **der abführenden Schlinge** efferent loop syndrome
~ **der blinden Schlinge** blind-loop syndrome
~ **der brennenden Füße** burning (painful) feet syndrome
~ **der eingedickten Galle** inspissated bile syndrome
~ **der Kindsmißhandlung** battered-child syndrome
~ **der mißhandelten Eltern** battered-parents syndrome
~ **der multiplen endokrinen Adenomatose** multiple endocrine adenomatosis syndrome, MEA syndrome
~ **der unbeweglichen Zilien** immotile cilia syndrome *(erblich bedingte fehlende Zilienaktivität z. B. bei Spermien)*
~ **der zuführenden Schlinge** afferent loop syndrome
~ **des bösartigen Karzinoids** carcinoid syndrome, carcinoidosis, functioning [carcinoid] syndrome
~ **des kurzen Darms** short-bowel syndrome, short-gut syndrome *(nach Darmresektion)*
~/**Frey-Baillargersches** *s.* ~/**aurikulotemporales**
~/**Heerfordtsches** *s.* Heerfordt-Mylius-Krankheit
~/**hepatorenales** hepatorenal (hepatourologic, urohepatic) syndrome

Syndrom

~/**Hurlersches** s. Pfaundler-Hurler-Syndrom
~/**hypokinetisches** hypokinetic syndrome
~/**Kelly-Pattersonsches** s. Plummer-Vinson-Syndrom
~/**Milroysches** s. Nonne-Meige-Milroy-Syndrom
~/**myasthenisches** myasthenic syndrome
~/**myeloproliferatives** myeloproliferative disorder
~/**nephrotisches** nephrotic syndrome, nephrosis
~/**okulopupilläres** Horner's [oculopupillary] syndrome
~/**postkommotionelles** postconcussion syndrome *(Regulationsstörung der Gehirndurchblutung nach einer Gehirnerschütterung)*
~/**postthrombotisches** postthrombotic (lower-leg) syndrome
~/**prämenstruelles** premenstruation syndrome, premenstrual tension
~/**psychoorganisches** acute [organic] brain syndrome
~/**Sylvestsches** s. Krankheit/Bornholmer
~/**Takayasusches** s. Takayasu-Krankheit
~/**thalamisches** thalamic syndrome
~/**Turnersches** s. Morgagni-Turner-Albright-Syndrom
~ **von Ehlers und Danlos** s. Ehlers-Danlos-Syndrom
~/**zervikobrachiales** cervicobrachial (cervical radicular) syndrome
synechial synechial
Synechie f synechia, adhesion
Synechiendurchtrennung f[/operative] s. Synechiotomie
Synechiotom n synech[i]otome
Synechiotomie f synech[i]otomy, division of a synechia; corelysis
Synenzephalie f synencephalia
Synenzephalus m synencephalus *(Mißgeburt)*
Synergismus m synergism *(z. B. von Muskeln)*
Synergist m synergist, synergistic muscle
synergistisch synergistic, synergetic, synergic
syngam syngamic, syngamous
Syngamie f syngamy
syngen syngeneic, syngenesious
Synhidrose f syn[h]idrosis
Synkanthus m syncanthus
Synkarion m synkarion, syncaryon
Synkinese f synkinesia, synkinesis, syncinesis, associated [automatic] movement, accessory movement
synkinetisch synkinetic
synklitisch synclitic
Synklitismus m synclitism *(Achseneinstellung des Kindskopfes bei der Geburt)*
Synklonus m synclonus
synkopal syncopal, syncopic
Synkope f syncope, faint; syncopal attack ● eine ~ haben to faint, to swoon, to suffer from a syncope
~/**orthostatische** orthostatic syncope
synkopenartig syncopal, syncopic
Synophrys f synophrys

Synophthalmie f synophthalmia, synopsia, cyclopia
Synophthalmus m synophthalmus, cyclops
Synoptometer n synoptometer *(ophthalmologisches Instrument)*
Synoptophor m synoptophore *(Instrument zur Diagnostik und Therapie des Schielens)*
Synorchidie f synorchi[di]sm
Synostose f synost[e]osis
~/**tribasilare** tribasilar synostosis *(vorzeitige Schädelbasisknochenverschmelzung)*
Synotie f synotia, teratic fusion of the ears
Synotus m synotus *(Mißgeburt)*
Synovektomie f synovectomy, excision of the synovial membrane
Synovia f synovia, synovial fluid
~ **articularis** joint synovia
Synovialauskleidung f synovial lining
Synovialchondromatose f synovial chondromatosis
Synovialdivertikulum n synovial diverticulum
Synovialfalte f synovial plica (fold)
Synovialflüssigkeit f s. Synovia
Synovialgelenk n synovial (diarthrodial) joint, coarticulation
Synovialhämangiom n synovial haemangioma
Synovialhaut f s. Synovialmembran
Synovialhernie f synovial hernia
Synovialhöhle f synovial cavity (space), synovial sac
Synovialhyperplasie f synovial hyperplasia
Synovialis f s. Synovialmembran
Synovialisendotheliom n synovioendothelioma
Synovialisentfernung f/operative s. Synovektomie
Synovialissarkom n synovial sarcoma
Synovialissarkomesotheliom n synovial sarcomesothelioma
Synovialmembran f synovial membrane (capsule), synovialis, synovium
Synovialom n synovialoma
Synovialscheide f synovial [tendon] sheath
Synovialscheidenhypertrophie f synovial sheath hypertrophy
Synovialzotte f synovial villus
Synovialzottenexzision f s. Synovektomie
Synovialzyste f synovial cyst
Synoviitis f s. Synovitis
Synoviom n synovioma
Synovitis f synovi[i]tis, inflammation of a synovial membrane
~/**akute eitrige** acute suppurative synovitis
~ **fungosa** fungous arthritis (synovitis)
~ **hyperplastica** hyperplastic synovitis
~/**seröse** serosynovitis
~ **villosa** villous synovitis
Synthetase f synthetase *(Enzym)*
synthetisieren/Verdauungsenzyme to synthesize (elaborate) digestive enzymes
Synzephalus m syncephalus, symphyocephalus
Synzytialzelle f syncytial cell
Synzytiolysin n syncytiolysin

Synzytiom n syncytioma
Synzytiotrophoblast m syn[cytio]trophoblast, syncytial trophoblast
synzytiotrophoblastisch syncytiotrophoblastic
Synzytium n syncytium *(mehrkerniger Zellverband ohne Zellgrenzen)*
Synzytiumzelle f syncytial cell
Syphilämie f syphilaemia
Syphilid n syphilid[e], syphiloderm[a]
~/**erosives** erosive syphilid
Syphilis f syphilis, lues, [Spanish] pox ● **nach einer** ~ **auftretend** metasyphilitic ● **von der** ~ **herrührend** syphilogenous
~/**angeborene** congenital (prenatal) syphilis
~ **des Nervensystems** neurosyphilis, neurolues
~ **des Zentralnervensystems** central nervous system syphilis
~/**endemische** endemic syphilis of the Bedouins, endemic non-venereal syphilis, bejel
~/**erworbene** acquired syphilis
~ **hepatitis** syphilis of the liver
~/**hereditäre** heredosyphilis, heredolues, hereditary syphilis
~ **im Stadium I** primary syphilis, protosyphilis
~ **im Stadium II** secondary syphilis
~ **im Stadium III** tertiary syphilis, tertiarism
~ **innocentum (insontium)** non-venereal syphilis
~/**nichtvenerische** non-venereal syphilis
~ **spinalis** myelosyphilis
syphilisartig syphiloid, resembling syphilis
Syphilisausbreitung f syphilization
syphilisauslösend syphilogenous
Syphilisbehandlung f syphilotherapy
Syphilisentwicklung f syphilogenesis, development of syphilis
Syphiliserkrankung f syphilopathy
~/**generalisierte** syphilosis
syphilisfrei non-syphilitic, non-luetic
syphilisfürchtend syphilophobic
Syphilisgewächs n syphilophyma
syphilishemmend antisyphilitic
Syphilisimpfung f syphilization, inoculation with Treponema pallidum
Syphilisinfektion f syphilitic (luetic) infection
Syphilisknoten m syphilitic node
Syphiliskomplementbindungstest m nach **Boerner und Lukens** Boerner-Lukens test
syphiliskrank syphilitic, syphilous
Syphiliskranker m syphilitic
Syphilispsychose f syphilopsychosis
Syphilisspezialist m syphilologist
Syphilisspirochäte f s. Treponema pallidum
Syphilistest m syphilis test
Syphilitiker m syphilitic
syphilitisch syphilitic, syphilous, luetic
Syphiloderma n syphiloderm[a]; dermosyphilopathy
syphilogen syphilogenous
Syphilogenese f syphilogenesis, development of syphilis
Syphiloid n syphiloid *(milde Syphilisform)*
Syphilologe m syphilologist

Syphilologie f syphilology
Syphilom n syphiloma, [syphilitic] gumma
Syphilomanie f syphilomania, overwhelming syphilophobia
syphilomatös syphilomatous
Syphilonychia f **exulcerans** syphilitic onychia with ulceration
~ **sicca** syphilis of the nail bed
Syphilopathie f syphilopathy, syphilitic disease
Syphilophobie f syphilophobia *(krankhafte Angst vor Syphilis)*
Syphilose f syphilosis, generalized syphilitic disease
Syringektomie f syringectomy, excision of the walls of a fistula
Syringitis f syringitis, salpingitis, inflammation of the Eustachian tube
Syringobulbie f syringobulbia *(Höhlenbildung im verlängerten Rückenmark)*
syringoid syringoid, resembling a tube; fistulous
Syringokarzinom n syringocarcinoma
Syringokystom n syringocystoma
Syringom n syringoma, syringocystadenoma, hydrocystadenoma
Syringomeningozele f s. Syringomyelozele
Syringomyelie f syringomyelia, myelosyringosis
Syringomyelitis f syringomyelitis, inflammation of the spinal cord with cavity formation
Syringomyelozele f syringomeningocele, syringomyelocele, myelosyringocele
Syringotom n syringotome
Syringozele f syringocele
Syringozystadenom n s. Syringom
systaltisch systaltic
System n system[a] *(s. a. unter Systema)*
~/**akrosomales** acrosomal system *(des Spermiums)*
~ **der Blutgruppeneigenschaften/Landsteinersches AB0** [blood group] system
~/**endokrines** endocrinium, endocrine (incretory) system
~/**extrapyramidales** extrapyramidal system
~/**Haverssches** Haversian system *(der Knochenkanäle)*
~/**hormonales** s. ~/endokrines
~/**kardiovaskuläres** cardiovascular system
~/**limbisches** limbic cortex (lobe, system) *(zur Steuerung vegetativer Vorgänge)*
~/**lokomotorisches** locomotor system
~/**lymphatisches** lymphatic system
~/**mikrozirkulatorisches** microcirculatory system
~/**perilymphatisches** perilymphatic system
~/**portales** portal system
~/**respiratorisches** respiratory system
~/**retikuloendotheliales** reticuloendothelial (reticular) system, RES
~/**vaskuläres** vascular system
~/**venöses** venous system
~/**vertebrobasiläres** vertebrobasilar system
Systema n system[a] *(s. a. unter System)*
~ **digestorium** digestive system
~ **nervosum** nervous system

Systema

- **nervosum autonomicum** autonomic nervous system
- **nervosum centrale** central nervous system
- **nervosum periphericum** peripheral nervous system
- **nervosum sympathicum** orthosympathetic (sympathetic nervous) system; sympathicus
- **urogenitale** urogenital system (tract)

systematisch systematic
systematisieren to systematize
Systemerkrankung f system disease; systemic disease
~/hämopoetische haemopoietic disease
~/retikuloendotheliale reticuloendothelial system disease
systemisch systemic
Systemkreislauf m systemic (greater) circulation
systemlos asystematic, asystemic
Systole f systole, miocardia ● am Anfang der ~ [liegend] protosystolic ● am Ende der ~ [liegend] telesystolic ● nach der ~ [liegend] postsystolic ● vor der ~ [liegend] presystolic ● während der gesamten ~ pansystolic
~/abgekürzte (abortive) aborted systole
~/arterielle arterial systole
~/vorzeitige premature systole
Systolenausfall m asystole, asystolia, asystolism (z. B. bei Herzblock); dropped [heart-]beat (bei AV-Block II. Grades)
Systolengeräusch n s. Systolikum
systolenlos asystolic
Systolenschwäche f hyposystole
Systolenverstärkung f hypersystole
Systolikum n systolic murmur (bruit)
~/rauhes coarse systolic murmur
systolisch systolic
S-Zacke f [im EKG] S wave [of the electrocardiogram]
Szintifotografie f scintiphotography
Szintigramm n scintigram, [scintillation] scan, scintiscan
Szintigraph m scintigraph
Szintigraphie f scintigraphy, [scintillation] scanning, scintiscanning (Isotopendiagnostik)
~/pulmonale pulmonary scintigraphy
szintigraphisch scintigraphic
Szintillationskamera f scintillation camera (Radiologie)
Szintillationsskotom n scintillating scotoma
Szintillationsspektrometer n scintillation spectrometer
Szintillationszähler m scintillation counter (detector)
szintillieren to scintillate
Szintillographie f s. Szintigraphie
Szintiscanner m s. Szintigraph
szirrhös scirrhous, scirrhoid, hard
Szirrhus m scirrhus, scirrhus cancer (carcinoma)

T

T_3 s. Trijodthyronin
T_4 s. Thyroxin
T n/koronares s. T-Welle/koronare
Tabacosis f s. Tabakvergiftung
Tabak-Alkohol-Amblyopie f tobacco [and alcohol] amblyopia
Tabaklunge f s. Tabakstaublungenerkrankung
Tabakmosaikvirus n tobacco mosaic virus
Tabaksbeutelnaht f purse-string suture, tobacco bag suture
Tabakstaublunge[nerkrankung] f tabacosis, tabacism; tabaco lung
Tabakvergiftung f tabac[co]ism, tabacosis, tabagism, poisoning by tobacco, nicotine poisoning
Tabardillofieber n tabardillo, epidemic typhus fever, Mexican typhus
Tabatière f snuff-box [space], anatomical (anatomist's) snuffbox, tabatière anatomique, radial fossa
Tabes f **dorsalis** tabes [dorsalis], tabetic (locomotor) ataxia; posterior spinal sclerosis, myelophthisis
~ optica optic tabes
Tabesarthropathie f tabetic [osteo]arthropathy; Charcot's joint
tabesartig tabetiform
tabeskrank tabetic, tabic, tabid
Tabeskranker m tabetic
Tabeskrise f tabetic crisis
Tabeslähmung f taboparalysis, taboparesis
Tabeszeichen n/**Gowerssches** Gowers' sign
Tabiker m tabetic
TAB-Impfstoff m T.A.B. vaccine, typhoid-paratyphoid A and B vaccine, tetravaccine (gegen Typhus, Paratyphus A und B sowie Cholera)
tabisch tabetic, tabic, tabid
Tablette f tablet; lozenge
~/kleine parvule
Tablettenhülle f coating
Tablettenröhrchen n tablet tube
Tablettensucht f pharmacomania
Taboparalyse f taboparalysis, taboparesis
Tabophobie f tabophobia (krankhafte Angst vor Tabes)
Tabula f table, tabula
~ externa outer table of the skull
~ interna (vitrea) inner table of the skull
Tabun n tabun (Nervenkampfstoff)
Tachistoskop n tachistoscope (Gerät zur Prüfung der Wahrnehmungsgeschwindigkeit)
tachistoskopisch tachistoscopic
Tachogramm n tachogram, tachygram
Tachyarrhythmie f tachyarrhythmia
Tachygraphie f tachygraphy, tachography
tachykard tachycardiac
Tachykardie f tachycardia, tachyrhythmia, tachysystole, synchopexia
~/idioventrikuläre idioventricular tachycardia
~/paroxysmale paroxysmal tachycardia

~/paroxysmale supraventrikuläre paroxysmal heart atrium tachycardia
~/paroxysmale ventrikuläre paroxysmal heart ventricle tachycardia
~/rezidivierende recurrent tachycardia
Tachylalie f tachylalia, tachylogia, tachyphemia, tachyphrasia, oxylalia
Tachyphagie f tachyphagia, rapid eating
Tachyphrenie f tachyphrenia, mental hyperactivity
Tachyphylaxie f tachyphylaxia, tachyphylaxis (z. B. eines Medikaments)
Tachypnoe f tachypnoea, accelerated respiration, polypnoea
tachypnoisch tachypnoeic
Tachysterol n tachysterol
Taenia f 1. taenia (Anatomie); 2. Taenia, tapeworm
~ acustica acoustic stria (Streifen am Boden der Rautengrube)
~ coli colon taenia
~ mesocolica mesocolic taenia (band)
~ omentalis omental taenia
~ saginata Taenia saginata
~ solium Taenia solium, pork tapeworm
~ thalami taenia of the third ventricle
~ ventriculi quarti taenia of the fourth ventricle
~ ventriculi tertii s. ~ thalami
Taenia... s. Bandwurm...
Taeniasis f taeniasis, tapeworm infestation
Taeniophobie f taeniophobia (krankhafte Angst vor Bandwurmbefall)
Tafel f/pseudoisochromatische pseudoisochromatic plate (zur Farbsinnprüfung)
Tafelknochen m tabular bone
Tagangst f day terrors, pavor diurnus
Tagblindheit f day blindness, hemeralopia
Tagesdienst m day duty
Tagesdosis f daily dose
Tageseinnässen n diurnal enuresis
Tageslichtadaption f photopia
Tageslichtscheu f phen[g]ophobia
Tagesmaximaldosis f maximum daily dose
Tagesperiodizität f diurnal periodicity (der Loa-loa-Filarien)
Tagessichtigkeit f day sightedness, photopia
täglich quaque die, q.d., in dies, in d., every day; quotidian
~/viermal quarter in die, q.i.d., four times a day
Taille f waist
Takata-[Ara-]Reaktion f Takata-Ara test, Jezler-Takata test (Serumlabilitätsprobe)
Takayasu-Krankheit f Takayasu's syndrome, aortic arch syndrome (arteritis, occlusive disease), young female syndrome
taktil tactile; palpable
Talalgie f talalgia, pain in the ankle (heel)
Talfieber n coccidio[ido]mycosis, desert fever (rheumatism), San Joaquin [Valley] fever, California (Posada's) disease (durch Coccidioides immitis)
Talg m sebum, tallow, sebaceous matter

talgabsondernd sebaceous, sebiferous, sebiparous
Talgabsonderung f seborrhoea, seborrhagia, steatorrhoea
~/vermehrte hypersteatosis
~/verminderte hyposteatosis
talgbildend sebiferous, sebiparous
Talgdrüse f sebaceous (pilous) gland, oil (hair) gland
Talgdrüsendifferenzierung f sebaceous gland differentiation
Talgdrüsenfollikel m sebaceous follicle
Talgdrüsensekretion f/fehlende asteatosis
Talgdrüsenstein m sebolith, sebolite
Talgdrüsenzyste f s. Talgzyste
Talgfluß m s. Talgabsonderung
talgig sebaceous
Talgproduktion f sebaceous secretion
talgsezernierend sebiferous, sebiparous
Talgzyste f sebaceous cyst, sebocystoma, [cysto]steatoma; wen (am Kopf)
Talipes m talipes [varus], pes varus, club-foot
~ arcuatus arcuate talipes
~ calcaneocavus [talipes] calcaneocavus (Form des Hackenfußes)
~ calcaneovalgus [talipes] calcaneovalgus (Form des Hackenfußes)
~ calcaneus [talipes] calcaneus, calcaneum
~ cavus [talipes] cavus, hollow (claw, contracted) foot, non-deforming club-foot
~ equinocavus equinocavus [deformity]
~ equinovalgus equinovalgus [deformity]
~ equinovarus equinovarus [deformity]
~ equinus equinus [deformity], horsefoot
~ valgus valgus [deformity], splayfoot
Talipomanus f talipomanus, manus vara, clubhand
Talkose f talcosis, talc dust pneumoconiosis
Talkstaublunge[nerkrankung] f s. Talkose
Talkum n talc (Magnesiumsilikat)
Talkumgranulom n talc (talcum-powder) granuloma, surgical-glove talc granuloma
talofibular talofibular, astragalofibular
talokalkaneal talocalcaneal, talocalcanean, astragalocalcanean, calcaneoastragalar
Talokalkanealband n/hinteres posterior talocalcaneal ligament
~/vorderes anterior talocalcaneal ligament
talokalkaneonavikular talocalcaneonavicular
talokrural talocrural, astragalocrural
talomalleolär talomalleolar
talonavikular talonavicular, taloscaphoid, astragaloscaphoid
talotibial talotibial, astragalotibial
Talus m s. Sprungbein
Tampon m tampon, plug, pack, pledget, swab
Tamponade f 1. tamponade, tamponage, surgical pack; 2. s. Tamponieren ● zu einer ~ führen to tamponade
Tamponadekatheter m tamponade (haemostatic) catheter

Tamponadestiel

Tamponadestiel *m* [tamponade] packer; uterine gauze packer
Tamponadestreifen *m s.* Tamponade 1.
Tamponhalter *m* tamponade (swab) holder
tamponieren to tampon[ade], to plug, to pack
Tamponieren *n* tamponing, tamponment, plugging, packing
Tamponzange *f* dressing (cotton swab) forceps; uterine dressing forceps
Tangentialperkussion *f* tangential percussion
Tänie *f s.* Taenia 2.
Täniose *f s.* Taeniasis
Tannase *f* tannase *(Enzym)*
Tannin *n* tannic acid *(Hautgerbungsmittel)*
Tannin[säure]gerbung *f der Haut* tanning *(z. B. bei Verbrennungstherapie)*
Tanzwut *f* tarant[ul]ism, dancing mania, choreomania
Tapetum *n* tapetum, lining [membrane], coat *(z. B. von Zellen)*
~ **alveoli** alveolar periosteum *(Knochenhaut der Zahnfächer)*
Taphophobie *f* taphephobia, taphiphobia, taphophobia *(krankhafte Angst vor dem Lebendigbegrabenwerden)*
Tapirlippe *f* tapir lip (mouth)
tapirlippenartig tapiroid
Tapirnase *f* tapir nose
Tapotement *n* tapotement, hacking, hackement, tapping *(Massage)*
Tarantismus *m s.* Tanzwut
tardiv tardive
Targetzelle *f* target (hat) cell, pessary corpuscle *(Erythrozytenform)*
Tarsadenitis *f* tarsadenitis, inflammation of the tarsal glands and tarsal plate
Tarsalgie *f* tarsalgia, pain in the tarsus
Tarsalplatte *f* tarsal plate, tarsus
Tarsaltunnelsyndrom *n* tarsal tunnel syndrome
Tarsektomie *f* tarsectomy, excision of the tarsal bone
Tarsitis *f* 1. tarsitis, inflammation of the tarsal bone; 2. tarsitis, inflammation of the tarsus of the eyelid; 3. *s.* Blepharitis
Tarsocheiloplastik *f* tarsocheiloplasty, marginoplasty
Tarsoklasie *f* tarsoclasis *(bei Klumpfuß)*
Tarsomalazie *f* tarsomalacia, softening of the tarsus of the eyelid
Tarsomegalie *f* tarsomegaly, enlargement of the tarsal bone
Tarsophym *n* tarsophyma
Tarsoplastik *f* tarsoplasty, tarsoplasia
Tarsoptose *f* tarsoptosia, tarsoptosis; flat foot
Tarsorrhaphie *f* tarsorrhaphy
Tarsotomie *f* 1. tarsotomy, incision into the tarsal bone; 2. tarsotomy, incision into the tarsus of the eyelid
Tarsus *m s.* 1. Fußwurzel; 2. Lidknorpel
Tarsus... *s. a.* Lidknorpel...
Tarsusbindehaut *f* tarsal conjunctiva
Tarsusbindehautentzündung *f* tarsal conjunctivitis

Tarsusdrüse *f* tarsal (Meibomian) gland, palpebral follicle
Tarsusdrüsenentzündung *f s.* Tarsadenitis
Tarsusknorpel *m s.* Lidknorpel
Tarsustumor *m* tarsophyma
Tartzelle *f* tart cell *(Leukozyt mit fremder Kernsubstanz)*
Tasche *f* pocket *(z. B. am Zahnfleisch)*; pouch *(z. B. des Peritoneums)*; sac[cus] *(z. B. des Zahnschmelzes)*; bursa *(Anatomie)*; cavity *(Höhle)*; sacculation *(Aussackung)*
~/**Morgagnische** ventricle of Morgagni (the larynx), laryngeal ventricle (sinus)
~/**Rathkesche** Rathke's (craniobuccal) pouch *(Aussackung der primären Mundhöhle)*
~/**Tröltschsche** Tröltsch's space
Taschenband *n* vestibular ligament
Taschenbildung *f* pocketing, pocket formation; sacculation
Taschenfalte *f* vestibular fold, false vocal cord
Taschenklappe *f* semilunar valve
Taschenmesserphänomen *n* clasp-knife phenomenon (rigidity, spasticity)
Taschkentgeschwür *n* Tashkent ulcer, paschacurda *(Hautleishmaniase)*
tastbar palpable; tactile
~/**nicht** impalpable
Tastbefund *m* palpatory findings
Tastblindheit *f* stereoagnosis, tactile agnosia, astereocognosy, astereognosis; stereoanaesthesia
Tastempfindlichkeit *f* tactile sensibility
Tastempfindung *f s.* Tastsinn
tasten to palpate, to touch, to feel
tastend palpating; haptic
Tastgefühl *n* palpation, touching, pselaphesis, sense of touch
~/**krankhaft gesteigertes** hyperpselaphesia
~/**krankhaft vermindertes** hypopselaphesia
Tastkörperchen *n* [/**Meissnersches**] tactile (touch, oval) corpuscle, Meissner's corpuscle, tactile end organ
~/**Vater-Pacinisches** Vater-Pacini corpuscle, lamellar corpuscle
Tastperkussion *f* palpatory percussion, palpatopercussion
Tastsinn *m* stereognosis, stereognostic (tactile) sense, sense of touch, pselaphesia, pselaphesis, thigm[o]aesthesia
Tastsinnempfindlichkeit *f* tactile sensibility
Tastsinnkörperchen *n s.* Tastkörperchen[/Meissnersches]
Tastsinnlähmung *f s.* Tastblindheit
Tastsinnstörung *f* paraphia, parapsis, morbid sense of touch, abnormality of the sense of touch, dysaesthesia
Tastsinnunterscheidung *f* tactile discrimination
Tastsinnverlust *m* apselaphesia, loss of the tactile sense, anaphia
tätowieren to tattoo

Tätowier[ungs]nadel f tattooing needle
taub 1. deaf *(Gehör)*; 2. numb *(Gefühl)* ● **~ machen** to deafen ● **~ werden** to become deaf
Taubheit f 1. deafness, surdity *(Gehör)*; 2. numbness *(Gefühl)*
~/otosklerotische otosclerotic deafness
~/psychogene psychic deafness
~/völlige anacousia, anacusis
~/zentrale cerebral deafness
Taubheitsareal n deaf field
Taubheitspunkt m deaf point
taubstumm deaf-mute, deaf and dumb, surdomute
Taubstummensprache f finger (deaf-and-dumb) language
Taubstummer m deaf-mute, deaf and dumb [person], surdomute
Taubstummheit f deaf-mutism, surdimutism
Taucherkonjunktivitis f diver's conjunctivitis
Taucherkrankheit f caisson disease, decompression sickness, compressed-air illness
Taucherlähmung f diver's palsy (paralysis)
Taucherneurose f diver's neurosis
Taucherohr n diver's ear
Tauchkropf m plunging (diving) goitre *(bei Struma)*
Taumeln n staggering, reeling; temulence, temulentia *(bei Alkoholabusus)*
Taurocholämie f taurocholaemia
Taurocholat n taurocholate
Taurocholsäure f taurocholic acid *(eine Gallensäure)*
Taurocholsäureausscheidung f taurocholaneresis *(mit der Galle)*
Taurocholsäurebildung f taurocholanopoiesis *(in der Leber)*
Taussig-Bing-Syndrom n Taussig-Bing complex (malformation) *(Ventrikelseptumdefekt, reitende Arteria pulmonalis und rechtsventrikuläre Aorta)*
Taxis f s. 1. Tropismus; 2. Reposition
taxonom taxonomic
TB s. Tuberkelbazillus
Tbc, Tbk s. Tuberkulose
T-Drain m[/Kehrscher] T tube *(Gallenchirurgie)*
T-Drainage f T-tube drainage
T-Drain-Cholangiographie f T-tube cholangiography
T-Drain-Dekompression f T-tube decompression
T-Drain-Ureterostomie f T-tube ureterostomy
T. E. s. Tonsillektomie
Technik f **des dicken Tropfens** thick-film method *(zum Malariaparasitennachweis)*
Tectum n tectum, roof, tegmen, cap *(s. a. unter Tegmen)*
~ mesencephali tectum of the mesencephalon
Teelöffelmenge f teaspoonful, tsp
Teerakne f tar acne
Teerekzem n tar itch
Teerkrebs m tar (pitch-worker's) cancer
Teerstuhl m tarry stool; mel[a]ena, melanorrhoea *(schwarzgefärbter Stuhl durch Blutbeimengung)*

teerstuhlähnlich melaenic, maelenic
Teevergiftung f the[in]ism
Tegmen n tegmen, cover[ing], tectum, roof, cap *(s. a. unter Tectum)*
~ mastoideum roof of the mastoid cells
~ tympani roof of the tympanic cavity, [tympanic] scute, scutum
~ ventriculi quarti roof of the fourth ventricle
Tegmentum n 1. tegmentum, covering; 2. s. **~ mesencephali**
~ mesencephali tegmentum
~ rhombencephali rhombencephalic tegmentum
Teichopsie f teichopsia, fortification spectrum; flittering (scintillating) scotoma
Teil... s. a. Partial...
Teilamputation f partial amputation
Teilanästhesie f partial anaesthesia
Teilankylose f partial ankylosis
Teilblindheit f meropia
Teilen/zu gleichen ana [partes], aa
teilend/sich komplett holoblastic *(z. B. Eizelle)*
~/sich partiell meroblastic *(z. B. Eizelle)*
Teilentwicklung f der Eizelle merogony
Teilfarbenblindheit f partial colour blindness
teilnahmslos apath[et]ic, lethargic; listless
Teilnahmslosigkeit f apathy, lethargic lethargy
Teilprothese f partial denture, bridgework *(Stomatologie)*
Teilresektion f partial resection
Teilschlaf m hypnosis, hypnotism, syngignoscism
~/künstlicher self-hypnosis, autohypnosis, autohypnotism
teilschlaferzeugend hypnogen[et]ic, hypnogenous
Teilschlaferzeugung f hypnogenesis
Teilung f 1. division *(z. B. von Zellen)*; fission *(Spaltung)*; cleavage *(Embryologie)*; segmentation *(z. B. der Eizelle)*; 2. graduation *(an Meßgeräten)*
~ des Golgi-Apparats division of the Golgi apparatus, dictyokinesis
Teilungsebene f plane of division; cleavage plane *(bei Mitose)*
Teilungskern m cleavage nucleus
Teilungsspindel f cleavage spindle
Teilverknöcherung f partial ossification
Teilverrenkung f partial dislocation
Tein n theine *(Alkaloid)*
Teinvergiftung f the[in]ism
Tektorialmembran f tectorial membrane *(der Halswirbelsäule)*
Tela f tela, tissue, web *(s. a. unter Gewebe)*
~ adiposa adipose (fatty) tissue
~ depurata mull
~ subcutanea subcutaneous [connective] tissue; superficial fascia
~ submucosa submucosa, submucous membrane
Telangioma n telangioma
Teleangiectasis f **lymphatica** lymphatic teleangiectasis

Teleangiektasie

Teleangiektasie f tel[e]angiectasia, telangiectasis, angiotelectasia
~/hereditäre hämorrhagische hereditary haemorrhagic telangiectasia, Rendu-Osler-Weber's disease, Osler-Weber-Rendu disease
~/intestinale intestinal teleangiectasia
teleangiektatisch telangiectatic, tel[e]angiectodes
Teleangiitis f telangitis, inflammation of the capillaries, capillaritis
Teleangiose f telangiosis, disease of the capillaries
telediastolisch telediastolic
Teleelektrokardiographie f s. Telekardiographie
Telefluoroskopie f telefluoroscopy
telefluoroskopisch telefluoroscopic
Telegrammstil m telegraphic language (style), agrammaphasia *(Sprachstörung)*
Telekardiogramm n tele[lectro]cardiogram
Telekardiographie f tele[lectro]cardiography
telekardiographisch tele[lectro]cardiographic
Telekardiophon n telecardiophone
Telekobaltbehandlung f telecobalt therapy
Telemetrie f telemetry
Teleneurit m s. Nervenendigung
telenzephal telencephal[ic]
Telenzephalon n telencephalon, endbrain
Telepath m telepathist
Telepathie f telepathy, thought reading (transference)
telepathisch telepathic
Teleradiographie f s. Teleröntgenographie
Teleradiologie f teleradiology
Teleradiumtherapie f teleradium therapy
Telerezeptor m tele[re]ceptor, teloreceptor
Teleröntgenbehandlung f teleroentgen therapy
Teleröntgenogramm n teleroentgenogram
Teleröntgenographie f tele[o]roentgenography, teleradiography
teleröntgenographisch teleroentgenographic
Telestereoröntgenographie f telestereoroentgenography
telesystolisch telesystolic
Teletherapie f teletherapy, teleotherapeutics
Telodendron n telodendr[i]on, teledendrite
Telolemma n telolemma
Telophase f telophase, teleomitosis
Telozöle f telocoele
Temperament n temperament
Temperatur f temperature ● **die ~ messen** to take the temperature ● **erhöhte ~ haben** to have a temperature
Temperaturabfall m drop (fall) in temperature
Temperaturdarstellung f thermography
Temperaturerhöhung f temperature rise, rise in temperature
temperaturgleich isothermal
Temperaturgleichheit f monothermia
Temperaturkurve f thermogram, temperature curve
Temperaturmessung f temperature measurement, thermometry

Temperaturregler m thermoregulator
Temperaturregulationszentrum n temperature regulatory centre
Temperaturschreiber m thermograph
Temperaturschwankung f variation of temperature
Temperatursinn m temperature sense
Temperatursinnmesser m thermaesthesiometer
Temperaturüberempfindlichkeit f thermohyperaesthesia
Temperaturunterempfindlichkeit f thermohypoaesthesia
Temperaturunterschied m difference in temperature
Temperaturwahrnehmung f s. Thermästhesie 1.
temporal temporal
Temporalarterie f temporal artery
Temporalarteriitis f temporal arteri[i]tis
Temporaldurchmesser m temporal diameter
Temporalgrube f temporal fossa
Temporalis m temporalis [muscle]
Temporalisfaszie f temporalis fascia
Temporallappen m temporal lobe ● **durch den ~ transtemporal**
Temporallappenanschwellung f temporal lobe swelling
Temporallappenentfernung f[/operative] temporal lobectomy
Temporallappenepilepsie f temporal lobe epilepsy
Temporallappenglioblastom n temporal glioblastoma
Temporallappenhernie f temporal lobe hernia
Temporallappenhirnrinde f temporal cortex
Temporallappenödem n temporal lobe oedema
Temporallappenpol m temporal pole
Temporallappenrinde f temporal cortex
Temporallappenschwellung f temporal lobe swelling
Temporallinie f temporal line
Temporalvene f temporal vein
~/mittlere middle temporal vein
Temporoparietalregion f temporoparietal region
Tempus n s. Schläfe
Temulenz f 1. temulence, temulentia, drunkenness; 2. temulence, temulentia, chronic alcoholism
Tenaculum n **linguae** linguotrite
Tenalgia f tenalgia, tenodynia, pain in a tendon, desmalgia, desmodynia
~ crepitans crepitant tenalgia
Tendinitis f tendinitis, ten[d]onitis, inflammation of a tendon, desmitis
~ ossificans teno[no]stosis
tendinoplastisch tendinoplastic
Tendo m tendo[n], tendineum, sinew, leader; ligament
~ Achilles s. ~ calcaneus
~ calcaneus calcaneal (Achilles) tendon, tendon Achilles
~ conjunctivus inguinal falx
~ crico-oesophageus crico-oesophageal tendon

~ **musculi bicipitis femoris** outer hamstring
~ **musculi flexoris radialis** flexor carpi radialis tendon
~ **musculi tensoris tympani** tensor tympani tendon
~ **musculi tricipitis surae [Achilli]** s. ~ calcaneus
Tendolyse f ten[d]olysis
Tendomuzin n tendomucin, tendomucoid
Tendon m s. Tendo
Tendoplastik f tendinoplasty, ten[d]oplasty
Tendosynovitis f s. Tendovaginitis
tendovaginal tendovaginal, tenosynovial
Tendovaginitis f ten[d]ovaginitis, ten[d]osynovitis, tendinous (vaginal) synovitis, inflammation of a tendon and its sheath
~ **adhaesiva** adhesive tendovaginitis
~ **crepitans** crepitant (fibrinous) tendovaginitis, crepitant tenalgia
~ **granulosa** granular tendovaginitis
~ **stenosans [de Quervain]** stenosing tendovaginitis, [de] Quervain's disease
Tenektomie f ten[on]ectomy, excision of a tendon
Tenesmus m tenesmus, [painful] straining
Tennisellenbogen m tennis elbow; radiohumeral bursitis
Tenodese f tenodesis, tendon suspension, fixation of a tendon
Tenodynie f s. Tenalgie
Tenomyoplastik f tenomyoplasty
Tenomyotomie f tenomyotomy *(zur Schielbehandlung)*
Tenonektomie f s. Tenektomie
Tenonitis f 1. tenonitis, inflammation of the Tenon's capsule; 2. s. Tendinitis
Tenorrhaphie f tenorrhaphy, ten[din]osuture, suture of a divided tendon; desmopexia
Tenosynovektomie f tenosynovectomy, vaginectomy, excision of the tendon sheath
Tenosynovitis f s. Tendovaginitis
Tenotom n tenotome, tenotomy knife
Tenotomie f tenotomy, desmotomy, cutting of a tendon
tenotomieren to tenotomize, to perform a tenotomy
Tension f 1. tension, stretching; 2. tension, partial pressure; 3. tension, mental (psychic) strain; physical strain
Tensionskopfschmerz m tension (muscle-contraction) headache
Tensor[muskel] m tensor [muscle]
Tentorium n s. ~ cerebelli ● **unter dem** ~ subtentorial ● **über dem** ~ supratentorial
~ **cerebelli** tentorium [cerebelli], cerebellar tentorium
Tentoriumdurchtrennung f[/operative] tentoriotomy
Tentoriumeinklemmung f tentorial coning (herniation); tentorial pressure cone
Tentoriumschlitz m tentorial notch, incisure of the tentorium ● **durch den** ~ transtentorial, across the tentorium

ter in die ter in die, t.i.d., three times a day
Teratismus m teratism, teratosis
Teratoblastom n teratoblastoma
teratogen teratogenous, teratogenic
Teratogenese f teratogeny, teratogenesis, formation of monsters
Teratogenizität f teratogenicity
teratoid teratoid
Teratokarzinom n teratocarcinoma
Teratologe m teratologist
Teratologie f teratology *(Lehre von den Mißbildungen)*
teratologisch teratologic
Teratom n teratoma, teratoid tumour, tridermoma, dysembryoma
~/**karzinomatöses** teratocarcinoma
teratomartig teratomatous
Teratophobie f teratophobia *(krankhafte Angst vor Mißbildungen)*
Terato[zoo]spermie f terato[zoo]spermia
Terminalganglion n terminal ganglion
Terminationes fpl nervorum liberae free nerve endings
Terpentinvergiftung f terebinthism, turpentine poisoning
Terrainbehandlung f terrain cure (treatment) *(z. B. bei Herzkrankheiten)*
Terry-Syndrom n Terry's syndrome, retrolental fibroplasia, retinopathia of prematurity
Tertiana f tertian fever (malaria)
Tertianaanfall m tertian ague *(im 48-Stunden-Intervall)*
Tertianaparasit m tertian parasite
Tertiärfollikel m tertiary (vesicular) follicle
Tertiärsequester m tertiary sequestrum
Tertiärstadium n tertiary stage
Tertiärsyphilid n tertiary syphilid
Tertiärsyphilis f tertiary syphilis, tertiarism
Tertigravida f tertigravida
Tertipara f tertipara
Tesla-Strom-Behandlung f [d']arsonvalization
Test m test, assay; trial; examination *(s. a. unter Versuch und Prüfung)*
~/**Albarranscher** Albarran's (polyuria) test
~/**Bauerscher** Bauer's (galactose tolerance) test
~/**Legalscher** Legal's test *(zum Nachweis von Azeton und Azetessigsäure im Harn)*
~/**Nelsonscher** Nelson's test *(zum serologischen Syphilisnachweis)*
~/**psychologischer** psychological test
~/**Queckenstedtscher** Queckenstedt manoeuvre (sign, test), jugular compression *(zur Überprüfung der Liquorpassage zwischen Gehirn und Rückenmark)*
~/**Sachs-Georgischer** Sachs-Georgi test *(serologische Flockungsreaktion zur Syphilisdiagnostik)*
~/**serologischer** serologic test *(z. B. auf Syphilis)*
~/**Tzanckscher** Tzanck smear (test) *(zum Nachweis von Pemphigus vulgaris)*
~/**van den Berghscher** van den Bergh's test [for serum bilirubin]

Testalgie

Testalgie f s. Hodenschmerz
Testantigen n test antigen
Testbuchstabe m test letter (type)
testen to test, to assay
Testikel m s. Testis
testikulär testicular
Testis m testis, testicle, orchis, didymus, male gonad, seminal gland *(s. a. unter Hoden)*
~ **inguinalis** inguinal testis, orchiocele
Testitis f s. Hodenentzündung
Testkarte f test card *(zur Visusprüfung)*
Testlösung f test solution, T.S.
Testmahlzeit f test meal
Testosteron n testosterone
Testosteronblutspiegel m testosterone blood level
Testserum n test serum
Testserumverdünnung f test serum dilution
Teststreifen m test strip *(z. B. zum Harnzuckernachweis)*
Testtafel f s. Testkarte
Tetania f **uteri** tetanic contraction of the uterus
Tetanie f tetany
~/**rachitogene** spasmophilia
~/**thyreoprive** thyroprival tetany
Tetaniekatarakt f tetanic cataract
Tetaniezeichen n/**Erbsches** Erb's sign
tetaniform tetaniform
tetanigen tetanigenous
tetanisch tetanic, tetanal
tetanisieren to tetanize
Tetanismus m tetanism
Tetanolyse f tetanolysis *(Hämolyse durch Tetanustoxin)*
Tetanolysin n tetanolysin *(Hämolysegift von Clostridium tetani)*
Tetanometer n tetanometer
tetanophil tetanophil[ic], tetanus-prone
Tetanophobie f tetanophobia *(krankhafte Angst vor Tetanus)*
Tetanospasmin n tetanospasmin *(Neurotoxin von Clostridium tetani)*
Tetanus m tetanus, tetany
~ **infantum** tetanus infantum (neonatorum), tetany of the newborn
~ **lateralis** pleurothotonus
~/**lokaler** localized tetanus
~ **neonatorum** s. ~ infantum
~/**toxischer** toxic tetanus
Tetanus-Aluminium-Adsorbat-Impfstoff m alum-adsorbed toxoid, alum-precipitated tetanal toxoid
Tetanusantiglobulin n antitetanus globulin
Tetanusantiserum n, **Tetanusantitoxin** n s. Tetanusserum
tetanusartig tetaniform, tetanoid
tetanusauslösend tetanigenous
Tetanusauslösung f tetanization
Tetanusbazillus m Clostridium tetani
tetanusbewirkend tetanigenous
Tetanusclostridium n Clostridium tetani
Tetanusglobulin n antitetanus globulin

Tetanusimmunisierung f/**aktive** tetanus vaccination (toxoid immunization)
Tetanus-Immunoglobulin n tetanus immune globulin, tetanal immunoglobulin
Tetanus-Immunserum n tetanus immune serum; antitetanus serum, A.T.S.
Tetanus[krampf]intervall n tetanode
Tetanusmesser m tetanometer
Tetanusprophylaxe f tetanus prophylaxis, prophylaxis of tetanus
Tetanusschutzimpfung f tetanus vaccination (toxoid immunization)
Tetanusserum n tetanus antitoxin, antitetanus (antitetanic) serum, A.T.S.
~ **vom Hammel** ovine antitetanic serum, antitetanus serum of ovine
~ **vom Pferd** equine antitetanic serum, antitetanic serum of equine
~ **vom Rind** bovine antitetanus serum, antitetanic serum of bovine
~ **vom Schaf** sheep antitetanus serum, antitetanic serum of sheep
Tetanustoxin n tetanus toxin
Tetanustoxoid n tetanus toxoid
Tetanustoxoid-Impfstoff m tetanus vaccine
Tetatoxoid n tetanus toxoid
Tetatoxoid-Immunisierung f tetanus vaccination (toxoid immunization)
tetrabrachial tetrabrachial
Tetrabrachius m tetrabrachius *(Mißgeburt)*
Tetracain n tetracaine *(Lokalanästhetikum)*
Tetrachirus m tetracheirus *(Mißgeburt)*
Tetrachlormethan n tetrachloromethane, carbon tetrachloride
Tetrade f tetrad *(bei der Zellkernteilung)*
Tetrajodthyronin n s. Thyroxin
Tetralogie f/**Fallotsche** tetralogy (tetrad) of Fallot *(Herzfehler mit Kammerseptumdefekt, Vorhofseptumdefekt, Rechtsherzhypertrophie und reitender Aorta)*
Tetramastie f tetramastia, tetramazia
Tetramelus m tetramelus *(Mißgeburt)*
Tetramethylthioninchlorid n methylene blue
Tetranopsie f tetranopsia *(Blindheit im Bereich eines Sehfeldquadranten)*
Tetraotus m tetr[a]otus
Tetraparese f s. Tetraplegie
Tetrapeptid n tetrapeptide
Tetraplegie f tetraplegia, tetraparesis, quadriplegia
tetraploid tetraploid *(Chromosomensatz)*
Tetrasa[c]charid n tetrasaccharide
tetrasom tetrasomic *(Chromosom)*
Tetrasomie f tetrasomy
Tetraster m tetraster *(Mitosefigur)*
Tetrastichiasis f tetrastichiasis *(Vorhandensein von vier Augenwimperreihen)*
Tetravakzine f s. TAB-Impfstoff
Tetrazyklin n tetracycline *(Antibiotikum)*
Tetrose f tetrose *(Monosaccharid)*
Teufelslachen n sardonic grin (laugh) *(Gesichtsstarre bei Tetanus)*

Teufelswahn m demonomania, demonopathy
Texasfieber n Texas (red-water) fever, bovine malaria (piroplasmosis)
Textur f texture, structure; tissue
textural textural, structural
T-Fraktur f T fracture
TGA s. Transposition der großen Arterien
Thalamenzephalon n thalamencephalon *(Teil des Zwischenhirns)*
Thalamonal n droperidol fentanyl compound
Thalamotomie f thalamotomy
Thalamus m thalamus ● **durch den ~** transthalamic ● **unter dem ~ [liegend]** subthalamic, hypothalamic
Thalamusapoplexie f thalamic apoplexy
Thalamuskern m thalamic nucleus
Thalamusschädigung f **durch Kälteanwendung** cryothalamotomy
Thalamusschmerz m thalamic pain
Thalamusseitenkern m lateral nucleus of the thalamus
Thalamusstiel m thalamic peduncle
Thalamusstrahlung f thalamic radiation
Thalamussyndrom n thalamic (Déjèrine-Roussy) syndrome
Thalassaemia f thalass[an]aemia, familial erythroblastic (microcytic) anaemia
~ major Cooley's anaemia (disease), Mediterranean (erythroblastic, target cell) anaemia
~ minor Cooley's trait, microcytic anaemia
Thalassophobie f thalassophobia *(krankhafte Angst vor Seereisen)*
Thalassotherapie f thalassotherapy
Thalidomid n thalidomide
Thalliumvergiftung f thallotoxicosis, poisoning by thallium
thanatobiologisch thanatobiologic
thanatognomonisch thanatognomonic, indicative of death
thanatognostisch thanatognostic
Thanatographie f thanatography
thanatoid thanatoid
Thanatologie f thanatology *(Lehre von den Todeszeichen)*
Thanatomanie f thanatomania
Thanatophobie f thanatophobia *(krankhafte Angst vor dem Tod)*
Thanatopsie f thanatopsy
Thebain n thebaine *(Opiumalkaloid)*
Thebainvergiftung f thebaism
Theca f theca; sheath
~ externa external theca
~ folliculi follicular theca
~ interna internal theca
Theileriasis f theileriasis *(Infektion mit Theileria)*
Thein n s. Tein
Theka f s. Theca
thekal thecal
Thekaluteinzelle f theca lutein cell
Thekazelltumor m thecoma
Thelalgie f thelalgia, pain in a nipple
Thelaziasis f thelaziasis *(Augenerkrankung durch Thelazia)*

Theleretismus m theleretism, thelotism, erection of a nipple
Thelitis f thelitis, inflammation of a nipple
Thelorrhagie f thelorrhagia, haemorrhage from the nipple
Thelotismus m s. Theleretismus
thelygen thelygenic
Thenar m thenar [eminence]
Theobromin n theobromine *(Alkaloid)*
Theomane m theomaniac
Theomanie f theomania, religious mania, hieromania, sebastomania
Theophobie f theophobia
Theophyllin n theophylline *(Alkaloid)*
Therapeut m therap[eut]ist
Therapeutik f therapeutics *(Lehre von der Krankheitsbehandlung)*
therapeutisch therapeutic
Therapie f therapy, treatment *(s. a. unter Behandlung)*
~/adjuvante adjuvant therapy
~/antikonvulsive anticonvulsant therapy
~/antimikrobielle antimicrobial therapy
~/antirheumatische antirheumatic therapy
~ der Wahl treatment of choice
~/immunosuppressive antirejection therapy *(z. B. bei Transplantatabstoßung)*
~/krampflösende anticonvulsant therapy
~/manuelle chiropractic
~/mikrobentötende antimicrobial therapy
~ mit elektrischen Bädern hydroelectric therapy
~/oberflächliche topical treatment
~/physikalische physical therapy, physiotherapy, physiatrics
~/tuberkulostatische antituberculous therapy
~/unterstützende supportive (supporting) therapy
Therapie... s. a. Behandlungs...
Therapieplan m therapeutical (treatment) plan, plan of therapy
Therapieresistenz f resistance to therapy
Therapieschema n therapeutical scheme, scheme of therapy
Therapiestandard m therapeutical (care) standard, standard of therapy
Therapieversagen n treatment failure
Therapiewirksamkeit f therapeutic efficacy
Therapiewirkung f therapeutic effect
Thermalgesie f therm[o]algesia
Thermalgie f thermalgia
Thermalschlamm m peloid
Thermanästhesie f thermanaesthesia, thermic anaesthesia
Thermästhesie f 1. thermaesthesia, temperature sensibility, temperature sense; 2. thermaesthesia, sensitiveness to heat
Thermästhesiometer n thermaesthesiometer
Thermatologie f thermatology *(Lehre von der Wärmebehandlung)*
thermatologisch thermatologic
thermisch stabil heat-stable
Thermoalgesie f therm[o]algesia

Thermoanalgesie

Thermoanalgesie f therm[o]analgesia
Thermobiologie f thermobiology
Thermodilution f thermodilution
Thermodilutionstechnik f thermodilution (thermal dilution) technique
thermogen thermogen[et]ic, thermogenous
Thermogenese f thermogenesis
Thermogramm n thermogram
Thermograph m thermograph
Thermographie f thermography
Thermohypästhesie f thermohypoaesthesia
Thermohyperalgesie f thermohyperalgesia
Thermohyperästhesie f thermohyperaesthesia, hyperthermalgesia, hyperthermo-aesthesia
thermoinhibitorisch thermoinhibitory
Thermokautern n thermocautery
Thermokoagulation f thermocoagulation
thermokoagulieren to thermocoagulate
thermolabil thermolabil
thermolytisch thermolytic
Thermomassage f thermomassage
Thermometer n thermometer
Thermometrie f thermometry, temperature measurement
thermometrisch thermometric
Thermoneurose f thermoneurosis
Thermopenetration f thermopenetration, medical diathermy, [short-wave] diathermy; electrothermy
thermophil thermophil[ic] (z. B. Bakterien)
Thermophobie f thermophobia (krankhafte Angst vor Hitze)
thermoplastisch thermoplastic
Thermopräzipitation f thermoprecipitation
Thermopräzipitin n thermoprecipitin (Antikörper)
Thermopunktion f thermopuncture
Thermoradiotherapie f thermoradiotherapy
Thermoregulation f thermoregulation
Thermoregulationsstörung f thermoregulation (heat) disorder
Thermoregulator m thermoregulator
thermoresistent thermoresistant, heat-resistant (Bakterien)
Thermosäule f thermopile
thermostabil thermostable, thermostabile, thermophylic
Thermostabilität f thermostability, heat stability
thermosystaltisch thermosystaltic
thermotaktisch thermotactic, thermotaxic
Thermotaxis f thermotaxis
Thermotherapie f thermotherapy
Thermotoxin n thermotoxin
Thermotropismus m thermotropism
Thesaurismose f thesaurismosis, storage disease
Theta-Welle f theta wave (im EEG)
Theta-Wellenrhythmus m theta rhythm (im EEG)
Thiamin n thiamin[e], aneurin, vitamin B_1
Thiaminase f thiaminase (Enzym)
Thiaminasekrankheit f Chastek paralysis (Vitamin B_1-Avitaminose)
Thiaminmangelkrankheit f athiaminosis

Thiaminpyrophosphat n thiamine pyrophosphate (Enzym)
Thiersch-Hautlappen m Thiersch graft
Thigmanästhesie f thigmanaesthesia, loss of superficial touch sensibility
Thigmoästhesie f thigmoaesthesia, superficial touch sensibility
Thigmotropismus m thigmotaxis, thigmotropism, stereotaxia, stereotropism (gezielte Bewegung auf Berührung)
Thiobakterien npl thiobacteria
Thiobarbiturat n thiobarbiturate
Thiobarbitursäure f thiobarbituric acid
Thioharnstoff m thiourea (schilddrüsenhemmender Stoff)
thiophil thiophil[e]
Thiourazil n thiouracil (schilddrüsenhemmender Stoff)
Thoma-Zeiss-Zählkammer f Thoma-Zeiss cell (counting chambre), Abbe-Zeiss [counting] cell (zur Blutuntersuchung)
Thorakal... s. a. Brust... und Brustkorb...
Thorakalgie f thoracalgia, thoracodynia, pain in the chest wall
Thorakektomie f thoracectomy
Thorakodelphus m thora[co]delphus (Mißgeburt mit vier Beinen, zwei Armen und einem Kopf)
Thorakodidymus m thoracodidymus (Mißgeburt)
Thorakodynie f s. Thorakalgie
Thorakogastrodidymus m thoracogastrodidymus (Doppelmißgeburt mit Verwachsungen an Brustkorb und Bauch)
Thorakogastroschisis f thoracogastroschisis, thoracocoeloschisis
Thorakolaparotomie f thoracolaparotomy, thoracocoeliotomy
Thorakolumbalfaszie f thoracolumbar (lumbodorsal) fascia
Thorakomelus m thoracomelus (Mißgeburt)
Thorakometer n thoracometer
Thorakometrie f thoracometry, measurement of the chest
Thorakomyotonie f thoracomyodynia, pain in the chest muscles
Thorakopagus m thoracopagus (Mißgeburt)
Thorakoparazephalus m thoracoparacephalus (Mißgeburt)
Thorakopathie f thoracopathy
Thorakoplastik f thoracoplasty
Thorakopneumoplastik f thoracopneumoplasty
Thorakoschisis f thoracoschisis, fissure of the thorax; fissured chest
Thorakoskop n thoracoscope
Thorakoskopie f thoracoscopy
Thorakostenosis f thoracostenosis; stenothorax
Thorakostomie f thoracostomy
Thorakostomiekatheter m thoracostomy catheter
Thorakotomie f thoracotomy, incision into the chest wall, pleuracotomy
Thorakozentese f thora[co]centesis, puncture (tapping) of the chest wall, pleuracentesis

Thorakozöliotomie f s. Thorakolaparotomie
Thorakozöloschisis f thoracocoeloschisis, thoracogastroschisis, fissure of the thorax and abdomen
Thorax m thorax, chest, rib (thoracic) cage, pectus *(Zusammensetzungen s. unter* Brustkorb *und* Pectus*)*
Thorax... *s. a.* Brustkorb...
Thoraxapertur f/**obere** thoracic inlet
Thoraxbinnendruck m intrathoracic pressure
Thoraxchirurg m thoracic surgeon, chest physician
Thoraxchirurgie f thoracic surgery
Thoraxdauerdrainage f continuous intercostal drainage
Thoraxdeformität f thoracic deformity, deformity of the thorax, thoracocyllosis; deformed thorax
Thoraxdrain n chest tube
Thoraxempyem n thoracic empyema
Thoraxhöhle f thoracic cavity (space)
Thoraxinstabilität f flail chest
Thoraxkyphose f thoracic kyphosis
Thorax-Lungen-Plastik f thoracopneumoplasty
Thoraxmagen m thoracic (upside-down) stomach
Thoraxmitte f midthorax
Thoraxoperation f thoracic operation
Thoraxorgan n thoracic organ
Thoraxplombe f plombage thoracoplasty
Thoraxprellung f contusion of the thorax
Thoraxröntgen n chest roentgenography (X-ray radiography)
Thoraxröntgenaufnahme f chest roentgenogram, X-ray photograph of the chest
~/anteroposteriore anteroposterior roentgenogram of the thorax, postero-anterior chest roentgenogram
~/seitliche lateral roentgenogram of the thorax, lateral chest roentgenogram
Thorax-Röntgen-Reihenuntersuchung f mass chest radiographic survey
Thoraxröntgenübersichtsaufnahme f chest survey X-ray photograph
Thoraxsaugdrain m intercostal drain (chest tube)
Thoraxsaugdrainage f/**geschlossene** closed intercostal [tube] drainage
Thoraxsegment n thoracic segment
Thoraxspiegel m thoracoscope
Thoraxspiegelung f thoracoscopy
Thoraxübersichtsaufnahme f chest survey X-ray photograph, plain radiograph of the thorax
Thoraxverletzung f thoracic injury
Thoraxwand f thoracic (chest) wall
Thoraxwanddeformität f chest wall deformity
Thoraxwunde f chest wound
~/offene (schlürfende) sucking chest wound
Thoraxzweiteingriff m rethoracotomy
ThPP s. Thiaminpyrophosphat
Thr s. Threonin
Threonin n threonine, α-amino-β-hydroxybutyric acid *(Aminosäure)*
Thrombangiitis f thromboangiitis

~ obliterans thromboangiitis obliterans, Buerger's disease, presenile spontaneous gangrene
Thrombase f s. Thrombin
Thrombasthenie f thromb[o]asthenia, functional deficiency of the blood platelets
Thrombektomie f thrombectomy, excision of a thrombus, thromboembolectomy
Thrombelastogramm n thrombelastogram
Thrombelastographie f thrombelastography
thrombenbildend thrombogenic
Thrombenbildung f thrombogenesis, clot formation; thrombogenicity
Thrombendarteriektomie f thromboendarterectomy
thrombenzerstörend thrombolytic, thromboclastic
Thrombin n thrombin, thrombase *(Enzym)*
Thrombinogen n s. Prothrombin
Thrombinspiegelerhöhung f **im Blut** hyperthrombinaemia
Thrombinzeit f thrombin time
Thromboangiitis f s. Thrombangiitis
Thromboarteri[i]tis f thrombo[end]arteritis
Thromboblast m thromboblast, mega[lo]karyocyte
Thromboembolektomie f s. Thrombektomie
Thromboembolie f thromboembolism; thromboembolization
thromboembolisch thromboembolic
Thromboembolus m thromboembolus
Thromboendokarditis f thromboendocarditis
Thrombogenese f thrombogenesis, clot formation
Thrombogenizität f thrombogenicity
Thromboglobulinspiegel m thromboglobulin level
Thrombokavernositis f thrombocavernositis
Thrombokinase f thrombokinase *(Enzym)*
Thrombolymphangitis f thrombolymphangitis
Thrombolyse f thrombolysis, dissolution of a thrombus
thrombolytisch thrombolytic, thromboclastic
Thrombopathie f 1. thrombopathy, deficiency of thrombus formation; 2. thrombopathy, disease of platelet function
Thrombopenie f thrombo[cyto]penia
thrombopenisch thrombocytopenic
Thrombophilie f thrombophilia, tendency to thrombosis
Thrombophlebitis f thrombophlebitis
~/floride florid thrombophlebitis
Thrombophthisis f thrombophthisis
Thromboplastin n thromboplastin, blood-clotting factor III
~/partielles partial thromboplastin
Thromboplastinmangel m thromboplastinopenia, deficiency of thromboplastin
Thromboplastinzeit f thromboplastin (prothrombin) time
~/partielle partial thromboplastin time, PTT
thromboplastisch thromboplastic
Thrombose f thrombosis
~/arterielle artery thrombosis

Thrombose

~/**intervillöse** intervillous thrombosis, placentosis
~/**marantische** marantic thrombosis *(Folge herabgesetzter Kreislauffunktion)*
~ **mit Arterienentzündung** thromboarteriitis, thromboendarteritis
~ **mit Blutgefäßentzündung** thromboangiitis
~ **mit Penisschwellkörperentzündung** thrombocavernositis
~/**umbiliko-portale** umbilical-portal thrombosis
~/**venöse** venous thrombosis
Thromboseneigung f thrombophilia, tendency to thrombosis
Thromboseprophylaxe f prophylaxis of thrombosis, thrombosis prophylaxis
thromboseverhindernd antithrombotic
thrombosieren 1. to thrombose, to form clots; 2. to thrombose, to form thrombosis
Thrombosinusitis f thrombosinusitis, thrombosis of a dural sinus
Thrombostase f thrombostasis
thrombotisch thrombotic
Thromboxan n thromboxane
Thrombozym n s. Prothrombin
Thrombozyt m thrombocyte, thromboplastid, [blood] platelet, blood plate (plaque), Deetjen's (elementary) body
~/**großer** macrothrombocyte
~/**thrombasthenischer** thrombasthenic platelet
Thrombozyten... s. a. Blutplättchen...
Thrombozytenabtrennung f **vom Blut** thrombocytopheresis
Thrombozytenadhäsivität f thrombocyte adhaesiveness
Thrombozytenaggregat n thrombocyte aggregate
Thrombozytenaggregation f thrombocyte aggregation
Thrombozytenkonzentrat n platelet pack
Thrombozytenkrankheit f thrombocytopathy
Thrombozytenkrise f thrombocytic crisis
Thrombozytenmangel m s. Thrombozytopenie
Thrombozytenschwäche f s. Thrombasthenie
Thrombozytentransfusion f platelet transfusion
Thrombozytenvermehrung f s. Thrombozythämie
Thrombozytenzahl f thrombocyte count
Thrombozytenzählrohr n thrombocytocrit
Thrombozythämie f thrombocytosis, [hyper]thrombocytohaemia
~/**hämorrhagische** haemorrhagic thrombocytohaemia
Thrombozytolyse f thrombocytolysis, dissolution (destruction) of the thrombocytes
Thrombozytolysin n thrombocytolysin *(thrombozytenauflösender Stoff)*
thrombozytolytisch thrombocytolytic
Thrombozytopathie f thrombocytopathy
thrombozytopathisch thrombocytopathic
Thrombozytopenie f thrombo[cyto]penia, plastocytopenia
~/**essentielle** essential thrombocytopenia, Werlhof's disease, land scurvy

~/**tropische** tropical thrombocytopenia, onyalai, onyalia
thrombozytopenisch thrombocytopenic
~/**nicht** non-thrombo[cyto]penic
Thrombozytopherese f thrombocytopheresis
Thrombozytophthisis f thrombophthisis
Thrombozytopoese f thrombo[cyto]poiesis
thrombozytopoetisch thrombocytopoietic
Thrombozytose f thrombocytosis, thrombocytohaemia
Thrombus m thrombus, clot [of blood]; embolus
● **einen ~ bilden** to form a thrombus
~/**marantischer** marantic thrombus
~/**muraler** s. ~ wandständiger
~/**parietaler** parietal (valvular) thrombus *(z. B. in Gefäßen)*
~/**postmortaler** post-mortem thrombus
~/**reitender** riding (saddle) thrombus
~/**roter** red thrombus
~/**wandständiger** lateral thrombus *(in Gefäßen)*; mural thrombus *(z. B. im Herzen)*
~/**weißer** white (platelet) thrombus
Thrombus... s. a. Blutgerinnsel... und Gerinnsel...
Thrombusbildung f thrombosis, thrombus formation, thrombogenesis
Thrombusbildungsstörung f thrombopathy, deficiency of thrombus formation
Thrombusbildungstendenz f thrombophilia
Thrombusbildungszeit f clot formation time
Thrombusextraktion f s. Thrombektomie
Thrombus- und Gefäßinnenhautentfernung f[/**operative**] thromboendarterectomy
Thromboszerstörung f thrombolysis
Thymektomie f thymectomy, excision of the thymus
thymektomieren to thymectomize, to excise (remove) the thymus gland
Thymergasie f thymergasia, affective illness
thymergastisch thymergastic
Thymidin n thymidine *(Nukleosid)*
Thymidinstoffwechsel m thymidine metabolism
thymikolymphatisch thymicolymphatic
Thymin n thymine *(Pyrimidinbase)*
Thymindesoxyribosid n thymidine *(Nukleosid)*
Thymitis f thymitis, inflammation of the thymus
thymogen thymogenic
Thymoleptikum n thymoleptic [agent]
thymoleptisch thymoleptic
Thymolflockungstest m thymol flocculation test
Thymoltrübungstest m thymol turbidity test *(zur Leberfunktionsprobe)*
Thymolysin n thymolysin
thymolytisch thymolytic
Thymom n thymoma
Thymonukleinsäure f thymonucleic (thymus nucleic) acid
Thymonukleodepolymerase f thymonucleodepolymerase *(Enzym)*
Thymopathie f 1. thymopathy, disease of the thymus; 2. thymopathy, disturbance of affectivity; mental affection; psychopathy

Thymopexie f thymopexy, fixation of the thymus
thymopriv thymoprivic, thymoprivous
thymotoxisch thymotoxic
thymotrop thymotropic
Thymozyt m thymocyte, thymic cell
Thymus m thymus [gland] ● **ohne ~** athymic ● **vom ~ ausgehend** thymogenic
~/vergrößerter megalothymus
Thymusaplasie f thymic aplasia, alymphoplasia, Di George's syndrome
thymusaplastisch thymus-aplastic
Thymusarterie f thymic artery
Thymusasthma n thymic asthma
Thymusdrüse f s. Thymus
Thymusentfernung f [/operative] s. Thymektomie
Thymusentzündung f s. Thymitis
Thymuserkrankung f s. Thymopathie 1.
Thymusfunktionsstörung f dysthymia, malfunction of the thymus
Thymusgeschwulst f thymoma
thymusgiftig thymotoxic
Thymushypertrophie f thymus hypertrophy; megalothymus
Thymuskörper m thymic body
Thymuskörperchen n thymic corpuscle
Thymusläppchen n lobule of the thymus
Thymuslappen m lobe of the thymus
thymuslos athymic
Thymuspersistenz f thymokesis, persistence of the thymus
Thymustod m thymic death
Thymusüberfunktion f hyperthymism
Thymusunterfunktion f hypothymism
Thymusvene f thymic vein
Thymusvergrößerung f enlargement of the thymus; megalothymus
Thymuszelle f thymocyte, thymic cell
thymuszerstörend thymolytic
Thymuszerstörung f thymolysis
Thyreo... s. a. Schilddrüsen...
Thyreochondrotomie f thyro[chondro]tomy, incision into the thyroid cartilage, laryngofissure
thyreogen thyr[e]ogenic, thyrogenous
Thyreoglobulin n thyroglobulin, thyroid-binding globulin
Thyreoglobulinantikörper m thyroglobulin antibody, TGA
Thyreoglobulinproteolyse f thyroglobulin proteolysis
thyreoglossal thyroglossal, thyrolingual
Thyreoglossusfistel f thyroglossal duct fistula
Thyreoglossuszyste f thyroglossal [duct] cyst
thyreohyoidal thyrohyoid, thyrohyal
Thyreohyoidmembran f thyrohyoid membrane
Thyreoid... s. a. Schilddrüsen...
Thyreoidea f thyroid [gland], thyroid body (Zusammensetzungen s. unter Schilddrüse)
Thyreoidektomie f s. Schilddrüsenentfernung
thyreoidektomieren to thyroidectomize, to perform a thyroidectomy
Thyreoiditis f thyroiditis, thyroadenitis, inflammation of the thyroid [gland]

~/chronisch schwielige ligneous thyroiditis (mit Bindegewebswucherung, Atrophie und Follikelschwund)
~/lymphozytäre struma lymphomatosa, Hashimoto's disease (struma)
~/Quervainsche (subakute) de Quervain's disease
Thyreoidotoxin n thyroidotoxin
thyreomimetisch thyromimetic
Thyreoparathyreoidektomie f thyroparathyroidectomy, excision of the thyroid and parathyroids
Thyreopathie f thyropathy, disease of the thyroid, thyroid disease; thyreosis
thyreopriv thyroprival, thyroprivic, thyroprivous, athyreotic; strumiprival, strumiprivic
Thyreoptose f thyroptosis
Thyreostatikum n antithyroid [agent]
Thyreotherapie f thyrotherapy, thyroidization
Thyreotom n thyrotome
Thyreotomie f 1. thyro[ido]tomy, incision into the thyroid [gland]; 2. s. Thyreochondrotomie
Thyreotoxikose f thyrotoxicosis, thyrotoxaemia, thyroid storm, hyperthyroid (thyrotoxic) crisis
thyreotoxikoseverhindernd antithyrotoxic
Thyreotoxin n thyrotoxin
thyreotoxisch thyrotoxic
thyreotrop[h] thyrotrop[h]ic
Thyreotropin n thyrotrop[h]in, thyrotropic (thyroid-stimulating) hormone
Thyreotropin-Freisetzungsfaktor m thyrotropin-releasing factor
Thyreotropinspiegelerhöhung f im Blut hyperthyrotropinaemia
Thyreotropismus m thyrotropism
Thyroaplasie f thyroaplasia
Thyroidotomie f s. Thyreotomie 1.
Thyroxin n thyroxine, tetraiodothyronine (Schilddrüsenhormon)
Thyroxinämie f thyroxinaemia
Thyroxindejodierung f deiodination of thyroxine
Thyroxin[spiegel]erhöhung f im Blut hyperthyroxinaemia
Tibia f tibia, shinbone, shank, cnemis
Tibia... s. a. Schienbein...
Tibiaabflachung f platycnemia
Tibiakopfschraube f tibial bolt
Tibialgie f tibialgia, pain in the shinbone; painful shin
Tibialis m 1. tibial (medial popliteal) nerve; 2. tibialis anterior [muscle]; 3. tibialis posterior [muscle]
Tibialis-anterior-Syndrom n anterior tibial syndrome
Tibialisphänomen n tibialis phenomenon, Strümpell's sign
Tibialis-posterior-Reflex m tibialis posterior reflex
Tibianagel m tibial nail
Tibiapunktion f tibial puncture
Tibiofibularband n/**hinteres** posterior tibiofibular ligament
~/vorderes anterior tibiofibular ligament

Tibiofibulargelenk 760

Tibiofibulargelenk *n*/**unteres** inferior (distal) tibiofibular joint
tibionavikular tibionavicular, tibioscaphoid
Tic *m* 1. tic, twitching; 2. tic, mimic (habit) spasm
~ **convulsif** convulsive tic
~ **douloureux** prosopospasm, tic douloureux, trigeminal [paroxysmal] neuralgia
~ **rotatoire** rotatory tic, spasmodic torticollis
Tick *m s.* Tic
Tickkranker *m* tiqueur
Tickkrankheit *f* convulsive tic
~/**allgemeine** Gilles de la Tourette disease (syndrome)
t. i. d. s. ter in die
Tidal-Drainage *f* tidal drainage
tief deep; sound *(Schlaf)*; low, profound *(tiefliegend)* ● ~ **atmen** to breath deeply, to suspire
Tiefe *f* intensity *(z. B. von Gefühlen)*
Tiefenanästhesie *f* bathyanaesthesia
Tiefenangst *f* bathmophobia
Tiefenbestrahlung *f* deep X-ray therapy
Tiefen[bestrahlungs]dosis *f* depth dose
Tiefenperkussion *f* deep percussion
Tiefenperzeption *f* depth perception
Tiefenpsychologie *f* depth psychology
Tiefenpsychotherapie *f* intensive psychotherapy
Tiefenreflex *m* deep reflex
tiefenrichtig orthoscopic
Tiefensehen *n* depth perception
Tiefensensibilität *f* deep sensibility, bath[y]aesthesia
Tiefensensibilitätsverlust *m* bathyanaesthesia
Tiefenwahrnehmung *f* depth perception
Tiemann-Katheter *m* Tiemann's catheter
Tierfellnävus *m* pilous naevus
Tiergift *n* venom, venenum, animal poison, zootoxin
Tierhalluzination *f* zoopsia *(Wahnvorstellung)*
tierisch animal
Tierkohle *f* animal charcoal
Tierliebe *f* zoophilia, zoophilism
~/**krankhafte** zoomania
tierliebend zoophilic
Tier-Mensch-Übertragung *f* animal-to-man transmission
Tierparasit *m* zooparasite
Tiertransplantat *n* zoograft, zooplastic graft
Tiertransplantatverpflanzung *f* zooplasty
Tierversuch *m* animal experiment; vivisection
Tietze-Syndrom *n* Tietze's disease (syndrome) *(schmerzhafte Schwellung der Rippenknorpel)*
Tigerherz *n* tiger heart; tigering of the heart muscle
tigroid tigroid, tiger-spotted
Tigroidsubstanz *f* tigroid bodies, Nissl bodies (granules) *(in Nervenzellen)*
Tigrolyse *f* tigrolysis *(Auflösung der Tigroidsubstanz)*
Tinctura *f* **jodi** iodine tincture
Tinea *f* tinea, ringworm *(s. a. unter* Flechte *und* Lichen*)*

~ **barbae** tinea barbae, barber's itch, ringworm of the beard, hyphogenic sycosis
~ **capitis** tinea capitis, ringworm of the scalp
~ **corporis** tinea corporis, ringworm of the body
~ **cruris** tinea cruris, laundryman's itch, gum (jock) itch, jockey[-strap] itch
~ **favosa** tinea favosa, favus, crusted ringworm, honeycomb ringworm (tetter)
~ **imbricata** tropical tinea circinata, Malabar itch, scaly ringworm *(Tropenkrankheit durch Trichophyton concentricum)*
~ **nodosa** tinea nodosa, piedra
~ **pedis** tinea pedis, ringworm of the foot; athletes' foot
~ **sycosis** *s.* ~ barbae
~ **versicolor** tinea versicolor, chromophytosis
tingiert/blutig blood-tinged
Tinktion *f* tinction *(Rezeptur)*
Tinktur *f* tincture, tinct., tr.
Tinnitus *m* **aurium** tinnitus [aurium], ringing in the ears
Tintometer *n* tintometer
Tintometrie *f* tintometry
Titer *m* titre
Titillatio *f* titillation, tickling
Titillomanie *f* titillomania, morbid desire to cratch
Titrieranalyse *f* titrimetric (volumetric) analysis
titrieren to titrate
Titrimetrie *f* titrimetry, volumetry
Titubation *f* titubation, unsteadiness of posture *(z. B. bei Kleinhirnerkrankung)*
T-Knochenbruch *m* T fracture
T-Lymphozyt *m* T (thymus-dependent) lymphocyte
TMD *s.* Tagesmaximaldosis
Tobiafieber *n*/**kolumbianisches** Columbian spotted fever
Tochterchromosom *n* chromatid
Tochtergeschwulst *f s.* Metastase
Tochterstern *m* daughter star, diaster *(Mitosefigur)*
Tochterzelle *f* daughter cell
Tochterzyste *f* daughter (secondary) cyst
Tod *m* death, exitus, mors ● **bei Eintritt des Todes** at death ● **den** ~ **feststellen** to certify death ● **nach dem Tode** post mortem, posthumous ● **vor dem** ~ antemortem ● **zum** ~ **führen** to lead to death
~/**klinischer** clinical death
~/**örtlicher** local death *(z. B. von Körperteilen)*
~/**plötzlicher** sudden death
~/**schmerzhafter** painful death, dysthanasia
~/**Schwarzer** Black Death, black plague
~/**sofortiger** immediate death
todanzeigend thanatognomonic
todbringend thanatophoric
Todesangst *f* agonia, agony
todesartig thanatoid
Todesbeschreibung *f* thanatography
Todeserklärung *f* declaration of death

Todesfall *m* case of death; fatality, fatal outcome *(z. B. nach Operationen)*; casuality *(Militärmedizin)*
Todesherbeiführung *f*/**willentliche** euthanasia
Todesinstinkt *m* thanatos
Todeskampf *m* throes of death, death struggle; agony, agonia ● **im ~** agonal
Todesrate *f* death rate
~/spezifische specific death rate
Todestrieb *m* death instinct, morbid desire for death, necromania
Todesursache *f* cause of death
Todesvortäuschung *f* simulation of death, necromimesis
Todeszeichen *n* sign of death
todkrank dangerously ill
tödlich fatal, deadly, mortal; lethal
Togavirus *n* togavirus
Tokelau *n s.* Tinea imbricata
Tokodynamometer *n* toco[dynamo]meter, TKD
Tokodynamometrie *f* tocodynamometry, tocotachography
Tokogramm *n* tocogram
Tokograph *m* tocograph, TKG
Tokographie *f* toco[tacho]graphy
tokographisch tocographic
Tokologie *f* tocology
Tokomanie *f* tocomania, puerperal psychosis (mania)
Tokometrie *f* tocometry
Tokopherol *n* tocopherol, vitamin E
Tokophobie *f* tocophobia *(krankhafte Angst vor der Geburt)*
Tolbutamid *n* tolbutamide *(Antidiabetikum)*
tolerant/immunologisch immunologically tolerant, hyposensitive
Toleranz *f*/**gekreuzte** cross[ed] tolerance
~/immunologische immunologic (immune) tolerance
Toleranzdosis *f* tolerance dose *(z. B. von Röntgenstrahlen)*
Toleranzschwelle *f* tolerance threshold
tolerierend/Kälte cryotolerant
Tollkirsche *f* belladonna
Tollkirschenalkaloid *n* belladonna alkaloid
Tollwut *f* [cyno]lyssa, rabies, hydrophobia, dumb-madness ● **die ~ haben** to be rabid ● **von ~ befallen** mad
tollwutähnlich lyssoid
Tollwutantiserum *n* antirabies [anti]serum
tollwutartig rabiform, lyssoid
Tollwutbehandlung *f* antirabies treatment
tollwutbekämpfend antirabic, antilyssic
tollwuterzeugend rabigenic
Tollwutfurcht *f* rabiesphobia, lyssophobia, hydrophobophobia
tollwütig rabid, rabic, hydrophobic, mad ● **~ sein** to be rabid
Tollwutimmunisierung *f* rabies immunization
Tollwutimpfstoff *m* [anti]rabies vaccine
Tollwutimpfung *f* [anti]rabies vaccination
Tollwutknötchen *npl* Babés nodules (tubercles)
Tollwutmittel *n* antirabic [agent]

Tollwutprophylaxe *f* rabies prophylaxis
Tollwutserum *n* [anti]rabies serum
Tollwutvirus *n* [street] rabies virus
tollwutvirustötend rabicidal
tollwutwirksam antirabic, antilyssic
Toluidin *n* toluidine
Toluidinblau *n* toluidine blue
Toluol *n* toluol, toluene
Tomogramm *n* tomogram, laminagram, planigram
Tomograph *m* tomograph, laminagraph
Tomographie *f* tomography, laminography, planigraphy, planography, stratigraphy
tomographieren to tomograph
tomographisch tomographic
Tomomanie *f* tomomania *(1. Sucht, operiert zu werden; 2. Drang nach operativer Therapie)*
Tomotokie *f* tomotocia, caesarean section, delivery by abdominal section
Ton *m* sound, tone
~/schnappender snap
Tonaphasie *f* tonaphasia, motor amusia
tönend sonorous, resonant
Tonikum *n* tonic
Tonikumbehandlung *f* tonic treatment
tonisch tonic
tonisch-klonisch tonic-clonic, ton[ic]oclonic
tonisierend tonic
Tonitrophobie *f* tonitrophobia *(krankhafte Angst vor Gewitter)*
Tonizität *f* tonicity
tonlos soundless, aphonic, aphonous; voiceless
Tonlosigkeit *f* aphonia, soundlessness; voicelessness
Tonnenzähne *mpl* Hutchinsonian teeth *(bei Syphilis)*
Tonofibrille *f* tonofibril, tenofibril
Tonofilament *n* tonofilament
Tonogramm *n* tonogram
Tonograph *m* tonograph
Tonographie *f* tonography
tonographisch tonographic
Tonometer *n* tonometer, teno[no]meter
~/Schiötzsches Schiötz tonometer
Tonometrie *f* tonometry
tonometrisch tonometric
Tonpfeifenstielarterie *f* pipe-stem artery
Tonpfeifenstielzirrhose *f* pipe-stem cirrhosis *(Leberzirrhose bei Bilharziose)*
Tonsilla *f* **cerebelli** cerebellar tonsil, tonsil of the cerebellum
~ lingualis lingual tonsil
~ palatina palatine (faucial) tonsil
~ pharyngica pharyngeal tonsil (adenoids)
~ tuberia tubal tonsil, Eustachian tonsil
Tonsille *f* tonsil[la], amygdala, paristhmion *(Zusammensetzungen s. unter Mandel)*
Tonsillektomie *f* tonsillectomy, excision of the tonsils, amygdaloidectomy
tonsillektomiert tonsilloprive
Tonsillen... *s. a.* Mandel...
Tonsillenausschälung *f s.* Tonsillektomie

Tonsillenelevatorium

Tonsillenelevatorium n tonsil dissector (elevator)
Tonsillenfibrosarkom n fibrosarcoma of tonsil
Tonsillengrube f tonsillar fossa
Tonsillenkrankheit f tonsillopathy, disease of the tonsils
Tonsillenlager n tonsil bed
Tonsillenloge f tonsil bed
Tonsillenmesser n s. Tonsillotom
Tonsillenmykose f tonsillomycosis; mycotic tonsillitis
Tonsillennadel f tonsil needle
Tonsillenschere f tonsil scissors
Tonsillenschlinge f tonsillar (amygdaline) snare
Tonsillenspritze f tonsil syringe
Tonsillitis f tonsillitis, tonsillar inflammation, amygdalitis, paristhmitis
~/**eitrige** quinzy
~ **follicularis** follicular tonsillitis; spotted sore
~ **lacunaris** lacunar tonsillitis *(Gaumenmandelentzündung mit Beteiligung der Gaumenbögen und der Rachenschleimhaut)*
~/**mykotische** mycotic tonsillitis
tonsillitisch tonsillitic
Tonsillolith m tonsillolith, tonsillar calculus, amygdalolith
Tonsillopathie f tonsillopathy, disease of the tonsils
Tonsillopharyngitis f tonsillopharyngitis, inflammation of the tonsils and the pharynx
Tonsillotom n tonsillotome, tonsil knife, tonsillectome, tonsilsector
Tonsillotomie f tonsillotomy, incision into the tonsils
Tontaubheit f tone deafness, asonia, sensory amusia
Tonus m tonus, tone *(z. B. der Muskeln)* ● **den gleichen ~ besitzend** isotonic
~/**gleicher** isotonia
Tonuserhöhung f hypertonia, hypertonicity; hypertonus
~ **der Muskulatur** spasticity
tonusgesteigert hypertonic *(z. B. Muskeln)*
Tonuslage f/**neurovegetative** neurotony
tonuslos atonic
Tonusmangel m lack of tonicity (tone)
tonusschwach hypotonic
Tonusschwäche f hypotonia, hypotonicity; hypotonus
Tonussteigerung f hypertonia, hypertonicity; hypertonus
Tonusstörung f dystonia
Tonusverlust m loss of tonicity (tone)
~/**affektiver** cataplexis
~ **des Herzens** cardianeuria
Topagnosie f topoanaesthesia, topagnosis
Topalgie f top[o]algia
Topästhesie f topaesthesia
Topektomie f topectomy
Tophus m 1. tophus, chalkstone; 2. tophus, tartar of the teeth
~ **arthriticus** s. Tophus 1.

Tophusgicht f chalk gout
topisch topical, local
Topoanästhesie f topoanaesthesia, topagnosis
Topognosis f topaesthesia
Topographie f topography
Toponeurose f toponeurosis
Topoparästhesie f topoparaesthesia, localized paraesthesia
Topophobie f topophobia *(krankhafte Angst vor bestimmten Orten)*
Torcular m **Herophili** torcular [Herophili], confluence of the sinuses
Torkildsen-Drainage f Torkildsen tube; ventriculocisternostomy, ventriculospinal-subarachnoid shunt *(bei Hydrozephalus)*
Tormina npl tormina, griping pains in the bowel
torpid torpid
Torpor m torpor, torpidity, torpescence; numbness; sluggishness; inactivity
~ **retinae** Berlin's disease *(partiell oder total)*
Torsion f torsion, twisting *(s. a. Drehung)*
Torsionsdystonie f torsion dystonia (spasm), dystonia musculorum deformans
Torsionsfraktur f torsion (spiral) fracture
Torso m torso, trunk
Torticollis m torticollis, wry-neck, loxia, trachelocyllosis
~/**hysterischer** hysterical torticollis
~/**labyrinthärer** labyrinthine torticollis
~/**myogener** myogenic torticollis
~/**neurogener** neurogenic torticollis
~/**reflektorischer** reflex torticollis
~/**spastischer** spasmodic (intermittent) torticollis, rotatory tic
Torulom n toruloma
Torulosis f torulosis, cryptococcosis *(durch Cryptococcus neoformans)*
Torulus m torulus, small elevation; papilla
Torus m torus, swelling
~ **genitalis** genital torus (ridge)
~ **occipitalis transversus** transverse occipital torus
~ **palatinus** palatine torus
~ **tubarius** tubal elevation, Eustachian cushion
tot dead ● **[für] ~ erklären** to declare dead
Totaladrenalektomie f bilateral adrenalectomy
Totalaphasie f total (complete) aphasia
Totalatelektase f total atelectasis (collapse)
Totalkapazität f total lung capacity
Totalophthalmoplegie f total ophthalmoplegia
Totalskotom n absolute scotoma
Tote m corpse, dead body
töten to kill, to deaden *(z. B. einen Nerven)*
~/**sich** to commit suicide, to take one's own life
Totenbett n deathbed
totenblaß deadly pale, pale as death
Totenblässe f deadly pallor (paleness)
tötend mortal, killing, thanatophoric
Totenflecken mpl livor [mortis]; postmortem (cadaveric) lividity
Totenfurcht f necrophobia
Totenkammer f morgue

Totenkopf *m* 1. death's head; 2. skull and crossbones *(Zeichen für Lebensgefahr)*
Totenladeneröffnung *f*/**operative** sequestrotomy
Totenschein *m* death certificate
Totenstarre *f* postmortem (cadaveric) rigidity, rigidity of death
Toterklärung *f* declaration of death
totgeboren stillborn
Totgeburt *f* stillbirth, dead birth; stillborn child
Totgeburtsrate *f* stillbirth rate, natimortality
Totraum *m* dead space
~/anatomischer anatomical dead space
~/physiologischer physiological dead space *(Atemwege)*
~/respiratorischer anatomical dead space
Totraumluft *f* dead space air
totscheinend mortisemblant
Tourniquet *m* tourniquet
Towey-Krankheit *f* Towey disease, maple bark [stripper's] disease
Tox... *s. a.* Gift...
Toxalbumin *n* toxalbumin
Toxalbumose *f* toxalbumose
Toxämie *f* tox[in]aemia, toxicaemia
toxämisch toxaemic
Toxidermie *f s.* Toxikodermatose
toxigen toxicogenic, producing toxins
Toxigenität *f* toxigenicity
Toxikämie *f s.* Toxämie
Toxikoderma *n s.* Toxikodermatose
Toxikodermatitis *f* toxi[co]dermatitis, skin inflammation due to poison
Toxikodermatose *f* toxicodermatosis, toxicodermia; toxicoderma
Toxikologe *m* toxicologist
Toxikologie *f* toxicology
toxikologisch toxicologic[al]
Toxikomane *m* toxicomaniac
Toxikomanie *f* toxicomania
Toxikopathie *f s.* Toxikose
Toxikophobie *f* toxi[co]phobia *(krankhafte Angst vor Giften)*
Toxikose *f* tox[ic]osis, toxinosis, toxonosis, toxicopathy
~/endogene endotoxicosis
Toxikum *n s.* Toxin
Toxin *n* toxin[um], poison, [in]toxicant
~/entgiftetes toxoid, anatoxin
~/pflanzliches phytotoxin
~/tierisches zootoxin, venenum, venom
Toxin... *s. a.* Gift...
Toxinabsorption *f* toxin absorption
Toxinämie *f* tox[in]aemia, toxicaemia
Toxin-Antitoxin *n* toxin-antitoxin, TAT
Toxin-Antitoxin-Reaktion *f* toxin-antitoxin reaction
Toxineinheit *f* toxin (toxic) unit
Toxinfixierung *f* toxicopexis
toxinogen *s.* toxinproduzierend
Toxinproduktion *f* toxin production
toxinproduzierend toxin-producing, toxigenic, toxinogenous

Toxinpsychose *f* toxic psychosis (insanity)
Toxinspezialist *m* toxicologist
toxinspezifisch toxignomic
toxintragend toxophorous, toxiphoric
toxisch poisonous, toxic, toxicant *(z. B. Substanzen)*; venenous, venomous *(z. B. Tiere)*
Toxisterin *n* toxisterol
Toxizität *f* poisonousness, toxicity *(von Substanzen)*; venomousness *(z. B. von Schlangen)*
Toxoid *n* toxoid, anatoxin
Toxolezithin *n* toxolecithin
toxophil toxophil[e]
toxophor toxophorous, toxiphoric
Toxophor *n* toxophore
Toxoplasma *n* **gondii (hominis)** Toxoplasma gondii *(Toxoplasmoseerreger)*
Toxoplasma-Antikörper *m* toxoplasma antibody
toxoplasmatisch toxoplasm[at]ic
Toxoplasmin *n* toxoplasmin
Toxoplasmin-Test *m* toxoplasmin [skin] test
Toxoplasmose *f* toxoplasmosis *(Infektionskrankheit durch Toxoplasma gondii)*
Toxoplasmose-Hauttest *m* toxoplasmin [skin] test
TPI *s.* Treponema-pallidum-Immobilisierungstest
TPN *s.* Triphosphopyridinnukleotid
Trabeculae *fpl* **carneae (cordis)** carneous trabeculae (columns), pectinate muscles
~ lienis splenic trabeculae
Trabekel *m* trabecula
Trabekelarterie *f* trabecular artery
Trabekelbildung *f* trabeculation *(in einem Organ)*
Trabekelgeflecht *n* trabecular meshwork
Trabekelpigmentierung *f* trabecular pigmentation
Trabekelschnitt *m* trabeculotomy
Trabekelstruktur *f* trabecularism
Trabekelvene *f* trabecular vein
trabekulär trabecular
Trabekulation *f* trabeculation *(in einem Organ)*
Trabekulektomie *f* trabeculectomy *(am Auge)*
Trabekulotomie *f* trabeculotomy
Tracer *m* tracer [element]
Trachea *f* trachea, windpipe
Trachea... *s. a.* Luftröhren...
Tracheadilatation *f* tracheaectasy, dilatation of the trachea
Tracheadilatator *m* tracheal dilator
Tracheaintubation *f* tracheal intubation
tracheal tracheal
Tracheal... *s. a.* Luftröhren...
Trachealabsaugung *f* tracheal aspiration
Trachealatmen *n* tracheal respiration
Trachealbifurkation *f* bifurcation of the trachea
Trachealektasie *f s.* Tracheadilatation
Trachealgie *f* trachealgia, pain in the trachea
Trachealhäkchen *n* trachea retractor (tenaculum)
Trachealintubation *f* tracheal intubation
Trachealkanüle *f* tracheotomy cannula, tracheostomy (tracheal) tube
Trachealkatheter *m* tracheal catheter, tracheo[s]tomy tube

Trachealknorpel

Trachealknorpel *m* tracheal cartilage (ring)
Trachealobstruktion *f* tracheal obstruction
Trachealödem *n* tracheal oedema
Trachealöffnung *f* tracheostoma, tracheostomy
Trachealrasseln *n* tracheal rale (breath sounds)
Trachealschleimfluß *m s.* Tracheoblennorrhoe
Trachealschleimhaut *f* tracheal mucosa, mucous membrane of the trachea
Trachealschleimhautdrüse *f* tracheal mucous gland
Trachealschleimhautentzündung *f s.* Tracheitis
Trachealschleimhautödem *n* tracheal oedema
Trachealstenose *f* tracheal stenosis, tracheostenosis
Trachealtubus *m* tubus, tube, [endo]tracheal tube
Trachealulkus *n* tracheal ulcer, trachielcus
Trachealulzeration *f* ulceration of the trachea, trachielcosis
Tracheaschichtbild *n* laminagram of the trachea
Tracheastenose *f s.* Tracheostenose
Tracheaverlegung *f* tracheal obstruction
Tracheaverschiebung *f* tracheal shift
Tracheitis *f* trach[e]itis, inflammation of the trachea
~ **purulenta** purulent tracheitis; tracheopyosis
Trachelagra *f* trachelagra, gout in the neck
Trachelektomie *f* trachelectomy, excision of the cervix uteri
Trachelismus *m* trachelism[us] *(bei Epilepsie)*
Trachelitis *f* trachelitis, inflammation of the neck of the uterus
Trachelodynie *f* trachelodynia, pain in the neck
Trachelokyphose *f* trachelokyphosis, anterior curvature of the cervical spine
Trachelomyositis *f* trachelomyitis, inflammation of the muscles of the neck
Tracheloparasit *m* tracheloparasitus *(Mißgeburt)*
Trachelopexie *f* trachelopexia, fixation of the cervix uteri
Tracheloplastik *f* tracheloplasty
Trachelorrhaphie *f* trachelorrhaphy, suture of the cervix uteri
Trachelorrhektor *m* trachelorrhector *(Instrument zur Halswirbelsäulendurchtrennung)*
Tracheloschisis *f* tracheloschisis, cervical fissure
Trachelosyringorrhaphie *f* trachelosyringorrhaphy
Trachelotomie *f* trachelotomy, incision into the cervix uteri
Trachelozele *f* trache[l]ocele
Trachelozystitis *f* trachelocystitis, inflammation of the neck of the bladder
Tracheoblennorrhoe *f* tracheoblennorrhoea, mucous discharge from the trachea
Tracheobronchialabsaugung *f* tracheobronchial aspiration (suction)
Tracheobronchialbaum *m* tracheobronchial tree (airways)
Tracheobronchialsekret *n* tracheobronchial secretion
Tracheobronchialtoilette *f* tracheobronchial toilet
Tracheobronchitis *f* tracheobronchitis, inflammation of the trachea and bronchi
Tracheobronchoskop *n* tracheobronchoscope
Tracheobronchoskopie *f* tracheobronchoscopy
Tracheogramm *n* tracheogram
Tracheographie *f* tracheography
Tracheolaryngotomie *f* tracheolaryngotomy, incision into the larynx and the trachea
Tracheomalazie *f* tracheomalacia, softening of the tracheal cartilages
Tracheopathie *f* tracheopathy, disease of the trachea
Tracheophonie *f* tracheophony
Tracheopyosis *f* tracheopyosis; purulent tracheitis
Tracheorrhagie *f* tracheorrhagia, haemorrhage from the trachea
Tracheorrhaphie *f* tracheorrhaphy, suture of the trachea
Tracheoschisis *f* tracheoschisis, tracheofissure, fissure of the trachea
Tracheoskop *n* tracheoscope
Tracheoskopie *f* tracheoscopy
tracheoskopisch tracheoscopic
Tracheostenose *f* tracheostenosis, tracheal stenosis
Tracheostoma *n* tracheostoma
Tracheostomie *f* tracheostomy
Tracheostomiekanülenentfernung *f* decannulation
Tracheotom *n* tracheotome
Tracheotomie *f* tracheotomy, incision into the trachea
~ **mit Ringknorpelspaltung** cricotracheotomy
~/**obere** superior (high) tracheotomy
~/**untere** inferior (low) tracheotomy
Tracheotomiebesteck *n* tracheotomy set (equipment)
Tracheotomiehaken *m* tracheotomy hook
Tracheotomiekanüle *f s.* Trachealkanüle
Tracheotomiemesser *n s.* Tracheotom
tracheotomieren to tracheotomize, to perform a tracheotomy
Tracheotomietubus *m* tracheotomy tube
Tracheozele *f* trache[l]ocele
Trachom *n* trachoma, trachomatous (trachoma inclusion) conjunctivitis, granular conjunctivitis (ophthalmia), Egyptian ophthalmia; granular lids
~ **im Stadium I** follicular trachoma
Trachomentropion *n* trachomatous entropion
Trachomkeratitis *f* trachomatous keratitis
Trachomkörner *npl* trachoma follicles
Trachomkörperchen *npl* trachoma (Prowazek-Halberstaedter) bodies, trachoma granulations
Trachompannus *m* trachomatous pannus
Trachyphonie *f* trachyphonia, roughness of the voice; hoarseness
Tractus *m* tract[us] *(s. a. unter Canalis und Ductus)*
~ **bulbocerebellaris** cerebellobulbar tract
~ **cerebellorubralis** cerebellorubral (dentatorubral) tract

- **cerebellothalamicus** cerebellothalamic tract
- **cerebellovestibularis** cerebellovestibular tract
- **corticobulbaris** corticobulbar tract
- **corticocerebellaris** corticocerebellar tract
- **corticohypothalamicus** corticohypothalamic tract
- **corticonigralis** corticonigral tract
- **corticonuclearis** corticonuclear tract
- **corticopallidalis** corticopallidal tract
- **corticopontinus** corticopontile (corticopontine) tract
- **corticorubralis** corticorubral tract
- **corticospinalis** corticospinal tract
- **corticospinalis anterior** anterior corticospinal tract, fascicle of Türck
- **corticospinalis lateralis** lateral corticospinal tract
- **corticothalamicus** corticothalamic tract
- **dorsolateralis** dorsolateral tract
- **frontopontinus** frontopontine tract
- **hypothalamohypophysialis** hypothalamohypophyseal tract, paraventriculohypophyseal tract
- **iliotibialis fasciae latae** iliotibial tract, Maissiat's band
- **lenticulothalamicus** lenticulothalamic tract
- **occipitopontinus** occipitopontine tract
- **olfactorius** olfactory tract
- **olivocerebellaris** olivocerebellar tract
- **olivospinalis** olivospinal (bulbospinal) tract, spinoolivary fasciculus, Helweg's bundle
- **opticus** optic (ophthalmic) tract
- **parietopontinus** parietopontine tract
- **pyramidalis** pyramidal tract
- **reticuloreticularis** reticuloreticular tract
- **reticulospinalis** reticulospinal tract
- **rubroreticularis** rubroreticular tract
- **rubrospinalis** rubrospinal tract
- **rubrotectalis** tectorubral tract
- **solitarius** solitary fasciculus (tract), Allen's tract
- **spinalis nervi trigemini** spinal tract of the trigeminal nerve
- **spinocerebellaris anterior** anterior spinocerebellar tract, ventral spinocerebellar fasciculus [of Gowers], Gowers' column (tract), anterolateral fasciculus of Gowers
- **spinocerebellaris posterior** posterior spinocerebellar tract, dorsal spinocerebellar fasciculus [of Flechsig], Flechsig's (direct cerebellar) tract
- **spinotectalis** spinotectal tract
- **spinothalamicus anterior** anterior spinothalamic tract
- **spinothalamicus lateralis** lateral spinothalamic tract
- **tectocerebellaris** tectocerebellar tract
- **tectospinalis** tectospinal tract
- **tegmentalis centralis** central tegmental tract
- **temporopontinus** temporopontine tract
- **vestibulocerebellaris** vestibulocerebellar tract
- **vestibulospinalis** vestibulospinal (spinal vestibular) tract, descending vestibular root (tract)

Tragbahre f stretcher, litter
träge 1. indolent, lazy; idle, inactive; slow; lethargic; 2. inert
Trage f stretcher, litter
Träger m carrier
trägerfrei carrier-free, c. f.
Trägerkultur f carrier culture
Trägersubstanz f vehicle, excipient *(z. B. für Medikamente)*
Tragevorrichtung f suspensorium, suspensory
Tragezeit f gestation[al] period
Trägheit f indolence, laziness; slowness, sluggishness; inactivity *(z. B. von Organen);* bradypragia, bradypraxia *(z. B. von Körperbewegungen)*
Tragophonie f tragophonia, tragophony
Tragus m tragus *(Vorsprung am äußeren Ohr)*
Tragusknorpel m tragal (tragic) cartilage
trainierbar trainable
Training n training, conditioning
Trainingsgerät n simulator
Trakt m tract; duct; canal *(Zusammensetzungen s. unter Tractus, Canalis und Ductus)*
Traktion f traction
Traktionsaneurysma n traction aneurysm
Traktionsdivertikel n traction (midthoracic) diverticulum *(in der Speiseröhre)*
Traktor m tractor
Traktotomie f tractotomy
Trance f trance
Träne f tear, lachryma, lacrima
tränen to tear, to run with tears, to water
Tränenabflußsystem n lacrimal drainage system
Tränenabsonderung f lachrymation, lacrimation, secretion of tears
Tränenapparat m lacrimal apparatus ● zum ~ und zur Nase gehörend lacrimonasal
Tränenapparatchirurgie f lacrimal surgery
Tränenbein n lacrimal bone
Tränenbucht f lacrimal bay
Tränendrainagesystem n lacrimal drainage system
Tränendrüse f lacrimal gland
Tränendrüsenarterie f lacrimal artery
Tränendrüsenentfernung f[/**operative**] dacryoadenectomy, excision of a lacrimal gland
Tränendrüsenentzündung f dacryoadenitis, inflammation of a lacrimal gland, lacrimal adenitis
~/eitrige dacryoblennorrhoea
Tränendrüsengeschwulst f dacryoma, lacrimal tumour
Tränendrüsengrube f lacrimal fossa
Tränendrüsenretentionszyste f dacryops
Tränendrüsenschmerz m dacry[o]adenalgia, pain in a lacrimal gland
Tränendrüsenzirrhus m dacryadenoscirrhus
Tränendrüsenvene f lacrimal vein
Tränendrüsenvereiterung f dacryoblennorrhoea
Tränenfilm m tear film
Tränenfistel f lacrimal fistula, dacryosyrinx
Tränenfluß m lacrimal flow, lachrymation, lacrimation, dacryorrhoea, flow of tears; epiphora
Tränenflüssigkeit f lacrimal fluid

Tränengang

Tränengang m lacrimal (lacrimonasal) canal, nasal (nasolacrimal) duct
Tränengangabflußblockade f nasolacrimal drainage system blockage
Tränengangentzündung f dacryocanaliculitis
Tränengangeröffnung f[/operative] lacrimotomy, canaliculotomy
Tränengangfistelung f in die Nasenhöhle [/operative] canaliculorhinostomy
Tränengang-Nasen-Fistel f canaliculorhinostomy
Tränengangobstruktion f dacry[o]agogatresia, obstruction of a lacrimal canaliculus
Tränengangspritze f dacryosyringe
Tränengangstein m rhinodacryolith
Tränengangvereng[er]ung f dacryo[cystorhino]stenosis, nasolacrimal duct stenosis
Tränengas n tear gas, lacrimator [gas]
Tränengrube f lacrimal fossa
Tränenkanal m s. Tränengang
Tränenkanälchen n lacrimal canaliculus
Tränenkanälchenampulle f ampulla of the lacrimal canaliculus (duct)
Tränenkanälchenentzündung f lacrimal canaliculus inflammation
Tränenkanälchenvereng[er]ung f lacrimal canaliculus stenosis
Tränenkanalschere f canalicular scissors
Tränenkanalwiederherstellung f[/operative] canaliculoplasty
Tränenleiste f lacrimal crest
~/**hintere** posterior lacrimal crest
~/**vordere** anterior lacrimal crest
Tränenlysozym n tear lysozyme (Enzym)
Tränenmangel m oligodacrya, deficiency of tears
Tränennasengang m s. Tränengang
Tränennerv m lacrimal nerve
Tränenorgane npl lacrimal apparatus
Tränenpapille f lacrimal papilla (tubercle)
Tränenpumpenmechanismus m lacrimal pump mechanism
Tränenpunkt m lacrimal point (punctum)
Tränenreflex m lacrimal reflex
Tränensack m lacrimal (tear) sac, dacryocyst[is]
Tränensackeiterung f dacryocystoblennorrhoea
Tränensackentfernung f[/operative] dacryocystectomy, tear-sac extirpation
Tränensackentzündung f dacryocystitis, inflammation of the lacrimal sac
~/**eitrige** dacryocystoblennorrhoea
Tränensackeröffnung f[/operative] dacryocystotomy
Tränensackerweiterung f dacryo[cyst]ectasia
Tränensackfistel f lacrimal sac fistula
Tränensackfistelung f[/operative] dacryocystostomy
Tränensackgrube f lacrimal sulcus (groove)
Tränensackmesser n lacrimotome
Tränensack-Nasen-Fistelung f dacryocystorhinostomy
Tränensackphlegmone f dacryophlegmon
Tränensackröntgen[kontrast]bild n dacryocystogram

Tränensackröntgen[kontrast]darstellung f dacryocystography
Tränensackschnitt m dacryocystotomy
Tränensacksenkung f dacryo[cysto]ptosis, prolapse of a lacrimal sac
Tränensackstein m dacryolith
Tränensackvereiterung f dacryocystoblennorrhoea
Tränensackvereng[er]ung f dacryocystostenosis
Tränensackvorfall m dacryo[cysto]cele
Tränensee m lacrimal lake
Tränensekretion f lachrymation, lacrimation, lacrimal (tear) secretion ● ~ **bewirkend** lacrimatory
Tränenstein m tear stone, lacrimal calculus, dacryolith
Tränensteinkrankheit f dacryolithiasis
Tränenträufeln n dacryorrhoea, epiphora; watery eye
tränentreibend dacryagogic, dacryagogue
Tränenwärzchen n lacrimal caruncle
Tränenwegchirurgie f lacrimal surgery
Tränenwege mpl lacrimal passages
Trank m potion, draught, drink
Tranquil[l]izer m tranquilizer
tranquillisieren to tranquilize
Transaminase f transaminase, aminotransferase, aminopherase, transpeptidase (Enzym)
Transaminierung f transamination
Transanimation f transanimation
Transduktion f transduction (genetischen Materials)
Transektion f transection
Transfer m transfer, transference
Transferase f transferase (Enzym)
Transfer-Rate f transfer rate
Transfer-Ribonukleinsäure f transfer ribonucleic acid, tRNA
Transferrin n transferrin, siderophilin (Eisentransporteiweiß)
Transferrinkomplex m transferrin complex
Transfixation f transfixion
Transfixationsnaht f figure-of-eight suture
transfixieren to transfix
Transforation f transforation, perforation of the foetal skull
Transformation f transformation (z. B. von Gewebe)
transfundieren to transfuse
Transfusion f transfusion; blood transfusion (s. a. unter Bluttransfusion) ● **vor der** ~ pretransfusion
~/**fetofetale** foetofoetal transfusion
~/**fetomaternale** foetomaternal transfusion
~/**intraarterielle** intraarterial transfusion
~/**intrauterine** intrauterine transfusion
~/**intravenöse** intravenous transfusion
~/**plazentale** placental transfusion
~/**reziproke** reciprocal transfusion
Transfusions... s. a. Bluttransfusions...
Transfusionsarzt m transfusionist
Transfusionsbesteck n transfusion set, blood transfusion instruments

Transfusionshepatitis f [post]transfusion hepatitis, posttransfusion viral hepatitis
Transfusionsikterus m transfusion icterus, posttransfusion jaundice
Transfusionsmalaria f transfusion malaria
Transfusionsreaktion f transfusion reaction
Transfusionszwischenfall m transfusion emergency, [blood] transfusion accident
Transillumination f transillumination
transilluminierbar transilluminable
transitorisch transient, transitional, transitory
Transkortin n transcortin *(Serumglobulin)*
Transkription f transcription *(genetischer Informationen)*
Translation f translation *(genetischer Informationen)*
Translokation f translocation *(z. B. von Chromosomen)*
transluzent translucent, translucid
Transmigration f transmigration
Transmission f s. Übertragung
Transmittersubstanz f transmitter substance *(z. B. für Nervenimpulse)*
transmural transmural *(z. B. Herzinfarkt)*
transparent transparent; translucent; pellucid
Transphosphorylase f transphosphorylase *(Enzym)*
Transphosphorylation f transphosphorylation
Transpiration f transpiration, sweating, [sensible] perspiration
~/pulmonale pulmonary transpiration
transpirierbar transpirable
transpirieren to transpire, to sweat, to perspire
Transplantat n transplant, graft
~/artfremdes s. ~/heterologes
~/artgleiches s. ~/homologes
~/heterologes heterotransplant, heterograft, heterologous graft, xenograft
~/homologes homotransplant, homograft, homologous graft
~/körpereigenes autograft, autogenous graft, autoplast
~/Reverdinsches Reverdin (pinch) graft
Transplantatabstoßung f transplant (graft) rejection
Transplantatempfänger m transplant patient, graft recipient, host
Transplantat-gegen-Empfänger-Reaktion f graft-versus-host disease (reaction)
Transplantation f transplantation, grafting, transplant operation; implantation
~ artfremden Gewebes s. ~/heterologe
~ artgleichen Gewebes s. ~/homologe
~/heterologe heterotransplantation, heteroplastic transplantation, heteroplasty
~/homologe hom[e]otransplantation, hom[e]oplastic transplantation, homoplasty
~ körpereigenen Gewebes autotransplantation, autoplasty
~/orthotope orthotopic (homoiotopic) transplantation
Transplantationsantigen n transplantation antigen

Transplantationsgewebe n/**artgleiches** homotransplant
~/körpereigenes autograft, autogenous graft, autoplast
Transplantationsgruppe f transplant team
Transplantationslunge f transplant lung
Transplantationsmetastase f transplantation metastasis
Transplantationsoperation f s. Transplantation
Transplantationspatient m transplant patient
Transplantatspender m transplant donor
Transplantatverwerfungszelle f graft rejection cell
transplantieren to transplant, to graft
transplantiert/erbgleich syngenesioplastic
transplazental transplacental
transponieren to transpose *(z. B. Gewebe)*
Transport m/**passiver** passive transport
Transportmedium n transport medium *(z. B. für Bakterien)*
Transportsubstanz f carrier, excipient *(für Arzneistoffe)*
Transposio f **viscerum** transposition of the viscera
Transposition f transposition
~ der Aorta transposition of the aorta
~ der großen Arterien (Gefäße) transposition of the great arteries (vessels), TGA
~ der Pulmonalarterie transposition of the pulmonary artery
Transrektalschnitt m rectus incision
~/oberer rechter upper right rectus-splitting incision
Transsakralblock m transsacral block
Transsexualismus m transsexualism; transves[ti]tism
Transsexueller m transsexual; transvestite
Transsudat n transudate
Transsudation f transudation
transsudieren to transudate
Transthermie f short-wave diathermy, electrothermy
transvers transverse, transversal
Transversektomie f transversectomy
Transversostomie f transversostomy
Transversotomie f transversotomy
Transvestismus m transves[ti]tism, transsexualism
Transvestit m transvestite, transsexual
Trapezband n trapezoid ligament
trapezförmig trapeziform, trapezoid
Trapezium n trapezium [bone]
Trapezkörper m trapezoid body
Trapezmuskel m trapezius [muscle] ● **unter dem ~** subtrapezial
trapezoid s. trapezförmig
Trapezoideum n trapezoid [bone]
traubenförmig racemose, acinose, staphyline *(z. B. Drüsen)*
Traubenhaut f s. Uvea
Traubenhautentzündung f s. Uveitis
Traubenmole f hydatid (cystic) mole, hydati[di]form mole; dropsical ovum

Traubenpilzkrankheit

Traubenpilzkrankheit f botryomycosis
Traubenzucker m glucose, glycose, dextrose
träufeln to drip, to dribble
Traum m dream
Trauma n trauma, injury; casualty ● **durch ~ bewirkt** traumatic
~/akustisches acoustic (auditory) trauma
~/psychisches psychic trauma, psychotrauma
~/renales renal injury
~/seelisches s. ~/psychisches
~/stumpfes blunt trauma, closed injury
Traumanalyse f oneiroscopy
traumartig dream-like, oneiric
Traumatherapie f trauma[to]therapy
traumatisch traumatic
traumatisieren to traumatize, to injure
traumatisierend/nicht atraumatic
Traumatisierung f traumatism, traumatosis
traumatogen traumatogenic
Traumatologe m traumatologist, fracture surgeon
Traumatologie f traumatology
traumatologisch traumatologic
Traumatopathie f traumatopathy
Traumatopnoe f traumatopnoea
Traumbild n vision, illusion
träumen to dream
träumend dreaming, somniative
traumhaft oneiric
Traumlehre f oneirology
Traumschmerz m hypnalgia
Traumzustand m dream state, oneirism
~/hypnotischer somnolism
traurig melancholic, sorrowful, sad
Traurigkeit f melancholia, sadness, depression, lypemania, dejection, depressive insanity *(psychische Störung)*
Trematode f trematode
Trematodeninfektion f trematodiasis
Tremogramm n tremogram
Tremograph m tremograph
tremolabil tremolabile
Tremophobie f tremophobia *(krankhafte Angst vor Tremor)*
Tremor m tremor, trembling
~/feinschlägiger fine tremor
~/grobschlägiger flapping tremor
~/intermittierender intermittent tremor
~/kinetischer kinetic tremor
~ mercurialis mercurial tremor *(Vergiftungssymptom)*
~ metallicus metallic tremor
~ potatorum tremor of drinkers
~/seniler senile tremor
Tremorschreiber m tremograph
tremostabil tremostable
trennen 1. to separate; to segregate, to isolate; 2. to divide; to split
~/im Gelenk to disarticulate
Trennung f separation; segregation, isolation *(Absonderung)*; sejunction *(von Assoziationsprozessen)*

Trennwand f diaphragm *(z. B. bei der Dialyse)*
Trepan m trepan, trephine, craniotome
Trepanation f trepanation, trephination
~/Elliotsche Elliot's operation
Trepanationsfräser m s. Trepan
Trepanationsloch n trepanation hole (opening), burr hole
trepanieren to trepan[ize], to trephine
Trepidation f 1. trepidatio[n], state of agitation; 2. trepidation, trembling
Treponema n treponema, spiroch[a]ete *(s. a. unter Spirochaeta)*
~ americanum (carateum) Treponema americanum (carateum, pintae) *(Erreger der Pinta)*
~ pallidum Treponema pallidum *(Erreger der Syphilis)*
~ pertenue Treponema pertenue *(Erreger der Frambösie)*
treponemal treponemal, spirochaetal
Treponema-pallidum-Antikörper m Treponema pallidum antibody
Treponema-pallidum-Hämagglutinationstest m Treponema pallidum haemagglutination test
Treponema-pallidum-Immobilisierungstest m Treponema pallidum immobilization test, TPI [test]
Treponema-pallidum-Komplementbindungsreaktion f Treponema pallidum complement fixation test
Treponemaspezialist m treponematologist
Treponematose f treponem[at]osis, treponemiasis, treponemal disease, spirochaetal infection
Treponemennachweistest m/serologischer treponemal serologic test
treponementötend treponemicidal, antitreponemal, spirochaeticidal
Treppe f scala *(im Innenohr)*
Triade f s. Trias
triangular triangular, triquetrous
Trias f triad
~/Charcotsche Charcot's triad *(Nystagmus, Intentionstremor und skandierende Sprache)*
~/Hornersche Horner's [oculopupillary] syndrome
~/Hutchinsonsche Hutchinson's triad *(Keratitis parenchymatosa, Hutchinsonsche Zähne, Labyrinthschwerhörigkeit)*
~/portale portal triad
~/Whipplesche triad of Whipple *(bei Hyperinsulinismus)*
triatrial triatrial
Tribade f tribade, lesbian
Tribadie f tribadism, lesbianism, sapphism
Tribasilarsynostose f tribasilar synostosis *(vorzeitige Schädelbasisknochenverschmelzung)*
tribrachial tribrachial, tribrachius
Trichalgie f trichalgia
Trichästhesie f trich[o]aesthesia, hair sensibility
Trichatrophie f trichatrophia
Trichiasis f trichiasis
Trichine f trichina, trichinella ● **von Trichinen durchsetzt** trichinous

Trichinenbefall *m* trichinization, trichinella infestation
trichinenhaltig trichiniferous
Trichinenkrankheit *f s.* Trichinose
Trichinenlarve *f* trichina larva
Trichinophobie *f* trichinophobia *(krankhafte Angst vor Trichinen)*
trichinös trichinous
Trichinose *f* trichinosis, trichiniasis
Trichitis *f* trichitis, inflammation of the hair bulbs
Trichlorazetaldehyd *m* trichloroacetic aldehyde, chloral
Trichlorazetaldehydhydrat *n* chloral hydrate
Trichlormethan *n* trichloromethane, chloroform *(Narkotikum)*
Trichoanästhesie *f* trichoanaesthesia, lack of hair sensibility
Trichoästhesiometer *n* trichoaesthesiometer
Trichobezoar *m* trichobezoar, hair ball, pilibezoar, egagropilus *(im Magen)*
Trichocephaliasis *f s.* Trichuriasis
Trichocephalus *m* trichuris, trichocephalus, whipworm
~ **dispar (trichiuris)** Trichocephalus dispar (trichiuris)
Trichoclasia *f idiopathica s.* Trichoklasie
Trichoepitheliom *n* trichoepithelioma
Trichoglossie *f* trichoglossia; hair[y] tongue
Trichohyalin *n* trichohyalin, hyalin of the hair
trichoid trichoid, hair-like, resembling hair
Trichokardie *f* trichocardia; hairy heart
Trichoklasie *f* trichoclasia, brittleness of the hairs
Trichokryptomanie *f* trichokryptomania, trichorrhexomania
Trichokryptose *f* trichocryptosis
Tricholith *m* tricholith
Trichologie *f* trichology
Trichom[a] *n* trichoma
Trichomanie *f* tricho[tillo]mania
trichomatös trichomatose
Trichomatose *f* trichomatosis
Trichomonade *f* trichomonad
Trichomonadeninfektion *f s.* Trichomoniasis
Trichomonadenmittel *n* antitrichomonal agent
trichomonadentötend trichomona[di]cidal
Trichomonadenvaginitis *f* trichomonad vaginitis
trichomonal trichomonal
trichomonazid trichomona[di]cidal
Trichomoniasis *f* trichomoniasis, trichomonal infection
Trichomycosis *f* trichomycetosis, trichomycosis
~ **axillaris** trichomycosis axillaris, chromotrichomycosis
~ **capillitii (circinata)** ringworm of the scalp
~ **favosa** favus
Trichomyzeten *mpl* Trichomycetes
Trichomyzeteninfektion *f s.* Trichomycosis
Trichonodose *f* trichonodosis; knotting hair
Trichonokardiose *f* trichonocardiasis *(Haarerkrankung durch Nocardia tenuis)*
Trichopathie *f* trichopathy, tricho[no]sis, disease of the hair
trichopathisch trichopathic
Trichopathophobie *f* trichopathophobia *(krankhafte Angst vor Haarerkrankung)*
Trichophagie *f* trichophagia, eating of hair
Trichophobie *f* trichophobia *(krankhafte Angst vor Haaren)*
Trichophyt *m* trichophyton, trichophyte
Trichophytid *n* trichophytid
Trichophytie *f* trichophytosis
Trichophytin *n* trichophytin *(Antigen)*
Trichophytobezoar *m* trichophytobezoar *(im Magen)*
Trichophyton *n* trichophyton, trichophyte
Trichophytonexanthem *n* trichophytid
Trichophytose *f* trichophytosis
Trichopoliose *f* trichopoliosis, canities
Trichoptilosis *f* trichoptilosis, trichoschisis, splitting of the hairs
Trichorrhexis *f* trichorrhexis, brittleness of the hair
~ **nodosa** trichonodosis; knotting hair
Trichorrhexomanie *f* trichorrhexomania, trichokryptomania
Trichosis *f s.* Trichopathie
Trichosporie *f s.* Trichosporose
Trichosporose *f* trichosporosis, Beigel's disease, piedra *(tropisches Haarpilzleiden)*
Trichostrongyliasis *f* trichostrongylosis
Trichotillomanie *f* tricho[tillo]mania
Trichotrophie *f* trichotrophy, nutrition of the hair
Trichozephalose *f s.* Trichuriasis
Trichozephalus *m s.* Trichuris
Trichroismus *m* trichroism, trichromatism *(z. B. von Kristallen)*
trichromat trichromatic, trichro[m]ic
Trichromat[er] *m* trichromat[e]
Trichromatopsie *f* trichromatopsia, trichromatism
Trichter *m* 1. funnel; 2. *s.* Infundibulum
Trichterafter *m* infundibuliform anus
Trichterbrust *f* funnel (cobber's) chest; koilosternia
trichterförmig 1. funnel-shaped; 2. infundibular, infundibuliform
Trichterstethoskop *n* bell type stethoscope
Trichuriasis *f* trichuriasis, trichocephaliasis, trichocephalosis
Trichuris *f* trichuris, trichocephalus, whipworm
tridaktyl tridactyl
Trieb *m* 1. instinct; 2. impulse; 3. mania
triebartig instinctive; impulsive
triebgestört erotopathic
triebhaft instinctive, impulsive; libidinal
Triebhandlung *f/***isolierte** monomania, monopsychosis
triebmäßig [bedingt] instinctive; psychomotor
Triefauge *n* blear eye; lippitude, lippitudo
triefäugig blear-eyed
Trifokalbrille *f* trifocal spectacles
Trifokallinse *f* trifocal lens
Trifurkation *f* trifurcation
Trigeminie *f* trigeminy

Trigeminus

Trigeminus *m* trigeminus, trigeminal nerve; 2. trigeminus, trigeminal pulse
Trigeminusdenervierung *f* trigeminal denervation
Trigeminusganglion *n* trigeminal ganglion
Trigeminuskern *m* trigeminal nucleus
Trigeminuslähmung *f* trigeminal paralysis
Trigeminusmesser *n* trigeminal knife
Trigeminusnervenausschaltung *f f* trigeminal denervation
Trigeminusneuralgie *f* trigeminal (facial) neuralgia, trifacial neuralgic syndrome, prosop[oneur]algia, prosopodynia
Trigeminusrhythmus *m* trigeminy
Triglyzerid *n* triglyceride *(Fettstoffwechsel)*
Triglyzerid[spiegel]erhöhung *f* im Blut hypertriglyceridaemia
Trigonitis *f* trigonitis
trigonozephal trigonocephalous
Trigonozephalie *f* trigonocephalia
Trigonozephalus *m* trigonocephalus
Trigonum *n* trigone, trigonum, triangle *(s. a. unter Dreieck)*
~ **caroticum** carotid triangle
~ **caroticum inferius** inferior carotid triangle, triangle of necessity
~ **caroticum superius** superior carotid triangle, triangle of election
~ **collaterale** collateral trigone
~ **deltoideopectorale** deltopectoral groove
~ **femorale** femoral (Scarpa's) triangle
~ **fibrosum cordis** fibrous trigone of the heart
~ **fibrosum cordis dextrum** right fibrous trigone of the heart
~ **fibrosum cordis sinistrum** left fibrous trigone of the heart
~ **habenulae** habenular trigone
~ **iliofemorale** iliofemoral (Bryant's) triangle
~ **inguinale** inguinal triangle (trigone), triangular area of Hesselbach
~ **lumbale [Petiti]** lumbar (Petit's) triangle
~ **lumbocostale** lumbocostal (vertebrocostal) triangle, foramen of Bochdalek, Bochdalek's foramen
~ **nervi hypoglossi** hypoglossal trigone
~ **olfactorium** olfactory trigone
~ **omoclaviculare** omoclavicular trigonum
~ **submandibulare** submandibular triangle
~ **urogenitale** urogenital triangle
~ **vesicae [Lientaudi]** vesical trigone, bladder (Lientaud's) triangle, trigone of the [urinary] bladder
Trijodmethan *n* triiodomethane, iodoform *(Wundantiseptikum)*
Trijodthyronin *n* triiodothyronine *(Schilddrüsenhormon)*
Trijodthyronin[spiegel]verminderung *f* im Blut hypotriiodothyroninaemia
Trikarboxylsäurezyklus *m* tricarboxylic-acid cycle
Trikorie *f* triplocoria
Trikotschlauch *m* stockinet

trikrot tricrotic *(Puls)*
Trikrotie *f* tricrotism *(Puls)*
Trikuspidalatresie *f* tricuspid [valve] atresia, atresia of the tricuspid orifice
Trikuspidalgeräusch *n* tricuspid murmur
Trikuspidalinsuffizienz *f* tricuspid insufficiency (regurgitation)
Trikuspidalis *f s.* Trikuspidalklappe
Trikuspidalklappe *f* tricuspid [valve], right atrioventricular valve
~/**reitende** straddling tricuspid valve *(bei Transposition der großen Arterien)*
Trikuspidalklappenerkrankung *f* tricuspid valvular disease
Trikuspidalklappensegel *n s.* Trikuspidalsegel
Trikuspidalklappenverschluß *m/angeborener* tricuspid atresia
Trikuspidalsegel *n* tricuspid leaflet
~/**hinteres** posterior tricuspid leaflet, posterior cusp of the right atrioventricular valve
~/**vorderes** anterior tricuspid leaflet, anterior cusp of the right atrioventricular valve
Trikuspidalsegelspalte *f* cleft tricuspid
Trikuspidalstenose *f* tricuspid stenosis
trilaminar trilaminar
trilobulär trilobate, trilobular
Trilogie *f* trilogy, triad
~/**Fallotsche** trilogy of Fallot *(Herzfehler mit Vorhofseptumdefekt, Rechtsherzhypertrophie und Pulmonalstenose)*
trimalleolar trimalleolar
Trimenon *n*, **Trimester** *n* trimenon, trimester *(z. B. der Schwangerschaft)*
trimorph trimorphic, trimorphous
trinken/an der Brust to suck the breast
Trinker *m* potator, alcoholic, alcohol addict, drunkard
Trinkerheilanstalt *f* inebriates' home
Trinkernase *f* toper's nose
Trinksucht *f* hydromania
Trinkwasserfluoridierung *f* fluoridation of the drinking water
Trinkwasserverunreinigung *f* contamination of the drinking water
triorchid triorchid, having three testes
Triorchid[er] *m* triorchid
Triorchidie *f* triorchi[di]sm
Tripara *f* tripara
Tripelniere *f* triple kidney
Tripelphosphatkristalle *mpl* triple phosphate crystals
Tripelureter *m* triple ureter
Tripeptid *n* tripeptid[e]
Triphalangismus *m* triphalangism, triphalangy
Triphosphopyridinnukleotid *n* triphosphopyridine nucleotide, TPN
Triplegie *f* triplegia
Triple-Vakzine *f* triple vaccine
triploblastisch triploblastic
triploid triploid *(Chromosomensatz)*
Triplokorie *f* triplocoria
Triplopie *f* triplopia

Trippelgang *m* festinating gait, festination *(z. B. bei Parkinsonismus)*
Tripper *m* gonorrhoea, clap, neisserosis *(Infektion durch Neisseria gonorrhoeae)*
Tripperfaden *m* gonorrhoeal thread
Trippergelenkentzündung *f* urethral synovitis
Triprosopie *f* triprosopia
Tripus *m* tripus, tripod
Triquetrum *n* triquetrum
triradiär triradial, triradiate
Trisa[c]charid *n* trisaccharide
Trismus *m* trismus, lockjaw
trisom trisomic *(Chromosomen)*
Trisomer *m* trisomic
Trisomie *f* trisomy
~ **13** trisomy 13 [syndrome], D trisomy, Pateau's syndrome
~ **18** trisomy 18 [syndrome], Edward's syndrome
~ **21** trisomy 21 [syndrome], Down's syndrome, Mongolian (mongoloid) idiocy, mongolism
Tristeza *f s.* Texasfieber
Tristichiasis *f* tristichia[sis]
Tritanomalie *f* tritanomaly
Tritanoper *m* tritanope
Tritanop[s]ie *f* tritanop[s]ia, blue[-yellow] blindness
Trituration *f* trituration, tripsis
Trizephalus *m* tricephalus *(Mißgeburt)*
Trizeps *m* triceps [muscle], tricipital muscle
Trizeps[sehnen]reflex *m* triceps jerk (reflex), elbow reflex
t-RNS *f s.* Transfer-Ribonukleinsäure
Trochanter *m* trochanter ● **unter dem** ~ subtrochanteric
~ **major** trochanter major, greater tuberosity (trochanter) of the femur
~ **minor** trochanter minor, lesser tuberosity (trochanter) of the femur, trochantin
Trochantergrube *f* trochanteric fossa
trochanterisch trochanteric
Trochiscus *m* trochiscus, troche
Trochlea *f* trochlea *(Anatomie)* ● **über der** ~ supratrochlear ● **unter der** ~ subtrochlear
~ **humeri** trochlea of the humerus
~ **musculi obliqui [oculi] superioris** trochlea of the superior oblique muscle of the eye
~ **peronealis** peroneal trochlea (tubercle) of the calcaneus
~ **tali** trochlea of the astragalus
trochleaförmig trochlear[iform], trochoid
Trochleariskern *m* trochlear nucleus
Trochoginglymus *m* trochoginglymus
trochoid trochoid
trochozephal trochocephalic
Trochozephalie *f* trochocephalia
Trochozephalus *m* trochocephalus
trocken 1. dry, xerotic *(z. B. die Haut)*; 2. unproductive *(Husten)*
Trockeneis *n* dry ice, carbon dioxide snow
trockengefroren freeze-dried *(z. B. Gewebe)*
Trockengewicht *n* dry weight *(z. B. von Gewebe)*
Trockenimpfstoff *m* dried vaccine

Trockenplasma *n* dried human plasma
Trockenspirometer *n* dry spirometer
trocknen to dry; to desiccate; to dehydrate
Trocknung *f* drying; desiccation; dehydration
~/**lyophile** lyophilization
Troikart *m s.* Trepan
Troissier-Hanot-Chauffard-Syndrom *n* Troissier's syndrome, diabetic cachexia with bronzed skin; bronze diabetes
Trokar *m s.* Trepan
Trombicula *f* **akamushi** Trombicula akamushi *(Überträger der Tsutsugamushikrankheit)*
~ **irritans** Trombicula irritans, harvest mite (bug)
Trombikulabefall *m* trombiculiasis, trombiculosis, trombidiosis, chigger infestation
Trommelbauch *m* pot-belly, aerenterectasia; meteorism
Trommelfell *n* eardrum, drum [membrane], drumhead, tympanic membrane, tympanum, myrinx ● **durch das** ~ transtympanic
trommelfellbildend tympanoplastic
Trommelfellblutung *f* haemotympanum
Trommelfellentfernung *f[/operative]* tympanectomy, excision of the tympanic membrane, myring[od]ectomy
Trommelfellentzündung *f s.* Tympanitis
Trommelfellepidermis *f* drumhead epidermis
Trommelfellhomotransplantat *n* tympanic membrane homograft
Trommelfellparazentese *f* paracentesis (puncture) of the eardrum, tympanotomy, myringotomy
Trommelfellperforation *f* [ear]drum perforation, tympanic [membrane] perforation
Trommelfellpilzinfektion *f* myringomycosis
Trommelfellreflex *m* cone of light, Politzer's cone
trommelfellrekonstruierend tympanoplastic
Trommelfellrekonstruktion *f[/plastische]* tympanoplasty, myringoplasty
Trommelfellring *m* tympanic ring
Trommelfellspanner *m* tensor tympani [muscle], tensor muscle of the drum, salpingomalleus [muscle]
Trommelfellspannersehne *f* tensor tympani tendon
Trommelfellspiegel *m* myringoscope
Trommelfellspiegelung *f* myringoscopy
Trommelfelltasche *f* recess of the tympanic cavity
Trommelfellzentrum *n* umbo of the tympanic membrane
Trommelschlegelfinger *m* clubbed (drumstick) finger; acropachy
Trommelschlegelfingerbildung *f* clubbing of digits, finger (digital) clubbing, [hypertrophic] pulmonary osteoarthropathy *(z. B. bei Herzfehlern)*
Trommelsucht *f* tympania, tympanism, tympanites, tympanosis, meteorism
Trommlerlähmung *f* drummer's palsy (paralysis)
Tromomanie *f* tromomania, delirium tremens

Tropakokain *n* tropacocaine *(Alkaloid)*
Tropenabszeß *m* tropical abscess
Tropenanämie *f*/**makrozytäre** tropical macrocytic (megaloblastic, megalocytic) anaemia
Tropenfieber *n* tropical fever, pernicious (malignant tertian) malaria
Tropengeschwür *n* tropical ulcer, tropical [sloughing] phagedaena
Tropenkoller *m* tropical frenzy
Tropenkrankheit *f* tropical disease
Tropenmedizin *f* tropical medicine
Tropenpemphigus *m* tropical pemphigus
Tropenruhr *f* tropical (amoebic) dysentery, amoebiasis, loeschiasis *(durch Entamoeba histolytica)*
Tropf *m* s. Tropfinfusion
Tröpfcheninfektion *f* droplet (airborne) infection
tropfen to drop, to drib[ble]; to tear *(Tränen)*
Tropfen *m* drop, gutta
~/dicker thick blood film *(beim Blutausstrich)*
~/hängender hanging drop *(zur Bakterienlebendbeobachtung)*
tropfenförmig drop-shaped, guttiform, guttate
Tropfenherz *n* drop (pendulous, hanging) heart
Tropfenzähler *m* stalagmometer
Tropfflasche *f* dropping bottle, dropper *(für Medikamente)*
Tropfinfusion *f* [intravenous] drip, drip infusion, phleboclysis
Tropfkammer *f* drip chamber *(des Infusionssystems)*
Tropfmetastase *f* drop metastasis
Tropfpipette *f* dropper pipet
trophisch trophic
Trophismus *m* 1. trophism; nutrition *(s. a. Ernährung)*; 2. trophism, trophicity
Trophoblast *m* trophoblast, trophoderm
trophoblastisch trophoblastic
Trophödem *n* trophoedema
Trophoderm *n* 1. trophoderm, ectoplacenta, placental trophoblast; 2. s. Trophoblast
Trophodermatoneurose *f* trophodermatoneurosis
Trophodynamik *f* trophodynamics
Trophologie *f* trophology
Trophoneurose *f* trophoneurosis *(Ernährungsstörung des Gewebes nach Nervenschädigung)*
trophoneurotisch trophoneurotic
Trophonukleus *m* trophonucleus, trophic nucleus
Trophopathie *f* trophopathy, trophonosis
Trophoplasma *n* trophoplasm
Trophospongium *n* trophospongium, Golgi apparatus (body, substance), Golgi complex (membrane, network)
Trophotherapie *f* trophotherapy
Trophozoit *m* trophozoite *(Malariaparasitenstadium)*
Trophozyt *m* trophocyte
Tropikaanfall *m* quotidian ague *(24-Stunden-Intervall des Malariafiebers)*
Tropin *n* tropin *(Atropinspaltprodukt)*

Tropismus *m* tropism, taxis *(von Zellen)*
Tropokollagen *n* tropocollagen *(Kollagenfaserbestandteil)*
Tropomyosin *n* tropomyosin *(Muskeleiweiß)*
Trotzreaktion *f* negativism, act (reaction) of defiance
trübe cloudy, turbid, opaque; clouded ● **~ werden** to go cloudy, to cloud, to opacify
Trübsinn *m* melancholia, dejection, lypemania
trübsinnig melancholic
Trübung *f* 1. clouding, opacification; 2. cloudiness, shadow *(z. B. auf Röntgenbildern)*; turbidity *(z. B. von Flüssigkeiten)*; opacity, opaqueness, dullness *(z. B. des Auges)*
~/Berlinsche Berlin's disease *(partiell oder total)*
~/pulmonale pulmonary opacification *(Röntgenologie)*
Trübungsmesser *m* turbidimeter, nephelometer
Trübungsmessung *f* turbidimetry, nephelometry
Trübungsreaktion *f* flocculation reaction
~/Meinickesche Meinicke's test *(zum serologischen Syphilisnachweis)*
Trübungstest *m* turbidity test
Trugbild *n* phantasm, phantom, vision; illusion, hallucination
Trugschluß *m* paralogism, erroneous conclusion, fallacy
Trümmerfraktur *f* comminuted (multiple) fracture
Truncus *m* trunk, truncus
~ arteriosus arterial trunk
~ arteriosus communis common arterial trunk; aorticopulmonary septal defect
~ brachiocephalicus brachiocephalic trunk, innominate artery, anonyma
~ bronchomediastinalis bronchomediastinal trunk
~ cerebri brain stem (axis)
~ coeliacus coeliac artery (axis, trunk)
~ corporis callosi trunk of the corpus callosi
~ costocervicalis costocervical trunk
~ inferior plexus brachialis inferior trunk of the brachial plexus
~ intestinalis intestinal trunk
~ jugularis jugular trunk
~ lumbalis lumbar trunk
~ lumbosacralis lumbosacral trunk
~ pulmonalis main pulmonary artery (trunk)
~ pulmonalis communis common pulmonary trunk
~ subclavius subclavian trunk
~ superior plexus brachialis superior trunk of the brachial plexus
~ sympathicus sympathetic [nerve] trunk
~ thyreocervicalis thyrocervical trunk
~ vagalis anterior anterior vagal trunk
~ vagalis posterior posterior vagal trunk
Truncus-coeliacus-Kompression *f* coeliac artery compression
Truncus-coeliacus-Kompressionssyndrom *n* coeliac artery compression syndrome
Truncus-coeliacus-Obstruktion *f* coeliac artery obstruction (occlusion)

trunkal truncal
Trunkenheit f drunkenness
Trunksucht f potomania, alcoholophilia
~/chronische alcoholism, inebriety
~/periodische dipsomania, posiomania
trunksüchtig dipsomaniac, intemperate
Trunksüchtiger m dipsomaniac, alcoholic, intemperate
trunkulär truncal
Trunkus m s. Truncus
Trypanblau n trypan blue *(trypanozider Farbstoff)*
Trypanolyse f trypanolysis, destruction of trypanosomes
Trypanolysin n trypanolysin
trypanolytisch trypanolytic
Trypanosoma n trypanosome *(geißeltragender Endoparasit)*
~ **brucei** Trypanosoma brucei *(Erreger der Naganaseuche)*
~ **cruzi** Trypanosoma cruzi *(Erreger der Chagaskrankheit)*
~ **gambiense** Trypanosoma gambiense *(Erreger der westafrikanischen Schlafkrankheit)*
~ **rhodesiense** Trypanosoma rhodesiense *(Erreger der ostafrikanischen Schlafkrankheit)*
Trypanosoma-gambiense-Infektion f s. Trypanosomiasis/westafrikanische
trypanosomal trypanosomal, trypanosomic
trypanosomalozid s. trypanosomenabtötend
trypanosomatotrop trypanosomatotropic
trypanosomenabtötend trypano[soma]cidal, antitrypanosomal
trypanosomenanziehend trypanosomatotropic
trypanosomenauflösend s. trypanolytisch
Trypanosomenerkrankung f s. Trypanosomiasis
Trypanosomenfieber n trypanosome fever
Trypanosomenmeningitis f trypanosome meningitis
Trypanosomenmittel n trypanocide [agent], antitrypanosomal [agent]
Trypanosomenschanker m trypanosomal chancre
Trypanosomenzerstörung f s. Trypanolyse
Trypanosomiasis f trypanosomiasis, trypanosom[at]osis, trypanosome fever, sleeping sickness
~/afrikanische African trypanosomiasis (sleeping sickness)
~/ostafrikanische Rhodesian trypanosomiasis, East African sleeping sickness
~/südamerikanische [South] American trypanosomiasis, Brazilian trypanosomiasis, barbeiro fever, Chagas' (Cruz') disease
~/westafrikanische West African trypanosomiasis (sleeping sickness)
Trypanosomiasisstadium n/**meningo-enzephalitisches** African meningitis *(Terminalstadium der Schlafkrankheit)*
Trypanosomid n trypanosomid *(Hautausschlag bei Trypanosomeninfektion)*
trypanozid trypano[soma]cidal, antitrypanosomal
Trypsin n trypsin, tryptase

trypsinartig trypsin-like
Trypsininhibitor m trypsin inhibitor, antitrypsin, antitryptase
Trypsinogen n trypsinogen *(Trypsinvorstufe)*
tryptisch tryptic
tryptolytisch tryptolytic
Tryptophan n tryptophan *(essentielle Aminosäure)*
Tryptophanämie f tryptophanaemia
Tryptophanase f tryptophanase *(Enzym)*
Tryptophanausscheidung f im Urin tryptophanuria
T-Schleife f T loop *(bei der Vektorkardiographie)*
Tsetsefliege f tsetse [fly] *(Überträger der Schlafkrankheit und der Naganaseuche)*
TSH s. Hormon/thyreotropes
Tsutsugamushikrankheit f tsutsugamushi disease (fever), tropical (rural, mite-borne) typhus, Malayan [scrub] typhus, Queensland coastal fever
T-Test m nach Student Student's t test *(Statistik)*
Tuba f s. 1. ~ auditiva; 2. ~ uteri
~ **auditiva** Eustachian (otopharyngeal) tube, tuba, [oto]salpinx, auditory (pharyngotympanic) tube
~ **auditiva Eustachii (pharyngo-tympanica)** s. ~ auditiva
~ **Falloppii** s. ~ uteri
~ **pharyngotympanica** s. ~ auditiva
~ **uteri** uterine (Fallopian) tube, tuba, oviduct, salpinx
~ **uterina [Falloppii]** s. ~ uteri
Tubakurarin n s. Tubokurare
Tubargravidität f s. Eileiterschwangerschaft
Tubbs-Dilatator m Tubbs dilator, dilator for mitral valve
Tube f s. 1. Tuba auditiva; 2. Tuba uteri
Tubektomie f tubectomy, salpingectomy, excision of a uterine tube
Tuben... s. a. 1. Eileiter...; 2. Ohrtrompeten...
Tubenbruch m salpingocele
Tubendermoid n tubal dermoid
Tubendivertikel n Eustachian diverticulum
Tubendurchblasung f tubal insufflation, perflation, pertubation
Tubendurchgängigkeit f tubal patency
Tubendurchgängigkeitsprobe f tubal patency testing
Tubenenge f isthmus of the auditory (Eustachian) tube *(Grenze von knöchernem und knorpeligem Teil der Ohrtrompete)*
Tubenfunktionsstörung f Eustachian tube dysfunction
Tubenhämatom n haemosalpinx; haemorrhagic salpingitis
Tubeninsufflation f tubal insufflation
Tubenisthmus m isthmus of the Fallopian (uterine) tube
Tubenkatarrh m 1. Eustachian salpingitis, syringitis, eustachitis; 2. s. Salpingitis 1.
Tubenkatheter m Eustachian catheter

Tubenkatheterismus

Tubenkatheterismus *m* salpingocatheterism
Tubenkoagulation *f* uterine tube coagulation
Tubenligatur *f* tubal (uterine tube) ligation
Tubenmandel *f* tubal (Eustachian) tonsil
Tubenmotilität *f* uterine tube motility
Tubenmukosa *f* uterine tube mucosa, mucous membrane of the uterine tube, endosalpinx
Tubenokklusion *f* uterine tube occlusion, tubal block
Tubenreimplantation *f* uterine tube reimplantation
Tubenruptur *f* tubal (uterine tube) rupture
Tubensterilisation *f* uterine tube sterilization
Tubentonsille *f* tubal (Eustachian) tonsil
Tubentransplantation *f* uterine tube transplantation
Tubenverschluß *m* 1. uterine tube occlusion, tubal block, salpingemphraxis; 2. Eustachian tube occlusion (blockage), tubal block
Tubenwulst *m* tubal elevation, Eustachian cushion
Tuber *m* tuber; tuberosity; eminence
~ **calcanei** calcaneal tuber[osity]
~ **frontale** frontal eminence
~ **ischiadicum** ischiadic tuber, sciatic tuberosity, tuberosity of the ischium
~ **maxillae** maxillary tuber (tuberosity)
~ **parietale** parietal eminence (boss)
Tuberculosis *f s.* Tuberkulose
~ **cutis** cutaneous (skin) tuberculosis
~ **cutis luposa** lupus [vulgaris]
~ **cutis verrucosa** necrogenic verruca, postmortem (pathologist's) wart
~ **ileocaecalis** ileocaecal tuberculosis
~ **intestinalis** intestinal tuberculosis
~ **laryngis** laryngeal tuberculosis
Tuberculum *n* tubercle, tuberculum *(1. kleiner Knochenvorsprung; 2. Tuberkuloseknötchen)*
~ **acusticum** acoustic tubercle
~ **adductorium** adductor tubercle
~ **anterius thalami** frontal extremity of the thalamus
~ **anterius vertebrarum cervicalium** anterior tubercle of the cervical vertebrae
~ **articulare ossis temporalis** articular eminence (tubercle of the temporal bone)
~ **caroticum [/Chassaignacsches]** carotid (Chassaignac's) tubercle
~ **caudatum** caudate lobe [of the liver]
~ **conoideum** conoid tubercle
~ **corniculatum** corniculate tubercle
~ **coronae dentis** dental tubercle, cusp of a tooth
~ **costae** costal tubercle
~ **cuneiforme** cuneiform tubercle
~ **epiglotticum** epiglottic tubercle
~ **genitale** genital tubercle
~ **ilicum** anterior inferior iliac spine
~ **infraglenoidale** infraglenoid tubercle (tuberosity)
~ **intercondylare laterale** lateral intercondylar tubercle [of the tibia]
~ **intercondylare mediale** medial intercondylar tubercle [of the tibia]
~ **intervenosum** intervenous tubercle
~ **jugulare [ossis occipitalis]** jugular tubercle
~ **labii superioris** labial tubercle
~ **majus humeri** greater tubercle of the humerus
~ **marginale ossis zygomatici** marginal tubercle of the zygomatic bone
~ **mentale mandibulae** mental tubercle
~ **minus humeri** lesser tubercle of the humerus
~ **musculi scaleni anterioris** scalene tubercle
~ **nuclei cuneati** cuneate tubercle
~ **obturatorium anterius** anterior obturator tubercle
~ **obturatorium posterius** posterior obturator tubercle
~ **pharyngeum** pharyngeal tubercle
~ **pubicum [ossis pubis]** pubic tubercle (spine)
~ **supraglenoidale** supraglenoid tubercle
Tuber-Gelenk-Winkel *m* tuber angle
Tuberkel *m s.* Tuberculum
~/**hirsekorngroßer** miliary tubercle
tuberkelartig tubercular, tuberculoid
Tuberkelbakterieneiweiß *n* tuberculoprotein
tuberkelbakterienhemmend tuberculostatic
tuberkelbakterientötend tuberculocidal
Tuberkelbakterium *n s.* Tuberkelbazillus
Tuberkelbazillenfärbung *f*/**Ziehl-Neelsensche** Ziehl-Neelsen stain [for tubercle bacilli], Ziehl-Neelsen staining procedure (technique)
Tuberkelbazillus *m* tubercle (Koch's) bacillus, t. b., Mycobacterium tuberculosis
Tuberkelbildung *f*, **Tuberkelentwicklung** *f* tubercul[iz]ation
tuberkelübersät tuberculated
tuberkular tubercular
Tuberkulid *n* tuberculid[e]
~/**papulonekrotisches** papulonecrotic (rosacea-like) tuberculid, folliclis; tuberculosis papulonecrotica
Tuberkulin *n* tuberculin *(zur Tuberkulosetestung)*
Tuberkulinallergie *f* tuberculin[-type] allergy
Tuberkulinantikörper *m* antituberculin
Tuberkulinapplikation *f* tuberculin[iz]ation
Tuberkulinbehandlung *f* tuberculinotherapy; tuberculination
Tuberkulindiagnostik *f* tuberculin[iz]ation
Tuberkulineinheit *f* tuberculin unit, TU
Tuberkulinhauttest *m* tuberculin skin test
tuberkulinnegativ tuberculin-negative
Tuberkulin-Pflasterprobe *f* tuberculin patch test
tuberkulinpositiv tuberculin-positive
Tuberkulinpräzipitation *f* tuberculin precipitation
Tuberkulinprobe *f* tuberculin test
~/**Mendel-Mantouxsche** Mantoux test
Tuberkulinreaktion *f* tuberculin reaction
~/**intrakutane** intradermal tuberculin reaction
Tuberkulinsofortreaktion *f* tuberculin-type sensitivity, tuberculin hypersensitivity
Tuberkulinspätreaktion *f* tuberculin-type allergy
Tuberkulinspätreaktionstyp *m* tuberculin[-type] allergy
Tuberkulinspritze *f* tuberculin syringe
Tuberkulintyp *m* tuberculin[-type] allergy

Tuberkuloderm[a] n tuberculoderm[a]
tuberkuloid tuberculoid
Tuberkulom n tuberculoma
Tuberkulomanie f tuberculomania
Tuberkulophobie f tuberculophobia *(krankhafte Angst vor Tuberkulose)*
Tuberkuloprotein n tuberculoprotein
tuberkulös tuberculous, tuberculose, consumptive, tubercular, tuberculoid
Tuberkulose f tuberculosis, TB, consumption, phthisis *(durch Mycobacterium tuberculosis) (s. a. unter Tuberculosis)*
~/**aktive** active [pulmonary] tuberculosis, open tuberculosis
~/**chronische** chronic (reinfection) tuberculosis, adult-type tuberculosis
~/**disseminierte** disseminated (acute miliary) tuberculosis
~/**extrapulmonale** extrapulmonary tuberculosis
~/**galoppierende** galloping consumption, florid phthisis
~/**generalisierte** s. ~/**disseminierte**
~/**geschlossene (inaktive)** closed (inactive pulmonary) tuberculosis, latent tuberculous disease
~/**käsige** caseous [pneumonic] tuberculosis
~/**kavernöse** cavitary [pulmonary] tuberculosis
~/**miliare** s. ~/**disseminierte**
~/**offene** s. ~/**aktive**
Tuberkulosebakterium n s. Tuberkelbazillus
Tuberkulosebehandlung f antituberculous therapy, phthisiotherapy
Tuberkulosebekämpfung f tuberculosis control
tuberkulosebewirkend tuberculigenous
Tuberkulosediathese f tuberculous diathesis
Tuberkuloseforschung f phthisiology
Tuberkulosegeschwulst f tuberculoma
Tuberkuloseheilstätte f tuberculosarium, sanatorium for the tuberculotics
tuberkulosehemmend tuberculostatic, antituberculous, antituberculotic
Tuberkuloseherd m tuberculous lesion
Tuberkuloseinfektion f tuberculous infection
Tuberkuloseknötchen n tubercle, tuberculum
Tuberkuloseknoten m tuberculoma
Tuberkulosekranker m tuberculotic, tuberculous
Tuberkuloselehre f phthisiology
Tuberkulosemorbiditätsrate f tuberculosis morbidity rate
Tuberkulosemortalitätsrate f tuberculosis mortality rate
Tuberkulosespezialist m phthisiologist
Tuberkulosetherapie f phthisiotherapy
Tuberkulosewahn m tuberculomania
Tuberkulosilikose f tuberculosilicosis
Tuberkulostatikum n tuberculostatic [agent], antituberculous drug
tuberkulostatisch tuberculostatic, antituberculous
tuberkulozid tuberculocidal
tuberös tuberous
Tuberositas f tuberosity, protuberance

~ **deltoidea** deltoid tuberosity (tubercle), deltoid ridge (crest)
~ **glutaea** glutaeal tuberosity
~ **iliaca** iliac tuberosity
~ **ossis cuboidei** tuberosity of the cuboid bone
~ **ossis navicularis** tuberosity of the navicular bone
~ **phalangis distalis** ungual tuberosity
~ **pterygoidea** pterygoid tubercle
~ **radii** radial tuberosity
~ **sacralis** sacral tuberosity
~ **tibiae** tibial tuberosity, tuberosity (condyle) of the tibia
~ **ulnae** tuberosity of the ulna
Tubokurare n, **Tubokurarin** n tubocurare, tubocurarine, tube curare *(Muskelrelaxans)*
Tuboovarialabszeß m tubo-ovarian abscess
Tuboovarialgravidität f tubo-ovarian pregnancy
Tuboovarialzyste f tubo-ovarian cyst
tubulär tubular
Tubuli mpl:
~ **lactiferi** excretory ducts of the mammary gland
~ **renales** renal tubules
~ **renales contorti** convoluted renal tubules
~ **renales recti** straight renal tubules
~ **seminiferi** seminiferous tubules
~ **seminiferi contorti** convoluted seminiferous tubules
~ **seminiferi recti** straight seminiferous tubules
tubuloalveolar tubuloalveolar
tubuloazinös tubuloacinous
tubulös tubulous
Tubulus m tubule, tubulus
Tubulusepithel n tubular epithelium
Tubulusfunktionsstörung f tubular malfunction
Tubuluskonvolut n/**proximales** proximal convoluted tubules
Tubulusnekrose f/**akute** acute tubular necrosis; lower nephron nephrosis (syndrome)
Tubulusschädigung f tubular injury (damage) *(der Niere)*
Tubulusstruktur f tubular structure
Tubus m 1. tubus, tube *(Anatomie)*; 2. tubus, [intubation] tube ● einen ~ einführen to intubate *(z. B. in die Luftröhre)*
~ **digestorius** digestive canal (tube, tract)
~/**intratrachealer** endotracheal tube
~/**nasaler** [nasal] airway
Tubuseinführung f intubation, tubage *(z. B. in die Luftröhre)*
~/**endotracheale** endotracheal intubation
Tubuseinführungsinstrument n intubator
Tubusentfernung f extubation
Tubushalter m holder for an endotracheal tube
Tubusmanschette f endotracheal tube cuff
Tubusstativ n tube fixation stand
Tubuszange f endotracheal tube introducing forceps
Tuch n/**steriles** sterile towel, sterilized cloth
Tuchklemme f towel (skin-holding) forceps
Tuchschlinge f [forearm] sling *(Verband)*
Tularämie f tularaemia, rabbit fever, deer-fly fever; Ohara's disease

Tularämiepneumonie

Tularämiepneumonie f tularaemic pneumonia
Tumeszenz f tumescence, tumefaction
Tumor m 1. tumour, growth, neoplasm; 2. swelling, lump ● **durch einen ~ verschlossen** obstructed by a tumour ● **zu einem ~ auswachsend** neoplastic
~/bösartiger malignant tumour
~/chromophiler chromophile tumour
~ cordis cardiac (heart) tumour
~/retroperitonealer retroperitoneal tumour
~/sanduhrförmiger hourglass tumour
~/Schlofferscher Schloffer's tumour *(nach Leistenbruchoperation)*
tumorabtötend cytostatic
tumoraffin tumouraffin
tumorartig tumourous, tumoural, tumour-like
tumorauflösend oncolytic; tumouricidal
Tumorausbreitung f**/intrakavitäre** intracavitary tumour spread
tumorbildend tumour-forming, tumourigenic, neoplastic
Tumorbildung f tumour formation, tumourigenesis, oncogenesis
Tumordiagnostik f tumour diagnosis
Tumordignität f tumour status
Tumorentfernung f**[/operative]** tumourectomy, tumour removal
Tumorfaßzange f tumour [grasping] forceps
tumorfrei tumour-free, free of tumours
Tumorgewebe n tumour tissue
Tumorgröße f tumour size (volume)
tumorhemmend cytostatic, oncostatic
Tumorinduktion f tumour induction
Tumorinfiltration f tumour infiltration
Tumorkrankheit f oncosis, tumour disease
Tumorlokalisation f tumour localization
Tumorpathologie f tumour pathology
Tumorrezidiv n tumour recurrence
Tumorsitz m tumour site
Tumorspezialist m oncologist
Tumortherapie f oncotherapy
Tumorversprengung f**/embolische** embolization of tumour emboli
Tumorwachstum n tumour growth
tumorwirksam tumouraffin
Tumorzange f tumour [grasping] forceps
Tumorzelle f tumour cell ● **Tumorzellen anziehend** oncotropic
Tumorzellenaussaat f dissemination of tumour cells
Tumorzellenvakzine f tumour cell vaccine
Tumorzerfall m oncolysis
tumorzerstörend tumouricidal, oncolytic
Tunga f penetrans Tunga penetrans
Tungiasis f tungiasis
Tunica f tunic[a]
Tunnelanämie f s. Ankylostomiasis
Tüpfel m dot, spot
Tüpfel mpl**/Maurersche** Maurer's dots *(der roten Blutkörperchen bei Malaria tropica)*
Tüpfelung f stippling
~/basophile basophilic stippling; punctate basophilia

~/Schüffnersche Schüffner's dots (stippling) *(der Erythrozyten bei Malaria)*
Tüpfelzelle f stipple cell
tupfen to sponge, to swap
Tupfer m swab, sponge, gauze pad, pledget, pack
~/mit Kochsalzlösung getränkter saline-soaked surgical sponge
Tupferhalter m sponge holder
Tupferklemme f dressing (sponge-holding) forceps
Tupfzytologie f brush cytology *(zur Zelluntersuchung)*
Turbidimeter n turbidimeter, nephelometer
Turbidimetrie f turbidimetry, nephelometry
turbidimetrisch turbidimetric
turbinal turbinal, turbinate
Turgeszenz f turgescence
Turgor m turgor, tissue tone (tension)
Türkensattel m sella turcica, pituitary fossa ● **neben dem ~** parasellar ● **über dem ~** suprasellar
Türkensattelabszeß m intrasellar abscess
Turmschädel m turricephalus, tower skull, steeple head, hypsicephalus
türmschädelig turricephalous, oxycephalous, pyrgocephalic, pyrgocephalous; hypsicephalic, hypsocephalous
Turmschädeligkeit f turricephalia, oxycephalia, pyrgocephalia; hypsicephalia
Turrizephalus m s. Turmschädel
Tussis f tussis, cough *(Zusammensetzungen s. unter Husten)*
~ convulsiva s. Keuchhusten
Tutor m cylinder cast
T-Verband m T (crucial) bandage
T-Welle f**/koronare** coronary (cove-plane) T wave
T-Wellenumkehrung f inversion of T wave *(im EKG)*
Tyloma n tyloma, callosity
Tylosis f tylosis
Tympanektomie f tympanectomy, excision of the tympanic membrane
Tympanie f tympania, tympanism, tympanites, tympanosis
tympanisch tympanous
Tympanitis f tympanitis, myringitis, inflammation of the tympanum
~/durch Pilze hervorgerufene mycomyringitis
tympanitisch tympanitic, tympanic, tympanal, resonant
Tympanodynamometrie f tympanodynamometry
tympano-eustachisch tympanoeustachian
Tympanogramm n tympanogram
Tympanomastoidektomie f tympanomastoidectomy
Tympanomastoiditis f tympanomastoiditis, inflammation of the tympanum and the mastoid cells
Tympanometrie f tympanometry
tympanometrisch tympanometric

Tympanophonie f tympanophonia, autophonia
Tympanoplastik f tympanoplasty, myringoplasty
tympanoplastisch tympanoplastic
Tympanosklerose f tympanosclerosis
tympanosklerotisch tympanosclerotic
Tympanotomie f tympanotomy, myringotomy, paracentesis (puncture) of the eardrum
Tyndallisation f tyndallization
Typhlatonie f typhlatonia, atonia of the caecum
Typhlektasie f typhlectasia, dilatation of the caecum
Typhlektomie f typhlectomy, excision of the caecum
Typhlitis f typhlitis, inflammation of the caecum
Typhloempyem n typhloempyema
Typhloenteritis f typhl[o]enteritis
Typhlokolitis f typhlocolitis
Typhlolithiasis f typhlolithiasis
Typhlologie f typhlology
Typhlomegalie f typhlomegaly, enlargement of the caecum
Typhlon n s. Zökum
Typhlopexie f typhlopexy, fixation of the caecum
Typhlophilie f typhlophilia
Typhloptosis f typhloptosis, prolapse of the caecum
Typhlorrhaphie f typhlorrhaphy, suture of the caecum
Typhlospasmus m typhlospasm, spasm of the caecum
Typhlostenose f typhlostenosis, stenosis of the caecum
Typhlostomie f typhlostomy, caecostomy, caecal colostomy
Typhlotomie f typhlotomy, caecotomy, incision into the caecum
Typhlozele f typhlocele
Typhobakterin n typhobacterin (Typhusimpfstoff)
Typhomanie f typhomania
typhös s. typhusartig
Typhus m [abdominalis] typhoid [fever], abdominal typhus, lent fever
~/**epidemischer** epidemic (classic) typhus
~ **exanthematicus** typhus [fever], petechial (exanthematous) typhus, ship (jail, prison) fever, fleckfieber, fleck (epidemic) typhus, sporadic (louse-borne) typhus
~/**mexikanischer** tabardillo, Mexican typhus
typhusartig typhoid[al], typhose, typhous, typhic
typhusauslösend typhogenic
Typhusbakterium n typhoid bacillus
Typhusdauerausscheider m [chronic] typhoid carrier
Typhusdauerausscheidung f typhoid carrier state
typhuserzeugend typhogenic
Typhusexanthem n typhoid (rose) spots
Typhusimpfstoff m typhoid vaccine
Typhusknoten m typhoid nodule
Typhuslethargie f typhomania
Typhusmilz f splenotyphoid

Typhusosteomyelitis f typhoid osteomyelitis
Typhus-Paratyphus-A-B-Vakzine f typhoid-paratyphoid A and B vaccine, T. A. B. vaccine
Typhuspleuritis f pleurotyphoid
Typhuspneumonie f typhoid pneumonia, typho-pneumonia; pneumotyphoid, pneumotyphus
Typhusroseole f typhoid roseola
Typhusschutzimpfung f typhoid vaccination
typisch typical; symptomatic, semeiotic
~/**für die Todesart** thanatognostic
typisieren to type (z. B. Nierenspender)
~/**den Zellkern** to karyotype
Tyramin n tyr[os]amine (biogenes Amin)
Tyremesis f tyremesis, vomiting of caseous matter
Tyroglyphus m **farinae** meal mite
tyroid tyroid, cheese-like
Tyroma n tyroma, caseous tumour
Tyrosamin n s. Tyramin
Tyrosin n tyrosine (Aminosäure)
Tyrosinämie f tyrosinaemia
Tyrosinase f tyrosinase, dopa oxidase, dopase (Enzym)
Tyrosinaseaktivität f tyrosinase (dopa-oxidase) activity
Tyrosinausscheidung f **im Urin** tyrosinuria
Tyrosinose f tyrosinosis (Stoffwechselkrankheit)
Tyrosinspiegelerhöhung f **im Blut** [hyper]tyrosinaemia
Tyrosis f tyrosis, caseation, cheesy (caseous) degeneration
Tysonitis f tysonitis, inflammation of Tyson's glands
T-Zacke f T wave [of the electrocardiogram], ventricular repolarization complex
T-Zacken-Veränderung f T-wave change
T-Zelle f T cell, T (thymus-dependent) lymphocyte
T-Zellen-Rosetten-Test m T-cell rosette test

U

übel nauseous; sick; bad
Übelkeit f nausea, sicchasia; sickness, malaise
● ~ **bewirkend** nauseant, nauseous
~/**morgendliche** matutinal nausea; morning sickness [of pregnancy]
übelriechend foul-smelling, malodorous; foul; putrid; pestilential
überaktiv hyperactive, overactive; hyperpragic
~/**geistig** hyperphrenic, mentally hyperactive
Überaktivität f hyperactivity, superactivity
~/**geistige** hyperphrenia, mental hyperactivity, excessive mental activity, tachyphrenia
überanstrengen to [over]strain
Überanstrengung f [over]strain (Überlastung); defatigation (Übermüdung); ponopathy (Überarbeitung)
Überbefruchtung f s. Überschwängerung
überbehaart hypertrichotic
Überbein n 1. ganglion, synovial cyst, weeping sinew; 2. s. Exostose

überbelüften

überbelüften/die Lunge to hyperventilate
Überbiß m overbite, supra[-oc]clusion
Überbrückungstransplantat n bridging graft
überdecken/mit Bauchfell to periton[eal]ize
überdeckt recessive (Erbanlagen); masked (z. B. ein Symptom)
Überdehnung f superdistension, overdistension, overstretching; overstraining; dilatation
~ **des linken Ventrikels** left ventricular dilatation
~ **des rechten Ventrikels** right ventricular dilatation
Überdehnungsemphysem n ectatic (compensatory) emphysema
überdosieren to overdose
Überdosierung f overdosage
Überdosis f overdose
Überdruckbeatmung f positive pressure breathing (respiration), hyperbaric ventilation
~**/intermittierende** intermittent positive-pressure breathing (respiration), IPPB
Überdruckkammer f hyperbaric chamber (zur Überdruckbehandlung)
Überdruckrespirator m positive pressure respirator (ventilator)
Übereinkunft f consent (Arzt–Patient)
überempfindlich hypersensitive, allergic; anaphylactic, hyperergic (gegenüber Antigenen); hyperalgetic, hyperalgesic (bei Schmerzen); [hyper]sensitive, hyperaesthetic (z. B. die Haut) ● ~ **sein gegenüber** to be hypersensitive to ● ~ **werden** to become hypersensitive (hypersusceptible)
~**/immunologisch** hypersensitive
Überempfindlichkeit f hypersensitivity, allergy; anaphylaxis, hyperergia (gegenüber Antigenen); hyperalg[es]ia (gegenüber Schmerzen); [hyper]sensitivity, hypersensibility (z. B. auf äußere Reize); hyperaesthesia, oxyaesthesia (z. B. der Haut)
~**/bakterielle** bacterial allergy
~**/erbliche** atopy
~**/immunologische** immunological hypersensitivity (hypersensitiveness)
~**/krankhafte** pathergia, pathergy (bei Allergie)
Überempfindlichkeitsreaktion f hypersensitivity reaction
überentwickelt overdeveloped, hyperplastic; hypertrophic; hypergenetic (s. a. überreif)
Überentwicklung f overdevelopment, hypergenesis, hyperplasia; hypertrophy, overgrowth (z. B. von Organen und Geweben); overmaturity (des Fetus)
~ **der Geschlechtsorgane** hypergenitalism
Überernährung f 1. overfeeding, hyperalimentation, superalimentation, hypernutrition, supernutrition, supralimentation; 2. polytrophy, hyperalimentation
Übererregbarkeit f hyperexcitability, erethism
übererregt excessive excited, hyperexcited; nervous
Übererregung f superexcitation, excessive excitement, surexcitation

Überforderungssyndrom n overwork syndrome
Überfüllung f repletion (z. B. von Organen)
Überfunktion f hyperfunction (z. B. eines Organs); hyperactivity
~ **der Leydigschen Zellen** hyperleydigism
überfüttern to overfeed
Überfütterung f s. Überernährung
Übergang m**/mukokutaner** mucocutaneous junction
Übergangsepithel n transitional epithelium
Übergangsepithelkarzinom n transitional cell carcinoma
Übergangsepithelpapillom n transitional cell papilloma
Übergangswirbel m transitional vertebra
Übergangszelle f transitional cell
Übergangszellenneoplasma n neoplasm of transitional cell type
übergeben/sich to vomit, to retch
Übergeben n s. Erbrechen
übergehen/in eine positive Stickstoffbilanz to pass into nitrogen anabolism
~**/in Fäulnis** to putrefy, to decay, to rot, to decompose
Übergewicht n overweight (z. B. körperlich); preponderance (geistig)
übergewichtig overweight
Übergießung f affusion
übergreifen to spread, to expand (z. B. eine Infektion)
Überhäutung f cutization, epidermization (z. B. einer Wunde)
überimpfbar inoculable
Überimpfbarkeit f inoculability
überimpfen to inoculate
Überkompensation f overcompensation (Psychiatrie)
überkompensieren to overcompensate
Überkorrektur f overcorrection (von Sehfehlern)
überkreuzen/sich to cross, to decussate (z. B. Hirnnerven)
Überkreuzung f 1. crossing-over; 2. criss-cross inheritance (Genetik)
überladen overloaded; pleonastic (z. B. Gewebe)
überlappen to overlap; to imbricate (z. B. eine Faszie)
Überlappung f overlapping; imbrication (Fasziennaht)
überlasten to overload; to [over]strain
Überlastung f overloading; [over]strain
überleben to survive, to outlive
~**/bis zum Erwachsenenalter** to survive to adolescence (adulthood) (z. B. Kinder mit Herzfehlern)
Überlebensaussicht f chance of survival
Überlebensmechanismus m survival mechanism
Überlebensrate f survival rate
Überlebenszahl f survival figure
Überlebenszeit f survival [time]
~**/mittlere** mean afterlifetime
Überleitung f**/atrioventrikuläre** atrioventricular conduction (des Herzens)

Überleitungsstörung f disturbed conduction *(des Herzens)*
Überleitungsstück n descending limb *(der Nierenkanälchen)*
Überleitungsverzögerung f delayed conduction
Überleitungszeit f/**atrioventrikuläre** atrioventricular conduction time, ventricular activation time
Übermüdung f overfatigue; apocamnosis *(bei Myasthenia gravis)*
Übermüdungsfraktur f stress fracture
übernähen/mit Bauchfell to periton[eal]ize
übernormal supernormal, hypernormal
Überperfusion f hyperperfusion
überpflanzen to transplant, to graft *(z. B. Gewebe)*
überpigmentiert hyperpigmented; melanodermic
Überpigmentierung f hyperpigmentation, superpigmentation, hyperchromatism, hyperchromatosis, hyperchromia; melanodermia *(der Haut)*
Überredung f persuasion *(bei Psychotherapie)*
überreif overripe, hypermature *(z. B. Katarakt)*; postmature *(Fetus)*
Überreizbarkeit f hyperexcitability, overexcitability
Überreizung f overexcitation, superexcitation, surexcitation; overexcitedness, excessive irritation
übersäuert hyperacid, superacid
überschatten to overshadow *(Radiologie)*
überschießend exuberant *(Gewebewachstum)*
Überschreibung f transcription *(genetischer Informationen)*
Überschwängerung f superfecundation, superfoetation, superimpregnation, multifoetation
überschwellig supraliminal *(Reizung)*
Übersegmentierung f hypersegmentation *(z. B. von Organen)*
Übersetzung f translation *(genetischer Informationen)*
übersichtig s. hyperop
Übersichts[röntgen]aufnahme f plain radiograph, survey roentgenogram, scout film
Übersichts[röntgen]darstellung f plain radiography, survey roentgenography
überspannt 1. eccentric *(psychisch)*; 2. s. überstreckt
überstrecken to hyperextend, to overextend, to overstretch
überstreckt hyperextended, superdistended, overstretched *(z. B. eine Sehne)*
Überstreckung f hyperextension, superextension, overextension *(z. B. eines Muskels)*
überstürzt precipitate, headlong, overhasty
übertragbar communicable, contagious; transmissible
Übertragbarkeit f contagiousness; transmissibility *(z. B. einer Infektion)*
übertragen 1. to transmit, to communicate, to mediate *(z. B. Bakterien)*; to transmit, to conduct *(z. B. Nervenreize)*; 2. to transfuse *(Blut)*; 3. to transpose *(z. B. Gewebe)*; to graft, to transplant *(z. B. Organe)*; 4. to confer *(z. B. Immunität)*
~/immunologische Spezifität to confer immunologic specificity
~ werden/auf dem Blutwege to be transmitted haematogenously
übertragen 1. transmitted; transferred; 2. transfused; 3. postmature *(Fetus)*
~/durch Blut blood-borne
~/durch den Knochen perosseous
~/durch Fliegen fly-borne
~/durch Insekten insect-borne, entomogenous
~/durch Komplement complement-mediated
~/durch Körperflüssigkeiten humoral
~/durch Luft air-borne
~/durch Lymphozyten lymphocyte-mediated
~/durch Milch milk-borne
~/durch Nahrungsmittel food-borne
~/durch Stechmücken mosquito-borne
~/durch Wasser water-borne *(z. B. Krankheiten)*
~/durch Zecken tick-borne, tick transmitted
Überträger m vector, carrier, mediator; transmitter; conductor *(gesunder Genträger)*
Überträgersubstanz f transmitter substance *(z. B. für Nervenimpulse)*
Übertragung f transmission, communication, transfer *(z. B. von Bakterien)*; transfusion *(von Blut)*; transmission, conduction *(z. B. von Nervenreizen)*; transposition *(z. B. von Gewebe)*; transplantation, grafting *(z. B. von Organen)*; transcription *(genetischer Informationen)*; transference *(psychisch)*
~/adrenerge adrenergic transmission
~/aerogene air-borne transmission
~ artfremden Gewebes heteroplasty
~ artgleichen Gewebes homoplasty
~ körpereigenen Gewebes autoplasty
~/passive passive transfer *(z. B. von Antikörpern)*
~/synaptische synaptic conduction
übertragungsfähig s. übertragbar
Übertragungsstadium n carrier state
Übertransfusion f overtransfusion
Übertreibungswahn m mythomania
übertreten to pass; to shunt *(z. B. Blut)*
überwachen to control; to monitor
Überwachung f control; observation *(z. B. von Frischoperierten)*; monitoring *(z. B. mit EKG-Gerät)*; follow-up *(ambulanter Patienten)*
~/antenatale antenatal monitoring
~/elektrokardiographische electrocardiographic monitoring
~/kardiale cardiac monitoring
~/kardiotokographische cardiotocographic monitoring
Überwachungsausrüstung f monitoring equipment
Überwachungsgerät n monitor
Überwässerung f hyperhydration, overhydration *(z. B. bei Infusionstherapie)*
Überwässerungssyndrom n overinfusion syndrome
überweisen/zum Facharzt to refer to the specialist

Überweisung

Überweisung f referral *(eines Patienten)*
überwinden/die Blut-Hirn-Schranke to penetrate the blood-brain barrier
Überzeugung f persuasion *(Psychotherapie)*
überziehen/mit einer Kruste to incrust
Überzug m coating *(z. B. von Pillen)*
Überzungenbeinregion f suprahyoid region
ubiquitär ubiquitous *(z. B. Bakterien)*
Übung f/**kreisende** circumduction exercise *(z. B. der Extremitäten)*
~/passive passive exercise
Übungsbehandlung f exercise treatment
UDPG s. Uridindiphosphatglukose
UDPG-Glykogen-Transglukosidase f glycogen synthetase *(Enzym)*
Uffelmann-Reaktion f Uffelmann's test *(zum Milchsäurenachweis)*
Uhrglasmagen m hour-glass stomach, bilocular stomach
~/physiologischer physiological hour-glass stomach
Uhrglasnagel m hour-glass nail
Ulalgie f ulalgia, pain in the gums
Ulcus n ulcer, ulcus; sore *(s. a. unter Geschwür)*
~ **ad pylorum** channel ulcer
~ **atheromatosum** atheromatous ulcer
~ **cancrosum** cancerous ulcer
~ **corneae** corneal ulcer
~ **cruris** varicose ulcer, ulcer of the leg *(Hautgeschwürbildung bei Krampfaderleiden)*
~ **duodeni** duodenal ulcer
~ **durum** hard ulcer (sore), hard (syphilitic) chancre, syphilelcos, syphilelcus
~ **exedens** s. ~ rodens
~ **marginale** marginal ulcer
~ **mercurialis** mercurial ulcer
~ **mixtum** mixed chancre *(bei gleichzeitiger Infektion mit Treponema pallidum und Haemophilus Ducreyi)*
~ **molle** soft chancre, chancroid, chancroidal ulcer
~ **penetrans** perforating ulcer
~ **pepticum** peptic ulcer
~ **rodens** rodent cancer (ulcer), phagedaena *(Basalzellenkarzinom der Haut)*
~ **rodens corneae** corneal rodent ulcer
~ **serpens [corneae]** serpiginous ulcer [of the cornea]
~ **tropicum** tropical ulcer, tropical [sloughing] phagedaena
~ **varicosum** s. ~ cruris
~ **venereum** s. 1. ~ durum; 2. ~ molle
~ **ventriculi** gastric ulcer
Ulegyrie f ulegyria *(infolge Narbenbildung)*
Ulektomie f ulectomy, gingivectomy
Ulerythema n ulerythema *(erythematöse Hauterkrankung mit Narbenbildung)*
~ **sycosiforme** ulerythema sycosiforme, keloid sycosis *(follikuläre Eiterbläschen der Wangen- und Bartgegend)*
Ulitis f s. Gingivitis
Ulkus... s. a. Geschwür...

Ulkusbehandlung f ulcer therapy
Ulkusgenese f ulcerogenesis, ulceration, formation of an ulcer
Ulkuskrater m ulcer crater
Ulkusnische f ulcer niche *(Radiologie)*
Ulkusschmerz m ulcer pain (distress)
Ullrich-Turner-Syndrom n Ullrich-Turner syndrome, [male] Turner's syndrome, gonadal dysgenesis syndrome
Ulna f s. Elle
Ulnaris m ulnar (cubital, musician's) nerve
Ulnarislähmung f ulnar nerve palsy (paralysis)
Ulnarisnerv m s. Ulnaris
Ulnariszeichen n/**Biernackisches** Biernacki's sign *(Ulnarnervenunempfindlichkeit bei Tabes)*
Ulnarückseite f posterior surface of the ulna
Ulnavorderseite f anterior surface of the ulna
Ulodermatitis f ulodermatitis, scar-forming inflammation of the skin
Uloglossitis f uloglossitis, inflammation of the gums and the tongue
Ulokarzinom n ulocarcinoma, carcinoma of the gums
Ulokaze f ulocace, ulceration of the gums
Ulonkus m uloncus, swelling of the gums
Ulorrhagie f ulorrhagia, ulorrhoea, bleeding from the gums
Ulotomie f ulotomy, incision into the gums
ultimobranchial ultimobranchial *(Embryologie)*
Ultimobranchialkörper m ultimobranchial (postbranchial) body, lateral thyroid
ultrabrachykranial ultrabrachycranial *(Schädelindex über 90,0)*
ultradolichokranial ultradolichocranial *(Schädelindex unter 64,9)*
ultradolichozephal ultradolichocephalic
Ultradünnschnitt m ultrathin section *(Histologie)*
Ultrafiltrat n ultrafiltrate
Ultrafiltration f ultrafiltration *(Dialysemethode)*
Ultramikroskop n ultramicroscope ● **mit dem ~ nicht sichtbar** amicroscopic
ultramikroskopisch ultramicroscopic[al]
Ultramikrotom n ultramicrotome *(Histologie)*
Ultraschall m ultrasound, ultrasonic sound
Ultraschallabtastung f ultrasonic scanning
Ultraschallbefund m ultrasonic findings
Ultraschallbehandlung f ultrasonic therapy
Ultraschallbestrahlung f ultrasonic irradiation
Ultraschallbild n [ultra]sonogram; ultrasonic image
Ultraschallbilddarstellung f ultrasonication, ultrasonic visualization *(z. B. von Organen)*
Ultraschallbildverfahren n ultrasonic scanning
Ultraschalldiagnostik f ultrasonic (pulse-echo) diagnosis
Ultraschall-Dopplertechnik f ultrasound Doppler technique
Ultraschallechographie f [ultra]sonography, ultrasound echography
Ultraschallecholaminographie f B-mode ultrasound [technique]
Ultraschallenzephalogramm n sonoencephalogram

Ultraschallenzephalographie f sonoencephalography
Ultraschallhypophysektomie f ultrasonic hypophysectomy
Ultraschallkardiographie f ultrasonic cardiography
Ultraschallkardiotomographie f ultrasonic cardiotomography, ultrasono-cardiotomography
Ultraschallsichtgerät n ultrasonoscope
Ultraschallsteinzertrümmerung f ultrasonic litholapaxy
Ultraschalltomographie f ultrasonic tomography
Ultraschalluntersuchung f ultrasonic examination
~ **des Auges** ophthalmosonometry
Ultraschallvernebler m ultrasonic nebulizer (atomizer)
Ultraschallwelle f ultrasonic wave
Ultrasonoskop n ultrasonoscope
ultrasteril ultrasterile
Ultrastruktur f ultrastructure, fine structure
Ultraviolettbestrahlung f ultraviolet irradiation
Ultraviolettstrahler m ultraviolet lamp
Ultraviolettstrahlung f ultraviolet radiation
Ultravirus n ultravirus *(sehr kleines Virus)*
ultravisibel ultravisible
ultrazytochemisch ultracytochemical
Ulzeration f ulceration, formation of an ulcer, ulcerogenesis
ulzerativ ulcerative, ulcerous, ulcerated
ulzerieren to ulcerate
ulzerierend ulcerative
ulzerogen ulcerogenic
ulzeroglandulär ulceroglandular
ulzerogranulomatös ulcerogranulomatous
ulzeromembranös ulceromembranous
ulzerös ulcerous, ulcerative; helcoid
Umbauzonen fpl/**Loosersche** Looser's [transformation] zones *(Knochenbereiche mit Auflockerung des kristalloiden Systems)*
umbilden to transform, to metamorphose
~/**sich zu Knorpel** to chondrify
Umbilektomie f umbilectomy, excision of the umbilicus (navel), omphalectomy
umbilikal umbilical, omphalic
Umbilikal... s. a. Nabel...
Umbilikalgeräusch n umbilical souffle
Umbilikalhernie f s. Nabelbruch
Umbilikalkreislauf m umbilical circulation, allantoic (chorionic) circulation
Umbilikalregion f umbilical region
Umbilikalvesikel f umbilical vesicle
Umbilikalzyste f umbilical cyst
Umbilikus m s. Nabel
Umbo m 1. umbo, boss, bosselation; 2. umbo, central convex eminence
~ **membranae tympani** umbo of the tympanic membrane
Umfang m/**okzipitofrontaler** occipitofrontal circumference, OFC
Umformung f transformation *(z. B. von Gewebe)*

umgebend:
~/**das Knochenmark** perimedullary
~/**das Rückenmark** perimedullary
~/**den Brustkorb** perithoracic
~/**den Knorpel** perichondr[i]al
~/**den Scheideneingang** perivulvar
~/**den Uterus** periuterine
~/**die Eingeweide** perivisceral
~/**die Harnblase** perivesical
~/**die Uvula** periuvular
~/**ein Samenkanälchen** perivesicular
~/**eine Herzkammer** periventricular
~/**eine Hirnkammer** periventricular
~/**einen Wirbel** perivertebral
Umgehungsanastomose f bypass anastomosis; short circuit
~/**aortoiliakale** aortoiliac bypass
Umgehungskreislauf m collateral circulation
Umgehungsoperation f bypass operation *(z. B. der Herzkranzgefäße)*; short-circuiting operation *(z. B. am Darm)*
Umgehungs[operations]verfahren n bypass procedure
umgestülpt everted, exstrophic *(nach außen)*; inverse *(nach innen)*
Umherblicken n/**krankhaftes** periblepsia *(bei Psychose)*
Umherspringen n saltation *(z. B. bei Chorea)*
Umhüllung f 1. velamen[tum], covering membrane; 2. covering, envelope; capsule *(z. B. eines Dragees)*
umkehrbar reversible
~/**nicht** irreversible
umkehren 1. to invert, to reverse in position; to reverse in relationship; 2. to invert, to subject to inversion
Umklammerungsreflex m/**Moroscher** [Moro's] embrace reflex
umklappen to ectropionize, to evert *(das Augenlid)*
umknicken to sprain *(mit dem Fuß)*
Umknickung f sprain, twisting; distortion *(z. B. in einem Gelenk)*; kinking *(z. B. eines Gefäßes)*
Umlauf m paronychia, panaris, panaritium, runaround, felon
umleiten to bypass; to shunt *(z. B. Blut)*
Umleitung f bypass; shunt *(z. B. von Blut)*
Umnachtung f mental derangement; mental clouding, obnubilation
Umschaltstelle f s. Synapse
Umschlag m compress; poultice, cataplasm *(als Brei)*; fomentation, dressing *(warmer feuchter oder kalter)*
umschlagen 1. to change; 2. to reflect *(z. B. das Bauchfell)*
Umschlagfalte f duplicature, duplication *(z. B. des Bauchfells)*; palpebral fold *(der Augenbindehaut)*
Umschlingung f cerclage *(z. B. mit Draht)*
umschneiden to circumcise, to peritomize *(z. B. eine Wunde)*
Umschneidung f circumcision, peritomy

umschrieben

umschrieben circumscribed, localized *(z. B. eine Entzündung)*
umsetzen to convert *(enzymatisch)*; to metabolize *(im Stoffwechsel)*
Umstechung *f* purse-string suture; purse-string ligation *(z. B. eines Gefäßes)*
Umstellung *f* 1. transposition *(örtlich)*; 2. change-over *(z. B. einer Behandlung)*
Umstimmung *f* change, alteration *(der Psyche)*; stimulation *(z. B. bei einer Allergie)*
Umstimmungsbehandlung *f* stimulation therapy
Umstimmungsmedikament *n* alterative [agent], alterant
umstülpen 1. to invert, to introvert, to turn outside in; 2. to evert, to extrovert, to turn inside out
Umstülpung *f* 1. inversion, turning inward; 2. eversion, turning outward; ex[s]trophy *(z. B. der Blase)*; ectropion *(des Augenlids)*
umwallt vallate *(z. B. Zungenpapillen)*
umwandeln to change, to transform; to assimilate *(z. B. Nährstoffe)*
~/in Hyalin to hyalinize
~/in Zucker to saccharify
~/sich zu Keratin to keratinize
Umwandlung *f* change, transformation *(z. B. von Gewebe)*; assimilation *(z. B. von Nährstoffen)*; transduction, transmutation *(genetischen Materials)*
~/hyaline hyaline degeneration, hyalinosis
Umwelt *f* environment; peristasis
Umweltanpassung *f* acclimatization
Umwelteinfluß *m* environmental influence
Umweltverschmutzung *f* environmental pollution
U-Naht *f* retention suture
Unangepaßtsein *n*/**soziales** social maladjustment
unartikuliert inarticulated
unauffällig not contributory *(z. B. Krankengeschichte)*; uneventful *(z. B. Krankheitsverlauf)*
unbedingt unconditioned *(Reflex)*
unbeeinflußbar uncurable *(z. B. eine Krankheit)*; intractable *(psychisch)*
unbefruchtet unfertilized
Unbehagen *n* discomfort
unbeherrscht intemperate; nervous
unbesonnen precipitate, hasty; thoughtless
unbeständig labile, inconstant *(psychisch)*; instable
Unbeständigkeit *f* lability *(der Psyche)*; instability
unbestimmt ambiguous, unsure; indefinable
unbeteiligt indifferent, uninterested; neutral
unbeweglich immobile, immovable; non-motile, amotile
unbewußt unvoluntary; subconscious, unconscious; instinctive
unblutig bloodless; non-operative; non-invasive
Uncinariasis *f s.* Ankylostomiasis
Uncinatusanfall *m* uncinate seizure (fit)
Uncinatusepilepsie *f* uncinate epilepsy
Uncus *m* uncus, hook

~ gyri hippocampi (parahippocampalis) uncus [of the hippocampal gyrus]
undifferenziert undifferentiated, not differentiated *(z. B. Gewebe)*
Undine *f* undine *(Augenspülglas)*
undulierend undulating, undulant; fluctuating
undurchdringlich impenetrable, impermeable, impervious
undurchgängig closed, obstructed
undurchlässig impermeable, impervious ● **für Röntgenstrahlen ~ sein** to be opaque to X-rays
undurchsichtig opaque
unecht spurious *(z. B. ein Aneurysma)*
unelastisch inelastic, not elastic, non-elastic
unempfänglich unreceptive *(für Reize)*; immune *(für Infektionen)*; insusceptible *(z. B. für Krankheiten)*; insensible, insensitive *(für Gefühle)*
unempfindlich insensible, insensitive, hyposensitive, refractory *(z. B. gegen Reize)*; anaesthetic, hypaesthesic, hypaesthetic *(z. B. gegenüber Berührung)*; indolent *(gegen Schmerzen)*; immune *(gegenüber Keimen)* ● **~ werden** to become insensitive; to become immune (resistant); to stupefy *(psychisch abstumpfen)*
Unempfindlichkeit *f* insensibility, insensitiveness, hyposensitivity *(z. B. gegen äußere Reize)*; anaesthesia, hypaesthesia *(z. B. gegen Berührung)*; indolence *(gegen Schmerzen)*; immunity *(gegen Keime)*; obdormition, numbness *(z. B. von Gliedmaßen)*
~/örtliche local immunity
unentwickelt undeveloped; primitive
Unersättlichkeit *f* acoria, morbid appetite
unerwartet unexpected; foudroyant *(z. B. Krankheitsverlauf)*
~ schnell fulminant, foudroyant
unfähig incompetent; unable; unfit
Unfall *m* accident, casualty *(s. a.* Trauma*)*
Unfallabteilung *f* emergency department, accident ward
Unfallarzt *m* traumatologist
unfallbedingt traumatogenic
Unfallbehandlung *f* trauma[to]therapy
Unfallchirurgie *f* emergency (accident) surgery
Unfallheilkunde *f* traumatology
Unfallkrankheit *f* traumatopathy
Unfallneurose *f* accident neurosis
Unfallschiene *f* leg splint
Unfallverletzter *m* casualty, victim of an accident
Unfallverletzung *f* accidental injury
Unförmigkeit *f* monstrosity
unfruchtbar sterile, infertile, not fertile; barren, acyetic *(Frau)* ● **~ machen** to sterilize, to render sterile, to render incapable of reproduction; to castrate
Unfruchtbarkeit *f* sterility, infecundity, infertility; barrenness *(der Frau)*
ungeboren unborn
ungehemmt uninhibited, not inhibited
ungeimpft unvaccinated, not inoculated
ungeordnet irregular; ataxic *(Bewegungen)*; incoherent *(Sprache)*
ungepaart 1. unmated; 2. *s.* unpaarig

ungerinnbar incoagulable
Ungerinnbarkeit f incoagulability *(des Bluts)*
ungeschlechtlich asexual
ungestielt sessile *(z. B. Geschwulst)*
ungesund unhealthy, unsound; diseased; injurious, noxious; insalubrious
Ungezieferveмnichtung f disinfestation; deinsectization
ungezielt non-specific *(z. B. eine Therapie)*
ungiftig atoxic, non-toxic
Ungleichfärbung f anisochrom[as]ia *(z. B. der roten Blutkörperchen)*
Ungleichgewicht n imbalance; disequilibrium *(z. B. im Elektrolythaushalt)*
~/hormonales hormonal imbalance
Ungleichheit f asymmetry *(z. B. beider Körperhälften)*
ungleichmäßig irregular *(z. B. Herzaktion)*; asymmetric *(Körperbau)*
Unguentum n s. Salbe
Unguis m s. Nagel
unheilbar incurable; irremediable, immedicable
Unheilbarer m incurable
Unheilbarkeit f incurability
unhygienisch insanitary, non-hygienic
Universalempfänger m universal recipient *(bei Blutgruppe AB)*
Universalspender m universal donor *(bei Blutgruppe 0 rh)*
Universitätsklinik f university hospital
unklar of unknown origin *(Fieber)*
unkompliziert simple, uncomplicated
unkoordiniert uncoordinated, ataxic *(z. B. Bewegungen)*
unlöslich insoluble
unmäßig excessive, intemperate
Unmäßigkeit f excess, intemperance
Unna-Thost-Syndrom n Unna-Thost syndrome, symmetrical hyperkeratosis of the palms and soles
unoperierbar inoperable
unpaarig unpaired; impar, azygous, azygos *(Anatomie)*
unpäßlich indisposed, unwell
Unpäßlichkeit f indisposition, malaise
unperforiert imperforate
unphysiologisch unphysiologic
unpigmentiert unpigmented
unregelmäßig irregular *(z. B. der Pulsschlag)*; anomalous
Unregelmäßigkeit f irregularity *(z. B. des Pulses)*; anomaly *(Mißbildung)*
unreif immature, unripe, not fully developed; indifferentiated; abortive; puerile
Unreife f immaturity *(z. B. des Fetus)*
Unreinheit f impurity *(z. B. der Haut)*
Unruhe f/**allgemeine körperliche** agitation, restlessness, unrest
~/nächtliche oneirodynia
unschädlich innocuous, innoxious, harmless, innocent
Unschuldswurm[fortsatz] m lily-white appendix
unsegmentiert non-segmented

unsicher doubtful, uncertain *(z. B. eine Diagnose)*; ataxic *(z. B. die Gangart)*; unsteady *(z. B. das Stehen)*; insecure *(psychisch)*
unspezifisch non-specific
unstet inconstant; restless
unstillbar uncontrollable *(z. B. eine Blutung)*; unquenchable *(z. B. der Durst)*
unsymmetrisch asymmetric
untätig inactive, passive, inert
Untätigkeit f inactivity, inertia *(z. B. von Organen)*
untauglich incompetent *(geistig)*; unfit *(körperlich)*
Untauglichkeit f incompetence *(geistige)*; unfitness *(körperliche)*
Unterarm m forearm, antebrachium, antibrachium, cubitus
Unterarmfaszie f antebrachial fascia
Unterarmhautnerv m/**seitlicher** lateral antebrachial cutaneous nerve
Unterarmrückseite f posterior surface of the forearm
Unterarmvorderseite f anterior surface of the forearm
Unterbauch m hypogastrium, hypogastric region
Unterbauchlängsschnitt m lower abdominal vertical incision
Unterbauchmittelschnitt m lower abdominal midline incision, midline lower abdominal incision
Unterbauchnerv m hypogastric nerve
Unterbauchquerschnitt m lower abdominal transverse incision
Unterbauchreflex m hypogastric (lower abdominal) reflex
Unterbauchregion f hypogastric region, hypogastrium
Unterbauchschmerz m lower abdominal pain
Unterbauchwechselschnitt m oblique muscle-splitting incision of McBurney, McBurney's incision *(bei Blinddarmentzündung)*
unterbelüften/die Lunge to hypoventilate
unterbewußt subconscious, unconscious, coconscious
Unterbewußtsein n subconscious, unconscious, coconscious; crypt[an]amnesia
unterbinden to ligate, to ligature, to tie up
Unterbindung f s. Ligatur
unterbrochen/periodisch intermittent *(z. B. Fieber)*
unterdosieren to underdose
Unterdosierung f underdosage
Unterdruck m negative pressure
Unterdruckdrainage f negative pressure drainage
unterdrücken to suppress
~/eine Krankheit im Anfangsstadium to abort a disease
unterdrückt/genetisch hypostatic, genetically suppressed
Unterdrückung f 1. suppression *(z. B. eines Reizes)*; repression *(z. B. von Konflikten)*; 2. hypostasis *(eines Gens)*

unterempfindlich hyposensitive
Unterempfindlichkeit f hyposensitivity, hyposensitiveness *(z. B. auf äußere Reize)*; hypoergia *(gegenüber Antigenen)*
unterentwickelt underdeveloped; hypotrophic; hypoplastic; hypogenetic; retarded
Unterentwicklung f underdevelopment; hypotrophy; hypoplasia *(von Organen und Geweben)*; hypogenesis
~ **der Geschlechtsorgane** hypogenitalism
~/**geistige** mental retardation (subnormality)
unterernährt undernourished, malnourished; hypotrophic
Unterernährung f undernourishment, undernutrition, malnutrition, subnutrition; hypoalimentation
Unterfeld n lower area *(der Lunge)*
Unterführungsnadel f/**Deschampssche** Deschamps' needle *(für Gefäßligaturen)*
Unterfunktion f hypofunction *(z. B. eines Organs)*
~ **der Leydigschen Zellen** hypoleydigismus
Untergrätenmuskel m infraspinatus [muscle]
Untergrätenmuskelreflex m infraspinatus reflex
Unterhaut f hypodermis, subcutis
Unterhautbindegewebe n subcutaneous connective tissue
Unterhautfettgewebe n subcutaneous fatty tissue; dermafat
Unterhautfettgewebeentzündung f panniculitis, adipositis
Unterhaut[zell]gewebe n subcutis, subcutaneous tissue, hypodermis
Unterhautzellgewebsentzündung f dermatocellulitis
Unterhorn n underhorn
Unterkiefer m mandible, inferior maxilla, submaxilla, [lower] jaw-bone ● **einen zurückstehenden ~ besitzend** hypognathous ● **über dem ~** supramandibular ● **unter dem ~** submandibular, submaxillary
Unterkiefer... s. a. Mandibula...
Unterkieferarterie f inferior alveolar artery
Unterkieferbasis f base of the mandible
Unterkieferbruch m fracture of the mandible, mandibular fracture
Unterkieferdreieck n submandibular triangle
Unterkieferentfernung f[/**operative**] mandibulectomy
Unterkieferkleinwuchs m opisthognathia, opisthogeny
Unterkiefernerv m mandibular nerve
Unterkiefernervengeflecht n inferior dental plexus
Unterkieferprothese f mandibular reconstructive device
Unterkieferregion f submandibular region
Unterkieferspeicheldrüse f [sub]mandibular gland
Unterkiefersymphyse f mandibular symphysis
Unterkieferteilresektion f hemimandibulectomy
Unterkiefervene f inferior alveolar vein
Unterkieferverkümmerung f opisthognathia, opisthogeny
Unterkieferverrenkung f dislocation of the mandible
Unterkiefervorbiß m mesio[oc]clusion
Unterkieferwinkel m mandibular angle, angle of the mandible (jaw)
Unterkinnarterie f submental artery
Unterkinnvene f submental vein
Unterkühlung f refrigeration *(Vorgang)*; hypothermia, hypothermy *(Zustand)*
~ **der Extremitäten** acrohypothermy
Unterkühlungsanästhesie f refrigeration anaesthesia
Unterlage f rubber square; mattress
Unterlappen m lower (inferior) lobe
Unterlappenbronchus m lower-lobe bronchus
Unterlappenhauptbronchus m main lower-lobe bronchus
Unterlappenlungenentzündung f basal pneumonia
Unterleib m lower abdomen
Unterleibstyphus m typhoid [fever], typhus [abdominalis], hospital (lent) fever
Unterlid n lower [eye]lid
Unterlidödem n lower lid oedema
Unterlidregion f region of the lower eyelid
Unterlidsenker m tarsalis inferior [muscle]
Unterlidvene f inferior palpebral vein
unterliegen/**dem Abbaustoffwechsel** to catabolize; to dissimilate
~/**dem Verfall** to degenerate
~/**der Hämolyse** to undergo haemolysis
~/**der Plasmolyse** to plasmolyze
Unterlippe f lower lip
Unterlippenarterie f inferior labial artery
Unterlippendeformierung f deformity of the lower lip
Unterlippenregion f region of the lower lip
Unterlippensenker m depressor labii inferioris [muscle], quadratus labii inferioris [muscle]
Unterlippenvene f inferior labial vein
Unterminieren n undercutting *(z. B. bei Operationen)*
unterpigmentiert hypopigmented
Unterpigmentierung f hypopigmentation
Unterrippenarterie f subcostal artery
Unterrippengegend f hypochondriac region, hypochondrium
Unterrippenvene f subcostal vein
Untersättigung f/**arterielle** arterial desaturation
unterscheiden/**durch Gramfärbung** to establish by gram stain
unterscheidend distinctive, diacritic[al]; diagnostic
Unterscheidungsschwelle f differential threshold
Unterschenkel m lower leg, crus, shank
Unterschenkelamputation f below-knee amputation, lower-leg amputation
Unterschenkelamputierter m below-knee amputee

Unterschenkelfaszie f crural fascia
Unterschenkelgeschwür n ulcer of the leg
Unterschenkelgips[verband] m lower-leg plaster cast, toe-to-knee plaster cast
Unterschenkelhautnerv m**/seitlicher** lateral sural cutaneous nerve
Unterschenkelmangelentwicklung f acnemia
Unterschenkelnagel m tibial nail
Unterschenkelsyndrom n lower-leg syndrome
Unterschenkelzinkleimverband m toe-to-knee flexible adhesive bandage
Unterschläfengrube f infratemporal (zygomatic) fossa
Unterschlüsselbeingrube f infraclavicular fossa
Unterschlüsselbeinmuskel m subclavius [muscle]
Unterschulterblattarterie f subscapular artery
Unterschulterblattmuskel m subscapularis [muscle]
unterschwellig subliminal, subthreshold
untersetzt pyknic, thickset, stocky
untersuchen to examine *(ärztlich)*; to inspect *(z. B. einen Patienten)*; to explore *(z. B. eine Körperhöhle)*; to palpate *(tastend)*; to percuss *(abklopfend)*
Untersuchung f examination *(z. B. durch den Arzt)*; inspection *(z. B. eines Patienten)*; exploration *(z. B. einer Körperhöhle)*; investigation *(z. B. einer Infektionsquelle)*
~/ambulante outpatient investigation
~/ärztliche medical checkup (examination)
~/bimanuelle bimanual examination (palpation); double touch
~/intensive thorough examination
~/koprologische coprologic study
~/körperliche physical examination
~/makroskopische macroscopic examination, macroscopy, macrographia
~/mikroskopische microscopic examination, microscopy, micrographia
~/rektale rectal examination (palpation)
~/urodynamische urodynamic investigation
Untersuchungsbefund m examination findings
Untersuchungsfinger m examining finger
Untersuchungsliege f bed for examination
Untersuchungsmaterial n specimen
Untersuchungsstuhl m examining-chair
Untersuchungstisch m examining-table
Untersuchungsvorgang m investigative process
untertreiben to dissimulate *(Krankheiten)*
Unterwasserbehandlung f underwater treatment
Unterwasserbewegungstherapie f hydrokinesitherapy
Unterwasserdarmbad n enterocleaner
Unterwasser-Dauersaugung f continuous water-seal suction
Unterwassergymnastik f hydrogymnastics, underwater exercises
Unterwassermassage f hydromassage, underwater massage
Unterwasser-Saugdrainage f underwater seal drainage

Unterwasserübungen fpl s. Unterwassergymnastik
Unterwässerung f hypohydration, hydropenia
Unterwurm m inferior vermis *(im Kleinhirn)*
Unterzungenarterie f sublingual artery
Unterzungenfalte f sublingual plica (fold)
Unterzungengewebeentzündung f hypoglossitis, inflammation of the sublingual tissue
Unterzungengrube f sublingual fossa
Unterzungennerv m s. Hypoglossus
Unterzungenspeicheldrüse f sublingual [salivary] gland
Unterzungenspeicheldrüsenentzündung f sublinguitis, inflammation of the sublingual gland
Unterzungenspeicheldrüsenzyste f sublingual cyst
Unterzungenvene f sublingual vein
unverdaulich indigestible
unverfälscht unadulterated, pure
unverletzt uninjured, unhurt, not damaged *(z. B. bei einem Unfall)*; intact *(z. B. die Haut)*
unvermindert unrelieved, unmitigated *(z. B. Schmerzen)*; continuous, undiminished *(z. B. Hustenreiz)*
unvermischt unmixed, unblended, pure
Unvermögen n inability; failure, inertia *(z. B. von Organen)*
unversorgt unattended *(z. B. ein Verletzter)*; undressed *(z. B. eine Wunde)*
unverträglich incompatible *(z. B. im Rh-System)*; insalubrious *(z. B. das Klima)*; intolerant *(z. B. Medikamente)*
Unverträglichkeit f incompatibility *(z. B. im Rh-System)*; insalubrity *(z. B. Klima)*; intolerance *(z. B. gegenüber Medikamenten)*
unverzerrt orthoscopic *(z. B. Netzhautabbildung)*
unwillkürlich involuntary; consensual, unconscious
unwirksam inactive, ineffective, inefficacious
Unwirksammachung f inactivation *(z. B. eines Serums)*; neutralization *(z. B. einer Giftwirkung durch ein Gegenmittel)*
unwohl unwell, indisposed
Unwohlsein n indisposition; malaise
~/morgendliches morning sickness [of pregnancy]
unzurechnungsfähig irresponsible, of unsound mind, criminally insane
Unzurechnungsfähigkeit f criminal irresponsibility, of unsound mindness, imputability
unzureichend insufficient *(z. B. die Ernährung)*
unzusammenhängend incoherent *(z. B. die Sprache)*; inconsequential *(z. B. Denkabläufe)*
Urachus m urachus
Urachusfistel f urachus (vesicoumbilical) fistula, umbilical urinary fistula
Urachusvereiterung f pyourachus
Urachuszyste f urachus cyst
Urämie f uraemia
~/extrarenale (prärenale) prerenal (extrarenal) uraemia
urämiebedingt uraemigenic

urämieerzeugend

urämieerzeugend uraemigenic
Urämiesyndrom n/**hämolytisches** haemolytic uraemia syndrome
urämisch uraemic
Uranismus m s. Homosexualität
Urano... s. a. Palato... und Gaumen...
Uranoplastik f urano[staphylo]plasty, staphyloplasty, palatoplasty
uranoplastisch uranoplastic
Uranoplegie f uranoplegia, palatoplegia, palatine paralysis
Urat n urate *(Salz der Harnsäure)*
Uratämie f urataemia
uratauflösend uratolytic, uricolytic
Uratauflösung f uratolysis, uricolysis
urataussscheidend uricosuric
Urataussscheidung f im Urin uraturia
urathaltig uratic
Uratstein m urate (uric acid) calculus
Urazil n uracil *(Nukleinsäurebestandteil)*
Urazilribosid n s. Uridin
Urbild n imago *(Psychoanalyse)*
Urdarm m primary (primitive) gut, archenteron, progaster *(Embryologie)*
Urea f s. Harnstoff
Urease f ur[e]ase *(Enzym)*
Urei n oogonium, ovogonium, primordial ovum
Ureter m ureter, urinary (metanephric) duct *(s. a. unter Harnleiter)*
~/**aberrierender** aberrant ureter
~ **trifidus (triplex)** triple ureter
Ureter... s. a. Harnleiter...
Ureteralgie f ureteralgia, pain in the ureter; neuralgia of the ureter
Ureterdilatation f ureteral dilatation; ureterectasia
Ureterdurchspülung f ureteral irrigation
Ureterektasie f ureterectasia, distention of the ureter
Ureterektomie f ureterectomy, excision of the ureter
Ureterimplantation f ureter implantation, implantation of the ureter
ureterisch ureteral, ureteric
Ureterknospe f ureteral bud *(Embryologie)*
Ureterkrankheit f ureteropathy, disease of the ureter
Uretermukosa f mucous membrane of the ureter
ureteroenterisch ureteroenteric, ureterointestinal
Ureteroenterostomie f ureteroenterostomy
Ureterogramm n ureterogram
Ureterographie f ureterography
ureterographisch ureterographic
Ureterohydronephrose f ureterohydronephrosis
uretero-ileal ureteroileal
Ureterolith m ureterolith, ureteral calculus
Ureterolithiasis f ureterolithiasis
Ureterolithotomie f ureterolithotomy
Ureterolyse f ureterolysis *(z. B. aus Verwachsungen)*
Ureteromeatotomie f ureteral meatotomy

Ureteromegalie f ureteromegaly
Ureteronephrektomie f ureteronephrectomy
ureteropelvin ureteropelvic
Ureteropelvineostomie f s. Ureteropyeloneostomie
Ureteropelvioplastik f ureteropelvioplasty
Ureteropyelitis f ureteropyelitis, inflammation of the ureter and the renal pelvis
Ureteropyelogramm n ureteropyelogram
Ureteropyelographie f ureteropyelography
Ureteropyeloneostomie f ureteropyeloneostomy, ureteropelvineostomy, uretero[neo]pyelostomy
Ureteropyelonephritis f ureteropyelonephritis
Ureteropyelonephrostomie f ureteropyelonephrostomy
Ureteropyeloplastik f ureteropyeloplasty
Ureteropyosis f ureteropyosis
Ureterorektostomie f ureterorectostomy
Ureterorrhagie f ureterorrhagia, haemorrhage from the ureter
Ureterorrhaphie f ureterorrhaphy, suture of the ureter
Ureterosigmoidostomie f ureterosigmoidostomy
Ureterostomie f ureterostomy
Ureterotomie f ureterotomy, incision into the ureter
Ureteroureterostomie f uretero-ureterostomy
Ureterozele f ureterocele
Ureterozelektomie f ureterocelectomy
Ureterozystoneostomie f ureterocystoneostomy, ureteroneocystostomy
Ureterozystoskop n ureterocystoscope
Ureterozystoskopie f ureter[o]cystoscopy
ureterozystoskopisch ureterocystoscopic
Ureterozystostomie f ureterocystostomy
Ureterschiene f ureter splint
Ureterstenose f ureterstenosis, ureteral stenosis
Ureterstoma n ureterostoma
Urethra f urethra *(s. a. unter Harnröhre)*
~ **membranacea** membranous urethra
Urethra... s. a. Harnröhren...
Urethradilatation f urethral dilatation
Urethraexsudat n urethral exudate
Urethrakarunkel f urethral caruncula
Urethrakondylome npl urethral condylomata
Urethralgie f urethralgia, urethrodynia, pain in the urethra
Urethraltumor m urethral tumour, urethrophyma
Urethramukosa f urethral mucosa
Urethramündung f urethral meatus (opening, orifice)
~/**seitliche** paraspadias
Urethramündungsstenose f urethral meatal stenosis
Urethrasphinkter m urethral sphincter, external urinary sphincter, sphincter urethrae [membranaceae]
Urethrektomie f urethrectomy, excision of the urethra
Urethritis f urethritis, inflammation of the urethra
~ **anterior** anterior urethritis

~ **gonorrhoica** gonococcal (venereal) urethritis
~ **posterior** posterior urethritis
~ **simplex** simple urethritis
~/**spezifische** specific urethritis
~/**unspezifische** non-specific (simple) urethritis, pseudogonorrhoea
Urethroblennorrhoe f urethroblennorrhoea
Urethrogramm n urethrogram
Urethrographie f urethrography
urethrographisch urethrographic
Urethroplastik f urethroplasty
Urethrorrhagie f urethrorrhagia, urethral haemorrhage (bleeding)
Urethrorrhoe f urethrorrhoea, urethral discharge
Urethroskop n urethroscope, meatoscope
Urethroskopie f urethroscopy, urethrascopy, meatoscopy
urethroskopisch urethroscopic
Urethrospasmus m urethrospasm
Urethrostoma n urethrostoma
Urethrostomie f urethrostomy
Urethrotom n urethrotome
Urethrotomie f urethrotomy, incision into the urethra
~/**perineale** perineal urethrotomy
Urethrotrigonitis f urethrotrigonitis
Urethrozele f urethrocele, urethral hernia
Urethrozystitis f urethrocystitis, inflammation of the urethra and the urinary bladder
Urethrozystogramm n urethrocystogram
Urethrozystographie f urethrocystography
Urethrozystozele f urethrocystocele
Urharnsack m s. Allantois
Urhidrosis f ur[h]idrosis
Urhirn n archencephalon *(Embryologie)*
Uridin n uridine, uracil riboside
Uridindiphosphatglukose f uridine diphosphate glucose, uridinediphosphoglucose, UDPG
Uridindiphosphatglukose-Epimerase f uridine diphosphate glucose epimerase *(Enzym)*
Uridindiphosphatglukose-Pyrophosphorylase f uridine diphosphate glucose pyrophosphorylase *(Enzym)*
Uridindiphosphat-Glukuronyltransferase f uridine diphosphate glucuronyl transferase *(Enzym)*
Urikämie f uricaemia, uricacidaemia, lithaemia
Urikase f uricase *(Enzym)*
Urikazidurie f uricaciduria, lithuria
Urikolyse f uricolysis, disintegration of uric acid
Urin m urine, water *(s. a. unter Harn)*
~/**blutiger** haemorrhagic (blood-tinged) urine, bloody urine; haematuria
~/**klarer** clear (limpid) urine
~/**trüber** cloudy (turbid) urine
Urin... s. a. Harn...
Urinal n urinal
Urinamylase f urinary amylase
urinartig urinose, urinous
urinausscheidend urinary, urinific, voiding; diuretic

Urinausscheidung f 1. urinary outflow (output, excretion); 2. discharge of urine; [di]uresis, urination, micturation
~ **beim Fasten/vermehrte** opsiuria
~/**forcierte** forced diuresis (uresis)
~/**vermehrte** polyuria, hyper[di]uresis, urorrhagia
~/**verminderte** oliguria, oliguresis, hypouresis, uropenia
Urinausscheidungshemmung f antidiuresis
Urinazidometer n urinacidometer, uroacidometer
urinazidometrisch urinacidometric
Urinbefund m urine (urinary) findings
Urindauerausscheider m chronic urinary carrier
Urindiagnostik f urinary diagnosis, urinology
Urindiagnostiker m urinologist
Urinentleerung f **aus dem After** urochesia
Urinfärbung f/**abnorme** chromaturia
Urinflasche f urine bottle; urinal [bottle]
Urinfluoreszenz f photuria, phosphorescence of urine
Uringeschwulst f urinoma
Uringläserprobe f [urine] glass test
Urinharnstoff m urine-urea
urinieren to urinate, to discharge (pass) urine, to micturate
urinierend urinating, micturating, urinific
Urininfiltration f urinary infiltration, urecchysis *(im Gewebe)*
Urinkatheter m urinary catheter
Urinkultur f urine culture
Urinlehre f urinology
Urinmangel m deficiency of urine, uropenia
urinophil urinophil[e] *(z. B. Bakterien)*
urinös urinose, urinous
Urinosmolalität f urine osmolality
Urinphlegmone f urinary abscess; urecchysis *(im Gewebe)*
Urinsand m urocheras, urinary sand (gravel), uropsammus
Urinstatus m urinary findings; urinalysis
Urinvolumen n urine volume
Urkeimzelle f primordial germ cell
Urkleinhirn n palaeocerebellum *(Embryologie)*
Urlinde f s. Urninde
Urmund m primitive mouth, archistome, blastopore, protostoma *(Embryologie)*
Urniere f mesonephros, embryonic (primordial, middle) kidney, Wolffian body *(Embryologie)*
Urnierenadenokarzinom n mesonephric adenocarcinoma
urnierenartig mesonephroid
Urnierenfalte f mesonephric fold (ridge)
Urnierengang m mesonephric (Wolffian) duct
Urnierenkanälchen n mesonephric tubule
Urnierenleiste f nephrogenic cord
Urninde f urlinde, urninde, female homosexual
Urning m urning, male homosexual
Uroazotometer n uroazotometer
Urobilin n urobilin *(Bilirubinabbauprodukt)*
Urobilinämie f urobilinaemia
urobilinartig urobilinoid
Urobilinausscheidung f **im Urin** urobilinuria

Urobilinikterus

Urobilinikterus m urobilinicterus, urobilin jaundice
Urobilinogen n urobilinogen
Urobilinogenämie f urobilinogenaemia
Urobilinogenausscheidung f im Urin urobilinogenuria
Urochezie f urochesia
Urochrom n urochrome *(Harnfarbstoff)*
Urochromogen n urochromogen *(Urochromvorstufe)*
Urodynie f urodynia
Uroerythrin n uroerythrin *(Harnfarbstoff)*
Uroflavin n uroflavin
Urofuszin n urofuscin *(Harnfarbstoff)*
urogen s. harnbildend
urogenital urogenital, genitourinary
Urogenitalapparat m urogenital system (tract)
Urogenitalbilharziose f urogenital schistosomiasis
Urogenitaldreieck n urogenital triangle
Urogenitalfalte f urogenital fold (ridge)
Urogenitalfistel f urogenital fistula
Urogenitalmembran f urogenital (urethral) membrane
Urogenitalregion f urogenital region
Urogenitalsinus m urogenital sinus
Urogenitalspalte f urogenital fissure, genitourinary slit
Urogenitalsystem n urogenital system, genitourinary tract
Urogenitaltuberkulose f urogenital [tract] tuberculosis
Urogramm n urogram
Urographie f urography
~/intravenöse intravenous urography
~/orale oral urography
~/retrograde retrograde urography *(nach Kontrastmittelgabe über Katheter)*
urographisch urographic
Urohämatin n urohaematin *(Harnfarbstoff)*
Urohämatonephrose f urohaematonephrosis
Urohämatoporphyrin n urohaematoporphyrin
Urokinase f urokinase *(Enzym)*
Urokinaseinhibitor m urokinase inhibitor
urokinetisch urokinetic
Urolith m urolith, urolite, urinary calculus
Urolithiasis f urolithiasis, urinary lithiasis
Urolithotomie f urolithotomy
Urologe m ur[in]ologist
Urologie f ur[in]ology *(Lehre von den Erkrankungen der Harnorgane)*
urologisch urologic[al]
Urolutein n urolutein *(Harnfarbstoff)*
Uromelanin n uromelanin *(Harnfarbstoff)*
Urometer n ur[in]ometer, urogravimeter
Urometrie f ur[in]ometry
urometrisch ur[in]ometric
Uronephrose f uronephrosis, nephrohydrosis, hydro[uretero]nephrosis
Uropathie f uropathy
Uropathologie f uropathology
Uropenie f uropenia, deficiency of urine

Urophobie f urophobia *(krankhafte Angst vor Urin)*
Uropoese f uropoiesis, urine production
Uroporphyrin n uroporphyrin
Uroporphyrinogen n uroporphyrinogen
Uroporphyrinogensynthetase f uroporphyrinogen synthetase *(Enzym)*
Uropterin n uropterin *(Harnfarbstoff)*
Uropyonephrose f uropyonephrosis
Urorektalseptum n urorectal (Douglas') septum *(Embryologie)*
Urorosein n urorosein *(Harnfarbstoff)*
Urorrhodin n urorrhodin *(Harnfarbstoff)*
Urorrhodinogen n urorrhodinogen *(Urorrhodinvorstufe)*
Urorubin n urorubin *(Harnfarbstoff)*
Urorubinogen n urorubinogen *(Urorubinvorstufe)*
Urosepsis f urosepsis
uroseptisch uroseptic
Uroskopie f ur[in]oscopy
uroskopisch ur[in]oscopic
Urotoxikose f urosepsis
Urotoxin n urotoxin
urotoxisch urotoxic
Uroxanthin n uroxanthin *(Harnfarbstoff)*
Urozyanose f urocyanosis
Ursache-Wirkung-Beziehung f cause-and-effect relationship
ursächlich aetiologic; causal, causative, autochthonous
Ursamenzelle f spermatogonium, sperm[at]ospore
Ursegment n somite, metamere, primitive (mesodermal, mesoblastic) segment
Ursprung m origin *(z. B. eines Muskels)* ● **ektodermalen Ursprungs sein** to be ectodermal in origin ● **gleichen Ursprungs** homologous; isogenic, isogenous, isologous
ursprünglich primordial, primary, primitive
Ursprungsaponeurose f aponeurosis of origin
Ursprungskern m nucleus of origin
~/Westphal-Edingerscher nucleus of Edinger-Westphal
Urticaria f s. Urtikaria
~ factitia factitious urticaria *(vasomotorisches Nachröten der Haut nach dem Bestreichen)*
~ pigmentosa xanthelasmoidea
~ solaris solar urticaria
Urtika f urtica, wheal, pomphus
Urtikaria f urticaria, urticarial rash, nettle [rash], hives *(s. a. unter Urticaria)*
~/allergische allergic urticaria
~/hämorrhagische haemorrhagic urticaria
~/medikamentöse medicamentous urticaria
urtikariaartig urticarial, urticarious
urtikariaerzeugend urticariogenic
Urwirbelsäule f notochord *(Embryologie)* ● **neben der ~** parachordal
Urwirbelsäulenkanal m notochordal canal
Usher-Syndrom n Usher's syndrome *(Retinitis pigmentosa mit Taubstummheit)*
Usur f defect *(z. B. an den Rippen)*

Uta-Geschwür n [/amerikanisches] uta ulcer (s. a. Espundia)
uterin uterine
Uteringeräusch n uterine souffle; placental murmur
Uterinsegment n uterine segment
~/oberes upper uterine segment
~/unteres lower uterine segment
Utero... s. a. Hystero... und Gebärmutter...
uterogen uterogenic
Uterometer n uterometer, hysterometer
Uterometrie f uterometry, hysterometry
uterometrisch uterometric, hysterometric
Uteropexie f uteropexia, uterofixation, hysteropexia (an die Bauchdecken)
Uterospasmus m hysterospasm, hysterotrism[us], uterine spasm
Uterotonikum n uterotonic [agent]
uterotonisch uterotonic
Uterus m uterus, womb, metra ● **im ~** intrauterine ● **mit gedoppeltem ~** didelphic ● **neben dem ~** para-uterine ● **ohne ~** ametrous ● **vom ~ ausgehend** uterogenic
~ bicornis bicornuate uterus
~ didelphys (duplex) duplex (double) uterus; didelphia, dimetria
~ septatus septate (bipartite) uterus
Uterus... s. a. Gebärmutter...
Uterusanämie f uterine anaemia, metranaemia
Uterusapoplexie f uterine apoplexy
Uterusausfluß m metrorrhoea, uterine discharge
Uterusausschabung f curettage, curettement
Uterusdilatator m uterine dilator
Uterusdislokation f metrectopia, uterine displacement
Uterusdysfunktion f uterine disorder
Uteruserweichung f uteromalacia, metromalacia, hysteromalacia, softening of the uterus
Uterusexstirpation f s. Hysterektomie
Uterusfaßzange f uterotractor, uterine elevating forceps, uterine tenaculum [forceps]
Uterusflexion f uterine flexion, metrocampsis
Uterushämatom n haematometra, haematometrium
Uterushernie f uterine hernia, hysterocele, metrocele
Uterushyperämie f hyperaemia of the uterus, metraemia
Uterushyperästhesie f metryperaesthesia, hyperaesthesia of the uterus
Uterushypertrophie f metrypertrophia, uterine hypertrophy, metrauxe
Uterushypoplasie f uterine hypoplasia
Uterusinnervation f uterine innervation
Uterusinvolution f involution of the uterus (z. B. nach einer Geburt)
Uteruskarzinom n uterine cancer, hysterocarcinoma, metrocarcinoma
Uteruslöffel m uterine scoop
Uterusmißbildung f uterine malformation, deformity of the uterus
Uterusmotilität f uterine motility

Uterusmuskulaturentzündung f s. Myometritis
Uterusprolaps m uterine prolapse, prolapse of the uterus, falling of the womb, hysteroptosis, metroptosis
Uterusretroflexion f uterine retroflexion, retroflexion of the uterus (Abknickung des Gebärmutterkörpers nach hinten)
Uterusruptur f uterine rupture, hysterorrhexis, metrorrhexis
Uterussekretlöffel m uterine secretion scoop
Uterussklerose f uterosclerosis
Uterusspekulum n uteroscope, hysteroscope
Uterusspritze f uterine syringe
Utriculus m s. 1. ~ masculinus; 2. ~ vestibuli
~ masculinus (prostaticus) [prostatic] utricle, utriculus [masculinus]
~ vestibuli utricle, utriculus (im Innenohr)
Utrikulusendolymphe f utricular endolymph
Utrikulusentzündung f 1. utriculitis, inflammation of the prostatic utricle; 2. utriculitis, inflammation of the utricle of the ear
UV-... s. Ultraviolett...
Uvea f uvea
Uveaektropium n ectropion of the uvea
Uveakolobom n uveal coloboma
Uveamelanom n uveal melanoma
Uveastaphylom n uveal staphyloma
Uveitis f uveitis, uveal inflammation, inflammation of the uvea, iridochoroiditis
Uveitiskatarakt f choroid cataract
Uveomeningoenzephalitis f uveo[meningo]encephalitis, idiopathic uveoneuraxitis, Harada's syndrome
Uveoparotitis f uveoparotitis, uveoparotid fever
Uvula f uvula, staphyle
~ bifida split (bifid) uvula
~ palatina s. Uvula
Uvula... s. a. Gaumenzäpfchen...
Uvulageschwulst f staphyloncus
Uvulahämatom n staphylhaematoma; haemorrhage from the uvula
Uvulaödem n uvular oedema, staphyloedema, staphylygroma, oedema of the uvula
Uvulaptose f uvuloptosis, staphyloptosis; pendulous uvula
Uvularesektion f uvulectomy, staphylectomy, excision of the uvula
Uvulitis f uvulitis, staphylitis, inflammation of the uvula, kionitis
Uvulotom n uvulotome, uvulatome
Uvulotomie f uvulotomy, staphylotomy, incision into the uvula, kiotomy
U-Welle f U wave [of the electrocardiogram]

V

V s. 1. Vena; 2. Visus; 3. Brustwandableitung
Vaccina f vaccina (Impfpustel)
Vaccinia fpl vaccinia, cowpox, bovine smallpox
Vagabundenhaut f vagabond's disease (pigmentation)

Vagabundenneurose

Vagabundenneurose f vagabond neurosis, vagabondage
vagal vagal
Vagandenhaut f s. Vagabundenhaut
Vagina f 1. vagina *(Anatomie)*; 2. vagina, sheath
● **durch die ~** transvaginal ● **innerhalb der ~** intravaginal ● **neben der ~ paravaginal** ● **oberhalb der ~** supravaginal
~ bulbi Tenon's capsule, fascia of the bulb
~ carotica [fasciae cervicalis] carotid sheath
~ duplex double vagina
~ musculi recti abdominis sheath of the rectus abdominis [muscle]
~ synovialis synovial [tendon] sheath
~ tendinis s. Sehnenscheide
Vagina... s. a. Scheiden...
Vaginalausstrich m vaginal smear
Vaginaldrüse f vaginal gland
Vaginaldusche f vaginal douche
Vaginalgel n vaginal gel
Vaginalgie f vaginalgia, vaginodynia, pain in the vagina, colpalgia, colpodynia
Vaginalhernie f vaginal hernia
Vaginalkarzinom n vaginal cancer (carcinoma)
Vaginalklemme f vaginal clamp
Vaginalplastik f vaginoplasty, colpoplasty
Vaginalsekret n vaginal secretion
Vaginalspekulum n vaginal speculum, vaginoscope, colposcope
~/Simssches Sims's speculum *(rinnenförmiges Doppelspekulum)*
Vaginaltampon m vaginal plug
Vaginal- und Abdominaluntersuchung f double touch
Vaginalzäpfchen n vaginal suppository (insert)
Vaginalzytologie f vaginal cytology
vaginaspiegelnd vaginoscopic
Vaginektomie f 1. vagin[al]ectomy, colpectomy, excision of the vagina; 2. vagin[al]ectomy, excision of the tunica vaginalis
Vaginismus m vaginism[us], vulvismus, vaginal spasm, colpospasm
~/psychischer mental vaginismus; psychologic dyspareunia *(infolge Abneigung gegen Geschlechtsverkehr)*
Vaginitis f 1. vaginitis, elytritis, [endo]colpitis, encolpitis, inflammation of the vagina; 2. vaginitis, inflammation of a sheath
~/emphysematöse emphysematous vaginitis
~ gonorrhoica gonococcal vaginitis
~/senile senile vaginitis
Vaginofixation f vaginofixation, vaginal hysteropexy
Vaginogramm n vaginogram
Vaginographie f vaginography
Vaginometer n vaginometer
Vaginomykose f vaginomycosis, fungous infection of the vagina
Vaginopathie f vaginopathy, colpopathy, vaginal disease
Vaginoperineorrhaphie f vaginoperineorrhaphy, colpoperineorrhaphy, episioperineorrhaphy

Vaginoperineotomie f vaginoperineotomy, episiotomy
Vaginopexie f vaginopexy, colpopexy
Vaginoskop n vaginoscope, colposcope
Vaginoskopie f vaginoscopy, colposcopy, inspection of the vagina
Vaginotom n vaginotome, colpotome
Vaginotomie f vaginotomy, colpotomy, coleotomy, incision of the vagina
Vaginozele f vaginocele, colpocele, vaginal hernia
Vagitus m vagitus, cry of an infant
Vagogramm n [electro]vagogram
Vagolyse f vagolysis, vagal denervation
vagolytisch vagolytic
vagomimetisch vagomimetic
vagopressorisch vagopressor
Vagotomie f vagotomy, division of the vagus nerve; vagus nerve resection; vagal denervation
~/trunkuläre truncal vagotomy, Dragstedt's operation
~/zervikale cervical vagotomy
vagotomieren to vagotomize, to perform a vagotomy
vagoton vagotonic
Vagotonie f vagotonia, parasympathicotonia *(Verschiebung des Gleichgewichts im vegetativen Nervensystem zugunsten des Parasympathikus)*
vagotrop vagotrope, vagotropic
Vagotropismus m vagotropism
vagovagal vagovagal
Vagus m vagus [nerve], parasympathetic (pneumogastric) nerve, cardiac inhibitory nerve, cranial nerve X ● **auf den ~ einwirkend** vagotrope, vagotropic
vagusdenervierend vagolytic
Vagusdenervierung f vagal denervation, vagolysis
Vagusdurchtrennung f[/operative] s. Vagotomie
vagushemmend vagolytic
Vagushemmung f vagolysis
Vaguskern m vagal nucleus
Vaguslähmung f vagal paralysis
Vagusnerv m s. Vagus
Vagusneuralgie f neuralgia of the vagus nerve, Arnold's neuralgia
Vaguspuls m vagus pulse
Vagusstamm m vagal trunk
vagusstimulierend vagomimetic
Vagusstumpf m vagal stump
Vagussystem n vagal system
vagustonuserhöhend vagotonic
Vagustonuserhöhung f vagotonia
Vaguswirkung f vagotropism
vakuolär vacuolar, vaculate
Vakuole f vacuole
Vakuolenbildung f vacuol[iz]ation
Vakuumextraktion f vacuum extraction *(des Fetus)*

Vakuumextraktor m vacuum extractor
Vakzin n s. Vakzine
vakzinal vaccinal
Vakzination f vaccination (s. a. unter Impfung)
~/**Jennersche** Jennerian vaccination
Vakzinationsbehandlung f s. Vakzinetherapie
Vakzine f vaccin[e], [vaccine] lymph
~/**fettlösliche** lipovaccine
~/**homologe** homologous (autogenous) vaccine
~/**Jennersche** Jennerian vaccine
vakzineproduzierend vacci[no]genous
Vakzinetherapie f vaccinotherapy, vaccine therapy (immunoprophylaxis)
~/**autogene** autogenous vaccine therapy
Vakziniavirus n vaccinia (vaccine) virus
vakzinieren 1. to vaccinate, to inoculate [with] vaccine, to administer vaccine; 2. to vaccinate, to inoculate with cowpox virus
vakziniform vacciniform, vaccinoid
vakzinogen vacci[no]genous
Vakzinophobie f vaccinophobia (krankhafte Angst vor Impfung)
Valeriansäure f valer[ian]ic acid
Valgusdeformität f valgus deformity
Valin n valine, α-aminoisovaleric acid, 2-amino-3-methylbutanoic acid (essentielle Aminosäure)
Vallecula f vallecula
~ **cerebelli** cerebellar vallecula (Spalte an der Kleinhirnunterfläche)
~ **epiglottica [linguae]** epiglottic vallecula
Valva f valve, valva (s. a. unter Valvula und Klappe)
~ **aortae** aortic valve
~ **atrioventricularis dextra** right atrioventricular valve, tricuspid valve
~ **atrioventricularis sinistra** left atrioventricular valve, mitral valve
~ **ileocaecalis** ileocaecal (Bauhin's) valve, [ileo]colic valve
~ **mitralis** s. ~ atrioventricularis sinistra
~ **trunci pulmonalis** pulmonary valve
valvär valv[ul]ar
Valvula f valvula (s. a. unter Valva und Klappe)
~ **analis** anal valve
~ **atrioventricularis** atrioventricular valve
~ **bicuspidalis** bicuspid valve (valvula)
~ **cordis** s. Herzklappe
~ **Eustachii** s. ~ venae cavae inferioris
~ **Heisteri** spiral valve [of Heister], Heister's valve
~ **ileocaecalis** ileocaecal valve, [ileo]colic valve
~ **mitralis** mitral (left atrioventricular) valve
~ **sinus coronarii** coronary (Thebesian) valve
~ **tricuspidalis** tricuspid [valve], right atrioventricular valve
~ **venae cavae inferioris** inferior vena cava valve, caval (Eustachian) valve
valvulär valv[ul]ar
Valvulektomie f valvulectomy, excision of a valve
Valvulitis f valvulitis, inflammation of a valve
Valvuloplastik f valvuloplasty
Valvulotom n valvulotome

Valvulotomie f valv[ul]otomy
Vanadiumvergiftung f vanadiumism
van-der-Hoeve-Syndrom n van-der-Hoeve's syndrome, osteogenesis imperfecta with deafness
Vanilledermatitis f vanilla dermatitis
Vanillevergiftung f vanillism
Vanillinmandelsäure f vanilylmandelic acid
Vankomyzin n vancomycin (Antibiotikum)
Vaporarium n vaporarium, vapour bath
Vaporisation f vaporization, vapocauterization (z. B. von Gewebe)
vaporisieren to vaporize
Vaporotherapie f vapotherapy
Varicella f **gangraenosa** gangrenous varicella
~ **inoculata** vaccination varicella
~ **pustulosa** pustular varicella
Varietät f variety
Varikektomie f varicectomy, varicotomy, phlebectomy, cirsectomy, excision of a varix (varicose vein)
Varikoblepharon n varicoblepharon
Varikogramm n varicogram
Varikographie f varicography
Varikomphalus m varicomphalus
Varikophlebitis f varicophlebitis
varikös varicose
Varikosis f varicosis
Varikosität f varicosity
Varikozele f varicocele, pampinocele
Varikozelenexstirpation f varicocelectomy
Variola f variola, smallpox, blattern (Zusammensetzungen s. unter Pocken)
Variolation f variol[iz]ation
Variolavakzine f variolovaccine
Variolavirus n variola virus
Variolois f varioloid, modified smallpox
Varix m varix, varicose vein
~ **lymphaticus** lymphatic varix
Varize f varix, varicose vein; phlebectasia
Varizellen pl varicella, chickenpox, sheep pox
~/**kindliche** childhood varicella
varizellenartig varicelliform, varicelloid
Varizellenenzephalitis f varicella encephalitis
Varizellenexanthem n varicellar rash
Varizellenimpfung f varicell[iz]ation
Varizellenpneumonie f varicella pneumonia
Varizellen-Zoster-Virus n varicella[-zoster] virus, V-Z virus
varizelliform varicelliform
Varizen... s. a. Krampfader...
Varizenbildung f varication; varicosis
varizendarstellend varicographic
varizenförmig variciform
Varizennabel m varicomphalus
Varizensklerosierung f varicosclerosation
Varizenstrippen n s. Varikektomie
Varolsbrücke f [Varolian] pons (Hirnteil oberhalb des verlängerten Rückenmarks)
Varusdeformität f varus deformity
Vas n vessel, vas (s. a. unter Gefäß)
~ **anastomoticum** anastomotic vessel
~ **capillare** capillary [vessel]

~ **collaterale** collateral vessel
~ **lymphaticum** s. Lymphgefäß
vasal s. vaskulär
Vasalgie f vasalgia, pain in a vessel
Vasculitis f vasculitis, inflammation of a vessel, angi[i]tis
~ **retinae** retinal vasculitis
Vasektomie f vasectomy, vasoresection, resection of the ductus deferens
vasektomieren to vasectomize
vaskulär vascular, vasal, angeial
Vaskularisation f vascularization
vaskularisieren to vascularize, to supply with vessels
Vaskulogenese f vasculogenesis
vaskulolymphatisch vasculolymphatic
Vaskulum n vasculum, small vessel
Vasodepressor m vasodepressor [agent]
vasodepressorisch vasodepressor
Vasodilatation f vasodila[ta]tion, dilatation of a vessel, angiohypotonia
Vasodilatator m vasodilator [agent]
~/**koronarer** coronary vasodilating agent
Vasodilatatorenfaser f vasodilator fibre
Vasodilatatorentherapie f vasodilator therapy
Vasodilatatorenzentrum n vasodilator centre
vasodilatatorisch vasodilator, vasodilative, vasohypotonic
Vasoepididymostomie f vasoepididymostomy
Vasographie f vasography, angiography
Vasoinhibitor m vasoinhibitor [agent]
vasoinhibitorisch vasoinhibitory
Vasokonstriktion f vasoconstriction, angiohypertonia
vasokonstriktiv s. vasokonstriktorisch
Vasokonstriktor m vasoconstrictor [agent], vasopressor
Vasokonstriktorenfaser f vasoconstrictor fibre
Vasokonstriktorenzentrum n vasoconstrictor centre
vasokonstriktorisch vasoconstrictor, vasoconstrictive, vasohypertonic
Vasoligatur f vasoligation, vasoligature, ligation of the vas deferens
Vasomotilität f vasomotion
Vasomotor m vasomotor nerve
Vasomotorenkollaps m vasomotor collapse
Vasomotorenlähmung f vasomotor paralysis, vasoparalysis
~/**inkomplette** vasoparesis, partial vasomotor paralysis, angioparesis
~/**komplette** vasoparalysis, [complete] vasomotor paralysis, angioparalysis
Vasomotorennerv m s. Vasomotor
Vasomotorenneurose f vasomotor neurosis, vasoneurosis, angioneurosis
Vasomotorenreflex m vasomotor reflex
Vasomotorensystem n vasomotor system
Vasomotorenzentrum n vasomotor centre, pressor area
vasomotorisch vasomotor[ial], vasomotory, vasculomotor, angiokinetic

Vasoneurose f s. Vasomotorenneurose
Vasoorchidostomie f vasoorchidostomy
Vasoparalyse f s. Vasomotorenlähmung/komplette
Vasoparese f s. Vasomotorenlähmung/inkomplette
Vasopressin n vasopressin, antidiuretic hormone (Hypophysenhinterlappenhormon)
Vasopressin[spiegel]verminderung f im Blut hypovasopressinaemia
vasopressorisch vasopressor
vasoproliferativ vasoproliferative
Vasorelaxation f vasorelaxation
Vasoresektion f s. Vasektomie
Vasorrhaphie f vasorrhaphy, suture of the vas deferens
vasosensorisch vasosensory
Vasospasmus m vasospasm
~/**zerebraler** cerebral vasospasm
vasospastisch vasospastic
Vasostimulans n vasostimulant [agent]
vasostimulierend vasostimulant
Vasostomie f vasostomy
Vasotomie f vasotomy, incision into the vas deferens
Vasotonikum n vasotonic [agent]
vasotroph vasotrophic
vasovagal vasovagal
Vasovasostomie f vasovasostomy
Vasovesikulektomie f vasovesiculectomy
Vasovesikulitis f vasovesiculitis
Vaterkomplex m father complex
väterlicherseits patrilineal
Vatermord m patricide
Vaterschaft f paternity
Vaterschaftsbestimmung f paternity (parentage) test; proof of paternity
vegetabil[isch] vegetable
Vegetarier m vegetarian
vegetarisch vegetarian
Vegetation f vegetation (z. B. an Herzklappen)
Vegetationen fpl/**adenoide** adenoids, adenoid vegetations (lymphatisches Gewebe im Nasenrachen)
Vehikel n vehicle; excipient (z. B. für Arzneistoffe)
Veitstanz m [dancing] chorea, Sydenham's chorea, Saint Vitus' (Anthony's) dance
~/**infektiös-toxischer** acute chorea
Vektion f vection, infection
Vektorkardiogramm n vectorcardiogram, V.C.G.
Vektorkardiograph m vectorcardiograph
Vektorkardiographie f vectorcardiography, cardiovectography
vektorkardiographisch vectorcardiographic
Velamen n velamen[tum], veil, covering membrane
~ **vulvae** vulvar velamen
velamentös velamentous
Velamentum n s. Velamen
Velum n velum, veil
~ **medullare anterius** s. ~ medullare superius

- ~ **medullare inferius (posterius)** inferior (posterior) medullary velum
- ~ **medullare superius** superior (anterior) medullary velum
- ~ **palatinum** palatine velum, soft palate, staphyle

Vena f vein, vena *(s.a. unter Vene)*
- ~ **alveolaris inferior** inferior alveolar vein
- ~ **anastomotica inferior** inferior anastomotic vein
- ~ **anastomotica superior** superior anastomotic vein
- ~ **angularis** angular vein
- ~ **anonyma** innominate vein
- ~ **appendicis vermiformis** appendicular vein
- ~ **appendicularis** appendicular vein
- ~ **arciformis (arcuata)** arcuate vein
- ~ **articularis mandibulae** vein of the temporomandibular joint
- ~ **auditiva interna** internal auditory vein
- ~ **auricularis anterior** anterior auricular vein
- ~ **auricularis posterior** posterior auricular vein
- ~ **axillaris** axillary vein
- ~ **azygos** azygous vein
- ~ **basalis** basal vein
- ~ **basalis communis** common basal vein
- ~ **basalis inferior** inferior basal vein
- ~ **basalis Rosenthal** basal vein
- ~ **basalis superior** superior basal vein
- ~ **basilica** basilic vein
- ~ **basivertebralis** basivertebral vein
- ~ **brachialis** brachial vein
- ~ **brachiocephalica dextra** right brachiocephalic vein, right innominate (anonymous) vein
- ~ **brachiocephalica sinistra** left brachiocephalic vein, left innominate (anonymous) vein
- ~ **bronchialis** bronchial vein
- ~ **canaliculi pterygoidei** vein of the pterygoid canal
- ~ **cava [vena] cava**, caval vein
- ~ **cava inferior** inferior vena cava, postcava
- ~ **cava superior** superior vena cava, precava
- ~ **centralis glandulae suprarenalis** central vein of the suprarenal gland
- ~ **centralis hepatis** central hepatic vein, central vein of the liver
- ~ **centralis retinae** central retinal vein, central vein of the retina
- ~ **cephalica** cephalic vein
- ~ **cephalica accessoria** accessory cephalic vein
- ~ **cerebelli inferior** inferior cerebellar vein
- ~ **cerebelli superior** superior cerebellar vein
- ~ **cerebri** cerebral vein
- ~ **cerebri anterior** anterior cerebral vein
- ~ **cerebri inferior** inferior cerebral vein
- ~ **cerebri interna** internal cerebral vein
- ~ **cerebri magna [Galeni]** great cerebral vein
- ~ **cerebri media** s. ~ cerebri media superficialis
- ~ **cerebri media profunda** deep medial cerebral vein
- ~ **cerebri media superficialis** superficial medial cerebral vein, Sylvian vein
- ~ **cerebri superior** superior cerebral vein
- ~ **cervicalis profunda** deep cervical vein
- ~ **ciliaris** ciliary vein
- ~ **circumflexa femoris lateralis** lateral femoral circumflex vein
- ~ **circumflexa femoris medialis** medial femoral circumflex vein
- ~ **colica dextra** right colic vein
- ~ **colica media** middle colic vein
- ~ **colica sinistra** left colic vein
- ~ **conjunctivalis** conjunctival vein
- ~ **cordis** cardiac vein, vein of the heart
- ~ **cordis anterior** anterior cardiac vein
- ~ **cordis magna** great cardiac vein
- ~ **cordis media** middle cardiac vein
- ~ **cordis parva** small cardiac vein
- ~ **coronaria** coronary vein
- ~ **coronaria ventriculi** coronary vein of the stomach
- ~ **cutanea** cutaneous vein
- ~ **cystica** cystic vein
- ~ **diploica frontalis** diploic vein of the frontal bone
- ~ **diploica occipitalis** diploic vein of the occipital bone
- ~ **dorsalis clitoridis [profunda]** [deep] dorsal vein of the clitoris
- ~ **dorsalis penis [profunda]** deep dorsal vein of the penis
- ~ **dorsalis penis superficialis** superficial dorsal vein of the penis
- ~ **duodenalis** duodenal vein
- ~ **emissaria** emissary vein
- ~ **emissaria condylaris** condyloid emissary vein
- ~ **emissaria mastoidea** mastoid emissary vein
- ~ **emissaria occipitalis** occipital emissary vein
- ~ **emissaria parietalis** parietal emissary vein
- ~ **epigastrica inferior** inferior epigastric vein
- ~ **epigastrica superficialis** superficial epigastric vein
- ~ **epigastrica superior** superior epigastric vein
- ~ **episcleralis** episcleral vein
- ~ **ethmoidalis** ethmoid vein
- ~ **ethmoidalis anterior** anterior ethmoid vein
- ~ **ethmoidalis posterior** posterior ethmoid vein
- ~ **facialis** facial vein
- ~ **facialis anterior** anterior facial vein
- ~ **facialis communis** common facial vein
- ~ **facialis posterior** posterior facial vein
- ~ **facialis profunda** deep facial vein
- ~ **femoralis** femoral vein
- ~ **femoropoplitea** femoropopliteal vein
- ~ **fibularis** fibular vein
- ~ **frontalis** frontal vein, vein of the forehead
- ~ **gastrica** gastric vein
- ~ **gastrica brevis** short gastric vein
- ~ **gastrica dextra** right gastric vein
- ~ **gastrica sinistra** left gastric vein
- ~ **gastroepiploica** gastroepiploic vein
- ~ **gastroepiploica dextra** right gastroepiploic vein
- ~ **gastroepiploica sinistra** left gastroepiploic vein

Vena

- ~ **genua** genicular vein
- ~ **glutaea inferior** inferior gluteal vein
- ~ **glutaea superior** superior gluteal vein
- ~ **haemorrhoidalis inferior** s. ~ rectalis inferior
- ~ **hemiazygos** hemiazygous vein
- ~ **hemiazygos accessoria** accessory hemiazygous vein
- ~ **hepatica** hepatic vein
- ~ **hepatica dextra** right hepatic vein
- ~ **hepatica media** middle hepatic vein
- ~ **hepatica sinistra** left hepatic vein
- ~ **hypogastrica** s. ~ iliaca interna
- ~ **ilei** ileal vein
- ~ **ileocolica** ileocolic vein
- ~ **iliaca communis** common iliac vein
- ~ **iliaca externa** external iliac vein
- ~ **iliaca interna** internal iliac vein, hypogastric vein
- ~ **iliofemoralis** iliofemoral vein
- ~ **iliolumbalis** iliolumbar vein
- ~ **intercostalis** intercostal vein
- ~ **intercostalis anterior** anterior intercostal vein
- ~ **intercostalis posterior** posterior intercostal vein
- ~ **intercostalis superior dextra** right intercostal superior vein
- ~ **intercostalis superior sinistra** left intercostal superior vein
- ~ **intercostalis suprema** highest intercostal vein
- ~ **interlobaris renis** interlobar vein of the kidney
- ~ **interlobularis [hepatis]** interlobular vein of the liver
- ~ **interlobularis renis** interlobular vein of the kidney
- ~ **intervertebralis** intervertebral vein
- ~ **intestinalis** intestinal vein
- ~ **jejunalis** jejunal vein
- ~ **jugularis** jugular vein
- ~ **jugularis anterior** anterior jugular vein
- ~ **jugularis externa** external jugular vein
- ~ **jugularis interna** internal jugular vein
- ~ **labialis inferior** inferior labial vein, vein of the lower lip
- ~ **labialis posterior** posterior labial vein
- ~ **labialis superior** superior labial vein, vein of the upper lip
- ~ **labyrynthi** labyrinthine vein
- ~ **lacrimalis** lacrimal vein
- ~ **laryngea inferior** inferior laryngeal vein
- ~ **laryngea superior** superior laryngeal vein
- ~ **lienalis** splenic vein
- ~ **lingualis** lingual vein
- ~ **lumbalis ascendens** ascendent lumbal vein, ascending lumbar vein
- ~ **mammaria interna** s. ~ thoracica interna
- ~ **masseterica** masseteric vein
- ~ **maxillaris** maxillary vein
- ~ **mediana antebrachii** median antebrachial vein
- ~ **mediana basilica** median basilic vein
- ~ **mediana cephalica** median cephalic vein
- ~ **mediana cubiti** median cubital vein
- ~ **mediastinalis** mediastinal vein
- ~ **meningea** meningeal vein
- ~ **meningea media** middle meningeal vein
- ~ **mesenterica** mesenteric vein
- ~ **mesenterica inferior** inferior mesenteric vein
- ~ **mesenterica superior** superior mesenteric vein
- ~ **metacarpea dorsalis** dorsal metacarpal vein
- ~ **metacarpea palmaris (ventralis, volaris)** palmar (volar) metacarpal vein
- ~ **metatarsea dorsalis pedis** dorsal metatarsal vein
- ~ **metatarsea plantaris** plantar metatarsal vein
- ~ **muscularis** muscular vein
- ~ **musculophrenica** musculophrenic vein
- ~ **nasofrontalis** nasofrontal vein
- ~ **obliqua atrii sinistri** oblique vein of Marshall (the left atrium)
- ~ **obturatoria** obturator vein
- ~ **occipitalis** occipital vein
- ~ **oesophagea** oesophageal vein
- ~ **omphalomesenterica** omphalomesenteric (vitelline) vein
- ~ **ophthalmica inferior** inferior ophthalmic vein
- ~ **ophthalmica superior** superior ophthalmic vein
- ~ **ophthalmomeningea** ophthalmomeningeal vein
- ~ **ovarica** ovaric vein
- ~ **ovarica dextra** right ovarian vein
- ~ **ovarica sinistra** left ovarian vein
- ~ **palatina externa** external palatine vein
- ~ **palpebralis** palpebral vein
- ~ **palpebralis inferior** inferior palpebral vein
- ~ **palpebralis superior** superior palpebral vein
- ~ **pancreatica** pancreatic vein
- ~ **pancreaticoduodenalis** pancreaticoduodenal vein
- ~ **paraumbilicalis [Sappeyi]** para-umbilical vein [of Sappey]
- ~ **parotidea** parotid vein
- ~ **pectoralis** pectoral vein
- ~ **pericardiacophrenica** pericardiacophrenic vein
- ~ **peronea** peroneal vein
- ~ **pharyngea** pharyngeal vein
- ~ **phrenica inferior** inferior phrenic vein
- ~ **phrenica superior** superior phrenic vein
- ~ **poplitea** popliteal vein
- ~ **portae** portal [vein], porta
- ~ **posterior ventriculi sinistri** posterior vein of the left ventricle
- ~ **praepylorica** prepyloric vein
- ~ **profunda clitoridis** deep vein of the clitoris
- ~ **profunda femoris** deep femoral vein
- ~ **profunda linguae** deep lingual vein
- ~ **profunda penis** deep vein of the penis
- ~ **pudenda externa** external pudendal vein
- ~ **pudenda interna** internal pudendal vein
- ~ **pulmonalis** pulmonary vein
- ~ **pulmonalis dextra** right pulmonary vein
- ~ **pulmonalis inferior dextra** inferior right pulmonary vein
- ~ **pulmonalis inferior sinistra** inferior left pulmonary vein
- ~ **pulmonalis sinistra** left pulmonary vein

Venenblutung

- ~ pulmonalis superior dextra superior right pulmonary vein
- ~ pulmonalis superior sinistra superior left pulmonary vein
- ~ radialis radial vein
- ~ rectalis inferior inferior rectal (haemorrhoidal) vein
- ~ rectalis media middle rectal (haemorrhoidal) vein
- ~ rectalis superior superior rectal (haemorrhoidal) vein
- ~ renalis (renis) renal vein
- ~ retromandibularis retromandibular vein
- ~ sacralis lateralis lateral sacral vein
- ~ sacralis mediana middle sacral vein
- ~ saphena saphena, saphenous vein
- ~ saphena accessoria accessory saphenous vein
- ~ saphena magna great (long) saphenous vein, internal saphenous vein
- ~ saphena parva small (short, external) saphenous vein
- ~ scapularis dorsalis dorsal scapular vein
- ~ scrotalis anterior anterior scrotal vein
- ~ scrotalis posterior posterior scrotal vein
- ~ sigmoidea sigmoid vein
- ~ spermatica dextra s. ~ testicularis dextra
- ~ spinalis spinal vein
- ~ spinalis externa anterior anterior external spinal vein
- ~ spinalis externa posterior posterior external spinal vein
- ~ spinalis interna internal spinal vein
- ~ stellata stellate vein
- ~ sternocleideomastoidea sternocleidomastoid vein
- ~ stylomastoidea stylomastoid vein
- ~ subclavia subclavian vein
- ~ subclavia dextra right subclavian vein
- ~ subclavia sinistra left subclavian vein
- ~ subcostalis subcostal vein
- ~ sublingualis sublingual vein
- ~ submentalis submental vein
- ~ supraorbitalis supra-orbital vein
- ~ suprarenalis suprarenal vein
- ~ suprarenalis dextra right suprarenal vein
- ~ suprarenalis sinistra left suprarenal vein
- ~ suprascapularis suprascapular vein
- ~ supratrochlearis supratrochlear vein
- ~ temporalis media middle temporal vein
- ~ temporalis profunda deep temporal vein
- ~ temporalis superficialis superficial temporal vein
- ~ testicularis dextra right testicular (spermatic) vein
- ~ testicularis sinistra left testicular (spermatic) vein
- ~ thoracica interna internal thoracic (mammary) vein
- ~ thoracica lateralis lateral thoracic vein
- ~ thoracica longitudinalis dextra azygous vein
- ~ thoracica longitudinalis sinistra hemiazygous vein
- ~ thoracica longitudinalis sinistra accessoria accessory hemiazygous vein
- ~ thoracoacromialis thoracoacromial (acromiothoracic) vein
- ~ thymica thymic vein
- ~ thyreoidea inferior inferior thyroid vein
- ~ thyreoidea media middle thyroid vein
- ~ thyreoidea superior superior thyroid vein
- ~ tibialis anterior anterior tibial vein
- ~ tibialis posterior posterior tibial vein
- ~ trachealis tracheal vein
- ~ transversa colli transverse cervical vein
- ~ transversa faciei transverse facial vein
- ~ tympanica tympanic vein
- ~ ulnaris ulnar vein
- ~ umbilicalis umbilical vein
- ~ uterina uterina vein
- ~ vertebralis vertebral vein
- ~ vertebralis accessoria accessory vertebral vein
- ~ vesicalis vesical vein
- ~ vestibularis vestibular vein
- ~ vorticosa vortex vein

Vena-angularis-Thrombophlebitis f angular vein thrombophlebitis
Vena-cava-inferior-Syndrom n inferior vena cava syndrome
Vena-cava-Kompressionssyndrom n vena cava compression syndrome, supine hypotension syndrome *(in der Schwangerschaft)*
Vena-cava-superior-Syndrom n superior vena cava syndrome
Venae fpl **perforantes** perforating veins
Venae punctio f venepuncture, venipuncture
Venae sectio f venesection, surgical (venous) cut-down, venotomy, phlebotomy ● eine ~ ausführen to cut down a vein
Venae-sectio-Besteck n venesection (cut-down) set
Vena-jugularis-Kompression f jugular compression
Vena-saphena-Zeichen n/**Cruveilhiersches** Cruveilhier's sign
Vene f vein, vena *(s. a. unter Vena)* ● in die ~ hinein intravenous, I.V., i.v. ● innerhalb der ~ intravenous, I.V., i.v. ● neben einer ~ paravenous ● von einer ~ ausgehend phlebogenous
~/kleine venule, venula
Venektasie f venectasia, phlebectasia, dilatation of a vein
Venektomie f venectomy, phlebectomy, excision of a vein
Venen... s. a. Phlebo...
Venenanästhesie f/**Biersche** Bier's anaesthesia
Venenanastomose f venovenostomy, phlebophlebostomy
Venenanordnung f venation
venenartig phleboid
Venenaußenhautentzündung f periphlebitis
Venenblut n venous blood
Venenblutfülle f venosity
Venenblutung f phleborrhagia, venous haemorrhage

venendarstellend

venendarstellend venographic, phlebographic
Venendruck *m* venous pressure, intravenous tension
~/zentraler central venous pressure, c.v.p.
Venendruckmessung *f* phlebopiezometry
Veneneinriß *m* phleborrhexis
Venenentfernung *f*[/operative] *s.* Venektomie
Venenentzündung *f* phlebitis
~ mit Blutgerinnselbildung thrombophlebitis
~/septische septicophlebitis
Veneneröffnung *f*[/operative] *s.* Venae sectio
Venenerweiterung *f s.* Venektasie
Venenexairese *f* phlebexeresis, excision of a vein
Venenfehlbildung *f* venous malformation
Venenfibrose *f* venofibrosis
Venenfreilegung *f* surgical cut-down
Venenfüllung *f* venous filling
Venengeflecht *n* venous plexus
Venenhaken *m* vein retractor
Venenhomotransplantat *n* vein homograft
Veneninfektion *f* infection of vein
Veneninfusion *f* venoclysis, phleboclysis
Veneninnenhautentzündung *f* endophlebitis
Veneninsuffizienz *f* venous insufficiency
Venenkatheter *m* venous (vein) catheter, intravenous portal (route)
~/zentraler central venous catheter
Venenklappe *f* venous valve [cusp]
Venenknoten *m s.* Varize
Venenkollaps *m* venous collapse
Venenkonstriktion *f* phlebostenosis, constriction of a vein
Venenkrampf *m* venospasm, venous spasm
Venenlehre *f* phlebology
venenlumenregulierend venomotor
venenlumenverengernd venopressor
Venenmesser *n* phlebotome
Venenmißbildung *f* venous malformation
Venenmuster *n* venation
Venennaht *f* venesuture, venisuture, phleborrhaphy, suture of a vein
Venenpatch *m* vein patch
Venenplastik *f* phleboplasty
Venenplexus *m* venous plexus
Venenpuls *m* venous pulse
venenpulsaufzeichnend phlebographic
Venenpulsaufzeichnung *f* phlebography
Venenpulskurve *f* phlebogram
Venenpunktion *f* venepuncture, venipuncture
venenreich venose
Venenreichtum *m* venosity
Venenrekonstruktion *f* phleboplasty
Venenresektion *f s.* Venektomie
Venenretraktor *m* vein retractor
Venenriß *m* phleborrhexis, rupture of a vein
Venenröntgen[kontrast]bild *n* venogram, phlebogram, roentgenogram of a vein
Venenröntgen[kontrast]darstellung *f* venography, phlebography
Venenschmerz *m* phlebalgia, venalgia, pain in a vein

Venenschnitt *m s.* Venae sectio
Venenschwäche *f* phlebasthenia
Venenskalpell *n* phlebotome
Venensklerose *f* venosclerosis, venous sclerosis, phlebosclerosis; hardening of a vein
Venenstein *m* phlebolith, vein stone
Venensteinbildung *f* phlebolithiasis
Venenstripper *m* vein stripper
Venenstrippung *f* vein stripping, phlebexeresis
Venenthrombose *f* venous thrombosis, phlebothrombosis
~/tiefe deep venous thrombosis
venenthrombosierend venothrombotic
Venentransplantat *n* vein graft
Venentransplantation *f* vein grafting
Venenüberdehnung *f* phlebismus
Venenum *n* venom, venenum, zootoxin
Venen- und Arterienerweiterung *f* phlebarteriectasia
venenverengernd venopressor, venoconstrictive
Venenvereng[er]ung *f* phlebostenosis
Venenverhärtung *f*[/bindegewebige] venofibrosis; hardening of a vein
Venenverkalkung *f* venosclerosis, phlebosclerosis
Venenverlagerung *f* phlebectopia, displacement of a vein
Venenverödung *f* phlebosclerozation
Venenverschluß *m* vein occlusion
Venenverschlußplethysmographie *f* vein-occlusion plethysmography
Venenverstopfung *f* phlebemphraxis, plugging of a vein *(z. B. durch Blutgerinnsel)*
Venenverteilung *f* venation
Venenverweilkanüle *f* indwelling venous cannula
Venenverzweigung *f* venation, branching (ramification) of veins
Venenwandschwäche *f* phlebasthenia
Venenzerreißung *f* phleborrhexis
Venenzugang *m* intravenous portal
Venerie *f* venereal disease, VD
venerisch venereal
~/nicht non-venereal
Venerologe *m* venereologist
Venerologie *f* venereology *(Lehre von den Geschlechtskrankheiten)*
venerologisch venereologic
Venerophobie *f* venereophobia *(krankhafte Angst vor Geschlechtskrankheiten)*
Venin *n* venin, venene, snake venom
Venole *f s.* Venula
Venolenendothel *n* venular endothelium
venomotorisch venomotor
venopressorisch venopressor
venös venous
Venospasmus *m* venospasm, venous spasm
Venotomie *f s.* Venae sectio
Venter *m* venter, belly
~ anterior musculi digastrici anterior belly of the digastric muscle

~ **frontalis musculi epicranii** frontal (anterior) belly of the epicranius muscle, frontalis muscle
~ **inferior musculi omohyoidei** inferior belly of the omohyoid muscle
~ **musculi** venter, belly of the muscle
~ **occipitalis musculi occipitofrontalis** occipital (posterior) belly of the epicranius muscle, occipitalis muscle
~ **posterior musculi digastrici** posterior belly of the digastric muscle
~ **superior musculi omohyoidei** superior belly of the omohyoid muscle
Ventilation f ventilation
~/**alveoläre** alveolar ventilation
~/**maximale willkürliche** maximal voluntary ventilation
Ventilationsbewegung f ventilatory movement
Ventilationskapazität f ventilatory capacity
Ventilationsleistungsquotient m air velocity index
Ventilationsstörung f ventilatory disorder
ventilieren 1. to ventilate, to renew the air; 2. to ventilate, to oxygenate the blood
Ventilpneumothorax m valvular pneumothorax
Ventilthrombus m ball-valve thrombus
ventral ventral
Ventriculus m 1. ventricle, ventriculus (s. a. unter Ventrikel); 2. ventriculus, stomach, gaster
~ **cerebri** cerebral ventricle, ventricle [of the brain]
~ **cordis** ventricle [of the heart], chamber of the heart, [cardiac] chamber
~ **encephali** s. ~ **cerebri**
~ **laryngis** laryngeal ventricle (sinus), sinus of the larynx, ventricle of Morgagni
~ **lateralis** lateral ventricle
~ **medius** middle ventricle
~ **quartus** fourth ventricle
~ **terminalis** terminal ventricle
~ **tertius** third ventricle
Ventrifixatio f uteri ventrohysteropexy
Ventrikel m ventricle, ventriculus (s. a. unter Ventriculus) ● **über einem** ~ supraventricular
~/**dominanter linker** dominant left ventricle
~/**linker** left ventricle of the heart, L. V.
~/**rechter** right ventricle of the heart, R. V.
Ventrikel... s. a. Herzkammer... und Kammer...
Ventrikel-Compliance f ventricular compliance
Ventrikeldepolarisation f ventricular depolarization
Ventrikeldruck m [intra]ventricular pressure
~/**linker** left ventricular pressure
Ventrikelfüllung f ventricular filling
Ventrikelfüllungston m ventricular filling sound
Ventrikelgalopp m ventricular gallop
Ventrikelkontraktion f ventricular contraction
Ventrikelpunktion f 1. cardiopuncture, cardi[o]centesis; 2. ventriculopuncture, cranial (ventricular) puncture
Ventrikelrelaxation f ventricular relaxation
Ventrikelseptum n [inter]ventricular septum
Ventrikelseptumdefekt m ventricular septal defect, Roger's disease

Ventrikelsystem n ventricular system
Ventrikelvergrößerung f ventricular enlargement
ventrikulär ventricular
Ventrikulitis f ventriculitis, inflammation of a [brain] ventricle
ventrikuloatrial ventriculoatrial
Ventrikuloatriostomie f ventriculoatriostomy (bei Hydrozephalus)
Ventrikulogramm n ventriculogram
Ventrikulographie f ventriculography
ventrikulographisch ventriculographic
ventrikulojugulär ventriculojugular
Ventrikulometrie f ventriculometry
ventrikulometrisch ventriculometric
ventrikuloperitoneal ventriculoperitoneal
Ventrikuloskop n ventriculoscope
Ventrikuloskopie f ventriculoscopy
ventrikuloskopisch ventriculoscopic
Ventrikulostomie f ventriculostomy
ventrikulovenös ventriculovenous
Ventrikulozisternostomie f ventriculocisternostomy, ventriculospinal-subarachnoid shunt
Ventriloquismus m ventriloquism
Ventrofixation f ventrohysteropexy, gastrohysteropexy, ventrifixation of the uterus
Ventrohysteropexie f s. Ventrofixation
ventroskopisch ventroscopic
Ventrozystorrhaphie f ventrocystorrhaphy
Venula f venule, venula, small vein
Venulae fpl **rectae renis** straight venules [of the kidney]
~ **stellatae** stellate venules [of the kidney]
Venusberg m mount of Venus
Venuskranz m crown of Venus (bei Syphilis)
verabfolgen to give, to administer (z. B. eine Medizin)
~/**durch intramuskuläre Injektion** to give by intramuscular injection
~/**eine Prämedikation** to premedicate
verabfolgt/durch den Mund peroral, by the mouth
verabreichen to administer, to give (z. B. eine Medizin)
~/**eine Injektion** to give an injection
~/**in Dosen** to dose
~/**per os** to administer orally
verändern/die Kindslage to turn (z. B. bei der Geburt)
~/**durch Opsonin** to opsonize (Bakterien im Blut)
~/**sich geschwürig** to ulcerate
verändernd/den Zustand metamorphic
~/**sich leicht** labile
Veränderung f **der Ernährung[sweise]** metatrophy
~/**elektrokardiographische** electrocardiographic change
~/**pigmentäre** pigmentary change
Veranlagung f [pre]disposition
Verarmung f depletion (z. B. an Glykogen)
Veraschungsbild n **eines Gewebes** spodogram
verästelt ramified, branched; dendritic, dendroid
Verätzung f 1. acid (caustic, chemical) burn; 2. cauterization (Vorgang)

Verbalagraphie

Verbalagraphie f verbal agraphia
Verbalsuggestion f verbal suggestion
Verband m dressing, bandage, strapping
~/**beidäugiger** binocle bandage
~/**provisorischer** temporary dressing
~/**ringförmiger** circular bandage, cingulum
~/**Schanzscher** cervical collar
Verbandgips m plaster of Paris, surgical plaster
Verbandkasten m first-aid box
Verbandlehre f desmurgia
Verbandmaterial n dressing (bandaging) material
Verbandmull m mull, aseptic gauze, [absorbent] gauze
Verbandschere f bandage [cutting] scissors, bandage shears, [curved] scissors
Verbandstoff m s. Verbandmaterial
Verbandstofftrommel f dressing [sterilizing] container
Verbandtasche f medical wallet
Verbandwagen m dressing trolley, trolley for dressing utensils
Verbandwechsel m change of dressing, redressement
Verbandzeug n s. Verbandmaterial
verbessern/die Nervenleitfähigkeit to canalize
Verbeugungsreflex m/**Gamperscher** Gamper's bowing reflex
Verbiegung f arcuation *(z. B. bei Knochen)*
~ **nach vorn** antecurvature
Verbigeration f verbigeration
verbinden 1. to bandage, to dress, to strap [up]; 2. s. ~/**miteinander**
~/**durch eine Synapse** to synapse
~/**miteinander** to anastomose *(z. B. Blutgefäße, Nerven)*
~/**mit Jod** to iodinate
Verbindung f 1. connection; 2. junction, junctura; articulation, joint *(Anatomie)*; 3. s. Commissura; 4. anastomosis *(operativ oder natürlich)*
~/**myoneurale** myoneural junction
~/**schmale** isthmus
Verbindungsgang m fistula
Verblitzung f flash blindness (ophthalmia), electric ophthalmia, photophthalmia; flasheye
Verblödung f s. Demenz
verbluten to bleed to death, to exsanguinate
Verblutung f bleeding to death, exsanguination
verborgen hidden, latent *(z. B. eine Infektion)*; larvate, larvaceous *(z. B. eine Erkrankung)*; occult *(z. B. eine Blutung)*
Verbrauch m consumption *(z. B. der Nahrung)*
verbrauchend consumptive
Verbrauchskoagulopathie f consumptive coagulopathy
Verbreitung f/**hämatogene** haematogenous spread[ing]
verbrennen/Leichen to cremate, to incinerate
~/**sich** to burn; to tan *(durch die Sonne)*
Verbrennung f 1. burn; cremation, incineration *(einer Leiche)*; 2. X-ray burn *(durch Röntgenstrahlen)*; electric contact burn ● **eine viertgradige ~ erleiden** to carbonize

~/**chemische** chemical burn
~ **dritten Grades** burn of third degree, third-degree burn
~ **ersten Grades** burn of first degree, first-degree burn
~ **vierten Grades** burn of fourth degree, fourth-degree burn, carbonization
~ **zweiten Grades** burn of second degree, second-degree burn
Verbrennungsbehandlung f burn management
Verbrennungsenzephalopathie f burn encephalopathy
Verbrennungsintensivstation f burn unit
Verbrennungskachexie f burn cachexia
Verbrennungskeloid n burn keloid
Verbrennungspatient m burn patient
Verbrennungsrekonvaleszentenserum n convalescent burn serum
Verbrennungsschock m burn shock
Verbrennungsschockvorbeugung f burn shock prevention
Verbrennungsschorf m burn eschar
Verbrennungsspezialklinik f burn centre
Verbrennungswärme f burn of combustion
Verbrennungswasser n water of combustion
Verbrennungswunde f burn wound
Verbrennungswundeninfektion f burn wound infection
verbrühen/sich to scald
Verbrühung f scald [burn]
verbunden/durch die Nabelschnurgefäße omphaloangiopagous *(Zwillingsmißbildung)*
Verdachtsdiagnose f tentative diagnosis
verdampfen to vaporize, to evaporate; to volatilize *(verflüchtigen)*
Verdampfer m evaporator, vaporizer
Verdampfung f vaporization, evaporation; volatilization
verdauen to digest
~/**durch Pepsin** to peptonize
verdauend digestive
verdaulich digestible
~/**gut** eupeptic
~/**leicht** easily digestible, light
~/**nicht** indigestible
~/**schwer** hard to digest, indigestible, heavy, rich, stodgy
Verdaulichkeit f digestibility
Verdauung f digestion ● **durch ~ entstanden** peptic
~/**gastrointestinale** gastrointestinal (primary) digestion
~/**gute (normale)** eupepsia
~/**peptische** peptic digestion
~/**tryptische** tryptic digestion
Verdauungsapparat m digestive (alimentary) system
Verdauungsdrüse f digestive gland
Verdauungsenzym n digestive enzyme
verdauungsfördernd promoting digestion, digestive, digestant, peptogenic, peptic
verdauungsgestört dyspeptic

Verdauungskanal m s. Verdauungstrakt
Verdauungsleukozytose f digestive leucocytosis
Verdauungsorgan n digestive organ
Verdauungsphysiologie f digestive physiology
Verdauungspräparat n digestive [agent], digestant, stomachic
Verdauungsstörung f digestive disturbance, indigestion, disturbed digestion, dyspepsia
Verdauungssystem n digestive (alimentary) system
Verdauungstrakt m digestive tract (canal, tube), alimentary (gastro-intestinal) tract ● **den ~ umgehend** parenteral, paraoral
Verdauungstraktfunktionsstörung f digestive tract dysfunction
Verdauungsvorgang m digestive process
verdichtet pyknotic (z. B. eine Zelle)
Verdichtung f consolidation, solidification (z. B. von Gewebe); condensation (z. B. einer Idee); densification (z. B. von Röntgenstrukturen)
verdickt/abnorm pachyntic
Verdickung f/**abnorme** pachynsis (z. B. einer Membran)
Verdoglobin n verdoglobin (Hämoglobinabbauprodukt)
~ CN cyanhaemoglobin
Verdoglobinämie f verdoglobinaemia; enterogenous cyanosis
Verdohämin n verdohaemin (Gallepigment)
Verdohämochromogen n verdohaemochromogen (Gallepigment)
Verdohämoglobin n verdohaemoglobin (Hämoglobinabbauprodukt)
Verdopp[e]lung f duplication; reduplication (z. B. der Chromosomen)
Verdrängung f 1. repression, suppression (z. B. eines Konflikts); 2. displacement (z. B. eines Organs)
verdreht twisted, torsive, tortuous; distorted
Verdrehung f twisting, torsion (z. B. des Darms); distortion, sprain (z. B. eines Gelenks)
verdünnen to dilute (z. B. Flüssigkeiten); to rarefy (z. B. Gase)
Verdünnung f dilution (z. B. von Flüssigkeiten); rarefaction (z. B. von Gasen)
Verdünnungsmittel n diluent
Verdünnungsversuch m/**Volhardscher** Volhard's (urine concentration) test
verdunsten to evaporate, to vaporize; to volatilize; to transpire (z. B. Schweiß)
Verdunstung f evaporation, vaporization; volatilization, transpiration (z. B. von Schweiß)
Verdunstungsmesser m psychrometer
Vereinsamungsfurcht f monophobia
vereinzelt solitary
vereitern to suppurate, to form pus, to produce matter
Vereiterung f suppuration, pyosis
~ des Recessus epitympanicus attic suppuration
~ einer Meibomschen Drüse Meibomian stye
verengen/sich to stenose, to narrow, to constrict

verengernd constrictive
Verengerung f 1. narrowing (z. B. durch Narbenzug); contraction (z. B. der Pupillen); 2. s. Verengung 1.
verengt narrowed; contracted; stenosed, stenotic, constricted, strictured; coarctate
Verengung f 1. stenosis (z. B. eines Gefäßes); constriction (z. B. des Rachens); stricture (z. B. der Harnröhre); [co]arctation (z. B. der Aorta); isthmus (z. B. der Eileiter); strait (z. B. des Beckens); 2. s. Verengerung 1.
~/narbige cicatricial narrowing
vererbbar hereditary, [in]heritable, transmissable
Vererbbarkeit f hereditariness, [in]heritability
vererbt hereditary, inherited
Vererbung f heredity, hereditary transmission, inheritance
~/autosomal-dominante autosomal dominant transmission
~/autosomal-rezessive autosomal recessive transmission
Vererbungslehre f genetics, genesiology
Verfahren n/**einzeitiges** one-stage procedure
~/Politzersches politzerization, Politzer's method of inflation (von Luft durch die Ohrtrompete in das Mittelohr)
Verfall m decay (z. B. von Zellen); degeneration (z. B. von Muskelgewebe); decline (z. B. der Gesundheit); marasmus (des Körpers); deterioration (des Geistes); senility (im Alter); (s. a. unter Degeneration und Marasmus) ● **dem ~ unterliegen** to degenerate
verfallen to decay (z. B. Zellen); to degenerate (z. B. Gewebe); to waste [away], to decline (gesundheitlich); to be marantic, to lose flesh (körperlich); to deteriorate (geistig); to become senile (altern)
verfallen 1. decayed; declined; degenerated; wasted, haggard; marantic, marasm[at]ic; deteriorated; 2. addicted (dem Rauschgift)
verfärben/sich to change colour (z. B. Gesicht); to discolour, to lose colour; to grow pale (erblassen)
verfärbt discoloured
~/blutig sanguinolent
Verfassung f state, condition (körperlich); constitution; predisposition (Krankheitsbereitschaft)
~/momentane disposition
~/psychische mental condition
verfaulen to putrefy, to rot, to decompose
verfaulend putrescent
verfestigen/sich to consolidate (z. B. ein Knochenbruch)
verfestigend consolidant
Verfestigung f consolidation
Verfestigungsnekrose f coagulation necrosis (durch Säureverätzung)
verfettend steatogenous
verfettet adipose, fatty, liparous (z. B. Organe); obese (Körper)
Verfettung f steatosis, fatty degeneration (z. B. von Organen); obesity (des Körpers)

verflüchtigen

verflüchtigen/sich to volat[il]ize; to evaporate
verflüssigen/sich to liquefy
verflüssigend/sich liquescent; colliquative *(z. B. durch Laugenverätzung)*
Verflüssigung *f* liquefaction; colliquation, colliquative softening *(von Geweben)*
Verflüssigungsmittel *n* liquefacient [agent]
Verflüssigungsnekrose *f* colliquative (liquefying) necrosis, liquefaction necrosis (degeneration)
Verfolgungswahn *m* delusion of persecution, persecution complex (mania), obsession
vergällen to denature
Vergällung *f* denatur[iz]ation
vergasen 1. to gasify, to vaporize *(Gas bilden)*; 2. to gas *(durch Giftgas)*; to disinfect by gas
Vergewaltigung *f* rape, violation
vergiften to poison, to intoxicate
~/sich to take poison, to poison
Vergiftung *f* poisoning, [in]toxication; venenation *(z. B. durch tierische Gifte)* ● **eine ~ bewirkend** intoxicant
~/äußere hetero-intoxication, exogenous toxicosis
~/innere endo-intoxication, auto-intoxication, endogenous toxicosis
Vergiftungsfurcht *f* toxi[co]phobia
Vergiftungskrankheit *f* tox[ic]osis, toxinosis, toxonosis, toxicopathy
Vergiftungsschwachsichtigkeit *f* toxic amblyopia
Vergiftungssymptom *n* intoxication sign (symptom)
Vergreisung *f* **im Kindesalter** childhood progeria, Hutchinson-Gilford disease, premature senility syndrome
Vergrößerung *f* growth *(durch Wachstum)*; enlargement *(z. B. eines Organs)*; hypertrophy *(z. B. eines Muskels)*; magnification *(z. B. eines Mikroskops)*; augmentation *(z. B. der Keimzahl)*
Verhakung *f* **der Wirbelsäulengelenkfortsätze** locking of the articular processes
Verhalten *n* behaviour, attitude
~/dramatisches dramatism
~/männliches masculinity
~/weibliches feminism
Verhaltensforschung *f* behavioural research
Verhaltenslehre *f* ethology
Verhaltensmuster *n* behaviour pattern
Verhaltenspsychologie *f* behaviouristic psychology
Verhaltensreflex *m* behaviour reflex
Verhaltensstörung *f* pathergasia, behavioural disorder, behaviour disturbance; personality maladjustment
~/aggressive aggressive behavioural disorder
Verhaltenstest *m* psychological test
Verhaltenstherapie *f* behaviour therapy
Verhaltensweise *f* behaviour [pattern]
Verhaltenswissenschaft *f* behavioural science
Verhaltung *f* retention, suppression *(z. B. von Körperflüssigkeiten)*

verhärten/sich to harden, to indurate *(z. B. Organe)*; to sclerose *(z. B. Gewebe)*
verhärtend indurative; sclerosing, sclerogenous
verhärtet indurative; sclerosed
Verhärtung *f* hardening, induration *(z. B. von Organen)*; sclerosis *(z. B. von Gewebe)*
~/vollständige pansclerosis
verheilen to heal [up] *(z. B. eine Wunde)*; to consolidate *(z. B. ein Knochenbruch)*
verheilend healing; consolidant
verhornen to become horny *(z. B. die Haut)*; to keratinize *(z. B. Gewebe)*
verhornt horny, cornified; keratose, keratinized, keratotic
Verhornung *f* 1. cornification, hornification *(z. B. der Haut)*; keratinization *(z. B. von Geweben)*; 2. keratosis *(z. B. der Hände und Füße)*
Verhornungsprozeß *m* keratinization [process]
Verhornungsstörung *f* **der Oberhaut** parakeratosis
verhungern to starve [to death]
Verhungern *n* starvation
verhütend preventive, prophylactic
Verhütung *f* prevention, prophylaxis
Verhütungsmittel *n* preventive [agent], prophylactic; contraceptive
verimpfbar inoculable
Verimpfbarkeit *f* inoculability
verimpfen to inoculate *(z. B. Serum)*
Verimpfung *f* inoculation *(z. B. von Serum)*
verkalken to calcify, to sclerose *(z. B. Gefäße)*
verkalkend calcareous, sclerosing
verkalkt calcareous, sclerotic
Verkalkung *f* 1. calcification; sclerosis; 2. *s.* Arteriosklerose; 3. calcinosis, calcium gout (thesaurismosis) *(durch Kalkablagerung)*
~ des Nervengewebes neurosclerosis
Verkalkungslinie *f* calcification line
verkappt larvate, larvaceous
verkäsen to caseate, to undergo caseous degeneration
Verkäsung *f* caseation, caseous degeneration, tyrosis
Verkäsungsabszeß *m* caseous (cheesy) abscess
Verkäsungsherd *m* caseous [pulmonary] focus, caseonecrotic focus *(bei Tuberkulose)*
Verkäsungslungentuberkulose *f* caseous pneumonic tuberculosis
Verkäsungsnekrose *f* caseation necrosis, caseous (cheesy) necrosis *(bei Tuberkulose)*
Verkehr *m***/sexueller** [sexual] intercourse
verkeilen/sich to become impacted *(z. B. ein Knochenbruch)*; to become locked *(z. B. bei der Geburt)*
Verkeilung *f* impaction *(z. B. eines Knochenbruchs)*; head lock *(bei der Geburt)*
verkleben to adhere *(z. B. Eingeweide)*; to obliterate *(z. B. Hohlräume)*; to clump, to agglutinate *(z. B. Erythrozyten)*; to conglutinate *(z. B. Oberflächen)*; to plaster up *(z. B. eine Wunde)*
~/die Eileiterfimbrien to fuse the fimbriae

verklebend adhesive; obliterant, obliterative; agglutinative; conglutinant, conglutinate
Verklebung f adhesion *(z. B. von Eingeweiden)*; obliteration *(z. B. von Hohlräumen)*; clumping, agglutination *(z. B. von Erythrozyten)*; conglutination *(z. B. von Oberflächen)*; synechia *(z. B. am Auge)*; concretion *(z. B. der Finger)*
verklumpen to clump, to agglutinate
Verklumpung f clumping, agglutination *(z. B. von Blutkörperchen)*
verknöchern to ossify, to form bone; to consolidate *(Knochenbruch)*
verknöchernd ossific; consolidant *(Knochenbruch)*
Verknöcherung f ossification, formation of bone; consolidation *(eines Knochenbruchs)*
~/elfenbeinähnliche eburnation; productive osteitis
Verknöcherungsstörung f dysostosis
Verknöcherungszentrum n centre of ossification, ossification point
verknorpeln to chondrify, to become cartilaginous, to convert into cartilage
verknorpelt chondrified, cartilaginous
Verknorpelung f chondrification, cartilaginification
verknüpfen 1. to knot, to tie [up] *(z. B. einen Faden)*; 2. to associate *(Gedanken)*
Verknüpfung f 1. knotting, tying [up] *(z. B. eines Fadens)*; 2. association *(z. B. von Gedanken)*
verkochen/elektrisch to electrocoagulate
Verkochung f/elektrische electrocoagulation
verkohlen to carbonize
Verkohlung f carbonization, burn of fourth degree, fourth-degree burn
verkrampft cramped, spastic, spasmodic
Verkrümmtsehen n metamorphopsia *(verzerrte Wahrnehmung von Gegenständen durch das Auge)*
Verkrümmung f arcuation *(z. B. von Knochen)*; curvature *(z. B. der Wirbelsäule)*; incurvation *(nach innen)*; excurvation *(nach außen)*
verkrüppeln to cripple, to stunt, to deform, to maim, to mutilate; to become crippled
verkrusten to incrust, to form crusts, to scab
Verkrustung f incrustation
verkümmern to atrophy, to become atrophied; to degenerate
verkümmert rudimentary; stunted, dwarfed
Verkümmerung f atrophy; degeneration; rudiment[um]
Verkupferung f des Auges chalcosis
verlagern to shift; to displace *(z. B. Organe)*; to transpose *(z. B. Gewebe)*; to repress *(z. B. Gedanken)*
Verlagerung f shift, dislocation; displacement, dystopia *(z. B. von Organen)*; transposition *(z. B. von Gewebe)*; repression *(z. B. von Gedanken)*
verlängern 1. to elongate, to lengthen *(z. B. den Gebärmutterhals)*; to extend *(z. B. einen Knochen)*; to prolongate *(z. B. ein Zeitintervall)*; 2. to protract *(z. B. die Wirkung von Arzneimitteln)*
Verlängerung f elongation *(z. B. des Gebärmutterhalses)*; extension *(z. B. eines Knochens)*; prolongation *(z. B. des zeitlichen Ablaufs)*
Verlangsamung f slowing *(z. B. der Blutzirkulation)*; retardation, backwardness *(der geistigen und körperlichen Entwicklung)*
~ **aller psychischen Leistungen** bradyphrenia
~ **der Herzfrequenz** bradycardia, brachycardia, bradyrhythmia
Verlauf m course, progress *(z. B. einer Krankheit)*; course *(z. B. von Gefäßen)*; path *(z. B. von Nervenbahnen)*
~/schleichender chronicity
verlaufend/abgekürzt abortive
~/heftig acute
~/in der Längsrichtung longitudinal
~/langsam chronic
~/leicht abortive
~/milde bland
~/ohne die üblichen Merkmale larvate, larvaceous
~/ruhig bland
~/schnell acute
~/schräg obliquus
~/tödlich lethal, l.; pernicious
Verlaufsuntersuchung f follow-up
verlaust lousy, lice-infested, pediculous
Verlausung f lousiness, pediculosis
verlegen 1. to obstruct *(z. B. den Darm)*; to block *(z. B. einen Gang)*; to obturate *(z. B. Hohlräume)* *(s. a. verschließen)*; 2. to transfer *(einen Patienten)*
verlegend obstructive, obstruent *(z. B. Gallensteine)*
Verlegung f 1. obstruction *(z. B. des Darms)*; blockage *(z. B. eines Gangs)*; obturation *(z. B. von Hohlräumen)*; 2. transfer *(eines Patienten)*
~ **der oberen Luftwege** upper airway obstruction
verleihen/Immunität to confer immunity
verletzbar vulnerable, damageable, sensive
Verletzbarkeit f vulnerability, sensitivity
verletzen to injure, to traumatize, to hurt, to wound, to violate, to vulnerate
verletzend/nicht atraumatic
Verletzter m injured (wounded) person; casualty
Verletzung f 1. injury, trauma; lesion, vulnus, wound *(s. a. unter Trauma)*; 2. traumatism, traumatosis; mutilation ● **innerhalb einer ~** intralesional
~ **durch Verkehrsunfall** traffic injury
verletzungsbedingt caused by an injury
Verletzungsfolge f traumatopathy
Verletzungspotential n demarcation (injury) potential *(Physiologie)*
Verletzungsschock m traumatic shock
Verletzungsstrom m demarcation (injury) current *(Physiologie)*
verlieren/das Augenlicht to become blind
~/das Bewußtsein to lose consciousness
~/das Gehör to become deaf

verlieren

~/die weiblichen Charakterzüge to defeminize
~/einen Patienten to lose a patient
Verlust *m*/**sanitärer** casualty *(Militärmedizin)*
vermännlichen to masculinize
vermännlichend virilizing, virilogenic
Vermännlichung *f* mascul[iniz]ation, virilization, virilescence
~/krankhafte virilism[us] *(bei Frauen)*
vermehren/sich to reproduce
Vermehrung *f* multiplication; reproduction
~/bakterielle bacterial multiplication
Vermeidensreaktion *f* avoidance reaction
vermiform worm-like, vermiform, vermicular, vermiculose, vermiculous, vermiculate
vermifug vermifugal
Vermifugum *n* vermifuge [agent]
vermilingual vermilingual
vermindern to lessen, to decrease, to diminish; to obtund *(z. B. die Sensibilität)*; to attenuate *(die Virulenz pathogener Keime)*
vermindernd/den Psychotonus psycholeptic
Verminderung *f* lessening, decrease, diminution; obtundation *(z. B. der Sensibilität)*; attenuation *(der Virulenz pathogener Keime)*
Vermiphobie *f* vermiphobia *(krankhafte Angst vor Würmern)*
Vermis *m* 1. worm, vermis, helminth; 2. *s.* ~ cerebelli
~ cerebelli [cerebellar] vermis, worm of the cerebellum
~ inferior inferior vermis *(im Kleinhirn)*
Vermis-Syndrom *n* vermis (flocculonodular) syndrome
vermizid vermicidal
Vermizidum *n* vermicide [agent]
vernarben to scar, to cicatrize
vernarbend scarring, cicatrizant, ulotic
Vernarbung *f* scarring, cicatrization, [ep]ulosis
Vernarbungsprozeß *m* scarring (cicatricial) process
vernebeln to nebulize, to aerosolize, to atomize
Vernebelungsgerät *n* nebulizer, atomizer
Verneinungswahn *m* delusion of negation, nihilism
vernichten to destroy; to eradicate, to exterminate
~/Krankheitsüberträger to eradicate [vectors]
Vernix *f* caseosa cheesy varnish
vernünftig sane, level-headed; sensible
Vernunftsabneigung *f* misology
Vernunftwidrigkeit *f* paralogia
veröden to sclerose *(z. B. Varizen)*; to obliterate *(z. B. Gefäße)*
verödend sclerosing; obliterative
Verödung *f* sclerosing, varicosclerozation, phlebosclerozation; obliteration *(z. B. von Gefäßen)*
verordnen to prescribe *(ein Medikament)*; to order *(z. B. Bettruhe)*
Verordnung *f* prescription *(durch Rezept)*; order
verpestet pestilential
verpflanzen/Gewebe to transplant, to graft

verpflanzend/artfremdes Gewebe heteroplastic
~/artgleiches Gewebe homoplastic
Verpflanzung *f s.* Transplantation
Verrauschen *n* masking *(bei der Audiometrie)*
verreiben to triturate, to grind [fine]
Verreibung *f* trituration, tripsis
verrenken to dislocate, to disjoint, to luxate; to sprain *(verstauchen)*
~/inkomplett to sublux
verrenkt dislocated, disjoint, luxated
~/unvollständig subluxated
Verrenkung *f* dislocation, luxation; sprain *(Verstauchung)*
~ im Atlantoaxialgelenk atlantoaxial dislocation
~/komplette complete dislocation
~/komplizierte (offene) compound dislocation *(z. B. eines Gelenks)*
~/subglenoidale subglenoid dislocation *(des Humeruskopfes)*
~/unvollständige incomplete dislocation, subluxation
verringern/die Widerstandskraft gegenüber einer Infektion to decrease resistance to infection
Verruca *f* verruca, wart
~ acuminata venereal verruca, fig wart
~ filiformis filiform verruca
~ necrogenica necrogenic verruca, anatomical (postmortem, prosector's) wart, dissection tubercle
~ peru[vi]ana *s.* Verruga peruviana
~ plantaris plantar (planter's) wart
~ senilis senile wart
~ vulgaris wart, common wart [of the skin]
verrückt crazy, mad, insane; manic, maniacal; paranoi[a]c, paranoid
Verrückter *m* madman, lunatic; maniac; paranoiac
Verrücktheit *f* craziness, madness, insanity, lunacy, mental derangement; mania; paranoia, paranoidism
Verruga *f* peruviana Peruvian wart, verruga peruviana, verruca peruana, haemorrhagic pian, Carrion's disease *(durch Bartonella bacilliformis)*
verrukös verrucous, warty
Versagen *n* **des linken Ventrikels** left ventricular [heart] failure, left heart failure
~ des rechten Ventrikels right ventricular [heart] failure, right [ventricular congestive] heart failure
~/kardiovaskuläres cardiovascular failure
~/renales renal (kidney) failure
verschatten to overshadow, to cloud *(Radiologie)*
Verschattung *f* overshadowing, clouding, shadow casting, cloudiness *(z. B. auf Röntgenaufnahmen)*
Verschiebelappen *m* sliding flap
Verschiebeosteotomie *f* displacement (sliding) osteotomy

Verschiebung f shift[ing] *(z. B. der Leukozyten)*; displacement *(z. B. eines Organs)*; distortion
~ **des Elektrolytgleichgewichts** distortion of electrolyte balance
~/**parallaktische** parallax
verschiedenartig heterogeneous
Verschiedenartigkeit f heterogeneity
verschiedenfarbig heterochromic; versicolour
Verschiedenfarbigkeit f heterochromia *(z. B. der Regenbogenhaut)*
verschiedenfingerig anisodactylous
verschiedengestaltig anisomorphic, anisomorphous, heteromorphic
verschiedenzehig anisodactylous
verschiedenzellig polymorphocellular
verschlechtern to aggravate, to make worse, to deteriorate
~/**sich** to worsen, to become worse, to deteriorate *(Zustand)*; to progress *(z. B. eine Krankheit)*; to exacerbate *(z. B. ein Krankheitsverlauf)*
verschlechternd/sich worsening, palindromic; progressive *(Krankheit)*
~/**sich wieder** recrudescent
Verschlechterung f worsening, aggravation, deterioration *(z. B. einer Krankheit)*; complication, change for the worse; augmentation *(z. B. von Symptomen)*; progression, palindromia *(eines Krankheitsgeschehens)*
~/**erneute** exacerbation
verschleiern/das klinische Bild to cloud (mask) the clinical picture
verschleimt congested with phlegm, suffering from phlegm; mucous, mucilaginous
Verschleimung f mucilaginousness, mucosity, mucous congestion, secretional obstruction
verschleppen to spread, to transmit *(z. B. eine Infektion)*; to protract *(eine Krankheit)*; to neglect *(vernachlässigen)*
verschließen to obstruct, to occlude *(z. B. ein Gefäß)*; to close *(z. B. eine Wunde)*; to obturate *(z. B. Hohlräume) (s. a. verlegen)*
verschließend closing; obstructive, occlusive; obturant, obturative; emphractic
verschlimmern s. verschlechtern
verschlossen atresic, atretic, impatent *(z. B. ein Ductus)*; imperforate *(z. B. natürliche Körperöffnungen)* ● ~ **sein** 1. to be impatent *(ein Ductus)*; 2. to introvert *(psychisch)*
verschlucken to swallow
Verschlucken n swallowing, deglutition
verschlungen convoluted *(z. B. Nierenkanälchen)*; twisted *(z. B. Darmschlingen)*
Verschluß m 1. occlusion, obturation, obstruction, emphraxis *(z. B. eines Ductus)*; obliteration *(z. B. eines Gefäßes)*; 2. closure *(z. B. einer Wunde)*
~/**aortoiliakaler** aortoiliac obstruction (occlusion)
verschlüsselt sein to be encoded in *(z. B. genetische Informationen)*

Verschlußhydrozephalus m obstructive (internal) hydrocephalus, non-communicating hydrocephalus
Verschlußikterus m obstructive jaundice, cholestatic (posthepatic) jaundice, resorptive (regurgitation) jaundice *(durch Galleabflußstauung)*
~/**extrahepatischer** extrahepatic obstructive jaundice
Verschlußkapazität f closing capacity *(der Lunge)*
Verschlußkrankheit f/**arterielle** occlusive arterial (vascular) disease, Buerger's disease
Verschlußplethysmographie f occlusion plethysmography
verschmelzen to fuse, to unite; to grow together, to coalesce; to obliterate *(z. B. der I. und II. Herzton)*
Verschmelzungsniere f fused kidney
verschmutzen to soil; to pollute *(z. B. das Trinkwasser)*; to contaminate *(z. B. eine Wunde)*
Verschmutzung f soiling; pollution *(z. B. des Trinkwassers)*; contamination *(z. B. einer Wunde)*
Verschmutzungsangst f molysmophobia, rhypophobia
verschnupft sein to have a cold [in one's head]
verschorfen to scab, to slough
verschorfend scabbing, sloughing; escharotic
Verschorfung f 1. scab formation; 2. cauterization, cautery *(z. B. mit einem elektrischen Messer)*
Verschorfungsmittel n escharotic [agent]
verschreiben to prescribe *(ein Medikament)*
verschroben queer, odd; schizoid
Verschüttungsanurie f compression anuria *(beim Crush-Syndrom)*
Verschüttungssyndrom n crush (compression) syndrome
verschwommen indistinct, blurred; oneiric *(Bewußtseinszustand)*
Versehrtensport m sport (athletics) for the disableds
verseifen to saponify
Verseifung f saponification *(z. B. bei Leichenzersetzung)*
versetzen/mit Kohlensäure to carbonate
~/**mit Neßlers Reagens** to nesslerize
~/**mit Zitrat** to citrate
verseuchen to infect *(z. B. mit Keimen)*; to infest *(z. B. mit Parasiten)*
~/**radioaktiv** to contaminate
verseuchend/Länder und Erdteile pandemic
Verseuchung f infection; infestation; contamination
~/**bakterielle** bacterial contamination
~/**radioaktive** [radioactive] contamination
versikolor versicolour
Versilberung f argentation, silver staining *(Histologie)*
Versio f version, turning *(s. a. unter Wendung)*
~ **spontanea** spontaneous version (turning) *(des Fetus)*

Versio

~ **uteri** uterine version (displacement)
versorgen 1. to perform a wound toilet; to dress, to bandage *(eine Wunde)*; 2. to provide, to supply *(z. B. mit Blut)*; to innervate *(z. B. mit Nerven)*
~/**provisorisch** to temporize *(z. B. eine Wunde)*
Versorgung f/**medizinische** medical care
~ **mit Nervenfasern** innervation
~/**provisorische** temporization *(z. B. einer Wunde)*
Versorgungsgebiet n circulation (supply) area *(eines Blutgefäßes)*; distribution area *(eines Nervs)*; catchment area *(eines Krankenhauses)*
versperren to occlude, to obstruct, to block *(z. B. einen Gang)*
versprühen to atomize, to spray *(Flüssigkeiten)*
Verstand m intellect, mind; intelligence ● **mit gesundem** ~ sane
~/**gesunder** sanity
verstandesmäßig intellectual; rational, reasonable
verstärken to strengthen, to reinforce; to intensify; to increase
~/**eine Wirkung** to activate, to intensify; to reinforce; to increase
Verstärkung f strengthening, reinforcement; intensification; increase
verstauchen to sprain, to twist
Verstauchung f sprain, distortion *(z. B. eines Gelenks)*
Verstauchungsbruch m sprain fracture
versteckt hidden, latent *(z. B. eine Krankheit)*; larvate, larvaceous, masked, concealed *(z. B. ein Symptom)*
versteifen to ankylose; to arthrodese *(operativ)*
versteift werden to be arthrodesed *(z. B. ein Gelenk)*
Versteifung f stiffening; ankylosis, acampsia *(z. B. eines Gelenks)*; arthrodesis *(operativ)*
Versteinerung f petrification *(z. B. eines Gewebes durch Kalkablagerung)*; petrifaction *(Zustand)*
verstoffwechseln to metabolize
verstopfen to obstruct, to occlude, to block *(z. B. einen Ductus)*; to obturate *(z. B. einen Hohlraum)*; to constipate, to obstipate *(den Darm)*; to become obliterated *(z. B. Gefäße)*
verstopfend obstructive, obstruent, occluding, blocking
verstopft obstructed, blocked; constipated, costive *(Darm)*; impatent
Verstopfung f obstruction, occlusion, blockage *(z. B. eines Ductus)*; constipation, obstipation, costiveness *(des Darms)*; obturation *(z. B. eines Hohlraums)*; obliteration *(eines Gefäßes)*
Verstopfungsatelektase f absorption atelectasis
verstreuen to scatter, to disseminate
~/**Sporen** to sporulate
verstümmeln to mutilate, to maim
Verstümmelung f mutilation; dismemberment
Versuch m experiment; trial, test *(s. a. unter* Test *und* Prüfung*)*

~/**Báránscher** Bárány's [caloric] test *(zur Überprüfung des Gleichgewichtsnervs)*
~/**Donath-Landsteinerscher** Donath-Landsteiner test *(zum Nachweis einer paroxysmalen Hämoglobinurie)*
~/**Rinnescher** Rinne's test *(Hörfähigkeitsvergleich zwischen Knochen- und Luftleitung)*
~/**Valsalvascher** Valsalva's manoeuvre *(zur Druckerhöhung in den Hohlvenen)*
~/**Weberscher** Weber's test *(Hörprobe mittels Stimmgabel)*
Versuchsperson f proband, test person
Versuchspräparat n test preparation
Versuchstier n experimental animal
Vertebra f vertebra, spondylus
~ **cervicalis** cervical vertebra
~ **coccygea** coccygeal vertebra
~ **dentata** odontoid vertebra
~ **lumbalis** lumbar vertebra
~ **plana Calvé** Calvé's vertebra plana; Calvé's disease
~ **prominens** seventh cervical vertebra
~ **sacralis** sacral vertebra
~ **thoracica** thoracic vertebra
Vertebral... *s. a.* Wirbel... *und* Spondyl...
Vertebralaponeurose f vertebral aponeurosis
Vertebralbogen m vertebral arch *(Anatomie)*; neural arch *(Embryologie)*
Vertebralis f vertebral artery
Vertebralisaneurysma n vertebral artery aneurysm
Vertebralisarteriogramm n vertebral arteriogram
Vertebralisarteriographie f vertebral arteriography (angiography)
Vertebralkanal m vertebral (spinal) canal *(Anatomie)*; neural canal *(Embryologie)*
Vertebralregion f vertebral region
Vertebrodidymie f vertebrodidymia
Vertebrodidymus m vertebrodidymus *(Mißgeburt)*
Vertebrokostaldreieck n vertebrocostal triangle
Verteilung f distribution *(z. B. von Nerven)*
Vertex m vertex
~ **cordis** vertex of the heart
~ **corneae** vertex of the cornea
~ **vesicae** apex of the bladder
Vertiefung f fossa; impression; recess[us]; lacuna, lake; cavity; sinus; crypt
vertiginös vertiginous, dizzy, giddy, dinic[al], light-headed
Vertigo f vertigo, dizziness, giddiness, light-headedness, lipothymia, dinus *(s. a. unter* Schwindel*)*
~ **auricularis** aural (auditory) vertigo
~ **ocularis** ocular vertigo
~ **stomachalis** stomachal vertigo
~ **tenebricosa** tenebric vertigo
Vertikalbeleuchtung f vertical illumination
Vertikalnystagmus m vertical (up-beat) nystagmus
~/**grobschlägiger** coarse up-beating nystagmus
Vertikalschielen n vertical squint (strabismus)

Vertikalschwindel *m* vertical vertigo
verträglich compatible
Verträglichkeit *f* compatibility
Vertrauensbereich *m* confidence limits *(Statistik)*
Vertrauensverhältnis *n* confidentiality *(Arzt–Patient)*
vertrocknen to dry up; to mummify
vertrocknend drying, xerantic
Vertrocknung *f* xeransis *(z. B. der Haut)*
Verunglückter *m* casualty
verunreinigen to soil; to pollute, to contaminate *(z. B. die Luft)*
verunreinigt/mit Krankheitserregern infectious, infective
Verunreinigung *f* soiling; pollution, contamination
~ **mit Krankheitskeimen** taint, contamination
Verunreinigungssubstanz *f* contaminant
verunstalten to deform, to disfigure
Verunstaltung *f* 1. deformation, disfigurement; 2. deformity
verursachen/allergische Reaktionen to produce allergic reactions
~/**eine Krankheit** to cause a disease
verursachend/Gicht gouty
~/**Kolik** griping
~/**Pellagra** pellagric
verursacht/durch aufrechtes Stehen ortho[sta]tic
~/**durch Insekten** entomogenous
~/**durch Mikroorganismen** microbial, microbic
~/**durch seelische Vorgänge** psychogen[et]ic
~/**körperlich** somatogen[et]ic
verwachsen to grow together; to heal up *(z. B. eine Wunde)*; to coalesce *(z. B. Knochen)*; to fuse *(z. B. beide Nieren)*; to adhere *(z. B. seröse Häute)*; to obliterate *(z. B. Hohlräume)*
~/**mit dem Hinterhauptbein** to occipitalize
verwachsen crooked, crippled, deformed; hunchbacked
Verwachsung *f* 1. union, closure *(z. B. einer Wunde)*; coalescence *(z. B. von Knochen)*; cicatrization *(z. B. einer Narbe)*; fusion *(z. B. beider Nieren)*; adhesion *(z. B. seröser Häute)*; obliteration *(z. B. von Hohlräumen)*; concretion *(z. B. der Finger)*; 2. synechia *(der Iris)*; synophrys *(der Augenbrauen)*; symphysis, synchondrosis *(Knorpelhaft)*
~ **mit dem Hinterhauptbein** occipitalization *(z. B. des Atlas)*
Verwachsungsnaht *f*[/**natürliche**] raphe
Verwachsungsstrang *m* bridle
Verwandlung *f* alteration, change, conversion; transformation; metamorphosis
Verwandtenheirat *f* intermarriage, consanguineous marriage
Verwandtschaft *f* relation
verweiblichen to feminize
Verweiblichung *f* 1. feminization; 2. feminism
verweigern to refuse, to reject *(z. B. Nahrung)*

Verweildauer *f* 1. retention time *(eines Pharmakons)*; 2. period of hospitalization
Verweilkanüle *f* indwelling cannula
Verweilkatheter *m* indwelling (self-retaining) catheter
verwesen to decay, to decompose, to rot, to putrefy
verwesend putrescent
verwest decomposed, rotten, putrid, putrefied
Verwesung *f* decay, decomposition, rot, putrefaction
verwirrt confused, disoriented, abalienated, light-headed *(Bewußtseinslage)*; incoherent *(z. B. die Sprache)*
Verwirrtheit *f* confusion, disorientation, light-headedness, amentia; incoherence *(z. B. der Sprache)*
Verwirrung *f*/**geistige** mental confusion (disorientation), obfuscation
verworren confused, intricate
verwundbar vulnerable
Verwundbarkeit *f* vulnerability
verwunden to injure, to wound, to vulnerate
Verwundeter *m* casualty, wounded person; wounded soldier
Verwundung *f* wound, hurt; [war] injury
verwurmt verminous, vermiculose, vermiculous
verzahnen to interdigitate
Verzahnung *f* interdigitation *(z. B. von Muskelfasern)*
verzerren to distort
Verzerrtsehen *n* metamorphopsia
Verzerrung *f* distortion *(z. B. von Bändern)*
verzögern to delay, to retard, to protract *(z. B. die Wirkung von Arzneimitteln)*
Verzögerungszeit *f* lag period *(Immunologie)*; latent period *(z. B. eines Reflexes)*
verzuckern to saccharify
Verzuckerung *f* saccharification
Verzückung *f* ecstasy
Verzweiflung *f* despair; hypothymia
verzweigen to branch, to ramify *(z. B. Gefäße)*
verzweigt branched, ramified, ramous, ramose; arborescent, dendritic, dendroid *(baumartig)*
Verzweigung *f* branching, ramification, arborization *(z. B. von Gefäßen)*; bifurcation *(z. B. der Luftröhre)*
Verzweigungsblock *m* arborization block *(im EKG)*
Vesania *f* vesania, unsoundness of mind
Vesica *f* vesica, bladder *(s. a. unter Blase)*
~ **felea** *s.* Gallenblase
~ **urinaria** *s.* Harnblase
Vesicans *n* vesicant [agent], blistering agent; blister gas
Vesicula *f* vesicle, vesicula *(s. a. unter Bläschen)*
~ **lenticularis** lens vesicle
~ **ophthalmica** optic (ophthalmic) vesicle *(Embryologie)*
~ **seminalis** *s.* Samenblase
vesikal vesical
Vesikel *f s.* Vesicula

vesikobullös

vesikobullös vesicobullous
vesikopustular vesicopustular
Vesikorektalfistel *f* vesicorectal fistula
Vesikorektovaginalfistel *f* vesicorectovaginal fistula
Vesikostomie *f* vesicostomy, cystostomy
Vesikotomie *f* vesicotomy, cystotomy, incision into the bladder
Vesikoumbilikalfistel *f* vesicoumbilical (umbilical urinary) fistula
Vesikovaginalseptum *n* vesicovaginal septum
Vesikozele *f* vesicocele, vesical (cystic) hernia
Vesikuläratemgeräusch *n* vesicular rale
Vesikuläratmen *n* vesicular respiration; vesicular resonance
Vesikularemphysem *n* vesicular emphysema
Vesikulektomie *f* vesiculectomy
Vesikulitis *f* vesiculitis, inflammation of the seminal vesicle, spermatocystitis
vesikulobullös vesicolobullous
Vesikulogramm *n* vesiculogram
Vesikulographie *f* vesiculography, radiography of the seminal vesicles
vesikulopapulös vesiculopapular
vesikulopustulös vesiculopustular
Vesikulotomie *f* vesiculotomy, incision into the seminal vesicle
Vestibularanfall *m* vestibular fit (seizure)
Vestibularapparat *m* vestibular apparatus (system), static organ
Vestibulardrüse *f* vestibular gland
Vestibularfalte *f* vestibular fold
Vestibularganglion *n* vestibular ganglion
Vestibularis *m* vestibular nerve
Vestibularisausfall *m* vestibular failure
Vestibulariskern *m* vestibular nucleus
Vestibulariskerndegeneration *f* vestibular nuclear degeneration
Vestibularisstimulation *f* vestibular stimulation
Vestibularisstörung *f* vestibular disorder
Vestibularmembran *f* vestibular membrane [of Reissner]
Vestibularnystagmus *m* vestibular (labyrinthine) nystagmus
Vestibularschwindel *m* vestibular vertigo
Vestibulookularreflex *m* vestibulo-ocular reflex
Vestibulotomie *f* vestibulotomy
Vestibulum *n* vestibule, vestibulum (s. a. unter Vorhof)
~ **auris interna** vestibule of the inner ear
~ **labyrinthi ossei** s. ~ auris interna
~ **laryngis** vestibule of the larynx
~ **nasi** vestibule of the nose
~ **oris** vestibule of the mouth, oral vestibule
~ **vaginae** vestibule of the vagina, vulvar canal
Vestibulumeröffnung *f* [/operative] vestibulotomy
Vestigium *n* vestige, vestigium, rudimentary organ
~ **processus vaginalis** vaginal ligament
via Anus by the anus, per anum
Via *f* **falsa** false passage

Vibices *fpl* vibices
vibrationsempfindend pallaesthetic
Vibrationsempfindung *f* 1. vibratory perception, pallaesthetic sensibility; 2. s. Vibrationssinn
Vibrationsgefühl *n* **der Knochen** bone sensibility, pallaesthesia *(Empfindungsqualität der Tiefensensibilität)*
Vibrationsmassage *f* vibratory massage, vibromassage, vibration treatment, seismotherapy
Vibrationssinn *m* vibratory sense, seismaesthesia
Vibrieren *n* vibration; fremitus *(bei Lungenauskultation)*; thrill *(Schwirren)*
Vibrio *m* **cholerae (comma)** cholera vibrio, comma bacillus
~ **El Tor** s. Vibrio cholerae
~ **septique** vibrion septique
Vibrissa *f* vibrissa, rhinotrix
Vicia-faba-Bohnen-Krankheit *f* favism, fabism[us] *(hämolytische Anämie infolge Enzymmangels)*
vieldrüsig polyglandular, multiglandular, polyadenous
Vieleckbein *n* multangular bone, multangulum
~/**großes** greater multangular [bone], trapezium [bone]
~/**kleines** lesser multangular [bone], trapezoid [bone]
Vielehe *f* polygamy
vielehig polygamous
vielfächerig multilocular
vielfarbig polychromatic, polychrome; versicolour
Vielfärbigkeit *f* polychromasia
Vielfüßigkeit *f* polypodia
vielgeißelig multiflagellate
vielgestaltig multiform, variform; polymorphic, pleomorphic, pleomorphous
Vielgestaltigkeit *f* polymorphism, pleomorphism
vielhändig polycheirous
vielherdig multifocal
vielkammerig multilocular
vielkernig multinuclear, multinucleate, polynuclear, polynucleate
vielknotig multinodular
vielköpfig multicipital *(z. B. Muskel)*
viellappig multilobar, multilobate, polylobular
vielpolig multipolar
vielporig polyporous
Vielreihigkeit *f* **der Wimpern** polystichia
vielrippig multicostate
vielzahnig multidentate
Vielzeller *m* metazoan
vielzellig polycellular, multicellular
vierarmig tetrabrachial
Vierbrüstigkeit *f* tetramastia, tetramazia
Viererrhythmus *m* quadruple rhythm *(des Herzens)*
Vierfachimpfstoff *m* tetravaccine *(gegen Typhus, Paratyphus A und B sowie Cholera)*
vierfingrig tetradactyl[ous], quadridigitate
vierfüßig tetrapus, quadrupedal

viergeißlig tetramastigote
vierhändig tetracheirous
vierhöckrig quadritubercular
Vier-Kammer-Herz n four-chambered heart
vierköpfig quadriceps
Vierlinge mpl quadruplets
viermal täglich four times a day, quarter in die, q.i.d.
vierohrig tetrotus
viersegelig quadricuspid
vierseitig quadrilateral
Viertage[wechsel]fieber n quartan fever (ague, malaria) (durch Plasmodium malariae)
viertägig quartan
Vierteljahr n trimenon, trimester (z. B. der Schwangerschaft)
viertgebärend quadriparous
Viertgebärende f quadripara, quartipara
Viertgeburt f quadriparity
vigil vigil, watchful, wakeful
Vigilambulismus m vigilambulism
Vigilanz f vigilance
vikariierend vicarious
Villi mpl **intestinales** intestinal villi
villös villous, villose, villiform
Villus m villus (s. a. unter Zotte)
~ **articularis** synovial villus
~ **duodenalis** duodenal villus
~ **pleuralis** pleural villus
~ **synovialis** synovial villus
Villusektomie f villusectomy
Vinblastin n vinblastine (Zytostatikum)
Vinculum n vinculum, band
~ **breve** short vinculum
~ **longum** long vinculum
Vinkristin n vincristine (Zytostatikum)
Vinyläther m vinyl ether (Narkotikum)
Violettblindheit f violet blindness, tritanop[s]ia, anianthinopsia
Violettsichtigkeit f ianthinopsia
Viomyzin n viomycin (Antibiotikum)
viral viral
Virämie f vir[us]aemia, viremia
virämisch viraemic
virginal virginal
Virginität f virginity, maidenhood
Virgo f virgin
Viridofulvin n viridofulvin (Antibiotikum)
viril virile
virilisieren to masculinize
virilisierend virilizing, viriligenic
Virilisierung f virilization, virilescence, masculinization
Virilismus m virilism (bei Frauen)
Virilität f virility
Virion n virion
virizid viricidal, virucidal
Virologe m virologist
Virologie f virology (Lehre von den Viren)
virulent virulent
Virulenz f virulence, potentiality of a virus ● **ohne** ~ avirulent

Virulenztest m virulence test
Virus n virus ● **an ein** ~ **gebunden** virus-bound
~/**abgeschwächtes** attenuated virus
~/**derm[at]otropes** dermotropic virus
~/**filtrierbares** filtrable virus
~/**neurotropes** neurotropic virus
virusabhängig virus-bound
Virusämie f s. Virämie
virusartig virus-like
Virusätiologie f virus aetiology
Virusausscheidung f virus excretion
Virusenteritis f virus diarrhoea
Virusenzephalitis f virus encephalitis
Viruserkrankung f virus disease
Virusfreisetzung f virus release
Virusgastroenteritis f virus gastroenteritis, abdominal influenza, winter vomiting disease
Virusgrippe f virus influenza
Virushaftung f viropexis
Virushepatitis f virus (acute infectious) hepatitis
Virusimpfstoff m/**abgeschwächter** attenuated virus vaccine
Virusinaktivierung f virus inactivation
Virusinfektion f virus infection
Virusinterferenz f virus interference
Virusisolierung f virus isolation
Viruskapsid n virus capsid
Virusklassifikation f virus classification
Viruskrupp m croupine
Viruskultur f virus culture
Virusmeningitis f virus (epidemic serous) meningitis, aseptic (abacterial, sterile) meningitis, acute benign lymphocytic meningitis
Virusneutralisation f virus neutralization
Virusneutralisationstest m virus neutralization test
Viruspartikel f virus particle
~/**infektiöse (reife)** virion
Viruspneumonie f virus pneumonia
Virusreplikation f virus replication
Virusreservoir n reservoir of virus
Virusschnupfen m pharyngoconjunctival fever
Virusschutzsubstanz f interferon
Virusspezialist m virologist
virusständig virus-bound
virustötend viricidal, virucidal
virustragend viruliferous
virusübertragend viruliferous
Virusvermehrung f/**gesteigerte** virus enhancement
Visio f vision, sight (s. a. unter Sehen)
~ **alternans** alternating vision
Visite f visit; [house] call ● ~ **machen** to make the rounds of the wards
viskös viscous, viscid, viscose
Viskosimetrie f viscosimetry
Viskosität f viscosity
Viskositätsmessung f viscosimetry
Viskus m viscus
visuell visual
visuomotorisch visuomotor
visuopsychisch visuopsychic

visuosensorisch

visuosensorisch visuosensory
Visus m visus, sight *(s. a. unter Sehen)*
~ **acris** acuteness of vision
~ **brevior** myopia, my.
~ **coloratus** chrom[at]opsia, chromatic vision
~ **debilitas** asthenopia
~ **decoloratus** achromatopsia, achromatic vision
~ **dimidiatus** hemianop[s]ia, hemiopia, hemiamblyopia, hemiablepsia, hemiscotosis
~ **duplicatus** diplopia, double vision
~ **hebetudo** amblyopia
~ **juvenum** myopia, my.
Visuskorrektur f correction of vision
Visusschwelle f visual threshold
Visusuntersuchung f sight-testing; sighting-test
Visusverbesserung f visual improvement
Visusverlust m visual loss
Viszera pl viscera *(s. a. Eingeweide)*
Viszeralbogen m visceral (branchial, pharyngeal) arch
Viszeralepilepsie f visceral epilepsy
Viszeralfurche f visceral groove
Viszeralgehirn n visceral brain; limbic lobe
Viszeralgie f visceralgia, pain in the viscera
Viszeralkrise f visceral crisis
Viszeralleishmaniasis f visceral leishmaniasis
Viszerallymphomatose f visceral lymphomatosis, big liver disease
Viszeralmuskel m visceral muscle
Viszeralnerv m visceral nerve
Viszeralnervensystem n visceral nervous system
Viszeralneuralgie f visceral neuralgia
Viszeralorgan n visceral organ
Viszeralreflex m visceral reflex
Viszeralschädel m visceral cranium
Viszeralschmerz m s. Viszeralgie
Viszeralspalte f visceral cleft, branchial cleft (duct)
Viszerogramm n viscerogram
Viszerographie f viscerography
viszeroinhibitorisch visceroinhibitory
viszerokardial viscerocardiac
Viszeromegalie f visceromegaly
viszeromotorisch visceromotor
viszeroparietal visceroparietal
viszeroperitoneal visceroperitoneal
viszeropleural visceropleural
Viszeroptose f visceroptosis, ptosis of a visceral organ; abdominal ptosis
viszerosensorisch viscerosensory
viszerosomatisch viscerosomatic
Viszerotom n viscerotome *(1. Instrument; 2. Eingeweideabschnitt)*
Viszerotomie f viscerotomy
viszerotonisch viscerotonic
viszerotrop viscerotropic
viszerotroph[isch] viscerotrophic
Viszerozeptor m visceroceptor
vital vital
Vitalamputation f [intra]vital pulpectomy *(Pulpaabtragung in Lokalanästhesie)*
Vitalfarbstoff m [intra]vital stain, vital dye

Vitalfärbung f [intra]vital staining, intra vitam staining
Vitalgefühl n vital sensibility
Vitalität f vitality
Vitalkapazität f vital capacity *(der Lunge)*
Vitalkapazitätstest m vital capacity test
Vitamin n vitamin, vitamine
~ **A** vitamin A, retinol, antixerophthalmic vitamin, antixerotic factor, biosterol
~/**antihämorrhagisches** s. ~ K
~/**antineuritisches** s. ~ B_1
~/**antirachitisches** s. ~ D
~/**antiskorbutisches** s. ~ C
~ B_1 vitamin B_1, thiamin[e], antineuritic (antiberiberi) vitamin
~ B_2 vitamin B_2, riboflavin, lactoflavin, hepatoflavin
~ B_6 vitamin B_6, pyridoxine, adermin
~ B_{12} vitamin B_{12}, cyanocobalamin, antipernicious-anaemia factor, antianaemia principle, [Castle's] extrinsic factor, erythrocyte-maturing factor
~ **C** vitamin C, antiscorbutic vitamin, ascorbic acid
~ **D** vitamin D, antirachitic vitamin (factor)
~ D_2 vitamin D_2, [ergo]calciferol, irradiated ergosterol
~ D_3 vitamin D_3, cholecalciferol
~ **E** vitamin E, tocopherol, fertility vitamin, antisterility factor
~ **F** vitamin F
~ **K** vitamin K, antihaemorrhagic (coagulation) vitamin, prothrombin factor
~ K_1 vitamin K_1, phytonadione
~ K_3 vitamin K_3, menadione
~ **P** vitamin P
Vitaminaktivität f vitamin activity
Vitamin-A-Mangel m retinol deficiency
Vitamin-A-Mangelkrankheit f hypovitaminosis A
Vitamin-A-Mangel-Xerophthalmie f vitamin A deficiency xerophthalmia, hypovitaminosis A xerophthalmia
Vitaminantagonist m antivitamin
vitaminarm vitamin-deficient, poor in vitamins
vitaminartig vitaminoid
Vitamin-B-Komplex m vitamin B complex
Vitamin-B_6-Mangel m pyridoxine deficiency
Vitamin-B_1-Mangelkrankheit f athiaminosis, endemic neuritis
Vitamin-B_2-Mangelkrankheit f s. Pellagra
Vitamin-B_{12}-Resorption f cyanocobalamin (vitamin B_{12}) absorption
Vitamin-B_{12}-Resorptionstest m Schilling test
Vitamin-C-Mangelkrankheit f s. Skorbut
Vitamin-D-Hypervitaminose f hypervitaminosis D
Vitaminkomplex m vitamin complex
Vitamin-K-Test m vitamin K test *(Leberfunktionsprobe)*
Vitaminlehre f vitaminology
Vitaminmangel m vitamin deficiency, subvitaminosis

Vitaminmangelkrankheit f vitamin deficiency disease, hypovitaminosis; avitaminosis
Vitaminpräparat n vitamin preparation
~/öliges oleovitamin
vitaminreich vitamin-rich, rich in vitamins
Vitaminüberschuß m hypervitaminosis
Vitellin n vitellin *(Dottereiweiß)*
vitellointestinal vitellointestinal
Vitellus m vitellus, deut[er]oplasm, yolk
vitiliginös vitiliginous
Vitiligo f vitiligo, white leprosy
Vitium n vitium, defect
Vitreoretinopathie f vitreoretinopathy, vitreoretinal disease
Vitrina f auditoria (auris) endolymph, otic fluid
Vivifikation f vivification, animation
vivipar viviparous
Vivisektion f vivisection
vivisezieren to vivisect
VK s. Vitalkapazität
VKG s. Vektorkardiogramm
Vogelgesicht n bird-face, micrognathic face
Vogelmilbenkrätze f gamasoidosis
vokal vocal
Vokalbildungsschwäche f mogiphonia
Vola f manus vola [manus], palm [of the hand]
~ pedis vola pedis, sole [of the foot]
volämisch volaemic
volar volar
Vollblut n whole blood
vollblütig plethoric
Vollblütigkeit f plethora, polyaemia
Vollbluttransfusion f whole-blood transfusion, full-blood transfusion
Vollblutverlust m whole-blood loss
vollbrüstig mammose, mastous
Vollhaut-Fettgewebe-Faszien-Transplantat n dermafat-fascia graft
Vollhaut-Fettgewebe-Lappen m/**gestielter** dermis-fat pedicle flap
Vollhaut-Fettgewebe-Transplantat n dermis-fat graft
Vollhautlappen m full-thickness [skin] graft, thick-split graft
Vollheparinisierung f systemic heparinization
Vollmondgesicht n moon[-shaped] face *(bei Nebennierenrindenüberfunktion)*
Vollnarkose f general anaesthesia
Vollnarkotikum n general anaesthetic
Vollprothese f full denture
Vollschwester f graduate (trained) nurse
Volumen n volume; capacity
~/mittleres korpuskulares mean corpuscular (cell) volume, MCV
Volumenauffüllung f volume replenishment *(z. B. bei Blutung)*
volumenbestimmend volumetric
Volumenexpander m [blood-]volume expander
Volumenmangelhypotonie f hypovolaemic hypotension
Volumenmangelschock m hypovolaemic (wound) shock

volumenmessend volumetric
Volumenpulskurve f plethysmogram
Volumenpulskurvenaufzeichnung f plethysmography
Volumenpulskurvenschreiber m plethysmograph
Volumenwiederauffüllung f volume replenishment *(z. B. bei Blutung)*
Volumenzunahme f swelling, intumescence, intumescentia
Volumeter n volumometer, inspirometer
Volumetrie f volumetric analysis
volumetrisch volumetric
Volvulus m volvulus, twisted bowel
Vomer m vomer
Vomitivum n vomitory, emetic
Vomitus m vomiting, vomit[us], vomiturition, emesis *(s. a. unter Erbrechen)*
~ cruentes s. Hämatemesis
~ marinus seasickness, pelagism *(Kinetose)*
~ niger s. Melanemesis
von-Baelz-Krankheit f Baelz' syndrome, glandular cheilitis
von-Baerensprung-Krankheit f Baerensprung's disease (erythrasma)
von-Willebrand-Jürgens-Syndrom n von Willebrand's disease, vascular haemophilia
voraseptisch preaseptic
vorausgehend prodromal, prodromic, prodromous *(z. B. ein Symptom)*
~/einer Operation preoperative
voraussagen to prognose, to prognosticate *(z. B. einen Krankheitsverlauf)*
voraussagend prognostic
Vorbehandlung f pretreatment; premedication
Vorbeizeigen n past pointing *(beim Finger-Nasen-Versuch)*
Vorbereitung f preparation *(z. B. auf eine Operation)*; premedication *(vor einer Narkose)*
vorbeugen to prevent, to guard
~/einem Rezidiv to prevent recurrence
vorbeugend prophylactic, preventive; sanitary
Vorbeugungsmaßnahme f preventive measure
Vorbeugungsreflex m bowing reflex
Vorbildung f preformation
Vorbote m prodrome, preliminary sign
Vordehnung f des Herzens preload *(durch Füllungsvolumen)*
Vorderdarm m foregut, protogaster, head gut
Vorderfuß m forefoot
Vorderhaupt n forehead
Vorderhauptslage f/erste (linke) left frontoanterior position of the foetus, L. F. A.
~/rechte (zweite) right frontoanterior position of the foetus, R. F. A.
Vorderhirn n prosencephalon, forebrain *(aus Dienzephalon und Telenzephalon)*
Vorderhirnbläschen n prosencephalic (anterior brain) vesicle, prosocoele
Vorderhirndysraphie f prosencephalic dysraphism

Vorderhorn

Vorderhorn n anterior horn [of the spinal medulla], ventral cornu (column)
Vorderhornsyndrom n anterior cornual syndrome
Vorderhornzelle f anterior cornual (horn) cell
~/**motorische** motor cell
Vorderkopf m sinciput
Vorderlappen m **des Kleinhirns** anterior lobe of the cerebellum
Vorderscheitelbeinstellung f anterior asynclitism, Naegele's (biparietal) obliquity *(Abweichung der Pfeilnaht aus der Beckenführungslinie nach hinten bei der Geburt)*
Vorderwandinfarkt m anterior myocardial infarct[ion]
Vorderwurzel f anterior (ventral) root
~/**motorische** motor root
vorehelich premarital
Vorenzym n proenzyme
Vorerziehung f propaedeutics
Vorfall m prolapse, prolapsus, procidentia *(Zusammensetzungen s. unter* Prolapsus*)*
vorfallen to prolapse; to herniate *(z. B. Organe)*
Vorfuß m forefoot
Vorfußabtragung f **im Chopartschen Gelenk** mediotarsal (midtarsal) amputation
Vorfußgangrän f forefoot gangrene
Vorgebirge n s. Promontorium
Vorgeburt f veil, caul
vorgeburtlich prenatal, antepartal
Vorgeburtsblutung f antepartum bleeding, prenatal haemorrhage
Vorgefühl n aura *(bei Epilepsie)*
Vorgehen n **der Wahl** regimen of choice *(bei Therapie)*
~/**einzeitiges** one-stage procedure
~/**therapeutisches** therapeutic approach
vorgelagert exstrophic *(z. B. die Harnblase)*
Vorgerinnung f preclotting, precoagulation *(z. B. bei Gefäßprothesenimplantation)*
Vorgeschichte f anamnesis, case history
vorhanden/in der Anlage rudimentary
~/**ohne typische Merkmale** latent
Vorhaut f foreskin, prepuce, praeputium *(s. a. unter* Praeputium*)*
~/**fehlende** aposthia
Vorhautbändchen n frenulum of the prepuce
Vorhautbeschneidung f circumcision, peritomy, excision of the prepuce, removal of the foreskin
Vorhautdrüse f preputial gland
Vorhautdrüsenzelle f preputial gland cell
Vorhautentzündung f posthitis, inflammation of the prepuce
Vorhautplastik f posthioplasty
Vorhautschnitt m preputiomy
Vorhautspalt m preputial space
Vorhautstein m postholith, preputial calculus (concretion), smegmolith
Vorhauttalg m smegma
Vorhautvereng[er]ung f phimosis
vorhergehend premonitory

Vorherrschen n prevalence *(z. B. einer Krankheit)*; dominance *(z. B. einer Hirnhälfte)*; preponderance *(z. B. einer Herzkammer)*
~ **des linken Herzens** dominant left ventricle
~ **einer Gehirnhälfte** hemispheric dominance
vorherrschend dominant
~/**nicht** non-dominant
Vorhof m vestibule, vestibulum, atrium, auricle *(s. a. unter* Vestibulum*)* ● **durch den** ~ transatrial ● **mit drei Vorhöfen** triatrial
~/**linker** left atrium of the heart, left auricle
~/**rechter** right atrium of the heart, right auricle
Vorhof... s. a. Herzvorhof...
Vorhofarrhythmie f atrial arrhythmia
Vorhofbogengangsapparat m vestibular apparatus (system) *(im Ohr)*
Vorhofdiastole f atrial diastole
Vorhofdruckkurve f atrial pressure curve
Vorhofeingang m entrance to the mastoid antrum
Vorhoferöffnung f[/**operative**] atriotomy
Vorhoferregbarkeit f atrial excitability
Vorhoffenster n oval (vestibular) window *(im Ohr)*
Vorhofflattern n atrial flutter
Vorhofflimmern n atrial fibrillation
Vorhofgalopp m atrial gallop [sound]
Vorhof-Kammer-Dissoziation f atrioventricular dissociation
Vorhof-Kammer-Scheidewand f atrioventricular septum
Vorhof-Kammer-Überleitung f atrioventricular conduction
Vorhof-Kammer-Überleitungszeit f atrioventricular conduction time
Vorhofkomplex m auricular complex
Vorhofkontraktion f atrial contraction
Vorhofmitteldruck m/**linker** mean left atrial pressure
~/**rechter** mean right atrial pressure
Vorhofmyxom n atrial myxoma, [heart] atrium myxoma
Vorhofschrittmacher m/**wandernder** wandering atrial pacemaker *(Herzreizleitung)*
Vorhofseptum n atrial septum
Vorhofseptumaneurysma n atrial septal aneurysm
Vorhofseptumanomalie f atrial septal anomaly
Vorhofseptumdefekt m atrial septal defect, heart atrium septum defect
~ **vom Secundum-Typ** secundum [type] atrial septal defect
Vorhofseptumverschluß m/**operativer** atrioseptopexy
Vorhofsschwelle f limen nasi *(Grenze zwischen Vorhof und eigentlicher Nasenhöhle)*
Vorhofstillstand m atrial standstill
Vorhofstreppe f vestibular scala *(im Ohr)*
Vorhofsystole f atrial (auricular) systole
Vorhoftachyarrhythmie f atrial tachyarrhythmia
Vorhoftachykardie f atrial tachycardia

~/**paroxysmale** paroxysmal atrial tachycardia, Bouveret's syndrome
Vorhofzacke *f* **im EKG** P wave [of the electrocardiogram]
Vorkeil *m* precuneus *(Rindenfeld)*
Vorkern *m* pronucleus, germ[inal] nucleus
vorklinisch preclinical
vorkommend/überall ubiquitous *(z. B. Bakterien)*
Vorlagerung *f* 1. exteriorization *(z. B. eines Organs)*; 2. ex[s]trophy *(z. B. der Blase)*
Vorlagerungsoperation *f* exteriorization [operation]
Vormauer *f* claustrum *(Gehirnabschnitt)*
vormedizinisch premedical
Vormilch *f* foremilk, colostrum, protogala, neogala
vorn anterior, anticus, a. ● **von ~ nach hinten** ventroposterior
~ **und außen** anteroexternal
~ **und hinten** anteroposterior, postero-anterior, ventrodorsal
~ **und in der Mitte** anteromedial, ventromedial
~ **und in der Mittellinie** anteromedian
~ **und innen** anterointerior
~ **und oben** anterosuperior
~ **und scheitel[bein]wärts** anteroparietal
~ **und seitlich** anterolateral, ventrolateral
~ **und unten** anteroinferior
vornehmen/eine Entlastungstrepanation to trepanize, to trephine
~/**eine Milzentfernung** to perform a splenectomy
~/**eine Operation** to operate
~/**eine Tracheotomie** to tracheotomize
Vorniere *f* s. Pronephros
Vornierengang *m* mesonephric duct
Voröstrogen *n* pro-oestrogen
Vorpubertätsperiode *f* prepuberty
Vorschlaf *m* predormition
Vorschlaginstrument *n* nail driver *(bei Osteosynthese)*
Vorschrift *f* prescription; recipe *(auf Rezepten)*
● **laut ärztlicher ~** according to doctor's order
● **nach ~ des Arztes bereitet** magistral *(Arzneimittel)*
Vorsensibilisierung *f* presensitization
Vorsorgeuntersuchung *f* preventive medical examination
Vorsprung *m* prominence, protuberance, protuberantia, eminence *(s. a. unter* Protuberantia, Prominentia *und* Eminentia*)*
~/**kleiner** tubercle, tuberculum
vorstehen to protrude *(z. B. die Zähne)*
Vorstehen *n* **des Oberkiefers** prognathism
~ **des Unterkiefers** progenia
Vorsteherdrüse *f* prostate [gland], prostata, prostatic gland
Vorsteherdrüsen... *s. a.* Prostata...
Vorsteherdrüseneiterung *f* prostatic abscess
Vorsteherdrüsenentfernung *f***/operative** prostatectomy, prostatic adenectomy
Vorsteherdrüsenentzündung *f* prostatitis, inflammation of the prostatic gland

Vorsteherdrüsenerkrankung *f* prostatic disease
Vorsteherdrüseninnervation *f* prostatic nerve supply
Vorsteherdrüsenkrebs *m* prostatic cancer, carcinoma of the prostata
Vorsteherdrüsenschmerz *m* prostatalgia, pain in the prostate, prostatodynia
Vorsteherdrüsensekret[aus]fluß *m* discharge from the prostata, prostatorrhoea
Vorsteherdrüsen- und Blasenentzündung *f* prostatocystitis
Vorsteherdrüsen- und Samenbläschenentfernung *f*[/**operative**] prostatovesiculectomy
Vorsteherdrüsen- und Samenbläschenentzündung *f* prostatovesiculitis, prostatoseminal vesiculitis
Vorsteherdrüsenvergrößerung *f* prostatauxe, enlargement of the prostate
Vorstellung *f* imagination
vorstülpen to protrude
vortäuschen to simulate, to malinger *(z. B. eine Krankheit)*
~/**eine Appendizitis** to mimic an appendicitis
Vortäuschung *f* simulation *(z. B. einer Krankheit)*
Vortex *m* vortex, whorl
~ **cordis** vortex of the heart
~ **lentis** vortex of the lens, lens vortex
Vortices *mpl* **pilorum** hair whorls
vorübergehend transient, ephemeral
Vorübung *f* propaedeutics
vorverdauen to predigest
Vorverdauung *f* predigestion
Vorwärtsbeugung *f* procurvation *(z. B. des Körpers)*
vorwölbend protrusive
Vorwölbung *f* protrusion
vorzeitig precocious, precox; premature
Vorzwickel *m* precuneus *(Rindenfeld)*
Vox *f* voice, vox *(s. a. unter* Stimme*)*
~ **abscissa** loss of voice
~ **capitis** falsetto voice
Voyeurismus *m* voyeurism
VSD *s.* Ventrikelseptumdefekt
vulnerabel vulnerable
Vulnerabilität *f* vulnerability
Vulnus *m* *s.* Wunde
Vulva *f* vulva, cunnus
Vulvaatresie *f* vulvar atresia (fusion)
Vulvabereich *m* vulvar area
Vulvablutung *f* episiorrhagia
Vulvaelephantiasis *f* vulvar elephantiasis
Vulvaentzündung *f* vulvitis, inflammation of the vulva
Vulvaesthiomene *n* vulvar esthiomene
Vulvaexstirpation *f* vulvectomy
Vulvakarzinom *n* vulvar carcinoma
Vulvanaht *f* episiorrhaphy
Vulvaplastik *f* episioplasty
vulvar vulvar, vulval
Vulvasarkom *n* vulvar sarcoma
Vulvaschmerz *m* vulvar pain
Vulvaspreizer *m* vulvar (vaginal) retractor

Vulvastenose

Vulvastenose f episiostenosis
Vulvaulzeration f vulvar ulceration
Vulvaverklebung f agglutination of the vulva
Vulvaverschluß m/**operativer** episioclisia
Vulvektomie f vulvectomy
Vulvitis f s. Vulvaentzündung
Vulvovaginitis f vulvovaginitis
~ **gonorrhoica** gonococcal vaginitis

W

Wabenlunge f honeycomb lung; end-staged lung
Wachanfall m sleep paralysis
wachsartig waxy, wax-like, ceraceous
wachsend/außen exogenous, exogen[et]ic
~/**innen** endogenous, endogen[et]ic
~/**langsam** dysgonic *(Bakterien)*
~/**nach außen** ectophytic
~/**nach innen** endophytic
~/**ungebremst** exuberant *(z. B. Gewebe)*
~/**üppig** luxuriant *(z. B. Zellen)*; eugonic *(z. B. Bakterien)*
Wachsentartung f amyloid degeneration *(s. a. Amyloidose)*
Wachsleber f waxy (amyloid) liver
Wachsmilz f waxy (amyloid, lardaceous) spleen
Wachsniere f waxy (amyloid) kidney
Wachspräparat n/**anatomisches** moulage, wax model
Wachstum n growth
~/**bakterielles** bacterial growth
~/**fetales** foetal growth
Wachstumsbeschleunigung f acceleration [of growth], hypergenesis
wachstumsfördernd growth-promoting, growth-stimulating
Wachstumsfuge f growth cartilage
wachstumshemmend antiblastic
Wachstumshemmung f inhibition of growth, hypogenesis
Wachstumshormon n growth (somatotropic) hormone, somatotrop[h]in, STH
Wachstumslinie f epiphyseal line
Wachstumspotential n plastodynamia
Wachstumsquotient m growth quotient
Wachstumsstörung f growth disturbance, disturbance of development; dysontogenesis *(z. B. von Gewebe)*
Wachtraum m daydream, waking dream
Wachzustand m wakefulness, wakeful state
Wackelgelenk n loose (mixed) joint, amphiarthrosis
Wackelknie n loose knee joint
Wade f calf [of the leg], sura
Wadenarterie f sural artery
Wadenbein n fibula, calf bone
Wadenbeinarterie f peroneal (fibular) artery
Wadenbeinhals m fibular neck
Wadenbeinköpfchen n head of the fibula
Wadenbeinleiste f/**vordere** anterior margin of the fibula
Wadenbeinmuskel m/**dritter** peroneus tertius [muscle]
~/**kurzer** peroneus brevis [muscle]
~/**langer** peroneus longus [muscle]
Wadenbeinnerv m common peroneal (popliteal) nerve
Wadenbeinschaft m shaft of the fibula
Wadenbeinvene f peroneal (fibular) vein
Wadendurchblutung f calf blood flow
Wadenkrampf m calf cramp, systremma
Wadenmuskel m calf (peroneal) muscle, gastrocnemius [muscle]
~/**dreiköpfiger** triceps surae muscle
Wadenmuskelatrophie f peroneal muscular atrophy
Wadenmuskelkontraktion f calf muscle contraction
Wadenmuskelsehne f s. Achillessehne
Wadenmuskulatur f calf musculature, muscles of the calf
Wadennerv m sural (peroneal) nerve
Wadenvene f calf (peroneal) vein
Wahn m delusion, mania
~/**katathymer** catathymia
Wahnbild n illusion; delusional image
Wahnfixierung f hyperprosexia *(z. B. bei Psychosen)*
Wahnsinn m madness, insanity, lunacy, phrenesis
wahnsinnig mad, insane, lunatic, crazy; phrenetic, vesanic; maniac[al]; paranoi[a]c, paranoid
Wahnsinniger m madman, insane person, lunatic; phrenesiac; maniac; paranoiac
~/**katathym** catathymic
Wahnvorstellung f delusion, delusional (fixed) idea
~/**einseitige** monomania, monopsychosis
wahrnehmbar perceptible; visible *(optisch)*; audible *(akustisch)*
~/**sinnlich** sensual
wahrnehmend perceptive, perceptual; cognitive
~/**körpereigene Reize** proprioceptive
~/**nicht** agnostic
~/**schnell** tachistoscopic
Wahrnehmung f perception; cognition
~/**bewußte** apperception
Wahrnehmungen fpl/**entoptische** entoptic imagery
Wahrnehmungsphysiologie f aesthesiophysiology
Wahrnehmungsschwelle f threshold of perception
Wahrnehmungsstörung f perceptive disorder
Wahrnehmungstäuschung f perceptive hallucination
Wahrnehmungszentrum n receptive centre
Waldpest f sylvatic plague
Wall m wall *(z. B. von Blutgefäßen)*
Wand f wall, paries ● **durch die** ~ transmural *(z. B. Herzinfarkt)*
~/**halbdurchlässige** semipermeable membrane
Wand... s. a. Parietal...

Wanderabszeß m wandering abscess
Wanderblinddarm m wandering caecum
Wandererysipel n wandering (migrant) erysipelas
Wanderfilarie f/**afrikanische** Loa, eye worm *(Erreger der Kalabarbeule)*
Wanderfurcht f dromophobia
Wanderherz n wandering heart
Wanderhoden m migrating testis
Wanderlappen m wandering flap
Wanderleber f wandering (floating) liver ; hepatoptosis
Wanderlinse f phacoplanesis
Wanderlust f apodemialgia, planomania
Wandermakrophage m wandering macrophage
Wandermilz f wandering (floating) spleen, prolapsed (ectopic) spleen
wandern/zur Verletzungsstelle to emigrate to the site of injury *(Leukozyten)*
wandernd migratory, migrant
Wanderniere f wandering (floating, movable) kidney; nephroptosis
Wandernierenfixierung f nephropexy
Wandernystagmus m wandering nystagmus
Wanderpneumonie f wandering (migratory) pneumonia *(mehrere Lungenlappen nacheinander befallende Lungenentzündung)*
Wandersüchtiger m poriomaniac
Wandertrieb m apodemialgia, wandering madness, dromomania, drapetomania; poriomania, ambulatory automatism *(motorische Unruhe bei Epileptikern)*
Wanderzelle f wandering (vagrant) cell *(z. B. ein Leukozyt)*
~/**ruhende** resting wandering cell, rhagiocrine cell, histiocyte *(im Bindegewebe)*
Wandlung f transduction *(z. B. genetischen Materials)*
Wandscherspannung f wall shear stress *(am Herzen)*
wandständig parietal, mural
Wandständigkeit f margination *(der Leukozyten bei Entzündung)*
Wandthrombus m parietal (mural) thrombus
Wange f cheek, bucca, gena, mala
Wangen fpl/**eingefallene** hollow cheeks
Wangen... s. a. Backen...
Wangenbrand m noma, gangrenous stomatitis
Wangenentzündung f melitis, inflammation of the cheek; gnathitis
Wangenepithelzelle f buccal epithelial cell
Wangenfettpfropf m sucking (suctorial) pad
Wangengegend f buccal region
Wangennerv m buccal nerve
Wangenohr n melotia *(Ohrmuschelmißbildung)*
Wangenoperation f/**plastische** s. Wangenplastik
Wangenplastik f meloplasty, genyplasty, gnathoplasty
Wangenschleimhaut f buccal mucosa
Wangenspalte f genal cleft (coloboma, fissure), meloschisis

~/**quere** macrostomia *(Hemmungsmißbildung)*
Wangentasche f buccal cavity, cheek pouch
Wangenzeichen n cheek sign (phenomenon)
wankend staggering
WaR s. Wassermann-Reaktion
Warmblüter m homeotherm
warmblütig warm-blooded, homothermal, homeothermic; haemothermal
wärmeableitend thermolytic
Wärmeabneigung f thermophobia
Wärmeanwendung f s. Wärmebehandlung
Wärmeaufzeichnung f thermography
Wärmeaustauscher m heat exchanger
Wärmebehandlung f thermotherapy
wärmebeständig thermostable, thermostabile, thermophylic, thermotolerant, heat-resistant
Wärmebeständigkeit f heat stability (resistance)
Wärmebett n incubator *(für Frühgeborene)*
Wärmebewegung f thermotaxis
Wärmedurchdringung f, **Wärmedurchflutung** f s. Thermopenetration
wärmedurchlässig diathermic, diathermanous, transcalent
Wärmeempfindlichkeit f thermaesthesia, temperature sensibility
Wärmeempfindlichkeitsmesser m thermaesthesiometer
Wärmeempfindung f thermaesthesia, sensitiveness to heat
~/**schmerzhafte** thermalgia
Wärmeempfindungsverlust m thermanaesthesia, thermic anaesthesia
wärmeerzeugend thermogen[et]ic, thermogenous, heat-producing
Wärmeerzeugung f thermogenesis
Wärmefällung f thermoprecipitation
wärmefest heat-stable
Wärmefestigkeit f heat-stability
Wärmegift n thermotoxin
wärmehemmend thermoinhibitory
Wärmekoagulation f thermocoagulation
Wärmekontraktion f thermosystaltism *(z. B. eines Muskels)*
wärmeleitend heat-conducting
wärmeliebend thermophil[ic] *(z. B. Bakterien)*
Wärmepackung f hot pack
Wärmeregulation f thermoregulation
Wärmeregulationszentrum n heat regulating centre, calorific centre
Wärmereiz m thermal stimulus
Wärmerezeptor m thermoreceptor
Wärmeschmerz m therm[o]algesia
Wärmeschmerzüberempfindlichkeit f thermohyperalgesia
Wärmeschmerzunempfindlichkeit f therm[o]analgesia
Wärmeschrank m incubator *(z. B. in der Mikrobiologie)*
Wärmesinn m s. Thermästhesie 1.
Wärmestabilität f thermostability, heat stability
Wärmestar m heat[-ray] cataract; glassblower's cataract

Wärmestauung

Wärmestauung f hyperthermia
Wärmetodzeit f thermal death time *(z. B. für Bakterien)*
wärmeunbeständig thermolabil
Wärmeunempfindlichkeit f thermanaesthesia, thermic anaesthesia
Wärmflasche f hot-water bottle; hot-water bag *(Gummi)*
Warm-Kalt-Wechselbad n contrast bath
Warmluftbehandlung f thermaerotherapy
Warteraum m waiting room
Warze f 1. wart, verruca *(s. a. unter* Verruca*)*; sycoma; thymion, cutaneous wart; 2. s. Papilla; 3. s. Brustwarze
~/gestielte acrochordon *(Hautpolyp an Augenlidern)*
warzenartig warty, verruciform, verrucoid; papillary
warzenförmig wart-shaped, verruciform, verrucous; papilliform; mamilliform
Warzenfortsatz m mastoid [process], mastoid bone ● **neben dem ~** paramastoid ● **über dem ~** supramastoid
Warzenfortsatz... s. a. Mastoid...
Warzenfortsatzaufmeißelung f masto[ido]tomy
Warzenfortsatzausräumung f[/**operative**] [tympano]mastoidectomy, antrectomy
Warzenfortsatzentfernung f/**radikale** radical mastoidectomy, mastoidotympanectomy
Warzenfortsatzentzündung f mastoiditis, inflammation of the mastoid antrum and air cells, otantritis
~ des Säuglings antritis
Warzenfortsatzeröffnung f[/**operative**] masto[ido]tomy, antrotomy
Warzenfortsatzhöhle f mastoid antrum *(vor der Paukenhöhle)*
Warzenfortsatzoperation f mastoid operation
Warzenfortsatzpneumatisation f mastoid pneumatization
Warzenfortsatzregion f mastoid region (area)
Warzenfortsatzschmerz m mastoidalgia, pain in the mastoid process
Warzenfortsatzzelle f mastoid [air] cell, mastoid sinus
Warzenfortsatzzelleneröffnung f[/**operative**] mastoideocentesis, paracentesis of the mastoid cells
Warzenfortsatzzellsystem n mastoid air cell system
warzenhaft verrucose
Warzenkrankheit f/**Peruanische** bartonelliasis, bartonellosis
Warzen[mutter]mal n naevus verrucosus, epidermal naevus
warzenreich verrucose
Warzen-Virus n wart virus
warzig warty, verrucose, verrucous
Waschfrauenekzem n washerwomen's itch
Waschfrauenhand f washerwoman's hand
Waschgeschirr n wash-basin
Waschraum m scrubbing-up room *(im Operationssaal)*

Waschzange f dressing forceps
Wasser n/**destilliertes** distilled water
~ zur Injektion [sterile] water for injection
Wasserabspaltung f anhydration
wasserabstoßend hydrophobic; water-repellent
Wasseranlagerung f hydration
Wasseransammlung f s. Ödem
wasseranziehend hydrophilic; hygroscopic
Wasseranziehungsvermögen n hydrophilism
wasseraufnehmend hydrophilic
Wasserauge n hydrophthalmos, buphthalmos
Wasserbauch m hydroabdomen, hydroperitoneum; ascites
Wasserbehandlung f water cure, hydrotherapy
Wasserbelastungsversuch m water loading test; drinking test *(z. B. der Niere)*
Wasserbett n water (hydrostatic) bed; water mattress
Wasserblase f water blister, hydrocyst; physaliphorous cell *(große blasige Zelle des Chordoms)*
Wasserbruch m s. Hydrozele
Wasserbruchoperation f hydrocelectomy
Wasserbrust f pleurorrhoea
Wassereinlagerung f water retention
Wasserentzug m dehydration; hydropenia
Wasserentzugserschöpfung f dehydration exhaustion
Wasserfieber n water fever, swamp (mud, slime) fever, harvest (field) fever *(Infektionskrankheit durch Leptospira grippotyphosa)*
Wasserfluß m hydrorrhoea
Wassergeschwulst f hygroma, hydroma
Wassergleichgewicht n water balance (equilibrium); isohydria *(z. B. des Körpers)*
Wasserhammerpuls m water-hammer[-type] pulse, trip-hammer pulse, Corrigan's (cannon ball) pulse *(bei Aorteninsuffizienz)*
Wasserharnruhr f diabetes
Wasserhaushalt m water metabolism
Wasserhaushaltsgleichgewicht n water balance (equilibrium)
Wasserhaut f s. Amnion
Wasserheilkunde f hydrotherapy, hydriatry, hydropathy
Wasserhirnbruch m hydro[en]cephalocele
Wasserkesselgeräusch n kettle-singing sound *(z. B. in der Lunge)*
Wasserkissen n water pillow, water-filled cushion
Wasserkopf m hydrocephalus
~/kommunizierender communicating hydrocephalus
~/nichtkommunizierender non-communicating hydrocephalus
wasserköpfig hydrocephalic, hydrocephaloid
Wasserkrebs m water cancer, gangrenous stomatitis, noma
Wasserkur f water cure
Wasserlassen n micturition, miction, voiding, urination, uresis
~/nächtliches nycturia, nocturia

~/schmerzhaftes painful micturition (urination), dysuria, urodynia, stranguria, odynuria
wasserlöslich water-soluble, hydrosoluble
Wassermangel m hydropenia, water lack (deficiency); hypohydration
Wassermann-Antikörper m Wassermann antibody *(bei Syphilis)*
Wassermann-beständig Wassermann-fast, seroresistant *(bei Syphilis)*
Wassermann-Reaktion f Wassermann reaction (test)
Wasserpfeifengeräusch n whistling sound *(z. B. der Lunge)*
Wasserpocken pl s. Windpocken
Wasserrückresorption f water reabsorption *(z. B. in der Niere)*
Wassersackniere f hydronephrosis
Wasserscheu f hydrophobia, aquaphobia
Wasserscheuer m hydrophobe
Wasserschierlingvergiftung f cicutism
Wasserspeiergesicht n gargoylism *(s. a. Krankheit/Hunter-Hurlersche)*
Wasserspritze f water syringe *(Stomatologie)*
Wasserstoffabspaltung f dehydrogenation
Wasserstoff[ionen]exponent m hydrogen ion exponent, pH value
Wasserstoffionenkonzentration f hydrogen-ion concentration
Wasserstoffperoxid n hydrogen peroxide
Wasserstrahlmassage f hydromassage
Wassersucht f dropsy, hydrops; oedema ● ~ erzeugend hydropigenous ● von ~ befallen hydropic
wassersüchtig hydropic, dropsical; oedematous
wassertreibend diuretic
Wassertrinksucht f hydrodipsomania
Wassertrinkversuch m drinking test
~/Volhardscher Volhard's (dilution) test *(zur Nierenfunktionsprobe)*
Wasserüberschuß m hyperhydration
Wasser- und Elektrolythaushalt m hydro-electrolytic metabolism
Wasserverdunstung f durch die Haut insensible water loss
Wasservergiftung f water intoxication *(des Körpers)*
Wasserzufuhr f water intake, hydration
Wasserzyste f hydrocyst
wäßrig aqueous
Waterhouse-Friderichsen-Syndrom n [Waterhouse-]Friderichsen syndrome, acute fulminating meningococcaemia, meningococcic adrenal syndrome, fulminating adrenal meningitis, adrenal haemorrhage [syndrome]
Watschelgang m waddling (waddle) gait
Watte f cotton wool
Wattebausch m wad of cotton wool, cotton swab
Wattepolster n pad
Wattepolsterung f wadding *(z. B. eines Gipsverbandes)*
Watteträger m cotton applicator, carrier

Wattetupfer m cotton swab
Weberkrampf m twister's cramp
Weber-Syndrom n Weber's syndrome, syndrome of cerebral peduncle, alternating oculomotor, hemiplegia, superior alternating hemiplegia
Wechselbad n contrast bath
Wechseldruckbeatmung f alternating positive-negative pressure breathing
Wechselfieber n 1. intermittent fever; 2. s. Malaria
Wechseljahre pl s. Klimakterium
wechselnd intermittent, alternate; phasic *(regelmäßig)*
Wechselschielen n bilateral strabismus
Wechselschnitt m gridiron (muscle-splinting) incision
Wechselsehen n alternating vision
wechselseitig mutual, reciprocal
wechselwarm[blütig] poikilothermal, poikilothermic
Weckeffekt m arousal reaction *(im Hirnrinden-EEG)*
Weckmittel n analeptic [agent], agrypnode, agrypnotic [agent]
Weg m/falscher false passage
wegbewegend abducent *(z. B. ein Muskel)*
wegführend efferent *(z. B. ein Nerv)*; abducent *(z. B. eine Bewegung)*
~/vom Gehirn cerebrifugal
~/vom Kleinhirn cerebellifugal
~/von der Leber hepatopetal
~/von der Zelle cellulifugal
Wegwerfblutlanzette f disposable blood lancet
Wegwerfkanüle f disposable needle
Wegwerfplastiksonde f disposable plastic tube
Wegwerfspritze f disposable syringe
Wegwerftransfusionsbeutel m disposable transfusion pack, disposable plastic transfusion set
Wehen fpl pains, labour pains ● ~ haben to be in labour (throes) ● in den ~ liegen to be in labour, to labour
~/atonische inert labour
~/heftige strong pains
~/vergebliche missed labour *(besonders bei abgestorbener reifer Frucht)*
wehenanregend oxytocic, ocyodinic, ecbolic
Wehenanregung f induction of labour
Wehenaufzeichnung f toco[tacho]graphy
Wehenaufzeichnungsgerät n tocograph
Wehenfurcht f tocophobia
Wehenkraftmesser m toco[dynamo]meter
Wehenkraftmessung f toco[dynamo]metry
Wehenkurve f tocogram
Wehenkurvenschreiber m tocograph
Wehenkurvenschreibung f toco[tacho]graphy
Wehenmittel n oxytocic [agent], ecbolic [agent], parturifacient [agent], uterotonic [agent]
Wehenschwäche f uterine inertia, bradytocia
Wehensturm m uterine tetanus
Weiberhaß m misogyny
weiblich feminine, female

Weichheit

Weichheit f softness, mollities
~ **des Pulsschlages** microsphygmy, microsphyxia
Weichselzopf m trichoma
Weichstrahlen mpl soft X-rays
Weichstrahlung f soft radiation
Weichteil n soft part
Weichteildefekt m soft-tissue defect
Weichteilinfektion f soft-tissue infection
Weichteilrheumatismus m non-articular rheumatism syndrome
Weichteilsarkom n soft-tissue sarcoma
Weichteilschaden m soft-tissue damage
Weichteilschwellung f soft-tissue swelling
Weichteilstruktur f soft-tissue structure
Weichteilverdickung f **des Körpers** pachysomia
Weichteilverletzung f soft-tissue injury
Weichteilwunde f soft-tissue wound
Weil-Felix-Reaktion f Weil-Felix reaction (test) *(zur Fleckfieberdiagnostik)*
Weinen n/**reflektorisches** reflex weeping
Weisheitszahn m wisdom tooth
weißäugig leucophthalmous
weißblütig leukaemic
Weißblütigkeit f s. Leukämie
Weißfleckenkrankheit f vitiligo, white leprosy
Weißfleckigkeit f **der Nägel** leuconychia, onychopacity; gift spots
Weißfluß m whites, leucorrhoea, leucorrhagia
Weißhaarigkeit f leucotrichia, whiteness of the hair
weißhäutig leucodermic, leucodermatous
weißlich whitish, albicans
Weißschwielenkrankheit f leucoplakia, leucoplasia, leucokeratosis; smoker's patches (tongue)
weitsichtig hyper[metr]opic, long-sighted, farsighted
Weitsichtiger m hyper[metr]ope
Weitsichtigkeit f hyper[metr]opia, long-sightedness, farsightedness
Weitwinkelglaukom n wide-angle glaucoma, open-angle glaucoma, non-congestive glaucoma, [chronic] simple glaucoma
Welch-Fraenkel-Gasbrandbazillus m Welch (gas gangrene) bacillus
Wellenbewegung f wave movement; fluctuation *(z. B. bei Perkussion)*
wellenförmig undulated
Wellennystagmus m undulatory nystagmus
Wellenschreibung f/**mechanische** kymography
Weltgesundheitsorganisation f World Health Organization, WHO
wenden to turn *(z. B. bei der Geburt)*
~/**nach außen** to extrovert
~/**nach innen** to introvert
~/**sich nach außen** to extrovert
~/**sich nach innen** to introvert *(z. B. auf das eigene Seelenleben)*
Wendung f version, turning *(s. a. unter Versio)*
~/**äußere** external (abdominal) version
~/**innere** internal version
~/**spontane** spontaneous version
Werner-Syndrom n Werner's (premature senility) syndrome, adult progeria
Wert m/**kalorischer** calori[fi]c value *(der Nahrung)*
West-Nile-Fieber n West Nile fever (encephalitis), Mediterranean dengue
West-Nile-Virus n West Nile virus
wetterfühlig meteorosensitive
Wetterfühligkeit f meteorosensitiveness; meteoropathy
Wetterkrankheit f meteoropathy
wetterunempfindlich meteororesistant
Wetzsteinkristall m whetstone crystal *(Harnsäurekristall)*
Whiskynase f whisky[-rum] nose
Wickel m pack[ing], wrap, compress
wickeln to pack *(s. a. bandagieren)*
Widal-Probe f Widal reaction (test) *(auf Typhus)*
Widerhallempfindung f echoacousia; resonance
widernatürlich preternatural
widerspiegeln to reflect
Widerstand m resistance *(z. B. eines Organs beim Abtasten)* ● ~ **bietend** resistant
~/**arterieller** artery resistance
~/**peripherer** peripheral (blood-vessel) resistance; afterload
~/**pulmonaler** pulmonary resistance
widerstandsfähig resistant *(z. B. Bakterien)*; refractory *(z. B. gegen Krankheiten)*; robust *(körperlich)*
~ **gegen Hitze** thermoduric, thermoresistant
Widerstandsfähigkeit f resistance
~/**bakterielle** bacterial resistance
Widerstandskraft f [power of] resistance *(eines Individuums)* ● **die ~ senken** to decrease resistance *(z. B. gegenüber einer Infektion)*
widerstehen/einer Infektion to resist infection
wiederanstecken to reinfect
Wiederansteckung f reinfection
wiederaufflackern to relapse, to exacerbate, to recur *(z. B. Krankheiten)*; to recrudesce *(von Epidemien)*
Wiederaufflackern n relapse, exacerbation, epicrisis *(z. B. einer Krankheit)*; recrudescence *(z. B. einer Epidemie)*
wiederauffrischend regenerative, anastatic
Wiederauffrischung f regeneration
Wiederauffrischungsimpfung f booster inoculation
Wiederauftreten n **eines Ahnenmerkmals** atavism
Wiederausgrabung f exhumation *(einer Leiche)*
wiederbelebbar resuscitable
~/**nicht** irresuscitable
wiederbeleben to resuscitate, to restore to life, to reanimate, to revive
wiederbelebend life-restoring, resuscitating; analeptic *(Medikament)*
Wiederbelebung f resuscitation, reanimation, revivification, transanimation
~/**kardiale** cardiac resuscitation

~/**kardiopulmonale** heart-lung resuscitation
~/**zerebrale** neuroresuscitation
Wiederbelebungsabteilung f resuscitation department (ward)
Wiederbelebungsapparat m resuscitator
Wiederbelebungsausrüstung f resuscitative (life-restoring) equipment
Wiederbelebungsmaßnahme f resuscitation measure
Wiederbelebungsmedikament n resuscitating drug
Wiederbelebungsversuch m attempt to restore to life
Wiederbrechen n/**operatives** refracture *(eines schlecht geheilten Knochenbruchs)*
Wiederdurchblutung f reperfusion, restoration of blood flow
Wiedereinfügung f reintegration *(Psychiatrie)*
wiedereingliedern to rehabilitate
Wiedereingliederung f rehabilitation; reintegration *(Psychiatrie)*
wiedereinheilen to reimplant
Wiedereinheilung f re[im]plantation
wiedereinlagern/Kalk to recalcify
wiedereinpflanzen to reimplant
Wiedereinpflanzung f re[im]plantation
wiedereinrenken to reduce *(z. B. ein Gelenk)*
Wiedereinrenkung f reduction *(z. B. eines Gelenks)*
wiedereinrichtbar reducible
Wiedereinrichtung f reposition *(z. B. eines Bruchs)*
Wiedereinstülpung f reinversion *(z. B. der Gebärmutter)*; reposition *(z. B. einer Hernie)*
Wiedererinnerung f palinmnesis
Wiedererkrankung f relapse, recurrence, recidivation
wiedererlangen/das Bewußtsein to recover (regain) consciousness
~/**die Gesundheit** to recuperate
wiedererweckbar/nicht irresuscitable
wiederherstellen to cure, to heal *(z. B. die Gesundheit)*; to [re]convalesce *(z. B. die Körperkräfte)*; to restore *(z. B. eine Organfunktion)*; to rehabilitate *(z. B. einen Kranken)*; to repair *(z. B. das Epithel)*; to consolidate *(z. B. die Knochenstruktur)*; to reconstruct *(z. B. Körperteile)*
~/**den Kreislauf** to re-establish circulation
~/**die Gefäßversorgung** to revascularize
wiederherstellend healing; rehabilitant; reparative; consolidant
~/**die Gesundheit** sanitary
Wiederherstellung f recovery *(z. B. der Gesundheit)*; [re]convalescence *(z. B. der Körperkraft)*; restoration *(z. B. einer Organfunktion)*; rehabilitation *(z. B. eines Kranken)*; repair *(z. B. des Epithels)*; reconstitution *(z. B. von Gewebe)*; consolidation *(z. B. der Knochenstruktur)*; reconstruction *(z. B. von Körperteilen)*
~ **der Arbeitsfähigkeit** rehabilitation
~ **der Gefäßversorgung** revascularization

~/**völlige** restitutio ad integrum
Wiederherstellungschirurg m plastic surgeon
Wiederherstellungschirurgie f plastic (reparative, reconstructive) surgery
Wiederherstellungsoperation f plastic (reconstructive) operation; anaplasty
Wiederholungsaphasie f repetition aphasia
Wiederholungsimpfung f re-inoculation, revaccination, repeated vaccination
Wiederholungszwang m perseveration *(z. B. gleicher Handlungen)*
Wiederintubation f reintubation
Wiederkauen n rumination, merycism
wiederkäuend ruminant
wiederkehren to recur, to relapse *(Krankheiten)*
wiederkehrend/in bestimmten Abständen phasic
Wiedervereinigung f recombination *(z. B. von Genen)*
Wiederverrenkung f redislocation, reluxation
Wiederverschlimmerung f recrudescence
Wiesendermatitis f grass dermatitis
willenlos[/krankhaft] aboulic
Willenlosigkeit f[/**krankhafte**] aboulia, aboulomania
Willenshemmung f dysboulia
Willenskraft f/**gestörte** dysboulia
Willensrichtung f intention
willensschwach dysboulic, hypoboulic
Willensschwäche f[/**krankhafte**] dysboulia, hypoboulia
Willensstärke f will-power, conation
~/**übermäßige** hyperboulia
Willensstörung f[/**krankhafte**] paraboulia
willkürlich voluntary
Willkürmuskel m voluntary muscle *(s. a. Muskel/quergestreifter)*
Willkürmuskellähmung f motor paralysis
Willkürmuskulatur f voluntary musculature (muscles)
Wilms-Tumor m Wilm'[s] tumour, nephrogenic dysembryoma, embryonal (mesoblastic) nephroma, adenosarcoma of the kidney
Wilson-Elektrode f Wilson central terminal (EKG)
Wimper f 1. eyelash; 2. cilium *(z. B. von Bakterien)* ● **die Wimpern verlierend** madarotic, madarous
Wimpernausfall m palpebral alopecia
Wimpern[balg]drüse f ciliary (palpebral, Zeis's) gland, [sebaceous] gland of Zeis
Wimperneinwärtskehrung f trichiasis
Wimpernreihe f/**doppelte** distichia[sis] *(Lidanomalie)*
Wimpernschlag m ciliary movement *(z. B. von Bakterien)*
Wimpernverlust m ptilosis, madarosis
Wind m s. Flatus ● **ein ~ geht ab** a flatus passes
Winddorn m tuberculous dactylitis; spina ventosa
Windelausschlag m napkin (diaper) rash; diaper (napkin area) dermatitis

Windkesselfunktion

Windkesselfunktion f windkessel function *(der Aorta)*
Windpocken pl chickenpox, varicella
Windpocken... s. a. Varizellen...
Windpockenimpfung f varicell[iz]ation
Windpockenvirus n varicella[-zoster] virus, V-Z virus
Windsucht f pneumatosis
windtreibend carminative
Windung f convolution, gyrus *(s. a. unter Gyrus)*
~/**Brocasche** left inferior frontal gyrus
Winkel m/**Brocascher** Broca's (parietal) angle
~/**epigastrischer** epigastric (infrasternal) angle, [sub]costal angle
~/**kostophrenischer** costophrenic angle
~/**kostovertebraler** costovertebral angle
~/**Louisscher** angle of the sternum (Louis, Ludwig)
~/**optischer** optic angle
~/**zerebellopontiner** pontocerebellar angle
Winkelbewegung f angular movement
Winkelblockglaukom n closed-angle glaucoma, narrow-angle glaucoma
Winkelgelenk n hinge joint, ginglymus
Winkelkatheter m elbow catheter
Winkelmesser m goniometer
Winkelnagel m/**Jewettscher** Jewett [angle] nail
Winkelplatte f angular nail plate *(Osteosynthese)*
Winterschlaf m/**künstlicher** artificial hibernation *(durch Unterkühlung des Körpers)*
Wirbel m 1. vertebra, spondylus *(Zusammensetzungen s. unter* Vertebra*)*; 2. vortex *(der Haare)*; 3. vertex, crown, top [of the head]
Wirbel... s. a. Vertebral... und Spondyl...
Wirbelabsenkung f spondyloptosis
Wirbelarterie f s. Vertebralis
Wirbelauflösung f spondylolysis, dissolution of a vertebra
Wirbelbereich m vertebral region
Wirbelbogen m vertebral arch
Wirbelbogendurchtrennung f[/operative] laminoctomy
Wirbelbogenentfernung f[/operative] laminectomy *(zur Freilegung des Rückenmarks)*
Wirbelbogenteilentfernung f[/operative] hemilaminectomy
Wirbelbruch m vertebral fracture
Wirbeldislokation f dislocation of a vertebra, spondylexarthrosis
Wirbeldrehmuskeln mpl rotatores spinae [muscles]
Wirbeldurchtrennung f[/operative] s. Spondylotomie
Wirbelentfernung f[/operative] vertebrectomy
Wirbelentzündung f s. Spondylitis
Wirbelerkrankung f spondylopathy
Wirbelerweichung f spondylomalacia, softening of the vertebrae
Wirbelfenstervergrößerung f[/operative] foraminotomy
Wirbelfortsatz m vertebral process

Wirbelfusion f spinal fusion
Wirbelgelenk n vertebral joint
Wirbelgelenkentzündung f s. Spondylarthritis
Wirbelgelenkfortsatz m articular process of the vertebra
~/**unterer** inferior articular process of the vertebra
Wirbelgelenkgicht f rachisagra, gout in the spine
Wirbelgleiten n s. Spondylolisthesis
wirbelgleitend spondylolisthetic
Wirbelkörper m vertebral body, body of the vertebra; neurocentrum *(Embryologie)* ● **oberhalb eines Wirbelkörpers** epineural
Wirbelkörperabflachung f[/angeborene] platyspondylia
Wirbelkörperosteomyelitis f vertebral osteomyelitis
Wirbelkörperresektion f vertebrectomy
Wirbelkörperspalte f butterfly (cleft) vertebra
Wirbelkörperspreizer m lamina spreader
Wirbelkörpervene f basivertebral vein
Wirbelkrankheit f spondylopathy, disease of a vertebra
Wirbelloch n vertebral (spinal) foramen
Wirbelosteomyelitis f vertebral osteomyelitis
Wirbelquerfortsatzentfernung f[/operative] transversectomy
wirbelreich vorticose
Wirbelsäule f vertebral (spinal) column, backbone, spine, rachis ● **neben der ~** paravertebral; juxtaspinal ● **über der ~** supraspinal ● **vor der ~** prevertebral
~/**Bechterewsche** poker back (spine); rheumatoid spondylitis
Wirbelsäulenaufrichtemuskel m erector spinae [muscle]
Wirbelsäulenbereich m vertebral region
Wirbelsäulenentzündung f s. Spondylitis
Wirbelsäulenextension f/**Glissonsche** Glisson's sling
Wirbelsäulenfehlbildung f atelorrhachidia
Wirbelsäulengelenkleiden n spondyloarthropathy
Wirbelsäulenkanal m spinal (craniovertebral) canal
Wirbelsäulenkanaleröffnung f[/operative] rachi[o]tomy
Wirbelsäulenkrümmung f rachiocampsis, curvature of the spinal column, spinal curvature
Wirbelsäulenkrümmungsmesser m rachiometer
Wirbelsäulenleiden n rachiopathy, disease of the spine; spondyloarthropathy
wirbelsäulenlos spineless, invertebral
Wirbelsäulenmesser n rachiotome
Wirbelsäulenmuskulatur f spinal musculature
wirbelsäulennah juxtaspinal
Wirbelsäulenschiefwuchs m scoliosis
Wirbelsäulenschmerz m rachialgia, spinalgia, pain in the vertebral column
Wirbelsäulenseitenverkrümmung f lateral curvature [of the spine]

Wirbelsäulenspalte f rachischisis, spinal dysraphism; bifid spine
~/unvollständige hemirachischisis
Wirbelsäulentuberkulose f spinal tuberculosis, spondyl[arthr]ocace, tuberculous spondylitis, caries (tuberculosis) of the spine
Wirbelsäulenunterentwicklung f atelorrhachidia
Wirbelsäulenverkrümmung f curvature of the spine (spinal column), rachiocampsis; kyphosis; kyphoscoliosis, scoliokyphosis
~/seitliche [rachio]scoliosis
Wirbelsäulenverletzung f spinal column injury
Wirbelsäulenversteifung f spondylo[syn]desis, spinal fusion
Wirbelsäulenversteifungsoperation f spinal fusion operation
Wirbelschmerz m spinalgia, rachiodynia, spondylalgia, spondylodynia
Wirbelspalte f rachischisis, spinal dysraphism; cleft vertebra
Wirbelspaltenplastik f/Bobroffsche Bobroff's operation
Wirbeltuberkulose f s. Wirbelsäulentuberkulose
Wirbelvene f 1. vertebral vein; 2. vortex vein *(am Auge)*
Wirbelvereinigung f spinal fusion
Wirbelvereiterung f spondylopyosis, suppuration of a vertebra
Wirbelverrenkung f spondylexarthrosis, dislocation of a vertebra
Wirbelverschiebung f s. Spondylolisthesis
Wirbelversteifung f s. Wirbelsäulenversteifung
Wirbelzerfall m spondylolysis, dissolution of a vertebra
Wirbelzusammenbruch m vertebra collapse
Wirkdosis f/minimale minimal effective dose, M.E.D.
wirkend:
~/antibiotisch antibiotic
~/auf das Nervensystem neurotrop[h]ic, neurotrope, neurophilic
~/auf den Sympathikus sympathicotropic
~/auf den Vagus[nerv] vagotrope, vagotropic
~/auf die Bauchspeicheldrüse pancrea[to]tropic
~/auf die Brustdrüse mammotropic
~/auf die Lunge pneumotropic
~/auf die Nebenniere adrenalotropic
~/auf die Nebennierenrinde adrenocorticotropic
~/auf die Nebenschilddrüse parathyrotropic
~/auf ein Organ organotropic
~/auf mehrere Gewebe pan[to]tropic
~/auf Schmarotzer parasitotrope, parasitotropic
~/äußerlich topical
~/gegen das retikulo-endotheliale System antireticular
~/gegen Erythrozyten antierythrogenic
~/gegen Gelbsucht anti-icteric
~/gegen Lepra antileprotic
~/gegen Malaria malariacidal
~/gegen mehrere Krankheitserreger polyvalent
~/gegen Nokardia antinocardial
~/gegen Spirochäten antispirochaetic

~/gegen Syphilis antiluetic
~/gegen Toxin antitoxic
~/gegen Treponemen antitreponemal
~/gegen Trichomonaden antitrichomonal
~/gegen Trypanosomen antitrypanosomal
~/im gleichen Sinne consensual
~/in kleinsten Mengen oligodynamic
~/stark intensive, intense *(z. B. Medikament)*
~/tödlich lethal, l.
~/von außen extrinsic
~/von innen intrinsic
~/wie eine Parasympathikusreizung parasympathicomimetic
Wirkfaktor m/mutationsauslösender mutagen
Wirkgruppe f/pharmakologische pharmacophore
wirksam/stark intensive, intense *(z. B. Medikament)*
Wirksamkeit f/relative biologische relative biologic effectiveness [of radiation], RBE
~/therapeutische therapeutic efficacy
Wirkspiegel m efficient level *(z. B. eines Medikaments)*
Wirkstoff m/antibiotischer antibiotic [agent]
~/chemischer chemical agent
Wirkung f/antikomplementäre anticomplementary action *(des Serums)*
~/entgegengesetzte antagonistic action
~/oligodynamische oligodynamic action *(keimhemmende Wirkung von Schwermetallionen)*
Wirkungsbereich m [activity] spectrum *(z. B. eines Antibiotikums)*
Wirkungsgruppe f prosthetic group
wirkungslos ineffective, inefficacious *(z. B. eine Therapie)*
Wirkungsverlust m/schneller tachyphylaxia, tachyphylaxis *(z. B. eines Medikaments)*
Wirkungszeit f action time
Wirt m host ● **nur einen ~ benötigend** monoxenic, monoxenous
Wirt-gegen-Transplantat-Reaktion f host-versus-graft reaction
Wirt-Parasit-Beziehung f host-parasite relationship
Wirt-Parasit-Gleichgewicht n host-parasite balance
Wirt-Parasit-Wechselbeziehung f host-parasite interaction
Wirtsorgan n organ of attachment *(z. B. der Bandwürmer)*
Wirtsorganismus m host organism
Wirtsresistenz f host resistance
Wirtszellenreaktivierung f host cell reactivation
Wismutvergiftung f bismuthism, bismuthosis
witterungsempfindlich meteorosensitive
witterungsunempfindlich meteororesistant
Witzelsucht f joking mania, moria
Wochenbett n childbed, puerperium, lying-in [period] ● **im ~ liegend** to be confined
Wochenbett... s. a. Puerperal... und Kindbett...
Wochenbettdepression f puerperal depression (melancholia)

Wochenbettthrombose

Wochenbettthrombose f puerperal venous thrombosis
Wochenfluß m lochia *(nach der Entbindung)*
~/**abnormer** lochiorrhagia, lochiorrhoea
~/**blutiger** lochia cruenta (rubra)
~/**wäßriger** lochia serosa
~/**weißer schleimiger** lochia alba
Wochenflußverhaltung f lochioschesis, lochiostasis
~ **in der Gebärmutter** lochiometra
~ **in der Scheide** lochiocolpos
Wöchnerin f puerpera, puerperant (lying-in) woman
Wöchnerinnenstation f maternity ward
Wöchnerinnentetanie f puerperal tetany
Wöchnerinnenzimmer n lying-in room
wogend undulant
Wohlbefinden n good health, well-being, euaesthesia
wohlgenährt well-nourished, well-fed; corpulent
Wohnungsmilbenbefall m grocer's itch
Wolf m s. Intertrigo
Wolff-Parkinson-White-Syndrom n Wolff-Parkinson-White syndrome, W-P-W syndrome, [ventricular] pre-excitation syndrome *(im EKG)*
Wolfshunger m bulimia, lycorexia
Wolfsrachen m wolfjaw, cheilognathopalatoschisis; cleft lip face palate
Wollfett n wool fat, adeps lanae, lanolin
~/**wasserhaltiges** hydrous wool fat
Wollhaar n lanugo *(des Fetus)*
wollhaarartig lanuginous
Wollust f voluptuousness, salacity
wollüstig voluptuous, lustful, salacious; libidinal
Wortamnesie f verbal amnesia
Wortblindheit f word (text) blindness, logagnosia, logamnesia
~/**kongenitale** congenital alexia; legasthenia
~/**zentrale** alexia, typhlolexia
Wortfindungsstörung f amnesic aphasia
Wortneubildung f paraphrasia
Wortsalat m word salad, schizophasia
Wortschreibunfähigkeit f verbal agraphia
Wortstummheit f motor aphasia, word dumbness; aphemia; logoplegia
Wortsuggestion f verbal suggestion
Worttaubheit f word deafness, logamnesia; sensory aphasia, logokophosis, kophemia, anacroasia, auditory aphasia
Wortverwechslung f paralalia *(Sprachstörung)*
Wortwiederholung f/monotone verbigeration
WPW-Syndrom n s. Wolff-Parkinson-White-Syndrom
Wuchereria bancrofti Wuchereria bancrofti *(Erreger der Elephantiasis)*
Wuchereriainfektion f wuchereriasis, bancroftosis, Bancroft's filariasis
wuchern to proliferate
wuchernd proliferative, proliferous, luxuriant *(z. B. Zellen)*
~/**stark** exuberant *(Gewebe)*

820

Wucherung f 1. proliferation *(z. B. von Zellen)*; 2. [adenoid] vegetation *(Rachenmandel)*; 3. s. Tumor 1.
~ **des lymphatischen Gewebes** lymphadenia
~ **des myeloiden Gewebes** myeloidosis
~/**pilzartige** fungosity
Wuchs m 1. stature; 2. s. Wachstum
Wulst m(f) torus, elevation, prominence
~/**idiomuskulärer** idiomuscular contracture
~/**kleiner** torulus, minute elevation
wulstig torose; swelled; thick, protruded *(z. B. die Lippen)*
Wulstnarbe f keloid, kelis, cheloid, keloma
wund sore, chafed, tender ● **sich ~ liegen** to get bedsore ● **~ werden** to gall
Wundbehandlung f wound treatment (management)
~/**antiseptische** antiseptic surgery (wound treatment)
~/**keimfreie** aseptic surgery (wound treatment)
~/**offene** air dressing
Wundbenzin n surgical spirit
Wundbrand m s. 1. Wunderysipel; 2. Gangrän
Wunddehiszenz f wound dehiscence (disruption)
Wunddiphtherie f wound (surgical) diphtheria
Wunde f wound, vulnus; injury, trauma; cut *(durch Schnitt)*; sore *(geschwürartig)*
~/**frische** recent wound
~/**infizierte** infected (septic) wound
~/**klaffende** gaping wound, gash; dehiscence
~/**vereiterte** suppurating (festering) wound
~/**verunreinigte** contaminated (dirty) wound
Wunderysipel n [surgical] erysipelas, traumatic erysipelas
Wundexzision f wound excision, debridement [of wound]
Wundfieber n wound (traumatic) fever
Wundflüssigkeitsabfluß m [wound] drainage
wundgelaufen footsore
wundgelegen bedsore
wundgerieben galled
Wundhaken m [wound] retractor; rib spreader
Wundheilung f wound healing
~/**primäre** healing by first intention
~/**sekundäre** healing by second intention
Wundheilungsprozeß m wound healing process
Wundinfektion f wound infection
Wundinfektionsbekämpfung f antisepsis
Wundklammer f wound-clip, suture clip
Wundklammerentfernung f suture clip removing
Wundklammersetzen n suture clip applying
Wundklammersetzer m clip applying forceps
Wundlefze f lip [of a wound], margin of wound
Wundliegen n decubitus, bedsore
Wundmal n stigma
Wundnaht f 1. [wound] suture; 2. s. Wundverschluß
Wundnahtbesteck n suturing instrument set
Wundpflaster n [adhesive] plaster
Wundpolizei f hospital infection committee *(verantwortlich für Erfassung von Wundinfektionen)*

Wundrand m wound edge, border of wound
Wundrand[anlege]pinzette f approximation forceps
Wundrandschere f scissors for wound edges
Wundreiben n attrition
Wundreinigung f s. Wundtoilette
Wundrose f s. Wunderysipel
Wundsalbe f healing ointment
Wundschock m wound shock
Wundschorf m scab, crust
Wundsein n diaper (napkin) rash *(beim Säugling)*; intertrigo; soreness
Wundsekret n ichor, wound exudation, sanies
Wundsekretableitung f [wound] drainage
Wundsekretfluß m/**jauchiger** ichorrhoea
Wundsepsis f wound sepsis
Wundspreizer m wound stretcher, [self-retaining] retractor; rib spreader
Wundspritze f wound syringe
Wundstarrkrampf m s. Tetanus
Wundstupor m traumatic anaesthesia
Wundtoilette f wound toilet, surgical cleansing; debridement [of wound]
Wundtuch n wound towel
Wundverschluß m wound closure, closure of a wound
~/**primärer** primary [wound] closure
~/**sekundärer** secondary [wound] closure
Würfelbein n cuboid [bone]
würfelförmig cuboid[al], cubiform
Würfelzelle f cuboidal cell
Würgeanfall m/**krampfartiger** pharyngeal crisis
Würgen n retching; vomiturition
Würgereflex m retching (gag, vomiting) reflex, pharyngeal reflex
Wurm m 1. worm, helminth; 2. vermis *(Anatomie)*; 3. s. Rotz
Wurmabszeß m worm (helminthic) abscess
wurmabtreibend anthelmint[h]ic, vermifugal
Wurmabtreibung f vermifuge treatment
Wurmabtreibungsmittel n s. Wurmmittel
Wurmangst f vermiphobia
wurmartig 1. worm-like, vermiform, vermicular, vermiculose, vermiculous, vermiculate, scolecoid; 2. peristaltic *(z. B. Magen- und Darmbewegung)*
Wurmbefall m worm infestation, [in]vermination, verminosis, helminthic infection
wurmbekämpfend anthelmint[h]ic
Wurmbekämpfungsmittel n s. Wurmmittel
Wurmerbrechen n helminthemesis, vomiting of worms
wurmförmig s. wurmartig
Wurmfortsatz m [vermiform] appendix, vermiform process, epithyphlon, caecal appendage
Wurmfortsatz... s. a. Appendix...
Wurmfortsatzabszeß m appendix abscess
Wurmfortsatzadenokarzinom n appendix adenocarcinoma
Wurmfortsatzadenom n appendix adenoma
Wurmfortsatzarterie f appendicular artery

Wurmfortsatz-Blasen-Kolon-Fistel f appendicovesicocolic fistula
Wurmfortsatzblutung f appendix haemorrhage
Wurmfortsatzentfernung f[/**operative**] append[ic]ectomy
Wurmfortsatzentzündung f appendicitis, inflammation of the appendix, epityphlitis, perityphlitis *(Zusammensetzungen s. unter* Appendizitis*)*
Wurmfortsatzerkrankung f appendicopathy
Wurmfortsatzfistelung f appendicostomy
Wurmfortsatzgangrän f gangrene of the appendix
Wurmfortsatzgekröse n mesoappendix, mesenteriolum
Wurmfortsatzgekröseentzündung f mesoappendicitis
Wurmfortsatzinversion f appendix inversion
Wurmfortsatzkarzinom n appendix carcinoma
Wurmfortsatzmukozele f appendix mucocele
Wurmfortsatzneurom n appendix neuroma
Wurmfortsatzobliteration f obliteration (obstruction) of the appendix, appendiclausis
Wurmfortsatzperforation f appendix perforation
Wurmfortsatzpolyp m appendix polyp
Wurmfortsatzröntgen[kontrast]darstellung f vermography
Wurmfortsatzruptur f appendix rupture
Wurmfortsatzschmerz m appendalgia
Wurmfortsatzstein m appendicolith
Wurmfortsatzvene f appendicular vein
Wurmfortsatzvolvulus m appendix volvulus
Wurmfortsatzzystadenom n appendix cystadenoma
Wurminfektion f worm (helminthic) infection
Wurminfestation f s. Wurmbefall
wurminfiziert verminous, vermiculose, vermiculous
Wurmkrankheit f [in]vermination, verminosis, helminthiasis, helminthism
Wurmmittel n anthelmintic [agent], helminthagogue, vermifuge [agent]; helminthicide [agent], vermicide [agent]
wurmtötend helminthicide, vermicidal
Wurstvergiftung f s. Botulismus
Wurzel f root, radix *(z. B. eines Nervs)*; root, fang *(z. B. eines Zahns) (s. a. unter* Radix*)*
~/**hintere** posterior root
~/**kleine** radicle
~/**motorische** motor root
~/**sensorische** sensory root
~/**vordere** anterior root
Wurzelarterie f radicular artery
wurzelartig root-like, rhizoid[al]
Wurzelbehandlung f root treatment
Wurzelbohrer m reamer
Wurzeldurchtrennung f[/**operative**] rhizotomy
Wurzelentfernung f[/**operative**] radicectomy
Wurzelfaser f fibril, rootlet
wurzelförmig radiciform, rhizomorphoid
Wurzelgranulom n apical (dental) granuloma
Wurzelhaut f root membrane, periodontal ligament, pericementum, odontoperiosteum

Wurzelhautatrophie

Wurzelhautatrophie f periodontal atrophy
Wurzelhautentzündung f periodontitis
Wurzelhautzerfall m pericementoclasia
Wurzelhautzyste f periodontal cyst
Wurzelheber m root elevator, elevator [for prizing out roots]
Wurzelkanal m root canal
Wurzelkanalbehandlung f root canal treatment
Wurzelkanalfüllung f root canal filling
Wurzelkaries f root caries
Wurzelscheide f root sheath
~/Huxleysche Hertwig's epithelial root sheath *(der Zahnkeime)*
Wurzelschmerz m root (radicular) pain
Wurzelspitzengranulom n periapical granuloma
Wurzelspitzenresektion f root amputation; rad[ic]ectomy
Wurzelzange f root (dental stump) forceps
Wurzelzyste f root (radicular) cyst
Wüstenfieber n desert fever (rheumatism), coccidio[ido]mycosis, San Joaquin [Valley] fever, California (Posada's) disease *(durch Coccidioides immitis)*
Wüstengeschwür n desert (veldt) sore
Wüstenrheumatismus m s. Wüstenfieber
Wut f rage, fury; frenzy, madness
Wutanfall m fit of rage
Wutausbruch m burst of fury, tantrum
Wutknötchen npl Babés nodules (tubercles)
Wutkrankheit f s. Tollwut
Wutreaktion f rage reaction

X

Xanthämie f xanthaemia *(Vorhandensein gelber Substanzen im Blut)*
Xanthelasma n [palpebrarum] xanthelasma *(Cholesterineinlagerung in den Lidern)*
Xanthelasmatose f xanthelasmatosis *(Häufung von Cholesterineinlagerungen in der Haut)*
Xanthin n xanthine
Xanthinausscheidung f im Urin xanthi[n]uria, xanthuria
Xanthinoxydase f xanthine oxidase
Xanthinstein m xanthic calculus
xanthochrom[atisch] xanthochrom[at]ic
Xanthochromie f xanthochromia *(z. B. der Gehirnflüssigkeit)*; aurantiasis, carotinoid pigmentation *(z. B. der Haut)*
xanthoderm xanthochroous, yellow-skinned
Xanthoderma n xanthoderma
Xanthodermie f xanthodermia; xanthochromia
Xanthogranulom n xanthogranuloma, juvenile xanthoma
xanthogranulomatös xanthogranulomatous
Xanthogranulomatose f xanthogranulomatosis
Xanthoma n xanthoma
~ palpebrarum palpebral xanthoma
xanthomatös xanthomatous
Xanthomatose f xanthomatosis

~/hypercholesterolämische hypercholesterolaemic xanthomatosis
Xanthomzelle f xanthoma (foam) cell
Xanthophyll n xanthophyll *(Lipochromfarbstoff)*
Xanthoprotein n xanthoprotein
Xanthoproteinreaktion f xanthoproteic reaction *(zum Tryptophan- und Tyrosinnachweis)*
Xanthoproteinsäure f xanthoproteic acid
Xanthopsie f xanthop[s]ia, yellow vision
Xanthopsin n xanthopsin, visual yellow
Xanthopterin n xanthopterin *(gelbes Pigment)*
Xanthorrhoe f xanthorrhoea, yellow discharge
Xanthose f xanthosis *(Gelbfärbung der Haut durch Karotin)*
Xanthosin n xanthosine *(Nukleosid)*
Xanthozyanopsie f xanthocyanop[s]ia, xanthokyanopsy
Xanthozyt m xanthocyte, yellow-pigmented cell
Xanthydrol n xanthydrol *(zum Harnstoffnachweis)*
X-Bazillus m x-bacillus
X-Bein n knock-knee, in-knee, genu valgum, baker leg; gonycrotesis
x-beinig knock-kneed, in-kneed, valgoid, valgus
X-Chromosom n X chromosome *(Geschlechtschromosom)* ● **an X-Chromosomen gebunden** X-linked
Xenoantigen n xenoantigen
Xenoantikörper m xenoantibody
Xenodiagnose f xenodiagnosis
Xenodiagnostik f xenodiagnosis
xenogen xenogenic, xenogenous
Xenogenese f xenogenesis *(Entstehung von Nachkommen ohne Elternähnlichkeit)*
Xenograft n xenograft
Xenologie f xenology
Xenomenia f xenomenia, vicarious menstruation
Xenophobie f xenophobia *(krankhafte Angst vor Fremden)*
Xenoplastik f xenoplasty
xenoplastisch xenoplastic
Xenopsylla f **cheopis** Xenopsylla cheopis, rat flea
Xerasie f xerasia
Xerocheilie f xerocheilia
Xeroderma n xeroderma, dry skin; dermatoxerasia
Xerodermie f xerodermia, xerosis
Xerophagie f xerophagy *(Ernährung durch getrocknete Nahrung)*
Xerophthalmie f xerophthalmia, ophthalmoxerosis; vitamin A deficiency xerophthalmia
xerophthalmieverhindernd antixerophthalmic
xerophthalmisch xerophthalmic
Xeroradiographie f xeroradiography
Xerosalgie f xerosalgia
Xerose f xerosis, dryness of a tissue; dryness of the body
Xerosis f **conjunctivae** conjunctival xerosis; Bitot's patches
Xerostomie f xerostomia; dry mouth

xerotisch xerotic, dry
Xerotokie f xerotocia, dry labour
X-Hormon n X factor
Xiphodymus m xiphodymus *(Mißgeburt)*
Xiphodynie f xiphodynia, pain in the xiphoid cartilage
xiphoid xiphoid, xyphoid, sword-shaped; ensiform
Xiphoid n xiphosternum, xiphoid [cartilage], xiphoid process (appendage)
Xiphoiditis f xiphoiditis, inflammation of the xiphoid process
Xiphoidwinkel m xiphoid angle
Xiphopagus m xiphopagus *(Mißgeburt)*
xiphosternal xiphosternal, xiphisternal
X-Krankheit f**/australische** [Australian] X disease, Australian X encephalitis
XO-Syndrom n XO syndrome, gonadal dysgenesis
X-Strahlen mpl s. Röntgenstrahlen
X-Trisomie f, **XXX-Syndrom** n triple-X syndrome *(Chromosomenanomalie)*
Xylokain n xylocaine, lidocaine, lignocaine *(Lokalanästhetikum)*
Xylol n xylene, xylol
Xylose f xylose, wood sugar
Xyloseausscheidung f im Urin xylosuria
Xyrospasmus m xyrospasm

Y

Yabapoxvirus n yaba [pox] virus
Y-Ableitung f **nach Roux** Roux-en-Y drainage
Y-Anastomose f **nach Roux** Roux-en-Y anastomosis
Yangtse-Flußfieber n Yangtze Valley fever, Katayama disease, hepatosplenic schistosomiasis
Y-Chromosom n Y chromosome *(Geschlechtschromosom)* ● **an Y-Chromosomen gebunden** Y-linked
Y-förmig triradial, triradiate
Y-Gastroenterostomie f **nach Roux** Roux's (Roux-en-Y) gastroenterostomy
Y-Infusionssystem n Y-type infusion pathway
Yohimbin n yohimbine, johimbine, quebrachine *(Alkaloid)*
Yoshida-Sarkom n Yoshida's sarcoma, Yoshida tumour
Y-Ösophagojejunostomie f **nach Roux** Roux-en-Y oesophagojejunostomy
Yperit n yperite, mustard gas *(hautschädigender Kampfstoff)*
Y-Schlinge f **nach Roux** Roux-en-Y loop (bypass)
Y-Stück n Y-shaped connecting piece; Y-type infusion pathway

Z

Zacke f peak *(z. B. einer Aktivitätskurve)*; spike *(z. B. im EEG)*
Zackensehen n s. Teichopsia
Zacke-Welle-Komplex m spike-and-wave *(im EEG)*
zäh[flüssig] viscous, viscid, viscose; ropy
Zähflüssigkeit f viscosity, viscidity
Zähigkeit f viscosity; toughness; tenacity
Zahl f**/phagozytische** phagocytic (opsonic) index
Zahlengedächtnis n memory for figures
Zählkammer f counting cell (chamber), haemocytometer
Zählunfähigkeit f anarithmia, inability to count
Zählzwang m arithmomania, morbid impulse to count
Zahn m tooth, dens *(s. a. unter Dens)* ● **neben einem ~ paradental** ● **unter einem ~ subdental**
~/bleibender permanent (succedent, second) tooth
~/einhöckriger unicuspid [tooth], unicuspidate
~/fehlstehender malposed (snaggle) tooth
~/gesunder sound tooth
~/kariöser carious (decayed) tooth
~/künstlicher artificial tooth, pontic, dummy
~/lebensfähiger vital tooth
~/lockerer loose tooth
~/plombierter filled tooth
~/zweihöckriger bicuspid [tooth], bicuspidate
Zahn... s. a. Dental...
Zahnabdruck m impression, die
Zahnabnormität f dental abnormality
Zahnabnutzung f odontotripsis
Zahnabszeß m dental (periodontal, alveolar) abscess; parulis, subperiosteal abscess
Zahnalveole f dental alveolus, tooth socket
Zahnalveolenentzündung f alveolitis, inflammation of a dental alveolus
Zahnamalgam n dental amalgam
Zahnanatomie f dental anatomy
Zahnanlage f dental germ
Zahnarterie f dental artery
zahnartig odont[in]oid, dentoid, tooth-like
Zahnarzt m dentist, dental surgeon, odontologist ● **beim ~ at the dentist's**
zahnärztlich dental
Zahnarztstuhl m dentist's chair
Zahnaufbohrung f dental excavation, odontotrypy
Zahnaufhängeapparat m parodontium, periodontium, attachment apparatus
Zahnauflösung f odontolysis
Zahnbehandlung f dental (tooth) treatment, odontotherapy ● **in ~ sein** to have one's teeth seen to; to get one's teeth fixed
Zahnbehandlungsangst f odontophobia
Zahnbein n dentin[e], ivory *(Zusammensetzungen s. unter Dentin)*
Zahnbein... s. Dentin...

Zahnbelag

Zahnbelag *m* [dental] film, coating [on the teeth], materia alba, dental deposit, dental (mucinous) plaques
Zahnbeschreibung *f* odontography
Zahnbetäubung *f* dental anaesthesia
Zahnbett *n* parodontium
Zahnbettentzündung *f* parodontitis, periodontitis, inflammation of the periodontium
Zahnbetterkrankung *f* parodontopathy
Zahnbild *n* odontogram
zahnbildend odontogenic, dentiparous
Zahnbildung *f* odontogenesis, odontosis, development of a tooth, dentification; dentition
Zahnbogen *m*/**oberer** superior dental arch, dental arch of the upper teeth
~/unterer inferior dental arch, dental arch of the lower teeth
Zahnbohrer *m* [dental] burr, drill, dental excavator
Zahnbrücke *f* bridge[work]; pontic; dummy; retainer
Zähnchen *n* denticle
Zahndeformierung *f* dental (tooth) deformity
Zahndurchbruch *m* teething, eruption (cutting) of the teeth, dentition, odontiasis, dentification
Zähne *mpl*: ● **mit großen Zähnen** macrodont ● **mit kleinen Zähnen** microdont ● **von den Zähnen ausgehend** odontogenic ● **zwischen zwei benachbarten Zähnen** interproximal, interproximate
~/bleibende permanent teeth; permanent dentition
~/Hutchinsonsche Hutchinsonian (notched) teeth *(bei Syphilis)*
Zahneinlage *f* inlay, filling
Zähneklappern *n* odonterism, chattering of the teeth
Zähneknirschen *n* odontoprisis, grinding (gnashing) of teeth, bruxism
~/krankhaftes bruxomania
Zahnemail *n s.* Zahnschmelz
zahnen to teethe, to cut teeth
Zahnentwicklung *f* odontogenesis, odontosis, development of the teeth
Zahnentzündung *f* odontitis, inflammation of a tooth
Zahnerkrankung *f* odontopathy
Zahnersatz *m* denture, dental prosthesis, [dental] plate
~/künstlicher set of artificial teeth
~/vorläufiger immediate denture; temporary teeth
Zahnersatzkunde *f* prosthodontia, prosthodontics, prosthetic dentistry
Zahnexostose *f* dental exostosis
Zahnextraktion *f* dental extraction, odontectomy, extraction of a tooth
Zahnextraktionslehre *f* exodontics
Zahnextraktionszange *f* dental [extraction] forceps, tooth forceps
Zähneziehen *n s.* Zahnextraktion
Zahnfach *n* dental alveolus, [tooth] socket

Zahnfachabszeß *m* dental (dentoalveolar) abscess
Zahnfachentzündung *f* alveolitis
Zahnfacheröffnung *f*[/**operative**] alveolotomy
Zahnfachscheidewand *f* interalveolar septum
Zahnfaser *f* dentinal fibre
Zahnfäule *f s.* Zahnkaries
Zahnfehlbildung *f* dental dysplasia, tooth malformation
Zahnfehlstellung *f* malalignment [of a tooth]
Zahnfissur *f* odontoschism, dental fissure, fissure of a tooth
Zahnfleisch *n* gingiva, gums, [o]ula ● **über dem ~** supragingival ● **unter dem ~** subgingival
Zahnfleisch... *s. a.* Gingiva...
Zahnfleischabszeß *m* gumboil; alveolar abscess
Zahnfleischblutung *f* bleeding from the gums, gingivorrhagia, ulorrhoea, [o]ulorrhagia
Zahnfleischeiterung *f* parulis, subperiosteal abscess
Zahnfleischentfernung *f*/**operative** gingivectomy, [o]ulectomy
Zahnfleischentzündung *f* gingivitis, [o]ulitis, inflammation of the gums
Zahnfleischfistel *f* gingival fistula
Zahnfleischgeschwulst *f* uloncus
Zahnfleischgeschwür *n* ulocace
Zahnfleischgranulationsgeschwulst *f* epulis
Zahnfleischinzision *f* ulotomy, incision into the gums
Zahnfleischjucken *n* odontocnesis, itching of the gums
Zahnfleischkappe *f* odontoclamis, tooth hood
Zahnfleischkrebs *m* ulocarcinoma, cancer of the gums
Zahnfleischmassage *f* ulotripsis, massage of the gums
Zahnfleischmukosa *f* gingival mucosa
Zahnfleischplastik *f* gingivoplasty
Zahnfleischrand *m* gingival margin; marginal gingiva
Zahnfleischresektion *f* gingivectomy, [o]ulectomy
Zahnfleischschmerz *m* gingivalgia, pain in the gingiva
Zahnfleischschwellung *f* gingival swelling, swelling of the gums; uloncus
Zahnfleischtasche *f* gingival (periodontal, gum) pocket, gingivodental crevice
Zahnfleisch- und Mundschleimhautentzündung *f* gingivostomatitis
Zahnfleisch- und Zungenentzündung *f* gingivoglossitis, uloglossitis
Zahnfleischverband *m* periodontal pack
Zahnfleischvereiterung *f* ulocace
Zahnfleischwucherung *f* epulis
Zahnformel *f* dental formula, dentition
zahnförmig tooth-shaped, odont[in]oid, dentiform
Zahnfraktur *f* tooth fracture
Zahnfraß *m s.* Zahnkaries
Zahnfüllmaterial *n* tooth-filling material

Zahnfüllung f 1. filling, stopping, plugging, odontoplerosis; 2. filling, inlay
Zahngeschwür n gumboil; parulis
Zahngranulom n apical (dental) granuloma
Zahnhals m dental neck, neck of the tooth
Zahnhalslinie f cervical line
Zahnhalteapparat m parodontium, periodontium, attachment apparatus
Zahnhebel m dental elevator
Zahnheilkunde f dentistry, odontiatria, odontology
~/konservierende endodontology, conservative dentistry, endodontia, endodontics
Zahnhöhle f pulp-cavity, cavity of a tooth, dental cavity
Zahnhöhlenvorbereitung f cavity preparation
Zahnhygiene f dental hygiene; dental prophylaxis
Zahnhypertrophie f macrodontia, megalodontia
Zahnhypotrophie f microdontia
Zahnindex m dental index
Zahninnervation f dental innervation
Zahninstrument n dental instrument
Zahnirregularität f odontoparallaxis, odontoloxia, irregularity of the teeth
Zahnkanal m 1. dentinal tubule; 2. s. Zahnwurzelkanal
Zahnkaries f [dental] caries, dental decay, saprodontia
Zahnkaries... s. Karies...
Zahnkeim m dental germ
Zahnkeimentfernung f[/operative] germectomy
Zahnklinik f dental hospital (clinic)
Zahnknospe f tooth bud
Zahnkrankheit f odontopathy, disease of the teeth
Zahnkrone f crown [of the tooth]
~/künstliche artificial crown
Zahnkronenodontom n coronal odontoma
Zahnkronenpulpa f coronal pulp
Zahnkunde f odontology
~/beschreibende odontography
Zahnlegierung f dental alloy
Zahnleiste f dental (dentogingival) lamina, dental ridge
Zahnlockerung f [a]gomphiasis, looseness of the teeth, periodontoclasia, odontoseisis
zahnlos toothless, agomphious, edentulous, edentate; anodont
Zahnloser m edentate
Zahnlosigkeit f agomphiasis, absence of the teeth, edentia
~/angeborene anodontia
Zahnlücke f diastema, gap [between the teeth]
Zahnmangel m/**angeborener** oligodontia
Zahnmark n s. Zahnpulpa
zahnmarkfrei pulpless
Zahnmarkhöhle f pulp cavity [of the tooth]
Zahnmedizin f/**vorbeugende** prophylactodontia
Zahnmißbildung f dental (tooth) malformation; imperfect odontogenesis
Zahn-Mund-Kiefer-Heilkunde f stomatology

Zahnneigung f inclination [of a tooth]
Zahnneuralgie f odontoneuralgia
Zahnpapille f dental papilla
Zahnpatient m dental patient
Zahnpflege f care of one's teeth; oral hygiene
Zahnplastik f odontoplasty *(Implantation von künstlichen Zähnen)*
Zahnplexus m dental plexus
Zahnprothese f [artificial] denture, dental prosthesis, [dental] plate; artificial teeth
Zahnprothetik f dental prosthetics
Zahnprothetiker m prosthodontist, prosthetist
Zahnpulpa f dental pulp, endodontium
Zahnpulpaentzündung f pulpitis, inflammation of the pulp, endodontitis
Zahnpulpahöhle f pulp cavity [of the tooth]
Zahnputzmittel n dentifrice
Zahnreguliervorrichtung f jackscrew *(mit Schraubenzug)*
Zahnreihe f row of teeth
Zahnreinigung f odontexesis
Zahnröntgenaufnahme f dental roentgenogram
Zahnröntgendarstellung f dental roentgenography
Zahnröntgendiagnostik f radiodontia, radiodontics
Zahnsäckchen n dental follicle (sac)
Zahnscheide f/**Neumannsche** Neumann's sheath
Zahnschlußebene f bite plane
Zahnschmelz m [dental] enamel, adamantine, odonthyalus
~/gefleckter mottled enamel
Zahnschmelz... s. a. Schmelz...
Zahnschmelzbildner m ameloblast, adamantoblast, ganoblast
Zahnschmelzbildung f amelogenesis, formation of enamel
Zahnschmelzgrenze f cementoenamel junction
Zahnschmelzzerstörung f s. Zahnkaries
Zahnschmerz m toothache, dentalgia, odont[oneur]algia, odontodynia
~ durch Luftdruckverminderung aerodontalgia
zahnschmerzlindernd antiodontalgic
Zahnspalte f odontoschism
Zahnspange f dental brace; jackscrew *(mit Schraubenzug)*
Zahnspiegel m odontoscope, dental mirror
Zahnspiegelung f odontoscopy
Zahnstatus m dental findings
Zahnstein m tartar [on the teeth], dental deposit, [dental] scale; odontolith, dental calculus
Zahnsteinentfernung f scaling, odontexesis
Zahnsteinleiden n odontolithiasis
Zahnstellungsabweichung f odontoparallaxis, odontoloxia
Zahnstift m dental pin, dowel, peg
Zahnstruktur f dental structure
Zahnsubstanz f tooth substance
Zahnsubstanzauflösung f odontolysis
Zahnsubstanzverlust m dental erosion

Zahntechniker

Zahntechniker *m* dental mechanic (technician); prosthodontist
Zahntrepanation *f* odontotomy
Zahnüberempfindlichkeit *f* odontohyperaesthesia
Zahnüberzahl *f* hyperodontia, poly[o]dontia
Zahnung *f s.* Zahndurchbruch
Zahnuntersuchung *f* dental checkup, tooth examination
Zahnunterzahl *f* hypodontia
Zahnvereiterung *f* dental (periodontal) abscess; dentoalveolar abscess
Zahnvergrößerung *f/abnorme* macrodontia, megalodontia
Zahnverkleinerung *f* microdontia
Zahnverlust *m* odontoptosis, dedentition, loss of the teeth
Zahnwechsel *m* diphyodontia, second dentition
Zahnweh *n s.* Zahnschmerz
Zahnwurzel *f* [tooth] root
~/**anatomische** anatomic root of a tooth
Zahnwurzelbehandlung *f* root canal treatment
Zahnwurzelentfernung *f*[/**operative**] *s.* Zahnwurzelresektion
Zahnwurzelgranulom *n* [peri]apical granuloma
Zahnwurzelhaut *f* odontoperiosteum, periodontium, paradentium, periodontal ligament (membrane)
Zahnwurzelhautentzündung *f* periodontitis, pericementitis, paradentitis, alveolodental osteoperiostitis
Zahnwurzelhautkrankheit *f* cementopathia, periodontia
Zahnwurzelhautspezialist *m* periodontist
Zahnwurzelkanal *m* root canal [of the tooth], pulp canal
Zahnwurzelkanalöffnung *f* apical foramen
Zahnwurzelkaries *f* root caries
Zahnwurzelpulpa *f* radicular pulp
Zahnwurzelresektion *f* root resection (amputation), rad[i]ectomy
Zahnwurzelspitzenabszeß *m* periapical abscess
Zahnwurzelspitzenentzündung *f* apicitis
Zahnwurzelspitzengranulom *n* [peri]apical granuloma
Zahnwurzelspitzenresektion *f* apic[o]ectomy, apiceotomy, apicotomy
Zahnwurzelspitzenzyste *f* periapical cyst
Zahnwurzeltasche *f* infrabony pocket
Zahnwurzelzyste *f* radicular (radiculodental) cyst
Zahnzange *f* dental [extraction] forceps
Zahnzement *m* [dental] cement, cementum
Zahnzementbildung *f* cementogenesis
~/**gesteigerte** hypercementosis
Zahnzementbildungszelle *f* cementoblast
Zahnzerfall *m* odontonecrosis, dental necrosis
Zahnziehen *n s.* Zahnextraktion
Zahnzwischenraum *m* interdentium
Zahnzyste *f* odontocele, [alveolo]dental cyst
zäkal *s.* zökal
Zäkum *n s.* Zökum
Zange *f* forceps

~/**Bartonsche** Barton's forceps *(Geburtshilfe)*
~/**hohe** high forceps
~/**kardiaerweiternde** cardiodilator
~/**Lüersche** Luer's bone plier (nibblers), bone nippers
~/**mittlere** mid[plane] forceps *(Geburtshilfe)*
~/**tiefe** low forceps *(Geburtshilfe)*
Zangenbiopsie *f* forceps biopsy
Zangenbiß *m* labidodontia
Zangenblatt *n,* **Zangenbranche** *f* [forceps] blade
Zangenentbindung *f* forceps delivery (operation), instrumental labour, embryulcia, [forceps] extraction of the foetus
Zangenextraktion *f* forceps extraction *(z. B. der Augenlinse)*
Zangengeburt *f s.* Zangenentbindung
Zangenwendung *f* forceps rotation
Zänogenese *f* caenogenesis
Zäpfchen *n* 1. *s.* Uvula; 2. suppository
Zäpfchenmuskel *m* staphylinus medius [muscle]
Zäpfchenspalte *f* cleft (bifid) uvula
Zapfen *m* 1. [retinal] cone; 2. pivot *(z. B. eines Gelenks)*
Zapfenadaptation *f* cone adaptation
Zapfendegeneration *f* retinal cone degeneration
Zapfendystrophie *f* cone dystrophy
Zapfenfaser *f* cone fibre
zapfenförmig piniform, cone-shaped
Zapfenopsin *n* cone opsin, photopsin *(Sehfarbstoff)*
Zapfenpigment *n* cone pigment
Zapfensehen *n* cone (photopic) vision
Zapfen- und Stäbchenschicht *f* layer of rods and cones *(der Netzhaut)*
Zapfenzelle *f* cone cell
zart tender, tenuous, thin *(z. B. Fasern)*; soft, delicate *(z. B. Gewebe)*; delicate *(z. B. die Gesundheit)*; slender, slight, fragile *(z. B. Gestalt)*; pale, subdued
Zartheit *f* tenderness, tenuity, thinness *(z. B. von Fasern)*; softness, delicacy *(z. B. des Gewebes)*; slenderness, fragility *(z. B. der Gestalt)*
Zebozephalie *f* cebocephalia
Zebozephalus *m* cebocephalus *(Mißgeburt)*
Zecke *f* tick, ixodid ● **durch Zecken übertragen** tick-borne, tick-transmitted, ixodic
Zeckenbefall *m* ixodiasis
Zeckenbißfieber *n* spotted disease (fever), tick[-]borne typhus] fever
~/**afrikanisches** African tick-borne typhus, African tick (relapsing) fever
~/**altweltliches** Marseille fever
~/**asiatisches** [North] Asian tick fever, [North] Asian tick-borne rickettsiosis, Siberian tick typhus *(durch Rickettsia sibirica)*
~/**neuweltliches** Brazilian (Columbian) spotted fever
~/**nordafrikanisches** North African tick-bite fever *(durch Rickettsia conori)*
~/**Omsker** Omsk haemorrhagic fever *(durch Arbovirus Gruppe B)*
~/**südafrikanisches** South African tick-bite fever

Zeckenenzephalitis f tick-borne encephalitis
~/russische Russian tick-borne encephalitis
Zeckenenzephalitisvirus n tick-borne encephalitis [flavi] virus
Zeckenfieber n/**amerikanisches** Rocky Mountain spotted fever, R.M.S.F., spotted (tick) fever of the Rocky Mountains
Zeckenlähmung f tick-bite paralysis
Zeckenrückfallfieber n s. Rückfallfieber
Zeh m s. Zehe
Zehe f toe, digit, dactyl[us]
~/dritte third toe
~/große big toe, hallux
~/kleine little toe
~/vierte fourth toe
~/zweite second toe
Zehen fpl digits of the foot, toes ● **mit einwärtsgerichteten ~** pigeon-toed ● **mit verwachsenen ~** syndactyl[ous]
Zehenamputation f toe (digital) amputation, amputation of a toe, dactylolysis
Zehenarterie f/**gemeinsame plantare** common plantar digital artery
Zehenbeuger m/**kurzer** flexor digitorum brevis [muscle]
~/langer flexor digitorum longus [muscle]
Zehenendglied n distal phalanx of the toe, ungual phalanx
Zehenentfernung f[/**operative**] s. Zehenamputation
Zehenentzündung f dactylitis, inflammation of a toe
Zehen-Fingergelenkpolster-Syndrom n knuckle-pads syndrome
zehenförmig digital, toe-shaped
Zehengangrän f digital gangrene, gangrene of a toe
Zehengelenk n interphalangeal joint [of a toe]
Zehengicht f podagra
Zehenglied n phalanx of the toe
Zehengrundgelenk n metatarsophalangeal articulation (joint)
Zehengrundglied n proximal phalanx of the toe
Zehenknochen m phalanx
Zehenknochenentzündung f phalangitis, inflammation of a phalanx
Zehenkrampf m dactylospasm, toe clonus
zehenlos adactylous
Zehenminderzahl f hypodactyly
Zehenmittelglied n middle phalanx of the toe
Zehennagel m toe-nail, onyx
~/eingewachsener ingrowing toe-nail
Zehennagelverkrümmung f gryposis
Zehenphänomen n/**Babinskisches** Babinski phenomenon (reflex), fanning sign of Babinski
Zehenreflex m toe (digital) reflex
Zehenrückenarterie f dorsal digital artery of the foot
Zehenrückennerven mpl dorsal digital nerves of the foot
Zehenschmerz m digitalgia, pain in a toe

Zehenstrecker m/**kurzer** extensor digitorum brevis [muscle]
~/langer extensor digitorum longus [muscle]
Zehenüberzahl f hyperdactylia, polydactyly
Zehenvergrößerung f dactylomegaly
Zehenverkrümmung f dactylogryposis
Zehenverkümmerung f perodactyly
Zehenverwachsung f ankylodactyly, syndactyly, symphysodactyly, dactylosymphysis
Zehenzeichen n/**Gordonsches** Gordon's reflex (sign) *(Pyramidenbahnsymptom)*
Zehngebärende f decipara
Zehrrose f discoid lupus erythematosus
Zeichen n 1. sign; phenomenon; 2. symptom; 3. mark
~/Abadiesches Abadie's sign *(1. Achillessehnenunempfindlichkeit bei Tabes dorsalis; 2. Augenlidheberkrampf bei Morbus Basedow)*
~/Bardsches Bard's sign *(Nystagmuszeichen)*
~/Bechterewsches Bechterew's sign *(1. Bechterewscher Reflex; 2. bei Amimie; 3. bei Tabes dorsalis)*
~/Bergara-Wartenbergsches Bergara-Wartenberg's sign, Wartenberg's phenomenon *(bei Fazialislähmung)*
~/Biernackisches Biernacki's sign *(bei Tabes dorsalis)*
~/Blumenbergsches Blumenberg's sign *(Appendizitiszeichen)*
~/Broadbentsches Broadbent's sign *(bei Pericarditis adhaesiva)*
~/Bumkesches Bumke's pupil (symptom) *(fehlende Pupillenkontraktion bei Lichteinfall)*
~/Chaddocksches Chaddock's reflex (sign), external malleolar sign *(Pyramidenbahnzeichen)*
~/Chvosteksches Chvostek's sign, facialis (face) phenomenon
~/Courvoisiersches Courvoisier's sign *(Gallenblasenzeichen)*
~/Cullensches Cullen's sign *(Braunfärbung des Nabels bei Bauchhöhlenschwangerschaft)*
~/Erbsches Erb's sign *(1. bei Tabes dorsalis; 2. Tetaniezeichen)*
~/Gowerssches Gowers's sign *(bei Tabes dorsalis)*
~/Graefesches [**von**] Graefe's sign, [eye]lid lag *(bei Hyperthyreose)*
~/Jellineksches Jellinek's sign *(Augenlidpigmentation bei Schilddrüsenüberfunktion)*
~/Lasèguesches Lasègue's sign *(bei Bandscheibenprolaps)*; straight-leg-raising test
~/McBurneysches McBurney's sign *(Appendizitiszeichen)*
~/Nikolskysches Nikolsky's sign *(bei Pemphigus vulgaris)*
~/Pastiasches Pastia's lines (sign) *(bei beginnendem Scharlach)*
~/Romañasches Romaña's sign *(Ober- und Unterlidödeme bei Chagaskrankheit)*
~/Rombergsches Romberg's sign *(Fallneigung bei Kleinhirnerkrankung)*
~/röntgenologisches radiographic sign

Zeichen

~/**Rovsingsches** Rovsing's sign *(Appendizitiszeichen)*
~/**Rumpel-Leedesches** Rumpel-Leede phenomenon (sign) *(Kapillarblutungen bei Thrombozytenmangel)*
~/**Schultz-Charltonsches** Schultz-Charlton blanching phenomenon *(bei Scharlach)*
~/**Stellwagsches** Stellwag's sign *(bei Hyperthyreose)*
~/**Strümpellsches** Strümpell's sign, anterior tibial syndrome, tibialis phenomenon
~ von **Wolff** Wolff-Parkinson-White syndrome, W-P-W syndrome *(im EKG)*
~/**Wintrichsches** Wintrich's sign *(bei Lungenkavernen)*
Zeichenunverständnis *n* asymboly, asemia
Zeichnen *n* show *(Blutabgang vor der Geburt)*
Zeichnung *f*/**bronchovaskuläre** bronchovascular markings *(auf Lungenröntgenbildern)*
Zeigefinger *m* index [finger], forefinger
Zeigefingerabzieher *m* abductor indicis [muscle]
Zeigefingerarterie *f*/**speichenseitige** radial artery of the index finger
Zeigefingerstrecker *m* extensor indicis [muscle], extensor indicis proprius [muscle]
Zeigeversuch *m*/**Báránykscher** Bárány's pointing test *(zur Kleinhirndiagnostik)*
Zeitbewußtsein *n* consciousness of time
Zeiterleben *n* time perception
Zell... s. a. **Zyto...**
Zellabwehr *f* cellular defence
Zellaktivität *f* cell activity, cytolergy
Zellanordnung *f* cell pattern; cytoarchitecture
Zelläquator *m* equator of a cell
zellarchitektonisch cytoarchitectonic
Zellarchitektur *f* cytoarchitecture
zellartig cellular, cell-like, cytoid
Zellatmung *f* cell respiration
Zellatypie *f* cellular atypia
zellauflösend cytolytic
Zellauflösung *f* cytolysis, cell lysis
~ durch **Licht** photolysis
Zellauskleidung *f* cell lining
Zellausscheidung *f* **im Urin** cyturia, urinary cellular excretion
Zellaustritt *m* [cellular] migration *(z. B. der Leukozyten)*; diapedesis
zellbeobachtend cytoscopic
Zellbeobachtung *f* cytoscopy, cytoscopic examination
Zellbestandteil *m* cell (cellular) constituent
Zellbeweglichkeit *f* cell motility
Zellbewegung *f* cytotaxis
Zellchemie *f* cytochemistry
Zellchemismus *m* cytochemism
Zelldetritus *m* cell detritus, cellular debris (detritus)
Zelldiagnostik *f* cytodiagnosis
Zelldifferenzierung *f* cell differentiation
Zelle *f* cell
~/**adelomorphe** adelomorphous (zymogenous) cell

828

~/**Alzheimersche** Alzheimer cell *(bei hepatolentikulärer Degeneration)*
~/**amakrine** amacrine (association) cell
~/**amöboide** amoeboid cell
~/**Anitschkowsche** Anitschkow cell (myocyte)
~/**argentaffine** argentaffine cell
~/**azidophile** acidophilic cell
~/**basophile** basophilic cell
~/**begeißelte** flagellate cell
~/**Cajalsche** Cajal's cell *(Nervenzelle in der Großhirnrinde)*
~/**chromaffine** chromaffin cell; phaeochromocyte *(z. B. im Nebennierenmark)*
~/**chromophile** chromophile [cell]
~/**chromophobe** chromophobe [cell]
~/**den Zellkern phagozytierende** karyophage
~/**eisenfreundliche** siderophil[e]
~/**eisenspeichernde** siderophage
~/**enterochromaffine** enterochromaffin cell *(im Verdauungskanal)*
~/**fettig degenerierte** bloated cell
~/**fettverzehrende** lipophage
~/**gelbpigmentierte** xanthocyte
~/**Hensensche** cell of Hensen *(im Cortischen Organ)*
~/**Hortegasche** Hortega cell *(Mikrogliazelle)*
~/**hyperchromatische** hyperchromatic cell
~/**immunokompetente** immunocompetent cell
~/**jugendliche** juvenile cell
~/**karyochrome** karyochromic cell
~/**keratinproduzierende** keratinocyte
~/**kernlose** akaryote, non-nucleated cell
~/**kleine** small cell, cellule, cellula
~/**leicht färbbare** chromophile [cell]
~/**lymphozytenähnliche** lymphoid cell
~/**melaninbildende** melanocyte, melanoblast
~/**Mottsche** morular cell of Mott
~/**mukoseröse** mucoserous cell
~/**myeloische** myeloid cell
~/**osteogene** osteogenic cell
~/**peptische** peptic cell
~/**pigmentbildende** melanocyte, melanoblast
~/**pigmentierte** pigmented cell
~/**pigmenttragende** pigmentophore
~/**polymorphkernige** polymorphonuclear cell, polymorphocyte
~/**Purkinjesche** Purkinje cell *(stark verzweigte Nervenzelle in der Kleinhirnrinde)*
~/**Reed-Sternbergsche** Reed-Sternberg cell *(bei Hodgkinscher Krankheit)*
~/**retikuloendotheliale** reticuloendothelial cell
~/**Rougetsche** Rouget's (adventitial) cell, pericyte
~/**salzsäureproduzierende** acid (parietal) cell, oxyntic (oxyphilic) cell *(der Magenschleimhaut)*
~/**schlecht färbbare** chromophobe
~/**seromuköse** mucoserous cell
~/**Sertolische** Sertoli cell *(im Hoden)*
~/**somatische** somatic (body) cell
~/**wasserhelle** water-clear cell *(in der Nebenschilddrüse)*
α-**Zelle** alpha cell *(z. B. des Pankreas)*

Zellpilzinfektion

Zelleinschluß *m* cell inclusion, endocyte
Zelleinschlüsse *mpl*/**Prowazeksche** Prowazek-Halberstaedter bodies *(in den Augenbindehautzellen bei Trachom)*
Zellelement *n* cellular element
zellenbildend cytogen[et]ic, cell-forming
Zellenbildung *f* cytogenesis, cytopoiesis, cell formation
zellenlos acellular
zellennah cytoproximal
Zellentdifferenzierung *f* anaplasia
Zellentwicklung *f* development of cells, cytogenesis, cytopoiesis
zellenvergiftend cytotoxic
Zellenzym *n* [intra]cellular enzyme, endoenzyme
Zellfarbstoff *m* cytochrome, cytopigment, histohaematin
Zellform *f* cell shape ● **mehrere Zellformen besitzend** polymorphocellular
zellförmig cell-shaped, celliform, cellular
Zellfortsatz *m* cell process, cytodendrite
zellfrei acellular, cell-free
zellfressend cytophagous
Zellfreßzelle *f* cytophage
Zellfusion *f* cell (cellular) fusion
zellgebunden cell-bound, cell-linked; cell-mediated
Zellgenetik *f* cytogenetics
Zellgerüst *n* cytoskeleton, cell framework
Zellgewebe *n* cell tissue
Zellgewebsentzündung *f* cellulitis
~/**eitrige** phlegmon
Zellgift *n* 1. cytotoxin, cell poison; necrocytotoxin *(infolge des Zelltodes)*; 2. cytocide
zellgiftig cytotoxic; cytocidal
Zellglobulin *n* cytoglobulin
Zellgrenzschicht *f* cell membrane
Zellhaufen *m* cell (cellular) cluster
zellhemmend cytostatic
Zellhemmung *f* cytostasis, cell inhibition
Zellhohlraum *m* vacuole
Zellhohlraumbildung *f* vacuol[iz]ation
Zellhypersensibilität *f* cell hypersensitivity
zellig cellular
zellig-faserig cellulofibrous
Zellimmunität *f* cell immunity
Zellinfiltrat *n* cell[ular] infiltrate
Zellinfiltration *f* cell[ular] infiltration
Zellinseln *fpl*/**Walthardsche** Walthard's islets *(im Eierstock)*
Zellkapsel *f* cell capsule
Zellkern *m* [cell] nucleus, karyoplast, karyon, cytoblast, endoplast ● **den ~ aufnehmend** karyophage
~/**diploider** diploid nucleus, amphikaryon
~/**großer** macronucleus
~/**kleiner** micronucleus
Zellkernabnormität *f* dyskaryosis
zellkernauflösend karyolytic
Zellkernauflösung *f* karyolysis
zellkernbildend karyogenic
Zellkernbildung *f* karyogenesis

Zellkernchromatinmangel *m* hypochromatism, hypochromatosis, hypochromia
Zellkernchromatinminderfärbung *f* amblychromasia
Zellkernchromatinvermehrung *f* hyperchromatism, hyperchromatosis, hyperchromia
Zellkerneinschlußkörper *m* intranuclear (cell nucleus) inclusion body
Zellkernentwicklung *f* karyogenesis, development of the cell nucleus
zellkernfärbend karyochrome
Zellkernfreßzelle *f* karyophage
Zellkernlehre *f* karyology
zellkernlos akaryote
Zellkernmembran *f* karyotheca
Zellkernmessung *f* karyometry
Zellkern[proto]plasma *n* nucleoplasm, karyoplasm
Zellkernsaft *m* karenchyma
Zellkernschrumpfung *f* pyknosis *(beim Absterben von Zellen)*
zellkernteilend karyomitotic
Zellkernteilung *f* [karyo]mitosis, karyokinesis, mitotic division
Zellkernteilungsindex *m* mitotic index
Zellkernverdichtung *f* pyknosis *(beim Absterben von Zellen)*
Zellkernvergrößerung *f* karyomegaly
zellkernverschmelzend karyogamic
Zellkern-Zellplasma-Verhältnis *n* nucleocytoplasmic ratio
Zellkinetik *f* cell (cellular) kinetics
Zellklon *m* cell (cellular) clone
Zellkomponente *f* cell (cellular) component
Zellkörper *m* cytosome, cell body
~/**Barrscher** Barr body, sex chromatin mass
Zellkörperchen *npl*/**Russellsche** Russel bodies *(der Plasmazellen)*
Zellkrankheit *f* cytopathy
Zellkultur *f* cell culture
Zellmembran *f* cell membrane (wall), cellular membrane
Zellmembranfunktion *f* cell-membrane function
Zellmorphologie *f* cytomorphology, cell morphology
Zellmund *m* cytostome, cell mouth
Zellnekrose *f s.* Zelltod
Zellnest *n* cell nest
Zellophanmakulopathie *f* cellophane maculopathy *(Augenerkrankung)*
Zellorganelle *f* cell organelle
Zellorganisation *f* cellular organization
Zellpackungsvolumen *n* packed cell volume, PCV
Zellparasitismus *m* cell parasitism
zellpathogen cytopathogenic
Zellpathologie *f* cytopathology, cell[ular] pathology
zellpathologisch cytopathologic[al]
Zellphysiologie *f* cytophysiology, cell[ular] physiology
Zellpilzinfektion *f* cytomycosis

Zellplasma

Zellplasma *n s.* Zytoplasma
Zellpopulation *f* cell population
Zellproliferation *f* cell (cellular) proliferation
Zellreplikation *f* cell (cellular) replication
Zellretikulum *n* cytoreticulum, cell (cellular) reticulum
Zellsaft *m* cell sap
Zellschädigung *f* cell damage, cellular injury
Zellschicht *f* cellular layer
Zellspezialist *m* cytologist
Zellstamm *m* cell (cellular) clone
zellständig intracellular; cell-bound, cell-linked; cell-mediated
Zellstern *m* cytaster
Zellstoff *m* 1. cellulose; 2. cellulose wadding *(Verbandstoff)*
Zellstoffschwämmchen *n* cellulose sponge *(zur Tamponade)*
Zellstoffwechsel *m* cell (cellular) metabolism
Zellsuspension *f* cell (cellular) suspension
Zellsynchronisation *f* cell (cellular) synchronization
Zellteilung *f* cell division, [cell] cleavage ● **zwischen der ~** intermitotic
~/direkte direct cell division, amitosis, amitotic division *(ohne Chromosomenausbildung)*
~/indirekte indirect cell division, karyokinesis, mitosis, mitotic division *(mit Chromosomenausbildung)*
~/krankhafte pathologic mitosis
Zellteilungsapparat *m* mitotic apparatus
zellteilungshemmend cytostatic
Zellteilungshemmung *f* cytostasis
Zellteilungsrate *f* mitotic index
Zelltod *m* cell death, cytoclasis, cytolysis, necrocytosis
Zelltransplantation *f* cell transplantation
Zelltransport *m* cytopempsis, transmission by cell
Zelltropismus *m* cytotropism
zellübertragen cell-mediated
zellulär cellular
zellulär-fibrös cellulofibrous
Zellulase *f* cellulase *(Enzym)*
zellulifugal cellulifugal
zellulipetal cellulipetal
Zellulitis *f* cellulitis, inflammation of subcutaneous tissue
Zellumbildung *f* cytomorphosis
Zelluntergang *m* cell destruction, cellular decay
Zellverbindung *f* cell (cellular) junction
zellverdickend karyopyknotic
Zellvermehrung *f* cell (cellular) proliferation; pleocytosis *(in der Gehirn- und Rückenmarkflüssigkeit)*; polycytosis *(im Blut)*
Zellvermehrungswachstum *n* hyperplasia, cell (cellular) overgrowth
Zellvermessung *f* cytometry
Zellverminderung *f* cytopenia, hypocytosis
zellvermittelt cell-mediated
Zellverschmelzung *f* cell fusion, cellular mating
Zellverwandlung *f* cytomorphosis

Zellvolumen *n*/**mittleres** mean cell (corpuscular) volume, MCV
~/relatives relative cell volume, RCV
Zellwachstum *n* cytotrophy, cell (cellular) growth
zellwachstumshemmend cytostatic
Zellwachstumshemmung *f* cytostasis
Zellwand *f* cell wall, cellular membrane
Zellwandantigen *n* cell wall antigen
Zellwandsynthese *f* cell wall synthesis
Zellzahlerhöhung *f* hypercytosis
Zellzählgerät *n* cytometer
Zellzählung *f* cytometry
Zellzahlverminderung *f* hypocytosis
Zellzerfall *m* cytolysis, cytoclasis, plasmoschisis
Zellzerreißung *f* plasmorrhexis
zellzerstörend cytoclastic; cellulicidal
Zellzerstörung *f* cellular destruction
Zellzyklus *m* cell (cellular) cycle
Zement *m* 1. *s.* Zahnzement; 2. cement[um] *(Anatomie)*
Zementexostose *f* cementoexostosis; cementicle
Zementhypertrophie *f* hypercementosis
Zementikel *n* cementicle
Zementkaries *f* [dental] cement caries
Zementoblast *m* cementoblast
Zementoblastom *n* cementoblastoma *(Zahnzementgeschwulst)*
Zementom *n* cementoma *(Zahnzementgeschwulst)*
Zentralarterie *f*/**Zinnsche** Zinn's central artery *(der Netzhaut)*
Zentralbeleuchtung *f* central illumination *(Mikroskopie)*
Zentralfibrillenmyopathie *f* central core disease *(Muskelerkrankung)*
Zentralfurche *f* central (Rolando's) fissure, central sulcus [of Rolando]
Zentralkanal *m* central canal [of the spinal cord], neurocanal
Zentralkörper *m*, **Zentralkörperchen** *n s.* Zentriol
Zentrallähmung *f* central paralysis
Zentralläppchen *n* central lobule *(im Kleinhirn)*
Zentralnekrose *f* central necrosis
Zentralnervensystem *n* central nervous system, CNS, encephalospinal (neural, cerebrospinal) axis, neuraxis
Zentralnervensystemabnormität *f* central nervous system abnormality
Zentralnervensystembeteiligung *f* central nervous system involvement
Zentralnervensystemfunktion *f* central nervous system function
Zentralnervensystemsyphilis *f* central nervous system syphilis
Zentralnervensystemtoxizität *f* central nervous system toxicity
Zentralnervensystem- und Gelenkerkrankung *f* neuroarthropathy

Zentralschluß *m* centric occlusion *(des Gebisses)*
Zentralsehen *n* central (direct) vision
Zentralsehne *f* central tendon *(des Zwerchfells)*
Zentralskotom *n* central scotoma (blindness)
Zentralspindel *f* central spindle *(bei der Zellteilung)*
Zentralstar *m* central cataract
Zentralvenendruck *m* central venous pressure, c.v.p.
Zentralvenendruckkatheter *m* central venous pressure cannula
Zentralvenendruckmessung *f* central venous pressure measurement
Zentralvenenkatheter *m* central venous catheter
zentralwärts centrad; axopetal, axipetal, centripetal
Zentralwindung *f*/**hintere** posterior central gyrus
~/vordere anterior central gyrus
zentrifugal centrifugal, axofugal, axifugal
Zentrifugenmikroskop *n* centrifuge microscope
zentrifugieren to centrifuge
Zentriol *n* centriole, central body, centrosome, kinocentrum, microcentrum, karyomicrosome *(im Zellkern)*; ovocentre *(während der Befruchtung)*
Zentriolenanhang *m* satellite
zentripetal centripetal, axopetal, axipetal
Zentrodesmose *f* centrodesmose, centrodesmus
Zentromer *n* centromere
Zentrosom *n s.* Zentriol
Zentrosphäre *f* centrosphere
Zentrum *n*/**autonomes** autonomic centre
~/Brocasches Broca's area (centre, convolution, gyrus), motor speech area
~/medizinisches medical centre
~/motorisches motor centre
~/rezeptives receptive centre
Zephal... *s. a.* Kephal...
Zephalgie *f* cephalgia, cephalodynia, headache *(Zusammensetzungen s. unter Kopfschmerz)*
zephalisch cephalic
Zephaloridin *n* cephaloridine *(Antibiotikum)*
Zephalosporin *n* cephalosporin *(Antibiotikum)*
Zephalosporininfektion *f* cephalosporiosis
Zephalotin *n* cephalothin *(Antibiotikum)*
Zephalozentese *f* cephalocentesis
zerbrechen to break, to fracture *(z. B. die Knochen)*; to break to pieces, to comminute
zerdrücken to crush
zerebellar cerebellar
zerebellifugal cerebellifugal
zerebellipetal cerebellipetal
Zerebellitis *f* cerebellitis, inflammation of the cerebellum
Zerebellum *n s.* Kleinhirn
zerebral cerebral
Zerebral... *s. a.* Hirn... *und* Gehirn...
Zerebralneurasthenie *f* cerebrasthenia, phrenasthenia
zerebralneurasthenisch phrenasthenic

Zerebralparagonimiasis *f* cerebral paragonimiasis
Zerebralsklerose *f* cerebral sclerosis, cerebrosclerosis, encephalosclerosis
~/Schildersche Schilder's cerebral (diffuse) sclerosis, sudanophilic diffuse sclerosis
zerebralsklerotisch cerebrosclerotic
Zerebralthrombose *f* cerebral thrombosis
zerebriform cerebriform, cerebroid
zerebrifugal cerebrifugal
zerebripetal cerebripetal
Zerebromeningitis *f* cerebromeningitis
Zerebron *n* cerebron *(Zerebrosid)*
zerebrookulär cerebro-ocular
zerebropontin cerebropontine
zerebroretinal cerebroretinal
Zerebrosid *n* cerebroside, galactolipid, galactolipin[e]
Zerebrosidspeicherkrankheit *f* cerebrosidosis, cerebroside lipidosis (thesaurismosis, storage disease)
Zerebrosidsulfatasemangel *m* cerebroside sulphatase deficiency
zerebrosklerotisch cerebrosclerotic
zerebrospinal cerebrospinal, encephalorachidian
Zerebrospinalflüssigkeit *f* cerebrospinal fluid, CSF, subarachnoid fluid
Zerebrospinalkanal *m* cerebrospinal canal
Zerebrospinalmeningitis *f* cerebrospinal meningitis (fever)
Zerebrospinalnerv *m* cerebrospinal nerve
Zerebrospinalsklerose *f* cerebrospinal sclerosis
Zerebrospinalsystem *n* cerebrospinal system
zerebrovaskulär cerebrovascular
zerebrozerebellär cerebrocerebellar
Zerebrum *n s.* Gehirn
zerfahren absent-minded, confused; incoherent
Zerfahrenheit *f* absent-mindedness, confusion; incoherence
Zerfall *m* decomposition, decay, disintegration ● **durch radioaktiven ~ entstanden** radiogenic
~/geschwüriger ulceration
~ in Bruchstücke fragmentation
zerfallen to decompose, to decay
~/ulzerös to ulcerate
zerfallend karyorrhectic *(Zellkern nach dem Zelltod)*
~/geschwürig ulcerative
Zerfallsgeschwindigkeit *f* decay (disintegration) rate *(radioaktiver Stoffe)*
Zerfallskonstante *f*/**radioaktive** [radioactive] decay constant, disintegration constant
Zerfallskurve *f* decay (disintegration) curve
Zerfallsprodukt *n* decay (disintegration) product *(radioaktiv)*; decomposition product
Zerfallsrate *f* rate of decay, disintegration rate
Zerfallsteilung *f* schizogenesis, schizogony
zerfressend/geschwürig rodent
zergliedern to section, to dissect, to dismember *(z. B. eine Leiche)*
Zergliederung *f* [dis]section, dismemberment
Zerkarie *f* cercarian

Zerkariendermatitis

Zerkariendermatitis f cercarial dermatitis
zerkarientötend cercaricidal
zerkauen to chew, to manducate
Zerklage f cerclage
zerklüftet fissured
zermahlend molar
Zermalmungssyndrom n crush syndrome
Zeroid n ceroid
Zeroidspeicherkrankheit f ceroid lipofuscinosis (storage disease)
zerpulvern to pulverize
zerquetschen to crush
zerreiben to grind, to triturate, to levigate
~/zu Pulver to pulverize
zerreißen to tear, to rupture, to lacerate
Zerreißung f 1. tearing, laceration, rupture, rhexis; 2. s. Riß
zerren to strain (z. B. einen Muskel); to stretch (z. B. eine Sehne)
zerrissen ruptured, lacerated
Zerrung f strain (z. B. eines Muskels)
zersetzen/sich to decompose, to decay; to disintegrate
Zersetzung f decomposition, decay; disintegration
Zersetzungsprodukt n decomposition product
Zersetzungsprozeß m process of decomposition
zersplittern to splinter, to fracture, to comminute (z. B. Knochen)
Zersplitterung f splintering, splitting, fragmentation, comminution (z. B. eines Knochens)
zerstäuben to atomize (Feststoffe) (s. a. versprühen)
Zerstäuber m atomizer; sprayer
zerstören to destroy (z. B. Organe); to ruin, to wreck (z. B. die Gesundheit)
zerstörend destructive; deleterious
Zerstörung f destruction; ruin (z. B. der Gesundheit); decay (z. B. der Zähne)
zerstoßen to crush, to pestle, to pound; to pulverize
Zerstreutheit f absent-mindedness, confusion
Zerstreuung f dispersion (z. B. von Keimen); dissemination (z. B. von Bakterien)
Zerstreuungslinse f dispersing (diverging) lens
Zerstreuungsspiegel m convex mirror
Zerstreuungswinkel m angle of dispersion
zerstückeln to divide, to cut up; to dismember (z. B. einen Körper)
Zerstückelung f dismemberment (z. B. des Körpers); morcellation (z. B. von Tumoren)
zertrümmern to crush (z. B. die Muskulatur); to comminute (z. B. einen Knochen)
Zertrümmerungsbruch m crush (comminuted) fracture
Zeruloplasmin n ceruloplasmin (Plasmakupferspeicher)
Zeruloplasmin[spiegel]erhöhung f im Blut hyperoeruloplasminaemia
Zerumen n cerumen, earwax
zeruminal ceruminous, ceruminal
Zeruminaldrüse f ceruminous gland

Zeruminalpfropf m ceruminous plug, ceruminoma
Zeruminose f ceruminosis
Zervikal... s. a. Zervix... und Gebärmutterhals...
Zervikalbandscheibe f cervical disk
Zervikalbandscheibenhernie f cervical disk hernia
Zervikaldivertikel n cervical diverticulum
Zervikalfissur f cervical fissure
Zervikalfistel f cervical fistula
Zervikalganglion n cervical ganglion
Zervikalhydrozele f cervical hydrocele
Zervikallymphknoten m cervical lymph node
Zervikalnerv m cervical nerve
Zervikalplexus m cervical plexus
Zervikalspondylose f cervical spondylosis
Zervikobrachialneuritis f cervicobrachial neuritis, cervical radicular syndrome
Zervikogramm n cervicogram
Zervikographie f cervicography
Zervikokolpitis f cervicocolpitis, cervicovaginitis, inflammation of the uterine cervix and vagina
Zerviko-Okzipital-Neuralgie f cervico-occipital neuralgia
Zervikovaginitis f s. Zervikokolpitis
Zervix f cervix [of the uterus], uterine neck, neck of the womb
Zervix... s. a. Zervikal... und Gebärmutterhals...
Zervixabort m cervical abortion
Zervixabstrich m cervical smear; cervical scrapings
Zervixamputation f cervicectomy, [hystero]trachelectomy, uterine cervix amputation
Zervixbiopsie f cervical (uterine cervix) biopsy
Zervixbiopsiezange f cervical punch [biopsy clamp]
Zervixcerclage f cervical cerclage
Zervixdehnung f cervical (uterine cervix) dilatation
Zervixgravidität f cervical (uterine cervix) pregnancy
Zervixinzision f trachelotomy
Zervixkarzinom n cervical cancer (carcinoma)
Zervixkonisation f uterine cervix conization, coning of the cervix, rotary coring of the cervix
Zervixpessar n uterine veil
Zervixpolyp m cervical (uterine cervix) polyp
Zervixschleim m cervical (uterine cervix) mucus
Zervixschleimpfropf m cervical [mucus] plug
Zervixsegment n lower uterine segment
Zervixstanze f cervical punch [biopsy clamp]
Zervixzange f cervical grasping forceps
Zestode m cestode (s. a. Bandwurm)
Zestodeninfestation f cestodiasis, infestation with tapeworms
Zestodensegment n cestode segment
zeugen to procreate, to reproduce, to generate
~/ein Kind to father a child
zeugend/weibliche Nachkommen thelygenic
Zeugung f procreation, generation, progenitre
zeugungsfähig potent, procreative

Zeugungsfähigkeit f potency, procreative power (capacity)
Zeugungsorgane npl reproductive organs, genitals, genitalia
zeugungsunfähig impotent
Zeugungsunfähigkeit f impotence
Ziegelmehlsediment n latericeous sediment *(im Urin)*
ziegelrot latericeous, lateritious *(z. B. Harnsediment)*
Ziegenfieber n goat fever *(s. a. Bruzellose)*
Ziegenmeckern n aegophonia *(bei Bronchophonie)*
Ziegenmilchanämie f goat's-milk anaemia *(durch Folsäuremangel)*
Ziegenpeter m *s.* Mumps
ziehen to draw, to pull *(z. B. einen Zahn)*; to extract *(z. B. eine Zahnwurzel)*
Ziehinstrument n tractor
Zielaufnahme f spot-film radiogram
Zieldrüse f target gland *(Endokrinologie)*
Zielorgan n target organ *(der Hormonwirkung)*
Zielzelle f target cell *(Immunologie)*
Zigarettendrain n cigarette (Penrose) drain
Zikatrikektomie f cicatricectomy
Ziliarapparat m ciliary apparatus
Ziliarbewegung f ciliary movement
Ziliarblepharitis f ciliary blepharitis
Ziliardrüse f ciliary gland
Ziliarepithel n ciliary (vibrating) epithelium
Ziliarfalte f ciliary plica (fold)
Ziliarfortsatz m ciliary process
Ziliarganglion n ciliary ganglion
Ziliarkörper m ciliary body
Ziliarkörperband n ciliary body band
Ziliarkörperentfernung f[/operative] cyclectomy, excision of the ciliary body
Ziliarkörperentzündung f cyclitis, inflammation of the ciliary body
Ziliarkörpergeschwulst f ciliary body tumour
Ziliarkörperkreislauf m ciliary body circulation
Ziliarkörperlähmung f cycloplegia, paralysis of the ciliary muscles
Ziliarkörpermelanom n ciliary body melanoma
Ziliarkörperschwellung f ciliary body swelling
Ziliarkörpervene f ciliary vein
Ziliarkörperzyste f ciliary body cyst
Ziliarmuskel m ciliary muscle
Ziliarmuskeldurchtrennung f[/operative] cycl[ic]otomy
ziliarmuskellähmend cycloplegic
Ziliarmuskellähmung f cycloplegia
~ durch Atropin atropine cycloplegia
Ziliarnerv m ciliary nerve
Ziliarneuralgie f ciliary neuralgia
Ziliarrand m ciliary margin (border) *(der Iris)*
Ziliarreflex m ciliary reflex
Ziliarregion f ciliary region
Ziliarring m ciliary ring
Ziliarstaphylom n ciliary staphyloma
Zilie f 1. cilium, vibratile process; 2. eyelash ● **mit Zilien besetzt** ciliated

Zilienbewegung f ciliary movement
Zilienpinzette f cilia forceps
Ziliospinalreflex m ciliospinal reflex
Zingulektomie f cingulectomy, excision of the cingulate gyrus
Zingulotraktotomie f cingulotractotomy
Zingulum n 1. cingulum, girdle, zone; 2. cingulate gyrus; 3. *s.* Herpes zoster
Zingulumentfernung f/**operative** *s.* Zingulektomie
Zinkfieber n zinc chills
Zinkleimverband m Unna's paste dressing; Unna's paste boot *(z. B. bei Knöchelfraktur)*
Zinkoxid n zinc oxide *(Dermatikum)*
Zink-Quecksilberoxid-Schrittmacherbatterie f zinc mercuric-oxide pacemaker battery
Zinksulfattrübungstest m zinc sulphate turbidity test *(zur Leberfunktionsprobe)*
Zinkvergiftung f zinc poisoning, brazier's disease
Zipfel m 1. cusp, cuspis *(an Herzklappen) (Zusammensetzungen s. unter Cuspis)*; 2. flap *(der Haut)*
zipflig cuspidate, cuspidal
Zipperlein n podagra, gout
Zirbeldrüse f pineal gland (body, appendage), epiphysis, false (cerebral) apophysis, conarium ● **über der ~** suprapineal
Zirbeldrüsen... *s. a.* Epiphysen...
Zirbeldrüsenentfernung f[/**operative**] pinealectomy, excision of the pineal body
Zirbeldrüsenerkrankung f pinealopathy, epiphysiopathy, disease of the pineal gland
Zirbeldrüseninsuffizienz f hypopinealism
Zirbeldrüsensyndrom n pineal syndrome
Zirbeldrüsenteratom n/**heterotopes** heterotopic pineal teratoma
Zirbeldrüsentumor m pineal tumour
Zirbeldrüsenüberfunktion f hyperpinealism
Zirbeldrüsenunterfunktion f hypopinealism
Zirbeldrüsenventrikel m pineal ventricle
Zirkadianrhythmus m circadian rhythm
Zirkadiansyndrom n jet travel syndrome
Zirkelschnitt m circular incision (cut)
Zirkulärnaht f circular suture
Zirkulärverband m circular bandage
Zirkulation f/**portale** portal circulation
Zirkumduktion f circumduction, helicopodia *(z. B. eines gelähmten Beins)*
Zirkumferenz f circumference
zirkumskript circumscribed, localized
zirkumzidieren to circumcise
Zirkumzision f 1. circumcision *(einer Wunde)*; 2. *s.* Beschneidung
zirrhös cirrhotic
Zirrhose f 1. cirrhosis; 2. *s.* Leberzirrhose
zirrhotisch cirrhotic
zirzinär circinate
Zisternenarachnoiditis f cisternal arachnoiditis
Zisternenpunktion f cisternal puncture
Zisternenröntgen[kontrast]bild n cisternogram
Zisternenröntgen[kontrast]darstellung f cisternography

Zisternogramm

Zisternogramm n cisternogram
Zisternographie f cisternography
Zitrat n citrate
Zitratblut n citrated blood *(ungerinnbar)*
Zitratplasma n citrated plasm
Zitratsynthase f citrate (citric) synthase, [citrate] condensing enzyme
Zitratzyklus m citric-acid cycle, tricarboxylic-acid cycle, TCA (Krebs) cycle
Zitronensäure f citric acid
Zitronensäurezyklus m s. Zitratzyklus
Zitrovorumfaktor m citrovorum factor, folinic acid
Zitrullin n citrulline
Zitrullinämie f citrullinaemia *(Aminosäurestoffwechselstörung)*
Zitterbewegung f tremor, trembling, tremulation, trepidation *(Zusammensetzungen s. unter Tremor)*
zittern 1. to tremble, to quiver, to shake, to shiver, to shudder; 2. to vibrate
zitternd 1. tremulous, trembling, trepident; 2. vibratory; oscillatory
Zitterpuls m trembling pulse
Zivilisationskrankheit f civilizational disease
Zivilisationsschaden m civilizational damage
Z-Lappenplastik f Z flap *(plastische Chirurgie)*
Z-Naht f Z stitch
ZNS s. Zentralnervensystem
Zoanthropie f zoanthropy *(Wahn, sich in ein Tier zu verwandeln)*
zökal caecal, coecal
Zökal... s. a. Zökum... und Blinddarm...
Zökalabszeß m typhloempyema
Zökalfalte f caecal plica
Zökalgeschwür n caecum ulcer
Zökalgrube f caecal fossa
Zökalstase f caecum stasis
Zökektomie f caecectomy, typhlectomy
Zökoileostomie f caecoileostomy, ileocaecostomy
Zökokolostomie f caecocolostomy, colocaecostomy
Zökopexie f caecopexy, caecofixation, typhlopexy
Zökoplikation f caecoplication
Zökoptosis f caecoptosis, typhloptosis
Zökorrhaphie f caecorrhaphy, typhlorrhaphy
Zökosigmoidostomie f caecosigmoidostomy
Zökostomie f caecostomy, typhlostomy
Zökotomie f caecotomy, typhlotomy
Zökum n caecum, typhlon, blind gut
~/ausgewalztes megacaecum
Zökumatonie f typhlatonia
Zökumbeweglichkeit f caecum mobility
Zökumbruch m caecocele, typhlocele
Zökumdilatation f typhlectasia
Zökumentzündung f caecitis, inflammation of the caecum; typhl[o]enteritis
Zökumfixation f caecopexy, typhlofixation
Zökumgekröse n mesocaecum
Zökum-Ileum-Anastomose f s. Zökoileostomie
Zökuminzision f typhlotomy
Zökumkarzinom n caecum cancer (carcinoma)
Zökum-Kolon-Anastomose f s. Zökokolostomie
Zökumleiomyom n caecum leiomyoma
Zökummobilität f caecum mobility
Zökumneurilemmom n caecum neurilemmoma
Zökumperforation f caecum perforation
Zökumraffung f caecoplication
Zökum-Sigma-Anastomose f caecosigmoidostomy
Zökumstauung f caecum stasis
Zökumsteinkrankheit f typhlolithiasis
Zökumstenose f typhlostenosis
Zökumtiefstand m caecoptosis
Zökumvergrößerung f typhlomegaly
Zökumvolvulus m caecum volvulus
zöliakal coeliac
Zöliakalganglion n coeliac ganglion
Zöliakie f [infantile] coeliac disease, coeliac syndrome (infantilism), Heubner-Herter disease, Gee-Herter disease, idiopathic infantile steatorrhoea, gluten-induced enteropathy; adult coeliac disease (syndrome)
Zöliakographie f coeliac angiography (arteriography)
Zöliektasie f coeliectasia, distension of the abdominal cavity
Zölioenterotomie f coelioenterotomy
Zöliogastrotomie f coeliogastrotomy
Zöliokolpotomie f coeliocolpotomy
Zöliomyomektomie f coeliomyomectomy
Zölioparazentese f coelioparacentesis
Zöliorrhaphie f coeliorrhaphy
Zölioskopie f coel[i]oscopy
Zöliotomie f coeliotomy
Zölitis f coelitis
Zollinger-Ellison-Syndrom n Zollinger-Ellison syndrome *(Magengeschwürbildung bei gastrinbildendem Tumor)*
Zölom n coelom, embryonic body cavity
Zölomausstülpung f coelomic pouch
Zölomspalte f coelomic cleft
Zölosom n coelosoma
Zona f 1. zona, zone, girdle, belt *(s. a. unter Zone)*; 2. s. Herpes zoster
~ **cartilaginea** limbus of the spiral lamina
~ **ciliaris** ciliary zone
~ **fasciculata** fasciculated zone *(der Nebenniere)*
~ **glomerulosa** glomerular zone *(der Nebenniere)*
~ **haemorrhoidalis** haemorrhoidal zone (ring)
~ **pellucida** pellucid zone
~ **pupillaris** pupillary zone
Zonästhesie f zonaesthesia, girdle sensation; girdle pain
Zone f zona, zone, area, region *(s. a. unter Zona)*
~/**androgene** androgenous zone
~/**chondrogene** chondrogenic zone
~/**epileptogene** epileptogenous zone
~/**erogene** ero[to]genous zone
~/**Headsche** Head's area (zone) *(der Haut)*
~/**hyperästhetische** hyperaesthetic zone
~/**hypnogene** hypnogenous zone
~/**hysterogene** hysterogenic zone

Zonula f zonule, zonula, small band
~ **ciliaris** ciliary zonule, zonule of Zinn, suspensory ligament of the lens
Zonulaapparat m s. Zonula ciliaris
Zonulaapparatkatarakt m ciliary zonule cataract
Zonulafasern fpl zonular fibres
Zonulitis f zonulitis, inflammation of the ciliary zonule
Zonulotomie f zonulotomy, cutting of the ciliary zonular fibres
Zooerastie f zooerastia, erotic zoophilism, sexual intercourse with animals
Zoogloea f zoogloea *(Interzellularsubstanz in Bakterienkolonien)*
Zoograft n zoograft, zooplastic graft
Zoomanie f zoomania *(krankhafte Tierliebe)*
zoonotisch zoonotic
Zooparasit m zooparasite
zooparasitisch zooparasitic
zoophag zoophagous
zoophil zoophilic, zoophile
Zoophilia f **erotica** s. Zooerastie
Zoophilie f zoophilia, zoophilism, love of animals
Zoophobie f zoophobia *(krankhafte Angst vor Tieren)*
Zooplastik f zooplasty, zoografting
Zoopsie f zoopsia, seeing of animals *(Wahnvorstellung)*
Zoospermie f zoospermia *(Vorhandensein von Samenfäden im Ejakulat)*
Zoospermium n zoosperm
Zoospore f zoospore, swarm spore (cell)
Zootoxin n zootoxin, animal toxin
Zoster m zoster, zona, shingles
~ **ophthalmicus** ophthalmic zoster
~/**viszeraler** visceral zoster
zosterartig zosteriform, zosteroid
Zoster-Immunglobulin n zoster immune globulin
Zotte f villus; fimbria, fringe *(s. a. unter Villus)*
~/**primäre** primary villus
~/**sekundäre** secondary villus
Zottenbildung f formation of villi ● **vor der** ~ previllous
Zottenentfernung f[/**operative**] fimbriectomy
Zottenfalte f villous fold
Zottenhaut f chorion ● **unter der** ~ subchorial, subchorionic
Zottenhautentstehung f choriogenesis
Zottenhautentzündung f chorionitis
Zottenherz n villous (hairy, shaggy) heart; trichocardia
Zottenkrebs m villous cancer (carcinoma)
Zottenperikard n shaggy pericardium; fibropericarditis, fibrinous pericarditis
zottenreich villous
Zottenreichtum m villosity
zottentragend villiferous
Zottenzwischenraum m intervillous space
Zottigkeit f villosity
Z-Plastik f Z-plastic relaxing operation
zubereiten/Arzneien to dispense *(nach Rezept)*

Zubereitung f 1. dispensation, preparation; 2. preparation, formulation
züchten to culture *(z. B. Bakterien)*
Züchtungsstamm m strain
zucken to jerk *(z. B. reflektorisch)*; to twitch *(z. B. ein Muskel)*; to vellicate, to twitch spasmodically; to winch with pain; to move convulsively
Zucker m sugar ● **in** ~ **umwandeln** to saccharify
~/**einfacher** monosaccharide, monose
zuckerartig saccharine
Zuckerausscheidung f **im Urin** saccharuria, glycosuria, mel[l]ituria
Zuckerausschwitzung f saccharephidrosis
zuckererzeugend sacchariferous
Zuckergehalt m sugar content
Zuckergehaltsbestimmung f saccharimetry
Zuckergußleber f zuckerguss (frosted) liver, [sugar-]icing liver
Zuckergußmilz f zuckerguss (iced, sugar-coated) spleen
zuckerhaltig sacchariferous, saccharine
Zuckerharnruhr f s. Diabetes mellitus
Zuckerkranker m s. Diabetiker
zuckerlösend saccharolytic
zuckerneubildend gluconeogenetic, glyconeogenetic
Zuckerneubildung f gluconeogenesis, neoglycogenesis *(aus Fett oder Eiweißen)*
Zuckerrohrstaublunge[nerkrankung] f bagasse disease, bagass[c]osis
zuckerspaltend saccharolytic
Zuckerstar m diabetic cataract
Zuckerstich m[/**Bernardscher**] diabetic (Bernard's) puncture
Zuckerstoffwechsel m saccharometabolism, glycometabolism
zuckerstoffwechselregulierend glycoregulatory
Zuckung f jerk, jump *(reflektorisch)*; twitching *(z. B. eines Muskels)*; contraction *(eines Muskels)*; convulsive tic *(des Gesichts)*; convulsion *(Krampf)*; palpitation, throbbing *(z. B. des Herzens)*
Zuckungsgesetz n/**Pflügersches** Pflüger's law *(Physiologie)*
Zuckungskrampf m convulsion
zufällig accidental, incidental, adventitious; random *(Statistik)*
Zufallssymptom n accidental symptom
Zufluß m afflux, influx; intake; supply
zuführen to supply *(z. B. Blut)*; to administer *(z. B. ein Medikament)*
~/**Atropin** to atropinize
~/**oral** to give by mouth, to administer orally
Zug m 1. pull, tug *(Ziehen)*; extension *(z. B. bei Knochenbruch)*; traction, tension *(z. B. durch Spannung)*; 2. feature *(des Gesichts)*; 3. trait, characteristic *(des Charakters)*
Zugang m 1. iter, passageway *(Anatomie)*; meatus, orifice *(Öffnung)*; aditus, entrance, aperture, introitus *(z. B. zu einer Körperhöhle)*; approach, access; 2. admission *(im K...)*

Zugang

~/**dauerhafter intravenöser** continuous intravenous access
~/**venöser** intravenous route (portal)
zugänglich approachable, accessible
Zugangsweg *m* approach, access *(z. B. bei einer Operation)*
Zügel *m* bridle; habena, frenum *(Anatomie)*
Zügelnaht *f* bridle suture
Zuggurtung *f* figure-of-eight suture
Zugmittel *n* epispastic [agent], vesicant [agent], blistering agent
Zugnaht *f* traction suture
Zugverband *m* traction (extension) bandage; traction (pulley) apparatus, tractor
zuletztgeboren ultimogenitary
zunehmen/an Gewicht to gain (put on) weight
Zunge *f* tongue, lingua, glossa *(s. a. unter Lingua)* ● **unter der ~** sublingual, subglossal
~/**belegte** furred (coated, dirty) tongue
~/**brennende** burning tongue
~/**feuchte** moist tongue
~/**gefurchte** furrowed (fissured) tongue
~/**glatte** bald tongue
~/**nicht belegte** clean tongue
~/**runzelige** wrinkled (scrotal, crocodile) tongue
~/**stark belegte** encrusted tongue
~/**trockene** dry tongue
~/**weißlich belegte** white tongue
Zungenabszeß *m* lingual abscess
Zungenaponeurose *f* lingual aponeurosis
Zungenapraxie *f* lingual (tongue) apraxia
Zungenarterie *f* lingual artery
~/**tiefe** deep lingual artery, profunda linguae artery
Zungenarteriennervengeflecht *n* lingual plexus
Zungenbändchen *n* frenulum of the tongue
Zungenbanddurchtrennung *f*[/**operative**] frenotomy
Zungenbandentfernung *f*[/**operative**] frenectomy
Zungenbandverkürzung *f*/**angeborene** tonguetie
Zungenbein *n* hyoid [bone] ● **über dem ~** suprahyoid ● **unter dem ~** subhyoid
Zungenbeinbogen *m* hyoid arch
Zungenbeinhorn *n*/**großes** greater horn of the hyoid bone, thyrohyal
~/**kleines** lesser horn of the hyoid bone
Zungenbeinknorpel *m* Reichert's cartilage
Zungenbeinregion *f* hyoid region
Zungenbeinschaft *m* basihyal
Zungenbein-Schildknorpel-Band *n* hyothyroid ligament
Zungenbein-Zungen-Muskel *m* hyoglossus [muscle]
Zungenbelag *m* fur (coating) of the tongue, sordes
Zungenbiß *m* odaxesmus, biting of the tongue
Zungenbrennen *n* glossopyrosis, pyroglossia, burning sensation of the tongue
Zungendeformierung *f* tongue malformation
Zungendepressorium *n* tongue depressor
Zungendrüse *f* lingual gland

~/**Blandinsche** Blandin's gland
Zungendrüsenspeichel *m* lingual saliva
Zungenentfernung *f*[/**operative**] glossectomy, glossosteresis, elinguation
Zungenentzündung *f* glossitis, inflammation of the tongue
~/**atrophische** atrophic (Hunter's) glossitis
Zungenerkrankung *f* glossopathy, disease of the tongue
Zungenfaßzange *f* tongue [seizing] forceps, linguotrite
Zungenfleischnerv *m* hypoglossal nerve, hypoglossus
zungenförmig tongue-shaped, linguiform, lingular
Zungen-Gaumen-Nerv *m* glossopalatine nerve
Zungengrundstruma *f* [sub]lingual goitre, lingual thyroid *(versprengtes Schilddrüsengewebe am Zungengrund)*
Zungenhochstand *m* elevation of the tongue
Zungenhypertrophie *f* macroglossia, megaloglossia
Zungenhypotrophie *f* microglossia
Zungeninspektion *f* glossoscopy
Zungeninzision *f* glossotomy
Zungen-Kehldeckel-Falte *f* glossoepiglottic fold
Zungen-Kehldeckel-Grube *f* glossoepiglottic fossa
Zungenkrampf *m* lingual spasm, glossospasm, spasm of the tongue
Zungenkrypten *fpl* crypts of the tongue
Zungenlähmung *f* lingual paralysis, glossoplegia, glossolysis, sausarism
~/**halbseitige** hemiglossoplegia
Zungenlaut *m* lingual [sound]
Zungenloser *m* aglossus
Zungenlosigkeit *f* aglossia
Zungenmandel *f* lingual tonsil
Zungenmilzbrandkarbunkel *m* glossanthrax
Zungenmißbildung *f* tongue malformation; ateloglossia
Zungenmuskel *m* lingualis [muscle], lingual muscle
~/**querer** transverse lingual muscle
Zungennaht *f* glossorrhaphy, suture of the tongue
Zungennerv *m* lingual nerve
Zungenoberfläche *f* lingual surface
Zungenoberseite *f s.* Zungenrücken
Zungenödem *n* lingual oedema, oedema of the tongue, glossocele
Zungenoperation *f*/**plastische** glossoplasty
Zungenosteom *n* osteoma of the tongue
Zungenpapille *f* lingual papilla
~/**umwallte** circumvallate papilla
Zungenpapillenentzündung *f* linguopapillitis
Zungenplastik *f* glossoplasty
Zungenpsoriasis *f* lingual psoriasis
Zungenrand *m* border of the tongue
~/**seitlicher** lateral border of the tongue
Zungenrekonstruktion *f* glossoplasty

Zungenrücken m dorsum (upper surface) of the tongue
Zungenscheidewand f lingual septum
Zungenschleimhaut f lingual mucosa, periglottis, mucous membrane of the tongue
Zungen-Schlund-Nerv m glossopharyngeal nerve
Zungen-Schlund-Nervenlähmung f glossopharyngeal paralysis
Zungen-Schlund-Nervenschmerz m glossopharyngeal neuralgia
Zungenschluß m lingual occlusion *(Stomatologie)*
Zungenschmerz m glossodynia, glossalgia, pain in the tongue
Zungenschwellung f lingual swelling, swelling of the tongue
Zungenseptum n lingual septum
Zungenspalte f glossoschisis, schistoglossia; bifid (cleft) tongue
Zungenspatel m tongue spatula; tongue depressor
Zungenspeichel m lingual saliva
Zungenspitze f tip of the tongue, proglossis
Zungenspitzendrüse f Nuhn's (anterior lingual) gland
Zungenteilentfernung f[/operative] hemiglossectomy
Zungentrockenheit f dryness of the tongue, sausarism
Zungen- und Mundschleimhautentzündung f stomatoglossitis
Zungenunterentwicklung f ateloglossia
Zungenunterseite f lower surface of the tongue, hypoglottis
Zungenuntersuchung f glossoscopy, inspection (examination) of the tongue
Zungenvene f lingual vein
~/tiefe deep lingual vein
Zungenverdickung f pachyglossia
Zungenwurm m linguatula, pentastome
Zungenwurmbefall m linguatuliasis, linguatulosis, pentastomiasis
Zungenwurzel f root of the tongue
Zungenzange f tongue [seizing] forceps
Zungenzurücksinken n glossoptosis, downward displacement of the tongue *(z. B. bei kleinem Unterkiefer)*
Zünglein n s. Lingula
zurechnungsfähig responsible, of sound (sane) mind
~/nicht irresponsible, of unsound mind
Zurechnungsfähigkeit f imputability, [criminal] responsibility
zureichen/die Instrumente to pass (hand) the instruments
zurückbeugen/sich to bend back, to tilt backward, to retrovert
zurückbilden/sich to regress, to recede, to remit
zurückbildend/sich re[tro]gressive
Zurückbildung f/**übermäßige** hyperinvolution *(z. B. von Organen)*

zurückbleiben to lag (fall) behind; to be retarded
zurückbleibend residual *(z. B. Krankheitsfolgen)*
zurückdrängen to push back, to drive back *(z. B. den Darm)*; to reduce *(z. B. eine Hernie)*; to repress *(z. B. Gefühle)*
Zurückfallen n **der Zunge** dropping backward of the tongue, tongue swallowing *(bei Bewußtlosigkeit)*
zurückfließen to flow back, to regurgitate *(z. B. Blut)*
zurückfließend regurgitant
zurückgeblieben infantile, backward *(z. B. ein Kind)*; underdeveloped, primitive *(in der Entwicklung)*; retarded *(im Wachstum)*
~/geistig mentally defective (retarded), subnormal
Zurückgebliebener m retardate
zurückgehen to regress, to recede, to disappear *(z. B. eine Symptomatik)*; to abate, to subside *(z. B. Schmerzen)*; to remit, to go back (down), to fall *(z. B. das Fieber)*; to fade, to disappear *(z. B. ein Exanthem)*
zurückgehend regressive *(z. B. Symptome)*; remittent *(z. B. das Fieber)*
zurückgeneigt recumbent *(z. B. die Körperhaltung)*
zurückhaltend[/willkürlich] continent
Zurückhaltung f 1. s. Retention 1.; 2. temperance *(z. B. gegenüber Alkohol)*
Zurückschneiden n **von Knochen** resection
Zurückstehen n **des Unterkiefers** retrognathia, retrognathism
zurückströmen to flow back, to regurgitate *(z. B. Blut)*
zurückweichen to recede *(z. B. das Zahnfleisch)*
Zurückweichen n recession *(z. B. des Zahnfleischrands)*
zurückwenden/sich to retrovert, to turn back, to tilt backward
zurückziehen/sich to draw back, to retract
Zurückziehen n retraction *(z. B. einer Sehne)*
zusammenballen/Erythrozyten to agglutinate erythrocytes
~/sich to agglomerate, to conglomerate
zusammenballend agglutinative
Zusammenballung f agglomeration, conglomeration, clumping, agglutination; aggregation
zusammenbrechen to break down *(z. B. der Blutkreislauf)*; to collapse; to crack up *(psychisch)*
Zusammenbruch m break down *(z. B. des Kreislaufs)*; collapse *(des Körpers)*; failure *(z. B. einer Organfunktion)*
zusammenfließend confluent
Zusammenfluß m **der Hirnblutleiter** confluence of the sinuses
zusammenfügen/sich to fit together *(z. B. Knochenteile)*; to unite, to join *(z. B. die Wundränder)*
zusammengeballt agglomerated, conglobated, clumped; convoluted

zusammenhanglos

zusammenhang[s]los disjointed, incoherent *(z. B. das Denken)*
Zusammenhangslosigkeit *f* disjointedness, incoherence *(z. B. des Denkens)*
zusammenlaufend convergent
Zusammenpressen *n* compression
~/digitales digital compression
zusammenschnüren to constrict; to ligate
zusammenschnürend constrictive
Zusammenschnürer *m* constrictor [muscle]
zusammenschnurren to retract *(z. B. ein Muskel)*
Zusammenschnürung *f* constriction; ligature, ligation
zusammenschrumpfen to shrink *(z. B. Organe)*
Zusammensinken *n* cataplexis *(z. B. des Körpers)*
zusammensinkend cataplectic
Zusammenspiel *n*/**geordnetes** coordination, synergy *(z. B. der Muskeln)*
~/mangelhaftes incoordination, asynergy *(z. B. der Muskeln)*
zusammenwachsen to grow together, to unite *(z. B. Knochenbruchteile)*; to close, to heal *(z. B. die Wundränder)*; to adhere *(z. B. Organe)*
~/wieder to coalesce
Zusammenwirken *n* synergia, synergism *(z. B. von Organen)*
zusammenwirkend synergistic, synerg[et]ic
zusammenziehbar contractile *(z. B. Muskeln)*
Zusammenziehbarkeit *f* contractility *(z. B. von Muskeln)*
zusammenziehen/sich to contract *(z. B. ein Muskel)*; to retract *(z. B. eine Sehne)*; to constrict *(z. B. eine Arterie) (s. a. schrumpfen, verengen/sich)*
~/sich krampfartig to vellicate, to twitch spasmodically
Zusammenziehen *n* contraction *(z. B. eines Muskels)*; retraction *(z. B. einer Sehne)*; constriction *(z. B. einer Arterie)*; syneresis *(z. B. von Blutgerinnseln)*
zusammenziehend astringent, [ad]stringent
~/sich contracting; retracting; constricting; systaltic
~/sich unter Wärmeeinwirkung thermosystaltic
Zusatzbewegung *f* accessory movement
Zusatzdrüse *f* accessory gland
zusätzlich additional, extra; supplemental *(z. B. Ausatmungsluft)*; supplementary *(z. B. ein Gelenk)*; accessory, supernumerary *(z. B. ein Organ)*; adjuvant *(z. B. eine Therapie)*; collateral *(z. B. Durchblutung)*
Zusatzmilz *f* accessory (supernumerary) spleen
Zusatzmuskel *m* accessory muscle
Zusatznerv *m* accessory nerve
Zusatzsymptom *n* accessory symptom
Zusatztherapie *f* adjuvant therapy
Zustand *m* state, status, condition *(s. a. unter Status)*; situation ● **den ~ verändernd** metamorphic
~/akuter acuity, acuteness, acute phase (stage)

~/amorpher amorphism, amorphia
~/ausgewachsener metaplasis
~/bewußtseinsklarer conscious state, consciousness
~/deliranter delirious (deliriant) state
~/depressiver depressive state
~/entzündlicher inflammatory condition
~/epidemischer epidemic state, epidemicity
~/fetaler foetalism, foetal condition *(Persistenz fetaler Zeichen nach der Geburt)*
~/formloser amorphism, amorphia
~/gesunder state of health, salubrity, salubrious state
~/hygienischer sanitation, sanitary (healthful) condition
~/hypnagoger hypnagogic state
~/hypnoleptischer hypnoleptic state
~/hypnopomper hypnopompic state
~/hysterischer hysterical state
~/knotiger nodosity, nodose state
~/konstitutionell psychopathischer constitutional psychopathic state
~/psychischer mental state
~/refraktärer refractory state
~/unhygienischer insanitation, insanitary (unhealthful) condition
~/unreifer immaturity, immature state *(z. B. des Fetus)*
~/variköser varicosity; varicose state
Zustrom *m* afflux; intake
zuträglich salubrious
zuziehen/einen Arzt to consult (call in) a doctor
~/sich eine Erkältung to catch a cold
~/sich eine Infektion to contract an infection
~/sich eine Verbrennung to burn
~/sich eine Verbrennung vierten Grades to carbonize
ZVD s. Venendruck/zentraler
ZVD-Messung *f* central venous pressure measurement
Zwang *m* compulsion, obsession; anankastia, anancastia
zwanghaft compulsive, obsessional, obsessive; anankastic
Zwangsantrieb *m* impulsion
Zwangsbefürchtung *f* phobia
Zwangsdenken *n* compulsive (obsessional) thinking
Zwangseinweisung *f* commitment, compulsory hospitalization *(psychisch Kranker)*
Zwangserbrechen *n* forcible vomiting
Zwangshandlung *f* compulsive (obsessional) act, compulsive ritual, anankastia
Zwangsidee *f* compulsive idea
Zwangsirresein *n* compulsive insanity
Zwangsjacke *f* straitjacket
Zwangslachen *n* compulsive laughter
Zwangsneurose *f* compulsion (obsessive-compulsive) neurosis
Zwangsneurotiker *m* [obsessive-]compulsive personality, anankastic personality
zwangsneurotisch obsessive-compulsive

Zwangspsychose f compulsive insanity
Zwangsvorstellung f obsession, compulsive idea
● **einer ~ unterliegend** obsessive, obsessional
zweckbewußt rational *(z. B. eine Therapie)*
zweiachsig biaxial
zweiarmig two-armed
zweiäugig binocular
Zweiäugigkeit f binocularity
zweibäuchig digastric, biventral, biventer
zweibeinig two-legged
zweieiig biovular, dizygotic
Zweifachunterbindung f double ligation (ligature)
zweifarbensichtig dichro[mat]ic
Zweifarbensichtigkeit f dichromatopsia, dichromasia, dichromatism
zweifarbig dichrom[at]ic, dichroic *(z. B. Kristalle)*
Zweifarbigkeit f dichro[mat]ism
zweifingerig bidigitate, bidactylar, didactylate
Zweifingerigkeit f bidactyly, didactylism
zweifüßig bipedal
Zweig m ramus, branch
zweigelenkig diarticular, diarthric, biarticular
Zweigelenkmuskel m two-joint muscle
zweigeschlechtlich bisexual, ambisexual, ambosexual
zweigeteilt bipartite, bifid; bifurcated
Zweigläserprobe f two-glass test
Zweigläserpyurie f two-glass pyuria
zweihändig bimanual, two-handed
zweihörnig bicornuate, bicornuous
Zweikammerherz n bilocular (biventricular) heart
~/funktionelles functional two-chambered heart
zweikammerig biventricular, bilocular, biloculate, two-chambered
zweikapselig bicapsular
zweikeimblättrig diploblastic
zweikeimig bigerminal
zweikernig binuclear, binucleate
zweiklappig bivalvular
zweiköpfig two-headed, bicephalous, bicapitate, dicephalous; bicipital, biceps *(z. B. ein Muskel)*
Zweiköpfigkeit f dicephalia, dicephalism
Zweikopfmuskel m bicipital muscle, biceps [muscle]
zweilappig bilobate, bilobular
zweiohrig binaural, biaural
Zweiolivenstethoskop n binaural stethoscope
Zweiphasenschlaf m two-phase sleep
zweipolig bipolar
Zweipunktediskriminierung f two-point discrimination (sensibility), spatial discrimination, double point threshold, limen of twoness
zweischichtig bilaminar
zweiseitig bilateral
Zweiseitigkeit f bilateralism
Zweistärkenbrille f bifocal spectacles (glasses)
Zweistärkenglas n bifocal lens
Zweistufenoperation f two-stage operation
Zweistufentest m two-step test

~/Masterscher Master's two-step test *(Belastungsprüfung im EKG)*
Zweiteilung f dichotomy, dichotomous division; bifurcation
zweitgebärend secundiparous, biparous
Zweitgebärende f secundipara, bipara, duipara
Zweitgebiß n secondary dentition
Zweitgeburt f secundiparity
Zweitimpfung f secondary vaccination
Zweitschwangere f secundigravida
zweizackig bifurcate
zweizellig bicellular
zweizipfelig bicuspidal, bicuspidate *(z. B. eine Klappe)*; bisferious *(z. B. eine Druckkurve)*
Zwerchfell n diaphragm[a], midriff ● **über dem ~** supradiaphragmatic, epiphrenic, epiphrenal ● **unter dem ~** subdiaphragmatic, subphrenic, hypodiaphragmatic
Zwerchfell... s. a. Diaphragma...
Zwerchfellähmung f phrenoparalysis, phrenoplegia
Zwerchfellarterie f [musculo]phrenic artery
~/obere superior phrenic artery
~/untere inferior phrenic artery
Zwerchfellatmer m diaphragmatic breather
Zwerchfellatmung f diaphragmatic respiration
Zwerchfellatmungstyp m diaphragmatic breathing type
Zwerchfellbruch m diaphragmatic hernia, diaphragmatocele
Zwerchfellentzündung f diaphragm[at]itis, inflammation of the diaphragm, phrenitis
Zwerchfellflattern n diaphragmatic flutter (tic)
Zwerchfellganglion n phrenic ganglion
Zwerchfellgeflecht n diaphragmatic (phrenic) plexus
Zwerchfellhälfte f hemidiaphragm
Zwerchfellhochstand m elevation of the diaphragm
Zwerchfell-Kolon-Band n phrenicocolic ligament
Zwerchfellkrampf m diaphragmatic spasm, phrenospasm
Zwerchfellkuppel f dome (cupula) of the diaphragm; subphrenic space
~/linke left dome of the diaphragm
~/rechte right dome of the diaphragm
Zwerchfellnerv m phrenic nerve
Zwerchfellnervendurchtrennung f phrenicotomy
Zwerchfellnervenlähmung f phrenic nerve paralysis
Zwerchfellnervenschmerz m phrenic neuralgia
Zwerchfellphänomen n diaphragmatic phenomenon
Zwerchfellpleura f diaphragmatic pleura
Zwerchfellpleuraentzündung f diaphragmatic pleurisy
Zwerchfellplexus m phrenic (diaphragmatic) plexus
Zwerchfellschenkel m diaphragmatic crus, crus of the diaphragm
~/linker left crus of the diaphragm
~/rechter right crus of the diaphragm

Zwerchfellschmerz *m* diaphragmalgia, phrenodynia, pain in the diaphragm
Zwerchfelltiefstand *m* phrenoptosis
Zwerchfellvene *f* [musculo]phrenic vein
~/**obere** superior phrenic vein
~/**untere** inferior phrenic vein
Zwerchfellzeichen *n* diaphragmatic sign
Zwerchfellzentralsehne *f* central (trefoil) tendon
Zwerchfellzucken *n* diaphragmatic flutter (tic)
Zwerchsackgeschwulst *f* hourglass tumour
Zwerg *m* dwarf, pygmy, midget, nanosomus, nanus
~/**achondroplastischer** achondroplastic dwarf
~/**chondrodystropher** achondroplastic dwarf
~/**hypophysärer** hypophysial (pituitary) dwarf
~/**mikromeler** micromelic dwarf
~/**rachitischer** rachitic dwarf
zwergartig dwarf-like, dwarfish, nanoid, nanous
Zwergäugiger *m* nanophthalmos, nanophthalmus *(Mißgeburt)*
Zwergbandwurmbefall *m* hymenolepiasis
Zwergbecken *n* dwarf pelvis
Zwergdarmegelbefall *m* metagonimiasis
zwergenhaft nanoid, nanous, dwarf-like
Zwergfadenwurm *m* strongyloid threadworm
Zwergkopf *m* nanocephalus
zwergköpfig nanocephalous
Zwergköpfigkeit *f* nanocephalia
Zwergwuchs *m* dwarfism, nanism, nanosomia, microsomia, microplasia
~/**greisenhafter** childhood progeria, Gilford-Hutchinson disease, Hutchinson-Gilford syndrome, premature senility syndrome
~/**renaler** renal dwarfism
Zwiebel *f* 1. bulb *(z. B. der Haarbalg)*; 2. onion
zwiebelartig bulb-like, bulbous, bulboid, bulbiform
Zwiebelschalendermatom *n* onion-peel dermatome
Zwiemilch *f* mixed milk *(für Säuglinge)*
Zwiespalt *m* conflict
Zwilling *m* twin, geminus
Zwillinge *mpl*/**eineiige** uniovular (monochorionic) twins, monozygotic (enzygotic) twins, similar (identical, conjoined) twins
~/**siamesische** Siamese twins
~/**zweieiige** biovular (dichorionic) twins, dizygotic twins, dissimilar (non-identical, fraternal) twins
Zwillingsbildung *f* diembryony *(eineiig)*
zwillingsgebärend biparous
Zwillingsgebärende *f* gemellipara
Zwillingsmißgeburt *f* twin (double) monster
Zwillingsmuskel *m* gastrocnemius [muscle] *(der Wade)*
Zwillingsmutter *f* gemellipara
Zwillingsschwangerschaft *f* twin (bigeminal, gemellery) pregnancy, double gestation
Zwillingsverhaken *n* locking of twins *(bei der Geburt)*
Zwinkerkrampf *m* winking spasm
zwinkern to wink, to blink, to palpebrate
Zwinkerreflex *m* winking reflex
Zwischenauswertervariabilität *f* between-observer variability
Zwischenblutung *f* intermenstrual bleeding (flow), spotting
Zwischenbrauenraum *m* intercilium, glabella
Zwischendornmuskeln *mpl* **der Brustwirbelsäule** interspinales muscles of the thoracic region
~ **der Halswirbelsäule** interspinales muscles of the neck
~ **der Lendenwirbelsäule** interspinales muscles of the lumbar region
Zwischenfingerraum *m* interdigit, interdigital space
zwischengeschlechtlich intersexual
Zwischengeschlechtlichkeit *f* intersexuality
Zwischenhirn *n* diencephalon, interbrain, betweenbrain
Zwischenhirnsyndrom *n* diencephalic syndrome
Zwischenkallus *m* intermediate callus
Zwischenkiefer[knochen] *m* incisive bone, intermaxillary [bone], intermaxilla, premaxilla
Zwischenkieferknochennaht *f* intermaxillary suture
Zwischenknochenarterie *f*/**gemeinsame** common interosseous artery
~/**hintere** posterior interosseous artery
~/**rückläufige** recurrent interosseous artery
~/**vordere** anterior interosseous artery
Zwischenknochenmesser *n* interosseous knife
Zwischenknochenmuskel *m* interosseus [muscle]
Zwischenknochenmuskeln *mpl* **der Hand/dorsale** dorsal interossei muscles of the hand
~ **des Fußes/dorsale** dorsal interossei muscles of the foot
~/**palmare** palmar interossei muscles
~/**plantare** plantar interossei muscles
Zwischenkörper *m* amboceptor, interbody *(Immunkörper)*; intermediate body [of Flemming] *(bei der Zellteilung)*
Zwischenneuron *n*/**inhibitorisches** inhibitory (intercalated) neuron
Zwischenraum *m* interstice, interspace, space, spatium *(Zusammensetzungen s. unter Spatium)*; interstitial tissue, interstitium *(z. B. der bindegewebige Raum um Gefäße)*
Zwischenrippen... s. Interkostal...
Zwischenscheitelbein *n* interparietal bone
Zwischenstoffwechsel *m* intermediary metabolism
Zwischensystole *f* intersystole
Zwischenwirbelknorpel *m* intervertebral cartilage
Zwischenwirbelloch *n* intervertebral foramen
Zwischenwirbelscheibe *f* intervertebral disk
Zwischenwirbelvene *f* intervertebral vein
Zwischenwirt *m* intermediate (alternate) host
Zwischenwurzelscheidewand *f* interradicular septum

Zwischenzehenraum *m* interdigit, interdigital space
Zwischenzelle *f*/**Leydigsche** Leydig (interstitial) cell
Zwischenzellenadenom *n*/**Leydigsches** Leydig-cell tumour, interstitial-cell tumour, interstitioma
Zwischenzellraum *m* intercellular space
Zwitter *m* hermaphrodite; gynandroid, androgyne, androgynus
zwitterig hermaphroditic; bisexual, intersexual, ambisexual, ambosexual; gynandroid, androgynous
Zwitterigkeit *f* hermaphrodi[ti]sm, intersexuality, ambisexuality
Zwitterzustand *m* gynandromorphy
Zwölffingerdarm *m* duodenum, dodecadactylon ● **durch den** ~ transduodenal ● **neben dem** ~ paraduodenal
Zwölffingerdarm... *s. a.* Duodenal...
Zwölffingerdarm-Darm-Anastomose *f* duodenoenterostomy
Zwölffingerdarmendoskopie *f* duodenoscopy
Zwölffingerdarmentfernung *f*[/**operative**] duodenectomy
Zwölffingerdarmentzündung *f* duodenitis, inflammation of the duodenum
Zwölffingerdarmerweiterung *f* duodenectasia; megaduodenum
Zwölffingerdarmflexur *f*/**untere** inferior duodenal flexure
Zwölffingerdarmgeschwür *n* duodenal ulcer
Zwölffingerdarm-Krummdarm-Anastomose *f* duodenoileostomy
Zwölffingerdarm-Leerdarm-Anastomose *f* duodenojejunostomy
Zwölffingerdarm-Leerdarm-Übergang *m* duodenojejunal flexure (angle, junction)
Zwölffingerdarmnaht *f* duodenorrhaphy, suture of the duodenum
Zwölffingerdarmrekonstruktion *f* duodenoplasty
Zwölffingerdarmröntgen[kontrast]bild *n* duodenogram
Zwölffingerdarmröntgen[kontrast]darstellung *f* duodenography
Zwölffingerdarmschleimhaut *f* duodenal mucosa
Zwölffingerdarm- und Bauchspeicheldrüsenentfernung *f*[/**operative**] duodenopancreatectomy, Whipple resection
Zwölffingerdarm- und Magenpförtnerentfernung *f*[/**operative**] duodenopylorectomy
Zwölffingerdarmvereng[er]ung *f* duodenal stenosis
Zwölffingerdarmverschluß *m*/**akuter** arteriomesenteric ileus
Zwölffingerdarm-Zwölffingerdarm-Anastomose *f* duodenoduodenostomy
Zyanephidrosis *f* cyan[ep]hidrosis
Zyanhämatin *n* cyanhaematin
Zyanhämoglobin *n* cyanhaemoglobin
Zyanidstruma *f* cyanide goitre

Zyanmethämoglobin *n* cyan[o]methaemoglobin
Zyanoderma *n* cyanoderma
Zyanokobalamin *n* cyanocobalamin, vitamin B₁₂, erythrocyte-maturing factor
Zyanokobalaminabsorption *f* cyanocobalamin absorption
Zyanopsie *f* cyanop[s]ia
Zyanopsin *n* cyanopsin *(Sehfarbstoff)*
Zyanose *f* cyanosis, cyanopathy ● **ohne** ~ acyanotic
~/**traumatische** traumatic cyanosis
zyanotisch cyanotic ● ~ **werden** to become cyanotic
~/**stark** hypercyanotic
Zyan[wasserstoff]vergiftung *f* hydrocyanism, cyanogen (hydrocyanic acid) poisoning
Zygoma *n s.* Jochbein
zygomatisch zygomatic
Zygomatitis *f* zygomatitis
Zygomyzeten *mpl* zygomycetes
Zygospore *f* zygospore
Zygote *f* zygote, oosperm, fertilized egg
zygotisch zygotic
Zyklektomie *f* cyclectomy
Zyklitis *f s.* Ziliarkörperentzündung
Zyklodialyse *f* cyclodialysis *(zur Druckentlastung durch Lederhautschnitt bei Glaukom)*
Zyklodiathermie[punktur] *f* cyclodiathermy
Zyklokryotherapie *f* cyclocryotherapy
zyklop cyclopic, cyclopean, monophthalmic
Zyklop *m* cyclops, monops, monoculus, synophthalmus
zyklophor cyclophoric
Zyklophorie *f* cyclophoria, rotational heterophoria
~/**akkommodative** accommodative cyclophoria
~ **nach außen** excyclophoria, positive (plus) cyclophoria
~ **nach innen** incyclophoria, negative (minus) cyclophoria
~/**permanente** permanent (essential) cyclophoria, cyclotropia
Zyklophorometer *n* cyclophorometer *(ophthalmologisches Instrument)*
Zyklophosphamid *n* cyclophosphamide *(Zytostatikum)*
Zyklophosphamidbehandlung *f* cyclophosphamide treatment
Zyklophrenie *f s.* Zyklothymie
Zyklopie *f* cyclopia, synophthalmia, synopsia, monophthalmia
zyklopisch *s.* zyklop
Zykloplegie *f* 1. cycloplegia, paralysis of accommodation; 2. cycloplegia, paralysis of the ciliary muscle
Zykloplegikum *n* cycloplegic [agent]
zykloplegisch cycloplegic
Zykloserin *n* cycloserine *(Tuberkulostatikum)*
Zykloskop *n* cycloscope
zyklothym cyclothymic, cyclophrenic
Zyklothymer *m* cyclothyme, cyclothymi[a]c, cycloid personality

Zyklothymie

Zyklothymie f cyclothymia, cyclophrenia, manic-depressive illness (reaction), cyclic insanity, circular psychosis (dementia)
Zyklotom n cyclotome *(ophthalmologisches Messer)*
Zyklotomie f cycl[ic]otomy
Zyklotropie f cyclotropia
Zyklozephalie f cyclocephalia *(Mißbildung mit verwachsenen Augäpfeln, fehlendem Riechhirn und gemeinsamer Orbita)*
Zyklozephalus m cyclocephalus *(Mißgeburt)*
Zyklus m/**anovulatorischer (monophasischer)** anovulatory cycle, anovular (non-ovulational) menstruation
Zyklusmitte f midcycle, midmenstrual cycle
Zylinder m cast *(z. B. im Nierenkanälchen)*
~/**hyaliner** hyaline cast
~/**Külzscher** coma cast *(bei Diabetes mellitus)*
Zylinderaneurysma n cylindrical aneurysm
zylinderartig cylindroid
Zylinderepithel n cylindrical epithelium
Zylinderepithelzelle f cylindrical (columnar) cell
zylinderförmig cylindriform
Zylinderglas n cylindrical lens
Zylinderlinse f cylindrical lens
Zylinderzelle f cylindrical (columnar) cell
Zylinderzellenkarzinom n cylindrical-cell cancer, columnar-cell carcinoma
Zylindrom n cylindroma, adenoid cystic carcinoma
~ **des harten Gaumens** hard palate cylindroma
Zylindrurie f cylindruria
Zymase f zymase *(Enzym)*
Zymbozephalie f cymbocephalia
Zymbozephalus m cymbocephalus *(Mißgeburt)*
zymogen zymogenic, zymogenous
Zymogen n zymogen
Zymogenkörnchen n zymogen granule *(z. B. in der Bauchspeicheldrüse)*
Zymohexase f zymohexase *(Enzym)*
Zymologie f zymology
zymologisch zymologic
Zymolyse f zymolysis
zymophor zymophoric, zymophorous
zymotisch zymotic, zymogenic, zymogenous
Zynophobie f cynophobia *(krankhafte Angst vor Hunden)*
Zynorexie f cynorexia
Zypridophobie f cypridophobia *(krankhafte Angst vor Geschlechtskrankheiten)*
Zyst... s. a. Cyst... und Kyst...
Zystadenolymphom n cystadenolymphoma, Whartin's tumour
Zystadenom n cyst[aden]oma, cystic adenoma, adenocystoma *(s. a. unter Cystadenoma)*
~/**pseudomuzinöses** pseudomucinous cystadenoma, colloid ovarian cystoma
~/**seröses** serous cystadenoma (cystoma)
Zystadenosarkom n cystadenosarcoma
Zystalgie f cystalgia, cystodynia, pain in the urinary bladder
Zystathionin n cystathionine

Zystathioninausscheidung f **im Urin** cystathioninuria *(angeborene Stoffwechselstörung)*
Zyste f cyst
~/**Bartholinische** Bartholin's cyst *(der Bartholinischen Drüsen)*
~/**branchiogene** branchial (cervical) cyst, branchial cleft (inclusion) cyst
~/**bronchogene** bronchogenic cyst
~/**Cowpersche** Cowper's cyst *(der Glandula bulbourethralis)*
~/**große** macrocyst
~/**kleine** microcyst
~/**Nabothsche** Nabothian cyst (follicle) *(der Gebärmutterhalsdrüsen)*
~/**periapikale** periapical cyst
Zystektasie f cystectasia, dilatation of a bladder
Zystektomie f 1. cystectomy, excision of a cyst; 2. cystectomy, excision of the gall-bladder
Zystenadamantinom n cystic adamantinoma
Zystenakne f cystic acne
zystenartig cystoid, cyst-like
Zystenaustritt m excystation *(z. B. Parasiten im Zystenstadium)*
Zystenbildung f cystogenesis, cyst formation
Zysteneierstock m polycystic ovary
Zysteneinschluß m encystation
Zystenentfernung f/**operative** s. Zystektomie 1.
zystenförmig cystiform
Zystenkropf m cystic goitre
Zystenleber f cystic liver
Zystenlunge f honeycomb lung
Zystenniere f polycystic kidney, [multi]cystic kidney
Zystennierenkrankheit f nephrocystosis, kidney polycystic disease, renal cystic dysplasia
Zystenstruma f cystic goitre
zystiform cystiform
Zystikus m cystic duct
Zystikusmyoblastom n cystic duct myoblastoma
Zystikusneurom n cystic duct neuroma
Zystikusstein m cystic duct stone
Zystin n cystine
Zystinämie f cystinaemia
Zystinaminopeptidase f cystine aminopeptidase *(Enzym)*
Zystinausscheidung f **im Urin** cystinuria
Zystinose f cystinosis, cystine storage disease, Abderhalden-Kaufmann-Lignac syndrome
Zystinspeicherkrankheit f s. Zystinose
Zystinstein m cystine calculus
zystisch cystic
Zystitis f cystitis, inflammation of the urinary bladder; endocystitis
~/**allergische** allergic cystitis
Zystitom n cystitome
Zystizerkeninfektion f cysticercosis
Zystizerkoid n cysticercoid *(Bandwurmentwicklungsstadium)*
Zystizerkose f cysticercosis
Zystizerkus m cysticercus, bladder worm *(Bandwurmentwicklungsstadium)*
Zystoduodenostomie f cystoduodenostomy

Zystodynie f s. Zystalgie
Zystoenterozele f cystoenterocele
Zystofibrom n cystofibroma
Zystofibrose f **der Bauchspeicheldrüse** fibrocystic disease of the pancreas, cystic fibrosis [of the pancreas]
Zystofotografie f cystophotography
Zystogenese f cystogenesis
Zystogramm n cystogram
Zystographie f cystography
zystographisch cystographic
Zystoid n cystoid
Zystojejunostomie f cystojejunostomy
Zystolith m cystolith
Zystolithektomie f cystolithectomy
Zystolithiasis f cystolithiasis
Zystom[a] n s. Zystadenom
Zystometer n cystometer
Zystometrie f cystometry
Zystometrogramm n cystometrogram
Zystopexie f cystopexy, vesicofixation
Zystophthise f cystophthisis
Zystoplastik f cystoplasty
Zystoplegie f cystoplegia, paralysis of the bladder
Zystoprostatektomie f cystoprostatectomy
Zystopyelitis f cystopyelitis, pyelocystitis
Zystopyelogramm n cystopyelogram
Zystopyelographie f cystopyelography
Zystopyelonephritis f cystopyelonephritis
Zystorektostomie f cystorectostomy
Zystorektozele f cystorectocele
Zystorrhagie f cystorrhagia, haemorrhage from the bladder
Zystorrhaphie f cystorrhaphy, suture of the urinary bladder
Zystoskop n cystoscope, lithoscope
Zystoskopie f cystoscopy
zystoskopisch cystoscopic
Zystosphinkterometrie f cystosphincterometry
Zystosteatom n cystosteatoma
Zystostomie f cystostomy
Zystotom n cystotome
Zystotomie f cystotomy
Zystoureterozele f cystoureterocele
Zystourethritis f cystourethritis
Zystourethrogramm n cystourethrogram
Zystourethrographie f cystourethrography
zystourethrographisch cystourethrographic
Zystourethropexie f cystourethropexy
Zystourethroskop n cystourethroscope
Zystourethroskopie f cystourethroscopy
zystourethroskopisch cystourethroscopic
Zystourethrozele f cystourethrocele
Zystozele f cystocele, vesicocele, vesical hernia
Zytaster m cytaster
Zytidin n cytidine
Zyto... s. a. Zell...
Zytoblast m cytoblast
Zytoblastem n cytoblastema
Zytochrom n cytochrome, histohaematin (Atmungsenzym)

Zytochromoxydase f cytochrome oxidase
Zytochromreduktase f cytochrome reductase
Zytochromreduktasemangel m cytochrome reductase deficiency
Zytogenese f cytogenesis, cytopoiesis, cell formation
Zytogenetik f cytogenetics
zytogenetisch cytogen[et]ic, cell-forming
Zytohämolyse f cythaemolysis
zytoid cytoid, cell-like, cellular
Zytokinese f cytokinesis
zytokinetisch cytokinetic
Zytoklase f cytoclasis, cell death
zytoklastisch cytoclastic
Zytokrinie f cytocrinia
Zytolipochrom n cytolipochrome
Zytologe m cytologist
Zytologie f cytology
zytologisch cytologic[al]
Zytolyse f cytolysis, dissolution of cells
Zytolysin n cytolysin (1. *die Zellen auflösender Giftstoff*; 2. *Immunstoff*)
Zytolysosom n cytolysosome
zytolytisch cytolytic
zytomegal cytomegalic
Zytomegalie f cytomegalic [inclusion body] disease, cytomegalovirus inclusion syndrome, salivary gland virus disease
Zytomegalievirus n cytomegalovirus, cytomegalic [inclusion body] virus
Zytomegalovirussyndrom n s. Zytomegalie
Zytometer n cytometer
Zytometrie f cytometry
zytometrisch cytometric
Zytomorphose f cytomorphosis
Zytomykose f cytomycosis
Zytopathie f cytopathy
zytopathisch cytopathic
Zytopempsis f cytopempsis, transmission by cell
Zytopenie f cytopenia, hypocytosis
zytophag cytophagous
Zytophag m cytophage
Zytophagie f cytophagy
zytophil cytophilic
Zytophotometer n cytophotometer
Zytophotometrie f cytophotometry
zytophotometrisch cytophotometric
Zytoplasma n cytoplasm, plasm[a], cell juice, bioplasm
Zytoplasmaaustritt m plasmoptysis
Zytoplasmaeinschluß m cytoplasmic inclusion
Zytoplasmaeinschlußkörper m cytoplasmic inclusion body
Zytoplasmafilament n cytoplasmic filament
Zytoplasmafortsatz m cytodendrite
Zytoplasmakörnchen n cytoplasmic granule
zytoplasmakörnerfrei agranulocytic
Zytoplasmamembran f cytoplasmic membrane
Zytoplasmaorganelle f cytoplasmic organelle
Zytoplasmateilung f cytokinesis, cytoplasmic cleavage

Zytoplasmaverschmelzung

Zytoplasmaverschmelzung f plasm[at]ogamy, plastogamy
Zytoplasmazerfall m plasmatorrhexis
Zytopoese f s. Zytogenese
Zytosiderin n cytosiderin *(eisenhaltiges Zellpigment)*
Zytosin n cytosine *(Nukleinsäurebestandteil)*
Zytosinarabinosid n cytosine arabinoside
Zytosindesoxyribonukleosid n deoxycytidine
Zytosinribosid n cytidine
Zytoskelett n cytoskeleton
Zytoskopie f cytoscopy, cytoscopic examination
zytoskopisch cytoscopic

Zytosom n cytosome
Zytostase f cytostasis, cell inhibition
Zytostatikum n cytostatic [agent]
zytostatisch cytostatic
Zytotaxis f cytotaxis
Zytotoxin n cytotoxin, cell poison
zytotoxisch cytotoxic; cytocidal
Zytotoxizität f cytotoxicity
zytotrop cytotropic
Zytotrophie f cytotrophy
Zytotrophoblast m cytotrophoblast
Zytotropismus m cytotropism
Zytozym n cytozyme *(Enzym)*

ANHANG

Hinweise zur Anwendung der IUPAC-Nomenklatur bei der Benennung chemischer Verbindungen

Mit der Anwendung der IUPAC-Nomenklaturregeln bei der Benennung chemischer Verbindungen ergeben sich hinsichtlich der bisherigen deutschen Schreibweise chemischer Namen vor allem folgende Änderungen:

1. Die Schreibweise von Verbindungs- und Elementnamen mit k, z oder c wird der englischen Schreibweise weitestgehend angeglichen:
   Acetat, Cadmium, Caesium, Calcium, Carbonyl-,
   Cresol, Cellulose, Cobalt, Cyan-, Cyclo- usw.;
   dagegen wie bisher:
   Azo-, Keto-, Alkali-, Kalium, Zink.

2. Trivialnamen aromatischer Kohlenwasserstoffe auf -ol werden zu -en geändert:
   Benzen, Toluen, Styren, Cumen, Cymen
   Naphthalen *statt* Naphthalin.

3. Trivialnamen mehrwertiger Alkohole und einer Reihe von Phenolen enden – wie die der einwertigen Akohole – konsequent auf -ol:
Glycerol	*statt*	Glyzerin
Sorbitol	*statt*	Sorbit
Mannitol	*statt*	Mannit
Resorcinol	*statt*	Resorzin.

4. Ethan *statt* Äthan
   (ebenso auch Ethen, Ethin, Ethyl- usw.).

5. Das Element Wismut wird in Angleichung an sein Symbol zu:
   Bismut.
   Name und Symbol des Jods werden gemäß der englischen Schreibweise (und dem griechischen Ursprungswort) zu:
   Iod, Symbol I.
   Die Elemente Ce, Cr, Nb, Nd, Pm, Ti, V und U erhalten wie im Englischen lateinische Endungen und werden zu:
   Cerium, Chromium, Niobium,
   Neodymium, Praseodymium,
   Titanium, Vanadium und
   Uranium.

6. Erscheinen im Namen einer Verbindung mehrere Präfixe für Substituenten, so werden sie *ohne* Berücksichtigung erforderlicher griechischer Zahlenpräfixe alphabetisch angeordnet.
   (Die bisherige Wahlmöglichkeit zwischen dieser Methode und der Ordnung von Substituenten nach steigender Größe oder Komplexität entfällt):
   Monochlortrifluorethen,
   2-Amino-4-ethyl-cyclohexandicarbonsäure
   2,3,6,7-Tetrabrom-1,4-dimethyl-naphthalen.

Anhang

7. Auch Stellungsangaben für funktionelle Gruppen und Lagebezeichnungen für Mehrfachverbindungen werden den kennzeichnenden Suffixen unmittelbar vorangestellt:
   4-Methyl-oct-2-en,
   2,3,5-Trimethyl-hept-2-en.
   Klein- und Großbuchstaben für Stellungsangaben wie o-, m-, p-, C-, S-, N- usw. werden nicht mehr durch eine andere Schriftart hervorgehoben.

Zur genaueren Information empfehlen wir:

1) LIEBSCHER, W., in Mitteilungsbl. Chem. Ges. DDR **25** (1978), S. 259–262.
2) HALLPAP, P., W. LIEBSCHER u. E. WIESNER, Nomenklatur organischer Verbindungen (Lehrprogrammbücher Hochschulstudium **8**), Leipzig 1978.
3) Handbuch zur Anwendung der Nomenklatur organisch-chemischer Verbindungen, hrsg. v. W. LIEBSCHER, Berlin 1979. (Dieses Werk unterrichtet auch über die noch gültigen Trivialnamen, deren Anzahl eingeschränkt wurde.)

Notizen

Notizen